The Sporting News

OFFICIAL
NBA REGISTER

2001-2002 EDITION

Editors/Official NBA Register
JEFF PAUR
DAVID WALTON
JOHN GARDELLA
JOHN HAREAS

Contributing Editors/Official NBA Register
CHRIS EKSTRAND
JAN HUBBARD
ROB REHEUSER
JED TAI

ON THE COVER: Vince Carter.
(Photo by Nathaniel S. Butler/NBA Photos)

Certain statistical data have been selected, compiled and exclusively supplied by NBA Properties, Inc.
Elias Sports Bureau, New York, is the official statistician of the NBA.

All photos supplied by NBA Photos.

Published by The Sporting News, a division of Vulcan Sports Media.
10176 Corporate Square Drive, Suite 200, St. Louis, MO 63132. Printed in the U.S.A.

ISBN:0-89204-655-4   10 9 8 7 6 5 4 3 2 1

CONTENTS

Veteran players **4**
This section includes veteran NBA players who appeared in at least one NBA game during the 2000-01 season or appeared on a roster as of August 29, 2001.

Individual career highs **275**
Regular-season and playoff highs for veteran NBA players.

Promising newcomers **285**

Head coaches **302**

All-time great players **334**
This section includes non-active players who reached one or more of the following plateaus: 17,000 NBA or NBA/ABA points; 10,000 rebounds; 5,000 assists and 10,000 points; named to either the 25th, 35th or 50th NBA Anniversary All-Time Teams; NBA or ABA Most Valuable Player; four-time first-, second- or third-team All-NBA selection or All NBA plus All ABA or All NBL; six NBA All-Star Games or NBA All-Defensive first-team selections; career scoring average of 23 points per game.

All-time great coaches **447**
This section includes non-active coaches who compiled 400 or more regular-season NBA victories.

National Basketball Association statistical leaders **472**

EXPLANATION OF FOOTNOTES AND ABBREVIATIONS

* Led league.
† Tied for league lead.
‡ College freshman or junior varsity statistics; not counted toward totals.
... Statistic unavailable, unofficial or mathematically impossible to calculate.
— Statistic inapplicable.

POSITIONS: C: center. **F:** forward. **G:** guard.

STATISTICS: APG: Assists per game. **Ast.:** Assists. **Blk.:** Blocked shots. **Def.:** Defensive rebounds. **Dq.:** Disqualifications. **FGA:** Field goals attempted. **FGM:** Field goals made. **FTA:** Free throws attempted. **FTM:** Free throws made. **G:** Games. **L:** Losses. **Min.:** Minutes. **Off.:** Offensive rebounds. **Pct.:** Percentage. **PF:** Personal fouls. **PPG:** Points per game. **Pts.:** Points. **Reb.:** Rebounds. **RPG:** Rebounds per game. **Stl.:** Steals. **TO:** Turnovers. **Tot.:** Total. **W:** Wins.

LEAGUES/ORGANIZATIONS: AABA: All-America Basketball Alliance. **ABA:** American Basketball Association. **ABL:** American Basketball League. **BAA:** Basketball Association of America. **CBA:** Continental Basketball Association. **EBL:** Eastern Basketball League. **IL:** Inter-State League. **MBL:** Metropolitan Basketball League. **NAIA:** National Association of Intercollegiate Athletics. **NBA:** National Basketball Association. **NBL:** National Basketball League or National League. **NCAA:** National Collegiate Athletic Association. **NIT:** National Invitation Tournament. **NYSL:** New York State League. **PBLA:** Professional Basketball League of America. **WBA:** Western Basketball Association.

TEAMS: Ala.: Alabama. **Al.:** Albany. **Amw. Zaragoza:** Amway Zaragoza. **And.:** Anderson. **Ark.:** Arkansas. **Atl.:** Atlanta. **Bakers.:** Bakersfield. **Balt.:** Baltimore. **Bay St.:** Bay State. **B., Bos.:** Boston. **Buck. Beer Bolo.:** Buckler Beer Bologna. **Buff.:** Buffalo. **Cha., Char.:** Charlotte. **Ch., Chi.:** Chicago. **Chip. Panionios:** Chipita Panionios. **Cin.:** Cincinnati. **Cl., Clev.:** Cleveland. **Col.:** Columbus. **Dal., Dall.:** Dallas. **Den.:** Denver. **Det.:** Detroit. **Fargo/Moor., F./M.:** Fargo-Moorhead. **Ft. Wayne, F.W.:** Fort Wayne. **Frank. & Marsh.:** Franklin & Marshall. **George Wash.:** George Washington. **Gold. St., G.S.:** Golden State. **G.R., Gr. Rap.:** Grand Rapids. **Grupo Ifa Espa.:** Grupo Ifa Espanol's. **Hfrd.:** Hartford. **Hou.:** Houston. **Ind.:** Indiana. **K.C.:** Kansas City. **K.C./O., K.C./Omaha:** Kansas City/Omaha. **L.A.:** Los Angeles. **L.A.C., LA Clip.:** Los Angeles Clippers. **La Cr.:** La Crosse. **L.A.L., LA Lak.:** Los Angeles Lakers. **Il Mess. Roma:** Il Meccaggero Roma. **Mil.:** Milwaukee. **Min., Minn.:** Minnesota. **Neptunas Klaib.:** Neptunas Klaibeda. **N.J.:** New Jersey. **N.O.:** New Orleans. **N.Y.:** New York. **N.C.:** North Carolina. **Okla. C., O.C.:** Oklahoma City. **Or., Orl.:** Orlando. **Penn.:** Pennsylvania. **Pens.:** Pensacola. **Pfizer R. Calabria:** Pfizer Reggio Calabria. **Phi., Phil.:** Philadelphia. **Phoe.:** Phoenix. **Pitt.:** Pittsburgh. **Port.:** Portland. **Quad C., Q.C.:** Quad City. **Rancho San.:** Rancho Santiago. **Rap. C., R.C.:** Rapid City. **Roch.:** Rochester. **Rock.:** Rockford. **S.A., San Ant.:** San Antonio. **Sac.:** Sacramento. **S.F., San Fran.:** San Francisco. **Sav.:** Savannah. **Sea.:** Seattle. **Shamp. C. Cantu:** Shampoo Clear Cantu. **Shb.:** Sheboygan. **Sioux F.:** Sioux Falls. **St.L.:** St. Louis. **Syr., Syrac.:** Syracuse. **Team. Fabriano:** Teamsystem Fabriano. **Tele. Brescia:** Telemarket Brescia. **Teore. Milan:** Teorematur Milan. **Top.:** Topeka. **Tri C.:** Tri-Cities. **Tul.:** Tulsa. **Va.:** Virginia. **W.:** Warren. **Wash.:** Washington. **Wash. & Jeff.:** Washington & Jefferson. **Wis., Wisc.:** Wisconsin. **Yak.:** Yakima.

BASEBALL STATISTICS: A.A.: American Association. **A:** Assists. **AB:** At-bats. **A.L.:** American League. **Avg.:** Average. **BB:** Bases on balls. **E:** Errors. **East.:** Eastern League. **ER:** Earned runs. **ERA:** Earned-run average. **G:** Games. **H:** Hits. **HR:** Home runs. **Int'l.:** International. **IP:** Innings pitched. **L:** Losses. **N.L.:** National League. **NYP:** New York-Pennsylvania. **OF:** Outfield. **Pct.:** Winning percentage. **PO:** Putouts. **Pos.:** Position. **R:** Runs. **RBI:** Runs batted in. **SB:** Stolen bases. **SO:** Strikeouts. **South.:** Southern Association. **SS:** Shortstop. **Sv.:** Saves. **W:** Wins. **1B:** First base. **2B:** Doubles or second base. **3B:** Triples or third base.

ABDUL-RAUF, MAHMOUD   G

PERSONAL: Born March 9, 1969, in Gulfport, Miss. ... 6-1/162. (1,85/73,5). ... Formerly known as Chris Jackson. ... Name pronounced MOCK-mood Abdul Rah-OOF.
HIGH SCHOOL: Gulfport (Miss.).
COLLEGE: Louisiana State.
TRANSACTIONS/CAREER NOTES: Selected after sophomore season by Denver Nuggets in first round (third pick overall) of 1990 NBA Draft. ... Traded by Nuggets to Sacramento Kings for G Sarunas Marciulionis and 1996 second-round draft choice (June 13, 1996). ... Played in Turkey (1998-99). ... Signed as free agent by Vancouver Grizzlies (August 20, 2000).

COLLEGIATE RECORD

NOTES: THE SPORTING NEWS All-America first team (1989). ... THE SPORTING NEWS All-America second team (1990).

Season Team	G	Min.	FGM	FGA	Pct.	FTM	FTA	Pct.	Reb.	Ast.	Pts.	RPG	APG	PPG
88-89—Louisiana State	32	1180	359	739	.486	163	200	.815	108	130	965	3.4	4.1	30.2
89-90—Louisiana State	32	1202	305	662	.461	191	210	.910	81	102	889	2.5	3.2	27.8
Totals	64	2382	664	1401	.474	354	410	.863	189	232	1854	3.0	3.6	29.0

Three-point field goals: 1988-89, 84-for-216 (.389). 1989-90, 88-for-246 (.358). Totals, 172-for-462 (.372).

NBA REGULAR-SEASON RECORD

HONORS: NBA Most Improved Player (1993). ... NBA All-Rookie second team (1991).

Season Team	G	Min.	FGM	FGA	Pct.	FTM	FTA	Pct.	Off.	Def.	Tot.	Ast.	St.	Blk.	TO	Pts.	RPG	APG	PPG
90-91—Denver	67	1505	417	1009	.413	84	98	.857	34	87	121	206	55	4	110	942	1.8	3.1	14.1
91-92—Denver	81	1538	356	845	.421	94	108	.870	22	92	114	192	44	4	117	837	1.4	2.4	10.3
92-93—Denver	81	2710	633	1407	.450	217	232	.935	51	174	225	344	84	8	187	1553	2.8	4.2	19.2
93-94—Denver	80	2617	588	1279	.460	219	229	*.956	27	141	168	362	82	10	151	1437	2.1	4.5	18.0
94-95—Denver	73	2082	472	1005	.470	138	156	.885	32	105	137	263	77	9	119	1165	1.9	3.6	16.0
95-96—Denver	57	2029	414	955	.434	146	157	*.930	26	112	138	389	64	3	115	1095	2.4	6.8	19.2
96-97—Sacramento	75	2131	411	924	.445	115	136	.846	16	106	122	189	56	6	119	1031	1.6	2.5	13.7
97-98—Sacramento	31	530	103	273	.377	16	16	1.000	6	31	37	58	16	1	19	227	1.2	1.9	7.3
00-01—Vancouver	41	486	120	246	.488	22	29	.759	5	20	25	76	9	1	26	266	0.6	1.9	6.5
Totals	586	15628	3514	7943	.442	1051	1161	.905	219	868	1087	2079	487	46	963	8553	1.9	3.5	14.6

Three-point field goals: 1990-91, 24-for-100 (.240). 1991-92, 31-for-94 (.330). 1992-93, 70-for-197 (.355). 1993-94, 42-for-133 (.316). 1994-95, 83-for-215 (.386). 1995-96, 121-for-309 (.392). 1996-97, 94-for-246 (.382). 1997-98, 5-for-31 (.161). 2000-01, 4-for-14 (.286). Totals, 474-for-1339 (.354).
Personal fouls/disqualifications: 1990-91, 149/2. 1991-92, 130/0. 1992-93, 179/0. 1993-94, 150/1. 1994-95, 126/0. 1995-96, 117/0. 1996-97, 174/3. 1997-98, 31/0. 2000-01, 50/0. Totals, 1106/6.

NBA PLAYOFF RECORD

Season Team	G	Min.	FGM	FGA	Pct.	FTM	FTA	Pct.	Off.	Def.	Tot.	Ast.	St.	Blk.	TO	Pts.	RPG	APG	PPG
93-94—Denver	12	339	57	154	.370	29	31	.935	3	15	18	30	5	1	14	155	1.5	2.5	12.9
94-95—Denver	3	76	12	33	.364	14	14	1.000	2	3	5	5	2	0	8	40	1.7	1.7	13.3
Totals	15	415	69	187	.369	43	45	.956	5	18	23	35	7	1	22	195	1.5	2.3	13.0

Three-point field goals: 1993-94, 12-for-37 (.324). 1994-95, 2-for-12 (.167). Totals, 14-for-49 (.286).
Personal fouls/disqualifications: 1993-94, 29/0. 1994-95, 8/0. Totals, 37/0.

TURKISH LEAGUE RECORD

Season Team	G	Min.	FGM	FGA	Pct.	FTM	FTA	Pct.	Reb.	Ast.	Pts.	RPG	APG	PPG
98-99—Fenerbache	5	155	31	73	.425	7	7	1.000	3	13	75	0.6	2.6	15.0

Three-point field goals: 1998-99, 6-for-24 (.250).

ABDUL-WAHAD, TARIQ   G/F   NUGGETS

PERSONAL: Born November 3, 1974, in Maisons Alfort, France. ... 6-6/223. (1,98/101,2). ... Fomerly known as Olivier Saint-Jean.
HIGH SCHOOL: Lycee Aristide Briand (Evreux, France).
COLLEGE: Michigan, then San Jose State.
TRANSACTIONS/CAREER NOTES: Selected after junior season by Sacramento Kings in first round (11th pick overall) of 1997 NBA Draft. ... Traded by Kings with future first-round draft choice to Orlando Magic for G/F Nick Anderson (August 3, 1999). ... Traded by Magic with F/C Chris Gatling, a future first round draft choice and cash considerations to Denver Nuggets for G Chauncey Billups, G/F Ron Mercer, F Johnny Taylor and draft considerations (February 1, 2000).

FRENCH LEAGUE RECORD

Season Team	G	Min.	FGM	FGA	Pct.	FTM	FTA	Pct.	Reb.	Ast.	Pts.	RPG	APG	PPG
90-91—Evreux	2	3	0	1	.000	0	0	...	0	0	0	0.0	0.0	0.0
91-92—Evreux	8	40	7	16	.438	1	3	.333	5	1	15	0.6	0.1	1.9
92-93—Evreux	17	238	40	80	.500	13	25	.520	64	8	93	3.8	0.5	5.5
Totals	27	281	47	97	.485	14	28	.500	69	9	108	2.6	0.3	4.0

COLLEGIATE RECORD

NOTES: Injured knee (1994-95); granted extra year of eligibility.

Season Team	G	Min.	FGM	FGA	Pct.	FTM	FTA	Pct.	Reb.	Ast.	Pts.	RPG	APG	PPG
												AVERAGES		
93-94—Michigan	32	418	49	96	.510	13	23	.565	72	17	115	2.3	0.5	3.6
94-95—Michigan	4	53	8	16	.500	2	2	1.000	13	0	19	3.3	0.0	4.8
95-96—San Jose State	25	698	148	332	.446	117	158	.741	157	64	431	6.3	2.6	17.2
96-97—San Jose State	26	868	225	457	.492	143	196	.730	229	28	619	8.8	1.1	23.8
Totals	87	2037	430	901	.477	275	379	.726	471	109	1184	5.4	1.3	13.6

Three-point field goals: 1993-94, 4-for-14 (.286). 1994-95, 1-for-2 (.500). 1995-96, 18-for-65 (.277). 1996-97, 26-for-71 (.366). Totals, 49-for-152 (.322).

NBA REGULAR-SEASON RECORD

Season Team	G	Min.	FGM	FGA	Pct.	FTM	FTA	Pct.	Off.	Def.	Tot.	Ast.	St.	Blk.	TO	Pts.	RPG	APG	PPG
									REBOUNDS								**AVERAGES**		
97-98—Sacramento	59	959	144	357	.403	84	125	.672	44	72	116	51	35	13	65	376	2.0	0.9	6.4
98-99—Sacramento	49	1205	177	407	.435	94	136	.691	72	114	186	50	50	16	70	454	3.8	1.0	9.3
99-00—Orl.-Den.	61	1578	274	646	.424	146	193	.756	101	190	291	98	59	28	106	697	4.8	1.6	11.4
00-01—Denver	29	420	43	111	.387	21	36	.583	14	45	59	22	14	13	34	111	2.0	0.8	3.8
Totals	198	4162	638	1521	.419	345	490	.704	231	421	652	221	158	70	275	1638	3.3	1.1	8.3

Three-point field goals: 1997-98, 4-for-19 (.211). 1998-99, 6-for-21 (.286). 1999-00, 3-for-23 (.130). 2000-01, 4-for-10 (.400). Totals, 17-for-73 (.233).
Personal fouls/disqualifications: 1997-98, 81/0. 1998-99, 121/0. 1999-00, 147/1. 2000-01, 54/0. Totals, 403/1.

NBA PLAYOFF RECORD

Season Team	G	Min.	FGM	FGA	Pct.	FTM	FTA	Pct.	Off.	Def.	Tot.	Ast.	St.	Blk.	TO	Pts.	RPG	APG	PPG
									REBOUNDS								**AVERAGES**		
98-99—Sacramento	5	99	15	33	.455	13	16	.813	6	13	19	4	4	4	3	43	3.8	0.8	8.6

Three-point field goals: 1998-99, 0-for-1.
Personal fouls/disqualifications: 1998-99, 8/0.

ABDUR-RAHIM, SHAREEF F   HAWKS

PERSONAL: Born December 11, 1976, in Marietta, Ga. ... 6-9/230. (2,06/104,3). ... Full Name: Julius Shareef Abdur-Rahim. ... Name pronounced shah-REEF ab-DOOR-Rah-heem.
HIGH SCHOOL: Wheeler (Marietta, Ga.).
COLLEGE: California.
TRANSACTIONS/CAREER NOTES: Selected after freshman season by Vancouver Grizzlies in first round (third pick overall) of 1996 NBA Draft. ... Grizzlies franchise moved to Memphis for 2001-02 season. ... Traded by Grizzlies with draft rights to G Jamaal Tinsley to Atlanta Hawks for F/C Lorenzen Wright, G Brevin Knight and draft rights to F Pau Gasol (July 19, 2001).
MISCELLANEOUS: Vancouver Grizzlies all-time scoring leader with 7,801 points, all-time leading rebounder with 3,070, all-time steals leader with 416 and all-time blocked shots leader with 374 (1996-97 through 2000-01). ... Member of gold-medal-winning U.S. Olympic team (2000).

COLLEGIATE RECORD

Season Team	G	Min.	FGM	FGA	Pct.	FTM	FTA	Pct.	Reb.	Ast.	Pts.	RPG	APG	PPG
												AVERAGES		
95-96—California	28	972	206	398	.518	170	249	.683	236	29	590	8.4	1.0	21.1

Three-point field goals: 1995-96, 8-for-21 (.381).

NBA REGULAR-SEASON RECORD

HONORS: NBA All-Rookie first team (1997).

Season Team	G	Min.	FGM	FGA	Pct.	FTM	FTA	Pct.	Off.	Def.	Tot.	Ast.	St.	Blk.	TO	Pts.	RPG	APG	PPG
									REBOUNDS								**AVERAGES**		
96-97—Vancouver	80	2802	550	1214	.453	387	519	.746	216	339	555	175	79	79	225	1494	6.9	2.2	18.7
97-98—Vancouver	82	2950	653	1347	.485	502	640	.784	227	354	581	213	89	76	257	1829	7.1	2.6	22.3
98-99—Vancouver	50	2021	386	893	.432	369	439	.841	114	260	374	172	69	55	*186	1152	7.5	3.4	23.0
99-00—Vancouver	82	3223	594	1277	.465	446	551	.809	218	607	825	271	89	87	249	1663	10.1	3.3	20.3
00-01—Vancouver	81	3241	604	1280	.472	443	531	.834	175	560	735	250	90	77	231	1663	9.1	3.1	20.5
Totals	375	14237	2787	6011	.464	2147	2680	.801	950	2120	3070	1081	416	374	1148	7801	8.2	2.9	20.8

Three-point field goals: 1996-97, 7-for-27 (.259). 1997-98, 21-for-51 (.412). 1998-99, 11-for-36 (.306). 1999-00, 29-for-96 (.302). 2000-01, 12-for-64 (.188). Totals, 80-for-274 (.292).
Personal fouls/disqualifications: 1996-97, 199/0. 1997-98, 201/0. 1998-99, 137/1. 1999-00, 244/3. 2000-01, 238/1. Totals, 1019/5.

ALEXANDER, CORY   G

PERSONAL: Born June 22, 1973, in Waynesboro, Va. ... 6-1/190. (1,85/86,2). ... Full Name: Cory Lynn Alexander.
HIGH SCHOOL: Oak Hill Academy (Mouth of Wilson, Va.).
COLLEGE: Virginia.
TRANSACTIONS/CAREER NOTES: Selected after junior season by San Antonio Spurs in first round (29th pick overall) of 1995 NBA Draft. ... Waived by Spurs (February 27, 1998). ... Signed as free agent by Denver Nuggets (March 4, 1998). ... Waived by Nuggets (October 30, 2000). ... Signed by Orlando Magic to the first of two consecutive 10-day contract (January 29, 2001). ... Re-signed by Magic for remainder of season (February 23, 2001).

COLLEGIATE RECORD

NOTES: Broke ankle (1993-94); granted extra year of eligibility.

Season Team	G	Min.	FGM	FGA	Pct.	FTM	FTA	Pct.	Reb.	Ast.	Pts.	RPG	APG	PPG
												AVERAGES		
91-92—Virginia	33	1037	127	338	.376	72	105	.686	106	145	370	3.2	4.4	11.2
92-93—Virginia	31	1118	213	470	.453	93	132	.705	107	144	583	3.5	4.6	18.8
93-94—Virginia	1	11	0	4	.000	0	2	.000	1	2	0	1.0	2.0	0.0
94-95—Virginia	20	692	119	263	.452	61	87	.701	84	110	333	4.2	5.5	16.7
Totals	85	2858	459	1075	.427	226	326	.693	298	401	1286	3.5	4.7	15.1

Three-point field goals: 1991-92, 44-for-149 (.295). 1992-93, 64-for-174 (.368). 1993-94, 0-for-2. 1994-95, 34-for-97 (.351). Totals, 142-for-422 (.336).

NBA REGULAR-SEASON RECORD

Season Team	G	Min.	FGM	FGA	Pct.	FTM	FTA	Pct.	REBOUNDS Off.	Def.	Tot.	Ast.	St.	Blk.	TO	Pts.	AVERAGES RPG	APG	PPG
95-96—San Antonio....	60	560	63	155	.406	16	25	.640	9	33	42	121	27	2	68	168	0.7	2.0	2.8
96-97—San Antonio....	80	1454	194	490	.396	95	129	.736	29	94	123	254	82	16	146	577	1.5	3.2	7.2
97-98—S.A.-Denver	60	1298	171	400	.428	80	102	.784	17	129	146	209	70	11	112	488	2.4	3.5	8.1
98-99—Denver	36	778	97	260	.373	37	44	.841	7	67	74	119	35	5	69	261	2.1	3.3	7.3
99-00—Denver	29	329	28	98	.286	17	22	.773	8	34	42	58	24	2	28	82	1.4	2.0	2.8
00-01—Orlando..........	26	227	18	56	.321	12	18	.667	0	25	25	36	16	0	25	52	1.0	1.4	2.0
Totals	291	4646	571	1459	.391	257	340	.756	70	382	452	797	254	36	448	1628	1.6	2.7	5.6

Three-point field goals: 1995-96, 26-for-66 (.394). 1996-97, 94-for-252 (.373). 1997-98, 66-for-176 (.375). 1998-99, 30-for-105 (.286). 1999-00, 9-for-35 (.257). 2000-01, 4-for-16 (.250). Totals, 229-for-650 (.352).

Personal fouls/disqualifications: 1995-96, 94/0. 1996-97, 148/0. 1997-98, 98/2. 1998-99, 77/0. 1999-00, 39/0. 2000-01, 29/0. Totals, 485/2.

NBA PLAYOFF RECORD

Season Team	G	Min.	FGM	FGA	Pct.	FTM	FTA	Pct.	REBOUNDS Off.	Def.	Tot.	Ast.	St.	Blk.	TO	Pts.	AVERAGES RPG	APG	PPG
95-96—San Antonio....	9	70	10	24	.417	5	7	.714	4	5	9	9	2	0	6	26	1.0	1.0	2.9

Three-point field goals: 1995-96, 1-for-5 (.200).
Personal fouls/disqualifications: 1995-96, 8/0.

ALEXANDER, COURTNEY   G   WIZARDS

PERSONAL: Born April 27, 1977, in Bridgeport, Conn. ... 6-5/205. (1,96/93,0). ... Full Name: Courtney Jason Alexander.
HIGH SCHOOL: Jordan (Durham, N.C.).
COLLEGE: Virginia, then Fresno State.
TRANSACTIONS/CAREER NOTES: Selected by Orlando Magic in first round (13th pick overall) of 2000 NBA Draft. ... Draft rights traded by Magic to Dallas Mavericks for a future first-round draft choice and cash (June 28, 2000). ... Traded by Mavericks with F/C Christian Laettner, F Loy Vaught, G Hubert Davis, F/C Etan Thomas and cash considerations to Washington Wizards for F Juwan Howard, C Calvin Booth and F Obinna Ekezie (February 22, 2001).

COLLEGIATE RECORD

NOTES: Led NCAA Division I with 24.8 points per game (2000).

Season Team	G	Min.	FGM	FGA	Pct.	FTM	FTA	Pct.	Reb.	Ast.	Pts.	AVERAGES RPG	APG	PPG
95-96—Virginia..........	27	727	147	302	.487	63	82	.768	122	36	375	4.5	1.3	13.9
96-97—Virginia..........	26	732	142	338	.420	60	79	.759	70	37	384	2.7	1.4	14.8
97-98—Fresno State					Did not play—transfer student.									
98-99—Fresno State	32	1023	264	563	.469	106	140	.757	121	82	684	3.8	2.6	21.4
99-00—Fresno State	27	974	252	564	.447	107	137	.781	128	94	669	4.7	3.5	24.8
Totals	112	3456	805	1767	.456	336	438	.767	441	249	2112	3.9	2.2	18.9

Three-point field goals: 1995-96, 18-for-35 (.514). 1996-97, 40-for-90 (.444). 1998-99, 50-for-158 (.316). 1999-00, 58-for-175 (.331). Totals, 166-for-458 (.362).

HONORS: NBA All-Rookie second team (2001).

NBA REGULAR-SEASON RECORD

Season Team	G	Min.	FGM	FGA	Pct.	FTM	FTA	Pct.	REBOUNDS Off.	Def.	Tot.	Ast.	St.	Blk.	TO	Pts.	AVERAGES RPG	APG	PPG
00-01—Dallas-Wash. ..	65	1382	239	573	.417	123	150	.820	42	101	143	62	45	5	75	618	2.2	1.0	9.5

Three-point field goals: 2000-01, 17-for-46 (.370).
Personal fouls/disqualifications: 2000-01, 139/1.

ALLEN, RAY   G   BUCKS

PERSONAL: Born July 20, 1975, in Merced, Calif. ... 6-5/205. (1,96/93,0). ... Full Name: Walter Ray Allen.
HIGH SCHOOL: Hillcrest (Dalzell, S.C.).
COLLEGE: Connecticut.
TRANSACTIONS/CAREER NOTES: Selected after junior season by Minnesota Timberwolves in first round (fifth pick overall) of 1996 NBA Draft. ... Draft rights traded by Timberwolves with future first-round draft choice to Milwaukee Bucks for draft rights to G Stephon Marbury (June 26, 1996).
MISCELLANEOUS: Member of gold-medal-winning U.S. Olympic team (2000).

COLLEGIATE RECORD

NOTES: The Sporting News All-America first team (1996).

Season Team	G	Min.	FGM	FGA	Pct.	FTM	FTA	Pct.	Reb.	Ast.	Pts.	AVERAGES RPG	APG	PPG
93-94—Connecticut	34	735	158	310	.510	80	101	.792	155	53	429	4.6	1.6	12.6
94-95—Connecticut	32	1051	255	521	.489	80	110	.727	218	75	675	6.8	2.3	21.1
95-96—Connecticut	35	1098	292	618	.472	119	147	.810	228	117	818	6.5	3.3	23.4
Totals	101	2884	705	1449	.487	279	358	.779	601	245	1922	6.0	2.4	19.0

Three-point field goals: 1993-94, 33-for-82 (.402). 1994-95, 85-for-191 (.445). 1995-96, 115-for-247 (.466). Totals, 233-for-520 (.448).

NBA REGULAR-SEASON RECORD

HONORS: All-NBA third team (2001). ... NBA All-Rookie second team (1997). ... Long Distance Shootout winner (2001).
NOTES: Led NBA with 172 three-point field goals made and 407 three-point field goals attempted (2000). ... Led NBA with 202 three-point field goals made and 467 three-point field goals attempted (2001).

									REBOUNDS								AVERAGES		
Season Team	G	Min.	FGM	FGA	Pct.	FTM	FTA	Pct.	Off.	Def.	Tot.	Ast.	St.	Blk.	TO	Pts.	RPG	APG	PPG
96-97—Milwaukee	82	2532	390	908	.430	205	249	.823	97	229	326	210	75	10	149	1102	4.0	2.6	13.4
97-98—Milwaukee	82	3287	563	1315	.428	342	391	.875	127	278	405	356	111	12	263	1602	4.9	4.3	19.5
98-99—Milwaukee	50	1719	303	673	.450	176	195	.903	57	155	212	178	53	7	122	856	4.2	3.6	17.1
99-00—Milwaukee	82	3070	642	1411	.455	353	398	.887	83	276	359	308	110	19	183	1809	4.4	3.8	22.1
00-01—Milwaukee	82	3129	628	1309	.480	348	392	.888	101	327	428	374	124	20	204	1806	5.2	4.6	22.0
Totals	378	13737	2526	5616	.450	1424	1625	.876	465	1265	1730	1426	473	68	921	7175	4.6	3.8	19.0

Three-point field goals: 1996-97, 117-for-298 (.393). 1997-98, 134-for-368 (.364). 1998-99, 74-for-208 (.356). 1999-00, 172-for-407 (.423). 2000-01, 202-for-467 (.433). Totals, 699-for-1748 (.400).

Personal fouls/disqualifications: 1996-97, 218/0. 1997-98, 244/2. 1998-99, 117/0. 1999-00, 187/1. 2000-01, 192/2. Totals, 958/5.

NBA PLAYOFF RECORD

NOTES: Shares single-game playoff record for most three-point field goals made in one quarter—5 (May 11, 1999, at Indiana).

									REBOUNDS								AVERAGES		
Season Team	G	Min.	FGM	FGA	Pct.	FTM	FTA	Pct.	Off.	Def.	Tot.	Ast.	St.	Blk.	TO	Pts.	RPG	APG	PPG
98-99—Milwaukee	3	120	25	47	.532	8	13	.615	8	14	22	13	3	1	11	67	7.3	4.3	22.3
99-00—Milwaukee	5	186	40	90	.444	20	22	.909	10	23	33	13	8	0	9	110	6.6	2.6	22.0
00-01—Milwaukee	18	768	158	331	.477	79	86	.919	19	55	74	108	24	10	43	452	4.1	6.0	25.1
Totals	26	1074	223	468	.476	107	121	.884	37	92	129	134	35	11	63	629	5.0	5.2	24.2

Three-point field goals: 1998-99, 9-for-19 (.474). 1999-00, 10-for-26 (.385). 2000-01, 57-for-119 (.479). Totals, 76-for-164 (.463).

Personal fouls/disqualifications: 1998-99, 9/0. 1999-00, 10/0. 2000-01, 44/0. Totals, 63/0.

NBA ALL-STAR GAME RECORD

							REBOUNDS								
Season Team	Min.	FGM	FGA	Pct.	FTM	FTA	Pct.	Off.	Def.	Tot.	Ast.	PF	Dq.	St.	Blk.	TO	Pts.
2000 —Milwaukee	17	4	13	.308	5	6	.833	1	0	1	2	2	0	3	1	3	14
2001 —Milwaukee	19	7	15	.467	0	0	...	1	2	3	2	0	0	1	1	1	15
Totals	36	11	28	.393	5	6	.833	2	2	4	4	2	0	4	2	4	29

Three-point field goals: 2000, 1-for-6 (.167). 2001, 1-for-7 (.143). Totals, 2-for-13 (.154).

ALSTON, RAFER   G   BUCKS

PERSONAL: Born July 24, 1976, in New York. ... 6-2/173. (1,88/78,5).
HIGH SCHOOL: Cardozo (Queens, N.Y.).
JUNIOR COLLEGE: Ventura College (Calif.), then Fresno (Calif.) Community College.
COLLEGE: Fresno State.
TRANSACTIONS/CAREER NOTES: Selected after junior season by Milwaukee Bucks in second round (39th pick overall) of 1998 NBA Draft. ... Played in Continental Basketball Association with Idaho Stampede (1998-99).

COLLEGIATE RECORD

											AVERAGES		
Season Team	G	Min.	FGM	FGA	Pct.	FTM	FTA	Pct.	Reb.	Ast.	Pts.	RPG	APG	PPG
94-95—Ventura College						Statistics unavailable.								
95-96—Fresno C.C.						Did not play.								
96-97—Fresno C.C.	32	...	197	395	.499	69	85	.812	64	275	554	2.0	8.6	17.3
97-98—Fresno State	33	1030	124	309	.401	50	66	.758	71	240	364	2.2	7.3	11.0
Junior College Totals	32	...	197	395	.499	69	85	.812	64	275	554	2.0	8.6	17.3
4-Year-College Totals	33	1030	124	309	.401	50	66	.758	71	240	364	2.2	7.3	11.0

Three-point field goals: 1996-97, 91-for-223 (.408). 1997-98, 66-for-196 (.337).

CBA REGULAR-SEASON RECORD

											AVERAGES		
Season Team	G	Min.	FGM	FGA	Pct.	FTM	FTA	Pct.	Reb.	Ast.	Pts.	RPG	APG	PPG
98-99—Idaho	17	427	45	116	.388	13	19	.684	33	106	111	1.9	6.2	6.5

Three-point field goals: 1998-99, 8-for-28 (.286).

NBA REGULAR-SEASON RECORD

									REBOUNDS								AVERAGES		
Season Team	G	Min.	FGM	FGA	Pct.	FTM	FTA	Pct.	Off.	Def.	Tot.	Ast.	St.	Blk.	TO	Pts.	RPG	APG	PPG
99-00—Milwaukee	27	361	27	95	.284	3	4	.750	5	18	23	70	12	0	29	60	0.9	2.6	2.2
00-01—Milwaukee	37	288	30	84	.357	9	13	.692	4	27	31	68	13	0	20	77	0.8	1.8	2.1
Totals	64	649	57	179	.318	12	17	.706	9	45	54	138	25	0	49	137	0.8	2.2	2.1

Three-point field goals: 1999-00, 3-for-14 (.214). 2000-01, 8-for-30 (.267). Totals, 11-for-44 (.250).

Personal fouls/disqualifications: 1999-00, 29/0. 2000-01, 27/0. Totals, 56/0.

NBA PLAYOFF RECORD

									REBOUNDS								AVERAGES		
Season Team	G	Min.	FGM	FGA	Pct.	FTM	FTA	Pct.	Off.	Def.	Tot.	Ast.	St.	Blk.	TO	Pts.	RPG	APG	PPG
99-00—Milwaukee	4	16	0	3	.000	0	2	.000	0	0	0	1	0	0	1	0	0.0	0.3	0.0
00-01—Milwaukee	5	8	0	1	.000	0	0	...	0	0	0	1	0	0	2	0	0.0	0.2	0.0
Totals	9	24	0	4	.000	0	2	.000	0	0	0	2	0	0	3	0	0.0	0.2	0.0

Three-point field goals: 1999-00, 0-for-1. Totals, 0-for-1 (.000).

DID YOU KNOW . . .

. . . that Shaquille O'Neal and Kobe Bryant last season became the first teammates to finish in the NBA's top five in scoring since Denver's Kiki Vandeweghe and Alex English in 1983-84?

AMAECHI, JOHN F/C JAZZ

PERSONAL: Born November 26, 1970, in Boston. ... 6-10/270. (2,08/122,5). ... Name pronounced uh-MAY-chee.
HIGH SCHOOL: St. John's (Toledo, Ohio).
COLLEGE: Vanderbilt, then Penn State.
TRANSACTIONS/CAREER NOTES: Not drafted by an NBA franchise. ... Signed as free agent by Cleveland Cavaliers (October 5, 1995). ... Waived by Cavaliers (July 31, 1996). ... Played in France (1995-96 and 1998-99). ... Played in Greece (1996-97). ... Played in Italy (1997-98). ... Played in Great Britain (1997-98). ... Signed as free agent by Orlando Magic (September 20, 1999). ... Signed as free agent by Utah Jazz (July 19, 2001).

COLLEGIATE RECORD

Season Team	G	Min.	FGM	FGA	Pct.	FTM	FTA	Pct.	Reb.	Ast.	Pts.	RPG	APG	PPG
90-91—Vanderbilt	24	311	26	57	.456	14	25	.560	65	6	66	2.7	0.3	2.8
91-92—Penn State						Did not play—transfer student.								
92-93—Penn State	27	897	114	241	.473	130	182	.714	206	20	373	7.6	0.7	13.8
93-94—Penn State	25	837	124	243	.510	171	245	.698	223	37	423	8.9	1.5	16.9
94-95—Penn State	32	1108	168	300	.560	176	260	.677	316	55	514	9.9	1.7	16.1
Totals	108	3153	432	841	.514	491	712	.690	810	118	1376	7.5	1.1	12.7

Three-point field goals: 1992-93, 15-for-48 (.313). 1993-94, 4-for-15 (.267). 1994-95, 2-for-6 (.333). Totals, 21-for-69 (.304).

FRENCH LEAGUE RECORD

Season Team	G	Min.	FGM	FGA	Pct.	FTM	FTA	Pct.	Reb.	Ast.	Pts.	RPG	APG	PPG
95-96—Cholet	2	...	17	27	.630	6	10	.600	22	3	40	11.0	1.5	20.0
98-99—Limoges	11	306	57	113	.504	18	33	.545	53	12	140	4.8	1.1	12.7
Totals	13	...	74	140	.529	24	43	.558	75	15	180	5.8	1.2	13.8

Three-point field goals: 1998-99, 8-for-20 (.400).

NBA REGULAR-SEASON RECORD

Season Team	G	Min.	FGM	FGA	Pct.	FTM	FTA	Pct.	Off.	Def.	Tot.	Ast.	St.	Blk.	TO	Pts.	RPG	APG	PPG
95-96—Cleveland	28	357	29	70	.414	19	33	.576	13	39	52	9	6	11	34	77	1.9	0.3	2.8
99-00—Orlando	80	1684	306	700	.437	223	291	.766	62	204	266	95	35	37	139	836	3.3	1.2	10.5
00-01—Orlando	82	1710	237	592	.400	176	279	.631	77	191	268	74	28	29	124	650	3.3	0.9	7.9
Totals	190	3751	572	1362	.420	418	603	.693	152	434	586	178	69	77	297	1563	3.1	0.9	8.2

Three-point field goals: 1999-00, 1-for-6 (.167). 2000-01, 0-for-7. Totals, 1-for-13 (.077).
Personal fouls/disqualifications: 1995-96, 49/1. 1999-00, 161/1. 2000-01, 175/1. Totals, 385/3.

NBA PLAYOFF RECORD

Season Team	G	Min.	FGM	FGA	Pct.	FTM	FTA	Pct.	Off.	Def.	Tot.	Ast.	St.	Blk.	TO	Pts.	RPG	APG	PPG
95-96—Cleveland	1	2	0	1	.000	0	0	...	0	0	0	0	0	0	0	0	0.0	0.0	0.0
00-01—Orlando	4	29	3	8	.375	3	4	.750	1	2	3	3	3	2	0	9	0.8	0.8	2.3
Totals	5	31	3	9	.333	3	4	.750	1	2	3	3	3	2	0	9	0.6	0.6	1.8

Personal fouls/disqualifications: 2000-01, 2/0. Totals, 2/0.

GREEK LEAGUE RECORD

Season Team	G	Min.	FGM	FGA	Pct.	FTM	FTA	Pct.	Reb.	Ast.	Pts.	RPG	APG	PPG
96-97—Panathinaikos	22	515	81	161	.503	55	78	.705	132	9	217	6.0	0.4	9.9

Three-point field goals: 1996-97, 0-for-1.

BRITISH LEAGUE RECORD

Season Team	G	Min.	FGM	FGA	Pct.	FTM	FTA	Pct.	Reb.	Ast.	Pts.	RPG	APG	PPG
97-98—Sheffield	18	701	117	224	.522	105	159	.660	170	41	402	9.4	2.3	22.3

ITALIAN LEAGUE RECORD

Season Team	G	Min.	FGM	FGA	Pct.	FTM	FTA	Pct.	Reb.	Ast.	Pts.	RPG	APG	PPG
97-98—Virtus Bologna	7	82	5	21	.238	15	26	.577	18	2	25	2.6	0.3	3.6

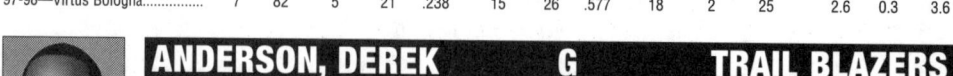

ANDERSON, DEREK G TRAIL BLAZERS

PERSONAL: Born July 18, 1974, in Louisville. ... 6-5/195. (1,96/88,5). ... Full Name: Derek Lamont Anderson.
HIGH SCHOOL: Doss (Louisville).
COLLEGE: Ohio State, then Kentucky.
TRANSACTIONS/CAREER NOTES: Selected by Cleveland Cavaliers in first round (13th pick overall) of 1997 NBA Draft. ... Traded by Cavaliers with F Johnny Newman to Los Angeles Clippers for F Lamond Murray (August 4, 1999). ... Signed as free agent by San Antonio Spurs (August 4, 2000). ... Traded by Spurs with G Steve Kerr and 2003 second-round draft choice to Portland Trail Blazers for G Steve Smith (July 25, 2001).

COLLEGIATE RECORD

NOTES: Member of NCAA Division I championship team (1996).

Season Team	G	Min.	FGM	FGA	Pct.	FTM	FTA	Pct.	Reb.	Ast.	Pts.	AVERAGES		
												RPG	APG	PPG
92-93—Ohio State	22	587	72	158	.456	72	89	.809	72	59	225	3.3	2.7	10.2
93-94—Ohio State	22	695	108	232	.466	92	113	.814	108	107	329	4.9	4.9	15.0
94-95—Kentucky						Did not play—transfer student.								
95-96—Kentucky	36	700	117	230	.509	80	102	.784	122	88	337	3.4	2.4	9.4
96-97—Kentucky	19	481	111	226	.491	77	95	.811	77	67	337	4.1	3.5	17.7
Totals	99	2463	408	846	.482	321	399	.805	379	321	1228	3.8	3.2	12.4

Three-point field goals: 1992-93, 9-for-35 (.257). 1993-94, 21-for-62 (.339). 1995-96, 23-for-59 (.390). 1996-97, 38-for-94 (.404). Totals, 91-for-250 (.364).

NBA REGULAR-SEASON RECORD

HONORS: NBA All-Rookie second team (1998).

Season Team	G	Min.	FGM	FGA	Pct.	FTM	FTA	Pct.	REBOUNDS			Ast.	St.	Blk.	TO	Pts.	AVERAGES		
									Off.	Def.	Tot.						RPG	APG	PPG
97-98—Cleveland	66	1839	239	586	.408	275	315	.873	55	132	187	227	86	13	128	770	2.8	3.4	11.7
98-99—Cleveland	38	978	125	314	.398	138	165	.836	20	89	109	145	48	4	82	409	2.9	3.8	10.8
99-00—L.A. Clippers	64	2201	377	860	.438	271	309	.877	80	178	258	220	90	11	167	1080	4.0	3.4	16.9
00-01—San Antonio	82	2859	413	993	.416	342	402	.851	75	288	363	301	120	14	165	1269	4.4	3.7	15.5
Totals	250	7877	1154	2753	.419	1026	1191	.861	230	687	917	893	344	42	542	3528	3.7	3.6	14.1

Three-point field goals: 1997-98, 17-for-84 (.202). 1998-99, 21-for-69 (.304). 1999-00, 55-for-178 (.309). 2000-01, 101-for-253 (.399). Totals, 194-for-584 (.332).

Personal fouls/disqualifications: 1997-98, 136/0. 1998-99, 73/0. 1999-00, 149/2. 2000-01, 188/1. Totals, 546/3.

NBA PLAYOFF RECORD

Season Team	G	Min.	FGM	FGA	Pct.	FTM	FTA	Pct.	REBOUNDS			Ast.	St.	Blk.	TO	Pts.	AVERAGES		
									Off.	Def.	Tot.						RPG	APG	PPG
97-98—Cleveland	4	103	10	22	.455	23	26	.885	0	9	9	11	5	1	12	43	2.3	2.8	10.8
00-01—San Antonio	7	194	16	61	.262	16	21	.762	3	16	19	17	3	0	15	54	2.7	2.4	7.7
Totals	11	297	26	83	.313	39	47	.830	3	25	28	28	8	1	27	97	2.5	2.5	8.8

Three-point field goals: 2000-01, 6-for-22 (.273). Totals, 6-for-22 (.273).
Personal fouls/disqualifications: 1997-98, 10/0. 2000-01, 10/0. Totals, 20/0.

ANDERSON, KENNY   G   CELTICS

PERSONAL: Born October 9, 1970, in Queens, N.Y. ... 6-1/168. (1,85/76,2). ... Full Name: Kenneth Anderson.
HIGH SCHOOL: Archbishop Molloy (Queens, N.Y.).
COLLEGE: Georgia Tech.
TRANSACTIONS/CAREER NOTES: Selected after sophomore season by New Jersey Nets in first round (second pick overall) of 1991 NBA Draft. ... Traded by Nets with G/F Gerald Glass to Charlotte Hornets for G Kendall Gill and G Khalid Reeves (January 19, 1996). ... Signed as free agent by Portland Trail Blazers (July 23, 1996). ... Traded by Trail Blazers with G Alvin Williams, F Gary Trent and two first-round draft choices to Toronto Raptors for G Damon Stoudamire, F Walt Williams and F Carlos Rogers (February 13, 1998). ... Traded by Raptors with C Zan Tabak and F Popeye Jones to Boston Celtics for G Chauncey Billups, G Dee Brown, F John Thomas and F Roy Rogers (February 18, 1998).
MISCELLANEOUS: Member of bronze-medal-winning U.S. World Championship team (1990). ... New Jersey Nets franchise all-time assists leader with 2,363 (1991-92 through 1995-96).

COLLEGIATE RECORD

NOTES: The Sporting News All-America second team (1990, 1991).

Season Team	G	Min.	FGM	FGA	Pct.	FTM	FTA	Pct.	Reb.	Ast.	Pts.	AVERAGES		
												RPG	APG	PPG
89-90—Georgia Tech	35	1321	283	549	.515	107	146	.733	193	285	721	5.5	8.1	20.6
90-91—Georgia Tech	30	1167	278	636	.437	155	187	.829	171	169	776	5.7	5.6	25.9
Totals	65	2488	561	1185	.473	262	333	.787	364	454	1497	5.6	7.0	23.0

Three-point field goals: 1989-90, 48-for-117 (.410). 1990-91, 65-for-185 (.351). Totals, 113-for-302 (.374).

NBA REGULAR-SEASON RECORD

Season Team	G	Min.	FGM	FGA	Pct.	FTM	FTA	Pct.	REBOUNDS			Ast.	St.	Blk.	TO	Pts.	AVERAGES		
									Off.	Def.	Tot.						RPG	APG	PPG
91-92—New Jersey	64	1086	187	480	.390	73	98	.745	38	89	127	203	67	9	97	450	2.0	3.2	7.0
92-93—New Jersey	55	2010	370	850	.435	180	232	.776	51	175	226	449	96	11	153	927	4.1	8.2	16.9
93-94—New Jersey	82	3135	576	1381	.417	346	423	.818	89	233	322	784	158	15	266	1538	3.9	9.6	18.8
94-95—New Jersey	72	2689	411	1031	.399	348	414	.841	73	177	250	680	103	14	225	1267	3.5	9.4	17.6
95-96—N.J.-Char.	69	2344	349	834	.418	260	338	.769	63	140	203	575	111	14	146	1050	2.9	8.3	15.2
96-97—Portland	82	3081	485	1137	.427	334	435	.768	91	272	363	584	162	15	193	1436	4.4	7.1	17.5
97-98—Port.-Boston	61	1858	268	674	.398	153	194	.789	39	134	173	345	87	1	143	746	2.8	5.7	12.2
98-99—Boston	34	1010	161	357	.451	84	101	.832	24	79	103	193	33	2	71	412	3.0	5.7	12.1
99-00—Boston	82	2593	434	986	.440	196	253	.775	55	170	225	420	139	8	130	1149	2.7	5.1	14.0
00-01—Boston	33	849	88	227	.388	59	71	.831	16	57	73	134	44	2	52	246	2.2	4.1	7.5
Totals	634	20655	3329	7957	.418	2033	2559	.794	539	1526	2065	4367	1000	91	1476	9221	3.3	6.9	14.5

Three-point field goals: 1991-92, 3-for-13 (.231). 1992-93, 7-for-25 (.280). 1993-94, 40-for-132 (.303). 1994-95, 97-for-294 (.330). 1995-96, 92-for-256 (.359). 1996-97, 132-for-366 (.361). 1997-98, 57-for-160 (.356). 1998-99, 6-for-24 (.250). 1999-00, 85-for-220 (.386). 2000-01, 11-for-33 (.333). Totals, 530-for-1523 (.348).

Personal fouls/disqualifications: 1991-92, 68/0. 1992-93, 140/1. 1993-94, 201/0. 1994-95, 184/1. 1995-96, 178/1. 1996-97, 222/2. 1997-98, 135/1. 1998-99, 78/1. 1999-00, 230/4. 2000-01, 62/0. Totals, 1498/11.

NBA PLAYOFF RECORD

Season Team	G	Min.	FGM	FGA	Pct.	FTM	FTA	Pct.	REBOUNDS Off.	Def.	Tot.	Ast.	St.	Blk.	TO	Pts.	RPG	APG	PPG
91-92—New Jersey.....	3	24	3	9	.333	2	2	1.000	1	2	3	3	1	0	1	8	1.0	1.0	2.7
93-94—New Jersey.....	4	181	19	54	.352	22	33	.667	2	10	12	27	9	0	9	63	3.0	6.8	15.8
96-97—Portland..........	4	169	22	46	.478	19	20	.950	2	15	17	19	7	1	11	68	4.3	4.8	17.0
Totals...................	11	374	44	109	.404	43	55	.782	5	27	32	49	17	1	21	139	2.9	4.5	12.6

Three-point field goals: 1993-94, 3-for-10 (.300). 1996-97, 5-for-19 (.263). Totals, 8-for-29 (.276).
Personal fouls/disqualifications: 1991-92, 1/0. 1993-94, 11/0. 1996-97, 10/0. Totals, 22/0.

NBA ALL-STAR GAME RECORD

Season Team	Min.	FGM	FGA	Pct.	FTM	FTA	Pct.	REBOUNDS Off.	Def.	Tot.	Ast.	PF	Dq.	St.	Blk.	TO	Pts.
1994 —New Jersey........	16	3	10	.300	0	0	...	1	3	4	3	2	0	0	0	4	6

Three-point field goals: 1994, 0-for-1.

ANDERSON, NICK   G/F   GRIZZLIES

PERSONAL: Born January 20, 1968, in Chicago.... 6-6/228. (1,98/103,4).... Full Name: Nelson Anderson.
HIGH SCHOOL: Prosser Vocational (Chicago), then Neal F. Simeon (Chicago).
COLLEGE: Illinois.
TRANSACTIONS/CAREER NOTES: Selected after junior season by Orlando Magic in first round (11th pick overall) of 1989 NBA Draft.... Traded by Magic to Sacramento Kings for G/F Tariq Abdul-Wahad and future first-round draft choice (August 3, 1999).... Traded by Kings with G Jason Williams to Vancouver Grizzlies for G Mike Bibby and G Brent Price (June 27, 2001).... Grizzlies franchise moved to Memphis for 2001-02 season.
MISCELLANEOUS: Orlando Magic all-time leading scorer with 10,650 points and all-time steals leader with 1,004 (1989-90 through 1998-99).

COLLEGIATE RECORD

Season Team	G	Min.	FGM	FGA	Pct.	FTM	FTA	Pct.	Reb.	Ast.	Pts.	AVERAGES RPG	APG	PPG
86-87—Illinois						Did not play—ineligible.								
87-88—Illinois	33	909	223	390	.572	77	120	.642	217	53	525	6.6	1.6	15.9
88-89—Illinois	36	1125	262	487	.538	99	148	.669	285	72	647	7.9	2.0	18.0
Totals	69	2034	485	877	.553	176	268	.657	502	125	1172	7.3	1.8	17.0

Three-point field goals: 1987-88, 2-for-6 (.333). 1988-89, 24-for-66 (.364). Totals, 26-for-72 (.361).

NBA REGULAR-SEASON RECORD

Season Team	G	Min.	FGM	FGA	Pct.	FTM	FTA	Pct.	REBOUNDS Off.	Def.	Tot.	Ast.	St.	Blk.	TO	Pts.	RPG	APG	PPG
89-90—Orlando..........	81	1785	372	753	.494	186	264	.705	107	209	316	124	69	34	138	931	3.9	1.5	11.5
90-91—Orlando..........	70	1971	400	857	.467	173	259	.668	92	294	386	106	74	44	113	990	5.5	1.5	14.1
91-92—Orlando..........	60	2203	482	1042	.463	202	303	.667	98	286	384	163	97	33	125	1196	6.4	2.7	19.9
92-93—Orlando..........	79	2920	594	1324	.449	298	402	.741	122	355	477	265	128	56	164	1574	6.0	3.4	19.9
93-94—Orlando..........	81	2811	504	1054	.478	168	250	.672	113	363	476	294	134	33	165	1277	5.9	3.6	15.8
94-95—Orlando..........	76	2588	439	923	.476	143	203	.704	85	250	335	314	125	22	141	1200	4.4	4.1	15.8
95-96—Orlando..........	77	2717	400	904	.442	166	240	.692	92	323	415	279	121	46	141	1134	5.4	3.6	14.7
96-97—Orlando..........	63	2163	288	725	.397	38	94	.404	66	238	304	182	120	32	86	757	4.8	2.9	12.0
97-98—Orlando..........	58	1701	343	754	.455	127	199	.638	98	199	297	119	72	23	85	890	5.1	·2.1	15.3
98-99—Orlando..........	47	1581	253	640	.395	99	162	.611	51	226	277	91	64	15	83	701	5.9	1.9	14.9
99-00—Sacramento	72	2094	306	782	.391	37	76	.487	83	256	339	123	94	16	95	781	4.7	1.7	10.8
00-01—Sacramento	21	169	14	57	.246	0	0	...	3	22	25	13	10	4	7	38	1.2	0.6	1.8
Totals	785	24703	4395	9815	.448	1637	2452	.668	1100	3021	4031	2073	1108	358	1343	11469	5.1	2.6	14.6

Three-point field goals: 1989-90, 1-for-17 (.059). 1990-91, 17-for-58 (.293). 1991-92, 30-for-85 (.353). 1992-93, 88-for-249 (.353). 1993-94, 101-for-314 (.322). 1994-95, 179-for-431 (.415). 1995-96, 168-for-430 (.391). 1996-97, 143-for-405 (.353). 1997-98, 77-for-214 (.360). 1998-99, 96-for-277 (.347). 1999-00, 132-for-397 (.332). 2000-01, 10-for-39 (.256). Totals, 1042-for-2916 (.357).
Personal fouls/disqualifications: 1989-90, 140/0. 1990-91, 145/0. 1991-92, 132/0. 1992-93, 200/1. 1993-94, 148/1. 1994-95, 124/0. 1995-96, 135/0. 1996-97, 160/1. 1997-98, 98/1. 1998-99, 72/0. 1999-00, 118/0. 2000-01, 13/0. Totals, 1485/4.

NBA PLAYOFF RECORD

NOTES: Holds NBA Finals single-game record for most three-point field goals attempted—12 (June 11, 1995, at Houston).

Season Team	G	Min.	FGM	FGA	Pct.	FTM	FTA	Pct.	REBOUNDS Off.	Def.	Tot.	Ast.	St.	Blk.	TO	Pts.	RPG	APG	PPG
93-94—Orlando..........	3	120	13	34	.382	9	12	.750	2	8	10	10	5	2	5	43	3.3	3.3	14.3
94-95—Orlando..........	21	814	107	239	.448	43	63	.683	21	79	100	65	33	10	30	298	4.8	3.1	14.2
95-96—Orlando..........	11	418	55	127	.433	28	45	.622	16	39	55	21	21	5	21	156	5.0	1.9	14.2
96-97—Orlando..........	5	130	12	36	.333	0	2	.000	3	26	29	3	3	9	6	28	5.8	0.6	5.6
98-99—Orlando..........	4	152	29	79	.367	14	19	.737	7	20	27	9	9	0	10	83	6.8	2.3	20.8
99-00—Sacramento	5	132	11	34	.324	7	8	.875	4	13	17	2	1	3	4	36	3.4	0.4	7.2
Totals	49	1766	227	549	.413	101	149	.678	53	185	238	110	72	29	76	644	4.9	2.2	13.1

Three-point field goals: 1993-94, 8-for-20 (.400). 1994-95, 41-for-107 (.383). 1995-96, 18-for-63 (.286). 1996-97, 4-for-15 (.267). 1998-99, 11-for-42 (.262). 1999-00, 7-for-20 (.350). Totals, 89-for-267 (.333).
Personal fouls/disqualifications: 1993-94, 8/0. 1994-95, 49/0. 1995-96, 22/0. 1996-97, 8/0. 1998-99, 12/1. 1999-00, 9/0. Totals, 108/1.

DID YOU KNOW . . .

. . . that Kareem Abdul-Jabbar's original first name was Ferdinand? He was born

Ferdinand Lewis Alcindor in 1947.

ANDERSON, SHANDON F KNICKS

PERSONAL: Born December 31, 1973, in Atlanta. ... 6-6/210. (1,98/95,3). ... Full Name: Shandon Rodriguez Anderson. ... Brother of Willie Anderson, guard/forward with San Antonio Spurs (1988-89 through 1994-95), Toronto Raptors (1995-96), New York Knicks (1995-96) and Miami Heat (1996-97).
HIGH SCHOOL: Crim (Atlanta).
COLLEGE: Georgia.
TRANSACTIONS/CAREER NOTES: Selected by Utah Jazz in second round (54th pick overall) of 1996 NBA Draft. ... Signed as free agent by Houston Rockets (September 29, 1999). ... Traded by Rockets to New York Knicks as part of three-team trade in which Knicks acquired G Howard Eisley from Mavericks, Mavericks acquired G Muggsy Bogues from Knicks and Rockets acquired F Glen Rice from Knicks and draft rights to G Kyle Hill from Mavericks (August 10, 2001).

COLLEGIATE RECORD

Season Team	G	Min.	FGM	FGA	Pct.	FTM	FTA	Pct.	Reb.	Ast.	Pts.	RPG	APG	PPG
92-93—Georgia	29	554	99	201	.493	64	105	.610	103	44	271	3.6	1.5	9.3
93-94—Georgia	30	859	157	324	.485	93	141	.660	168	114	413	5.6	3.8	13.8
94-95—Georgia	28	827	149	315	.473	59	95	.621	145	83	371	5.2	3.0	13.3
95-96—Georgia	31	891	176	327	.538	94	143	.657	171	83	462	5.5	2.7	14.9
Totals	118	3131	581	1167	.498	310	484	.640	587	324	1517	5.0	2.7	12.9

Three-point field goals: 1992-93, 9-for-26 (.346). 1993-94, 6-for-34 (.176). 1994-95, 17-for-53 (.321). 1995-96, 16-for-52 (.308). Totals, 48-for-165 (.291).

NBA REGULAR-SEASON RECORD

Season Team	G	Min.	FGM	FGA	Pct.	FTM	FTA	Pct.	REBOUNDS Off.	Def.	Tot.	Ast.	St.	Blk.	TO	Pts.	RPG	APG	PPG
96-97—Utah	65	1066	147	318	.462	68	99	.687	52	127	179	49	27	8	73	386	2.8	0.8	5.9
97-98—Utah	82	1602	269	500	.538	136	185	.735	86	141	227	89	66	18	92	681	2.8	1.1	8.3
98-99—Utah	50	1072	162	363	.446	89	125	.712	49	83	132	56	39	10	66	427	2.6	1.1	8.5
99-00—Houston	82	2700	368	778	.473	194	253	.767	91	293	384	239	96	32	194	1009	4.7	2.9	12.3
00-01—Houston	82	2396	263	590	.446	138	188	.734	72	261	333	189	82	40	131	710	4.1	2.3	8.7
Totals	361	8836	1209	2549	.474	625	850	.735	350	905	1255	622	310	108	556	3213	3.5	1.7	8.9

Three-point field goals: 1996-97, 24-for-47 (.511). 1997-98, 7-for-32 (.219). 1998-99, 14-for-41 (.341). 1999-00, 79-for-225 (.351). 2000-01, 46-for-170 (.271). Totals, 170-for-515 (.330).
Personal fouls/disqualifications: 1996-97, 113/0. 1997-98, 145/0. 1998-99, 89/0. 1999-00, 182/0. 2000-01, 202/0. Totals, 731/0.

NBA PLAYOFF RECORD

Season Team	G	Min.	FGM	FGA	Pct.	FTM	FTA	Pct.	REBOUNDS Off.	Def.	Tot.	Ast.	St.	Blk.	TO	Pts.	RPG	APG	PPG
96-97—Utah	18	296	29	66	.439	20	28	.714	20	28	48	13	11	1	13	83	2.7	0.7	4.6
97-98—Utah	20	378	53	103	.515	25	37	.676	26	37	63	19	5	1	30	134	3.2	1.0	6.7
98-99—Utah	11	297	37	77	.481	24	34	.706	8	33	41	13	6	3	14	104	3.7	1.2	9.5
Totals	49	971	119	246	.484	69	99	.697	54	98	152	45	22	5	57	321	3.1	0.9	6.6

Three-point field goals: 1996-97, 5-for-12 (.417). 1997-98, 3-for-11 (.273). 1998-99, 6-for-14 (.429). Totals, 14-for-37 (.378).
Personal fouls/disqualifications: 1996-97, 28/0. 1997-98, 30/0. 1998-99, 34/2. Totals, 92/2.

ANTHONY, GREG G BULLS

PERSONAL: Born November 15, 1967, in Las Vegas. ... 6-1/180. (1,85/81,6). ... Full Name: Gregory C. Anthony.
HIGH SCHOOL: Rancho (North Las Vegas).
COLLEGE: Portland, then UNLV.
TRANSACTIONS/CAREER NOTES: Selected by New York Knicks in first round (12th pick overall) of 1991 NBA Draft. ... Selected by Vancouver Grizzlies from Knicks in NBA Expansion Draft (June 24, 1995). ... Signed as free agent by Seattle SuperSonics (October 9, 1997). ... Rights renounced by SuperSonics (January 22, 1999). ... Signed as free agent by Portland Trail Blazers (January 22, 1999). ... Traded by Trail Blazers to Chicago Bulls for future second-round draft choice (July 20, 2001).

COLLEGIATE RECORD

NOTES: Member of NCAA Division I championship team (1990).

Season Team	G	Min.	FGM	FGA	Pct.	FTM	FTA	Pct.	Reb.	Ast.	Pts.	RPG	APG	PPG
86-87—Portland	28	923	147	369	.398	100	144	.694	121	112	429	4.3	4.0	15.3
87-88—UNLV					Did not play—transfer student.									
88-89—UNLV	36	1025	155	350	.443	107	153	.699	102	239	464	2.8	6.6	12.9
89-90—UNLV	39	1160	145	317	.457	101	148	.682	116	289	436	3.0	7.4	11.2
90-91—UNLV	35	1100	141	309	.456	79	102	.775	89	310	406	2.5	8.9	11.6
Totals	138	4208	588	1345	.437	387	547	.707	428	950	1735	3.1	6.9	12.6

Three-point field goals: 1986-87, 35-for-95 (.368). 1988-89, 47-for-125 (.376). 1989-90, 45-for-120 (.375). 1990-91, 45-for-114 (.395). Totals, 172-for-454 (.379).

NBA REGULAR-SEASON RECORD

Season Team	G	Min.	FGM	FGA	Pct.	FTM	FTA	Pct.	REBOUNDS Off.	Def.	Tot.	Ast.	St.	Blk.	TO	Pts.	RPG	APG	PPG
91-92—New York	82	1510	161	435	.370	117	158	.741	33	103	136	314	59	9	98	447	1.7	3.8	5.5
92-93—New York	70	1699	174	419	.415	107	159	.673	42	128	170	398	113	12	104	459	2.4	5.7	6.6
93-94—New York	80	1994	225	571	.394	130	168	.774	43	146	189	365	114	13	127	628	2.4	4.6	7.9
94-95—New York	61	943	128	293	.437	60	76	.789	7	57	64	160	50	7	57	372	1.0	2.6	6.1
95-96—Vancouver	69	2096	324	781	.415	229	297	.771	29	145	174	476	116	11	160	967	2.5	6.9	14.0
96-97—Vancouver	65	1863	199	507	.393	130	178	.730	25	159	184	407	129	4	129	616	2.8	6.3	9.5

Season Team	G	Min.	FGM	FGA	Pct.	FTM	FTA	Pct.	Off.	Def.	Tot.	Ast.	St.	Blk.	TO	Pts.	RPG	APG	PPG
97-98—Seattle	80	1021	150	349	.430	53	80	.663	18	93	111	205	64	3	91	419	1.4	2.6	5.2
98-99—Portland	50	806	104	251	.414	62	89	.697	14	49	63	100	66	3	55	319	1.3	2.0	6.4
99-00—Portland	82	1548	169	416	.406	88	114	.772	17	116	133	208	59	9	85	514	1.6	2.5	6.3
00-01—Portland	58	856	97	253	.383	23	35	.657	21	40	61	82	40	3	43	282	1.1	1.4	4.9
Totals	697	14336	1731	4275	.405	999	1354	.738	249	1036	1285	2715	810	74	949	5023	1.8	3.9	7.2

Three-point field goals: 1991-92, 8-for-55 (.145). 1992-93, 4-for-30 (.133). 1993-94, 48-for-160 (.300). 1994-95, 56-for-155 (.361). 1995-96, 90-for-271 (.332). 1996-97, 88-for-238 (.370). 1997-98, 66-for-159 (.415). 1998-99, 49-for-125 (.392). 1999-00, 88-for-233 (.378). 2000-01, 65-for-159 (.409). Totals, 562-for-1585 (.355).

Personal fouls/disqualifications: 1991-92, 170/0. 1992-93, 141/0. 1993-94, 163/1. 1994-95, 99/1. 1995-96, 137/1. 1996-97, 122/0. 1997-98, 97/0. 1998-99, 75/0. 1999-00, 143/0. 2000-01, 63/0. Totals, 1210/3.

NBA PLAYOFF RECORD

Season Team	G	Min.	FGM	FGA	Pct.	FTM	FTA	Pct.	Off.	Def.	Tot.	Ast.	St.	Blk.	TO	Pts.	RPG	APG	PPG
91-92—New York	12	213	19	46	.413	20	33	.606	4	13	17	41	16	1	13	63	1.4	3.4	5.3
92-93—New York	15	240	24	60	.400	8	14	.571	4	26	30	52	13	1	11	59	2.0	3.5	3.9
93-94—New York	25	436	45	128	.352	14	24	.583	9	18	27	59	19	8	31	122	1.1	2.4	4.9
94-95—New York	11	135	15	38	.395	10	11	.909	2	8	10	15	2	2	6	47	0.9	1.4	4.3
97-98—Seattle	9	118	12	40	.300	3	8	.375	3	7	10	10	5	1	11	32	1.1	1.1	3.6
98-99—Portland	13	225	18	55	.327	23	34	.676	4	10	14	32	13	1	9	67	1.1	2.5	5.2
99-00—Portland	15	213	19	52	.365	12	16	.750	2	14	16	25	13	4	12	60	1.1	1.7	4.0
00-01—Portland	2	17	2	6	.333	0	0	...	0	0	0	0	1	0	1	5	0.0	0.0	2.5
Totals	102	1597	154	425	.362	90	140	.643	28	96	124	234	82	18	94	455	1.2	2.3	4.5

Three-point field goals: 1991-92, 5-for-12 (.417). 1992-93, 3-for-14 (.214). 1993-94, 18-for-61 (.295). 1994-95, 7-for-23 (.304). 1997-98, 5-for-19 (.263). 1998-99, 8-for-31 (.258). 1999-00, 10-for-31 (.323). 2000-01, 1-for-3 (.333). Totals, 57-for-194 (.294).

Personal fouls/disqualifications: 1991-92, 28/0. 1992-93, 26/0. 1993-94, 55/0. 1994-95, 27/0. 1997-98, 17/1. 1998-99, 25/0. 1999-00, 27/0. 2000-01, 2/0. Totals, 207/1.

ARMSTRONG, DARRELL   G   MAGIC

PERSONAL: Born June 22, 1968, in Gastonia, N.C. ... 6-1/180. (1,85/81,6).
HIGH SCHOOL: Ashbrook (Gastonia, N.C.).
COLLEGE: Fayetteville State.
TRANSACTIONS/CAREER NOTES: Not drafted by an NBA franchise. ... Played in Global Basketball Association with South Georgia (1991-92 and 1992-93). ... Played in United States Basketball League with Atlanta Trojans (1992 through 1994). ... Played in Continental Basketball Association with Capital Region Pontiacs (1992-93). ... Played in Cyprus (1993-94). ... Played in Spain (1994-95). ... Signed as free agent by Orlando Magic (April 8, 1995).

COLLEGIATE RECORD

Season Team	G	Min.	FGM	FGA	Pct.	FTM	FTA	Pct.	Reb.	Ast.	Pts.	RPG	APG	PPG
87-88—Fayetteville State							Did not play.							
88-89—Fayetteville State	27	662	131	255	.514	93	116	.802	80	58	369	3.0	2.1	13.7
89-90—Fayetteville State	27	800	125	235	.532	83	106	.783	140	125	350	5.2	4.6	13.0
90-91—Fayetteville State	24	643	117	233	.502	115	152	.757	86	113	393	3.6	4.7	16.4
Totals	78	2105	373	723	.516	291	374	.778	306	296	1112	3.9	3.8	14.3

Three-point field goals: 1988-89, 14-for-40 (.350). 1989-90, 17-for-40 (.425). 1990-91, 44-for-107 (.411). Totals, 75-for-187 (.401).

CBA REGULAR-SEASON RECORD

Season Team	G	Min.	FGM	FGA	Pct.	FTM	FTA	Pct.	Reb.	Ast.	Pts.	RPG	APG	PPG
92-93—Capital Region	2	13	1	3	.333	0	0	...	1	1	2	0.5	0.5	1.0

Three-point field goals: 1992-93, 0-for-2.

NBA REGULAR-SEASON RECORD

HONORS: NBA Sixth Man Award (1999). ... NBA Most Improved Player (1999).

Season Team	G	Min.	FGM	FGA	Pct.	FTM	FTA	Pct.	Off.	Def.	Tot.	Ast.	St.	Blk.	TO	Pts.	RPG	APG	PPG
94-95—Orlando	3	8	3	8	.375	2	2	1.000	1	0	1	3	1	0	1	10	0.3	1.0	3.3
95-96—Orlando	13	41	16	32	.500	4	4	1.000	0	2	2	5	6	0	6	42	0.2	0.4	3.2
96-97—Orlando	67	1010	132	345	.383	92	106	.868	35	41	76	175	61	9	99	411	1.1	2.6	6.1
97-98—Orlando	48	1236	156	380	.411	105	123	.854	65	94	159	236	58	5	112	442	3.3	4.9	9.2
98-99—Orlando	50	1502	230	522	.441	161	178	.904	53	127	180	335	108	4	158	690	3.6	6.7	13.8
99-00—Orlando	82	2590	484	1119	.433	225	247	.911	65	205	270	501	169	9	248	1330	3.3	6.1	16.2
00-01—Orlando	75	2767	413	1002	.412	220	249	.884	94	249	343	524	135	13	200	1189	4.6	7.0	15.9
Totals	338	9154	1434	3408	.421	809	909	.890	313	718	1031	1779	538	40	824	4114	3.1	5.3	12.2

Three-point field goals: 1994-95, 2-for-6 (.333). 1995-96, 6-for-12 (.500). 1996-97, 55-for-181 (.304). 1997-98, 25-for-68 (.368). 1998-99, 69-for-189 (.365). 1999-00, 137-for-403 (.340). 2000-01, 143-for-403 (.355). Totals, 437-for-1262 (.346).

Personal fouls/disqualifications: 1994-95, 3/0. 1995-96, 4/0. 1996-97, 114/1. 1997-98, 96/1. 1998-99, 90/0. 1999-00, 137/0. 2000-01, 155/2. Totals, 599/4.

NBA PLAYOFF RECORD

Season Team	G	Min.	FGM	FGA	Pct.	FTM	FTA	Pct.	Off.	Def.	Tot.	Ast.	St.	Blk.	TO	Pts.	RPG	APG	PPG
96-97—Orlando	5	143	20	42	.476	11	13	.846	3	18	21	17	8	1	7	57	4.2	3.4	11.4
98-99—Orlando	4	163	17	46	.370	16	16	1.000	6	14	20	25	9	0	25	59	5.0	6.3	14.8
00-01—Orlando	4	167	17	45	.378	12	13	.923	5	17	22	19	8	2	11	53	5.5	4.8	13.3
Totals	13	473	54	133	.406	39	42	.929	14	49	63	61	25	3	43	169	4.8	4.7	13.0

Three-point field goals: 1996-97, 6-for-18 (.333). 1998-99, 9-for-24 (.375). 2000-01, 7-for-19 (.368). Totals, 22-for-61 (.361).
Personal fouls/disqualifications: 1996-97, 6/0. 1998-99, 16/1. 2000-01, 10/0. Totals, 32/1.

Season Team	G	Min.	FGM	FGA	Pct.	FTM	FTA	Pct.	Reb.	Ast.	Pts.	RPG	APG	PPG
94-95—Coren Orense	38	1481	309	631	.490	176	293	.601	170	94	936	4.5	2.5	24.6

Three-point field goals: 1994-95, 142-for-338 (.420).

ARTEST, RON — G/F — BULLS

PERSONAL: Born November 13, 1979, in Queensbridge, N.Y. ... 6-7/247. (2,01/112,0). ... Full Name: Ronald William Artest.
HIGH SCHOOL: La Salle Academy (New York, N.Y.).
COLLEGE: St. John's.
TRANSACTIONS/CAREER NOTES: Selected after sophomore season by Chicago Bulls in first round (16th pick overall) of 1999 NBA Draft.

COLLEGIATE RECORD

Season Team	G	Min.	FGM	FGA	Pct.	FTM	FTA	Pct.	Reb.	Ast.	Pts.	RPG	APG	PPG
97-98—St. John's	32	870	139	335	.415	60	114	.526	201	62	372	6.3	1.9	11.6
98-99—St. John's	37	1265	196	418	.469	85	132	.644	232	156	535	6.3	4.2	14.5
Totals	69	2135	335	753	.445	145	246	.589	433	218	907	6.3	3.2	13.1

Three-point field goals: 1997-98, 34-for-104 (.327). 1998-99, 58-for-155 (.374). Totals, 92-for-259 (.355).

NBA REGULAR-SEASON RECORD

HONORS: NBA All-Rookie second team (2000).

Season Team	G	Min.	FGM	FGA	Pct.	FTM	FTA	Pct.	REBOUNDS Off.	Def.	Tot.	Ast.	St.	Blk.	TO	Pts.	RPG	APG	PPG
99-00—Chicago	72	2238	309	759	.407	188	279	.674	62	246	308	202	119	39	166	866	4.3	2.8	12.0
00-01—Chicago	76	2363	327	815	.401	210	280	.750	59	235	294	228	152	45	159	907	3.9	3.0	11.9
Totals	148	4601	636	1574	.404	398	559	.712	121	481	602	430	271	84	325	1773	4.1	2.9	12.0

Three-point field goals: 1999-00, 60-for-191 (.314). 2000-01, 43-for-148 (.291). Totals, 103-for-339 (.304).
Personal fouls/disqualifications: 1999-00, 159/0. 2000-01, 254/7. Totals, 413/7.

ATKINS, CHUCKY — G — PISTONS

PERSONAL: Born August 14, 1974, in Orlando, Fla. ... 5-11/160. (1,80/72,6). ... Full Name: Kenneth Lavon Atkins.
HIGH SCHOOL: Evans (Orlando, Fla.).
COLLEGE: South Florida.
TRANSACTIONS/CAREER NOTES: Not drafted by an NBA franchise. ... Played in Continental Basketball Association with LaCrosse Catbirds (1996-97). ... Played in Croatia (1997-98 and 1998-99). ... Signed as free agent by Orlando Magic (September 20, 1999). ... Traded by Magic with F Ben Wallace to Detroit Pistons for F Grant Hill (August 3, 2000).

COLLEGIATE RECORD

Season Team	G	Min.	FGM	FGA	Pct.	FTM	FTA	Pct.	Reb.	Ast.	Pts.	RPG	APG	PPG
92-93—South Florida.................	27	867	94	221	.425	46	72	.639	93	108	275	3.4	4.0	10.2
93-94—South Florida.................	26	787	96	269	.357	70	94	.745	62	105	299	2.4	4.0	11.5
94-95—South Florida.................	30	1067	161	389	.414	98	131	.748	96	196	504	3.2	6.5	16.8
95-96—South Florida.................	28	1064	175	405	.432	109	141	.773	85	111	541	3.0	4.0	19.3
Totals	111	3785	526	1284	.410	323	438	.737	336	520	1619	3.0	4.7	14.6

Three-point field goals: 1992-93, 41-for-101 (.406). 1993-94, 37-for-134 (.276). 1994-95, 84-for-219 (.384). 1995-96, 82-for-220 (.373). Totals, 244-for-674 (.362).

CBA REGULAR-SEASON RECORD

NOTES: CBA All-Rookie first team (1997).

Season Team	G	Min.	FGM	FGA	Pct.	FTM	FTA	Pct.	Reb.	Ast.	Pts.	RPG	APG	PPG
96-97—La Crosse	50	1907	288	644	.447	148	189	.783	139	375	812	2.8	7.5	16.2

Three-point field goals: 1996-97, 88-for-240 (.367).

CROATIAN LEAGUE RECORD

Season Team	G	Min.	FGM	FGA	Pct.	FTM	FTA	Pct.	Reb.	Ast.	Pts.	RPG	APG	PPG
97-98—Cibona Zagreb	26	603	108	190	.568	76	98	.776	98	97	318	3.8	3.7	12.2
98-99—Cibona Zagreb	20	512	84	145	.579	40	56	.714	24	49	225	1.2	2.5	11.3
Totals	46	1115	192	335	.573	116	154	.753	122	146	543	2.7	3.2	11.8

Three-point field goals: 1997-98, 26-for-59 (.441). 1998-99, 17-for-48 (.354). Totals, 43-for-107 (.402).

NBA REGULAR-SEASON RECORD

HONORS: NBA All-Rookie second team (2000).

Season Team	G	Min.	FGM	FGA	Pct.	FTM	FTA	Pct.	REBOUNDS Off.	Def.	Tot.	Ast.	St.	Blk.	TO	Pts.	RPG	APG	PPG
99-00—Orlando..........	82	1626	314	741	.424	97	133	.729	20	106	126	306	52	3	142	782	1.5	3.7	9.5
00-01—Detroit	81	2363	380	952	.399	90	130	.692	28	145	173	330	67	5	149	971	2.1	4.1	12.0
Totals	163	3989	694	1693	.410	187	263	.711	48	251	299	636	119	8	291	1753	1.8	3.9	10.8

Three-point field goals: 1999-00, 57-for-163 (.350). 2000-01, 121-for-339 (.357). Totals, 178-for-502 (.355).
Personal fouls/disqualifications: 1999-00, 137/1. 2000-01, 184/2. Totals, 321/3.

AUGMON, STACEY   F   HORNETS

PERSONAL: Born August 1, 1968, in Pasadena, Calif. ... 6-8/205. (2,03/93,0). ... Full Name: Stacey Orlando Augmon. ... Name pronounced AWG-men.
HIGH SCHOOL: John Muir (Pasadena, Calif.).
COLLEGE: UNLV.
TRANSACTIONS/CAREER NOTES: Selected by Atlanta Hawks in first round (ninth pick overall) of 1991 NBA Draft. ... Traded by Hawks with F Grant Long to Detroit Pistons for three conditional draft choices (July 15, 1996). ... Traded by Pistons to Portland Trail Blazers for G Aaron McKie, G Randolph Childress and G Reggie Jordan (January 24, 1997). ... Traded by Trail Blazers with C Kelvin Cato, G/F Walt Williams, G Brian Shaw, G Ed Gray and F/C Carlos Rogers to Houston Rockets for F Scottie Pippen (October 2, 1999). ... Waived by Rockets (October 12, 1999). ... Signed as free agent by Trail Blazers (October 18, 1999). ... Signed as free agent by Charlotte Hornets (July 25, 2001).
MISCELLANEOUS: Member of bronze-medal-winning U.S. Olympic team (1988).

COLLEGIATE RECORD

NOTES: THE SPORTING NEWS All-America first team (1991). ... Member of NCAA Division I championship team (1990).

Season Team	G	Min.	FGM	FGA	Pct.	FTM	FTA	Pct.	Reb.	Ast.	Pts.	RPG	APG	PPG
86-87—UNLV						Did not play—ineligible.								
87-88—UNLV	34	884	117	204	.574	75	116	.647	206	64	311	6.1	1.9	9.1
88-89—UNLV	37	1091	210	405	.519	106	160	.663	274	101	567	7.4	2.7	15.3
89-90—UNLV	39	1246	210	380	.553	118	176	.670	270	143	554	6.9	3.7	14.2
90-91—UNLV	35	1062	220	375	.587	101	139	.727	255	125	579	7.3	3.6	16.5
Totals	145	4283	757	1364	.555	400	591	.677	1005	433	2011	6.9	3.0	13.9

Three-point field goals: 1987-88, 2-for-2. 1988-89, 41-for-98 (.418). 1989-90, 16-for-50 (.320). 1990-91, 38-for-81 (.469). Totals, 97-for-231 (.420).

NBA REGULAR-SEASON RECORD

HONORS: NBA All-Rookie first team (1992).

Season Team	G	Min.	FGM	FGA	Pct.	FTM	FTA	Pct.	REBOUNDS Off.	Def.	Tot.	Ast.	St.	Blk.	TO	Pts.	RPG	APG	PPG
91-92—Atlanta	82	2505	440	899	.489	213	320	.666	191	229	420	201	124	27	181	1094	5.1	2.5	13.3
92-93—Atlanta	73	2112	397	792	.501	227	307	.739	141	146	287	170	91	18	157	1021	3.9	2.3	14.0
93-94—Atlanta	82	2605	439	861	.510	333	436	.764	178	216	394	187	149	45	147	1212	4.8	2.3	14.8
94-95—Atlanta	76	2362	397	876	.453	252	346	.728	157	211	368	197	100	47	152	1053	4.8	2.6	13.9
95-96—Atlanta	77	2294	362	738	.491	251	317	.792	137	167	304	137	106	31	138	976	3.9	1.8	12.7
96-97—Portland	60	942	105	220	.477	69	97	.711	47	91	138	56	42	17	64	279	2.3	0.9	4.7
97-98—Portland	71	1445	154	372	.414	94	156	.603	104	131	235	88	57	32	81	403	3.3	1.2	5.7
98-99—Portland	48	874	78	174	.448	52	76	.684	47	78	125	58	57	18	30	208	2.6	1.2	4.3
99-00—Portland	59	692	83	175	.474	37	55	.673	42	74	116	53	27	11	38	203	2.0	0.9	3.4
00-01—Portland	66	1182	127	266	.477	57	87	.655	60	99	159	98	48	21	48	311	2.4	1.5	4.7
Totals	694	17013	2582	5373	.481	1585	2197	.721	1104	1442	2546	1245	801	267	1036	6760	3.7	1.8	9.7

Three-point field goals: 1991-92, 1-for-6 (.167). 1992-93, 0-for-4. 1993-94, 1-for-7 (.143). 1994-95, 7-for-26 (.269). 1995-96, 1-for-4 (.250). 1997-98, 1-for-7 (.143). 1998-99, 0-for-2. 1999-00, 0-for-2. 2000-01, 0-for-4. Totals, 11-for-62 (.177).
Personal fouls/disqualifications: 1991-92, 161/0. 1992-93, 141/1. 1993-94, 179/0. 1994-95, 163/0. 1995-96, 188/1. 1996-97, 87/0. 1997-98, 144/0. 1998-99, 81/0. 1999-00, 69/0. 2000-01, 105/0. Totals, 1318/2.

NBA PLAYOFF RECORD

Season Team	G	Min.	FGM	FGA	Pct.	FTM	FTA	Pct.	REBOUNDS Off.	Def.	Tot.	Ast.	St.	Blk.	TO	Pts.	RPG	APG	PPG
92-93—Atlanta	3	93	14	31	.452	8	12	.667	3	5	8	5	4	0	4	36	2.7	1.7	12.0
93-94—Atlanta	11	324	46	89	.517	27	38	.711	13	16	29	28	7	2	15	119	2.6	2.5	10.8
94-95—Atlanta	3	52	6	14	.429	9	12	.750	3	4	7	5	3	0	2	21	2.3	1.7	7.0
95-96—Atlanta	10	314	35	72	.486	33	40	.825	9	27	36	27	11	6	17	103	3.6	2.7	10.3
96-97—Portland	4	35	2	6	.333	3	4	.750	1	0	1	3	1	0	1	7	0.3	0.8	1.8
97-98—Portland	4	28	2	4	.500	1	2	.500	1	2	3	1	2	1	2	5	0.8	0.3	1.3
98-99—Portland	13	176	10	28	.357	15	18	.833	10	23	33	5	8	3	3	35	2.5	0.4	2.7
99-00—Portland	7	34	4	12	.333	1	2	.500	0	2	2	0	0	0	0	9	0.3	0.0	1.3
00-01—Portland	2	28	4	10	.400	2	2	1.000	1	3	4	4	1	0	1	10	2.0	2.0	5.0
Totals	57	1084	123	266	.462	99	130	.762	41	82	123	78	37	12	45	345	2.2	1.4	6.1

Three-point field goals: 1995-96, 0-for-1. 1998-99, 0-for-1. Totals, 0-for-2 (.000).
Personal fouls/disqualifications: 1992-93, 7/0. 1993-94, 26/0. 1994-95, 8/0. 1995-96, 26/0. 1996-97, 6/0. 1997-98, 2/0. 1998-99, 15/0. 1999-00, 6/0. 2000-01, 3/0. Totals, 99/0.

AUSTIN, ISAAC   C   GRIZZLIES

PERSONAL: Born August 18, 1969, in Gridley, Calif. ... 6-10/270. (2,08/122,5). ... Full Name: Isaac Edward Austin.
HIGH SCHOOL: Las Plumas (Oroville, Calif.).
JUNIOR COLLEGE: Kings River College.
COLLEGE: Arizona State.
TRANSACTIONS/CAREER NOTES: Selected by Utah Jazz in second round (48th pick overall) of 1991 NBA Draft. ... Waived by Jazz (November 2, 1993). ... Played in Continental Basketball Association with Oklahoma City Cavalry (1993-94). ... Signed by Philadelphia 76ers to first of two consecutive 10-day contracts (March 22, 1994). ... Signed by 76ers for remainder of season (April 11, 1994). ... Played in France (1994-95). ... Played in Turkey (1995-96). ... Signed as free agent by Miami Heat (October 2, 1996). ... Traded by Heat with G Charles Smith and 1998 first-round draft choice to Los Angeles Clippers for G Brent Barry (February 19, 1998). ... Signed as free agent by Orlando Magic (January 21, 1999). ... Traded by Magic to Washington Wizards for F/C Terry Davis, F Ben Wallace, G Tim Legler and G Jeff McInnis (August 11, 1999). ... Traded by Wizards to Vancouver Grizzlies for G/F Dennis Scott, F/C Cherokee Parks, F Obinna Ekezie and G Felipe Lopez (August 22, 2000). ... Grizzlies franchise moved to Memphis for 2001-02 season.

COLLEGIATE RECORD

Season Team	G	Min.	FGM	FGA	Pct.	FTM	FTA	Pct.	Reb.	Ast.	Pts.	RPG	APG	PPG
87-88—Kings River College........	32	...	113	231	.489	62	87	.713	182	...	288	5.7	...	9.0
88-89—Kings River College........	31	...	215	405	.531	131	182	.720	279	...	561	9.0	...	18.1
89-90—Arizona State	31	848	164	300	.547	97	150	.647	192	27	425	6.2	0.9	13.7
90-91—Arizona State	30	906	189	331	.571	112	178	.629	262	57	490	8.7	1.9	16.3
Junior College Totals.............	63	...	328	636	.516	193	269	.717	461	...	849	7.3	...	13.5
4-Year-College Totals............	61	1754	353	631	.559	209	328	.637	454	84	915	7.4	1.4	15.0

Three-point field goals: 1989-90, 0-for-1. 1990-91, 0-for-1. Totals, 0-for-2 (.000).

HONORS: NBA Most Improved Player (1997).

A

NBA REGULAR-SEASON RECORD

									REBOUNDS								AVERAGES		
Season Team	G	Min.	FGM	FGA	Pct.	FTM	FTA	Pct.	Off.	Def.	Tot.	Ast.	St.	Blk.	TO	Pts.	RPG	APG	PPG
91-92—Utah	31	112	21	46	.457	19	30	.633	11	24	35	5	2	2	8	61	1.1	0.2	2.0
92-93—Utah	46	306	50	112	.446	29	44	.659	38	41	79	6	8	14	23	129	1.7	0.1	2.8
93-94—Philadelphia	14	201	29	66	.439	14	23	.609	25	44	69	17	5	10	17	72	4.9	1.2	5.1
96-97—Miami	82	1881	321	639	.502	150	226	.664	136	342	478	101	45	43	161	792	5.8	1.2	9.7
97-98—Mia.-L.A.C.	78	2266	406	871	.466	243	363	.669	199	358	557	175	61	56	206	1055	7.1	2.2	13.5
98-99—Orlando	49	1259	185	453	.408	105	157	.669	83	154	237	89	47	35	114	477	4.8	1.8	9.7
99-00—Washington	59	1173	151	352	.429	94	137	.686	64	218	282	74	17	38	107	397	4.8	1.3	6.7
00-01—Vancouver	52	845	96	270	.356	28	40	.700	50	172	222	58	20	23	54	226	4.3	1.1	4.3
Totals	411	8043	1259	2809	.448	682	1020	.669	606	1353	1959	525	205	221	690	3209	4.8	1.3	7.8

Three-point field goals: 1992-93, 0-for-1. 1993-94, 0-for-1. 1996-97, 0-for-3. 1997-98, 0-for-8. 1998-99, 2-for-7 (.286). 1999-00, 1-for-4 (.250). 2000-01, 6-for-24 (.250). Totals, 9-for-48 (.188).
Personal fouls/disqualifications: 1991-92, 20/0. 1992-93, 60/1. 1993-94, 29/0. 1996-97, 244/4. 1997-98, 231/5. 1998-99, 125/1. 1999-00, 128/0. 2000-01, 94/0. Totals, 931/11.

NBA PLAYOFF RECORD

									REBOUNDS								AVERAGES		
Season Team	G	Min.	FGM	FGA	Pct.	FTM	FTA	Pct.	Off.	Def.	Tot.	Ast.	St.	Blk.	TO	Pts.	RPG	APG	PPG
92-93—Utah	1	3	1	2	.500	0	0	...	0	1	1	0	0	1	0	2	1.0	0.0	2.0
96-97—Miami	15	287	36	81	.444	25	31	.806	16	50	66	6	6	7	22	98	4.4	0.4	6.5
98-99—Orlando	4	112	9	23	.391	8	12	.667	7	9	16	8	4	3	8	26	4.0	2.0	6.5
Totals	20	402	46	106	.434	33	43	.767	23	60	83	14	10	11	30	126	4.2	0.7	6.3

Three-point field goals: 1996-97, 1-for-4 (.250). 1998-99, 0-for-2. Totals, 1-for-6 (.167).
Personal fouls/disqualifications: 1992-93, 1/0. 1996-97, 50/0. 1998-99, 14/0. Totals, 50/0.

CBA REGULAR-SEASON RECORD

Season Team	G	Min.	FGM	FGA	Pct.	FTM	FTA	Pct.	Reb.	Ast.	Pts.	RPG	APG	PPG
93-94—Oklahoma City	26	787	155	300	.517	99	150	.660	216	50	409	8.3	1.9	15.7

Three-point field goals: 1993-94, 0-for-1.

FRENCH LEAGUE RECORD

Season Team	G	Min.	FGM	FGA	Pct.	FTM	FTA	Pct.	Reb.	Ast.	Pts.	RPG	APG	PPG
94-95—Lyon	11	...	...	...	...	...	...	...	96	20	159	8.7	1.8	14.5

TURKISH LEAGUE RECORD

Season Team	G	Min.	FGM	FGA	Pct.	FTM	FTA	Pct.	Reb.	Ast.	Pts.	RPG	APG	PPG
95-96—Tuborg Izmir..................	61	...	...	...	...	...	...	...	...	...	...	13.9	...	22.3

AVERY, WILLIAM   G   TIMBERWOLVES

PERSONAL: Born August 8, 1979, in Augusta, Ga. ... 6-2/180. (1,88/81,6).
HIGH SCHOOL: Westside (Augusta, Ga.).
COLLEGE: Duke.
TRANSACTIONS/CAREER NOTES: Selected after sophomore season by Minnesota Timberwolves in first round (14th pick overall) of 1999 NBA Draft.

COLLEGIATE RECORD

Season Team	G	Min.	FGM	FGA	Pct.	FTM	FTA	Pct.	Reb.	Ast.	Pts.	RPG	APG	PPG
97-98—Duke.............................	35	674	102	239	.427	61	82	.744	69	87	297	2.0	2.5	8.5
98-99—Duke.............................	39	1210	201	416	.483	102	126	.810	137	196	580	3.5	5.0	14.9
Totals	74	1884	303	655	.463	163	208	.784	206	283	877	2.8	3.8	11.0

Three-point field goals: 1997-98, 32-for-108 (.296). 1998-99, 76-for-185 (.411). Totals, 108-for-293 (.369).

NBA REGULAR-SEASON RECORD

									REBOUNDS								AVERAGES		
Season Team	G	Min.	FGM	FGA	Pct.	FTM	FTA	Pct.	Off.	Def.	Tot.	Ast.	St.	Blk.	TO	Pts.	RPG	APG	PPG
99-00—Minnesota.......	59	484	56	181	.309	24	36	.667	8	32	40	88	14	2	42	154	0.7	1.5	2.6
00-01—Minnesota.......	55	463	55	144	.382	28	36	.778	5	24	29	75	13	4	45	154	0.5	1.4	2.8
Totals	114	947	111	325	.342	52	72	.722	13	56	69	163	27	6	87	308	0.6	1.4	2.7

Three-point field goals: 1999-00, 18-for-63 (.286). 2000-01, 16-for-59 (.271). Totals, 34-for-122 (.279).
Personal fouls/disqualifications: 1999-00, 60/0. 2000-01, 48/0. Totals, 108/0.

NBA PLAYOFF RECORD

									REBOUNDS								AVERAGES		
Season Team	G	Min.	FGM	FGA	Pct.	FTM	FTA	Pct.	Off.	Def.	Tot.	Ast.	St.	Blk.	TO	Pts.	RPG	APG	PPG
00-01—Minnesota.......	2	12	3	6	.500	0	0	...	0	1	1	2	0	1	0	7	0.5	1.0	3.5

Three-point field goals: 2000-01, 1-for-2 (.500).

BAGARIC, DALIBOR　　　C　　　BULLS

PERSONAL: Born February 7, 1980, in Croatia. ... 7-1/290. (2,16/131,5).
TRANSACTIONS/CAREER NOTES: Played in Croatia (1997-98 through 1999-2000). ... Selected by Chicago Bulls in first round (24th pick overall) of 2000 NBA Draft.

CROATIAN LEAGUE RECORD

Season Team	G	Min.	FGM	FGA	Pct.	FTM	FTA	Pct.	Reb.	Ast.	Pts.	RPG	APG	PPG
97-98—Benston Zagreb	25	383	57	100	.570	35	40	.875	72	9	149	2.9	0.4	6.0
98-99—Cibona Zagreb	11	189	27	39	.692	21	26	.808	54	4	75	4.9	0.4	6.8
99-00—Benston Zagreb	22	682	147	251	.586	109	167	.653	228	15	403	10.4	0.7	18.3
Totals	58	1254	231	390	.592	165	233	.708	354	28	627	6.1	0.5	10.8

Three-point field goals: 1997-98, 0-for-1. 1999-00, 0-for-2. Totals, 0-for-3 (.000).

NBA REGULAR-SEASON RECORD

Season Team	G	Min.	FGM	FGA	Pct.	FTM	FTA	Pct.	REBOUNDS Off.	Def.	Tot.	Ast.	St.	Blk.	TO	Pts.	RPG	APG	PPG
00-01—Chicago	35	259	17	65	.262	13	28	.464	22	34	56	10	9	16	21	47	1.6	0.3	1.3

Three-point field goals: 2000-01, 0-for-1.
Personal fouls/disqualifications: 2000-01, 44/0.

BAKER, VIN　　　F　　　SUPERSONICS

PERSONAL: Born November 23, 1971, in Lake Wales, Fla. ... 6-11/250. (2,11/113,4). ... Full Name: Vincent Lamont Baker.
HIGH SCHOOL: Old Saybrook (Conn.).
COLLEGE: Hartford.
TRANSACTIONS/CAREER NOTES: Selected by Milwaukee Bucks in first round (eighth pick overall) of 1993 NBA Draft. ... Traded by Bucks to Seattle SuperSonics in three-way deal in which SuperSonics sent F Shawn Kemp to Cavaliers and Bucks sent G Sherman Douglas to Cleveland Cavaliers for G Terrell Brandon and F Tyrone Hill (September 25, 1997); Bucks also received 1998 conditional first-round draft choice from Cavaliers.
MISCELLANEOUS: Member of gold-medal-winning U.S. Olympic team (2000).

COLLEGIATE RECORD

Season Team	G	Min.	FGM	FGA	Pct.	FTM	FTA	Pct.	Reb.	Ast.	Pts.	RPG	APG	PPG
89-90—Hartford	28	374	58	94	.617	16	41	.390	82	7	132	2.9	0.3	4.7
90-91—Hartford	29	899	216	440	.491	137	202	.678	302	18	569	10.4	0.6	19.6
91-92—Hartford	27	997	281	638	.440	142	216	.657	267	36	745	9.9	1.3	27.6
92-93—Hartford	28	1019	305	639	.477	150	240	.625	300	54	792	10.7	1.9	28.3
Totals	112	3289	860	1811	.475	445	699	.637	951	115	2238	8.5	1.0	20.0

Three-point field goals: 1991-92, 41-for-214 (.192). 1992-93, 32-for-119 (.269). Totals, 73-for-333 (.219).

NBA REGULAR-SEASON RECORD

HONORS: All-NBA second team (1998). ... All-NBA third team (1997). ... NBA All-Rookie first team (1994).

Season Team	G	Min.	FGM	FGA	Pct.	FTM	FTA	Pct.	REBOUNDS Off.	Def.	Tot.	Ast.	St.	Blk.	TO	Pts.	RPG	APG	PPG
93-94—Milwaukee	82	2560	435	869	.501	234	411	.569	277	344	621	163	60	114	162	1105	7.6	2.0	13.5
94-95—Milwaukee	82	*3361	594	1229	.483	256	432	.593	289	557	846	296	86	116	221	1451	10.3	3.6	17.7
95-96—Milwaukee	82	3319	699	1429	.489	321	479	.670	263	545	808	212	68	91	216	1729	9.9	2.6	21.1
96-97—Milwaukee	78	3159	632	1251	.505	358	521	.687	267	537	804	211	81	112	245	1637	10.3	2.7	21.0
97-98—Seattle	82	2944	631	1164	.542	311	526	.591	286	370	656	152	91	86	174	1574	8.0	1.9	19.2
98-99—Seattle	34	1162	198	437	.453	72	160	.450	86	125	211	56	32	34	76	468	6.2	1.6	13.8
99-00—Seattle	79	2849	514	1129	.455	281	412	.682	227	378	605	148	47	66	213	1311	7.7	1.9	16.6
00-01—Seattle	76	2129	347	822	.422	232	321	.723	179	251	430	90	38	73	158	927	5.7	1.2	12.2
Totals	595	21483	4050	8330	.486	2065	3262	.633	1874	3107	4981	1328	503	692	1465	10202	8.4	2.2	17.1

Three-point field goals: 1993-94, 1-for-5 (.200). 1994-95, 7-for-24 (.292). 1995-96, 10-for-48 (.208). 1996-97, 15-for-54 (.278). 1997-98, 1-for-7 (.143). 1998-99, 0-for-3. 1999-00, 2-for-8 (.250). 2000-01, 1-for-16 (.063). Totals, 37-for-165 (.224).
Personal fouls/disqualifications: 1993-94, 231/3. 1994-95, 277/5. 1995-96, 272/3. 1996-97, 275/8. 1997-98, 278/7. 1998-99, 121/2. 1999-00, 288/6. 2000-01, 264/2. Totals, 2006/36.

NBA PLAYOFF RECORD

Season Team	G	Min.	FGM	FGA	Pct.	FTM	FTA	Pct.	REBOUNDS Off.	Def.	Tot.	Ast.	St.	Blk.	TO	Pts.	RPG	APG	PPG
97-98—Seattle	10	371	71	134	.530	16	38	.421	41	53	94	18	18	15	22	158	9.4	1.8	15.8
99-00—Seattle	5	177	30	75	.400	10	17	.588	16	22	38	10	5	2	16	70	7.6	2.0	14.0
Totals	15	548	101	209	.483	26	55	.473	57	75	132	28	23	17	38	228	8.8	1.9	15.2

Three-point field goals: 1999-00, 0-for-1. Totals, 0-for-1 (.000).
Personal fouls/disqualifications: 1997-98, 38/1. 1999-00, 19/0. Totals, 57/1.

NBA ALL-STAR GAME RECORD

Season Team	Min.	FGM	FGA	Pct.	FTM	FTA	Pct.	REBOUNDS Off.	Def.	Tot.	Ast.	PF	Dq.	St.	Blk.	TO	Pts.
1995 —Milwaukee	11	0	2	.000	2	4	.500	2	0	2	0	1	0	0	1	1	2
1996 —Milwaukee	14	2	5	.400	2	2	1.000	1	1	2	2	4	0	1	0	0	6
1997 —Milwaukee	24	8	12	.667	3	4	.750	7	5	12	1	2	0	0	0	0	19
1998 —Seattle	21	3	12	.250	2	2	1.000	6	2	8	0	1	0	1	0	0	8
Totals	70	13	31	.419	9	12	.750	16	8	24	3	8	0	2	1	1	35

BARKLEY, ERICK　　　G　　　TRAIL BLAZERS

PERSONAL: Born February 21, 1978, in Queens, N.Y. ... 6-1/177. (1,85/80,3).
HIGH SCHOOL: Christ the King (Queens, N.Y.), then Maine Central Institute (Pittsfield, Maine).
COLLEGE: St. John's.
TRANSACTIONS/CAREER NOTES: Selected after sophomore season by Portland Trail Blazers in first round (28th pick overall) of 2000 NBA Draft.

COLLEGIATE RECORD

Season Team	G	Min.	FGM	FGA	Pct.	FTM	FTA	Pct.	Reb.	Ast.	Pts.	RPG	APG	PPG
98-99—St. John's	37	1228	157	397	.395	129	167	.772	118	175	500	3.2	4.7	13.5
99-00—St. John's	28	1033	159	400	.398	81	122	.664	84	127	449	3.0	4.5	16.0
Totals	65	2261	316	797	.396	210	289	.727	202	302	949	3.1	4.6	14.6

Three-point field goals: 1998-99, 57-for-166 (.343). 1999-00, 50-for-160 (.313). Totals, 107-for-326 (.328).

NBA REGULAR-SEASON RECORD

Season Team	G	Min.	FGM	FGA	Pct.	FTM	FTA	Pct.	Off.	Def.	Tot.	Ast.	St.	Blk.	TO	Pts.	RPG	APG	PPG
00-01—Portland	8	38	8	22	.364	0	0	...	0	3	3	6	2	0	5	19	0.4	0.8	2.4

Three-point field goals: 2000-01, 3-for-8 (.375).
Personal fouls/disqualifications: 2000-01, 2/0.

BARROS, DANA　　　G

PERSONAL: Born April 13, 1967, in Boston. ... 5-11/163. (1,80/73,9). ... Full Name: Dana Bruce Barros.
HIGH SCHOOL: Xaverian Brothers (Westwood, Mass.).
COLLEGE: Boston College.
TRANSACTIONS/CAREER NOTES: Selected by Seattle SuperSonics in first round (16th pick overall) of 1989 NBA Draft. ... Traded by SuperSonics with F Eddie Johnson and option to switch 1994 first-round draft choices to Charlotte Hornets for G Kendall Gill (September 1, 1993). ... Traded by Hornets with F Sidney Green, draft rights to G Greg Graham and option to switch 1994 first-round draft choices to Philadelphia 76ers for G Hersey Hawkins (September 3, 1993). ... Signed as unrestricted free agent by Boston Celtics (September 22, 1995). ... Traded by Celtics to Dallas Mavericks as part of four-team deal in which Celtics received G Robert Pack, C John Williams and cash considerations from Mavericks and a conditional first-round draft choice from Utah Jazz, Mavericks received F Bill Curley from Golden State Warriors and G Howard Eisley from Jazz, Jazz received F Donyell Marshall from Warriors and C Bruno Sundov from Mavericks and Warriors received F Danny Fortson from Celtics and F Adam Keefe from Jazz (August 16, 2000). ... Traded by Mavericks with F Ansu Sesay to Detroit Pistons for F Loy Vaught (October 17, 2000).

COLLEGIATE RECORD

Season Team	G	Min.	FGM	FGA	Pct.	FTM	FTA	Pct.	Reb.	Ast.	Pts.	RPG	APG	PPG
85-86—Boston College	28	971	158	330	.479	68	86	.791	78	97	384	2.8	3.5	13.7
86-87—Boston College	29	1145	194	424	.458	85	100	.850	85	110	543	2.9	3.8	18.7
87-88—Boston College	33	1223	242	504	.480	130	153	.850	113	135	723	3.4	4.1	21.9
88-89—Boston College	29	1096	230	484	.475	120	140	.857	103	96	692	3.6	3.3	23.9
Totals	119	4435	824	1742	.473	403	479	.841	379	438	2342	3.2	3.7	19.7

Three-point field goals: 1986-87, 70-for-173 (.405). 1987-88, 109-for-240 (.454). 1988-89, 112-for-261 (.429). Totals, 291-for-674 (.432).

NBA REGULAR-SEASON RECORD

RECORDS: Holds career record for most consecutive games with one or more three-point field goals made—89 (December 23, 1994-January 10, 1996).
HONORS: NBA Most Improved Player (1995).
NOTES: Led NBA with .446 three-point field goal percentage (1992).

Season Team	G	Min.	FGM	FGA	Pct.	FTM	FTA	Pct.	Off.	Def.	Tot.	Ast.	St.	Blk.	TO	Pts.	RPG	APG	PPG
89-90—Seattle	81	1630	299	738	.405	89	110	.809	35	97	132	205	53	1	123	782	1.6	2.5	9.7
90-91—Seattle	66	750	154	311	.495	78	85	.918	17	54	71	111	23	1	54	418	1.1	1.7	6.3
91-92—Seattle	75	1331	238	493	.483	60	79	.759	17	64	81	125	51	4	56	619	1.1	1.7	8.3
92-93—Seattle	69	1243	214	474	.451	49	59	.831	18	89	107	151	63	3	58	541	1.6	2.2	7.8
93-94—Philadelphia	81	2519	412	878	.469	116	145	.800	28	168	196	424	107	5	167	1075	2.4	5.2	13.3
94-95—Philadelphia	82	3318	571	1165	.490	347	386	.899	27	247	274	619	149	4	242	1686	3.3	7.5	20.6
95-96—Boston	80	2328	379	806	.470	130	147	.884	21	171	192	306	58	3	120	1038	2.4	3.8	13.0
96-97—Boston	24	708	110	253	.435	37	43	.860	5	43	48	81	26	6	39	300	2.0	3.4	12.5
97-98—Boston	80	1686	281	609	.461	122	144	.847	28	125	153	286	83	6	107	784	1.9	3.6	9.8
98-99—Boston	50	1156	168	371	.453	64	73	.877	16	89	105	208	52	5	88	464	2.1	4.2	9.3
99-00—Boston	72	1139	196	435	.451	66	76	.868	13	86	99	133	31	4	66	517	1.4	1.8	7.2
00-01—Detroit	60	1079	183	412	.444	68	80	.850	6	88	94	110	30	2	60	478	1.6	1.8	8.0
Totals	820	18887	3205	6945	.461	1226	1427	.859	231	1321	1552	2759	726	44	1180	8702	1.9	3.4	10.6

Three-point field goals: 1989-90, 95-for-238 (.399). 1990-91, 32-for-81 (.395). 1991-92, 83-for-186 (.446). 1992-93, 64-for-169 (.379). 1993-94, 135-for-354 (.381). 1994-95, 197-for-425 (.464). 1995-96, 150-for-368 (.408). 1996-97, 43-for-105 (.410). 1997-98, 100-for-246 (.407). 1998-99, 64-for-160 (.400). 1999-00, 59-for-144 (.410). 2000-01, 44-for-105 (.419). Totals, 1066-for-2581 (.413).

Personal fouls/disqualifications: 1989-90, 97/0. 1990-91, 40/0. 1991-92, 84/0. 1992-93, 78/0. 1993-94, 96/0. 1994-95, 159/1. 1995-96, 116/1. 1996-97, 34/0. 1997-98, 124/0. 1998-99, 64/1. 1999-00, 80/0. 2000-01, 63/0. Totals, 1035/3.

NBA PLAYOFF RECORD

Season Team	G	Min.	FGM	FGA	Pct.	FTM	FTA	Pct.	REBOUNDS Off.	Def.	Tot.	Ast.	St.	Blk.	TO	Pts.	RPG	APG	PPG
90-91—Seattle	3	25	9	13	.692	3	4	.750	1	3	4	5	3	0	3	23	1.3	1.7	7.7
91-92—Seattle	7	96	21	40	.525	0	0	...	1	6	7	8	4	0	6	52	1.0	1.1	7.4
92-93—Seattle	16	136	22	47	.468	6	8	.750	0	12	12	12	5	0	8	55	0.8	0.8	3.4
Totals	26	257	52	100	.520	9	12	.750	2	21	23	25	12	0	17	130	0.9	1.0	5.0

Three-point field goals: 1990-91, 2-for-5 (.400). 1991-92, 10-for-17 (.588). 1992-93, 5-for-16 (.313). Totals, 17-for-38 (.447).
Personal fouls/disqualifications: 1990-91, 1/0. 1991-92, 11/0. 1992-93, 6/0. Totals, 18/0.

NBA ALL-STAR GAME RECORD

Season Team	Min.	FGM	FGA	Pct.	FTM	FTA	Pct.	REBOUNDS Off.	Def.	Tot.	Ast.	PF	Dq.	St.	Blk.	TO	Pts.
1995 —Philadelphia.......	11	2	5	.400	0	0	...	0	1	1	3	0	0	0	0	0	5

Three-point field goals: 1995, 1-for-3 (.333).

BARRY, BRENT   G   SUPERSONICS

PERSONAL: Born December 31, 1971, in Hempstead, N.Y. ... 6-6/215. (1,98/97,5). ... Full Name: Brent Robert Barry. ... Son of Rick Barry, forward with San Francisco/Golden State Warriors (1965-66, 1966-67 and 1972-73 through 1977-78) and Houston Rockets of NBA (1978-79 and 1979-80) and three American Basketball Association teams (1968-69 through 1971-72) and member of Naismith Memorial Basketball Hall of Fame; brother of Jon Barry, guard, Sacramento Kings; brother of Drew Barry, guard with Atlanta Hawks (1997-98 and 1999-2000), Seattle SuperSonics (1998-99) and Golden State Warriors (1999-2000).

HIGH SCHOOL: De La Salle Catholic (Concord, Calif.).

COLLEGE: Oregon State.

TRANSACTIONS/CAREER NOTES: Selected by Denver Nuggets in first round (15th pick overall) of 1995 NBA Draft. ... Draft rights traded by Nuggets with F Rodney Rogers to Los Angeles Clippers for G Randy Woods and draft rights to F Antonio McDyess (June 28, 1995). ... Traded by Clippers to Miami Heat for C Isaac Austin, G Charles Smith and 1998 first-round draft choice (February 19, 1998). ... Signed as free agent by Chicago Bulls (January 25, 1999). ... Traded by Bulls to Seattle SuperSonics for G Hersey Hawkins and G James Cotton (August 12, 1999).

COLLEGIATE RECORD

Season Team	G	Min.	FGM	FGA	Pct.	FTM	FTA	Pct.	Reb.	Ast.	Pts.	AVERAGES RPG	APG	PPG
90-91—Oregon State						Did not play—redshirted.								
91-92—Oregon State	31	545	57	136	.419	22	33	.667	47	70	161	1.5	2.3	5.2
92-93—Oregon State	23	607	55	134	.410	40	47	.851	49	83	165	2.1	3.6	7.2
93-94—Oregon State	27	959	144	289	.498	85	112	.759	141	94	411	5.2	3.5	15.2
94-95—Oregon State	27	1012	181	352	.514	153	186	.823	159	104	567	5.9	3.9	21.0
Totals	108	3123	437	911	.480	300	378	.794	396	351	1304	3.7	3.3	12.1

Three-point field goals: 1991-92, 25-for-77 (.325). 1992-93, 15-for-64 (.234). 1993-94, 38-for-104 (.365). 1994-95, 52-for-132 (.394). Totals, 130-for-377 (.345).

NBA REGULAR-SEASON RECORD

HONORS: Slam Dunk championship winner (1996). ... NBA All-Rookie second team (1996).
NOTES: Led NBA with .476 three-point field goal percentage (2001).

Season Team	G	Min.	FGM	FGA	Pct.	FTM	FTA	Pct.	REBOUNDS Off.	Def.	Tot.	Ast.	St.	Blk.	TO	Pts.	AVERAGES RPG	APG	PPG
95-96—L.A. Clippers...	79	1898	283	597	.474	111	137	.810	38	130	168	230	95	22	120	800	2.1	2.9	10.1
96-97—L.A. Clippers ...	59	1094	155	379	.409	76	93	.817	30	80	110	154	51	15	76	442	1.9	2.6	7.5
97-98—L.A.C.-Miami...	58	1600	213	506	.421	115	134	.858	29	142	171	153	64	27	104	631	2.9	2.6	10.9
98-99—Chicago	37	1181	141	356	.396	78	101	.772	39	105	144	116	42	11	72	412	3.9	3.1	11.1
99-00—Seattle	80	2726	327	707	.463	127	157	.809	50	322	372	291	103	31	142	945	4.7	3.6	11.8
00-01—Seattle	67	1778	198	401	.494	84	103	.816	33	178	211	225	80	14	86	589	3.1	3.4	8.8
Totals	380	10277	1317	2946	.447	591	725	.815	219	957	1176	1169	435	120	600	3819	3.1	3.1	10.1

Three-point field goals: 1995-96, 123-for-296 (.416). 1996-97, 56-for-173 (.324). 1997-98, 90-for-229 (.393). 1998-99, 52-for-172 (.302). 1999-00, 164-for-399 (.411). 2000-01, 109-for-229 (.476). Totals, 594-for-1498 (.397).
Personal fouls/disqualifications: 1995-96, 196/2. 1996-97, 88/1. 1997-98, 118/0. 1998-99, 98/2. 1999-00, 228/4. 2000-01, 126/1. Totals, 854/10.

NBA PLAYOFF RECORD

Season Team	G	Min.	FGM	FGA	Pct.	FTM	FTA	Pct.	REBOUNDS Off.	Def.	Tot.	Ast.	St.	Blk.	TO	Pts.	AVERAGES RPG	APG	PPG
96-97—L.A. Clippers...	3	84	11	27	.407	8	9	.889	1	6	7	10	4	0	4	35	2.3	3.3	11.7
99-00—Seattle	5	155	12	33	.364	10	14	.714	3	10	13	15	3	3	7	42	2.6	3.0	8.4
Totals	8	239	23	60	.383	18	23	.783	4	16	20	25	7	3	11	77	2.5	3.1	9.6

Three-point field goals: 1996-97, 5-for-11 (.455). 1999-00, 8-for-20 (.400). Totals, 13-for-31 (.419).
Personal fouls/disqualifications: 1996-97, 10/0. 1999-00, 20/2. Totals, 30/2.

BARRY, JON   G   KINGS

PERSONAL: Born July 25, 1969, in Oakland. ... 6-5/210. (1,96/95,3). ... Full Name: Jon Alan Barry. ... Son of Rick Barry, forward with San Francisco/Golden State Warriors (1965-66, 1966-67 and 1972-73 through 1977-78) and Houston Rockets of NBA (1978-79 and 1979-80) and three American Basketball Association teams (1968-69 through 1971-72), and member of Naismith Memorial Basketball Hall of Fame; brother of Brent Barry, guard, Seattle SuperSonics; and brother of Drew Barry, guard with Atlanta Hawks (1997-98 and 1999-2000), Seattle SuperSonics (1998-99) and Golden State Warriors (1999-2000).

HIGH SCHOOL: De La Salle Catholic (Concord, Calif.).

JUNIOR COLLEGE: Paris (Texas) Junior College.

COLLEGE: Pacific, then Georgia Tech.

TRANSACTIONS/CAREER NOTES: Selected by Boston Celtics in first round (21st pick overall) of 1992 NBA Draft. ... Traded by Celtics to Milwaukee Bucks for F Alaa Abdelnaby (December 4, 1992). ... Signed as unrestricted free agent by Golden State Warriors (October 4, 1995). ... Signed as free agent by Atlanta Hawks (August 13, 1996). ... Signed as free agent by Los Angeles Lakers (August 27, 1997). ... Signed as free agent by Sacramento Kings (January 22, 1999).

COLLEGIATE RECORD

Season Team	G	Min.	FGM	FGA	Pct.	FTM	FTA	Pct.	Reb.	Ast.	Pts.	RPG	APG	PPG
87-88—Pacific	29	809	100	269	.372	53	71	.746	74	108	275	2.6	3.7	9.5
88-89—Paris Junior College							Did not play.							
89-90—Paris Junior College	30	...	204	358	.570	58	73	.795	108	90	513	3.6	3.0	17.1
90-91—Georgia Tech	30	1088	180	405	.444	41	56	.732	110	110	478	3.7	3.7	15.9
91-92—Georgia Tech	35	1231	201	468	.429	101	145	.697	152	207	602	4.3	5.9	17.2
Junior College Totals	30	...	204	358	.570	58	73	.795	108	90	513	3.6	3.0	17.1
4-Year-College Totals	94	3128	481	1142	.421	195	272	.717	336	425	1355	3.6	4.5	14.4

Three-point field goals: 1987-88, 22-for-59 (.373). 1990-91, 77-for-209 (.368). 1991-92, 99-for-265 (.374). Totals, 198-for-533 (.371).

NBA REGULAR-SEASON RECORD

Season Team	G	Min.	FGM	FGA	Pct.	FTM	FTA	Pct.	Off.	Def.	Tot.	Ast.	St.	Blk.	TO	Pts.	RPG	APG	PPG
92-93—Milwaukee	47	552	76	206	.369	33	49	.673	10	33	43	68	35	3	42	206	0.9	1.4	4.4
93-94—Milwaukee	72	1242	158	382	.414	97	122	.795	36	110	146	168	102	17	83	445	2.0	2.3	6.2
94-95—Milwaukee	52	602	57	134	.425	61	80	.763	15	34	49	85	30	4	41	191	0.9	1.6	3.7
95-96—Golden State	68	712	91	185	.492	31	37	.838	17	46	63	85	33	11	42	257	0.9	1.3	3.8
96-97—Atlanta	58	965	100	246	.407	37	46	.804	26	73	99	115	55	3	59	285	1.7	2.0	4.9
97-98—L.A. Lakers	49	374	38	104	.365	27	29	.931	8	29	37	51	24	3	22	121	0.8	1.0	2.5
98-99—Sacramento	43	736	59	138	.428	71	84	.845	25	71	96	112	53	5	47	213	2.2	2.6	5.0
99-00—Sacramento	62	1281	161	346	.465	107	116	.922	38	121	159	150	75	7	85	495	2.6	2.4	8.0
00-01—Sacramento	62	1010	103	255	.404	64	73	.877	16	78	94	130	28	6	53	316	1.5	2.1	5.1
Totals	513	7474	843	1996	.422	528	636	.830	191	595	786	964	435	59	474	2529	1.5	1.9	4.9

Three-point field goals: 1992-93, 21-for-63 (.333). 1993-94, 32-for-115 (.278). 1994-95, 16-for-48 (.333). 1995-96, 44-for-93 (.473). 1996-97, 48-for-124 (.387). 1997-98, 18-for-61 (.295). 1998-99, 24-for-79 (.304). 1999-00, 66-for-154 (.429). 2000-01, 46-for-132 (.348). Totals, 315-for-869 (.362).

Personal fouls/disqualifications: 1992-93, 57/0. 1993-94, 110/0. 1994-95, 54/0. 1995-96, 51/1. 1996-97, 56/0. 1997-98, 33/0. 1998-99, 61/1. 1999-00, 104/1. 2000-01, 66/0. Totals, 592/3.

NBA PLAYOFF RECORD

Season Team	G	Min.	FGM	FGA	Pct.	FTM	FTA	Pct.	Off.	Def.	Tot.	Ast.	St.	Blk.	TO	Pts.	RPG	APG	PPG
96-97—Atlanta	2	9	0	3	.000	0	0	...	0	0	0	0	0	0	0	0	0.0	0.0	0.0
97-98—L.A. Lakers	7	18	0	8	.000	0	0	...	0	2	2	0	1	0	0	0	0.3	0.0	0.0
98-99—Sacramento	5	112	12	34	.353	11	12	.917	3	7	10	9	6	1	9	40	2.0	1.8	8.0
99-00—Sacramento	5	102	9	21	.429	14	16	.875	2	10	12	12	3	0	4	39	2.4	2.4	7.8
00-01—Sacramento	7	55	7	17	.412	0	0	...	3	0	3	4	1	0	3	16	0.4	0.6	2.3
Totals	26	296	28	83	.337	25	28	.893	8	19	27	25	11	1	16	95	1.0	1.0	3.7

Three-point field goals: 1997-98, 0-for-5. 1998-99, 5-for-19 (.263). 1999-00, 7-for-12 (.583). 2000-01, 2-for-7 (.286). Totals, 14-for-43 (.326).

Personal fouls/disqualifications: 1997-98, 1/0. 1998-99, 9/0. 1999-00, 7/0. 2000-01, 7/0. Totals, 24/0.

BATTIE, TONY — C/F — CELTICS

PERSONAL: Born February 11, 1976, in Dallas. ... 6-11/240. (2,11/108,9). ... Full Name: Demetrius Antonio Battie.

HIGH SCHOOL: South Oak Cliff (Dallas).

COLLEGE: Texas Tech.

TRANSACTIONS/CAREER NOTES: Selected after junior season by Denver Nuggets in first round (fifth pick overall) of 1997 NBA Draft. ... Traded by Nuggets with draft rights to G Tyronn Lue to Los Angeles Lakers for G Nick Van Exel (June 24, 1998). ... Traded by Lakers to Boston Celtics for C Travis Knight (January 21, 1999).

COLLEGIATE RECORD

Season Team	G	Min.	FGM	FGA	Pct.	FTM	FTA	Pct.	Reb.	Ast.	Pts.	RPG	APG	PPG
94-95—Texas Tech	29	368	47	96	.490	18	27	.667	129	17	112	4.4	0.6	3.9
95-96—Texas Tech	30	806	114	221	.516	60	95	.632	266	32	292	8.9	1.1	9.7
96-97—Texas Tech	28	978	206	356	.579	107	163	.656	329	23	525	11.8	0.8	18.8
Totals	87	2152	367	673	.545	185	285	.649	724	72	929	8.3	0.8	10.7

Three-point field goals: 1994-95, 0-for-6. 1995-96, 4-for-14 (.286). 1996-97, 6-for-16 (.375). Totals, 10-for-36 (.278).

NBA REGULAR-SEASON RECORD

Season Team	G	Min.	FGM	FGA	Pct.	FTM	FTA	Pct.	Off.	Def.	Tot.	Ast.	St.	Blk.	TO	Pts.	RPG	APG	PPG
97-98—Denver	65	1506	234	525	.446	73	104	.702	138	213	351	60	54	69	98	544	5.4	0.9	8.4
98-99—Boston	50	1121	147	283	.519	41	61	.672	96	204	300	53	29	71	45	335	6.0	1.1	6.7
99-00—Boston	82	1505	219	459	.477	102	151	.675	152	258	410	63	47	70	67	541	5.0	0.8	6.6
00-01—Boston	40	845	108	201	.537	44	69	.638	73	160	233	16	27	60	37	260	5.8	0.4	6.5
Totals	237	4977	708	1468	.482	260	385	.675	459	835	1294	192	157	270	247	1680	5.5	0.8	7.1

Three-point field goals: 1997-98, 3-for-14 (.214). 1998-99, 0-for-3. 1999-00, 1-for-8 (.125). 2000-01, 0-for-3. Totals, 4-for-28 (.143).

Personal fouls/disqualifications: 1997-98, 199/6. 1998-99, 159/1. 1999-00, 249/4. 2000-01, 126/3. Totals, 733/14.

BELL, RAJA   G   76ERS

PERSONAL: Born September 19, 1976, in St. Croix, Virgin Islands. ... 6-5/215. (1,96/97,5).
HIGH SCHOOL: Killian (Miami).
COLLEGE: Boston University, then Florida International.
TRANSACTIONS/CAREER NOTES: Not drafted by an NBA franchise. ... Played in Continental Basketball Association with Yakima Sun Kings (1999-2000 and 2000-01). ... Signed as free agent by San Antonio Spurs (August 2, 2000). ... Waived by Spurs (October 30, 2000). ... Signed by Philadelphia 76ers to 10-day contract (April 6, 2001). ... Re-signed by 76ers for remainder of season (April 16, 2001).

COLLEGIATE RECORD

Season Team	G	Min.	FGM	FGA	Pct.	FTM	FTA	Pct.	Reb.	Ast.	Pts.	RPG	APG	PPG
94-95—Boston University	30	866	119	291	.409	59	81	.728	127	37	330	4.2	1.2	11.0
95-96—Boston University	28	932	155	360	.431	74	112	.661	114	52	421	4.1	1.9	15.0
96-97—Florida International						Did not play—transfer student.								
97-98—Florida International	29	855	165	373	.442	112	146	.767	118	65	481	4.1	2.2	16.6
98-99—Florida International	29	1011	167	366	.456	102	137	.745	124	79	484	4.3	2.7	16.7
Totals	116	3664	606	1390	.436	347	476	.729	483	233	1716	4.2	2.0	14.8

Three-point field goals: 1994-95, 33-for-77 (.429). 1995-96, 37-for-112 (.330). 1997-98, 39-for-121 (.322). 1998-99, 48-for-138 (.348). Totals, 157-for-448 (.350).

CBA REGULAR-SEASON RECORD

Season Team	G	Min.	FGM	FGA	Pct.	FTM	FTA	Pct.	Reb.	Ast.	Pts.	RPG	APG	PPG
99-00—Yakima	52	1494	238	464	.513	104	137	.759	146	142	597	2.8	2.7	11.5
00-01—Yakima	9	293	58	124	.468	44	57	.772	39	37	172	4.3	4.1	19.1
Totals	61	1787	296	588	.503	148	194	.763	185	179	769	3.0	2.9	12.6

Three-point field goals: 1999-00, 17-for-46 (.370). 2000-01, 12-for-36 (.333). Totals, 29-for-82 (.354).

NBA REGULAR-SEASON RECORD

Season Team	G	Min.	FGM	FGA	Pct.	FTM	FTA	Pct.	Off.	Def.	Tot.	Ast.	St.	Blk.	TO	Pts.	RPG	APG	PPG
00-01—Philadelphia	5	30	2	7	.286	0	0	...	0	1	1	0	1	0	2	5	0.2	0.0	1.0

Three-point field goals: 2000-01, 1-for-3 (.333).
Personal fouls/disqualifications: 2000-01, 1/0.

NBA PLAYOFF RECORD

Season Team	G	Min.	FGM	FGA	Pct.	FTM	FTA	Pct.	Off.	Def.	Tot.	Ast.	St.	Blk.	TO	Pts.	RPG	APG	PPG
00-01—Philadelphia	15	124	12	27	.444	8	14	.571	4	9	13	7	15	0	5	34	0.9	0.5	2.3

Three-point field goals: 2000-01, 2-for-8 (.250).
Personal fouls/disqualifications: 2000-01, 20/0.

BENDER, JONATHAN   F   PACERS

PERSONAL: Born January 30, 1981, in Picayune, Miss. ... 6-11/202. (2,11/91,6). ... Full Name: Jonathan Rene Bender.
HIGH SCHOOL: Picayune (Miss.) Memorial.
COLLEGE: Did not attend college.
TRANSACTIONS/CAREER NOTES: Selected out of high school by Toronto Raptors in first round (fifth pick overall) of 1999 NBA Draft. ... Draft rights traded by Raptors to Indiana Pacers for F/C Antonio Davis (August 1, 1999).

NBA REGULAR-SEASON RECORD

Season Team	G	Min.	FGM	FGA	Pct.	FTM	FTA	Pct.	Off.	Def.	Tot.	Ast.	St.	Blk.	TO	Pts.	RPG	APG	PPG
99-00—Indiana	24	130	23	70	.329	16	24	.667	4	17	21	3	1	5	7	64	0.9	0.1	2.7
00-01—Indiana	59	574	66	186	.355	50	68	.735	14	60	74	32	7	28	42	193	1.3	0.5	3.3
Totals	83	704	89	256	.348	66	92	.717	18	77	95	35	8	33	49	257	1.1	0.4	3.1

Three-point field goals: 1999-00, 2-for-12 (.167). 2000-01, 11-for-41 (.268). Totals, 13-for-53 (.245).
Personal fouls/disqualifications: 1999-00, 18/0. 2000-01, 73/0. Totals, 91/0.

NBA PLAYOFF RECORD

Season Team	G	Min.	FGM	FGA	Pct.	FTM	FTA	Pct.	Off.	Def.	Tot.	Ast.	St.	Blk.	TO	Pts.	RPG	APG	PPG
99-00—Indiana	9	21	4	6	.667	3	6	.500	0	3	3	0	1	0	0	12	0.3	0.0	1.3
00-01—Indiana	1	4	0	1	.000	0	0	...	0	0	0	0	0	0	0	0	0.0	0.0	0.0
Totals	10	25	4	7	.571	3	6	.500	0	3	3	0	1	0	0	12	0.3	0.0	1.2

Three-point field goals: 1999-00, 1-for-1. Totals, 1-for-1 (1.000).
Personal fouls/disqualifications: 1999-00, 2/0. 2000-01, 1/0. Totals, 3/0.

BENJAMIN, COREY   G

PERSONAL: Born February 24, 1978, in Compton, Calif. ... 6-6/205. (1,98/93,0).
HIGH SCHOOL: Fontana (Calif.).
COLLEGE: Oregon State.
TRANSACTIONS/CAREER NOTES: Selected after sophomore season by Chicago Bulls in first round (28th pick overall) of 1998 NBA Draft.

COLLEGIATE RECORD

Season Team	G	Min.	FGM	FGA	Pct.	FTM	FTA	Pct.	Reb.	Ast.	Pts.	RPG	APG	PPG
96-97—Oregon	23	601	121	280	.432	66	101	.653	92	31	343	4.0	1.3	14.9
97-98—Oregon	25	673	185	343	.539	97	136	.713	125	56	496	5.0	2.2	19.8
Totals	48	1274	306	623	.491	163	237	.688	217	87	839	4.5	1.8	17.5

Three-point field goals: 1996-97, 35-for-111 (.315). 1997-98, 29-for-99 (.293). Totals, 64-for-210 (.305).

NBA REGULAR-SEASON RECORD

Season Team	G	Min.	FGM	FGA	Pct.	FTM	FTA	Pct.	Off.	Def.	Tot.	Ast.	St.	Blk.	TO	Pts.	RPG	APG	PPG
98-99—Chicago	31	320	44	117	.376	27	40	.675	15	25	40	10	11	8	21	118	1.3	0.3	3.8
99-00—Chicago	48	862	145	350	.414	49	82	.598	21	67	88	54	31	22	74	370	1.8	1.1	7.7
00-01—Chicago	65	857	115	302	.381	56	83	.675	38	62	100	69	28	16	63	307	1.5	1.1	4.7
Totals	144	2039	304	769	.395	132	205	.644	74	154	228	133	70	46	158	795	1.6	0.9	5.5

Three-point field goals: 1998-99, 3-for-14 (.214). 1999-00, 31-for-89 (.348). 2000-01, 21-for-81 (.259). Totals, 55-for-184 (.299).
Personal fouls/disqualifications: 1998-99, 46/0. 1999-00, 122/2. 2000-01, 128/2. Totals, 296/4.

BENOIT, DAVID   F

PERSONAL: Born May 9, 1968, in Lafayette, La. ... 6-8/220. (2,03/99,8). ... Name pronounced ben-WAH.
HIGH SCHOOL: Lafayette (La.).
JUNIOR COLLEGE: Tyler (Texas) Junior College.
COLLEGE: Alabama.
TRANSACTIONS/CAREER NOTES: Not drafted by an NBA franchise. ... Played in Spain (1990-91). ... Signed as free agent by Utah Jazz (August 7, 1991). ... Signed as free agent by New Jersey Nets (August 7, 1996). ... Traded by Nets with G Kevin Edwards, C Yinka Dare and 1998 first-round draft choice to Orlando Magic for C Rony Seikaly and F Brian Evans (February 19, 1998). ... Played in Israel (1998-99). ... Signed as free agent by Jazz (October 3, 2000).

COLLEGIATE RECORD

Season Team	G	Min.	FGM	FGA	Pct.	FTM	FTA	Pct.	Reb.	Ast.	Pts.	RPG	APG	PPG
86-87—Tyler Junior College						Statistics unavailable.								
87-88—Tyler Junior College						Statistics unavailable.								
88-89—Alabama	31	913	136	268	.507	62	84	.738	248	20	335	8.0	0.6	10.8
89-90—Alabama	35	920	156	303	.515	46	60	.767	212	29	367	6.1	0.8	10.5
Totals	66	1833	292	571	.511	108	144	.750	460	49	702	7.0	0.7	10.6

Three-point field goals: 1988-89, 1-for-3 (.333). 1989-90, 9-for-20 (.450). Totals, 10-for-23 (.435).

SPANISH LEAGUE RECORD

Season Team	G	Min.	FGM	FGA	Pct.	FTM	FTA	Pct.	Reb.	Ast.	Pts.	RPG	APG	PPG
90-91—Malaga	34	1235	302	609	.496	128	165	.776	349	22	749	10.3	0.6	22.0

Three-point field goals: 1990-91, 17-for-52 (.327).

NBA REGULAR-SEASON RECORD

Season Team	G	Min.	FGM	FGA	Pct.	FTM	FTA	Pct.	Off.	Def.	Tot.	Ast.	St.	Blk.	TO	Pts.	RPG	APG	PPG
91-92—Utah	77	1161	175	375	.467	81	100	.810	105	191	296	34	19	44	71	434	3.8	0.4	5.6
92-93—Utah	82	1712	258	592	.436	114	152	.750	116	276	392	43	45	43	90	664	4.8	0.5	8.1
93-94—Utah	55	1070	139	361	.385	68	88	.773	89	171	260	23	23	37	37	358	4.7	0.4	6.5
94-95—Utah	71	1841	285	587	.486	132	157	.841	96	272	368	58	45	47	75	740	5.2	0.8	10.4
95-96—Utah	81	1961	255	581	.439	87	112	.777	90	293	383	82	43	49	71	661	4.7	1.0	8.2
96-97—New Jersey						Did not play—injured.													
97-98—N.J.-Orlando	77	1123	152	408	.373	61	74	.824	60	143	203	25	35	20	52	420	2.6	0.3	5.5
00-01—Utah	49	446	71	147	.483	31	39	.795	20	61	81	22	6	6	28	178	1.7	0.4	3.6
Totals	492	9314	1335	3051	.438	574	722	.795	576	1407	1983	287	216	246	424	3455	4.0	0.6	7.0

Three-point field goals: 1991-92, 3-for-14 (.214). 1992-93, 34-for-98 (.347). 1993-94, 12-for-59 (.203). 1994-95, 38-for-115 (.330). 1995-96, 64-for-192 (.333). 1997-98, 55-for-170 (.324). 2000-01, 5-for-13 (.385). Totals, 211-for-661 (.319).
Personal fouls/disqualifications: 1991-92, 124/0. 1992-93, 201/2. 1993-94, 115/0. 1994-95, 183/1. 1995-96, 166/2. 1997-98, 157/0. 2000-01, 75/0. Totals, 1021/5.

NBA PLAYOFF RECORD

Season Team	G	Min.	FGM	FGA	Pct.	FTM	FTA	Pct.	Off.	Def.	Tot.	Ast.	St.	Blk.	TO	Pts.	RPG	APG	PPG
91-92—Utah	13	257	36	84	.429	11	11	1.000	18	32	50	6	6	5	10	89	3.8	0.5	6.8
92-93—Utah	5	136	13	41	.317	9	13	.692	7	17	24	5	3	6	2	37	4.8	1.0	7.4
93-94—Utah	16	357	48	122	.393	16	25	.640	23	44	67	10	7	11	16	115	4.2	0.6	7.2
94-95—Utah	5	167	21	45	.467	6	9	.667	7	21	28	4	2	4	10	59	5.6	0.8	11.8
95-96—Utah	14	259	33	70	.471	7	9	.778	6	31	37	7	1	3	14	87	2.6	0.5	6.2
00-01—Utah	4	61	7	19	.368	7	7	1.000	1	6	7	2	0	2	2	23	1.8	0.5	5.8
Totals	57	1237	158	381	.415	56	74	.757	62	151	213	34	19	31	54	410	3.7	0.6	7.2

Three-point field goals: 1991-92, 6-for-13 (.462). 1992-93, 2-for-9 (.222). 1993-94, 3-for-16 (.188). 1994-95, 11-for-25 (.440). 1995-96, 14-for-28 (.500). 2000-01, 2-for-6 (.333). Totals, 38-for-97 (.392).
Personal fouls/disqualifications: 1991-92, 30/0. 1992-93, 17/0. 1993-94, 31/0. 1994-95, 10/0. 1995-96, 17/0. 2000-01, 6/0. Totals, 111/0.

ISRAELI LEAGUE RECORD

Season Team	G	Min.	FGM	FGA	Pct.	FTM	FTA	Pct.	Reb.	Ast.	Pts.	RPG	APG	PPG
98-99—Maccabi Ramat Gan	12	327	64	115	.557	29	36	.806	79	11	167	6.6	0.9	13.9

Three-point field goals: 1998-99, 10-for-29 (.345).

BEST, TRAVIS — G — PACERS

PERSONAL: Born July 12, 1972, in Springfield, Mass. ... 5-11/182. (1,80/82,6). ... Full Name: Travis Eric Best.
HIGH SCHOOL: Springfield (Mass.) Central.
COLLEGE: Georgia Tech.
TRANSACTIONS/CAREER NOTES: Selected by Indiana Pacers in first round (23rd pick overall) of 1995 NBA Draft.

B

COLLEGIATE RECORD

Season Team	G	Min.	FGM	FGA	Pct.	FTM	FTA	Pct.	Reb.	Ast.	Pts.	AVERAGES RPG	APG	PPG
91-92—Georgia Tech	35	1227	151	336	.449	72	98	.735	89	198	430	2.5	5.7	12.3
92-93—Georgia Tech	30	1075	163	345	.472	82	109	.752	94	176	488	3.1	5.9	16.3
93-94—Georgia Tech	29	1087	180	390	.462	123	142	.866	104	167	532	3.6	5.8	18.3
94-95—Georgia Tech	30	1115	209	469	.446	116	137	.847	95	151	607	3.2	5.0	20.2
Totals	124	4504	703	1540	.456	393	486	.809	382	692	2057	3.1	5.6	16.6

Three-point field goals: 1991-92, 56-for-145 (.386). 1992-93, 80-for-175 (.457). 1993-94, 49-for-144 (.340). 1994-95, 73-for-192 (.380). Totals, 258-for-656 (.393).

NBA REGULAR-SEASON RECORD

Season Team	G	Min.	FGM	FGA	Pct.	FTM	FTA	Pct.	REBOUNDS Off.	Def.	Tot.	Ast.	St.	Blk.	TO	Pts.	AVERAGES RPG	APG	PPG
95-96—Indiana	59	571	69	163	.423	75	90	.833	11	33	44	97	20	3	63	221	0.7	1.6	3.7
96-97—Indiana	76	2064	274	620	.442	149	197	.756	36	130	166	318	98	5	153	754	2.2	4.2	9.9
97-98—Indiana	82	1547	201	480	.419	112	131	.855	28	94	122	281	85	5	111	535	1.5	3.4	6.5
98-99—Indiana	49	1043	127	305	.416	70	83	.843	19	61	80	169	42	4	62	346	1.6	3.4	7.1
99-00—Indiana	82	1691	271	561	.483	156	190	.821	16	126	142	272	76	5	107	733	1.7	3.3	8.9
00-01—Indiana	77	2457	347	788	.440	187	226	.827	38	184	222	473	110	11	127	918	2.9	6.1	11.9
Totals	425	9373	1289	2917	.442	749	917	.817	148	628	776	1610	431	33	623	3507	1.8	3.8	8.3

Three-point field goals: 1995-96, 8-for-25 (.320). 1996-97, 57-for-155 (.368). 1997-98, 21-for-70 (.300). 1998-99, 22-for-59 (.373). 1999-00, 35-for-93 (.376). 2000-01, 37-for-97 (.381). Totals, 180-for-499 (.361).
Personal fouls/disqualifications: 1995-96, 80/0. 1996-97, 221/3. 1997-98, 193/3. 1998-99, 111/2. 1999-00, 204/1. 2000-01, 246/10. Totals, 1055/19.

NBA PLAYOFF RECORD

Season Team	G	Min.	FGM	FGA	Pct.	FTM	FTA	Pct.	REBOUNDS Off.	Def.	Tot.	Ast.	St.	Blk.	TO	Pts.	AVERAGES RPG	APG	PPG
95-96—Indiana	5	84	11	22	.500	6	7	.857	3	8	11	9	6	0	10	29	2.2	1.8	5.8
97-98—Indiana	16	280	27	72	.375	38	43	.884	1	15	16	31	11	3	19	97	1.0	1.9	6.1
98-99—Indiana	11	150	16	46	.348	12	13	.923	7	10	17	21	4	1	14	46	1.5	1.9	4.2
99-00—Indiana	23	463	77	179	.430	37	44	.841	15	42	57	66	19	4	25	204	2.5	2.9	8.9
00-01—Indiana	4	163	17	39	.436	4	4	1.000	6	13	19	37	4	0	6	39	4.8	9.3	9.8
Totals	59	1140	148	358	.413	97	111	.874	32	88	120	164	44	8	74	415	2.0	2.8	7.0

Three-point field goals: 1995-96, 1-for-6 (.167). 1997-98, 5-for-18 (.278). 1998-99, 2-for-10 (.200). 1999-00, 13-for-30 (.433). 2000-01, 1-for-3 (.333). Totals, 22-for-67 (.328).
Personal fouls/disqualifications: 1995-96, 10/0. 1997-98, 36/0. 1998-99, 34/1. 1999-00, 61/1. 2000-01, 15/1. Totals, 156/3.

BIBBY, MIKE — G — KINGS

PERSONAL: Born May 13, 1978, in Cherry Hill, N.J. ... 6-1/190. (1,85/86,2). ... Full Name: Michael Bibby. ... Son of Henry Bibby, guard with New York Knicks (1972-73 through 1974-75), New Orleans Jazz (1974-75 and 1975-76), Philadelphia 76ers (1976-77 through 1979-80) and San Diego Clippers (1980-81).
HIGH SCHOOL: Shadow Mountain (Phoenix).
COLLEGE: Arizona.
TRANSACTIONS/CAREER NOTES: Selected after sophomore season by Vancouver Grizzlies in first round (second pick overall) of 1998 NBA Draft. ... Traded by Grizzlies with G Brent Price to Sacramento Kings for G Jason Williams and G/F Nick Anderson (June 27, 2001).
MISCELLANEOUS: Vancouver Grizzlies all-time assists leader with 1,675 (1998-99 through 2000-01).

COLLEGIATE RECORD

NOTES: Member of NCAA Division I championship team (1997). ... THE SPORTING NEWS All-America first team (1998).

Season Team	G	Min.	FGM	FGA	Pct.	FTM	FTA	Pct.	Reb.	Ast.	Pts.	AVERAGES RPG	APG	PPG
96-97—Arizona	34	1110	151	339	.445	89	127	.701	109	176	458	3.2	5.2	13.5
97-98—Arizona	35	1124	209	450	.464	108	143	.755	106	199	603	3.0	5.7	17.2
Totals	69	2234	360	789	.456	197	270	.730	215	375	1061	3.1	5.4	15.4

Three-point field goals: 1996-97, 67-for-170 (.394). 1997-98, 77-for-199 (.387). Totals, 144-for-369 (.390).

NBA REGULAR-SEASON RECORD

HONORS: NBA All-Rookie first team (1999).

Season Team	G	Min.	FGM	FGA	Pct.	FTM	FTA	Pct.	REBOUNDS Off.	Def.	Tot.	Ast.	St.	Blk.	TO	Pts.	AVERAGES RPG	APG	PPG
98-99—Vancouver	50	1758	260	605	.430	127	169	.751	30	106	136	325	78	5	146	662	2.7	6.5	13.2
99-00—Vancouver	82	3155	459	1031	.445	195	250	.780	73	233	306	665	132	15	247	1190	3.7	8.1	14.5
00-01—Vancouver	82	3190	525	1157	.454	143	188	.761	47	257	304	685	107	12	248	1301	3.7	8.4	15.9
Totals	214	8103	1244	2793	.445	465	607	.766	150	596	746	1675	317	32	641	3153	3.5	7.8	14.7

Three-point field goals: 1998-99, 15-for-74 (.203). 1999-00, 77-for-212 (.363). 2000-01, 108-for-285 (.379). Totals, 200-for-571 (.350).
Personal fouls/disqualifications: 1998-99, 122/0. 1999-00, 171/1. 2000-01, 148/1. Totals, 441/2.

BILLUPS, CHAUNCEY   G   TIMBERWOLVES

PERSONAL: Born September 25, 1976, in Denver. ... 6-3/202. (1,91/91,6). ... Full Name: Chauncey Ray Billups.
HIGH SCHOOL: George Washington (Denver).
COLLEGE: Colorado.
TRANSACTIONS/CAREER NOTES: Selected after sophomore season by Boston Celtics in first round (third pick overall) of 1997 NBA Draft. ... Traded by Celtics with G Dee Brown, F John Thomas and F Roy Rogers to Toronto Raptors for G Kenny Anderson, C Zan Tabak and F Popeye Jones (February 18, 1998). ... Traded by Raptors with draft rights to G Tyson Wheeler to Denver Nuggets in three-way deal in which Raptors received 1999 first-round draft choice from Nuggets and draft rights to F Zeljko Rebraca, G Micheal Williams and 1999 or 2000 first-round draft choice from Minnesota Timberwolves and Timberwolves received C Dean Garrett and G Bobby Jackson from Nuggets (January 21, 1999). ... Traded by Nuggets with G/F Ron Mercer, F Johnny Taylor and draft considerations to Orlando Magic for F/C Chris Gatling, F Tariq Abdul-Wahad, a future first-round draft pick and cash considerations (February 1, 2000). ... Signed as free agent by Timberwolves (August 8, 2000).

COLLEGIATE RECORD

NOTES: THE SPORTING NEWS All-America second team (1997).

												AVERAGES		
Season Team	G	Min.	FGM	FGA	Pct.	FTM	FTA	Pct.	Reb.	Ast.	Pts.	RPG	APG	PPG
95-96—Colorado	26	919	145	351	.413	130	151	.861	165	143	465	6.3	5.5	17.9
96-97—Colorado	29	947	152	368	.413	176	206	.854	141	139	555	4.9	4.8	19.1
Totals	55	1866	297	719	.413	306	357	.857	306	282	1020	5.6	5.1	18.5

Three-point field goals: 1995-96, 45-for-127 (.354). 1996-97, 75-for-187 (.401). Totals, 120-for-314 (.382).

NBA REGULAR-SEASON RECORD

									REBOUNDS								AVERAGES		
Season Team	G	Min.	FGM	FGA	Pct.	FTM	FTA	Pct.	Off.	Def.	Tot.	Ast.	St.	Blk.	TO	Pts.	RPG	APG	PPG
97-98—Bos.-Tor.	80	2216	280	749	.374	226	266	.850	62	128	190	314	107	4	174	893	2.4	3.9	11.2
98-99—Denver	45	1488	191	495	.386	157	172	.913	24	72	96	173	58	14	98	624	2.1	3.8	13.9
99-00—Den.-Orl.	13	305	34	101	.337	37	44	.841	8	26	34	39	10	2	24	112	2.6	3.0	8.6
00-01—Minnesota	77	1790	248	587	.422	144	171	.842	32	126	158	260	51	11	111	713	2.1	3.4	9.3
Totals	215	5799	753	1932	.390	564	653	.864	126	352	478	786	226	31	407	2342	2.2	3.7	10.9

Three-point field goals: 1997-98, 107-for-325 (.329). 1998-99, 85-for-235 (.362). 1999-00, 7-for-41 (.171). 2000-01, 73-for-194 (.376). Totals, 272-for-795 (.342).
Personal fouls/disqualifications: 1997-98, 172/2. 1998-99, 115/0. 1999-00, 27/0. 2000-01, 178/2. Totals, 492/4.

NBA PLAYOFF RECORD

									REBOUNDS								AVERAGES		
Season Team	G	Min.	FGM	FGA	Pct.	FTM	FTA	Pct.	Off.	Def.	Tot.	Ast.	St.	Blk.	TO	Pts.	RPG	APG	PPG
00-01—Minnesota	3	26	1	6	.167	1	1	1.000	1	4	5	2	0	0	1	3	1.7	0.7	1.0

Three-point field goals: 2000-01, 0-for-1.
Personal fouls/disqualifications: 2000-01, 5/0.

BLAYLOCK, MOOKIE   G   WARRIORS

PERSONAL: Born March 20, 1967, in Garland, Texas. ... 6-1/185. (1,85/83,9). ... Full Name: Daron Oshay Blaylock.
HIGH SCHOOL: Garland (Texas).
JUNIOR COLLEGE: Midland (Texas) College.
COLLEGE: Oklahoma.
TRANSACTIONS/CAREER NOTES: Selected by New Jersey Nets in first round (12th pick overall) of 1989 NBA Draft. ... Traded by Nets with F Roy Hinson to Atlanta Hawks for G Rumeal Robinson (November 3, 1992). ... Traded by Hawks with 1999 first-round draft choice to Golden State Warriors for G Bimbo Coles, F Duane Ferrell and 1999 first-round draft choice (June 29, 1999).
MISCELLANEOUS: Atlanta Hawks franchise all-time steals leader with 1,321 (1992-93 through 1998-99).

COLLEGIATE RECORD

NOTES: THE SPORTING NEWS All-America second team (1989). ... Holds NCAA Division I career record for for most steals per game—3.8. ... Holds NCAA Division I single-season record for most steals—150 (1988). ... Holds NCAA Division I single-game record for most steals—13 (December 12, 1987, vs. Centenary; and December 17, 1988, vs. Loyola Marymount).

												AVERAGES		
Season Team	G	Min.	FGM	FGA	Pct.	FTM	FTA	Pct.	Reb.	Ast.	Pts.	RPG	APG	PPG
85-86—Midland College	34	...	254	449	.566	62	84	.738	109	158	570	3.2	4.6	16.8
86-87—Midland College	33	...	258	500	.516	60	83	.723	138	161	647	4.2	4.9	19.6
87-88—Oklahoma	39	1347	241	624	.460	78	114	.604	102	232	638	4.2	5.9	16.4
88-89—Oklahoma	35	1359	272	598	.455	65	100	.650	164	233	700	4.7	6.7	20.0
Junior College Totals	67	...	512	949	.540	122	167	.731	247	319	1217	3.7	4.8	18.2
4-Year-College Totals	74	2706	513	1122	.457	143	214	.668	326	465	1338	4.4	6.3	18.1

Three-point field goals: 1987-88, 78-for-201 (.388). 1988-89, 91-for-245 (.371). Totals, 169-for-446 (.379).

NBA REGULAR-SEASON RECORD

RECORDS: Shares career record for most consecutive seasons leading league in steals—2 (1996-97 and 1997-98).
HONORS: NBA All-Defensive first team (1994, 1995). ... NBA All-Defensive second team (1996, 1997, 1998, 1999).
NOTES: Led NBA with 2.72 steals per game (1997) and 2.61 steals per game (1998).

									REBOUNDS								AVERAGES		
Season Team	G	Min.	FGM	FGA	Pct.	FTM	FTA	Pct.	Off.	Def.	Tot.	Ast.	St.	Blk.	TO	Pts.	RPG	APG	PPG
89-90—New Jersey	50	1267	212	571	.371	63	81	.778	42	98	140	210	82	14	111	505	2.8	4.2	10.1
90-91—New Jersey	72	2585	432	1039	.416	139	176	.790	67	182	249	441	169	40	207	1017	3.5	6.1	14.1
91-92—New Jersey	72	2548	429	993	.432	126	177	.712	101	168	269	492	170	40	152	996	3.7	6.8	13.8
92-93—Atlanta	80	2820	414	964	.429	123	169	.728	89	191	280	671	203	23	187	1069	3.5	8.4	13.4
93-94—Atlanta	81	2915	444	1079	.411	116	159	.730	117	307	424	789	212	44	196	1118	5.2	9.7	13.8

B

Season Team	G	Min.	FGM	FGA	Pct.	FTM	FTA	Pct.	Off.	Def.	Tot.	Ast.	St.	Blk.	TO	Pts.	RPG	APG	PPG
94-95—Atlanta	80	3069	509	1198	.425	156	214	.729	117	276	393	616	200	26	242	1373	4.9	7.7	17.2
95-96—Atlanta	81	2893	455	1123	.405	127	170	.747	110	222	332	478	212	17	188	1268	4.1	5.9	15.7
96-97—Atlanta	78	3056	501	1159	.432	131	174	.753	114	299	413	463	*212	20	185	1354	5.3	5.9	17.4
97-98—Atlanta	70	2700	368	938	.392	95	134	.709	81	260	341	469	*183	21	176	921	4.9	6.7	13.2
98-99—Atlanta	48	1763	247	651	.379	69	91	.758	45	179	224	278	99	9	115	640	4.7	5.8	13.3
99-00—Golden State	73	2459	327	837	.391	67	95	.705	55	215	270	489	146	22	143	822	3.7	6.7	11.3
00-01—Golden State	69	2352	317	801	.396	53	76	.697	71	201	272	462	163	20	128	760	3.9	6.7	11.0
Totals	854	30427	4655	11353	.410	1265	1716	.737	1009	2598	3607	5858	2051	296	2030	11843	4.2	6.9	13.9

Three-point field goals: 1989-90, 18-for-80 (.225). 1990-91, 14-for-91 (.154). 1991-92, 12-for-54 (.222). 1992-93, 118-for-315 (.375). 1993-94, 114-for-341 (.334). 1994-95, 199-for-555 (.359). 1995-96, 231-for-623 (.371). 1996-97, 221-for-604 (.366). 1997-98, 90-for-334 (.269). 1998-99, 77-for-251 (.307). 1999-00, 101-for-301 (.336). 2000-01, 73-for-225 (.324). Totals, 1268-for-3774 (.336).

Personal fouls/disqualifications: 1989-90, 110/0. 1990-91, 180/0. 1991-92, 182/1. 1992-93, 156/0. 1993-94, 144/0. 1994-95, 164/3. 1995-96, 151/1. 1996-97, 141/0. 1997-98, 122/0. 1998-99, 61/0. 1999-00, 122/0. 2000-01, 134/1. Totals, 1667/6.

NBA PLAYOFF RECORD

Season Team	G	Min.	FGM	FGA	Pct.	FTM	FTA	Pct.	Off.	Def.	Tot.	Ast.	St.	Blk.	TO	Pts.	RPG	APG	PPG
91-92—New Jersey	4	148	17	55	.309	3	4	.750	5	11	16	31	15	2	7	38	4.0	7.8	9.5
92-93—Atlanta	3	99	9	25	.360	5	6	.833	2	11	13	13	3	4	11	27	4.3	4.3	9.0
93-94—Atlanta	11	415	48	141	.340	25	30	.833	16	39	55	98	24	5	32	143	5.0	8.9	13.0
94-95—Atlanta	3	121	18	49	.367	7	11	.636	7	6	13	17	4	0	9	54	4.3	5.7	18.0
95-96—Atlanta	10	426	61	145	.421	16	24	.667	13	30	43	64	22	8	29	171	4.3	6.4	17.1
96-97—Atlanta	10	441	61	154	.396	14	21	.667	12	58	70	65	21	2	35	164	7.0	6.5	16.4
97-98—Atlanta	4	153	22	53	.415	7	12	.583	6	14	20	33	9	1	9	59	5.0	8.3	14.8
98-99—Atlanta	9	358	44	135	.326	7	15	.467	6	30	36	36	18	2	30	113	4.0	4.0	12.6
Totals	54	2161	280	757	.370	84	123	.683	67	199	266	357	116	24	162	769	4.9	6.6	14.2

Three-point field goals: 1991-92, 1-for-6 (.167). 1992-93, 4-for-12 (.333). 1993-94, 22-for-64 (.344). 1994-95, 11-for-28 (.393). 1995-96, 33-for-84 (.393). 1996-97, 28-for-85 (.329). 1997-98, 8-for-27 (.296). 1998-99, 18-for-51 (.353). Totals, 125-for-357 (.350).

Personal fouls/disqualifications: 1991-92, 16/0. 1992-93, 9/0. 1993-94, 22/0. 1994-95, 6/0. 1995-96, 15/0. 1996-97, 15/0. 1997-98, 8/0. 1998-99, 11/0. Totals, 102/0.

NBA ALL-STAR GAME RECORD

Season Team	Min.	FGM	FGA	Pct.	FTM	FTA	Pct.	Off.	Def.	Tot.	Ast.	PF	Dq.	St.	Blk.	TO	Pts.
1994 —Atlanta	16	2	5	.400	0	0	...	0	1	1	2	3	0	0	0	1	5

Three-point field goals: 1994, 1-for-2 (.500).

BLOUNT, CORIE   F   WARRIORS

PERSONAL: Born January 4, 1969, in Monrovia, Calif. ... 6-10/242. (2,08/109,8). ... Full Name: Corie Kasoun Blount. ... Name pronounced BLUNT.

HIGH SCHOOL: Monrovia (Calif.).

JUNIOR COLLEGE: Rancho Santiago (Calif.) Community College.

COLLEGE: Cincinnati.

TRANSACTIONS/CAREER NOTES: Selected by Chicago Bulls in first round (25th pick overall) of 1993 NBA Draft. ... Traded by Bulls to Los Angeles Lakers for cash (June 30, 1995). ... Waived by Lakers (March 10, 1999). ... Signed as free agent by Cleveland Cavaliers (March 13, 1999). ... Signed as free agent by Phoenix Suns (September 8, 1999). ... Traded by Suns with F Ruben Garces and G Paul McPherson to Golden State Warriors for G Vinny Del Negro (January 26, 2001).

NOTES: Broke foot (1988-89); granted extra year of eligibility.

COLLEGIATE RECORD

Season Team	G	Min.	FGM	FGA	Pct.	FTM	FTA	Pct.	Reb.	Ast.	Pts.	RPG	APG	PPG
88-89—Rancho Santiago C.C.	4	...	8	16	.500	3	5	.600	15	2	19	3.8	0.5	4.8
89-90—Rancho Santiago C.C.	34	...	200	373	.536	72	123	.585	279	56	472	8.2	1.6	13.9
90-91—Rancho Santiago C.C.	37	...	301	511	.589	121	182	.665	333	108	723	9.0	2.9	19.5
91-92—Cincinnati	34	864	114	238	.479	50	90	.556	213	69	278	6.3	2.0	8.2
92-93—Cincinnati	21	588	104	189	.550	30	53	.566	170	47	238	8.1	2.2	11.3
Junior College Totals	75	...	509	900	.566	196	310	.632	627	166	1214	8.4	2.2	16.2
4-Year-College Totals	55	1452	218	427	.511	80	143	.559	383	116	516	7.0	2.1	9.4

Three-point field goals: 1991-92, 0-for-2.

NBA REGULAR-SEASON RECORD

Season Team	G	Min.	FGM	FGA	Pct.	FTM	FTA	Pct.	Off.	Def.	Tot.	Ast.	St.	Blk.	TO	Pts.	RPG	APG	PPG
93-94—Chicago	67	690	76	174	.437	46	75	.613	76	118	194	56	19	33	52	198	2.9	0.8	3.0
94-95—Chicago	68	889	100	210	.476	38	67	.567	107	133	240	60	26	33	59	238	3.5	0.9	3.5
95-96—L.A. Lakers	57	715	79	167	.473	25	44	.568	69	101	170	42	25	35	47	183	3.0	0.7	3.2
96-97—L.A. Lakers	58	1009	92	179	.514	56	83	.675	113	163	276	35	22	26	50	241	4.8	0.6	4.2
97-98—L.A. Lakers	70	1029	107	187	.572	39	78	.500	114	184	298	37	29	25	51	253	4.3	0.5	3.6
98-99—L.A.L.-Cleve.	34	530	36	100	.360	28	54	.519	58	93	151	12	19	16	21	100	4.4	0.4	2.9
99-00—Phoenix	38	446	44	89	.494	19	33	.576	52	61	113	10	15	7	28	107	3.0	0.3	2.8
00-01—Phoenix-G.S.	68	1305	130	294	.442	51	82	.614	181	219	400	59	42	22	73	313	5.9	0.9	4.6
Totals	460	6613	664	1400	.474	302	517	.584	770	1072	1842	311	197	197	381	1633	4.0	0.7	3.6

Three-point field goals: 1994-95, 0-for-2. 1995-96, 0-for-2. 1996-97, 1-for-3 (.333). 1997-98, 0-for-4. 1998-99, 0-for-1. 1999-00, 0-for-2. 2000-01, 2-for-8 (.250). Totals, 3-for-22 (.136).

Personal fouls/disqualifications: 1993-94, 93/0. 1994-95, 146/0. 1995-96, 109/2. 1996-97, 121/2. 1997-98, 157/2. 1998-99, 74/0. 1999-00, 78/0. 2000-01, 165/3. Totals, 943/9.

Season Team	G	Min.	FGM	FGA	Pct.	FTM	FTA	Pct.	REBOUNDS Off.	Def.	Tot.	Ast.	St.	Blk.	TO	Pts.	AVERAGES RPG	APG	PPG
94-95—Chicago	8	20	0	3	.000	0	0	...	1	4	5	0	0	0	1	0	0.6	0.0	0.0
96-97—L.A. Lakers	3	8	1	1	1.000	1	2	.500	2	2	2	1	0	0	0	3	0.7	0.3	1.0
97-98—L.A. Lakers	12	209	12	24	.500	7	11	.636	24	40	64	7	6	4	3	31	5.3	0.6	2.6
99-00—Phoenix	9	162	17	31	.548	10	18	.556	25	31	56	3	6	6	13	44	6.2	0.3	4.9
Totals	32	399	30	59	.508	18	31	.581	50	77	127	11	12	10	17	78	4.0	0.3	2.4

Three-point field goals: 1994-95, 0-for-1. Totals, 0-for-1 (.000).
Personal fouls/disqualifications: 1994-95, 5/0. 1996-97, 2/0. 1997-98, 27/1. 1999-00, 36/0. Totals, 70/1.

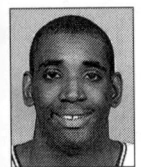

BLOUNT, MARK   C   CELTICS

B

PERSONAL: Born November 30, 1975, in Dobbs Ferry, N.Y. ... 7-0/230. (2,13/104,3). ... Full Name: Mark D. Blount.
HIGH SCHOOL: Oak Hill Academy (Mouth of Wilson, Va.), then Sacred Heart (Yonkers, N.Y.), then Dobbs Ferry (N.Y.).
COLLEGE: Pittsburgh.
TRANSACTIONS/CAREER NOTES: Selected after sophomore season by Seattle SuperSonics in second round (55th pick overall) of 1997 NBA Draft. ... Waived by SuperSonics (October 7, 1997). ... Played in Continental Basketball Association with Yakima Sun Kings (1997-98). ... Signed as free agent by Los Angeles Clippers (January 22, 1999). ... Waived by Clippers (January 31, 1999). ... Played in International Basketball League with Baltimore Bayrunners (1999-2000). ... Signed as free agent by Boston Celtics (August 1, 2000).

COLLEGIATE RECORD

Season Team	G	Min.	FGM	FGA	Pct.	FTM	FTA	Pct.	Reb.	Ast.	Pts.	AVERAGES RPG	APG	PPG
95-96—Pittsburgh	27	389	35	85	.412	26	48	.542	80	9	96	3.0	0.3	3.6
96-97—Pittsburgh	29	760	101	207	.488	61	120	.508	198	30	264	6.8	1.0	9.1
Totals	56	1149	136	292	.466	87	168	.518	278	39	360	5.0	0.7	6.4

Three-point field goals: 1996-97, 1-for-2 (.500).

CBA REGULAR-SEASON RECORD

Season Team	G	Min.	FGM	FGA	Pct.	FTM	FTA	Pct.	Reb.	Ast.	Pts.	AVERAGES RPG	APG	PPG
97-98—Yakima	5	64	8	22	.364	2	2	1.000	9	0	18	1.8	0.0	3.6

IBL REGULAR SEASON RECORD

Season Team	G	Min.	FGM	FGA	Pct.	FTM	FTA	Pct.	Reb.	Ast.	Pts.	AVERAGES RPG	APG	PPG
99-00—Baltimore	54	1077	189	352	.537	98	152	.645	274	44	471	5.1	0.8	8.7

Three-point field goals: 1999-00, 0-for-1.

NBA REGULAR-SEASON RECORD

Season Team	G	Min.	FGM	FGA	Pct.	FTM	FTA	Pct.	REBOUNDS Off.	Def.	Tot.	Ast.	St.	Blk.	TO	Pts.	AVERAGES RPG	APG	PPG
00-01—Boston	64	1098	101	200	.505	46	66	.697	97	134	231	32	39	76	62	248	3.6	0.5	3.9

Personal fouls/disqualifications: 2000-01, 183/0.

BOGUES, MUGGSY   G   MAVERICKS

PERSONAL: Born January 9, 1965, in Baltimore. ... 5-3/141. (1,60/64,0). ... Full Name: Tyrone Curtis Bogues. ... Name pronounced rhymes with rogues.
HIGH SCHOOL: Dunbar (Baltimore).
COLLEGE: Wake Forest.
TRANSACTIONS/CAREER NOTES: Selected by Washington Bullets in first round (12th pick overall) of 1987 NBA Draft. ... Played in United States Basketball League with Rhode Island Gulls (1987). ... Selected by Charlotte Hornets from Bullets in NBA Expansion Draft (June 23, 1988). ... Traded by Hornets with G Tony Delk to Golden State Warriors for G B.J. Armstrong (November 7, 1997). ... Signed as free agent by Toronto Raptors (September 23, 1999). ... Traded by Raptors with G Mark Jackson to New York Knicks for G Chris Childs and 2001 first-round draft choice (February 22, 2001). ... Traded by Knicks to Dallas Mavericks as part of three-team trade in which Knicks acquired F Shandon Anderson from Houston Rockets and G Howard Eisley from Mavericks and Rockets acquired F Glen Rice from Knicks and draft rights to G Kyle Hill from Mavericks (August 10, 2001).
MISCELLANEOUS: Member of gold-medal-winning U.S. World Championship team (1986). ... Charlotte Hornets all-time assists leader with 5,557 and all-time steals leader with 1,067 (1988-89 through 1997-98).

COLLEGIATE RECORD

NOTES: Frances Pomeroy Naismith Award winner (1987).

Season Team	G	Min.	FGM	FGA	Pct.	FTM	FTA	Pct.	Reb.	Ast.	Pts.	AVERAGES RPG	APG	PPG
83-84—Wake Forest	32	312	14	46	.304	9	13	.692	21	53	37	0.7	1.7	1.2
84-85—Wake Forest	29	1025	81	162	.500	30	44	.682	69	207	192	2.4	7.1	6.6
85-86—Wake Forest	29	1101	132	290	.455	65	89	.730	90	245	329	3.1	8.4	11.3
86-87—Wake Forest	29	1130	159	318	.500	75	93	.806	110	276	428	3.8	9.5	14.8
Totals	119	3568	386	816	.473	179	239	.749	290	781	986	2.4	6.6	8.3

Three-point field goals: 1986-87, 35-for-79 (.443).

NBA REGULAR-SEASON RECORD

Season Team	G	Min.	FGM	FGA	Pct.	FTM	FTA	Pct.	REBOUNDS Off.	Def.	Tot.	Ast.	St.	Blk.	TO	Pts.	AVERAGES RPG	APG	PPG
87-88—Washington	79	1628	166	426	.390	58	74	.784	35	101	136	404	127	3	101	393	1.7	5.1	5.0
88-89—Charlotte	79	1755	178	418	.426	66	88	.750	53	112	165	620	111	7	124	423	2.1	7.8	5.4
89-90—Charlotte	81	2743	326	664	.491	106	134	.791	48	159	207	867	166	3	146	763	2.6	10.7	9.4
90-91—Charlotte	81	2299	241	524	.460	86	108	.796	58	158	216	669	137	3	120	568	2.7	8.3	7.0
91-92—Charlotte	82	2790	317	671	.472	94	120	.783	58	177	235	743	170	6	156	730	2.9	9.1	8.9
92-93—Charlotte	81	2833	331	730	.453	140	168	.833	51	247	298	711	161	5	154	808	3.7	8.8	10.0
93-94—Charlotte	77	2746	354	751	.471	125	155	.806	78	235	313	780	133	2	171	835	4.1	10.1	10.8
94-95—Charlotte	78	2629	348	730	.477	160	180	.889	51	206	257	675	103	0	132	862	3.3	8.7	11.1
95-96—Charlotte	6	77	6	16	.375	2	2	1.000	6	1	7	19	2	0	6	14	1.2	3.2	2.3
96-97—Charlotte	65	1880	204	443	.460	54	64	.844	25	116	141	469	82	2	108	522	2.2	7.2	8.0
97-98—Char.-G.S.	61	1570	141	323	.437	61	68	.897	30	102	132	331	67	3	105	347	2.2	5.4	5.7
98-99—Golden State ...	36	714	76	154	.494	31	36	.861	16	57	73	134	43	1	47	183	2.0	3.7	5.1
99-00—Toronto	80	1731	157	358	.439	79	87	.908	25	110	135	299	65	4	59	410	1.7	3.7	5.1
00-01—Tor.-N.Y.	3	34	0	2	.000	0	0	.000	0	3	3	5	2	0	4	0	1.0	1.7	0.0
Totals	889	25429	2845	6210	.458	1062	1284	.827	534	1784	2318	6726	1369	39	1433	6858	2.6	7.5	7.7

Three-point field goals: 1987-88, 3-for-16 (.188). 1988-89, 1-for-13 (.077). 1989-90, 5-for-26 (.192). 1990-91, 0-for-12. 1991-92, 2-for-27 (.074). 1992-93, 6-for-26 (.231). 1993-94, 2-for-12 (.167). 1994-95, 6-for-30 (.200). 1995-96, 0-for-1. 1996-97, 60-for-144 (.417). 1997-98, 4-for-16 (.250). 1998-99, 0-for-6. 1999-00, 17-for-51 (.333). 2000-01, 0-for-1. Totals, 106-for-381 (.278).

Personal fouls/disqualifications: 1987-88, 138/1. 1988-89, 141/1. 1989-90, 168/1. 1990-91, 160/2. 1991-92, 156/0. 1992-93, 179/0. 1993-94, 147/1. 1994-95, 151/0. 1995-96, 4/0. 1996-97, 114/0. 1997-98, 58/0. 1998-99, 44/0. 1999-00, 117/0. 2000-01, 3/0. Totals, 1582/6.

NBA PLAYOFF RECORD

Season Team	G	Min.	FGM	FGA	Pct.	FTM	FTA	Pct.	REBOUNDS Off.	Def.	Tot.	Ast.	St.	Blk.	TO	Pts.	AVERAGES RPG	APG	PPG
87-88—Washington	1	2	0	0	...	0	0	...	0	0	0	2	0	0	1	0	0.0	2.0	0.0
92-93—Charlotte	9	346	39	82	.476	10	14	.714	6	30	36	70	24	0	17	88	4.0	7.8	9.8
94-95—Charlotte	4	145	14	45	.311	5	5	1.000	3	3	6	25	4	0	9	34	1.5	6.3	8.5
96-97—Charlotte	2	58	11	19	.579	4	4	1.000	1	2	3	5	1	0	6	32	1.5	2.5	16.0
99-00—Toronto	3	87	6	21	.286	1	3	.333	3	3	6	5	4	0	4	16	2.0	1.7	5.3
Totals	19	638	70	167	.419	20	26	.769	13	38	51	107	33	0	37	170	2.7	5.6	8.9

Three-point field goals: 1992-93, 0-for-2. 1994-95, 1-for-3 (.333). 1996-97, 6-for-7 (.857). 1999-00, 3-for-9 (.333). Totals, 10-for-21 (.476).
Personal fouls/disqualifications: 1992-93, 21/0. 1994-95, 8/0. 1996-97, 3/0. 1999-00, 4/0. Totals, 36/0.

BOHANNON, ETDRICK   F

PERSONAL: Born May 29, 1973, in San Bernardino, Calif. ... 6-9/235. (2,06/106,6).
HIGH SCHOOL: Maine Central Institute (Pittsfield, Maine).
COLLEGE: Arizona, then Tennessee, then Auburn-Montgomery (Ala.).
TRANSACTIONS/CAREER NOTES: Not drafted by an NBA franchise. ... Signed as free agent by Indiana Pacers (July 10, 1997). ... Signed as free agent by Washington Wizards (January 21, 1999). ... Waived by Wizards (February 19, 1999). ... Played in Continental Basketball Association with Fort Wayne Fury (1999-2000). ... Signed by New York Knicks to first of two consecutive 10-day contracts (February 20, 2000). ... Signed by Los Angeles Clippers to 10-day contract (March 27, 2000). ... Re-signed by Clippers for remainder of season (April 6, 2000). ... Waived by Clippers (October 25, 2000). ... Played in Spain (2000-01). ... Played in American Basketball Association 2000 with Los Angeles Stars (2000-01). ... Signed by Cleveland Cavaliers to first of two consecutive 10-day contracts (January 7, 2001).

COLLEGIATE RECORD

Season Team	G	Min.	FGM	FGA	Pct.	FTM	FTA	Pct.	Reb.	Ast.	Pts.	AVERAGES RPG	APG	PPG
92-93—Arizona	24	203	23	52	.442	17	31	.548	52	12	63	2.2	0.5	2.6
93-94—Tennessee						Did not play—transfer student.								
94-95—Tennessee	14	182	79	135	.585	56	97	.577	122	9	55	8.7	0.6	3.9
95-96—Auburn-Montgomery......	12	327	79	135	.585	56	97	.577	122	17	214	10.2	1.4	17.8
96-97—Auburn-Montgomery......	24	750	140	234	.598	92	166	.554	225	20	372	9.4	0.8	15.5
Totals	74	1462	321	556	.577	221	391	.565	521	58	704	7.0	0.8	9.5

NBA REGULAR-SEASON RECORD

Season Team	G	Min.	FGM	FGA	Pct.	FTM	FTA	Pct.	REBOUNDS Off.	Def.	Tot.	Ast.	St.	Blk.	TO	Pts.	RPG	APG	PPG
97-98—Indiana...........	5	11	0	4	.000	0	0	...	2	4	6	1	0	2	3	0	1.2	0.2	0.0
98-99—Washington	2	4	0	0	...	0	0	...	0	0	0	0	0	0	0	0	0.0	0.0	0.0
99-00—N.Y.-L.A.C.	13	118	7	13	.538	15	24	.625	13	18	31	5	2	6	10	29	2.4	0.4	2.2
00-01—Cleveland	6	19	2	4	.500	4	4	1.000	3	4	7	0	0	2	1	8	1.2	0.0	1.3
Totals	26	152	9	21	.429	19	28	.679	18	26	44	6	2	10	14	37	1.7	0.2	1.4

Personal fouls/disqualifications: 1997-98, 3/0. 1999-00, 25/0. 2000-01, 4/0. Totals, 32/0.

CBA REGULAR-SEASON RECORD

Season Team	G	Min.	FGM	FGA	Pct.	FTM	FTA	Pct.	Reb.	Ast.	Pts.	AVERAGES RPG	APG	PPG
99-00—Fort Wayne...................	39	1257	193	353	.547	101	169	.598	417	25	487	10.7	0.6	12.5

Three-point field goals: 1999-00, 0-for-1.

ABA 2000 LEAGUE RECORD

Season Team	G	Min.	FGM	FGA	Pct.	FTM	FTA	Pct.	Reb.	Ast.	Pts.	AVERAGES RPG	APG	PPG
00-01—Los Angeles	4	98	11	20	.550	9	15	.600	26	3	32	6.5	0.7	8.0

Three-point field goals: 2000-01, 0-for-1.

SPANISH LEAGUE RECORD

Season Team	G	Min.	FGM	FGA	Pct.	FTM	FTA	Pct.	Reb.	Ast.	Pts.	AVERAGES RPG	APG	PPG
00-01—Baloncesto Girona..........	14	358	48	98	.490	35	66	.530	97	7	131	6.9	0.5	9.4

B

BOOTH, CALVIN   C   SUPERSONICS

PERSONAL: Born May 7, 1976, in Reynoldsburg, Ohio ... 6-11/241. (2,11/109,3). ... Full Name: Calvin L. Booth.
HIGH SCHOOL: Groveport Madison (Reynoldsburg, Ohio).
COLLEGE: Penn State.
TRANSACTIONS/CAREER NOTES: Selected by Washington Wizards in second round (35th pick overall) of 1999 NBA Draft. ... Traded by Wizards with F Juwan Howard and F Obinna Ekezie to Dallas Mavericks for F/C Christian Laettner, G Courtney Alexander, F Loy Vaught, G Hubert Davis, F/C Etan Thomas and cash considerations (February 22, 2001). ... Signed as free agent by Seattle SuperSonics (July 31, 2001).

B

COLLEGIATE RECORD

Season Team	G	Min.	FGM	FGA	Pct.	FTM	FTA	Pct.	Reb.	Ast.	Pts.	RPG	APG	PPG
94-95—Penn State						Did not play—redshirted.								
95-96—Penn State	28	670	100	182	.549	61	96	.635	150	35	261	5.4	1.3	9.3
96-97—Penn State	27	706	87	204	.426	61	84	.726	134	15	236	5.0	0.6	8.7
97-98—Penn State	32	955	156	294	.531	65	97	.670	208	8	377	6.5	0.3	11.8
98-99—Penn State	27	942	157	306	.513	100	129	.775	236	24	414	8.7	0.9	15.3
Totals	114	3273	500	986	.507	287	406	.707	728	82	1288	6.4	0.7	11.3

Three-point field goals: 1996-97, 1-for-3 (.333). 1997-98, 0-for-1. 1998-99, 0-for-6. Totals, 1-for-10 (.100).

NBA REGULAR-SEASON RECORD

Season Team	G	Min.	FGM	FGA	Pct.	FTM	FTA	Pct.	Off.	Def.	Tot.	Ast.	St.	Blk.	TO	Pts.	RPG	APG	PPG
99-00—Washington	11	143	16	46	.348	10	14	.714	17	17	32	7	3	11	6	42	2.9	0.6	3.8
00-01—Wash.-Dallas	55	933	120	252	.476	53	78	.679	77	169	246	42	29	111	53	293	4.5	0.8	5.3
Totals	66	1076	136	298	.456	63	92	.685	92	186	278	49	32	125	59	335	4.2	0.7	5.1

Personal fouls/disqualifications: 1999-00, 23/0. 2000-01, 146/1. Totals, 169/1.

NBA PLAYOFF RECORD

Season Team	G	Min.	FGM	FGA	Pct.	FTM	FTA	Pct.	Off.	Def.	Tot.	Ast.	St.	Blk.	TO	Pts.	RPG	APG	PPG
00-01—Dallas	10	137	15	37	.405	8	9	.889	16	12	28	2	7	6	4	38	2.8	0.2	3.8

Personal fouls/disqualifications: 2000-01, 29/0.

BOWDLER, CAL   F   HAWKS

PERSONAL: Born March 31, 1977, in Sharps, Va. ... 6-10/245. (2,08/111,1). ... Full Name: James Calloway Bowdler II.
HIGH SCHOOL: Rappahannock (Warsaw, Va.).
COLLEGE: Old Dominion.
TRANSACTIONS/CAREER NOTES: Selected by Atlanta Hawks in first round (17th pick overall) of 1999 NBA Draft.

COLLEGIATE RECORD

Season Team	G	Min.	FGM	FGA	Pct.	FTM	FTA	Pct.	Reb.	Ast.	Pts.	RPG	APG	PPG
95-96—Old Dominion	23	204	16	47	.340	9	13	.692	38	14	49	1.7	0.6	2.1
96-97—Old Dominion	33	626	65	150	.433	39	80	.488	161	11	183	4.9	0.3	5.5
97-98—Old Dominion	28	830	102	242	.421	74	133	.556	245	15	285	8.8	0.5	10.2
98-99—Old Dominion	34	1021	177	364	.492	133	182	.731	339	43	500	10.0	1.3	14.7
Totals	118	2681	362	803	.451	255	408	.625	783	83	1017	6.6	0.7	8.6

Three-point field goals: 1995-96, 8-for-26 (.308). 1996-97, 14-for-44 (.318). 1997-98, 7-for-39 (.179). 1998-99, 9-for-35 (.257). Totals, 38-for-144 (.264).

NBA REGULAR-SEASON RECORD

Season Team	G	Min.	FGM	FGA	Pct.	FTM	FTA	Pct.	Off.	Def.	Tot.	Ast.	St.	Blk.	TO	Pts.	RPG	APG	PPG
99-00—Atlanta	46	423	49	115	.426	24	38	.632	22	63	85	14	14	9	21	122	1.8	0.3	2.7
00-01—Atlanta	44	375	53	114	.465	33	40	.825	30	47	77	4	10	21	11	140	1.8	0.1	3.2
Totals	90	798	102	229	.445	57	78	.731	52	110	162	18	24	30	32	262	1.8	0.2	2.9

Three-point field goals: 1999-00, 0-for-1. 2000-01, 1-for-5 (.200). Totals, 1-for-6 (.167).
Personal fouls/disqualifications: 1999-00, 46/1. 2000-01, 45/0. Totals, 91/1.

BOWEN, BRUCE   G   SPURS

PERSONAL: Born June 14, 1971, in Merced, Calif. ... 6-7/200. (2,01/90,7).
HIGH SCHOOL: Edison (Fresno, Calif.).
COLLEGE: Cal State Fullerton.
TRANSACTIONS/CAREER NOTES: Not drafted by an NBA franchise. ... Played in France (1994-95 and 1996-97). ... Signed as free agent by Miami Heat (October 5, 1995). ... Waived by Heat (October 13, 1995). ... Played in Continental Basketball Association with Fort Wayne Fury (1995-96) and Rockford Lightning (1995-96 and 1996-97). ... Signed by Heat to 10-day contract (March 15, 1997). ... Signed by Heat for remainder of season (March 25, 1997). ... Signed as free agent by Boston Celtics (July 28, 1997). ... Signed as free agent by Philadelphia 76ers (September 16, 1999). ... Traded by 76ers to Chicago Bulls for F Toni Kukoc in three-way deal in which 76ers sent G Larry Hughes and F/G Billy Owens to Golden State Warriors and Warriors sent G John Starks and future first-round draft choice to Bulls (February 16, 2000). ... Waived by Bulls (February 18, 2000). ... Signed as free agent by Heat (February 23, 2000). ... Signed as free agent by San Antonio Spurs (July 31, 2001).

COLLEGIATE RECORD

Season Team	G	Min.	FGM	FGA	Pct.	FTM	FTA	Pct.	Reb.	Ast.	Pts.	RPG	APG	PPG
89-90—Cal State Full.	18	98	9	22	.409	10	13	.769	18	4	31	1.0	0.2	1.7
90-91—Cal State Full.	28	849	89	236	.377	83	120	.692	196	75	275	7.0	2.7	9.8
91-92—Cal State Full.	28	969	138	311	.444	120	161	.745	196	75	408	7.0	2.7	14.6
92-93—Cal State Full.	27	987	148	318	.465	131	201	.652	176	62	441	6.5	2.3	16.3
Totals	101	2903	384	887	.433	344	495	.695	586	216	1155	5.8	2.1	11.4

Three-point field goals: 1989-90, 3-for-5 (.600). 1990-91, 14-for-60 (.233). 1991-92, 12-for-44 (.273). 1992-93, 14-for-43 (.326). Totals, 43-for-152 (.283).

FRENCH LEAGUE RECORD

Season Team	G	Min.	FGM	FGA	Pct.	FTM	FTA	Pct.	Reb.	Ast.	Pts.	RPG	APG	PPG
94-95—Evreux	21	...	...	...	...	...	...	...	79	21	642	3.8	1.0	30.6
96-97—Bescanson	20	768	173	333	.520	97	142	.683	70	55	509	3.5	2.8	25.5
Totals	41	...	...	...	...	...	...	...	149	76	1151	3.6	1.9	28.1

Three-point field goals: 1996-97, 25-for-67 (.373).

HONORS: NBA All-Defensive second team (2001).

NBA REGULAR-SEASON RECORD

Season Team	G	Min.	FGM	FGA	Pct.	FTM	FTA	Pct.	REBOUNDS Off.	Def.	Tot.	Ast.	St.	Blk.	TO	Pts.	RPG	APG	PPG
96-97—Miami	1	1	0	0	...	0	0	...	0	0	0	0	0	1	0	0	0.0	0.0	0.0
97-98—Boston	61	1305	122	298	.409	76	122	.623	79	95	174	81	87	29	52	340	2.9	1.3	5.6
98-99—Boston	30	494	26	93	.280	11	24	.458	15	37	52	28	21	9	13	70	1.7	0.9	2.3
99-00—Phil.-Miami	69	878	72	194	.371	25	43	.581	27	69	96	34	23	15	19	196	1.4	0.5	2.8
00-01—Miami	82	2685	211	581	.363	98	161	.609	45	200	245	132	83	53	74	623	3.0	1.6	7.6
Totals	243	5363	431	1166	.370	210	350	.600	166	401	567	275	214	107	158	1229	2.3	1.1	5.1

Three-point field goals: 1997-98, 20-for-59 (.339). 1998-99, 7-for-26 (.269). 1999-00, 27-for-58 (.466). 2000-01, 103-for-307 (.336). Totals, 157-for-450 (.349).
Personal fouls/disqualifications: 1997-98, 174/0. 1998-99, 51/2. 1999-00, 118/0. 2000-01, 269/8. Totals, 612/10.

NBA PLAYOFF RECORD

Season Team	G	Min.	FGM	FGA	Pct.	FTM	FTA	Pct.	REBOUNDS Off.	Def.	Tot.	Ast.	St.	Blk.	TO	Pts.	RPG	APG	PPG
99-00—Miami	10	157	10	27	.370	10	16	.625	1	9	10	8	7	4	6	35	1.0	0.8	3.5
00-01—Miami	3	58	5	16	.313	0	0	...	1	1	2	2	2	2	2	12	0.7	0.7	4.0
Totals	13	215	15	43	.349	10	16	.625	2	10	12	10	9	6	8	47	0.9	0.8	3.6

Three-point field goals: 1999-00, 5-for-22 (.227). 2000-01, 2-for-8 (.250). Totals, 7-for-30 (.233).
Personal fouls/disqualifications: 1999-00, 27/1. 2000-01, 8/0. Totals, 35/1.

CBA REGULAR-SEASON RECORD

Season Team	G	Min.	FGM	FGA	Pct.	FTM	FTA	Pct.	Reb.	Ast.	Pts.	RPG	APG	PPG
95-96—Fort Wayne-Rockford	46	1228	182	404	.451	133	191	.696	160	59	510	3.5	1.3	11.1
96-97—Rockford	16	619	94	206	.456	75	98	.765	70	45	277	4.4	2.8	17.3
Totals	62	1847	276	610	.452	208	289	.720	230	104	787	3.7	1.7	12.7

Three-point field goals: 1995-96, 13-for-55 (.236). 1996-97, 14-for-43 (.326). Totals, 27-for-98 (.276).

BOWEN, RYAN   F   NUGGETS

PERSONAL: Born November 20, 1975, in Fort Madison, Iowa. ... 6-7/220. (2,01/99,8). ... Full Name: Ryan Cleo Bowen.
HIGH SCHOOL: Fort Madison (Iowa).
COLLEGE: Iowa.
TRANSACTIONS/CAREER NOTES: Selected by Denver Nuggets in second round (55th pick overall) of 1998 NBA Draft. ... Played in Turkey (1998-99).

COLLEGIATE RECORD

Season Team	G	Min.	FGM	FGA	Pct.	FTM	FTA	Pct.	Reb.	Ast.	Pts.	RPG	APG	PPG
94-95—Iowa	33	647	58	110	.527	35	59	.593	148	16	151	4.5	0.5	4.6
95-96—Iowa	27	554	55	91	.604	39	58	.672	121	16	149	4.5	0.6	5.5
96-97—Iowa	29	827	120	217	.553	93	135	.689	264	35	343	9.1	1.2	11.8
97-98—Iowa	31	852	164	272	.603	111	161	.689	271	48	447	8.7	1.5	14.4
Totals	120	2880	397	690	.575	278	413	.673	804	115	1090	6.7	1.0	9.1

Three-point field goals: 1994-95, 0-for-1. 1996-97, 10-for-32 (.313). 1997-98, 8-for-15 (.533). Totals, 18-for-48 (.375).

TURKISH LEAGUE RECORD

Season Team	G	Min.	FGM	FGA	Pct.	FTM	FTA	Pct.	Reb.	Ast.	Pts.	RPG	APG	PPG
98-99—Oyak Renau	23	873	139	271	.513	64	80	.800	189	39	370	8.2	1.7	16.1

Three-point field goals: 1998-99, 28-for-84 (.333).

NBA REGULAR-SEASON RECORD

Season Team	G	Min.	FGM	FGA	Pct.	FTM	FTA	Pct.	REBOUNDS Off.	Def.	Tot.	Ast.	St.	Blk.	TO	Pts.	RPG	APG	PPG
99-00—Denver	52	589	46	117	.393	38	53	.717	75	39	114	20	39	13	14	131	2.2	0.4	2.5
00-01—Denver	57	696	80	144	.556	27	44	.614	62	51	113	30	37	12	24	191	2.0	0.5	3.4
Totals	109	1285	126	261	.483	65	97	.670	137	90	227	50	76	25	38	322	2.1	0.5	3.0

Three-point field goals: 1999-00, 1-for-9 (.111). 2000-01, 4-for-11 (.364). Totals, 5-for-20 (.250).
Personal fouls/disqualifications: 1999-00, 95/0. 2000-01, 95/0. Totals, 190/0.

BOWMAN, IRA   G

PERSONAL: Born June 11, 1973, in Newark, N.J. ... 6-5/195. (1,96/88,5).
HIGH SCHOOL: Seton Hall Preparatory (West Orange, N.J.).
COLLEGE: Providence, then Pennsylvania.
TRANSACTIONS/CAREER NOTES: Not drafted by an NBA franchise. ... Played in Continental Basketball Association with Connecticut Pride (1996-97 through 2000-01). ... Signed as free agent by Philadelphia 76ers (February 24, 2000). ... Signed as free agent by Utah Jazz (October 2, 2000). ... Waived by Jazz (October 25, 2000). ... Played in International Basketball League with Connecticut Pride (2000-01). ... Signed by Atlanta Hawks to 10-day contract (February 16, 2001). ... Signed to play for Napoli in Italy for 2001-02 season.

COLLEGIATE RECORD

Season Team	G	Min.	FGM	FGA	Pct.	FTM	FTA	Pct.	Reb.	Ast.	Pts.	RPG	APG	PPG
91-92—Providence	28	354	40	82	.488	46	72	.639	22	35	127	0.8	1.3	4.5
92-93—Providence	15	136	17	29	.586	12	18	.667	23	5	46	1.5	0.3	3.1
93-94—Pennsylvania					Did not play—transfer student.									
94-95—Pennsylvania	28	558	120	210	.571	50	76	.658	85	46	301	3.0	1.6	10.8
95-96—Pennsylvania	27	950	149	328	.454	118	166	.711	135	142	444	5.0	5.3	16.4
Totals	98	1998	326	649	.502	226	332	.681	265	228	918	2.7	2.3	9.4

Three-point field goals: 1991-92, 1-for-5 (.200). 1994-95, 11-for-34 (.324). 1995-96, 28-for-76 (.368). Totals, 40-for-115 (.348).

NOTES: CBA All-Defensive Team (2000).

CBA REGULAR-SEASON RECORD

Season Team	G	Min.	FGM	FGA	Pct.	FTM	FTA	Pct.	Reb.	Ast.	Pts.	RPG	APG	PPG
96-97—Connecticut	7	172	28	58	.483	15	27	.556	14	16	71	2.0	2.3	10.1
97-98—Connecticut	55	1634	268	558	.480	194	267	.727	139	200	765	2.5	3.6	13.9
98-99—Connecticut	56	1844	265	594	.446	207	267	.775	148	166	775	2.6	3.0	13.8
99-00—Connecticut	40	1374	164	346	.474	147	203	.724	142	213	497	3.6	5.3	12.4
00-01—Connecticut	25	964	108	263	.411	102	139	.734	108	190	338	4.3	7.6	13.5
Totals	183	5988	833	1819	.458	665	903	.736	551	785	2446	3.0	4.3	13.4

Three-point field goals: 1996-97, 0-for-3. 1997-98, 35-for-116 (.302). 1998-99, 38-for-119 (.319). 1999-00, 22-for-67 (.328). 2000-01, 20-for-71 (.282). Totals, 115-for-376 (.306).

IBL REGULAR-SEASON RECORD

Season Team	G	Min.	FGM	FGA	Pct.	FTM	FTA	Pct.	Reb.	Ast.	Pts.	RPG	APG	PPG
00-01—Connecticut	19	656	68	154	.442	62	86	.721	65	150	207	3.4	7.9	10.9

Three-point field goals: 2000-01, 9-for-49 (.184).

NBA REGULAR-SEASON RECORD

Season Team	G	Min.	FGM	FGA	Pct.	FTM	FTA	Pct.	Off.	Def.	Tot.	Ast.	St.	Blk.	TO	Pts.	RPG	APG	PPG
99-00—Philadelphia	11	20	2	2	1.000	1	2	.500	0	2	2	1	1	0	1	5	0.2	0.1	0.5
00-01—Atlanta	3	19	0	2	.000	0	0	...	1	1	2	7	0	0	1	0	0.7	2.3	0.0
Totals	14	39	2	4	.500	1	2	.500	1	3	4	8	1	0	2	5	0.3	0.6	0.4

NBA PLAYOFF RECORD

Season Team	G	Min.	FGM	FGA	Pct.	FTM	FTA	Pct.	Off.	Def.	Tot.	Ast.	St.	Blk.	TO	Pts.	RPG	APG	PPG
99-00—Philadelphia	7	11	0	2	.000	0	2	.000	0	0	0	2	0	0	0	0	0.0	0.3	0.0

Three-point field goals: 1999-00, 0-for-1.

BOYKINS, EARL   G   CLIPPERS

PERSONAL: Born June 2, 1976, in Cleveland. ... 5-5/133. (1,65/60,3). ... Full Name: Earl Antoine Boykins.
HIGH SCHOOL: Central Catholic (Cleveland).
COLLEGE: Eastern Michigan.
TRANSACTIONS/CAREER NOTES: Not drafted by an NBA franchise. ... Played in Continental Basketball Association with Rockford Lightning (1998-99 and 1999-2000). ... Signed as free agent by New Jersey Nets (January 21, 1999). ... Waived by Nets (February 19, 1999). ... Signed by Cleveland Cavaliers to 10-day contract (March 10, 1999). ... Waived by Cavaliers (March 19, 1999). ... Re-signed by Cavaliers to 10-day contract (March 23, 1999). ... Signed by Cavaliers for remainder of the season (April 2, 1999). ... Waived by Cavaliers (October 28, 1999). ... Signed as free agent by Orlando Magic (November 15, 1999). ... Waived by Magic (December 20, 1999). ... Signed by Cavaliers to first of two consecutive 10-day contracts (February 8, 2000). ... Re-signed by Cavaliers for remainder of season (February 28, 2000). ... Signed as free agent by Los Angeles Clippers (September 29, 2000).

COLLEGIATE RECORD

NOTES: Frances Pomeroy Naismith Award winner (1998).

Season Team	G	Min.	FGM	FGA	Pct.	FTM	FTA	Pct.	Reb.	Ast.	Pts.	RPG	APG	PPG
94-95—Eastern Michigan	30	976	129	312	.413	83	118	.703	73	136	375	2.4	4.5	12.5
95-96—Eastern Michigan	31	1029	156	361	.432	144	179	.804	71	181	479	2.3	5.8	15.5
96-97—Eastern Michigan	32	1163	208	492	.423	156	183	.852	67	147	611	2.1	4.6	19.1
97-98—Eastern Michigan	29	1070	266	563	.472	129	158	.816	66	160	746	2.3	5.5	25.7
Totals	122	4238	759	1728	.439	512	638	.803	277	624	2211	2.3	5.1	18.1

Three-point field goals: 1994-95, 34-for-99 (.343). 1995-96, 23-for-75 (.307). 1996-97, 39-for-130 (.300). 1997-98, 85-for-209 (.407). Totals, 181-for-513 (.353).

CBA REGULAR-SEASON RECORD

Season Team	G	Min.	FGM	FGA	Pct.	FTM	FTA	Pct.	Reb.	Ast.	Pts.	AVERAGES		
												RPG	APG	PPG
98-99—Rockford	29	503	85	209	.407	32	37	.865	40	106	215	1.4	3.7	7.4
99-00—Rockford	18	681	147	302	.487	74	88	.841	64	167	389	3.6	9.3	21.6
Totals	47	1184	232	511	.454	106	125	.848	104	273	604	2.2	5.8	12.9

Three-point field goals: 1998-99, 13-for-47 (.277). 1999-00, 21-for-59 (.356). Totals, 34-for-106 (.321).

NBA REGULAR-SEASON RECORD

Season Team	G	Min.	FGM	FGA	Pct.	FTM	FTA	Pct.	REBOUNDS			Ast.	St.	Blk.	TO	Pts.	AVERAGES		
									Off.	Def.	Tot.						RPG	APG	PPG
98-99—N.J.-Cleve.	22	221	30	79	.380	2	3	.667	7	10	17	33	6	0	20	65	0.8	1.5	3.0
99-00—Orlando-Cleve.	26	261	56	116	.483	18	23	.783	12	14	26	48	12	1	17	138	1.0	1.8	5.3
00-01—L.A. Clippers	10	149	25	63	.397	14	17	.824	4	7	11	32	5	0	9	65	1.1	3.2	6.5
Totals	58	631	111	258	.430	34	43	.791	23	31	54	113	23	1	46	268	0.9	1.9	4.6

Three-point field goals: 1998-99, 3-for-18 (.167). 1999-00, 8-for-20 (.400). 2000-01, 1-for-8 (.125). Totals, 12-for-46 (.261).
Personal fouls/disqualifications: 1998-99, 20/0. 1999-00, 23/0. 2000-01, 9/0. Totals, 52/0.

BRADLEY, SHAWN   C   MAVERICKS

PERSONAL: Born March 22, 1972, in Landstuhl, West Germany. ... 7-6/265. (2,29/120,2). ... Full Name: Shawn Paul Bradley.
HIGH SCHOOL: Emery County (Castle Dale, Utah).
COLLEGE: Brigham Young.
TRANSACTIONS/CAREER NOTES: Selected after freshman season by Philadelphia 76ers in first round (second pick overall) of 1993 NBA Draft. ... Traded by 76ers with F Tim Perry and G Greg Graham to New Jersey Nets for F Derrick Coleman, F Sean Higgins and G Rex Walters (November 30, 1995). ... Traded by Nets with F Ed O'Bannon, G Khalid Reeves and G Robert Pack to Dallas Mavericks for C Eric Montross, G Jim Jackson, F/C Chris Gatling, F/G George McCloud and G Sam Cassell (February 17, 1997).

COLLEGIATE RECORD

NOTES: Shares NCAA Division I single-game record for most blocked shots—14 (December 7, 1990, vs. Eastern Kentucky). ... Led NCAA Division I with 5.2 blocked shots per game (1991).

Season Team	G	Min.	FGM	FGA	Pct.	FTM	FTA	Pct.	Reb.	Ast.	Pts.	AVERAGES		
												RPG	APG	PPG
90-91—Brigham Young	34	984	187	361	.518	128	185	.692	262	41	503	7.7	1.2	14.8
91-92—Brigham Young					Did not play—on Mormon mission.									
92-93—Brigham Young					Did not play—on Mormon mission.									
Totals	34	984	187	361	.518	128	185	.692	262	41	503	7.7	1.2	14.8

Three-point field goals: 1990-91, 1-for-1.

NBA REGULAR-SEASON RECORD

HONORS: NBA All-Rookie second team (1994).
NOTES: Led NBA with 338 personal fouls and 18 disqualifications (1995). ... Led NBA with 3.40 blocks per game (1997).

Season Team	G	Min.	FGM	FGA	Pct.	FTM	FTA	Pct.	REBOUNDS			Ast.	St.	Blk.	TO	Pts.	AVERAGES		
									Off.	Def.	Tot.						RPG	APG	PPG
93-94—Philadelphia	49	1385	201	491	.409	102	168	.607	98	208	306	98	45	147	148	504	6.2	2.0	10.3
94-95—Philadelphia	82	2365	315	693	.455	148	232	.638	243	416	659	53	54	274	142	778	8.0	0.6	9.5
95-96—Phil.-N.J.	79	2329	387	873	.443	169	246	.687	221	417	638	63	49	288	179	944	8.1	0.8	11.9
96-97—N.J.-Dal.	73	2288	406	905	.449	149	228	.654	221	390	611	52	40	248	134	961	8.4	0.7	13.2
97-98—Dallas	64	1822	300	711	.422	130	180	.722	164	354	518	60	51	214	96	731	8.1	0.9	11.4
98-99—Dallas	49	1294	167	348	.480	86	115	.748	130	262	392	40	35	159	56	420	8.0	0.8	8.6
99-00—Dallas	77	1901	266	555	.479	114	149	.765	160	337	497	60	71	190	74	647	6.5	0.8	8.4
00-01—Dallas	82	2001	219	447	.490	140	178	.787	160	448	608	38	36	†228	88	579	7.4	0.5	7.1
Totals	555	15385	2261	5023	.450	1038	1496	.694	1397	2832	4229	464	381	1748	917	5564	7.6	0.8	10.0

Three-point field goals: 1993-94, 0-for-3. 1994-95, 0-for-3. 1995-96, 1-for-4 (.250). 1996-97, 0-for-8. 1997-98, 1-for-3 (.333). 1998-99, 0-for-4. 1999-00, 1-for-5 (.200). 2000-01, 1-for-6 (.167). Totals, 4-for-36 (.111).
Personal fouls/disqualifications: 1993-94, 170/3. 1994-95, 338/18. 1995-96, 286/5. 1996-97, 237/7. 1997-98, 214/9. 1998-99, 153/2. 1999-00, 260/7. 2000-01, 256/6. Totals, 1914/57.

NBA PLAYOFF RECORD

Season Team	G	Min.	FGM	FGA	Pct.	FTM	FTA	Pct.	REBOUNDS			Ast.	St.	Blk.	TO	Pts.	AVERAGES		
									Off.	Def.	Tot.						RPG	APG	PPG
00-01—Dallas	10	256	27	51	.529	10	13	.769	24	47	71	5	4	30	10	64	7.1	0.5	6.4

Personal fouls/disqualifications: 2000-01, 37/1.

BRAND, ELTON   F   CLIPPERS

PERSONAL: Born March 11, 1979, in Cortland, N.Y. ... 6-8/275. (2,03/124,7). ... Full Name: Elton Tyron Brand.
HIGH SCHOOL: Peekskill (Peekskill, N.Y.).
COLLEGE: Duke.
TRANSACTIONS/CAREER NOTES: Selected after sophomore season by Chicago Bulls in first round (first pick overall) of 1999 NBA Draft. ... Traded by Bulls to Los Angeles Clippers for F Brian Skinner and draft rights to C Tyson Chandler (June 27, 2001).

COLLEGIATE RECORD

NOTES: THE SPORTING NEWS College Player of the Year (1999). ... Wooden Award winner (1999). ... Naismith Award winner (1999). ... THE SPORTING NEWS All-America first team (1999).

Season Team	G	Min.	FGM	FGA	Pct.	FTM	FTA	Pct.	Reb.	Ast.	Pts.	AVERAGES		
												RPG	APG	PPG
97-98—Duke................	21	493	100	169	.592	81	134	.604	154	10	281	7.3	0.5	13.4
98-99—Duke................	39	1141	255	411	.620	181	256	.707	382	41	691	9.8	1.1	17.7
Totals	60	1634	355	580	.612	262	390	.672	536	51	972	8.9	0.9	16.2

NBA REGULAR-SEASON RECORD

HONORS: NBA co-Rookie of the Year (2000). ... NBA All-Rookie first team (2000).

Season Team	G	Min.	FGM	FGA	Pct.	FTM	FTA	Pct.	REBOUNDS			Ast.	St.	Blk.	TO	Pts.	AVERAGES		
									Off.	Def.	Tot.						RPG	APG	PPG
99-00—Chicago	81	2999	630	1306	.482	367	536	.685	*348	462	810	155	66	132	228	1627	10.0	1.9	20.1
00-01—Chicago	74	2906	578	1215	.476	334	472	.708	285	461	746	240	71	118	219	1490	10.1	3.2	20.1
Totals	155	5905	1208	2521	.479	701	1008	.695	633	923	1556	395	137	250	447	3117	10.0	2.5	20.1

Three-point field goals: 1999-00, 0-for-2. 2000-01, 0-for-2. Totals, 0-for-4 (.000).
Personal fouls/disqualifications: 1999-00, 259/3. 2000-01, 243/4. Totals, 502/7.

BRANDON, TERRELL   G   TIMBERWOLVES

PERSONAL: Born May 20, 1970, in Portland, Ore. ... 5-11/173. (1,80/78,5). ... Full Name: Thomas Terrell Brandon. ... Name pronounced Tur-RELL.
HIGH SCHOOL: Grant (Portland, Ore.).
COLLEGE: Oregon.
TRANSACTIONS/CAREER NOTES: Selected after junior season by Cleveland Cavaliers in first round (11th pick overall) of 1991 NBA Draft. ... Traded by Cavaliers with F Tyrone Hill to Milwaukee Bucks in three-way deal in which Bucks sent G Sherman Douglas to Cavaliers and sent F Vin Baker to Seattle SuperSonics for F Shawn Kemp (September 25, 1997); Bucks also received 1998 conditional first-round draft choice from Cavaliers. ... Traded by Bucks to Minnesota Timberwolves in three-way deal in which Timberwolves also received F Brian Evans, 1999 first-round draft choice and an undisclosed draft choice from Nets, Nets sent G Sam Cassell and F/C Chris Gatling to Bucks, Timberwolves sent G Stephon Marbury, G Chris Carr and F Bill Curley to Nets and Timberwolves sent C Paul Grant to Bucks (March 11, 1999).

COLLEGIATE RECORD

Season Team	G	Min.	FGM	FGA	Pct.	FTM	FTA	Pct.	Reb.	Ast.	Pts.	AVERAGES		
												RPG	APG	PPG
88-89—Oregon						Did not play—ineligible.								
89-90—Oregon	29	1067	190	401	.474	97	129	.752	106	174	518	3.7	6.0	17.9
90-91—Oregon	28	1108	273	556	.491	159	187	.850	101	141	745	3.6	5.0	26.6
Totals	57	2175	463	957	.484	256	316	.810	207	315	1263	3.6	5.5	22.2

Three-point field goals: 1989-90, 41-for-94 (.436). 1990-91, 40-for-119 (.336). Totals, 81-for-213 (.380).

NBA REGULAR-SEASON RECORD

HONORS: NBA Sportsmanship Award (1997). ... NBA All-Rookie second team (1992).

Season Team	G	Min.	FGM	FGA	Pct.	FTM	FTA	Pct.	REBOUNDS			Ast.	St.	Blk.	TO	Pts.	AVERAGES		
									Off.	Def.	Tot.						RPG	APG	PPG
91-92—Cleveland	82	1605	252	601	.419	100	124	.806	49	113	162	316	81	22	136	605	2.0	3.9	7.4
92-93—Cleveland	82	1622	297	621	.478	118	143	.825	37	142	179	302	79	27	107	725	2.2	3.7	8.8
93-94—Cleveland	73	1548	230	548	.420	139	162	.858	38	121	159	277	84	16	111	606	2.2	3.8	8.3
94-95—Cleveland	67	1961	341	762	.448	159	186	.855	35	151	186	363	107	14	144	889	2.8	5.4	13.3
95-96—Cleveland	75	2570	510	1096	.465	338	381	.887	47	201	248	487	132	33	142	1449	3.3	6.5	19.3
96-97—Cleveland	78	2868	575	1313	.438	268	297	.902	48	253	301	490	138	30	178	1519	3.9	6.3	19.5
97-98—Milwaukee	50	1784	339	731	.464	132	156	.846	23	153	176	387	111	17	145	841	3.5	7.7	16.8
98-99—Mil.-Min.	36	1217	212	507	.418	65	78	.833	27	107	134	309	63	10	74	501	3.7	8.6	13.9
99-00—Minnesota	71	2587	486	1042	.466	187	208	.899	44	194	238	629	134	30	184	1212	3.4	8.9	17.1
00-01—Minnesota	78	2821	511	1134	.451	195	224	.871	60	238	298	583	161	21	155	1250	3.8	7.5	16.0
Totals	692	20583	3753	8355	.449	1701	1959	.868	408	1673	2081	4143	1090	220	1376	9597	3.0	6.0	13.9

Three-point field goals: 1991-92, 1-for-23 (.043). 1992-93, 13-for-42 (.310). 1993-94, 7-for-32 (.219). 1994-95, 48-for-121 (.397). 1995-96, 91-for-235 (.387). 1996-97, 101-for-271 (.373). 1997-98, 31-for-93 (.333). 1998-99, 12-for-47 (.255). 1999-00, 53-for-132 (.402). 2000-01, 33-for-91 (.363). Totals, 390-for-1087 (.359).
Personal fouls/disqualifications: 1991-92, 107/0. 1992-93, 122/1. 1993-94, 108/0. 1994-95, 118/0. 1995-96, 146/1. 1996-97, 177/1. 1997-98, 120/1. 1998-99, 82/0. 1999-00, 158/1. 2000-01, 138/1. Totals, 1276/6.

NBA PLAYOFF RECORD

Season Team	G	Min.	FGM	FGA	Pct.	FTM	FTA	Pct.	REBOUNDS			Ast.	St.	Blk.	TO	Pts.	AVERAGES		
									Off.	Def.	Tot.						RPG	APG	PPG
91-92—Cleveland	12	157	22	55	.400	3	4	.750	4	18	22	30	3	1	11	47	1.8	2.5	3.9
92-93—Cleveland	8	132	20	46	.435	9	9	1.000	4	13	17	17	7	3	14	51	2.1	2.1	6.4
93-94—Cleveland	3	56	12	19	.632	2	3	.667	1	3	4	5	1	0	1	26	1.3	1.7	8.7
95-96—Cleveland	3	125	21	47	.447	13	15	.867	1	8	9	24	4	1	11	58	3.0	8.0	19.3
98-99—Minnesota	4	161	31	69	.449	12	13	.923	2	28	30	28	9	2	14	77	7.5	7.0	19.3
99-00—Minnesota	4	162	32	63	.508	10	11	.909	4	19	23	34	3	0	8	78	5.8	8.5	19.5
00-01—Minnesota	4	153	27	62	.435	3	3	1.000	2	15	17	25	4	2	8	61	4.3	6.3	15.3
Totals	38	946	165	361	.457	52	58	.897	18	104	122	163	31	9	67	398	3.2	4.3	10.5

Three-point field goals: 1991-92, 0-for-3. 1992-93, 2-for-5 (.400). 1995-96, 3-for-9 (.333). 1998-99, 3-for-5 (.600). 1999-00, 4-for-11 (.364). 2000-01, 4-for-9 (.444). Totals, 16-for-42 (.381).
Personal fouls/disqualifications: 1991-92, 17/0. 1992-93, 6/0. 1993-94, 1/0. 1995-96, 10/0. 1998-99, 11/0. 1999-00, 11/0. 2000-01, 10/0. Totals, 66/0.

NBA ALL-STAR GAME RECORD

Season Team	Min.	FGM	FGA	Pct.	FTM	FTA	Pct.	REBOUNDS			Ast.	PF	Dq.	St.	Blk.	TO	Pts.
								Off.	Def.	Tot.							
1996 —Cleveland..........	20	4	10	.400	2	2	1.000	1	0	1	3	1	0	1	1	3	11
1997 —Cleveland..........	17	4	11	.364	0	0	...	1	2	3	8	2	0	2	0	0	10
Totals........................	37	8	21	.381	2	2	1.000	2	2	4	11	3	0	3	1	3	21

Three-point field goals: 1996, 1-for-4 (.250). 1997, 2-for-4 (.500). Totals, 3-for-8 (.375).

BROWN, CHUCKY F

PERSONAL: Born February 29, 1968, in New York. ... 6-8/220. (2,03/99,8). ... Full Name: Clarence Brown.
HIGH SCHOOL: North Brunswick (Leland, N.C.).
COLLEGE: North Carolina State.
TRANSACTIONS/CAREER NOTES: Selected by Cleveland Cavaliers in second round (43rd pick overall) of 1989 NBA Draft. ... Waived by Cavaliers (December 2, 1991). ... Signed as free agent by Los Angeles Lakers (December 5, 1991). ... Played in Italy (1992-93). ... Signed as free agent by New Jersey Nets (October 7, 1992). ... Signed as free agent by Dallas Mavericks (November 12, 1993). ... Waived by Mavericks (November 23, 1993). ... Signed as free agent by Miami Heat (October 4, 1994). ... Waived by Heat (November 1, 1994). ... Played in Continental Basketball Association with Grand Rapids Hoops (1993-94) and Yakima Sun Kings (1993-94 and 1994-95). ... Signed by Houston Rockets to first of two consecutive 10-day contracts (February 2, 1995). ... Re-signed by Rockets for remainder of season (February 25, 1995). ... Traded by Rockets with G Sam Cassell, F Robert Horry and F Mark Bryant to Phoenix Suns for F Charles Barkley and 1999 second-round draft choice (August 19, 1996). ... Traded by Suns to Milwaukee Bucks for G/F Darrin Hancock and 1997, 1998 or 1999 second-round draft choice (December 4, 1996). ... Signed as free agent by Atlanta Hawks (October 2, 1997). ... Signed as free agent by Charlotte Hornets (January 21, 1999). ... Signed as free agent by San Antonio Spurs (October 1, 1999). ... Waived by Spurs (February 4, 2000). ... Signed as free agent by Charlotte Hornets (February 8, 2000). ... Signed by Golden State Warriors to first of two consecutive 10-day contracts (January 13, 2001). ... Waived by Warriors (January 26, 2001). ... Signed by Cavaliers to the first of two consecutive 10-day contract (January 29, 2001). ... Re-signed by Cavaliers for remainder of season (February 22, 2001).
MISCELLANEOUS: Member of NBA championship team (1995).

COLLEGIATE RECORD

Season Team	G	Min.	FGM	FGA	Pct.	FTM	FTA	Pct.	Reb.	Ast.	Pts.	RPG	APG	PPG
85-86—North Carolina State.......	31	310	38	80	.475	21	34	.618	67	13	97	2.2	0.4	3.1
86-87—North Carolina State.......	34	629	81	138	.587	61	80	.763	145	12	223	4.3	0.4	6.6
87-88—North Carolina State.......	32	1024	226	395	.572	77	121	.636	193	27	530	6.0	0.8	16.6
88-89—North Carolina State.......	31	1051	210	383	.548	81	125	.648	274	42	507	8.8	1.4	16.4
Totals	128	3014	555	996	.557	240	360	.667	679	94	1357	5.3	0.7	10.6

Three-point field goals: 1986-87, 0-for-1. 1987-88, 1-for-6 (.167). 1988-89, 6-for-21 (.286). Totals, 7-for-28 (.250).

NBA REGULAR-SEASON RECORD

Season Team	G	Min.	FGM	FGA	Pct.	FTM	FTA	Pct.	Off.	Def.	Tot.	Ast.	St.	Blk.	TO	Pts.	RPG	APG	PPG
89-90—Cleveland	75	1339	210	447	.470	125	164	.762	83	148	231	50	33	26	69	545	3.1	0.7	7.3
90-91—Cleveland	74	1485	263	502	.524	101	144	.701	78	135	213	80	26	24	94	627	2.9	1.1	8.5
91-92—Clev.-L.A.L.	42	431	60	128	.469	30	49	.612	31	51	82	26	12	7	29	150	2.0	0.6	3.6
92-93—New Jersey	77	1186	160	331	.483	71	98	.724	88	144	232	51	20	24	56	391	3.0	0.7	5.1
93-94—Dallas.............	1	10	1	1	1.000	1	1	1.000	0	1	1	0	0	0	0	3	1.0	0.0	3.0
94-95—Houston	41	814	105	174	.603	38	62	.613	64	125	189	30	11	14	29	249	4.6	0.7	6.1
95-96—Houston	82	2019	300	555	.541	104	150	.693	134	307	441	89	47	38	94	705	5.4	1.1	8.6
96-97—Phoe.-Mil.	70	757	78	154	.506	47	70	.671	41	107	148	28	9	22	19	204	2.1	0.4	2.9
97-98—Atlanta	77	1202	161	372	.433	63	87	.724	57	126	183	55	23	13	51	387	2.4	0.7	5.0
98-99—Charlotte........	48	1192	176	373	.472	40	59	.678	36	138	174	57	16	19	38	407	3.6	1.2	8.5
99-00—S.A.-Char.	63	1096	148	328	.451	36	52	.692	35	132	167	66	20	18	45	334	2.7	1.0	5.3
00-01—G.S.-Cleveland .	26	339	40	95	.421	22	34	.647	8	46	54	11	9	7	8	102	2.1	0.4	3.9
Totals	676	11870	1702	3460	.492	678	970	.699	655	1460	2115	543	226	212	532	4104	3.1	0.8	6.1

Three-point field goals: 1989-90, 0-for-7. 1990-91, 0-for-4. 1991-92, 0-for-3. 1992-93, 0-for-5. 1994-95, 1-for-3 (.333). 1995-96, 1-for-8 (.125). 1996-97, 1-for-6 (.167). 1997-98, 2-for-8 (.250). 1998-99, 15-for-40 (.375). 1999-00, 2-for-10 (.200). 2000-01, 0-for-3. Totals, 22-for-97 (.227).

Personal fouls/disqualifications: 1989-90, 148/0. 1990-91, 150/0. 1991-92, 48/0. 1992-93, 112/0. 1993-94, 2/0. 1994-95, 105/0. 1995-96, 163/0. 1996-97, 100/1. 1997-98, 100/0. 1998-99, 106/0. 1999-00, 114/1. 2000-01, 37/0. Totals, 1165/2.

NBA PLAYOFF RECORD

Season Team	G	Min.	FGM	FGA	Pct.	FTM	FTA	Pct.	Off.	Def.	Tot.	Ast.	St.	Blk.	TO	Pts.	RPG	APG	PPG
91-92—L.A. Lakers	3	44	8	19	.421	3	6	.500	3	8	11	2	0	2	1	19	3.7	0.7	6.3
92-93—New Jersey	4	62	9	22	.409	6	7	.857	3	6	9	1	3	3	2	24	2.3	0.3	6.0
94-95—Houston	21	326	34	76	.447	25	37	.676	20	45	65	7	9	2	12	94	3.1	0.3	4.5
95-96—Houston	8	168	25	45	.556	15	18	.833	6	18	24	5	3	0	4	65	3.0	0.6	8.1
97-98—Atlanta	4	50	7	15	.467	1	2	.500	1	5	6	4	0	0	2	16	1.5	1.0	4.0
Totals	40	650	83	177	.469	50	70	.714	33	82	115	19	15	7	21	218	2.9	0.5	5.5

Three-point field goals: 1991-92, 0-for-1. 1994-95, 1-for-2 (.500). 1997-98, 1-for-2 (.500). Totals, 2-for-5 (.400).

Personal fouls/disqualifications: 1991-92, 3/0. 1992-93, 2/0. 1994-95, 46/2. 1995-96, 17/0. 1997-98, 5/0. Totals, 73/2.

ITALIAN LEAGUE RECORD

Season Team	G	Min.	FGM	FGA	Pct.	FTM	FTA	Pct.	Reb.	Ast.	Pts.	RPG	APG	PPG
92-93—Panna Firenze................	3	111	16	36	.444	11	17	.647	22	3	47	7.3	1.0	15.7

Three-point field goals: 1992-93, 4-for-9 (.444).

CBA REGULAR-SEASON RECORD

NOTES: CBA All-League first team (1995).

Season Team	G	Min.	FGM	FGA	Pct.	FTM	FTA	Pct.	Reb.	Ast.	Pts.	RPG	APG	PPG
93-94—Grand Rapids-Yakima.....	46	1372	251	513	.489	110	150	.733	278	60	612	6.0	1.3	13.3
94-95—Yakima	31	1107	262	459	.571	122	162	.753	171	51	659	5.5	1.6	21.3
Totals	77	2479	513	972	.528	232	312	.744	449	111	1271	5.8	1.4	16.5

Three-point field goals: 1993-94, 0-for-4. 1994-95, 13-for-32 (.406). Totals, 13-for-36 (.361).

BROWN, DEE G

PERSONAL: Born November 29, 1968, in Jacksonville. ... 6-2/205. (1,88/93,0). ... Full Name: DeCovan Kadell Brown.
HIGH SCHOOL: The Bolles School (Jacksonville).
COLLEGE: Jacksonville.
TRANSACTIONS/CAREER NOTES: Selected by Boston Celtics in first round (19th pick overall) of 1990 NBA Draft. ... Traded by Celtics with G Chauncey Billups, F John Thomas and F Roy Rogers to Toronto Raptors for G Kenny Anderson, C Zan Tabak and F Popeye Jones (February 18, 1998). ... Signed as free agent by Orlando Magic (August 3, 2000). ... Announced retirement (August 29, 2001).

COLLEGIATE RECORD

Season Team	G	Min.	FGM	FGA	Pct.	FTM	FTA	Pct.	Reb.	Ast.	Pts.	RPG	APG	PPG
86-87—Jacksonville	21	186	28	65	.431	13	22	.591	28	17	71	1.3	0.8	3.4
87-88—Jacksonville	28	764	108	239	.452	54	66	.818	125	56	282	4.5	2.0	10.1
88-89—Jacksonville	30	1133	219	447	.490	108	131	.824	228	112	589	7.6	3.7	19.6
89-90—Jacksonville	29	1052	231	466	.496	69	101	.683	192	151	561	6.6	5.2	19.3
Totals	108	3135	586	1217	.482	244	320	.763	573	336	1503	5.3	3.1	13.9

Three-point field goals: 1986-87, 2-for-12 (.167). 1987-88, 12-for-45 (.267). 1988-89, 43-for-101 (.426). 1989-90, 30-for-80 (.375). Totals, 87-for-238 (.366).

NBA REGULAR-SEASON RECORD

HONORS: Slam Dunk championship winner (1991). ... NBA All-Rookie first team (1991).
NOTES: Led NBA with 135 three-point field goals made and 349 three-point field goals attempted (1999).

Season Team	G	Min.	FGM	FGA	Pct.	FTM	FTA	Pct.	Off.	Def.	Tot.	Ast.	St.	Blk.	TO	Pts.	RPG	APG	PPG
90-91—Boston	82	1945	284	612	.464	137	157	.873	41	141	182	344	83	14	137	712	2.2	4.2	8.7
91-92—Boston	31	883	149	350	.426	60	78	.769	15	64	79	164	33	7	59	363	2.5	5.3	11.7
92-93—Boston	80	2254	328	701	.468	192	242	.793	45	201	246	461	138	32	136	874	3.1	5.8	10.9
93-94—Boston	77	2867	490	1021	.480	182	219	.831	63	237	300	347	156	47	126	1192	3.9	4.5	15.5
94-95—Boston	79	2792	437	977	.447	236	277	.852	63	186	249	301	110	49	146	1236	3.2	3.8	15.6
95-96—Boston	65	1591	246	616	.399	135	158	.854	36	100	136	146	80	12	74	695	2.1	2.2	10.7
96-97—Boston	21	522	61	166	.367	18	22	.818	8	40	48	67	31	7	24	160	2.3	3.2	7.6
97-98—Bos.-Tor.	72	1719	246	562	.438	58	71	.817	24	128	152	154	82	23	73	658	2.1	2.1	9.1
98-99—Toronto	49	1377	187	495	.378	40	55	.727	15	88	103	143	56	8	80	549	2.1	2.9	11.2
99-00—Toronto	38	673	93	258	.360	11	16	.688	9	45	54	86	24	5	39	264	1.4	2.3	6.9
00-01—Orlando	7	155	16	44	.364	4	5	.800	0	11	11	12	4	0	7	48	1.6	1.7	6.9
Totals	601	16778	2537	5802	.437	1073	1300	.825	319	1241	1560	2225	797	204	901	6751	2.6	3.7	11.2

Three-point field goals: 1990-91, 7-for-34 (.206). 1991-92, 5-for-22 (.227). 1992-93, 26-for-82 (.317). 1993-94, 30-for-96 (.313). 1994-95, 126-for-327 (.385). 1995-96, 68-for-220 (.309). 1996-97, 20-for-65 (.308). 1997-98, 108-for-271 (.399). 1998-99, 135-for-349 (.387). 1999-00, 67-for-187 (.358). 2000-01, 12-for-32 (.375). Totals, 604-for-1685 (.358).
Personal fouls/disqualifications: 1990-91, 161/0. 1991-92, 74/0. 1992-93, 203/2. 1993-94, 207/3. 1994-95, 181/0. 1995-96, 119/0. 1996-97, 45/0. 1997-98, 123/1. 1998-99, 75/0. 1999-00, 62/1. 2000-01, 10/0. Totals, 1260/7.

NBA PLAYOFF RECORD

Season Team	G	Min.	FGM	FGA	Pct.	FTM	FTA	Pct.	Off.	Def.	Tot.	Ast.	St.	Blk.	TO	Pts.	RPG	APG	PPG
90-91—Boston	11	284	53	108	.491	28	34	.824	9	36	45	41	11	6	22	134	4.1	3.7	12.2
91-92—Boston	6	120	22	44	.500	4	6	.667	3	9	12	31	1	4	7	48	2.0	5.2	8.0
92-93—Boston	4	133	15	41	.366	14	14	1.000	2	4	6	15	2	4	6	45	1.5	3.8	11.3
94-95—Boston	4	172	26	62	.419	14	16	.875	6	14	20	19	5	1	7	75	5.0	4.8	18.8
99-00—Toronto	3	19	0	4	.000	0	0	...	0	2	2	2	2	0	1	0	0.7	0.7	0.0
00-01—Orlando	3	54	6	13	.462	0	0	...	0	3	3	4	2	0	1	18	1.0	1.3	6.0
Totals	31	782	122	272	.449	60	70	.857	20	68	88	112	23	15	44	320	2.8	3.6	10.3

Three-point field goals: 1990-91, 0-for-5. 1991-92, 0-for-3. 1992-93, 1-for-7 (.143). 1994-95, 9-for-26 (.346). 1999-00, 0-for-3. 2000-01, 6-for-11 (.545). Totals, 16-for-55 (.291).
Personal fouls/disqualifications: 1990-91, 32/0. 1991-92, 16/2. 1992-93, 11/0. 1994-95, 13/1. 1999-00, 4/0. 2000-01, 3/0. Totals, 79/3.

BROWN, P.J. F HORNETS

PERSONAL: Born October 14, 1969, in Detroit. ... 6-11/240. (2,11/108,9). ... Full Name: Collier Brown Jr.
HIGH SCHOOL: Winnfield (La.) Senior.
COLLEGE: Louisiana Tech.
TRANSACTIONS/CAREER NOTES: Selected by New Jersey Nets in second round (29th pick overall) of 1992 NBA Draft. ... Played in Greece (1992-93). ... Signed as free agent by Miami Heat (July 18, 1996). ... Traded by Heat with F Jamal Mashburn, F/C Otis Thorpe, F Tim James and G/F Rodney Buford to Charlotte Hornets for G Eddie Jones, F Anthony Mason, G Ricky Davis and G/F Dale Ellis (August 1, 2000).

COLLEGIATE RECORD

Season Team	G	Min.	FGM	FGA	Pct.	FTM	FTA	Pct.	Reb.	Ast.	Pts.	RPG	APG	PPG
88-89—Louisiana Tech	32	569	61	147	.415	25	44	.568	178	36	149	5.6	1.1	4.7
89-90—Louisiana Tech	27	672	94	204	.461	48	81	.593	230	29	239	8.5	1.1	8.9
90-91—Louisiana Tech	31	936	170	315	.540	98	150	.653	301	58	445	9.7	1.9	14.4
91-92—Louisiana Tech	31	931	151	309	.489	84	115	.730	308	53	395	9.9	1.7	12.7
Totals	121	3108	476	975	.488	255	390	.654	1017	176	1228	8.4	1.5	10.1

Three-point field goals: 1988-89, 2-for-3 (.667). 1989-90, 3-for-5 (.600). 1990-91, 7-for-20 (.350). 1991-92, 9-for-25 (.360). Totals, 21-for-53 (.396).

GREEK LEAGUE RECORD

Season Team	G	Min.	FGM	FGA	Pct.	FTM	FTA	Pct.	Reb.	Ast.	Pts.	RPG	APG	PPG
92-93—Panionios	26	...	164	299	.548	107	151	.709	357	...	441	13.7	...	17.0

HONORS: J. Walter Kennedy Citizenship Award (1997). ... NBA All-Defensive second team (1997, 1999, 2001).

Season Team	G	Min.	FGM	FGA	Pct.	FTM	FTA	Pct.	Off.	Def.	Tot.	Ast.	St.	Blk.	TO	Pts.	RPG	APG	PPG
93-94—New Jersey.....	79	1950	167	402	.415	115	152	.757	188	305	493	93	71	93	72	450	6.2	1.2	5.7
94-95—New Jersey.....	80	2466	254	570	.446	139	207	.671	178	309	487	135	69	135	80	651	6.1	1.7	8.1
95-96—New Jersey.....	81	2942	354	798	.444	204	265	.770	215	345	560	165	79	100	133	915	6.9	2.0	11.3
96-97—Miami	80	2592	300	656	.457	161	220	.732	239	431	670	92	85	98	113	761	8.4	1.2	9.5
97-98—Miami	74	2362	278	590	.471	151	197	.766	235	400	635	103	66	98	97	707	8.6	1.4	9.6
98-99—Miami	50	1611	229	477	.480	113	146	.774	115	231	346	66	46	48	69	571	6.9	1.3	11.4
99-00—Miami	80	2302	322	671	.480	120	159	.755	216	384	600	145	65	61	100	764	7.5	1.8	9.6
00-01—Charlotte........	80	2811	249	561	.444	178	209	.852	257	485	742	127	78	92	108	676	9.3	1.6	8.5
Totals	604	19036	2153	4725	.456	1181	1555	.759	1643	2890	4533	926	559	725	772	5495	7.5	1.5	9.1

Three-point field goals: 1993-94, 1-for-6 (.167). 1994-95, 4-for-24 (.167). 1995-96, 3-for-15 (.200). 1996-97, 0-for-2. 1999-00, 0-for-1. 2000-01, 0-for-4. Totals, 8-for-52 (.154).

Personal fouls/disqualifications: 1993-94, 177/1. 1994-95, 262/8. 1995-96, 249/5. 1996-97, 283/7. 1997-98, 264/9. 1998-99, 166/2. 1999-00, 264/4. 2000-01, 260/6. Totals, 1925/42.

NBA PLAYOFF RECORD

Season Team	G	Min.	FGM	FGA	Pct.	FTM	FTA	Pct.	Off.	Def.	Tot.	Ast.	St.	Blk.	TO	Pts.	RPG	APG	PPG
93-94—New Jersey.....	4	56	2	9	.222	8	8	1.000	4	4	8	3	0	2	3	12	2.0	0.8	3.0
96-97—Miami	15	451	42	103	.408	38	53	.717	48	81	129	10	9	20	16	122	8.6	0.7	8.1
97-98—Miami	5	190	19	37	.514	8	22	.364	15	29	44	4	7	3	6	46	8.8	0.8	9.2
98-99—Miami	5	144	21	45	.467	9	10	.900	14	17	31	5	2	2	3	51	6.2	1.0	10.2
99-00—Miami	10	308	35	82	.427	5	6	.833	26	56	82	11	8	4	11	75	8.2	1.1	7.5
00-01—Charlotte........	10	385	28	67	.418	24	29	.828	41	59	100	11	12	14	12	80	10.0	1.1	8.0
Totals	49	1534	147	343	.429	92	128	.719	148	246	394	44	38	45	51	386	8.0	0.9	7.9

Three-point field goals: 1998-99, 0-for-1. Totals, 0-for-1 (.000).

Personal fouls/disqualifications: 1993-94, 13/0. 1996-97, 40/0. 1997-98, 22/1. 1998-99, 17/0. 1999-00, 42/3. 2000-01, 31/1. Totals, 165/5.

BROWN, RANDY — G — CELTICS

PERSONAL: Born May 22, 1968, in Chicago. ... 6-2/190. (1,88/86,2).
HIGH SCHOOL: Collins (Chicago).
JUNIOR COLLEGE: Howard College (Texas).
COLLEGE: Houston, then New Mexico State.
TRANSACTIONS/CAREER NOTES: Selected by Sacramento Kings in second round (31st pick overall) of 1991 NBA Draft. ... Signed as unrestricted free agent by Chicago Bulls (October 5, 1995). ... Signed as free agent by Boston Celtics (August 3, 2000).
MISCELLANEOUS: Member of NBA championship team (1996, 1997, 1998).

COLLEGIATE RECORD

Season Team	G	Min.	FGM	FGA	Pct.	FTM	FTA	Pct.	Reb.	Ast.	Pts.	RPG	APG	PPG
86-87—Houston	28	578	42	83	.506	21	36	.583	75	81	105	2.7	2.9	3.8
87-88—Houston	29	998	64	142	.451	75	100	.750	83	162	203	2.9	5.6	7.0
88-89—Howard College.............						Did not play.								
89-90—New Mexico State	31	907	131	294	.446	131	184	.712	106	109	409	3.4	3.5	13.2
90-91—New Mexico State	29	917	110	276	.399	121	175	.691	116	187	351	4.0	6.4	12.1
4-Year-College Totals.............	117	3400	347	795	.436	348	495	.703	380	539	1068	3.2	4.6	9.1

Three-point field goals: 1986-87, 0-for-2. 1987-88, 0-for-4. 1989-90, 16-for-42 (.381). 1990-91, 10-for-36 (.278). Totals, 26-for-84 (.310).

NBA REGULAR-SEASON RECORD

Season Team	G	Min.	FGM	FGA	Pct.	FTM	FTA	Pct.	Off.	Def.	Tot.	Ast.	St.	Blk.	TO	Pts.	RPG	APG	PPG
91-92—Sacramento	56	535	77	169	.456	38	58	.655	26	43	69	59	35	12	42	192	1.2	1.1	3.4
92-93—Sacramento	75	1726	225	486	.463	115	157	.732	75	137	212	196	108	34	120	567	2.8	2.6	7.6
93-94—Sacramento	61	1041	110	251	.438	53	87	.609	40	72	112	133	63	14	75	273	1.8	2.2	4.5
94-95—Sacramento	67	1086	124	287	.432	55	82	.671	24	84	108	133	99	19	78	317	1.6	2.0	4.7
95-96—Chicago	68	671	78	192	.406	28	46	.609	17	49	66	73	57	12	31	185	1.0	1.1	2.7
96-97—Chicago	72	1057	140	333	.420	57	84	.679	34	77	111	133	81	17	58	341	1.5	1.8	4.7
97-98—Chicago	71	1147	116	302	.384	56	78	.718	34	60	94	151	71	12	63	288	1.3	2.1	4.1
98-99—Chicago	39	1139	132	319	.414	78	103	.757	27	105	132	149	68	8	80	342	3.4	3.8	8.8
99-00—Chicago	59	1625	157	435	.361	62	84	.738	23	121	144	202	61	15	105	379	2.4	3.4	6.4
00-01—Boston	54	1238	100	237	.422	23	40	.575	23	76	99	154	62	10	56	223	1.8	2.9	4.1
Totals	622	11265	1259	3011	.418	565	819	.690	323	824	1147	1383	705	153	708	3107	1.8	2.2	5.0

Three-point field goals: 1991-92, 0-for-6. 1992-93, 2-for-6 (.333). 1993-94, 0-for-4. 1994-95, 14-for-47 (.298). 1995-96, 1-for-11 (.091). 1996-97, 4-for-22 (.182). 1997-98, 0-for-5. 1998-99, 0-for-1. 1999-00, 3-for-6 (.500). 2000-01, 0-for-3. Totals, 24-for-111 (.216).

Personal fouls/disqualifications: 1991-92, 68/0. 1992-93, 206/4. 1993-94, 132/2. 1994-95, 153/0. 1995-96, 88/0. 1996-97, 116/0. 1997-98, 118/0. 1998-99, 93/1. 1999-00, 120/1. 2000-01, 132/1. Totals, 1226/9.

NBA PLAYOFF RECORD

Season Team	G	Min.	FGM	FGA	Pct.	FTM	FTA	Pct.	Off.	Def.	Tot.	Ast.	St.	Blk.	TO	Pts.	RPG	APG	PPG
95-96—Chicago	16	112	16	28	.571	9	12	.750	3	7	10	7	5	1	7	44	0.6	0.4	2.8
96-97—Chicago	17	98	9	30	.300	3	5	.600	3	7	10	6	8	2	4	21	0.6	0.4	1.2
97-98—Chicago	14	71	2	12	.167	5	6	.833	3	6	9	9	2	0	7	9	0.6	0.6	0.6
Totals	47	281	27	70	.386	17	23	.739	9	20	29	22	15	3	18	74	0.6	0.5	1.6

Three-point field goals: 1995-96, 3-for-6 (.500). Totals, 3-for-6 (.500).

Personal fouls/disqualifications: 1995-96, 18/0. 1996-97, 22/0. 1997-98, 6/0. Totals, 46/0.

B

BRUNSON, RICK   G

PERSONAL: Born June 14, 1972, in Syracuse, N.Y. ... 6-4/190. (1,93/86,2). ... Full Name: Rick Daniel Brunson.
HIGH SCHOOL: Salem (Mass.).
COLLEGE: Temple.
TRANSACTIONS/CAREER NOTES: Not drafted by an NBA franchise. ... Played in Australia (1995-96). ... Played in Continental Basketball Association with Quad City Thunder (1996-97) and Connecticut Pride (1997-98 and 1998-99). ... Signed as free agent by Orlando Magic (September 30, 1997). ... Waived by Magic (October 20, 1997). ... Signed as free agent by New York Knicks (October 23, 1997). ... Waived by Knicks (October 30, 1997). ... Signed as free agent by Portland Trail Blazers (December 2, 1997). ... Signed as free agent by Knicks (January 21, 1999). ... Signed as free agent by Miami Heat (September 28, 2000). ... Waived by Heat (October 20, 2000). ... Signed as free agent by Boston Celtics (November 6, 2000). ... Waived by Celtics (November 21, 2000). ... Claimed on waivers by Knicks (November 27, 2000).

B

COLLEGIATE RECORD

Season Team	G	Min.	FGM	FGA	Pct.	FTM	FTA	Pct.	Reb.	Ast.	Pts.	RPG	APG	PPG
91-92—Temple	30	537	41	128	.320	53	87	.609	79	56	147	2.6	1.9	4.9
92-93—Temple	33	1205	147	371	.396	112	171	.655	98	149	463	3.0	4.5	14.0
93-94—Temple	31	1221	128	346	.370	77	119	.647	127	142	383	4.1	4.6	12.4
94-95—Temple	30	1149	164	448	.366	100	143	.699	177	123	500	5.9	4.1	16.7
Totals	124	4112	480	1293	.371	342	520	.658	481	470	1493	3.9	3.8	12.0

Three-point field goals: 1991-92, 12-for-53 (.226). 1992-93, 57-for-177 (.322). 1993-94, 50-for-167 (.299). 1994-95, 72-for-252 (.286). Totals, 191-for-649 (.294).

CBA REGULAR-SEASON RECORD

Season Team	G	Min.	FGM	FGA	Pct.	FTM	FTA	Pct.	Reb.	Ast.	Pts.	RPG	APG	PPG
96-97—Quad City	56	1953	231	567	.407	148	198	.747	218	380	652	3.9	6.8	11.6
97-98—Connecticut	8	333	66	133	.496	45	54	.833	29	53	191	3.6	6.6	23.9
98-99—Connecticut	21	817	134	332	.404	73	101	.723	48	154	367	2.3	7.3	17.5
Totals	85	3103	431	1032	.418	266	353	.754	275	587	1210	3.5	6.9	14.2

Three-point field goals: 1996-97, 42-for-154 (.273). 1997-98, 14-for-40 (.350). 1998-99, 26-for-82 (.317). Totals, 82-for-276 (.297).

NBA REGULAR-SEASON RECORD

Season Team	G	Min.	FGM	FGA	Pct.	FTM	FTA	Pct.	Off.	Def.	Tot.	Ast.	St.	Blk.	TO	Pts.	RPG	APG	PPG
97-98—Portland	38	622	49	141	.348	42	62	.677	14	42	56	100	25	3	52	162	1.5	2.6	4.3
98-99—New York	17	95	6	21	.286	5	18	.278	3	7	10	19	9	0	12	17	0.6	1.1	1.0
99-00—New York	37	289	29	70	.414	11	18	.611	3	24	27	49	9	1	31	71	0.7	1.3	1.9
00-01—Boston-N.Y.	22	208	18	54	.333	8	15	.533	5	16	21	31	8	1	17	46	1.0	1.4	2.1
Totals	114	1214	102	286	.357	66	113	.584	25	89	114	199	51	5	112	296	1.0	1.7	2.6

Three-point field goals: 1997-98, 22-for-61 (.361). 1998-99, 0-for-5. 1999-00, 2-for-13 (.154). 2000-01, 2-for-14 (.143). Totals, 26-for-93 (.280).
Personal fouls/disqualifications: 1997-98, 55/0. 1998-99, 8/0. 1999-00, 35/0. 2000-01, 21/0. Totals, 119/0.

NBA PLAYOFF RECORD

Season Team	G	Min.	FGM	FGA	Pct.	FTM	FTA	Pct.	Off.	Def.	Tot.	Ast.	St.	Blk.	TO	Pts.	RPG	APG	PPG
98-99—New York	9	18	2	5	.400	2	2	1.000	1	0	1	2	0	0	4	6	0.1	0.2	0.7
99-00—New York	3	4	0	1	.000	0	0	...	0	0	0	1	1	0	0	0	0.0	0.3	0.0
00-01—New York	2	4	0	1	.000	3	4	.750	0	0	0	0	0	1	3	0.0	0.0	1.5
Totals	14	26	2	7	.286	5	6	.833	1	0	1	3	1	0	5	9	0.1	0.2	0.6

Personal fouls/disqualifications: 1998-99, 3/0. 1999-00, 2/0. Totals, 5/0.

BRYANT, KOBE   G   LAKERS

PERSONAL: Born August 23, 1978, in Philadelphia. ... 6-7/215. (2,01/97,5). ... Full Name: Kobe B. Bryant. ... Son of Joe "Jelly Bean" Bryant, forward with Philadelphia 76ers (1975-75 through 1978-79), San Diego Clippers (1980-81 through 1981-82) and Houston Rockets (1982-83). ... Name pronounced Co-bee.
HIGH SCHOOL: Lower Merion (Pa.).
COLLEGE: Did not attend college.
TRANSACTIONS/CAREER NOTES: Selected out of high school by Charlotte Hornets in first round (13th pick overall) of 1996 NBA Draft. ... Draft rights traded by Hornets to Los Angeles Lakers for C Vlade Divac (July 11, 1996).
MISCELLANEOUS: Member of NBA championship team (2000, 2001).

NBA REGULAR-SEASON RECORD

HONORS: Slam Dunk championship winner (1997). ... All-NBA second team (2000, 2001). ... All-NBA third team (1999). ... NBA All-Defensive first team (2000). ... NBA All-Defensive second team (2001). ... NBA All-Rookie second team (1997).

Season Team	G	Min.	FGM	FGA	Pct.	FTM	FTA	Pct.	Off.	Def.	Tot.	Ast.	St.	Blk.	TO	Pts.	RPG	APG	PPG
96-97—L.A. Lakers	71	1103	176	422	.417	136	166	.819	47	85	132	91	49	23	112	539	1.9	1.3	7.6
97-98—L.A. Lakers	79	2056	391	913	.428	363	457	.794	79	163	242	199	74	40	157	1220	3.1	2.5	15.4
98-99—L.A. Lakers	50	1896	362	779	.465	245	292	.839	53	211	264	190	72	50	157	996	5.3	3.8	19.9
99-00—L.A. Lakers	66	2524	554	1183	.468	331	403	.821	108	308	416	323	106	62	182	1485	6.3	4.9	22.5
00-01—L.A. Lakers	68	2783	701	1510	.464	475	557	.853	104	295	399	338	114	43	220	1938	5.9	5.0	28.5
Totals	334	10362	2184	4807	.454	1550	1875	.827	391	1062	1453	1141	415	218	828	6178	4.4	3.4	18.5

Three-point field goals: 1996-97, 51-for-136 (.375). 1997-98, 75-for-220 (.341). 1998-99, 27-for-101 (.267). 1999-00, 46-for-144 (.319). 2000-01, 61-for-200 (.305). Totals, 260-for-801 (.325).
Personal fouls/disqualifications: 1996-97, 102/0. 1997-98, 180/1. 1998-99, 153/0. 1999-00, 220/4. 2000-01, 222/3. Totals, 877/11.

NBA PLAYOFF RECORD

Season Team	G	Min.	FGM	FGA	Pct.	FTM	FTA	Pct.	REBOUNDS Off.	Def.	Tot.	Ast.	St.	Blk.	TO	Pts.	AVERAGES RPG	APG	PPG
96-97—L.A. Lakers	9	133	21	55	.382	26	30	.867	1	10	11	11	3	2	14	74	1.2	1.2	8.2
97-98—L.A. Lakers	11	220	31	76	.408	31	45	.689	7	14	21	16	3	8	11	96	1.9	1.5	8.7
98-99—L.A. Lakers	8	315	61	142	.430	28	35	.800	13	42	55	37	15	10	31	158	6.9	4.6	19.8
99-00—L.A. Lakers	22	857	174	394	.442	95	126	.754	26	72	98	97	32	32	55	465	4.5	4.4	21.1
00-01—L.A. Lakers	16	694	168	358	.469	124	151	.821	29	87	116	97	25	12	51	471	7.3	6.1	29.4
Totals	**66**	**2219**	**455**	**1025**	**.444**	**304**	**387**	**.786**	**76**	**225**	**301**	**258**	**78**	**64**	**162**	**1264**	**4.6**	**3.9**	**19.2**

Three-point field goals: 1996-97, 6-for-23 (.261). 1997-98, 3-for-14 (.214). 1998-99, 8-for-23 (.348). 1999-00, 22-for-64 (.344). 2000-01, 11-for-34 (.324). Totals, 50-for-158 (.316).

Personal fouls/disqualifications: 1996-97, 23/0. 1997-98, 28/0. 1998-99, 24/1. 1999-00, 89/1. 2000-01, 53/0. Totals, 217/2.

NBA ALL-STAR GAME RECORD

Season Team	Min.	FGM	FGA	Pct.	FTM	FTA	Pct.	REBOUNDS Off.	Def.	Tot.	Ast.	PF	Dq.	St.	Blk.	TO	Pts.
1998 —L.A. Lakers	22	7	16	.438	2	2	1.000	2	4	6	1	1	...	2	0	1	18
2000 —L.A. Lakers	28	7	16	.438	0	0	...	1	0	1	3	3	0	2	0	1	15
2001 —L.A. Lakers	30	9	17	.529	0	0	...	2	2	4	7	3	0	1	0	3	19
Totals	**80**	**23**	**49**	**.469**	**2**	**2**	**1.000**	**5**	**6**	**11**	**11**	**7**	**0**	**5**	**0**	**5**	**52**

Three-point field goals: 1998, 2-for-3 (.667). 2000, 1-for-4 (.250). 2001, 1-for-2 (.500). Totals, 4-for-9 (.444).

BRYANT, MARK   F/C   SPURS

PERSONAL: Born April 25, 1965, in Glen Ridge, N.J. ... 6-9/250. (2,06/113,4). ... Full Name: Mark Craig Bryant.
HIGH SCHOOL: Columbia (Maplewood, N.J.).
COLLEGE: Seton Hall.
TRANSACTIONS/CAREER NOTES: Selected by Portland Trail Blazers in first round (21st pick overall) of 1988 NBA Draft. ... Signed as unrestricted free agent by Houston Rockets (September 29, 1995). ... Traded by Rockets with G Sam Cassell, F Chucky Brown and F Robert Horry to Phoenix Suns for F Charles Barkley and 1999 second-round draft choice (August 19, 1996). ... Traded by Suns with F Martin Muursepp, G/F Bubba Wells and conditional first-round draft choice to Chicago Bulls for C Luc Longley (January 23, 1999). ... Signed as free agent by Cleveland Cavaliers (August 12, 1999). ... Waived by Cavaliers (November 15, 2000). ... Signed as free agent by Dallas Mavericks (November 28, 2000). ... Signed as free agent by San Antonio Spurs (August 1, 2001).

COLLEGIATE RECORD

Season Team	G	Min.	FGM	FGA	Pct.	FTM	FTA	Pct.	Reb.	Ast.	Pts.	AVERAGES RPG	APG	PPG
84-85—Seton Hall......................	26	774	122	257	.475	74	114	.649	177	16	318	6.8	0.6	12.2
85-86—Seton Hall......................	30	901	169	323	.523	82	121	.678	226	16	420	7.5	0.5	14.0
86-87—Seton Hall......................	28	891	171	345	.496	127	180	.706	198	23	470	7.1	0.8	16.8
87-88—Seton Hall......................	34	1105	267	473	.564	163	218	.748	311	32	698	9.1	0.9	20.5
Totals	**118**	**3671**	**729**	**1398**	**.521**	**446**	**633**	**.705**	**912**	**87**	**1906**	**7.7**	**0.7**	**16.2**

Three-point field goals: 1986-87, 1-for-1. 1987-88, 1-for-2 (.500). Totals, 2-for-3 (.667).

NBA REGULAR-SEASON RECORD

Season Team	G	Min.	FGM	FGA	Pct.	FTM	FTA	Pct.	REBOUNDS Off.	Def.	Tot.	Ast.	St.	Blk.	TO	Pts.	AVERAGES RPG	APG	PPG
88-89—Portland	56	803	120	247	.486	40	69	.580	65	114	179	33	20	7	41	280	3.2	0.6	5.0
89-90—Portland	58	562	70	153	.458	28	50	.560	54	92	146	13	18	9	25	168	2.5	0.2	2.9
90-91—Portland	53	781	99	203	.488	74	101	.733	65	125	190	27	15	12	33	272	3.6	0.5	5.1
91-92—Portland	56	800	95	198	.480	40	60	.667	87	114	201	41	26	8	30	230	3.6	0.7	4.1
92-93—Portland	80	1396	186	370	.503	104	148	.703	132	192	324	41	37	23	65	476	4.1	0.5	6.0
93-94—Portland	79	1441	185	384	.482	72	104	.692	117	198	315	37	32	29	66	442	4.0	0.5	5.6
94-95—Portland	49	658	101	192	.526	41	63	.651	55	106	161	28	19	16	39	244	3.3	0.6	5.0
95-96—Houston	71	1587	242	446	.543	127	177	.718	131	220	351	52	31	19	85	611	4.9	0.7	8.6
96-97—Phoenix	41	1018	152	275	.553	76	108	.704	67	145	212	47	22	5	46	380	5.2	1.1	9.3
97-98—Phoenix	70	1110	109	225	.484	73	95	.768	92	152	244	46	36	15	58	291	3.5	0.7	4.2
98-99—Chicago	45	1204	168	348	.483	71	110	.645	92	140	232	48	34	16	68	407	5.2	1.1	9.0
99-00—Cleveland	75	1712	174	346	.503	76	94	.809	126	226	352	61	31	31	87	424	4.7	0.8	5.7
00-01—Cleve.-Dallas ..	18	101	8	20	.400	3	5	.600	4	17	21	3	1	2	5	19	1.2	0.2	1.1
Totals	**751**	**13173**	**1709**	**3407**	**.502**	**825**	**1184**	**.697**	**1087**	**1841**	**2928**	**477**	**322**	**192**	**648**	**4244**	**3.9**	**0.6**	**5.7**

Three-point field goals: 1990-91, 0-for-1. 1991-92, 0-for-3. 1992-93, 0-for-1. 1993-94, 0-for-1. 1994-95, 1-for-2 (.500). 1995-96, 0-for-2. 1997-98, 0-for-1. 1998-99, 0-for-1. Totals, 1-for-12 (.083).

Personal fouls/disqualifications: 1988-89, 144/3. 1989-90, 93/0. 1990-91, 120/0. 1991-92, 105/0. 1992-93, 226/1. 1993-94, 187/0. 1994-95, 109/1. 1995-96, 234/4. 1996-97, 136/4. 1997-98, 180/3. 1998-99, 149/2. 1999-00, 250/5. 2000-01, 29/1. Totals, 1962/24.

NBA PLAYOFF RECORD

Season Team	G	Min.	FGM	FGA	Pct.	FTM	FTA	Pct.	REBOUNDS Off.	Def.	Tot.	Ast.	St.	Blk.	TO	Pts.	AVERAGES RPG	APG	PPG
89-90—Portland	13	160	18	33	.545	6	8	.750	9	20	29	3	3	2	12	42	2.2	0.2	3.2
90-91—Portland	14	137	10	22	.455	14	16	.875	14	18	32	2	2	1	4	34	2.3	0.1	2.4
91-92—Portland	12	116	10	29	.345	3	4	.750	11	18	29	1	3	0	9	23	2.4	0.1	1.9
92-93—Portland	4	83	17	37	.459	5	5	1.000	10	8	18	0	0	3	6	39	4.5	0.0	9.8
93-94—Portland	4	64	5	17	.294	0	0	...	6	6	12	2	2	2	3	10	3.0	0.5	2.5
94-95—Portland	2	6	1	2	.500	0	2	.000	1	1	2	0	0	0	2	2	1.0	0.0	1.0
95-96—Houston	8	145	21	35	.600	12	15	.800	7	20	27	4	1	2	3	54	3.4	0.5	6.8
96-97—Phoenix	4	36	4	10	.400	3	3	1.000	1	3	4	0	0	0	2	11	1.0	0.0	2.8
97-98—Phoenix	4	93	17	34	.500	6	12	.500	9	14	23	1	4	2	3	40	5.8	0.3	10.0
00-01—Dallas.............	4	34	1	2	.500	0	0	...	3	3	6	0	1	0	1	2	1.5	0.0	0.5
Totals	**69**	**874**	**104**	**221**	**.471**	**49**	**65**	**.754**	**71**	**111**	**182**	**13**	**16**	**12**	**43**	**257**	**2.6**	**0.2**	**3.7**

Three-point field goals: 1993-94, 0-for-2. Totals, 0-for-2 (.000).

Personal fouls/disqualifications: 1989-90, 27/1. 1990-91, 25/0. 1991-92, 22/0. 1992-93, 14/0. 1993-94, 7/0. 1994-95, 1/0. 1995-96, 21/0. 1996-97, 4/0. 1997-98, 16/1. 2000-01, 6/0. Totals, 143/2.

BUCKNER, GREG G MAVERICKS

PERSONAL: Born September 16, 1976, in Hopkinsville, Ky. ... 6-4/210. (1,93/95,3). ... Full Name: Gregory Derayle Buckner.
HIGH SCHOOL: University Heights Academy (Hopkinsville, Ky.).
COLLEGE: Clemson.
TRANSACTIONS/CAREER NOTES: Selected by Dallas Mavericks in second round (53rd pick overall) of 1998 NBA Draft. ... Played in Continental Basketball Association with Grand Rapids Hoops (1998-99). ... Waived by Mavericks (February 2, 1999). ... Re-signed as free agent by Mavericks (August 3, 1999). ... Waived by Mavericks (November 1, 1999). ... Signed by Mavericks to the first of two consecutive 10-day contracts (January 6, 2000). ... Re-signed by Mavericks for remainder of season January 26, 2000).

COLLEGIATE RECORD

Season Team	G	Min.	FGM	FGA	Pct.	FTM	FTA	Pct.	Reb.	Ast.	Pts.	RPG	APG	PPG
94-95—Clemson	28	911	141	268	.526	41	80	.513	165	58	336	5.9	2.1	12.0
95-96—Clemson	29	950	144	305	.472	92	137	.672	147	48	381	5.1	1.7	13.1
96-97—Clemson	33	1071	190	393	.483	119	168	.708	150	63	516	4.5	1.9	15.6
97-98—Clemson	32	1022	204	380	.537	94	135	.696	130	83	521	4.1	2.6	16.3
Totals	122	3954	679	1346	.504	346	520	.665	592	252	1754	4.9	2.1	14.4

Three-point field goals: 1994-95, 13-for-44 (.295). 1995-96, 1-for-25 (.040). 1996-97, 17-for-54 (.315). 1997-98, 19-for-58 (.328). Totals, 50-for-181 .276).

CBA REGULAR-SEASON RECORD

Season Team	G	Min.	FGM	FGA	Pct.	FTM	FTA	Pct.	Reb.	Ast.	Pts.	RPG	APG	PPG
98-99—Grand Rapids	47	1064	161	365	.441	64	81	.790	182	96	406	3.9	2.0	8.6

Three-point field goals: 1998-99, 20-for-87 (.230).

NBA REGULAR-SEASON RECORD

Season Team	G	Min.	FGM	FGA	Pct.	FTM	FTA	Pct.	Off.	Def.	Tot.	Ast.	St.	Blk.	TO	Pts.	RPG	APG	PPG
99-00—Dallas	48	923	111	233	.476	43	63	.683	56	118	174	55	38	20	36	275	3.6	1.1	5.7
00-01—Dallas	37	820	84	192	.438	59	81	.728	60	97	157	49	33	9	27	229	4.2	1.3	6.2
Totals	85	1743	195	425	.459	102	144	.708	116	215	331	104	71	29	63	504	3.9	1.2	5.9

Three-point field goals: 1999-00, 10-for-26 (.385). 2000-01, 2-for-7 (.286). Totals, 12-for-33 (.364).
Personal fouls/disqualifications: 1999-00, 148/1. 2000-01, 118/2. Totals, 266/3.

NBA PLAYOFF RECORD

Season Team	G	Min.	FGM	FGA	Pct.	FTM	FTA	Pct.	Off.	Def.	Tot.	Ast.	St.	Blk.	TO	Pts.	RPG	APG	PPG
00-01—Dallas	5	75	11	23	.478	7	10	.700	8	13	21	3	5	0	2	30	4.2	0.6	6.0

Three-point field goals: 2000-01, 1-for-3 (.333).
Personal fouls/disqualifications: 2000-01, 12/0.

BUECHLER, JUD G/F SUNS

PERSONAL: Born June 19, 1968, in San Diego. ... 6-6/228. (1,98/103,4). ... Full Name: Judson Donald Buechler. ... Name pronounced Boosh-ler.
HIGH SCHOOL: Poway (Calif.).
COLLEGE: Arizona.
TRANSACTIONS/CAREER NOTES: Selected by Seattle SuperSonics in second round (38th pick overall) of 1990 NBA Draft. ... Draft rights traded by SuperSonics to New Jersey Nets in exchange for Nets agreement not to select G/F Dennis Scott in 1990 draft (June 27, 1990). ... Claimed on waivers by San Antonio Spurs (November 12, 1991). ... Waived by Spurs (December 17, 1991). ... Signed as free agent by Golden State Warriors (December 22, 1991). ... Signed as free agent by Chicago Bulls (September 16, 1994). ... Signed as free agent by Detroit Pistons (January 22, 1999). ... Traded by Pistons with F John Wallace to Phoenix Suns for F Clifford Robinson (June 29, 2001).
MISCELLANEOUS: Member of NBA championship team (1996, 1997, 1998).

COLLEGIATE RECORD

Season Team	G	Min.	FGM	FGA	Pct.	FTM	FTA	Pct.	Reb.	Ast.	Pts.	RPG	APG	PPG
86-87—Arizona	30	474	54	111	.486	16	28	.571	68	35	134	2.3	1.2	4.5
87-88—Arizona	36	422	64	124	.516	38	58	.655	87	41	170	2.4	1.1	4.7
88-89—Arizona	33	962	139	229	.607	84	103	.816	219	51	363	6.6	1.5	11.0
89-90—Arizona	32	1072	182	338	.538	88	115	.765	264	129	477	8.3	4.0	14.9
Totals	131	2930	439	802	.547	226	304	.743	638	256	1144	4.9	2.0	8.7

Three-point field goals: 1986-87, 10-for-25 (.400). 1987-88, 4-for-9 (.444). 1988-89, 1-for-5 (.200). 1989-90, 25-for-66 (.379). Totals, 40-for-105 (.381).

NBA REGULAR-SEASON RECORD

Season Team	G	Min.	FGM	FGA	Pct.	FTM	FTA	Pct.	Off.	Def.	Tot.	Ast.	St.	Blk.	TO	Pts.	RPG	APG	PPG
90-91—New Jersey	74	859	94	226	.416	43	66	.652	61	80	141	51	33	15	26	232	1.9	0.7	3.1
91-92—NJ-SA-GS	28	290	29	71	.408	12	21	.571	18	34	52	23	19	7	13	70	1.9	0.8	2.5
92-93—Golden State	70	1287	176	403	.437	65	87	.747	81	114	195	94	47	19	55	437	2.8	1.3	6.2
93-94—Golden State	36	218	42	84	.500	10	20	.500	13	19	32	16	8	1	12	106	0.9	0.4	2.9
94-95—Chicago	57	605	90	183	.492	22	39	.564	36	62	98	50	24	12	30	217	1.7	0.9	3.8
95-96—Chicago	74	740	112	242	.463	14	22	.636	45	66	111	56	34	7	39	278	1.5	0.8	3.8
96-97—Chicago	76	703	58	158	.367	5	14	.357	45	81	126	60	23	21	27	139	1.7	0.8	1.8

Season Team	G	Min.	FGM	FGA	Pct.	FTM	FTA	Pct.	REBOUNDS Off.	Def.	Tot.	Ast.	St.	Blk.	TO	Pts.	AVERAGES RPG	APG	PPG
97-98—Chicago	74	608	85	176	.483	3	6	.500	24	53	77	49	22	15	21	198	1.0	0.7	2.7
98-99—Detroit	50	1056	100	240	.417	13	18	.722	29	104	133	57	37	13	21	274	2.7	1.1	5.5
99-00—Detroit	58	657	55	156	.353	2	7	.286	30	61	91	33	25	16	13	130	1.6	0.6	2.2
00-01—Detroit	57	737	76	164	.463	9	12	.750	20	74	94	39	21	10	25	193	1.6	0.7	3.4
Totals	654	7760	917	2103	.436	198	312	.635	402	748	1150	528	293	136	282	2274	1.8	0.8	3.5

Three-point field goals: 1990-91, 1-for-4 (.250). 1991-92, 0-for-1. 1992-93, 20-for-59 (.339). 1993-94, 12-for-29 (.414). 1994-95, 15-for-48 (.313). 1995-96, 40-for-90 (.444). 1996-97, 18-for-54 (.333). 1997-98, 25-for-65 (.385). 1998-99, 61-for-148 (.412). 1999-00, 18-for-83 (.217). 2000-01, 32-for-77 (.416). Totals, 242-for-658 (.368).

Personal fouls/disqualifications: 1990-91, 79/0. 1991-92, 31/0. 1992-93, 98/0. 1993-94, 24/0. 1994-95, 64/0. 1995-96, 70/0. 1996-97, 50/0. 1997-98, 47/0. 1998-99, 83/0. 1999-00, 50/1. 2000-01, 83/0. Totals, 679/1.

NBA PLAYOFF RECORD

Season Team	G	Min.	FGM	FGA	Pct.	FTM	FTA	Pct.	REBOUNDS Off.	Def.	Tot.	Ast.	St.	Blk.	TO	Pts.	AVERAGES RPG	APG	PPG
94-95—Chicago	10	104	9	21	.429	2	4	.500	11	9	20	5	4	3	3	20	2.0	0.5	2.0
95-96—Chicago	17	127	18	38	.474	2	4	.500	2	8	10	6	7	0	8	46	0.6	0.4	2.7
96-97—Chicago	18	138	13	31	.419	3	5	.600	9	14	23	5	3	1	1	33	1.3	0.3	1.8
97-98—Chicago	16	64	4	11	.364	0	0	...	4	7	11	3	3	1	1	11	0.7	0.2	0.7
98-99—Detroit	5	84	3	15	.200	0	0	...	4	9	13	3	3	1	3	8	2.6	0.6	1.6
99-00—Detroit	3	34	2	7	.286	0	0	...	0	4	4	1	0	1	0	6	1.3	0.3	2.0
Totals	69	551	49	123	.398	7	13	.538	30	51	81	23	20	7	16	124	1.2	0.3	1.8

Three-point field goals: 1994-95, 0-for-2. 1995-96, 8-for-21 (.381). 1996-97, 4-for-12 (.333). 1997-98, 3-for-5 (.600). 1998-99, 2-for-8 (.250). 1999-00, 2-for-5 (.400). Totals, 19-for-53 (.358).

Personal fouls/disqualifications: 1994-95, 15/0. 1995-96, 13/0. 1996-97, 15/0. 1997-98, 7/0. 1998-99, 6/0. 1999-00, 4/0. Totals, 60/0.

BUFORD, RODNEY   G/F

PERSONAL: Born November 2, 1977, in Milwaukee. ... 6-5/189. (1,96/85,7). ... Full Name: Rodney Alan Buford.
HIGH SCHOOL: Milwaukee (Wis.) Vincent.
COLLEGE: Creighton.
TRANSACTIONS/CAREER NOTES: Selected by Miami Heat in second round (53rd pick overall) of 1999 NBA Draft. ... Traded by Heat with F P.J. Brown, F Jamal Mashburn, F/C Otis Thorpe and F Tim James to Charlotte Hornets for G Eddie Jones, F Anthony Mason, G Ricky Davis and G/F Dale Ellis (August 1, 2000). ... Waived by Hornets (October 2, 2000). ... Played in Italy (2000-01). ... Signed as free agent by Philadelphia 76ers (December 22, 2000).

COLLEGIATE RECORD

Season Team	G	Min.	FGM	FGA	Pct.	FTM	FTA	Pct.	Reb.	Ast.	Pts.	AVERAGES RPG	APG	PPG
95-96—Creighton	29	752	158	342	.462	59	81	.728	122	41	421	4.2	1.4	14.5
96-97—Creighton	30	947	225	512	.439	81	110	.736	168	48	589	5.6	1.6	19.6
97-98—Creighton	28	864	189	446	.424	99	138	.717	204	58	530	7.3	2.1	18.9
98-99—Creighton	31	1011	206	439	.469	109	133	.820	222	68	576	7.2	2.2	18.6
Totals	118	3574	778	1739	.447	348	462	.753	716	215	2116	6.1	1.8	17.9

Three-point field goals: 1995-96, 46-for-118 (.390). 1996-97, 58-for-153 (.379). 1997-98, 53-for-162 (.327). 1998-99, 55-for-125 (.440). Totals, 212-for-558 (.380).

NBA REGULAR-SEASON RECORD

Season Team	G	Min.	FGM	FGA	Pct.	FTM	FTA	Pct.	REBOUNDS Off.	Def.	Tot.	Ast.	St.	Blk.	TO	Pts.	AVERAGES RPG	APG	PPG
99-00—Miami	34	386	62	151	.411	16	22	.727	10	38	48	21	10	8	9	147	1.4	0.6	4.3
00-01—Philadelphia	47	573	104	241	.432	24	29	.828	16	58	74	17	17	6	29	248	1.6	0.4	5.3
Totals	81	959	166	392	.423	40	51	.784	26	96	122	38	27	14	38	395	1.5	0.5	4.9

Three-point field goals: 1999-00, 7-for-29 (.241). 2000-01, 16-for-38 (.421). Totals, 23-for-67 (.343).
Personal fouls/disqualifications: 1999-00, 44/0. 2000-01, 68/0. Totals, 112/0.

NBA PLAYOFF RECORD

Season Team	G	Min.	FGM	FGA	Pct.	FTM	FTA	Pct.	REBOUNDS Off.	Def.	Tot.	Ast.	St.	Blk.	TO	Pts.	AVERAGES RPG	APG	PPG
99-00—Miami	1	16	4	8	.500	2	2	1.000	0	1	1	1	0	0	0	11	1.0	1.0	11.0
00-01—Philadelphia	15	72	8	24	.333	2	2	1.000	5	7	12	3	4	1	4	21	0.8	0.2	1.4
Totals	16	88	12	32	.375	4	4	1.000	5	8	13	4	4	1	4	32	0.8	0.3	2.0

Three-point field goals: 1999-00, 1-for-2 (.500). 2000-01, 3-for-6 (.500). Totals, 4-for-8 (.500).
Personal fouls/disqualifications: 1999-00, 3/0. 2000-01, 15/0. Totals, 18/0.

ITALIAN LEAGUE RECORD

Season Team	G	Min.	FGM	FGA	Pct.	FTM	FTA	Pct.	Reb.	Ast.	Pts.	AVERAGES RPG	APG	PPG
00-01—Basket Rimini	10	364	87	179	.486	40	50	.800	52	21	241	5.2	2.1	24.1

Three-point field goals: 2000-01, 27-for-65 (.415).

BULLARD, MATT   F   HORNETS

PERSONAL: Born June 5, 1967, in West Des Moines, Iowa. ... 6-10/235. (2,08/106,6). ... Full Name: Matthew Gordon Bullard. ... Name pronounced BULL-ard.
HIGH SCHOOL: Valley (West Des Moines, Iowa).
COLLEGE: Colorado, then Iowa.

TRANSACTIONS/CAREER NOTES: Not drafted by an NBA franchise. ... Signed as free agent by Houston Rockets (August 22, 1990). ... Traded by Rockets with F Robert Horry and two future second-round draft choices to Detroit Pistons for F Sean Elliott (February 4, 1994); trade voided when Elliott failed physical (February 7, 1994). ... Played in Greece (1994-95). ... Signed as free agent by Atlanta Hawks (October 5, 1995). ... Signed as free agent by Rockets (September 27, 1996). ... Signed as free agent by Charlotte Hornets (August 13, 2001).
MISCELLANEOUS: Member of NBA championship team (1994).

COLLEGIATE RECORD

Season Team	G	Min.	FGM	FGA	Pct.	FTM	FTA	Pct.	Reb.	Ast.	Pts.	AVERAGES RPG	APG	PPG
85-86—Colorado	28	869	142	235	.604	72	88	.818	179	86	356	6.4	3.1	12.7
86-87—Colorado	28	938	182	349	.521	95	128	.742	280	61	464	10.0	2.2	16.6
87-88—Iowa						Did not play—transfer student.								
88-89—Iowa	20	498	66	117	.564	32	40	.800	123	37	181	6.2	1.9	9.1
89-90—Iowa	18	366	72	166	.434	36	50	.720	53	24	205	2.9	1.3	11.4
Totals	94	2671	462	867	.533	235	306	.768	635	208	1206	6.8	2.2	12.8

Three-point field goals: 1986-87, 5-for-26 (.192). 1988-89, 17-for-43 (.395). 1989-90, 25-for-71 (.352). Totals, 47-for-140 (.336).

NBA REGULAR-SEASON RECORD

Season Team	G	Min.	FGM	FGA	Pct.	FTM	FTA	Pct.	REBOUNDS Off.	Def.	Tot.	Ast.	St.	Blk.	TO	Pts.	AVERAGES RPG	APG	PPG
90-91—Houston	18	63	14	31	.452	11	17	.647	6	8	14	2	3	0	3	39	0.8	0.1	2.2
91-92—Houston	80	1278	205	447	.459	38	50	.760	73	150	223	75	26	21	56	512	2.8	0.9	6.4
92-93—Houston	79	1356	213	494	.431	58	74	.784	66	156	222	110	30	11	57	575	2.8	1.4	7.3
93-94—Houston	65	725	78	226	.345	20	26	.769	23	61	84	64	14	6	28	226	1.3	1.0	3.5
95-96—Atlanta	46	460	66	162	.407	16	20	.800	18	42	60	18	17	11	24	174	1.3	0.4	3.8
96-97—Houston	71	1025	114	284	.401	25	34	.735	13	104	117	67	21	18	38	320	1.6	0.9	4.5
97-98—Houston	67	1190	175	389	.450	20	27	.741	25	121	146	60	31	24	39	466	2.2	0.9	7.0
98-99—Houston	41	413	43	114	.377	7	10	.700	9	33	42	18	13	4	14	117	1.0	0.4	2.9
99-00—Houston	56	1024	139	340	.409	25	30	.833	13	125	138	63	19	13	36	382	2.5	1.1	6.8
00-01—Houston	61	1000	129	305	.423	10	14	.714	22	108	130	42	10	9	12	354	2.1	0.7	5.8
Totals	584	8534	1176	2792	.421	230	302	.762	268	908	1176	519	184	117	307	3165	2.0	0.9	5.4

Three-point field goals: 1990-91, 0-for-3. 1991-92, 64-for-166 (.386). 1992-93, 91-for-243 (.374). 1993-94, 50-for-154 (.325). 1995-96, 26-for-72 (.361). 1996-97, 67-for-183 (.366). 1997-98, 96-for-231 (.416). 1998-99, 24-for-62 (.387). 1999-00, 79-for-177 (.446). 2000-01, 86-for-213 (.404). Totals, 583-for-1504 (.388).

Personal fouls/disqualifications: 1990-91, 10/0. 1991-92, 129/1. 1992-93, 129/0. 1993-94, 67/0. 1995-96, 50/0. 1996-97, 68/0. 1997-98, 104/0. 1998-99, 28/0. 1999-00, 85/0. 2000-01, 76/0. Totals, 746/1.

NBA PLAYOFF RECORD

Season Team	G	Min.	FGM	FGA	Pct.	FTM	FTA	Pct.	REBOUNDS Off.	Def.	Tot.	Ast.	St.	Blk.	TO	Pts.	AVERAGES RPG	APG	PPG
92-93—Houston	12	169	20	42	.476	6	6	1.000	4	19	23	13	4	5	9	61	1.9	1.1	5.1
93-94—Houston	10	55	4	19	.211	6	8	.750	2	8	10	0	1	2	0	16	1.0	0.0	1.6
95-96—Atlanta	4	51	4	12	.333	2	4	.500	0	6	6	0	0	2	2	14	1.5	0.0	3.5
96-97—Houston	2	7	2	2	1.000	0	0	—	1	1	2	0	0	0	0	6	1.0	0.0	3.0
97-98—Houston	5	70	6	18	.333	2	2	1.000	3	5	8	5	1	0	0	17	1.6	1.0	3.4
98-99—Houston	2	8	2	2	1.000	2	2	1.000	0	0	0	1	0	0	0	7	0.0	0.5	3.5
Totals	35	360	38	95	.400	18	22	.818	10	39	49	19	6	9	11	121	1.4	0.5	3.5

Three-point field goals: 1992-93, 15-for-28 (.536). 1993-94, 2-for-10 (.200). 1995-96, 4-for-8 (.500). 1996-97, 2-for-2. 1997-98, 3-for-10 (.300). 1998-99, 1-for-1. Totals, 27-for-59 (.458).

Personal fouls/disqualifications: 1992-93, 11/0. 1993-94, 6/0. 1995-96, 6/0. 1996-97, 1/0. 1997-98, 5/0. Totals, 29/0.

GREEK LEAGUE RECORD

Season Team	G	Min.	FGM	FGA	Pct.	FTM	FTA	Pct.	Reb.	Ast.	Pts.	AVERAGES RPG	APG	PPG
94-95—PAOK	...	...	...	...	...	...	...	...	...	...	...	11.6	...	18.5

BURRELL, SCOTT G/F

PERSONAL: Born January 12, 1971, in New Haven, Conn. ... 6-7/218. (2,01/98,9). ... Full Name: Scott David Burrell.
HIGH SCHOOL: Hamden (Conn.).
COLLEGE: Connecticut.
TRANSACTIONS/CAREER NOTES: Selected by Charlotte Hornets in first round (20th pick overall) of 1993 NBA Draft. ... Traded by Hornets to Golden State Warriors for F Donald Royal (February 20, 1997). ... Traded by Warriors to Chicago Bulls for F Dickey Simpkins (September 22, 1997). ... Signed as free agent by New Jersey Nets (February 3, 1999). ... Signed as free agent by Hornets for remainder of season (April 10, 2001).
MISCELLANEOUS: Member of NBA championship team (1998). ... Only athlete ever to be drafted in the first round of two professional sports.

COLLEGIATE RECORD

Season Team	G	Min.	FGM	FGA	Pct.	FTM	FTA	Pct.	Reb.	Ast.	Pts.	AVERAGES RPG	APG	PPG
89-90—Connecticut	32	826	88	228	.386	66	106	.623	177	57	262	5.5	1.8	8.2
90-91—Connecticut	31	1075	136	309	.440	84	142	.592	234	95	393	7.5	3.1	12.7
91-92—Connecticut	30	1059	175	386	.453	77	126	.611	183	87	488	6.1	2.9	16.3
92-93—Connecticut	26	861	145	353	.411	79	104	.760	156	54	419	6.0	2.1	16.1
Totals	119	3821	544	1276	.426	306	478	.640	750	293	1562	6.3	2.5	13.1

Three-point field goals: 1989-90, 20-for-64 (.313). 1990-91, 37-for-108 (.343). 1991-92, 61-for-154 (.396). 1992-93, 50-for-145 (.345). Totals, 168-for-471 (.357).

NBA REGULAR-SEASON RECORD

Season Team	G	Min.	FGM	FGA	Pct.	FTM	FTA	Pct.	Off.	Def.	Tot.	Ast.	St.	Blk.	TO	Pts.	RPG	APG	PPG
93-94—Charlotte........	51	767	98	234	.419	46	70	.657	46	86	132	62	37	16	45	244	2.6	1.2	4.8
94-95—Charlotte........	65	2014	277	593	.467	100	144	.694	96	272	368	161	75	40	85	750	5.7	2.5	11.5
95-96—Charlotte........	20	693	92	206	.447	42	56	.750	26	72	98	47	27	13	43	263	4.9	2.4	13.2
96-97—Char.-G.S........	57	939	98	271	.362	57	76	.750	49	109	158	74	28	19	53	294	2.8	1.3	5.2
97-98—Chicago	80	1096	159	375	.424	47	64	.734	80	118	198	65	64	37	50	416	2.5	0.8	5.2
98-99—New Jersey.....	32	706	75	208	.361	34	42	.810	32	87	119	45	40	11	23	212	3.7	1.4	6.6
99-00—New Jersey.....	74	1336	165	419	.394	39	50	.780	65	191	256	72	67	44	38	451	3.5	1.0	6.1
00-01—Charlotte........	4	41	7	15	.467	1	4	.250	1	2	3	1	3	0	0	17	0.8	0.3	4.3
Totals	383	7592	971	2321	.418	366	506	.723	395	937	1332	527	341	180	337	2647	3.5	1.4	6.9

Three-point field goals: 1993-94, 2-for-6 (.333). 1994-95, 96-for-235 (.409). 1995-96, 37-for-98 (.378). 1996-97, 41-for-116 (.353). 1997-98, 51-for-144 (.354). 1998-99, 28-for-72 (.389). 1999-00, 82-for-232 (.353). 2000-01, 2-for-6 (.333). Totals, 339-for-909 (.373).

Personal fouls/disqualifications: 1993-94, 88/0. 1994-95, 187/1. 1995-96, 76/2. 1996-97, 120/0. 1997-98, 131/1. 1998-99, 82/2. 1999-00, 173/1. 2000-01, 8/0. Totals, 865/7.

NBA PLAYOFF RECORD

Season Team	G	Min.	FGM	FGA	Pct.	FTM	FTA	Pct.	Off.	Def.	Tot.	Ast.	St.	Blk.	TO	Pts.	RPG	APG	PPG
97-98—Chicago	21	261	32	73	.438	10	11	.909	11	32	43	10	19	3	11	80	2.0	0.5	3.8
00-01—Charlotte........	2	12	2	3	.667	1	2	.500	0	3	3	1	2	0	0	5	1.5	0.5	2.5
Totals	23	273	34	76	.447	11	13	.846	11	35	46	11	21	3	11	85	2.0	0.5	3.7

Three-point field goals: 1997-98, 6-for-20 (.300). 2000-01, 0-for-1. Totals, 6-for-21 (.286).
Personal fouls/disqualifications: 1997-98, 33/0. Totals, 33/0.

RECORD AS BASEBALL PLAYER

TRANSACTIONS/CAREER NOTES: Threw right, batted right. ... Selected by Seattle Mariners organization in first round (26th pick overall) of free-agent draft (June 5, 1989); did not sign. ... Selected by Toronto Blue Jays organization in fifth round of free-agent draft (June 4, 1990). ... On St. Catharines temporarily inactive list (June 17-30, 1991). ... On Myrtle Beach temporarily inactive list (April 9-June 30, 1992). ... On Dunedin disabled list (August 27, 1992-remainder of season). ... On Syracuse temporarily inactive list (April 8-July 2, 1993). ... On Syracuse restricted list (July 2, 1993).

Year Team (League)	W	L	Pct.	ERA	G	GS	CG	ShO	Sv.	IP	H	R	ER	BB	SO
1990—St. Catharines (NYP)	1	4	.200	5.86	7	7	0	0	0	27⅔	29	20	18	15	24
1991—St. Catharines (NYP)	0	2	.000	1.50	2	2	0	0	0	6	3	3	1	3	5
Myrtle Beach (S. Atl.)	1	0	1.000	2.00	5	5	0	0	0	27	18	6	6	13	31
1992—									Did not play.						

CAFFEY, JASON   F   BUCKS

PERSONAL: Born June 12, 1973, in Mobile, Ala. ... 6-8/256. (2,03/116,1). ... Full Name: Jason Andre Caffey.
HIGH SCHOOL: Davidson (Mobile, Ala.).
COLLEGE: Alabama.
TRANSACTIONS/CAREER NOTES: Selected by Chicago Bulls in first round (20th pick overall) of 1995 NBA Draft. ... Traded by Bulls to Golden State Warriors for F David Vaughn and 1998 and 2000 second-round draft choices (February 19, 1998). ... Traded by Warriors with F/G Billy Owens to Milwaukee Bucks as part of three-way deal in which Bucks traded F/C J.R. Reid and F Robert Traylor to Cleveland Cavaliers, Cavaliers traded G Bob Sura to Golden State Warriors and Bucks traded G Vinny Del Negro to Warriors (June 27, 2000).
MISCELLANEOUS: Member of NBA championship team (1996, 1997).

COLLEGIATE RECORD

Season Team	G	Min.	FGM	FGA	Pct.	FTM	FTA	Pct.	Reb.	Ast.	Pts.	RPG	APG	PPG
91-92—Alabama	30	331	31	73	.425	10	30	.333	67	10	72	2.2	0.3	2.4
92-93—Alabama	29	847	169	326	.518	80	130	.615	252	39	421	8.7	1.3	14.5
93-94—Alabama	29	784	140	269	.520	90	143	.629	183	20	371	6.3	0.7	12.8
94-95—Alabama	31	933	148	291	.509	79	145	.545	249	51	375	8.0	1.6	12.1
Totals	119	2895	488	959	.509	259	448	.578	751	120	1239	6.3	1.0	10.4

Three-point field goals: 1991-92, 0-for-1. 1992-93, 3-for-11 (.273). 1993-94, 1-for-2 (.500). 1994-95, 0-for-4. Totals, 4-for-18 (.222).

NBA REGULAR-SEASON RECORD

Season Team	G	Min.	FGM	FGA	Pct.	FTM	FTA	Pct.	Off.	Def.	Tot.	Ast.	St.	Blk.	TO	Pts.	RPG	APG	PPG
95-96—Chicago	57	545	71	162	.438	40	68	.588	51	60	111	24	12	7	48	182	1.9	0.4	3.2
96-97—Chicago	75	1405	205	385	.532	139	211	.659	135	166	301	89	25	9	97	549	4.0	1.2	7.3
97-98—Chi-Gold.St.....	80	1423	226	466	.485	131	200	.655	160	184	344	67	25	20	105	583	4.3	0.8	7.3
98-99—Golden State ..	35	876	123	277	.444	62	98	.633	79	126	205	18	24	9	75	308	5.9	0.5	8.8
99-00—Golden State ...	71	2159	323	675	.479	206	345	.597	189	293	482	119	62	20	170	852	6.8	1.7	12.0
00-01—Milwaukee	70	1460	179	367	.488	142	211	.673	135	218	353	53	38	25	77	500	5.0	0.8	7.1
Totals	388	7868	1127	2332	.483	720	1133	.635	749	1047	1796	370	186	90	572	2974	4.6	1.0	7.7

Three-point field goals: 1995-96, 0-for-1. 1996-97, 0-for-1. 1997-98, 0-for-2. 1998-99, 0-for-1. 1999-00, 0-for-2. Totals, 0-for-7 (.000).
Personal fouls/disqualifications: 1995-96, 91/3. 1996-97, 149/0. 1997-98, 181/4. 1998-99, 113/1. 1999-00, 269/11. 2000-01, 184/8. Totals, 987/27.

NBA PLAYOFF RECORD

Season Team	G	Min.	FGM	FGA	Pct.	FTM	FTA	Pct.	Off.	Def.	Tot.	Ast.	St.	Blk.	TO	Pts.	RPG	APG	PPG
96-97—Chicago	17	167	15	33	.455	11	14	.786	25	17	42	15	3	3	12	41	2.5	0.9	2.4
00-01—Milwaukee	18	297	24	63	.381	20	31	.645	31	43	74	14	3	5	15	68	4.1	0.8	3.8
Totals	35	464	39	96	.406	31	45	.689	56	60	116	29	6	8	27	109	3.3	0.8	3.1

Personal fouls/disqualifications: 1996-97, 27/0. 2000-01, 44/0. Totals, 71/0.

CAMBY, MARCUS   F/C   KNICKS

PERSONAL: Born March 22, 1974, in Hartford. ... 6-11/225. (2,11/102,1). ... Full Name: Marcus D. Camby.
HIGH SCHOOL: Hartford Public (Conn.).
COLLEGE: Massachusetts.
TRANSACTIONS/CAREER NOTES: Selected after junior season by Toronto Raptors in first round (second pick overall) of 1996 NBA Draft. ... Traded by Raptors to New York Knicks for F Charles Oakley, draft rights to F/C Sean Marks and cash (June 25, 1998).
MISCELLANEOUS: Toronto Raptors all-time blocked shots leader with 360 (1996-97 and 1997-98).

COLLEGIATE RECORD

NOTES: The Sporting News College Player of the Year (1996). ... Naismith Award winner (1996). ... Wooden Award winner (1996). ... The Sporting News All-America first team (1996).

Season Team	G	Min.	FGM	FGA	Pct.	FTM	FTA	Pct.	Reb.	Ast.	Pts.	RPG	APG	PPG
93-94—Massachusetts	29	634	117	237	.494	62	104	.596	185	36	296	6.4	1.2	10.2
94-95—Massachusetts	30	679	166	302	.550	83	129	.643	186	37	416	6.2	1.2	13.9
95-96—Massachusetts	33	1011	256	537	.477	163	233	.700	271	58	675	8.2	1.8	20.5
Totals	92	2324	539	1076	.501	308	466	.661	642	131	1387	7.0	1.4	15.1

Three-point field goals: 1993-94, 0-for-4. 1994-95, 1-for-1. 1995-96, 0-for-8. Totals, 1-for-13 (.077).

NBA REGULAR-SEASON RECORD

HONORS: NBA All-Rookie first team (1997).
NOTES: Led NBA with 3.65 blocks per game (1998).

Season Team	G	Min.	FGM	FGA	Pct.	FTM	FTA	Pct.	REBOUNDS Off.	Def.	Tot.	Ast.	St.	Blk.	TO	Pts.	RPG	APG	PPG
96-97—Toronto	63	1897	375	778	.482	183	264	.693	131	263	394	97	66	130	134	935	6.3	1.5	14.8
97-98—Toronto	63	2002	308	747	.412	149	244	.611	203	263	466	111	68	230	134	765	7.4	1.8	12.1
98-99—New York	46	945	136	261	.521	57	103	.553	102	151	253	12	29	74	39	329	5.5	0.3	7.2
99-00—New York	59	1548	226	471	.480	148	221	.670	174	287	461	49	43	116	72	601	7.8	0.8	10.2
00-01—New York	63	2127	304	580	.524	150	225	.667	196	527	723	52	66	136	63	759	11.5	0.8	12.0
Totals	294	8519	1349	2837	.476	687	1057	.650	806	1491	2297	321	272	686	442	3389	7.8	1.1	11.5

Three-point field goals: 1996-97, 2-for-14 (.143). 1997-98, 0-for-2. 1999-00, 1-for-2 (.500). 2000-01, 1-for-8 (.125). Totals, 4-for-26 (.154).
Personal fouls/disqualifications: 1996-97, 214/7. 1997-98, 200/1. 1998-99, 131/2. 1999-00, 204/5. 2000-01, 205/4. Totals, 954/19.

NBA PLAYOFF RECORD

Season Team	G	Min.	FGM	FGA	Pct.	FTM	FTA	Pct.	REBOUNDS Off.	Def.	Tot.	Ast.	St.	Blk.	TO	Pts.	RPG	APG	PPG
98-99—New York	20	509	81	143	.566	45	73	.616	51	102	153	6	24	38	15	207	7.7	0.3	10.4
99-00—New York	16	386	29	86	.337	19	31	.613	35	77	112	6	8	23	12	77	7.0	0.4	4.8
00-01—New York	4	141	10	26	.385	5	13	.385	4	28	32	7	2	9	2	25	8.0	1.8	6.3
Totals	40	1036	120	255	.471	69	117	.590	90	207	297	19	34	70	29	309	7.4	0.5	7.7

Three-point field goals: 1998-99, 0-for-1. 1999-00, 0-for-1. Totals, 0-for-2 (.000).
Personal fouls/disqualifications: 1998-99, 76/2. 1999-00, 51/1. 2000-01, 18/1. Totals, 145/4.

CAMPBELL, ELDEN   C   HORNETS

PERSONAL: Born July 23, 1968, in Los Angeles. ... 7-0/275. (2,13/124,7). ... Full Name: Elden Jerome Campbell.
HIGH SCHOOL: Morningside (Inglewood, Calif.).
COLLEGE: Clemson.
TRANSACTIONS/CAREER NOTES: Selected by Los Angeles Lakers in first round (27th pick overall) of 1990 NBA Draft. ... Traded by Lakers with G Eddie Jones to Charlotte Hornets for F Glen Rice, F/C J.R. Reid and G B.J. Armstrong (March 10, 1999).

COLLEGIATE RECORD

Season Team	G	Min.	FGM	FGA	Pct.	FTM	FTA	Pct.	Reb.	Ast.	Pts.	RPG	APG	PPG
86-87—Clemson	31	534	107	193	.554	59	84	.702	126	20	273	4.1	0.6	8.8
87-88—Clemson	28	808	217	345	.629	91	147	.619	207	15	525	7.4	0.5	18.8
88-89—Clemson	29	814	205	373	.550	95	138	.688	222	34	507	7.7	1.2	17.5
89-90—Clemson	35	1038	205	431	.522	124	207	.599	281	44	575	8.0	1.3	16.4
Totals	123	3194	754	1342	.562	369	576	.641	836	113	1880	6.8	0.9	15.3

Three-point field goals: 1987-88, 0-for-4. 1988-89, 2-for-5 (.400). 1989-90, 1-for-1. Totals, 3-for-10 (.300).

NBA REGULAR-SEASON RECORD

NOTES: Tied for NBA lead with 300 personal fouls (1996).

Season Team	G	Min.	FGM	FGA	Pct.	FTM	FTA	Pct.	REBOUNDS Off.	Def.	Tot.	Ast.	St.	Blk.	TO	Pts.	RPG	APG	PPG
90-91—L.A. Lakers	52	380	56	123	.455	32	49	.653	40	56	96	10	11	38	16	144	1.8	0.2	2.8
91-92—L.A. Lakers	81	1876	220	491	.448	138	223	.619	155	268	423	59	53	159	73	578	5.2	0.7	7.1
92-93—L.A. Lakers	79	1551	238	520	.458	130	204	.637	127	205	332	48	59	100	69	606	4.2	0.6	7.7
93-94—L.A. Lakers	76	2253	373	808	.462	188	273	.689	167	352	519	86	64	146	98	934	6.8	1.1	12.3
94-95—L.A. Lakers	73	2076	360	785	.459	193	290	.666	168	277	445	92	69	132	98	913	6.1	1.3	12.5
95-96—L.A. Lakers	82	2699	447	888	.503	249	349	.713	162	461	623	181	88	212	137	1143	7.6	2.2	13.9
96-97—L.A. Lakers	77	2516	442	942	.469	263	370	.711	207	408	615	126	46	117	130	1148	8.0	1.6	14.9
97-98—L.A. Lakers	81	1784	289	624	.463	237	342	.693	143	312	455	78	35	102	115	816	5.6	1.0	10.1
98-99—L.A.L.-Char.	49	1459	222	465	.477	172	269	.639	126	271	397	69	39	73	80	616	8.1	1.4	12.6
99-00—Charlotte	78	2538	370	829	.446	247	358	.690	168	422	590	129	56	150	127	987	7.6	1.7	12.7
00-01—Charlotte	78	2337	367	834	.440	288	406	.709	157	451	608	104	60	140	144	1022	7.8	1.3	13.1
Totals	806	21469	3384	7309	.463	2137	3133	.682	1620	3483	5103	982	580	1369	1087	8907	6.3	1.2	11.1

Three-point field goals: 1991-92, 0-for-2. 1992-93, 0-for-3. 1993-94, 0-for-2. 1994-95, 0-for-1. 1995-96, 0-for-5. 1996-97, 1-for-4 (.250). 1997-98, 1-for-2 (.500). 1998-99, 0-for-1. 1999-00, 0-for-6. 2000-01, 0-for-6. Totals, 2-for-32 (.063).

Personal fouls/disqualifications: 1990-91, 71/1. 1991-92, 203/1. 1992-93, 165/0. 1993-94, 241/2. 1994-95, 246/4. 1995-96, 300/4. 1996-97, 276/6. 1997-98, 209/1. 1998-99, 159/3. 1999-00, 269/6. 2000-01, 280/1. Totals, 2419/29.

NBA PLAYOFF RECORD

Season Team	G	Min.	FGM	FGA	Pct.	FTM	FTA	Pct.	Off.	Def.	Tot.	Ast.	St.	Blk.	TO	Pts.	RPG	APG	PPG
90-91—L.A. Lakers	14	138	25	38	.658	7	15	.467	8	21	29	3	6	8	6	57	2.1	0.2	4.1
91-92—L.A. Lakers	4	117	14	37	.378	12	18	.667	9	16	25	6	3	6	4	40	6.3	1.5	10.0
92-93—L.A. Lakers	5	178	29	69	.420	12	24	.500	17	25	42	7	6	12	12	70	8.4	1.4	14.0
94-95—L.A. Lakers	10	376	64	132	.485	29	44	.659	26	47	73	16	4	30	15	157	7.3	1.6	15.7
95-96—L.A. Lakers	4	129	20	39	.513	8	16	.500	3	29	32	8	1	9	10	48	8.0	2.0	12.0
96-97—L.A. Lakers	9	278	37	93	.398	31	38	.816	14	25	39	9	7	13	14	106	4.3	1.0	11.8
97-98—L.A. Lakers	13	180	23	51	.451	22	34	.647	17	28	45	8	3	12	13	68	3.5	0.6	5.2
99-00—Charlotte........	4	150	22	47	.468	13	14	.929	9	24	33	4	2	4	8	57	8.3	1.0	14.3
00-01—Charlotte........	10	287	42	106	.396	37	49	.755	27	52	79	7	5	11	17	121	7.9	0.7	12.1
Totals	**73**	**1833**	**276**	**612**	**.451**	**171**	**252**	**.679**	**130**	**267**	**397**	**68**	**37**	**105**	**99**	**724**	**5.4**	**0.9**	**9.9**

Three-point field goals: 1995-96, 0-for-1. 1996-97, 1-for-1. 1999-00, 0-for-1. Totals, 1-for-3 (.333).

Personal fouls/disqualifications: 1990-91, 23/1. 1991-92, 14/0. 1992-93, 15/0. 1994-95, 44/2. 1995-96, 17/1. 1996-97, 30/0. 1997-98, 27/0. 1999-00, 16/0. 2000-01, 37/1. Totals, 223/5.

CARDINAL, BRIAN   F

PERSONAL: Born May 2, 1977, in Tolono, Ill. ... 6-8/245. (2,03/111,1). ... Full Name: Brian Lee Cardinal.
HIGH SCHOOL: Unity (Tolono, Ill.).
COLLEGE: Purdue.
TRANSACTIONS/CAREER NOTES: Selected by Detroit Pistons in second round (44th pick overall) of 2000 NBA Draft.

COLLEGIATE RECORD

Season Team	G	Min.	FGM	FGA	Pct.	FTM	FTA	Pct.	Reb.	Ast.	Pts.	RPG	APG	PPG
95-96—Purdue							Did not play—redshirted.							
96-97—Purdue	30	865	100	220	.455	98	139	.705	182	58	319	6.1	1.9	10.6
97-98—Purdue	36	925	140	275	.509	122	155	.787	178	66	432	4.9	1.8	12.0
98-99—Purdue	34	960	118	246	.480	114	147	.776	186	82	387	5.5	2.4	11.4
99-00—Purdue	32	943	137	333	.411	130	169	.769	203	71	446	6.3	2.2	13.9
Totals	**132**	**3693**	**495**	**1074**	**.461**	**464**	**610**	**.761**	**749**	**277**	**1584**	**5.7**	**2.1**	**12.0**

Three-point field goals: 1996-97, 21-for-63 (.333). 1997-98, 30-for-70 (.429). 1998-99, 37-for-99 (.374). 1999-00, 42-for-124 (.339). Totals, 130-for-356 (.365).

NBA REGULAR-SEASON RECORD

Season Team	G	Min.	FGM	FGA	Pct.	FTM	FTA	Pct.	Off.	Def.	Tot.	Ast.	St.	Blk.	TO	Pts.	RPG	APG	PPG
00-01—Detroit	15	126	10	31	.323	11	18	.611	8	15	23	3	7	2	9	31	1.5	0.2	2.1

Three-point field goals: 2000-01, 0-for-5.
Personal fouls/disqualifications: 2000-01, 27/0.

CARR, CHRIS   G

PERSONAL: Born March 12, 1974, in Ironton, Mo. ... 6-6/220. (1,98/99,8). ... Full Name: Chris Dean Carr.
HIGH SCHOOL: Arcadia Valley (Pilot Knob, Mo.).
COLLEGE: Southern Illinois.
TRANSACTIONS/CAREER NOTES: Selected after junior season by Phoenix Suns in second round (56th pick overall) of 1995 NBA Draft. ... Signed as free agent by Minnesota Timberwolves (July 19, 1996). ... Traded by Timberwolves with F Bill Curley and G Stephon Marbury to New Jersey Nets in three-way deal in which Nets also received G Elliot Perry from Milwaukee Bucks, Timberwolves received F Brian Evans, 1999 first-round draft choice and an undisclosed draft choice from Nets, Bucks sent G Terrell Brandon to Timberwolves, Timberwolves sent C Paul Grant to Bucks and Nets sent G Sam Cassell and F/C Chris Gatling to Bucks (March 11, 1999). ... Signed as free agent by Golden State Warriors (December 1, 1999). ... Waived by Warriors (December 16, 1999). ... Signed by Chicago Bulls to the first of two consecutive 10-day contracts (January 10, 2000). ... Re-signed by Bulls for remainder of season (January 30, 2000). ... Signed as free agent by Boston Celtics (August 21, 2000).

COLLEGIATE RECORD

Season Team	G	Min.	FGM	FGA	Pct.	FTM	FTA	Pct.	Reb.	Ast.	Pts.	RPG	APG	PPG
92-93—Southern Illinois............	31	353	52	88	.591	18	33	.545	110	15	122	3.5	0.5	3.9
93-94—Southern Illinois............	30	946	156	301	.518	88	109	.807	197	55	424	6.6	1.8	14.1
94-95—Southern Illinois............	32	1069	250	521	.480	165	214	.771	232	68	705	7.3	2.1	22.0
Totals	**93**	**2368**	**458**	**910**	**.503**	**271**	**356**	**.761**	**539**	**138**	**1251**	**5.8**	**1.5**	**13.5**

Three-point field goals: 1992-93, 0-for-4. 1993-94, 24-for-74 (.324). 1994-95, 40-for-101 (.396). Totals, 64-for-179 (.358).

NBA REGULAR-SEASON RECORD

Season Team	G	Min.	FGM	FGA	Pct.	FTM	FTA	Pct.	Off.	Def.	Tot.	Ast.	St.	Blk.	TO	Pts.	RPG	APG	PPG
95-96—Phoenix	60	590	90	217	.415	49	60	.817	27	75	102	43	10	5	40	240	1.7	0.7	4.0
96-97—Minnesota.......	55	830	125	271	.461	56	73	.767	31	82	113	48	24	10	37	337	2.1	0.9	6.1
97-98—Minnesota.......	51	1165	190	452	.420	84	99	.848	43	112	155	85	17	11	69	504	3.0	1.7	9.9
98-99—Minn.-N.J.......	39	445	76	205	.371	27	40	.675	23	48	71	23	8	2	28	207	1.8	0.6	5.3
99-00—Gold.St.-Chi. ...	57	1166	196	496	.395	107	125	.856	41	132	173	84	30	15	117	531	3.0	1.5	9.3
00-01—Boston	35	309	53	112	.473	46	60	.767	11	33	44	11	4	3	19	169	1.3	0.3	4.8
Totals	**297**	**4505**	**730**	**1753**	**.416**	**369**	**457**	**.807**	**176**	**482**	**658**	**294**	**93**	**46**	**310**	**1988**	**2.2**	**1.0**	**6.7**

Three-point field goals: 1995-96, 11-for-42 (.262). 1996-97, 31-for-88 (.352). 1997-98, 40-for-127 (.315). 1998-99, 28-for-75 (.373). 1999-00, 32-for-101 (.317). 2000-01, 17-for-37 (.459). Totals, 159-for-470 (.338).
Personal fouls/disqualifications: 1995-96, 77/1. 1996-97, 93/0. 1997-98, 129/1. 1998-99, 45/0. 1999-00, 113/0. 2000-01, 45/1. Totals, 502/3.

NBA PLAYOFF RECORD

Season Team	G	Min.	FGM	FGA	Pct.	FTM	FTA	Pct.	Off.	Def.	Tot.	Ast.	St.	Blk.	TO	Pts.	RPG	APG	PPG
95-96—Phoenix	3	36	9	14	.643	4	5	.800	3	4	7	4	2	1	4	24	2.3	1.3	8.0
96-97—Minnesota.......	1	8	0	2	.000	0	0	...	0	2	2	1	0	0	1	0	2.0	1.0	0.0
Totals	4	44	9	16	.563	4	5	.800	3	6	9	5	2	1	5	24	2.3	1.3	6.0

Three-point field goals: 1995-96, 2-for-3 (.667). 1996-97, 0-for-2. Totals, 2-for-5 (.400).
Personal fouls/disqualifications: 1995-96, 6/0. Totals, 6/0.

CARTER, ANTHONY   G   HEAT

PERSONAL: Born June 16, 1975, in Atlanta. ... 6-1/190. (1,85/86,2). ... Full Name: Anthony Bernard Carter.
HIGH SCHOOL: Alonzo A. Crim (Atlanta).
JUNIOR COLLEGE: Saddleback Community College (Calif.).
COLLEGE: Hawaii.
TRANSACTIONS/CAREER NOTES: Not drafted by an NBA franchise. ... Played in Continental Basketball Association with Yakima Sun Kings (1998-99). ... Signed as free agent by Miami Heat (August 6, 1999).

COLLEGIATE RECORD

Season Team	G	Min.	FGM	FGA	Pct.	FTM	FTA	Pct.	Reb.	Ast.	Pts.	RPG	APG	PPG
94-95—Saddleback C.C.	33	...	261	508	.514	100	146	.685	203	116	641	6.2	3.5	19.4
95-96—Saddleback C.C.	33	...	324	668	.485	209	278	.752	216	178	889	6.5	5.4	26.9
96-97—Hawaii	29	1005	211	426	.495	89	138	.645	107	191	543	3.7	6.6	18.7
97-98—Hawaii	29	1041	191	422	.453	111	142	.782	152	212	527	5.2	7.3	18.2
Junior College Totals........	66	...	585	1176	.497	309	424	.729	419	294	1530	6.3	4.5	23.2
4-Year-College Totals............	58	2046	402	848	.474	200	280	.962	259	403	1070	4.5	6.9	18.4

Three-point field goals: 1994-95, 19-for-81 (.235). 1995-96, 32-for-110 (.291). 1996-97, 32-for-90 (.356). 1997-98, 34-for-110 (.309). Totals, 51-for-191 (.267).

CBA REGULAR-SEASON RECORD

Season Team	G	Min.	FGM	FGA	Pct.	FTM	FTA	Pct.	Reb.	Ast.	Pts.	RPG	APG	PPG
98-99—Yakima	48	1202	220	502	.438	101	141	.716	130	209	555	2.7	4.4	11.6

Three-point field goals: 1998-99, 14-for-63 (.222).

NBA REGULAR-SEASON RECORD

Season Team	G	Min.	FGM	FGA	Pct.	FTM	FTA	Pct.	Off.	Def.	Tot.	Ast.	St.	Blk.	TO	Pts.	RPG	APG	PPG
99-00—Miami	79	1859	201	509	.395	93	124	.750	48	151	199	378	93	5	173	498	2.5	4.8	6.3
00-01—Miami	72	1630	195	480	.406	65	103	.631	46	134	180	268	73	10	119	461	2.5	3.7	6.4
Totals	151	3489	396	989	.400	158	227	.696	94	285	379	646	166	15	292	959	2.5	4.3	6.4

Three-point field goals: 1999-00, 3-for-23 (.130). 2000-01, 6-for-40 (.150). Totals, 9-for-63 (.143).
Personal fouls/disqualifications: 1999-00, 167/0. 2000-01, 154/1. Totals, 321/1.

NBA PLAYOFF RECORD

Season Team	G	Min.	FGM	FGA	Pct.	FTM	FTA	Pct.	Off.	Def.	Tot.	Ast.	St.	Blk.	TO	Pts.	RPG	APG	PPG
99-00—Miami	10	275	32	77	.416	12	16	.750	8	32	40	56	12	2	23	77	4.0	5.6	7.7
00-01—Miami	3	69	9	19	.474	0	0	...	0	6	6	11	2	1	10	18	2.0	3.7	6.0
Totals	13	344	41	96	.427	12	16	.750	8	38	46	67	14	3	33	95	3.5	5.2	7.3

Three-point field goals: 1999-00, 1-for-6 (.167). 2000-01, 0-for-1. Totals, 1-for-7 (.143).
Personal fouls/disqualifications: 1999-00, 22/0. 2000-01, 9/0. Totals, 31/0.

CARTER, VINCE   G/F   RAPTORS

PERSONAL: Born January 26, 1977, in Daytona Beach, Fla. ... 6-6/225. (1,98/102,1). ... Full Name: Vincent Lamar Carter.
HIGH SCHOOL: Daytona Beach (Fla.) Mainland.
COLLEGE: North Carolina.
TRANSACTIONS/CAREER NOTES: Selected after junior season by Golden State Warriors in first round (fifth pick overall) of 1998 NBA Draft. ... Draft rights traded by Warriors with cash to Toronto Raptors for draft rights to F Antawn Jamison (June 24, 1998).
MISCELLANEOUS: Member of gold-medal-winning U.S. Olympic team (2000). ... Toronto Raptors all-time points leader with 5,090 (1998-99 through 2000-01).

COLLEGIATE RECORD

NOTES: THE SPORTING NEWS All-America second team (1998).

Season Team	G	Min.	FGM	FGA	Pct.	FTM	FTA	Pct.	Reb.	Ast.	Pts.	RPG	APG	PPG
95-96—North Carolina...............	31	555	91	185	.492	31	45	.689	119	40	232	3.8	1.3	7.5
96-97—North Carolina...............	34	937	166	316	.525	75	100	.750	152	83	443	4.5	2.4	13.0
97-98—North Carolina...............	38	1185	224	379	.591	100	147	.680	195	74	592	5.1	1.9	15.6
Totals	103	2677	481	880	.547	206	292	.705	466	197	1267	4.5	1.9	12.3

Three-point field goals: 1995-96, 19-for-55 (.345). 1996-97, 38-for-107 (.355). 1997-98, 44-for-107 (.411). Totals, 101-for-269 (.375).

NBA REGULAR-SEASON RECORD

HONORS: NBA Rookie of the Year (1999). ... All-NBA second team (2001). ... All-NBA third team (2000). ... NBA All-Rookie first team (1999). ... Slam Dunk championship winner (2000).

Season Team	G	Min.	FGM	FGA	Pct.	FTM	FTA	Pct.	Off.	Def.	Tot.	Ast.	St.	Blk.	TO	Pts.	RPG	APG	PPG
									REBOUNDS								**AVERAGES**		
98-99—Toronto	50	1760	345	766	.450	204	268	.761	94	189	283	149	55	77	110	913	5.7	3.0	18.3
99-00—Toronto	82	3126	788	1696	.465	436	551	.791	150	326	476	322	110	92	178	2107	5.8	3.9	25.7
00-01—Toronto	75	2979	762	1656	.460	384	502	.765	176	240	416	291	114	82	167	2070	5.5	3.9	27.6
Totals	207	7865	1895	4118	.460	1024	1321	.775	420	755	1175	762	279	251	455	5090	5.7	3.7	24.6

Three-point field goals: 1998-99, 19-for-66 (.288). 1999-00, 95-for-236 (.403). 2000-01, 162-for-397 (.408). Totals, 276-for-699 (.395).
Personal fouls/disqualifications: 1998-99, 140/2. 1999-00, 263/2. 2000-01, 205/1. Totals, 608/5.

NBA PLAYOFF RECORD

NOTES: Holds single-game record for most three-point field goals made in one half—8 (May 11, 2001, vs. Philadelphia). ... Shares single-game record for most three-point field goals made in one quarter—5 (May 11, 2001, vs. Philadelphia).

Season Team	G	Min.	FGM	FGA	Pct.	FTM	FTA	Pct.	Off.	Def.	Tot.	Ast.	St.	Blk.	TO	Pts.	RPG	APG	PPG
									REBOUNDS								**AVERAGES**		
99-00—Toronto	3	119	15	50	.300	27	31	.871	9	9	18	19	3	4	8	58	6.0	6.3	19.3
00-01—Toronto	12	539	122	280	.436	58	74	.784	37	41	78	56	20	20	27	327	6.5	4.7	27.3
Totals	15	658	137	330	.415	85	105	.810	46	50	96	75	23	24	35	385	6.4	5.0	25.7

Three-point field goals: 1999-00, 1-for-10 (.100). 2000-01, 25-for-61 (.410). Totals, 26-for-71 (.366).
Personal fouls/disqualifications: 1999-00, 12/0. 2000-01, 45/1. Totals, 57/1.

NBA ALL-STAR GAME RECORD

Season Team	Min.	FGM	FGA	Pct.	FTM	FTA	Pct.	Off.	Def.	Tot.	Ast.	PF	Dq.	St.	Blk.	TO	Pts.
								REBOUNDS									
2000 —Toronto	28	6	11	.545	0	0		2	2	4	2	0	0	2	0	2	12
2001 —Toronto	24	7	18	.389	1	1	1.000	1	2	3	4	1	0	1	1	3	16
Totals	52	13	29	.448	1	1	1.000	3	4	7	6	1	0	3	1	5	28

Three-point field goals: 2000, 0-for-2. 2001, 1-for-4 (.250). Totals, 1-for-6 (.167).

C

CASSELL, SAM   G   BUCKS

PERSONAL: Born November 18, 1969, in Baltimore. ... 6-3/185. (1,91/83,9). ... Full Name: Samuel James Cassell. ... Name pronounced KUH-sell.
HIGH SCHOOL: Dunbar (Baltimore).
JUNIOR COLLEGE: San Jacinto College (Texas).
COLLEGE: Florida State.
TRANSACTIONS/CAREER NOTES: Selected by Houston Rockets in first round (24th pick overall) of 1993 NBA Draft. ... Traded by Rockets with F Chucky Brown, F Robert Horry and F Mark Bryant to Phoenix Suns for F Charles Barkley and 1999 second-round draft choice (August 19, 1996). ... Traded by Suns with F A.C. Green, F Michael Finley and 1997 or 1998 conditional second-round draft choice to Dallas Mavericks for G Jason Kidd, F Tony Dumas and C Loren Meyer (December 26, 1996). ... Traded by Mavericks with C Eric Montross, G Jim Jackson, F/C Chris Gatling and F/G George McCloud to New Jersey Nets for C Shawn Bradley, F Ed O'Bannon, G Khalid Reeves and G Robert Pack (February 17, 1997). ... Traded by Nets with F Chris Gatling to Milwaukee Bucks in three-way deal in which Bucks also received C Paul Grant from Minnesota Timberwolves, Timberwolves received F Brian Evans, 1999 first-round draft choice and an undisclosed draft choice from Nets, Bucks sent G Terrell Brandon to Timberwolves and Timberwolves sent G Stephon Marbury, G Chris Carr and F Bill Curley to Nets and Nets received G Elliot Perry from Bucks (March 11, 1999).
MISCELLANEOUS: Member of NBA championship team (1994, 1995).

COLLEGIATE RECORD

Season Team	G	Min.	FGM	FGA	Pct.	FTM	FTA	Pct.	Reb.	Ast.	Pts.	RPG	APG	PPG
												AVERAGES		
89-90—San Jacinto College	38	1061	296	597	.496	136	170	.800	208	200	810	5.5	5.3	21.3
90-91—San Jacinto College	31	864	233	471	.495	198	246	.805	157	237	727	5.1	7.6	23.5
91-92—Florida State	31	1046	206	454	.454	100	142	.704	141	119	570	4.5	3.8	18.4
92-93—Florida State	35	1298	234	466	.502	123	162	.759	152	170	641	4.3	4.9	18.3
Junior college totals	69	1925	529	1068	.495	334	416	.803	365	437	1537	5.3	6.3	22.3
4-year-college totals	66	2344	440	920	.478	223	304	.734	293	289	1211	4.4	4.4	18.3

Three-point field goals: 1989-90, 82-for-184 (.446). 1990-91, 63-for-160 (.394). 1991-92, 58-for-164 (.354). 1992-93, 50-for-131 (.382). Totals, 108-for-295 (.366).

NBA REGULAR-SEASON RECORD

Season Team	G	Min.	FGM	FGA	Pct.	FTM	FTA	Pct.	Off.	Def.	Tot.	Ast.	St.	Blk.	TO	Pts.	RPG	APG	PPG
									REBOUNDS								**AVERAGES**		
93-94—Houston	66	1122	162	388	.418	90	107	.841	25	109	134	192	59	7	94	440	2.0	2.9	6.7
94-95—Houston	82	1882	253	593	.427	214	254	.843	38	173	211	405	94	14	167	783	2.6	4.9	9.5
95-96—Houston	61	1682	289	658	.439	235	285	.825	51	137	188	278	53	4	157	886	3.1	4.6	14.5
96-97—Pho.-Dal.-N.J.	61	1714	337	783	.430	212	251	.845	47	135	182	305	77	19	168	967	3.0	5.0	15.9
97-98—New Jersey	75	2606	510	1156	.441	436	507	.860	73	155	228	603	121	20	269	1471	3.0	8.0	19.6
98-99—N.J.-Mil.	8	199	39	93	.419	47	50	.940	5	10	15	36	9	0	20	127	1.9	4.5	15.9
99-00—Milwaukee	81	2899	545	1170	.466	390	445	.876	69	232	301	729	102	8	267	1506	3.7	9.0	18.6
00-01—Milwaukee	76	2709	537	1132	.474	277	323	.858	46	244	290	580	88	8	220	1381	3.8	7.6	18.2
Totals	510	14813	2672	5973	.447	1901	2222	.856	354	1195	1549	3128	603	80	1362	7561	3.0	6.1	14.8

Three-point field goals: 1993-94, 26-for-88 (.295). 1994-95, 63-for-191 (.330). 1995-96, 73-for-210 (.348). 1996-97, 81-for-231 (.351). 1997-98, 15-for-80 (.188). 1998-99, 2-for-10 (.200). 1999-00, 26-for-90 (.289). 2000-01, 30-for-98 (.306). Totals, 316-for-998 (.317).
Personal fouls/disqualifications: 1993-94, 136/1. 1994-95, 209/3. 1995-96, 166/2. 1996-97, 200/9. 1997-98, 262/5. 1998-99, 22/1. 1999-00, 255/5. 2000-01, 214/5. Totals, 1464/31.

Season Team	G	Min.	FGM	FGA	Pct.	FTM	FTA	Pct.	REBOUNDS Off.	Def.	Tot.	Ast.	St.	Blk.	TO	Pts.	AVERAGES RPG	APG	PPG
93-94—Houston	22	478	63	160	.394	64	74	.865	19	40	59	93	21	5	47	207	2.7	4.2	9.4
94-95—Houston	22	485	74	169	.438	71	85	.835	8	34	42	89	21	2	33	243	1.9	4.0	11.0
95-96—Houston	8	206	26	81	.321	23	29	.793	1	16	17	34	6	1	18	83	2.1	4.3	10.4
97-98—New Jersey	3	26	3	9	.333	0	0	...	1	2	3	5	0	1	2	6	1.0	1.7	2.0
98-99—Milwaukee	3	102	16	32	.500	14	16	.875	0	6	6	26	3	0	7	46	2.0	8.7	15.3
99-00—Milwaukee	5	178	30	72	.417	18	21	.857	0	17	17	45	4	0	9	79	3.4	9.0	15.8
00-01—Milwaukee	18	682	110	278	.396	84	97	.866	12	71	83	120	19	3	52	314	4.6	6.7	17.4
Totals	81	2157	322	801	.402	274	322	.851	41	186	227	412	74	12	168	978	2.8	5.1	12.1

Three-point field goals: 1993-94, 17-for-45 (.378). 1994-95, 24-for-60 (.400). 1995-96, 8-for-29 (.276). 1998-99, 0-for-1. 1999-00, 1-for-5 (.200). 2000-01, 10-for-30 (.333). Totals, 60-for-170 (.353).

Personal fouls/disqualifications: 1993-94, 62/1. 1994-95, 66/1. 1995-96, 20/0. 1997-98, 7/0. 1998-99, 14/1. 1999-00, 19/1. 2000-01, 76/2. Totals, 264/6.

CATO, KELVIN   C   ROCKETS

PERSONAL: Born August 26, 1974, in Atlanta. ... 6-11/255. (2,11/115,7). ... Full Name: Kelvin T. Cato.
HIGH SCHOOL: Lithonia (Decatur, Ga.).
COLLEGE: South Alabama, then Iowa State.
TRANSACTIONS/CAREER NOTES: Selected by Dallas Mavericks in first round (15th pick overall) of 1997 NBA Draft. ... Draft rights traded by Mavericks to Portland Trail Blazers for draft rights to C Chris Anstey and cash (June 25, 1997). ... Traded by Trail Blazers with F Stacy Augmon, G/F Walt Williams, G Brian Shaw, G Ed Gray and F/C Carlos Rogers to Houston Rockets for F Scottie Pippen (October 2, 1999).

COLLEGIATE RECORD

Season Team	G	Min.	FGM	FGA	Pct.	FTM	FTA	Pct.	Reb.	Ast.	Pts.	AVERAGES RPG	APG	PPG
92-93—South Alabama						Did not play—ineligible.								
93-94—South Alabama	24	433	49	123	.398	45	79	.570	138	17	143	5.8	0.7	6.0
94-95—Iowa State						Did not play—transfer student.								
95-96—Iowa State	27	697	94	187	.503	71	111	.640	209	17	259	7.7	0.6	9.6
96-97—Iowa State	28	801	128	234	.547	61	113	.540	235	15	317	8.4	0.5	11.3
Totals	79	1931	271	544	.498	177	303	.584	582	49	719	7.4	0.6	9.1

Three-point field goals: 1996-97, 0-for-1.

NBA REGULAR-SEASON RECORD

Season Team	G	Min.	FGM	FGA	Pct.	FTM	FTA	Pct.	REBOUNDS Off.	Def.	Tot.	Ast.	St.	Blk.	TO	Pts.	AVERAGES RPG	APG	PPG
97-98—Portland	74	1007	98	229	.428	86	125	.688	91	161	252	23	29	94	44	282	3.4	0.3	3.8
98-99—Portland	43	545	58	129	.450	34	67	.507	49	101	150	19	23	56	27	151	3.5	0.4	3.5
99-00—Houston	65	1581	216	402	.537	135	208	.649	102	287	389	26	33	124	71	567	6.0	0.4	8.7
00-01—Houston	35	624	64	111	.577	37	57	.649	47	94	141	11	13	31	25	165	4.0	0.3	4.7
Totals	217	3757	436	871	.501	292	457	.639	289	643	932	79	98	305	167	1165	4.3	0.4	5.4

Three-point field goals: 1997-98, 0-for-3. 1998-99, 1-for-1. 1999-00, 0-for-4. Totals, 1-for-8 (.125).
Personal fouls/disqualifications: 1997-98, 164/3. 1998-99, 175/1. 1999-00, 89/1. Totals, 528/8.

NBA PLAYOFF RECORD

Season Team	G	Min.	FGM	FGA	Pct.	FTM	FTA	Pct.	REBOUNDS Off.	Def.	Tot.	Ast.	St.	Blk.	TO	Pts.	AVERAGES RPG	APG	PPG
97-98—Portland	4	58	9	17	.529	8	11	.727	3	9	12	1	1	7	4	26	3.0	0.3	6.5
98-99—Portland	8	43	1	9	.111	4	10	.400	6	1	7	2	1	1	2	6	0.9	0.3	0.8
Totals	12	101	10	26	.385	12	21	.571	9	10	19	3	2	8	6	32	1.6	0.3	2.7

Three-point field goals: 1997-98, 0-for-1. Totals, 0-for-1 (.000).
Personal fouls/disqualifications: 1997-98, 12/0. 1998-99, 13/0. Totals, 25/0.

CAUSWELL, DUANE   C

PERSONAL: Born May 31, 1968, in Queens Village, N.Y. ... 7-0/255. (2,13/115,7).
HIGH SCHOOL: Benjamin Cardozo (Bayside, N.Y.).
COLLEGE: Temple.
TRANSACTIONS/CAREER NOTES: Selected by Sacramento Kings in first round (18th pick overall) of 1990 NBA Draft. ... Traded by Kings with 1994, 1995 and 1996 second-round draft choices to Detroit Pistons for C Olden Polynice and F David Wood (February 16, 1994); trade voided when Causwell failed physical (February 19, 1994). ... Traded by Kings to Miami Heat for G Gary Grant, C Matt Fish and 1998 conditional second-round draft choice (August 12, 1997).

COLLEGIATE RECORD

Season Team	G	Min.	FGM	FGA	Pct.	FTM	FTA	Pct.	Reb.	Ast.	Pts.	AVERAGES RPG	APG	PPG
86-87—Temple						Did not play—redshirted.								
87-88—Temple	33	399	27	55	.491	13	30	.433	85	3	67	2.6	0.1	2.0
88-89—Temple	30	1081	128	249	.514	84	123	.683	267	19	340	8.9	0.6	11.3
89-90—Temple	12	416	52	107	.486	31	52	.596	99	9	135	8.3	0.8	11.3
Totals	75	1896	207	411	.504	128	205	.624	451	31	542	6.0	0.4	7.2

Three-point field goals: 1988-89, 0-for-1.

NBA REGULAR-SEASON RECORD

Season Team	G	Min.	FGM	FGA	Pct.	FTM	FTA	Pct.	Off.	Def.	Tot.	Ast.	St.	Blk.	TO	Pts.	RPG	APG	PPG
90-91—Sacramento	76	1719	210	413	.508	105	165	.636	141	250	391	69	49	148	96	525	5.1	0.9	6.9
91-92—Sacramento	80	2291	250	455	.549	136	222	.613	196	384	580	59	47	215	124	636	7.3	0.7	8.0
92-93—Sacramento	55	1211	175	321	.545	103	165	.624	112	191	303	35	32	87	58	453	5.5	0.6	8.2
93-94—Sacramento	41	674	71	137	.518	40	68	.588	68	118	186	11	19	49	33	182	4.5	0.3	4.4
94-95—Sacramento	58	820	76	147	.517	57	98	.582	57	117	174	15	14	80	33	209	3.0	0.3	3.6
95-96—Sacramento	73	1044	90	216	.417	70	96	.729	86	162	248	20	27	78	53	250	3.4	0.3	3.4
96-97—Sacramento	46	581	48	94	.511	20	37	.541	57	70	127	20	15	38	34	118	2.8	0.4	2.6
97-98—Miami	37	363	37	89	.416	15	26	.577	29	70	99	5	7	27	18	89	2.7	0.1	2.4
98-99—Miami	19	137	20	35	.571	4	12	.333	14	21	35	2	0	11	18	44	1.8	0.1	2.3
99-00—Miami	25	185	20	37	.541	26	38	.684	11	36	47	2	2	16	10	66	1.9	0.1	2.6
00-01—Miami	31	384	32	85	.376	12	25	.480	23	60	83	5	8	18	23	76	2.7	0.2	2.5
Totals	541	9409	1029	2029	.507	588	952	.618	794	1479	2273	243	220	767	500	2648	4.2	0.4	4.9

Three-point field goals: 1991-92, 0-for-1. 1992-93, 0-for-1. 1994-95, 0-for-1. 1995-96, 1-for-1. 1996-97, 2-for-3 (.667). Totals, 2-for-7 (.286).

Personal fouls/disqualifications: 1990-91, 225/4. 1991-92, 281/4. 1992-93, 192/7. 1993-94, 109/2. 1994-95, 146/4. 1995-96, 173/2. 1996-97, 131/5. 1997-98, 73/0. 1998-99, 32/1. 1999-00, 42/0. 2000-01, 67/0. Totals, 1471/29.

NBA PLAYOFF RECORD

Season Team	G	Min.	FGM	FGA	Pct.	FTM	FTA	Pct.	Off.	Def.	Tot.	Ast.	St.	Blk.	TO	Pts.	RPG	APG	PPG
95-96—Sacramento	2	25	1	3	.333	3	4	.750	1	4	5	1	0	0	2	5	2.5	0.5	2.5
97-98—Miami	1	5	0	0	...	0	0	...	0	2	2	0	0	0	1	0	2.0	0.0	0.0
98-99—Miami	4	20	1	2	.500	4	6	.667	0	2	2	1	1	0	0	6	0.5	0.3	1.5
00-01—Miami	1	5	0	1	.000	0	0	...	0	3	3	0	0	0	0	0	3.0	0.0	0.0
Totals	8	55	2	6	.333	7	10	.700	1	11	12	2	1	0	3	11	1.5	0.3	1.4

Three-point field goals: 1995-96, 0-for-1. Totals, 0-for-1 (.000).

Personal fouls/disqualifications: 1995-96, 3/0. 1998-99, 2/0. 2000-01, 1/0. Totals, 6/0.

CEBALLOS, CEDRIC F

PERSONAL: Born August 2, 1969, in Maui, Hawaii. ... 6-7/220. (2,01/99,8). ... Full Name: Cedric Z. Ceballos. ... Name pronounced SED-rick se-BAHL-ose.
HIGH SCHOOL: Dominquez (Compton, Calif.).
JUNIOR COLLEGE: Ventura (Calif.) College.
COLLEGE: Cal State Fullerton.
TRANSACTIONS/CAREER NOTES: Selected by Phoenix Suns in second round (48th pick overall) of 1990 NBA Draft. ... Traded by Suns to Los Angeles Lakers for 1995 first-round draft choice (September 23, 1994). ... Traded by Lakers with G Rumeal Robinson to Suns for F Robert Horry and C Joe Kleine (January 10, 1997). ... Traded by Suns to Dallas Mavericks for F Dennis Scott (February 18, 1998). ... Traded by Mavericks with F John Wallace and G Eric Murdock to Detroit Pistons for F/C Christian Laettner and F Terry Mills (August 29, 2000). ... Traded by Pistons to Miami Heat for conditional second-round draft choice (November 26, 2000).

COLLEGIATE RECORD

Season Team	G	Min.	FGM	FGA	Pct.	FTM	FTA	Pct.	Reb.	Ast.	Pts.	RPG	APG	PPG
86-87—Ventura College							Statistics unavailable.							
87-88—Ventura College							Statistics unavailable.							
88-89—Cal State Fullerton	29	986	241	545	.442	117	174	.672	256	43	615	8.8	1.5	21.2
89-90—Cal State Fullerton	29	1071	247	509	.485	144	215	.670	362	50	669	12.5	1.7	23.1
4-Year-College Totals	58	2057	488	1054	.463	261	389	.671	618	93	1284	10.7	1.6	22.1

Three-point field goals: 1988-89, 16-for-58 (.276). 1989-90, 31-for-96 (.323). Totals, 47-for-154 (.305).

HONORS: Slam Dunk championship winner (1992).

NBA REGULAR-SEASON RECORD

Season Team	G	Min.	FGM	FGA	Pct.	FTM	FTA	Pct.	Off.	Def.	Tot.	Ast.	St.	Blk.	TO	Pts.	RPG	APG	PPG
90-91—Phoenix	63	730	204	419	.487	110	166	.663	77	73	150	35	22	5	69	519	2.4	0.6	8.2
91-92—Phoenix	64	725	176	365	.482	109	148	.736	60	92	152	50	16	11	71	462	2.4	0.8	7.2
92-93—Phoenix	74	1607	381	662	.576	187	258	.725	172	236	408	77	54	28	106	949	5.5	1.0	12.8
93-94—Phoenix	53	1602	425	795	.535	160	221	.724	153	191	344	91	59	23	93	1010	6.5	1.7	19.1
94-95—L.A. Lakers	58	2029	497	977	.509	209	292	.716	169	295	464	105	60	19	143	1261	8.0	1.8	21.7
95-96—L.A. Lakers	78	2628	638	1203	.530	329	409	.804	215	321	536	119	94	22	167	1656	6.9	1.5	21.2
96-97—L.A.L.-Phoe. ...	50	1426	282	617	.457	139	186	.747	102	228	330	64	33	23	85	729	6.6	1.3	14.6
97-98—Pho.-Dal.	47	990	204	415	.492	107	145	.738	75	146	221	60	33	16	72	536	4.7	1.3	11.4
98-99—Dallas	13	352	59	140	.421	34	49	.694	23	62	85	12	7	5	28	163	6.5	0.9	12.5
99-00—Dallas	69	2064	447	1002	.446	209	248	.843	172	290	462	90	56	24	125	1147	6.7	1.3	16.6
00-01—Detroit-Miami .	40	559	101	229	.441	37	43	.860	34	72	106	20	16	7	32	261	2.7	0.5	6.5
Totals	609	14712	3414	6824	.500	1630	2165	.753	1252	2006	3258	723	450	183	991	8693	5.3	1.2	14.3

Three-point field goals: 1990-91, 1-for-6 (.167). 1991-92, 1-for-6 (.167). 1992-93, 0-for-2. 1993-94, 0-for-0. 1994-95, 58-for-146 (.397). 1995-96, 51-for-184 (.277). 1996-97, 26-for-102 (.255). 1997-98, 21-for-70 (.300). 1998-99, 11-for-28 (.393). 1999-00, 44-for-134 (.328). 2000-01, 22-for-73 (.301). Totals, 235-for-760 (.309).

Personal fouls/disqualifications: 1990-91, 70/0. 1991-92, 52/0. 1992-93, 103/1. 1993-94, 124/0. 1994-95, 131/1. 1995-96, 144/0. 1996-97, 113/0. 1997-98, 88/0. 1998-99, 23/1. 1999-00, 165/3. 2000-01, 61/0. Totals, 1074/6.

DID YOU KNOW . . .

. . . that Paul Pierce attempted more free throws last season (738) than any player in Celtics history?

NBA PLAYOFF RECORD

								REBOUNDS								AVERAGES		
Season Team	G	Min.	FGM	FGA	Pct.	FTM	FTA	Pct.	Off.	Def.	Tot.	Ast.	St.	Blk.	TO	Pts.	RPG	APG	PPG
90-91—Phoenix	3	24	7	12	.583	2	6	.333	3	2	5	2	2	0	1	16	1.7	0.7	5.3
91-92—Phoenix	8	188	44	80	.550	20	30	.667	20	31	51	12	6	6	11	108	6.4	1.5	13.5
92-93—Phoenix	16	185	40	70	.571	16	22	.727	13	24	37	13	5	7	5	96	2.3	0.8	6.0
93-94—Phoenix	10	212	43	93	.462	15	18	.833	16	28	44	8	8	2	11	101	4.4	0.8	10.1
94-95—L.A. Lakers	10	340	48	126	.381	28	38	.737	11	50	61	18	12	7	21	142	6.1	1.8	14.2
95-96—L.A. Lakers	4	142	30	62	.484	11	12	.917	11	22	33	5	4	1	8	76	8.3	1.3	19.0
96-97—Phoenix	5	107	11	33	.333	8	8	1.000	9	17	26	3	4	3	8	33	5.2	0.6	6.6
00-01—Miami	3	15	2	7	.286	1	2	.500	3	3	6	1	0	0	1	5	2.0	0.3	1.7
Totals	59	1213	225	483	.466	101	136	.743	86	177	263	62	41	26	66	577	4.5	1.1	9.8

Three-point field goals: 1993-94, 0-for-2. 1994-95, 18-for-50 (.360). 1995-96, 5-for-16 (.313). 1996-97, 3-for-12 (.250). Totals, 26-for-80 (.325).
Personal fouls/disqualifications: 1991-92, 14/0. 1992-93, 12/0. 1993-94, 2/0. 1994-95, 21/0. 1995-96, 9/0. 1996-97, 12/0. 2000-01, 3/0. Totals, 80/0.

NBA ALL-STAR GAME RECORD

							REBOUNDS								
Season Team	Min.	FGM	FGA	Pct.	FTM	FTA	Pct.	Off.	Def.	Tot.	Ast.	PF	Dq.	St.	Blk.	TO	Pts.
1995 —Los Angeles							Selected, did not play—injured.									

CHEANEY, CALBERT   G/F   NUGGETS

PERSONAL: Born July 17, 1971, in Evansville, Ind. ... 6-7/217. (2,01/98,4). ... Full Name: Calbert N. Cheaney. ... Name pronounced CHAIN-ee.
HIGH SCHOOL: Harrison (Evansville, Ind.).
COLLEGE: Indiana.
TRANSACTIONS/CAREER NOTES: Selected by Washington Bullets in first round (sixth pick overall) of 1993 NBA Draft. ... Bullets franchise renamed Washington Wizards for 1997-98 season. ... Signed as free agent by Boston Celtics (August 5, 1999). ... Traded by Celtics with G Robert Pack to Denver Nuggets for G Chris Herren and G Bryant Stith (October 16, 2000).

COLLEGIATE RECORD

NOTES: THE SPORTING NEWS College Player of the Year (1993). ... Naismith Award winner (1993). ... Wooden Award winner (1993). ... THE SPORTING NEWS All-America first team (1993). ... THE SPORTING NEWS All-America third team (1991).

											AVERAGES		
Season Team	G	Min.	FGM	FGA	Pct.	FTM	FTA	Pct.	Reb.	Ast.	Pts.	RPG	APG	PPG
89-90—Indiana	29	928	199	348	.572	72	96	.750	133	48	495	4.6	1.7	17.1
90-91—Indiana	34	1029	289	485	.596	113	141	.801	188	47	734	5.5	1.4	21.6
91-92—Indiana	34	991	227	435	.522	112	140	.800	166	48	599	4.9	1.4	17.6
92-93—Indiana	35	1181	303	552	.549	132	166	.795	223	84	785	6.4	2.4	22.4
Totals	132	4129	1018	1820	.559	429	543	.790	710	227	2613	5.4	1.7	19.8

Three-point field goals: 1989-90, 25-for-51 (.490). 1990-91, 43-for-91 (.473). 1991-92, 33-for-86 (.384). 1992-93, 47-for-110 (.427). Totals, 148-for-338 (.438).

NBA REGULAR-SEASON RECORD

								REBOUNDS								AVERAGES		
Season Team	G	Min.	FGM	FGA	Pct.	FTM	FTA	Pct.	Off.	Def.	Tot.	Ast.	St.	Blk.	TO	Pts.	RPG	APG	PPG
93-94—Washington	65	1604	327	696	.470	124	161	.770	88	102	190	126	63	10	108	779	2.9	1.9	12.0
94-95—Washington	78	2651	512	1129	.453	173	213	.812	105	216	321	177	80	21	151	1293	4.1	2.3	16.6
95-96—Washington	70	2324	426	905	.471	151	214	.706	67	172	239	154	67	18	129	1055	3.4	2.2	15.1
96-97—Washington	79	2411	369	730	.505	95	137	.693	70	198	268	114	77	18	94	837	3.4	1.4	10.6
97-98—Washington	82	2841	448	981	.457	139	215	.647	82	242	324	173	96	36	104	1050	4.0	2.1	12.8
98-99—Washington	50	1266	172	415	.414	33	67	.493	33	108	141	73	39	16	42	385	2.8	1.5	7.7
99-00—Boston	67	1309	120	273	.440	9	21	.429	23	115	138	80	44	14	46	267	2.1	1.2	4.0
00-01—Denver	9	153	10	30	.333	1	2	.500	5	15	20	9	4	2	5	21	2.2	1.0	2.3
Totals	500	14559	2384	5159	.462	725	1030	.704	473	1168	1641	906	470	135	679	5687	3.3	1.8	11.4

Three-point field goals: 1993-94, 1-for-23 (.043). 1994-95, 96-for-283 (.339). 1995-96, 52-for-154 (.338). 1996-97, 4-for-30 (.133). 1997-98, 15-for-53 (.283). 1998-99, 8-for-37 (.216). 1999-00, 18-for-54 (.333). Totals, 194-for-634 (.306).
Personal fouls/disqualifications: 1993-94, 148/0. 1994-95, 215/0. 1995-96, 205/1. 1996-97, 226/3. 1997-98, 264/4. 1998-99, 146/0. 1999-00, 158/3. 2000-01, 14/0. Totals, 1376/11.

NBA PLAYOFF RECORD

								REBOUNDS								AVERAGES		
Season Team	G	Min.	FGM	FGA	Pct.	FTM	FTA	Pct.	Off.	Def.	Tot.	Ast.	St.	Blk.	TO	Pts.	RPG	APG	PPG
96-97—Washington	3	120	18	41	.439	9	12	.750	6	5	11	4	3	2	5	45	3.7	1.3	15.0

Three-point field goals: 1996-97, 0-for-2.
Personal fouls/disqualifications: 1996-97, 10/0.

CHILDS, CHRIS   G   RAPTORS

PERSONAL: Born November 20, 1967, in Bakersfield, Calif. ... 6-3/195. (1,91/88,5).
HIGH SCHOOL: Foothill (Bakersfield, Calif.).
COLLEGE: Boise State.
TRANSACTIONS/CAREER NOTES: Not drafted by an NBA franchise. ... Played in Continental Basketball Association with Columbus Horizon (1989-90 and 1990-91), Rapid City Thrillers (1989-90), La Crosse Catbirds (1990-91), Rockford Lightning (1990-91 and 1991-92), Bakersfield Jammers (1991-92) and Quad City Thunder (1992-93 and 1993-94). ... Played in United States Basketball League with Miami Tropics (1993, 1994). ... Signed as free agent by San Antonio Spurs (August 16, 1993). ... Waived by Spurs (October 25, 1993). ... Signed as free agent by New Jersey Nets (July 29, 1994). ... Signed as free agent by New York Knicks (July 14, 1996). ... Traded by Knicks with 2001 first-round draft choice to Toronto Raptors for G Mark Jackson and G Muggsy Bogues (February 22, 2001).

COLLEGIATE RECORD

Season Team	G	Min.	FGM	FGA	Pct.	FTM	FTA	Pct.	Reb.	Ast.	Pts.	AVERAGES RPG	APG	PPG
85-86—Boise State	28	792	109	264	.413	72	91	.791	87	84	300	3.1	3.0	10.7
86-87—Boise State	30	945	153	344	.445	109	132	.826	77	87	462	2.6	2.9	15.4
87-88—Boise State	30	944	147	316	.465	81	95	.853	79	99	429	2.6	3.3	14.3
88-89—Boise State	30	929	131	295	.444	97	121	.802	101	122	411	3.4	4.1	13.7
Totals	118	3610	540	1219	.443	359	439	.818	344	392	1602	2.9	3.3	13.6

Three-point field goals: 1985-86, 10-for-31 (.323). 1986-87, 47-for-116 (.405). 1987-88, 54-for-120 (.450). 1988-89, 52-for-119 (.437). Totals, 163-for-386 (.422).

CBA REGULAR-SEASON RECORD

NOTES: Member of CBA championship team (1994). ... CBA Playoff Most Valuable Player (1994).

Season Team	G	Min.	FGM	FGA	Pct.	FTM	FTA	Pct.	Reb.	Ast.	Pts.	AVERAGES RPG	APG	PPG
89-90—Columbus-Rapid City	21	531	55	136	.404	38	46	.826	61	158	158	2.9	7.5	7.5
90-91—Col.-La Crosse-Rockford	33	717	100	228	.439	84	105	.800	94	165	297	2.8	5.0	9.0
91-92—Bakersfield-Rockford	47	1379	205	443	.463	159	183	.869	174	357	585	3.7	7.6	12.4
92-93—Quad City	50	1624	226	497	.455	130	157	.828	173	292	597	3.5	5.8	11.9
93-94—Quad City	56	2143	368	772	.477	246	281	.875	220	423	1003	3.9	7.6	17.9
Totals	207	6394	954	2076	.460	657	772	.851	722	1395	2640	3.5	6.7	12.8

Three-point field goals: 1989-90, 10-for-30 (.333). 1990-91, 13-for-41 (.317). 1991-92, 16-for-64 (.250). 1992-93, 15-for-62 (.242). 1993-94, 21-for-88 (.239). Totals, 75-for-285 (.263).

NBA REGULAR-SEASON RECORD

Season Team	G	Min.	FGM	FGA	Pct.	FTM	FTA	Pct.	REBOUNDS Off.	Def.	Tot.	Ast.	St.	Blk.	TO	Pts.	AVERAGES RPG	APG	PPG
94-95—New Jersey	53	1021	106	279	.380	55	73	.753	14	55	69	219	42	3	76	308	1.3	4.1	5.8
95-96—New Jersey	78	2408	324	778	.416	259	304	.852	51	194	245	548	111	8	230	1002	3.1	7.0	12.8
96-97—New York	65	2076	211	510	.414	113	149	.758	22	169	191	398	78	11	180	605	2.9	6.1	9.3
97-98—New York	68	1599	149	354	.421	104	126	.825	29	133	162	268	56	6	103	429	2.4	3.9	6.3
98-99—New York	48	1297	114	267	.427	64	78	.821	18	115	133	193	44	1	85	328	2.8	4.0	6.8
99-00—New York	71	1675	146	357	.409	47	59	.797	17	130	147	285	36	4	105	376	2.1	4.0	5.3
00-01—N.Y.-Tor.	77	1859	135	335	.403	60	71	.845	24	178	202	355	59	15	156	362	2.6	4.6	4.7
Totals	460	11935	1185	2880	.411	702	860	.816	175	974	1149	2266	426	48	935	3410	2.5	4.9	7.4

Three-point field goals: 1994-95, 41-for-125 (.328). 1995-96, 95-for-259 (.367). 1996-97, 70-for-181 (.387). 1997-98, 27-for-87 (.310). 1998-99, 36-for-94 (.383). 1999-00, 37-for-104 (.356). 2000-01, 32-for-106 (.302). Totals, 338-for-956 (.354).

Personal fouls/disqualifications: 1994-95, 116/1. 1995-96, 246/3. 1996-97, 213/6. 1997-98, 179/2. 1998-99, 156/0. 1999-00, 240/4. 2000-01, 242/3. Totals, 1392/19.

NBA PLAYOFF RECORD

Season Team	G	Min.	FGM	FGA	Pct.	FTM	FTA	Pct.	REBOUNDS Off.	Def.	Tot.	Ast.	St.	Blk.	TO	Pts.	AVERAGES RPG	APG	PPG
96-97—New York	10	328	38	87	.437	19	23	.826	9	40	49	59	20	0	28	104	4.9	5.9	10.4
97-98—New York	10	254	24	58	.414	11	15	.733	5	20	25	33	6	0	23	63	2.5	3.3	6.3
98-99—New York	20	494	33	93	.355	19	26	.731	8	39	47	73	13	1	30	94	2.4	3.7	4.7
99-00—New York	16	334	27	70	.386	24	28	.857	1	36	37	39	7	0	14	87	2.3	2.4	5.4
00-01—Toronto	12	380	37	90	.411	20	23	.870	2	36	38	72	18	3	35	109	3.2	6.5	9.1
Totals	68	1790	159	398	.399	93	115	.809	25	171	196	282	58	4	130	457	2.9	4.1	6.7

Three-point field goals: 1996-97, 9-for-26 (.346). 1997-98, 4-for-13 (.308). 1998-99, 9-for-28 (.321). 1999-00, 9-for-28 (.321). 2000-01, 15-for-36 (.417). Totals, 46-for-131 (.351).

Personal fouls/disqualifications: 1996-97, 39/1. 1997-98, 29/0. 1998-99, 64/2. 1999-00, 53/1. 2000-01, 48/2. Totals, 233/6.

CHRISTIE, DOUG   G/F   KINGS

PERSONAL: Born May 9, 1970, in Seattle. ... 6-6/205. (1,98/93,0). ... Full Name: Douglas Dale Christie. ... Name pronounced CHRIS-tee.

HIGH SCHOOL: Rainier Beach (Seattle).

COLLEGE: Pepperdine.

TRANSACTIONS/CAREER NOTES: Selected by Seattle SuperSonics in first round (17th pick overall) of 1992 NBA Draft. ... Traded by SuperSonics with C Benoit Benjamin to Los Angeles Lakers for F/C Sam Perkins (February 22, 1993). ... Traded by Lakers to New York Knicks for two future second-round draft choices (October 13, 1994). ... Traded by Knicks with C/F Herb Williams and cash to Toronto Raptors for G Willie Anderson and F/C Victor Alexander (February 18, 1996). ... Traded by Raptors to Sacramento Kings for F Corliss Williamson (September 29, 2000).

MISCELLANEOUS: Toronto Raptors all-time steals leader with 664 (1995-96 through 1999-2000).

COLLEGIATE RECORD

Season Team	G	Min.	FGM	FGA	Pct.	FTM	FTA	Pct.	Reb.	Ast.	Pts.	AVERAGES RPG	APG	PPG
88-89—Pepperdine						Did not play—ineligible.								
89-90—Pepperdine	28	687	84	167	.503	70	98	.714	115	112	250	4.1	4.0	8.9
90-91—Pepperdine	28	913	188	401	.469	143	187	.765	145	134	536	5.2	4.8	19.1
91-92—Pepperdine	31	1058	211	453	.466	144	193	.746	183	149	606	5.9	4.8	19.5
Totals	87	2658	483	1021	.473	357	478	.747	443	395	1392	5.1	4.5	16.0

Three-point field goals: 1989-90, 12-for-47 (.255). 1990-91, 17-for-65 (.262). 1991-92, 40-for-120 (.333). Totals, 69-for-232 (.297).

NBA REGULAR-SEASON RECORD

RECORDS: Shares single-game record for most steals in one half—8 (April 2, 1997, at Philadelphia).

HONORS: NBA All-Defensive second team (2001).

Season Team	G	Min.	FGM	FGA	Pct.	FTM	FTA	Pct.	REBOUNDS Off.	Def.	Tot.	Ast.	St.	Blk.	TO	Pts.	AVERAGES RPG	APG	PPG
92-93—L.A. Lakers	23	332	45	106	.425	50	66	.758	24	27	51	53	22	5	50	142	2.2	2.3	6.2
93-94—L.A. Lakers	65	1515	244	562	.434	145	208	.697	93	142	235	136	89	28	140	672	3.6	2.1	10.3
94-95—New York	12	79	5	22	.227	4	5	.800	3	10	13	8	2	1	13	15	1.1	0.7	1.3
95-96—N.Y.-Tor.	55	1036	150	337	.445	69	93	.742	34	120	154	117	70	19	95	415	2.8	2.1	7.5
96-97—Toronto	81	3127	396	949	.417	237	306	.775	85	347	432	315	201	45	200	1176	5.3	3.9	14.5
97-98—Toronto	78	2939	458	1071	.428	271	327	.829	94	310	404	282	190	57	228	1287	5.2	3.6	16.5
98-99—Toronto	50	1768	252	650	.388	207	246	.841	59	148	207	187	113	26	119	760	4.1	3.7	15.2
99-00—Toronto	73	2264	311	764	.407	182	216	.843	63	222	285	321	102	43	144	903	3.9	4.4	12.4
00-01—Sacramento	81	2939	311	788	.395	280	312	.897	95	260	355	289	*183	45	154	996	4.4	3.6	12.3
Totals	518	15999	2172	5249	.414	1445	1779	.812	550	1586	2136	1708	972	269	1143	6366	4.1	3.8	12.3

Three-point field goals: 1992-93, 2-for-12 (.167). 1993-94, 39-for-119 (.328). 1994-95, 1-for-7 (.143). 1995-96, 46-for-106 (.434). 1996-97, 147-for-383 (.384). 1997-98, 100-for-307 (.326). 1998-99, 49-for-161 (.304). 1999-00, 99-for-275 (.360). 2000-01, 94-for-250 (.376). Totals, 577-for-1620 (.356).

Personal fouls/disqualifications: 1992-93, 53/0. 1993-94, 186/2. 1994-95, 18/1. 1995-96, 141/5. 1996-97, 245/6. 1997-98, 198/3. 1998-99, 111/1. 1999-00, 167/1. 2000-01, 224/2. Totals, 1343/21.

NBA PLAYOFF RECORD

Season Team	G	Min.	FGM	FGA	Pct.	FTM	FTA	Pct.	REBOUNDS Off.	Def.	Tot.	Ast.	St.	Blk.	TO	Pts.	AVERAGES RPG	APG	PPG
92-93—L.A. Lakers	5	39	4	11	.364	0	0	...	1	3	4	6	2	2	4	9	0.8	1.2	1.8
94-95—New York	2	6	0	4	.000	0	0	...	0	0	0	0	0	0	1	0	0.0	0.0	0.0
99-00—Toronto	3	61	3	13	.231	3	6	.500	1	4	5	6	4	1	4	12	1.7	2.0	4.0
00-01—Sacramento	8	304	25	68	.368	24	29	.828	7	28	35	26	20	9	19	79	4.4	3.3	9.9
Totals	18	410	32	96	.333	27	35	.771	9	35	44	38	26	12	28	100	2.4	2.1	5.6

Three-point field goals: 1992-93, 1-for-3 (.333). 1999-00, 3-for-8 (.375). 2000-01, 5-for-17 (.294). Totals, 9-for-28 (.321).
Personal fouls/disqualifications: 1992-93, 5/0. 1994-95, 3/0. 1999-00, 10/0. 2000-01, 31/1. Totals, 49/1.

CLARK, KEON   F/C   RAPTORS

PERSONAL: Born April 16, 1975, in Danville, Ill. ... 6-11/220. (2,11/99,8). ... Full Name: Arian Keon Clark.
HIGH SCHOOL: Danville (Ill.).
JUNIOR COLLEGE: Irvine Valley College (Calif.), then Dixie College (Utah).
COLLEGE: UNLV.
TRANSACTIONS/CAREER NOTES: Selected by Orlando Magic in first round (13th pick overall) of 1998 NBA Draft. ... Draft rights traded by Magic with F Johnny Taylor to Denver Nuggets for 1999 first-round draft choice (January 21, 1999). ... Traded by Nuggets with F Tracy Murray and C Mamadou N'diaye to Toronto Raptors for F/C Kevin Willis, C Aleksandar Radojevic, C Garth Joseph and 2001 or 2002 second-round draft choice (January 12, 2001).

COLLEGIATE RECORD

Season Team	G	Min.	FGM	FGA	Pct.	FTM	FTA	Pct.	Reb.	Ast.	Pts.	AVERAGES RPG	APG	PPG
94-95—Irvine Valley College	23	...	211	312	.676	97	148	.655	471	...	520	20.5	...	22.6
95-96—Dixie College	17	...	105	161	.652	49	79	.620	188	23	259	11.1	1.4	15.2
96-97—UNLV	29	816	168	302	.556	88	140	.629	289	32	430	10.0	1.1	14.8
97-98—UNLV	10	320	57	104	.548	30	45	.667	86	19	148	8.6	1.9	14.8
Junior college Totals	40	...	316	473	.668	146	227	.643	659	...	779	16.5	...	19.5
4-Year-College Totals	39	1136	225	406	.554	118	185	.638	375	51	578	9.6	1.3	14.8

Three-point field goals: 1994-95, 1-for-1. 1995-96, 0-for-1. 1996-97, 6-for-19 (.316). 1997-98, 4-for-8 (.500). Totals, 10-for-27 (.370).

NBA REGULAR-SEASON RECORD

Season Team	G	Min.	FGM	FGA	Pct.	FTM	FTA	Pct.	REBOUNDS Off.	Def.	Tot.	Ast.	St.	Blk.	TO	Pts.	AVERAGES RPG	APG	PPG
98-99—Denver	28	409	36	80	.450	21	37	.568	36	60	96	10	10	31	21	93	3.4	0.4	3.3
99-00—Denver	81	1850	286	528	.542	121	176	.688	162	343	505	71	45	114	125	694	6.2	0.9	8.6
00-01—Den.-Toronto ..	81	1720	249	519	.480	142	240	.592	136	298	434	72	32	154	90	640	5.4	0.9	7.9
Totals	190	3979	571	1127	.507	284	453	.627	334	701	1035	153	87	299	236	1427	5.4	0.8	7.5

Three-point field goals: 1998-99, 0-for-1. 1999-00, 1-for-8 (.125). 2000-01, 0-for-1. Totals, 1-for-10 (.100).
Personal fouls/disqualifications: 1998-99, 52/0. 1999-00, 231/1. 2000-01, 244/6. Totals, 527/7.

NBA PLAYOFF RECORD

Season Team	G	Min.	FGM	FGA	Pct.	FTM	FTA	Pct.	REBOUNDS Off.	Def.	Tot.	Ast.	St.	Blk.	TO	Pts.	AVERAGES RPG	APG	PPG
00-01—Toronto	11	103	11	30	.367	13	20	.650	7	16	23	6	2	3	4	35	2.1	0.5	3.2

Personal fouls/disqualifications: 2000-01, 16/0.

CLEAVES, MATEEN   G   PISTONS

PERSONAL: Born September 7, 1977, in Flint, Mich. ... 6-3/210. (1,91/95,3).
HIGH SCHOOL: Northern (Flint, Mich.).
COLLEGE: Michigan State.
TRANSACTIONS/CAREER NOTES: Selected by Detroit Pistons in first round (14th pick overall) of 2000 NBA Draft.

COLLEGIATE RECORD

NOTES: Member of NCAA Division I championship team (2000). ... NCAA Division I Tournament Most Outstanding Player (2000). ... THE SPORTING NEWS All-America first team (2000). ... THE SPORTING NEWS All-America second team (1999).

Season Team	G	Min.	FGM	FGA	Pct.	FTM	FTA	Pct.	Reb.	Ast.	Pts.	AVERAGES RPG	APG	PPG
96-97—Michigan State	29	750	111	277	.401	57	79	.722	73	146	297	2.5	5.0	10.2
97-98—Michigan State	30	1005	161	403	.400	111	158	.703	75	217	484	2.5	7.2	16.1
98-99—Michigan State	38	1185	159	392	.406	85	108	.787	62	274	445	1.6	7.2	11.7
99-00—Michigan State	26	820	109	259	.421	65	86	.756	46	179	315	1.8	6.9	12.1
Totals	123	3760	540	1331	.406	318	431	.738	256	816	1541	2.1	6.6	12.5

Three-point field goals: 1996-97, 18-for-76 (.237). 1997-98, 51-for-152 (.336). 1998-99, 42-for-144 (.292). 1999-00, 32-for-85 (.376). Totals, 143-for-457 (.313).

NBA REGULAR-SEASON RECORD

Season Team	G	Min.	FGM	FGA	Pct.	FTM	FTA	Pct.	REBOUNDS Off.	Def.	Tot.	Ast.	St.	Blk.	TO	Pts.	AVERAGES RPG	APG	PPG
00-01—Detroit	78	1268	160	400	.400	97	137	.708	26	106	132	207	49	1	139	422	1.7	2.7	5.4

Three-point field goals: 2000-01, 5-for-17 (.294).
Personal fouls/disqualifications: 2000-01, 153/1.

COKER, JOHN C

PERSONAL: Born October 28, 1971, in Richland, Wash. ... 7-1/253. (2,16/114,8). ... Full Name: John Michael Coker.
HIGH SCHOOL: Olympic (Bremerton, Wash.).
COLLEGE: Boise State.
TRANSACTIONS/CAREER NOTES: Not drafted by an NBA franchise. ... Signed as free agent by Phoenix Suns (September 25, 1995). ... Waived by Suns (October 29, 1996). ... Played in Continental Basketball Association with Connecticut Pride (1996-97) and Quad City Thunder (2000-01). ... Played in Croatia (1996-97). ... Signed as free agent by Toronto Raptors (October 2, 1997). ... Waived by Raptors (October 17, 1997). ... Played in Spain (1997-98). ... Signed as free agent by Houston Rockets (January 21, 1999). ... Waived by Rockets (February 17, 1999). ... Signed by Washington Wizards to the first of two consecutive 10-day contracts (March 18, 1999). ... Re-signed by Wizards for remainder of season (April 8, 1999). ... Played in American Basketball Association 2000 with Memphis HoundDawgs (2000-01). ... Signed as free agent by Minnesota Timberwolves (October 26, 2000). ... Waived by Timberwolves (October 30, 2000). ... Played in International Basketball League with Sioux Falls Skyforce (2000-01). ... Signed as free agent by Golden State Warriors (December 20, 2000). ... Waived by Warriors (January 3, 2001). ... Re-signed by Warriors to 10-day contract (January 8, 2001).

COLLEGIATE RECORD

Season Team	G	Min.	FGM	FGA	Pct.	FTM	FTA	Pct.	Reb.	Ast.	Pts.	AVERAGES RPG	APG	PPG
90-91—Boise State						Did not play—redshirted.								
91-92—Boise State	11	98	14	25	.560	1	5	.200	17	3	29	1.5	0.3	2.6
92-93—Boise State	22	298	65	125	.520	18	26	.692	86	13	148	3.9	0.6	6.7
93-94—Boise State	30	866	231	403	.573	59	117	.504	203	39	521	6.8	1.3	17.4
94-95—Boise State	21	573	129	244	.529	76	112	.679	153	17	334	7.3	0.8	15.9
Totals	84	1835	439	797	.551	154	260	.592	459	72	1032	5.5	0.9	12.3

NBA REGULAR-SEASON RECORD

Season Team	G	Min.	FGM	FGA	Pct.	FTM	FTA	Pct.	REBOUNDS Off.	Def.	Tot.	Ast.	St.	Blk.	TO	Pts.	AVERAGES RPG	APG	PPG
95-96—Phoenix	5	11	4	5	.800	0	0	...	2	0	2	1	0	1	0	8	0.4	0.2	1.6
98-99—Washington	14	98	13	31	.419	5	6	.833	7	15	22	0	1	2	2	31	1.6	0.0	2.2
00-01—Golden State	6	32	1	8	.125	0	0	...	3	2	5	2	1	0	2	2	0.8	0.3	0.3
Totals	25	141	18	44	.409	5	6	.833	12	17	29	3	2	3	4	41	1.2	0.1	1.6

Personal fouls/disqualifications: 1995-96, 1/0. 1998-99, 17/0. 2000-01, 4/0. Totals, 22/0.

CBA REGULAR-SEASON RECORD

Season Team	G	Min.	FGM	FGA	Pct.	FTM	FTA	Pct.	Reb.	Ast.	Pts.	AVERAGES RPG	APG	PPG
96-97—Connecticut	5	28	0	5	.000	0	0	...	9	0	0	1.8	0.0	0.0
00-01—Quad City	4	149	39	73	.534	6	12	.500	47	3	84	11.8	0.8	21.0
Totals	9	177	39	78	.500	6	12	.500	56	3	84	6.2	0.3	9.3

IBL REGULAR-SEASON RECORD

Season Team	G	Min.	FGM	FGA	Pct.	FTM	FTA	Pct.	Reb.	Ast.	Pts.	AVERAGES RPG	APG	PPG
00-01—Sioux Falls	10	214	36	90	.400	10	10	1.000	43	6	83	4.3	0.6	8.3

Three-point field goals: 2000-01, 1-for-5 (.200).

SPANISH LEAGUE RECORD

Season Team	G	Min.	FGM	FGA	Pct.	FTM	FTA	Pct.	Reb.	Ast.	Pts.	AVERAGES RPG	APG	PPG
97-98—Xacabeo	10	193	38	81	.469	4	10	.400	46	2	80	4.6	0.2	8.0

ABA 2000 LEAGUE RECORD

Season Team	G	Min.	FGM	FGA	Pct.	FTM	FTA	Pct.	Reb.	Ast.	Pts.	AVERAGES RPG	APG	PPG
00-01—Memphis	13	283	47	109	.431	18	26	.692	77	6	117	5.9	0.5	9.0

Three-point field goals: 2000-01, 5-for-11 (.455).

DID YOU KNOW . . .

. . . that Elvin Hayes played exactly 50,000 regular-season minutes during his NBA career?

COLEMAN, DERRICK   F   HORNETS

PERSONAL: Born June 21, 1967, in Mobile, Ala. ... 6-10/270. (2,08/122,5). ... Full Name: Derrick D. Coleman.
HIGH SCHOOL: Northern (Detroit).
COLLEGE: Syracuse.
TRANSACTIONS/CAREER NOTES: Selected by New Jersey Nets in first round (first pick overall) of 1990 NBA Draft. ... Traded by Nets with F Sean Higgins and G Rex Walters to Philadelphia 76ers for C Shawn Bradley, F Tim Perry and G Greg Graham (November 30, 1995). ... Signed as free agent by Charlotte Hornets (January 21, 1999).
MISCELLANEOUS: Member of gold-medal-winning U.S. World Championship team (1994).

COLLEGIATE RECORD

NOTES: The Sporting News All-America first team (1990). ... 1986-87 minutes played totals are missing one game.

Season Team	G	Min.	FGM	FGA	Pct.	FTM	FTA	Pct.	Reb.	Ast.	Pts.	RPG	APG	PPG
86-87—Syracuse	38	1163	173	309	.560	107	156	.686	333	45	453	8.8	1.2	11.9
87-88—Syracuse	35	1133	176	300	.587	121	192	.630	384	76	474	11.0	2.2	13.5
88-89—Syracuse	37	1226	227	395	.575	171	247	.692	422	106	625	11.4	2.9	16.9
89-90—Syracuse	33	1166	194	352	.551	188	263	.715	398	95	591	12.1	2.9	17.9
Totals	143	4688	770	1356	.568	587	858	.684	1537	322	2143	10.7	2.3	15.0

Three-point field goals: 1987-88, 1-for-6 (.167). 1988-89, 0-for-8. 1989-90, 15-for-41 (.366). Totals, 16-for-55 (.291).

NBA REGULAR-SEASON RECORD

HONORS: NBA Rookie of the Year (1991). ... All-NBA third team (1993, 1994). ... NBA All-Rookie first team (1991).

Season Team	G	Min.	FGM	FGA	Pct.	FTM	FTA	Pct.	REBOUNDS Off.	Def.	Tot.	Ast.	St.	Blk.	TO	Pts.	RPG	APG	PPG
90-91—New Jersey	74	2602	514	1100	.467	323	442	.731	269	490	759	163	71	99	217	1364	10.3	2.2	18.4
91-92—New Jersey	65	2207	483	958	.504	300	393	.763	203	415	618	205	54	98	248	1289	9.5	3.2	19.8
92-93—New Jersey	76	2759	564	1226	.460	421	521	.808	247	605	852	276	92	126	243	1572	11.2	3.6	20.7
93-94—New Jersey	77	2778	541	1209	.447	439	567	.774	262	608	870	262	68	142	208	1559	11.3	3.4	20.2
94-95—New Jersey	56	2103	371	874	.424	376	490	.767	167	424	591	187	35	94	172	1146	10.6	3.3	20.5
95-96—Philadelphia	11	294	48	118	.407	20	32	.625	13	59	72	31	4	10	28	123	6.5	2.8	11.2
96-97—Philadelphia	57	2102	364	836	.435	272	365	.745	157	416	573	193	50	75	184	1032	10.1	3.4	18.1
97-98—Philadelphia	59	2135	356	867	.411	302	391	.772	149	438	587	145	46	68	157	1040	9.9	2.5	17.6
98-99—Charlotte	37	1178	168	406	.414	143	190	.753	76	252	328	78	24	42	90	486	8.9	2.1	13.1
99-00—Charlotte	74	2347	446	979	.456	296	377	.785	124	508	632	175	34	130	173	1239	8.5	2.4	16.7
00-01—Charlotte	34	683	97	255	.380	63	92	.685	46	138	184	39	10	21	42	277	5.4	1.1	8.1
Totals	620	21188	3952	8829	.448	2955	3860	.766	1713	4353	6066	1754	488	905	1762	11127	9.8	2.8	17.9

Three-point field goals: 1990-91, 13-for-38 (.342). 1991-92, 23-for-76 (.303). 1992-93, 23-for-99 (.232). 1993-94, 38-for-121 (.314). 1994-95, 28-for-120 (.233). 1995-96, 7-for-21 (.333). 1996-97, 32-for-119 (.269). 1997-98, 26-for-98 (.265). 1998-99, 7-for-33 (.212). 1999-00, 51-for-141 (.362). 2000-01, 20-for-51 (.392). Totals, 268-for-917 (.292).

Personal fouls/disqualifications: 1990-91, 217/3. 1991-92, 168/2. 1992-93, 210/1. 1993-94, 209/2. 1994-95, 162/2. 1995-96, 30/0. 1996-97, 164/1. 1997-98, 144/1. 1998-99, 96/1. 1999-00, 195/2. 2000-01, 53/1. Totals, 1648/16.

NBA PLAYOFF RECORD

Season Team	G	Min.	FGM	FGA	Pct.	FTM	FTA	Pct.	REBOUNDS Off.	Def.	Tot.	Ast.	St.	Blk.	TO	Pts.	RPG	APG	PPG
91-92—New Jersey	4	162	36	74	.486	16	21	.762	13	32	45	21	7	4	11	89	11.3	5.3	22.3
92-93—New Jersey	5	225	50	94	.532	29	36	.806	13	54	67	23	6	13	13	134	13.4	4.6	26.8
93-94—New Jersey	4	173	27	68	.397	39	50	.780	19	38	57	10	2	5	18	98	14.3	2.5	24.5
99-00—Charlotte	4	169	27	57	.474	22	28	.786	10	40	50	14	3	12	13	81	12.5	3.5	20.3
00-01—Charlotte	5	88	9	34	.265	7	9	.778	9	16	25	6	4	2	5	27	5.0	1.2	5.4
Totals	22	817	149	327	.456	113	144	.785	64	180	244	74	22	36	60	429	11.1	3.4	19.5

Three-point field goals: 1991-92, 1-for-6 (.167). 1992-93, 5-for-12 (.417). 1993-94, 5-for-9 (.556). 1999-00, 5-for-16 (.313). 2000-01, 2-for-8 (.250). Totals, 18-for-51 (.353).

Personal fouls/disqualifications: 1991-92, 12/0. 1992-93, 18/0. 1993-94, 12/0. 1999-00, 11/1. 2000-01, 12/0. Totals, 65/1.

NBA ALL-STAR GAME RECORD

Season Team	Min.	FGM	FGA	Pct.	FTM	FTA	Pct.	REBOUNDS Off.	Def.	Tot.	Ast.	PF	Dq.	St.	Blk.	TO	Pts.
1994 —New Jersey	18	1	6	.167	0	0	...	1	2	3	1	3	0	1	1	0	2

Three-point field goals: 1994, 0-for-2.

COLES, BIMBO   G   CAVALIERS

PERSONAL: Born April 22, 1968, in Covington, Va. ... 6-2/182. (1,88/82,6). ... Full Name: Vernell Eufaye Coles.
HIGH SCHOOL: Greenbriar East (Lewisburg, W.Va.).
COLLEGE: Virginia Tech.
TRANSACTIONS/CAREER NOTES: Selected by Sacramento Kings in second round (40th pick overall) of 1990 NBA Draft. ... Draft rights traded by Kings to Miami Heat for G Rory Sparrow (June 27, 1990). ... Traded by Heat with F/C Kevin Willis to Golden State Warriors for G Tim Hardaway and F/C Chris Gatling (February 22, 1996). ... Traded by Warriors with F Duane Ferrell and 1999 first-round draft choice to Atlanta Hawks for G Mookie Blaylock and 1999 first-round draft choice (June 29, 1999). ... Signed as free agent by Cleveland Cavaliers (August 12, 2000).
MISCELLANEOUS: Member of bronze-medal-winning U.S. Olympic team (1988). ... Selected by California Angels organization in 54th round of free-agent draft (June 4, 1990); did not sign.

COLLEGIATE RECORD

Season Team	G	Min.	FGM	FGA	Pct.	FTM	FTA	Pct.	Reb.	Ast.	Pts.	RPG	APG	PPG
86-87—Virginia Tech	28	752	101	245	.412	78	109	.716	85	112	280	3.0	4.0	10.0
87-88—Virginia Tech	29	990	241	544	.443	200	270	.741	103	172	702	3.6	5.9	24.2
88-89—Virginia Tech	27	924	249	547	.455	157	200	.785	111	141	717	4.1	5.2	26.6
89-90—Virginia Tech	31	1147	280	693	.404	158	214	.738	147	122	785	4.7	3.9	25.3
Totals	115	3813	871	2029	.429	593	793	.748	446	547	2484	3.9	4.8	21.6

Three-point field goals: 1986-87, 0-for-14. 1987-88, 20-for-62 (.323). 1988-89, 62-for-166 (.373). 1989-90, 67-for-218 (.307). Totals, 149-for-460 (.324).

NBA REGULAR-SEASON RECORD

Season Team	G	Min.	FGM	FGA	Pct.	FTM	FTA	Pct.	REBOUNDS Off.	Def.	Tot.	Ast.	St.	Blk.	TO	Pts.	AVERAGES RPG	APG	PPG
90-91—Miami	82	1355	162	393	.412	71	95	.747	56	97	153	232	65	12	98	401	1.9	2.8	4.9
91-92—Miami	81	1976	295	649	.455	216	262	.824	69	120	189	366	73	13	167	816	2.3	4.5	10.1
92-93—Miami	81	2232	318	686	.464	177	220	.805	58	108	166	373	80	11	108	855	2.0	4.6	10.6
93-94—Miami	76	1726	233	519	.449	102	131	.779	50	109	159	263	75	12	107	588	2.1	3.5	7.7
94-95—Miami	68	2207	261	607	.430	141	174	.810	46	145	191	416	99	13	156	679	2.8	6.1	10.0
95-96—Mia.-G.S.	81	2615	318	777	.409	168	211	.796	49	211	260	422	94	17	171	892	3.2	5.2	11.0
96-97—Golden State	51	1183	122	314	.389	37	49	.755	39	79	118	149	35	7	59	311	2.3	2.9	6.1
97-98—Golden State	53	1471	166	438	.379	78	88	.886	17	106	123	248	51	13	89	423	2.3	4.7	8.0
98-99—Golden State	48	1272	183	414	.442	83	101	.822	21	96	117	222	45	11	82	455	2.4	4.6	9.5
99-00—Atlanta	80	1924	276	607	.455	85	104	.817	30	142	172	290	58	11	103	645	2.2	3.6	8.1
00-01—Cleveland	47	804	91	239	.381	48	56	.857	9	39	48	138	27	6	59	232	1.0	2.9	4.9
Totals	748	18765	2425	5643	.430	1206	1491	.809	444	1252	1696	3119	702	126	1199	6297	2.3	4.2	8.4

Three-point field goals: 1990-91, 6-for-34 (.176). 1991-92, 10-for-52 (.192). 1992-93, 42-for-137 (.307). 1993-94, 20-for-99 (.202). 1994-95, 16-for-76 (.211). 1995-96, 88-for-254 (.346). 1996-97, 30-for-102 (.294). 1997-98, 13-for-57 (.228). 1998-99, 6-for-25 (.240). 1999-00, 8-for-39 (.205). 2000-01, 2-for-16 (.125). Totals, 241-for-891 (.270).

Personal fouls/disqualifications: 1990-91, 149/0. 1991-92, 151/3. 1992-93, 199/4. 1993-94, 132/0. 1994-95, 185/1. 1995-96, 253/5. 1996-97, 96/0. 1997-98, 135/2. 1998-99, 113/2. 1999-00, 178/1. 2000-01, 87/0. Totals, 1678/18.

NBA PLAYOFF RECORD

Season Team	G	Min.	FGM	FGA	Pct.	FTM	FTA	Pct.	REBOUNDS Off.	Def.	Tot.	Ast.	St.	Blk.	TO	Pts.	AVERAGES RPG	APG	PPG
91-92—Miami	3	45	7	10	.700	8	10	.800	2	5	7	6	3	0	5	23	2.3	2.0	7.7
93-94—Miami	5	140	25	47	.532	18	23	.783	2	12	14	17	7	1	11	69	2.8	3.4	13.8
Totals	8	185	32	57	.561	26	33	.788	4	17	21	23	10	1	16	92	2.6	2.9	11.5

Three-point field goals: 1991-92, 1-for-1. 1993-94, 1-for-4 (.250). Totals, 2-for-5 (.400).
Personal fouls/disqualifications: 1991-92, 5/0. 1993-94, 15/0. Totals, 20/0.

COLLIER, JASON   F/C   ROCKETS

PERSONAL: Born September 8, 1977, in Springfield, Ohio. ... 7-0/260. (2,13/117,9). ... Full Name: Jason Jeffrey Collier.
HIGH SCHOOL: Catholic Central (Springfield, Ohio).
COLLEGE: Indiana, then Georgia Tech.
TRANSACTIONS/CAREER NOTES: Selected by Milwaukee Bucks in first round (15th pick overall) of 2000 NBA Draft. ... Draft rights traded by Bucks with a future first-round choice to Houston Rockets for draft rights to C Joel Przybilla (June 28, 2000).

COLLEGIATE RECORD

Season Team	G	Min.	FGM	FGA	Pct.	FTM	FTA	Pct.	Reb.	Ast.	Pts.	AVERAGES RPG	APG	PPG
96-97—Indiana	33	778	112	258	.434	80	117	.684	188	24	310	5.7	0.7	9.4
97-98—Indiana	9	226	36	64	.563	24	36	.667	47	9	96	5.2	1.0	10.7
98-99—Georgia Tech	25	849	153	347	.441	92	128	.719	182	36	430	7.3	1.4	17.2
99-00—Georgia Tech	30	975	178	376	.473	122	166	.735	276	49	509	9.2	1.6	17.0
Totals	97	2828	479	1045	.458	318	447	.711	693	118	1345	7.1	1.2	13.9

Three-point field goals: 1996-97, 6-for-13 (.462). 1998-99, 32-for-90 (.356). 1999-00, 31-for-84 (.369). Totals, 69-for-187 (.369).

NBA REGULAR-SEASON RECORD

Season Team	G	Min.	FGM	FGA	Pct.	FTM	FTA	Pct.	REBOUNDS Off.	Def.	Tot.	Ast.	St.	Blk.	TO	Pts.	AVERAGES RPG	APG	PPG
00-01—Houston	23	222	27	71	.380	17	24	.708	12	25	37	6	2	3	11	71	1.6	0.3	3.1

Three-point field goals: 2000-01, 0-for-1.
Personal fouls/disqualifications: 2000-01, 27/1.

COLSON, SEAN   G

PERSONAL: Born July 1, 1975 ... 6-0/165. (1,83/74,8). ... Full Name: Sean Tyree Colson.
HIGH SCHOOL: Franklin Learning Center (Philadelphia), then Maine Central Institute (Pittsfield, Maine).
JUNIOR COLLEGE: Hagerstown (Md.).
COLLEGE: Rhode Island, then UNC Charlotte.
TRANSACTIONS/CAREER NOTES: Not drafted by an NBA franchise. ... Played in Continental Basketball Association with Grand Rapids Hoops (1998-99 through 2000-01). ... Signed by Atlanta Hawks to 10-day contract (January 18, 2001). ... Waived by Hawks (January 25, 2001). ... Played in International Basketball League with Grand Rapids Hoops (2000-01). ... Signed by Houston Rockets to the first of two consecutive 10-day contracts (February 28, 2001). ... Re-signed by Rockets for remainder of season (March 20, 2001).

COLLEGIATE RECORD

Season Team	G	Min.	FGM	FGA	Pct.	FTM	FTA	Pct.	Reb.	Ast.	Pts.	AVERAGES RPG	APG	PPG
93-94—Rhode Island						Did not play—redshirted.								
94-95—Rhode Island	26	354	38	144	.264	30	37	.811	36	53	122	1.4	2.0	4.7
95-96—Hagerstown J.C.	30	603	166	311	.534	56	75	.747	99	253	462	3.3	8.4	15.4
96-97—Charlotte	31	1022	142	368	.386	107	139	.770	100	196	438	3.2	6.3	14.1
97-98—Charlotte	29	1004	146	381	.383	105	119	.882	90	231	451	3.1	8.0	15.6
Junior College Totals	30	603	166	311	.534	56	75	.747	99	253	462	3.3	8.4	15.4
4-Year-College Totals	86	2380	326	893	.365	242	295	.820	226	480	1011	2.6	5.6	11.8

Three-point field goals: 1994-95, 16-for-81 (.198). 1995-96, 74-for-164 (.451). 1996-97, 47-for-147 (.320). 1997-98, 54-for-171 (.316). Totals, 117-for-399 (.293).

Season Team	G	Min.	FGM	FGA	Pct.	FTM	FTA	Pct.	Reb.	Ast.	Pts.	RPG	APG	PPG
98-99—Grand Rapids	28	640	88	211	.417	69	74	.932	75	150	265	2.7	5.4	9.5
99-00—Grand Rapids	55	1491	325	706	.460	142	160	.888	143	311	825	2.6	5.7	15.0
00-01—Grand Rapids	21	848	163	392	.416	96	113	.850	81	160	461	3.9	7.6	22.0
Totals	104	2979	576	1309	.440	307	347	.885	299	621	1551	2.9	6.0	14.9

Three-point field goals: 1998-99, 20-for-60 (.333). 1999-00, 33-for-87 (.379). 2000-01, 39-for-111 (.351). Totals, 92-for-258 (.357).

IBL REGULAR-SEASON RECORD

												AVERAGES		
Season Team	G	Min.	FGM	FGA	Pct.	FTM	FTA	Pct.	Reb.	Ast.	Pts.	RPG	APG	PPG
00-01—Grand Rapids	4	175	28	30	.42	25	28	.893	21	36	118	5.3	9.0	29.5

Three-point field goals: 2000-01, 17-for-40 (.425).

NBA REGULAR-SEASON RECORD

								REBOUNDS								AVERAGES		
Season Team	G	Min.	FGM	FGA	Pct.	FTM	FTA	Pct.	Off.	Def.	Tot.	Ast.	St.	Blk.	TO	Pts.	RPG	APG	PPG
00-01—Atlanta-Hou. ...	13	44	6	24	.250	2	4	.500	2	4	6	10	1	0	2	15	0.5	0.8	1.2

Three-point field goals: 2000-01, 1-for-5 (.200).
Personal fouls/disqualifications: 2000-01, 6/0.

CORBIN, TYRONE F

PERSONAL: Born December 31, 1962, in Columbia, S.C. ... 6-6/225. (1,98/102,1). ... Full Name: Tyrone Kennedy Corbin.
HIGH SCHOOL: A.C. Flora (Columbia, S.C.).
COLLEGE: DePaul.
TRANSACTIONS/CAREER NOTES: Selected by San Antonio Spurs in second round (35th pick overall) of 1985 NBA Draft. ... Waived by Spurs (January 21, 1987). ... Signed as free agent by Cleveland Cavaliers (January 24, 1987). ... Traded by Cavaliers with G Kevin Johnson, F/C Mark West, 1988 first- and second-round draft choices and 1989 second-round draft choice to Phoenix Suns for F Larry Nance, F Mike Sanders and 1988 first-round draft choice (February 25, 1988). ... Selected by Minnesota Timberwolves from Suns in NBA Expansion Draft (June 15, 1989). ... Traded by Timberwolves to Utah Jazz for F Thurl Bailey and 1992 second-round draft choice (November 25, 1991). ... Traded by Jazz with 1995 second-round draft choice to Atlanta Hawks for F Adam Keefe (September 16, 1994). ... Traded by Hawks to Sacramento Kings for G Spud Webb (June 29, 1995). ... Traded by Kings with F/G Walt Williams to Miami Heat for G/F Billy Owens and G/F Kevin Gamble (February 22, 1996). ... Signed as free agent by Atlanta Hawks (September 12, 1996). ... Waived by Hawks (August 16, 1999). ... Signed as free agent by Kings (October 2, 1999). ... Signed as free agent by Toronto Raptors (October 20, 2000). ... Traded by Raptors with F Corliss Williamson, F Kornel David and future first-round draft choice to Detroit Pistons for F Jerome Williams and C Eric Montross (February 22, 2001). ... Waived by Pistons (February 23, 2001).

COLLEGIATE RECORD

											AVERAGES		
Season Team	G	Min.	FGM	FGA	Pct.	FTM	FTA	Pct.	Reb.	Ast.	Pts.	RPG	APG	PPG
81-82—DePaul	28	602	43	103	.417	56	78	.718	172	30	142	6.1	1.1	5.1
82-83—DePaul	33	1060	124	263	.471	102	132	.773	262	39	350	7.9	1.2	10.6
83-84—DePaul	30	1070	166	316	.525	93	125	.744	223	89	425	7.4	3.0	14.2
84-85—DePaul	29	1004	189	354	.534	83	102	.814	236	69	461	8.1	2.4	15.9
Totals	120	3736	522	1036	.504	334	437	.764	893	227	1378	7.4	1.9	11.5

NBA REGULAR-SEASON RECORD

									REBOUNDS								AVERAGES		
Season Team	G	Min.	FGM	FGA	Pct.	FTM	FTA	Pct.	Off.	Def.	Tot.	Ast.	St.	Blk.	TO	Pts.	RPG	APG	PPG
85-86—San Antonio	16	174	27	64	.422	10	14	.714	11	14	25	11	11	2	12	64	1.6	0.7	4.0
86-87—S.A.-Clev.	63	1170	156	381	.409	91	124	.734	88	127	215	97	55	5	66	404	3.4	1.5	6.4
87-88—Cleve.-Phoenix	84	1739	257	525	.490	110	138	.797	127	223	350	115	72	18	104	625	4.2	1.4	7.4
88-89—Phoenix	77	1655	245	454	.540	141	179	.788	176	222	398	118	82	13	92	631	5.2	1.5	8.2
89-90—Minnesota	82	3011	521	1083	.481	161	209	.770	219	385	604	216	175	41	143	1203	7.4	2.6	14.7
90-91—Minnesota	82	3196	587	1311	.448	296	371	.798	185	404	589	347	162	53	209	1472	7.2	4.2	18.0
91-92—Minn.-Utah	80	2207	303	630	.481	174	201	.866	163	309	472	140	82	20	97	780	5.9	1.8	9.8
92-93—Utah	82	2555	385	766	.503	180	218	.826	194	325	519	173	108	32	108	950	6.3	2.1	11.6
93-94—Utah	82	2149	268	588	.456	117	144	.813	150	239	389	122	99	24	92	659	4.7	1.5	8.0
94-95—Atlanta	81	1389	205	464	.442	78	114	.684	98	164	262	67	55	16	74	502	3.2	0.8	6.2
95-96—Sac.-Mia.	71	1284	155	351	.442	100	120	.833	81	163	244	84	63	20	67	413	3.4	1.2	5.8
96-97—Atlanta	70	2305	253	600	.422	86	108	.796	76	218	294	124	90	7	85	666	4.2	1.8	9.5
97-98—Atlanta	79	2699	328	747	.439	101	128	.789	78	284	362	173	105	7	86	806	4.6	2.2	10.2
98-99—Atlanta	47	1066	131	335	.391	52	80	.650	37	108	145	43	31	7	43	352	3.1	0.9	7.5
99-00—Sacramento	54	941	88	247	.356	33	39	.846	40	125	165	60	36	5	29	219	3.1	1.1	4.1
00-01—Toronto	15	117	9	38	.237	2	4	.500	3	10	13	4	2	0	3	20	0.9	0.3	1.3
Totals	1065	27657	3918	8584	.456	1732	2191	.791	1726	3320	5046	1894	1228	270	1310	9766	4.7	1.8	9.2

Three-point field goals: 1985-86, 0-for-1. 1986-87, 1-for-4 (.250). 1987-88, 1-for-6 (.167). 1988-89, 0-for-2. 1989-90, 0-for-11. 1990-91, 2-for-10 (.200). 1991-92, 0-for-4. 1992-93, 0-for-5. 1993-94, 6-for-29 (.207). 1994-95, 14-for-56 (.250). 1995-96, 3-for-18 (.167). 1996-97, 74-for-208 (.356). 1997-98, 49-for-141 (.348). 1998-99, 38-for-119 (.319). 1999-00, 10-for-44 (.227). 2000-01, 0-for-5. Totals, 198-for-663 (.299).
Personal fouls/disqualifications: 1985-86, 21/0. 1986-87, 219/0. 1987-88, 181/2. 1988-89, 222/2. 1989-90, 288/5. 1990-91, 257/3. 1991-92, 193/1. 1992-93, 252/3. 1993-94, 212/0. 1994-95, 161/1. 1995-96, 147/1. 1996-97, 176/1. 1997-98, 197/1. 1998-99, 74/0. 1999-00, 99/2. 2000-01, 18/0. Totals, 2627/22.

NBA PLAYOFF RECORD

									REBOUNDS								AVERAGES		
Season Team	G	Min.	FGM	FGA	Pct.	FTM	FTA	Pct.	Off.	Def.	Tot.	Ast.	St.	Blk.	TO	Pts.	RPG	APG	PPG
85-86—San Antonio	1	14	0	4	.000	0	0	...	0	1	1	1	0	0	0	0	1.0	1.0	0.0
88-89—Phoenix	12	310	45	86	.523	19	25	.760	43	42	85	26	24	4	14	109	7.1	2.2	9.1
91-92—Utah	16	447	69	137	.504	42	54	.778	39	49	88	17	12	3	17	180	5.5	1.1	11.3

Season Team	G	Min.	FGM	FGA	Pct.	FTM	FTA	Pct.	REBOUNDS Off.	Def.	Tot.	Ast.	St.	Blk.	TO	Pts.	AVERAGES RPG	APG	PPG
92-93—Utah	5	161	24	52	.462	9	13	.692	16	22	38	9	3	1	7	59	7.6	1.8	11.8
93-94—Utah	16	413	41	106	.387	14	15	.933	25	54	79	15	21	3	11	100	4.9	0.9	6.3
94-95—Atlanta	3	79	12	26	.462	8	9	.889	6	4	10	2	2	1	2	34	3.3	0.7	11.3
95-96—Miami	2	34	1	5	.200	3	4	.750	4	3	7	1	2	0	1	5	3.5	0.5	2.5
96-97—Atlanta	10	364	42	92	.457	9	9	1.000	12	31	43	20	4	2	14	106	4.3	2.0	10.6
97-98—Atlanta	4	113	7	25	.280	0	0	...	3	12	15	4	6	1	3	15	3.8	1.0	3.8
98-99—Atlanta	9	268	30	72	.417	3	4	.750	7	26	33	16	6	0	8	69	3.7	1.8	7.7
99-00—Sacramento	3	23	2	5	.400	1	1	1.000	1	4	5	3	0	0	0	4	1.7	1.0	1.3
Totals	81	2226	273	610	.448	107	134	.799	156	248	404	114	80	15	77	681	5.0	1.4	8.4

Three-point field goals: 1991-92, 0-for-2. 1993-94, 4-for-12 (.333). 1994-95, 2-for-6 (.333). 1996-97, 13-for-37 (.351). 1997-98, 1-for-6 (.167). 1998-99, 6-for-23 (.261). 1999-00, 0-for-2. Totals, 26-for-88 (.295).

Personal fouls/disqualifications: 1988-89, 37/0. 1991-92, 45/0. 1992-93, 15/0. 1993-94, 31/0. 1994-95, 10/0. 1995-96, 3/0. 1996-97, 29/0. 1997-98, 10/0. 1998-99, 20/0. 1999-00, 2/0. Totals, 202/0.

C

CRAWFORD, CHRIS   F   HAWKS

PERSONAL: Born May 13, 1975, in Kalamazoo, Mich. ... 6-9/235. (2,06/106,6). ... Full Name: Christopher Lee Crawford.
HIGH SCHOOL: Comstock (Kalamazoo, Mich.).
COLLEGE: Marquette.
TRANSACTIONS/CAREER NOTES: Selected by Atlanta Hawks in second round (51st pick overall) of 1997 NBA Draft.

COLLEGIATE RECORD

Season Team	G	Min.	FGM	FGA	Pct.	FTM	FTA	Pct.	Reb.	Ast.	Pts.	AVERAGES RPG	APG	PPG
93-94—Marquette	18	116	9	25	.360	9	13	.692	11	3	33	0.6	0.2	1.8
94-95—Marquette	33	611	72	163	.442	43	67	.642	89	16	204	2.7	0.5	6.2
95-96—Marquette	31	798	118	280	.421	83	116	.716	126	29	348	4.1	0.9	11.2
96-97—Marquette	31	961	165	352	.469	100	130	.769	165	45	463	5.3	1.5	14.9
Totals	113	2486	364	820	.444	235	326	.721	391	93	1048	3.5	0.8	9.3

Three-point field goals: 1993-94, 6-for-13 (.462). 1994-95, 17-for-45 (.378). 1995-96, 29-for-84 (.345). 1996-97, 33-for-86 (.384). Totals, 85-for-228 (.373).

NBA REGULAR-SEASON RECORD

Season Team	G	Min.	FGM	FGA	Pct.	FTM	FTA	Pct.	REBOUNDS Off.	Def.	Tot.	Ast.	St.	Blk.	TO	Pts.	AVERAGES RPG	APG	PPG
97-98—Atlanta	40	256	46	110	.418	57	68	.838	20	21	41	9	12	7	18	150	1.0	0.2	3.8
98-99—Atlanta	42	784	110	255	.431	57	70	.814	37	53	90	24	10	13	48	288	2.1	0.6	6.9
99-00—Atlanta	55	668	91	229	.397	63	81	.778	51	48	99	33	17	16	37	252	1.8	0.6	4.6
00-01—Atlanta	47	901	122	270	.452	68	83	.819	28	82	110	37	21	16	62	318	2.3	0.8	6.8
Totals	184	2609	369	864	.427	245	302	.811	136	204	340	103	60	52	165	1008	1.8	0.6	5.5

Three-point field goals: 1997-98, 1-for-3 (.333). 1998-99, 11-for-33 (.333). 1999-00, 7-for-27 (.259). 2000-01, 6-for-22 (.273). Totals, 25-for-85 (.294).
Personal fouls/disqualifications: 1997-98, 27/0. 1998-99, 106/1. 1999-00, 83/1. 2000-01, 117/3. Totals, 333/5.

NBA PLAYOFF RECORD

Season Team	G	Min.	FGM	FGA	Pct.	FTM	FTA	Pct.	REBOUNDS Off.	Def.	Tot.	Ast.	St.	Blk.	TO	Pts.	AVERAGES RPG	APG	PPG
97-98—Atlanta	1	4	0	0	...	2	2	1.000	1	1	2	0	0	1	2	2	2.0	0.0	2.0
98-99—Atlanta	6	125	16	48	.333	23	26	.885	6	13	19	5	1	1	6	59	3.2	0.8	9.8
Totals	7	129	16	48	.333	25	28	.893	7	14	21	5	1	2	8	61	3.0	0.7	8.7

Three-point field goals: 1998-99, 4-for-14 (.286). Totals, 4-for-14 (.286).
Personal fouls/disqualifications: 1997-98, 2/0. 1998-99, 19/2. Totals, 21/2.

CRAWFORD, JAMAL   G   BULLS

PERSONAL: Born March 20, 1980, in Seattle. ... 6-5/175. (1,96/79,4).
HIGH SCHOOL: Rainer Beach (Renton, Wash.).
COLLEGE: Michigan.
TRANSACTIONS/CAREER NOTES: Selected after freshman season by Cleveland Cavaliers in first round (eighth pick overall) of 2000 NBA Draft. ... Draft rights traded by Cavaliers with cash to Chicago Bulls for draft rights to C Chris Mihm (June 28, 2000).

COLLEGIATE RECORD

Season Team	G	Min.	FGM	FGA	Pct.	FTM	FTA	Pct.	Reb.	Ast.	Pts.	AVERAGES RPG	APG	PPG
99-00—Michigan	17	577	105	255	.412	40	51	.784	47	76	283	2.8	4.5	16.6

Three-point field goals: 1999-00, 33-for-101 (.327).

NBA REGULAR-SEASON RECORD

Season Team	G	Min.	FGM	FGA	Pct.	FTM	FTA	Pct.	REBOUNDS Off.	Def.	Tot.	Ast.	St.	Blk.	TO	Pts.	AVERAGES RPG	APG	PPG
00-01—Chicago	61	1050	107	304	.352	27	34	.794	9	80	89	141	43	14	85	282	1.5	2.3	4.6

Three-point field goals: 2000-01, 41-for-117 (.350).
Personal fouls/disqualifications: 2000-01, 68/0.

CROSHERE, AUSTIN   F   PACERS

PERSONAL: Born May 1, 1975, in Los Angeles. ... 6-9/235. (2,06/106,6). ... Full Name: Austin Nathan Croshere.
HIGH SCHOOL: Crossroads (Santa Monica).
COLLEGE: Providence.
TRANSACTIONS/CAREER NOTES: Selected by Indiana Pacers in first round (12th pick overall) of 1997 NBA Draft.

COLLEGIATE RECORD

Season Team	G	Min.	FGM	FGA	Pct.	FTM	FTA	Pct.	Reb.	Ast.	Pts.	RPG	APG	PPG
93-94—Providence	25	233	38	95	.400	29	40	.725	55	3	115	2.2	0.1	4.6
94-95—Providence	30	570	106	231	.459	66	85	.776	147	33	307	4.9	1.1	10.2
95-96—Providence	30	863	151	359	.421	109	128	.852	173	33	458	5.8	1.1	15.3
96-97—Providence	36	1192	200	440	.455	182	205	.888	270	54	643	7.5	1.5	17.9
Totals	121	2858	495	1125	.440	386	458	.843	645	123	1523	5.3	1.0	12.6

Three-point field goals: 1993-94, 10-for-31 (.323). 1994-95, 29-for-85 (.341). 1995-96, 47-for-141 (.333). 1996-97, 61-for-175 (.349). Totals, 147-for-432 (.340).

NBA REGULAR-SEASON RECORD

Season Team	G	Min.	FGM	FGA	Pct.	FTM	FTA	Pct.	REBOUNDS Off.	Def.	Tot.	Ast.	St.	Blk.	TO	Pts.	AVERAGES RPG	APG	PPG
97-98—Indiana	26	243	32	86	.372	8	14	.571	10	35	45	8	9	5	13	76	1.7	0.3	2.9
98-99—Indiana	27	249	32	75	.427	20	23	.870	16	29	45	10	7	8	23	92	1.7	0.4	3.4
99-00—Indiana	81	1885	288	653	.441	196	231	.848	135	381	516	89	44	60	121	835	6.4	1.1	10.3
00-01—Indiana	81	1874	276	701	.394	200	231	.866	123	264	387	92	36	50	136	822	4.8	1.1	10.1
Totals	215	4251	628	1515	.415	424	499	.850	284	709	993	199	96	123	293	1825	4.6	0.9	8.5

Three-point field goals: 1997-98, 4-for-13 (.308). 1998-99, 8-for-29 (.276). 1999-00, 63-for-174 (.362). 2000-01, 70-for-207 (.338). Totals, 145-for-423 (.343).

Personal fouls/disqualifications: 1997-98, 32/1. 1998-99, 32/0. 1999-00, 203/2. 2000-01, 180/1. Totals, 447/4.

NBA PLAYOFF RECORD

NOTES: Shares NBA Finals single-game record for most free throws made in one quarter—9 (June 16, 2000, vs. Los Angeles Lakers).

Season Team	G	Min.	FGM	FGA	Pct.	FTM	FTA	Pct.	REBOUNDS Off.	Def.	Tot.	Ast.	St.	Blk.	TO	Pts.	AVERAGES RPG	APG	PPG
98-99—Indiana	1	1	0	1	.000	2	2	1.000	1	0	1	0	0	0	2	1.0	0.0	2.0	
99-00—Indiana	23	490	64	153	.418	73	87	.839	31	78	109	19	9	16	25	216	4.7	0.8	9.4
00-01—Indiana	4	129	14	35	.400	13	15	.867	5	15	20	6	4	2	9	43	5.0	1.5	10.8
Totals	28	620	78	189	.413	88	104	.846	37	93	130	25	13	18	34	261	4.6	0.9	9.3

Three-point field goals: 1999-00, 15-for-37 (.405). 2000-01, 2-for-10 (.200). Totals, 17-for-47 (.362).
Personal fouls/disqualifications: 1999-00, 51/0. 2000-01, 15/1. Totals, 66/1.

CROTTY, JOHN   G   JAZZ

PERSONAL: Born July 15, 1969, in Orange, N.J. ... 6-2/194. (1,88/88,0). ... Full Name: John Kevin Crotty.
HIGH SCHOOL: Christian Brothers Academy (Lincroft, N.J.).
COLLEGE: Virginia.
TRANSACTIONS/CAREER NOTES: Not drafted by an NBA franchise. ... Played in Global Basketball Association with Greenville Spinners (1991-92). ... Signed as free agent by Utah Jazz (September 4, 1992). ... Signed as free agent by Cleveland Cavaliers (October 23, 1995). ... Signed by Miami Heat to first of two consecutive 10-day contracts (January 6, 1997). ... Signed by Heat for remainder of season (January 25, 1997). ... Signed as free agent by Portland Trail Blazers (September 23, 1997). ... Waived by Trail Blazers (March 18, 1999). ... Signed as free agent by Seattle SuperSonics for remainder of season (March 23, 1999). ... Signed as free agent by Detroit Pistons (November 13, 1999). ... Signed as free agent by Jazz (August 10, 2000).

COLLEGIATE RECORD

Season Team	G	Min.	FGM	FGA	Pct.	FTM	FTA	Pct.	Reb.	Ast.	Pts.	RPG	APG	PPG
87-88—Virginia	31	717	59	163	.362	51	87	.586	70	92	195	2.3	3.0	6.3
88-89—Virginia	33	1143	136	309	.440	113	169	.669	85	208	426	2.6	6.3	12.9
89-90—Virginia	32	1176	156	401	.389	134	191	.702	94	214	512	2.9	6.7	16.0
90-91—Virginia	33	1138	176	397	.443	115	148	.777	78	169	513	2.4	5.1	15.5
Totals	129	4174	527	1270	.415	413	595	.694	327	683	1646	2.5	5.3	12.8

Three-point field goals: 1987-88, 26-for-75 (.347). 1988-89, 41-for-112 (.366). 1989-90, 66-for-194 (.340). 1990-91, 46-for-136 (.338). Totals, 179-for-517 (.346).

NBA REGULAR-SEASON RECORD

Season Team	G	Min.	FGM	FGA	Pct.	FTM	FTA	Pct.	REBOUNDS Off.	Def.	Tot.	Ast.	St.	Blk.	TO	Pts.	AVERAGES RPG	APG	PPG
92-93—Utah	40	243	37	72	.514	26	38	.684	4	13	17	55	11	0	30	102	0.4	1.4	2.6
93-94—Utah	45	313	45	99	.455	31	36	.861	11	20	31	77	15	1	27	132	0.7	1.7	2.9
94-95—Utah	80	1019	93	231	.403	98	121	.810	27	70	97	205	39	6	70	295	1.2	2.6	3.7
95-96—Cleveland	58	617	51	114	.447	62	72	.861	20	34	54	102	22	6	51	172	0.9	1.8	3.0
96-97—Miami	48	659	79	154	.513	54	64	.844	15	32	47	102	18	0	42	232	1.0	2.1	4.8
97-98—Portland	26	379	29	90	.322	32	34	.941	4	28	32	63	10	1	42	96	1.2	2.4	3.7
98-99—Port.-Seattle	27	382	51	124	.411	43	50	.860	8	23	31	63	11	0	33	159	1.1	2.3	5.9
99-00—Detroit	69	937	106	251	.422	80	93	.860	17	58	75	128	27	5	54	325	1.1	1.9	4.7
00-01—Utah	31	264	22	65	.338	17	19	.895	13	15	28	34	6	0	19	65	0.9	1.1	2.1
Totals	424	4813	513	1200	.428	443	527	.841	119	293	412	829	159	19	368	1578	1.0	2.0	3.7

Three-point field goals: 1992-93, 2-for-14 (.143). 1993-94, 11-for-24 (.458). 1994-95, 11-for-36 (.306). 1995-96, 8-for-27 (.296). 1996-97, 20-for-49 (.408). 1997-98, 6-for-20 (.300). 1998-99, 14-for-36 (.389). 1999-00, 33-for-80 (.413). 2000-01, 4-for-7 (.571). Totals, 109-for-293 (.372).

Personal fouls/disqualifications: 1992-93, 29/0. 1993-94, 36/0. 1994-95, 105/0. 1995-96, 60/0. 1996-97, 79/0. 1997-98, 28/0. 1998-99, 31/0. 1999-00, 104/0. 2000-01, 32/0. Totals, 504/0.

Season Team	G	Min.	FGM	FGA	Pct.	FTM	FTA	Pct.	REBOUNDS Off.	Def.	Tot.	Ast.	St.	Blk.	TO	Pts.	AVERAGES RPG	APG	PPG
92-93—Utah	1	3	2	2	1.000	0	0	...	1	0	1	1	0	0	0	4	1.0	1.0	4.0
93-94—Utah	8	38	4	11	.364	2	2	1.000	0	3	3	9	1	0	1	12	0.4	1.1	1.5
94-95—Utah	3	24	2	3	.667	3	5	.600	0	0	0	6	1	0	0	7	0.0	2.0	2.3
95-96—Cleveland	2	9	0	0	...	2	2	1.000	1	0	1	1	1	1	1	2	0.5	0.5	1.0
96-97—Miami	15	125	13	33	.394	6	7	.857	5	6	11	11	4	0	14	37	0.7	0.7	2.5
99-00—Detroit	3	51	2	10	.200	2	2	1.000	0	4	4	4	1	1	4	6	1.3	1.3	2.0
00-01—Utah	4	19	0	3	.000	3	3	1.000	1	2	3	3	1	1	0	3	0.8	0.8	0.8
Totals	36	269	23	62	.371	18	21	.857	8	15	23	35	9	3	20	71	0.6	1.0	2.0

Three-point field goals: 1993-94, 2-for-2. 1996-97, 5-for-12 (.417). 1999-00, 0-for-3. Totals, 7-for-17 (.412).
Personal fouls/disqualifications: 1993-94, 6/0. 1994-95, 2/0. 1996-97, 15/0. 1999-00, 4/0. 2000-01, 3/0. Totals, 30/0.

CUMMINGS, VONTEEGO   G   WARRIORS

PERSONAL: Born February 29, 1976, in Thomson, Ga. ... 6-3/190. (1,91/86,2). ... Full Name: Vonteego Marfeek Cummings.
HIGH SCHOOL: Thomson (Ga.).
COLLEGE: Pittsburgh.
TRANSACTIONS/CAREER NOTES: Selected by Indiana Pacers in first round (26th pick overall) of 1999 NBA Draft. ... Draft rights traded by Pacers with future first-round draft choice to Golden State Warriors for F/C Jeff Foster (June 30, 1999).

COLLEGIATE RECORD

Season Team	G	Min.	FGM	FGA	Pct.	FTM	FTA	Pct.	Reb.	Ast.	Pts.	AVERAGES RPG	APG	PPG
95-96—Pittsburgh	18	438	39	117	.333	28	42	.667	62	52	116	3.4	2.9	6.4
96-97—Pittsburgh	33	1129	189	414	.457	119	167	.713	137	140	539	4.2	4.2	16.3
97-98—Pittsburgh	26	1042	173	406	.426	120	173	.694	107	154	507	4.1	5.9	19.5
98-99—Pittsburgh	26	923	153	372	.411	72	103	.699	106	112	419	4.1	4.3	16.1
Totals	103	3532	554	1309	.423	339	485	.699	412	458	1581	4.0	4.4	15.3

Three-point field goals: 1995-96, 10-for-42 (.238). 1996-97, 42-for-105 (.400). 1997-98, 41-for-130 (.315). 1998-99, 41-for-124 (.331). Totals, 134-for-401 (.334).

NBA REGULAR-SEASON RECORD

Season Team	G	Min.	FGM	FGA	Pct.	FTM	FTA	Pct.	REBOUNDS Off.	Def.	Tot.	Ast.	St.	Blk.	TO	Pts.	AVERAGES RPG	APG	PPG
99-00—Golden State	75	1793	265	655	.405	127	169	.751	57	127	184	247	91	13	132	706	3.3	3.3	9.4
00-01—Golden State	66	1495	178	517	.344	79	116	.681	47	90	137	227	67	14	91	483	2.1	3.4	7.3
Totals	141	3288	443	1172	.378	206	285	.723	104	217	321	474	158	27	223	1189	2.3	3.4	8.4

Three-point field goals: 1999-00, 49-for-151 (.325). 2000-01, 48-for-143 (.336). Totals, 97-for-294 (.330).
Personal fouls/disqualifications: 1999-00, 174/4. 2000-01, 160/2. Totals, 334/6.

CURLEY, BILL   F

PERSONAL: Born May 29, 1972, in Boston. ... 6-9/245. (2,06/111,1). ... Full Name: William Michael Curley.
HIGH SCHOOL: Duxbury (Mass.).
COLLEGE: Boston College.
TRANSACTIONS/CAREER NOTES: Selected by San Antonio Spurs in first round (22nd pick overall) of 1994 NBA Draft. ... Draft rights traded by Spurs with 1997 second-round draft choice to Detroit Pistons for F Sean Elliott (July 19, 1994). ... Traded by Pistons with draft rights to G Randolph Childress to Portland Trail Blazers for F Otis Thorpe (September 20, 1995). ... Traded by Trail Blazers with G James Robinson and 1997 or 1998 first-round draft choice to Minnesota Timberwolves for G Isaiah Rider (July 23, 1996). ... Traded by Timberwolves with G Stephon Marbury and G Chris Carr to New Jersey Nets in three-way deal in which Nets also received G Elliot Perry from Milwaukee Bucks, Timberwolves received F Brian Evans, 1999 first-round draft choice and an undisclosed draft choice from Nets, Bucks sent G Terrell Brandon to Timberwolves, Timberwolves sent C Paul Grant to Bucks and Nets sent G Sam Cassell and F/C Chris Gatling to Bucks (March 11, 1999). ... Waived by Nets (March 13, 1999). ... Signed by Timberwolves for remainder of season (March 17, 1999). ... Signed as free agent by Golden State Warriors (October 4, 1999). ... Waived by Warriors (November 1, 1999). ... Re-signed as free agent by Warriors (December 6, 1999). ... Waived by Warriors (January 5, 2000). ... Signed by Houston Rockets to the first of two consecutive 10-day contracts (January 13, 2000). ... Signed by Warriors for remainder of season (March 21, 2000). ... Traded by Warriors to Dallas Mavericks as part of four-team deal in which Boston Celtics received G Robert Pack, C John Williams and cash considerations from Mavericks and a conditional first-round draft choice from Utah Jazz, Mavericks received G Dana Barros from Celtics, and G Howard Eisley from Jazz, Jazz received F Donyell Marshall from Warriors and C Bruno Sundov from Mavericks and Warriors received F Danny Fortson from Celtics and F Adam Keefe from Jazz (August 16, 2000). ... Waived by Mavericks (November 28, 2000). ... Signed as free agent by Warriors (December 1, 2000). ... Waived by Warriors (January 3, 2001). ... Signed by Warriors to the first of two consecutive 10-day contracts (January 5, 2001).

COLLEGIATE RECORD

Season Team	G	Min.	FGM	FGA	Pct.	FTM	FTA	Pct.	Reb.	Ast.	Pts.	AVERAGES RPG	APG	PPG
90-91—Boston College	30	873	141	260	.542	96	139	.691	206	38	378	6.9	1.3	12.6
91-92—Boston College	31	1051	187	324	.577	178	230	.774	250	29	552	8.1	0.9	17.8
92-93—Boston College	31	1052	181	312	.580	129	152	.849	235	37	491	7.6	1.2	15.8
93-94—Boston College	34	1140	233	418	.557	215	271	.793	305	54	681	9.0	1.6	20.0
Totals	126	4116	742	1314	.565	618	792	.780	996	158	2102	7.9	1.3	16.7

Three-point field goals: 1990-91, 0-for-3. 1991-92, 0-for-1. 1993-94, 0-for-1. Totals, 0-for-5 (.000).

NBA REGULAR-SEASON RECORD

								REBOUNDS								AVERAGES		
Season Team	G	Min.	FGM	FGA	Pct.	FTM	FTA	Pct.	Off.	Def.	Tot.	Ast.	St.	Blk.	TO	Pts.	RPG	APG	PPG
94-95—Detroit	53	595	58	134	.433	27	36	.750	54	70	124	25	21	21	25	143	2.3	0.5	2.7
95-96—Portland							Did not play—injured.												
96-97—Minnesota							Did not play—injured.												
97-98—Minnesota......	11	146	16	33	.485	2	3	.667	11	17	28	4	3	1	3	34	2.5	0.4	3.1
98-99—Minnesota......	35	372	29	72	.403	19	22	.864	20	31	51	14	17	9	10	78	1.5	0.4	2.2
99-00—Houston-G.S...	28	309	29	68	.426	18	25	.720	18	32	50	14	13	4	21	76	1.8	0.5	2.7
00-01—Dallas-G.S......	20	192	25	47	.532	12	19	.632	21	16	37	3	7	9	16	63	1.9	0.2	3.2
Totals	147	1614	157	354	.444	78	105	.743	124	166	290	60	61	44	75	394	2.0	0.4	2.7

Three-point field goals: 1997-98, 0-for-1. 1998-99, 1-for-5 (.200). 1999-00, 0-for-1. 2000-01, 1-for-2 (.500). Totals, 2-for-9 (.222).
Personal fouls/disqualifications: 1994-95, 128/3. 1997-98, 28/1. 1998-99, 83/1. 1999-00, 61/2. 2000-01, 45/1. Totals, 345/8.

NBA PLAYOFF RECORD

								REBOUNDS								AVERAGES		
Season Team	G	Min.	FGM	FGA	Pct.	FTM	FTA	Pct.	Off.	Def.	Tot.	Ast.	St.	Blk.	TO	Pts.	RPG	APG	PPG
97-98—Minnesota.......	2	7	0	0	...	0	0	...	0	0	0	0	0	0	0	0	0.0	0.0	0.0

CURRY, DELL   G   RAPTORS

PERSONAL: Born June 25, 1964, in Harrisonburg, Va. ... 6-5/205. (1,96/93,0). ... Full Name: Wardell Stephen Curry. ... Cousin of Reggie Harris, pitcher with four major league baseball teams (1990-91 and 1996-99).
HIGH SCHOOL: Fort Defiance (Va.).
COLLEGE: Virginia Tech.
TRANSACTIONS/CAREER NOTES: Selected by Utah Jazz in first round (15th pick overall) of 1986 NBA Draft. ... Traded by Jazz with F/C Kent Benson and future second-round draft considerations to Cleveland Cavaliers for C Darryl Dawkins, C Mel Turpin and future second-round draft considerations (October 8, 1987). ... Selected by Charlotte Hornets from Cavaliers in NBA Expansion Draft (June 23, 1988). ... Signed as free agent by Milwaukee Bucks (January 22, 1999). ... Signed as free agent by Toronto Raptors (August 5, 1999).
MISCELLANEOUS: Charlotte Hornets all-time leading scorer with 9,839 points (1988-89 through 1997-98). ... Selected by Baltimore Orioles organization in 14th round of free-agent baseball draft (June 3, 1985); did not sign.

COLLEGIATE RECORD

NOTES: THE SPORTING NEWS All-America second team (1986).

												AVERAGES		
Season Team	G	Min.	FGM	FGA	Pct.	FTM	FTA	Pct.	Reb.	Ast.	Pts.	RPG	APG	PPG
82-83—Virginia Tech	32	1024	198	417	.475	68	80	.850	95	107	464	3.0	3.3	14.5
83-84—Virginia Tech	35	1166	293	561	.522	88	116	.759	143	96	674	4.1	2.7	19.3
84-85—Virginia Tech	29	968	225	467	.482	75	99	.758	169	91	529	5.8	3.1	18.2
85-86—Virginia Tech	30	1117	305	577	.529	112	142	.789	203	113	722	6.8	3.8	24.1
Totals	126	4275	1021	2022	.505	343	437	.785	610	407	2389	4.8	3.2	19.0

Three-point field goals: 1984-85, 4-for-7 (.571).

NBA REGULAR-SEASON RECORD

HONORS: NBA Sixth Man Award (1994).
NOTES: Led NBA with .476 three-point field goal percentage (1999).

								REBOUNDS								AVERAGES		
Season Team	G	Min.	FGM	FGA	Pct.	FTM	FTA	Pct.	Off.	Def.	Tot.	Ast.	St.	Blk.	TO	Pts.	RPG	APG	PPG
86-87—Utah...............	67	636	139	326	.426	30	38	.789	30	48	78	58	27	4	44	325	1.2	0.9	4.9
87-88—Cleveland	79	1499	340	742	.458	79	101	.782	43	123	166	149	94	22	108	787	2.1	1.9	10.0
88-89—Charlotte	48	813	256	521	.491	40	46	.870	26	78	104	50	42	4	44	571	2.2	1.0	11.9
89-90—Charlotte	67	1860	461	990	.466	96	104	.923	31	137	168	159	98	26	100	1070	2.5	2.4	16.0
90-91—Charlotte	76	1515	337	715	.471	96	114	.842	47	152	199	166	75	25	80	802	2.6	2.2	10.6
91-92—Charlotte	77	2020	504	1038	.486	127	152	.836	57	202	259	177	93	20	134	1209	3.4	2.3	15.7
92-93—Charlotte	80	2094	498	1102	.452	136	157	.866	51	235	286	180	87	23	129	1227	3.6	2.3	15.3
93-94—Charlotte	82	2173	533	1171	.455	117	134	.873	71	191	262	221	98	27	120	1335	3.2	2.7	16.3
94-95—Charlotte	69	1718	343	778	.441	95	111	.856	41	127	168	113	55	18	98	935	2.4	1.6	13.6
95-96—Charlotte	82	2371	441	974	.453	146	171	.854	68	196	264	176	108	25	130	1192	3.2	2.1	14.5
96-97—Charlotte	68	2078	384	836	.459	114	142	.803	40	171	211	118	60	14	93	1008	3.1	1.7	14.8
97-98—Charlotte	52	971	194	434	.447	41	52	.788	26	75	101	69	31	4	54	490	1.9	1.3	9.4
98-99—Milwaukee	42	864	163	336	.485	28	34	.824	18	67	85	48	36	3	45	423	2.0	1.1	10.1
99-00—Toronto	67	1095	194	454	.427	24	32	.750	11	89	100	89	32	9	40	507	1.5	1.3	7.6
00-01—Toronto	71	956	162	382	.424	43	51	.843	16	69	85	75	27	8	39	429	1.2	1.1	6.0
Totals	1027	22663	4949	10799	.458	1212	1439	.842	576	1960	2536	1848	963	232	1258	12310	2.5	1.8	12.0

Three-point field goals: 1986-87, 17-for-60 (.283). 1987-88, 28-for-81 (.346). 1988-89, 19-for-55 (.345). 1989-90, 52-for-147 (.354). 1990-91, 32-for-86 (.372). 1991-92, 74-for-183 (.404). 1992-93, 95-for-237 (.401). 1993-94, 152-for-378 (.402). 1994-95, 154-for-361 (.427). 1995-96, 164-for-406 (.404). 1996-97, 126-for-296 (.426). 1997-98, 61-for-145 (.421). 1998-99, 69-for-145 (.476). 1999-00, 95-for-242 (.393). 2000-01, 62-for-145 (.428). Totals, 1200-for-2967 (.404).
Personal fouls/disqualifications: 1986-87, 86/0. 1987-88, 128/0. 1988-89, 68/0. 1989-90, 148/0. 1990-91, 125/0. 1991-92, 156/1. 1992-93, 150/1. 1993-94, 161/0. 1994-95, 144/1. 1995-96, 173/2. 1996-97, 147/0. 1997-98, 85/2. 1998-99, 42/0. 1999-00, 66/0. 2000-01, 66/0. Totals, 1745/7.

NBA PLAYOFF RECORD

								REBOUNDS								AVERAGES		
Season Team	G	Min.	FGM	FGA	Pct.	FTM	FTA	Pct.	Off.	Def.	Tot.	Ast.	St.	Blk.	TO	Pts.	RPG	APG	PPG
86-87—Utah...............	2	4	0	3	.000	0	1	.000	0	0	0	0	0	0	0	0	0.0	0.0	0.0
87-88—Cleveland	2	17	1	4	.250	0	0	...	1	0	1	2	0	1	0	2	0.5	1.0	1.0
92-93—Charlotte	9	222	42	97	.433	9	11	.818	11	21	32	18	13	0	13	99	3.6	2.0	11.0
94-95—Charlotte	4	107	16	34	.471	10	11	.909	5	4	9	6	0	0	6	51	2.3	1.5	12.8
96-97—Charlotte	3	50	5	17	.294	3	3	1.000	1	0	1	5	4	0	1	14	0.3	1.7	4.7

Season Team	G	Min.	FGM	FGA	Pct.	FTM	FTA	Pct.	Off.	Def.	Tot.	Ast.	St.	Blk.	TO	Pts.	RPG	APG	PPG
97-98—Charlotte	9	171	21	52	.404	6	7	.857	6	13	19	10	7	3	5	52	2.1	1.1	5.8
98-99—Milwaukee	3	49	2	15	.133	4	4	1.000	0	4	4	1	3	0	0	9	1.3	0.3	3.0
99-00—Toronto	3	30	2	4	.500	1	2	.500	1	1	2	1	2	0	2	7	0.7	0.3	2.3
00-01—Toronto	12	182	27	64	.422	10	12	.833	2	12	14	10	6	1	11	78	1.2	0.8	6.5
Totals	47	832	116	290	.400	43	51	.843	27	55	82	53	35	5	38	312	1.7	1.1	6.6

Three-point field goals: 1986-87, 0-for-1. 1987-88, 0-for-1. 1992-93, 6-for-21 (.286). 1994-95, 9-for-21 (.429). 1996-97, 1-for-4 (.250). 1997-98, 4-for-16 (.250). 1998-99, 1-for-8 (.125). 1999-00, 2-for-3 (.667). 2000-01, 14-for-37 (.378). Totals, 37-for-112 (.330).

Personal fouls/disqualifications: 1986-87, 1/0. 1987-88, 1/0. 1992-93, 19/0. 1994-95, 11/0. 1996-97, 5/0. 1997-98, 21/0. 1998-99, 5/0. 1999-00, 4/0. 2000-01, 10/0. Totals, 77/0.

CURRY, MICHAEL   G   PISTONS

PERSONAL: Born August 22, 1968, in Anniston, Ala. ... 6-5/227. (1,96/103,0).
HIGH SCHOOL: Glenn Hills (Augusta, Ga.).
COLLEGE: Georgia Southern.
TRANSACTIONS/CAREER NOTES: Not drafted by an NBA franchise. ... Played in Germany, Belgium and France (1990-91 and 1991-92). ... Played in United States Basketball League with Long Island Surf (1992). ... Played in Continental Basketball Association with Capital Region Pontiacs (1992-93) and Omaha Racers (1995-96). ... Signed as free agent by Philadelphia 76ers (October 7, 1993). ... Waived by 76ers (December 29, 1993). ... Played in Italy (1993-94). ... Played in Spain (1994-95). ... Signed by Washington Bullets to 10-day contract (January 12, 1996). ... Signed by Detroit Pistons to first of two consecutive 10-day contracts (January 31, 1996). ... Re-signed by Pistons for remainder of season (February 22, 1996). ... Signed as free agent by Milwaukee Bucks (July 30, 1997). ... Signed as free agent by Pistons (August 2, 1999).

COLLEGIATE RECORD

Season Team	G	Min.	FGM	FGA	Pct.	FTM	FTA	Pct.	Reb.	Ast.	Pts.	RPG	APG	PPG
86-87—Georgia Southern	31	594	59	116	.509	31	45	.689	87	29	149	2.8	0.9	4.8
87-88—Georgia Southern	31	836	82	151	.543	33	51	.647	154	44	198	5.0	1.4	6.4
88-89—Georgia Southern	29	1014	117	219	.534	75	108	.694	211	89	309	7.3	3.1	10.7
89-90—Georgia Southern	28	926	164	264	.621	137	170	.806	196	58	465	7.0	2.1	16.6
Totals	119	3370	422	750	.563	276	374	.738	648	220	1121	5.4	1.8	9.4

Three-point field goals: 1987-88, 1-for-6 (.167). 1988-89, 0-for-3. 1989-90, 0-for-3. Totals, 1-for-12 (.083).

CBA REGULAR-SEASON RECORD

Season Team	G	Min.	FGM	FGA	Pct.	FTM	FTA	Pct.	Reb.	Ast.	Pts.	RPG	APG	PPG
92-93—Capital Region	36	1391	268	482	.556	161	200	.805	179	75	698	5.0	2.1	19.4
95-96—Omaha	11	404	84	153	.549	46	61	.754	37	44	237	3.4	4.0	21.5
Totals	47	1795	352	635	.554	207	261	.793	216	119	935	4.6	2.5	19.9

Three-point field goals: 1992-93, 1-for-7 (.143). 1995-96, 23-for-55 (.418). Totals, 24-for-62 (.387).

ITALIAN LEAGUE RECORD

Season Team	G	Min.	FGM	FGA	Pct.	FTM	FTA	Pct.	Reb.	Ast.	Pts.	RPG	APG	PPG
93-94—S. Clear	15	581	110	206	.534	72	87	.828	74	21	323	4.9	1.4	21.5

NBA REGULAR-SEASON RECORD

Season Team	G	Min.	FGM	FGA	Pct.	FTM	FTA	Pct.	Off.	Def.	Tot.	Ast.	St.	Blk.	TO	Pts.	RPG	APG	PPG
93-94—Philadelphia	10	43	3	14	.214	3	4	.750	0	1	1	1	1	0	3	9	0.1	0.1	0.9
95-96—Was.-Det.	46	783	73	161	.453	45	62	.726	27	58	85	27	24	2	24	211	1.8	0.6	4.6
96-97—Detroit	81	1217	99	221	.448	97	108	.898	23	96	119	43	31	12	28	318	1.5	0.5	3.9
97-98—Milwaukee	82	1978	196	418	.469	147	176	.835	26	72	98	137	56	14	77	543	1.2	1.7	6.6
98-99—Milwaukee	50	1146	90	206	.437	63	79	.797	19	89	108	78	42	7	37	244	2.2	1.6	4.9
99-00—Detroit	82	1611	182	379	.480	141	168	.839	21	83	104	87	33	5	73	506	1.3	1.1	6.2
00-01—Detroit	68	1485	145	319	.455	62	73	.849	21	100	121	132	27	3	61	356	1.8	1.9	5.2
Totals	419	8263	788	1718	.459	558	670	.833	137	499	636	505	214	43	303	2187	1.5	1.2	5.2

Three-point field goals: 1993-94, 0-for-0. 1995-96, 20-for-53 (.377). 1996-97, 23-for-77 (.299). 1997-98, 4-for-9 (.444). 1998-99, 1-for-15 (.067). 1999-00, 1-for-5 (.200). 2000-01, 4-for-9 (.444). Totals, 53-for-170 (.312).

Personal fouls/disqualifications: 1995-96, 92/1. 1996-97, 128/0. 1997-98, 218/1. 1998-99, 135/0. 1999-00, 209/3. 2000-01, 173/0. Totals, 955/5.

NBA PLAYOFF RECORD

Season Team	G	Min.	FGM	FGA	Pct.	FTM	FTA	Pct.	Off.	Def.	Tot.	Ast.	St.	Blk.	TO	Pts.	RPG	APG	PPG
95-96—Detroit	3	43	3	7	.429	0	0	...	1	2	3	1	1	1	0	6	1.0	0.3	2.0
96-97—Detroit	2	7	1	2	.500	0	1	.000	0	1	1	0	0	0	2	2	0.5	0.0	1.0
98-99—Milwaukee	3	59	7	12	.583	6	6	1.000	1	3	4	3	2	1	2	20	1.3	1.0	6.7
99-00—Detroit	3	79	12	23	.522	4	6	.667	0	3	3	3	1	1	2	28	1.0	1.0	9.3
Totals	11	188	23	44	.523	10	13	.769	2	9	11	7	4	3	4	56	1.0	0.6	5.1

Three-point field goals: 1995-96, 0-for-1. 1998-99, 0-for-1. 1999-00, 0-for-2 (.000). Totals, 0-for-4 (.000).

Personal fouls/disqualifications: 1995-96, 5/0. 1996-97, 5/0. 1998-99, 8/0. 1999-00, 5/0. Totals, 19/0.

SPANISH LEAGUE RECORD

Season Team	G	Min.	FGM	FGA	Pct.	FTM	FTA	Pct.	Reb.	Ast.	Pts.	RPG	APG	PPG
94-95—Valvi Girona	38	1371	216	456	.474	171	214	.799	128	60	672	3.4	1.6	17.7

Three-point field goals: 1994-95, 69-for-176 (.392).

DAMPIER, ERICK　　　C　　　WARRIORS

PERSONAL: Born July 14, 1974, in Jackson, Miss. ... 6-11/265. (2,11/120,2). ... Full Name: Erick Trevez Dampier.
HIGH SCHOOL: Lawrence County (Monticello, Miss.).
COLLEGE: Mississippi State.
TRANSACTIONS/CAREER NOTES: Selected after junior season by Indiana Pacers in first round (10th pick overall) of 1996 NBA Draft. ... Traded by Pacers with F Duane Ferrell to Golden State Warriors for F Chris Mullin (August 12, 1997).

COLLEGIATE RECORD

Season Team	G	Min.	FGM	FGA	Pct.	FTM	FTA	Pct.	Reb.	Ast.	Pts.	RPG	APG	PPG
93-94—Mississippi State...........	29	678	133	226	.588	78	159	.491	251	23	344	8.7	0.8	11.9
94-95—Mississippi State...........	30	853	153	239	.640	87	146	.596	291	28	393	9.7	0.9	13.1
95-96—Mississippi State...........	34	1112	195	354	.551	104	170	.612	317	77	494	9.3	2.3	14.5
Totals	93	2643	481	819	.587	269	475	.566	859	128	1231	9.2	1.4	13.2

NBA REGULAR-SEASON RECORD

Season Team	G	Min.	FGM	FGA	Pct.	FTM	FTA	Pct.	Off.	Def.	Tot.	Ast.	St.	Blk.	TO	Pts.	RPG	APG	PPG
96-97—Indiana...........	72	1052	131	336	.390	107	168	.637	96	198	294	43	19	73	84	370	4.1	0.6	5.1
97-98—Golden State...	82	2656	352	791	.445	267	399	.669	272	443	715	94	39	139	175	971	8.7	1.1	11.8
98-99—Golden State...	50	1414	161	414	.389	120	204	.588	164	218	382	54	26	58	92	442	7.6	1.1	8.8
99-00—Golden State...	21	495	70	173	.405	27	51	.529	48	86	134	19	8	15	29	167	6.4	0.9	8.0
00-01—Golden State...	43	1038	126	314	.401	67	126	.532	97	153	250	59	17	58	82	319	5.8	1.4	7.4
Totals	268	6655	840	2028	.414	588	948	.620	677	1098	1775	269	109	343	462	2269	6.6	1.0	8.5

Three-point field goals: 1996-97, 1-for-1. 1997-98, 0-for-2. 2000-01, 0-for-2. Totals, 1-for-5 (.200).
Personal fouls/disqualifications: 1996-97, 153/1. 1997-98, 281/6. 1998-99, 165/2. 1999-00, 75/1. 2000-01, 123/3. Totals, 797/13.

DANIELS, ANTONIO　　　G　　　SPURS

D

PERSONAL: Born March 19, 1975, in Columbus, Ohio. ... 6-4/205. (1,93/93,0). ... Full Name: Antonio Robert Daniels.
HIGH SCHOOL: St. Francis DeSales (Columbus, Ohio).
COLLEGE: Bowling Green State.
TRANSACTIONS/CAREER NOTES: Selected by Vancouver Grizzlies in first round (fourth pick overall) of 1997 NBA Draft. ... Traded by Grizzlies to San Antonio Spurs for F Carl Herrera and draft rights to G Felipe Lopez (June 24, 1998).
MISCELLANEOUS: Member of NBA championship team (1999).

COLLEGIATE RECORD

Season Team	G	Min.	FGM	FGA	Pct.	FTM	FTA	Pct.	Reb.	Ast.	Pts.	RPG	APG	PPG
93-94—Bowling Green State.......	28	864	132	258	.512	84	103	.816	81	110	354	2.9	3.9	12.6
94-95—Bowling Green State.......	26	753	97	196	.495	58	83	.699	73	100	268	2.8	3.8	10.3
95-96—Bowling Green State.......	25	922	142	297	.478	99	137	.723	77	147	400	3.1	5.9	16.0
96-97—Bowling Green State.......	32	1161	279	510	.547	164	211	.777	90	216	767	2.8	6.8	24.0
Totals	111	3700	650	1261	.515	405	534	.758	321	573	1789	2.9	5.2	16.1

Three-point field goals: 1993-94, 4-for-17 (.235). 1994-95, 16-for-38 (.421). 1995-96, 17-for-37 (.459). 1996-97, 45-for-104 (.433). Totals, 82-for-196 (.418).

NBA REGULAR-SEASON RECORD

Season Team	G	Min.	FGM	FGA	Pct.	FTM	FTA	Pct.	Off.	Def.	Tot.	Ast.	St.	Blk.	TO	Pts.	RPG	APG	PPG
97-98—Vancouver.......	74	1956	228	548	.416	112	170	.659	22	121	143	334	55	10	164	579	1.9	4.5	7.8
98-99—San Antonio....	47	614	83	183	.454	49	65	.754	13	41	54	106	30	6	44	220	1.1	2.3	4.7
99-00—San Antonio....	68	1195	163	344	.474	72	101	.713	16	70	86	177	55	5	58	420	1.3	2.6	6.2
00-01—San Antonio....	79	2060	275	588	.468	121	156	.776	26	137	163	304	61	14	109	745	2.1	3.8	9.4
Totals	268	5825	749	1663	.450	354	492	.720	77	369	446	921	201	35	375	1964	1.7	3.4	7.3

Three-point field goals: 1997-98, 11-for-52 (.212). 1998-99, 5-for-17 (.294). 1999-00, 22-for-66 (.333). 2000-01, 74-for-183 (.404). Totals, 112-for-318 (.352).
Personal fouls/disqualifications: 1997-98, 88/0. 1998-99, 39/0. 1999-00, 73/0. 2000-01, 120/0. Totals, 320/0.

NBA PLAYOFF RECORD

Season Team	G	Min.	FGM	FGA	Pct.	FTM	FTA	Pct.	Off.	Def.	Tot.	Ast.	St.	Blk.	TO	Pts.	RPG	APG	PPG
98-99—San Antonio....	15	106	9	21	.429	5	6	.833	1	9	10	16	4	0	10	27	0.7	1.1	1.8
99-00—San Antonio....	4	82	9	23	.391	9	13	.692	2	8	10	6	7	0	6	29	2.5	1.5	7.3
00-01—San Antonio....	13	406	63	131	.481	33	35	.943	4	22	26	38	7	1	13	176	2.0	2.9	13.5
Totals	32	594	81	175	.463	47	54	.870	7	39	46	60	18	1	29	232	1.4	1.9	7.3

Three-point field goals: 1998-99, 4-for-6 (.667). 1999-00, 2-for-8 (.250). 2000-01, 17-for-46 (.370). Totals, 23-for-60 (.383).
Personal fouls/disqualifications: 1998-99, 7/0. 1999-00, 5/0. 2000-01, 22/0. Totals, 34/0.

DAVID, KORNEL　　　F

PERSONAL: Born October 22, 1971, in Hungary. ... 6-9/230. (2,06/104,3).
COLLEGE: Budapest AEH.
TRANSACTIONS/CAREER NOTES: Not drafted by an NBA franchise. ... Signed as free agent by Chicago Bulls (October 1, 1997). ... Waived by Bulls (October 28, 1997). ... Played in Continental Basketball Association with Rockford Lightning (1997-98). ... Played in Hungary (1997-98 and 1999-2000). ... Signed as free agent by Bulls (January 21, 1999). ... Waived by Bulls (January 3, 2000). ... Signed by Cleveland Cavaliers to the first of two consecutive 10-day contracts (January 6, 2000). ... Signed as free agent by Toronto Raptors (August 25, 2000). ... Traded by Raptors with F Corliss Williamson, F Tyrone Corbin and future first-round draft choice to Detroit Pistons for F Jerome Williams and C Eric Montross (February 22, 2001).

CBA REGULAR-SEASON RECORD

Season Team	G	Min.	FGM	FGA	Pct.	FTM	FTA	Pct.	Reb.	Ast.	Pts.	RPG	APG	PPG
												AVERAGES		
97-98—Rockford	1	4	0	0	...	0	0	...	1	1	0	1.0	1.0	0.0

HUNGARIAN LEAGUE RECORD

Season Team	G	Min.	FGM	FGA	Pct.	FTM	FTA	Pct.	Reb.	Ast.	Pts.	RPG	APG	PPG
												AVERAGES		
97-98—Albacomp-SZUV	32	1188	274	507	.540	150	203	.739	263	83	714	8.2	2.6	22.3
99-00—Albacomp-SZUV	2	49	10	17	.588	11	16	.688	12	4	31	6.0	2.0	15.5
Totals	34	1237	284	524	.542	161	219	.735	275	87	745	8.1	2.6	21.9

Three-point field goals: 1997-98, 16-for-46 (.348). 1999-00, 0-for-1. Totals, 16-for-47 (.340).

NBA REGULAR-SEASON RECORD

Season Team	G	Min.	FGM	FGA	Pct.	FTM	FTA	Pct.	Off.	Def.	Tot.	Ast.	St.	Blk.	TO	Pts.	RPG	APG	PPG
									REBOUNDS								AVERAGES		
98-99—Chicago	50	902	109	243	.449	90	111	.811	70	103	173	40	23	17	48	308	3.5	0.8	6.2
99-00—Chi.-Clev.	32	474	67	157	.427	45	56	.804	26	55	81	17	17	3	33	179	2.5	0.5	5.6
00-01—Tor.-Detroit	27	209	25	51	.490	12	13	.923	15	37	52	7	6	4	11	62	1.9	0.3	2.3
Totals	109	1585	201	451	.446	147	180	.817	111	195	306	64	46	24	92	549	2.8	0.6	5.0

Three-point field goals: 1998-99, 0-for-1. 1999-00, 0-for-3. Totals, 0-for-4 (.000).
Personal fouls/disqualifications: 1998-99, 88/0. 1999-00, 56/0. 2000-01, 28/0. Totals, 172/0.

DAVIS, ANTONIO   F/C   RAPTORS

PERSONAL: Born October 31, 1968, in Oakland. ... 6-9/230. (2,06/104,3). ... Full Name: Antonio Lee Davis.
HIGH SCHOOL: McClymonds (Oakland).
COLLEGE: Texas-El Paso.
TRANSACTIONS/CAREER NOTES: Selected by Indiana Pacers in second round (45th pick overall) of 1990 NBA Draft. ... Played in Greece (1990-91 and 1991-92). ... Played in Italy (1992-93). ... Traded by Pacers to Toronto Raptors for draft rights to F Jonathan Bender (August 1, 1999).

COLLEGIATE RECORD

Season Team	G	Min.	FGM	FGA	Pct.	FTM	FTA	Pct.	Reb.	Ast.	Pts.	RPG	APG	PPG
												AVERAGES		
86-87—Texas-El Paso	28	240	11	32	.344	13	30	.433	51	4	35	1.8	0.1	1.3
87-88—Texas-El Paso	30	907	108	183	.590	63	115	.548	195	20	279	6.5	0.7	9.3
88-89—Texas-El Paso	32	1014	162	298	.544	135	218	.619	255	14	459	8.0	0.4	14.3
89-90—Texas-El Paso	32	991	119	228	.522	106	165	.642	243	21	344	7.6	0.7	10.8
Totals	122	3152	400	741	.540	317	528	.600	744	59	1117	6.1	0.5	9.2

Three-point field goals: 1988-89, 0-for-1. 1989-90, 0-for-1. Totals, 0-for-2 (.000).

ITALIAN LEAGUE RECORD

Season Team	G	Min.	FGM	FGA	Pct.	FTM	FTA	Pct.	Reb.	Ast.	Pts.	RPG	APG	PPG
												AVERAGES		
92-93—Philips Milano	29	892	121	195	.621	81	130	.623	286	5	323	9.9	0.2	11.1

Three-point field goals: 1992-93, 0-for-1.

NBA REGULAR-SEASON RECORD

Season Team	G	Min.	FGM	FGA	Pct.	FTM	FTA	Pct.	Off.	Def.	Tot.	Ast.	St.	Blk.	TO	Pts.	RPG	APG	PPG
									REBOUNDS								AVERAGES		
93-94—Indiana	81	1732	216	425	.508	194	302	.642	190	315	505	55	45	84	107	626	6.2	0.7	7.7
94-95—Indiana	44	1030	109	245	.445	117	174	.672	105	175	280	25	19	29	64	335	6.4	0.6	7.6
95-96—Indiana	82	2092	236	482	.490	246	345	.713	188	313	501	43	33	66	87	719	6.1	0.5	8.8
96-97—Indiana	82	2335	308	641	.480	241	362	.666	190	408	598	65	42	84	141	858	7.3	0.8	10.5
97-98—Indiana	82	2191	254	528	.481	277	398	.696	192	368	560	61	45	72	103	785	6.8	0.7	9.6
98-99—Indiana	49	1271	164	348	.471	135	192	.703	116	228	344	33	22	42	50	463	7.0	0.7	9.4
99-00—Toronto	79	2479	313	712	.440	284	371	.765	235	461	696	105	38	100	121	910	8.8	1.3	11.5
00-01—Toronto	78	2729	375	866	.433	319	423	.754	274	513	787	106	22	151	135	1069	10.1	1.4	13.7
Totals	577	15859	1975	4247	.465	1813	2567	.706	1490	2781	4271	493	266	628	808	5765	7.4	0.9	10.0

Three-point field goals: 1993-94, 0-for-1. 1995-96, 1-for-2 (.500). 1996-97, 1-for-14 (.071). 1997-98, 0-for-3. 2000-01, 0-for-1. Totals, 2-for-21 (.095).
Personal fouls/disqualifications: 1993-94, 189/1. 1994-95, 134/2. 1995-96, 248/6. 1996-97, 260/4. 1997-98, 234/6. 1998-99, 136/3. 1999-00, 267/2. 2000-01, 230/4. Totals, 1698/28.

NBA PLAYOFF RECORD

Season Team	G	Min.	FGM	FGA	Pct.	FTM	FTA	Pct.	Off.	Def.	Tot.	Ast.	St.	Blk.	TO	Pts.	RPG	APG	PPG
									REBOUNDS								AVERAGES		
93-94—Indiana	16	401	48	89	.539	37	66	.561	37	69	106	7	11	18	22	134	6.6	0.4	8.4
94-95—Indiana	17	367	32	71	.451	37	59	.627	38	59	97	7	9	11	23	101	5.7	0.4	5.9
95-96—Indiana	5	127	13	25	.520	13	15	.867	12	19	31	3	3	6	10	39	6.2	0.6	7.8
97-98—Indiana	16	459	42	91	.462	63	94	.670	37	71	108	14	12	18	25	147	6.8	0.9	9.2
98-99—Indiana	13	326	31	75	.413	41	62	.661	23	69	92	8	5	14	20	103	7.1	0.6	7.9
99-00—Toronto	3	105	14	24	.583	11	14	.786	7	18	25	3	1	4	4	39	8.3	1.0	13.0
00-01—Toronto	12	485	77	154	.500	43	53	.811	41	92	133	23	10	22	21	197	11.1	1.9	16.4
Totals	82	2270	257	529	.486	245	363	.675	195	397	592	65	51	93	125	760	7.2	0.8	9.3

Three-point field goals: 1993-94, 1-for-1. Totals, 1-for-1 (1.000).
Personal fouls/disqualifications: 1993-94, 47/0. 1994-95, 61/0. 1995-96, 12/0. 1997-98, 65/5. 1998-99, 39/0. 1999-00, 9/0. 2000-01, 35/0. Totals, 268/5.

NBA ALL-STAR GAME RECORD

Season Team	Min.	FGM	FGA	Pct.	FTM	FTA	Pct.	Off.	Def.	Tot.	Ast.	PF	Dq.	St.	Blk.	TO	Pts.
								REBOUNDS									
2001 —Toronto	20	4	11	.364	0	0	...	7	2	9	0	0	0	1	1	0	8

DAVIS, BARON　　　　　　　G　　　　　　　HORNETS

PERSONAL: Born April 13, 1979, in Los Angeles. ... 6-3/212. (1,91/96,2).
HIGH SCHOOL: Crossroads (Santa Monica, Calif.).
COLLEGE: UCLA.
TRANSACTIONS/CAREER NOTES: Selected after sophomore season by Charlotte Hornets in first round (third pick overall) of 1999 NBA Draft.

COLLEGIATE RECORD

Season Team	G	Min.	FGM	FGA	Pct.	FTM	FTA	Pct.	Reb.	Ast.	Pts.	RPG	APG	PPG
97-98—UCLA	32	1003	137	259	.529	75	111	.676	129	161	373	4.0	5.0	11.7
98-99—UCLA	27	828	150	312	.481	94	157	.599	97	97	429	3.6	3.6	15.9
Totals	59	1831	287	571	.503	169	268	.631	226	258	802	3.8	4.4	13.6

Three-point field goals: 1997-98, 24-for-78 (.308). 1998-99, 59-for-180 (.328). Totals, 83-for-258 (.322).

NBA REGULAR-SEASON RECORD

Season Team	G	Min.	FGM	FGA	Pct.	FTM	FTA	Pct.	Off.	Def.	Tot.	Ast.	St.	Blk.	TO	Pts.	RPG	APG	PPG
99-00—Charlotte	82	1523	182	433	.420	97	153	.634	48	117	165	309	97	19	140	486	2.0	3.8	5.9
00-01—Charlotte	82	3192	409	957	.427	228	337	.677	129	279	408	598	170	36	226	1131	5.0	7.3	13.8
Totals	164	4715	591	1390	.425	325	490	.663	177	396	573	907	267	55	366	1617	3.5	5.5	9.9

Three-point field goals: 1999-00, 25-for-111 (.225). 2000-01, 85-for-274 (.310). Totals, 110-for-385 (.286).
Personal fouls/disqualifications: 1999-00, 201/1. 2000-01, 267/1. Totals, 468/2.

NBA PLAYOFF RECORD

Season Team	G	Min.	FGM	FGA	Pct.	FTM	FTA	Pct.	Off.	Def.	Tot.	Ast.	St.	Blk.	TO	Pts.	RPG	APG	PPG
99-00—Charlotte	4	57	10	23	.435	2	4	.500	3	3	6	6	4	0	3	23	1.5	1.5	5.8
00-01—Charlotte	10	397	59	123	.480	40	56	.714	9	35	44	58	28	5	22	178	4.4	5.8	17.8
Totals	14	454	69	146	.473	42	60	.700	12	38	50	64	32	5	25	201	3.6	4.6	14.4

Three-point field goals: 1999-00, 1-for-6 (.167). 2000-01, 20-for-50 (.400). Totals, 21-for-56 (.375).
Personal fouls/disqualifications: 1999-00, 6/0. 2000-01, 33/0. Totals, 39/0.

DAVIS, DALE　　　　　　　F　　　　　　TRAIL BLAZERS

PERSONAL: Born March 25, 1969, in Toccoa, Ga. ... 6-11/252. (2,11/114,3). ... Full Name: Elliott Lydell Davis.
HIGH SCHOOL: Stephens County (Toccoa, Ga.).
COLLEGE: Clemson.
TRANSACTIONS/CAREER NOTES: Selected by Indiana Pacers in first round (13th pick overall) of 1991 NBA Draft. ... Traded by Pacers to Portland Trail Blazers for F Jermaine O'Neal and C Joe Kleine (August 31, 2000).

COLLEGIATE RECORD

Season Team	G	Min.	FGM	FGA	Pct.	FTM	FTA	Pct.	Reb.	Ast.	Pts.	RPG	APG	PPG
87-88—Clemson	29	714	91	171	.532	45	89	.506	223	10	227	7.7	0.3	7.8
88-89—Clemson	29	736	146	218	.670	93	144	.646	258	16	385	8.9	0.6	13.3
89-90—Clemson	35	1077	205	328	.625	127	213	.596	395	21	537	11.3	0.6	15.3
90-91—Clemson	28	971	191	359	.532	119	205	.580	340	37	501	12.1	1.3	17.9
Totals	121	3498	633	1076	.588	384	651	.590	1216	84	1650	10.0	0.7	13.6

Three-point field goals: 1989-90, 0-for-1. 1990-91, 0-for-2. Totals, 0-for-3 (.000).

NBA REGULAR-SEASON RECORD

Season Team	G	Min.	FGM	FGA	Pct.	FTM	FTA	Pct.	Off.	Def.	Tot.	Ast.	St.	Blk.	TO	Pts.	RPG	APG	PPG
91-92—Indiana	64	1301	154	279	.552	87	152	.572	158	252	410	30	27	74	49	395	6.4	0.5	6.2
92-93—Indiana	82	2264	304	535	.568	119	225	.529	291	432	723	69	63	148	79	727	8.8	0.8	8.9
93-94—Indiana	66	2292	308	582	.529	155	294	.527	280	438	718	100	48	106	102	771	10.9	1.5	11.7
94-95—Indiana	74	2346	324	576	.563	138	259	.533	259	437	696	58	72	116	124	786	9.4	0.8	10.6
95-96—Indiana	78	2617	334	599	.558	135	289	.467	252	457	709	76	56	112	119	803	9.1	1.0	10.3
96-97—Indiana	80	2589	370	688	.538	92	215	.428	301	471	772	59	60	77	108	832	9.7	0.7	10.4
97-98—Indiana	78	2174	273	498	.548	80	172	.465	233	378	611	70	51	87	73	626	7.8	0.9	8.0
98-99—Indiana	50	1374	161	302	.533	76	123	.618	155	261	416	22	20	57	43	398	8.3	0.4	8.0
99-00—Indiana	74	2127	302	602	.502	139	203	.685	256	473	729	64	52	94	91	743	9.9	0.9	10.0
00-01—Portland	81	2162	242	487	.497	96	152	.632	233	373	606	103	44	76	67	580	7.5	1.3	7.2
Totals	727	21246	2772	5148	.538	1117	2084	.536	2418	3972	6390	651	493	947	855	6661	8.8	0.9	9.2

Three-point field goals: 1991-92, 0-for-1. 1993-94, 0-for-1. 1994-95, 0-for-1. 2000-01, 0-for-4. Totals, 0-for-7 (.000).
Personal fouls/disqualifications: 1991-92, 191/2. 1992-93, 274/5. 1993-94, 214/1. 1994-95, 222/2. 1995-96, 238/0. 1996-97, 233/3. 1997-98, 209/1. 1998-99, 115/0. 1999-00, 203/1. 2000-01, 199/0. Totals, 2098/15.

NBA PLAYOFF RECORD

Season Team	G	Min.	FGM	FGA	Pct.	FTM	FTA	Pct.	Off.	Def.	Tot.	Ast.	St.	Blk.	TO	Pts.	RPG	APG	PPG
91-92—Indiana	3	69	4	10	.400	0	0	...	5	14	19	2	0	5	1	8	6.3	0.7	2.7
92-93—Indiana	4	117	8	12	.667	1	4	.250	4	28	32	4	4	4	3	17	8.0	1.0	4.3
93-94—Indiana	16	578	56	106	.528	11	36	.306	63	96	159	11	18	17	30	123	9.9	0.7	7.7
94-95—Indiana	17	490	56	105	.533	23	47	.489	53	83	136	6	7	14	22	135	8.0	0.4	7.9
95-96—Indiana	5	184	16	31	.516	4	11	.364	20	36	56	4	3	6	10	36	11.2	0.8	7.2
97-98—Indiana	16	466	56	86	.651	29	64	.453	44	76	120	12	5	18	21	141	7.5	0.8	8.8

Season Team	G	Min.	FGM	FGA	Pct.	FTM	FTA	Pct.	REBOUNDS Off.	Def.	Tot.	Ast.	St.	Blk.	TO	Pts.	AVERAGES RPG	APG	PPG
98-99—Indiana	13	394	45	77	.584	28	50	.560	45	87	132	11	10	18	21	118	10.2	0.8	9.1
99-00—Indiana	23	714	79	151	.523	32	59	.542	83	180	263	17	11	31	18	190	11.4	0.7	8.3
00-01—Portland	2	20	0	2	.000	1	2	.500	3	1	4	0	1	0	1	1	2.0	0.0	0.5
Totals	99	3032	320	580	.552	129	273	.473	320	601	921	67	59	113	127	769	9.3	0.7	7.8

Three-point field goals: 1993-94, 0-for-1. 2000-01, 0-for-1. Totals, 0-for-2 (.000).

Personal fouls/disqualifications: 1991-92, 8/0. 1992-93, 15/0. 1993-94, 52/0. 1994-95, 56/0. 1995-96, 16/0. 1997-98, 42/0. 1998-99, 42/0. 1999-00, 83/4. 2000-01, 7/1. Totals, 321/5.

NBA ALL-STAR GAME RECORD

Season Team	Min.	FGM	FGA	Pct.	FTM	FTA	Pct.	REBOUNDS Off.	Def.	Tot.	Ast.	PF	Dq.	St.	Blk.	TO	Pts.
2000 —Indiana	14	2	3	.667	0	0	...	3	5	8	1	0	...	0	0	0	4

DAVIS, EMANUAL   G   HAWKS

PERSONAL: Born August 27, 1968, in Philadelphia. ... 6-5/195. (1,96/88,5).
HIGH SCHOOL: Kensington (Philadelphia).
COLLEGE: Delaware State.
TRANSACTIONS/CAREER NOTES: Not drafted by an NBA franchise. ... Played in United States Basketball League with Philadelphia Spirit (1991). ... Signed as free agent by New Jersey Nets (September 30, 1991). ... Waived by Nets (October 25, 1991). ... Played in American Basketball Association with Allentown Jets (1992-93). ... Played in Continental Basketball Association with Yakima Sun Kings (1992-93) and Rockford Lightning (1993-94 and 1995-96). ... Played in Italy (1994-95). ... Signed as free agent by Milwaukee Bucks (October 5, 1995). ... Waived by Bucks (October 25, 1995). ... Signed as free agent by Houston Rockets (June 26, 1996). ... Played in France (1998-99). ... Signed as free agent by Seattle SuperSonics (August 20, 1999). ... Traded by SuperSonics to Los Angeles Lakers as part of four-team trade in which Knicks acquired F Glen Rice, C Luc Longley, F/C Travis Knight, G Vernon Maxwell, C Vladimir Stepania, F Lazaro Borrell, two 2001 first-round draft choices and two 2001 second-round draft choices, SuperSonics acquired C Patrick Ewing, Phoenix Suns acquired C Chris Dudley and 2001 first-round draft choice and Lakers acquired F Horace Grant, C Greg Foster and F Chuck Person (September 20, 2000). ... Waived by Lakers (October 25, 2000). ... Claimed on waivers by SuperSonics (October 27, 2000). ... Signed as free agent by Atlanta Hawks (July 27, 2001).

COLLEGIATE RECORD

Season Team	G	Min.	FGM	FGA	Pct.	FTM	FTA	Pct.	Reb.	Ast.	Pts.	AVERAGES RPG	APG	PPG
88-89—Delaware State	19	...	126	285	.442	80	119	.672	128	83	390	6.7	4.4	20.5
89-90—Delaware State	28	...	119	259	.459	94	126	.746	135	156	386	4.8	5.6	13.8
90-91—Delaware State	25	838	165	328	.503	122	163	.748	118	139	493	4.7	5.6	19.7
Totals	72	...	410	872	.470	296	408	.725	381	378	1269	5.3	5.3	17.6

Three-point field goals: 1988-89, 58-for-172 (.337). 1989-90, 54-for-138 (.391). 1990-91, 41-for-106 (.387). Totals, 153-for-416 (.368).

CBA REGULAR-SEASON RECORD

NOTES: CBA Defensive Player of the Year (1996). ... CBA All-League first team (1996). ... CBA All-Defensive team (1996).

Season Team	G	Min.	FGM	FGA	Pct.	FTM	FTA	Pct.	Reb.	Ast.	Pts.	AVERAGES RPG	APG	PPG
92-93—Yakima	7	78	13	28	.464	7	8	.875	9	12	33	1.3	1.7	4.7
93-94—Rockford	34	700	89	184	.484	54	66	.818	116	129	243	3.4	3.8	7.1
95-96—Rockford	52	1936	258	543	.475	157	203	.773	259	342	720	5.0	6.6	13.8
Totals	93	2714	360	755	.477	218	277	.787	384	483	996	4.1	5.2	10.7

Three-point field goals: 1993-94, 11-for-29 (.379). 1995-96, 47-for-138 (.341). Totals, 58-for-167 (.347).

ITALIAN LEAGUE RECORD

Season Team	G	Min.	FGM	FGA	Pct.	FTM	FTA	Pct.	Reb.	Ast.	Pts.	AVERAGES RPG	APG	PPG
94-95—Rimini	33	1070	140	215	.651	89	113	.788	198	68	436	6.0	2.1	13.2

NBA REGULAR-SEASON RECORD

Season Team	G	Min.	FGM	FGA	Pct.	FTM	FTA	Pct.	REBOUNDS Off.	Def.	Tot.	Ast.	St.	Blk.	TO	Pts.	AVERAGES RPG	APG	PPG
96-97—Houston	13	230	24	54	.444	5	8	.625	2	20	22	26	9	2	17	65	1.7	2.0	5.0
97-98—Houston	45	599	63	142	.444	31	37	.838	10	37	47	59	17	3	52	184	1.0	1.3	4.1
99-00—Seattle	54	701	80	220	.364	26	38	.684	15	85	100	70	38	5	44	217	1.9	1.3	4.0
00-01—Seattle	62	1290	133	318	.418	45	55	.818	28	126	154	137	64	12	77	361	2.5	2.2	5.8
Totals	174	2820	300	734	.409	107	138	.775	55	268	323	292	128	22	190	827	1.9	1.7	4.8

Three-point field goals: 1996-97, 12-for-27 (.444). 1997-98, 27-for-72 (.375). 1999-00, 31-for-103 (.301). 2000-01, 50-for-127 (.394). Totals, 120-for-329 (.365).

Personal fouls/disqualifications: 1996-97, 20/0. 1997-98, 55/0. 1999-00, 72/0. 2000-01, 101/0. Totals, 248/0.

FRENCH LEAGUE RECORD

Season Team	G	Min.	FGM	FGA	Pct.	FTM	FTA	Pct.	Reb.	Ast.	Pts.	AVERAGES RPG	APG	PPG
98-99—Pau Orthez	12	309	49	94	.521	15	22	.682	43	41	120	3.6	3.4	10.0

Three-point field goals: 1998-99, 7-for-23 (.304).

DID YOU KNOW . . .

... that the Los Angeles Clippers played five overtime games in February 2001? It was the most of any NBA team in one month since the Rochester Royals played five OT games in January 1953.

DAVIS, HUBERT　　　　　　　G　　　　　　WIZARDS

PERSONAL: Born May 17, 1970, in Winston-Salem, N.C. ... 6-5/183. (1,96/83,0). ... Full Name: Hubert Ira Davis Jr. ... Nephew of Walter Davis, forward/guard with Phoenix Suns (1977-78 through 1987-88), Denver Nuggets (1988-89 through 1990-91 and 1991-92) and Portland Trail Blazers (1990-91).
HIGH SCHOOL: Lake Braddock Secondary School (Burke, Va.).
COLLEGE: North Carolina.
TRANSACTIONS/CAREER NOTES: Selected by New York Knicks in first round (20th pick overall) of 1992 NBA Draft. ... Traded by Knicks to Toronto Raptors for 1997 first-round draft choice (July 24, 1996). ... Signed as free agent by Dallas Mavericks (September 4, 1997). ... Traded by Mavericks with F/C Christian Laettner, G Courtney Alexander, F Loy Vaught, F/C Etan Thomas and cash considerations to Washington Wizards for F Juwan Howard, C Calvin Booth and F Obinna Ekezie (February 22, 2001).

COLLEGIATE RECORD

Season Team	G	Min.	FGM	FGA	Pct.	FTM	FTA	Pct.	Reb.	Ast.	Pts.	RPG	APG	PPG
88-89—North Carolina	35	248	44	86	.512	24	31	.774	27	9	116	0.8	0.3	3.3
89-90—North Carolina	34	725	111	249	.446	59	74	.797	60	52	325	1.8	1.5	9.6
90-91—North Carolina	35	851	161	309	.521	81	97	.835	85	66	467	2.4	1.9	13.3
91-92—North Carolina	33	1095	241	474	.508	140	169	.828	76	52	707	2.3	1.6	21.4
Totals	137	2919	557	1118	.498	304	371	.819	248	179	1615	1.8	1.3	11.8

Three-point field goals: 1988-89, 4-for-13 (.308). 1989-90, 44-for-111 (.396). 1990-91, 64-for-131 (.489). 1991-92, 85-for-198 (.429). Totals, 197-for-453 (.435).

NBA REGULAR-SEASON RECORD

NOTES: Led NBA with .491 three-point field goal percentage (2000).

Season Team	G	Min.	FGM	FGA	Pct.	FTM	FTA	Pct.	Off.	Def.	Tot.	Ast.	St.	Blk.	TO	Pts.	RPG	APG	PPG
92-93—New York	50	815	110	251	.438	43	54	.796	13	43	56	83	22	4	45	269	1.1	1.7	5.4
93-94—New York	56	1333	238	505	.471	85	103	.825	23	44	67	165	40	4	76	614	1.2	2.9	11.0
94-95—New York	82	1697	296	617	.480	97	120	.808	30	80	110	150	35	11	87	820	1.3	1.8	10.0
95-96—New York	74	1773	275	566	.486	112	129	.868	35	88	123	103	31	8	63	789	1.7	1.4	10.7
96-97—Toronto	36	623	74	184	.402	17	23	.739	11	29	40	34	11	2	21	181	1.1	0.9	5.0
97-98—Dallas	81	2378	350	767	.456	97	116	.836	34	135	169	157	43	5	88	898	2.1	1.9	11.1
98-99—Dallas	50	1378	174	397	.438	44	50	.880	3	83	86	89	21	3	57	457	1.7	1.8	9.1
99-00—Dallas	79	1817	217	464	.468	67	77	.870	17	117	134	141	24	3	70	583	1.7	1.8	7.4
00-01—Dallas-Wash.	66	1692	196	433	.453	54	62	.871	28	111	139	110	35	1	81	524	2.1	1.7	7.9
Totals	574	13506	1930	4184	.461	616	734	.839	194	730	924	1032	262	41	588	5135	1.6	1.8	8.9

Three-point field goals: 1992-93, 6-for-19 (.316). 1993-94, 53-for-132 (.402). 1994-95, 131-for-288 (.455). 1995-96, 127-for-267 (.476). 1996-97, 16-for-70 (.229). 1997-98, 101-for-230 (.439). 1998-99, 65-for-144 (.451). 1999-00, 82-for-167 (.491). 2000-01, 78-for-171 (.456). Totals, 659-for-1488 (.443).

Personal fouls/disqualifications: 1992-93, 71/1. 1993-94, 118/0. 1994-95, 146/1. 1995-96, 120/1. 1996-97, 40/0. 1997-98, 117/0. 1998-99, 76/0. 1999-00, 109/0. 2000-01, 121/0. Totals, 918/3.

NBA PLAYOFF RECORD

Season Team	G	Min.	FGM	FGA	Pct.	FTM	FTA	Pct.	Off.	Def.	Tot.	Ast.	St.	Blk.	TO	Pts.	RPG	APG	PPG
92-93—New York	7	96	14	25	.560	2	3	.667	1	5	6	5	6	0	9	31	0.9	0.7	4.4
93-94—New York	23	396	44	121	.364	23	32	.719	5	16	21	26	5	3	23	121	0.9	1.1	5.3
94-95—New York	11	184	17	48	.354	2	2	1.000	0	7	7	9	1	5	9	46	0.6	0.8	4.2
95-96—New York	8	145	17	31	.548	9	11	.818	4	8	12	4	0	0	7	53	1.5	0.5	6.6
Totals	49	821	92	225	.409	36	48	.750	10	36	46	44	12	8	48	251	0.9	0.9	5.1

Three-point field goals: 1992-93, 1-for-2 (.500). 1993-94, 10-for-35 (.286). 1994-95, 10-for-27 (.370). 1995-96, 10-for-19 (.526). Totals, 31-for-83 (.373).

Personal fouls/disqualifications: 1992-93, 8/0. 1993-94, 43/0. 1994-95, 20/0. 1995-96, 12/0. Totals, 83/0.

DAVIS, RICKY　　　　　　　G　　　　　　HEAT

PERSONAL: Born September 23, 1979, in Las Vegas. ... 6-7/197. (2,01/89,4). ... Full Name: Tyree Ricardo Davis.
HIGH SCHOOL: North (Davenport, Iowa).
COLLEGE: Iowa.
TRANSACTIONS/CAREER NOTES: Selected after freshman season by Charlotte Hornets in first round (21st pick overall) of 1998 NBA Draft. ... Traded by Hornets with G Eddie Jones, F Anthony Mason and G/F Dale Ellis to Miami Heat for F P.J. Brown, F Jamal Mashburn, F/C Otis Thorpe, F Tim James and G/F Rodney Buford (August 1, 2000).

COLLEGIATE RECORD

Season Team	G	Min.	FGM	FGA	Pct.	FTM	FTA	Pct.	Reb.	Ast.	Pts.	RPG	APG	PPG
97-98—Iowa	31	825	173	371	.466	90	129	.698	148	74	464	4.8	2.4	15.0

Three-point field goals: 1997-98, 28-for-91 (.308).

NBA REGULAR-SEASON RECORD

Season Team	G	Min.	FGM	FGA	Pct.	FTM	FTA	Pct.	Off.	Def.	Tot.	Ast.	St.	Blk.	TO	Pts.	RPG	APG	PPG
98-99—Charlotte	46	557	81	200	.405	45	59	.763	40	44	84	58	30	7	54	209	1.8	1.3	4.5
99-00—Charlotte	48	570	94	187	.503	39	51	.765	29	54	83	62	30	8	46	227	1.7	1.3	4.7
00-01—Miami	7	70	12	29	.414	7	8	.875	1	6	7	11	5	2	5	32	1.0	1.6	4.6
Totals	101	1197	187	416	.450	91	118	.771	70	104	174	131	65	17	105	468	1.7	1.3	4.6

Three-point field goals: 1998-99, 2-for-12 (.167). 1999-00, 0-for-4. 2000-01, 1-for-1. Totals, 3-for-17 (.176).
Personal fouls/disqualifications: 1998-99, 46/0. 1999-00, 39/0. 2000-01, 7/0. Totals, 92/0.

DAVIS, TERRY   F/C

PERSONAL: Born June 17, 1967, in Danville, Va. ... 6-10/250. (2,08/113,4). ... Full Name: Terry Raymond Davis.
HIGH SCHOOL: George Washington (Danville, Va.).
COLLEGE: Virginia Union.
TRANSACTIONS/CAREER NOTES: Not drafted by an NBA franchise. ... Signed as free agent by Miami Heat (September 28, 1989). ... Signed as unrestricted free agent by Dallas Mavericks (August 6, 1991). ... Waived by Mavericks (October 29, 1996). ... Signed as free agent by Washington Wizards (October 27, 1997). ... Traded by Wizards with F Ben Wallace, G Tim Legler and G Jeff McInnis to Orlando Magic for C Isaac Austin (August 11, 1999). ... Waived by Magic (October 29, 1999). ... Signed as free agent by Denver Nuggets (September 26, 2000).

COLLEGIATE RECORD

Season Team	G	Min.	FGM	FGA	Pct.	FTM	FTA	Pct.	Reb.	Ast.	Pts.	RPG	APG	PPG
85-86—Virginia Union	27	...	42	91	.462	26	43	.605	116	9	110	4.3	0.3	4.1
86-87—Virginia Union	32	...	135	259	.521	98	142	.690	360	23	368	11.3	0.7	11.5
87-88—Virginia Union	31	...	257	454	.566	191	267	.715	338	...	705	10.9	...	22.7
88-89—Virginia Union	31	1034	272	442	.615	148	217	.682	369	40	692	11.9	1.3	22.3
Totals	121	...	706	1246	.567	463	669	.692	1183	...	1875	9.8	...	15.5

Three-point field goals: 1988-89, 0-for-1.

NBA REGULAR-SEASON RECORD

Season Team	G	Min.	FGM	FGA	Pct.	FTM	FTA	Pct.	REBOUNDS			Ast.	St.	Blk.	TO	Pts.	AVERAGES		
									Off.	Def.	Tot.						RPG	APG	PPG
89-90—Miami	63	884	122	262	.466	54	87	.621	93	136	229	25	25	28	68	298	3.6	0.4	4.7
90-91—Miami	55	996	115	236	.487	69	124	.556	107	159	266	39	18	28	36	300	4.8	0.7	5.5
91-92—Dallas	68	2149	256	531	.482	181	285	.635	228	444	672	57	26	29	117	693	9.9	0.8	10.2
92-93—Dallas	75	2462	393	863	.455	167	281	.594	259	442	701	68	36	28	160	955	9.3	0.9	12.7
93-94—Dallas	15	286	24	59	.407	8	12	.667	30	44	74	6	9	1	5	56	4.9	0.4	3.7
94-95—Dallas	46	580	49	113	.434	42	66	.636	63	93	156	10	6	3	30	140	3.4	0.2	3.0
95-96—Dallas	28	501	55	108	.509	27	47	.574	43	74	117	21	10	4	25	137	4.2	0.8	4.9
97-98—Washington	74	1705	127	256	.496	69	119	.580	209	271	480	30	41	24	56	323	6.5	0.4	4.4
98-99—Washington	37	578	49	92	.533	28	38	.737	50	89	139	10	11	3	16	126	3.8	0.3	3.4
00-01—Denver	19	228	12	25	.480	9	22	.409	24	29	53	7	1	1	5	33	2.8	0.4	1.7
Totals	480	10369	1202	2545	.472	654	1081	.605	1106	1781	2887	273	183	149	518	3061	6.0	0.6	6.4

Three-point field goals: 1989-90, 0-for-1. 1990-91, 1-for-2 (.500). 1991-92, 0-for-5. 1992-93, 2-for-8 (.250). 1994-95, 0-for-2. 1997-98, 0-for-1. Totals, 3-for-19 (.158).

Personal fouls/disqualifications: 1989-90, 171/2. 1990-91, 129/2. 1991-92, 202/1. 1992-93, 199/3. 1993-94, 27/0. 1994-95, 76/2. 1995-96, 66/2. 1997-98, 193/4. 1998-99, 79/0. 2000-01, 34/0. Totals, 1176/16.

D

DAY, TODD   G/F

PERSONAL: Born January 7, 1970, in Decatur, Ill. ... 6-6/188. (1,98/85,3). ... Full Name: Todd Fitzgerald Day.
HIGH SCHOOL: Hamilton (Memphis).
COLLEGE: Arkansas.
TRANSACTIONS/CAREER NOTES: Selected by Milwaukee Bucks in first round (eighth pick overall) of 1992 NBA Draft. ... Traded by Bucks with C Alton Lister to Boston Celtics for G Sherman Douglas (November 26, 1995). ... Signed as free agent by Miami Heat (September 17, 1997). ... Waived by Heat (November 22, 1997). ... Played in Italy (1997-98). ... Played in Continental Basketball Association with La Crosse Bobcats (1998-99). ... Signed as free agent by Phoenix Suns (October 4, 1999). ... Signed as free agent by Minnesota Timberwolves (October 3, 2000). ... Waived by Timberwolves (February 27, 2001).
MISCELLANEOUS: Member of bronze-medal-winning U.S. World Championship team (1990).

COLLEGIATE RECORD

NOTES: THE SPORTING NEWS All-America second team (1992).

Season Team	G	Min.	FGM	FGA	Pct.	FTM	FTA	Pct.	Reb.	Ast.	Pts.	RPG	APG	PPG
88-89—Arkansas	32	741	148	328	.451	98	137	.715	129	49	425	4.0	1.5	13.3
89-90—Arkansas	35	1008	237	483	.491	139	183	.760	188	89	684	5.4	2.5	19.5
90-91—Arkansas	38	1121	277	586	.473	165	221	.747	201	111	786	5.3	2.9	20.7
91-92—Arkansas	22	711	173	347	.499	97	127	.764	155	70	500	7.0	3.2	22.7
Totals	127	3581	835	1744	.479	499	668	.747	673	319	2395	5.3	2.5	18.9

Three-point field goals: 1988-89, 31-for-90 (.344). 1989-90, 71-for-176 (.403). 1990-91, 67-for-189 (.354). 1991-92, 57-for-133 (.429). Totals, 226-for-588 (.384).

NBA REGULAR-SEASON RECORD

Season Team	G	Min.	FGM	FGA	Pct.	FTM	FTA	Pct.	REBOUNDS			Ast.	St.	Blk.	TO	Pts.	AVERAGES		
									Off.	Def.	Tot.						RPG	APG	PPG
92-93—Milwaukee	71	1931	358	828	.432	213	297	.717	144	147	291	117	75	48	118	983	4.1	1.6	13.8
93-94—Milwaukee	76	2127	351	845	.415	231	331	.698	115	195	310	138	103	52	129	966	4.1	1.8	12.7
94-95—Milwaukee	82	2717	445	1049	.424	257	341	.754	95	227	322	134	104	63	157	1310	3.9	1.6	16.0
95-96—Mil.-Boston	79	1807	299	817	.366	224	287	.780	70	154	224	107	81	51	109	922	2.8	1.4	11.7
96-97—Boston	81	2277	398	999	.398	256	331	.773	109	221	330	117	108	48	127	1178	4.1	1.4	14.5
97-98—Miami	5	69	11	31	.355	9	9	.667	4	2	6	7	7	0	3	30	1.2	1.4	6.0
99-00—Phoenix	58	941	130	330	.394	72	108	.667	31	98	129	65	44	22	50	396	2.2	1.1	6.8
00-01—Minnesota	31	345	44	118	.373	18	23	.783	10	27	37	28	10	7	24	132	1.2	0.9	4.3
Totals	483	12214	2036	5017	.406	1277	1727	.739	578	1071	1649	713	532	291	717	5917	3.4	1.5	12.3

Three-point field goals: 1992-93, 54-for-184 (.293). 1993-94, 33-for-148 (.223). 1994-95, 163-for-418 (.390). 1995-96, 100-for-302 (.331). 1996-97, 126-for-348 (.362). 1997-98, 2-for-12 (.167). 1999-00, 64-for-165 (.388). 2000-01, 26-for-69 (.377). Totals, 568-for-1646 (.345).

Personal fouls/disqualifications: 1992-93, 222/1. 1993-94, 221/4. 1994-95, 283/6. 1995-96, 225/2. 1996-97, 208/0. 1997-98, 10/0. 1999-00, 127/1. 2000-01, 52/0. Totals, 1348/14.

Season Team	G	Min.	FGM	FGA	Pct.	FTM	FTA	Pct.	REBOUNDS Off.	Def.	Tot.	Ast.	St.	Blk.	TO	Pts.	AVERAGES RPG	APG	PPG
99-00—Phoenix	9	100	16	35	.457	5	10	.500	6	4	10	4	4	1	4	42	1.1	0.4	4.7

Three-point field goals: 1999-00, 5-for-16 (.313).
Personal fouls/disqualifications: 1999-00, 24/0.

ITALIAN LEAGUE RECORD

Season Team	G	Min.	FGM	FGA	Pct.	FTM	FTA	Pct.	Reb.	Ast.	Pts.	AVERAGES RPG	APG	PPG
97-98—Scavolini Pesaro............	13	419	50	129	.388	41	59	.695	59	4	202	4.5	0.3	15.5

Three-point field goals: 1997-98, 20-for-74 (.270).

CBA REGULAR-SEASON RECORD

Season Team	G	Min.	FGM	FGA	Pct.	FTM	FTA	Pct.	Reb.	Ast.	Pts.	AVERAGES RPG	APG	PPG
98-99—La Crosse	21	828	132	352	.375	116	160	.725	106	66	416	5.1	3.1	19.8

Three-point field goals: 1998-99, 36-for-112 (.321).

DeCLERCQ, ANDREW   F/C   MAGIC

PERSONAL: Born February 1, 1973, in Detroit. ... 6-10/255. (2,08/115,7). ... Name pronounced Dah-CLAIR-k.
HIGH SCHOOL: Countryside (Clearwater, Fla.).
COLLEGE: Florida.
TRANSACTIONS/CAREER NOTES: Selected by Golden State Warriors in second round (34th pick overall) of 1995 NBA Draft. ... Signed as free agent by Boston Celtics (July 28, 1997). ... Traded by Celtics with 1999 first-round draft choice to Cleveland Cavaliers for C/F Vitaly Potapenko (March 11, 1999). ... Traded by Cavaliers to Orlando Magic for F Matt Harpring (August 3, 2000).

COLLEGIATE RECORD

Season Team	G	Min.	FGM	FGA	Pct.	FTM	FTA	Pct.	Reb.	Ast.	Pts.	AVERAGES RPG	APG	PPG
91-92—Florida	33	825	117	231	.506	57	87	.655	203	26	291	6.2	0.8	8.8
92-93—Florida	28	715	118	208	.567	59	101	.584	198	15	295	7.1	0.5	10.5
93-94—Florida	37	998	129	237	.544	68	104	.654	292	54	327	7.9	1.5	8.8
94-95—Florida	30	966	138	270	.511	115	159	.723	265	42	396	8.8	1.4	13.2
Totals	128	3504	502	946	.531	299	451	.663	958	137	1309	7.5	1.1	10.2

Three-point field goals: 1993-94, 1-for-3 (.333). 1994-95, 5-for-15 (.333). Totals, 6-for-18 (.333).

NBA REGULAR-SEASON RECORD

Season Team	G	Min.	FGM	FGA	Pct.	FTM	FTA	Pct.	REBOUNDS Off.	Def.	Tot.	Ast.	St.	Blk.	TO	Pts.	AVERAGES RPG	APG	PPG
95-96—Golden State ...	22	203	24	50	.480	11	19	.579	18	21	39	9	7	5	4	59	1.8	0.4	2.7
96-97—Golden State ...	71	1065	142	273	.520	91	151	.603	122	176	298	32	33	27	76	375	4.2	0.5	5.3
97-98—Boston	81	1523	169	340	.497	101	168	.601	180	212	392	59	85	49	84	439	4.8	0.7	5.4
98-99—Boston-Cleve..	47	1102	138	276	.500	95	141	.674	104	151	255	31	50	29	54	371	5.4	0.7	7.9
99-00—Cleveland	82	1831	225	443	.508	94	160	.588	156	283	439	58	63	66	108	544	5.4	0.7	6.6
00-01—Orlando..........	67	903	107	193	.554	47	82	.573	91	145	236	32	41	33	51	261	3.5	0.5	3.9
Totals	370	6627	805	1575	.511	439	721	.609	671	988	1659	221	279	209	377	2049	4.5	0.6	5.5

Three-point field goals: 1995-96, 0-for-1. 1997-98, 0-for-1. Totals, 0-for-2 (.000).
Personal fouls/disqualifications: 1995-96, 30/0. 1996-97, 229/3. 1997-98, 277/3. 1998-99, 161/3. 1999-00, 275/6. 2000-01, 198/2. Totals, 1170/17.

NBA PLAYOFF RECORD

Season Team	G	Min.	FGM	FGA	Pct.	FTM	FTA	Pct.	REBOUNDS Off.	Def.	Tot.	Ast.	St.	Blk.	TO	Pts.	AVERAGES RPG	APG	PPG
00-01—Orlando..........	4	54	8	14	.571	4	8	.500	7	9	16	1	2	2	2	20	4.0	0.3	5.0

Personal fouls/disqualifications: 2000-01, 17/1.

DEL NEGRO, VINNY   G   SUNS

PERSONAL: Born August 9, 1966, in Springfield, Mass. ... 6-4/200. (1,93/90,7). ... Full Name: Vincent Joseph Del Negro.
HIGH SCHOOL: Suffield (Conn.) Academy.
COLLEGE: North Carolina State.
TRANSACTIONS/CAREER NOTES: Selected by Sacramento Kings in second round (29th pick overall) of 1988 NBA Draft. ... Played in Italy (1990-91, 1991-92 and 1998-99). ... Signed as free agent by San Antonio Spurs (July 30, 1992). ... Played in Italy (1998-99). ... Signed as free agent by Milwaukee Bucks (February 2, 1999). ... Traded by Bucks to Golden State Warriors as part of three-way deal in which Warriors traded F Jason Caffey and F/G Billy Owens to Milwaukee Bucks, Bucks traded F/C J.R. Reid and F Robert Traylor to Cleveland Cavaliers and Cavaliers traded G Bob Sura to Warriors (June 27, 2000). ... Traded by Warriors to Phoenix Suns for F Corie Blount, F Reuben Garces and G Paul McPherson (January 26, 2001).

COLLEGIATE RECORD

Season Team	G	Min.	FGM	FGA	Pct.	FTM	FTA	Pct.	Reb.	Ast.	Pts.	AVERAGES RPG	APG	PPG
84-85—North Carolina State.......	19	125	12	21	.571	15	23	.652	14	22	39	0.7	1.2	2.1
85-86—North Carolina State.......	17	139	11	30	.367	7	11	.636	14	31	29	0.8	1.8	1.7
86-87—North Carolina State.......	35	918	133	269	.494	63	71	.887	115	102	365	3.3	2.9	10.4
87-88—North Carolina State.......	32	1093	187	363	.515	104	124	.839	158	115	509	4.9	3.6	15.9
Totals	103	2275	343	683	.502	189	229	.825	301	270	942	2.9	2.6	9.1

Three-point field goals: 1986-87, 36-for-72 (.500). 1987-88, 31-for-78 (.397). Totals, 67-for-150 (.447).

NBA REGULAR-SEASON RECORD

Season Team	G	Min.	FGM	FGA	Pct.	FTM	FTA	Pct.	REBOUNDS Off.	Def.	Tot.	Ast.	St.	Blk.	TO	Pts.	AVERAGES RPG	APG	PPG
88-89—Sacramento	80	1556	239	503	.475	85	100	.850	48	123	171	206	65	14	77	569	2.1	2.6	7.1
89-90—Sacramento	76	1858	297	643	.462	135	155	.871	39	159	198	250	64	10	111	739	2.6	3.3	9.7
92-93—San Antonio	73	1526	218	430	.507	101	117	.863	19	144	163	291	44	1	92	543	2.2	4.0	7.4
93-94—San Antonio	77	1949	309	634	.487	140	170	.824	27	134	161	320	64	1	102	773	2.1	4.2	10.0
94-95—San Antonio	75	2360	372	766	.486	128	162	.790	28	164	192	226	61	14	56	938	2.6	3.0	12.5
95-96—San Antonio	82	2766	478	962	.497	178	214	.832	36	236	272	315	85	6	100	1191	3.3	3.8	14.5
96-97—San Antonio	72	2243	365	781	.467	112	129	.868	39	171	210	231	59	7	92	886	2.9	3.2	12.3
97-98—San Antonio	54	1721	211	479	.441	74	93	.796	13	139	152	183	39	6	53	513	2.8	3.4	9.5
98-99—Milwaukee	48	1093	114	270	.422	40	50	.800	14	88	102	174	33	3	55	281	2.1	3.6	5.9
99-00—Milwaukee	67	1211	153	325	.471	35	39	.897	9	98	107	160	36	0	48	349	1.6	2.4	5.2
00-01—G.S.-Phoenix ..	65	922	106	234	.453	41	44	.932	12	70	82	126	26	3	34	254	1.3	1.9	3.9
Totals	769	19205	2862	6027	.475	1069	1273	.840	284	1526	2482	576	65	820	7036	2.4	3.2	9.1

Three-point field goals: 1988-89, 6-for-20 (.300). 1989-90, 10-for-32 (.313). 1992-93, 6-for-24 (.250). 1993-94, 15-for-43 (.349). 1994-95, 66-for-162 (.407). 1995-96, 57-for-150 (.380). 1996-97, 44-for-140 (.314). 1997-98, 17-for-39 (.436). 1998-99, 13-for-30 (.433). 1999-00, 8-for-24 (.333). 2000-01, 1-for-13 (.077). Totals, 243-for-677 (.359).

Personal fouls/disqualifications: 1988-89, 160/2. 1989-90, 182/2. 1992-93, 146/0. 1993-94, 168/0. 1994-95, 179/0. 1995-96, 166/0. 1996-97, 131/0. 1997-98, 113/0. 1998-99, 62/0. 1999-00, 81/0. 2000-01, 78/0. Totals, 1466/4.

NBA PLAYOFF RECORD

Season Team	G	Min.	FGM	FGA	Pct.	FTM	FTA	Pct.	REBOUNDS Off.	Def.	Tot.	Ast.	St.	Blk.	TO	Pts.	AVERAGES RPG	APG	PPG
92-93—San Antonio....	8	112	17	38	.447	4	4	1.000	6	13	19	24	1	1	3	40	2.4	3.0	5.0
93-94—San Antonio	4	93	12	27	.444	3	5	.600	1	6	7	18	1	0	6	29	1.8	4.5	7.3
94-95—San Antonio	15	382	51	118	.432	20	24	.833	4	28	32	37	8	2	16	131	2.1	2.5	8.7
95-96—San Antonio	10	379	57	124	.460	13	19	.684	4	22	26	29	13	3	6	143	2.6	2.9	14.3
97-98—San Antonio	9	283	39	81	.481	16	17	.941	2	22	24	29	8	0	13	96	2.7	3.2	10.7
99-00—Milwaukee	5	93	13	30	.433	0	0	...	0	8	8	9	3	0	3	26	1.6	1.8	5.2
00-01—Phoenix	3	26	4	7	.571	0	0	...	0	2	2	5	0	0	0	8	0.7	1.7	2.7
Totals	54	1368	193	425	.454	56	69	.812	17	101	118	151	34	6	47	473	2.2	2.8	8.8

Three-point field goals: 1992-93, 2-for-9 (.222). 1993-94, 2-for-4 (.500). 1994-95, 9-for-20 (.450). 1995-96, 16-for-27 (.593). 1997-98, 2-for-10 (.200). 1999-00, 0-for-2. Totals, 31-for-72 (.431).

Personal fouls/disqualifications: 1992-93, 13/0. 1993-94, 6/0. 1994-95, 23/0. 1995-96, 19/0. 1997-98, 30/0. 1999-00, 4/0. 2000-01, 2/0. Totals, 97/0.

ITALIAN LEAGUE RECORD

Season Team	G	Min.	FGM	FGA	Pct.	FTM	FTA	Pct.	Reb.	Ast.	Pts.	AVERAGES RPG	APG	PPG
90-91—Benetton Treviso	35	1345	271	455	.596	214	263	.814	146	...	894	4.2	...	25.5
91-92—Benetton Treviso	30	1148	284	492	.577	167	183	.913	141	111	755	4.7	3.7	25.2
98-99—Teamsystem Bologna	4	92	12	28	.429	5	8	.625	4	9	32	1.0	2.3	8.0
Totals	69	2585	567	975	.582	386	454	.850	291	...	1681	4.2	...	24.4

Three-point field goals: 1991-92, 20-for-59 (.339). 1998-99, 3-for-5 (.600). Totals, 23-for-64 (.359).

DELK, TONY   G   SUNS

PERSONAL: Born January 28, 1974, in Covington, Tenn. ... 6-2/189. (1,88/85,7). ... Full Name: Tony Lorenzo Delk.
HIGH SCHOOL: Haywood (Brownsville, Tenn.).
COLLEGE: Kentucky.
TRANSACTIONS/CAREER NOTES: Selected by Charlotte Hornets in first round (16th pick overall) of 1996 NBA Draft. ... Traded by Hornets with G Muggsy Bogues to Golden State Warriors for G B.J. Armstrong (November 7, 1997). ... Signed as free agent by Sacramento Kings (August 16, 1999). ... Signed as free agent by Phoenix Suns (August 1, 2000).

COLLEGIATE RECORD

NOTES: Member of NCAA Division I championship team (1996). ... THE SPORTING NEWS All-America second team (1996). ... NCAA Division I Tournament Most Outstanding Player (1996).

Season Team	G	Min.	FGM	FGA	Pct.	FTM	FTA	Pct.	Reb.	Ast.	Pts.	AVERAGES RPG	APG	PPG
92-93—Kentucky	30	287	47	104	.452	24	33	.727	57	22	136	1.9	0.7	4.5
93-94—Kentucky	34	957	200	440	.455	69	108	.639	153	59	564	4.5	1.7	16.6
94-95—Kentucky	33	960	207	433	.478	60	89	.674	110	65	551	3.3	2.0	16.7
95-96—Kentucky	36	947	229	464	.494	88	110	.800	150	64	639	4.2	1.8	17.8
Totals	133	3151	683	1441	.474	241	340	.709	470	210	1890	3.5	1.6	14.2

Three-point field goals: 1992-93, 18-for-51 (.353). 1993-94, 95-for-254 (.374). 1994-95, 77-for-197 (.391). 1995-96, 93-for-210 (.443). Totals, 283-for-712 (.397).

NBA REGULAR-SEASON RECORD

Season Team	G	Min.	FGM	FGA	Pct.	FTM	FTA	Pct.	REBOUNDS Off.	Def.	Tot.	Ast.	St.	Blk.	TO	Pts.	AVERAGES RPG	APG	PPG
96-97—Charlotte	61	867	119	256	.465	42	51	.824	31	68	99	99	36	6	68	332	1.6	1.6	5.4
97-98—Char.-G.S.	77	1681	314	798	.393	111	151	.735	38	134	172	172	73	12	109	781	2.2	2.2	10.1
98-99—Golden State ...	36	630	92	253	.364	46	71	.648	11	43	54	95	16	6	45	246	1.5	2.6	6.8
99-00—Sacramento	46	682	120	279	.430	47	59	.797	36	52	88	55	35	5	32	296	1.9	1.2	6.4
00-01—Phoenix	82	2288	383	923	.415	185	235	.787	76	185	261	160	75	17	101	1005	3.2	2.0	12.3
Totals	302	6148	1028	2509	.410	431	567	.760	192	482	674	581	235	46	355	2660	2.2	1.9	8.8

Three-point field goals: 1996-97, 52-for-112 (.464). 1997-98, 42-for-157 (.268). 1998-99, 16-for-66 (.242). 1999-00, 9-for-40 (.225). 2000-01, 54-for-168 (.321). Totals, 173-for-543 (.319).

Personal fouls/disqualifications: 1996-97, 71/1. 1997-98, 96/0. 1998-99, 47/0. 1999-00, 58/0. 2000-01, 171/1. Totals, 443/2.

D

NBA PLAYOFF RECORD

Season Team	G	Min.	FGM	FGA	Pct.	FTM	FTA	Pct.	REBOUNDS Off.	Def.	Tot.	Ast.	St.	Blk.	TO	Pts.	AVERAGES RPG	APG	PPG
96-97—Charlotte........	3	85	13	31	.419	0	0	...	5	5	10	6	2	0	2	31	3.3	2.0	10.3
99-00—Sacramento	5	101	18	41	.439	17	23	.739	11	7	18	7	3	0	8	56	3.6	1.4	11.2
00-01—Phoenix	4	114	18	43	.419	7	11	.636	5	11	16	4	3	0	5	47	4.0	1.0	11.8
Totals	12	300	49	115	.426	24	34	.706	21	23	44	17	8	0	15	134	3.7	1.4	11.2

Three-point field goals: 1996-97, 5-for-13 (.385). 1999-00, 3-for-5 (.600). 2000-01, 4-for-10 (.400). Totals, 12-for-28 (.429).
Personal fouls/disqualifications: 1996-97, 10/0. 1999-00, 11/0. 2000-01, 7/0. Totals, 28/0.

DIAL, DERRICK　　　　G

PERSONAL: Born December 20, 1975, in Detroit. ... 6-4/184. (1,93/83,5). ... Full Name: Derrick Jonathon Dial.
HIGH SCHOOL: Cass Tech (Detroit).
COLLEGE: Eastern Michigan.
TRANSACTIONS/CAREER NOTES: Selected by San Antonio Spurs in second round (52nd pick overall) of 1998 NBA Draft. ... Played in Greece (1998-99).

COLLEGIATE RECORD

Season Team	G	Min.	FGM	FGA	Pct.	FTM	FTA	Pct.	Reb.	Ast.	Pts.	AVERAGES RPG	APG	PPG
93-94—Eastern Michigan...........						Did not play—redshirted.								
94-95—Eastern Michigan...........	30	767	104	258	.403	53	69	.768	154	40	294	5.1	1.3	9.8
95-96—Eastern Michigan...........	31	915	161	332	.485	56	80	.700	178	63	425	5.7	2.0	13.7
96-97—Eastern Michigan...........	32	1099	204	392	.520	102	125	.816	165	73	565	5.2	2.3	17.7
97-98—Eastern Michigan...........	29	1030	222	459	.484	84	107	.785	195	67	607	6.7	2.3	20.9
Totals	122	3811	691	1441	.480	295	381	.774	692	243	1891	5.7	2.0	15.5

Three-point field goals: 1994-95, 33-for-113 (.292). 1995-96, 47-for-127 (.370). 1996-97, 55-for-130 (.423). 1997-98, 79-for-198 (.399). Totals, 214-for-568 (.377).

GREEK LEAGUE RECORD

Season Team	G	Min.	FGM	FGA	Pct.	FTM	FTA	Pct.	Reb.	Ast.	Pts.	AVERAGES RPG	APG	PPG
98-99—Peristeri Nikas...............	21	772	135	326	.414	82	107	.766	101	36	393	4.8	1.7	18.7

Three-point field goals: 1998-99, 41-for-118 (.347).

NBA REGULAR-SEASON RECORD

Season Team	G	Min.	FGM	FGA	Pct.	FTM	FTA	Pct.	REBOUNDS Off.	Def.	Tot.	Ast.	St.	Blk.	TO	Pts.	AVERAGES RPG	APG	PPG
99-00—San Antonio....	8	95	17	46	.370	3	5	.600	14	12	26	5	1	1	6	40	3.3	0.6	5.0
00-01—San Antonio....	33	207	36	83	.434	12	21	.571	12	26	38	21	4	6	12	86	1.2	0.6	2.6
Totals	41	302	53	129	.411	15	26	.577	26	38	64	26	5	7	18	126	1.6	0.6	3.1

Three-point field goals: 1999-00, 3-for-12 (.250). 2000-01, 2-for-10 (.200). Totals, 5-for-22 (.227).
Personal fouls/disqualifications: 1999-00, 10/0. 2000-01, 22/0. Totals, 32/0.

NBA PLAYOFF RECORD

Season Team	G	Min.	FGM	FGA	Pct.	FTM	FTA	Pct.	REBOUNDS Off.	Def.	Tot.	Ast.	St.	Blk.	TO	Pts.	AVERAGES RPG	APG	PPG
99-00—San Antonio....	2	8	2	4	.500	1	2	.500	2	0	2	0	0	0	0	5	1.0	0.0	2.5

Personal fouls/disqualifications: 1999-00, 1/0.

DICKERSON, MICHAEL　　G　　　　GRIZZLIES

PERSONAL: Born June 25, 1975, in Greenville, S.C. ... 6-5/190. (1,96/86,2). ... Full Name: Michael DeAngelo Dickerson.
HIGH SCHOOL: Federal Way (Seattle).
COLLEGE: Arizona.
TRANSACTIONS/CAREER NOTES: Selected by Houston Rockets in first round (14th pick overall) of 1998 NBA Draft. ... Traded by Rockets with F/C Othella Harrington, G Brent Price, F/C Antoine Carr and future first-round draft choice to Vancouver Grizzlies as part of three-way deal in which Rockets received draft rights to G Steve Francis and F Tony Massenburg from Grizzlies and F Don MacLean and future first-round draft choice from Orlando Magic and Magic received F Michael Smith, G/F Rodrick Rhodes, G Lee Mayberry and F Makhtar Ndiaye from Grizzles (August 27, 1999). ... Grizzlies franchise moved to Memphis for 2001-02 season.

COLLEGIATE RECORD

NOTES: Member of NCAA Division I championship team (1997).

Season Team	G	Min.	FGM	FGA	Pct.	FTM	FTA	Pct.	Reb.	Ast.	Pts.	AVERAGES RPG	APG	PPG
94-95—Arizona	29	330	50	93	.538	28	41	.683	58	18	138	2.0	0.6	4.8
95-96—Arizona	32	736	144	329	.438	62	84	.738	113	59	381	3.5	1.8	11.9
96-97—Arizona	34	1079	233	565	.412	121	170	.712	153	51	642	4.5	1.5	18.9
97-98—Arizona	35	993	241	473	.510	91	120	.758	156	62	630	4.5	1.8	18.0
Totals	130	3138	668	1460	.458	302	415	.728	480	190	1791	3.7	1.5	13.8

Three-point field goals: 1994-95, 10-for-19 (.526). 1995-96, 31-for-91 (.341). 1996-97, 55-for-166 (.331). 1997-98, 57-for-141 (.404). Totals, 153-for-417 (.367).

D

NBA REGULAR-SEASON RECORD

HONORS: NBA All-Rookie second team (1999).

Season Team	G	Min.	FGM	FGA	Pct.	FTM	FTA	Pct.	Off.	Def.	Tot.	Ast.	St.	Blk.	TO	Pts.	RPG	APG	PPG
									REBOUNDS								AVERAGES		
98-99—Houston.........	50	1558	215	462	.465	46	72	.639	26	57	83	95	27	11	66	547	1.7	1.9	10.9
99-00—Vancouver......	82	3103	554	1270	.436	269	324	.830	78	201	279	208	116	45	165	1496	3.4	2.5	18.2
00-01—Vancouver......	70	2618	425	1020	.417	206	270	.763	70	159	229	233	62	27	162	1142	3.3	3.3	16.3
Totals	202	7279	1194	2752	.434	521	666	.782	174	417	591	536	205	83	393	3185	2.9	2.7	15.8

Three-point field goals: 1998-99, 71-for-164 (.433). 1999-00, 119-for-291 (.409). 2000-01, 86-for-230 (.374). Totals, 276-for-685 (.403).
Personal fouls/disqualifications: 1998-99, 90/0. 1999-00, 226/0. 2000-01, 207/0. Totals, 523/0.

NBA PLAYOFF RECORD

Season Team	G	Min.	FGM	FGA	Pct.	FTM	FTA	Pct.	Off.	Def.	Tot.	Ast.	St.	Blk.	TO	Pts.	RPG	APG	PPG
									REBOUNDS								AVERAGES		
98-99—Houston.........	4	82	6	22	.273	2	4	.500	2	2	4	3	2	3	2	17	1.0	0.8	4.3

Three-point field goals: 1998-99, 3-for-8 (.375).
Personal fouls/disqualifications: 1998-99, 8/0.

DIVAC, VLADE   C   KINGS

PERSONAL: Born February 3, 1968, in Prijepolje, Yugoslavia. ... 7-1/260. (2,16/117,9). ... Name pronounced Vlah-day De-vats.

HIGH SCHOOL: Belgrade (Yugoslavia).

COLLEGE: Did not attend college.

TRANSACTIONS/CAREER NOTES: Selected by Los Angeles Lakers in first round (26th pick overall) of 1989 NBA Draft. ... Traded by Lakers to Charlotte Hornets for draft rights to G Kobe Bryant (July 11, 1996). ... Signed as free agent by Sacramento Kings (January 22, 1999).

MISCELLANEOUS: Member of silver-medal-winning Yugoslavian Olympic teams (1988, 1996).

NBA REGULAR-SEASON RECORD

HONORS: J. Walter Kennedy Citizenship Award (2000). ... NBA All-Rookie first team (1990).

Season Team	G	Min.	FGM	FGA	Pct.	FTM	FTA	Pct.	Off.	Def.	Tot.	Ast.	St.	Blk.	TO	Pts.	RPG	APG	PPG
									REBOUNDS								AVERAGES		
89-90—L.A. Lakers	82	1611	274	549	.499	153	216	.708	167	345	512	75	79	114	110	701	6.2	0.9	8.5
90-91—L.A. Lakers	82	2310	360	637	.565	196	279	.703	205	461	666	92	106	127	146	921	8.1	1.1	11.2
91-92—L.A. Lakers	36	979	157	317	.495	86	112	.768	87	160	247	60	55	35	88	405	6.9	1.7	11.3
92-93—L.A. Lakers	82	2525	397	819	.485	235	341	.689	220	509	729	232	128	140	214	1050	8.9	2.8	12.8
93-94—L.A. Lakers	79	2685	453	895	.506	208	303	.686	282	569	851	307	92	112	191	1123	10.8	3.9	14.2
94-95—L.A. Lakers	80	2807	485	957	.507	297	382	.777	261	568	829	329	109	174	205	1277	10.4	4.1	16.0
95-96—L.A. Lakers	79	2470	414	807	.513	189	295	.641	198	481	679	261	76	131	199	1020	8.6	3.3	12.9
96-97—Charlotte........	81	2840	418	847	.494	177	259	.683	241	484	725	301	103	180	193	1024	9.0	3.7	12.6
97-98—Charlotte........	64	1805	267	536	.498	130	188	.691	183	335	518	172	83	94	114	667	8.1	2.7	10.4
98-99—Sacramento	50	1761	262	557	.470	179	255	.702	140	361	501	215	44	51	131	714	10.0	4.3	14.3
99-00—Sacramento	82	2374	384	764	.503	230	333	.691	174	482	656	244	103	103	190	1005	8.0	3.0	12.3
00-01—Sacramento	81	2420	364	755	.482	242	350	.691	207	466	673	231	87	93	192	974	8.3	2.9	12.0
Totals	878	26587	4235	8440	.502	2322	3313	.701	2365	5221	7586	2519	1065	1354	1973	10881	8.6	2.9	12.4

Three-point field goals: 1989-90, 0-for-5. 1990-91, 5-for-14 (.357). 1991-92, 5-for-19 (.263). 1992-93, 21-for-75 (.280). 1993-94, 9-for-47 (.191). 1994-95, 10-for-53 (.189). 1995-96, 3-for-18 (.167). 1996-97, 11-for-47 (.234). 1997-98, 3-for-14 (.214). 1998-99, 11-for-43 (.256). 1999-00, 7-for-26 (.269). 2000-01, 4-for-14 (.286). Totals, 89-for-375 (.237).
Personal fouls/disqualifications: 1989-90, 240/2. 1990-91, 247/3. 1991-92, 114/3. 1992-93, 311/7. 1993-94, 288/5. 1994-95, 305/8. 1995-96, 274/5. 1996-97, 277/6. 1997-98, 179/1. 1998-99, 166/2. 1999-00, 251/2. 2000-01, 242/5. Totals, 2894/49.

NBA PLAYOFF RECORD

Season Team	G	Min.	FGM	FGA	Pct.	FTM	FTA	Pct.	Off.	Def.	Tot.	Ast.	St.	Blk.	TO	Pts.	RPG	APG	PPG
									REBOUNDS								AVERAGES		
89-90—L.A. Lakers	9	175	32	44	.727	17	19	.895	16	32	48	10	8	15	13	82	5.3	1.1	9.1
90-91—L.A. Lakers	19	609	97	172	.564	57	71	.803	49	78	127	21	27	41	41	252	6.7	1.1	13.3
91-92—L.A. Lakers	4	143	15	43	.349	9	10	.900	6	16	22	15	5	3	18	39	5.5	3.8	9.8
92-93—L.A. Lakers	5	167	37	74	.500	12	22	.545	17	30	47	28	6	12	11	90	9.4	5.6	18.0
94-95—L.A. Lakers	10	388	57	122	.467	40	62	.645	34	51	85	31	8	13	28	156	8.5	3.1	15.6
95-96—L.A. Lakers	4	115	15	35	.429	5	8	.625	11	19	30	8	0	5	8	36	7.5	2.0	9.0
96-97—Charlotte........	3	116	21	46	.457	12	15	.800	13	13	26	10	3	6	6	54	8.7	3.3	18.0
97-98—Charlotte........	9	345	42	87	.483	20	33	.606	25	73	98	31	7	14	22	104	10.9	3.4	11.6
98-99—Sacramento	5	198	25	56	.446	30	36	.833	9	41	50	23	8	4	19	81	10.0	4.6	16.2
99-00—Sacramento	5	160	20	56	.357	16	23	.696	9	27	36	14	7	4	9	56	7.2	2.8	11.2
00-01—Sacramento	8	225	28	80	.350	29	38	.763	20	47	67	19	8	12	18	86	8.4	2.4	10.8
Totals	81	2641	389	815	.477	247	337	.733	209	427	636	210	87	129	193	1036	7.9	2.6	12.8

Three-point field goals: 1989-90, 1-for-2 (.500). 1990-91, 1-for-6 (.167). 1991-92, 0-for-2. 1992-93, 4-for-9 (.444). 1994-95, 2-for-9 (.222). 1995-96, 1-for-5 (.200). 1996-97, 0-for-3. 1997-98, 0-for-1. 1998-99, 1-for-5 (.200). 1999-00, 0-for-2. 2000-01, 1-for-3 (.333). Totals, 11-for-47 (.234).
Personal fouls/disqualifications: 1989-90, 27/1. 1990-91, 65/2. 1991-92, 17/1. 1992-93, 22/0. 1994-95, 44/2. 1995-96, 10/0. 1996-97, 11/0. 1997-98, 34/1. 1998-99, 17/0. 1999-00, 22/0. 2000-01, 25/1. Totals, 294/8.

NBA ALL-STAR GAME RECORD

Season Team	Min.	FGM	FGA	Pct.	FTM	FTA	Pct.	Off.	Def.	Tot.	Ast.	PF	Dq.	St.	Blk.	TO	Pts.
								REBOUNDS									
2001 —Sacramento.......	9	4	6	.667	0	0	...	1	2	3	1	0	0	2	0	1	8

DOLEAC, MICHAEL — C — CAVALIERS

PERSONAL: Born June 15, 1977, in San Antonio. ... 6-11/262. (2,11/118,8). ... Full Name: Michael Scott Doleac.
HIGH SCHOOL: Central Catholic (Portland, Ore.).
COLLEGE: Utah.
TRANSACTIONS/CAREER NOTES: Selected by Orlando Magic in first round (12th pick overall) of 1998 NBA Draft. ... Traded by Magic to Cleveland Cavaliers for draft rights to C Brendan Haywood (June 27, 2001).

COLLEGIATE RECORD

Season Team	G	Min.	FGM	FGA	Pct.	FTM	FTA	Pct.	Reb.	Ast.	Pts.	RPG	APG	PPG
94-95—Utah	32	547	81	179	.453	72	97	.742	144	6	234	4.5	0.2	7.3
95-96—Utah	34	819	101	218	.463	92	116	.793	261	26	294	7.7	0.8	8.6
96-97—Utah	33	876	166	309	.537	135	174	.776	253	25	475	7.7	0.8	14.4
97-98—Utah	32	876	165	338	.488	173	215	.805	228	17	516	7.1	0.5	16.1
Totals	131	3118	513	1044	.491	472	602	.784	886	74	1519	6.8	0.6	11.6

Three-point field goals: 1994-95, 0-for-1. 1995-96, 0-for-1. 1996-97, 8-for-18 (.444). 1997-98, 13-for-32 (.406). Totals, 21-for-52 (.404).

HONORS: NBA All-Rookie second team (1999).

NBA REGULAR-SEASON RECORD

Season Team	G	Min.	FGM	FGA	Pct.	FTM	FTA	Pct.	Off.	Def.	Tot.	Ast.	St.	Blk.	TO	Pts.	RPG	APG	PPG
98-99—Orlando	49	780	125	267	.468	54	80	.675	66	82	148	20	19	17	26	304	3.0	0.4	6.2
99-00—Orlando	81	1335	242	535	.452	80	95	.842	89	245	334	63	29	34	65	565	4.1	0.8	7.0
00-01—Orlando	77	1398	220	527	.417	50	59	.847	70	203	273	65	37	41	59	490	3.5	0.8	6.4
Totals	207	3513	587	1329	.442	184	234	.786	225	530	755	148	85	92	150	1359	3.6	0.7	6.6

Three-point field goals: 1999-00, 1-for-2 (.500). 2000-01, 0-for-3. 1-for-5 (.200).
Personal fouls/disqualifications: 1998-99, 117/1. 1999-00, 224/3. 2000-01, 239/10. Totals, 580/14.

NBA PLAYOFF RECORD

Season Team	G	Min.	FGM	FGA	Pct.	FTM	FTA	Pct.	Off.	Def.	Tot.	Ast.	St.	Blk.	TO	Pts.	RPG	APG	PPG
98-99—Orlando	4	43	5	18	.278	7	9	.778	5	7	12	0	0	1	3	17	3.0	0.0	4.3
00-01—Orlando	4	45	6	16	.375	0	0		4	10	14	1	3	0	2	12	3.5	0.3	3.0
Totals	8	88	11	34	.324	7	9	.778	9	17	26	1	3	1	5	29	3.3	0.1	3.6

Three-point field goals: 1998-99, 0-for-1. Totals, 0-for-1 (.000).
Personal fouls/disqualifications: 1998-99, 6/0. 2000-01, 10/0. Totals, 16/0.

DOOLING, KEYON — G — CLIPPERS

PERSONAL: Born May 8, 1980, in Fort Lauderdale, Fla. ... 6-3/184. (1,91/83,5). ... Full Name: Keyon Latwae Dooling.
HIGH SCHOOL: Dillard (Fort Lauderdale, Fla.).
COLLEGE: Missouri.
TRANSACTIONS/CAREER NOTES: Selected after sophomore season by Orlando Magic in first round (10th pick overall) of 2000 NBA Draft. ... Draft rights traded by Magic with F Corey Maggette and F Derek Strong to Los Angeles Clippers for a future first-round draft choice (June 28, 2000).

COLLEGIATE RECORD

Season Team	G	Min.	FGM	FGA	Pct.	FTM	FTA	Pct.	Reb.	Ast.	Pts.	RPG	APG	PPG
98-99—Missouri	28	676	78	170	.459	79	110	.718	58	85	243	2.1	3.0	8.7
99-00—Missouri	31	983	145	373	.389	124	167	.743	84	113	473	2.7	3.6	15.3
Totals	59	1659	223	543	.411	203	277	.733	142	198	716	2.4	3.4	12.1

Three-point field goals: 1998-99, 8-for-28 (.286). 1999-00, 59-for-170 (.347). Totals, 67-for-198 (.338).

NBA REGULAR-SEASON RECORD

Season Team	G	Min.	FGM	FGA	Pct.	FTM	FTA	Pct.	Off.	Def.	Tot.	Ast.	St.	Blk.	TO	Pts.	RPG	APG	PPG
00-01—L.A. Clippers	76	1237	148	362	.409	125	179	.698	8	81	89	177	41	11	94	449	1.2	2.3	5.9

Three-point field goals: 2000-01, 28-for-80 (.350).
Personal fouls/disqualifications: 2000-01, 107/0.

DOUGLAS, SHERMAN — G

PERSONAL: Born September 15, 1966, in Washington, D.C. ... 6-1/195. (1,85/88,5).
HIGH SCHOOL: Spingarn (Washington, D.C.).
COLLEGE: Syracuse.
TRANSACTIONS/CAREER NOTES: Selected by Miami Heat in second round (28th pick overall) of 1989 NBA Draft. ... Traded by Heat to Boston Celtics for G Brian Shaw (January 10, 1992). ... Traded by Celtics to Milwaukee Bucks for G Todd Day and C Alton Lister (November 26, 1995). ... Traded by Bucks to Cleveland Cavaliers in three-way deal in which Cavaliers sent G Terrell Brandon and F Tyrone Hill to Bucks and Bucks sent F Vin Baker to Seattle SuperSonics for F Shawn Kemp (September 25, 1997); Bucks received 1998 conditional first-round draft choice from Cavaliers. ... Traded by Cavaliers with a 2000 second-round draft choice to Denver Nuggets for G Greg Graham (October 20, 1997). ... Waived by Nuggets (October 27, 1997). ... Signed as free agent by New Jersey Nets (October 31, 1997). ... Signed as free agent by Los Angeles Clippers (February 4, 1999). ... Signed as free agent by Nets (October 21, 1999).

COLLEGIATE RECORD

NOTES: Shares NCAA Division I single-game record for most assists—22 (January 28, 1989, vs. Providence). ... 1986-87 minutes played totals are missing one game.

Season Team	G	Min.	FGM	FGA	Pct.	FTM	FTA	Pct.	Reb.	Ast.	Pts.	RPG	APG	PPG
85-86—Syracuse	27	307	57	93	.613	32	44	.727	33	57	146	1.2	2.1	5.4
86-87—Syracuse	38	1240	246	463	.531	151	203	.744	97	289	659	2.6	7.6	17.3
87-88—Syracuse	35	1195	222	428	.519	104	150	.693	76	288	562	2.2	8.2	16.1
88-89—Syracuse	38	1348	272	498	.546	110	174	.632	93	326	693	2.4	8.6	18.2
Totals	138	4090	797	1482	.538	397	571	.695	299	960	2060	2.2	7.0	14.9

Three-point field goals: 1986-87, 16-for-49 (.327). 1987-88, 14-for-53 (.264). 1988-89, 39-for-106 (.368). Totals, 69-for-208 (.332).

NBA REGULAR-SEASON RECORD

HONORS: NBA All-Rookie first team (1990).

Season Team	G	Min.	FGM	FGA	Pct.	FTM	FTA	Pct.	Off.	Def.	Tot.	Ast.	St.	Blk.	TO	Pts.	RPG	APG	PPG
89-90—Miami	81	2470	463	938	.494	224	326	.687	70	136	206	619	145	10	246	1155	2.5	7.6	14.3
90-91—Miami	73	2562	532	1055	.504	284	414	.686	78	131	209	624	121	5	270	1352	2.9	8.5	18.5
91-92—Miami-Boston	42	752	117	253	.462	73	107	.682	13	50	63	172	25	9	68	308	1.5	4.1	7.3
92-93—Boston	79	1932	264	530	.498	84	150	.560	65	97	162	508	49	10	161	618	2.1	6.4	7.8
93-94—Boston	78	2789	425	919	.462	177	276	.641	70	123	193	683	89	11	233	1040	2.5	8.8	13.3
94-95—Boston	65	2048	365	769	.475	204	296	.689	48	122	170	446	80	2	162	954	2.6	6.9	14.7
95-96—Bos.-Mil.	79	2335	345	685	.504	160	219	.731	55	125	180	436	63	5	194	890	2.3	5.5	11.3
96-97—Milwaukee	79	2316	306	610	.502	114	171	.667	57	136	193	427	78	10	153	764	2.4	5.4	9.7
97-98—New Jersey	80	1699	255	515	.495	115	172	.669	52	83	135	319	55	7	110	639	1.7	4.0	8.0
98-99—L.A. Clippers	30	842	96	219	.438	55	87	.632	16	42	58	124	27	3	61	247	1.9	4.1	8.2
99-00—New Jersey	20	309	45	90	.500	25	28	.893	13	16	29	34	17	0	24	120	1.5	1.7	6.0
00-01—New Jersey	59	1094	122	303	.403	86	115	.748	21	53	74	144	36	4	79	338	1.3	2.4	5.7
Totals	765	21148	3335	6886	.484	1601	2361	.678	558	1114	1672	4536	785	76	1761	8425	2.2	5.9	11.0

Three-point field goals: 1989-90, 5-for-31 (.161). 1990-91, 4-for-31 (.129). 1991-92, 1-for-10 (.100). 1992-93, 6-for-29 (.207). 1993-94, 13-for-56 (.232). 1994-95, 20-for-82 (.244). 1995-96, 40-for-110 (.364). 1996-97, 38-for-114 (.333). 1997-98, 14-for-46 (.304). 1998-99, 0-for-11. 1999-00, 5-for-16 (.313). 2000-01, 8-for-40 (.200). Totals, 154-for-576 (.267).

Personal fouls/disqualifications: 1989-90, 187/0. 1990-91, 178/2. 1991-92, 78/0. 1992-93, 166/1. 1993-94, 171/2. 1994-95, 152/0. 1995-96, 163/0. 1996-97, 191/0. 1997-98, 156/2. 1998-99, 54/0. 1999-00, 26/0. 2000-01, 93/0. Totals, 1615/7.

NBA PLAYOFF RECORD

Season Team	G	Min.	FGM	FGA	Pct.	FTM	FTA	Pct.	Off.	Def.	Tot.	Ast.	St.	Blk.	TO	Pts.	RPG	APG	PPG
91-92—Boston	6	65	9	25	.360	1	2	.500	1	3	4	10	0	0	4	19	0.7	1.7	3.2
92-93—Boston	4	166	17	45	.378	10	15	.667	12	14	26	38	4	0	12	44	6.5	9.5	11.0
94-95—Boston	4	168	24	68	.353	8	11	.727	4	16	20	33	4	1	17	60	5.0	8.3	15.0
97-98—New Jersey	3	125	23	44	.523	7	10	.700	1	7	8	25	6	0	13	55	2.7	8.3	18.3
Totals	17	524	73	182	.401	26	38	.684	18	40	58	106	14	1	46	178	3.4	6.2	10.5

Three-point field goals: 1991-92, 0-for-2. 1992-93, 0-for-3. 1994-95, 4-for-12 (.333). 1997-98, 2-for-5 (.400). Totals, 6-for-22 (.273).

Personal fouls/disqualifications: 1991-92, 8/0. 1992-93, 10/0. 1994-95, 12/0. 1997-98, 5/0. Totals, 35/0.

DREW, BRYCE   G   HORNETS

PERSONAL: Born September 21, 1974, in Baton Rouge, La. ... 6-3/185. (1,91/83,9). ... Full Name: Bryce Homer Drew.
HIGH SCHOOL: Valparaiso (Ind.).
COLLEGE: Valparaiso.
TRANSACTIONS/CAREER NOTES: Selected by Houston Rockets in first round (16th pick overall) of 1998 NBA Draft. ... Traded by Rockets to Chicago Bulls for conditional future first-round draft choice and two future second-round draft choices (September 28, 2000). ... Signed as free agent by Charlotte Hornets (July 24, 2001).

COLLEGIATE RECORD

Season Team	G	Min.	FGM	FGA	Pct.	FTM	FTA	Pct.	Reb.	Ast.	Pts.	RPG	APG	PPG
94-95—Valparaiso	27	943	117	267	.438	49	65	.754	64	162	361	2.4	6.0	13.4
95-96—Valparaiso	32	1136	178	401	.444	103	119	.866	92	164	551	2.9	5.1	17.2
96-97—Valparaiso	31	1078	193	419	.461	131	149	.879	94	145	617	3.0	4.7	19.9
97-98—Valparaiso	31	1114	208	462	.450	103	130	.792	130	155	613	4.2	5.0	19.8
Totals	121	4271	696	1549	.449	386	463	.834	380	626	2142	3.1	5.2	17.7

Three-point field goals: 1994-95, 78-for-170 (.459). 1995-96, 92-for-231 (.398). 1996-97, 100-for-219 (.457). 1997-98, 94-for-217 (.433). Totals, 364-for-837 (.435).

NBA REGULAR-SEASON RECORD

Season Team	G	Min.	FGM	FGA	Pct.	FTM	FTA	Pct.	Off.	Def.	Tot.	Ast.	St.	Blk.	TO	Pts.	RPG	APG	PPG
98-99—Houston	34	441	47	129	.364	8	8	1.000	3	29	32	52	12	4	31	118	0.9	1.5	3.5
99-00—Houston	72	1293	158	413	.383	45	53	.849	23	80	103	162	41	1	66	420	1.4	2.3	5.8
00-01—Chicago	48	1305	124	327	.379	14	19	.737	12	57	69	185	32	3	68	302	1.4	3.9	6.3
Totals	154	3039	329	869	.379	67	80	.838	38	166	204	399	85	8	165	840	1.3	2.6	5.5

Three-point field goals: 1998-99, 16-for-49 (.327). 1999-00, 59-for-163 (.362). 2000-01, 40-for-105 (.381). Totals, 115-for-317 (.363).

Personal fouls/disqualifications: 1998-99, 61/2. 1999-00, 79/0. 2000-01, 99/1. Totals, 239/3.

NBA PLAYOFF RECORD

Season Team	G	Min.	FGM	FGA	Pct.	FTM	FTA	Pct.	Off.	Def.	Tot.	Ast.	St.	Blk.	TO	Pts.	RPG	APG	PPG
98-99—Houston	1	4	1	1	1.000	0	2	.000	1	2	3	2	0	0	0	2	3.0	2.0	2.0

Personal fouls/disqualifications: 1998-99, 1/0.

PERSONAL: Born February 22, 1965, in Stamford, Conn. ... 6-11/260. (2,11/117,9). ... Full Name: Christen Guilford Dudley.

HIGH SCHOOL: Torrey Pines (Encinitas, Calif.).

COLLEGE: Yale.

TRANSACTIONS/CAREER NOTES: Selected by Cleveland Cavaliers in fourth round (75th pick overall) of 1987 NBA Draft. ... Traded by Cavaliers to New Jersey Nets for 1991 and 1993 second-round draft choices (February 21, 1990). ... Signed as unrestricted free agent by Portland Trail Blazers (August 3, 1993). ... Contract disallowed by NBA (August 5, 1993); contract upheld by NBA special master (September 2, 1993). ... Traded by Trail Blazers to New York Knicks for 1998 first-round draft choice in three-way deal in which Knicks traded F John Wallace to Toronto Raptors for 1998 first-round draft choice and Raptors sent future second-round choice to Trail Blazers (October 10, 1997). ... Traded by Knicks with 2001 first-round draft choice to Phoenix Suns as part of four-team trade in which Knicks acquired F Glen Rice, C Luc Longley, F/C Travis Knight, G Vernon Maxwell, C Vladimir Stepania, F Lazaro Borrell, two 2001 first-round draft choices and two 2001 second-round draft choices, Seattle SuperSonics acquired C Patrick Ewing and Los Angeles Lakers acquired F Horace Grant, C Greg Foster, F Chuck Person and G Emanual Davis (September 20, 2000). ... Traded by Suns with G Jason Kidd to New Jersey Nets for G Stephon Marbury, F Johnny Newman and C Soumaila Samake (July 18, 2001). ... Waived by Nets (August 15, 2001).

COLLEGIATE RECORD

Season Team	G	Min.	FGM	FGA	Pct.	FTM	FTA	Pct.	Reb.	Ast.	Pts.	RPG	APG	PPG
83-84—Yale	26	498	45	97	.464	28	60	.467	132	10	118	5.1	0.4	4.5
84-85—Yale	26	795	131	294	.446	65	122	.533	266	22	327	10.2	0.8	12.6
85-86—Yale	26	756	171	317	.539	80	166	.482	256	17	422	9.8	1.0	16.2
86-87—Yale	24	749	165	290	.569	96	177	.542	320	14	426	13.3	0.6	17.8
Totals	102	2798	512	998	.513	269	525	.512	974	73	1293	9.5	0.7	12.7

NBA REGULAR-SEASON RECORD

HONORS: J. Walter Kennedy Citizenship Award (1996).

Season Team	G	Min.	FGM	FGA	Pct.	FTM	FTA	Pct.	Off.	Def.	Tot.	Ast.	St.	Blk.	TO	Pts.	RPG	APG	PPG
87-88—Cleveland	55	513	65	137	.474	40	71	.563	74	70	144	23	13	19	31	170	2.6	0.4	3.1
88-89—Cleveland	61	544	73	168	.435	39	107	.364	72	85	157	21	9	23	44	185	2.6	0.3	3.0
89-90—Clev.-N.J.	64	1356	146	355	.411	58	182	.319	174	249	423	39	41	72	84	350	6.6	0.6	5.5
90-91—New Jersey	61	1560	170	417	.408	94	176	.534	229	282	511	37	39	153	80	434	8.4	0.6	7.1
91-92—New Jersey	82	1902	190	472	.403	80	171	.468	343	396	739	58	38	179	79	460	9.0	0.7	5.6
92-93—New Jersey	71	1398	94	266	.353	57	110	.518	215	298	513	16	17	103	54	245	7.2	0.2	3.5
93-94—Portland	6	86	6	25	.240	2	4	.500	16	8	24	5	4	3	2	14	4.0	0.8	2.3
94-95—Portland	82	2245	181	446	.406	85	183	.464	325	439	764	34	43	126	81	447	9.3	0.4	5.5
95-96—Portland	80	1924	162	358	.453	80	157	.510	239	481	720	37	41	100	79	404	9.0	0.5	5.1
96-97—Portland	81	1840	126	293	.430	65	137	.474	204	389	593	41	39	96	80	317	7.3	0.5	3.9
97-98—New York	51	858	58	143	.406	41	92	.446	108	167	275	21	13	51	44	157	5.4	0.4	3.1
98-99—New York	46	685	48	109	.440	19	40	.475	79	114	193	7	13	38	24	115	4.2	0.2	2.5
99-00—New York	47	459	23	67	.343	9	27	.333	63	73	136	5	7	21	18	55	2.9	0.1	1.2
00-01—Phoenix	53	613	29	73	.397	14	36	.389	64	119	183	18	14	29	26	72	3.5	0.3	1.4
Totals	840	15983	1371	3329	.412	683	1493	.457	2205	3170	5375	362	331	1013	726	3425	6.4	0.4	4.1

Three-point field goals: 1988-89, 0-for-1. 1994-95, 0-for-1. 1995-96, 0-for-1. Totals, 0-for-3 (.000).

Personal fouls/disqualifications: 1987-88, 87/2. 1988-89, 82/0. 1989-90, 164/2. 1990-91, 217/6. 1991-92, 275/5. 1992-93, 195/5. 1993-94, 18/0. 1994-95, 286/6. 1995-96, 251/4. 1996-97, 247/3. 1997-98, 139/4. 1998-99, 116/1. 1999-00, 95/2. 2000-01, 111/1. Totals, 2283/41.

NBA PLAYOFF RECORD

Season Team	G	Min.	FGM	FGA	Pct.	FTM	FTA	Pct.	Off.	Def.	Tot.	Ast.	St.	Blk.	TO	Pts.	RPG	APG	PPG
87-88—Cleveland	4	24	2	4	.500	1	2	.500	4	2	6	2	0	0	1	5	1.5	0.5	1.3
88-89—Cleveland	1	4	0	1	.000	0	0	...	0	0	0	0	0	0	1	0	0.0	0.0	0.0
91-92—New Jersey	4	77	5	14	.357	4	8	.500	13	12	25	3	2	10	1	14	6.3	0.8	3.5
93-94—Portland	4	81	4	10	.400	1	2	.500	5	10	15	0	6	0	1	9	3.8	0.0	2.3
94-95—Portland	3	59	2	3	.667	3	8	.375	6	9	15	1	0	1	3	7	5.0	0.3	2.3
95-96—Portland	5	92	5	13	.385	4	6	.667	9	18	27	1	2	2	4	14	5.4	0.2	2.8
96-97—Portland	4	69	5	11	.455	2	6	.333	10	18	28	3	2	5	0	12	7.0	0.8	3.0
97-98—New York	6	53	3	9	.333	2	4	.500	6	12	18	0	2	1	2	8	3.0	0.0	1.3
98-99—New York	18	294	16	38	.421	11	28	.393	27	55	82	5	9	8	9	43	4.6	0.3	2.4
99-00—New York	5	43	1	2	.500	2	2	1.000	5	7	12	2	1	1	1	4	2.4	0.4	0.8
00-01—Phoenix	3	26	1	2	.500	0	0	...	4	3	7	0	1	1	4	2	2.3	0.0	0.7
Totals	57	822	44	107	.411	30	66	.455	88	147	235	17	25	29	27	118	4.1	0.3	2.1

Personal fouls/disqualifications: 1987-88, 3/0. 1988-89, 1/0. 1991-92, 14/1. 1993-94, 16/0. 1994-95, 8/0. 1995-96, 18/0. 1996-97, 19/1. 1997-98, 16/0. 1998-99, 63/2. 1999-00, 11/0. 2000-01, 1/0. Totals, 170/4.

PERSONAL: Born April 25, 1976, in St. Croix, Virgin Islands. ... 7-0/260. (2,13/117,9). ... Full Name: Timothy Theodore Duncan.

HIGH SCHOOL: St. Dunstan's Episcopal High (Virgin Islands).

COLLEGE: Wake Forest.

TRANSACTIONS/CAREER NOTES: Selected by San Antonio Spurs in first round (first pick overall) of 1997 NBA Draft.

MISCELLANEOUS: Member of NBA championship team (1999).

COLLEGIATE RECORD

NOTES: The Sporting News College Player of the Year (1997). ... Naismith Award winner (1997). ... Wooden Award winner (1997). ... The Sporting News All-America first team (1996 and 1997). ... Holds NCAA Division I career record for most rebounds in four-year career (since 1973)—1,570. ... Led NCAA Division I with 14.7 rebounds per game (1997).

Season Team	G	Min.	FGM	FGA	Pct.	FTM	FTA	Pct.	Reb.	Ast.	Pts.	AVERAGES		
												RPG	APG	PPG
93-94—Wake Forest	33	997	120	220	.545	82	110	.745	317	30	323	9.6	0.9	9.8
94-95—Wake Forest	32	1168	208	352	.591	118	159	.742	401	67	537	12.5	2.1	16.8
95-96—Wake Forest	32	1190	228	411	.555	149	217	.687	395	93	612	12.3	2.9	19.1
96-97—Wake Forest	31	1137	234	385	.608	171	269	.636	457	98	645	14.7	3.2	20.8
Totals	128	4492	790	1368	.577	520	755	.689	1570	288	2117	12.3	2.3	16.5

Three-point field goals: 1993-94, 1-for-1. 1994-95, 3-for-7 (.429). 1995-96, 7-for-23 (.304). 1996-97, 6-for-22 (.273). Totals, 17-for-53 (.321).

NBA REGULAR-SEASON RECORD

HONORS: NBA Rookie of the Year (1998). ... All-NBA first team (1998, 1999, 2000, 2001). ... NBA All-Defensive first team (1999, 2000, 2001). ... NBA All-Defensive second team (1998). ... NBA All-Rookie first team (1998).

Season Team	G	Min.	FGM	FGA	Pct.	FTM	FTA	Pct.	REBOUNDS			Ast.	St.	Blk.	TO	Pts.	AVERAGES		
									Off.	Def.	Tot.						RPG	APG	PPG
97-98—San Antonio	82	3204	706	1287	.549	319	482	.662	274	703	977	224	55	206	279	1731	11.9	2.7	21.1
98-99—San Antonio	50	1963	418	845	.495	247	358	.690	159	412	571	121	45	126	146	1084	11.4	2.4	21.7
99-00—San Antonio	74	2875	628	1281	.490	459	603	.761	262	656	918	234	66	165	242	1716	12.4	3.2	23.2
00-01—San Antonio	82	3174	702	1406	.499	409	662	.618	259	738	997	245	70	192	242	1820	12.2	3.0	22.2
Totals	288	11216	2454	4819	.509	1434	2105	.681	954	2509	3463	824	236	689	909	6351	12.0	2.9	22.1

Three-point field goals: 1997-98, 0-for-10. 1998-99, 1-for-7 (.143). 1999-00, 1-for-11 (.091). 2000-01, 7-for-27 (.259). Totals, 9-for-55 (.164).
Personal fouls/disqualifications: 1997-98, 254/1. 1998-99, 147/2. 1999-00, 210/1. 2000-01, 247/0. Totals, 858/4.

NBA PLAYOFF RECORD

NOTES: NBA Finals Most Valuable Player (1999).

Season Team	G	Min.	FGM	FGA	Pct.	FTM	FTA	Pct.	REBOUNDS			Ast.	St.	Blk.	TO	Pts.	AVERAGES		
									Off.	Def.	Tot.						RPG	APG	PPG
97-98—San Antonio	9	374	73	140	.521	40	60	.667	20	61	81	17	5	23	25	186	9.0	1.9	20.7
98-99—San Antonio	17	733	144	282	.511	107	143	.748	55	140	195	48	13	45	52	395	11.5	2.8	23.2
00-01—San Antonio	13	526	120	246	.488	76	119	.639	54	134	188	49	14	35	50	317	14.5	3.8	24.4
Totals	39	1633	337	668	.504	223	322	.693	129	335	464	114	32	103	127	898	11.9	2.9	23.0

Three-point field goals: 1997-98, 0-for-1. 1998-99, 0-for-3. 2000-01, 1-for-1. Totals, 1-for-5 (.200).
Personal fouls/disqualifications: 1997-98, 24/1. 1998-99, 50/1. 2000-01, 43/0. Totals, 117/2.

NBA ALL-STAR GAME RECORD

NOTES: NBA All-Star Game co-Most Valuable Player (2000).

Season Team	Min.	FGM	FGA	Pct.	FTM	FTA	Pct.	REBOUNDS			Ast.	PF	Dq.	St.	Blk.	TO	Pts.
								Off.	Def.	Tot.							
1998 —San Antonio	14	1	4	.250	0	0	...	1	10	11	1	0	0	0	0	2	2
2000 —San Antonio	33	12	14	.857	0	0	...	7	7	14	4	3	0	1	1	2	24
2001 —San Antonio	28	5	11	.455	4	4	1.000	4	10	14	1	1	0	2	1	2	14
Totals	75	18	29	.621	4	4	1.000	12	27	39	6	4	0	3	2	6	40

Three-point field goals: 1998, 0-for-1. Totals, 0-for-1 (.000).

D E

EDNEY, TYUS   G

PERSONAL: Born February 14, 1973, in Gardena, Calif. ... 5-10/152. (1,78/68,9). ... Full Name: Tyus Dwayne Edney. ... Name pronounced TIE-us ED-knee.

HIGH SCHOOL: Long Beach (Calif.) Polytechnic.

COLLEGE: UCLA.

TRANSACTIONS/CAREER NOTES: Selected by Sacramento Kings in second round (47th pick overall) of 1995 NBA Draft. ... Signed as free agent by Boston Celtics (August 22, 1997). ... Played in Lithuania (1998-99). ... Played in Italy (1999-2000). ... Signed as free agent by Indiana Pacers (September 22, 2000). ... Signed to play for Benetton Treviso in Italy for 2001-02 season.

COLLEGIATE RECORD

NOTES: Frances Pomeroy Naismith Award winner (1995). ... Member of NCAA Division I championship team (1995).

Season Team	G	Min.	FGM	FGA	Pct.	FTM	FTA	Pct.	Reb.	Ast.	Pts.	AVERAGES		
												RPG	APG	PPG
91-92—UCLA	32	586	59	125	.472	47	59	.797	67	88	179	2.1	2.8	5.6
92-93—UCLA	33	1207	142	294	.483	132	157	.841	117	186	450	3.5	5.6	13.6
93-94—UCLA	28	891	137	294	.466	132	161	.820	96	162	430	3.4	5.8	15.4
94-95—UCLA	32	976	146	294	.497	139	182	.764	99	216	456	3.1	6.8	14.3
Totals	125	3660	484	1007	.481	450	559	.805	379	652	1515	3.0	5.2	12.1

Three-point field goals: 1991-92, 14-for-41 (.341). 1992-93, 34-for-82 (.415). 1993-94, 24-for-64 (.375). 1994-95, 25-for-66 (.379). Totals, 97-for-253 (.383).

NBA REGULAR-SEASON RECORD

HONORS: NBA All-Rookie second team (1996).

Season Team	G	Min.	FGM	FGA	Pct.	FTM	FTA	Pct.	REBOUNDS			Ast.	St.	Blk.	TO	Pts.	AVERAGES		
									Off.	Def.	Tot.						RPG	APG	PPG
95-96—Sacramento	80	2481	305	740	.412	197	252	.782	63	138	201	491	89	3	192	860	2.5	6.1	10.8
96-97—Sacramento	70	1376	150	391	.384	177	215	.823	34	79	113	226	60	2	112	485	1.6	3.2	6.9
97-98—Boston	52	623	93	216	.431	88	111	.793	20	35	55	139	51	1	66	277	1.1	2.7	5.3
00-01—Indiana	24	263	35	91	.385	35	39	.897	5	19	24	54	17	0	25	106	1.0	2.3	4.4
Totals	226	4743	583	1438	.405	497	617	.806	122	271	393	910	217	6	395	1728	1.7	4.0	7.6

Three-point field goals: 1995-96, 53-for-144 (.368). 1996-97, 8-for-42 (.190). 1997-98, 3-for-10 (.300). 2000-01, 1-for-6 (.167). Totals, 65-for-202 (.322).

Personal fouls/disqualifications: 1995-96, 203/2. 1996-97, 98/0. 1997-98, 69/0. 2000-01, 17/0. Totals, 387/2.

NBA PLAYOFF RECORD

Season Team	G	Min.	FGM	FGA	Pct.	FTM	FTA	Pct.	Off.	Def.	Tot.	Ast.	St.	Blk.	TO	Pts.	RPG	APG	PPG
95-96—Sacramento	4	121	18	42	.429	10	12	.833	2	10	12	11	8	0	9	48	3.0	2.8	12.0
00-01—Indiana...........	2	10	2	7	.286	0	1	.000	0	0	0	3	1	0	0	4	0.0	1.5	2.0
Totals	6	131	20	49	.408	10	13	.769	2	10	12	14	9	0	9	52	2.0	2.3	8.7

Three-point field goals: 1995-96, 2-for-8 (.250). 2000-01, 0-for-1. Totals, 2-for-9 (.222).
Personal fouls/disqualifications: 1995-96, 11/1. 2000-01, 1/0. Totals, 12/1.

LITHUANIAN LEAGUE RECORD

Season Team	G	Min.	FGM	FGA	Pct.	FTM	FTA	Pct.	Reb.	Ast.	Pts.	RPG	APG	PPG
98-99—Zalgiris Kaunas..............	17	392	66	128	.516	38	48	.792	35	77	179	2.1	4.5	10.5

Three-point field goals: 1998-99, 9-for-20 (.450).

ITALIAN LEAGUE RECORD

Season Team	G	Min.	FGM	FGA	Pct.	FTM	FTA	Pct.	Reb.	Ast.	Pts.	RPG	APG	PPG
99-00—Benetton Treviso	29	890	140	303	.462	90	109	.826	69	85	410	2.4	2.9	14.1

Three-point field goals: 1999-00, 40-for-81 (.494).

EDWARDS, KEVIN   G

PERSONAL: Born October 30, 1965, in Cleveland Heights, Ohio. ... 6-3/210. (1,91/95,3). ... Full Name: Kevin Durell Edwards.
HIGH SCHOOL: St. Joseph Academy (Cleveland).
JUNIOR COLLEGE: Lakeland Community College (Ohio).
COLLEGE: DePaul.
TRANSACTIONS/CAREER NOTES: Selected by Miami Heat in first round (20th pick overall) of 1988 NBA Draft. ... Signed as free agent by New Jersey Nets (July 8, 1993). ... Traded by Nets with F David Benoit, C Yinka Dare and 1998 first-round draft choice to Orlando Magic for C Rony Seikaly and F Brian Evans (February 19, 1998). ... Rights renounced by Magic (January 21, 1999). ... Signed as free agent by Vancouver Grizzlies (October 1, 2000).

COLLEGIATE RECORD

Season Team	G	Min.	FGM	FGA	Pct.	FTM	FTA	Pct.	Reb.	Ast.	Pts.	RPG	APG	PPG
84-85—Lakeland C.C.	33	...	256	435	.589	103	144	.715	178	95	615	5.4	2.9	18.6
85-86—Lakeland C.C.	32	...	325	519	.626	121	159	.761	239	154	771	7.5	4.8	24.1
86-87—DePaul..........................	31	1060	184	343	.536	63	78	.808	156	98	447	5.0	3.2	14.4
87-88—DePaul..........................	30	999	220	413	.533	83	106	.783	158	117	548	5.3	3.9	18.3
Junior College Totals.............	65	...	581	954	.609	224	303	.739	417	249	1386	6.4	3.8	21.3
4-Year-College Totals	61	2059	404	756	.534	146	184	.793	314	215	995	5.1	3.5	16.3

Three-point field goals: 1986-87, 16-for-36 (.444). 1987-88, 25-for-56 (.446). Totals, 41-for-92 (.446).

HONORS: NBA All-Rookie second team (1989).

NBA REGULAR-SEASON RECORD

Season Team	G	Min.	FGM	FGA	Pct.	FTM	FTA	Pct.	Off.	Def.	Tot.	Ast.	St.	Blk.	TO	Pts.	RPG	APG	PPG
88-89—Miami	79	2349	470	1105	.425	154	193	.746	85	177	262	349	139	27	246	1094	3.3	4.4	13.8
89-90—Miami	78	2211	395	959	.412	139	183	.760	77	205	282	252	125	33	180	938	3.6	3.2	12.0
90-91—Miami	79	2000	380	927	.410	171	213	.803	80	125	205	240	129	46	163	955	2.6	3.0	12.1
91-92—Miami	81	1840	325	716	.454	162	191	.848	56	155	211	170	99	20	120	819	2.6	2.1	10.1
92-93—Miami	40	1134	216	462	.468	119	141	.844	48	73	121	120	68	12	75	556	3.0	3.0	13.9
93-94—New Jersey	82	2727	471	1028	.458	167	217	.770	94	187	281	232	120	34	135	1144	3.4	2.8	14.0
94-95—New Jersey	14	466	69	154	.448	40	42	.952	10	27	37	27	19	5	35	196	2.6	1.9	14.0
95-96—New Jersey	34	1007	142	390	.364	68	84	.810	14	61	75	71	54	7	68	394	2.2	2.1	11.6
96-97—New Jersey	32	477	69	183	.377	37	43	.860	9	34	43	57	17	4	49	190	1.3	1.8	5.9
97-98—N.J.-Orlando	39	487	57	165	.345	30	35	.857	20	34	54	39	26	1	30	150	1.4	1.0	3.8
00-01—Vancouver.......	46	634	56	170	.329	43	53	.811	23	59	82	52	29	8	37	160	1.8	1.1	3.5
Totals	604	15332	2650	6259	.423	1120	1395	.803	516	1137	1653	1609	825	197	1138	6596	2.7	2.7	10.9

Three-point field goals: 1988-89, 10-for-37 (.270). 1989-90, 9-for-30 (.300). 1990-91, 24-for-84 (.286). 1991-92, 7-for-32 (.219). 1992-93, 5-for-17 (.294). 1993-94, 35-for-99 (.354). 1994-95, 18-for-45 (.400). 1995-96, 42-for-104 (.404). 1996-97, 15-for-43 (.349). 1997-98, 6-for-15 (.400). 2000-01, 5-for-19 (.263). Totals, 176-for-525 (.335).
Personal fouls/disqualifications: 1988-89, 154/0. 1989-90, 149/1. 1990-91, 151/2. 1991-92, 138/1. 1992-93, 69/0. 1993-94, 150/0. 1994-95, 42/0. 1995-96, 67/0. 1996-97, 34/0. 1997-98, 28/0. 2000-01, 46/0. Totals, 1028/4.

NBA PLAYOFF RECORD

Season Team	G	Min.	FGM	FGA	Pct.	FTM	FTA	Pct.	Off.	Def.	Tot.	Ast.	St.	Blk.	TO	Pts.	RPG	APG	PPG
91-92—Miami	3	55	5	13	.385	5	8	.625	1	6	7	7	2	0	5	15	2.3	2.3	5.0
93-94—New Jersey	4	148	18	50	.360	13	14	.929	8	8	16	9	5	1	9	49	4.0	2.3	12.3
Totals	7	203	23	63	.365	18	22	.818	9	14	23	16	7	1	14	64	3.3	2.3	9.1

Three-point field goals: 1993-94, 0-for-2. Totals, 0-for-2 (.000).
Personal fouls/disqualifications: 1991-92, 3/0. 1993-94, 9/0. Totals, 12/0.

DID YOU KNOW . . .

. . . that Kareem Abdul-Jabbar, Michael Jordan, Oscar Robertson and Mitch Richmond are the only players to average at least 21 points per game in each of their first 10 NBA seasons?

PERSONAL: Born December 4, 1972, in Detroit. ... 6-2/180. (1,88/81,6). ... Full Name: Howard Jonathan Eisley.
HIGH SCHOOL: Southwestern (Detroit).
COLLEGE: Boston College.
TRANSACTIONS/CAREER NOTES: Selected by Minnesota Timberwolves in second round (30th pick overall) of 1994 NBA Draft. ... Waived by Timberwolves (February 13, 1995). ... Signed by San Antonio Spurs to first of two consecutive 10-day contracts (February 26, 1995). ... Signed by Spurs for remainder of season (March 18, 1995). ... Waived by Spurs (April 17, 1995). ... Signed as free agent by Utah Jazz (October 5, 1995). ... Waived by Jazz (October 30, 1995). ... Played in Continental Basketball Association with Rockford Lightning (1995-96). ... Signed as free agent by Jazz (December 7, 1995). ... Traded by Jazz to Dallas Mavericks as part of four-team deal in which Boston Celtics received G Robert Pack, C John Williams and cash considerations from Mavericks and a conditional first-round draft choice from Jazz, Mavericks received G Dana Barros from Celtics, F Bill Curley from Golden State Warriors, Jazz received F Donyell Marshall and C Bruno Sundov from Mavericks and Warriors received F Danny Fortson from Celtics and F Adam Keefe from Jazz (August 16, 2000). ... Traded by Mavericks to New York Knicks as part of three-team trade in which Knicks acquired F Shandon Anderson from Houston Rockets, Mavericks acquired G Muggsy Bogues from Knicks and Rockets acquired F Glen Rice from Knicks and draft rights to G Kyle Hill from Mavericks (August 10, 2001).

COLLEGIATE RECORD

Season Team	G	Min.	FGM	FGA	Pct.	FTM	FTA	Pct.	Reb.	Ast.	Pts.	AVERAGES RPG	APG	PPG
90-91—Boston College	30	1011	95	264	.360	81	108	.750	79	100	297	2.6	3.3	9.9
91-92—Boston College	31	1071	118	242	.488	88	118	.746	111	135	361	3.6	4.4	11.6
92-93—Boston College	31	1162	131	296	.443	121	145	.834	107	153	426	3.5	4.9	13.7
93-94—Boston College	34	1203	529	1191	.444	373	476	.784	116	156	544	3.4	4.6	16.0
Totals	126	4447	873	1993	.438	663	847	.783	413	544	1628	3.3	4.3	12.9

Three-point field goals: 1990-91, 26-for-74 (.351). 1991-92, 37-for-75 (.493). 1992-93, 43-for-104 (.413). 1993-94, 91-for-188 (.484). Totals, 197-for-441 (.447).

NBA REGULAR-SEASON RECORD

Season Team	G	Min.	FGM	FGA	Pct.	FTM	FTA	Pct.	REBOUNDS Off.	Def.	Tot.	Ast.	St.	Blk.	TO	Pts.	AVERAGES RPG	APG	PPG
94-95—Minn.-San Ant.	49	552	40	122	.328	31	40	.775	12	36	48	95	18	6	50	120	1.0	1.9	2.4
95-96—Utah	65	961	104	242	.430	65	77	.844	22	56	78	146	29	3	77	287	1.2	2.2	4.4
96-97—Utah	82	1083	139	308	.451	70	89	.787	20	64	84	198	44	10	110	368	1.0	2.4	4.5
97-98—Utah	82	1726	229	519	.441	127	149	.852	25	141	166	346	54	13	160	633	2.0	4.2	7.7
98-99—Utah	50	1038	140	314	.446	67	80	.838	12	82	94	185	30	2	109	368	1.9	3.7	7.4
99-00—Utah	82	2096	282	675	.418	84	102	.824	23	147	170	347	59	9	132	708	2.1	4.2	8.6
00-01—Dallas	82	2426	265	675	.393	104	126	.825	23	174	197	295	99	12	102	741	2.4	3.6	9.0
Totals	492	9882	1199	2855	.420	548	663	.827	137	700	837	1612	333	55	740	3225	1.7	3.3	6.6

Three-point field goals: 1994-95, 9-for-37 (.243). 1995-96, 14-for-62 (.226). 1996-97, 20-for-72 (.278). 1997-98, 48-for-118 (.407). 1998-99, 21-for-50 (.420). 1999-00, 60-for-163 (.368). 2000-01, 107-for-269 (.398). Totals, 279-for-771 (.362).
Personal fouls/disqualifications: 1994-95, 81/0. 1995-96, 130/0. 1996-97, 141/0. 1997-98, 182/3. 1998-99, 122/0. 1999-00, 223/2. 2000-01, 218/3. Totals, 1097/8.

NBA PLAYOFF RECORD

Season Team	G	Min.	FGM	FGA	Pct.	FTM	FTA	Pct.	REBOUNDS Off.	Def.	Tot.	Ast.	St.	Blk.	TO	Pts.	AVERAGES RPG	APG	PPG
95-96—Utah	18	202	16	42	.381	18	22	.818	4	18	22	44	3	2	11	53	1.2	2.4	2.9
96-97—Utah	20	217	38	76	.500	27	28	.964	4	14	18	40	3	0	17	112	0.9	2.0	5.6
97-98—Utah	20	366	46	125	.368	12	13	.923	4	36	40	81	12	5	31	112	2.0	4.1	5.6
98-99—Utah	11	241	26	71	.366	24	29	.828	3	17	20	32	7	3	20	81	1.8	2.9	7.4
99-00—Utah	10	200	17	55	.309	8	9	.889	1	17	18	19	6	1	13	51	1.8	1.9	5.1
00-01—Dallas	9	194	19	53	.358	4	4	1.000	1	11	12	17	5	1	13	52	1.3	1.9	5.8
Totals	88	1420	162	422	.384	93	105	.886	17	113	130	233	36	12	105	461	1.5	2.6	5.2

Three-point field goals: 1995-96, 3-for-9 (.333). 1996-97, 9-for-19 (.474). 1997-98, 8-for-27 (.296). 1998-99, 5-for-24 (.208). 1999-00, 9-for-19 (.474). 2000-01, 10-for-26 (.385). Totals, 44-for-124 (.355).
Personal fouls/disqualifications: 1995-96, 29/0. 1996-97, 27/1. 1997-98, 42/0. 1998-99, 27/0. 1999-00, 24/0. 2000-01, 18/0. Totals, 167/1.

CBA REGULAR-SEASON RECORD

Season Team	G	Min.	FGM	FGA	Pct.	FTM	FTA	Pct.	Reb.	Ast.	Pts.	AVERAGES RPG	APG	PPG
95-96—Rockford	7	168	32	58	.552	17	17	1.000	16	23	87	2.3	3.3	12.4

Three-point field goals: 1995-96, 6-for-15 (.400).

PERSONAL: Born August 22, 1975, in Port Harcourt, Nigeria. ... 6-9/270. (2,06/122,5). ... Full Name: Obinna Ralph Ekezie.
HIGH SCHOOL: Worcester (Mass.) Academy.
COLLEGE: Maryland.
TRANSACTIONS/CAREER NOTES: Selected by Vancouver Grizzlies in second round (37th pick overall) of 1999 NBA Draft. ... Traded by Grizzlies with G/F Dennis Scott, F/C Cherokee Parks and G Felipe Lopez to Washington Wizards for C Ike Austin (August 22, 2000). ... Traded by Wizards with F/C Cherokee Parks to Los Angeles Clippers for F Tyrone Nesby (November 28, 2000). ... Claimed on waivers by Wizards (December 1, 2000). ... Traded by Wizards with F Juwan Howard and C Calvin Booth to Dallas Mavericks for F/C Christian Laettner, G Courtney Alexander, F Loy Vaught, G Hubert Davis, F/C Etan Thomas and cash considerations (February 22, 2001).

Season Team	G	Min.	FGM	FGA	Pct.	FTM	FTA	Pct.	Reb.	Ast.	Pts.	AVERAGES RPG	APG	PPG
95-96—Maryland	30	463	51	108	.472	33	60	.550	111	10	135	3.7	0.3	4.5
96-97—Maryland	32	858	115	209	.550	92	144	.639	212	22	322	6.6	0.7	10.1
97-98—Maryland	32	895	138	285	.484	134	200	.670	207	51	410	6.5	1.6	12.8
98-99—Maryland	24	614	104	213	.488	97	140	.693	141	21	305	5.9	0.9	12.7
Totals	118	2830	408	815	.501	356	544	.654	671	104	1172	5.7	0.9	9.9

Three-point field goals: 1998-99, 0-for-2.

NBA REGULAR-SEASON RECORD

Season Team	G	Min.	FGM	FGA	Pct.	FTM	FTA	Pct.	REBOUNDS Off.	Def.	Tot.	Ast.	St.	Blk.	TO	Pts.	AVERAGES RPG	APG	PPG
99-00—Vancouver	39	351	41	88	.466	43	64	.672	34	58	92	8	9	4	26	125	2.4	0.2	3.2
00-01—Wash.-Dallas	33	281	32	81	.395	37	53	.698	31	47	78	9	5	5	14	101	2.4	0.3	3.1
Totals	72	632	73	169	.432	80	117	.684	65	105	170	17	14	9	40	226	2.4	0.2	3.1

Personal fouls/disqualifications: 1999-00, 61/0. 2000-01, 48/0. Totals, 109/0.

EL-AMIN, KHALID   G   MAVERICKS

PERSONAL: Born April 25, 1979, in Minneapolis. ... 5-9/200. (1,75/90,7).
HIGH SCHOOL: North (Minneapolis).
COLLEGE: Connecticut.
TRANSACTIONS/CAREER NOTES: Selected after junior season by Chicago Bulls in second round (34th pick overall) of 2000 NBA Draft. ... Waived by Bulls (March 20, 2001). ... Signed as free agent by Dallas Mavericks (August 2, 2001).

COLLEGIATE RECORD

NOTES: Member of NCAA Division I championship team (1999).

Season Team	G	Min.	FGM	FGA	Pct.	FTM	FTA	Pct.	Reb.	Ast.	Pts.	AVERAGES RPG	APG	PPG
97-98—Connecticut	37	1105	211	498	.424	90	113	.796	108	156	593	2.9	4.2	16.0
98-99—Connecticut	36	1031	174	422	.412	98	126	.778	101	140	497	2.8	3.9	13.8
99-00—Connecticut	35	1118	195	475	.411	107	120	.892	110	183	560	3.1	5.2	16.0
Totals	108	3254	580	1395	.416	295	359	.822	319	479	1650	3.0	4.4	15.3

Three-point field goals: 1997-98, 81-for-222 (.365). 1998-99, 51-for-151 (.338). 1999-00, 63-for-177 (.356). Totals, 195-for-550 (.355).

NBA REGULAR-SEASON RECORD

Season Team	G	Min.	FGM	FGA	Pct.	FTM	FTA	Pct.	REBOUNDS Off.	Def.	Tot.	Ast.	St.	Blk.	TO	Pts.	AVERAGES RPG	APG	PPG
00-01—Chicago	50	936	115	311	.370	56	72	.778	21	60	81	145	48	2	54	314	1.6	2.9	6.3

Three-point field goals: 2000-01, 28-for-84 (.333).
Personal fouls/disqualifications: 2000-01, 99/0.

ELIE, MARIO   F/G

PERSONAL: Born November 26, 1963, in New York. ... 6-5/225. (1,96/102,1). ... Full Name: Mario Antoine Elie. ... Name pronounced MERRY-O EL-ee.
HIGH SCHOOL: Power Memorial (New York).
COLLEGE: American International (Mass.).
TRANSACTIONS/CAREER NOTES: Selected by Milwaukee Bucks in seventh round (160th pick overall) of 1985 NBA Draft. ... Waived by Bucks (July 25, 1985). ... Played in Portugal, Argentina and Ireland (1985-86 through 1988-89). ... Played in United States Basketball League with Miami Tropics (1987). ... Played in Continental Basketball Association with Albany Patroons (1989-90 and 1990-91). ... Played in World Basketball League with Youngstown Pride (1990). ... Signed as free agent by Los Angeles Lakers (October 2, 1990). ... Waived by Lakers (October 15, 1990). ... Signed by Philadelphia 76ers to 10-day contract (December 28, 1990). ... Signed by Golden State Warriors to 10-day contract (February 23, 1991). ... Signed by Warriors for remainder of season (March 5, 1991). ... Signed as free agent by Portland Trail Blazers (August 4, 1992); Warriors waived their right of first refusal. ... Traded by Trail Blazers to Houston Rockets for 1995 second-round draft choice (August 2, 1993). ... Signed as free agent by San Antonio Spurs (January 21, 1999). ... Signed as free agent by Phoenix Suns (September 15, 2000).
MISCELLANEOUS: Member of NBA championship team (1994, 1995, 1999).

COLLEGIATE RECORD

Season Team	G	Min.	FGM	FGA	Pct.	FTM	FTA	Pct.	Reb.	Ast.	Pts.	AVERAGES RPG	APG	PPG
81-82—American Int'l College	25	754	157	268	.586	72	97	.742	207	50	386	8.3	2.0	15.4
82-83—American Int'l College	31	1060	188	357	.527	116	157	.739	239	99	492	7.7	3.2	15.9
83-84—American Int'l College	31	1174	225	398	.565	135	170	.794	256	59	585	8.3	1.9	18.9
84-85—American Int'l College	33	1208	252	459	.549	157	202	.777	299	124	661	9.1	3.8	20.0
Totals	120	4196	822	1482	.555	480	626	.767	1001	332	2124	8.3	2.8	17.7

CBA REGULAR-SEASON RECORD

NOTES: CBA All-League first team (1991).

Season Team	G	Min.	FGM	FGA	Pct.	FTM	FTA	Pct.	Reb.	Ast.	Pts.	AVERAGES RPG	APG	PPG
89-90—Albany	56	1772	367	654	.561	259	295	.878	339	193	1022	6.1	3.4	18.3
90-91—Albany	41	1451	352	658	.535	270	302	.894	235	197	1002	5.7	4.8	24.4
Totals	97	3223	719	1312	.548	529	597	.886	574	390	2024	5.9	4.0	20.9

Three-point field goals: 1989-90, 29-for-76 (.382). 1990-91, 28-for-87 (.322). Totals, 57-for-163 (.350).

E

Season Team	G	Min.	FGM	FGA	Pct.	FTM	FTA	Pct.	REBOUNDS			Ast.	St.	Blk.	TO	Pts.	AVERAGES		
									Off.	Def.	Tot.						RPG	APG	PPG
90-91—Phil.-G.S.	33	644	79	159	.497	75	89	.843	46	64	110	45	19	10	30	237	3.3	1.4	7.2
91-92—Golden State	79	1677	221	424	.521	155	182	.852	69	158	227	174	68	15	83	620	2.9	2.2	7.8
92-93—Portland	82	1757	240	524	.458	183	214	.855	59	157	216	177	74	20	89	708	2.6	2.2	8.6
93-94—Houston	67	1606	208	466	.446	154	179	.860	28	153	181	208	50	8	109	626	2.7	3.1	9.3
94-95—Houston	81	1896	243	487	.499	144	171	.842	50	146	196	189	65	12	104	710	2.4	2.3	8.8
95-96—Houston	45	1385	180	357	.504	98	115	.852	47	108	155	138	45	11	59	499	3.4	3.1	11.1
96-97—Houston	78	2687	291	585	.497	207	237	.896	60	175	235	310	92	12	135	909	3.0	4.0	11.7
97-98—Houston	73	1988	206	456	.452	145	174	.833	39	117	156	221	81	8	100	612	2.1	3.0	8.4
98-99—San Antonio	47	1291	156	331	.471	103	119	.866	36	101	137	89	46	12	61	455	2.9	1.9	9.7
99-00—San Antonio	79	2217	195	457	.427	126	149	.846	48	201	249	193	73	9	130	590	3.2	2.4	7.5
00-01—Phoenix	68	1506	104	246	.423	55	69	.797	38	117	155	131	58	12	60	299	2.3	1.9	4.4
Totals	732	18654	2123	4492	.473	1445	1692	.854	520	1497	2017	1875	671	129	960	6265	2.8	2.6	8.6

Three-point field goals: 1990-91, 4-for-10 (.400). 1991-92, 23-for-70 (.329). 1992-93, 45-for-129 (.349). 1993-94, 56-for-167 (.335). 1994-95, 80-for-201 (.398). 1995-96, 41-for-127 (.323). 1996-97, 120-for-286 (.420). 1997-98, 55-for-189 (.291). 1998-99, 40-for-107 (.374). 1999-00, 74-for-186 (.398). 2000-01, 36-for-100 (.360). Totals, 574-for-1572 (.365).

Personal fouls/disqualifications: 1990-91, 85/1. 1991-92, 159/3. 1992-93, 145/0. 1993-94, 124/0. 1994-95, 158/0. 1995-96, 93/0. 1996-97, 200/2. 1997-98, 115/0. 1998-99, 91/0. 1999-00, 156/0. 2000-01, 112/0. Totals, 1438/6.

NBA PLAYOFF RECORD

Season Team	G	Min.	FGM	FGA	Pct.	FTM	FTA	Pct.	REBOUNDS			Ast.	St.	Blk.	TO	Pts.	AVERAGES		
									Off.	Def.	Tot.						RPG	APG	PPG
90-91—Golden State	9	197	28	56	.500	27	32	.844	17	15	32	13	5	1	10	84	3.6	1.4	9.3
91-92—Golden State	4	80	23	36	.639	2	3	.667	11	11	22	10	5	0	6	50	5.5	2.5	12.5
92-93—Portland	4	52	5	10	.500	8	9	.889	2	4	6	4	2	1	5	20	1.5	1.0	5.0
93-94—Houston	23	382	42	106	.396	40	47	.851	9	31	40	38	8	3	21	134	1.7	1.7	5.8
94-95—Houston	22	635	69	137	.504	35	44	.795	19	43	62	54	21	1	21	201	2.8	2.5	9.1
95-96—Houston	8	233	29	66	.439	11	12	.917	6	16	22	14	7	3	5	78	2.8	1.8	9.8
96-97—Houston	16	598	54	116	.466	52	62	.839	19	37	56	61	14	4	30	184	3.5	3.8	11.5
97-98—Houston	5	133	12	27	.444	6	9	.667	3	10	13	6	2	0	5	33	2.6	1.2	6.6
98-99—San Antonio	17	526	43	112	.384	41	49	.837	9	50	59	50	22	2	25	135	3.5	2.9	7.9
99-00—San Antonio	4	115	6	22	.273	17	18	.944	5	12	17	7	5	0	12	30	4.3	1.8	7.5
00-01—Phoenix	4	103	14	31	.452	6	8	.750	2	11	13	7	3	1	2	36	3.3	1.8	9.0
Totals	116	3054	325	719	.452	245	293	.836	102	240	342	264	94	16	142	985	2.9	2.3	8.5

Three-point field goals: 1990-91, 1-for-1. 1991-92, 2-for-2. 1992-93, 2-for-2. 1993-94, 10-for-32 (.313). 1994-95, 28-for-65 (.431). 1995-96, 9-for-24 (.375). 1996-97, 24-for-60 (.400). 1997-98, 3-for-9 (.333). 1998-99, 8-for-30 (.267). 1999-00, 1-for-7 (.143). 2000-01, 2-for-13 (.154). Totals, 90-for-245 (.367).

Personal fouls/disqualifications: 1990-91, 32/0. 1991-92, 11/1. 1992-93, 1/0. 1993-94, 30/0. 1994-95, 55/0. 1995-96, 17/0. 1996-97, 52/3. 1997-98, 10/0. 1998-99, 42/0. 1999-00, 4/0. 2000-01, 6/0. Totals, 260/4.

ELLIOTT, SEAN   F

E

PERSONAL: Born February 2, 1968, in Tucson, Ariz. ... 6-8/220. (2,03/99,8). ... Full Name: Sean Michael Elliott.
HIGH SCHOOL: Cholla (Tucson, Ariz.).
COLLEGE: Arizona.
TRANSACTIONS/CAREER NOTES: Selected by San Antonio Spurs in first round (third pick overall) of 1989 NBA Draft. ... Traded by Spurs with F David Wood to Detroit Pistons for F Dennis Rodman (October 1, 1993). ... Traded by Pistons to Houston Rockets for F Robert Horry, F Matt Bullard and two future second-round draft choices (February 4, 1994); trade voided when Elliott failed physical (February 7, 1994). ... Traded by Pistons to Spurs for draft rights to C Bill Curley and 1997 second-round draft choice (July 19, 1994).
MISCELLANEOUS: Member of NBA championship team (1999). ... Member of gold-medal-winning U.S. World Championship team (1986).

COLLEGIATE RECORD
NOTES: Wooden Award winner (1989). ... THE SPORTING NEWS All-America first team (1988, 1989).

Season Team	G	Min.	FGM	FGA	Pct.	FTM	FTA	Pct.	Reb.	Ast.	Pts.	AVERAGES		
												RPG	APG	PPG
85-86—Arizona	32	1079	187	385	.486	125	167	.749	171	70	499	5.3	2.2	15.6
86-87—Arizona	30	1046	209	410	.510	127	165	.770	181	110	578	6.0	3.7	19.3
87-88—Arizona	38	1249	263	461	.570	176	222	.793	219	137	743	5.8	3.6	19.6
88-89—Arizona	33	1125	237	494	.480	195	232	.841	237	134	735	7.2	4.1	22.3
Totals	133	4499	896	1750	.512	623	786	.793	808	451	2555	6.1	3.4	19.2

Three-point field goals: 1986-87, 33-for-89 (.371). 1987-88, 41-for-87 (.471). 1988-89, 66-for-151 (.437). Totals, 140-for-327 (.428).

HONORS: NBA All-Rookie second team (1990).

NBA REGULAR-SEASON RECORD

Season Team	G	Min.	FGM	FGA	Pct.	FTM	FTA	Pct.	REBOUNDS			Ast.	St.	Blk.	TO	Pts.	AVERAGES		
									Off.	Def.	Tot.						RPG	APG	PPG
89-90—San Antonio	81	2032	311	647	.481	187	216	.866	127	170	297	154	45	14	112	810	3.7	1.9	10.0
90-91—San Antonio	82	3044	478	976	.490	325	402	.808	142	314	456	238	69	33	147	1301	5.6	2.9	15.9
91-92—San Antonio	82	3120	514	1040	.494	285	331	.861	143	296	439	214	84	29	152	1338	5.4	2.6	16.3
92-93—San Antonio	70	2604	451	918	.491	268	337	.795	85	237	322	265	68	28	152	1207	4.6	3.8	17.2
93-94—Detroit	73	2409	360	791	.455	139	173	.803	68	195	263	197	54	27	129	885	3.6	2.7	12.1
94-95—San Antonio	81	2858	502	1072	.468	326	404	.807	63	224	287	206	78	38	151	1466	3.5	2.5	18.1
95-96—San Antonio	77	2901	525	1127	.466	326	423	.771	69	327	396	211	69	33	198	1537	5.1	2.7	20.0
96-97—San Antonio	39	1393	196	464	.422	148	196	.755	48	142	190	124	24	24	89	582	4.9	3.2	14.9
97-98—San Antonio	36	1012	122	303	.403	56	78	.718	16	108	124	62	24	14	57	334	3.4	1.7	9.3
98-99—San Antonio	50	1509	208	507	.410	106	140	.757	35	178	213	117	26	17	71	561	4.3	2.3	11.2
99-00—San Antonio	19	391	38	106	.358	25	32	.781	6	41	47	28	12	2	19	114	2.5	1.5	6.0
00-01—San Antonio	52	1229	147	339	.434	60	84	.714	17	153	170	81	23	25	51	409	3.3	1.6	7.9
Totals	742	24502	3852	8290	.465	2251	2816	.799	819	2385	3204	1897	576	284	1328	10544	4.3	2.6	14.2

Three-point field goals: 1989-90, 1-for-9 (.111). 1990-91, 20-for-64 (.313). 1991-92, 25-for-82 (.305). 1992-93, 37-for-104 (.356). 1993-94, 26-for-87 (.299). 1994-95, 136-for-333 (.408). 1995-96, 161-for-392 (.411). 1996-97, 42-for-126 (.333). 1997-98, 34-for-90 (.378). 1998-99, 39-for-119 (.328). 1999-00, 13-for-37 (.351). 2000-01, 55-for-129 (.426). Totals, 589-for-1572 (.375).

Personal fouls/disqualifications: 1989-90, 172/0. 1990-91, 190/2. 1991-92, 149/0. 1992-93, 132/1. 1993-94, 174/3. 1994-95, 216/2. 1995-96, 178/1. 1996-97, 105/1. 1997-98, 92/1. 1998-99, 104/1. 1999-00, 34/0. 2000-01, 80/0. Totals, 1626/12.

NBA PLAYOFF RECORD

									REBOUNDS									AVERAGES		
Season Team	G	Min.	FGM	FGA	Pct.	FTM	FTA	Pct.	Off.	Def.	Tot.	Ast.	St.	Blk.	TO	Pts.	RPG	APG	PPG
89-90—San Antonio....	10	291	53	96	.552	21	29	.724	11	30	41	18	9	6	15	127	4.1	1.8	12.7
90-91—San Antonio....	4	132	17	40	.425	25	32	.781	8	14	22	16	4	1	9	59	5.5	4.0	14.8
91-92—San Antonio....	3	137	19	40	.475	16	18	.889	4	9	13	8	3	4	6	59	4.3	2.7	19.7
92-93—San Antonio....	10	381	59	125	.472	37	40	.925	8	40	48	36	8	3	22	158	4.8	3.6	15.8
94-95—San Antonio....	15	574	87	200	.435	66	85	.776	23	49	72	40	10	7	27	260	4.8	2.7	17.3
95-96—San Antonio....	10	389	47	117	.402	51	64	.797	11	28	39	25	11	4	30	155	3.9	2.5	15.5
98-99—San Antonio....	17	574	68	153	.444	45	59	.763	11	47	58	45	9	4	21	203	3.4	2.6	11.9
99-00—San Antonio....	4	119	15	40	.375	5	8	.625	1	21	22	5	0	2	4	40	5.5	1.3	10.0
00-01—San Antonio....	12	239	19	51	.373	11	11	1.000	3	23	26	14	5	6	13	57	2.2	1.2	4.8
Totals	85	2836	384	862	.445	277	346	.801	80	261	341	207	59	37	147	1118	4.0	2.4	13.2

Three-point field goals: 1989-90, 0-for-1. 1990-91, 0-for-3. 1991-92, 5-for-8 (.625). 1992-93, 3-for-14 (.214). 1994-95, 20-for-55 (.364). 1995-96, 10-for-34 (.294). 1998-99, 22-for-55 (.400). 1999-00, 5-for-13 (.385). 2000-01, 8-for-22 (.364). Totals, 73-for-205 (.356).

Personal fouls/disqualifications: 1989-90, 37/0. 1990-91, 9/0. 1991-92, 6/0. 1992-93, 22/0. 1994-95, 38/0. 1995-96, 24/0. 1998-99, 50/0. 1999-00, 13/0. 2000-01, 21/0. Totals, 220/0.

NBA ALL-STAR GAME RECORD

								REBOUNDS									
Season Team	Min.	FGM	FGA	Pct.	FTM	FTA	Pct.	Off.	Def.	Tot.	Ast.	PF	Dq.	St.	Blk.	TO	Pts.
1993 —San Antonio	15	1	6	.167	3	4	.750	1	1	2	0	1	0	0	0	1	5
1996 —San Antonio	22	5	12	.417	1	1	1.000	2	3	5	2	4	0	0	0	2	13
Totals...........................	37	6	18	.333	4	5	.800	3	4	7	2	5	0	0	0	3	18

Three-point field goals: 1996, 2-for-6 (.333). Totals, 2-for-6 (.333).

ELLIS, LaPHONSO   F   HEAT

PERSONAL: Born May 5, 1970, in East St. Louis, Ill. ... 6-8/240. (2,03/108,9). ... Full Name: LaPhonso Darnell Ellis. ... Name pronounced la-FON-zo.
HIGH SCHOOL: Lincoln (East St. Louis, Ill.).
COLLEGE: Notre Dame.
TRANSACTIONS/CAREER NOTES: Selected by Denver Nuggets in first round (fifth pick overall) of 1992 NBA Draft. ... Signed as free agent by Atlanta Hawks (January 30, 1999). ... Signed as free agent by Minnesota Timberwolves (October 4, 2000). ... Signed as free agent by Miami Heat (July 28, 2001).

COLLEGIATE RECORD

											AVERAGES		
Season Team	G	Min.	FGM	FGA	Pct.	FTM	FTA	Pct.	Reb.	Ast.	Pts.	RPG	APG	PPG
88-89—Notre Dame	27	819	156	277	.563	52	76	.684	254	31	365	9.4	1.1	13.5
89-90—Notre Dame	22	712	114	223	.511	79	117	.675	278	33	309	12.6	1.5	14.0
90-91—Notre Dame	15	495	90	157	.573	58	81	.716	158	26	246	10.5	1.7	16.4
91-92—Notre Dame	33	1194	227	360	.631	127	194	.655	385	51	585	11.7	1.5	17.7
Totals	97	3220	587	1017	.577	316	468	.675	1075	141	1505	11.1	1.5	15.5

Three-point field goals: 1988-89, 1-for-1. 1989-90, 2-for-6 (.333). 1990-91, 8-for-17 (.471). 1991-92, 4-for-9 (.444). Totals, 15-for-33 (.455).

NBA REGULAR-SEASON RECORD

HONORS: NBA All-Rookie first team (1993).

									REBOUNDS									AVERAGES		
Season Team	G	Min.	FGM	FGA	Pct.	FTM	FTA	Pct.	Off.	Def.	Tot.	Ast.	St.	Blk.	TO	Pts.	RPG	APG	PPG
92-93—Denver	82	2749	483	958	.504	237	317	.748	274	470	744	151	72	111	153	1205	9.1	1.8	14.7
93-94—Denver	79	2699	483	963	.502	242	359	.674	220	462	682	167	63	80	172	1215	8.6	2.1	15.4
94-95—Denver	6	58	9	25	.360	6	6	1.000	7	10	17	4	1	5	5	24	2.8	0.7	4.0
95-96—Denver	45	1269	189	432	.438	89	148	.601	93	229	322	74	36	33	83	471	7.2	1.6	10.5
96-97—Denver	55	2002	445	1014	.439	218	282	.773	107	279	386	131	44	41	117	1203	7.0	2.4	21.9
97-98—Denver	76	2575	410	1007	.407	206	256	.805	146	398	544	213	65	49	173	1083	7.2	2.8	14.3
98-99—Atlanta	20	539	80	190	.421	43	61	.705	25	84	109	18	8	7	34	204	5.5	0.9	10.2
99-00—Atlanta	58	1309	209	464	.450	66	95	.695	98	192	290	59	32	25	52	487	5.0	1.0	8.4
00-01—Minnesota.......	82	1948	298	642	.464	169	214	.790	199	295	494	93	67	74	108	772	6.0	1.1	9.4
Totals	503	15148	2606	5695	.458	1276	1738	.734	1169	2419	3588	910	388	425	897	6664	7.1	1.8	13.2

Three-point field goals: 1992-93, 2-for-13 (.154). 1993-94, 7-for-23 (.304). 1995-96, 4-for-22 (.182). 1996-97, 95-for-259 (.367). 1997-98, 57-for-201 (.284). 1998-99, 1-for-5 (.200). 1999-00, 3-for-21 (.143). 2000-01, 7-for-22 (.318). Totals, 176-for-566 (.311).

Personal fouls/disqualifications: 1992-93, 293/8. 1993-94, 304/6. 1994-95, 12/0. 1995-96, 163/3. 1996-97, 181/7. 1997-98, 226/2. 1998-99, 48/1. 1999-00, 133/1. 2000-01, 290/7. Totals, 1650/35.

NBA PLAYOFF RECORD

									REBOUNDS									AVERAGES		
Season Team	G	Min.	FGM	FGA	Pct.	FTM	FTA	Pct.	Off.	Def.	Tot.	Ast.	St.	Blk.	TO	Pts.	RPG	APG	PPG
93-94—Denver	12	436	68	142	.479	38	54	.704	27	70	97	26	9	11	19	177	8.1	2.2	14.8
00-01—Minnesota.......	4	77	9	23	.391	6	8	.750	7	7	14	0	1	3	5	24	3.5	0.0	6.0
Totals	16	513	77	165	.467	44	62	.710	34	77	111	26	10	14	24	201	6.9	1.6	12.6

Three-point field goals: 1993-94, 3-for-6 (.500). 2000-01, 0-for-1. Totals, 3-for-7 (.429).
Personal fouls/disqualifications: 1993-94, 46/2. 2000-01, 13/0. Totals, 59/2.

E

ELLISON, PERVIS F/C

PERSONAL: Born April 3, 1967, in Savannah, Ga. ... 6-10/242. (2,08/109,8).
HIGH SCHOOL: Savannah (Ga.).
COLLEGE: Louisville.
TRANSACTIONS/CAREER NOTES: Selected by Sacramento Kings in first round (first pick overall) of 1989 NBA Draft. ... Traded by Kings to Washington Bullets in three-way deal in which Bullets sent G Jeff Malone to Utah Jazz and Jazz sent G Bobby Hansen, F/C Eric Leckner and 1990 first- and second-round draft choices to Kings (June 25, 1990); Jazz also received 1990 second-round draft choice from Kings and Kings also received 1991 second-round draft choice from Bullets. ... Signed as unrestricted free agent by Boston Celtics (August 1, 1994). ... Signed as free agent by Seattle SuperSonics (October 2, 2000). ... Waived by SuperSonics (December 18, 2000).

COLLEGIATE RECORD

NOTES: The Sporting News All-America second team (1989). ... NCAA Division I Tournament Most Outstanding Player (1986). ... Member of NCAA Division I championship team (1986).

Season Team	G	Min.	FGM	FGA	Pct.	FTM	FTA	Pct.	Reb.	Ast.	Pts.	RPG	APG	PPG
85-86—Louisville	39	1194	210	379	.554	90	132	.682	318	78	510	8.2	2.0	13.1
86-87—Louisville	31	952	185	347	.533	100	139	.719	270	56	470	8.7	1.8	15.2
87-88—Louisville	35	1175	235	391	.601	146	211	.692	291	108	617	8.3	3.1	17.6
88-89—Louisville	31	1014	227	369	.615	92	141	.652	270	78	546	8.7	2.5	17.6
Totals	136	4335	857	1486	.577	428	623	.687	1149	320	2143	8.4	2.4	15.8

Three-point field goals: 1987-88, 1-for-2 (.500). 1988-89, 0-for-1. Totals, 1-for-3 (.333).

NBA REGULAR-SEASON RECORD

HONORS: NBA Most Improved Player (1992).

Season Team	G	Min.	FGM	FGA	Pct.	FTM	FTA	Pct.	Off.	Def.	Tot.	Ast.	St.	Blk.	TO	Pts.	RPG	APG	PPG
89-90—Sacramento	34	866	111	251	.442	49	78	.628	64	132	196	65	16	57	62	271	5.8	1.9	8.0
90-91—Washington	76	1942	326	636	.513	139	214	.650	224	361	585	102	49	157	146	791	7.7	1.3	10.4
91-92—Washington	66	2511	547	1014	.539	227	312	.728	217	523	740	190	62	177	196	1322	11.2	2.9	20.0
92-93—Washington	49	1701	341	655	.521	170	242	.702	138	295	433	117	45	108	110	852	8.8	2.4	17.4
93-94—Washington	47	1178	137	292	.469	70	97	.722	77	165	242	70	25	50	73	344	5.1	1.5	7.3
94-95—Boston	55	1083	152	300	.507	71	99	.717	124	185	309	34	22	54	76	375	5.6	0.6	6.8
95-96—Boston	69	1431	145	295	.492	75	117	.641	151	300	451	62	39	99	84	365	6.5	0.9	5.3
96-97—Boston	6	125	6	16	.375	3	5	.600	9	17	26	4	5	9	7	15	4.3	0.7	2.5
97-98—Boston	33	447	40	70	.571	20	34	.588	52	57	109	31	20	31	28	100	3.3	0.9	3.0
98-99—Boston							Did not play—injured.												
99-00—Boston	30	269	19	43	.442	15	21	.714	29	38	67	13	10	8	13	53	2.2	0.4	1.8
00-01—Seattle	9	40	2	7	.286	2	2	1.000	2	10	12	3	0	2	3	6	1.3	0.3	0.7
Totals	474	11593	1826	3579	.510	841	1221	.689	1087	2083	3170	691	293	752	798	4494	6.7	1.5	9.5

Three-point field goals: 1989-90, 0-for-2. 1990-91, 0-for-6. 1991-92, 1-for-3 (.333). 1992-93, 0-for-4. 1993-94, 0-for-3. 1994-95, 0-for-2. Totals, 1-for-20 (.050).

Personal fouls/disqualifications: 1989-90, 132/4. 1990-91, 268/6. 1991-92, 222/2. 1992-93, 154/3. 1993-94, 140/3. 1994-95, 179/5. 1995-96, 207/2. 1996-97, 21/1. 1997-98, 90/2. 1999-00, 67/1. 2000-01, 13/0. Totals, 1493/29.

NBA PLAYOFF RECORD

Season Team	G	Min.	FGM	FGA	Pct.	FTM	FTA	Pct.	Off.	Def.	Tot.	Ast.	St.	Blk.	TO	Pts.	RPG	APG	PPG
94-95—Boston	4	68	11	19	.579	2	2	1.000	11	6	17	2	2	5	4	24	4.3	0.5	6.0

Personal fouls/disqualifications: 1994-95, 17/1.

ESCHMEYER, EVAN C MAVERICKS

PERSONAL: Born May 30, 1975, in New Knoxville, Ohio. ... 6-11/255. (2,11/115,7). ... Full Name: Evan Bruce Eschmeyer.
HIGH SCHOOL: New Knoxville (Ohio).
COLLEGE: Northwestern.
TRANSACTIONS/CAREER NOTES: Selected by New Jersey Nets in second round (34th pick overall) of 1999 NBA Draft. ... Signed as free agent by Dallas Mavericks (August 25, 2001).

COLLEGIATE RECORD

NOTES: The Sporting News All-America second team (1999).

Season Team	G	Min.	FGM	FGA	Pct.	FTM	FTA	Pct.	Reb.	Ast.	Pts.	RPG	APG	PPG
93-94—Northwestern						Did not play—redshirted.								
94-95—Northwestern						Did not play—redshirted.								
95-96—Northwestern	27	691	94	168	.560	54	106	.509	178	16	242	6.6	0.6	9.0
96-97—Northwestern	29	805	147	240	.613	116	178	.652	235	47	410	8.1	1.6	14.1
97-98—Northwestern	27	1015	200	328	.610	185	302	.613	290	67	585	10.7	2.5	21.7
98-99—Northwestern	29	938	180	308	.584	208	273	.762	292	76	568	10.1	2.6	19.6
Totals	112	3449	621	1044	.595	563	859	.655	995	206	1805	8.9	1.8	16.1

NBA REGULAR-SEASON RECORD

Season Team	G	Min.	FGM	FGA	Pct.	FTM	FTA	Pct.	Off.	Def.	Tot.	Ast.	St.	Blk.	TO	Pts.	RPG	APG	PPG
99-00—New Jersey	31	373	38	72	.528	15	30	.500	40	68	108	21	8	21	21	91	3.5	0.7	2.9
00-01—New Jersey	74	1331	92	200	.460	67	102	.657	135	231	366	40	41	58	53	251	4.9	0.5	3.4
Totals	105	1704	130	272	.478	82	132	.621	175	299	474	61	49	79	74	342	4.5	0.6	3.3

Personal fouls/disqualifications: 1999-00, 84/2. 2000-01, 220/5. Totals, 304/7.

PERSONAL: Born August 5, 1962, in Kingston, Jamaica. ... 7-0/255. (2,13/115,7). ... Full Name: Patrick Aloysius Ewing.
HIGH SCHOOL: Cambridge (Mass.) Rindge & Latin School.
COLLEGE: Georgetown.
TRANSACTIONS/CAREER NOTES: Selected by New York Knicks in first round (first pick overall) of 1985 NBA Draft. ... Traded by Knicks to Seattle SuperSonics as part of four-team trade in which Knicks acquired F Glen Rice, C Luc Longley, F/C Travis Knight, G Vernon Maxwell, C Vladimir Stepania, F Lazaro Borrell, two 2001 first-round draft choices and two 2001 second-round draft choices, Phoenix Suns acquired C Chris Dudley and 2001 first-round draft choice and Los Angeles Lakers acquired F Horace Grant, C Greg Foster, F Chuck Person and G Emanual Davis (September 20, 2000). ... Signed as free agent by Orlando Magic (July 18, 2001).
CAREER HONORS: NBA 50th Anniversary All-Time Team (1996).
MISCELLANEOUS: Member of gold-medal-winning U.S. Olympic teams (1984, 1992). ... New York Knicks all-time leading scorer with 23,665 points, all-time leading rebounder with 10,759, all-time steals leader with 1,061 and all-time blocked shots leader with 2,758 (1985-86 through 1999-2000).

COLLEGIATE RECORD

NOTES: THE SPORTING NEWS College Player of the Year (1985). ... Naismith Award winner (1985). ... THE SPORTING NEWS All-America first team (1985). ... THE SPORTING NEWS All-America second team (1983, 1984). ... NCAA Division I Tournament Most Outstanding Player (1984). ... Member of NCAA Division I championship team (1984).

Season Team	G	Min.	FGM	FGA	Pct.	FTM	FTA	Pct.	Reb.	Ast.	Pts.	RPG	APG	PPG
81-82—Georgetown	37	1064	183	290	.631	103	167	.617	279	23	469	7.5	0.6	12.7
82-83—Georgetown	32	1024	212	372	.570	141	224	.629	325	26	565	10.2	0.8	17.7
83-84—Georgetown	37	1179	242	368	.658	124	189	.656	371	31	608	10.0	0.8	16.4
84-85—Georgetown	37	1132	220	352	.625	102	160	.638	341	48	542	9.2	1.3	14.6
Totals	143	4399	857	1382	.620	470	740	.635	1316	128	2184	9.2	0.9	15.3

NBA REGULAR-SEASON RECORD

HONORS: NBA Rookie of the Year (1986). ... All-NBA first team (1990). ... All-NBA second team (1988, 1989, 1991, 1992, 1993, 1997). ... NBA All-Defensive second team (1988, 1989, 1992). ... NBA All-Rookie team (1986).
NOTES: Led NBA with 332 personal fouls (1988).

Season Team	G	Min.	FGM	FGA	Pct.	FTM	FTA	Pct.	Off.	Def.	Tot.	Ast.	St.	Blk.	TO	Pts.	RPG	APG	PPG
85-86—New York	50	1771	386	814	.474	226	306	.739	124	327	451	102	54	103	172	998	9.0	2.0	20.0
86-87—New York	63	2206	530	1053	.503	296	415	.713	157	398	555	104	89	147	229	1356	8.8	1.7	21.5
87-88—New York	82	2546	656	1183	.555	341	476	.716	245	431	676	125	104	245	287	1653	8.2	1.5	20.2
88-89—New York	80	2896	727	1282	.567	361	484	.746	213	527	740	188	117	281	266	1815	9.3	2.4	22.7
89-90—New York	82	3165	922	1673	.551	502	648	.775	235	658	893	182	78	327	278	2347	10.9	2.2	28.6
90-91—New York	81	3104	845	1645	.514	464	623	.745	194	711	905	244	80	258	291	2154	11.2	3.0	26.6
91-92—New York	82	3150	796	1525	.522	377	511	.738	228	693	921	156	88	245	209	1970	11.2	1.9	24.0
92-93—New York	81	3003	779	1550	.503	400	556	.719	191	*789	980	151	74	161	265	1959	12.1	1.9	24.2
93-94—New York	79	2972	745	1503	.496	445	582	.765	219	666	885	179	90	217	260	1939	11.2	2.3	24.5
94-95—New York	79	2920	730	1452	.503	420	560	.750	157	710	867	212	68	159	256	1886	11.0	2.7	23.9
95-96—New York	76	2783	678	1456	.466	351	461	.761	157	649	806	160	68	184	221	1711	10.6	2.1	22.5
96-97—New York	78	2887	655	1342	.488	439	582	.754	175	659	834	156	69	189	269	1751	10.7	2.0	22.4
97-98—New York	26	848	203	403	.504	134	186	.720	59	206	265	28	16	58	77	540	10.2	1.1	20.8
98-99—New York	38	1300	247	568	.435	163	231	.706	74	303	377	43	30	100	99	657	9.9	1.1	17.3
99-00—New York	62	2035	361	775	.466	207	283	.731	140	464	604	58	36	84	142	929	9.7	0.9	15.0
00-01—Seattle	79	2107	294	684	.430	172	251	.685	124	461	585	92	53	91	151	760	7.4	1.2	9.6
Totals	1118	39693	9554	18908	.505	5298	7155	.740	2692	8652	11344	2180	1114	2849	3472	24425	10.1	1.9	21.8

Three-point field goals: 1985-86, 0-for-5. 1986-87, 0-for-7. 1987-88, 0-for-3. 1988-89, 0-for-6. 1989-90, 1-for-4 (.250). 1990-91, 0-for-6. 1991-92, 1-for-6 (.167). 1992-93, 1-for-7 (.143). 1993-94, 4-for-14 (.286). 1994-95, 6-for-21 (.286). 1995-96, 4-for-28 (.143). 1996-97, 2-for-9 (.222). 1997-98, 0-for-2. 1998-99, 0-for-2. 1999-00, 0-for-2. 2000-01, 0-for-2. Totals, 19-for-124 (.153).

Personal fouls/disqualifications: 1985-86, 191/7. 1986-87, 248/5. 1987-88, 332/5. 1988-89, 311/5. 1989-90, 325/7. 1990-91, 287/3. 1991-92, 277/2. 1992-93, 286/2. 1993-94, 275/3. 1994-95, 272/3. 1995-96, 247/2. 1996-97, 250/2. 1997-98, 74/0. 1998-99, 105/1. 1999-00, 196/1. 2000-01, 229/1. Totals, 3905/49.

NBA PLAYOFF RECORD

NOTES: Holds NBA Finals single-series record for most blocked shots—30 (1994, vs. Houston). ... Shares NBA Finals single-game record for most blocked shots—8 (June 17, 1994, vs. Houston).

Season Team	G	Min.	FGM	FGA	Pct.	FTM	FTA	Pct.	Off.	Def.	Tot.	Ast.	St.	Blk.	TO	Pts.	RPG	APG	PPG
87-88—New York	4	153	28	57	.491	19	22	.864	16	35	51	10	6	13	11	75	12.8	2.5	18.8
88-89—New York	9	340	70	144	.486	39	52	.750	23	67	90	20	9	18	15	179	10.0	2.2	19.9
89-90—New York	10	395	114	219	.521	65	79	.823	21	84	105	31	13	20	27	294	10.5	3.1	29.4
90-91—New York	3	110	18	45	.400	14	18	.778	2	28	30	6	1	5	11	50	10.0	2.0	16.7
91-92—New York	12	482	109	239	.456	54	73	.740	33	100	133	27	7	31	23	272	11.1	2.3	22.7
92-93—New York	15	604	165	322	.512	51	80	.638	43	121	164	36	17	31	39	382	10.9	2.4	25.5
93-94—New York	25	1032	210	481	.437	123	163	.755	88	205	293	65	32	76	83	547	11.7	2.6	21.9
94-95—New York	11	399	80	156	.513	48	70	.686	17	89	106	27	6	25	30	209	9.6	2.5	19.0
95-96—New York	8	328	65	137	.474	41	63	.651	11	74	85	15	1	25	30	172	10.6	1.9	21.5
96-97—New York	9	357	88	167	.527	27	42	.643	26	69	95	17	3	22	27	203	10.6	1.9	22.6
97-98—New York	4	132	20	56	.357	16	27	.593	9	23	32	5	3	5	10	56	8.0	1.3	14.0
98-99—New York	11	347	58	135	.430	28	36	.778	14	82	96	6	7	8	10	144	8.7	0.5	13.1
99-00—New York	14	461	71	170	.418	62	89	.697	29	104	133	6	16	20	27	204	9.5	0.4	14.6
Totals	135	5140	1096	2328	.471	587	814	.721	332	1081	1413	271	121	299	343	2787	10.5	2.0	20.6

Three-point field goals: 1987-88, 0-for-1. 1989-90, 1-for-2 (.500). 1991-92, 0-for-1. 1992-93, 1-for-1. 1993-94, 4-for-11 (.364). 1994-95, 1-for-3 (.333). 1995-96, 1-for-2 (.500). 1996-97, 0-for-1. Totals, 8-for-22 (.364).

Personal fouls/disqualifications: 1987-88, 17/0. 1988-89, 35/0. 1989-90, 41/0. 1990-91, 12/0. 1991-92, 49/1. 1992-93, 60/2. 1993-94, 94/1. 1994-95, 51/1. 1995-96, 22/0. 1996-97, 30/0. 1997-98, 16/0. 1998-99, 35/0. 1999-00, 48/0. Totals, 510/5.

NBA ALL-STAR GAME RECORD

Season Team	Min.	FGM	FGA	Pct.	FTM	FTA	Pct.	REBOUNDS Off.	Def.	Tot.	Ast.	PF	Dq.	St.	Blk.	TO	Pts.
1986 —New York							Selected, did not play—injured.										
1988 —New York	16	4	8	.500	1	1	1.000	1	5	6	0	1	0	0	1	1	9
1989 —New York	17	2	8	.250	0	4	.000	1	5	6	2	2	0	1	2	3	4
1990 —New York	27	5	9	.556	2	2	1.000	1	9	10	1	5	0	1	5	5	12
1991 —New York	30	8	10	.800	2	2	1.000	2	8	10	0	5	0	1	4	2	18
1992 —New York	17	4	7	.571	2	5	.400	2	2	4	0	3	0	2	1	2	10
1993 —New York	25	7	11	.636	1	1	1.000	3	7	10	1	4	0	2	2	4	15
1994 —New York	24	7	15	.467	6	7	.857	4	4	8	1	2	0	0	0	1	20
1995 —New York	22	4	7	.571	2	2	1.000	0	3	3	1	3	0	1	0	5	10
1996 —New York	12	3	7	.429	2	2	1.000	1	2	3	1	2	0	3	1	0	8
1997 —New York							Selected, did not play—injured.										
Totals.........................	190	44	82	.537	18	26	.692	15	45	60	7	27	0	11	16	23	106

FEICK, JAMIE   F/C   NETS

PERSONAL: Born July 3, 1974, in Lexington, Ohio. ... 6-8/255. (2,03/115,7).
HIGH SCHOOL: Lexington (Lexington, Ohio).
COLLEGE: Michigan State.
TRANSACTIONS/CAREER NOTES: Selected by Philadelphia 76ers in second round (48th pick overall) of 1996 NBA Draft. ... Waived by 76ers (October 27, 1996). ... Played in Continental Basketball Association with Oklahoma City Cavalry (1996-97). ... Signed by Charlotte Hornets to first of two consecutive 10-day contracts (January 6, 1997). ... Signed by San Antonio Spurs to first of two consecutive 10-day contracts (January 28, 1997). ... Re-signed by Spurs for remainder of season (February 20, 1997). ... Played in Spain (1997-98). ... Signed as free agent by Milwaukee Bucks (October 2, 1997). ... Signed as free agent by Phoenix Suns (January 24, 1999). ... Waived by Suns (January 29, 1999). ... Claimed on waivers by Bucks (February 3, 1999). ... Waived by Bucks (February 18, 1999). ... Signed by New Jersey Nets to first of two consecutive 10-day contracts (March 22, 1999). ... Signed by Nets for remainder of season (April 11, 1999). ... Signed as free agent by Nets (August 1, 1999).

COLLEGIATE RECORD

Season Team	G	Min.	FGM	FGA	Pct.	FTM	FTA	Pct.	Reb.	Ast.	Pts.	AVERAGES RPG	APG	PPG
92-93—Michigan State	14	55	2	15	.133	1	4	.250	20	1	5	1.4	0.1	0.4
93-94—Michigan State	32	506	38	69	.551	20	41	.488	104	23	96	3.3	0.7	3.0
94-95—Michigan State	28	875	111	180	.617	54	93	.581	281	29	276	10.0	1.0	9.9
95-96—Michigan State	32	986	116	268	.433	71	115	.617	303	75	323	9.5	2.3	10.1
Totals	106	2422	267	532	.502	146	253	.577	708	128	700	6.7	1.2	6.6

Three-point field goals: 1992-93, 0-for-1. 1993-94, 0-for-2. 1995-96, 20-for-65 (.308). Totals, 20-for-68 (.294).

CBA REGULAR-SEASON RECORD

Season Team	G	Min.	FGM	FGA	Pct.	FTM	FTA	Pct.	Reb.	Ast.	Pts.	AVERAGES RPG	APG	PPG
96-97—Oklahoma City	13	410	57	117	.487	21	36	.583	140	14	139	10.8	1.1	10.7

Three-point field goals: 1996-97, 4-for-11 (.364).

NBA REGULAR-SEASON RECORD

Season Team	G	Min.	FGM	FGA	Pct.	FTM	FTA	Pct.	REBOUNDS Off.	Def.	Tot.	Ast.	St.	Blk.	TO	Pts.	AVERAGES RPG	APG	PPG
96-97—Char.-San Ant.	41	624	56	157	.357	34	67	.507	82	132	214	26	16	14	31	151	5.2	0.6	3.7
97-98—Milwaukee	45	450	39	90	.433	20	41	.488	45	79	124	16	25	17	21	102	2.8	0.4	2.3
98-99—Mil.-N.J.	28	852	67	134	.500	43	60	.717	112	176	288	24	25	18	34	177	10.3	0.9	6.3
99-00—New Jersey	81	2241	181	423	.428	94	133	.707	264	491	755	68	43	38	59	459	9.3	0.8	5.7
00-01—New Jersey	6	149	8	23	.348	6	12	.500	12	44	56	5	8	3	7	22	9.3	0.8	3.7
Totals	201	4316	351	827	.424	197	313	.629	515	922	1437	139	117	90	152	911	7.1	0.7	4.5

Three-point field goals: 1996-97, 5-for-14 (.357). 1997-98, 4-for-13 (.308). 1999-00, 3-for-3. Totals, 12-for-30 (.400).
Personal fouls/disqualifications: 1996-97, 78/0. 1997-98, 67/0. 1998-99, 73/0. 1999-00, 206/2. 2000-01, 15/0. Totals, 439/2.

SPANISH LEAGUE RECORD

Season Team	G	Min.	FGM	FGA	Pct.	FTM	FTA	Pct.	Reb.	Ast.	Pts.	AVERAGES RPG	APG	PPG
97-98—Unicaja	1	30	2	10	.200	1	2	.500	5	0	5	5.0	0.0	5.0

Three-point field goals: 1997-98, 0-for-3.

FERRY, DANNY   F   SPURS

PERSONAL: Born October 17, 1966, in Hyattsville, Md. ... 6-10/235. (2,08/106,6). ... Full Name: Daniel John Willard Ferry. ... Son of Bob Ferry, center/forward with St. Louis Hawks (1959-60), Detroit Pistons (1960-61 through 1963-64) and Baltimore Bullets (1964-65 through 1968-69).
HIGH SCHOOL: DeMatha Catholic (Hyattsville, Md.).
COLLEGE: Duke.
TRANSACTIONS/CAREER NOTES: Selected by Los Angeles Clippers in first round (second pick overall) of 1989 NBA Draft. ... Played in Italy (1989-90). ... Draft rights traded by Clippers with G Reggie Williams to Cleveland Cavaliers for G Ron Harper, 1990 and 1992 first-round draft choices and 1991 second-round draft choice (November 16, 1989). ... Signed as free agent by San Antonio Spurs (August 10, 2000).

COLLEGIATE RECORD
NOTES: Naismith Award winner (1989). ... THE SPORTING NEWS All-America first team (1988, 1989).

E
F

Season Team	G	Min.	FGM	FGA	Pct.	FTM	FTA	Pct.	Reb.	Ast.	Pts.	RPG	APG	PPG
												AVERAGES		
85-86—Duke	40	912	91	198	.460	54	86	.628	221	60	236	5.5	1.5	5.9
86-87—Duke	33	1094	172	383	.449	92	109	.844	256	141	461	7.8	4.3	14.0
87-88—Duke	35	1138	247	519	.476	135	163	.828	266	139	667	7.6	4.0	19.1
88-89—Duke	35	1163	300	575	.522	146	193	.756	260	166	791	7.4	4.7	22.6
Totals	143	4307	810	1675	.484	427	551	.775	1003	506	2155	7.0	3.5	15.1

Three-point field goals: 1986-87, 25-for-63 (.397). 1987-88, 38-for-109 (.349). 1988-89, 45-for-106 (.425). Totals, 108-for-278 (.388).

ITALIAN LEAGUE RECORD

Season Team	G	Min.	FGM	FGA	Pct.	FTM	FTA	Pct.	Reb.	Ast.	Pts.	RPG	APG	PPG
												AVERAGES		
89-90—Il Messaggero Roma	30	1090	203	370	.549	125	168	.744	195	...	878	6.5	...	29.3

Three-point field goals: 1989-90, 49-for-118 (.415).

NBA REGULAR-SEASON RECORD

Season Team	G	Min.	FGM	FGA	Pct.	FTM	FTA	Pct.	Off.	Def.	Tot.	Ast.	St.	Blk.	TO	Pts.	RPG	APG	PPG
									REBOUNDS								AVERAGES		
90-91—Cleveland	81	1661	275	643	.428	124	152	.816	99	187	286	142	43	25	120	697	3.5	1.8	8.6
91-92—Cleveland	68	937	134	328	.409	61	73	.836	53	160	213	75	22	15	46	346	3.1	1.1	5.1
92-93—Cleveland	76	1461	220	459	.479	99	113	.876	81	198	279	137	29	49	83	573	3.7	1.8	7.5
93-94—Cleveland	70	965	149	334	.446	38	43	.884	47	94	141	74	28	22	41	350	2.0	1.1	5.0
94-95—Cleveland	82	1290	223	500	.446	74	84	.881	30	113	143	96	27	22	59	614	1.7	1.2	7.5
95-96—Cleveland	82	2680	422	919	.459	103	134	.769	71	238	309	191	57	37	122	1090	3.8	2.3	13.3
96-97—Cleveland	82	2633	341	794	.429	74	87	.851	82	255	337	151	56	32	94	870	4.1	1.8	10.6
97-98—Cleveland	69	1034	113	286	.395	32	40	.800	23	91	114	59	26	17	53	291	1.7	0.9	4.2
98-99—Cleveland	50	1058	141	296	.476	29	33	.879	16	86	102	53	23	10	39	349	2.0	1.1	7.0
99-00—Cleveland	63	1326	189	380	.497	52	57	.912	55	183	238	67	22	24	55	463	3.8	1.1	7.3
00-01—San Antonio	80	1688	178	375	.475	22	30	.733	55	168	223	71	28	21	50	448	2.8	0.9	5.6
Totals	803	16733	2385	5314	.449	708	846	.837	612	1773	2385	1116	361	274	762	6091	3.0	1.4	7.6

Three-point field goals: 1990-91, 23-for-77 (.299). 1991-92, 17-for-48 (.354). 1992-93, 34-for-82 (.415). 1993-94, 14-for-51 (.275). 1994-95, 94-for-233 (.403). 1995-96, 143-for-363 (.394). 1996-97, 114-for-284 (.401). 1997-98, 33-for-99 (.333). 1998-99, 38-for-97 (.392). 1999-00, 33-for-75 (.440). 2000-01, 70-for-156 (.449). Totals, 613-for-1565 (.392).

Personal fouls/disqualifications: 1990-91, 230/1. 1991-92, 135/0. 1992-93, 171/1. 1993-94, 113/0. 1994-95, 131/0. 1995-96, 233/3. 1996-97, 245/1. 1997-98, 118/0. 1998-99, 113/0. 1999-00, 181/1. 2000-01, 169/1. Totals, 1839/8.

NBA PLAYOFF RECORD

Season Team	G	Min.	FGM	FGA	Pct.	FTM	FTA	Pct.	Off.	Def.	Tot.	Ast.	St.	Blk.	TO	Pts.	RPG	APG	PPG
									REBOUNDS								AVERAGES		
91-92—Cleveland	9	55	7	15	.467	4	4	1.000	7	9	16	1	1	1	2	19	1.8	0.1	2.1
92-93—Cleveland	8	118	13	34	.382	9	10	.900	4	21	25	14	4	3	7	39	3.1	1.8	4.9
93-94—Cleveland	1	4	0	0	...	0	0	...	0	0	0	1	0	0	1	0	0.0	1.0	0.0
94-95—Cleveland	4	67	13	25	.520	4	6	.667	0	3	3	6	2	0	0	38	0.8	1.5	9.5
95-96—Cleveland	3	117	14	41	.341	0	0	...	1	14	15	9	3	2	4	29	5.0	3.0	9.7
97-98—Cleveland	3	10	0	2	.000	0	0	...	0	1	1	0	0	0	0	0	0.3	0.0	0.0
00-01—San Antonio	13	334	27	68	.397	0	0	...	8	33	41	17	4	1	6	75	3.2	1.3	5.8
Totals	41	705	74	185	.400	17	20	.850	20	81	101	48	14	7	20	200	2.5	1.2	4.9

Three-point field goals: 1991-92, 1-for-3 (.333). 1992-93, 4-for-9 (.444). 1994-95, 8-for-15 (.533). 1995-96, 1-for-16 (.063). 1997-98, 0-for-2. 2000-01, 21-for-46 (.457). Totals, 35-for-91 (.385).
Personal fouls/disqualifications: 1991-92, 7/0. 1992-93, 14/0. 1993-94, 1/0. 1994-95, 9/0. 1995-96, 13/1. 1997-98, 1/0. 2000-01, 32/0. Totals, 77/1.

FINLEY, MICHAEL   G/F   MAVERICKS

PERSONAL: Born March 6, 1973, in Melrose Park, Ill. ... 6-7/215. (2,01/97,5). ... Full Name: Michael H. Finley.
HIGH SCHOOL: Proviso East (Maywood, Ill.).
COLLEGE: Wisconsin.
TRANSACTIONS/CAREER NOTES: Selected by Phoenix Suns in first round (21st pick overall) of 1995 NBA Draft. ... Traded by Suns with G Sam Cassell, F A.C. Green and 1997 or 1998 conditional second-round draft choice to Dallas Mavericks for G Jason Kidd, F Tony Dumas and C Loren Meyer (December 26, 1996).

COLLEGIATE RECORD

Season Team	G	Min.	FGM	FGA	Pct.	FTM	FTA	Pct.	Reb.	Ast.	Pts.	RPG	APG	PPG
												AVERAGES		
91-92—Wisconsin	31	920	130	287	.453	95	128	.742	152	85	381	4.9	2.7	12.3
92-93—Wisconsin	28	979	223	478	.467	111	144	.771	161	86	620	5.8	3.1	22.1
93-94—Wisconsin	29	1046	208	446	.466	110	140	.786	194	92	592	6.7	3.2	20.4
94-95—Wisconsin	27	1000	178	470	.379	140	181	.773	141	108	554	5.2	4.0	20.5
Totals	115	3945	739	1681	.440	456	593	.769	648	371	2147	5.6	3.2	18.7

Three-point field goals: 1991-92, 26-for-72 (.361). 1992-93, 63-for-173 (.364). 1993-94, 66-for-182 (.363). 1994-95, 58-for-204 (.284). Totals, 213-for-631 (.338).

HONORS: NBA All-Rookie first team (1996).

NBA REGULAR-SEASON RECORD

Season Team	G	Min.	FGM	FGA	Pct.	FTM	FTA	Pct.	Off.	Def.	Tot.	Ast.	St.	Blk.	TO	Pts.	RPG	APG	PPG
									REBOUNDS								AVERAGES		
95-96—Phoenix	82	3212	465	976	.476	242	323	.749	139	235	374	289	85	31	133	1233	4.6	3.5	15.0
96-97—Pho.-Dal.	83	2790	475	1071	.444	198	245	.808	88	284	372	224	68	24	164	1249	4.5	2.7	15.0
97-98—Dallas	82	*3394	675	1505	.449	326	416	.784	149	289	438	405	130	30	219	1763	5.3	4.9	21.5
98-99—Dallas	50	2051	389	876	.444	186	226	.823	69	194	263	218	66	15	107	1009	5.3	4.4	20.2
99-00—Dallas	82	3464	748	1636	.457	260	317	.820	122	396	518	438	109	32	196	1855	6.3	5.3	22.6
00-01—Dallas	82	*3443	711	1552	.458	252	325	.775	109	316	425	360	118	32	190	1765	5.2	4.4	21.5
Totals	461	18354	3463	7616	.455	1464	1852	.790	676	1714	2390	1934	578	164	1009	8874	5.2	4.2	19.2

Three-point field goals: 1995-96, 61-for-186 (.328). 1996-97, 101-for-280 (.361). 1997-98, 87-for-244 (.357). 1998-99, 45-for-136 (.331). 1999-00, 99-for-247 (.401). 2000-01, 91-for-263 (.346). Totals, 484-for-1356 (.357).
Personal fouls/disqualifications: 1995-96, 199/1. 1996-97, 138/0. 1997-98, 163/0. 1998-99, 96/1. 1999-00, 171/1. 2000-01, 174/2. Totals, 941/5.

NBA PLAYOFF RECORD

Season Team	G	Min.	FGM	FGA	Pct.	FTM	FTA	Pct.	REBOUNDS Off.	Def.	Tot.	Ast.	St.	Blk.	TO	Pts.	AVERAGES RPG	APG	PPG
00-01—Dallas.............	10	434	72	200	.360	36	44	.818	13	40	53	44	12	2	24	197	5.3	4.4	19.7

Three-point field goals: 2000-01, 17-for-47 (.362).
Personal fouls/disqualifications: 2000-01, 23/0.

NBA ALL-STAR GAME RECORD

Season Team	Min.	FGM	FGA	Pct.	FTM	FTA	Pct.	REBOUNDS Off.	Def.	Tot.	Ast.	PF	Dq.	St.	Blk.	TO	Pts.
2000 —Dallas...............	10	5	6	.833	0	0	...	0	1	1	0	0	0	0	0	1	11
2001 —Dallas...............	19	5	15	.333	2	2	1.000	2	1	3	5	0	0	0	0	1	12
Totals..................	29	10	21	.476	2	2	1.000	2	2	4	5	0	0	0	2	23

Three-point field goals: 2000, 1-for-2 (.500). 2001, 0-for-2. Totals, 1-for-4 (.250).

FISHER, DEREK   G   LAKERS

PERSONAL: Born August 9, 1974, in Little Rock, Ark. ... 6-1/200. (1,85/90,7). ... Full Name: Derek Fisher. ... Brother of Duane Washington, guard with New Jersey Nets (1987-88) and Los Angeles Clippers (1992-93).
HIGH SCHOOL: Parkview (Little Rock, Ark.).
COLLEGE: Arkansas-Little Rock.
TRANSACTIONS/CAREER NOTES: Selected by Los Angeles Lakers in first round (24th pick overall) of 1996 NBA Draft.
MISCELLANEOUS: Member of NBA championship team (2000, 2001).

COLLEGIATE RECORD

Season Team	G	Min.	FGM	FGA	Pct.	FTM	FTA	Pct.	Reb.	Ast.	Pts.	AVERAGES RPG	APG	PPG
92-93—Arkansas-Little Rock	27	749	57	138	.413	71	92	.772	89	92	194	3.3	3.4	7.2
93-94—Arkansas-Little Rock	28	888	94	212	.443	72	93	.774	109	102	283	3.9	3.6	10.1
94-95—Arkansas-Little Rock	27	938	153	386	.396	130	180	.722	135	124	479	5.0	4.6	17.7
95-96—Arkansas-Little Rock	30	1041	128	313	.409	126	169	.746	155	154	437	5.2	5.1	14.6
Totals	112	3616	432	1049	.412	399	534	.747	488	472	1393	4.4	4.2	12.4

Three-point field goals: 1992-93, 9-for-31 (.290). 1993-94, 23-for-55 (.418). 1994-95, 43-for-113 (.381). 1995-96, 50-for-130 (.385). Totals, 125-for-329 (.380).

NBA REGULAR-SEASON RECORD

Season Team	G	Min.	FGM	FGA	Pct.	FTM	FTA	Pct.	REBOUNDS Off.	Def.	Tot.	Ast.	St.	Blk.	TO	Pts.	AVERAGES RPG	APG	PPG
96-97—L.A. Lakers	80	921	104	262	.397	79	120	.658	25	72	97	119	41	5	71	309	1.2	1.5	3.9
97-98—L.A. Lakers	82	1760	164	378	.434	115	152	.757	38	155	193	333	75	5	119	474	2.4	4.1	5.8
98-99—L.A. Lakers	50	1131	99	263	.376	60	79	.759	21	70	91	197	61	3	77	296	1.8	3.9	5.9
99-00—L.A. Lakers	78	1803	167	483	.346	105	145	.724	22	121	143	216	80	3	75	491	1.8	2.8	6.3
00-01—L.A. Lakers	20	709	77	187	.412	50	62	.806	5	54	59	87	39	2	29	229	3.0	4.4	11.5
Totals	310	6324	611	1573	.388	409	558	.733	111	472	583	952	296	16	371	1799	1.9	3.1	5.8

Three-point field goals: 1996-97, 22-for-73 (.301). 1997-98, 31-for-81 (.383). 1998-99, 38-for-97 (.392). 1999-00, 52-for-166 (.313). 2000-01, 25-for-63 (.397). Totals, 168-for-480 (.350).
Personal fouls/disqualifications: 1996-97, 87/0. 1997-98, 126/1. 1998-99, 95/0. 1999-00, 150/1. 2000-01, 50/0. Totals, 508/2.

NBA PLAYOFF RECORD

Season Team	G	Min.	FGM	FGA	Pct.	FTM	FTA	Pct.	REBOUNDS Off.	Def.	Tot.	Ast.	St.	Blk.	TO	Pts.	AVERAGES RPG	APG	PPG
96-97—L.A. Lakers	6	34	3	11	.273	2	3	.667	0	3	3	6	1	0	6	8	0.5	1.0	1.3
97-98—L.A. Lakers	13	278	27	68	.397	18	29	.621	2	23	25	49	17	0	15	78	1.9	3.8	6.0
98-99—L.A. Lakers	8	238	28	67	.418	12	15	.800	6	23	29	39	8	0	11	78	3.6	4.9	9.8
99-00—L.A. Lakers	21	322	34	79	.430	19	25	.760	4	18	22	41	11	1	9	99	1.0	2.0	4.7
00-01—L.A. Lakers	16	576	77	159	.484	26	34	.765	5	56	61	48	21	1	12	215	3.8	3.0	13.4
Totals	64	1448	169	384	.440	77	106	.726	17	123	140	183	58	2	53	478	2.2	2.9	7.5

Three-point field goals: 1996-97, 0-for-5. 1997-98, 6-for-20 (.300). 1998-99, 10-for-29 (.345). 1999-00, 12-for-29 (.414). 2000-01, 35-for-68 (.515). Totals, 63-for-151 (.417).
Personal fouls/disqualifications: 1996-97, 4/0. 1997-98, 33/0. 1998-99, 20/1. 1999-00, 30/0. 2000-01, 44/1. Totals, 131/2.

FIZER, MARCUS   F   BULLS

PERSONAL: Born August 10, 1978, in Detroit. ... 6-8/260. (2,03/117,9). ... Full Name: Darnell Marcus Lamar Fizer.
HIGH SCHOOL: Arcadia (La.).
COLLEGE: Iowa State.
TRANSACTIONS/CAREER NOTES: Selected after junior season by Chicago Bulls in first round (fourth pick overall) of 2000 NBA Draft.

COLLEGIATE RECORD

NOTES: THE SPORTING NEWS All-America second team (2000).

Season Team	G	Min.	FGM	FGA	Pct.	FTM	FTA	Pct.	Reb.	Ast.	Pts.	AVERAGES RPG	APG	PPG
97-98—Iowa State	30	784	173	365	.474	101	164	.616	202	19	447	6.7	0.6	14.9
98-99—Iowa State	30	961	190	422	.450	153	208	.736	229	34	539	7.6	1.1	18.0
99-00—Iowa State	37	1243	327	562	.582	175	239	.732	285	41	844	7.7	1.1	22.8
Totals	97	2988	690	1349	.511	429	611	.702	716	94	1830	7.4	1.0	18.9

Three-point field goals: 1997-98, 0-for-2. 1998-99, 6-for-28 (.214). 1999-00, 15-for-42 (.357). Totals, 21-for-72 (.292).

F

HONORS: NBA All-Rookie second team (2001).

Season Team	G	Min.	FGM	FGA	Pct.	FTM	FTA	Pct.	REBOUNDS Off.	Def.	Tot.	Ast.	St.	Blk.	TO	Pts.	AVERAGES RPG	APG	PPG
00-01—Chicago	72	1580	278	646	.430	117	161	.727	76	237	313	76	30	19	124	683	4.3	1.1	9.5

Three-point field goals: 2000-01, 10-for-39 (.256).
Personal fouls/disqualifications: 2000-01, 175/0.

FORTSON, DANNY F WARRIORS

PERSONAL: Born March 27, 1976, in Philadelphia. ... 6-8/260. (2,03/117,9). ... Full Name: Daniel Anthony Fortson.
HIGH SCHOOL: Altoona (Pa.), then Shaler (Pittsburgh).
COLLEGE: Cincinnati.
TRANSACTIONS/CAREER NOTES: Selected after junior season by Milwaukee Bucks in first round (10th pick overall) of 1997 NBA Draft. ... Draft rights traded by Bucks with F Johnny Newman and F/C Joe Wolf to Denver Nuggets for C Ervin Johnson (June 25, 1997). ... Traded by Nuggets with F Eric Williams, G Eric Washington and first-round draft choice within the next three years to Boston Celtics for G/F Ron Mercer, F Popeye Jones and C Dwayne Schintzius (August 3, 1999). ... Traded by Celtics with a future draft choice to Toronto Raptors for G Alvin Williams, F/C Sean Marks and cash considerations (February 9, 2000); trade later voided because Williams failed physical. ... Traded by Celtics to Golden State Warriors as part of four-team deal in which Celtics received G Robert Pack, C John Williams and cash considerations from Dallas Mavericks and a conditional first-round draft choice from Utah Jazz, Mavericks received G Dana Barros from Celtics, F Bill Curley from Warriors and G Howard Eisley from Jazz, Jazz received F Donyell Marshall from Warriors and C Bruno Sundov from Mavericks and Warriors received F Adam Keefe from Jazz (August 16, 2000).

COLLEGIATE RECORD

NOTES: The Sporting News All-America second team (1996). ... The Sporting News All-America first team (1997).

Season Team	G	Min.	FGM	FGA	Pct.	FTM	FTA	Pct.	Reb.	Ast.	Pts.	AVERAGES RPG	APG	PPG
94-95—Cincinnati	34	797	190	355	.535	134	196	.684	258	38	514	7.6	1.1	15.1
95-96—Cincinnati	33	909	222	413	.538	220	292	.753	316	45	664	9.6	1.4	20.1
96-97—Cincinnati	33	986	243	392	.620	217	281	.772	299	36	703	9.1	1.1	21.3
Totals	100	2692	655	1160	.565	571	769	.743	873	119	1881	8.7	1.2	18.8

Three-point field goals: 1994-95, 0-for-1. 1995-96, 0-for-1. 1996-97, 0-for-1. Totals, 0-for-3 (.000).

NBA REGULAR-SEASON RECORD

NOTES: Led NBA with 212 personal fouls (1999) and tied for NBA lead with nine disqualifications (1999).

Season Team	G	Min.	FGM	FGA	Pct.	FTM	FTA	Pct.	REBOUNDS Off.	Def.	Tot.	Ast.	St.	Blk.	TO	Pts.	AVERAGES RPG	APG	PPG
97-98—Denver	80	1811	276	611	.452	263	339	.776	182	266	448	76	44	30	157	816	5.6	1.0	10.2
98-99—Denver	50	1417	191	386	.495	168	231	.727	*210	371	581	32	31	22	77	550	11.6	0.6	11.0
99-00—Boston	55	856	140	265	.528	139	189	.735	141	225	366	29	20	5	67	419	6.7	0.5	7.6
00-01—Golden State ...	6	203	29	50	.580	42	54	.778	29	69	98	5	2	0	10	100	16.3	0.8	16.7
Totals	191	4287	636	1312	.485	612	813	.753	562	931	1493	142	97	57	311	1885	7.8	0.7	9.9

Three-point field goals: 1997-98, 1-for-3 (.333). 1998-99, 0-for-3. Totals, 1-for-6 (.167).
Personal fouls/disqualifications: 1997-98, 314/7. 1998-99, 212/9. 1999-00, 180/4. 2000-01, 22/1. Totals, 728/21.

FOSTER, GREG C BUCKS

PERSONAL: Born October 3, 1968, in Oakland. ... 6-11/250. (2,11/113,4). ... Full Name: Gregory Clinton Foster.
HIGH SCHOOL: Skyline (Oakland).
COLLEGE: UCLA, then Texas-El Paso.
TRANSACTIONS/CAREER NOTES: Played in Spain (1989-90). ... Selected by Washington Bullets in second round (35th pick overall) of 1990 NBA Draft. ... Waived by Bullets (December 1, 1992). ... Signed as free agent by Atlanta Hawks (December 16, 1992). ... Waived by Hawks (November 2, 1993). ... Signed as free agent by Milwaukee Bucks (November 19, 1993). ... Waived by Bucks (December 3, 1993). ... Signed as free agent by Chicago Bulls (September 27, 1994). ... Waived by Bulls (December 12, 1994). ... Signed by Minnesota Timberwolves (December 16, 1994). ... Signed as unrestricted free agent by Utah Jazz (October 6, 1995). ... Traded by Jazz with F Chris Morris and 1998 first-round draft choice to Orlando Magic for C Rony Seikaly (February 16, 1998); Jazz voided trade because Seikaly failed to report (February 18, 1998). ... Signed as free agent by Seattle SuperSonics (August 17, 1999). ... Traded by SuperSonics to Los Angeles Lakers as part of four-team trade in which Knicks acquired F Glen Rice, C Luc Longley, F/C Travis Knight, G Vernon Maxwell, C Vladimir Stepania, F Lazaro Borrell, two 2001 first-round draft choices and two 2001 second-round draft choices, SuperSonics acquired C Patrick Ewing, Phoenix Suns acquired C Chris Dudley and 2001 first-round draft choice and Lakers acquired F Horace Grant, F Chuck Person and G Emanual Davis (September 20, 2000). ... Traded by Lakers to Bucks for G Lindsey Hunter (June 28, 2001).
MISCELLANEOUS: Member of NBA championship team (2001).

COLLEGIATE RECORD

Season Team	G	Min.	FGM	FGA	Pct.	FTM	FTA	Pct.	Reb.	Ast.	Pts.	AVERAGES RPG	APG	PPG
86-87—UCLA	31	441	44	88	.500	13	26	.500	76	25	101	2.5	0.8	3.3
87-88—UCLA	11	292	39	74	.527	16	37	.432	61	13	94	5.5	1.2	8.5
88-89—Texas-El Paso	26	728	117	242	.483	54	83	.651	189	18	288	7.3	0.7	11.1
89-90—Texas-El Paso	32	837	133	286	.465	73	90	.811	198	31	339	6.2	1.0	10.6
Totals	100	2298	333	690	.483	156	236	.661	524	87	822	5.2	0.9	8.2

Three-point field goals: 1988-89, 0-for-1. 1989-90, 0-for-2. Totals, 0-for-3 (.000).

Season Team	G	Min.	FGM	FGA	Pct.	FTM	FTA	Pct.	Reb.	Ast.	Pts.	AVERAGES		
												RPG	APG	PPG
89-90—DYC Breogan	3	97	19	42	.452	12	16	.750	31	2	50	10.3	0.7	16.7

NBA REGULAR-SEASON RECORD

Season Team	G	Min.	FGM	FGA	Pct.	FTM	FTA	Pct.	REBOUNDS			Ast.	St.	Blk.	TO	Pts.	AVERAGES		
									Off.	Def.	Tot.						RPG	APG	PPG
90-91—Washington	54	606	97	211	.460	42	61	.689	52	99	151	37	12	22	45	236	2.8	0.7	4.4
91-92—Washington	49	548	89	193	.461	35	49	.714	43	102	145	35	6	12	36	213	3.0	0.7	4.3
92-93—Wash.-Atlanta .	43	298	55	120	.458	15	21	.714	32	51	83	21	3	14	25	125	1.9	0.5	2.9
93-94—Milwaukee	3	19	4	7	.571	2	2	1.000	0	3	3	0	0	1	1	10	1.0	0.0	3.3
94-95—Chicago-Minn.	78	1144	150	318	.472	78	111	.703	85	174	259	39	15	28	71	385	3.3	0.5	4.9
95-96—Utah	73	803	107	244	.439	61	72	.847	53	125	178	25	7	22	58	276	2.4	0.3	3.8
96-97—Utah	79	920	111	245	.453	54	65	.831	56	131	187	31	10	20	54	278	2.4	0.4	3.5
97-98—Utah	78	1446	186	418	.445	67	87	.770	85	188	273	51	15	28	68	441	3.5	0.7	5.7
98-99—Utah	42	458	52	138	.377	13	21	.619	28	55	83	25	6	8	24	118	2.0	0.6	2.8
99-00—Seattle	60	718	91	224	.406	18	28	.643	16	91	107	41	10	18	28	203	1.8	0.7	3.4
00-01—L.A. Lakers	62	451	56	133	.421	10	14	.714	29	83	112	32	9	12	25	125	1.8	0.5	2.0
Totals	621	7411	998	2251	.443	395	531	.744	479	1102	1581	337	93	185	435	2410	2.5	0.5	3.9

Three-point field goals: 1990-91, 0-for-5. 1991-92, 0-for-1. 1992-93, 0-for-4. 1993-94, 1-for-4. 1994-95, 7-for-23 (.304). 1995-96, 1-for-8 (.125). 1996-97, 2-for-3 (.667). 1997-98, 2-for-9 (.222). 1998-99, 1-for-4 (.250). 1999-00, 3-for-15 (.200). 2000-01, 3-for-9 (.333). Totals, 19-for-81 (.235).

Personal fouls/disqualifications: 1990-91, 112/1. 1991-92, 83/0. 1992-93, 58/0. 1993-94, 3/0. 1994-95, 183/0. 1995-96, 120/0. 1996-97, 145/0. 1997-98, 187/2. 1998-99, 63/1. 1999-00, 105/0. 2000-01, 76/0. Totals, 1135/4.

NBA PLAYOFF RECORD

Season Team	G	Min.	FGM	FGA	Pct.	FTM	FTA	Pct.	REBOUNDS			Ast.	St.	Blk.	TO	Pts.	AVERAGES		
									Off.	Def.	Tot.						RPG	APG	PPG
92-93—Atlanta	1	5	1	3	.333	3	4	.750	0	1	1	0	0	0	0	5	1.0	0.0	5.0
95-96—Utah	12	76	11	22	.500	6	10	.600	6	6	12	2	1	2	5	28	1.0	0.2	2.3
96-97—Utah	20	309	28	72	.389	26	30	.867	15	41	56	11	4	7	11	84	2.8	0.6	4.2
97-98—Utah	20	335	39	86	.453	3	5	.600	20	47	67	5	2	5	18	82	3.4	0.3	4.1
98-99—Utah	8	70	8	19	.421	0	0	...	1	7	8	1	1	0	3	16	1.0	0.1	2.0
99-00—Seattle	5	68	7	19	.368	2	2	1.000	0	10	11	1	0	1	3	18	2.2	0.2	3.6
00-01—L.A. Lakers	1	3	0	0	...	0	0	...	0	1	1	0	0	0	0	0	1.0	0.0	0.0
Totals	67	866	94	221	.425	40	51	.784	43	113	156	20	8	15	40	233	2.3	0.3	3.5

Three-point field goals: 1996-97, 2-for-8 (.250). 1997-98, 1-for-2 (.500). 1999-00, 2-for-5 (.400). Totals, 5-for-15 (.333).

Personal fouls/disqualifications: 1995-96, 16/0. 1996-97, 53/0. 1997-98, 55/0. 1998-99, 11/0. 1999-00, 14/0. 2000-01, 1/0. Totals, 150/0.

FOSTER, JEFF   F   PACERS

PERSONAL: Born January 16, 1977, in San Antonio. ... 6-11/230. (2,11/104,3). ... Full Name: Jeffrey Douglas Foster.
HIGH SCHOOL: James Madison (San Antonio).
COLLEGE: Southwest Texas State.
TRANSACTIONS/CAREER NOTES: Selected by Golden State Warriors in first round (21st pick overall) of 1999 NBA Draft. ... Draft rights traded by Warriors to Indiana Pacers for draft rights to G Vonteego Cummings and future first-round draft choice (June 30, 1999).

COLLEGIATE RECORD

Season Team	G	Min.	FGM	FGA	Pct.	FTM	FTA	Pct.	Reb.	Ast.	Pts.	AVERAGES		
												RPG	APG	PPG
95-96—Southwest Texas State ...	26	340	31	70	.443	19	39	.487	108	19	82	4.2	0.7	3.2
96-97—Southwest Texas State ...	29	637	87	170	.512	71	110	.645	222	25	248	7.7	0.9	8.6
97-98—Southwest Texas State ...	28	816	140	263	.532	77	126	.611	285	44	357	10.2	1.6	12.8
98-99—Southwest Texas State ...	28	787	142	285	.498	113	163	.693	316	43	397	11.3	1.5	14.2
Totals	111	2580	400	788	.508	280	438	.639	931	131	1084	8.4	1.2	9.8

Three-point field goals: 1995-96, 1-for-1. 1996-97, 3-for-3. Totals, 4-for-4 (1.000).

NBA REGULAR-SEASON RECORD

Season Team	G	Min.	FGM	FGA	Pct.	FTM	FTA	Pct.	REBOUNDS			Ast.	St.	Blk.	TO	Pts.	AVERAGES		
									Off.	Def.	Tot.						RPG	APG	PPG
99-00—Indiana	19	86	13	23	.565	17	25	.680	12	20	32	5	5	1	2	43	1.7	0.3	2.3
00-01—Indiana	71	1152	100	213	.469	47	91	.516	144	245	389	33	39	28	52	249	5.5	0.5	3.5
Totals	90	1238	113	236	.479	64	116	.552	156	265	421	38	44	29	54	292	4.7	0.4	3.2

Three-point field goals: 1999-00, 0-for-1. 2000-01, 2-for-7 (.286). Totals, 2-for-8 (.250).
Personal fouls/disqualifications: 1999-00, 18/0. 2000-01, 152/3. Totals, 170/3.

NBA PLAYOFF RECORD

Season Team	G	Min.	FGM	FGA	Pct.	FTM	FTA	Pct.	REBOUNDS			Ast.	St.	Blk.	TO	Pts.	AVERAGES		
									Off.	Def.	Tot.						RPG	APG	PPG
00-01—Indiana	4	52	4	9	.444	2	2	1.000	3	9	12	2	0	3	4	10	3.0	0.5	2.5

Personal fouls/disqualifications: 2000-01, 8/0.

FOX, RICK   F   LAKERS

PERSONAL: Born July 24, 1969, in Toronto. ... 6-7/242. (2,01/109,8). ... Full Name: Ulrich Alexander Fox.
HIGH SCHOOL: Warsaw (Ind.) Community.
COLLEGE: North Carolina.
TRANSACTIONS/CAREER NOTES: Selected by Boston Celtics in first round (24th pick overall) of 1991 NBA Draft. ... Signed as free agent by Los Angeles Lakers (August 28, 1997).
MISCELLANEOUS: Member of NBA championship team (2000, 2001).

COLLEGIATE RECORD

NOTES: THE SPORTING NEWS All-America third team (1991).

Season Team	G	Min.	FGM	FGA	Pct.	FTM	FTA	Pct.	Reb.	Ast.	Pts.	RPG	APG	PPG
												AVERAGES		
87-88—North Carolina	34	371	59	94	.628	15	30	.500	63	32	136	1.9	0.9	4.0
88-89—North Carolina	37	829	165	283	.583	83	105	.790	142	76	426	3.8	2.1	11.5
89-90—North Carolina	34	981	203	389	.522	75	102	.735	157	84	551	4.6	2.5	16.2
90-91—North Carolina	35	999	206	455	.453	111	138	.804	232	131	590	6.6	3.7	16.9
Totals	140	3180	633	1221	.518	284	375	.757	594	323	1703	4.2	2.3	12.2

Three-point field goals: 1987-88, 3-for-9 (.333). 1988-89, 13-for-29 (.448). 1989-90, 70-for-160 (.438). 1990-91, 67-for-196 (.342). Totals, 153-for-394 (.388).

HONORS: NBA All-Rookie second team (1992).

NBA REGULAR-SEASON RECORD

Season Team	G	Min.	FGM	FGA	Pct.	FTM	FTA	Pct.	Off.	Def.	Tot.	Ast.	St.	Blk.	TO	Pts.	RPG	APG	PPG
									REBOUNDS								**AVERAGES**		
91-92—Boston	81	1535	241	525	.459	139	184	.755	73	147	220	126	78	30	123	644	2.7	1.6	8.0
92-93—Boston	71	1082	184	380	.484	81	101	.802	55	104	159	113	61	21	77	453	2.2	1.6	6.4
93-94—Boston	82	2096	340	728	.467	174	230	.757	105	250	355	217	81	52	158	887	4.3	2.6	10.8
94-95—Boston	53	1039	169	351	.481	95	123	.772	61	94	155	139	52	19	78	464	2.9	2.6	8.8
95-96—Boston	81	2588	421	928	.454	196	254	.772	158	292	450	369	113	41	216	1137	5.6	4.6	14.0
96-97—Boston	76	2650	433	950	.456	207	263	.787	114	280	394	286	167	40	178	1174	5.2	3.8	15.4
97-98—L.A. Lakers	82	2709	363	771	.471	171	230	.743	78	280	358	276	100	48	201	983	4.4	3.4	12.0
98-99—L.A. Lakers	44	944	148	330	.448	66	89	.742	26	63	89	28	10	56	394	2.0	2.0	9.0
99-00—L.A. Lakers	82	1473	206	498	.414	63	78	.808	63	135	198	138	52	26	87	534	2.4	1.7	6.5
00-01—L.A. Lakers	82	2291	287	646	.444	95	122	.779	80	245	325	262	70	29	136	787	4.0	3.2	9.6
Totals	734	18407	2792	6107	.457	1287	1674	.769	813	1890	2703	2015	802	316	1310	7457	3.7	2.7	10.2

Three-point field goals: 1991-92, 23-for-70 (.329). 1992-93, 4-for-23 (.174). 1993-94, 33-for-100 (.330). 1994-95, 31-for-75 (.413). 1995-96, 99-for-272 (.364). 1996-97, 101-for-278 (.363). 1997-98, 86-for-265 (.325). 1998-99, 32-for-95 (.337). 1999-00, 59-for-181 (.326). 2000-01, 118-for-300 (.393). Totals, 586-for-1659 (.353).

Personal fouls/disqualifications: 1991-92, 230/3. 1992-93, 133/1. 1993-94, 244/4. 1994-95, 154/1. 1995-96, 290/5. 1996-97, 279/4. 1997-98, 309/4. 1998-99, 114/1. 1999-00, 203/1. 2000-01, 225/1. Totals, 2181/25.

NBA PLAYOFF RECORD

Season Team	G	Min.	FGM	FGA	Pct.	FTM	FTA	Pct.	Off.	Def.	Tot.	Ast.	St.	Blk.	TO	Pts.	RPG	APG	PPG
									REBOUNDS								**AVERAGES**		
91-92—Boston	8	67	11	23	.478	4	4	1.000	3	3	6	4	2	2	2	29	0.8	0.5	3.6
92-93—Boston	4	71	7	25	.280	2	2	1.000	8	11	19	5	2	1	4	17	4.8	1.3	4.3
97-98—L.A. Lakers	13	428	51	114	.447	19	23	.826	18	40	58	51	11	3	21	142	4.5	3.9	10.9
98-99—L.A. Lakers	8	181	24	60	.400	1	1	1.000	9	13	22	12	4	5	14	53	2.8	1.5	6.6
99-00—L.A. Lakers	23	331	33	73	.452	16	21	.762	11	27	38	28	9	0	16	100	1.7	1.2	4.3
00-01—L.A. Lakers	16	573	58	129	.450	26	30	.867	13	66	79	57	31	7	36	160	4.9	3.6	10.0
Totals	72	1651	184	424	.434	68	81	.840	62	160	222	157	59	18	93	501	3.1	2.2	7.0

Three-point field goals: 1991-92, 3-for-6 (.500). 1992-93, 1-for-3 (.333). 1997-98, 21-for-53 (.396). 1998-99, 4-for-21 (.190). 1999-00, 18-for-39 (.462). 2000-01, 18-for-57 (.316). Totals, 65-for-179 (.363).

Personal fouls/disqualifications: 1991-92, 11/0. 1992-93, 7/0. 1997-98, 47/2. 1998-99, 26/1. 1999-00, 68/1. 2000-01, 55/1. Totals, 214/5.

FOYLE, ADONAL — F/C — WARRIORS

PERSONAL: Born March 9, 1975, in Island of Canouan, Grenadines. ... 6-10/250. (2,08/113,4). ... Full Name: Adonal David Foyle.
HIGH SCHOOL: Hamilton (N.Y.).
COLLEGE: Colgate.
TRANSACTIONS/CAREER NOTES: Selected after junior season by Golden State Warriors in first round (eighth pick overall) of 1997 NBA Draft.

COLLEGIATE RECORD

NOTES: Holds NCAA Division I career record for most blocked shots—492. ... Holds NCAA Division I single-season record for highest blocked-shots-per-game average-6.4 (1997). ... Led NCAA Division I with 6.4 blocked shots per game (1997).

Season Team	G	Min.	FGM	FGA	Pct.	FTM	FTA	Pct.	Reb.	Ast.	Pts.	RPG	APG	PPG
												AVERAGES		
94-95—Colgate	30	1063	207	370	.559	95	190	.500	371	36	682	12.4	1.2	22.7
95-96—Colgate	29	1060	228	441	.517	129	264	.489	364	44	585	12.6	1.5	20.2
96-97—Colgate	28	1055	277	490	.565	127	261	.487	368	54	682	13.1	1.9	24.4
Totals	87	3178	712	1301	.547	351	715	.491	1103	134	1949	12.7	1.5	22.4

Three-point field goals: 1995-96, 0-for-3. 1996-97, 1-for-10 (.100). Totals, 1-for-13 (.077).

NBA REGULAR-SEASON RECORD

Season Team	G	Min.	FGM	FGA	Pct.	FTM	FTA	Pct.	Off.	Def.	Tot.	Ast.	St.	Blk.	TO	Pts.	RPG	APG	PPG
									REBOUNDS								**AVERAGES**		
97-98—Golden State	55	656	69	170	.406	27	62	.435	73	111	184	14	13	52	50	165	3.3	0.3	3.0
98-99—Golden State	44	614	52	121	.430	25	51	.490	79	115	194	18	15	43	31	129	4.4	0.4	2.9
99-00—Golden State	76	1654	193	380	.508	34	90	.378	174	250	424	42	26	136	71	420	5.6	0.6	5.5
00-01—Golden State	58	1457	156	375	.416	30	68	.441	156	249	405	48	31	156	79	342	7.0	0.8	5.9
Totals	233	4381	470	1046	.449	116	271	.428	482	725	1207	122	85	387	231	1056	5.2	0.5	4.5

Three-point field goals: 1997-98, 0-for-1. Totals, 0-for-1 (.000).

Personal fouls/disqualifications: 1997-98, 94/0. 1998-99, 90/0. 1999-00, 218/2. 2000-01, 136/0. Totals, 538/2.

FRANCIS, STEVE   G   ROCKETS

PERSONAL: Born February 21, 1977, in Silver Spring, Md. ... 6-3/193. (1,91/87,5). ... Full Name: Steve D'Shawn Francis.
HIGH SCHOOL: Montgomery Blair (Silver Spring, Md.).
JUNIOR COLLEGE: San Jacinto College (Texas), then Allegany (Md.) Community College.
COLLEGE: Maryland.
TRANSACTIONS/CAREER NOTES: Selected after junior season by Vancouver Grizzlies in first round (second pick overall) of 1999 NBA Draft. ... Draft rights traded by Grizzlies with F Tony Massenburg to Houston Rockets as part of three-way deal in which Grizzlies received G Michael Dickerson, F/C Othella Harrington, G Brent Price, F/C Antoine Carr and future first-round draft choice from Rockets, Rockets received F Don MacLean and future first-round draft choice from Orlando Magic, and Magic received G Michael Smith, G/F Rodrick Rhodes, G Lee Mayberry and F Makhtar Ndiaye from Grizzles (August 27, 1999).

COLLEGIATE RECORD

NOTES: THE SPORTING NEWS All-America second team (1999).

Season Team	G	Min.	FGM	FGA	Pct.	FTM	FTA	Pct.	Reb.	Ast.	Pts.	RPG	APG	PPG
96-97—San Jacinto College........	35	971	138	248	.556	146	184	.793	263	264	437	7.5	7.5	12.5
97-98—Allegany C.C.	35	...	295	561	.526	204	248	.823	248	304	885	7.1	8.7	25.3
98-99—Maryland	34	1044	205	392	.523	124	157	.790	154	152	579	4.5	4.5	17.0
Junior College Totals.............	70	...	433	809	.535	250	432	.579	511	568	1322	7.3	8.1	18.9
4-Year-College Totals	34	1044	205	392	.523	124	157	.790	154	152	579	4.5	4.5	17.0

Three-point field goals: 1996-97, 15-for-39 (.385). 1997-98, 91-for-241 (.378). 1998-99, 45-for-116 (.388).

NBA REGULAR-SEASON RECORD

HONORS: NBA Co-Rookie of the Year (2000). ... NBA All-Rookie first team (2000).

Season Team	G	Min.	FGM	FGA	Pct.	FTM	FTA	Pct.	Off.	Def.	Tot.	Ast.	St.	Blk.	TO	Pts.	RPG	APG	PPG
99-00—Houston..........	77	2776	497	1117	.445	287	365	.786	152	257	409	507	118	29	306	1388	5.3	6.6	18.0
00-01—Houston..........	80	3194	550	1219	.451	358	438	.817	190	363	553	517	141	31	265	1591	6.9	6.5	19.9
Totals	157	5970	1047	2336	.448	645	803	.803	342	620	962	1024	259	60	571	2979	6.1	6.5	19.0

Three-point field goals: 1999-00, 107-for-310 (.345). 2000-01, 133-for-336 (.396). Totals, 240-for-646 (.372).
Personal fouls/disqualifications: 1999-00, 231/2. 2000-01, 274/7. Totals, 505/9.

FULLER, TODD   C

PERSONAL: Born July 25, 1974, in Fayetteville, N.C. ... 7-0/268. (2,13/121,6). ... Full Name: Todd Douglas Fuller.
HIGH SCHOOL: Charlotte Christian.
COLLEGE: North Carolina State.
TRANSACTIONS/CAREER NOTES: Selected by Golden State Warriors in first round (11th pick overall) of 1996 NBA Draft. ... Traded by Warriors to Utah Jazz for 2000 second-round draft choice (February 4, 1999). ... Signed as free agent by Charlotte Hornets (August 18, 1999). ... Signed as free agent by Miami Heat (September 13, 2000).

COLLEGIATE RECORD

Season Team	G	Min.	FGM	FGA	Pct.	FTM	FTA	Pct.	Reb.	Ast.	Pts.	RPG	APG	PPG
92-93—North Carolina State.......	27	413	53	116	.457	34	44	.773	97	6	141	3.6	0.2	5.2
93-94—North Carolina State.......	30	875	144	299	.482	67	89	.753	253	33	355	8.4	1.1	11.8
94-95—North Carolina State.......	27	816	164	316	.519	116	138	.841	229	35	440	8.5	1.3	16.3
95-96—North Carolina State.......	31	1044	225	445	.506	183	229	.799	308	39	649	9.9	1.3	20.9
Totals	115	3148	586	1176	.498	400	500	.800	887	113	1585	7.7	1.0	13.8

Three-point field goals: 1992-93, 1-for-2 (.500). 1993-94, 0-for-1. 1994-95, 0-for-9. 1995-96, 16-for-43 (.372). Totals, 17-for-55 (.309).

NBA REGULAR-SEASON RECORD

Season Team	G	Min.	FGM	FGA	Pct.	FTM	FTA	Pct.	Off.	Def.	Tot.	Ast.	St.	Blk.	TO	Pts.	RPG	APG	PPG
96-97—Golden State ...	75	949	114	266	.429	76	110	.691	108	141	249	24	10	20	52	304	3.3	0.3	4.1
97-98—Golden State ...	57	613	86	205	.420	55	80	.688	61	135	196	10	6	16	37	227	3.4	0.2	4.0
98-99—Utah	42	462	56	124	.452	30	50	.600	28	73	101	6	6	14	27	142	2.4	0.1	3.4
99-00—Charlotte	41	399	51	122	.418	32	53	.604	36	74	110	5	9	8	27	134	2.7	0.1	3.3
00-01—Miami	10	77	10	35	.286	8	8	1.000	7	11	18	1	3	2	3	28	1.8	0.1	2.8
Totals	225	2500	317	752	.422	201	301	.668	240	434	674	46	34	60	146	835	3.0	0.2	3.7

Three-point field goals: 1997-98, 0-for-4. Totals, 0-for-4 (.000).
Personal fouls/disqualifications: 1996-97, 146/0. 1997-98, 89/0. 1998-99, 60/0. 1999-00, 46/0. 2000-01, 10/0. Totals, 351/0.

NBA PLAYOFF RECORD

Season Team	G	Min.	FGM	FGA	Pct.	FTM	FTA	Pct.	Off.	Def.	Tot.	Ast.	St.	Blk.	TO	Pts.	RPG	APG	PPG
98-99—Utah...............	10	105	10	26	.385	6	10	.600	8	20	28	0	0	2	5	26	2.8	0.0	2.6

Personal fouls/disqualifications: 1998-99, 21/0.

FUNDERBURKE, LAWRENCE   F   KINGS

PERSONAL: Born December 15, 1970, in Columbus, Ohio. ... 6-9/230. (2,06/104,3).
HIGH SCHOOL: Worthington (Ohio) Christian, then Wehrle (Columbus, Ohio).
JUNIOR COLLEGE: St. Catharine College (Ky.).
COLLEGE: Indiana, then Ohio State.
TRANSACTIONS/CAREER NOTES: Selected by Sacramento Kings in second round (51st pick overall) on 1994 NBA Draft. ... Played in Greece (1994-95 and 1995-96). ... Played in France (1996-97).

COLLEGIATE RECORD

												AVERAGES		
Season Team	G	Min.	FGM	FGA	Pct.	FTM	FTA	Pct.	Reb.	Ast.	Pts.	RPG	APG	PPG
89-90—Indiana	6	144	28	57	.491	14	27	.519	40	8	70	6.7	1.3	11.7
89-90—St. Catharine..................							Did not play.							
90-91—Ohio State						Did not play—transfer student.								
91-92—Ohio State	23	668	115	210	.548	51	78	.654	149	18	281	6.5	0.8	12.2
92-93—Ohio State	28	878	186	349	.533	84	135	.622	190	34	457	6.8	1.2	16.3
93-94—Ohio State	29	847	188	345	.545	63	106	.594	190	28	441	6.6	1.0	15.2
Totals	86	2537	517	961	.538	212	346	.613	569	88	1249	6.6	1.0	14.5

Three-point field goals: 1992-93, 1-for-3 (.333). 1993-94, 2-for-7 (.286). Totals, 3-for-10 (.300).

GREEK LEAGUE RECORD

												AVERAGES		
Season Team	G	Min.	FGM	FGA	Pct.	FTM	FTA	Pct.	Reb.	Ast.	Pts.	RPG	APG	PPG
94-95—Ampelokipi Afisorama	25	971	236	473	.499	141	192	.734	189	26	627	7.6	1.0	25.1
95-96—PAOK	14	...	...	...	...	...	...	...	121	20	244	8.6	1.4	17.4
Totals	39	...	...	...	...	...	...	...	310	46	871	7.9	1.2	22.3

Three-point field goals: 1994-95, 14-for-55 (.255).

FRENCH LEAGUE RECORD

												AVERAGES		
Season Team	G	Min.	FGM	FGA	Pct.	FTM	FTA	Pct.	Reb.	Ast.	Pts.	RPG	APG	PPG
96-97—Pau Orthez.....................	20	889	181	283	.640	59	82	.720	155	37	444	7.8	1.9	22.2

NBA REGULAR-SEASON RECORD

									REBOUNDS								AVERAGES		
Season Team	G	Min.	FGM	FGA	Pct.	FTM	FTA	Pct.	Off.	Def.	Tot.	Ast.	St.	Blk.	TO	Pts.	RPG	APG	PPG
97-98—Sacramento	52	1094	191	390	.490	110	162	.679	80	154	234	63	19	15	62	493	4.5	1.2	9.5
98-99—Sacramento	47	936	167	299	.559	85	120	.708	101	121	222	30	22	23	52	420	4.7	0.6	8.9
99-00—Sacramento	75	1026	184	352	.523	115	163	.706	98	136	234	33	32	20	40	483	3.1	0.4	6.4
00-01—Sacramento	59	698	120	242	.496	48	77	.623	74	122	196	17	9	13	32	288	3.3	0.3	4.9
Totals	233	3754	662	1283	.516	358	522	.686	353	533	886	143	82	71	186	1684	3.8	0.6	7.2

Three-point field goals: 1997-98, 1-for-7 (.143). 1998-99, 1-for-5 (.200). 1999-00, 0-for-2. Totals, 2-for-14 (.143).
Personal fouls/disqualifications: 1997-98, 56/0. 1998-99, 77/0. 1999-00, 91/0. 2000-01, 44/0. Totals, 268/0.

NBA PLAYOFF RECORD

									REBOUNDS								AVERAGES		
Season Team	G	Min.	FGM	FGA	Pct.	FTM	FTA	Pct.	Off.	Def.	Tot.	Ast.	St.	Blk.	TO	Pts.	RPG	APG	PPG
98-99—Sacramento	3	31	5	12	.417	0	0	...	2	2	4	1	3	0	3	10	1.3	0.3	3.3
99-00—Sacramento	4	34	4	9	.444	2	4	.500	4	7	11	0	1	0	0	10	2.8	0.0	2.5
00-01—Sacramento	3	17	3	8	.375	1	1	1.000	4	2	6	0	2	2	1	7	2.0	0.0	2.3
Totals	10	82	12	29	.414	3	5	.600	10	11	21	1	6	2	4	27	2.1	0.1	2.7

Personal fouls/disqualifications: 1998-99, 3/0. 2000-01, 4/0. Totals, 7/0.

GARCES, RUBEN   F

PERSONAL: Born October 17, 1973, in Colon, Panama. ... 6-9/235. (2,06/106,6). ... Full Name: Ruben Santiago Garces.
HIGH SCHOOL: Colegio Abel Bravo (Panama).
JUNIOR COLLEGE: Navarro College (Texas).
COLLEGE: Providence.
TRANSACTIONS/CAREER NOTES: Not drafted by an NBA franchise. ... Played in Continental Basketball Association with Quad City Thunder (1998-99) and LaCrosse Bobcats (1999-2000). ... Played in Argentina (1999-2000). ... Played in France (2000-01). ... Played in Venezuela (2000-01). ... Signed as free agent by Phoenix Suns (August 3, 2000). ... Traded by Suns with F Corie Blount and G Paul McPherson to Golden State Warriors for G Vinny Del Negro (January 26, 2001). ... Waived by Warriors (February 28, 2001). ... Signed to play for Forum Valladolid in Spain for 2001-02 season.

COLLEGIATE RECORD

											AVERAGES		
Season Team	G	Min.	FGM	FGA	Pct.	FTM	FTA	Pct.	Reb.	Ast.	Pts.	RPG	APG	PPG
92-93—Navarro College.............						Did not play—redshirted.								
93-94—Navarro College.............						Statistics unavailable.								
94-95—Navarro College.............						Statistics unavailable.								
95-96—Providence	30	671	94	191	.492	24	60	.400	225	20	212	7.5	0.7	7.1
96-97—Providence	35	902	149	277	.538	35	84	.417	272	23	333	7.8	0.7	9.5
Totals	65	1573	243	468	.519	59	144	.410	497	43	545	7.6	0.7	8.4

CBA REGULAR-SEASON RECORD

											AVERAGES		
Season Team	G	Min.	FGM	FGA	Pct.	FTM	FTA	Pct.	Reb.	Ast.	Pts.	RPG	APG	PPG
98-99—Quad City-La Crosse	25	417	61	125	.488	18	36	.500	138	7	140	5.5	0.3	5.6
99-00—La Crosse	26	600	88	160	.550	33	65	.508	236	11	209	9.1	0.4	8.0
Totals	51	1017	149	285	.523	51	101	.505	374	18	349	6.9	0.4	6.8

ARGENTINIAN LEAGUE RECORD

											AVERAGES		
Season Team	G	Min.	FGM	FGA	Pct.	FTM	FTA	Pct.	Reb.	Ast.	Pts.	RPG	APG	PPG
99-00—Boca	2	55	12	20	.600	2	4	.500	11	2	26	5.5	1.0	13.0

F

G

Season Team	G	Min.	FGM	FGA	Pct.	FTM	FTA	Pct.	Reb.	Ast.	Pts.	AVERAGES		
												RPG	APG	PPG
00-01—Villeurbanne	11	252	51	95	.537	26	44	.591	82	5	128	7.5	0.5	11.6

Three-point field goals: 2000-01, 0-for-1.

NBA REGULAR-SEASON RECORD

Season Team	G	Min.	FGM	FGA	Pct.	FTM	FTA	Pct.	REBOUNDS			Ast.	St.	Blk.	TO	Pts.	AVERAGES		
									Off.	Def.	Tot.						RPG	APG	PPG
00-01—Phoenix-G.S.	13	73	7	22	.318	2	8	.250	16	13	29	5	3	2	5	16	2.2	0.4	1.2

Personal fouls/disqualifications: 2000-01, 14/0.

VENEZUELAN LEAGUE RECORD

Season Team	G	Min.	FGM	FGA	Pct.	FTM	FTA	Pct.	Reb.	Ast.	Pts.	AVERAGES		
												RPG	APG	PPG
00-01—Toros	32	...	...	...	...	...	...	...	320	...	544	10.0	...	17.0

GARNER, CHRIS   G

PERSONAL: Born February 2, 1975, in Memphis. ... 5-10/156. (1,78/70,8).
HIGH SCHOOL: Treadwell (Memphis).
COLLEGE: Memphis.
TRANSACTIONS/CAREER NOTES: Not drafted by an NBA franchise. ... Signed as free agent by Toronto Raptors (October 31, 1997). ... Played in Continental Basketball Association with Idaho Stampede (1998-99), Fort Wayne Fury (1998-99) and Quad City Thunder (1999-2000 and 2000-01). ... Signed as free agent by San Antonio Spurs (January 22, 1999). ... Waived by Spurs (February 2, 1999). ... Played in Lithuania (1999-2000). ... Played in American Basketball Association 2000 with Memphis HoundDawgs (2000-01). ... Signed by Golden State Warriors to 10-day contract (April 6, 2001). ... Re-signed by Warriors for remainder of season (April 16, 2001).

COLLEGIATE RECORD

Season Team	G	Min.	FGM	FGA	Pct.	FTM	FTA	Pct.	Reb.	Ast.	Pts.	AVERAGES		
												RPG	APG	PPG
93-94—Memphis	28	733	70	179	.391	26	40	.650	78	124	179	2.8	4.4	6.4
94-95—Memphis	34	1165	85	202	.421	48	99	.485	114	217	225	3.4	6.4	6.6
95-96—Memphis	30	1014	92	201	.458	26	46	.565	104	171	228	3.5	5.7	7.6
96-97—Memphis	31	1005	85	194	.438	18	26	.692	81	127	211	2.6	4.1	6.8
Totals	123	3917	332	776	.428	118	211	.559	377	639	843	3.1	5.2	6.9

Three-point field goals: 1993-94, 13-for-52 (.250). 1994-95, 7-for-49 (.143). 1995-96, 18-for-49 (.367). 1996-97, 23-for-83 (.277). Totals, 61-for-233 (.262).

NBA REGULAR-SEASON RECORD

Season Team	G	Min.	FGM	FGA	Pct.	FTM	FTA	Pct.	REBOUNDS			Ast.	St.	Blk.	TO	Pts.	AVERAGES		
									Off.	Def.	Tot.						RPG	APG	PPG
97-98—Toronto	38	293	23	70	.329	3	7	.429	7	17	24	45	21	4	25	53	0.6	1.2	1.4
00-01—Golden State	8	149	7	37	.189	5	6	.833	2	10	12	18	7	1	9	19	1.5	2.3	2.4
Totals	46	442	30	107	.280	8	13	.615	9	27	36	63	28	5	34	72	0.8	1.4	1.6

Three-point field goals: 1997-98, 4-for-14 (.286). 2000-01, 0-for-7. Totals, 4-for-21 (.190).
Personal fouls/disqualifications: 1997-98, 50/0. 2000-01, 18/0. Totals, 68/0.

CBA REGULAR-SEASON RECORD

Season Team	G	Min.	FGM	FGA	Pct.	FTM	FTA	Pct.	Reb.	Ast.	Pts.	AVERAGES		
												RPG	APG	PPG
98-99—Idaho-Fort Wayne	47	1495	163	450	.362	55	73	.753	131	267	424	2.8	5.7	9.0
99-00—Quad City	6	105	12	29	.414	2	3	.667	15	18	26	2.5	3.0	4.3
00-01—Quad City	21	831	119	273	.436	55	78	.705	78	148	312	3.7	7.0	14.9
Totals	74	2431	294	752	.391	112	154	.727	224	433	762	3.0	5.9	10.3

Three-point field goals: 1998-99, 43-for-131 (.328). 1999-00, 0-for-1. 2000-01, 19-for-72 (.264). Totals, 62-for-204 (.304).

LITHUANIAN LEAGUE RECORD

Season Team	G	Min.	FGM	FGA	Pct.	FTM	FTA	Pct.	Reb.	Ast.	Pts.	AVERAGES		
												RPG	APG	PPG
99-00—Zalgiris Kaunas	24	556	46	113	.407	8	11	.727	61	70	114	2.5	2.9	4.8

Three-point field goals: 1999-00, 14-for-40 (.350).

ABA 2000 LEAGUE RECORD

Season Team	G	Min.	FGM	FGA	Pct.	FTM	FTA	Pct.	Reb.	Ast.	Pts.	AVERAGES		
												RPG	APG	PPG
00-01—Memphis	19	605	67	187	.358	22	30	.733	70	118	178	3.7	6.2	9.4

Three-point field goals: 2000-01, 22-for-77 (.286).

GARNETT, KEVIN   F   TIMBERWOLVES

PERSONAL: Born May 19, 1976, in Mauldin, S.C. ... 6-11/220. (2,11/99,8).
HIGH SCHOOL: Mauldin (S.C.), then Farragut Academy (Chicago).
COLLEGE: Did not attend college.
TRANSACTIONS/CAREER NOTES: Selected out of high school by Minnesota Timberwolves in first round (fifth pick overall) of 1995 NBA Draft.
MISCELLANEOUS: Member of gold-medal-winning U.S. Olympic team (2000). ... Minnesota Timberwolves all-time points leader with 8,280, all-time rebounds leader with 4,271, all-time steals leader with 639, and all-time blocked shots leader with 798 (1995-96 through 2000-01).

G

NBA REGULAR-SEASON RECORD

HONORS: All-NBA first team (2000). ... All-NBA second team (2001). ... All-NBA third team (1999). ... NBA All-Defensive first team (2000, 2001). ... NBA All-Rookie second team (1996).

Season Team	G	Min.	FGM	FGA	Pct.	FTM	FTA	Pct.	REB Off.	REB Def.	REB Tot.	Ast.	St.	Blk.	TO	Pts.	RPG	APG	PPG
95-96—Minnesota	80	2293	361	735	.491	105	149	.705	175	326	501	145	86	131	110	835	6.3	1.8	10.4
96-97—Minnesota	77	2995	549	1100	.499	205	272	.754	190	428	618	236	105	163	175	1309	8.0	3.1	17.0
97-98—Minnesota	82	3222	635	1293	.491	245	332	.738	222	564	786	348	139	150	192	1518	9.6	4.2	18.5
98-99—Minnesota	47	1780	414	900	.460	145	206	.704	166	323	489	202	78	83	135	977	10.4	4.3	20.8
99-00—Minnesota	81	3243	759	1526	.497	309	404	.765	223	733	956	401	120	126	268	1857	11.8	5.0	22.9
00-01—Minnesota	81	3202	704	1475	.477	357	467	.764	219	702	921	401	111	145	230	1784	11.4	5.0	22.0
Totals	448	16735	3422	7029	.487	1366	1830	.746	1195	3076	4271	1733	639	798	1110	8280	9.5	3.9	18.5

Three-point field goals: 1995-96, 8-for-28 (.286). 1996-97, 6-for-21 (.286). 1997-98, 3-for-16 (.188). 1998-99, 4-for-14 (.286). 1999-00, 30-for-81 (.370). 2000-01, 19-for-66 (.288). Totals, 70-for-226 (.310).

Personal fouls/disqualifications: 1995-96, 189/2. 1996-97, 199/2. 1997-98, 224/1. 1998-99, 152/5. 1999-00, 205/1. 2000-01, 204/0. Totals, 1173/11.

NBA PLAYOFF RECORD

Season Team	G	Min.	FGM	FGA	Pct.	FTM	FTA	Pct.	REB Off.	REB Def.	REB Tot.	Ast.	St.	Blk.	TO	Pts.	RPG	APG	PPG
96-97—Minnesota	3	125	24	51	.471	3	3	1.000	14	14	28	11	4	3	4	52	9.3	3.7	17.3
97-98—Minnesota	5	194	36	75	.480	7	9	.778	17	31	48	20	4	12	22	79	9.6	4.0	15.8
98-99—Minnesota	4	170	35	79	.443	17	23	.739	16	32	48	15	7	8	13	87	12.0	3.8	21.8
99-00—Minnesota	4	171	30	78	.385	13	16	.813	13	30	43	35	5	3	11	75	10.8	8.8	18.8
00-01—Minnesota	4	165	27	58	.466	30	36	.833	10	38	48	17	4	6	6	84	12.0	4.3	21.0
Totals	20	825	152	341	.446	70	87	.805	70	145	215	98	24	32	56	377	10.8	4.9	18.9

Three-point field goals: 1996-97, 1-for-1. 1998-99, 0-for-2. 1999-00, 2-for-3 (.667). 2000-01, 0-for-3. Totals, 3-for-9 (.333).

Personal fouls/disqualifications: 1996-97, 6/0. 1997-98, 17/0. 1998-99, 10/0. 1999-00, 12/0. 2000-01, 13/0. Totals, 58/0.

NBA ALL-STAR GAME RECORD

Season Team	Min.	FGM	FGA	Pct.	FTM	FTA	Pct.	REB Off.	REB Def.	REB Tot.	Ast.	PF	Dq.	St.	Blk.	TO	Pts.
1997—Minnesota	18	1	7	.143	4	4	1.000	1	8	9	1	2	0	0	1	0	6
1998—Minnesota	21	6	11	.545	0	0	...	1	3	4	2	0	...	2	1	3	12
2000—Minnesota	35	10	19	.526	4	4	1.000	3	7	10	5	1	0	1	1	0	24
2001—Minnesota	27	7	12	.583	0	0	...	1	3	4	4	0	0	1	3	2	14
Totals	101	24	49	.490	8	8	1.000	6	21	27	12	3	0	4	6	5	56

Three-point field goals: 1998, 0-for-1. 1900, 0-for-1. Totals, 0-for-2 (.000).

GARRETT, DEAN   C   TIMBERWOLVES

PERSONAL: Born November 27, 1966, in Los Angeles. ... 6-11/250. (2,11/113,4).
HIGH SCHOOL: San Clemente (Calif.).
JUNIOR COLLEGE: San Francisco City College.
COLLEGE: Indiana.
TRANSACTIONS/CAREER NOTES: Selected by Phoenix Suns in second round (38th pick overall) of 1988 NBA Draft. ... Played in Italy (1989-90 through 1994-95). ... Played in Greece (1995-96). ... Signed as free agent by Minnesota Timberwolves (September 18, 1996). ... Signed as free agent by Denver Nuggets (September 5, 1997). ... Traded by Nuggets with G Bobby Jackson to Timberwolves in three-way deal in which Nuggets received G Chauncey Billups and draft rights to G Tyson Wheeler from Toronto Raptors and Raptors received 1999 first-round draft choice from Nuggets and draft rights to F Zeljiko Rebraca, G Micheal Williams and 1999 or 2000 first-round draft choice from Timberwolves (January 21, 1999).

COLLEGIATE RECORD

NOTES: Member of NCAA Division I championship team (1987).

Season Team	G	Min.	FGM	FGA	Pct.	FTM	FTA	Pct.	Reb.	Ast.	Pts.	RPG	APG	PPG
84-85—San Francisco City College						Statistics unavailable.								
85-86—San Francisco City College						Statistics unavailable.								
86-87—Indiana	34	952	163	301	.542	61	96	.635	288	21	387	8.5	0.6	11.4
87-88—Indiana	29	957	184	344	.535	99	142	.697	246	13	467	8.5	0.4	16.1
4-Year-College Totals	63	1909	347	645	.538	160	238	.672	534	34	854	8.5	0.5	13.6

NBA REGULAR-SEASON RECORD

Season Team	G	Min.	FGM	FGA	Pct.	FTM	FTA	Pct.	REB Off.	REB Def.	REB Tot.	Ast.	St.	Blk.	TO	Pts.	RPG	APG	PPG
88-89—Phoenix						Did not play—injured.													
96-97—Minnesota	68	1665	223	389	.573	96	138	.606	140	346	405	30	40	95	34	542	7.3	0.8	8.0
97-98—Denver	82	2632	242	565	.428	114	176	.648	227	417	644	90	57	133	84	598	7.9	1.1	7.3
98-99—Minnesota	49	1054	116	231	.502	38	51	.745	99	158	257	28	30	45	29	270	5.2	0.6	5.5
99-00—Minnesota	56	604	48	108	.444	18	26	.692	41	99	140	19	8	40	21	114	2.5	0.3	2.0
00-01—Minnesota	70	831	75	156	.481	27	39	.692	65	152	217	24	26	49	25	177	3.1	0.3	2.5
Totals	325	6786	704	1449	.486	293	430	.681	581	1172	1753	199	161	362	193	1701	5.4	0.6	5.2

Personal fouls/disqualifications: 1996-97, 158/1. 1997-98, 197/0. 1998-99, 113/0. 1999-00, 94/1. 2000-01, 93/0. Totals, 655/2.

NBA PLAYOFF RECORD

Season Team	G	Min.	FGM	FGA	Pct.	FTM	FTA	Pct.	REB Off.	REB Def.	REB Tot.	Ast.	St.	Blk.	TO	Pts.	RPG	APG	PPG
96-97—Minnesota	3	118	15	29	.517	8	10	.800	19	16	35	4	2	3	1	38	11.7	1.3	12.7
98-99—Minnesota	4	92	10	18	.556	2	5	.400	9	7	16	5	2	3	2	22	4.0	1.3	5.5
99-00—Minnesota	3	16	1	2	.500	1	2	.500	1	1	2	0	0	1	0	3	0.7	0.0	1.0
00-01—Minnesota	3	41	4	12	.333	5	6	.833	2	7	9	0	1	1	0	13	3.0	0.0	4.3
Totals	13	267	30	61	.492	16	23	.696	31	31	62	9	5	8	3	76	4.8	0.7	5.8

Personal fouls/disqualifications: 1996-97, 11/0. 1998-99, 16/1. 1999-00, 2/0. 2000-01, 6/0. Totals, 35/1.

G

Season Team	G	Min.	FGM	FGA	Pct.	FTM	FTA	Pct.	Reb.	Ast.	Pts.	AVERAGES RPG	APG	PPG
93-94—Scavolini Pesaro............	27	...	...	...	...	...	...	...	276	9	376	10.2	0.3	13.9
94-95—Scavolini Pesaro............	32	...	...	...	...	...	...	...	314	10	302	9.8	0.3	9.4
Totals	59	...	...	...	...	...	...	...	590	19	678	10.0	0.3	11.5

GREEK LEAGUE RECORD

Season Team	G	Min.	FGM	FGA	Pct.	FTM	FTA	Pct.	Reb.	Ast.	Pts.	AVERAGES RPG	APG	PPG
95-96—PAOK.............................	19	...	...	...	...	...	...	...	164	12	206	8.6	0.6	10.8

GARRITY, PAT F MAGIC

PERSONAL: Born August 23, 1976, in Las Vegas. ... 6-9/238. (2,06/108,0). ... Full Name: Patrick Joseph Garrity.
HIGH SCHOOL: Lewis Palmer (Monument, Colo.).
COLLEGE: Notre Dame.
TRANSACTIONS/CAREER NOTES: Selected by Milwaukee Bucks in first round (19th pick overall) of 1998 NBA Draft. ... Draft rights traded by Bucks with draft rights to C Dirk Nowitzki to Dallas Mavericks for draft rights to F Robert Traylor (June 24, 1998). ... Draft rights traded by Mavericks with F Martin Muursepp, G/F Bubba Wells and 1999 first-round draft choice to Phoenix Suns for G Steve Nash (June 24, 1998). ... Traded by Suns with F/C Danny Manning and two future first-round draft choices to Orlando Magic for G Anfernee Hardaway (August 5, 1999).

COLLEGIATE RECORD

NOTES: The Sporting News All-America second team (1998).

Season Team	G	Min.	FGM	FGA	Pct.	FTM	FTA	Pct.	Reb.	Ast.	Pts.	AVERAGES RPG	APG	PPG
94-95—Notre Dame..................	27	744	136	260	.523	82	107	.766	137	34	361	5.1	1.3	13.4
95-96—Notre Dame..................	27	893	177	372	.476	96	140	.686	193	38	464	7.1	1.4	17.2
96-97—Notre Dame..................	30	1056	221	457	.484	152	196	.776	221	84	633	7.4	2.8	21.1
97-98—Notre Dame..................	27	956	214	445	.481	159	212	.750	225	66	627	8.3	2.4	23.2
Totals	111	3649	748	1534	.488	489	655	.747	776	222	2085	7.0	2.0	18.8

Three-point field goals: 1994-95, 7-for-18 (.389). 1995-96, 14-for-51 (.275). 1996-97, 39-for-102 (.382). 1997-98, 40-for-108 (.370). Totals, 100-for-279 (.358).

NBA REGULAR-SEASON RECORD

Season Team	G	Min.	FGM	FGA	Pct.	FTM	FTA	Pct.	REBOUNDS Off.	Def.	Tot.	Ast.	St.	Blk.	TO	Pts.	AVERAGES RPG	APG	PPG
98-99—Phoenix	39	538	85	170	.500	40	56	.714	26	49	75	18	8	3	20	217	1.9	0.5	5.6
99-00—Orlando..........	82	1479	258	585	.441	80	111	.721	44	166	210	58	31	19	85	675	2.6	0.7	8.2
00-01—Orlando..........	76	1579	223	576	.387	85	98	.867	51	159	210	51	40	15	68	628	2.8	0.7	8.3
Totals	197	3596	566	1331	.425	205	265	.774	121	374	495	127	79	37	173	1520	2.5	0.6	7.7

Three-point field goals: 1998-99, 7-for-18 (.389). 1999-00, 79-for-197 (.401). 2000-01, 97-for-224 (.433). Totals, 183-for-439 (.417).
Personal fouls/disqualifications: 1998-99, 62/0. 1999-00, 197/1. 2000-01, 241/3. Totals, 500/4.

NBA PLAYOFF RECORD

Season Team	G	Min.	FGM	FGA	Pct.	FTM	FTA	Pct.	REBOUNDS Off.	Def.	Tot.	Ast.	St.	Blk.	TO	Pts.	AVERAGES RPG	APG	PPG
98-99—Phoenix	3	52	9	17	.529	6	6	1.000	6	3	9	1	1	1	3	27	3.0	0.3	9.0
00-01—Orlando..........	4	117	17	36	.472	4	5	.800	1	4	5	2	0	1	2	48	1.3	0.5	12.0
Totals	7	169	26	53	.491	10	11	.909	7	7	14	3	1	2	5	75	2.0	0.4	10.7

Three-point field goals: 1998-99, 3-for-3. 2000-01, 10-for-20 (.500). Totals, 13-for-23 (.565).
Personal fouls/disqualifications: 1998-99, 9/0. 2000-01, 11/0. Totals, 20/0.

G

GATLING, CHRIS F/C

PERSONAL: Born September 3, 1967, in Elizabeth, N.J. ... 6-10/230. (2,08/104,3). ... Full Name: Chris Raymond Gatling.
HIGH SCHOOL: Elizabeth (N.J.).
COLLEGE: Pittsburgh, then Old Dominion.
TRANSACTIONS/CAREER NOTES: Selected by Golden State Warriors in first round (16th pick overall) of 1991 NBA Draft. ... Traded by Warriors with G Tim Hardaway to Miami Heat for F/C Kevin Willis and G Bimbo Coles (February 22, 1996). ... Signed as free agent by Dallas Mavericks (July 16, 1996). ... Traded by Mavericks with C Eric Montross, G Jim Jackson, F/G George McCloud and G Sam Cassell to New Jersey Nets for C Shawn Bradley, F Ed O'Bannon, G Khalid Reeves and G Robert Pack (February 17, 1997). ... Traded by Nets with G Sam Cassell to Milwaukee Bucks in three-way deal in which Bucks also received C Paul Grant from Minnesota Timberwolves, Timberwolves received F Brian Evans, 1999 first-round draft choice and an undisclosed future draft choice from Nets, Bucks sent G Terrell Brandon to Timberwolves and Timberwolves sent G Stephon Marbury, G Chris Carr and F Bill Curley to Nets and Nets received G Elliot Perry from Bucks (March 11, 1999). ... Traded by Bucks with F Armen Gilliam to Orlando Magic for F/C Danny Manning and G/F Dale Ellis (August 19, 1999). ... Traded by Magic with F Tariq Abdul-Wahad, a future first-round draft choice and cash considerations to Denver Nuggets for G Chauncey Billups, G/F Ron Mercer, F Johnny Taylor and draft considerations (February 1, 2000). ... Traded by Nuggets with a 2000 second-round draft choice to Miami Heat for G Voshon Lenard and F Mark Strickland (June 27, 2000). ... Traded by Heat to Cleveland Cavaliers as part of three-way deal in which Cavaliers sent F Shawn Kemp to Portland Trail Blazers, Trail Blazers sent F Brian Grant to Heat, Heat sent F Clarence Weatherspoon, future first-round draft choice and cash Cavaliers and Trail Blazers sent G Gary Grant to Cavaliers (August 30, 2000).
MISCELLANEOUS: Member of bronze-medal-winning U.S. World Championship team (1990).

COLLEGIATE RECORD

Season Team	G	Min.	FGM	FGA	Pct.	FTM	FTA	Pct.	Reb.	Ast.	Pts.	RPG	APG	PPG
86-87—Pittsburgh							Did not play.							
87-88—Old Dominion						Did not play—transfer student.								
88-89—Old Dominion	27	839	239	388	.616	126	179	.704	244	26	604	9.0	1.0	22.4
89-90—Old Dominion	26	822	207	357	.580	120	179	.670	259	25	534	10.0	1.0	20.5
90-91—Old Dominion	32	1002	251	405	.620	171	247	.692	356	24	673	11.1	0.8	21.0
Totals	85	2663	697	1150	.606	417	605	.689	859	75	1811	10.1	0.9	21.3

Three-point field goals: 1990-91, 0-for-1.

NBA REGULAR-SEASON RECORD

Season Team	G	Min.	FGM	FGA	Pct.	FTM	FTA	Pct.	Off.	Def.	Tot.	Ast.	St.	Blk.	TO	Pts.	RPG	APG	PPG
91-92—Golden State ...	54	612	117	206	.568	72	109	.661	75	107	182	16	31	36	44	306	3.4	0.3	5.7
92-93—Golden State ...	70	1248	249	462	.539	150	207	.725	129	191	320	40	44	53	102	648	4.6	0.6	9.3
93-94—Golden State ...	82	1296	271	461	.588	129	208	.620	143	254	397	41	40	63	84	671	4.8	0.5	8.2
94-95—Golden State ...	58	1470	324	512	*.633	148	250	.592	144	299	443	51	39	52	117	796	7.6	0.9	13.7
95-96—G.S.-Miami	71	1427	326	567	.575	139	207	.671	129	288	417	43	36	40	95	791	5.9	0.6	11.1
96-97—Dallas-N.J.	47	1283	327	623	.525	236	329	.717	134	236	370	28	39	31	120	891	7.9	0.6	19.0
97-98—New Jersey	57	1359	248	545	.455	159	265	.600	118	216	334	53	52	29	99	656	5.9	0.9	11.5
98-99—N.J.-Mil.	48	775	117	265	.442	37	93	.398	52	127	179	32	32	10	62	272	3.7	0.7	5.7
99-00—Orl.-Den.	85	1811	365	802	.455	266	373	.713	154	348	502	71	82	23	169	1014	5.9	0.8	11.9
00-01—Cleveland	74	1670	329	733	.449	156	228	.684	99	292	391	61	52	27	119	842	5.3	0.8	11.4
Totals	646	12951	2673	5176	.516	1492	2269	.658	1177	2358	3535	436	447	364	1011	6887	5.5	0.7	10.7

Three-point field goals: 1991-92, 0-for-4. 1992-93, 0-for-6. 1993-94, 0-for-1. 1994-95, 0-for-1. 1995-96, 0-for-1. 1996-97, 1-for-6 (.167). 1997-98, 1-for-4 (.250). 1998-99, 1-for-8 (.125). 1999-00, 18-for-70 (.257). 2000-01, 28-for-92 (.304). Totals, 49-for-193 (.254).

Personal fouls/disqualifications: 1991-92, 101/0. 1992-93, 197/2. 1993-94, 223/5. 1994-95, 184/4. 1995-96, 217/0. 1996-97, 138/1. 1997-98, 152/2. 1998-99, 118/0. 1999-00, 246/2. 2000-01, 185/0. Totals, 1761/16.

NBA PLAYOFF RECORD

Season Team	G	Min.	FGM	FGA	Pct.	FTM	FTA	Pct.	Off.	Def.	Tot.	Ast.	St.	Blk.	TO	Pts.	RPG	APG	PPG
91-92—Golden State ...	4	81	18	29	.621	14	22	.636	9	16	25	0	2	10	1	50	6.3	0.0	12.5
93-94—Golden State ...	3	54	8	13	.615	10	13	.769	7	10	17	4	2	1	2	26	5.7	1.3	8.7
95-96—Miami	3	68	6	22	.273	6	12	.500	10	14	24	1	2	0	8	18	8.0	0.3	6.0
97-98—New Jersey	3	81	19	38	.500	8	12	.667	6	4	10	2	2	2	3	46	3.3	0.7	15.3
98-99—Milwaukee	2	12	0	2	.000	0	2	.000	1	2	3	0	1	0	2	0	1.5	0.0	0.0
Totals	15	296	51	104	.490	38	61	.623	33	46	79	7	9	13	16	140	5.3	0.5	9.3

Personal fouls/disqualifications: 1991-92, 14/0. 1993-94, 10/0. 1995-96, 8/1. 1997-98, 9/0. 1998-99, 3/0. Totals, 44/1.

NBA ALL-STAR GAME RECORD

Season Team	Min.	FGM	FGA	Pct.	FTM	FTA	Pct.	Off.	Def.	Tot.	Ast.	PF	Dq.	St.	Blk.	TO	Pts.
1997 —Dallas	12	1	8	.125	0	0	...	0	2	2	0	1	0	1	0	0	2

GEIGER, MATT   F/C   76ERS

PERSONAL: Born September 10, 1969, in Salem, Mass. ... 7-1/248. (2,16/112,5). ... Full Name: Matthew Allen Geiger. ... Name pronounced GUY-gher.
HIGH SCHOOL: Countryside Senior (Clearwater, Fla.).
COLLEGE: Auburn, then Georgia Tech.
TRANSACTIONS/CAREER NOTES: Selected by Miami Heat in second round (42nd pick overall) of 1992 NBA Draft. ... Traded by Heat with G/F Glen Rice, G Khalid Reeves and 1996 first-round draft choice to Charlotte Hornets for C Alonzo Mourning, C LeRon Ellis and G Pete Myers (November 3, 1995). ... Signed as free agent by Philadelphia 76ers (January 21, 1999).

COLLEGIATE RECORD

Season Team	G	Min.	FGM	FGA	Pct.	FTM	FTA	Pct.	Reb.	Ast.	Pts.	RPG	APG	PPG
87-88—Auburn	30	597	80	156	.513	33	50	.660	124	24	193	4.1	0.8	6.4
88-89—Auburn	28	807	170	337	.504	106	154	.688	186	31	446	6.6	1.1	15.9
89-90—Georgia Tech					Did not play—transfer student.									
90-91—Georgia Tech	27	711	130	237	.549	49	73	.671	172	26	309	6.4	1.0	11.4
91-92—Georgia Tech	35	952	165	270	.611	84	119	.706	254	37	414	7.3	1.1	11.8
Totals	120	3067	545	1000	.545	272	396	.687	736	118	1362	6.1	1.0	11.4

Three-point field goals: 1988-89, 0-for-3. 1990-91, 0-for-3. 1991-92, 0-for-2. Totals, 0-for-9 (.000).

NBA REGULAR-SEASON RECORD

NOTES: Led NBA with 11 disqualifications (1996).

Season Team	G	Min.	FGM	FGA	Pct.	FTM	FTA	Pct.	Off.	Def.	Tot.	Ast.	St.	Blk.	TO	Pts.	RPG	APG	PPG
92-93—Miami	48	554	76	145	.524	62	92	.674	46	74	120	14	15	18	36	214	2.5	0.3	4.5
93-94—Miami	72	1199	202	352	.574	116	149	.779	119	184	303	32	36	29	61	521	4.2	0.4	7.2
94-95—Miami	74	1712	260	485	.536	93	143	.650	146	267	413	55	41	51	113	617	5.6	0.7	8.3
95-96—Charlotte	77	2349	357	666	.536	149	205	.727	201	448	649	60	46	63	137	866	8.4	0.8	11.2
96-97—Charlotte	49	1044	171	350	.489	89	127	.701	100	158	258	38	20	27	67	437	5.3	0.8	8.9
97-98—Charlotte	78	1839	358	709	.505	168	236	.712	196	325	521	78	68	87	111	885	6.7	1.0	11.3
98-99—Philadelphia	50	1540	266	555	.479	141	177	.797	137	225	362	58	39	40	101	674	7.2	1.2	13.5
99-00—Philadelphia	65	1406	260	589	.441	109	140	.779	154	233	387	39	29	22	91	629	6.0	0.6	9.7
00-01—Philadelphia	35	542	88	224	.393	37	54	.685	50	89	139	14	12	8	25	213	4.0	0.4	6.1
Totals	548	12185	2038	4075	.500	964	1323	.729	1149	2003	3152	388	306	345	742	5056	5.8	0.7	9.2

Three-point field goals: 1992-93, 0-for-4. 1993-94, 1-for-5 (.200). 1994-95, 4-for-10 (.400). 1995-96, 3-for-8 (.375). 1996-97, 6-for-20 (.300). 1997-98, 1-for-11 (.091). 1998-99, 1-for-5 (.200). 1999-00, 0-for-4. 2000-01, 0-for-2. Totals, 16-for-69 (.232).

Personal fouls/disqualifications: 1992-93, 123/6. 1993-94, 201/2. 1994-95, 245/5. 1995-96, 290/11. 1996-97, 153/1. 1997-98, 191/1. 1998-99, 157/2. 1999-00, 194/1. 2000-01, 73/0. Totals, 1627/29.

G

NBA PLAYOFF RECORD

Season Team	G	Min.	FGM	FGA	Pct.	FTM	FTA	Pct.	REBOUNDS Off.	Def.	Tot.	Ast.	St.	Blk.	TO	Pts.	AVERAGES RPG	APG	PPG
93-94—Miami	2	11	0	2	.000	1	2	.500	0	4	4	0	0	0	0	1	2.0	0.0	0.5
96-97—Charlotte	3	31	2	3	.667	2	2	1.000	4	4	8	2	2	1	2	6	2.7	0.7	2.0
97-98—Charlotte	4	22	1	6	.167	0	0	...	3	2	5	1	0	0	1	2	1.3	0.3	0.5
98-99—Philadelphia	8	239	42	96	.438	24	29	.828	23	38	61	6	9	6	13	108	7.6	0.8	13.5
99-00—Philadelphia	8	128	25	50	.500	20	25	.800	17	23	40	2	5	2	5	70	5.0	0.3	8.8
00-01—Philadelphia	12	100	17	29	.586	4	4	1.000	10	8	18	7	2	0	5	38	1.5	0.6	3.2
Totals	37	531	87	186	.468	51	62	.823	57	79	136	18	18	9	26	225	3.7	0.5	6.1

Three-point field goals: 1998-99, 0-for-1. Totals, 0-for-1 (.000).
Personal fouls/disqualifications: 1993-94, 1/0. 1996-97, 5/0. 1997-98, 2/0. 1998-99, 29/0. 1999-00, 23/0. 2000-01, 30/2. Totals, 90/2.

GEORGE, DEVEAN　　　　　G/F　　　　　LAKERS

PERSONAL: Born August 29, 1977, in Minneapolis. ... 6-8/220. (2,03/99,8). ... Full Name: Devean Jamar George.
HIGH SCHOOL: Benilde-St. Margaret (St. Louis Park, Minn.).
COLLEGE: Augsburg (Minn.).
TRANSACTIONS/CAREER NOTES: Selected by Los Angeles Lakers in first round (23rd pick overall) of 1999 NBA Draft.
MISCELLANEOUS: Member of NBA championship team (2000, 2001).

COLLEGIATE RECORD

Season Team	G	Min.	FGM	FGA	Pct.	FTM	FTA	Pct.	Reb.	Ast.	Pts.	AVERAGES RPG	APG	PPG
95-96—Augsburg (Minn.)..........	17	500	93	185	.503	55	78	.705	111	28	258	6.5	1.6	15.2
96-97—Augsburg (Minn.)..........	25	766	207	419	.494	109	152	.717	178	39	566	7.1	1.6	22.6
97-98—Augsburg (Minn.)..........	26	751	218	433	.503	185	246	.752	262	31	664	10.1	1.2	25.5
98-99—Augsburg (Minn.)..........	28	969	281	542	.518	163	213	.765	317	58	770	11.3	2.1	27.5
Totals	96	2986	799	1579	.506	512	689	.743	868	156	2258	9.0	1.6	23.5

Three-point field goals: 1995-96, 17-for-40 (.425). 1996-97, 43-for-129 (.333). 1997-98, 43-for-134 (.321). 1998-99, 45-for-138 (.326). Totals, 148-for-441 (.336).

NBA REGULAR-SEASON RECORD

Season Team	G	Min.	FGM	FGA	Pct.	FTM	FTA	Pct.	REBOUNDS Off.	Def.	Tot.	Ast.	St.	Blk.	TO	Pts.	AVERAGES RPG	APG	PPG
99-00—L.A. Lakers	49	345	56	144	.389	27	41	.659	29	46	75	12	10	4	21	155	1.5	0.2	3.2
00-01—L.A. Lakers	59	593	64	207	.309	39	55	.709	35	75	110	19	15	15	34	182	1.9	0.3	3.1
Totals	108	938	120	351	.342	66	96	.688	64	121	185	31	25	19	55	337	1.7	0.3	3.1

Three-point field goals: 1999-00, 16-for-47 (.340). 2000-01, 15-for-68 (.221). Totals, 31-for-115 (.270).
Personal fouls/disqualifications: 1999-00, 54/0. 2000-01, 87/1. Totals, 141/1.

NBA PLAYOFF RECORD

Season Team	G	Min.	FGM	FGA	Pct.	FTM	FTA	Pct.	REBOUNDS Off.	Def.	Tot.	Ast.	St.	Blk.	TO	Pts.	AVERAGES RPG	APG	PPG
99-00—L.A. Lakers	9	45	7	19	.368	6	11	.545	4	6	10	2	1	0	3	22	1.1	0.2	2.4
00-01—L.A. Lakers	7	27	6	12	.500	1	2	.500	3	2	5	1	0	0	3	14	0.7	0.1	2.0
Totals	16	72	13	31	.419	7	13	.538	7	8	15	3	1	0	6	36	0.9	0.2	2.3

Three-point field goals: 1999-00, 2-for-10 (.200). 2000-01, 1-for-2 (.500). Totals, 3-for-12 (.250).
Personal fouls/disqualifications: 1999-00, 5/0. 2000-01, 6/0. Totals, 11/0.

GILL, EDDIE　　　　　G

PERSONAL: Born August 16, 1978, in Aurora, Colo. ... 6-0/190. (1,83/86,2).
HIGH SCHOOL: Overland (Colo.).
JUNIOR COLLEGE: Eastern Utah, then Salt Lake Community College.
COLLEGE: Weber State.
TRANSACTIONS/CAREER NOTES: Not drafted by an NBA franchise. ... Played in Italy (2000-01). ... Played in International Basketball League with Las Vegas Bandits (2000-01). ... Played in American Basketball Association 2000 with Kansas City Knights (2000-01). ... Signed by New Jersey Nets to the first of two consecutive 10-day contracts (March 29, 2001).

COLLEGIATE RECORD

Season Team	G	Min.	FGM	FGA	Pct.	FTM	FTA	Pct.	Reb.	Ast.	Pts.	AVERAGES RPG	APG	PPG
96-97—College of Eastern Utah..	33	...	70	165	.424	32	55	.582	62	79	200	1.9	2.4	6.1
97-98—Salt Lake C.C..............	31	...	148	325	.455	144	184	.783	131	197	507	4.2	6.4	16.4
98-99—Weber State.................	33	1145	141	331	.426	97	111	.874	129	150	462	3.9	4.5	14.0
99-00—Weber State.................	28	1009	128	325	.394	149	173	.861	179	194	457	6.4	6.9	16.3
Junior College Totals............	64	...	218	490	.445	176	239	.736	193	276	707	3.0	4.3	11.0
4-Year-College Totals	61	2154	269	656	.410	246	284	.866	308	344	919	5.0	5.6	15.1

Three-point field goals: 1996-97, 28-for-73 (.384). 1997-98, 67-for-159 (.421). 1998-99, 83-for-203 (.409). 1999-00, 52-for-142 (.366). Totals, 95-for-232 (.409) Totals, 135-for-345 (.391).

ABA 2000 LEAGUE RECORD

Season Team	G	Min.	FGM	FGA	Pct.	FTM	FTA	Pct.	Reb.	Ast.	Pts.	AVERAGES RPG	APG	PPG
00-01—Kansas City	2	51	5	12	.417	1	2	.500	7	18	12	3.5	9.0	6.0

Three-point field goals: 2000-01, 1-for-4 (.250).

G

IBL REGULAR SEASON RECORD

Season Team	G	Min.	FGM	FGA	Pct.	FTM	FTA	Pct.	Reb.	Ast.	Pts.	AVERAGES		
												RPG	APG	PPG
00-01—Las Vegas......................	31	1169	134	324	.414	113	156	.724	129	213	436	4.2	6.9	14.1

Three-point field goals: 2000-01, 55-for-139 (.396).

ITALIAN LEAGUE RECORD

Season Team	G	Min.	FGM	FGA	Pct.	FTM	FTA	Pct.	Reb.	Ast.	Pts.	AVERAGES		
												RPG	APG	PPG
00-01—Fortitudo Bologna..........	1	29	2	8	.250	7	8	.875	4	4	12	4.0	4.0	12.0

Three-point field goals: 2000-01, 1-for-5 (.200).

NBA REGULAR-SEASON RECORD

Season Team	G	Min.	FGM	FGA	Pct.	FTM	FTA	Pct.	REBOUNDS			Ast.	St.	Blk.	TO	Pts.	AVERAGES		
									Off.	Def.	Tot.						RPG	APG	PPG
00-01—New Jersey.....	8	152	16	41	.390	4	5	.800	0	9	9	24	4	1	10	39	1.1	3.0	4.9

Three-point field goals: 2000-01, 3-for-9 (.333).
Personal fouls/disqualifications: 2000-01, 9/0.

GILL, KENDALL   G   HEAT

PERSONAL: Born May 25, 1968, in Chicago. ... 6-5/216. (1,96/98,0). ... Full Name: Kendall Cedric Gill.
HIGH SCHOOL: Rich Central (Olympia Fields, Ill.).
COLLEGE: Illinois.
TRANSACTIONS/CAREER NOTES: Selected by Charlotte Hornets in first round (fifth pick overall) of 1990 NBA Draft. ... Traded by Hornets to Seattle SuperSonics for F Eddie Johnson, G Dana Barros and option to switch 1994 first-round draft choices (September 1, 1993). ... Traded by SuperSonics to Hornets for G Hersey Hawkins and G/F David Wingate (June 27, 1995). ... Traded by Hornets with G Khalid Reeves to New Jersey Nets for G Kenny Anderson and G/F Gerald Glass (January 19, 1996). ... Signed as free agent by Miami Heat (August 5, 2001).

COLLEGIATE RECORD

NOTES: The Sporting News All-America third team (1990).

Season Team	G	Min.	FGM	FGA	Pct.	FTM	FTA	Pct.	Reb.	Ast.	Pts.	AVERAGES		
												RPG	APG	PPG
86-87—Illinois	31	345	40	83	.482	34	53	.642	42	27	114	1.4	0.9	3.7
87-88—Illinois	33	946	128	272	.471	67	89	.753	73	138	344	2.2	4.2	10.4
88-89—Illinois	24	681	143	264	.542	46	58	.793	70	91	370	2.9	3.8	15.4
89-90—Illinois	29	1000	211	422	.500	136	175	.777	143	96	581	4.9	3.3	20.0
Totals	117	2972	522	1041	.501	283	375	.755	328	352	1409	2.8	3.0	12.0

Three-point field goals: 1986-87, 0-for-1. 1987-88, 21-for-69 (.304). 1988-89, 38-for-83 (.458). 1989-90, 23-for-66 (.348). Totals, 82-for-219 (.374).

NBA REGULAR-SEASON RECORD

RECORDS: Shares single-game record for most steals—11 (April 3, 1999, vs. Miami).
HONORS: NBA All-Rookie first team (1991).
NOTES: Led NBA with 2.68 steals per game (1999).

Season Team	G	Min.	FGM	FGA	Pct.	FTM	FTA	Pct.	REBOUNDS			Ast.	St.	Blk.	TO	Pts.	AVERAGES		
									Off.	Def.	Tot.						RPG	APG	PPG
90-91—Charlotte	82	1944	376	836	.450	152	182	.835	105	158	263	303	104	39	163	906	3.2	3.7	11.0
91-92—Charlotte	79	2906	666	1427	.467	284	381	.745	165	237	402	329	154	46	180	1622	5.1	4.2	20.5
92-93—Charlotte	69	2430	463	1032	.449	224	290	.772	120	220	340	268	98	36	174	1167	4.9	3.9	16.9
93-94—Seattle	79	2435	429	969	.443	215	275	.782	91	177	268	275	151	32	143	1111	3.4	3.5	14.1
94-95—Seattle	73	2125	392	858	.457	155	209	.742	99	191	290	192	117	28	138	1002	4.0	2.6	13.7
95-96—Charlotte-N.J...	47	1683	246	524	.469	138	176	.784	72	160	232	260	64	24	131	656	4.9	5.5	14.0
96-97—New Jersey	82	3199	644	1453	.443	427	536	.797	183	316	499	326	154	46	218	1789	6.1	4.0	21.8
97-98—New Jersey	81	2733	418	974	.429	225	327	.688	112	279	391	200	156	64	124	1087	4.8	2.5	13.4
98-99—New Jersey	50	1606	236	593	.398	114	167	.683	61	183	244	132	*134	26	71	588	4.9	2.5	11.8
99-00—New Jersey	76	2355	396	956	.414	181	255	.710	82	201	283	210	139	41	89	993	3.7	2.8	13.1
00-01—New Jersey	31	892	107	323	.331	65	90	.722	32	99	131	87	47	7	48	283	4.2	2.8	9.1
Totals	749	24308	4373	9945	.440	2180	2888	.755	1122	2221	3343	2573	1318	389	1479	11204	4.5	3.4	15.0

Three-point field goals: 1990-91, 2-for-14 (.143). 1991-92, 6-for-25 (.240). 1992-93, 17-for-62 (.274). 1993-94, 38-for-120 (.317). 1994-95, 63 for 171 (.368). 1995-96, 26-for-79 (.329). 1996-97, 74-for-220 (.336). 1997-98, 26-for-101 (.257). 1998-99, 2-for-17 (.118). 1999-00, 20-for-78 (.256). 2000-01, 4-for-14 (.286). Totals, 278-for-901 (.309).

Personal fouls/disqualifications: 1990-91, 186/0. 1991-92, 237/1. 1992-93, 191/2. 1993-94, 194/1. 1994-95, 186/0. 1995-96, 131/2. 1996-97, 225/2. 1997-98, 268/4. 1998-99, 162/4. 1999-00, 211/3. 2000-01, 64/0. Totals, 2055/19.

NBA PLAYOFF RECORD

Season Team	G	Min.	FGM	FGA	Pct.	FTM	FTA	Pct.	REBOUNDS			Ast.	St.	Blk.	TO	Pts.	AVERAGES		
									Off.	Def.	Tot.						RPG	APG	PPG
92-93—Charlotte	9	353	65	162	.401	25	35	.714	26	20	46	26	21	6	19	156	5.1	2.9	17.3
93-94—Seattle	5	153	26	60	.433	13	21	.619	7	17	24	10	6	1	6	67	4.8	2.0	13.4
94-95—Seattle	4	72	9	25	.360	5	8	.625	1	3	4	10	4	1	4	25	1.0	2.5	6.3
97-98—New Jersey	3	100	18	40	.450	7	8	.875	3	10	13	3	4	1	4	43	4.3	1.0	14.3
Totals	21	678	118	287	.411	50	72	.694	37	50	87	49	35	9	33	291	4.1	2.3	13.9

Three-point field goals: 1992-93, 1-for-6 (.167). 1993-94, 2-for-9 (.222). 1994-95, 2-for-8 (.250). Totals, 5-for-23 (.217).
Personal fouls/disqualifications: 1992-93, 29/0. 1993-94, 12/0. 1994-95, 6/0. 1997-98, 15/1. Totals, 62/1.

G

GLOVER, DION G HAWKS

PERSONAL: Born October 22, 1978, in Marietta, Ga. ... 6-5/228. (1,96/103,4). ... Full Name: Micaiah Diondae Glover.
HIGH SCHOOL: Cedar Grove (Decatur, Ga.).
COLLEGE: Georgia Tech.
TRANSACTIONS/CAREER NOTES: Selected after redshirt sophomore season by Atlanta Hawks in first round (20th pick overall) of 1999 NBA Draft.

COLLEGIATE RECORD

Season Team	G	Min.	FGM	FGA	Pct.	FTM	FTA	Pct.	Reb.	Ast.	Pts.	AVERAGES RPG	APG	PPG
97-98—Georgia Tech	33	1163	222	503	.441	119	186	.640	166	86	608	5.0	2.6	18.4
98-99—Georgia Tech						Did not play—redshirted.								
Totals	33	1163	222	503	.441	119	186	.640	166	86	608	5.0	2.6	18.4

Three-point field goals: 1997-98, 45-for-166 (.271).

NBA REGULAR-SEASON RECORD

Season Team	G	Min.	FGM	FGA	Pct.	FTM	FTA	Pct.	REBOUNDS Off.	Def.	Tot.	Ast.	St.	Blk.	TO	Pts.	AVERAGES RPG	APG	PPG
99-00—Atlanta	30	446	66	171	.386	51	70	.729	15	23	38	27	15	4	28	195	1.3	0.9	6.5
00-01—Atlanta	57	929	141	336	.420	47	69	.681	39	92	131	69	49	10	54	338	2.3	1.2	5.9
Totals	87	1375	207	507	.408	98	139	.705	54	115	169	96	64	14	82	533	1.9	1.1	6.1

Three-point field goals: 1999-00, 12-for-45 (.267). 2000-01, 9-for-46 (.196). Totals, 21-for-91 (.231).
Personal fouls/disqualifications: 1999-00, 28/0. 2000-01, 92/1. Totals, 120/1.

GOLDWIRE, ANTHONY G

PERSONAL: Born September 6, 1971, in West Palm Beach, Fla. ... 6-2/182. (1,88/82,6).
HIGH SCHOOL: Suncoast (Riviera Beach, Fla.).
JUNIOR COLLEGE: Pensacola Junior College (Fla.).
COLLEGE: Houston.
TRANSACTIONS/CAREER NOTES: Selected by Phoenix Suns in second round (52nd pick overall) of 1994 NBA Draft. ... Waived by Suns (November 1, 1994). ... Played in Continental Basketball Association with Yakima Sun Kings (1994-95 and 1995-96). ... Signed by Charlotte Hornets to 10-day contract (January 22, 1996). ... Re-signed by Hornets for remainder of season (January 31, 1996). ... Traded by Hornets with C George Zidek to Denver Nuggets for G Ricky Pierce (February 20, 1997). ... Played in Greece (1998-99). ... Played in Spain (1999-2000). ... Signed as free agent by Nuggets (October 2, 2000). ... Waived by Nuggets (October 25, 2000). ... Played in American Basketball Association 2000 with Kansas City Knights (2000-01). ... Signed by Nuggets to first of two consecutive 10-day contracts (January 29, 2001). ... Signed by Nuggets for remainder of season (February 18, 2001).

COLLEGIATE RECORD

Season Team	G	Min.	FGM	FGA	Pct.	FTM	FTA	Pct.	Reb.	Ast.	Pts.	AVERAGES RPG	APG	PPG
90-91—Pensacola J.C.	30	...	105	234	.449	84	104	.808	91	169	305	3.0	5.6	10.2
91-92—Pensacola J.C.	31	...	155	360	.431	128	168	.762	128	241	477	4.1	7.8	15.4
92-93—Houston	30	1110	139	313	.444	124	158	.785	92	170	427	3.1	5.7	14.2
93-94—Houston	27	995	144	366	.393	138	171	.807	100	164	463	3.7	6.1	17.1
Junior College Totals	61	...	260	594	.438	212	272	.779	219	410	782	3.6	6.7	12.8
4-Year-College Totals	57	2105	283	679	.417	262	329	.796	192	334	890	3.4	5.9	15.6

Three-point field goals: 1990-91, 11-for-39 (.282). 1991-92, 39-for-95 (.411). 1992-93, 25-for-88 (.284). 1993-94, 37-for-123 (.301). Totals, 50-for-134 (.373) Totals, 62-for-211 (.294).

CBA REGULAR-SEASON RECORD

NOTES: Member of CBA championship team (1995). ... CBA All-Rookie second team (1995).

Season Team	G	Min.	FGM	FGA	Pct.	FTM	FTA	Pct.	Reb.	Ast.	Pts.	AVERAGES RPG	APG	PPG
94-95—Yakima	55	1121	150	312	.481	119	160	.744	83	217	439	1.5	3.9	8.0
95-96—Yakima	27	977	171	373	.458	139	163	.853	96	189	519	3.6	7.0	19.2
Totals	82	2098	321	685	.469	258	323	.799	179	406	958	2.2	5.0	11.7

Three-point field goals: 1994-95, 20-for-60 (.333). 1995-96, 38-for-99 (.384). Totals, 58-for-159 (.365).

NBA REGULAR-SEASON RECORD

Season Team	G	Min.	FGM	FGA	Pct.	FTM	FTA	Pct.	REBOUNDS Off.	Def.	Tot.	Ast.	St.	Blk.	TO	Pts.	AVERAGES RPG	APG	PPG
95-96—Charlotte	42	621	76	189	.402	46	60	.767	8	35	43	112	16	0	63	231	1.0	2.7	5.5
96-97—Char.-Denver	60	1188	131	330	.397	61	78	.782	12	72	84	219	33	2	76	387	1.4	3.7	6.5
97-98—Denver	82	2212	269	636	.423	150	186	.806	40	107	147	277	86	7	85	751	1.8	3.4	9.2
00-01—Denver	20	201	30	80	.375	13	17	.765	1	11	12	34	9	0	15	82	0.6	1.7	4.1
Totals	204	4222	506	1235	.410	270	341	.792	61	225	286	642	144	9	239	1451	1.4	3.1	7.1

Three-point field goals: 1995-96, 33-for-83 (.398). 1996-97, 64-for-153 (.418). 1997-98, 63-for-164 (.384). 2000-01, 9-for-34 (.265). Totals, 169-for-434 (.389).
Personal fouls/disqualifications: 1995-96, 79/0. 1996-97, 104/1. 1997-98, 149/0. 2000-01, 13/0. Totals, 345/1.

GREEK LEAGUE RECORD

Season Team	G	Min.	FGM	FGA	Pct.	FTM	FTA	Pct.	Reb.	Ast.	Pts.	AVERAGES RPG	APG	PPG
98-99—Olympiakos S.F.P.	25	784	95	227	.419	58	80	.725	38	60	295	1.5	2.4	11.8

Three-point field goals: 1998-99, 47-for-108 (.435).

G

Season Team	G	Min.	FGM	FGA	Pct.	FTM	FTA	Pct.	Reb.	Ast.	Pts.	AVERAGES		
												RPG	APG	PPG
99-00—FC Barcelona	33	750	114	266	.429	80	97	.825	56	60	363	1.7	1.8	11.0

Three-point field goals: 1999-00, 55-for-144 (.382).

ABA 2000 LEAGUE RECORD

Season Team	G	Min.	FGM	FGA	Pct.	FTM	FTA	Pct.	Reb.	Ast.	Pts.	AVERAGES		
												RPG	APG	PPG
00-01—Kansas City	14	504	98	216	.454	47	49	.959	44	68	290	3.1	4.9	20.7

Three-point field goals: 2000-01, 41-for-98 (.418).

GOODRICH, STEVE   F/C

PERSONAL: Born March 18, 1976, in Brussels, Belgium. ... 6-10/220. (2,08/99,8). ... Full Name: Steven Withington Goodrich.
HIGH SCHOOL: William Penn Charter (Philadelphia).
COLLEGE: Princeton.
TRANSACTIONS/CAREER NOTES: Not drafted by an NBA franchise. ... Played in Spain (1998-99). ... Played in International Basketball League with Baltimore Bayrunners (1999-2000). ... Signed as free agent by New Jersey Nets (January 21, 1999). ... Waived by Nets (February 1, 1999). ... Signed as free agent by Chicago Bulls (October 2, 2000). ... Waived by Bulls (October 30, 2000). ... Played in Italy (2000-01). ... Re-signed as free agent by Bulls (March 27, 2001).

COLLEGIATE RECORD

Season Team	G	Min.	FGM	FGA	Pct.	FTM	FTA	Pct.	Reb.	Ast.	Pts.	AVERAGES		
												RPG	APG	PPG
94-95—Princeton......................	26	518	72	141	.511	39	55	.709	80	35	185	3.1	1.3	7.1
95-96—Princeton......................	29	822	129	212	.608	63	87	.724	109	52	337	3.8	1.8	11.6
96-97—Princeton......................	28	729	117	190	.616	50	71	.704	90	48	297	3.2	1.7	10.6
97-98—Princeton......................	29	904	152	256	.594	53	82	.646	128	99	388	4.4	3.4	13.4
Totals	112	2973	470	799	.588	205	295	.695	407	234	1207	3.6	2.1	10.8

Three-point field goals: 1994-95, 2-for-8 (.250). 1995-96, 16-for-39 (.410). 1996-97, 13-for-40 (.325). 1997-98, 31-for-73 (.425). Totals, 62-for-160 (.388).

SPANISH LEAGUE RECORD

Season Team	G	Min.	FGM	FGA	Pct.	FTM	FTA	Pct.	Reb.	Ast.	Pts.	AVERAGES		
												RPG	APG	PPG
98-99—Baloncesto Girona..........	5	131	13	35	.371	8	12	.667	22	3	37	4.4	0.6	7.4

Three-point field goals: 1998-99, 3-for-11 (.273).

IBL REGULAR SEASON RECORD

Season Team	G	Min.	FGM	FGA	Pct.	FTM	FTA	Pct.	Reb.	Ast.	Pts.	AVERAGES		
												RPG	APG	PPG
99-00—Baltimore......................	64	2053	268	503	.533	125	205	.610	282	79	692	4.4	1.2	10.8

Three-point field goals: 1999-00, 31-for-84 (.369).

ITALIAN LEAGUE RECORD

Season Team	G	Min.	FGM	FGA	Pct.	FTM	FTA	Pct.	Reb.	Ast.	Pts.	AVERAGES		
												RPG	APG	PPG
00-01—Olimpia Milano..............	24	489	84	147	.571	24	31	.774	75	16	215	3.1	0.7	9.0

Three-point field goals: 2000-01, 23-for-51 (.451).

NBA REGULAR-SEASON RECORD

Season Team	G	Min.	FGM	FGA	Pct.	FTM	FTA	Pct.	REBOUNDS			Ast.	St.	Blk.	TO	Pts.	AVERAGES		
									Off.	Def.	Tot.						RPG	APG	PPG
00-01—Chicago	12	133	7	18	.389	4	7	.571	7	14	21	6	2	1	8	19	1.8	0.5	1.6

Three-point field goals: 2000-01, 1-for-3 (.333).
Personal fouls/disqualifications: 2000-01, 14/0.

GRANT, BRIAN   F   HEAT

PERSONAL: Born March 5, 1972, in Columbus, Ohio. ... 6-9/254. (2,06/115,2). ... Full Name: Brian Wade Grant.
HIGH SCHOOL: Georgetown (Ohio).
COLLEGE: Xavier.
TRANSACTIONS/CAREER NOTES: Selected by Sacramento Kings in first round (eighth pick overall) of 1994 NBA Draft. ... Signed as free agent by Portland Trail Blazers (August 23, 1997). ... Traded by Trail Blazers to Miami Heat as part of three-way deal in which Heat sent F/C Chris Gatling, F Clarence Weatherspoon, future first-round draft choice and cash to Cleveland Cavaliers, Cavaliers sent F Shawn Kemp to Trail Blazers and Trail Blazers sent G Gary Grant to Cavaliers (August 30, 2000).

COLLEGIATE RECORD

Season Team	G	Min.	FGM	FGA	Pct.	FTM	FTA	Pct.	Reb.	Ast.	Pts.	AVERAGES		
												RPG	APG	PPG
90-91—Xavier	32	932	135	236	.572	100	144	.694	273	20	370	8.5	0.6	11.6
91-92—Xavier	26	729	117	203	.576	74	127	.583	237	23	308	9.1	0.9	11.8
92-93—Xavier	30	944	223	341	.654	110	159	.692	283	46	556	9.4	1.5	18.5
93-94—Xavier	29	894	181	324	.559	122	171	.713	287	47	485	9.9	1.6	16.7
Totals	117	3499	656	1104	.594	406	601	.676	1080	136	1719	9.2	1.2	14.7

Three-point field goals: 1993-94, 1-for-3 (.333).

G

NBA REGULAR-SEASON RECORD

HONORS: J. Walter Kennedy Citizenship Award (1999). ... NBA All-Rookie first team (1995).

Season Team	G	Min.	FGM	FGA	Pct.	FTM	FTA	Pct.	Off.	Def.	Tot.	Ast.	St.	Blk.	TO	Pts.	RPG	APG	PPG
									REBOUNDS								**AVERAGES**		
94-95—Sacramento	80	2289	413	809	.511	231	363	.636	207	391	598	99	49	116	163	1058	7.5	1.2	13.2
95-96—Sacramento	78	2398	427	842	.507	262	358	.732	175	370	545	127	40	103	185	1120	7.0	1.6	14.4
96-97—Sacramento	24	607	91	207	.440	70	90	.778	49	93	142	28	19	25	44	252	5.9	1.2	10.5
97-98—Portland	61	1921	283	557	.508	171	228	.750	197	358	555	86	44	45	110	737	9.1	1.4	12.1
98-99—Portland	48	1525	183	382	.479	184	226	.814	173	297	470	67	21	34	96	550	9.8	1.4	11.5
99-00—Portland	63	1322	173	352	.491	112	166	.675	121	223	344	64	32	28	84	459	5.5	1.0	7.3
00-01—Miami	82	2771	484	1010	.479	282	354	.797	217	501	718	101	60	71	170	1250	8.8	1.2	15.2
Totals	436	12833	2054	4159	.494	1312	1785	.735	1139	2233	3372	572	265	422	852	5426	7.7	1.3	12.4

Three-point field goals: 1994-95, 1-for-4 (.250). 1995-96, 4-for-17 (.235). 1997-98, 0-for-1. 1999-00, 1-for-2 (.500). 2000-01, 0-for-1. Totals, 6-for-25 (.240).

Personal fouls/disqualifications: 1994-95, 276/4. 1995-96, 269/9. 1996-97, 75/0. 1997-98, 184/3. 1998-99, 136/1. 1999-00, 166/2. 2000-01, 293/5. Totals, 1399/24.

NBA PLAYOFF RECORD

Season Team	G	Min.	FGM	FGA	Pct.	FTM	FTA	Pct.	Off.	Def.	Tot.	Ast.	St.	Blk.	TO	Pts.	RPG	APG	PPG
									REBOUNDS								**AVERAGES**		
95-96—Sacramento	4	124	16	42	.381	7	14	.500	7	13	20	4	2	7	13	39	5.0	1.0	9.8
97-98—Portland	4	135	19	36	.528	15	18	.833	18	25	43	6	4	3	5	53	10.8	1.5	13.3
98-99—Portland	13	482	63	119	.529	45	72	.625	34	85	119	14	10	16	21	171	9.2	1.1	13.2
99-00—Portland	16	320	29	65	.446	29	39	.744	37	55	92	8	6	6	17	87	5.8	0.5	5.4
00-01—Miami	3	84	10	24	.417	10	14	.714	6	18	24	1	0	5	6	30	8.0	0.3	10.0
Totals	40	1145	137	286	.479	106	157	.675	102	196	298	33	22	37	62	380	7.5	0.8	9.5

Personal fouls/disqualifications: 1995-96, 14/1. 1997-98, 20/0. 1998-99, 48/1. 1999-00, 53/1. 2000-01, 9/0. Totals, 144/3.

GRANT, GARY   G

PERSONAL: Born April 21, 1965, in Canton, Ohio. ... 6-3/185. (1,91/83,9).

HIGH SCHOOL: McKinley (Canton, Ohio).

COLLEGE: Michigan.

TRANSACTIONS/CAREER NOTES: Selected by Seattle SuperSonics in first round (15th pick overall) of 1988 NBA Draft. ... Draft rights traded by SuperSonics with 1989 first-round draft choice to Los Angeles Clippers for F Michael Cage (June 28, 1988). ... Signed as free agent by New York Knicks (November 9, 1995). ... Signed as free agent by Miami Heat (August 12, 1996). ... Traded by Heat with C Matt Fish and 1998 conditional second-round draft choice to Sacramento Kings for C Duane Causwell (August 12, 1997). ... Waived by Kings (September 5, 1997). ... Played in Continental Basketball Association with Yakima Sun Kings (1997-98). ... Signed by Portland Trail Blazers to first of two consecutive 10-day contracts (March 5, 1998). ... Signed by Trail Blazers for remainder of season (March 25, 1998). ... Played in Greece (1998-99). ... Signed by Trail Blazers for remainder of season (April 24, 1999). ... Signed as free agent by Trail Blazers (August 5, 1999). ... Traded by Trail Blazers to Cleveland Cavaliers as part of three-way deal in which Cavaliers sent F Shawn Kemp to Trail Blazers, Trail Blazers sent F Brian Grant to Heat and Heat sent F/C Chris Gatling, F Clarence Weatherspoon, future first-round draft choice and cash Cavaliers (August 30, 2000). ... Waived by Cavaliers (September 19, 2000). ... Signed as free agent by Trail Blazers (September 29, 2000). ... Waived by Trail Blazers (March 5, 2001).

COLLEGIATE RECORD

NOTES: The Sporting News All-America second team (1988).

Season Team	G	Min.	FGM	FGA	Pct.	FTM	FTA	Pct.	Reb.	Ast.	Pts.	RPG	APG	PPG
													AVERAGES	
84-85—Michigan	30	950	169	307	.550	49	60	.817	76	140	387	2.5	4.7	12.9
85-86—Michigan	33	1010	172	348	.494	58	78	.744	104	185	402	3.2	5.6	12.2
86-87—Michigan	32	1088	286	533	.537	111	142	.782	159	172	716	5.0	5.4	22.4
87-88—Michigan	34	1190	269	508	.530	135	167	.808	116	234	717	3.4	6.9	21.1
Totals	129	4238	896	1696	.528	353	447	.790	455	731	2222	3.5	5.7	17.2

Three-point field goals: 1986-87, 33-for-68 (.485). 1987-88, 44-for-99 (.444). Totals, 77-for-167 (.461).

NBA REGULAR-SEASON RECORD

Season Team	G	Min.	FGM	FGA	Pct.	FTM	FTA	Pct.	Off.	Def.	Tot.	Ast.	St.	Blk.	TO	Pts.	RPG	APG	PPG
									REBOUNDS								**AVERAGES**		
88-89—L.A. Clippers...	71	1924	361	830	.435	119	162	.735	80	158	238	506	144	9	258	846	3.4	7.1	11.9
89-90—L.A. Clippers...	44	1529	241	517	.466	88	113	.779	59	136	195	442	108	5	206	575	4.4	10.0	13.1
90-91—L.A. Clippers...	68	2105	265	587	.451	51	74	.689	69	140	209	587	103	12	210	590	3.1	8.6	8.7
91-92—L.A. Clippers...	78	2049	275	595	.462	44	54	.815	34	150	184	538	138	14	187	609	2.4	6.9	7.8
92-93—L.A. Clippers...	74	1624	210	476	.441	55	74	.743	27	112	139	353	106	9	129	486	1.9	4.8	6.6
93-94—L.A. Clippers...	78	1533	253	563	.449	65	76	.855	42	100	142	291	119	12	136	588	1.8	3.7	7.5
94-95—L.A. Clippers...	33	470	78	166	.470	45	55	.818	8	27	35	93	29	3	44	205	1.1	2.8	6.2
95-96—New York	47	596	88	181	.486	48	58	.828	12	40	52	69	39	3	45	232	1.1	1.5	4.9
96-97—Miami	28	365	39	110	.355	18	22	.818	8	30	38	45	16	0	27	110	1.4	1.6	3.9
97-98—Portland	22	359	43	93	.462	12	14	.857	8	40	48	84	17	2	24	105	2.2	3.8	4.8
98-99—Portland	2	7	0	1	.000	0	0	...	0	0	0	3	1	0	0	0	0.0	1.5	0.0
99-00—Portland	3	24	6	14	.429	0	0	...	0	3	3	1	1	0	2	12	1.0	0.3	4.0
00-01—Portland	4	17	5	7	.714	0	0	...	0	1	1	1	0	0	0	10	0.3	0.3	2.5
Totals	552	12602	1864	4140	.450	545	702	.776	347	936	1283	3013	821	69	1268	4368	2.3	5.5	7.9

Three-point field goals: 1988-89, 5-for-22 (.227). 1989-90, 5-for-21 (.238). 1990-91, 9-for-39 (.231). 1991-92, 15-for-51 (.294). 1992-93, 11-for-42 (.262). 1993-94, 17-for-62 (.274). 1994-95, 4-for-16 (.250). 1995-96, 8-for-24 (.333). 1996-97, 14-for-46 (.304). 1997-98, 7-for-19 (.368). Totals, 95-for-342 (.278).

Personal fouls/disqualifications: 1988-89, 170/1. 1989-90, 120/1. 1990-91, 192/4. 1991-92, 181/4. 1992-93, 168/2. 1993-94, 139/1. 1994-95, 66/0. 1995-96, 91/0. 1996-97, 39/0. 1997-98, 30/0. 1999-00, 3/0. 2000-01, 1/0. Totals, 1200/13.

G

NBA PLAYOFF RECORD

| | | | | | | | | | REBOUNDS | | | | | | | | AVERAGES | | |
Season Team	G	Min.	FGM	FGA	Pct.	FTM	FTA	Pct.	Off.	Def.	Tot.	Ast.	St.	Blk.	TO	Pts.	RPG	APG	PPG
91-92—L.A. Clippers...	5	77	10	21	.476	2	2	1.000	0	4	4	18	3	2	8	22	0.8	3.6	4.4
92-93—L.A. Clippers...	5	101	10	31	.323	1	2	.500	1	1	2	23	3	0	7	21	0.4	4.6	4.2
95-96—New York.......	1	8	2	5	.400	0	0	...	2	1	3	0	1	0	1	6	3.0	0.0	6.0
97-98—Portland.........	4	27	2	7	.286	0	0	...	2	3	5	7	1	1	2	5	1.3	1.8	1.3
99-00—Portland.........	2	8	0	2	.000	1	2	.500	0	0	0	1	0	0	0	1	0.0	0.5	0.5
Totals	17	221	24	66	.364	4	6	.667	5	9	14	49	8	3	18	55	0.8	2.9	3.2

Three-point field goals: 1991-92, 0-for-2. 1995-96, 2-for-3 (.667). 1997-98, 1-for-4 (.250). Totals, 3-for-9 (.333).
Personal fouls/disqualifications: 1991-92, 10/0. 1992-93, 13/0. 1997-98, 2/0. Totals, 25/0.

CBA REGULAR-SEASON RECORD

| | | | | | | | | | | | AVERAGES | | |
Season Team	G	Min.	FGM	FGA	Pct.	FTM	FTA	Pct.	Reb.	Ast.	Pts.	RPG	APG	PPG
97-98—Yakima	7	221	37	80	.463	34	38	.895	31	41	112	4.4	5.9	16.0

Three-point field goals: 1997-98, 4-for-5 (.800).

GREEK LEAGUE RECORD

| | | | | | | | | | | | AVERAGES | | |
Season Team	G	Min.	FGM	FGA	Pct.	FTM	FTA	Pct.	Reb.	Ast.	Pts.	RPG	APG	PPG
98-99—Aris...............................	18	664	125	270	.463	67	82	.817	80	63	336	4.4	3.5	18.7

Three-point field goals: 1998-99, 19-for-52 (.365).

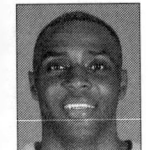

GRANT, HORACE   F   MAGIC

PERSONAL: Born July 4, 1965, in Augusta, Ga. ... 6-10/245. (2,08/111,1). ... Full Name: Horace Junior Grant. ... Twin brother of Harvey Grant, forward with Washington Bullets/Wizards (1988-89 though 1992-93, 1996-97 and 1997-98), Portland Trail Blazers (1993-94 through 1995-96) and Philadelphia 76ers (1998-99).
HIGH SCHOOL: Hancock Central (Sparta, Ga.).
COLLEGE: Clemson.
TRANSACTIONS/CAREER NOTES: Selected by Chicago Bulls in first round (10th pick overall) of 1987 NBA Draft. ... Signed as unrestricted free agent by Orlando Magic (July 30, 1994). ... Contract disallowed by NBA (August 2, 1994). ... Re-signed by Magic (September 19, 1994). ... Traded by Magic with 2001 and 2002 second-round draft choices to Seattle SuperSonics for F/G Billy Owens, G/F Dale Ellis, F Don MacLean and draft rights to F Corey Maggette (June 30, 1999). ... Traded by SuperSonics to Los Angeles Lakers as part of four-team trade in which Knicks acquired F Glen Rice, C Luc Longley, F/C Travis Knight, G Vernon Maxwell, C Vladimir Stepania, F Lazaro Borrell, two 2001 first-round draft choices and two 2001 second-round draft choices, SuperSonics acquired C Patrick Ewing, Phoenix Suns acquired C Chris Dudley and 2001 first-round draft choice and Lakers acquired C Greg Foster, F Chuck Person and G Emanual Davis (September 20, 2000). ... Signed as free agent by Magic (July 19, 2001).
MISCELLANEOUS: Member of NBA championship team (1991, 1992, 1993, 2001).

COLLEGIATE RECORD

| | | | | | | | | | | | | AVERAGES | | |
Season Team	G	Min.	FGM	FGA	Pct.	FTM	FTA	Pct.	Reb.	Ast.	Pts.	RPG	APG	PPG
83-84—Clemson	28	551	64	120	.533	32	43	.744	129	49	160	4.6	1.8	5.7
84-85—Clemson	29	703	132	238	.555	65	102	.637	196	32	329	6.8	1.1	11.3
85-86—Clemson	34	1099	208	356	.584	140	193	.725	357	62	556	10.5	1.8	16.4
86-87—Clemson	31	1010	256	390	.656	138	195	.708	299	63	651	9.6	2.0	21.0
Totals	122	3363	660	1104	.598	375	533	.704	981	206	1696	8.0	1.7	13.9

Three-point field goals: 1986-87, 1-for-2 (.500).

NBA REGULAR-SEASON RECORD

HONORS: NBA All-Defensive second team (1993, 1994, 1995, 1996).

| | | | | | | | | | REBOUNDS | | | | | | | | AVERAGES | | |
Season Team	G	Min.	FGM	FGA	Pct.	FTM	FTA	Pct.	Off.	Def.	Tot.	Ast.	St.	Blk.	TO	Pts.	RPG	APG	PPG
87-88—Chicago	81	1827	254	507	.501	114	182	.626	155	292	447	89	51	53	86	622	5.5	1.1	7.7
88-89—Chicago	79	2809	405	781	.519	140	199	.704	240	441	681	168	86	62	128	950	8.6	2.1	12.0
89-90—Chicago	80	2753	446	853	.523	179	256	.699	236	393	629	227	92	84	110	1071	7.9	2.8	13.4
90-91—Chicago	78	2641	401	733	.547	197	277	.711	266	393	659	178	95	69	92	1000	8.4	2.3	12.8
91-92—Chicago	81	2859	457	790	.578	235	317	.741	344	463	807	217	100	131	94	1149	10.0	2.7	14.2
92-93—Chicago	77	2745	421	829	.508	174	281	.619	341	388	729	201	89	96	110	1017	9.5	2.6	13.2
93-94—Chicago	70	2570	460	878	.524	137	230	.596	306	463	769	236	74	84	109	1057	11.0	3.4	15.1
94-95—Orlando	74	2693	401	707	.567	146	211	.692	223	492	715	173	76	88	85	948	9.7	2.3	12.8
95-96—Orlando	63	2286	347	677	.513	152	207	.734	178	402	580	170	62	74	64	847	9.2	2.7	13.4
96-97—Orlando	67	2496	358	695	.515	128	179	.715	206	394	600	163	101	65	99	845	9.0	2.4	12.6
97-98—Orlando	76	2803	393	857	.459	135	199	.678	228	390	618	172	81	79	88	921	8.1	2.3	12.1
98-99—Orlando	50	1660	198	456	.434	47	70	.671	117	234	351	90	46	60	44	443	7.0	1.8	8.9
99-00—Seattle	76	2688	266	599	.444	80	111	.721	167	424	591	188	55	60	61	612	7.8	2.5	8.1
00-01—L.A. Lakers	77	2390	263	569	.462	131	169	.775	220	325	545	121	51	61	48	657	7.1	1.6	8.5
Totals	1029	35220	5070	9931	.511	1995	2888	.691	3227	5494	8721	2393	1059	1066	1222	12139	8.5	2.3	11.8

Three-point field goals: 1987-88, 0-for-2. 1988-89, 0-for-5. 1990-91, 1-for-6 (.167). 1991-92, 0-for-2. 1992-93, 1-for-5 (.200). 1993-94, 0-for-6. 1994-95, 0-for-8. 1995-96, 1-for-6 (.167). 1996-97, 1-for-6 (.167). 1997-98, 0-for-7. 1998-99, 0-for-4. 1999-00, 0-for-3. 2000-01, 0-for-3. Totals, 4-for-62 (.065).
Personal fouls/disqualifications: 1987-88, 221/3. 1988-89, 251/1. 1989-90, 230/1. 1990-91, 203/2. 1991-92, 196/0. 1992-93, 218/4. 1993-94, 164/0. 1994-95, 203/2. 1995-96, 144/1. 1996-97, 157/1. 1997-98, 180/0. 1998-99, 99/0. 1999-00, 192/0. 2000-01, 181/2. Totals, 2639/17.

NBA PLAYOFF RECORD

| | | | | | | | | | REBOUNDS | | | | | | | | AVERAGES | | |
Season Team	G	Min.	FGM	FGA	Pct.	FTM	FTA	Pct.	Off.	Def.	Tot.	Ast.	St.	Blk.	TO	Pts.	RPG	APG	PPG
87-88—Chicago	10	299	46	81	.568	9	15	.600	25	45	70	16	14	2	7	101	7.0	1.6	10.1
88-89—Chicago	17	625	72	139	.518	40	50	.800	53	114	167	35	11	16	31	184	9.8	2.1	10.8

G

Season Team	G	Min.	FGM	FGA	Pct.	FTM	FTA	Pct.	Off.	Def.	Tot.	Ast.	St.	Blk.	TO	Pts.	RPG	APG	PPG
89-90—Chicago	16	616	81	159	.509	33	53	.623	73	86	159	40	18	18	26	195	9.9	2.5	12.2
90-91—Chicago	17	666	91	156	.583	44	60	.733	56	82	138	38	15	6	20	226	8.1	2.2	13.3
91-92—Chicago	22	856	99	183	.541	51	76	.671	76	118	194	66	24	39	21	249	8.8	3.0	11.3
92-93—Chicago	19	651	83	152	.546	37	54	.685	61	95	156	44	23	23	17	203	8.2	2.3	10.7
93-94—Chicago	10	393	65	120	.542	31	42	.738	30	44	74	26	10	18	10	162	7.4	2.6	16.2
94-95—Orlando	21	869	121	224	.540	45	59	.763	74	145	219	39	21	24	26	287	10.4	1.9	13.7
95-96—Orlando..........	9	334	61	94	.649	13	15	.867	31	63	94	13	7	6	6	135	10.4	1.4	15.0
98-99—Orlando	4	128	11	30	.367	5	8	.625	14	14	28	5	2	2	2	27	7.0	1.3	6.8
99-00—Seattle	5	185	11	27	.407	2	4	.500	8	23	31	10	8	5	1	24	6.2	2.0	4.8
00-01—L.A. Lakers	16	423	37	96	.385	22	30	.733	40	56	96	19	15	13	15	96	6.0	1.2	6.0
Totals	166	6045	778	1461	.533	332	466	.712	541	885	1426	351	168	172	182	1889	8.6	2.1	11.4

Three-point field goals: 1987-88, 0-for-1. 1989-90, 0-for-2. 1991-92, 0-for-2. 1993-94, 1-for-1. 1994-95, 0-for-2. Totals, 1-for-8 (.125).
Personal fouls/disqualifications: 1987-88, 35/2. 1988-89, 68/2. 1989-90, 51/1. 1990-91, 45/0. 1991-92, 68/1. 1992-93, 60/1. 1993-94, 23/0. 1994-95, 68/1. 1995-96, 23/0. 1998-99, 12/0. 1999-00, 12/0. 2000-01, 43/0. Totals, 508/8.

NBA ALL-STAR GAME RECORD

Season Team	Min.	FGM	FGA	Pct.	FTM	FTA	Pct.	Off.	Def.	Tot.	Ast.	PF	Dq.	St.	Blk.	TO	Pts.
1994 —Chicago	17	2	8	.250	0	0	...	6	2	8	2	0	0	1	0	1	4

GREEN, A.C.   F

PERSONAL: Born October 4, 1963, in Portland, Ore. ... 6-9/225. (2,06/102,1). ... Full Name: A.C. Green Jr.
HIGH SCHOOL: Benson Polytechnic (Portland, Ore.).
COLLEGE: Oregon State.
TRANSACTIONS/CAREER NOTES: Selected by Los Angeles Lakers in first round (23rd pick overall) of 1985 NBA Draft. ... Signed as unrestricted free agent by Phoenix Suns (September 28, 1993). ... Traded by Suns with G Sam Cassell, F Michael Finley and 1997 or 1998 conditional second-round draft choice to Dallas Mavericks for G Jason Kidd, F Tony Dumas and C Loren Meyer (December 26, 1996). ... Traded by Mavericks to Lakers for C Sean Rooks and 2000 second-round draft choice (September 1, 1999). ... Waived by Lakers (June 28, 2000). ... Signed as free agent by Miami Heat (October 31, 2000).
MISCELLANEOUS: Member of NBA championship team (1987, 1988, 2000).

COLLEGIATE RECORD

Season Team	G	Min.	FGM	FGA	Pct.	FTM	FTA	Pct.	Reb.	Ast.	Pts.	RPG	APG	PPG
81-82—Oregon State	30	895	99	161	.615	61	100	.610	158	32	259	5.3	1.1	8.6
82-83—Oregon State	31	1113	162	290	.559	111	161	.689	235	53	435	7.6	1.7	14.0
83-84—Oregon State	23	853	134	204	.657	141	183	.770	201	38	409	8.7	1.7	17.8
84-85—Oregon State	31	1191	217	362	.599	157	231	.680	286	62	591	9.2	2.0	19.1
Totals	115	4052	612	1017	.602	470	675	.696	880	185	1694	7.7	1.6	14.7

NBA REGULAR-SEASON RECORD

RECORDS: Holds NBA record for most consecutive games played—1,192 (November 19, 1986 to present).
HONORS: NBA All-Defensive second team (1989).

Season Team	G	Min.	FGM	FGA	Pct.	FTM	FTA	Pct.	Off.	Def.	Tot.	Ast.	St.	Blk.	TO	Pts.	RPG	APG	PPG
85-86—L.A. Lakers	82	1542	209	388	.539	102	167	.611	160	221	381	54	49	49	99	521	4.6	0.7	6.4
86-87—L.A. Lakers	79	2240	316	587	.538	220	282	.780	210	405	615	84	70	80	102	852	7.8	1.1	10.8
87-88—L.A. Lakers	82	2636	322	640	.503	293	379	.773	245	465	710	93	87	45	120	937	8.7	1.1	11.4
88-89—L.A. Lakers	82	2510	401	758	.529	282	359	.786	258	481	739	103	94	55	119	1088	9.0	1.3	13.3
89-90—L.A. Lakers	82	2709	385	806	.478	278	370	.751	262	450	712	90	66	50	116	1061	8.7	1.1	12.9
90-91—L.A. Lakers	82	2164	258	542	.476	223	302	.738	201	315	516	71	59	23	99	750	6.3	0.9	9.1
91-92—L.A. Lakers	82	2902	382	803	.476	340	457	.744	306	456	762	117	91	36	111	1116	9.3	1.4	13.6
92-93—L.A. Lakers	82	2819	379	706	.537	277	375	.739	287	424	711	116	88	39	116	1051	8.7	1.4	12.8
93-94—Phoenix	82	2825	465	926	.502	266	362	.735	275	478	753	137	70	38	100	1204	9.2	1.7	14.7
94-95—Phoenix	82	2687	311	617	.504	251	343	.732	194	475	669	127	55	31	114	916	8.2	1.5	11.2
95-96—Phoenix	82	2113	215	444	.484	168	237	.709	166	388	554	72	45	23	79	612	6.8	0.9	7.5
96-97—Pho.-Dal.	83	2492	234	484	.483	128	197	.650	222	434	656	69	70	16	74	597	7.9	0.8	7.2
97-98—Dallas..............	82	2649	242	534	.453	116	162	.716	219	449	668	123	78	27	68	600	8.1	1.5	7.3
98-99—Dallas..............	50	924	108	256	.422	30	52	.577	82	146	228	25	28	8	19	246	4.6	0.5	4.9
99-00—Dallas..............	82	1929	173	387	.447	66	95	.695	160	326	486	80	53	18	53	413	5.9	1.0	5.0
00-01—Miami	82	1411	144	324	.444	79	111	.712	107	206	313	39	30	8	45	367	3.8	0.5	4.5
Totals	1278	36552	4544	9202	.494	3119	4250	.734	3354	6119	9473	1400	1033	546	1434	12331	7.4	1.1	9.6

Three-point field goals: 1985-86, 1-for-6 (.167). 1986-87, 0-for-5. 1987-88, 0-for-2. 1988-89, 4-for-17 (.235). 1989-90, 13-for-46 (.283). 1990-91, 11-for-55 (.200). 1991-92, 12-for-56 (.214). 1992-93, 16-for-46 (.348). 1993-94, 8-for-35 (.229). 1994-95, 43-for-127 (.339). 1995-96, 14-for-52 (.269). 1996-97, 1-for-20 (.050). 1997-98, 0-for-4. 1998-99, 0-for-8. 1999-00, 1-for-4 (.250). 2000-01, 0-for-6. Totals, 124-for-489 (.254).
Personal fouls/disqualifications: 1985-86, 229/2. 1986-87, 171/0. 1987-88, 204/0. 1988-89, 172/0. 1989-90, 207/0. 1990-91, 117/0. 1991-92, 141/0. 1992-93, 149/0. 1993-94, 142/0. 1994-95, 146/0. 1995-96, 141/1. 1996-97, 145/0. 1997-98, 157/0. 1998-99, 69/0. 1999-00, 127/0. 2000-01, 119/0. Totals, 2436/3.

NBA PLAYOFF RECORD

Season Team	G	Min.	FGM	FGA	Pct.	FTM	FTA	Pct.	Off.	Def.	Tot.	Ast.	St.	Blk.	TO	Pts.	RPG	APG	PPG
85-86—L.A. Lakers	9	106	9	17	.529	4	9	.444	3	13	16	0	1	3	4	22	1.8	0.0	2.4
86-87—L.A. Lakers	18	505	71	130	.546	65	87	.747	54	88	142	11	9	8	17	207	7.9	0.6	11.5
87-88—L.A. Lakers	24	746	92	169	.544	55	73	.753	57	118	175	20	11	12	26	239	7.3	0.8	10.0
88-89—L.A. Lakers	15	502	47	114	.412	58	76	.763	38	99	137	18	16	6	23	152	9.1	1.2	10.1
89-90—L.A. Lakers	9	252	41	79	.519	24	32	.750	34	47	81	9	5	4	14	106	9.0	1.0	11.8
90-91—L.A. Lakers	19	400	41	97	.423	38	54	.704	46	56	102	9	12	3	19	124	5.4	0.5	6.5

G

Season Team	G	Min.	FGM	FGA	Pct.	FTM	FTA	Pct.	Off.	Def.	Tot.	Ast.	St.	Blk.	TO	Pts.	RPG	APG	PPG
									REBOUNDS								AVERAGES		
91-92—L.A. Lakers	4	153	16	39	.410	19	23	.826	15	21	36	7	7	0	5	51	9.0	1.8	12.8
92-93—L.A. Lakers	5	220	18	42	.429	13	21	.619	26	47	73	13	7	3	9	49	14.6	2.6	9.8
93-94—Phoenix	10	350	40	83	.482	38	62	.613	29	55	84	13	10	2	7	125	8.4	1.3	12.5
94-95—Phoenix	10	368	36	78	.462	55	63	.873	38	82	120	13	6	2	10	128	12.0	1.3	12.8
95-96—Phoenix	4	87	6	17	.353	7	8	.875	6	12	18	2	1	0	2	19	4.5	0.5	4.8
99-00—L.A. Lakers	23	429	37	90	.411	16	23	.696	43	53	96	13	14	3	9	90	4.2	0.6	3.9
00-01—Miami	3	21	1	3	.333	1	1	1.000	1	3	4	2	1	0	1	3	1.3	0.7	1.0
Totals	153	4119	455	958	.475	393	532	.739	390	694	1084	130	100	46	146	1315	7.1	0.8	8.6

Three-point field goals: 1988-89, 0-for-3. 1990-91, 4-for-8 (.500). 1992-93, 0-for-5. 1993-94, 7-for-17 (.412). 1994-95, 1-for-12 (.083). 1995-96, 0-for-3. Totals, 12-for-48 (.250).

Personal fouls/disqualifications: 1985-86, 13/0. 1986-87, 47/0. 1987-88, 61/0. 1988-89, 37/1. 1989-90, 22/0. 1990-91, 37/0. 1991-92, 10/0. 1992-93, 14/1. 1993-94, 22/0. 1994-95, 22/0. 1995-96, 7/0. 1999-00, 44/0. 2000-01, 4/0. Totals, 340/2.

NBA ALL-STAR GAME RECORD

Season Team	Min.	FGM	FGA	Pct.	FTM	FTA	Pct.	Off.	Def.	Tot.	Ast.	PF	Dq.	St.	Blk.	TO	Pts.
								REBOUNDS									
1990 —L.A. Lakers	12	0	3	.000	0	0	...	0	3	3	1	1	0	0	1	1	0

GRIFFIN, ADRIAN   G/F   MAVERICKS

PERSONAL: Born July 4, 1974, in Wichita, Kan. ... 6-5/215. (1,96/97,5).
HIGH SCHOOL: Wichita East (Kansas).
COLLEGE: Seton Hall.
TRANSACTIONS/CAREER NOTES: Not drafted by an NBA franchise. ... Played in Continental Basketball Association with Connecticut Pride (1996-97 through 1998-99). ... Played in Italy (1998-99). ... Signed by Miami Heat (January 21, 1999). ... Waived by Heat (February 1, 1999). ... Signed as free agent by Boston Celtics (August 1, 1999). ... Signed as free agent by Dallas Mavericks (July 27, 2001).

COLLEGIATE RECORD

Season Team	G	Min.	FGM	FGA	Pct.	FTM	FTA	Pct.	Reb.	Ast.	Pts.	RPG	APG	PPG
												AVERAGES		
92-93—Seton Hall....................	35	465	44	87	.506	31	53	.585	123	29	29	3.5	0.8	0.8
93-94—Seton Hall....................	30	893	106	224	.473	76	126	.603	233	66	290	7.8	2.2	9.7
94-95—Seton Hall....................	30	949	184	332	.554	86	119	.723	216	85	460	7.2	2.8	15.3
95-96—Seton Hall....................	28	983	213	438	.486	107	161	.665	231	86	454	8.3	3.1	16.2
Totals	123	3290	547	1081	.506	300	459	.654	803	266	1233	6.5	2.2	10.0

Three-point field goals: 1992-93, 0-for-2. 1993-94, 2-for-6 (.333). 1994-95, 6-for-20 (.300). 1995-96, 12-for-44 (.273). Totals, 20-for-72 (.278).

CBA REGULAR-SEASON RECORD

NOTES: Member of CBA championship team (1999). ... CBA Most Valuable Player (1999). ... CBA Finals MVP (1999). ... CBA All-League first team (1998, 1999). ... CBA All-Defensive team (1998, 1999). ... CBA All-Rookie first team (1997).

Season Team	G	Min.	FGM	FGA	Pct.	FTM	FTA	Pct.	Reb.	Ast.	Pts.	RPG	APG	PPG
												AVERAGES		
96-97—Connecticut	54	1894	312	621	.502	127	169	.751	361	116	751	6.7	2.1	13.9
97-98—Connecticut	56	2157	391	798	.490	165	213	.775	376	188	961	6.7	3.4	17.2
98-99—Connecticut	47	1758	319	699	.456	222	261	.851	358	159	888	7.6	3.4	18.9
Totals	157	5809	1022	2118	.483	514	643	.799	1095	463	2600	7.0	2.9	16.6

Three-point field goals: 1996-97, 0-for-9. 1997-98, 14-for-52 (.269). 1998-99, 28-for-84 (.333). Totals, 42-for-145 (.290).

ITALIAN LEAGUE RECORD

Season Team	G	Min.	FGM	FGA	Pct.	FTM	FTA	Pct.	Reb.	Ast.	Pts.	RPG	APG	PPG
												AVERAGES		
98-99—Cordivari........................	8	226	41	71	.577	19	30	.633	48	7	103	6.0	0.9	12.9

Three-point field goals: 1998-99, 2-for-6 (.333).

NBA REGULAR-SEASON RECORD

Season Team	G	Min.	FGM	FGA	Pct.	FTM	FTA	Pct.	Off.	Def.	Tot.	Ast.	St.	Blk.	TO	Pts.	RPG	APG	PPG
									REBOUNDS								AVERAGES		
99-00—Boston	72	1927	175	413	.424	119	158	.753	128	244	372	177	116	15	93	485	5.2	2.5	6.7
00-01—Boston	44	377	33	97	.340	18	24	.750	27	60	87	27	18	5	18	93	2.0	0.6	2.1
Totals	116	2304	208	510	.408	137	182	.753	155	304	459	204	134	20	111	578	4.0	1.8	5.0

Three-point field goals: 1999-00, 16-for-57 (.281). 2000-01, 9-for-26 (.346). Totals, 25-for-83 (.301).
Personal fouls/disqualifications: 1999-00, 222/3. 2000-01, 45/0. Totals, 267/3.

GUGLIOTTA, TOM   F   SUNS

PERSONAL: Born December 19, 1969, in Huntington Station, N.Y. ... 6-10/240. (2,08/108,9). ... Full Name: Thomas James Gugliotta. ... Name pronounced GOOG-lee-ah-tah.
HIGH SCHOOL: Walt Whitman (Huntington Station, N.Y.).
COLLEGE: North Carolina State.
TRANSACTIONS/CAREER NOTES: Selected by Washington Bullets in first round (sixth pick overall) of 1992 NBA Draft. ... Traded by Bullets with 1996, 1998 and 2000 first-round draft choices to Golden State Warriors for F Chris Webber (November 17, 1994). ... Traded by Warriors to Minnesota Timberwolves for F Donyell Marshall (February 18, 1995). ... Signed as free agent by Phoenix Suns (January 23, 1999).

G

COLLEGIATE RECORD

Season Team	G	Min.	FGM	FGA	Pct.	FTM	FTA	Pct.	Reb.	Ast.	Pts.	RPG	APG	PPG
												AVERAGES		
88-89—North Carolina State.......	21	171	18	42	.429	19	29	.655	35	5	56	1.7	0.2	2.7
89-90—North Carolina State.......	30	886	135	268	.504	41	61	.672	211	47	334	7.0	1.6	11.1
90-91—North Carolina State.......	31	1123	170	340	.500	65	101	.644	281	87	471	9.1	2.8	15.2
91-92—North Carolina State.......	30	1107	240	534	.449	102	149	.685	293	92	675	9.8	3.1	22.5
Totals	112	3287	563	1184	.476	227	340	.668	820	231	1536	7.3	2.1	13.7

Three-point field goals: 1988-89, 1-for-2 (.500). 1989-90, 23-for-47 (.489). 1990-91, 66-for-166 (.398). 1991-92, 93-for-233 (.399). Totals, 183-for-448 (.408).

NBA REGULAR-SEASON RECORD

HONORS: NBA All-Rookie first team (1993).

Season Team	G	Min.	FGM	FGA	Pct.	FTM	FTA	Pct.	REBOUNDS Off.	Def.	Tot.	Ast.	St.	Blk.	TO	Pts.	AVERAGES RPG	APG	PPG
92-93—Washington	81	2795	484	1135	.426	181	281	.644	219	562	781	306	134	35	230	1187	9.6	3.8	14.7
93-94—Washington	78	2795	540	1159	.466	213	311	.685	189	539	728	276	172	51	247	1333	9.3	3.5	17.1
94-95—Was.-G.S.-Minn.	77	2568	371	837	.443	174	252	.690	165	407	572	279	132	62	189	976	7.4	3.6	12.7
95-96—Minnesota.......	78	2835	473	1004	.471	289	374	.773	176	514	690	238	139	96	234	1261	8.8	3.1	16.2
96-97—Minnesota.......	81	3131	592	1339	.442	464	566	.820	187	515	702	335	130	89	293	1672	8.7	4.1	20.6
97-98—Minnesota.......	41	1582	319	635	.502	183	223	.821	106	250	356	167	61	22	109	823	8.7	4.1	20.1
98-99—Phoenix	43	1563	277	573	.483	173	218	.794	131	250	381	121	59	21	88	729	8.9	2.8	17.0
99-00—Phoenix	54	1767	310	645	.481	117	151	.775	141	284	425	124	80	31	106	738	7.9	2.3	13.7
00-01—Phoenix	57	1159	149	380	.392	61	77	.792	76	179	255	55	47	21	51	362	4.5	1.0	6.4
Totals	590	20195	3515	7707	.456	1855	2453	.756	1390	3500	4890	1901	954	428	1547	9081	8.3	3.2	15.4

Three-point field goals: 1992-93, 38-for-135 (.281). 1993-94, 40-for-148 (.270). 1994-95, 60-for-186 (.323). 1995-96, 26-for-86 (.302). 1996-97, 24-for-93 (.258). 1997-98, 2-for-17 (.118). 1998-99, 2-for-7 (.286). 1999-00, 1-for-8 (.125). 2000-01, 3-for-12 (.250). Totals, 196-for-692 (.283).

Personal fouls/disqualifications: 1992-93, 195/0. 1993-94, 174/0. 1994-95, 203/2. 1995-96, 265/1. 1996-97, 237/3. 1997-98, 102/0. 1998-99, 110/0. 1999-00, 152/2. 2000-01, 110/0. Totals, 1548/8.

NBA PLAYOFF RECORD

Season Team	G	Min.	FGM	FGA	Pct.	FTM	FTA	Pct.	REBOUNDS Off.	Def.	Tot.	Ast.	St.	Blk.	TO	Pts.	AVERAGES RPG	APG	PPG
96-97—Minnesota.......	3	121	23	52	.442	6	10	.600	2	14	16	13	7	2	6	55	5.3	4.3	18.3
98-99—Phoenix	3	118	13	35	.371	6	8	.750	6	19	25	10	4	3	8	32	8.3	3.3	10.7
00-01—Phoenix	4	86	8	26	.308	7	9	.778	4	11	15	3	8	1	5	23	3.8	0.8	5.8
Totals	10	325	44	113	.389	19	27	.704	12	44	56	26	19	6	19	110	5.6	2.6	11.0

Three-point field goals: 1996-97, 3-for-4 (.750). Totals, 3-for-4 (.750).
Personal fouls/disqualifications: 1996-97, 13/0. 1998-99, 10/0. 2000-01, 9/0. Totals, 32/0.

NBA ALL-STAR GAME RECORD

Season Team	Min.	FGM	FGA	Pct.	FTM	FTA	Pct.	REBOUNDS Off.	Def.	Tot.	Ast.	PF	Dq.	St.	Blk.	TO	Pts.
1997 —Minnesota	19	3	7	.429	3	4	.750	1	7	8	3	3	0	2	0	3	9

Three-point field goals: 1997, 0-for-1.

GUYTON, A.J.   G   BULLS

PERSONAL: Born February 13, 1978, in Peoria, Ill. ... 6-2/185. (1,88/83,9). ... Full Name: Arthur James Guyton.
HIGH SCHOOL: Central (Peoria, Ill.).
COLLEGE: Indiana.
TRANSACTIONS/CAREER NOTES: Selected by Chicago Bulls in second round (32nd pick overall) of 2000 NBA Draft.

COLLEGIATE RECORD

NOTES: The Sporting News All-America first team (2000).

Season Team	G	Min.	FGM	FGA	Pct.	FTM	FTA	Pct.	Reb.	Ast.	Pts.	AVERAGES RPG	APG	PPG
96-97—Indiana	33	1107	157	361	.435	80	94	.851	110	129	450	3.3	3.9	13.6
97-98—Indiana	32	1088	188	402	.468	82	107	.766	112	118	537	3.5	3.7	16.8
98-99—Indiana	34	1158	198	435	.455	71	94	.755	117	88	543	3.4	2.6	16.0
99-00—Indiana	29	995	204	444	.459	90	114	.789	90	68	570	3.1	2.3	19.7
Totals	128	4348	747	1642	.455	323	409	.790	429	403	2100	3.4	3.1	16.4

Three-point field goals: 1996-97, 56-for-145 (.386). 1997-98, 79-for-180 (.439). 1998-99, 76-for-187 (.406). 1999-00, 72-for-172 (.419). Totals, 283-for-684 (.414).

NBA REGULAR-SEASON RECORD

Season Team	G	Min.	FGM	FGA	Pct.	FTM	FTA	Pct.	REBOUNDS Off.	Def.	Tot.	Ast.	St.	Blk.	TO	Pts.	AVERAGES RPG	APG	PPG
00-01—Chicago	33	630	78	192	.406	15	18	.833	10	26	36	64	9	5	24	198	1.1	1.9	6.0

Three-point field goals: 2000-01, 27-for-69 (.391).
Personal fouls/disqualifications: 2000-01, 35/0.

HAM, DARVIN   F   BUCKS

PERSONAL: Born July 23, 1973, in Saginaw, Mich. ... 6-7/240. (2,01/108,9).
HIGH SCHOOL: Saginaw (Mich.).
JUNIOR COLLEGE: Otero Junior College (Colo.).
COLLEGE: Texas Tech.
TRANSACTIONS/CAREER NOTES: Not drafted by an NBA franchise. ... Played in United States Basketball League with Florida Sharks (1996). ... Signed as free agent by Denver Nuggets (October 1, 1996). ... Traded by Nuggets to Indiana Pacers for G Jerome Allen (February 20, 1997). ... Signed as free agent by Washington Wizards (September 30, 1997). ... Played in Spain (1998-99). ... Signed as free agent by Milwaukee Bucks (September 22, 1999).

G
H

COLLEGIATE RECORD

Season Team	G	Min.	FGM	FGA	Pct.	FTM	FTA	Pct.	Reb.	Ast.	Pts.	RPG	APG	PPG
92-93—Otero Junior College	...	...	...	...	.580	...	...	.780	...	...	...	9.0	...	...
93-94—Texas Tech....................	28	668	97	157	.618	36	72	.500	152	34	230	5.4	1.2	8.2
94-95—Texas Tech....................	30	638	78	131	.595	50	85	.588	129	26	206	4.3	0.9	6.9
95-96—Texas Tech....................	32	752	115	198	.581	61	138	.442	181	31	291	5.7	1.0	9.1
Junior College Totals.............	...	...	...	...	.580	...	...	.780	...	...	...	9.0	...	...
4-Year-College Totals.............	90	2058	290	486	.597	147	295	.498	462	91	727	5.1	1.0	8.1

Three-point field goals: 1995-96, 0-for-1.

NBA REGULAR-SEASON RECORD

									REBOUNDS						AVERAGES		
Season Team	G	Min.	FGM	FGA	Pct.	FTM	FTA	Pct.	Off.	Def.	Tot.	Ast.	St.	Blk.	TO	Pts.	RPG APG PPG
96-97—Den.-Indiana ...	36	318	33	62	.532	17	35	.486	29	27	56	14	9	8	22	83	1.6 0.4 2.3
97-98—Washington	71	635	55	104	.529	35	74	.473	72	59	131	16	21	25	37	145	1.8 0.2 2.0
99-00—Milwaukee	35	792	71	128	.555	35	78	.449	85	87	172	42	29	29	29	177	4.9 1.2 5.1
00-01—Milwaukee	29	540	39	80	.488	29	49	.592	56	65	121	25	17	21	33	109	4.2 0.9 3.8
Totals	171	2285	198	374	.529	116	236	.492	242	238	480	97	76	83	121	514	2.8 0.6 3.0

Three-point field goals: 1999-00, 0-for-1. 2000-01, 2-for-3 (.667). Totals, 2-for-4 (.500).
Personal fouls/disqualifications: 1996-97, 57/3. 1997-98, 118/1. 1999-00, 102/1. 2000-01, 85/0. Totals, 362/5.

NBA PLAYOFF RECORD

									REBOUNDS						AVERAGES		
Season Team	G	Min.	FGM	FGA	Pct.	FTM	FTA	Pct.	Off.	Def.	Tot.	Ast.	St.	Blk.	TO	Pts.	RPG APG PPG
99-00—Milwaukee	5	144	11	17	.647	3	9	.333	17	12	29	7	1	8	7	25	5.8 1.4 5.0
00-01—Milwaukee	14	132	9	15	.600	11	20	.550	10	9	19	5	4	7	6	29	1.4 0.4 2.1
Totals	19	276	20	32	.625	14	29	.483	27	21	48	12	5	15	13	54	2.5 0.6 2.8

Three-point field goals: 1999-00, 0-for-1. Totals, 0-for-1 (.000).
Personal fouls/disqualifications: 1999-00, 22/0. 2000-01, 31/1. Totals, 53/1.

SPANISH LEAGUE RECORD

Season Team	G	Min.	FGM	FGA	Pct.	FTM	FTA	Pct.	Reb.	Ast.	Pts.	RPG	APG	PPG
98-99—Coviran-C.Alhambra	12	398	58	100	.580	24	54	.444	84	15	140	7.0	1.3	11.7

Three-point field goals: 1998-99, 0-for-1.

HAMILTON, RICHARD   G/F   WIZARDS

PERSONAL: Born February 14, 1978, in Coatesville, Pa. ... 6-6/185. (1,98/83,9). ... Full Name: Richard Clay Hamilton.
HIGH SCHOOL: Coatesville (Pa.) Area.
COLLEGE: Connecticut.
TRANSACTIONS/CAREER NOTES: Selected after junior season by Washington Wizards in first round (seventh pick overall) of 1999 NBA Draft.

COLLEGIATE RECORD

NOTES: Member of NCAA Division I championship team (1999). ... NCAA Division I Tournament Most Outstanding Player (1999). ... THE SPORTING NEWS All-America first team (1999). ... THE SPORTING NEWS All-America second team (1998).

Season Team	G	Min.	FGM	FGA	Pct.	FTM	FTA	Pct.	Reb.	Ast.	Pts.	RPG	APG	PPG
96-97—Connecticut	32	980	174	451	.386	91	116	.784	138	88	509	4.3	2.8	15.9
97-98—Connecticut	37	1203	270	614	.440	156	185	.843	163	87	795	4.4	2.4	21.5
98-99—Connecticut	34	1091	247	557	.443	170	204	.833	163	91	732	4.8	2.7	21.5
Totals	103	3274	691	1622	.426	417	505	.826	464	266	2036	4.5	2.6	19.8

Three-point field goals: 1996-97, 70-for-186 (.376). 1997-98, 99-for-245 (.404). 1998-99, 68-for-196 (.347). Totals, 237-for-627 (.378).

NBA REGULAR-SEASON RECORD

									REBOUNDS						AVERAGES		
Season Team	G	Min.	FGM	FGA	Pct.	FTM	FTA	Pct.	Off.	Def.	Tot.	Ast.	St.	Blk.	TO	Pts.	RPG APG PPG
99-00—Washington	71	1373	254	605	.420	103	133	.774	38	91	129	108	28	6	84	639	1.8 1.5 9.0
00-01—Washington	78	2519	547	1249	.438	277	319	.868	75	163	238	224	75	10	201	1411	3.1 2.9 18.1
Totals	149	3892	801	1854	.432	380	452	.841	113	254	367	332	103	16	285	2050	2.5 2.2 13.8

Three-point field goals: 1999-00, 28-for-77 (.364). 2000-01, 40-for-146 (.274). Totals, 68-for-223 (.305).
Personal fouls/disqualifications: 1999-00, 142/2. 2000-01, 203/2. Totals, 345/4.

HAMILTON, ZENDON   C

PERSONAL: Born April 29, 1975, in Queens, N.Y. ... 6-11/240. (2,11/108,9).
HIGH SCHOOL: Sewanhaka (Floral Park, N.Y.).
COLLEGE: St. John's.
TRANSACTIONS/CAREER NOTES: Not drafted by an NBA franchise. ... Played in Spain (1998-99). ... Signed as free agent by Dallas Mavericks (October 4, 1999). ... Waived by Mavericks (October 15, 1999). ... Played in Greece (1999-2000). ... Signed as free agent by Los Angeles Clippers (September 29, 2000).

COLLEGIATE RECORD

Season Team	G	Min.	FGM	FGA	Pct.	FTM	FTA	Pct.	Reb.	Ast.	Pts.	RPG	APG	PPG
94-95—St. John's	28	...	112	214	.523	95	154	.617	141	18	319	5.0	0.6	11.4
95-96—St. John's	27	...	179	368	.486	204	256	.797	277	21	542	10.3	0.8	20.1
96-97—St. John's	27	...	132	306	.431	173	242	.715	254	11	437	9.4	0.4	16.2
97-98—St. John's	32	...	161	341	.472	170	260	.654	277	12	492	8.7	0.4	15.4
Totals	114	...	584	1229	.475	642	912	.704	949	62	1790	8.3	0.5	15.7

Three-point field goals: 1994-95, 0-for-1. 1995-96, 0-for-4. 1996-97, 0-for-1. Totals, 0-for-6 (.000).

H

SPANISH LEAGUE RECORD

Season Team	G	Min.	FGM	FGA	Pct.	FTM	FTA	Pct.	Reb.	Ast.	Pts.	AVERAGES RPG	APG	PPG
98-99—Forum Valladolid	18	443	84	175	.480	67	100	.670	111	6	235	6.2	0.3	13.1

Three-point field goals: 1998-99, 0-for-2.

GREEK LEAGUE RECORD

Season Team	G	Min.	FGM	FGA	Pct.	FTM	FTA	Pct.	Reb.	Ast.	Pts.	AVERAGES RPG	APG	PPG
99-00—Dafni..............................	21	620	109	245	.445	88	119	.739	143	13	310	6.8	0.6	14.8

Three-point field goals: 1999-00, 4-for-15 (.267).

NBA REGULAR-SEASON RECORD

Season Team	G	Min.	FGM	FGA	Pct.	FTM	FTA	Pct.	REBOUNDS Off.	Def.	Tot.	Ast.	St.	Blk.	TO	Pts.	AVERAGES RPG	APG	PPG
00-01—L.A. Clippers...	3	19	2	9	.222	5	8	.625	3	5	8	0	0	0	2	9	2.7	0.0	3.0

Personal fouls/disqualifications: 2000-01, 4/0.

HAMMONDS, TOM   F ·   TIMBERWOLVES

PERSONAL: Born March 27, 1967, in Fort Walton Beach, Fla. ... 6-9/225. (2,06/102,1). ... Full Name: Tom Edward Hammonds.
HIGH SCHOOL: Crestview (Fla.).
COLLEGE: Georgia Tech.
TRANSACTIONS/CAREER NOTES: Selected by Washington Bullets in first round (ninth pick overall) of 1989 NBA Draft. ... Traded by Bullets to Charlotte Hornets for G Rex Chapman (February 19, 1992). ... Waived by Hornets (January 26, 1993). ... Signed as free agent by Denver Nuggets (February 5, 1993). ... Waived by Nuggets (September 5, 1997). ... Signed as free agent by Minnesota Timberwolves (November 25, 1997).
MISCELLANEOUS: Member of gold-medal-winning U.S. World Championship team (1986).

COLLEGIATE RECORD

Season Team	G	Min.	FGM	FGA	Pct.	FTM	FTA	Pct.	Reb.	Ast.	Pts.	AVERAGES RPG	APG	PPG
85-86—Georgia Tech	34	1112	168	276	.609	80	98	.816	219	37	416	6.4	1.1	12.2
86-87—Georgia Tech	29	1088	206	362	.569	59	74	.797	208	41	471	7.2	1.4	16.2
87-88—Georgia Tech	30	1076	229	403	.568	109	132	.826	216	40	567	7.2	1.3	18.9
88-89—Georgia Tech	30	1111	250	465	.538	126	163	.773	242	51	627	8.1	1.7	20.9
Totals	123	4387	853	1506	.566	374	467	.801	885	169	2081	7.2	1.4	16.9

Three-point field goals: 1988-89, 1-for-3 (.333).

NBA REGULAR-SEASON RECORD

Season Team	G	Min.	FGM	FGA	Pct.	FTM	FTA	Pct.	REBOUNDS Off.	Def.	Tot.	Ast.	St.	Blk.	TO	Pts.	AVERAGES RPG	APG	PPG
89-90—Washington	61	805	129	295	.437	63	98	.643	61	107	168	51	11	14	46	321	2.8	0.8	5.3
90-91—Washington	70	1023	155	336	.461	57	79	.722	58	148	206	43	15	7	54	367	2.9	0.6	5.2
91-92—Washington	37	984	195	400	.488	50	82	.610	49	136	185	36	22	13	58	440	5.0	1.0	11.9
92-93—Char.-Denver ...	54	713	105	221	.475	38	62	.613	38	89	127	24	18	12	34	248	2.4	0.4	4.6
93-94—Denver	74	877	115	230	.500	71	104	.683	62	137	199	34	20	12	41	301	2.7	0.5	4.1
94-95—Denver	70	956	139	260	.535	132	177	.746	55	167	222	36	11	14	56	410	3.2	0.5	5.9
95-96—Denver	71	1045	127	268	.474	88	115	.765	85	138	223	23	23	13	48	342	3.1	0.3	4.8
96-97—Denver	81	1758	191	398	.480	124	172	.721	135	266	401	64	16	24	88	506	5.0	0.8	6.2
97-98—Minnesota	57	1140	127	246	.516	92	132	.697	100	171	271	36	15	17	48	346	4.8	0.6	6.1
98-99—Minnesota	49	716	82	179	.458	48	75	.640	54	82	136	20	8	7	32	212	2.8	0.4	4.3
99-00—Minnesota	56	372	42	97	.433	33	56	.589	34	67	101	10	8	3	21	117	1.8	0.2	2.1
00-01—Minnesota	7	30	3	10	.300	1	2	.500	2	2	4	1	0	0	3	7	0.6	0.1	1.0
Totals	687	10419	1410	2940	.480	797	1154	.691	733	1510	2243	378	167	136	529	3617	3.3	0.6	5.3

Three-point field goals: 1989-90, 0-for-1. 1990-91, 0-for-4. 1991-92, 0-for-1. 1992-93, 0-for-1. 1994-95, 0-for-1. 1996-97, 0-for-2. 1997-98, 0-for-1. Totals, 0-for-11 (.000).

Personal fouls/disqualifications: 1989-90, 98/0. 1990-91, 108/0. 1991-92, 118/1. 1992-93, 77/0. 1993-94, 91/0. 1994-95, 132/1. 1995-96, 137/0. 1996-97, 205/0. 1997-98, 127/1. 1998-99, 88/1. 1999-00, 55/0. 2000-01, 8/1. Totals, 1244/5.

NBA PLAYOFF RECORD

Season Team	G	Min.	FGM	FGA	Pct.	FTM	FTA	Pct.	REBOUNDS Off.	Def.	Tot.	Ast.	St.	Blk.	TO	Pts.	AVERAGES RPG	APG	PPG
93-94—Denver	8	49	2	9	.222	5	6	.833	5	8	13	2	0	0	1	9	1.6	0.3	1.1
94-95—Denver	3	44	9	14	.643	2	6	.333	3	4	7	1	0	2	4	20	2.3	0.3	6.7
97-98—Minnesota	5	113	12	28	.429	12	16	.750	10	12	22	2	0	1	4	36	4.4	0.4	7.2
98-99—Minnesota	4	18	0	0	...	4	4	1.000	0	2	2	0	0	0	1	4	0.5	0.0	1.0
99-00—Minnesota	1	2	0	0	...	0	0	...	0	0	0	0	0	0	0	0	0.0	0.0	0.0
Totals	21	226	23	51	.451	23	32	.719	18	26	44	5	0	3	10	69	2.1	0.2	3.3

Personal fouls/disqualifications: 1993-94, 6/0. 1994-95, 12/0. 1997-98, 18/0. 1998-99, 4/0. Totals, 40/0.

HARDAWAY, ANFERNEE   G/F   SUNS

H

PERSONAL: Born July 18, 1971, in Memphis. ... 6-7/215. (2,01/97,5). ... Full Name: Anfernee Deon Hardaway. ... Name pronounced ANN-fur-nee. ... Nickname: Penny.
HIGH SCHOOL: Treadwell (Memphis).
COLLEGE: Memphis.
TRANSACTIONS/CAREER NOTES: Selected after junior season by Golden State Warriors in first round (third pick overall) of 1993 NBA Draft. ... Draft rights traded by Warriors with 1996, 1998 and 2000 first-round draft choices to Orlando Magic for draft rights F/C Chris Webber (June 30, 1993). ... Traded by Magic to Phoenix Suns for F/C Danny Manning, F Pat Garrity and two future first-round draft choices (August 5, 1999).
MISCELLANEOUS: Member of gold-medal-winning U.S. Olympic team (1996).

COLLEGIATE RECORD

NOTES: The Sporting News All-America first team (1993).

Season Team	G	Min.	FGM	FGA	Pct.	FTM	FTA	Pct.	Reb.	Ast.	Pts.	RPG	APG	PPG
90-91—Memphis						Did not play—ineligible.								
91-92—Memphis	34	1224	209	483	.433	103	158	.652	237	188	590	7.0	5.5	17.4
92-93—Memphis	32	1196	249	522	.477	158	206	.767	273	204	729	8.5	6.4	22.8
Totals	66	2420	458	1005	.456	261	364	.717	510	392	1319	7.7	5.9	20.0

Three-point field goals: 1991-92, 69-for-190 (.363). 1992-93, 73-for-220 (.332). Totals, 142-for-410 (.346).

NBA REGULAR-SEASON RECORD

HONORS: All-NBA first team (1995, 1996). ... All-NBA third team (1997). ... NBA All-Rookie first team (1994). ... MVP of Rookie Game (1994).

Season Team	G	Min.	FGM	FGA	Pct.	FTM	FTA	Pct.	REBOUNDS			Ast.	St.	Blk.	TO	Pts.	AVERAGES		
									Off.	Def.	Tot.						RPG	APG	PPG
93-94—Orlando	82	3015	509	1092	.466	245	330	.742	192	247	439	544	190	51	292	1313	5.4	6.6	16.0
94-95—Orlando	77	2901	585	1142	.512	356	463	.769	139	197	336	551	130	26	258	1613	4.4	7.2	20.9
95-96—Orlando	82	3015	623	1215	.513	445	580	.767	129	225	354	582	166	41	229	1780	4.3	7.1	21.7
96-97—Orlando	59	2221	421	941	.447	283	345	.820	82	181	263	332	93	35	145	1210	4.5	5.6	20.5
97-98—Orlando	19	625	103	273	.377	90	118	.763	8	68	76	68	28	15	46	311	4.0	3.6	16.4
98-99—Orlando	50	1944	301	717	.420	149	211	.706	74	210	284	266	111	23	150	791	5.7	5.3	15.8
99-00—Phoenix	60	2253	378	798	.474	226	286	.790	91	256	347	315	94	38	153	1015	5.8	5.3	16.9
00-01—Phoenix	4	112	15	36	.417	7	11	.636	5	13	18	15	6	1	3	39	4.5	3.8	9.8
Totals	433	16086	2935	6214	.472	1801	2344	.768	720	1397	2117	2673	818	230	1276	8072	4.9	6.2	18.6

Three-point field goals: 1993-94, 50-for-187 (.267). 1994-95, 87-for-249 (.349). 1995-96, 89-for-283 (.314). 1996-97, 85-for-267 (.318). 1997-98, 15-for-50 (.300). 1998-99, 40-for-140 (.286). 1999-00, 33-for-102 (.324). 2000-01, 2-for-8 (.250). Totals, 401-for-1286 (.312).

Personal fouls/disqualifications: 1993-94, 205/2. 1994-95, 158/1. 1995-96, 160/0. 1996-97, 123/1. 1997-98, 45/0. 1998-99, 111/0. 1999-00, 164/1. 2000-01, 6/0. Totals, 972/5.

NBA PLAYOFF RECORD

Season Team	G	Min.	FGM	FGA	Pct.	FTM	FTA	Pct.	REBOUNDS			Ast.	St.	Blk.	TO	Pts.	AVERAGES		
									Off.	Def.	Tot.						RPG	APG	PPG
93-94—Orlando	3	133	22	50	.440	7	10	.700	8	12	20	21	5	6	20	56	6.7	7.0	18.7
94-95—Orlando	21	849	144	305	.472	84	111	.757	30	49	79	162	40	15	73	412	3.8	7.7	19.6
95-96—Orlando	12	473	101	217	.465	58	78	.744	20	36	56	72	20	4	26	280	4.7	6.0	23.3
96-97—Orlando	5	220	52	111	.468	40	54	.741	7	23	30	17	12	7	9	155	6.0	3.4	31.0
98-99—Orlando	4	167	20	57	.351	30	39	.769	9	11	20	22	9	1	12	76	5.0	5.5	19.0
99-00—Phoenix	9	386	67	145	.462	44	62	.710	14	30	44	51	14	9	25	183	4.9	5.7	20.3
Totals	54	2228	406	885	.459	263	354	.743	88	161	249	345	100	42	165	1162	4.6	6.4	21.5

Three-point field goals: 1993-94, 5-for-11 (.455). 1994-95, 40-for-99 (.404). 1995-96, 20-for-55 (.364). 1996-97, 11-for-30 (.367). 1998-99, 6-for-13 (.462). 1999-00, 5-for-19 (.263). Totals, 87-for-227 (.383).

Personal fouls/disqualifications: 1993-94, 10/0. 1994-95, 70/0. 1995-96, 27/1. 1996-97, 14/0. 1998-99, 13/0. 1999-00, 29/0. Totals, 163/1.

NBA ALL-STAR GAME RECORD

Season Team	Min.	FGM	FGA	Pct.	FTM	FTA	Pct.	REBOUNDS			Ast.	PF	Dq.	St.	Blk.	TO	Pts.
								Off.	Def.	Tot.							
1995 —Orlando	31	4	9	.444	4	6	.667	4	1	5	11	1	0	0	0	3	12
1996 —Orlando	31	6	8	.750	4	4	1.000	0	0	0	7	0	0	2	0	3	18
1997 —Orlando	24	7	10	.700	2	2	1.000	4	3	7	3	2	0	2	0	1	19
1998 —Orlando	12	3	5	.600	0	0	...	0	0	0	3	0	0	0	0	1	6
Totals	98	20	32	.625	10	12	.833	8	4	12	24	3	0	4	0	8	55

Three-point field goals: 1995, 0-for-2. 1996, 2-for-4 (.500). 1997, 3-for-5 (.600). 1998, 0-for-1. Totals, 5-for-12 (.417).

HARDAWAY, TIM   G   MAVERICKS

PERSONAL: Born September 1, 1966, in Chicago ... 6-0/195. (1,83/88,5). ... Full Name: Timothy Duane Hardaway.
HIGH SCHOOL: Carver (Chicago).
COLLEGE: Texas-El Paso.
TRANSACTIONS/CAREER NOTES: Selected by Golden State Warriors in first round (14th pick overall) of 1989 NBA Draft. ... Traded by Warriors with F/C Chris Gatling to Miami Heat for F/C Kevin Willis and G Bimbo Coles (February 22, 1996). ... Traded by Heat to Dallas Mavericks for 2003 or 2004 second-round draft choice (August 22, 2001).
MISCELLANEOUS: Member of gold-medal-winning U.S. Olympic team (2000). ... Member of gold-medal-winning U.S. World Championship team (1994). ... Miami Heat all-time assists leader with 2,867 (1995-96 through 2000-01).

COLLEGIATE RECORD

NOTES: Frances Pomeroy Naismith Award winner (1989).

Season Team	G	Min.	FGM	FGA	Pct.	FTM	FTA	Pct.	Reb.	Ast.	Pts.	RPG	APG	PPG
85-86—Texas-El Paso	28	435	37	71	.521	41	63	.651	35	53	115	1.3	1.9	4.1
86-87—Texas-El Paso	31	922	120	245	.490	67	101	.663	62	148	310	2.0	4.8	10.0
87-88—Texas-El Paso	32	1036	159	354	.449	98	130	.754	93	183	434	2.9	5.7	13.6
88-89—Texas-El Paso	33	1182	255	509	.501	169	228	.741	131	179	727	4.0	5.4	22.0
Totals	124	3575	571	1179	.484	375	522	.718	321	563	1586	2.6	4.5	12.8

Three-point field goals: 1986-87, 3-for-12 (.250). 1987-88, 18-for-53 (.340). 1988-89, 48-for-131 (.366). Totals, 69-for-196 (.352).

NBA REGULAR-SEASON RECORD

RECORDS: Holds single-game record for most field goals attempted, none made—17 (December 27, 1991, OT, at San Antonio).
HONORS: All-NBA first team (1997). ... All-NBA second team (1992, 1998, 1999). ... All-NBA third team (1993). ... NBA All-Rookie first team (1990).

H

Season Team	G	Min.	FGM	FGA	Pct.	FTM	FTA	Pct.	REBOUNDS Off.	Def.	Tot.	Ast.	St.	Blk.	TO	Pts.	AVERAGES RPG	APG	PPG
89-90—Golden State ...	79	2663	464	985	.471	211	276	.764	57	253	310	689	165	12	260	1162	3.9	8.7	14.7
90-91—Golden State ...	82	3215	739	1551	.476	306	381	.803	87	245	332	793	214	12	270	1881	4.0	9.7	22.9
91-92—Golden State ...	81	3332	734	1592	.461	298	389	.766	81	229	310	807	164	13	267	1893	3.8	10.0	23.4
92-93—Golden State ...	66	2609	522	1168	.447	273	367	.744	60	203	263	699	116	12	220	1419	4.0	10.6	21.5
93-94—Golden State ...						Did not play—knee injury.													
94-95—Golden State ...	62	2321	430	1007	.427	219	288	.760	46	144	190	578	88	12	214	1247	3.1	9.3	20.1
95-96—G.S.-Miami	80	2534	419	992	.422	241	305	.790	35	194	229	640	132	17	235	1217	2.9	8.0	15.2
96-97—Miami	81	3136	575	1384	.415	291	364	.799	49	228	277	695	151	9	230	1644	3.4	8.6	20.3
97-98—Miami	81	3031	558	1296	.431	257	329	.781	48	251	299	672	136	16	224	1528	3.7	8.3	18.9
98-99—Miami	48	1772	301	752	.400	121	149	.812	15	137	152	352	57	6	131	835	3.2	7.3	17.4
99-00—Miami	52	1672	246	638	.386	110	133	.827	25	125	150	385	49	4	119	696	2.9	7.4	13.4
00-01—Miami	77	2613	408	1042	.392	145	181	.801	26	178	204	483	90	6	189	1150	2.6	6.3	14.9
Totals	789	28898	5396	12407	.435	2472	3162	.782	529	2187	2716	6793	1362	119	2359	14672	3.4	8.6	18.6

Three-point field goals: 1989-90, 23-for-84 (.274). 1990-91, 97-for-252 (.385). 1991-92, 127-for-376 (.338). 1992-93, 102-for-309 (.330). 1994-95, 168-for-444 (.378). 1995-96, 138-for-379 (.364). 1996-97, 203-for-590 (.344). 1997-98, 155-for-442 (.351). 1998-99, 112-for-311 (.360). 1999-00, 94-for-256 (.367). 2000-01, 189-for-517 (.366). Totals, 1408-for-3960 (.356).

Personal fouls/disqualifications: 1989-90, 232/6. 1990-91, 228/7. 1991-92, 208/1. 1992-93, 152/0. 1994-95, 155/1. 1995-96, 201/3. 1996-97, 165/2. 1997-98, 200/2. 1998-99, 102/1. 1999-00, 112/0. 2000-01, 155/1. Totals, 1910/24.

NBA PLAYOFF RECORD

Season Team	G	Min.	FGM	FGA	Pct.	FTM	FTA	Pct.	REBOUNDS Off.	Def.	Tot.	Ast.	St.	Blk.	TO	Pts.	AVERAGES RPG	APG	PPG
90-91—Golden State ...	9	396	90	185	.486	30	38	.789	5	28	33	101	28	7	25	227	3.7	11.2	25.2
91-92—Golden State ...	4	176	32	80	.400	24	37	.649	6	9	15	29	13	0	14	98	3.8	7.3	24.5
95-96—Miami	3	110	20	43	.465	5	7	.714	1	4	5	17	3	0	15	53	1.7	5.7	17.7
96-97—Miami	17	701	103	287	.359	70	88	.795	13	56	69	119	27	1	53	318	4.1	7.0	18.7
97-98—Miami	5	222	42	94	.447	29	37	.784	3	14	17	33	6	0	18	130	3.4	6.6	26.0
98-99—Miami	5	182	15	56	.268	10	16	.625	3	11	14	32	5	1	18	45	2.8	6.4	9.0
99-00—Miami	7	182	20	68	.294	7	10	.700	1	14	15	33	5	0	11	54	2.1	4.7	7.7
00-01—Miami	2	36	2	9	.222	0	0	...	1	1	2	9	0	0	8	5	1.0	4.5	2.5
Totals	52	2005	324	822	.394	175	233	.751	33	137	170	373	87	9	162	930	3.3	7.2	17.9

Three-point field goals: 1990-91, 17-for-48 (.354). 1991-92, 10-for-29 (.345). 1995-96, 8-for-22 (.364). 1996-97, 42-for-134 (.313). 1997-98, 17-for-39 (.436). 1998-99, 5-for-25 (.200). 1999-00, 7-for-34 (.206). 2000-01, 1-for-3 (.333). Totals, 107-for-334 (.320).

Personal fouls/disqualifications: 1990-91, 22/0. 1991-92, 14/0. 1995-96, 10/0. 1996-97, 37/0. 1997-98, 9/0. 1998-99, 14/0. 1999-00, 10/0. 2000-01, 4/0. Totals, 120/0.

NBA ALL-STAR GAME RECORD

Season	Team	Min.	FGM	FGA	Pct.	FTM	FTA	Pct.	REBOUNDS Off.	Def.	Tot.	Ast.	PF	Dq.	St.	Blk.	TO	Pts.
1991	—Golden State	12	2	7	.286	0	0	...	2	1	3	4	1	0	2	0	0	5
1992	—Golden State	20	5	10	.500	2	2	1.000	0	0	0	7	2	0	1	0	2	14
1993	—Golden State	21	3	9	.333	9	12	.750	1	5	6	4	1	0	1	0	3	16
1997	—Miami	14	4	10	.400	0	0	...	0	3	3	2	0	0	1	0	2	10
1998	—Miami	17	3	8	.375	0	0	...	0	1	1	6	0	0	0	0	6	8
Totals		84	17	44	.386	11	14	.786	3	10	13	23	5	0	5	0	13	53

Three-point field goals: 1991, 1-for-2 (.500). 1992, 2-for-5 (.400). 1993, 1-for-3 (.333). 1997, 2-for-6 (.333). 1998, 2-for-5 (.400). Totals, 8-for-21 (.381).

HARPER, RON   G

PERSONAL: Born January 20, 1964, in Dayton, Ohio. ... 6-6/215. (1,98/97,5). ... Full Name: Ronald Harper.
HIGH SCHOOL: Kiser (Dayton, Ohio).
COLLEGE: Miami of Ohio.
TRANSACTIONS/CAREER NOTES: Selected by Cleveland Cavaliers in first round (eighth pick overall) of 1986 NBA Draft. ... Traded by Cavaliers with 1990 and 1992 first-round draft choices and 1991 second-round draft choice to Los Angeles Clippers for G Reggie Williams and draft rights to F Danny Ferry (November 16, 1989). ... Signed as unrestricted free agent by Chicago Bulls (September 15, 1994). ... Signed as free agent by Los Angeles Lakers (October 13, 1999).
MISCELLANEOUS: Member of NBA championship team (1996, 1997, 1998, 2000, 2001).

COLLEGIATE RECORD

NOTES: THE SPORTING NEWS All-America second team (1986).

Season Team	G	Min.	FGM	FGA	Pct.	FTM	FTA	Pct.	Reb.	Ast.	Pts.	AVERAGES RPG	APG	PPG
82-83—Miami of Ohio	28	887	148	298	.497	64	95	.674	195	62	360	7.0	2.2	12.9
83-84—Miami of Ohio	30	989	197	367	.537	94	165	.570	229	64	488	7.6	2.1	16.3
84-85—Miami of Ohio	31	1144	312	577	.541	148	224	.661	333	79	772	10.7	2.5	24.9
85-86—Miami of Ohio	31	1144	312	572	.545	133	200	.665	362	133	757	11.7	4.3	24.4
Totals ....……...........	120	4164	969	1814	.534	439	684	.642	1119	338	2377	9.3	2.8	19.8

HONORS: NBA All-Rookie team (1987).

NBA REGULAR-SEASON RECORD

Season Team	G	Min.	FGM	FGA	Pct.	FTM	FTA	Pct.	REBOUNDS Off.	Def.	Tot.	Ast.	St.	Blk.	TO	Pts.	AVERAGES RPG	APG	PPG
86-87—Cleveland	82	3064	734	1614	.455	386	564	.684	169	223	392	394	209	84	*345	1874	4.8	4.8	22.9
87-88—Cleveland	57	1830	340	732	.464	196	278	.705	64	159	223	281	122	52	158	879	3.9	4.9	15.4
88-89—Cleveland	82	2851	587	1149	.511	323	430	.751	122	287	409	434	185	74	230	1526	5.0	5.3	18.6
89-90—Cleve.-L.A.C. ...	35	1367	301	637	.473	182	231	.788	74	132	206	182	81	41	100	798	5.9	5.2	22.8
90-91—L.A. Clippers ...	39	1383	285	729	.391	145	217	.668	58	130	188	209	66	35	129	763	4.8	5.4	19.6
91-92—L.A. Clippers ...	82	3144	569	1292	.440	293	398	.736	120	327	447	417	152	72	252	1495	5.5	5.1	18.2
92-93—L.A. Clippers ...	80	2970	542	1203	.451	307	399	.769	117	308	425	360	177	73	222	1443	5.3	4.5	18.0

H

Season Team	G	Min.	FGM	FGA	Pct.	FTM	FTA	Pct.	Off.	Def.	Tot.	Ast.	St.	Blk.	TO	Pts.	RPG	APG	PPG
93-94—L.A. Clippers...	75	2856	569	1335	.426	299	418	.715	129	331	460	344	144	54	242	1508	6.1	4.6	20.1
94-95—Chicago	77	1536	209	491	.426	81	131	.618	51	129	180	157	97	27	100	530	2.3	2.0	6.9
95-96—Chicago	80	1886	234	501	.467	98	139	.705	74	139	213	208	105	32	73	594	2.7	2.6	7.4
96-97—Chicago	76	1740	177	406	.436	58	82	.707	46	147	193	191	86	38	50	480	2.5	2.5	6.3
97-98—Chicago	82	2284	293	665	.441	162	216	.750	107	183	290	241	108	48	91	764	3.5	2.9	9.3
98-99—Chicago	35	1107	147	390	.377	71	101	.703	49	131	180	115	60	35	65	392	5.1	3.3	11.2
99-00—L.A. Lakers	80	2042	212	531	.399	100	147	.680	96	241	337	270	85	39	132	557	4.2	3.4	7.0
00-01—L.A. Lakers	47	1139	127	271	.469	34	48	.708	46	120	166	113	39	25	62	307	3.5	2.4	6.5
Totals	1009	31199	5326	11946	.446	2735	3799	.720	1322	2987	4309	3916	1716	729	2251	13910	4.3	3.9	13.8

Three-point field goals: 1986-87, 20-for-94 (.213). 1987-88, 3-for-20 (.150). 1988-89, 29-for-116 (.250). 1989-90, 14-for-51 (.275). 1990-91, 48-for-148 (.324). 1991-92, 64-for-211 (.303). 1992-93, 52-for-186 (.280). 1993-94, 71-for-236 (.301). 1994-95, 31-for-110 (.282). 1995-96, 28-for-104 (.269). 1996-97, 68-for-188 (.362). 1997-98, 16-for-84 (.190). 1998-99, 27-for-85 (.318). 1999-00, 33-for-106 (.311). 2000-01, 19-for-72 (.264). Totals, 523-for-1811 (.289).

Personal fouls/disqualifications: 1986-87, 247/3. 1987-88, 157/3. 1988-89, 224/1. 1989-90, 105/1. 1990-91, 111/0. 1991-92, 199/0. 1992-93, 212/1. 1993-94, 167/0. 1994-95, 132/1. 1995-96, 137/0. 1996-97, 138/0. 1997-98, 181/0. 1998-99, 164/0. 2000-01, 70/0. Totals, 2324/10.

NBA PLAYOFF RECORD

Season Team	G	Min.	FGM	FGA	Pct.	FTM	FTA	Pct.	Off.	Def.	Tot.	Ast.	St.	Blk.	TO	Pts.	RPG	APG	PPG
87-88—Cleveland	4	134	30	63	.476	11	16	.688	4	16	20	15	11	4	11	71	5.0	3.8	17.8
88-89—Cleveland	5	189	39	69	.565	20	26	.769	7	14	21	20	11	4	7	98	4.2	4.0	19.6
91-92—L.A. Clippers ...	5	206	39	87	.448	11	14	.786	10	22	32	23	5	4	15	90	6.4	4.6	18.0
92-93—L.A. Clippers ...	5	174	37	78	.474	11	17	.647	4	16	20	16	15	10	11	90	4.0	3.2	18.0
94-95—Chicago	6	40	6	14	.429	0	0	...	2	4	6	4	3	1	1	12	1.0	0.7	2.0
95-96—Chicago	18	494	57	134	.425	29	42	.690	26	41	67	45	25	7	18	158	3.7	2.5	8.8
96-97—Chicago	19	515	50	125	.400	21	28	.750	20	61	81	57	24	11	14	143	4.3	3.0	7.5
97-98—Chicago	21	563	56	122	.459	24	39	.615	22	55	77	48	20	18	18	141	3.7	2.3	6.7
99-00—L.A. Lakers	23	643	78	181	.431	33	47	.702	30	55	85	73	23	13	28	198	3.7	3.2	8.6
00-01—L.A. Lakers	6	42	5	10	.500	2	3	.667	1	7	8	4	4	1	1	13	1.3	0.7	2.2
Totals	112	3000	397	883	.450	162	232	.698	126	291	417	305	141	76	121	1013	3.7	2.7	9.0

Three-point field goals: 1987-88, 0-for-2. 1988-89, 0-for-2. 1991-92, 1-for-9 (.111). 1992-93, 5-for-10 (.500). 1994-95, 0-for-2. 1995-96, 15-for-47 (.319). 1996-97, 21-for-61 (.344). 1997-98, 5-for-19 (.263). 1999-00, 9-for-39 (.231). 2000-01, 1-for-4 (.250). Totals, 57-for-195 (.292).

Personal fouls/disqualifications: 1987-88, 9/0. 1988-89, 20/1. 1991-92, 13/0. 1992-93, 7/0. 1994-95, 6/0. 1995-96, 38/0. 1996-97, 43/1. 1997-98, 42/0. 1999-00, 63/0. 2000-01, 4/0. Totals, 245/2.

HARPRING, MATT   F   76ERS

PERSONAL: Born May 31, 1976, in Cincinnati. ... 6-7/231. (2,01/104,8). ... Full Name: Matthew Joseph Harpring.
HIGH SCHOOL: Marist (Atlanta).
COLLEGE: Georgia Tech.
TRANSACTIONS/CAREER NOTES: Selected by Orlando Magic in first round (15th pick overall) of 1998 NBA Draft. ... Traded by Magic to Cleveland Cavaliers for F/C Andrew DeClercq (August 3, 2000). ... Traded by Cavaliers with F Cedric Henderson and F/C Robert Traylor to Philadelphia 76ers for F Tyrone Hill and F Jumaine Jones (August 3, 2001).

COLLEGIATE RECORD

Season Team	G	Min.	FGM	FGA	Pct.	FTM	FTA	Pct.	Reb.	Ast.	Pts.	RPG	APG	PPG
94-95—Georgia Tech	29	966	121	250	.484	81	110	.736	180	68	351	6.2	2.3	12.1
95-96—Georgia Tech	36	1328	233	457	.510	138	181	.762	293	79	670	8.1	2.2	18.6
96-97—Georgia Tech	27	1015	169	410	.412	110	163	.675	222	60	513	8.2	2.2	19.0
97-98—Georgia Tech	32	1163	230	504	.456	179	221	.810	302	82	691	9.4	2.6	21.6
Totals	124	4472	753	1621	.465	508	675	.753	997	289	2225	8.0	2.3	17.9

Three-point field goals: 1994-95, 28-for-73 (.384). 1995-96, 66-for-154 (.429). 1996-97, 65-for-190 (.342). 1997-98, 52-for-168 (.310). Totals, 211-for-585 (.361).

NBA REGULAR-SEASON RECORD

HONORS: NBA All-Rookie first team (1999).

Season Team	G	Min.	FGM	FGA	Pct.	FTM	FTA	Pct.	Off.	Def.	Tot.	Ast.	St.	Blk.	TO	Pts.	RPG	APG	PPG
98-99—Orlando..........	50	1114	148	320	.463	102	143	.713	88	126	214	45	30	6	73	408	4.3	0.9	8.2
99-00—Orlando..........	4	63	4	17	.235	5	7	.857	5	7	12	8	5	1	1	16	3.0	2.0	4.0
00-01—Cleveland	56	1615	238	524	.454	134	165	.812	90	152	242	102	42	17	90	623	4.3	1.8	11.1
Totals	110	2792	390	861	.453	242	315	.768	183	285	468	155	77	24	164	1047	4.3	1.4	9.5

Three-point field goals: 1998-99, 10-for-25 (.400). 1999-00, 2-for-2. 2000-01, 13-for-52 (.250). Totals, 25-for-79 (.316).
Personal fouls/disqualifications: 1998-99, 112/0. 1999-00, 7/0. 2000-01, 161/1. Totals, 280/1.

NBA PLAYOFF RECORD

Season Team	G	Min.	FGM	FGA	Pct.	FTM	FTA	Pct.	Off.	Def.	Tot.	Ast.	St.	Blk.	TO	Pts.	RPG	APG	PPG
98-99—Orlando..........	4	82	12	26	.462	8	11	.727	7	13	20	7	1	0	5	33	5.0	1.8	8.3

Three-point field goals: 1998-99, 1-for-5 (.200).
Personal fouls/disqualifications: 1998-99, 9/0.

H

DID YOU KNOW . . .

. . . that Elgin Baylor and Wilt Chamberlain are the only players to average 34 points per game in three different seasons?

HARRINGTON, AL   F   PACERS

PERSONAL: Born February 17, 1980, in Los Angeles. ... 6-9/230. (2,06/104,3). ... Full Name: Albert Harrington.
HIGH SCHOOL: Roselle (N.J.), then St. Patrick's (Elizabeth, N.J.).
COLLEGE: Did not attend college.
TRANSACTIONS/CAREER NOTES: Selected out of high school by Indiana Pacers in first round (25th pick overall) of 1998 NBA Draft.

NBA REGULAR-SEASON RECORD

Season Team	G	Min.	FGM	FGA	Pct.	FTM	FTA	Pct.	Off.	Def.	Tot.	Ast.	St.	Blk.	TO	Pts.	RPG	APG	PPG
98-99—Indiana	21	160	18	56	.321	9	15	.600	20	19	39	5	4	2	11	45	1.9	0.2	2.1
99-00—Indiana	50	854	121	264	.458	78	111	.703	47	112	159	38	25	9	65	328	3.2	0.8	6.6
00-01—Indiana	78	1892	241	543	.444	103	157	.656	119	262	381	130	63	18	148	586	4.9	1.7	7.5
Totals	149	2906	380	863	.440	190	283	.671	186	393	579	173	92	29	224	959	3.9	1.2	6.4

Three-point field goals: 1998-99, 0-for-5. 1999-00, 8-for-34 (.235). 2000-01, 1-for-7 (.143). Totals, 9-for-46 (.196).
Personal fouls/disqualifications: 1998-99, 26/0. 1999-00, 130/0. 2000-01, 223/2. Totals, 379/2.

NBA PLAYOFF RECORD

Season Team	G	Min.	FGM	FGA	Pct.	FTM	FTA	Pct.	Off.	Def.	Tot.	Ast.	St.	Blk.	TO	Pts.	RPG	APG	PPG
00-01—Indiana	3	40	2	13	.154	1	2	.500	3	1	4	3	0	0	1	5	1.3	1.0	1.7

Three-point field goals: 2000-01, 0-for-2.
Personal fouls/disqualifications: 2000-01, 8/0.

HARRINGTON, OTHELLA   F   KNICKS

PERSONAL: Born January 31, 1974, in Jackson, Miss. ... 6-9/235. (2,06/106,6).
HIGH SCHOOL: Murrah (Jackson, Miss.).
COLLEGE: Georgetown.
TRANSACTIONS/CAREER NOTES: Selected by Houston Rockets in second round (30th pick overall) of 1996 NBA Draft. ... Traded by Rockets with G Michael Dickerson, G Brent Price, F/C Antoine Carr and future first-round draft choice to Vancouver Grizzlies as part of three-way deal in which Rockets received draft rights to G Steve Francis and F Tony Massenburg from Grizzlies and Magic received F Michael Smith, G/F Rodrick Rhodes, G Lee Mayberry and F Makhtar Ndiaye from Grizzles (August 27, 1999). ... Traded by Grizzlies to New York Knicks for G Erick Strickland, 2001 first-round draft choice and 2001 second-round draft choice (January 30, 2001).

COLLEGIATE RECORD

Season Team	G	Min.	FGM	FGA	Pct.	FTM	FTA	Pct.	Reb.	Ast.	Pts.	RPG	APG	PPG
92-93—Georgetown	33	1075	205	358	.573	144	193	.746	291	32	554	8.8	1.0	16.8
93-94—Georgetown	31	897	152	276	.551	151	206	.733	248	36	455	8.0	1.2	14.7
94-95—Georgetown	31	767	132	236	.559	115	163	.706	187	25	379	6.0	0.8	12.2
95-96—Georgetown	37	983	161	288	.559	129	174	.741	257	44	451	6.9	1.2	12.2
Totals	132	3722	650	1158	.561	539	736	.732	983	137	1839	7.4	1.0	13.9

NBA REGULAR-SEASON RECORD

Season Team	G	Min.	FGM	FGA	Pct.	FTM	FTA	Pct.	Off.	Def.	Tot.	Ast.	St.	Blk.	TO	Pts.	RPG	APG	PPG
96-97—Houston	57	860	112	204	.549	49	81	.605	75	123	198	18	12	22	57	273	3.5	0.3	4.8
97-98—Houston	58	903	129	266	.485	92	122	.754	73	134	207	24	10	27	47	350	3.6	0.4	6.0
98-99—Houston	41	903	156	304	.513	88	122	.721	72	174	246	15	6	25	61	400	6.0	0.4	9.8
99-00—Vancouver	82	2677	420	830	.506	236	298	.792	196	367	563	97	36	58	217	1076	6.9	1.2	13.1
00-01—Van.-N.Y.	74	1815	247	507	.487	171	224	.763	139	249	388	56	34	45	145	665	5.2	0.8	9.0
Totals	312	7158	1064	2111	.504	636	847	.751	555	1047	1602	210	98	177	527	2764	5.1	0.7	8.9

Three-point field goals: 1996-97, 0-for-3. 1997-98, 0-for-1. 1999-00, 0-for-2. 2000-01, 0-for-3. Totals, 0-for-9 (.000).
Personal fouls/disqualifications: 1996-97, 112/2. 1997-98, 112/1. 1998-99, 103/0. 1999-00, 287/3. 2000-01, 237/4. Totals, 851/10.

NBA PLAYOFF RECORD

Season Team	G	Min.	FGM	FGA	Pct.	FTM	FTA	Pct.	Off.	Def.	Tot.	Ast.	St.	Blk.	TO	Pts.	RPG	APG	PPG
96-97—Houston	7	15	1	2	.500	7	10	.700	1	3	4	0	0	0	2	9	0.6	0.0	1.3
97-98—Houston	3	23	6	12	.500	4	5	.800	3	4	7	0	0	1	0	16	2.3	0.0	5.3
98-99—Houston	4	42	9	14	.643	4	6	.667	5	9	14	1	0	1	3	22	3.5	0.3	5.5
00-01—New York	5	77	7	14	.500	4	5	.800	7	8	15	2	4	2	3	18	3.0	0.4	3.6
Totals	19	157	23	42	.548	19	26	.731	16	24	40	3	4	4	8	65	2.1	0.2	3.4

Three-point field goals: 1997-98, 0-for-1. Totals, 0-for-1 (.000).
Personal fouls/disqualifications: 1996-97, 1/0. 1997-98, 1/0. 1998-99, 2/0. 2000-01, 16/1. Totals, 20/1.

HARRIS, LUCIOUS   G   NETS

PERSONAL: Born December 18, 1970, in Los Angeles. ... 6-5/205. (1,96/93,0). ... Full Name: Lucious H. Harris Jr. ... Name pronounced LOO-shus.
HIGH SCHOOL: Cleveland (Los Angeles).
COLLEGE: Long Beach State.
TRANSACTIONS/CAREER NOTES: Selected by Dallas Mavericks in second round (28th pick overall) of 1993 NBA Draft. ... Signed as free agent by Philadelphia 76ers (July 23, 1996). ... Traded by 76ers with C Michael Cage, F Don MacLean and draft rights to F Keith Van Horn to New Jersey Nets for draft rights to F Tim Thomas, draft rights to G Anthony Parker, G Jim Jackson and C Eric Montross (June 27, 1997).

H

COLLEGIATE RECORD

Season Team	G	Min.	FGM	FGA	Pct.	FTM	FTA	Pct.	Reb.	Ast.	Pts.	RPG	APG	PPG
												AVERAGES		
89-90—Long Beach State	32	945	147	342	.430	118	170	.694	152	52	457	4.8	1.6	14.3
90-91—Long Beach State	28	940	181	457	.396	140	200	.700	131	69	552	4.7	2.5	19.7
91-92—Long Beach State	30	1132	197	418	.471	127	173	.734	129	97	564	4.3	3.2	18.8
92-93—Long Beach State	32	1166	251	478	.525	164	212	.774	169	79	739	5.3	2.5	23.1
Totals	122	4183	776	1695	.458	549	755	.727	581	297	2312	4.8	2.4	19.0

Three-point field goals: 1989-90, 45-for-136 (.331). 1990-91, 50-for-153 (.327). 1991-92, 43-for-117 (.368). 1992-93, 73-for-177 (.412). Totals, 211-for-583 (.362).

NBA REGULAR-SEASON RECORD

Season Team	G	Min.	FGM	FGA	Pct.	FTM	FTA	Pct.	REBOUNDS Off.	Def.	Tot.	Ast.	St.	Blk.	TO	Pts.	AVERAGES RPG	APG	PPG
93-94—Dallas..............	77	1165	162	385	.421	87	119	.731	45	112	157	106	49	10	78	418	2.0	1.4	5.4
94-95—Dallas..............	79	1695	280	610	.459	136	170	.800	85	135	220	132	58	14	77	751	2.8	1.7	9.5
95-96—Dallas..............	61	1016	183	397	.461	68	87	.782	41	81	122	79	35	3	46	481	2.0	1.3	7.9
96-97—Philadelphia	54	813	112	294	.381	33	47	.702	27	44	71	50	41	3	34	293	1.3	0.9	5.4
97-98—New Jersey	50	671	69	177	.390	41	55	.745	21	31	52	42	42	5	21	191	1.0	0.8	3.8
98-99—New Jersey	36	602	73	181	.403	36	48	.750	21	46	67	31	18	7	18	193	1.9	0.9	5.4
99-00—New Jersey	77	1510	198	463	.428	79	99	.798	53	134	187	100	65	6	42	513	2.4	1.3	6.7
00-01—New Jersey	73	2071	265	624	.425	107	139	.770	71	217	288	135	74	16	64	683	3.9	1.8	9.4
Totals	507	9543	1342	3131	.429	587	764	.768	364	800	1164	675	382	64	380	3523	2.3	1.3	6.9

Three-point field goals: 1993-94, 7-for-33 (.212). 1994-95, 55-for-142 (.387). 1995-96, 47-for-125 (.376). 1996-97, 36-for-99 (.364). 1997-98, 12-for-39 (.308). 1998-99, 11-for-50 (.220). 1999-00, 38-for-115 (.330). 2000-01, 46-for-132 (.348). Totals, 252-for-735 (.343).

Personal fouls/disqualifications: 1993-94, 117/0. 1994-95, 105/0. 1995-96, 56/0. 1996-97, 49/0. 1997-98, 77/0. 1998-99, 52/1. 1999-00, 98/0. 2000-01, 127/1. Totals, 677/2.

NBA PLAYOFF RECORD

Season Team	G	Min.	FGM	FGA	Pct.	FTM	FTA	Pct.	REBOUNDS Off.	Def.	Tot.	Ast.	St.	Blk.	TO	Pts.	AVERAGES RPG	APG	PPG
97-98—New Jersey	3	52	2	6	.333	5	6	.833	1	7	8	1	2	0	2	9	2.7	0.3	3.0

Three-point field goals: 1997-98, 0-for-2.
Personal fouls/disqualifications: 1997-98, 11/0.

HART, JASON   G   BUCKS

PERSONAL: Born April 29, 1978, in Los Angeles. ... 6-3/185. (1,91/83,9). ... Full Name: Jason Keema Hart.
HIGH SCHOOL: Inglewood (Calif.).
COLLEGE: Syracuse.
TRANSACTIONS/CAREER NOTES: Selected by Milwaukee Bucks in second round (49th pick overall) of 2000 NBA Draft.

COLLEGIATE RECORD

Season Team	G	Min.	FGM	FGA	Pct.	FTM	FTA	Pct.	Reb.	Ast.	Pts.	RPG	APG	PPG
												AVERAGES		
96-97—Syracuse	32	1142	113	298	.379	58	84	.690	113	184	307	3.5	5.8	9.6
97-98—Syracuse	35	1198	120	328	.366	91	133	.684	126	174	356	3.6	5.0	10.2
98-99—Syracuse	33	1068	167	407	.410	71	96	.740	98	143	458	3.0	4.3	13.9
99-00—Syracuse	32	1083	125	304	.411	94	128	.734	96	208	382	3.0	6.5	11.9
Totals	132	4491	525	1337	.393	314	441	.712	433	709	1503	3.3	5.4	11.4

Three-point field goals: 1996-97, 23-for-70 (.329). 1997-98, 25-for-96 (.260). 1998-99, 53-for-145 (.366). Totals, 101-for-311 (.325).

NBA REGULAR-SEASON RECORD

Season Team	G	Min.	FGM	FGA	Pct.	FTM	FTA	Pct.	REBOUNDS Off.	Def.	Tot.	Ast.	St.	Blk.	TO	Pts.	AVERAGES RPG	APG	PPG
00-01—Milwaukee	1	10	1	1	1.000	0	0	...	0	0	0	1	0	0	2	2	0.0	1.0	2.0

HARVEY, ANTONIO   F

PERSONAL: Born July 6, 1970, in Pascagoula, Miss. ... 6-11/250. (2,11/113,4).
HIGH SCHOOL: Pascagoula (Miss.).
JUNIOR COLLEGE: Connors State College (Okla.).
COLLEGE: Southern Illinois, then Georgia, then Pfeiffer (N.C.).
TRANSACTIONS/CAREER NOTES: Not drafted by an NBA franchise. ... Played in United States Basketball League with Atlanta Eagles (1993) ... Signed as free agent by Los Angeles Lakers (July 15, 1993) ... Selected by Vancouver Grizzlies from Lakers in NBA Expansion Draft (June 24, 1995). ... Waived by Grizzlies (December 28, 1995). ... Signed as free agent by Los Angeles Clippers for remainder of season (January 3, 1996). ... Signed as free agent by Seattle SuperSonics (November 15, 1996). ... Waived by SuperSonics (January 5, 1997). ... Played in Italy (1996-97). ... Played in Greece (1997-98 and 1998-99). ... Played in Spain (1998-99). ... Signed as free agent by Portland Trail Blazers (October 5, 1999).

COLLEGIATE RECORD

NOTES: Led NCAA Division II with 5.3 blocked shots per game (1993).

Season Team	G	Min.	FGM	FGA	Pct.	FTM	FTA	Pct.	Reb.	Ast.	Pts.	RPG	APG	PPG
												AVERAGES		
88-89—Southern Illinois............	34	718	102	220	.464	31	64	.484	178	21	235	5.2	0.6	6.9
89-90—Connors State College....								Did not play.						
90-91—Georgia	29	570	87	191	.455	36	71	.507	125	21	210	4.3	0.7	7.2
91-92—Pfeiffer	29	...	163	306	.533	70	101	.693	234	21	398	8.1	0.7	13.7
92-93—Pfeiffer	29	...	218	415	.525	89	155	.574	294	36	530	10.1	1.2	18.3
4-Year-College Totals	121	570		1132	.504	226	391	.578	831	99	1373	6.9	0.8	11.3

Three-point field goals: 1990-91, 0-for-4. 1991-92, 4-for-8 (.500). 1992-93, 5-for-12 (.417). Totals, 9-for-24 (.375).

H

NBA REGULAR-SEASON RECORD

Season Team	G	Min.	FGM	FGA	Pct.	FTM	FTA	Pct.	REBOUNDS Off.	Def.	Tot.	Ast.	St.	Blk.	TO	Pts.	AVERAGES RPG	APG	PPG
93-94—L.A. Lakers	27	247	29	79	.367	12	26	.462	26	33	59	5	8	19	17	70	2.2	0.2	2.6
94-95—L.A. Lakers	59	572	77	176	.438	24	45	.533	39	63	102	23	15	41	25	179	1.7	0.4	3.0
95-96—Van.-L.A.C.	55	821	83	224	.371	38	83	.458	69	131	200	15	27	47	44	204	3.6	0.3	3.7
96-97—Seattle	6	26	5	11	.455	5	6	.833	2	8	10	1	0	4	1	15	1.7	0.2	2.5
99-00—Portland	19	137	17	30	.567	7	12	.583	8	25	33	5	1	6	12	41	1.7	0.3	2.2
00-01—Portland	12	72	13	28	.464	5	6	.833	5	9	14	4	1	6	3	31	1.2	0.3	2.6
Totals	178	1875	224	548	.409	91	178	.511	149	269	418	53	52	123	102	540	2.3	0.3	3.0

Three-point field goals: 1994-95, 1-for-1. 1995-96, 0-for-2. Totals, 1-for-3 (.333).
Personal fouls/disqualifications: 1993-94, 39/0. 1994-95, 87/0. 1995-96, 76/0. 1996-97, 8/0. 1999-00, 20/0. 2000-01, 10/0. Totals, 240/0.

NBA PLAYOFF RECORD

Season Team	G	Min.	FGM	FGA	Pct.	FTM	FTA	Pct.	REBOUNDS Off.	Def.	Tot.	Ast.	St.	Blk.	TO	Pts.	AVERAGES RPG	APG	PPG
94-95—L.A. Lakers	3	4	0	0	...	0	0	...	0	1	1	0	0	0	0	0	0.3	0.0	0.0
00-01—Portland	2	14	0	1	.000	0	0	...	1	5	6	0	0	0	1	0	3.0	0.0	0.0
Totals	5	18	0	1	.000	0	0	...	1	6	7	0	0	0	1	0	1.4	0.0	0.0

Personal fouls/disqualifications: 2000-01, 4/0. Totals, 4/0.

ITALIAN LEAGUE RECORD

Season Team	G	Min.	FGM	FGA	Pct.	FTM	FTA	Pct.	Reb.	Ast.	Pts.	AVERAGES RPG	APG	PPG
96-97—Montecatini	5	163	20	39	.513	1	5	.200	47	4	41	9.4	0.8	8.2

Three-point field goals: 1996-97, 0-for-2.

GREEK LEAGUE RECORD

Season Team	G	Min.	FGM	FGA	Pct.	FTM	FTA	Pct.	Reb.	Ast.	Pts.	AVERAGES RPG	APG	PPG
97-98—Panionios	19	645	123	252	.488	24	47	.511	179	29	270	9.4	1.5	14.2
98-99—Irakleio	21	724	119	237	.502	32	64	.500	185	22	270	8.8	1.0	12.9
Totals	40	1369	242	489	.495	56	111	.505	411	51	540	9.1	1.3	13.5

Three-point field goals: 1997-98, 0-for-11.

SPANISH LEAGUE RECORD

Season Team	G	Min.	FGM	FGA	Pct.	FTM	FTA	Pct.	Reb.	Ast.	Pts.	AVERAGES RPG	APG	PPG
98-99—Coviran-C.Alhambra	4	129	19	40	.475	5	10	.500	37	2	44	9.3	0.5	11.0

Three-point field goals: 1998-99, 1-for-2 (.500).

HARVEY, DONNELL   F   MAVERICKS

PERSONAL: Born August 26, 1980, in Shellman, Ga. ... 6-8/216. (2,03/98,0). ... Full Name: Donnell Eugene Harvey.
HIGH SCHOOL: Randolph Clay (Cuthbert, Ga.).
COLLEGE: Florida.
TRANSACTIONS/CAREER NOTES: Selected after freshman season by New York Knicks in first round (22nd pick overall) of 2000 NBA Draft. ... Draft rights traded by Knicks with F John Wallace to Dallas Mavericks for G Erick Strickland and draft rights to F Pete Mickeal (June 28, 2000).

COLLEGIATE RECORD

Season Team	G	Min.	FGM	FGA	Pct.	FTM	FTA	Pct.	Reb.	Ast.	Pts.	AVERAGES RPG	APG	PPG
99-00—Florida	37	746	144	284	.507	86	141	.610	258	37	374	7.0	1.0	10.1

NBA REGULAR-SEASON RECORD

Season Team	G	Min.	FGM	FGA	Pct.	FTM	FTA	Pct.	REBOUNDS Off.	Def.	Tot.	Ast.	St.	Blk.	TO	Pts.	AVERAGES RPG	APG	PPG
00-01—Dallas..............	18	65	8	14	.571	6	16	.375	6	14	20	2	3	1	7	22	1.1	0.1	1.2

Personal fouls/disqualifications: 2000-01, 15/0.

HAWKINS, HERSEY   G

PERSONAL: Born September 29, 1966, in Chicago. ... 6-3/200. (1,91/90,7). ... Full Name: Hersey R. Hawkins Jr. ... Name pronounced Her-see.
HIGH SCHOOL: Westinghouse Vocational (Chicago).
COLLEGE: Bradley.
TRANSACTIONS/CAREER NOTES: Selected by Los Angeles Clippers in first round (sixth pick overall) of 1988 NBA Draft. ... Draft rights traded by Clippers with 1989 first-round draft choice to Philadelphia 76ers for draft rights to F Charles Smith (June 28, 1988). ... Traded by 76ers to Charlotte Hornets for G Dana Barros, F Sidney Green, draft rights to G Greg Graham and option to switch 1994 first-round draft choices (September 3, 1993). ... Traded by Hornets with G/F David Wingate to Seattle SuperSonics for G Kendall Gill (June 27, 1995). ... Traded by SuperSonics with G James Cotton to Chicago Bulls for G Brent Barry (August 12, 1999). ... Waived by Bulls (September 19, 2000). ... Signed as free agent by Hornets (September 21, 2000).
MISCELLANEOUS: Member of bronze-medal-winning U.S. Olympic team (1988).

COLLEGIATE RECORD

NOTES: THE SPORTING NEWS College Player of the Year (1988). ... THE SPORTING NEWS All-America first team (1988). ... Led NCAA Division I with 36.3 points per game (1988).

Season Team	G	Min.	FGM	FGA	Pct.	FTM	FTA	Pct.	Reb.	Ast.	Pts.	AVERAGES RPG	APG	PPG
84-85—Bradley	30	1121	179	308	.581	81	105	.771	182	82	439	6.1	2.7	14.6
85-86—Bradley	35	1291	250	461	.542	156	203	.768	200	104	656	5.7	3.0	18.7
86-87—Bradley	29	1102	294	552	.533	169	213	.793	195	103	788	6.7	3.6	27.2
87-88—Bradley	31	1202	377	720	.524	284	335	.848	241	111	1125	7.8	3.6	36.3
Totals	125	4716	1100	2041	.539	690	856	.806	818	400	3008	6.5	3.2	24.1

Three-point field goals: 1986-87, 31-for-108 (.287). 1987-88, 87-for-221 (.394). Totals, 118-for-329 (.359).

NBA REGULAR-SEASON RECORD

HONORS: NBA Sportsmanship Award (1999). ... NBA All-Rookie first team (1989).

Season Team	G	Min.	FGM	FGA	Pct.	FTM	FTA	Pct.	REBOUNDS Off.	Def.	Tot.	Ast.	St.	Blk.	TO	Pts.	AVERAGES RPG	APG	PPG
88-89—Philadelphia	79	2577	442	971	.455	241	290	.831	51	174	225	239	120	37	158	1196	2.8	3.0	15.1
89-90—Philadelphia	82	2856	522	1136	.460	387	436	.888	85	219	304	261	130	28	185	1515	3.7	3.2	18.5
90-91—Philadelphia	80	3110	590	1251	.472	479	550	.871	48	262	310	299	178	39	213	1767	3.9	3.7	22.1
91-92—Philadelphia	81	3013	521	1127	.462	403	461	.874	53	218	271	248	157	43	189	1536	3.3	3.1	19.0
92-93—Philadelphia	81	2977	551	1172	.470	419	487	.860	91	255	346	317	137	30	180	1643	4.3	3.9	20.3
93-94—Charlotte	82	2648	395	859	.460	312	362	.862	89	288	377	216	135	22	158	1180	4.6	2.6	14.4
94-95—Charlotte	82	2731	390	809	.482	261	301	.867	60	254	314	262	122	18	150	1172	3.8	3.2	14.3
95-96—Seattle	82	2823	443	936	.473	249	285	.874	86	211	297	218	149	14	164	1281	3.6	2.7	15.6
96-97—Seattle	82	2755	369	795	.464	258	295	.875	92	228	320	250	159	12	130	1139	3.9	3.0	13.9
97-98—Seattle	82	2597	280	636	.440	177	204	.868	71	263	334	221	148	17	102	862	4.1	2.7	10.5
98-99—Seattle	50	1644	171	408	.419	119	132	.902	51	150	201	123	80	18	80	516	4.0	2.5	10.3
99-00—Chicago	61	1622	159	375	.424	107	119	.899	31	144	175	134	74	15	100	480	2.9	2.2	7.9
00-01—Charlotte	59	681	56	137	.409	54	63	.857	17	63	80	72	33	9	19	183	1.4	1.2	3.1
Totals	983	32034	4889	10612	.461	3466	3985	.870	825	2729	3554	2860	1622	302	1828	14470	3.6	2.9	14.7

Three-point field goals: 1988-89, 71-for-166 (.428). 1989-90, 84-for-200 (.420). 1990-91, 108-for-270 (.400). 1991-92, 91-for-229 (.397). 1992-93, 122-for-307 (.397). 1993-94, 78-for-235 (.332). 1994-95, 131-for-298 (.440). 1995-96, 146-for-380 (.384). 1996-97, 143-for-355 (.403). 1997-98, 125-for-301 (.415). 1998-99, 55-for-180 (.306). 1999-00, 55-for-141 (.390). 2000-01, 17-for-46 (.370). Totals, 1226-for-3108 (.394).

Personal fouls/disqualifications: 1988-89, 184/0. 1989-90, 217/2. 1990-91, 182/0. 1991-92, 174/0. 1992-93, 189/0. 1993-94, 167/2. 1994-95, 178/1. 1995-96, 172/0. 1996-97, 146/1. 1997-98, 153/0. 1998-99, 90/1. 1999-00, 146/1. 2000-01, 45/0. Totals, 2043/8.

NBA PLAYOFF RECORD

Season Team	G	Min.	FGM	FGA	Pct.	FTM	FTA	Pct.	REBOUNDS Off.	Def.	Tot.	Ast.	St.	Blk.	TO	Pts.	AVERAGES RPG	APG	PPG
88-89—Philadelphia	3	72	3	24	.125	2	2	1.000	1	4	5	4	3	1	3	8	1.7	1.3	2.7
89-90—Philadelphia	10	415	81	163	.497	59	63	.937	8	23	31	36	12	7	31	235	3.1	3.6	23.5
90-91—Philadelphia	8	329	47	101	.465	59	63	.937	8	38	46	27	20	10	16	167	5.8	3.4	20.9
94-95—Charlotte	4	130	13	32	.406	15	17	.882	5	16	21	8	6	2	9	45	5.3	2.0	11.3
95-96—Seattle	21	713	76	168	.452	85	95	.895	17	46	63	46	27	4	33	259	3.0	2.2	12.3
96-97—Seattle	12	483	62	132	.470	32	35	.914	17	37	54	34	30	4	21	183	4.5	2.8	15.3
97-98—Seattle	10	337	41	88	.466	35	40	.875	17	40	57	36	18	1	9	134	5.7	3.6	13.4
00-01—Charlotte	6	50	3	8	.375	5	7	.714	1	8	9	4	3	0	0	12	1.5	0.7	2.0
Totals	74	2529	326	716	.455	292	322	.907	74	212	286	195	119	29	122	1043	3.9	2.6	14.1

Three-point field goals: 1988-89, 0-for-5. 1989-90, 14-for-36 (.389). 1990-91, 14-for-26 (.538). 1994-95, 4-for-13 (.308). 1995-96, 22-for-64 (.344). 1996-97, 27-for-59 (.458). 1997-98, 17-for-43 (.395). 2000-01, 1-for-4 (.250). Totals, 99-for-250 (.396).

Personal fouls/disqualifications: 1988-89, 6/0. 1989-90, 25/0. 1990-91, 29/1. 1994-95, 13/1. 1995-96, 55/0. 1996-97, 32/0. 1997-98, 24/0. 2000-01, 4/0. Totals, 188/2.

NBA ALL-STAR GAME RECORD

Season Team	Min.	FGM	FGA	Pct.	FTM	FTA	Pct.	REBOUNDS Off.	Def.	Tot.	Ast.	PF	Dq.	St.	Blk.	TO	Pts.
1991 —Philadelphia	14	3	5	.600	0	0	...	0	0	0	1	1	0	0	0	1	6

Three-point field goals: 1991, 0-for-1.

HAWKINS, MICHAEL   G

PERSONAL: Born October 28, 1972, in Canton, Ohio. ... 6-0/180. (1,83/81,6). ... Full Name: Steve Michael Hawkins.
HIGH SCHOOL: McKinley (Canton, Ohio).
COLLEGE: Xavier (Ohio).
TRANSACTIONS/CAREER NOTES: Not drafted by an NBA franchise. ... Signed as free agent by Portland Trail Blazers (October 10, 1995). ... Waived by Trail Blazers (November 2, 1995). ... Played in Continental Basketball Association with Rockford Lightning and Sioux Falls Skyforce (1995-96, 1996-97, 1998-99 and 2000-01). ... Signed as free agent by Philadelphia 76ers (October 1, 1996). ... Waived by 76ers (October 17, 1996). ... Signed by Boston Celtics to first of two consecutive 10-day contracts (February 8, 1997). ... Re-signed by Celtics for remainder of season (March 7, 1997). ... Played in Greece (1997-98). ... Signed as free agent by Portland Trail Blazers (January 21, 1999). ... Waived by Trail Blazers (February 18, 1999). ... Signed as free agent by Sacramento Kings (February 22, 1999). ... Signed as free agent by Detroit Pistons (October 4, 1999). ... Waived by Pistons (October 25, 1999). ... Signed as free agent by Charlotte Hornets (November 9, 1999). ... Signed as free agent by Atlanta Hawks (October 3, 2000). ... Waived by Hawks (October 8, 2000). ... Signed as free agent by Cleveland Cavaliers (October 16, 2000). ... Waived by Cavaliers (October 26, 2000). ... Signed as free agent by Cavaliers (November 22, 2000). ... Waived by Cavaliers (January 2, 2001). ... Played in Spain (2001). ... Signed to play for Slask Wroclaw in Poland for 2001-02 season.
MISCELLANEOUS: Member of bronze-medal-winning U.S. World Championship team (1998).

COLLEGIATE RECORD

Season Team	G	Min.	FGM	FGA	Pct.	FTM	FTA	Pct.	Reb.	Ast.	Pts.	AVERAGES RPG	APG	PPG
91-92—Xavier	27	743	76	185	.411	35	54	.648	75	118	209	2.8	4.4	7.7
92-93—Xavier	28	771	80	174	.460	32	41	.780	71	104	228	2.5	3.7	8.1
93-94—Xavier	29	570	68	182	.374	23	36	.639	61	64	196	2.1	2.2	6.8
94-95—Xavier	28	922	117	274	.427	103	130	.792	93	162	396	3.3	5.8	14.1
Totals	112	3006	341	815	.418	193	261	.739	300	448	1029	2.7	4.0	9.2

Three-point field goals: 1991-92, 22-for-63 (.349). 1992-93, 36-for-88 (.409). 1993-94, 37-for-100 (.370). 1994-95, 59-for-152 (.388). Totals, 154-for-403 (.382).

H

CBA REGULAR-SEASON RECORD

NOTES: CBA All-League second team (1997). ... CBA All-Defensive team (1997). ... Led CBA with 2.34 steals per game (1997).

Season Team	G	Min.	FGM	FGA	Pct.	FTM	FTA	Pct.	Reb.	Ast.	Pts.	AVERAGES RPG	APG	PPG
95-96—Rockford	53	1000	92	248	.371	48	69	.696	86	201	251	1.6	3.8	4.7
96-97—Rockford	35	1417	198	412	.481	77	98	.786	137	325	560	3.9	9.3	16.0
98-99—Rockford	23	836	101	217	.465	35	45	.778	78	158	261	3.4	6.9	11.3
00-01—Sioux Falls	13	459	59	135	.437	31	42	.738	49	97	167	3.8	7.5	12.8
Totals	124	3712	450	1012	.445	191	254	.752	350	781	1239	2.9	6.3	10.0

Three-point field goals: 1995-96, 19-for-58 (.328). 1996-97, 87-for-186 (.468). 1998-99, 24-for-68 (.353). 2000-01, 18-for-46 (.391). Totals, 148-for-358 (.413).

NBA REGULAR-SEASON RECORD

Season Team	G	Min.	FGM	FGA	Pct.	FTM	FTA	Pct.	REBOUNDS Off.	Def.	Tot.	Ast.	St.	Blk.	TO	Pts.	AVERAGES RPG	APG	PPG
96-97—Boston	29	326	29	68	.426	12	15	.800	9	22	31	64	16	1	28	80	1.1	2.2	2.8
98-99—Sacramento	24	203	14	40	.350	3	3	1.000	10	15	25	27	3	1	13	36	1.0	1.1	1.5
99-00—Charlotte	12	36	3	13	.231	1	2	.500	0	7	7	13	0	0	3	8	0.6	1.1	0.7
00-01—Cleveland	10	76	3	9	.333	0	0	...	2	3	5	13	2	0	6	8	0.5	1.3	0.8
Totals	75	641	49	130	.377	16	20	.800	21	47	68	117	21	2	50	132	0.9	1.6	1.8

Three-point field goals: 1996-97, 10-for-31 (.323). 1998-99, 5-for-19 (.263). 1999-00, 1-for-5 (.200). 2000-01, 2-for-4 (.500). Totals, 18-for-59 (.305).
Personal fouls/disqualifications: 1996-97, 40/0. 1998-99, 14/0. 1999-00, 2/0. 2000-01, 13/0. Totals, 69/0.

NBA PLAYOFF RECORD

Season Team	G	Min.	FGM	FGA	Pct.	FTM	FTA	Pct.	REBOUNDS Off.	Def.	Tot.	Ast.	St.	Blk.	TO	Pts.	AVERAGES RPG	APG	PPG
98-99—Sacramento	2	10	0	1	.000	2	2	1.000	0	0	0	0	0	0	0	2	0.0	0.0	1.0

Three-point field goals: 1998-99, 0-for-1.
Personal fouls/disqualifications: 1998-99, 1/0.

GREEK LEAGUE RECORD

Season Team	G	Min.	FGM	FGA	Pct.	FTM	FTA	Pct.	Reb.	Ast.	Pts.	AVERAGES RPG	APG	PPG
97-98—Olympiakos S.F.P.	24	661	73	172	.424	30	39	.769	63	71	207	2.6	3.0	8.6

Three-point field goals: 1997-98, 31-for-77 (.403).

SPANISH LEAGUE RECORD

Season Team	G	Min.	FGM	FGA	Pct.	FTM	FTA	Pct.	Reb.	Ast.	Pts.	AVERAGES RPG	APG	PPG
0-01—FC Barcelona	15	294	32	76	.421	10	22	.455	16	42	87	1.1	2.8	5.8

Three-point field goals: 2000-01, 13-for-28 (.464).

HENDERSON, ALAN   F   HAWKS

PERSONAL: Born December 2, 1972, in Indianapolis. ... 6-9/235. (2,06/106,6). ... Full Name: Alan Lybrooks Henderson.
HIGH SCHOOL: Brebeuf Prep (Indianapolis).
COLLEGE: Indiana.
TRANSACTIONS/CAREER NOTES: Selected by Atlanta Hawks in first round (16th pick overall) of 1995 NBA Draft.

COLLEGIATE RECORD

Season Team	G	Min.	FGM	FGA	Pct.	FTM	FTA	Pct.	Reb.	Ast.	Pts.	AVERAGES RPG	APG	PPG
91-92—Indiana	33	783	151	297	.508	80	121	.661	238	17	383	7.2	0.5	11.6
92-93—Indiana	30	737	130	267	.487	72	113	.637	243	27	333	8.1	0.9	11.1
93-94—Indiana	30	983	198	373	.531	136	207	.657	308	36	534	10.3	1.2	17.8
94-95—Indiana	31	1093	284	476	.597	159	251	.633	302	54	729	9.7	1.7	23.5
Totals	124	3596	763	1413	.540	447	692	.646	1091	134	1979	8.8	1.1	16.0

Three-point field goals: 1991-92, 1-for-4 (.250). 1992-93, 1-for-6 (.167). 1993-94, 2-for-6 (.333). 1994-95, 2-for-10 (.200). Totals, 6-for-26 (.231).

HONORS: NBA Most Improved Player (1998).

NBA REGULAR-SEASON RECORD

Season Team	G	Min.	FGM	FGA	Pct.	FTM	FTA	Pct.	REBOUNDS Off.	Def.	Tot.	Ast.	St.	Blk.	TO	Pts.	AVERAGES RPG	APG	PPG
95-96—Atlanta	79	1416	192	434	.442	119	200	.595	164	192	356	51	44	43	87	503	4.5	0.6	6.4
96-97—Atlanta	30	501	77	162	.475	45	75	.600	47	69	116	23	21	6	29	199	3.9	0.8	6.6
97-98—Atlanta	69	2000	365	753	.485	253	388	.652	199	243	442	73	42	36	110	986	6.4	1.1	14.3
98-99—Atlanta	38	1142	187	423	.442	100	149	.671	100	150	250	28	33	19	58	474	6.6	0.7	12.5
99-00—Atlanta	82	2775	429	930	.461	224	334	.671	265	306	571	77	81	54	139	1083	7.0	0.9	13.2
00-01—Atlanta	73	1810	298	671	.444	173	271	.638	180	226	406	50	51	29	126	769	5.6	0.7	10.5
Totals	371	9644	1548	3373	.459	914	1417	.645	955	1186	2141	302	272	187	549	4014	5.8	0.8	10.8

Three-point field goals: 1995-96, 0-for-3. 1997-98, 3-for-6 (.500). 1998-99, 0-for-1. 1999-00, 1-for-10 (.100). 2000-01, 0-for-1. Totals, 4-for-21 (.190).
Personal fouls/disqualifications: 1995-96, 217/5. 1996-97, 73/1. 1997-98, 175/1. 1998-99, 96/1. 1999-00, 233/3. 2000-01, 164/2. Totals, 958/13.

NBA PLAYOFF RECORD

Season Team	G	Min.	FGM	FGA	Pct.	FTM	FTA	Pct.	REBOUNDS Off.	Def.	Tot.	Ast.	St.	Blk.	TO	Pts.	AVERAGES RPG	APG	PPG
95-96—Atlanta	10	145	23	40	.575	7	10	.700	17	10	27	7	1	4	9	53	2.7	0.7	5.3
96-97—Atlanta	10	136	19	34	.559	20	26	.769	11	22	33	0	1	3	7	58	3.3	0.0	5.8
97-98—Atlanta	4	126	20	38	.526	11	18	.611	10	12	22	4	3	1	6	51	5.5	1.0	12.8
98-99—Atlanta	1	4	0	0	...	0	0	...	0	0	0	0	0	0	0	0	0.0	0.0	0.0
Totals	25	411	62	112	.554	38	54	.704	38	44	82	11	5	8	22	162	3.3	0.4	6.5

Three-point field goals: 1997-98, 0-for-1. Totals, 0-for-1 (.000).
Personal fouls/disqualifications: 1995-96, 20/0. 1996-97, 26/0. 1997-98, 13/0. 1998-99, 1/0. Totals, 60/0.

H

HENDERSON, CEDRIC　　F　　76ERS

PERSONAL: Born March 11, 1975, in Memphis. ... 6-7/225. (2,01/102,1). ... Full Name: Cedric Earl Henderson.
HIGH SCHOOL: East (Memphis).
COLLEGE: Memphis.
TRANSACTIONS/CAREER NOTES: Selected by Cleveland Cavaliers in second round (45th pick overall) of 1997 NBA Draft. ... Traded by Cavaliers with F Matt Harpring and F/C Robert Traylor to Philadelphia 76ers for F Tyrone Hill and F Jumaine Jones (August 3, 2001).

COLLEGIATE RECORD

Season Team	G	Min.	FGM	FGA	Pct.	FTM	FTA	Pct.	Reb.	Ast.	Pts.	RPG	APG	PPG
93-94—Memphis	28	902	160	344	.465	45	75	.600	142	52	383	5.1	1.9	13.7
94-95—Memphis	34	1061	174	395	.441	67	115	.583	172	48	438	5.1	1.4	12.9
95-96—Memphis	30	877	146	297	.492	57	93	.613	120	38	379	4.0	1.3	12.6
96-97—Memphis	31	1069	184	441	.417	104	151	.689	203	43	497	6.5	1.4	16.0
Totals	123	3909	664	1477	.450	273	434	.629	637	181	1697	5.2	1.5	13.8

Three-point field goals: 1993-94, 18-for-67 (.269). 1994-95, 23-for-77 (.299). 1995-96, 30-for-77 (.390): 1996-97, 25-for-95 (.263). Totals, 96-for-316 (.304).

HONORS: NBA All-Rookie second team (1998).

NBA REGULAR-SEASON RECORD

Season Team	G	Min.	FGM	FGA	Pct.	FTM	FTA	Pct.	REBOUNDS Off.	Def.	Tot.	Ast.	St.	Blk.	TO	Pts.	RPG	APG	PPG
97-98—Cleveland	82	2527	348	725	.480	136	190	.716	71	254	325	168	96	45	165	832	4.0	2.0	10.1
98-99—Cleveland	50	1517	189	453	.417	74	91	.813	45	152	197	113	58	24	97	454	3.9	2.3	9.1
99-00—Cleveland	61	1107	129	326	.396	69	104	.663	34	106	140	55	39	17	68	328	2.3	0.9	5.4
00-01—Cleveland	55	961	102	262	.389	30	46	.652	19	71	90	79	29	23	63	235	1.6	1.4	4.3
Totals	248	6112	768	1766	.435	309	431	.717	169	583	752	415	222	109	393	1849	3.0	1.7	7.5

Three-point field goals: 1997-98, 0-for-4. 1998-99, 2-for-12 (.167). 1999-00, 1-for-15 (.067). 2000-01, 1-for-8 (.125). Totals, 4-for-39 (.103).
Personal fouls/disqualifications: 1997-98, 238/3. 1998-99, 136/2. 1999-00, 99/0. 2000-01, 101/0. Totals, 574/5.

NBA PLAYOFF RECORD

Season Team	G	Min.	FGM	FGA	Pct.	FTM	FTA	Pct.	REBOUNDS Off.	Def.	Tot.	Ast.	St.	Blk.	TO	Pts.	RPG	APG	PPG
97-98—Cleveland	4	157	11	28	.393	8	13	.615	4	13	17	11	6	0	13	30	4.3	2.8	7.5

Three-point field goals: 1997-98, 0-for-1.
Personal fouls/disqualifications: 1997-98, 14/0.

HERREN, CHRIS　　G

PERSONAL: Born September 27, 1975, in Fall River, Mass. ... 6-2/190. (1,88/86,2). ... Full Name: Chris Albert Herren.
HIGH SCHOOL: Durfee (Fall River, Mass.).
COLLEGE: Boston College, then Fresno State.
TRANSACTIONS/CAREER NOTES: Selected by Denver Nuggets in second round (33rd pick overall) of 1999 NBA Draft. ... Traded by Nuggets with G Bryant Stith to Boston Celtics for G Robert Pack and F Calbert Cheaney (October 16, 2000). ... Signed to play for Fortitudo Bologna in Italy for 2001-02 season.

COLLEGIATE RECORD

NOTES: Injured wrist (1994-95); granted extra year of eligibility.

Season Team	G	Min.	FGM	FGA	Pct.	FTM	FTA	Pct.	Reb.	Ast.	Pts.	RPG	APG	PPG
94-95—Boston College	1	21	3	4	.750	8	8	1.000	2	6	14	2.0	6.0	14.0
95-96—Fresno State					Did not play—transfer student.									
96-97—Fresno State	32	971	194	408	.475	104	159	.654	74	146	560	2.3	4.6	17.5
97-98—Fresno State	29	953	162	347	.467	75	133	.564	67	138	453	2.3	4.8	15.6
98-99—Fresno State	25	685	91	223	.408	58	85	.682	41	181	284	1.6	7.2	11.4
Totals	87	2630	450	982	.458	245	385	.636	184	471	1311	2.1	5.4	15.1

Three-point field goals: 1996-97, 68-for-188 (.362). 1997-98, 54-for-149 (.362). 1998-99, 44-for-115 (.383). Totals, 166-for-452 (.367).

NBA REGULAR-SEASON RECORD

Season Team	G	Min.	FGM	FGA	Pct.	FTM	FTA	Pct.	REBOUNDS Off.	Def.	Tot.	Ast.	St.	Blk.	TO	Pts.	RPG	APG	PPG
99-00—Denver	45	597	45	124	.363	27	40	.675	12	40	52	111	15	2	42	141	1.2	2.6	3.1
00-01—Boston	25	408	29	96	.302	9	12	.750	4	17	21	56	14	0	20	83	0.8	2.2	3.3
Totals	70	1005	74	220	.336	36	52	.692	16	57	73	167	29	2	62	224	1.0	2.4	3.2

Three-point field goals: 1999-00, 24-for-67 (.358). 2000-01, 16-for-55 (.291). Totals, 40-for-122 (.328).
Personal fouls/disqualifications: 1999-00, 74/0. 2000-01, 43/0. Totals, 117/0.

HILL, GRANT　　F　　MAGIC

PERSONAL: Born October 5, 1972, in Dallas. ... 6-8/225. (2,03/102,1). ... Full Name: Grant Henry Hill. ... Son of Calvin Hill, running back with three NFL teams (1969-74 and 1976-81) and the Hawaii Hawaiians of the World Football League (1975).
HIGH SCHOOL: South Lakes (Reston, Va.).
COLLEGE: Duke.
TRANSACTIONS/CAREER NOTES: Selected by Detroit Pistons in first round (third pick overall) of 1994 NBA Draft. ... Traded by Pistons to Orlando Magic for G Chucky Atkins and F Ben Wallace (August 3, 2000).
MISCELLANEOUS: Member of gold-medal-winning U.S. Olympic team (1996).

H

NOTES: The Sporting News All-America first team (1994). ... Member of NCAA Division I championship team (1991, 1992).

Season Team	G	Min.	FGM	FGA	Pct.	FTM	FTA	Pct.	Reb.	Ast.	Pts.	AVERAGES		
												RPG	APG	PPG
90-91—Duke	36	887	160	310	.516	81	133	.609	185	79	402	5.1	2.2	11.2
91-92—Duke	33	1000	182	298	.611	99	135	.733	187	134	463	5.7	4.1	14.0
92-93—Duke	26	822	185	320	.578	94	126	.746	166	72	468	6.4	2.8	18.0
93-94—Duke	34	1213	218	472	.462	116	165	.703	233	176	591	6.9	5.2	17.4
Totals	129	3922	745	1400	.532	390	559	.698	771	461	1924	6.0	3.6	14.9

Three-point field goals: 1990-91, 1-for-2 (.500). 1991-92, 0-for-14. 1992-93, 4-for-14 (.286). 1993-94, 39-for-100 (.390). Totals, 44-for-117 (.376).

NBA REGULAR-SEASON RECORD

HONORS: NBA Co-Rookie of the Year (1995). ... IBM Award, for all-around contributions to team's success (1997). ... All-NBA first team (1997). ... All-NBA second team (1996, 1998, 1999, 2000). ... NBA All-Rookie first team (1995).

Season Team	G	Min.	FGM	FGA	Pct.	FTM	FTA	Pct.	REBOUNDS			Ast.	St.	Blk.	TO	Pts.	AVERAGES		
									Off.	Def.	Tot.						RPG	APG	PPG
94-95—Detroit	70	2678	508	1064	.477	374	511	.732	125	320	445	353	124	62	202	1394	6.4	5.0	19.9
95-96—Detroit	80	3260	564	1221	.462	485	646	.751	127	656	783	548	100	48	263	1618	9.8	6.9	20.2
96-97—Detroit	80	3147	625	1259	.496	450	633	.711	123	598	721	583	144	48	259	1710	9.0	7.3	21.4
97-98—Detroit	81	3294	615	1361	.452	479	647	.740	93	530	623	551	143	53	285	1712	7.7	6.8	21.1
98-99—Detroit	50	1852	384	802	.479	285	379	.752	65	290	355	300	80	27	184	1053	7.1	6.0	21.1
99-00—Detroit	74	2776	696	1422	.489	480	604	.795	97	393	490	385	103	43	240	1906	6.6	5.2	25.8
00-01—Orlando	4	133	19	43	.442	16	26	.615	8	17	25	25	5	2	11	55	6.3	6.3	13.8
Totals	439	17140	3411	7172	.476	2569	3446	.746	638	2804	3442	2745	699	283	1444	9448	7.8	6.3	21.5

Three-point field goals: 1994-95, 4-for-27 (.148). 1995-96, 5-for-26 (.192). 1996-97, 10-for-33 (.303). 1997-98, 3-for-21 (.143). 1998-99, 0-for-14. 1999-00, 34-for-98 (.347). 2000-01, 1-for-1. Totals, 57-for-220 (.259).

Personal fouls/disqualifications: 1994-95, 203/1. 1995-96, 242/1. 1996-97, 186/0. 1997-98, 196/1. 1998-99, 114/0. 1999-00, 190/0. 2000-01, 9/0. Totals, 1140/3.

NBA PLAYOFF RECORD

Season Team	G	Min.	FGM	FGA	Pct.	FTM	FTA	Pct.	REBOUNDS			Ast.	St.	Blk.	TO	Pts.	AVERAGES		
									Off.	Def.	Tot.						RPG	APG	PPG
95-96—Detroit	3	115	22	39	.564	12	14	.857	4	18	22	11	3	0	8	57	7.3	3.7	19.0
96-97—Detroit	5	203	45	103	.437	28	39	.718	13	21	34	27	4	5	19	118	6.8	5.4	23.6
98-99—Detroit	5	176	42	92	.457	13	16	.813	7	29	36	37	10	2	12	97	7.2	7.4	19.4
99-00—Detroit	2	55	6	16	.375	9	10	.900	0	11	11	9	1	0	10	22	5.5	4.5	11.0
Totals	15	549	115	250	.460	62	79	.785	24	79	103	84	18	7	49	294	6.9	5.6	19.6

Three-point field goals: 1995-96, 1-for-2 (.500). 1998-99, 0-for-1. 1999-00, 1-for-2 (.500). Totals, 2-for-5 (.400).

Personal fouls/disqualifications: 1995-96, 13/0. 1996-97, 14/0. 1998-99, 12/0. 1999-00, 7/0. Totals, 46/0.

NBA ALL-STAR GAME RECORD

Season Team	Min.	FGM	FGA	Pct.	FTM	FTA	Pct.	REBOUNDS			Ast.	PF	Dq.	St.	Blk.	TO	Pts.
								Off.	Def.	Tot.							
1995 —Detroit	20	5	8	.625	0	4	.000	0	0	0	3	2	0	2	0	1	10
1996 —Detroit	26	6	10	.600	2	2	1.000	1	2	3	2	1	0	1	0	2	14
1997 —Detroit	22	4	7	.571	3	4	.750	2	1	3	2	2	0	1	1	3	11
1998 —Detroit	28	7	11	.636	0	0	...	0	3	3	5	1	0	1	0	0	15
2000 —Detroit	19	3	7	.429	1	1	1.000	0	3	3	5	0	0	1	0	3	7
2001 —Orlando	Selected, did not play—injured.																
Totals	115	25	43	.581	6	11	.545	3	9	12	17	6	0	6	1	9	57

Three-point field goals: 1998, 1-for-1. 1900, 0-for-1. Totals, 1-for-2 (.500).

HILL, TYRONE   F   CAVALIERS

PERSONAL: Born March 19, 1968, in Cincinnati. ... 6-9/250. (2,06/113,4).

HIGH SCHOOL: Withrow (Cincinnati).

COLLEGE: Xavier.

TRANSACTIONS/CAREER NOTES: Selected by Golden State Warriors in first round (11th pick overall) of 1990 NBA Draft. ... Traded by Warriors to Cleveland Cavaliers for 1994 first-round draft choice (July 15, 1993). ... Traded by Cavaliers with G Terrell Brandon to Milwaukee Bucks in three-way deal in which Bucks sent G Sherman Douglas to Cavaliers and sent F Vin Baker to Seattle SuperSonics for F Shawn Kemp (September 25, 1997); Bucks also received 1998 conditional first-round draft choice from Cavaliers. ... Traded by Bucks with F/G Jerald Honeycutt to Philadelphia 76ers for F Tim Thomas and C/F Scott Williams (March 11, 1999). ... Traded by 76ers with F Jumaine Jones to Cavaliers for F Matt Harpring, F Cedric Henderson and F/C Robert Traylor (August 3, 2001).

COLLEGIATE RECORD

Season Team	G	Min.	FGM	FGA	Pct.	FTM	FTA	Pct.	Reb.	Ast.	Pts.	AVERAGES		
												RPG	APG	PPG
86-87—Xavier	31	881	95	172	.552	84	125	.672	261	7	274	8.4	0.2	8.8
87-88—Xavier	30	858	172	309	.557	114	153	.745	314	21	458	10.5	0.7	15.3
88-89—Xavier	33	1094	235	388	.606	155	221	.701	403	45	625	12.2	1.4	18.9
89-90—Xavier	32	1063	250	430	.581	146	222	.658	402	49	646	12.6	1.5	20.2
Totals	126	3896	752	1299	.579	499	721	.692	1380	122	2003	11.0	1.0	15.9

Three-point field goals: 1989-90, 0-for-2.

NBA REGULAR-SEASON RECORD

NOTES: Led NBA with 315 personal fouls (1992).

H

Season Team	G	Min.	FGM	FGA	Pct.	FTM	FTA	Pct.	Off.	Def.	Tot.	Ast.	St.	Blk.	TO	Pts.	RPG	APG	PPG
90-91—Golden State ...	74	1192	147	299	.492	96	152	.632	157	226	383	19	33	30	72	390	5.2	0.3	5.3
91-92—Golden State ..	82	1886	254	487	.522	163	235	.694	182	411	593	47	73	43	106	671	7.2	0.6	8.2
92-93—Golden State ..	74	2070	251	494	.508	138	221	.624	255	499	754	68	41	40	92	640	10.2	0.9	8.6
93-94—Cleveland	57	1447	216	398	.543	171	256	.668	184	315	499	46	53	35	78	603	8.8	0.8	10.6
94-95—Cleveland	70	2397	350	694	.504	263	397	.662	269	496	765	55	55	41	151	963	10.9	0.8	13.8
95-96—Cleveland	44	929	130	254	.512	81	135	.600	94	150	244	33	31	20	64	341	5.5	0.8	7.8
96-97—Cleveland	74	2582	357	595	.600	241	381	.633	259	477	736	92	63	30	147	955	9.9	1.2	12.9
97-98—Milwaukee	57	2064	208	418	.498	155	255	.608	212	396	608	88	67	30	106	571	10.7	1.5	10.0
98-99—Mil.-Phil.	38	1104	122	268	.455	81	150	.540	115	172	287	35	34	16	59	325	7.6	0.9	8.6
99-00—Philadelphia ..	68	2155	318	656	.485	179	259	.691	220	405	625	52	64	27	124	815	9.2	0.8	12.0
00-01—Philadelphia ..	76	2363	278	587	.474	172	273	.630	239	448	687	48	37	27	127	728	9.0	0.6	9.6
Totals	714	20189	2631	5150	.511	1740	2714	.641	2186	3995	6181	583	551	339	1126	7002	8.7	0.8	9.8

Three-point field goals: 1991-92, 0-for-1. 1992-93, 0-for-4. 1993-94, 0-for-2. 1994-95, 0-for-1. 1996-97, 0-for-1. 1997-98, 0-for-1. 1999-00, 0-for-1. 2000-01, 0-for-1. Totals, 0-for-12 (.000).
Personal fouls/disqualifications: 1990-91, 264/8. 1991-92, 315/7. 1992-93, 320/8. 1993-94, 193/5. 1994-95, 245/4. 1995-96, 144/3. 1996-97, 268/6. 1997-98, 230/8. 1998-99, 145/2. 1999-00, 243/3. 2000-01, 242/2. Totals, 2609/56.

NBA PLAYOFF RECORD

Season Team	G	Min.	FGM	FGA	Pct.	FTM	FTA	Pct.	Off.	Def.	Tot.	Ast.	St.	Blk.	TO	Pts.	RPG	APG	PPG
90-91—Golden State ...	9	80	9	14	.643	4	6	.667	7	16	23	2	3	4	2	22	2.6	0.2	2.4
91-92—Golden State ...	4	47	3	7	.429	0	2	.000	3	5	8	1	2	0	3	6	2.0	0.3	1.5
93-94—Cleveland	3	123	11	27	.407	20	37	.541	14	17	31	4	1	1	8	42	10.3	1.3	14.0
94-95—Cleveland	4	139	9	29	.310	16	25	.640	8	15	23	3	7	1	10	34	5.8	0.8	8.5
95-96—Cleveland	3	53	9	12	.750	7	9	.778	7	8	15	0	0	0	3	25	5.0	0.0	8.3
98-99—Philadelphia ..	8	196	19	39	.487	7	19	.368	19	40	59	0	3	2	6	45	7.4	0.0	5.6
99-00—Philadelphia	10	352	46	100	.460	31	44	.705	36	61	97	9	9	1	12	123	9.7	0.9	12.3
00-01—Philadelphia	23	742	65	159	.409	36	53	.679	54	114	168	10	13	12	26	166	7.3	0.4	7.2
Totals	64	1732	171	387	.442	121	195	.621	148	276	424	29	38	21	70	463	6.6	0.5	7.2

Three-point field goals: 1990-91, 0-for-1. 1994-95, 0-for-1. 1999-00, 0-for-1. 2000-01, 0-for-1. Totals, 0-for-4 (.000).
Personal fouls/disqualifications: 1990-91, 25/2. 1991-92, 12/0. 1993-94, 14/1. 1994-95, 18/1. 1995-96, 11/1. 1998-99, 33/1. 1999-00, 38/0. 2000-01, 80/0. Totals, 231/6.

NBA ALL-STAR GAME RECORD

Season	Team	Min.	FGM	FGA	Pct.	FTM	FTA	Pct.	Off.	Def.	Tot.	Ast.	PF	Dq.	St.	Blk.	TO	Pts.
1995	—Cleveland...........	6	1	1	1.000	0	0	...	2	2	4	0	1	0	0	0	0	2

HOIBERG, FRED   G

PERSONAL: Born October 15, 1972, in Lincoln, Neb. ... 6-4/203. (1,93/92,1). ... Full Name: Fredrick Kristian Hoiberg. ... Nickname: The Mayor. ... Name pronounced HOY-berg.
HIGH SCHOOL: Ames (Iowa).
COLLEGE: Iowa State.
TRANSACTIONS/CAREER NOTES: Selected by Indiana Pacers in second round (52nd pick overall) of 1995 NBA Draft. ... Signed as free agent by Chicago Bulls (September 14, 1999).

COLLEGIATE RECORD

Season Team	G	Min.	FGM	FGA	Pct.	FTM	FTA	Pct.	Reb.	Ast.	Pts.	RPG	APG	PPG
91-92—Iowa State	34	1037	161	281	.573	75	93	.806	181	85	410	5.3	2.5	12.1
92-93—Iowa State	31	1018	127	231	.550	84	103	.816	194	93	360	6.3	3.0	11.6
93-94—Iowa State	27	971	177	331	.535	133	154	.864	181	97	546	6.7	3.6	20.2
94-95—Iowa State	34	1252	207	473	.438	174	202	.861	192	75	677	5.6	2.2	19.9
Totals	126	4278	672	1316	.511	466	552	.844	748	350	1993	5.9	2.8	15.8

Three-point field goals: 1991-92, 13-for-50 (.260). 1992-93, 22-for-60 (.367). 1993-94, 59-for-131 (.450). 1994-95, 89-for-216 (.412). Totals, 183-for-457 (.400).

NBA REGULAR-SEASON RECORD

Season Team	G	Min.	FGM	FGA	Pct.	FTM	FTA	Pct.	Off.	Def.	Tot.	Ast.	St.	Blk.	TO	Pts.	RPG	APG	PPG
95-96—Indiana...........	15	85	8	19	.421	15	18	.833	4	5	9	8	6	1	7	32	0.6	0.5	2.1
96-97—Indiana...........	47	572	67	156	.429	61	77	.792	13	68	81	41	27	6	22	224	1.7	0.9	4.8
97-98—Indiana...........	65	874	85	222	.383	59	69	.855	14	100	123	46	40	3	22	261	1.9	0.7	4.0
98-99—Indiana...........	12	87	6	21	.286	6	6	1.000	2	9	11	4	0	0	3	19	0.9	0.3	1.6
99-00—Chicago	31	845	89	230	.387	69	76	.908	7	103	110	85	40	2	43	279	3.5	2.7	9.0
00-01—Chicago	74	2247	217	495	.438	136	157	.866	21	287	308	263	98	12	74	673	4.2	3.6	9.1
Totals	244	4710	472	1143	.413	346	403	.859	61	581	642	446	211	24	171	1488	2.6	1.8	6.1

Three-point field goals: 1995-96, 1-for-3 (.333). 1996-97, 29-for-70 (.414). 1997-98, 32-for-85 (.376). 1998-99, 1-for-9 (.111). 1999-00, 32-for-94 (.340). 2000-01, 103-for-250 (.412). Totals, 198-for-511 (.387).
Personal fouls/disqualifications: 1995-96, 12/0. 1996-97, 51/0. 1997-98, 101/0. 1998-99, 11/0. 1999-00, 66/0. 2000-01, 155/0. Totals, 396/0.

NBA PLAYOFF RECORD

Season Team	G	Min.	FGM	FGA	Pct.	FTM	FTA	Pct.	Off.	Def.	Tot.	Ast.	St.	Blk.	TO	Pts.	RPG	APG	PPG
97-98—Indiana...........	2	20	3	8	.375	2	2	1.000	1	3	4	1	1	0	0	9	2.0	0.5	4.5
98-99—Indiana...........	4	20	2	4	.500	0	0	...	0	3	3	2	3	0	0	4	0.8	0.5	1.0
Totals	6	40	5	12	.417	2	2	1.000	1	6	7	3	4	0	0	13	1.2	0.5	2.2

Three-point field goals: 1997-98, 1-for-2 (.500). Totals, 1-for-2 (.500).
Personal fouls/disqualifications: 1997-98, 2/0. 1998-99, 1/0. Totals, 3/0.

H

HORRY, ROBERT   F   LAKERS

PERSONAL: Born August 25, 1970, in Hartford, Md. ... 6-10/235. (2,08/106,6). ... Full Name: Robert Keith Horry. ... Name pronounced OR-ee.
HIGH SCHOOL: Andalusia (Ala.).
COLLEGE: Alabama.
TRANSACTIONS/CAREER NOTES: Selected by Houston Rockets in first round (11th pick overall) of 1992 NBA Draft. ... Traded by Rockets with F Matt Bullard and two future second-round draft choices to Detroit Pistons for F Sean Elliott (February 4, 1994); trade voided when Elliott failed physical (February 7, 1994). ... Traded by Rockets with G Sam Cassell, F Chucky Brown and F Mark Bryant to Phoenix Suns for F Charles Barkley and 1999 second-round draft choice (August 19, 1996). ... Traded by Suns with C Joe Kleine to Los Angeles Lakers for F Cedric Ceballos and G Rumeal Robinson (January 10, 1997).
MISCELLANEOUS: Member of NBA championship team (1994, 1995, 2000, 2001).

COLLEGIATE RECORD

Season Team	G	Min.	FGM	FGA	Pct.	FTM	FTA	Pct.	Reb.	Ast.	Pts.	RPG	APG	PPG
88-89—Alabama	31	590	79	185	.427	38	59	.644	156	35	200	5.0	1.1	6.5
89-90—Alabama	35	1022	164	351	.467	79	104	.760	217	9	457	6.2	0.3	13.1
90-91—Alabama	32	959	133	296	.449	82	102	.804	260	56	381	8.1	1.8	11.9
91-92—Alabama	35	1185	196	417	.470	120	165	.727	296	88	554	8.5	2.5	15.8
Totals	133	3756	572	1249	.458	319	430	.742	929	188	1592	7.0	1.4	12.0

Three-point field goals: 1988-89, 4-for-13 (.308). 1989-90, 50-for-117 (.427). 1990-91, 33-for-98 (.337). 1991-92, 42-for-120 (.350). Totals, 129-for-348 (.371).

HONORS: NBA All-Rookie second team (1993).

NBA REGULAR-SEASON RECORD

Season Team	G	Min.	FGM	FGA	Pct.	FTM	FTA	Pct.	Off.	Def.	Tot.	Ast.	St.	Blk.	TO	Pts.	RPG	APG	PPG
92-93—Houston	79	2330	323	682	.474	143	200	.715	113	279	392	191	80	83	156	801	5.0	2.4	10.1
93-94—Houston	81	2370	322	702	.459	115	157	.732	128	312	440	231	119	75	137	803	5.4	2.9	9.9
94-95—Houston	64	2074	240	537	.447	86	113	.761	81	243	324	216	94	76	122	652	5.1	3.4	10.2
95-96—Houston	71	2634	300	732	.410	111	143	.776	97	315	412	281	116	109	160	853	5.8	4.0	12.0
96-97—Phoenix-L.A.L.	54	1395	157	360	.436	60	90	.667	68	169	237	110	66	55	72	423	4.4	2.0	7.8
97-98—L.A. Lakers	72	2192	200	420	.476	117	169	.692	186	356	542	163	112	94	99	536	7.5	2.3	7.4
98-99—L.A. Lakers	38	744	67	146	.459	34	46	.739	56	96	152	56	36	39	49	188	4.0	1.5	4.9
99-00—L.A. Lakers	76	1685	159	363	.438	89	113	.788	133	228	361	118	84	80	73	436	4.8	1.6	5.7
00-01—L.A. Lakers	79	1587	147	380	.387	59	83	.711	93	203	296	128	54	54	79	407	3.7	1.6	5.2
Totals	614	17011	1915	4322	.443	814	1114	.731	955	2201	3156	1494	761	665	947	5099	5.1	2.4	8.3

Three-point field goals: 1992-93, 12-for-47 (.255). 1993-94, 44-for-136 (.324). 1994-95, 86-for-227 (.379). 1995-96, 142-for-388 (.366). 1996-97, 49-for-154 (.318). 1997-98, 19-for-93 (.204). 1998-99, 20-for-45 (.444). 1999-00, 29-for-94 (.309). 2000-01, 54-for-156 (.346). Totals, 455-for-1340 (.340).
Personal fouls/disqualifications: 1992-93, 210/1. 1993-94, 186/0. 1994-95, 161/0. 1995-96, 197/3. 1996-97, 153/2. 1997-98, 238/5. 1998-99, 103/2. 1999-00, 189/0. 2000-01, 210/3. Totals, 1647/16.

NBA PLAYOFF RECORD

NOTES: Holds NBA Finals single-game record for most steals—7 (June 9, 1995, at Orlando). ... Holds single-game playoff records for most three-point field goals, none missed—7 (May 6, 1997, vs. Utah). ... Shares single-game playoff record for most three-point field goals made in one quarter—5 (May 12, 1996, vs. Seattle).

Season Team	G	Min.	FGM	FGA	Pct.	FTM	FTA	Pct.	Off.	Def.	Tot.	Ast.	St.	Blk.	TO	Pts.	RPG	APG	PPG
92-93—Houston	12	374	47	101	.465	20	27	.741	14	48	62	38	18	16	28	123	5.2	3.2	10.3
93-94—Houston	23	778	98	226	.434	39	51	.765	40	101	141	82	35	20	27	269	6.1	3.6	11.7
94-95—Houston	22	841	93	209	.445	58	78	.744	40	115	155	76	32	26	25	288	7.0	3.5	13.1
95-96—Houston	8	308	37	91	.407	10	23	.435	15	42	57	24	21	13	15	105	7.1	3.0	13.1
96-97—L.A. Lakers	9	279	17	38	.447	14	18	.778	12	36	48	13	10	7	11	60	5.3	1.4	6.7
97-98—L.A. Lakers	13	422	39	70	.557	28	41	.683	34	50	84	40	14	14	18	112	6.5	3.1	8.6
98-99—L.A. Lakers	8	177	12	26	.462	11	14	.786	10	26	36	11	6	6	7	40	4.5	1.4	5.0
99-00—L.A. Lakers	23	618	59	145	.407	40	57	.702	38	85	123	58	20	19	30	175	5.3	2.5	7.6
00-01—L.A. Lakers	16	382	32	87	.368	13	22	.591	30	53	83	31	22	16	18	94	5.2	1.9	5.9
Totals	134	4179	434	993	.437	233	331	.704	233	556	789	373	178	137	179	1266	5.9	2.8	9.4

Three-point field goals: 1992-93, 9-for-30 (.300). 1993-94, 34-for-89 (.382). 1994-95, 44-for-110 (.400). 1995-96, 21-for-53 (.396). 1996-97, 12-for-28 (.429). 1997-98, 6-for-17 (.353). 1998-99, 5-for-12 (.417). 1999-00, 17-for-59 (.288). 2000-01, 17-for-47 (.362). Totals, 165-for-445 (.371).
Personal fouls/disqualifications: 1992-93, 30/1. 1993-94, 68/0. 1994-95, 69/2. 1995-96, 29/1. 1996-97, 27/0. 1997-98, 45/0. 1998-99, 29/1. 1999-00, 88/3. 2000-01, 50/0. Totals, 435/8.

HOUSE, EDDIE   G   HEAT

PERSONAL: Born May 14, 1978, in Berkeley, Calif. ... 6-0/176. (1,83/79,8). ... Full Name: Edward L. House II.
HIGH SCHOOL: Hayward (Union City, Calif.).
COLLEGE: Arizona State.
TRANSACTIONS/CAREER NOTES: Selected by Miami Heat in second round (37th pick overall) of 2000 NBA Draft.

COLLEGIATE RECORD

Season Team	G	Min.	FGM	FGA	Pct.	FTM	FTA	Pct.	Reb.	Ast.	Pts.	RPG	APG	PPG
96-97—Arizona State	30	886	151	363	.416	18	28	.643	84	108	377	2.8	3.6	12.6
97-98—Arizona State	32	983	143	331	.432	22	29	.759	96	93	363	3.0	2.9	11.3
98-99—Arizona State	30	1106	206	477	.432	91	115	.791	147	93	568	4.9	3.1	18.9
99-00—Arizona State	32	1189	263	623	.422	137	164	.835	175	111	736	5.5	3.5	23.0
Totals	124	4164	763	1794	.425	268	336	.798	502	405	2044	4.0	3.3	16.5

Three-point field goals: 1996-97, 57-for-179 (.318). 1997-98, 55-for-137 (.401). 1998-99, 65-for-167 (.389). 1999-00, 73-for-200 (.365). Totals, 250-for-683 (.366).

H

NBA REGULAR-SEASON RECORD

								REBOUNDS								AVERAGES		
Season Team	G	Min.	FGM	FGA	Pct.	FTM	FTA	Pct.	Off.	Def.	Tot.	Ast.	St.	Blk.	TO	Pts.	RPG	APG	PPG
00-01—Miami	50	550	104	247	.421	24	35	.686	5	37	42	52	13	0	35	251	0.8	1.0	5.0

Three-point field goals: 2000-01, 19-for-55 (.345).
Personal fouls/disqualifications: 2000-01, 58/0.

NBA PLAYOFF RECORD

								REBOUNDS								AVERAGES		
Season Team	G	Min.	FGM	FGA	Pct.	FTM	FTA	Pct.	Off.	Def.	Tot.	Ast.	St.	Blk.	TO	Pts.	RPG	APG	PPG
00-01—Miami	3	64	16	40	.400	4	5	.800	1	4	5	5	3	1	5	38	1.7	1.7	12.7

Three-point field goals: 2000-01, 2-for-7 (.286).
Personal fouls/disqualifications: 2000-01, 7/0.

HOUSTON, ALLAN　　　　G　　　　KNICKS

PERSONAL: Born April 20, 1971, in Louisville, Ky. ... 6-6/200. (1,98/90,7). ... Full Name: Allan Wade Houston.
HIGH SCHOOL: Ballard (Louisville, Ky.).
COLLEGE: Tennessee.
TRANSACTIONS/CAREER NOTES: Selected by Detroit Pistons in first round (11th pick overall) of 1993 NBA Draft. ... Signed as free agent by New York Knicks (July 14, 1996).
MISCELLANEOUS: Member of gold-medal-winning U.S. Olympic team (2000).

COLLEGIATE RECORD

NOTES: The Sporting News All-America second team (1993).

											AVERAGES		
Season Team	G	Min.	FGM	FGA	Pct.	FTM	FTA	Pct.	Reb.	Ast.	Pts.	RPG	APG	PPG
89-90—Tennessee	30	1083	203	465	.437	120	149	.805	88	127	609	2.9	4.2	20.3
90-91—Tennessee	34	1212	265	550	.482	177	205	.863	104	131	806	3.1	3.9	23.7
91-92—Tennessee	34	1236	223	492	.453	189	225	.840	180	110	717	5.3	3.2	21.1
92-93—Tennessee	30	1075	211	454	.465	165	188	.878	145	92	669	4.8	3.1	22.3
Totals	128	4606	902	1961	.460	651	767	.849	517	460	2801	4.0	3.6	21.9

Three-point field goals: 1989-90, 83-for-192 (.432). 1990-91, 99-for-231 (.429). 1991-92, 82-for-196 (.418). 1992-93, 82-for-198 (.414). Totals, 346-for-817 (.424).

NBA REGULAR-SEASON RECORD

								REBOUNDS								AVERAGES		
Season Team	G	Min.	FGM	FGA	Pct.	FTM	FTA	Pct.	Off.	Def.	Tot.	Ast.	St.	Blk.	TO	Pts.	RPG	APG	PPG
93-94—Detroit	79	1519	272	671	.405	89	108	.824	19	101	120	100	34	13	99	668	1.5	1.3	8.5
94-95—Detroit	76	1996	398	859	.463	147	171	.860	29	138	167	164	61	14	113	1101	2.2	2.2	14.5
95-96—Detroit	82	3072	564	1244	.453	298	362	.823	54	246	300	250	61	16	233	1617	3.7	3.0	19.7
96-97—New York	81	2681	437	1032	.423	175	218	.803	43	197	240	179	41	18	167	1197	3.0	2.2	14.8
97-98—New York	82	2848	571	1277	.447	285	335	.851	43	231	274	212	63	24	200	1509	3.3	2.6	18.4
98-99—New York	50	1815	294	703	.418	168	195	.862	20	132	152	137	35	9	130	813	3.0	2.7	16.3
99-00—New York	82	3169	614	1271	.483	280	334	.838	38	233	271	224	65	14	186	1614	3.3	2.7	19.7
00-01—New York	78	2858	542	1208	.449	279	307	.909	20	263	283	173	52	10	161	1459	3.6	2.2	18.7
Totals	610	19958	3692	8265	.447	1721	2030	.848	266	1541	1807	1439	412	118	1289	9978	3.0	2.4	16.4

Three-point field goals: 1993-94, 35-for-117 (.299). 1994-95, 158-for-373 (.424). 1995-96, 191-for-447 (.427). 1996-97, 148-for-384 (.385). 1997-98, 82-for-213 (.385). 1998-99, 57-for-140 (.407). 1999-00, 106-for-243 (.436). 2000-01, 96-for-252 (.381). Totals, 873-for-2169 (.402).
Personal fouls/disqualifications: 1993-94, 165/2. 1994-95, 182/0. 1995-96, 233/1. 1996-97, 233/6. 1997-98, 207/2. 1998-99, 115/1. 1999-00, 219/1. 2000-01, 190/5. Totals, 1544/18.

NBA PLAYOFF RECORD

								REBOUNDS								AVERAGES		
Season Team	G	Min.	FGM	FGA	Pct.	FTM	FTA	Pct.	Off.	Def.	Tot.	Ast.	St.	Blk.	TO	Pts.	RPG	APG	PPG
95-96—Detroit	3	136	25	58	.431	18	20	.900	1	7	8	6	0	1	11	75	2.7	2.0	25.0
96-97—New York	9	360	58	133	.436	31	35	.886	3	20	23	21	6	3	24	173	2.6	2.3	19.2
97-98—New York	10	403	76	175	.434	50	58	.862	6	32	38	28	5	1	32	211	3.8	2.8	21.1
98-99—New York	20	783	135	305	.443	91	103	.883	6	48	54	51	8	1	50	370	2.7	2.6	18.5
99-00—New York	16	654	103	235	.438	56	65	.862	3	49	52	26	19	3	36	281	3.3	1.6	17.6
00-01—New York	5	189	38	64	.594	22	22	1.000	0	9	9	7	5	1	10	104	1.8	1.4	20.8
Totals	63	2525	435	970	.448	268	303	.884	19	165	184	139	43	10	163	1214	2.9	2.2	19.3

Three-point field goals: 1995-96, 7-for-21 (.333). 1996-97, 26-for-52 (.500). 1997-98, 9-for-23 (.391). 1998-99, 9-for-36 (.250). 1999-00, 19-for-38 (.500). 2000-01, 8-for-11 (.545). Totals, 78-for-181 (.420).
Personal fouls/disqualifications: 1995-96, 11/0. 1996-97, 14/0. 1997-98, 27/0. 1998-99, 40/0. 1999-00, 42/0. 2000-01, 17/0. Totals, 151/0.

NBA ALL-STAR GAME RECORD

							REBOUNDS								
Season Team	Min.	FGM	FGA	Pct.	FTM	FTA	Pct.	Off.	Def.	Tot.	Ast.	PF	Dq.	St.	Blk.	TO	Pts.
2000 —New York...........	18	3	10	.300	4	4	1.000	0	0	0	2	1	0	1	0	1	11
2001 —New York...........	15	2	5	.400	0	0	...	0	3	3	3	0	0	0	0	1	5
Totals...........................	33	5	15	.333	4	4	1.000	0	3	3	5	1	0	1	0	2	16

Three-point field goals: 2000, 1-for-3 (.333). 2001, 1-for-2 (.500). Totals, 2-for-5 (.400).

DID YOU KNOW . . .

. . . that Houston's Steve Francis was the only NBA player last season to lead his team in points,

rebounds and assists?

H

HOWARD, JUWAN   F   MAVERICKS

PERSONAL: Born February 7, 1973, in Chicago. ... 6-9/250. (2,06/113,4). ... Full Name: Juwan Antonio Howard.
HIGH SCHOOL: Vocational (Chicago).
COLLEGE: Michigan.
TRANSACTIONS/CAREER NOTES: Selected after junior season by Washington Bullets in first round (fifth pick overall) of 1994 NBA Draft. ... Signed as free agent by Miami Heat (July 15, 1996). ... Contract disallowed by NBA (July 31, 1996). ... Re-signed as free agent by Bullets (August 5, 1996). ... Bullets franchise renamed Washington Wizards for 1997-98 season. ... Traded by Wizards with C Calvin Booth and F Obinna Ekezie to Dallas Mavericks for F/C Christian Laettner, G Courtney Alexander, F Loy Vaught, G Hubert Davis, F/C Etan Thomas and cash considerations (February 22, 2001).

COLLEGIATE RECORD

Season Team	G	Min.	FGM	FGA	Pct.	FTM	FTA	Pct.	Reb.	Ast.	Pts.	RPG	APG	PPG
91-92—Michigan	34	956	150	333	.450	77	112	.688	212	62	377	6.2	1.8	11.1
92-93—Michigan	36	1095	206	407	.506	112	160	.700	267	69	524	7.4	1.9	14.6
93-94—Michigan	30	1020	261	469	.557	102	151	.675	266	71	625	8.9	2.4	20.8
Totals	100	3071	617	1209	.510	291	423	.688	745	202	1526	7.5	2.0	15.3

Three-point field goals: 1991-92, 0-for-2. 1992-93, 0-for-2. 1993-94, 1-for-7 (.143). Totals, 1-for-11 (.091).

NBA REGULAR-SEASON RECORD

HONORS: All-NBA third team (1996). ... NBA All-Rookie second team (1995).

Season Team	G	Min.	FGM	FGA	Pct.	FTM	FTA	Pct.	Off.	Def.	Tot.	Ast.	St.	Blk.	TO	Pts.	RPG	APG	PPG
94-95—Washington	65	2348	455	931	.489	194	292	.664	184	361	545	165	52	15	166	1104	8.4	2.5	17.0
95-96—Washington	81	3294	733	1500	.489	319	426	.749	188	472	660	360	67	39	303	1789	8.1	4.4	22.1
96-97—Washington	82	3324	638	1313	.486	294	389	.756	202	450	652	311	93	23	246	1570	8.0	3.8	19.1
97-98—Washington	64	2559	463	991	.467	258	358	.721	161	288	449	208	82	23	185	1184	7.0	3.3	18.5
98-99—Washington	36	1430	286	604	.474	110	146	.753	90	203	293	107	42	14	95	682	8.1	3.0	18.9
99-00—Washington	82	2909	509	1108	.459	202	275	.735	132	338	470	247	67	21	225	1220	5.7	3.0	14.9
00-01—Wash.-Dallas	81	2974	583	1218	.479	296	383	.773	171	401	572	224	75	37	242	1462	7.1	2.8	18.0
Totals	491	18838	3667	7665	.478	1673	2269	.737	1128	2513	3641	1622	478	172	1462	9011	7.4	3.3	18.4

Three-point field goals: 1994-95, 0-for-7. 1995-96, 4-for-13 (.308). 1996-97, 0-for-2. 1997-98, 0-for-2. 1998-99, 0-for-3. 1999-00, 0-for-7. 2000-01, 0-for-3. Totals, 4-for-37 (.108).
Personal fouls/disqualifications: 1994-95, 236/2. 1995-96, 269/3. 1996-97, 259/3. 1997-98, 225/3. 1998-99, 130/1. 1999-00, 299/2. 2000-01, 292/2. Totals, 1710/16.

NBA PLAYOFF RECORD

Season Team	G	Min.	FGM	FGA	Pct.	FTM	FTA	Pct.	Off.	Def.	Tot.	Ast.	St.	Blk.	TO	Pts.	RPG	APG	PPG
96-97—Washington	3	129	20	43	.465	16	18	.889	10	8	18	5	2	2	3	56	6.0	1.7	18.7
00-01—Dallas	10	391	49	136	.360	36	45	.800	29	54	83	14	6	5	14	134	8.3	1.4	13.4
Totals	13	520	69	179	.385	52	63	.825	39	62	101	19	8	7	17	190	7.8	1.5	14.6

Personal fouls/disqualifications: 1996-97, 9/0. 2000-01, 38/0. Totals, 47/0.

NBA ALL-STAR GAME RECORD

Season Team	Min.	FGM	FGA	Pct.	FTM	FTA	Pct.	Off.	Def.	Tot.	Ast.	PF	Dq.	St.	Blk.	TO	Pts.
1996 —Washington	16	1	5	.200	0	0	...	4	2	6	2	3	0	1	0	0	2

HUDSON, TROY   G

PERSONAL: Born March 13, 1976, in Carbondale, Ill. ... 6-1/170. (1,85/77,1).
HIGH SCHOOL: Carbondale (Ill.).
COLLEGE: Missouri, then Southern Illinois.
TRANSACTIONS/CAREER NOTES: Not drafted by an NBA franchise. ... Signed as free agent by Utah Jazz (October 3, 1997). ... Waived by Jazz (December 28, 1997). ... Played in Continental Basketball Association with Yakima Sun Kings (1997-98) and Sioux Falls Skyforce (1997-98 and 1998-99). ... Signed as free agent by Minnesota Timberwolves (January 22, 1999). ... Waived by Timberwolves (February 3, 1999). ... Signed by Los Angeles Clippers to first of two consecutive 10-day contracts (March 23, 1999). ... Re-signed by Clippers for remainder of season (April 13, 1999). ... Waived by Clippers (March 27, 2000). ... Signed as free agent by Orlando Magic (August 10, 2000).

COLLEGIATE RECORD

Season Team	G	Min.	FGM	FGA	Pct.	FTM	FTA	Pct.	Reb.	Ast.	Pts.	RPG	APG	PPG
94-95—Missouri	2	20	4	10	.400	1	2	.500	2	4	10	1.0	2.0	5.0
95-96—Southern Illinois	25	812	179	459	.390	82	103	.796	110	38	533	4.4	1.5	21.3
96-97—Southern Illinois	30	1075	209	534	.391	79	96	.823	107	83	631	3.6	2.8	21.0
Totals	57	1907	392	1003	.391	162	201	.806	219	125	1174	3.8	2.2	20.6

Three-point field goals: 1994-95, 1-for-6 (.167). 1995-96, 82-for-103 (.796). 1996-97, 134-for-362 (.370). Totals, 217-for-471 (.461).

CBA REGULAR-SEASON RECORD

Season Team	G	Min.	FGM	FGA	Pct.	FTM	FTA	Pct.	Reb.	Ast.	Pts.	RPG	APG	PPG
97-98—Yakima-Sioux Falls	22	399	71	163	.436	25	31	.806	46	38	199	2.1	1.7	9.0
98-99—Sioux Falls	37	1213	173	449	.385	52	60	.867	113	170	461	3.1	4.6	12.5
Totals	59	1612	244	612	.399	77	91	.846	159	208	660	2.7	3.5	11.2

Three-point field goals: 1997-98, 32-for-78 (.410). 1997-98, 10-for-20 (.500). 1998-99, 63-for-205 (.307). Totals, 105-for-303 (.347).

H

Season Team	G	Min.	FGM	FGA	Pct.	FTM	FTA	Pct.	REBOUNDS Off.	Def.	Tot.	Ast.	St.	Blk.	TO	Pts.	AVERAGES RPG	APG	PPG
97-98—Utah................	8	23	6	14	.429	0	0	...	1	1	2	4	2	0	1	12	0.3	0.5	1.5
98-99—L.A. Clippers ...	25	524	60	150	.400	34	38	.895	15	40	55	92	11	2	38	169	2.2	3.7	6.8
99-00—L.A. Clippers ...	62	1592	204	541	.377	77	95	.811	28	120	148	242	43	0	108	545	2.4	3.9	8.8
00-01—Orlando..........	75	1008	125	372	.336	85	104	.817	38	67	105	162	37	3	92	357	1.4	2.2	4.8
Totals	170	3147	395	1077	.367	196	237	.827	82	228	310	500	93	5	239	1083	1.8	2.9	6.4

Three-point field goals: 1997-98, 0-for-3. 1998-99, 15-for-47 (.319). 1999-00, 60-for-193 (.311). 2000-01, 22-for-109 (.202). Totals, 97-for-352 (.276).
Personal fouls/disqualifications: 1997-98, 1/0. 1998-99, 28/1. 1999-00, 65/0. 2000-01, 82/0. Totals, 176/1.

NBA PLAYOFF RECORD

Season Team	G	Min.	FGM	FGA	Pct.	FTM	FTA	Pct.	REBOUNDS Off.	Def.	Tot.	Ast.	St.	Blk.	TO	Pts.	AVERAGES RPG	APG	PPG
00-01—Orlando..........	4	56	6	21	.286	5	6	.833	5	4	9	9	1	0	3	17	2.3	2.3	4.3

Three-point field goals: 2000-01, 0-for-3.
Personal fouls/disqualifications: 2000-01, 3/0.

HUGHES, LARRY　　　G　　　WARRIORS

PERSONAL: Born January 23, 1979, in St. Louis. ... 6-5/184. (1,96/83,5). ... Full Name: Larry Darnell Hughes.
HIGH SCHOOL: Christian Brothers (St. Louis).
COLLEGE: Saint Louis.
TRANSACTIONS/CAREER NOTES: Selected after freshman season by Philadelphia 76ers in first round (eighth pick overall) of 1998 NBA Draft. ... Traded by 76ers with F/G Billy Owens to Golden State Warriors in three-way deal in which Warriors sent G John Starks and a future first-round draft choice to Chicago Bulls and 76ers sent F Bruce Bowen to Bulls for F Toni Kukoc (February 16, 2000).

COLLEGIATE RECORD

NOTES: The Sporting News Freshman of the Year (1998).

Season Team	G	Min.	FGM	FGA	Pct.	FTM	FTA	Pct.	Reb.	Ast.	Pts.	AVERAGES RPG	APG	PPG
97-98—St. Louis........................	32	1038	224	540	.415	180	260	.692	162	77	670	5.1	2.4	20.9

Three-point field goals: 1997-98, 42-for-145 (.290).

NBA REGULAR-SEASON RECORD

Season Team	G	Min.	FGM	FGA	Pct.	FTM	FTA	Pct.	REBOUNDS Off.	Def.	Tot.	Ast.	St.	Blk.	TO	Pts.	AVERAGES RPG	APG	PPG
98-99—Philadelphia	50	988	170	414	.411	107	151	.709	83	106	189	77	44	14	68	455	3.8	1.5	9.1
99-00—Phil.-G.S.	82	2324	459	1147	.400	279	377	.740	113	236	349	205	115	28	195	1226	4.3	2.5	15.0
00-01—Golden State ...	50	1846	308	805	.383	193	252	.766	76	200	276	223	96	29	152	823	5.5	4.5	16.5
Totals	182	5158	937	2366	.396	579	780	.742	272	542	814	505	255	71	415	2504	4.5	2.8	13.8

Three-point field goals: 1998-99, 8-for-52 (.154). 1999-00, 29-for-125 (.232). 2000-01, 14-for-75 (.187). Totals, 51-for-252 (.202).
Personal fouls/disqualifications: 1998-99, 97/0. 1999-00, 191/2. 2000-01, 147/2. Totals, 435/4.

NBA PLAYOFF RECORD

Season Team	G	Min.	FGM	FGA	Pct.	FTM	FTA	Pct.	REBOUNDS Off.	Def.	Tot.	Ast.	St.	Blk.	TO	Pts.	AVERAGES RPG	APG	PPG
98-99—Philadelphia	8	198	31	77	.403	20	24	.833	17	20	37	16	15	9	12	82	4.6	2.0	10.3

Three-point field goals: 1998-99, 0-for-7.
Personal fouls/disqualifications: 1998-99, 21/0.

HUNTER, LINDSEY　　　G　　　LAKERS

PERSONAL: Born December 3, 1970, in Utica, Miss. ... 6-2/195. (1,88/88,5). ... Full Name: Lindsey Benson Hunter Jr.
HIGH SCHOOL: Murrah (Jackson, Miss.).
COLLEGE: Alcorn State, then Jackson State.
TRANSACTIONS/CAREER NOTES: Selected by Detroit Pistons in first round (10th pick overall) of 1993 NBA Draft. ... Traded by Pistons to Milwaukee Bucks for F Billy Owens (August 22, 2000). ... Traded by Bucks to Los Angeles Lakers for G Greg Foster (June 28, 2001).

COLLEGIATE RECORD

NOTES: Holds NCAA Division I single-game record for most three-point field goals attempted—26 (December 27, 1992, vs. Kansas, 11 made).

Season Team	G	Min.	FGM	FGA	Pct.	FTM	FTA	Pct.	Reb.	Ast.	Pts.	AVERAGES RPG	APG	PPG
88-89—Alcorn State...................	27	624	70	178	.393	23	32	.719	67	99	167	2.5	3.7	6.2
89-90—Jackson State................						Did not play—transfer student.								
90-91—Jackson State................	30	1042	229	560	.409	82	118	.695	100	105	626	3.3	3.5	20.9
91-92—Jackson State................	28	960	249	605	.412	100	157	.637	96	121	693	3.4	4.3	24.8
92-93—Jackson State................	34	1152	320	777	.412	155	201	.771	115	115	907	3.4	3.4	26.7
Totals	119	3778	868	2120	.409	360	508	.709	378	440	2393	3.2	3.7	20.1

Three-point field goals: 1988-89, 4-for-21 (.190). 1990-91, 86-for-235 (.366). 1991-92, 95-for-257 (.370). 1992-93, 112-for-328 (.341). Totals, 297-for-841 (.353).

NBA REGULAR-SEASON RECORD

HONORS: NBA All-Rookie second team (1994).

H

Season Team	G	Min.	FGM	FGA	Pct.	FTM	FTA	Pct.	REBOUNDS Off.	Def.	Tot.	Ast.	St.	Blk.	TO	Pts.	AVERAGES RPG	APG	PPG
93-94—Detroit	82	2172	335	893	.375	104	142	.732	47	142	189	390	121	10	184	843	2.3	4.8	10.3
94-95—Detroit	42	944	119	318	.374	40	55	.727	24	51	75	159	51	7	79	314	1.8	3.8	7.5
95-96—Detroit	80	2138	239	628	.381	84	120	.700	44	150	194	188	84	18	80	679	2.4	2.4	8.5
96-97—Detroit	82	3023	421	1042	.404	158	203	.778	59	174	233	154	129	24	96	1166	2.8	1.9	14.2
97-98—Detroit	71	2505	316	826	.383	145	196	.740	61	186	247	224	123	10	110	862	3.5	3.2	12.1
98-99—Detroit	49	1755	228	524	.435	67	89	.753	26	142	168	193	86	8	92	582	3.4	3.9	11.9
99-00—Detroit	82	2919	379	892	.425	117	154	.760	35	215	250	327	129	22	145	1043	3.0	4.0	12.7
00-01—Milwaukee	82	2002	298	783	.381	77	96	.802	32	137	169	222	102	12	68	825	2.1	2.7	10.1
Totals	570	17458	2335	5906	.395	792	1055	.751	328	1197	1525	1857	825	111	854	6314	2.7	3.3	11.1

Three-point field goals: 1993-94, 69-for-207 (.333). 1994-95, 36-for-108 (.333). 1995-96, 117-for-289 (.405). 1996-97, 166-for-468 (.355). 1997-98, 85-for-265 (.321). 1998-99, 59-for-153 (.386). 1999-00, 168-for-389 (.432). 2000-01, 152-for-407 (.373). Totals, 852-for-2286 (.373).

Personal fouls/disqualifications: 1993-94, 174/1. 1994-95, 94/1. 1995-96, 185/0. 1996-97, 206/1. 1997-98, 174/3. 1998-99, 126/2. 1999-00, 216/2. 2000-01, 172/1. Totals, 1347/11.

NBA PLAYOFF RECORD

Season Team	G	Min.	FGM	FGA	Pct.	FTM	FTA	Pct.	REBOUNDS Off.	Def.	Tot.	Ast.	St.	Blk.	TO	Pts.	AVERAGES RPG	APG	PPG
95-96—Detroit	2	36	2	8	.250	1	2	.500	1	1	2	1	1	0	0	6	1.0	0.5	3.0
96-97—Detroit	5	201	29	66	.439	5	7	.714	4	14	18	6	6	1	1	75	3.6	1.2	15.0
98-99—Detroit	5	180	14	53	.264	5	5	1.000	5	10	15	12	7	0	7	36	3.0	2.4	7.2
99-00—Detroit	3	93	10	32	.313	4	6	.667	0	7	7	5	5	1	5	25	2.3	1.7	8.3
00-01—Milwaukee	18	289	24	99	.242	8	11	.727	2	29	31	34	14	3	13	64	1.7	1.9	3.6
Totals	33	799	79	258	.306	23	31	.742	12	61	73	58	33	5	26	206	2.2	1.8	6.2

Three-point field goals: 1995-96, 1-for-4 (.250). 1996-97, 12-for-29 (.414). 1998-99, 3-for-11 (.273). 1999-00, 1-for-9 (.111). 2000-01, 8-for-53 (.151). Totals, 25-for-106 (.236).

Personal fouls/disqualifications: 1995-96, 2/0. 1996-97, 9/0. 1998-99, 11/0. 1999-00, 4/0. 2000-01, 24/0. Totals, 50/0.

ILGAUSKAS, ZYDRUNAS   C   CAVALIERS

PERSONAL: Born June 5, 1975, in Kaunas, Lithuania. ... 7-3/260. (2,21/117,9). ... Name pronounced ZHEE-drew-nus ill-GAUS-kus.

TRANSACTIONS/CAREER NOTES: Played in Lithuania (1994-95 and 1995-96). ... Selected by Cleveland Cavaliers in first round (20th pick overall) of 1996 NBA Draft.

LITHUANIAN LEAGUE RECORD

Season Team	G	Min.	FGM	FGA	Pct.	FTM	FTA	Pct.	Reb.	Ast.	Pts.	AVERAGES RPG	APG	PPG
94-95—Atletas	36	1091	303	504	.601	123	180	.683	460	26	731	12.8	0.7	20.3
95-96—Atletas						Did not play—injured.								
Totals	36	1091	303	504	.601	123	180	.683	460	26	731	12.8	0.7	20.3

Three-point field goals: 1994-95, 2-for-9 (.222).

NBA REGULAR-SEASON RECORD

HONORS: NBA All-Rookie first team (1998). ... MVP of Rookie game (1998).

Season Team	G	Min.	FGM	FGA	Pct.	FTM	FTA	Pct.	REBOUNDS Off.	Def.	Tot.	Ast.	St.	Blk.	TO	Pts.	AVERAGES RPG	APG	PPG
96-97—Cleveland						Did not play—injured.													
97-98—Cleveland	82	2379	454	876	.518	230	302	.762	279	444	723	71	52	135	146	1139	8.8	0.9	13.9
98-99—Cleveland	5	171	29	57	.509	18	30	.600	17	27	44	4	4	7	9	76	8.8	0.8	15.2
99-00—Cleveland						Did not play—injured.													
00-01—Cleveland	24	616	114	234	.487	53	78	.679	65	95	160	18	15	37	60	281	6.7	0.8	11.7
Totals	111	3166	597	1167	.512	301	410	.734	361	566	927	93	71	179	215	1496	8.4	0.8	13.5

Three-point field goals: 1997-98, 1-for-4 (.250). 2000-01, 0-for-2. Totals, 1-for-6 (.167).

Personal fouls/disqualifications: 1997-98, 288/4. 1998-99, 24/1. 2000-01, 78/0. Totals, 390/5.

NBA PLAYOFF RECORD

Season Team	G	Min.	FGM	FGA	Pct.	FTM	FTA	Pct.	REBOUNDS Off.	Def.	Tot.	Ast.	St.	Blk.	TO	Pts.	AVERAGES RPG	APG	PPG
97-98—Cleveland	4	147	28	49	.571	13	25	.520	14	16	30	2	2	5	10	69	7.5	0.5	17.3

Personal fouls/disqualifications: 1997-98, 22/2.

IVERSON, ALLEN   G   76ERS

PERSONAL: Born June 7, 1975, in Hampton, Va. ... 6-0/165. (1,83/74,8).
HIGH SCHOOL: Bethel (Hampton, Va.).
COLLEGE: Georgetown.
TRANSACTIONS/CAREER NOTES: Selected after sophomore season by Philadelphia 76ers in first round (first pick overall) of 1996 NBA Draft.

COLLEGIATE RECORD

NOTES: The Sporting News All-America first team (1996).

Season Team	G	Min.	FGM	FGA	Pct.	FTM	FTA	Pct.	Reb.	Ast.	Pts.	AVERAGES RPG	APG	PPG
94-95—Georgetown...................	30	966	203	520	.390	172	250	.688	99	134	613	3.3	4.5	20.4
95-96—Georgetown...................	37	1213	312	650	.480	215	317	.678	141	173	926	3.8	4.7	25.0
Totals	67	2179	515	1170	.440	387	567	.683	240	307	1539	3.6	4.6	23.0

Three-point field goals: 1994-95, 35-for-151 (.232). 1995-96, 87-for-238 (.366). Totals, 122-for-389 (.314).

NBA REGULAR-SEASON RECORD

HONORS: NBA Most Valuable Player (2001). ... NBA Rookie of the Year (1997). ... All-NBA first team (1999, 2001). ... All-NBA second team (2000). ... NBA All-Rookie first team (1997). ... MVP of Rookie Game (1997).

NOTES: Led NBA with 2.51 steals per game (2001).

									REBOUNDS								AVERAGES		
Season Team	G	Min.	FGM	FGA	Pct.	FTM	FTA	Pct.	Off.	Def.	Tot.	Ast.	St.	Blk.	TO	Pts.	RPG	APG	PPG
96-97—Philadelphia....	76	3045	625	1504	.416	382	544	.702	115	197	312	567	157	24	*337	1787	4.1	7.5	23.5
97-98—Philadelphia....	80	3150	649	1407	.461	390	535	.729	86	210	296	494	176	25	244	1758	3.7	6.2	22.0
98-99—Philadelphia....	48	1990	435	*1056	.412	356	474	.751	66	170	236	223	110	7	167	1284	4.9	4.6	*26.8
99-00—Philadelphia....	70	2853	729	1733	.421	442	620	.713	71	196	267	328	144	5	230	1989	3.8	4.7	28.4
00-01—Philadelphia....	71	2979	762	1813	.420	585	719	.814	50	223	273	325	178	20	237	2207	3.8	4.6	*31.1
Totals	345	14017	3200	7513	.426	2155	2892	.745	388	996	1384	1937	765	81	1215	9025	4.0	5.6	26.2

Three-point field goals: 1996-97, 155-for-455 (.341). 1997-98, 70-for-235 (.298). 1998-99, 58-for-199 (.291). 1999-00, 89-for-261 (.341). 2000-01, 98-for-306 (.320). Totals, 470-for-1456 (.323).

Personal fouls/disqualifications: 1996-97, 233/5. 1997-98, 200/2. 1998-99, 98/0. 1999-00, 162/1. 2000-01, 147/0. Totals, 840/8.

NBA PLAYOFF RECORD

NOTES: Holds single-game playoff record for most steals—10 (May 13, 1999, vs. Orlando). ... Shares NBA Finals single-game record for most free throws made in one quarter—9 (June 10, 2001, vs. Los Angeles Lakers).

									REBOUNDS								AVERAGES		
Season Team	G	Min.	FGM	FGA	Pct.	FTM	FTA	Pct.	Off.	Def.	Tot.	Ast.	St.	Blk.	TO	Pts.	RPG	APG	PPG
98-99—Philadelphia....	8	358	88	214	.411	37	52	.712	14	19	33	39	20	2	24	228	4.1	4.9	28.5
99-00—Philadelphia....	10	444	91	237	.384	68	92	.739	14	26	40	45	12	1	32	262	4.0	4.5	26.2
00-01—Philadelphia....	22	1016	257	661	.389	161	208	.774	15	89	104	134	52	7	63	723	4.7	6.1	32.9
Totals	40	1818	436	1112	.392	266	352	.756	43	134	177	218	84	10	119	1213	4.4	5.5	30.3

Three-point field goals: 1998-99, 15-for-53 (.283). 1999-00, 12-for-39 (.308). 2000-01, 48-for-142 (.338). Totals, 75-for-234 (.321).
Personal fouls/disqualifications: 1998-99, 19/0. 1999-00, 24/0. 2000-01, 55/0. Totals, 98/0.

NBA ALL-STAR GAME RECORD

NOTES: NBA All-Star Game Most Valuable Player (2001).

								REBOUNDS								
Season Team	Min.	FGM	FGA	Pct.	FTM	FTA	Pct.	Off.	Def.	Tot.	Ast.	PF	Dq.	St.	Blk.	TO	Pts.
2000 —Philadelphia......	28	10	18	.556	4	5	.800	2	0	2	9	0	0	2	0	5	26
2001 —Philadelphia......	27	9	21	.429	6	6	1.000	0	2	2	5	0	0	4	0	4	25
Totals........................	55	19	39	.487	10	11	.909	2	2	4	14	0	0	6	0	9	51

Three-point field goals: 2000, 2-for-2. 2001, 1-for-1. Totals, 3-for-3 (1.000).

JACKSON, BOBBY G KINGS

PERSONAL: Born March 13, 1973, in East Spencer, N.C. ... 6-1/185. (1,85/83,9).
HIGH SCHOOL: Salisbury (N.C.).
JUNIOR COLLEGE: Western Nebraska Community College.
COLLEGE: Minnesota.
TRANSACTIONS/CAREER NOTES: Selected by Seattle SuperSonics in first round (23rd pick overall) of 1997 NBA Draft. ... Draft rights traded by SuperSonics to Denver Nuggets for draft rights to G James Cotton and 1998 second-round draft choice (June 25, 1997). ... Traded to Nuggets with C Dean Garrett to Minnesota Timberwolves in three-way deal in which Nuggets received G Chauncey Billups and draft rights to G Tyson Wheeler from Toronto Raptors and Raptors received 1999 first-round draft choice from Nuggets and draft rights to F Zeljko Rebraca, G Michael Williams and 1999 or 2000 first-round draft choice from Timberwolves (January 21, 1999). ... Signed as free agent by Sacramento Kings (August 1, 2000).

COLLEGIATE RECORD

												AVERAGES		
Season Team	G	Min.	FGM	FGA	Pct.	FTM	FTA	Pct.	Reb.	Ast.	Pts.	RPG	APG	PPG
93-94—Western Nebraska.........	39	...	155	298	.520	98	136	.721	158	105	413	4.1	2.7	10.6
94-95—Western Nebraska.........	32	...	166	302	.550	52	79	.658	161	143	406	5.0	4.5	12.7
95-96—Minnesota	25	683	115	283	.406	74	94	.787	119	68	332	4.8	2.7	13.3
96-97—Minnesota	35	1101	191	433	.441	121	154	.786	213	139	534	6.1	4.0	15.3
Junior College Totals..............	71		321	600	.535	150	215	.698	319	248	819	4.5	3.5	11.5
4-Year-College Totals	60	1784	306	716	.427	195	248	.786	332	207	866	5.5	3.5	14.4

Three-point field goals: 1993-94, 5-for-28 (.179). 1994-95, 22-for-67 (.328). 1995-96, 28-for-95 (.295). 1996-97, 31-for-97 (.320). Totals, 27-for-95 (.284) Totals, 59-for-192 (.307).

NBA REGULAR-SEASON RECORD

HONORS: NBA All-Rookie second team (1998).

									REBOUNDS								AVERAGES		
Season Team	G	Min.	FGM	FGA	Pct.	FTM	FTA	Pct.	Off.	Def.	Tot.	Ast.	St.	Blk.	TO	Pts.	RPG	APG	PPG
97-98—Denver	68	2042	310	791	.392	149	183	.814	78	224	302	317	105	11	184	790	4.4	4.7	11.6
98-99—Minnesota.......	50	941	141	348	.405	61	79	.772	43	92	135	167	39	3	75	353	2.7	3.3	7.1
99-00—Minnesota.......	73	1034	140	346	.405	76	98	.776	50	103	153	172	48	7	58	369	2.1	2.4	5.1
00-01—Sacramento.....	79	1648	231	526	.439	65	88	.739	74	172	246	161	87	7	103	566	3.1	2.0	7.2
Totals	270	5665	822	2011	.409	351	448	.783	245	591	836	817	279	28	420	2078	3.1	3.0	7.7

Three-point field goals: 1997-98, 21-for-81 (.259). 1998-99, 10-for-27 (.370). 1999-00, 13-for-46 (.283). 2000-01, 39-for-104 (.375). Totals, 83-for-258 (.322).

Personal fouls/disqualifications: 1997-98, 160/0. 1998-99, 75/1. 1999-00, 114/0. 2000-01, 139/0. Totals, 488/1.

NBA PLAYOFF RECORD

									REBOUNDS								AVERAGES		
Season Team	G	Min.	FGM	FGA	Pct.	FTM	FTA	Pct.	Off.	Def.	Tot.	Ast.	St.	Blk.	TO	Pts.	RPG	APG	PPG
98-99—Minnesota.......	4	27	2	10	.200	0	0	...	1	3	4	2	0	0	1	4	1.0	0.5	1.0
99-00—Minnesota.......	3	30	4	8	.500	6	6	1.000	0	5	5	4	2	1	2	15	1.7	1.3	5.0
00-01—Sacramento	8	182	21	48	.438	10	14	.714	6	20	26	18	8	0	7	56	3.3	2.3	7.0
Totals	15	239	27	66	.409	16	20	.800	7	28	35	24	10	1	10	75	2.3	1.6	5.0

Three-point field goals: 1998-99, 0-for-3. 1999-00, 1-for-3 (.333). 2000-01, 4-for-14 (.286). Totals, 5-for-20 (.250).
Personal fouls/disqualifications: 1998-99, 3/0. 1999-00, 4/0. 2000-01, 18/0. Totals, 25/0.

JACKSON, JAREN   G

PERSONAL: Born October 27, 1967, in New Orleans. ... 6-6/225. (1,98/102,1).
HIGH SCHOOL: Walter Cohen (New Orleans).
COLLEGE: Georgetown.
TRANSACTIONS/CAREER NOTES: Not drafted by an NBA franchise. ... Signed as free agent by New Jersey Nets (October 3, 1989). ... Waived by Nets (February 27, 1990). ... Played in Continental Basketball Association with Wichita Falls Texans (1990-91), La Crosse Catbirds (1991-92 and 1993-94), Pittsburgh Piranhas (1994-95) and Fort Wayne Fury (1995-96). ... Played in World Basketball League with Dayton Wings (1991). ... Signed by Golden State Warriors to first of two consecutive 10-day contracts (January 24, 1992). ... Signed as free agent by Los Angeles Clippers (October 7, 1992). ... Signed as free agent by Chicago Bulls (October 7, 1993). ... Waived by Bulls (October 28, 1993). ... Signed as free agent by Portland Trail Blazers (December 21, 1993). ... Waived by Trail Blazers (November 1, 1994). ... Signed as free agent by Philadelphia 76ers (November 15, 1994). ... Waived by 76ers (January 4, 1995). ... Signed by Houston Rockets to first of two consecutive 10-day contracts (February 22, 1996). ... Signed as free agent by Washington Bullets (October 2, 1996). ... Bullets franchise renamed Washington Wizards for 1997-98 season. ... Signed as free agent by San Antonio Spurs (September 29, 1997). ... Waived by Spurs (August 29, 2001).
MISCELLANEOUS: Member of NBA championship team (1999).

COLLEGIATE RECORD

Season Team	G	Min.	FGM	FGA	Pct.	FTM	FTA	Pct.	Reb.	Ast.	Pts.	RPG	APG	PPG
85-86—Georgetown	32	283	42	97	.433	18	22	.818	49	19	102	1.5	0.6	3.2
86-87—Georgetown	34	387	68	148	.459	37	52	.712	69	26	193	2.0	0.8	5.7
87-88—Georgetown	30	558	100	243	.412	42	56	.750	88	46	262	2.9	1.5	8.7
88-89—Georgetown	34	923	161	357	.451	59	90	.656	176	62	417	5.2	1.8	12.3
Totals	130	2151	371	845	.439	156	220	.709	382	153	974	2.9	1.2	7.5

Three-point field goals: 1986-87, 20-for-48 (.417). 1987-88, 20-for-73 (.274). 1988-89, 36-for-87 (.414). Totals, 76-for-208 (.365).

NBA REGULAR-SEASON RECORD

Season Team	G	Min.	FGM	FGA	Pct.	FTM	FTA	Pct.	Off.	Def.	Tot.	Ast.	St.	Blk.	TO	Pts.	RPG	APG	PPG
89-90—New Jersey	28	160	25	69	.362	17	21	.810	16	8	24	13	13	1	18	67	0.9	0.5	2.4
91-92—Golden State	5	54	11	23	.478	4	6	.667	5	5	10	3	2	0	4	26	2.0	0.6	5.2
92-93—L.A. Clippers	34	350	53	128	.414	23	27	.852	19	20	39	35	19	5	17	131	1.1	1.0	3.9
93-94—Portland	29	187	34	87	.391	12	14	.857	6	11	17	27	4	2	14	80	0.6	0.9	2.8
94-95—Philadelphia	21	257	25	68	.368	16	24	.667	18	24	42	19	9	5	17	70	2.0	0.9	3.3
95-96—Houston	4	33	0	8	.000	8	10	.800	0	3	3	0	1	0	0	8	0.8	0.0	2.0
96-97—Washington	75	1133	134	329	.407	53	69	.768	31	101	132	65	45	16	60	374	1.8	0.9	5.0
97-98—San Antonio	82	2226	258	654	.394	94	118	.797	55	155	210	156	60	8	104	722	2.6	1.9	8.8
98-99—San Antonio	47	861	108	284	.380	32	39	.821	21	78	99	49	41	9	37	301	2.1	1.0	6.4
99-00—San Antonio	81	1691	186	488	.381	33	51	.647	34	147	181	118	54	7	66	513	2.2	1.5	6.3
00-01—San Antonio	16	114	16	40	.400	2	2	.000	1	11	12	7	5	0	3	39	0.8	0.4	2.4
Totals	422	7066	850	2178	.390	292	381	.766	206	563	769	492	253	53	340	2331	1.8	1.2	5.5

Three-point field goals: 1989-90, 0-for-3. 1992-93, 2-for-5 (.400). 1993-94, 0-for-6. 1994-95, 4-for-15 (.267). 1995-96, 0-for-5. 1996-97, 53-for-158 (.335). 1997-98, 112-for-297 (.377). 1998-99, 53-for-147 (.361). 1999-00, 108-for-306 (.353). 2000-01, 7-for-18 (.389). Totals, 339-for-960 (.353).
Personal fouls/disqualifications: 1989-90, 16/0. 1991-92, 7/1. 1992-93, 45/1. 1993-94, 20/0. 1994-95, 33/0. 1995-96, 5/0. 1996-97, 131/0. 1997-98, 222/3. 1998-99, 63/0. 1999-00, 157/1. 2000-01, 13/0. Totals, 712/6.

NBA PLAYOFF RECORD

Season Team	G	Min.	FGM	FGA	Pct.	FTM	FTA	Pct.	Off.	Def.	Tot.	Ast.	St.	Blk.	TO	Pts.	RPG	APG	PPG
92-93—L.A. Clippers	4	28	5	13	.385	0	0	...	4	1	5	2	2	0	3	10	1.3	0.5	2.5
93-94—Portland	1	1	0	0	...	0	0	...	0	0	0	0	0	0	0	0	0.0	0.0	0.0
96-97—Washington	3	11	0	0	...	0	2	.000	1	1	2	1	0	0	2	0	0.7	0.3	0.0
97-98—San Antonio	9	319	30	88	.341	14	19	.737	4	35	39	14	5	1	12	92	4.3	1.6	10.2
98-99—San Antonio	17	345	50	131	.382	9	13	.692	6	35	41	18	13	0	20	140	2.4	1.1	8.2
99-00—San Antonio	2	19	0	3	.000	2	4	.500	0	1	1	2	1	0	0	2	0.5	1.0	1.0
Totals	36	723	85	235	.362	25	38	.658	15	73	88	37	21	1	37	244	2.4	1.0	6.8

Three-point field goals: 1992-93, 0-for-1. 1997-98, 18-for-59 (.305). 1998-99, 31-for-86 (.360). 1999-00, 0-for-1. Totals, 49-for-147 (.333).
Personal fouls/disqualifications: 1992-93, 6/0. 1996-97, 7/0. 1997-98, 31/1. 1998-99, 33/0. 1999-00, 1/0. Totals, 78/1.

CBA REGULAR-SEASON RECORD

Season Team	G	Min.	FGM	FGA	Pct.	FTM	FTA	Pct.	Reb.	Ast.	Pts.	RPG	APG	PPG
90-91—Wichita Falls	51	1099	233	525	.444	113	165	.685	214	74	597	4.2	1.5	11.7
91-92—La Crosse	43	1596	314	674	.466	147	184	.799	215	157	785	5.0	3.7	18.3
93-94—La Crosse	14	530	114	251	.454	63	78	.808	58	35	298	4.1	2.5	21.3
94-95—Pittsburgh	22	687	118	274	.431	55	70	.786	109	101	310	5.0	4.6	14.1
95-96—Fort Wayne	24	695	135	256	.527	50	66	.758	107	57	346	4.5	2.4	14.4
Totals	154	4607	914	1980	.462	428	563	.760	703	424	2336	4.6	2.8	15.2

Three-point field goals: 1990-91, 18-for-55 (.327). 1991-92, 10-for-37 (.270). 1993-94, 7-for-24 (.292). 1994-95, 19-for-62 (.306). 1995-96, 26-for-50 (.520). Totals, 80-for-228 (.351).

JACKSON, JIM   G

PERSONAL: Born October 14, 1970, in Toledo, Ohio. ... 6-6/220. (1,98/99,8). ... Full Name: James Arthur Jackson.
HIGH SCHOOL: Macomber-Whitney (Toledo, Ohio).
COLLEGE: Ohio State.
TRANSACTIONS/CAREER NOTES: Selected after junior season by Dallas Mavericks in first round (fourth pick overall) of 1992 NBA Draft. ... Traded by Mavericks with C Eric Montross, F/C Chris Gatling, F/G George McCloud and G Sam Cassell to New Jersey Nets for C Shawn Bradley, F Ed O'Bannon, G Khalid Reeves and G Robert Pack (February 17, 1997). ...

Traded by Nets with draft rights to F Tim Thomas, draft rights to G Anthony Parker and C Eric Montross to Philadelphia 76ers for C Michael Cage, G Lucious Harris, F Don MacLean and draft rights to F Keith Van Horn (June 27, 1997). ... Traded by 76ers with F Clarence Weatherspoon to Golden State Warriors for F Joe Smith and G Brian Shaw (February 17, 1998). ... Signed as free agent by Portland Trail Blazers (February 2, 1999). ... Traded by Trail Blazers with G Isaiah Rider to Atlanta Hawks for G Steve Smith and G Ed Gray (August 2, 1999). ... Traded by Hawks with G Anthony Johnson and F/G Larry Robinson to Cleveland Cavaliers for G Brevin Knight (January 2, 2001).

COLLEGIATE RECORD

NOTES: The Sporting News All-America first team (1992). ... The Sporting News All-America third team (1991).

Season Team	G	Min.	FGM	FGA	Pct.	FTM	FTA	Pct.	Reb.	Ast.	Pts.	RPG	APG	PPG
89-90—Ohio State	30	1035	194	389	.499	73	93	.785	166	110	482	5.5	3.7	16.1
90-91—Ohio State	31	997	228	441	.517	112	149	.752	169	133	585	5.5	4.3	18.9
91-92—Ohio State	32	1133	264	535	.493	146	180	.811	217	129	718	6.8	4.0	22.4
Totals	93	3165	686	1365	.503	331	422	.784	552	372	1785	5.9	4.0	19.2

Three-point field goals: 1989-90, 21-for-59 (.356). 1990-91, 17-for-51 (.333). 1991-92, 44-for-108 (.407). Totals, 82-for-218 (.376).

NBA REGULAR-SEASON RECORD

Season Team	G	Min.	FGM	FGA	Pct.	FTM	FTA	Pct.	Off.	Def.	Tot.	Ast.	St.	Blk.	TO	Pts.	RPG	APG	PPG
92-93—Dallas	28	938	184	466	.395	68	92	.739	42	80	122	131	40	11	115	457	4.4	4.7	16.3
93-94—Dallas	82	3066	637	1432	.445	285	347	.821	169	219	388	374	87	25	*334	1576	4.7	4.6	19.2
94-95—Dallas	51	1982	484	1026	.472	306	380	.805	120	140	260	191	28	12	160	1309	5.1	3.7	25.7
95-96—Dallas	82	2820	569	1308	.435	345	418	.825	173	237	410	235	47	22	191	1604	5.0	2.9	19.6
96-97—Dallas-N.J.	77	2831	444	1029	.431	252	310	.813	132	279	411	316	86	32	208	1226	5.3	4.1	15.9
97-98—Phil.-G.S.	79	3046	476	1107	.430	229	282	.812	130	270	400	381	79	8	263	1242	5.1	4.8	15.7
98-99—Portland	49	1175	152	370	.411	85	101	.842	36	123	159	128	43	6	82	414	3.2	2.6	8.4
99-00—Atlanta	79	2767	507	1235	.411	186	212	.877	101	293	394	230	57	10	185	1317	5.0	2.9	16.7
00-01—Atlanta-Cleve.	56	1690	239	632	.378	139	169	.822	53	171	224	163	53	10	130	643	4.0	2.9	11.5
Totals	583	20315	3692	8605	.429	1895	2311	.820	956	1812	2768	2149	520	136	1668	9788	4.7	3.7	16.8

Three-point field goals: 1992-93, 21-for-73 (.288). 1993-94, 17-for-60 (.283). 1994-95, 35-for-110 (.318). 1995-96, 121-for-333 (.363). 1996-97, 86-for-247 (.348). 1997-98, 61-for-191 (.319). 1998-99, 25-for-90 (.278). 1999-00, 117-for-303 (.386). 2000-01, 26-for-80 (.325). Totals, 509-for-1487 (.342).

Personal fouls/disqualifications: 1992-93, 80/0. 1993-94, 161/0. 1994-95, 92/0. 1995-96, 165/0. 1996-97, 194/0. 1997-98, 186/0. 1998-99, 80/0. 1999-00, 167/0. 2000-01, 139/0. Totals, 1264/0.

NBA PLAYOFF RECORD

Season Team	G	Min.	FGM	FGA	Pct.	FTM	FTA	Pct.	Off.	Def.	Tot.	Ast.	St.	Blk.	TO	Pts.	RPG	APG	PPG
98-99—Portland	13	265	26	72	.361	38	42	.905	8	22	30	19	7	1	18	95	2.3	1.5	7.3

Three-point field goals: 1998-99, 5-for-18 (.278).
Personal fouls/disqualifications: 1998-99, 26/0.

JACKSON, MARC   F/C

PERSONAL: Born January 16, 1975, in Philadelphia. ... 6-10/270. (2,08/122,5). ... Full Name: Marc Anthony Jackson.
HIGH SCHOOL: Roman Catholic (Philadelphia).
COLLEGE: Virginia Commonwealth, then Temple.
TRANSACTIONS/CAREER NOTES: Selected after junior season by Golden State Warriors in second round (38th pick overall) of 1997 NBA Draft. ... Played in Turkey (1997-98). ... Played in Spain (1998-99 and 1999-2000).

COLLEGIATE RECORD

Season Team	G	Min.	FGM	FGA	Pct.	FTM	FTA	Pct.	Reb.	Ast.	Pts.	RPG	APG	PPG
93-94—Virginia Commonwealth	22	277	23	52	.442	12	21	.571	67	9	58	3.0	0.4	2.6
94-95—Temple						Did not play—transfer student.								
95-96—Temple	32	1117	183	384	.477	133	199	.668	287	24	501	9.0	0.8	15.7
96-97—Temple	31	1201	175	366	.478	148	193	.767	278	38	500	9.0	1.2	16.1
Totals	85	2595	381	802	.475	293	413	.709	632	71	1059	7.4	0.8	12.5

Three-point field goals: 1995-96, 2-for-4 (.500). 1996-97, 2-for-6 (.333). Totals, 4-for-10 (.400).

TURKISH LEAGUE RECORD

Season Team	G	Min.	FGM	FGA	Pct.	FTM	FTA	Pct.	Reb.	Ast.	Pts.	RPG	APG	PPG
97-98—Tofas Bursa	27	...	179	316	.566	155	206	.752	293	39	518	10.9	1.4	19.2

Three-point field goals: 1997-98, 7-for-15 (.467).

SPANISH LEAGUE RECORD

Season Team	G	Min.	FGM	FGA	Pct.	FTM	FTA	Pct.	Reb.	Ast.	Pts.	RPG	APG	PPG
98-99—Lobos Caja Cantabria	14	505	119	254	.469	60	79	.759	130	27	298	9.3	1.9	21.3
99-00—Cantabria Lobos	23	852	156	315	.495	108	168	.643	192	27	427	8.3	1.2	18.6
Totals	37	1357	275	569	.483	168	247	.680	322	54	725	8.7	1.5	19.6

Three-point field goals: 1998-99, 0-for-9. 1999-00, 7-for-17 (.412). Totals, 7-for-26 (.269).

NBA REGULAR-SEASON RECORD

HONORS: NBA All-Rookie first team (2001).

Season Team	G	Min.	FGM	FGA	Pct.	FTM	FTA	Pct.	Off.	Def.	Tot.	Ast.	St.	Blk.	TO	Pts.	RPG	APG	PPG
00-01—Golden State	48	1410	237	508	.467	154	192	.802	119	242	361	59	34	27	93	633	7.5	1.2	13.2

Three-point field goals: 2000-01, 5-for-23 (.217).
Personal fouls/disqualifications: 2000-01, 138/1.

JACKSON, MARK   G   KNICKS

PERSONAL: Born April 1, 1965, in Brooklyn, N.Y. ... 6-3/205. (1,91/93,0). ... Full Name: Mark A. Jackson.
HIGH SCHOOL: Bishop Loughlin Memorial (Brooklyn, N.Y.).
COLLEGE: St. John's.
TRANSACTIONS/CAREER NOTES: Selected by New York Knicks in first round (18th pick overall) of 1987 NBA Draft. ... Traded by Knicks with 1995 second-round draft choice to Los Angeles Clippers in three-way deal in which Clippers also received C Stanley Roberts from Orlando Magic, Knicks received G Doc Rivers, F Charles Smith and G Bo Kimble from Clippers and Magic received 1993 first-round draft choice from Knicks and 1994 first-round draft choice from Clippers (September 22, 1992). ... Traded by Clippers with draft rights to G Greg Minor to Indiana Pacers for G Pooh Richardson, F Malik Sealy and draft rights to F Eric Piatkowski (June 30, 1994). ... Traded by Pacers with G Ricky Pierce and 1996 first-round draft choice to Denver Nuggets for G Jalen Rose, F Reggie Williams and 1996 first-round draft choice (June 13, 1996). ... Traded by Nuggets with F/C LaSalle Thompson to Pacers for G Vincent Askew, F Eddie Johnson and 1997 and 1998 second-round draft choices (February 20, 1997). ... Signed as free agent by Toronto Raptors (August 11, 2000). ... Traded by Raptors with G Muggsy Bogues to Knicks for G Chris Childs and 2001 first-round draft choice (February 22, 2001).

COLLEGIATE RECORD

NOTES: THE SPORTING NEWS All-America second team (1987). ... Led NCAA Division I with 9.11 assists per game (1986).

Season Team	G	Min.	FGM	FGA	Pct.	FTM	FTA	Pct.	Reb.	Ast.	Pts.	RPG	APG	PPG
83-84—St. John's	30	855	61	106	.575	53	77	.688	59	108	175	2.0	3.6	5.8
84-85—St. John's	35	601	57	101	.564	66	91	.725	44	109	180	1.3	3.1	5.1
85-86—St. John's	36	1340	151	316	.478	105	142	.739	125	328	407	3.5	9.1	11.3
86-87—St. John's	30	1184	196	389	.504	125	155	.806	110	193	566	3.7	6.4	18.9
Totals	131	3980	465	912	.510	349	465	.751	338	738	1328	2.6	5.6	10.1

Three-point field goals: 1986-87, 49-for-117 (.419).

NBA REGULAR-SEASON RECORD

RECORDS: Holds single-season record for most assists by a rookie—868 (1988).
HONORS: NBA Rookie of the Year (1988). ... NBA All-Rookie team (1988).

Season Team	G	Min.	FGM	FGA	Pct.	FTM	FTA	Pct.	REBOUNDS Off.	Def.	Tot.	Ast.	St.	Blk.	TO	Pts.	AVERAGES RPG	APG	PPG
87-88—New York	82	3249	438	1013	.432	206	266	.774	120	276	396	868	205	6	258	1114	4.8	10.6	13.6
88-89—New York	72	2477	479	1025	.467	180	258	.698	106	235	341	619	139	7	226	1219	4.7	8.6	16.9
89-90—New York	82	2428	327	749	.437	120	165	.727	106	212	318	604	109	4	211	809	3.9	7.4	9.9
90-91—New York	72	1595	250	508	.492	117	160	.731	62	135	197	452	60	9	135	630	2.7	6.3	8.8
91-92—New York	81	2461	367	747	.491	171	222	.770	95	210	305	694	112	13	211	916	3.8	8.6	11.3
92-93—L.A. Clippers	82	3117	459	945	.486	241	300	.803	129	259	388	724	136	12	220	1181	4.7	8.8	14.4
93-94—L.A. Clippers	79	2711	331	732	.452	167	211	.791	107	241	348	678	120	6	232	865	4.4	8.6	10.9
94-95—Indiana	82	2402	239	566	.422	119	153	.778	73	233	306	616	105	16	210	624	3.7	7.5	7.6
95-96—Indiana	81	2643	296	626	.473	150	191	.785	66	241	307	635	100	5	201	806	3.8	7.8	10.0
96-97—Denver-Ind.	82	3054	289	679	.426	168	213	.789	91	304	395	*935	97	12	274	812	4.8	*11.4	9.9
97-98—Indiana	82	2413	249	598	.416	137	180	.761	67	255	322	713	84	2	174	678	3.9	8.7	8.3
98-99—Indiana	49	1382	138	329	.419	65	79	.823	33	151	184	386	42	3	99	373	3.8	7.9	7.6
99-00—Indiana	81	2190	246	570	.432	79	98	.806	63	233	296	650	76	10	174	660	3.7	8.0	8.1
00-01—Tor.-N.Y.	*83	2588	244	583	.419	73	93	.785	63	242	305	661	84	7	175	631	3.7	8.0	7.6
Totals	1090	34710	4352	9670	.450	1993	2589	.770	1181	3227	4408	9235	1469	112	2800	11318	4.0	8.5	10.4

Three-point field goals: 1987-88, 32-for-126 (.254). 1988-89, 81-for-240 (.338). 1989-90, 35-for-131 (.267). 1990-91, 13-for-51 (.255). 1991-92, 11-for-43 (.256). 1992-93, 22-for-82 (.268). 1993-94, 36-for-127 (.283). 1994-95, 27-for-87 (.310). 1995-96, 64-for-149 (.430). 1996-97, 66-for-178 (.371). 1997-98, 43-for-137 (.314). 1998-99, 32-for-103 (.311). 1999-00, 89-for-221 (.403). 2000-01, 70-for-207 (.338). Totals, 621-for-1882 (.330).
Personal fouls/disqualifications: 1987-88, 244/2. 1988-89, 163/1. 1989-90, 121/0. 1990-91, 81/0. 1991-92, 153/0. 1992-93, 158/0. 1993-94, 115/0. 1994-95, 148/0. 1995-96, 153/0. 1996-97, 161/0. 1997-98, 132/0. 1998-99, 58/0. 1999-00, 111/0. 2000-01, 139/0. Totals, 1937/3.

NBA PLAYOFF RECORD

Season Team	G	Min.	FGM	FGA	Pct.	FTM	FTA	Pct.	REBOUNDS Off.	Def.	Tot.	Ast.	St.	Blk.	TO	Pts.	AVERAGES RPG	APG	PPG
87-88—New York	4	171	22	60	.367	8	11	.727	6	13	19	39	10	0	14	57	4.8	9.8	14.3
88-89—New York	9	336	51	100	.510	19	28	.679	7	24	31	91	10	3	28	132	3.4	10.1	14.7
89-90—New York	9	81	13	31	.419	8	11	.727	1	4	5	21	2	0	7	34	0.6	2.3	3.8
90-91—New York	3	36	1	3	.333	0	0	...	0	0	0	8	1	1	5	2	0.0	2.7	0.7
91-92—New York	12	368	37	92	.402	22	27	.815	12	15	27	86	10	0	30	100	2.3	7.2	8.3
92-93—L.A. Clippers	5	188	28	64	.438	19	22	.864	8	21	29	38	8	1	13	76	5.8	7.6	15.2
94-95—Indiana	17	553	59	130	.454	34	46	.739	27	62	89	121	15	0	41	168	5.2	7.1	9.9
95-96—Indiana	5	186	18	51	.353	13	17	.765	3	22	25	30	6	0	13	53	5.0	6.0	10.6
97-98—Indiana	16	494	53	127	.417	27	34	.794	18	55	73	133	23	0	47	147	4.6	8.3	9.2
98-99—Indiana	13	451	51	103	.495	30	42	.714	14	45	59	112	14	1	35	146	4.5	8.6	11.2
99-00—Indiana	23	634	69	176	.392	28	31	.903	12	74	86	178	19	2	43	187	3.7	7.7	8.1
00-01—New York	5	156	20	40	.500	3	3	1.000	3	23	26	26	8	0	10	45	5.2	5.2	9.0
Totals	121	3654	422	977	.432	211	272	.776	111	358	469	883	126	8	286	1147	3.9	7.3	9.5

Three-point field goals: 1987-88, 5-for-12 (.417). 1988-89, 11-for-28 (.393). 1989-90, 0-for-2. 1991-92, 4-for-21 (.190). 1992-93, 1-for-2 (.500). 1994-95, 16-for-40 (.400). 1995-96, 4-for-18 (.222). 1997-98, 14-for-37 (.378). 1998-99, 14-for-34 (.412). 1999-00, 21-for-67 (.313). 2000-01, 2-for-8 (.250). Totals, 92-for-269 (.342).
Personal fouls/disqualifications: 1987-88, 13/0. 1988-89, 9/0. 1989-90, 5/0. 1990-91, 1/0. 1991-92, 26/0. 1992-93, 8/0. 1994-95, 34/0. 1995-96, 9/0. 1997-98, 28/0. 1998-99, 32/0. 1999-00, 42/0. 2000-01, 6/0. Totals, 213/0.

NBA ALL-STAR GAME RECORD

Season Team	Min.	FGM	FGA	Pct.	FTM	FTA	Pct.	REBOUNDS Off.	Def.	Tot.	Ast.	PF	Dq.	St.	Blk.	TO	Pts.
1989 —New York	16	3	5	.600	2	4	.500	1	1	2	4	1	0	1	1	2	9

Three-point field goals: 1989, 1-for-1.

JACKSON, STEPHEN   G/F   SPURS

PERSONAL: Born April 5, 1978, in Houston. ... 6-8/218. (2,03/98,9). ... Full Name: Stephen Jesse Jackson.
HIGH SCHOOL: Oak Hill Academy (Mouth of Wilson, Va.).
JUNIOR COLLEGE: Butler County Community College, Kan. (did not play basketball).
TRANSACTIONS/CAREER NOTES: Selected after freshman season by Phoenix Suns in second round (43rd pick overall) of 1997 NBA Draft. ... Waived by Suns (October 30, 1997). ... Played in Continental Basketball Association with La Crosse Bobcats (1997-98) and Fort Wayne Fury (1999-2000). ... Played in Venezuela (1999-2000). ... Signed as free agent by Vancouver Grizzlies (October 4, 1999). ... Waived by Grizzlies (October 28, 1999). ... Signed as free agent by New Jersey Nets (October 2, 2000). ... Signed as free agent by San Antonio Spurs (August 2, 2001).

CBA REGULAR-SEASON RECORD

Season Team	G	Min.	FGM	FGA	Pct.	FTM	FTA	Pct.	Reb.	Ast.	Pts.	RPG	APG	PPG
97-98—La Crosse	6	76	8	20	.400	0	0	...	2	4	16	0.3	0.7	2.7
99-00—Fort Wayne	5	84	12	31	.387	2	3	.667	8	5	26	1.6	1.0	5.2
Totals	11	160	20	51	.392	2	3	.667	10	9	42	0.9	0.8	3.8

Three-point field goals: 1997-98, 0-for-1. 1999-00, 0-for-2. Totals, 0-for-3 (.000).

VENEZUELAN LEAGUE RECORD

Season Team	G	Min.	FGM	FGA	Pct.	FTM	FTA	Pct.	Reb.	Ast.	Pts.	RPG	APG	PPG
99-00—Marinos	50	1776	437	756	.578	191	265	.721	143	197	1153	2.9	3.9	23.1

Three-point field goals: 1999-00, 88-for-199 (.442).

NBA REGULAR-SEASON RECORD

Season Team	G	Min.	FGM	FGA	Pct.	FTM	FTA	Pct.	Off.	Def.	Tot.	Ast.	St.	Blk.	TO	Pts.	RPG	APG	PPG
00-01—New Jersey	77	1660	243	572	.425	97	135	.719	41	167	208	140	86	14	130	635	2.7	1.8	8.2

Three-point field goals: 2000-01, 52-for-155 (.335).
Personal fouls/disqualifications: 2000-01, 166/2.

JACOBSON, SAM   G/F

PERSONAL: Born July 22, 1975, in Cottage Grove, Minn. ... 6-4/219. (1,93/99,3). ... Full Name: Samuel Ryan Jacobson.
HIGH SCHOOL: Park-Cottage Grove (Minn.).
COLLEGE: Minnesota.
TRANSACTIONS/CAREER NOTES: Selected by Los Angeles Lakers in first round (26th pick overall) of 1998 NBA Draft. ... Waived by Lakers (November 12, 1999). ... Signed by Golden State Warriors to the first of two consecutive 10-day contracts (January 11, 2000). ... Re-signed by Warriors for remainder of season (January 31, 2000). ... Signed as free agent by Minnesota Timberwolves (October 17, 2000).

COLLEGIATE RECORD

Season Team	G	Min.	FGM	FGA	Pct.	FTM	FTA	Pct.	Reb.	Ast.	Pts.	RPG	APG	PPG
94-95—Minnesota	31	589	92	198	.465	38	57	.667	149	37	239	4.8	1.2	7.7
95-96—Minnesota	32	853	143	347	.412	75	95	.789	154	64	408	4.8	2.0	12.8
96-97—Minnesota	35	847	188	411	.457	43	67	.642	158	58	480	4.5	1.7	13.7
97-98—Minnesota	32	995	215	505	.426	104	143	.727	165	57	582	5.2	1.8	18.2
Totals	130	3284	638	1461	.437	260	362	.718	626	216	1709	4.8	1.7	13.1

Three-point field goals: 1994-95, 17-for-53 (.321). 1995-96, 47-for-118 (.398). 1996-97, 61-for-155 (.394). 1997-98, 48-for-148 (.324). Totals, 173-for-474 (.365).

NBA REGULAR-SEASON RECORD

Season Team	G	Min.	FGM	FGA	Pct.	FTM	FTA	Pct.	Off.	Def.	Tot.	Ast.	St.	Blk.	TO	Pts.	RPG	APG	PPG
98-99—L.A. Lakers	2	12	3	5	.600	2	2	1.000	0	3	3	0	0	0	1	8	1.5	0.0	4.0
99-00—L.A.L.-G.S.	52	681	108	212	.509	30	41	.732	25	46	71	32	30	3	33	255	1.4	0.6	4.9
00-01—Minnesota	14	59	9	18	.500	2	3	.667	3	3	6	4	3	0	0	20	0.4	0.3	1.4
Totals	68	752	120	235	.511	34	46	.739	28	52	80	36	33	3	34	283	1.2	0.5	4.2

Three-point field goals: 1998-99, 0-for-1. 1999-00, 9-for-24 (.375). Totals, 9-for-25 (.360).
Personal fouls/disqualifications: 1998-99, 2/0. 1999-00, 113/3. 2000-01, 19/0. Totals, 134/3.

JAMES, TIM   F   HORNETS

PERSONAL: Born December 25, 1976, in Miami. ... 6-7/214. (2,01/97,1). ... Full Name: Tim O'Connor James.
HIGH SCHOOL: Miami Northwestern.
COLLEGE: Miami (Fla.).
TRANSACTIONS/CAREER NOTES: Selected by Miami Heat in first round (25th pick overall) of 1999 NBA Draft. ... Traded by Heat with F P.J. Brown, F Jamal Mashburn, F/C Otis Thorpe, F Tim James and G/F Rodney Buford to Charlotte Hornets for G Eddie Jones, F Anthony Mason, G Ricky Davis and G/F Dale Ellis (August 1, 2000).

COLLEGIATE RECORD

Season Team	G	Min.	FGM	FGA	Pct.	FTM	FTA	Pct.	Reb.	Ast.	Pts.	RPG	APG	PPG
95-96—Miami (Fla.)	28	625	117	221	.529	46	85	.541	151	12	282	5.4	0.4	10.1
96-97—Miami (Fla.)	29	900	165	380	.434	73	120	.608	196	35	405	6.8	1.2	14.0
97-98—Miami (Fla.)	28	890	184	379	.485	97	144	.674	263	12	469	9.4	0.4	16.8
98-99—Miami (Fla.)	30	956	215	451	.477	115	165	.697	246	24	557	8.2	0.8	18.6
Totals	115	3371	681	1431	.476	331	514	.644	856	83	1713	7.4	0.7	14.9

Three-point field goals: 1995-96, 2-for-6 (.333). 1996-97, 2-for-8 (.250). 1997-98, 4-for-17 (.235). 1998-99, 12-for-41 (.293). Totals, 20-for-72 (.278).

NBA REGULAR-SEASON RECORD

								REBOUNDS								AVERAGES		
Season Team	G	Min.	FGM	FGA	Pct.	FTM	FTA	Pct.	Off.	Def.	Tot.	Ast.	St.	Blk.	TO	Pts.	RPG	APG	PPG
99-00—Miami	4	23	5	14	.357	1	3	.333	3	1	4	2	0	3	2	11	1.0	0.5	2.8
00-01—Charlotte	30	197	16	52	.308	12	14	.857	15	20	35	8	2	5	8	45	1.2	0.3	1.5
Totals	34	220	21	66	.318	13	17	.765	18	21	39	10	2	8	10	56	1.1	0.3	1.6

Three-point field goals: 2000-01, 1-for-3 (.333). Totals, 1-for-3 (.333).
Personal fouls/disqualifications: 1999-00, 1/0. 2000-01, 27/0. Totals, 28/0.

JAMISON, ANTAWN　　　F　　　WARRIORS

PERSONAL: Born June 12, 1976, in Shreveport, La. ... 6-9/223. (2,06/101,2). ... Full Name: Antawn Cortez Jamison.
HIGH SCHOOL: Providence (Charlotte).
COLLEGE: North Carolina.
TRANSACTIONS/CAREER NOTES: Selected after junior season by Toronto Raptors in first round (fourth pick overall) of 1998 NBA Draft. ... Draft rights traded by Raptors to Golden State Warriors for draft rights to G Vince Carter and cash (June 24, 1998).

COLLEGIATE RECORD

NOTES: THE SPORTING NEWS College Player of the Year (1998). ... Naismith Award winner (1998). ... Wooden Award winner (1998). ... THE SPORTING NEWS All-America first team (1998). ... THE SPORTING NEWS All-America second team (1997).

												AVERAGES		
Season Team	G	Min.	FGM	FGA	Pct.	FTM	FTA	Pct.	Reb.	Ast.	Pts.	RPG	APG	PPG
95-96—North Carolina	32	1052	201	322	.624	82	156	.526	309	33	484	9.7	1.0	15.1
96-97—North Carolina	35	1199	270	496	.544	126	203	.621	329	30	668	9.4	0.9	19.1
97-98—North Carolina	37	1227	316	546	.579	184	276	.667	389	30	822	10.5	0.8	22.2
Totals	104	3478	787	1364	.577	392	635	.617	1027	93	1974	9.9	0.9	19.0

Three-point field goals: 1995-96, 0-for-1. 1996-97, 2-for-11 (.182). 1997-98, 6-for-15 (.400). Totals, 8-for-27 (.296).

NBA REGULAR-SEASON RECORD

HONORS: NBA All-Rookie second team (1999).

								REBOUNDS								AVERAGES		
Season Team	G	Min.	FGM	FGA	Pct.	FTM	FTA	Pct.	Off.	Def.	Tot.	Ast.	St.	Blk.	TO	Pts.	RPG	APG	PPG
98-99—Golden State	47	1058	178	394	.452	90	153	.588	131	170	301	34	38	16	68	449	6.4	0.7	9.6
99-00—Golden State	43	1556	356	756	.471	127	208	.611	172	187	359	90	30	15	113	841	8.3	2.1	19.6
00-01—Golden State	82	3394	800	1812	.442	382	534	.715	280	435	715	164	114	28	199	2044	8.7	2.0	24.9
Totals	172	6008	1334	2962	.450	599	895	.669	583	792	1375	288	182	59	380	3334	8.0	1.7	19.4

Three-point field goals: 1998-99, 3-for-10 (.300). 1999-00, 2-for-7 (.286). 2000-01, 62-for-205 (.302). Totals, 67-for-222 (.302).
Personal fouls/disqualifications: 1998-99, 102/1. 1999-00, 115/0. 2000-01, 225/2. Totals, 442/3.

JOHNSON, ANTHONY　　　G

PERSONAL: Born October 10, 1974, in Charleston, S.C. ... 6-3/190. (1,91/86,2). ... Full Name: Anthony Mark Johnson.
HIGH SCHOOL: Stall (Charleston, S.C.).
COLLEGE: College of Charleston.
TRANSACTIONS/CAREER NOTES: Selected by Sacramento Kings in second round (40th pick overall) of 1997 NBA Draft. ... Signed as free agent by Atlanta Hawks (January 21, 1999). ... Traded by Hawks to Orlando Magic for condidtional second-round draft choice (February 24, 2000). ... Signed as free agent by Hawks (August 21, 2000). ... Traded by Hawks with G Jim Jackson and F/G Larry Robinson to Cleveland Cavaliers for G Brevin Knight (January 2, 2001).

COLLEGIATE RECORD

												AVERAGES		
Season Team	G	Min.	FGM	FGA	Pct.	FTM	FTA	Pct.	Reb.	Ast.	Pts.	RPG	APG	PPG
92-93—College of Charleston	27	273	23	58	.397	37	52	.712	44	30	84	1.6	1.1	3.1
93-94—College of Charleston						Did not play—redshirted.								
94-95—College of Charleston	29	490	34	87	.391	22	34	.647	53	68	100	1.8	2.3	3.4
95-96—College of Charleston	29	946	119	259	.459	65	97	.670	92	193	329	3.2	6.7	11.3
96-97—College of Charleston	32	1138	158	313	.505	100	126	.794	113	229	446	3.5	7.2	13.9
Totals	117	2847	334	717	.466	224	309	.725	302	520	959	2.6	4.4	8.2

Three-point field goals: 1992-93, 1-for-3 (.333). 1994-95, 10-for-25 (.400). 1995-96, 26-for-64 (.406). 1996-97, 30-for-74 (.405). Totals, 67-for-166 (.404).

NBA REGULAR-SEASON RECORD

								REBOUNDS								AVERAGES		
Season Team	G	Min.	FGM	FGA	Pct.	FTM	FTA	Pct.	Off.	Def.	Tot.	Ast.	St.	Blk.	TO	Pts.	RPG	APG	PPG
97-98—Sacramento	77	2266	226	609	.371	80	110	.727	51	120	171	329	64	6	120	574	2.2	4.3	7.5
98-99—Atlanta	49	885	91	225	.404	57	82	.695	16	59	75	107	35	7	65	244	1.5	2.2	5.0
99-00—Atlanta-Orl.	56	637	62	164	.378	28	39	.718	21	30	51	72	33	4	32	154	0.9	1.3	2.8
00-01—Atlanta-Cleve.	53	511	53	152	.349	23	33	.697	10	34	44	78	23	6	34	130	0.8	1.5	2.5
Totals	235	4299	432	1150	.376	188	264	.712	98	243	341	586	155	23	251	1102	1.5	2.5	4.7

Three-point field goals: 1997-98, 42-for-128 (.328). 1998-99, 5-for-19 (.263). 1999-00, 2-for-11 (.182). 2000-01, 1-for-5 (.200). Totals, 50-for-163 (.307).
Personal fouls/disqualifications: 1997-98, 188/1. 1998-99, 67/0. 1999-00, 58/0. 2000-01, 62/0. Totals, 375/1.

NBA PLAYOFF RECORD

								REBOUNDS								AVERAGES		
Season Team	G	Min.	FGM	FGA	Pct.	FTM	FTA	Pct.	Off.	Def.	Tot.	Ast.	St.	Blk.	TO	Pts.	RPG	APG	PPG
98-99—Atlanta	9	111	8	29	.276	7	10	.700	3	6	9	10	1	1	5	24	1.0	1.1	2.7

Three-point field goals: 1998-99, 1-for-2 (.500).
Personal fouls/disqualifications: 1998-99, 9/0.

JOHNSON, AVERY　　　　G　　　　NUGGETS

PERSONAL: Born March 25, 1965, in New Orleans. ... 5-11/180. (1,80/81,6).
HIGH SCHOOL: St. Augustine (New Orleans).
JUNIOR COLLEGE: New Mexico Junior College.
COLLEGE: Cameron (Okla.), then Southern (La.).
TRANSACTIONS/CAREER NOTES: Not drafted by an NBA franchise. ... Played in United States Basketball League with Palm Beach Stingrays (1988). ... Signed as free agent by Seattle SuperSonics (August 2, 1988). ... Traded by SuperSonics to Denver Nuggets for 1997 second-round draft choice (October 24, 1990). ... Waived by Nuggets (December 24, 1990). ... Signed as free agent by San Antonio Spurs (January 17, 1991). ... Waived by Spurs (December 17, 1991). ... Signed by Houston Rockets to first of two consecutive 10-day contracts (January 10, 1992). ... Re-signed by Rockets for remainder of season (January 31, 1992). ... Signed as free agent by Spurs (November 19, 1992). ... Signed as free agent by Golden State Warriors (October 25, 1993). ... Signed as unrestricted free agent by Spurs (July 21, 1994). ... Signed as free agent by Nuggets (July 18, 2001).
MISCELLANEOUS: Member of NBA championship team (1999). ... San Antonio Spurs all-time assist leader with 4,474 (1990-91 through 1992-93, and 1994-95 through 2000-01).

COLLEGIATE RECORD

NOTES: Holds NCAA Division I career record for highest assists-per-game average—12.0. ... Holds NCAA Division I single-season record for highest assists-per-game average—13.3 (1988). ... Shares NCAA Division I single-game record for most assists—22 (January 25, 1988, vs. Texas Southern). ... Led NCAA Division I with 10.74 assists per game (1987) and 13.30 assists per game (1988).

													AVERAGES		
Season Team	G	Min.	FGM	FGA	Pct.	FTM	FTA	Pct.	Reb.	Ast.	Pts.		RPG	APG	PPG
83-84—New Mexico J.C.	26	583	66	102	.647	28	39	.718	30	159	160		1.2	6.1	6.2
84-85—Cameron	33	...	54	106	.509	34	55	.618	31	111	142		0.9	3.4	4.3
85-86—Southern						Did not play—transfer student.									
86-87—Southern	31	1111	86	196	.439	40	65	.615	73	333	219		2.4	10.7	7.1
87-88—Southern	30	1145	138	257	.537	44	64	.688	84	399	342		2.8	13.3	11.4
4-Year-College Totals	94	...	278	559	.497	118	184	.641	188	843	703		2.0	9.0	7.5

Three-point field goals: 1986-87, 7-for-24 (.292). 1987-88, 22-for-47 (.468). Totals, 29-for-71 (.408).

NBA REGULAR-SEASON RECORD

HONORS: NBA Sportsmanship Award (1998).

									REBOUNDS								AVERAGES		
Season Team	G	Min.	FGM	FGA	Pct.	FTM	FTA	Pct.	Off.	Def.	Tot.	Ast.	St.	Blk.	TO	Pts.	RPG	APG	PPG
88-89—Seattle	43	291	29	83	.349	9	16	.563	11	13	24	73	21	3	18	68	0.6	1.7	1.6
89-90—Seattle	53	575	55	142	.387	29	40	.725	21	22	43	162	26	1	48	140	0.8	3.1	2.6
90-91—Denver-San Ant.	68	959	130	277	.469	59	87	.678	22	55	77	230	47	4	74	320	1.1	3.4	4.7
91-92—S.A.-Hou.	69	1235	158	330	.479	66	101	.653	13	67	80	266	61	9	110	386	1.2	3.9	5.6
92-93—San Antonio	75	2030	256	510	.502	144	182	.791	20	126	146	561	85	16	145	656	1.9	7.5	8.7
93-94—Golden State ...	82	2332	356	724	.492	178	253	.704	41	135	176	433	113	8	172	890	2.1	5.3	10.9
94-95—San Antonio	82	3011	448	863	.519	202	295	.685	49	159	208	670	114	13	207	1101	2.5	8.2	13.4
95-96—San Antonio	82	3084	438	887	.494	189	262	.721	37	169	206	789	119	21	195	1071	2.5	9.6	13.1
96-97—San Antonio	76	2472	327	685	.477	140	203	.690	32	115	147	513	96	15	146	800	1.9	6.8	10.5
97-98—San Antonio	75	2674	321	671	.478	122	168	.726	30	120	150	591	84	18	165	766	2.0	7.9	10.2
98-99—San Antonio	50	1672	218	461	.473	50	88	.568	22	96	118	369	51	11	112	487	2.4	7.4	9.7
99-00—San Antonio	82	2571	402	850	.473	114	155	.735	33	125	158	491	76	18	140	919	1.9	6.0	11.2
00-01—San Antonio	55	1290	134	300	.447	41	60	.683	21	64	85	237	33	4	60	310	1.5	4.3	5.6
Totals	892	24196	3272	6783	.482	1343	1910	.703	352	1266	1618	5385	926	141	1592	7914	1.8	6.0	8.9

Three-point field goals: 1988-89, 1-for-9 (.111). 1989-90, 1-for-4 (.250). 1990-91, 1-for-9 (.111). 1991-92, 4-for-15 (.267). 1992-93, 0-for-8. 1993-94, 0-for-12. 1994-95, 3-for-22 (.136). 1995-96, 6-for-31 (.194). 1996-97, 6-for-26 (.231). 1997-98, 2-for-13 (.154). 1998-99, 1-for-12 (.083). 1999-00, 1-for-9 (.111). 2000-01, 1-for-6 (.167). Totals, 27-for-176 (.153).

Personal fouls/disqualifications: 1988-89, 34/0. 1989-90, 55/0. 1990-91, 62/0. 1991-92, 89/1. 1992-93, 141/0. 1993-94, 160/0. 1994-95, 154/0. 1995-96, 179/1. 1996-97, 158/1. 1997-98, 140/0. 1998-99, 101/0. 1999-00, 150/0. 2000-01, 90/0. Totals, 1513/3.

NBA PLAYOFF RECORD

									REBOUNDS								AVERAGES		
Season Team	G	Min.	FGM	FGA	Pct.	FTM	FTA	Pct.	Off.	Def.	Tot.	Ast.	St.	Blk.	TO	Pts.	RPG	APG	PPG
88-89—Seattle	6	31	5	12	.417	1	2	.500	2	2	4	5	4	0	0	11	0.7	0.8	1.8
90-91—San Antonio	3	19	0	5	.000	2	2	1.000	0	0	0	4	1	0	0	2	0.0	1.3	0.7
92-93—San Antonio	10	314	36	70	.514	10	14	.714	8	23	31	81	10	1	23	82	3.1	8.1	8.2
93-94—Golden State ...	3	41	9	17	.529	0	0	...	0	3	3	10	4	1	3	18	1.0	3.3	6.0
94-95—San Antonio	15	575	91	176	.517	36	58	.621	9	23	32	125	20	6	30	218	2.1	8.3	14.5
95-96—San Antonio	10	407	52	121	.430	19	27	.704	6	30	36	94	20	1	24	123	3.6	9.4	12.3
97-98—San Antonio	9	342	61	101	.604	34	51	.667	3	10	13	55	9	0	21	156	1.4	6.1	17.3
98-99—San Antonio	17	653	91	187	.487	32	47	.681	9	33	42	126	20	1	50	215	2.5	7.4	12.6
99-00—San Antonio	4	144	19	42	.452	10	14	.714	2	7	9	21	4	0	10	48	2.3	5.3	12.0
00-01—San Antonio	13	281	34	88	.386	8	15	.533	3	13	16	41	10	1	10	76	1.2	3.2	5.8
Totals	90	2807	398	819	.486	152	230	.661	42	144	186	562	102	11	171	949	2.1	6.2	10.5

Three-point field goals: 1988-89, 0-for-4. 1990-91, 0-for-1. 1992-93, 0-for-1. 1993-94, 0-for-1. 1994-95, 0-for-1. 1995-96, 0-for-2. 1997-98, 1998-99, 1-for-3 (.333). 2000-01, 0-for-1. Totals, 1-for-16 (.063).

Personal fouls/disqualifications: 1988-89, 1/0. 1990-91, 3/0. 1992-93, 27/0. 1993-94, 2/0. 1994-95, 29/0. 1995-96, 21/0. 1997-98, 27/0. 1998-99, 30/0. 1999-00, 10/0. 2000-01, 24/1. Totals, 174/1.

JOHNSON, DERMARR　　　　G　　　　HAWKS

PERSONAL: Born May 5, 1980, in Washington, D.C. ... 6-9/201. (2,06/91,2). ... Full Name: DerMarr Miles Johnson.
HIGH SCHOOL: Bladensburg (Md.), then Parkdale (Riverdale, Md.), then The Newport School (Kensington, Md.), then Maine Central Institute (Pittsfield, Maine).
COLLEGE: Cincinnati.
TRANSACTIONS/CAREER NOTES: Selected after freshman season by Atlanta Hawks in first round (sixth pick overall) of 2000 NBA Draft.

COLLEGIATE RECORD

												AVERAGES		
Season Team	G	Min.	FGM	FGA	Pct.	FTM	FTA	Pct.	Reb.	Ast.	Pts.	RPG	APG	PPG
99-00—Cincinnati	32	879	140	293	.478	70	95	.737	123	45	402	3.8	1.4	12.6

Three-point field goals: 1999-00, 52-for-140 (.371).

NBA REGULAR-SEASON RECORD

									REBOUNDS								AVERAGES		
Season Team	G	Min.	FGM	FGA	Pct.	FTM	FTA	Pct.	Off.	Def.	Tot.	Ast.	St.	Blk.	TO	Pts.	RPG	APG	PPG
00-01—Atlanta	78	1313	146	390	.374	64	87	.736	56	122	178	64	43	30	93	397	2.3	0.8	5.1

Three-point field goals: 2000-01, 41-for-127 (.323).
Personal fouls/disqualifications: 2000-01, 134/0.

JOHNSON, ERVIN   C   BUCKS

PERSONAL: Born December 21, 1967, in New Orleans. ... 6-11/255. (2,11/115,7). ... Full Name: Ervin Johnson Jr.
HIGH SCHOOL: Block (Jonesville, La.).
COLLEGE: New Orleans.
TRANSACTIONS/CAREER NOTES: Selected by Seattle SuperSonics in first round (23rd pick overall) of 1993 NBA Draft. ... Signed as free agent by Denver Nuggets (July 17, 1996). ... Traded by Nuggets to Milwaukee Bucks for F Johnny Newman, F/C Joe Wolf and draft rights to F Danny Fortson (June 25, 1997).

COLLEGIATE RECORD

												AVERAGES		
Season Team	G	Min.	FGM	FGA	Pct.	FTM	FTA	Pct.	Reb.	Ast.	Pts.	RPG	APG	PPG
88-89—New Orleans						Did not play—redshirted.									
89-90—New Orleans	32	757	84	145	.579	32	57	.561	218	29	200	6.8	0.9	6.3
90-91—New Orleans	30	899	162	283	.572	58	108	.537	367	34	382	12.2	1.1	12.7
91-92—New Orleans	32	1073	185	317	.584	122	171	.713	356	56	492	11.1	1.8	15.4
92-93—New Orleans	29	965	208	336	.619	118	175	.674	346	16	534	11.9	0.6	18.4
Totals	123	3694	639	1081	.591	330	511	.646	1287	135	1608	10.5	1.1	13.1

NBA REGULAR-SEASON RECORD

NOTES: Led NBA with 321 personal fouls (1998).

									REBOUNDS								AVERAGES		
Season Team	G	Min.	FGM	FGA	Pct.	FTM	FTA	Pct.	Off.	Def.	Tot.	Ast.	St.	Blk.	TO	Pts.	RPG	APG	PPG
93-94—Seattle	45	280	44	106	.415	29	46	.630	48	70	118	7	10	22	24	117	2.6	0.2	2.6
94-95—Seattle	64	907	85	192	.443	29	46	.630	101	188	289	16	17	67	54	199	4.5	0.3	3.1
95-96—Seattle	81	1519	180	352	.511	85	127	.669	129	304	433	48	40	129	98	446	5.3	0.6	5.5
96-97—Denver	82	2599	243	467	.520	96	156	.615	231	*682	913	71	65	227	118	582	11.1	0.9	7.1
97-98—Milwaukee	81	2261	253	471	.537	143	238	.601	242	443	685	59	79	158	117	649	8.5	0.7	8.0
98-99—Milwaukee	50	1027	96	189	.508	64	105	.610	120	200	320	19	29	57	47	256	6.4	0.4	5.1
99-00—Milwaukee	80	2129	144	279	.516	95	157	.605	233	415	648	44	81	127	80	383	8.1	0.6	4.8
00-01—Milwaukee	82	1981	108	198	.545	50	93	.538	205	408	613	40	44	97	47	266	7.5	0.5	3.2
Totals	565	12703	1153	2254	.512	591	968	.611	1309	2710	4019	304	365	884	585	2898	7.1	0.5	5.1

Three-point field goals: 1994-95, 0-for-1. 1995-96, 1-for-3 (.333). 1996-97, 0-for-2. 1999-00, 0-for-1. Totals, 1-for-7 (.143).
Personal fouls/disqualifications: 1993-94, 45/0. 1994-95, 163/1. 1995-96, 245/3. 1996-97, 288/5. 1997-98, 321/7. 1998-99, 151/1. 1999-00, 298/6. 2000-01, 257/4. Totals, 1768/27.

NBA PLAYOFF RECORD

									REBOUNDS								AVERAGES		
Season Team	G	Min.	FGM	FGA	Pct.	FTM	FTA	Pct.	Off.	Def.	Tot.	Ast.	St.	Blk.	TO	Pts.	RPG	APG	PPG
93-94—Seattle	2	8	0	1	.000	0	0		0	4	4	0	0	0	1	0	2.0	0.0	0.0
94-95—Seattle	4	54	4	14	.286	6	6	1.000	8	13	21	0	1	4	1	14	5.3	0.0	3.5
95-96—Seattle	18	253	23	62	.371	9	11	.818	28	42	70	7	6	15	14	55	3.9	0.4	3.1
98-99—Milwaukee	3	92	6	13	.462	1	2	.500	8	10	18	1	2	5	0	13	6.0	0.3	4.3
99-00—Milwaukee	5	155	10	20	.500	11	18	.611	14	35	49	2	6	6	3	31	9.8	0.4	6.2
00-01—Milwaukee	18	577	39	68	.574	20	32	.625	59	135	194	10	9	37	12	98	10.8	0.6	5.4
Totals	50	1139	82	178	.461	47	69	.681	117	239	356	20	24	67	31	211	7.1	0.4	4.2

Personal fouls/disqualifications: 1993-94, 1/0. 1994-95, 16/0. 1995-96, 45/0. 1998-99, 9/0. 1999-00, 19/0. 2000-01, 52/1. Totals, 142/1.

JOHNSON, LARRY   F   KNICKS

PERSONAL: Born March 14, 1969, in Tyler, Texas. ... 6-7/235. (2,01/106,6). ... Full Name: Larry Demetric Johnson.
HIGH SCHOOL: Skyline (Dallas).
JUNIOR COLLEGE: Odessa (Texas) College.
COLLEGE: UNLV.
TRANSACTIONS/CAREER NOTES: Selected by Charlotte Hornets in first round (first pick overall) of 1991 NBA Draft. ... Traded by Hornets to New York Knicks for F Anthony Mason and F Brad Lohaus (July 14, 1996).
MISCELLANEOUS: Member of gold-medal-winning U.S. World Championship team (1994). ... Charlotte Hornets all-time leading rebounder with 3,479 (1991-92 through 1995-96).

COLLEGIATE RECORD

NOTES: Member of NCAA Division I championship team (1990). ... THE SPORTING NEWS College Player of the Year (1991). ... Naismith Award winner (1991). ... Wooden Award winner (1991). ... THE SPORTING NEWS All-America first team (1990, 1991).

Season Team	G	Min.	FGM	FGA	Pct.	FTM	FTA	Pct.	Reb.	Ast.	Pts.	AVERAGES		
												RPG	APG	PPG
87-88—Odessa Junior College....	35	...	324	499	.649	131	167	.784	430	...	779	12.3	...	22.3
88-89—Odessa Junior College....	35	...	422	646	.653	196	258	.760	380	69	1043	10.9	2.0	29.8
89-90—UNLV	40	1259	304	487	.624	201	262	.767	457	84	822	11.4	2.1	20.6
90-91—UNLV	35	1113	308	465	.662	162	198	.818	380	104	795	10.9	3.0	22.7
Junior College Totals	70	...	746	1145	.652	327	425	.769	810	...	1822	11.6	...	26.0
4-Year-College Totals	75	2372	612	952	.643	363	460	.789	837	188	1617	11.2	2.5	21.6

Three-point field goals: 1987-88, 0-for-1. 1988-89, 3-for-11 (.273). 1989-90, 13-for-38 (.342). 1990-91, 17-for-48 (.354). Totals, 3-for-12 (.250) Totals, 30-for-86 (.349).

NBA REGULAR-SEASON RECORD

HONORS: NBA Rookie of the Year (1992). ... All-NBA second team (1993). ... NBA All-Rookie first team (1992).

Season Team	G	Min.	FGM	FGA	Pct.	FTM	FTA	Pct.	REBOUNDS			Ast.	St.	Blk.	TO	Pts.	AVERAGES		
									Off.	Def.	Tot.						RPG	APG	PPG
91-92—Charlotte	82	3047	616	1258	.490	339	409	.829	323	576	899	292	81	51	160	1576	11.0	3.6	19.2
92-93—Charlotte	82	*3323	728	1385	.526	336	438	.767	281	583	864	353	53	27	227	1810	10.5	4.3	22.1
93-94—Charlotte	51	1757	346	672	.515	137	197	.695	143	305	448	184	29	14	116	834	8.8	3.6	16.4
94-95—Charlotte	81	3234	585	1219	.480	274	354	.774	190	395	585	369	78	28	207	1525	7.2	4.6	18.8
95-96—Charlotte	81	3274	583	1225	.476	247	564	.757	249	434	683	355	55	43	182	1660	8.4	4.4	20.5
96-97—New York	76	2613	376	735	.512	190	274	.693	165	228	393	174	64	36	136	976	5.2	2.3	12.8
97-98—New York	70	2412	429	884	.485	214	283	.756	175	226	401	150	40	13	127	1087	5.7	2.1	15.5
98-99—New York	49	1639	210	458	.459	134	164	.817	91	193	284	119	34	10	89	587	5.8	2.4	12.0
99-00—New York	70	2281	282	652	.433	128	167	.766	87	293	380	175	42	7	94	750	5.4	2.5	10.7
00-01—New York	65	2105	246	598	.411	102	128	.797	90	273	363	127	39	29	97	645	5.6	2.0	9.9
Totals	707	25685	4401	9086	.484	2200	2978	.766	1794	3506	5300	2298	515	258	1435	11450	7.5	3.3	16.2

Three-point field goals: 1991-92, 5-for-22 (.227). 1992-93, 18-for-71 (.254). 1993-94, 5-for-21 (.238). 1994-95, 81-for-210 (.386). 1995-96, 67-for-183 (.366). 1996-97, 34-for-105 (.324). 1997-98, 15-for-63 (.238). 1998-99, 33-for-92 (.359). 1999-00, 58-for-174 (.333). 2000-01, 51-for-163 (.313). Totals, 367-for-1104 (.332).

Personal fouls/disqualifications: 1991-92, 225/3. 1992-93, 187/0. 1993-94, 131/0. 1994-95, 174/2. 1995-96, 173/0. 1996-97, 249/3. 1997-98, 193/2. 1998-99, 147/1. 1999-00, 205/1. 2000-01, 209/2. Totals, 1893/14.

NBA PLAYOFF RECORD

Season Team	G	Min.	FGM	FGA	Pct.	FTM	FTA	Pct.	REBOUNDS			Ast.	St.	Blk.	TO	Pts.	AVERAGES		
									Off.	Def.	Tot.						RPG	APG	PPG
92-93—Charlotte	9	348	68	122	.557	41	52	.788	19	43	62	30	5	2	19	178	6.9	3.3	19.8
94-95—Charlotte	4	172	31	65	.477	20	25	.800	10	13	23	11	4	2	6	83	5.8	2.8	20.8
96-97—New York	9	295	43	77	.558	32	38	.842	11	25	36	23	7	1	15	124	4.0	2.6	13.8
97-98—New York	8	310	52	107	.486	37	50	.740	25	28	53	13	10	3	25	143	6.6	1.6	17.9
98-99—New York	20	683	87	204	.426	31	46	.674	22	75	97	31	21	1	33	229	4.9	1.6	11.5
99-00—New York	16	589	70	152	.461	27	34	.794	15	65	80	26	8	2	23	180	5.0	1.6	11.3
Totals	66	2397	351	727	.483	188	245	.767	102	249	351	134	55	11	121	937	5.3	2.0	14.2

Three-point field goals: 1992-93, 1-for-4 (.250). 1994-95, 1-for-9 (.111). 1996-97, 6-for-17 (.353). 1997-98, 2-for-10 (.200). 1998-99, 24-for-82 (.293). 1999-00, 13-for-33 (.394). Totals, 47-for-155 (.303).

Personal fouls/disqualifications: 1992-93, 27/0. 1994-95, 7/0. 1996-97, 27/0. 1997-98, 30/0. 1998-99, 64/2. 1999-00, 47/1. Totals, 202/3.

NBA ALL-STAR GAME RECORD

Season Team	Min.	FGM	FGA	Pct.	FTM	FTA	Pct.	REBOUNDS			Ast.	PF	Dq.	St.	Blk.	TO	Pts.
								Off.	Def.	Tot.							
1993 —Charlotte	16	2	6	.333	0	0		3	1	4	0	1	0	0	0	0	4
1995 —Charlotte	20	2	3	.667	2	2	1.000	1	3	4	2	0	0	0	0	1	7
Totals	36	4	9	.444	2	2	1.000	4	4	8	2	1	0	0	0	1	11

Three-point field goals: 1995, 1-for-1. Totals, 1-for-1 (1.000).

JONES, DAMON   G

PERSONAL: Born August 25, 1976, in Galveston, Texas. ... 6-3/185. (1,91/83,9).
HIGH SCHOOL: Ball (Galveston, Texas).
COLLEGE: Houston.
TRANSACTIONS/CAREER NOTES: Not drafted by an NBA franchise. ... Played in International Basketball Association with Black Hills Posse (1997-98). ... Played in Continental Basketball Association with Idaho Stampede (1998-99). ... Signed as free agent by Orlando Magic (January 21, 1999). ... Waived by Magic (February 2, 1999). ... Signed as free agent by New Jersey Nets (February 16, 1999). ... Waived by Nets (March 8, 1999). ... Signed by Boston Celtics to first of two consecutive 10-day contracts (April 14, 1999). ... Re-signed by Celtics for remainder of season (May 4, 1999). ... Signed as free agent by Golden State Warriors (October 4, 1999). ... Waived by Warriors (November 30, 1999). ... Signed as free agent by Dallas Mavericks (December 2, 1999). ... Waived by Mavericks (January 5, 2000) Signed by Mavericks to first of two consecutive 10-day contracts (January 8, 2000). ... Re-signed by Mavericks for remainder of season (January 28, 2000). ... Signed as free agent by Vancouver Grizzlies (August 8, 2000).

COLLEGIATE RECORD

Season Team	G	Min.	FGM	FGA	Pct.	FTM	FTA	Pct.	Reb.	Ast.	Pts.	AVERAGES		
												RPG	APG	PPG
94-95—Houston	27	781	91	262	.347	40	64	.625	92	77	277	3.4	2.9	10.3
95-96—Houston	27	857	115	266	.432	34	51	.667	111	105	321	4.1	3.9	11.9
96-97—Houston	27	968	159	341	.466	55	78	.705	120	132	443	4.4	4.9	16.4
Totals	81	2606	365	869	.420	129	193	.668	323	314	1041	4.0	3.9	12.9

Three-point field goals: 1994-95, 55-for-168 (.327). 1995-96, 57-for-167 (.341). 1996-97, 70-for-186 (.376). Totals, 182-for-521 (.349).

IBA REGULAR-SEASON RECORD

Season Team	G	Min.	FGM	FGA	Pct.	FTM	FTA	Pct.	Reb.	Ast.	Pts.	AVERAGES		
												RPG	APG	PPG
97-98—Black Hills	34	726	148	330	.448	53	75	.707	84	115	423	2.5	3.4	12.4

Three-point field goals: 1997-98, 74-for-200 (.370).

CBA REGULAR-SEASON RECORD

NOTES: CBA Newcomer of the Year (1999). ... CBA All-League first team (1999). ... Led CBA with 120 three-point field goals made and 336 three-point field goals attempted (1999).

Season Team	G	Min.	FGM	FGA	Pct.	FTM	FTA	Pct.	Reb.	Ast.	Pts.	AVERAGES RPG	APG	PPG
98-99—Idaho	35	1400	269	645	.417	100	130	.769	137	222	758	3.9	6.3	21.7

Three-point field goals: 1998-99, 120-for-336 (.357).

NBA REGULAR-SEASON RECORD

Season Team	G	Min.	FGM	FGA	Pct.	FTM	FTA	Pct.	REBOUNDS Off.	Def.	Tot.	Ast.	St.	Blk.	TO	Pts.	AVERAGES RPG	APG	PPG
98-99—N.J.-Boston	24	344	43	119	.361	14	17	.824	6	38	44	42	13	0	17	125	1.8	1.8	5.2
99-00—G.S.-Dallas	55	612	80	208	.385	32	48	.667	12	43	55	96	18	1	40	233	1.0	1.7	4.2
00-01—Vancouver	71	1415	170	416	.409	37	52	.712	16	108	124	224	36	1	76	461	1.7	3.2	6.5
Totals	150	2371	293	743	.394	83	117	.709	34	189	223	362	67	2	133	819	1.5	2.4	5.5

Three-point field goals: 1998-99, 25-for-62 (.403). 1999-00, 41-for-114 (.360). 2000-01, 84-for-231 (.364). Totals, 150-for-407 (.369).
Personal fouls/disqualifications: 1998-99, 23/0. 1999-00, 34/0. 2000-01, 58/0. Totals, 115/0.

JONES, EDDIE   G   HEAT

PERSONAL: Born October 20, 1971, in Pompano Beach, Fla. ... 6-7/194. (2,01/88,0). ... Full Name: Eddie Charles Jones.
HIGH SCHOOL: Ely (Pompano Beach, Fla.).
COLLEGE: Temple.
TRANSACTIONS/CAREER NOTES: Selected by Los Angeles Lakers in first round (10th pick overall) of 1994 NBA Draft. ... Traded by Lakers with F/C Elden Campbell to Charlotte Hornets for F Glen Rice, F/C J.R. Reid and G B.J. Armstrong (March 10, 1999). ... Traded by Hornets with F Anthony Mason, G Ricky Davis and G/F Dale Ellis to Miami Heat for F P.J. Brown, F Jamal Mashburn, F/C Otis Thorpe, F Tim James and G/F Rodney Buford (August 1, 2000).

COLLEGIATE RECORD

Season Team	G	Min.	FGM	FGA	Pct.	FTM	FTA	Pct.	Reb.	Ast.	Pts.	AVERAGES RPG	APG	PPG
90-91—Temple					Did not play—ineligible.									
91-92—Temple	29	764	122	279	.437	41	75	.547	122	30	332	4.2	1.0	11.4
92-93—Temple	32	1169	212	463	.458	70	116	.603	225	56	543	7.0	1.8	17.0
93-94—Temple	31	1184	231	491	.470	88	133	.662	210	58	595	6.8	1.9	19.2
Totals	92	3117	565	1233	.458	199	324	.614	557	144	1470	6.1	1.6	16.0

Three-point field goals: 1991-92, 47-for-134 (.351). 1992-93, 49-for-141 (.348). 1993-94, 45-for-128 (.352). Totals, 141-for-403 (.350).

NBA REGULAR-SEASON RECORD

HONORS: All-NBA third team (2000). ... NBA All-Defensive second team (1998, 1999, 2000). ... NBA All-Rookie first team (1995). ... MVP of Rookie Game (1995).
NOTES: Led NBA with 2.7 steals per game (2000).

Season Team	G	Min.	FGM	FGA	Pct.	FTM	FTA	Pct.	REBOUNDS Off.	Def.	Tot.	Ast.	St.	Blk.	TO	Pts.	AVERAGES RPG	APG	PPG
94-95—L.A. Lakers	64	1981	342	744	.460	122	169	.722	79	170	249	128	131	41	75	897	3.9	2.0	14.0
95-96—L.A. Lakers	70	2184	337	685	.492	136	184	.739	45	188	233	246	129	45	99	893	3.3	3.5	12.8
96-97—L.A. Lakers	80	2998	473	1081	.438	276	337	.819	90	236	326	270	189	49	169	1374	4.1	3.4	17.2
97-98—L.A. Lakers	80	2910	486	1005	.484	234	306	.765	85	217	302	246	160	55	146	1349	3.8	3.1	16.9
98-99—L.A.L.-Char.	50	1881	260	595	.437	212	271	.782	50	144	194	186	125	58	93	780	3.9	3.7	15.6
99-00—Charlotte	72	2807	478	1119	.427	362	419	.864	81	262	343	305	*192	49	160	1446	4.8	4.2	20.1
00-01—Miami	63	2282	388	871	.445	258	270	.844	75	217	292	171	110	58	135	1094	4.6	2.7	17.4
Totals	479	17043	2764	6100	.453	1570	1956	.803	505	1434	1939	1552	1036	355	877	7833	4.0	3.2	16.4

Three-point field goals: 1994-95, 91-for-246 (.370). 1995-96, 83-for-227 (.366). 1996-97, 152-for-389 (.391). 1997-98, 143-for-368 (.389). 1998-99, 48-for-142 (.338). 1999-00, 128-for-341 (.375). 2000-01, 90-for-238 (.378). Totals, 735-for-1951 (.377).
Personal fouls/disqualifications: 1994-95, 175/1. 1995-96, 162/0. 1996-97, 226/3. 1997-98, 164/0. 1998-99, 128/1. 1999-00, 176/1. 2000-01, 183/5. Totals, 1214/11.

NBA PLAYOFF RECORD

Season Team	G	Min.	FGM	FGA	Pct.	FTM	FTA	Pct.	REBOUNDS Off.	Def.	Tot.	Ast.	St.	Blk.	TO	Pts.	AVERAGES RPG	APG	PPG
94-95—L.A. Lakers	10	286	30	80	.375	15	21	.714	7	25	32	20	8	9	17	87	3.2	2.0	8.7
95-96—L.A. Lakers	4	155	27	49	.551	5	8	.625	7	14	21	6	8	1	4	69	5.3	1.5	17.3
96-97—L.A. Lakers	9	283	33	72	.458	26	35	.742	8	23	31	29	9	4	13	101	3.4	3.2	11.2
97-98—L.A. Lakers	13	476	69	148	.466	63	76	.829	12	39	51	32	26	21	17	221	3.9	2.5	17.0
99-00—Charlotte	4	171	22	58	.379	15	16	.938	4	16	20	19	10	3	5	68	5.0	4.8	17.0
00-01—Miami	3	108	22	44	.500	6	7	.857	2	16	18	7	3	1	7	57	6.0	2.3	19.0
Totals	43	1479	203	451	.450	130	163	.798	40	133	173	113	64	39	63	603	4.0	2.6	14.0

Three-point field goals: 1994-95, 12-for-27 (.444). 1995-96, 10-for-19 (.526). 1996-97, 9-for-24 (.375). 1997-98, 20-for-48 (.417). 1999-00, 9-for-26 (.346). 2000-01, 7-for-16 (.438). Totals, 67-for-160 (.419).
Personal fouls/disqualifications: 1994-95, 27/0. 1995-96, 16/0. 1996-97, 24/0. 1997-98, 37/0. 1999-00, 12/0. 2000-01, 9/0. Totals, 125/0.

NBA ALL-STAR GAME RECORD

Season Team	Min.	FGM	FGA	Pct.	FTM	FTA	Pct.	REBOUNDS Off.	Def.	Tot.	Ast.	PF	Dq.	St.	Blk.	TO	Pts.
1997 —L.A. Lakers	17	3	4	.750	4	7	.571	1	0	1	1	1	0	1	2	3	10
1998 —L.A. Lakers	25	7	19	.368	1	2	.500	7	4	11	1	1	0	2	0	0	15
2000 —Charlotte	21	4	7	.571	0	0	...	1	3	4	3	1	0	1	0	1	10
Totals	63	14	30	.467	5	9	.556	9	7	16	5	3	0	4	2	4	35

Three-point field goals: 1997, 0-for-1. 1998, 0-for-7. 1900, 2-for-3 (.667). Totals, 2-for-11 (.182).

JONES, JUMAINE F CAVALIERS

PERSONAL: Born February 10, 1979, in Cocoa, Fla. ... 6-8/218. (2,03/98,9). ... Full Name: Jumaine Lanard Jones.
HIGH SCHOOL: Mitchell-Baker (Camilla, Ga.).
COLLEGE: Georgia.
TRANSACTIONS/CAREER NOTES: Selected after sophomore season by Atlanta Hawks in first round (27th pick overall) of 1999 NBA Draft. ... Draft rights traded by Hawks to Philadelphia 76ers for future first-round draft choice (June 30, 1999). ... Traded by 76ers with F Tyrone Hill to Cleveland Cavaliers for F Matt Harpring, F Cedric Henderson and F/C Robert Traylor (August 3, 2001).

COLLEGIATE RECORD

Season Team	G	Min.	FGM	FGA	Pct.	FTM	FTA	Pct.	Reb.	Ast.	Pts.	RPG	APG	PPG
97-98—Georgia	35	1031	188	415	.453	95	121	.785	299	30	515	8.5	0.9	14.7
98-99—Georgia	30	1032	197	443	.445	122	168	.726	284	30	564	9.5	1.0	18.8
Totals	65	2063	385	858	.449	217	289	.751	583	60	1079	9.0	0.9	16.6

Three-point field goals: 1997-98, 44-for-124 (.355). 1998-99, 48-for-138 (.348). Totals, 92-for-262 (.351).

NBA REGULAR-SEASON RECORD

Season Team	G	Min.	FGM	FGA	Pct.	FTM	FTA	Pct.	Off.	Def.	Tot.	Ast.	St.	Blk.	TO	Pts.	RPG	APG	PPG
99-00—Philadelphia	33	138	22	58	.379	11	18	.611	16	22	38	5	6	5	14	57	1.2	0.2	1.7
00-01—Philadelphia	65	866	122	275	.444	40	53	.755	63	126	189	32	30	15	39	304	2.9	0.5	4.7
Totals	98	1004	144	333	.432	51	71	.718	79	148	227	37	36	20	53	361	2.3	0.4	3.7

Three-point field goals: 1999-00, 2-for-4 (.500). 2000-01, 20-for-60 (.333). Totals, 22-for-64 (.344).
Personal fouls/disqualifications: 1999-00, 10/0. 2000-01, 68/0. Totals, 78/0.

NBA PLAYOFF RECORD

Season Team	G	Min.	FGM	FGA	Pct.	FTM	FTA	Pct.	Off.	Def.	Tot.	Ast.	St.	Blk.	TO	Pts.	RPG	APG	PPG
99-00—Philadelphia	4	8	1	3	.333	0	0	...	0	0	0	0	0	0	0	2	0.0	0.0	0.5
00-01—Philadelphia	23	447	52	125	.416	15	21	.714	35	49	84	17	10	11	14	127	3.7	0.7	5.5
Totals	27	455	53	128	.414	15	21	.714	35	49	84	17	10	11	14	129	3.1	0.6	4.8

Three-point field goals: 1999-00, 0-for-2. 2000-01, 8-for-32 (.250). Totals, 8-for-34 (.235).
Personal fouls/disqualifications: 2000-01, 33/0. Totals, 33/0.

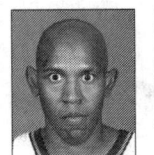

JONES, POPEYE F WIZARDS

PERSONAL: Born June 17, 1970, in Dresden, Tenn. ... 6-8/250. (2,03/113,4). ... Full Name: Ronald Jerome Jones.
HIGH SCHOOL: Dresden (Tenn.).
COLLEGE: Murray State.
TRANSACTIONS/CAREER NOTES: Selected by Houston Rockets in second round (41st pick overall) of 1992 NBA Draft. ... Played in Italy (1992-93). ... Draft rights traded by Rockets to Dallas Mavericks for draft rights to C Eric Riley (June 30, 1993). ... Traded by Mavericks with 1997 first-round draft choice to Toronto Raptors for G Jimmy King and 1997 and 1998 second-round draft choices (July 23, 1996). ... Traded by Raptors with G Kenny Anderson and C Zan Tabak to Boston Celtics for G Chauncey Billups, G Dee Brown, F John Thomas and F Roy Rogers (February 18, 1998). ... Traded by Celtics with G/F Ron Mercer and C Dwayne Schintzius to Denver Nuggets for F Danny Fortson, F Eric Williams, G Eric Washington and first-round draft choice within the next three years (August 3, 1999). ... Traded by Nuggets with second-round draft choice to Washington Wizards for F Tracy Murray (September 25, 2000).

COLLEGIATE RECORD

NOTES: Led NCAA Division I with 14.4 rebounds per game (1992).

Season Team	G	Min.	FGM	FGA	Pct.	FTM	FTA	Pct.	Reb.	Ast.	Pts.	RPG	APG	PPG
88-89—Murray State	30	518	65	133	.489	43	57	.754	138	21	173	4.6	0.7	5.8
89-90—Murray State	30	1038	217	434	.500	137	181	.757	336	59	586	11.2	2.0	19.5
90-91—Murray State	33	1052	268	544	.493	123	173	.711	469	69	666	14.2	2.1	20.2
91-92—Murray State	30	994	232	475	.488	161	207	.778	431	72	632	14.4	2.4	21.1
Totals	123	3602	782	1586	.493	464	618	.751	1374	221	2057	11.2	1.8	16.7

Three-point field goals: 1989-90, 15-for-34 (.441). 1990-91, 7-for-32 (.219). 1991-92, 7-for-18 (.389). Totals, 29-for-84 (.345).

ITALIAN LEAGUE RECORD

Season Team	G	Min.	FGM	FGA	Pct.	FTM	FTA	Pct.	Reb.	Ast.	Pts.	RPG	APG	PPG
92-93—Teorematour Milan	30	1094	217	353	.615	145	189	.767	398	37	633	13.3	1.2	21.1

Three-point field goals: 1992-93, 18-for-65 (.277).

NBA REGULAR-SEASON RECORD

Season Team	G	Min.	FGM	FGA	Pct.	FTM	FTA	Pct.	Off.	Def.	Tot.	Ast.	St.	Blk.	TO	Pts.	RPG	APG	PPG
93-94—Dallas	81	1773	195	407	.479	78	107	.729	299	306	605	99	61	31	94	468	7.5	1.2	5.8
94-95—Dallas	80	2385	372	839	.443	80	124	.645	*329	515	844	163	35	27	124	825	10.6	2.0	10.3
95-96—Dallas	68	2322	327	733	.446	102	133	.767	260	477	737	132	54	27	109	770	10.8	1.9	11.3
96-97—Toronto	79	2421	258	537	.480	99	121	.818	270	410	680	84	58	39	116	616	8.6	1.1	7.8
97-98—Toronto	14	352	52	127	.409	14	19	.737	50	52	102	18	10	3	16	118	7.3	1.3	8.6
98-99—Boston	18	206	20	51	.392	14	17	.824	28	24	52	15	5	0	7	54	2.9	0.8	3.0
99-00—Denver	40	330	44	104	.423	14	19	.737	41	62	103	19	3	6	13	104	2.6	0.5	2.6
00-01—Washington	45	638	60	153	.392	41	55	.745	83	137	220	31	19	8	21	162	4.9	0.7	3.6
Totals	425	10427	1328	2951	.450	442	595	.743	1360	1983	3343	561	245	141	500	3119	7.9	1.3	7.3

Three-point field goals: 1993-94, 0-for-1. 1994-95, 1-for-12 (.083). 1995-96, 14-for-39 (.359). 1996-97, 1-for-13 (.077). 1997-98, 2-for-3 (.667). 1998-99, 0-for-1. 1999-00, 2-for-3 (.667). 2000-01, 1-for-6 (.167). Totals, 21-for-78 (.269).
Personal fouls/disqualifications: 1993-94, 246/2. 1994-95, 267/5. 1995-96, 262/8. 1996-97, 269/3. 1997-98, 39/0. 1998-99, 31/0. 1999-00, 50/1. 2000-01, 95/0. Totals, 1259/19.

JOSEPH, GARTH   C

PERSONAL: Born August 8, 1973, in Roseau, Dominica. ... 7-2/315. (2,18/142,9). ... Full Name: Garth McArthur Fitzgerald Joseph.
HIGH SCHOOL: St. Mary's (Roseau, Dominica).
COLLEGE: College of St. Rose (N.Y.).
TRANSACTIONS/CAREER NOTES: Not drafted by an NBA franchise. ... Played in Greece (1997-98). ... Played in International Basketball Association with Mansfield Hawks (1998-99). ... Played in International Basketball League with Trenton Stars (1999-2000). ... Signed as free agent by Toronto Raptors (October 2, 2000). ... Traded by Raptors with F/C Kevin Willis, C Aleksandar Radojevic and future second-round draft choice to Denver Nuggets for F/C Keon Clark, F Tracy Murray and C Mamadou N'Diaye (January 12, 2001). ... Waived by Nuggets (January 29, 2001).

COLLEGIATE RECORD

Season Team	G	Min.	FGM	FGA	Pct.	FTM	FTA	Pct.	Reb.	Ast.	Pts.	RPG	APG	PPG
94-95—College of Saint Rose.....	31	891	184	271	.679	73	135	.541	396	19	441	12.8	0.6	14.2
95-96—College of Saint Rose.....	24	699	147	223	.659	84	144	.583	284	14	378	11.8	0.6	15.8
96-97—College of Saint Rose.....	34	947	195	306	.637	80	138	.580	392	59	470	11.5	1.7	13.8
Totals	89	2537	526	800	.658	237	417	.568	1072	92	1289	12.0	1.0	14.5

Three-point field goals: 1996-97, 0-for-1.

GREEK LEAGUE RECORD

Season Team	G	Min.	FGM	FGA	Pct.	FTM	FTA	Pct.	Reb.	Ast.	Pts.	RPG	APG	PPG
97-98—Peristeri........................	10	277	29	48	.604	9	28	.321	64	6	67	6.4	0.6	6.7

IBL REGULAR SEASON RECORD

Season Team	G	Min.	FGM	FGA	Pct.	FTM	FTA	Pct.	Reb.	Ast.	Pts.	RPG	APG	PPG
99-00—Trenton	62	1415	185	311	.595	59	102	.578	429	51	429	6.9	0.8	6.9

NBA REGULAR-SEASON RECORD

Season Team	G	Min.	FGM	FGA	Pct.	FTM	FTA	Pct.	Off.	Def.	Tot.	Ast.	St.	Blk.	TO	Pts.	RPG	APG	PPG
00-01—Tor.-Denver.....	4	16	1	5	.200	0	2	.000	2	0	2	1	0	1	2	2	0.5	0.3	0.5

Personal fouls/disqualifications: 2000-01, 1/0.

KEEFE, ADAM   F

PERSONAL: Born February 22, 1970, in Irvine, Calif. ... 6-9/230. (2,06/104,3). ... Full Name: Adam Thomas Keefe.
HIGH SCHOOL: Woodbridge (Irvine, Calif.).
COLLEGE: Stanford.
TRANSACTIONS/CAREER NOTES: Selected by Atlanta Hawks in first round (10th pick overall) of 1992 NBA Draft. ... Traded by Hawks to Utah Jazz for F Tyrone Corbin and 1995 second-round draft choice (September 16, 1994). ... Traded by Jazz to Golden State Warriors as part of four-team deal in which Boston Celtics received G Robert Pack, C John Williams and cash considerations from Dallas Mavericks and a conditional first-round draft choice from Jazz, Mavericks received G Dana Barros from Celtics, F Bill Curley from Golden State Warriors and G Howard Eisley from Utah Jazz, Jazz received F Donyell Marshall from Warriors and C Bruno Sundov from Mavericks and Warriors received F Danny Fortson from Celtics (August 16, 2000). ... Signed to play for Girona in Spain for 2001-02 season.

COLLEGIATE RECORD

Season Team	G	Min.	FGM	FGA	Pct.	FTM	FTA	Pct.	Reb.	Ast.	Pts.	RPG	APG	PPG
88-89—Stanford	33	653	93	147	.633	91	132	.689	179	22	277	5.4	0.7	8.4
89-90—Stanford	30	1065	210	335	.627	179	247	.725	272	41	599	9.1	1.4	20.0
90-91—Stanford	33	1204	252	414	.609	203	267	.760	313	61	709	9.5	1.8	21.5
91-92—Stanford	29	1080	275	488	.564	179	240	.746	355	86	734	12.2	3.0	25.3
Totals	125	4002	830	1384	.600	652	886	.736	1119	210	2319	9.0	1.7	18.6

Three-point field goals: 1990-91, 2-for-4 (.500). 1991-92, 5-for-11 (.455). Totals, 7-for-15 (.467).

NBA REGULAR-SEASON RECORD

Season Team	G	Min.	FGM	FGA	Pct.	FTM	FTA	Pct.	Off.	Def.	Tot.	Ast.	St.	Blk.	TO	Pts.	RPG	APG	PPG
92-93—Atlanta	82	1549	188	376	.500	166	237	.700	171	261	432	80	57	16	100	542	5.3	1.0	6.6
93-94—Atlanta	63	763	96	213	.451	81	111	.730	77	124	201	34	20	9	60	273	3.2	0.5	4.3
94-95—Utah	75	1270	172	298	.577	117	173	.676	135	192	327	30	36	25	62	461	4.4	0.4	6.1
95-96—Utah	82	1708	180	346	.520	139	201	.692	176	279	455	64	51	41	88	499	5.5	0.8	6.1
96-97—Utah	62	915	82	160	.513	71	103	.689	75	141	216	32	30	13	45	235	3.5	0.5	3.8
97-98—Utah	80	2047	229	424	.540	162	200	.810	179	259	438	89	52	24	71	620	5.5	1.1	7.8
98-99—Utah	44	642	56	124	.452	62	89	.697	51	91	142	28	16	12	33	174	3.2	0.6	4.0
99-00—Utah	62	604	53	130	.408	29	36	.806	45	91	136	34	17	13	46	135	2.2	0.5	2.2
00-01—Golden State ...	67	836	64	159	.403	39	63	.619	90	119	209	36	28	20	40	168	3.1	0.5	2.5
Totals	617	10334	1120	2230	.502	866	1213	.714	999	1557	2556	427	307	173	545	3107	4.1	0.7	5.0

Three-point field goals: 1992-93, 0-for-1. 1995-96, 0-for-4. 1996-97, 0-for-1. 1998-99, 0-for-4. 1999-00, 1-for-3. 2000-01, 1-for-3 (.333). Totals, 1-for-14 (.071).

Personal fouls/disqualifications: 1992-93, 195/1. 1993-94, 80/0. 1994-95, 141/0. 1995-96, 174/0. 1996-97, 97/0. 1997-98, 172/0. 1998-99, 63/0. 1999-00, 90/0. 2000-01, 102/0. Totals, 1114/1.

NBA PLAYOFF RECORD

Season Team	G	Min.	FGM	FGA	Pct.	FTM	FTA	Pct.	REBOUNDS Off.	Def.	Tot.	Ast.	St.	Blk.	TO	Pts.	AVERAGES RPG	APG	PPG
92-93—Atlanta	3	53	7	13	.538	4	6	.667	4	9	13	6	1	0	3	18	4.3	2.0	6.0
93-94—Atlanta	7	62	6	10	.600	4	9	.444	3	10	13	2	1	1	4	16	1.9	0.3	2.3
94-95—Utah	4	69	7	12	.583	4	6	.667	8	9	17	2	5	1	0	18	4.3	0.5	4.5
95-96—Utah	17	178	23	34	.676	11	17	.647	9	24	33	2	3	1	8	58	1.9	0.1	3.4
96-97—Utah	8	59	2	6	.333	4	6	.667	3	13	16	2	2	1	2	8	2.0	0.3	1.0
97-98—Utah	15	154	10	29	.345	11	17	.647	13	21	34	2	4	2	3	31	2.3	0.1	2.1
98-99—Utah	10	101	18	30	.600	5	5	1.000	7	17	24	3	4	3	8	41	2.4	0.3	4.1
Totals	64	676	73	134	.545	43	66	.652	47	103	150	19	20	9	28	190	2.3	0.3	3.0

Three-point field goals: 1995-96, 1-for-2 (.500). Totals, 1-for-2 (.500).
Personal fouls/disqualifications: 1992-93, 7/0. 1993-94, 9/0. 1994-95, 4/0. 1995-96, 23/0. 1996-97, 5/0. 1997-98, 18/0. 1998-99, 17/0. Totals, 83/0.

KEMP, SHAWN   F   TRAIL BLAZERS

K

PERSONAL: Born November 26, 1969, in Elkhart, Ind. ... 6-10/280. (2,08/127,0). ... Full Name: Shawn T. Kemp.
HIGH SCHOOL: Concord (Elkhart, Ind.).
COLLEGE: Kentucky (did not play basketball).
TRANSACTIONS/CAREER NOTES: Selected after freshman year by Seattle SuperSonics in first round (17th pick overall) of 1989 NBA Draft. ... Traded by SuperSonics to Cleveland Cavaliers in three-way deal in which Cavaliers sent G Terrell Brandon and F Tyrone Hill to Milwaukee Bucks for G Sherman Douglas and Bucks sent F Vin Baker to SuperSonics (September 25, 1997); Bucks also received 1998 first-round draft choice from Cavaliers. ... Traded by Cavaliers to Portland Trail Blazers as part of three-way deal in which Trail Blazers sent F Brian Grant to Miami Heat, Heat sent F/C Chris Gatling, F Clarence Weatherspoon, future first-round draft choice and cash Cavaliers and Trail Blazers sent G Gary Grant to Cavaliers (August 30, 2000).
MISCELLANEOUS: Member of gold-medal-winning U.S. World Championship team (1994). ... Seattle SuperSonics franchise all-time blocked shots leader with 959 (1989-90 through 1996-97).

NBA REGULAR-SEASON RECORD

RECORDS: Holds career record for most seasons leading league in disqualifications—5. ... Shares career record for most seasons leading league in personal fouls—3.
HONORS: All-NBA second team (1994, 1995, 1996).
NOTES: Led NBA with 13 disqualifications (1992), 11 disqualifications (1994), and 15 disqualifications (1998). ... Led NBA with 312 personal fouls (1994), 320 personal fouls (1997) and 371 personal fouls (2000). ... Tied for NBA lead with 11 disqualifications (1997) and 13 disqualifications (2000).

Season Team	G	Min.	FGM	FGA	Pct.	FTM	FTA	Pct.	REBOUNDS Off.	Def.	Tot.	Ast.	St.	Blk.	TO	Pts.	AVERAGES RPG	APG	PPG
89-90—Seattle	81	1120	203	424	.479	117	159	.736	146	200	346	26	47	70	107	525	4.3	0.3	6.5
90-91—Seattle	81	2442	462	909	.508	288	436	.661	267	412	679	144	77	123	202	1214	8.4	1.8	15.0
91-92—Seattle	64	1808	362	718	.504	270	361	.748	264	401	665	86	70	124	156	994	10.4	1.3	15.5
92-93—Seattle	78	2582	515	1047	.492	358	503	.712	287	546	833	155	119	146	217	1388	10.7	2.0	17.8
93-94—Seattle	79	2597	533	990	.538	364	491	.741	312	539	851	207	142	166	259	1431	10.8	2.6	18.1
94-95—Seattle	82	2679	545	997	.547	438	585	.749	318	575	893	149	102	122	259	1530	10.9	1.8	18.7
95-96—Seattle	79	2631	526	937	.561	493	664	.742	276	628	904	173	93	127	315	1550	11.4	2.2	19.6
96-97—Seattle	81	2750	526	1032	.510	452	609	.742	275	532	807	156	125	81	280	1516	10.0	1.9	18.7
97-98—Cleveland	80	2769	518	1164	.445	404	556	.727	219	526	745	197	108	90	271	1442	9.3	2.5	18.0
98-99—Cleveland	42	1475	277	575	.482	307	389	.789	131	257	388	101	48	45	127	862	9.2	2.4	20.5
99-00—Cleveland	82	2492	484	1160	.417	493	635	.776	231	494	725	138	100	96	291	1463	8.8	1.7	17.8
00-01—Portland	68	1083	168	413	.407	101	131	.771	63	196	259	65	45	23	99	441	3.8	1.0	6.5
Totals	897	26428	5119	10366	.494	4085	5519	.740	2789	5306	8095	1597	1076	1213	2583	14356	9.0	1.8	16.0

Three-point field goals: 1989-90, 2-for-12 (.167). 1990-91, 2-for-12 (.167). 1991-92, 0-for-3. 1992-93, 0-for-4. 1993-94, 1-for-4 (.250). 1994-95, 2-for-7 (.286). 1995-96, 5-for-12 (.417). 1996-97, 12-for-33 (.364). 1997-98, 2-for-8 (.250). 1998-99, 1-for-2 (.500). 1999-00, 2-for-6 (.333). 2000-01, 4-for-11 (.364). Totals, 33-for-114 (.289).
Personal fouls/disqualifications: 1989-90, 204/5. 1990-91, 319/11. 1991-92, 261/13. 1992-93, 327/13. 1993-94, 312/11. 1994-95, 337/9. 1995-96, 299/6. 1996-97, 320/11. 1997-98, 310/15. 1998-99, 159/2. 2000-01, 371/13. 2000-01, 184/3. Totals, 3403/112.

NBA PLAYOFF RECORD

Season Team	G	Min.	FGM	FGA	Pct.	FTM	FTA	Pct.	REBOUNDS Off.	Def.	Tot.	Ast.	St.	Blk.	TO	Pts.	AVERAGES RPG	APG	PPG
90-91—Seattle	5	149	22	57	.386	22	27	.815	13	23	36	6	3	4	16	66	7.2	1.2	13.2
91-92—Seattle	9	338	48	101	.475	61	80	.763	47	63	110	4	5	14	27	157	12.2	0.4	17.4
92-93—Seattle	19	663	110	215	.512	93	115	.809	80	110	190	49	29	40	54	313	10.0	2.6	16.5
93-94—Seattle	5	206	26	70	.371	22	33	.667	20	29	49	17	10	12	14	74	9.8	3.4	14.8
94-95—Seattle	4	160	33	57	.579	32	39	.821	17	31	48	11	8	7	15	99	12.0	2.8	24.8
95-96—Seattle	20	720	147	258	.570	124	156	.795	66	142	208	30	24	40	80	418	10.4	1.5	20.9
96-97—Seattle	12	442	85	175	.486	87	105	.829	52	96	148	36	14	16	47	259	12.3	3.0	21.6
97-98—Cleveland	4	152	33	71	.465	38	45	.844	16	25	41	8	5	4	16	104	10.3	2.0	26.0
Totals	78	2830	504	1004	.502	479	600	.798	311	519	830	161	98	137	269	1490	10.6	2.1	19.1

Three-point field goals: 1990-91, 0-for-1. 1994-95, 1-for-1. 1995-96, 0-for-3. 1996-97, 2-for-10 (.200). Totals, 3-for-15 (.200).
Personal fouls/disqualifications: 1990-91, 20/1. 1991-92, 41/0. 1992-93, 78/2. 1993-94, 18/0. 1994-95, 17/0. 1995-96, 84/3. 1996-97, 55/2. 1997-98, 12/0. Totals, 325/8.

NBA ALL-STAR GAME RECORD

Season Team	Min.	FGM	FGA	Pct.	FTM	FTA	Pct.	REBOUNDS Off.	Def.	Tot.	Ast.	PF	Dq.	St.	Blk.	TO	Pts.
1993 —Seattle	9	0	2	.000	0	0	...	2	0	2	0	3	0	0	0	0	0
1994 —Seattle	22	3	11	.273	0	0	...	6	6	12	4	4	0	0	3	6	6
1995 —Seattle	23	4	6	.667	5	6	.833	0	2	2	2	5	0	1	0	4	13
1996 —Seattle	22	6	12	.500	1	2	.500	2	2	4	1	4	0	0	1	3	13
1997 —Seattle	19	4	7	.571	1	2	.500	1	3	4	1	1	0	1	0	1	10
1998 —Cleveland	25	5	10	.500	2	2	1.000	2	9	11	2	2	...	4	0	4	12
Totals	120	22	48	.458	9	12	.750	13	22	35	10	19	0	6	4	18	54

Three-point field goals: 1996, 0-for-2. 1997, 1-for-2 (.500). 1998, 0-for-1. Totals, 1-for-5 (.200).

KERR, STEVE — G — TRAIL BLAZERS

PERSONAL: Born September 27, 1965, in Beirut, Lebanon. ... 6-3/180. (1,91/81,6). ... Full Name: Stephen Douglas Kerr.
HIGH SCHOOL: Pacific Palisades (Calif.).
COLLEGE: Arizona.
TRANSACTIONS/CAREER NOTES: Selected by Phoenix Suns in second round (50th pick overall) of 1988 NBA Draft. ... Traded by Suns to Cleveland Cavaliers for 1993 second-round draft choice (September 5, 1989). ... Traded by Cavaliers to Orlando Magic for 1996 second-round draft choice (December 2, 1992). ... Signed as free agent by Chicago Bulls (September 29, 1993). ... Traded by Bulls to San Antonio Spurs for F Chuck Person, conditional first-round draft choice and future considerations (January 22, 1999). ... Traded by Spurs with G Derek Anderson and 2003 second-round draft choice to Portland Trail Blazers for G Steve Smith (July 25, 2001).
MISCELLANEOUS: Member of NBA championship team (1996, 1997, 1998, 1999). ... Member of gold-medal-winning U.S. World Championship team (1986).

COLLEGIATE RECORD

NOTES: Holds NCAA Division I single-season record for most consecutive games with a three-point field goal made—38 (November 27, 1987, to April 2, 1988).

Season Team	G	Min.	FGM	FGA	Pct.	FTM	FTA	Pct.	Reb.	Ast.	Pts.	AVERAGES RPG	APG	PPG
83-84—Arizona	28	633	81	157	.516	36	52	.692	33	35	198	1.2	1.3	7.1
84-85—Arizona	31	1036	126	222	.568	57	71	.803	73	123	309	2.4	4.0	10.0
85-86—Arizona	32	1228	195	361	.540	71	79	.899	101	135	461	3.2	4.2	14.4
86-87—Arizona						Did not play—knee injury.								
87-88—Arizona	38	1239	151	270	.559	61	74	.824	76	150	477	2.0	3.9	12.6
Totals	129	4136	553	1010	.548	225	276	.815	283	443	1445	2.2	3.4	11.2

Three-point field goals: 1987-88, 114-for-199 (.573).

NBA REGULAR-SEASON RECORD

RECORDS: Holds career record for highest three-point field goal percentage (minimum 250 made)—.462. ... Shares career record for most seasons leading league in three-point field goal percentage—2. ... Holds single-season record for highest three-point field goal percentage—.524 (1995).
HONORS: Long Distance Shootout winner (1997).
NOTES: Led NBA with .507 three-point field goal percentage (1990) and .524 three-point field goal percentage (1995).

Season Team	G	Min.	FGM	FGA	Pct.	FTM	FTA	Pct.	REBOUNDS Off.	Def.	Tot.	Ast.	St.	Blk.	TO	Pts.	AVERAGES RPG	APG	PPG
88-89—Phoenix	26	157	20	46	.435	6	9	.667	3	14	17	24	7	0	6	54	0.7	0.9	2.1
89-90—Cleveland	78	1664	192	432	.444	63	73	.863	12	86	98	248	45	7	74	520	1.3	3.2	6.7
90-91—Cleveland	57	905	99	223	.444	45	53	.849	5	32	37	131	29	4	40	271	0.6	2.3	4.8
91-92—Cleveland	48	847	121	237	.511	45	54	.833	14	64	78	110	27	10	31	319	1.6	2.3	6.6
92-93—Clev.-Orlando	52	481	53	122	.434	22	24	.917	5	40	45	70	10	1	27	134	0.9	1.3	2.6
93-94—Chicago	82	2036	287	577	.497	83	97	.856	26	105	131	210	75	3	57	709	1.6	2.6	8.6
94-95—Chicago	82	1839	261	495	.527	63	81	.778	20	99	119	151	44	3	48	674	1.5	1.8	8.2
95-96—Chicago	82	1919	244	482	.506	78	84	.929	25	85	110	192	63	2	42	688	1.3	2.3	8.4
96-97—Chicago	82	1861	249	467	.533	54	67	.806	29	101	130	175	67	3	43	662	1.6	2.1	8.1
97-98—Chicago	50	1119	137	302	.454	45	49	.918	14	63	77	96	26	5	27	376	1.5	1.9	7.5
98-99—San Antonio	44	734	68	174	.391	31	35	.886	6	38	44	49	23	3	22	192	1.0	1.1	4.4
99-00—San Antonio	32	268	32	74	.432	9	11	.818	3	16	19	12	4	0	7	89	0.6	0.4	2.8
00-01—San Antonio	55	650	67	159	.421	14	15	.933	6	29	35	57	16	1	21	181	0.6	1.0	3.3
Totals	770	14480	1830	3790	.483	558	652	.856	168	772	940	1525	436	42	445	4869	1.2	2.0	6.3

Three-point field goals: 1988-89, 8-for-17 (.471). 1989-90, 73-for-144 (.507). 1990-91, 28-for-62 (.452). 1991-92, 32-for-74 (.432). 1992-93, 6-for-26 (.231). 1993-94, 52-for-124 (.419). 1994-95, 89-for-170 (.524). 1995-96, 122-for-237 (.515). 1996-97, 110-for-237 (.464). 1997-98, 57-for-130 (.438). 1998-99, 25-for-80 (.313). 1999-00, 16-for-31 (.516). 2000-01, 33-for-77 (.429). Totals, 651-for-1409 (.462).
Personal fouls/disqualifications: 1988-89, 12/0. 1989-90, 59/0. 1990-91, 52/0. 1991-92, 29/0. 1992-93, 36/0. 1993-94, 97/0. 1994-95, 114/0. 1995-96, 109/0. 1996-97, 98/0. 1997-98, 71/0. 1998-99, 28/0. 1999-00, 14/0. 2000-01, 30/0. Totals, 749/0.

NBA PLAYOFF RECORD

Season Team	G	Min.	FGM	FGA	Pct.	FTM	FTA	Pct.	REBOUNDS Off.	Def.	Tot.	Ast.	St.	Blk.	TO	Pts.	AVERAGES RPG	APG	PPG
89-90—Cleveland	5	73	4	14	.286	0	0	...	1	5	6	10	4	0	2	8	1.2	2.0	1.6
91-92—Cleveland	12	149	18	41	.439	5	5	1.000	1	5	6	10	5	0	4	44	0.5	0.8	3.7
93-94—Chicago	10	186	13	36	.361	3	3	1.000	2	12	14	10	7	0	1	35	1.4	1.0	3.5
94-95—Chicago	10	193	19	40	.475	5	5	1.000	1	5	6	15	1	0	0	51	0.6	1.5	5.1
95-96—Chicago	18	357	39	87	.448	27	31	.871	3	15	18	31	14	0	13	122	1.0	1.7	6.8
96-97—Chicago	19	341	33	77	.429	13	14	.929	4	14	18	20	17	2	8	95	0.9	1.1	5.0
97-98—Chicago	21	415	33	76	.434	18	22	.818	8	9	17	35	7	0	5	103	0.8	1.7	4.9
98-99—San Antonio	11	97	8	30	.267	5	6	.833	3	6	9	8	2	0	4	24	0.8	0.7	2.2
00-01—San Antonio	9	101	12	25	.480	1	2	.500	3	6	9	6	4	1	2	30	1.0	0.7	3.3
Totals	115	1912	179	426	.420	77	88	.875	26	77	103	145	61	3	39	512	0.9	1.3	4.5

Three-point field goals: 1989-90, 0-for-3. 1991-92, 3-for-11 (.273). 1993-94, 6-for-16 (.375). 1994-95, 8-for-19 (.421). 1995-96, 17-for-53 (.321). 1996-97, 16-for-42 (.381). 1997-98, 19-for-41 (.463). 1998-99, 3-for-13 (.231). 2000-01, 5-for-15 (.333). Totals, 77-for-213 (.362).
Personal fouls/disqualifications: 1989-90, 6/0. 1991-92, 12/0. 1993-94, 13/0. 1994-95, 14/0. 1995-96, 21/0. 1996-97, 25/0. 1997-98, 26/0. 1998-99, 5/0. 2000-01, 8/0. Totals, 130/0.

KERSEY, JEROME — F

PERSONAL: Born June 26, 1962, in Clarksville, Va. ... 6-7/245. (2,01/111,1).
HIGH SCHOOL: Bluestone Senior (Skipwith, Va.).
COLLEGE: Longwood (Va.).
TRANSACTIONS/CAREER NOTES: Selected by Portland Trail Blazers in second round (46th pick overall) of 1984 NBA Draft. ... Selected by Toronto Raptors from Trail Blazers in NBA Expansion Draft (June 24, 1995). ... Signed as free agent by Golden State Warriors (October 18, 1995). ... Signed as free agent by Los Angeles Lakers (August 12, 1996). ... Signed as free agent by Seattle SuperSonics (September 24, 1997). ... Signed as free agent by San Antonio Spurs (January 22, 1999). ... Signed as free agent by Milwaukee Bucks (November 24, 2000).
MISCELLANEOUS: Member of NBA championship team (1999).

COLLEGIATE RECORD

NOTES: Led NCAA Division II with 14.2 rebounds per game (1984).

												AVERAGES		
Season Team	G	Min.	FGM	FGA	Pct.	FTM	FTA	Pct.	Reb.	Ast.	Pts.	RPG	APG	PPG
80-81—Longwood (Va.)	28	...	197	313	.629	78	133	.586	249	30	472	8.9	1.1	16.9
81-82—Longwood (Va.)	23	...	165	282	.585	62	98	.633	260	61	392	11.3	2.7	17.0
82-83—Longwood (Va.)	25	...	144	257	.560	76	125	.608	270	77	364	10.8	3.1	14.6
83-84—Longwood (Va.)	27	...	214	411	.521	100	165	.606	383	98	528	14.2	3.6	19.6
Totals	103	...	720	1263	.570	316	521	.607	1162	266	1756	11.3	2.6	17.0

NBA REGULAR-SEASON RECORD

									REBOUNDS								AVERAGES		
Season Team	G	Min.	FGM	FGA	Pct.	FTM	FTA	Pct.	Off.	Def.	Tot.	Ast.	St.	Blk.	TO	Pts.	RPG	APG	PPG
84-85—Portland	77	958	178	372	.478	117	181	.646	95	111	206	63	49	29	66	473	2.7	0.8	6.1
85-86—Portland	79	1217	258	470	.549	156	229	.681	137	156	293	83	85	32	113	672	3.7	1.1	8.5
86-87—Portland	82	2088	373	733	.509	262	364	.720	201	295	496	194	122	77	149	1009	6.0	2.4	12.3
87-88—Portland	79	2888	611	1225	.499	291	396	.735	211	446	657	243	127	65	161	1516	8.3	3.1	19.2
88-89—Portland	76	2716	533	1137	.469	258	372	.694	246	383	629	243	137	84	167	1330	8.3	3.2	17.5
89-90—Portland	82	2843	519	1085	.478	269	390	.690	251	439	690	188	121	63	144	1310	8.4	2.3	16.0
90-91—Portland	73	2359	424	887	.478	232	327	.709	169	312	481	227	101	76	149	1084	6.6	3.1	14.8
91-92—Portland	77	2553	398	852	.467	174	262	.664	241	392	633	243	114	71	151	971	8.2	3.2	12.6
92-93—Portland	65	1719	281	642	.438	116	183	.634	126	280	406	121	80	41	84	686	6.2	1.9	10.6
93-94—Portland	78	1276	203	469	.433	101	135	.748	130	201	331	75	71	49	63	508	4.2	1.0	6.5
94-95—Portland	63	1143	203	489	.415	95	124	.766	93	163	256	82	52	35	64	508	4.1	1.3	8.1
95-96—Golden State	76	1620	205	500	.410	97	147	.660	154	209	363	114	91	45	75	510	4.8	1.5	6.7
96-97—L.A. Lakers	70	1766	194	449	.432	71	118	.602	112	251	363	89	119	49	74	476	5.2	1.3	6.8
97-98—Seattle	37	717	97	233	.416	39	65	.600	56	79	135	44	52	14	36	234	3.6	1.2	6.3
98-99—San Antonio	45	699	68	200	.340	6	14	.429	42	88	130	41	37	14	30	145	2.9	0.9	3.2
99-00—San Antonio	72	1310	146	354	.412	29	41	.707	58	167	225	69	67	47	51	321	3.1	1.0	4.5
00-01—Milwaukee	22	243	32	69	.464	8	16	.500	8	37	45	15	14	8	6	72	2.0	0.7	3.3
Totals	1153	28115	4723	10166	.465	2321	3364	.690	2330	4009	6339	2134	1439	799	1583	11825	5.5	1.9	10.3

Three-point field goals: 1984-85, 0-for-3. 1985-86, 0-for-6. 1986-87, 1-for-23 (.043). 1987-88, 3-for-15 (.200). 1988-89, 6-for-21 (.286). 1989-90, 3-for-20 (.150). 1990-91, 4-for-13 (.308). 1991-92, 1-for-8 (.125). 1992-93, 8-for-28 (.286). 1993-94, 1-for-8 (.125). 1994-95, 7-for-27 (.259). 1995-96, 3-for-17 (.176). 1996-97, 17-for-65 (.262). 1997-98, 1-for-10 (.100). 1998-99, 3-for-14 (.214). 1999-00, 0-for-9. 2000-01, 0-for-1. Totals, 58-for-288 (.201).

Personal fouls/disqualifications: 1984-85, 147/1. 1985-86, 208/2. 1986-87, 328/5. 1987-88, 302/8. 1988-89, 277/6. 1989-90, 304/7. 1990-91, 251/4. 1991-92, 254/1. 1992-93, 181/2. 1993-94, 213/1. 1994-95, 173/1. 1995-96, 205/2. 1996-97, 219/0. 1997-98, 104/1. 1998-99, 92/1. 1999-00, 161/0. 2000-01, 36/1. Totals, 3455/43.

NBA PLAYOFF RECORD

									REBOUNDS								AVERAGES		
Season Team	G	Min.	FGM	FGA	Pct.	FTM	FTA	Pct.	Off.	Def.	Tot.	Ast.	St.	Blk.	TO	Pts.	RPG	APG	PPG
84-85—Portland	8	60	16	31	.516	6	8	.750	5	4	9	6	7	2	2	38	1.1	0.8	4.8
85-86—Portland	4	60	9	22	.409	4	4	1.000	7	8	15	4	1	4	6	22	3.8	1.0	5.5
86-87—Portland	4	50	10	25	.400	4	4	1.000	6	13	19	3	5	1	6	24	4.8	0.8	6.0
87-88—Portland	4	127	32	65	.492	15	21	.714	17	13	30	9	7	4	5	79	7.5	2.3	19.8
88-89—Portland	3	117	23	47	.489	15	19	.789	11	13	24	7	10	1	4	61	8.0	2.3	20.3
89-90—Portland	21	831	166	361	.460	103	144	.715	66	108	174	45	34	20	45	435	8.3	2.1	20.7
90-91—Portland	16	588	105	226	.465	76	101	.752	52	59	111	49	28	7	17	286	6.9	3.1	17.9
91-92—Portland	21	756	131	257	.510	79	114	.693	59	103	162	75	41	19	53	341	7.7	3.6	16.2
92-93—Portland	4	98	22	42	.524	12	17	.706	10	24	34	4	4	2	2	57	8.5	1.0	14.3
93-94—Portland	3	38	5	16	.313	1	5	.200	5	4	9	0	1	1	0	11	3.0	0.0	3.7
94-95—Portland	3	63	16	28	.571	6	9	.667	2	6	8	3	3	1	0	38	2.7	1.0	12.7
96-97—L.A. Lakers	9	210	17	35	.486	15	19	.789	14	34	48	14	9	6	3	49	5.3	1.6	5.4
97-98—Seattle	10	213	31	72	.431	16	19	.842	17	23	40	9	10	10	13	78	4.0	0.9	7.8
98-99—San Antonio	14	152	15	43	.349	5	7	.714	10	20	30	4	6	1	6	36	2.1	0.3	2.6
99-00—San Antonio	2	25	1	7	.143	0	0		2	2	4	1	2	1	1	2	2.0	0.5	1.0
Totals	126	3394	599	1277	.469	357	491	.727	283	434	717	233	168	80	163	1557	5.7	1.8	12.4

Three-point field goals: 1985-86, 0-for-1. 1987-88, 0-for-1. 1988-89, 0-for-2. 1989-90, 0-for-3. 1991-92, 0-for-3. 1992-93, 1-for-1. 1994-95, 0-for-2. 1996-97, 0-for-1. 1997-98, 0-for-3. 1998-99, 1-for-4 (.250). Totals, 2-for-21 (.095).

Personal fouls/disqualifications: 1984-85, 11/0. 1985-86, 13/0. 1986-87, 13/0. 1987-88, 17/1. 1988-89, 12/0. 1989-90, 87/2. 1990-91, 68/2. 1991-92, 85/2. 1992-93, 15/0. 1993-94, 5/0. 1994-95, 11/1. 1996-97, 34/2. 1997-98, 32/0. 1998-99, 19/0. 1999-00, 5/0. Totals, 427/10.

KETNER, LARI   F/C

PERSONAL: Born February 1, 1977, in Philadelphia. ... 6-10/285. (2,08/129,3). ... Full Name: Lari Arthur Ketner.
HIGH SCHOOL: Roman Catholic (Philadelphia).
COLLEGE: Massachusetts.
TRANSACTIONS/CAREER NOTES: Selected by Chicago Bulls in second round (49th pick overall) of 1999 NBA Draft. ... Waived by Bulls (December 20, 1999). ... Played in Continental Basketball Association with Fort Wayne Fury (1999-2000). ... Signed by Cleveland Cavaliers to first of two consecutive 10-day contracts (February 22, 2000). ... Re-signed by Cavaliers for remainder of season (March 13, 2000). ... Signed as free agent by Indiana Pacers (October 3, 2000).

COLLEGIATE RECORD

												AVERAGES		
Season Team	G	Min.	FGM	FGA	Pct.	FTM	FTA	Pct.	Reb.	Ast.	Pts.	RPG	APG	PPG
95-96—Massachusetts					Did not play—ineligible.									
96-97—Massachusetts	33	792	141	253	.557	67	114	.588	175	23	349	5.3	0.7	10.6
97-98—Massachusetts	32	968	195	373	.523	96	149	.644	238	16	486	7.4	0.5	15.2
98-99—Massachusetts	29	879	128	303	.422	57	102	.559	242	35	313	8.3	1.2	10.8
Totals	94	2639	464	929	.499	220	365	.603	655	74	1148	7.0	0.8	12.2

Three-point field goals: 1996-97, 0-for-1.

CBA REGULAR-SEASON RECORD

Season Team	G	Min.	FGM	FGA	Pct.	FTM	FTA	Pct.	Reb.	Ast.	Pts.	AVERAGES RPG	APG	PPG
99-00—Fort Wayne	24	577	112	238	.471	32	62	.516	140	7	256	5.8	0.3	10.7

NBA REGULAR-SEASON RECORD

Season Team	G	Min.	FGM	FGA	Pct.	FTM	FTA	Pct.	REBOUNDS Off.	Def.	Tot.	Ast.	St.	Blk.	TO	Pts.	AVERAGES RPG	APG	PPG
99-00—Chi.-Clev.	22	132	13	32	.406	8	12	.667	12	22	34	1	4	3	10	34	1.5	0.0	1.5
00-01—Indiana	3	7	0	0	...	0	0	...	0	0	0	1	0	0	2	0	0.0	0.3	0.0
Totals	25	139	13	32	.406	8	12	.667	12	22	34	2	4	3	12	34	1.4	0.1	1.4

Personal fouls/disqualifications: 1999-00, 20/1. Totals, 20/1.

KIDD, JASON   G   NETS

PERSONAL: Born March 23, 1973, in San Francisco. ... 6-4/212. (1,93/96,2). ... Full Name: Jason Frederick Kidd.
HIGH SCHOOL: St. Joseph of Notre Dame (Alameda, Calif.).
COLLEGE: California.
TRANSACTIONS/CAREER NOTES: Selected after sophomore season by Dallas Mavericks in first round (second pick overall) of 1994 NBA Draft. ... Traded by Mavericks with G Tony Dumas and C Loren Meyer to Phoenix Suns for G Sam Cassell, F A.C. Green, F Michael Finley and 1997 or 1998 conditional second-round draft choice (December 26, 1996). ... Traded by Suns with C Chris Dudley to New Jersey Nets for G Stephon Marbury, F Johnny Newman and C Soumaila Samake (July 18, 2001).
K MISCELLANEOUS: Member of gold-medal-winning U.S. Olympic team.

COLLEGIATE RECORD

NOTES: THE SPORTING NEWS All-America first team (1994). ... Led NCAA Division I with 3.8 steals per game (1993). ... Led NCAA Division I with 9.1 assists per game (1994).

Season Team	G	Min.	FGM	FGA	Pct.	FTM	FTA	Pct.	Reb.	Ast.	Pts.	AVERAGES RPG	APG	PPG
92-93—California	29	922	133	287	.463	88	134	.657	142	222	378	4.9	7.7	13.0
93-94—California	30	1053	166	352	.472	117	169	.692	207	272	500	6.9	9.1	16.7
Totals	59	1975	299	639	.468	205	303	.677	349	494	878	5.9	8.4	14.9

Three-point field goals: 1992-93, 24-for-84 (.286). 1993-94, 51-for-141 (.362). Totals, 75-for-225 (.333).

NBA REGULAR-SEASON RECORD

RECORDS: Shares single-game record for most turnovers—14 (November 17, 2000, vs. New York).
HONORS: NBA Co-Rookie of the Year (1995). ... All-NBA first team (1999, 2000, 2001). ... NBA All-Defensive first team (1999, 2001). ... NBA All-Defensive second team (2000). ... NBA All-Rookie first team (1995).

Season Team	G	Min.	FGM	FGA	Pct.	FTM	FTA	Pct.	REBOUNDS Off.	Def.	Tot.	Ast.	St.	Blk.	TO	Pts.	AVERAGES RPG	APG	PPG
94-95—Dallas	79	2668	330	857	.385	192	275	.698	152	278	430	607	151	24	250	922	5.4	7.7	11.7
95-96—Dallas	81	3034	493	1293	.381	229	331	.692	203	350	553	783	175	26	*328	1348	6.8	9.7	16.6
96-97—Dal.-Pho.	55	1964	213	529	.403	112	165	.679	64	185	249	496	124	20	142	599	4.5	9.0	10.9
97-98—Phoenix	82	3118	357	859	.416	167	209	.799	108	402	510	745	162	26	261	954	6.2	9.1	11.6
98-99—Phoenix	50	*2060	310	698	.444	181	239	.757	87	252	339	*539	114	19	150	846	6.8	*10.8	16.9
99-00—Phoenix	67	2616	350	855	.409	203	245	.829	96	387	483	678	134	28	226	959	7.2	*10.1	14.3
00-01—Phoenix	77	3065	451	1097	.411	328	403	.814	91	403	494	*753	166	23	286	1299	6.4	*9.8	16.9
Totals	491	18525	2504	6188	.405	1412	1867	.756	801	2257	3058	4601	1026	166	1643	6927	6.2	9.4	14.1

Three-point field goals: 1994-95, 70-for-257 (.272). 1995-96, 133-for-396 (.336). 1996-97, 61-for-165 (.370). 1997-98, 73-for-233 (.313). 1998-99, 45-for-123 (.366). 1999-00, 56-for-166 (.337). 2000-01, 69-for-232 (.297). Totals, 507-for-1572 (.323).
Personal fouls/disqualifications: 1994-95, 146/0. 1995-96, 155/0. 1996-97, 114/0. 1997-98, 142/0. 1998-99, 108/1. 1999-00, 148/2. 2000-01, 171/1. Totals, 984/4.

NBA PLAYOFF RECORD

Season Team	G	Min.	FGM	FGA	Pct.	FTM	FTA	Pct.	REBOUNDS Off.	Def.	Tot.	Ast.	St.	Blk.	TO	Pts.	AVERAGES RPG	APG	PPG
96-97—Phoenix	5	207	21	53	.396	10	19	.526	4	26	30	49	11	2	13	60	6.0	9.8	12.0
97-98—Phoenix	4	171	22	58	.379	13	16	.813	5	18	23	31	16	2	12	57	5.8	7.8	14.3
98-99—Phoenix	3	126	18	43	.419	5	7	.714	1	6	7	31	5	1	9	45	2.3	10.3	15.0
99-00—Phoenix	6	229	22	55	.400	7	9	.778	8	32	40	53	11	1	23	59	6.7	8.8	9.8
00-01—Phoenix	4	166	22	69	.319	9	12	.750	9	15	24	53	8	0	12	57	6.0	13.3	14.3
Totals	22	899	105	278	.378	44	63	.698	27	97	124	217	51	6	69	278	5.6	9.9	12.6

Three-point field goals: 1996-97, 8-for-22 (.364). 1997-98, 0-for-7. 1998-99, 4-for-16 (.250). 1999-00, 8-for-22 (.364). 2000-01, 4-for-17 (.235). Totals, 24-for-84 (.286).
Personal fouls/disqualifications: 1996-97, 11/0. 1997-98, 13/0. 1998-99, 12/0. 1999-00, 14/0. 2000-01, 13/0. Totals, 63/0.

NBA ALL-STAR GAME RECORD

Season Team	Min.	FGM	FGA	Pct.	FTM	FTA	Pct.	REBOUNDS Off.	Def.	Tot.	Ast.	PF	Dq.	St.	Blk.	TO	Pts.
1996 —Dallas	22	3	4	.750	0	0	...	2	4	6	10	1	0	2	0	2	7
1998 —Phoenix	19	0	1	.000	0	0	...	0	1	1	9	2	0	0	0	2	0
2000 —Phoenix	34	4	9	.444	0	0	...	0	5	5	14	0	0	4	0	6	11
2001 —Phoenix	30	4	6	.667	0	0	...	0	4	4	2	3	0	1	0	5	11
Totals	105	11	20	.550	0	0	...	2	14	16	35	6	0	7	0	15	29

Three-point field goals: 1996, 1-for-2 (.500). 1900, 3-for-6 (.500). 1901, 3-for-4 (.750). Totals, 7-for-12 (.583).

KING, GERARD — F

PERSONAL: Born November 25, 1972, in New Orleans. ... 6-9/250. (2,06/113,4).
HIGH SCHOOL: McDonogh 35 (New Orleans).
COLLEGE: Nicholls State.
TRANSACTIONS/CAREER NOTES: Not drafted by an NBA franchise. ... Played with United States Basketball League with Miami Tropics (1995). ... Signed as free agent by Los Angeles Lakers (September 29, 1995). ... Waived by Lakers (October 31, 1995). ... Played in Continental Basketball Association with Quad City Thunder (1995-96). ... Played in Italy (1996-97 and 1997-98). ... Signed as free agent by San Antonio Spurs (January 21, 1999). ... Signed as free agent by Washington Wizards (September 20, 1999). ... Waived by Wizards (February 22, 2001).
MISCELLANEOUS: Member of NBA championship team (1999). ... Member of bronze-medal-winning U.S. World Championship team (1998).

COLLEGIATE RECORD

Season Team	G	Min.	FGM	FGA	Pct.	FTM	FTA	Pct.	Reb.	Ast.	Pts.	RPG	APG	PPG
90-91—Nicholls State	27	708	133	257	.518	92	151	.609	182	23	358	6.7	0.9	13.3
91-92—Nicholls State	28	708	137	274	.500	98	153	.641	147	28	372	5.3	1.0	13.3
92-93—Nicholls State						Did not play—medical redshirt.								
93-94—Nicholls State	27	871	186	351	.530	127	205	.620	239	54	499	8.9	2.0	18.5
94-95—Nicholls State	28	860	238	423	.563	128	182	.703	218	30	605	7.8	1.1	21.6
Totals	110	3147	694	1305	.532	445	691	.644	786	135	1834	7.1	1.2	16.7

Three-point field goals: 1990-91, 0-for-4. 1991-92, 0-for-1. 1994-95, 1-for-1. Totals, 1-for-6 (.167).

CBA REGULAR-SEASON RECORD

Season Team	G	Min.	FGM	FGA	Pct.	FTM	FTA	Pct.	Reb.	Ast.	Pts.	RPG	APG	PPG
95-96—Quad City	23	626	111	186	.597	40	60	.667	206	33	262	9.0	1.4	11.4

ITALIAN LEAGUE RECORD

Season Team	G	Min.	FGM	FGA	Pct.	FTM	FTA	Pct.	Reb.	Ast.	Pts.	RPG	APG	PPG
96-97—Fontanafredda Siena	28	955	164	276	.594	112	152	.737	287	15	440	10.3	0.5	15.7
97-98—Fontanafredda Siena	31	1129	199	356	.559	119	161	.739	319	24	517	10.3	0.8	16.7
Totals	59	2084	363	632	.574	231	313	.738	606	39	957	10.3	0.7	16.2

NBA REGULAR-SEASON RECORD

Season Team	G	Min.	FGM	FGA	Pct.	FTM	FTA	Pct.	Off.	Def.	Tot.	Ast.	St.	Blk.	TO	Pts.	RPG	APG	PPG
98-99—San Antonio	19	63	6	14	.429	11	18	.611	6	8	14	4	2	1	4	23	0.7	0.2	1.2
99-00—Washington	62	1060	139	277	.502	49	66	.742	84	166	250	49	34	15	41	327	4.0	0.8	5.3
00-01—Washington	45	706	90	176	.511	36	45	.800	39	90	129	31	14	11	47	216	2.9	0.7	4.8
Totals	126	1829	235	467	.503	96	129	.744	129	264	393	84	50	27	92	566	3.1	0.7	4.5

Personal fouls/disqualifications: 1998-99, 12/0. 1999-00, 132/1. 2000-01, 94/2. Totals, 238/3.

NBA PLAYOFF RECORD

Season Team	G	Min.	FGM	FGA	Pct.	FTM	FTA	Pct.	Off.	Def.	Tot.	Ast.	St.	Blk.	TO	Pts.	RPG	APG	PPG
98-99—San Antonio	8	14	2	4	.500	0	0	...	0	4	4	1	0	1	1	4	0.5	0.1	0.5

Personal fouls/disqualifications: 1998-99, 2/0.

KITTLES, KERRY — G — NETS

PERSONAL: Born June 12, 1974, in Dayton, Ohio. ... 6-5/180. (1,96/81,6).
HIGH SCHOOL: St. Augustine (New Orleans).
COLLEGE: Villanova.
TRANSACTIONS/CAREER NOTES: Selected by New Jersey Nets in first round (eighth pick overall) of 1996 NBA Draft.

COLLEGIATE RECORD

NOTES: THE SPORTING NEWS All-America first team (1996).

Season Team	G	Min.	FGM	FGA	Pct.	FTM	FTA	Pct.	Reb.	Ast.	Pts.	RPG	APG	PPG
92-93—Villanova	27	875	108	224	.482	37	55	.673	94	79	294	3.5	2.9	10.9
93-94—Villanova	32	1258	233	516	.452	91	129	.705	207	109	630	6.5	3.4	19.7
94-95—Villanova	33	1218	264	504	.524	92	120	.767	201	115	706	6.1	3.5	21.4
95-96—Villanova	30	1059	216	475	.455	103	145	.710	213	105	613	7.1	3.5	20.4
Totals	122	4410	821	1719	.478	323	449	.719	715	408	2243	5.9	3.3	18.4

Three-point field goals: 1992-93, 41-for-95 (.432). 1993-94, 73-for-209 (.349). 1994-95, 86-for-209 (.411). 1995-96, 78-for-193 (.404). Totals, 278-for-706 (.394).

NBA REGULAR-SEASON RECORD

RECORDS: Holds single-season record for most three-point field goals made by a rookie—158 (1997).
HONORS: NBA All-Rookie second team (1997).

Season Team	G	Min.	FGM	FGA	Pct.	FTM	FTA	Pct.	Off.	Def.	Tot.	Ast.	St.	Blk.	TO	Pts.	RPG	APG	PPG
96-97—New Jersey	82	3012	507	1189	.426	175	227	.771	106	213	319	249	157	35	127	1347	3.9	3.0	16.4
97-98—New Jersey	77	2814	508	1154	.440	202	250	.808	132	230	362	176	132	37	106	1328	4.7	2.3	17.2
98-99—New Jersey	46	1570	227	613	.370	88	114	.772	52	139	191	116	79	26	66	592	4.2	2.5	12.9
99-00—New Jersey	62	1896	305	698	.437	101	127	.795	46	179	225	142	79	19	56	807	3.6	2.3	13.0
00-01—New Jersey						Did not play—injured.													
Totals	267	9292	1547	3654	.423	566	718	.788	336	761	1097	683	447	117	355	4074	4.1	2.6	15.3

Three-point field goals: 1996-97, 158-for-419 (.377). 1997-98, 110-for-263 (.418). 1998-99, 50-for-158 (.316). 1999-00, 96-for-240 (.400). Totals, 414-for-1080 (.383).

Personal fouls/disqualifications: 1996-97, 165/1. 1997-98, 152/0. 1998-99, 82/0. 1999-00, 120/0. Totals, 519/1.

									REBOUNDS								AVERAGES		
Season Team	G	Min.	FGM	FGA	Pct.	FTM	FTA	Pct.	Off.	Def.	Tot.	Ast.	St.	Blk.	TO	Pts.	RPG	APG	PPG
97-98—New Jersey	3	126	17	40	.425	10	11	.909	0	15	15	8	4	2	7	49	5.0	2.7	16.3

Three-point field goals: 1997-98, 5-for-13 (.385).
Personal fouls/disqualifications: 1997-98, 12/1.

KNIGHT, BREVIN   G   GRIZZLIES

PERSONAL: Born November 8, 1975, in Livingston, N.J. ... 5-10/170. (1,78/77,1).
HIGH SCHOOL: Seton Hall Prep (East Orange, N.J.).
COLLEGE: Stanford.
TRANSACTIONS/CAREER NOTES: Selected by Cleveland Cavaliers in first round (16th pick overall) of 1997 NBA Draft. ... Traded by Cavaliers to Atlanta Hawks for G Jim Jackson, G Anthony Johnson and F/G Larry Robinson (January 2, 2001). ... Traded by Hawks with F/C Lorenzen Wright and draft rights to Pau Gasol to Memphis Grizzlies for F Shareef Abdur-Rahim and draft rights to G Jamaal Tinsley (July 19, 2001).

COLLEGIATE RECORD

NOTES: Frances Pomeroy Naismith Award winner (1997). ... THE SPORTING NEWS All-America first team (1997).

												AVERAGES		
Season Team	G	Min.	FGM	FGA	Pct.	FTM	FTA	Pct.	Reb.	Ast.	Pts.	RPG	APG	PPG
93-94—Stanford	28	916	90	254	.354	121	160	.756	108	150	312	3.9	5.4	11.1
94-95—Stanford	28	912	146	321	.455	153	204	.750	109	184	464	3.9	6.6	16.6
95-96—Stanford	29	915	140	323	.433	151	178	.848	110	212	449	3.8	7.3	15.5
96-97—Stanford	30	960	139	341	.408	166	199	.834	111	234	489	3.7	7.8	16.3
Totals	115	3703	515	1239	.416	591	741	.798	438	780	1714	3.8	6.8	14.9

Three-point field goals: 1993-94, 11-for-55 (.200). 1994-95, 19-for-51 (.373). 1995-96, 18-for-61 (.295). 1996-97, 45-for-110 (.409). Totals, 93-for-277 (.336).

NBA REGULAR-SEASON RECORD

HONORS: NBA All-Rookie first team (1998).

									REBOUNDS								AVERAGES		
Season Team	G	Min.	FGM	FGA	Pct.	FTM	FTA	Pct.	Off.	Def.	Tot.	Ast.	St.	Blk.	TO	Pts.	RPG	APG	PPG
97-98—Cleveland	80	2483	261	592	.441	201	251	.801	67	186	253	656	*196	18	194	723	3.2	8.2	9.0
98-99—Cleveland	39	1186	134	315	.425	105	141	.745	16	115	131	302	70	7	105	373	4.4	7.7	9.6
99-00—Cleveland	65	1754	230	558	.412	140	184	.761	38	155	193	458	107	21	157	602	3.0	7.0	9.3
00-01—Clev.-Atl.	53	1457	139	371	.375	54	66	.818	23	145	168	311	101	4	91	333	3.2	5.9	6.3
Totals	237	6880	764	1836	.416	500	642	.779	144	601	745	1727	474	50	547	2031	3.1	7.3	8.6

Three-point field goals: 1997-98, 0-for-7. 1998-99, 0-for-5. 1999-00, 2-for-10 (.200). 2000-01, 1-for-10 (.100). Totals, 3-for-32 (.094).
Personal fouls/disqualifications: 1997-98, 271/5. 1998-99, 115/1. 1999-00, 185/2. 2000-01, 155/2. Totals, 726/10.

NBA PLAYOFF RECORD

									REBOUNDS								AVERAGES		
Season Team	G	Min.	FGM	FGA	Pct.	FTM	FTA	Pct.	Off.	Def.	Tot.	Ast.	St.	Blk.	TO	Pts.	RPG	APG	PPG
97-98—Cleveland	4	132	6	21	.286	6	10	.600	0	16	16	23	10	1	8	18	4.0	5.8	4.5

Personal fouls/disqualifications: 1997-98, 16/1.

KNIGHT, TRAVIS   F/C   KNICKS

PERSONAL: Born September 13, 1974, in Salt Lake City. ... 7-0/235. (2,13/106,6). ... Full Name: Travis James Knight.
HIGH SCHOOL: Alta (Sandy, Utah).
COLLEGE: Connecticut.
TRANSACTIONS/CAREER NOTES: Selected by Chicago Bulls in first round (29th pick overall) of 1996 NBA Draft. ... Draft rights renounced by Bulls (July 12, 1996). ... Signed as free agent by Los Angeles Lakers (July 31, 1996). ... Signed as free agent by Boston Celtics (July 7, 1997). ... Traded by Celtics to Lakers for C/F Tony Battie (January 21, 1999). ... Traded by Lakers to New York Knicks as part of four-team trade in which Knicks acquired F Glen Rice, C Luc Longley, G Vernon Maxwell, C Vladimir Stepania, F Lazaro Borrell, two 2001 first-round draft choices and two 2001 second-round draft choices, Seattle SuperSonics acquired C Patrick Ewing, Phoenix Suns acquired C Chris Dudley and 2001 first-round draft choice and Lakers acquired F Horace Grant, C Greg Foster, F Chuck Person and G Emanual Davis (September 20, 2000).
MISCELLANEOUS: Member of NBA championship team (2000).

COLLEGIATE RECORD

												AVERAGES		
Season Team	G	Min.	FGM	FGA	Pct.	FTM	FTA	Pct.	Reb.	Ast.	Pts.	RPG	APG	PPG
92-93—Connecticut	24	278	29	63	.460	11	27	.407	61	9	69	2.5	0.4	2.9
93-94—Connecticut	33	390	36	82	.439	9	18	.500	97	24	81	2.9	0.7	2.5
94-95—Connecticut	33	768	129	231	.558	41	63	.651	272	38	299	8.2	1.2	9.1
95-96—Connecticut	34	854	126	242	.521	59	85	.694	317	71	311	9.3	2.1	9.1
Totals	124	2290	320	618	.518	120	193	.622	747	142	760	6.0	1.1	6.1

Three-point field goals: 1992-93, 0-for-5.

DID YOU KNOW . . .

. . . that the Miami Heat enter the 2001-02 season having hit at least one 3-point field goal
in a record 589 consecutive games?

NBA REGULAR-SEASON RECORD

◄HONORS: NBA All-Rookie second team (1997).

								REBOUNDS								AVERAGES		
Season Team	G	Min.	FGM	FGA	Pct.	FTM	FTA	Pct.	Off.	Def.	Tot.	Ast.	St.	Blk.	TO	Pts.	RPG	APG	PPG
96-97—L.A. Lakers	71	1156	140	275	.509	62	100	.620	130	189	319	39	31	58	49	342	4.5	0.5	4.8
97-98—Boston	74	1503	193	438	.441	81	103	.786	146	219	365	104	54	82	87	482	4.9	1.4	6.5
98-99—L.A. Lakers	37	525	67	130	.515	22	29	.759	34	94	128	31	21	27	35	156	3.5	0.8	4.2
99-00—L.A. Lakers	63	410	46	118	.390	17	28	.607	46	83	129	23	6	23	26	109	2.0	0.4	1.7
00-01—New York	45	256	10	53	.189	9	18	.500	19	34	53	5	5	11	10	29	1.2	0.1	0.6
Totals	290	3850	456	1014	.450	191	278	.687	375	619	994	202	117	201	207	1118	3.4	0.7	3.9

Three-point field goals: 1997-98, 15-for-55 (.273). 1998-99, 0-for-1. 2000-01, 0-for-1. Totals, 15-for-57 (.263).
Personal fouls/disqualifications: 1996-97, 170/2. 1997-98, 253/3. 1998-99, 108/2. 1999-00, 88/1. 2000-01, 47/0. Totals, 666/8.

NBA PLAYOFF RECORD

NOTES: Shares single-game playoff record for fewest minutes played, disqualified player—7 (May 23, 1999, vs. San Antonio).

								REBOUNDS								AVERAGES		
Season Team	G	Min.	FGM	FGA	Pct.	FTM	FTA	Pct.	Off.	Def.	Tot.	Ast.	St.	Blk.	TO	Pts.	RPG	APG	PPG
96-97—L.A. Lakers	9	93	8	10	.800	3	4	.750	3	15	18	3	3	3	2	19	2.0	0.3	2.1
98-99—L.A. Lakers	3	10	1	3	.333	1	2	.500	0	5	5	1	0	0	3	3	1.7	0.3	1.0
99-00—L.A. Lakers	14	48	8	15	.533	2	6	.333	3	2	5	0	1	3	6	18	0.4	0.0	1.3
00-01—New York	1	1	0	0	...	0	0	...	0	0	0	0	0	0	0	0	0.0	0.0	0.0
Totals	27	152	17	28	.607	6	12	.500	6	22	28	4	4	6	11	40	1.0	0.1	1.5

Personal fouls/disqualifications: 1996-97, 16/0. 1998-99, 7/1. 1999-00, 16/0. 2000-01, 1/0. Totals, 40/1.

KUKOC, TONI   F   HAWKS

PERSONAL: Born September 18, 1968, in Split, Croatia. ... 6-11/235. (2,11/106,6). ... Name pronounced COO-coach.
TRANSACTIONS/CAREER NOTES: Played in Yugoslavia (1989-90 and 1990-91). ... Selected by Chicago Bulls in second round (29th pick overall) of 1990 NBA Draft. ... Played in Italy (1991-92 and 1992-93). ... Traded by Bulls to Philadelphia 76ers for F Bruce Bowen in three-way deal in which 76ers sent G Larry Hughes and F/G Billy Owens to Golden State Warriors and Warriors sent G John Starks and future first-round draft choice to Bulls (February 16, 2000). ... Traded by 76ers with F/C Theo Ratliff, C Nazr Mohammed and G Pepe Sanchez to Atlanta Hawks for C Dikembe Mutombo and F Roshown McLeod (February 22, 2001).
MISCELLANEOUS: Member of NBA championship team (1996, 1997, 1998). ... Member of silver-medal-winning Yugoslavian Olympic team (1988). ... Member of silver-medal-winning Croatian Olympic team (1992). ... Member of Croatian Olympic team (1996).

ITALIAN LEAGUE RECORD

												AVERAGES		
Season Team	G	Min.	FGM	FGA	Pct.	FTM	FTA	Pct.	Reb.	Ast.	Pts.	RPG	APG	PPG
91-92—Benetton Treviso	22	826	173	313	.553	59	89	.663	118	121	464	5.4	5.5	21.1
92-93—Benetton Treviso	29	1084	191	363	.526	117	150	.780	187	152	551	6.4	5.2	19.0
Totals	51	1910	364	676	.538	176	239	.736	305	273	1015	6.0	5.4	19.9

Three-point field goals: 1991-92, 59-for-130 (.454). 1992-93, 52-for-130 (.400). Totals, 111-for-260 (.427).

NBA REGULAR-SEASON RECORD

HONORS: NBA Sixth Man Award (1996). ... NBA All-Rookie second team (1994).

								REBOUNDS								AVERAGES		
Season Team	G	Min.	FGM	FGA	Pct.	FTM	FTA	Pct.	Off.	Def.	Tot.	Ast.	St.	Blk.	TO	Pts.	RPG	APG	PPG
93-94—Chicago	75	1808	313	726	.431	156	210	.743	98	199	297	252	81	33	167	814	4.0	3.4	10.9
94-95—Chicago	81	2584	487	967	.504	235	314	.748	155	285	440	372	102	16	165	1271	5.4	4.6	15.7
95-96—Chicago	81	2103	386	787	.490	206	267	.772	115	208	323	287	64	28	114	1065	4.0	3.5	13.1
96-97—Chicago	57	1610	285	605	.471	134	174	.770	94	167	261	256	60	29	91	754	4.6	4.5	13.2
97-98—Chicago	74	2235	383	841	.455	155	219	.708	121	206	327	314	76	37	154	984	4.4	4.2	13.3
98-99—Chicago	44	1654	315	750	.420	159	215	.740	65	245	310	235	49	11	121	828	7.0	5.3	18.8
99-00—Chi.-Phil.	56	1784	297	728	.408	192	265	.725	75	198	273	265	77	28	146	830	4.9	4.7	14.8
00-01—Phil.a-Atlanta	65	1597	275	582	.473	101	160	.631	66	193	259	199	48	11	111	721	4.0	3.1	11.1
Totals	533	15375	2741	5986	.458	1338	1824	.734	789	1701	2490	2180	557	193	1069	7267	4.7	4.1	13.6

Three-point field goals: 1993-94, 32-for-118 (.271). 1994-95, 62-for-198 (.313). 1995-96, 87-for-216 (.403). 1996-97, 50-for-151 (.331). 1997-98, 63-for-174 (.362). 1998-99, 39-for-137 (.285). 1999-00, 44-for-168 (.262). 2000-01, 70-for-157 (.446). Totals, 447-for-1319 (.339).
Personal fouls/disqualifications: 1993-94, 122/0. 1994-95, 163/1. 1995-96, 160/0. 1996-97, 97/1. 1997-98, 149/0. 1998-99, 82/0. 1999-00, 112/0. 2000-01, 98/0. Totals, 973/2.

NBA PLAYOFF RECORD

								REBOUNDS								AVERAGES		
Season Team	G	Min.	FGM	FGA	Pct.	FTM	FTA	Pct.	Off.	Def.	Tot.	Ast.	St.	Blk.	TO	Pts.	RPG	APG	PPG
93-94—Chicago	10	194	30	67	.448	25	34	.735	11	29	40	36	5	3	17	93	4.0	3.6	9.3
94-95—Chicago	10	372	53	111	.477	18	26	.692	20	48	68	57	10	2	19	138	6.8	5.7	13.8
95-96—Chicago	15	439	59	151	.391	31	37	.838	19	44	63	58	14	4	26	162	4.2	3.9	10.8
96-97—Chicago	19	423	45	125	.360	41	58	.707	13	41	54	54	13	4	17	150	2.8	2.8	7.9
97-98—Chicago	21	637	106	218	.486	40	62	.645	24	57	81	60	26	10	27	275	3.9	2.9	13.1
99-00—Philadelphia	10	257	36	93	.387	10	17	.588	7	30	37	17	10	3	15	93	3.7	1.7	9.3
Totals	85	2322	329	765	.430	165	234	.705	94	249	343	282	78	26	121	911	4.0	3.3	10.7

Three-point field goals: 1993-94, 8-for-19 (.421). 1994-95, 14-for-32 (.438). 1995-96, 13-for-68 (.191). 1996-97, 19-for-53 (.358). 1997-98, 23-for-61 (.377). 1999-00, 11-for-34 (.324). Totals, 88-for-267 (.330).
Personal fouls/disqualifications: 1993-94, 15/0. 1994-95, 23/0. 1995-96, 33/0. 1996-97, 30/0. 1997-98, 57/1. 1999-00, 26/0. Totals, 184/1.

LAETTNER, CHRISTIAN   F/C   WIZARDS

PERSONAL: Born August 17, 1969, in Angola, N.Y. ... 6-11/245. (2,11/111,1). ... Full Name: Christian Donald Laettner. ... Name pronounced LATE-ner.
HIGH SCHOOL: Nichols School (Buffalo).
COLLEGE: Duke.
TRANSACTIONS/CAREER NOTES: Selected by Minnesota Timberwolves in first round (third pick overall) of 1992 NBA Draft. ... Traded by Timberwolves with C Sean Rooks to Atlanta Hawks for G Spud Webb and C Andrew Lang (February 22, 1996). ... Traded by Hawks to Detroit Pistons for C Scot Pollard and 1999 first-round draft choice (January 22, 1999). ... Traded by Pistons with F Terry Mills to Dallas Mavericks for F Cedric Ceballos, F John Wallace and G Eric Murdock (August 29, 2000). ... Traded by Mavericks with G Courtney Alexander, F Loy Vaught, G Hubert Davis, F/C Etan Thomas and cash considerations to Washington Wizards for F Juwan Howard, C Calvin Booth and F Obinna Ekezie (February 22, 2001).
MISCELLANEOUS: Member of gold-medal-winning U.S. Olympic team (1992). ... Member of bronze-medal-winning U.S. World Championship team (1990).

COLLEGIATE RECORD

NOTES: THE SPORTING NEWS College Player of the Year (1992). ... Naismith Award winner (1992). ... Wooden Award winner (1992). ... THE SPORTING NEWS All-America first team (1992). ... THE SPORTING NEWS All-America second team (1991). ... THE SPORTING NEWS All-America third team (1990). ... NCAA Division I Tournament Most Outstanding Player (1991). ... Member of NCAA Division I championship team (1991, 1992).

Season Team	G	Min.	FGM	FGA	Pct.	FTM	FTA	Pct.	Reb.	Ast.	Pts.	RPG	APG	PPG
88-89—Duke	36	607	115	159	.723	88	121	.727	170	44	319	4.7	1.2	8.9
89-90—Duke	38	1135	194	380	.511	225	269	.836	364	84	619	9.6	2.2	16.3
90-91—Duke	39	1178	271	471	.575	211	263	.802	340	76	771	8.7	1.9	19.8
91-92—Duke	35	1128	254	442	.575	189	232	.815	275	69	751	7.9	2.0	21.5
Totals	148	4048	834	1452	.574	713	885	.806	1149	273	2460	7.8	1.8	16.6

Three-point field goals: 1988-89, 1-for-1. 1989-90, 6-for-12 (.500). 1990-91, 18-for-53 (.340). 1991-92, 54-for-97 (.557). Totals, 79-for-163 (.485).

HONORS: NBA All-Rookie first team (1993).

NBA REGULAR-SEASON RECORD

Season Team	G	Min.	FGM	FGA	Pct.	FTM	FTA	Pct.	Off.	Def.	Tot.	Ast.	St.	Blk.	TO	Pts.	RPG	APG	PPG
92-93—Minnesota	81	2823	503	1061	.474	462	553	.835	171	537	708	223	105	83	275	1472	8.7	2.8	18.2
93-94—Minnesota	70	2428	396	883	.448	375	479	.783	160	442	602	307	87	86	259	1173	8.6	4.4	16.8
94-95—Minnesota	81	2770	450	920	.489	409	500	.818	164	449	613	234	101	87	225	1322	7.6	2.9	16.3
95-96—Minn.-Atl.	74	2495	442	907	.487	324	396	.818	184	354	538	197	71	71	187	1217	7.3	2.7	16.4
96-97—Atlanta	82	3140	548	1128	.486	359	440	.816	212	508	720	223	102	64	218	1486	8.8	2.7	18.1
97-98—Atlanta	74	2282	354	730	.485	306	354	.864	142	345	487	190	71	73	183	1020	6.6	2.6	13.8
98-99—Detroit	16	337	38	106	.358	44	57	.772	21	33	54	24	15	12	19	121	3.4	1.5	7.6
99-00—Detroit	82	2443	379	801	.473	237	292	.812	175	378	553	186	83	45	186	1002	6.7	2.3	12.2
00-01—Dallas-Wash.	78	1663	277	551	.503	170	204	.833	118	247	365	124	71	46	137	728	4.7	1.6	9.3
Totals	638	20381	3387	7087	.478	2686	3275	.820	1347	3293	4640	1708	706	567	1689	9541	7.3	2.7	15.0

Three-point field goals: 1992-93, 4-for-40 (.100). 1993-94, 6-for-25 (.240). 1994-95, 13-for-40 (.325). 1995-96, 9-for-39 (.231). 1996-97, 31-for-88 (.352). 1997-98, 6-for-27 (.222). 1998-99, 1-for-3 (.333). 1999-00, 7-for-24 (.292). 2000-01, 4-for-13 (.308). Totals, 81-for-299 (.271).

Personal fouls/disqualifications: 1992-93, 290/4. 1993-94, 264/6. 1994-95, 302/4. 1995-96, 276/7. 1996-97, 277/8. 1997-98, 246/6. 1998-99, 30/0. 1999-00, 326/10. 2000-01, 242/1. Totals, 2253/46.

NBA PLAYOFF RECORD

Season Team	G	Min.	FGM	FGA	Pct.	FTM	FTA	Pct.	Off.	Def.	Tot.	Ast.	St.	Blk.	TO	Pts.	RPG	APG	PPG
95-96—Atlanta	10	334	59	122	.484	38	54	.704	27	42	69	15	12	10	21	157	6.9	1.5	15.7
96-97—Atlanta	10	403	62	153	.405	48	56	.857	19	53	72	26	10	8	31	176	7.2	2.6	17.6
97-98—Atlanta	4	87	12	35	.343	15	17	.882	3	14	17	4	6	1	8	39	4.3	1.0	9.8
98-99—Detroit	5	123	20	47	.426	11	14	.786	6	8	14	11	4	1	3	51	2.8	2.2	10.2
99-00—Detroit	3	75	7	17	.412	6	8	.750	2	13	15	6	0	1	3	20	5.0	2.0	6.7
Totals	32	1022	160	374	.428	118	149	.792	57	130	187	62	32	21	66	443	5.8	1.9	13.8

Three-point field goals: 1995-96, 1-for-3 (.333). 1996-97, 4-for-21 (.190). 1997-98, 0-for-3. Totals, 5-for-27 (.185).

Personal fouls/disqualifications: 1995-96, 41/1. 1996-97, 32/0. 1997-98, 16/1. 1998-99, 14/0. 1999-00, 14/0. Totals, 117/2.

NBA ALL-STAR GAME RECORD

Season Team	Min.	FGM	FGA	Pct.	FTM	FTA	Pct.	Off.	Def.	Tot.	Ast.	PF	Dq.	St.	Blk.	TO	Pts.
1997 —Atlanta	24	3	5	.600	1	1	1.000	4	7	11	2	4	0	1	1	2	7

LaFRENTZ, RAEF   F/C   NUGGETS

PERSONAL: Born May 29, 1976, in Hampton, Iowa. ... 6-11/240. (2,11/108,9). ... Full Name: Raef Andrew LaFrentz.
HIGH SCHOOL: Mar-Mac (Monona, Iowa).
COLLEGE: Kansas.
TRANSACTIONS/CAREER NOTES: Selected by Denver Nuggets in first round (third pick overall) of 1998 NBA Draft.

COLLEGIATE RECORD

NOTES: THE SPORTING NEWS All-America first team (1998). ... THE SPORTING NEWS All-America second team (1997).

Season Team	G	Min.	FGM	FGA	Pct.	FTM	FTA	Pct.	Reb.	Ast.	Pts.	RPG	APG	PPG
94-95—Kansas	31	732	143	268	.534	65	102	.637	231	17	353	7.5	0.5	11.4
95-96—Kansas	34	917	189	348	.543	74	112	.661	278	14	454	8.2	0.4	13.4
96-97—Kansas	36	1041	261	447	.584	143	188	.761	335	25	666	9.3	0.7	18.5
97-98—Kansas	30	906	232	423	.548	121	164	.738	342	30	593	11.4	1.0	19.8
Totals	131	3596	825	1486	.555	403	566	.712	1186	86	2066	9.1	0.7	15.8

Three-point field goals: 1994-95, 2-for-5 (.400). 1995-96, 1-for-5 (.200). 1996-97, 1-for-3 (.333). 1997-98, 8-for-17 (.471). Totals, 12-for-30 (.400).

NBA REGULAR-SEASON RECORD

									REBOUNDS								AVERAGES		
Season Team	G	Min.	FGM	FGA	Pct.	FTM	FTA	Pct.	Off.	Def.	Tot.	Ast.	St.	Blk.	TO	Pts.	RPG	APG	PPG
98-99—Denver	12	387	59	129	.457	36	48	.750	33	58	91	8	9	17	9	166	7.6	0.7	13.8
99-00—Denver	81	2435	392	879	.446	162	236	.686	170	471	641	97	42	180	96	1006	7.9	1.2	12.4
00-01—Denver	78	2457	387	812	.477	183	262	.698	173	434	607	107	37	206	97	1008	7.8	1.4	12.9
Totals	171	5279	838	1820	.460	381	546	.698	376	963	1339	212	88	403	202	2180	7.8	1.2	12.7

Three-point field goals: 1998-99, 12-for-31 (.387). 1999-00, 60-for-183 (.328). 2000-01, 51-for-139 (.367). Totals, 123-for-353 (.348).
Personal fouls/disqualifications: 1998-99, 38/2. 1999-00, 292/6. 2000-01, 290/9. Totals, 620/17.

LANGDON, TRAJAN   G   CAVALIERS

PERSONAL: Born May 13, 1976, in Palo Alto, Calif. ... 6-3/197. (1,91/89,4). ... Full Name: Trajan Shaka Langdon.
HIGH SCHOOL: Anchorage (Alaska) Christian.
COLLEGE: Duke.
TRANSACTIONS/CAREER NOTES: Selected by Cleveland Cavaliers in first round (11th pick overall) of 1999 NBA Draft.
MISCELLANEOUS: Member of bronze-medal-winning U.S. World Championship team (1998).

COLLEGIATE RECORD

NOTES: The Sporting News All-America second team (1998 and 1999).

												AVERAGES		
Season Team	G	Min.	FGM	FGA	Pct.	FTM	FTA	Pct.	Reb.	Ast.	Pts.	RPG	APG	PPG
94-95—Duke	31	797	124	274	.453	44	56	.786	65	48	351	2.1	1.5	11.3
95-96—Duke						Did not play—medical redshirt.								
96-97—Duke	33	972	137	308	.445	113	126	.897	97	68	473	2.9	2.1	14.3
97-98—Duke	36	1035	171	385	.444	101	114	.886	104	70	528	2.9	1.9	14.7
98-99—Duke	36	1117	191	413	.462	128	152	.842	123	69	622	3.4	1.9	17.3
Totals	136	3921	623	1380	.451	386	448	.862	389	255	1974	2.9	1.9	14.5

Three-point field goals: 1994-95, 59-for-138 (.428). 1996-97, 86-for-195 (.441). 1997-98, 85-for-215 (.395). 1998-99, 112-for-254 (.441). Totals, 342-for-802 (.426).

NBA REGULAR-SEASON RECORD

									REBOUNDS								AVERAGES		
Season Team	G	Min.	FGM	FGA	Pct.	FTM	FTA	Pct.	Off.	Def.	Tot.	Ast.	St.	Blk.	TO	Pts.	RPG	APG	PPG
99-00—Cleveland	10	145	15	40	.375	11	11	1.000	4	11	15	11	5	0	6	49	1.5	1.1	4.9
00-01—Cleveland	65	1116	135	313	.431	68	76	.895	12	77	89	81	38	9	52	389	1.4	1.2	6.0
Totals	75	1261	150	353	.425	79	87	.908	16	88	104	92	43	9	58	438	1.4	1.2	5.8

Three-point field goals: 1999-00, 8-for-19 (.421). 2000-01, 51-for-124 (.411). Totals, 59-for-143 (.413).
Personal fouls/disqualifications: 1999-00, 16/0. 2000-01, 114/0. Totals, 130/0.

LANGHI, DAN   F   ROCKETS

PERSONAL: Born November 28, 1977, in Chicago. ... 6-11/220. (2,11/99,8). ... Full Name: Daniel Matthew Langhi.
HIGH SCHOOL: Marshall County (Benton, Ky.).
COLLEGE: Vanderbilt.
TRANSACTIONS/CAREER NOTES: Selected by Dallas Mavericks in second round (31st pick overall) of 2000 NBA Draft. ... Draft rights traded by Mavericks to Houston Rockets for draft rights to F Eduardo Najera and a future second-round draft choice (June 28, 2000).

COLLEGIATE RECORD

												AVERAGES		
Season Team	G	Min.	FGM	FGA	Pct.	FTM	FTA	Pct.	Reb.	Ast.	Pts.	RPG	APG	PPG
96-97—Vanderbilt	32	477	33	76	.434	55	74	.743	76	9	130	2.4	0.3	4.1
97-98—Vanderbilt	31	492	68	162	.420	36	47	.766	91	14	196	2.9	0.5	6.3
98-99—Vanderbilt	29	954	162	338	.479	141	167	.844	211	36	512	7.3	1.2	17.7
99-00—Vanderbilt	30	1033	222	465	.477	162	186	.871	181	24	664	6.0	0.8	22.1
Totals	122	2956	485	1041	.466	394	474	.831	559	83	1502	4.6	0.7	12.3

Three-point field goals: 1996-97, 9-for-27 (.333). 1997-98, 24-for-67 (.358). 1998-99, 47-for-122 (.385). 1999-00, 58-for-144 (.403). Totals, 138-for-360 (.383).

NBA REGULAR-SEASON RECORD

									REBOUNDS								AVERAGES		
Season Team	G	Min.	FGM	FGA	Pct.	FTM	FTA	Pct.	Off.	Def.	Tot.	Ast.	St.	Blk.	TO	Pts.	RPG	APG	PPG
00-01—Houston	33	241	37	99	.374	16	29	.552	13	28	41	4	7	1	8	90	1.2	0.1	2.7

Three-point field goals: 2000-01, 0-for-1.
Personal fouls/disqualifications: 2000-01, 16/0.

LENARD, VOSHON   G   NUGGETS

PERSONAL: Born May 14, 1973, in Detroit. ... 6-4/205. (1,93/93,0). ... Full Name: Voshon Kelan Lenard. ... Name pronounced Va-SHON.
HIGH SCHOOL: Southwestern (Detroit).
COLLEGE: Minnesota.
TRANSACTIONS/CAREER NOTES: Selected after junior season by Milwaukee Bucks in second round (46th pick overall) of 1994 NBA Draft. ... Returned to college for senior season (1994-95). ... Waived by Bucks (October 25, 1995). ... Played in Continental Basketball Association with Oklahoma City Cavalry (1995-96). ... Signed as free agent by Miami Heat for remainder of season (December 29, 1995). ... Traded by Heat with F Mark Strickland to Denver Nuggets for F/C Chris Gatling and a 2000 second-round draft choice (June 27, 2000).

Season Team	G	Min.	FGM	FGA	Pct.	FTM	FTA	Pct.	Reb.	Ast.	Pts.	RPG	APG	PPG
91-92—Minnesota	32	868	139	330	.421	82	101	.812	118	86	411	3.7	2.7	12.8
92-93—Minnesota	31	883	192	399	.481	89	111	.802	113	82	531	3.6	2.6	17.1
93-94—Minnesota	33	1029	218	462	.472	103	122	.844	123	74	625	3.7	2.2	18.9
94-95—Minnesota	31	992	174	422	.412	107	141	.759	134	80	536	4.3	2.6	17.3
Totals	127	3772	723	1613	.448	381	475	.802	488	322	2103	3.8	2.5	16.6

Three-point field goals: 1991-92, 51-for-144 (.354). 1992-93, 58-for-158 (.367). 1993-94, 86-for-209 (.411). 1994-95, 81-for-244 (.332). Totals, 276-for-755 (.366).

CBA REGULAR-SEASON RECORD

Season Team	G	Min.	FGM	FGA	Pct.	FTM	FTA	Pct.	Reb.	Ast.	Pts.	RPG	APG	PPG
95-96—Oklahoma City	18	711	189	387	.488	75	100	.750	60	70	541	3.3	3.9	30.1

Three-point field goals: 1995-96, 88-for-203 (.433).

NBA REGULAR-SEASON RECORD

Season Team	G	Min.	FGM	FGA	Pct.	FTM	FTA	Pct.	REBOUNDS Off.	Def.	Tot.	Ast.	St.	Blk.	TO	Pts.	RPG	APG	PPG
95-96—Miami	30	323	53	141	.376	34	43	.791	12	40	52	31	6	1	23	176	1.7	1.0	5.9
96-97—Miami	73	2111	314	684	.459	86	105	.819	38	179	217	161	50	18	109	897	3.0	2.2	12.3
97-98—Miami	81	2621	363	854	.425	141	179	.788	72	220	292	180	58	16	99	1020	3.6	2.2	12.6
98-99—Miami	12	190	31	79	.392	8	11	.727	4	12	16	10	3	1	7	82	1.3	0.8	6.8
99-00—Miami	53	1434	228	560	.407	84	106	.792	37	116	153	136	41	15	80	629	2.9	2.6	11.9
00-01—Denver	80	2331	336	846	.397	153	192	.797	47	184	231	190	65	18	102	972	2.9	2.4	12.2
Totals	329	9010	1325	3164	.419	506	636	.796	210	751	961	708	223	69	420	3776	2.9	2.2	11.5

Three-point field goals: 1995-96, 36-for-101 (.356). 1996-97, 183-for-442 (.414). 1997-98, 153-for-378 (.405). 1998-99, 12-for-35 (.343). 1999-00, 89-for-228 (.390). 2000-01, 147-for-382 (.385). Totals, 620-for-1566 (.396).

Personal fouls/disqualifications: 1995-96, 31/0. 1996-97, 168/1. 1997-98, 219/0. 1998-99, 18/0. 1999-00, 127/2. 2000-01, 170/1. Totals, 733/4.

NBA PLAYOFF RECORD

Season Team	G	Min.	FGM	FGA	Pct.	FTM	FTA	Pct.	REBOUNDS Off.	Def.	Tot.	Ast.	St.	Blk.	TO	Pts.	RPG	APG	PPG
96-97—Miami	17	548	63	155	.406	32	37	.865	12	38	50	36	11	3	30	194	2.9	2.1	11.4
97-98—Miami	5	186	24	52	.462	15	20	.750	1	18	19	7	1	2	11	72	3.8	1.4	14.4
98-99—Miami	4	57	12	22	.545	4	4	1.000	0	1	1	3	0	1	1	37	0.3	0.8	9.3
Totals	26	791	99	229	.432	51	61	.836	13	57	70	46	12	6	42	303	2.7	1.8	11.7

Three-point field goals: 1996-97, 36-for-91 (.396). 1997-98, 9-for-26 (.346). 1998-99, 9-for-14 (.643). Totals, 54-for-131 (.412).

Personal fouls/disqualifications: 1996-97, 49/0. 1997-98, 20/0. 1998-99, 4/0. Totals, 73/0.

LEWIS, QUINCY   F   JAZZ

PERSONAL: Born June 26, 1977, in Little Rock, Ark. ... 6-7/215. (2,01/97,5). ... Full Name: Quincy Lavell Lewis.
HIGH SCHOOL: Parkview Arts/Science Magnet (Little Rock, Ark.).
COLLEGE: Minnesota.
TRANSACTIONS/CAREER NOTES: Selected by Utah Jazz in first round (19th pick overall) of 1999 NBA Draft.

COLLEGIATE RECORD

Season Team	G	Min.	FGM	FGA	Pct.	FTM	FTA	Pct.	Reb.	Ast.	Pts.	RPG	APG	PPG
95-96—Minnesota	30	407	76	167	.455	24	36	.667	56	35	202	1.9	1.2	6.7
96-97—Minnesota	35	618	110	230	.478	45	70	.643	91	51	281	2.6	1.5	8.0
97-98—Minnesota	35	1044	197	431	.457	80	118	.678	195	66	506	5.6	1.9	14.5
98-99—Minnesota	27	913	226	495	.457	120	148	.811	160	38	625	5.9	1.4	23.1
Totals	127	2982	609	1323	.460	269	372	.723	502	190	1614	4.0	1.5	12.7

Three-point field goals: 1995-96, 26-for-71 (.366). 1996-97, 32-for-107 (.299). 1997-98, 32-for-107 (.299). 1998-99, 53-for-133 (.398). Totals, 143-for-418 (.342).

NBA REGULAR-SEASON RECORD

Season Team	G	Min.	FGM	FGA	Pct.	FTM	FTA	Pct.	REBOUNDS Off.	Def.	Tot.	Ast.	St.	Blk.	TO	Pts.	RPG	APG	PPG
99-00—Utah	74	896	111	298	.372	38	52	.731	46	67	113	40	24	15	46	283	1.5	0.5	3.8
00-01—Utah	35	402	50	123	.407	15	21	.714	14	33	47	18	10	10	17	124	1.3	0.5	3.5
Totals	109	1298	161	421	.382	53	73	.726	60	100	160	58	34	25	63	407	1.5	0.5	3.7

Three-point field goals: 1999-00, 23-for-63 (.365). 2000-01, 9-for-25 (.360). Totals, 32-for-88 (.364).

Personal fouls/disqualifications: 1999-00, 158/0. 2000-01, 78/1. Totals, 236/1.

NBA PLAYOFF RECORD

Season Team	G	Min.	FGM	FGA	Pct.	FTM	FTA	Pct.	REBOUNDS Off.	Def.	Tot.	Ast.	St.	Blk.	TO	Pts.	RPG	APG	PPG
99-00—Utah	8	106	10	27	.370	4	5	.800	2	13	15	2	3	7	3	26	1.9	0.3	3.3

Three-point field goals: 1999-00, 2-for-6 (.333).
Personal fouls/disqualifications: 1999-00, 24/0.

LEWIS, RASHARD   F   SUPERSONICS

PERSONAL: Born August 8, 1979, in Pineville, La. ... 6-10/215. (2,08/97,5). ... Full Name: Rashard Quovon Lewis.
HIGH SCHOOL: Alief (Texas) Elsik.
COLLEGE: Did not attend college.
TRANSACTIONS/CAREER NOTES: Selected out of high school by Seattle SuperSonics in second round (32nd pick overall) of 1998 NBA Draft.

NBA REGULAR-SEASON RECORD

Season Team	G	Min.	FGM	FGA	Pct.	FTM	FTA	Pct.	REBOUNDS Off.	Def.	Tot.	Ast.	St.	Blk.	TO	Pts.	AVERAGES RPG	APG	PPG
98-99—Seattle	20	145	19	52	.365	8	14	.571	13	12	25	4	8	1	20	47	1.3	0.2	2.4
99-00—Seattle	82	1575	275	566	.486	84	123	.683	127	209	336	70	62	36	78	674	4.1	0.9	8.2
00-01—Seattle	78	2720	426	887	.480	176	213	.826	143	398	541	125	91	45	129	1151	6.9	1.6	14.8
Totals	180	4440	720	1505	.478	268	350	.766	283	619	902	199	161	82	227	1872	5.0	1.1	10.4

Three-point field goals: 1998-99, 1-for-6 (.167). 1999-00, 40-for-120 (.333). 2000-01, 123-for-285 (.432). Totals, 164-for-411 (.399).
Personal fouls/disqualifications: 1998-99, 19/0. 1999-00, 163/0. 2000-01, 191/2. Totals, 373/2.

NBA PLAYOFF RECORD

Season Team	G	Min.	FGM	FGA	Pct.	FTM	FTA	Pct.	REBOUNDS Off.	Def.	Tot.	Ast.	St.	Blk.	TO	Pts.	AVERAGES RPG	APG	PPG
99-00—Seattle	5	157	26	59	.441	16	20	.800	12	19	31	3	5	3	10	77	6.2	0.6	15.4

Three-point field goals: 1999-00, 9-for-19 (.474).
Personal fouls/disqualifications: 1999-00, 11/0.

LIVINGSTON, RANDY   G

PERSONAL: Born April 2, 1975, in New Orleans. ... 6-4/209. (1,93/94,8). ... Full Name: Randy Anthony Livingston.
HIGH SCHOOL: Newman (New Orleans).
COLLEGE: Louisiana State.
TRANSACTIONS/CAREER NOTES: Selected after sophomore season by Houston Rockets in second round (42nd pick overall) of 1996 NBA Draft. ... Waived by Rockets (October 30, 1997). ... Signed as free agent by Atlanta Hawks (November 7, 1997). ... Waived by Hawks (November 20, 1997). ... Played in Continental Basketball Association with Sioux Falls Skyforce (1997-98 and 1998-99) and Idaho Stampede (2000-01). ... Re-signed as free agent by Hawks (December 9, 1997). ... Waived by Hawks (December 19, 1997). ... Re-signed by Hawks to 10-day contract (January 10, 1998). ... Signed as free agent by Miami Heat (January 21, 1999). ... Waived by Heat (January 30, 1999). ... Signed as free agent by Phoenix Suns for remainder of season (May 4, 1999). ... Waived by Suns (August 31, 2000). ... Signed as free agent by Seattle SuperSonics (October 2, 2000). ... Claimed on waivers by Orlando Magic (October 13, 2000). ... Waived by Magic (October 30, 2000). ... Signed as free agent by Golden State Warriors (November 15, 2000). ... Waived by Warriors (November 21, 2000). ... Played in International Basketball League with Sioux Falls Sky Force (2000-01).

COLLEGIATE RECORD

Season Team	G	Min.	FGM	FGA	Pct.	FTM	FTA	Pct.	Reb.	Ast.	Pts.	AVERAGES RPG	APG	PPG
93-94—Louisiana State..............							Did not play—redshirted.							
94-95—Louisiana State..............	16	550	81	185	.438	42	62	.677	64	151	224	4.0	9.4	14.0
95-96—Louisiana State..............	13	318	24	83	.289	30	38	.789	30	69	79	2.3	5.3	6.1
Totals	29	868	105	268	.392	72	100	.720	94	220	303	3.2	7.6	10.4

Three-point field goals: 1994-95, 20-for-65 (.308). 1995-96, 1-for-20 (.050). Totals, 21-for-85 (.247).

NBA REGULAR-SEASON RECORD

Season Team	G	Min.	FGM	FGA	Pct.	FTM	FTA	Pct.	REBOUNDS Off.	Def.	Tot.	Ast.	St.	Blk.	TO	Pts.	AVERAGES RPG	APG	PPG
96-97—Houston.........	64	981	100	229	.437	42	65	.646	32	62	94	155	39	12	102	251	1.5	2.4	3.9
97-98—Atlanta	12	82	3	12	.250	4	5	.800	1	5	6	5	7	2	6	10	0.5	0.4	0.8
98-99—Phoenix	1	22	5	8	.625	2	2	1.000	0	2	2	3	2	0	1	12	2.0	3.0	12.0
99-00—Phoenix	79	1081	155	373	.416	52	62	.839	25	105	130	170	49	13	92	381	1.6	2.2	4.8
00-01—Golden State ...	2	7	0	2	.000	0	0	...	0	1	1	1	0	0	0	0	0.5	0.5	0.0
Totals	158	2173	263	624	.421	100	134	.746	58	175	233	334	97	27	201	654	1.5	2.1	4.1

Three-point field goals: 1996-97, 9-for-22 (.409). 1999-00, 19-for-55 (.345). 2000-01, 0-for-1. Totals, 28-for-78 (.359).
Personal fouls/disqualifications: 1996-97, 107/0. 1997-98, 6/0. 98-99, 1/0. 1999-00, 129/1. Totals, 243/1.

NBA PLAYOFF RECORD

Season Team	G	Min.	FGM	FGA	Pct.	FTM	FTA	Pct.	REBOUNDS Off.	Def.	Tot.	Ast.	St.	Blk.	TO	Pts.	AVERAGES RPG	APG	PPG
96-97—Houston.........	2	15	1	4	.250	0	0	...	0	0	0	4	1	0	1	3	0.0	2.0	1.5
98-99—Phoenix	3	24	6	15	.400	4	4	1.000	5	2	7	2	1	0	2	16	2.3	0.7	5.3
99-00—Phoenix	7	63	6	27	.222	0	0	...	2	5	7	4	4	1	4	14	1.0	0.6	2.0
Totals	12	102	13	46	.283	4	4	1.000	7	7	14	10	6	1	7	33	1.2	0.8	2.8

Three-point field goals: 1996-97, 1-for-1. 1998-99, 0-for-1. 1999-00, 2-for-6 (.333). Totals, 3-for-8 (.375).
Personal fouls/disqualifications: 1996-97, 1/0. 1998-99, 6/0. 1999-00, 6/0. Totals, 13/0.

NOTES: CBA All-League second team (1999).

CBA REGULAR-SEASON RECORD

Season Team	G	Min.	FGM	FGA	Pct.	FTM	FTA	Pct.	Reb.	Ast.	Pts.	AVERAGES RPG	APG	PPG
97-98—Sioux Falls.....................	28	1049	160	387	.413	91	128	.711	151	187	424	5.4	6.7	15.1
98-99—Sioux Falls.....................	40	1321	196	483	.406	128	159	.805	168	259	546	4.2	6.5	13.7
00-01—Idaho..........................	24	892	128	328	.390	56	65	.862	87	174	339	3.6	7.3	14.1
Totals	92	3262	484	1198	.404	275	352	.781	406	620	1309	4.4	6.7	14.2

Three-point field goals: 1997-98, 13-for-57 (.228). 1998-99, 26-for-101 (.257). 190-01, 27-for-105 (.257). Totals, 66-for-263 (.251).

IBL REGULAR-SEASON RECORD

Season Team	G	Min.	FGM	FGA	Pct.	FTM	FTA	Pct.	Reb.	Ast.	Pts.	AVERAGES RPG	APG	PPG
00-01—Sioux Falls.....................	26	885	138	335	.412	74	88	.841	100	164	400	4.2	6.3	15.4

Three-point field goals: 2000-01, 50-for-126 (.397).

L

LONG, ART   F

PERSONAL: Born October 1, 1973, in Rochester, N.Y. ... 6-9/250. (2,06/113,4). ... Full Name: Arthur Donnell Long.
HIGH SCHOOL: East (Rochester, N.Y.).
JUNIOR COLLEGE: Independence (Kan.) Community College, then Dodge City (Kan.) Community College, then Southeastern (Iowa) Community College.
COLLEGE: Cincinnati.
TRANSACTIONS/CAREER NOTES: Not drafted by an NBA franchise. ... Played in Portugal (1996-97). ... Played in France (1996-97 and 2000-01). ... Played in Argentina (1996-97). ... Played in Continental Basketball Association with Idaho Stampede (1998-99) and Yakima Sun Kings (1999-2000). ... Played in Cyprus (1998-99). ... Signed as free agent by Portland Trail Blazers (January 22, 1999). ... Waived by Trail Blazers (February 18, 1999). ... Signed as free agent by Sacramento Kings (October 1, 1999). ... Waived by Kings (October 29, 1999). ... Played in Puerto Rico (1999-2000 and 2000-01). ... Signed by Kings to first of two consecutive 10-day contracts (February 18, 2001). ... Re-signed by Kings for remainder of season (March 12, 2001).

COLLEGIATE RECORD

Season Team	G	Min.	FGM	FGA	Pct.	FTM	FTA	Pct.	Reb.	Ast.	Pts.	RPG	APG	PPG
91-92—Independence C.C.							Did not play.							
92-93—Dodge City C.C.	27	...	177	300	.590	49	100	.490	243	26	403	9.0	1.0	14.9
93-94—Southeastern Iowa C.C...	34	934	335	523	.641	107	180	.594	352	60	778	10.4	1.8	22.9
94-95—Cincinnati	32	881	171	326	.525	46	84	.548	266	40	389	8.3	1.3	12.2
95-96—Cincinnati	33	813	124	277	.448	48	85	.565	296	21	296	9.0	0.6	9.0
Junior College Totals............	61		512	823	.622	156	280	.557	595	86	1181	9.8	1.4	19.4
4-Year-College Totals	65	1694	295	603	.489	94	169	.556	562	61	685	8.6	0.9	10.5

Three-point field goals: 1992-93, 0-for-8. 1993-94, 1-for-9 (.111). 1994-95, 1-for-5 (.200). 1995-96, 0-for-4. Totals, 1-for-17 (.059) Totals, 1-for-9 (.111).

ARGENTINIAN LEAGUE RECORD

Season Team	G	Min.	FGM	FGA	Pct.	FTM	FTA	Pct.	Reb.	Ast.	Pts.	RPG	APG	PPG
96-97—Gimnasia Comodoro	6	194	44	81	.543	10	27	.370	39	4	98	6.5	0.7	16.3

Three-point field goals: 1996-97, 0-for-6.

FRENCH LEAGUE RECORD

Season Team	G	Min.	FGM	FGA	Pct.	FTM	FTA	Pct.	Reb.	Ast.	Pts.	RPG	APG	PPG
96-97—Pau Orthez..................	4	76	11	23	.478	2	8	.250	12	6	24	3.0	1.5	6.0
00-01—Villeurbanne	13	342	91	144	.632	27	43	.628	112	18	209	8.6	1.4	16.1
Totals	17	418	102	167	.611	29	51	.569	124	24	233	7.3	1.4	13.7

Three-point field goals: 2000-01, 0-for-3.

CBA REGULAR-SEASON RECORD

Season Team	G	Min.	FGM	FGA	Pct.	FTM	FTA	Pct.	Reb.	Ast.	Pts.	RPG	APG	PPG
98-99—Idaho	10	268	48	107	.449	21	31	.677	88	7	117	8.8	0.7	11.7
99-00—Yakima	45	1223	302	573	.527	136	213	.638	401	65	745	8.9	1.4	16.6
Totals	55	1491	350	680	.515	157	244	.643	489	72	862	8.9	1.3	15.7

Three-point field goals: 1998-99, 0-for-3. 1999-00, 5-for-19 (.263). Totals, 5-for-22 (.227).

PUERTO RICAN LEAGUE RECORD

Season Team	G	Min.	FGM	FGA	Pct.	FTM	FTA	Pct.	Reb.	Ast.	Pts.	RPG	APG	PPG
00-01—Guayama	8	227	53	92	.576	10	18	.556	83	17	121	10.4	2.1	15.1

Three-point field goals: 2000-01, 5-for-21 (.238).

NBA REGULAR-SEASON RECORD

Season Team	G	Min.	FGM	FGA	Pct.	FTM	FTA	Pct.	REBOUNDS Off.	Def.	Tot.	Ast.	St.	Blk.	TO	Pts.	RPG	APG	PPG
00-01—Sacramento	9	20	0	4	.000	0	2	.000	2	6	8	1	0	3	2	0	0.9	0.1	0.0

Personal fouls/disqualifications: 2000-01, 5/0.

LONG, GRANT   F   GRIZZLIES

PERSONAL: Born March 12, 1966, in Wayne, Mich. ... 6-9/248. (2,06/112,5). ... Full Name: Grant Andrew Long. ... Nephew of John Long, guard with five NBA teams (1978-79 through 1990-91 and 1996-97); and cousin of Terry Mills, forward, Indiana Pacers.
HIGH SCHOOL: Romulus (Mich.).
COLLEGE: Eastern Michigan.
TRANSACTIONS/CAREER NOTES: Selected by Miami Heat in second round (33rd pick overall) of 1988 NBA Draft. ... Traded by Heat with G Steve Smith and conditional second-round draft choice to Atlanta Hawks for F Kevin Willis and conditional first-round draft choice (November 7, 1994). ... Traded by Hawks with G Stacey Augmon to Detroit Pistons for four conditional draft choices (July 15, 1996). ... Signed as free agent by Hawks (February 1, 1999). ... Signed as free agent by Vancouver Grizzlies (September 16, 1999). ... Grizzlies franchise moved to Memphis for 2001-02 season.
MISCELLANEOUS: Miami Heat all-time steals leader with 666 (1988-89 through 1994-95).

COLLEGIATE RECORD

Season Team	G	Min.	FGM	FGA	Pct.	FTM	FTA	Pct.	Reb.	Ast.	Pts.	RPG	APG	PPG
84-85—Eastern Michigan............	28	551	44	78	.564	28	46	.609	112	10	116	4.0	0.4	4.1
85-86—Eastern Michigan............	27	803	92	175	.526	47	73	.644	178	52	231	6.6	1.9	8.6
86-87—Eastern Michigan............	29	879	169	308	.549	95	131	.725	260	83	433	9.0	2.9	14.9
87-88—Eastern Michigan............	30	1026	237	427	.555	215	281	.765	313	66	689	10.4	2.2	23.0
Totals	114	3259	542	988	.549	385	531	.725	863	211	1469	7.6	1.9	12.9

NBA REGULAR-SEASON RECORD

NOTES: Led NBA with 337 personal fouls (1989). ... Tied for NBA lead with 11 disqualifications (1990).

									REBOUNDS								AVERAGES		
Season Team	G	Min.	FGM	FGA	Pct.	FTM	FTA	Pct.	Off.	Def.	Tot.	Ast.	St.	Blk.	TO	Pts.	RPG	APG	PPG
88-89—Miami	82	2435	336	692	.486	304	406	.749	240	306	546	149	122	48	201	976	6.7	1.8	11.9
89-90—Miami	81	1856	257	532	.483	172	241	.714	156	246	402	96	91	38	139	686	5.0	1.2	8.5
90-91—Miami	80	2514	276	561	.492	181	230	.787	225	343	568	176	119	43	156	734	7.1	2.2	9.2
91-92—Miami	82	3063	440	890	.494	326	404	.807	259	432	691	225	125	40	185	1212	8.4	2.7	14.8
92-93—Miami	76	2728	397	847	.469	261	341	.765	197	371	568	182	104	31	133	1061	7.5	2.4	14.0
93-94—Miami	69	2201	300	672	.446	187	238	.786	190	305	495	170	89	26	125	788	7.2	2.5	11.4
94-95—Miami-Atlanta .	81	2641	342	716	.478	244	325	.751	191	415	606	131	109	34	155	939	7.5	1.6	11.6
95-96—Atlanta	82	3008	395	838	.471	257	337	.763	248	540	788	183	108	34	157	1078	9.6	2.2	13.1
96-97—Detroit	65	1166	123	275	.447	63	84	.750	88	134	222	39	43	6	48	326	3.4	0.6	5.0
97-98—Detroit	40	739	50	117	.427	41	57	.719	57	93	150	25	29	12	22	141	3.8	0.6	3.5
98-99—Atlanta	50	1380	151	359	.421	184	235	.783	100	196	296	53	57	16	74	489	5.9	1.1	9.8
99-00—Vancouver......	42	920	74	167	.443	55	71	.775	86	148	234	43	45	10	49	203	5.6	1.0	4.8
00-01—Vancouver......	66	1507	140	319	.439	112	157	.713	76	198	274	83	72	15	62	396	4.2	1.3	6.0
Totals	896	26158	3281	6985	.470	2387	3126	.764	2113	3727	5840	1555	1127	353	1506	9029	6.5	1.7	10.1

Three-point field goals: 1988-89, 0-for-5. 1989-90, 0-for-3. 1990-91, 1-for-6 (.167). 1991-92, 6-for-22 (.273). 1992-93, 6-for-26 (.231). 1993-94, 1-for-6 (.167). 1994-95, 11-for-31 (.355). 1995-96, 31-for-86 (.360). 1996-97, 17-for-47 (.362). 1997-98, 0-for-4. 1998-99, 3-for-18 (.167). 1999-00, 0-for-4. 2000-01, 4-for-15 (.267). Totals, 80-for-273 (.293).
Personal fouls/disqualifications: 1988-89, 337/13. 1989-90, 300/11. 1990-91, 295/10. 1991-92, 248/2. 1992-93, 264/8. 1993-94, 244/5. 1994-95, 243/3. 1995-96, 233/3. 1996-97, 106/0. 1997-98, 91/2. 1998-99, 143/0. 1999-00, 108/1. 2000-01, 160/2. Totals, 2772/60.

NBA PLAYOFF RECORD

									REBOUNDS								AVERAGES		
Season Team	G	Min.	FGM	FGA	Pct.	FTM	FTA	Pct.	Off.	Def.	Tot.	Ast.	St.	Blk.	TO	Pts.	RPG	APG	PPG
91-92—Miami	3	120	15	36	.417	7	10	.700	7	8	15	8	5	0	5	37	5.0	2.7	12.3
93-94—Miami	4	110	14	36	.389	21	27	.778	10	8	18	7	3	2	10	49	4.5	1.8	12.3
94-95—Atlanta	3	110	14	28	.500	13	18	.722	13	21	34	4	4	1	8	41	11.3	1.3	13.7
95-96—Atlanta	10	362	44	111	.396	20	25	.800	30	56	86	28	7	3	19	114	8.6	2.8	11.4
96-97—Detroit	5	86	8	18	.444	9	11	.818	4	7	11	3	4	0	0	25	2.2	0.6	5.0
98-99—Atlanta	9	358	36	88	.409	32	44	.727	28	46	74	8	18	4	23	105	8.2	0.9	11.7
Totals	34	1146	131	317	.413	102	135	.756	92	146	238	58	41	10	65	371	7.0	1.7	10.9

Three-point field goals: 1991-92, 0-for-4. 1994-95, 0-for-1. 1995-96, 6-for-24 (.250). 1996-97, 0-for-2. 1998-99, 1-for-4 (.250). Totals, 7-for-35 (.200).
Personal fouls/disqualifications: 1991-92, 11/0. 1993-94, 16/1. 1994-95, 11/0. 1995-96, 27/1. 1996-97, 11/0. 1998-99, 27/0. Totals, 103/2.

LONGLEY, LUC   C   KNICKS

PERSONAL: Born January 19, 1969, in Melbourne, Australia. ... 7-2/260. (2,18/117,9). ... Full Name: Lucien James Longley. ... Name pronounced LUKE.
HIGH SCHOOL: Scotch College (Perth, Australia).
COLLEGE: New Mexico.
TRANSACTIONS/CAREER NOTES: Selected by Minnesota Timberwolves in first round (seventh pick overall) of 1991 NBA Draft. ... Traded by Timberwolves to Chicago Bulls for F/C Stacey King (February 23, 1994). ... Traded by Bulls to Phoenix Suns for F/C Mark Bryant, F Martin Muursepp, G/F Bubba Wells and conditional first-round draft choice (January 23, 1999). ... Traded by Suns to New York Knicks as part of four-team trade in which Knicks acquired F Glen Rice, F/C Travis Knight, G Vernon Maxwell, C Vladimir Stepania, F Lazaro Borrell, two 2001 first-round draft choices and two 2001 second-round draft choices, Seattle SuperSonics acquired C Patrick Ewing, Suns acquired C Chris Dudley and 2001 first-round draft choice and Los Angeles Lakers acquired F Horace Grant, C Greg Foster, F Chuck Person and G Emanual Davis (September 20, 2000).
MISCELLANEOUS: Member of NBA championship team (1996, 1997, 1998). ... Member of Australian Olympic team (1988, 1992).

COLLEGIATE RECORD

											AVERAGES		
Season Team	G	Min.	FGM	FGA	Pct.	FTM	FTA	Pct.	Reb.	Ast.	Pts.	RPG	APG	PPG
87-88—New Mexico..................	35	424	60	120	.500	20	51	.392	94	22	140	2.7	0.6	4.0
88-89—New Mexico..................	33	966	174	301	.578	80	104	.769	223	78	428	6.8	2.4	13.0
89-90—New Mexico..................	34	1192	233	417	.559	161	196	.821	330	108	627	9.7	3.2	18.4
90-91—New Mexico..................	30	1067	229	349	.656	116	162	.716	275	109	574	9.2	3.6	19.1
Totals	132	3649	696	1187	.586	377	513	.735	922	317	1769	7.0	2.4	13.4

Three-point field goals: 1990-91, 0-for-2.

NBA REGULAR-SEASON RECORD

									REBOUNDS								AVERAGES		
Season Team	G	Min.	FGM	FGA	Pct.	FTM	FTA	Pct.	Off.	Def.	Tot.	Ast.	St.	Blk.	TO	Pts.	RPG	APG	PPG
91-92—Minnesota.......	66	991	114	249	.458	53	80	.663	67	190	257	53	35	64	83	281	3.9	0.8	4.3
92-93—Minnesota.......	55	1045	133	292	.455	53	74	.716	71	169	240	51	47	77	88	319	4.4	0.9	5.8
93-94—Minn.-Chi.......	76	1502	219	465	.471	90	125	.720	129	304	433	109	45	79	119	528	5.7	1.4	6.9
94-95—Chicago	55	1001	135	302	.447	88	107	.822	82	181	263	73	24	45	86	358	4.8	1.3	6.5
95-96—Chicago	62	1641	242	502	.482	80	103	.777	104	214	318	119	22	84	114	564	5.1	1.9	9.1
96-97—Chicago	59	1472	221	485	.456	95	120	.792	121	211	332	141	23	66	111	537	5.6	2.4	9.1
97-98—Chicago	58	1703	277	609	.455	109	148	.736	113	228	341	161	34	62	130	663	5.9	2.8	11.4
98-99—Phoenix	39	933	140	290	.483	59	76	.776	59	162	221	45	23	21	53	339	5.7	1.2	8.7
99-00—Phoenix	72	1417	186	399	.466	80	97	.825	100	223	323	77	22	42	136	452	4.5	1.1	6.3
00-01—New York	25	301	18	54	.333	13	17	.765	26	40	66	7	3	9	22	49	2.6	0.3	2.0
Totals	567	12006	1685	3647	.462	720	947	.760	872	1922	2794	836	278	549	942	4090	4.9	1.5	7.2

Three-point field goals: 1993-94, 0-for-1. 1994-95, 0-for-2. 1996-97, 0-for-2. Totals, 0-for-5 (.000).
Personal fouls/disqualifications: 1991-92, 157/0. 1992-93, 169/4. 1993-94, 216/3. 1994-95, 177/5. 1995-96, 223/4. 1996-97, 191/5. 1997-98, 206/7. 1998-99, 119/0. 1999-00, 221/1. 2000-01, 51/0. Totals, 1730/29.

NBA PLAYOFF RECORD

Season Team	G	Min.	FGM	FGA	Pct.	FTM	FTA	Pct.	REBOUNDS			Ast.	St.	Blk.	TO	Pts.	AVERAGES		
									Off.	Def.	Tot.						RPG	APG	PPG
93-94—Chicago	10	170	25	50	.500	13	18	.722	13	32	45	18	6	8	21	63	4.5	1.8	6.3
94-95—Chicago	10	204	24	50	.480	8	10	.800	6	26	32	11	7	5	10	56	3.2	1.1	5.6
95-96—Chicago	18	439	61	130	.469	28	37	.757	34	48	82	28	7	25	38	150	4.6	1.6	8.3
96-97—Chicago	19	432	57	104	.548	10	26	.385	39	45	84	35	7	16	28	124	4.4	1.8	6.5
97-98—Chicago	18	456	54	120	.450	34	39	.872	34	56	90	35	12	15	36	142	5.0	1.9	7.9
98-99—Phoenix	3	51	2	12	.167	0	0	...	2	7	9	1	3	0	2	4	3.0	0.3	1.3
99-00—Phoenix	9	162	18	51	.353	2	3	.667	12	18	30	8	4	4	10	38	3.3	0.9	4.2
Totals	87	1914	241	517	.466	95	133	.714	140	232	372	136	46	73	145	577	4.3	1.6	6.6

Personal fouls/disqualifications: 1993-94, 38/0. 1994-95, 41/1. 1995-96, 83/4. 1996-97, 65/0. 1997-98, 73/2. 1998-99, 2/0. 1999-00, 36/1. Totals, 338/8.

LOPEZ, FELIPE   G   TIMBERWOLVES

PERSONAL: Born December 19, 1974, in Santo Domingo, Dominican Republic. ... 6-5/195. (1,96/88,5). ... Full Name: Luis Felipe Lopez.
HIGH SCHOOL: Rice (New York).
COLLEGE: St. John's.
TRANSACTIONS/CAREER NOTES: Selected by San Antonio Spurs in first round (24th pick overall) of 1998 NBA Draft. ... Draft rights traded by Spurs with F Carl Herrera to Vancouver Grizzlies for G Antonio Daniels (June 24, 1998). ... Traded by Grizzlies with G/F Dennis Scott, F/C Cherokee Parks and F Obinna Ekezie to Washington Wizards for C Ike Austin (August 22, 2000). ... Waived by Wizards (February 22, 2001). ... Signed as free agent by Minnesota Timberwolves (February 28, 2001).

COLLEGIATE RECORD

Season Team	G	Min.	FGM	FGA	Pct.	FTM	FTA	Pct.	Reb.	Ast.	Pts.	AVERAGES		
												RPG	APG	PPG
94-95—St. John's	28	966	166	404	.411	131	174	.753	160	77	498	5.7	2.8	17.8
95-96—St. John's	27	905	156	384	.406	99	145	.683	168	51	437	6.2	1.9	16.2
96-97—St. John's	27	955	142	349	.407	119	192	.620	183	61	430	6.8	2.3	15.9
97-98—St. John's	32	1108	206	478	.431	90	157	.573	152	85	562	4.8	2.7	17.6
Totals	114	3934	670	1615	.415	439	668	.657	663	274	1927	5.8	2.4	16.9

Three-point field goals: 1994-95, 35-for-114 (.307). 1995-96, 26-for-100 (.260). 1996-97, 27-for-108 (.250). 1997-98, 60-for-178 (.337). Totals, 148-for-500 (.296).

NBA REGULAR-SEASON RECORD

Season Team	G	Min.	FGM	FGA	Pct.	FTM	FTA	Pct.	REBOUNDS			Ast.	St.	Blk.	TO	Pts.	AVERAGES		
									Off.	Def.	Tot.						RPG	APG	PPG
98-99—Vancouver	47	1218	169	379	.446	87	135	.644	69	97	166	62	49	14	82	437	3.5	1.3	9.3
99-00—Vancouver	65	781	111	261	.425	67	109	.615	59	65	124	44	32	17	53	292	1.9	0.7	4.5
00-01—Wash.-Minn.	70	1565	211	478	.441	109	156	.699	55	179	234	107	62	30	83	550	3.3	1.5	7.9
Totals	182	3564	491	1118	.439	263	400	.658	183	341	524	213	143	61	218	1279	2.9	1.2	7.0

Three-point field goals: 1998-99, 12-for-44 (.273). 1999-00, 3-for-18 (.167). 2000-01, 19-for-52 (.365). Totals, 34-for-114 (.298).
Personal fouls/disqualifications: 1998-99, 128/0. 1999-00, 94/0. 2000-01, 156/0. Totals, 378/0.

NBA PLAYOFF RECORD

Season Team	G	Min.	FGM	FGA	Pct.	FTM	FTA	Pct.	REBOUNDS			Ast.	St.	Blk.	TO	Pts.	AVERAGES		
									Off.	Def.	Tot.						RPG	APG	PPG
00-01—Minnesota	4	55	7	22	.318	2	3	.667	4	7	11	5	4	0	2	17	2.8	1.3	4.3

Three-point field goals: 2000-01, 1-for-5 (.200).
Personal fouls/disqualifications: 2000-01, 5/0.

LUE, TYRONN   G   WIZARDS

PERSONAL: Born May 3, 1977, in Mexico, Mo. ... 6-0/178. (1,83/80,7). ... Full Name: Tyronn Jamar Lue.
HIGH SCHOOL: Raytown (Kansas City, Mo.).
COLLEGE: Nebraska.
TRANSACTIONS/CAREER NOTES: Selected after junior season by Denver Nuggets in first round (23rd pick overall) of 1998 NBA Draft. ... Draft rights traded by Nuggets with F Tony Battie to Los Angeles Lakers for G Nick Van Exel (June 24, 1998). ... Signed as free agent by Washington Wizards (July 18, 2001).
MISCELLANEOUS: Member of NBA championship team (2000, 2001).

COLLEGIATE RECORD

Season Team	G	Min.	FGM	FGA	Pct.	FTM	FTA	Pct.	Reb.	Ast.	Pts.	AVERAGES		
												RPG	APG	PPG
95-96—Nebraska	35	1033	105	232	.453	66	96	.688	106	144	296	3.0	4.1	8.5
96-97—Nebraska	32	1150	215	476	.452	126	155	.813	93	136	603	2.9	4.3	18.8
97-98—Nebraska	32	1149	240	547	.439	120	145	.828	137	152	678	4.3	4.8	21.2
Totals	99	3332	560	1255	.446	312	396	.788	336	432	1577	3.4	4.4	15.9

Three-point field goals: 1995-96, 20-for-61 (.328). 1996-97, 47-for-137 (.343). 1997-98, 78-for-209 (.373). Totals, 145-for-407 (.356).

NBA REGULAR-SEASON RECORD

Season Team	G	Min.	FGM	FGA	Pct.	FTM	FTA	Pct.	REBOUNDS			Ast.	St.	Blk.	TO	Pts.	AVERAGES		
									Off.	Def.	Tot.						RPG	APG	PPG
98-99—L.A. Lakers	15	188	28	65	.431	12	21	.571	2	4	6	25	5	0	11	75	0.4	1.7	5.0
99-00—L.A. Lakers	8	146	19	39	.487	6	8	.750	2	10	12	17	3	0	9	48	1.5	2.1	6.0
00-01—L.A. Lakers	38	468	50	117	.427	19	24	.792	5	27	32	45	19	0	27	130	0.8	1.2	3.4
Totals	61	802	97	221	.439	37	53	.698	9	41	50	87	27	0	47	253	0.8	1.4	4.1

Three-point field goals: 1998-99, 7-for-16 (.438). 1999-00, 4-for-8 (.500). 2000-01, 11-for-34 (.324). Totals, 22-for-58 (.379).
Personal fouls/disqualifications: 1998-99, 28/0. 1999-00, 17/0. 2000-01, 54/1. Totals, 99/1.

NBA PLAYOFF RECORD

Season Team	G	Min.	FGM	FGA	Pct.	FTM	FTA	Pct.	REBOUNDS Off.	Def.	Tot.	Ast.	St.	Blk.	TO	Pts.	AVERAGES RPG	APG	PPG
98-99—L.A. Lakers	3	33	7	17	.412	0	0	...	0	2	2	6	2	0	4	14	0.7	2.0	4.7
00-01—L.A. Lakers	15	131	10	29	.345	4	5	.800	1	9	10	10	12	1	8	29	0.7	0.7	1.9
Totals	18	164	17	46	.370	4	5	.800	1	11	12	16	14	1	12	43	0.7	0.9	2.4

Three-point field goals: 1998-99, 0-for-2. 2000-01, 5-for-13 (.385). Totals, 5-for-15 (.333).
Personal fouls/disqualifications: 1998-99, 4/0. 2000-01, 11/0. Totals, 15/0.

LYNCH, GEORGE   F   76ERS

PERSONAL: Born September 3, 1970, in Roanoke, Va. ... 6-8/228. (2,03/103,4). ... Full Name: George DeWitt Lynch III.
HIGH SCHOOL: Patrick Henry (Roanoke, Va.), then Flint Hill Prep (Oakton, Va.).
COLLEGE: North Carolina.
TRANSACTIONS/CAREER NOTES: Selected by Los Angeles Lakers in first round (12th pick overall) of 1993 NBA Draft. ... Traded by Lakers with G Anthony Peeler and 1997 and 1998 second-round draft choices to Vancouver Grizzlies for 1997 and 1998 second-round draft choices (July 16, 1996). ... Signed as free agent by Philadelphia 76ers (January 21, 1999).

COLLEGIATE RECORD

NOTES: Member of NCAA Division I championship team (1993).

Season Team	G	Min.	FGM	FGA	Pct.	FTM	FTA	Pct.	Reb.	Ast.	Pts.	AVERAGES RPG	APG	PPG
89-90—North Carolina	34	663	112	215	.521	67	101	.663	183	34	292	5.4	1.0	8.6
90-91—North Carolina	35	912	172	329	.523	85	135	.630	258	41	436	7.4	1.2	12.5
91-92—North Carolina	33	982	192	356	.539	74	114	.649	291	86	459	8.8	2.6	13.9
92-93—North Carolina	38	1148	235	469	.501	88	132	.667	365	72	560	9.6	1.9	14.7
Totals	140	3705	711	1369	.519	314	482	.651	1097	233	1747	7.8	1.7	12.5

Three-point field goals: 1989-90, 1-for-3 (.333). 1990-91, 7-for-10 (.700). 1991-92, 1-for-8 (.125). 1992-93, 2-for-11 (.182). Totals, 11-for-32 (.344).

NBA REGULAR-SEASON RECORD

Season Team	G	Min.	FGM	FGA	Pct.	FTM	FTA	Pct.	REBOUNDS Off.	Def.	Tot.	Ast.	St.	Blk.	TO	Pts.	AVERAGES RPG	APG	PPG
93-94—L.A. Lakers	71	1762	291	573	.508	99	166	.596	220	190	410	96	102	27	87	681	5.8	1.4	9.6
94-95—L.A. Lakers	56	953	138	295	.468	62	86	.721	75	109	184	62	51	10	73	341	3.3	1.1	6.1
95-96—L.A. Lakers	76	1012	117	272	.430	53	80	.663	82	127	209	51	47	10	40	291	2.8	0.7	3.8
96-97—Vancouver	41	1059	137	291	.471	60	97	.619	98	163	261	76	63	17	64	342	6.4	1.9	8.3
97-98—Vancouver	82	1493	248	516	.481	111	158	.703	147	215	362	122	65	41	104	616	4.4	1.5	7.5
98-99—Philadelphia	43	1315	147	349	.421	53	84	.631	110	169	279	76	85	22	79	356	6.5	1.8	8.3
99-00—Philadelphia	75	2416	297	644	.461	113	183	.617	216	366	582	136	119	38	120	722	7.8	1.8	9.6
00-01—Philadelphia	82	2649	274	616	.445	123	171	.719	200	390	590	139	99	30	109	686	7.2	1.7	8.4
Totals	526	12659	1649	3556	.464	674	1025	.658	1148	1729	2877	758	631	195	676	4035	5.5	1.4	7.7

Three-point field goals: 1993-94, 0-for-5. 1994-95, 3-for-21 (.143). 1995-96, 4-for-13 (.308). 1996-97, 8-for-31 (.258). 1997-98, 9-for-30 (.300). 1998-99, 9-for-23 (.391). 1999-00, 15-for-36 (.417). 2000-01, 15-for-57 (.263). Totals, 63-for-216 (.292).
Personal fouls/disqualifications: 1993-94, 177/1. 1994-95, 86/0. 1995-96, 106/0. 1996-97, 97/1. 1997-98, 161/0. 1998-99, 142/2. 1999-00, 231/2. 2000-01, 222/2. Totals, 1222/8.

NBA PLAYOFF RECORD

Season Team	G	Min.	FGM	FGA	Pct.	FTM	FTA	Pct.	REBOUNDS Off.	Def.	Tot.	Ast.	St.	Blk.	TO	Pts.	AVERAGES RPG	APG	PPG
94-95—L.A. Lakers	10	136	15	32	.469	13	20	.650	13	17	30	7	8	0	9	44	3.0	0.7	4.4
95-96—L.A. Lakers	2	15	2	4	.500	0	0	...	0	3	3	1	0	0	2	4	1.5	0.5	2.0
98-99—Philadelphia	8	249	29	65	.446	12	17	.706	28	25	53	16	18	2	13	72	6.6	2.0	9.0
99-00—Philadelphia	10	293	22	65	.338	14	18	.778	26	45	71	14	9	5	8	59	7.1	1.4	5.9
00-01—Philadelphia	10	222	24	50	.480	9	14	.643	20	31	51	12	13	2	13	57	5.1	1.2	5.7
Totals	40	915	92	216	.426	48	69	.696	87	121	208	50	48	9	45	236	5.2	1.3	5.9

Three-point field goals: 1994-95, 1-for-5 (.200). 1995-96, 0-for-1. 1998-99, 2-for-6 (.333). 1999-00, 1-for-7 (.143). 2000-01, 0-for-1. Totals, 4-for-20 (.200).
Personal fouls/disqualifications: 1994-95, 22/0. 1995-96, 4/0. 1998-99, 30/1. 1999-00, 33/1. 2000-01, 30/0. Totals, 119/2.

MacCULLOCH, TODD   C   NETS

PERSONAL: Born January 27, 1976, in Winnipeg, Man. ... 7-0/280. (2,13/127,0). ... Full Name: Todd Carlyle MacCulloch.
HIGH SCHOOL: Shaftesbury (Winnipeg, Man.).
COLLEGE: Washington.
TRANSACTIONS/CAREER NOTES: Selected by Philadelphia 76ers in second round (47th pick overall) of 1999 NBA Draft. ... Signed as free agent by New Jersey Nets (July 19, 2001).

COLLEGIATE RECORD

NOTES: Led NCAA Division I with .676 field goal percentage (1997), .664 field goal percentage (1998) and .662 field goal percentage (1999).

Season Team	G	Min.	FGM	FGA	Pct.	FTM	FTA	Pct.	Reb.	Ast.	Pts.	AVERAGES RPG	APG	PPG
95-96—Washington	28	419	104	154	.675	38	59	.644	134	4	246	4.8	0.1	8.8
96-97—Washington	28	614	163	241	.676	72	98	.735	204	12	398	7.3	0.4	14.2
97-98—Washington	30	848	492	741	.664	107	152	.704	292	11	557	9.7	0.4	18.6
98-99—Washington	29	904	210	317	.662	122	204	.598	345	24	542	11.9	0.8	18.7
Totals	115	2785	969	1453	.667	339	513	.661	975	51	1743	8.5	0.4	15.2

L

M

NBA REGULAR-SEASON RECORD

Season Team	G	Min.	FGM	FGA	Pct.	FTM	FTA	Pct.	REBOUNDS Off.	Def.	Tot.	Ast.	St.	Blk.	TO	Pts.	AVERAGES RPG	APG	PPG
99-00—Philadelphia	56	528	89	161	.553	28	54	.519	48	98	146	13	11	37	26	206	2.6	0.2	3.7
00-01—Philadelphia	63	597	109	185	.589	42	66	.636	69	99	168	10	7	19	27	260	2.7	0.2	4.1
Totals	119	1125	198	346	.572	70	120	.583	117	197	314	23	18	56	53	466	2.6	0.2	3.9

Personal fouls/disqualifications: 1999-00, 94/0. 2000-01, 96/0. Totals, 190/0.

NBA PLAYOFF RECORD

Season Team	G	Min.	FGM	FGA	Pct.	FTM	FTA	Pct.	REBOUNDS Off.	Def.	Tot.	Ast.	St.	Blk.	TO	Pts.	AVERAGES RPG	APG	PPG
99-00—Philadelphia	5	24	2	3	.667	4	6	.667	3	6	9	0	0	0	0	8	1.8	0.0	1.6
00-01—Philadelphia	18	109	24	38	.632	8	10	.800	17	12	29	4	0	3	4	56	1.6	0.2	3.1
Totals	23	133	26	41	.634	12	16	.750	20	18	38	4	0	3	4	64	1.7	0.2	2.8

Personal fouls/disqualifications: 1999-00, 2/0. 2000-01, 14/0. Totals, 16/0.

MacLEAN, DON   F   HEAT

PERSONAL: Born January 16, 1970, in Palo Alto, Calif. ... 6-10/235. (2,08/106,6). ... Full Name: Donald James MacLean. ... Name pronounced ma-CLAYNE.
HIGH SCHOOL: Simi Valley (Calif.).
COLLEGE: UCLA.
TRANSACTIONS/CAREER NOTES: Selected by Detroit Pistons in first round (19th pick overall) of 1992 NBA Draft. ... Draft rights traded by Pistons with C William Bedford to Los Angeles Clippers for C Olden Polynice and 1996 and 1997 second-round draft choices (June 24, 1992). ... Draft rights traded by Clippers with C William Bedford to Washington Bullets for F John Williams (October 8, 1992). ... Traded by Bullets with G Doug Overton to Denver Nuggets for G Robert Pack (October 30, 1995). ... Signed as free agent by Philadelphia 76ers (July 16, 1996). ... Traded by 76ers with C Michael Cage, G Lucious Harris and draft rights to F Keith Van Horn to New Jersey Nets for draft rights to F Tim Thomas, draft rights to G Anthony Parker, G Jim Jackson and C Eric Montross (June 27, 1997). ... Traded by Nets with F/C Michael Cage to Seattle SuperSonics for C Jim McIlvaine (January 21, 1999). ... Traded by SuperSonics with F/G Billy Owens, G/F Dale Ellis and draft rights to F Corey Maggette to Orlando Magic for F Horace Grant and 2001 and 2002 second-round draft choices (June 30, 1999). ... Traded to Magic with future first-round draft choice to Houston Rockets as part of three-way deal in which Rockets also received draft rights to G Steve Francis and F Tony Massenburg from Vancouver Grizzlies, Magic received F Michael Smith, G/F Rodrick Rhodes, G Lee Mayberry and F Makhtar Ndiaye from Grizzlies, and Grizzlies received G Michael Dickerson, F/C Othella Harrington, G Brent Price, F/C Antoine Carr and future first-round draft choice from Rockets (August 27, 1999). ... Waived by Rockets (November 1, 1999). ... Signed by Phoenix Suns to first of two consecutive 10-day contracts (March 13, 2000). ... Re-signed by Suns for remainder of season (April 2, 2000). ... Signed as free agent by Miami Heat (September 13, 2000).

COLLEGIATE RECORD

NOTES: The Sporting News All-America second team (1992). ... Led NCAA Division I with .921 free throw percentage (1992).

Season Team	G	Min.	FGM	FGA	Pct.	FTM	FTA	Pct.	Reb.	Ast.	Pts.	AVERAGES RPG	APG	PPG
88-89—UCLA	31	999	217	391	.555	142	174	.816	231	37	577	7.5	1.2	18.6
89-90—UCLA	33	1111	238	461	.516	179	211	.848	287	35	656	8.7	1.1	19.9
90-91—UCLA	31	1008	259	470	.551	193	228	.846	226	62	714	7.3	2.0	23.0
91-92—UCLA	32	1033	229	454	.504	197	214	.921	248	66	661	7.8	2.1	20.7
Totals	127	4151	943	1776	.531	711	827	.860	992	200	2608	7.8	1.6	20.5

Three-point field goals: 1988-89, 1-for-3 (.333). 1989-90, 1-for-2 (.500). 1990-91, 3-for-13 (.231). 1991-92, 6-for-17 (.353). Totals, 11-for-35 (.314).

NBA REGULAR-SEASON RECORD

HONORS: NBA Most Improved Player (1994).

Season Team	G	Min.	FGM	FGA	Pct.	FTM	FTA	Pct.	REBOUNDS Off.	Def.	Tot.	Ast.	St.	Blk.	TO	Pts.	AVERAGES RPG	APG	PPG
92-93—Washington	62	674	157	361	.435	90	111	.811	33	89	122	39	11	4	42	407	2.0	0.6	6.6
93-94—Washington	75	2487	517	1030	.502	328	398	.824	140	327	467	160	47	22	152	1365	6.2	2.1	18.2
94-95—Washington	39	1052	158	361	.438	104	136	.765	46	119	165	51	15	3	44	430	4.2	1.3	11.0
95-96—Denver	56	1107	233	547	.426	145	198	.732	62	143	205	89	21	5	68	625	3.7	1.6	11.2
96-97—Philadelphia	37	733	163	365	.447	64	97	.660	41	99	140	37	12	10	47	402	3.8	1.0	10.9
97-98—New Jersey	9	42	1	10	.100	0	0		3	2	5	0	0	0	2	3	0.6	0.0	0.3
98-99—Seattle	17	365	63	159	.396	50	80	.625	18	47	65	16	5	5	25	185	3.8	0.9	10.9
99-00—Phoenix	16	143	18	49	.367	4	6	.667	6	17	23	8	2	1	8	42	1.4	0.5	2.6
00-01—Miami	8	76	10	20	.500	9	12	.750	7	11	18	4	5	1	10	31	2.3	0.5	3.9
Totals	319	6679	1320	2902	.455	794	1038	.765	356	854	1210	404	118	51	398	3490	3.8	1.3	10.9

Three-point field goals: 1992-93, 3-for-6 (.500). 1993-94, 3-for-21 (.143). 1994-95, 10-for-40 (.250). 1995-96, 14-for-49 (.286). 1996-97, 12-for-38 (.316). 1997-98, 1-for-2 (.500). 1998-99, 9-for-33 (.273). 1999-00, 2-for-6 (.333). 2000-01, 2-for-2. Totals, 56-for-197 (.284).

Personal fouls/disqualifications: 1992-93, 82/0. 1993-94, 169/0. 1994-95, 97/0. 1995-96, 105/1. 1996-97, 71/0. 1997-98, 7/0. 1998-99, 34/0. 1999-00, 24/0. 2000-01, 9/0. Totals, 598/1.

MADSEN, MARK   F   LAKERS

PERSONAL: Born January 28, 1976, in Walnut Creek, Calif. ... 6-9/240. (2,06/108,9). ... Full Name: Mark Ellsworth Madsen.
HIGH SCHOOL: San Ramon Valley (Danville, Calif.).
COLLEGE: Stanford.
TRANSACTIONS/CAREER NOTES: Selected by Los Angeles Lakers in first round (29th pick overall) of 2000 NBA Draft.
MISCELLANEOUS: Member of NBA championship team (2001).

COLLEGIATE RECORD

Season Team	G	Min.	FGM	FGA	Pct.	FTM	FTA	Pct.	Reb.	Ast.	Pts.	AVERAGES RPG	APG	PPG
96-97—Stanford	25	410	51	95	.537	45	74	.608	126	8	147	5.0	0.3	5.9
97-98—Stanford	27	706	116	197	.589	83	132	.629	220	20	315	8.1	0.7	11.7
98-99—Stanford	33	969	153	253	.605	127	218	.583	297	16	433	9.0	0.5	13.1
99-00—Stanford	23	628	108	184	.587	65	113	.575	214	25	281	9.3	1.1	12.2
Totals	108	2713	428	729	.587	320	537	.596	857	69	1176	7.9	0.6	10.9

Three-point field goals: 1997-98, 0-for-1. 1998-99, 0-for-1. Totals, 0-for-2 (.000).

NBA REGULAR-SEASON RECORD

Season Team	G	Min.	FGM	FGA	Pct.	FTM	FTA	Pct.	REBOUNDS Off.	Def.	Tot.	Ast.	St.	Blk.	TO	Pts.	AVERAGES RPG	APG	PPG
00-01—L.A. Lakers	70	641	55	113	.487	26	37	.703	74	78	152	24	8	8	27	137	2.2	0.3	2.0

Three-point field goals: 2000-01, 1-for-1.
Personal fouls/disqualifications: 2000-01, 111/2.

NBA PLAYOFF RECORD

Season Team	G	Min.	FGM	FGA	Pct.	FTM	FTA	Pct.	REBOUNDS Off.	Def.	Tot.	Ast.	St.	Blk.	TO	Pts.	AVERAGES RPG	APG	PPG
00-01—L.A. Lakers	13	48	1	13	.077	3	5	.600	6	4	10	4	0	2	2	5	0.8	0.3	0.4

Personal fouls/disqualifications: 2000-01, 4/0.

MAGGETTE, COREY   F   CLIPPERS

PERSONAL: Born November 12, 1979, in Melrose Park, Ill. ... 6-6/218. (1,98/98,9). ... Full Name: Corey Antoine Maggette.
HIGH SCHOOL: Fenwick (Oak Park, Ill.).
COLLEGE: Duke.
TRANSACTIONS/CAREER NOTES: Selected after freshman season by Seattle SuperSonics in first round (13th pick overall) of 1999 NBA Draft. ... Draft rights traded by SuperSonics with F/G Billy Owens, G/F Dale Ellis and F Don MacLean to Orlando Magic for F Horace Grant and 2001 and 2002 second-round draft choices (June 30, 1999). ... Traded by Magic with F Derek Strong and draft rights to G Keyon Dooling to Los Angeles Clippers for a future first-round draft choice (June 28, 2000).

COLLEGIATE RECORD

Season Team	G	Min.	FGM	FGA	Pct.	FTM	FTA	Pct.	Reb.	Ast.	Pts.	AVERAGES RPG	APG	PPG
98-99—Duke	39	691	137	261	.525	111	155	.716	151	59	414	3.9	1.5	10.6

Three-point field goals: 1998-99, 29-for-84 (.345).

NBA REGULAR-SEASON RECORD

Season Team	G	Min.	FGM	FGA	Pct.	FTM	FTA	Pct.	REBOUNDS Off.	Def.	Tot.	Ast.	St.	Blk.	TO	Pts.	AVERAGES RPG	APG	PPG
99-00—Orlando	77	1370	224	469	.478	196	261	.751	123	180	303	61	24	26	138	646	3.9	0.8	8.4
00-01—L.A. Clippers	69	1359	225	487	.462	223	288	.774	88	203	291	82	35	9	106	690	4.2	1.2	10.0
Totals	146	2729	449	956	.470	419	549	.763	211	383	594	143	59	35	244	1336	4.1	1.0	9.2

Three-point field goals: 1999-00, 2-for-11 (.182). 2000-01, 17-for-56 (.304). Totals, 19-for-67 (.284).
Personal fouls/disqualifications: 1999-00, 169/1. 2000-01, 140/1. Totals, 309/2.

MAGLOIRE, JAMAAL   C   HORNETS

PERSONAL: Born May 21, 1978, in Toronto. ... 6-10/260. (2,08/117,9). ... Full Name: Jamaal Dane Magloire.
HIGH SCHOOL: Eastern School of Commerce (Toronto).
COLLEGE: Kentucky.
TRANSACTIONS/CAREER NOTES: Selected by Charlotte Hornets in first round (19th pick overall) of 2000 NBA Draft.

COLLEGIATE RECORD
NOTES: Member of NCAA Division I championship team (1998).

Season Team	G	Min.	FGM	FGA	Pct.	FTM	FTA	Pct.	Reb.	Ast.	Pts.	AVERAGES RPG	APG	PPG
96-97—Kentucky	40	626	75	153	.490	45	82	.549	177	15	195	4.4	0.4	4.9
97-98—Kentucky	38	526	77	158	.487	43	64	.672	161	11	197	4.2	0.3	5.2
98-99—Kentucky	34	668	94	177	.531	49	85	.576	151	18	237	4.4	0.5	7.0
99-00—Kentucky	33	978	148	296	.500	139	203	.685	300	18	435	9.1	0.5	13.2
Totals	145	2798	394	784	.503	276	434	.636	789	62	1064	5.4	0.4	7.3

NBA REGULAR-SEASON RECORD

Season Team	G	Min.	FGM	FGA	Pct.	FTM	FTA	Pct.	REBOUNDS Off.	Def.	Tot.	Ast.	St.	Blk.	TO	Pts.	AVERAGES RPG	APG	PPG
00-01—Charlotte	74	1095	122	271	.450	95	145	.655	103	192	295	27	18	78	61	339	4.0	0.4	4.6

Three-point field goals: 2000-01, 0-for-2.
Personal fouls/disqualifications: 2000-01, 139/0.

NBA PLAYOFF RECORD

Season Team	G	Min.	FGM	FGA	Pct.	FTM	FTA	Pct.	REBOUNDS Off.	Def.	Tot.	Ast.	St.	Blk.	TO	Pts.	AVERAGES RPG	APG	PPG
00-01—Charlotte	10	110	16	28	.571	7	23	.304	8	20	28	3	0	6	4	39	2.8	0.3	3.9

Personal fouls/disqualifications: 2000-01, 20/0.

M

MAJERLE, DAN　　　　G/F　　　　SUNS

PERSONAL: Born September 9, 1965, in Traverse City, Mich. ... 6-6/222. (1,98/100,7). ... Full Name: Daniel Lewis Majerle. ... Name pronounced MAR-lee.
HIGH SCHOOL: Traverse City (Mich.) Senior.
COLLEGE: Central Michigan.
TRANSACTIONS/CAREER NOTES: Selected by Phoenix Suns in first round (14th pick overall) of 1988 NBA Draft. ... Traded by Suns with F Antonio Lang and 1996, 1997 or 1998 first-round draft choice to Cleveland Cavaliers for F/C John Williams (October 7, 1995). ... Signed as free agent by Miami Heat (August 22, 1996). ... Signed as free agent by Suns (July 19, 2001).
MISCELLANEOUS: Member of bronze-medal-winning U.S. Olympic team (1988). ... Member of gold-medal-winning U.S. World Championship team (1994).

COLLEGIATE RECORD

Season Team	G	Min.	FGM	FGA	Pct.	FTM	FTA	Pct.	Reb.	Ast.	Pts.	RPG	APG	PPG
83-84—Central Michigan						Did not play—back injury.								
84-85—Central Michigan	12	360	92	162	.568	39	67	.582	80	24	223	6.7	2.0	18.6
85-86—Central Michigan	27	1002	228	433	.527	122	170	.718	212	51	578	7.9	1.9	21.4
86-87—Central Michigan	23	824	191	344	.555	101	183	.552	196	53	485	8.5	2.3	21.1
87-88—Central Michigan	32	1197	279	535	.521	156	242	.645	346	81	759	10.8	2.5	23.7
Totals	94	3383	790	1474	.536	418	662	.631	834	209	2045	8.9	2.2	21.8

Three-point field goals: 1986-87, 2-for-8 (.250). 1987-88, 45-for-101 (.446). Totals, 47-for-109 (.431).

NBA REGULAR-SEASON RECORD

RECORDS: Shares record for most seasons leading league in three-point field goals made—2.
HONORS: NBA All-Defensive second team (1991, 1993).
NOTES: Led NBA with 167 three-point field goals made (1993) and 192 three-point field goals made (1994).

Season Team	G	Min.	FGM	FGA	Pct.	FTM	FTA	Pct.	REBOUNDS Off.	Def.	Tot.	Ast.	St.	Blk.	TO	Pts.	RPG	APG	PPG
88-89—Phoenix	54	1354	181	432	.419	78	127	.614	62	147	209	130	63	14	48	467	3.9	2.4	8.6
89-90—Phoenix	73	2244	296	698	.424	198	260	.762	144	286	430	188	100	32	82	809	5.9	2.6	11.1
90-91—Phoenix	77	2281	397	821	.484	227	298	.762	168	250	418	216	106	40	114	1051	5.4	2.8	13.6
91-92—Phoenix	82	2853	551	1153	.478	229	303	.756	148	335	483	274	131	43	101	1418	5.9	3.3	17.3
92-93—Phoenix	82	3199	509	1096	.464	203	261	.778	120	263	383	311	138	33	133	1388	4.7	3.8	16.9
93-94—Phoenix	80	3207	476	1138	.418	176	238	.739	120	229	349	275	129	43	137	1320	4.4	3.4	16.5
94-95—Phoenix	82	3091	438	1031	.425	206	282	.730	104	271	375	340	96	38	105	1284	4.6	4.1	15.6
95-96—Cleveland	82	2367	303	748	.405	120	169	.710	70	235	305	214	81	34	93	872	3.7	2.6	10.6
96-97—Miami	36	1264	141	347	.406	40	59	.678	45	117	162	116	54	14	50	390	4.5	3.2	10.8
97-98—Miami	72	1928	184	439	.419	40	51	.784	48	220	268	157	68	15	65	519	3.7	2.2	7.2
98-99—Miami	48	1624	118	298	.396	33	46	.717	21	187	208	150	38	7	55	337	4.3	3.1	7.0
99-00—Miami	69	2308	170	422	.403	56	69	.812	27	306	333	206	89	17	62	506	4.8	3.0	7.3
00-01—Miami	53	1306	87	259	.336	36	44	.818	20	146	166	88	53	15	35	267	3.1	1.7	5.0
Totals	890	29026	3851	8882	.434	1642	2207	.744	1097	2992	4089	2665	1146	345	1080	10625	4.6	3.0	11.9

Three-point field goals: 1988-89, 27-for-82 (.329). 1989-90, 19-for-80 (.238). 1990-91, 30-for-86 (.349). 1991-92, 87-for-228 (.382). 1992-93, 167-for-438 (.381). 1993-94, 192-for-503 (.382). 1994-95, 199-for-548 (.363). 1995-96, 146-for-414 (.353). 1996-97, 68-for-201 (.338). 1997-98, 111-for-295 (.376). 1998-99, 68-for-203 (.335). 1999-00, 110-for-304 (.362). 2000-01, 57-for-181 (.315). Totals, 1281-for-3563 (.360).
Personal fouls/disqualifications: 1988-89, 139/1. 1989-90, 177/5. 1990-91, 162/0. 1991-92, 158/0. 1992-93, 180/0. 1993-94, 153/0. 1994-95, 155/0. 1995-96, 131/0. 1996-97, 75/0. 1997-98, 139/2. 1998-99, 100/0. 1999-00, 156/1. 2000-01, 90/0. Totals, 1823/9.

NBA PLAYOFF RECORD

NOTES: Shares NBA Finals single-series record for most three-point field goals made—17 (1993, vs. Chicago). ... Holds NBA Finals single-game records for most minutes played, no personal fouls—59; and most minutes played, no turnovers—59 (June 13, 1993, at Chicago, 3 OT). ... Holds single-game playoff records for most minutes played, no personal fouls—59; and most minutes played, no turnovers—59 (June 13, 1993, at Chicago, 3 OT).

Season Team	G	Min.	FGM	FGA	Pct.	FTM	FTA	Pct.	REBOUNDS Off.	Def.	Tot.	Ast.	St.	Blk.	TO	Pts.	RPG	APG	PPG
88-89—Phoenix	12	352	63	144	.438	38	48	.792	22	35	57	14	13	4	15	172	4.8	1.2	14.3
89-90—Phoenix	16	479	73	150	.487	51	65	.785	30	51	81	34	20	2	18	201	5.1	2.1	12.6
90-91—Phoenix	4	110	12	32	.375	14	19	.737	6	9	15	7	5	1	2	42	3.8	1.8	10.5
91-92—Phoenix	7	266	48	111	.432	25	26	.962	13	31	44	20	10	0	9	130	6.3	2.9	18.6
92-93—Phoenix	24	1071	134	311	.431	48	69	.696	29	111	140	88	33	28	32	370	5.8	3.7	15.4
93-94—Phoenix	10	410	46	127	.362	11	16	.688	15	28	43	24	11	4	10	123	4.3	2.4	12.3
94-95—Phoenix	10	307	27	73	.370	12	17	.706	8	23	31	17	14	3	9	82	3.1	1.7	8.2
95-96—Cleveland	3	91	16	36	.444	8	9	.889	2	10	12	9	4	2	3	50	4.0	3.0	16.7
96-97—Miami	17	496	46	117	.393	19	28	.679	16	56	72	43	21	4	13	136	4.2	2.5	8.0
97-98—Miami	2	62	3	8	.375	1	2	.500	1	4	5	5	4	1	1	9	2.5	2.5	4.5
98-99—Miami	5	152	5	26	.192	5	7	.714	3	26	29	6	5	2	3	20	5.8	1.2	4.0
99-00—Miami	10	372	30	71	.423	10	14	.714	5	65	70	32	21	1	11	90	7.0	3.2	9.0
00-01—Miami	3	71	5	16	.313	2	4	.500	3	7	10	5	3	0	2	16	3.3	1.7	5.3
Totals	123	4239	508	1222	.416	244	324	.753	153	456	609	304	164	52	128	1441	5.0	2.5	11.7

Three-point field goals: 1988-89, 8-for-28 (.286). 1989-90, 4-for-12 (.333). 1990-91, 4-for-11 (.364). 1991-92, 9-for-33 (.273). 1992-93, 54-for-137 (.394). 1993-94, 20-for-59 (.339). 1994-95, 16-for-44 (.364). 1995-96, 10-for-23 (.435). 1996-97, 25-for-74 (.338). 1997-98, 2-for-6 (.333). 1998-99, 5-for-22 (.227). 1999-00, 20-for-50 (.400). 2000-01, 4-for-14 (.286). Totals, 181-for-513 (.353).
Personal fouls/disqualifications: 1988-89, 28/0. 1989-90, 34/0. 1990-91, 12/0. 1991-92, 11/0. 1992-93, 57/0. 1993-94, 23/0. 1994-95, 24/0. 1995-96, 6/0. 1996-97, 31/0. 1997-98, 3/0. 1998-99, 15/0. 1999-00, 34/0. 2000-01, 7/0. Totals, 285/0.

NBA ALL-STAR GAME RECORD

Season Team	Min.	FGM	FGA	Pct.	FTM	FTA	Pct.	REBOUNDS Off.	Def.	Tot.	Ast.	PF	Dq.	St.	Blk.	TO	Pts.
1992 —Phoenix	12	2	5	.400	0	0	...	0	3	3	2	0	0	0	0	1	4
1993 —Phoenix	26	6	11	.545	3	4	.750	2	5	7	3	2	0	1	0	0	18
1995 —Phoenix	20	4	12	.333	0	0	...	1	4	5	3	1	0	0	0	0	10
Totals	58	12	28	.429	3	4	.750	3	12	15	8	3	0	1	2	1	32

Three-point field goals: 1992, 0-for-2. 1993, 3-for-6 (.500). 1995, 2-for-7 (.286). Totals, 5-for-15 (.333).

MALONE, KARL   F   JAZZ

PERSONAL: Born July 24, 1963, in Summerfield, La. ... 6-9/256. (2,06/116,1). ... Nickname: The Mailman.
HIGH SCHOOL: Summerfield (La.).
COLLEGE: Louisiana Tech.
TRANSACTIONS/CAREER NOTES: Selected after junior season by Utah Jazz in first round (13th pick overall) of 1985 NBA Draft.
CAREER HONORS: NBA 50th Anniversary All-Time Team (1996).
MISCELLANEOUS: Member of gold-medal-winning U.S. Olympic teams (1992, 1996). ... Utah Jazz franchise all-time leading scorer with 32,919 points and all-time leading rebounder with 13,287 (1985-86 through 2000-01).

COLLEGIATE RECORD

Season Team	G	Min.	FGM	FGA	Pct.	FTM	FTA	Pct.	Reb.	Ast.	Pts.	RPG	APG	PPG
81-82—Louisiana Tech						Did not play—redshirted.								
82-83—Louisiana Tech	28	894	217	373	.582	152	244	.623	289	10	586	10.3	0.4	20.9
83-84—Louisiana Tech	32	1011	220	382	.576	161	236	.682	282	42	601	8.8	1.3	18.8
84-85—Louisiana Tech	32	926	216	399	.541	97	170	.571	288	73	529	9.0	2.3	16.5
Totals	**92**	**2831**	**653**	**1154**	**.566**	**410**	**650**	**.631**	**859**	**125**	**1716**	**9.3**	**1.4**	**18.7**

NBA REGULAR-SEASON RECORD

RECORDS: Holds career records for most seasons with 2,000 or more points—12 (1987-88 through 1997-98 and 1999-2000); most consecutive seasons with 2,000 or more points—11 (1987-88 through 1997-98); most free throws made—8,636; most seasons leading league in free throws made—8; most consecutive seasons leading league in free throws made—5; and most turnovers—3,948.

HONORS: NBA Most Valuable Player (1997, 1999). ... IBM Award, for all-around contributions to team's success (1998). ... All-NBA first team (1989, 1990, 1991, 1992, 1993, 1994, 1995, 1996, 1997, 1998, 1999). ... All-NBA second team (1988, 2000). ... All-NBA third team (2001). ... NBA All-Defensive first team (1997, 1998, 1999). ... NBA All-Defensive second team (1988). ... NBA All-Rookie team (1986).

Season Team	G	Min.	FGM	FGA	Pct.	FTM	FTA	Pct.	REBOUNDS Off.	Def.	Tot.	Ast.	St.	Blk.	TO	Pts.	RPG	APG	PPG
85-86—Utah	81	2475	504	1016	.496	195	405	.481	174	544	718	236	105	44	279	1203	8.9	2.9	14.9
86-87—Utah	82	2857	728	1422	.512	323	540	.598	278	577	855	158	104	60	237	1779	10.4	1.9	21.7
87-88—Utah	82	3198	858	1650	.520	552	789	.700	277	709	986	199	117	50	*325	2268	12.0	2.4	27.7
88-89—Utah	80	3126	809	1559	.519	*703	*918	.766	259	594	853	219	144	70	285	2326	10.7	2.7	29.1
89-90—Utah	82	3122	914	1627	.562	*696	*913	.762	232	679	911	226	121	50	304	2540	11.1	2.8	31.0
90-91—Utah	82	3302	847	1608	.527	*684	*888	.770	236	*731	967	270	89	79	244	2382	11.8	3.3	29.0
91-92—Utah	81	3054	798	1516	.526	*673	*865	.778	225	684	909	241	108	51	248	2272	11.2	3.0	28.0
92-93—Utah	82	3099	797	1443	.552	*619	*836	.740	227	692	919	308	124	85	240	2217	11.2	3.8	27.0
93-94—Utah	82	3329	772	1552	.497	511	736	.694	235	705	940	328	125	126	234	2063	11.5	4.0	25.2
94-95—Utah	82	3126	830	1548	.536	516	695	.742	156	*715	871	285	129	85	236	2187	10.6	3.5	26.7
95-96—Utah	82	3113	789	1520	.519	512	708	.723	175	629	804	345	138	56	199	2106	9.8	4.2	25.7
96-97—Utah	82	2998	864	1571	.550	*521	*690	.755	193	616	809	368	113	48	233	2249	9.9	4.5	27.4
97-98—Utah	81	3030	780	1472	.530	*628	*825	.761	189	645	834	316	96	70	247	2190	10.3	3.9	27.0
98-99—Utah	49	1832	393	797	.493	*378	480	.788	107	356	463	201	62	28	162	1164	9.4	4.1	23.8
99-00—Utah	82	2947	752	1476	.509	589	739	.797	169	610	779	304	79	71	231	2095	9.5	3.7	25.5
00-01—Utah	81	2895	670	1345	.498	536	676	.793	114	555	669	361	93	62	244	1878	8.3	4.5	23.2
Totals	**1273**	**47503**	**12105**	**23122**	**.524**	**8636**	**11703**	**.738**	**3246**	**10041**	**13287**	**4365**	**1747**	**1035**	**3948**	**32919**	**10.4**	**3.4**	**25.9**

Three-point field goals: 1985-86, 0-for-2. 1986-87, 0-for-7. 1987-88, 0-for-5. 1988-89, 5-for-16 (.313). 1989-90, 16-for-43 (.372). 1990-91, 4-for-14 (.286). 1991-92, 3-for-17 (.176). 1992-93, 4-for-20 (.200). 1993-94, 8-for-32 (.250). 1994-95, 11-for-41 (.268). 1995-96, 16-for-40 (.400). 1996-97, 0-for-13. 1997-98, 2-for-6 (.333). 1998-99, 0-for-1. 1999-00, 2-for-8 (.250). 2000-01, 2-for-5 (.400). Totals, 73-for-270 (.270).

Personal fouls/disqualifications: 1985-86, 295/2. 1986-87, 323/6. 1987-88, 296/2. 1988-89, 286/3. 1989-90, 259/1. 1990-91, 268/2. 1991-92, 226/2. 1992-93, 261/2. 1993-94, 268/2. 1994-95, 269/2. 1995-96, 245/1. 1996-97, 217/0. 1997-98, 237/0. 1998-99, 134/0. 1999-00, 229/1. 2000-01, 216/0. Totals, 4029/26.

NBA PLAYOFF RECORD

NOTES: Holds single-game playoff record for most free throws made, none missed—18 (May 10, 1997, at L.A. Lakers). ... Shares single-game playoff record for most free throws made in one half—19 (May 9, 1991, vs. Portland).

Season Team	G	Min.	FGM	FGA	Pct.	FTM	FTA	Pct.	REBOUNDS Off.	Def.	Tot.	Ast.	St.	Blk.	TO	Pts.	RPG	APG	PPG
85-86—Utah	4	144	38	72	.528	11	26	.423	6	24	30	4	8	0	6	87	7.5	1.0	21.8
86-87—Utah	5	200	37	88	.420	26	36	.722	15	33	48	6	11	4	17	100	9.6	1.2	20.0
87-88—Utah	11	494	123	255	.482	81	112	.723	33	97	130	17	13	7	39	327	11.8	1.5	29.7
88-89—Utah	3	136	33	66	.500	26	32	.813	22	27	49	4	3	1	13	92	16.3	1.3	30.7
89-90—Utah	5	203	46	105	.438	34	45	.756	16	35	51	11	11	5	12	126	10.2	2.2	25.2
90-91—Utah	9	303	95	209	.455	77	91	.840	23	97	120	29	9	11	28	267	13.3	3.2	29.7
91-92—Utah	16	688	148	284	.521	169	210	.805	43	138	181	42	22	19	46	465	11.3	2.6	29.1
92-93—Utah	5	216	44	97	.454	31	38	.816	12	40	52	10	6	2	20	120	10.4	2.0	24.0
93-94—Utah	16	703	158	338	.467	118	160	.738	52	146	198	54	23	13	34	434	12.4	3.4	27.1
94-95—Utah	5	216	48	103	.466	54	78	.692	15	51	66	19	7	2	14	151	13.2	3.8	30.2
95-96—Utah	18	725	188	401	.469	101	176	.574	47	139	186	79	34	10	45	477	10.3	4.4	26.5
96-97—Utah	20	816	187	430	.435	144	200	.720	60	168	228	57	27	15	54	519	11.4	2.9	26.0
97-98—Utah	20	795	198	420	.471	130	165	.788	47	170	217	68	22	20	60	526	10.9	3.4	26.3
98-99—Utah	11	451	86	206	.417	68	86	.791	36	88	124	52	13	8	40	240	11.3	4.7	21.8
99-00—Utah	10	386	103	198	.520	64	79	.810	19	70	89	31	7	7	27	272	8.9	3.1	27.2
00-01—Utah	5	199	49	121	.405	39	49	.796	9	35	44	17	5	4	19	138	8.8	3.4	27.6
Totals	**163**	**6755**	**1581**	**3393**	**.466**	**1173**	**1583**	**.741**	**455**	**1358**	**1813**	**500**	**221**	**128**	**472**	**4341**	**11.1**	**3.1**	**26.6**

Three-point field goals: 1987-88, 0-for-1. 1989-90, 0-for-1. 1990-91, 0-for-8. 1991-92, 0-for-2. 1992-93, 1-for-2 (.500). 1993-94, 1-for-5 (.200). 1994-95, 1-for-3 (.333). 1995-96, 0-for-3. 1996-97, 1-for-3 (.333). 1997-98, 0-for-3. 1998-99, 0-for-1. 1999-00, 2-for-2 (.500). 2000-01, 1-for-2 (.500). Totals, 6-for-34 (.176).

Personal fouls/disqualifications: 1985-86, 18/1. 1986-87, 20/1. 1987-88, 35/0. 1988-89, 16/1. 1989-90, 22/1. 1990-91, 35/0. 1991-92, 57/0. 1992-93, 21/0. 1993-94, 59/2. 1994-95, 18/0. 1995-96, 61/0. 1996-97, 59/0. 1997-98, 69/0. 1998-99, 37/0. 1999-00, 31/0. 2000-01, 13/0. Totals, 571/6.

M

NOTES: NBA All-Star Game Most Valuable Player (1989). ... NBA All-Star Game co-Most Valuable Player (1993).

Season Team	Min.	FGM	FGA	Pct.	FTM	FTA	Pct.	REBOUNDS Off.	Def.	Tot.	Ast.	PF	Dq.	St.	Blk.	TO	Pts.
1988 —Utah	33	9	19	.474	4	5	.800	4	6	10	2	4	0	2	0	3	22
1989 —Utah	26	12	17	.706	4	6	.667	4	5	9	3	3	0	2	0	2	28
1990 —Utah							Selected, did not play—injured.										
1991 —Utah	31	6	11	.545	4	6	.667	4	7	11	4	1	0	1	1	3	16
1992 —Utah	19	5	7	.714	1	2	.500	0	7	7	3	1	0	1	1	1	11
1993 —Utah	34	11	17	.647	6	9	.667	3	7	10	0	3	0	1	2	3	28
1994 —Utah	21	3	9	.333	0	0	...	3	4	7	2	2	0	1	0	1	6
1995 —Utah	16	6	6	1.000	3	4	.750	0	3	3	1	0	0	0	0	1	15
1996 —Utah	20	2	6	.333	7	8	.875	0	9	9	2	1	0	1	0	1	11
1997 —Utah	20	2	8	.250	0	0	...	1	3	4	0	0	0	1	1	0	4
1998 —Utah	17	2	4	.500	0	0	...	0	3	3	2	1	0	...	2	0	4
2000 —Utah	3	0	1	.000	0	0	...	0	0	0	0	0	0	0	0	0	0
2001 —Utah	4	0	2	.000	0	0	...	0	1	1	0	0	0	0	0	0	0
Totals	244	58	107	.542	29	40	.725	19	55	74	19	16	0	12	5	15	145

MALONEY, MATT   G

PERSONAL: Born December 6, 1971, in Silver Spring, Md. ... 6-3/200. (1,91/90,7).
HIGH SCHOOL: Memorial (Haddonfield, N.J.).
COLLEGE: Vanderbilt, then Pennsylvania.
TRANSACTIONS/CAREER NOTES: Not drafted by an NBA franchise. ... Signed as free agent by Golden State Warriors (October 6, 1995). ... Waived by Warriors (November 1, 1995). ... Played in Continental Basketball Association with Grand Rapids Mackers (1995-96). ... Signed as free agent by Houston Rockets (October 1, 1996). ... Waived by Rockets (November 1, 1999). ... Signed as free agent by Chicago Bulls (January 7, 2000). ... Signed as free agent Atlanta Hawks (October 3, 2000).

COLLEGIATE RECORD

Season Team	G	Min.	FGM	FGA	Pct.	FTM	FTA	Pct.	Reb.	Ast.	Pts.	AVERAGES RPG	APG	PPG
90-91—Vanderbilt	30	557	41	100	.410	11	14	.786	45	51	122	1.5	1.7	4.1
91-92—Pennsylvania						Did not play—transfer student.								
92-93—Pennsylvania	27	954	148	359	.412	52	67	.776	88	96	439	3.3	3.6	16.3
93-94—Pennsylvania	28	918	133	338	.393	61	68	.897	74	105	393	2.6	3.8	14.0
94-95—Pennsylvania	28	886	144	314	.459	41	59	.695	78	121	416	2.8	4.3	14.9
Totals	113	3315	466	1111	.419	165	208	.793	285	373	1370	2.5	3.3	12.1

Three-point field goals: 1990-91, 29-for-69 (.420). 1992-93, 91-for-205 (.444). 1993-94, 66-for-202 (.327). 1994-95, 87-for-198 (.439). Totals, 273-for-674 (.405).

NOTES: CBA All-Rookie second team (1996).

CBA REGULAR-SEASON RECORD

Season Team	G	Min.	FGM	FGA	Pct.	FTM	FTA	Pct.	Reb.	Ast.	Pts.	AVERAGES RPG	APG	PPG
95-96—Grand Rapids	56	1659	239	569	.420	95	105	.905	142	310	678	2.5	5.5	12.1

Three-point field goals: 1995-96, 105-for-259 (.405).

HONORS: NBA All-Rookie second team (1996).

NBA REGULAR-SEASON RECORD

Season Team	G	Min.	FGM	FGA	Pct.	FTM	FTA	Pct.	REBOUNDS Off.	Def.	Tot.	Ast.	St.	Blk.	TO	Pts.	AVERAGES RPG	APG	PPG
96-97—Houston	82	2386	271	615	.441	71	93	.763	19	141	160	303	82	1	122	767	2.0	3.7	9.4
97-98—Houston	78	2217	239	586	.408	65	78	.833	16	126	142	219	62	5	107	669	1.8	2.8	8.6
98-99—Houston	15	186	5	28	.179	10	11	.909	2	8	10	21	4	0	14	21	0.7	1.4	1.4
99-00—Chicago	51	1175	114	318	.358	37	45	.822	10	54	64	138	32	3	63	327	1.3	2.7	6.4
00-01—Atlanta	55	1403	146	348	.420	26	34	.765	14	103	117	154	56	5	70	369	2.1	2.8	6.7
Totals	281	7367	775	1895	.409	209	261	.801	61	432	493	835	236	14	376	2153	1.8	3.0	7.7

Three-point field goals: 1996-97, 154-for-381 (.404). 1997-98, 126-for-346 (.364). 1998-99, 1-for-15 (.067). 1999-00, 62-for-174 (.356). 2000-01, 51-for-142 (.359). Totals, 394-for-1058 (.372).
Personal fouls/disqualifications: 1996-97, 125/0. 1997-98, 99/0. 1998-99, 7/0. 1999-00, 42/0. 2000-01, 94/1. Totals, 367/1.

NBA PLAYOFF RECORD

Season Team	G	Min.	FGM	FGA	Pct.	FTM	FTA	Pct.	REBOUNDS Off.	Def.	Tot.	Ast.	St.	Blk.	TO	Pts.	AVERAGES RPG	APG	PPG
96-97—Houston	16	526	61	153	.399	14	21	.667	1	18	19	50	10	3	38	179	1.2	3.1	11.2
97-98—Houston	5	165	10	30	.333	8	9	.889	0	8	8	18	2	2	4	33	1.6	3.6	6.6
Totals	21	691	71	183	.388	22	30	.733	1	26	27	68	12	5	42	212	1.3	3.2	10.1

Three-point field goals: 1996-97, 43-for-108 (.398). 1997-98, 5-for-20 (.250). Totals, 48-for-128 (.375).
Personal fouls/disqualifications: 1996-97, 31/0. 1997-98, 11/0. Totals, 42/0.

MANNING, DANNY   F   MAVERICKS

PERSONAL: Born May 17, 1966, in Hattiesburg, Miss. ... 6-10/234. (2,08/106,1). ... Full Name: Daniel Ricardo Manning. ... Son of Ed Manning, forward with Baltimore Bullets (1967-68 through 1969-70), Chicago Bulls (1969-70) and Portland Trail Blazers (1970-71) and three American Basketball Association teams (1971-72 through 1975-76).
HIGH SCHOOL: Page (Greensboro, N.C.), then Lawrence (Kan.).
COLLEGE: Kansas.

M

TRANSACTIONS/CAREER NOTES: Selected by Los Angeles Clippers in first round (first pick overall) of 1988 NBA Draft. ... Traded by Clippers to Atlanta Hawks for F Dominique Wilkins and 1994 or 1995 conditional first-round draft choice (February 24, 1994). ... Signed as unrestricted free agent by Phoenix Suns (September 3, 1994). ... Traded by Suns with F Pat Garrity and two future first-round draft choices to Orlando Magic for G Anfernee Hardaway (August 5, 1999). ... Traded by Magic with G/F Dale Ellis to Milwaukee Bucks for F/C Chris Gatling and F Armen Gilliam (August 19, 1999). ... Waived by Bucks (August 2, 2000). ... Signed as free agent by Utah Jazz (August 11, 2000). ... Signed as free agent by Dallas Mavericks (August 2, 2001).

MISCELLANEOUS: Member of bronze-medal-winning U.S. Olympic team (1988).

COLLEGIATE RECORD

NOTES: Member of NCAA Division I championship team (1988). ... Naismith Award winner (1988). ... Wooden Award winner (1988). ... NCAA Division I Tournament Most Outstanding Player (1988). ... THE SPORTING NEWS All-America first team (1987, 1988). ... Holds NCAA Division I career record for most games scoring in double figures—132.

Season Team	G	Min.	FGM	FGA	Pct.	FTM	FTA	Pct.	Reb.	Ast.	Pts.	RPG	APG	PPG
84-85—Kansas	34	1120	209	369	.566	78	102	.765	258	108	496	7.6	3.2	14.6
85-86—Kansas	39	1256	279	465	.600	95	127	.748	245	93	653	6.3	2.4	16.7
86-87—Kansas	36	1249	347	562	.617	165	226	.730	342	64	860	9.5	1.8	23.9
87-88—Kansas	38	1336	381	653	.583	171	233	.734	342	77	942	9.0	2.0	24.8
Totals	147	4961	1216	2049	.593	509	688	.740	1187	342	2951	8.1	2.3	20.1

Three-point field goals: 1986-87, 1-for-3 (.333). 1987-88, 9-for-26 (.346). Totals, 10-for-29 (.345).

NBA REGULAR-SEASON RECORD

HONORS: NBA Sixth Man Award (1998).

Season Team	G	Min.	FGM	FGA	Pct.	FTM	FTA	Pct.	Off.	Def.	Tot.	Ast.	St.	Blk.	TO	Pts.	RPG	APG	PPG
88-89—L.A. Clippers	26	950	177	358	.494	79	103	.767	70	101	171	81	44	25	93	434	6.6	3.1	16.7
89-90—L.A. Clippers	71	2269	440	826	.533	274	370	.741	142	280	422	187	91	39	188	1154	5.9	2.6	16.3
90-91—L.A. Clippers	73	2197	470	905	.519	219	306	.716	169	257	426	196	117	62	188	1159	5.8	2.7	15.9
91-92—L.A. Clippers	82	2904	650	1199	.542	279	385	.725	229	335	564	285	135	122	210	1579	6.9	3.5	19.3
92-93—L.A. Clippers	79	2761	702	1379	.509	388	484	.802	198	322	520	207	108	101	230	1800	6.6	2.6	22.8
93-94—L.A.C.-Atl.	68	2520	586	1201	.488	228	341	.669	131	334	465	261	99	82	233	1403	6.8	3.8	20.6
94-95—Phoenix	46	1510	340	622	.547	136	202	.673	97	179	276	154	41	57	121	822	6.0	3.3	17.9
95-96—Phoenix	33	816	178	388	.459	82	109	.752	30	113	143	65	38	24	77	441	4.3	2.0	13.4
96-97—Phoenix	77	2134	426	795	.536	181	251	.721	137	332	469	173	81	74	161	1040	6.1	2.2	13.5
97-98—Phoenix	70	1794	390	756	.516	167	226	.739	110	282	392	139	71	46	100	947	5.6	2.0	13.5
98-99—Phoenix	50	1184	187	386	.484	78	112	.696	62	157	219	113	36	38	69	453	4.4	2.3	9.1
99-00—Milwaukee	72	1217	149	339	.440	34	52	.654	50	158	208	73	62	29	55	333	2.9	1.0	4.6
00-01—Utah	82	1305	247	500	.494	102	140	.729	66	148	214	92	47	29	96	603	2.6	1.1	7.4
Totals	829	23561	4942	9654	.512	2247	3081	.729	1491	2998	4489	2026	970	728	1821	12168	5.4	2.4	14.7

Three-point field goals: 1988-89, 1-for-5 (.200). 1989-90, 0-for-5. 1990-91, 0-for-3. 1991-92, 0-for-5. 1992-93, 8-for-30 (.267). 1993-94, 3-for-17 (.176). 1994-95, 6-for-21 (.286). 1995-96, 3-for-14 (.214). 1996-97, 7-for-36 (.194). 1997-98, 0-for-7. 1998-99, 1-for-9 (.111). 1999-00, 1-for-4 (.250). 2000-01, 7-for-28 (.250). Totals, 37-for-184 (.201).

Personal fouls/disqualifications: 1988-89, 89/1. 1989-90, 261/4. 1990-91, 281/5. 1991-92, 293/5. 1992-93, 323/8. 1993-94, 260/2. 1994-95, 176/1. 1995-96, 121/2. 1996-97, 268/7. 1997-98, 201/2. 1998-99, 129/1. 1999-00, 183/2. 2000-01, 219/0. Totals, 2804/40.

NBA PLAYOFF RECORD

Season Team	G	Min.	FGM	FGA	Pct.	FTM	FTA	Pct.	Off.	Def.	Tot.	Ast.	St.	Blk.	TO	Pts.	RPG	APG	PPG
91-92—L.A. Clippers	5	194	46	81	.568	20	31	.645	15	13	28	14	5	4	13	113	5.6	2.8	22.6
92-93—L.A. Clippers	5	171	35	85	.412	21	26	.808	12	24	36	8	7	5	13	91	7.2	1.6	18.2
93-94—Atlanta	11	426	84	172	.488	52	66	.788	28	49	77	37	15	9	26	220	7.0	3.4	20.0
95-96—Phoenix	4	90	22	48	.458	5	8	.625	4	7	11	5	4	1	6	49	2.8	1.3	12.3
96-97—Phoenix	5	116	26	45	.578	14	15	.933	4	26	30	7	4	7	8	66	6.0	1.4	13.2
98-99—Phoenix	3	79	14	24	.583	10	13	.769	0	5	5	6	4	0	3	38	1.7	2.0	12.7
99-00—Milwaukee	1	5	0	1	.000	0	0	...	0	1	1	0	0	0	0	0	1.0	0.0	0.0
00-01—Utah	5	96	19	34	.559	9	12	.750	2	9	11	3	3	4	7	49	2.2	0.6	9.8
Totals	39	1177	246	490	.502	131	171	.766	65	134	199	80	42	30	76	626	5.1	2.1	16.1

Three-point field goals: 1991-92, 1-for-3 (.333). 1992-93, 0-for-2. 1995-96, 0-for-1. 1996-97, 0-for-3. 2000-01, 2-for-2. Totals, 3-for-11 (.273).

Personal fouls/disqualifications: 1991-92, 21/1. 1992-93, 19/0. 1993-94, 39/0. 1995-96, 15/1. 1996-97, 21/1. 1998-99, 12/0. 2000-01, 21/0. Totals, 148/3.

NBA ALL-STAR GAME RECORD

Season Team	Min.	FGM	FGA	Pct.	FTM	FTA	Pct.	Off.	Def.	Tot.	Ast.	PF	Dq.	St.	Blk.	TO	Pts.
1993 —L.A. Clippers	18	5	5	1.000	0	0	...	1	3	4	1	1	0	0	0	0	10
1994 —L.A. Clippers	17	4	7	.571	0	0	...	0	4	4	2	4	0	0	1	0	8
Totals	35	9	12	.750	0	0	...	1	7	8	3	5	0	0	1	0	18

M

MARBURY, STEPHON G SUNS

PERSONAL: Born February 20, 1977, in Brooklyn, N.Y. ... 6-2/180. (1,88/81,6). ... Cousin of Jamel Thomas, forward with Boston Celtics (1999-2000), Golden State Warriors (1999-2000), Portland Trail Blazers (1999-2000) and New Jersey Nets (2000-01).

HIGH SCHOOL: Abraham Lincoln (Brooklyn, N.Y.).

COLLEGE: Georgia Tech.

TRANSACTIONS/CAREER NOTES: Selected after freshman season by Milwaukee Bucks in first round (fourth pick overall) of 1996 NBA Draft. ... Draft rights traded by Bucks to Minnesota Timberwolves for draft rights to G Ray Allen and a first-round draft choice (June 26, 1996). ... Traded by Timberwolves with F Bill Curley and G Chris Carr to New Jersey Nets in three-way deal in which Nets also received G Elliot Perry from Milwaukee Bucks, Timberwolves received F Brian Evans, 1999 first-round draft choice and an undisclosed draft choice from Nets, Bucks sent G Terrell Brandon to Timberwolves, Timberwolves sent C Paul Grant to Bucks and Nets sent G Sam Cassell and F/C Chris Gatling to Bucks (March 11, 1999). ... Traded by Nets with F Johnny Newman and C Soumaila Samake to Phoenix Suns for G Jason Kidd and C Chris Dudley (July 18, 2001).

COLLEGIATE RECORD

Season Team	G	Min.	FGM	FGA	Pct.	FTM	FTA	Pct.	Reb.	Ast.	Pts.	AVERAGES		
												RPG	APG	PPG
95-96—Georgia Tech	36	1345	235	514	.457	121	164	.738	113	161	679	3.1	4.5	18.9

Three-point field goals: 1995-96, 88-for-238 (.370).

HONORS: All-NBA third team (2000). ... NBA All-Rookie first team (1997).

NBA REGULAR-SEASON RECORD

Season Team	G	Min.	FGM	FGA	Pct.	FTM	FTA	Pct.	REBOUNDS			Ast.	St.	Blk.	TO	Pts.	AVERAGES		
									Off.	Def.	Tot.						RPG	APG	PPG
96-97—Minnesota......	67	2324	355	871	.408	245	337	.727	54	130	184	522	67	19	210	1057	2.7	7.8	15.8
97-98—Minnesota......	82	3112	513	1237	.415	329	450	.731	58	172	230	704	104	7	256	1450	2.8	8.6	17.7
98-99—Minn.-N.J....	49	1895	378	883	.428	222	278	.799	37	105	142	437	59	8	164	1044	2.9	8.9	21.3
99-00—New Jersey....	74	2881	569	1317	.432	436	536	.813	61	179	240	622	112	15	270	1640	3.2	8.4	22.2
00-01—New Jersey....	67	2557	563	1277	.441	362	458	.790	53	152	205	506	79	5	197	1598	3.1	7.6	23.9
Totals	339	12769	2378	5585	.426	1594	2059	.774	263	738	1001	2791	421	54	1097	6789	3.0	8.2	20.0

Three-point field goals: 1996-97, 102-for-288 (.354). 1997-98, 95-for-304 (.313). 1998-99, 66-for-197 (.335). 1999-00, 66-for-233 (.283). 2000-01, 110-for-335 (.328). Totals, 439-for-1357 (.324).
Personal fouls/disqualifications: 1996-97, 159/2. 1997-98, 222/0. 1998-99, 125/0. 1999-00, 195/4. 2000-01, 150/1. Totals, 851/7.

NBA PLAYOFF RECORD

Season Team	G	Min.	FGM	FGA	Pct.	FTM	FTA	Pct.	REBOUNDS			Ast.	St.	Blk.	TO	Pts.	AVERAGES		
									Off.	Def.	Tot.						RPG	APG	PPG
96-97—Minnesota......	3	117	26	65	.400	6	10	.600	2	10	12	23	2	0	9	64	4.0	7.7	21.3
97-98—Minnesota......	5	209	22	72	.306	18	23	.783	5	11	16	38	12	0	18	69	3.2	7.6	13.8
Totals	8	326	48	137	.350	24	33	.727	7	21	28	61	14	0	27	133	3.5	7.6	16.6

Three-point field goals: 1996-97, 6-for-20 (.300). 1997-98, 7-for-25 (.280). Totals, 13-for-45 (.289).
Personal fouls/disqualifications: 1996-97, 9/0. 1997-98, 16/0. Totals, 25/0.

NBA ALL-STAR GAME RECORD

Season Team	Min.	FGM	FGA	Pct.	FTM	FTA	Pct.	REBOUNDS			Ast.	PF	Dq.	St.	Blk.	TO	Pts.
								Off.	Def.	Tot.							
2001 —New Jersey........	18	5	9	.556	0	2	.000	0	0	0	4	2	0	0	0	3	12

Three-point field goals: 2001, 2-for-3 (.667).

MARION, SHAWN　　　　F　　　　SUNS

PERSONAL: Born May 7, 1978, in Chicago. ... 6-7/215. (2,01/97,5). ... Full Name: Shawn Dwayne Marion.
HIGH SCHOOL: Clarksville (Tenn.).
JUNIOR COLLEGE: Vincennes (Ind.) University.
COLLEGE: UNLV.
TRANSACTIONS/CAREER NOTES: Selected after junior season by Phoenix Suns in first round (ninth pick overall) of 1999 NBA Draft.

COLLEGIATE RECORD

Season Team	G	Min.	FGM	FGA	Pct.	FTM	FTA	Pct.	Reb.	Ast.	Pts.	AVERAGES		
												RPG	APG	PPG
96-97—Vincennes......................	36	...	346	581	.596	124	178	.697	462	124	838	12.8	3.4	23.3
97-98—Vincennes......................	36	...	352	605	.582	122	163	.748	471	99	847	13.1	2.8	23.5
98-99—UNLV	29	954	221	418	.529	81	111	.730	269	36	543	9.3	1.2	18.7
Junior College Totals.............	72	...	698	1186	.589	246	341	.721	933	223	1685	13.0	3.1	23.4
4-Year-College Totals	29	954	221	418	.529	81	111	.730	269	36	543	9.3	1.2	18.7

Three-point field goals: 1996-97, 22-for-65 (.338). 1997-98, 21-for-56 (.375). 1998-99, 20-for-67 (.299). Totals, 43-for-121 (.355).

HONORS: NBA All-Rookie second team (2000).

NBA REGULAR-SEASON RECORD

Season Team	G	Min.	FGM	FGA	Pct.	FTM	FTA	Pct.	REBOUNDS			Ast.	St.	Blk.	TO	Pts.	AVERAGES		
									Off.	Def.	Tot.						RPG	APG	PPG
99-00—Phoenix	51	1260	222	471	.471	72	85	.847	105	227	332	69	38	53	51	520	6.5	1.4	10.2
00-01—Phoenix	79	2857	557	1160	.480	234	289	.810	220	628	848	160	132	108	129	1369	10.7	2.0	17.3
Totals	130	4117	779	1631	.478	306	374	.818	325	855	1180	229	170	161	180	1889	9.1	1.8	14.5

Three-point field goals: 1999-00, 4-for-22 (.182). 2000-01, 21-for-82 (.256). Totals, 25-for-104 (.240).
Personal fouls/disqualifications: 1999-00, 113/0. 2000-01, 211/2. Totals, 324/2.

NBA PLAYOFF RECORD

Season Team	G	Min.	FGM	FGA	Pct.	FTM	FTA	Pct.	REBOUNDS			Ast.	St.	Blk.	TO	Pts.	AVERAGES		
									Off.	Def.	Tot.						RPG	APG	PPG
99-00—Phoenix	9	281	36	86	.419	9	11	.818	21	58	79	7	6	14	7	82	8.8	0.8	9.1
00-01—Phoenix	4	139	23	62	.371	12	14	.857	10	23	33	3	6	6	6	59	8.3	0.8	14.8
Totals	13	420	59	148	.399	21	25	.840	31	81	112	10	12	20	13	141	8.6	0.8	10.8

Three-point field goals: 1999-00, 1-for-6 (.167). 2000-01, 1-for-1. Totals, 2-for-7 (.286).
Personal fouls/disqualifications: 1999-00, 17/0. 2000-01, 13/0. Totals, 30/0.

MARSHALL, DONYELL　　　　F　　　　JAZZ

PERSONAL: Born May 18, 1973, in Reading, Pa. ... 6-9/230. (2,06/104,3). ... Full Name: Donyell Lamar Marshall. ... Name pronounced Don-YELL.
HIGH SCHOOL: Reading (Pa.).
COLLEGE: Connecticut.
TRANSACTIONS/CAREER NOTES: Selected after junior season by Minnesota Timberwolves in first round (fourth pick overall) of 1994 NBA Draft. ... Traded by Timberwolves to Golden State Warriors for F Tom Gugliotta (February 18, 1995). ... Traded by Warriors to Utah Jazz as part of four-team deal in which Boston Celtics received G Robert Pack, C John

M

Williams and cash considerations from Dallas Mavericks and a conditional first-round draft choice from Jazz, Mavericks received G Dana Barros from Celtics, F Bill Curley from Warriors and G Howard Eisley from Jazz, Jazz received C Bruno Sundov from Mavericks and Warriors received F Danny Fortson from Celtics and F Adam Keefe from Jazz (August 16, 2000).

COLLEGIATE RECORD

NOTES: THE SPORTING NEWS All-America first team (1994).

Season Team	G	Min.	FGM	FGA	Pct.	FTM	FTA	Pct.	Reb.	Ast.	Pts.	RPG	APG	PPG
91-92—Connecticut	30	806	125	295	.424	69	93	.742	183	45	334	6.1	1.5	11.1
92-93—Connecticut	27	854	166	332	.500	107	129	.829	210	30	459	7.8	1.1	17.0
93-94—Connecticut	34	1157	306	599	.511	200	266	.752	302	56	853	8.9	1.6	25.1
Totals	91	2817	597	1226	.487	376	488	.770	695	131	1646	7.6	1.4	18.1

Three-point field goals: 1991-92, 15-for-62 (.242). 1992-93, 20-for-54 (.370). 1993-94, 41-for-132 (.311). Totals, 76-for-248 (.306).

NBA REGULAR-SEASON RECORD

HONORS: NBA All-Rookie second team (1995).

Season Team	G	Min.	FGM	FGA	Pct.	FTM	FTA	Pct.	Off.	Def.	Tot.	Ast.	St.	Blk.	TO	Pts.	RPG	APG	PPG
94-95—Minn.-G.S.	72	2086	345	876	.394	147	222	.662	137	268	405	105	45	88	115	906	5.6	1.5	12.6
95-96—Golden State	62	934	125	314	.398	64	83	.771	65	148	213	49	22	31	48	342	3.4	0.8	5.5
96-97—Golden State	61	1022	174	421	.413	61	98	.622	92	184	276	54	25	46	55	444	4.5	0.9	7.3
97-98—Golden State	73	2611	451	1091	.413	158	216	.731	210	418	628	159	95	73	147	1123	8.6	2.2	15.4
98-99—Golden State	48	1250	208	494	.421	88	121	.727	115	227	342	66	47	37	80	530	7.1	1.4	11.0
99-00—Golden State	64	2071	331	840	.394	199	255	.780	189	448	637	167	68	68	123	910	10.0	2.6	14.2
00-01—Utah	81	2326	427	849	.503	205	273	.751	172	394	566	133	85	78	128	1100	7.0	1.6	13.6
Totals	461	12300	2061	4885	.422	922	1268	.727	980	2087	3067	733	387	421	696	5355	6.7	1.6	11.6

Three-point field goals: 1994-95, 69-for-243 (.284). 1995-96, 28-for-94 (.298). 1996-97, 35-for-111 (.315). 1997-98, 63-for-201 (.313). 1998-99, 26-for-72 (.361). 1999-00, 49-for-138 (.355). 2000-01, 41-for-128 (.320). Totals, 311-for-987 (.315).

Personal fouls/disqualifications: 1994-95, 157/1. 1995-96, 83/0. 1996-97, 96/0. 1997-98, 226/1. 1998-99, 123/1. 1999-00, 180/1. 2000-01, 196/0. Totals, 1061/4.

NBA PLAYOFF RECORD

Season Team	G	Min.	FGM	FGA	Pct.	FTM	FTA	Pct.	Off.	Def.	Tot.	Ast.	St.	Blk.	TO	Pts.	RPG	APG	PPG
00-01—Utah	5	160	22	54	.407	7	9	.778	13	25	38	8	2	5	9	52	7.6	1.6	10.4

Three-point field goals: 2000-01, 1-for-8 (.125).
Personal fouls/disqualifications: 2000-01, 19/1.

MARTIN, DARRICK   G   MAVERICKS

PERSONAL: Born March 6, 1971, in Denver. ... 5-11/170. (1,80/77,1).
HIGH SCHOOL: St. Anthony (Long Beach, Calif.).
COLLEGE: UCLA.
TRANSACTIONS/CAREER NOTES: Not drafted by an NBA franchise. ... Played with Magic Johnson All-Stars (1992-93 and 1993-94). ... Played in Continental Basketball Association with Sioux Falls Skyforce (1994-95). ... Signed by Minnesota Timberwolves to first of two consecutive 10-day contracts (February 13, 1995). ... Re-signed by Timberwolves for remainder of season (March 7, 1995). ... Signed as free agent by Vancouver Grizzlies (November 3, 1995). ... Traded by Grizzlies to Timberwolves for 1996 second-round draft choice (January 12, 1996). ... Signed as free agent by Los Angeles Clippers (September 19, 1996). ... Signed as free agent by Sacramento Kings (August 4, 1999). ... Signed as free agent by Dallas Mavericks (August 2, 2001).

M

COLLEGIATE RECORD

Season Team	G	Min.	FGM	FGA	Pct.	FTM	FTA	Pct.	Reb.	Ast.	Pts.	RPG	APG	PPG
88-89—UCLA	31	929	92	203	.453	68	91	.747	59	90	265	1.9	2.9	8.5
89-90—UCLA	33	1069	132	283	.466	90	126	.714	71	199	374	2.2	6.0	11.3
90-91—UCLA	32	1030	129	278	.464	90	120	.750	77	217	371	2.4	6.8	11.6
91-92—UCLA	33	642	52	120	.433	68	82	.829	43	130	185	1.3	3.9	5.6
Totals	129	3670	405	884	.458	316	419	.754	250	636	1195	1.9	4.9	9.3

Three-point field goals: 1988-89, 13-for-37 (.351). 1989-90, 20-for-63 (.317). 1990-91, 23-for-79 (.291). 1991-92, 13-for-35 (.371). Totals, 69-for-214 (.322).

CBA REGULAR-SEASON RECORD

NOTES: CBA All-League second team (1995).

Season Team	G	Min.	FGM	FGA	Pct.	FTM	FTA	Pct.	Reb.	Ast.	Pts.	RPG	APG	PPG
94-95—Sioux Falls	37	1422	285	518	.550	196	226	.867	96	289	777	2.6	7.8	21.0

Three-point field goals: 1994-95, 11-for-39 (.282).

NBA REGULAR-SEASON RECORD

Season Team	G	Min.	FGM	FGA	Pct.	FTM	FTA	Pct.	Off.	Def.	Tot.	Ast.	St.	Blk.	TO	Pts.	RPG	APG	PPG
94-95—Minnesota	34	803	95	233	.408	57	65	.877	14	50	64	133	34	0	62	254	1.9	3.9	7.5
95-96—Van.-Minn.	59	1149	147	362	.406	101	120	.842	16	66	82	217	53	3	107	415	1.4	3.7	7.0
96-97—L.A. Clippers	82	1820	292	718	.407	218	250	.872	26	87	113	339	57	2	127	893	1.4	4.1	10.9
97-98—L.A. Clippers	82	2299	275	730	.377	184	217	.848	19	145	164	331	82	10	154	841	2.0	4.0	10.3
98-99—L.A. Clippers	37	941	102	278	.367	61	76	.803	5	43	48	144	43	4	67	296	1.3	3.9	8.0
99-00—Sacramento	71	893	133	350	.380	98	119	.824	7	37	44	122	28	2	62	402	0.6	1.7	5.7
00-01—Sacramento	31	176	29	76	.382	31	35	.886	2	14	16	14	7	0	10	103	0.5	0.5	3.3
Totals	396	8081	1073	2747	.391	750	882	.850	89	442	531	1300	304	21	589	3204	1.3	3.3	8.1

Three-point field goals: 1994-95, 7-for-38 (.184). 1995-96, 20-for-69 (.290). 1996-97, 91-for-234 (.389). 1997-98, 107-for-293 (.365). 1998-99, 31-for-106 (.292). 1999-00, 38-for-124 (.306). 2000-01, 14-for-27 (.519). Totals, 308-for-891 (.346).

Personal fouls/disqualifications: 1994-95, 88/0. 1995-96, 123/0. 1996-97, 165/1. 1997-98, 198/2. 1998-99, 82/1. 1999-00, 89/0. 2000-01, 27/0. Totals, 772/4.

Season Team	G	Min.	FGM	FGA	Pct.	FTM	FTA	Pct.	REBOUNDS Off.	Def.	Tot.	Ast.	St.	Blk.	TO	Pts.	AVERAGES RPG	APG	PPG
96-97—L.A. Clippers...	3	77	11	25	.440	6	9	.667	1	1	2	13	0	0	2	33	0.7	4.3	11.0
99-00—Sacramento	2	21	3	9	.333	3	4	.750	1	2	3	2	1	0	3	10	1.5	1.0	5.0
00-01—Sacramento	2	9	0	6	.000	0	0	...	0	0	0	3	0	0	1	0	0.0	1.5	0.0
Totals	7	107	14	40	.350	9	13	.692	2	3	5	18	1	0	6	43	0.7	2.6	6.1

Three-point field goals: 1996-97, 5-for-9 (.556). 1999-00, 1-for-3 (.333). 2000-01, 0-for-2. Totals, 6-for-14 (.429).
Personal fouls/disqualifications: 1996-97, 9/0. 1999-00, 4/0. 2000-01, 1/0. Totals, 14/0.

MARTIN, KENYON   F/C   NETS

PERSONAL: Born December 30, 1977, in Saginaw, Mich. ... 6-9/230. (2,06/104,3). ... Full Name: Kenyon Lee Martin.
HIGH SCHOOL: Bryan Adams (Dallas).
COLLEGE: Cincinnati.
TRANSACTIONS/CAREER NOTES: Selected by New Jersey Nets in first round (first pick overall) of 2000 NBA Draft.

COLLEGIATE RECORD

NOTES: The Sporting News College Player of the Year (2000). ... Wooden Award winner (2000). ... Naismith Award winner (2000). ... The Sporting News All-America first team (2000).

Season Team	G	Min.	FGM	FGA	Pct.	FTM	FTA	Pct.	Reb.	Ast.	Pts.	AVERAGES RPG	APG	PPG
96-97—Cincinnati	22	233	26	40	.650	10	32	.313	74	10	62	3.4	0.5	2.8
97-98—Cincinnati	30	858	124	198	.626	50	105	.476	267	41	298	8.9	1.4	9.9
98-99—Cincinnati	33	900	142	248	.573	50	89	.562	228	49	334	6.9	1.5	10.1
99-00—Cincinnati	31	909	221	389	.568	141	206	.684	300	42	585	9.7	1.4	18.9
Totals	116	2900	513	875	.586	251	432	.581	869	142	1279	7.5	1.2	11.0

Three-point field goals: 1997-98, 0-for-1. 1998-99, 0-for-1. 1999-00, 2-for-7 (.286). Totals, 2-for-9 (.222).

NBA REGULAR-SEASON RECORD

HONORS: NBA All-Rookie first team (2001).

Season Team	G	Min.	FGM	FGA	Pct.	FTM	FTA	Pct.	REBOUNDS Off.	Def.	Tot.	Ast.	St.	Blk.	TO	Pts.	AVERAGES RPG	APG	PPG
00-01—New Jersey.....	68	2272	346	777	.445	121	192	.630	137	365	502	131	78	113	138	814	7.4	1.9	12.0

Three-point field goals: 2000-01, 1-for-11 (.091).
Personal fouls/disqualifications: 2000-01, 281/10.

M

MASHBURN, JAMAL   F   HORNETS

PERSONAL: Born November 29, 1972, in New York. ... 6-8/241. (2,03/109,3).
HIGH SCHOOL: Cardinal Hayes (Bronx, N.Y.).
COLLEGE: Kentucky.
TRANSACTIONS/CAREER NOTES: Selected after junior season by Dallas Mavericks in first round (fourth pick overall) of 1993 NBA Draft. ... Traded by Mavericks to Miami Heat for G Sasha Danilovic, F Kurt Thomas and F Martin Muursepp (February 14, 1997). ... Traded by Heat with F P.J. Brown, F/C Otis Thorpe, F Tim James and G/F Rodney Buford to Charlotte Hornets for G Eddie Jones, F Anthony Mason, G Ricky Davis and G/F Dale Ellis (August 1, 2000).

COLLEGIATE RECORD

NOTES: The Sporting News All-America first team (1993).

Season Team	G	Min.	FGM	FGA	Pct.	FTM	FTA	Pct.	Reb.	Ast.	Pts.	AVERAGES RPG	APG	PPG
90-91—Kentucky	28	677	137	289	.474	64	88	.727	195	42	362	7.0	1.5	12.9
91-92—Kentucky	36	1176	279	492	.567	151	213	.709	281	52	767	7.8	1.4	21.3
92-93—Kentucky	34	1109	259	526	.492	130	194	.670	284	124	714	8.4	3.6	21.0
Totals	98	2962	675	1307	.516	345	495	.697	760	218	1843	7.8	2.2	18.8

Three-point field goals: 1990-91, 23-for-82 (.280). 1991-92, 58-for-132 (.439). 1992-93, 66-for-180 (.367). Totals, 147-for-394 (.373).

NBA REGULAR-SEASON RECORD

HONORS: NBA All-Rookie first team (1994).

Season Team	G	Min.	FGM	FGA	Pct.	FTM	FTA	Pct.	REBOUNDS Off.	Def.	Tot.	Ast.	St.	Blk.	TO	Pts.	AVERAGES RPG	APG	PPG
93-94—Dallas.............	79	2896	561	1382	.406	306	438	.699	107	246	353	266	89	14	245	1513	4.5	3.4	19.2
94-95—Dallas.............	80	2980	683	1566	.436	447	605	.739	116	215	331	298	82	8	235	1926	4.1	3.7	24.1
95-96—Dallas.............	18	669	145	383	.379	97	133	.729	37	60	97	50	14	3	55	422	5.4	2.8	23.4
96-97—Dallas-Miami...	69	2164	286	743	.385	160	228	.702	69	225	294	204	78	12	114	822	4.3	3.0	11.9
97-98—Miami	48	1729	251	577	.435	184	231	.797	72	164	236	132	43	14	108	723	4.9	2.8	15.1
98-99—Miami	24	855	134	297	.451	75	104	.721	24	122	146	75	20	3	60	356	6.1	3.1	14.8
99-00—Miami	76	2828	515	1158	.445	186	239	.778	64	317	381	298	79	14	180	1328	5.0	3.9	17.5
00-01—Charlotte........	76	2989	573	1388	.413	279	364	.766	92	484	576	411	85	13	211	1528	7.6	5.4	20.1
Totals	470	17110	3148	7494	.420	1734	2342	.740	581	1833	2414	1734	490	81	1208	8618	5.1	3.7	18.3

Three-point field goals: 1993-94, 85-for-299 (.284). 1994-95, 113-for-344 (.328). 1995-96, 35-for-102 (.343). 1996-97, 90-for-277 (.325). 1997-98, 37-for-122 (.303). 1998-99, 13-for-30 (.433). 1999-00, 112-for-278 (.403). 2000-01, 103-for-289 (.356). Totals, 588-for-1741 (.338).
Personal fouls/disqualifications: 1993-94, 205/0. 1994-95, 190/0. 1995-96, 39/0. 1996-97, 186/4. 1997-98, 137/1. 1998-99, 58/0. 1999-00, 215/3. 2000-01, 185/1. Totals, 1215/9.

NBA PLAYOFF RECORD

Season Team	G	Min.	FGM	FGA	Pct.	FTM	FTA	Pct.	Off.	Def.	Tot.	Ast.	St.	Blk.	TO	Pts.	RPG	APG	PPG
96-97—Miami	17	554	65	168	.387	26	40	.650	22	62	84	35	17	2	30	178	4.9	2.1	10.5
97-98—Miami	5	129	12	45	.267	3	4	.750	4	18	22	9	3	1	9	31	4.4	1.8	6.2
98-99—Miami	5	152	19	49	.388	6	9	.667	4	9	13	10	2	0	10	50	2.6	2.0	10.0
99-00—Miami	10	423	63	157	.401	36	42	.857	9	37	46	32	11	2	24	175	4.6	3.2	17.5
00-01—Charlotte	10	419	84	208	.404	74	88	.841	18	44	62	57	12	3	30	249	6.2	5.7	24.9
Totals	47	1677	243	627	.388	145	183	.792	57	170	227	143	45	8	103	683	4.8	3.0	14.5

Three-point field goals: 1996-97, 22-for-62 (.355). 1997-98, 4-for-11 (.364). 1998-99, 6-for-14 (.429). 1999-00, 13-for-33 (.394). 2000-01, 7-for-21 (.333). Totals, 52-for-141 (.369).
Personal fouls/disqualifications: 1996-97, 58/2. 1997-98, 21/2. 1998-99, 11/0. 1999-00, 30/0. 2000-01, 24/0. Totals, 144/4.

MASON, ANTHONY   F

PERSONAL: Born December 14, 1966, in Miami. ... 6-8/260. (2,03/117,9). ... Full Name: Anthony George Douglas Mason.
HIGH SCHOOL: Springfield Gardens (N.Y.).
COLLEGE: Tennessee State.
TRANSACTIONS/CAREER NOTES: Selected by Portland Trail Blazers in third round (53rd pick overall) of 1988 NBA Draft. ... Played in Turkey (1988-89). ... Draft rights renounced by Trail Blazers (June 30, 1989). ... Signed as free agent by New Jersey Nets (September 19, 1989). ... Waived by Nets (October 30, 1990). ... Played in Continental Basketball Association with Tulsa Fast Breakers (1990-91). ... Signed by Denver Nuggets to first of two consecutive 10-day contracts (December 28, 1990). ... Played in United States Basketball League with Long Island Surf (1991). ... Signed as free agent by New York Knicks (July 30, 1991). ... Traded by Knicks with F Brad Lohaus to Charlotte Hornets for F Larry Johnson (July 14, 1996). ... Traded by Hornets with G Eddie Jones, G Ricky Davis and G/F Dale Ellis to Miami Heat for F P.J. Brown, F Jamal Mashburn, F/C Otis Thorpe, F Tim James and G/F Rodney Buford (August 1, 2000).

COLLEGIATE RECORD

Season Team	G	Min.	FGM	FGA	Pct.	FTM	FTA	Pct.	Reb.	Ast.	Pts.	RPG	APG	PPG
84-85—Tennessee State	28	801	100	213	.469	79	122	.648	148	46	279	5.3	1.6	10.0
85-86—Tennessee State	28	913	206	427	.482	93	130	.715	192	69	505	6.9	2.5	18.0
86-87—Tennessee State	27	951	201	449	.448	89	135	.659	262	68	508	9.7	2.5	18.8
87-88—Tennessee State	28	1064	276	608	.454	191	247	.773	292	85	783	10.4	3.0	28.0
Totals	111	3729	783	1697	.461	452	634	.713	894	268	2075	8.1	2.4	18.7

Three-point field goals: 1986-87, 17-for-49 (.347). 1987-88, 40-for-81 (.494). Totals, 57-for-130 (.438).

NBA REGULAR-SEASON RECORD

HONORS: NBA Sixth Man Award (1995). ... All-NBA third team (1997). ... NBA All-Defensive second team (1997).

Season Team	G	Min.	FGM	FGA	Pct.	FTM	FTA	Pct.	Off.	Def.	Tot.	Ast.	St.	Blk.	TO	Pts.	RPG	APG	PPG
89-90—New Jersey	21	108	14	40	.350	9	15	.600	11	23	34	7	2	2	11	37	1.6	0.3	1.8
90-91—Denver	3	21	2	4	.500	6	8	.750	3	2	5	0	1	0	0	10	1.7	0.0	3.3
91-92—New York	82	2198	203	399	.509	167	260	.642	216	357	573	106	46	20	101	573	7.0	1.3	7.0
92-93—New York	81	2482	316	629	.502	199	292	.682	231	409	640	170	43	19	137	831	7.9	2.1	10.3
93-94—New York	73	1903	206	433	.476	116	161	.720	158	269	427	151	31	9	107	528	5.8	2.1	7.2
94-95—New York	77	2496	287	507	.566	191	298	.641	182	468	650	240	69	21	123	765	8.4	3.1	9.9
95-96—New York	82	*3457	449	798	.563	298	414	.720	220	544	764	363	69	34	211	1196	9.3	4.4	14.6
96-97—Charlotte	73	3143	433	825	.525	319	428	.745	186	643	829	414	76	33	165	1186	11.4	5.7	16.2
97-98—Charlotte	81	3148	389	764	.509	261	402	.649	177	649	826	342	68	18	146	1039	10.2	4.2	12.8
98-99—Charlotte						Did not play—injured.													
99-00—Charlotte	82	3133	317	661	.480	314	421	.746	145	554	699	367	74	29	160	948	8.5	4.5	11.6
00-01—Miami	80	3254	460	954	.482	370	474	.781	169	601	770	248	80	25	179	1290	9.6	3.1	16.1
Totals	735	25343	3076	6014	.511	2250	3173	.709	1698	4519	6217	2408	559	210	1340	8403	8.5	3.3	11.4

Three-point field goals: 1993-94, 0-for-1. 1994-95, 0-for-1. 1996-97, 1-for-3 (.333). 1997-98, 0-for-4. 1999-00, 0-for-1. Totals, 1-for-10 (.100).
Personal fouls/disqualifications: 1989-90, 20/0. 1990-91, 6/0. 1991-92, 229/0. 1992-93, 240/2. 1993-94, 190/2. 1994-95, 253/3. 1995-96, 246/3. 1996-97, 202/3. 1997-98, 182/1. 1999-00, 220/0. 2000-01, 231/5. Totals, 2019/19.

NBA PLAYOFF RECORD

Season Team	G	Min.	FGM	FGA	Pct.	FTM	FTA	Pct.	Off.	Def.	Tot.	Ast.	St.	Blk.	TO	Pts.	RPG	APG	PPG
91-92—New York	12	288	19	43	.442	22	28	.786	28	48	76	10	2	8	11	60	6.3	0.8	5.0
92-93—New York	15	510	72	122	.590	43	68	.632	55	54	109	41	10	6	23	187	7.3	2.7	12.5
93-94—New York	25	660	67	137	.489	55	77	.714	53	93	146	46	15	5	36	189	5.8	1.8	7.6
94-95—New York	11	352	31	51	.608	43	69	.623	23	45	68	24	6	6	26	105	6.2	2.2	9.5
95-96—New York	8	350	41	78	.526	19	28	.679	17	45	62	26	4	1	20	101	7.8	3.3	12.6
96-97—Charlotte	3	131	16	38	.421	7	13	.538	8	28	36	9	1	1	9	39	12.0	3.0	13.0
97-98—Charlotte	9	367	57	99	.576	25	42	.595	17	54	71	31	8	0	22	139	7.9	3.4	15.4
99-00—Charlotte	4	179	18	38	.474	14	20	.700	16	23	39	22	4	0	13	50	9.8	5.5	12.5
00-01—Miami	3	98	5	13	.385	6	6	1.000	9	8	4	9	1	0	7	16	3.0	1.3	5.3
Totals	90	2935	326	619	.527	234	351	.667	218	398	616	213	51	27	167	886	6.8	2.4	9.8

Three-point field goals: 1994-95, 0-for-1. 1997-98, 0-for-1. 1999-00, 0-for-1. 2000-01, 0-for-1. Totals, 0-for-4 (.000).
Personal fouls/disqualifications: 1991-92, 34/0. 1992-93, 50/2. 1993-94, 66/0. 1994-95, 28/0. 1995-96, 20/0. 1996-97, 6/0. 1997-98, 17/0. 1999-00, 13/0. 2000-01, 6/0. Totals, 240/2.

NBA ALL-STAR GAME RECORD

Season Team	Min.	FGM	FGA	Pct.	FTM	FTA	Pct.	Off.	Def.	Tot.	Ast.	PF	Dq.	St.	Blk.	TO	Pts.
2001 —Miami	20	0	3	.000	0	0	...	2	2	4	1	2	0	1	0	2	0

CBA REGULAR-SEASON RECORD

Season Team	G	Min.	FGM	FGA	Pct.	FTM	FTA	Pct.	Reb.	Ast.	Pts.	RPG	APG	PPG
90-91—Tulsa	26	1074	256	456	.561	266	370	.719	384	102	778	14.8	3.9	29.9

MASON, DESMOND   G/F   SUPERSONICS

PERSONAL: Born October 11, 1977, in Waxahachie, Texas. ... 6-5/215. (1,96/97,5). ... Full Name: Desmond Tremaine Mason.
HIGH SCHOOL: Waxahachie (Texas).
COLLEGE: Oklahoma State.
TRANSACTIONS/CAREER NOTES: Selected by Seattle SuperSonics in first round (17th pick overall) of 2000 NBA Draft.

COLLEGIATE RECORD

Season Team	G	Min.	FGM	FGA	Pct.	FTM	FTA	Pct.	Reb.	Ast.	Pts.	RPG	APG	PPG
96-97—Oklahoma State	32	539	52	138	.377	23	37	.622	80	22	144	2.5	0.7	4.5
97-98—Oklahoma State	29	947	157	299	.525	86	126	.683	223	45	422	7.7	1.6	14.6
98-99—Oklahoma State	34	1180	196	408	.480	106	142	.746	267	28	525	7.9	0.8	15.4
99-00—Oklahoma State	34	1202	211	423	.499	125	163	.767	225	52	611	6.6	1.5	18.0
Totals	129	3868	616	1268	.486	340	468	.726	795	147	1702	6.2	1.1	13.2

Three-point field goals: 1996-97, 17-for-52 (.327). 1997-98, 22-for-69 (.319). 1998-99, 27-for-79 (.342). 1999-00, 64-for-149 (.430). Totals, 130-for-349 (.372).

NBA REGULAR-SEASON RECORD

HONORS: NBA All-Rookie second team (2001). ... Slam Dunk championship winner (2001).

Season Team	G	Min.	FGM	FGA	Pct.	FTM	FTA	Pct.	Off.	Def.	Tot.	Ast.	St.	Blk.	TO	Pts.	RPG	APG	PPG
00-01—Seattle	78	1522	189	439	.431	67	91	.736	72	177	249	63	39	20	53	463	3.2	0.8	5.9

Three-point field goals: 2000-01, 18-for-67 (.269).
Personal fouls/disqualifications: 2000-01, 146/0.

MASSENBURG, TONY   F   GRIZZLIES

PERSONAL: Born July 31, 1967, in Sussex, Va. ... 6-9/250. (2,06/113,4). ... Full Name: Tony Arnel Massenburg.
HIGH SCHOOL: Sussex (Va.) Central.
COLLEGE: Maryland.
TRANSACTIONS/CAREER NOTES: Selected by San Antonio Spurs in second round (43rd pick overall) of 1990 NBA Draft. ... Waived by Spurs (December 2, 1991). ... Played in Italy (1991-92). ... Signed as free agent by Charlotte Hornets (December 11, 1991). ... Waived by Hornets (January 7, 1992). ... Signed by Boston Celtics to first of two consecutive 10-day contracts (January 10, 1992). ... Signed by Golden State Warriors to first of two consecutive 10-day contracts (February 13, 1992). ... Played in Spain (1992-93 and 1993-94). ... Signed as free agent by Los Angeles Clippers (June 27, 1994). ... Selected by Toronto Raptors from Clippers in NBA Expansion Draft (June 24, 1995). ... Traded by Raptors with F Ed Pinckney and right to swap 1996 or 1997 first-round draft choices to Philadelphia 76ers for F Sharone Wright (February 22, 1996). ... Signed as free agent by New Jersey Nets (September 10, 1996). ... Traded by Celtics with future second-round draft choice to Vancouver Grizzlies for F Roy Rogers (October 28, 1997). ... Traded by Grizzlies with draft rights to G Steve Francis as part of three-way deal in which Grizzlies received G Michael Dickerson, F/C Othella Harrington, G Brent Price, F/C Antoine Carr and future first-round draft choice from Rockets, Rockets received F Don MacLean and future first-round draft choice from Orlando Magic, and Magic received G Michael Smith, G/F Rodrick Rhodes, G Lee Mayberry and F Makhtar Ndiaye from Grizzlies (August 27, 1999). ... Signed as free agent by Grizzlies (August 8, 2000). ... Grizzlies franchise moved to Memphis for 2001-02 season.

COLLEGIATE RECORD

Season Team	G	Min.	FGM	FGA	Pct.	FTM	FTA	Pct.	Reb.	Ast.	Pts.	RPG	APG	PPG
85-86—Maryland	29	349	28	56	.500	27	48	.563	60	0	83	2.1	0.0	2.9
86-87—Maryland						Did not play.								
87-88—Maryland	23	616	93	179	.520	47	82	.573	122	10	233	5.3	0.4	10.1
88-89—Maryland	29	1001	197	358	.550	87	145	.600	226	21	481	7.8	0.7	16.6
89-90—Maryland	31	973	206	408	.505	145	201	.721	314	20	557	10.1	0.6	18.0
Totals	112	2939	524	1001	.523	306	476	.643	722	51	1354	6.4	0.5	12.1

Three-point field goals: 1988-89, 0-for-1. 1989-90, 0-for-2. Totals, 0-for-3 (.000).

NBA REGULAR-SEASON RECORD

Season Team	G	Min.	FGM	FGA	Pct.	FTM	FTA	Pct.	Off.	Def.	Tot.	Ast.	St.	Blk.	TO	Pts.	RPG	APG	PPG
90-91—San Antonio	35	161	27	60	.450	28	45	.622	23	35	58	4	4	9	13	82	1.7	0.1	2.3
91-92—SA-Char.-Bos.-GS	18	90	10	25	.400	9	15	.600	7	18	25	0	1	1	9	29	1.4	0.0	1.6
94-95—L.A. Clippers	80	2127	282	601	.469	177	235	.753	160	295	455	67	48	58	118	741	5.7	0.8	9.3
95-96—Tor.-Phil.	54	1463	214	432	.495	111	157	.707	127	225	352	30	28	20	73	539	6.5	0.6	10.0
96-97—New Jersey	79	1954	219	452	.485	130	206	.631	222	295	517	23	38	50	91	568	6.5	0.3	7.2
97-98—Vancouver	61	894	148	309	.479	100	137	.730	80	152	232	21	25	24	60	396	3.8	0.3	6.5
98-99—Vancouver	43	1143	189	388	.487	103	155	.665	83	174	257	23	26	39	64	481	6.0	0.5	11.2
99-00—Houston	10	109	16	36	.444	14	16	.875	7	20	27	3	2	5	9	46	2.7	0.3	4.6
00-01—Vancouver	52	823	92	199	.462	49	70	.700	75	135	210	9	10	28	48	233	4.0	0.2	4.5
Totals	432	8764	1197	2502	.478	721	1036	.696	784	1349	2133	180	182	234	485	3115	4.9	0.4	7.2

Three-point field goals: 1994-95, 0-for-3. 1995-96, 0-for-3. 1996-97, 0-for-1. 1998-99, 0-for-2. Totals, 0-for-9 (.000).
Personal fouls/disqualifications: 1990-91, 26/0. 1991-92, 21/0. 1994-95, 253/2. 1995-96, 140/0. 1996-97, 217/2. 1997-98, 123/0. 1998-99, 108/0. 1999-00, 13/0. 2000-01, 122/0. Totals, 1023/4.

NBA PLAYOFF RECORD

Season Team	G	Min.	FGM	FGA	Pct.	FTM	FTA	Pct.	Off.	Def.	Tot.	Ast.	St.	Blk.	TO	Pts.	RPG	APG	PPG
90-91—San Antonio	1	1	0	0	...	0	0	...	0	0	0	0	0	0	0	0	0.0	0.0	0.0

M

ITALIAN LEAGUE RECORD

Season Team	G	Min.	FGM	FGA	Pct.	FTM	FTA	Pct.	Reb.	Ast.	Pts.	AVERAGES RPG	APG	PPG
91-92—Sidis Reggio Emilia	4	133	35	60	.583	21	33	.636	40	0	91	10.0	0.0	22.8

SPANISH LEAGUE RECORD

Season Team	G	Min.	FGM	FGA	Pct.	FTM	FTA	Pct.	Reb.	Ast.	Pts.	AVERAGES RPG	APG	PPG
92-93—Unicaja-Mayoral	30	1008	195	351	.556	72	106	.679	293	10	462	9.8	0.3	15.4
93-94—Barcelona	25	759	150	264	.568	88	127	.693	199	12	388	8.0	0.5	15.5
Totals	55	1767	345	615	.561	160	233	.687	492	22	850	8.9	0.4	15.5

MAXWELL, VERNON   G

PERSONAL: Born September 12, 1965, in Gainesville, Fla. ... 6-4/190. (1,93/86,2).
HIGH SCHOOL: Buchholz (Gainesville, Fla.).
COLLEGE: Florida.
TRANSACTIONS/CAREER NOTES: Selected by Denver Nuggets in second round (47th pick overall) of 1988 NBA Draft. ... Draft rights traded by Nuggets to San Antonio Spurs for 1989 second-round draft choice (June 28, 1988). ... Traded by Spurs to Houston Rockets for cash (February 21, 1990). ... Waived by Rockets (June 30, 1995). ... Signed as free agent by Philadelphia 76ers (September 26, 1995). ... Signed as free agent by Spurs (August 29, 1996). ... Signed by Orlando Magic to 10-day contract (January 5, 1998). ... Signed by Charlotte Hornets to 10-day contract (February 2, 1998). ... Re-signed by Hornets for remainder of season (February 13, 1998). ... Signed as free agent by Sacramento Kings (January 22, 1999). ... Signed as free agent by Seattle SuperSonics (August 9, 1999). ... Traded by SuperSonics to New York Knicks as part of four-team trade in which Knicks acquired F Glen Rice, C Luc Longley, F/C Travis Knight, C Vladimir Stepania, F Lazaro Borrell, two 2001 first-round draft choices and two 2001 second-round draft choices, SuperSonics acquired C Patrick Ewing, Phoenix Suns acquired C Chris Dudley and 2001 first-round draft choice and Los Angeles Lakers acquired F Horace Grant, C Greg Foster, F Chuck Person and G Emanual Davis (September 20, 2000). ... Waived by Knicks (October 5, 2000). ... Signed as free agent by 76ers (October 28, 2000). ... Waived by 76ers (December 22, 2000). ... Signed as free agent by Dallas Mavericks (February 28, 2001).
MISCELLANEOUS: Member of NBA championship team (1994, 1995).

COLLEGIATE RECORD

Season Team	G	Min.	FGM	FGA	Pct.	FTM	FTA	Pct.	Reb.	Ast.	Pts.	AVERAGES RPG	APG	PPG
84-85—Florida	30	752	163	366	.445	72	105	.686	72	40	398	2.4	1.3	13.3
85-86—Florida	33	1142	262	566	.463	124	177	.701	147	81	648	4.5	2.5	19.6
86-87—Florida	34	1086	266	548	.485	161	217	.742	125	123	738	3.7	3.6	21.7
87-88—Florida	33	1214	230	515	.447	148	207	.715	138	142	666	4.2	4.3	20.2
Totals	130	4194	921	1995	.462	505	706	.715	482	386	2450	3.7	3.0	18.8

Three-point field goals: 1986-87, 45-for-128 (.352). 1987-88, 58-for-147 (.395). Totals, 103-for-275 (.375).

NBA REGULAR-SEASON RECORD

RECORDS: Shares record for most seasons leading league in three-point field goals made—2.
NOTES: Led NBA with 172 three-point field goals made (1991) and 162 three-point field goals (1992).

Season Team	G	Min.	FGM	FGA	Pct.	FTM	FTA	Pct.	REBOUNDS Off.	Def.	Tot.	Ast.	St.	Blk.	TO	Pts.	AVERAGES RPG	APG	PPG
88-89—San Antonio	79	2065	357	827	.432	181	243	.745	49	153	202	301	86	8	178	927	2.6	3.8	11.7
89-90—S.A.-Hou........	79	1987	275	627	.439	136	211	.645	50	178	228	296	84	10	143	714	2.9	3.7	9.0
90-91—Houston	82	2870	504	1247	.404	217	296	.733	41	197	238	303	127	15	171	1397	2.9	3.7	17.0
91-92—Houston	80	2700	502	1216	.413	206	267	.772	37	206	243	326	104	28	178	1372	3.0	4.1	17.2
92-93—Houston	71	2251	349	858	.407	164	228	.719	29	192	221	297	86	8	140	982	3.1	4.2	13.8
93-94—Houston	75	2571	380	976	.389	143	191	.749	42	187	229	380	125	20	185	1023	3.1	5.1	13.6
94-95—Houston	64	2038	306	777	.394	99	144	.688	18	146	164	274	75	13	137	854	2.6	4.3	13.3
95-96—Philadelphia ...	75	2467	410	1052	.390	251	332	.756	39	190	229	330	96	12	215	1217	3.1	4.4	16.2
96-97—San Antonio ...	72	2068	340	906	.375	134	180	.744	27	132	159	153	87	19	121	929	2.2	2.1	12.9
97-98—Orlando-Char. .	42	636	103	258	.399	48	60	.800	14	43	57	52	16	4	40	291	1.4	1.2	6.9
98-99—Sacramento	46	1007	164	421	.390	84	114	.737	13	72	85	76	30	3	67	492	1.8	1.7	10.7
99-00—Seattle	47	989	169	490	.345	108	148	.730	15	64	79	75	38	9	53	513	1.7	1.6	10.9
00-01—Phil.-Dallas	43	660	73	223	.327	21	32	.656	4	62	66	49	21	3	35	201	1.5	1.1	4.7
Totals	855	24309	3932	9878	.398	1792	2446	.733	378	1822	2200	2912	975	152	1663	10912	2.6	3.4	12.8

Three-point field goals: 1988-89, 32-for-129 (.248). 1989-90, 28-for-105 (.267). 1990-91, 172-for-510 (.337). 1991-92, 162-for-473 (.342). 1992-93, 120-for-361 (.332). 1993-94, 120-for-403 (.298). 1994-95, 143-for-441 (.324). 1995-96, 146-for-460 (.317). 1996-97, 115-for-372 (.309). 1997-98, 37-for-112 (.330). 1998-99, 80-for-231 (.346). 1999-00, 67-for-223 (.300). 2000-01, 34-for-111 (.306). Totals, 1256-for-3931 (.320).
Personal fouls/disqualifications: 1988-89, 136/0. 1989-90, 148/0. 1990-91, 179/2. 1991-92, 200/3. 1992-93, 124/1. 1993-94, 143/0. 1994-95, 157/1. 1995-96, 182/1. 1996-97, 168/1. 1997-98, 71/1. 1998-99, 111/1. 1999-00, 83/0. 2000-01, 64/0. Totals, 1766/11.

NBA PLAYOFF RECORD

Season Team	G	Min.	FGM	FGA	Pct.	FTM	FTA	Pct.	REBOUNDS Off.	Def.	Tot.	Ast.	St.	Blk.	TO	Pts.	AVERAGES RPG	APG	PPG
89-90—Houston	4	159	30	81	.370	11	21	.524	5	7	12	17	5	0	6	79	3.0	4.3	19.8
90-91—Houston	3	113	23	56	.411	1	2	.500	1	7	8	9	2	1	7	56	2.7	3.0	18.7
92-93—Houston	9	308	47	117	.402	21	24	.875	3	19	22	32	11	2	17	126	2.4	3.6	14.0
93-94—Houston	23	880	118	314	.376	37	54	.685	12	69	81	96	20	2	49	318	3.5	4.2	13.8
94-95—Houston	1	16	1	7	.143	1	1	1.000	0	3	3	1	0	0	1	3	3.0	1.0	3.0
98-99—Sacramento	5	129	19	60	.317	7	10	.700	4	7	11	5	6	0	6	56	2.2	1.0	11.2
00-01—Dallas..............	4	43	2	10	.200	0	0	...	1	5	6	5	0	0	2	4	1.5	1.3	1.0
Totals	49	1648	240	645	.372	78	112	.696	26	117	143	165	44	5	88	642	2.9	3.4	13.1

Three-point field goals: 1989-90, 8-for-26 (.308). 1990-91, 9-for-27 (.333). 1992-93, 11-for-46 (.239). 1993-94, 45-for-138 (.326). 1994-95, 0-for-2. 1998-99, 11-for-35 (.314). 2000-01, 0-for-5. Totals, 84-for-279 (.301).
Personal fouls/disqualifications: 1989-90, 12/0. 1990-91, 8/0. 1992-93, 17/0. 1993-94, 55/1. 1994-95, 1/0. 1998-99, 12/0. 2000-01, 6/0. Totals, 111/1.

M

McCARTY, WALTER F CELTICS

PERSONAL: Born February 1, 1974, in Evansville, Ind. ... 6-10/230. (2,08/104,3). ... Full Name: Walter Lee McCarty.
HIGH SCHOOL: Harrison (Evansville, Ind.).
COLLEGE: Kentucky.
TRANSACTIONS/CAREER NOTES: Selected by New York Knicks in first round (19th pick overall) of 1996 NBA Draft. ... Traded by Knicks with F Dontae' Jones, F John Thomas, G Scott Brooks and two future second-round draft choices to Boston Celtics for F Chris Mills (October 22, 1997).

COLLEGIATE RECORD

NOTES: Member of NCAA Division I championship team (1996).

Season Team	G	Min.	FGM	FGA	Pct.	FTM	FTA	Pct.	Reb.	Ast.	Pts.	AVERAGES RPG	APG	PPG
92-93—Kentucky						Did not play—ineligible.								
93-94—Kentucky	34	484	72	153	.471	31	56	.554	131	39	194	3.9	1.1	5.7
94-95—Kentucky	33	744	128	251	.510	61	84	.726	185	50	345	5.6	1.5	10.5
95-96—Kentucky	36	888	152	280	.543	75	104	.721	206	92	407	5.7	2.6	11.3
Totals	103	2116	352	684	.515	167	244	.684	522	181	946	5.1	1.8	9.2

Three-point field goals: 1993-94, 19-for-50 (.380). 1994-95, 28-for-77 (.364). 1995-96, 28-for-60 (.467). Totals, 75-for-187 (.401).

NBA REGULAR-SEASON RECORD

Season Team	G	Min.	FGM	FGA	Pct.	FTM	FTA	Pct.	REBOUNDS Off.	Def.	Tot.	Ast.	St.	Blk.	TO	Pts.	AVERAGES RPG	APG	PPG
96-97—New York	35	192	26	68	.382	8	14	.571	8	15	23	13	7	9	17	64	0.7	0.4	1.8
97-98—Boston	82	2340	295	730	.404	144	194	.742	141	223	364	177	110	44	141	788	4.4	2.2	9.6
98-99—Boston	32	659	64	177	.362	40	57	.702	36	79	115	40	24	13	40	181	3.6	1.3	5.7
99-00—Boston	61	879	78	230	.339	39	54	.722	33	77	110	70	24	23	67	229	1.8	1.1	3.8
00-01—Boston	60	478	45	126	.357	22	28	.786	24	57	81	39	14	7	20	131	1.4	0.7	2.2
Totals	270	4548	508	1331	.382	253	347	.729	242	451	693	339	179	96	285	1393	2.6	1.3	5.2

Three-point field goals: 1996-97, 4-for-14 (.286). 1997-98, 54-for-175 (.309). 1998-99, 13-for-50 (.260). 1999-00, 34-for-110 (.309). 2000-01, 19-for-56 (.339). Totals, 124-for-405 (.306).

Personal fouls/disqualifications: 1996-97, 38/0. 1997-98, 274/6. 1998-99, 88/0. 1999-00, 83/1. 2000-01, 82/0. Totals, 565/7.

NBA PLAYOFF RECORD

Season Team	G	Min.	FGM	FGA	Pct.	FTM	FTA	Pct.	REBOUNDS Off.	Def.	Tot.	Ast.	St.	Blk.	TO	Pts.	AVERAGES RPG	APG	PPG
96-97—New York	2	4	2	2	1.000	0	0	...	0	0	0	1	0	0	4	0.0	0.0	2.0

McCLINTOCK, DAN C

M

PERSONAL: Born April 19, 1977, in Fountain Valley, Calif. ... 7-0/260. (2,13/117,9). ... Full Name: Daniel Raymond McClintock.
HIGH SCHOOL: Visalia (Calif.).
COLLEGE: Northern Arizona.
TRANSACTIONS/CAREER NOTES: Selected by Denver Nuggets in second round (53rd pick overall) of 2000 NBA Draft. ... Waived by Nuggets (October 30, 2000). ... Played in American Basketball Association 2000 with Kansas City Knights (2000-01). ... Re-signed by Nuggets for remainder of season (April 4, 2001).

COLLEGIATE RECORD

Season Team	G	Min.	FGM	FGA	Pct.	FTM	FTA	Pct.	Reb.	Ast.	Pts.	AVERAGES RPG	APG	PPG
96-97—Northern Arizona	28	510	117	178	.657	58	95	.611	90	13	292	3.2	0.5	10.4
97-98—Northern Arizona	29	463	110	175	.629	59	94	.628	90	17	279	3.1	0.6	9.6
98-99—Northern Arizona	27	452	125	187	.668	59	88	.670	104	13	309	3.9	0.5	11.4
99-00—Northern Arizona	31	754	190	318	.597	103	151	.682	202	36	483	6.5	1.2	15.6
Totals	115	2179	542	858	.632	279	428	.652	486	79	1363	4.2	0.7	11.9

Three-point field goals: 1997-98, 0-for-1.

ABA 2000 LEAGUE RECORD

Season Team	G	Min.	FGM	FGA	Pct.	FTM	FTA	Pct.	Reb.	Ast.	Pts.	AVERAGES RPG	APG	PPG
00-01—Kansas City	27	476	63	129	.488	23	46	.500	91	14	149	3.4	0.5	5.5

NBA REGULAR-SEASON RECORD

Season Team	G	Min.	FGM	FGA	Pct.	FTM	FTA	Pct.	REBOUNDS Off.	Def.	Tot.	Ast.	St.	Blk.	TO	Pts.	AVERAGES RPG	APG	PPG
00-01—Denver	6	58	9	18	.500	0	5	.000	10	7	17	1	0	2	3	18	2.8	0.2	3.0

Personal fouls/disqualifications: 2000-01, 11/1.

McCLOUD, GEORGE F NUGGETS

PERSONAL: Born May 27, 1967, in Daytona Beach, Fla. ... 6-8/225. (2,03/102,1). ... Full Name: George Aaron McCloud.
HIGH SCHOOL: Mainland (Daytona Beach, Fla.).
COLLEGE: Florida State.
TRANSACTIONS/CAREER NOTES: Selected by Indiana Pacers in first round (seventh pick overall) of 1989 NBA Draft. ... Played in Italy (1993-94). ... Played in Continental Basketball Association with Rapid City Thrillers (1994-95). ... Signed by Dallas Mavericks to first of two consecutive 10-day contracts (January 30, 1995). ... Re-signed by Mavericks for remainder of season (February 22, 1995). ... Traded by Mavericks with C Eric Montross, G Jim Jackson, F/C Chris Gatling and G Sam Cassell

to New Jersey Nets for C Shawn Bradley, F Ed O'Bannon, G Khalid Reeves and G Robert Pack (February 17, 1997). ... Traded by Nets to Los Angeles Lakers for C Joe Kleine, 1997 first-round draft choice and conditional second-round draft choice (February 20, 1997). ... Signed as free agent by Phoenix Suns (September 2, 1997). ... Signed as free agent by Denver Nuggets (August 3, 1999).

COLLEGIATE RECORD

| | | | | | | | | | | | | AVERAGES | | |
Season Team	G	Min.	FGM	FGA	Pct.	FTM	FTA	Pct.	Reb.	Ast.	Pts.	RPG	APG	PPG
85-86—Florida State	27	283	42	87	.483	31	49	.633	49	13	115	1.8	0.5	4.3
86-87—Florida State	30	590	87	197	.442	42	68	.618	126	18	230	4.2	0.6	7.7
87-88—Florida State	30	902	193	403	.479	88	112	.786	111	48	546	3.7	1.6	18.2
88-89—Florida State	30	1067	207	462	.448	154	176	.875	109	125	683	3.6	4.2	22.8
Totals	117	2842	529	1149	.460	315	405	.778	395	204	1574	3.4	1.7	13.5

Three-point field goals: 1986-87, 14-for-47 (.298). 1987-88, 72-for-159 (.453). 1988-89, 115-for-262 (.439). Totals, 201-for-468 (.429).

NBA REGULAR-SEASON RECORD

RECORDS: Holds single-season record for most three-point field goals attempted—678 (1996). ... Holds single-game record for most three-point field goals attempted, none made—10 (March 10, 1996, vs. Toronto).

| | | | | | | | | | REBOUNDS | | | | | | | | AVERAGES | | |
Season Team	G	Min.	FGM	FGA	Pct.	FTM	FTA	Pct.	Off.	Def.	Tot.	Ast.	St.	Blk.	TO	Pts.	RPG	APG	PPG
89-90—Indiana	44	413	45	144	.313	15	19	.789	12	30	42	45	19	3	36	118	1.0	1.0	2.7
90-91—Indiana	74	1070	131	351	.373	38	49	.776	35	83	118	150	40	11	91	343	1.6	2.0	4.6
91-92—Indiana	51	892	128	313	.409	50	64	.781	45	87	132	116	26	11	62	338	2.6	2.3	6.6
92-93—Indiana	78	1500	216	525	.411	75	102	.735	60	145	205	192	53	11	107	565	2.6	2.5	7.2
94-95—Dallas	42	802	144	328	.439	80	96	.833	82	65	147	53	23	9	40	402	3.5	1.3	9.6
95-96—Dallas	79	2846	530	1281	.414	180	224	.804	116	263	379	212	113	38	166	1497	4.8	2.7	18.9
96-97—Dallas-L.A.L.	64	1493	238	578	.412	83	101	.822	36	143	179	109	61	8	61	658	2.8	1.7	10.3
97-98—Phoenix	63	1213	173	427	.405	39	51	.765	45	173	218	84	54	13	63	456	3.5	1.3	7.2
98-99—Phoenix	48	1245	142	324	.438	75	87	.862	34	128	162	79	45	14	49	428	3.4	1.6	8.9
99-00—Denver	78	2118	266	638	.417	148	181	.818	72	213	285	246	48	26	134	787	3.7	3.2	10.1
00-01—Denver	76	2007	250	655	.382	152	181	.840	55	169	224	279	53	27	117	729	2.9	3.7	9.6
Totals	697	15599	2263	5564	.407	935	1155	.810	592	1499	2091	1565	535	171	926	6321	3.0	2.2	9.1

Three-point field goals: 1989-90, 13-for-40 (.325). 1990-91, 43-for-124 (.347). 1991-92, 32-for-94 (.340). 1992-93, 58-for-181 (.320). 1994-95, 34-for-89 (.382). 1995-96, 257-for-678 (.379). 1996-97, 99-for-254 (.390). 1997-98, 71-for-208 (.341). 1998-99, 69-for-166 (.416). 1999-00, 107-for-283 (.378). 2000-01, 77-for-234 (.329). Totals, 860-for-2351 (.366).

Personal fouls/disqualifications: 1989-90, 56/0. 1990-91, 141/1. 1991-92, 95/1. 1992-93, 165/0. 1994-95, 71/0. 1995-96, 212/1. 1996-97, 126/1. 1997-98, 132/1. 1998-99, 128/0. 1999-00, 180/2. 2000-01, 165/1. Totals, 1471/8.

NBA PLAYOFF RECORD

| | | | | | | | | | REBOUNDS | | | | | | | | AVERAGES | | |
Season Team	G	Min.	FGM	FGA	Pct.	FTM	FTA	Pct.	Off.	Def.	Tot.	Ast.	St.	Blk.	TO	Pts.	RPG	APG	PPG
89-90—Indiana	1	4	1	2	.500	0	0	...	0	1	1	0	0	0	1	2	1.0	0.0	2.0
91-92—Indiana	2	53	6	12	.500	8	11	.727	0	2	2	6	2	1	3	23	1.0	3.0	11.5
92-93—Indiana	4	79	8	23	.348	1	4	.250	3	8	11	14	4	1	5	19	2.8	3.5	4.8
97-98—Phoenix	4	126	21	41	.512	3	4	.750	2	17	19	8	1	1	6	57	4.8	2.0	14.3
98-99—Phoenix	3	80	13	30	.433	7	10	.700	2	11	13	2	5	0	3	42	4.3	0.7	14.0
Totals	14	342	49	108	.454	19	29	.655	8	38	46	30	12	3	18	143	3.3	2.1	10.2

Three-point field goals: 1991-92, 3-for-6 (.500). 1992-93, 2-for-12 (.167). 1997-98, 12-for-21 (.571). 1998-99, 9-for-20 (.450). Totals, 26-for-59 (.441).
Personal fouls/disqualifications: 1989-90, 2/0. 1991-92, 5/0. 1992-93, 14/0. 1997-98, 15/0. 1998-99, 13/0. Totals, 49/0.

ITALIAN LEAGUE RECORD

| | | | | | | | | | | | | AVERAGES | | |
Season Team	G	Min.	FGM	FGA	Pct.	FTM	FTA	Pct.	Reb.	Ast.	Pts.	RPG	APG	PPG
93-94—Scavolini Pesaro	30	1093	198	394	.503	98	124	.790	163	31	565	5.4	1.0	18.8

Three-point field goals: 1993-94, 71-for-168 (.423).

CBA REGULAR-SEASON RECORD

| | | | | | | | | | | | | AVERAGES | | |
Season Team	G	Min.	FGM	FGA	Pct.	FTM	FTA	Pct.	Reb.	Ast.	Pts.	RPG	APG	PPG
94-95—Rapid City	32	1177	225	469	.480	187	214	.874	229	109	679	7.2	3.4	21.2

Three-point field goals: 1994-95, 42-for-123 (.341).

McCOY, JELANI   C

PERSONAL: Born December 6, 1977, in Oakland. ... 6-10/245. (2,08/111,1). ... Full Name: Jelani Marwan McCoy.
HIGH SCHOOL: St. Augustine (San Diego).
COLLEGE: UCLA.
TRANSACTIONS/CAREER NOTES: Selected after junior season by Seattle SuperSonics in second round (33rd pick overall) of 1998 NBA Draft.

COLLEGIATE RECORD

| | | | | | | | | | | | | AVERAGES | | |
Season Team	G	Min.	FGM	FGA	Pct.	FTM	FTA	Pct.	Reb.	Ast.	Pts.	RPG	APG	PPG
95-96—UCLA	31	921	138	204	.676	40	92	.435	214	28	316	6.9	0.9	10.2
96-97—UCLA	32	846	152	201	.756	45	101	.446	207	48	349	6.5	1.5	10.9
97-98—UCLA	15	319	57	95	.600	35	67	.522	107	13	149	7.1	0.9	9.9
Totals	78	2086	347	500	.694	120	260	.462	528	89	814	6.8	1.1	10.4

Season Team	G	Min.	FGM	FGA	Pct.	FTM	FTA	Pct.	REBOUNDS Off.	Def.	Tot.	Ast.	St.	Blk.	TO	Pts.	AVERAGES RPG	APG	PPG
98-99—Seattle	26	331	56	76	.737	21	42	.500	27	52	79	4	11	20	10	133	3.0	0.2	5.1
99-00—Seattle	58	746	102	177	.576	45	91	.495	54	125	179	24	15	46	45	249	3.1	0.4	4.3
00-01—Seattle	70	1143	138	264	.523	41	93	.441	92	159	251	57	18	49	75	317	3.6	0.8	4.5
Totals	154	2220	296	517	.573	107	226	.473	173	336	509	85	44	115	130	699	3.3	0.6	4.5

Personal fouls/disqualifications: 1998-99, 42/0. 1999-00, 127/0. 2000-01, 141/0. Totals, 310/0.

NBA PLAYOFF RECORD

Season Team	G	Min.	FGM	FGA	Pct.	FTM	FTA	Pct.	REBOUNDS Off.	Def.	Tot.	Ast.	St.	Blk.	TO	Pts.	AVERAGES RPG	APG	PPG
99-00—Seattle	3	26	2	5	.400	0	3	.000	0	6	6	2	0	0	2	4	2.0	0.7	1.3

Personal fouls/disqualifications: 1999-00, 6/0.

McDYESS, ANTONIO   F   NUGGETS

PERSONAL: Born September 7, 1974, in Quitman, Miss. ... 6-9/245. (2,06/111,1). ... Full Name: Antonio Keithflen McDyess. ... Name pronounced mick-DICE.
HIGH SCHOOL: Quitman (Miss.).
COLLEGE: Alabama.
TRANSACTIONS/CAREER NOTES: Selected after sophomore season by Los Angeles Clippers in first round (second pick overall) of 1995 NBA Draft. ... Draft rights traded by Clippers with G Randy Woods to Denver Nuggets for F Rodney Rogers and draft rights to G Brent Barry (June 28, 1995). ... Traded by Nuggets to Phoenix Suns for a minimum of three first-round draft choices and two second-round draft choices (October 1, 1997). ... Signed as free agent by Nuggets (January 22, 1999).
MISCELLANEOUS: Member of gold-medal-winning U.S. Olympic team (2000).

COLLEGIATE RECORD

Season Team	G	Min.	FGM	FGA	Pct.	FTM	FTA	Pct.	Reb.	Ast.	Pts.	AVERAGES RPG	APG	PPG
93-94—Alabama	26	618	132	234	.564	32	60	.533	210	11	296	8.1	0.4	11.4
94-95—Alabama	33	861	185	361	.512	88	132	.667	337	21	458	10.2	0.6	13.9
Totals	59	1479	317	595	.533	120	192	.625	547	32	754	9.3	0.5	12.8

Three-point field goals: 1994-95, 0-for-1.

NBA REGULAR-SEASON RECORD

HONORS: All-NBA third team (1999). ... NBA All-Rookie first team (1996).

Season Team	G	Min.	FGM	FGA	Pct.	FTM	FTA	Pct.	REBOUNDS Off.	Def.	Tot.	Ast.	St.	Blk.	TO	Pts.	AVERAGES RPG	APG	PPG
95-96—Denver	76	2280	427	881	.485	166	243	.683	229	343	572	75	54	114	154	1020	7.5	1.0	13.4
96-97—Denver	74	2565	536	1157	.463	274	387	.708	155	382	537	106	62	126	199	1352	7.3	1.4	18.3
97-98—Phoenix	81	2441	497	927	.536	231	329	.702	206	407	613	106	100	135	142	1225	7.6	1.3	15.1
98-99—Denver	50	1937	415	882	.471	230	338	.680	168	369	537	82	73	115	138	1061	10.7	1.6	21.2
99-00—Denver	81	2698	614	1211	.507	323	516	.626	234	451	685	159	69	139	230	1551	8.5	2.0	19.1
00-01—Denver	70	2555	577	1165	.495	304	434	.700	240	605	845	146	43	102	162	1458	12.1	2.1	20.8
Totals	432	14476	3066	6223	.493	1528	2247	.680	1232	2557	3789	674	401	731	1025	7667	8.8	1.6	17.7

Three-point field goals: 1995-96, 0-for-4. 1996-97, 6-for-35 (.171). 1997-98, 0-for-2. 1998-99, 1-for-9 (.111). 1999-00, 0-for-2. Totals, 7-for-52 (.135).
Personal fouls/disqualifications: 1995-96, 250/4. 1996-97, 276/9. 1997-98, 292/6. 1998-99, 175/5. 1999-00, 316/12. 2000-01, 220/2. Totals, 1529/38.

NBA PLAYOFF RECORD

Season Team	G	Min.	FGM	FGA	Pct.	FTM	FTA	Pct.	REBOUNDS Off.	Def.	Tot.	Ast.	St.	Blk.	TO	Pts.	AVERAGES RPG	APG	PPG
97-98—Phoenix	4	147	31	65	.477	9	14	.643	18	35	53	4	2	6	5	71	13.3	1.0	17.8

Personal fouls/disqualifications: 1997-98, 12/0.

NBA ALL-STAR GAME RECORD

Season Team	Min.	FGM	FGA	Pct.	FTM	FTA	Pct.	REBOUNDS Off.	Def.	Tot.	Ast.	PF	Dq.	St.	Blk.	TO	Pts.
2001 —Denver	15	4	9	.444	0	0	...	3	5	8	2	2	0	1	0	0	8

McGRADY, TRACY   G/F   MAGIC

PERSONAL: Born May 24, 1979, in Bartow, Fla. ... 6-8/210. (2,03/95,3). ... Full Name: Tracy Lamar McGrady Jr.
HIGH SCHOOL: Mount Zion Christian Academy (Durham, N.C.).
COLLEGE: Did not attend college.
TRANSACTIONS/CAREER NOTES: Selected out of high school by Toronto Raptors in first round (ninth pick overall) of 1997 NBA Draft. ... Traded by Raptors to Orlando Magic for future first-round draft choice (August 3, 2000).

NBA REGULAR-SEASON RECORD

HONORS: NBA Most Improved Player Award (2001). ... All-NBA second team (2001).

Season Team	G	Min.	FGM	FGA	Pct.	FTM	FTA	Pct.	REBOUNDS Off.	Def.	Tot.	Ast.	St.	Blk.	TO	Pts.	AVERAGES RPG	APG	PPG
97-98—Toronto	64	1179	179	398	.450	79	111	.712	105	164	269	98	49	61	66	451	4.2	1.5	7.0
98-99—Toronto	49	1106	168	385	.436	114	157	.726	120	158	278	113	52	66	80	458	5.7	2.3	9.3
99-00—Toronto	79	2462	459	1018	.451	277	392	.707	188	313	501	263	90	151	160	1213	6.3	3.3	15.4
00-01—Orlando	77	3087	788	1724	.457	430	587	.733	192	388	580	352	116	118	198	2065	7.5	4.6	26.8
Totals	269	7834	1594	3525	.452	900	1247	.722	605	1023	1628	826	307	396	504	4187	6.1	3.1	15.6

Three-point field goals: 1997-98, 14-for-41 (.341). 1998-99, 8-for-35 (.229). 1999-00, 18-for-65 (.277). 2000-01, 59-for-166 (.355). Totals, 99-for-307 (.322).

Personal fouls/disqualifications: 1997-98, 86/0. 1998-99, 94/1. 1999-00, 201/2. 2000-01, 160/0. Totals, 541/3.

								REBOUNDS							AVERAGES		
Season Team	G	Min.	FGM	FGA	Pct.	FTM	FTA	Pct.	Off.	Def.	Tot.	Ast.	St.	Blk.	TO	Pts.	RPG	APG	PPG
99-00—Toronto..........	3	111	17	44	.386	14	16	.875	10	11	21	9	3	3	10	50	7.0	3.0	16.7
00-01—Orlando..........	4	178	51	123	.415	31	38	.816	6	20	26	33	7	5	8	135	6.5	8.3	33.8
Totals	7	289	68	167	.407	45	54	.833	16	31	47	42	10	8	18	185	6.7	6.0	26.4

Three-point field goals: 1999-00, 2-for-7 (.286). 2000-01, 2-for-10 (.200). Totals, 4-for-17 (.235).
Personal fouls/disqualifications: 1999-00, 10/0. 2000-01, 11/0. Totals, 21/0.

NBA ALL-STAR GAME RECORD

							REBOUNDS								
Season Team	Min.	FGM	FGA	Pct.	FTM	FTA	Pct.	Off.	Def.	Tot.	Ast.	PF	Dq.	St.	Blk.	TO	Pts.
2001 —Toronto..............	21	1	4	.250	0	0	...	1	0	1	0	0	0	2	1	4	2

Three-point field goals: 2001, 0-for-1.

McILVAINE, JIM   C   NETS

PERSONAL: Born July 30, 1972, in Racine, Wis. ... 7-1/264. (2,16/119,7). ... Full Name: James Michael McIlvaine. ... Name pronounced Mac-il-vane.
HIGH SCHOOL: St. Catherine (Racine, Wis.).
COLLEGE: Marquette.
TRANSACTIONS/CAREER NOTES: Selected by Washington Bullets in second round (32nd pick overall) of 1994 NBA Draft. ... Signed as free agent by Seattle SuperSonics (July 22, 1996). ... Traded by SuperSonics to New Jersey Nets for F/C Michael Cage and F Don MacLean (January 21, 1999).

COLLEGIATE RECORD

											AVERAGES		
Season Team	G	Min.	FGM	FGA	Pct.	FTM	FTA	Pct.	Reb.	Ast.	Pts.	RPG	APG	PPG
90-91—Marquette.....................	28	540	84	145	.579	55	92	.598	132	14	223	4.7	0.5	8.0
91-92—Marquette.....................	29	701	102	187	.545	95	126	.754	134	16	299	4.6	0.6	10.3
92-93—Marquette.....................	28	532	111	192	.578	85	119	.714	134	21	307	4.8	0.8	11.0
93-94—Marquette.....................	33	946	170	322	.528	109	164	.665	273	43	449	8.3	1.3	13.6
Totals	118	2719	467	846	.552	344	501	.687	673	94	1278	5.7	0.8	10.8

NBA REGULAR-SEASON RECORD

								REBOUNDS								AVERAGES		
Season Team	G	Min.	FGM	FGA	Pct.	FTM	FTA	Pct.	Off.	Def.	Tot.	Ast.	St.	Blk.	TO	Pts.	RPG	APG	PPG
94-95—Washington	55	534	34	71	.479	28	41	.683	40	65	105	10	10	60	19	96	1.9	0.2	1.7
95-96—Washington	80	1195	62	145	.428	58	105	.552	66	164	230	11	21	166	36	182	2.9	0.1	2.3
96-97—Seattle	82	1477	130	276	.471	53	107	.495	132	198	330	23	39	164	62	314	4.0	0.3	3.8
97-98—Seattle	78	1211	101	223	.453	45	81	.556	96	163	259	19	24	137	54	247	3.3	0.2	3.2
98-99—New Jersey	22	269	22	51	.431	4	6	.667	31	23	54	2	9	32	13	48	2.5	0.1	2.2
99-00—New Jersey	66	1048	64	154	.416	29	56	.518	106	124	230	36	26	117	38	157	3.5	0.5	2.4
00-01—New Jersey	18	193	10	28	.357	8	12	.667	8	27	35	4	7	15	9	28	1.9	0.2	1.6
Totals	401	5927	423	948	.446	225	408	.551	479	764	1243	105	136	691	231	1072	3.1	0.3	2.7

Three-point field goals: 1996-97, 1-for-7 (.143). 1997-98, 0-for-3. Totals, 1-for-10 (.100).
Personal fouls/disqualifications: 1994-95, 95/0. 1995-96, 171/0. 1996-97, 247/4. 1997-98, 240/3. 1998-99, 59/1. 1999-00, 205/2. 2000-01, 35/0. Totals, 1052/10.

NBA PLAYOFF RECORD

								REBOUNDS								AVERAGES		
Season Team	G	Min.	FGM	FGA	Pct.	FTM	FTA	Pct.	Off.	Def.	Tot.	Ast.	St.	Blk.	TO	Pts.	RPG	APG	PPG
96-97—Seattle	5	28	4	7	.571	1	2	.500	1	1	2	0	1	2	1	9	0.4	0.0	1.8
97-98—Seattle	6	59	6	20	.300	1	2	.500	7	3	10	1	2	6	1	13	1.7	0.2	2.2
Totals	11	87	10	27	.370	2	4	.500	8	4	12	1	3	8	2	22	1.1	0.1	2.0

Three-point field goals: 1997-98, 0-for-1. Totals, 0-for-1 (.000).
Personal fouls/disqualifications: 1996-97, 7/0. 1997-98, 22/1. Totals, 29/1.

McINNIS, JEFF   G   CLIPPERS

PERSONAL: Born October 22, 1974, in Charlotte. ... 6-4/190. (1,93/86,2). ... Full Name: Jeff Lemans McInnis.
HIGH SCHOOL: West Charlotte (Charlotte), then Oak Hill Academy (Mouth of Wilson, Va).
COLLEGE: North Carolina.
TRANSACTIONS/CAREER NOTES: Selected after junior season by Denver Nuggets in second round (37th pick overall) of 1996 NBA Draft. ... Waived by Nuggets (December 12, 1996). ... Played in Greece (1996-97). ... Played in Continental Basketball Association with Quad City Thunder (1997-98 through 1999-2000). ... Signed as free agent by Washington Wizards (January 21, 1999). ... Traded by Wizards with F/C Terry Davis, F Ben Wallace and G Tim Legler to Orlando Magic C Isaac Austin (August 11, 1999). ... Waived by Magic (September 16, 1999). ... Signed by Los Angeles Clippers to first of two consecutive 10-day contracts (February 26, 2000). ... Re-signed by Clippers for remainder of season (March 16, 2000).

COLLEGIATE RECORD

											AVERAGES		
Season Team	G	Min.	FGM	FGA	Pct.	FTM	FTA	Pct.	Reb.	Ast.	Pts.	RPG	APG	PPG
93-94—North Carolina...............	35	512	70	153	.458	30	47	.638	58	85	197	1.7	2.4	5.6
94-95—North Carolina...............	34	981	155	316	.491	66	99	.667	138	180	420	4.1	5.3	12.4
95-96—North Carolina...............	31	1067	178	409	.435	88	110	.800	81	170	511	2.6	5.5	16.5
Totals	100	2560	403	878	.459	184	256	.719	277	435	1128	2.8	4.4	11.3

Three-point field goals: 1993-94, 27-for-65 (.415). 1994-95, 44-for-112 (.393). 1995-96, 67-for-171 (.392). Totals, 138-for-348 (.397).

GREEK LEAGUE RECORD

Season Team	G	Min.	FGM	FGA	Pct.	FTM	FTA	Pct.	Reb.	Ast.	Pts.	AVERAGES RPG	APG	PPG
96-97—Panionios	6	...	...	...	...	...	...	...	19	22	123	3.2	3.7	20.5

NBA REGULAR-SEASON RECORD

Season Team	G	Min.	FGM	FGA	Pct.	FTM	FTA	Pct.	REBOUNDS Off.	Def.	Tot.	Ast.	St.	Blk.	TO	Pts.	AVERAGES RPG	APG	PPG
96-97—Denver	13	117	23	49	.469	7	10	.700	2	4	6	18	2	1	13	65	0.5	1.4	5.0
98-99—Washington	35	427	50	134	.373	21	28	.750	9	12	21	73	19	1	30	130	0.6	2.1	3.7
99-00—L.A. Clippers	25	597	80	186	.430	13	17	.765	18	54	72	89	15	2	27	180	2.9	3.6	7.2
00-01—L.A. Clippers	81	2831	432	933	.463	130	161	.807	41	179	220	447	75	7	113	1046	2.7	5.5	12.9
Totals	154	3972	585	1302	.449	171	216	.792	70	249	319	627	111	11	183	1421	2.1	4.1	9.2

Three-point field goals: 1996-97, 12-for-26 (.462). 1998-99, 9-for-35 (.257). 1999-00, 7-for-21 (.333). 2000-01, 52-for-144 (.361). Totals, 80-for-226 (.354).

Personal fouls/disqualifications: 1996-97, 16/0. 1998-99, 36/0. 1999-00, 55/0. 2000-01, 199/2. Totals, 306/2.

CBA REGULAR-SEASON RECORD

NOTES: Member of CBA championship team (1998). ... CBA Newcomer of the Year (1998). ... CBA All-League second team (1998). ... CBA All-Defensive team (1998). ... CBA Most Valuable Player (2000). ... CBA All-League first team (2000).

Season Team	G	Min.	FGM	FGA	Pct.	FTM	FTA	Pct.	Reb.	Ast.	Pts.	AVERAGES RPG	APG	PPG
97-98—Quad City	56	1734	315	705	.447	168	206	.816	135	316	834	2.4	5.6	14.9
98-99—Quad City	21	825	175	348	.503	65	88	.739	54	119	442	2.6	5.7	21.0
99-00—Quad City	41	1629	316	719	.439	123	149	.826	136	319	807	3.3	7.8	19.7
Totals	118	4188	806	1772	.455	356	443	.804	325	754	2083	2.8	6.4	17.7

Three-point field goals: 1997-98, 36-for-119 (.303). 1998-99, 27-for-77 (.351). 1999-00, 52-for-167 (.311). Totals, 115-for-363 (.317).

McKEY, DERRICK   F   PACERS

PERSONAL: Born October 10, 1966, in Meridian, Miss. ... 6-10/225. (2,08/102,1). ... Full Name: Derrick Wayne McKey.
HIGH SCHOOL: Meridian (Miss.).
COLLEGE: Alabama.
TRANSACTIONS/CAREER NOTES: Selected after junior season by Seattle SuperSonics in first round (ninth pick overall) of 1987 NBA Draft. ... Traded by SuperSonics with F Gerald Paddio to Indiana Pacers for F Detlef Schrempf (November 1, 1993).

MISCELLANEOUS: Member of gold-medal-winning U.S. World Championship team (1986).

COLLEGIATE RECORD

NOTES: THE SPORTING NEWS All-America second team (1987).

Season Team	G	Min.	FGM	FGA	Pct.	FTM	FTA	Pct.	Reb.	Ast.	Pts.	AVERAGES RPG	APG	PPG
84-85—Alabama	33	728	74	155	.477	20	33	.606	134	44	168	4.1	1.3	5.1
85-86—Alabama	33	1117	178	280	.636	92	117	.786	262	29	448	7.9	0.9	13.6
86-87—Alabama	33	1199	247	425	.581	100	116	.862	247	59	615	7.5	1.8	18.6
Totals	99	3044	499	860	.580	212	266	.797	643	132	1231	6.5	1.3	12.4

Three-point field goals: 1986-87, 21-for-50 (.420).

NBA REGULAR-SEASON RECORD

HONORS: NBA All-Defensive second team (1995, 1996). ... NBA All-Rookie team (1988).

Season Team	G	Min.	FGM	FGA	Pct.	FTM	FTA	Pct.	REBOUNDS Off.	Def.	Tot.	Ast.	St.	Blk.	TO	Pts.	AVERAGES RPG	APG	PPG
87-88—Seattle	82	1706	255	519	.491	173	224	.772	115	213	328	107	70	63	108	694	4.0	1.3	8.5
88-89—Seattle	82	2804	487	970	.502	301	375	.803	167	297	464	219	105	70	188	1305	5.7	2.7	15.9
89-90—Seattle	80	2748	468	949	.493	315	403	.782	170	319	489	187	87	81	192	1254	6.1	2.3	15.7
90-91—Seattle	73	2503	438	847	.517	235	278	.845	172	251	423	169	91	56	158	1115	5.8	2.3	15.3
91-92—Seattle	52	1757	285	604	.472	188	222	.847	95	173	268	120	61	47	114	777	5.2	2.3	14.9
92-93—Seattle	77	2439	387	780	.496	220	297	.741	121	206	327	197	105	58	152	1034	4.2	2.6	13.4
93-94—Indiana	76	2613	355	710	.500	192	254	.756	129	273	402	327	111	49	228	911	5.3	4.3	12.0
94-95—Indiana	81	2805	411	833	.493	221	297	.744	125	269	394	276	125	49	168	1075	4.9	3.4	13.3
95-96—Indiana	75	2440	346	712	.486	170	221	.769	123	238	361	262	83	44	143	879	4.8	3.5	11.7
96-97—Indiana	50	1449	148	379	.391	89	123	.724	80	161	241	135	47	30	83	400	4.8	2.7	8.0
97-98—Indiana	57	1316	150	327	.459	55	77	.714	74	137	211	88	57	30	79	359	3.7	1.5	6.3
98-99—Indiana	13	244	23	52	.442	14	17	.824	18	23	41	13	12	4	12	60	3.2	1.0	4.6
99-00—Indiana	32	634	43	108	.398	43	56	.768	29	106	135	35	29	13	19	139	4.2	1.1	4.3
00-01—Indiana	66	987	60	136	.441	21	27	.778	49	127	176	74	48	13	47	145	2.7	1.1	2.2
Totals	896	26445	3856	7926	.487	2237	2871	.779	1467	2793	4260	2209	1031	607	1691	10147	4.8	2.5	11.3

Three-point field goals: 1987-88, 11-for-30 (.367). 1988-89, 30-for-89 (.337). 1989-90, 3-for-23 (.130). 1990-91, 4-for-19 (.211). 1991-92, 19-for-50 (.380). 1992-93, 40-for-112 (.357). 1993-94, 9-for-31 (.290). 1994-95, 32-for-89 (.360). 1995-96, 17-for-68 (.250). 1996-97, 15-for-58 (.259). 1997-98, 4-for-17 (.235). 1998-99, 0-for-1. 1999-00, 10-for-23 (.435). 2000-01, 4-for-20 (.200). Totals, 198-for-630 (.314).

Personal fouls/disqualifications: 1987-88, 237/3. 1988-89, 264/4. 1989-90, 247/2. 1990-91, 220/2. 1991-92, 142/2. 1992-93, 208/5. 1993-94, 248/1. 1994-95, 260/5. 1995-96, 246/4. 1996-97, 141/1. 1997-98, 156/1. 1998-99, 24/0. 1999-00, 81/0. 2000-01, 136/1. Totals, 2610/31.

NBA PLAYOFF RECORD

Season Team	G	Min.	FGM	FGA	Pct.	FTM	FTA	Pct.	REBOUNDS Off.	Def.	Tot.	Ast.	St.	Blk.	TO	Pts.	AVERAGES RPG	APG	PPG
87-88—Seattle	5	109	24	38	.632	10	17	.588	7	13	20	8	3	5	5	60	4.0	1.6	12.0
88-89—Seattle	8	286	44	89	.494	17	21	.810	21	31	52	18	6	15	23	106	6.5	2.3	13.3
90-91—Seattle	4	114	16	28	.571	6	11	.545	7	16	23	8	3	0	6	38	5.8	2.0	9.5
91-92—Seattle	9	315	52	99	.525	38	45	.844	17	27	44	24	7	12	22	147	4.9	2.7	16.3

M

Season Team	G	Min.	FGM	FGA	Pct.	FTM	FTA	Pct.	Off.	Def.	Tot.	Ast.	St.	Blk.	TO	Pts.	RPG	APG	PPG
92-93—Seattle	19	647	83	158	.525	46	69	.667	51	47	98	71	12	17	36	214	5.2	3.7	11.3
93-94—Indiana	16	587	58	142	.408	31	47	.660	32	66	98	67	26	9	40	155	6.1	4.2	9.7
94-95—Indiana	17	592	76	174	.437	54	62	.871	29	52	81	64	17	11	36	217	4.8	3.8	12.8
95-96—Indiana	5	180	24	57	.421	11	13	.846	8	25	33	10	7	1	14	64	6.6	2.0	12.8
97-98—Indiana	15	284	23	69	.333	18	23	.783	8	32	40	11	9	8	11	67	2.7	0.7	4.5
98-99—Indiana	13	245	15	40	.375	17	26	.654	17	26	43	19	12	4	11	47	3.3	1.5	3.6
99-00—Indiana	23	352	15	32	.469	16	20	.800	25	54	79	14	7	4	19	47	3.4	0.6	2.0
00-01—Indiana	4	35	2	5	.400	1	2	.500	4	5	9	4	1	0	1	6	2.3	1.0	1.5
Totals	138	3746	432	931	.464	265	356	.744	226	394	620	318	110	86	224	1168	4.5	2.3	8.5

Three-point field goals: 1987-88, 2-for-6 (.333). 1988-89, 1-for-9 (.111). 1990-91, 0-for-1. 1991-92, 5-for-16 (.313). 1992-93, 2-for-5 (.400). 1993-94, 8-for-24 (.333). 1994-95, 11-for-35 (.314). 1995-96, 5-for-12 (.417). 1997-98, 3-for-10 (.300). 1998-99, 0-for-4. 1999-00, 1-for-6 (.167). 2000-01, 1-for-1. Totals, 39-for-129 (.302).

Personal fouls/disqualifications: 1987-88, 12/0. 1988-89, 33/1. 1990-91, 13/0. 1991-92, 37/1. 1992-93, 51/0. 1993-94, 59/1. 1994-95, 65/2. 1995-96, 20/0. 1997-98, 50/0. 1998-99, 39/0. 1999-00, 45/0. 2000-01, 7/0. Totals, 431/5.

McKIE, AARON   G   76ERS

PERSONAL: Born October 2, 1972, in Philadelphia. ... 6-5/209. (1,96/94,8). ... Full Name: Aaron Fitzgerald McKie. ... Name pronounced mik-KEY.
HIGH SCHOOL: Simon Gratz (Philadelphia).
COLLEGE: Temple.
TRANSACTIONS/CAREER NOTES: Selected by Portland Trail Blazers in first round (17th pick overall) of 1994 NBA Draft. ... Traded by Trail Blazers with G Randolph Childress and G Reggie Jordan to Detroit Pistons for F Stacey Augmon (January 24, 1997). ... Traded by Pistons with C Theo Ratliff and conditional first-round draft choice to Philadelphia 76ers for G Jerry Stackhouse and C Eric Montross (December 18, 1997).

COLLEGIATE RECORD

Season Team	G	Min.	FGM	FGA	Pct.	FTM	FTA	Pct.	Reb.	Ast.	Pts.	RPG	APG	PPG
90-91—Temple						Did not play—ineligible.								
91-92—Temple	28	1011	130	300	.433	86	114	.754	167	94	388	6.0	3.4	13.9
92-93—Temple	33	1272	240	555	.432	123	156	.788	195	109	680	5.9	3.3	20.6
93-94—Temple	31	1214	193	481	.401	137	168	.815	224	98	582	7.2	3.2	18.8
Totals	92	3497	563	1336	.421	346	438	.790	586	301	1650	6.4	3.3	17.9

Three-point field goals: 1991-92, 42-for-131 (.321). 1992-93, 77-for-196 (.393). 1993-94, 59-for-159 (.371). Totals, 178-for-486 (.366).

NBA REGULAR-SEASON RECORD

HONORS: NBA Sixth Man Award (2001).

Season Team	G	Min.	FGM	FGA	Pct.	FTM	FTA	Pct.	Off.	Def.	Tot.	Ast.	St.	Blk.	TO	Pts.	RPG	APG	PPG
94-95—Portland	45	827	116	261	.444	50	73	.685	35	94	129	89	36	16	39	293	2.9	2.0	6.5
95-96—Portland	81	2259	337	722	.467	152	199	.764	86	218	304	205	92	21	135	864	3.8	2.5	10.7
96-97—Port.-Detroit	83	1625	150	365	.411	92	110	.836	40	181	221	161	77	22	90	433	2.7	1.9	5.2
97-98—Det.-Phila.	81	1813	139	381	.365	42	55	.764	58	173	231	175	101	13	76	332	2.9	2.2	4.1
98-99—Philadelphia	50	959	95	237	.401	44	62	.710	27	113	140	100	63	3	57	240	2.8	2.0	4.8
99-00—Philadelphia	82	1952	244	593	.411	121	146	.829	47	199	246	240	108	18	113	653	3.0	2.9	8.0
00-01—Philadelphia	76	2394	338	714	.473	149	194	.768	33	278	311	377	106	8	203	878	4.1	5.0	11.6
Totals	498	11829	1419	3273	.434	650	839	.775	326	1256	1582	1347	583	101	713	3693	3.2	2.7	7.4

Three-point field goals: 1994-95, 11-for-28 (.393). 1995-96, 38-for-117 (.325). 1996-97, 41-for-103 (.398). 1997-98, 12-for-63 (.190). 1998-99, 6-for-31 (.194). 1999-00, 44-for-121 (.364). 2000-01, 53-for-170 (.312). Totals, 205-for-633 (.324).

Personal fouls/disqualifications: 1994-95, 97/1. 1995-96, 205/5. 1996-97, 130/1. 1997-98, 164/0. 1998-99, 90/1. 1999-00, 194/3. 2000-01, 178/3. Totals, 1058/14.

NBA PLAYOFF RECORD

Season Team	G	Min.	FGM	FGA	Pct.	FTM	FTA	Pct.	Off.	Def.	Tot.	Ast.	St.	Blk.	TO	Pts.	RPG	APG	PPG
94-95—Portland	3	34	8	14	.571	0	0	...	0	2	2	1	3	0	0	17	0.7	0.3	5.7
95-96—Portland	5	134	11	30	.367	7	9	.778	4	14	18	9	6	2	9	31	3.6	1.8	6.2
96-97—Detroit	5	97	7	20	.350	0	0	...	1	9	10	10	6	2	3	15	2.0	2.0	3.0
98-99—Philadelphia	6	97	7	23	.304	6	7	.857	4	11	15	11	4	0	1	20	2.5	1.8	3.3
99-00—Philadelphia	10	331	50	103	.485	26	31	.839	4	32	36	46	4	2	16	138	3.6	4.6	13.8
00-01—Philadelphia	23	892	125	301	.415	59	75	.787	24	95	119	121	34	3	46	336	5.2	5.3	14.6
Totals	52	1585	208	491	.424	98	122	.803	37	163	200	198	57	9	75	557	3.8	3.8	10.7

Three-point field goals: 1994-95, 1-for-2 (.500). 1995-96, 2-for-8 (.250). 1996-97, 1-for-5 (.200). 1998-99, 0-for-1. 1999-00, 12-for-35 (.343). 2000-01, 27-for-64 (.422). Totals, 43-for-115 (.374).

Personal fouls/disqualifications: 1994-95, 4/0. 1995-96, 13/0. 1996-97, 12/0. 1998-99, 17/0. 1999-00, 26/0. 2000-01, 67/0. Totals, 139/0.

M

McLEOD, ROSHOWN   F   CELTICS

PERSONAL: Born November 17, 1975, in Jersey City, N.J. ... 6-8/221. (2,03/100,2).
HIGH SCHOOL: St. Anthony (Jersey City, N.J.).
COLLEGE: St. John's, then Duke.
TRANSACTIONS/CAREER NOTES: Selected by Atlanta Hawks in first round (20th pick overall) of 1998 NBA Draft. ... Traded by Hawks with C Dikembe Mutombo to Philadelphia 76ers for F/C Theo Ratliff, F/G Toni Kukoc, C Nazr Mohammed and G Pepe Sanchez (February 22, 2001). ... Traded by 76ers with conditional first-round draft choice to Boston Celtics for F Jerome Moiso (August 3, 2001).

Season Team	G	Min.	FGM	FGA	Pct.	FTM	FTA	Pct.	Reb.	Ast.	Pts.	AVERAGES RPG	APG	PPG
93-94—St. John's	29	542	77	179	.430	39	53	.736	110	34	193	3.8	1.2	6.7
94-95—St. John's	28	563	86	179	.480	44	62	.710	219	31	219	7.8	1.1	7.8
95-96—Duke						Did not play—transfer student.								
96-97—Duke	33	797	142	290	.490	81	102	.794	175	29	392	5.3	0.9	11.9
97-98—Duke	36	852	196	397	.494	113	160	.706	201	49	549	5.6	1.4	15.3
Totals	126	2754	501	1045	.479	277	377	.735	705	143	1353	5.6	1.1	10.7

Three-point field goals: 1993-94, 0-for-5. 1994-95, 3-for-9 (.333). 1996-97, 27-for-72 (.375). 1997-98, 44-for-107 (.411). Totals, 74-for-193 (.383).

NBA REGULAR-SEASON RECORD

Season Team	G	Min.	FGM	FGA	Pct.	FTM	FTA	Pct.	REBOUNDS Off.	Def.	Tot.	Ast.	St.	Blk.	TO	Pts.	AVERAGES RPG	APG	PPG
98-99—Atlanta	34	348	62	163	.380	37	45	.822	12	38	50	14	2	1	23	162	1.5	0.4	4.8
99-00—Atlanta	44	860	131	332	.395	54	70	.771	41	97	138	52	16	5	59	318	3.1	1.2	7.2
00-01—Atlanta-Phil.	35	922	145	332	.437	45	51	.882	38	82	120	58	23	8	58	337	3.4	1.7	9.6
Totals	113	2130	338	827	.409	136	166	.819	91	217	308	124	41	14	140	817	2.7	1.1	7.2

Three-point field goals: 1998-99, 1-for-10 (.100). 1999-00, 2-for-13 (.154). 2000-01, 2-for-22 (.091). Totals, 5-for-45 (.111).
Personal fouls/disqualifications: 1998-99, 24/0. 1999-00, 84/0. 2000-01, 90/0. Totals, 198/0.

NBA PLAYOFF RECORD

Season Team	G	Min.	FGM	FGA	Pct.	FTM	FTA	Pct.	REBOUNDS Off.	Def.	Tot.	Ast.	St.	Blk.	TO	Pts.	AVERAGES RPG	APG	PPG
98-99—Atlanta	6	49	11	21	.524	4	4	1.000	1	2	3	1	1	1	1	26	0.5	0.2	4.3

Personal fouls/disqualifications: 1998-99, 3/0.

McPHERSON, PAUL G/F

PERSONAL: Born July 3, 1978, in Chicago. ... 6-4/210. (1,93/95,3). ... Full Name: Paul L. McPherson.
HIGH SCHOOL: South Shore (Chicago).
JUNIOR COLLEGE: Tallahasee Community College, then Kennedy King College (Ill.).
COLLEGE: DePaul.
TRANSACTIONS/CAREER NOTES: Not drafted by an NBA franchise. ... Signed as free agent by Phoenix Suns (August 23, 2000). ... Traded by Suns with F Corie Blount and F Ruben Garces to Golden State Warriors for G Vinny Del Negro (January 26, 2001).

COLLEGIATE RECORD

Season Team	G	Min.	FGM	FGA	Pct.	FTM	FTA	Pct.	Reb.	Ast.	Pts.	AVERAGES RPG	APG	PPG
96-97—Tallahassee C.C.	35	...	230	320	.719	104	156	.667	227	75	570	6.5	2.1	16.3
97-98—						Did not play.								
98-99—Kennedy-King J.C.						Statistics unavailable.								
99-00—DePaul	32	878	149	281	.530	56	89	.629	149	59	359	4.7	1.8	11.2
Junior College Totals	35	...	230	320	.719	104	156	.667	227	75	570	6.5	2.1	16.3
4-Year-College Totals	32	878	149	281	.530	56	89	.629	149	59	359	4.7	1.8	11.2

Three-point field goals: 1996-97, 6-for-12 (.500). 1999-00, 5-for-16 (.313).

NBA REGULAR-SEASON RECORD

Season Team	G	Min.	FGM	FGA	Pct.	FTM	FTA	Pct.	REBOUNDS Off.	Def.	Tot.	Ast.	St.	Blk.	TO	Pts.	AVERAGES RPG	APG	PPG
00-01—Pho.-G.S.	55	595	109	216	.505	42	58	.724	40	39	79	38	25	4	47	262	1.4	0.7	4.8

Three-point field goals: 2000-01, 2-for-12 (.167).
Personal fouls/disqualifications: 2000-01, 80/0.

MEDVEDENKO, STANISLAV F LAKERS

PERSONAL: Born April 4, 1979, in Ukraine. ... 6-9/250. (2,06/113,4).
TRANSACTIONS/CAREER NOTES: Not drafted by an NBA franchise. ... Played in Lithuania (1998-99). ... Played in Ukraine (1999-2000). ... Signed as free agent by Los Angeles Lakers (August 15, 2000).
MISCELLANEOUS: Member of NBA Championship Team (2001).

LITHUANIAN LEAGUE RECORD

Season Team	G	Min.	FGM	FGA	Pct.	FTM	FTA	Pct.	Reb.	Ast.	Pts.	AVERAGES RPG	APG	PPG
98-99—Alytus Alita	24	698	166	300	.553	75	97	.773	180	25	410	7.5	1.0	17.1

Three-point field goals: 1998-99, 3-for-8 (.375).

UKRAINIAN LEAGUE RECORD

Season Team	G	Min.	FGM	FGA	Pct.	FTM	FTA	Pct.	Reb.	Ast.	Pts.	AVERAGES RPG	APG	PPG
99-00—Kyiv Kiev	19	554	169	337	.501	64	95	.674	143	21	405	7.5	1.1	21.3

Three-point field goals: 1999-00, 3-for-18 (.167).

NBA REGULAR-SEASON RECORD

Season Team	G	Min.	FGM	FGA	Pct.	FTM	FTA	Pct.	REBOUNDS Off.	Def.	Tot.	Ast.	St.	Blk.	TO	Pts.	AVERAGES RPG	APG	PPG
00-01—L.A. Lakers	7	39	12	25	.480	7	12	.583	1	8	9	2	1	1	3	32	1.3	0.3	4.6

Three-point field goals: 2000-01, 1-for-1.
Personal fouls/disqualifications: 2000-01, 9/0.

M

MERCER, RON   G   BULLS

PERSONAL: Born May 18, 1976, in Nashville. ... 6-7/210. (2,01/95,3). ... Full Name: Ronald Eugene Mercer.
HIGH SCHOOL: Oak Hill Academy (Mouth of Wilson, Va.).
COLLEGE: Kentucky.
TRANSACTIONS/CAREER NOTES: Selected after sophomore season by Boston Celtics in first round (sixth pick overall) of 1997 NBA Draft. ... Traded by Celtics with F Popeye Jones and C Dwayne Schintzius to Denver Nuggets for F Danny Fortson, F Eric Williams, G Eric Washington and first-round draft choice within the next three years (August 3, 1999). ... Traded by Nuggets with G Chauncey Billups, F Johnny Taylor and draft considerations to Orlando Magic for F/C Chris Gatling, F Tariq Abdul-Wahad, a future first-round draft pick and cash considerations (February 1, 2000). ... Signed as free agent by Chicago Bulls (August 1, 2000).

COLLEGIATE RECORD

NOTES: Member of NCAA Division I championship team (1996). ... THE SPORTING NEWS All-America second team (1997).

Season Team	G	Min.	FGM	FGA	Pct.	FTM	FTA	Pct.	Reb.	Ast.	Pts.	RPG	APG	PPG
												AVERAGES		
95-96—Kentucky	36	677	107	234	.457	51	65	.785	104	50	288	2.9	1.4	8.0
96-97—Kentucky	40	1299	297	603	.493	82	105	.781	210	97	725	5.3	2.4	18.1
Totals	76	1976	404	837	.483	133	170	.782	314	147	1013	4.1	1.9	13.3

Three-point field goals: 1995-96, 23-for-68 (.338). 1996-97, 49-for-141 (.348). Totals, 72-for-209 (.344).

NBA REGULAR-SEASON RECORD

HONORS: NBA All-Rookie first team (1998).

Season Team	G	Min.	FGM	FGA	Pct.	FTM	FTA	Pct.	Off.	Def.	Tot.	Ast.	St.	Blk.	TO	Pts.	RPG	APG	PPG
									REBOUNDS								**AVERAGES**		
97-98—Boston	80	2662	515	1145	.450	188	224	.839	109	171	280	176	125	17	132	1221	3.5	2.2	15.3
98-99—Boston	41	1551	305	707	.431	83	105	.790	37	118	155	104	67	12	89	698	3.8	2.5	17.0
99-00—Den.-Orl.	68	2377	460	1080	.426	213	270	.789	64	186	250	158	75	23	151	1148	3.7	2.3	16.9
00-01—Chicago	61	2535	500	1121	.446	188	228	.825	72	164	236	201	78	27	129	1202	3.9	3.3	19.7
Totals	250	9125	1780	4053	.439	672	827	.813	282	639	921	639	345	79	501	4269	3.7	2.6	17.1

Three-point field goals: 1997-98, 3-for-28 (.107). 1998-99, 5-for-30 (.167). 1999-00, 15-for-48 (.313). 2000-01, 14-for-46 (.304). Totals, 37-for-152 (.243).
Personal fouls/disqualifications: 1997-98, 213/2. 1998-99, 81/1. 1999-00, 151/2. 2000-01, 148/3. Totals, 593/8.

MIHM, CHRIS   C   CAVALIERS

PERSONAL: Born July 16, 1979, in Milwaukee. ... 7-0/265. (2,13/120,2). ... Full Name: Christopher Steven Mihm.
HIGH SCHOOL: Westlake (Austin, Texas).
COLLEGE: Texas.
TRANSACTIONS/CAREER NOTES: Selected after junior season by Chicago Bulls in first round (seventh pick overall) of 2000 NBA Draft. ... Draft rights traded by Bulls to Cleveland Cavaliers for draft rights to G Jamal Crawford and cash (June 28, 2000).

COLLEGIATE RECORD

NOTES: THE SPORTING NEWS All-America second team (2000).

Season Team	G	Min.	FGM	FGA	Pct.	FTM	FTA	Pct.	Reb.	Ast.	Pts.	RPG	APG	PPG
												AVERAGES		
97-98—Texas	31	769	148	288	.514	86	133	.647	248	14	384	8.0	0.5	12.4
98-99—Texas	32	1027	144	321	.449	149	218	.683	351	19	437	11.0	0.6	13.7
99-00—Texas	33	1014	206	394	.523	164	232	.707	346	22	583	10.5	0.7	17.7
Totals	96	2810	498	1003	.497	399	583	.684	945	55	1404	9.8	0.6	14.6

Three-point field goals: 1997-98, 2-for-11 (.182). 1998-99, 0-for-4. 1999-00, 7-for-15 (.467). Totals, 9-for-30 (.300).

NBA REGULAR-SEASON RECORD

HONORS: NBA All-Rookie second team (2001).

Season Team	G	Min.	FGM	FGA	Pct.	FTM	FTA	Pct.	Off.	Def.	Tot.	Ast.	St.	Blk.	TO	Pts.	RPG	APG	PPG
									REBOUNDS								**AVERAGES**		
00-01—Cleveland	59	1166	173	391	.442	100	126	.794	106	174	280	16	20	53	80	446	4.7	0.3	7.6

Three-point field goals: 2000-01, 0-for-1.
Personal fouls/disqualifications: 2000-01, 156/2.

MILES, DARIUS   F   CLIPPERS

PERSONAL: Born October 9, 1981, in Belleville, Ill. ... 6-9/202. (2,06/91,6). ... Full Name: Darius LaVar Miles.
HIGH SCHOOL: East St. Louis (Ill.).
COLLEGE: Did not attend college.
TRANSACTIONS/CAREER NOTES: Selected out of high school by Los Angeles Clippers in first round (third pick overall) of 2000 NBA Draft.

NBA REGULAR-SEASON RECORD

HONORS: NBA All-Rookie first team (2001).

Season Team	G	Min.	FGM	FGA	Pct.	FTM	FTA	Pct.	Off.	Def.	Tot.	Ast.	St.	Blk.	TO	Pts.	RPG	APG	PPG
									REBOUNDS								**AVERAGES**		
00-01—L.A. Clippers	81	2133	318	630	.505	124	238	.521	127	350	477	99	51	125	147	761	5.9	1.2	9.4

Three-point field goals: 2000-01, 1-for-19 (.053).
Personal fouls/disqualifications: 2000-01, 191/1.

M

MILLER, ANDRE　　　　　G　　　　　CAVALIERS

PERSONAL: Born March 19, 1976, in Los Angeles. ... 6-2/200. (1,88/90,7). ... Full Name: Andre Lloyd Miller.
HIGH SCHOOL: Verbum Dei (Los Angeles).
COLLEGE: Utah.
TRANSACTIONS/CAREER NOTES: Selected by Cleveland Cavaliers in first round (eighth pick overall) of 1999 NBA Draft.

COLLEGIATE RECORD

NOTES: THE SPORTING NEWS All-America first team (1999).

Season Team	G	Min.	FGM	FGA	Pct.	FTM	FTA	Pct.	Reb.	Ast.	Pts.	AVERAGES RPG	APG	PPG
94-95—Utah						Did not play—ineligible.								
95-96—Utah	34	872	104	195	.533	78	113	.690	126	157	292	3.7	4.6	8.6
96-97—Utah	33	974	121	249	.486	71	122	.582	154	201	323	4.7	6.1	9.8
97-98—Utah	34	1076	173	315	.549	117	162	.722	185	177	483	5.4	5.2	14.2
98-99—Utah	33	1092	190	387	.491	118	171	.690	178	186	520	5.4	5.6	15.8
Totals	134	4014	588	1146	.513	384	568	.676	643	721	1618	4.8	5.4	12.1

Three-point field goals: 1995-96, 6-for-19 (.316). 1996-97, 10-for-35 (.286). 1997-98, 20-for-60 (.333). 1998-99, 22-for-83 (.265). Totals, 58-for-197 (.294).

HONORS: NBA All-Rookie first team (2000).

NBA REGULAR-SEASON RECORD

Season Team	G	Min.	FGM	FGA	Pct.	FTM	FTA	Pct.	REBOUNDS Off.	Def.	Tot.	Ast.	St.	Blk.	TO	Pts.	AVERAGES RPG	APG	PPG
99-00—Cleveland	82	2093	339	755	.449	226	292	.774	85	195	280	476	84	17	166	914	3.4	5.8	11.1
00-01—Cleveland	82	2848	452	999	.452	375	450	.833	94	266	360	657	119	28	265	1296	4.4	8.0	15.8
Totals	164	4941	791	1754	.451	601	742	.810	179	461	640	1133	203	45	431	2210	3.9	6.9	13.5

Three-point field goals: 1999-00, 10-for-49 (.204). 2000-01, 17-for-64 (.266). Totals, 27-for-113 (.239).
Personal fouls/disqualifications: 1999-00, 194/1. 2000-01, 229/0. Totals, 423/1.

MILLER, ANTHONY　　　　　F

PERSONAL: Born October 22, 1971, in Benton Harbor, Mich. ... 6-9/255. (2,06/115,7). ... Nickname: Pig.
HIGH SCHOOL: Benton Harbor (Mich.).
COLLEGE: Michigan State.
TRANSACTIONS/CAREER NOTES: Selected by Golden State Warriors in second round (39th pick overall) of 1994 NBA Draft. ... Draft rights traded by Warriors to Los Angeles Lakers for 1995 second-round draft choice (July 1, 1994). ... Signed as free agent by Seattle SuperSonics (September 30, 1996). ... Waived by SuperSonics (October 26, 1996). ... Signed as free agent by Atlanta Hawks (November 14, 1996). ... Waived by Hawks (November 16, 1996). ... Played in Continental Basketball Association with Florida Beachdogs (1996-97). ... Signed as free agent by Hawks (September 26, 1997). ... Signed as free agent by Houston Rockets (January 21, 1999). ... Signed as free agent by Minnesota Timberwolves (October 18, 1999). ... Waived by Timberwolves (October 21, 1999). ... Signed by Houston Rockets to the first of two consecutive 10-day contracts (January 6, 2000). ... Re-signed by Rockets for remainder of season (January 26, 2000). ... Signed as free agent by Hawks (October 3, 2000). ... Waived by Hawks (November 8, 2000). ... Signed as free agent by Rockets (December 8, 2000). ... Waived by Rockets (December 28, 2000). ... Signed as free agent by Philadelphia 76ers (March 7, 2001). ... Waived by 76ers (March 15, 2001).

COLLEGIATE RECORD

Season Team	G	Min.	FGM	FGA	Pct.	FTM	FTA	Pct.	Reb.	Ast.	Pts.	AVERAGES RPG	APG	PPG
90-91—Michigan State						Did not play—ineligible.								
91-92—Michigan State	30	555	83	154	.539	50	80	.625	156	24	216	5.2	0.8	7.2
92-93—Michigan State	27	474	76	124	.613	26	48	.542	139	12	179	5.1	0.4	6.6
93-94—Michigan State	32	910	162	249	.651	78	136	.574	287	30	402	9.0	0.9	12.6
Totals	89	1939	321	527	.609	154	264	.583	582	66	797	6.5	0.7	9.0

Three-point field goals: 1992-93, 1-for-1. 1993-94, 0-for-1. Totals, 1-for-2 (.500).

NBA REGULAR-SEASON RECORD

Season Team	G	Min.	FGM	FGA	Pct.	FTM	FTA	Pct.	REBOUNDS Off.	Def.	Tot.	Ast.	St.	Blk.	TO	Pts.	AVERAGES RPG	APG	PPG
94-95—L.A. Lakers	46	527	70	132	.530	47	76	.618	67	85	152	35	20	7	38	189	3.3	0.8	4.1
95-96—L.A. Lakers	27	123	15	35	.429	6	10	.600	11	14	25	4	4	1	8	36	0.9	0.1	1.3
96-97—Atlanta	1	14	0	5	.000	0	0	...	2	5	7	0	0	0	0	0	7.0	0.0	0.0
97-98—Atlanta	37	228	29	52	.558	21	39	.538	30	40	70	3	15	3	14	79	1.9	0.1	2.1
98-99—Houston	29	249	28	60	.467	14	22	.636	26	41	67	7	7	5	9	70	2.3	0.2	2.4
99-00—Houston	35	476	52	97	.536	26	51	.510	49	115	164	16	11	10	19	130	4.7	0.5	3.7
00-01—Atl.-Hou.-Phil.	4	11	1	2	.500	0	0	...	0	2	2	0	0	0	1	2	0.5	0.0	0.5
Totals	179	1628	195	383	.509	114	198	.576	185	302	487	65	57	26	89	506	2.7	0.4	2.8

Three-point field goals: 1994-95, 2-for-5 (.400). 1995-96, 0-for-2. 1998-99, 0-for-1. Totals, 2-for-8 (.250).
Personal fouls/disqualifications: 1994-95, 77/2. 1995-96, 19/0. 1996-97, 2/0. 1997-98, 41/0. 1998-99, 34/0. 1999-00, 68/1. 2000-01, 1/0. Totals, 242/3.

NBA PLAYOFF RECORD

Season Team	G	Min.	FGM	FGA	Pct.	FTM	FTA	Pct.	REBOUNDS Off.	Def.	Tot.	Ast.	St.	Blk.	TO	Pts.	AVERAGES RPG	APG	PPG
94-95—L.A. Lakers	4	15	0	2	.000	0	0	...	2	4	6	1	1	0	1	0	1.5	0.3	0.0
97-98—Atlanta	4	33	3	8	.375	2	2	1.000	5	4	9	1	2	1	3	8	2.3	0.3	2.0
Totals	8	48	3	10	.300	2	2	1.000	7	8	15	2	3	1	4	8	1.9	0.3	1.0

Personal fouls/disqualifications: 1994-95, 2/0. 1997-98, 5/0. Totals, 7/0.

CBA REGULAR-SEASON RECORD

Season Team	G	Min.	FGM	FGA	Pct.	FTM	FTA	Pct.	Reb.	Ast.	Pts.	AVERAGES RPG	APG	PPG
96-97—Florida	16	334	51	102	.500	27	40	.675	135	3	129	8.4	0.2	8.1

Three-point field goals: 1996-97, 0-for-1.

M

MILLER, BRAD   C   BULLS

PERSONAL: Born April 12, 1976, in Fort Wayne, Ind. ... 7-0/261. (2,13/118,4). ... Full Name: Bradley Alan Miller.
HIGH SCHOOL: East Noble (Berwick, Maine), Maine Central Institute (Pittsfield, Maine).
COLLEGE: Purdue.
TRANSACTIONS/CAREER NOTES: Not drafted by an NBA franchise. ... Played in Italy (1998-99). ... Signed as free agent by Charlotte Hornets (January 21, 1999). ... Signed as free agent by Chicago Bulls (September 7, 2000).
MISCELLANEOUS: Member of bronze-medal-winning U.S. World Championship team (1998).

COLLEGIATE RECORD

Season Team	G	Min.	FGM	FGA	Pct.	FTM	FTA	Pct.	Reb.	Ast.	Pts.	RPG	APG	PPG
94-95—Purdue	32	574	71	122	.582	66	100	.660	153	39	208	4.8	1.2	6.5
95-96—Purdue	32	682	100	193	.518	107	145	.738	158	46	308	4.9	1.4	9.6
96-97—Purdue	30	929	128	239	.536	171	220	.777	249	86	430	8.3	2.9	14.3
97-98—Purdue	33	964	186	291	.639	196	251	.781	291	84	571	8.8	2.5	17.3
Totals	127	3149	485	845	.574	540	716	.754	851	255	1517	6.7	2.0	11.9

Three-point field goals: 1995-96, 1-for-6 (.167). 1996-97, 3-for-11 (.273). 1997-98, 3-for-9 (.333). Totals, 7-for-26 (.269).

ITALIAN LEAGUE RECORD

Season Team	G	Min.	FGM	FGA	Pct.	FTM	FTA	Pct.	Reb.	Ast.	Pts.	RPG	APG	PPG
98-99—Bini Viaggi	16	484	95	170	.559	61	73	.836	140	17	253	8.8	1.1	15.8

NBA REGULAR-SEASON RECORD

Season Team	G	Min.	FGM	FGA	Pct.	FTM	FTA	Pct.	Off.	Def.	Tot.	Ast.	St.	Blk.	TO	Pts.	RPG	APG	PPG
98-99—Charlotte	38	469	78	138	.565	81	102	.794	35	82	117	22	9	18	32	238	3.1	0.6	6.3
99-00—Charlotte	55	961	135	293	.461	153	195	.785	113	180	293	45	23	35	48	423	5.3	0.8	7.7
00-01—Chicago	57	1434	168	386	.435	168	226	.743	144	275	419	107	33	38	73	505	7.4	1.9	8.9
Totals	150	2864	381	817	.466	402	523	.769	292	537	829	174	65	91	153	1166	5.5	1.2	7.8

Three-point field goals: 1998-99, 1-for-2 (.500). 1999-00, 0-for-2. 2000-01, 1-for-5 (.200). Totals, 2-for-9 (.222).
Personal fouls/disqualifications: 1998-99, 65/0. 1999-00, 111/1. 2000-01, 176/5. Totals, 352/6.

NBA PLAYOFF RECORD

Season Team	G	Min.	FGM	FGA	Pct.	FTM	FTA	Pct.	Off.	Def.	Tot.	Ast.	St.	Blk.	TO	Pts.	RPG	APG	PPG
99-00—Charlotte	4	62	9	17	.529	12	15	.800	8	5	13	3	0	3	9	30	3.3	0.8	7.5

Personal fouls/disqualifications: 1999-00, 11/0.

MILLER, MIKE   F   MAGIC

M

PERSONAL: Born February 19, 1980, in Mitchell, S.D. ... 6-9/211. (2,06/95,7). ... Full Name: Michael Lloyd Miller.
HIGH SCHOOL: Mitchell (S.D.).
COLLEGE: Florida.
TRANSACTIONS/CAREER NOTES: Selected after sophomore season by Orlando Magic in first round (fifth pick overall) of 2000 NBA Draft.

COLLEGIATE RECORD

Season Team	G	Min.	FGM	FGA	Pct.	FTM	FTA	Pct.	Reb.	Ast.	Pts.	RPG	APG	PPG
98-99—Florida	28	677	115	233	.494	80	114	.702	146	58	341	5.2	2.1	12.2
99-00—Florida	37	1058	175	368	.476	124	170	.729	243	91	521	6.6	2.5	14.1
Totals	65	1735	290	601	.483	204	284	.718	389	149	862	6.0	2.3	13.3

Three-point field goals: 1998-99, 31-for-87 (.356). 1999-00, 47-for-139 (.338). Totals, 78-for-226 (.345).

NBA REGULAR-SEASON RECORD

HONORS: NBA Rookie of the Year (2001). ... NBA All-Rookie first team (2001).

Season Team	G	Min.	FGM	FGA	Pct.	FTM	FTA	Pct.	Off.	Def.	Tot.	Ast.	St.	Blk.	TO	Pts.	RPG	APG	PPG
00-01—Orlando	82	2390	368	845	.436	91	128	.711	66	261	327	140	51	19	97	975	4.0	1.7	11.9

Three-point field goals: 2000-01, 148-for-364 (.407).
Personal fouls/disqualifications: 2000-01, 200/2.

NBA PLAYOFF RECORD

Season Team	G	Min.	FGM	FGA	Pct.	FTM	FTA	Pct.	Off.	Def.	Tot.	Ast.	St.	Blk.	TO	Pts.	RPG	APG	PPG
00-01—Orlando	4	112	19	48	.396	3	4	.750	5	13	18	7	0	3	3	48	4.5	1.8	12.0

Three-point field goals: 2000-01, 7-for-18 (.389).
Personal fouls/disqualifications: 2000-01, 13/0.

MILLER, REGGIE   G   PACERS

PERSONAL: Born August 24, 1965, in Riverside, Calif. ... 6-7/190. (2,01/86,2). ... Full Name: Reginald Wayne Miller. ... Brother of Darrell Miller, outfielder/catcher with California Angels (1984-88); and brother of Cheryl Miller, member of gold-medal-winning U.S. Olympic women's basketball team (1984), and head coach and general manager, Phoenix Mercury (1997-2000).
HIGH SCHOOL: Riverside (Calif.) Polytechnic.
COLLEGE: UCLA.
TRANSACTIONS/CAREER NOTES: Selected by Indiana Pacers in first round (11th pick overall) of 1987 NBA Draft.

MISCELLANEOUS: Member of gold-medal-winning U.S. Olympic team (1996). ... Member of gold-medal-winning U.S. World Championship team (1994). ... Indiana Pacers franchise all-time leading scorer with 21,319 points and all-time steals leader with 1,240 (1987-88 through 2000-01).

COLLEGIATE RECORD

Season Team	G	Min.	FGM	FGA	Pct.	FTM	FTA	Pct.	Reb.	Ast.	Pts.	RPG	APG	PPG
83-84—UCLA	28	384	56	110	.509	18	28	.643	42	21	130	1.5	0.8	4.6
84-85—UCLA	33	1174	192	347	.553	119	148	.804	141	86	503	4.3	2.6	15.2
85-86—UCLA	29	1112	274	493	.556	202	229	.882	153	69	750	5.3	2.4	25.9
86-87—UCLA	32	1166	247	455	.543	149	179	.832	173	71	712	5.4	2.2	22.3
Totals	122	3836	769	1405	.547	488	584	.836	509	247	2095	4.2	2.0	17.2

Three-point field goals: 1986-87, 69-for-157 (.439).

NBA REGULAR-SEASON RECORD

RECORDS: Holds career record for most three-point field goals made—2,037; and most three-point field goals attempted—5,093. ... Shares NBA record for most seasons leading league in three-point field goals made—2.

HONORS: All-NBA third team (1995, 1996, 1998).

NOTES: Led NBA with 167 three-point field goals made (1993) and 229 three-point field goals made (1997).

Season Team	G	Min.	FGM	FGA	Pct.	FTM	FTA	Pct.	REBOUNDS Off.	Def.	Tot.	Ast.	St.	Blk.	TO	Pts.	RPG	APG	PPG
87-88—Indiana	82	1840	306	627	.488	149	186	.801	95	95	190	132	53	19	101	822	2.3	1.6	10.0
88-89—Indiana	74	2536	398	831	.479	287	340	.844	73	219	292	227	93	29	143	1181	3.9	3.1	16.0
89-90—Indiana	82	3192	661	1287	.514	544	627	.868	95	200	295	311	110	18	222	2016	3.6	3.8	24.6
90-91—Indiana	82	2972	596	1164	.512	551	600	*.918	81	200	281	331	109	13	163	1855	3.4	4.0	22.6
91-92—Indiana	82	3120	562	1121	.501	442	515	.858	82	236	318	314	105	26	157	1695	3.9	3.8	20.7
92-93—Indiana	82	2954	571	1193	.479	427	485	.880	67	191	258	262	120	26	145	1736	3.1	3.2	21.2
93-94—Indiana	79	2638	524	1042	.503	403	444	.908	30	182	212	248	119	24	175	1574	2.7	3.1	19.9
94-95—Indiana	81	2665	505	1092	.462	383	427	.897	30	180	210	242	98	16	151	1588	2.6	3.0	19.6
95-96—Indiana	76	2621	504	1066	.473	430	498	.863	38	176	214	253	77	13	189	1606	2.8	3.3	21.1
96-97—Indiana	81	2966	552	1244	.444	418	475	.880	53	233	286	273	75	25	166	1751	3.5	3.4	21.6
97-98—Indiana	81	2795	516	1081	.477	382	440	.868	46	186	232	171	78	11	128	1578	2.9	2.1	19.5
98-99—Indiana	50	1787	294	671	.438	226	247	*.915	25	110	135	112	37	9	76	920	2.7	2.2	18.4
99-00—Indiana	81	2987	466	1041	.448	373	406	.919	50	189	239	187	85	25	129	1470	3.0	2.3	18.1
00-01—Indiana	81	3181	517	1176	.440	323	348	*.928	38	247	285	260	81	15	133	1527	3.5	3.2	18.9
Totals	1094	38254	6972	14636	.476	5338	6038	.884	803	2644	3447	3323	1240	269	2078	21319	3.2	3.0	19.5

Three-point field goals: 1987-88, 61-for-172 (.355). 1988-89, 98-for-244 (.402). 1989-90, 150-for-362 (.414). 1990-91, 112-for-322 (.348). 1991-92, 129-for-341 (.378). 1992-93, 167-for-419 (.399). 1993-94, 123-for-292 (.421). 1994-95, 195-for-470 (.415). 1995-96, 168-for-410 (.410). 1996-97, 229-for-536 (.427). 1997-98, 164-for-382 (.429). 1998-99, 106-for-275 (.385). 1999-00, 165-for-404 (.408). 2000-01, 170-for-464 (.366). Totals, 2037-for-5093 (.400).

Personal fouls/disqualifications: 1987-88, 157/0. 1988-89, 170/2. 1989-90, 175/1. 1990-91, 165/1. 1991-92, 210/1. 1992-93, 182/0. 1993-94, 193/2. 1994-95, 157/0. 1995-96, 175/0. 1996-97, 172/1. 1997-98, 148/2. 1998-99, 101/1. 1999-00, 126/0. 2000-01, 162/0. Totals, 2293/11.

NBA PLAYOFF RECORD

NOTES: Shares single-game playoff record most three-point field goals made in one quarter—5 (June 1, 1994, at New York).

Season Team	G	Min.	FGM	FGA	Pct.	FTM	FTA	Pct.	REBOUNDS Off.	Def.	Tot.	Ast.	St.	Blk.	TO	Pts.	RPG	APG	PPG
89-90—Indiana	3	125	20	35	.571	19	21	.905	1	11	12	6	3	0	3	62	4.0	2.0	20.7
90-91—Indiana	5	193	34	70	.486	32	37	.865	5	11	16	14	8	2	12	108	3.2	2.8	21.6
91-92—Indiana	3	130	25	43	.581	24	30	.800	4	3	7	14	4	0	4	81	2.3	4.7	27.0
92-93—Indiana	4	175	40	75	.533	36	38	.947	4	8	12	11	3	0	10	126	3.0	2.8	31.5
93-94—Indiana	16	576	121	270	.448	94	112	.839	11	37	48	46	21	4	32	371	3.0	2.9	23.2
94-95—Indiana	17	641	138	290	.476	104	121	.860	9	52	61	36	15	4	39	434	3.6	2.1	25.5
95-96—Indiana	1	31	7	17	.412	13	15	.867	1	0	1	1	0	0	0	29	1.0	1.0	29.0
97-98—Indiana	16	628	98	230	.426	85	94	.904	5	23	28	32	19	3	27	319	1.8	2.0	19.9
98-99—Indiana	13	481	79	199	.397	77	86	.895	13	38	51	34	9	3	21	263	3.9	2.6	20.2
99-00—Indiana	22	892	174	385	.452	121	129	.938	9	44	53	60	23	10	28	527	2.4	2.7	24.0
00-01—Indiana	4	177	41	90	.456	28	30	.933	7	13	20	10	3	2	11	125	5.0	2.5	31.3
Totals	104	4049	877	1704	.456	633	713	.888	69	240	309	264	109	28	187	2445	3.0	2.5	23.5

Three-point field goals: 1989-90, 3-for-7 (.429). 1990-91, 8-for-19 (.421). 1991-92, 7-for-11 (.636). 1992-93, 10-for-19 (.526). 1993-94, 35-for-83 (.422). 1994-95, 54-for-128 (.422). 1995-96, 2-for-6 (.333). 1997-98, 38-for-95 (.400). 1998-99, 28-for-84 (.333). 1999-00, 58-for-147 (.395). 2000-01, 15-for-35 (.429). Totals, 258-for-634 (.407).

Personal fouls/disqualifications: 1989-90, 6/0. 1990-91, 14/0. 1991-92, 12/1. 1992-93, 11/0. 1993-94, 34/0. 1994-95, 35/0. 1995-96, 1/0. 1997-98, 26/0. 1998-99, 26/0. 1999-00, 37/0. 2000-01, 3/0. Totals, 205/1.

NBA ALL-STAR GAME RECORD

Season Team	Min.	FGM	FGA	Pct.	FTM	FTA	Pct.	REBOUNDS Off.	Def.	Tot.	Ast.	PF	Dq.	St.	Blk.	TO	Pts.
1990 —Indiana	14	2	3	.667	0	0	...	0	1	1	3	1	0	1	0	0	4
1995 —Indiana	23	3	9	.333	0	0	...	0	0	0	2	0	0	1	1	1	9
1996 —Indiana	18	4	8	.500	0	0	...	0	0	0	2	2	0	1	0	1	8
1998 —Indiana	20	6	8	.750	1	2	.500	0	0	0	0	2	...	1	0	0	14
2000 —Indiana	21	1	7	.143	2	2	1.000	0	2	2	3	1	0	1	0	1	5
Totals	96	16	35	.457	3	4	.750	0	3	3	10	6	0	5	1	3	40

Three-point field goals: 1990, 0-for-1. 1995, 3-for-6 (.500). 1996, 0-for-4. 1998, 1-for-2 (.500). 1900, 1-for-6 (.167). Totals, 5-for-19 (.263).

DID YOU KNOW . . .

. . . that Minnesota's 47 wins last season were the most ever by a No. 8 playoff seed?

MILLS, CHRIS   F   WARRIORS

PERSONAL: Born January 25, 1970, in Los Angeles. ... 6-7/216. (2,01/98,0). ... Full Name: Christopher Lemonte Mills.
HIGH SCHOOL: Fairfax (Los Angeles).
COLLEGE: Kentucky, then Arizona.
TRANSACTIONS/CAREER NOTES: Selected by Cleveland Cavaliers in first round (22nd pick overall) of 1993 NBA Draft. ... Signed as free agent by Boston Celtics (August 22, 1997). ... Traded by Celtics with two future second-round draft choices to New York Knicks for F Walter McCarty, F Dontae' Jones, F John Thomas and G Scott Brooks (October 22, 1997). ... Traded by Knicks with G John Starks and F Terry Cummings to Golden State Warriors for G Latrell Sprewell (January 21, 1999).

COLLEGIATE RECORD

Season Team	G	Min.	FGM	FGA	Pct.	FTM	FTA	Pct.	Reb.	Ast.	Pts.	RPG	APG	PPG
88-89—Kentucky	32	1124	180	372	.484	82	115	.713	277	92	459	8.7	2.9	14.3
89-90—Arizona						Did not play—transfer student.								
90-91—Arizona	35	1025	206	397	.519	91	122	.746	216	66	545	6.2	1.9	15.6
91-92—Arizona	31	984	198	391	.506	80	103	.777	244	73	504	7.9	2.4	16.3
92-93—Arizona	28	870	211	406	.520	92	110	.836	222	53	570	7.9	1.9	20.4
Totals	126	4003	795	1566	.508	345	450	.767	959	284	2078	7.6	2.3	16.5

Three-point field goals: 1988-89, 17-for-54 (.315). 1990-91, 42-for-122 (.344). 1991-92, 28-for-89 (.315). 1992-93, 56-for-116 (.483). Totals, 143-for-381 (.375).

NBA REGULAR-SEASON RECORD

Season Team	G	Min.	FGM	FGA	Pct.	FTM	FTA	Pct.	REBOUNDS Off.	Def.	Tot.	Ast.	St.	Blk.	TO	Pts.	AVERAGES RPG	APG	PPG
93-94—Cleveland	79	2022	284	677	.419	137	176	.778	134	267	401	128	54	50	89	743	5.1	1.6	9.4
94-95—Cleveland	80	2814	359	855	.420	174	213	.817	99	267	366	154	59	35	120	986	4.6	1.9	12.3
95-96—Cleveland	80	3060	454	971	.468	218	263	.829	112	331	443	188	73	52	121	1205	5.5	2.4	15.1
96-97—Cleveland	80	3167	405	894	.453	176	209	.842	118	379	497	198	86	41	120	1072	6.2	2.5	13.4
97-98—New York	80	2183	292	675	.433	152	189	.804	120	288	408	133	45	30	107	776	5.1	1.7	9.7
98-99—Golden State	47	1395	186	453	.411	79	96	.823	49	188	237	103	39	14	58	483	5.0	2.2	10.3
99-00—Golden State	20	649	123	292	.421	68	84	.810	46	77	123	47	18	4	25	322	6.2	2.4	16.1
00-01—Golden State	15	493	71	191	.372	31	36	.861	24	69	93	18	9	5	20	180	6.2	1.2	12.0
Totals	481	15783	2174	5008	.434	1035	1266	.818	702	1866	2568	969	383	231	660	5767	5.3	2.0	12.0

Three-point field goals: 1993-94, 38-for-122 (.311). 1994-95, 94-for-240 (.392). 1995-96, 79-for-210 (.376). 1996-97, 86-for-220 (.391). 1997-98, 40-for-137 (.292). 1998-99, 32-for-115 (.278). 1999-00, 8-for-30 (.267). 2000-01, 7-for-25 (.280). Totals, 384-for-1099 (.349).
Personal fouls/disqualifications: 1993-94, 232/3. 1994-95, 242/2. 1995-96, 241/1. 1996-97, 222/1. 1997-98, 218/3. 1998-99, 125/1. 1999-00, 60/0. 2000-01, 43/1. Totals, 1383/12.

NBA PLAYOFF RECORD

Season Team	G	Min.	FGM	FGA	Pct.	FTM	FTA	Pct.	REBOUNDS Off.	Def.	Tot.	Ast.	St.	Blk.	TO	Pts.	AVERAGES RPG	APG	PPG
93-94—Cleveland	3	112	19	38	.500	9	11	.818	10	13	23	8	7	1	5	51	7.7	2.7	17.0
94-95—Cleveland	4	139	20	37	.541	5	5	1.000	2	14	16	11	3	2	6	53	4.0	2.8	13.3
95-96—Cleveland	3	105	11	33	.333	1	1	1.000	5	11	16	5	2	2	3	23	5.3	1.7	7.7
97-98—New York	9	168	15	35	.429	10	12	.833	8	19	27	5	8	2	6	44	3.0	0.6	4.9
Totals	19	524	65	143	.455	25	29	.862	25	57	82	29	20	7	20	171	4.3	1.5	9.0

Three-point field goals: 1993-94, 4-for-5 (.800). 1994-95, 8-for-14 (.571). 1995-96, 0-for-5. 1997-98, 4-for-10 (.400). Totals, 16-for-34 (.471).
Personal fouls/disqualifications: 1993-94, 9/0. 1994-95, 18/1. 1995-96, 10/0. 1997-98, 21/0. Totals, 58/1.

M

MILLS, TERRY   F

PERSONAL: Born December 21, 1967, in Romulus, Mich. ... 6-10/250. (2,08/113,4). ... Full Name: Terry Richard Mills. ... Nephew of John Long, guard with five NBA teams (1978-79 through 1990-91 and 1996-97); and cousin of Grant Long, forward, Memphis Grizzlies.
HIGH SCHOOL: Romulus (Mich.).
COLLEGE: Michigan.
TRANSACTIONS/CAREER NOTES: Selected by Milwaukee Bucks in first round (16th pick overall) of 1990 NBA Draft. ... Traded by Bucks to Denver Nuggets for C Danny Schayes (August 1, 1990). ... Traded by Nuggets to New Jersey Nets in three-way deal in which Nets sent F Greg Anderson to Nuggets, Nuggets sent G Walter Davis to Portland Trail Blazers and Trail Blazers sent G Drazen Petrovic to Nets (January 23, 1991); Nuggets also received 1992 first-round draft choice from Nets and 1993 second-round draft choice from Trail Blazers and Trail Blazers also received 1992 second-round draft choice from Nuggets. ... Signed as free agent by Detroit Pistons (October 1, 1992). ... Signed as free agent by Miami Heat (August 20, 1997). ... Signed as free agent by Pistons (September 20, 1999). ... Traded by Pistons with F/C Christian Laettner to Dallas Mavericks for F Cedric Ceballos, F John Wallace and G Eric Murdock (August 29, 2000). ... Waived by Mavericks (October 2, 2000). ... Signed as free agent by Indiana Pacers (October 5, 2000).

COLLEGIATE RECORD

NOTES: Member of NCAA Division I championship team (1989).

Season Team	G	Min.	FGM	FGA	Pct.	FTM	FTA	Pct.	Reb.	Ast.	Pts.	RPG	APG	PPG
86-87—Michigan						Did not play—ineligible.								
87-88—Michigan	34	884	181	341	.531	51	70	.729	216	56	413	6.4	1.6	12.1
88-89—Michigan	37	999	180	319	.564	70	91	.769	218	104	430	5.9	2.8	11.6
89-90—Michigan	31	961	237	405	.585	88	116	.759	247	68	562	8.0	2.2	18.1
Totals	102	2844	598	1065	.562	209	277	.755	681	228	1405	6.7	2.2	13.8

Three-point field goals: 1987-88, 0-for-2. 1988-89, 0-for-2. Totals, 0-for-4 (.000).

NBA REGULAR-SEASON RECORD

RECORDS: Shares single-season record for most consecutive three-point field goals made without a miss—13 (December 4-7, 1996).

Season Team	G	Min.	FGM	FGA	Pct.	FTM	FTA	Pct.	REBOUNDS Off.	Def.	Tot.	Ast.	St.	Blk.	TO	Pts.	RPG	APG	PPG
90-91—Denver-N.J......	55	819	134	288	.465	47	66	.712	82	147	229	33	35	29	43	315	4.2	0.6	5.7
91-92—New Jersey.....	82	1714	310	670	.463	114	152	.750	187	266	453	84	48	41	82	742	5.5	1.0	9.0
92-93—Detroit	81	2183	494	1072	.461	201	254	.791	176	296	472	111	44	50	142	1199	5.8	1.4	14.8
93-94—Detroit	80	2773	588	1151	.511	181	227	.797	193	479	672	177	64	62	153	1381	8.4	2.2	17.3
94-95—Detroit	72	2514	417	933	.447	175	219	.799	124	434	558	160	68	33	144	1118	7.8	2.2	15.5
95-96—Detroit	82	1656	283	675	.419	121	157	.771	108	244	352	98	42	20	98	769	4.3	1.2	9.4
96-97—Detroit	79	1997	312	702	.444	58	70	.829	68	309	377	99	35	27	85	857	4.8	1.3	10.8
97-98—Miami	50	782	81	206	.393	25	33	.758	34	118	152	39	19	9	45	212	3.0	0.8	4.2
98-99—Miami	1	29	3	8	.375	1	2	.500	3	1	4	0	1	0	3	9	4.0	0.0	9.0
99-00—Detroit	82	1842	214	488	.439	25	34	.735	50	340	390	85	38	24	46	548	4.8	1.0	6.7
00-01—Indiana...........	14	113	11	34	.324	0	0	...	4	17	21	5	3	1	10	25	1.5	0.4	1.8
Totals	678	16422	2847	6227	.457	948	1214	.781	1029	2651	3680	891	397	296	851	7175	5.4	1.3	10.6

Three-point field goals: 1990-91, 0-for-4. 1991-92, 8-for-23 (.348). 1992-93, 10-for-36 (.278). 1993-94, 24-for-73 (.329). 1994-95, 109-for-285 (.382). 1995-96, 82-for-207 (.396). 1996-97, 175-for-415 (.422). 1997-98, 25-for-81 (.309). 1998-99, 2-for-4 (.500). 1999-00, 95-for-242 (.393). 2000-01, 3-for-17 (.176). Totals, 533-for-1387 (.384).

Personal fouls/disqualifications: 1990-91, 100/0. 1991-92, 200/3. 1992-93, 282/6. 1993-94, 309/6. 1994-95, 253/5. 1995-96, 197/0. 1996-97, 161/1. 1997-98, 129/1. 1998-99, 3/0. 1999-00, 242/4. 2000-01, 20/1. Totals, 1896/27.

NBA PLAYOFF RECORD

Season Team	G	Min.	FGM	FGA	Pct.	FTM	FTA	Pct.	REBOUNDS Off.	Def.	Tot.	Ast.	St.	Blk.	TO	Pts.	RPG	APG	PPG
91-92—New Jersey.....	4	77	10	27	.370	7	11	.636	9	15	24	8	1	2	7	27	6.0	2.0	6.8
95-96—Detroit	3	48	5	20	.250	5	6	.833	3	2	5	4	1	0	1	16	1.7	1.3	5.3
96-97—Detroit	5	196	24	55	.436	2	4	.500	4	31	35	7	6	0	4	59	7.0	1.4	11.8
97-98—Miami	2	11	1	5	.200	1	2	.500	0	3	3	0	0	0	0	4	1.5	0.0	2.0
99-00—Detroit	3	77	9	15	.600	1	2	.500	0	6	6	1	2	0	2	25	2.0	0.3	8.3
Totals	17	409	49	122	.402	16	25	.640	16	57	73	20	10	2	14	131	4.3	1.2	7.7

Three-point field goals: 1991-92, 0-for-1. 1995-96, 1-for-8 (.125). 1996-97, 9-for-26 (.346). 1997-98, 1-for-4 (.250). 1999-00, 6-for-9 (.667). Totals, 17-for-48 (.354).

Personal fouls/disqualifications: 1991-92, 18/0. 1995-96, 6/0. 1996-97, 14/0. 1997-98, 3/0. 1999-00, 12/1. Totals, 53/1.

MITCHELL, SAM   F   TIMBERWOLVES

PERSONAL: Born September 2, 1963, in Columbus, Ga. ... 6-7/215. (2,01/97,5). ... Full Name: Samuel E. Mitchell Jr.
HIGH SCHOOL: Columbus (Ga.).
COLLEGE: Mercer (Ga.).
TRANSACTIONS/CAREER NOTES: Selected by Houston Rockets in third round (54th pick overall) of 1985 NBA Draft. ... Waived by Rockets (October 22, 1985). ... Played in Continental Basketball Association with Wisconsin Flyers (1985-86 and 1986-87) and Rapid City Thrillers (1986-87). ... Played in United States Basketball League with Tampa Bay Flash (1986). ... Signed as free agent by Rockets (October 7, 1986). ... Waived by Rockets (October 28, 1986). ... Played in France (1987-88 and 1988-89). ... Signed as free agent by Minnesota Timberwolves (July 23, 1989). ... Traded by Timberwolves with G Pooh Richardson to Indiana Pacers for F Chuck Person and G Micheal Williams (September 8, 1992). ... Signed as unrestricted free agent by Timberwolves (September 29, 1995).

COLLEGIATE RECORD

Season Team	G	Min.	FGM	FGA	Pct.	FTM	FTA	Pct.	Reb.	Ast.	Pts.	RPG	APG	PPG
81-82—Mercer...........................	27	...	77	155	.497	38	53	.717	100	13	192	3.7	0.5	7.1
82-83—Mercer...........................	28	964	178	343	.519	105	134	.784	164	47	461	5.9	1.7	16.5
83-84—Mercer...........................	26	935	219	432	.507	121	155	.781	184	46	559	7.1	1.8	21.5
84-85—Mercer...........................	31	1157	294	570	.516	186	248	.750	255	43	774	8.2	1.4	25.0
Totals	112	...	768	1500	.512	450	590	.763	703	149	1986	6.3	1.3	17.7

CBA REGULAR-SEASON RECORD

Season Team	G	Min.	FGM	FGA	Pct.	FTM	FTA	Pct.	Reb.	Ast.	Pts.	RPG	APG	PPG
85-86—Wisconsin	13	450	107	238	.450	55	83	.663	95	16	270	7.3	1.2	20.8
86-87—Wisconsin-Rapid City.....	42	1370	253	554	.457	154	210	.733	256	31	663	6.1	0.7	15.8
Totals	55	1820	360	792	.455	209	293	.713	351	47	933	6.4	0.9	17.0

Three-point field goals: 1985-86, 1-for-3 (.333). 1986-87, 3-for-12 (.250). Totals, 4-for-15 (.267).

NBA REGULAR-SEASON RECORD

NOTES: Led NBA with 338 personal fouls (1991).

Season Team	G	Min.	FGM	FGA	Pct.	FTM	FTA	Pct.	REBOUNDS Off.	Def.	Tot.	Ast.	St.	Blk.	TO	Pts.	RPG	APG	PPG
89-90—Minnesota.......	80	2414	372	834	.446	268	349	.768	180	282	462	89	66	54	96	1012	5.8	1.1	12.7
90-91—Minnesota.......	82	3121	445	1010	.441	307	396	.775	188	332	520	133	66	57	104	1197	6.3	1.6	14.6
91-92—Minnesota.......	82	2151	307	725	.423	209	266	.786	158	315	473	94	53	39	97	825	5.8	1.1	10.1
92-93—Indiana...........	81	1402	215	483	.445	150	185	.811	93	155	248	76	23	10	51	584	3.1	0.9	7.2
93-94—Indiana...........	75	1084	140	306	.458	82	110	.745	71	119	190	65	33	9	50	362	2.5	0.9	4.8
94-95—Indiana...........	81	1377	201	413	.487	126	174	.724	95	148	243	61	43	20	54	529	3.0	0.8	6.5
95-96—Minnesota.......	78	2145	303	618	.490	237	291	.814	107	232	339	74	49	26	87	844	4.3	0.9	10.8
96-97—Minnesota.......	82	2044	269	603	.446	224	295	.759	112	214	326	79	51	20	93	766	4.0	1.0	9.3
97-98—Minnesota.......	81	2239	371	800	.464	243	292	.832	118	267	385	107	64	22	66	1000	4.8	1.3	12.3
98-99—Minnesota.......	50	1344	213	522	.408	126	165	.764	55	127	182	98	35	16	34	561	3.6	2.0	11.2
99-00—Minnesota.......	66	1227	168	376	.447	81	92	.880	28	110	138	111	27	14	44	427	2.1	1.7	6.5
00-01—Minnesota.......	82	983	118	289	.408	40	55	.727	28	95	123	57	26	10	36	285	1.5	0.7	3.5
Totals	920	21531	3122	6979	.447	2093	2670	.784	1233	2396	3629	1044	536	297	812	8392	3.9	1.1	9.1

M

Three-point field goals: 1989-90, 0-for-9. 1990-91, 0-for-9. 1991-92, 2-for-11 (.182). 1992-93, 4-for-23 (.174). 1993-94, 0-for-5. 1994-95, 1-for-10 (.100). 1995-96, 1-for-18 (.056). 1996-97, 4-for-25 (.160). 1997-98, 15-for-43 (.349). 1998-99, 9-for-38 (.237). 1999-00, 10-for-23 (.435). 2000-01, 9-for-43 (.209). Totals, 55-for-257 (.214).

Personal fouls/disqualifications: 1989-90, 301/7. 1990-91, 338/13. 1991-92, 230/3. 1992-93, 207/1. 1993-94, 152/1. 1994-95, 206/0. 1995-96, 220/3. 1996-97, 232/1. 1997-98, 200/0. 1998-99, 111/1. 1999-00, 116/0. 2000-01, 117/0. Totals, 2430/30.

NBA PLAYOFF RECORD

Season Team	G	Min.	FGM	FGA	Pct.	FTM	FTA	Pct.	REBOUNDS Off.	Def.	Tot.	Ast.	St.	Blk.	TO	Pts.	AVERAGES RPG	APG	PPG
92-93—Indiana...........	4	25	5	8	.625	2	2	1.000	0	1	1	0	0	0	2	12	0.3	0.0	3.0
93-94—Indiana...........	15	99	9	26	.346	3	4	.750	5	12	17	5	2	2	4	21	1.1	0.3	1.4
94-95—Indiana.......	17	223	23	64	.359	22	28	.786	17	31	48	6	3	1	14	68	2.8	0.4	4.0
96-97—Minnesota......	3	47	6	13	.462	5	8	.625	2	5	7	1	1	1	1	17	2.3	0.3	5.7
97-98—Minnesota......	5	177	26	58	.448	17	19	.895	7	20	27	8	1	1	5	72	5.4	1.6	14.4
98-99—Minnesota......	4	131	15	40	.375	9	12	.750	5	9	14	6	1	2	8	40	3.5	1.5	10.0
99-00—Minnesota......	4	68	9	18	.500	3	3	1.000	2	5	7	2	0	1	4	23	1.8	0.5	5.8
00-01—Minnesota......	4	50	2	10	.200	2	2	1.000	1	6	7	3	1	0	1	6	1.8	0.8	1.5
Totals	56	820	95	237	.401	63	78	.808	39	89	128	31	9	8	39	259	2.3	0.6	4.6

Three-point field goals: 1993-94, 0-for-1. 1994-95, 0-for-2. 1997-98, 3-for-14 (.214). 1998-99, 1-for-6 (.167). 1999-00, 2-for-5 (.400). 2000-01, 0-for-1. Totals, 6-for-29 (.207).

Personal fouls/disqualifications: 1992-93, 4/0. 1993-94, 22/0. 1994-95, 41/0. 1996-97, 9/0. 1997-98, 18/0. 1998-99, 13/0. 1999-00, 5/0. 2000-01, 5/0. Totals, 117/0.

MOBLEY, CUTTINO   G   ROCKETS

PERSONAL: Born September 1, 1974, in Philadelphia. ... 6-4/190. (1,93/86,2). ... Full Name: Cuttino Rashawn Mobley.
HIGH SCHOOL: Cardinal Dougherty (Philadelphia), then Maine Central Institute (Pittsfield, Maine).
COLLEGE: Rhode Island.
TRANSACTIONS/CAREER NOTES: Selected by Houston Rockets in second round (41st pick overall) of 1998 NBA Draft.

COLLEGIATE RECORD

NOTES: Granted medical redshirt (1995-96).

Season Team	G	Min.	FGM	FGA	Pct.	FTM	FTA	Pct.	Reb.	Ast.	Pts.	AVERAGES RPG	APG	PPG
93-94—Rhode Island						Did not play—redshirted.								
94-95—Rhode Island	27	864	126	334	.377	63	81	.778	129	39	358	4.8	1.4	13.3
95-96—Rhode Island	2	35	9	14	.643	1	2	.500	0	5	24	0.0	2.5	12.0
96-97—Rhode Island	30	730	138	315	.438	61	76	.803	117	44	366	3.9	1.5	12.2
97-98—Rhode Island	34	1133	193	402	.480	131	153	.856	147	88	586	4.3	2.6	17.2
Totals	93	2762	466	1065	.438	256	312	.821	393	176	1334	4.2	1.9	14.3

Three-point field goals: 1994-95, 43-for-142 (.303). 1995-96, 5-for-7 (.714). 1996-97, 29-for-97 (.299). 1997-98, 69-for-166 (.416). Totals, 146-for-412 (.354).

HONORS: NBA All-Rookie second team (1999).

NBA REGULAR-SEASON RECORD

Season Team	G	Min.	FGM	FGA	Pct.	FTM	FTA	Pct.	REBOUNDS Off.	Def.	Tot.	Ast.	St.	Blk.	TO	Pts.	AVERAGES RPG	APG	PPG
98-99—Houston.........	49	1456	172	405	.425	90	110	.818	22	89	111	121	44	23	79	487	2.3	2.5	9.9
99-00—Houston.........	81	2496	437	1016	.430	299	353	.847	59	229	288	208	87	32	186	1277	3.6	2.6	15.8
00-01—Houston.........	79	3002	527	1214	.434	394	474	.831	83	314	397	195	84	26	165	1538	5.0	2.5	19.5
Totals	209	6954	1136	2635	.431	783	937	.836	164	632	796	524	215	81	430	3302	3.8	2.5	15.8

Three-point field goals: 1998-99, 53-for-148 (.358). 1999-00, 104-for-292 (.356). 2000-01, 90-for-252 (.357). Totals, 247-for-692 (.357).

Personal fouls/disqualifications: 1998-99, 98/0. 1999-00, 171/0. 2000-01, 169/1. Totals, 438/1.

NBA PLAYOFF RECORD

Season Team	G	Min.	FGM	FGA	Pct.	FTM	FTA	Pct.	REBOUNDS Off.	Def.	Tot.	Ast.	St.	Blk.	TO	Pts.	AVERAGES RPG	APG	PPG
98-99—Houston.........	4	94	7	15	.467	10	11	.909	0	4	4	11	2	0	5	28	1.0	2.8	7.0

Three-point field goals: 1998-99, 4-for-7 (.571).

Personal fouls/disqualifications: 1998-99, 11/0.

MOHAMMED, NAZR   C   HAWKS

PERSONAL: Born September 5, 1977, in Chicago. ... 6-10/240. (2,08/108,9). ... Full Name: Nazr Tahiru Mohammed. ... Name pronounced NAH-zee.
HIGH SCHOOL: Kenwood (Chicago).
COLLEGE: Kentucky.
TRANSACTIONS/CAREER NOTES: Selected after junior season by Utah Jazz in first round (29th pick overall) of 1998 NBA Draft. ... Draft rights traded by Jazz to Philadelphia 76ers for future first-round draft choice (June 24, 1998). ... Traded by 76ers with F/C Theo Ratliff, F/G Toni Kukoc and G Pepe Sanchez to Atlanta Hawks for C Dikembe Mutombo and F Roshown McLeod (February 22, 2001).

COLLEGIATE RECORD

NOTES: Member of NCAA Division I championship team (1996 and 1998).

Season Team	G	Min.	FGM	FGA	Pct.	FTM	FTA	Pct.	Reb.	Ast.	Pts.	AVERAGES RPG	APG	PPG
95-96—Kentucky	16	88	13	29	.448	11	24	.458	24	3	37	1.5	0.2	2.3
96-97—Kentucky	39	617	132	259	.510	45	89	.506	226	12	309	5.8	0.3	7.9
97-98—Kentucky	39	819	190	318	.597	88	135	.652	282	28	468	7.2	0.7	12.0
Totals	94	1524	335	606	.553	144	248	.581	532	43	814	5.7	0.5	8.7

Three-point field goals: 1996-97, 0-for-2.

NBA REGULAR-SEASON RECORD

									REBOUNDS								AVERAGES		
Season Team	G	Min.	FGM	FGA	Pct.	FTM	FTA	Pct.	Off.	Def.	Tot.	Ast.	St.	Blk.	TO	Pts.	RPG	APG	PPG
98-99—Philadelphia....	26	121	15	42	.357	12	21	.571	18	19	37	2	5	4	12	42	1.4	0.1	1.6
99-00—Philadelphia....	28	190	21	54	.389	12	22	.545	16	34	50	2	4	12	18	54	1.8	0.1	1.9
00-01—Phil.-Atlanta..	58	912	176	369	.477	89	126	.706	115	192	307	19	29	35	64	441	5.3	0.3	7.6
Totals	112	1223	212	465	.456	113	169	.669	149	245	394	23	38	51	94	537	3.5	0.2	4.8

Three-point field goals: 2000-01, 0-for-1. Totals, 0-for-1 (.000).
Personal fouls/disqualifications: 1998-99, 22/0. 1999-00, 29/0. 2000-01, 113/0. Totals, 164/0.

NBA PLAYOFF RECORD

									REBOUNDS								AVERAGES		
Season Team	G	Min.	FGM	FGA	Pct.	FTM	FTA	Pct.	Off.	Def.	Tot.	Ast.	St.	Blk.	TO	Pts.	RPG	APG	PPG
98-99—Philadelphia....	3	3	0	0	...	0	0	...	0	0	0	0	0	0	0	0	0.0	0.0	0.0

MOISO, JEROME   F   76ERS

PERSONAL: Born June 15, 1978, in Paris, France. ... 6-10/232. (2,08/105,2).
HIGH SCHOOL: INSEP (Paris, France), then Milford (Conn.) Academy.
COLLEGE: UCLA.
TRANSACTIONS/CAREER NOTES: Selected after sophomore season by Boston Celtics in first round (11th pick overall) of 2000 NBA Draft. ... Traded by Celtics to Philadelphia 76ers for F Roshown McLeod and conditional first-round draft choice (August 3, 2001).

COLLEGIATE RECORD

											AVERAGES		
Season Team	G	Min.	FGM	FGA	Pct.	FTM	FTA	Pct.	Reb.	Ast.	Pts.	RPG	APG	PPG
98-99—UCLA.............................	29	689	131	269	.487	48	78	.615	169	26	314	5.8	0.9	10.8
99-00—UCLA.............................	33	972	170	339	.501	87	142	.613	252	40	428	7.6	1.2	13.0
Totals	62	1661	301	608	.495	135	220	.614	421	66	742	6.8	1.1	12.0

Three-point field goals: 1998-99, 4-for-16 (.250). 1999-00, 1-for-6 (.167). Totals, 5-for-22 (.227).

NBA REGULAR-SEASON RECORD

									REBOUNDS								AVERAGES		
Season Team	G	Min.	FGM	FGA	Pct.	FTM	FTA	Pct.	Off.	Def.	Tot.	Ast.	St.	Blk.	TO	Pts.	RPG	APG	PPG
00-01—Boston	24	135	12	30	.400	11	26	.423	12	30	42	3	3	4	18	35	1.8	0.1	1.5

Three-point field goals: 2000-01, 0-for-1.
Personal fouls/disqualifications: 2000-01, 29/0.

M

MONTROSS, ERIC   C   RAPTORS

PERSONAL: Born September 23, 1971, in Indianapolis. ... 7-0/270. (2,13/122,5). ... Full Name: Eric Scott Montross. ... Grandson of Johnny Townsend, forward with Hammond Ciesar All-Americans (1938-39), Indianapolis Kautskys (1941-42), Toledo Jim White Chevrolets (1942-43) and Oshkosh All-Stars (1943-44) of the National Basketball League. ... Name pronounced MON-tross.
HIGH SCHOOL: Lawrence North (Indianapolis).
COLLEGE: North Carolina.
TRANSACTIONS/CAREER NOTES: Selected by Boston Celtics in first round (ninth pick overall) of 1994 NBA Draft. ... Traded by Celtics with 1996 first-round draft choice to Dallas Mavericks for 1996 and 1997 first-round draft choices (June 21, 1996). ... Traded by Mavericks with G Jim Jackson, F/C Chris Gatling, F/G George McCloud and G Sam Cassell to New Jersey Nets for C Shawn Bradley, F Ed O'Bannon, G Khalid Reeves and G Robert Pack (February 17, 1997). ... Traded by Nets with draft rights to F Tim Thomas, draft rights to G Anthony Parker and G Jim Jackson to Philadelphia 76ers for C Michael Cage, G Lucious Harris, F Don MacLean and draft rights to F Keith Van Horn (June 27, 1997). ... Traded by 76ers with G Jerry Stackhouse to Detroit Pistons for C Theo Ratliff, G Aaron McKie and conditional first-round draft choice (December 18, 1997). ... Traded by Pistons with F Jerome Williams to Toronto Raptors for F Corliss Williamson, F Tyrone Corbin, F Kornel David and future first-round draft choice (February 22, 2001).

COLLEGIATE RECORD

NOTES: THE SPORTING NEWS All-America second team (1993, 1994). ... Member of NCAA Division I championship team (1993).

											AVERAGES		
Season Team	G	Min.	FGM	FGA	Pct.	FTM	FTA	Pct.	Reb.	Ast.	Pts.	RPG	APG	PPG
90-91—North Carolina...............	35	531	81	138	.587	41	67	.612	148	11	203	4.2	0.3	5.8
91-92—North Carolina...............	31	784	140	244	.574	68	109	.624	218	18	348	7.0	0.6	11.2
92-93—North Carolina...............	38	1076	222	361	.615	156	228	.684	290	28	600	7.6	0.7	15.8
93-94—North Carolina...............	35	1110	183	327	.560	110	197	.558	285	29	476	8.1	0.8	13.6
Totals	139	3501	626	1070	.585	375	601	.624	941	86	1627	6.8	0.6	11.7

NBA REGULAR-SEASON RECORD

HONORS: NBA All-Rookie second team (1995).

									REBOUNDS								AVERAGES		
Season Team	G	Min.	FGM	FGA	Pct.	FTM	FTA	Pct.	Off.	Def.	Tot.	Ast.	St.	Blk.	TO	Pts.	RPG	APG	PPG
94-95—Boston	78	2315	307	575	.534	167	263	.635	196	370	566	36	29	61	112	781	7.3	0.5	10.0
95-96—Boston	61	1432	196	346	.566	50	133	.376	119	233	352	43	19	29	83	442	5.8	0.7	7.2
96-97—Dallas-N.J...	78	1828	159	349	.456	21	62	.339	181	337	518	61	20	73	77	339	6.6	0.8	4.3
97-98—Phila.-Det........	48	691	61	144	.424	16	40	.400	69	130	199	11	13	27	29	138	4.1	0.2	2.9
98-99—Detroit	46	577	42	80	.525	11	32	.344	45	94	139	14	12	27	16	95	3.0	0.3	2.1
99-00—Detroit	51	332	17	55	.309	6	12	.500	18	54	72	7	6	9	22	40	1.4	0.1	0.8
00-01—Detroit-Tor.	54	649	56	138	.406	8	31	.258	52	121	173	19	11	26	41	120	3.2	0.4	2.2
Totals	416	7824	838	1687	.497	279	573	.487	680	1339	2019	191	110	252	380	1955	4.9	0.5	4.7

Three-point field goals: 1994-95, 0-for-1. 1998-99, 0-for-1. Totals, 0-for-2 (.000).
Personal fouls/disqualifications: 1994-95, 299/10. 1995-96, 181/1. 1996-97, 268/5. 1997-98, 127/1. 1998-99, 107/1. 1999-00, 81/0. 2000-01, 115/0. Totals, 1178/18.

NBA PLAYOFF RECORD

Season Team	G	Min.	FGM	FGA	Pct.	FTM	FTA	Pct.	REBOUNDS Off.	Def.	Tot.	Ast.	St.	Blk.	TO	Pts.	AVERAGES RPG	APG	PPG
94-95—Boston	4	62	5	11	.455	3	6	.500	7	2	9	0	0	0	8	13	2.3	0.0	3.3
98-99—Detroit	5	70	3	6	.500	1	2	.500	3	10	13	0	0	2	0	7	2.6	0.0	1.4
99-00—Detroit	2	5	0	0	...	0	0	...	0	2	2	0	0	0	0	0	1.0	0.0	0.0
00-01—Toronto	5	31	2	5	.400	0	0	...	5	5	10	1	0	3	2	4	2.0	0.2	0.8
Totals	16	168	10	22	.455	4	8	.500	15	19	34	1	0	5	10	24	2.1	0.1	1.5

Personal fouls/disqualifications: 1994-95, 13/0. 1998-99, 15/0. 1999-00, 2/0. 2000-01, 6/0. Totals, 36/0.

MOORE, MIKKI   C   PISTONS

PERSONAL: Born November 4, 1975, in Orangeburg, S.C. ... 7-0/225. (2,13/102,1).
HIGH SCHOOL: Blackburg (Gaffney, S.C.).
COLLEGE: Nebraska.
TRANSACTIONS/CAREER NOTES: Not drafted by an NBA franchise. ... Signed as free agent by Minnesota Timberwolves (September 30, 1997). ... Waived by Timberwolves (October 28, 1997). ... Played in Continental Basketball Association with Fort Wayne Fury (1997-98 and 1998-99). ... Played in Greece (1998-99). ... Signed as free agent by Minnesota Timberwolves (January 21, 1999). ... Waived by Timberwolves (January 27, 1999). ... Signed as free agent by Detroit Pistons (January 29, 1999). ... Waived by Pistons (February 18, 1999). ... Signed as free agent by Pistons (October 5, 1999).

COLLEGIATE RECORD

Season Team	G	Min.	FGM	FGA	Pct.	FTM	FTA	Pct.	Reb.	Ast.	Pts.	AVERAGES RPG	APG	PPG
93-94—Nebraska	14	87	10	22	.455	11	18	.611	13	1	31	0.9	0.1	2.2
94-95—Nebraska	32	788	102	205	.498	49	89	.551	198	25	255	6.2	0.8	8.0
95-96—Nebraska	35	968	118	202	.584	79	115	.687	205	36	315	5.9	1.0	9.0
96-97—Nebraska	33	1011	144	247	.583	96	137	.701	245	43	385	7.4	1.3	11.7
Totals	114	2854	374	676	.553	235	359	.655	661	105	986	5.8	0.9	8.6

Three-point field goals: 1993-94, 0-for-2. 1994-95, 2-for-8 (.250). 1996-97, 1-for-2 (.500). Totals, 3-for-12 (.250).

CBA REGULAR-SEASON RECORD

NOTES: CBA All-League first team (1999). ... CBA All-Defensive team (1999). ... CBA All-Rookie team (1998).

Season Team	G	Min.	FGM	FGA	Pct.	FTM	FTA	Pct.	Reb.	Ast.	Pts.	AVERAGES RPG	APG	PPG
97-98—Fort Wayne	55	1478	262	450	.582	122	174	.701	346	60	647	6.3	1.1	11.8
98-99—Fort Wayne	29	1026	156	277	.563	143	195	.733	219	41	455	7.6	1.4	15.7
Totals	84	2504	418	727	.575	265	369	.718	565	101	1102	6.7	1.2	13.1

Three-point field goals: 1997-98, 1-for-9 (.111).

GREEK LEAGUE RECORD

Season Team	G	Min.	FGM	FGA	Pct.	FTM	FTA	Pct.	Reb.	Ast.	Pts.	AVERAGES RPG	APG	PPG
98-99—Papagou	9	283	39	71	.549	22	29	.759	78	8	106	8.7	0.9	11.8

Three-point field goals: 1998-99, 6-for-12 (.500).

NBA REGULAR-SEASON RECORD

Season Team	G	Min.	FGM	FGA	Pct.	FTM	FTA	Pct.	REBOUNDS Off.	Def.	Tot.	Ast.	St.	Blk.	TO	Pts.	AVERAGES RPG	APG	PPG
98-99—Detroit	2	6	1	1	1.000	2	2	1.000	0	1	1	0	0	0	0	4	0.5	0.0	2.0
99-00—Detroit	29	488	87	140	.621	54	68	.794	44	68	112	17	9	31	23	228	3.9	0.6	7.9
00-01—Detroit	81	1154	132	268	.493	95	130	.731	121	195	316	33	24	61	74	359	3.9	0.4	4.4
Totals	112	1648	220	409	.538	151	200	.755	165	264	429	50	33	92	97	591	3.8	0.4	5.3

Three-point field goals: 2000-01, 0-for-1. Totals, 0-for-1 (.000).
Personal fouls/disqualifications: 1999-00, 104/5. 2000-01, 202/2. Totals, 306/7.

NBA PLAYOFF RECORD

Season Team	G	Min.	FGM	FGA	Pct.	FTM	FTA	Pct.	REBOUNDS Off.	Def.	Tot.	Ast.	St.	Blk.	TO	Pts.	AVERAGES RPG	APG	PPG
99-00—Detroit	3	42	5	12	.417	8	8	1.000	7	5	12	3	1	0	4	18	4.0	1.0	6.0

Personal fouls/disqualifications: 1999-00, 9/0.

MOTTOLA, HANNO   F   HAWKS

PERSONAL: Born September 9, 1976, in Helsinki, Finland. ... 6-11/247. (2,11/112,0). ... Full Name: Hanno Aleksanteri Mottola.
HIGH SCHOOL: Makelanrinne (Helsinki, Finland).
COLLEGE: Utah.
TRANSACTIONS/CAREER NOTES: Selected by Atlanta Hawks in second round (40th pick overall) of 2000 NBA Draft.

COLLEGIATE RECORD

Season Team	G	Min.	FGM	FGA	Pct.	FTM	FTA	Pct.	Reb.	Ast.	Pts.	AVERAGES RPG	APG	PPG
96-97—Utah	32	560	78	133	.586	48	77	.623	91	29	204	2.8	0.9	6.4
97-98—Utah	34	958	158	323	.489	92	122	.754	181	27	424	5.3	0.8	12.5
98-99—Utah	33	1023	186	386	.482	100	120	.833	178	47	506	5.4	1.4	15.3
99-00—Utah	21	579	116	233	.498	105	127	.827	101	36	358	4.8	1.7	17.0
Totals	120	3120	538	1075	.500	345	446	.774	551	139	1492	4.6	1.2	12.4

Three-point field goals: 1996-97, 0-for-2. 1997-98, 16-for-55 (.291). 1998-99, 34-for-96 (.354). 1999-00, 21-for-60 (.350). Totals, 71-for-213 (.333).

M

NBA REGULAR-SEASON RECORD

Season Team	G	Min.	FGM	FGA	Pct.	FTM	FTA	Pct.	REBOUNDS Off.	Def.	Tot.	Ast.	St.	Blk.	TO	Pts.	AVERAGES RPG	APG	PPG
00-01—Atlanta	73	989	123	277	.444	73	90	.811	49	125	174	25	11	9	67	319	2.4	0.3	4.4

Three-point field goals: 2000-01, 0-for-3.
Personal fouls/disqualifications: 2000-01, 163/3.

MOURNING, ALONZO   C   HEAT

PERSONAL: Born February 8, 1970, in Chesapeake, Va. ... 6-10/261. (2,08/118,4).
HIGH SCHOOL: Indian River (Chesapeake, Va.).
COLLEGE: Georgetown.
TRANSACTIONS/CAREER NOTES: Selected by Charlotte Hornets in first round (second pick overall) of 1992 NBA Draft. ... Traded by Hornets with C LeRon Ellis and G Pete Myers to Miami Heat for G/F Glen Rice, G Khalid Reeves, C Matt Geiger and 1996 first-round draft choice (November 3, 1995).
MISCELLANEOUS: Member of gold-medal-winning U.S. Olympic team (2000). ... Member of bronze-medal-winning U.S. World Championship team (1990) and gold-medal-winning U.S. World Championship team (1994). ... Charlotte Hornets all-time blocked shots leader with 684 (1992-93 through 1994-95). ... Miami Heat all-time blocked shots leader with 1,013 (1995-96 through 2000-01).

COLLEGIATE RECORD

NOTES: THE SPORTING NEWS All-America second team (1990, 1992). ... Led NCAA Division I with 4.97 blocked shots per game (1989). ... Led NCAA Division I in blocked shots with 169 (1989) and 160 (1992).

Season Team	G	Min.	FGM	FGA	Pct.	FTM	FTA	Pct.	Reb.	Ast.	Pts.	AVERAGES RPG	APG	PPG
88-89—Georgetown...................	34	962	158	262	.603	130	195	.667	248	24	447	7.3	0.7	13.1
89-90—Georgetown...................	31	937	145	276	.525	220	281	.783	265	36	510	8.5	1.2	16.5
90-91—Georgetown...................	23	682	105	201	.522	149	188	.793	176	25	363	7.7	1.1	15.8
91-92—Georgetown...................	32	1051	204	343	.595	272	359	.758	343	53	681	10.7	1.7	21.3
Totals	120	3632	612	1082	.566	771	1023	.754	1032	138	2001	8.6	1.2	16.7

Three-point field goals: 1988-89, 1-for-4 (.250). 1989-90, 0-for-2. 1990-91, 4-for-13 (.308). 1991-92, 6-for-23 (.261). Totals, 11-for-42 (.262).

NBA REGULAR-SEASON RECORD

HONORS: NBA Defensive Player of the Year (1999, 2000). ... All-NBA first team (1999). ... All-NBA second team (2000). ... NBA All-Defensive first team (1999, 2000). ... NBA All-Rookie first team (1993).
NOTES: Led NBA with 3.91 blocked shots per game (1999) and 3.7 blocks per game (2000).

Season Team	G	Min.	FGM	FGA	Pct.	FTM	FTA	Pct.	REBOUNDS Off.	Def.	Tot.	Ast.	St.	Blk.	TO	Pts.	AVERAGES RPG	APG	PPG
92-93—Charlotte........	78	2644	572	1119	.511	495	634	.781	263	542	805	76	27	271	236	1639	10.3	1.0	21.0
93-94—Charlotte........	60	2018	427	845	.505	433	568	.762	177	433	610	86	27	188	199	1287	10.2	1.4	21.5
94-95—Charlotte........	77	2941	571	1101	.519	490	644	.761	200	561	761	111	49	225	241	1643	9.9	1.4	21.3
95-96—Miami	70	2671	563	1076	.523	488	712	.685	218	509	727	159	70	189	262	1623	10.4	2.3	23.2
96-97—Miami	66	2320	473	885	.534	363	565	.642	189	467	656	104	56	189	226	1310	9.9	1.6	19.8
97-98—Miami	58	1939	403	732	.551	309	465	.665	193	365	558	52	40	130	179	1115	9.6	0.9	19.2
98-99—Miami	46	1753	324	634	.511	276	423	.652	166	341	507	74	34	*180	139	924	11.0	1.6	20.1
99-00—Miami	79	2748	652	1184	.551	414	582	.711	215	538	753	123	40	*294	217	1718	9.5	1.6	21.7
00-01—Miami	13	306	73	141	.518	31	55	.564	35	66	101	12	4	31	28	177	7.8	0.9	13.6
Totals	547	19340	4058	7717	.526	3299	4648	.710	1656	3822	5478	797	347	1697	1727	11436	10.0	1.5	20.9

Three-point field goals: 1992-93, 0-for-3. 1993-94, 0-for-2. 1994-95, 11-for-34 (.324). 1995-96, 9-for-30 (.300). 1996-97, 1-for-9 (.111). 1998-99, 0-for-2. 1999-00, 0-for-4. 2000-01, 0-for-1. Totals, 21-for-85 (.247).
Personal fouls/disqualifications: 1992-93, 286/6. 1993-94, 207/3. 1994-95, 275/5. 1995-96, 245/5. 1996-97, 272/9. 1997-98, 208/4. 1998-99, 161/1. 1999-00, 308/8. 2000-01, 24/0. Totals, 1986/41.

NBA PLAYOFF RECORD

Season Team	G	Min.	FGM	FGA	Pct.	FTM	FTA	Pct.	REBOUNDS Off.	Def.	Tot.	Ast.	St.	Blk.	TO	Pts.	AVERAGES RPG	APG	PPG
92-93—Charlotte........	9	367	71	148	.480	72	93	.774	28	61	89	13	6	31	37	214	9.9	1.4	23.8
94-95—Charlotte........	4	174	24	57	.421	36	43	.837	14	39	53	11	3	13	14	88	13.3	2.8	22.0
95-96—Miami	3	92	17	35	.486	20	28	.714	3	15	18	4	2	3	16	54	6.0	1.3	18.0
96-97—Miami	17	630	107	218	.491	86	155	.555	44	129	173	18	11	46	70	303	10.2	1.1	17.8
97-98—Miami	4	138	29	56	.518	19	29	.655	10	24	34	5	3	10	8	77	8.5	1.3	19.3
98-99—Miami	5	194	38	73	.521	32	49	.653	7	34	41	4	8	14	12	108	8.2	0.8	21.6
99-00—Miami	10	376	76	157	.484	64	96	.667	31	69	100	14	2	33	24	216	10.0	1.4	21.6
00-01—Miami	3	91	12	25	.480	11	19	.579	3	13	16	3	0	5	5	35	5.3	1.0	11.7
Totals	55	2062	374	769	.486	340	512	.664	140	384	524	72	35	155	186	1095	9.5	1.3	19.9

Three-point field goals: 1992-93, 0-for-2. 1994-95, 4-for-8 (.500). 1996-97, 3-for-8 (.375). 1999-00, 0-for-1. Totals, 7-for-19 (.368).
Personal fouls/disqualifications: 1992-93, 37/1. 1994-95, 17/0. 1995-96, 13/1. 1996-97, 73/2. 1997-98, 18/0. 1998-99, 19/0. 1999-00, 40/1. 2000-01, 9/0. Totals, 226/5.

NBA ALL-STAR GAME RECORD

Season Team	Min.	FGM	FGA	Pct.	FTM	FTA	Pct.	REBOUNDS Off.	Def.	Tot.	Ast.	PF	Dq.	St.	Blk.	TO	Pts.
1994 —Charlotte						Selected, did not play—injured.											
1995 —Charlotte..........	19	4	9	.444	2	3	.667	0	8	8	1	5	0	0	1	1	10
1996 —Miami................	13	1	6	.167	0	0	...	0	1	1	0	2	0	0	1	2	2
1997 —Miami................						Selected, did not play—injured.											
2000 —Miami................	27	7	11	.636	1	2	.500	2	5	7	1	4	0	3	4	1	15
2001 —Miami................						Selected, did not play—injured.											
Totals	59	12	26	.462	3	5	.600	2	14	16	2	11	0	3	6	4	27

Three-point field goals: 1995, 0-for-1. Totals, 0-for-1 (.000).

MULLIN, CHRIS F

PERSONAL: Born July 30, 1963, in New York. ... 6-7/215. (2,01/97,5). ... Full Name: Christopher Paul Mullin.
HIGH SCHOOL: Power Memorial (New York), then Xaverian (Brooklyn, N.Y.).
COLLEGE: St. John's.
TRANSACTIONS/CAREER NOTES: Selected by Golden State Warriors in first round (seventh pick overall) of 1985 NBA Draft. ... Traded by Warriors to Indiana Pacers for C Erick Dampier and F Duane Ferrell (August 12, 1997). ... Waived by Pacers (September 12, 2000). ... Signed as free agent by Warriors (September 28, 2000).
MISCELLANEOUS: Member of gold-medal-winning U.S. Olympic team (1984, 1992). ... Golden State Warriors franchise all-time steals leader with 1,376 (1985-86 through 1996-97 and 2000-01).

COLLEGIATE RECORD

NOTES: Wooden Award winner (1985). ... THE SPORTING NEWS All-America first team (1985). ... THE SPORTING NEWS All-America second team (1984).

Season Team	G	Min.	FGM	FGA	Pct.	FTM	FTA	Pct.	Reb.	Ast.	Pts.	RPG	APG	PPG
81-82—St. John's	30	1061	175	328	.534	148	187	.791	97	92	498	3.2	3.1	16.6
82-83—St. John's	33	1210	228	395	.577	173	197	.878	123	101	629	3.7	3.1	19.1
83-84—St. John's	27	1070	225	394	.571	169	187	.904	120	109	619	4.4	4.0	22.9
84-85—St. John's	35	1327	251	482	.521	192	233	.824	169	151	694	4.8	4.3	19.8
Totals	125	4668	879	1599	.550	682	804	.848	509	453	2440	4.1	3.6	19.5

NBA REGULAR-SEASON RECORD

HONORS: All-NBA first team (1992). ... All-NBA second team (1989, 1991). ... All-NBA third team (1990).

Season Team	G	Min.	FGM	FGA	Pct.	FTM	FTA	Pct.	Off.	Def.	Tot.	Ast.	St.	Blk.	TO	Pts.	RPG	APG	PPG
85-86—Golden State	55	1391	287	620	.463	189	211	.896	42	73	115	105	70	23	75	768	2.1	1.9	14.0
86-87—Golden State	82	2377	477	928	.514	269	326	.825	39	142	181	261	98	36	154	1242	2.2	3.2	15.1
87-88—Golden State	60	2033	470	926	.508	239	270	.885	58	147	205	290	113	32	156	1213	3.4	4.8	20.2
88-89—Golden State	82	3093	830	1630	.509	493	553	.892	152	331	483	415	176	39	296	2176	5.9	5.1	26.5
89-90—Golden State	78	2830	682	1272	.536	505	568	.889	130	333	463	319	123	45	239	1956	5.9	4.1	25.1
90-91—Golden State	82	*3315	777	1449	.536	513	580	.884	141	302	443	329	173	63	245	2107	5.4	4.0	25.7
91-92—Golden State	81	*3346	830	1584	.524	350	420	.833	127	323	450	286	173	62	202	2074	5.6	3.5	25.6
92-93—Golden State	46	1902	474	930	.510	183	226	.810	42	190	232	166	68	41	139	1191	5.0	3.6	25.9
93-94—Golden State	62	2324	410	869	.472	165	219	.753	64	281	345	315	107	53	178	1040	5.6	5.1	16.8
94-95—Golden State	25	890	170	348	.489	94	107	.879	25	90	115	125	38	19	93	476	4.6	5.0	19.0
95-96—Golden State	55	1617	269	539	.499	137	160	.856	44	115	159	194	75	32	122	734	2.9	3.5	13.3
96-97—Golden State	79	2733	438	792	.553	184	213	.864	75	242	317	322	130	33	192	1143	4.0	4.1	14.5
97-98—Indiana	82	2177	333	692	.481	154	164	*.939	38	211	249	186	95	39	117	921	3.0	2.3	11.3
98-99—Indiana	50	1179	177	371	.477	80	92	.870	25	135	160	81	47	13	60	507	3.2	1.6	10.1
99-00—Indiana	47	582	80	187	.428	37	41	.902	14	62	76	37	28	9	28	242	1.6	0.8	5.1
00-01—Golden State	20	374	36	106	.340	24	28	.857	10	31	41	19	16	10	19	115	2.1	1.0	5.8
Totals	986	32163	6740	13243	.509	3616	4178	.865	1026	3008	4034	3450	1530	549	2315	17911	4.1	3.5	18.2

Three-point field goals: 1985-86, 5-for-27 (.185). 1986-87, 19-for-63 (.302). 1987-88, 34-for-97 (.351). 1988-89, 23-for-100 (.230). 1989-90, 87-for-234 (.372). 1990-91, 40-for-133 (.301). 1991-92, 64-for-175 (.366). 1992-93, 60-for-133 (.451). 1993-94, 55-for-151 (.364). 1994-95, 42-for-93 (.452). 1995-96, 59-for-150 (.393). 1996-97, 83-for-202 (.411). 1997-98, 107-for-243 (.440). 1998-99, 73-for-157 (.465). 1999-00, 45-for-110 (.409). 2000-01, 19-for-52 (.365). Totals, 815-for-2120 (.384).

Personal fouls/disqualifications: 1985-86, 130/1. 1986-87, 217/1. 1987-88, 136/3. 1988-89, 178/1. 1989-90, 142/1. 1990-91, 176/2. 1991-92, 171/1. 1992-93, 76/0. 1993-94, 114/0. 1994-95, 53/0. 1995-96, 127/0. 1996-97, 155/0. 1997-98, 186/0. 1998-99, 101/0. 1999-00, 60/0. 2000-01, 28/0. Totals, 2050/10.

NBA PLAYOFF RECORD

Season Team	G	Min.	FGM	FGA	Pct.	FTM	FTA	Pct.	Off.	Def.	Tot.	Ast.	St.	Blk.	TO	Pts.	RPG	APG	PPG
86-87—Golden State	10	262	49	98	.500	12	16	.750	2	13	15	23	9	2	16	113	1.5	2.3	11.3
88-89—Golden State	8	341	88	163	.540	58	67	.866	11	36	47	36	14	11	32	235	5.9	4.5	29.4
90-91—Golden State	8	366	69	131	.527	43	50	.860	9	49	58	23	15	12	25	190	7.3	2.9	23.8
91-92—Golden State	4	168	27	63	.429	13	14	.929	3	9	12	12	5	2	8	71	3.0	3.0	17.8
93-94—Golden State	3	135	30	51	.588	10	11	.909	4	10	14	11	0	5	7	76	4.7	3.7	25.3
97-98—Indiana	16	412	52	113	.460	18	21	.857	13	44	57	23	15	9	24	142	3.6	1.4	8.9
98-99—Indiana	13	283	41	100	.410	20	23	.870	2	18	20	15	10	3	20	124	1.5	1.2	9.5
99-00—Indiana	9	90	10	21	.476	9	11	.818	2	12	14	5	6	1	4	31	1.6	0.6	3.4
Totals	71	2057	366	740	.495	183	213	.860	46	101	237	148	74	45	136	902	3.3	2.1	13.8

Three-point field goals: 1986-87, 3-for-4 (.750). 1988-89, 1-for-8 (.125). 1990-91, 9-for-13 (.692). 1991-92, 4-for-12 (.333). 1993-94, 6-for-12 (.500). 1997-98, 20-for-52 (.385). 1998-99, 22-for-55 (.400). 1999-00, 2-for-8 (.250). Totals, 67-for-164 (.409).

Personal fouls/disqualifications: 1986-87, 31/0. 1988-89, 19/0. 1990-91, 23/0. 1991-92, 8/0. 1993-94, 4/0. 1997-98, 32/0. 1998-99, 21/0. 1999-00, 7/0. Totals, 145/0.

NBA ALL-STAR GAME RECORD

Season Team	Min.	FGM	FGA	Pct.	FTM	FTA	Pct.	Off.	Def.	Tot.	Ast.	PF	Dq.	St.	Blk.	TO	Pts.
1989 —Golden State	14	1	4	.250	2	2	1.000	2	0	2	2	0	0	0	0	1	4
1990 —Golden State	16	1	5	.200	1	2	.500	1	2	3	1	0	0	2	1	1	3
1991 —Golden State	24	4	8	.500	4	4	1.000	0	2	2	2	2	0	2	0	2	13
1992 —Golden State	24	6	7	.857	0	0	...	0	1	1	3	0	0	0	0	1	13
1993 —Golden State							Selected, did not play—injured.										
Totals	78	12	24	.500	7	8	.875	3	5	8	8	2	0	4	1	5	33

Three-point field goals: 1991, 1-for-1. 1992, 1-for-1. Totals, 2-for-2 (1.000).

M

MURRAY, LAMOND F CAVALIERS

PERSONAL: Born April 20, 1973, in Pasadena, Calif. ... 6-7/236. (2,01/107,0). ... Full Name: Lamond Maurice Murray. ... Cousin of Tracy Murray, forward, Toronto Raptors.
HIGH SCHOOL: John Kennedy (Fremont, Calif.).
COLLEGE: California.
TRANSACTIONS/CAREER NOTES: Selected after junior season by Los Angeles Clippers in first round (seventh pick overall) of 1994 NBA Draft. ... Traded by Clippers to Cleveland Cavaliers for G Derek Anderson and F Johnny Newman (August 4, 1999).

COLLEGIATE RECORD

Season Team	G	Min.	FGM	FGA	Pct.	FTM	FTA	Pct.	Reb.	Ast.	Pts.	RPG	APG	PPG
91-92—California	28	745	152	321	.474	66	93	.710	171	56	387	6.1	2.0	13.8
92-93—California	30	897	230	445	.517	76	121	.628	189	41	572	6.3	1.4	19.1
93-94—California	30	1047	262	550	.476	159	208	.764	236	63	729	7.9	2.1	24.3
Totals	88	2689	644	1316	.489	301	422	.713	596	160	1688	6.8	1.8	19.2

Three-point field goals: 1991-92, 17-for-56 (.304). 1992-93, 36-for-99 (.364). 1993-94, 46-for-139 (.331). Totals, 99-for-294 (.337).

NBA REGULAR-SEASON RECORD

Season Team	G	Min.	FGM	FGA	Pct.	FTM	FTA	Pct.	Off.	Def.	Tot.	Ast.	St.	Blk.	TO	Pts.	RPG	APG	PPG
94-95—L.A. Clippers	81	2556	439	1093	.402	199	264	.754	132	222	354	133	72	55	163	1142	4.4	1.6	14.1
95-96—L.A. Clippers	77	1816	257	575	.447	99	132	.750	89	157	246	84	61	25	108	650	3.2	1.1	8.4
96-97—L.A. Clippers	74	1295	181	435	.416	156	211	.739	85	148	233	57	53	29	86	549	3.1	0.8	7.4
97-98—L.A. Clippers	79	2579	473	984	.481	220	294	.748	172	312	484	142	118	54	171	1220	6.1	1.8	15.4
98-99—L.A. Clippers	50	1317	226	578	.391	126	157	.803	59	136	195	61	58	20	99	612	3.9	1.2	12.2
99-00—Cleveland	74	2365	460	1019	.451	204	268	.761	127	296	423	132	105	36	184	1175	5.7	1.8	15.9
00-01—Cleveland	78	2225	391	925	.423	155	211	.735	104	236	340	124	83	27	141	998	4.4	1.6	12.8
Totals	513	14153	2427	5609	.433	1159	1537	.754	768	1507	2275	733	550	246	952	6346	4.4	1.4	12.4

Three-point field goals: 1994-95, 65-for-218 (.298). 1995-96, 37-for-116 (.319). 1996-97, 31-for-91 (.341). 1997-98, 54-for-153 (.353). 1998-99, 34-for-103 (.330). 1999-00, 51-for-139 (.367). 2000-01, 61-for-165 (.370). Totals, 333-for-985 (.338).
Personal fouls/disqualifications: 1994-95, 180/3. 1995-96, 151/0. 1996-97, 113/3. 1997-98, 193/3. 1998-99, 107/1. 1999-00, 208/2. 2000-01, 173/0. Totals, 1125/12.

NBA PLAYOFF RECORD

Season Team	G	Min.	FGM	FGA	Pct.	FTM	FTA	Pct.	Off.	Def.	Tot.	Ast.	St.	Blk.	TO	Pts.	RPG	APG	PPG
96-97—L.A. Clippers	3	65	6	20	.300	7	7	1.000	2	9	11	3	2	3	4	21	3.7	1.0	7.0

Three-point field goals: 1996-97, 2-for-8 (.250).
Personal fouls/disqualifications: 1996-97, 7/0.

M

MURRAY, TRACY F RAPTORS

PERSONAL: Born July 25, 1971, in Los Angeles. ... 6-7/228. (2,01/103,4). ... Full Name: Tracy Lamonte Murray. ... Cousin of Lamond Murray, forward, Cleveland Cavaliers.
HIGH SCHOOL: Glendora (Calif.).
COLLEGE: UCLA.
TRANSACTIONS/CAREER NOTES: Selected after junior season by San Antonio Spurs in first round (18th pick overall) of 1992 NBA Draft. ... Draft rights traded by Spurs to Milwaukee Bucks for G/F Dale Ellis (July 1, 1992). ... Draft rights traded by Bucks to Portland Trail Blazers for F Alaa Abdelnaby (July 1, 1992). ... Traded by Trail Blazers with G Clyde Drexler to Houston Rockets for F Otis Thorpe, rights to F Marcelo Nicola and 1995 first-round draft choice (February 14, 1995). ... Signed as free agent by Toronto Raptors (November 1, 1995). ... Signed as free agent by Washington Bullets (July 15, 1996). ... Bullets franchise renamed Washington Wizards for 1997-98 season. ... Traded by Wizards to Denver Nuggets F Popeye Jones and second-round draft choice (September 25, 2000). ... Traded by Nuggets with F/C Keon Clark and C Mamadou N'diaye to Toronto Raptors for F/C Kevin Willis, C Aleksandar Radojevic, C Garth Joseph and 2001 or 2002 second-round draft choice (January 12, 2001).

COLLEGIATE RECORD

Season Team	G	Min.	FGM	FGA	Pct.	FTM	FTA	Pct.	Reb.	Ast.	Pts.	RPG	APG	PPG
89-90—UCLA	33	863	146	330	.442	69	90	.767	182	41	407	5.5	1.2	12.3
90-91—UCLA	32	1003	247	491	.503	112	141	.794	213	43	679	6.7	1.3	21.2
91-92—UCLA	33	1083	240	446	.538	148	185	.800	232	59	706	7.0	1.8	21.4
Totals	98	2949	633	1267	.500	329	416	.791	627	143	1792	6.4	1.5	18.3

Three-point field goals: 1989-90, 46-for-134 (.343). 1990-91, 73-for-189 (.386). 1991-92, 78-for-156 (.500). Totals, 197-for-479 (.411).

NBA REGULAR-SEASON RECORD

NOTES: Led NBA with .459 three-point field goal percentage (1994).

Season Team	G	Min.	FGM	FGA	Pct.	FTM	FTA	Pct.	Off.	Def.	Tot.	Ast.	St.	Blk.	TO	Pts.	RPG	APG	PPG
92-93—Portland	48	495	108	260	.415	35	40	.875	40	43	83	11	8	5	31	272	1.7	0.2	5.7
93-94—Portland	66	820	167	355	.470	50	72	.694	43	68	111	31	21	20	37	434	1.7	0.5	6.6
94-95—Port.-Houston	54	516	95	233	.408	33	42	.786	20	39	59	14	4	35	258	1.1	0.4	4.8
95-96—Toronto	82	2458	496	1092	.454	182	219	.831	114	238	352	131	87	40	132	1325	4.3	1.6	16.2
96-97—Washington	82	1814	288	678	.425	135	161	.839	84	169	253	78	69	19	86	817	3.1	1.0	10.0
97-98—Washington	82	2227	449	1007	.446	182	209	.871	75	202	277	84	67	25	102	1238	3.4	1.0	15.1
98-99—Washington	36	653	83	237	.350	34	42	.810	18	63	81	27	21	6	29	233	2.3	0.8	6.5
99-00—Washington	80	1831	290	670	.433	120	141	.851	63	208	271	72	45	24	84	813	3.4	0.9	10.2
00-01—Denver-Tor.	51	588	94	248	.379	33	42	.786	22	59	81	23	12	7	26	257	1.6	0.5	5.0
Totals	581	11402	2070	4780	.433	804	968	.831	479	1089	1568	476	344	150	562	5647	2.7	0.8	9.7

Three-point field goals: 1992-93, 21-for-70 (.300). 1993-94, 50-for-109 (.459). 1994-95, 35-for-86 (.407). 1995-96, 151-for-358 (.422). 1996-97, 106-for-300 (.353). 1997-98, 158-for-403 (.392). 1998-99, 33-for-103 (.320). 1999-00, 113-for-263 (.430). 2000-01, 36-for-103 (.350). Totals, 703-for-1795 (.392).

Personal fouls/disqualifications: 1992-93, 59/0. 1993-94, 76/0. 1994-95, 73/0. 1995-96, 208/2. 1996-97, 150/1. 1997-98, 167/0. 1998-99, 65/0. 1999-00, 185/2. 2000-01, 53/0. Totals, 1036/5.

NBA PLAYOFF RECORD

								REBOUNDS							AVERAGES		
Season Team	G	Min.	FGM	FGA	Pct.	FTM	FTA	Pct.	Off.	Def.	Tot.	Ast.	St.	Blk.	TO	Pts.	RPG APG PPG
93-94—Portland.........	2	11	3	6	.500	0	0	...	3	0	3	1	1	0	0	6	1.5 0.5 3.0
96-97—Washington	3	87	17	30	.567	16	17	.941	3	6	9	2	4	2	0	55	3.0 0.7 18.3
00-01—Toronto..........	2	5	1	3	.333	0	0	...	0	0	0	1	0	2	2	2	0.0 0.0 1.0
Totals	7	103	21	39	.538	16	17	.941	6	6	12	3	6	2	2	63	1.7 0.4 9.0

Three-point field goals: 1993-94, 0-for-1. 1996-97, 5-for-10 (.500). 2000-01, 0-for-2. Totals, 5-for-13 (.385).
Personal fouls/disqualifications: 1993-94, 3/0. 1996-97, 10/0. 2000-01, 1/0. Totals, 14/0.

MUTOMBO, DIKEMBE   C   76ERS

PERSONAL: Born June 25, 1966, in Kinshasa, Zaire. ... 7-2/261. (2,18/118,4). ... Name pronounced di-KEM-bay moo-TUM-bow.
HIGH SCHOOL: Institute Boboto (Kinshasa, Zaire).
COLLEGE: Georgetown.
TRANSACTIONS/CAREER NOTES: Selected by Denver Nuggets in first round (fourth pick overall) of 1991 NBA Draft. ... Signed as free agent by Atlanta Hawks (July 15, 1996). ... Traded by Hawks with F Roshown McLeod to Philadelphia 76ers for F/C Theo Ratliff, F/G Toni Kukoc, G Nazr Mohammed and G Pepe Sanchez (February 22, 2001).
MISCELLANEOUS: Denver Nuggets franchise all-time blocked shots leader with 1,486 (1991-92 through 1995-96).

COLLEGIATE RECORD

NOTES: THE SPORTING NEWS All-America third team (1991).

											AVERAGES		
Season Team	G	Min.	FGM	FGA	Pct.	FTM	FTA	Pct.	Reb.	Ast.	Pts.	RPG APG PPG
87-88—Georgetown..................							Did not play.					
88-89—Georgetown..................	33	374	53	75	.707	23	48	.479	109	5	129	3.3 0.2 3.9
89-90—Georgetown..................	31	797	129	182	.709	73	122	.598	325	18	331	10.5 0.6 10.7
90-91—Georgetown..................	32	1090	170	290	.586	147	209	.703	389	52	487	12.2 1.6 15.2
Totals	96	2261	352	547	.644	243	379	.641	823	75	947	8.6 0.8 9.9

NBA REGULAR-SEASON RECORD

RECORDS: Holds career record for most consecutive seasons leading league in blocked shots per game—3 (1993-94 through 1995-96).
HONORS: J. Walter Kennedy Citizenship Award (2001). ... NBA Defensive Player of the Year (1995, 1997, 1998, 2001). ... IBM Award, for all-around contributions to team's success (1999). ... All-NBA second team (2001). ... All-NBA third team (1998). ... NBA All-Defensive first team (1997, 1998, 2001). ... NBA All-Defensive second team (1995, 1999). ... NBA All-Rookie first team (1992).
NOTES: Led NBA with 4.10 blocked shots per game (1994), 3.91 blocked shots per game (1995) and 4.49 blocked shots per game (1996).

									REBOUNDS								AVERAGES		
Season Team	G	Min.	FGM	FGA	Pct.	FTM	FTA	Pct.	Off.	Def.	Tot.	Ast.	St.	Blk.	TO	Pts.	RPG	APG	PPG
91-92—Denver	71	2716	428	869	.493	321	500	.642	316	554	870	156	43	210	252	1177	12.3	2.2	16.6
92-93—Denver	82	3029	398	781	.510	335	492	.681	344	726	1070	147	43	287	216	1131	13.0	1.8	13.8
93-94—Denver	82	2853	365	642	.569	256	439	.583	286	685	971	127	59	*336	206	986	11.8	1.5	12.0
94-95—Denver	82	3100	349	628	.556	248	379	.654	319	710	*1029	113	40	*321	192	946	12.5	1.4	11.5
95-96—Denver	74	2713	284	569	.499	246	354	.695	249	622	871	108	38	*332	150	814	11.8	1.5	11.0
96-97—Atlanta	80	2973	380	721	.527	306	434	.705	268	661	929	110	49	*264	186	1066	11.6	1.4	13.3
97-98—Atlanta	82	2917	399	743	.537	303	452	.670	276	656	932	82	34	277	168	1101	11.4	1.0	13.4
98-99—Atlanta	50	1829	173	338	.512	195	285	.684	192	*418	*610	57	16	147	94	541	12.2	1.1	10.8
99-00—Atlanta	82	2984	322	573	.562	298	421	.708	304	*853	*1157	105	27	269	174	942	*14.1	1.3	11.5
00-01—Atlanta-Phil.	75	2591	269	556	.484	211	291	.725	*307	708	1015	76	29	203	144	749	*13.5	1.0	10.0
Totals	760	27705	3367	6420	.524	2719	4047	.672	2861	6593	9454	1081	378	2646	1782	9453	12.4	1.4	12.4

Three-point field goals: 1993-94, 0-for-1. 1995-96, 0-for-1. Totals, 0-for-2 (.000).
Personal fouls/disqualifications: 1991-92, 273/1. 1992-93, 284/5. 1993-94, 262/2. 1994-95, 284/2. 1995-96, 258/4. 1996-97, 249/3. 1997-98, 254/1. 1998-99, 145/2. 1999-00, 248/3. 2000-01, 204/2. Totals, 2461/25.

NBA PLAYOFF RECORD

									REBOUNDS								AVERAGES		
Season Team	G	Min.	FGM	FGA	Pct.	FTM	FTA	Pct.	Off.	Def.	Tot.	Ast.	St.	Blk.	TO	Pts.	RPG	APG	PPG
93-94—Denver	12	511	50	108	.463	59	98	.602	40	104	144	21	8	69	30	159	12.0	1.8	13.3
94-95—Denver	3	84	6	10	.600	6	9	.667	4	15	19	1	0	7	7	18	6.3	0.3	6.0
96-97—Atlanta	10	415	54	86	.628	46	64	.719	37	86	123	13	1	26	20	154	12.3	1.3	15.4
97-98—Atlanta	4	136	11	24	.458	10	16	.625	13	38	51	1	0	9	8	32	12.8	0.3	8.0
98-99—Atlanta	9	380	40	71	.563	33	47	.702	36	89	125	11	5	23	18	113	13.9	1.2	12.6
00-01—Philadelphia	23	981	102	208	.490	115	148	.777	113	203	316	17	15	72	36	319	13.7	0.7	13.9
Totals	61	2507	263	507	.519	269	382	.704	243	535	778	64	30	206	119	795	12.8	1.0	13.0

Three-point field goals: 2000-01, 0-for-1. Totals, 0-for-1 (.000).
Personal fouls/disqualifications: 1993-94, 42/0. 1994-95, 15/1. 1996-97, 30/0. 1997-98, 10/0. 1998-99, 28/0. 2000-01, 56/1. Totals, 181/2.

NBA ALL-STAR GAME RECORD

							REBOUNDS									
Season Team	Min.	FGM	FGA	Pct.	FTM	FTA	Pct.	Off.	Def.	Tot.	Ast.	PF	Dq.	St.	Blk.	TO	Pts.
1992 —Denver..............	10	2	4	.500	0	0	...	1	1	2	1	0	0	1	0	2	4
1995 —Denver..............	20	6	8	.750	0	0	...	3	5	8	1	3	0	0	4	0	12
1996 —Denver..............	11	2	4	.500	0	0	...	6	3	9	0	3	0	0	3	0	4
1997 —Atlanta..............	15	1	5	.200	1	2	.500	2	6	8	0	0	0	0	1	1	3
1998 —Atlanta..............	19	4	5	.800	1	2	.500	1	6	7	0	3	...	0	1	0	9
2000 —Atlanta..............	16	2	4	.500	0	0	...	2	6	8	0	0	0	0	0	2	4
2001 —Atlanta..............	28	2	2	1.000	2	2	1.000	3	19	22	0	5	0	2	3	2	6
Totals..............	119	19	32	.594	4	6	.667	18	46	64	2	14	0	3	9	10	42

N'DIAYE, MAMADOU   C   RAPTORS

PERSONAL: Born June 16, 1975, in Dakar, Senegal. ... 7-0/255. (2,13/115,7).
HIGH SCHOOL: Delafosse (Dakar, Senegal), then Maine Central Institute (Pittsfield, Maine).
COLLEGE: Auburn.
TRANSACTIONS/CAREER NOTES: Selected by Denver Nuggets in first round (26th pick overall) of 2000 NBA Draft. ... Traded by Nuggets with F Tracy Murray, F/C Keon Clark to Toronto Raptors for F/C Kevin Willis, C Aleksandar Radojevic, C Garth Joseph and 2001 or 2002 second-round draft choice (January 12, 2001).

COLLEGIATE RECORD

Season Team	G	Min.	FGM	FGA	Pct.	FTM	FTA	Pct.	Reb.	Ast.	Pts.	RPG	APG	PPG
96-97—Auburn	31	350	42	86	.488	10	19	.526	76	7	94	2.5	0.2	3.0
97-98—Auburn	30	747	89	177	.503	61	99	.616	208	22	239	6.9	0.7	8.0
98-99—Auburn	33	785	88	180	.489	63	97	.649	247	29	239	7.5	0.9	7.2
99-00—Auburn	34	903	100	187	.535	103	155	.665	267	18	303	7.9	0.5	8.9
Totals	128	2785	319	630	.506	237	370	.641	798	76	875	6.2	0.6	6.8

Three-point field goals: 1996-97, 0-for-1. 1998-99, 0-for-1. Totals, 0-for-2 (.000).

NBA REGULAR-SEASON RECORD

Season Team	G	Min.	FGM	FGA	Pct.	FTM	FTA	Pct.	Off.	Def.	Tot.	Ast.	St.	Blk.	TO	Pts.	RPG	APG	PPG
00-01—Toronto	3	10	1	4	.250	2	2	1.000	1	1	2	0	0	0	0	4	0.7	0.0	1.3

Personal fouls/disqualifications: 2000-01, 3/0.

NAILON, LEE   F   HORNETS

PERSONAL: Born February 22, 1975, in South Bend, Ind. ... 6-8/241. (2,03/109,3).
HIGH SCHOOL: Clay (South Bend, Ind.).
JUNIOR COLLEGE: Southeastern Community College (Iowa), then Butler County Community College (Kan.).
COLLEGE: Texas Christian.
TRANSACTIONS/CAREER NOTES: Selected by Charlotte Hornets in second round (43rd pick overall) of 1999 NBA Draft. ... Played in Italy (1999-2000).

COLLEGIATE RECORD

Season Team	G	Min.	FGM	FGA	Pct.	FTM	FTA	Pct.	Reb.	Ast.	Pts.	RPG	APG	PPG
95-96—Southeastern C.C.	31	892	311	500	.622	112	155	.723	252	83	735	8.1	2.7	23.7
96-97—Butler County C.C.	34	887	292	443	.659	101	154	.656	250	117	686	7.4	3.4	20.2
97-98—Texas Christian	32	1066	329	594	.554	137	184	.745	285	61	796	8.9	1.9	24.9
98-99—Texas Christian	31	990	266	524	.508	171	239	.715	288	79	707	9.3	2.5	22.8
Junior College Totals	65	1779	603	943	.639	213	309	.689	502	200	1421	7.7	3.1	21.9
4-Year-College Totals	63	2056	595	1118	.532	308	423	.728	573	140	1503	9.1	2.2	23.9

Three-point field goals: 1995-96, 1-for-13 (.077). 1996-97, 0-for-1. 1997-98, 1-for-2 (.500). 1998-99, 4-for-15 (.267). Totals, 1-for-14 (.071) Totals, 5-for-17 (.294).

ITALIAN LEAGUE RECORD

Season Team	G	Min.	FGM	FGA	Pct.	FTM	FTA	Pct.	Reb.	Ast.	Pts.	RPG	APG	PPG
99-00—Milano	18	584	139	260	.535	45	61	.738	79	30	327	4.4	1.7	18.2

NBA REGULAR-SEASON RECORD

Season Team	G	Min.	FGM	FGA	Pct.	FTM	FTA	Pct.	Off.	Def.	Tot.	Ast.	St.	Blk.	TO	Pts.	RPG	APG	PPG
00-01—Charlotte	42	469	66	136	.485	32	43	.744	29	63	92	24	9	5	27	164	2.2	0.6	3.9

Three-point field goals: 2000-01, 0-for-1.
Personal fouls/disqualifications: 2000-01, 60/0.

NAJERA, EDUARDO   F   MAVERICKS

PERSONAL: Born July 11, 1976, in Meoqui, Chihuahua, Mexico. ... 6-8/240. (2,03/108,9). ... Full Name: Eduardo Alonso Najera.
HIGH SCHOOL: Cornerstone Christian Academy (San Antonio).
COLLEGE: Oklahoma.
TRANSACTIONS/CAREER NOTES: Selected by Houston Rockets in second round (38th pick overall) of 2000 NBA Draft. ... Draft rights traded by Rockets with a future second-round draft pick to Dallas Mavericks for draft rights to F Dan Langhi (June 28, 2000).

COLLEGIATE RECORD

Season Team	G	Min.	FGM	FGA	Pct.	FTM	FTA	Pct.	Reb.	Ast.	Pts.	RPG	APG	PPG
96-97—Oklahoma	30	739	72	178	.404	64	92	.696	167	32	211	5.6	1.1	7.0
97-98—Oklahoma	30	855	119	280	.425	64	101	.634	163	42	315	5.4	1.4	10.5
98-99—Oklahoma	32	1100	187	451	.415	70	109	.642	266	69	495	8.3	2.2	15.5
99-00—Oklahoma	34	1162	234	514	.455	139	202	.688	314	72	625	9.2	2.1	18.4
Totals	126	3856	612	1423	.430	337	504	.669	910	215	1646	7.2	1.7	13.1

Three-point field goals: 1996-97, 3-for-15 (.200). 1997-98, 13-for-49 (.265). 1998-99, 51-for-149 (.342). 1999-00, 18-for-82 (.220). Totals, 85-for-295 (.288).

Season Team	G	Min.	FGM	FGA	Pct.	FTM	FTA	Pct.	REBOUNDS Off.	Def.	Tot.	Ast.	St.	Blk.	TO	Pts.	AVERAGES RPG	APG	PPG
00-01—Dallas	40	431	58	111	.523	14	33	.424	41	54	95	27	13	8	17	131	2.4	0.7	3.3

Three-point field goals: 2000-01, 1-for-3 (.333).
Personal fouls/disqualifications: 2000-01, 48/0.

NBA PLAYOFF RECORD

Season Team	G	Min.	FGM	FGA	Pct.	FTM	FTA	Pct.	REBOUNDS Off.	Def.	Tot.	Ast.	St.	Blk.	TO	Pts.	AVERAGES RPG	APG	PPG
00-01—Dallas	7	44	9	17	.529	0	0	...	7	8	15	1	1	1	1	21	2.1	0.1	3.0

Three-point field goals: 2000-01, 3-for-4 (.750).
Personal fouls/disqualifications: 2000-01, 8/0.

NASH, STEVE   G   MAVERICKS

PERSONAL: Born February 7, 1974, in Johannesburg, South Africa. ... 6-3/195. (1,91/88,5). ... Full Name: Stephen John Nash.
HIGH SCHOOL: St. Michael's Victoria (British Columbia).
COLLEGE: Santa Clara.
TRANSACTIONS/CAREER NOTES: Selected by Phoenix Suns in first round (15th pick overall) of 1996 NBA Draft. ... Traded by Suns to Dallas Mavericks for F Martin Muursepp, G/F Bubba Wells, draft rights to F Pat Garrity and 1999 first-round draft choice (June 24, 1998).

COLLEGIATE RECORD

Season Team	G	Min.	FGM	FGA	Pct.	FTM	FTA	Pct.	Reb.	Ast.	Pts.	AVERAGES RPG	APG	PPG
92-93—Santa Clara	31	743	78	184	.424	47	57	.825	79	67	252	2.5	2.2	8.1
93-94—Santa Clara	26	778	122	295	.414	69	83	.831	65	95	380	2.5	3.7	14.6
94-95—Santa Clara	27	902	164	369	.444	153	174	.879	102	174	565	3.8	6.4	20.9
95-96—Santa Clara	29	979	164	381	.430	101	113	.894	102	174	492	3.5	6.0	17.0
Totals	113	3402	528	1229	.430	370	427	.867	348	510	1689	3.1	4.5	14.9

Three-point field goals: 1992-93, 49-for-120 (.408). 1993-94, 67-for-168 (.399). 1994-95, 84-for-185 (.454). 1995-96, 63-for-183 (.344). Totals, 263-for-656 (.401).

NBA REGULAR-SEASON RECORD

Season Team	G	Min.	FGM	FGA	Pct.	FTM	FTA	Pct.	REBOUNDS Off.	Def.	Tot.	Ast.	St.	Blk.	TO	Pts.	AVERAGES RPG	APG	PPG
96-97—Phoenix	65	684	74	175	.423	42	51	.824	16	47	63	138	20	0	63	213	1.0	2.1	3.3
97-98—Phoenix	76	1664	268	584	.459	74	86	.860	32	128	160	262	63	4	98	691	2.1	3.4	9.1
98-99—Dallas	40	1269	114	314	.363	38	46	.826	32	82	114	219	37	2	83	315	2.9	5.5	7.9
99-00—Dallas	56	1532	173	363	.477	75	85	.882	34	87	121	272	37	3	102	481	2.2	4.9	8.6
00-01—Dallas	70	2387	386	792	.487	231	258	.895	46	177	223	509	72	5	205	1092	3.2	7.3	15.6
Totals	307	7536	1015	2228	.456	460	526	.875	160	521	681	1400	229	14	551	2792	2.2	4.6	9.1

Three-point field goals: 1996-97, 23-for-55 (.418). 1997-98, 81-for-195 (.415). 1998-99, 49-for-131 (.374). 1999-00, 60-for-149 (.403). 2000-01, 89-for-219 (.406). Totals, 302-for-749 (.403).
Personal fouls/disqualifications: 1996-97, 92/1. 1997-98, 145/1. 1998-99, 98/2. 1999-00, 122/1. 2000-01, 158/0. Totals, 615/5.

NBA PLAYOFF RECORD

Season Team	G	Min.	FGM	FGA	Pct.	FTM	FTA	Pct.	REBOUNDS Off.	Def.	Tot.	Ast.	St.	Blk.	TO	Pts.	AVERAGES RPG	APG	PPG
96-97—Phoenix	4	15	2	9	.222	0	0	...	1	0	1	1	1	1	2	5	0.3	0.3	1.3
97-98—Phoenix	4	51	8	18	.444	5	8	.625	2	8	10	7	2	0	3	22	2.5	1.8	5.5
00-01—Dallas	10	370	45	108	.417	30	34	.882	6	26	32	64	6	1	25	136	3.2	6.4	13.6
Totals	18	436	55	135	.407	35	42	.833	9	34	43	72	9	2	30	163	2.4	4.0	9.1

Three-point field goals: 1996-97, 1-for-4 (.250). 1997-98, 1-for-5 (.200). 2000-01, 16-for-39 (.410). Totals, 18-for-48 (.375).
Personal fouls/disqualifications: 1996-97, 5/0. 1997-98, 7/0. 2000-01, 19/0. Totals, 31/0.

N

NESBY, TYRONE   F   WIZARDS

PERSONAL: Born January 31, 1976, in Cairo, Ill. ... 6-6/245. (1,98/111,1). ... Full Name: Tyrone Lamont Nesby.
HIGH SCHOOL: Cairo (Ill.).
JUNIOR COLLEGE: Vincennes (Ind.) University.
COLLEGE: UNLV.
TRANSACTIONS/CAREER NOTES: Not drafted by an NBA franchise. ... Played in Continental Basketball Association with Sioux Falls Skyforce (1998-99). ... Signed as free agent by Los Angeles Clippers (January 21, 1999). ... Traded by Clippers to Washington Wizards for F/C Cherokee Parks and F Obinna Ekezie (November 28, 2000).

COLLEGIATE RECORD

Season Team	G	Min.	FGM	FGA	Pct.	FTM	FTA	Pct.	Reb.	Ast.	Pts.	AVERAGES RPG	APG	PPG
94-95—Vincennes	37	...	215	425	.506	145	209	.694	317	92	589	8.6	2.5	15.9
95-96—Vincennes	22	...	181	338	.536	79	112	.705	166	38	465	7.5	1.7	21.1
96-97—UNLV	32	1063	190	482	.394	108	150	.720	228	60	529	7.1	1.9	16.5
97-98—UNLV	33	1082	187	486	.385	95	134	.709	185	40	521	5.6	1.2	15.8
Junior College Totals	59	...	396	763	.519	224	321	.698	483	130	1054	8.2	2.2	17.9
4-Year-College Totals	65	2145	377	968	.389	203	284	.715	413	100	1050	6.4	1.5	16.2

Three-point field goals: 1994-95, 14-for-53 (.264). 1995-96, 24-for-56 (.429). 1996-97, 41-for-147 (.279). 1997-98, 52-for-156 (.333). Totals, 38-for-109 (.349) Totals, 93-for-303 (.307).

CBA REGULAR-SEASON RECORD

Season Team	G	Min.	FGM	FGA	Pct.	FTM	FTA	Pct.	Reb.	Ast.	Pts.	RPG	APG	PPG
												AVERAGES		
98-99—Sioux Falls....................	26	451	99	234	.423	44	59	.746	86	32	261	3.3	1.2	10.0

Three-point field goals: 1998-99, 19-for-69 (.275).

NBA REGULAR-SEASON RECORD

Season Team	G	Min.	FGM	FGA	Pct.	FTM	FTA	Pct.	Off.	Def.	Tot.	Ast.	St.	Blk.	TO	Pts.	RPG	APG	PPG
									REBOUNDS								AVERAGES		
98-99—L.A. Clippers...	50	1288	182	405	.449	104	133	.782	57	118	175	82	77	20	53	503	3.5	1.6	10.1
99-00—L.A. Clippers...	73	2317	364	915	.398	151	191	.791	82	193	275	121	75	31	102	973	3.8	1.7	13.3
00-01—L.A.C.-Wash....	62	1556	189	530	.357	85	106	.802	51	122	173	76	51	20	65	512	2.8	1.2	8.3
Totals	185	5161	735	1850	.397	340	430	.791	190	433	623	279	203	71	220	1988	3.4	1.5	10.7

Three-point field goals: 1998-99, 35-for-96 (.365). 1999-00, 94-for-281 (.335). 2000-01, 49-for-180 (.272). Totals, 178-for-557 (.320).
Personal fouls/disqualifications: 1998-99, 143/2. 1999-00, 205/5. 2000-01, 155/1. Totals, 503/8.

NESTEROVIC, RASHO   C   TIMBERWOLVES

PERSONAL: Born May 30, 1976, in Ljubljana, Slovenia. ... 7-0/250. (2,13/113,4). ... Full Name: Radoslav Nesterovic.
HIGH SCHOOL: Gymnasium (Sremski Karlovci, Slovenia).
TRANSACTIONS/CAREER NOTES: Played in Slovenia (1996-97). ... Played in Italy (1997-98 and 1998-99). ... Selected by Minnesota Timberwolves in first round (17th pick overall) of 1998 NBA Draft.

ITALIAN LEAGUE RECORD

Season Team	G	Min.	FGM	FGA	Pct.	FTM	FTA	Pct.	Reb.	Ast.	Pts.	RPG	APG	PPG
												AVERAGES		
97-98—Virtus Kinder Bologna	26	587	84	124	.677	13	30	.433	139	3	181	5.3	0.1	7.0
98-99—Virtus Roma	26	852	152	233	.652	47	79	.595	162	11	351	6.2	0.4	13.5
Totals	52	1439	236	357	.661	60	109	.550	301	14	532	5.8	0.3	10.2

Three-point field goals: 1997-98, 0-for-1.

NBA REGULAR-SEASON RECORD

Season Team	G	Min.	FGM	FGA	Pct.	FTM	FTA	Pct.	Off.	Def.	Tot.	Ast.	St.	Blk.	TO	Pts.	RPG	APG	PPG
									REBOUNDS								AVERAGES		
98-99—Minnesota.......	2	30	3	12	.250	2	2	1.000	4	3	7	3	0	0	1	8	4.0	0.5	4.0
99-00—Minnesota.......	82	1723	206	433	.476	59	103	.573	135	244	379	93	21	85	71	471	4.6	1.1	5.7
00-01—Minnesota.......	73	1233	147	319	.461	34	65	.523	99	187	286	45	25	63	55	328	3.9	0.6	4.5
Totals	157	2986	356	764	.466	95	170	.559	237	436	673	139	46	148	127	807	4.3	0.9	5.1

Three-point field goals: 1999-00, 0-for-2. 2000-01, 0-for-1. Totals, 0-for-3 (.000).
Personal fouls/disqualifications: 1998-99, 5/0. 1999-00, 262/9. 2000-01, 189/3. Totals, 456/12.

NBA PLAYOFF RECORD

Season Team	G	Min.	FGM	FGA	Pct.	FTM	FTA	Pct.	Off.	Def.	Tot.	Ast.	St.	Blk.	TO	Pts.	RPG	APG	PPG
									REBOUNDS								AVERAGES		
98-99—Minnesota.......	3	29	4	8	.500	0	0	...	4	3	7	3	0	0	1	8	2.3	1.0	2.7
99-00—Minnesota.......	4	126	11	25	.440	3	6	.500	5	8	13	6	3	7	4	25	3.3	1.5	6.3
00-01—Minnesota.......	4	49	5	13	.385	0	0	...	5	7	12	3	1	3	3	10	3.0	0.8	2.5
Totals	11	204	20	46	.435	3	6	.500	14	18	32	12	4	10	8	43	2.9	1.1	3.9

Personal fouls/disqualifications: 1998-99, 4/0. 1999-00, 20/1. 2000-01, 9/0. Totals, 33/1.

N

NEWBLE, IRA   F

PERSONAL: Born January 20, 1975, in Detroit. ... 6-7/220. (2,01/99,8).
HIGH SCHOOL: Southfield (Mich.).
JUNIOR COLLEGE: Mississippi Gulf Coast Junior College.
COLLEGE: Miami of Ohio.
TRANSACTIONS/CAREER NOTES: Not drafted by an NBA franchise. ... Played in International Basketball Association with Wisconsin Blast (1997-98). ... Played in Continental Basketball Association with Idaho Stampede (1997-98 through 1999-2000). ... Signed as free agent by San Antonio Spurs (September 25, 1999). ... Waived by Spurs (October 27, 1999). ... Played in Cyprus (1999-2000). ... Re-signed by Spurs (August 12, 2000).

COLLEGIATE RECORD

Season Team	G	Min.	FGM	FGA	Pct.	FTM	FTA	Pct.	Reb.	Ast.	Pts.	RPG	APG	PPG
												AVERAGES		
93-94—Mississippi Gulf Coast....					Statistics unavailable.									
94-95—Mississippi Gulf Coast....					Statistics unavailable.									
95-96—Miami of Ohio	29	452	86	178	.483	14	24	.583	152	12	186	5.2	0.4	6.4
96-97—Miami of Ohio	29	756	138	231	.597	49	74	.662	218	35	329	7.5	1.2	11.3
4-Year-College Totals	58	1208	224	409	.548	63	98	.643	370	47	515	6.4	0.8	8.9

Three-point field goals: 1995-96, 0-for-7. 1996-97, 4-for-10 (.400). Totals, 4-for-17 (.235).

CBA REGULAR-SEASON RECORD

Season Team	G	Min.	FGM	FGA	Pct.	FTM	FTA	Pct.	Reb.	Ast.	Pts.	RPG	APG	PPG
												AVERAGES		
97-98—Idaho	16	260	50	87	.575	20	29	.690	66	10	123	4.1	0.6	7.7
98-99—Idaho	31	838	148	267	.554	57	85	.671	141	37	359	4.5	1.2	11.6
99-00—Idaho	53	2026	330	622	.531	133	174	.764	369	149	818	7.0	2.8	15.4
Totals	100	3124	528	976	.541	210	288	.729	576	196	1300	5.8	2.0	13.0

Three-point field goals: 1997-98, 3-for-6 (.500). 1998-99, 6-for-25 (.240). 1999-00, 25-for-67 (.373). Totals, 34-for-98 (.347).

NBA REGULAR-SEASON RECORD

								REBOUNDS							AVERAGES		
Season Team	G	Min.	FGM	FGA	Pct.	FTM	FTA	Pct.	Off.	Def.	Tot.	Ast.	St.	Blk.	TO	Pts.	RPG APG PPG
00-01—San Antonio....	27	184	21	55	.382	8	16	.500	13	22	35	6	2	4	7	54	1.3 0.2 2.0

Three-point field goals: 2000-01, 4-for-9 (.444).
Personal fouls/disqualifications: 2000-01, 18/0.

NEWMAN, JOHNNY   F   SUNS

PERSONAL: Born November 28, 1963, in Danville, Va. ... 6-7/210. (2,01/95,3). ... Full Name: John Sylvester Newman Jr.
HIGH SCHOOL: George Washington (Danville, Va.).
COLLEGE: Richmond.
TRANSACTIONS/CAREER NOTES: Selected by Cleveland Cavaliers in second round (29th pick overall) of 1986 NBA Draft. ... Waived by Cavaliers (November 5, 1987). ... Signed as free agent by New York Knicks (November 12, 1987). ... Signed as unrestricted free agent by Charlotte Hornets (July 28, 1990). ... Traded by Hornets to New Jersey Nets for G Rumeal Robinson (December 10, 1993). ... Signed as free agent by Milwaukee Bucks (October 7, 1994). ... Traded by Bucks with F/C Joe Wolf and draft rights to F Danny Fortson to Denver Nuggets for C Ervin Johnson (June 25, 1997). ... Signed as free agent by Cavaliers (January 24, 1999). ... Traded by Cavaliers with G Derek Anderson to Los Angeles Clippers for F Lamond Murray (August 4, 1999). ... Traded by Clippers to New Jersey Nets for G Eric Murdock (September 23, 1999). ... Traded by Nets with G Stephon Marbury and C Soumaila Samake to Phoenix Suns for G Jason Kidd and C Chris Dudley (July 18, 2001).

COLLEGIATE RECORD

												AVERAGES		
Season Team	G	Min.	FGM	FGA	Pct.	FTM	FTA	Pct.	Reb.	Ast.	Pts.	RPG	APG	PPG
82-83—Richmond......................	28	763	137	259	.529	69	96	.719	87	24	343	3.1	0.9	12.3
83-84—Richmond......................	32	1189	273	517	.528	155	197	.787	196	31	701	6.1	1.0	21.9
84-85—Richmond......................	32	1128	270	490	.551	140	181	.773	166	38	680	5.2	1.2	21.3
85-86—Richmond......................	30	1123	253	489	.517	153	172	.890	219	28	659	7.3	0.9	22.0
Totals	122	4203	933	1755	.532	517	646	.800	668	121	2383	5.5	1.0	19.5

NBA REGULAR-SEASON RECORD

RECORDS: Shares single-game records for most free throws made in one quarter—14; and most free throws attempted in one quarter—16 (February 10, 1998, vs. Boston).

									REBOUNDS								AVERAGES		
Season Team	G	Min.	FGM	FGA	Pct.	FTM	FTA	Pct.	Off.	Def.	Tot.	Ast.	St.	Blk.	TO	Pts.	RPG	APG	PPG
86-87—Cleveland	59	630	113	275	.411	66	76	.868	36	34	70	27	20	7	46	293	1.2	0.5	5.0
87-88—New York........	77	1589	270	620	.435	207	246	.841	87	72	159	62	72	11	103	773	2.1	0.8	10.0
88-89—New York........	81	2336	455	957	.475	286	351	.815	93	113	206	162	111	23	153	1293	2.5	2.0	16.0
89-90—New York........	80	2277	374	786	.476	239	299	.799	60	131	191	180	95	22	143	1032	2.4	2.3	12.9
90-91—Charlotte........	81	2477	478	1017	.470	385	476	.809	94	160	254	188	100	17	189	1371	3.1	2.3	16.9
91-92—Charlotte........	55	1651	295	618	.477	236	308	.766	71	108	179	146	70	14	129	839	3.3	2.7	15.3
92-93—Charlotte........	64	1471	279	534	.522	194	240	.808	72	71	143	117	45	19	90	764	2.2	1.8	11.9
93-94—Charlotte-N.J..	81	1697	313	664	.471	182	225	.809	86	94	180	72	69	27	90	832	2.2	0.9	10.3
94-95—Milwaukee	82	1896	226	488	.463	137	171	.801	72	101	173	91	69	13	86	634	2.1	1.1	7.7
95-96—Milwaukee	82	2690	321	649	.495	186	232	.802	66	134	200	154	90	15	108	889	2.4	1.9	10.8
96-97—Milwaukee	82	2060	246	547	.450	189	247	.765	66	120	186	116	73	17	115	715	2.3	1.4	8.7
97-98—Denver	74	2176	344	799	.431	365	445	.820	50	91	141	138	77	24	147	1089	1.9	1.9	14.7
98-99—Cleveland	50	949	106	251	.422	68	84	.810	15	60	75	41	28	12	41	303	1.5	0.8	6.1
99-00—New Jersey.....	82	1763	278	623	.446	192	229	.838	39	115	154	65	53	11	89	820	1.9	0.8	10.0
00-01—New Jersey.....	82	2049	291	695	.419	254	297	.855	34	142	176	115	63	10	106	895	2.1	1.4	10.9
Totals	1112	27711	4389	9523	.461	3186	3926	.812	941	1546	2487	1635	1042	242	1635	12542	2.2	1.5	11.3

Three-point field goals: 1986-87, 1-for-22 (.045). 1987-88, 26-for-93 (.280). 1988-89, 97-for-287 (.338). 1989-90, 45-for-142 (.317). 1990-91, 30-for-84 (.357). 1991-92, 13-for-46 (.283). 1992-93, 12-for-45 (.267). 1993-94, 24-for-90 (.267). 1994-95, 45-for-128 (.352). 1995-96, 61-for-162 (.377). 1996-97, 34-for-98 (.347). 1997-98, 36-for-105 (.343). 1998-99, 23-for-61 (.377). 1999-00, 72-for-190 (.379). 2000-01, 59-for-176 (.335). Totals, 578-for-1729 (.334).

Personal fouls/disqualifications: 1986-87, 67/0. 1987-88, 204/5. 1988-89, 259/4. 1989-90, 254/3. 1990-91, 278/7. 1991-92, 181/4. 1992-93, 154/1. 1993-94, 196/3. 1994-95, 234/3. 1995-96, 257/4. 1996-97, 257/4. 1997-98, 208/2. 1998-99, 126/2. 1999-00, 207/0. 2000-01, 229/3. Totals, 3111/45.

NBA PLAYOFF RECORD

									REBOUNDS								AVERAGES		
Season Team	G	Min.	FGM	FGA	Pct.	FTM	FTA	Pct.	Off.	Def.	Tot.	Ast.	St.	Blk.	TO	Pts.	RPG	APG	PPG
87-88—New York........	4	113	31	68	.456	14	16	.875	8	3	11	7	6	1	6	76	2.8	1.8	19.0
88-89—New York........	9	258	50	107	.467	38	49	.776	13	12	25	17	8	1	18	145	2.8	1.9	16.1
89-90—New York........	10	231	38	85	.447	37	49	.755	11	10	21	10	9	3	17	117	2.1	1.0	11.7
92-93—Charlotte........	9	173	28	55	.509	11	16	.688	7	12	19	18	10	1	15	68	2.1	2.0	7.6
93-94—New Jersey.....	4	54	3	13	.231	5	7	.714	2	3	5	2	2	2	3	12	1.3	0.5	3.0
Totals	36	829	150	328	.457	105	137	.766	41	40	81	54	35	8	59	418	2.3	1.5	11.6

Three-point field goals: 1987-88, 0-for-9. 1988-89, 7-for-28 (.250). 1989-90, 4-for-10 (.400). 1992-93, 1-for-5 (.200). 1993-94, 1-for-4 (.250). Totals, 13-for-56 (.232).

Personal fouls/disqualifications: 1987-88, 16/0. 1988-89, 27/1. 1989-90, 41/1. 1992-93, 19/0. 1993-94, 11/0. Totals, 114/2.

NORRIS, MOOCHIE   G

PERSONAL: Born July 27, 1973, in Washington, D.C. ... 6-1/175. (1,85/79,4). ... Full Name: Martyn Norris.
HIGH SCHOOL: Cardoza (Washington, D.C.).
JUNIOR COLLEGE: Odessa (Texas) Junior College.
COLLEGE: Auburn, then West Florida.
TRANSACTIONS/CAREER NOTES: Selected by Milwaukee Bucks in second round (33rd pick overall) of 1996 NBA Draft. ... Waived by Bucks (November 22, 1996). ... Played in Continental Basketball Association with Florida Beachdogs (1996-

97) and Fort Wayne Fury (1996-97 through 1999-2000). ... Signed as free agent by Vancouver Grizzlies (December 12, 1996). ... Waived by Grizzlies (December 30, 1996). ... Played in France (1997-98). ... Signed as free agent by Seattle SuperSonics (January 21, 1999). ... Waived by SuperSonics (March 23, 1999). ... Played in Venezuela (1999-2000). ... Signed by Houston Rockets to first of two consecutive 10-day contracts (February 8, 2000). ... Re-signed by Rockets for remainder of season (February 28, 2000).

COLLEGIATE RECORD

Season Team	G	Min.	FGM	FGA	Pct.	FTM	FTA	Pct.	Reb.	Ast.	Pts.	RPG	APG	PPG
92-93—Odessa Junior College....	32	...	160	290	.552	121	171	.708	91	225	459	2.8	7.0	14.3
93-94—Odessa Junior College....	27	...	147	264	.557	83	120	.692	104	214	401	3.9	7.9	14.9
94-95—Auburn	29	1009	124	312	.397	58	83	.699	116	143	363	4.0	4.9	12.5
95-96—West Florida	16	615	121	265	.457	86	113	.761	92	143	378	5.8	8.9	23.6
Junior College Totals.............	59	...	307	554	.554	204	291	.701	195	439	860	3.3	7.4	14.6
4-Year-College Totals.............	29	1009	124	312	.397	58	83	.699	116	143	363	4.0	4.9	12.5

Three-point field goals: 1992-93, 18-for-43 (.419). 1993-94, 24-for-60 (.400). 1994-95, 57-for-161 (.354). 1995-96, 50-for-118 (.424). Totals, 42-for-103 (.408).

CBA REGULAR-SEASON RECORD

NOTES: CBA All-League second team (1998). ... CBA All-Rookie second team (1997). ... CBA All-League first team (2000).

Season Team	G	Min.	FGM	FGA	Pct.	FTM	FTA	Pct.	Reb.	Ast.	Pts.	RPG	APG	PPG
96-97—Florida-Fort Wayne........	31	745	97	226	.429	58	81	.716	82	94	273	2.6	3.0	8.8
97-98—Fort Wayne....................	46	1413	208	404	.515	126	167	.754	226	244	552	4.9	5.3	12.0
98-99—Fort Wayne....................	18	669	95	189	.503	80	97	.825	105	144	278	5.8	8.0	15.4
99-00—Fort Wayne....................	33	1372	239	488	.490	165	202	.817	166	200	664	5.0	6.1	20.1
Totals....................................	128	4199	639	1307	.489	429	547	.784	579	682	1767	4.5	5.3	13.8

Three-point field goals: 1996-97, 21-for-76 (.276). 1997-98, 10-for-39 (.256). 1998-99, 8-for-16 (.500). 1999-00, 21-for-61 (.344). Totals, 60-for-192 (.313).

NBA REGULAR-SEASON RECORD

Season Team	G	Min.	FGM	FGA	Pct.	FTM	FTA	Pct.	Off.	Def.	Tot.	Ast.	St.	Blk.	TO	Pts.	RPG	APG	PPG
									REBOUNDS								AVERAGES		
96-97—Vancouver.......	8	89	4	22	.182	2	5	.400	3	9	12	23	4	0	5	12	1.5	2.9	1.5
98-99—Seattle	12	140	13	40	.325	6	16	.375	4	16	20	24	7	0	16	38	1.7	2.0	3.2
99-00—Houston	30	502	69	159	.434	57	73	.781	16	52	68	94	23	1	30	207	2.3	3.1	6.9
00-01—Houston	82	1654	184	413	.446	151	194	.778	44	154	198	283	69	2	107	544	2.4	3.5	6.6
Totals....................	132	2385	270	634	.426	216	288	.750	67	231	298	424	103	3	158	801	2.3	3.2	6.1

Three-point field goals: 1996-97, 2-for-10 (.200). 1998-99, 6-for-15 (.400). 1999-00, 12-for-29 (.414). 2000-01, 25-for-89 (.281). Totals, 45-for-143 (.315).

Personal fouls/disqualifications: 1996-97, 5/0. 1998-99, 17/0. 1999-00, 32/0. 2000-01, 84/0. Totals, 138/0.

FRENCH LEAGUE RECORD

Season Team	G	Min.	FGM	FGA	Pct.	FTM	FTA	Pct.	Reb.	Ast.	Pts.	RPG	APG	PPG
97-98—Pau Orthez.....................	8	177	26	45	.578	24	33	.727	33	21	79	4.1	2.6	9.9

VENEZUELAN LEAGUE RECORD

Season Team	G	Min.	FGM	FGA	Pct.	FTM	FTA	Pct.	Reb.	Ast.	Pts.	RPG	APG	PPG
99-00—Gaiteros.........................	6	217	44	86	.512	37	64	.578	17	48	136	2.8	8.0	22.7

Three-point field goals: 1999-00, 7-for-22 (.318).

NOWITZKI, DIRK   F   MAVERICKS

PERSONAL: Born June 19, 1978, in Wurzburg, Germany. ... 7-0/250. (2,13/113,4).
HIGH SCHOOL: Rontgen Gymnasium (Wurzburg, Germany).
TRANSACTIONS/CAREER NOTES: Played in Germany (1997-98 and 1998-99). ... Selected by Milwaukee Bucks in first round (ninth pick overall) of 1998 NBA Draft. ... Draft rights traded by Bucks with draft rights to F Pat Garrity to Dallas Mavericks for draft rights to F Robert Traylor (June 24, 1998).

GERMAN LEAGUE RECORD

Season Team	G	Min.	FGM	FGA	Pct.	FTM	FTA	Pct.	Reb.	Ast.	Pts.	RPG	APG	PPG
97-98—DJK Wurzburg...............	20	699	206	367	.561	135	177	.763	198	20	565	9.9	1.0	28.3
98-99—DJK Wurzburg...............	16	599	123	275	.447	100	128	.781	135	50	366	8.4	3.1	22.9
Totals......................................	36	1298	329	642	.512	235	305	.770	333	70	931	9.3	1.9	25.9

Three-point field goals: 1997-98, 18-for-54 (.333). 1998-99, 20-for-76 (.263). Totals, 38-for-130 (.292).

HONORS: All-NBA third team (2001).

NBA REGULAR-SEASON RECORD

Season Team	G	Min.	FGM	FGA	Pct.	FTM	FTA	Pct.	Off.	Def.	Tot.	Ast.	St.	Blk.	TO	Pts.	RPG	APG	PPG
									REBOUNDS								AVERAGES		
98-99—Dallas.............	47	958	136	336	.405	99	128	.773	41	121	162	47	29	27	73	385	3.4	1.0	8.2
99-00—Dallas.............	82	2938	515	1118	.461	289	348	.830	102	430	532	203	63	68	141	1435	6.5	2.5	17.5
00-01—Dallas.............	82	3125	591	1247	.474	451	538	.838	119	635	754	173	79	101	156	1784	9.2	2.1	21.8
Totals....................	211	7021	1242	2701	.460	839	1014	.827	262	1186	1448	423	171	196	370	3604	6.9	2.0	17.1

Three-point field goals: 1998-99, 14-for-68 (.206). 1999-00, 116-for-306 (.379). 2000-01, 151-for-390 (.387). Totals, 281-for-764 (.368).
Personal fouls/disqualifications: 1998-99, 105/5. 1999-00, 256/4. 2000-01, 245/1. Totals, 606/10.

NBA PLAYOFF RECORD

Season Team	G	Min.	FGM	FGA	Pct.	FTM	FTA	Pct.	Off.	Def.	Tot.	Ast.	St.	Blk.	TO	Pts.	RPG	APG	PPG
									REBOUNDS								AVERAGES		
00-01—Dallas.............	10	399	69	163	.423	83	94	.883	14	67	81	14	11	8	14	234	8.1	1.4	23.4

Three-point field goals: 2000-01, 13-for-46 (.283).
Personal fouls/disqualifications: 2000-01, 37/1.

OAKLEY, CHARLES   F   BULLS

PERSONAL: Born December 18, 1963, in Cleveland. ... 6-9/245. (2,06/111,1).

HIGH SCHOOL: John Hay (Cleveland).

COLLEGE: Virginia Union.

TRANSACTIONS/CAREER NOTES: Selected by Cleveland Cavaliers in first round (ninth pick overall) of 1985 NBA Draft. ... Draft rights traded by Cavaliers with draft rights to G Calvin Duncan to Chicago Bulls for G Ennis Whatley and draft rights to F Keith Lee (June 18, 1985). ... Traded by Bulls with 1988 first- and third-round draft choices to New York Knicks for C Bill Cartwright and 1988 first- and third-round draft choices (June 27, 1988). ... Traded by Knicks with draft rights to F/C Sean Marks and cash to Toronto Raptors for F Marcus Camby (June 25, 1998). ... Traded by Raptors with 2002 second-round draft choice to Bulls for F/C Brian Skinner (July 18, 2001).

MISCELLANEOUS: Toronto Raptors all-time rebounds leader with 1,655 (1998-99 through 2000-01).

COLLEGIATE RECORD

NOTES: Led NCAA Division II with 17.3 rebounds per game (1985).

Season Team	G	Min.	FGM	FGA	Pct.	FTM	FTA	Pct.	Reb.	Ast.	Pts.	RPG	APG	PPG
81-82—Virginia Union	28	...	169	274	.617	106	174	.609	349	...	444	12.5	...	15.9
82-83—Virginia Union	28	...	220	378	.582	100	170	.588	365	28	540	13.0	1.0	19.3
83-84—Virginia Union	30	...	256	418	.612	139	224	.621	393	...	651	13.1	...	21.7
84-85—Virginia Union	31	...	283	453	.625	178	266	.669	535	66	744	17.3	2.1	24.0
Totals	117	...	928	1523	.609	523	834	.627	1642	...	2379	14.0	...	20.3

NBA REGULAR-SEASON RECORD

HONORS: NBA All-Defensive first team (1994). ... NBA All-Defensive second team (1998). ... NBA All-Rookie team (1986).

									REBOUNDS							AVERAGES		
Season Team	G	Min.	FGM	FGA	Pct.	FTM	FTA	Pct.	Off.	Def.	Tot.	Ast.	St.	Blk.	TO	Pts.	RPG	APG	PPG
85-86—Chicago	77	1772	281	541	.519	178	269	.662	255	409	664	133	68	30	175	740	8.6	1.7	9.6
86-87—Chicago	82	2980	468	1052	.445	245	357	.686	299	*775	*1074	296	85	36	299	1192	13.1	3.6	14.5
87-88—Chicago	82	2816	375	776	.483	261	359	.727	326	*740	*1066	248	68	28	241	1014	13.0	3.0	12.4
88-89—New York	82	2604	426	835	.510	197	255	.773	343	518	861	187	104	14	248	1061	10.5	2.3	12.9
89-90—New York	61	2196	336	641	.524	217	285	.761	258	469	727	146	64	16	165	889	11.9	2.4	14.6
90-91—New York	76	2739	307	595	.516	239	305	.784	305	615	920	204	62	17	215	853	12.1	2.7	11.2
91-92—New York	82	2309	210	402	.522	86	117	.735	256	444	700	133	67	15	123	506	8.5	1.6	6.2
92-93—New York	82	2230	219	431	.508	127	176	.722	288	420	708	126	85	15	124	565	8.6	1.5	6.9
93-94—New York	82	2932	363	760	.478	243	313	.776	349	616	965	218	110	18	193	969	11.8	2.7	11.8
94-95—New York	50	1567	192	393	.489	119	150	.793	155	290	445	126	60	7	103	506	8.9	2.5	10.1
95-96—New York	53	1775	211	448	.471	175	210	.833	162	298	460	137	58	14	104	604	8.7	2.6	11.4
96-97—New York	80	2873	339	694	.488	181	224	.808	246	535	781	221	111	21	171	864	9.8	2.8	10.8
97-98—New York	79	2734	307	698	.440	97	114	.851	218	506	724	201	123	22	126	711	9.2	2.5	9.0
98-99—Toronto	50	1633	140	327	.428	67	83	.807	96	278	374	168	46	21	96	348	7.5	3.4	7.0
99-00—Toronto	80	2431	234	560	.418	66	85	.776	117	423	540	253	102	45	154	548	6.8	3.2	6.9
00-01—Toronto	80	2767	305	786	.388	127	152	.836	142	599	741	264	76	48	139	748	9.5	3.4	9.6
Totals	1176	38508	4713	9939	.474	2625	3454	.760	3815	7935	11750	3061	1289	367	2676	12118	10.0	2.6	10.3

Three-point field goals: 1985-86, 0-for-3. 1986-87, 11-for-30 (.367). 1987-88, 3-for-12 (.250). 1988-89, 12-for-48 (.250). 1989-90, 0-for-3. 1990-91, 0-for-2. 1991-92, 0-for-3. 1992-93, 0-for-1. 1993-94, 0-for-3. 1994-95, 3-for-12 (.250). 1995-96, 7-for-26 (.269). 1996-97, 5-for-19 (.263). 1997-98, 0-for-6. 1998-99, 1-for-5 (.200). 1999-00, 14-for-41 (.341). 2000-01, 11-for-49 (.224). Totals, 67-for-263 (.255).

Personal fouls/disqualifications: 1985-86, 250/9. 1986-87, 315/4. 1987-88, 272/2. 1988-89, 270/1. 1989-90, 220/3. 1990-91, 288/4. 1991-92, 258/2. 1992-93, 289/5. 1993-94, 293/4. 1994-95, 179/3. 1995-96, 195/6. 1996-97, 305/4. 1997-98, 280/4. 1998-99, 182/4. 1999-00, 294/6. 2000-01, 258/0. Totals, 4148/61.

NBA PLAYOFF RECORD

									REBOUNDS							AVERAGES		
Season Team	G	Min.	FGM	FGA	Pct.	FTM	FTA	Pct.	Off.	Def.	Tot.	Ast.	St.	Blk.	TO	Pts.	RPG	APG	PPG
85-86—Chicago	3	88	11	21	.524	8	13	.615	10	20	30	3	6	2	5	30	10.0	1.0	10.0
86-87—Chicago	3	129	19	50	.380	20	24	.833	17	29	46	6	4	1	8	60	15.3	2.0	20.0
87-88—Chicago	10	373	40	91	.440	21	24	.875	39	89	128	32	6	4	18	101	12.8	3.2	10.1
88-89—New York	9	299	35	73	.479	16	24	.667	43	58	101	11	12	1	22	87	11.2	1.2	9.7
89-90—New York	10	336	43	84	.512	34	52	.654	39	71	110	27	11	2	22	121	11.0	2.7	12.1
90-91—New York	3	100	10	21	.476	3	6	.500	15	16	31	3	2	1	7	23	10.3	1.0	7.7
91-92—New York	12	354	22	58	.379	20	27	.741	44	64	108	8	8	5	15	64	9.0	0.7	5.3
92-93—New York	15	507	63	131	.481	40	55	.727	71	94	165	17	16	2	36	166	11.0	1.1	11.1
93-94—New York	25	992	125	262	.477	79	102	.775	116	176	292	59	35	5	65	329	11.7	2.4	13.2
94-95—New York	11	421	49	109	.450	42	51	.824	31	62	93	41	19	6	24	144	8.5	3.7	13.1
95-96—New York	8	308	39	78	.500	25	36	.694	28	41	69	14	8	0	28	105	8.6	1.8	13.1
96-97—New York	10	358	38	86	.442	22	29	.759	23	65	88	16	22	3	18	98	8.8	1.6	9.8
97-98—New York	10	342	29	71	.408	23	25	.920	21	64	85	14	11	2	13	81	8.5	1.4	8.1
99-00—Toronto	3	110	14	29	.483	0	1	1.000	2	21	23	11	6	1	5	30	7.7	3.7	10.0
00-01—Toronto	12	391	47	108	.435	14	17	.824	20	56	76	21	12	7	22	111	6.3	1.8	9.3
Totals	144	5108	584	1272	.459	367	486	.755	519	926	1445	283	178	42	308	1550	10.0	2.0	10.8

Three-point field goals: 1986-87, 2-for-4 (.500). 1987-88, 0-for-2. 1988-89, 1-for-2 (.500). 1989-90, 1-for-1. 1994-95, 4-for-10 (.400). 1995-96, 2-for-6 (.333). 1996-97, 0-for-1. 1999-00, 0-for-7 (.286). 2000-01, 3-for-8 (.375). Totals, 15-for-41 (.366).

Personal fouls/disqualifications: 1985-86, 13/0. 1986-87, 13/0. 1987-88, 33/0. 1988-89, 31/1. 1989-90, 33/1. 1990-91, 13/0. 1991-92, 36/0. 1992-93, 51/1. 1993-94, 87/1. 1994-95, 42/0. 1995-96, 33/1. 1996-97, 37/0. 1997-98, 38/1. 1999-00, 14/0. 2000-01, 29/0. Totals, 503/6.

NBA ALL-STAR GAME RECORD

							REBOUNDS									
Season Team	Min.	FGM	FGA	Pct.	FTM	FTA	Pct.	Off.	Def.	Tot.	Ast.	PF	Dq.	St.	Blk.	TO	Pts.
1994 —New York	11	1	3	.333	0	0	...	1	2	3	3	3	0	0	0	0	2

O

ODOM, LAMAR   F   CLIPPERS

PERSONAL: Born November 6, 1979, in Jamaica, N.Y. ... 6-10/220. (2,08/99,8). ... Full Name: Lamar Joseph Odom.
HIGH SCHOOL: Christian Redemption Academy (Troy, N.Y.), then Christ the King (Middlevillage Queens, N.Y.), then St. Thomas Aquinas (New Britain, Conn.).
COLLEGE: UNLV, then Rhode Island.
TRANSACTIONS/CAREER NOTES: Selected after sophomore season by Los Angeles Clippers in first round (fourth pick overall) of 1999 NBA Draft.

COLLEGIATE RECORD

Season Team	G	Min.	FGM	FGA	Pct.	FTM	FTA	Pct.	Reb.	Ast.	Pts.	RPG	APG	PPG
97-98—Rhode Island							Did not play.							
98-99—Rhode Island	32	1116	203	421	.482	125	182	.687	302	122	564	9.4	3.8	17.6
Totals	32	1116	203	421	.482	125	182	.687	302	122	564	9.4	3.8	17.6

Three-point field goals: 1998-99, 33-for-100 (.330).

HONORS: NBA All-Rookie first team (2000).
NOTES: Tied for NBA lead with 13 disqualifications (2000).

NBA REGULAR-SEASON RECORD

Season Team	G	Min.	FGM	FGA	Pct.	FTM	FTA	Pct.	REBOUNDS Off.	Def.	Tot.	Ast.	St.	Blk.	TO	Pts.	RPG	APG	PPG
99-00—L.A. Clippers	76	2767	449	1024	.438	302	420	.719	159	436	595	317	91	95	258	1259	7.8	4.2	16.6
00-01—L.A. Clippers	76	2836	481	1046	.460	262	386	.679	110	482	592	392	74	122	264	1304	7.8	5.2	17.2
Totals	152	5603	930	2070	.449	564	806	.700	269	918	1187	709	165	217	522	2563	7.8	4.7	16.9

Three-point field goals: 1999-00, 59-for-164 (.360). 2000-01, 80-for-253 (.316). Totals, 139-for-417 (.333).
Personal fouls/disqualifications: 1999-00, 291/13. 2000-01, 236/4. Totals, 527/17.

OLAJUWON, HAKEEM   C   RAPTORS

PERSONAL: Born January 21, 1963, in Lagos, Nigeria. ... 7-0/255. (2,13/115,7). ... Full Name: Hakeem Abdul Olajuwon. ... Known as Akeem Olajuwon until March 9, 1991. ... Nickname: The Dream. ... Name pronounced ah-KEEM a-lie-shoe-on.
HIGH SCHOOL: Muslim Teachers College (Lagos, Nigeria).
COLLEGE: Houston.
TRANSACTIONS/CAREER NOTES: Selected by Houston Rockets in first round (first pick overall) of 1984 NBA Draft. ... Traded by Rockets to Toronto Raptors for 2002 first-round draft choice and 2002 second-round draft choice (August 2, 2001).
CAREER HONORS: NBA 50th Anniversary All-Time Team (1996).
MISCELLANEOUS: Member of NBA championship team (1994, 1995). ... Member of gold-medal-winning U.S. Olympic team (1996). ... Houston Rockets franchise all-time leading scorer with 26,511 points, all-time leading rebounder with 13,382, all-time steals leader with 2,088 and all-time blocked shots leader with 3,740 (1984-85 through 2000-01).

COLLEGIATE RECORD

NOTES: THE SPORTING NEWS All-America first team (1984). ... NCAA Division I Tournament Most Outstanding Player (1983). ... Led NCAA Division I with .675 field goal percentage (1984). ... Led NCAA Division I with 13.5 rebounds per game (1984). ... Led NCAA Division I with 5.6 blocked shots per game (1984).

Season Team	G	Min.	FGM	FGA	Pct.	FTM	FTA	Pct.	Reb.	Ast.	Pts.	RPG	APG	PPG
80-81—Houston							Did not play.							
81-82—Houston	29	529	91	150	.607	58	103	.563	179	11	240	6.2	0.4	8.3
82-83—Houston	34	932	192	314	.611	88	148	.595	388	29	472	11.4	0.9	13.9
83-84—Houston	37	1260	249	369	.675	122	232	.526	500	48	620	13.5	1.3	16.8
Totals	100	2721	532	833	.639	268	483	.555	1067	88	1332	10.7	0.9	13.3

NBA REGULAR-SEASON RECORD

RECORDS: Holds career record for most blocked shots—3,740.
HONORS: NBA Most Valuable Player (1994). ... NBA Defensive Player of the Year (1993, 1994). ... IBM Award, for all-around contributions to team's success (1993). ... All-NBA first team (1987, 1988, 1993, 1994, 1997). ... All-NBA second team (1986, 1990, 1996). ... All-NBA third team (1991, 1995, 1999). ... NBA All-Defensive first team (1987, 1988, 1990, 1993, 1994). ... NBA All-Defensive second team (1985, 1991, 1996, 1997). ... NBA All-Rookie team (1985).
NOTES: Led NBA with 4.59 blocked shots per game (1990), 3.95 blocked shots per game (1991) and 4.17 blocked shots per game (1993). ... Led NBA with 344 personal fouls (1985).

Season Team	G	Min.	FGM	FGA	Pct.	FTM	FTA	Pct.	REBOUNDS Off.	Def.	Tot.	Ast.	St.	Blk.	TO	Pts.	RPG	APG	PPG
84-85—Houston	82	2914	677	1258	.538	338	551	.613	*440	534	974	111	99	220	234	1692	11.9	1.4	20.6
85-86—Houston	68	2467	625	1188	.526	347	538	.645	333	448	781	137	134	231	195	1597	11.5	2.0	23.5
86-87—Houston	75	2760	677	1332	.508	400	570	.702	315	543	858	220	140	254	228	1755	11.4	2.9	23.4
87-88—Houston	79	2825	712	1385	.514	381	548	.695	302	657	959	163	162	214	243	1805	12.1	2.1	22.8
88-89—Houston	82	3024	790	1556	.508	454	652	.696	338	*767	*1105	149	213	282	275	2034	*13.5	1.8	24.8
89-90—Houston	82	3124	806	1609	.501	382	536	.713	299	*850	*1149	234	174	*376	316	1995	*14.0	2.9	24.3
90-91—Houston	56	2062	487	959	.508	213	277	.769	219	551	770	131	121	221	174	1187	13.8	2.3	21.2
91-92—Houston	70	2636	591	1177	.502	328	428	.766	246	599	845	157	127	304	187	1510	12.1	2.2	21.6
92-93—Houston	82	3242	848	1603	.529	444	570	.779	283	785	1068	291	150	*342	262	2140	13.0	3.5	26.1
93-94—Houston	80	3277	894	*1694	.528	388	542	.716	229	726	955	287	128	297	271	2184	11.9	3.6	27.3
94-95—Houston	72	2853	798	1545	.517	406	537	.756	172	603	775	255	133	242	237	2005	10.8	3.5	27.8
95-96—Houston	72	2797	768	1494	.514	397	548	.724	176	608	784	257	113	207	247	1936	10.9	3.6	26.9
96-97—Houston	78	2852	727	1426	.510	351	446	.787	173	543	716	236	117	173	281	1810	9.2	3.0	23.2
97-98—Houston	47	1633	306	633	.483	160	212	.755	116	344	460	143	84	96	126	772	9.8	3.0	16.4
98-99—Houston	50	1784	373	725	.514	195	272	.717	106	372	478	88	82	123	139	945	9.6	1.8	18.9
99-00—Houston	44	1049	193	421	.458	69	112	.616	65	209	274	61	41	70	73	455	6.2	1.4	10.3
00-01—Houston	58	1545	283	568	.498	123	198	.621	124	307	431	72	70	88	81	689	7.4	1.2	11.9
Totals	1177	42844	10555	20573	.513	5376	7537	.713	3936	9446	13382	2992	2088	3740	3569	26511	11.4	2.5	22.5

O

Three-point field goals: 1986-87, 1-for-5 (.200). 1987-88, 0-for-4. 1988-89, 0-for-10. 1989-90, 1-for-6 (.167). 1990-91, 0-for-4. 1991-92, 0-for-1. 1992-93, 0-for-8. 1993-94, 8-for-19 (.421). 1994-95, 3-for-16 (.188). 1995-96, 3-for-14 (.214). 1996-97, 5-for-16 (.313). 1997-98, 0-for-3. 1998-99, 4-for-13 (.308). 1999-00, 0-for-2. 2000-01, 0-for-1. Totals, 25-for-122 (.205).

Personal fouls/disqualifications: 1984-85, 344/10. 1985-86, 271/9. 1986-87, 294/8. 1987-88, 324/7. 1988-89, 329/10. 1989-90, 314/6. 1990-91, 221/5. 1991-92, 263/7. 1992-93, 305/5. 1993-94, 289/4. 1994-95, 250/3. 1995-96, 242/0. 1996-97, 249/3. 1997-98, 152/0. 1998-99, 160/3. 1999-00, 88/0. 2000-01, 141/0. Totals, 4236/80.

NBA PLAYOFF RECORD

NOTES: NBA Finals Most Valuable Player (1994, 1995). ... Shares NBA Finals single-game record for most blocked shots—8 (June 5, 1986, vs. Boston). ... Shares single-game playoff record for most blocked shots—10 (April 29, 1990, vs. Los Angeles Lakers).

Season Team	G	Min.	FGM	FGA	Pct.	FTM	FTA	Pct.	Off.	Def.	Tot.	Ast.	St.	Blk.	TO	Pts.	RPG	APG	PPG
84-85—Houston	5	187	42	88	.477	22	46	.478	33	32	65	7	7	13	11	106	13.0	1.4	21.2
85-86—Houston	20	766	205	387	.530	127	199	.638	101	135	236	39	40	69	43	537	11.8	2.0	26.9
86-87—Houston	10	389	110	179	.615	72	97	.742	39	74	113	25	13	43	36	292	11.3	2.5	29.2
87-88—Houston	4	162	56	98	.571	38	43	.884	20	47	67	7	9	11	9	150	16.8	1.8	37.5
88-89—Houston	4	162	42	81	.519	17	25	.680	14	38	52	12	10	11	10	101	13.0	3.0	25.3
89-90—Houston	4	161	31	70	.443	12	17	.706	15	31	46	8	10	23	11	74	11.5	2.0	18.5
90-91—Houston	3	129	26	45	.578	14	17	.824	12	32	44	6	4	8	8	66	14.7	2.0	22.0
92-93—Houston	12	518	123	238	.517	62	75	.827	52	116	168	57	21	59	45	308	14.0	4.8	25.7
93-94—Houston	23	989	267	514	.519	128	161	.795	55	199	254	98	40	92	83	664	11.0	4.3	28.9
94-95—Houston	22	929	306	576	.531	111	163	.681	44	183	227	98	26	62	69	725	10.3	4.5	33.0
95-96—Houston	8	329	75	147	.510	29	40	.725	17	56	73	31	15	17	29	179	9.1	3.9	22.4
96-97—Houston	16	629	147	249	.590	76	104	.731	46	128	174	54	33	41	46	370	10.9	3.4	23.1
97-98—Houston	5	190	39	99	.394	24	33	.727	9	45	54	12	5	16	13	102	10.8	2.4	20.4
98-99—Houston	4	123	23	54	.426	7	8	.875	5	24	29	2	5	3	5	53	7.3	0.5	13.3
Totals	140	5663	1492	2825	.528	739	1028	.719	462	1140	1602	456	238	468	418	3727	11.4	3.3	26.6

Three-point field goals: 1985-86, 0-for-1. 1986-87, 0-for-1. 1987-88, 0-for-1. 1990-91, 0-for-1. 1992-93, 0-for-1. 1993-94, 2-for-4 (.500). 1994-95, 2-for-4 (.500). 1995-96, 0-for-1. 1996-97, 0-for-3. 1997-98, 0-for-1. Totals, 4-for-18 (.222).

Personal fouls/disqualifications: 1984-85, 22/0. 1985-86, 87/3. 1986-87, 44/1. 1987-88, 14/0. 1988-89, 17/0. 1989-90, 19/0. 1990-91, 11/0. 1992-93, 37/0. 1993-94, 82/0. 1994-95, 95/0. 1995-96, 28/1. 1996-97, 61/0. 1997-98, 18/0. 1998-99, 18/0. Totals, 553/5.

NBA ALL-STAR GAME RECORD

NOTES: Shares single-game records for most offensive rebounds—9 (1990); and most blocked shots in one half—4 (1994).

Season Team	Min.	FGM	FGA	Pct.	FTM	FTA	Pct.	Off.	Def.	Tot.	Ast.	PF	Dq.	St.	Blk.	TO	Pts.
1985 —Houston	15	2	2	1.000	2	6	.333	2	3	5	1	1	0	0	2	0	6
1986 —Houston	15	1	8	.125	1	2	.500	1	4	5	0	3	0	1	2	1	3
1987 —Houston	26	2	6	.333	6	8	.750	4	9	13	2	6	1	0	3	1	10
1988 —Houston	28	8	13	.615	5	7	.714	7	2	9	2	3	0	2	2	4	21
1989 —Houston	25	5	12	.417	2	3	.667	4	3	7	3	2	0	3	2	3	12
1990 —Houston	31	2	14	.143	4	10	.400	9	7	16	2	1	0	1	1	4	8
1992 —Houston	20	3	6	.500	1	2	.500	0	4	4	2	3	0	2	1	3	7
1993 —Houston	21	1	5	.200	1	2	.500	2	5	7	1	3	0	2	2	3	3
1994 —Houston	30	8	15	.533	3	6	.500	4	7	11	2	4	0	2	5	3	19
1995 —Houston	25	6	13	.462	2	2	.000	4	7	11	1	2	0	2	2	3	13
1996 —Houston	14	2	8	.250	0	0	...	1	2	3	0	2	0	0	0	0	4
1997 —Houston	20	5	8	.625	1	2	.500	0	3	3	1	1	0	0	1	1	11
Totals	270	45	110	.409	26	50	.520	38	56	94	17	31	1	15	23	26	117

Three-point field goals: 1995, 1-for-1. Totals, 1-for-1 (1.000).

OLLIE, KEVIN   G

PERSONAL: Born December 27, 1972, in Dallas. ... 6-4/195. (1,93/88,5). ... Full Name: Kevin Jermaine Ollie.
HIGH SCHOOL: Crenshaw (Los Angeles).
COLLEGE: Connecticut.
TRANSACTIONS/CAREER NOTES: Not drafted by an NBA franchise. ... Signed as free agent by Golden State Warriors (October 4, 1995). ... Waived by Warriors (October 11, 1995). ... Played in Continental Basketball Association with Connecticut Pride (1995-96 through 1997-98 and 1999-2000). ... Signed as free agent by Dallas Mavericks (October 7, 1997). ... Waived by Mavericks (December 17, 1997). ... Signed by Orlando Magic to first of two consecutive 10-day contracts (March 2, 1998). ... Signed by Magic for remainder of season (March 22, 1998). ... Signed as free agent by Sacramento Kings (January 21, 1999). ... Waived by Kings (February 19, 1999). ... Re-signed by Magic to 10-day contract (March 8, 1999). ... Waived by Magic (March 14, 1999). ... Signed as free agent by Mavericks (October 6, 1999). ... Waived by Mavericks (October 29, 1999). ... Signed as free agent by Philadelphia 76ers (November 24, 1999). ... Signed as free agent by New Jersey Nets (October 3, 2000). ... Waived by Nets (December 15, 2000). ... Signed as free agent by 76ers (December 22, 2000).

COLLEGIATE RECORD

Season Team	G	Min.	FGM	FGA	Pct.	FTM	FTA	Pct.	Reb.	Ast.	Pts.	RPG	APG	PPG
91-92—Connecticut	29	294	17	45	.378	28	39	.718	23	40	62	0.8	1.4	2.1
92-93—Connecticut	28	864	69	176	.392	81	109	.743	64	158	220	2.3	5.6	7.9
93-94—Connecticut	34	973	73	155	.471	71	97	.732	83	209	219	2.4	6.1	6.4
94-95—Connecticut	33	1025	112	222	.505	87	108	.806	82	212	324	2.5	6.4	9.8
Totals	124	3156	271	598	.453	267	353	.756	252	619	825	2.0	5.0	6.7

Three-point field goals: 1992-93, 1-for-9 (.111). 1993-94, 2-for-10 (.200). 1994-95, 13-for-42 (.310). Totals, 16-for-61 (.262).

CBA REGULAR-SEASON RECORD

NOTES: Member of CBA championship team (1999).

Season Team	G	Min.	FGM	FGA	Pct.	FTM	FTA	Pct.	Reb.	Ast.	Pts.	RPG	APG	PPG
95-96—Connecticut	56	1448	161	378	.426	134	178	.753	154	226	459	2.8	4.0	8.2
96-97—Connecticut	52	2226	277	565	.490	204	251	.813	202	300	763	3.9	5.8	14.7
97-98—Connecticut	24	886	177	379	.467	108	136	.794	77	118	474	3.2	4.9	19.8
99-00—Connecticut	2	81	12	24	.500	15	16	.938	7	15	40	3.5	7.5	20.0
Totals	134	4641	627	1346	.466	461	581	.793	440	659	1736	3.3	4.9	13.0

Three-point field goals: 1995-96, 3-for-18 (.167). 1996-97, 5-for-14 (.357). 1997-98, 12-for-34 (.353). 1999-00, 1-for-2 (.500). Totals, 21-for-68 (.309).

NBA REGULAR-SEASON RECORD

Season Team	G	Min.	FGM	FGA	Pct.	FTM	FTA	Pct.	REBOUNDS Off.	Def.	Tot.	Ast.	St.	Blk.	TO	Pts.	RPG	APG	PPG
97-98—Dallas-Orlando	35	430	37	98	.378	49	70	.700	9	30	39	65	13	0	44	123	1.1	1.9	3.5
98-99—Sac.-Orlando	8	72	4	14	.286	5	7	.714	0	7	7	3	3	1	3	13	0.9	0.4	1.6
99-00—Philadelphia	40	290	22	49	.449	28	37	.757	4	27	31	46	10	0	10	72	0.8	1.2	1.8
00-01—N.J.-Phila.	70	925	76	192	.396	63	89	.708	16	79	95	146	30	1	49	216	1.4	2.1	3.1
Totals	153	1717	139	353	.394	145	203	.714	29	143	172	260	56	2	106	424	1.1	1.7	2.8

Three-point field goals: 1997-98, 0-for-1. 1998-99, 5-for-7 (.714). 2000-01, 1-for-3 (.333). Totals, 6-for-11 (.545).
Personal fouls/disqualifications: 1997-98, 31/0. 1998-99, 9/0. 1999-00, 27/0. 2000-01, 84/0. Totals, 151/0.

NBA PLAYOFF RECORD

Season Team	G	Min.	FGM	FGA	Pct.	FTM	FTA	Pct.	REBOUNDS Off.	Def.	Tot.	Ast.	St.	Blk.	TO	Pts.	RPG	APG	PPG
99-00—Philadelphia	10	65	6	12	.500	8	9	.889	0	5	5	12	2	0	3	20	0.5	1.2	2.0
00-01—Philadelphia	23	123	10	27	.370	13	14	.929	2	7	9	23	0	0	8	33	0.4	1.0	1.4
Totals	33	188	16	39	.410	21	23	.913	2	12	14	35	2	0	11	53	0.4	1.1	1.6

Personal fouls/disqualifications: 1999-00, 5/0. 2000-01, 12/0. Totals, 17/0.

OLOWOKANDI, MICHAEL   C   CLIPPERS

PERSONAL: Born April 3, 1975, in Lagos, Nigeria. ... 7-0/269. (2,13/122,0).
HIGH SCHOOL: Newlands Manor School (East Sussex, England).
COLLEGE: Brunel (Middlesex, England); did not play basketball, then Pacific.
TRANSACTIONS/CAREER NOTES: Selected by Los Angeles Clippers in first round (first pick overall) of 1998 NBA Draft. ... Played in Italy (1998-99).

COLLEGIATE RECORD

Season Team	G	Min.	FGM	FGA	Pct.	FTM	FTA	Pct.	Reb.	Ast.	Pts.	RPG	APG	PPG
95-96—Pacific	25	257	40	76	.526	20	36	.556	84	4	100	3.4	0.2	4.0
96-97—Pacific	19	433	94	165	.570	19	57	.333	126	8	207	6.6	0.4	10.9
97-98—Pacific	33	1046	309	508	.608	114	235	.485	369	26	732	11.2	0.8	22.2
Totals	77	1736	443	749	.591	153	328	.466	579	38	1039	7.5	0.5	13.5

ITALIAN LEAGUE RECORD

Season Team	G	Min.	FGM	FGA	Pct.	FTM	FTA	Pct.	Reb.	Ast.	Pts.	RPG	APG	PPG
98-99—Bologna Arimo	3	52	6	14	.429	2	4	.500	17	1	14	5.7	0.3	4.7

HONORS: NBA All-Rookie second team (1999).

NBA REGULAR-SEASON RECORD

Season Team	G	Min.	FGM	FGA	Pct.	FTM	FTA	Pct.	REBOUNDS Off.	Def.	Tot.	Ast.	St.	Blk.	TO	Pts.	RPG	APG	PPG
98-99—L.A. Clippers	45	1279	172	399	.431	57	118	.483	120	237	357	25	27	55	85	401	7.9	0.6	8.9
99-00—L.A. Clippers	80	2493	330	756	.437	123	189	.651	194	462	656	38	35	140	177	783	8.2	0.5	9.8
00-01—L.A. Clippers	82	2127	308	708	.435	85	156	.545	168	357	525	46	30	108	169	701	6.4	0.6	8.5
Totals	207	5899	810	1863	.435	265	463	.572	482	1056	1538	109	92	303	431	1885	7.4	0.5	9.1

Personal fouls/disqualifications: 1998-99, 137/2. 1999-00, 304/10. 2000-01, 250/4. Totals, 691/16.

O

O'NEAL, JERMAINE   F/C   PACERS

PERSONAL: Born October 13, 1978, in Columbia, S.C. ... 6-11/230. (2,11/104,3).
HIGH SCHOOL: Eau Claire (Columbia, S.C.).
COLLEGE: Did not attend college.
TRANSACTIONS/CAREER NOTES: Selected out of high school by Portland Trail Blazers in first round (17th pick overall) of 1996 NBA Draft. ... Traded by Trail Blazers with C Joe Kleine to Indiana Pacers for F Dale Davis (August 31, 2000).

NBA REGULAR-SEASON RECORD

Season Team	G	Min.	FGM	FGA	Pct.	FTM	FTA	Pct.	REBOUNDS Off.	Def.	Tot.	Ast.	St.	Blk.	TO	Pts.	RPG	APG	PPG
96-97—Portland	45	458	69	153	.451	47	78	.603	39	85	124	8	2	26	27	185	2.8	0.2	4.1
97-98—Portland	60	808	112	231	.485	45	89	.506	80	121	201	17	15	58	55	269	3.4	0.3	4.5
98-99—Portland	36	311	36	83	.434	18	35	.514	42	55	97	13	4	14	14	90	2.7	0.4	2.5
99-00—Portland	70	859	108	222	.486	57	98	.582	97	132	229	18	11	55	47	273	3.3	0.3	3.9
00-01—Indiana	81	2641	404	868	.465	229	545	.601	249	545	794	98	49	*228	161	1041	9.8	1.2	12.9
Totals	292	5077	729	1557	.468	400	688	.581	507	938	1445	154	81	381	304	1858	4.9	0.5	6.4

Three-point field goals: 1996-97, 0-for-1. 1997-98, 0-for-2. 1998-99, 0-for-1. 1999-00, 0-for-1. 2000-01, 0-for-5. Totals, 0-for-10 (.000).
Personal fouls/disqualifications: 1996-97, 46/0. 1997-98, 101/0. 1998-99, 41/0. 1999-00, 127/1. 2000-01, 280/5. Totals, 595/6.

NBA PLAYOFF RECORD

									REBOUNDS							AVERAGES		
Season Team	G	Min.	FGM	FGA	Pct.	FTM	FTA	Pct.	Off.	Def.	Tot.	Ast.	St.	Blk.	TO	Pts.	RPG	APG	PPG
96-97—Portland.........	2	4	0	2	.000	0	2	.000	0	1	1	0	0	1	0	0	0.5	0.0	0.0
97-98—Portland.........	1	3	0	3	.000	0	0	...	1	0	1	0	0	2	0	0	1.0	0.0	0.0
98-99—Portland.........	9	55	4	10	.400	6	12	.500	8	9	17	1	0	3	2	14	1.9	0.1	1.6
99-00—Portland.........	8	38	3	11	.273	6	9	.667	2	5	7	1	0	3	0	12	0.9	0.1	1.5
00-01—Indiana...........	4	157	17	39	.436	5	10	.500	12	38	50	7	0	10	7	39	12.5	1.8	9.8
Totals	24	257	24	65	.369	17	33	.515	23	53	76	9	0	19	9	65	3.2	0.4	2.7

Three-point field goals: 1996-97, 0-for-1. 1997-98, 0-for-1. 2000-01, 0-for-1. Totals, 0-for-3 (.000).
Personal fouls/disqualifications: 1997-98, 1/0. 1998-99, 11/0. 1999-00, 9/0. 2000-01, 13/0. Totals, 34/0.

O'NEAL, SHAQUILLE   C   LAKERS

PERSONAL: Born March 6, 1972, in Newark, N.J. ... 7-1/315. (2,16/142,9). ... Full Name: Shaquille Rashaun O'Neal. ... Nickname: Shaq. ... Name pronounced shuh-KEEL.
HIGH SCHOOL: Cole (San Antonio).
COLLEGE: Louisiana State.
TRANSACTIONS/CAREER NOTES: Selected after junior season by Orlando Magic in first round (first pick overall) of 1992 NBA Draft. ... Signed as free agent by Los Angeles Lakers (July 18, 1996).
CAREER HONORS: NBA 50th Anniversary All-Time Team (1996).
MISCELLANEOUS: Member of NBA championship team (2000, 2001). ... Member of gold-medal-winning U.S. Olympic team (1996). ... Member of gold-medal-winning U.S. World Championship team (1994). ... Orlando Magic all-time leading rebounder with 3,691 and all-time blocked shots leader with 824 (1992-93 through 1995-96).

COLLEGIATE RECORD

NOTES: The Sporting News All-America first team (1991, 1992). ... Led NCAA Division I with 14.7 rebounds per game (1991). ... Led NCAA Division I with 5.2 blocked shots per game (1992).

												AVERAGES		
Season Team	G	Min.	FGM	FGA	Pct.	FTM	FTA	Pct.	Reb.	Ast.	Pts.	RPG	APG	PPG
89-90—Louisiana State..............	32	901	180	314	.573	85	153	.556	385	61	445	12.0	1.9	13.9
90-91—Louisiana State..............	28	881	312	497	.628	150	235	.638	411	45	774	14.7	1.6	27.6
91-92—Louisiana State..............	30	959	294	478	.615	134	254	.528	421	46	722	14.0	1.5	24.1
Totals	90	2741	786	1289	.610	369	642	.575	1217	152	1941	13.5	1.7	21.6

NBA REGULAR-SEASON RECORD

RECORDS: Holds single-game record for most free throws attempted, none made—11 (December 8, 2000, vs. Seattle).
HONORS: NBA Most Valuable Player (2000). ... NBA Rookie of the Year (1993). ... IBM Award, for all-around contributions to team's success (2000, 2001). ... All-NBA first team (1998, 2000, 2001). ... All-NBA second team (1995, 1999). ... All-NBA third team (1994, 1996, 1997). ... NBA All-Defensive second team (2000, 2001). ... NBA All-Rookie first team (1993).

									REBOUNDS								AVERAGES		
Season Team	G	Min.	FGM	FGA	Pct.	FTM	FTA	Pct.	Off.	Def.	Tot.	Ast.	St.	Blk.	TO	Pts.	RPG	APG	PPG
92-93—Orlando..........	81	3071	733	1304	.562	427	721	.592	342	780	1122	152	60	286	*307	1893	13.9	1.9	23.4
93-94—Orlando..........	81	3224	*953	1591	*.599	471	850	.554	384	688	1072	195	76	231	222	2377	13.2	2.4	29.3
94-95—Orlando..........	79	2923	*930	*1594	.583	455	*854	.533	328	573	901	214	73	192	204	*2315	11.4	2.7	*29.3
95-96—Orlando..........	54	1946	592	1033	.573	249	511	.487	182	414	596	155	34	115	155	1434	11.0	2.9	26.6
96-97—L.A. Lakers.....	51	1941	552	991	.557	232	479	.484	195	445	640	159	46	147	146	1336	12.5	3.1	26.2
97-98—L.A. Lakers.....	60	2175	670	1147	*.584	359	681	.527	208	473	681	142	39	144	175	1699	11.4	2.4	28.3
98-99—L.A. Lakers.....	49	1705	*510	885	*.576	269	*498	.540	187	338	525	114	36	82	122	*1289	10.7	2.3	26.3
99-00—L.A. Lakers.....	79	3163	*956	*1665	*.574	*432	*824	.524	336	742	1078	299	36	239	223	*2344	13.6	3.8	*29.7
00-01—L.A. Lakers.....	74	2924	*813	1422	*.572	499	*972	.513	291	649	940	277	47	204	218	2125	12.7	3.7	28.7
Totals	608	23072	6709	11632	.577	3393	6390	.531	2453	5102	7555	1707	447	1640	1772	16812	12.4	2.8	27.7

Three-point field goals: 1992-93, 0-for-2. 1993-94, 0-for-2. 1994-95, 0-for-5. 1995-96, 1-for-2 (.500). 1996-97, 0-for-4. 1998-99, 0-for-1. 1999-00, 0-for-1. 2000-01, 0-for-2. Totals, 1-for-19 (.053).
Personal fouls/disqualifications: 1992-93, 321/8. 1993-94, 281/3. 1994-95, 258/1. 1995-96, 193/1. 1996-97, 180/2. 1997-98, 193/1. 1998-99, 155/4. 1999-00, 255/2. 2000-01, 256/6. Totals, 2092/28.

NBA PLAYOFF RECORD

NOTES: NBA Finals Most Valuable Player (2000, 2001). ... Holds NBA Finals single-game record for most free throws attempted in one quarter—16; most free throws made in one half—13; and most free throws attempted in one game—39 (June 9, 2000, vs. Indiana). ... Shares NBA Finals single-game records for most free throws made in one quarter—9 (June 9, 2000, vs. Indiana); and most blocked shots—8 (June 8, 2001, vs. Philadelphia). ... Holds single-game playoff record for most free throws attempted—39 (June 9, 2000, vs. Indiana); most free throws attempted in one half—27; and most free throws attempted in one quarter—25 (May 20, 2000, vs. Portland).

									REBOUNDS								AVERAGES		
Season Team	G	Min.	FGM	FGA	Pct.	FTM	FTA	Pct.	Off.	Def.	Tot.	Ast.	St.	Blk.	TO	Pts.	RPG	APG	PPG
93-94—Orlando..........	3	126	23	45	.511	16	34	.471	17	23	40	7	2	9	10	62	13.3	2.3	20.7
94-95—Orlando..........	21	805	195	338	.577	149	261	.571	95	155	250	70	18	40	73	539	11.9	3.3	25.7
95-96—Orlando..........	12	459	131	216	.606	48	122	.393	49	71	120	55	9	15	44	310	10.0	4.6	25.8
96-97—L.A. Lakers.....	9	326	89	173	.514	64	105	.610	38	57	95	29	5	17	22	242	10.6	3.2	26.9
97-98—L.A. Lakers.....	13	501	158	258	.612	80	159	.503	48	84	132	38	7	34	43	396	10.2	2.9	30.5
98-99—L.A. Lakers.....	8	315	79	155	.510	55	118	.466	44	49	93	18	7	23	18	213	11.6	2.3	26.6
99-00—L.A. Lakers.....	23	1000	286	505	.566	135	296	.456	119	236	355	71	13	55	56	707	15.4	3.1	30.7
00-01—L.A. Lakers.....	16	676	191	344	.555	105	200	.525	91	156	247	51	7	38	57	487	15.4	3.2	30.4
Totals	105	4208	1152	2034	.566	652	1295	.503	501	831	1332	339	68	231	323	2956	12.7	3.2	28.2

Personal fouls/disqualifications: 1993-94, 13/0. 1994-95, 84/1. 1995-96, 40/0. 1996-97, 37/1. 1997-98, 41/1. 1998-99, 29/0. 1999-00, 67/1. 2000-01, 55/2. Totals, 366/6.

NOTES: NBA All-Star Game co-Most Valuable Player (2000).

Season	Team	Min.	FGM	FGA	Pct.	FTM	FTA	Pct.	REBOUNDS Off.	Def.	Tot.	Ast.	PF	Dq.	St.	Blk.	TO	Pts.
1993	—Orlando	25	4	9	.444	6	9	.667	3	4	7	0	3	0	0	0	0	14
1994	—Orlando	26	2	12	.167	4	11	.364	4	6	10	0	2	0	1	4	1	8
1995	—Orlando	26	9	16	.563	4	7	.571	4	3	7	1	2	0	3	2	2	22
1996	—Orlando	28	10	16	.625	5	11	.455	3	7	10	1	3	0	1	2	2	25
1997	—L.A. Lakers							Selected, did not play—injured.										
1998	—L.A. Lakers	18	5	10	.500	2	4	.500	2	2	4	1	2	...	0	0	2	12
2000	—L.A. Lakers	25	11	20	.550	0	2	.000	4	5	9	3	2	0	0	3	4	22
2001	—L.A. Lakers							Selected, did not play—injured.										
	Totals........................	148	41	83	.494	21	44	.477	20	27	47	6	14	0	5	11	11	103

Three-point field goals: 1995, 0-for-1. Totals, 0-for-1 (.000).

OSTERTAG, GREG　　　　　C　　　　　JAZZ

PERSONAL: Born March 6, 1973, in Dallas. ... 7-2/280. (2,18/127,0). ... Full Name: Gregory Donovan Ostertag. ... Name pronounced OH-stir-tag.
HIGH SCHOOL: Duncanville (Texas).
COLLEGE: Kansas.
TRANSACTIONS/CAREER NOTES: Selected by Utah Jazz in first round (28th pick overall) of 1995 NBA Draft.

COLLEGIATE RECORD

Season Team	G	Min.	FGM	FGA	Pct.	FTM	FTA	Pct.	Reb.	Ast.	Pts.	AVERAGES RPG	APG	PPG
91-92—Kansas	32	311	61	112	.545	32	49	.653	112	5	154	3.5	0.2	4.8
92-93—Kansas	29	389	61	118	.517	33	55	.600	118	11	155	4.1	0.4	5.3
93-94—Kansas	35	739	145	272	.533	70	111	.631	307	12	360	8.8	0.3	10.3
94-95—Kansas	31	603	121	203	.596	57	103	.553	233	13	299	7.5	0.4	9.6
Totals	127	2042	388	705	.550	192	318	.604	770	41	968	6.1	0.3	7.6

Three-point field goals: 1991-92, 0-for-1. 1993-94, 0-for-2. Totals, 0-for-3 (.000).

NBA REGULAR-SEASON RECORD

Season Team	G	Min.	FGM	FGA	Pct.	FTM	FTA	Pct.	REBOUNDS Off.	Def.	Tot.	Ast.	St.	Blk.	TO	Pts.	AVERAGES RPG	APG	PPG
95-96—Utah	57	661	86	182	.473	36	54	.667	57	118	175	5	5	63	25	208	3.1	0.1	3.6
96-97—Utah	77	1818	210	408	.515	139	205	.678	180	385	565	27	24	152	74	559	7.3	0.4	7.3
97-98—Utah	63	1288	115	239	.481	67	140	.479	134	240	374	25	28	132	74	297	5.9	0.4	4.7
98-99—Utah	48	1340	99	208	.476	75	121	.620	105	243	348	23	12	131	45	273	7.3	0.5	5.7
99-00—Utah	81	1606	124	267	.464	119	187	.636	172	310	482	18	20	172	79	367	6.0	0.2	4.5
00-01—Utah	81	1491	139	281	.495	84	151	.556	164	251	415	22	22	142	63	363	5.1	0.3	4.5
Totals	407	8204	773	1585	.488	520	858	.606	812	1547	2359	120	111	792	360	2067	5.8	0.3	5.1

Three-point field goals: 1996-97, 0-for-4. 1999-00, 0-for-1. 2000-01, 1-for-2 (.500). Totals, 1-for-7 (.143).
Personal fouls/disqualifications: 1995-96, 91/1. 1996-97, 233/2. 1997-98, 166/1. 1998-99, 140/2. 1999-00, 196/2. 2000-01, 215/3. Totals, 1041/11.

NBA PLAYOFF RECORD

Season Team	G	Min.	FGM	FGA	Pct.	FTM	FTA	Pct.	REBOUNDS Off.	Def.	Tot.	Ast.	St.	Blk.	TO	Pts.	AVERAGES RPG	APG	PPG
95-96—Utah	15	212	20	45	.444	13	21	.619	18	32	50	1	2	21	4	53	3.3	0.1	3.5
96-97—Utah	20	459	34	83	.410	26	35	.743	52	85	137	6	10	47	18	94	6.9	0.3	4.7
97-98—Utah	19	336	26	46	.565	12	25	.480	25	56	81	5	7	37	12	64	4.3	0.3	3.4
98-99—Utah	11	261	13	35	.371	18	28	.643	18	47	65	6	2	24	8	44	5.9	0.5	4.0
99-00—Utah	8	172	10	19	.526	10	22	.455	19	26	45	2	2	17	8	30	5.6	0.3	3.8
00-01—Utah	5	64	4	11	.364	0	4	.000	6	12	18	1	0	2	2	8	3.6	0.2	1.6
Totals	78	1504	107	239	.448	79	135	.585	138	258	396	21	23	148	52	293	5.1	0.3	3.8

Personal fouls/disqualifications: 1995-96, 28/0. 1996-97, 76/3. 1997-98, 51/0. 1998-99, 27/0. 1999-00, 20/0. 2000-01, 10/1. Totals, 212/4.

OUTLAW, BO　　　　　F　　　　　MAGIC

PERSONAL: Born April 13, 1971, in San Antonio. ... 6-8/210. (2,03/95,3). ... Full Name: Charles Outlaw. ... Nickname: Bo.
HIGH SCHOOL: John Jay (San Antonio).
JUNIOR COLLEGE: South Plains College (Texas).
COLLEGE: Houston.
TRANSACTIONS/CAREER NOTES: Not drafted by an NBA franchise. ... Played in Spain (1993-94). ... Played in Continental Basketball Association with Grand Rapids Hoops (1993-94). ... Signed by Los Angeles Clippers to first of two consecutive 10-day contracts (February 14, 1994). ... Re-signed by Clippers for remainder of season (March 8, 1994). ... Signed as free agent by Orlando Magic (September 5, 1997).

COLLEGIATE RECORD

NOTES: Led NCAA Division I with .684 field goal percentage (1992) and .658 field goal percentage (1993).

Season Team	G	Min.	FGM	FGA	Pct.	FTM	FTA	Pct.	Reb.	Ast.	Pts.	AVERAGES RPG	APG	PPG
89-90—South Plains College	30	...	147	261	.563	69	136	.507	289	54	364	9.6	1.8	12.1
90-91—South Plains College	30	...	160	242	.661	70	122	.574	326	87	395	10.9	2.9	13.2
91-92—Houston	31	970	156	228	.684	57	129	.442	254	81	369	8.2	2.6	11.9
92-93—Houston	30	1055	196	298	.658	95	192	.495	301	99	487	10.0	3.3	16.2
Junior College Totals.............	60	...	307	503	.610	139	258	.539	615	141	759	10.3	2.4	12.7
4-Year-College Totals	61	2025	352	526	.669	152	321	.474	555	180	856	9.1	3.0	14.0

Three-point field goals: 1989-90, 0-for-1. 1990-91, 5-for-10 (.500). Totals, 5-for-11 (.455).

CBA REGULAR-SEASON RECORD

NOTES: Led CBA with 3.8 blocked shots per game (1994). ... CBA All-League second team (1994). ... CBA All-Defensive team (1994). ... CBA All-Rookie first team (1994).

Season Team	G	Min.	FGM	FGA	Pct.	FTM	FTA	Pct.	Reb.	Ast.	Pts.	AVERAGES RPG	APG	PPG
93-94—Grand Rapids	32	1211	167	243	.687	83	160	.519	349	56	417	10.9	1.8	13.0

Three-point field goals: 1993-94, 0-for-1.

NBA REGULAR-SEASON RECORD

Season Team	G	Min.	FGM	FGA	Pct.	FTM	FTA	Pct.	REBOUNDS Off.	Def.	Tot.	Ast.	St.	Blk.	TO	Pts.	AVERAGES RPG	APG	PPG
93-94—L.A. Clippers	37	871	98	167	.587	61	103	.592	81	131	212	36	36	37	31	257	5.7	1.0	6.9
94-95—L.A. Clippers	81	1655	170	325	.523	82	186	.441	121	192	313	84	90	151	78	422	3.9	1.0	5.2
95-96—L.A. Clippers	80	985	107	186	.575	72	162	.444	87	113	200	50	44	91	45	286	2.5	0.6	3.6
96-97—L.A. Clippers	82	2195	254	417	.609	117	232	.504	174	280	454	157	94	142	107	625	5.5	1.9	7.6
97-98—Orlando	82	2953	301	543	.554	180	313	.575	255	382	637	216	107	181	175	783	7.8	2.6	9.5
98-99—Orlando	31	851	84	154	.545	35	81	.432	54	113	167	56	40	43	58	203	5.4	1.8	6.5
99-00—Orlando	82	2326	204	339	.602	82	162	.506	202	323	525	245	113	148	133	490	6.4	3.0	6.0
00-01—Orlando	80	2534	226	368	.614	129	225	.573	211	408	619	225	105	137	141	582	7.7	2.8	7.3
Totals	555	14370	1444	2499	.578	758	1464	.518	1185	1942	3127	1069	629	930	768	3648	5.6	1.9	6.6

Three-point field goals: 1993-94, 0-for-2. 1994-95, 0-for-5. 1995-96, 0-for-3. 1996-97, 0-for-8. 1997-98, 1-for-4 (.250). 1998-99, 0-for-3. 1999-00, 0-for-3. 2000-01, 1-for-2 (.500). Totals, 2-for-30 (.067).
Personal fouls/disqualifications: 1993-94, 94/1. 1994-95, 227/4. 1995-96, 127/0. 1996-97, 227/5. 1997-98, 260/1. 1998-99, 79/1. 1999-00, 203/0. 2000-01, 241/4. Totals, 1458/16.

NBA PLAYOFF RECORD

Season Team	G	Min.	FGM	FGA	Pct.	FTM	FTA	Pct.	REBOUNDS Off.	Def.	Tot.	Ast.	St.	Blk.	TO	Pts.	AVERAGES RPG	APG	PPG
96-97—L.A. Clippers	3	66	6	11	.545	3	10	.300	6	8	14	4	1	2	3	15	4.7	1.3	5.0
98-99—Orlando	4	83	6	10	.600	6	13	.462	3	12	15	2	1	8	6	18	3.8	0.5	4.5
00-01—Orlando	4	134	16	26	.615	2	11	.182	11	31	42	9	5	6	9	34	10.5	2.3	8.5
Totals	11	283	28	47	.596	11	34	.324	20	51	71	15	7	16	18	67	6.5	1.4	6.1

Three-point field goals: 1996-97, 0-for-1. Totals, 0-for-1 (.000).
Personal fouls/disqualifications: 1996-97, 5/0. 1998-99, 9/0. 2000-01, 15/0. Totals, 29/0.

SPANISH LEAGUE RECORD

Season Team	G	Min.	FGM	FGA	Pct.	FTM	FTA	Pct.	Reb.	Ast.	Pts.	AVERAGES RPG	APG	PPG
93-94—Estudiante Caja Postal	2	10	0	3	.000	0	2	.000	2	0	0	1.0	0.0	0.0

OVERTON, DOUG   G

PERSONAL: Born August 3, 1969, in Philadelphia. ... 6-3/190. (1,91/86,2). ... Full Name: Douglas M. Overton.
HIGH SCHOOL: Dobbins Area Vocational Technical School (Philadelphia).
COLLEGE: La Salle.
TRANSACTIONS/CAREER NOTES: Selected by Detroit Pistons in second round (40th pick overall) of 1991 NBA Draft. ... Waived by Pistons (October 29, 1991). ... Played in Continental Basketball Association with Rockford Lightning (1991-92). ... Signed as free agent by Washington Bullets (October 19, 1992). ... Traded by Bullets with F Don MacLean to Denver Nuggets for G Robert Pack (October 30, 1995). ... Signed as free agent by Philadelphia 76ers (October 3, 1996). ... Signed as free agent by Orlando Magic (January 20, 1999). ... Waived by Magic (February 26, 1999). ... Signed as free agent by New Jersey Nets (March 3, 1999). ... Waived by Nets (March 10, 1999). ... Re-signed by Nets to 10-day contract (March 12, 1999). ... Signed by 76ers to first of two consecutive 10-day contracts (March 27, 1999). ... Re-signed by 76ers for remainder of season (April 16, 1999). ... Waived by 76ers (October 28, 1999). ... Signed as free agent by Boston Celtics (November 8, 1999). ... Waived by Celtics (October 29, 2000). ... Re-signed as free agent by Celtics (November 21, 2000). ... Waived by Celtics (December 7, 2000). ... Played in American Basketball Association 2000 with Kansas City Knights (2000-01). ... Signed by Charlotte Hornets to 10-day contract (January 26, 2001). ... Signed by Nets to first of two consecutive 10-day contracts (March 22, 2001). ... Signed by Nets for remainder of season (April 11, 2001).

COLLEGIATE RECORD

Season Team	G	Min.	FGM	FGA	Pct.	FTM	FTA	Pct.	Reb.	Ast.	Pts.	AVERAGES RPG	APG	PPG
87-88—La Salle	34	918	110	221	.498	37	44	.841	81	91	265	2.4	2.7	7.8
88-89—La Salle	32	1221	174	352	.494	47	59	.797	101	244	421	3.2	7.6	13.2
89-90—La Salle	32	1202	201	387	.519	95	119	.798	133	212	551	4.2	6.6	17.2
90-91—La Salle	25	959	199	447	.445	106	128	.828	103	124	558	4.1	5.0	22.3
Totals	123	4300	684	1407	.486	285	350	.814	418	671	1795	3.4	5.5	14.6

Three-point field goals: 1987-88, 8-for-27 (.296). 1988-89, 26-for-65 (.400). 1989-90, 54-for-124 (.435). 1990-91, 54-for-160 (.338). Totals, 142-for-376 (.378).

CBA REGULAR-SEASON RECORD

Season Team	G	Min.	FGM	FGA	Pct.	FTM	FTA	Pct.	Reb.	Ast.	Pts.	AVERAGES RPG	APG	PPG
91-92—Rockford	28	1071	194	396	.490	72	85	.847	123	170	463	4.4	6.1	16.5

Three-point field goals: 1991-92, 3-for-5 (.600).

NBA REGULAR-SEASON RECORD

Season Team	G	Min.	FGM	FGA	Pct.	FTM	FTA	Pct.	REBOUNDS Off.	Def.	Tot.	Ast.	St.	Blk.	TO	Pts.	AVERAGES RPG	APG	PPG
92-93—Washington	45	990	152	323	.471	59	81	.728	25	81	106	157	31	6	72	366	2.4	3.5	8.1
93-94—Washington	61	749	87	216	.403	43	52	.827	19	50	69	92	21	1	54	218	1.1	1.5	3.6
94-95—Washington	82	1704	207	498	.416	109	125	.872	26	117	143	246	53	2	104	576	1.7	3.0	7.0

Season Team	G	Min.	FGM	FGA	Pct.	FTM	FTA	Pct.	REBOUNDS Off.	Def.	Tot.	Ast.	St.	Blk.	TO	Pts.	AVERAGES RPG	APG	PPG
95-96—Denver............	55	607	67	178	.376	40	55	.727	8	55	63	106	13	5	40	182	1.1	1.9	3.3
96-97—Philadelphia....	61	634	81	190	.426	45	48	.938	18	50	68	101	24	0	39	217	1.1	1.7	3.6
97-98—Philadelphia....	23	277	24	63	.381	14	16	.875	2	12	14	37	8	1	23	62	0.6	1.6	2.7
98-99—Orl.-N.J.-Phil...	24	244	36	84	.429	18	20	.900	7	14	21	23	5	1	20	92	0.9	1.0	3.8
99-00—Boston............	48	432	61	154	.396	20	21	.952	14	19	33	53	10	0	20	152	0.7	1.1	3.2
00-01—Bos.-Char.-N.J.	21	475	52	139	.374	10	16	.625	4	35	39	72	8	0	31	125	1.9	3.4	6.0
Totals	420	6112	767	1845	.416	358	434	.825	123	433	556	887	173	16	403	1990	1.3	2.1	4.7

Three-point field goals: 1992-93, 3-for-13 (.231). 1993-94, 1-for-11 (.091). 1994-95, 53-for-125 (.424). 1995-96, 8-for-26 (.308). 1996-97, 10-for-40 (.250). 1997-98, 0-for-3. 1998-99, 2-for-7 (.286). 1999-00, 10-for-28 (.357). 2000-01, 11-for-36 (.306). Totals, 98-for-289 (.339).

Personal fouls/disqualifications: 1992-93, 81/0. 1993-94, 48/0. 1994-95, 126/1. 1995-96, 49/0. 1996-97, 44/0. 1997-98, 34/0. 1998-99, 18/0. 1999-00, 46/0. 2000-01, 37/0. Totals, 483/1.

ABA 2000 LEAGUE RECORD

Season Team	G	Min.	FGM	FGA	Pct.	FTM	FTA	Pct.	Reb.	Ast.	Pts.	AVERAGES RPG	APG	PPG
00-01—Kansas City	15	586	101	216	.468	48	51	.941	63	97	320	4.2	6.5	21.3

Three-point field goals: 2000-01, 50-for-101 (.495).

OWENS, BILLY   F/G

PERSONAL: Born May 1, 1969, in Carlisle, Pa. ... 6-9/235. (2,06/106,6). ... Full Name: Billy Eugene Owens.
HIGH SCHOOL: Carlisle (Pa.).
COLLEGE: Syracuse.
TRANSACTIONS/CAREER NOTES: Selected after junior season by Sacramento Kings in first round (third pick overall) of 1991 NBA Draft. ... Traded by Kings to Golden State Warriors for G Mitch Richmond and C Les Jepsen (November 1, 1991). ... Traded by Warriors with rights to G Predrag Danilovic to Miami Heat for C Rony Seikaly (November 2, 1994). ... Traded by Heat with G/F Kevin Gamble to Sacramento Kings for F/G Walt Williams and F Tyrone Corbin (February 22, 1996). ... Signed as free agent by Seattle SuperSonics (January 22, 1999). ... Traded by SuperSonics with draft rights to F Corey Maggette, G/F Dale Ellis and F Don MacLean to Orlando Magic for F Horace Grant and 2001 and 2002 second-round draft choices (June 30, 1999). ... Traded by Magic to Philadelphia 76ers for F Harvey Grant and G Anthony Parker (August 13, 1999). ... Traded by 76ers with G Larry Hughes to Warriors in three-way deal in which Warriors sent G John Starks and future first-round draft choice to Chicago Bulls and 76ers sent F Bruce Bowen to Bulls for F Toni Kukoc (February 16. 2000). ... Traded by Warriors with F Jason Caffey to Milwaukee Bucks as part of three-way deal in which Bucks traded F/C J.R. Reid and F Robert Traylor to Cleveland Cavaliers, Cavaliers traded G Bob Sura to Golden Warriors and Bucks traded G Vinny Del Negro to Warriors (June 27, 2000). ... Traded by Bucks to Detroit Pistons for G Lindsey Hunter (August 22, 2000).
MISCELLANEOUS: Member of bronze-medal-winning U.S. World Championship team (1990).

COLLEGIATE RECORD

NOTES: THE SPORTING NEWS All-America second team (1991).

Season Team	G	Min.	FGM	FGA	Pct.	FTM	FTA	Pct.	Reb.	Ast.	Pts.	AVERAGES RPG	APG	PPG
88-89—Syracuse	38	1215	196	376	.521	94	145	.648	263	119	494	6.9	3.1	13.0
89-90—Syracuse	33	1188	228	469	.486	127	176	.722	276	151	602	8.4	4.6	18.2
90-91—Syracuse	32	1215	282	554	.509	157	233	.674	371	111	744	11.6	3.5	23.3
Totals	103	3618	706	1399	.505	378	554	.682	910	381	1840	8.8	3.7	17.9

Three-point field goals: 1988-89, 8-for-36 (.222). 1989-90, 19-for-60 (.317). 1990-91, 23-for-58 (.397). Totals, 50-for-154 (.325).

NBA REGULAR-SEASON RECORD

HONORS: NBA All-Rookie first team (1992).

Season Team	G	Min.	FGM	FGA	Pct.	FTM	FTA	Pct.	REBOUNDS Off.	Def.	Tot.	Ast.	St.	Blk.	TO	Pts.	AVERAGES RPG	APG	PPG
91-92—Golden State...	80	2510	468	891	.525	204	312	.654	243	396	639	188	90	65	179	1141	8.0	2.4	14.3
92-93—Golden State...	37	1201	247	493	.501	117	183	.639	108	156	264	144	35	28	106	612	7.1	3.9	16.5
93-94—Golden State...	79	2738	492	971	.507	199	326	.610	230	410	640	326	83	60	214	1186	8.1	4.1	15.0
94-95—Miami	70	2296	403	820	.491	194	313	.620	203	299	502	246	80	30	204	1002	7.2	3.5	14.3
96-97—Sacramento	66	1995	299	640	.467	101	145	.697	134	258	392	187	62	25	133	724	5.9	2.8	11.0
97-98—Sacramento	78	2348	338	728	.464	116	197	.589	170	412	582	219	93	38	153	818	7.5	2.8	10.5
98-99—Seattle	21	451	65	165	.394	28	35	.800	35	45	80	38	12	4	33	163	3.8	1.8	7.8
99-00—Phil.-G.S.	62	1305	150	358	.419	63	106	.594	99	202	301	97	33	21	85	374	4.9	1.6	6.0
00-01—Detroit	45	793	88	230	.383	19	40	.475	84	121	205	55	32	12	39	198	4.6	1.2	4.4
Totals	538	15637	2550	5296	.481	1041	1657	.628	1306	2299	3605	1500	520	283	1146	6218	6.7	2.8	11.6

Three-point field goals: 1991-92, 1-for-9 (.111). 1992-93, 1-for-11 (.091). 1993-94, 3-for-15 (.200). 1994-95, 2-for-22 (.091). 1996-97, 25-for-72 (.347). 1997-98, 26-for-70 (.371). 1998-99, 5-for-11 (.455). 1999-00, 11-for-34 (.324). 2000-01, 3-for-20 (.150). Totals, 77-for-264 (.292).

Personal fouls/disqualifications: 1991-92, 276/4. 1992-93, 105/1. 1993-94, 269/5. 1994-95, 205/6. 1996-97, 187/4. 1997-98, 231/5. 1998-99, 37/0. 1999-00, 166/1. 2000-01, 93/0. Totals, 1569/26.

NBA PLAYOFF RECORD

Season Team	G	Min.	FGM	FGA	Pct.	FTM	FTA	Pct.	REBOUNDS Off.	Def.	Tot.	Ast.	St.	Blk.	TO	Pts.	AVERAGES RPG	APG	PPG
91-92—Golden State ...	4	157	30	57	.526	17	27	.630	13	20	33	13	8	2	6	77	8.3	3.3	19.3
93-94—Golden State ...	3	127	25	50	.500	9	12	.750	12	18	30	13	4	2	7	59	10.0	4.3	19.7
95-96—Sacramento	4	131	15	34	.441	3	6	.500	5	21	26	14	4	1	11	33	6.5	3.5	8.3
Totals	11	415	70	141	.496	29	45	.644	30	59	89	40	16	5	24	169	8.1	3.6	15.4

Three-point field goals: 1993-94, 0-for-1. 1995-96, 0-for-4. Totals, 0-for-5 (.000).
Personal fouls/disqualifications: 1991-92, 14/0. 1993-94, 11/0. 1995-96, 17/1. Totals, 42/1.

OYEDEJI, OLUMIDE   F/C   SUPERSONICS

PERSONAL: Born May 11, 1981, in Ibadan, Nigeria. ... 6-10/240. (2,08/108,9). ... Name pronounced o-LOOM-o-day o-YA-degee.
HIGH SCHOOL: Community (Ibadan, Nigeria).
TRANSACTIONS/CAREER NOTES: Played in Germany (1998-99 and 1999-2000). ... Selected by Seattle SuperSonics in second round (42nd pick overall) of 2000 NBA Draft.

GERMAN LEAGUE RECORD

Season Team	G	Min.	FGM	FGA	Pct.	FTM	FTA	Pct.	Reb.	Ast.	Pts.	RPG	APG	PPG
98-99—DJK Wurzburg	23	468	75	131	.573	32	51	.627	176	12	184	7.7	0.5	8.0
99-00—DJK Wurzburg	26	824	119	217	.548	77	145	.531	380	15	315	14.6	0.6	12.1
Totals	49	1292	194	348	.557	109	196	.556	556	27	499	11.3	0.6	10.2

Three-point field goals: 1998-99, 2-for-5 (.400). 1999-00, 0-for-2. Totals, 2-for-7 (.286).

NBA REGULAR-SEASON RECORD

Season Team	G	Min.	FGM	FGA	Pct.	FTM	FTA	Pct.	Off.	Def.	Tot.	Ast.	St.	Blk.	TO	Pts.	RPG	APG	PPG
00-01—Seattle	30	221	18	37	.486	9	12	.750	24	43	67	2	7	10	11	45	2.2	0.1	1.5

Personal fouls/disqualifications: 2000-01, 40/0.

PACK, ROBERT   G

PERSONAL: Born February 3, 1969, in New Orleans. ... 6-2/190. (1,88/86,2). ... Full Name: Robert John Pack Jr.
HIGH SCHOOL: Lawless (New Orleans).
JUNIOR COLLEGE: Tyler (Texas) Junior College.
COLLEGE: Southern California.
TRANSACTIONS/CAREER NOTES: Not drafted by an NBA franchise. ... Signed as free agent by Portland Trail Blazers (September 16, 1991). ... Traded by Trail Blazers to Denver Nuggets for 1993 second-round draft choice (October 23, 1992). ... Traded by Nuggets to Washington Bullets for G Doug Overton and F Don MacLean (October 30, 1995). ... Signed as free agent by New Jersey Nets (July 31, 1996). ... Traded by Nets with C Shawn Bradley, F Ed O'Bannon and G Khalid Reeves to Dallas Mavericks for C Eric Montross, G Jim Jackson, F/C Chris Gatling, F/G George McCloud and G Sam Cassell (February 17, 1997). ... Traded by Mavericks to Boston Celtics as part of four-team deal in which Celtics received C John Williams and cash considerations from Mavericks and a conditional first-round draft choice from Utah Jazz, Mavericks received G Dana Barros from Celtics, F Bill Curley from Warriors and G Howard Eisley from Jazz, Jazz received F Donyell Marshall from Warriors and C Bruno Sundov from Mavericks and Warriors received F Danny Fortson from Celtics and F Adam Keefe from Jazz (August 16, 2000). ... Traded by Celtics with F Calbert Cheaney to Nuggets for G Chris Herren and G Bryant Stith (October 16, 2000).

COLLEGIATE RECORD

Season Team	G	Min.	FGM	FGA	Pct.	FTM	FTA	Pct.	Reb.	Ast.	Pts.	RPG	APG	PPG
87-88—Tyler Junior College			Statistics unavailable.											
88-89—Tyler Junior College			Statistics unavailable.											
89-90—Southern California	28	883	118	250	.472	84	124	.677	67	165	339	2.4	5.9	12.1
90-91—Southern California	29	941	145	302	.480	123	155	.794	93	154	427	3.2	5.3	14.7
Totals	57	1824	263	552	.476	207	279	.742	160	319	766	2.8	5.6	13.4

Three-point field goals: 1989-90, 19-for-57 (.333). 1990-91, 14-for-55 (.255). Totals, 33-for-112 (.295).

NBA REGULAR-SEASON RECORD

Season Team	G	Min.	FGM	FGA	Pct.	FTM	FTA	Pct.	Off.	Def.	Tot.	Ast.	St.	Blk.	TO	Pts.	RPG	APG	PPG
91-92—Portland	72	894	115	272	.423	102	127	.803	32	65	97	140	40	4	92	332	1.3	1.9	4.6
92-93—Denver	77	1579	285	606	.470	239	311	.768	52	108	160	335	81	10	185	810	2.1	4.4	10.5
93-94—Denver	66	1382	223	503	.443	179	236	.758	25	98	123	356	81	9	204	631	1.9	5.4	9.6
94-95—Denver	42	1144	170	395	.430	137	175	.783	19	94	113	290	61	6	134	507	2.7	6.9	12.1
95-96—Washington	31	1084	190	444	.428	154	182	.846	29	103	132	242	62	1	114	560	4.3	7.8	18.1
96-97—N.J.-Dal.	54	1782	272	693	.392	196	243	.807	28	118	146	452	94	6	217	771	2.7	8.4	14.3
97-98—Dallas	12	292	33	98	.337	25	36	.694	8	26	34	42	20	1	38	94	2.8	3.5	7.8
98-99—Dallas	25	468	75	174	.431	72	88	.818	9	27	36	81	20	1	49	222	1.4	3.2	8.9
99-00—Dallas	29	665	96	230	.417	63	78	.808	7	35	42	168	31	3	76	259	1.4	5.8	8.0
00 01—Denver	74	1260	181	426	.425	105	137	.766	30	107	137	293	65	1	135	479	1.9	4.0	6.5
Totals	482	10550	1640	3841	.427	1272	1613	.789	239	781	1020	2399	555	42	1244	4665	2.1	5.0	9.7

Three-point field goals: 1991-92, 0-for-0. 1992-93, 1-for-8 (.125). 1993-94, 6-for-29 (.207). 1994-95, 30-for-72 (.417). 1995-96, 26-for-98 (.265). 1996-97, 31-for-112 (.277). 1997-98, 3-for-6 (.500). 1998-99, 0-for-4. 1999-00, 4-for-11 (.364). 2000-01, 12-for-31 (.387). Totals, 113-for-381 (.297).
Personal fouls/disqualifications: 1991-92, 101/0. 1992-93, 182/1. 1993-94, 147/1. 1994-95, 101/1. 1995-96, 68/0. 1996-97, 139/0. 1997-98, 17/0. 1998-99, 41/0. 1999-00, 44/0. 2000-01, 114/0. Totals, 954/3.

NBA PLAYOFF RECORD

Season Team	G	Min.	FGM	FGA	Pct.	FTM	FTA	Pct.	Off.	Def.	Tot.	Ast.	St.	Blk.	TO	Pts.	RPG	APG	PPG
91-92—Portland	14	52	4	18	.222	3	4	.750	2	4	6	7	5	1	3	11	0.4	0.5	0.8
93-94—Denver	12	332	48	118	.407	39	55	.709	5	23	28	51	18	6	46	141	2.3	4.3	11.8
Totals	26	384	52	136	.382	42	59	.712	7	27	34	58	23	7	49	152	1.3	2.2	5.8

Three-point field goals: 1993-94, 6-for-20 (.300). Totals, 6-for-20 (.300).
Personal fouls/disqualifications: 1991-92, 10/0. 1993-94, 41/0. Totals, 51/0.

O
P

PADGETT, SCOTT   F   JAZZ

PERSONAL: Born April 19, 1976, in Louisville, Ky. ... 6-9/240. (2,06/108,9). ... Full Name: Scott Anthony Padgett.
HIGH SCHOOL: St. Xavier (Louisville, Ky.).
COLLEGE: Kentucky.
TRANSACTIONS/CAREER NOTES: Selected by Utah Jazz in first round (28th pick overall) of 1999 NBA Draft.

COLLEGIATE RECORD

NOTES: Member of NCAA Division I championship team (1998).

Season Team	G	Min.	FGM	FGA	Pct.	FTM	FTA	Pct.	Reb.	Ast.	Pts.	RPG	APG	PPG
94-95—Kentucky	14	57	7	27	.259	10	12	.833	17	4	28	1.2	0.3	2.0
95-96—Kentucky						Did not play—ineligible.								
96-97—Kentucky	32	759	100	244	.410	61	80	.763	162	56	308	5.1	1.8	9.6
97-98—Kentucky	39	1089	161	338	.476	87	102	.853	255	82	449	6.5	2.1	11.5
98-99—Kentucky	37	1075	156	335	.466	94	138	.681	217	96	467	5.9	2.6	12.6
Totals	122	2980	424	944	.449	252	332	.759	651	238	1252	5.3	2.0	10.3

Three-point field goals: 1994-95, 4-for-13 (.308). 1996-97, 47-for-138 (.341). 1997-98, 40-for-107 (.374). 1998-99, 61-for-160 (.381). Totals, 152-for-418 (.364).

NBA REGULAR-SEASON RECORD

Season Team	G	Min.	FGM	FGA	Pct.	FTM	FTA	Pct.	REBOUNDS Off.	Def.	Tot.	Ast.	St.	Blk.	TO	Pts.	RPG	APG	PPG
99-00—Utah	47	432	44	140	.314	19	27	.704	24	64	88	25	14	8	22	120	1.9	0.5	2.6
00-01—Utah	27	127	18	43	.419	15	20	.750	19	20	39	5	6	3	10	56	1.4	0.2	2.1
Totals	74	559	62	183	.339	34	47	.723	43	84	127	30	20	11	32	176	1.7	0.4	2.4

Three-point field goals: 1999-00, 13-for-44 (.295). 2000-01, 5-for-9 (.556). Totals, 18-for-53 (.340).
Personal fouls/disqualifications: 1999-00, 55/1. 2000-01, 21/0. Totals, 76/1.

NBA PLAYOFF RECORD

Season Team	G	Min.	FGM	FGA	Pct.	FTM	FTA	Pct.	REBOUNDS Off.	Def.	Tot.	Ast.	St.	Blk.	TO	Pts.	RPG	APG	PPG
99-00—Utah	8	59	6	16	.375	0	0	...	3	14	17	5	1	2	4	15	2.1	0.6	1.9

Three-point field goals: 1999-00, 3-for-9 (.333).
Personal fouls/disqualifications: 1999-00, 10/0.

PALACIO, MILT   G   CELTICS

PERSONAL: Born February 7, 1978, in Los Angeles. ... 6-3/195. (1,91/88,5). ... Full Name: Milton S. Palacio.
HIGH SCHOOL: Gardena (Los Angeles).
JUNIOR COLLEGE: Midland (Texas) College.
COLLEGE: Colorado State.
TRANSACTIONS/CAREER NOTES: Not drafted by an NBA franchise. ... Signed as free agent by Vancouver Grizzlies (September 29, 1999). ... Signed as free agent by Washington Wizards (October 2, 2000). ... Waived by Wizards (October 16, 2000). ... Signed as free agent by Boston Celtics (December 7, 2000). ... Waived by Celtics (January 5, 2001). ... Re-signed by Celtics to the first of two consecutive 10-day contracts (January 10, 2001). ... Signed by Celtics for remainder of season (January 29, 2001).

COLLEGIATE RECORD

Season Team	G	Min.	FGM	FGA	Pct.	FTM	FTA	Pct.	Reb.	Ast.	Pts.	RPG	APG	PPG
95-96—Midland	29	...	83	167	.497	65	84	.774	114	142	254	3.9	4.9	8.8
96-97—Colorado State	29	898	75	151	.497	62	89	.697	111	147	230	3.8	5.1	7.9
97-98—Colorado State	29	957	98	205	.478	64	97	.660	103	148	283	3.6	5.1	9.8
98-99—Colorado State	30	1073	188	418	.450	135	179	.754	154	130	552	5.1	4.3	18.4
Junior College Totals	29	...	83	167	.497	65	84	.774	114	142	254	3.9	4.9	8.8
4-Year-College Totals	88	2928	361	774	.466	261	365	.715	368	425	1065	4.2	4.8	12.1

Three-point field goals: 1995-96, 23-for-57 (.404). 1996-97, 18-for-47 (.383). 1997-98, 23-for-61 (.377). 1998-99, 41-for-119 (.345). Totals, 82-for-227 (.361).

NBA REGULAR-SEASON RECORD

Season Team	G	Min.	FGM	FGA	Pct.	FTM	FTA	Pct.	REBOUNDS Off.	Def.	Tot.	Ast.	St.	Blk.	TO	Pts.	RPG	APG	PPG
99-00—Vancouver	53	394	43	98	.439	22	37	.595	17	34	51	48	20	0	44	108	1.0	0.9	2.0
00-01—Boston	58	1141	126	267	.472	78	92	.848	25	77	102	151	48	0	80	342	1.8	2.6	5.9
Totals	111	1535	169	365	.463	100	129	.775	42	111	153	199	68	0	124	450	1.4	1.8	4.1

Three-point field goals: 1999-00, 0-for-2. 2000-01, 12-for-36 (.333). Totals, 12-for-38 (.316).
Personal fouls/disqualifications: 1999-00, 32/0. 2000-01, 83/0. Totals, 115/0.

P

PANKO, ANDY   F

PERSONAL: Born November 29, 1977, in Harrisburg, Pa. ... 6-9/230. (2,06/104,3). ... Full Name: Andrew John Panko III.
HIGH SCHOOL: Bishop McDevitt (Harrisburg, Pa.).
COLLEGE: Lebanon Valley.
TRANSACTIONS/CAREER NOTES: Not drafted by an NBA franchise. ... Played in International Basketball League with New Mexico Slam (1999-2000 and 2000-01). ... Signed as free agent by Los Angeles Lakers (August 23, 2000). ... Waived by Lakers (October 29, 2000). ... Signed as free agent by Atlanta Hawks to 10-day contract (January 5, 2001). ... Waived by Hawks (January 13, 2001). ... Signed to play for Napoli in Italy for 2001-02 season.

COLLEGIATE RECORD

Season Team	G	Min.	FGM	FGA	Pct.	FTM	FTA	Pct.	Reb.	Ast.	Pts.	AVERAGES RPG	APG	PPG
95-96—Lebanon Valley	25	677	139	286	.486	57	78	.731	127	27	369	5.1	1.1	14.8
96-97—Lebanon Valley	28	992	237	435	.545	190	216	.880	208	79	703	7.4	2.8	25.1
97-98—Lebanon Valley	28	921	240	437	.549	200	244	.820	237	59	715	8.5	2.1	25.5
98-99—Lebanon Valley	28	968	232	420	.552	220	270	.815	257	96	728	9.2	3.4	26.0
Totals	109	3558	848	1578	.537	667	808	.825	829	261	2515	7.6	2.4	23.1

Three-point field goals: 1995-96, 34-for-96 (.354). 1996-97, 39-for-116 (.336). 1997-98, 35-for-114 (.307). 1998-99, 44-for-120 (.367). Totals, 152-for-446 (.341).

IBL REGULAR SEASON RECORD

Season Team	G	Min.	FGM	FGA	Pct.	FTM	FTA	Pct.	Reb.	Ast.	Pts.	AVERAGES RPG	APG	PPG
99-00—New Mexico	62	1351	245	560	.438	258	320	.806	199	80	834	3.2	1.3	13.5
00-01—New Mexico	42	1476	253	545	.464	293	353	.830	278	78	852	6.6	1.9	20.3
Totals	104	2827	498	1105	.451	551	673	.819	477	158	1686	4.6	1.5	16.2

Three-point field goals: 1999-00, 86-for-247 (.348). 2000-01, 53-for-173 (.306). Totals, 139-for-420 (.331).

NBA REGULAR-SEASON RECORD

Season Team	G	Min.	FGM	FGA	Pct.	FTM	FTA	Pct.	REBOUNDS Off.	Def.	Tot.	Ast.	St.	Blk.	TO	Pts.	AVERAGES RPG	APG	PPG
00-01—Atlanta	1	1	0	0	...	0	0	...	0	0	0	0	0	0	0	0	0.0	0.0	0.0

PARKS, CHEROKEE   F/C   SPURS

PERSONAL: Born October 11, 1972, in Huntington Beach, Calif. ... 6-11/230. (2,11/104,3). ... Full Name: Cherokee Bryan Parks.
HIGH SCHOOL: Marina (Huntington Beach, Calif.).
COLLEGE: Duke.
TRANSACTIONS/CAREER NOTES: Selected by Dallas Mavericks in first round (12th pick overall) of 1995 NBA Draft. ... Traded by Mavericks to Minnesota Timberwolves in exchange for Minnesota removing the 2-6 lottery protection on 1997 first-round draft choice Dallas acquired from Minnesota in 1994 trade involving C Sean Rooks (June 29, 1996). ... Signed as free agent by Vancouver Grizzlies (January 22, 1999). ... Traded by Grizzlies with G/F Dennis Scott, F Obinna Ekezie and G Felipe Lopez to Washington Wizards for C Ike Austin (August 22, 2000). ... Traded by Wizards with F Obinna Ekezie to Los Angeles Clippers for F Tyrone Nesby (November 28, 2000). ... Signed as free agent by San Antonio Spurs (August 3, 2001).

COLLEGIATE RECORD

NOTES: Member of NCAA Division I championship team (1992).

Season Team	G	Min.	FGM	FGA	Pct.	FTM	FTA	Pct.	Reb.	Ast.	Pts.	AVERAGES RPG	APG	PPG
91-92—Duke	34	435	60	105	.571	50	69	.725	81	13	170	2.4	0.4	5.0
92-93—Duke	32	899	161	247	.652	72	100	.720	220	14	394	6.9	0.4	12.3
93-94—Duke	34	1038	186	347	.536	115	149	.772	284	31	490	8.4	0.9	14.4
94-95—Duke	31	1091	222	443	.501	114	147	.776	289	45	589	9.3	1.5	19.0
Totals	131	3463	629	1142	.551	351	465	.755	874	103	1643	6.7	0.8	12.5

Three-point field goals: 1993-94, 3-for-17 (.176). 1994-95, 31-for-85 (.365). Totals, 34-for-102 (.333).

NBA REGULAR-SEASON RECORD

Season Team	G	Min.	FGM	FGA	Pct.	FTM	FTA	Pct.	REBOUNDS Off.	Def.	Tot.	Ast.	St.	Blk.	TO	Pts.	AVERAGES RPG	APG	PPG
95-96—Dallas	64	869	101	247	.409	41	62	.661	66	150	216	29	25	32	31	250	3.4	0.5	3.9
96-97—Minnesota	76	961	103	202	.510	46	76	.605	83	112	195	34	41	48	32	252	2.6	0.4	3.3
97-98—Minnesota	79	1703	224	449	.499	110	169	.651	140	297	437	53	36	86	66	558	5.5	0.7	7.1
98-99—Vancouver	48	1118	118	275	.429	30	55	.545	75	168	243	36	28	28	49	266	5.1	0.8	5.5
99-00—Vancouver	56	808	72	145	.497	24	37	.649	55	128	183	35	29	45	28	168	3.3	0.6	3.0
00-01—Wash.-LAC	65	1054	134	274	.489	31	44	.705	71	158	229	46	25	36	41	299	3.5	0.7	4.6
Totals	388	6513	752	1592	.472	282	443	.637	490	1013	1503	233	184	275	247	1793	3.9	0.6	4.6

Three-point field goals: 1995-96, 7-for-26 (.269). 1996-97, 0-for-1. 1997-98, 0-for-1. 1998-99, 0-for-1. 1999-00, 0-for-1. 2000-01, 0-for-6. Totals, 7-for-36 (.194).
Personal fouls/disqualifications: 1995-96, 100/0. 1996-97, 150/2. 1997-98, 237/4. 1998-99, 114/0. 1999-00, 115/2. 2000-01, 122/0. Totals, 838/8.

NBA PLAYOFF RECORD

Season Team	G	Min.	FGM	FGA	Pct.	FTM	FTA	Pct.	REBOUNDS Off.	Def.	Tot.	Ast.	St.	Blk.	TO	Pts.	AVERAGES RPG	APG	PPG
96-97—Minnesota	1	11	2	3	.667	0	0	...	0	5	5	0	1	0	0	4	5.0	0.0	4.0
97-98—Minnesota	1	1	0	0	...	0	0	...	0	0	0	0	0	0	0	0	0.0	0.0	0.0
Totals	2	12	2	3	.667	0	0	...	0	5	5	0	1	0	0	4	2.5	0.0	2.0

Personal fouls/disqualifications: 1996-97, 5/0. Totals, 5/0.

PATTERSON, ANDRAE   F

PERSONAL: Born November 12, 1975, in Riverside, Calif. ... 6-9/238. (2,06/108,0). ... Full Name: Andrae Malone Patterson.
HIGH SCHOOL: Cooper (Abilene, Texas).
COLLEGE: Indiana.
TRANSACTIONS/CAREER NOTES: Selected by Minnesota Timberwolves in second round (46th pick overall) of 1998 NBA Draft. ... Signed to play for Estudiantes in Spain for 2001-02 season.

P

COLLEGIATE RECORD

Season Team	G	Min.	FGM	FGA	Pct.	FTM	FTA	Pct.	Reb.	Ast.	Pts.	AVERAGES		
												RPG	APG	PPG
94-95—Indiana	28	540	84	170	.494	31	45	.689	108	21	203	3.9	0.8	7.3
95-96—Indiana	31	803	130	282	.461	70	95	.737	191	46	350	6.2	1.5	11.3
96-97—Indiana	30	829	151	321	.470	97	128	.758	201	43	410	6.7	1.4	13.7
97-98—Indiana	32	815	152	307	.495	88	111	.793	187	46	402	5.8	1.4	12.6
Totals	121	2987	517	1080	.479	286	379	.755	687	156	1365	5.7	1.3	11.3

Three-point field goals: 1994-95, 4-for-8 (.500). 1995-96, 20-for-57 (.351). 1996-97, 11-for-43 (.256). 1997-98, 10-for-36 (.278). Totals, 45-for-144 (.313).

NBA REGULAR-SEASON RECORD

Season Team	G	Min.	FGM	FGA	Pct.	FTM	FTA	Pct.	REBOUNDS			Ast.	St.	Blk.	TO	Pts.	AVERAGES		
									Off.	Def.	Tot.						RPG	APG	PPG
98-99—Minnesota	35	284	43	97	.443	28	36	.778	30	35	65	15	19	7	22	114	1.9	0.4	3.3
99-00—Minnesota	5	20	3	4	.750	0	0	...	1	1	2	1	1	0	1	6	0.4	0.2	1.2
00-01—Minnesota								Did not play—injured.											
Totals	40	304	46	101	.455	28	36	.778	31	36	67	16	20	7	23	120	1.7	0.4	3.0

Three-point field goals: 1998-99, 0-for-5. Totals, 0-for-5 (.000).
Personal fouls/disqualifications: 1998-99, 62/1. 1999-00, 4/0. Totals, 66/1.

NBA PLAYOFF RECORD

Season Team	G	Min.	FGM	FGA	Pct.	FTM	FTA	Pct.	REBOUNDS			Ast.	St.	Blk.	TO	Pts.	AVERAGES		
									Off.	Def.	Tot.						RPG	APG	PPG
98-99—Minnesota	2	7	0	0	...	0	0	...	1	3	4	2	0	0	1	0	2.0	1.0	0.0

Personal fouls/disqualifications: 1998-99, 1/0.

PATTERSON, RUBEN   F   TRAIL BLAZERS

PERSONAL: Born July 31, 1975, in Cleveland. ... 6-5/224. (1,96/101,6). ... Full Name: Ruben Nathaniel Patterson.
HIGH SCHOOL: John Hay (Cleveland).
JUNIOR COLLEGE: Independence (Kan.) Community College.
COLLEGE: Cincinnati.
TRANSACTIONS/CAREER NOTES: Selected by Los Angeles Lakers in second round (31st pick overall) of 1998 NBA Draft. ... Played in Greece (1998-99). ... Signed as free agent by Seattle SuperSonics (August 10, 1999). ... Signed as free agent by Portland Trail Blazers (July 30, 2001).

COLLEGIATE RECORD

Season Team	G	Min.	FGM	FGA	Pct.	FTM	FTA	Pct.	Reb.	Ast.	Pts.	AVERAGES		
												RPG	APG	PPG
94-95—Independence C.C.	33	...	274	417	.657	132	220	.600	210	48	690	6.4	1.5	20.9
95-96—Independence C.C.	32	...	296	464	.638	260	382	.681	298	79	868	9.3	2.5	27.1
96-97—Cincinnati	31	723	164	299	.548	87	144	.604	174	44	426	5.6	1.4	13.7
97-98—Cincinnati	19	530	109	231	.472	77	126	.611	119	41	313	6.3	2.2	16.5
Junior College Totals	65		570	881	.647	392	602	.651	508	127	1558	7.8	2.0	24.0
4-Year-College Totals	50	1253	273	530	.515	164	270	.607	293	85	739	5.9	1.7	14.8

Three-point field goals: 1994-95, 10-for-18 (.556). 1995-96, 16-for-39 (.410). 1996-97, 11-for-39 (.282). 1997-98, 18-for-67 (.269). Totals, 26-for-57 (.456) Totals, 29-for-106 (.274).

GREEK LEAGUE RECORD

Season Team	G	Min.	FGM	FGA	Pct.	FTM	FTA	Pct.	Reb.	Ast.	Pts.	AVERAGES		
												RPG	APG	PPG
98-99—A.E.K.	10	275	45	93	.484	28	42	.667	34	20	124	3.4	2.0	12.4

Three-point field goals: 1998-99, 6-for-23 (.261).

NBA REGULAR-SEASON RECORD

Season Team	G	Min.	FGM	FGA	Pct.	FTM	FTA	Pct.	REBOUNDS			Ast.	St.	Blk.	TO	Pts.	AVERAGES		
									Off.	Def.	Tot.						RPG	APG	PPG
98-99—L.A. Lakers	24	144	21	51	.412	22	31	.710	17	13	30	2	5	3	12	65	1.3	0.1	2.7
99-00—Seattle	81	2097	354	661	.536	222	321	.692	218	216	434	126	94	40	144	942	5.4	1.6	11.6
00-01—Seattle	76	2059	370	749	.494	246	361	.681	183	199	382	161	103	45	155	988	5.0	2.1	13.0
Totals	181	4300	745	1461	.510	490	713	.687	418	428	846	289	202	88	311	1995	4.7	1.6	11.0

Three-point field goals: 1998-99, 1-for-6 (.167). 1999-00, 12-for-27 (.444). 2000-01, 2-for-36 (.056). Totals, 15-for-69 (.217).
Personal fouls/disqualifications: 1998-99, 16/0. 1999-00, 190/0. 2000-01, 176/1. Totals, 382/1.

NBA PLAYOFF RECORD

Season Team	G	Min.	FGM	FGA	Pct.	FTM	FTA	Pct.	REBOUNDS			Ast.	St.	Blk.	TO	Pts.	AVERAGES		
									Off.	Def.	Tot.						RPG	APG	PPG
98-99—L.A. Lakers	3	5	0	1	.000	0	0	...	0	0	0	0	0	0	1	0	0.0	0.0	0.0
99-00—Seattle	5	84	14	26	.538	13	15	.867	9	6	15	2	3	2	8	41	3.0	0.4	8.2
Totals	8	89	14	27	.519	13	15	.867	9	6	15	2	3	2	9	41	1.9	0.3	5.1

Three-point field goals: 1999-00, 0-for-2. Totals, 0-for-2 (.000).
Personal fouls/disqualifications: 1999-00, 6/0. Totals, 6/0.

P

DID YOU KNOW . . .

. . . that basketball Hall of Famer Dave DeBusschere won three games as a pitcher with the Chicago White Sox in 1963?

PAYTON, GARY   G   SUPERSONICS

PERSONAL: Born July 23, 1968, in Oakland. ... 6-4/180. (1,93/81,6). ... Full Name: Gary Dwayne Payton.
HIGH SCHOOL: Skyline (Oakland).
COLLEGE: Oregon State.
TRANSACTIONS/CAREER NOTES: Selected by Seattle SuperSonics in first round (second pick overall) of 1990 NBA Draft.
MISCELLANEOUS: Member of gold-medal-winning U.S. Olympic team (1996, 2000). ... Seattle SuperSonics franchise all-time points leader with 15,308, all-time assists leader with 6,190 and all-time steals leader with 1,883 (1990-91 through 2000-01).

COLLEGIATE RECORD

NOTES: THE SPORTING NEWS All-America first team (1990).

Season Team	G	Min.	FGM	FGA	Pct.	FTM	FTA	Pct.	Reb.	Ast.	Pts.	RPG	APG	PPG
86-87—Oregon State	30	1115	153	333	.459	55	82	.671	120	229	374	4.0	7.6	12.5
87-88—Oregon State	31	1178	180	368	.489	58	83	.699	103	230	449	3.3	7.4	14.5
88-89—Oregon State	30	1140	208	438	.475	105	155	.677	122	244	603	4.1	8.1	20.1
89-90—Oregon State	29	1095	288	571	.504	118	171	.690	135	235	746	4.7	8.1	25.7
Totals	120	4528	829	1710	.485	336	491	.684	480	938	2172	4.0	7.8	18.1

Three-point field goals: 1986-87, 13-for-35 (.371). 1987-88, 31-for-78 (.397). 1988-89, 82-for-213 (.385). 1989-90, 52-for-156 (.333). Totals, 178-for-482 (.369).

NBA REGULAR-SEASON RECORD

HONORS: NBA Defensive Player of the Year (1996). ... All-NBA first team (1998, 2000). ... All-NBA second team (1995, 1996, 1997, 1999). ... All-NBA third team (1994, 2001). ... NBA All-Defensive first team (1994, 1995, 1996, 1997, 1998, 1999, 2000, 2001). ... NBA All-Rookie second team (1991).
NOTES: Led NBA with 2.85 steals per game (1996).

									REBOUNDS							AVERAGES		
Season Team	G	Min.	FGM	FGA	Pct.	FTM	FTA	Pct.	Off.	Def.	Tot.	Ast.	St.	Blk.	TO	Pts.	RPG APG PPG
90-91—Seattle	82	2244	259	575	.450	69	97	.711	108	135	243	528	165	15	180	588	3.0 6.4 7.2
91-92—Seattle	81	2549	331	734	.451	99	148	.669	123	172	295	506	147	21	174	764	3.6 6.2 9.4
92-93—Seattle	82	2548	476	963	.494	151	196	.770	95	186	281	399	177	21	148	1110	3.4 4.9 13.5
93-94—Seattle	82	2881	584	1159	.504	166	279	.595	105	164	269	494	188	19	173	1349	3.3 6.0 16.5
94-95—Seattle	82	3015	685	1345	.509	249	348	.716	108	173	281	583	204	13	201	1689	3.4 7.1 20.6
95-96—Seattle	81	3162	618	1276	.484	229	306	.748	104	235	339	608	*231	19	260	1563	4.2 7.5 19.3
96-97—Seattle	82	3213	706	1482	.476	254	355	.715	106	272	378	583	197	13	215	1785	4.6 7.1 21.8
97-98—Seattle	82	3145	579	1278	.453	279	375	.744	77	299	376	679	185	18	220	1571	4.6 8.3 19.2
98-99—Seattle	50	2008	401	923	.434	199	276	.721	62	182	244	436	109	12	154	1084	4.9 8.7 21.7
99-00—Seattle	82	3425	747	1666	.448	311	423	.735	100	429	529	*732	153	18	224	1982	6.5 8.9 24.2
00-01—Seattle	79	3244	725	1591	.456	271	354	.766	73	288	361	642	127	26	209	1823	4.6 8.1 23.1
Totals	865	31434	6111	12992	.470	2277	3157	.721	1061	2535	3596	6190	1883	195	2167	15308	4.2 7.2 17.7

Three-point field goals: 1990-91, 1-for-13 (.077). 1991-92, 3-for-23 (.130). 1992-93, 7-for-34 (.206). 1993-94, 15-for-54 (.278). 1994-95, 70-for-232 (.302). 1995-96, 98-for-299 (.328). 1996-97, 119-for-368 (.313). 1997-98, 134-for-397 (.338). 1998-99, 83-for-281 (.295). 1999-00, 177-for-520 (.340). 2000-01, 102-for-272 (.375). Totals, 809-for-2505 (.323).
Personal fouls/disqualifications: 1990-91, 249/3. 1991-92, 248/0. 1992-93, 250/1. 1993-94, 227/0. 1994-95, 206/1. 1995-96, 221/1. 1996-97, 208/1. 1997-98, 195/0. 1998-99, 115/0. 1999-00, 178/0. 2000-01, 184/0. Totals, 2281/7.

NBA PLAYOFF RECORD

NOTES: Holds single-game playoff record for most three-point field goal attempts in one half—11 (May 4, 1996, vs. Houston). ... Shares single-game playoff record for most three-point field goals made in one quarter—5 (April 29, 1997, at Phoenix).

									REBOUNDS							AVERAGES		
Season Team	G	Min.	FGM	FGA	Pct.	FTM	FTA	Pct.	Off.	Def.	Tot.	Ast.	St.	Blk.	TO	Pts.	RPG APG PPG
90-91—Seattle	5	135	11	27	.407	2	2	1.000	5	8	13	32	8	1	9	24	2.6 6.4 4.8
91-92—Seattle	8	221	27	58	.466	7	12	.583	6	15	21	38	8	2	10	61	2.6 4.8 7.6
92-93—Seattle	19	605	104	235	.443	25	37	.676	22	41	63	70	34	3	34	234	3.3 3.7 12.3
93-94—Seattle	5	181	34	69	.493	8	19	.421	6	11	17	28	8	2	8	79	3.4 5.6 15.8
94-95—Seattle	4	172	32	67	.478	5	12	.417	6	4	10	21	5	0	8	71	2.5 5.3 17.8
95-96—Seattle	21	911	162	334	.485	69	109	.633	19	89	108	143	37	7	62	434	5.1 6.8 20.7
96-97—Seattle	12	546	105	255	.412	50	61	.820	20	45	65	104	26	4	35	285	5.4 8.7 23.8
97-98—Seattle	10	428	87	183	.475	47	50	.940	9	25	34	70	18	1	26	240	3.4 7.0 24.0
99-00—Seattle	5	221	50	113	.442	20	26	.769	8	30	38	37	9	1	18	129	7.6 7.4 25.8
Totals	89	3420	612	1341	.456	233	328	.710	101	268	369	543	153	21	210	1557	4.1 6.1 17.5

Three-point field goals: 1990-91, 0-for-1. 1991-92, 0-for-2. 1992-93, 1-for-6 (.167). 1993-94, 3-for-9 (.333). 1994-95, 2-for-10 (.200). 1995-96, 41-for-100 (.410). 1996-97, 25-for-75 (.333). 1997-98, 19-for-50 (.380). 1999-00, 9-for-23 (.391). Totals, 100-for-276 (.362).
Personal fouls/disqualifications: 1990-91, 16/0. 1991-92, 26/1. 1992-93, 64/1. 1993-94, 15/0. 1994-95, 13/0. 1995-96, 69/0. 1996-97, 26/0. 1997-98, 31/1. 1999-00, 16/0. Totals, 276/3.

NBA ALL-STAR GAME RECORD

							REBOUNDS									
Season Team	Min.	FGM	FGA	Pct.	FTM	FTA	Pct.	Off.	Def.	Tot.	Ast.	PF	Dq.	St.	Blk.	TO	Pts.
1994 —Seattle	17	3	4	.750	0	0	...	2	4	6	9	2	0	0	0	0	6
1995 —Seattle	23	3	10	.300	0	0	...	3	2	5	15	1	0	3	0	3	6
1996 —Seattle	28	6	10	.600	6	6	1.000	3	2	5	5	1	0	5	0	6	18
1997 —Seattle	28	7	15	.467	2	2	1.000	0	1	1	10	2	0	2	0	4	17
1998 —Seattle	24	3	7	.429	0	0	...	2	1	3	13	0	0	2	0	4	7
2000 —Seattle	20	1	8	.125	3	3	1.000	0	4	4	8	1	0	2	0	2	5
2001 —Seattle	18	0	5	.000	0	0	...	2	2	4	5	2	0	2	0	1	0
Totals	158	23	59	.390	11	11	1.000	12	16	28	65	9	0	16	0	20	59

Three-point field goals: 1995, 0-for-3. 1996, 0-for-1. 1997, 1-for-5 (.200). 1998, 1-for-3 (.333). 1900, 0-for-4. Totals, 2-for-16 (.125).

P

PEELER, ANTHONY   G   TIMBERWOLVES

PERSONAL: Born November 25, 1969, in Kansas City, Mo. ... 6-4/208. (1,93/94,3). ... Full Name: Anthony Eugene Peeler.
HIGH SCHOOL: Paseo (Kansas City, Mo.).
COLLEGE: Missouri.
TRANSACTIONS/CAREER NOTES: Selected by Los Angeles Lakers in first round (15th pick overall) of 1992 NBA Draft. ... Traded by Lakers with F George Lynch and 1997 and 1998 second-round draft choices to Vancouver Grizzlies for 1997 and 1998 second-round draft choices (July 16, 1996). ... Traded by Grizzlies to Minnesota Timberwolves for G Doug West (February 18, 1998).
MISCELLANEOUS: Selected by Texas Rangers organization in 41st round of free-agent draft (June 1, 1988); did not sign.

COLLEGIATE RECORD

Season Team	G	Min.	FGM	FGA	Pct.	FTM	FTA	Pct.	Reb.	Ast.	Pts.	RPG	APG	PPG
88-89—Missouri	36	801	130	258	.504	89	118	.754	134	102	362	3.7	2.8	10.1
89-90—Missouri	31	1031	184	413	.446	130	169	.769	168	179	522	5.4	5.8	16.8
90-91—Missouri	21	725	134	282	.475	116	151	.768	131	104	408	6.2	5.0	19.4
91-92—Missouri	29	1026	218	475	.459	187	232	.806	160	112	678	5.5	3.9	23.4
Totals	117	3583	666	1428	.466	522	670	.779	593	497	1970	5.1	4.2	16.8

Three-point field goals: 1988-89, 13-for-37 (.351). 1989-90, 24-for-68 (.353). 1990-91, 24-for-58 (.414). 1991-92, 55-for-132 (.417). Totals, 116-for-295 (.393).

NBA REGULAR-SEASON RECORD

Season Team	G	Min.	FGM	FGA	Pct.	FTM	FTA	Pct.	REBOUNDS Off.	Def.	Tot.	Ast.	St.	Blk.	TO	Pts.	RPG	APG	PPG
92-93—L.A. Lakers	77	1656	297	634	.468	162	206	.786	64	115	179	166	60	14	123	802	2.3	2.2	10.4
93-94—L.A. Lakers	30	923	176	409	.430	57	71	.803	48	61	109	94	43	8	59	423	3.6	3.1	14.1
94-95—L.A. Lakers	73	1559	285	659	.432	102	128	.797	62	106	168	122	52	13	82	756	2.3	1.7	10.4
95-96—L.A. Lakers	73	1608	272	602	.452	61	86	.709	45	92	137	118	59	10	56	710	1.9	1.6	9.7
96-97—Vancouver	72	2291	402	1011	.398	109	133	.820	54	193	247	256	105	17	157	1041	3.4	3.6	14.5
97-98—Van.-Minn.	38	1193	190	420	.452	36	47	.766	37	86	123	137	61	6	51	469	3.2	3.6	12.3
98-99—Minnesota	28	810	103	272	.379	30	41	.732	30	54	84	78	35	6	38	270	3.0	2.8	9.6
99-00—Minnesota	82	2073	316	725	.436	87	109	.798	58	174	232	195	62	10	85	804	2.8	2.4	9.8
00-01—Minnesota	75	2126	308	732	.421	75	87	.862	44	148	192	192	91	18	105	791	2.6	2.6	10.5
Totals	548	14239	2349	5464	.430	719	908	.792	442	1029	1471	1358	568	102	756	6066	2.7	2.5	11.1

Three-point field goals: 1992-93, 46-for-118 (.390). 1993-94, 14-for-63 (.222). 1994-95, 84-for-216 (.389). 1995-96, 105-for-254 (.413). 1996-97, 128-for-343 (.373). 1997-98, 53-for-125 (.424). 1998-99, 34-for-114 (.298). 1999-00, 85-for-255 (.333). 2000-01, 100-for-256 (.391). Totals, 649-for-1744 (.372).

Personal fouls/disqualifications: 1992-93, 193/0. 1993-94, 93/0. 1994-95, 143/1. 1995-96, 139/0. 1996-97, 168/0. 1997-98, 97/0. 1998-99, 60/0. 1999-00, 171/1. 2000-01, 166/1. Totals, 1230/3.

NBA PLAYOFF RECORD

Season Team	G	Min.	FGM	FGA	Pct.	FTM	FTA	Pct.	REBOUNDS Off.	Def.	Tot.	Ast.	St.	Blk.	TO	Pts.	RPG	APG	PPG
94-95—L.A. Lakers	10	268	32	79	.405	17	22	.773	8	20	28	25	10	2	12	89	2.8	2.5	8.9
95-96—L.A. Lakers	3	72	9	27	.333	4	4	1.000	2	6	8	3	6	0	3	28	2.7	1.0	9.3
97-98—Minnesota	5	213	31	77	.403	4	4	1.000	16	22	38	18	10	3	8	81	7.6	3.6	16.2
98-99—Minnesota	4	125	11	35	.314	0	0	...	7	9	16	6	4	0	4	27	4.0	1.5	6.8
99-00—Minnesota	4	90	11	24	.458	6	8	.750	2	7	9	5	3	1	1	30	2.3	1.3	7.5
00-01—Minnesota	4	137	14	53	.264	0	0	...	3	11	14	7	7	1	6	34	3.5	1.8	8.5
Totals	30	905	108	295	.366	31	38	.816	38	75	113	64	40	7	34	289	3.8	2.1	9.6

Three-point field goals: 1994-95, 8-for-31 (.258). 1995-96, 6-for-14 (.429). 1997-98, 15-for-31 (.484). 1998-99, 5-for-13 (.385). 1999-00, 2-for-10 (.200). 2000-01, 6-for-17 (.353). Totals, 42-for-116 (.362).

Personal fouls/disqualifications: 1994-95, 23/0. 1995-96, 6/0. 1997-98, 15/0. 1998-99, 12/1. 1999-00, 9/0. 2000-01, 10/0. Totals, 75/1.

PENBERTHY, MIKE   G

PERSONAL: Born November 29, 1973 ... 6-3/185. (1,91/83,9).
HIGH SCHOOL: Hoover (Fresno, Calif.).
COLLEGE: The Masters College (Calif.).
TRANSACTIONS/CAREER NOTES: Not drafted by an NBA franchise. ... Played in Germany (1997-98 and 1999-2000). ... Played in Continental Basketball Association with Quad City Thunder (1998-99). ... Played in Venezuela (1999-2000). ... Signed as free agent by Los Angeles Lakers (October 2, 2000).
MISCELLANEOUS: Member of NBA Championship team (2001).

COLLEGIATE RECORD

Season Team	G	Min.	FGM	FGA	Pct.	FTM	FTA	Pct.	Reb.	Ast.	Pts.	RPG	APG	PPG
93-94—The Master's College	32	...	103	210	.490	59	72	.819	52	85	316	1.6	2.7	9.9
94-95—The Master's College	36	...	212	448	.473	110	121	.909	129	235	660	3.6	6.5	18.3
95-96—The Master's College	34	...	242	507	.477	178	203	.877	105	146	789	3.1	4.3	23.2
96-97—The Master's College	31	...	271	552	.491	169	192	.880	69	119	852	2.2	3.8	27.5
Totals	133	...	828	1717	.482	516	588	.878	355	585	2617	2.6	4.4	19.7

Three-point field goals: 1993-94, 51-for-118 (.432). 1994-95, 126-for-279 (.452). 1995-96, 127-for-290 (.438). 1996-97, 141-for-330 (.427). Totals, 445-for-1017 (.438).

P

GERMAN LEAGUE RECORD

Season Team	G	Min.	FGM	FGA	Pct.	FTM	FTA	Pct.	Reb.	Ast.	Pts.	RPG	APG	PPG
97-98—BC Hamburg..................						Statistics unavailable.								
99-00—BC Hamburg..................	22	809	138	303	.455	45	56	.804	68	61	390	3.1	2.8	17.7
Totals	22	809	138	303	.455	45	56	.804	68	61	390	3.1	2.8	17.7

Three-point field goals: 1999-00, 69-for-161 (.429).

CBA REGULAR-SEASON RECORD

Season Team	G	Min.	FGM	FGA	Pct.	FTM	FTA	Pct.	Reb.	Ast.	Pts.	RPG	APG	PPG
98-99—Quad City.......................	4	79	11	30	.367	2	2	1.000	8	8	28	2.0	2.0	7.0

Three-point field goals: 1998-99, 4-for-17 (.235).

VENEZUELAN LEAGUE RECORD

Season Team	G	Min.	FGM	FGA	Pct.	FTM	FTA	Pct.	Reb.	Ast.	Pts.	RPG	APG	PPG
99-00—Cocodrilos.....................	9	299	64	140	.457	19	23	.826	8	17	172	0.9	1.9	19.1

Three-point field goals: 1999-00, 25-for-67 (.373).

NBA REGULAR-SEASON RECORD

Season Team	G	Min.	FGM	FGA	Pct.	FTM	FTA	Pct.	Off.	Def.	Tot.	Ast.	St.	Blk.	TO	Pts.	RPG	APG	PPG
00-01—L.A. Lakers	53	851	92	222	.414	28	31	.903	10	53	63	71	22	2	34	267	1.2	1.3	5.0

Three-point field goals: 2000-01, 55-for-139 (.396).
Personal fouls/disqualifications: 2000-01, 57/0.

PERDUE, WILL   C   TRAIL BLAZERS

PERSONAL: Born August 29, 1965, in Melbourne, Fla. ... 7-0/240. (2,13/108,9). ... Full Name: William Edward Perdue III.
HIGH SCHOOL: Merritt Island (Fla.).
COLLEGE: Vanderbilt.
TRANSACTIONS/CAREER NOTES: Selected by Chicago Bulls in first round (11th pick overall) of 1988 NBA Draft. ... Traded by Bulls to San Antonio Spurs for F Dennis Rodman (October 2, 1995). ... Signed as free agent by Bulls (August 25, 1999). ... Waived by Bulls (June 26, 2000). ... Signed as free agent by Portland Trail Blazers (September 13, 2000).
MISCELLANEOUS: Member of NBA championship team (1991, 1992, 1993, 1999).

COLLEGIATE RECORD

Season Team	G	Min.	FGM	FGA	Pct.	FTM	FTA	Pct.	Reb.	Ast.	Pts.	RPG	APG	PPG
83-84—Vanderbilt..................	17	111	21	45	.467	4	9	.444	38	2	46	2.2	0.1	2.7
84-85—Vanderbilt..................						Did not play—redshirted.								
85-86—Vanderbilt..................	22	181	31	53	.585	14	32	.438	61	4	76	2.8	0.2	3.5
86-87—Vanderbilt..................	34	1033	233	389	.599	126	204	.618	295	50	592	8.7	1.5	17.4
87-88—Vanderbilt..................	31	1013	234	369	.634	99	147	.673	314	81	567	10.1	2.6	18.3
Totals	104	2338	519	856	.606	243	392	.620	708	137	1281	6.8	1.3	12.3

NBA REGULAR-SEASON RECORD

Season Team	G	Min.	FGM	FGA	Pct.	FTM	FTA	Pct.	Off.	Def.	Tot.	Ast.	St.	Blk.	TO	Pts.	RPG	APG	PPG
88-89—Chicago	30	190	29	72	.403	8	14	.571	18	27	45	11	4	6	15	66	1.5	0.4	2.2
89-90—Chicago	77	884	111	268	.414	72	104	.692	88	126	214	46	19	26	65	294	2.8	0.6	3.8
90-91—Chicago	74	972	116	235	.494	75	112	.670	122	214	336	47	23	57	75	307	4.5	0.6	4.1
91-92—Chicago	77	1007	152	278	.547	45	91	.495	108	204	312	80	16	43	72	350	4.1	1.0	4.5
92-93—Chicago	72	998	137	246	.557	67	111	.604	103	184	287	74	22	47	74	341	4.0	1.0	4.7
93-94—Chicago	43	397	47	112	.420	23	32	.719	40	86	126	34	8	11	42	117	2.9	0.8	2.7
94-95—Chicago	78	1592	254	459	.553	113	194	.582	211	311	522	90	26	56	116	621	6.7	1.2	8.0
95-96—San Antonio ...	80	1396	173	331	.523	67	125	.536	175	310	485	33	28	75	86	413	6.1	0.4	5.2
96-97—San Antonio ...	65	1918	233	410	.568	99	171	.579	251	387	638	38	32	102	87	565	9.8	0.6	8.7
97-98—San Antonio ...	79	1491	162	295	.549	70	133	.526	177	358	535	57	22	50	81	394	6.8	0.7	5.0
98-99—San Antonio ...	37	445	38	60	.633	14	26	.538	33	105	138	18	9	10	22	90	3.7	0.5	2.4
99-00—Chicago	67	1012	59	168	.351	50	105	.476	88	174	262	65	14	42	78	168	3.9	1.0	2.5
00-01—Portland	13	58	6	9	.667	2	4	.500	6	12	18	2	3	2	0	14	1.4	0.2	1.1
Totals	792	12360	1517	2943	.515	705	1222	.577	1420	2498	3918	595	226	527	813	3740	4.9	0.8	4.7

Three-point field goals: 1989-90, 0-for-5. 1990-91, 0-for-3. 1991-92, 1-for-2 (.500). 1992-93, 0-for-1. 1993-94, 0-for-1. 1994-95, 0-for-1. 1995-96, 0-for-1. 1997-98, 0-for-1. Totals, 1-for-15 (.067).
Personal fouls/disqualifications: 1988-89, 38/0. 1989-90, 150/0. 1990-91, 147/1. 1991-92, 133/1. 1992-93, 139/2. 1993-94, 61/0. 1994-95, 220/3. 1995-96, 183/0. 1996-97, 184/2. 1997-98, 137/0. 1998-99, 63/0. 1999-00, 126/1. 2000-01, 8/0. Totals, 1589/10.

NBA PLAYOFF RECORD

Season Team	G	Min.	FGM	FGA	Pct.	FTM	FTA	Pct.	Off.	Def.	Tot.	Ast.	St.	Blk.	TO	Pts.	RPG	APG	PPG
88-89—Chicago	3	22	6	9	.667	2	3	.667	3	3	6	2	0	0	0	14	2.0	0.7	4.7
89-90—Chicago	13	78	13	28	.464	13	18	.722	7	12	19	2	0	5	4	40	1.5	0.2	3.1
90-91—Chicago	17	198	29	53	.547	12	22	.545	32	33	65	4	2	8	14	70	3.8	0.2	4.1
91-92—Chicago	18	157	18	37	.486	9	20	.450	18	22	40	9	3	10	12	45	2.2	0.5	2.5
92-93—Chicago	13	101	10	20	.500	5	10	.500	15	15	30	5	1	2	8	25	2.3	0.4	1.9
94-95—Chicago	10	176	19	37	.514	12	21	.571	18	30	48	6	1	3	10	50	4.8	0.6	5.0
95-96—San Antonio	10	242	29	42	.690	16	20	.800	26	53	79	5	2	4	11	74	7.9	0.5	7.4
97-98—San Antonio	9	191	9	27	.333	18	21	.857	24	36	60	1	6	9	11	36	6.7	0.1	4.0
98-99—San Antonio	12	86	6	11	.545	1	2	.500	9	19	28	0	0	1	3	13	2.3	0.0	1.1
00-01—Portland	3	5	0	0	...	0	2	.000	1	1	2	0	0	0	0	0	0.7	0.0	0.0
Totals	108	1256	139	264	.527	88	139	.633	153	224	377	34	15	42	73	367	3.5	0.3	3.4

Three-point field goals: 1988-89, 0-for-1. 1989-90, 1-for-2 (.500). 1991-92, 0-for-1. Totals, 1-for-4 (.250).
Personal fouls/disqualifications: 1988-89, 4/0. 1989-90, 13/0. 1990-91, 41/1. 1991-92, 34/1. 1992-93, 18/0. 1994-95, 27/0. 1995-96, 24/0. 1997-98, 26/0. 1998-99, 19/0. Totals, 206/2.

PERKINS, SAM   F/C   PACERS

PERSONAL: Born June 14, 1961, in Brooklyn, N.Y. ... 6-9/260. (2,06/117,9). ... Full Name: Samuel Bruce Perkins.
HIGH SCHOOL: Shaker (Latham, N.Y.).
COLLEGE: North Carolina.
TRANSACTIONS/CAREER NOTES: Selected by Dallas Mavericks in first round (fourth pick overall) of 1984 NBA Draft. ... Signed as unrestricted free agent by Los Angeles Lakers (August 6, 1990). ... Traded by Lakers to Seattle SuperSonics for C Benoit Benjamin and G/F Doug Christie (February 22, 1993). ... Signed as free agent by Indiana Pacers (January 21, 1999).
MISCELLANEOUS: Member of gold-medal-winning U.S. Olympic team (1984).

COLLEGIATE RECORD

NOTES: THE SPORTING NEWS All-America first team (1984). ... THE SPORTING NEWS All-America second team (1982, 1983). ... Member of NCAA Division I championship team (1982).

Season Team	G	Min.	FGM	FGA	Pct.	FTM	FTA	Pct.	Reb.	Ast.	Pts.	AVERAGES RPG	APG	PPG
80-81—North Carolina	37	1115	199	318	.626	152	205	.741	289	27	550	7.8	0.7	14.9
81-82—North Carolina	32	1141	174	301	.578	109	142	.768	250	35	457	7.8	1.1	14.3
82-83—North Carolina	35	1174	218	414	.527	145	177	.819	330	47	593	9.4	1.3	16.9
83-84—North Carolina	31	1029	195	331	.589	155	181	.856	298	51	545	9.6	1.6	17.6
Totals	135	4459	786	1364	.576	561	705	.796	1167	160	2145	8.6	1.2	15.9

Three-point field goals: 1982-83, 12-for-28 (.429).

NBA REGULAR-SEASON RECORD

RECORDS: Shares single-game record for most three-point field goals without a miss—8 (January 15, 1997, vs. Toronto).
HONORS: NBA All-Rookie team (1985).

Season Team	G	Min.	FGM	FGA	Pct.	FTM	FTA	Pct.	REBOUNDS Off.	Def.	Tot.	Ast.	St.	Blk.	TO	Pts.	AVERAGES RPG	APG	PPG
84-85—Dallas	82	2317	347	736	.471	200	244	.820	189	416	605	135	63	63	102	903	7.4	1.6	11.0
85-86—Dallas	80	2626	458	910	.503	307	377	.814	195	490	685	153	75	94	145	1234	8.6	1.9	15.4
86-87—Dallas	80	2687	461	957	.482	245	296	.828	197	419	616	146	109	77	132	1186	7.7	1.8	14.8
87-88—Dallas	75	2499	394	876	.450	273	332	.822	201	400	601	118	74	54	119	1066	8.0	1.6	14.2
88-89—Dallas	78	2860	445	959	.464	274	329	.833	235	453	688	127	76	92	141	1171	8.8	1.6	15.0
89-90—Dallas	76	2668	435	883	.493	330	424	.778	209	363	572	175	88	64	148	1206	7.5	2.3	15.9
90-91—L.A. Lakers	73	2504	368	744	.495	229	279	.821	167	371	538	108	64	78	103	983	7.4	1.5	13.5
91-92—L.A. Lakers	63	2332	361	803	.450	304	372	.817	192	364	556	141	64	62	83	1041	8.8	2.2	16.5
92-93—L.A.L.-Seattle	79	2351	381	799	.477	250	305	.820	163	361	524	156	60	82	108	1036	6.6	2.0	13.1
93-94—Seattle	81	2170	341	779	.438	218	272	.801	120	246	366	111	67	31	103	999	4.5	1.4	12.3
94-95—Seattle	82	2356	346	742	.466	215	269	.799	96	302	398	135	72	45	77	1043	4.9	1.6	12.7
95-96—Seattle	82	2169	325	797	.408	191	241	.793	101	266	367	120	83	48	82	970	4.5	1.5	11.8
96-97—Seattle	81	1976	290	661	.439	187	229	.817	74	226	300	103	69	49	77	889	3.7	1.3	11.0
97-98—Seattle	81	1675	196	471	.416	101	128	.789	53	202	255	113	62	29	62	580	3.1	1.4	7.2
98-99—Indiana	48	789	80	200	.400	43	60	.717	36	102	138	25	15	14	22	238	2.9	0.5	5.0
99-00—Indiana	81	1620	184	441	.417	80	97	.825	64	225	289	68	31	33	63	537	3.6	0.8	6.6
00-01—Indiana	64	999	86	226	.381	32	38	.842	32	136	168	41	33	18	19	242	2.6	0.6	3.8
Totals	1286	36598	5498	11984	.459	3479	4292	.811	2324	5342	7666	1975	1105	933	1586	15324	6.0	1.5	11.9

Three-point field goals: 1984-85, 9-for-36 (.250). 1985-86, 11-for-33 (.333). 1986-87, 19-for-54 (.352). 1987-88, 5-for-30 (.167). 1988-89, 7-for-38 (.184). 1989-90, 6-for-28 (.214). 1990-91, 18-for-64 (.281). 1991-92, 15-for-69 (.217). 1992-93, 24-for-71 (.338). 1993-94, 99-for-270 (.367). 1994-95, 136-for-343 (.397). 1995-96, 129-for-363 (.355). 1996-97, 122-for-309 (.395). 1997-98, 87-for-222 (.392). 1998-99, 35-for-90 (.389). 1999-00, 89-for-218 (.408). 2000-01, 38-for-110 (.345). Totals, 849-for-2348 (.362).

Personal fouls/disqualifications: 1984-85, 236/1. 1985-86, 212/2. 1986-87, 269/6. 1987-88, 227/2. 1988-89, 224/1. 1989-90, 225/4. 1990-91, 247/2. 1991-92, 192/1. 1992-93, 225/0. 1993-94, 197/0. 1994-95, 186/0. 1995-96, 174/1. 1996-97, 134/0. 1997-98, 158/0. 1998-99, 74/0. 1999-00, 136/0. 2000-01, 61/0. Totals, 3177/20.

NBA PLAYOFF RECORD

Season Team	G	Min.	FGM	FGA	Pct.	FTM	FTA	Pct.	REBOUNDS Off.	Def.	Tot.	Ast.	St.	Blk.	TO	Pts.	AVERAGES RPG	APG	PPG
84-85—Dallas	4	169	24	49	.490	26	34	.765	16	35	51	11	2	1	3	75	12.8	2.8	18.8
85-86—Dallas	10	347	57	133	.429	33	43	.767	30	53	83	24	9	14	16	149	8.3	2.4	14.9
86-87—Dallas	4	133	26	52	.500	16	23	.696	12	22	34	5	4	1	9	68	8.5	1.3	17.0
87-88—Dallas	17	572	88	195	.451	53	66	.803	39	73	112	31	25	17	30	230	6.6	1.8	13.5
89-90—Dallas	3	118	16	36	.444	13	17	.765	10	12	22	8	3	2	7	45	7.3	2.7	15.0
90-91—L.A. Lakers	19	752	121	221	.548	83	109	.761	41	116	157	33	15	27	37	336	8.3	1.7	17.7
92-93—Seattle	19	626	98	225	.436	48	55	.873	33	100	133	37	19	25	21	274	7.0	1.9	14.4
93-94—Seattle	5	141	14	42	.333	15	17	.882	6	30	36	4	4	2	6	49	7.2	0.8	9.8
94-95—Seattle	4	141	21	48	.438	2	2	1.000	6	25	31	13	3	5	9	54	7.8	3.3	13.5
95-96—Seattle	21	654	90	196	.459	46	61	.754	21	69	90	35	15	6	30	258	4.3	1.7	12.3
96-97—Seattle	12	340	31	92	.337	25	29	.862	15	38	53	15	12	12	13	101	4.4	1.3	8.4
97-98—Seattle	10	210	16	42	.381	12	20	.600	6	26	32	14	3	5	11	54	3.2	1.4	5.4
98-99—Indiana	13	146	18	35	.514	6	9	.667	2	23	25	6	0	3	7	53	1.9	0.5	4.1
99-00—Indiana	23	417	34	105	.324	19	21	.905	17	56	73	10	4	6	8	110	3.2	0.4	4.8
00-01—Indiana	3	19	2	8	.250	0	0	...	1	3	4	0	0	0	0	5	1.3	0.0	1.7
Totals	167	4785	656	1479	.444	397	506	.785	255	681	936	246	118	126	207	1861	5.6	1.5	11.1

Three-point field goals: 1984-85, 1-for-4 (.250). 1985-86, 2-for-8 (.250). 1986-87, 0-for-4. 1987-88, 1-for-7 (.143). 1989-90, 0-for-1. 1990-91, 11-for-30 (.367). 1992-93, 30-for-79 (.380). 1993-94, 6-for-14 (.429). 1994-95, 10-for-22 (.455). 1995-96, 32-for-87 (.368). 1996-97, 14-for-45 (.311). 1997-98, 10-for-24 (.417). 1998-99, 11-for-24 (.458). 1999-00, 23-for-66 (.348). 2000-01, 1-for-4 (.250). Totals, 152-for-419 (.363).

Personal fouls/disqualifications: 1984-85, 13/1. 1985-86, 32/0. 1986-87, 16/0. 1987-88, 51/1. 1989-90, 17/2. 1990-91, 69/0. 1992-93, 55/0. 1993-94, 15/0. 1994-95, 12/0. 1995-96, 44/0. 1996-97, 34/1. 1997-98, 22/0. 1998-99, 13/0. 1999-00, 45/1. 2000-01, 3/0. Totals, 441/6.

P

PERRY, ELLIOT　　　　　G

PERSONAL: Born March 28, 1969, in Memphis. ... 6-0/152. (1,83/68,9). ... Full Name: Elliot Lamonte Perry.
HIGH SCHOOL: Treadwell (Memphis).
COLLEGE: Memphis.
TRANSACTIONS/CAREER NOTES: Selected by Los Angeles Clippers in second round (37th pick overall) of 1991 NBA Draft. ... Waived by Clippers (November 25, 1991). ... Played in Continental Basketball Association with La Crosse Catbirds (1991-92 and 1992-93), Rochester Renegades (1992-93) and Grand Rapids Hoops (1993-94). ... Signed as free agent by Charlotte Hornets (December 9, 1991). ... Signed as free agent by Portland Trail Blazers (October 7, 1992). ... Waived by Trail Blazers (November 2, 1992). ... Re-signed by Trail Blazers (August 5, 1993). ... Waived by Trail Blazers (November 3, 1993). ... Signed by Phoenix Suns to first of two consecutive 10-day contracts (January 22, 1994). ... Signed by Suns for remainder of season (February 11, 1994). ... Traded by Suns to Milwaukee Bucks for F Marty Conlon and conditional first-round draft choice (September 25, 1996). ... Traded by Bucks to New Jersey Nets in three-way deal in which Nets also received G Stephon Marbury, F Billy Curley and G Chris Carr from Minnesota Timberwolves, Nets sent F Brian Evans, 1999 first-round draft choice and an undisclosed draft choice to Timberwolves, Bucks sent G Terrell Brandon to Timberwolves, Timberwolves sent C Paul Grant to Bucks and Nets sent G Sam Cassell and F/C Chris Gatling to Bucks (March 11, 1999). ... Waived by Nets (October 30, 2000). ... Signed as free agent by Orlando Magic (November 2, 2000). ... Waived by Magic (November 30, 2000). ... Signed as free agent by Suns (December 8, 2000). ... Waived by Suns (January 5, 2001). ... Signed by Suns to 10-day contract (January 17, 2001). ... Re-signed by Suns for remainder of season (February 6, 2001).

COLLEGIATE RECORD

Season Team	G	Min.	FGM	FGA	Pct.	FTM	FTA	Pct.	Reb.	Ast.	Pts.	RPG	APG	PPG
												AVERAGES		
87-88—Memphis	32	968	140	336	.417	87	108	.806	113	130	420	3.5	4.1	13.1
88-89—Memphis	32	1017	202	437	.462	192	234	.821	109	118	620	3.4	3.7	19.4
89-90—Memphis	30	970	175	419	.418	137	182	.753	110	150	504	3.7	5.0	16.8
90-91—Memphis	32	1169	235	507	.464	146	184	.793	111	148	665	3.5	4.6	20.8
Totals	126	4124	752	1699	.443	562	708	.794	443	546	2209	3.5	4.3	17.5

Three-point field goals: 1987-88, 53-for-136 (.390). 1988-89, 24-for-76 (.316). 1989-90, 17-for-66 (.258). 1990-91, 49-for-136 (.360). Totals, 143-for-414 (.345).

CBA REGULAR-SEASON RECORD

Season Team	G	Min.	FGM	FGA	Pct.	FTM	FTA	Pct.	Reb.	Ast.	Pts.	RPG	APG	PPG
												AVERAGES		
91-92—La Crosse	2	59	8	18	.444	11	13	.846	2	9	27	1.0	4.5	13.5
92-93—La Crosse-Rochester	52	1682	259	543	.477	114	153	.745	136	240	633	2.6	4.6	12.2
93-94—Grand Rapids	28	933	151	283	.534	82	102	.804	99	179	387	3.5	6.4	13.8
Totals	82	2674	418	844	.495	207	268	.772	237	428	1047	2.9	5.2	12.8

Three-point field goals: 1991-92, 0-for-3. 1992-93, 1-for-13 (.077). 1993-94, 3-for-5 (.600). Totals, 4-for-21 (.190).

NBA REGULAR-SEASON RECORD

Season Team	G	Min.	FGM	FGA	Pct.	FTM	FTA	Pct.	Off.	Def.	Tot.	Ast.	St.	Blk.	TO	Pts.	RPG	APG	PPG
									REBOUNDS								AVERAGES		
91-92—L.A.C.-Char.	50	437	49	129	.380	27	41	.659	14	25	39	78	34	3	50	126	0.8	1.6	2.5
93-94—Phoenix	27	432	42	113	.372	21	28	.750	12	27	39	125	25	1	43	105	1.4	4.6	3.9
94-95—Phoenix	82	1977	306	588	.520	158	195	.810	51	100	151	394	156	4	163	795	1.8	4.8	9.7
95-96—Phoenix	81	1668	261	549	.475	151	194	.778	34	102	136	353	87	5	146	697	1.7	4.4	8.6
96-97—Milwaukee	82	1595	217	458	.474	79	106	.745	24	100	124	247	98	3	111	562	1.5	3.0	6.9
97-98—Milwaukee	81	1752	241	561	.430	92	109	.844	21	87	108	230	90	2	128	591	1.3	2.8	7.3
98-99—Mil.-N.J.	35	290	39	103	.379	10	14	.714	7	27	34	47	20	0	34	98	1.0	1.3	2.8
99-00—New Jersey	60	803	128	294	.435	50	62	.806	13	48	61	139	39	1	60	317	1.0	2.3	5.3
00-01—Orl.-Phoenix	49	499	65	140	.464	16	22	.727	9	37	46	79	22	1	38	147	0.9	1.6	3.0
Totals	547	9453	1348	2935	.459	604	771	.783	185	553	738	1692	571	20	773	3438	1.3	3.1	6.3

Three-point field goals: 1991-92, 1-for-7 (.143). 1993-94, 0-for-3. 1994-95, 25-for-60 (.417). 1995-96, 24-for-59 (.407). 1996-97, 49-for-137 (.358). 1997-98, 17-for-50 (.340). 1998-99, 10-for-24 (.417). 1999-00, 11-for-39 (.282). 2000-01, 1-for-5 (.200). Totals, 138-for-384 (.359).
Personal fouls/disqualifications: 1991-92, 36/0. 1993-94, 36/0. 1994-95, 142/0. 1995-96, 140/1. 1996-97, 117/0. 1997-98, 129/1. 1998-99, 25/0. 1999-00, 47/0. 2000-01, 29/0. Totals, 701/2.

NBA PLAYOFF RECORD

Season Team	G	Min.	FGM	FGA	Pct.	FTM	FTA	Pct.	Off.	Def.	Tot.	Ast.	St.	Blk.	TO	Pts.	RPG	APG	PPG
									REBOUNDS								AVERAGES		
93-94—Phoenix	4	13	1	7	.143	0	0	...	0	0	0	1	1	0	1	2	0.0	0.3	0.5
94-95—Phoenix	9	106	20	42	.476	20	25	.800	3	7	10	12	5	0	9	62	1.1	1.3	6.9
95-96—Phoenix	4	51	7	14	.500	0	1	.000	0	2	2	12	2	0	14	14	0.5	3.0	3.5
00-01—Phoenix	2	17	6	10	.600	1	1	1.000	1	3	4	4	2	0	0	13	2.0	2.0	6.5
Totals	19	187	34	73	.466	21	27	.778	4	12	16	29	10	0	10	91	0.8	1.5	4.8

Three-point field goals: 1994-95, 2-for-5 (.400). 2000-01, 0-for-1. Totals, 2-for-6 (.333).
Personal fouls/disqualifications: 1993-94, 2/0. 1994-95, 8/0. 1995-96, 3/0. Totals, 13/0.

PERSON, WESLEY　　　　G/F　　　　CAVALIERS

PERSONAL: Born March 28, 1971, in Crenshaw, Ala. ... 6-6/200. (1,98/90,7). ... Full Name: Wesley Lavon Person. ... Brother of Chuck Person, forward with Indiana Pacers (1986-87 through 1991-92), Minnesota Timberwolves (1992-93 and 1993-94), San Antonio Spurs (1994-95 through 1997-98) and Charlotte Hornets (1998-99).
HIGH SCHOOL: Brantley (Ala.).
COLLEGE: Auburn.
TRANSACTIONS/CAREER NOTES: Selected by Phoenix Suns in first round (23rd pick overall) of 1994 NBA Draft. ... Traded by Suns with G Tony Dumas to Cleveland Cavaliers for first-round draft choice no earlier than 2000 (October 1, 1997).

P

COLLEGIATE RECORD

Season Team	G	Min.	FGM	FGA	Pct.	FTM	FTA	Pct.	Reb.	Ast.	Pts.	AVERAGES RPG	APG	PPG
90-91—Auburn	26	857	153	325	.471	52	68	.765	147	48	400	5.7	1.8	15.4
91-92—Auburn	27	955	208	411	.506	53	73	.726	183	55	538	6.8	2.0	19.9
92-93—Auburn	27	957	194	349	.556	61	79	.772	192	102	507	7.1	3.8	18.8
93-94—Auburn	28	1006	217	448	.484	94	128	.734	179	79	621	6.4	2.8	22.2
Totals	108	3775	772	1533	.504	260	348	.747	701	284	2066	6.5	2.6	19.1

Three-point field goals: 1990-91, 42-for-118 (.356). 1991-92, 69-for-141 (.489). 1992-93, 58-for-125 (.464). 1993-94, 93-for-210 (.443). Totals, 262-for-594 (.441).

NBA REGULAR-SEASON RECORD

HONORS: NBA All-Rookie second team (1995).
NOTES: Led NBA with 192 three-point field goals made (1998).

Season Team	G	Min.	FGM	FGA	Pct.	FTM	FTA	Pct.	REBOUNDS Off.	Def.	Tot.	Ast.	St.	Blk.	TO	Pts.	AVERAGES RPG	APG	PPG
94-95—Phoenix	78	1800	309	638	.484	80	101	.792	67	134	201	105	48	24	79	814	2.6	1.3	10.4
95-96—Phoenix	82	2609	390	877	.445	148	192	.771	56	265	321	138	55	22	89	1045	3.9	1.7	12.7
96-97—Phoenix	80	2326	409	903	.453	91	114	.798	68	224	292	123	86	20	76	1080	3.7	1.5	13.5
97-98—Cleveland	82	3198	440	957	.460	132	170	.776	65	298	363	188	129	49	110	1204	4.4	2.3	14.7
98-99—Cleveland	45	1342	198	437	.453	32	53	.604	19	123	142	80	37	16	41	503	3.2	1.8	11.2
99-00—Cleveland	79	2056	280	654	.428	61	77	.792	44	223	267	146	40	19	60	727	3.4	1.8	9.2
00-01—Cleveland	44	958	128	292	.438	24	30	.800	11	119	130	64	27	11	40	314	3.0	1.5	7.1
Totals	490	14289	2154	4758	.453	568	737	.771	330	1386	1716	844	422	161	495	5687	3.5	1.7	11.6

Three-point field goals: 1994-95, 116-for-266 (.436). 1995-96, 117-for-313 (.374). 1996-97, 171-for-414 (.413). 1997-98, 192-for-447 (.430). 1998-99, 75-for-200 (.375). 1999-00, 106-for-250 (.424). 2000-01, 34-for-84 (.405). Totals, 811-for-1974 (.411).

Personal fouls/disqualifications: 1994-95, 149/0. 1995-96, 148/0. 1996-97, 102/0. 1997-98, 108/0. 1998-99, 52/0. 1999-00, 119/1. 2000-01, 62/0. Totals, 740/1.

NBA PLAYOFF RECORD

Season Team	G	Min.	FGM	FGA	Pct.	FTM	FTA	Pct.	REBOUNDS Off.	Def.	Tot.	Ast.	St.	Blk.	TO	Pts.	AVERAGES RPG	APG	PPG
94-95—Phoenix	10	247	34	83	.410	11	12	.917	9	12	21	11	3	2	9	96	2.1	1.1	9.6
95-96—Phoenix	4	183	22	56	.393	4	5	.800	8	15	23	3	3	1	5	57	5.8	0.8	14.3
96-97—Phoenix	5	163	25	53	.472	14	18	.778	5	28	33	6	4	3	4	78	6.6	1.2	15.6
97-98—Cleveland	4	136	11	29	.379	3	4	.750	2	7	9	10	3	0	1	32	2.3	2.5	8.0
Totals	23	729	92	221	.416	32	39	.821	24	62	86	30	13	6	19	263	3.7	1.3	11.4

Three-point field goals: 1994-95, 17-for-45 (.378). 1995-96, 9-for-29 (.310). 1996-97, 14-for-33 (.424). 1997-98, 7-for-19 (.368). Totals, 47-for-126 (.373).

Personal fouls/disqualifications: 1994-95, 19/0. 1995-96, 7/0. 1996-97, 5/0. 1997-98, 5/0. Totals, 36/0.

PETERSON, MORRIS   G/F   RAPTORS

PERSONAL: Born August 26, 1977, in Flint, Mich. ... 6-7/215. (2,01/97,5).
HIGH SCHOOL: Northwestern (Flint, Mich.).
COLLEGE: Michigan State.
TRANSACTIONS/CAREER NOTES: Selected by Toronto Raptors in first round (21st pick overall) of 2000 NBA Draft.

COLLEGIATE RECORD

NOTES: Member of NCAA Division I championship team (2000). ... The Sporting News All-America first team (2000).

Season Team	G	Min.	FGM	FGA	Pct.	FTM	FTA	Pct.	Reb.	Ast.	Pts.	AVERAGES RPG	APG	PPG
95-96—Michigan State	4	12	1	1	1.000	0	1	.000	3	2	2	0.8	0.5	0.5
96-97—Michigan State	29	518	72	166	.434	36	51	.706	97	18	196	3.3	0.6	6.8
97-98—Michigan State	27	503	81	182	.445	32	58	.552	94	24	217	3.5	0.9	8.0
98-99—Michigan State	38	907	190	343	.554	114	140	.814	216	36	516	5.7	0.9	13.6
99-00—Michigan State	39	1136	218	469	.465	136	176	.773	235	49	657	6.0	1.3	16.8
Totals	137	3076	562	1161	.484	318	426	.746	645	129	1588	4.7	0.9	11.6

Three-point field goals: 1996-97, 16-for-59 (.271). 1997-98, 23-for-69 (.333). 1998-99, 22-for-59 (.373). 1999-00, 85-for-200 (.425). Totals, 146-for-387 (.377).

NBA REGULAR-SEASON RECORD

HONORS: NBA All-Rookie first team (2001).

Season Team	G	Min.	FGM	FGA	Pct.	FTM	FTA	Pct.	REBOUNDS Off.	Def.	Tot.	Ast.	St.	Blk.	TO	Pts.	AVERAGES RPG	APG	PPG
00-01—Toronto	80	1809	290	673	.431	104	145	.717	112	147	259	105	63	20	78	747	3.2	1.3	9.3

Three-point field goals: 2000-01, 63-for-165 (.382).
Personal fouls/disqualifications: 2000-01, 164/0.

NBA PLAYOFF RECORD

Season Team	G	Min.	FGM	FGA	Pct.	FTM	FTA	Pct.	REBOUNDS Off.	Def.	Tot.	Ast.	St.	Blk.	TO	Pts.	AVERAGES RPG	APG	PPG
00-01—Toronto	8	110	18	35	.514	3	4	.750	2	10	12	15	6	0	6	43	1.5	1.9	5.4

Three-point field goals: 2000-01, 4-for-9 (.444).
Personal fouls/disqualifications: 2000-01, 10/0.

P

DID YOU KNOW . . .

. . . that Rick Barry was the youngest player in NBA history to score 50 points in a game?

PIATKOWSKI, ERIC G/F CLIPPERS

PERSONAL: Born September 30, 1970, in Steubenville, Ohio. ... 6-7/215. (2,01/97,5). ... Full Name: Eric Todd Piatkowski. ... Son of Walt Piatkowski, forward with Denver Rockets and Miami Floridians of American Basketball Association (1968-69 through 1971-1972). ... Name pronounced pie-it-COW-ski.
HIGH SCHOOL: Stevens (Rapid City, S.D.).
COLLEGE: Nebraska.
TRANSACTIONS/CAREER NOTES: Selected by Indiana Pacers in first round (15th pick overall) of 1994 NBA Draft. ... Draft rights traded by Pacers with F Malik Sealy and G Pooh Richardson to Los Angeles Clippers for G Mark Jackson and draft rights to G Greg Minor (June 30, 1994).

COLLEGIATE RECORD

Season Team	G	Min.	FGM	FGA	Pct.	FTM	FTA	Pct.	Reb.	Ast.	Pts.	RPG	APG	PPG
89-90—Nebraska						Did not play—redshirted.								
90-91—Nebraska	34	679	128	275	.465	72	86	.837	125	68	372	3.7	2.0	10.9
91-92—Nebraska	29	873	144	338	.426	79	109	.725	184	97	414	6.3	3.3	14.3
92-93—Nebraska	30	894	178	367	.485	98	129	.760	171	75	502	5.7	2.5	16.7
93-94—Nebraska	30	972	226	456	.496	131	165	.794	189	82	646	6.3	2.7	21.5
Totals	123	3418	676	1436	.471	380	489	.777	669	322	1934	5.4	2.6	15.7

Three-point field goals: 1990-91, 44-for-127 (.346). 1991-92, 47-for-136 (.346). 1992-93, 48-for-129 (.372). 1993-94, 63-for-172 (.366). Totals, 202-for-564 (.358).

NBA REGULAR-SEASON RECORD

Season Team	G	Min.	FGM	FGA	Pct.	FTM	FTA	Pct.	Off.	Def.	Tot.	Ast.	St.	Blk.	TO	Pts.	RPG	APG	PPG
94-95—L.A. Clippers	81	1208	201	456	.441	90	115	.783	63	70	133	77	37	15	63	566	1.6	1.0	7.0
95-96—L.A. Clippers	65	784	98	242	.405	67	82	.817	40	63	103	48	24	10	45	301	1.6	0.7	4.6
96-97—L.A. Clippers	65	747	134	298	.450	69	84	.821	49	56	105	52	33	10	46	388	1.6	0.8	6.0
97-98—L.A. Clippers	67	1740	257	568	.452	140	170	.824	70	166	236	85	51	12	80	760	3.5	1.3	11.3
98-99—L.A. Clippers	49	1242	180	417	.432	88	102	.863	39	101	140	53	44	6	53	513	2.9	1.1	10.5
99-00—L.A. Clippers	75	1712	238	573	.415	85	100	.850	74	148	222	81	44	13	57	654	3.0	1.1	8.7
00-01—L.A. Clippers	81	2144	291	672	.433	158	181	.873	54	187	241	96	46	19	76	860	3.0	1.2	10.6
Totals	483	9577	1399	3226	.434	697	834	.836	389	791	1180	492	279	85	420	4042	2.4	1.0	8.4

Three-point field goals: 1994-95, 74-for-198 (.374). 1995-96, 38-for-114 (.333). 1996-97, 51-for-120 (.425). 1997-98, 106-for-259 (.409). 1998-99, 65-for-165 (.394). 1999-00, 93-for-243 (.383). 2000-01, 120-for-297 (.404). Totals, 547-for-1396 (.392).
Personal fouls/disqualifications: 1994-95, 150/1. 1995-96, 83/0. 1996-97, 85/0. 1997-98, 137/0. 1998-99, 86/0. 1999-00, 140/0. 2000-01, 123/0. Totals, 804/1.

NBA PLAYOFF RECORD

Season Team	G	Min.	FGM	FGA	Pct.	FTM	FTA	Pct.	Off.	Def.	Tot.	Ast.	St.	Blk.	TO	Pts.	RPG	APG	PPG
96-97—L.A. Clippers	3	38	4	11	.364	6	7	.857	1	1	2	0	1	0	0	16	0.7	0.0	5.3

Three-point field goals: 1996-97, 2-for-5 (.400).
Personal fouls/disqualifications: 1996-97, 5/0.

PIERCE, PAUL F CELTICS

PERSONAL: Born October 13, 1977, in Oakland. ... 6-6/230. (1,98/104,3). ... Full Name: Paul Anthony Pierce.
HIGH SCHOOL: Inglewood (Calif.).
COLLEGE: Kansas.
TRANSACTIONS/CAREER NOTES: Selected after junior season by Boston Celtics in first round (10th pick oveall) of 1998 NBA Draft.

COLLEGIATE RECORD

NOTES: The Sporting News All-America first team (1998).

Season Team	G	Min.	FGM	FGA	Pct.	FTM	FTA	Pct.	Reb.	Ast.	Pts.	RPG	APG	PPG
95-96—Kansas	34	862	143	341	.419	83	137	.606	180	61	404	5.3	1.8	11.9
96-97—Kansas	36	1013	215	441	.488	124	173	.717	243	77	587	6.8	2.1	16.3
97-98—Kansas	38	1155	287	559	.513	163	221	.738	253	98	777	6.7	2.6	20.4
Totals	108	3030	645	1341	.481	370	531	.697	676	236	1768	6.3	2.2	16.4

Three-point field goals: 1995-96, 35-for-115 (.304). 1996-97, 33-for-71 (.465). 1997-98, 40-for-116 (.345). Totals, 108-for-302 (.358).

NBA REGULAR-SEASON RECORD

HONORS: NBA All-Rookie first team (1999).

Season Team	G	Min.	FGM	FGA	Pct.	FTM	FTA	Pct.	Off.	Def.	Tot.	Ast.	St.	Blk.	TO	Pts.	RPG	APG	PPG
98-99—Boston	48	1632	284	647	.439	139	195	.713	117	192	309	115	82	50	113	791	6.4	2.4	16.5
99-00—Boston	73	2583	486	1099	.442	359	450	.798	83	313	396	221	152	62	178	1427	5.4	3.0	19.5
00-01—Boston	82	3120	687	1513	.454	550	738	.745	94	428	522	253	138	69	262	2071	6.4	3.1	25.3
Totals	203	7335	1457	3259	.447	1048	1383	.758	294	933	1227	589	372	181	553	4289	6.0	2.9	21.1

Three-point field goals: 1998-99, 84-for-204 (.412). 1999-00, 96-for-280 (.343). 2000-01, 147-for-384 (.383). Totals, 327-for-868 (.377).
Personal fouls/disqualifications: 1998-99, 139/1. 1999-00, 237/5. 2000-01, 251/3. Totals, 627/9.

P

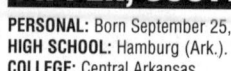

PIPPEN, SCOTTIE   F   TRAIL BLAZERS

PERSONAL: Born September 25, 1965, in Hamburg, Ark. ... 6-7/228. (2,01/103,4).
HIGH SCHOOL: Hamburg (Ark.).
COLLEGE: Central Arkansas.
TRANSACTIONS/CAREER NOTES: Selected by Seattle SuperSonics in first round (fifth pick overall) of 1987 NBA Draft. ... Draft rights traded by SuperSonics to Chicago Bulls for draft rights to F/C Olden Polynice, 1988 or 1989 second-round draft choice and option to exchange 1989 first-round draft choices (June 22, 1987). ... Traded by Bulls to Houston Rockets for F Roy Rogers and 1999 or 2000 second-round draft choice (January 22, 1999). ... Traded by Rockets to Portland Trail Blazers for C Kelvin Cato, F Stacy Augmon, G/F Walt Williams, G Brian Shaw, G Ed Gray and F/C Carlos Rogers (October 2, 1999).
CAREER HONORS: NBA 50th Anniversary All-Time Team (1996).
MISCELLANEOUS: Member of NBA championship team (1991, 1992, 1993, 1996, 1997, 1998). ... Member of gold-medal-winning U.S. Olympic teams (1992, 1996).

COLLEGIATE RECORD

Season Team	G	Min.	FGM	FGA	Pct.	FTM	FTA	Pct.	Reb.	Ast.	Pts.	RPG	APG	PPG
83-84—Central Arkansas	20	...	36	79	.456	13	19	.684	59	14	85	3.0	0.7	4.3
84-85—Central Arkansas	19	...	141	250	.564	69	102	.676	175	30	351	9.2	1.6	18.5
85-86—Central Arkansas	29	...	229	412	.556	116	169	.686	266	102	574	9.2	3.5	19.8
86-87—Central Arkansas	25	...	231	390	.592	105	146	.719	249	107	590	10.0	4.3	23.6
Totals	93		637	1131	.563	303	436	.695	749	253	1600	8.1	2.7	17.2

Three-point field goals: 1986-87, 23-for-40 (.575).

NBA REGULAR-SEASON RECORD

HONORS: All-NBA first team (1994, 1995, 1996). ... All-NBA second team (1992, 1997). ... All-NBA third team (1993, 1998). ... NBA All-Defensive first team (1992, 1993, 1994, 1995, 1996, 1997, 1998, 1999). ... NBA All-Defensive second team (1991, 2000).
NOTES: Led NBA with 2.94 steals per game (1995).

Season Team	G	Min.	FGM	FGA	Pct.	FTM	FTA	Pct.	Off.	Def.	Tot.	Ast.	St.	Blk.	TO	Pts.	RPG	APG	PPG
87-88—Chicago	79	1650	261	564	.463	99	172	.576	115	183	298	169	91	52	131	625	3.8	2.1	7.9
88-89—Chicago	73	2413	413	867	.476	201	301	.668	138	307	445	256	139	61	199	1048	6.1	3.5	14.4
89-90—Chicago	82	3148	562	1150	.489	199	295	.675	150	397	547	444	211	101	278	1351	6.7	5.4	16.5
90-91—Chicago	82	3014	600	1153	.520	240	340	.706	163	432	595	511	193	93	232	1461	7.3	6.2	17.8
91-92—Chicago	82	3164	687	1359	.506	330	434	.760	185	445	630	572	155	93	253	1720	7.7	7.0	21.0
92-93—Chicago	81	3123	628	1327	.473	232	350	.663	203	418	621	507	173	73	246	1510	7.7	6.3	18.6
93-94—Chicago	72	2759	627	1278	.491	270	409	.660	173	456	629	403	211	58	232	1587	8.7	5.6	22.0
94-95—Chicago	79	3014	634	1320	.480	315	440	.716	175	464	639	409	*232	89	271	1692	8.1	5.2	21.4
95-96—Chicago	77	2825	563	1216	.463	220	324	.679	152	344	496	452	133	57	207	1496	6.4	5.9	19.4
96-97—Chicago	82	3095	648	1366	.474	204	291	.701	160	371	531	467	154	45	214	1656	6.5	5.7	20.2
97-98—Chicago	44	1652	315	704	.447	150	193	.777	53	174	227	254	79	43	109	841	5.2	5.8	19.1
98-99—Houston	50	2011	261	604	.432	132	183	.721	63	260	323	293	98	37	159	726	6.5	5.9	14.5
99-00—Portland	82	2749	388	860	.451	160	223	.717	114	399	513	406	117	41	208	1022	6.3	5.0	12.5
00-01—Portland	64	2133	269	596	.451	119	161	.739	70	263	333	294	94	35	154	721	5.2	4.6	11.3
Totals	1029	36750	6856	14364	.477	2871	4116	.698	1914	4913	6827	5437	2080	878	2893	17456	6.6	5.3	17.0

Three-point field goals: 1987-88, 4-for-23 (.174). 1988-89, 22-for-56 (.273). 1989-90, 28-for-112 (.250). 1990-91, 21-for-68 (.309). 1991-92, 16-for-80 (.200). 1992-93, 22-for-93 (.237). 1993-94, 63-for-197 (.320). 1994-95, 109-for-316 (.345). 1995-96, 150-for-401 (.374). 1996-97, 156-for-424 (.368). 1997-98, 61-for-192 (.318). 1998-99, 72-for-212 (.340). 1999-00, 86-for-263 (.327). 2000-01, 64-for-186 (.344). Totals, 873-for-2644 (.330).
Personal fouls/disqualifications: 1987-88, 214/3. 1988-89, 261/8. 1989-90, 298/6. 1990-91, 270/3. 1991-92, 242/2. 1992-93, 219/3. 1993-94, 227/1. 1994-95, 238/4. 1995-96, 198/0. 1996-97, 213/2. 1997-98, 116/0. 1998-99, 90/0. 1999-00, 208/0. 2000-01, 158/2. Totals, 2980/34.

NBA PLAYOFF RECORD

NOTES: Holds NBA Finals career record for most three-point field goals attempted—117. ... Shares NBA Finals single-game record for most three-point field goals made in one game—7 (June 6, 1997, vs. Utah). ... Holds career playoff record for most three-point field goals attempted—640.

Season Team	G	Min.	FGM	FGA	Pct.	FTM	FTA	Pct.	Off.	Def.	Tot.	Ast.	St.	Blk.	TO	Pts.	RPG	APG	PPG
87-88—Chicago	10	294	46	99	.465	5	7	.714	24	28	52	24	8	8	26	100	5.2	2.4	10.0
88-89—Chicago	17	619	84	182	.462	32	50	.640	34	95	129	67	23	16	41	222	7.6	3.9	13.1
89-90—Chicago	15	612	104	210	.495	71	100	.710	33	75	108	83	31	19	49	289	7.2	5.5	19.3
90-91—Chicago	17	704	142	282	.504	80	101	.792	37	114	151	99	42	19	55	368	8.9	5.8	21.6
91-92—Chicago	22	899	152	325	.468	118	155	.761	59	134	193	147	41	25	70	428	8.8	6.7	19.5
92-93—Chicago	19	789	152	327	.465	74	116	.638	37	95	132	107	41	13	71	381	6.9	5.6	20.1
93-94—Chicago	10	384	85	196	.434	46	52	.885	17	66	83	46	24	7	37	228	8.3	4.6	22.8
94-95—Chicago	10	396	58	131	.443	48	71	.676	24	62	86	58	14	10	27	178	8.6	5.8	17.8
95-96—Chicago	18	742	112	287	.390	51	80	.638	62	91	153	107	47	16	41	305	8.5	5.9	16.9
96-97—Chicago	19	753	129	309	.417	68	86	.791	36	93	129	72	28	18	55	365	6.8	3.8	19.2
97-98—Chicago	21	836	122	294	.415	91	134	.679	49	101	150	110	45	20	51	353	7.1	5.2	16.8
98-99—Houston	4	172	23	70	.329	21	26	.808	20	27	47	22	7	3	13	73	11.8	5.5	18.3
99-00—Portland	16	614	83	198	.419	52	70	.743	22	92	114	69	32	7	37	239	7.1	4.3	14.9
00-01—Portland	3	117	16	38	.421	6	9	.667	2	15	17	7	8	2	12	41	5.7	2.3	13.7
Totals	201	7931	1308	2948	.444	763	1057	.722	456	1088	1544	1018	391	183	585	3570	7.7	5.1	17.8

Three-point field goals: 1987-88, 3-for-6 (.500). 1988-89, 22-for-56 (.393). 1989-90, 10-for-31 (.323). 1990-91, 4-for-17 (.235). 1991-92, 6-for-24 (.250). 1992-93, 3-for-17 (.176). 1993-94, 12-for-45 (.267). 1994-95, 14-for-38 (.368). 1995-96, 30-for-105 (.286). 1996-97, 39-for-113 (.345). 1997-98, 18-for-79 (.228). 1998-99, 6-for-22 (.273). 1999-00, 21-for-70 (.300). 2000-01, 4-for-17 (.176). Totals, 191-for-640 (.298).
Personal fouls/disqualifications: 1987-88, 33/1. 1988-89, 63/2. 1989-90, 62/0. 1990-91, 58/1. 1991-92, 72/1. 1992-93, 62/0. 1993-94, 33/1. 1994-95, 40/1. 1995-96, 51/0. 1996-97, 49/0. 1997-98, 66/1. 1998-99, 12/0. 1999-00, 43/1. 2000-01, 14/1. Totals, 664/10.

NBA ALL-STAR GAME RECORD

NOTES: NBA All-Star Game Most Valuable Player (1994). ... Holds career record for most three-point field goal attempts—22. ... Holds sin-

P

gle-game record for most three-point field goal attempts in one half—7 (1994). ... Shares single-game record for most three-point field goal attempts—9 (1994).

Season	Team	Min.	FGM	FGA	Pct.	FTM	FTA	Pct.	Off.	Def.	Tot.	Ast.	PF	Dq.	St.	Blk.	TO	Pts.
1990	—Chicago	12	2	4	.500	0	0	...	0	1	1	0	1	0	1	1	1	4
1992	—Chicago	21	6	13	.462	2	3	.667	4	0	4	1	0	0	2	1	1	14
1993	—Chicago	29	4	14	.286	2	3	.667	2	3	5	4	4	0	5	2	0	10
1994	—Chicago	31	9	15	.600	6	10	.600	0	11	11	2	2	0	4	1	2	29
1995	—Chicago	30	5	15	.333	0	0	...	0	7	7	3	1	0	2	1	4	12
1996	—Chicago	25	4	7	.571	0	0	...	2	6	8	5	0	0	3	0	6	8
1997	—Chicago	25	4	9	.444	0	0	...	0	3	3	2	0	0	0	0	2	8
Totals		173	34	77	.442	10	16	.625	8	31	39	17	8	0	17	6	16	85

Three-point field goals: 1990, 0-for-1. 1993, 0-for-2. 1994, 5-for-9 (.556). 1995, 2-for-6 (.333). 1996, 0-for-1. 1997, 0-for-3. Totals, 7-for-22 (.318).

POLLARD, SCOT   F/C   KINGS

PERSONAL: Born February 12, 1975, in Murray, Utah ... 6-11/265. (2,11/120,2).
HIGH SCHOOL: Torrey Pines (San Diego).
COLLEGE: Kansas.
TRANSACTIONS/CAREER NOTES: Selected by Detroit Pistons in first round (19th pick overall) of 1997 NBA Draft. ... Traded by Pistons with 1999 first-round draft choice to Atlanta Hawks for F/C Christian Laettner (January 22, 1999). ... Waived by Hawks (February 19, 1999). ... Signed as free agent by Sacramento Kings (February 24, 1999).

COLLEGIATE RECORD

Season Team	G	Min.	FGM	FGA	Pct.	FTM	FTA	Pct.	Reb.	Ast.	Pts.	RPG	APG	PPG
93-94—Kansas	35	597	95	175	.543	74	108	.685	173	13	264	4.9	0.4	7.5
94-95—Kansas	31	620	113	203	.557	89	136	.654	192	17	315	6.2	0.5	10.2
95-96—Kansas	34	835	123	218	.564	96	151	.636	253	10	342	7.4	0.3	10.1
96-97—Kansas	28	702	94	178	.528	99	140	.707	232	19	288	8.3	0.7	10.3
Totals	128	2754	425	774	.549	358	535	.669	850	59	1209	6.6	0.5	9.4

Three-point field goals: 1996-97, 1-for-1.

NBA REGULAR-SEASON RECORD

Season Team	G	Min.	FGM	FGA	Pct.	FTM	FTA	Pct.	Off.	Def.	Tot.	Ast.	St.	Blk.	TO	Pts.	RPG	APG	PPG
97-98—Detroit	33	317	35	70	.500	19	23	.826	34	40	74	9	8	10	12	89	2.2	0.3	2.7
98-99—Sacramento	16	259	33	61	.541	16	23	.696	38	44	82	4	8	18	5	82	5.1	0.3	5.1
99-00—Sacramento	76	1336	149	283	.527	114	159	.717	168	236	404	43	55	59	50	412	5.3	0.6	5.4
00-01—Sacramento	77	1658	185	395	.468	128	171	.749	173	292	465	47	48	97	66	498	6.0	0.6	6.5
Totals	202	3570	402	809	.497	277	376	.737	413	612	1025	103	119	184	133	1081	5.1	0.5	5.4

Three-point field goals: 2000-01, 0-for-2. Totals, 0-for-2 (.000).
Personal fouls/disqualifications: 1997-98, 48/0. 1998-99, 41/0. 1999-00, 213/3. 2000-01, 206/4. Totals, 508/7.

NBA PLAYOFF RECORD

Season Team	G	Min.	FGM	FGA	Pct.	FTM	FTA	Pct.	Off.	Def.	Tot.	Ast.	St.	Blk.	TO	Pts.	RPG	APG	PPG
98-99—Sacramento	5	74	6	9	.667	3	5	.600	5	6	11	1	4	6	2	15	2.2	0.2	3.0
99-00—Sacramento	5	70	9	16	.563	2	6	.333	6	10	16	1	2	1	3	20	3.2	0.2	4.0
00-01—Sacramento	8	141	19	30	.633	10	17	.588	23	32	55	2	1	7	6	48	6.9	0.3	6.0
Totals	18	285	34	55	.618	15	28	.536	34	48	82	4	7	14	11	83	4.6	0.2	4.6

Personal fouls/disqualifications: 1998-99, 13/0. 1999-00, 18/1. 2000-01, 30/0. Totals, 61/1.

POLYNICE, OLDEN   F/C

PERSONAL: Born November 21, 1964, in Port-au-Prince, Haiti. ... 7-0/250. (2,13/113,4). ... Name pronounced OLD-n Pol-a-neece.
HIGH SCHOOL: All Hallows Institute (Bronx, N.Y.).
COLLEGE: Virginia.
TRANSACTIONS/CAREER NOTES: Played in Italy after junior season (1986-87). ... Selected by Chicago Bulls in first round (eighth pick overall) of 1987 NBA Draft. ... Draft rights traded by Bulls with 1988 or 1989 second-round draft choice and option to exchange 1989 first-round draft choices to Seattle SuperSonics for draft rights to F Scottie Pippen (June 22, 1987). ... Traded by SuperSonics with 1991 first-round draft choice and 1993 or 1994 first-round draft choice to Los Angeles Clippers for C/F Benoit Benjamin (February 20, 1991). ... Traded by Clippers with 1996 and 1997 second-round draft choices to Detroit Pistons for C William Bedford and draft rights to F Don MacLean (June 24, 1992). ... Traded by Pistons with F David Wood to Sacramento Kings for C Duane Causwell and 1994, 1995 and 1996 second-round draft choices (February 16, 1994); trade voided when Causwell failed physical (February 19, 1994). ... Traded by Pistons to Sacramento Kings for F/C Pete Chilcutt, 1994 second-round draft choice and conditional first-round draft choice (February 20, 1994). ... Signed as free agent by SuperSonics (January 21, 1999). ... Signed as free agent by Utah Jazz (August 27, 1999).

COLLEGIATE RECORD

Season Team	G	Min.	FGM	FGA	Pct.	FTM	FTA	Pct.	Reb.	Ast.	Pts.	RPG	APG	PPG
83-84—Virginia	33	866	98	178	.551	57	97	.588	184	20	253	5.6	0.6	7.7
84-85—Virginia	32	1095	161	267	.603	94	157	.599	243	16	416	7.6	0.5	13.0
85-86—Virginia	30	1074	183	320	.572	116	182	.637	240	16	482	8.0	0.5	16.1
Totals	95	3035	442	765	.578	267	436	.612	667	52	1151	7.0	0.5	12.1

P

ITALIAN LEAGUE RECORD

Season Team	G	Min.	FGM	FGA	Pct.	FTM	FTA	Pct.	Reb.	Ast.	Pts.	AVERAGES RPG	APG	PPG
86-87—Rimini	30	968	214	378	.566	82	137	.599	330	...	518	11.0	...	17.3

NBA REGULAR-SEASON RECORD

Season Team	G	Min.	FGM	FGA	Pct.	FTM	FTA	Pct.	REBOUNDS Off.	Def.	Tot.	Ast.	St.	Blk.	TO	Pts.	AVERAGES RPG	APG	PPG
87-88—Seattle	82	1080	118	254	.465	101	158	.639	122	208	330	33	32	26	81	337	4.0	0.4	4.1
88-89—Seattle	80	835	91	180	.506	51	86	.593	98	108	206	21	37	30	46	233	2.6	0.3	2.9
89-90—Seattle	79	1085	156	289	.540	47	99	.475	128	172	300	15	25	21	35	360	3.8	0.2	4.6
90-91—Seattle-L.A.C.	79	2092	316	564	.560	146	252	.579	220	333	553	42	43	32	88	778	7.0	0.5	9.8
91-92—L.A. Clippers	76	1834	244	470	.519	125	201	.622	195	341	536	46	45	20	83	613	7.1	0.6	8.1
92-93—Detroit	67	1299	210	429	.490	66	142	.465	181	237	418	29	31	21	54	486	6.2	0.4	7.3
93-94—Detroit-Sac.	68	2402	346	662	.523	97	191	.508	299	510	809	41	42	67	78	789	11.9	0.6	11.6
94-95—Sacramento	81	2534	376	691	.544	124	194	.639	277	448	725	62	48	52	113	877	9.0	0.8	10.8
95-96—Sacramento	81	2441	431	818	.527	122	203	.601	257	507	764	58	52	66	127	985	9.4	0.7	12.2
96-97—Sacramento	82	2893	442	967	.457	141	251	.562	272	500	772	178	46	80	166	1025	9.4	2.2	12.5
97-98—Sacramento	70	1458	249	542	.459	52	115	.452	173	266	439	107	30	45	98	550	6.3	1.5	7.9
98-99—Seattle	48	1481	169	358	.472	29	94	.309	184	241	425	43	20	30	49	368	8.9	0.9	7.7
99-00—Utah	82	1819	203	398	.510	28	90	.311	166	287	453	37	30	84	70	435	5.5	0.5	5.3
00-01—Utah	81	1619	206	415	.496	17	65	.262	157	221	378	31	27	77	78	429	4.7	0.4	5.3
Totals	1056	24872	3557	7037	.505	1146	2141	.535	2729	4379	7108	743	515	651	1166	8265	6.7	0.7	7.8

Three-point field goals: 1987-88, 0-for-2. 1988-89, 0-for-1. 1989-90, 1-for-2 (.500). 1990-91, 0-for-1. 1991-92, 0-for-1. 1992-93, 0-for-1. 1993-94, 0-for-2. 1994-95, 1-for-1. 1995-96, 1-for-3 (.333). 1996-97, 0-for-6. 1997-98, 0-for-1. 1998-99, 1-for-1. 1999-00, 1-for-2 (.500). 2000-01, 0-for-1. Totals, 5-for-26 (.192).

Personal fouls/disqualifications: 1987-88, 215/1. 1988-89, 164/0. 1989-90, 187/0. 1990-91, 192/1. 1991-92, 165/0. 1992-93, 126/0. 1993-94, 189/2. 1994-95, 238/0. 1995-96, 250/3. 1996-97, 298/4. 1997-98, 158/0. 1998-99, 150/0. 1999-00, 260/1. 2000-01, 241/2. Totals, 2833/14.

NBA PLAYOFF RECORD

Season Team	G	Min.	FGM	FGA	Pct.	FTM	FTA	Pct.	REBOUNDS Off.	Def.	Tot.	Ast.	St.	Blk.	TO	Pts.	AVERAGES RPG	APG	PPG
87-88—Seattle	5	44	5	11	.455	0	2	.000	2	6	8	0	3	0	1	10	1.6	0.0	2.0
88-89—Seattle	8	162	25	41	.610	7	13	.538	27	35	62	1	6	4	5	57	7.8	0.1	7.1
91-92—L.A. Clippers	5	63	7	12	.583	2	6	.333	2	16	18	2	1	1	1	16	3.6	0.4	3.2
95-96—Sacramento	4	141	24	46	.522	6	9	.667	16	32	48	3	1	7	3	55	12.0	0.8	13.8
99-00—Utah	10	260	28	52	.538	3	6	.500	24	42	66	5	3	8	13	59	6.6	0.5	5.9
00-01—Utah	5	100	16	30	.533	7	10	.700	16	3	19	1	1	2	6	39	3.8	0.2	7.8
Totals	37	770	105	192	.547	25	46	.543	87	134	221	12	15	22	29	236	6.0	0.3	6.4

Three-point field goals: 1995-96, 1-for-1. 2000-01, 0-for-1. Totals, 1-for-2 (.500).

Personal fouls/disqualifications: 1987-88, 6/0. 1988-89, 32/1. 1991-92, 11/0. 1995-96, 15/0. 1999-00, 36/1. 2000-01, 12/0. Totals, 112/2.

POPE, MARK   F

PERSONAL: Born September 11, 1972, in Omaha, Neb. ... 6-10/235. (2,08/106,6). ... Full Name: Mark Edward Pope.
HIGH SCHOOL: Newport (Bellevue, Wash.).
COLLEGE: Washington, then Kentucky.
TRANSACTIONS/CAREER NOTES: Selected by Indiana Pacers in second round (52nd pick overall) of 1996 NBA Draft. ... Played in Turkey (1996-97 and 1999-2000). ... Waived by Pacers (October 30, 1999). ... Played in Continental Basketball Association with LaCrosse Bobcats (1999-2000). ... Signed as free agent by Milwaukee Bucks (September 27, 2000).

COLLEGIATE RECORD

NOTES: Member of NCAA Division I championship team (1996).

Season Team	G	Min.	FGM	FGA	Pct.	FTM	FTA	Pct.	Reb.	Ast.	Pts.	AVERAGES RPG	APG	PPG
91-92—Washington	29	872	110	190	.579	74	92	.804	234	58	300	8.1	2.0	10.3
92-93—Washington	27	868	106	201	.527	112	130	.862	217	34	329	8.0	1.3	12.2
94-95—Kentucky	33	728	89	173	.514	72	99	.727	207	29	271	6.3	0.9	8.2
95-96—Kentucky	36	716	94	195	.482	71	104	.683	187	37	275	5.2	1.0	7.6
Totals	125	3184	399	759	.526	329	425	.774	845	158	1175	6.8	1.3	9.4

Three-point field goals: 1991-92, 21-for-44 (.477). 1992-93, 5-for-20 (.250). 1994-95, 21-for-44 (.477). 1995-96, 16-for-45 (.356). Totals, 63-for-153 (.412).

TURKISH LEAGUE RECORD

Season Team	G	Min.	FGM	FGA	Pct.	FTM	FTA	Pct.	Reb.	Ast.	Pts.	AVERAGES RPG	APG	PPG
96-97—Efes Pilsen	9	182	17	42	.405	10	11	.909	30	6	51	3.3	0.7	5.7
99-00—Ulker	15	493	71	146	.486	27	46	.587	113	17	188	7.5	1.1	12.5
Totals	24	675	88	188	.468	37	57	.649	143	23	239	6.0	1.0	10.0

Three-point field goals: 1996-97, 7-for-19 (.368). 1999-00, 19-for-50 (.380). Totals, 26-for-69 (.377).

NBA REGULAR-SEASON RECORD

Season Team	G	Min.	FGM	FGA	Pct.	FTM	FTA	Pct.	REBOUNDS Off.	Def.	Tot.	Ast.	St.	Blk.	TO	Pts.	AVERAGES RPG	APG	PPG
97-98—Indiana	28	193	14	41	.341	10	17	.588	9	17	26	7	3	6	10	39	0.9	0.3	1.4
98-99—Indiana	4	26	1	7	.143	0	1	.000	2	2	4	0	0	0	1	2	1.0	0.0	0.5
00-01—Milwaukee	63	942	62	142	.437	22	35	.629	56	91	147	38	16	26	17	151	2.3	0.6	2.4
Totals	95	1161	77	190	.405	32	53	.604	67	110	177	45	19	32	28	192	1.9	0.5	2.0

Three-point field goals: 1997-98, 1-for-3 (.333). 1998-99, 0-for-4. 2000-01, 5-for-24 (.208). Totals, 6-for-31 (.194).

Personal fouls/disqualifications: 1997-98, 36/0. 1998-99, 6/0. 2000-01, 140/2. Totals, 182/2.

P

NBA PLAYOFF RECORD

Season Team	G	Min.	FGM	FGA	Pct.	FTM	FTA	Pct.	REBOUNDS Off.	Def.	Tot.	Ast.	St.	Blk.	TO	Pts.	AVERAGES RPG	APG	PPG
97-98—Indiana...........	7	42	4	6	.667	1	1	1.000	2	3	5	1	1	0	1	9	0.7	0.1	1.3
00-01—Milwaukee	6	46	5	10	.500	0	0	...	5	7	12	2	2	0	0	10	2.0	0.3	1.7
Totals	13	88	9	16	.563	1	1	1.000	7	10	17	3	3	0	1	19	1.3	0.2	1.5

Three-point field goals: 1997-98, 0-for-1. 2000-01, 0-for-1. Totals, 0-for-2 (.000).
Personal fouls/disqualifications: 1997-98, 8/0. 2000-01, 6/0. Totals, 14/0.

CBA REGULAR-SEASON RECORD

Season Team	G	Min.	FGM	FGA	Pct.	FTM	FTA	Pct.	Reb.	Ast.	Pts.	AVERAGES RPG	APG	PPG
99-00—La Crosse	9	305	38	83	.458	11	16	.688	79	18	89	8.8	2.0	9.9

Three-point field goals: 1999-00, 2-for-8 (.250).

PORTER, CHRIS F WARRIORS

PERSONAL: Born May 9, 1978, in Abbeville, Ala. ... 6-7/218. (2,01/98,9).
HIGH SCHOOL: Abbeville (Ala.).
JUNIOR COLLEGE: Chipola Junior College (Fla.).
COLLEGE: Auburn.
TRANSACTIONS/CAREER NOTES: Selected by Golden State Warriors in second round (55th pick overall) of 2000 NBA Draft.

COLLEGIATE RECORD

NOTES: The Sporting News All-America second team (1999).

Season Team	G	Min.	FGM	FGA	Pct.	FTM	FTA	Pct.	Reb.	Ast.	Pts.	AVERAGES RPG	APG	PPG
96-97—Chipola College (Fla.)	29	...	260	398	.653	99	139	.712	312	42	624	10.8	1.4	21.5
97-98—Chipola College (Fla.)	30	...	289	449	.644	138	190	.726	355	82	722	11.8	2.7	24.1
98-99—Auburn	30	862	179	381	.470	113	179	.631	259	34	479	8.6	1.1	16.0
99-00—Auburn	26	755	141	304	.464	94	139	.676	191	30	380	7.3	1.2	14.6
Junior College Totals..............	59		549	847	.648	237	329	.720	667	124	1346	11.3	2.1	22.8
4-Year-College Totals..............	56	1617	320	685	.467	207	318	.651	450	64	859	8.0	1.1	15.3

Three-point field goals: 1996-97, 5-for-10 (.500). 1997-98, 6-for-13 (.462). 1998-99, 8-for-22 (.364). 1999-00, 4-for-17 (.235). Totals, 11-for-23 (.478). Totals, 12-for-39 (.308).

NBA REGULAR-SEASON RECORD

Season Team	G	Min.	FGM	FGA	Pct.	FTM	FTA	Pct.	REBOUNDS Off.	Def.	Tot.	Ast.	St.	Blk.	TO	Pts.	AVERAGES RPG	APG	PPG
00-01—Golden State ...	51	1147	173	445	.389	94	141	.667	89	100	189	61	45	6	59	440	3.7	1.2	8.6

Three-point field goals: 2000-01, 0-for-5.
Personal fouls/disqualifications: 2000-01, 111/2.

PORTER, TERRY G SPURS

PERSONAL: Born April 8, 1963, in Milwaukee. ... 6-3/205. (1,91/93,0).
HIGH SCHOOL: South Division (Milwaukee).
COLLEGE: Wisconsin-Stevens Point.
TRANSACTIONS/CAREER NOTES: Selected by Portland Trail Blazers in first round (24th pick overall) of 1985 NBA Draft. ... Signed as free agent by Minnesota Timberwolves (October 14, 1995). ... Signed as free agent by Miami Heat (January 22, 1999). ... Signed as free agent by San Antonio Spurs (August 5, 1999).
MISCELLANEOUS: Portland Trail Blazers all-time assists leader with 5,319 (1985-86 through 1994-95).

COLLEGIATE RECORD

Season Team	G	Min.	FGM	FGA	Pct.	FTM	FTA	Pct.	Reb.	Ast.	Pts.	AVERAGES RPG	APG	PPG
81-82—Wis.-Stevens Point........	25	273	21	57	.368	9	13	.692	13	21	51	0.5	0.8	2.0
82-83—Wis.-Stevens Point........	30	949	140	229	.611	62	89	.697	117	157	342	3.9	5.2	11.4
83-84—Wis.-Stevens Point........	32	1040	244	392	.622	112	135	.830	165	133	600	5.2	4.2	18.8
84-85—Wis.-Stevens Point........	30	1042	233	405	.575	126	151	.834	155	129	592	5.2	4.3	19.7
Totals	117	3304	638	1083	.589	309	388	.796	450	440	1585	3.8	3.8	13.5

NBA REGULAR-SEASON RECORD

HONORS: J. Walter Kennedy Citizenship Award (1993).

Season Team	G	Min.	FGM	FGA	Pct.	FTM	FTA	Pct.	REBOUNDS Off.	Def.	Tot.	Ast.	St.	Blk.	TO	Pts.	AVERAGES RPG	APG	PPG
85-86—Portland.........	79	1214	212	447	.474	125	155	.806	35	82	117	198	81	1	106	562	1.5	2.5	7.1
86-87—Portland.........	80	2714	376	770	.488	280	334	.838	70	267	337	715	159	9	255	1045	4.2	8.9	13.1
87-88—Portland.........	82	2991	462	890	.519	274	324	.846	65	313	378	831	150	16	244	1222	4.6	10.1	14.9
88-89—Portland.........	81	3102	540	1146	.471	272	324	.840	85	282	367	770	146	8	248	1431	4.5	9.5	17.7
89-90—Portland.........	80	2781	448	969	.462	421	472	.892	59	213	272	726	151	4	245	1406	3.4	9.1	17.6
90-91—Portland.........	81	2665	486	944	.515	279	339	.823	52	230	282	649	158	4	189	1381	3.5	8.0	17.0
91-92—Portland.........	82	2784	521	1129	.461	315	368	.856	51	204	255	477	127	12	188	1485	3.1	5.8	18.1
92-93—Portland.........	81	2883	503	1108	.454	327	388	.843	58	258	316	419	101	10	199	1476	3.9	5.2	18.2
93-94—Portland.........	77	2074	348	836	.416	204	234	.872	45	170	215	401	79	18	166	1010	2.8	5.2	13.1
94-95—Portland.........	35	770	105	267	.393	58	82	.707	18	63	81	133	30	2	58	312	2.3	3.8	8.9
95-96—Minnesota.......	82	2072	269	608	.442	164	209	.785	36	176	212	452	89	15	173	773	2.6	5.5	9.4

P

Season Team	G	Min.	FGM	FGA	Pct.	FTM	FTA	Pct.	REBOUNDS Off.	Def.	Tot.	Ast.	St.	Blk.	TO	Pts.	AVERAGES RPG	APG	PPG
96-97—Minnesota......	82	1568	187	449	.416	127	166	.765	31	145	176	295	54	11	128	568	2.1	3.6	6.9
97-98—Minnesota......	82	1786	259	577	.449	167	195	.856	37	131	168	271	63	16	104	777	2.0	3.3	9.5
98-99—Miami	50	1365	172	370	.465	123	148	.831	13	127	140	146	48	11	74	525	2.8	2.9	10.5
99-00—San Antonio	68	1613	207	463	.447	137	170	.806	24	167	191	221	50	9	100	641	2.8	3.3	9.4
00-01—San Antonio	80	1678	197	440	.448	92	116	.793	24	177	201	251	52	11	104	573	2.5	3.1	7.2
Totals	1202	34060	5292	11413	.464	3365	4024	.836	703	3005	3708	6955	1538	165	2581	15187	3.1	5.8	12.6

Three-point field goals: 1985-86, 13-for-42 (.310). 1986-87, 13-for-60 (.217). 1987-88, 24-for-69 (.348). 1988-89, 79-for-219 (.361). 1989-90, 89-for-238 (.374). 1990-91, 130-for-313 (.415). 1991-92, 128-for-324 (.395). 1992-93, 143-for-345 (.414). 1993-94, 110-for-282 (.390). 1994-95, 44-for-114 (.386). 1995-96, 71-for-226 (.314). 1996-97, 67-for-200 (.335). 1997-98, 92-for-233 (.395). 1998-99, 58-for-141 (.411). 1999-00, 90-for-207 (.435). 2000-01, 87-for-205 (.424). Totals, 1238-for-3218 (.385).

Personal fouls/disqualifications: 1985-86, 136/0. 1986-87, 192/0. 1987-88, 204/1. 1988-89, 187/1. 1989-90, 150/0. 1990-91, 151/2. 1991-92, 155/1. 1992-93, 122/0. 1993-94, 132/0. 1994-95, 60/0. 1995-96, 154/0. 1996-97, 104/0. 1997-98, 103/0. 1998-99, 97/0. 1999-00, 79/0. 2000-01, 88/1. Totals, 2114/6.

NBA PLAYOFF RECORD

NOTES: Holds NBA Finals single-game record for most free throws made, none missed—15 (June 7, 1990, at Detroit, OT).

Season Team	G	Min.	FGM	FGA	Pct.	FTM	FTA	Pct.	REBOUNDS Off.	Def.	Tot.	Ast.	St.	Blk.	TO	Pts.	AVERAGES RPG	APG	PPG
85-86—Portland	4	68	12	27	.444	2	4	.500	1	4	5	12	3	2	6	27	1.3	3.0	6.8
86-87—Portland	4	150	24	50	.480	18	20	.900	1	18	19	40	10	2	13	68	4.8	10.0	17.0
87-88—Portland	4	149	29	52	.558	9	13	.692	4	10	14	28	10	0	13	68	3.5	7.0	17.0
88-89—Portland	3	124	26	52	.500	10	12	.833	6	10	16	25	1	1	7	66	5.3	8.3	22.0
89-90—Portland	21	815	127	274	.464	139	165	.842	9	52	61	155	28	3	62	433	2.9	7.4	20.6
90-91—Portland	16	595	102	204	.500	68	79	.861	8	36	44	105	24	1	32	289	2.8	6.6	18.1
91-92—Portland	21	870	147	285	.516	119	143	.832	25	72	97	141	22	3	46	450	4.6	6.7	21.4
92-93—Portland	4	152	27	68	.397	9	11	.818	4	16	20	8	4	0	6	66	5.0	2.0	16.5
93-94—Portland	4	76	12	35	.343	11	14	.786	1	11	12	9	4	0	2	41	3.0	2.3	10.3
94-95—Portland	3	21	7	13	.538	3	5	.600	1	1	2	4	0	0	1	19	0.7	1.3	6.3
96-97—Minnesota	3	46	5	13	.385	3	4	.750	1	2	3	9	2	2	2	16	1.0	3.0	5.3
97-98—Minnesota	5	188	27	63	.429	15	18	.833	7	18	25	16	5	0	4	79	5.0	3.2	15.8
98-99—Miami	5	139	15	32	.469	12	15	.800	3	16	19	15	3	0	8	45	3.8	3.0	9.0
99-00—San Antonio	4	89	8	31	.258	0	0	...	0	1	1	5	6	0	7	20	0.3	1.3	5.0
00-01—San Antonio	13	326	39	86	.453	17	22	.773	1	23	24	44	11	0	22	108	1.8	3.4	8.3
Totals	114	3808	607	1285	.472	435	525	.829	72	290	362	616	133	14	231	1795	3.2	5.4	15.7

Three-point field goals: 1985-86, 1-for-6 (.167). 1986-87, 2-for-5 (.400). 1987-88, 1-for-3 (.333). 1988-89, 4-for-11 (.364). 1989-90, 40-for-102 (.392). 1990-91, 17-for-47 (.362). 1991-92, 37-for-78 (.474). 1992-93, 3-for-19 (.158). 1993-94, 6-for-14 (.429). 1994-95, 2-for-5 (.400). 1996-97, 3-for-9 (.333). 1997-98, 10-for-25 (.400). 1998-99, 3-for-12 (.250). 1999-00, 4-for-14 (.286). 2000-01, 13-for-39 (.333). Totals, 146-for-389 (.375).

Personal fouls/disqualifications: 1985-86, 10/0. 1986-87, 14/0. 1987-88, 13/0. 1988-89, 8/0. 1989-90, 51/1. 1990-91, 32/0. 1991-92, 49/0. 1992-93, 10/0. 1993-94, 3/0. 1994-95, 6/0. 1996-97, 2/0. 1997-98, 10/0. 1998-99, 8/0. 1999-00, 4/0. 2000-01, 15/0. Totals, 235/1.

NBA ALL-STAR GAME RECORD

Season Team	Min.	FGM	FGA	Pct.	FTM	FTA	Pct.	REBOUNDS Off.	Def.	Tot.	Ast.	PF	Dq.	St.	Blk.	TO	Pts.
1991 —Portland	15	2	6	.333	0	0	...	1	2	3	4	2	0	2	1	3	4
1993 —Portland	19	3	8	.375	0	0	...	0	0	0	3	1	0	1	0	1	7
Totals	34	5	14	.357	0	0	...	1	2	3	7	3	0	3	1	4	11

Three-point field goals: 1991, 0-for-2. 1993, 1-for-5 (.200). Totals, 1-for-7 (.143).

POSEY, JAMES   G/F   NUGGETS

PERSONAL: Born January 13, 1977, in Cleveland. ... 6-8/215. (2,03/97,5). ... Full Name: James Mikley Mantell Posey.
HIGH SCHOOL: R.B. Chamberlain (Twinsburg, Ohio).
COLLEGE: Xavier.
TRANSACTIONS/CAREER NOTES: Selected by Denver Nuggets in first round (18th pick overall) of 1999 NBA Draft.

COLLEGIATE RECORD

Season Team	G	Min.	FGM	FGA	Pct.	FTM	FTA	Pct.	Reb.	Ast.	Pts.	AVERAGES RPG	APG	PPG
95-96—Xavier						Did not play—ineligible.								
96-97—Xavier	29	780	130	232	.560	121	155	.781	226	40	387	7.8	1.4	13.3
97-98—Xavier	30	864	145	261	.556	150	182	.824	253	39	459	8.4	1.3	15.3
98-99—Xavier	36	1268	191	391	.488	179	220	.814	322	84	609	8.9	2.3	16.9
Totals	95	2912	466	884	.527	450	557	.808	801	163	1455	8.4	1.7	15.3

Three-point field goals: 1996-97, 6-for-32 (.188). 1997-98, 19-for-59 (.322). 1998-99, 48-for-131 (.366). Totals, 73-for-222 (.329).

HONORS: NBA All-Rookie second team (2000).

NBA REGULAR-SEASON RECORD

Season Team	G	Min.	FGM	FGA	Pct.	FTM	FTA	Pct.	REBOUNDS Off.	Def.	Tot.	Ast.	St.	Blk.	TO	Pts.	AVERAGES RPG	APG	PPG
99-00—Denver	81	2052	230	536	.429	120	150	.800	85	232	317	146	98	33	95	662	3.9	1.8	8.2
00-01—Denver	82	2255	243	590	.412	115	141	.816	125	306	431	163	93	40	102	666	5.3	2.0	8.1
Totals	163	4307	473	1126	.420	235	291	.808	210	538	748	309	191	73	197	1328	4.6	1.9	8.1

Three-point field goals: 1999-00, 82-for-220 (.373). 2000-01, 65-for-217 (.300). Totals, 147-for-437 (.336).
Personal fouls/disqualifications: 1999-00, 207/1. 2000-01, 226/2. Totals, 433/3.

DID YOU KNOW . . .

. . . that Hall of Famer Moses Malone played on nine different teams in his 21-year pro career?

P

POSTELL, LAVOR　　　　G/F　　　　KNICKS

PERSONAL: Born February 26, 1978, in Albany, Ga. ... 6-5/205. (1,96/93,0). ... Full Name: Andre Lavor Postell.
HIGH SCHOOL: Westover (Albany, Ga.).
COLLEGE: St. John's.
TRANSACTIONS/CAREER NOTES: Selected by New York Knicks in second round (39th pick overall) of 2000 NBA Draft.

COLLEGIATE RECORD

Season Team	G	Min.	FGM	FGA	Pct.	FTM	FTA	Pct.	Reb.	Ast.	Pts.	RPG	APG	PPG
96-97—St. John's	27	689	51	140	.364	41	62	.661	89	60	152	3.3	2.2	5.6
97-98—St. John's	32	931	100	221	.452	100	121	.826	162	50	317	5.1	1.6	9.9
98-99—St. John's	37	1001	172	387	.444	100	126	.794	236	35	485	6.4	0.9	13.1
99-00—St. John's	33	1155	171	400	.428	106	131	.809	229	60	473	6.9	1.8	14.3
Totals	129	3776	494	1148	.430	347	440	.789	716	205	1427	5.6	1.6	11.1

Three-point field goals: 1996-97, 9-for-47 (.191). 1997-98, 17-for-51 (.333). 1998-99, 41-for-99 (.414). 1999-00, 25-for-85 (.294). Totals, 92-for-282 (.326).

NBA REGULAR-SEASON RECORD

Season Team	G	Min.	FGM	FGA	Pct.	FTM	FTA	Pct.	Off.	Def.	Tot.	Ast.	St.	Blk.	TO	Pts.	RPG	APG	PPG
00-01—New York	26	169	17	54	.315	22	27	.815	8	17	25	5	4	2	17	59	1.0	0.2	2.3

Three-point field goals: 2000-01, 3-for-11 (.273).
Personal fouls/disqualifications: 2000-01, 12/0.

POTAPENKO, VITALY　　　　F/C　　　　CELTICS

PERSONAL: Born March 21, 1975, in Kiev, Ukraine. ... 6-10/285. (2,08/129,3). ... Full Name: Vitaly Nikolaevich Potapenko. ... Name pronounced VEE-tal-lee poe-TAH-pen-koe.
COLLEGE: Wright State.
TRANSACTIONS/CAREER NOTES: Selected after junior season by Cleveland Cavaliers in first round (12th pick overall) of 1996 NBA Draft. ... Traded by Cavaliers to Boston Celtics for F/C Andrew DeClercq and a 1999 first-round draft choice (March 11, 1999).

COLLEGIATE RECORD

Season Team	G	Min.	FGM	FGA	Pct.	FTM	FTA	Pct.	Reb.	Ast.	Pts.	RPG	APG	PPG
94-95—Wright State	30	900	212	352	.602	151	206	.733	193	41	575	6.4	1.4	19.2
95-96—Wright State	25	807	197	322	.612	139	195	.713	182	36	534	7.3	1.4	21.4
Totals	55	1707	409	674	.607	290	401	.723	375	77	1109	6.8	1.4	20.2

Three-point field goals: 1995-96, 1-for-6 (.167).

NBA REGULAR-SEASON RECORD

Season Team	G	Min.	FGM	FGA	Pct.	FTM	FTA	Pct.	Off.	Def.	Tot.	Ast.	St.	Blk.	TO	Pts.	RPG	APG	PPG
96-97—Cleveland	80	1238	186	423	.440	92	125	.736	105	112	217	40	26	34	109	465	2.7	0.5	5.8
97-98—Cleveland	80	1412	234	488	.480	102	144	.708	110	203	313	57	27	28	132	570	3.9	0.7	7.1
98-99—Cleve.-Boston	50	1394	204	412	.495	91	155	.587	114	218	332	75	35	36	100	499	6.6	1.5	10.0
99-00—Boston	79	1797	307	615	.499	109	160	.681	182	317	499	77	41	29	145	723	6.3	1.0	9.2
00-01—Boston	82	1901	248	521	.476	115	158	.728	206	289	495	64	52	23	105	611	6.0	0.8	7.5
Totals	371	7742	1179	2459	.479	509	742	.686	717	1139	1856	313	181	150	591	2868	5.0	0.8	7.7

Three-point field goals: 1996-97, 1-for-2 (.500). 1997-98, 0-for-1. 1998-99, 0-for-1. 1999-00, 0-for-1. Totals, 1-for-5 (.200).
Personal fouls/disqualifications: 1996-97, 216/3. 1997-98, 196/4. 1998-99, 169/4. 1999-00, 239/4. 2000-01, 228/2. Totals, 1050/15.

NBA PLAYOFF RECORD

Season Team	G	Min.	FGM	FGA	Pct.	FTM	FTA	Pct.	Off.	Def.	Tot.	Ast.	St.	Blk.	TO	Pts.	RPG	APG	PPG
97-98—Cleveland	4	70	6	15	.400	5	10	.500	3	8	11	3	2	0	6	17	2.8	0.8	4.3

Personal fouls/disqualifications: 1997-98, 8/0.

PRICE, BRENT　　　　G　　　　KINGS

PERSONAL: Born December 9, 1968, in Shawnee, Okla. ... 6-1/185. (1,85/83,9). ... Full Name: Hartley Brent Price. ... Brother of Mark Price, guard with Cleveland Cavaliers (1986-87 through 1994-95), Washington Bullets (1995-96), Golden State Warriors (1996-97) and Orlando Magic (1997-98).
HIGH SCHOOL: Enid (Okla.).
COLLEGE: South Carolina, then Oklahoma.
TRANSACTIONS/CAREER NOTES: Selected by Washington Bullets in second round (32nd pick overall) of 1992 NBA Draft. ... Waived by Bullets (April 19, 1995). ... Re-signed as free agent by Bullets (October 3, 1995). ... Signed as free agent by Houston Rockets (July 15, 1996). ... Traded by Rockets with G Michael Dickerson, F/C Othella Harrington, F/C Antoine Carr and future first-round draft choice to Vancouver Grizzlies as part of three-way deal in which Rockets received draft rights to G Steve Francis and F Tony Massenburg from Grizzlies and F Don MacLean and future first-round draft choice from Orlando Magic, and Magic received F Michael Smith, G/F Rodrick Rhodes, G Lee Mayberry and F Makhtar Ndiaye from Grizzlies (August 27, 1999). ... Traded by Grizzlies with G Mike Bibby to Sacramento Kings for G Jason Williams and G/F Nick Anderson (June 27, 2001).

P

Season Team	G	Min.	FGM	FGA	Pct.	FTM	FTA	Pct.	Reb.	Ast.	Pts.	AVERAGES RPG	APG	PPG
87-88—South Carolina	29	643	98	213	.460	66	77	.857	47	78	311	1.6	2.7	10.7
88-89—South Carolina	30	952	144	294	.490	76	90	.844	75	128	432	2.5	4.3	14.4
89-90—Oklahoma					Did not play—transfer student.									
90-91—Oklahoma	35	1197	178	428	.416	166	198	.838	127	192	613	3.6	5.5	17.5
91-92—Oklahoma	30	1064	182	391	.465	120	152	.789	111	185	560	3.7	6.2	18.7
Totals	124	3856	602	1326	.454	428	517	.828	360	583	1916	2.9	4.7	15.5

Three-point field goals: 1987-88, 49-for-112 (.438). 1988-89, 68-for-139 (.489). 1990-91, 91-for-244 (.373). 1991-92, 76-for-194 (.392). Totals, 284-for-689 (.412).

NBA REGULAR-SEASON RECORD

RECORDS: Shares single-season record for most consecutive three-point field goals made without a miss—13 (January 15-19, 1996).

Season Team	G	Min.	FGM	FGA	Pct.	FTM	FTA	Pct.	REBOUNDS Off.	Def.	Tot.	Ast.	St.	Blk.	TO	Pts.	AVERAGES RPG	APG	PPG
92-93—Washington	68	859	100	279	.358	54	68	.794	28	75	103	154	56	3	85	262	1.5	2.3	3.9
93-94—Washington	65	1035	141	326	.433	68	87	.782	31	59	90	213	55	2	119	400	1.4	3.3	6.2
94-95—Washington					Did not play—injured.														
95-96—Washington	81	2042	252	534	.472	167	191	.874	38	190	228	416	78	4	153	810	2.8	5.1	10.0
96-97—Houston	25	390	44	105	.419	21	21	1.000	10	19	29	65	17	0	32	126	1.2	2.6	5.0
97-98—Houston	72	1332	128	310	.413	77	98	.786	37	70	107	192	52	4	111	406	1.5	2.7	5.6
98-99—Houston	40	806	100	207	.483	46	61	.754	18	60	78	113	33	1	65	292	2.0	2.8	7.3
99-00—Vancouver	41	424	41	119	.345	34	39	.872	8	29	37	69	17	1	47	141	0.9	1.7	3.4
00-01—Vancouver	6	30	3	11	.273	6	7	.857	1	3	4	5	2	0	4	13	0.7	0.8	2.2
Totals	398	6918	809	1891	.428	473	572	.827	171	505	676	1227	310	15	616	2450	1.7	3.1	6.2

Three-point field goals: 1992-93, 8-for-48 (.167). 1993-94, 50-for-150 (.333). 1995-96, 139-for-301 (.462). 1996-97, 17-for-53 (.321). 1997-98, 73-for-187 (.390). 1998-99, 46-for-112 (.411). 1999-00, 25-for-68 (.368). 2000-01, 1-for-4 (.250). Totals, 359-for-923 (.389).
Personal fouls/disqualifications: 1992-93, 90/0. 1993-94, 114/1. 1995-96, 184/3. 1996-97, 34/0. 1997-98, 163/3. 1998-99, 90/0. 1999-00, 63/0. 2000-01, 8/0. Totals, 746/7.

NBA PLAYOFF RECORD

Season Team	G	Min.	FGM	FGA	Pct.	FTM	FTA	Pct.	REBOUNDS Off.	Def.	Tot.	Ast.	St.	Blk.	TO	Pts.	AVERAGES RPG	APG	PPG
97-98—Houston	5	75	6	15	.400	2	3	.667	1	8	9	6	4	0	6	19	1.8	1.2	3.8
98-99—Houston	4	98	11	24	.458	6	6	1.000	3	5	8	14	4	1	6	33	2.0	3.5	8.3
Totals	9	173	17	39	.436	8	9	.889	4	13	17	20	8	1	12	52	1.9	2.2	5.8

Three-point field goals: 1997-98, 5-for-13 (.385). 1998-99, 5-for-14 (.357). Totals, 10-for-27 (.370).
Personal fouls/disqualifications: 1997-98, 12/1. 1998-99, 5/0. Totals, 17/1.

PROFIT, LARON   G/F   MAGIC

PERSONAL: Born August 5, 1977, in Charleston, S.C. ... 6-5/204. (1,96/92,5). ... Full Name: Bronta Laron Profit.
HIGH SCHOOL: Caesar Rodney (Dover, Del.).
COLLEGE: Maryland.
TRANSACTIONS/CAREER NOTES: Selected by Orlando Magic in second round (38th pick overall) of 1999 NBA Draft. ... Draft rights traded by Magic to Washington Wizards for conditional 2001 second-round draft choice (September 22, 1999). ... Traded by Wizards with future first-round draft choice to Magic for draft rights to C Brendan Haywood (August 1, 2001).

COLLEGIATE RECORD

Season Team	G	Min.	FGM	FGA	Pct.	FTM	FTA	Pct.	Reb.	Ast.	Pts.	AVERAGES RPG	APG	PPG
95-96—Maryland	27	366	54	112	.482	34	45	.756	74	32	154	2.7	1.2	5.7
96-97—Maryland	32	1033	160	337	.475	57	91	.626	171	78	412	5.3	2.4	12.9
97-98—Maryland	32	1008	184	412	.447	104	147	.707	165	104	506	5.2	3.3	15.8
98-99—Maryland	34	982	185	368	.503	100	148	.676	162	73	494	4.8	2.1	14.5
Totals	125	3389	583	1229	.474	295	431	.684	572	287	1566	4.6	2.3	12.5

Three-point field goals: 1995-96, 12-for-33 (.364). 1996-97, 35-for-99 (.354). 1997-98, 34-for-117 (.291). 1998-99, 24-for-77 (.312). Totals, 105-for-326 (.322).

NBA REGULAR-SEASON RECORD

Season Team	G	Min.	FGM	FGA	Pct.	FTM	FTA	Pct.	REBOUNDS Off.	Def.	Tot.	Ast.	St.	Blk.	TO	Pts.	AVERAGES RPG	APG	PPG
99-00—Washington	33	225	21	59	.356	4	10	.400	2	24	26	25	7	4	19	49	0.8	0.8	1.5
00-01—Washington	35	605	56	142	.394	33	45	.733	18	46	64	89	36	11	46	152	1.8	2.5	4.3
Totals	68	830	77	201	.383	37	55	.673	20	70	90	114	43	15	65	201	1.3	1.7	3.0

Three-point field goals: 1999-00, 3-for-17 (.176). 2000-01, 7-for-26 (.269). Totals, 10-for-43 (.233).
Personal fouls/disqualifications: 1999-00, 26/0. 2000-01, 43/0. Totals, 69/0.

PRZYBILLA, JOEL   C   BUCKS

PERSONAL: Born October 10, 1979, in Monticello, Minn. ... 7-1/255. (2,16/115,7). ... Full Name: Joel Anthony Przybilla.
HIGH SCHOOL: Monticello (Minn.).
COLLEGE: Minnesota.
TRANSACTIONS/CAREER NOTES: Selected after sophomore season by Houston Rockets in first round (ninth pick overall) of 2000 NBA Draft. ... Draft rights traded by Rockets to Milwaukee Bucks for draft rights to C Jason Collier and a future first-round draft choice (June 28, 2000).

COLLEGIATE RECORD

												AVERAGES		
Season Team	G	Min.	FGM	FGA	Pct.	FTM	FTA	Pct.	Reb.	Ast.	Pts.	RPG	APG	PPG
98-99—Minnesota	28	713	79	141	.560	30	52	.577	163	41	188	5.8	1.5	6.7
99-00—Minnesota	21	638	122	199	.613	55	111	.495	176	50	299	8.4	2.4	14.2
Totals	49	1351	201	340	.591	85	163	.521	339	91	487	6.9	1.9	9.9

NBA REGULAR-SEASON RECORD

									REBOUNDS								AVERAGES		
Season Team	G	Min.	FGM	FGA	Pct.	FTM	FTA	Pct.	Off.	Def.	Tot.	Ast.	St.	Blk.	TO	Pts.	RPG	APG	PPG
00-01—Milwaukee	33	270	12	35	.343	3	11	.273	29	42	71	2	3	30	13	27	2.2	0.1	0.8

Personal fouls/disqualifications: 2000-01, 56/0.

NBA PLAYOFF RECORD

									REBOUNDS								AVERAGES		
Season Team	G	Min.	FGM	FGA	Pct.	FTM	FTA	Pct.	Off.	Def.	Tot.	Ast.	St.	Blk.	TO	Pts.	RPG	APG	PPG
00-01—Milwaukee	1	2	0	0	...	0	0	...	0	0	0	0	0	0	0	0	0.0	0.0	0.0

RADOJEVIC, ALEKSANDAR C　　　　NUGGETS

PERSONAL: Born August 8, 1976, in Hercg-Novi, Yugoslavia ... 7-3/250. (2,21/113,4).
HIGH SCHOOL: Maldost-Bajela (Montenegro).
JUNIOR COLLEGE: Barton County Community College (Kan.).
TRANSACTIONS/CAREER NOTES: Selected after sophomore season by Toronto Raptors in first round (12th pick overall) of 1999 NBA Draft. ... Traded by Raptors with F/C Kevin Willis, C Garth Joseph and 2001 or 2002 second-round draft choice to Denver Nuggets for F Tracy Murray, F/C Keon Clark and C Mamadou N'diaye (January 12, 2001).

COLLEGIATE RECORD

												AVERAGES		
Season Team	G	Min.	FGM	FGA	Pct.	FTM	FTA	Pct.	Reb.	Ast.	Pts.	RPG	APG	PPG
97-98—Barton County C.C.	33	...	140	241	.581	60	102	.588	198	23	340	6.0	0.7	10.3
98-99—Barton County C.C.	38	1072	231	381	.606	121	191	.634	342	49	585	9.0	1.3	15.4
Junior College Totals	71	...	371	622	.596	181	293	.618	540	72	925	7.6	1.0	13.0

Three-point field goals: 1997-98, 0-for-1. 1998-99, 2-for-3 (.667). Totals, 2-for-4 (.500).

NBA REGULAR-SEASON RECORD

									REBOUNDS								AVERAGES		
Season Team	G	Min.	FGM	FGA	Pct.	FTM	FTA	Pct.	Off.	Def.	Tot.	Ast.	St.	Blk.	TO	Pts.	RPG	APG	PPG
99-00—Toronto	3	24	2	7	.286	3	6	.500	2	6	8	1	2	1	5	7	2.7	0.3	2.3
00-01—Tor.-Denver								Did not play—injured.											
Totals	3	24	2	7	.286	3	6	.500	2	6	8	1	2	1	5	7	2.7	0.3	2.3

Personal fouls/disqualifications: 1999-00, 5/0. Totals, 5/0.

RATLIFF, THEO　　　　C/F　　　　HAWKS

PERSONAL: Born April 17, 1973, in Demopolis, Ala. ... 6-10/225. (2,08/102,1). ... Full Name: Theo Curtis Ratliff.
HIGH SCHOOL: Demopolis (Ala.).
COLLEGE: Wyoming.
TRANSACTIONS/CAREER NOTES: Selected by Detroit Pistons in first round (18th pick overall) of 1995 NBA Draft. ... Traded by Pistons with G Aaron McKie and conditional first-round draft choice to Philadelphia 76ers for G Jerry Stackhouse and C Eric Montross (December 18, 1997). ... Traded by 76ers with F/G Toni Kukoc, C Nazr Mohammed and G Pepe Sanchez to Atlanta Hawks for C Dikembe Mutombo and F Roshown McLeod (February 22, 2001).

COLLEGIATE RECORD

NOTES: Led NCAA Division I with 4.4 blocked shots per game (1993).

												AVERAGES		
Season Team	G	Min.	FGM	FGA	Pct.	FTM	FTA	Pct.	Reb.	Ast.	Pts.	RPG	APG	PPG
91-92—Wyoming	27	298	14	32	.438	21	36	.583	54	8	49	2.0	0.3	1.8
92-93—Wyoming	28	824	99	184	.538	60	116	.517	173	8	258	6.2	0.3	9.2
93-94—Wyoming	28	892	160	281	.569	111	171	.649	217	27	431	7.8	1.0	15.4
94-95—Wyoming	28	912	148	272	.544	107	169	.633	211	31	404	7.5	1.1	14.4
Totals	111	2926	421	760	.647	299	492	.000	655	74	1142	5.9	0.7	10.3

Three-point field goals: 1992-93, 0-for-1. 1993-94, 0-for-1. 1994-95, 1-for-5 (.200). Totals, 1-for-7 (.143).

NBA REGULAR-SEASON RECORD

HONORS: NBA All-Defensive second team (1999).
NOTES: Led NBA with 3.74 blocks per game (2001).

									REBOUNDS								AVERAGES		
Season Team	G	Min.	FGM	FGA	Pct.	FTM	FTA	Pct.	Off.	Def.	Tot.	Ast.	St.	Blk.	TO	Pts.	RPG	APG	PPG
95-96—Detroit	75	1305	128	230	.557	85	120	.708	110	187	297	13	16	116	56	341	4.0	0.2	4.5
96-97—Detroit	76	1292	179	337	.531	81	109	.698	109	147	256	13	29	111	56	439	3.4	0.2	5.8
97-98—Det.-Phila.	82	2447	306	597	.513	197	281	.701	221	326	547	57	50	258	116	809	6.7	0.7	9.9
98-99—Philadelphia	50	1627	197	419	.470	166	229	.725	139	268	407	30	45	149	92	560	8.1	0.6	11.2
99-00—Philadelphia	57	1795	247	491	.503	182	236	.771	140	295	435	36	32	171	108	676	7.6	0.6	11.9
00-01—Philadelphia	50	1800	228	457	.499	165	217	.760	125	288	413	58	30	187	126	621	8.3	1.2	12.4
Totals	390	10266	1285	2531	.508	876	1199	.731	844	1511	2355	207	202	992	554	3446	6.0	0.5	8.8

Three-point field goals: 1995-96, 0-for-1. Totals, 0-for-1 (.000).
Personal fouls/disqualifications: 1995-96, 144/1. 1996-97, 181/2. 1997-98, 292/8. 1998-99, 180/8. 1999-00, 185/4. 2000-01, 165/3. Totals, 1147/26.

NBA PLAYOFF RECORD

Season Team	G	Min.	FGM	FGA	Pct.	FTM	FTA	Pct.	REBOUNDS Off.	Def.	Tot.	Ast.	St.	Blk.	TO	Pts.	AVERAGES RPG	APG	PPG
95-96—Detroit	1	4	0	0	...	0	0	...	0	0	0	0	0	0	0	0	0.0	0.0	0.0
96-97—Detroit	3	18	3	4	.750	2	4	.500	2	2	4	1	1	4	3	8	1.3	0.3	2.7
98-99—Philadelphia	7	204	20	43	.465	11	19	.579	23	28	51	6	5	18	7	51	7.3	0.9	7.3
99-00—Philadelphia	10	374	48	101	.475	34	47	.723	28	51	79	9	10	30	17	130	7.9	0.9	13.0
Totals	21	600	71	148	.480	47	70	.671	53	81	134	16	16	52	27	189	6.4	0.8	9.0

Personal fouls/disqualifications: 1996-97, 5/0. 1998-99, 19/0. 1999-00, 35/1. Totals, 59/1.

NBA ALL-STAR GAME RECORD

Season Team	Min.	FGM	FGA	Pct.	FTM	FTA	Pct.	REBOUNDS Off.	Def.	Tot.	Ast.	PF	Dq.	St.	Blk.	TO	Pts.
2001 —Philadelphia								Selected, did not play—injured.									

RECASNER, ELDRIDGE   G   HORNETS

PERSONAL: Born December 14, 1967, in New Orleans. ... 6-4/192. (1,93/87,1). ... Full Name: Eldridge David Recasner. ... Name pronounced rah-CAZ-ner.
HIGH SCHOOL: Alfred Lawless (New Orleans).
COLLEGE: Washington.
TRANSACTIONS/CAREER NOTES: Not drafted by an NBA franchise. ... Played in Germany (1990-91). ... Played in Global Basketball Association with Louisville Shooters (1991-92). ... Played in Continental Basketball Association with Yakima Sun Kings (1992-93 through 1994-95). ... Played in Turkey (1993-94). ... Signed by Denver Nuggets to 10-day contract (March 3, 1995). ... Signed as free agent by Houston Rockets (September 25, 1995). ... Signed as free agent by Atlanta Hawks (September 27, 1996). ... Signed as free agent by Charlotte Hornets (January 21, 1999).

COLLEGIATE RECORD

Season Team	G	Min.	FGM	FGA	Pct.	FTM	FTA	Pct.	Reb.	Ast.	Pts.	AVERAGES RPG	APG	PPG
85-86—Washington						Did not play—redshirted.								
86-87—Washington	35	1124	111	234	.474	69	99	.697	131	103	294	3.7	2.9	8.4
87-88—Washington	28	1061	173	338	.512	105	128	.820	107	78	477	3.8	2.8	17.0
88-89—Washington	28	1011	175	352	.497	106	128	.828	95	107	508	3.4	3.8	18.1
89-90—Washington	26	981	142	326	.436	99	112	.884	101	88	421	3.9	3.4	16.2
Totals	117	4177	601	1250	.481	379	467	.812	434	376	1700	3.7	3.2	14.5

Three-point field goals: 1986-87, 3-for-14 (.214). 1987-88, 36-for-67 (.537). 1988-89, 52-for-116 (.448). 1989-90, 38-for-103 (.369). Totals, 129-for-300 (.430).

CBA REGULAR-SEASON RECORD

NOTES: Member of CBA championship team (1995). ... CBA Most Valuable Player (1995). ... CBA All-League first team (1995).

Season Team	G	Min.	FGM	FGA	Pct.	FTM	FTA	Pct.	Reb.	Ast.	Pts.	AVERAGES RPG	APG	PPG
92-93—Yakima	44	1473	296	605	.489	140	158	.886	150	137	763	3.4	3.1	17.3
93-94—Yakima	25	841	171	317	.539	70	76	.921	76	70	427	3.0	2.8	17.1
94-95—Yakima	48	1779	356	640	.556	184	204	.902	180	246	981	3.8	5.1	20.4
Totals	117	4093	823	1562	.527	394	438	.900	406	453	2171	3.5	3.9	18.6

Three-point field goals: 1992-93, 31-for-90 (.344). 1993-94, 15-for-47 (.319). 1994-95, 85-for-172 (.494). Totals, 131-for-309 (.424).

NBA REGULAR-SEASON RECORD

Season Team	G	Min.	FGM	FGA	Pct.	FTM	FTA	Pct.	REBOUNDS Off.	Def.	Tot.	Ast.	St.	Blk.	TO	Pts.	AVERAGES RPG	APG	PPG
94-95—Denver	3	13	1	6	.167	4	4	1.000	0	2	2	1	3	0	2	6	0.7	0.3	2.0
95-96—Houston	63	1275	149	359	.415	57	66	.864	31	113	144	170	23	5	61	436	2.3	2.7	6.9
96-97—Atlanta	71	1207	148	350	.423	51	58	.879	35	80	115	94	38	4	65	405	1.6	1.3	5.7
97-98—Atlanta	59	1454	206	452	.456	74	79	.937	32	110	142	117	41	1	91	548	2.4	2.0	9.3
98-99—Charlotte	44	708	82	184	.446	34	39	.872	20	57	77	91	17	1	58	222	1.8	2.1	5.0
99-00—Charlotte	7	28	3	7	.429	0	0	...	0	4	4	5	0	0	0	7	0.6	0.7	1.0
00-01—Charlotte	43	403	38	114	.333	14	18	.778	13	37	50	39	6	1	27	103	1.2	0.9	2.4
Totals	290	5088	627	1472	.426	234	264	.886	131	403	534	517	128	12	304	1727	1.8	1.8	6.0

Three-point field goals: 1994-95, 0-for-1. 1995-96, 81-for-191 (.424). 1996-97, 58-for-140 (.414). 1997-98, 62-for-148 (.419). 1998-99, 24-for-60 (.400). 1999-00, 1-for-4 (.250). 2000-01, 13-for-39 (.333). Totals, 239-for-583 (.410).
Personal fouls/disqualifications: 1995-96, 111/1. 1996-97, 97/0. 1997-98, 94/0. 1998-99, 66/0. 1999-00, 1/0. 2000-01, 30/0. Totals, 399/1.

NBA PLAYOFF RECORD

Season Team	G	Min.	FGM	FGA	Pct.	FTM	FTA	Pct.	REBOUNDS Off.	Def.	Tot.	Ast.	St.	Blk.	TO	Pts.	AVERAGES RPG	APG	PPG
95-96—Houston	1	8	0	3	.000	0	0	...	0	1	1	2	0	0	1	0	1.0	2.0	0.0
96-97—Atlanta	10	121	11	26	.423	5	8	.625	3	8	11	9	2	0	7	31	1.1	0.9	3.1
97-98—Atlanta	4	89	10	25	.400	2	2	1.000	0	4	4	8	2	0	2	29	1.0	2.0	7.3
00-01—Charlotte	2	9	0	1	.000	3	4	.750	0	1	1	2	0	0	1	3	0.5	1.0	1.5
Totals	17	227	21	55	.382	10	14	.714	3	14	17	21	4	0	11	63	1.0	1.2	3.7

Three-point field goals: 1995-96, 0-for-1. 1996-97, 4-for-11 (.364). 1997-98, 7-for-12 (.583). Totals, 11-for-24 (.458).
Personal fouls/disqualifications: 1996-97, 9/0. 1997-98, 7/0. Totals, 16/0.

DID YOU KNOW . . .

. . . that Kareem Abdul-Jabbar and David Robinson are the only players to lead the NBA in scoring, rebounding and blocked shots?

REDD, MICHAEL G BUCKS

PERSONAL: Born August 24, 1979, in Columbus, Ohio. ... 6-6/214. (1,98/97,1). ... Full Name: Michael Wesley Redd.
HIGH SCHOOL: West (Columbus).
COLLEGE: Ohio State.
TRANSACTIONS/CAREER NOTES: Selected after junior season by Milwaukee Bucks in second round (43rd pick overall) of 2000 NBA Draft.

COLLEGIATE RECORD

Season Team	G	Min.	FGM	FGA	Pct.	FTM	FTA	Pct.	Reb.	Ast.	Pts.	AVERAGES RPG	APG	PPG
97-98—Ohio State	30	1137	241	550	.438	130	211	.616	194	91	658	6.5	3.0	21.9
98-99—Ohio State	36	1183	261	560	.466	135	220	.614	203	85	703	5.6	2.4	19.5
99-00—Ohio State	30	1004	197	452	.436	90	116	.776	196	62	518	6.5	2.1	17.3
Totals	96	3324	699	1562	.448	355	547	.649	593	238	1879	6.2	2.5	19.6

Three-point field goals: 1997-98, 46-for-152 (.303). 1998-99, 46-for-135 (.341). 1999-00, 31-for-99 (.313). Totals, 123-for-386 (.319).

NBA REGULAR-SEASON RECORD

Season Team	G	Min.	FGM	FGA	Pct.	FTM	FTA	Pct.	REBOUNDS Off.	Def.	Tot.	Ast.	St.	Blk.	TO	Pts.	AVERAGES RPG	APG	PPG
00-01—Milwaukee	6	35	5	19	.263	3	6	.500	3	1	4	1	1	0	1	13	0.7	0.2	2.2

Three-point field goals: 2000-01, 0-for-3.
Personal fouls/disqualifications: 2000-01, 2/0.

REEVES, BRYANT C GRIZZLIES

PERSONAL: Born June 8, 1973, in Fort Smith, Ark. ... 7-0/280. (2,13/127,0). ... Nickname: Big Country.
HIGH SCHOOL: Gans (Okla.).
COLLEGE: Oklahoma State.
TRANSACTIONS/CAREER NOTES: Selected by Vancouver Grizzlies in first round (sixth pick overall) of 1995 NBA Draft. ... Grizzlies franchise moved to Memphis for 2001-02 season.

COLLEGIATE RECORD

Season Team	G	Min.	FGM	FGA	Pct.	FTM	FTA	Pct.	Reb.	Ast.	Pts.	AVERAGES RPG	APG	PPG
91-92—Oklahoma State	36	763	111	213	.521	69	109	.633	182	24	291	5.1	0.7	8.1
92-93—Oklahoma State	29	944	210	338	.621	145	223	.650	291	36	566	10.0	1.2	19.5
93-94—Oklahoma State	34	1170	264	451	.585	185	311	.595	329	52	713	9.7	1.5	21.0
94-95—Oklahoma State	37	1288	289	493	.586	219	310	.706	350	30	797	9.5	0.8	21.5
Totals	136	4165	874	1495	.585	618	953	.648	1152	142	2367	8.5	1.0	17.4

Three-point field goals: 1992-93, 1-for-2 (.500). 1993-94, 0-for-1. 1994-95, 0-for-5. Totals, 1-for-8 (.125).

HONORS: NBA All-Rookie second team (1996).

NBA REGULAR-SEASON RECORD

Season Team	G	Min.	FGM	FGA	Pct.	FTM	FTA	Pct.	REBOUNDS Off.	Def.	Tot.	Ast.	St.	Blk.	TO	Pts.	AVERAGES RPG	APG	PPG
95-96—Vancouver	77	2460	401	877	.457	219	299	.732	178	392	570	109	43	55	157	1021	7.4	1.4	13.3
96-97—Vancouver	75	2777	498	1025	.486	216	307	.704	174	436	610	160	29	67	175	1213	8.1	2.1	16.2
97-98—Vancouver	74	2527	492	941	.523	223	316	.706	196	389	585	155	39	80	156	1207	7.9	2.1	16.3
98-99—Vancouver	25	702	102	251	.406	67	116	.578	50	88	138	37	13	8	47	271	5.5	1.5	10.8
99-00—Vancouver	69	1773	252	562	.448	107	165	.648	126	264	390	82	33	38	119	611	5.7	1.2	8.9
00-01—Vancouver	75	1832	254	552	.460	113	142	.796	132	320	452	80	43	54	90	622	6.0	1.1	8.3
Totals	395	12071	1999	4208	.475	945	1345	.703	856	1889	2745	623	200	302	744	4945	6.9	1.6	12.5

Three-point field goals: 1995-96, 0-for-3. 1996-97, 1-for-11 (.091). 1997-98, 0-for-4. 1998-99, 0-for-1. 1999-00, 0-for-4. 2000-01, 1-for-4 (.250). Totals, 2-for-27 (.074).
Personal fouls/disqualifications: 1995-96, 226/2. 1996-97, 270/3. 1997-98, 278/6. 1998-99, 103/3. 1999-00, 245/8. 2000-01, 243/5. Totals, 1365/27.

REID, DON F MAGIC

PERSONAL: Born December 30, 1973, in Washington, D.C. ... 6-8/250. (2,03/113,4).
HIGH SCHOOL: Largo (Md.).
COLLEGE: Georgetown.
TRANSACTIONS/CAREER NOTES: Selected by Detroit Pistons in second round (58th pick overall) of 1995 NBA Draft. ... Waived by Pistons (March 9, 2000). ... Signed as free agent by Washington Wizards (March 13, 2000). ... Signed as free agent by Orlando Magic (August 15, 2000).

COLLEGIATE RECORD

Season Team	G	Min.	FGM	FGA	Pct.	FTM	FTA	Pct.	Reb.	Ast.	Pts.	AVERAGES RPG	APG	PPG
91-92—Georgetown	28	215	13	30	.433	18	30	.600	59	7	44	2.1	0.3	1.6
92-93—Georgetown	32	279	18	43	.419	14	31	.452	68	4	50	2.1	0.1	1.6
93-94—Georgetown	31	713	90	140	.643	58	92	.630	182	27	238	5.9	0.9	7.7
94-95—Georgetown	31	731	88	148	.595	47	91	.516	178	26	223	5.7	0.8	7.2
Totals	122	1938	209	361	.579	137	244	.561	487	64	555	4.0	0.5	4.5

NBA REGULAR-SEASON RECORD

Season Team	G	Min.	FGM	FGA	Pct.	FTM	FTA	Pct.	REBOUNDS Off.	Def.	Tot.	Ast.	St.	Blk.	TO	Pts.	AVERAGES RPG	APG	PPG
95-96—Detroit	69	997	106	187	.567	51	77	.662	78	125	203	11	47	40	41	263	2.9	0.2	3.8
96-97—Detroit	47	462	54	112	.482	24	32	.750	36	65	101	14	16	15	23	132	2.1	0.3	2.8
97-98—Detroit	68	994	94	176	.534	50	71	.704	77	98	175	26	25	55	28	238	2.6	0.4	3.5
98-99—Detroit	47	935	97	174	.557	48	79	.608	66	104	170	33	27	43	36	242	3.6	0.7	5.1
99-00—Detroit-Wash..	38	498	60	112	.536	24	34	.706	31	71	102	11	24	31	23	144	2.7	0.3	3.8
00-01—Orlando...........	65	764	82	145	.566	46	75	.613	84	158	242	21	23	54	48	210	3.7	0.3	3.7
Totals	334	4650	493	906	.544	243	368	.660	372	621	993	116	162	238	199	1229	3.0	0.3	3.7

Three-point field goals: 1996-97, 0-for-1. Totals, 0-for-1 (.000).
Personal fouls/disqualifications: 1995-96, 199/2. 1996-97, 105/1. 1997-98, 183/2. 1998-99, 156/2. 1999-00, 118/5. 2000-01, 190/4. Totals, 951/16.

NBA PLAYOFF RECORD

Season Team	G	Min.	FGM	FGA	Pct.	FTM	FTA	Pct.	REBOUNDS Off.	Def.	Tot.	Ast.	St.	Blk.	TO	Pts.	AVERAGES RPG	APG	PPG
95-96—Detroit	3	26	1	3	.333	1	3	.333	0	1	1	1	0	2	1	3	0.3	0.3	1.0
98-99—Detroit	4	21	2	3	.667	0	0	...	2	2	4	1	0	0	0	4	1.0	0.3	1.0
00-01—Orlando...........	3	25	4	5	.800	2	6	.333	5	6	11	0	1	2	2	10	3.7	0.0	3.3
Totals	10	72	7	11	.636	3	9	.333	7	9	16	2	1	4	3	17	1.6	0.2	1.7

Three-point field goals: 2000-01, 0-for-1. Totals, 0-for-1 (.000).
Personal fouls/disqualifications: 1995-96, 8/0. 1998-99, 2/0. 2000-01, 9/0. Totals, 19/0.

REID, J.R.   F/C

PERSONAL: Born March 31, 1968, in Virginia Beach, Va. ... 6-10/250. (2,08/113,4). ... Full Name: Herman Reid Jr.
HIGH SCHOOL: Kempsville (Virginia Beach, Va.).
COLLEGE: North Carolina.
TRANSACTIONS/CAREER NOTES: Selected after junior season by Charlotte Hornets in first round (fifth pick overall) of 1989 NBA Draft. ... Traded by Hornets to San Antonio Spurs for F Sidney Green, 1993 first-round draft choice and 1996 second-round draft choice (December 9, 1992). ... Traded by Spurs with F/C Brad Lohaus and 1996 first-round draft choice to New York Knicks for F Charles Smith and F Monty Williams (February 8, 1996). ... Played in France (1996-97). ... Signed as free agent by Hornets (July 16, 1997). ... Traded by Hornets with F Glen Rice and G B.J. Armstrong to Los Angeles Lakers for G Eddie Jones and F/C Elden Campbell (March 10, 1999). ... Signed as free agent by Milwaukee Bucks (August 20, 1999). ... Traded by Bucks with F Robert Traylor to Cleveland Cavaliers as part of three-way deal in which Cavaliers traded G Bob Sura to Golden State Warriors, Warriors traded F Jason Caffey and F/G Billy Owens to Bucks and Bucks traded G Vinny Del Negro to Warriors (June 27, 2000). ... Waived by Cavaliers (January 2, 2001). ... Signed to play for Strasbourg in France for 2001-02 season.
MISCELLANEOUS: Member of bronze-medal-winning U.S. Olympic team (1988).

COLLEGIATE RECORD

NOTES: THE SPORTING NEWS All-America second team (1988).

Season Team	G	Min.	FGM	FGA	Pct.	FTM	FTA	Pct.	Reb.	Ast.	Pts.	AVERAGES RPG	APG	PPG
86-87—North Carolina	36	1030	198	339	.584	132	202	.653	268	66	528	7.4	1.8	14.7
87-88—North Carolina	33	1042	222	366	.607	151	222	.680	293	57	595	8.9	1.7	18.0
88-89—North Carolina	27	716	164	267	.614	101	151	.669	170	36	429	6.3	1.3	15.9
Totals	96	2788	584	972	.601	384	575	.668	731	159	1552	7.6	1.7	16.2

NBA REGULAR-SEASON RECORD

HONORS: NBA All-Rookie second team (1990).

Season Team	G	Min.	FGM	FGA	Pct.	FTM	FTA	Pct.	REBOUNDS Off.	Def.	Tot.	Ast.	St.	Blk.	TO	Pts.	AVERAGES RPG	APG	PPG
89-90—Charlotte........	82	2757	358	814	.440	192	289	.664	199	492	691	101	92	54	172	908	8.4	1.2	11.1
90-91—Charlotte........	80	2467	360	773	.466	182	259	.703	154	348	502	89	87	47	153	902	6.3	1.1	11.3
91-92—Charlotte........	51	1257	213	435	.490	134	190	.705	96	221	317	81	49	23	84	560	6.2	1.6	11.0
92-93—Char.-San Ant.	83	1887	283	595	.476	214	280	.764	120	336	456	80	47	31	125	780	5.5	1.0	9.4
93-94—San Antonio ...	70	1344	260	530	.491	107	153	.699	91	129	220	73	43	25	84	627	3.1	1.0	9.0
94-95—San Antonio ...	81	1566	201	396	.508	160	233	.687	120	273	393	55	60	32	113	563	4.9	0.7	7.0
95-96—San Ant.-N.Y..	65	1313	160	324	.494	107	142	.754	73	182	255	42	43	17	79	427	3.9	0.6	6.6
97-98—Charlotte........	79	1109	146	318	.459	89	122	.730	72	138	210	51	35	19	65	384	2.7	0.6	4.9
98-99—Char.-L.A.L....	41	1029	132	277	.477	105	137	.766	45	167	212	48	37	10	51	369	5.2	1.2	9.0
99-00—Milwaukee	34	602	53	127	.417	43	56	.768	29	88	117	18	19	5	20	150	3.4	0.5	4.4
00-01—Cleveland	6	39	2	5	.400	5	8	.750	5	3	8	1	2	1	1	10	1.3	0.2	1.7
Totals	672	15370	2168	4594	.472	1339	1869	.716	1004	2377	3381	639	514	264	947	5680	5.0	1.0	8.5

Three-point field goals: 1989-90, 0-for-5. 1990-91, 0-for-2. 1991-92, 0-for-3. 1992-93, 0-for-5. 1993-94, 0-for-3. 1994-95, 1-for-2 (.500). 1995-96, 0-for-1. 1997-98, 3-for-8 (.375). 1998-99, 0-for-1. 1999-00, 1-for-7 (.143). Totals, 5-for-37 (.135).
Personal fouls/disqualifications: 1989-90, 292/7. 1990-91, 286/6. 1991-92, 159/0. 1992-93, 266/3. 1993-94, 165/0. 1994-95, 230/2. 1995-96, 187/0. 1997-98, 172/1. 1998-99, 135/3. 1999-00, 81/2. 2000-01, 4/0. Totals, 1977/24.

NBA PLAYOFF RECORD

Season Team	G	Min.	FGM	FGA	Pct.	FTM	FTA	Pct.	REBOUNDS Off.	Def.	Tot.	Ast.	St.	Blk.	TO	Pts.	AVERAGES RPG	APG	PPG
92-93—San Antonio	10	220	29	60	.483	27	35	.771	16	34	50	15	8	8	13	85	5.0	1.5	8.5
93-94—San Antonio	4	56	6	21	.286	3	5	.600	3	9	12	3	1	2	1	15	3.0	0.8	3.8
94-95—San Antonio	15	209	29	59	.492	33	39	.846	14	28	42	9	7	4	15	91	2.8	0.6	6.1
95-96—New York	1	7	1	1	1.000	0	0	...	0	1	1	1	0	0	1	2	1.0	1.0	2.0
96-97—Detroit	1	3	0	0	...	4	4	1.000	0	1	1	0	0	0	0	4	1.0	0.0	4.0
97-98—Charlotte........	9	114	11	28	.393	8	10	.800	7	13	20	2	3	2	11	30	2.2	0.2	3.3
98-99—L.A. Lakers	8	178	10	28	.357	6	8	.750	9	33	42	3	4	5	2	26	5.3	0.4	3.3
Totals	48	787	86	197	.437	81	101	.802	49	119	168	33	23	21	43	253	3.5	0.7	5.3

Three-point field goals: 1992-93, 0-for-2. 1997-98, 0-for-1. Totals, 0-for-3 (.000).
Personal fouls/disqualifications: 1992-93, 31/0. 1993-94, 10/0. 1994-95, 36/0. 1995-96, 2/0. 1997-98, 23/0. 1998-99, 33/1. Totals, 135/1.

FRENCH LEAGUE RECORD

Season Team	G	Min.	FGM	FGA	Pct.	FTM	FTA	Pct.	Reb.	Ast.	Pts.	AVERAGES RPG	APG	PPG
96-97—Paris Racing	22	...	...	...	...	...	...	...	187	44	374	8.5	2.0	17.0

R

PERSONAL: Born May 28, 1967, in Flint, Mich. ... 6-8/220. (2,03/99,8). ... Full Name: Glen Anthony Rice.
HIGH SCHOOL: Northwestern Community (Flint, Mich.).
COLLEGE: Michigan.
TRANSACTIONS/CAREER NOTES: Selected by Miami Heat in first round (fourth pick overall) of 1989 NBA Draft. ... Traded by Heat with G Khalid Reeves, C Matt Geiger and 1996 first-round draft choice to Charlotte Hornets for C Alonzo Mourning, C LeRon Ellis and G Pete Myers (November 3, 1995). ... Traded by Hornets with F/C J.R. Reid and G B.J. Armstrong to Los Angeles Lakers for G Eddie Jones and F/C Elden Campbell (March 10, 1999). ... Traded by Lakers to New York Knicks as part of four-team trade in which Knicks acquired C Luc Longley, F/C Travis Knight, G Vernon Maxwell, C Vladimir Stepania, F Lazaro Borrell, two 2001 first-round draft choices and two 2001 second-round draft choices, Seattle SuperSonics acquired C Patrick Ewing, Phoenix Suns acquired C Chris Dudley and 2001 first-round draft choice and Lakers acquired F Horace Grant, C Greg Foster, F Chuck Person and G Emanual Davis (September 20, 2000). ... Traded by Knicks to Houston Rockets as part of three-team trade in which Knicks acquired F Shandon Anderson from Rockets and G Howard Eisley from Mavericks, Mavericks acquired G Muggsy Bogues from Knicks and Rockets acquired draft rights to G Kyle Hill from Mavericks (August 10, 2001).
MISCELLANEOUS: Member of NBA championship team (2000). ... Miami Heat all-time leading scorer with 9,248 points (1989-90 through 1994-95).

COLLEGIATE RECORD

NOTES: Member of NCAA Division I championship team (1989). ... THE SPORTING NEWS All-America second team (1989). ... NCAA Division I Tournament Most Outstanding Player (1989).

Season Team	G	Min.	FGM	FGA	Pct.	FTM	FTA	Pct.	Reb.	Ast.	Pts.	AVERAGES RPG	APG	PPG
85-86—Michigan	32	520	105	191	.550	15	25	.600	97	21	225	3.0	0.7	7.0
86-87—Michigan	32	1056	226	402	.562	85	108	.787	294	76	540	9.2	2.4	16.9
87-88—Michigan	33	1155	308	539	.571	79	98	.806	236	92	728	7.2	2.8	22.1
88-89—Michigan	37	1258	363	629	.577	124	149	.832	232	85	949	6.3	2.3	25.6
Totals	134	3989	1002	1761	.569	303	380	.797	859	274	2442	6.4	2.0	18.2

Three-point field goals: 1986-87, 3-for-12 (.250). 1987-88, 33-for-77 (.429). 1988-89, 99-for-192 (.516). Totals, 135-for-281 (.480).

NBA REGULAR-SEASON RECORD

HONORS: Long Distance Shootout winner (1995). ... All-NBA second team (1997). ... All-NBA third team (1998). ... NBA All-Rookie second team (1990).
NOTES: Led NBA with .470 three-point field goal percentage (1997).

Season Team	G	Min.	FGM	FGA	Pct.	FTM	FTA	Pct.	REBOUNDS Off.	Def.	Tot.	Ast.	St.	Blk.	TO	Pts.	AVERAGES RPG	APG	PPG
89-90—Miami	77	2311	470	1071	.439	91	124	.734	100	252	352	138	67	27	113	1048	4.6	1.8	13.6
90-91—Miami	77	2646	550	1193	.461	171	209	.818	85	296	381	189	101	26	166	1342	4.9	2.5	17.4
91-92—Miami	79	3007	672	1432	.469	266	318	.836	84	310	394	184	90	35	145	1765	5.0	2.3	22.3
92-93—Miami	82	3082	582	1324	.440	242	295	.820	92	332	424	180	92	25	157	1554	5.2	2.2	19.0
93-94—Miami	81	2999	663	1421	.467	250	284	.880	76	358	434	184	110	32	130	1708	5.4	2.3	21.1
94-95—Miami	82	3014	667	1403	.475	312	365	.855	99	279	378	192	112	14	153	1831	4.6	2.3	22.3
95-96—Charlotte	79	3142	610	1296	.471	319	381	.837	86	292	378	232	91	19	163	1710	4.8	2.9	21.6
96-97—Charlotte	79	*3362	722	1513	.477	464	535	.867	67	251	318	160	72	26	177	2115	4.0	2.0	26.8
97-98—Charlotte	82	3295	634	1386	.457	428	504	.849	89	264	353	182	77	22	182	1826	4.3	2.2	22.3
98-99—L.A. Lakers	27	985	171	396	.432	77	90	.856	9	90	99	71	17	6	45	472	3.7	2.6	17.5
99-00—L.A. Lakers	80	2530	421	980	.430	346	396	.874	56	271	327	176	47	12	114	1272	4.1	2.2	15.9
00-01—New York	75	2212	331	752	.440	155	182	.852	61	246	307	89	41	13	96	899	4.1	1.2	12.0
Totals	900	32585	6493	14167	.458	3121	3683	.847	904	3241	4145	1977	917	257	1641	17542	4.6	2.2	19.5

Three-point field goals: 1989-90, 17-for-69 (.246). 1990-91, 71-for-184 (.386). 1991-92, 155-for-396 (.391). 1992-93, 148-for-386 (.383). 1993-94, 132-for-346 (.382). 1994-95, 185-for-451 (.410). 1995-96, 171-for-403 (.424). 1996-97, 207-for-440 (.470). 1997-98, 130-for-300 (.433). 1998-99, 53-for-135 (.393). 1999-00, 84-for-229 (.367). 2000-01, 82-for-211 (.389). Totals, 1435-for-3550 (.404).

Personal fouls/disqualifications: 1989-90, 198/1. 1990-91, 216/0. 1991-92, 170/0. 1992-93, 201/0. 1993-94, 186/0. 1994-95, 231/0. 1995-96, 217/1. 1996-97, 190/0. 1997-98, 200/0. 1998-99, 67/1. 1999-00, 179/1. 2000-01, 179/1. Totals, 2206/5.

NBA PLAYOFF RECORD

Season Team	G	Min.	FGM	FGA	Pct.	FTM	FTA	Pct.	REBOUNDS Off.	Def.	Tot.	Ast.	St.	Blk.	TO	Pts.	AVERAGES RPG	APG	PPG
91-92—Miami	3	119	24	64	.375	6	7	.857	3	7	10	5	2	0	6	57	3.3	1.7	19.0
93-94—Miami	5	195	26	68	.382	6	8	.750	6	30	36	10	11	2	14	65	7.2	2.0	13.0
96-97—Charlotte	3	137	28	57	.491	21	23	.913	1	10	11	11	4	1	4	83	3.7	3.7	27.7
97-98—Charlotte	9	369	82	173	.474	30	36	.833	11	40	51	13	5	3	13	205	5.7	1.4	22.8
98-99—L.A. Lakers	7	307	45	101	.446	28	29	.966	4	23	27	11	5	1	9	128	3.9	1.6	18.3
99-00—L.A. Lakers	23	766	93	228	.408	71	89	.798	10	82	92	48	15	4	36	285	4.0	2.1	12.4
00-01—New York	5	144	24	52	.462	7	8	.875	3	19	22	3	3	1	7	61	4.4	0.6	12.2
Totals	55	2037	322	743	.433	169	200	.845	38	211	249	101	45	12	89	884	4.5	1.8	16.1

Three-point field goals: 1991-92, 3-for-12 (.250). 1993-94, 7-for-23 (.304). 1996-97, 6-for-16 (.375). 1997-98, 11-for-36 (.306). 1998-99, 10-for-28 (.357). 1999-00, 28-for-67 (.418). 2000-01, 6-for-14 (.429). Totals, 71-for-196 (.362).

Personal fouls/disqualifications: 1991-92, 7/0. 1993-94, 14/0. 1996-97, 11/0. 1997-98, 26/0. 1998-99, 15/0. 1999-00, 50/0. 2000-01, 10/0. Totals, 133/0.

NBA ALL-STAR GAME RECORD

NOTES: NBA All-Star Game Most Valuable Player (1997). ... Holds single-game records for most points in one half—24; most points in one quarter—20; most field-goal attempts in one half—17; and most three-point field goals made in one quarter—4 (1997). ... Shares single-game record for most field goals made in one quarter—8 (1997).

Season Team	Min.	FGM	FGA	Pct.	FTM	FTA	Pct.	REBOUNDS Off.	Def.	Tot.	Ast.	PF	Dq.	St.	Blk.	TO	Pts.
1996 —Charlotte	15	1	5	.200	4	4	1.000	0	0	0	2	2	0	0	0	2	7
1997 —Charlotte	25	10	24	.417	2	2	1.000	1	1	2	1	2	0	2	0	1	26
1998 —Charlotte	16	6	14	.429	0	0	...	1	0	1	0	0	0	0	0	1	16
Totals	56	17	43	.395	6	6	1.000	2	1	3	3	4	0	2	0	4	49

Three-point field goals: 1996, 1-for-2 (.500). 1997, 4-for-7 (.571). 1998, 4-for-6 (.667). Totals, 9-for-15 (.600).

RICHARDSON, QUENTIN　　G　　CLIPPERS

PERSONAL: Born April 13, 1980, in Chicago. ... 6-6/223. (1,98/101,2). ... Full Name: Quentin L. Richardson.
HIGH SCHOOL: Whitney Young (Chicago).
COLLEGE: DePaul.
TRANSACTIONS/CAREER NOTES: Selected after sophomore season by Los Angeles Clippers in first round (18th pick overall) of 2000 NBA Draft.

COLLEGIATE RECORD

NOTES: THE SPORTING NEWS Freshman of the Year (1999).

Season Team	G	Min.	FGM	FGA	Pct.	FTM	FTA	Pct.	Reb.	Ast.	Pts.	RPG	APG	PPG
98-99—DePaul	31	1040	203	425	.478	136	183	.743	327	32	586	10.5	1.0	18.9
99-00—DePaul	33	1150	202	468	.432	84	119	.706	325	72	561	9.8	2.2	17.0
Totals	64	2190	405	893	.454	220	302	.728	652	104	1147	10.2	1.6	17.9

Three-point field goals: 1998-99, 44-for-127 (.346). 1999-00, 73-for-190 (.384). Totals, 117-for-317 (.369).

NBA REGULAR-SEASON RECORD

Season Team	G	Min.	FGM	FGA	Pct.	FTM	FTA	Pct.	Off.	Def.	Tot.	Ast.	St.	Blk.	TO	Pts.	RPG	APG	PPG
00-01—L.A. Clippers	76	1358	232	525	.442	99	158	.627	105	152	257	62	42	7	64	613	3.4	0.8	8.1

Three-point field goals: 2000-01, 50-for-151 (.331).
Personal fouls/disqualifications: 2000-01, 98/0.

RICHMOND, MITCH　　G　　LAKERS

PERSONAL: Born June 30, 1965, in Fort Lauderdale. ... 6-5/220. (1,96/99,8). ... Full Name: Mitchell James Richmond.
HIGH SCHOOL: Boyd Anderson (Fort Lauderdale).
JUNIOR COLLEGE: Moberly (Mo.) Area Junior College.
COLLEGE: Kansas State.
TRANSACTIONS/CAREER NOTES: Selected by Golden State Warriors in first round (fifth pick overall) of 1988 NBA Draft. ... Traded by Warriors with C Les Jepsen to Sacramento Kings for F/G Billy Owens (November 1, 1991). ... Traded by Kings with F Otis Thorpe to Washington Wizards for F Chris Webber (May 14, 1998). ... Waived by Wizards (July 2, 2001). ... Signed as free agent by Los Angeles Lakers (July 20, 2001).
MISCELLANEOUS: Member of bronze-medal-winning U.S. Olympic team (1988) and gold-medal-winning U.S. Olympic team (1996).

COLLEGIATE RECORD

NOTES: THE SPORTING NEWS All-America second team (1988).

Season Team	G	Min.	FGM	FGA	Pct.	FTM	FTA	Pct.	Reb.	Ast.	Pts.	RPG	APG	PPG
84-85—Moberly Area J.C.	40	...	180	375	.480	55	85	.647	185	98	415	4.6	2.5	10.4
85-86—Moberly Area J.C.	38	...	242	506	.478	124	180	.689	251	99	608	6.6	2.6	16.0
86-87—Kansas State	30	964	201	450	.447	118	155	.761	170	80	559	5.7	2.7	18.6
87-88—Kansas State	34	1200	268	521	.514	186	240	.775	213	125	768	6.3	3.7	22.6
Junior College Totals	78	...	422	881	.479	179	265	.675	436	197	1023	5.6	2.5	13.1
4-Year-College Totals	64	2164	469	971	.483	304	395	.770	383	205	1327	6.0	3.2	20.7

Three-point field goals: 1986-87, 39-for-108 (.361). 1987-88, 46-for-98 (.469). Totals, 85-for-206 (.413).

NBA REGULAR-SEASON RECORD

HONORS: NBA Rookie of the Year (1989). ... All-NBA second team (1994, 1995, 1997). ... All-NBA third team (1996, 1998). ... NBA All-Rookie first team (1989).

Season Team	G	Min.	FGM	FGA	Pct.	FTM	FTA	Pct.	Off.	Def.	Tot.	Ast.	St.	Blk.	TO	Pts.	RPG	APG	PPG
88-89—Golden State	79	2717	649	1386	.468	410	506	.810	158	310	468	334	82	13	269	1741	5.9	4.2	22.0
89-90—Golden State	78	2799	640	1287	.497	406	469	.866	98	262	360	223	98	24	201	1720	4.6	2.9	22.1
90-91—Golden State	77	3027	703	1424	.494	394	465	.847	147	305	452	238	126	34	230	1840	5.9	3.1	23.9
91-92—Sacramento	80	3095	685	1465	.468	330	406	.813	62	257	319	411	92	34	247	1803	4.0	5.1	22.5
92-93—Sacramento	45	1728	371	782	.474	197	233	.845	18	136	154	221	53	9	130	987	3.4	4.9	21.9
93-94—Sacramento	78	2897	635	1428	.445	426	511	.834	70	216	286	313	103	17	216	1823	3.7	4.0	23.4
94-95—Sacramento	82	3172	668	1497	.446	375	445	.843	69	288	357	311	91	29	234	1867	4.4	3.8	22.8
95-96—Sacramento	81	2946	611	1368	.447	425	491	.866	54	215	269	255	125	19	220	1872	3.3	3.1	23.1
96-97—Sacramento	81	3125	717	1578	.454	457	531	.861	59	260	319	338	118	24	237	2095	3.9	4.2	25.9
97-98—Sacramento	70	2569	543	1220	.445	407	471	.864	50	179	229	279	88	15	181	1623	3.3	4.0	23.2
98-99—Washington	50	1912	331	803	.412	251	293	.857	30	142	172	122	64	10	136	983	3.4	2.4	19.7
99-00—Washington	74	2397	447	1049	.426	298	340	.876	37	176	213	185	110	13	154	1285	2.9	2.5	17.4
00-01—Washington	37	1216	205	504	.407	143	160	.894	15	94	109	111	43	7	84	598	2.9	3.0	16.2
Totals	912	33600	7205	15791	.456	4519	5321	.849	867	2840	3707	3341	1193	248	2539	20237	4.1	3.7	22.2

Three-point field goals: 1988-89, 33-for-90 (.367). 1989-90, 34-for-95 (.358). 1990-91, 40-for-115 (.348). 1991-92, 103-for-268 (.384). 1992-93, 48-for-130 (.369). 1993-94, 127-for-312 (.407). 1994-95, 156-for-424 (.368). 1995-96, 225-for-515 (.437). 1996-97, 204-for-477 (.428). 1997-98, 130-for-334 (.389). 1998-99, 70-for-221 (.317). 1999-00, 93-for-241 (.386). 2000-01, 45-for-133 (.338). Totals, 1308-for-3355 (.390).
Personal fouls/disqualifications: 1988-89, 223/5. 1989-90, 210/3. 1990-91, 207/0. 1991-92, 231/1. 1992-93, 137/3. 1993-94, 211/3. 1994-95, 227/2. 1995-96, 233/6. 1996-97, 211/1. 1997-98, 154/0. 1998-99, 121/1. 1999-00, 86/0. Totals, 2442/27.

NBA PLAYOFF RECORD

Season Team	G	Min.	FGM	FGA	Pct.	FTM	FTA	Pct.	Off.	Def.	Tot.	Ast.	St.	Blk.	TO	Pts.	RPG	APG	PPG
88-89—Golden State	8	314	62	135	.459	34	38	.895	10	25	35	14	1	24	161	7.3	4.4	20.1
90-91—Golden State	9	372	85	169	.503	23	24	.958	10	37	47	22	5	6	17	201	5.2	2.4	22.3
95-96—Sacramento	4	146	24	54	.444	28	35	.800	3	14	17	12	3	0	15	84	4.3	3.0	21.0
Totals	21	832	171	358	.478	85	97	.876	23	99	122	69	22	7	56	446	5.8	3.3	21.2

Three-point field goals: 1988-89, 3-for-16 (.188). 1990-91, 8-for-24 (.333). 1995-96, 8-for-23 (.348). Totals, 19-for-63 (.302).
Personal fouls/disqualifications: 1988-89, 25/0. 1990-91, 28/1. 1995-96, 11/0. Totals, 64/1.

NBA ALL-STAR GAME RECORD

NOTES: NBA All-Star Game Most Valuable Player (1995).

Season Team	Min.	FGM	FGA	Pct.	FTM	FTA	Pct.	REBOUNDS Off.	Def.	Tot.	Ast.	PF	Dq.	St.	Blk.	TO	Pts.
1993 —Sacramento......							Selected, did not play—injured.										
1994 —Sacramento......	24	5	16	.313	0	0	...	0	2	2	3	0	0	0	0	0	10
1995 —Sacramento......	22	10	13	.769	0	0	...	3	1	4	2	0	0	0	0	0	23
1996 —Sacramento......	25	3	10	.300	1	2	.500	0	2	2	2	0	0	1	0	2	7
1997 —Sacramento......	22	3	7	.429	0	0	...	1	2	3	4	1	0	0	0	1	9
1998 —Sacramento......	17	4	11	.364	0	0	...	0	1	1	2	0	...	0	0	0	8
Totals	110	25	57	.439	1	2	.500	4	8	12	13	1	0	1	0	3	57

Three-point field goals: 1995, 3-for-3. 1996, 0-for-3. 1997, 3-for-4 (.750). 1998, 0-for-2. Totals, 6-for-12 (.500).

RIDER, ISAIAH   G

PERSONAL: Born March 12, 1971, in Oakland. ... 6-5/215. (1,96/97,5). ... Full Name: Isaiah Rider Jr. ... Nickname: J.R.
HIGH SCHOOL: Encinal (Alameda, Calif.).
COLLEGE: UNLV.
TRANSACTIONS/CAREER NOTES: Selected by Minnesota Timberwolves in first round (fifth pick overall) of 1993 NBA Draft. ... Traded by Timberwolves to Portland Trail Blazers for F Bill Curley, G James Robinson and 1997 or 1998 first-round draft choice (July 23, 1996). ... Traded by Trail Blazers with G Jim Jackson to Atlanta Hawks for G Steve Smith and G Ed Gray (August 2, 1999). ... Waived by Hawks (March 20, 2000). ... Signed as free agent by Los Angeles Lakers (August 25, 2000).
MISCELLANEOUS: Member of NBA Championship Team (2001).

COLLEGIATE RECORD

Season Team	G	Min.	FGM	FGA	Pct.	FTM	FTA	Pct.	Reb.	Ast.	Pts.	AVERAGES RPG	APG	PPG
89-90—Allen County C.C.	30	...	340	...	...	154	...	...	...	...	929	...	...	31.0
90-91—Antelope Valley..............	24	...	319	535	.596	117	159	.736	273	92	806	11.4	3.8	33.6
91-92—UNLV	27	922	206	420	.490	65	87	.747	141	87	558	5.2	3.2	20.7
92-93—UNLV	28	992	282	548	.515	195	236	.826	250	71	814	8.9	2.5	29.1
Junior College Totals..............	54	...	659	...	...	271	...	...	...	...	1735	...	...	32.1
4-Year-College Totals	55	1914	488	968	.504	260	323	.806	391	158	1372	7.1	2.9	24.9

Three-point field goals: 1990-91, 51-for-138 (.370). 1991-92, 81-for-202 (.401). 1992-93, 55-for-137 (.401). Totals, 136-for-339 (.401).

NBA REGULAR-SEASON RECORD

HONORS: Slam Dunk championship winner (1994). ... NBA All-Rookie first team (1994).

Season Team	G	Min.	FGM	FGA	Pct.	FTM	FTA	Pct.	REBOUNDS Off.	Def.	Tot.	Ast.	St.	Blk.	TO	Pts.	AVERAGES RPG	APG	PPG
93-94—Minnesota......	79	2415	522	1115	.468	215	265	.811	118	197	315	202	54	28	218	1313	4.0	2.6	16.6
94-95—Minnesota......	75	2645	558	1249	.447	277	339	.817	90	159	249	245	69	23	232	1532	3.3	3.3	20.4
95-96—Minnesota......	75	2594	560	1206	.464	248	296	.838	99	210	309	213	48	23	201	1470	4.1	2.8	19.6
96-97—Portland..........	76	2563	456	983	.464	212	261	.812	94	210	304	198	45	19	212	1223	4.0	2.6	16.1
97-98—Portland..........	74	2786	551	1302	.423	221	267	.828	99	247	346	231	55	19	187	1458	4.7	3.1	19.7
98-99—Portland..........	47	1385	249	605	.412	111	147	.755	59	137	196	104	25	9	95	651	4.2	2.2	13.9
99-00—Atlanta	60	2084	449	1072	.419	204	260	.785	63	195	258	219	41	6	168	1158	4.3	3.7	19.3
00-01—L.A. Lakers	67	1206	201	472	.426	71	83	.855	44	112	156	111	27	7	98	507	2.3	1.7	7.6
Totals..............	553	17678	3546	8004	.443	1559	1918	.813	666	1467	2133	1523	364	134	1411	9312	3.9	2.8	16.8

Three-point field goals: 1993-94, 54-for-150 (.360). 1994-95, 139-for-396 (.351). 1995-96, 102-for-275 (.371). 1996-97, 99-for-257 (.385). 1997-98, 135-for-420 (.321). 1998-99, 42-for-111 (.378). 1999-00, 56-for-180 (.311). 2000-01, 34-for-92 (.370). Totals, 661-for-1881 (.351).
Personal fouls/disqualifications: 1993-94, 194/0. 1994-95, 194/3. 1995-96, 204/2. 1996-97, 199/2. 1997-98, 188/1. 1998-99, 100/0. 1999-00, 132/3. 2000-01, 105/0. Totals, 1316/11.

NBA PLAYOFF RECORD

Season Team	G	Min.	FGM	FGA	Pct.	FTM	FTA	Pct.	REBOUNDS Off.	Def.	Tot.	Ast.	St.	Blk.	TO	Pts.	AVERAGES RPG	APG	PPG
96-97—Portland..........	4	161	16	43	.372	15	17	.882	1	7	8	17	3	0	12	53	2.0	4.3	13.3
97-98—Portland..........	4	166	28	67	.418	20	26	.769	7	13	20	17	5	0	16	77	5.0	4.3	19.3
98-99—Portland..........	13	426	70	163	.429	63	71	.887	17	33	50	31	11	0	33	214	3.8	2.4	16.5
Totals..................	21	753	114	273	.418	98	114	.860	25	53	78	65	19	0	61	344	3.7	3.1	16.4

Three-point field goals: 1996-97, 6-for-16 (.375). 1997-98, 1-for-11 (.091). 1998-99, 11-for-26 (.423). Totals, 18-for-53 (.340).
Personal fouls/disqualifications: 1996-97, 11/0. 1997-98, 11/0. 1998-99, 30/0. Totals, 52/0.

ROBERSON, TERRANCE   F

PERSONAL: Born December 30, 1976, in Saginaw, Mich. ... 6-7/215. (2,00/97,5).
HIGH SCHOOL: Buvna Vista (Saginaw, Mich.).
COLLEGE: Fresno State.
TRANSACTIONS/CAREER NOTES: Not drafted by an NBA franchise. ... Signed as free agent by Charlotte Hornets (October 2, 2000). ... Waived by Hornets (December 19, 2000). ... Played in Continental Basketball Association with Idaho Stampede (2000-01). ... Played in International Basketball Association with Trenton Stars (2000-01).

COLLEGIATE RECORD

Season Team	G	Min.	FGM	FGA	Pct.	FTM	FTA	Pct.	Reb.	Ast.	Pts.	AVERAGES RPG	APG	PPG
95-96—Fresno State						Did not play—ineligible.								
96-97—Fresno State	28	589	92	185	.497	34	51	.667	120	31	252	4.3	1.1	9.0
97-98—Fresno State	34	1096	180	391	.460	48	84	.571	165	77	495	4.9	2.3	14.6
98-99—Fresno State	33	1016	145	367	.395	53	77	.688	194	68	405	5.9	2.1	12.3
99-00—Fresno State	33	1132	181	426	.425	88	104	.846	163	136	538	4.9	4.1	16.3
Totals	128	3833	598	1369	.437	223	316	.706	642	312	1690	5.0	2.4	13.2

Three-point field goals: 1996-97, 34-for-69 (.493). 1997-98, 87-for-213 (.408). 1998-99, 62-for-210 (.295). 1999-00, 88-for-241 (.365). Totals, 271-for-733 (.370).

CBA REGULAR-SEASON RECORD

											AVERAGES		
Season Team	G	Min.	FGM	FGA	Pct.	FTM	FTA	Pct.	Reb.	Ast.	Pts.	RPG	APG	PPG
00-01—Idaho	10	204	43	92	.467	17	26	.654	57	13	109	5.7	1.3	10.9

Three-point field goals: 2000-01, 6-for-23 (.261).

IBL REGULAR SEASON RECORD

											AVERAGES		
Season Team	G	Min.	FGM	FGA	Pct.	FTM	FTA	Pct.	Reb.	Ast.	Pts.	RPG	APG	PPG
00-01—Trenton	15	263	52	123	.423	18	21	.857	29	14	138	1.9	0.9	9.2

Three-point field goals: 2000-01, 16-for-42 (.381).

NBA REGULAR-SEASON RECORD

							REBOUNDS								AVERAGES		
Season Team	G	Min.	FGM	FGA	Pct.	FTM	FTA	Pct.	Off.	Def.	Tot.	Ast.	St.	Blk.	TO	Pts.	RPG	APG	PPG
00-01—Charlotte	3	13	0	2	.000	0	0	...	0	1	1	1	0	0	2	0	0.3	0.3	0.0

Three-point field goals: 2000-01, 0-for-1.
Personal fouls/disqualifications: 2000-01, 3/0.

ROBINSON, CLIFFORD   F   PISTONS

PERSONAL: Born December 16, 1966, in Buffalo. ... 6-10/225. (2,08/102,1). ... Full Name: Clifford Ralph Robinson.
HIGH SCHOOL: Riverside (Buffalo).
COLLEGE: Connecticut.
TRANSACTIONS/CAREER NOTES: Selected by Portland Trail Blazers in second round (36th pick overall) of 1989 NBA Draft. ... Signed as free agent by Phoenix Suns (August 25, 1997). ... Traded by Suns to Detroit Pistons for G/F Jud Buechler and F John Wallace (June 29, 2001).

COLLEGIATE RECORD

												AVERAGES		
Season Team	G	Min.	FGM	FGA	Pct.	FTM	FTA	Pct.	Reb.	Ast.	Pts.	RPG	APG	PPG
85-86—Connecticut	28	442	60	164	.366	36	59	.610	88	14	156	3.1	0.5	5.6
86-87—Connecticut	16	556	107	255	.420	69	121	.570	119	32	289	7.4	2.0	18.1
87-88—Connecticut	34	1079	222	463	.479	156	238	.655	233	44	600	6.9	1.3	17.6
88-89—Connecticut	31	974	235	500	.470	145	212	.684	228	46	619	7.4	1.5	20.0
Totals	109	3051	624	1382	.452	406	630	.644	668	136	1664	6.1	1.2	15.3

Three-point field goals: 1986-87, 6-for-18 (.333). 1988-89, 4-for-12 (.333). Totals, 10-for-30 (.333).

NBA REGULAR-SEASON RECORD

HONORS: NBA Sixth Man Award (1993). ... NBA All-Defensive second team (2000).

								REBOUNDS								AVERAGES		
Season Team	G	Min.	FGM	FGA	Pct.	FTM	FTA	Pct.	Off.	Def.	Tot.	Ast.	St.	Blk.	TO	Pts.	RPG	APG	PPG
89-90—Portland	82	1565	298	751	.397	138	251	.550	110	198	308	72	53	53	129	746	3.8	0.9	9.1
90-91—Portland	82	1940	373	806	.463	205	314	.653	123	226	349	151	78	76	133	957	4.3	1.8	11.7
91-92—Portland	82	2124	398	854	.466	219	330	.664	140	276	416	137	85	107	154	1016	5.1	1.7	12.4
92-93—Portland	82	2575	632	1336	.473	287	416	.690	165	377	542	182	98	163	173	1570	6.6	2.2	19.1
93-94—Portland	82	2853	641	1404	.457	352	460	.765	164	386	550	159	118	111	169	1647	6.7	1.9	20.1
94-95—Portland	75	2725	597	1320	.452	265	382	.694	152	271	423	198	79	82	158	1601	5.6	2.6	21.3
95-96—Portland	78	2980	553	1306	.423	360	542	.664	123	320	443	190	86	68	194	1644	5.7	2.4	21.1
96-97—Portland	81	3077	444	1043	.426	215	309	.696	90	231	321	261	99	66	172	1224	4.0	3.2	15.1
97-98—Phoenix	80	2359	429	895	.479	248	360	.689	152	258	410	170	92	90	140	1133	5.1	2.1	14.2
98-99—Phoenix	50	1740	299	629	.475	163	234	.697	69	158	227	128	75	59	88	819	4.5	2.6	16.4
99-00—Phoenix	80	2839	530	1142	.464	298	381	.782	105	254	359	224	90	61	166	1478	4.5	2.8	18.5
00-01—Phoenix	82	2751	501	1186	.422	253	357	.709	105	229	334	237	87	82	186	1345	4.1	2.9	16.4
Totals	936	29528	5695	12672	.449	3003	4336	.693	1498	3184	4682	2109	1040	1018	1862	15180	5.0	2.3	16.2

Three-point field goals: 1989-90, 12-for-44 (.273). 1990-91, 6-for-19 (.316). 1991-92, 1-for-11 (.091). 1992-93, 19-for-77 (.247). 1993-94, 13-for-53 (.245). 1994-95, 142-for-383 (.371). 1995-96, 178-for-471 (.378). 1996-97, 121-for-350 (.346). 1997-98, 27-for-84 (.321). 1998-99, 58-for-139 (.417). 1999-00, 120-for-324 (.370). 2000-01, 90-for-249 (.361). Totals, 787-for-2204 (.357).
Personal fouls/disqualifications: 1989-90, 226/4. 1990-91, 263/2. 1991-92, 274/11. 1992-93, 287/8. 1993-94, 263/0. 1994-95, 240/3. 1995-96, 248/3. 1996-97, 251/6. 1997-98, 249/5. 1998-99, 153/2. 1999-00, 239/3. 2000-01, 258/6. Totals, 2951/53.

NBA PLAYOFF RECORD

								REBOUNDS								AVERAGES		
Season Team	G	Min.	FGM	FGA	Pct.	FTM	FTA	Pct.	Off.	Def.	Tot.	Ast.	St.	Blk.	TO	Pts.	RPG	APG	PPG
89-90—Portland	21	391	54	151	.358	29	52	.558	32	55	87	23	19	24	25	137	4.1	1.1	6.5
90-91—Portland	16	354	63	117	.538	38	69	.551	24	39	63	18	7	16	25	165	3.9	1.1	10.3
91-92—Portland	21	522	91	197	.462	44	77	.571	25	63	88	43	22	21	28	227	4.2	2.0	10.8
92-93—Portland	4	131	16	61	.262	9	22	.409	10	7	17	6	6	7	8	41	4.3	1.5	10.3
93-94—Portland	4	149	28	68	.412	7	8	.875	11	14	25	10	3	6	11	65	6.3	2.5	16.3
94-95—Portland	3	119	17	47	.362	9	16	.563	7	12	19	8	2	1	8	47	6.3	2.7	15.7
95-96—Portland	5	181	21	61	.344	28	37	.757	4	14	18	8	7	5	16	76	3.6	1.6	15.2
96-97—Portland	4	161	17	47	.362	11	16	.688	12	15	27	12	2	4	10	48	6.8	3.0	12.0
97-98—Phoenix	4	92	9	33	.273	7	9	.778	6	6	12	3	3	2	5	25	3.0	0.8	6.3
98-99—Phoenix	3	117	19	40	.475	7	11	.636	7	9	16	8	6	1	7	47	5.3	2.7	15.7
99-00—Phoenix	9	333	56	145	.386	33	45	.733	18	36	54	19	11	7	18	158	6.0	2.1	17.6
00-01—Phoenix	4	114	21	50	.420	14	22	.636	6	10	16	4	6	2	9	60	4.0	1.0	15.0
Totals	98	2664	412	1017	.405	236	384	.615	162	280	442	162	94	96	170	1096	4.5	1.7	11.2

Three-point field goals: 1989-90, 0-for-4. 1990-91, 1-for-3 (.333). 1991-92, 1-for-6 (.167). 1992-93, 0-for-1. 1993-94, 2-for-9 (.222). 1994-95, 4-for-17 (.235). 1995-96, 6-for-23 (.261). 1996-97, 3-for-16 (.188). 1997-98, 0-for-1. 1998-99, 2-for-9 (.222). 1999-00, 13-for-40 (.325). 2000-01, 4-for-16 (.250). Totals, 36-for-145 (.248).

Personal fouls/disqualifications: 1989-90, 71/1. 1990-91, 47/1. 1991-92, 84/3. 1992-93, 17/1. 1993-94, 13/0. 1994-95, 13/0. 1995-96, 19/0. 1996-97, 13/0. 1997-98, 19/1. 1998-99, 12/1. 1999-00, 35/0. 2000-01, 14/0. Totals, 357/8.

NBA ALL-STAR GAME RECORD

								REBOUNDS									
Season Team	Min.	FGM	FGA	Pct.	FTM	FTA	Pct.	Off.	Def.	Tot.	Ast.	PF	Dq.	St.	Blk.	TO	Pts.
1994 —Portland	18	5	8	.625	0	0	...	1	1	2	5	0	0	1	0	0	10

Three-point field goals: 1994, 0-for-1.

ROBINSON, DAVID   C   SPURS

PERSONAL: Born August 6, 1965, in Key West, Fla. ... 7-1/250. (2,16/113,4). ... Full Name: David Maurice Robinson. ... Nickname: The Admiral.
HIGH SCHOOL: Osbourn Park (Manassas, Va.).
COLLEGE: Navy.
TRANSACTIONS/CAREER NOTES: Selected by San Antonio Spurs in first round (first pick overall) of 1987 NBA Draft.
CAREER HONORS: NBA 50th Anniversary All-Time Team (1996).
MISCELLANEOUS: Member of NBA championship team (1999). ... Member of bronze-medal-winning U.S. Olympic team (1988) and gold-medal-winning U.S. Olympic teams (1992, 1996). ... Member of gold-medal winning U.S. World Championship team (1986). ... San Antonio Spurs all-time points leader with 19,293, all-time rebound leader with 9,342, all-time steals leader with 1,250 and all-time blocked shots leader with 2,703 (1989-90 through 2000-01).

COLLEGIATE RECORD

NOTES: THE SPORTING NEWS College Player of the Year (1987). ... Naismith Award winner (1987). ... Wooden Award winner (1987). ... THE SPORTING NEWS All-America first team (1986, 1987). ... Holds NCAA Division I single-season records for most blocked shots—207 (1986). ... Shares NCAA Division I single-game record for most blocked shots—14 (January 4, 1986, vs. UNC Wilmington). ... Led NCAA Division I with 13.0 rebounds per game (1986). ... Led NCAA Division I with 5.91 blocked shots per game (1986) and 4.50 blocked shots per game (1987).

												AVERAGES		
Season Team	G	Min.	FGM	FGA	Pct.	FTM	FTA	Pct.	Reb.	Ast.	Pts.	RPG	APG	PPG
83-84—Navy	28	372	86	138	.623	42	73	.575	111	6	214	4.0	0.2	7.6
84-85—Navy	32	1075	302	469	.644	152	243	.626	370	19	756	11.6	0.6	23.6
85-86—Navy	35	1187	294	484	.607	208	331	.628	455	24	796	13.0	0.7	22.7
86-87—Navy	32	1107	350	592	.591	202	317	.637	378	33	903	11.8	1.0	28.2
Totals	127	3741	1032	1683	.613	604	964	.627	1314	82	2669	10.3	0.6	21.0

Three-point field goals: 1986-87, 1-for-1.

NBA REGULAR-SEASON RECORD

HONORS: NBA Most Valuable Player (1995). ... NBA Defensive Player of the Year (1992). ... NBA Rookie of the Year (1990). ... IBM Award, for all-around contributions to team's success (1990, 1991, 1994, 1995, 1996). ... All-NBA first team (1991, 1992, 1995, 1996). ... All-NBA second team (1994, 1998). ... All-NBA third team (1990, 1993, 2000, 2001). ... NBA All-Defensive first team (1991, 1992, 1995, 1996). ... NBA All-Defensive second team (1990, 1993, 1994, 1998). ... NBA All-Rookie first team (1990).
NOTES: Led NBA with 4.49 blocked shots per game (1992).

								REBOUNDS								AVERAGES		
Season Team	G	Min.	FGM	FGA	Pct.	FTM	FTA	Pct.	Off.	Def.	Tot.	Ast.	St.	Blk.	TO	Pts.	RPG	APG	PPG
87-88—San Antonio					Did not play—in military service.														
88-89—San Antonio					Did not play—in military service.														
89-90—San Antonio	82	3002	690	1300	.531	613	837	.732	303	680	983	164	138	319	257	1993	12.0	2.0	24.3
90-91—San Antonio	82	3095	754	1366	.552	592	777	.762	335	728	*1063	208	127	*320	270	2101	*13.0	2.5	25.6
91-92—San Antonio	68	2564	592	1074	.551	393	561	.701	261	568	829	181	158	*305	182	1578	12.2	2.7	23.2
92-93—San Antonio	82	3211	676	1348	.501	561	766	.732	229	727	956	301	127	264	241	1916	11.7	3.7	23.4
93-94—San Antonio	80	3241	840	1658	.507	*693	*925	.749	241	614	855	381	139	265	*2383	2383	10.7	4.8	*29.8
94-95—San Antonio	81	3074	788	1487	.530	*656	847	.774	234	643	877	236	134	262	233	2238	10.8	2.9	27.6
95-96—San Antonio	82	3019	711	1378	.516	*626	*823	.761	319	*681	*1000	247	111	271	190	2051	12.2	3.0	25.0
96-97—San Antonio	6	147	36	72	.500	34	52	.654	19	32	51	8	6	6	8	106	8.5	1.3	17.7
97-98—San Antonio	73	2457	544	1065	.511	485	660	.735	239	536	775	199	64	192	202	1574	10.6	2.7	21.6
98-99—San Antonio	49	1554	268	527	.509	239	363	.658	148	344	492	103	69	119	108	775	10.0	2.1	15.8
99-00—San Antonio	80	2557	528	1031	.512	371	511	.726	193	577	770	142	97	183	164	1427	9.6	1.8	17.8
00-01—San Antonio	80	2371	400	823	.486	351	470	.747	208	483	691	116	80	197	122	1151	8.6	1.5	14.4
Totals	845	30292	6827	13129	.520	5614	7592	.739	2729	6613	9342	2286	1250	2703	2230	19293	11.1	2.7	22.8

Three-point field goals: 1989-90, 0-for-4. 1990-91, 1-for-7 (.143). 1991-92, 1-for-8 (.125). 1992-93, 3-for-17 (.176). 1993-94, 10-for-29 (.345). 1994-95, 6-for-20 (.300). 1995-96, 3-for-9 (.333). 1997-98, 1-for-4 (.250). 1998-99, 0-for-1. 1999-00, 0-for-2. 2000-01, 0-for-1. Totals, 25-for-100 (.250).
Personal fouls/disqualifications: 1989-90, 259/3. 1990-91, 264/5. 1991-92, 219/2. 1992-93, 239/5. 1993-94, 228/3. 1994-95, 230/2. 1995-96, 262/1. 1996-97, 9/0. 1997-98, 204/2. 1998-99, 143/0. 1999-00, 247/1. 2000-01, 212/1. Totals, 2516/25.

NBA PLAYOFF RECORD

								REBOUNDS								AVERAGES		
Season Team	G	Min.	FGM	FGA	Pct.	FTM	FTA	Pct.	Off.	Def.	Tot.	Ast.	St.	Blk.	TO	Pts.	RPG	APG	PPG
89-90—San Antonio....	10	375	89	167	.533	65	96	.677	36	84	120	23	11	40	24	243	12.0	2.3	24.3
90-91—San Antonio....	4	166	35	51	.686	33	38	.868	11	43	54	8	6	15	15	103	13.5	2.0	25.8
92-93—San Antonio....	10	421	79	170	.465	73	110	.664	29	97	126	40	10	36	25	231	12.6	4.0	23.1
93-94—San Antonio....	4	146	30	73	.411	20	27	.741	13	27	40	14	3	10	9	80	10.0	3.5	20.0
94-95—San Antonio....	15	623	129	289	.446	121	149	.812	57	125	182	47	22	39	56	380	12.1	3.1	25.3
95-96—San Antonio....	10	353	83	161	.516	70	105	.667	37	64	101	24	15	25	24	236	10.1	2.4	23.6
97-98—San Antonio....	9	353	57	134	.425	61	96	.635	41	86	127	23	11	30	25	175	14.1	2.6	19.4
98-99—San Antonio....	17	600	87	180	.483	91	126	.722	36	132	168	43	28	40	40	265	9.9	2.5	15.6
99-00—San Antonio....	4	155	31	83	.373	32	42	.762	17	38	55	10	7	12	8	94	13.8	2.5	23.5
00-01—San Antonio....	13	409	75	159	.472	66	95	.695	39	114	153	22	17	31	28	216	11.8	1.7	16.6
Totals	96	3601	695	1467	.474	632	884	.715	316	810	1126	254	130	278	254	2023	11.7	2.6	21.1

Three-point field goals: 1990-91, 0-for-1. 1992-93, 0-for-1. 1993-94, 0-for-1. 1994-95, 1-for-5 (.200). 1999-00, 0-for-1. 2000-01, 0-for-1. Totals, 1-for-10 (.100).
Personal fouls/disqualifications: 1989-90, 35/1. 1990-91, 11/0. 1992-93, 39/0. 1993-94, 14/0. 1994-95, 63/1. 1995-96, 38/2. 1997-98, 28/1. 1998-99, 61/1. 1999-00, 15/0. 2000-01, 42/0. Totals, 346/6.

NBA ALL-STAR GAME RECORD

Season	Team	Min.	FGM	FGA	Pct.	FTM	FTA	Pct.	Off.	Def.	Tot.	Ast.	PF	Dq.	St.	Blk.	TO	Pts.
1990	—San Antonio	25	7	12	.583	1	2	.500	2	8	10	1	1	0	2	1	1	15
1991	—San Antonio	18	6	13	.462	4	5	.800	3	3	6	0	5	0	2	3	2	16
1992	—San Antonio	18	7	9	.778	5	8	.625	1	4	5	2	3	0	3	1	0	19
1993	—San Antonio	26	7	10	.700	7	12	.583	2	8	10	1	4	0	0	1	1	21
1994	—San Antonio	21	6	13	.462	7	10	.700	3	2	5	0	2	0	0	2	1	19
1995	—San Antonio	14	3	5	.600	4	6	.667	0	3	3	2	2	0	2	1	1	10
1996	—San Antonio	23	8	13	.615	2	2	1.000	6	5	11	2	4	0	2	2	1	18
1998	—San Antonio	22	3	4	.750	9	10	.900	2	4	6	0	1	...	2	2	2	15
2000	—San Antonio	7	0	1	.000	0	0	...	1	1	2	0	1	0	0	0	1	0
2001	—San Antonio	10	3	5	.600	2	4	.500	2	2	4	0	3	0	0	0	1	8
Totals	....	184	50	85	.588	41	59	.695	22	40	62	8	26	0	13	13	11	141

ROBINSON, EDDIE   F/G   BULLS

PERSONAL: Born April 10, 1976, in Flint, Mich. ... 6-9/205. (2,06/93,0). ... Full Name: Eddie B. Robinson Jr.
HIGH SCHOOL: Flint Northern (Flint, Mich.).
JUNIOR COLLEGE: Trinity Valley Community College (Texas), then Brown Mackie College (Kan.).
COLLEGE: Central Oklahoma.
TRANSACTIONS/CAREER NOTES: Not drafted by an NBA franchise. ... Signed as free agent by Charlotte Hornets (August 17, 1999). ... Signed as free agent by Chicago Bulls (July 18, 2001).

COLLEGIATE RECORD

NOTES: Led NCAA Division II with 28.0 points per game (1999).

												AVERAGES		
Season Team	G	Min.	FGM	FGA	Pct.	FTM	FTA	Pct.	Reb.	Ast.	Pts.	RPG	APG	PPG
94-95—Trinity Valley C.C.						Statistics unavailable.								
96-97—Brown Mackie J.C.	35	...	318	596	.534	58	97	.598	182	86	795	5.2	2.5	22.7
97-98—Central Oklahoma..........	27	690	170	331	.514	33	49	.673	200	21	400	7.4	0.8	14.8
98-99—Central Oklahoma..........	26	872	305	550	.555	95	123	.772	246	40	729	9.5	1.5	28.0
Junior College Totals..............	35	...	318	596	.534	58	97	.598	182	86	795	5.2	2.5	22.7
4-Year-College Totals	53	1562	475	881	.539	128	172	.744	446	61	1129	8.4	1.2	21.3

Three-point field goals: 1996-97, 101-for-229 (.441). 1997-98, 27-for-101 (.267). 1998-99, 24-for-74 (.324). Totals, 51-for-175 (.291).

NBA REGULAR-SEASON RECORD

									REBOUNDS								AVERAGES		
Season Team	G	Min.	FGM	FGA	Pct.	FTM	FTA	Pct.	Off.	Def.	Tot.	Ast.	St.	Blk.	TO	Pts.	RPG	APG	PPG
99-00—Charlotte........	67	1112	212	386	.549	47	64	.734	54	130	184	32	48	25	39	471	2.7	0.5	7.0
00-01—Charlotte........	67	1201	216	407	.531	64	88	.727	60	138	198	59	50	32	43	498	3.0	0.9	7.4
Totals	134	2313	428	793	.540	111	152	.730	114	268	382	91	98	57	82	969	2.9	0.7	7.2

Three-point field goals: 1999-00, 0-for-4. 2000-01, 2-for-4 (.500). Totals, 2-for-8 (.250).
Personal fouls/disqualifications: 1999-00, 67/0. 2000-01, 66/0. Totals, 133/0.

NBA PLAYOFF RECORD

									REBOUNDS								AVERAGES		
Season Team	G	Min.	FGM	FGA	Pct.	FTM	FTA	Pct.	Off.	Def.	Tot.	Ast.	St.	Blk.	TO	Pts.	RPG	APG	PPG
99-00—Charlotte........	4	45	5	12	.417	2	2	1.000	1	2	3	4	2	1	1	12	0.8	1.0	3.0
00-01—Charlotte........	10	192	31	60	.517	6	6	1.000	9	24	33	9	4	4	5	69	3.3	0.9	6.9
Totals	14	237	36	72	.500	8	8	1.000	10	26	36	13	6	5	6	81	2.6	0.9	5.8

Three-point field goals: 2000-01, 1-for-3 (.333). Totals, 1-for-3 (.333).
Personal fouls/disqualifications: 1999-00, 2/0. 2000-01, 12/0. Totals, 14/0.

ROBINSON, GLENN   F   BUCKS

PERSONAL: Born January 10, 1973, in Gary, Ind. ... 6-7/230. (2,01/104,3). ... Full Name: Glenn A. Robinson. ... Nickname: Big Dog.
HIGH SCHOOL: Roosevelt (Gary, Ind.).
COLLEGE: Purdue.
TRANSACTIONS/CAREER NOTES: Selected after junior season by Milwaukee Bucks in first round (first pick overall) of 1994 NBA Draft.

COLLEGIATE RECORD

NOTES: THE SPORTING NEWS College Player of the Year (1994). ... Naismith Award winner (1994). ... Wooden Award winner (1994). ... THE SPORTING NEWS All-America first team (1994). ... THE SPORTING NEWS All-America second team (1993). ... Led NCAA Division I with 30.3 points per game (1994).

											AVERAGES		
Season Team	G	Min.	FGM	FGA	Pct.	FTM	FTA	Pct.	Reb.	Ast.	Pts.	RPG	APG	PPG
91-92—Purdue	4					Did not play—ineligible.								
92-93—Purdue	28	1010	246	519	.474	152	205	.741	258	49	676	9.2	1.8	24.1
93-94—Purdue	34	1166	368	762	.483	215	270	.796	344	66	1030	10.1	1.9	30.3
Totals	62	2176	614	1281	.479	367	475	.773	602	115	1706	9.7	1.9	27.5

Three-point field goals: 1992-93, 32-for-80 (.400). 1993-94, 79-for-208 (.380). Totals, 111-for-288 (.385).

NBA REGULAR-SEASON RECORD

HONORS: NBA All-Rookie first team (1995).

Season Team	G	Min.	FGM	FGA	Pct.	FTM	FTA	Pct.	Off.	Def.	Tot.	Ast.	St.	Blk.	TO	Pts.	RPG	APG	PPG
94-95—Milwaukee	80	2958	636	1410	.451	397	499	.796	169	344	513	197	115	22	*313	1755	6.4	2.5	21.9
95-96—Milwaukee	82	3249	627	1382	.454	316	389	.812	136	368	504	293	95	42	282	1660	6.1	3.6	20.2
96-97—Milwaukee	80	3114	669	1438	.465	288	364	.791	130	372	502	248	103	68	269	1689	6.3	3.1	21.1
97-98—Milwaukee	56	2294	534	1136	.470	215	266	.808	82	225	307	158	69	34	200	1308	5.5	2.8	23.4
98-99—Milwaukee	47	1579	347	756	.459	140	161	.870	73	203	276	100	46	41	106	865	5.9	2.1	18.4
99-00—Milwaukee	81	2909	690	1461	.472	227	283	.802	107	378	485	193	78	41	223	1693	6.0	2.4	20.9
00-01—Milwaukee	76	2813	684	1460	.468	251	306	.820	124	402	526	252	86	62	219	1674	6.9	3.3	22.0
Totals	502	18916	4187	9043	.463	1834	2268	.809	821	2292	3113	1441	592	310	1612	10644	6.2	2.9	21.2

Three-point field goals: 1994-95, 86-for-268 (.321). 1995-96, 90-for-263 (.342). 1996-97, 63-for-180 (.350). 1997-98, 25-for-65 (.385). 1998-99, 31-for-79 (.392). 1999-00, 86-for-237 (.363). 2000-01, 55-for-184 (.299). Totals, 436-for-1276 (.342).

Personal fouls/disqualifications: 1994-95, 234/2. 1995-96, 236/2. 1996-97, 225/5. 1997-98, 164/2. 1998-99, 114/1. 1999-00, 212/3. 2000-01, 191/2. Totals, 1376/17.

NBA PLAYOFF RECORD

Season Team	G	Min.	FGM	FGA	Pct.	FTM	FTA	Pct.	Off.	Def.	Tot.	Ast.	St.	Blk.	TO	Pts.	RPG	APG	PPG
98-99—Milwaukee	3	118	21	51	.412	16	18	.889	4	21	25	5	3	2	10	62	8.3	1.7	20.7
99-00—Milwaukee	5	174	32	79	.405	11	13	.846	0	21	21	13	8	4	15	77	4.2	2.6	15.4
00-01—Milwaukee	18	687	138	322	.429	50	56	.893	26	90	116	60	11	24	46	350	6.4	3.3	19.4
Totals	26	979	191	452	.423	77	87	.885	30	132	162	78	22	30	71	489	6.2	3.0	18.8

Three-point field goals: 1998-99, 4-for-8 (.500). 1999-00, 2-for-7 (.286). 2000-01, 24-for-62 (.387). Totals, 30-for-77 (.390).
Personal fouls/disqualifications: 1998-99, 5/0. 1999-00, 18/0. 2000-01, 43/1. Totals, 66/1.

NBA ALL-STAR GAME RECORD

Season Team	Min.	FGM	FGA	Pct.	FTM	FTA	Pct.	Off.	Def.	Tot.	Ast.	PF	Dq.	St.	Blk.	TO	Pts.
2000 —Milwaukee	17	5	10	.500	0	0	...	2	4	6	0	0	0	0	0	0	10
2001 —Milwaukee	18	4	7	.571	0	0	...	1	3	4	1	0	0	1	1	0	8
Totals	35	9	17	.529	0	0	...	3	7	10	1	0	0	1	1	0	18

ROBINSON, JAMAL   F

PERSONAL: Born December 27, 1973, in San Diego. ... 6-7/195. (2,01/88,5). ... Full Name: Jamal Tyrone Robinson.
HIGH SCHOOL: Monsignor McClancy (N.Y.).
COLLEGE: Virginia.
TRANSACTIONS/CAREER NOTES: Not drafted by an NBA franchise. ... Played in France (1998-99). ... Played in Lebanon (1999-2000). ... Signed as free agent by Miami Heat (September 28, 2000). ... Waived by Heat (November 26, 2000). ... Played in Continental Basketball Association with Sioux Falls Skyforce (2000-01). ... Played in International Basketball League with Sioux Falls Sky Force (2000-01). ... Signed to play for Avellino in Italy for 2001-02 season.

COLLEGIATE RECORD

Season Team	G	Min.	FGM	FGA	Pct.	FTM	FTA	Pct.	Reb.	Ast.	Pts.	RPG	APG	PPG
93-94—Virginia	31	618	85	200	.425	33	46	.717	95	30	221	3.1	1.0	7.1
94-95—Virginia	34	643	66	182	.363	36	43	.837	98	45	184	2.9	1.3	5.4
95-96—Virginia	26	620	77	169	.456	35	57	.614	139	65	191	5.3	2.5	7.3
96-97—Virginia	31	690	73	183	.399	25	58	.431	149	60	171	4.8	1.9	5.5
Totals	122	2571	301	734	.410	129	204	.632	481	200	767	3.9	1.6	6.3

Three-point field goals: 1993-94, 18-for-56 (.321). 1994-95, 16-for-57 (.281). 1995-96, 7-for-29 (.241). 1996-97, 2-for-17 (.118). Totals, 43-for-159 (.270).

CBA REGULAR-SEASON RECORD

Season Team	G	Min.	FGM	FGA	Pct.	FTM	FTA	Pct.	Reb.	Ast.	Pts.	RPG	APG	PPG
00-01—Sioux Falls....................	21	820	144	312	.462	53	79	.671	141	85	367	6.7	4.0	17.5

Three-point field goals: 2000-01, 26-for-71 (.366).

IBL REGULAR-SEASON RECORD

Season Team	G	Min.	FGM	FGA	Pct.	FTM	FTA	Pct.	Reb.	Ast.	Pts.	RPG	APG	PPG
00-01—Sioux Falls....................	27	904	147	340	.432	60	78	.769	113	77	396	4.2	2.9	14.7

Three-point field goals: 2000-01, 42-for-121 (.347).

NBA REGULAR-SEASON RECORD

Season Team	G	Min.	FGM	FGA	Pct.	FTM	FTA	Pct.	Off.	Def.	Tot.	Ast.	St.	Blk.	TO	Pts.	RPG	APG	PPG
00-01—Miami	6	72	3	22	.136	0	0	...	3	8	11	2	6	0	3	6	1.8	0.3	1.0

Three-point field goals: 2000-01, 0-for-2.
Personal fouls/disqualifications: 2000-01, 7/0.

ROBINSON, JAMES   G

PERSONAL: Born August 31, 1970, in Jackson, Miss. ... 6-2/180. (1,88/81,6).
HIGH SCHOOL: Murrah (Jackson, Miss.).
COLLEGE: Alabama.
TRANSACTIONS/CAREER NOTES: Selected after junior season by Portland Trail Blazers in first round (21st pick overall) of 1993 NBA Draft. ... Traded by Trail Blazers with F Bill Curley and 1997 or 1998 first-round draft choice to Minnesota Timberwolves for G Isaiah Rider (July 23, 1996). ... Signed as free agent by Los Angeles Clippers (August 16, 1997). ...

Waived by Clippers (March 18, 1999). ... Signed by Minnesota Timberwolves to first of two consecutive 10-day contracts (March 26, 1999). ... Re-signed by Timberwolves for remainder of season (April 19, 1999). ... Played in Greece (1999-2000). ... Signed as free agent by Seattle SuperSonics (October 2, 2000). ... Waived by SuperSonics (October 7, 2000). ... Signed by Orlando Magic to first of two consecutive 10-day contracts (January 7, 2001).

R

COLLEGIATE RECORD

Season Team	G	Min.	FGM	FGA	Pct.	FTM	FTA	Pct.	Reb.	Ast.	Pts.	RPG	APG	PPG
89-90—Alabama						Did not play—redshirted.								
90-91—Alabama	33	917	194	413	.470	102	146	.699	130	40	554	3.9	1.2	16.8
91-92—Alabama	34	1217	237	533	.445	104	146	.712	138	79	661	4.1	2.3	19.4
92-93—Alabama	29	1000	202	481	.420	116	170	.682	130	68	598	4.5	2.3	20.6
Totals	96	3134	633	1427	.444	322	462	.697	398	187	1813	4.1	1.9	18.9

Three-point field goals: 1990-91, 64-for-153 (.418). 1991-92, 83-for-232 (.358). 1992-93, 78-for-222 (.351). Totals, 225-for-607 (.371).

NBA REGULAR-SEASON RECORD

Season Team	G	Min.	FGM	FGA	Pct.	FTM	FTA	Pct.	Off.	Def.	Tot.	Ast.	St.	Blk.	TO	Pts.	RPG	APG	PPG
93-94—Portland	58	673	104	285	.365	45	67	.672	34	44	78	68	30	15	52	276	1.3	1.2	4.8
94-95—Portland	71	1539	255	624	.409	65	110	.591	42	90	132	180	48	13	127	651	1.9	2.5	9.2
95-96—Portland	76	1627	229	574	.399	89	135	.659	44	113	157	150	34	16	111	649	2.1	2.0	8.5
96-97—Minnesota	69	1309	196	482	.407	78	114	.684	24	88	112	126	30	8	69	572	1.6	1.8	8.3
97-98—L.A. Clippers	70	1231	195	501	.389	77	107	.720	37	74	111	135	37	10	97	541	1.6	1.9	7.7
98-99—L.A.C.-Minn.	31	506	67	185	.362	28	41	.683	18	44	62	56	22	8	44	183	2.0	1.8	5.9
00-01—Orlando	6	50	4	11	.364	0	0	...	0	8	8	0	4	1	4	10	1.3	0.0	1.7
Totals	381	6935	1050	2662	.394	382	574	.666	199	461	660	715	205	71	504	2882	1.7	1.9	7.6

Three-point field goals: 1993-94, 23-for-73 (.315). 1994-95, 76-for-223 (.341). 1995-96, 102-for-284 (.359). 1996-97, 102-for-267 (.382). 1997-98, 74-for-225 (.329). 1998-99, 21-for-74 (.284). 2000-01, 2-for-5 (.400). Totals, 400-for-1151 (.348).

Personal fouls/disqualifications: 1993-94, 69/0. 1994-95, 142/0. 1995-96, 146/0. 1996-97, 125/1. 1997-98, 101/0. 1998-99, 60/0. 2000-01, 5/0. Totals, 648/1.

NBA PLAYOFF RECORD

Season Team	G	Min.	FGM	FGA	Pct.	FTM	FTA	Pct.	Off.	Def.	Tot.	Ast.	St.	Blk.	TO	Pts.	RPG	APG	PPG
93-94—Portland	4	28	4	10	.400	1	2	.500	2	1	3	6	1	1	0	10	0.8	1.5	2.5
94-95—Portland	2	4	2	3	.667	0	0	...	0	0	0	1	0	0	0	6	0.0	0.5	3.0
95-96—Portland	2	26	3	10	.300	0	0	...	0	1	1	3	1	1	3	8	0.5	1.5	4.0
96-97—Minnesota	2	31	5	12	.417	0	0	...	1	2	3	3	2	0	1	14	1.5	1.5	7.0
98-99—Minnesota	4	10	1	4	.250	0	0	...	0	1	1	0	0	0	3	3	0.3	0.0	0.8
Totals	14	99	15	39	.385	1	2	.500	3	5	8	13	4	2	7	41	0.6	0.9	2.9

Three-point field goals: 1993-94, 1-for-2 (.500). 1994-95, 2-for-3 (.667). 1995-96, 2-for-6 (.333). 1996-97, 4-for-10 (.400). 1998-99, 1-for-3 (.333). Totals, 10-for-24 (.417).

Personal fouls/disqualifications: 1993-94, 2/0. 1995-96, 4/0. 1996-97, 4/0. 1998-99, 3/0. Totals, 13/0.

GREEK LEAGUE RECORD

Season Team	G	Min.	FGM	FGA	Pct.	FTM	FTA	Pct.	Reb.	Ast.	Pts.	RPG	APG	PPG
99-00—Olympiakos S.F.P.	26	855	136	287	.474	57	82	.695	69	74	381	2.7	2.8	14.7

Three-point field goals: 1999-00, 52-for-133 (.391).

ROBINSON, LARRY   F/G   HAWKS

PERSONAL: Born January 11, 1968, in Bossier City, La. ... 6-5/180. (1,96/81,6). ... Second cousin of Robert Parish, center with Golden State Warriors (1976-77 through 1979-80), Boston Celtics (1980-81 through 1993-94), Charlotte Hornets (1994-95 and 1995-96) and Chicago Bulls (1996-97).

HIGH SCHOOL: Airline (Bossier City, La.).

COLLEGE: Eastern Oklahoma State, then Centenary (La.).

TRANSACTIONS/CAREER NOTES: Not drafted by an NBA franchise. ... Signed as free agent by Washington Bullets (September 25, 1990). ... Waived by Bullets (December 10, 1990). ... Signed by Golden State Warriors to 10-day contract (January 8, 1991). ... Re-signed by Warriors for remainder of season (January 11, 1991). ... Waived by Warriors (March 19, 1991). ... Signed by Bullets for remainder of season (April 18, 1991). ... Re-signed by Bullets (September 30, 1991). ... Waived by Bullets (October 25, 1991). ... Signed as free agent by Boston Celtics (October 29, 1991). ... Waived by Celtics (November 11, 1991). ... Played in Continental Basketball Association with Rapid City Thrillers (1991-92 through 1993-94), Yakima Sun Kings (1993-94 and 1994-95), Florida Beachdogs (1996-97) and Rockford Lightning (1997-98 and 1998-99). ... Played in World Basketball League with Hamilton Skyhawks (1992). ... Played in France (1992-93). ... Signed by Bullets to 10-day contract (March 8, 1993). ... Signed by Houston Rockets to first of two consecutive 10-day contracts (April 1, 1994). ... Re-signed by Rockets for remainder of season (April 21, 1994). ... Waived by Rockets (October 31, 1994). ... Played in Spain (1995-96). ... Signed by Vancouver Grizzlies to first of two consecutive 10-day contracts (March 27, 1998). ... Re-signed by Grizzlies for remainder of season (April 16, 1998). ... Played in Venezuela (1999-2000). ... Played in International Basketball League with Richmond Rhythm (1999-2000) and Trenton Stars (2000-01). ... Signed as free agent by Atlanta Hawks (October 3, 2000). ... Traded by Hawks with G Jim Jackson and G Anthony Johnson to Cleveland Cavaliers for G Brevin Knight (January 2, 2001). ... Waived by Cavaliers (January 5, 2001). ... Signed by Hawks to 10-day contract (February 15, 2001).

COLLEGIATE RECORD

Season Team	G	Min.	FGM	FGA	Pct.	FTM	FTA	Pct.	Reb.	Ast.	Pts.	RPG	APG	PPG
86-87—Eastern Oklahoma State						Statistics unavailable.								
87-88—Eastern Oklahoma State						Statistics unavailable.								
88-89—Centenary	30	1038	228	461	.495	87	124	.702	202	61	558	6.7	2.0	18.6
89-90—Centenary	30	1042	280	521	.537	117	168	.696	212	91	689	7.1	3.0	23.0
4-Year-College Totals	60	2080	508	982	.517	204	292	.699	414	152	1247	6.9	2.5	20.8

Three-point field goals: 1988-89, 15-for-48 (.313). 1989-90, 12-for-40 (.300). Totals, 27-for-88 (.307).

NBA REGULAR-SEASON RECORD

								REBOUNDS							AVERAGES		
Season Team	G	Min.	FGM	FGA	Pct.	FTM	FTA	Pct.	Off.	Def.	Tot.	Ast.	St.	Blk.	TO	Pts.	RPG	APG	PPG
90-91—G.S.-Wash.	36	425	62	150	.413	15	27	.556	29	22	51	35	16	1	27	139	1.4	1.0	3.9
91-92—Boston	1	6	1	5	.200	0	0	....	2	0	2	1	0	0	1	2	2.0	1.0	2.0
92-93—Washington	4	33	6	16	.375	3	5	.600	1	2	3	3	1	1	1	15	0.8	0.8	3.8
93-94—Houston.........	6	55	10	20	.500	3	8	.375	4	6	10	6	7	0	10	25	1.7	1.0	4.2
97-98—Vancouver......	6	41	6	19	.316	2	2	1.000	2	10	12	1	4	0	2	17	2.0	0.2	2.8
00-01—Clev.-Atla.	34	632	67	184	.364	21	24	.875	23	64	87	36	28	2	25	199	2.6	1.1	5.9
Totals	87	1192	152	394	.386	44	66	.667	61	104	165	82	56	4	66	397	1.9	0.9	4.6

Three-point field goals: 1990-91, 0-for-1. 1992-93, 0-for-1. 1993-94, 2-for-8 (.250). 1997-98, 3-for-6 (.500). 2000-01, 44-for-116 (.379). Totals, 49-for-132 (.371).

Personal fouls/disqualifications: 1990-91, 49/0. 1991-92, 3/0. 1993-94, 8/0. 2000-01, 46/0. Totals, 106/0.

CBA REGULAR-SEASON RECORD

NOTES: Member of CBA championship team (1995).

												AVERAGES		
Season Team	G	Min.	FGM	FGA	Pct.	FTM	FTA	Pct.	Reb.	Ast.	Pts.	RPG	APG	PPG
91-92—Rapid City......................	52	1372	291	608	.479	75	117	.641	209	102	709	4.0	2.0	13.6
92-93—Rapid City......................	43	1340	285	602	.473	84	122	.689	155	96	715	3.6	2.2	16.6
93-94—Rapid City-Yakima.........	47	1645	329	723	.455	109	163	.669	184	129	818	3.9	2.7	17.4
94-95—Yakima	55	1868	372	811	.459	170	235	.723	217	183	1006	3.9	3.3	18.3
96-97—Florida	48	937	144	362	.398	55	90	.611	89	68	396	1.9	1.4	8.3
97-98—Rockford	28	1126	214	499	.429	66	89	.742	131	95	575	4.7	3.4	20.5
98-99—Rockford	27	983	141	345	.409	42	54	.778	98	66	396	3.6	2.4	14.7
Totals	300	9271	1776	3950	.450	601	870	.691	1083	739	4615	3.6	2.5	15.4

Three-point field goals: 1991-92, 52-for-115 (.452). 1992-93, 61-for-161 (.379). 1993-94, 51-for-151 (.338). 1994-95, 92-for-236 (.390). 1996-97, 53-for-145 (.366). 1997-98, 81-for-202 (.401). 1998-99, 72-for-189 (.381). Totals, 462-for-1199 (.385).

FRENCH LEAGUE RECORD

												AVERAGES		
Season Team	G	Min.	FGM	FGA	Pct.	FTM	FTA	Pct.	Reb.	Ast.	Pts.	RPG	APG	PPG
92-93—Levallois	12	426	95	202	.470	31	49	.633	52	18	248	4.3	1.5	20.7

Three-point field goals: 1992-93, 27-for-69 (.391).

SPANISH LEAGUE RECORD

												AVERAGES		
Season Team	G	Min.	FGM	FGA	Pct.	FTM	FTA	Pct.	Reb.	Ast.	Pts.	RPG	APG	PPG
95-96—Valvi Girona..................	26	907	166	357	.465	77	114	.675	89	37	441	3.4	1.4	17.0

Three-point field goals: 1995-96, 32-for-110 (.291).

IBL REGULAR SEASON RECORD

												AVERAGES		
Season Team	G	Min.	FGM	FGA	Pct.	FTM	FTA	Pct.	Reb.	Ast.	Pts.	RPG	APG	PPG
99-00—Richmond......................	38	811	117	273	.429	49	56	.875	87	67	337	2.3	1.8	8.9
00-01—Trenton	1	18	3	8	.375	1	2	.500	3	1	7	3.0	1.0	7.0
Totals	39	829	120	281	.427	50	58	.862	90	68	344	2.3	1.7	8.8

Three-point field goals: 1999-00, 54-for-140 (.386).

VENEZUELAN LEAGUE RECORD

												AVERAGES		
Season Team	G	Min.	FGM	FGA	Pct.	FTM	FTA	Pct.	Reb.	Ast.	Pts.	RPG	APG	PPG
99-00—Miranda	10	283	56	101	.554	10	17	.588	35	45	148	3.5	4.5	14.8

Three-point field goals: 1999-00, 26-for-47 (.553).

ROGERS, CARLOS   F/C

PERSONAL: Born February 6, 1971, in Detroit. ... 6-10/232. (2,08/105,2). ... Full Name: Carlos Deon Rogers.
HIGH SCHOOL: Northwestern (Detroit).
COLLEGE: Arkansas-Little Rock, then Tennessee State.
TRANSACTIONS/CAREER NOTES: Selected by Seattle SuperSonics in first round (11th pick overall) of 1994 NBA Draft. ... Draft rights traded by SuperSonics with G Ricky Pierce and two 1995 second-round draft choices to Golden State Warriors for G Sarunas Marciulionis and F Byron Houston (July 10, 1994). ... Traded by Warriors with C Victor Alexander and draft rights to F Dwayne Whitfield, G/F Martin Lewis and C Michael McDonald to Toronto Raptors for G B.J. Armstrong (September 18, 1995). ... Traded by Raptors with G Damon Stoudamire and F Walt Williams to Portland Trail Blazers for G Kenny Anderson, G Alvin Williams, F Gary Trent and two first-round draft choices (February 13, 1998). ... Traded by Trail Blazers with C Kelvin Cato, F Stacy Augmon, G/F Walt Williams, G Brian Shaw and G Ed Gray to Houston Rockets for F Scottie Pippen (October 2, 1999).

COLLEGIATE RECORD

											AVERAGES		
Season Team	G	Min.	FGM	FGA	Pct.	FTM	FTA	Pct.	Reb.	Ast.	Pts.	RPG	APG	PPG
89-90—Arkansas-Little Rock					Did not play—ineligible.									
90-91—Arkansas-Little Rock	19	393	64	126	.508	31	56	.554	132	22	159	6.9	1.2	8.4
91-92—Tennessee State					Did not play—transfer student.									
92-93—Tennessee State	29	918	239	385	.621	111	178	.624	339	30	589	11.7	1.0	20.3
93-94—Tennessee State	31	1052	288	469	.614	179	276	.649	358	47	759	11.5	1.5	24.5
Totals	79	2363	591	980	.603	321	510	.629	829	99	1507	10.5	1.3	19.1

Three-point field goals: 1992-93, 0-for-3. 1993-94, 4-for-13 (.308). Totals, 4-for-16 (.250).

NBA REGULAR-SEASON RECORD

								REBOUNDS								AVERAGES		
Season Team	G	Min.	FGM	FGA	Pct.	FTM	FTA	Pct.	Off.	Def.	Tot.	Ast.	St.	Blk.	TO	Pts.	RPG	APG	PPG
94-95—Golden State...	49	1017	180	340	.529	76	146	.521	108	170	278	37	22	52	84	438	5.7	0.8	8.9
95-96—Toronto	56	1043	178	344	.517	71	130	.546	80	90	170	35	25	48	61	430	3.0	0.6	7.7
96-97—Toronto	56	1397	212	404	.525	102	170	.600	120	184	304	37	42	69	53	551	5.4	0.7	9.8
97-98—Tor.-Port.	21	376	47	91	.516	18	32	.563	35	32	67	18	10	8	14	112	3.2	0.9	5.3
98-99—Portland	2	8	2	2	1.000	1	4	.250	0	1	1	1	0	0	0	5	0.5	0.5	2.5
99-00—Houston	53	1101	170	324	.525	81	137	.591	98	177	275	42	14	34	63	422	5.2	0.8	8.0
00-01—Houston	39	544	75	110	.682	29	52	.558	48	91	139	9	10	18	17	179	3.6	0.2	4.6
Totals	276	5486	864	1615	.535	378	671	.563	489	745	1234	179	123	229	292	2137	4.5	0.6	7.7

Three-point field goals: 1994-95, 2-for-14 (.143). 1995-96, 3-for-21 (.143). 1996-97, 25-for-66 (.379). 1997-98, 0-for-2. 1999-00, 1-for-14 (.071). 2000-01, 0-for-1. Totals, 31-for-118 (.263).

Personal fouls/disqualifications: 1994-95, 124/2. 1995-96, 87/0. 1996-97, 140/1. 1997-98, 35/0. 1998-99, 2/0. 1999-00, 77/0. 2000-01, 33/0. Totals, 498/3.

ROGERS, RODNEY   F   SUNS

PERSONAL: Born June 20, 1971, in Durham, N.C. ... 6-7/255. (2,01/115,7). ... Full Name: Rodney Ray Rogers Jr.
HIGH SCHOOL: Hillside (Durham, N.C.).
COLLEGE: Wake Forest.
TRANSACTIONS/CAREER NOTES: Selected after junior season by Denver Nuggets in first round (ninth pick overall) of 1993 NBA Draft. ... Traded by Nuggets with draft rights to G Brent Barry to Los Angeles Clippers for G Randy Woods and draft rights to F Antonio McDyess (June 28, 1995). ... Signed as free agent by Phoenix Suns (August 3, 1999).

COLLEGIATE RECORD

NOTES: The Sporting News All-America second team (1993).

												AVERAGES		
Season Team	G	Min.	FGM	FGA	Pct.	FTM	FTA	Pct.	Reb.	Ast.	Pts.	RPG	APG	PPG
90-91—Wake Forest	30	895	199	349	.570	81	121	.669	237	46	489	7.9	1.5	16.3
91-92—Wake Forest	29	945	245	399	.614	86	126	.683	247	81	595	8.5	2.8	20.5
92-93—Wake Forest	30	981	239	431	.555	134	187	.717	221	68	636	7.4	2.3	21.2
Totals	89	2821	683	1179	.579	301	434	.694	705	195	1720	7.9	2.2	19.3

Three-point field goals: 1990-91, 10-for-35 (.286). 1991-92, 19-for-50 (.380). 1992-93, 24-for-67 (.358). Totals, 53-for-152 (.349).

NBA REGULAR-SEASON RECORD

HONORS: NBA Sixth Man Award (2000).

								REBOUNDS								AVERAGES		
Season Team	G	Min.	FGM	FGA	Pct.	FTM	FTA	Pct.	Off.	Def.	Tot.	Ast.	St.	Blk.	TO	Pts.	RPG	APG	PPG
93-94—Denver	79	1406	239	545	.439	127	189	.672	90	136	226	101	63	48	131	640	2.9	1.3	8.1
94-95—Denver	80	2142	375	769	.488	179	275	.651	132	253	385	161	95	46	173	979	4.8	2.0	12.2
95-96—L.A. Clippers	67	1950	306	641	.477	113	180	.628	113	173	286	167	75	35	144	774	4.3	2.5	11.6
96-97—L.A. Clippers	81	2480	408	884	.462	191	288	.663	137	274	411	222	88	61	221	1072	5.1	2.7	13.2
97-98—L.A. Clippers	76	2499	426	935	.456	225	328	.686	155	269	424	202	93	38	193	1149	5.6	2.7	15.1
98-99—L.A. Clippers	47	968	131	297	.441	68	101	.673	65	114	179	77	47	22	66	348	3.8	1.6	7.4
99-00—Phoenix	82	2286	428	881	.486	159	249	.639	138	309	447	170	94	47	163	1130	5.5	2.1	13.8
00-01—Phoenix	82	2183	377	876	.430	188	247	.761	94	265	359	180	97	47	157	998	4.4	2.2	12.2
Totals	594	15914	2690	5828	.462	1250	1857	.673	924	1793	2717	1280	652	344	1248	7090	4.6	2.2	11.9

Three-point field goals: 1993-94, 35-for-92 (.380). 1994-95, 50-for-148 (.338). 1995-96, 49-for-153 (.320). 1996-97, 65-for-180 (.361). 1997-98, 72-for-212 (.340). 1998-99, 18-for-63 (.286). 1999-00, 115-for-262 (.439). 2000-01, 56-for-189 (.296). Totals, 460-for-1299 (.354).

Personal fouls/disqualifications: 1993-94, 195/3. 1994-95, 281/7. 1995-96, 216/2. 1996-97, 272/5. 1997-98, 242/5. 1998-99, 140/2. 1999-00, 290/5. 2000-01, 269/5. Totals, 1905/34.

NBA PLAYOFF RECORD

								REBOUNDS								AVERAGES		
Season Team	G	Min.	FGM	FGA	Pct.	FTM	FTA	Pct.	Off.	Def.	Tot.	Ast.	St.	Blk.	TO	Pts.	RPG	APG	PPG
93-94—Denver	12	190	19	49	.388	17	27	.630	8	13	21	16	7	6	8	61	1.8	1.3	5.1
94-95—Denver	3	76	12	22	.545	1	4	.250	1	11	12	5	3	4	5	26	4.0	1.7	8.7
96-97—L.A. Clippers	3	85	12	29	.414	6	8	.750	3	4	7	6	4	3	7	32	2.3	2.0	10.7
99-00—Phoenix	9	263	48	115	.417	23	31	.742	16	45	61	14	10	10	15	127	6.8	1.6	14.1
00-01—Phoenix	4	82	12	40	.300	9	14	.643	3	11	14	2	2	3	5	35	3.5	0.5	8.8
Totals	31	696	103	255	.404	56	84	.667	31	84	115	43	26	26	40	281	3.7	1.4	9.1

Three-point field goals: 1993-94, 6-for-19 (.316). 1994-95, 1-for-4 (.250). 1996-97, 2-for-10 (.200). 1999-00, 8-for-36 (.222). 2000-01, 2-for-10 (.200). Totals, 19-for-79 (.241).

Personal fouls/disqualifications: 1993-94, 25/0. 1994-95, 13/1. 1996-97, 13/0. 1999-00, 31/1. 2000-01, 16/0. Totals, 98/2.

ROOKS, SEAN   C   CLIPPERS

PERSONAL: Born September 9, 1969, in New York. ... 6-10/260. (2,08/117,9). ... Full Name: Sean Lester Rooks.
HIGH SCHOOL: Fontana (Calif.).
COLLEGE: Arizona.
TRANSACTIONS/CAREER NOTES: Selected by Dallas Mavericks in second round (30th pick overall) of 1992 NBA Draft. ... Traded by Mavericks to Minnesota Timberwolves for conditional 1996 first-round draft choice (November 1, 1994). ... Traded by Timberwolves with F Christian Laettner to Atlanta Hawks for G Spud Webb and C Andrew Lang (February 22, 1996). ... Signed as free agent by Los Angeles Lakers (July 16, 1996). ... Traded by Lakers with 2000 second-round draft choice to Mavericks for F A.C. Green (September 1, 1999). ... Traded by Mavericks to Los Angeles Clippers for G Eric Murdock (June 28, 2000).

COLLEGIATE RECORD

												AVERAGES		
Season Team	G	Min.	FGM	FGA	Pct.	FTM	FTA	Pct.	Reb.	Ast.	Pts.	RPG	APG	PPG
87-88—Arizona						Did not play—redshirted.								
88-89—Arizona	32	362	70	117	.598	40	65	.615	88	18	180	2.8	0.6	5.6
89-90—Arizona	31	684	140	263	.532	114	161	.708	151	31	394	4.9	1.0	12.7
90-91—Arizona	35	800	159	283	.562	98	149	.658	198	43	418	5.7	1.2	11.9
91-92—Arizona	31	878	181	323	.560	140	215	.651	214	54	505	6.9	1.7	16.3
Totals	129	2724	550	986	.558	392	590	.664	651	146	1497	5.0	1.1	11.6

Three-point field goals: 1990-91, 2-for-4 (.500). 1991-92, 3-for-5 (.600). Totals, 5-for-9 (.556).

NBA REGULAR-SEASON RECORD

									REBOUNDS									AVERAGES		
Season Team	G	Min.	FGM	FGA	Pct.	FTM	FTA	Pct.	Off.	Def.	Tot.	Ast.	St.	Blk.	TO	Pts.	RPG	APG	PPG
92-93—Dallas	72	2087	368	747	.493	234	389	.602	196	340	536	95	38	81	160	970	7.4	1.3	13.5
93-94—Dallas	47	1255	193	393	.491	150	210	.714	84	175	259	49	21	44	80	536	5.5	1.0	11.4
94-95—Minnesota	80	2405	289	615	.470	290	381	.761	165	321	486	97	29	71	142	868	6.1	1.2	10.9
95-96—Minn.-Atl.	65	1117	144	285	.505	135	202	.668	81	174	255	47	23	42	80	424	3.9	0.7	6.5
96-97—L.A. Lakers	69	735	87	185	.470	91	130	.700	56	107	163	42	17	38	51	265	2.4	0.6	3.8
97-98—L.A. Lakers	41	425	46	101	.455	47	79	.595	46	72	118	24	2	23	19	139	2.9	0.6	3.4
98-99—L.A. Lakers	36	315	32	79	.405	34	48	.708	33	39	72	9	2	9	21	98	2.0	0.3	2.7
99-00—Dallas	71	1001	122	283	.431	65	89	.730	82	166	248	68	29	52	70	309	3.5	1.0	4.4
00-01—L.A. Clippers	82	1553	169	395	.428	107	143	.748	91	212	303	77	34	64	73	446	3.7	0.9	5.4
Totals	563	10893	1450	3083	.470	1153	1671	.690	834	1606	2440	508	195	424	696	4055	4.3	0.9	7.2

Three-point field goals: 1992-93, 0-for-2. 1993-94, 0-for-1. 1994-95, 0-for-5. 1995-96, 1-for-7 (.143). 1996-97, 0-for-1. 1998-99, 0-for-2. 2000-01, 1-for-2 (.500). Totals, 2-for-20 (.100).

Personal fouls/disqualifications: 1992-93, 204/2. 1993-94, 109/0. 1994-95, 208/1. 1995-96, 141/0. 1996-97, 123/1. 1997-98, 68/0. 1998-99, 61/0. 1999-00, 169/0. 2000-01, 197/2. Totals, 1280/6.

NBA PLAYOFF RECORD

									REBOUNDS									AVERAGES		
Season Team	G	Min.	FGM	FGA	Pct.	FTM	FTA	Pct.	Off.	Def.	Tot.	Ast.	St.	Blk.	TO	Pts.	RPG	APG	PPG
95-96—Atlanta	10	140	16	28	.571	13	21	.619	13	14	27	7	4	4	9	45	2.7	0.7	4.5
96-97—L.A. Lakers	8	54	4	9	.444	6	8	.750	5	7	12	1	3	3	3	14	1.5	0.1	1.8
97-98—L.A. Lakers	4	11	2	6	.333	0	0		1	0	1	0	0	3	0	4	0.3	0.0	1.0
98-99—L.A. Lakers	7	48	2	6	.333	5	6	.833	1	1	2	3	0	1	1	9	0.3	0.4	1.3
Totals	29	253	24	49	.490	24	35	.686	20	22	42	11	7	11	13	72	1.4	0.4	2.5

Personal fouls/disqualifications: 1995-96, 35/0. 1996-97, 10/0. 1997-98, 2/0. 1998-99, 13/0. Totals, 60/0.

ROSE, JALEN   G   PACERS

PERSONAL: Born January 30, 1973, in Detroit. ... 6-8/210. (2,03/95,3). ... Son of Jimmy Walker, guard with Detroit Pistons (1967-68 through 1971-72), Houston Rockets (1972-73 and 1973-74), Kansas City/Omaha Kings (1973-74 and 1974-75) and Kansas City Kings (1975-76). ... Name pronounced JAY-lin.

HIGH SCHOOL: Southwestern (Detroit).

COLLEGE: Michigan.

TRANSACTIONS/CAREER NOTES: Selected after junior season by Denver Nuggets in first round (13th pick overall) of 1994 NBA Draft. ... Traded by Nuggets with F Reggie Williams and 1996 first-round draft choice to Indiana Pacers for G Mark Jackson, G Ricky Pierce and 1996 first-round draft choice (June 13, 1996).

COLLEGIATE RECORD

NOTES: THE SPORTING NEWS All-America first team (1994).

												AVERAGES		
Season Team	G	Min.	FGM	FGA	Pct.	FTM	FTA	Pct.	Reb.	Ast.	Pts.	RPG	APG	PPG
91-92—Michigan	34	1126	206	424	.486	149	197	.756	146	135	597	4.3	4.0	17.6
92-93—Michigan	36	1232	203	455	.446	116	161	.720	150	140	555	4.2	3.9	15.4
93-94—Michigan	32	1152	220	477	.461	141	192	.734	181	126	636	5.7	3.9	19.9
Totals	102	3510	629	1356	.464	406	550	.738	477	401	1788	4.7	3.9	17.5

Three-point field goals: 1991-92, 36-for-111 (.324). 1992-93, 33-for-103 (.320). 1993-94, 55-for-155 (.355). Totals, 124-for-369 (.336).

NBA REGULAR-SEASON RECORD

HONORS: NBA Most Improved Player (2000). ... NBA All-Rookie second team (1995).

									REBOUNDS									AVERAGES		
Season Team	G	Min.	FGM	FGA	Pct.	FTM	FTA	Pct.	Off.	Def.	Tot.	Ast.	St.	Blk.	TO	Pts.	RPG	APG	PPG
94-95—Denver	81	1798	227	500	.454	173	234	.739	57	160	217	389	65	22	160	663	2.7	4.8	8.2
95-96—Denver	80	2134	290	604	.480	191	277	.690	46	214	260	495	53	39	234	803	3.3	6.2	10.0
96-97—Indiana	66	1188	172	377	.456	117	156	.750	27	94	121	155	57	18	107	482	1.8	2.3	7.3
97-98—Indiana	82	1706	290	607	.478	166	228	.728	28	167	195	155	56	14	132	771	2.4	1.9	9.4
98-99—Indiana	49	1238	200	496	.403	125	158	.791	34	120	154	93	50	15	72	542	3.1	1.9	11.1
99-00—Indiana	80	2978	563	1196	.471	254	307	.827	42	345	387	320	84	49	188	1457	4.8	4.0	18.2
00-01—Indiana	72	2943	567	1242	.457	285	344	.828	37	322	359	435	65	43	211	1478	5.0	6.0	20.5
Totals	510	13985	2309	5022	.460	1311	1704	.769	271	1422	1693	2042	430	200	1104	6196	3.3	4.0	12.1

Three-point field goals: 1994-95, 36-for-114 (.316). 1995-96, 32-for-108 (.296). 1996-97, 21-for-72 (.292). 1997-98, 25-for-73 (.342). 1998-99, 17-for-65 (.262). 1999-00, 77-for-196 (.393). 2000-01, 59-for-174 (.339). Totals, 267-for-802 (.333).

Personal fouls/disqualifications: 1994-95, 206/0. 1995-96, 229/3. 1996-97, 136/1. 1997-98, 171/0. 1998-99, 128/0. 1999-00, 234/1. 2000-01, 230/2. Totals, 1334/7.

R

NBA PLAYOFF RECORD

Season Team	G	Min.	FGM	FGA	Pct.	FTM	FTA	Pct.	Off.	Def.	Tot.	Ast.	St.	Blk.	TO	Pts.	RPG	APG	PPG
94-95—Denver	3	99	13	28	.464	3	5	.600	4	7	11	18	3	2	9	30	3.7	6.0	10.0
97-98—Indiana	15	293	48	100	.480	20	27	.741	1	26	27	28	11	6	25	122	1.8	1.9	8.1
98-99—Indiana	13	355	61	138	.442	28	34	.824	11	20	31	32	13	5	25	158	2.4	2.5	12.2
99-00—Indiana	23	964	171	391	.437	107	133	.805	10	91	101	78	16	11	50	479	4.4	3.4	20.8
00-01—Indiana	4	164	30	79	.380	7	7	1.000	3	15	18	11	6	1	9	72	4.5	2.8	18.0
Totals	58	1875	323	736	.439	165	206	.801	29	159	188	167	49	25	118	861	3.2	2.9	14.8

Three-point field goals: 1994-95, 1-for-4 (.250). 1997-98, 6-for-16 (.375). 1998-99, 8-for-23 (.348). 1999-00, 30-for-70 (.429). 2000-01, 5-for-16 (.313). Totals, 50-for-129 (.388).

Personal fouls/disqualifications: 1994-95, 9/0. 1997-98, 37/0. 1998-99, 39/0. 1999-00, 71/0. 2000-01, 18/0. Totals, 174/0.

ROSE, MALIK   F   SPURS

PERSONAL: Born November 23, 1974, in Philadelphia. ... 6-7/255. (2,01/115,7). ... Full Name: Malik Jabari Rose. ... Name pronounced Ma-leek.
HIGH SCHOOL: Overbrook (Philadelphia).
COLLEGE: Drexel.
TRANSACTIONS/CAREER NOTES: Selected by Charlotte Hornets in second round (44th pick overall) of 1996 NBA Draft. ... Signed as free agent by San Antonio Spurs (September 29, 1997).
MISCELLANEOUS: Member of NBA championship team (1999).

COLLEGIATE RECORD

Season Team	G	Min.	FGM	FGA	Pct.	FTM	FTA	Pct.	Reb.	Ast.	Pts.	RPG	APG	PPG
92-93—Drexel	29	820	144	287	.502	107	190	.563	330	10	395	11.4	0.3	13.6
93-94—Drexel	30	875	154	296	.520	110	202	.545	371	20	418	12.4	0.7	13.9
94-95—Drexel	30	984	216	384	.563	152	213	.714	404	36	584	13.5	1.2	19.5
95-96—Drexel	31	972	219	368	.595	182	255	.714	409	53	627	13.2	1.7	20.2
Totals	120	3651	733	1335	.549	551	860	.641	1514	119	2024	12.6	1.0	16.9

Three-point field goals: 1994-95, 0-for-3. 1995-96, 7-for-21 (.333). Totals, 7-for-24 (.292).

NBA REGULAR-SEASON RECORD

Season Team	G	Min.	FGM	FGA	Pct.	FTM	FTA	Pct.	Off.	Def.	Tot.	Ast.	St.	Blk.	TO	Pts.	RPG	APG	PPG
96-97—Charlotte	54	525	61	128	.477	38	62	.613	70	94	164	32	28	17	41	160	3.0	0.6	3.0
97-98—San Antonio	53	429	59	136	.434	39	61	.639	40	50	90	19	21	7	44	158	1.7	0.4	3.0
98-99—San Antonio	47	608	93	201	.463	98	146	.671	90	92	182	29	40	22	56	284	3.9	0.6	6.0
99-00—San Antonio	74	1341	176	385	.457	143	198	.722	133	202	335	47	35	52	99	496	4.5	0.6	6.7
00-01—San Antonio	57	1219	160	368	.435	114	160	.713	95	213	308	48	59	40	74	437	5.4	0.8	7.7
Totals	285	4122	549	1218	.451	432	627	.689	428	651	1079	175	183	138	314	1535	3.8	0.6	5.4

Three-point field goals: 1996-97, 0-for-2. 1997-98, 1-for-3 (.333). 1998-99, 0-for-1. 1999-00, 1-for-3 (.333). 2000-01, 3-for-17 (.176). Totals, 5-for-26 (.192).

Personal fouls/disqualifications: 1996-97, 114/3. 1997-98, 79/1. 1998-99, 120/0. 1999-00, 232/2. 2000-01, 148/1. Totals, 693/7.

NBA PLAYOFF RECORD

Season Team	G	Min.	FGM	FGA	Pct.	FTM	FTA	Pct.	Off.	Def.	Tot.	Ast.	St.	Blk.	TO	Pts.	RPG	APG	PPG
96-97—Charlotte	2	12	2	4	.500	0	0		4	1	5	1	0	0	2	4	2.5	0.5	2.0
97-98—San Antonio	5	18	4	6	.667	2	4	.500	3	4	7	1	1	0	4	10	1.4	0.2	2.0
98-99—San Antonio	17	194	14	38	.368	18	26	.692	17	22	39	3	7	4	10	46	2.3	0.2	2.7
99-00—San Antonio	4	83	8	18	.444	5	9	.556	5	14	19	1	2	3	7	21	4.8	0.3	5.3
00-01—San Antonio	13	215	23	55	.418	17	20	.850	16	33	49	4	3	1	10	64	3.8	0.3	4.9
Totals	41	522	51	121	.421	42	59	.712	45	74	119	10	13	8	33	145	2.9	0.2	3.5

Three-point field goals: 2000-01, 1-for-3 (.333). Totals, 1-for-3 (.333).
Personal fouls/disqualifications: 1996-97, 2/0. 1997-98, 2/0. 1998-99, 52/0. 1999-00, 12/0. 2000-01, 38/0. Totals, 106/0.

RUFFIN, MICHAEL   F   BULLS

PERSONAL: Born January 21, 1977, in Denver. ... 6-8/248. (2,03/112,5). ... Full Name: Michael David Ruffin.
HIGH SCHOOL: Cherry Creek (Englewood, Colo.).
COLLEGE: Tulsa.
TRANSACTIONS/CAREER NOTES: Selected by Chicago Bulls in second round (32nd overall) of 1999 NBA Draft.

COLLEGIATE RECORD

Season Team	G	Min.	FGM	FGA	Pct.	FTM	FTA	Pct.	Reb.	Ast.	Pts.	RPG	APG	PPG
95-96—Tulsa	30	689	78	146	.534	57	123	.463	232	22	213	7.7	0.7	7.1
96-97—Tulsa	34	965	98	174	.563	95	150	.633	341	37	291	10.0	1.1	8.6
97-98—Tulsa	31	1030	109	217	.502	104	154	.675	296	46	322	9.5	1.5	10.4
98-99—Tulsa	33	1063	117	222	.527	149	247	.603	342	45	383	10.4	1.4	11.6
Totals	128	3747	402	759	.530	405	674	.601	1211	150	1209	9.5	1.2	9.4

Three-point field goals: 1995-96, 0-for-1. 1996-97, 0-for-1. 1997-98, 0-for-4. 1998-99, 0-for-4. Totals, 0-for-10 (.000).

NBA REGULAR-SEASON RECORD

Season Team	G	Min.	FGM	FGA	Pct.	FTM	FTA	Pct.	Off.	Def.	Tot.	Ast.	St.	Blk.	TO	Pts.	RPG	APG	PPG
99-00—Chicago	71	975	58	138	.420	43	88	.489	117	133	250	44	26	26	59	159	3.5	0.6	2.2
00-01—Chicago	45	879	40	90	.444	39	77	.506	101	161	262	39	30	38	46	119	5.8	0.9	2.6
Totals	116	1854	98	228	.430	82	165	.497	218	294	512	83	56	64	105	278	4.4	0.7	2.4

Personal fouls/disqualifications: 1999-00, 170/1. 2000-01, 131/2. Totals, 301/3.

RUSSELL, BRYON   F   JAZZ

PERSONAL: Born December 31, 1970, in San Bernardino, Calif. ... 6-7/225. (2,01/102,1). ... Full Name: Bryon Demetrise Russell.
HIGH SCHOOL: San Bernardino (Calif.).
COLLEGE: Long Beach State.
TRANSACTIONS/CAREER NOTES: Selected by Utah Jazz in second round (45th pick overall) of 1993 NBA Draft.

COLLEGIATE RECORD

Season Team	G	Min.	FGM	FGA	Pct.	FTM	FTA	Pct.	Reb.	Ast.	Pts.	RPG	APG	PPG
89-90—Long Beach State						Did not play—ineligible.								
90-91—Long Beach State	28	552	83	193	.430	45	69	.652	162	41	220	5.8	1.5	7.9
91-92—Long Beach State	26	776	126	227	.555	99	151	.656	192	30	362	7.4	1.2	13.9
92-93—Long Beach State	32	1006	153	285	.537	104	143	.727	213	66	421	6.7	2.1	13.2
Totals	86	2334	362	705	.513	248	363	.683	567	137	1003	6.6	1.6	11.7

Three-point field goals: 1990-91, 9-for-28 (.321). 1991-92, 11-for-28 (.393). 1992-93, 11-for-34 (.324). Totals, 31-for-90 (.344).

NBA REGULAR-SEASON RECORD

Season Team	G	Min.	FGM	FGA	Pct.	FTM	FTA	Pct.	Off.	Def.	Tot.	Ast.	St.	Blk.	TO	Pts.	RPG	APG	PPG
93-94—Utah	67	1121	135	279	.484	62	101	.614	61	120	181	54	68	19	55	334	2.7	0.8	5.0
94-95—Utah	63	860	104	238	.437	62	93	.667	44	97	141	34	48	11	42	283	2.2	0.5	4.5
95-96—Utah	59	577	56	142	.394	48	67	.716	28	62	90	29	29	8	36	174	1.5	0.5	2.9
96-97—Utah	81	2525	297	620	.479	171	244	.701	79	252	331	123	129	27	94	873	4.1	1.5	10.8
97-98—Utah	82	2219	226	525	.430	213	278	.766	78	248	326	101	90	31	81	738	4.0	1.2	9.0
98-99—Utah	50	1770	217	468	.464	136	171	.795	65	201	266	74	76	15	76	622	5.3	1.5	12.4
99-00—Utah	82	2900	408	914	.446	237	316	.750	99	328	427	158	128	23	101	1159	5.2	1.9	14.1
00-01—Utah	78	2473	308	700	.440	222	285	.779	94	236	330	160	96	20	113	933	4.2	2.1	12.0
Totals	562	14445	1751	3886	.451	1151	1555	.740	548	1544	2092	733	664	154	598	5116	3.7	1.3	9.1

Three-point field goals: 1993-94, 2-for-22 (.091). 1994-95, 13-for-44 (.295). 1995-96, 14-for-40 (.350). 1996-97, 108-for-264 (.409). 1997-98, 73-for-214 (.341). 1998-99, 52-for-147 (.354). 1999-00, 106-for-268 (.396). 2000-01, 95-for-230 (.413). Totals, 463-for-1229 (.377).

Personal fouls/disqualifications: 1993-94, 138/0. 1994-95, 101/0. 1995-96, 66/0. 1996-97, 237/2. 1997-98, 229/2. 1998-99, 154/3. 1999-00, 255/3. 2000-01, 229/1. Totals, 1409/11.

NBA PLAYOFF RECORD

Season Team	G	Min.	FGM	FGA	Pct.	FTM	FTA	Pct.	Off.	Def.	Tot.	Ast.	St.	Blk.	TO	Pts.	RPG	APG	PPG
93-94—Utah	6	36	4	10	.400	6	6	1.000	4	5	9	3	0	0	1	16	1.5	0.5	2.7
94-95—Utah	2	13	4	7	.571	1	2	.500	1	1	2	3	1	0	0	11	1.0	1.5	5.5
95-96—Utah	18	459	58	124	.468	31	38	.816	17	58	75	22	23	9	10	172	4.2	1.2	9.6
96-97—Utah	20	758	89	193	.461	31	43	.721	18	74	92	27	21	6	20	245	4.6	1.4	12.3
97-98—Utah	20	698	69	147	.469	58	81	.716	12	81	93	22	21	5	17	219	4.7	1.1	11.0
98-99—Utah	11	387	49	115	.426	26	36	.722	17	50	67	13	20	2	11	133	6.1	1.2	12.1
99-00—Utah	10	371	48	114	.421	31	41	.756	9	43	52	21	16	5	15	140	5.2	2.1	14.0
00-01—Utah	5	214	25	56	.446	11	12	.917	4	32	36	15	3	1	2	71	7.2	3.0	14.2
Totals	92	2936	346	766	.452	195	259	.753	82	344	426	126	105	28	76	1007	4.6	1.4	10.9

Three-point field goals: 1993-94, 2-for-3 (.667). 1994-95, 2-for-4 (.500). 1995-96, 25-for-53 (.472). 1996-97, 36-for-101 (.356). 1997-98, 23-for-63 (.365). 1998-99, 9-for-36 (.250). 1999-00, 13-for-45 (.289). 2000-01, 10-for-22 (.455). Totals, 120-for-327 (.367).

Personal fouls/disqualifications: 1993-94, 3/0. 1994-95, 2/0. 1995-96, 42/0. 1996-97, 57/1. 1997-98, 49/0. 1998-99, 37/0. 1999-00, 27/0. 2000-01, 13/0. Totals, 232/1.

SABONIS, ARVYDAS   C   TRAIL BLAZERS

PERSONAL: Born December 19, 1964, in Kaunas, Lithuania. ... 7-3/292. (2,21/132,4). ... Name pronounced UHR-VEE-dus suh-BONE-is.
TRANSACTIONS/CAREER NOTES: Selected by Atlanta Hawks in fourth round (77th pick overall) of 1985 NBA Draft. ... Declared ineligible for 1985 NBA draft. ... Played in USSR (1984-85 through 1986-87 and 1988-89). ... Selected by Portland Trail Blazers in first round (24th pick overall) of 1986 NBA Draft. ... Played in Spain (1989-90 through 1994-95). ... Signed by Trail Blazers (September 29, 1995).
MISCELLANEOUS: Member of gold-medal-winning Soviet Union Olympic team (1988). ... Member of bronze-medal-winning Lithuanian Olympic teams (1992, 1996).

SPANISH LEAGUE RECORD

Season Team	G	Min.	FGM	FGA	Pct.	FTM	FTA	Pct.	Reb.	Ast.	Pts.	RPG	APG	PPG
89-90—Forum Valladolid	35	1174	324	661	.490	134	190	.705	456	65	809	13.0	1.9	23.1
90-91—Forum Valladolid	32	1004	237	460	.515	102	144	.708	337	61	590	10.5	1.9	18.4
91-92—Forum Valladolid	32	1032	268	498	.538	139	185	.751	425	75	696	13.3	2.3	21.8
92-93—Real Madrid	30	956	203	361	.562	87	118	.737	345	38	514	11.5	1.3	17.1
93-94—Real Madrid	27	856	181	290	.624	101	126	.802	303	54	478	11.2	2.0	17.7
94-95—Real Madrid	34	1188	300	511	.587	153	196	.781	448	82	778	13.2	2.4	22.9
Totals	190	6210	1513	2781	.544	716	959	.747	2314	375	3865	12.2	2.0	20.3

Three-point field goals: 1989-90, 27-for-65 (.415). 1990-91, 14-for-48 (.292). 1991-92, 21-for-51 (.412). 1992-93, 21-for-43 (.488). 1993-94, 15-for-36 (.417). 1994-95, 25-for-74 (.338). Totals, 123-for-317 (.388).

NBA REGULAR-SEASON RECORD

Season Team	G	Min.	FGM	FGA	Pct.	FTM	FTA	Pct.	Off.	Def.	Tot.	Ast.	St.	Blk.	TO	Pts.	RPG	APG	PPG
95-96—Portland	73	1735	394	723	.545	231	305	.757	147	441	588	130	64	78	154	1058	8.1	1.8	14.5
96-97—Portland	69	1762	328	658	.498	223	287	.777	114	433	547	146	63	84	151	928	7.9	2.1	13.4
97-98—Portland	73	2333	407	826	.493	323	405	.798	149	580	729	218	65	80	190	1167	10.0	3.0	16.0
98-99—Portland	50	1349	232	478	.485	135	175	.771	88	305	393	119	34	63	85	606	7.9	2.4	12.1
99-00—Portland	66	1688	302	598	.505	167	198	.843	97	416	513	118	43	78	97	778	7.8	1.8	11.8
00-01—Portland	61	1299	247	516	.479	121	156	.776	51	280	331	91	40	62	85	616	5.4	1.5	10.1
Totals	392	10166	1910	3799	.503	1200	1526	.786	646	2455	3101	822	309	445	762	5153	7.9	2.1	13.1

Three-point field goals: 1995-96, 39-for-104 (.375). 1996-97, 49-for-132 (.371). 1997-98, 30-for-115 (.261). 1998-99, 7-for-24 (.292). 1999-00, 7-for-19 (.368). 2000-01, 1-for-15 (.067). Totals, 133-for-409 (.325).

Personal fouls/disqualifications: 1995-96, 211/2. 1996-97, 203/4. 1997-98, 267/7. 1998-99, 147/2. 1999-00, 184/3. 2000-01, 137/2. Totals, 1149/20.

NBA PLAYOFF RECORD

Season Team	G	Min.	FGM	FGA	Pct.	FTM	FTA	Pct.	Off.	Def.	Tot.	Ast.	St.	Blk.	TO	Pts.	RPG	APG	PPG
95-96—Portland	5	177	35	81	.432	43	60	.717	12	39	51	9	4	3	10	118	10.2	1.8	23.6
96-97—Portland	4	108	18	42	.429	7	8	.875	8	18	26	9	3	3	9	45	6.5	2.3	11.3
97-98—Portland	4	107	18	40	.450	12	14	.857	7	24	31	6	7	3	10	49	7.8	1.5	12.3
98-99—Portland	13	392	45	113	.398	39	43	.907	12	102	114	29	15	15	19	130	8.8	2.2	10.0
99-00—Portland	16	493	68	150	.453	39	49	.796	19	88	107	31	14	13	26	181	6.7	1.9	11.3
00-01—Portland	3	104	14	29	.483	6	8	.750	8	17	25	8	1	7	2	34	8.3	2.7	11.3
Totals	45	1381	198	455	.435	146	182	.802	66	288	354	92	44	44	76	557	7.9	2.0	12.4

Three-point field goals: 1995-96, 5-for-9 (.556). 1996-97, 2-for-8 (.250). 1997-98, 1-for-2 (.500). 1998-99, 1-for-5 (.200). 1999-00, 6-for-21 (.286). 2000-01, 0-for-2. Totals, 15-for-47 (.319).

Personal fouls/disqualifications: 1995-96, 17/0. 1996-97, 19/1. 1997-98, 19/1. 1998-99, 35/0. 1999-00, 59/2. 2000-01, 12/0. Totals, 161/4.

SAMAKE, SOUMAILA   C   SUNS

PERSONAL: Born March 18, 1978, in Bougouni, Mali. ... 7-0/230. (2,13/104,3).
TRANSACTIONS/CAREER NOTES: Played in Slovenia (1998-99). ... Played in International Basketball League with Cincinnati Stuff (1999-2000). ... Selected by New Jersey Nets in second round (36th pick overall) of 2000 NBA Draft. ... Traded by Nets with G Stephon Marbury and F Johnny Newman to Phoenix Suns for G Jason Kidd and C Chris Dudley (July 18, 2001).

SLOVENIAN LEAGUE RECORD

Season Team	G	Min.	FGM	FGA	Pct.	FTM	FTA	Pct.	Reb.	Ast.	Pts.	RPG	APG	PPG
98-99—Slovan	30	601	81	123	.659	49	86	.570	147	4	211	4.9	0.1	7.0

Three-point field goals: 1998-99, 0-for-1.

IBL REGULAR SEASON RECORD

Season Team	G	Min.	FGM	FGA	Pct.	FTM	FTA	Pct.	Reb.	Ast.	Pts.	RPG	APG	PPG
99-00—Cincinnati	60	1745	235	413	.569	114	165	.691	458	39	584	7.6	0.7	9.7

Three-point field goals: 1999-00, 0-for-2.

NBA REGULAR-SEASON RECORD

Season Team	G	Min.	FGM	FGA	Pct.	FTM	FTA	Pct.	Off.	Def.	Tot.	Ast.	St.	Blk.	TO	Pts.	RPG	APG	PPG
00-01—New Jersey	34	226	18	48	.375	10	24	.417	22	31	53	1	2	14	4	46	1.6	0.0	1.4

Personal fouls/disqualifications: 2000-01, 23/0.

SANCHEZ, PEPE   G

PERSONAL: Born May 8, 1977, in Bahia Blanca, Argentina ... 6-4/195. (1,93/88,5). ... Full Name: Juan Ignacio Sanchez.
HIGH SCHOOL: EEM No. 3 (Argentina).
COLLEGE: Temple.
TRANSACTIONS/CAREER NOTES: Not drafted by an NBA franchise. ... Signed as free agent by Philadelphia 76ers (October 2, 2001). ... Traded by 76ers with F/C Theo Ratiff, F/G Toni Kukoc, and C Nazr Mohammed to Atlanta Hawks for C Dikembe Mutombo and F Roshown McLeod (February 22, 2001). ... Waived by Hawks (March 12, 2001). ... Signed as free agent by 76ers (March 15, 2001).

COLLEGIATE RECORD

Season Team	G	Min.	FGM	FGA	Pct.	FTM	FTA	Pct.	Reb.	Ast.	Pts.	RPG	APG	PPG
96-97—Temple	31	1185	113	318	.355	29	44	.659	130	163	311	4.2	5.3	10.0
97-98—Temple	27	849	87	266	.327	52	70	.743	111	133	258	4.1	4.9	9.6
98-99—Temple	33	1186	91	263	.346	55	75	.733	172	192	272	5.2	5.8	8.2
99-00—Temple	25	839	46	142	.324	22	28	.786	138	201	141	5.5	8.0	5.6
Totals	116	4059	337	989	.341	158	217	.728	551	689	982	4.8	5.9	8.5

Three-point field goals: 1996-97, 56-for-175 (.320). 1997-98, 32-for-119 (.269). 1998-99, 35-for-134 (.261). 1999-00, 27-for-80 (.338). Totals, 150-for-508 (.295).

NBA REGULAR-SEASON RECORD

Season Team	G	Min.	FGM	FGA	Pct.	FTM	FTA	Pct.	Off.	Def.	Tot.	Ast.	St.	Blk.	TO	Pts.	RPG	APG	PPG
00-01—Phila.-Atl.	29	150	9	28	.321	2	2	1.000	3	12	15	41	11	1	6	20	0.5	1.4	0.7

Three-point field goals: 2000-01, 0-for-1.
Personal fouls/disqualifications: 2000-01, 21/0.

SANTIAGO, DANIEL   C

PERSONAL: Born June 24, 1976, in Lubbock, Texas. ... 7-1/250. (2,16/113,4). ... Full Name: Daniel Gregg Santiago.
HIGH SCHOOL: Del Norte (Albuquerque, N.M.).
JUNIOR COLLEGE: New Mexico Military Institute.
COLLEGE: New Mexico, then St. Vincent College (Pa.).
TRANSACTIONS/CAREER NOTES: Not drafted by an NBA franchise. ... Played in Italy (1998-99 and 1999-2000). ... Signed as free agent by Phoenix Suns (August 2, 2000).

COLLEGIATE RECORD

Season Team	G	Min.	FGM	FGA	Pct.	FTM	FTA	Pct.	Reb.	Ast.	Pts.	RPG	APG	PPG
94-95—New Mexico Mil. Inst.	31	...	198	319	.621	98	151	.649	256	47	494	8.3	1.5	15.9
95-96—New Mexico..................	33	224	36	51	.706	35	48	.729	51	4	107	1.5	0.1	3.2
96-97—New Mexico..................	23	173	29	40	.725	29	37	.784	35	9	87	1.5	0.4	3.8
97-98—St. Vincent....................	33	833	239	355	.673	117	174	.672	301	48	595	9.1	1.5	18.0
Junior College Totals............	31		198	319	.621	98	151	.649	256	47	494	8.3	1.5	15.9
4-Year-College Totals.............	56	397	65	91	.714	64	85	.753	86	13	194	1.5	0.2	3.5

Three-point field goals: 1996-97, 0-for-1.

ITALIAN LEAGUE RECORD

Season Team	G	Min.	FGM	FGA	Pct.	FTM	FTA	Pct.	Reb.	Ast.	Pts.	RPG	APG	PPG
98-99—Pall. Varese	25	460	49	82	.598	54	79	.684	89	4	152	3.6	0.2	6.1
99-00—Pall. Varese	24	717	118	210	.562	72	112	.643	177	16	309	7.4	0.7	12.9
Totals	49	1177	167	292	.572	126	191	.660	266	20	461	5.4	0.4	9.4

Three-point field goals: 1999-00, 1-for-3 (.333).

NBA REGULAR-SEASON RECORD

Season Team	G	Min.	FGM	FGA	Pct.	FTM	FTA	Pct.	REBOUNDS Off.	Def.	Tot.	Ast.	St.	Blk.	TO	Pts.	RPG	APG	PPG
00-01—Phoenix	54	581	64	134	.478	42	61	.689	35	67	102	11	17	21	47	170	1.9	0.2	3.1

Personal fouls/disqualifications: 2000-01, 101/1.

NBA PLAYOFF RECORD

Season Team	G	Min.	FGM	FGA	Pct.	FTM	FTA	Pct.	REBOUNDS Off.	Def.	Tot.	Ast.	St.	Blk.	TO	Pts.	RPG	APG	PPG
00-01—Phoenix	1	12	1	2	.500	0	0	...	1	4	5	0	0	2	1	2	5.0	0.0	2.0

Personal fouls/disqualifications: 2000-01, 2/0.

SCHREMPF, DETLEF   F   TRAIL BLAZERS

PERSONAL: Born January 21, 1963, in Leverkusen, Germany. ... 6-10/235. (2,08/106,6). ... Name pronounced Det-lef.
HIGH SCHOOL: Centralia (Wash.).
COLLEGE: Washington.
TRANSACTIONS/CAREER NOTES: Selected by Dallas Mavericks in first round (eighth pick overall) of 1985 NBA Draft. ... Traded by Mavericks with 1990 or 1991 second-round draft choice to Indiana Pacers for C/F Herb Williams (February 21, 1989). ... Traded by Pacers to Seattle SuperSonics for F Derrick McKey and F Gerald Paddio (November 1, 1993). ... Signed as free agent by Portland Trail Blazers (August 1, 1999).
MISCELLANEOUS: Member of West German Olympic team (1984). ... Member of German Olympic team (1992).

COLLEGIATE RECORD

NOTES: THE SPORTING NEWS All-America second team (1985).

Season Team	G	Min.	FGM	FGA	Pct.	FTM	FTA	Pct.	Reb.	Ast.	Pts.	RPG	APG	PPG
81-82—Washington	28	314	33	73	.452	26	47	.553	56	13	92	2.0	0.5	3.3
82-83—Washington	31	958	124	266	.466	81	113	.717	211	44	329	6.8	1.4	10.6
83-84—Washington	31	1186	195	362	.539	131	178	.736	230	93	521	7.4	3.0	16.8
84-85—Washington	32	1180	191	342	.558	125	175	.714	255	134	507	8.0	4.2	15.8
Totals	122	3638	543	1043	.521	363	513	.708	752	284	1449	6.2	2.3	11.9

NBA REGULAR-SEASON RECORD

HONORS: NBA Sixth Man Award (1991, 1992). ... All-NBA third team (1995).

Season Team	G	Min.	FGM	FGA	Pct.	FTM	FTA	Pct.	REBOUNDS Off.	Def.	Tot.	Ast.	St.	Blk.	TO	Pts	RPG	APG	PPG
85-86—Dallas............	64	969	142	315	.451	110	152	.724	70	128	198	88	23	10	84	397	3.1	1.4	6.2
86-87—Dallas............	81	1711	265	561	.472	193	260	.742	87	216	303	161	50	16	110	756	3.7	2.0	9.3
87-88—Dallas............	82	1587	246	539	.456	201	266	.756	102	177	279	159	42	32	108	698	3.4	1.9	8.5
88-89—Dallas-Indiana.	69	1850	274	578	.474	273	350	.780	126	269	395	179	53	19	133	828	5.7	2.6	12.0
89-90—Indiana...........	78	2573	424	822	.516	402	490	.820	149	471	620	247	59	16	180	1267	7.9	3.2	16.2
90-91—Indiana...........	82	2632	432	831	.520	441	539	.818	178	482	660	301	58	22	175	1320	8.0	3.7	16.1
91-92—Indiana...........	80	2605	496	925	.536	365	441	.828	202	568	770	312	62	37	191	1380	9.6	3.9	17.3
92-93—Indiana...........	82	3098	517	1085	.476	525	653	.804	210	570	780	493	79	27	243	1567	9.5	6.0	19.1
93-94—Seattle	81	2728	445	903	.493	300	390	.769	144	310	454	275	73	9	173	1212	5.6	3.4	15.0
94-95—Seattle	82	2886	521	997	.523	437	521	.839	135	373	508	310	93	35	176	1572	6.2	3.8	19.2
95-96—Seattle	63	2200	360	740	.486	287	370	.776	73	255	328	276	56	8	146	1080	5.2	4.4	17.1
96-97—Seattle	61	2192	356	724	.492	253	316	.801	87	307	394	266	63	16	150	1022	6.5	4.4	16.8
97-98—Seattle	78	2742	447	898	.487	297	352	.844	135	419	554	341	60	19	168	1232	7.1	4.4	15.8
98-99—Seattle	50	1765	259	549	.472	200	243	.823	77	293	370	184	41	26	103	752	7.4	3.7	15.0
99-00—Portland.........	77	1662	187	433	.432	179	215	.833	79	253	332	197	37	17	100	574	4.3	2.6	7.5
00-01—Portland.........	26	397	39	95	.411	23	27	.852	17	61	78	44	7	3	28	104	3.0	1.7	4.0
Totals	1136	33597	5400	10995	.491	4486	5585	.803	1871	5152	7023	3833	856	312	2268	15761	6.2	3.4	13.9

Three-point field goals: 1985-86, 3-for-7 (.429). 1986-87, 33-for-69 (.478). 1987-88, 5-for-32 (.156). 1988-89, 7-for-35 (.200). 1989-90, 17-for-48 (.354). 1990-91, 15-for-40 (.375). 1991-92, 23-for-71 (.324). 1992-93, 8-for-52 (.154). 1993-94, 22-for-68 (.324). 1994-95, 93-for-181 (.514). 1995-96, 73-for-179 (.408). 1996-97, 57-for-161 (.354). 1997-98, 61-for-147 (.415). 1998-99, 34-for-86 (.395). 1999-00, 21-for-52 (.404). 2000-01, 3-for-8 (.375). Totals, 475-for-1236 (.384).

Personal fouls/disqualifications: 1985-86, 166/1. 1986-87, 224/2. 1987-88, 189/0. 1988-89, 220/3. 1989-90, 271/6. 1990-91, 262/3. 1991-92, 286/4. 1992-93, 305/3. 1993-94, 273/3. 1994-95, 252/0. 1995-96, 179/0. 1996-97, 151/0. 1997-98, 205/0. 1998-99, 152/0. 1999-00, 182/0. 2000-01, 43/0. Totals, 3360/25.

NBA PLAYOFF RECORD

Season Team	G	Min.	FGM	FGA	Pct.	FTM	FTA	Pct.	Off.	Def.	Tot.	Ast.	St.	Blk.	TO	Pts.	RPG	APG	PPG
85-86—Dallas	10	120	13	28	.464	11	17	.647	7	16	23	14	2	1	10	37	2.3	1.4	3.7
86-87—Dallas	4	97	13	35	.371	5	11	.455	4	8	12	6	3	2	6	31	3.0	1.5	7.8
87-88—Dallas	15	274	40	86	.465	36	51	.706	25	30	55	24	8	7	21	117	3.7	1.6	7.8
89-90—Indiana	3	125	23	47	.489	15	16	.938	5	17	22	5	2	1	10	61	7.3	1.7	20.3
90-91—Indiana	5	179	27	57	.474	25	30	.833	10	26	36	11	2	0	11	79	7.2	2.2	15.8
91-92—Indiana	3	120	18	47	.383	25	28	.893	12	27	39	7	2	1	7	63	13.0	2.3	21.0
92-93—Indiana	4	165	25	64	.391	28	36	.778	3	20	23	29	1	2	17	78	5.8	7.3	19.5
93-94—Seattle	5	174	26	50	.520	39	45	.867	8	19	27	10	1	3	8	93	5.4	2.0	18.6
94-95—Seattle	4	153	23	57	.404	19	24	.792	2	17	19	12	3	2	11	75	4.8	3.0	18.8
95-96—Seattle	21	789	123	259	.475	69	92	.750	19	86	105	67	14	5	67	336	5.0	3.2	16.0
96-97—Seattle	12	459	67	142	.472	53	65	.815	20	49	69	41	13	1	18	203	5.8	3.4	16.9
97-98—Seattle	10	375	64	125	.512	31	38	.816	18	59	77	39	7	1	22	161	7.7	3.9	16.1
99-00—Portland	15	276	22	56	.393	39	47	.830	10	43	53	30	4	0	15	84	3.5	2.0	5.6
00-01—Portland	3	32	4	6	.667	4	6	.667	0	5	5	1	0	0	2	14	1.7	0.3	4.7
Totals	114	3338	488	1059	.461	399	506	.789	143	422	565	296	62	26	225	1432	5.0	2.6	12.6

Three-point field goals: 1985-86, 0-for-1. 1986-87, 0-for-3. 1987-88, 1-for-3 (.333). 1989-90, 0-for-3. 1990-91, 0-for-4. 1991-92, 2-for-4 (.500). 1992-93, 0-for-2. 1993-94, 2-for-6 (.333). 1994-95, 10-for-18 (.556). 1995-96, 21-for-57 (.368). 1996-97, 16-for-29 (.552). 1997-98, 2-for-14 (.143). 1999-00, 1-for-6 (.167). 2000-01, 2-for-3 (.667). Totals, 57-for-153 (.373).

Personal fouls/disqualifications: 1985-86, 24/0. 1986-87, 13/0. 1987-88, 29/0. 1989-90, 13/0. 1990-91, 17/0. 1991-92, 10/0. 1992-93, 14/0. 1993-94, 21/1. 1994-95, 12/0. 1995-96, 63/1. 1996-97, 40/0. 1997-98, 21/0. 1999-00, 29/0. 2000-01, 3/0. Totals, 309/2.

NBA ALL-STAR GAME RECORD

Season Team	Min.	FGM	FGA	Pct.	FTM	FTA	Pct.	Off.	Def.	Tot.	Ast.	PF	Dq.	St.	Blk.	TO	Pts.
1993 —Indiana	13	1	3	.333	1	2	.500	0	3	3	0	4	0	0	0	1	3
1995 —Seattle	18	4	11	.364	0	0	...	0	4	4	5	2	0	0	0	0	9
1997 —Seattle	20	5	8	.625	0	1	.000	1	3	4	2	3	0	0	1	1	11
Totals	51	10	22	.455	1	3	.333	1	10	11	7	9	0	0	1	2	23

Three-point field goals: 1993, 0-for-1. 1995, 1-for-4 (.250). 1997, 1-for-3 (.333). Totals, 2-for-8 (.250).

SCOTT, SHAWNELLE   C

PERSONAL: Born June 16, 1972, in New York. ... 6-11/250. (2,11/113,4).
HIGH SCHOOL: All Hallows (Bronx, N.Y.).
COLLEGE: St. John's.
TRANSACTIONS/CAREER NOTES: Selected by Portland Trail Blazers in second round (43rd pick overall) of 1994 NBA Draft. Waived by Blazers (October 28, 1994) ... Played in Continental Basketball Association with Oklahoma City Cavalry (1994-95) and Connecticut Pride (1995-96, 1998-99 and 1999-2000). ... Signed as free agent by Cleveland Cavaliers (August 28, 1996). ... Waived by Cavaliers (June 29, 1998). ... Signed as free agent by Utah Jazz (January 21, 1999). ... Waived by Jazz (February 2, 1999). ... Signed as free agent by Denver Nuggets (September 2, 1999). ... Waived by Nuggets (October 26, 1999). ... Signed as free agent by San Antonio Spurs (August 11, 2000).

COLLEGIATE RECORD

Season Team	G	Min.	FGM	FGA	Pct.	FTM	FTA	Pct.	Reb.	Ast.	Pts.	RPG	APG	PPG
90-91—St. John's	32	526	69	138	.500	27	51	.529	115	7	165	3.6	0.2	5.2
91-92—St. John's	30	738	110	218	.505	49	81	.605	167	19	269	5.6	0.6	9.0
92-93—St. John's	29	830	169	289	.585	60	116	.517	225	33	398	7.8	1.1	13.7
93-94—St. John's	22	727	141	266	.530	69	117	.590	203	28	351	9.2	1.3	16.0
Totals	113	2821	489	911	.537	205	365	.562	710	87	1183	6.3	0.8	10.5

Three-point field goals: 1992-93, 0-for-2. 1993-94, 0-for-1. Totals, 0-for-3 (.000).

CBA REGULAR-SEASON RECORD

NOTES: Member of CBA championship team (1999).

Season Team	G	Min.	FGM	FGA	Pct.	FTM	FTA	Pct.	Reb.	Ast.	Pts.	RPG	APG	PPG
94-95—Oklahoma City	50	374	64	113	.566	29	53	.547	102	7	158	2.0	0.1	3.2
95-96—Connecticut	56	868	128	246	.520	47	82	.573	347	30	303	6.2	0.5	5.4
98-99—Connecticut	15	268	46	77	.597	19	37	.514	121	16	111	8.1	1.1	7.4
99-00—Connecticut	50	1266	178	319	.558	36	82	.439	568	42	393	11.4	0.8	7.9
Totals	171	2776	416	755	.551	131	254	.516	1138	95	965	6.7	0.6	5.6

Three-point field goals: 1994-95, 1-for-3 (.333). 1995-96, 0-for-3. 1999-00, 1-for-1. Totals, 2-for-7 (.286).

NBA REGULAR-SEASON RECORD

Season Team	G	Min.	FGM	FGA	Pct.	FTM	FTA	Pct.	Off.	Def.	Tot.	Ast.	St.	Blk.	TO	Pts.	RPG	APG	PPG
96-97—Cleveland	16	50	8	16	.500	4	11	.364	8	8	16	0	0	3	0	20	1.0	0.0	1.3
97-98—Cleveland	41	188	16	36	.444	12	18	.667	20	39	59	8	6	8	10	44	1.4	0.2	1.1
00-01—San Antonio	27	144	17	41	.415	9	22	.409	23	27	50	4	5	6	11	43	1.9	0.1	1.6
Totals	84	382	41	93	.441	25	51	.490	51	74	125	12	11	17	21	107	1.5	0.1	1.3

Personal fouls/disqualifications: 1996-97, 6/0. 1997-98, 45/0. 2000-01, 23/0. Totals, 74/0.

NBA PLAYOFF RECORD

									REBOUNDS								AVERAGES		
Season Team	G	Min.	FGM	FGA	Pct.	FTM	FTA	Pct.	Off.	Def.	Tot.	Ast.	St.	Blk.	TO	Pts.	RPG	APG	PPG
97-98—Cleveland	1	3	1	2	.500	0	0	...	0	0	0	0	0	1	1	2	0.0	0.0	2.0
00-01—San Antonio	7	13	1	4	.250	1	1	1.000	0	2	2	0	0	0	3	3	0.3	0.0	0.4
Totals	8	16	2	6	.333	1	1	1.000	0	2	2	0	0	1	4	5	0.3	0.0	0.6

Three-point field goals: 2000-01, 0-for-2. Totals, 0-for-2 (.000).
Personal fouls/disqualifications: 2000-01, 2/0. Totals, 2/0.

SHAW, BRIAN   G   LAKERS

PERSONAL: Born March 22, 1966, in Oakland. ... 6-6/200. (1,98/90,7). ... Full Name: Brian K. Shaw.
HIGH SCHOOL: Bishop O'Dowd (Oakland).
COLLEGE: St. Mary's (Calif.), then UC Santa Barbara.
TRANSACTIONS/CAREER NOTES: Selected by Boston Celtics in first round (24th pick overall) of 1988 NBA Draft. ... Played in Italy (1989-90). ... Traded by Celtics to Miami Heat for G Sherman Douglas (January 10, 1992). ... Signed as unrestricted free agent by Orlando Magic (September 22, 1994). ... Traded by Magic with F David Vaughn to Golden State Warriors for G Mark Price (October 28, 1997). ... Traded by Warriors with F Joe Smith to Philadelphia 76ers for F Clarence Weatherspoon and G Jim Jackson (February 17, 1998). ... Signed as free agent by Portland Trail Blazers to 10-day contract (April 6, 1999). ... Signed by Trail Blazers for remainder of season (April 13, 1999). ... Traded by Trail Blazers with C Kelvin Cato, F Stacy Augmon, G/F Walt Williams, G Ed Gray and F/C Carlos Rogers to Houston Rockets for F Scottie Pippen (October 2, 1999). ... Waived by Rockets (October 4, 1999). ... Signed as free agent by Los Angeles Lakers (October 20, 1999).
MISCELLANEOUS: Member of NBA championship team (2000, 2001). ... Member of gold-medal-winning U.S. World Championship team (1986).

COLLEGIATE RECORD

												AVERAGES		
Season Team	G	Min.	FGM	FGA	Pct.	FTM	FTA	Pct.	Reb.	Ast.	Pts.	RPG	APG	PPG
83-84—St. Mary's (Calif.)	14	129	13	36	.361	14	19	.737	12	23	40	0.9	1.6	2.9
84-85—St. Mary's (Calif.)	27	976	99	246	.402	55	76	.724	142	142	253	5.3	5.3	9.4
85-86—UC Santa Barbara					Did not play—transfer student.									
86-87—UC Santa Barbara..........	29	1013	125	288	.434	47	66	.712	224	193	315	7.7	6.7	10.9
87-88—UC Santa Barbara..........	30	1073	151	324	.466	71	96	.740	260	182	399	8.7	6.1	13.3
Totals	100	3191	388	894	.434	187	257	.728	640	540	1007	6.4	5.4	10.1

Three-point field goals: 1986-87, 18-for-42 (.429). 1987-88, 26-for-74 (.351). Totals, 44-for-116 (.379).

NBA REGULAR-SEASON RECORD

HONORS: NBA All-Rookie second team (1989).

									REBOUNDS								AVERAGES		
Season Team	G	Min.	FGM	FGA	Pct.	FTM	FTA	Pct.	Off.	Def.	Tot.	Ast.	St.	Blk.	TO	Pts.	RPG	APG	PPG
88-89—Boston...........	82	2301	297	686	.433	109	132	.826	119	257	376	472	78	27	188	703	4.6	5.8	8.6
90-91—Boston...........	79	2772	442	942	.469	204	249	.819	104	266	370	602	105	34	223	1091	4.7	7.6	13.8
91-92—Boston-Miami.	63	1423	209	513	.407	72	91	.791	50	154	204	250	57	22	99	495	3.2	4.0	7.9
92-93—Miami	68	1603	197	501	.393	61	78	.782	70	187	257	235	48	19	96	498	3.8	3.5	7.3
93-94—Miami	77	2037	278	667	.417	64	89	.719	104	246	350	385	71	21	173	693	4.5	5.0	9.0
94-95—Orlando..........	78	1836	192	494	.389	70	95	.737	52	189	241	406	73	18	184	502	3.1	5.2	6.4
95-96—Orlando..........	75	1679	182	486	.374	91	114	.798	58	166	224	336	58	11	173	496	3.0	4.5	6.6
96-97—Orlando..........	77	1867	189	516	.366	111	140	.793	47	147	194	319	67	26	170	552	2.5	4.1	7.2
97-98—G.S.-Phil........	59	1530	154	446	.345	36	52	.692	37	178	215	261	49	17	99	372	3.6	4.4	6.3
98-99—Portland.........	1	5	0	1	.000	0	0	...	0	1	1	1	0	0	1	0	1.0	1.0	0.0
99-00—L.A. Lakers	74	1249	123	322	.382	41	54	.759	45	171	216	201	35	14	75	305	2.9	2.7	4.1
00-01—L.A. Lakers	80	1833	164	411	.399	51	64	.797	48	256	304	258	49	27	97	421	3.8	3.2	5.3
Totals	813	20135	2427	5985	.406	910	1158	.786	734	2218	2952	3726	690	236	1578	6128	3.6	4.6	7.5

Three-point field goals: 1988-89, 0-for-13. 1990-91, 3-for-27 (.111). 1991-92, 5-for-23 (.217). 1992-93, 43-for-130 (.331). 1993-94, 73-for-216 (.338). 1994-95, 48-for-184 (.261). 1995-96, 41-for-144 (.285). 1996-97, 63-for-194 (.325). 1997-98, 28-for-95 (.295). 1999-00, 18-for-58 (.310). 2000-01, 42-for-135 (.311). Totals, 364-for-1219 (.299).
Personal fouls/disqualifications: 1988-89, 211/1. 1990-91, 206/1. 1991-92, 115/0. 1992-93, 163/2. 1993-94, 195/1. 1994-95, 184/1. 1995-96, 160/1. 1996-97, 197/3. 1997-98, 148/4. 1998-99, 1/0. 1999-00, 105/0. 2000-01, 159/1. Totals, 1844/15.

NBA PLAYOFF RECORD

									REBOUNDS								AVERAGES		
Season Team	G	Min.	FGM	FGA	Pct.	FTM	FTA	Pct.	Off.	Def.	Tot.	Ast.	St.	Blk.	TO	Pts.	RPG	APG	PPG
88-89—Boston...........	3	124	22	43	.512	7	9	.778	2	15	17	19	3	0	6	51	5.7	6.3	17.0
90-91—Boston...........	11	316	47	100	.470	26	30	.867	8	30	38	51	10	1	25	121	3.5	4.6	11.0
91-92—Miami	3	85	14	30	.467	5	8	.625	2	11	13	12	2	0	7	36	4.3	4.0	12.0
93-94—Miami	5	112	16	41	.390	7	12	.583	3	17	20	9	4	1	13	39	4.0	1.8	7.8
94-95—Orlando..........	21	355	48	123	.390	20	32	.625	17	45	62	66	11	4	26	138	3.0	3.1	6.6
95-96—Orlando..........	10	217	18	52	.346	3	4	.750	6	15	21	46	5	0	19	47	2.1	4.6	4.7
96-97—Orlando..........	5	82	3	19	.158	2	4	.500	1	8	9	8	1	1	8	10	1.8	1.6	2.0
99-00—L.A. Lakers	22	408	45	107	.421	13	16	.813	7	44	51	67	11	4	17	119	2.3	3.0	5.4
00-01—L.A. Lakers	16	290	27	72	.375	6	9	.667	10	45	55	43	10	1	16	70	3.4	2.7	4.4
Totals	96	1989	240	587	.409	89	124	.718	56	230	286	321	57	12	137	631	3.0	3.3	6.6

Three-point field goals: 1988-89, 0-for-1. 1990-91, 1-for-3 (.333). 1991-92, 3-for-5 (.600). 1993-94, 0-for-13. 1994-95, 22-for-57 (.386). 1995-96, 8-for-22 (.364). 1996-97, 2-for-6 (.333). 1999-00, 16-for-48 (.333). 2000-01, 10-for-29 (.345). Totals, 62-for-184 (.337).
Personal fouls/disqualifications: 1988-89, 11/0. 1990-91, 34/0. 1991-92, 13/0. 1993-94, 8/0. 1994-95, 49/0. 1995-96, 27/0. 1996-97, 5/0. 1999-00, 46/1. 2000-01, 37/0. Totals, 230/1.

ITALIAN LEAGUE RECORD

											AVERAGES		
Season Team	G	Min.	FGM	FGA	Pct.	FTM	FTA	Pct.	Reb.	Ast.	Pts.	RPG	APG	PPG
89-90—Il Messaggero Roma......	30	1144	244	418	.584	111	139	.799	274	...	749	9.1	...	25.0

Three-point field goals: 1989-90, 50-for-140 (.357).

SKINNER, BRIAN   F/C   RAPTORS

PERSONAL: Born May 19, 1976, in Temple, Texas. ... 6-9/255. (2,06/115,7).
HIGH SCHOOL: Temple (Texas).
COLLEGE: Baylor.
TRANSACTIONS/CAREER NOTES: Selected by Los Angeles Clippers in first round (22nd pick overall) of 1998 NBA Draft. ... Traded by Clippers with rights to C Tyson Chandler to Chicago Bulls for F Elton Brand (June 27, 2001). ... Traded by Bulls to Toronto Raptors for F Charles Oakley and 2002 second-round draft choice (July 18, 2001).

COLLEGIATE RECORD

Season Team	G	Min.	FGM	FGA	Pct.	FTM	FTA	Pct.	Reb.	Ast.	Pts.	RPG	APG	PPG
94-95—Baylor	18	501	98	164	.598	40	95	.421	147	9	236	8.2	0.5	13.1
95-96—Baylor	27	900	187	311	.601	101	163	.620	250	16	475	9.3	0.6	17.6
96-97—Baylor	30	973	196	349	.562	92	172	.535	253	26	484	8.4	0.9	16.1
97-98—Baylor	28	908	192	347	.553	123	208	.591	265	15	507	9.5	0.5	18.1
Totals	103	3282	673	1171	.575	356	638	.558	915	66	1702	8.9	0.6	16.5

NBA REGULAR-SEASON RECORD

Season Team	G	Min.	FGM	FGA	Pct.	FTM	FTA	Pct.	REBOUNDS Off.	Def.	Tot.	Ast.	St.	Blk.	TO	Pts.	AVERAGES RPG	APG	PPG
98-99—L.A. Clippers	21	258	33	71	.465	20	33	.606	20	33	53	1	10	13	19	86	2.5	0.0	4.1
99-00—L.A. Clippers	33	775	68	134	.507	43	65	.662	63	138	201	11	16	44	37	179	6.1	0.3	5.4
00-01—L.A. Clippers	39	584	64	161	.398	32	59	.542	55	113	168	18	14	11	32	160	4.3	0.5	4.1
Totals	93	1617	165	366	.451	95	157	.605	138	284	422	30	40	68	88	425	4.5	0.3	4.6

Personal fouls/disqualifications: 1998-99, 20/0. 1999-00, 75/0. 2000-01, 61/0. Totals, 156/0.

SLATER, REGGIE   F

PERSONAL: Born August 27, 1970, in Houston. ... 6-7/255. (2,01/115,7). ... Full Name: Reginald Dwayne Slater.
HIGH SCHOOL: Kashmere (Houston).
COLLEGE: Wyoming.
TRANSACTIONS/CAREER NOTES: Not drafted by an NBA franchise. ... Played in Spain (1992-93 and 1993-94). ... Signed as free agent by Denver Nuggets (August 2, 1994). ... Selected by Vancouver Grizzlies from Nuggets in NBA Expansion Draft (June 24, 1995). ... Signed as free agent by Portland Trail Blazers (October 1, 1995). ... Waived by Trail Blazers (December 8, 1995). ... Played in Continental Basketball Association with Chicago Rockers (1995-96) and La Crosse Bobcats (1996-97). ... Signed as free agent by Nuggets (December 26, 1995). ... Waived by Nuggets (January 5, 1996). ... Signed by Dallas Mavericks to first of two consecutive 10-day contracts (January 10, 1996). ... Waived by Mavericks (January 27, 1996). ... Signed by Toronto Raptors to 10-day contract (January 25, 1997). ... Re-signed by Raptors for remainder of season (February 3, 1997). ... Played in Italy (1999-2000). ... Signed as free agent by Minnesota Timberwolves (October 3, 2000).

COLLEGIATE RECORD

Season Team	G	Min.	FGM	FGA	Pct.	FTM	FTA	Pct.	Reb.	Ast.	Pts.	RPG	APG	PPG
88-89—Wyoming	31	703	66	117	.564	61	102	.598	211	6	193	6.8	0.2	6.2
89-90—Wyoming	29	977	170	294	.578	145	198	.732	328	29	485	11.3	1.0	16.7
90-91—Wyoming	32	1141	224	370	.605	165	217	.760	331	39	613	10.3	1.2	19.2
91-92—Wyoming	29	1049	184	320	.575	150	210	.714	327	57	518	11.3	2.0	17.9
Totals	121	3870	644	1101	.585	521	727	.717	1197	131	1809	9.9	1.1	15.0

Three-point field goals: 1988-89, 0-for-1.

SPANISH LEAGUE RECORD

Season Team	G	Min.	FGM	FGA	Pct.	FTM	FTA	Pct.	Reb.	Ast.	Pts.	RPG	APG	PPG
92-93—Argal Huesca	31	1126	230	428	.537	133	197	.675	271	57	593	8.7	1.8	19.1
93-94—Valvi Girona	27	884	181	320	.566	108	150	.720	180	57	470	6.7	2.1	17.4
Totals	58	2010	411	748	.549	241	347	.695	451	114	1063	7.8	2.0	18.3

Three-point field goals: 1992-93, 0-for-1.

NBA REGULAR-SEASON RECORD

Season Team	G	Min.	FGM	FGA	Pct.	FTM	FTA	Pct.	REBOUNDS Off.	Def.	Tot.	Ast.	St.	Blk.	TO	Pts.	AVERAGES RPG	APG	PPG
94-95—Denver	25	236	40	81	.494	40	55	.727	21	36	57	12	7	3	26	120	2.3	0.5	4.8
95-96—Port.-Den.-Dal.	11	72	14	27	.519	3	7	.429	4	11	15	2	2	3	9	31	1.4	0.2	2.8
96-97—Toronto	26	406	82	149	.550	39	75	.520	40	55	95	21	9	6	29	203	3.7	0.8	7.8
97-98—Toronto	78	1662	211	459	.460	203	322	.630	134	171	305	74	45	30	102	625	3.9	0.9	8.0
98-99—Toronto	30	263	31	81	.383	53	85	.624	36	34	70	5	3	3	25	115	2.3	0.2	3.8
00-01—Minnesota	55	686	90	175	.514	74	110	.673	78	108	186	26	18	9	43	254	3.4	0.5	4.6
Totals	225	3325	468	972	.481	412	654	.630	313	415	728	140	84	54	234	1348	3.2	0.6	6.0

Three-point field goals: 1996-97, 0-for-2. Totals, 0-for-2 (.000).
Personal fouls/disqualifications: 1994-95, 47/0. 1995-96, 11/0. 1996-97, 34/0. 1997-98, 201/4. 1998-99, 50/0. 2000-01, 126/1. Totals, 469/5.

NBA PLAYOFF RECORD

Season Team	G	Min.	FGM	FGA	Pct.	FTM	FTA	Pct.	REBOUNDS Off.	Def.	Tot.	Ast.	St.	Blk.	TO	Pts.	AVERAGES RPG	APG	PPG
00-01—Minnesota	4	52	6	16	.375	1	2	.500	5	9	14	0	2	3	13	13	3.5	0.0	3.3

Personal fouls/disqualifications: 2000-01, 15/1.

NOTES: CBA All-League first team (1997).

Season Team	G	Min.	FGM	FGA	Pct.	FTM	FTA	Pct.	Reb.	Ast.	Pts.	AVERAGES RPG	APG	PPG
95-96—Chicago	5	107	29	45	.644	25	33	.758	39	7	83	7.8	1.4	16.6
96-97—La Crosse	30	1117	258	423	.610	155	232	.668	269	103	671	9.0	3.4	22.4
Totals	35	1224	287	468	.613	180	265	.679	308	110	754	8.8	3.1	21.5

Three-point field goals: 1996-97, 0-for-2.

ITALIAN LEAGUE RECORD

Season Team	G	Min.	FGM	FGA	Pct.	FTM	FTA	Pct.	Reb.	Ast.	Pts.	AVERAGES RPG	APG	PPG
99-00—Montecatini	30	987	187	336	.557	105	144	.729	183	38	480	6.1	1.3	16.0

Three-point field goals: 1999-00, 1-for-3 (.333).

SMITH, CHARLES   G   SPURS   S

PERSONAL: Born August 22, 1975, in Fort Worth, Texas. ... 6-4/194. (1,93/88,0). ... Full Name: Charles Cornelius Smith.
HIGH SCHOOL: Dunbar (Fort Worth, Texas).
COLLEGE: New Mexico.
TRANSACTIONS/CAREER NOTES: Selected by Miami Heat in first round (26th pick overall) of 1997 NBA Draft. ... Traded by Heat with C Isaac Austin and 1998 first-round draft choice to Los Angeles Clippers for G Brent Barry (February 19, 1998). ... Waived by Clippers (October 28, 1999). ... Played in Continental Basketball Association with Rockford Lightning (1999-2000) and La Crosse Bobcats (2000-01). ... Played in Italy (1999-2000 and 2000-01). ... Signed as free agent by San Antonio Spurs (August 2, 2001).

COLLEGIATE RECORD

Season Team	G	Min.	FGM	FGA	Pct.	FTM	FTA	Pct.	Reb.	Ast.	Pts.	AVERAGES RPG	APG	PPG
93-94—New Mexico	31	799	121	290	.417	31	51	.608	113	68	313	3.6	2.2	10.1
94-95—New Mexico	29	929	180	400	.450	70	105	.667	127	95	461	4.4	3.3	15.9
95-96—New Mexico	33	1083	233	506	.460	107	132	.811	153	102	642	4.6	3.1	19.5
96-97—New Mexico	33	972	203	444	.457	104	139	.748	181	93	577	5.5	2.8	17.5
Totals	126	3783	737	1640	.449	312	427	.731	574	358	1993	4.6	2.8	15.8

Three-point field goals: 1993-94, 40-for-119 (.336). 1994-95, 31-for-116 (.267). 1995-96, 69-for-188 (.367). 1996-97, 67-for-182 (.368). Totals, 207-for-605 (.342).

NBA REGULAR-SEASON RECORD

Season Team	G	Min.	FGM	FGA	Pct.	FTM	FTA	Pct.	REBOUNDS Off.	Def.	Tot.	Ast.	St.	Blk.	TO	Pts.	AVERAGES RPG	APG	PPG
97-98—Mia.-L.A.C.	34	292	49	125	.392	6	11	.545	13	14	27	21	12	6	27	119	0.8	0.6	3.5
98-99—L.A. Clippers	23	317	35	97	.361	7	16	.438	7	17	24	13	17	14	20	84	1.0	0.6	3.7
Totals	57	609	84	222	.378	13	27	.481	20	31	51	34	29	20	47	203	0.9	0.6	3.6

Three-point field goals: 1997-98, 15-for-47 (.319). 1998-99, 7-for-33 (.212). Totals, 22-for-80 (.275).
Personal fouls/disqualifications: 1997-98, 24/0. 1998-99, 35/0. Totals, 59/0.

CBA REGULAR-SEASON RECORD

NOTES: CBA Newcomer of the Year (2000). ... CBA All-League second team (2000).

Season Team	G	Min.	FGM	FGA	Pct.	FTM	FTA	Pct.	Reb.	Ast.	Pts.	AVERAGES RPG	APG	PPG
99-00—Rockford	56	1786	376	804	.468	124	179	.693	...	119	936	3.6	2.1	16.7
00-01—La Crosse	5	165	32	65	.492	14	21	.667	...	44	80	4.4	8.8	16.0
Totals	61	1951	408	869	.470	138	200	.690	...	163	1016	...	2.7	16.7

Three-point field goals: 1999-00, 60-for-183 (.328). 2000-01, 2-for-13 (.154). Totals, 62-for-196 (.316).

ITALIAN LEAGUE RECORD

Season Team	G	Min.	FGM	FGA	Pct.	FTM	FTA	Pct.	Reb.	Ast.	Pts.	AVERAGES RPG	APG	PPG
99-00—Snaidero Udine	3	106	32	53	.604	1	4	.250	10	4	76	3.3	1.3	25.3
00-01—Snaidero Udine	34	1113	303	630	.481	124	170	.729	155	25	820	4.6	0.7	24.1
Totals	37	1219	335	683	.490	125	174	.718	165	29	896	4.5	0.8	24.2

Three-point field goals: 1999-00, 11-for-20 (.550). 2000-01, 92-for-243 (.379). Totals, 103-for-263 (.392).

SMITH, JABARI   C

PERSONAL: Born February 12, 1977, in Atlanta. ... 6 11/240. (2,11/108,9). ... Full Name: Jabari Montsho Smith.
HIGH SCHOOL: Booker T. Washington (Atlanta).
JUNIOR COLLEGE: Atlanta Metropolitan College.
COLLEGE: Louisiana State.
TRANSACTIONS/CAREER NOTES: Selected by Sacramento Kings in second round (45th pick overall) of 2000 NBA Draft.

COLLEGIATE RECORD

Season Team	G	Min.	FGM	FGA	Pct.	FTM	FTA	Pct.	Reb.	Ast.	Pts.	AVERAGES RPG	APG	PPG
95-96—Atlanta College	32	...	182	314	.580	142	179	.793	380	100	506	11.9	3.1	15.8
96-97—Atlanta College	24	...	...	...	...	158	213	.742	312	73	467	13.0	3.0	19.5
97-98—Atlanta College						Did not play.								
98-99—Louisiana State	27	808	115	227	.507	100	145	.690	262	51	342	9.7	1.9	12.7
99-00—Louisiana State	34	969	156	282	.553	100	168	.595	239	75	425	7.0	2.2	12.5
Junior College Totals	56	...	...	...	...	300	392	.765	692	173	973	12.4	3.1	17.4
4-Year-College Totals	61	1777	271	509	.532	200	313	.639	501	126	767	8.2	2.1	12.6

Three-point field goals: 1998-99, 12-for-49 (.245). 1999-00, 13-for-35 (.371). Totals, 25-for-84 (.298).

NBA REGULAR-SEASON RECORD

Season Team	G	Min.	FGM	FGA	Pct.	FTM	FTA	Pct.	Off.	Def.	Tot.	Ast.	St.	Blk.	TO	Pts.	RPG	APG	PPG
									REBOUNDS								AVERAGES		
00-01—Sacramento	9	66	11	22	.500	4	6	.667	1	7	8	6	4	0	3	26	0.9	0.7	2.9

Personal fouls/disqualifications: 2000-01, 7/0.

SMITH, JOE   F   TIMBERWOLVES

PERSONAL: Born July 26, 1975, in Norfolk, Va. ... 6-10/225. (2,08/102,1). ... Full Name: Joseph Leynard Smith.
HIGH SCHOOL: Maury (Norfolk, Va.).
COLLEGE: Maryland.
TRANSACTIONS/CAREER NOTES: Selected after sophomore season by Golden State Warriors in first round (first pick overall) of 1995 NBA Draft. ... Traded by Warriors with G Brian Shaw to Philadelphia 76ers for F Clarence Weatherspoon and G Jim Jackson (February 17, 1998). ... Signed as free agent by Minnesota Timberwolves (January 22, 1999). ... Contract voided by NBA (October 25, 2000). ... Signed as free agent by Detroit Pistons (November 20, 2000). ... Signed as free agent by Timberwolves (July 30, 2001).

COLLEGIATE RECORD

NOTES: Naismith Award winner (1995). ... THE SPORTING NEWS All-America second team (1995).

Season Team	G	Min.	FGM	FGA	Pct.	FTM	FTA	Pct.	Reb.	Ast.	Pts.	RPG	APG	PPG
												AVERAGES		
93-94—Maryland	30	988	206	395	.522	168	229	.734	321	25	582	10.7	0.8	19.4
94-95—Maryland	34	1110	245	424	.578	209	282	.741	362	40	708	10.6	1.2	20.8
Totals	64	2098	451	819	.551	377	511	.738	683	65	1290	10.7	1.0	20.2

Three-point field goals: 1993-94, 2-for-5 (.400). 1994-95, 9-for-21 (.429). Totals, 11-for-26 (.423).

NBA REGULAR-SEASON RECORD

HONORS: NBA All-Rookie first team (1996).

Season Team	G	Min.	FGM	FGA	Pct.	FTM	FTA	Pct.	Off.	Def.	Tot.	Ast.	St.	Blk.	TO	Pts.	RPG	APG	PPG
									REBOUNDS								AVERAGES		
95-96—Golden State ...	82	2821	469	1024	.458	303	392	.773	300	417	717	79	85	134	138	1251	8.7	1.0	15.3
96-97—Golden State ...	80	3086	587	1293	.454	307	377	.814	261	418	679	125	74	86	192	1493	8.5	1.6	18.7
97-98—G.S.-Phil.	79	2344	464	1070	.434	227	293	.775	199	272	471	94	62	51	158	1155	6.0	1.2	14.6
98-99—Minnesota.......	43	1418	223	522	.427	142	188	.755	154	200	354	68	32	66	66	588	8.2	1.6	13.7
99-00—Minnesota	78	1975	289	623	.464	195	258	.756	186	298	484	88	45	85	119	774	6.2	1.1	9.9
00-01—Detroit	69	1941	308	765	.403	231	287	.805	160	331	491	79	47	50	88	847	7.1	1.1	12.3
Totals	431	13585	2340	5297	.442	1405	1795	.783	1260	1936	3196	533	345	472	761	6108	7.4	1.2	14.2

Three-point field goals: 1995-96, 10-for-28 (.357). 1996-97, 12-for-46 (.261). 1997-98, 0-for-8. 1998-99, 0-for-3. 1999-00, 1-for-1. 2000-01, 0-for-5. Totals, 23-for-91 (.253).
Personal fouls/disqualifications: 1995-96, 224/5. 1996-97, 244/3. 1997-98, 263/2. 1998-99, 147/3. 1999-00, 302/8. 2000-01, 258/5. Totals, 1438/26.

NBA PLAYOFF RECORD

Season Team	G	Min.	FGM	FGA	Pct.	FTM	FTA	Pct.	Off.	Def.	Tot.	Ast.	St.	Blk.	TO	Pts.	RPG	APG	PPG
									REBOUNDS								AVERAGES		
98-99—Minnesota.......	4	120	11	37	.297	8	11	.727	10	16	26	5	2	8	5	30	6.5	1.3	7.5
99-00—Minnesota.......	4	79	8	17	.471	2	2	1.000	7	5	12	1	3	1	4	18	3.0	0.3	4.5
Totals	8	199	19	54	.352	10	13	.769	17	21	38	6	5	9	9	48	4.8	0.8	6.0

Three-point field goals: 1999-00, 0-for-1. Totals, 0-for-1 (.000).
Personal fouls/disqualifications: 1998-99, 15/0. 1999-00, 15/0. Totals, 30/0.

SMITH, MICHAEL   F

PERSONAL: Born March 28, 1972, in Washington, D.C. ... 6-8/240. (2,03/108,9). ... Full Name: Michael John Smith.
HIGH SCHOOL: Dunbar (Washington, D.C.).
COLLEGE: Providence.
TRANSACTIONS/CAREER NOTES: Selected by Sacramento Kings in second round (35th pick overall) of 1994 NBA Draft. ... Traded by Kings with G Bobby Hurley to Vancouver Grizzlies for F Otis Thorpe and G Chris Robinson (February 18, 1998). ... Traded by Grizzlies with G/F Rodrick Rhodes, G Lee Mayberry and F Makhtar Ndiaye to Orlando Magic as part of three-way deal in which Grizzlies received G Michael Dickerson, F/C Othella Harrington, G Brent Price, F/C Antoine Carr and future first-round draft choice from Rockets, and Rockets received draft rights to G Steve Francis and F Tony Massenburg from Grizzlies and F Don MacLean and future first-round draft choice from Magic (August 27, 1999). ... Waived by Magic (September 29, 1999). ... Signed as free agent by Washington Wizards (October 1, 1999). ... Waived by Wizards (July 25, 2001).

COLLEGIATE RECORD

Season Team	G	Min.	FGM	FGA	Pct.	FTM	FTA	Pct.	Reb.	Ast.	Pts.	RPG	APG	PPG
												AVERAGES		
90-91—Providence						Did not play—ineligible.								
91-92—Providence	31	876	108	218	.495	117	202	.579	319	41	333	10.3	1.3	10.7
92-93—Providence	33	976	125	243	.514	119	218	.546	375	38	389	11.4	1.2	11.8
93-94—Providence	30	872	144	238	.605	100	140	.714	344	25	388	11.5	0.8	12.9
Totals	94	2724	377	699	.539	336	560	.600	1038	104	1110	11.0	1.1	11.8

Three-point field goals: 1991-92, 0-for-1. 1993-94, 0-for-1. Totals, 0-for-2 (.000).

NBA REGULAR-SEASON RECORD

Season Team	G	Min.	FGM	FGA	Pct.	FTM	FTA	Pct.	Off.	Def.	Tot.	Ast.	St.	Blk.	TO	Pts.	RPG	APG	PPG
									REBOUNDS								AVERAGES		
94-95—Sacramento	82	1736	220	406	.542	127	262	.485	174	312	486	67	61	49	106	567	5.9	0.8	6.9
95-96—Sacramento	65	1384	144	238	.605	68	177	.384	143	246	389	110	47	46	72	357	6.0	1.7	5.5

Season Team	G	Min.	FGM	FGA	Pct.	FTM	FTA	Pct.	Off.	Def.	Tot.	Ast.	St.	Blk.	TO	Pts.	RPG	APG	PPG
96-97—Sacramento	81	2526	202	375	.539	128	258	.496	257	512	769	191	82	60	130	532	9.5	2.4	6.6
97-98—Sac.-Van.	48	1053	93	194	.479	65	103	.631	120	186	306	88	41	15	51	251	6.4	1.8	5.2
98-99—Vancouver.......	48	1098	77	144	.535	76	128	.594	135	215	350	48	46	18	60	230	7.3	1.0	4.8
99-00—Washington	46	1145	108	192	.563	73	101	.723	121	210	331	56	27	23	45	289	7.2	1.2	6.3
00-01—Washington	79	1610	106	218	.486	89	154	.578	172	390	562	101	57	37	62	301	7.1	1.3	3.8
Totals	449	10552	950	1767	.538	626	1183	.529	1122	2071	3193	661	361	248	526	2527	7.1	1.5	5.6

Three-point field goals: 1994-95, 0-for-2. 1995-96, 1-for-1. 1997-98, 0-for-1. 1998-99, 0-for-1. 1999-00, 0-for-1. 2000-01, 0-for-1. Totals, 1-for-7 (.143).
Personal fouls/disqualifications: 1994-95, 235/1. 1995-96, 166/0. 1996-97, 251/3. 1997-98, 95/0. 1998-99, 107/0. 1999-00, 127/0. 2000-01, 156/0.
Totals, 1137/4.

NBA PLAYOFF RECORD

Season Team	G	Min.	FGM	FGA	Pct.	FTM	FTA	Pct.	Off.	Def.	Tot.	Ast.	St.	Blk.	TO	Pts.	RPG	APG	PPG
95-96—Sacramento	4	87	7	12	.583	5	11	.455	7	15	22	8	1	2	2	19	5.5	2.0	4.8

Personal fouls/disqualifications: 1995-96, 14/0.

SMITH, MIKE   F

PERSONAL: Born April 15, 1976, in West Monroe, La. ... 6-8/195. (2,03/88,5).
HIGH SCHOOL: West Monroe (La.).
JUNIOR COLLEGE: Bossier Parish Community College (La.).
COLLEGE: Louisiana-Monroe.
TRANSACTIONS/CAREER NOTES: Selected by Washington Wizards in second round (35th pick overall) of 2000 NBA Draft. ... Waived by Wizards (February 22, 2001). ... Re-signed as free agent by Wizards (March 2, 2001).

COLLEGIATE RECORD

Season Team	G	Min.	FGM	FGA	Pct.	FTM	FTA	Pct.	Reb.	Ast.	Pts.	RPG	APG	PPG
96-97—Bossier Parish................						Statistics unavailable.								
97-98—Bossier Parish................	28	...	212	454	.467	53	90	.589	240	42	568	8.6	1.5	20.3
98-99—Louisiana-Monroe	27	927	166	383	.433	113	153	.739	185	51	500	6.9	1.9	18.5
99-00—Louisiana-Monroe	28	1011	187	441	.424	113	141	.801	264	96	562	9.4	3.4	20.1
Junior College Totals.............	28	...	212	454	.467	53	90	.589	240	42	568	8.6	1.5	20.3
4-Year-College Totals..........	55	1938	353	824	.428	226	294	.769	449	147	1062	8.2	2.7	19.3

Three-point field goals: 1997-98, 91-for-265 (.343). 1998-99, 55-for-187 (.294). 1999-00, 75-for-222 (.338). Totals, 130-for-409 (.318).

NBA REGULAR-SEASON RECORD

Season Team	G	Min.	FGM	FGA	Pct.	FTM	FTA	Pct.	Off.	Def.	Tot.	Ast.	St.	Blk.	TO	Pts.	RPG	APG	PPG
00-01—Washington	17	180	19	59	.322	10	16	.625	10	12	22	10	5	3	7	51	1.3	0.6	3.0

Three-point field goals: 2000-01, 3-for-18 (.167).
Personal fouls/disqualifications: 2000-01, 8/0.

SMITH, STEVE   G   SPURS

PERSONAL: Born March 31, 1969, in Highland Park, Mich. ... 6-8/221. (2,03/100,2). ... Full Name: Steven Delano Smith.
HIGH SCHOOL: Pershing (Detroit).
COLLEGE: Michigan State.
TRANSACTIONS/CAREER NOTES: Selected by Miami Heat in first round (fifth pick overall) of 1991 NBA Draft. ... Traded by Heat with F Grant Long and conditional second-round draft choice to Atlanta Hawks for F Kevin Willis and conditional first-round draft choice (November 7, 1994). ... Traded by Hawks with G Ed Gray to Portland Trail Blazers for G Isaiah Rider and G Jim Jackson (August 2, 1999). ... Traded by Trail Blazers to San Antonio Spurs for G Derek Anderson, G Steve Kerr and 2003 second-round draft choice (July 25, 2001).
MISCELLANEOUS: Member of gold-medal-winning U.S. Olympic team (2000). ... Member of gold-medal-winning U.S. World Championship team (1994).

COLLEGIATE RECORD

NOTES: The Sporting News All-America first team (1990, 1991).

Season Team	G	Min.	FGM	FGA	Pct.	FTM	FTA	Pct.	Reb.	Ast.	Pts.	RPG	APG	PPG
87-88—Michigan State	28	812	108	232	.466	69	91	.758	112	82	299	4.0	2.9	10.7
88-89—Michigan State	33	1168	217	454	.478	129	169	.763	229	112	585	6.9	3.4	17.7
89-90—Michigan State	31	1081	233	443	.526	116	167	.695	216	150	627	7.0	4.8	20.2
90-91—Michigan State	30	1134	268	566	.473	150	187	.802	183	109	752	6.1	3.6	25.1
Totals	122	4195	826	1695	.487	464	614	.756	740	453	2263	6.1	3.7	18.5

Three-point field goals: 1987-88, 14-for-30 (.467). 1988-89, 22-for-63 (.349). 1989-90, 45-for-98 (.459). 1990-91, 66-for-162 (.407). Totals, 147-for-353 (.416).

NBA REGULAR-SEASON RECORD

RECORDS: Shares single-game record for most three-point field goals made in one quarter—7 (March 14, 1997, vs. Seattle).
HONORS: J. Walter Kennedy Citizenship Award (1998). ... NBA All-Rookie first team (1992).

Season Team	G	Min.	FGM	FGA	Pct.	FTM	FTA	Pct.	Off.	Def.	Tot.	Ast.	St.	Blk.	TO	Pts.	RPG	APG	PPG
91-92—Miami	61	1806	297	654	.454	95	127	.748	81	107	188	278	59	19	152	729	3.1	4.6	12.0
92-93—Miami	48	1610	279	619	.451	155	197	.787	56	141	197	267	50	16	129	766	4.1	5.6	16.0
93-94—Miami	78	2776	491	1076	.456	273	327	.835	156	196	352	394	84	35	202	1346	4.5	5.1	17.3
94-95—Miami-Atlanta .	80	2665	428	1005	.426	312	371	.841	104	172	276	274	62	33	155	1305	3.5	3.4	16.3

Season Team	G	Min.	FGM	FGA	Pct.	FTM	FTA	Pct.	REBOUNDS Off.	Def.	Tot.	Ast.	St.	Blk.	TO	Pts.	RPG	APG	PPG
95-96—Atlanta	80	2856	494	1143	.432	318	385	.826	124	202	326	224	68	17	151	1446	4.1	2.8	18.1
96-97—Atlanta	72	2818	491	1145	.429	333	393	.847	90	148	238	305	62	23	176	1445	3.3	4.2	20.1
97-98—Atlanta	73	2857	489	1101	.444	389	455	.855	133	176	309	292	75	29	176	1464	4.2	4.0	20.1
98-99—Atlanta	36	1314	217	540	.402	191	225	.849	50	101	151	118	36	11	99	672	4.2	3.3	18.7
99-00—Portland........	82	2689	420	900	.467	289	340	.850	123	190	313	209	71	31	117	1225	3.8	2.5	14.9
00-01—Portland........	81	2542	359	788	.456	309	347	.890	87	185	272	213	48	24	137	1105	3.4	2.6	13.6
Totals	691	23933	3965	8971	.442	2664	3167	.841	1004	1618	2622	2574	615	238	1494	11503	3.8	3.7	16.6

Three-point field goals: 1991-92, 40-for-125 (.320). 1992-93, 53-for-132 (.402). 1993-94, 91-for-262 (.347). 1994-95, 137-for-416 (.329). 1995-96, 140-for-423 (.331). 1996-97, 130-for-388 (.335). 1997-98, 97-for-276 (.351). 1998-99, 47-for-139 (.338). 1999-00, 96-for-241 (.398). 2000-01, 78-for-230 (.339). Totals, 909-for-2632 (.345).

Personal fouls/disqualifications: 1991-92, 162/1. 1992-93, 148/3. 1993-94, 217/6. 1994-95, 225/2. 1995-96, 207/1. 1996-97, 173/2. 1997-98, 219/4. 1998-99, 100/2. 1999-00, 214/0. 2000-01, 203/0. Totals, 1868/21.

NBA PLAYOFF RECORD

Season Team	G	Min.	FGM	FGA	Pct.	FTM	FTA	Pct.	REBOUNDS Off.	Def.	Tot.	Ast.	St.	Blk.	TO	Pts.	RPG	APG	PPG
91-92—Miami	3	100	18	34	.529	5	6	.833	3	3	6	15	4	1	3	48	2.0	5.0	16.0
93-94—Miami	5	192	33	80	.413	21	25	.840	17	13	30	11	4	2	10	96	6.0	2.2	19.2
94-95—Atlanta	3	108	17	43	.395	16	19	.842	1	7	8	6	6	1	3	57	2.7	2.0	19.0
95-96—Atlanta	10	421	75	171	.439	42	52	.808	15	26	41	32	13	13	16	217	4.1	3.2	21.7
96-97—Atlanta	10	421	55	139	.396	61	74	.824	12	27	39	17	4	1	28	189	3.9	1.7	18.9
97-98—Atlanta	4	160	39	68	.574	11	16	.688	2	9	11	9	2	3	5	99	2.8	2.3	24.8
98-99—Atlanta	9	356	54	153	.353	39	43	.907	14	17	31	30	14	2	21	156	3.4	3.3	17.3
99-00—Portland........	16	604	88	181	.486	69	78	.885	13	27	40	44	19	4	27	224	2.5	2.8	17.1
00-01—Portland........	3	122	16	34	.471	15	16	.938	5	8	13	7	2	1	10	51	4.3	2.3	17.0
Totals	63	2484	395	903	.437	279	329	.848	82	137	219	171	68	28	123	1187	3.5	2.7	18.8

Three-point field goals: 1991-92, 7-for-11 (.636). 1993-94, 9-for-22 (.409). 1994-95, 7-for-18 (.389). 1995-96, 25-for-61 (.410). 1996-97, 18-for-55 (.327). 1997-98, 10-for-20 (.500). 1998-99, 9-for-33 (.273). 1999-00, 29-for-53 (.547). 2000-01, 4-for-11 (.364). Totals, 118-for-284 (.415).

Personal fouls/disqualifications: 1991-92, 2/0. 1993-94, 12/0. 1994-95, 11/0. 1995-96, 31/0. 1996-97, 38/0. 1997-98, 17/1. 1998-99, 32/0. 1999-00, 44/0. 2000-01, 3/0. Totals, 193/1.

NBA ALL-STAR GAME RECORD

Season Team	Min.	FGM	FGA	Pct.	FTM	FTA	Pct.	REBOUNDS Off.	Def.	Tot.	Ast.	PF	Dq.	St.	Blk.	TO	Pts.
1998 —Atlanta...............	16	6	12	.500	0	0	...	2	1	3	0	0	...	0	0	0	14

Three-point field goals: 1998, 2-for-5 (.400).

SMITH, TONY G

PERSONAL: Born June 14, 1968, in Wauwatosa, Wis. ... 6-4/205. (1,93/93,0). ... Full Name: Charles Anton Smith.
HIGH SCHOOL: East (Wauwatosa, Wis.).
COLLEGE: Marquette.
TRANSACTIONS/CAREER NOTES:: Selected by Los Angeles Lakers in second round (51st pick overall) of 1990 NBA Draft. ... Signed as unrestricted free agent by Phoenix Suns (November 1, 1995). ... Traded by Suns to Miami Heat for G Terrence Rencher (February 22, 1996). ... Signed as free agent by Charlotte Hornets (October 19, 1996). ... Played in Spain (1997-98 and 1998-99). ... Signed as free agent by Milwaukee Bucks (December 13, 1997). ... Waived by Bucks (January 7, 1998). ... Signed as free agent by Cleveland Cavaliers (October 4, 1999). ... Waived by Cavaliers (October 14, 1999). ... Signed by Atlanta Hawks to 10-day contract (January 25, 2001). ... Played in Italy (2000-01). ... Played in Continental Basketball Association with Rockford Lightning (2000-01).

COLLEGIATE RECORD

Season Team	G	Min.	FGM	FGA	Pct.	FTM	FTA	Pct.	Reb.	Ast.	Pts.	AVERAGES RPG	APG	PPG
86-87—Marquette.....................	29	722	86	161	.534	61	81	.753	96	62	234	3.3	2.1	8.1
87-88—Marquette.....................	28	894	136	260	.523	88	119	.739	126	82	367	4.5	2.9	13.1
88-89—Marquette.....................	28	943	153	275	.556	84	115	.730	109	158	398	3.9	5.6	14.2
89-90—Marquette.....................	29	1131	240	485	.495	173	202	.856	137	167	689	4.7	5.8	23.8
Totals	114	3690	615	1181	.521	406	517	.785	468	469	1688	4.1	4.1	14.8

Three-point field goals: 1986-87, 1-for-3 (.333). 1987-88, 7-for-19 (.368). 1988-89, 8-for-12 (.667). 1989-90, 36-for-87 (.414). Totals, 52-for-121 (.430).

NBA REGULAR-SEASON RECORD

Season Team	G	Min.	FGM	FGA	Pct.	FTM	FTA	Pct.	REBOUNDS Off.	Def.	Tot.	Ast.	St.	Blk.	TO	Pts.	RPG	APG	PPG
90-91—L.A. Lakers	64	695	97	220	.441	40	57	.702	24	47	71	135	28	12	69	234	1.1	2.1	3.7
91-92—L.A. Lakers	63	820	113	283	.399	49	75	.653	31	45	76	109	39	8	50	275	1.2	1.7	4.4
92-93—L.A. Lakers	55	752	133	275	.484	62	82	.756	46	41	87	63	50	7	40	330	1.6	1.1	6.0
93-94—L.A. Lakers	73	1617	272	617	.441	85	119	.714	106	89	195	148	59	14	76	645	2.7	2.0	8.8
94-95—L.A. Lakers	61	1024	132	309	.427	44	63	.698	43	64	107	102	46	7	50	340	1.8	1.7	5.6
95-96—Phoe.-Mia......	59	938	116	274	.423	28	46	.609	30	65	95	154	37	10	66	298	1.6	2.6	5.1
96-97—Charlotte........	69	1291	138	337	.409	38	59	.644	38	56	94	150	48	19	73	346	1.4	2.2	5.0
97-98—Milwaukee	7	80	8	24	.333	3	4	.750	4	3	7	10	5	2	9	19	1.0	1.4	2.7
00-01—Atlanta	6	78	8	23	.348	1	2	.500	2	1	3	10	7	0	9	17	0.5	1.7	2.8
Totals	457	7295	1017	2362	.431	350	507	.690	324	411	735	881	319	79	442	2504	1.6	1.9	5.5

Three-point field goals: 1990-91, 0-for-7. 1991-92, 0-for-11. 1992-93, 2-for-11 (.182). 1993-94, 16-for-50 (.320). 1994-95, 32-for-91 (.352). 1995-96, 38-for-116 (.328). 1996-97, 32-for-99 (.323). 1997-98, 0-for-4. 2000-01, 0-for-2. Totals, 120-for-391 (.307).

Personal fouls/disqualifications: 1990-91, 80/0. 1991-92, 91/0. 1992-93, 72/1. 1993-94, 128/1. 1994-95, 111/0. 1995-96, 106/2. 1996-97, 110/2. 1997-98, 7/0. 2000-01, 12/0. Totals, 717/6.

NBA PLAYOFF RECORD

Season Team	G	Min.	FGM	FGA	Pct.	FTM	FTA	Pct.	REBOUNDS Off.	Def.	Tot.	Ast.	St.	Blk.	TO	Pts.	AVERAGES RPG	APG	PPG
90-91—L.A. Lakers	7	40	6	13	.462	2	3	.667	3	0	3	2	1	0	6	14	0.4	0.3	2.0
91-92—L.A. Lakers	4	40	3	10	.300	1	2	.500	1	1	2	5	4	0	3	7	0.5	1.3	1.8
92-93—L.A. Lakers	5	73	13	25	.520	6	9	.667	5	3	8	2	1	1	3	34	1.6	0.4	6.8
94-95—L.A. Lakers	6	27	3	13	.231	0	2	.000	1	2	3	0	0	0	4	9	0.5	0.5	1.5
95-96—Miami	3	61	9	19	.474	0	0	...	3	1	4	8	4	0	3	22	1.3	2.7	7.3
96-97—Charlotte	2	9	0	1	.000	1	2	.500	0	1	1	2	1	0	3	1	0.5	1.0	0.5
Totals	27	250	34	81	.420	10	18	.556	13	8	21	22	11	1	22	87	0.8	0.8	3.2

Three-point field goals: 1991-92, 0-for-2. 1992-93, 2-for-4 (.500). 1994-95, 3-for-10 (.300). 1995-96, 4-for-10 (.400). 1996-97, 0-for-1. Totals, 9-for-27 (.333).

Personal fouls/disqualifications: 1990-91, 6/1. 1991-92, 5/0. 1992-93, 14/0. 1994-95, 1/0. 1995-96, 7/0. 1996-97, 1/0. Totals, 34/1.

SPANISH LEAGUE RECORD

Season Team	G	Min.	FGM	FGA	Pct.	FTM	FTA	Pct.	Reb.	Ast.	Pts.	AVERAGES RPG	APG	PPG
97-98—Tau Ceramica........	8	225	29	66	.439	8	15	.533	18	25	76	2.3	3.1	9.5
98-99—Recreativos Orenes	11	392	76	160	.475	36	44	.818	27	34	207	2.5	3.1	18.8
Totals	19	617	105	226	.465	44	59	.746	45	59	283	2.3	3.1	14.9

Three-point field goals: 1997-98, 10-for-21 (.476). 1998-99, 19-for-44 (.432). Totals, 29-for-65 (.446).

CBA REGULAR-SEASON RECORD

Season Team	G	Min.	FGM	FGA	Pct.	FTM	FTA	Pct.	Reb.	Ast.	Pts.	AVERAGES RPG	APG	PPG
00-01—Rockford	19	660	120	254	.472	49	58	.845	69	107	300	3.6	5.6	15.8

Three-point field goals: 2000-01, 11-for-31 (.355).

ITALIAN LEAGUE RECORD

Season Team	G	Min.	FGM	FGA	Pct.	FTM	FTA	Pct.	Reb.	Ast.	Pts.	AVERAGES RPG	APG	PPG
00-01—Basket Rimini................	5	167	28	66	.424	7	9	.778	18	9	73	3.6	1.8	14.6

Three-point field goals: 2000-01, 10-for-24 (.417).

SNOW, ERIC — G — 76ERS

PERSONAL: Born April 24, 1973, in Canton, Ohio. ... 6-3/204. (1,91/92,5). ... Brother of Percy Snow, linebacker with Kansas City Chiefs (1990 through 1992), Chicago Bears (1993) and Rhein Fire of World League (1996).
HIGH SCHOOL: McKinley (Canton, Ohio).
COLLEGE: Michigan State.
TRANSACTIONS/CAREER NOTES: Selected by Milwaukee Bucks in second round (43rd pick overall) of 1995 NBA Draft. ... Draft rights traded by Bucks to Seattle SuperSonics for draft rights to C Aurelijius Zukauskas and 1996 second-round draft choice (June 28, 1995). ... Traded by SuperSonics to Philadelphia 76ers for 1998 second-round draft choice (January 18, 1998).

COLLEGIATE RECORD

Season Team	G	Min.	FGM	FGA	Pct.	FTM	FTA	Pct.	Reb.	Ast.	Pts.	AVERAGES RPG	APG	PPG
91-92—Michigan State	25	144	12	25	.480	3	15	.200	15	24	27	0.6	1.0	1.1
92-93—Michigan State	28	798	53	97	.546	15	56	.268	73	145	121	2.6	5.2	4.3
93-94—Michigan State	32	992	91	177	.514	22	49	.449	111	213	217	3.5	6.7	6.8
94-95—Michigan State	28	916	117	225	.520	62	102	.608	92	217	303	3.3	7.8	10.8
Totals	113	2850	273	524	.521	102	222	.459	291	599	668	2.6	5.3	5.9

Three-point field goals: 1991-92, 0-for-2. 1992-93, 0-for-5. 1993-94, 13-for-45 (.289). 1994-95, 7-for-24 (.292). Totals, 20-for-76 (.263).

HONORS: NBA Sportsmanship Award (2000).

NBA REGULAR-SEASON RECORD

Season Team	G	Min.	FGM	FGA	Pct.	FTM	FTA	Pct.	REBOUNDS Off.	Def.	Tot.	Ast.	St.	Blk.	TO	Pts.	AVERAGES RPG	APG	PPG
95-96—Seattle	43	389	42	100	.420	29	49	.592	9	34	43	73	28	0	38	115	1.0	1.7	2.7
96-97—Seattle	67	775	74	164	.451	47	66	.712	17	53	70	159	37	3	48	199	1.0	2.4	3.0
97-98—Seattle-Phil.	64	918	79	184	.429	49	71	.690	19	62	81	177	60	5	63	209	1.3	2.8	3.3
98-99—Philadelphia ..	48	1716	149	348	.428	110	150	.733	25	137	162	301	100	1	111	413	3.4	6.3	8.6
99-00—Philadelphia ..	82	2866	257	597	.430	126	177	.712	42	219	261	624	140	8	162	651	3.2	7.6	7.9
00-01—Philadelphia ..	50	1740	182	435	.418	122	154	.792	27	139	166	369	77	7	124	491	3.3	7.4	9.8
Totals	354	8404	783	1828	.428	667	724	...	139	644	783	1703	442	24	546	2078	2.2	4.8	5.9

Three-point field goals: 1995-96, 2-for-10 (.200). 1996-97, 4-for-15 (.267). 1997-98, 2-for-17 (.118). 1998-99, 5-for-21 (.238). 1999-00, 11-for-45 (.244). 2000-01, 5-for-19 (.263). Totals, 29-for-127 (.228).

Personal fouls/disqualifications: 1995-96, 53/0. 1996-97, 94/0. 1997-98, 114/0. 1998-99, 149/2. 1999-00, 243/2. 2000-01, 123/1. Totals, 776/5.

NBA PLAYOFF RECORD

Season Team	G	Min.	FGM	FGA	Pct.	FTM	FTA	Pct.	REBOUNDS Off.	Def.	Tot.	Ast.	St.	Blk.	TO	Pts.	AVERAGES RPG	APG	PPG
95-96—Seattle	10	24	1	7	.143	0	0	...	0	4	4	6	2	0	4	2	0.4	0.6	0.2
96-97—Seattle	8	48	5	11	.455	1	2	.500	0	2	2	12	4	0	0	13	0.3	1.5	1.6
98-99—Philadelphia	8	306	37	88	.420	22	27	.815	3	30	33	57	8	1	25	99	4.1	7.1	12.4
99-00—Philadelphia	5	138	15	31	.484	4	4	1.000	0	10	10	35	4	1	7	37	2.0	7.0	7.4
00-01—Philadelphia	23	717	87	210	.414	40	55	.727	26	60	86	104	27	2	45	214	3.7	4.5	9.3
Totals	54	1233	145	347	.418	67	88	.761	29	106	135	214	45	4	81	365	2.5	4.0	6.8

Three-point field goals: 1995-96, 0-for-2. 1996-97, 2-for-4 (.500). 1998-99, 3-for-13 (.231). 1999-00, 3-for-4 (.750). 2000-01, 0-for-7. Totals, 8-for-30 (.267).

Personal fouls/disqualifications: 1995-96, 3/0. 1996-97, 7/0. 1998-99, 26/0. 1999-00, 14/0. 2000-01, 63/0. Totals, 113/0.

SPENCER, FELTON C

PERSONAL: Born January 5, 1968, in Louisville, Ky. ... 7-0/265. (2,13/120,2). ... Full Name: Felton LaFrance Spencer.
HIGH SCHOOL: Eastern (Middletown, Ky.).
COLLEGE: Louisville.
TRANSACTIONS/CAREER NOTES: Selected by Minnesota Timberwolves in first round (sixth pick overall) of 1990 NBA Draft. ... Traded by Timberwolves to Utah Jazz for F Mike Brown (June 30, 1993). ... Traded by Jazz to Orlando Magic for G Brooks Thompson, F Kenny Gattison and undisclosed first-round draft choice (August 9, 1996). ... Traded by Magic with C Jon Koncak and F Donald Royal to Golden State Warriors for C Rony Seikaly, C Clifford Rozier and future second-round draft choice (November 2, 1996). ... Signed as free agent by San Antonio Spurs (August 31, 1999). ... Signed as free agent by New York Knicks (October 3, 2000).

COLLEGIATE RECORD

Season Team	G	Min.	FGM	FGA	Pct.	FTM	FTA	Pct.	Reb.	Ast.	Pts.	RPG	APG	PPG
86-87—Louisville	31	356	43	78	.551	32	65	.492	83	12	118	2.7	0.4	3.8
87-88—Louisville	35	532	93	157	.592	73	114	.640	146	18	259	4.2	0.5	7.4
88-89—Louisville	33	581	85	140	.607	99	135	.733	169	20	269	5.1	0.6	8.2
89-90—Louisville	35	995	188	276	.681	146	204	.716	296	45	522	8.5	1.3	14.9
Totals	134	2464	409	651	.628	350	518	.676	694	95	1168	5.2	0.7	8.7

HONORS: NBA All-Rookie second team (1991).

NBA REGULAR-SEASON RECORD

Season Team	G	Min.	FGM	FGA	Pct.	FTM	FTA	Pct.	Off.	Def.	Tot.	Ast.	St.	Blk.	TO	Pts.	RPG	APG	PPG
90-91—Minnesota	81	2099	195	381	.512	182	252	.722	272	369	641	25	48	121	77	572	7.9	0.3	7.1
91-92—Minnesota	61	1481	141	331	.426	123	178	.691	167	268	435	53	27	79	70	405	7.1	0.9	6.6
92-93—Minnesota	71	1296	105	226	.465	83	127	.654	134	190	324	17	23	66	70	293	4.6	0.2	4.1
93-94—Utah	79	2210	256	507	.505	165	272	.607	235	423	658	43	41	67	127	677	8.3	0.5	8.6
94-95—Utah	34	905	105	215	.488	107	135	.793	90	170	260	17	12	32	68	317	7.6	0.5	9.3
95-96—Utah	71	1267	146	281	.520	104	151	.689	100	206	306	11	20	54	77	396	4.3	0.2	5.6
96-97—Orlando-G.S.	73	1558	139	284	.489	94	161	.584	157	259	416	22	34	50	88	372	5.7	0.3	5.1
97-98—Golden State	68	813	59	129	.457	44	79	.557	93	133	226	17	23	37	49	162	3.3	0.3	2.4
98-99—Golden State	26	159	15	33	.455	12	26	.462	18	28	46	0	5	10	9	42	1.8	0.0	1.6
99-00—San Antonio	26	149	15	33	.455	20	30	.667	15	24	39	3	6	8	9	50	1.5	0.1	1.9
00-01—New York	18	113	12	20	.600	15	25	.600	16	19	35	2	2	2	11	39	1.9	0.1	2.2
Totals	608	12050	1188	2440	.487	949	1436	.661	1297	2089	3386	210	241	526	655	3325	5.6	0.3	5.5

Three-point field goals: 1990-91, 0-for-1. Totals, 0-for-1 (.000).

Personal fouls/disqualifications: 1990-91, 337/14. 1991-92, 241/7. 1992-93, 243/10. 1993-94, 304/5. 1994-95, 131/3. 1995-96, 240/1. 1996-97, 275/7. 1997-98, 175/3. 1998-99, 41/0. 1999-00, 32/0. 2000-01, 24/0. Totals, 2043/50.

NBA PLAYOFF RECORD

Season Team	G	Min.	FGM	FGA	Pct.	FTM	FTA	Pct.	Off.	Def.	Tot.	Ast.	St.	Blk.	TO	Pts.	RPG	APG	PPG
93-94—Utah	16	492	47	105	.448	33	50	.660	61	74	135	7	3	20	24	127	8.4	0.4	7.9
95-96—Utah	18	276	23	53	.434	5	9	.556	26	28	54	2	5	22	19	51	3.0	0.1	2.8
00-01—New York	2	4	0	0	...	0	0	...	0	0	0	0	0	0	0	0	0.0	0.0	0.0
Totals	36	772	70	158	.443	38	59	.644	87	102	189	9	8	42	43	178	5.3	0.3	4.9

Three-point field goals: 1995-96, 0-for-1. Totals, 0-for-1 (.000).

Personal fouls/disqualifications: 1993-94, 73/3. 1995-96, 58/0. 2000-01, 2/0. Totals, 133/3.

SPREWELL, LATRELL G/F KNICKS

PERSONAL: Born September 8, 1970, in Milwaukee. ... 6-5/190. (1,96/86,2). ... Full Name: Latrell Fontaine Sprewell. ... Name pronounced Lah-TRELL SPREE-well.
HIGH SCHOOL: Washington (Milwaukee).
JUNIOR COLLEGE: Three Rivers Community College (Mo.).
COLLEGE: Alabama.
TRANSACTIONS/CAREER NOTES: Selected by Golden State Warriors in first round (24th pick overall) of 1992 NBA Draft. ... Contract terminated (December 3, 1997). ... Contract reinstated by arbitrator (March 4, 1998). ... Suspended for remainder of 1997-98 season. ... Traded by Warriors to New York Knicks for G John Starks, F Chris Mills and F Terry Cummings (January 21, 1999).

COLLEGIATE RECORD

Season Team	G	Min.	FGM	FGA	Pct.	FTM	FTA	Pct.	Reb.	Ast.	Pts.	RPG	APG	PPG
88-89—Three Rivers C.C.	26	...	169	327	.517	88	133	.662	218	45	429	8.4	1.7	16.5
89-90—Three Rivers C.C.	40	...	421	827	.509	217	281	.772	365	81	1064	9.1	2.0	26.6
90-91—Alabama	33	865	116	217	.535	58	84	.690	165	62	295	5.0	1.9	8.9
91-92—Alabama	35	1266	227	460	.493	101	131	.771	183	74	623	5.2	2.1	17.8
Junior College Totals	66	...	590	1154	.511	305	414	.737	583	126	1493	8.8	1.9	22.6
4-Year-College Totals	68	2131	343	677	.507	159	215	.740	348	136	918	5.1	2.0	13.5

Three-point field goals: 1988-89, 3-for-4 (.750). 1989-90, 5-for-17 (.294). 1990-91, 5-for-12 (.417). 1991-92, 68-for-171 (.398). Totals, 8-for-21 (.381) Totals, 73-for-183 (.399).

NBA REGULAR-SEASON RECORD

HONORS: All-NBA first team (1994). ... NBA All-Defensive second team (1994). ... NBA All-Rookie second team (1993).

Season Team	G	Min.	FGM	FGA	Pct.	FTM	FTA	Pct.	Off.	Def.	Tot.	Ast.	St.	Blk.	TO	Pts.	RPG	APG	PPG
92-93—Golden State...	77	2741	449	968	.464	211	283	.746	79	192	271	295	126	52	203	1182	3.5	3.8	15.4
93-94—Golden State...	82	*3533	613	1417	.433	353	456	.774	80	321	401	385	180	76	226	1720	4.9	4.7	21.0
94-95—Golden State..	69	2771	490	1171	.418	350	448	.781	58	198	256	279	112	46	230	1420	3.7	4.0	20.6
95-96—Golden State..	78	3064	515	1202	.428	352	446	.789	124	256	380	328	127	45	222	1473	4.9	4.2	18.9
96-97—Golden State..	80	3353	649	1444	.449	493	585	.843	58	308	366	507	132	45	322	1938	4.6	6.3	24.2
97-98—Golden State..	14	547	110	277	.397	70	94	.745	7	44	51	68	19	5	44	299	3.6	4.9	21.4
98-99—New York.......	37	1233	215	518	.415	155	191	.812	41	115	156	91	46	2	79	606	4.2	2.5	16.4
99-00—New York......	82	3276	568	1305	.435	344	397	.866	49	300	349	332	109	22	226	1524	4.3	4.0	18.6
00-01—New York.......	77	3017	524	1219	.430	275	351	.783	49	298	347	269	106	28	218	1364	4.5	3.5	17.7
Totals	596	23535	4133	9521	.434	2603	3251	.801	545	2032	2577	2554	957	321	1770	11526	4.3	4.3	19.3

Three-point field goals: 1992-93, 73-for-158 (.369). 1993-94, 141-for-391 (.361). 1994-95, 90-for-326 (.276). 1995-96, 91-for-282 (.323). 1996-97, 147-for-415 (.354). 1997-98, 9-for-48 (.188). 1998-99, 21-for-77 (.273). 1999-00, 44-for-127 (.346). 2000-01, 41-for-135 (.304). Totals, 657-for-1999 (.329).

Personal fouls/disqualifications: 1992-93, 166/2. 1993-94, 158/0. 1994-95, 108/0. 1995-96, 150/1. 1996-97, 153/0. 1997-98, 26/0. 1998-99, 65/0. 1999-00, 184/0. 2000-01, 159/1. Totals, 1169/4.

NBA PLAYOFF RECORD

Season Team	G	Min.	FGM	FGA	Pct.	FTM	FTA	Pct.	Off.	Def.	Tot.	Ast.	St.	Blk.	TO	Pts.	RPG	APG	PPG
93-94—Golden State ...	3	122	26	60	.433	8	12	.667	1	8	9	21	2	3	9	68	3.0	7.0	22.7
98-99—New York........	20	743	145	346	.419	113	133	.850	24	72	96	43	19	6	58	407	4.8	2.2	20.4
99-00—New York........	16	700	110	266	.414	69	88	.784	12	58	70	58	18	5	37	299	4.4	3.6	18.7
00-01—New York.......	5	212	35	86	.407	19	25	.760	3	12	15	17	5	1	20	92	3.0	3.4	18.4
Totals	44	1777	316	758	.417	209	258	.810	40	150	190	139	44	15	124	866	4.3	3.2	19.7

Three-point field goals: 1993-94, 8-for-23 (.348). 1998-99, 4-for-25 (.160). 1999-00, 10-for-30 (.333). 2000-01, 3-for-14 (.214). Totals, 25-for-92 (.272).
Personal fouls/disqualifications: 1993-94, 15/0. 1998-99, 40/1. 1999-00, 28/0. 2000-01, 17/0. Totals, 100/1.

NBA ALL-STAR GAME RECORD

Season Team	Min.	FGM	FGA	Pct.	FTM	FTA	Pct.	Off.	Def.	Tot.	Ast.	PF	Dq.	St.	Blk.	TO	Pts.
1994 —Golden State......	15	3	8	.375	3	7	.429	4	3	7	1	1	0	0	0	2	9
1995 —Golden State......	22	4	9	.444	1	1	1.000	2	2	4	0	0	0	3	0	1	9
1997 —Golden State......	25	7	12	.583	4	6	.667	1	2	3	1	2	0	2	0	1	19
2001 —New York..........	15	3	6	.500	1	3	.333	1	0	1	4	1	0	0	0	1	7
Totals........................	77	17	35	.486	9	17	.529	8	7	15	10	4	0	5	0	5	44

Three-point field goals: 1994, 0-for-2. 1995, 0-for-2. 1997, 1-for-3 (.333). 2001, 0-for-1. Totals, 1-for-8 (.125).

STACKHOUSE, JERRY   G/F   PISTONS

PERSONAL: Born November 5, 1974, in Kinston, N.C. ... 6-6/218. (1,98/98,9). ... Full Name: Jerry Darnell Stackhouse. ... Brother of Tony Dawson, forward with Sacramento Kings (1990-91) and Boston Celtics (1994-95).
HIGH SCHOOL: Kinston (N.C.), then Oak Hill Academy (Mouth of Wilson, Va.).
COLLEGE: North Carolina.
TRANSACTIONS/CAREER NOTES: Selected after sophomore season by Philadelphia 76ers in first round (third pick overall) of 1995 NBA Draft. ... Traded by 76ers with C Eric Montross to Detroit Pistons for C Theo Ratliff, G Aaron McKie and conditional first-round draft choice (December 18, 1997).

COLLEGIATE RECORD

NOTES: The Sporting News All-America second team (1995).

Season Team	G	Min.	FGM	FGA	Pct.	FTM	FTA	Pct.	Reb.	Ast.	Pts.	RPG	APG	PPG
93-94—North Carolina...............	35	734	138	296	.466	150	205	.732	176	69	428	5.0	2.0	12.2
94-95—North Carolina...............	34	1170	215	416	.517	185	260	.712	280	93	652	8.2	2.7	19.2
Totals	69	1904	353	712	.496	335	465	.720	456	162	1080	6.6	2.3	15.7

Three-point field goals: 1993-94, 2-for-20 (.100). 1994-95, 37-for-90 (.411). Totals, 39-for-110 (.355).

NBA REGULAR-SEASON RECORD

HONORS: NBA All-Rookie first team (1996).

Season Team	G	Min.	FGM	FGA	Pct.	FTM	FTA	Pct.	Off.	Def.	Tot.	Ast.	St.	Blk.	TO	Pts.	RPG	APG	PPG
95-96—Philadelphia	72	2701	452	1091	.414	387	518	.747	90	175	265	278	76	79	252	1384	3.7	3.9	19.2
96-97—Philadelphia	81	3166	533	1308	.407	511	667	.766	156	182	338	253	93	63	316	1679	4.2	3.1	20.7
97-98—Phila.-Det........	79	2545	424	975	.435	354	450	.787	105	161	266	241	89	59	224	1249	3.4	3.1	15.8
98-99—Detroit	42	1188	181	488	.371	210	247	.860	26	81	107	118	34	19	121	607	2.5	2.8	14.5
99-00—Detroit	82	3148	619	1447	.428	618	758	.815	118	197	315	365	103	36	*311	1939	3.8	4.5	23.6
00-01—Detroit	80	3215	774	*1927	.402	*666	810	.822	99	216	315	410	97	54	*326	*2380	3.9	5.1	29.8
Totals	436	15963	2983	7236	.412	2746	3450	.796	594	1012	1606	1665	492	310	1550	9238	3.7	3.8	21.2

Three-point field goals: 1995-96, 93-for-292 (.318). 1996-97, 102-for-342 (.298). 1997-98, 47-for-195 (.241). 1998-99, 35-for-126 (.278). 1999-00, 83-for-288 (.288). 2000-01, 166-for-473 (.351). Totals, 526-for-1716 (.307).
Personal fouls/disqualifications: 1995-96, 179/0. 1996-97, 219/2. 1997-98, 175/2. 1998-99, 79/0. 1999-00, 188/1. 2000-01, 160/1. Totals, 1000/6.

NBA PLAYOFF RECORD

Season Team	G	Min.	FGM	FGA	Pct.	FTM	FTA	Pct.	Off.	Def.	Tot.	Ast.	St.	Blk.	TO	Pts.	RPG	APG	PPG
98-99—Detroit	5	124	18	46	.391	12	14	.857	3	5	8	6	2	1	10	50	1.6	1.2	10.0
99-00—Detroit	3	120	24	59	.407	23	31	.742	1	11	12	10	2	0	14	74	4.0	3.3	24.7
Totals	8	244	42	105	.400	35	45	.778	4	16	20	16	4	1	24	124	2.5	2.0	15.5

Three-point field goals: 1998-99, 2-for-8 (.250). 1999-00, 3-for-7 (.429). Totals, 5-for-15 (.333).
Personal fouls/disqualifications: 1998-99, 11/0. 1999-00, 4/0. Totals, 15/0.

Season Team	Min.	FGM	FGA	Pct.	FTM	FTA	Pct.	REBOUNDS Off.	Def.	Tot.	Ast.	PF	Dq.	St.	Blk.	TO	Pts.
2000 —Detroit	14	4	7	.571	0	0	...	0	1	1	2	2	0	0	0	1	8
2001 —Detroit	15	3	8	.375	0	2	.000	2	0	2	2	1	0	0	0	0	7
Totals	29	7	15	.467	0	2	.000	2	1	3	4	3	0	0	0	1	15

Three-point field goals: 2001, 1-for-1. Totals, 1-for-1 (1.000).

STARKS, JOHN G JAZZ

PERSONAL: Born August 10, 1965, in Tulsa, Okla. ... 6-5/190. (1,96/86,2). ... Full Name: John Levell Starks.
HIGH SCHOOL: Tulsa (Okla.) Central.
JUNIOR COLLEGE: Northern Oklahoma College, then Rogers State College (Okla.), then Oklahoma Junior College.
COLLEGE: Oklahoma State.
TRANSACTIONS/CAREER NOTES: Not drafted by an NBA franchise. ... Signed as free agent by Golden State Warriors (September 29, 1988). ... Played in Continental Basketball Association with Cedar Rapids Silver Bullets (1989-90). ... Played in World Basketball League with Memphis Rockers (1990). ... Signed as unrestricted free agent by New York Knicks (October 1, 1990). ... Traded by Knicks with F Chris Mills and F Terry Cummings to Warriors for G Latrell Sprewell (January 21, 1999). ... Traded by Warriors with future first-round draft choice to Chicago Bulls in three-way deal in which Bulls sent F Toni Kukoc to Philadelphia 76ers and 76ers sent G Larry Hughes and F/G Billy Owens to Warriors and 76ers sent F Bruce Bowen to Bulls (February 16, 2000). ... Waived by Bulls (March 21, 2000). ... Signed as free agent by Utah Jazz (August 2, 2000).

COLLEGIATE RECORD

Season Team	G	Min.	FGM	FGA	Pct.	FTM	FTA	Pct.	Reb.	Ast.	Pts.	AVERAGES RPG	APG	PPG
84-85—Northern Okla. College ...	14	...	57	123	.463	41	53	.774	33	...	155	2.4	...	11.1
85-86—Rogers State College						Statistics unavailable.								
86-87—Oklahoma J.C.						Statistics unavailable.								
87-88—Oklahoma State	30	982	154	310	.497	114	136	.838	141	137	463	4.7	4.6	15.4
Junior College Totals	14	...	57	123	.463	41	53	.774	33	...	155	2.4	...	11.1
4-Year-College Totals	30	982	154	310	.497	114	136	.838	141	137	463	4.7	4.6	15.4

Three-point field goals: 1987-88, 41-for-108 (.380).

NBA REGULAR-SEASON RECORD

HONORS: NBA Sixth Man Award (1997). ... NBA All-Defensive second team (1993).

Season Team	G	Min.	FGM	FGA	Pct.	FTM	FTA	Pct.	REBOUNDS Off.	Def.	Tot.	Ast.	St.	Blk.	TO	Pts.	AVERAGES RPG	APG	PPG
88-89—Golden State ...	36	316	51	125	.408	34	52	.654	15	26	41	27	23	3	39	146	1.1	0.8	4.1
90-91—New York	61	1173	180	410	.439	79	105	.752	30	101	131	204	59	17	74	466	2.1	3.3	7.6
91-92—New York	82	2118	405	902	.449	235	302	.778	45	146	191	276	103	18	150	1139	2.3	3.4	13.9
92-93—New York	80	2477	513	1199	.428	263	331	.795	54	150	204	404	91	12	173	1397	2.6	5.1	17.5
93-94—New York	59	2057	410	977	.420	187	248	.754	37	148	185	348	95	6	184	1120	3.1	5.9	19.0
94-95—New York	80	2725	419	1062	.395	168	228	.737	34	185	219	411	92	4	160	1223	2.7	5.1	15.3
95-96—New York	81	2491	375	846	.443	131	174	.753	31	206	237	315	103	11	156	1024	2.9	3.9	12.6
96-97—New York	77	2042	369	856	.431	173	225	.769	36	169	205	217	90	11	158	1061	2.7	2.8	13.8
97-98—New York	82	2188	372	947	.393	185	235	.787	48	182	230	219	78	5	143	1059	2.8	2.7	12.9
98-99—Golden State ...	50	1686	269	728	.370	74	100	.740	33	130	163	235	69	5	83	690	3.3	4.7	13.8
99-00—Gold.St.-Chi. ...	37	1190	203	542	.375	50	59	.847	10	91	101	181	42	4	67	515	2.7	4.9	13.9
00-01—Utah	75	2122	273	686	.398	89	111	.802	29	125	154	178	73	10	94	699	2.1	2.4	9.3
Totals	800	22585	3839	9280	.414	1668	2170	.769	402	1659	2061	3015	918	106	1481	10539	2.6	3.8	13.2

Three-point field goals: 1988-89, 10-for-26 (.385). 1990-91, 27-for-93 (.290). 1991-92, 94-for-270 (.348). 1992-93, 108-for-336 (.321). 1993-94, 113-for-337 (.335). 1994-95, 217-for-611 (.355). 1995-96, 143-for-396 (.361). 1996-97, 150-for-407 (.369). 1997-98, 130-for-398 (.327). 1998-99, 78-for-269 (.290). 1999-00, 59-for-171 (.345). 2000-01, 64-for-182 (.352). Totals, 1193-for-3496 (.341).

Personal fouls/disqualifications: 1988-89, 36/0. 1990-91, 137/1. 1991-92, 231/4. 1992-93, 234/3. 1993-94, 191/4. 1994-95, 257/3. 1995-96, 226/2. 1996-97, 196/2. 1997-98, 205/2. 1998-99, 135/3. 1999-00, 102/1. 2000-01, 217/2. Totals, 2167/27.

NBA PLAYOFF RECORD

NOTES: Holds NBA Finals single-series record for most three-point field goals attempted—50 (1994, vs. Houston).

Season Team	G	Min.	FGM	FGA	Pct.	FTM	FTA	Pct.	REBOUNDS Off.	Def.	Tot.	Ast.	St.	Blk.	TO	Pts.	AVERAGES RPG	APG	PPG
90-91—New York	3	28	2	5	.400	2	2	1.000	1	2	3	6	0	0	6	6	1.0	2.0	2.0
91-92—New York	12	295	46	123	.374	42	52	.808	7	23	30	38	17	0	22	145	2.5	3.2	12.1
92-93—New York	15	575	88	200	.440	43	60	.717	4	48	52	96	15	3	55	247	3.5	6.4	16.5
93-94—New York	25	840	110	289	.381	97	126	.770	9	49	58	114	35	2	57	364	2.3	4.6	14.6
94-95—New York	11	380	58	129	.450	26	42	.619	2	23	25	57	13	1	26	172	2.3	5.2	15.6
95-96—New York	8	314	39	87	.448	29	39	.744	3	26	29	33	13	1	25	128	3.6	4.1	16.0
96-97—New York	9	253	44	99	.444	25	31	.806	7	24	31	25	10	0	20	126	3.4	2.8	14.0
97-98—New York	10	314	59	125	.472	21	24	.875	4	36	40	23	16	1	11	164	4.0	2.3	16.4
00-01—Utah	3	36	4	12	.333	2	2	1.000	0	3	3	1	1	1	2	11	1.0	0.3	3.7
Totals	96	3035	450	1069	.421	287	378	.759	37	234	271	393	120	9	224	1363	2.8	4.1	14.2

Three-point field goals: 1991-92, 11-for-46 (.239). 1992-93, 28-for-75 (.373). 1993-94, 47-for-132 (.356). 1994-95, 30-for-73 (.411). 1995-96, 21-for-45 (.467). 1996-97, 13-for-41 (.317). 1997-98, 25-for-59 (.424). 2000-01, 1-for-4 (.250). Totals, 176-for-475 (.371).

Personal fouls/disqualifications: 1990-91, 4/0. 1991-92, 45/1. 1992-93, 57/0. 1993-94, 86/1. 1994-95, 40/0. 1995-96, 26/0. 1996-97, 25/1. 1997-98, 35/1. 2000-01, 5/0. Totals, 323/4.

NBA ALL-STAR GAME RECORD

Season Team	Min.	FGM	FGA	Pct.	FTM	FTA	Pct.	REBOUNDS Off.	Def.	Tot.	Ast.	PF	Dq.	St.	Blk.	TO	Pts.
1994 —New York	20	4	9	.444	0	0	...	1	2	3	3	1	0	1	0	2	9

Three-point field goals: 1994, 1-for-3 (.333).

CBA REGULAR-SEASON RECORD

Season Team	G	Min.	FGM	FGA	Pct.	FTM	FTA	Pct.	Reb.	Ast.	Pts.	AVERAGES RPG	APG	PPG
89-90—Cedar Rapids	46	1670	385	801	.481	179	240	.746	246	255	997	5.3	5.5	21.7

Three-point field goals: 1989-90, 48-for-138 (.348).

STEPANIA, VLADIMIR   C

PERSONAL: Born May 8, 1976, in Tbilisi, Republic of Georgia. ... 7-0/236. (2,13/107,0).
TRANSACTIONS/CAREER NOTES: Played in Slovenia (1996-97 and 1997-98). ... Selected by Seattle SuperSonics in first round (27th pick overall) of 1998 NBA Draft. ... Traded by SuperSonics to New York Knicks as part of four-team trade in which Knicks acquired F Glen Rice, C Luc Longley, F/C Travis Knight, G Vernon Maxwell, F Lazaro Borrell, two 2001 first-round draft choices and two 2001 second-round draft choices, SuperSonics acquired C Patrick Ewing, Phoenix Suns acquired C Chris Dudley and 2001 first-round draft choice and Los Angeles Lakers acquired F Horace Grant, C Greg Foster, F Chuck Person and G Emanual Davis (September 20, 2000). ... Claimed on waivers by Toronto Raptors (October 25, 2000). ... Waived by Raptors (October 30, 2000). ... Signed as free agent by New Jersey Nets (December 15, 2000).

SLOVENIAN LEAGUE RECORD

												AVERAGES		
Season Team	G	Min.	FGM	FGA	Pct.	FTM	FTA	Pct.	Reb.	Ast.	Pts.	RPG	APG	PPG
96-97—Union Olimpija Ljubljana	23	...	58	111	.523	42	61	.689	99	5	159	4.3	0.2	6.9
97-98—Union Olimpija Ljubljana	17	404	60	135	.444	44	71	.620	97	9	170	5.7	0.5	10.0
Totals	40	...	118	246	.480	86	132	.652	196	14	329	4.9	0.4	8.2

Three-point field goals: 1996-97, 1-for-1. 1997-98, 6-for-16 (.375). Totals, 7-for-17 (.412).

NBA REGULAR-SEASON RECORD

									REBOUNDS								AVERAGES		
Season Team	G	Min.	FGM	FGA	Pct.	FTM	FTA	Pct.	Off.	Def.	Tot.	Ast.	St.	Blk.	TO	Pts.	RPG	APG	PPG
98-99—Seattle	23	313	53	125	.424	21	40	.525	27	48	75	12	10	23	32	127	3.3	0.5	5.5
99-00—Seattle	30	202	29	79	.367	17	36	.472	21	26	47	3	10	11	22	75	1.6	0.1	2.5
00-01—New Jersey	29	280	28	88	.318	25	34	.735	35	74	109	16	10	11	19	82	3.8	0.6	2.8
Totals	82	795	110	292	.377	63	110	.573	83	148	231	31	30	45	73	284	2.8	0.4	3.5

Three-point field goals: 1998-99, 0-for-3. 1999-00, 0-for-6. 2000-01, 1-for-4 (.250). Totals, 1-for-13 (.077).
Personal fouls/disqualifications: 1998-99, 58/0. 1999-00, 44/0. 2000-01, 47/0. Totals, 149/0.

STEVENSON, DeSHAWN   G   JAZZ

PERSONAL: Born April 3, 1981, in Fresno, Calif. ... 6-5/210. (1,96/95,3).
HIGH SCHOOL: Washington Union (Fresno, Calif.).
COLLEGE: Did not attend college.
TRANSACTIONS/CAREER NOTES: Selected out of high school by Utah Jazz in first round (23rd pick overall) of 2000 NBA Draft.

NBA REGULAR-SEASON RECORD

									REBOUNDS								AVERAGES		
Season Team	G	Min.	FGM	FGA	Pct.	FTM	FTA	Pct.	Off.	Def.	Tot.	Ast.	St.	Blk.	TO	Pts.	RPG	APG	PPG
00-01—Utah	40	293	31	91	.341	26	38	.684	9	19	28	18	10	2	28	89	0.7	0.5	2.2

Three-point field goals: 2000-01, 1-for-12 (.083).
Personal fouls/disqualifications: 2000-01, 29/0.

NBA PLAYOFF RECORD

									REBOUNDS								AVERAGES		
Season Team	G	Min.	FGM	FGA	Pct.	FTM	FTA	Pct.	Off.	Def.	Tot.	Ast.	St.	Blk.	TO	Pts.	RPG	APG	PPG
00-01—Utah	1	8	1	2	.500	0	0	...	0	1	1	0	0	0	1	2	1.0	0.0	2.0

STEWART, MICHAEL   C   RAPTORS

PERSONAL: Born April 24, 1975, in Cutq Trepied Stella Plage, France. ... 6-10/230. (2,08/104,3). ... Full Name: Michael Curtis Stewart.
HIGH SCHOOL: Kennedy (Sacramento).
COLLEGE: California.
TRANSACTIONS/CAREER NOTES: Not drafted by an NBA franchise. ... Signed as free agent by Sacramento Kings (September 11, 1997). ... Signed as free agent by Toronto Raptors (January 21, 1999).

COLLEGIATE RECORD

												AVERAGES		
Season Team	G	Min.	FGM	FGA	Pct.	FTM	FTA	Pct.	Reb.	Ast.	Pts.	RPG	APG	PPG
93-94—California	30	696	40	85	.471	31	65	.477	152	9	111	5.1	0.3	3.7
94-95—California	27	470	43	85	.506	18	39	.462	116	7	104	4.3	0.3	3.9
95-96—California	28	440	35	65	.538	12	27	.444	121	8	82	4.3	0.3	2.9
96-97—California	32	659	83	159	.522	36	68	.529	160	8	202	5.0	0.3	6.3
Totals	117	2265	201	394	.510	97	199	.487	549	32	499	4.7	0.3	4.3

NBA REGULAR-SEASON RECORD

									REBOUNDS								AVERAGES		
Season Team	G	Min.	FGM	FGA	Pct.	FTM	FTA	Pct.	Off.	Def.	Tot.	Ast.	St.	Blk.	TO	Pts.	RPG	APG	PPG
97-98—Sacramento	81	1761	155	323	.480	65	142	.458	197	339	536	61	29	195	85	375	6.6	0.8	4.6
98-99—Toronto	42	394	22	53	.415	17	25	.680	43	56	99	5	4	28	12	61	2.4	0.1	1.5
99-00—Toronto	42	389	20	53	.377	18	32	.563	33	61	94	6	5	19	17	58	2.2	0.1	1.4
00-01—Toronto	26	123	11	34	.324	11	18	.611	16	13	29	2	4	3	5	33	1.1	0.1	1.3
Totals	191	2667	208	463	.449	111	217	.512	289	469	758	74	42	245	119	527	4.0	0.4	2.8

Personal fouls/disqualifications: 1997-98, 251/6. 1998-99, 76/0. 1999-00, 81/3. 2000-01, 19/0. Totals, 427/9.

NBA PLAYOFF RECORD

									REBOUNDS								AVERAGES		
Season Team	G	Min.	FGM	FGA	Pct.	FTM	FTA	Pct.	Off.	Def.	Tot.	Ast.	St.	Blk.	TO	Pts.	RPG	APG	PPG
00-01—Toronto	2	4	0	1	.000	0	0	...	1	0	1	0	0	0	0	0	0.5	0.0	0.0

STITH, BRYANT　　　　　　　　G　　　　　　　　CAVALIERS

PERSONAL: Born December 10, 1970, in Emporia, Va. ... 6-5/210. (1,96/95,3). ... Full Name: Bryant Lamonica Stith.
HIGH SCHOOL: Brunswick (Lawrenceville, Va.).
COLLEGE: Virginia.
TRANSACTIONS/CAREER NOTES: Selected by Denver Nuggets in first round (13th pick overall) of 1992 NBA Draft. ... Traded by Nuggets with G Chris Herren to Boston Celtics for G Robert Pack and F Calbert Cheaney (October 16, 2000). ... Signed as free agent by Cleveland Cavaliers (August 13, 2001).
MISCELLANEOUS: Member of bronze-medal winning U.S. World Championship team (1990).

COLLEGIATE RECORD

Season Team	G	Min.	FGM	FGA	Pct.	FTM	FTA	Pct.	Reb.	Ast.	Pts.	RPG	APG	PPG
88-89—Virginia	33	942	181	330	.548	150	195	.769	216	50	513	6.5	1.5	15.5
89-90—Virginia	32	1127	217	451	.481	192	247	.777	221	53	666	6.9	1.7	20.8
90-91—Virginia	33	1120	228	484	.471	159	201	.791	203	41	653	6.2	1.2	19.8
91-92—Virginia	33	1202	230	509	.452	189	232	.815	219	72	684	6.6	2.2	20.7
Totals	131	4391	856	1774	.483	690	875	.789	859	216	2516	6.6	1.6	19.2

Three-point field goals: 1988-89, 1-for-1. 1989-90, 40-for-102 (.392). 1990-91, 38-for-125 (.304). 1991-92, 35-for-95 (.368). Totals, 114-for-323 (.353).

NBA REGULAR-SEASON RECORD

Season Team	G	Min.	FGM	FGA	Pct.	FTM	FTA	Pct.	Off.	Def.	Tot.	Ast.	St.	Blk.	TO	Pts.	RPG	APG	PPG
92-93—Denver	39	865	124	278	.446	99	119	.832	39	85	124	49	24	5	44	347	3.2	1.3	8.9
93-94—Denver	82	2853	365	811	.450	291	351	.829	119	230	349	199	116	16	131	1023	4.3	2.4	12.5
94-95—Denver	81	2329	312	661	.472	267	324	.824	95	173	268	153	91	18	110	911	3.3	1.9	11.2
95-96—Denver	82	2810	379	911	.416	320	379	.844	125	275	400	241	114	16	157	1119	4.9	2.9	13.6
96-97—Denver	52	1788	251	603	.416	202	234	.863	74	143	217	133	60	20	101	774	4.2	2.6	14.9
97-98—Denver	31	718	75	225	.333	75	86	.872	15	50	65	50	21	8	35	235	2.1	1.6	7.6
98-99—Denver	46	1194	114	290	.393	61	71	.859	30	77	107	82	28	15	45	320	2.3	1.8	7.0
99-00—Denver	45	691	86	189	.455	64	77	.831	23	61	84	61	18	12	33	253	1.9	1.4	5.6
00-01—Boston	78	2504	245	611	.401	175	207	.845	65	219	284	168	93	14	90	756	3.6	2.2	9.7
Totals	536	15752	1951	4579	.426	1554	1848	.841	585	1313	1898	1136	565	124	746	5738	3.5	2.1	10.7

Three-point field goals: 1992-93, 0-for-4. 1993-94, 2-for-9 (.222). 1994-95, 20-for-68 (.294). 1995-96, 41-for-148 (.277). 1996-97, 70-for-182 (.385). 1997-98, 10-for-48 (.208). 1998-99, 31-for-106 (.292). 1999-00, 17-for-56 (.304). 2000-01, 91-for-242 (.376). Totals, 282-for-863 (.327).

Personal fouls/disqualifications: 1992-93, 82/0. 1993-94, 165/0. 1994-95, 142/0. 1995-96, 187/3. 1996-97, 119/1. 1997-98, 52/0. 1998-99, 65/0. 1999-00, 56/0. 2000-01, 182/0. Totals, 1050/4.

NBA PLAYOFF RECORD

Season Team	G	Min.	FGM	FGA	Pct.	FTM	FTA	Pct.	Off.	Def.	Tot.	Ast.	St.	Blk.	TO	Pts.	RPG	APG	PPG
93-94—Denver	12	413	43	102	.422	50	60	.833	23	33	56	26	11	2	14	136	4.7	2.2	11.3
94-95—Denver	3	85	17	32	.531	15	19	.789	3	6	9	7	1	1	0	50	3.0	2.3	16.7
Totals	15	498	60	134	.448	65	79	.823	26	39	65	33	12	3	14	186	4.3	2.2	12.4

Three-point field goals: 1993-94, 0-for-1. 1994-95, 1-for-6 (.167). Totals, 1-for-7 (.143).
Personal fouls/disqualifications: 1993-94, 23/0. 1994-95, 7/0. Totals, 30/0.

STOCKTON, JOHN　　　　　　　G　　　　　　　　JAZZ

PERSONAL: Born March 26, 1962, in Spokane, Wash. ... 6-1/175. (1,85/79,4). ... Full Name: John Houston Stockton.
HIGH SCHOOL: Gonzaga Prep School (Spokane, Wash.).
COLLEGE: Gonzaga.
TRANSACTIONS/CAREER NOTES: Selected by Utah Jazz in first round (16th pick overall) of 1984 NBA Draft.
CAREER HONORS: NBA 50th Anniversary All-Time Team (1996).
MISCELLANEOUS: Member of gold-medal-winning U.S. Olympic teams (1992, 1996). ... Utah Jazz franchise all-time assists leader with 14,503 and all-time steals leader with 2,976 (1984-85 through 2000-01).

COLLEGIATE RECORD

Season Team	G	Min.	FGM	FGA	Pct.	FTM	FTA	Pct.	Reb.	Ast.	Pts.	RPG	APG	PPG
80-81—Gonzaga	25	235	26	45	.578	26	35	.743	11	34	78	0.4	1.4	3.1
81-82—Gonzaga	27	1054	117	203	.576	69	102	.676	67	135	303	2.5	5.0	11.2
82-83—Gonzaga	27	1036	142	274	.518	91	115	.791	87	184	375	3.2	6.8	13.9
83-84—Gonzaga	28	1053	229	397	.577	126	182	.692	66	201	584	2.4	7.2	20.9
Totals	107	3378	514	919	.559	312	434	.719	231	554	1340	2.2	5.2	12.5

NBA REGULAR-SEASON RECORD

RECORDS: Holds career records for most seasons leading league in assists—9; most consecutive seasons leading league in assists—9 (1987-88 through 1995-96); most assists—14,503; and most steals—2,976. ... Holds single-season records for most assists—1,164 (1991); and highest assists-per-game average (minimum 70 games)—14.5 (1990).
HONORS: All-NBA first team (1994, 1995). ... All-NBA second team (1988, 1989, 1990, 1992, 1993, 1996). ... All-NBA third team (1991, 1997, 1999). ... NBA All-Defensive second team (1989, 1991, 1992, 1995, 1997).
NOTES: Led NBA with 3.21 steals per game (1989) and 2.98 steals per game (1992).

Season Team	G	Min.	FGM	FGA	Pct.	FTM	FTA	Pct.	Off.	Def.	Tot.	Ast.	St.	Blk.	TO	Pts.	RPG	APG	PPG
84-85—Utah	82	1490	157	333	.471	142	193	.736	26	79	105	415	109	11	150	458	1.3	5.1	5.6
85-86—Utah	82	1935	228	466	.489	172	205	.839	33	146	179	610	157	10	168	630	2.2	7.4	7.7
86-87—Utah	82	1858	231	463	.499	179	229	.782	32	119	151	670	177	14	164	648	1.8	8.2	7.9
87-88—Utah	82	2842	454	791	.574	272	324	.840	54	183	237	*1128	242	16	262	1204	2.9	*13.8	14.7

Season Team	G	Min.	FGM	FGA	Pct.	FTM	FTA	Pct.	REBOUNDS Off.	Def.	Tot.	Ast.	St.	Blk.	TO	Pts.	AVERAGES RPG	APG	PPG
88-89—Utah	82	3171	497	923	.538	390	452	.863	83	165	248	*1118	*263	14	308	1400	3.0	*13.6	17.1
89-90—Utah	78	2915	472	918	.514	354	432	.819	57	149	206	*1134	207	18	272	1345	2.6	*14.5	17.2
90-91—Utah	82	3103	496	978	.507	363	434	.836	46	191	237	*1164	234	16	298	1413	2.9	*14.2	17.2
91-92—Utah	82	3002	453	939	.482	308	366	.842	68	202	270	*1126	*244	22	*286	1297	3.3	*13.7	15.8
92-93—Utah	82	2863	437	899	.486	293	367	.798	64	173	237	*987	199	21	266	1239	2.9	*12.0	15.1
93-94—Utah	82	2969	458	868	.528	272	338	.805	72	186	258	*1031	199	22	266	1236	3.1	*12.6	15.1
94-95—Utah	82	2867	429	791	.542	246	306	.804	57	194	251	*1011	194	22	267	1206	3.1	*12.3	14.7
95-96—Utah	82	2915	440	818	.538	234	282	.830	54	172	226	*916	140	15	246	1209	2.8	*11.2	14.7
96-97—Utah	82	2896	416	759	.548	275	325	.846	45	183	228	860	166	15	248	1183	2.8	10.5	14.4
97-98—Utah	64	1858	270	511	.528	191	231	.827	35	131	166	543	89	10	161	770	2.6	8.5	12.0
98-99—Utah	50	1410	200	410	.488	137	169	.811	31	115	146	374	81	13	110	553	2.9	7.5	11.1
99-00—Utah	82	2432	363	725	.501	221	257	.860	45	170	215	703	143	15	179	990	2.6	8.6	12.1
00-01—Utah	82	2397	328	651	.504	227	278	.817	54	173	227	713	132	21	203	944	2.8	8.7	11.5
Totals	1340	42923	6329	12243	.517	4276	5188	.824	856	2731	3587	14503	2976	275	3854	17725	2.7	10.8	13.2

Three-point field goals: 1984-85, 2-for-11 (.182). 1985-86, 2-for-15 (.133). 1986-87, 7-for-38 (.184). 1987-88, 24-for-67 (.358). 1988-89, 16-for-66 (.242). 1989-90, 47-for-113 (.416). 1990-91, 58-for-168 (.345). 1991-92, 83-for-204 (.407). 1992-93, 72-for-187 (.385). 1993-94, 48-for-149 (.322). 1994-95, 102-for-227 (.449). 1995-96, 95-for-225 (.422). 1996-97, 76-for-180 (.422). 1997-98, 39-for-91 (.429). 1998-99, 16-for-50 (.320). 1999-00, 43-for-121 (.355). 2000-01, 61-for-132 (.462). Totals, 791-for-2044 (.387).

Personal fouls/disqualifications: 1984-85, 203/3. 1985-86, 227/2. 1986-87, 224/1. 1987-88, 247/5. 1988-89, 241/3. 1989-90, 233/3. 1990-91, 233/1. 1991-92, 234/3. 1992-93, 224/2. 1993-94, 236/3. 1994-95, 215/3. 1995-96, 207/1. 1996-97, 194/2. 1997-98, 138/0. 1998-99, 107/0. 1999-00, 192/0. 2000-01, 194/1. Totals, 3549/33.

NBA PLAYOFF RECORD

NOTES: Shares NBA Finals single-game record for most assists in one quarter—8 (June 10, 1998, at Chicago). ... Holds single-game playoff record for most assists in one quarter—11 (May 5, 1994, vs. San Antonio). ... Shares single-game playoff record for most assists—24 (May 17, 1988, vs. Los Angeles Lakers).

Season Team	G	Min.	FGM	FGA	Pct.	FTM	FTA	Pct.	REBOUNDS Off.	Def.	Tot.	Ast.	St.	Blk.	TO	Pts.	AVERAGES RPG	APG	PPG
84-85—Utah	10	186	21	45	.467	26	35	.743	7	21	28	43	11	2	16	68	2.8	4.3	6.8
85-86—Utah	4	73	9	17	.529	8	9	.889	3	3	6	14	5	0	4	27	1.5	3.5	6.8
86-87—Utah	5	157	18	29	.621	10	13	.769	2	9	11	40	15	1	11	50	2.2	8.0	10.0
87-88—Utah	11	478	68	134	.507	75	91	.824	14	31	45	163	37	3	48	215	4.1	14.8	19.5
88-89—Utah	3	139	30	59	.508	19	21	.905	2	8	10	41	11	5	11	82	3.3	13.7	27.3
89-90—Utah	5	194	29	69	.420	16	20	.800	4	12	16	75	6	0	14	75	3.2	15.0	15.0
90-91—Utah	9	373	58	108	.537	37	44	.841	10	32	42	124	20	2	32	164	4.7	13.8	18.2
91-92—Utah	16	623	77	182	.423	65	78	.833	10	37	47	217	34	5	58	237	2.9	13.6	14.8
92-93—Utah	5	193	23	51	.451	15	18	.833	5	7	12	55	12	0	15	66	2.4	11.0	13.2
93-94—Utah	16	597	88	193	.456	51	63	.810	14	38	52	157	27	8	40	231	3.3	9.8	14.4
94-95—Utah	5	193	34	74	.459	13	17	.765	6	11	17	51	7	1	14	89	3.4	10.2	17.8
95-96—Utah	18	679	70	157	.446	48	59	.814	14	44	58	195	29	7	58	199	3.2	10.8	11.1
96-97—Utah	20	739	113	217	.521	77	90	.856	18	60	78	191	33	5	62	322	3.9	9.6	16.1
97-98—Utah	20	596	81	164	.494	51	71	.718	16	44	60	155	31	3	48	222	3.0	7.8	11.1
98-99—Utah	11	352	42	105	.400	34	46	.739	11	25	36	92	18	1	31	122	3.3	8.4	11.1
99-00—Utah	10	350	41	89	.461	23	30	.767	7	23	30	103	13	2	26	112	3.0	10.3	11.2
00-01—Utah	5	186	17	37	.459	15	21	.714	11	17	28	57	10	3	7	49	5.6	11.4	9.8
Totals	173	6108	819	1730	.473	583	726	.803	154	422	576	1773	319	48	495	2330	3.3	10.2	13.5

Three-point field goals: 1984-85, 0-for-2. 1985-86, 1-for-1. 1986-87, 4-for-5 (.800). 1987-88, 2-for-7 (.286). 1988-89, 3-for-4 (.750). 1989-90, 1-for-13 (.077). 1990-91, 11-for-27 (.407). 1991-92, 18-for-58 (.310). 1992-93, 5-for-13 (.385). 1993-94, 4-for-24 (.167). 1994-95, 8-for-20 (.400). 1995-96, 11-for-38 (.289). 1996-97, 19-for-50 (.380). 1997-98, 9-for-26 (.346). 1998-99, 4-for-12 (.333). 1999-00, 7-for-18 (.389). 2000-01, 0-for-8. Totals, 109-for-333 (.327).

Personal fouls/disqualifications: 1984-85, 30/0. 1985-86, 10/0. 1986-87, 18/0. 1987-88, 36/0. 1988-89, 15/0. 1989-90, 20/0. 1990-91, 33/0. 1991-92, 38/0. 1992-93, 16/0. 1993-94, 44/0. 1994-95, 13/0. 1995-96, 50/0. 1996-97, 52/0. 1997-98, 54/0. 1998-99, 32/0. 1999-00, 30/0. 2000-01, 19/0. Totals, 510/0.

NBA ALL-STAR GAME RECORD

NOTES: NBA All-Star Game Co-Most Valuable Player (1993). ... Holds single-game record for most assists in one quarter—9 (1989).

Season Team	Min.	FGM	FGA	Pct.	FTM	FTA	Pct.	REBOUNDS Off.	Def.	Tot.	Ast.	PF	Dq.	St.	Blk.	TO	Pts.
1989 —Utah	32	5	6	.833	0	0	...	0	2	2	17	4	0	5	0	12	11
1990 —Utah	15	1	4	.250	0	0	...	0	0	0	6	1	0	1	1	3	2
1991 —Utah	12	1	6	.167	2	4	.500	0	1	1	2	2	0	0	0	0	4
1992 —Utah	18	5	8	.625	0	0	...	0	1	1	5	2	0	3	0	3	12
1993 —Utah	31	3	6	.500	2	2	1.000	0	6	6	15	3	0	2	0	6	9
1994 —Utah	26	6	10	.600	0	0	...	1	4	5	10	2	0	1	0	4	13
1995 —Utah	14	2	6	.333	0	0	...	1	0	1	6	0	0	2	0	0	4
1996 —Utah	18	2	9	.222	0	0	...	0	1	1	3	2	0	0	1	0	4
1997 —Utah	20	5	6	.833	0	0	...	0	0	0	5	2	0	1	0	1	12
2000 —Utah	11	5	5	1.000	0	0	...	0	0	0	2	2	0	1	0	0	10
Totals	197	35	66	.530	4	6	.667	2	15	17	71	20	0	16	1	29	81

Three-point field goals: 1989, 1 for 1. 1990, 0-for-1. 1992, 2-for-3 (.667). 1993, 1-for-2 (.500). 1994, 1-for-1. 1995, 0-for-3. 1996, 0-for-7. 1997, 2-for-2. Totals, 7-for-20 (.350).

DID YOU KNOW . . .

. . . that Tim Duncan, Antonio McDyess and Shaquille O'Neal were the only players to have at least two 20-point/20-rebound games during the 2000-01 season?

STOJAKOVIC, PREDRAG F KINGS

PERSONAL: Born June 9, 1977, in Belgrade, Yugoslavia. ... 6-9/229. (2,06/103,9). ... Nickname: Peja.
COLLEGE: PAOK (Greece).
TRANSACTIONS/CAREER NOTES: Played in Greece (1995-96 through 1997-98). ... Selected by Sacramento Kings in first round (14th pick overall) of 1996 NBA Draft.

GREEK LEAGUE RECORD

Season Team	G	Min.	FGM	FGA	Pct.	FTM	FTA	Pct.	Reb.	Ast.	Pts.	AVERAGES RPG	APG	PPG
95-96—PAOK	31	...	185	343	.539	115	145	.793	159	47	523	5.1	1.5	16.9
96-97—PAOK	16	554	110	218	.505	71	82	.866	74	17	324	4.6	1.1	20.3
97-98—PAOK	24	884	187	405	.462	131	147	.891	118	59	574	4.9	2.5	23.9
Totals	71	...	482	966	.499	317	374	.848	351	123	1421	4.9	1.7	20.0

Three-point field goals: 1995-96, 38-for-98 (.388). 1996-97, 33-for-86 (.384). 1997-98, 69-for-170 (.406). Totals, 140-for-354 (.395).

NBA REGULAR-SEASON RECORD

Season Team	G	Min.	FGM	FGA	Pct.	FTM	FTA	Pct.	REBOUNDS Off.	Def.	Tot.	Ast.	St.	Blk.	TO	Pts.	AVERAGES RPG	APG	PPG
98-99—Sacramento	48	1025	141	373	.378	63	74	.851	43	100	143	72	41	7	53	402	3.0	1.5	8.4
99-00—Sacramento	74	1749	321	717	.448	135	153	.882	74	202	276	106	52	7	88	877	3.7	1.4	11.9
00-01—Sacramento	75	2905	559	1189	.470	267	312	.856	93	341	434	164	91	13	146	1529	5.8	2.2	20.4
Totals	197	5679	1021	2279	.448	465	539	.863	210	643	853	342	184	27	287	2808	4.3	1.7	14.3

Three-point field goals: 1998-99, 57-for-178 (.320). 1999-00, 100-for-267 (.375). 2000-01, 144-for-360 (.400). Totals, 301-for-805 (.374).
Personal fouls/disqualifications: 1998-99, 43/0. 1999-00, 97/0. 2000-01, 144/0. Totals, 284/0.

NBA PLAYOFF RECORD

Season Team	G	Min.	FGM	FGA	Pct.	FTM	FTA	Pct.	REBOUNDS Off.	Def.	Tot.	Ast.	St.	Blk.	TO	Pts.	AVERAGES RPG	APG	PPG
98-99—Sacramento	5	108	9	26	.346	3	3	1.000	12	7	19	2	3	0	6	24	3.8	0.4	4.8
99-00—Sacramento	5	129	16	40	.400	6	9	.667	2	15	17	3	4	0	5	44	3.4	0.6	8.8
00-01—Sacramento	8	307	52	128	.406	60	62	.968	17	34	51	3	5	3	18	173	6.4	0.4	21.6
Totals	18	544	77	194	.397	69	74	.932	31	56	87	8	12	3	29	241	4.8	0.4	13.4

Three-point field goals: 1998-99, 3-for-14 (.214). 1999-00, 6-for-13 (.462). 2000-01, 9-for-26 (.346). Totals, 18-for-53 (.340).
Personal fouls/disqualifications: 1998-99, 7/0. 1999-00, 7/0. 2000-01, 17/0. Totals, 31/0.

STOUDAMIRE, DAMON G TRAIL BLAZERS

PERSONAL: Born September 3, 1973, in Portland, Ore. ... 5-10/171. (1,78/77,6). ... Full Name: Damon Lamon Stoudamire. ... Name pronounced DAY-min STOD-a-mire.
HIGH SCHOOL: Woodrow Wilson (Portland, Ore.).
COLLEGE: Arizona.
TRANSACTIONS/CAREER NOTES: Selected by Toronto Raptors in first round (seventh pick overall) of 1995 NBA Draft. ... Traded by Raptors with F Walt Williams and F Carlos Rogers to Portland Trail Blazers for G Kenny Anderson, G Alvin Williams, F Gary Trent and two first-round draft choices (February 13, 1998).
MISCELLANEOUS: Toronto Raptors all-time assists leader with 1,761 (1995-96 through 1997-98).

COLLEGIATE RECORD

NOTES: THE SPORTING NEWS All-America first team (1995).

Season Team	G	Min.	FGM	FGA	Pct.	FTM	FTA	Pct.	Reb.	Ast.	Pts.	AVERAGES RPG	APG	PPG
91-92—Arizona	30	540	76	167	.455	37	48	.771	65	76	217	2.2	2.5	7.2
92-93—Arizona	28	870	99	226	.438	72	91	.791	116	159	309	4.1	5.7	11.0
93-94—Arizona	35	1164	217	484	.448	112	140	.800	157	208	639	4.5	5.9	18.3
94-95—Arizona	30	1092	222	466	.476	128	155	.826	128	220	684	4.3	7.3	22.8
Totals	123	3666	614	1343	.457	349	434	.804	466	663	1849	3.8	5.4	15.0

Three-point field goals: 1991-92, 28-for-69 (.406). 1992-93, 39-for-102 (.382). 1993-94, 93-for-265 (.351). 1994-95, 112-for-241 (.465). Totals, 272-for-677 (.402).

NBA REGULAR-SEASON RECORD

HONORS: NBA Rookie of the Year (1996). ... NBA All-Rookie first team (1996).

Season Team	G	Min.	FGM	FGA	Pct.	FTM	FTA	Pct.	REBOUNDS Off.	Def.	Tot.	Ast.	St.	Blk.	TO	Pts.	AVERAGES RPG	APG	PPG
95-96—Toronto	70	2865	481	1129	.426	236	296	.797	59	222	281	653	98	19	267	1331	4.0	9.3	19.0
96-97—Toronto	81	3311	564	1407	.401	330	401	.823	86	244	330	709	123	13	288	1634	4.1	8.8	20.2
97-98—Tor.-Port.	71	2839	448	1091	.411	238	287	.829	87	211	298	580	113	7	223	1225	4.2	8.2	17.3
98-99—Portland	50	1673	249	629	.396	89	122	.730	41	126	167	312	49	4	110	631	3.3	6.2	12.6
99-00—Portland	78	2372	386	894	.432	122	145	.841	61	182	243	405	77	1	149	954	3.1	5.2	12.5
00-01—Portland	82	2655	406	935	.434	172	207	.831	69	234	303	468	106	8	191	1066	3.7	5.7	13.0
Totals	432	15715	2534	6085	.416	1187	1458	.814	403	1219	1622	3127	566	52	1228	6861	3.8	7.2	15.9

Three-point field goals: 1995-96, 133-for-337 (.395). 1996-97, 176-for-496 (.355). 1997-98, 91-for-304 (.299). 1998-99, 44-for-142 (.310). 1999-00, 80-for-212 (.377). 2000-01, 82-for-219 (.374). Totals, 606-for-1710 (.354).
Personal fouls/disqualifications: 1995-96, 166/0. 1996-97, 162/1. 1997-98, 150/0. 1998-99, 173/0. 1999-00, 202/1. Totals, 934/2.

NBA PLAYOFF RECORD

Season Team	G	Min.	FGM	FGA	Pct.	FTM	FTA	Pct.	REBOUNDS Off.	Def.	Tot.	Ast.	St.	Blk.	TO	Pts.	AVERAGES RPG	APG	PPG
97-98—Portland	4	166	25	63	.397	13	13	1.000	6	11	17	38	5	1	16	71	4.3	9.5	17.8
98-99—Portland	13	403	49	129	.380	24	34	.706	7	34	41	73	8	1	38	132	3.2	5.6	10.2
99-00—Portland	16	447	56	135	.415	20	24	.833	8	34	42	58	8	4	19	142	2.6	3.6	8.9
00-01—Portland	3	114	19	46	.413	13	13	1.000	1	8	9	13	2	1	9	53	3.0	4.3	17.7
Totals	36	1130	149	373	.399	70	84	.833	22	87	109	182	23	7	82	398	3.0	5.1	11.1

Three-point field goals: 1997-98, 8-for-22 (.364). 1998-99, 10-for-22 (.455). 1999-00, 10-for-30 (.333). 2000-01, 2-for-13 (.154). Totals, 30-for-87 (.345).

Personal fouls/disqualifications: 1997-98, 13/0. 1998-99, 31/0. 1999-00, 43/1. 2000-01, 6/0. Totals, 93/1.

STRICKLAND, ERICK   G

S

PERSONAL: Born November 25, 1973, in Opelika, Ala. ... 6-3/210. (1,91/95,3). ... Full Name: Demerick Montae Strickland.

HIGH SCHOOL: West (Bellevue, Neb.).

COLLEGE: Nebraska.

TRANSACTIONS/CAREER NOTES: Not drafted by an NBA franchise. ... Signed as free agent by Dallas Mavericks (October 1, 1996). ... Waived by Mavericks (January 7, 1997). ... Played in Continental Basketball Association with Oklahoma City Cavalry (1996-97) and Quad City Thunder (1996-97). ... Signed by Mavericks to 10-day contract (February 17, 1997). ... Signed by Mavericks for remainder of season (February 25, 1997). ... Traded by Mavericks with draft rights to F Pete Mickeal to New York Knicks for F John Wallace and draft rights to F Donnell Harvey (June 28, 2000). ... Traded by Knicks with 2001 first-round draft choice and 2001 second-round draft choice to Vancouver Grizzlies for F Othella Harrington (January 30, 2001).

COLLEGIATE RECORD

Season Team	G	Min.	FGM	FGA	Pct.	FTM	FTA	Pct.	Reb.	Ast.	Pts.	AVERAGES RPG	APG	PPG
92-93—Nebraska	31	534	84	185	.454	43	59	.729	63	66	243	2.0	2.1	7.8
93-94—Nebraska	30	672	102	241	.423	77	95	.811	103	96	322	3.4	3.2	10.7
94-95—Nebraska	31	942	175	394	.444	101	139	.727	167	133	505	5.4	4.3	16.3
95-96—Nebraska	35	1087	174	399	.436	116	141	.823	170	119	516	4.9	3.4	14.7
Totals	127	3235	535	1219	.439	337	434	.776	503	414	1586	4.0	3.3	12.5

Three-point field goals: 1992-93, 32-for-88 (.364). 1993-94, 41-for-117 (.350). 1994-95, 54-for-160 (.338). 1995-96, 52-for-148 (.351). Totals, 179-for-513 (.349).

CBA REGULAR-SEASON RECORD

Season Team	G	Min.	FGM	FGA	Pct.	FTM	FTA	Pct.	Reb.	Ast.	Pts.	AVERAGES RPG	APG	PPG
96-97—Okla. City-Quad City	16	303	59	118	.500	42	49	.857	53	51	187	3.3	3.2	11.7

Three-point field goals: 1996-97, 27-for-61 (.443).

NBA REGULAR-SEASON RECORD

Season Team	G	Min.	FGM	FGA	Pct.	FTM	FTA	Pct.	REBOUNDS Off.	Def.	Tot.	Ast.	St.	Blk.	TO	Pts.	AVERAGES RPG	APG	PPG
96-97—Dallas	28	759	102	256	.398	65	80	.813	21	69	90	68	27	5	66	297	3.2	2.4	10.6
97-98—Dallas	67	1505	199	558	.357	65	84	.774	35	126	161	167	56	8	106	511	2.4	2.5	7.6
98-99—Dallas	33	567	89	221	.403	53	65	.815	12	71	83	64	40	2	36	249	2.5	1.9	7.5
99-00—Dallas	68	2025	316	730	.433	162	195	.831	69	254	323	211	105	13	102	867	4.8	3.1	12.8
00-01—N.Y.-Van	50	830	81	267	.303	68	79	.861	18	110	128	95	44	2	48	260	2.6	1.9	5.2
Totals	246	5686	787	2032	.387	413	503	.821	155	630	785	605	272	30	358	2184	3.2	2.5	8.9

Three-point field goals: 1996-97, 28-for-92 (.304). 1997-98, 48-for-163 (.294). 1998-99, 18-for-59 (.305). 1999-00, 73-for-186 (.392). 2000-01, 30-for-95 (.316). Totals, 197-for-595 (.331).

Personal fouls/disqualifications: 1996-97, 75/3. 1997-98, 140/1. 1998-99, 44/0. 1999-00, 190/3. 2000-01, 88/0. Totals, 537/7.

RECORD AS BASEBALL PLAYER

TRANSACTIONS/CAREER NOTES: Threw right, batted left. ... Selected by Florida Marlins organization in 31st round of free agent draft (June 1, 1992).

Season Team	Pos.	G.	AB	R	H	2B	3B	HR	RBI	Avg.	BB	SO	SB	FIELDING PO	A	E	Avg.
1992—GC Marlins (GCL)	OF	44	150	21	40	3	2	0	23	.267	20	26	11	64	3	2	.971
1993—Elmira (NY-Penn)	OF	59	212	30	55	11	3	4	34	.259	35	32	8	90	2	3	.968

STRICKLAND, MARK   F

PERSONAL: Born July 14, 1970, in Atlanta. ... 6-10/215. (2,08/97,5).

HIGH SCHOOL: Mcnair (Atlanta).

COLLEGE: Temple.

TRANSACTIONS/CAREER NOTES: Not drafted by an NBA franchise. ... Played in United States Basketball League with Philadelphia Spirit (1992), Atlanta Eagles/Trojans (1993 and 1994) and Atlantic City Seagulls (1996). ... Signed as free agent by Atlanta Hawks (September 16, 1992). ... Waived by Hawks (October 16, 1992). ... Played in Continental Basketball Association with Fort Wayne Fury (1994-95) and Yakima Sun Kings (1995-96). ... Signed by Indiana Pacers to first of two consecutive 10-day contracts (March 4, 1995). ... Waived by Pacers (March 24, 1995). ... Signed as free agent by Pacers (October 5, 1995). ... Waived by Pacers (October 23, 1995). ... Signed as free agent by Miami Heat (October 3, 1996). ... Waived by Heat (January 7, 1997). ... Re-signed by Heat to first of two consecutive 10-day contracts (January 12, 1997). ... Signed by Heat for remainder of season (February 1, 1997). ... Traded by Heat with G Voshon Lenard to Denver Nuggets for F/C Chris Gatling and a 2000 second-round draft choice (June 27, 2000). ... Waived by Nuggets (March 22, 2001). ... Signed by New Jersey Nets to first of two consecutive 10-day contracts (March 28, 2001). ... Re-signed by Nets for remainder of season (April 17, 2001).

COLLEGIATE RECORD

Season Team	G	Min.	FGM	FGA	Pct.	FTM	FTA	Pct.	Reb.	Ast.	Pts.	RPG	APG	PPG
88-89—Temple..........						Did not play—ineligible.								
89-90—Temple..........	31	679	68	127	.535	18	49	.367	161	6	154	5.2	0.2	5.0
90-91—Temple..........	34	1143	113	229	.493	35	82	.427	236	10	261	6.9	0.3	7.7
91-92—Temple..........	30	988	127	239	.531	39	91	.429	179	6	293	6.0	0.2	9.8
Totals	95	2810	308	595	.518	92	222	.414	576	22	708	6.1	0.2	7.5

Three-point field goals: 1989-90, 0-for-3.

CBA REGULAR-SEASON RECORD

Season Team	G	Min.	FGM	FGA	Pct.	FTM	FTA	Pct.	Reb.	Ast.	Pts.	RPG	APG	PPG
94-95—Fort Wayne	44	1542	301	512	.588	106	154	.688	321	44	708	7.3	1.0	16.1
95-96—Yakima	56	1661	312	585	.533	100	155	.645	439	45	724	7.8	0.8	12.9
Totals	100	3203	613	1097	.559	206	309	.667	760	89	1432	7.6	0.9	14.3

Three-point field goals: 1995-96, 0-for-2.

NBA REGULAR-SEASON RECORD

Season Team	G	Min.	FGM	FGA	Pct.	FTM	FTA	Pct.	Off.	Def.	Tot.	Ast.	St.	Blk.	TO	Pts.	RPG	APG	PPG
94-95—Indiana..........	4	9	1	3	.333	1	2	.500	2	2	4	0	0	1	1	3	1.0	0.0	0.8
96-97—Miami	31	153	25	60	.417	12	21	.571	16	21	37	1	4	10	15	62	1.2	0.0	2.0
97-98—Miami	51	847	145	269	.539	59	82	.720	80	133	213	26	18	34	47	349	4.2	0.5	6.8
98-99—Miami	32	357	50	101	.495	19	26	.731	26	52	78	9	7	8	13	119	2.4	0.3	3.7
99-00—Miami	58	663	122	224	.545	40	56	.714	44	96	140	22	15	18	24	284	2.4	0.4	4.9
00-01—Denver-N.J.	55	719	103	239	.431	45	70	.643	54	107	161	24	16	22	34	252	2.9	0.4	4.6
Totals	231	2748	446	896	.498	176	257	.685	222	411	633	82	60	93	134	1069	2.7	0.4	4.6

Three-point field goals: 1996-97, 0-for-1. 1997-98, 0-for-1. 1998-99, 0-for-1. 2000-01, 1-for-2 (.500). Totals, 1-for-5 (.200).
Personal fouls/disqualifications: 1996-97, 17/0. 1997-98, 87/0. 1998-99, 28/0. 1999-00, 68/0. 2000-01, 72/0. Totals, 272/0.

NBA PLAYOFF RECORD

Season Team	G	Min.	FGM	FGA	Pct.	FTM	FTA	Pct.	Off.	Def.	Tot.	Ast.	St.	Blk.	TO	Pts.	RPG	APG	PPG
96-97—Miami	4	16	4	8	.500	0	2	.000	0	3	3	1	1	0	2	8	0.8	0.3	2.0
97-98—Miami	3	28	4	5	.800	1	2	.500	2	5	7	0	0	1	0	9	2.3	0.0	3.0
98-99—Miami	2	8	1	2	.500	2	2	1.000	1	2	3	0	1	0	1	4	1.5	0.0	2.0
99-00—Miami	1	10	1	3	.333	0	2	.000	0	0	0	0	2	0	1	2	0.0	0.0	2.0
Totals	10	62	10	18	.556	3	8	.375	3	10	13	1	4	1	4	23	1.3	0.1	2.3

Personal fouls/disqualifications: 1997-98, 4/0. Totals, 4/0.

STRICKLAND, ROD   G

PERSONAL: Born July 11, 1966, in Bronx, N.Y. ... 6-3/185. (1,91/83,9). ... Full Name: Rodney Strickland.
HIGH SCHOOL: Harry S. Truman (Bronx, N.Y.), then Oak Hill Academy (Mouth of Wilson, Va.).
COLLEGE: DePaul.
TRANSACTIONS/CAREER NOTES: Selected after junior season by New York Knicks in first round (19th pick overall) of 1988 NBA Draft. ... Traded by Knicks to San Antonio Spurs for G Maurice Cheeks (February 21, 1990). ... Signed as free agent by Portland Trail Blazers (July 3, 1992). ... Traded by Trail Blazers with F Harvey Grant to Washington Bullets for F Rasheed Wallace and G Mitchell Butler (July 15, 1996). ... Bullets franchise renamed Washington Wizards for 1997-98 season. ... Waived by Wizards (March 1, 2001). ... Signed as free agent by Trail Blazers (March 5, 2001).

COLLEGIATE RECORD

NOTES: The Sporting News All-America first team (1988).

Season Team	G	Min.	FGM	FGA	Pct.	FTM	FTA	Pct.	Reb.	Ast.	Pts.	RPG	APG	PPG
85-86—DePaul..........	31	1063	176	354	.497	85	126	.675	84	159	437	2.7	5.1	14.1
86-87—DePaul..........	30	980	188	323	.582	106	175	.606	113	196	490	3.8	6.5	16.3
87-88—DePaul..........	26	837	207	392	.528	83	137	.606	98	202	521	3.8	7.8	20.0
Totals	87	2880	571	1069	.534	274	438	.626	295	557	1448	3.4	6.4	16.6

Three-point field goals: 1986-87, 8-for-15 (.533). 1987-88, 24-for-54 (.444). Totals, 32-for-69 (.464).

NBA REGULAR-SEASON RECORD

HONORS: All-NBA second team (1998). ... NBA All-Rookie second team (1989).

Season Team	G	Min.	FGM	FGA	Pct.	FTM	FTA	Pct.	Off.	Def.	Tot.	Ast.	St.	Blk.	TO	Pts.	RPG	APG	PPG
88-89—New York	81	1358	265	567	.467	172	231	.745	51	109	160	319	98	3	148	721	2.0	3.9	8.9
89-90—N.Y.-San Ant. ..	82	2140	343	756	.454	174	278	.626	90	169	259	468	127	14	170	868	3.2	5.7	10.6
90-91—San Antonio	58	2076	314	651	.482	161	211	.763	57	162	219	463	117	11	156	800	3.8	8.0	13.8
91-92—San Antonio	57	2053	300	659	.455	182	265	.687	92	173	265	491	118	17	160	787	4.6	8.6	13.8
92-93—Portland	78	2474	396	816	.485	273	381	.717	120	217	337	559	131	24	199	1069	4.3	7.2	13.7
93-94—Portland	82	2889	528	1093	.483	353	471	.749	122	248	370	740	147	24	257	1411	4.5	9.0	17.2
94-95—Portland	64	2267	441	946	.466	283	380	.745	73	244	317	562	123	9	209	1211	5.0	8.8	18.9
95-96—Portland	67	2526	471	1023	.460	276	423	.652	89	208	297	640	97	16	255	1256	4.4	9.6	18.7
96-97—Washington	82	2997	515	1105	.466	367	497	.738	95	240	335	727	143	14	270	1410	4.1	8.9	17.2
97-98—Washington	76	3020	490	1130	.434	357	492	.726	112	293	405	*801	126	25	266	1349	5.3	*10.5	17.8
98-99—Washington	44	1632	251	603	.416	176	236	.746	56	156	212	434	76	5	142	690	4.8	9.9	15.7
99-00—Washington	69	2188	327	762	.429	214	305	.702	73	186	259	519	94	18	187	869	3.8	7.5	12.6
00-01—Wash.-Port.	54	1371	182	429	.424	130	173	.751	36	104	140	303	53	5	107	498	2.6	5.6	9.2
Totals	894	28991	4823	10540	.458	3118	4343	.718	1066	2509	3575	7026	1450	185	2526	12939	4.0	7.9	14.5

Three-point field goals: 1988-89, 19-for-59 (.322). 1989-90, 8-for-30 (.267). 1990-91, 11-for-33 (.333). 1991-92, 5-for-15 (.333). 1992-93, 4-for-30 (.133). 1993-94, 2-for-10 (.200). 1994-95, 46-for-123 (.374). 1995-96, 38-for-111 (.342). 1996-97, 13-for-77 (.169). 1997-98, 12-for-48 (.250). 1998-99, 12-for-42 (.286). 1999-00, 1-for-21 (.048). 2000-01, 4-for-17 (.235). Totals, 175-for-616 (.284).

Personal fouls/disqualifications: 1988-89, 142/2. 1989-90, 160/3. 1990-91, 125/0. 1991-92, 122/0. 1992-93, 153/1. 1993-94, 171/0. 1994-95, 118/0. 1995-96, 135/2. 1996-97, 166/2. 1997-98, 182/2. 1998-99, 91/0. 1999-00, 147/1. 2000-01, 76/0. Totals, 1788/13.

NBA PLAYOFF RECORD

Season Team	G	Min.	FGM	FGA	Pct.	FTM	FTA	Pct.	Off.	Def.	Tot.	Ast.	St.	Blk.	TO	Pts.	RPG	APG	PPG
88-89—New York	9	111	22	49	.449	9	17	.529	6	7	13	25	4	1	13	54	1.4	2.8	6.0
89-90—San Antonio	10	384	54	127	.425	15	27	.556	22	31	53	112	14	0	34	123	5.3	11.2	12.3
90-91—San Antonio	4	168	29	67	.433	17	21	.810	5	16	21	35	9	0	13	75	5.3	8.8	18.8
91-92—San Antonio	2	80	13	22	.591	5	8	.625	0	7	7	19	3	2	6	31	3.5	9.5	15.5
92-93—Portland	4	156	22	52	.423	10	12	.833	9	17	26	37	5	2	7	54	6.5	9.3	13.5
93-94—Portland	4	154	36	72	.500	22	27	.815	3	13	16	39	4	2	10	94	4.0	9.8	23.5
94-95—Portland	3	126	27	65	.415	14	18	.778	1	11	12	37	3	2	10	70	4.0	12.3	23.3
95-96—Portland	5	202	37	84	.440	23	36	.639	12	19	31	42	5	0	12	103	6.2	8.4	20.6
96-97—Washington	3	124	22	52	.423	14	19	.737	5	13	18	25	3	0	11	59	6.0	8.3	19.7
00-01—Portland	2	19	2	6	.333	4	6	.667	2	2	4	2	2	0	1	8	2.0	1.0	4.0
Totals	46	1524	264	596	.443	133	191	.696	65	136	201	373	52	9	117	671	4.4	8.1	14.6

Three-point field goals: 1988-89, 1-for-1. 1989-90, 0-for-7. 1990-91, 0-for-6. 1992-93, 0-for-1. 1993-94, 0-for-1. 1994-95, 2-for-5 (.400). 1995-96, 6-for-12 (.500). 1996-97, 1-for-2 (.500). Totals, 10-for-35 (.286).

Personal fouls/disqualifications: 1988-89, 21/0. 1989-90, 30/2. 1990-91, 14/0. 1991-92, 8/0. 1992-93, 10/0. 1993-94, 13/0. 1994-95, 11/0. 1995-96, 14/0. 1996-97, 8/0. 2000-01, 1/0. Totals, 130/2.

STRONG, DEREK   F   CLIPPERS

PERSONAL: Born February 9, 1968, in Los Angeles. ... 6-9/240. (2,06/108,9). ... Full Name: Derek Lamar Strong.
HIGH SCHOOL: Pacific Palisades (Calif.).
COLLEGE: Xavier.
TRANSACTIONS/CAREER NOTES: Selected by Philadelphia 76ers in second round (47th pick overall) of 1990 NBA Draft. ... Played in Spain (1990-91). ... Played in United States Basketball League with Miami Tropics (1991). ... Waived by 76ers (March 5, 1992). ... Signed by Washington Bullets to 10-day contract (March 13, 1992). ... Signed as free agent by Bullets (October 5, 1992). ... Waived by Bullets (October 14, 1992). ... Played in Continental Basketball Association with Quad City Thunder (1992-93). ... Signed by Milwaukee Bucks to first of two consecutive 10-day contracts (February 22, 1993). ... Signed by Bucks for remainder of season (March 14, 1993). ... Traded by Bucks with G/F Blue Edwards to Boston Celtics for F Ed Pinckney and draft rights to F Andrei Fetisov (June 29, 1994). ... Signed as unrestricted free agent by Los Angeles Lakers (October 26, 1995). ... Signed as free agent by Orlando Magic (August 26, 1996). ... Traded by Magic with F Corey Maggette and draft rights to G Keyon Dooling to Los Angeles Clippers for a future first-round draft pick (June 28, 2000).

COLLEGIATE RECORD

Season Team	G	Min.	FGM	FGA	Pct.	FTM	FTA	Pct.	Reb.	Ast.	Pts.	RPG	APG	PPG
86-87—Xavier						Did not play—ineligible.								
87-88—Xavier	30	668	112	197	.569	94	131	.718	213	23	318	7.1	0.8	10.6
88-89—Xavier	33	983	163	264	.617	178	218	.817	264	17	504	8.0	0.5	15.3
89-90—Xavier	33	981	146	274	.533	177	211	.839	328	31	469	9.9	0.9	14.2
Totals	96	2632	421	735	.573	449	560	.802	805	71	1291	8.4	0.7	13.4

SPANISH LEAGUE RECORD

Season Team	G	Min.	FGM	FGA	Pct.	FTM	FTA	Pct.	Reb.	Ast.	Pts.	RPG	APG	PPG
90-91—Huesca La Magia	22	721	147	292	.503	67	84	.798	220	11	363	10.0	0.5	16.5

Three-point field goals: 1990-91, 2-for-4 (.500).

NBA REGULAR-SEASON RECORD

Season Team	G	Min.	FGM	FGA	Pct.	FTM	FTA	Pct.	Off.	Def.	Tot.	Ast.	St.	Blk.	TO	Pts.	RPG	APG	PPG
91-92—Washington	1	12	0	4	.000	3	4	.750	1	4	5	1	0	0	1	3	5.0	1.0	3.0
92-93—Milwaukee	23	339	42	92	.457	68	85	.800	40	75	115	14	11	1	13	156	5.0	0.6	6.8
93-94—Milwaukee	67	1131	141	341	.413	159	206	.772	109	172	281	48	38	14	61	444	4.2	0.7	6.6
94-95—Boston	70	1344	149	329	.453	141	172	.820	136	239	375	44	24	13	79	441	5.4	0.6	6.3
95-96—L.A. Lakers	63	746	72	169	.426	69	85	.812	60	118	178	32	18	12	20	214	2.8	0.5	3.4
96-97—Orlando	82	2004	262	586	.447	175	218	.803	174	345	519	73	47	20	102	699	6.3	0.9	8.5
97-98—Orlando	58	1638	259	617	.420	218	279	.781	152	275	427	51	31	24	74	736	7.4	0.9	12.7
98-99—Orlando	44	695	76	180	.422	71	99	.717	66	05	161	17	15	7	37	223	3.7	0.4	5.1
99-00—Orlando	20	148	21	48	.438	11	14	.786	11	33	44	4	5	2	12	54	2.2	0.2	2.7
00-01—L.A. Clippers	28	491	45	117	.385	28	37	.757	34	74	108	7	14	1	22	118	3.9	0.3	4.2
Totals	456	8548	1067	2483	.430	943	1199	.786	783	1430	2213	291	203	94	421	3088	4.9	0.6	6.8

Three-point field goals: 1992-93, 4-for-8 (.500). 1993-94, 3-for-13 (.231). 1994-95, 2-for-7 (.286). 1995-96, 1-for-9 (.111). 1996-97, 0-for-13. 1997-98, 0-for-4. 1998-99, 0-for-2. 1999-00, 1-for-4 (.250). 2000-01, 0-for-1. Totals, 11-for-61 (.180).

Personal fouls/disqualifications: 1991-92, 1/0. 1992-93, 20/0. 1993-94, 69/1. 1994-95, 143/0. 1995-96, 80/1. 1996-97, 196/2. 1997-98, 122/0. 1998-99, 64/0. 1999-00, 15/0. 2000-01, 30/0. Totals, 740/4.

NBA PLAYOFF RECORD

Season Team	G	Min.	FGM	FGA	Pct.	FTM	FTA	Pct.	Off.	Def.	Tot.	Ast.	St.	Blk.	TO	Pts.	RPG	APG	PPG
94-95—Boston	4	81	4	12	.333	3	6	.500	13	11	24	3	3	1	5	11	6.0	0.8	2.8
96-97—Orlando	5	195	21	40	.525	19	25	.760	20	30	50	4	2	2	14	61	10.0	0.8	12.2
98-99—Orlando	1	16	1	2	.500	2	2	1.000	0	0	0	0	1	0	1	4	0.0	0.0	4.0
Totals	10	292	26	54	.481	24	33	.727	33	41	74	7	6	3	20	76	7.4	0.7	7.6

Three-point field goals: 1996-97, 0-for-1. Totals, 0-for-1 (.000).
Personal fouls/disqualifications: 1994-95, 7/0. 1996-97, 20/1. 1998-99, 2/0. Totals, 29/1.

CBA REGULAR-SEASON RECORD

NOTES: CBA Most Valuable Player (1993). ... CBA Newcomer of the Year (1993). ... CBA All-League first team (1993). ... CBA All-Defensive team (1989, 1993).

Season Team	G	Min.	FGM	FGA	Pct.	FTM	FTA	Pct.	Reb.	Ast.	Pts.	AVERAGES RPG	APG	PPG
92-93—Quad City	43	1513	271	487	.556	319	375	.851	485	81	861	11.3	1.9	20.0

Three-point field goals: 1992-93, 0-for-4.

SUNDOV, BRUNO C PACERS

PERSONAL: Born February 10, 1980, in Split, Croatia. ... 7-2/239. (2,18/108,4).
HIGH SCHOOL: Winchendon Prep School (Mass.).
TRANSACTIONS/CAREER NOTES: Selected by Dallas Mavericks in second round (35th pick overall) of 1998 NBA Draft. ... Traded by Mavericks to Utah Jazz as part of four-team deal in which Boston Celtics received G Robert Pack, C John Williams and cash considerations from Mavericks and a conditional first-round draft choice from Jazz, Mavericks received G Dana Barros from Celtics, F Bill Curley from Golden State Warriors and G Howard Eisley from Jazz, Jazz received F Donyell Marshall from Warriors and Warriors received F Danny Fortson from Celtics and F Adam Keefe from Jazz (August 16, 2000). ... Waived by Jazz (September 26, 2000). ... Signed as free agent by Indiana Pacers (October 3, 2000).

NBA REGULAR-SEASON RECORD

Season Team	G	Min.	FGM	FGA	Pct.	FTM	FTA	Pct.	REBOUNDS Off.	Def.	Tot.	Ast.	St.	Blk.	TO	Pts.	AVERAGES RPG	APG	PPG
98-99—Dallas	3	11	2	7	.286	0	0	...	0	0	0	1	0	0	1	4	0.0	0.3	1.3
99-00—Dallas	14	61	12	31	.387	2	2	1.000	5	7	12	2	2	2	4	26	0.9	0.1	1.9
00-01—Indiana	11	120	20	41	.488	3	5	.600	4	19	23	2	2	4	3	43	2.1	0.2	3.9
Totals	28	192	34	79	.430	5	7	.714	9	26	35	5	4	6	8	73	1.3	0.2	2.6

Three-point field goals: 2000-01, 0-for-4. Totals, 0-for-4 (.000).
Personal fouls/disqualifications: 1998-99, 4/0. 1999-00, 16/0. 2000-01, 21/1. Totals, 41/1.

SURA, BOB G WARRIORS

PERSONAL: Born March 25, 1973, in Wilkes-Barre, Pa. ... 6-5/200. (1,96/90,7). ... Full Name: Robert Sura Jr.
HIGH SCHOOL: G.A.R. Memorial (Wilkes-Barre, Pa.).
COLLEGE: Florida State.
TRANSACTIONS/CAREER NOTES: Selected by Cleveland Cavaliers in first round (17th pick overall) of 1995 NBA Draft. ... Traded by Cavaliers to Golden State Warriors as part of three-way deal in which Warriors received G Vinny Del Negro from Milwaukee Bucks, Bucks traded F/C J.R. Reid and F Robert Traylor to Cavaliers and Warriors traded F Jason Caffey and F/G Billy Owens to Bucks (June 27, 2000).

COLLEGIATE RECORD

Season Team	G	Min.	FGM	FGA	Pct.	FTM	FTA	Pct.	Reb.	Ast.	Pts.	AVERAGES RPG	APG	PPG
91-92—Florida State	31	872	124	269	.461	94	150	.627	107	76	380	3.5	2.5	12.3
92-93—Florida State	34	1213	241	533	.452	120	188	.638	209	92	675	6.1	2.7	19.9
93-94—Florida State	27	932	202	431	.469	117	179	.654	213	121	573	7.9	4.5	21.2
94-95—Florida State	27	981	164	393	.417	123	179	.687	185	146	502	6.9	5.4	18.6
Totals	119	3998	731	1626	.450	454	696	.652	714	435	2130	6.0	3.7	17.9

Three-point field goals: 1991-92, 38-for-98 (.388). 1992-93, 73-for-220 (.332). 1993-94, 52-for-164 (.317). 1994-95, 51-for-158 (.323). Totals, 214-for-640 (.334).

NBA REGULAR-SEASON RECORD

Season Team	G	Min.	FGM	FGA	Pct.	FTM	FTA	Pct.	REBOUNDS Off.	Def.	Tot.	Ast.	St.	Blk.	TO	Pts.	AVERAGES RPG	APG	PPG
95-96—Cleveland	79	1150	148	360	.411	99	141	.702	34	101	135	233	56	21	115	422	1.7	2.9	5.3
96-97—Cleveland	82	2269	253	587	.431	196	319	.614	76	232	308	390	90	33	181	755	3.8	4.8	9.2
97-98—Cleveland	46	942	87	231	.377	74	131	.565	25	69	94	171	44	7	93	267	2.0	3.7	5.8
98-99—Cleveland	50	841	70	210	.333	65	103	.631	21	81	102	152	46	14	67	214	2.0	3.0	4.3
99-00—Cleveland	73	2216	356	815	.437	175	251	.697	50	238	288	284	91	19	148	1009	3.9	3.9	13.8
00-01—Golden State	53	1684	202	518	.390	135	189	.714	54	173	227	242	54	8	160	586	4.3	4.6	11.1
Totals	383	9102	1116	2721	.410	744	1134	.656	260	894	1154	1472	381	102	764	3253	3.0	3.8	8.5

Three-point field goals: 1995-96, 27-for-78 (.346). 1996-97, 53-for-164 (.323). 1997-98, 19-for-60 (.317). 1998-99, 9-for-45 (.200). 1999-00, 122-for-332 (.367). 2000-01, 47-for-172 (.273). Totals, 277-for-851 (.325).
Personal fouls/disqualifications: 1995-96, 126/1. 1996-97, 218/3. 1997-98, 113/0. 1998-99, 98/1. 1999-00, 201/0. 2000-01, 127/0. Totals, 883/5.

NBA PLAYOFF RECORD

Season Team	G	Min.	FGM	FGA	Pct.	FTM	FTA	Pct.	REBOUNDS Off.	Def.	Tot.	Ast.	St.	Blk.	TO	Pts.	AVERAGES RPG	APG	PPG
95-96—Cleveland	3	18	2	3	.667	0	0	...	0	1	1	3	1	0	4	4	0.3	1.0	1.3
97-98—Cleveland	3	31	1	5	.200	2	3	.667	0	3	3	4	1	0	2	4	1.0	1.3	1.3
Totals	6	49	3	8	.375	2	3	.667	0	4	4	7	2	0	6	8	0.7	1.2	1.3

Three-point field goals: 1997-98, 0-for-2. Totals, 0-for-2 (.000).
Personal fouls/disqualifications: 1995-96, 4/0. 1997-98, 4/0. Totals, 8/0.

DID YOU KNOW . . .

... that Kevin McHale is the only player in NBA history to shoot better than 60 percent from the floor and 80 percent from the free-throw line in the same season?

SWIFT, STROMILE   F   GRIZZLIES

PERSONAL: Born November 21, 1979, in Shreveport, La. ... 6-10/220. (2,08/99,8).
HIGH SCHOOL: Fair Park (Shreveport, La.).
COLLEGE: Louisiana State.
TRANSACTIONS/CAREER NOTES: Selected after sophomore season by Vancouver Grizzlies in first round (second pick overall) of 2000 NBA Draft. ... Grizzlies franchise moved to Memphis for 2001-02 season.

COLLEGIATE RECORD

Season Team	G	Min.	FGM	FGA	Pct.	FTM	FTA	Pct.	Reb.	Ast.	Pts.	RPG	APG	PPG
98-99—Louisiana State	16	319	45	110	.409	30	50	.600	69	5	121	4.3	0.3	7.6
99-00—Louisiana State	34	1013	208	342	.608	127	206	.617	279	32	550	8.2	0.9	16.2
Totals	50	1332	253	452	.560	157	256	.613	348	37	671	7.0	0.7	13.4

Three-point field goals: 1998-99, 1-for-8 (.125). 1999-00, 7-for-25 (.280). Totals, 8-for-33 (.242).

NBA REGULAR-SEASON RECORD

Season Team	G	Min.	FGM	FGA	Pct.	FTM	FTA	Pct.	Off.	Def.	Tot.	Ast.	St.	Blk.	TO	Pts.	RPG	APG	PPG
00-01—Vancouver	80	1312	153	339	.451	85	141	.603	109	175	284	28	62	82	64	391	3.6	0.4	4.9

Three-point field goals: 2000-01, 0-for-4.
Personal fouls/disqualifications: 2000-01, 160/0.

SZCZERBIAK, WALLY   F   TIMBERWOLVES

PERSONAL: Born March 5, 1977, in Madrid, Spain. ... 6-7/244. (2,01/110,7). ... Full Name: Walter Robert Szczerbiak. ... Son of Walter Szczerbiak, forward with Pittsburgh Condors of American Basketball Association (1971-72) and Real Madrid of Spanish League.
HIGH SCHOOL: Cold Spring Harbor (N.Y.).
COLLEGE: Miami of Ohio.
TRANSACTIONS/CAREER NOTES: Selected by Minnesota Timberwolves in first round (sixth pick overall) of 1999 NBA Draft.

COLLEGIATE RECORD

NOTES: THE SPORTING NEWS All-America first team (1999).

Season Team	G	Min.	FGM	FGA	Pct.	FTM	FTA	Pct.	Reb.	Ast.	Pts.	RPG	APG	PPG
95-96—Miami of Ohio	22	382	66	127	.520	22	28	.786	72	23	176	3.3	1.0	8.0
96-97—Miami of Ohio	30	927	150	316	.475	28	39	.718	162	63	384	5.4	2.1	12.8
97-98—Miami of Ohio	21	803	185	350	.529	79	98	.806	160	52	512	7.6	2.5	24.4
98-99—Miami of Ohio	32	1081	270	517	.522	172	207	.831	272	93	775	8.5	2.9	24.2
Totals	105	3193	671	1310	.512	301	372	.809	666	231	1847	6.3	2.2	17.6

Three-point field goals: 1995-96, 22-for-47 (.468). 1996-97, 56-for-121 (.463). 1997-98, 63-for-128 (.492). 1998-99, 63-for-177 (.356). Totals, 204-for-473 (.431).

NBA REGULAR-SEASON RECORD

HONORS: NBA All-Rookie first team (2000).

Season Team	G	Min.	FGM	FGA	Pct.	FTM	FTA	Pct.	Off.	Def.	Tot.	Ast.	St.	Blk.	TO	Pts.	RPG	APG	PPG
99-00—Minnesota	73	2171	342	669	.511	133	161	.826	89	183	272	201	58	23	83	845	3.7	2.8	11.6
00-01—Minnesota	82	2856	469	920	.510	181	208	.870	133	314	447	260	59	33	138	1145	5.5	3.2	14.0
Totals	155	5027	811	1589	.510	314	369	.851	222	497	719	461	117	56	221	1990	4.6	3.0	12.8

Three-point field goals: 1999-00, 28-for-78 (.359). 2000-01, 26-for-77 (.338). Totals, 54-for-155 (.348).
Personal fouls/disqualifications: 1999-00, 175/3. 2000-01, 226/4. Totals, 401/7.

NBA PLAYOFF RECORD

Season Team	G	Min.	FGM	FGA	Pct.	FTM	FTA	Pct.	Off.	Def.	Tot.	Ast.	St.	Blk.	TO	Pts.	RPG	APG	PPG
99-00—Minnesota	4	94	12	30	.400	0	0	...	2	6	8	2	3	1	1	24	2.0	0.5	6.0
00-01—Minnesota	4	143	18	37	.486	20	25	.800	4	14	18	10	5	3	12	56	4.5	2.5	14.0
Totals	8	237	30	67	.448	20	25	.800	6	20	26	12	8	4	13	80	3.3	1.5	10.0

Three-point field goals: 1999-00, 0-for-3. 2000-01, 0-for-1. Totals, 0-for-4 (.000).
Personal fouls/disqualifications: 1999-00, 7/0. 2000-01, 6/0. Totals, 13/0.

TABAK, ZAN   C

PERSONAL: Born June 15, 1970, in Split, Croatia. ... 7-0/257. (2,13/116,6). ... Name pronounced Zhawn Ta-BOK.
HIGH SCHOOL: Split (Croatia).
TRANSACTIONS/CAREER NOTES: Selected by Houston Rockets in second round (51st pick overall) of 1991 NBA Draft. ... Played in Croatia (1991-92). ... Played in Italy (1992-93 and 1993-94). ... Signed by Rockets (July 20, 1994). ... Selected by Toronto Raptors from Rockets in NBA Expansion Draft (June 24, 1995). ... Traded by Raptors with G Kenny Anderson and F Popeye Jones to Boston Celtics for G Chauncey Billups, G Dee Brown, F John Thomas and F Roy Rogers (February 18, 1998). ... Played in Turkey (1998-99). ... Signed as free agent by Indiana Pacers (October 1, 1999). ... Signed to play with Real Madrid in Spain for 2001-02 season.
MISCELLANEOUS: Member of NBA championship team (1995). ... Member of Croatian Olympic team (1996).

S
T

Season Team	G	Min.	FGM	FGA	Pct.	FTM	FTA	Pct.	Reb.	Ast.	Pts.	AVERAGES		
												RPG	APG	PPG
92-93—Livorno	30	1030	185	212	.873	90	129	.698	305	12	460	10.2	0.4	15.3
93-94—Milano	25	785	145	235	.617	76	116	.655	266	16	366	10.6	0.6	14.6
Totals	55	1815	330	447	.738	166	245	.678	571	28	826	10.4	0.5	15.0

Three-point field goals: 1992-93, 0-for-1. 1993-94, 0-for-1. Totals, 0-for-2 (.000).

NBA REGULAR-SEASON RECORD

Season Team	G	Min.	FGM	FGA	Pct.	FTM	FTA	Pct.	REBOUNDS			Ast.	St.	Blk.	TO	Pts.	AVERAGES		
									Off.	Def.	Tot.						RPG	APG	PPG
94-95—Houston	37	182	24	53	.453	27	44	.614	23	34	57	4	2	7	18	75	1.5	0.1	2.0
95-96—Toronto	67	1332	225	414	.543	64	114	.561	117	203	320	62	24	31	101	514	4.8	0.9	7.7
96-97—Toronto	13	218	32	71	.451	20	29	.690	20	29	49	14	6	11	21	84	3.8	1.1	6.5
97-98—Tor.-Bos.	57	984	142	304	.467	23	61	.377	84	128	212	48	20	38	61	307	3.7	0.8	5.4
99-00—Indiana	18	114	16	34	.471	5	8	.625	16	16	32	4	3	9	11	37	1.8	0.2	2.1
00-01—Indiana	55	777	98	186	.527	20	47	.426	65	148	213	33	10	30	57	216	3.9	0.6	3.9
Totals	247	3607	537	1062	.506	159	303	.525	325	558	883	165	65	126	269	1233	3.6	0.7	5.0

Three-point field goals: 1994-95, 0-for-1. 1995-96, 0-for-1. 1997-98, 0-for-1. Totals, 0-for-3 (.000).

Personal fouls/disqualifications: 1994-95, 37/0. 1995-96, 204/2. 1996-97, 35/0. 1997-98, 163/2. 1999-00, 13/0. 2000-01, 125/0. Totals, 577/4.

NBA PLAYOFF RECORD

Season Team	G	Min.	FGM	FGA	Pct.	FTM	FTA	Pct.	REBOUNDS			Ast.	St.	Blk.	TO	Pts.	AVERAGES		
									Off.	Def.	Tot.						RPG	APG	PPG
94-95—Houston	8	31	2	5	.400	2	2	1.000	1	0	1	1	1	3	2	6	0.1	0.1	0.8
99-00—Indiana	10	47	4	8	.500	4	4	1.000	4	12	16	0	0	2	1	12	1.6	0.0	1.2
00-01—Indiana	2	10	0	4	.000	1	2	.500	3	0	3	0	0	0	0	1	1.5	0.0	0.5
Totals	20	88	6	17	.353	7	8	.875	8	12	20	1	1	5	3	19	1.0	0.1	1.0

Personal fouls/disqualifications: 1994-95, 5/0. 1999-00, 10/0. 2000-01, 2/0. Totals, 17/0.

TURKISH LEAGUE RECORD

Season Team	G	Min.	FGM	FGA	Pct.	FTM	FTA	Pct.	Reb.	Ast.	Pts.	AVERAGES		
												RPG	APG	PPG
98-99—Fenerbache	31	989	186	281	.662	33	62	.532	307	47	405	9.9	1.5	13.1

TARLAC, DRAGAN   F/C

PERSONAL: Born May 9, 1973, in Belgrade, Yugoslavia. ... 6-10/260. (2,08/117,9).

TRANSACTIONS/CAREER NOTES: Played in Greece (1992-93 through 1999-2000). ... Selected by Chicago Bulls in second round (31st pick overall) of 1995 NBA Draft. ... Signed to play for Real Madrid in Spain for 2001-02 season.

GREEK LEAGUE RECORD

Season Team	G	Min.	FGM	FGA	Pct.	FTM	FTA	Pct.	Reb.	Ast.	Pts.	AVERAGES		
												RPG	APG	PPG
92-93—Olympiakos S.F.P.	25	758	116	202	.574	102	134	.761	201	15	334	8.0	0.6	13.4
93-94—Olympiakos S.F.P.	2	5	1	1	1.000	0	0	...	1	0	2	0.5	0.0	1.0
94-95—Olympiakos S.F.P.	23	523	97	151	.642	64	92	.696	180	14	258	7.8	0.6	11.2
95-96—Olympiakos S.F.P.						Statistics unavailable.								
96-97—Olympiakos S.F.P.	17	499	75	115	.652	42	54	.778	136	20	192	8.0	1.2	11.3
97-98—Olympiakos S.F.P.	11	332	51	85	.600	41	65	.631	91	14	143	8.3	1.3	13.0
98-99—Olympiakos S.F.P.	24	647	98	147	.667	71	97	.732	159	36	267	6.6	1.5	11.1
99-00—Olympiakos S.F.P.	24	731	86	155	.555	61	81	.753	193	32	234	8.0	1.3	9.8
Totals	126	3495	524	856	.612	381	523	.728	961	131	1430	7.6	1.0	11.3

Three-point field goals: 1996-97, 0-for-1. 1998-99, 0-for-1. 1999-00, 1-for-1. Totals, 1-for-3 (.333).

NBA REGULAR-SEASON RECORD

Season Team	G	Min.	FGM	FGA	Pct.	FTM	FTA	Pct.	REBOUNDS			Ast.	St.	Blk.	TO	Pts.	AVERAGES		
									Off.	Def.	Tot.						RPG	APG	PPG
00-01—Chicago	43	598	39	99	.394	25	33	.758	37	85	122	31	7	19	38	103	2.8	0.7	2.4

Personal fouls/disqualifications: 2000-01, 95/2.

TAYLOR, MAURICE   F   ROCKETS

PERSONAL: Born October 30, 1976, in Detroit. ... 6-9/260. (2,06/117,9). ... Full Name: Maurice De Shawn Taylor.

HIGH SCHOOL: Henry Ford (Detroit).

COLLEGE: Michigan.

TRANSACTIONS/CAREER NOTES: Selected after junior season by Los Angeles Clippers in first round (14th pick overall) of 1997 NBA Draft. ... Signed as free agent by Houston Rockets (August 25, 2000).

COLLEGIATE RECORD

Season Team	G	Min.	FGM	FGA	Pct.	FTM	FTA	Pct.	Reb.	Ast.	Pts.	AVERAGES		
												RPG	APG	PPG
94-95—Michigan	30	830	157	332	.473	59	98	.602	151	31	376	5.0	1.0	12.5
95-96—Michigan	32	908	194	380	.511	58	98	.592	223	42	447	7.0	1.3	14.0
96-97—Michigan	35	1055	173	341	.507	84	117	.718	218	40	431	6.2	1.1	12.3
Totals	97	2793	524	1053	.498	201	313	.642	592	113	1254	6.1	1.2	12.9

Three-point field goals: 1994-95, 3-for-7 (.429). 1995-96, 1-for-4 (.250). 1996-97, 1-for-5 (.200). Totals, 5-for-16 (.313).

HONORS: NBA All-Rookie second team (1998).

Season Team	G	Min.	FGM	FGA	Pct.	FTM	FTA	Pct.	REBOUNDS Off.	Def.	Tot.	Ast.	St.	Blk.	TO	Pts.	AVERAGES RPG	APG	PPG
97-98—L.A. Clippers ...	71	1513	321	675	.476	173	244	.709	118	178	296	53	34	40	107	815	4.2	0.7	11.5
98-99—L.A. Clippers ...	46	1505	311	675	.461	150	206	.728	100	142	242	67	16	29	120	773	5.3	1.5	16.8
99-00—L.A. Clippers ...	62	2227	458	988	.464	143	201	.711	96	304	400	101	51	48	169	1060	6.5	1.6	17.1
00-01—Houston	69	1972	390	797	.489	119	162	.735	109	269	378	104	28	38	125	899	5.5	1.5	13.0
Totals	248	7217	1480	3135	.472	585	813	.720	423	893	1316	325	129	155	521	3547	5.3	1.3	14.3

Three-point field goals: 1997-98, 0-for-1. 1998-99, 1-for-6 (.167). 1999-00, 1-for-8 (.125). 2000-01, 0-for-4. Totals, 2-for-19 (.105).
Personal fouls/disqualifications: 1997-98, 222/7. 1998-99, 179/5. 1999-00, 217/4. 2000-01, 208/3. Totals, 826/19.

TERRY, JASON   G   HAWKS

PERSONAL: Born September 15, 1977, in Seattle. ... 6-2/176. (1,88/79,8). ... Full Name: Jason Eugene Terry.
HIGH SCHOOL: Franklin (Seattle).
COLLEGE: Arizona.
TRANSACTIONS/CAREER NOTES: Selected by Atlanta Hawks in first round (10th pick overall) of 1999 NBA Draft.

COLLEGIATE RECORD

NOTES: Member of NCAA Division I championship team (1997). ... THE SPORTING NEWS All-America first team (1999).

Season Team	G	Min.	FGM	FGA	Pct.	FTM	FTA	Pct.	Reb.	Ast.	Pts.	AVERAGES RPG	APG	PPG
95-96—Arizona	31	303	32	59	.542	16	27	.593	23	35	95	0.7	1.1	3.1
96-97—Arizona	34	1037	124	280	.443	72	101	.713	91	150	360	2.7	4.4	10.6
97-98—Arizona	35	797	124	294	.422	62	75	.827	84	149	371	2.4	4.3	10.6
98-99—Arizona	29	1107	209	472	.443	141	168	.839	97	159	635	3.3	5.5	21.9
Totals	129	3244	489	1105	.443	291	371	.784	295	493	1461	2.3	3.8	11.3

Three-point field goals: 1995-96, 15-for-26 (.577). 1996-97, 40-for-121 (.331). 1997-98, 61-for-176 (.347). 1998-99, 76-for-191 (.398). Totals, 192-for-514 (.374).

NBA REGULAR-SEASON RECORD

HONORS: NBA All-Rookie second team (2000).

Season Team	G	Min.	FGM	FGA	Pct.	FTM	FTA	Pct.	REBOUNDS Off.	Def.	Tot.	Ast.	St.	Blk.	TO	Pts.	AVERAGES RPG	APG	PPG
99-00—Atlanta	81	1888	249	600	.415	113	140	.807	24	142	166	346	90	10	156	657	2.0	4.3	8.1
00-01—Atlanta	82	3089	596	1367	.436	303	358	.846	42	227	269	403	104	12	239	1619	3.3	4.9	19.7
Totals	163	4977	845	1967	.430	416	498	.835	66	369	435	749	194	22	395	2276	2.7	4.6	14.0

Three-point field goals: 1999-00, 46-for-157 (.293). 2000-01, 124-for-314 (.395). Totals, 170-for-471 (.361).
Personal fouls/disqualifications: 1999-00, 133/0. 2000-01, 204/2. Totals, 337/2.

THOMAS, JAMEL   F

PERSONAL: Born July 19, 1976, in Brooklyn, N.Y. ... 6-6/219. (1,98/99,3). ... Cousin of Stephon Marbury, guard, Phoenix Suns.
HIGH SCHOOL: Lincoln (Brooklyn, N.Y.).
COLLEGE: Providence.
TRANSACTIONS/CAREER NOTES: Not drafted by an NBA franchise. ... Played in Continental Basketball Association with Quad City Thunder (1999-2000 and 2000-01). ... Signed as free agent by Cleveland Cavaliers (October 4, 1999). ... Waived by Cavaliers (October 28, 1999). ... Signed as free agent by Boston Celtics (December 13, 1999). ... Waived by Celtics (December 23, 1999). ... Signed as free agent by Golden State Warriors (December 29, 1999). ... Waived by Warriors (January 3, 2000). ... Signed by Warriors to 10-day contract (January 9, 2000). ... Waived by Warriors (January 18, 2000). ... Signed as free agent by Portland Trail Blazers for remainder of season (April 14, 2000). ... Waived by Trail Blazers (October 26, 2000). ... Played in American Basketball Association 2000 with Memphis HoundDawgs (2000-01). ... Signed as free agent by New Jersey Nets (April 6, 2001).

COLLEGIATE RECORD

Season Team	G	Min.	FGM	FGA	Pct.	FTM	FTA	Pct.	Reb.	Ast.	Pts.	AVERAGES RPG	APG	PPG
95-96—Providence	29	606	105	232	.453	36	58	.621	132	44	270	4.6	1.5	9.3
96-97—Providence	36	1101	187	429	.436	65	96	.677	184	76	504	5.1	2.1	14.0
97-98—Providence	29	1016	163	455	.358	156	200	.780	200	59	536	6.9	2.0	18.5
98-99—Providence	30	984	225	532	.423	153	203	.754	217	63	661	7.2	2.1	22.0
Totals	124	3707	680	1648	.413	410	557	.736	733	242	1971	5.9	2.0	15.9

Three-point field goals: 1995-96, 24-for-64 (.375). 1996-97, 65-for-162 (.401). 1997-98, 54-for-178 (.303). 1998-99, 58-for-183 (.317). Totals, 201-for-587 (.342).

CBA REGULAR-SEASON RECORD

NOTES: CBA Rookie of the Year (2000). ... CBA All-Rookie team (2000).

Season Team	G	Min.	FGM	FGA	Pct.	FTM	FTA	Pct.	Reb.	Ast.	Pts.	AVERAGES RPG	APG	PPG
99-00—Quad City.......................	29	941	199	441	.451	120	153	.784	139	86	553	4.8	3.0	19.1
00-01—Quad City.......................	21	814	189	441	.429	79	104	.760	131	80	491	6.2	3.8	23.4
Totals	50	1755	388	882	.440	199	257	.774	270	166	1044	5.4	3.3	20.9

Three-point field goals: 1999-00, 35-for-93 (.376). 2000-01, 34-for-75 (.453). Totals, 69-for-168 (.411).

NBA REGULAR-SEASON RECORD

Season Team	G	Min.	FGM	FGA	Pct.	FTM	FTA	Pct.	REBOUNDS Off.	Def.	Tot.	Ast.	St.	Blk.	TO	Pts.	AVERAGES RPG	APG	PPG
99-00—Bos.-G.S.-Port.	7	46	8	18	.444	1	1	1.000	1	4	5	6	1	0	5	17	0.7	0.9	2.4
00-01—New Jersey	5	56	6	19	.316	0	0	...	4	5	9	0	3	0	6	13	1.8	0.0	2.6
Totals	12	102	14	37	.378	1	1	1.000	5	9	14	6	4	0	11	30	1.2	0.5	2.5

Three-point field goals: 1999-00, 0-for-3. 2000-01, 1-for-3 (.333). Totals, 1-for-6 (.167).
Personal fouls/disqualifications: 1999-00, 2/0. 2000-01, 6/0. Totals, 8/0.

ABA 2000 REGULAR-SEASON RECORD

Season Team	G	Min.	FGM	FGA	Pct.	FTM	FTA	Pct.	Reb.	Ast.	Pts.	AVERAGES RPG	APG	PPG
00-01—Memphis	13	492	106	240	.442	54	68	.794	89	32	295	6.8	2.5	22.7

Three-point field goals: 2000-01, 29-for-93 (.312).

THOMAS, KENNY F ROCKETS

PERSONAL: Born July 25, 1977, in Atlanta. ... 6-8/260. (2,03/117,9). ... Full Name: Kenneth Cornelius Thomas.
HIGH SCHOOL: El Paso (Texas), then Albuquerque (N.M.).
COLLEGE: New Mexico.
TRANSACTIONS/CAREER NOTES: Selected by Houston Rockets in first round (22nd pick overall) of 1999 NBA Draft.

COLLEGIATE RECORD
NOTES: THE SPORTING NEWS All-America second team (1998).

Season Team	G	Min.	FGM	FGA	Pct.	FTM	FTA	Pct.	Reb.	Ast.	Pts.	AVERAGES RPG	APG	PPG
95-96—New Mexico	33	981	170	294	.578	144	203	.709	256	53	484	7.8	1.6	14.7
96-97—New Mexico	32	1000	139	264	.527	155	206	.752	220	63	444	6.9	2.0	13.9
97-98—New Mexico	32	1047	195	385	.506	122	159	.767	297	95	539	9.3	3.0	16.8
98-99—New Mexico	26	903	162	297	.545	113	154	.734	259	51	464	10.0	2.0	17.8
Totals	123	3931	666	1240	.537	534	722	.740	1032	262	1931	8.4	2.1	15.7

Three-point field goals: 1995-96, 0-for-3. 1996-97, 11-for-36 (.306). 1997-98, 27-for-72 (.375). 1998-99, 27-for-73 (.370). Totals, 65-for-184 (.353).

NBA REGULAR-SEASON RECORD

Season Team	G	Min.	FGM	FGA	Pct.	FTM	FTA	Pct.	REBOUNDS Off.	Def.	Tot.	Ast.	St.	Blk.	TO	Pts.	AVERAGES RPG	APG	PPG
99-00—Houston	72	1797	212	531	.399	138	209	.660	147	290	437	113	54	22	112	594	6.1	1.6	8.3
00-01—Houston	74	1820	206	465	.443	91	126	.722	122	295	417	77	40	43	116	528	5.6	1.0	7.1
Totals	146	3617	418	996	.420	229	335	.684	269	585	854	190	94	65	228	1122	5.8	1.3	7.7

Three-point field goals: 1999-00, 32-for-122 (.262). 2000-01, 25-for-92 (.272). Totals, 57-for-214 (.266).
Personal fouls/disqualifications: 1999-00, 167/0. 2000-01, 178/4. Totals, 345/4.

THOMAS, KURT F KNICKS

PERSONAL: Born October 4, 1972, in Dallas. ... 6-9/230. (2,06/104,3). ... Full Name: Kurt Vincent Thomas.
HIGH SCHOOL: Hillcrest (Dallas).
COLLEGE: Texas Christian.
TRANSACTIONS/CAREER NOTES: Selected by Miami Heat in first round (10th pick overall) of 1995 NBA Draft. ... Traded by Heat with G Sasha Danilovic and F Martin Muursepp to Dallas Mavericks for F Jamal Mashburn (February 14, 1997). ... Signed as free agent by New York Knicks (January 22, 1999).

NOTES: Led NCAA Division I with 28.9 points per game and 14.6 rebounds per game (1995). ... One of only three players in NCAA history to lead nation in both scoring and rebounding in same season (1995).

Season Team	G	Min.	FGM	FGA	Pct.	FTM	FTA	Pct.	Reb.	Ast.	Pts.	AVERAGES RPG	APG	PPG
90-91—Texas Christian	28	42	8	18	.444	7	14	.500	13	2	23	0.5	0.1	0.8
91-92—Texas Christian	21	347	58	119	.487	34	51	.667	114	24	150	5.4	1.1	7.1
92-93—Texas Christian						Did not play—leg injury.								
93-94—Texas Christian	27	805	224	440	.509	98	152	.645	262	50	558	9.7	1.9	20.7
94-95—Texas Christian	27	872	288	526	.548	202	283	.714	393	32	781	14.6	1.2	28.9
Totals	103	2066	578	1103	.524	341	500	.682	782	108	1512	7.6	1.0	14.7

Three-point field goals: 1990-91, 0-for-2. 1993-94, 12-for-46 (.261). 1994-95, 3-for-12 (.250). Totals, 15-for-60 (.250).

NBA REGULAR-SEASON RECORD

Season Team	G	Min.	FGM	FGA	Pct.	FTM	FTA	Pct.	REBOUNDS Off.	Def.	Tot.	Ast.	St.	Blk.	TO	Pts.	AVERAGES RPG	APG	PPG
95-96—Miami	74	1655	274	547	.501	118	178	.663	122	317	439	46	47	36	98	666	5.9	0.6	9.0
96-97—Miami	18	374	39	105	.371	35	46	.761	31	76	107	9	12	9	25	113	5.9	0.5	6.3
97-98—Dallas	5	73	17	45	.378	3	3	1.000	8	16	24	3	1	0	10	37	4.8	0.6	7.4
98-99—New York	50	1182	170	368	.462	66	108	.611	82	204	286	55	45	17	73	406	5.7	1.1	8.1
99-00—New York	80	1971	270	535	.505	100	128	.781	144	361	505	82	51	42	105	641	6.3	1.0	8.0
00-01—New York	77	2125	314	614	.511	171	210	.814	172	343	515	63	61	69	99	800	6.7	0.8	10.4
Totals	304	7380	1084	2214	.490	493	673	.733	559	1317	1876	258	217	173	410	2663	6.2	0.8	8.8

Three-point field goals: 1995-96, 0-for-2. 1996-97, 0-for-1. 1998-99, 0-for-1. 1999-00, 1-for-3 (.333). 2000-01, 1-for-3 (.333). Totals, 2-for-10 (.200).
Personal fouls/disqualifications: 1995-96, 271/7. 1996-97, 67/3. 1997-98, 19/1. 1998-99, 159/3. 1999-00, 278/6. 2000-01, 287/6. Totals, 1081/26.

Season Team	G	Min.	FGM	FGA	Pct.	FTM	FTA	Pct.	REBOUNDS Off.	Def.	Tot.	Ast.	St.	Blk.	TO	Pts.	AVERAGES RPG	APG	PPG
95-96—Miami	3	60	4	10	.400	4	4	1.000	4	12	16	3	2	1	5	12	5.3	1.0	4.0
98-99—New York	20	419	45	118	.381	16	23	.696	38	72	110	7	15	12	19	106	5.5	0.4	5.3
99-00—New York	16	251	31	61	.508	7	10	.700	18	32	50	5	3	6	14	69	3.1	0.3	4.3
00-01—New York	5	186	25	47	.532	22	31	.710	17	39	56	9	2	5	9	72	11.2	1.8	14.4
Totals	44	916	105	236	.445	49	68	.721	77	155	232	24	22	24	47	259	5.3	0.5	5.9

Personal fouls/disqualifications: 1995-96, 13/1. 1998-99, 76/0. 1999-00, 44/1. 2000-01, 26/1. Totals, 159/3.

THOMAS, TIM   F   BUCKS

PERSONAL: Born February 26, 1977, in Paterson, N.J. ... 6-10/230. (2,08/104,3). ... Full Name: Timothy Mark Thomas.
HIGH SCHOOL: Paterson Catholic (Paterson, N.J.).
COLLEGE: Villanova.
TRANSACTIONS/CAREER NOTES: Selected after freshman season by New Jersey Nets in first round (seventh pick overall) of 1997 NBA Draft. ... Draft rights traded by Nets with draft rights to G Anthony Parker, G Jim Jackson and C Eric Montross to Philadelphia 76ers for C Michael Cage, G Lucious Harris, F Don MacLean and draft rights to F Keith Van Horn (June 27, 1997). ... Traded by 76ers with C/F Scott Williams to Milwaukee Bucks for F Tyrone Hill and F/G Jerald Honeycutt (March 11, 1999).

T

COLLEGIATE RECORD

NOTES: THE SPORTING NEWS Freshman of the Year (1997).

Season Team	G	Min.	FGM	FGA	Pct.	FTM	FTA	Pct.	Reb.	Ast.	Pts.	AVERAGES RPG	APG	PPG
96-97—Villanova........................	32	1005	187	416	.450	121	152	.796	193	66	542	6.0	2.1	16.9

Three-point field goals: 1996-97, 47-for-140 (.336).

NBA REGULAR-SEASON RECORD

RECORDS: Holds single-game record for most three-point field goals made in one half—8 (January 5, 2001, vs. Portland).
HONORS: NBA All-Rookie second team (1998).

Season Team	G	Min.	FGM	FGA	Pct.	FTM	FTA	Pct.	REBOUNDS Off.	Def.	Tot.	Ast.	St.	Blk.	TO	Pts.	AVERAGES RPG	APG	PPG
97-98—Philadelphia	77	1779	306	684	.447	171	231	.740	107	181	288	90	54	17	118	845	3.7	1.2	11.0
98-99—Phil.-Mil..........	50	812	132	279	.473	73	112	.652	49	77	126	46	26	12	46	358	2.5	0.9	7.2
99-00—Milwaukee	80	2093	347	753	.461	188	243	.774	100	232	332	113	59	31	129	945	4.2	1.4	11.8
00-01—Milwaukee	76	2086	326	758	.430	195	253	.771	79	234	313	138	78	45	114	954	4.1	1.8	12.6
Totals	283	6770	1111	2474	.449	627	839	.747	335	724	1059	387	217	105	407	3102	3.7	1.4	11.0

Three-point field goals: 1997-98, 62-for-171 (.363). 1998-99, 21-for-68 (.309). 1999-00, 63-for-182 (.346). 2000-01, 107-for-260 (.412). Totals, 253-for-681 (.372).
Personal fouls/disqualifications: 1997-98, 185/2. 1998-99, 107/2. 1999-00, 227/3. 2000-01, 194/5. Totals, 713/12.

NBA PLAYOFF RECORD

Season Team	G	Min.	FGM	FGA	Pct.	FTM	FTA	Pct.	REBOUNDS Off.	Def.	Tot.	Ast.	St.	Blk.	TO	Pts.	AVERAGES RPG	APG	PPG
98-99—Milwaukee	3	60	8	18	.444	7	12	.583	4	8	12	1	1	1	5	23	4.0	0.3	7.7
99-00—Milwaukee	5	142	29	59	.492	14	17	.824	6	18	24	10	1	4	1	77	4.8	2.0	15.4
00-01—Milwaukee	18	479	64	143	.448	53	65	.815	22	59	81	29	9	10	21	203	4.5	1.6	11.3
Totals	26	681	101	220	.459	74	94	.787	32	85	117	40	11	15	27	303	4.5	1.5	11.7

Three-point field goals: 1998-99, 0-for-2. 1999-00, 5-for-15 (.333). 2000-01, 22-for-51 (.431). Totals, 27-for-68 (.397).
Personal fouls/disqualifications: 1998-99, 11/0. 1999-00, 14/0. 2000-01, 52/1. Totals, 77/1.

THORPE, OTIS   F/C

PERSONAL: Born August 5, 1962, in Boynton Beach, Fla. ... 6-10/248. (2,08/112,5). ... Full Name: Otis Henry Thorpe.
HIGH SCHOOL: Lake Worth (Fla.) Community.
COLLEGE: Providence.
TRANSACTIONS/CAREER NOTES: Selected by Kansas City Kings in first round (ninth pick overall) of 1984 NBA Draft. ... Kings franchise moved from Kansas City to Sacramento for 1985-86 season. ... Traded by Kings to Houston Rockets for F/G Rodney McCray and F/C Jim Petersen (October 11, 1988). ... Traded by Rockets with rights to F Marcelo Nicola and 1995 first-round draft choice to Portland Trail Blazers for G Clyde Drexler and F Tracy Murray (February 14, 1995). ... Traded by Trail Blazers to Detroit Pistons for F Bill Curley and draft rights to G Randolph Childress (September 20, 1995). ... Traded by Pistons to Vancouver Grizzlies for first-round draft choice between 1998 and 2003 (August 7, 1997). ... Traded by Grizzlies with G Chris Robinson to Sacramento Kings for G Bobby Hurley and F Michael Smith (February 18, 1998). ... Traded by Kings with G Mitch Richmond to Washington Wizards for F Chris Webber (May 14, 1998). ... Signed as free agent by Miami Heat (August 4, 1999). ... Traded by Heat with F P.J. Brown, F Jamal Mashburn, F Tim James and G/F Rodney Buford to Charlotte Hornets for G Eddie Jones, F Anthony Mason, G Ricky Davis and G/F Dale Ellis (August 1, 2000).
MISCELLANEOUS: Member of NBA championship team (1994).

COLLEGIATE RECORD

Season Team	G	Min.	FGM	FGA	Pct.	FTM	FTA	Pct.	Reb.	Ast.	Pts.	AVERAGES RPG	APG	PPG
80-81—Providence	26	668	100	194	.515	50	76	.658	137	11	250	5.3	0.4	9.6
81-82—Providence	27	942	153	283	.541	74	115	.643	216	36	380	8.0	1.3	14.1
82-83—Providence	31	1041	204	321	.636	91	138	.659	249	24	499	8.0	0.8	16.1
83-84—Providence	29	1051	167	288	.580	162	248	.653	300	36	496	10.3	1.2	17.1
Totals	113	3702	624	1086	.575	377	577	.653	902	107	1625	8.0	0.9	14.4

NBA REGULAR-SEASON RECORD

NOTES: Tied for NBA lead with 300 personal fouls (1996) and nine disqualifications (1999).

Season Team	G	Min.	FGM	FGA	Pct.	FTM	FTA	Pct.	Off.	Def.	Tot.	Ast.	St.	Blk.	TO	Pts.	RPG	APG	PPG
84-85—Kansas City.....	82	1918	411	685	.600	230	371	.620	187	369	556	111	34	37	187	1052	6.8	1.4	12.8
85-86—Sacramento	75	1675	289	492	.587	164	248	.661	137	283	420	84	35	34	123	742	5.6	1.1	9.9
86-87—Sacramento	82	2956	567	1050	.540	413	543	.761	259	560	819	201	46	60	189	1547	10.0	2.5	18.9
87-88—Sacramento	82	3072	622	1226	.507	460	609	.755	279	558	837	266	62	56	228	1704	10.2	3.2	20.8
88-89—Houston.........	82	3135	521	961	.542	328	450	.729	272	515	787	202	82	37	225	1370	9.6	2.5	16.7
89-90—Houston.........	82	2947	547	998	.548	307	446	.688	258	476	734	261	66	24	229	1401	9.0	3.2	17.1
90-91—Houston.........	82	3039	549	988	.556	334	480	.696	287	559	846	197	73	20	217	1435	10.3	2.4	17.5
91-92—Houston.........	82	3056	558	943	.592	304	463	.657	285	577	862	250	52	37	237	1420	10.5	3.0	17.3
92-93—Houston.........	72	2357	385	690	.558	153	256	.598	219	370	589	181	43	19	151	923	8.2	2.5	12.8
93-94—Houston.........	82	2909	449	801	.561	251	382	.657	271	599	870	189	66	28	185	1149	10.6	2.3	14.0
94-95—Hou.-Port.......	70	2096	385	681	.565	167	281	.594	202	356	558	112	41	28	132	937	8.0	1.6	13.4
95-96—Detroit	82	2841	452	853	.530	257	362	.710	211	477	688	158	53	39	195	1161	8.4	1.9	14.2
96-97—Detroit	79	2661	419	787	.532	198	303	.653	226	396	622	133	59	17	145	1036	7.9	1.7	13.1
97-98—Van.-Sac.	74	2197	294	624	.471	164	240	.683	151	386	537	222	48	30	152	752	7.3	3.0	10.2
98-99—Washington	49	1539	240	440	.545	74	106	.698	96	238	334	101	42	19	88	554	6.8	2.1	11.3
99-00—Miami	51	777	125	243	.514	29	48	.604	56	110	166	33	26	9	59	279	3.3	0.6	5.5
00-01—Charlotte	49	647	59	131	.450	20	24	.833	50	95	145	29	12	7	32	138	3.0	0.6	2.8
Totals	1257	39822	6872	12593	.546	3853	5612	.687	3446	6924	10370	2730	840	501	2774	17600	8.2	2.2	14.0

Three-point field goals: 1984-85, 0-for-2. 1986-87, 0-for-3. 1987-88, 0-for-6. 1988-89, 0-for-2. 1989-90, 0-for-10. 1990-91, 3-for-7 (.429). 1991-92, 0-for-7. 1992-93, 0-for-2. 1993-94, 0-for-2. 1994-95, 0-for-7. 1995-96, 0-for-4. 1996-97, 0-for-2. 1997-98, 0-for-5. 1998-99, 0-for-2. 1999-00, 0-for-3. Totals, 3-for-64 (.047).

Personal fouls/disqualifications: 1984-85, 256/2. 1985-86, 233/3. 1986-87, 292/11. 1987-88, 264/3. 1988-89, 259/6. 1989-90, 270/5. 1990-91, 278/10. 1991-92, 307/7. 1992-93, 234/3. 1993-94, 253/1. 1994-95, 224/3. 1995-96, 300/7. 1996-97, 298/7. 1997-98, 238/4. 1998-99, 196/9. 1999-00, 136/4. 2000-01, 108/0. Totals, 4146/85.

NBA PLAYOFF RECORD

Season Team	G	Min.	FGM	FGA	Pct.	FTM	FTA	Pct.	Off.	Def.	Tot.	Ast.	St.	Blk.	TO	Pts.	RPG	APG	PPG
85-86—Sacramento	3	35	3	13	.231	6	13	.462	8	4	12	0	0	1	1	12	4.0	0.0	4.0
88-89—Houston.........	4	152	24	37	.649	16	21	.762	6	14	20	12	5	1	15	64	5.0	3.0	16.0
89-90—Houston.........	4	164	27	45	.600	26	38	.684	14	19	33	7	5	0	9	80	8.3	1.8	20.0
90-91—Houston.........	3	116	22	38	.579	3	6	.500	7	18	25	8	2	0	6	47	8.3	2.7	15.7
92-93—Houston.........	12	419	73	115	.635	28	43	.651	36	67	103	31	6	1	17	174	8.6	2.6	14.5
93-94—Houston.........	23	854	111	194	.572	38	67	.567	68	160	228	54	13	10	37	261	9.9	2.3	11.3
94-95—Portland	3	66	12	21	.571	7	10	.700	5	8	13	2	0	0	3	31	4.3	0.7	10.3
95-96—Detroit	3	101	13	24	.542	9	12	.750	14	21	35	7	0	0	7	35	11.7	2.3	11.7
96-97—Detroit	5	152	21	41	.512	7	9	.778	12	20	32	4	2	0	9	49	6.4	0.8	9.8
99-00—Miami	10	136	13	27	.481	7	14	.500	6	23	29	3	0	2	11	33	2.9	0.3	3.3
00-01—Charlotte	8	57	2	9	.222	0	0	...	6	11	17	0	0	0	2	4	2.1	0.0	0.5
Totals	78	2252	321	564	.569	147	233	.631	182	365	547	128	33	15	117	790	7.0	1.6	10.1

Three-point field goals: 1993-94, 1-for-2 (.500). 1999-00, 0-for-1. Totals, 1-for-3 (.333).

Personal fouls/disqualifications: 1985-86, 4/0. 1988-89, 17/1. 1989-90, 12/0. 1990-91, 8/0. 1992-93, 35/0. 1993-94, 86/2. 1994-95, 12/1. 1995-96, 9/0. 1996-97, 21/0. 1999-00, 29/0. 2000-01, 8/0. Totals, 241/4.

NBA ALL-STAR GAME RECORD

Season Team	Min.	FGM	FGA	Pct.	FTM	FTA	Pct.	Off.	Def.	Tot.	Ast.	PF	Dq.	St.	Blk.	TO	Pts.
1992 —Houston	4	1	1	1.000	0	0	...	0	0	0	0	0	0	0	0	0	2

TRAYLOR, ROBERT   F/C   76ERS

PERSONAL: Born February 1, 1977, in Detroit. ... 6-8/284. (2,03/128,8). ... Full Name: Robert DeShaun Traylor.
HIGH SCHOOL: Murray-Wright (Detroit).
COLLEGE: Michigan.
TRANSACTIONS/CAREER NOTES: Selected after junior season by Dallas Mavericks in first round (sixth pick overall) of 1998 NBA Draft. ... Draft rights traded by Mavericks to Milwaukee Bucks for draft rights to C Dirk Nowitzki and F Pat Garrity (June 24, 1998). ... Traded by Bucks with F/C J.R. Reid to Cleveland Cavaliers as part of three-way deal in which Cavaliers traded G Bob Sura to Golden State Warriors, Warriors traded F Jason Caffey and F/G Billy Owens to Bucks and Bucks traded G Vinny Del Negro to Warriors (June 27, 2000). ... Traded by Cavaliers with F Matt Harpring and F Cedric Henderson to Philadelphia 76ers for F Tyrone Hill and F Jumaine Jones (August 3, 2001).

COLLEGIATE RECORD

Season Team	G	Min.	FGM	FGA	Pct.	FTM	FTA	Pct.	Reb.	Ast.	Pts.	RPG	APG	PPG
95-96—Michigan	22	438	82	148	.554	34	62	.548	130	12	198	5.9	0.5	9.0
96-97—Michigan	35	955	190	342	.556	80	176	.455	271	33	460	7.7	0.9	13.1
97-98—Michigan	34	1090	224	387	.579	104	162	.642	344	88	552	10.1	2.6	16.2
Totals	91	2483	496	877	.566	218	400	.545	745	133	1210	8.2	1.5	13.3

Three-point field goals: 1997-98, 0-for-1.

NBA REGULAR-SEASON RECORD

Season Team	G	Min.	FGM	FGA	Pct.	FTM	FTA	Pct.	Off.	Def.	Tot.	Ast.	St.	Blk.	TO	Pts.	RPG	APG	PPG
98-99—Milwaukee	49	786	108	201	.537	43	80	.538	80	102	182	38	44	44	42	259	3.7	0.8	5.3
99-00—Milwaukee	44	447	58	122	.475	41	68	.603	50	65	115	20	25	25	27	157	2.6	0.5	3.6
00-01—Cleveland	70	1212	161	324	.497	80	141	.567	124	176	300	63	49	76	98	402	4.3	0.9	5.7
Totals	163	2445	327	647	.505	164	289	.567	254	343	597	121	118	145	167	818	3.7	0.7	5.0

Three-point field goals: 1998-99, 0-for-1. 1999-00, 0-for-4. 2000-01, 0-for-2. Totals, 0-for-7 (.000).

Personal fouls/disqualifications: 1998-99, 140/4. 1999-00, 79/0. 2000-01, 204/3. Totals, 423/7.

NBA PLAYOFF RECORD

								REBOUNDS								AVERAGES		
Season Team	G	Min.	FGM	FGA	Pct.	FTM	FTA	Pct.	Off.	Def.	Tot.	Ast.	St.	Blk.	TO	Pts.	RPG	APG	PPG
98-99—Milwaukee	3	45	7	9	.778	2	4	.500	6	6	12	2	2	4	4	16	4.0	0.7	5.3
99-00—Milwaukee	1	4	0	1	.000	0	0	...	1	1	2	1	0	1	0	0	2.0	1.0	0.0
Totals	4	49	7	10	.700	2	4	.500	7	7	14	3	2	5	4	16	3.5	0.8	4.0

Personal fouls/disqualifications: 1998-99, 15/1. 1999-00, 2/0. Totals, 17/1.

TRENT, GARY   F

PERSONAL: Born September 22, 1974, in Columbus, Ohio. ... 6-8/250. (2,03/113,4). ... Full Name: Gary Dajaun Trent.
HIGH SCHOOL: Hamilton Township (Columbus, Ohio).
COLLEGE: Ohio University.
TRANSACTIONS/CAREER NOTES: Selected after junior season by Milwaukee Bucks in first round (11th pick overall) of 1995 NBA Draft. ... Draft rights traded by Bucks with conditional 1996 first-round draft choice to Portland Trail Blazers for draft rights to G Shawn Respert (June 28, 1995). ... Traded by Trail Blazers with G Kenny Anderson, G Alvin Williams and two first-round draft choices to Toronto Raptors for G Damon Stoudamire, F Walt Williams and F Carlos Rogers (February 13, 1998). ... Signed as free agent by Dallas Mavericks (January 23, 1999).

COLLEGIATE RECORD

											AVERAGES		
Season Team	G	Min.	FGM	FGA	Pct.	FTM	FTA	Pct.	Reb.	Ast.	Pts.	RPG	APG	PPG
92-93—Ohio University..............	27	892	194	298	.651	126	181	.696	250	42	514	9.3	1.6	19.0
93-94—Ohio University..............	33	1119	309	536	.576	210	291	.722	377	65	837	11.4	2.0	25.4
94-95—Ohio University..............	33	1134	293	556	.527	163	254	.642	423	79	757	12.8	2.4	22.9
Totals	93	3145	796	1390	.573	499	726	.687	1050	186	2108	11.3	2.0	22.7

Three-point field goals: 1992-93, 0-for-1. 1993-94, 9-for-33 (.273). 1994-95, 8-for-35 (.229). Totals, 17-for-69 (.246).

NBA REGULAR-SEASON RECORD

								REBOUNDS								AVERAGES		
Season Team	G	Min.	FGM	FGA	Pct.	FTM	FTA	Pct.	Off.	Def.	Tot.	Ast.	St.	Blk.	TO	Pts.	RPG	APG	PPG
95-96—Portland.........	69	1219	220	429	.513	78	141	.553	84	154	238	50	25	11	92	518	3.4	0.7	7.5
96-97—Portland.........	82	1918	361	674	.536	160	229	.699	156	272	428	87	48	35	129	882	5.2	1.1	10.8
97-98—Portland-Tor....	54	1360	241	505	.477	144	212	.679	123	215	338	72	35	27	94	630	6.3	1.3	11.7
98-99—Dallas.............	45	1362	287	602	.477	145	235	.617	127	224	351	77	29	23	66	719	7.8	1.7	16.0
99-00—Dallas.............	11	301	70	142	.493	11	21	.524	20	32	52	22	8	3	25	151	4.7	2.0	13.7
00-01—Dallas.............	33	319	57	130	.438	19	36	.528	39	53	92	10	13	8	22	133	2.8	0.3	4.0
Totals	294	6479	1236	2482	.498	557	874	.637	549	950	1499	318	158	107	428	3033	5.1	1.1	10.3

Three-point field goals: 1995-96, 0-for-9. 1996-97, 0-for-11. 1997-98, 4-for-12 (.333). 1998-99, 0-for-5. 1999-00, 0-for-2. 2000-01, 0-for-1. Totals, 4-for-40 (.100).
Personal fouls/disqualifications: 1995-96, 116/0. 1996-97, 186/2. 1997-98, 161/3. 1998-99, 122/1. 1999-00, 28/0. 2000-01, 52/0. Totals, 665/6.

NBA PLAYOFF RECORD

								REBOUNDS								AVERAGES		
Season Team	G	Min.	FGM	FGA	Pct.	FTM	FTA	Pct.	Off.	Def.	Tot.	Ast.	St.	Blk.	TO	Pts.	RPG	APG	PPG
95-96—Portland.........	2	10	1	4	.250	0	0	...	0	1	1	0	1	0	0	2	0.5	0.0	1.0
96-97—Portland.........	4	61	13	29	.448	6	11	.545	5	7	12	4	0	1	6	32	3.0	1.0	8.0
Totals	6	71	14	33	.424	6	11	.545	5	8	13	4	1	1	6	34	2.2	0.7	5.7

Three-point field goals: 1996-97, 0-for-1. Totals, 0-for-1 (.000).
Personal fouls/disqualifications: 1995-96, 3/0. 1996-97, 11/0. Totals, 14/0.

TSAKALIDIS, IAKOVOS   C   SUNS

PERSONAL: Born June 10, 1979, in Rustavi, Republic of Georgia. ... 7-2/285. (2,18/129,3). ... Nickname: Jake.
TRANSACTIONS/CAREER NOTES: Played in Greece (1996-97 through 1999-2000). ... Selected by Phoenix Suns in first round (25th overall) of 2000 NBA Draft.

GREEK LEAGUE RECORD

											AVERAGES		
Season Team	G	Min.	FGM	FGA	Pct.	FTM	FTA	Pct.	Reb.	Ast.	Pts.	RPG	APG	PPG
96-97—A.E.K.	1	13	1	2	.500	2	2	1.000	4	0	4	4.0	0.0	4.0
97-98—A.E.K.	18	336	35	63	.556	24	43	.558	101	4	94	5.6	0.2	5.2
98-99—A.E.K.	25	515	63	121	.521	35	55	.636	149	5	161	6.0	0.2	6.4
99-00—A.E.K.	22	563	73	123	.593	57	103	.553	153	14	203	7.0	0.6	9.2
Totals	66	1427	172	309	.557	118	203	.581	407	23	462	6.2	0.3	7.0

NBA REGULAR-SEASON RECORD

								REBOUNDS								AVERAGES		
Season Team	G	Min.	FGM	FGA	Pct.	FTM	FTA	Pct.	Off.	Def.	Tot.	Ast.	St.	Blk.	TO	Pts.	RPG	APG	PPG
00-01—Phoenix	57	947	101	215	.470	54	91	.593	83	159	242	19	10	55	66	256	4.2	0.3	4.5

Personal fouls/disqualifications: 2000-01, 137/1.

NBA PLAYOFF RECORD

								REBOUNDS								AVERAGES		
Season Team	G	Min.	FGM	FGA	Pct.	FTM	FTA	Pct.	Off.	Def.	Tot.	Ast.	St.	Blk.	TO	Pts.	RPG	APG	PPG
00-01—Phoenix	4	75	6	16	.375	0	0	...	10	18	28	0	0	7	1	12	7.0	0.0	3.0

Personal fouls/disqualifications: 2000-01, 11/0.

TURKOGLU, HIDAYET   F   KINGS

PERSONAL: Born March 19, 1979, in Istanbul, Turkey. ... 6-8/220. (2,03/99,8). ... Nickname: Hedo.
TRANSACTIONS/CAREER NOTES: Played in Turkey (1996-97 through 1999-2000). ... Selected by Sacramento Kings in first round (16th pick overall) of 2000 NBA Draft.

TURKISH LEAGUE RECORD

Season Team	G	Min.	FGM	FGA	Pct.	FTM	FTA	Pct.	Reb.	Ast.	Pts.	RPG	APG	PPG
96-97—Efes Pilsen	11	...	27	38	.711	8	16	.500	30	17	83	2.7	1.5	7.5
97-98—Efes Pilsen	29	386	45	93	.484	25	38	.658	87	35	121	3.0	1.2	4.2
98-99—Efes Pilsen	23	575	69	146	.473	33	42	.786	95	37	192	4.1	1.6	8.3
99-00—Efes Pilsen	24	812	110	211	.521	66	88	.750	129	53	328	5.4	2.2	13.7
Totals	87	...	251	488	.514	132	184	.717	341	142	724	3.9	1.6	8.3

Three-point field goals: 1996-97, 7-for-17 (.412). 1997-98, 6-for-22 (.273). 1998-99, 21-for-65 (.323). 1999-00, 42-for-81 (.519). Totals, 76-for-185 (.411).

HONORS: NBA All-Rookie second team (2001).

NBA REGULAR-SEASON RECORD

Season Team	G	Min.	FGM	FGA	Pct.	FTM	FTA	Pct.	Off.	Def.	Tot.	Ast.	St.	Blk.	TO	Pts.	RPG	APG	PPG
00-01—Sacramento	74	1245	138	335	.412	87	112	.777	49	161	210	69	52	24	55	391	2.8	0.9	5.3

Three-point field goals: 2000-01, 28-for-86 (.326).
Personal fouls/disqualifications: 2000-01, 139/1.

NBA PLAYOFF RECORD

Season Team	G	Min.	FGM	FGA	Pct.	FTM	FTA	Pct.	Off.	Def.	Tot.	Ast.	St.	Blk.	TO	Pts.	RPG	APG	PPG
00-01—Sacramento	8	141	20	46	.435	12	12	1.000	7	21	28	11	3	1	6	60	3.5	1.4	7.5

Three-point field goals: 2000-01, 8-for-14 (.571).
Personal fouls/disqualifications: 2000-01, 18/0.

VAN EXEL, NICK   G   NUGGETS

PERSONAL: Born November 27, 1971, in Kenosha, Wis. ... 6-1/190. (1,85/86,2). ... Full Name: Nickey Maxwell Van Exel. ... Name pronounced van EX-el.
HIGH SCHOOL: St. Joseph's (Kenosha, Wis.).
JUNIOR COLLEGE: Trinity Valley Community College (Texas).
COLLEGE: Cincinnati.
TRANSACTIONS/CAREER NOTES: Selected by Los Angeles Lakers in second round (37th pick overall) of 1993 NBA Draft. ... Traded by Lakers to Denver Nuggets for F Tony Battie and draft rights to G Tyronn Lue (June 24, 1998).

COLLEGIATE RECORD

Season Team	G	Min.	FGM	FGA	Pct.	FTM	FTA	Pct.	Reb.	Ast.	Pts.	RPG	APG	PPG
89-90—Trinity Valley (Texas) C.C.	31	...	200	415	.482	88	128	.688	101	166	542	3.3	5.4	17.5
90-91—Trinity Valley (Texas) C.C.	27	...	190	441	.431	105	147	.714	110	185	551	4.1	6.9	20.4
91-92—Cincinnati	34	834	144	323	.446	68	101	.673	87	99	418	2.6	2.9	12.3
92-93—Cincinnati	31	1049	198	513	.386	87	120	.725	75	138	568	2.4	4.5	18.3
Junior College Totals	58	...	390	856	.456	193	275	.702	211	351	1093	3.6	6.1	18.8
4-Year-College Totals	65	1883	342	836	.409	155	221	.701	162	237	986	2.5	3.6	15.2

Three-point field goals: 1989-90, 71-for-186 (.382). 1990-91, 66-for-186 (.355). 1991-92, 62-for-163 (.380). 1992-93, 85-for-248 (.343). Totals, 137-for-372 (.368) Totals, 147-for-411 (.358).

HONORS: NBA All-Rookie second team (1994).

NBA REGULAR-SEASON RECORD

Season Team	G	Min.	FGM	FGA	Pct.	FTM	FTA	Pct.	Off.	Def.	Tot.	Ast.	St.	Blk.	TO	Pts.	RPG	APG	PPG
93-94—L.A. Lakers	81	2700	413	1049	.394	150	192	.781	47	191	238	466	85	8	145	1099	2.9	5.8	13.6
94-95—L.A. Lakers	80	2944	465	1107	.420	235	300	.783	27	196	223	660	97	6	220	1348	2.8	8.3	16.9
95-96—L.A. Lakers	74	2513	396	950	.417	163	204	.799	29	152	181	509	70	10	156	1099	2.4	6.9	14.9
96-97—L.A. Lakers	79	2937	432	1075	.402	165	200	.825	44	182	226	672	75	10	212	1206	2.9	8.5	15.3
97-98—L.A. Lakers	64	2053	311	743	.419	136	172	.791	31	163	194	442	64	6	104	881	3.0	6.9	13.8
98-99—Denver	50	1802	306	769	.398	142	175	.811	14	99	113	368	40	3	121	826	2.3	7.4	16.5
99-00—Denver	79	2950	473	1213	.390	196	240	.817	34	277	311	714	68	11	221	1275	3.9	9.0	16.1
00-01—Denver	71	2688	460	1112	.414	204	249	.819	44	197	241	600	61	18	165	1259	3.4	8.5	17.7
Totals	578	20587	3256	8018	.406	1391	1732	.803	270	1457	1727	4431	560	72	1344	8993	3.0	7.7	15.6

Three-point field goals: 1993-94, 123-for-364 (.338). 1994-95, 183-for-511 (.358). 1995-96, 144-for-403 (.357). 1996-97, 177-for-468 (.378). 1997-98, 123-for-316 (.389). 1998-99, 72-for-234 (.308). 1999-00, 133-for-401 (.332). 2000-01, 135-for-358 (.377). Totals, 1090-for-3055 (.357).
Personal fouls/disqualifications: 1993-94, 154/1. 1994-95, 157/0. 1995-96, 115/0. 1996-97, 110/0. 1997-98, 120/0. 1998-99, 90/0. 1999-00, 148/0. 2000-01, 109/1. Totals, 1003/2.

NBA PLAYOFF RECORD

Season Team	G	Min.	FGM	FGA	Pct.	FTM	FTA	Pct.	Off.	Def.	Tot.	Ast.	St.	Blk.	TO	Pts.	RPG	APG	PPG
94-95—L.A. Lakers	10	464	67	162	.414	45	59	.763	9	29	38	73	21	3	22	200	3.8	7.3	20.0
95-96—L.A. Lakers	4	137	16	54	.296	10	13	.769	4	12	16	27	2	0	11	47	4.0	6.8	11.8
96-97—L.A. Lakers	9	353	45	119	.378	28	34	.824	6	25	31	58	10	0	18	130	3.4	6.4	14.4
97-98—L.A. Lakers	13	367	50	151	.331	29	40	.725	9	23	32	54	8	1	22	151	2.5	4.2	11.6
Totals	36	1321	178	486	.366	112	146	.767	28	89	117	212	41	4	73	528	3.3	5.9	14.7

Three-point field goals: 1994-95, 21-for-66 (.318). 1995-96, 5-for-16 (.313). 1996-97, 12-for-44 (.273). 1997-98, 22-for-70 (.314). Totals, 60-for-196 (.306).
Personal fouls/disqualifications: 1994-95, 33/0. 1995-96, 10/0. 1996-97, 19/0. 1997-98, 30/0. Totals, 92/0.

NBA ALL-STAR GAME RECORD

Season Team	Min.	FGM	FGA	Pct.	FTM	FTA	Pct.	Off.	Def.	Tot.	Ast.	PF	Dq.	St.	Blk.	TO	Pts.
1998 —L.A. Lakers........	20	5	14	.357	2	2	1.000	1	2	3	2	0	...	0	0	2	13

Three-point field goals: 1998, 1-for-6 (.167).

VAN HORN, KEITH   F   NETS

PERSONAL: Born October 23, 1975, in Fullerton, Calif. ... 6-10/240. (2,08/108,9). ... Full Name: Keith Adam Van Horn.
HIGH SCHOOL: Diamond Bar (Calif.).
COLLEGE: Utah.
TRANSACTIONS/CAREER NOTES: Selected by Philadelphia 76ers in first round (second pick overall) of 1997 NBA Draft. ... Draft rights traded by 76ers with C Michael Cage, G Lucious Harris and F Don MacLean to New Jersey Nets for draft rights to F Tim Thomas, draft rights to G Anthony Parker, G Jim Jackson and C Eric Montross (June 27, 1997).

COLLEGIATE RECORD

NOTES: The Sporting News All-America first team (1997). ... The Sporting News All-America second team (1996).

Season Team	G	Min.	FGM	FGA	Pct.	FTM	FTA	Pct.	Reb.	Ast.	Pts.	RPG	APG	PPG
93-94—Utah	25	740	161	312	.516	100	129	.775	208	21	457	8.3	0.8	18.3
94-95—Utah	33	994	246	451	.545	143	167	.856	280	45	694	8.5	1.4	21.0
95-96—Utah	32	990	236	439	.538	160	188	.851	283	31	686	8.8	1.0	21.4
96-97—Utah	32	1008	248	504	.492	151	167	.904	303	45	705	9.5	1.4	22.0
Totals	122	3732	891	1706	.522	554	651	.851	1074	142	2542	8.8	1.2	20.8

Three-point field goals: 1993-94, 35-for-79 (.443). 1994-95, 59-for-153 (.386). 1995-96, 54-for-132 (.409). 1996-97, 58-for-150 (.387). Totals, 206-for-514 (.401).

NBA REGULAR-SEASON RECORD

HONORS: NBA All-Rookie first team (1998).

Season Team	G	Min.	FGM	FGA	Pct.	FTM	FTA	Pct.	Off.	Def.	Tot.	Ast.	St.	Blk.	TO	Pts.	RPG	APG	PPG
97-98—New Jersey	62	2325	446	1047	.426	258	305	.846	142	266	408	106	64	25	164	1219	6.6	1.7	19.7
98-99—New Jersey	42	1576	322	752	.428	256	298	.859	114	244	358	65	43	53	133	916	8.5	1.5	21.8
99-00—New Jersey	80	2782	559	1257	.445	333	393	.847	200	476	676	158	64	60	245	1535	8.5	2.0	19.2
00-01—New Jersey	49	1733	308	708	.435	150	186	.806	78	269	347	82	40	20	103	831	7.1	1.7	17.0
Totals	233	8416	1635	3764	.434	997	1182	.843	534	1255	1789	411	211	158	645	4501	7.7	1.8	19.3

Three-point field goals: 1997-98, 69-for-224 (.308). 1998-99, 16-for-53 (.302). 1999-00, 84-for-228 (.368). 2000-01, 65-for-170 (.382). Totals, 234-for-675 (.347).

Personal fouls/disqualifications: 1997-98, 216/0. 1998-99, 134/2. 1999-00, 258/5. 2000-01, 150/4. Totals, 758/11.

NBA PLAYOFF RECORD

Season Team	G	Min.	FGM	FGA	Pct.	FTM	FTA	Pct.	Off.	Def.	Tot.	Ast.	St.	Blk.	TO	Pts.	RPG	APG	PPG
97-98—New Jersey	3	77	13	29	.448	12	15	.800	2	7	9	1	0	0	2	38	3.0	0.3	12.7

Three-point field goals: 1997-98, 0-for-2.
Personal fouls/disqualifications: 1997-98, 7/0.

VANTERPOOL, DAVID   G

PERSONAL: Born March 31, 1973, in Dayton Beach, Fla. ... 6-5/190. (1,96/86,2).
HIGH SCHOOL: Montgomery Blair (Silver Spring, Md.).
COLLEGE: St. Bonaventure.
TRANSACTIONS/CAREER NOTES: Not drafted by an NBA franchise. ... Played in Italy (1996-97). ... Played in China (1997-98 and 1998-99). ... Played in Continental Basketball Association with Yakima Sun Kings (1999-2000 and 2000-01). ... Signed as free agent by Detroit Pistons (October 2, 2000). ... Waived by Pistons (October 28, 2000). ... Played in American Basketball Association 2000 with Kansas City Knights (2000-01). ... Signed by Washington Wizards to the first of two consecutive 10-day contracts (March 6, 2001). ... Signed by Wizards for remainder of season (March 26, 2001).

COLLEGIATE RECORD

Season Team	G	Min.	FGM	FGA	Pct.	FTM	FTA	Pct.	Reb.	Ast.	Pts.	RPG	APG	PPG
91-92—St. Bonaventure.............	27	802	74	176	.420	82	114	.719	133	96	239	4.9	3.6	8.0
92-93—St. Bonaventure.............	27	913	111	253	.439	115	156	.737	159	116	358	5.9	4.3	13.3
93-94—St. Bonaventure.............	27	891	108	271	.399	96	137	.701	169	95	335	6.3	3.5	12.4
94-95—St. Bonaventure.............	31	1029	176	396	.444	137	182	.753	169	94	542	5.5	3.0	17.5
Totals	112	3635	469	1096	.428	430	589	.730	630	401	1474	5.6	3.6	13.2

Three-point field goals: 1991-92, 9-for-40 (.225). 1992-93, 21-for-60 (.350). 1993-94, 23-for-72 (.319). 1994-95, 53-for-154 (.344). Totals, 106-for-326 (.325).

CBA REGULAR-SEASON RECORD

NOTES: Member of CBA championship team (2000). ... CBA All-Defensive team (2000).

Season Team	G	Min.	FGM	FGA	Pct.	FTM	FTA	Pct.	Reb.	Ast.	Pts.	RPG	APG	PPG
99-00—Yakima	55	1644	253	518	.488	205	302	.679	364	318	722	6.6	5.8	13.1
00-01—Yakima	22	888	173	385	.449	120	153	.784	185	185	480	8.4	8.4	21.8
Totals	77	2532	426	903	.472	325	455	.714	549	503	1202	7.1	6.5	15.6

Three-point field goals: 1999-00, 11-for-31 (.355). 2000-01, 14-for-40 (.350). Totals, 25-for-71 (.352).

Season Team	G	Min.	FGM	FGA	Pct.	FTM	FTA	Pct.	Reb.	Ast.	Pts.	AVERAGES		
												RPG	APG	PPG
00-01—Kansas City	10	375	61	145	.421	55	64	.859	69	44	182	6.9	4.4	18.2

Three-point field goals: 2000-01, 5-for-24 (.208).

NBA REGULAR-SEASON RECORD

Season Team	G	Min.	FGM	FGA	Pct.	FTM	FTA	Pct.	REBOUNDS			Ast.	St.	Blk.	TO	Pts.	AVERAGES		
									Off.	Def.	Tot.						RPG	APG	PPG
00-01—Washington	22	411	46	110	.418	30	50	.600	15	22	37	66	23	3	37	122	1.7	3.0	5.5

Three-point field goals: 2000-01, 0-for-6.
Personal fouls/disqualifications: 2000-01, 44/0.

VAUGHN, JACQUE   G   HAWKS

PERSONAL: Born February 11, 1975, in Los Angeles. ... 6-1/190. (1,85/86,2).
HIGH SCHOOL: John Muir (Pasadena, Calif.).
COLLEGE: Kansas.
TRANSACTIONS/CAREER NOTES: Selected by Utah Jazz in first round (27th pick overall) of 1997 NBA Draft. ... Signed as free agent by Atlanta Hawks (July 30, 2001).

COLLEGIATE RECORD

NOTES: THE SPORTING NEWS All-America first team (1997). ... THE SPORTING NEWS All-America second team (1996).

Season Team	G	Min.	FGM	FGA	Pct.	FTM	FTA	Pct.	Reb.	Ast.	Pts.	AVERAGES		
												RPG	APG	PPG
93-94—Kansas	35	896	91	195	.467	63	94	.670	89	181	273	2.5	5.2	7.8
94-95—Kansas	31	1046	94	208	.452	92	134	.687	116	238	300	3.7	7.7	9.7
95-96—Kansas	34	1045	120	249	.482	91	131	.695	106	223	370	3.1	6.6	10.9
96-97—Kansas	26	820	79	185	.427	88	113	.779	62	162	264	2.4	6.2	10.2
Totals	126	3807	384	837	.459	334	472	.708	373	804	1207	3.0	6.4	9.6

Three-point field goals: 1993-94, 28-for-70 (.400). 1994-95, 20-for-58 (.345). 1995-96, 39-for-92 (.424). 1996-97, 18-for-54 (.333). Totals, 105-for-274 (.383).

NBA REGULAR-SEASON RECORD

Season Team	G	Min.	FGM	FGA	Pct.	FTM	FTA	Pct.	REBOUNDS			Ast.	St.	Blk.	TO	Pts.	AVERAGES		
									Off.	Def.	Tot.						RPG	APG	PPG
97-98—Utah	45	419	44	122	.361	48	68	.706	4	34	38	84	9	1	56	139	0.8	1.9	3.1
98-99—Utah	19	87	11	30	.367	20	24	.833	1	10	11	12	5	0	14	44	0.6	0.6	2.3
99-00—Utah	78	884	109	262	.416	57	76	.750	11	54	65	121	32	0	77	289	0.8	1.6	3.7
00-01—Utah	82	1620	170	393	.433	128	164	.780	18	132	150	323	48	3	129	498	1.8	3.9	6.1
Totals	224	3010	334	807	.414	253	332	.762	34	230	264	540	94	4	276	970	1.2	2.4	4.3

Three-point field goals: 1997-98, 3-for-8 (.375). 1998-99, 2-for-8 (.250). 1999-00, 14-for-34 (.412). 2000-01, 30-for-78 (.385). Totals, 49-for-128 (.383).
Personal fouls/disqualifications: 1997-98, 63/1. 1998-99, 14/0. 1999-00, 92/0. 2000-01, 145/0. Totals, 314/1.

NBA PLAYOFF RECORD

Season Team	G	Min.	FGM	FGA	Pct.	FTM	FTA	Pct.	REBOUNDS			Ast.	St.	Blk.	TO	Pts.	AVERAGES		
									Off.	Def.	Tot.						RPG	APG	PPG
97-98—Utah	7	24	2	10	.200	2	2	1.000	0	3	3	4	0	0	4	7	0.4	0.6	1.0
98-99—Utah	2	6	1	2	.500	0	0	...	0	0	0	2	0	0	3	3	0.0	1.0	1.5
99-00—Utah	7	67	10	28	.357	7	8	.875	4	8	12	11	4	1	9	28	1.7	1.6	4.0
00-01—Utah	5	57	1	10	.100	0	0	...	0	2	2	8	0	1	1	3	0.4	1.6	0.6
Totals	21	154	14	50	.280	9	10	.900	4	13	17	25	4	2	14	41	0.8	1.2	2.0

Three-point field goals: 1997-98, 1-for-2 (.500). 1998-99, 1-for-1. 1999-00, 1-for-2 (.500). 2000-01, 1-for-2 (.500). Totals, 4-for-7 (.571).
Personal fouls/disqualifications: 1998-99, 2/0. 1999-00, 5/0. 2000-01, 13/0. Totals, 20/0.

VAUGHT, LOY   F   WIZARDS

PERSONAL: Born February 27, 1968, in Grand Rapids, Mich. ... 6-9/240. (2,06/108,9). ... Full Name: Loy Stephen Vaught. ... Name pronounced VAWT.
HIGH SCHOOL: East Kentwood (Mich.).
COLLEGE: Michigan.
TRANSACTIONS/CAREER NOTES: Selected by Los Angeles Clippers in first round (13th pick overall) of 1990 NBA Draft. ... Signed as free agent by Detroit Pistons (January 22, 1999). ... Traded by Pistons to Dallas Mavericks for G Dana Barros and F Ansu Sesay (October 17, 2000). ... Traded by Mavericks with F/C Christian Laettner, G Courtney Alexander, G Hubert Davis, F/C Etan Thomas and cash considerations to Washington Wizards for F Juwan Howard, C Calvin Booth and F Obinna Ekezie (February 22, 2001).
MISCELLANEOUS: Los Angeles Clippers franchise all-time leading rebounder with 4,471 (1990-91 through 1997-98).

COLLEGIATE RECORD

NOTES: Member of NCAA Division I championship team (1989).

Season Team	G	Min.	FGM	FGA	Pct.	FTM	FTA	Pct.	Reb.	Ast.	Pts.	AVERAGES		
												RPG	APG	PPG
85-86—Michigan					Did not play—redshirted.									
86-87—Michigan	32	416	68	122	.557	11	22	.500	125	12	147	3.9	0.4	4.6
87-88—Michigan	34	748	151	243	.621	55	76	.724	150	22	357	4.4	0.6	10.5
88-89—Michigan	37	851	201	304	.661	63	81	.778	296	36	467	8.0	1.0	12.6
89-90—Michigan	31	930	197	331	.595	86	107	.804	346	30	480	11.2	1.0	15.5
Totals	134	2945	617	1000	.617	215	286	.752	917	100	1451	6.8	0.7	10.8

Three-point field goals: 1988-89, 2-for-5 (.400). 1989-90, 0-for-1. Totals, 2-for-6 (.333).

NBA REGULAR-SEASON RECORD

Season Team	G	Min.	FGM	FGA	Pct.	FTM	FTA	Pct.	Off.	Def.	Tot.	Ast.	St.	Blk.	TO	Pts.	RPG	APG	PPG
90-91—L.A. Clippers...	73	1178	175	359	.487	49	74	.662	124	225	349	40	20	23	49	399	4.8	0.5	5.5
91-92—L.A. Clippers...	79	1687	271	551	.492	55	69	.797	160	352	512	71	37	31	66	601	6.5	0.9	7.6
92-93—L.A. Clippers...	79	1653	313	616	.508	116	155	.748	164	328	492	54	55	39	83	743	6.2	0.7	9.4
93-94—L.A. Clippers...	75	2118	373	695	.537	131	182	.720	218	438	656	74	76	22	96	877	8.7	1.0	11.7
94-95—L.A. Clippers...	80	2966	609	1185	.514	176	248	.710	261	511	772	139	104	29	166	1401	9.7	1.7	17.5
95-96—L.A. Clippers...	80	2966	571	1087	.525	149	205	.727	204	604	808	112	87	40	158	1298	10.1	1.4	16.2
96-97—L.A. Clippers...	82	2838	542	1084	.500	134	191	.702	222	595	817	110	85	25	137	1220	10.0	1.3	14.9
97-98—L.A. Clippers...	10	265	36	84	.429	3	8	.375	16	49	65	7	4	2	13	75	6.5	0.7	7.5
98-99—Detroit	37	481	59	155	.381	9	14	.643	36	110	146	11	15	6	17	127	3.9	0.3	3.4
99-00—Detroit	43	292	32	89	.360	11	16	.688	26	65	91	11	6	4	11	75	2.1	0.3	1.7
00-01—Dallas-Wash. ...	51	549	80	169	.473	8	10	.800	51	122	173	23	21	7	26	168	3.4	0.5	3.3
Totals	689	16993	3061	6074	.504	841	1172	.718	1482	3399	4881	652	510	228	822	6984	7.1	0.9	10.1

Three-point field goals: 1990-91, 0-for-2. 1991-92, 4-for-5 (.800). 1992-93, 1-for-4 (.250). 1993-94, 0-for-5. 1994-95, 7-for-33 (.212). 1995-96, 7-for-19 (.368). 1996-97, 2-for-12 (.167). 1997-98, 0-for-2. 1998-99, 0-for-1. 1999-00, 0-for-3. Totals, 21-for-86 (.244).

Personal fouls/disqualifications: 1990-91, 135/2. 1991-92, 165/1. 1992-93, 172/2. 1993-94, 221/5. 1994-95, 243/4. 1995-96, 241/4. 1996-97, 241/3. 1997-98, 33/0. 1998-99, 54/0. 1999-00, 45/0. 2000-01, 74/0. Totals, 1624/21.

NBA PLAYOFF RECORD

Season Team	G	Min.	FGM	FGA	Pct.	FTM	FTA	Pct.	Off.	Def.	Tot.	Ast.	St.	Blk.	TO	Pts.	RPG	APG	PPG
91-92—L.A. Clippers...	5	36	7	11	.636	2	2	1.000	2	10	12	4	1	1	1	17	2.4	0.8	3.4
92-93—L.A. Clippers...	3	50	6	15	.400	4	5	.800	4	14	18	0	4	1	3	16	6.0	0.0	5.3
96-97—L.A. Clippers...	3	90	19	31	.613	6	9	.667	5	22	27	2	3	2	6	45	9.0	0.7	15.0
98-99—Detroit	2	15	2	4	.500	0	0	...	0	1	1	0	1	0	0	4	0.5	0.0	2.0
99-00—Detroit	2	16	0	3	.000	0	0	...	1	5	6	0	2	0	1	0	3.0	0.0	0.0
Totals	15	207	34	64	.531	12	16	.750	12	52	64	6	11	4	11	82	4.3	0.4	5.5

Three-point field goals: 1991-92, 1-for-1. 1996-97, 1-for-3 (.333). Totals, 2-for-4 (.500).
Personal fouls/disqualifications: 1991-92, 3/0. 1992-93, 7/0. 1996-97, 12/1. 1998-99, 1/0. 1999-00, 1/0. Totals, 24/1.

VOSKUHL, JAKE　　C　　BULLS

PERSONAL: Born November 1, 1977, in Tulsa, Okla. ... 6-11/245. (2,11/111,1). ... Full Name: Robert Jake Voskuhl.
HIGH SCHOOL: Strake Jesuit College Prep (Houston).
COLLEGE: Connecticut.
TRANSACTIONS/CAREER NOTES: Selected by Chicago Bulls in second round (33rd pick overall) of 2000 NBA Draft.

COLLEGIATE RECORD

NOTES: Member of NCAA Division I championship team (1999).

Season Team	G	Min.	FGM	FGA	Pct.	FTM	FTA	Pct.	Reb.	Ast.	Pts.	RPG	APG	PPG
96-97—Connecticut	33	678	48	99	.485	36	57	.632	181	20	132	5.5	0.6	4.0
97-98—Connecticut	37	877	100	177	.565	56	83	.675	262	27	256	7.1	0.7	6.9
98-99—Connecticut	34	728	66	129	.512	54	87	.621	218	38	186	6.4	1.1	5.5
99-00—Connecticut	34	778	109	191	.571	71	104	.683	219	39	289	6.4	1.1	8.5
Totals	138	3061	323	596	.542	217	331	.656	880	124	863	6.4	0.9	6.3

NBA REGULAR-SEASON RECORD

Season Team	G	Min.	FGM	FGA	Pct.	FTM	FTA	Pct.	Off.	Def.	Tot.	Ast.	St.	Blk.	TO	Pts.	RPG	APG	PPG
00-01—Chicago	16	143	11	25	.440	8	14	.571	12	22	34	5	5	6	12	30	2.1	0.3	1.9

Personal fouls/disqualifications: 2000-01, 38/0.

WALKER, ANTOINE　　F　　CELTICS

PERSONAL: Born August 12, 1976, in Chicago. ... 6-9/245. (2,06/111,1). ... Full Name: Antoine Devon Walker.
HIGH SCHOOL: Mt. Carmel (Chicago).
COLLEGE: Kentucky.
TRANSACTIONS/CAREER NOTES: Selected after sophomore season by Boston Celtics in first round (sixth pick overall) of 1996 NBA Draft.

COLLEGIATE RECORD

NOTES: Member of NCAA Division I championship team (1996).

Season Team	G	Min.	FGM	FGA	Pct.	FTM	FTA	Pct.	Reb.	Ast.	Pts.	RPG	APG	PPG
94-95—Kentucky	33	479	95	227	.419	52	73	.712	148	47	259	4.5	1.4	7.8
95-96—Kentucky	36	971	228	492	.463	82	130	.631	302	104	547	8.4	2.9	15.2
Totals	69	1450	323	719	.449	134	203	.660	450	151	806	6.5	2.2	11.7

Three-point field goals: 1994-95, 17-for-55 (.309). 1995-96, 9-for-48 (.188). Totals, 26-for-103 (.252).

NBA REGULAR-SEASON RECORD

HONORS: NBA All-Rookie first team (1997).
NOTES: Led NBA with 221 three-point field goals made and 603 three-point field goals attempted (2001).

Season Team	G	Min.	FGM	FGA	Pct.	FTM	FTA	Pct.	REBOUNDS Off.	Def.	Tot.	Ast.	St.	Blk.	TO	Pts.	AVERAGES RPG	APG	PPG
96-97—Boston	82	2970	576	1354	.425	231	366	.631	288	453	741	262	105	53	230	1435	9.0	3.2	17.5
97-98—Boston	82	3268	722	1705	.423	305	473	.645	270	566	836	273	142	60	*292	1840	10.2	3.3	22.4
98-99—Boston	42	1549	303	735	.412	113	202	.559	106	253	359	130	63	28	119	784	8.5	3.1	18.7
99-00—Boston	82	3003	648	1506	.430	311	445	.699	199	453	652	305	117	32	259	1680	8.0	3.7	20.5
00-01—Boston	81	3396	711	1720	.413	249	348	.716	151	568	719	445	138	49	301	1892	8.9	5.5	23.4
Totals	369	14186	2960	7020	.422	1209	1834	.659	1014	2293	3307	1415	565	222	1201	7631	9.0	3.8	20.7

Three-point field goals: 1996-97, 52-for-159 (.327). 1997-98, 91-for-292 (.312). 1998-99, 65-for-176 (.369). 1999-00, 73-for-285 (.256). 2000-01, 221-for-603 (.367). Totals, 502-for-1515 (.331).

Personal fouls/disqualifications: 1996-97, 271/1. 1997-98, 262/2. 1998-99, 142/2. 1999-00, 263/4. 2000-01, 251/2. Totals, 1189/11.

NBA ALL-STAR GAME RECORD

Season Team	Min.	FGM	FGA	Pct.	FTM	FTA	Pct.	REBOUNDS Off.	Def.	Tot.	Ast.	PF	Dq.	St.	Blk.	TO	Pts.
1998 —Boston	15	2	8	.250	0	0	...	1	2	3	3	0	0	1	0	1	4

Three-point field goals: 1998, 0-for-3.

WALKER, SAMAKI   F   LAKERS

PERSONAL: Born February 25, 1976, in Columbus, Ohio. ... 6-9/260. (2,06/117,9). ... Full Name: Samaki Ijuma Walker. ... Name pronounced Suh-MAH-kee.

HIGH SCHOOL: Whitehall (Columbus, Ohio).

COLLEGE: Louisville.

TRANSACTIONS/CAREER NOTES: Selected after sophomore season by Dallas Mavericks in first round (ninth pick overall) of 1996 NBA Draft. ... Signed as free agent by San Antonio Spurs (August 26, 1999). ... Waived by Spurs (June 29, 2001). ... Signed as free agent by Los Angeles Lakers (July 20, 2001).

COLLEGIATE RECORD

Season Team	G	Min.	FGM	FGA	Pct.	FTM	FTA	Pct.	Reb.	Ast.	Pts.	AVERAGES RPG	APG	PPG
94-95—Louisville	29	841	153	279	.548	88	164	.537	210	37	396	7.2	1.3	13.7
95-96—Louisville	21	634	124	207	.599	70	114	.614	157	23	318	7.5	1.1	15.1
Totals	50	1475	277	486	.570	158	278	.568	367	60	714	7.3	1.2	14.3

Three-point field goals: 1994-95, 2-for-6 (.333). 1995-96, 0-for-1. Totals, 2-for-7 (.286).

NBA REGULAR-SEASON RECORD

Season Team	G	Min.	FGM	FGA	Pct.	FTM	FTA	Pct.	REBOUNDS Off.	Def.	Tot.	Ast.	St.	Blk.	TO	Pts.	AVERAGES RPG	APG	PPG
96-97—Dallas	43	602	83	187	.444	48	74	.649	47	100	147	17	15	22	39	214	3.4	0.4	5.0
97-98—Dallas	41	1027	156	321	.486	53	97	.546	96	206	302	24	30	40	61	365	7.4	0.6	8.9
98-99—Dallas	39	568	88	190	.463	53	98	.541	46	97	143	6	9	16	37	229	3.7	0.2	5.9
99-00—San Antonio	71	980	137	305	.449	86	126	.683	77	195	272	38	10	35	64	360	3.8	0.5	5.1
00-01—San Antonio	61	963	121	252	.480	78	124	.629	67	176	243	29	10	41	68	321	4.0	0.5	5.3
Totals	255	4140	585	1255	.466	318	519	.613	333	774	1107	114	74	154	269	1489	4.3	0.4	5.8

Three-point field goals: 1996-97, 0-for-1. 1997-98, 0-for-1. 1998-99, 0-for-1. 2000-01, 1-for-3 (.333). Totals, 1-for-6 (.167).

Personal fouls/disqualifications: 1996-97, 71/0. 1997-98, 127/2. 1998-99, 87/3. 1999-00, 108/1. 2000-01, 103/0. Totals, 496/6.

NBA PLAYOFF RECORD

Season Team	G	Min.	FGM	FGA	Pct.	FTM	FTA	Pct.	REBOUNDS Off.	Def.	Tot.	Ast.	St.	Blk.	TO	Pts.	AVERAGES RPG	APG	PPG
99-00—San Antonio	4	121	14	31	.452	8	12	.667	13	32	45	2	1	12	8	36	11.3	0.5	9.0
00-01—San Antonio	12	76	5	15	.333	4	8	.500	5	9	14	3	1	1	1	14	1.2	0.3	1.2
Totals	16	197	19	46	.413	12	20	.600	18	41	59	5	2	13	9	50	3.7	0.3	3.1

Personal fouls/disqualifications: 1999-00, 13/0. 2000-01, 12/0. Totals, 25/0.

WALLACE, BEN   F/C   PISTONS

PERSONAL: Born September 10, 1974, in White Hall, Ala. ... 6-9/240. (2,06/108,9).

HIGH SCHOOL: Central (Ala.).

JUNIOR COLLEGE: Cuyahoga Community College (Ohio).

COLLEGE: Virginia Union.

TRANSACTIONS/CAREER NOTES: Not drafted by an NBA franchise. ... Signed as free agent by Washington Bullets (October 2, 1996). ... Bullets franchise renamed Washington Wizards for 1997-98 season. ... Traded by Wizards with F/C Terry Davis, G Tim Legler and G Jeff McInnis to Orlando Magic for C Isaac Austin (August 11, 1999). ... Traded by Magic with G Chucky Atkins to Detroit Pistons for F Grant Hill (August 3, 2000).

COLLEGIATE RECORD

Season Team	G	Min.	FGM	FGA	Pct.	FTM	FTA	Pct.	Reb.	Ast.	Pts.	AVERAGES RPG	APG	PPG
92-93—Cuyahoga					Statistics unavailable.									
93-94—Cuyahoga					Statistics unavailable.									
94-95—Virginia Union	31	858	180	330	.545	85	209	.407	295	27	445	9.5	0.9	14.4
95-96—Virginia Union	31	902	159	318	.500	70	187	.374	325	18	388	10.5	0.6	12.5
4-Year-College Totals	62	1760	339	648	.523	155	396	.391	620	45	833	10.0	0.7	13.4

NBA REGULAR-SEASON RECORD

Season Team	G	Min.	FGM	FGA	Pct.	FTM	FTA	Pct.	Off.	Def.	Tot.	Ast.	St.	Blk.	TO	Pts.	RPG	APG	PPG
									REBOUNDS								AVERAGES		
96-97—Washington	34	197	16	46	.348	6	20	.300	25	33	58	2	8	11	18	38	1.7	0.1	1.1
97-98—Washington	67	1124	85	164	.518	35	98	.357	112	212	324	18	61	72	28	205	4.8	0.3	3.1
98-99—Washington	46	1231	115	199	.578	47	132	.356	137	247	384	18	50	90	36	277	8.3	0.4	6.0
99-00—Orlando..........	81	1959	168	334	.503	54	114	.474	211	454	665	67	72	130	67	390	8.2	0.8	4.8
00-01—Detroit	80	2760	215	439	.490	80	238	.336	303	*749	*1052	123	107	186	117	511	13.2	1.5	6.4
Totals	308	7271	599	1182	.507	222	602	.369	788	1695	2483	228	298	489	266	1421	8.1	0.7	4.6

Three-point field goals: 2000-01, 1-for-4 (.250). Totals, 1-for-4 (.250).
Personal fouls/disqualifications: 1996-97, 27/0. 1997-98, 116/1. 1998-99, 111/0. 1999-00, 162/0. 2000-01, 192/0. Totals, 608/1.

WALLACE, JOHN F SUNS

PERSONAL: Born February 9, 1974, in Rochester, N.Y. ... 6-9/225. (2,06/102,1).
HIGH SCHOOL: Greece-Athena (Rochester, N.Y.).
COLLEGE: Syracuse.
TRANSACTIONS/CAREER NOTES: Selected by New York Knicks in first round (18th pick overall) of 1996 NBA Draft. ... Traded by Knicks to Toronto Raptors for 1998 first-round draft choice in three-way deal in which Portland Trail Blazers traded C Chris Dudley to Knicks for 1998 first-round draft choice and Raptors sent future second-round draft choice to Trail Blazers (October 10, 1997). ... Signed as free agent by Knicks (August 6, 1999). ... Traded by Knicks with draft rights to F Donnell Harvey to Dallas Mavericks for G Erick Strickland and draft rights to F Pete Mickeal (June 28, 2000). ... Traded by Mavericks with F Cedric Ceballos and G Eric Murdock to Detroit Pistons for F/C Christian Laettner and F Terry Mills (August 29, 2000). ... Traded by Pistons with G/F Jud Buechler to Phoenix Suns for F Clifford Robinson (June 29, 2001).

COLLEGIATE RECORD

NOTES: THE SPORTING NEWS All-America second team (1996).

Season Team	G	Min.	FGM	FGA	Pct.	FTM	FTA	Pct.	Reb.	Ast.	Pts.	RPG	APG	PPG
												AVERAGES		
92-93—Syracuse	29	839	130	247	.526	61	85	.718	221	38	321	7.6	1.3	11.1
93-94—Syracuse	30	979	164	290	.566	121	159	.761	270	50	449	9.0	1.7	15.0
94-95—Syracuse	30	990	197	335	.588	106	156	.679	245	77	504	8.2	2.6	16.8
95-96—Syracuse	38	1379	293	599	.489	222	291	.763	329	90	845	8.7	2.4	22.2
Totals	127	4187	784	1471	.533	510	691	.738	1065	255	2119	8.4	2.0	16.7

Three-point field goals: 1992-93, 0-for-1. 1993-94, 0-for-2. 1994-95, 4-for-14 (.286). 1995-96, 37-for-88 (.420). Totals, 41-for-105 (.390).

NBA REGULAR-SEASON RECORD

Season Team	G	Min.	FGM	FGA	Pct.	FTM	FTA	Pct.	Off.	Def.	Tot.	Ast.	St.	Blk.	TO	Pts.	RPG	APG	PPG
									REBOUNDS								AVERAGES		
96-97—New York	68	787	122	236	.517	79	110	.718	51	104	155	37	21	25	76	325	2.3	0.5	4.8
97-98—Toronto	82	2361	468	979	.478	210	293	.717	117	256	373	110	62	101	172	1147	4.5	1.3	14.0
98-99—Toronto	48	812	153	354	.432	105	150	.700	54	117	171	46	12	43	70	411	3.6	1.0	8.6
99-00—New York	60	798	155	332	.467	82	102	.804	42	93	135	22	10	14	63	392	2.3	0.4	6.5
00-01—Detroit	40	527	100	236	.424	35	45	.778	25	58	83	23	13	16	36	237	2.1	0.6	5.9
Totals	298	5285	998	2137	.467	511	700	.730	289	628	917	238	118	199	417	2512	3.1	0.8	8.4

Three-point field goals: 1996-97, 2-for-4 (.500). 1997-98, 1-for-2 (.500). 1999-00, 0-for-3. 2000-01, 2-for-15 (.133). Totals, 5-for-24 (.208).
Personal fouls/disqualifications: 1996-97, 102/0. 1997-98, 239/7. 1998-99, 92/0. 1999-00, 103/0. 2000-01, 72/1. Totals, 608/8.

NBA PLAYOFF RECORD

Season Team	G	Min.	FGM	FGA	Pct.	FTM	FTA	Pct.	Off.	Def.	Tot.	Ast.	St.	Blk.	TO	Pts.	RPG	APG	PPG
									REBOUNDS								AVERAGES		
96-97—New York	4	40	4	15	.267	2	2	1.000	2	5	7	5	1	2	2	10	1.8	1.3	2.5
99-00—New York	1	4	0	2	.000	0	0	...	0	1	1	0	1	0	1	0	1.0	0.0	0.0
Totals	5	44	4	17	.235	2	2	1.000	2	6	8	5	2	2	3	10	1.6	1.0	2.0

Three-point field goals: 1996-97, 0-for-1. Totals, 0-for-1 (.000).
Personal fouls/disqualifications: 1996-97, 6/0. 1999-00, 1/0. Totals, 7/0.

WALLACE, RASHEED F/C TRAIL BLAZERS

PERSONAL: Born September 17, 1974, in Philadelphia. ... 6-11/230. (2,11/104,3). ... Full Name: Rasheed Abdul Wallace.
HIGH SCHOOL: Simon Gratz (Philadelphia).
COLLEGE: North Carolina.
TRANSACTIONS/CAREER NOTES: Selected after sophomore season by Washington Bullets in first round (fourth pick overall) of 1995 NBA Draft. ... Traded by Bullets with G Mitchell Butler to Portland Trail Blazers for G Rod Strickland and F Harvey Grant (July 15, 1996).

COLLEGIATE RECORD

NOTES: THE SPORTING NEWS All-America first team (1995).

Season Team	G	Min.	FGM	FGA	Pct.	FTM	FTA	Pct.	Reb.	Ast.	Pts.	RPG	APG	PPG
												AVERAGES		
93-94—North Carolina...............	35	732	139	230	.604	55	91	.604	232	18	333	6.6	0.5	9.5
94-95—North Carolina...............	34	1030	238	364	.654	89	141	.631	279	35	566	8.2	1.0	16.6
Totals	69	1762	377	594	.635	144	232	.621	511	53	899	7.4	0.8	13.0

Three-point field goals: 1993-94, 0-for-1. 1994-95, 1-for-3 (.333). Totals, 1-for-4 (.250).

HONORS: NBA All-Rookie second team (1996).

Season Team	G	Min.	FGM	FGA	Pct.	FTM	FTA	Pct.	REBOUNDS			Ast.	St.	Blk.	TO	Pts.	AVERAGES		
									Off.	Def.	Tot.						RPG	APG	PPG
95-96—Washington	65	1788	275	565	.487	78	120	.650	93	210	303	85	42	54	103	655	4.7	1.3	10.1
96-97—Portland.........	62	1892	380	681	.558	169	265	.638	122	297	419	74	48	59	114	938	6.8	1.2	15.1
97-98—Portland.........	77	2896	466	875	.533	184	278	.662	132	346	478	195	75	88	167	1124	6.2	2.5	14.6
98-99—Portland.........	49	1414	242	476	.508	131	179	.732	57	184	241	60	48	54	80	628	4.9	1.2	12.8
99-00—Portland.........	81	2845	542	1045	.519	233	331	.704	129	437	566	142	87	107	157	1325	7.0	1.8	16.4
00-01—Portland.........	77	2940	590	1178	.501	245	320	.766	147	455	602	212	90	135	158	1477	7.8	2.8	19.2
Totals	411	13775	2495	4820	.518	1040	1493	.697	680	1929	2609	768	390	497	779	6147	6.3	1.9	15.0

Three-point field goals: 1995-96, 27-for-82 (.329). 1996-97, 9-for-33 (.273). 1997-98, 8-for-39 (.205). 1998-99, 13-for-31 (.419). 1999-00, 8-for-50 (.160). 2000-01, 52-for-162 (.321). Totals, 117-for-397 (.295).

Personal fouls/disqualifications: 1995-96, 206/4. 1996-97, 198/1. 1997-98, 268/6. 1998-99, 175/6. 1999-00, 216/2. 2000-01, 206/2. Totals, 1269/21.

Season Team	G	Min.	FGM	FGA	Pct.	FTM	FTA	Pct.	REBOUNDS			Ast.	St.	Blk.	TO	Pts.	AVERAGES		
									Off.	Def.	Tot.						RPG	APG	PPG
96-97—Portland.........	4	148	33	56	.589	11	20	.550	8	16	24	6	2	2	6	79	6.0	1.5	19.8
97-98—Portland.........	4	157	23	47	.489	8	16	.500	7	12	19	11	2	2	5	58	4.8	2.8	14.5
98-99—Portland.........	13	468	75	146	.514	42	58	.724	17	46	63	20	20	11	16	193	4.8	1.5	14.8
99-00—Portland.........	16	605	110	225	.489	58	75	.773	31	72	103	28	15	20	23	286	6.4	1.8	17.9
00-01—Portland.........	3	128	19	51	.373	8	14	.571	5	19	24	7	1	3	4	50	8.0	2.3	16.7
Totals	40	1506	260	525	.495	127	183	.694	68	165	233	72	40	38	54	666	5.8	1.8	16.7

Three-point field goals: 1996-97, 2-for-5 (.400). 1997-98, 4-for-5 (.800). 1998-99, 1-for-9 (.111). 1999-00, 8-for-13 (.615). 2000-01, 4-for-11 (.364). Totals, 19-for-43 (.442).

Personal fouls/disqualifications: 1996-97, 17/1. 1997-98, 16/0. 1998-99, 50/1. 1999-00, 52/0. 2000-01, 9/0. Totals, 144/2.

Season Team	Min.	FGM	FGA	Pct.	FTM	FTA	Pct.	REBOUNDS			Ast.	PF	Dq.	St.	Blk.	TO	Pts.
								Off.	Def.	Tot.							
2000 —Portland	21	3	6	.500	3	4	.750	2	2	4	0	0	0	1	1	0	9
2001 —Portland	21	1	7	.143	0	0	...	1	3	4	2	0	0	1	0	2	2
Totals	42	4	13	.308	3	4	.750	3	5	8	2	0	0	2	1	2	11

Three-point field goals: 1901, 0-for-1. Totals, 0-for-1 (.000).

WARD, CHARLIE   G   KNICKS

W

PERSONAL: Born October 12, 1970, in Thomasville, Ga. ... 6-2/190. (1,88/86,2). ... Full Name: Charlie Ward Jr.
HIGH SCHOOL: Thomasville (Ga.) Central.
JUNIOR COLLEGE: Tallahassee (Fla.) Community College.
COLLEGE: Florida State.
TRANSACTIONS/CAREER NOTES: Selected by New York Knicks in first round (26th pick overall) of 1994 NBA Draft. ... Played in United States Basketball League with Jacksonville Hooters (1994).

MISCELLANEOUS: Heisman Trophy winner (1993). ... Named College Football Player of the Year by THE SPORTING NEWS (1993). ... Named quarterback on THE SPORTING NEWS college All-America first team (1993). ... Named quarterback on THE SPORTING NEWS college All-America second team (1992). ... Selected by Milwaukee Brewers organization in 59th round of free-agent draft (June 3, 1993); did not sign. ... ... Selected by New York Yankees organization in 18th round of free-agent draft (June 2, 1994); did not sign.

Season Team	G	Min.	FGM	FGA	Pct.	FTM	FTA	Pct.	Reb.	Ast.	Pts.	AVERAGES		
												RPG	APG	PPG
88-89—Tallahassee C.C.							Did not play.							
89-90—Florida State							Did not play.							
90-91—Florida State	30	715	81	178	.455	62	87	.713	89	103	239	3.0	3.4	8.0
91-92—Florida State	28	841	72	145	.497	35	66	.530	90	122	201	3.2	4.4	7.2
92-93—Florida State	17	557	49	106	.462	18	27	.667	45	93	132	2.6	5.5	7.8
93-94—Florida State	16	574	61	167	.365	25	40	.625	39	78	168	2.4	4.9	10.5
4-Year-College Totals	91	2687	263	596	.441	140	220	.636	263	396	740	2.9	4.4	8.1

Three-point field goals: 1990-91, 15-for-48 (.313). 1991-92, 22-for-48 (.458). 1992-93, 16-for-50 (.320). 1993-94, 21-for-83 (.253). Totals, 74-for-229 (.323).

Season Team	G	Min.	FGM	FGA	Pct.	FTM	FTA	Pct.	REBOUNDS			Ast.	St.	Blk.	TO	Pts.	AVERAGES		
									Off.	Def.	Tot.						RPG	APG	PPG
94-95—New York	10	44	4	19	.211	7	10	.700	1	5	6	4	2	0	8	16	0.6	0.4	1.6
95-96—New York	62	787	87	218	.399	37	54	.685	29	73	102	132	54	6	79	244	1.6	2.1	3.9
96-97—New York	79	1763	133	337	.395	95	125	.760	45	175	220	326	83	15	147	409	2.8	4.1	5.2
97-98—New York	82	2317	235	516	.455	91	113	.805	32	242	274	466	144	37	175	642	3.3	5.7	7.8
98-99—New York	50	1556	135	334	.404	55	78	.705	23	149	172	271	103	8	131	378	3.4	5.4	7.6
99-00—New York	72	1986	189	447	.423	48	58	.828	22	206	228	300	95	16	102	528	3.2	4.2	7.3
00-01—New York	61	1492	155	373	.416	56	70	.800	32	127	159	273	70	10	112	433	2.6	4.5	7.1
Totals	416	9945	938	2244	.418	389	508	.766	184	977	1161	1772	551	92	754	2650	2.8	4.3	6.4

Three-point field goals: 1994-95, 1-for-10 (.100). 1995-96, 33-for-99 (.333). 1996-97, 48-for-154 (.312). 1997-98, 81-for-215 (.377). 1998-99, 53-for-149 (.356). 1999-00, 102-for-264 (.386). 2000-01, 67-for-175 (.383). Totals, 385-for-1066 (.361).

Personal fouls/disqualifications: 1994-95, 7/0. 1995-96, 98/0. 1996-97, 188/2. 1997-98, 195/3. 1998-99, 105/0. 1999-00, 176/3. 2000-01, 132/0. Totals, 901/8.

Season Team	G	Min.	FGM	FGA	Pct.	FTM	FTA	Pct.	REBOUNDS Off.	Def.	Tot.	Ast.	St.	Blk.	TO	Pts.	AVERAGES RPG	APG	PPG
95-96—New York	7	92	13	27	.481	3	7	.429	2	7	9	17	11	0	6	32	1.3	2.4	4.6
96-97—New York	9	182	8	27	.296	3	4	.750	3	22	25	39	13	0	15	20	2.8	4.3	2.2
97-98—New York	10	261	23	55	.418	11	16	.688	3	25	28	60	20	2	17	66	2.8	6.0	6.6
98-99—New York	20	494	34	93	.366	6	8	.750	12	34	46	75	35	3	24	92	2.3	3.8	4.6
99-00—New York	16	439	57	113	.504	15	21	.714	11	57	68	65	22	5	20	150	4.3	4.1	9.4
00-01—New York	5	86	8	27	.296	6	6	1.000	2	5	7	7	2	0	8	25	1.4	1.4	5.0
Totals	67	1554	143	342	.418	44	62	.710	33	150	183	263	103	10	90	385	2.7	3.9	5.7

Three-point field goals: 1995-96, 3-for-12 (.250). 1996-97, 1-for-9 (.111). 1997-98, 9-for-21 (.429). 1998-99, 18-for-56 (.321). 1999-00, 21-for-53 (.396). 2000-01, 3-for-12 (.250). Totals, 55-for-163 (.337).

Personal fouls/disqualifications: 1995-96, 9/0. 1996-97, 18/1. 1997-98, 24/0. 1998-99, 45/0. 1999-00, 40/1. 2000-01, 8/0. Totals, 144/2.

WEATHERSPOON, CLARENCE F   KNICKS

PERSONAL: Born September 8, 1970, in Crawford, Miss. ... 6-7/265. (2,01/120,2).
HIGH SCHOOL: Motley (Columbus, Miss.).
COLLEGE: Southern Mississippi.
TRANSACTIONS/CAREER NOTES: Selected by Philadelphia 76ers in first round (ninth pick overall) of 1992 NBA Draft. ... Traded by 76ers with C/F Michael Cage to Boston Celtics for C/F Dino Radja (June 20, 1997); trade voided because Radja failed physical (June 24, 1997). ... Traded by 76ers with G Jim Jackson to Golden State Warriors for F Joe Smith and G Brian Shaw (February 17, 1998). ... Signed as free agent by Miami Heat (January 24, 1999). ... Traded by Heat to Cleveland Cavaliers as part of three-way deal in which Cavaliers sent F Shawn Kemp to Portland Trail Blazers, Trail Blazers sent F Brian Grant to Heat, Heat sent F/C Chris Gatling, future first-round draft choice and cash Cavaliers and Trail Blazers sent G Gary Grant to Cavaliers (August 30, 2000). ... Signed as free agent by New York Knicks (July 20, 2001).

COLLEGIATE RECORD

Season Team	G	Min.	FGM	FGA	Pct.	FTM	FTA	Pct.	Reb.	Ast.	Pts.	AVERAGES RPG	APG	PPG
88-89—Southern Mississippi	27	915	152	279	.545	92	156	.590	289	30	397	10.7	1.1	14.7
89-90—Southern Mississippi	32	1166	205	339	.605	159	230	.691	371	28	569	11.6	0.9	17.8
90-91—Southern Mississippi	29	1019	195	331	.589	120	161	.745	355	66	517	12.2	2.3	17.8
91-92—Southern Mississippi	29	1057	246	437	.563	131	194	.675	305	47	647	10.5	1.6	22.3
Totals	117	4157	798	1386	.576	502	741	.677	1320	171	2130	11.3	1.5	18.2

Three-point field goals: 1988-89, 1-for-3 (.333). 1989-90, 0-for-2. 1990-91, 7-for-14 (.500). 1991-92, 24-for-53 (.453). Totals, 32-for-72 (.444).

NBA REGULAR-SEASON RECORD

HONORS: NBA All-Rookie second team (1993).

Season Team	G	Min.	FGM	FGA	Pct.	FTM	FTA	Pct.	REBOUNDS Off.	Def.	Tot.	Ast.	St.	Blk.	TO	Pts.	AVERAGES RPG	APG	PPG
92-93—Philadelphia	82	2654	494	1053	.469	291	408	.713	179	410	589	147	85	67	176	1280	7.2	1.8	15.6
93-94—Philadelphia	82	3147	602	1246	.483	298	430	.693	254	578	832	192	100	116	195	1506	10.1	2.3	18.4
94-95—Philadelphia	76	2991	543	1238	.439	283	377	.751	144	382	526	215	115	67	191	1373	6.9	2.8	18.1
95-96—Philadelphia	78	3096	491	1015	.484	318	426	.746	237	516	753	158	112	108	179	1300	9.7	2.0	16.7
96-97—Philadelphia	82	2949	398	811	.491	206	279	.738	219	460	679	140	74	86	137	1003	8.3	1.7	12.2
97-98—Phil.-G.S.	79	2325	268	608	.441	200	277	.722	198	396	594	89	85	74	119	736	7.5	1.1	9.3
98-99—Miami	49	1040	141	264	.534	115	143	.804	72	171	243	34	28	17	61	397	5.0	0.7	8.1
99-00—Miami	78	1615	215	419	.513	135	183	.738	128	321	449	93	51	49	100	565	5.8	1.2	7.2
00-01—Cleveland	82	2774	347	692	.501	230	291	.790	223	573	796	103	85	105	112	924	9.7	1.3	11.3
Totals	688	22591	3499	7346	.476	2076	2814	.738	1654	3807	5461	1171	735	689	1270	9084	7.9	1.7	13.2

Three-point field goals: 1992-93, 1-for-4 (.250). 1993-94, 4-for-17 (.235). 1994-95, 4-for-21 (.190). 1995-96, 0-for-2. 1996-97, 1-for-6 (.167). Totals, 10-for-50 (.200).

Personal fouls/disqualifications: 1992-93, 188/1. 1993-94, 152/0. 1994-95, 195/1. 1995-96, 214/3. 1996-97, 187/0. 1997-98, 194/2. 1998-99, 107/0. 1999-00, 165/1. 2000-01, 171/0. Totals, 1573/8.

NBA PLAYOFF RECORD

Season Team	G	Min.	FGM	FGA	Pct.	FTM	FTA	Pct.	REBOUNDS Off.	Def.	Tot.	Ast.	St.	Blk.	TO	Pts.	AVERAGES RPG	APG	PPG
98-99—Miami	5	112	9	26	.346	11	17	.647	4	17	21	2	7	1	3	29	4.2	0.4	5.8
99-00—Miami	10	170	25	60	.417	14	24	.583	18	23	41	1	4	3	8	64	4.1	0.1	6.4
Totals	15	282	34	86	.395	25	41	.610	22	40	62	3	11	4	11	93	4.1	0.2	6.2

Personal fouls/disqualifications: 1998-99, 8/0. 1999-00, 23/0. Totals, 31/0.

WEBBER, CHRIS   F   KINGS

PERSONAL: Born March 1, 1973, in Detroit. ... 6-10/245. (2,08/111,1). ... Full Name: Mayce Edward Christopher Webber III.
HIGH SCHOOL: Detroit Country Day (Beverly Hills, Mich.).
COLLEGE: Michigan.
TRANSACTIONS/CAREER NOTES: Selected after sophomore season by Orlando Magic in first round (first pick overall) of 1993 NBA Draft. ... Draft rights traded by Magic to Golden State Warriors for draft rights to G Anfernee Hardaway and 1996, 1998 and 2000 first-round draft choices (June 30, 1993). ... Traded by Warriors to Washington Bullets for F Tom Gugliotta and 1996, 1998 and 2000 first-round draft choices (November 17, 1994). ... Bullets franchise renamed Wizards for 1997-98 season. ... Traded by Wizards to Sacramento Kings for G Mitch Richmond and F Otis Thorpe (May 14, 1998).

COLLEGIATE RECORD

NOTES: THE SPORTING NEWS All-America first team (1993).

Season Team	G	Min.	FGM	FGA	Pct.	FTM	FTA	Pct.	Reb.	Ast.	Pts.	AVERAGES RPG	APG	PPG
91-92—Michigan	34	1088	229	412	.556	56	113	.496	340	76	528	10.0	2.2	15.5
92-93—Michigan	36	1143	281	454	.619	101	183	.552	362	90	690	10.1	2.5	19.2
Totals	70	2231	510	866	.589	157	296	.530	702	166	1218	10.0	2.4	17.4

Three-point field goals: 1991-92, 14-for-54 (.259). 1992-93, 27-for-80 (.338). Totals, 41-for-134 (.306).

NBA REGULAR-SEASON RECORD

HONORS: NBA Rookie of the Year (1994). ... All-NBA first team (2001). ... All-NBA second team (1999). ... All-NBA third team (2000). ... NBA All-Rookie first team (1994).

Season Team	G	Min.	FGM	FGA	Pct.	FTM	FTA	Pct.	REBOUNDS Off.	Def.	Tot.	Ast.	St.	Blk.	TO	Pts.	AVERAGES RPG	APG	PPG
93-94—Golden State	76	2438	572	1037	.552	189	355	.532	305	389	694	272	93	164	206	1333	9.1	3.6	17.5
94-95—Washington	54	2067	464	938	.495	117	233	.502	200	318	518	256	83	85	167	1085	9.6	4.7	20.1
95-96—Washington	15	558	150	276	.543	41	69	.594	37	77	114	75	27	9	49	356	7.6	5.0	23.7
96-97—Washington	72	2806	604	1167	.518	177	313	.565	238	505	743	331	122	137	230	1445	10.3	4.6	20.1
97-98—Washington	71	2809	647	1341	.482	196	333	.589	176	498	674	273	111	124	185	1555	9.5	3.8	21.9
98-99—Sacramento	42	1719	378	778	.486	79	174	.454	149	396	545	173	60	89	148	839	*13.0	4.1	20.0
99-00—Sacramento	75	2880	748	1548	.483	311	414	.751	189	598	787	345	120	128	218	1834	10.5	4.6	24.5
00-01—Sacramento	70	2836	786	1635	.481	324	461	.703	179	598	777	294	93	118	195	1898	11.1	4.2	27.1
Totals	475	18113	4349	8720	.499	1434	2352	.610	1473	3379	4852	2019	709	854	1398	10345	10.2	4.3	21.8

Three-point field goals: 1993-94, 0-for-14. 1994-95, 40-for-145 (.276). 1995-96, 15-for-34 (.441). 1996-97, 60-for-151 (.397). 1997-98, 65-for-205 (.317). 1998-99, 4-for-34 (.118). 1999-00, 27-for-95 (.284). 2000-01, 2-for-28 (.071). Totals, 213-for-706 (.302).

Personal fouls/disqualifications: 1993-94, 247/4. 1994-95, 186/2. 1995-96, 51/1. 1996-97, 258/6. 1997-98, 269/4. 1998-99, 145/1. 1999-00, 264/7. 2000-01, 226/1. Totals, 1646/26.

NBA PLAYOFF RECORD

Season Team	G	Min.	FGM	FGA	Pct.	FTM	FTA	Pct.	REBOUNDS Off.	Def.	Tot.	Ast.	St.	Blk.	TO	Pts.	AVERAGES RPG	APG	PPG
93-94—Golden State	3	109	22	40	.550	3	10	.300	13	13	26	27	3	9	9	47	8.7	9.0	15.7
96-97—Washington	3	106	19	30	.633	4	8	.500	7	17	24	10	2	7	16	47	8.0	3.3	15.7
98-99—Sacramento	5	192	31	80	.388	10	25	.400	13	34	47	20	9	5	20	74	9.4	4.0	14.8
99-00—Sacramento	5	196	47	110	.427	27	34	.794	14	34	48	27	8	10	8	122	9.6	5.4	24.4
00-01—Sacramento	8	348	76	196	.388	34	49	.694	34	58	92	25	9	8	31	186	11.5	3.1	23.3
Totals	24	951	195	456	.428	78	126	.619	81	156	237	109	31	39	84	476	9.9	4.5	19.8

Three-point field goals: 1993-94, 0-for-2. 1996-97, 5-for-11 (.455). 1998-99, 2-for-7 (.286). 1999-00, 1-for-5 (.200). 2000-01, 0-for-1. Totals, 8-for-26 (.308).

Personal fouls/disqualifications: 1993-94, 11/0. 1996-97, 18/3. 1998-99, 20/1. 1999-00, 14/1. 2000-01, 29/0. Totals, 92/5.

NBA ALL-STAR GAME RECORD

Season Team	Min.	FGM	FGA	Pct.	FTM	FTA	Pct.	REBOUNDS Off.	Def.	Tot.	Ast.	PF	Dq.	St.	Blk.	TO	Pts.
1997 —Washington	14	1	4	.250	0	0	...	1	3	4	3	3	0	1	0	3	2
2000 —Sacramento	13	3	10	.300	0	0	...	3	5	8	3	2	0	1	0	2	6
2001 —Sacramento	29	6	14	.429	2	4	.500	4	5	9	3	2	0	1	0	1	14
Totals	56	10	28	.357	2	4	.500	8	13	21	9	7	0	3	0	6	22

Three-point field goals: 20001, 0-for-1.

WELLS, BONZI   G/F   TRAIL BLAZERS

PERSONAL: Born September 20, 1976, in Muncie, Ind. ... 6-5/210. (1,96/95,3). ... Full Name: Gawen Deangelo Wells.
HIGH SCHOOL: Central (Muncie, Ind.).
COLLEGE: Ball State.
TRANSACTIONS/CAREER NOTES: Selected by Detroit Pistons in first round (11th pick overall) of 1998 NBA Draft. ... Rights traded by Pistons to Portland Trail Blazers for conditional first-round draft choice (January 21, 1999); Pistons received 2000 second-round draft choice to complete deal (June 13, 2000).

COLLEGIATE RECORD

NOTES: Led NCAA Division I with 3.6 steals per game (1998).

Season Team	G	Min.	FGM	FGA	Pct.	FTM	FTA	Pct.	Reb.	Ast.	Pts.	AVERAGES RPG	APG	PPG
94-95—Ball State	30	887	177	380	.466	87	141	.617	183	84	474	6.1	2.8	15.8
95-96—Ball State	28	910	269	544	.494	143	202	.708	246	80	712	8.8	2.9	25.4
96-97—Ball State	29	900	229	492	.465	154	223	.691	230	127	637	7.9	4.4	22.0
97-98—Ball State	29	843	238	486	.490	133	193	.689	184	95	662	6.3	3.3	22.8
Totals	116	3540	913	1902	.480	517	759	.681	843	386	2485	7.3	3.3	21.4

Three-point field goals: 1994-95, 33-for-99 (.333). 1995-96, 31-for-92 (.337). 1996-97, 25-for-104 (.240). 1997-98, 53-for-142 (.373). Totals, 142-for-437 (.325).

NBA REGULAR-SEASON RECORD

Season Team	G	Min.	FGM	FGA	Pct.	FTM	FTA	Pct.	REBOUNDS Off.	Def.	Tot.	Ast.	St.	Blk.	TO	Pts.	AVERAGES RPG	APG	PPG
98-99—Portland	7	35	11	20	.550	8	18	.444	4	5	9	3	1	1	6	31	1.3	0.4	4.4
99-00—Portland	66	1162	236	480	.492	88	129	.682	78	104	182	97	69	12	97	580	2.8	1.5	8.8
00-01—Portland	75	1995	387	726	.533	159	240	.663	120	247	367	208	94	20	169	950	4.9	2.8	12.7
Totals	148	3192	634	1226	.517	255	387	.659	202	356	558	308	164	33	272	1561	3.8	2.1	10.5

Three-point field goals: 1998-99, 1-for-3 (.333). 1999-00, 20-for-53 (.377). 2000-01, 17-for-50 (.340). Totals, 38-for-106 (.358).

Personal fouls/disqualifications: 1998-99, 5/0. 1999-00, 153/3. 2000-01, 203/1. Totals, 361/4.

W

NBA PLAYOFF RECORD

								REBOUNDS							AVERAGES		
Season Team	G	Min.	FGM	FGA	Pct.	FTM	FTA	Pct.	Off.	Def.	Tot.	Ast.	St.	Blk.	TO	Pts.	RPG	APG	PPG
99-00—Portland.........	14	188	37	83	.446	29	41	.707	12	23	35	13	7	0	16	105	2.5	0.9	7.5

Three-point field goals: 1999-00, 2-for-10 (.200).
Personal fouls/disqualifications: 1999-00, 33/0.

WESLEY, DAVID   G   HORNETS

PERSONAL: Born November 14, 1970, in San Antonio. ... 6-1/211. (1,85/95,7). ... Full Name: David Barakau Wesley.
HIGH SCHOOL: Longview (Texas).
JUNIOR COLLEGE: Temple (Texas) Junior College.
COLLEGE: Baylor.
TRANSACTIONS/CAREER NOTES: Not drafted by an NBA franchise. ... Played in Continental Basketball Association with Wichita Falls Texans (1992-93). ... Signed as free agent by New Jersey Nets (July 27, 1993). ... Signed as unrestricted free agent by Boston Celtics (July 20, 1994). ... Signed as free agent by Charlotte Hornets (July 1, 1997).

COLLEGIATE RECORD

											AVERAGES		
Season Team	G	Min.	FGM	FGA	Pct.	FTM	FTA	Pct.	Reb.	Ast.	Pts.	RPG	APG	PPG
88-89—Temple Junior College....	31	...	155	331	.468	88	125	.704	106	184	455	3.4	5.9	14.7
89-90—Baylor........................	18	394	61	134	.455	61	73	.836	39	37	208	2.2	2.1	11.6
90-91—Baylor........................	26	837	133	314	.424	125	149	.839	76	148	430	2.9	5.7	16.5
91-92—Baylor........................	28	1020	174	387	.450	179	219	.817	136	131	586	4.9	4.7	20.9
Junior College Totals.............	31	...	155	331	.468	88	125	.704	106	184	455	3.4	5.9	14.7
4-Year-College Totals............	72	2251	368	835	.441	365	441	.828	251	316	1224	3.5	4.4	17.0

Three-point field goals: 1989-90, 25-for-56 (.446). 1990-91, 39-for-114 (.342). 1991-92, 59-for-156 (.378). Totals, 123-for-326 (.377).

NOTES: CBA All-Rookie first team (1993).

CBA REGULAR-SEASON RECORD

											AVERAGES		
Season Team	G	Min.	FGM	FGA	Pct.	FTM	FTA	Pct.	Reb.	Ast.	Pts.	RPG	APG	PPG
92-93—Wichita Falls..................	55	1830	350	759	.461	282	360	.783	218	225	948	4.0	4.1	17.2

Three-point field goals: 1992-93, 34-for-93 (.366).

NBA REGULAR-SEASON RECORD

								REBOUNDS								AVERAGES		
Season Team	G	Min.	FGM	FGA	Pct.	FTM	FTA	Pct.	Off.	Def.	Tot.	Ast.	St.	Blk.	TO	Pts.	RPG	APG	PPG
93-94—New Jersey.....	60	542	64	174	.368	44	53	.830	10	34	44	123	38	4	52	183	0.7	2.1	3.1
94-95—Boston...........	51	1380	128	313	.409	71	94	.755	31	86	117	266	82	9	87	378	2.3	5.2	7.4
95-96—Boston...........	82	2104	338	736	.459	217	288	.753	68	196	264	390	100	11	159	1009	3.2	4.8	12.3
96-97—Boston...........	74	2991	456	974	.468	225	288	.781	67	197	264	537	162	13	211	1240	3.6	7.3	16.8
97-98—Charlotte........	81	2845	383	864	.443	229	288	.795	49	164	213	529	140	30	226	1054	2.6	6.5	13.0
98-99—Charlotte........	50	1848	243	545	.446	159	191	.832	23	138	161	322	100	10	142	706	3.2	6.4	14.1
99-00—Charlotte........	82	2760	407	955	.426	214	275	.778	39	186	225	463	109	11	159	1116	2.7	5.6	13.6
00-01—Charlotte........	82	3106	523	1239	.422	271	339	.799	64	160	224	361	128	16	171	1414	2.7	4.4	17.2
Totals	562	17576	2542	5800	.438	1430	1816	.787	351	1161	1512	2991	859	104	1207	7100	2.7	5.3	12.6

Three-point field goals: 1993-94, 11-for-47 (.234). 1994-95, 51-for-119 (.429). 1995-96, 116-for-272 (.426). 1996-97, 103-for-286 (.360). 1997-98, 59-for-170 (.347). 1998-99, 61-for-170 (.359). 1999-00, 88-for-248 (.355). 2000-01, 97-for-258 (.376). Totals, 586-for-1570 (.373).
Personal fouls/disqualifications: 1993-94, 47/0. 1994-95, 144/0. 1995-96, 207/0. 1996-97, 221/1. 1997-98, 229/3. 1998-99, 130/2. 1999-00, 186/2. 2000-01, 220/2. Totals, 1384/10.

NBA PLAYOFF RECORD

								REBOUNDS								AVERAGES		
Season Team	G	Min.	FGM	FGA	Pct.	FTM	FTA	Pct.	Off.	Def.	Tot.	Ast.	St.	Blk.	TO	Pts.	RPG	APG	PPG
93-94—New Jersey.....	3	18	3	7	.429	2	2	1.000	0	0	0	3	2	0	4	9	0.0	1.0	3.0
97-98—Charlotte........	9	285	33	83	.398	15	21	.714	5	13	18	60	7	0	19	90	2.0	6.7	10.0
99-00—Charlotte........	4	152	16	48	.333	9	9	1.000	3	9	12	19	8	0	6	44	3.0	4.8	11.0
00-01—Charlotte........	10	394	63	134	.470	31	41	.756	4	26	30	39	16	1	14	170	3.0	3.9	17.0
Totals	26	849	115	272	.423	57	73	.781	12	48	60	121	33	1	43	313	2.3	4.7	12.0

Three-point field goals: 1993-94, 1-for-4 (.250). 1997-98, 9-for-21 (.429). 1999-00, 3-for-10 (.300). 2000-01, 13-for-33 (.394). Totals, 26-for-68 (.382).
Personal fouls/disqualifications: 1997-98, 25/0. 1999-00, 17/0. 2000-01, 28/0. Totals, 70/0.

WEST, DOUG   G/F

PERSONAL: Born May 27, 1967, in Altoona, Pa. ... 6-6/225. (1,98/102,1). ... Full Name: Jeffery Douglas West.
HIGH SCHOOL: Altoona (Pa.) Area.
COLLEGE: Villanova.
TRANSACTIONS/CAREER NOTES: Selected by Minnesota Timberwolves in second round (38th pick overall) of 1989 NBA Draft. ... Traded by Timberwolves to Vancouver Grizzlies for G Anthony Peeler (February 18, 1998).

COLLEGIATE RECORD

											AVERAGES		
Season Team	G	Min.	FGM	FGA	Pct.	FTM	FTA	Pct.	Reb.	Ast.	Pts.	RPG	APG	PPG
85-86—Villanova.......................	37	995	158	307	.515	60	88	.682	136	16	376	3.7	0.4	10.2
86-87—Villanova.......................	31	1022	180	376	.479	94	129	.729	151	9	470	4.9	0.3	15.2
87-88—Villanova.......................	37	1281	215	433	.497	92	127	.724	181	82	583	4.9	2.2	15.8
88-89—Villanova.......................	33	1137	226	488	.463	90	125	.720	162	92	608	4.9	2.8	18.4
Totals	138	4435	779	1604	.486	336	469	.716	630	199	2037	4.6	1.4	14.8

Three-point field goals: 1986-87, 16-for-43 (.372). 1987-88, 61-for-143 (.427). 1988-89, 66-for-177 (.373). Totals, 143-for-363 (.394).

NBA REGULAR-SEASON RECORD

Season Team	G	Min.	FGM	FGA	Pct.	FTM	FTA	Pct.	REBOUNDS Off.	Def.	Tot.	Ast.	St.	Blk.	TO	Pts.	RPG	APG	PPG
89-90—Minnesota......	52	378	53	135	.393	26	32	.813	24	46	70	18	10	6	31	135	1.3	0.3	2.6
90-91—Minnesota......	75	824	118	246	.480	58	84	.690	56	80	136	48	35	23	41	294	1.8	0.6	3.9
91-92—Minnesota......	80	2540	463	894	.518	186	231	.805	107	150	257	281	66	26	120	1116	3.2	3.5	14.0
92-93—Minnesota......	80	3104	646	1249	.517	249	296	.841	89	158	247	235	85	21	165	1543	3.1	2.9	19.3
93-94—Minnesota......	72	2182	434	891	.487	187	231	.810	61	170	231	172	65	24	137	1056	3.2	2.4	14.7
94-95—Minnesota......	71	2328	351	762	.461	206	246	.837	60	167	227	185	65	24	126	919	3.2	2.6	12.9
95-96—Minnesota......	73	1639	175	393	.445	114	144	.792	48	113	161	119	30	17	81	465	2.2	1.6	6.4
96-97—Minnesota......	68	1920	226	484	.467	64	94	.681	37	111	148	113	61	24	66	531	2.2	1.7	7.8
97-98—Minnesota......	38	688	64	171	.374	29	40	.725	23	59	82	45	11	5	21	157	2.2	1.2	4.1
98-99—Vancouver......	14	294	31	65	.477	19	25	.760	5	20	25	19	16	7	12	81	1.8	1.4	5.8
99-00—Vancouver......	38	581	59	145	.407	34	40	.850	18	53	71	43	12	8	19	152	1.9	1.1	4.0
00-01—Vancouver......	15	171	11	38	.289	6	7	.857	4	11	15	14	3	4	4	28	1.0	0.9	1.9
Totals	676	16649	2631	5473	.481	1178	1470	.801	532	1138	1670	1292	459	189	823	6477	2.5	1.9	9.6

Three-point field goals: 1989-90, 3-for-11 (.273). 1990-91, 0-for-1. 1991-92, 4-for-23 (.174). 1992-93, 2-for-23 (.087). 1993-94, 1-for-8 (.125). 1994-95, 11-for-61 (.180). 1995-96, 1-for-13 (.077). 1996-97, 15-for-45 (.333). 1997-98, 0-for-2. 1998-99, 0-for-2. 1999-00, 0-for-3. 2000-01, 0-for-2. Totals, 37-for-194 (.191).

Personal fouls/disqualifications: 1989-90, 61/0. 1990-91, 115/0. 1991-92, 239/1. 1992-93, 279/1. 1993-94, 236/3. 1994-95, 250/4. 1995-96, 228/2. 1996-97, 218/3. 1997-98, 97/1. 1998-99, 38/1. 1999-00, 80/1. 2000-01, 21/0. Totals, 1862/17.

NBA PLAYOFF RECORD

Season Team	G	Min.	FGM	FGA	Pct.	FTM	FTA	Pct.	REBOUNDS Off.	Def.	Tot.	Ast.	St.	Blk.	TO	Pts.	RPG	APG	PPG
96-97—Minnesota......	3	87	12	22	.545	9	9	1.000	0	4	4	6	2	1	1	33	1.3	2.0	11.0

Three-point field goals: 1996-97, 0-for-2.
Personal fouls/disqualifications: 1996-97, 11/0.

WHITE, JAHIDI   C   WIZARDS

PERSONAL: Born February 19, 1976, in St. Louis. ... 6-9/290. (2,06/131,5).
HIGH SCHOOL: Cardinal Ritter (St. Louis).
COLLEGE: Georgetown.
TRANSACTIONS/CAREER NOTES: Selected by Washington Wizards in second round (43rd pick overall) of 1998 NBA Draft.

COLLEGIATE RECORD

Season Team	G	Min.	FGM	FGA	Pct.	FTM	FTA	Pct.	Reb.	Ast.	Pts.	RPG	APG	PPG
94-95—Georgetown..................	26	201	24	56	.429	13	35	.371	46	2	61	1.8	0.1	2.3
95-96—Georgetown..................	37	409	70	125	.560	43	89	.483	138	5	183	3.7	0.1	4.9
96-97—Georgetown..................	30	607	84	164	.512	50	103	.485	193	14	218	6.4	0.5	7.3
97-98—Georgetown..................	12	259	52	82	.634	22	50	.440	100	2	126	8.3	0.2	10.5
Totals	105	1476	230	427	.539	128	277	.462	477	23	588	4.5	0.2	5.6

NBA REGULAR-SEASON RECORD

Season Team	G	Min.	FGM	FGA	Pct.	FTM	FTA	Pct.	REBOUNDS Off.	Def.	Tot.	Ast.	St.	Blk.	TO	Pts.	RPG	APG	PPG
98-99—Washington	20	191	17	32	.531	15	35	.429	23	35	58	1	3	11	16	49	2.9	0.1	2.5
99-00—Washington	80	1537	228	450	.507	113	211	.536	202	351	553	15	31	83	94	569	6.9	0.2	7.1
00-01—Washington	68	1609	203	408	.498	177	312	.567	178	343	521	20	32	111	136	583	7.7	0.3	8.6
Totals	168	3337	448	890	.503	305	558	.547	403	729	1132	36	66	205	246	1201	6.7	0.2	7.1

Three-point field goals: 2000-01, 0-for-1. Totals, 0-for-1 (.000).
Personal fouls/disqualifications: 1998-99, 39/1. 1999-00, 234/0. 2000-01, 211/3. Totals, 484/6.

WHITNEY, CHRIS   G   WIZARDS

PERSONAL: Born October 5, 1971, in Hopkinsville, Ky. ... 6-0/175. (1,83/79,4). ... Full Name: Christopher Antoine Whitney.
HIGH SCHOOL: Christian County (Hopkinsville, Ky.).
JUNIOR COLLEGE: Lincoln Trail Community College (Ill.).
COLLEGE: Clemson.
TRANSACTIONS/CAREER NOTES: Selected by San Antonio Spurs in second round (47th pick overall) of 1993 NBA Draft. ... Waived by Spurs (February 23, 1995). ... Played in Continental Basketball Association with Rapid City Thrillers (1994-95) and Florida Beachdogs (1995-96). ... Signed by Washington Bullets to first of two consecutive 10-day contracts (March 3, 1996). ... Signed by Bullets for remainder of season (March 23, 1996). ... Bullets franchise renamed Washington Wizards for 1997-98 season.

COLLEGIATE RECORD

Season Team	G	Min.	FGM	FGA	Pct.	FTM	FTA	Pct.	Reb.	Ast.	Pts.	RPG	APG	PPG
89-90—Lincoln Trail C.C.	33	...	120	253	.474	74	91	.813	...	...	335	...	...	10.2
90-91—Lincoln Trail C.C.	32	...	230	447	.515	134	158	.848	154	202	653	4.8	6.3	20.4
91-92—Clemson	28	982	119	290	.410	56	73	.767	92	161	374	3.3	5.8	13.4
92-93—Clemson	30	1126	149	338	.441	85	106	.802	122	193	470	4.1	6.4	15.7
Junior College Totals.............	65	...	350	700	.500	208	249	.835	...	...	988	...	...	15.2
4-Year-College Totals.............	58	2108	268	628	.427	141	179	.788	214	354	844	3.7	6.1	14.6

Three-point field goals: 1989-90, 21-for-57 (.368). 1990-91, 59-for-135 (.437). 1991-92, 80-for-191 (.419). 1992-93, 87-for-213 (.408). Totals, 80-for-192 (.417) Totals, 167-for-404 (.413).

NBA REGULAR-SEASON RECORD

Season Team	G	Min.	FGM	FGA	Pct.	FTM	FTA	Pct.	REBOUNDS Off.	Def.	Tot.	Ast.	St.	Blk.	TO	Pts.	AVERAGES RPG	APG	PPG
93-94—San Antonio....	40	339	25	82	.305	12	15	.800	5	24	29	53	11	1	37	72	0.7	1.3	1.8
94-95—San Antonio....	25	179	14	47	.298	11	11	1.000	4	9	13	28	4	0	18	42	0.5	1.1	1.7
95-96—Washington ...	21	335	45	99	.455	41	44	.932	2	31	33	51	18	1	23	150	1.6	2.4	7.1
96-97—Washington ...	82	1117	139	330	.421	94	113	.832	13	91	104	182	49	4	68	430	1.3	2.2	5.2
97-98—Washington ...	82	1073	126	355	.355	118	129	.915	16	99	115	196	34	6	65	422	1.4	2.4	5.1
98-99—Washington ...	39	441	64	156	.410	27	31	.871	8	39	47	69	18	2	36	187	1.2	1.8	4.8
99-00—Washington ...	82	1627	217	521	.417	112	132	.848	20	114	134	313	55	5	107	642	1.6	3.8	7.8
00-01—Washington ...	59	1532	182	470	.387	101	113	.894	12	94	106	248	55	3	103	558	1.8	4.2	9.5
Totals	430	6643	812	2060	.394	516	588	.878	80	501	581	1140	244	22	457	2503	1.4	2.7	5.8

Three-point field goals: 1993-94, 10-for-30 (.333). 1994-95, 3-for-19 (.158). 1995-96, 19-for-44 (.432). 1996-97, 58-for-163 (.356). 1997-98, 52-for-169 (.308). 1998-99, 32-for-95 (.337). 1999-00, 96-for-255 (.376). 2000-01, 93-for-248 (.375). Totals, 363-for-1023 (.355).

Personal fouls/disqualifications: 1993-94, 53/0. 1994-95, 34/1. 1995-96, 46/0. 1996-97, 100/0. 1997-98, 106/0. 1998-99, 49/0. 1999-00, 166/1. 2000-01, 150/5. Totals, 704/7.

NBA PLAYOFF RECORD

Season Team	G	Min.	FGM	FGA	Pct.	FTM	FTA	Pct.	REBOUNDS Off.	Def.	Tot.	Ast.	St.	Blk.	TO	Pts.	AVERAGES RPG	APG	PPG
96-97—Washington	3	20	2	5	.400	1	1	1.000	0	2	2	2	0	0	5	7	0.7	0.7	2.3

Three-point field goals: 1996-97, 2-for-4 (.500).

Personal fouls/disqualifications: 1996-97, 1/0.

CBA REGULAR-SEASON RECORD

Season Team	G	Min.	FGM	FGA	Pct.	FTM	FTA	Pct.	Reb.	Ast.	Pts.	AVERAGES RPG	APG	PPG
94-95—Rapid City	7	190	29	83	.349	23	25	.920	26	22	92	3.7	3.1	13.1
95-96—Florida	34	896	141	304	.464	91	114	.798	74	192	432	2.2	5.6	12.7
Totals	41	1086	170	387	.439	114	139	.820	100	214	524	2.4	5.2	12.8

Three-point field goals: 1994-95, 11-for-36 (.306). 1995-96, 59-for-134 (.440). Totals, 70-for-170 (.412).

WILLIAMS, AARON   F   NETS

PERSONAL: Born October 2, 1971, in Evanston, Ill. ... 6-9/225. (2,06/102,1).
HIGH SCHOOL: Rolling Meadows (Ill.).
COLLEGE: Xavier.
TRANSACTIONS/CAREER NOTES: Not drafted by an NBA franchise. ... Played in Continental Basketball Association with Grand Rapids Hoops (1993-94) and Connecticut Pride (1995-96 and 1996-97). ... Played in Italy (1993-94). ... Signed as free agent by Utah Jazz (November 29, 1993). ... Waived by Jazz (December 27, 1993). ... Signed as free agent by Milwaukee Bucks (October 6, 1994). ... Waived by Bucks (November 7, 1994). ... Re-signed as free agent by Bucks (November 9, 1994). ... Waived by Bucks (March 22, 1995). ... Played in Greece (1995-96). ... Signed as free agent by Denver Nuggets (December 22, 1996). ... Waived by Nuggets (January 6, 1997). ... Signed by Vancouver Grizzlies to first of two consecutive 10-day contracts (January 29, 1997). ... Signed by Grizzlies for remainder of season (February 20, 1997). ... Signed as free agent by Seattle SuperSonics (August 11, 1997). ... Signed as free agent by Washington Wizards (August 17, 1999). ... Signed as free agent by New Jersey Nets (August 5, 2000).

COLLEGIATE RECORD

Season Team	G	Min.	FGM	FGA	Pct.	FTM	FTA	Pct.	Reb.	Ast.	Pts.	AVERAGES RPG	APG	PPG
89-90—Xavier	28	278	27	47	.574	8	20	.400	76	6	62	2.7	0.2	2.2
90-91—Xavier	32	278	27	47	.574	8	20	.400	209	33	309	6.5	1.0	9.7
91-92—Xavier	27	786	148	253	.585	79	113	.699	215	31	375	8.0	1.1	13.9
92-93—Xavier	30	843	127	247	.514	73	94	.777	213	54	327	7.1	1.8	10.9
Totals	117	2185	329	594	.554	168	247	.680	713	124	1073	6.1	1.1	9.2

NOTES: CBA All-Rookie second team (1994).

CBA REGULAR-SEASON RECORD

Season Team	G	Min.	FGM	FGA	Pct.	FTM	FTA	Pct.	Reb.	Ast.	Pts.	AVERAGES RPG	APG	PPG
93-94—Grand Rapids	43	863	149	267	.558	81	105	.771	242	38	379	5.6	0.9	8.8
95-96—Connecticut	13	235	51	90	.567	8	16	.500	80	4	110	6.2	0.3	8.5
96-97—Connecticut	25	968	174	316	.551	73	101	.723	247	42	421	9.9	1.7	16.8
Totals	81	2066	374	673	.556	162	222	.730	569	84	910	7.0	1.0	11.2

Three-point field goals: 1993-94, 0-for-2. 1996-97, 0-for-2. Totals, 0-for-4 (.000).

ITALIAN LEAGUE RECORD

Season Team	G	Min.	FGM	FGA	Pct.	FTM	FTA	Pct.	Reb.	Ast.	Pts.	AVERAGES RPG	APG	PPG
93-94—Teorematour Milan	6	...	...	...	...	...	...	...	71	2	83	11.8	0.3	13.8

NOTES: Led NBA with 319 personal fouls (2001).

NBA REGULAR-SEASON RECORD

Season Team	G	Min.	FGM	FGA	Pct.	FTM	FTA	Pct.	REBOUNDS Off.	Def.	Tot.	Ast.	St.	Blk.	TO	Pts.	AVERAGES RPG	APG	PPG
93-94—Utah	6	12	2	8	.250	0	1	.000	1	2	3	1	0	0	1	4	0.5	0.2	0.7
94-95—Milwaukee	15	72	8	24	.333	8	12	.667	5	14	19	0	2	6	7	24	1.3	0.0	1.6
96-97—Denver-Van.....	33	563	85	148	.574	33	49	.673	62	81	143	15	16	29	32	203	4.3	0.5	6.2
97-98—Seattle	65	757	115	220	.523	66	85	.776	48	99	147	14	19	38	50	296	2.3	0.2	4.6
98-99—Seattle	40	458	52	123	.423	54	74	.730	54	74	128	22	14	24	30	158	3.2	0.6	4.0

W

Season Team	G	Min.	FGM	FGA	Pct.	FTM	FTA	Pct.	Off.	Def.	Tot.	Ast.	St.	Blk.	TO	Pts.	RPG	APG	PPG
									REBOUNDS								**AVERAGES**		
99-00—Washington	81	1545	235	450	.522	146	201	.726	159	250	409	58	41	92	80	616	5.0	0.7	7.6
00-01—New Jersey	82	2336	297	650	.457	244	310	.787	211	379	590	88	59	113	132	838	7.2	1.1	10.2
Totals	322	5743	794	1623	.489	551	732	.753	540	899	1439	198	151	302	332	2139	4.5	0.6	6.6

Three-point field goals: 1994-95, 0-for-1. 1996-97, 0-for-1. 1997-98, 0-for-1. 1998-99, 0-for-1. 1999-00, 0-for-3. 2000-01, 0-for-2. Totals, 0-for-9 (.000).
Personal fouls/disqualifications: 1993-94, 4/0. 1994-95, 14/0. 1996-97, 72/1. 1997-98, 119/0. 1998-99, 75/1. 1999-00, 234/3. 2000-01, 319/9. Totals, 837/14.

NBA PLAYOFF RECORD

Season Team	G	Min.	FGM	FGA	Pct.	FTM	FTA	Pct.	Off.	Def.	Tot.	Ast.	St.	Blk.	TO	Pts.	RPG	APG	PPG
									REBOUNDS								**AVERAGES**		
97-98—Seattle	3	7	0	3	.000	2	2	1.000	1	0	1	0	0	1	1	2	0.3	0.0	0.7

GREEK LEAGUE RECORD

Season Team	G	Min.	FGM	FGA	Pct.	FTM	FTA	Pct.	Reb.	Ast.	Pts.	RPG	APG	PPG
												AVERAGES		
95-96—Ambelokipi	13	...	...	...	...	...	...	...	111	11	178	8.5	0.8	13.7

WILLIAMS, ALVIN   G   RAPTORS

PERSONAL: Born August 6, 1974, in Philadelphia. ... 6-5/185. (1,96/83,9). ... Full Name: Alvin Leon Williams.
HIGH SCHOOL: Germantown Academy (Philadelphia).
COLLEGE: Villanova.
TRANSACTIONS/CAREER NOTES: Selected by Portland Trail Blazers in second round (48th pick overall) of 1997 NBA Draft. ... Traded by Trail Blazers with G Kenny Anderson, F Gary Trent and two first-round draft choices to Toronto Raptors for G Damon Stoudamire, F Walt Williams and F Carlos Rogers (February 13, 1998). ... Traded by Raptors with F/C Sean Marks and cash considerations to Boston Celtics for F Danny Fortson and a future draft choice (February 9, 2000); trade later voided because Williams failed physical.

COLLEGIATE RECORD

Season Team	G	Min.	FGM	FGA	Pct.	FTM	FTA	Pct.	Reb.	Ast.	Pts.	RPG	APG	PPG
												AVERAGES		
93-94—Villanova........................	31	721	79	203	.389	67	96	.698	87	88	245	2.8	2.8	7.9
94-95—Villanova........................	33	963	79	195	.405	61	82	.744	116	159	234	3.5	4.8	7.1
95-96—Villanova........................	33	1078	129	284	.454	71	100	.710	117	177	364	3.5	5.4	11.0
96-97—Villanova........................	34	1163	198	412	.481	121	163	.742	169	129	580	5.0	3.8	17.1
Totals	131	3925	485	1094	.443	320	441	.726	489	553	1423	3.7	4.2	10.9

Three-point field goals: 1993-94, 20-for-51 (.392). 1994-95, 15-for-57 (.263). 1995-96, 35-for-101 (.347). 1996-97, 63-for-171 (.368). Totals, 133-for-380 (.350).

NBA REGULAR-SEASON RECORD

Season Team	G	Min.	FGM	FGA	Pct.	FTM	FTA	Pct.	Off.	Def.	Tot.	Ast.	St.	Blk.	TO	Pts.	RPG	APG	PPG
									REBOUNDS								**AVERAGES**		
97-98—Portland-Tor....	54	1071	125	282	.443	65	90	.722	24	57	81	103	38	3	58	324	1.5	1.9	6.0
98-99—Toronto	50	1051	95	237	.401	44	52	.846	19	63	82	130	51	12	56	248	1.6	2.6	5.0
99-00—Toronto	55	779	114	287	.397	48	65	.738	27	58	85	126	34	11	47	292	1.5	2.3	5.3
00-01—Toronto	82	2394	330	767	.430	109	145	.752	50	162	212	407	123	26	103	802	2.6	5.0	9.8
Totals	241	5295	664	1573	.422	266	352	.756	120	340	460	766	246	52	264	1666	1.9	3.2	6.9

Three-point field goals: 1997-98, 9-for-28 (.321). 1998-99, 14-for-42 (.333). 1999-00, 16-for-55 (.291). 2000-01, 33-for-108 (.306). Totals, 72-for-233 (.309).
Personal fouls/disqualifications: 1997-98, 79/0. 1998-99, 94/1. 1999-00, 78/0. 2000-01, 171/1. Totals, 422/2.

NBA PLAYOFF RECORD

Season Team	G	Min.	FGM	FGA	Pct.	FTM	FTA	Pct.	Off.	Def.	Tot.	Ast.	St.	Blk.	TO	Pts.	RPG	APG	PPG
									REBOUNDS								**AVERAGES**		
99-00—Toronto	1	1	0	0	...	0	0	...	0	0	0	0	0	0	0	0	0.0	0.0	0.0
00-01—Toronto	12	486	69	160	.431	17	25	.680	6	29	35	50	15	8	16	165	2.9	4.2	13.8
Totals	13	487	69	160	.431	17	25	.680	6	29	35	50	15	8	16	165	2.7	3.8	12.7

Three-point field goals: 2000-01, 10-for-28 (.357). Totals, 10-for-28 (.357).
Personal fouls/disqualifications: 2000-01, 34/0. Totals, 34/0.

WILLIAMS, ERIC   F   CELTICS

PERSONAL: Born July 17, 1972, in Newark, N.J. ... 6-8/220. (2,03/99,8). ... Full Name: Eric C. Williams.
HIGH SCHOOL: M.X. Shabazz (Newark, N.J.).
JUNIOR COLLEGE: Burlington County (N.J.) College, then Vincennes (Ind.) University.
COLLEGE: Providence.
TRANSACTIONS/CAREER NOTES: Selected by Boston Celtics in first round (14th pick overall) of 1995 NBA Draft. ... Traded by Celtics to Denver Nuggets for a second-round draft choice in 1999 and a second-round draft choice in 2001 (August 21, 1997). ... Traded by Nuggets with F Danny Fortson, G Eric Washington and first-round draft choice within the next three years to Celtics for G/F Ron Mercer, F Popeye Jones and C Dwayne Schintzius (August 3, 1999).

Season Team	G	Min.	FGM	FGA	Pct.	FTM	FTA	Pct.	Reb.	Ast.	Pts.	AVERAGES RPG	APG	PPG
90-91—Burlington County J.C. ...						Did not play.								
91-92—Vincennes	25	...	167	271	.616	103	154	.669	189	...	437	7.6	...	17.5
92-93—Vincennes	35	...	273	485	.563	182	273	.667	323	96	729	9.2	2.7	20.8
93-94—Providence	30	781	166	327	.508	138	209	.660	151	37	470	5.0	1.2	15.7
94-95—Providence	30	1041	184	445	.413	134	195	.687	201	75	531	6.7	2.5	17.7
Junior College Totals	60	...	440	756	.582	285	427	.667	512	...	1166	8.5	...	19.4
4-Year-College Totals	60	1822	350	772	.453	272	404	.673	352	112	1001	5.9	1.9	16.7

Three-point field goals: 1991-92, 0-for-1. 1992-93, 1-for-2 (.500). 1993-94, 0-for-5. 1994-95, 29-for-78 (.372). Totals, 1-for-3 (.333) Totals, 29-for-83 (.349).

NBA REGULAR-SEASON RECORD

Season Team	G	Min.	FGM	FGA	Pct.	FTM	FTA	Pct.	REBOUNDS Off.	Def.	Tot.	Ast.	St.	Blk.	TO	Pts.	AVERAGES RPG	APG	PPG
95-96—Boston	64	1470	241	546	.441	200	298	.671	92	125	217	70	56	11	88	685	3.4	1.1	10.7
96-97—Boston	72	2435	374	820	.456	328	436	.752	126	203	329	129	72	13	139	1078	4.6	1.8	15.0
97-98—Denver	4	145	24	61	.393	31	45	.689	10	11	21	12	4	0	9	79	5.3	3.0	19.8
98-99—Denver	38	780	80	219	.365	111	139	.799	34	47	81	37	27	8	49	277	2.1	1.0	7.3
99-00—Boston	68	1378	165	386	.427	134	169	.793	55	101	156	93	44	16	66	489	2.3	1.4	7.2
00-01—Boston	81	1745	162	448	.362	165	231	.714	64	143	207	112	64	13	76	535	2.6	1.4	6.6
Totals	327	7953	1046	2480	.422	969	1318	.735	381	630	1011	453	267	61	427	3143	3.1	1.4	9.6

Three-point field goals: 1995-96, 3-for-10 (.300). 1996-97, 2-for-8 (.250). 1998-99, 6-for-26 (.231). 1999-00, 25-for-72 (.347). 2000-01, 46-for-139 (.331). Totals, 82-for-255 (.322).

Personal fouls/disqualifications: 1995-96, 147/1. 1996-97, 213/0. 1997-98, 9/0. 1998-99, 76/0. 1999-00, 165/3. 2000-01, 179/1. Totals, 789/5.

WILLIAMS, JASON   G   GRIZZLIES

PERSONAL: Born November 18, 1975, in Belle, W.Va. ... 6-1/190. (1,85/86,2). ... Full Name: Jason Chandler Williams.
HIGH SCHOOL: Dupont (Belle, W.Va.).
COLLEGE: Marshall (W.Va.), then Florida.
TRANSACTIONS/CAREER NOTES: Selected after junior season by Sacramento Kings in first round (seventh pick overall) of 1998 NBA Draft. ... Traded by Kings with G/F Nick Anderson to Vancouver Grizzlies for G Mike Bibby and G Brent Price (June 27, 2001). ... Grizzlies franchise moved to Memphis for 2001-02 season.

COLLEGIATE RECORD

Season Team	G	Min.	FGM	FGA	Pct.	FTM	FTA	Pct.	Reb.	Ast.	Pts.	AVERAGES RPG	APG	PPG
94-95—Marshall						Did not play—redshirted.								
95-96—Marshall	28	816	144	276	.522	52	70	.743	99	178	375	3.5	6.4	13.4
96-97—Florida						Did not play—transfer student.								
97-98—Florida	20	635	112	254	.441	63	75	.840	59	134	341	3.0	6.7	17.1
Totals	48	1451	256	530	.483	115	145	.793	158	312	716	3.3	6.5	14.9

Three-point field goals: 1995-96, 35-for-92 (.380). 1997-98, 54-for-134 (.403). Totals, 89-for-226 (.394).

HONORS: NBA All-Rookie first team (1999).

Season Team	G	Min.	FGM	FGA	Pct.	FTM	FTA	Pct.	REBOUNDS Off.	Def.	Tot.	Ast.	St.	Blk.	TO	Pts.	AVERAGES RPG	APG	PPG
98-99—Sacramento	50	1805	231	617	.374	79	105	.752	14	139	153	299	95	1	143	641	3.1	6.0	12.8
99-00—Sacramento	81	2760	363	973	.373	128	170	.753	22	208	230	589	117	8	296	999	2.8	7.3	12.3
00-01—Sacramento	77	2290	281	690	.407	60	76	.789	19	166	185	416	94	9	160	720	2.4	5.4	9.4
Totals	208	6855	875	2280	.384	267	351	.761	55	513	568	1304	306	18	599	2360	2.7	6.3	11.3

Three-point field goals: 1998-99, 100-for-323 (.310). 1999-00, 145-for-505 (.287). 2000-01, 98-for-311 (.315). Totals, 343-for-1139 (.301).

Personal fouls/disqualifications: 1998-99, 91/0. 1999-00, 140/0. 2000-01, 114/0. Totals, 345/0.

NBA PLAYOFF RECORD

Season Team	G	Min.	FGM	FGA	Pct.	FTM	FTA	Pct.	REBOUNDS Off.	Def.	Tot.	Ast.	St.	Blk.	TO	Pts.	AVERAGES RPG	APG	PPG
98-99—Sacramento	5	163	16	45	.356	9	9	1.000	2	16	18	20	8	1	13	50	3.6	4.0	10.0
99-00—Sacramento	5	145	18	48	.375	8	10	.800	1	7	8	12	3	0	8	52	1.6	2.4	10.4
00-01—Sacramento	8	191	26	61	.426	7	7	1.000	0	18	18	23	8	0	21	70	2.3	2.9	8.8
Totals	18	499	60	154	.390	24	26	.923	3	41	44	55	19	1	42	172	2.4	3.1	9.6

Three-point field goals: 1998-99, 9-for-29 (.310). 1999-00, 8-for-25 (.320). 2000-01, 11-for-30 (.367). Totals, 28-for-84 (.333).

Personal fouls/disqualifications: 1998-99, 15/0. 1999-00, 8/0. 2000-01, 14/0. Totals, 37/0.

WILLIAMS, JEROME   F   RAPTORS

PERSONAL: Born May 10, 1973, in Washington, D.C. ... 6-9/206. (2,06/93,4).
HIGH SCHOOL: Magruder (Germantown, Md.).
JUNIOR COLLEGE: Montgomery College (Md.).
COLLEGE: Georgetown.
TRANSACTIONS/CAREER NOTES: Selected by Detroit Pistons in first round (26th pick overall) of 1996 NBA Draft. ... Traded by Pistons with C Eric Montross to Toronto Raptors for F Corliss Williamson, F Tyrone Corbin, F Kornel David and future first-round draft choice (February 22, 2001).

W

Season Team	G	Min.	FGM	FGA	Pct.	FTM	FTA	Pct.	Reb.	Ast.	Pts.	AVERAGES RPG	APG	PPG
92-93—Montgomery College.....						Statistics unavailable.								
93-94—Montgomery College.....						Statistics unavailable.								
94-95—Georgetown..................	31	939	126	252	.500	83	132	.629	310	45	337	10.0	1.5	10.9
95-96—Georgetown..................	37	1016	147	250	.588	85	133	.639	324	51	380	8.8	1.4	10.3
4-Year-College Totals...........	68	1955	273	502	.544	168	265	.634	634	96	717	9.3	1.4	10.5

Three-point field goals: 1994-95, 2-for-11 (.182). 1995-96, 1-for-7 (.143). Totals, 3-for-18 (.167).

NBA REGULAR-SEASON RECORD

Season Team	G	Min.	FGM	FGA	Pct.	FTM	FTA	Pct.	REBOUNDS Off.	Def.	Tot.	Ast.	St.	Blk.	TO	Pts.	AVERAGES RPG	APG	PPG
96-97—Detroit	33	177	20	51	.392	9	17	.529	22	28	50	7	13	1	13	49	1.5	0.2	1.5
97-98—Detroit	77	1305	151	288	.524	108	166	.651	170	209	379	48	51	10	60	410	4.9	0.6	5.3
98-99—Detroit	50	1154	124	248	.500	107	159	.673	158	191	349	23	63	7	41	355	7.0	0.5	7.1
99-00—Detroit	82	2102	257	456	.564	175	284	.616	277	512	789	68	95	21	105	689	9.6	0.8	8.4
00-01—Detroit-Tor.	59	1182	136	294	.463	100	135	.741	133	249	382	45	57	20	63	372	6.5	0.8	6.3
Totals	301	5920	688	1337	.515	499	761	.656	760	1189	1949	191	279	59	282	1875	6.5	0.6	6.2

Three-point field goals: 1997-98, 0-for-1. 1999-00, 0-for-3. 2000-01, 0-for-3. Totals, 0-for-7 (.000).
Personal fouls/disqualifications: 1996-97, 18/0. 1997-98, 144/1. 1998-99, 108/0. 1999-00, 196/0. 2000-01, 124/0. Totals, 590/1.

NBA PLAYOFF RECORD

Season Team	G	Min.	FGM	FGA	Pct.	FTM	FTA	Pct.	REBOUNDS Off.	Def.	Tot.	Ast.	St.	Blk.	TO	Pts.	AVERAGES RPG	APG	PPG
96-97—Detroit	1	5	2	2	1.000	0	0	...	0	3	3	0	1	0	1	4	3.0	0.0	4.0
98-99—Detroit	5	123	12	27	.444	7	9	.778	12	20	32	4	4	0	4	31	6.4	0.8	6.2
99-00—Detroit	3	73	7	14	.500	1	8	.125	7	14	21	2	3	0	3	15	7.0	0.7	5.0
00-01—Toronto	11	164	12	24	.500	11	22	.500	20	25	45	9	10	6	6	35	4.1	0.8	3.2
Totals	20	365	33	67	.493	19	39	.487	39	62	101	15	18	6	14	85	5.1	0.8	4.3

Personal fouls/disqualifications: 1998-99, 7/0. 1999-00, 8/0. 2000-01, 23/0. Totals, 38/0.

WILLIAMS, MONTY   F

PERSONAL: Born October 8, 1971, in Fredericksburg, Va. ... 6-8/225. (2,03/102,1). ... Full Name: Tavares Montgomery Williams.
HIGH SCHOOL: Potomac (Oxon Hill, Md.).
COLLEGE: Notre Dame.
TRANSACTIONS/CAREER NOTES: Selected by New York Knicks in first round (24th pick overall) of 1994 NBA Draft. ... Traded by Knicks with F Charles Smith to San Antonio Spurs for F J.R. Reid, C Brad Lohaus and 1996 first-round draft choice (February 8, 1996). ... Signed as free agent by Denver Nuggets (January 23, 1999). ... Waived by Nuggets (February 19, 1999). ... Signed as free agent by Orlando Magic (September 17, 1999).

W

COLLEGIATE RECORD

Season Team	G	Min.	FGM	FGA	Pct.	FTM	FTA	Pct.	Reb.	Ast.	Pts.	AVERAGES RPG	APG	PPG
89-90—Notre Dame...................	29	588	83	172	.483	54	73	.740	108	31	222	3.7	1.1	7.7
90-91—Notre Dame...................						Did not play—heart problem.								
91-92—Notre Dame...................						Did not play—heart problem.								
92-93—Notre Dame...................	27	942	177	384	.461	121	153	.791	251	39	500	9.3	1.4	18.5
93-94—Notre Dame...................	29	1000	237	464	.511	143	205	.698	239	68	649	8.2	2.3	22.4
Totals	85	2530	497	1020	.487	318	431	.738	598	138	1371	7.0	1.6	16.1

Three-point field goals: 1989-90, 2-for-10 (.200). 1992-93, 25-for-74 (.338). 1993-94, 32-for-78 (.410). Totals, 59-for-162 (.364).

NBA REGULAR-SEASON RECORD

Season Team	G	Min.	FGM	FGA	Pct.	FTM	FTA	Pct.	REBOUNDS Off.	Def.	Tot.	Ast.	St.	Blk.	TO	Pts.	AVERAGES RPG	APG	PPG
94-95—New York	41	503	60	133	.451	17	38	.447	42	56	98	49	20	4	41	137	2.4	1.2	3.3
95-96—N.Y.-San Ant...	31	184	27	68	.397	14	20	.700	20	20	40	8	6	2	18	68	1.3	0.3	2.2
96-97—San Antonio....	65	1345	234	460	.509	120	186	.645	98	108	206	91	55	52	116	588	3.2	1.4	9.0
97-98—San Antonio....	72	1314	165	368	.448	122	182	.670	67	112	179	89	34	24	82	453	2.5	1.2	6.3
98-99—Denver............	1	6	0	2	.000	1	2	.500	0	0	0	0	0	0	0	1	0.0	0.0	1.0
99-00—Orlando...........	75	1501	263	538	.489	123	166	.741	96	154	250	106	46	17	109	651	3.3	1.4	8.7
00-01—Orlando...........	82	1211	162	364	.445	85	133	.639	86	157	243	79	29	16	85	410	3.0	1.0	5.0
Totals	367	6064	911	1933	.471	482	727	.663	409	607	1016	422	190	115	451	2308	2.8	1.1	6.3

Three-point field goals: 1994-95, 0-for-8. 1995-96, 0-for-1. 1996-97, 0-for-1. 1997-98, 1-for-2 (.500). 1999-00, 2-for-5 (.400). 2000-01, 1-for-13 (.077). Totals, 4-for-30 (.133).
Personal fouls/disqualifications: 1994-95, 87/0. 1995-96, 26/0. 1996-97, 161/1. 1997-98, 133/1. 1999-00, 187/1. 2000-01, 136/1. Totals, 730/4.

NBA PLAYOFF RECORD

Season Team	G	Min.	FGM	FGA	Pct.	FTM	FTA	Pct.	REBOUNDS Off.	Def.	Tot.	Ast.	St.	Blk.	TO	Pts.	AVERAGES RPG	APG	PPG
94-95—New York	1	4	2	2	1.000	0	0	...	0	0	0	0	0	0	0	4	0.0	0.0	4.0
95-96—San Antonio....	7	29	2	9	.222	3	6	.500	3	4	7	0	0	0	4	7	1.0	0.0	1.0
97-98—San Antonio....	5	28	5	8	.625	2	3	.667	2	4	6	1	0	0	4	12	1.2	0.2	2.4
00-01—Orlando...........	3	14	3	4	.750	1	3	.333	4	2	6	0	0	2	1	7	2.0	0.0	2.3
Totals	16	75	12	23	.522	6	12	.500	9	10	19	1	0	2	9	30	1.2	0.1	1.9

Personal fouls/disqualifications: 1994-95, 1/0. 1995-96, 4/0. 1997-98, 2/0. 2000-01, 2/0. Totals, 9/0.

WILLIAMS, SCOTT   C/F   BUCKS

PERSONAL: Born March 21, 1968, in Hacienda Heights, Calif. ... 6-10/245. (2,08/111,1). ... Full Name: Scott Christopher Williams.
HIGH SCHOOL: Woodrow Wilson (Los Angeles).
COLLEGE: North Carolina.
TRANSACTIONS/CAREER NOTES: Not drafted by an NBA franchise. ... Signed as free agent by Chicago Bulls (July 20, 1990). ... Signed as unrestricted free agent by Philadelphia 76ers (July 28, 1994). ... Traded by 76ers with F Tim Thomas to Milwaukee Bucks for F Tyrone Hill and F/G Jerald Honeycutt (March 11, 1999).
MISCELLANEOUS: Member of NBA championship team (1991, 1992, 1993).

COLLEGIATE RECORD

Season Team	G	Min.	FGM	FGA	Pct.	FTM	FTA	Pct.	Reb.	Ast.	Pts.	AVERAGES RPG	APG	PPG
86-87—North Carolina	36	540	78	157	.497	43	77	.558	150	31	199	4.2	0.9	5.5
87-88—North Carolina	34	900	162	283	.572	107	159	.673	217	42	434	6.4	1.2	12.8
88-89—North Carolina	35	802	165	297	.556	68	104	.654	254	26	398	7.3	0.7	11.4
89-90—North Carolina	33	813	190	343	.554	96	156	.615	240	25	477	7.3	0.8	14.5
Totals	138	3055	595	1080	.551	314	496	.633	861	124	1508	6.2	0.9	10.9

Three-point field goals: 1986-87, 0-for-1. 1987-88, 3-for-7 (.429). 1988-89, 0-for-2. 1989-90, 1-for-7 (.143). Totals, 4-for-17 (.235).

NBA REGULAR-SEASON RECORD

Season Team	G	Min.	FGM	FGA	Pct.	FTM	FTA	Pct.	REBOUNDS Off.	Def.	Tot.	Ast.	St.	Blk.	TO	Pts.	AVERAGES RPG	APG	PPG
90-91—Chicago	51	337	53	104	.510	20	28	.714	42	56	98	16	12	13	23	127	1.9	0.3	2.5
91-92—Chicago	63	690	83	172	.483	48	74	.649	90	157	247	50	13	36	35	214	3.9	0.8	3.4
92-93—Chicago	71	1369	166	356	.466	90	126	.714	168	283	451	68	55	66	73	422	6.4	1.0	5.9
93-94—Chicago	38	638	114	236	.483	60	98	.612	69	112	181	39	16	21	44	289	4.8	1.0	7.6
94-95—Philadelphia	77	1781	206	434	.475	79	107	.738	173	312	485	59	71	40	84	491	6.3	0.8	6.4
95-96—Philadelphia	13	193	15	29	.517	10	12	.833	13	33	46	5	6	7	8	40	3.5	0.4	3.1
96-97—Philadelphia	62	1317	162	318	.509	38	55	.691	155	242	397	41	44	41	50	362	6.4	0.7	5.8
97-98—Philadelphia	58	801	93	213	.437	51	63	.810	87	124	211	29	17	21	30	237	3.6	0.5	4.1
98-99—Phil.-Mil.	7	46	5	17	.294	4	7	.571	3	11	14	1	3	2	4	14	2.0	0.1	2.0
99-00—Milwaukee	68	1488	213	426	.500	94	129	.729	177	271	448	28	40	66	65	520	6.6	0.4	7.6
00-01—Milwaukee	66	1272	171	361	.474	60	70	.857	97	267	364	35	48	32	41	403	5.5	0.5	6.1
Totals	574	9932	1281	2666	.480	554	769	.720	1074	1868	2942	371	325	345	457	3119	5.1	0.6	5.4

Three-point field goals: 1990-91, 1-for-2 (.500). 1991-92, 0-for-3. 1992-93, 0-for-7. 1993-94, 1-for-5 (.200). 1994-95, 0-for-7. 1995-96, 0-for-2. 1996-97, 0-for-2. 1997-98, 0-for-5. 2000-01, 1-for-4 (.250). Totals, 3-for-37 (.081).
Personal fouls/disqualifications: 1990-91, 51/0. 1991-92, 122/0. 1992-93, 230/3. 1993-94, 112/1. 1994-95, 237/4. 1995-96, 27/0. 1996-97, 206/5. 1997-98, 132/0. 1998-99, 9/0. 1999-00, 230/3. 2000-01, 178/1. Totals, 1534/17.

NBA PLAYOFF RECORD

Season Team	G	Min.	FGM	FGA	Pct.	FTM	FTA	Pct.	REBOUNDS Off.	Def.	Tot.	Ast.	St.	Blk.	TO	Pts.	AVERAGES RPG	APG	PPG
90-91—Chicago	12	72	6	13	.462	11	20	.550	4	16	20	3	1	3	4	23	1.7	0.3	1.9
91-92—Chicago	22	321	34	70	.486	20	28	.714	33	62	95	7	6	18	15	88	4.3	0.3	4.0
92-93—Chicago	19	395	44	87	.506	16	29	.552	40	71	111	26	7	17	24	104	5.8	1.4	5.5
93-94—Chicago	10	151	24	57	.421	15	21	.714	15	24	39	7	7	3	9	63	3.9	0.7	6.3
99-00—Milwaukee	5	93	23	36	.639	5	6	.833	9	19	28	2	2	5	4	51	5.6	0.4	10.2
00-01—Milwaukee	17	378	59	120	.492	16	28	.571	45	77	122	12	11	24	12	134	7.2	0.7	7.9
Totals	85	1410	190	383	.496	83	132	.629	146	269	415	57	34	70	68	463	4.9	0.7	5.4

Three-point field goals: 1990-91, 0-for-1. 1991-92, 0-for-1. 1992-93, 0-for-2. Totals, 0-for-4 (.000).
Personal fouls/disqualifications: 1990-91, 15/0. 1991-92, 65/0. 1992-93, 58/2. 1993-94, 23/0. 1999-00, 16/0. 2000-01, 57/1. Totals, 234/3.

WILLIAMS, SHAMMOND   G

PERSONAL: Born April 5, 1975, in Bronx, N.Y. ... 6-1/201. (1,85/91,2). ... Full Name: Shammond Omar Williams.
HIGH SCHOOL: Southside (Greenville, N.C.), then Fork Union (Va.) Military Academy.
COLLEGE: North Carolina.
TRANSACTIONS/CAREER NOTES: Selected by Chicago Bulls in second round (34th pick overall) of 1998 NBA Draft. ... Draft rights traded by Bulls to Atlanta Hawks for draft rights to G Cory Carr and 1999 and 2000 second-round draft choices (June 24, 1998). ... Played in Turkey (1998-99). ... Waived by Hawks (February 19, 1999). ... Signed as free agent by Seattle SuperSonics (August 12, 1999).

COLLEGIATE RECORD

Season Team	G	Min.	FGM	FGA	Pct.	FTM	FTA	Pct.	Reb.	Ast.	Pts.	AVERAGES RPG	APG	PPG
94-95—North Carolina	29	132	12	31	.387	18	21	.857	12	20	48	0.4	0.7	1.7
95-96—North Carolina	32	663	84	186	.452	53	69	.768	82	65	267	2.6	2.0	8.3
96-97—North Carolina	35	1146	155	367	.422	88	108	.815	115	153	493	3.3	4.4	14.1
97-98—North Carolina	38	1250	209	428	.488	133	146	.911	123	161	637	3.2	4.2	16.8
Totals	134	3191	460	1012	.455	292	344	.849	332	399	1445	2.5	3.0	10.8

Three-point field goals: 1994-95, 6-for-20 (.300). 1995-96, 46-for-116 (.397). 1996-97, 95-for-227 (.419). 1997-98, 86-for-215 (.400). Totals, 233-for-578 (.403).

Season Team	G	Min.	FGM	FGA	Pct.	FTM	FTA	Pct.	REBOUNDS Off.	Def.	Tot.	Ast.	St.	Blk.	TO	Pts.	AVERAGES RPG	APG	PPG
98-99—Atlanta	2	4	0	1	.000	3	4	.750	0	0	0	1	0	0	0	3	0.0	0.5	1.5
99-00—Seattle	43	517	84	225	.373	33	51	.647	12	40	52	78	18	0	40	225	1.2	1.8	5.2
00-01—Seattle	69	1238	161	368	.438	84	96	.875	34	98	132	190	31	4	82	467	1.9	2.8	6.8
Totals	114	1759	245	594	.412	120	151	.795	46	138	184	269	49	4	122	695	1.6	2.4	6.1

Three-point field goals: 1999-00, 24-for-81 (.296). 2000-01, 61-for-133 (.459). Totals, 85-for-214 (.397).

Personal fouls/disqualifications: 1999-00, 39/0. 2000-01, 83/0. Totals, 122/0.

NBA PLAYOFF RECORD

Season Team	G	Min.	FGM	FGA	Pct.	FTM	FTA	Pct.	REBOUNDS Off.	Def.	Tot.	Ast.	St.	Blk.	TO	Pts.	AVERAGES RPG	APG	PPG
99-00—Seattle	5	99	18	33	.545	8	11	.727	2	9	11	18	8	0	6	51	2.2	3.6	10.2

Three-point field goals: 1999-00, 7-for-11 (.636).

Personal fouls/disqualifications: 1999-00, 3/0.

TURKISH LEAGUE RECORD

Season Team	G	Min.	FGM	FGA	Pct.	FTM	FTA	Pct.	Reb.	Ast.	Pts.	AVERAGES RPG	APG	PPG
98-99—Ulker..............................	4	130	17	27	.630	10	15	.667	17	20	74	4.3	5.0	18.5

Three-point field goals: 1998-99, 10-for-20 (.500).

WILLIAMS, WALT   F/G   ROCKETS

PERSONAL: Born April 16, 1970, in Washington, D.C. ... 6-8/230. (2,03/104,3). ... Full Name: Walter Ander Williams.
HIGH SCHOOL: Crossland (Temple Hills, Md.).
COLLEGE: Maryland.
TRANSACTIONS/CAREER NOTES: Selected by Sacramento Kings in first round (seventh pick overall) of 1992 NBA Draft. ... Traded by Kings with F Tyrone Corbin to Miami Heat for G/F Billy Owens and G/F Kevin Gamble (February 22, 1996). ... Signed as free agent by Toronto Raptors (August 29, 1996). ... Traded by Raptors with G Damon Stoudamire and F Carlos Rogers to Portland Trail Blazers for G Kenny Anderson, G Alvin Williams, F Gary Trent and two first-round draft choices (February 13, 1998). ... Traded by Trail Blazers with C Kelvin Cato, F Stacy Augmon, G Brian Shaw, G Ed Gray and F/C Carlos Rogers to Houston Rockets for F Scottie Pippen (October 2, 1999).

COLLEGIATE RECORD

NOTES: THE SPORTING NEWS All-America first team (1992).

Season Team	G	Min.	FGM	FGA	Pct.	FTM	FTA	Pct.	Reb.	Ast.	Pts.	AVERAGES RPG	APG	PPG
88-89—Maryland	26	617	75	170	.441	33	53	.623	92	66	190	3.5	2.5	7.3
89-90—Maryland	33	993	143	296	.483	104	134	.776	138	149	420	4.2	4.5	12.7
90-91—Maryland	17	537	109	243	.449	72	86	.837	86	91	318	5.1	5.4	18.7
91-92—Maryland	29	1042	256	542	.472	175	231	.758	162	104	776	5.6	3.6	26.8
Totals	105	3189	583	1251	.466	384	504	.762	478	410	1704	4.6	3.9	16.2

Three-point field goals: 1988-89, 7-for-27 (.259). 1989-90, 30-for-67 (.448). 1990-91, 28-for-95 (.295). 1991-92, 89-for-240 (.371). Totals, 154-for-429 (.359).

NBA REGULAR-SEASON RECORD

HONORS: NBA All-Rookie second team (1993).
NOTES: Tied for NBA lead with 11 disqualifications (1997).

Season Team	G	Min.	FGM	FGA	Pct.	FTM	FTA	Pct.	REBOUNDS Off.	Def.	Tot.	Ast.	St.	Blk.	TO	Pts.	AVERAGES RPG	APG	PPG
92-93—Sacramento	59	1673	358	823	.435	224	302	.742	115	150	265	178	66	29	179	1001	4.5	3.0	17.0
93-94—Sacramento	57	1356	226	580	.390	148	233	.635	71	164	235	132	52	30	145	638	4.1	2.3	11.2
94-95—Sacramento	77	2739	445	990	.446	266	364	.731	100	245	345	316	123	63	243	1259	4.5	4.1	16.4
95-96—Sac.-Mia.	73	2169	359	808	.444	163	232	.703	99	220	319	230	85	58	151	995	4.4	3.2	13.6
96-97—Toronto	73	2647	419	982	.427	186	243	.765	103	264	367	197	97	62	174	1199	5.0	2.7	16.4
97-98—Tor.-Port.	59	1470	210	544	.386	108	125	.864	50	150	200	122	59	35	92	608	3.4	2.1	10.3
98-99—Portland	48	1044	147	347	.424	89	107	.832	36	107	143	80	37	28	63	446	3.0	1.7	9.3
99-00—Houston	76	1859	312	681	.458	101	123	.821	69	237	306	157	49	44	113	827	4.0	2.1	10.9
00-01—Houston	72	1583	202	513	.394	97	126	.770	31	214	245	97	30	28	73	599	3.4	1.3	8.3
Totals	594	16540	2678	6276	.427	1382	1855	.745	674	1751	2425	1509	598	370	1233	7572	4.1	2.5	12.7

Three-point field goals: 1992-93, 61-for-191 (.319). 1993-94, 38-for-132 (.288). 1994-95, 103-for-296 (.348). 1995-96, 114-for-293 (.389). 1996-97, 175-for-437 (.400). 1997-98, 80-for-219 (.365). 1998-99, 63-for-144 (.438). 1999-00, 102-for-261 (.391). 2000-01, 98-for-248 (.395). Totals, 834-for-2221 (.376).

Personal fouls/disqualifications: 1992-93, 209/6. 1993-94, 200/6. 1994-95, 265/3. 1995-96, 238/0. 1996-97, 282/11. 1997-98, 161/2. 1998-99, 101/2. 1999-00, 190/2. 2000-01, 153/2. Totals, 1799/34.

NBA PLAYOFF RECORD

Season Team	G	Min.	FGM	FGA	Pct.	FTM	FTA	Pct.	REBOUNDS Off.	Def.	Tot.	Ast.	St.	Blk.	TO	Pts.	AVERAGES RPG	APG	PPG
95-96—Miami	3	70	6	18	.333	1	2	.500	3	9	12	5	1	1	3	14	4.0	1.7	4.7
97-98—Portland	4	102	17	31	.548	11	14	.786	3	11	14	9	1	0	1	53	3.5	2.3	13.3
98-99—Portland	13	185	21	58	.362	8	14	.571	5	11	16	11	7	3	11	63	1.2	0.8	4.8
Totals	20	357	44	107	.411	20	30	.667	11	31	42	25	9	4	15	130	2.1	1.3	6.5

Three-point field goals: 1995-96, 1-for-9 (.111). 1997-98, 8-for-15 (.533). 1998-99, 13-for-32 (.406). Totals, 22-for-56 (.393).

Personal fouls/disqualifications: 1995-96, 4/0. 1997-98, 18/2. 1998-99, 27/0. Totals, 49/2.

WILLIAMSON, CORLISS   F   PISTONS

PERSONAL: Born December 4, 1973, in Russellville, Ark. ... 6-7/245. (2,01/111,1). ... Full Name: Corliss Mondari Williamson.

HIGH SCHOOL: Russellville (Ark.).

COLLEGE: Arkansas.

TRANSACTIONS/CAREER NOTES: Selected after junior season by Sacramento Kings in first round (13th pick overall) of 1995 NBA Draft. ... Traded by Kings to Toronto Raptors for G/F Doug Christie (September 29, 2000). ... Traded by Raptors with F Tyrone Corbin, F Kornel David and future first-round draft choice to Detroit Pistons for F Jerome Williams and C Eric Montross (February 22, 2001).

COLLEGIATE RECORD

NOTES: Member of NCAA Division I championship team (1994). ... THE SPORTING NEWS All-America first team (1995). ... NCAA Division I Tournament Most Outstanding Player (1994).

Season Team	G	Min.	FGM	FGA	Pct.	FTM	FTA	Pct.	Reb.	Ast.	Pts.	RPG	APG	PPG
												AVERAGES		
92-93—Arkansas	18	454	101	176	.574	61	98	.622	92	30	263	5.1	1.7	14.6
93-94—Arkansas	34	989	273	436	.626	149	213	.700	262	74	695	7.7	2.2	20.4
94-95—Arkansas	39	1208	283	515	.550	203	304	.668	293	89	770	7.5	2.3	19.7
Totals	91	2651	657	1127	.583	413	615	.672	647	193	1728	7.1	2.1	19.0

Three-point field goals: 1994-95, 1-for-6 (.167).

NBA REGULAR-SEASON RECORD

Season Team	G	Min.	FGM	FGA	Pct.	FTM	FTA	Pct.	Off.	Def.	Tot.	Ast.	St.	Blk.	TO	Pts.	RPG	APG	PPG
									REBOUNDS								**AVERAGES**		
95-96—Sacramento	53	609	125	268	.466	47	84	.560	56	58	114	23	11	9	76	297	2.2	0.4	5.6
96-97—Sacramento	79	1992	371	745	.498	173	251	.689	139	187	326	124	60	49	157	915	4.1	1.6	11.6
97-98—Sacramento	79	2819	561	1134	.495	279	443	.630	162	284	446	230	76	48	199	1401	5.6	2.9	17.7
98-99—Sacramento	50	1374	269	555	.485	120	188	.638	85	121	206	66	30	8	75	659	4.1	1.3	13.2
99-00—Sacramento	76	1707	311	622	.500	163	212	.769	122	168	290	82	38	19	110	785	3.8	1.1	10.3
00-01—Tor.-Detroit	69	1686	325	647	.502	151	237	.637	110	211	321	61	50	21	110	801	4.7	0.9	11.6
Totals	406	10187	1962	3971	.494	933	1415	.659	674	1029	1703	586	265	154	727	4858	4.2	1.4	12.0

Three-point field goals: 1995-96, 0-for-3. 1996-97, 0-for-3. 1997-98, 0-for-9. 1998-99, 1-for-5 (.200). 2000-01, 0-for-2. Totals, 1-for-22 (.045).
Personal fouls/disqualifications: 1995-96, 115/2. 1996-97, 263/4. 1997-98, 252/4. 1998-99, 118/1. 1999-00, 192/0. 2000-01, 185/0. Totals, 1125/11.

NBA PLAYOFF RECORD

Season Team	G	Min.	FGM	FGA	Pct.	FTM	FTA	Pct.	Off.	Def.	Tot.	Ast.	St.	Blk.	TO	Pts.	RPG	APG	PPG
									REBOUNDS								**AVERAGES**		
95-96—Sacramento	1	2	0	1	.000	1	1	1.000	0	0	0	0	0	0	0	1	0.0	0.0	1.0
98-99—Sacramento	5	130	23	40	.575	7	10	.700	7	9	16	6	2	1	6	53	3.2	1.2	10.6
99-00—Sacramento	5	87	11	16	.688	11	12	.917	4	11	15	1	1	0	5	33	3.0	0.2	6.6
Totals	11	219	34	57	.596	19	23	.826	11	20	31	7	3	1	11	87	2.8	0.6	7.9

Personal fouls/disqualifications: 1998-99, 13/0. 1999-00, 8/0. Totals, 21/0.

WILLIS, KEVIN   F/C   NUGGETS

PERSONAL: Born September 6, 1962, in Los Angeles. ... 7-0/245. (2,13/111,1). ... Full Name: Kevin Alvin Willis.

HIGH SCHOOL: Pershing (Detroit).

JUNIOR COLLEGE: Jackson Community College (Mich.).

COLLEGE: Michigan State.

TRANSACTIONS/CAREER NOTES: Selected by Atlanta Hawks in first round (11th pick overall) of 1984 NBA Draft. ... Traded by Hawks with conditional first-round draft choice to Miami Heat for G Steve Smith, F Grant Long and conditional second-round draft choice (November 7, 1994). ... Traded by Heat with G Bimbo Coles to Golden State Warriors for G Tim Hardaway and F/C Chris Gatling (February 22, 1996). ... Signed as free agent by Houston Rockets (August 19, 1996). ... Traded by Rockets to Toronto Raptors for F Roy Rogers and two first-round picks in 1998 draft (June 9, 1998). ... Traded by Raptors with C Aleksander Radojevic, C Garth Joseph and 2001 or 2002 second-round draft choice to Denver Nuggets for F Tracy Murray, F/C Keon Clark and C Mamadou N'diaye (January 12, 2001).

COLLEGIATE RECORD

Season Team	G	Min.	FGM	FGA	Pct.	FTM	FTA	Pct.	Reb.	Ast.	Pts.	RPG	APG	PPG
												AVERAGES		
80-81—Jackson C.C.	...	...	...	...	...	...	...	...	...	...	...	...	...	19.0
81-82—Michigan State	27	518	73	164	.474	17	30	.567	113	2	163	4.2	0.1	6.0
82-83—Michigan State	27	865	162	272	.596	36	70	.514	258	8	360	9.6	0.3	13.3
83-84—Michigan State	25	738	118	240	.492	39	59	.661	192	7	275	7.7	0.3	11.0
4-Year-College Totals	79	2121	353	666	.530	92	159	.579	563	17	798	7.1	0.2	10.1

Three-point field goals: 1982-83, 0-for-1.

NBA REGULAR-SEASON RECORD

HONORS: All-NBA third team (1992).

Season Team	G	Min.	FGM	FGA	Pct.	FTM	FTA	Pct.	Off.	Def.	Tot.	Ast.	St.	Blk.	TO	Pts.	RPG	APG	PPG
									REBOUNDS								**AVERAGES**		
84-85—Atlanta	82	1785	322	690	.467	119	181	.657	177	345	522	36	31	49	104	765	6.4	0.4	9.3
85-86—Atlanta	82	2300	419	811	.517	172	263	.654	243	461	704	45	66	44	177	1010	8.6	0.5	12.3
86-87—Atlanta	81	2626	538	1003	.536	227	320	.709	321	528	849	62	65	61	173	1304	10.5	0.8	16.1
87-88—Atlanta	75	2091	356	687	.518	159	245	.649	235	312	547	28	68	42	138	871	7.3	0.4	11.6
88-89—Atlanta					Did not play—injured.														
89-90—Atlanta	81	2273	418	805	.519	168	246	.683	253	392	645	57	63	47	144	1006	8.0	0.7	12.4
90-91—Atlanta	80	2373	444	881	.504	159	238	.668	259	445	704	99	60	40	153	1051	8.8	1.2	13.1

W

Season Team	G	Min.	FGM	FGA	Pct.	FTM	FTA	Pct.	Off.	Def.	Tot.	Ast.	St.	Blk.	TO	Pts.	RPG	APG	PPG
91-92—Atlanta	81	2962	591	1224	.483	292	363	.804	418	840	1258	173	72	54	197	1480	15.5	2.1	18.3
92-93—Atlanta	80	2878	616	1218	.506	196	300	.653	335	693	1028	165	68	41	213	1435	12.9	2.1	17.9
93-94—Atlanta	80	2867	627	1257	.499	268	376	.713	335	628	963	150	79	38	188	1531	12.0	1.9	19.1
94-95—Atlanta-Miami .	67	2390	473	1015	.466	205	297	.690	227	505	732	86	60	36	162	1154	10.9	1.3	17.2
95-96—Mia.-G.S.	75	2135	325	712	.456	143	202	.708	208	430	638	53	32	41	161	794	8.5	0.7	10.6
96-97—Houston	75	1964	350	728	.481	140	202	.693	146	415	561	71	42	32	119	842	7.5	0.9	11.2
97-98—Houston	81	2528	531	1041	.510	242	305	.793	232	447	679	78	55	38	170	1305	8.4	1.0	16.1
98-99—Toronto	42	1216	187	447	.418	130	155	.839	109	241	350	67	28	28	86	504	8.3	1.6	12.0
99-00—Toronto	79	1679	236	569	.415	131	164	.799	201	281	482	49	36	48	98	604	6.1	0.6	7.6
00-01—Tor.-Denver	78	1830	304	690	.441	113	147	.769	177	355	532	50	52	52	87	722	6.8	0.6	9.3
Totals	1219	35897	6737	13778	.489	2864	4004	.715	3876	731811194	1269	882	691	2370	16378	9.2	1.0	13.4

Three-point field goals: 1984-85, 2-for-9 (.222). 1985-86, 0-for-6. 1986-87, 1-for-4 (.250). 1987-88, 0-for-2. 1989-90, 2-for-7 (.286). 1990-91, 4-for-10 (.400). 1991-92, 6-for-37 (.162). 1992-93, 7-for-29 (.241). 1993-94, 9-for-24 (.375). 1994-95, 3-for-15 (.200). 1995-96, 1-for-9 (.111). 1996-97, 2-for-14 (.143). 1997-98, 1-for-7 (.143). 1998-99, 0-for-2. 1999-00, 1-for-3 (.333). 2000-01, 1-for-6 (.167). Totals, 40-for-184 (.217).

Personal fouls/disqualifications: 1984-85, 226/4. 1985-86, 294/6. 1986-87, 313/4. 1987-88, 240/2. 1989-90, 259/4. 1990-91, 235/2. 1991-92, 223/0. 1992-93, 264/1. 1993-94, 250/2. 1994-95, 215/3. 1995-96, 253/4. 1996-97, 216/1. 1997-98, 235/1. 1998-99, 134/1. 1999-00, 256/3. 2000-01, 216/0. Totals, 3829/38.

NBA PLAYOFF RECORD

| | | | | | | | | | REBOUNDS | | | | | | | | AVERAGES | | |
Season Team	G	Min.	FGM	FGA	Pct.	FTM	FTA	Pct.	Off.	Def.	Tot.	Ast.	St.	Blk.	TO	Pts.	RPG	APG	PPG
85-86—Atlanta	9	280	55	98	.561	15	23	.652	31	34	65	5	7	8	15	125	7.2	0.6	13.9
86-87—Atlanta	9	356	60	115	.522	21	31	.677	33	50	83	6	9	7	17	141	9.2	0.7	15.7
87-88—Atlanta	12	462	80	138	.580	34	50	.680	36	72	108	11	10	10	25	194	9.0	0.9	16.2
90-91—Atlanta	5	159	27	67	.403	21	30	.700	18	27	45	5	3	1	2	77	9.0	1.0	15.4
92-93—Atlanta	3	103	21	45	.467	8	14	.571	13	13	26	3	2	0	7	50	8.7	1.0	16.7
93-94—Atlanta	11	362	59	129	.457	16	21	.762	38	81	119	11	8	5	19	134	10.8	1.0	12.2
96-97—Houston	16	295	38	95	.400	26	38	.684	22	53	75	11	9	4	22	102	4.7	0.7	6.4
97-98—Houston	5	168	22	55	.400	12	16	.750	18	35	53	5	8	3	12	56	10.6	1.0	11.2
99-00—Toronto	3	76	12	33	.364	15	20	.750	6	20	26	1	2	0	2	39	8.7	0.3	13.0
Totals	73	2261	374	775	.483	168	243	.691	215	385	600	58	58	38	121	918	8.2	0.8	12.6

Three-point field goals: 1987-88, 0-for-1. 1990-91, 2-for-3 (.667). 1992-93, 0-for-1. 1993-94, 0-for-5. 1996-97, 0-for-1. 1997-98, 0-for-1. Totals, 2-for-12 (.167).

Personal fouls/disqualifications: 1985-86, 38/2. 1986-87, 33/0. 1987-88, 51/1. 1990-91, 22/0. 1992-93, 13/0. 1993-94, 37/0. 1996-97, 47/0. 1997-98, 21/0. 1999-00, 11/0. Totals, 273/3.

NBA ALL-STAR GAME RECORD

| | | | | | | | | REBOUNDS | | | | | | | | |
Season Team	Min.	FGM	FGA	Pct.	FTM	FTA	Pct.	Off.	Def.	Tot.	Ast.	PF	Dq.	St.	Blk.	TO	Pts.
1992 —Atlanta..............	14	4	10	.400	0	0	...	4	0	4	0	1	0	0	0	0	8

WINGATE, DAVID   G/F

PERSONAL: Born December 15, 1963, in Baltimore. ... 6-5/187. (1,96/84,8). ... Full Name: David Grover Stacey Wingate Jr.
HIGH SCHOOL: Dunbar (Baltimore).
COLLEGE: Georgetown.
TRANSACTIONS/CAREER NOTES: Selected by Philadelphia 76ers in second round (44th pick overall) of 1986 NBA Draft. ... Traded by 76ers with G Maurice Cheeks and C Christian Welp to San Antonio Spurs for G Johnny Dawkins and F Jay Vincent (August 28, 1989). ... Waived by Spurs (June 28, 1991). ... Signed as free agent by Washington Bullets (September 30, 1991). ... Signed as free agent by Charlotte Hornets (November 18, 1992). ... Traded by Hornets with G Hersey Hawkins to Seattle SuperSonics for G Kendall Gill (June 27, 1995). ... Signed as free agent by New York Knicks (February 1, 1999). ... Signed as free agent by SuperSonics (October 2, 2000).

COLLEGIATE RECORD

NOTES: Member of NCAA Division I championship team (1984).

| | | | | | | | | | | | | AVERAGES | | |
Season Team	G	Min.	FGM	FGA	Pct.	FTM	FTA	Pct.	Reb.	Ast.	Pts.	RPG	APG	PPG
82-83—Georgetown..................	32	855	149	335	.445	87	124	.702	95	69	385	3.0	2.2	12.0
83-84—Georgetown..................	37	1005	161	370	.435	93	129	.721	135	99	415	3.6	2.7	11.2
84-85—Georgetown..................	38	1128	191	395	.484	91	132	.689	135	121	473	3.6	3.2	12.4
85-86—Georgetown..................	32	956	196	394	.497	117	155	.755	129	75	509	4.0	2.3	15.9
Totals	139	3944	697	1494	.467	388	540	.719	494	364	1782	3.6	2.6	12.8

NBA REGULAR-SEASON RECORD

| | | | | | | | | | REBOUNDS | | | | | | | | AVERAGES | | |
Season Team	G	Min.	FGM	FGA	Pct.	FTM	FTA	Pct.	Off.	Def.	Tot.	Ast.	St.	Blk.	TO	Pts.	RPG	APG	PPG
86-87—Philadelphia	77	1612	259	602	.430	149	201	.741	70	86	156	155	93	19	128	680	2.0	2.0	8.8
87-88—Philadelphia	61	1419	218	545	.400	99	132	.750	44	57	101	119	47	22	104	545	1.7	2.0	8.9
88-89—Philadelphia	33	372	54	115	.470	27	34	.794	12	25	37	73	9	2	35	137	1.1	2.2	4.2
89-90—San Antonio	78	1856	220	491	.448	87	112	.777	62	133	195	208	89	18	127	527	2.5	2.7	6.8
90-91—San Antonio	25	563	53	138	.384	29	41	.707	24	51	75	46	19	5	42	136	3.0	1.8	5.4
91-92—Washington	81	2127	266	572	.465	105	146	.719	80	189	269	247	123	21	124	638	3.3	3.0	7.9
92-93—Charlotte	72	1471	180	336	.536	79	107	.738	49	125	174	183	66	9	89	440	2.4	2.5	6.1
93-94—Charlotte	50	1005	136	283	.481	34	51	.667	30	104	134	104	42	6	53	310	2.7	2.1	6.2
94-95—Charlotte	52	515	50	122	.410	18	24	.750	11	49	60	56	19	6	27	122	1.2	1.1	2.3
95-96—Seattle	60	695	88	212	.415	32	41	.780	17	39	56	58	20	4	42	223	0.9	1.0	3.7
96-97—Seattle	65	929	89	214	.416	33	40	.825	23	51	74	80	44	5	37	236	1.1	1.2	3.6
97-98—Seattle	58	546	66	140	.471	15	29	.517	19	60	79	37	21	3	37	150	1.4	0.6	2.6
98-99—New York	20	92	7	16	.438	0	0	...	3	5	8	5	4	0	6	14	0.4	0.3	0.7
99-00—New York	7	32	1	9	.111	0	0	...	1	1	2	3	1	2	2	2	0.3	0.4	0.3
00-01—Seattle	1	9	3	3	1.000	0	0	...	0	0	0	2	0	0	0	6	0.0	2.0	6.0
Totals	740	13243	1690	3798	.445	707	958	.738	445	975	1420	1376	597	122	853	4166	1.9	1.9	5.6

W

Three-point field goals: 1986-87, 13-for-52 (.250). 1987-88, 10-for-40 (.250). 1988-89, 2-for-6 (.333). 1989-90, 0-for-13. 1990-91, 1-for-9 (.111). 1991-92, 1-for-18 (.056). 1992-93, 1-for-6 (.167). 1993-94, 4-for-12 (.333). 1994-95, 4-for-22 (.182). 1995-96, 15-for-34 (.441). 1996-97, 25-for-71 (.352). 1997-98, 3-for-7 (.429). Totals, 79-for-290 (.272).

Personal fouls/disqualifications: 1986-87, 169/1. 1987-88, 125/0. 1988-89, 43/0. 1989-90, 154/2. 1990-91, 66/0. 1991-92, 162/1. 1992-93, 135/1. 1993-94, 85/0. 1994-95, 60/0. 1995-96, 66/0. 1996-97, 108/0. 1997-98, 58/0. 1998-99, 10/0. 1999-00, 7/0. 2000-01, 1/0. Totals, 1249/5.

NBA PLAYOFF RECORD

								REBOUNDS								AVERAGES		
Season Team	G	Min.	FGM	FGA	Pct.	FTM	FTA	Pct.	Off.	Def.	Tot.	Ast.	St.	Blk.	TO	Pts.	RPG	APG	PPG
86-87—Philadelphia....	5	90	15	37	.405	9	14	.643	5	7	12	9	5	1	9	41	2.4	1.8	8.2
89-90—San Antonio....	10	293	40	77	.519	9	12	.750	9	28	37	38	18	3	14	91	3.7	3.8	9.1
90-91—San Antonio....	3	38	6	12	.500	2	3	.667	1	2	3	1	1	0	1	14	1.0	0.3	4.7
92-93—Charlotte........	9	117	8	22	.364	3	8	.375	4	8	12	15	4	1	1	19	1.3	1.7	2.1
94-95—Charlotte........	4	73	13	27	.481	4	6	.667	3	3	6	15	4	0	4	32	1.5	3.8	8.0
95-96—Seattle	13	68	7	16	.438	4	4	1.000	1	2	3	0	0	0	4	19	0.2	0.0	1.5
96-97—Seattle	12	192	28	66	.424	9	13	.692	13	24	37	14	5	3	9	77	3.1	1.2	6.4
97-98—Seattle	3	13	2	5	.400	4	6	.667	2	2	4	2	1	0	1	8	1.3	0.7	2.7
Totals	59	884	119	262	.454	44	66	.667	38	76	114	94	38	8	43	301	1.9	1.6	5.1

Three-point field goals: 1986-87, 2-for-2. 1989-90, 2-for-3 (.667). 1994-95, 2-for-6 (.333). 1995-96, 1-for-2 (.500). 1996-97, 12-for-31 (.387). Totals, 19-for-44 (.432).

Personal fouls/disqualifications: 1986-87, 11/1. 1989-90, 34/1. 1990-91, 8/1. 1992-93, 9/0. 1994-95, 14/0. 1995-96, 16/0. 1996-97, 22/0. 1997-98, 1/0. Totals, 115/3.

WOLKOWYSKI, RUBEN   F   MAVERICKS

PERSONAL: Born September 30, 1973, in Juan Jose Castelli Pavincia Chaco, Argentina. ... 6-10/270. (2,08/122,5).
HIGH SCHOOL: Quilmes (Buenos Aires, Argentina).
TRANSACTIONS/CAREER NOTES: Not drafted by an NBA franchise. ... Played in Argentina (1995-96 through 1999-2000). ... Signed as free agent by Seattle SuperSonics (September 7, 2000). ... Waived by SuperSonics (July 30, 2001). ... Signed as free agent by Dallas Mavericks (August 2001).

NBA REGULAR-SEASON RECORD

								REBOUNDS								AVERAGES		
Season Team	G	Min.	FGM	FGA	Pct.	FTM	FTA	Pct.	Off.	Def.	Tot.	Ast.	St.	Blk.	TO	Pts.	RPG	APG	PPG
00-01—Seattle	34	305	25	79	.316	25	34	.735	12	34	46	3	6	18	12	75	1.4	0.1	2.2

Three-point field goals: 2000-01, 0-for-2.
Personal fouls/disqualifications: 2000-01, 38/0.

WRIGHT, LORENZEN   F/C   GRIZZLIES

PERSONAL: Born November 4, 1975, in Memphis. ... 6-11/240. (2,11/108,9). ... Full Name: Lorenzen Vern-Gagne Wright.
HIGH SCHOOL: Booker T. Washington (Memphis).
COLLEGE: Memphis.
TRANSACTIONS/CAREER NOTES: Selected after sophomore season by Los Angeles Clippers in first round (seventh pick overall) of 1996 NBA Draft. ... Traded by Clippers to Atlanta Hawks for two future first-round draft choices (August 8, 1999). ... Traded by Hawks with G Brevin Knight and draft rights to Pau Gasol to Memphis Grizzlies for F Shareef Abdur-Rahim and draft rights to G Jamaal Tinsley (July 19, 2001).

COLLEGIATE RECORD

											AVERAGES		
Season Team	G	Min.	FGM	FGA	Pct.	FTM	FTA	Pct.	Reb.	Ast.	Pts.	RPG	APG	PPG
94-95—Memphis	34	1170	198	353	.561	107	171	.626	345	50	503	10.1	1.5	14.8
95-96—Memphis	30	1058	207	382	.542	109	169	.645	313	35	523	10.4	1.2	17.4
Totals	64	2228	405	735	.551	216	340	.635	658	85	1026	10.3	1.3	16.0

Three-point field goals: 1994-95, 0-for-1. 1995-96, 0-for-1. Totals, 0-for-2 (.000).

NBA REGULAR-SEASON RECORD

								REBOUNDS								AVERAGES		
Season Team	G	Min.	FGM	FGA	Pct.	FTM	FTA	Pct.	Off.	Def.	Tot.	Ast.	St.	Blk.	TO	Pts.	RPG	APG	PPG
96-97—L.A. Clippers...	77	1936	236	491	.481	88	150	.587	206	265	471	49	48	60	79	561	6.1	0.6	7.3
97-98—L.A. Clippers...	69	2067	241	542	.445	141	214	.659	180	426	606	55	55	87	81	623	8.8	0.8	9.0
98-99—L.A. Clippers...	48	1135	119	260	.458	81	117	.692	142	219	361	33	26	36	48	319	7.5	0.7	6.6
99-00—Atlanta	75	1205	180	361	.499	87	135	.644	117	188	305	21	29	40	66	448	4.1	0.3	6.0
00-01—Atlanta	71	1988	363	811	.448	155	216	.718	180	355	535	87	42	63	125	881	7.5	1.2	12.4
Totals	340	8331	1139	2465	.462	552	832	.663	825	1453	2278	245	200	286	399	2832	6.7	0.7	8.3

Three-point field goals: 1996-97, 1-for-4 (.250). 1997-98, 0-for-2. 1998-99, 0-for-1. 1999-00, 1-for-3 (.333). 2000-01, 0-for-2. Totals, 2-for-12 (.167).
Personal fouls/disqualifications: 1996-97, 211/2. 1997-98, 237/2. 1998-99, 162/2. 1999-00, 203/3. 2000-01, 232/2. Totals, 1045/11.

NBA PLAYOFF RECORD

								REBOUNDS								AVERAGES		
Season Team	G	Min.	FGM	FGA	Pct.	FTM	FTA	Pct.	Off.	Def.	Tot.	Ast.	St.	Blk.	TO	Pts.	RPG	APG	PPG
96-97—L.A. Clippers...	3	92	13	32	.406	5	5	1.000	7	15	22	2	3	2	1	31	7.3	0.7	10.3

Personal fouls/disqualifications: 1996-97, 6/0.

DID YOU KNOW . . .

. . . that Nets rookie Eddie Gill scored the 8,000,000th point in NBA history on April 15, 2001 against Boston?

ZHI ZHI, WANG　　　　　　C　　　　　　MAVERICKS

PERSONAL: Born July 8, 1977, in Beijing, China. ... 7-0/255. (2,13/115,7).
COLLEGE: Beijing (China).
TRANSACTIONS/CAREER NOTES: Played in China (1996-97 through 2000-01). ... Selected by Dallas Mavericks in second round (36th pick overall) of 1999 NBA Draft.
MISCELLANEOUS: Member of Chinese Olympic team (1996, 2000).

CHINESE REGULAR-SEASON RECORD

Season Team	G	Min.	FGM	FGA	Pct.	FTM	FTA	Pct.	Reb.	Ast.	Pts.	AVERAGES		
												RPG	APG	PPG
96-97—Bayi	26	...	163	298	.547	97	117	.829	189	26	429	7.3	1.0	16.5
97-98—Bayi	29	...	253	442	.572	125	152	.822	269	33	643	9.3	1.1	22.2
98-99—Bayi	30	...	262	456	.575	112	135	.830	184	24	656	6.1	0.8	21.9
99-00—Bayi	30	...	340	610	.557	104	125	.832	301	23	809	10.0	0.8	27.0
00-01—Bayi	31	...	330	539	.612	93	123	.756	354	51	773	11.4	1.6	24.9
Totals	146	...	1348	2345	.575	531	652	.814	1297	157	3310	8.9	1.1	22.7

Three-point field goals: 1997-98, 16-for-42 (.381).

NBA REGULAR-SEASON RECORD

Season Team	G	Min.	FGM	FGA	Pct.	FTM	FTA	Pct.	REBOUNDS			Ast.	St.	Blk.	TO	Pts.	AVERAGES		
									Off.	Def.	Tot.						RPG	APG	PPG
00-01—Dallas	5	38	8	19	.421	8	10	.800	1	6	7	0	0	0	1	24	1.4	0.0	4.8

Three-point field goals: 2000-01, 0-for-2.
Personal fouls/disqualifications: 2000-01, 8/0.

NBA PLAYOFF RECORD

Season Team	G	Min.	FGM	FGA	Pct.	FTM	FTA	Pct.	REBOUNDS			Ast.	St.	Blk.	TO	Pts.	AVERAGES		
									Off.	Def.	Tot.						RPG	APG	PPG
00-01—Dallas	5	23	3	8	.375	3	3	1.000	0	2	2	1	1	1	1	10	0.4	0.2	2.0

Three-point field goals: 2000-01, 1-for-2 (.500).
Personal fouls/disqualifications: 2000-01, 1/0.

Z

INDIVIDUAL CAREER HIGHS

Player	FGM	FGA	FTM	FTA	REB	AST	STL	BLK	PTS
Abdul-Rauf, Mahmoud	17	32	10	13	9	20	5	2	51
Abdul-Wahad, Tariq	12	20	9	10	17	5	6	3	31
Abdur-Rahim, Shareef	15	31	16	19	22	13	6	6	39
Alexander, Cory	10	19	7	8	11	12	5	2	28
Alexander, Courtney	14	25	11	11	9	4	6	1	33
Allen, Ray	17	27	19	20	11	13	6	2	43
Alston, Rafer	5	10	2	2	6	8	3	0	12
Amaechi, John	12	24	13	18	10	4	3	3	31
Anderson, Derek	14	23	16	17	12	14	5	2	35
Anderson, Kenny	17	33	20	23	13	18	6	2	45
Anderson, Nick	17	33	14	15	15	12	8	4	50
Anderson, Shandon	12	21	13	15	13	8	6	3	35
Anthony, Greg	11	20	14	16	10	15	7	2	32
Armstrong, Darrell	13	24	11	11	12	16	7	2	34
Artest, Ron	12	20	15	17	10	9	8	4	29
Atkins, Chucky	15	28	7	8	7	13	5	2	36
Augmon, Stacey	14	23	13	16	12	7	7	4	36
Austin, Isaac	12	29	9	13	22	6	5	4	33
Avery, Will	6	12	5	7	5	8	2	2	16
Bagaric, Dalibor	2	6	2	6	8	3	2	3	5
Baker, Vin	16	31	15	21	21	12	5	7	41
Barkley, Erick	4	7	0	0	3	1	1	0	9
Barros, Dana	21	26	11	12	13	19	7	2	50
Barry, Brent	10	20	10	11	13	11	6	2	30
Barry, Jon	8	17	11	13	8	10	5	2	23
Battie, Tony	9	18	7	10	15	5	3	8	19
Bell, Raja	1	4	0	0	1	0	1	0	3
Bender, Jonathan	5	11	8	9	5	3	1	4	20
Benjamin, Corey	8	25	6	7	7	6	4	3	21
Benoit, David	10	17	13	18	17	5	3	5	24
Best, Travis	12	20	12	15	11	13	6	1	30
Bibby, Mike	14	25	11	12	11	18	7	2	37
Billups, Chauncey	11	20	13	16	9	13	7	2	32
Blaylock, Mookie	15	26	8	11	13	23	10	3	39
Blount, Corie	7	13	9	13	17	7	5	3	17
Blount, Mark	5	7	6	7	11	3	3	5	12
Bogues, Muggsy	11	20	10	11	10	19	7	2	24
Bohannon, Etdrick	2	3	5	8	6	1	1	2	7
Booth, Calvin	7	11	4	6	11	3	3	6	18
Bowdler, Cal	6	10	4	4	8	2	2	3	15
Bowen, Bruce	7	16	6	9	9	5	6	4	20
Bowen, Ryan	5	9	4	6	11	2	5	2	12
Bowman, Ira	1	2	1	2	2	5	1	0	2
Boykins, Earl	8	14	5	6	5	10	3	1	22
Bradley, Shawn	14	25	10	12	22	7	5	13	32
Brand, Elton	18	26	13	19	21	8	4	8	44
Brandon, Terrell	15	28	14	15	12	16	8	5	34
Brown, Chucky	12	17	10	10	14	6	4	3	30
Brown, P.J.	13	18	11	12	20	8	5	6	30
Brown, Dee	15	26	14	15	10	18	7	4	41
Brown, Randy	10	18	8	11	11	10	8	4	27
Brunson, Rick	6	15	6	8	6	12	4	1	19
Bryant, Kobe	20	35	23	26	14	12	6	5	51
Bryant, Mark	12	19	8	13	15	4	4	4	30
Buckner, Greg	9	13	7	8	11	5	6	3	25
Buechler, Jud	8	16	5	9	10	6	4	3	19
Buford, Rodney	8	13	4	5	8	5	3	2	17
Bullard, Matt	11	18	5	5	9	6	4	4	28
Burrell, Scott	10	19	7	10	11	7	6	4	26
Caffey, Jason	12	21	10	17	16	6	3	2	28
Camby, Marcus	16	28	13	16	23	7	4	11	37
Campbell, Elden	15	27	15	19	20	9	6	9	40
Cardinal, Brian	3	7	3	5	4	1	3	1	9
Carr, Chris	9	19	9	12	11	5	3	5	24
Carter, Anthony	9	15	7	8	8	13	5	2	21
Carter, Vince	20	36	22	27	15	11	4	6	51
Cassell, Sam	18	27	19	20	10	19	6	3	40
Cato, Kelvin	11	16	8	8	15	3	3	8	27
Causwell, Duane	10	17	8	12	16	5	5	9	22
Ceballos, Cedric	21	31	17	20	17	7	6	3	50
Chapman, Rex	17	32	13	13	11	11	5	3	39
Cheaney, Calbert	14	26	9	11	13	9	5	4	32
Childs, Chris	10	23	13	14	11	17	5	2	30
Christie, Doug	13	25	14	16	15	13	9	7	35
Clark, Keon	13	20	6	10	22	5	3	12	29

INDIVIDUAL CAREER HIGHS

Player	FGM	FGA	FTM	FTA	REB	AST	STL	BLK	PTS
Cleaves, Mateen	7	14	6	8	7	9	5	1	19
Coker, John	4	9	2	2	5	1	1	2	8
Coleman, Derrick	15	28	18	20	24	11	6	9	42
Coles, Bimbo	11	20	12	13	9	15	7	2	26
Collier, Jason	5	10	6	8	4	2	1	2	12
Colson, Sean	3	5	1	2	2	6	1	0	6
Corbin, Tyrone	15	27	9	11	19	10	8	5	36
Crawford, Chris	10	17	9	10	9	5	3	4	27
Crawford, Jamal	7	16	6	7	7	7	5	2	17
Croshere, Austin	11	20	15	16	13	5	4	5	32
Crotty, John	8	12	9	10	6	11	4	1	19
Cummings, Vonteego	10	21	13	14	8	13	5	2	23
Curley, Bill	6	11	6	6	10	3	3	3	15
Curry, Michael	11	15	8	8	7	8	4	2	25
Curry, Dell	15	26	9	12	11	10	7	3	38
Dampier, Erick	9	19	12	16	18	6	3	6	23
Daniels, Antonio	10	18	8	10	10	12	4	3	26
David, Kornel	8	15	11	16	11	3	4	2	20
Davis, Antonio	13	22	15	17	19	6	5	6	31
Davis, Baron	9	18	9	12	10	14	7	3	28
Davis, Dale	11	17	11	18	22	6	5	7	28
Davis, Emanual	7	13	6	6	7	8	4	3	19
Davis, Hubert	12	20	9	9	8	8	3	2	32
Davis, Terry	13	21	9	15	21	4	5	3	35
Davis, Ricky	12	20	8	9	9	6	3	2	32
Day, Todd	13	29	14	18	11	6	7	4	41
DeClercq, Andrew	9	15	7	10	17	5	5	4	19
Delk, Tony	20	27	13	15	11	13	5	3	53
Del Negro, Vinny	13	20	12	15	10	13	5	2	31
Dial, Derrick	6	10	2	4	7	4	1	1	15
Dickerson, Michael	17	28	11	12	9	10	4	5	40
Divac, Vlade	15	26	14	19	24	13	6	12	34
Doleac, Michael	11	21	6	9	13	5	3	4	25
Dooling, Keyon	5	10	6	8	6	7	4	2	14
Douglas, Sherman	15	26	13	17	10	22	6	2	42
Drew, Bryce	10	20	4	6	6	11	3	2	24
Dudley, Chris	7	16	9	18	21	4	4	7	20
Duncan, Tim	19	31	16	24	23	11	8	8	46
Edney, Tyus	8	17	15	15	8	14	5	1	23
Edwards, Kevin	14	26	13	15	12	12	6	4	34
Eisley, Howard	9	20	7	8	10	13	4	2	27
Ekezie, Obinna	6	11	7	9	8	3	3	1	13
El-Amin, Khalid	8	16	10	10	7	9	4	1	21
Elie, Mario	10	17	11	12	15	13	6	3	27
Elliott, Sean	16	26	14	16	17	12	6	4	41
Ellis, LaPhonso	14	27	12	16	19	8	4	6	39
Ellison, Pervis	14	28	12	14	22	7	5	8	31
Eschmeyer, Evan	5	10	4	7	13	4	3	4	12
Ewing, Patrick	22	37	18	23	26	11	5	9	51
Feick, Jamie	8	14	7	11	25	4	4	4	17
Ferry, Danny	12	21	9	10	16	8	5	4	32
Finley, Michael	16	36	12	16	14	13	10	3	39
Fisher, Derek	8	16	8	10	11	13	6	1	26
Fizer, Marcus	12	24	6	8	13	4	3	3	26
Fortson, Danny	11	20	13	19	24	5	3	3	26
Foster, Greg	8	14	7	8	15	4	2	3	18
Foster, Jeff	6	10	5	9	14	2	2	2	15
Fox, Rick	14	23	17	18	16	10	6	4	34
Foyle, Adonal	9	16	4	7	17	3	2	8	20
Francis, Steve	13	25	14	15	17	14	6	4	36
Fuller, Todd	7	14	10	10	15	3	3	3	18
Funderburke, Lawrence	9	15	8	10	15	4	2	3	18
Garces, Ruben	3	8	1	4	11	1	1	1	6
Garner, Chris	6	11	2	2	4	7	3	1	13
Garnett, Kevin	17	33	13	18	23	11	7	8	40
Garrett, Dean	11	15	7	8	21	4	4	7	25
Garrity, Pat	12	17	5	9	8	5	3	2	32
Gatling, Chris	17	26	12	16	20	5	4	4	38
Geiger, Matt	14	26	11	12	21	6	5	5	29
George, Devean	5	13	5	6	9	4	2	2	14
Gill, Eddie	4	7	2	2	2	5	1	1	9
Gill, Kendall	17	27	18	22	13	12	11	6	41
Glover, Dion	10	20	7	9	9	5	4	2	28
Goldwire, Anthony	9	21	8	10	7	15	4	1	22
Goodrich, Steve	1	3	1	2	7	3	1	1	4
Grant, Brian	14	23	14	17	24	6	5	6	34
Grant, Gary	13	23	9	10	11	21	8	3	31
Grant, Horace	15	22	13	14	23	10	5	7	31
Green, A.C.	14	23	17	21	20	8	6	5	35
Griffin, Adrian	7	15	9	12	15	7	5	3	23
Gugliotta, Tom	17	28	18	20	20	11	8	5	39
Guyton, A.J.	8	18	4	4	4	5	2	1	24
Ham, Darvin	6	9	7	10	13	5	4	3	13

Player	FGM	FGA	FTM	FTA	REB	AST	STL	BLK	PTS
Hamilton, Richard	17	27	14	14	9	8	3	2	41
Hamilton, Zendon	1	6	3	4	4	0	0	0	5
Hammonds, Tom	14	24	11	14	17	5	3	3	31
Hardaway, Anfernee	17	27	17	20	13	19	7	4	42
Hardaway, Tim	17	33	15	19	11	22	8	3	45
Harper, Ron	19	31	16	20	16	15	10	5	40
Harpring, Matt	9	18	10	12	12	7	4	3	28
Harrington, Al	9	19	9	12	16	7	5	2	22
Harrington, Othella	11	20	13	14	20	4	4	4	27
Harris, Lucious	12	23	10	10	12	7	5	2	31
Hart, Jason	1	1	0	0	0	1	0	0	2
Harvey, Antonio	8	15	4	8	11	3	3	3	18
Harvey, Donnell	2	4	3	4	4	1	1	1	5
Hawkins, Hersey	14	25	15	17	14	11	9	3	43
Hawkins, Michael	5	10	4	4	5	10	3	1	14
Henderson, Alan	16	21	11	18	15	5	6	4	39
Henderson, Cedric	12	21	9	12	10	5	4	3	30
Herren, Chris	5	11	5	6	7	9	3	1	18
Hill, Grant	17	35	18	22	18	14	6	4	46
Hill, Tyrone	12	20	11	16	20	5	5	3	29
Hoiberg, Fred	9	18	11	11	10	13	5	3	28
Horry, Robert	16	26	9	12	15	10	6	6	40
House, Eddie	10	17	3	4	5	8	2	0	23
Houston, Allan	16	30	14	15	11	8	4	3	39
Howard, Juwan	19	29	15	17	15	9	5	5	42
Hudson, Troy	12	22	8	9	7	14	3	1	30
Hughes, Larry	16	32	12	15	12	11	7	4	44
Hunter, Lindsey	12	26	16	18	11	15	7	2	35
Ilgauskas, Zydrunas	12	21	10	13	18	5	3	6	32
Iverson, Allen	20	40	17	23	11	15	9	3	54
Jackson, Bobby	11	20	8	8	13	14	6	1	28
Jackson, Jim	17	36	16	18	14	12	7	3	50
Jackson, Jaren	11	20	7	8	8	8	5	3	31
Jackson, Marc	12	19	15	16	16	6	3	5	31
Jackson, Mark	14	27	12	15	16	22	8	2	34
Jackson, Stephen	9	18	6	8	11	6	4	1	25
Jacobson, Sam	7	11	5	6	7	4	4	1	19
James, Tim	2	5	2	4	4	2	1	2	6
Jamison, Antawn	23	36	13	18	21	7	5	3	51
Johnson, Anthony	9	19	6	8	5	11	4	2	22
Johnson, Avery	12	20	12	13	10	20	6	3	29
Johnson, DerMarr	8	17	6	7	9	5	5	4	19
Johnson, Ervin	10	16	8	11	26	5	4	8	28
Johnson, Larry	16	27	18	19	23	14	5	3	44
Jones, Damon	8	18	5	5	7	13	3	1	25
Jones, Eddie	14	24	15	17	13	12	9	4	35
Jones, Jumaine	7	15	8	8	13	4	3	2	26
Jones, Popeye	11	20	8	10	28	7	5	5	25
Joseph, Garth	1	2	0	2	1	1	0	1	2
Keefe, Adam	12	14	9	12	17	6	4	3	30
Kemp, Shawn	15	29	20	22	22	12	7	10	42
Kerr, Steve	9	16	7	9	6	11	6	2	24
Kersey, Jerome	15	26	15	16	20	10	6	5	36
Ketner, Lari	2	5	2	2	8	1	2	1	6
Kidd, Jason	16	34	14	22	16	25	6	4	43
King, Gerard	9	15	6	8	16	4	4	2	20
Kittles, Kerry	14	27	13	15	13	9	6	4	40
Knight, Brevin	11	24	12	15	9	20	8	2	31
Knight, Travis	10	17	7	9	15	7	4	4	21
Kukoc, Toni	13	26	14	20	14	13	5	4	34
Laettner, Christian	12	25	18	21	19	9	6	5	37
LaFrentz, Raef	13	28	10	12	20	4	3	9	32
Langdon, Trajan	11	16	6	6	7	5	3	1	31
Langhi, Dan	5	11	4	5	5	1	1	1	13
Lenard, Voshon	13	21	9	10	12	8	3	2	38
Lewic, Quincy	6	14	5	6	8	3	2	2	14
Lewis, Rashard	14	27	8	8	14	6	5	4	30
Livingston, Randy	10	20	6	6	7	7	3	2	23
Long, Art	0	1	0	2	2	1	0	1	0
Long, Grant	13	23	12	15	21	9	7	6	33
Longley, Luc	10	23	8	9	19	8	5	7	24
Lopez, Felipe	10	20	8	10	11	6	4	3	26
Lue, Tyronn	5	10	4	6	7	6	3	0	15
Lynch, George	12	19	8	10	20	6	7	4	30
MacCulloch, Todd	8	12	6	8	13	3	2	5	21
MacLean, Don	14	27	13	16	15	7	3	2	38
Madsen, Mark	6	9	3	4	10	2	2	1	15
Maggette, Corey	9	14	10	14	15	5	2	2	23
Magloire, Jamaal	5	10	7	10	10	2	2	6	16
Majerle, Dan	15	27	14	15	15	13	6	4	37
Malone, Karl	22	34	20	28	23	10	7	5	61
Maloney, Matt	10	18	11	13	7	12	4	2	24
Manning, Danny	21	32	15	19	18	11	7	6	43

Player	FGM	FGA	FTM	FTA	REB	AST	STL	BLK	PTS
Marbury, Stephon	17	34	15	20	11	20	5	2	50
Marion, Shawn	16	23	11	13	19	8	6	6	38
Marshall, Donyell	16	26	11	14	23	7	5	6	37
Martin, Darrick	10	21	15	15	6	13	6	2	38
Martin, Kenyon	12	20	6	10	15	11	6	5	26
Mashburn, Jamal	19	37	15	18	15	14	5	3	50
Mason, Anthony	12	21	15	16	22	12	5	4	31
Mason, Desmond	11	19	4	6	17	4	4	3	25
Massenburg, Tony	13	27	10	14	16	3	4	4	34
Maxwell, Vernon	15	33	19	22	11	14	6	3	51
McCarty, Walter	9	16	10	11	13	6	5	3	27
McClintock, Dan	4	6	0	4	8	1	0	1	8
McCloud, George	14	28	8	10	12	22	7	3	37
McCoy, Jelani	6	10	4	8	13	4	2	5	15
McDyess, Antonio	17	32	15	21	21	7	5	7	46
McGrady, Tracy	19	35	15	19	15	11	5	7	49
McIlvaine, Jim	5	10	6	8	16	3	4	9	12
McInnis, Jeff	14	24	8	9	12	13	5	2	33
McKey, Derrick	15	25	15	15	17	11	5	6	34
McKie, Aaron	10	19	7	9	12	14	7	3	25
McLeod, Roshown	11	22	6	6	10	6	3	3	24
McPherson, Paul	11	14	6	7	6	4	4	1	26
Medvedenko, Stanislav	5	8	3	4	4	1	1	1	10
Mercer, Ron	16	32	11	12	10	10	7	3	39
Mihm, Chris	8	17	7	8	15	2	3	5	18
Miles, Darius	12	19	8	12	13	4	3	8	26
Miller, Andre	12	24	12	15	10	17	4	2	30
Miller, Anthony	8	14	7	9	15	4	5	2	19
Miller, Brad	9	19	14	17	16	5	3	3	32
Miller, Mike	11	21	6	7	11	6	3	2	28
Miller, Reggie	16	29	21	23	12	11	6	3	57
Mills, Chris	11	21	10	12	17	8	5	4	30
Mills, Terry	16	28	11	13	19	9	3	4	41
Mitchell, Sam	14	24	13	15	17	7	6	5	37
Mobley, Cuttino	14	29	14	16	11	11	5	3	41
Mohammed, Nazr	10	17	8	10	19	2	3	5	24
Moiso, Jerome	2	6	3	4	5	1	1	2	5
Montross, Eric	13	17	9	13	18	4	3	5	28
Moore, Mikki	7	10	8	10	12	3	2	4	16
Mottola, Hanno	5	10	4	6	7	2	2	1	11
Mourning, Alonzo	19	34	17	24	22	7	4	9	50
Mullin, Chris	19	32	17	19	18	14	7	4	47
Murray, Lamond	15	27	9	12	17	7	6	5	38
Murray, Tracy	18	29	9	11	12	5	5	3	50
Mutombo, Dikembe	14	28	15	21	31	7	5	12	39
Nailon, Lee	6	11	4	4	7	3	2	1	15
Najera, Eduardo	4	9	4	7	12	3	2	1	10
Nash, Steve	12	22	10	11	8	17	5	1	31
N'diaye, Mamadou	1	2	2	2	2	0	0	0	2
Nesby, Tyrone	13	23	13	13	12	8	7	2	30
Nesterovic, Rasho	11	16	5	8	13	4	2	8	23
Newble, Ira	5	11	3	4	7	2	1	2	14
Newman, Johnny	14	25	18	22	11	8	7	3	41
Norris, Moochie	10	20	8	9	8	10	4	1	28
Nowitzki, Dirk	13	26	15	17	17	8	5	5	38
Oakley, Charles	14	27	13	15	35	15	5	6	35
Odom, Lamar	13	24	14	15	16	11	5	9	34
Olajuwon, Hakeem	24	40	17	20	25	12	8	12	52
Ollie, Kevin	6	11	6	7	10	10	3	1	14
Olowokandi, Michael	12	20	7	10	20	4	3	7	27
O'Neal, Jermaine	14	25	10	14	20	5	3	8	30
O'Neal, Shaquille	24	40	19	31	28	9	5	15	61
Ostertag, Greg	10	15	9	13	20	4	3	11	25
Outlaw, Bo	11	17	8	12	17	10	6	9	29
Overton, Doug	11	17	8	9	8	18	6	1	30
Owens, Billy	15	27	9	14	22	11	6	4	34
Oyedeji, Olumide	4	6	2	2	14	2	1	2	10
Pack, Robert	13	27	14	16	10	22	6	3	35
Padgett, Scott	5	10	5	6	10	3	2	2	16
Palacio, Milt	7	12	7	9	7	7	3	0	19
Panko, Andy	0	0	0	0	0	0	0	0	0
Parks, Cherokee	10	17	8	10	14	5	4	5	25
Patterson, Andrae	5	10	6	8	7	3	3	1	12
Patterson, Ruben	12	21	11	13	15	8	6	4	32
Payton, Gary	18	32	14	20	16	17	8	3	44
Peeler, Anthony	13	28	13	13	10	10	6	3	40
Penberthy, Mike	7	9	5	6	4	5	2	1	16
Perdue, Will	9	14	9	14	23	5	3	9	21
Perkins, Sam	19	29	14	16	20	10	7	5	45
Perry, Elliot	14	22	9	10	7	17	6	1	35
Person, Wesley	14	23	11	11	15	7	6	4	33
Peterson, Morris	10	19	8	10	9	6	3	2	29
Piatkowski, Eric	11	19	12	13	13	6	5	3	35

Player	FGM	FGA	FTM	FTA	REB	AST	STL	BLK	PTS
Pierce, Paul	16	30	18	21	15	9	9	4	44
Pippen, Scottie	19	34	13	21	18	15	9	5	47
Pollard, Scot	10	15	10	12	18	4	5	5	22
Polynice, Olden	13	22	9	13	25	8	4	7	30
Pope, Mark	4	8	4	6	7	3	1	4	10
Porter, Chris	9	21	7	9	11	5	4	2	24
Porter, Terry	15	26	14	16	13	19	8	3	40
Posey, James	9	17	10	11	19	9	5	4	25
Postell, Lavor	3	5	5	6	3	2	2	1	10
Potapenko, Vitaly	10	21	11	12	18	7	5	3	26
Price, Brent	10	18	9	12	9	14	5	2	30
Profit, Laron	8	17	12	12	8	14	7	2	18
Przybilla, Joel	1	3	1	3	9	1	1	3	3
Radojevic, Aleksandar	2	5	2	4	8	1	1	1	6
Ratliff, Theo	12	17	11	14	17	4	4	9	27
Recasner, Eldridge	9	15	8	8	11	12	4	1	26
Redd, Michael	3	11	2	4	3	1	1	0	8
Reeves, Bryant	18	28	14	18	18	7	4	7	41
Reid, Don	10	15	5	8	17	5	4	5	25
Reid, J.R.	12	22	11	16	20	6	6	4	29
Rice, Glen	20	36	16	18	17	9	6	4	56
Richardson, Quentin	8	18	5	7	11	4	4	1	21
Richmond, Mitch	18	34	16	19	13	13	7	3	47
Rider, Isaiah	18	36	15	18	15	11	4	3	42
Roberson, Terrance	0	1	0	0	1	1	0	0	0
Robinson, Clifford	18	30	15	19	16	9	6	7	50
Robinson, David	26	41	18	25	24	11	7	12	71
Robinson, Eddie	10	16	5	7	10	4	4	3	21
Robinson, Glenn	19	33	17	20	17	10	5	4	45
Robinson, Jamal	1	8	0	0	3	1	2	0	2
Robinson, James	12	22	9	11	8	11	4	2	30
Robinson, Larry	8	14	4	5	8	5	4	1	21
Rogers, Carlos	12	20	8	12	17	7	4	7	28
Rogers, Rodney	14	23	11	14	21	9	6	5	36
Rooks, Sean	12	21	10	14	18	6	5	5	28
Rose, Jalen	17	34	15	15	13	20	4	6	42
Rose, Malik	10	16	12	14	14	4	4	5	26
Ruffin, Michael	5	7	8	16	18	4	3	5	14
Russell, Bryon	10	19	12	12	15	6	6	3	25
Sabonis, Arvydas	11	20	12	16	20	9	5	6	33
Samake, Soumaila	2	5	2	4	7	1	1	2	5
Sanchez, Pepe	2	3	2	2	3	6	3	1	4
Santiago, Daniel	7	13	5	6	8	2	2	3	15
Schrempf, Detlef	14	25	22	23	23	14	4	3	36
Scott, Shawnelle	4	12	6	8	14	1	2	4	14
Shaw, Brian	14	24	10	12	15	17	7	4	32
Skinner, Brian	8	15	7	10	17	2	3	4	23
Slater, Reggie	9	18	9	12	11	5	3	3	21
Smith, Tony	11	23	9	12	10	9	5	2	25
Smith, Jabari	4	8	2	2	4	3	4	0	9
Smith, Joe	16	28	13	15	20	6	5	6	38
Smith, Michael	9	15	9	12	18	7	7	4	20
Smith, Mike	5	9	4	4	3	3	1	1	11
Smith, Steve	14	28	18	21	14	15	5	4	41
Snow, Eric	9	19	10	11	8	15	6	3	25
Spencer, Felton	9	19	10	12	19	4	3	7	23
Sprewell, Latrell	18	31	22	25	13	13	8	5	46
Stackhouse, Jerry	21	36	18	21	15	11	7	5	57
Starks, John	15	36	12	15	10	14	7	3	39
Stepania, Vladimir	5	13	7	11	10	3	3	3	17
Stevenson, DeShawn	4	8	4	6	4	3	2	1	11
Stewart, Michael	6	12	5	6	19	4	2	9	14
Stith, Bryant	14	21	16	16	12	8	5	3	37
Stockton, John	14	22	15	16	9	28	9	3	34
Stojakovic, Predrag	14	29	11	12	17	7	5	2	39
Stoudamire, Damon	15	37	14	15	12	19	5	2	36
Strickland, Erick	12	20	13	17	11	11	7	2	36
Strickland, Mark	11	18	6	8	13	4	3	4	23
Strickland, Rod	15	25	16	18	12	20	6	3	37
Strong, Derek	10	23	11	12	16	4	3	2	27
Sundov, Bruno	8	14	2	2	9	1	1	1	17
Sura, Bob	13	25	9	12	13	13	6	3	31
Swift, Stromile	7	11	5	8	11	3	4	5	17
Szczerbiak, Wally	13	21	9	10	12	10	4	2	28
Tabak, Zan	12	16	5	8	16	6	3	4	26
Tarlac, Dragan	4	7	4	6	9	4	1	3	10
Taylor, Maurice	13	24	12	15	20	5	4	3	34
Terry, Jason	14	27	12	12	8	13	6	2	38
Thomas, Jamel	4	10	1	1	7	2	1	0	9
Thomas, Kenny	9	18	8	12	22	6	4	3	22
Thomas, Kurt	11	24	10	12	18	5	4	4	29
Thomas, Tim	13	21	10	13	12	6	4	4	39
Thorpe, Otis	15	27	14	19	26	11	6	4	40

Player	FGM	FGA	FTM	FTA	REB	AST	STL	BLK	PTS
Traylor, Robert	7	11	8	12	10	3	4	6	17
Trent, Gary	14	25	13	20	16	7	3	3	33
Tsakalidis, Iakovos	6	10	6	8	12	2	2	5	17
Turkoglu, Hidayet	6	12	11	11	12	4	3	3	18
Van Exel, Nick	16	32	14	15	10	23	5	3	44
Van Horn, Keith	13	30	15	17	18	5	4	6	35
Vanterpool, David	7	11	7	7	6	7	2	2	21
Vaughn, Jacque	6	13	11	12	8	15	3	2	18
Vaught, Loy	15	26	12	13	21	7	6	4	33
Voskuhl, Jake	3	6	2	2	5	2	1	2	6
Walker, Antoine	21	36	16	18	21	13	6	4	49
Walker, Samaki	11	22	8	10	20	4	3	5	26
Wallace, Ben	9	14	6	16	28	6	6	8	20
Wallace, John	14	28	11	12	12	6	4	5	30
Wallace, Rasheed	17	27	12	17	18	7	6	6	42
Wang, Zhizhi	5	10	3	4	3	0	0	0	13
Ward, Charlie	8	18	8	8	11	17	6	4	25
Weatherspoon, Clarence	14	26	12	19	23	13	7	7	35
Webber, Chris	24	47	17	23	26	13	8	9	51
Wells, Bonzi	12	20	10	12	14	7	7	2	29
Wesley, David	15	22	13	13	10	15	7	2	37
West, Doug	16	26	10	12	11	9	4	3	39
White, Jahidi	9	16	10	15	16	2	3	7	23
Whitney, Chris	11	20	11	12	7	14	6	1	29
Williams, Aaron	11	18	9	10	19	6	4	5	27
Williams, Alvin	10	19	7	9	10	14	4	3	23
Williams, Eric	12	20	13	19	11	6	5	2	31
Williams, Jason	12	25	9	10	9	18	5	2	28
Williams, Jerome	11	16	10	14	21	4	7	3	26
Williams, Scott	12	18	9	12	20	5	4	4	24
Williams, Shammond	9	18	6	8	7	10	4	1	28
Williams, Monty	14	26	10	12	10	6	3	4	30
Williams, Walt	13	29	14	17	15	9	6	6	40
Williamson, Corliss	16	27	12	15	16	7	5	3	40
Willis, Kevin	16	31	12	16	33	8	5	6	39
Wingate, David	11	24	11	13	13	15	7	3	28
Wolkowyski, Ruben	3	7	5	5	4	1	1	2	7
Wright, Lorenzen	12	22	9	14	25	5	4	5	32

CAREER SINGLE-GAME HIGHS, PLAYOFFS
THROUGH 2000-01 SEASON

Player	FGM	FGA	FTM	FTA	REB	AST	STL	BLK	PTS
Abdul-Rauf, Mahmoud	9	21	6	6	4	6	1	1	23
Abdul-Wahad, Tariq	5	9	6	6	5	3	3	1	16
Alexander, Cory	3	6	2	2	3	3	1	0	8
Allen, Ray	15	25	11	13	11	10	3	2	41
Alston, Rafer	0	2	0	2	0	1	0	0	0
Amaechi, John	2	4	3	4	2	2	2	2	5
Anderson, Derek	6	16	8	10	5	6	2	1	18
Anderson, Kenny	9	15	9	13	5	11	3	1	30
Anderson, Nick	10	26	8	10	12	7	6	3	29
Anderson, Shandon	7	13	6	8	11	3	2	1	17
Anthony, Greg	5	13	5	7	6	8	4	1	16
Armstrong, Darrell	6	14	7	7	10	8	4	1	21
Augmon, Stacey	7	14	9	11	8	6	3	2	23
Austin, Isaac	5	9	6	8	8	4	3	2	12
Avery, Will	3	5	0	0	1	1	0	1	7
Baker, Vin	12	20	7	12	12	3	4	3	28
Barros, Dana	5	9	3	4	3	4	3	0	12
Barry, Brent	5	12	7	8	7	4	2	3	17
Barry, Jon	6	12	6	8	5	4	2	1	17
Bell, Raja	4	6	2	6	4	2	3	0	10
Bender, Jonathan	2	3	3	4	1	0	1	0	4
Benoit, David	8	16	5	6	11	3	2	3	20
Best, Travis	8	15	11	12	11	12	4	1	24
Billups, Chauncey	1	4	1	1	4	2	0	0	3
Blaylock, Mookie	11	25	9	9	12	18	8	3	31
Blount, Corie	4	6	3	6	11	2	3	3	8
Bogues, Muggsy	7	14	4	6	9	15	5	0	19
Booth, Calvin	7	10	2	2	6	1	2	2	16
Bowen, Bruce	3	8	3	4	3	2	2	2	11
Bowman, Ira	0	1	0	2	0	1	0	0	0
Bradley, Shawn	5	9	7	9	12	1	1	6	10
Brandon, Terrell	10	19	7	8	9	12	4	2	28
Brown, Chucky	6	11	4	6	8	2	3	2	16
Brown, P.J.	8	17	8	10	16	3	3	4	20
Brown, Dee	9	17	8	10	9	10	2	2	22
Brown, Randy	4	10	4	4	5	3	2	1	9
Brunson, Rick	2	2	3	4	1	1	1	0	4
Bryant, Kobe	19	35	17	19	16	11	4	4	48

Player	FGM	FGA	FTM	FTA	REB	AST	STL	BLK	PTS
Bryant, Mark	8	16	5	6	9	1	2	3	21
Buckner, Greg	4	7	5	8	12	2	2	0	14
Buechler, Jud	4	7	2	2	6	2	2	2	8
Buford, Rodney	4	8	2	2	3	1	2	1	11
Bullard, Matt	3	9	4	4	5	4	1	2	12
Burrell, Scott	9	11	2	2	9	4	2	2	23
Caffey, Jason	6	8	8	8	11	4	1	2	13
Camby, Marcus	9	15	9	13	18	4	4	6	21
Campbell, Elden	12	22	11	12	18	4	3	5	29
Carr, Chris	6	9	3	3	4	3	2	1	17
Carter, Anthony	6	13	4	4	7	13	4	2	15
Carter, Vince	19	31	13	16	10	9	4	4	50
Cassell, Sam	10	23	13	15	16	13	3	2	33
Cato, Kelvin	3	6	4	5	4	1	1	3	10
Causwell, Duane	1	2	4	4	3	1	1	0	4
Ceballos, Cedric	10	20	8	10	12	6	4	3	25
Chapman, Rex	12	22	9	12	5	5	2	0	42
Cheaney, Calbert	10	18	6	6	5	2	2	1	26
Childs, Chris	9	17	6	7	9	10	5	1	25
Christie, Doug	5	13	5	8	8	5	4	2	17
Clark, Keon	2	7	7	8	6	1	1	1	9
Coleman, Derrick	13	26	21	25	21	9	3	9	33
Coles, Bimbo	7	13	5	7	6	7	4	1	18
Corbin, Tyrone	11	16	8	8	14	6	5	2	28
Crawford, Chris	7	14	9	11	6	2	1	1	26
Croshere, Austin	7	15	12	12	11	5	3	2	24
Crotty, John	3	6	3	3	3	5	1	1	8
Curley, Bill	0	0	0	0	0	0	0	0	0
Curry, Michael	5	11	4	6	2	2	1	1	14
Curry, Dell	12	17	4	4	7	5	6	1	27
Daniels, Antonio	9	16	12	12	5	9	3	1	24
Davis, Antonio	11	16	9	12	15	4	3	4	23
Davis, Baron	10	16	7	9	8	8	6	3	29
Davis, Dale	8	13	6	10	18	3	4	5	20
Davis, Emanual	0	0	0	0	0	0	0	0	0
Davis, Hubert	5	10	6	7	4	4	3	2	15
Davis, Ricky	0	0	0	0	0	0	0	0	0
Day, Todd	5	9	5	8	5	2	2	1	16
DeClercq, Andrew	3	5	2	4	6	1	2	1	6
Delk, Tony	8	15	7	10	7	4	2	0	18
Del Negro, Vinny	13	19	5	5	7	8	3	1	29
Dial, Derrick	2	4	1	2	2	0	0	0	5
Dickerson, Michael	4	9	1	2	2	2	1	1	11
Divac, Vlade	12	22	10	15	19	8	3	5	30
Doleac, Michael	4	9	3	4	7	1	1	1	11
Douglas, Sherman	9	22	6	7	9	15	4	1	21
Drew, Bryce	1	1	0	2	3	2	0	0	2
Dudley, Chris	6	7	3	6	12	2	3	4	14
Duncan, Tim	15	26	19	23	22	7	4	6	40
Edney, Tyus	7	13	5	6	6	5	3	0	17
Edwards, Kevin	6	15	5	5	5	3	3	1	16
Eisley, Howard	9	15	5	5	4	9	3	2	21
Elie, Mario	11	16	10	10	9	11	4	1	22
Elliott, Sean	9	21	14	16	11	8	3	2	26
Ellis, LaPhonso	10	20	9	10	17	4	2	3	27
Ellison, Pervis	5	8	2	2	10	1	1	3	10
Ewing, Patrick	18	34	17	18	22	10	7	8	45
Ferry, Danny	7	17	3	4	6	4	2	2	20
Finley, Michael	13	24	9	11	12	10	4	1	33
Fisher, Derek	11	13	6	6	8	10	4	1	28
Foster, Greg	6	10	6	7	6	2	1	2	17
Foster, Jeff	2	5	2	2	5	2	0	2	4
Fox, Rick	8	14	7	7	10	10	5	3	24
Fuller, Todd	3	4	3	4	6	0	0	1	7
Funderburke, Lawrence	4	11	1	2	6	1	3	2	8
Garnett, Kevin	11	22	8	12	18	11	3	5	25
Garrett, Dean	11	17	4	5	15	3	2	2	26
Garrity, Pat	6	11	3	3	6	2	1	1	16
Gatling, Chris	10	18	6	9	12	2	2	3	24
Geiger, Matt	10	18	6	8	13	2	2	2	23
George, Devean	3	5	1	2	2	1	1	0	7
Gill, Kendall	12	24	6	9	10	6	6	2	30
Grant, Brian	10	14	9	13	15	3	2	3	23
Grant, Gary	3	10	2	2	3	8	2	1	6
Grant, Horace	14	17	8	9	20	7	6	5	29
Green, A.C.	9	16	10	15	20	7	3	3	25
Gugliotta, Tom	10	21	5	6	10	5	4	3	27
Ham, Darvin	4	6	4	8	8	3	1	4	9
Hammonds, Tom	5	11	5	6	7	2	0	1	12
Hardaway, Anfernee	16	30	13	17	12	15	5	3	42
Hardaway, Tim	15	29	9	15	8	20	8	2	38
Harper, Ron	12	25	7	10	12	9	6	4	31
Harpring, Matt	4	11	6	7	10	3	1	0	10

Player	FGM	FGA	FTM	FTA	REB	AST	STL	BLK	PTS
Harrington, Al	1	5	1	2	2	2	0	0	3
Harrington, Othella	5	8	4	4	9	1	3	1	12
Harris, Lucious	2	3	3	4	6	1	2	0	4
Harvey, Antonio	0	1	0	0	4	0	0	0	0
Hawkins, Hersey	14	26	15	15	10	8	6	4	39
Hawkins, Michael	0	1	2	2	0	0	0	0	2
Henderson, Alan	9	15	5	6	9	2	2	2	22
Henderson, Cedric	4	9	5	8	6	5	4	0	9
Hill, Grant	11	27	11	13	14	11	3	2	28
Hill, Tyrone	8	14	10	14	15	2	4	3	20
Hoiberg, Fred	2	7	2	2	3	1	2	0	6
Horry, Robert	10	18	7	11	17	8	7	5	24
House, Eddie	6	18	3	3	3	2	1	1	16
Houston, Allan	14	25	12	12	9	6	4	1	34
Howard, Juwan	8	18	7	9	12	3	1	2	21
Hudson, Troy	2	7	3	4	6	3	1	0	6
Hughes, Larry	5	12	6	6	8	3	3	3	14
Hunter, Lindsey	11	17	3	5	9	5	3	1	26
Ilgauskas, Zydrunas	10	14	5	8	10	2	1	2	25
Iverson, Allen	21	41	13	16	12	16	10	2	54
Jackson, Bobby	6	9	4	6	9	5	4	1	16
Jackson, Jim	4	10	9	9	4	6	2	1	17
Jackson, Jaren	9	15	4	6	11	4	3	1	22
Jackson, Mark	11	24	10	11	14	17	5	1	28
Johnson, Anthony	2	7	2	2	4	4	1	1	7
Johnson, Avery	12	18	8	12	8	18	6	2	30
Johnson, Ervin	6	9	8	10	17	3	2	5	12
Johnson, Larry	11	20	10	13	13	6	4	1	31
Jones, Eddie	12	21	10	14	11	8	5	6	32
Jones, Jumaine	6	15	4	8	9	3	2	2	16
Keefe, Adam	8	11	4	7	8	4	3	2	18
Kemp, Shawn	13	24	14	16	20	6	6	7	33
Kerr, Steve	5	9	6	6	4	6	3	1	15
Kersey, Jerome	14	23	12	15	16	8	6	4	34
Kidd, Jason	9	22	4	7	12	16	6	2	23
King, Gerard	1	2	0	0	1	1	0	1	2
Kittles, Kerry	9	17	4	4	7	4	2	1	23
Knight, Brevin	4	8	3	6	7	7	4	1	11
Knight, Travis	4	5	2	2	5	1	1	1	9
Kukoc, Toni	11	17	7	9	11	11	4	3	30
Laettner, Christian	11	25	10	12	12	6	5	3	26
Lenard, Voshon	10	17	8	9	7	5	2	2	28
Lewis, Quincy	2	9	2	3	4	2	1	3	6
Lewis, Rashard	8	17	8	8	10	2	2	2	20
Livingston, Randy	4	6	4	4	4	3	2	1	12
Long, Grant	10	16	12	14	14	6	6	2	26
Longley, Luc	8	13	7	8	10	6	2	6	19
Lopez, Felipe	3	7	1	2	3	3	2	0	8
Lue, Tyronn	6	16	3	3	3	6	5	1	12
Lynch, George	7	12	5	6	14	6	4	2	17
MacCulloch, Todd	5	9	3	4	5	3	0	1	13
Madsen, Mark	1	6	2	3	5	2	0	1	3
Magloire, Jamaal	3	4	2	8	8	1	0	2	8
Majerle, Dan	12	24	10	12	12	9	5	5	34
Malone, Karl	18	32	22	24	22	9	6	5	50
Maloney, Matt	9	19	5	6	4	6	2	2	26
Manning, Danny	14	25	9	13	12	8	3	3	35
Marbury, Stephon	10	25	6	8	5	13	4	0	28
Marion, Shawn	9	19	5	5	14	3	4	4	21
Marshall, Donyell	8	14	3	4	10	4	1	2	17
Martin, Darrick	5	12	5	7	3	6	1	0	16
Mashburn, Jamal	15	26	13	15	9	9	3	1	36
Mason, Anthony	13	18	8	12	15	7	5	2	29
Massenburg, Tony	0	0	0	0	0	0	0	0	0
Maxwell, Vernon	14	25	7	8	9	9	3	2	34
McCarty, Walter	1	1	0	0	0	0	1	0	2
McCloud, George	8	13	4	7	9	6	3	1	22
McCoy, Jelani	1	3	0	2	5	1	0	0	2
McDyess, Antonio	11	23	5	7	19	2	1	4	26
McGrady, Tracy	15	34	14	18	10	10	3	2	42
McIlvaine, Jim	4	7	1	2	3	1	1	3	8
McKey, Derrick	12	19	8	11	13	8	4	5	27
McKie, Aaron	9	20	9	9	10	13	4	2	25
McLeod, Roshown	4	9	2	2	1	1	1	1	10
Miller, Anthony	2	5	2	2	4	1	1	1	4
Miller, Brad	3	8	7	8	6	2	0	2	13
Miller, Mike	9	18	2	2	6	3	0	2	22
Miller, Reggie	15	27	17	19	11	7	4	2	41
Mills, Chris	10	17	5	6	10	5	5	2	25
Mills, Terry	7	14	4	6	10	4	3	1	17
Mitchell, Sam	7	14	5	6	7	3	1	1	19
Mobley, Cuttino	3	5	6	7	2	6	1	0	13
Mohammed, Nazr	0	0	0	0	0	0	0	0	0

Player	FGM	FGA	FTM	FTA	REB	AST	STL	BLK	PTS
Montross, Eric	2	4	2	2	6	1	0	2	6
Moore, Mikki	2	5	6	6	6	1	1	0	8
Mourning, Alonzo	13	26	15	18	20	4	3	9	34
Mullin, Chris	16	30	16	19	11	7	5	5	41
Murray, Lamond	4	10	5	5	5	1	2	2	15
Murray, Tracy	8	14	10	11	5	2	2	1	22
Mutombo, Dikembe	13	14	13	19	22	5	3	8	28
Najera, Eduardo	4	7	0	0	7	1	1	1	10
Nash, Steve	8	15	7	7	7	14	2	1	27
Nesterovic, Rasho	4	7	1	2	6	3	2	2	8
Newman, Johnny	14	25	10	14	6	6	3	2	34
Nowitzki, Dirk	14	24	14	18	18	2	6	2	42
Oakley, Charles	10	20	10	12	24	8	5	3	26
Olajuwon, Hakeem	20	34	18	20	26	10	6	10	49
Ollie, Kevin	3	5	6	6	4	4	2	0	8
O'Neal, Jermaine	8	16	3	6	20	3	0	6	16
O'Neal, Shaquille	21	33	18	39	24	9	4	8	46
Ostertag, Greg	7	10	7	7	15	2	2	9	16
Outlaw, Bo	8	10	3	6	14	3	4	4	17
Owens, Billy	13	23	8	10	17	6	3	1	27
Pack, Robert	8	15	11	12	4	8	6	1	23
Padgett, Scott	3	6	0	0	5	2	1	1	8
Parks, Cherokee	2	3	0	0	5	0	1	0	4
Patterson, Andrae	0	0	0	0	2	1	0	0	0
Patterson, Ruben	5	8	5	5	5	1	1	1	15
Payton, Gary	12	29	12	16	11	14	6	2	35
Peeler, Anthony	10	21	6	6	14	6	5	2	28
Perdue, Will	8	10	6	9	12	4	2	4	17
Perkins, Sam	13	22	11	13	19	5	4	5	29
Perry, Elliot	5	9	9	9	5	6	2	0	14
Person, Wesley	10	19	7	8	10	4	2	2	29
Peterson, Morris	7	11	2	2	4	7	2	0	17
Piatkowski, Eric	3	5	5	6	2	0	1	0	8
Pippen, Scottie	13	35	11	14	18	13	6	5	37
Pollard, Scot	5	8	4	6	14	1	2	3	11
Polynice, Olden	8	16	5	6	16	2	2	3	18
Pope, Mark	2	4	1	1	7	2	1	0	5
Porter, Terry	13	19	15	16	8	15	5	2	41
Potapenko, Vitaly	3	5	3	8	4	2	1	0	8
Price, Brent	6	9	4	4	4	7	4	1	18
Przybilla, Joel	0	0	0	0	0	0	0	0	0
Ratliff, Theo	10	16	6	7	12	2	3	6	26
Recasner, Eldridge	4	9	3	4	4	4	2	0	12
Reid, Don	3	4	4	4	5	1	1	2	8
Reid, J.R.	6	14	10	11	12	5	3	2	17
Rice, Glen	15	26	15	17	13	9	3	1	39
Richmond, Mitch	13	29	9	12	13	8	4	2	37
Rider, Isaiah	10	19	14	14	10	8	3	0	27
Robinson, Clifford	12	25	9	14	10	6	3	6	32
Robinson, David	14	27	18	23	22	11	4	8	40
Robinson, Eddie	7	9	2	2	6	3	2	1	14
Robinson, Glenn	11	22	7	8	12	11	4	3	29
Robinson, James	4	7	1	2	2	2	1	1	11
Rogers, Rodney	9	18	5	8	10	4	4	3	23
Rooks, Sean	4	8	4	4	7	2	2	2	10
Rose, Jalen	16	23	11	14	9	10	4	2	40
Rose, Malik	4	9	5	6	10	2	2	1	13
Russell, Bryon	12	20	9	11	12	5	4	2	29
Sabonis, Arvydas	10	22	16	20	15	8	3	4	27
Santiago, Daniel	1	2	0	0	5	0	0	2	2
Schrempf, Detlef	12	22	13	18	16	9	3	3	29
Scott, Shawnelle	1	2	1	1	1	0	0	1	3
Shaw, Brian	9	21	7	8	8	11	4	1	22
Slater, Reggie	3	8	1	2	6	0	1	2	6
Smith, Tony	5	10	4	5	3	3	2	1	15
Smith, Joe	5	14	3	4	10	3	1	3	12
Smith, Michael	2	5	3	6	9	3	1	2	7
Smith, Steve	13	31	12	14	9	9	4	3	35
Snow, Eric	7	17	6	9	7	13	3	1	20
Spencer, Felton	6	11	5	6	15	1	2	4	15
Sprewell, Latrell	13	27	15	19	10	10	5	2	35
Stackhouse, Jerry	10	22	11	13	7	4	1	1	26
Starks, John	11	21	11	14	11	12	5	1	30
Stevenson, DeShawn	1	2	0	0	1	0	0	0	2
Stewart, Michael	0	1	0	0	1	0	0	0	0
Stith, Bryant	7	13	14	14	8	5	2	2	22
Stockton, John	13	21	16	19	11	24	6	3	34
Stojakovic, Predrag	10	18	14	14	10	2	2	1	37
Stoudamire, Damon	10	22	7	8	7	14	2	1	25
Strickland, Mark	4	5	2	2	7	1	2	1	9
Strickland, Rod	12	23	10	11	10	17	4	2	30
Strong, Derek	6	14	7	9	16	2	1	1	18
Sura, Bob	2	4	2	3	3	4	1	0	4

– 283 –

Player	FGM	FGA	FTM	FTA	REB	AST	STL	BLK	PTS
Szczerbiak, Wally	6	12	8	11	6	3	2	2	20
Tabak, Zan	2	4	2	2	7	1	1	1	6
Thomas, Kurt	7	14	9	12	16	5	4	3	23
Thomas, Tim	8	16	9	10	12	4	1	2	19
Thorpe, Otis	12	17	11	14	17	6	4	2	28
Traylor, Robert	5	6	1	2	5	1	1	3	10
Trent, Gary	5	10	5	7	6	2	1	1	10
Tsakalidis, Iakovos	3	6	0	0	12	0	0	3	6
Turkoglu, Hidayet	8	10	4	4	6	3	1	1	22
Van Exel, Nick	13	23	9	13	8	12	4	1	34
Van Horn, Keith	5	12	8	11	5	1	0	0	18
Vaughn, Jacque	4	10	2	2	5	4	3	1	11
Vaught, Loy	9	15	3	4	11	2	3	1	20
Walker, Samaki	5	8	4	6	16	2	1	8	13
Wallace, Ben	0	0	0	0	0	0	0	0	0
Wallace, John	2	8	2	2	4	2	1	2	4
Wallace, Rasheed	13	26	11	13	13	5	5	4	34
Wang, Zhizhi	2	5	2	2	1	1	1	1	7
Ward, Charlie	8	13	4	4	7	14	6	2	20
Weatherspoon, Clarence	8	11	5	6	10	1	3	1	18
Webber, Chris	13	32	10	14	18	13	4	7	34
Wells, Bonzi	8	13	6	8	6	3	2	0	20
Wesley, David	9	17	6	10	5	12	5	1	27
West, Doug	6	10	6	6	2	3	1	1	16
Whitney, Chris	2	3	1	1	1	1	0	0	6
Williams, Aaron	0	2	2	2	1	0	0	1	2
Williams, Alvin	10	19	7	7	5	8	3	3	23
Williams, Jason	8	16	4	4	8	6	2	1	20
Williams, Jerome	5	10	4	7	10	3	3	2	11
Williams, Scott	9	14	5	6	16	4	3	4	21
Williams, Shammond	9	14	3	4	6	10	4	0	23
Williams, Monty	3	4	2	3	4	1	0	1	7
Williams, Walt	6	12	4	6	8	4	2	1	17
Williamson, Corliss	8	11	4	4	4	2	1	1	18
Willis, Kevin	12	24	8	11	16	4	4	4	27
Wingate, David	6	14	5	6	10	6	4	2	19
Wright, Lorenzen	6	13	5	5	9	1	2	2	17

PROMISING NEWCOMERS

ALLEN, MALIK   F   HEAT

PERSONAL: Born June 27, 1978, in Medford, N.J. ... 6-10/265. (2,08/120,2).
HIGH SCHOOL: Shawnee (Medford, N.J.).
COLLEGE: Villanova.
TRANSACTIONS/CAREER NOTES: Not drafted by an NBA franchise. ... Played in American Basketball Association 2000 with San Diego Wildfire (2000-01). ... Played in International Basketball League with Trenton Stars (2000-01). ... Signed as free agent by Miami Heat (July 20, 2001).

COLLEGIATE RECORD

Season Team	G	Min.	FGM	FGA	Pct.	FTM	FTA	Pct.	Reb.	Ast.	Pts.	RPG	APG	PPG
96-97—Villanova	33	357	24	51	.471	19	45	.422	96	13	67	2.9	0.4	2.0
97-98—Villanova	29	715	91	194	.469	58	80	.725	168	22	240	5.8	0.8	8.3
98-99—Villanova	32	887	136	241	.564	85	107	.794	201	31	357	6.3	1.0	11.2
99-00—Villanova	33	1103	184	360	.511	99	143	.692	243	32	467	7.4	1.0	14.2
Totals	127	3062	435	846	.514	261	375	.696	708	98	1131	5.6	0.8	8.9

INTERNATIONAL LEAGUE RECORD

Season Team	G	Min.	FGM	FGA	Pct.	FTM	FTA	Pct.	Reb.	Ast.	Pts.	RPG	APG	PPG
00-01—Trenton	5	93	16	32	.500	3	4	.750	24	5	37	9.8	1.0	7.4

Three-point field goals: 2000-01, 16-for-42 (.381).

ABA 2000 LEAGUE RECORD

Season Team	G	Min.	FGM	FGA	Pct.	FTM	FTA	Pct.	Reb.	Ast.	Pts.	RPG	APG	PPG
00-01—San Diego	31	1066	208	424	.491	85	112	.759	242	50	506	7.8	1.6	16.3

Three-point field goals: 2000-01, 4-for-8 (.500).

ARENAS, GILBERT   G   WARRIORS

PERSONAL: Born January 6, 1982, in Los Angeles. ... 6-3/191. (1,91/86,6). ... Full Name: Gilbert Jay Arenas.
HIGH SCHOOL: Grant (Calif.).
COLLEGE: Arizona.
TRANSACTIONS/CAREER NOTES: Selected after sophomore season by Golden State Warriors in first round (31st pick overall) of 2001 NBA Draft.

COLLEGIATE RECORD

Season Team	G	Min.	FGM	FGA	Pct.	FTM	FTA	Pct.	Reb.	Ast.	Pts.	RPG	APG	PPG
99-00—Arizona	34	1093	187	413	.453	111	148	.750	138	71	523	4.1	2.1	15.4
00-01—Arizona	36	1044	208	434	.479	97	134	.724	131	84	582	3.6	2.3	16.2
Totals	70	2137	395	847	.466	208	282	.738	269	155	1105	3.8	2.2	15.8

Three-point field goals: 1999-00, 38-for-130 (.292). 2000-01, 69-for-166 (.416). Totals, 107-for-296 (.361).

ARMSTRONG, BRANDON   G   NETS

PERSONAL: Born June 16, 1980, in San Francisco. ... 6-5/185. (1,96/83,9). ... Full Name: Brandon Simone Armstrong.
HIGH SCHOOL: Vallejo (Calif.).
COLLEGE: Pepperdine.
TRANSACTIONS/CAREER NOTES: Selected after junior season by Houston Rockets in first round (23rd pick overall) of 2001 NBA Draft. ... Draft rights traded by Rockets with draft rights to F Richard Jefferson and C Jason Collins to New Jersey Nets for draft rights to F Eddie Griffin (June 27, 2001).

COLLEGIATE RECORD

Season Team	G	Min.	FGM	FGA	Pct.	FTM	FTA	Pct.	Reb.	Ast.	Pts.	RPG	APG	PPG
98-99—Pepperdine						Did not play—ineligible.								
99-00—Pepperdine	34	947	190	443	.429	45	55	.818	108	50	491	3.2	1.5	14.4
00-01—Pepperdine	31	1027	240	537	.447	128	155	.826	101	46	684	3.3	1.5	22.1
Totals	65	1974	430	980	.439	173	210	.824	209	96	1175	3.2	1.5	18.1

Three-point field goals: 1999-00, 66-for-165 (.400). 2000-01, 76-for-198 (.384). Totals, 142-for-363 (.391).

BATTIER, SHANE   F   GRIZZLIES

PERSONAL: Born September 9, 1978, in Birmingham, Mich. ... 6-8/220. (2,03/99,8). ... Full Name: Shane Courtney Battier.
HIGH SCHOOL: Country Day (Detroit).
COLLEGE: Duke.
TRANSACTIONS/CAREER NOTES: Selected by Vancover Grizzlies in first round (sixth pick overall) of 2001 NBA Draft. ... Grizzlies franchise moved to Memphis for 2001-02 season.

COLLEGIATE RECORD

NOTES: Member of NCAA Division I championship team (2001). ... THE SPORTING NEWS All-America first team (2001). ... THE SPORTING NEWS College Player of the Year (2001). ... Naismith Award Winner (2001). ... Wooden Award winner (2001). ... NCAA Division I Tournament Most Outstanding Player (2001).

Season Team	G	Min.	FGM	FGA	Pct.	FTM	FTA	Pct.	Reb.	Ast.	Pts.	AVERAGES RPG	APG	PPG
97-98—Duke	36	887	96	178	.539	79	108	.731	230	40	275	6.4	1.1	7.6
98-99—Duke	37	881	114	209	.545	71	98	.724	180	55	338	4.9	1.5	9.1
99-00—Duke	34	1206	190	383	.496	134	164	.817	192	72	593	5.6	2.1	17.4
00-01—Duke	39	1363	251	533	.471	152	191	.796	285	72	778	7.3	1.8	19.9
Totals	146	4337	651	1303	.500	436	561	.777	887	239	1984	6.1	1.6	13.6

Three-point field goals: 1997-98, 4-for-24 (.167). 1998-99, 39-for-94 (.415). 1999-00, 79-for-178 (.444). 2000-01, 124-for-296 (.419). Totals, 246-for-592 (.416).

BELL, CHARLIE   G   SUNS

PERSONAL: Born March 12, 1979, in Flint, Mich. ... 6-3/200. (1,91/90,7).
HIGH SCHOOL: Southwestern Academy (Mich.).
COLLEGE: Michigan State.
TRANSACTIONS/CAREER NOTES: Not drafted by an NBA franchise. ... Signed as free agent by Phoenix Suns (August 1, 2001).

COLLEGIATE RECORD

Season Team	G	Min.	FGM	FGA	Pct.	FTM	FTA	Pct.	Reb.	Ast.	Pts.	AVERAGES RPG	APG	PPG
97-98—Michigan State	30	725	94	216	.435	69	87	.793	133	40	276	4.4	1.3	9.2
98-99—Michigan State	38	861	116	243	.477	16	45	.356	146	39	297	3.8	1.0	7.8
99-00—Michigan State	39	1078	159	351	.453	93	116	.802	190	123	449	4.9	3.2	11.5
00-01—Michigan State	33	1034	150	373	.402	94	122	.770	155	169	446	4.7	5.1	13.5
Totals	140	3698	519	1183	.439	272	370	.735	624	371	1468	4.5	2.7	10.5

Three-point field goals: 1997-98, 19-for-56 (.339). 1998-99, 16-for-45 (.356). 1999-00, 38-for-111 (.342). 190-01, 52-for-152 (.342). Totals, 125-for-364 (.343).

BOUMTJE-BOUMTJE, RUBEN C   TRAIL BLAZERS

PERSONAL: Born May 20, 1978, in Edda, Cameroon. ... 7-0/257. (2,13/116,6). ... Full Name: Ruben Bertrand Boumtje-Boumtje.
HIGH SCHOOL: Archbishop Caroll (Washington, D.C.).
COLLEGE: Georgetown.
TRANSACTIONS/CAREER NOTES: Selected by Portland Trail Blazers in second round (50th pick overall) of 2001 NBA Draft.

COLLEGIATE RECORD

Season Team	G	Min.	FGM	FGA	Pct.	FTM	FTA	Pct.	Reb.	Ast.	Pts.	AVERAGES RPG	APG	PPG
97-98—Georgetown	6	80	7	20	.350	2	7	.286	28	4	16	4.7	0.7	2.7
98-99—Georgetown	31	854	100	215	.465	62	113	.549	217	34	262	7.0	1.1	8.5
99-00—Georgetown	31	816	133	279	.477	130	182	.714	240	23	396	7.7	0.7	12.8
00-01—Georgetown	33	713	105	203	.517	89	124	.718	225	30	299	6.8	0.9	9.1
Totals	101	2463	345	717	.481	283	426	.664	710	91	973	7.0	0.9	9.6

Three-point field goals: 1997-98, 0-for-1. 1998-99, 0-for-1. Totals, 0-for-2 (.000).

BRACEY, BRYAN   F   SPURS

PERSONAL: Born August 5, 1978, in Chicago. ... 6-7/210. (2,01/95,3). ... Full Name: Bryan Patrick Bracey.
HIGH SCHOOL: Oak Park (Ill.).
JUNIOR COLLEGE: Triton College (Ill.), then Malcolm X College (Chicago).
COLLEGE: Wisconsin-Platteville, then Oregon.
TRANSACTIONS/CAREER NOTES: Selected by San Antonio Spurs in second round (58th pick overall) of 2001 NBA Draft.

COLLEGIATE RECORD

Season Team	G	Min.	FGM	FGA	Pct.	FTM	FTA	Pct.	Reb.	Ast.	Pts.	AVERAGES RPG	APG	PPG
96-97—Wisconsin-Platteville	1	8	2	2	1.000	0	0	...	2	0	4	2.0	0.0	4.0
97-98—Triton Junior College							Did not play.							
98-99—Malcolm X J.C.	28	...	243	498	.488	86	107	.804	291	65	647	10.4	2.3	23.1
99-00—Oregon	30	498	91	158	.576	60	85	.706	109	10	244	3.6	0.3	8.1
00-01—Oregon	28	858	177	359	.493	130	165	.788	200	29	522	7.1	1.0	18.6
Junior College Totals	28	...	243	498	.488	86	107	.804	291	65	647	10.4	2.3	23.1
4-Year-College Totals	59	1364	270	519	.520	190	250	.760	311	39	770	5.3	0.7	13.1

Three-point field goals: 1998-99, 75-for-158 (.475). 1999-00, 2-for-5 (.400). 2000-01, 38-for-89 (.427). Totals, 40-for-94 (.426).

DID YOU KNOW . . .

. . . that Dolph Schayes was the first player in NBA history to play 1,000 games with his first team?

BRADLEY, MICHAEL   F   RAPTORS

PERSONAL: Born April 18, 1979, in Worcester, Mass. ... 6-10/245. (2,08/111,1). ... Full Name: Michael Thomas Bradley.
HIGH SCHOOL: Burncoat (Mass.).
COLLEGE: Kentucky, then Villanova.
TRANSACTIONS/CAREER NOTES: Selected after junior season by Toronto Raptors in first round (17th pick overall) of 2001 NBA Draft.

COLLEGIATE RECORD

NOTES: The Sporting News All-America second team (2001).

Season Team	G	Min.	FGM	FGA	Pct.	FTM	FTA	Pct.	Reb.	Ast.	Pts.	RPG	APG	PPG
97-98—Kentucky	32	221	30	45	.667	18	35	.514	55	15	78	1.7	0.5	2.4
98-99—Kentucky	37	811	157	239	.657	50	110	.455	182	37	364	4.9	1.0	9.8
99-00—Villanova						Did not play—transfer student.								
00-01—Villanova	31	1053	254	367	.692	125	212	.590	303	81	645	9.8	2.6	20.8
Totals	100	2085	441	651	.677	193	357	.541	540	133	1087	5.4	1.3	10.9

Three-point field goals: 2000-01, 12-for-34 (.353).

BREWER, JAMISON   G   PACERS

PERSONAL: Born November 19, 1980, in Esa Point, Ga. ... 6-5/180. (1,96/81,6). ... Full Name: Jamison Rudy Van Brewer.
HIGH SCHOOL: Newport (Md.).
COLLEGE: Auburn.
TRANSACTIONS/CAREER NOTES: Selected after sophomore season by Indiana Pacers in second round (41st pick overall) of 2001 NBA Draft.

COLLEGIATE RECORD

Season Team	G	Min.	FGM	FGA	Pct.	FTM	FTA	Pct.	Reb.	Ast.	Pts.	RPG	APG	PPG
99-00—Auburn	26	312	22	54	.407	13	25	.520	43	49	60	1.7	1.9	2.3
00-01—Auburn	32	1035	97	207	.469	64	121	.529	230	187	268	7.2	5.8	8.4
Totals	58	1347	119	261	.456	77	146	.527	273	236	328	4.7	4.1	5.7

Three-point field goals: 1999-00, 3-for-15 (.200). 2000-01, 10-for-44 (.227). Totals, 13-for-59 (.220).

BREZEC, PRIMOZ   C   PACERS

PERSONAL: Born October 2, 1979, in Postojna, Slovenia ... 7-1/243. (2,16/110,2).
TRANSACTIONS/CAREER NOTES: Played in Slovenia (1997-98 through 2000-01). ... Selected by Indiana Pacers in first round (27th pick overall) of 2000 NBA Draft.

SLOVENIAN LEAGUE RECORD

Season Team	G	Min.	FGM	FGA	Pct.	FTM	FTA	Pct.	Reb.	Ast.	Pts.	RPG	APG	PPG
96-97—Kraski	30	...	164	283	.580	201	258	.779	207	12	577	6.9	0.4	19.2
97-98—Kraski	12	...	36	47	.766	28	41	.683	38	4	100	3.2	0.3	8.3
98-99—Olimpija Ljubljana	23	203	40	52	.769	31	45	.689	40	4	111	1.7	0.2	4.8
99-00—Olimpija Ljubljana	30	609	111	150	.740	76	105	.724	155	5	298	5.2	0.2	9.9
00-01—Olimpija Ljubljana	30	618	132	190	.695	78	122	.639	127	19	342	4.2	0.6	11.4
Totals	125	...	483	722	.669	414	571	.725	567	44	1428	4.5	0.4	11.4

Three-point field goals: 1996-97, 16-for-52 (.308).

BROWN, ERNEST   C   HEAT

PERSONAL: Born May 17, 1979, in Bronx, N.Y. ... 7-0/255. (2,13/115,7).
HIGH SCHOOL: St. Raymond's (Bronx, N.Y.).
JUNIOR COLLEGE: Mesa (Ariz.) Community College, then Indian Hills Community College (Iowa).
TRANSACTIONS/CAREER NOTES: Selected after sophomore season by Miami Heat in second round (52nd pick overall) of 2000 NBA Draft. ... Played in American Basketball Association 2000 with Kansas City Knights (2000-01).

COLLEGIATE RECORD

Season Team	G	Min.	FGM	FGA	Pct.	FTM	FTA	Pct.	Reb.	Ast.	Pts.	RPG	APG	PPG
98-99—Mesa CC	29	...	283	361	.784	92	152	.605	444	20	658	15.3	0.7	22.7
99-00—Indian Hills CC	33	...	168	276	.609	59	113	.522	227	21	395	6.9	0.6	12.0
Junior College Totals	62	...	451	637	.708	151	265	.570	671	41	1053	10.8	0.7	17.0

ABA 2000 LEAGUE RECORD

Season Team	G	Min.	FGM	FGA	Pct.	FTM	FTA	Pct.	Reb.	Ast.	Pts.	RPG	APG	PPG
00-01—Kansas City	6	55	11	22	.500	4	8	.500	16	0	26	2.7	0.0	4.3

BROWN, DAMONE   F   76ERS

PERSONAL: Born June 28, 1979, in Buffalo. ... 6-9/200. (2,06/90,7). ... Full Name: Damone Lamar Brown.
HIGH SCHOOL: Seneca Vocational (N.Y.).
COLLEGE: Syracuse.
TRANSACTIONS/CAREER NOTES: Selected by Philadelphia 76ers in second round (37th pick overall) of 2001 NBA Draft.

COLLEGIATE RECORD

Season Team	G	Min.	FGM	FGA	Pct.	FTM	FTA	Pct.	Reb.	Ast.	Pts.	AVERAGES RPG	APG	PPG
97-98—Syracuse	15	54	10	24	.417	5	10	.500	13	1	26	0.9	0.1	1.7
98-99—Syracuse	33	815	128	256	.500	45	60	.750	180	42	314	5.5	1.3	9.5
99-00—Syracuse	31	807	137	268	.511	55	82	.671	190	42	331	6.1	1.4	10.7
00-01—Syracuse	34	1242	215	437	.492	158	300	.527	300	56	559	8.8	1.6	16.4
Totals	113	2918	490	985	.497	263	452	.582	683	141	1230	6.0	1.2	10.9

Three-point field goals: 1997-98, 1-for-6 (.167). 1998-99, 13-for-57 (.228). 1999-00, 2-for-12 (.167). 2000-01, 4-for-14 (.286). Totals, 20-for-89 (.225).

BROWN, KEDRICK   F   CELTICS

PERSONAL: Born March 18, 1981, in Zachary, La. ... 6-7/222. (2,01/100,7). ... Full Name: Albert Kedrick Brown.
HIGH SCHOOL: Zachary (La.).
JUNIOR COLLEGE: Okaloosa-Walton Community College (Fla.).
TRANSACTIONS/CAREER NOTES: Selected after sophomore season by Boston Celtics in first round (11th pick overall) of 2001 NBA Draft.

COLLEGIATE RECORD

Season Team	G	Min.	FGM	FGA	Pct.	FTM	FTA	Pct.	Reb.	Ast.	Pts.	AVERAGES RPG	APG	PPG
99-00—Okaloosa-Walton J.C.	30	...	187	332	.563	87	110	.791	317	111	499	10.6	3.7	16.6
00-01—Okaloosa-Walton J.C.	32	...	266	504	.528	124	169	.734	280	97	732	8.8	3.0	22.9
Junior College Totals	62	...	453	836	.542	211	279	.756	597	208	1231	9.6	3.4	19.9

Three-point field goals: 1999-00, 38-for-106 (.358). 2000-01, 76-for-188 (.404). Totals, 114-for-294 (.388).

BROWN, KWAME   C/F   WIZARDS

PERSONAL: Born March 10, 1982, in Charleston, S.C. ... 6-11/240. (2,11/108,9).
HIGH SCHOOL: Glynn Academy (Ga.).
COLLEGE: Did not attend college.
TRANSACTIONS/CAREER NOTES: Selected out of high school by Washington Wizards in first round (first pick overall) of 2001 NBA Draft.

CHANDLER, TYSON   F   BULLS

PERSONAL: Born October 2, 1982, in Hanford, Calif. ... 7-0/235. (2,13/106,6). ... Full Name: Tyson Cleotis Chandler.
HIGH SCHOOL: Dominguez (Calif.).
COLLEGE: Did not attend college.
TRANSACTIONS/CAREER NOTES: Selected out of high school by Los Angeles Clippers in first round (second pick overall) of 2001 NBA Draft. ... Draft rights traded by Clippers with F Brian Skinner to Chicago Bulls for F Elton Brand (June 27, 2001).

CHENOWITH, ERIC   C   KNICKS

PERSONAL: Born March 9, 1979, in Orange, Calif. ... 7-1/270. (2,16/122,5). ... Full Name: Eric Robert Chenowith.
HIGH SCHOOL: Villa Park (Calif.).
COLLEGE: Kansas.
TRANSACTIONS/CAREER NOTES: Selected by New York Knicks in second round (43rd pick overall) of 2001 NBA Draft.

COLLEGIATE RECORD

Season Team	G	Min.	FGM	FGA	Pct.	FTM	FTA	Pct.	Reb.	Ast.	Pts.	AVERAGES RPG	APG	PPG
97-98—Kansas	39	664	89	196	.454	52	76	.684	191	29	230	4.9	0.7	5.9
98-99—Kansas	33	948	165	368	.448	113	153	.739	301	32	444	9.1	1.0	13.5
99-00—Kansas	34	748	113	247	.457	93	136	.684	250	36	292	7.4	1.1	8.6
00-01—Kansas	33	746	111	243	.457	93	136	.684	250	28	315	7.6	0.8	9.5
Totals	139	3106	478	1054	.454	351	501	.701	992	125	1281	7.1	0.9	9.2

Three-point field goals: 1997-98, 0-for-1. 1998-99, 1-for-5 (.200). 1999-00, 0-for-2. 2000-01, 0-for-2. Totals, 1-for-10 (.100).

DID YOU KNOW . . .

. . . that Chuck Daly (at age 59 in 1990) was the oldest coach to win an NBA championship?

CISSE, OUSMANE   F   MAVERICKS

PERSONAL: Born October 20, 1982, in Bamako, Mali. ... 6-9/250. (2,06/113,4).
HIGH SCHOOL: Montgomery Catholic (Ala.), then St. Jude (Ala.).
COLLEGE: Did not attend college.
TRANSACTIONS/CAREER NOTES: Selected out of high school by Denver Nuggets in second round (47th pick overall) of 2001 NBA Draft.

CLAXTON, CRAIG   G   76ERS

PERSONAL: Born May 8, 1978, in Hempstead, N.Y. ... 5-11/166. (1,80/75,3). ... Nickname: Speedy.
HIGH SCHOOL: Christ the King (Queens, N.Y.).
COLLEGE: Hofstra.
TRANSACTIONS/CAREER NOTES: Selected by Philadelphia 76ers in first round (20th pick overall) of 2000 NBA Draft.

COLLEGIATE RECORD

Season Team	G	Min.	FGM	FGA	Pct.	FTM	FTA	Pct.	Reb.	Ast.	Pts.	RPG	APG	PPG
96-97—Hofstra	27	916	134	310	.432	132	187	.706	123	91	406	4.6	3.4	15.0
97-98—Hofstra	31	1081	182	375	.485	138	189	.730	144	224	504	4.6	7.2	16.3
98-99—Hofstra	30	970	136	282	.482	121	151	.801	131	159	399	4.4	5.3	13.3
99-00—Hofstra	31	1089	253	538	.470	149	195	.764	168	186	706	5.4	6.0	22.8
Totals	119	4056	705	1505	.468	540	722	.748	566	660	2015	4.8	5.5	16.9

Three-point field goals: 1996-97, 6-for-38 (.158). 1997-98, 2-for-11 (.182). 1998-99, 6-for-19 (.316). 1999-00, 51-for-134 (.381). Totals, 65-for-202 (.322).

NBA REGULAR-SEASON RECORD

Season Team	G	Min.	FGM	FGA	Pct.	FTM	FTA	Pct.	Off.	Def.	Tot.	Ast.	St.	Blk.	TO	Pts.	RPG	APG	PPG
2000—Philadelphia							Did not play—injured.												

COLLINS, JARRON   F   JAZZ

PERSONAL: Born December 2, 1978, in Northridge, Calif. ... 6-11/255. (2,11/115,7). ... Full Name: Jarron Thomas Collins. ... Twin brother of Jason Collins, center, New Jersey Nets.
HIGH SCHOOL: Harvard-Westlake (Calif.).
COLLEGE: Stanford.
TRANSACTIONS/CAREER NOTES: Selected by Utah Jazz in second round (53rd pick overall) of 2001 NBA Draft.

COLLEGIATE RECORD

Season Team	G	Min.	FGM	FGA	Pct.	FTM	FTA	Pct.	Reb.	Ast.	Pts.	RPG	APG	PPG
97-98—Stanford	34	460	44	83	.530	39	64	.609	119	18	128	3.5	0.5	3.8
98-99—Stanford	30	516	58	117	.496	60	101	.594	157	53	176	5.2	1.8	5.9
99-00—Stanford	31	850	114	235	.485	113	157	.720	201	53	342	6.5	1.7	11.0
00-01—Stanford	34	963	154	276	.558	125	182	.687	229	47	435	6.7	1.4	12.8
Totals	129	2789	370	711	.520	337	504	.669	706	171	1081	5.5	1.3	8.4

Three-point field goals: 1997-98, 1-for-5 (.200). 1998-99, 0-for-1. 1999-00, 1-for-4 (.250). 2000-01, 2-for-6 (.333). Totals, 4-for-16 (.250).

COLLINS, JASON   C   NETS

PERSONAL: Born December 2, 1978, in Northridge, Calif. ... 7-0/260. (2,13/117,9). ... Full Name: Jason Paul Collins. ... Twin brother of Jarron Collins, forward, Utah Jazz.
HIGH SCHOOL: Harvard-Westlake (Calif.).
COLLEGE: Stanford.
TRANSACTIONS/CAREER NOTES: Selected after sophomore season by Houston Rockets in first round (18th pick overall) of 2001 NBA Draft. ... Draft rights traded by Rockets with draft rights to F Richard Jefferson and G Brandon Armstrong to New Jersey Nets for draft rights to F Eddie Griffin (June 27, 2001).

COLLEGIATE RECORD

Season Team	G	Min.	FGM	FGA	Pct.	FTM	FTA	Pct.	Reb.	Ast.	Pts.	RPG	APG	PPG
97-98—Stanford	1	15	1	4	.250	5	7	.714	6	0	7	6.0	0.0	7.0
98-99—Stanford	7	89	9	18	.500	11	23	.478	23	2	29	3.3	0.3	4.1
99-00—Stanford	31	607	84	135	.622	88	133	.662	190	20	256	6.1	0.6	8.3
00-01—Stanford	34	895	168	271	.620	145	185	.784	265	51	493	7.8	1.5	14.5
Totals	73	1606	262	428	.612	249	348	.716	484	73	785	6.6	1.0	10.8

Three-point field goals: 1999-00, 0-for-1. 2000-01, 12-for-26 (.462). Totals, 12-for-27 (.444).

COOK, OMAR   G   NUGGETS

PERSONAL: Born January 28, 1982, in Brooklyn, N.Y. ... 6-1/190. (1,85/86,2).
HIGH SCHOOL: Christ the King (N.Y.).
COLLEGE: St. John's.
TRANSACTIONS/CAREER NOTES: Selected after freshman season by Orlando Magic in second round (32nd pick overall) of 2001 NBA Draft. ... Draft rights traded by Magic to Denver Nuggets for future first-round draft choice (June 27, 2001).

COLLEGIATE RECORD

Season Team	G	Min.	FGM	FGA	Pct.	FTM	FTA	Pct.	Reb.	Ast.	Pts.	AVERAGES RPG	APG	PPG
00-01—St. John's	29	1107	141	392	.360	95	128	.742	88	252	445	3.0	8.7	15.3

Three-point field goals: 2000-01, 68-for-220 (.309).

CURRY, EDDY   F/C   BULLS

PERSONAL: Born December 5, 1982, in Harvey, Ill. ... 6-11/285. (2,11/129,3). ... Full Name: Eddy Curry Jr.
HIGH SCHOOL: Thornwood (Ill.).
COLLEGE: Did not attend college.
TRANSACTIONS/CAREER NOTES: Selected out of high school by Chicago Bulls in first round (fourth pick overall) of 2001 NBA Draft.

DALEMBERT, SAMUEL   C   76ERS

PERSONAL: Born May 10, 1981, in Port-Au-Prince, Haiti. ... 6-11/250. (2,11/113,4). ... Full Name: Samuel Davis Dalembert.
HIGH SCHOOL: Surenpagge (Montreal), then St. Patrick's (N.J.).
COLLEGE: Seton Hall.
TRANSACTIONS/CAREER NOTES: Selected after sophomore season by Philadelphia 76ers in first round (26th pick overall) of 2001 NBA Draft.

COLLEGIATE RECORD

Season Team	G	Min.	FGM	FGA	Pct.	FTM	FTA	Pct.	Reb.	Ast.	Pts.	AVERAGES RPG	APG	PPG
99-00—Seton Hall	30	643	75	149	.503	29	56	.518	179	10	179	6.0	0.3	6.0
00-01—Seton Hall	29	622	100	177	.565	40	72	.556	166	9	240	5.7	0.3	8.3
Totals	59	1265	175	326	.537	69	128	.539	345	19	419	5.8	0.3	7.1

DIOP, DeSAGANA   C   CAVALIERS

PERSONAL: Born January 30, 1983, in Dakar, Senegal. ... 7-0/315. (2,13/142,9). ... Full Name: DeSagana Ngagne Diop.
HIGH SCHOOL: Oak Hill Academy (Mouth of Wilson, Va.).
COLLEGE: Did not attend college.
TRANSACTIONS/CAREER NOTES: Selected out of high school by Cleveland Cavaliers in first round (eighth pick overall) of 2001 NBA Draft.

EVANS, MAURICE   G   TIMBERWOLVES

PERSONAL: Born November 8, 1978, in Wichita, Kan. ... 6-5/220. (1,96/99,8). ... Full Name: Maurice Eugene Evans.
HIGH SCHOOL: Wichita Collegiate (Wichita, Kan.).
COLLEGE: Wichita State, then Texas.
TRANSACTIONS/CAREER NOTES: Not drafted by an NBA franchise. ... Signed as free agent by Minnesota Timberwolves (July 23, 2001).

COLLEGIATE RECORD

Season Team	G	Min.	FGM	FGA	Pct.	FTM	FTA	Pct.	Reb.	Ast.	Pts.	AVERAGES RPG	APG	PPG
97-98—Wichita State	31	761	130	339	.383	66	98	.673	141	27	375	4.5	0.9	12.1
98-99—Wichita State	28	903	211	458	.461	141	178	.792	130	57	632	4.6	2.0	22.6
99-00—Texas					Did not play—transfer student									
00-01—Texas	34	1122	181	411	.440	84	111	.757	179	56	532	5.3	1.6	15.6
Totals	93	2786	522	1208	.432	291	387	.752	450	140	1539	4.8	1.5	16.5

Three-point field goals: 1997-98, 49-for-149 (.329). 1998-99, 69-for-164 (.421). 2000-01, 86-for-221 (.389). Totals, 204-for-534 (.382).

DID YOU KNOW . . .

... that the Sacramento Kings won an NBA-record nine overtime games last season?

FORD, ALTON　　　　　F　　　　　SUNS

PERSONAL: Born May 29, 1981, in Houston. ... 6-9/275. (2,06/124,7). ... Full Name: Alton Ford Jr.
HIGH SCHOOL: Milby (Houston).
COLLEGE: Houston.
TRANSACTIONS/CAREER NOTES: Selected after freshman season by Phoenix Suns in second round (51st pick overall) of 2001 NBA Draft.

COLLEGIATE RECORD

Season Team	G	Min.	FGM	FGA	Pct.	FTM	FTA	Pct.	Reb.	Ast.	Pts.	AVERAGES RPG	APG	PPG
00-01—Houston	26	663	95	220	.432	81	133	.609	154	17	280	5.9	0.7	10.8

Three-point field goals: 2000-01, 9-for-34 (.265).

FORTE, JOSEPH　　　　　G　　　　　CELTICS

PERSONAL: Born March 23, 1981, in Atlanta. ... 6-4/192. (1,93/87,1). ... Full Name: Joseph Xavier Forte.
HIGH SCHOOL: DeMatha Catholic (Md.).
COLLEGE: North Carolina.
TRANSACTIONS/CAREER NOTES: Selected after sophomore season by Boston Celtics in first round (21st pick overall) of 2001 NBA Draft.

COLLEGIATE RECORD

NOTES: THE SPORTING NEWS All-America first team (2001).

Season Team	G	Min.	FGM	FGA	Pct.	FTM	FTA	Pct.	Reb.	Ast.	Pts.	AVERAGES RPG	APG	PPG
99-00—North Carolina	36	1195	228	497	.459	88	117	.752	198	94	600	5.5	2.6	16.7
00-01—North Carolina	33	1145	251	558	.450	133	156	.853	201	116	690	6.1	3.5	20.9
Totals	69	2340	479	1055	.454	221	273	.810	399	210	1290	5.8	3.0	18.7

Three-point field goals: 1999-00, 56-for-156 (.359). 2000-01, 55-for-146 (.377). Totals, 111-for-302 (.368).

FOTSIS, ANTONIS　　　　　F　　　　　GRIZZLIES

PERSONAL: Born April 1, 1981, in Athens, Greece. ... 6-10/219. (2,08/99,3).
TRANSACTIONS/CAREER NOTES: Played in Greece (1997-98 through 2000-01). ... Selected by Vancouver Grizzlies in second round (48th pick overall) of 2001 NBA Draft. ... Grizzlies franchise moved to Memphis for 2001-02 season.

GREEK LEAGUE RECORD

Season Team	G	Min.	FGM	FGA	Pct.	FTM	FTA	Pct.	Reb.	Ast.	Pts.	AVERAGES RPG	APG	PPG
97-98—Panathinaikos	6	24	6	9	.667	5	6	.833	1	0	20	0.2	0.0	3.3
98-99—Panathinaikos	7	56	7	11	.636	10	15	.667	8	3	33	1.1	0.4	4.7
99-00—Panathinaikos	24	434	39	76	.513	29	36	.806	80	21	164	3.3	0.9	6.8
00-01—Panathinaikos	24	502	69	151	.457	33	45	.733	110	21	191	4.6	0.9	8.0
Totals	61	1016	121	247	.490	77	102	.755	199	45	408	3.3	0.7	6.7

Three-point field goals: 1997-98, 1-for-1. 1998-99, 3-for-4 (.750). 1999-00, 19-for-43 (.442). 2000-01, 20-for-64 (.313). Totals, 43-for-112 (.384).

GASOL, PAU　　　　　F　　　　　GRIZZLIES

PERSONAL: Born July 6, 1980, in Barcelona, Spain. ... 7-0/227. (2,13/103,0).
COLLEGE: Did not attend college.
TRANSACTIONS/CAREER NOTES: Played in Spain (1998-99 through 2000-01). ... Selected by Atlanta Hawks in first round (third pick overall) of 2001 NBA Draft. ... Draft rights traded by Hawks with F/C Lorenzen Wright and G Brevin Knight to Memphis Grizzlies for F Shareef Abdur-Rahim and draft rights to G Jamaal Tinsley (July 19, 2001).

SPANISH LEAGUE RECORD

Season Team	G	Min.	FGM	FGA	Pct.	FTM	FTA	Pct.	Reb.	Ast.	Pts.	AVERAGES RPG	APG	PPG
98-99—FC Barcelona	2	11	2	4	.500	1	3	.333	2	1	6	1.0	0.5	3.0
99-00—FC Barcelona	26	385	40	79	.506	23	44	.523	68	12	109	2.6	0.5	4.2
00-01—FC Barcelona	30	716	129	235	.549	70	119	.588	156	23	328	5.2	0.8	10.9
Totals	58	1112	171	318	.538	94	166	.566	226	36	443	3.9	0.6	7.6

Three-point field goals: 1998-99, 1-for-3 (.333). 1999-00, 6-for-20 (.300). 2000-01, 15-for-43 (.349). Totals, 22-for-66 (.333).

GRIFFIN, EDDIE　　　　　F　　　　　ROCKETS

PERSONAL: Born May 30, 1982, in Philadelphia. ... 6-9/220. (2,06/99,8). ... Full Name: Eddie J. Griffin.
HIGH SCHOOL: Roman Catholic (Philadelphia).
COLLEGE: Seton Hall.
TRANSACTIONS/CAREER NOTES: Selected after freshman season by New Jersey Nets in first round (seventh pick overall) of 2001 NBA Draft. ... Draft rights traded by Nets to Houston Rockets for draft rights to F Richard Jefferson, C Jason Collins and G Brandon Armstrong (June 27, 2001).

PROMISING NEWCOMERS

NOTES: THE SPORTING NEWS Freshman of the Year (2001).

Season Team	G	Min.	FGM	FGA	Pct.	FTM	FTA	Pct.	Reb.	Ast.	Pts.	AVERAGES RPG	APG	PPG
00-01—Seton Hall......................	30	979	206	480	.429	80	109	.734	323	49	533	10.8	1.6	17.8

Three-point field goals: 2000-01, 41-for-128 (.320).

HASSELL, TRENTON   G   BULLS

PERSONAL: Born March 4, 1979, in Clarksville, Tenn. ... 6-2/200. (1,88/90,7). ... Full Name: Trenton Lavar Hassell.
HIGH SCHOOL: Clarksville (Tenn.).
COLLEGE: Austin Peay.
TRANSACTIONS/CAREER NOTES: Selected after junior season by Chicago Bulls in second round (30th pick overall) of 2001 NBA Draft.

COLLEGIATE RECORD

Season Team	G	Min.	FGM	FGA	Pct.	FTM	FTA	Pct.	Reb.	Ast.	Pts.	AVERAGES RPG	APG	PPG
97-98—Austin Peay						Did not play—ineligible.								
98-99—Austin Peay	25	963	166	369	.450	107	140	.764	251	102	481	10.0	4.1	19.2
99-00—Austin Peay	25	868	167	352	.474	91	118	.771	185	129	452	7.4	5.2	18.1
00-01—Austin Peay	32	1213	246	507	.485	148	186	.796	249	144	693	7.8	4.5	21.7
Totals	82	3044	579	1228	.471	346	444	.779	685	375	1626	8.4	4.6	19.8

Three-point field goals: 1998-99, 42-for-136 (.309). 1999-00, 27-for-82 (.329). 2000-01, 53-for-136 (.390). Totals, 122-for-354 (.345).

HASTON, KIRK   F   HORNETS

PERSONAL: Born March 10, 1979, in Lobleville, Tenn. ... 6-10/240. (2,08/108,9).
HIGH SCHOOL: Perry County (Tenn.).
COLLEGE: Indiana.
TRANSACTIONS/CAREER NOTES: Selected after junior season by Charlotte Hornets in first round (16th pick overall) of 2001 NBA Draft.

COLLEGIATE RECORD

Season Team	G	Min.	FGM	FGA	Pct.	FTM	FTA	Pct.	Reb.	Ast.	Pts.	AVERAGES RPG	APG	PPG
97-98—Indiana						Did not play—redshirted.								
98-99—Indiana	34	760	133	259	.514	70	93	.753	220	30	336	6.5	0.9	9.9
99-00—Indiana	29	794	168	339	.496	108	148	.730	240	40	444	8.3	1.4	15.3
00-01—Indiana	33	1018	243	552	.440	114	166	.687	288	41	626	8.7	1.2	19.0
Totals	96	2572	544	1150	.473	292	407	.717	748	111	1406	7.8	1.2	14.6

Three-point field goals: 1999-00, 0-for-2. 2000-01, 26-for-69 (.377). Totals, 26-for-71 (.366).

HAYWOOD, BRENDAN   C   WIZARDS

PERSONAL: Born November 11, 1979, in New York. ... 7-0/268. (2,13/121,6). ... Full Name: Brendan Todd Haywood.
HIGH SCHOOL: Dudley (N.C.).
COLLEGE: North Carolina.
TRANSACTIONS/CAREER NOTES: Selected by Cleveland Cavaliers in first round (20th pick overall) of 2001 NBA Draft. ... Draft rights traded by Cavaliers to Orlando Magic for C Michael Doleac (June 27, 2001). ... Draft rights traded by Magic to Washington Wizards for G/F Laron Profit and future first-round draft choice (August 1, 2001).

COLLEGIATE RECORD

NOTES: THE SPORTING NEWS All-America second team (2001).

Season Team	G	Min.	FGM	FGA	Pct.	FTM	FTA	Pct.	Reb.	Ast.	Pts.	AVERAGES RPG	APG	PPG
97-98—North Carolina...............	38	308	35	66	.530	40	63	.635	91	6	110	2.4	0.2	2.9
98-99—North Carolina...............	34	1035	160	247	.648	88	131	.672	235	33	408	6.9	1.0	12.0
99-00—North Carolina...............	36	1071	191	274	.697	106	179	.592	271	37	488	7.5	1.0	13.6
00-01—North Carolina...............	33	901	155	262	.592	95	184	.516	242	42	405	7.3	1.3	12.3
Totals	141	3315	541	849	.637	329	557	.591	839	118	1411	6.0	0.8	10.0

HILL, KYLE   G   ROCKETS

PERSONAL: Born April 7, 1979, in Summit, Ill. ... 6-2/180. (1,88/81,6).
HIGH SCHOOL: Argo (Ill.).
COLLEGE: Eastern Illinois.
TRANSACTIONS/CAREER NOTES: Selected by Dallas Mavericks in second round (44th pick overall) in 2001 NBA Draft. ... Draft rights traded by Mavericks to Houston Rockets as part of three-team trade in which Knicks acquired F Shandon Anderson from Rockets and G Howard Eisley from Mavericks and Rockets acquired F Glen Rice from Knicks (August 10, 2001).

COLLEGIATE RECORD

Season Team	G	Min.	FGM	FGA	Pct.	FTM	FTA	Pct.	Reb.	Ast.	Pts.	AVERAGES RPG	APG	PPG
97-98—Eastern Illinois	9	85	18	43	.419	10	12	.833	19	3	49	2.1	0.3	5.4
98-99—Eastern Illinois	29	853	175	393	.445	67	94	.713	124	78	480	4.3	2.7	16.6
99-00—Eastern Illinois	29	209	209	444	.471	76	113	.673	128	104	553	4.4	3.6	19.1
00-01—Eastern Illinois	31	1042	250	529	.473	151	180	.839	151	125	737	4.9	4.0	23.8
Totals	98	2189	652	1409	.463	304	399	.762	422	310	1819	4.2	3.2	18.6

Three-point field goals: 1997-98, 3-for-15 (.200). 1998-99, 63-for-169 (.373). 1999-00, 59-for-157 (.376). 2000-01, 86-for-199 (.432). Totals, 211-for-540 (.391).

HUNTER, STEVEN   C   MAGIC

PERSONAL: Born October 31, 1981, in Chicago. ... 7-0/220. (2,13/99,8). ... Full Name: Steven D. Hunter.
HIGH SCHOOL: Proviso East (Ill.).
COLLEGE: DePaul.
TRANSACTIONS/CAREER NOTES: Selected after sophomore season by Orlando Magic in first round (15th pick overall) of 2001 NBA Draft.

COLLEGIATE RECORD

Season Team	G	Min.	FGM	FGA	Pct.	FTM	FTA	Pct.	Reb.	Ast.	Pts.	AVERAGES RPG	APG	PPG
99-00—DePaul	33	744	114	197	.579	53	75	.707	128	9	281	3.9	0.3	8.5
00-01—DePaul	30	808	138	233	.592	67	125	.536	169	15	343	5.6	0.5	11.4
Totals	63	1552	252	430	.586	120	200	.600	297	24	624	4.7	0.4	9.9

Three-point field goals: 1999-00, 0-for-2.

HUTSON, ANDRE   F   BUCKS

PERSONAL: Born January 12, 1979, in Dayton, Ohio. ... 6-8/240. (2,03/108,9). ... Full Name: Andre Davon Hutson.
HIGH SCHOOL: Trotwood-Madison (Ohio).
COLLEGE: Michigan State.
TRANSACTIONS/CAREER NOTES: Selected by Milwaukee Bucks in second round (51st pick overall) of 2001 NBA Draft.

COLLEGIATE RECORD

Season Team	G	Min.	FGM	FGA	Pct.	FTM	FTA	Pct.	Reb.	Ast.	Pts.	AVERAGES RPG	APG	PPG
97-98—Michigan State	30	631	87	142	.613	52	69	.754	156	25	226	5.2	0.8	7.5
98-99—Michigan State	37	926	111	180	.617	107	137	.781	192	23	329	5.2	0.6	8.9
99-00—Michigan State	39	1056	147	251	.586	103	154	.669	243	57	397	6.2	1.5	10.2
00-01—Michigan State	32	956	173	278	.622	95	131	.725	244	61	441	7.6	1.9	13.8
Totals	138	3569	518	851	.609	357	491	.727	835	166	1393	6.1	1.2	10.1

Three-point field goals: 1999-00, 0-for-1.

JAMES, MIKE   G   HEAT

PERSONAL: Born June 23, 1975, in Amityville, N.Y. ... 6-2/188. (1,88/85,3). ... Full Name: Michael Lamont James.
HIGH SCHOOL: Amityville (N.Y.).
COLLEGE: Duquesne.
TRANSACTIONS/CAREER NOTES: Not drafted by an NBA franchise. ... Played in Austria (1998-99). ... Played in France (1999-2000 and 2000-01). ... Signed as free agent by Miami Heat (July 20, 2001).

COLLEGIATE RECORD

Season Team	G	Min.	FGM	FGA	Pct.	FTM	FTA	Pct.	Reb.	Ast.	Pts.	AVERAGES RPG	APG	PPG
94-95—Duquesne	27	381	55	123	.447	24	35	.686	36	27	135	1.3	1.0	5.0
95-96—Duquesne	27	843	151	318	.475	79	108	.731	94	106	384	3.5	3.9	14.2
96-97—Duquesne	27	862	141	325	.434	60	84	.714	93	76	366	3.4	2.8	13.6
97-98—Duquesne	30	1029	190	443	.429	81	109	.743	106	104	526	3.5	3.5	17.5
Totals	111	3115	537	1209	.444	244	336	.726	329	313	1411	3.0	2.8	12.7

Three-point field goals: 1994-95, 1-for-13 (.077). 1995-96, 3-for-19 (.158). 1996-97, 24-for-67 (.358). 1997-98, 65-for-184 (.353). Totals, 93-for-283 (.329).

AUSTRIAN LEAGUE RECORD

Season Team	G	Min.	FGM	FGA	Pct.	FTM	FTA	Pct.	Reb.	Ast.	Pts.	AVERAGES RPG	APG	PPG
98-99—St. Polten	15	556	103	217	.475	61	80	.763	83	110	282	5.5	7.3	18.8

Three-point field goals: 2000-01, 15-for-56 (.268).

FRENCH LEAGUE RECORD

Season Team	G	Min.	FGM	FGA	Pct.	FTM	FTA	Pct.	Reb.	Ast.	Pts.	AVERAGES RPG	APG	PPG
99-00—ESPE Basket Chalons	30	1061	196	422	.464	104	124	.839	91	144	536	3.0	4.8	17.9
00-01—SLUC Basket Nancy	30	1028	169	360	.469	67	90	.744	109	154	451	3.6	5.1	15.0
Totals	60	2089	365	782	.467	171	214	.799	200	298	987	3.3	5.0	16.5

Three-point field goals: 1999-00, 40-for-99 (.404). 2000-01, 46-for-125 (.368). Totals, 86-for-224 (.384).

JAVTOKAS, ROBERTAS   F   SPURS

PERSONAL: Born March 20, 1980, in Siauliai, Lithuania. ... 6-10/205. (2,08/93,0).
HIGH SCHOOL: Bishop McGuiness (N.C.), then St. Mary's (Ohio).
COLLEGE: Arizona.
TRANSACTIONS/CAREER NOTES: Played in Lithuania (1996-97, 1999-2000 and 2000-01). ... Selected by San Antonio Spurs in second round (56th pick overall) of 2001 NBA Draft.

LITHUANIAN LEAGUE RECORD

Season Team	G	Min.	FGM	FGA	Pct.	FTM	FTA	Pct.	Reb.	Ast.	Pts.	RPG	APG	PPG
96-97—Siauliai	2	5	0	0	...	1	2	.500	0	0	1	0.0	0.0	0.5
99-00—Lietuvos Rytas	21	359	47	78	.603	27	52	.519	109	8	121	5.2	0.4	5.8
00-01—Lietuvos Rytas	27	660	122	220	.555	100	223	.448	223	15	300	8.3	0.6	11.1
Totals	50	1024	169	298	.567	128	277	.462	332	23	422	6.6	0.5	8.4

Three-point field goals: 2000-01, 2-for-3 (.667).

COLLEGIATE RECORD

Season Team	G	Min.	FGM	FGA	Pct.	FTM	FTA	Pct.	Reb.	Ast.	Pts.	RPG	APG	PPG
99-00—Arizona	8	55	3	8	.375	0	5	.000	10	0	6	1.3	0.0	0.8

JEFFERS, MAURICE   G   KINGS

PERSONAL: Born April 3, 1979, in Morrilton, Ark. ... 6-4/195. (1,93/88,5).
HIGH SCHOOL: Morrilton (Ark.).
JUNIOR COLLEGE: Westark Community College (Ark.).
COLLEGE: Saint Louis.
TRANSACTIONS/CAREER NOTES: Selected by Sacramento Kings in second round (55th pick overall) of 2001 NBA Draft.

COLLEGIATE RECORD

Season Team	G	Min.	FGM	FGA	Pct.	FTM	FTA	Pct.	Reb.	Ast.	Pts.	RPG	APG	PPG
97-98—Westark C.C.						Statistics unavailable.								
98-99—Westark C.C.	24	...	171	317	.539	111	171	.649	221	56	464	9.2	2.3	19.3
99-00—St. Louis	33	851	82	195	.421	46	76	.605	142	55	219	4.3	1.7	6.6
00-01—St. Louis	31	1012	158	352	.449	160	206	.777	190	76	497	6.1	2.5	16.0
Junior College Totals	24	...	171	317	.539	111	171	.649	221	56	464	9.2	2.3	19.3
4-Year-College Totals	64	1863	240	547	.439	206	282	.730	332	131	716	5.2	2.0	11.2

Three-point field goals: 1998-99, 11-for-34 (.324). 1999-00, 9-for-35 (.257). 2000-01, 21-for-48 (.438). Totals, 30-for-83 (.361).

JEFFERSON, RICHARD   F   NETS

PERSONAL: Born June 21, 1980, in Los Angeles. ... 6-7/222. (2,01/100,7). ... Full Name: Richard Allen Jefferson.
HIGH SCHOOL: Moon Valley (Phoenix).
COLLEGE: Arizona.
TRANSACTIONS/CAREER NOTES: Selected after junior season by Houston Rockets in first round (13th pick overall) of 2001 NBA Draft. ... Draft rights traded by Rockets with draft rights to C Jason Collins and G Brandon Armstrong to New Jersey Nets for draft rights to F Eddie Griffin (June 27, 2001).

COLLEGIATE RECORD

Season Team	G	Min.	FGM	FGA	Pct.	FTM	FTA	Pct.	Reb.	Ast.	Pts.	RPG	APG	PPG
98-99—Arizona	28	755	104	210	.495	97	125	.776	134	80	317	4.8	2.9	11.3
99-00—Arizona	21	495	84	167	.503	45	63	.714	92	58	230	4.4	2.8	11.0
00-01—Arizona	35	961	147	307	.479	72	110	.655	190	94	397	5.4	2.7	11.3
Totals	84	2211	335	684	.490	214	298	.718	416	232	944	5.0	2.8	11.2

Three-point field goals: 1998-99, 12-for-33 (.364). 1999-00, 17-for-40 (.425). 2000-01, 31-for-90 (.344). Totals, 60-for-163 (.368).

JOHNSON, JOE   G/F   CELTICS

PERSONAL: Born July 29, 1981, in Little Rock, Ark. ... 6-8/225. (2,03/102,1). ... Full Name: Joe Marcus Johnson.
HIGH SCHOOL: Little Rock Central (Ark.).
COLLEGE: Arkansas.
TRANSACTIONS/CAREER NOTES: Selected after sophomore season by Boston Celtics in first round (10th pick overall) of 2001 NBA Draft.

COLLEGIATE RECORD

Season Team	G	Min.	FGM	FGA	Pct.	FTM	FTA	Pct.	Reb.	Ast.	Pts.	RPG	APG	PPG
99-00—Arkansas	23	732	140	302	.464	60	79	.759	132	50	368	5.7	2.2	16.0
00-01—Arkansas	30	873	162	346	.468	68	91	.747	193	77	427	6.4	2.6	14.2
Totals	53	1605	302	648	.466	128	170	.753	325	127	795	6.1	2.4	15.0

Three-point field goals: 1999-00, 28-for-76 (.368). 2000-01, 35-for-79 (.443). Totals, 63-for-155 (.406).

JOHNSON, KEN　　　　C　　　　HEAT

PERSONAL: Born February 1, 1978, in Detroit. ... 6-11/235. (2,11/106,6). ... Full Name: Kenyata Allen Johnson.
HIGH SCHOOL: Henry Ford (Detroit).
COLLEGE: Ohio State.
TRANSACTIONS/CAREER NOTES: Selected by Miami Heat in second round (49th pick overall) of 2001 NBA Draft. ... Signed to play for Avellino in Italy for 2001-02 season.

COLLEGIATE RECORD

Season Team	G	Min.	FGM	FGA	Pct.	FTM	FTA	Pct.	Reb.	Ast.	Pts.	RPG	APG	PPG
96-97—Ohio State						Did not play—ineligible.								
97-98—Ohio State	30	811	162	488	.332	45	73	.616	127	16	203	4.2	0.5	6.8
98-99—Ohio State	36	951	98	188	.521	35	72	.486	204	8	231	5.7	0.2	6.4
99-00—Ohio State	30	885	94	170	.553	47	74	.635	182	9	235	6.1	0.3	7.8
00-01—Ohio State	31	916	145	251	.578	96	135	.711	226	25	386	7.3	0.8	12.5
Totals	127	3563	499	1097	.455	223	354	.630	739	58	1055	5.8	0.5	8.3

JONES, ALVIN　　　　C　　　　76ERS

PERSONAL: Born September 9, 1978, in Luxembourg. ... 6-11/265. (2,11/120,2). ... Full Name: Alvin Robert Lamar Jones III.
HIGH SCHOOL: Kathleen (Fla.).
COLLEGE: Georgia Tech.
TRANSACTIONS/CAREER NOTES: Selected by Philadelphia 76ers in second round (57th pick overall) of 2001 NBA Draft.

COLLEGIATE RECORD

Season Team	G	Min.	FGM	FGA	Pct.	FTM	FTA	Pct.	Reb.	Ast.	Pts.	RPG	APG	PPG
97-98—Georgia Tech	33	1009	80	161	.497	64	115	.557	...	28	224	6.7	0.8	6.8
98-99—Georgia Tech	31	1085	145	277	.523	105	201	.522	302	53	395	9.7	1.7	12.7
99-00—Georgia Tech	30	911	91	205	.444	110	179	.615	241	43	292	8.0	1.4	9.7
00-01—Georgia Tech	30	875	134	278	.482	133	223	.596	312	46	401	10.4	1.5	13.4
Totals	124	3880	450	921	.489	412	718	.574	...	170	1312	...	1.4	10.6

Three-point field goals: 1997-98, 0-for-1. 1999-00, 0-for-1. 2000-01, 0-for-2. Totals, 0-for-4 (.000).

KIRILENKO, ANDREI　　　　F　　　　JAZZ

PERSONAL: Born February 18, 1981, in Russia. ... 6-9/210. (2,06/95,3).
TRANSACTIONS/CAREER NOTES: Played in Russia (1996-97 through 2000-01). ... Selected by Utah Jazz in first round (24th pick overall) of 1999 NBA Draft.

RUSSIAN LEAGUE RECORD

Season Team	G	Min.	FGM	FGA	Pct.	FTM	FTA	Pct.	Reb.	Ast.	Pts.	RPG	APG	PPG
96-97—Spartak St. Petersburg	3	16	2	5	.400	2	4	.500	4	1	6	1.3	0.3	2.0
97-98—Spartak St. Petersburg	41	993	164	315	.521	143	223	.641	188	58	486	4.6	1.4	11.9
98-99—CSKA	26	495	116	178	.652	86	125	.688	110	54	323	4.2	2.1	12.4
99-00—CSKA	37	841	173	235	.736	131	185	.708	227	94	488	6.1	2.5	13.2
00-01—CSKA	20	540	97	161	.602	78	122	.639	172	43	281	8.6	2.2	14.1
Totals	127	2885	552	894	.617	440	659	.668	701	250	1584	5.5	2.0	12.5

Three-point field goals: 1996-97, 0-for-1. 1997-98, 15-for-48 (.313). 1998-99, 5-for-11 (.455). 1999-00, 11-for-24 (.458). 2000-01, 9-for-31 (.290). Totals, 40-for-115 (.348).

LAMPLEY, SEAN　　　　F　　　　BULLS

PERSONAL: Born September 9, 1979, in Harvey, Ill. ... 6-7/225. (2,01/102,1). ... Full Name: Sean James Lampley.
HIGH SCHOOL: St. Francis DeSales (Chicago).
COLLEGE: California.
TRANSACTIONS/CAREER NOTES: Selected by Chicago Bulls in second round (45th pick overall) of 2001 NBA Draft.

COLLEGIATE RECORD

Season Team	G	Min.	FGM	FGA	Pct.	FTM	FTA	Pct.	Reb.	Ast.	Pts.	RPG	APG	PPG
97-98—California	27	664	89	198	.449	43	73	.589	141	45	226	5.2	1.7	8.4
98-99—California	32	912	151	307	.492	90	142	.634	280	45	396	8.8	1.4	12.4
99-00—California	33	1101	212	417	.508	124	192	.646	244	103	549	7.4	3.1	16.6
00-01—California	31	1073	209	416	.502	180	244	.738	224	102	605	7.2	3.3	19.5
Totals	123	3750	661	1338	.494	437	651	.671	889	295	1776	7.2	2.4	14.4

Three-point field goals: 1997-98, 5-for-19 (.263). 1998-99, 4-for-12 (.333). 1999-00, 1-for-17 (.059). 2000-01, 7-for-33 (.212). Totals, 17-for-81 (.210).

PROMISING NEWCOMERS

LOPEZ, RAUL G JAZZ

PERSONAL: Born April 15, 1980, in Vic, Spain. ... 6-0/180. (1,83/81,6).

TRANSACTIONS/CAREER NOTES: Played in Spain (1997-98 through 2000-01). ... Selected by Utah Jazz in first round (24th pick overall) of 2001 NBA Draft.

SPANISH LEAGUE RECORD

Season Team	G	Min.	FGM	FGA	Pct.	FTM	FTA	Pct.	Reb.	Ast.	Pts.	AVERAGES RPG	APG	PPG
97-98—Festina Andorra	1	17	3	6	.500	1	2	.500	2	4	10	2.0	4.0	10.0
98-99—Joventut Badalona	34	500	44	113	.389	49	65	.754	42	54	149	1.2	1.6	4.4
99-00—Joventut Badalona	32	757	116	246	.472	61	73	.836	50	90	323	1.6	2.8	10.1
00-01—Real Madrid	32	654	73	157	.465	48	65	.738	48	79	225	1.5	2.5	7.0
Totals	99	1928	236	522	.452	159	205	.776	142	227	707	1.4	2.3	7.1

Three-point field goals: 1997-98, 3-for-3. 1998-99, 12-for-30 (.400). 1999-00, 30-for-79 (.380). 2000-01, 31-for-79 (.392). Totals, 76-for-191 (.398).

MORRIS, TERENCE F ROCKETS

PERSONAL: Born January 11, 1979, in Frederick, Md. ... 6-9/221. (2,06/100,2). ... Full Name: Terence Darea Morris.
HIGH SCHOOL: Thomas Johnson (Md.).
COLLEGE: Maryland.
TRANSACTIONS/CAREER NOTES: Selected by Atlanta Hawks in second round (34th pick overall) of 2001 NBA Draft. ... Draft rights traded by Hawks to Houston Rockets for future first-round draft choice (June 27, 2001).

COLLEGIATE RECORD

Season Team	G	Min.	FGM	FGA	Pct.	FTM	FTA	Pct.	Reb.	Ast.	Pts.	AVERAGES RPG	APG	PPG
97-98—Maryland	32	511	91	174	.523	41	59	.695	113	25	236	3.5	0.8	7.4
98-99—Maryland	34	999	195	354	.551	104	126	.825	242	56	521	7.1	1.6	15.3
99-00—Maryland	34	1103	200	406	.493	102	134	.761	293	80	537	8.6	2.4	15.8
00-01—Maryland	36	993	158	366	.432	97	122	.795	277	68	439	7.7	1.9	12.2
Totals	136	3606	644	1300	.495	344	441	.780	925	229	1733	6.8	1.7	12.7

Three-point field goals: 1997-98, 13-for-37 (.351). 1998-99, 27-for-76 (.355). 1999-00, 35-for-96 (.365). 2000-01, 26-for-90 (.289). Totals, 101-for-299 (.338).

MURPHY, TROY F WARRIORS

PERSONAL: Born May 2, 1980, in Sparta, N.J. ... 6-11/245. (2,11/111,1). ... Full Name: Troy Brandon Murphy.
HIGH SCHOOL: Delbarton (N.J.).
COLLEGE: Notre Dame.
TRANSACTIONS/CAREER NOTES: Selected after junior season by Golden State Warriors in first round (14th pick overall) of 2001 NBA Draft.

COLLEGIATE RECORD

NOTES: The Sporting News All-America first team (2001).

Season Team	G	Min.	FGM	FGA	Pct.	FTM	FTA	Pct.	Reb.	Ast.	Pts.	AVERAGES RPG	APG	PPG
98-99—Notre Dame	27	890	180	340	.529	149	201	.741	267	38	519	9.9	1.4	19.2
99-00—Notre Dame	37	1318	274	557	.492	261	323	.808	380	58	839	10.3	1.6	22.7
00-01—Notre Dame	30	1090	223	473	.471	177	231	.766	277	62	653	9.2	2.1	21.8
Totals	94	3298	677	1370	.494	587	755	.777	924	158	2011	9.8	1.7	21.4

Three-point field goals: 1998-99, 4-for-13 (.308). 1999-00, 30-for-92 (.326). 2000-01, 30-for-86 (.349). Totals, 64-for-191 (.335).

OKUR, MEHMET F/C PISTONS

PERSONAL: Born May 26, 1979, in Yalova, Turkey. ... 6-11/249. (2,11/112,9).
HIGH SCHOOL: Cem Sultan (Gazcilar Bursa).
TRANSACTIONS/CAREER NOTES: Played in Turkey (1997-98 through 2000-01). ... Selected by Detroit Pistons in second round (38th pick overall) of 2001 NBA Draft.

TURKISH LEAGUE RECORD

Season Team	G	Min.	FGM	FGA	Pct.	FTM	FTA	Pct.	Reb.	Ast.	Pts.	AVERAGES RPG	APG	PPG
97-98—Oyak Renau	25	332	47	108	.435	17	26	.654	81	18	111	3.2	0.7	4.4
98-99—Tofas Bursa	33	440	55	112	.491	29	42	.690	142	12	155	4.3	0.4	4.7
99-00—Tofas Bursa	37	731	94	212	.443	35	50	.700	210	32	243	5.7	0.9	6.6
00-01—Efes Pilsen	26	477	91	163	.558	35	42	.833	161	12	231	6.2	0.5	8.9
Totals	121	1980	287	595	.482	116	160	.725	594	74	740	4.9	0.6	6.1

Three-point field goals: 1998-99, 16-for-31 (.516). 1999-00, 20-for-60 (.333). 2000-01, 14-for-27 (.519). Totals, 50-for-118 (.424).

PARKER, TONY   G   SPURS

PERSONAL: Born May 17, 1982, in Bruges, Belgium. ... 6-2/177. (1,88/80,3). ... Full Name: William Anthony Parker.
HIGH SCHOOL: INSEP (Paris, France).
TRANSACTIONS/CAREER NOTES: Played in France (1997-98 through 2000-01). ... Selected by San Antonio Spurs in first round (28th pick overall) of 2001 NBA Draft.

FRENCH LEAGUE RECORD

Season Team	G	Min.	FGM	FGA	Pct.	FTM	FTA	Pct.	Reb.	Ast.	Pts.	RPG	APG	PPG
97-98—Centre Federal	29	...	146	292	.500	97	145	.669	78	162	426	2.7	5.6	14.7
98-99—Centre Federal	30	...	252	488	.516	113	173	.653	120	195	663	4.0	6.5	22.1
99-00—Paris Racing	23	231	33	76	.434	13	26	.500	20	40	90	0.9	1.7	3.9
00-01—Paris Racing	30	992	163	333	.489	80	107	.748	82	168	440	2.7	5.6	14.7
Totals	112	...	594	1189	.500	303	451	.672	300	565	1619	2.7	5.0	14.5

Three-point field goals: 1997-98, 37-for-108 (.343). 1998-99, 46-for-156 (.295). 1999-00, 11-for-34 (.324). 2000-01, 34-for-112 (.304). Totals, 128-for-410 (.312).

RADMANOVIC, VLADIMIR   F   SUPERSONICS

PERSONAL: Born November 19, 1980, in Trebinje, Yugoslavia. ... 6-10/227. (2,08/103,0).
TRANSACTIONS/CAREER NOTES: Played in Yugoslavia (1998-99 through 2000-01). ... Selected by Seattle SuperSonics in first round (12th pick overall) of 2001 NBA Draft.

YUGOSLAVIAN LEAGUE RECORD

Season Team	G	Min.	FGM	FGA	Pct.	FTM	FTA	Pct.	Reb.	Ast.	Pts.	RPG	APG	PPG
98-99—Crvena Zveda Belgrade	10	150	23	35	.657	6	8	.750	28	8	59	2.8	0.8	5.9
99-00—Crvena Zveda Belgrade	12	...	54	113	.478	33	45	.733	115	31	152	9.6	2.6	12.7
00-01—FMP Zeleznik	19	623	119	216	.551	33	85	.388	139	51	327	7.3	2.7	17.2
Totals	41	...	196	364	.538	72	138	.522	282	90	538	6.9	2.2	13.1

Three-point field goals: 1998-99, 7-for-10 (.700). 1999-00, 11-for-44 (.250). 2000-01, 33-for-85 (.388). Totals, 51-for-139 (.367).

RANDOLPH, ZACH   F   TRAIL BLAZERS

PERSONAL: Born July 16, 1981, in Marion, Ind. ... 6-9/270. (2,06/122,5). ... Full Name: Zachary Randolph.
HIGH SCHOOL: Marion (Ind.).
COLLEGE: Michigan State.
TRANSACTIONS/CAREER NOTES: Selected after freshman season by Portland Trail Blazers in first round (19th pick overall) of 2001 NBA Draft.

COLLEGIATE RECORD

Season Team	G	Min.	FGM	FGA	Pct.	FTM	FTA	Pct.	Reb.	Ast.	Pts.	RPG	APG	PPG
00-01—Michigan State	33	654	138	235	.587	80	126	.635	221	34	356	6.7	1.0	10.8

Three-point field goals: 2000-01, 0-for-1.

REBRACA, ZELJKO   F   PISTONS

PERSONAL: Born April 9, 1972, in Prigrevica, Yugoslavia. ... 6-11/240. (2,11/108,4). ... Name pronounced Reh-bhra-tcha.
TRANSACTIONS/CAREER NOTES: Played in Yugoslavia (1993-94 and 1994-95). ... Selected by Seattle SuperSonics in second round (54th pick overall) of 1994 NBA Draft. ... Draft rights traded by SuperSonics to Minnesota Timberwolves for 1996 second-round draft choice (June 30, 1994). ... Played in Italy (1995-96 through 1998-99). ... Played in Greece (1999-2000 and 2000-01). ... Traded by Timberwolves with G Micheal Williams and 1999 or 2000 first-round draft choice to Toronto Raptors in three-way deal in which Raptors also received 1999 first-round draft choice from Denver Nuggets, Timberwolves received C Dean Garrett and G Bobby Jackson from Nuggets and Nuggets received G Chauncey Billups and draft rights to G Tyson Wheeler from Raptors (January 21, 1999). ... Traded by Raptors to Detroit Pistons for 2002 second-round draft choice (July 18, 2001).

YUGOSLAVIAN LEAGUE RECORD

Season Team	G	Min.	FGM	FGA	Pct.	FTM	FTA	Pct.	Reb.	Ast.	Pts.	RPG	APG	PPG
93-94—Belgrade Partizan	20	...	114	251	.454	60	82	.732	131	8	288	6.6	0.4	14.4
94-95—Belgrade Partizan	20	...	...	...	...	...	...	...	136	...	518	6.8	...	25.9
Totals	40	...	...	...	...	...	...	...	267	...	806	6.7	...	20.2

Three-point field goals: 1993-94, 0-for-1.

ITALIAN LEAGUE RECORD

Season Team	G	Min.	FGM	FGA	Pct.	FTM	FTA	Pct.	Reb.	Ast.	Pts.	RPG	APG	PPG
95-96—Benetton	40	1149	241	362	.666	106	137	.774	262	15	588	6.6	0.4	14.7
96-97—Benetton	38	1057	202	335	.603	120	156	.769	255	17	526	6.7	0.4	13.8
97-98—Benetton	30	931	201	320	.628	107	136	.787	217	23	509	7.2	0.8	17.0
98-99—Benetton	34	880	145	237	.612	116	147	.789	184	26	406	5.4	0.8	11.9
Totals	142	4017	789	1254	.629	449	576	.780	918	81	2029	6.5	0.6	14.3

Three-point field goals: 1995-96, 0-for-1. 1996-97, 2-for-3 (.667). 1997-98, 0-for-1. Totals, 2-for-5 (.400).

PROMISING NEWCOMERS

Season Team	G	Min.	FGM	FGA	Pct.	FTM	FTA	Pct.	Reb.	Ast.	Pts.	AVERAGES		
												RPG	APG	PPG
99-00—Panathinaikos..............	24	666	116	191	.607	54	74	.730	156	20	287	6.5	0.8	12.0
00-01—Panathinaikos..............	21	414	79	121	.653	47	63	.746	148	19	205	7.0	0.9	9.8
Totals	45	1080	195	312	.625	101	137	.737	304	39	492	6.8	0.9	10.9

Three-point field goals: 1999-00, 1-for-1.

RICHARDSON, JASON   G/F   WARRIORS

PERSONAL: Born January 20, 1981, in Saginaw, Mich. ... 6-6/220. (1,98/99,8). ... Full Name: Jason Anthony Richardson.
HIGH SCHOOL: Arthur Hill (Saginaw, Mich.).
COLLEGE: Michigan State.
TRANSACTIONS/CAREER NOTES: Selected after sophomore season by Golden State Warriors in first round (fifth pick overall) of 2001 NBA Draft.

COLLEGIATE RECORD

NOTES: THE SPORTING NEWS All-America second team (2001).

Season Team	G	Min.	FGM	FGA	Pct.	FTM	FTA	Pct.	Reb.	Ast.	Pts.	AVERAGES		
												RPG	APG	PPG
99-00—Michigan State	37	582	79	157	.503	23	42	.548	153	23	189	4.1	0.6	5.1
00-01—Michigan State	33	940	182	362	.503	73	106	.689	195	73	486	5.9	2.2	14.7
Totals	70	1522	261	519	.503	96	148	.649	348	96	675	5.0	1.4	9.6

Three-point field goals: 1999-00, 8-for-27 (.296). 2000-01, 49-for-122 (.402). Totals, 57-for-149 (.383).

SASSER, JERYL   G   MAGIC

PERSONAL: Born February 13, 1979, in Dallas. ... 6-6/200. (1,98/90,7). ... Full Name: Jeryl Henry Braxton Sasser Jr.
HIGH SCHOOL: Kimball (Dallas).
COLLEGE: Southern Methodist.
TRANSACTIONS/CAREER NOTES: Selected by Orlando Magic in first round (22nd pick overall) of 2001 NBA Draft.

COLLEGIATE RECORD

Season Team	G	Min.	FGM	FGA	Pct.	FTM	FTA	Pct.	Reb.	Ast.	Pts.	AVERAGES		
												RPG	APG	PPG
97-98—Southern Methodist.......	28	935	135	346	.390	122	170	.718	231	104	420	8.3	3.7	15.0
98-99—Southern Methodist.......	30	1042	188	455	.413	153	212	.722	254	106	562	8.5	3.5	18.7
99-00—Southern Methodist.......	30	1064	181	479	.378	119	175	.680	249	137	518	8.3	4.6	17.3
00-01—Southern Methodist.......	29	1011	170	431	.394	117	163	.718	242	22	492	8.3	0.8	17.0
Totals	117	4052	674	1711	.394	511	720	.710	976	369	1992	8.3	3.2	17.0

Three-point field goals: 1997-98, 28-for-107 (.262). 1998-99, 33-for-113 (.292). 1999-00, 37-for-133 (.278). 2000-01, 35-for-122 (.287). Totals, 133-for-475 (.280).

SATTERFIELD, KENNY   G   MAVERICKS

PERSONAL: Born April 12, 1981, in New York. ... 6-2/186. (1,88/84,4). ... Full Name: Kenneth Satterfield.
HIGH SCHOOL: Brother Rice (New York).
COLLEGE: Cincinnati.
TRANSACTIONS/CAREER NOTES: Selected after sophomore season by Dallas Mavericks in second round (54th pick overall) of 2001 NBA Draft.

COLLEGIATE RECORD

Season Team	G	Min.	FGM	FGA	Pct.	FTM	FTA	Pct.	Reb.	Ast.	Pts.	AVERAGES		
												RPG	APG	PPG
99-00—Cincinnati	33	939	104	242	.430	79	103	.767	113	178	304	3.4	5.4	9.2
00-01—Cincinnati	35	1203	163	421	.387	130	165	.788	165	177	504	4.7	5.1	14.4
Totals	68	2142	267	663	.403	209	268	.780	278	355	808	4.1	5.2	11.9

Three-point field goals: 1999-00, 17-for-57 (.298). 2000-01, 48-for-144 (.333). Totals, 65-for-201 (.323).

SCALABRINE, BRIAN   F   NETS

PERSONAL: Born March 18, 1978, in Long Beach, Calif. ... 6-9/240. (2,06/108,9). ... Full Name: Brian David Scalabrine.
HIGH SCHOOL: Enumclaw (Wash.).
JUNIOR COLLEGE: Highline College (Wash.).
COLLEGE: Southern California.
TRANSACTIONS/CAREER NOTES: Selected by New Jersey Nets in second round (35th pick overall) of 2001 NBA Draft.

COLLEGIATE RECORD

Season Team	G	Min.	FGM	FGA	Pct.	FTM	FTA	Pct.	Reb.	Ast.	Pts.	AVERAGES		
												RPG	APG	PPG
96-97—Highline College	32	932	207	350	.591	108	144	.750	308	94	522	9.6	2.9	16.3
97-98—Highline College					Did not play—redshirted.									
98-99—Southern California	28	869	152	286	.531	103	130	.792	178	68	408	6.4	2.4	14.6
99-00—Southern California	30	1052	203	382	.531	103	144	.715	180	85	534	6.0	2.8	17.8
00-01—Southern California	34	1116	173	362	.478	133	166	.801	202	96	499	5.9	2.8	14.7
Junior College Totals...............	32	932	207	350	.591	108	144	.750	308	94	522	9.6	2.9	16.3
4-Year-College Totals	92	3037	528	1030	.513	339	440	.770	560	249	1441	6.1	2.7	15.7

Three-point field goals: 1996-97, 0-for-6. 1998-99, 1-for-6 (.167). 1999-00, 25-for-62 (.403). 2000-01, 20-for-66 (.303). Totals, 46-for-134 (.343).

PROMISING NEWCOMERS

SIMMONS, BOBBY   G/F   WIZARDS

PERSONAL: Born June 2, 1980, in Chicago. ... 6-7/210. (2,01/95,3).
HIGH SCHOOL: Simeon (Chicago).
COLLEGE: DePaul.
TRANSACTIONS/CAREER NOTES: Selected after junior season by Seattle SuperSonics in second round (42nd pick overall) of 2001 NBA Draft. ... Draft rights traded by SuperSonics to Washington Wizards for draft rights to C Predrag Drobnjak (June 27, 2001).

COLLEGIATE RECORD

Season Team	G	Min.	FGM	FGA	Pct.	FTM	FTA	Pct.	Reb.	Ast.	Pts.	RPG	APG	PPG
98-99—DePaul	31	949	112	300	.373	92	116	.793	190	82	347	6.1	2.6	11.2
99-00—DePaul	33	1009	142	308	.461	120	158	.759	262	53	433	7.9	1.6	13.1
00-01—DePaul	29	981	149	333	.447	124	155	.800	248	72	483	8.6	2.5	16.7
Totals	93	2939	403	941	.428	336	429	.783	700	207	1263	7.5	2.2	13.6

Three-point field goals: 1998-99, 31-for-112 (.277). 1999-00, 29-for-89 (.326). 2000-01, 61-for-165 (.370). Totals, 121-for-366 (.331).

SOLOMON, WILL   G   GRIZZLIES

PERSONAL: Born July 20, 1978, in Hartford, Conn. ... 6-1/185. (1,85/83,9). ... Full Name: William James Solomon.
HIGH SCHOOL: Windsor (Conn.).
COLLEGE: Clemson.
TRANSACTIONS/CAREER NOTES: Selected after junior season by Vancouver Grizzlies in second round (33rd pick overall) of 2001 NBA Draft. ... Grizzlies franchise moved to Memphis for 2001-02 season.

COLLEGIATE RECORD

Season Team	G	Min.	FGM	FGA	Pct.	FTM	FTA	Pct.	Reb.	Ast.	Pts.	RPG	APG	PPG
98-99—Clemson	34	662	73	203	.360	41	66	.621	50	49	213	1.5	1.4	6.3
99-00—Clemson	30	1079	213	531	.401	108	158	.684	123	95	627	4.1	3.2	20.9
00-01—Clemson	30	998	183	461	.397	130	165	.788	86	102	591	2.9	3.4	19.7
Totals	94	2739	469	1195	.392	279	389	.717	259	246	1431	2.8	2.6	15.2

Three-point field goals: 1998-99, 26-for-85 (.306). 1999-00, 93-for-248 (.375). 2000-01, 95-for-252 (.377). Totals, 214-for-585 (.366).

THOMAS, ETAN   F/C   WIZARDS

PERSONAL: Born April 1, 1978, in Harlem, N.Y. ... 6-9/256. (2,06/116,1). ... Full Name: Dedreck Etan Thomas.
HIGH SCHOOL: Booker T. Washington (Tulsa, Okla.).
COLLEGE: Syracuse.
TRANSACTIONS/CAREER NOTES: Selected by Dallas Mavericks in first round (12th pick overall) of 2000 NBA Draft. ... Traded by Mavericks with F/C Christian Laettner, G Courtney Alexander, F Loy Vaught, G Hubert Davis and cash considerations to Washington Wizards for F Juwan Howard, C Calvin Booth and F Obinna Ekezie (February 22, 2001).

COLLEGIATE RECORD

Season Team	G	Min.	FGM	FGA	Pct.	FTM	FTA	Pct.	Reb.	Ast.	Pts.	RPG	APG	PPG
96-97—Syracuse	25	408	55	103	.534	33	71	.465	105	3	143	4.2	0.1	5.7
97-98—Syracuse	35	1009	144	236	.610	109	178	.612	230	15	397	6.6	0.4	11.3
98-99—Syracuse	33	913	148	240	.617	109	190	.574	243	17	405	7.4	0.5	12.3
99-00—Syracuse	29	940	148	246	.602	99	146	.678	269	16	395	9.3	0.6	13.6
Totals	122	3270	495	825	.600	350	585	.598	847	51	1340	6.9	0.4	11.0

NBA REGULAR-SEASON RECORD

Season Team	G	Min.	FGM	FGA	Pct.	FTM	FTA	Pct.	Off.	Def.	Tot.	Ast.	St.	Blk.	TO	Pts.	RPG	APG	PPG
00-01—Dal.-Wash.								Did not play—injured.											

TINSLEY, JAMAAL   G   PACERS

PERSONAL: Born February 28, 1978, in Brooklyn, N.Y. ... 6-3/185. (1,91/83,9).
HIGH SCHOOL: Tilden (N.Y.).
JUNIOR COLLEGE: Mount San Jacinto Community College (Calif.).
COLLEGE: Iowa State.
TRANSACTIONS/CAREER NOTES: Selected by Vancouver Grizzlies in first round (27th pick overall) of 2001 NBA Draft. ... Draft rights traded by Grizzlies with F Shareef Abdur-Rahim to Atlanta Hawks for F/C Lorenzen Wright, G Brevin Knight and draft rights to F Pau Gasol (July 19, 2001). ... Draft rights traded by Hawks to Indiana Pacers for future first-round draft choice (July 19, 2001).

DID YOU KNOW . . .

. . . that Paul Arizin was the first NBA player to score 10,000 points in a career?

NOTES: The Sporting News All-America second team (2001).

Season Team	G	Min.	FGM	FGA	Pct.	FTM	FTA	Pct.	Reb.	Ast.	Pts.	AVERAGES		
												RPG	APG	PPG
97-98—Mount San Jacinto	36	...	194	403	.481	94	159	.591	153	341	509	4.3	9.5	14.1
98-99—Mount San Jacinto	37	...	281	502	.560	201	287	.700	160	362	814	4.3	9.8	22.0
99-00—Iowa	37	1212	145	384	.378	102	151	.675	189	244	407	5.1	6.6	11.0
00-01—Iowa	31	999	139	348	.399	128	185	.692	117	187	443	3.8	6.0	14.3
Junior College Totals	73	...	475	905	.525	295	446	.661	313	703	1323	4.3	9.6	18.1
4-Year-College Totals	68	2211	284	732	.388	230	336	.685	306	431	850	4.5	6.3	12.5

Three-point field goals: 1997-98, 27-for-100 (.270). 1998-99, 51-for-139 (.367). 1999-00, 15-for-62 (.242). 2000-01, 37-for-97 (.381). Totals, 78-for-239 (.326) Totals, 52-for-159 (.327).

TREPAGNIER, JEFF　　　G　　　CAVALIERS

PERSONAL: Born July 11, 1979, in Los Angeles. ... 6-4/200. (1,93/90,7). ... Full Name: Jeffery Trepagnier.
HIGH SCHOOL: Compton (Calif.).
COLLEGE: Southern California.
TRANSACTIONS/CAREER NOTES: Selected by Cleveland Cavaliers in second round (36th pick overall) of 2001 NBA Draft.

COLLEGIATE RECORD

Season Team	G	Min.	FGM	FGA	Pct.	FTM	FTA	Pct.	Reb.	Ast.	Pts.	AVERAGES		
												RPG	APG	PPG
97-98—Southern California	28	460	52	129	.403	40	63	.635	98	21	149	3.5	0.8	5.3
98-99—Southern California	28	764	125	254	.492	62	87	.713	150	28	330	5.4	1.0	11.8
99-00—Southern California	29	1054	182	373	.488	66	100	.660	191	60	460	6.6	2.1	15.9
00-01—Southern California	21	621	72	159	.453	37	61	.607	107	33	189	5.1	1.6	9.0
Totals	106	2899	431	915	.471	205	311	.659	546	142	1128	5.2	1.3	10.6

Three-point field goals: 1997-98, 5-for-25 (.200). 1998-99, 18-for-67 (.269). 1999-00, 30-for-79 (.380). 2000-01, 8-for-34 (.235). Totals, 61-for-205 (.298).

VARDA, RATKO　　　C　　　PISTONS

PERSONAL: Born June 5, 1979, in Bosanka Gradiska. ... 7-1/260. (2,16/117,9).
TRANSACTIONS/CAREER NOTES: Not drafted by an NBA franchise. ... Played in Yugoslavia (1996-97 through 2000-01). ... Signed as free agent by Detroit Pistons (July 24, 2001).

YUGOSLAVIAN LEAGUE RECORD

Season Team	G	Min.	FGM	FGA	Pct.	FTM	FTA	Pct.	Reb.	Ast.	Pts.	AVERAGES		
												RPG	APG	PPG
96-97—Partizan	6	9	0	0	...	0	2	.000	1	0	0	0.2	0.0	0.0
97-98—Partizan	24	129	13	29	.448	10	18	.556	28	3	36	1.2	0.1	1.5
98-99—Partizan	19	224	37	60	.617	10	15	.667	54	5	84	2.8	0.3	4.4
99-00—Partizan	19	387	60	93	.645	28	45	.622	75	6	153	3.9	0.3	8.1
00-01—Partizan	19	298	41	88	.466	16	24	.667	69	9	99	3.6	0.5	5.2
Totals	87	1047	151	270	.559	64	104	.615	227	23	372	2.6	0.3	4.3

Three-point field goals: 1997-98, 0-for-1. 1998-99, 0-for-2. 1999-00, 5-for-10 (.500). 2000-01, 1-for-9 (.111). Totals, 6-for-22 (.273).

WALLACE, GERALD　　　F　　　KINGS

PERSONAL: Born July 23, 1982, in Sylacauga, Ala. ... 6-7/215. (2,01/97,5). ... Full Name: Gerald Jermaine Wallace.
HIGH SCHOOL: Childersburg (Ala.).
COLLEGE: Alabama.
TRANSACTIONS/CAREER NOTES: Selected after freshman season by Sacramento Kings in first round (25th pick overall) of 2001 NBA Draft.

COLLEGIATE RECORD

Season Team	G	Min.	FGM	FGA	Pct.	FTM	FTA	Pct.	Reb.	Ast.	Pts.	AVERAGES		
												RPG	APG	PPG
00-01—Alabama	36	824	126	288	.438	88	155	.568	216	55	351	6.0	1.5	9.8

Three-point field goals: 2000-01, 11-for-63 (.175).

WATSON, EARL　　　G　　　SUPERSONICS

PERSONAL: Born June 12, 1979, in Kansas City, Kan. ... 6-1/195. (1,85/88,5). ... Full Name: Earl Joseph Watson.
HIGH SCHOOL: Washington (Kan.).
COLLEGE: UCLA.
TRANSACTIONS/CAREER NOTES: Selected by Seattle SuperSonics in second round (40th pick overall) of 2001 NBA Draft.

PROMISING NEWCOMERS

COLLEGIATE RECORD

												AVERAGES		
Season Team	G	Min.	FGM	FGA	Pct.	FTM	FTA	Pct.	Reb.	Ast.	Pts.	RPG	APG	PPG
97-98—UCLA	33	1057	65	166	.392	40	66	.606	122	104	191	3.7	3.2	5.8
98-99—UCLA	31	1053	144	331	.435	90	128	.703	116	142	411	3.7	4.6	13.3
99-00—UCLA	33	1146	137	304	.451	61	94	.649	129	195	376	3.9	5.9	11.4
00-01—UCLA	32	1115	172	349	.493	89	140	.636	117	166	471	3.7	5.2	14.7
Totals	129	4371	518	1150	.450	280	428	.654	484	607	1449	3.8	4.7	11.2

Three-point field goals: 1997-98, 21-for-65 (.323). 1998-99, 33-for-103 (.320). 1999-00, 41-for-114 (.360). 2000-01, 38-for-108 (.352). Totals, 133-for-390 (.341).

WHITE, RODNEY   F   PISTONS

PERSONAL: Born June 28, 1980, in Philadelphia. ... 6-9/238. (2,06/108,0). ... Full Name: Rodney Charles White.
HIGH SCHOOL: J.P. Stevens (N.J.), then St. Peter's (N.J.), then Mt. Zion Christian Academy (N.C.), then George Washington (Denver).
COLLEGE: Charlotte.
TRANSACTIONS/CAREER NOTES: Selected after freshman season by Detroit Pistons in first round (ninth pick overall) of 2001 NBA Draft.

COLLEGIATE RECORD

												AVERAGES		
Season Team	G	Min.	FGM	FGA	Pct.	FTM	FTA	Pct.	Reb.	Ast.	Pts.	RPG	APG	PPG
00-01—Charlotte	28	865	188	386	.487	114	160	.713	182	41	523	6.5	1.5	18.7

Three-point field goals: 2000-01, 33-for-95 (.347).

WOODS, LOREN   C   TIMBERWOLVES

PERSONAL: Born June 21, 1978, in St. Louis. ... 7-1/245. (2,16/111,1). ... Full Name: Loren Gerard Woods.
HIGH SCHOOL: Cardinal Ritter (St. Louis).
COLLEGE: Wake Forest, then Arizona.
TRANSACTIONS/CAREER NOTES: Selected by Minnesota Timberwolves in second round (46th pick overall) of 2001 NBA Draft.

COLLEGIATE RECORD

												AVERAGES		
Season Team	G	Min.	FGM	FGA	Pct.	FTM	FTA	Pct.	Reb.	Ast.	Pts.	RPG	APG	PPG
96-97—Wake Forest	30	525	71	147	.483	63	93	.677	157	16	205	5.2	0.5	6.8
97-98—Wake Forest	22	554	63	157	.401	67	100	.670	157	19	194	7.1	0.9	8.8
98-99—Arizona					Did not play—transfer student.									
99-00—Arizona	26	820	154	286	.538	97	128	.758	194	38	405	7.5	1.5	15.6
00-01—Arizona	29	879	133	264	.504	117	141	.830	189	62	384	6.5	2.1	13.2
Totals	107	2778	421	854	.493	344	462	.745	697	135	1188	6.5	1.3	11.1

Three-point field goals: 1997-98, 1-for-4 (.250). 1999-00, 0-for-2. 2000-01, 1-for-3 (.333). Totals, 2-for-9 (.222).

WRIGHT, MICHAEL   F   KNICKS

PERSONAL: Born January 7, 1980, in Chicago. ... 6-7/238. (2,01/108,0).
HIGH SCHOOL: Farragut Academy (Chicago).
COLLEGE: Arizona.
TRANSACTIONS/CAREER NOTES: Selected after junior season by New York Knicks in second round (39th pick overall) of 2001 NBA Draft.

COLLEGIATE RECORD

												AVERAGES		
Season Team	G	Min.	FGM	FGA	Pct.	FTM	FTA	Pct.	Reb.	Ast.	Pts.	RPG	APG	PPG
98-99—Arizona	29	791	135	243	.556	134	182	.736	254	8	404	8.8	0.3	13.9
99-00—Arizona	34	1059	190	334	.569	145	203	.714	297	21	526	8.7	0.6	15.5
00-01—Arizona	36	1004	202	340	.594	157	197	.797	281	11	561	7.8	0.3	15.6
Totals	99	2854	527	917	.575	436	582	.749	832	40	1491	8.4	0.4	15.1

Three-point field goals: 1998-99, 0-for-2. 1999-00, 1-for-1. 2000-01, 0-for-3. Totals, 1 for 6 (.167).

ADELMAN, RICK KINGS

PERSONAL: Born June 16, 1946, in Lynwood, Calif. ... 6-2/180. (1,88/81,6). ... Full name: Richard Leonard Adelman. ... Name pronounced ADD-el-mun.
HIGH SCHOOL: St. Pius X (Downey, Calif.).
COLLEGE: Loyola Marymount.
TRANSACTIONS/CAREER NOTES: Selected by San Diego Rockets in seventh round (79th pick overall) of 1968 NBA Draft. ... Selected by Portland Trail Blazers from Rockets in NBA expansion draft (May 11, 1970). ... Traded by Trail Blazers to Chicago Bulls for cash and 1974 second-round draft choice (September 14, 1973). ... Traded by Bulls to New Orleans Jazz for F/C John Block (November 11, 1974). ... Traded by Jazz with F Ollie Johnson to Kansas City/Omaha Kings for F Nate Williams (February 1, 1975). ... Kings franchise moved from Kansas City/Omaha to Kansas City for 1975-76 season. ... Released by Kings (October 21, 1975).

COLLEGIATE RECORD

Season Team	G	Min.	FGM	FGA	Pct.	FTM	FTA	Pct.	Reb.	Ast.	Pts.	RPG	APG	PPG
64-65—Loyola (Calif.)‡						Freshman team statistics unavailable.								
65-66—Loyola (Calif.)	26	...	149	376	.396	129	152	.849	113	...	427	4.3	...	16.4
66-67—Loyola (Calif.)	25	...	151	349	.433	171	214	.799	124	...	473	5.0	...	18.9
67-68—Loyola (Calif.)	25	...	177	420	.421	171	216	.792	127	...	525	5.1	...	21.0
Varsity totals	76	...	477	1145	.417	471	582	.809	364	...	1425	4.8	...	18.8

NBA REGULAR-SEASON RECORD

Season Team	G	Min.	FGM	FGA	Pct.	FTM	FTA	Pct.	Reb.	Ast.	PF	Dq.	Pts.	RPG	APG	PPG
68-69—San Diego	77	1448	177	449	.394	131	204	.642	216	238	158	1	485	2.8	3.1	6.3
69-70—San Diego	35	717	96	247	.389	68	91	.747	81	113	90	0	260	2.3	3.2	7.4
70-71—Portland	81	2303	378	895	.422	267	369	.724	282	380	214	2	1023	3.5	4.7	12.6
71-72—Portland	80	2445	329	753	.437	151	201	.751	229	413	209	2	808	2.9	5.2	10.1
72-73—Portland	76	1822	214	525	.408	73	102	.716	157	294	155	2	591	2.1	3.9	7.8

| | | | | | | | | | REBOUNDS | | | | | | AVERAGES | | |
Season Team	G	Min.	FGM	FGA	Pct.	FTM	FTA	Pct.	Off.	Def.	Tot.	Ast.	St.	Blk.	TO	Pts.	RPG	APG	PPG
73-74—Chicago	55	618	64	170	.376	54	76	.711	16	53	69	56	36	1	...	182	1.3	1.0	3.3
74-75—Ch-NO-KC/O	58	1074	123	291	.423	73	103	.709	25	70	95	112	70	8	...	319	1.6	1.9	5.5
Totals	462	10427	1381	3330	.415	817	1146	.713	...	...	1129	1606	106	9	...	3668	2.4	3.5	7.9

Personal fouls/disqualifications: 1973-74, 63/0. 1974-75, 101/1. Totals, 990/8.

NBA PLAYOFF RECORD

Season Team	G	Min.	FGM	FGA	Pct.	FTM	FTA	Pct.	Reb.	Ast.	PF	Dq.	Pts.	RPG	APG	PPG
68-69—San Diego	6	187	24	53	.453	22	37	.595	15	29	18	0	70	2.5	4.8	11.7

| | | | | | | | | | REBOUNDS | | | | | | AVERAGES | | |
Season Team	G	Min.	FGM	FGA	Pct.	FTM	FTA	Pct.	Off.	Def.	Tot.	Ast.	St.	Blk.	TO	Pts.	RPG	APG	PPG
73-74—Chicago	9	108	16	34	.471	7	11	.636	1	9	10	7	7	0	...	39	1.1	0.8	4.3
74-75—K.C./Omaha	6	34	3	9	.333	6	8	.750	1	1	2	3	1	0	...	12	0.3	0.5	2.0
Totals	21	329	43	96	.448	35	56	.625	...	...	27	39	8	0	...	121	1.3	1.9	5.8

Personal fouls/disqualifications: 1973-74, 5/0. 1974-75, 9/0. Totals, 32/0.

HEAD COACHING RECORD

BACKGROUND: Head coach, Chemeketa Community College, Ore. (1977-78 through 1982-83; record: 141-39, .783). ... Assistant coach, Portland Trail Blazers (1983-84 to February 18, 1989).

NBA COACHING RECORD

	REGULAR SEASON				PLAYOFFS		
Season Team	W	L	Pct.	Finish	W	L	Pct.
88-89 —Portland	14	21	.400	5th/Pacific Division	0	3	.000
89-90 —Portland	59	23	.720	2nd/Pacific Division	12	9	.571
90-91 —Portland	63	19	.768	1st/Pacific Division	9	7	.563
91-92 —Portland	57	25	.695	1st/Pacific Division	13	8	.619
92-93 —Portland	51	31	.622	3rd/Pacific Division	1	3	.250
93-94 —Portland	47	35	.573	4th/Pacific Division	1	3	.250
95-96 —Golden State	36	46	.439	6th/Pacific Division	—	—	—
96-97 —Golden State	30	52	.366	7th Pacific Divison	—	—	—
98-99 —Sacramento	27	23	.540	T3rd/Pacific Division	2	3	.400
99-00 —Sacramento	44	38	.537	5th/Pacific Division	2	3	.400
00-01 —Sacramento	55	27	.671	2nd/Pacific Division	3	5	.375
Totals (11 years)	483	340	.587	**Totals (9 years)**	43	44	.494

NOTES:
1989—Replaced Mike Schuler as Portland head coach (February 18), with record of 25-22. Lost to Los Angeles Lakers in Western Conference first round.
1990—Defeated Dallas, 3-0, in Western Conference first round; defeated San Antonio, 4-3, in Western Conference semifinals; defeated Phoenix, 4-2, in Western Conference finals; lost to Detroit, 4-1, in NBA Finals.
1991—Defeated Seattle, 3-2, in Western Conference first round; defeated Utah, 4-1, in Western Conference semifinals; lost to Los Angeles Lakers, 4-2, in Western Conference finals.
1992—Defeated Los Angeles Lakers, 3-1, in Western Conference first round; defeated Phoenix, 4-1, in Western Conference semifinals; defeated Utah, 4-2, in Western Conference finals; lost to Chicago, 4-2, in NBA Finals.
1993—Lost to San Antonio in Western Conference first round.
1994—Lost to Houston in Western Conference first round.
1999—Lost to Utah in Western Conference first round.
2000—Lost to Los Angeles Lakers in Western Conference first round.
2001—Defeated Phoenix, 3-1, in Western Conference first round; lost to Los Angeles Lakers, 4-0, in Western Conference semifinals.

BROWN, LARRY   76ERS

PERSONAL: Born September 14, 1940, in Brooklyn, N.Y. ... 5-9/160. (1,76/72,6). ... Full name: Lawrence Harvey Brown. ... Brother of Herb Brown, head coach with Detroit Pistons (1975-76 through 1977-78).
HIGH SCHOOL: Long Beach (N.Y.).
COLLEGE: North Carolina.
TRANSACTIONS/CAREER NOTES: Signed by New Orleans Buccaneers of American Basketball Association (1967). ... Traded by Buccaneers with F/G Doug Moe to Oakland Oaks for F Steve Jones, F Ron Franz and G Barry Leibowitz (June 18, 1968). ... Oaks franchise moved from Oakland to Washington and renamed Capitols for 1969-70 season. ... Capitols franchise moved from Washington to Virginia and renamed Squires for 1970-71 season. ... Contract sold by Squires to Denver Rockets (January 23, 1971).
MISCELLANEOUS: Member of gold-medal-winning U.S. Olympic team (1964).

COLLEGIATE RECORD

Season Team	G	Min.	FGM	FGA	Pct.	FTM	FTA	Pct.	Reb.	Ast.	Pts.	RPG	APG	PPG
59-60—North Carolina‡	15	...	88	...	...	100	143	.699	...	...	276	...	...	18.4
60-61—North Carolina	18	...	28	54	.519	25	34	.735	28	...	81	1.6	...	4.5
61-62—North Carolina	17	...	90	204	.441	101	127	.795	52	...	281	3.1	...	16.5
62-63—North Carolina	21	...	102	231	.442	95	122	.779	50	...	299	2.4	...	14.2
Varsity totals	56	...	220	489	.450	221	283	.781	130	...	661	2.3	...	11.8

AMATEUR PLAYING RECORD

Season Team	G	Min.	FGM	FGA	Pct.	FTM	FTA	Pct.	Reb.	Ast.	Pts.	RPG	APG	PPG
63-64—Akron (Ohio)	33	...	149	...	...	31	...	...	...	...	329	...	...	10.0
64-65—Akron (Ohio)	32	...	144	297	.485	139	167	.832	90	...	427	2.8	...	13.3
Totals	65	...	293	...	...	170	...	...	...	...	756	...	...	11.6

ABA REGULAR-SEASON RECORD

NOTES: ABA All-Star second team (1968). ... Member of ABA championship team (1969). ... Holds single-game record for most assists—23 (February 20, 1972, vs. Pittsburgh).

			2-POINT			3-POINT									AVERAGES		
Season Team	G	Min.	FGM	FGA	Pct.	FGM	FGA	Pct.	FTM	FTA	Pct.	Reb.	Ast.	Pts.	RPG	APG	PPG
67-68—New Orleans	78	2807	311	812	.383	19	89	.213	366	450	.813	249	*506	1045	3.2	6.5	13.4
68-69—Oakland	77	2381	300	671	.447	8	35	.229	301	379	.794	235	*544	925	3.1	7.1	12.0
69-70—Washington	82	2766	366	815	.449	10	39	.256	362	439	.825	246	*580	1124	3.0	7.1	13.7
70-71—Virginia-Denver	63	1343	171	319	.379	6	21	.286	186	225	.827	109	330	446	1.7	5.2	7.1
71-72—Denver	76	2012	238	531	.448	5	25	.200	198	244	.811	166	549	689	2.2	7.2	9.1
Totals	376	11309	1336	3148	.424	48	209	.230	1413	1737	.813	1005	2509	4229	2.7	6.7	11.2

ABA PLAYOFF RECORD

			2-POINT			3-POINT									AVERAGES		
Season Team	G	Min.	FGM	FGA	Pct.	FGM	FGA	Pct.	FTM	FTA	Pct.	Reb.	Ast.	Pts.	RPG	APG	PPG
67-68—New Orleans	17	696	86	194	.443	4	18	.222	100	122	.820	59	129	284	3.5	7.6	16.7
68-69—Oakland	16	534	74	170	.435	0	3	.000	76	90	.844	52	87	224	3.3	5.4	14.0
69-70—Washington	7	269	32	68	.471	1	5	.200	30	34	.882	35	68	97	5.0	9.7	13.9
71-72—Denver	7	211	21	47	.447	0	3	.000	23	24	.958	10	36	65	1.4	5.1	9.3
Totals	47	1710	213	479	.445	5	29	.172	229	270	.848	156	320	670	3.3	6.8	14.3

ABA ALL-STAR GAME RECORD

NOTES: ABA All-Star Game Most Valuable Player (1968).

		2-POINT			3-POINT								
Season Team	Min.	FGM	FGA	Pct.	FGM	FGA	Pct.	FTM	FTA	Pct.	Reb.	Ast.	Pts.
1968—New Orleans	22	5	7	.714	2	2	1.000	1	1	1.000	3	5	17
1969—Oakland	25	1	6	.167	0	1	.000	3	5	.600	0	7	5
1970—Washington	15	0	2	.000	0	0	...	3	3	1.000	3	3	3
Totals	62	6	15	.400	2	3	.667	7	9	.778	6	15	25

HEAD COACHING RECORD

BACKGROUND: Assistant coach, University of North Carolina (1965-66 and 1966-67). ... Assistant coach, U.S. Olympic team (1980).
HONORS: ABA Coach of the Year (1973, 1975, 1976). ... NBA Coach of the Year (2001).

ABA COACHING RECORD

	REGULAR SEASON				PLAYOFFS		
Season Team	W	L	Pct.	Finish	W	L	Pct.
72-73 —Carolina	57	27	.679	1st/Eastern Division	7	5	.583
73-74 —Carolina	47	37	.560	3rd/Eastern Division	0	4	.000
74-75 —Denver	65	19	.774	1st/Western Division	7	6	.538
75-76 —Denver	60	24	.714	1st/Western Division	6	7	.462
Totals (4 years)	229	107	.682	Totals (4 years)	20	22	.476

NBA COACHING RECORD

	REGULAR SEASON				PLAYOFFS		
Season Team	W	L	Pct.	Finish	W	L	Pct.
76-77 —Denver	50	32	.610	1st/Midwest Division	2	4	.500
77-78 —Denver	48	34	.585	1st/Midwest Division	6	7	.462
78-79 —Denver	28	25	.528		—	—	—
81-82 —New Jersey	44	38	.537	3rd/Atlantic Division	0	2	.000
82-83 —New Jersey	47	29	.618		—	—	—
88-89 —San Antonio	21	61	.256	5th/Midwest Division	—	—	—
89-90 —San Antonio	56	26	.683	1st/Midwest Division	6	4	.600

		REGULAR SEASON					PLAYOFFS		
Season Team	W	L	Pct.	Finish			W	L	Pct.
90-91 —San Antonio	55	27	.671	1st/Midwest Division			1	3	.250
91-92 —San Antonio	21	17	.553				—	—	—
—Los Angeles Clippers	23	12	.657	5th/Pacific Division			2	3	.400
92-93 —Los Angeles Clippers	41	41	.500	4th/Pacific Division			2	3	.400
93-94 —Indiana	47	35	.573	T3rd/Central Division			10	6	.625
94-95 —Indiana	52	30	.634	1st/Central Division			10	7	.588
95-96 —Indiana	52	30	.634	2nd/Central Division			2	3	.400
96-97 —Indiana	39	43	.476	6th/Central Division			—	—	—
97-98 —Philadelphia	31	51	.378	7th/Atlantic Division			—	—	—
98-99 —Philadelphia	28	22	.560	3rd/Atlantic Division			3	5	.375
99-00 —Philadelphia	49	33	.598	3rd/Atlantic Division			5	5	.500
00-01 —Philadelphia	56	26	.683	1st/Atlantic Division			12	11	.522
Totals (18 years)	**788**	**612**	**.563**	**Totals (13 years)**			**62**	**63**	**.496**

COLLEGIATE COACHING RECORD

Season Team	W	L	Pct.	Finish
79-80 —UCLA	22	10	.688	4th/Pacific-10 Conference
80-81 —UCLA	20	7	.741	3rd/Pacific-10 Conference
83-84 —Kansas	22	10	.688	2nd/Big Eight Conference
84-85 —Kansas	26	8	.765	2nd/Big Eight Conference
85-86 —Kansas	35	4	.897	1st/Big Eight Conference
86-87 —Kansas	25	11	.694	T2nd/Big Eight Conference
87-88 —Kansas	27	11	.711	3rd/Big Eight Conference
Totals (7 years)	**177**	**61**	**.744**	

NOTES:

1973—Defeated New York, 4-1, in Eastern Division semifinals; lost to Kentucky, 4-3, in Eastern Division finals.

1974—Lost to Kentucky in Eastern Division semifinals.

1975—Defeated Utah, 4-2, in Western Division semifinals; lost to Indiana, 4-3, in Western Division finals.

1976—Defeated Kentucky, 4-3, in semifinals; lost to New York, 4-2, in ABA Finals.

1977—Lost to Portland in Western Conference semifinals.

1978—Defeated Milwaukee, 4-3, in Western Conference semifinals; lost to Seattle, 4-2, in Western Conference finals.

1979—Resigned as Denver head coach (February 1); replaced by Donnie Walsh with club in second place.

1980—Defeated Old Dominion, 87-74, in NCAA Tournament first round; defeated DePaul, 77-71, in second round; defeated Ohio State, 72-68, in regional semifinals; defeated Clemson, 85-74, in regional finals; defeated Purdue, 67-62, in semifinals; lost to Louisville, 59-54, in championship game.

1981—Lost to Brigham Young, 78-55, in NCAA Tournament second round.

1982—Lost to Washington in Eastern Conference first round.

1983—Resigned as New Jersey head coach (April 7); replaced by Bill Blair with club in third place.

1984—Defeated Alcorn State, 57-56, in NCAA Tournament first round; lost to Wake Forest, 69-59, in second round.

1985—Defeated Ohio University, 49-38, in NCAA Tournament first round; lost to Auburn, 66-64, in second round.

1986—Defeated North Carolina A&T, 71-46, in NCAA Tournament first round; defeated Temple, 65-43, in second round; defeated Michigan State, 96-86, in regional semifinals; defeated North Carolina State, 75-67, in regional finals; lost to Duke, 71-67, in semifinals.

1987—Defeated Houston, 66-55, in NCAA Tournament first round; defeated Southwest Missouri State, 67-63, in second round; lost to Georgetown, 70-57, in regional semifinals.

1988—Defeated Xavier, 85-72, in NCAA Tournament first round; defeated Murray State, 61-58, in second round; defeated Vanderbilt, 77-64, in regional semifinals; defeated Kansas State, 71-58, in regional finals; defeated Duke, 66-59, in semifinals; defeated Oklahoma, 83-79, in championship game.

1990—Defeated Denver, 3-0, in Western Conference first round; lost to Portland, 4-3, in Western Conference semifinals.

1991—Lost to Golden State in Western Conference first round.

1992—Replaced as San Antonio head coach by Bob Bass with club in second place (January 21); replaced Mike Schuler (21-24) and Mack Calvin (interim head coach, 1-1) as Los Angeles Clippers head coach (February 6), with record of 22-25 and club in sixth place. Lost to Utah in Western Conference first round.

1993—Lost to Houston in Western Conference first round.

1994—Defeated Orlando, 3-0, in Eastern Conference first round; defeated Atlanta, 4-2, in Eastern Conference semifinals; lost to New York, 4-3, in Eastern Conference finals.

1995—Defeated Atlanta, 3-0, in Eastern Conference first round; defeated New York, 4-3, Eastern Conference semifinals; lost to Orlando, 4-3, in Eastern Conference finals.

1996—Lost to Atlanta in Eastern Conference first round.

1999—Defeated Orlando, 3-1, in Eastern Conference first round; lost to Indiana, 4-0, in Eastern Conference semifinals.

2000—Defeated Charlotte, 3-1, in Eastern Conference first round; lost to Indiana, 4-2, in Eastern Conference semifinals.

2001—Defeated Indiana, 3-1, in Eastern Conference first round; defeated Toronto, 4-3, in Eastern Conference semifinals; defeated Milwaukee, 4-3, in Eastern Conferene finals; lost to Los Angeles Lakers, 4-1, in NBA Finals.

CARLISLE, RICK   PISTONS

PERSONAL: Born October 27, 1959, in Ogdensburg, N.Y. ... 6-5/210. (1,96/95,3). ... Full Name: Richard Preston Carlisle.
HIGH SCHOOL: Central.
COLLEGE: Maine, then Virginia.
TRANSACTIONS/CAREER NOTES: Selected by Boston Celtics in third round (69th pick overall) of 1984 NBA Draft. ... Waived by Celtics (November 3, 1987). ... Signed as free agent by New York Knicks (November 30, 1987). ... Played in Continental Basketball Association with Albany Patroons (1987-88). ... Signed as free agent by New Jersey Nets (October 4, 1989). ... Waived by Nets (December 1, 1989).

COLLEGIATE RECORD

Season Team	G	Min.	FGM	FGA	Pct.	FTM	FTA	Pct.	Reb.	Ast.	Pts.	RPG	APG	PPG
79-80—Maine	28	...	131	236	.555	83	97	.856	96	118	345	3.4	4.2	12.3
80-81—Maine	28	...	176	322	.547	102	126	.810	118	132	454	4.2	4.7	16.2
81-82—Virginia							Did not play.							
82-83—Virginia	33	956	142	277	.513	87	104	.837	100	98	379	3.0	3.0	11.5
83-84—Virginia	33	959	149	289	.516	67	96	.698	93	95	365	2.8	2.9	11.1
Totals	122	...	598	1124	.532	339	423	.801	407	443	1543	3.3	3.6	12.6

Three-point field goals: 1982-83, 8-for-12 (.667).

NBA REGULAR-SEASON RECORD

Season Team	G	Min.	FGM	FGA	Pct.	FTM	FTA	Pct.	REBOUNDS Off.	Def.	Tot.	Ast.	St.	Blk.	TO	Pts.	AVERAGES RPG	APG	PPG
84-85—Boston	38	179	26	67	.388	15	17	.882	8	13	21	25	3	0	...	67	0.6	0.7	1.8
85-86—Boston	77	760	92	189	.487	15	23	.652	22	55	77	104	19	4	...	199	1.0	1.4	2.6
86-87—Boston	42	297	30	92	.326	15	20	.750	8	22	30	35	8	0	...	80	0.7	0.8	1.9
87-88—New York	26	204	29	67	.433	10	11	.909	6	7	13	32	11	4	...	74	0.5	1.2	2.8
89-90—New Jersey	5	21	1	7	.143	0	0	...	0	0	0	5	1	1	...	2	0.0	1.0	0.4
Totals	188	1461	178	422	.422	55	71	.775	44	97	141	201	42	9	...	422	0.8	1.1	2.2

Three-point field goals: 1984-85, 0-for-2. 1985-86, 0-for-10. 1986-87, 5-for-16 (.313). 1987-88, 6-for-17 (.353). 1989-90, 0-for-3. Totals, 11-for-48 (.229).

Personal fouls/disqualifications: 1984-85, 21/0. 1985-86, 92/1. 1986-87, 28/0. 1987-88, 39/1. 1989-90, 7/0. Totals, 187/2.

NBA PLAYOFF RECORD

Season Team	G	Min.	FGM	FGA	Pct.	FTM	FTA	Pct.	REBOUNDS Off.	Def.	Tot.	Ast.	St.	Blk.	TO	Pts.	AVERAGES RPG	APG	PPG
85-86—Boston	10	54	8	15	.533	3	4	.750	3	2	5	8	2	0	...	19	0.5	0.8	1.9
87-88—New York	2	8	1	4	.250				1	1	2	0	1	0	...	2	1.0	0.0	1.0
Totals	12	62	9	19	.474	3	4	.750	4	3	7	8	3	0	...	21	0.6	0.7	1.8

Three-point field goals: 1987-88, 0-for-2. Totals, 0-for-2 (.000).

Personal fouls/disqualifications: 1985-86, 9/0. 1987-88, 1/0. Totals, 10/0.

CBA REGULAR-SEASON RECORD

Season Team	G	Min.	FGM	FGA	Pct.	FTM	FTA	Pct.	Reb.	Ast.	Pts.	RPG	APG	PPG
87-88—Albany	6	172	38	74	.514	16	19	.842	11	14	104	1.8	2.3	17.3

Three-point field goals: 1987-88, 4-for-8 (.500).

HEAD COACHING RECORD

NOTES: Assistant coach, New Jersey Nets (1989-90 through 1993-94). ... Assistant coach, Portland Trailblazers (1994-95 through 1996-97). ... Assistant coach, Indiana Pacers (1997-98 through 2000-01).

CHEEKS, MAURICE — TRAILBLAZERS

PERSONAL: Born September 8, 1956, in Chicago. ... 6-1/180. (1,85/81,6). ... Full name: Maurice Edward Cheeks.

HIGH SCHOOL: Du Sable (Chicago).

COLLEGE: West Texas State.

TRANSACTIONS: Selected by Philadelphia 76ers in second round (36th pick overall) of 1978 NBA Draft. ... Traded by 76ers with C Christian Welp and G David Wingate to San Antonio Spurs for G Johnny Dawkins and F Jay Vincent (August 28, 1989). ... Traded by Spurs to New York Knicks for G Rod Strickland (February 21, 1990). ... Traded by Knicks to Atlanta Hawks for C Tim McCormick (October 3, 1991). ... Signed as free agent by New Jersey Nets (January 7, 1993).

CAREER NOTES: Assistant coach, 76ers (1994-95 to 2000-01).

MISCELLANEOUS: Member of NBA championship team (1983). ... Philadelphia 76ers franchise all-time assists leader with 6,212 and all-time steals leader with 1,942 (1978-79 through 1988-89).

COLLEGIATE RECORD

Season Team	G	Min.	FGM	FGA	Pct.	FTM	FTA	Pct.	Reb.	Ast.	Pts.	RPG	APG	PPG
74-75—West Texas State	26	...	35	75	.467	31	53	.585	56	...	101	2.2	...	3.9
75-76—West Texas State	23	767	102	170	.600	52	84	.619	91	...	256	4.0	...	11.1
76-77—West Texas State	30	1095	149	246	.606	119	169	.704	119	212	417	4.0	7.1	13.9
77-78—West Texas State	27	941	174	319	.545	105	147	.714	152	153	453	5.6	5.7	16.8
Totals	106	...	460	810	.568	307	453	.678	418	...	1227	3.9	...	11.6

NBA REGULAR-SEASON RECORD

HONORS: NBA All-Defensive first team (1983, 1984, 1985, 1986). ... NBA All-Defensive second team (1987).

Season Team	G	Min.	FGM	FGA	Pct.	FTM	FTA	Pct.	REBOUNDS Off.	Def.	Tot.	Ast.	St.	Blk.	TO	Pts.	AVERAGES RPG	APG	PPG
78-79—Philadelphia	82	2409	292	572	.510	101	140	.721	63	191	254	431	174	12	193	685	3.1	5.3	8.4
79-80—Philadelphia	79	2623	357	661	.540	180	231	.779	75	199	274	556	183	32	216	898	3.5	7.0	11.4
80-81—Philadelphia	81	2415	310	581	.534	140	178	.787	67	178	245	560	193	39	174	763	3.0	6.9	9.4
81-82—Philadelphia	79	2498	352	676	.521	171	220	.777	51	197	248	667	209	33	184	881	3.1	8.4	11.2
82-83—Philadelphia	79	2465	404	745	.542	181	240	.754	53	156	209	543	184	31	179	990	2.6	6.9	12.5
83-84—Philadelphia	75	2494	386	702	.550	170	232	.733	44	161	205	478	171	20	182	950	2.7	6.4	12.7
84-85—Philadelphia	78	2616	422	741	.570	175	199	.879	54	163	217	497	169	24	155	1025	2.8	6.4	13.1

Season Team	G	Min.	FGM	FGA	Pct.	FTM	FTA	Pct.	REBOUNDS Off.	Def.	Tot.	Ast.	St.	Blk.	TO	Pts.	RPG	APG	PPG
85-86—Philadelphia	82	*3270	490	913	.537	282	335	.842	55	180	235	753	207	27	238	1266	2.9	9.2	15.4
86-87—Philadelphia	68	2624	415	788	.527	227	292	.777	47	168	215	538	180	15	173	1061	3.2	7.9	15.6
87-88—Philadelphia	79	2871	428	865	.495	227	275	.825	59	194	253	635	167	22	160	1086	3.2	8.0	13.7
88-89—Philadelphia	71	2298	336	696	.483	151	195	.774	39	144	183	554	105	17	116	824	2.6	7.8	11.6
89-90—S.A.-N.Y.	81	2519	307	609	.504	171	202	.847	50	190	240	453	124	10	121	789	3.0	5.6	9.7
90-91—New York	76	2147	241	483	.499	105	129	.814	22	151	173	435	128	10	108	592	2.3	5.7	7.8
91-92—Atlanta	56	1086	115	249	.462	26	43	.605	29	66	95	185	83	0	36	259	1.7	3.3	4.6
92-93—New Jersey	35	510	51	93	.548	24	27	.889	5	37	42	107	33	2	33	126	1.2	3.1	3.6
Totals	1101	34845	4906	9374	.523	2331	2938	.793	713	2375	3088	7392	2310	294	2268	12195	2.8	6.7	11.1

Three-point field goals: 1979-80, 4-for-9 (.444). 1980-81, 3-for-8 (.375). 1981-82, 6-for-22 (.273). 1982-83, 1-for-6 (.167). 1983-84, 8-for-20 (.400). 1984-85, 6-for-26 (.231). 1985-86, 4-for-17 (.235). 1986-87, 4-for-22 (.235). 1987-88, 3-for-22 (.136). 1988-89, 1-for-13 (.077). 1989-90, 4-for-16 (.250). 1990-91, 5-for-20 (.250). 1991-92, 3-for-6 (.500). 1992-93, 0-for-2. Totals, 52-for-204 (.255).

Personal fouls/disqualifications: 1978-79, 198/2. 1979-80, 197/1. 1980-81, 231/1. 1981-82, 247/0. 1982-83, 182/0. 1983-84, 196/1. 1984-85, 184/0. 1985-86, 160/0. 1986-87, 109/0. 1987-88, 116/0. 1988-89, 114/0. 1989-90, 78/0. 1990-91, 138/0. 1991-92, 73/0. 1992-93, 35/0. Totals, 2258/5.

NBA PLAYOFF RECORD

Season Team	G	Min.	FGM	FGA	Pct.	FTM	FTA	Pct.	REBOUNDS Off.	Def.	Tot.	Ast.	St.	Blk.	TO	Pts.	RPG	APG	PPG
78-79—Philadelphia	9	330	66	121	.545	37	56	.661	13	22	35	63	37	4	29	169	3.9	7.0	18.8
79-80—Philadelphia	18	675	89	174	.512	29	41	.707	22	52	74	111	45	4	45	208	4.1	6.2	11.6
80-81—Philadelphia	16	513	68	125	.544	32	42	.762	4	47	51	116	40	12	36	168	3.2	7.3	10.5
81-82—Philadelphia	21	765	125	265	.472	50	65	.769	15	47	62	172	48	6	49	301	3.0	8.2	14.3
82-83—Philadelphia	13	483	83	165	.503	45	64	.703	11	28	39	91	26	2	34	212	3.0	7.0	16.3
83-84—Philadelphia	5	171	35	67	.522	13	15	.867	2	10	12	19	13	0	10	83	2.4	3.8	16.6
84-85—Philadelphia	13	483	81	153	.529	36	42	.857	12	34	46	67	31	5	34	198	3.5	5.2	15.2
85-86—Philadelphia	12	519	94	182	.516	62	73	.849	13	43	56	85	13	3	32	250	4.7	7.1	20.8
86-87—Philadelphia	5	210	35	66	.530	18	21	.857	1	12	13	44	9	4	12	88	2.6	8.8	17.6
88-89—Philadelphia	3	128	21	41	.512	11	13	.846	3	8	11	39	7	1	3	53	3.7	13.0	17.7
89-90—New York	10	388	50	104	.481	28	31	.903	12	27	39	85	17	2	19	128	3.9	8.5	12.8
90-91—New York	3	101	14	23	.609	1	2	.500	3	6	9	16	3	1	8	30	3.0	5.3	10.0
92-93—New Jersey	5	82	11	23	.478	0	1	.000	3	3	6	14	6	1	7	22	1.2	2.8	4.4
Totals	133	4848	772	1509	.512	362	466	.777	114	339	453	922	295	45	318	1910	3.4	6.9	14.4

Three-point field goals: 1979-80, 1-for-5 (.200). 1980-81, 0-for-3. 1981-82, 1-for-9 (.111). 1982-83, 1-for-2 (.500). 1983-84, 0-for-1. 1984-85, 0-for-5. 1985-86, 0-for-7. 1986-87, 0-for-1. 1988-89, 0-for-1. 1989-90, 0-for-4. 1990-91, 1-for-3 (.333). Totals, 4-for-41 (.098).

Personal fouls/disqualifications: 1978-79, 29/0. 1979-80, 43/0. 1980-81, 55/1. 1981-82, 58/0. 1982-83, 23/0. 1983-84, 18/0. 1984-85, 29/0. 1985-86, 18/0. 1986-87, 14/0. 1988-89, 4/0. 1989-90, 21/0. 1990-91, 9/0. 1992-93, 3/0. Totals, 324/1.

NBA ALL-STAR GAME RECORD

Season Team	Min.	FGM	FGA	Pct.	FTM	FTA	Pct.	REBOUNDS Off.	Def.	Tot.	Ast.	PF	Dq.	St.	Blk.	TO	Pts.
1983 —Philadelphia	18	3	8	.375	0	0	...	0	1	1	1	0	0	0	0	0	6
1986 —Philadelphia	14	3	6	.500	0	0	...	0	0	0	2	1	0	0	2	0	6
1987 —Philadelphia	8	1	2	.500	2	2	1.000	0	0	0	0	1	0	1	0	1	4
1988 —Philadelphia	4	0	0	...	0	0	...	0	2	2	1	0	0	0	0	0	0
Totals	44	7	16	.438	2	2	1.000	0	3	3	4	2	0	3	0	4	16

COLLINS, DOUG   WIZARDS

PERSONAL: Born July 28, 1951, in Christopher, Ill. ... 6-6/180. (1,98/81,6). ... Full name: Paul Douglas Collins.
HIGH SCHOOL: Benton (Ill.).
COLLEGE: Illinois State.
TRANSACTIONS/CAREER NOTES: Selected by Philadelphia 76ers in first round (first pick overall) of 1973 NBA Draft.
MISCELLANEOUS: Member of silver-medal-winning U.S. Olympic team (1972). ... Broadcaster, CBS Sports (1984-85 and 1985-86). ... Broadcaster, Turner Sports (1989-90 through 1994-95). ... Broadcaster, NBC Sports (1998-99 through 2000-01).

COLLEGIATE RECORD

NOTES: THE SPORTING NEWS All-America second team (1973).

Season Team	G	Min.	FGM	FGA	Pct.	FTM	FTA	Pct.	Reb.	Ast.	Pts.	RPG	APG	PPG
69-70—Illinois State‡	21	...	173	376	.460	95	113	.841	196	...	441	9.3	...	21.0
70-71—Illinois State	26	...	273	609	.448	197	235	.838	166	...	743	6.4	...	28.6
71-72—Illinois State	26	...	352	704	.500	143	177	.808	133	...	847	5.1	...	32.6
72-73—Illinois State	25	...	269	565	.476	112	137	.818	126	...	650	5.0	...	26.0
Varsity totals	77	...	894	1878	.476	452	549	.823	425	...	2240	5.5	...	29.1

NBA REGULAR-SEASON RECORD

Season Team	G	Min.	FGM	FGA	Pct.	FTM	FTA	Pct.	REBOUNDS Off.	Def.	Tot.	Ast.	St.	Blk.	TO	Pts.	RPG	APG	PPG
73-74—Philadelphia ..	25	436	72	194	.371	55	72	.764	7	39	46	40	13	2	...	199	1.8	1.6	8.0
74-75—Philadelphia ..	81	2820	561	1150	.488	331	392	.844	104	211	315	213	108	17	...	1453	3.9	2.6	17.9
75-76—Philadelphia ..	77	2995	614	1196	.513	372	445	.836	126	181	307	191	110	24	...	1600	4.0	2.5	20.8
76-77—Philadelphia ..	58	2037	426	823	.518	210	250	.840	64	131	195	271	70	15	...	1062	3.4	4.7	18.3
77-78—Philadelphia ..	79	2770	643	1223	.526	267	329	.812	87	143	230	320	129	25	250	1553	2.9	4.1	19.7
78-79—Philadelphia ..	47	1595	358	717	.499	201	247	.814	36	87	123	191	52	20	131	917	2.6	4.1	19.5
79-80—Philadelphia ..	36	963	191	410	.466	113	124	.911	29	65	94	100	30	7	82	495	2.6	2.8	13.8
80-81—Philadelphia ..	12	329	62	126	.492	24	29	.828	6	23	29	42	7	4	22	148	2.4	3.5	12.3
Totals	415	13945	2927	5839	.501	1573	1888	.833	459	880	1339	1368	519	114	485	7427	3.2	3.3	17.9

Three-point field goals: 1979-80, 0-for-1.
Personal fouls/disqualifications: 1973-74, 65/1. 1974-75, 291/6. 1975-76, 249/2. 1976-77, 174/2. 1977-78, 228/2. 1978-79, 139/1. 1979-80, 76/0. 1980-81, 23/0. Totals, 1245/14.

NBA PLAYOFF RECORD

Season Team	G	Min.	FGM	FGA	Pct.	FTM	FTA	Pct.	REBOUNDS Off.	Def.	Tot.	Ast.	St.	Blk.	TO	Pts.	AVERAGES RPG	APG	PPG
75-76—Philadelphia ..	3	117	23	53	.434	12	14	.857	13	8	21	10	3	1	...	58	7.0	3.3	19.3
76-77—Philadelphia ..	19	759	177	318	.557	71	96	.740	30	49	79	74	28	3	...	425	4.2	3.9	22.4
77-78—Philadelphia ..	10	342	82	165	.497	40	49	.816	8	23	31	27	3	0	...	204	3.1	2.7	20.4
Totals	32	1218	282	536	.526	123	159	.774	51	80	131	111	34	4	34	687	4.1	3.5	21.5

Personal fouls/disqualifications: 1975-76, 9/0. 1976-77, 57/0. 1977-78, 29/0. Totals, 95/0.

NBA ALL-STAR GAME RECORD

Season Team	Min.	FGM	FGA	Pct.	FTM	FTA	Pct.	REBOUNDS Off.	Def.	Tot.	Ast.	PF	Dq.	St.	Blk.	TO	Pts.
1977 —Philadelphia.......	20	5	10	.500	2	2	1.000	2	4	6	3	3	0	3	0	...	12
1978 —Philadelphia.......	21	3	6	.500	2	2	1.000	1	1	2	6	2	0	1	0	...	8
1979 —Philadelphia.......	27	3	8	.375	8	11	.727	4	1	5	8	3	0	2	0	...	14
1980 —Philadelphia							Selected, did not play—injured.										
Totals..........................	68	11	24	.458	12	15	.800	7	6	13	17	8	0	6	0	...	34

HEAD COACHING RECORD

BACKGROUND: Assistant coach, University of Pennsylvania (1981-82). ... Assistant coach, Arizona State (1982-83 and 1983-84).

NBA COACHING RECORD

Season Team	REGULAR SEASON W	L	Pct.	Finish	PLAYOFFS W	L	Pct.
86-87 —Chicago	40	42	.488	5th/Central Division	0	3	.000
87-88 —Chicago	50	32	.610	2nd/Central Division	4	6	.400
88-89 —Chicago	47	35	.573	5th/Central Division	9	8	.529
95-96 —Detroit	46	36	.561	4th/Central Division	0	3	.000
96-97 —Detroit	54	28	.659	4th/Central Division	2	3	.400
97-98 —Detroit	21	24	.467		—	—	—
Totals (5 years)....................................	258	197	.521	Totals (5 years).......	15	23	.395

NOTES:

1987—Lost to Boston in Eastern Conference first round.

1988—Defeated Cleveland, 3-2, in Eastern Conference first round; lost to Detroit, 4-1, in Eastern Conference semifinals.

1989—Defeated Cleveland, 3-2, in Eastern Conference first round; defeated New York, 4-2, in Eastern Conference semifinals; lost to Detroit, 4-2, in Eastern Conference finals.

1996—Lost to Orlando in Eastern Conference first round.

1997—Lost to Atlanta in Eastern Conference first round.

1998—Replaced as Detroit head coach by Alvin Gentry (February 2) with club in seventh place.

COWENS, DAVE — WARRIORS

PERSONAL: Born October 25, 1948, in Newport, Ky. ... 6-9/230. (2,05/104,3). ... Full name: David William Cowens.
HIGH SCHOOL: Newport (Ky.) Central Catholic.
COLLEGE: Florida State.
TRANSACTIONS/CAREER NOTES: Selected by Boston Celtics in first round (fourth pick overall) of 1970 NBA Draft. ... Traded by Celtics to Milwaukee Bucks for G Quinn Buckner (September 9, 1982).
CAREER HONORS: Elected to Naismith Memorial Basketball Hall of Fame (1990). ... One of the 50 Greatest Players in NBA History (1996).
MISCELLANEOUS: Member of NBA championship team (1974, 1976).

COLLEGIATE RECORD

NOTES: The Sporting News All-America second team (1970).

Season Team	G	Min.	FGM	FGA	Pct.	FTM	FTA	Pct.	Reb.	Ast.	Pts.	AVERAGES RPG	APG	PPG
66-67—Florida State‡................	18	...	105	208	.505	49	90	.544	357	...	259	19.8	...	14.4
67-68—Florida State	27	...	206	383	.538	96	131	.733	456	...	508	16.9	...	18.8
68-69—Florida State	25	...	202	384	.526	104	164	.634	437	...	508	17.5	...	20.3
69-70—Florida State	26	...	174	355	.490	115	169	.680	447	...	463	17.2	...	17.8
Varsity totals.........................	78	...	582	1122	.519	315	464	.679	1340	...	1479	17.2	...	19.0

NBA REGULAR-SEASON RECORD

HONORS: NBA Most Valuable Player (1973). ... NBA co-Rookie of the Year (1971). ... All-NBA second team (1973, 1975, 1976). ... NBA All-Defensive first team (1976). ... NBA All-Defensive second team (1975, 1980). ... NBA All-Rookie team (1971).

Season Team	G	Min.	FGM	FGA	Pct.	FTM	FTA	Pct.	Reb.	Ast.	PF	Dq.	Pts.	AVERAGES RPG	APG	PPG
70-71—Boston	81	3076	550	1302	.422	273	373	.732	1216	228	*350	15	1373	15.0	2.8	17.0
71-72—Boston	79	3186	657	1357	.484	175	243	.720	1203	245	*314	10	1489	15.2	3.1	18.8
72-73—Boston	82	3425	740	1637	.452	204	262	.779	1329	333	311	7	1684	16.2	4.1	20.5

Season Team	G	Min.	FGM	FGA	Pct.	FTM	FTA	Pct.	REBOUNDS Off.	Def.	Tot.	Ast.	St.	Blk.	TO	Pts.	AVERAGES RPG	APG	PPG
73-74—Boston	80	3352	645	1475	.437	228	274	.832	264	993	1257	354	95	101	...	1518	15.7	4.4	19.0
74-75—Boston	65	2632	569	1199	.475	191	244	.783	229	729	958	296	87	73	...	1329	14.7	4.6	20.4
75-76—Boston	78	3101	611	1305	.468	257	340	.756	335	911	1246	325	94	71	...	1479	16.0	4.2	19.0
76-77—Boston	50	1888	328	756	.434	162	198	.818	147	550	697	248	46	49	...	818	13.9	5.0	16.4
77-78—Boston	77	3215	598	1220	.490	239	284	.842	248	830	1078	351	102	67	217	1435	14.0	4.6	18.6
78-79—Boston	68	2517	488	1010	.483	151	187	.807	152	500	652	242	76	51	174	1127	9.6	3.6	16.6
79-80—Boston	66	2159	422	932	.453	95	122	.779	126	408	534	206	69	61	108	940	8.1	3.1	14.2
80-81—							Did not play—retired.												
81-82—							Did not play—retired.												
82-83—Milwaukee......	40	1014	136	306	.444	52	63	.825	73	201	274	82	30	15	44	324	6.9	2.1	8.1
Totals	766	29565	5744	12499	.460	2027	2590	.783	...		10444	2910	599	488	543	13516	13.6	3.8	17.6

Three-point field goals: 1979-80, 1-for-12 (.083). 1982-83, 0-for-2. Totals, 1-for-14 (.071).

Personal fouls/disqualifications: 1973-74, 294/7. 1974-75, 243/7. 1975-76, 314/10. 1976-77, 181/7. 1977-78, 297/5. 1978-79, 263/16. 1979-80, 216/2. 1982-83, 137/4. Totals, 2920/90.

NBA PLAYOFF RECORD

NOTES: Shares single-game playoff record for most defensive rebounds—20 (April 22, 1975, vs. Houston; and May 1, 1977, vs. Philadelphia).

Season Team	G	Min.	FGM	FGA	Pct.	FTM	FTA	Pct.	Reb.	Ast.	PF	Dq.	Pts.	AVERAGES RPG	APG	PPG
71-72—Boston	11	441	71	156	.455	28	47	.596	152	33	50	2	170	13.8	3.0	15.5
72-73—Boston	13	598	129	273	.473	27	41	.659	216	48	54	2	285	16.6	3.7	21.9

Season Team	G	Min.	FGM	FGA	Pct.	FTM	FTA	Pct.	REBOUNDS Off.	Def.	Tot.	Ast.	St.	Blk.	TO	Pts.	AVERAGES RPG	APG	PPG
73-74—Boston	18	772	161	370	.435	47	59	.797	60	180	240	66	21	17	...	369	13.3	3.7	20.5
74-75—Boston	11	479	101	236	.428	23	26	.885	49	132	181	46	18	6	...	225	16.5	4.2	20.5
75-76—Boston	18	798	156	341	.457	66	87	.759	87	209	296	83	22	13	...	378	16.4	4.6	21.0
76-77—Boston	9	379	66	148	.446	17	22	.773	29	105	134	36	8	13	...	149	14.9	4.0	16.6
79-80—Boston	9	301	49	103	.476	10	11	.909	18	48	66	21	9	7	8	108	7.3	2.3	12.0
Totals	89	3768	733	1627	.451	218	293	.744	...	...	1285	333	78	56	8	1684	14.4	3.7	18.9

Three-point field goals: 1979-80, 0-for-2.

Personal fouls/disqualifications: 1973-74, 85/2. 1974-75, 50/2. 1975-76, 85/4. 1976-77, 37/3. 1979-80, 37/0. Totals, 398/15.

NBA ALL-STAR GAME RECORD

NOTES: NBA All-Star Game Most Valuable Player (1973).

Season Team	Min.	FGM	FGA	Pct.	FTM	FTA	Pct.	Reb	Ast.	PF	Dq.	Pts.
1972 —Boston	32	5	12	.417	4	5	.800	20	1	4	0	14
1973 —Boston	30	7	15	.467	1	1	1.000	13	1	2	0	15

Season Team	Min.	FGM	FGA	Pct.	FTM	FTA	Pct.	REBOUNDS Off.	Def.	Tot.	Ast.	PF	Dq.	St.	Blk.	TO	Pts.
1974 —Boston	26	5	10	.500	1	3	.333	6	6	12	1	3	0	0	1	...	11
1975 —Boston	15	3	7	.429	0	0		0	6	6	3	4	0	1	0	...	6
1976 —Boston	23	6	13	.462	4	5	.800	8	8	16	1	3	0	1	0	...	16
1977 —Boston								Selected, did not play—injured.									
1978 —Boston	28	7	9	.778	0	0		6	8	14	5	5	0	2	0	2	14
Totals	154	33	66	.500	10	14	.714	...	...	81	12	21	0	4	1	2	76

HEAD COACHING RECORD

BACKGROUND: Assistant coach, San Antonio Spurs (1994-95 and 1995-96). ... Assistant coach, Golden State Warriors (January 31-April 20, 2000).

NBA COACHING RECORD

Season Team	REGULAR SEASON W	L	Pct.	Finish	PLAYOFFS W	L	Pct.
78-79 —Boston	27	41	.397	5th/Atlantic Division	—	—	—
96-97 —Charlotte	54	28	.659	6th/Central Division	0	3	.000
97-98 —Charlotte	51	31	.622	3rd/Central Division	4	5	.444
98-99 —Charlotte	4	11	.267		—	—	—
00-01 —Golden State	17	65	.207	7th/Pacific Division	—	—	—
Totals (5 years)	153	176	.465	**Totals (2 years)**	4	8	.333

CBA COACHING RECORD

Season Team	REGULAR SEASON W	L	Pct.	Finish	PLAYOFFS W	L	Pct.
84-85 —Bay State	20	28	.417	6th/Atlantic Division	—	—	—

NOTES:

1978—Replaced Tom Sanders as Boston head coach (November), with record of 2-12.

1997—Lost to New York in Eastern Conference First Round.

1998—Defeated New Jersey, 3-1, in Eastern Conference First Round; lost to Chicago, 4-1, in Eastern Conference Semifinals.

1999—Resigned as Charlotte head coach (March 7); replaced by Paul Silas with club in seventh place.

FLOYD, TIM   BULLS

PERSONAL: Born February 25, 1954, in Hattiesburg, Miss. ... Full name: Timothy Fitzpatrick Floyd.
HIGH SCHOOL: Oak Grove (Hattiesburg, Miss.).
COLLEGE: Lousiana Tech.

HEAD COACHING RECORD

BACKGROUND: Assistant coach, University of Texas-El Paso (1977-78 through 1985-86). ... Director of Basketball Operations, Chicago Bulls (1998-99 to present).

COLLEGIATE COACHING RECORD

Season Team	W	L	Pct.	Finish
86-87 —Idaho	16	14	.533	T5th/Big Sky Conference
87-88 —Idaho	19	11	.633	2nd/Big Sky Conference
88-89 —New Orleans	19	11	.633	1st/American South Conference
89-90 —New Orleans	21	11	.656	T1st/American South Conference
90-91 —New Orleans	23	8	.742	T1st/American South Conference
91-92 —New Orleans	18	14	.563	7th/Sun Belt Conference
92-93 —New Orleans	26	4	.867	1st/Sun Belt Conference
93-94 —New Orleans	20	10	.667	3rd/Sun Belt Conference

Season Team	W	L	Pct.	Finish
94-95 —Iowa State	23	11	.676	5th/Big Eight Conference
95-96 —Iowa State	24	9	.727	2nd/Big Eight Conference
96-97 —Iowa State	22	9	.710	3rd/Big Eight Conference
97-98 —Iowa State	12	18	.400	11th/Big Twelve Conference
Totals (12 years)	243	130	.651	

NBA COACHING RECORD

		REGULAR SEASON				PLAYOFFS		
Season Team	W	L	Pct.	Finish		W	L	Pct.
98-99 —Chicago	13	37	.260	8th/Central Division		—	—	—
99-00 —Chicago	17	65	.207	8th/Central Division		—	—	—
00-01 —Chicago	15	67	.183	8th/Central Division		—	—	—
Totals (3 years)	45	169	.210					

NOTES:

1989—Lost to Wisconsin, 63-61, in NIT first round.

1990—Defeated James Madison, 78-74, in NIT first round; defeated Mississippi State, 65-60, in NIT second round; lost to Vanderbilt, 88-65, in NIT quarterfinals.

1991—Lost to Kansas, 55-49, in NCAA Tournament first round.

1993—Lost to Xavier, 73-55, in NCAA Tournament first round.

1994—Defeated Texas A&M, 79-73, in NIT first round; lost to Vanderbilt, 78-59, in NIT second round.

1995—Defeated Florida, 64-61, in NCAA Tournament first round; lost to North Carolina, 73-51, in NCAA Tournament second round.

1996—Defeated California, 74-64, in NCAA Tournament first round; lost to Utah, 73-67, in NCAA Tournament second round.

1997—Defeated Illinois State, 69-57, in NCAA Tournament first round; defeated Cincinnati, 67-66, in NCAA Tournament second round; lost to UCLA, 74-73, in NCAA Tournament regional semifinals.

GENTRY, ALVIN — CLIPPERS

PERSONAL: Born November 5, 1954, in Shelby, N.C. ... 6-4/218. (1,93/98,9). ... Cousin of David Thompson, guard with Denver Nuggets of ABA (1975-76), and Denver Nuggets (1976-77 through 1981-82) and Seattle SuperSonics (1982-83 and 1983-84) of NBA.

HIGH SCHOOL: Shelby (N.C.).

COLLEGE: Appalachian State (degree in management), then Colorado.

COLLEGIATE RECORD

												AVERAGES		
Season Team	G	Min.	FGM	FGA	Pct.	FTM	FTA	Pct.	Reb.	Ast.	Pts.	RPG	APG	PPG
73-74—Appalachian State	25	...	75	146	.514	55	77	.714	53	...	205	2.1	...	8.2
74-75—Appalachian State	8	...	17	29	.586	10	16	.625	15	...	42	1.8	...	5.3
75-76—Appalachian State	25	...	49	115	.426	49	71	.690	61	...	147	2.4	...	5.9
76-77—Appalachian State	23	...	35	67	.522	24	35	.686	30	20	95	1.3	0.9	4.1
Totals	81	...	176	357	.493	138	199	.693	159	...	489	2.0	...	6.0

HEAD COACHING RECORD

BACKGROUND: Graduate assistant, University of Colorado (1977-78). ... Assistant coach, Baylor University (1980-81). ... Assistant coach, University of Colorado (1981-82 through 1984-85). ... Assistant coach, University of Kansas (1985-86 through 1987-88). ... Assistant coach, San Antonio Spurs (1988-89 and 1989-90). ... Assistant coach, Los Angeles Clippers (1990-91). ... Assistant coach, Miami Heat (1991-92 through 1994-95). ... Assistant coach, Detroit Pistons (1995-96 to February 2, 1998).

NBA COACHING RECORD

		REGULAR SEASON				PLAYOFFS		
Season Team	W	L	Pct.	Finish		W	L	Pct.
94-95 —Miami	15	21	.417	4th/Atlantic Division		—	—	—
97-98 —Detroit	16	21	.432	6th/Central Division		—	—	—
98-99 —Detroit	29	21	.580	3rd/Central Division		2	3	.400
99-00 —Detroit	28	30	.483			—	—	—
00-01 —Los Angeles Clippers	31	51	.378	6th/Pacific Division		—	—	—
Totals (5 years)	119	144	.453		Totals (1 year)	2	3	.400

NOTES:

1995—Replaced Kevin Loughery as Miami head coach (February 14) with record of 17-29 and club in sixth place.

1998—Replaced Doug Collins as Detroit head coach (February 2) with record of 21-24 and club in seventh place.

1999—Lost to Atlanta in Eastern Conference first round.

2000 Replaced as Detroit head coach by George Irvine (March 6) with club in fourth place.

ISSEL, DAN — NUGGETS

PERSONAL: Born October 25, 1948, in Batavia, Ill. ... 6-9/240. (2,06/108,4). ... Full name: Daniel Paul Issel.

HIGH SCHOOL: Batavia (Ill.).

COLLEGE: Kentucky.

TRANSACTIONS: Selected by Detroit Pistons in eighth round (122nd pick overall) of 1970 NBA Draft. ... Selected by Kentucky Colonels in first round of 1970 ABA draft. ... Traded by Colonels to Baltimore Claws for C Tom Owens and cash (September 19, 1975). ... Traded by Claws to Denver Nuggets for C Dave Robisch and cash (October 8, 1975). ... Nuggets franchise became part of NBA for 1976-77 season.

CAREER HONORS: Elected to Naismith Memorial Basketball Hall of Fame (1993).

MISCELLANEOUS: Denver Nuggets franchise all-time leading rebounder with 6,630 (1976-77 through 1984-85).

CAREER NOTES: Vice president, Denver Nuggets (March 1998 to August 2001).

COLLEGIATE RECORD

NOTES: The Sporting News All-America first team (1970). ... The Sporting News All-America second team (1969).

Season Team	G	Min.	FGM	FGA	Pct.	FTM	FTA	Pct.	Reb.	Ast.	Pts.	AVERAGES RPG	APG	PPG
66-67—Kentucky‡	20	...	168	332	.506	80	111	.721	355	...	416	17.8	...	20.8
67-68—Kentucky	27	836	171	390	.438	102	154	.662	328	10	444	12.1	0.4	16.4
68-69—Kentucky	28	1063	285	534	.534	176	232	.759	381	49	746	13.6	1.8	26.6
69-70—Kentucky	28	1044	369	667	.553	210	275	.764	369	39	948	13.2	1.4	33.9
Varsity totals	83	2943	825	1591	.519	488	661	.738	1078	98	2138	13.0	1.2	25.8

ABA REGULAR-SEASON RECORD

NOTES: ABA co-Rookie of the Year (1971). ... ABA All-Star first team (1972). ... ABA All-Star second team (1971, 1973, 1974, 1976). ... ABA All-Rookie team (1971). ... Member of ABA championship team (1975). ... Holds single-season record for most points—2,538 (1972).

Season Team	G	Min.	2-POINT FGM	FGA	Pct.	3-POINT FGM	FGA	Pct.	FTM	FTA	Pct.	Reb.	Ast.	Pts.	AVERAGES RPG	APG	PPG
70-71—Kentucky	83	3274	938	1989	.472	0	5	.000	604	748	.807	1093	162	*2480	13.2	2.0	*29.9
71-72—Kentucky	83	3570	969	1990	.487	3	11	.273	591	*753	.785	931	195	*2538	11.2	2.3	30.6
72-73—Kentucky	84	*3531	899	1742	.516	3	15	.200	485	635	.764	922	220	*2292	11.0	2.6	27.3
73-74—Kentucky	83	3347	826	1709	.483	3	17	.176	457	581	.787	847	137	2118	10.2	1.7	25.5
74-75—Kentucky	83	2864	614	1298	.473	0	5	.000	237	321	.738	710	188	1465	8.6	2.3	17.7
75-76—Denver	84	2858	751	1468	.512	1	4	.250	425	521	.816	923	201	1930	11.0	2.4	23.0
Totals	500	19444	4997	10196	.490	10	57	.175	2799	3559	.786	5426	1103	12823	10.9	2.2	25.6

ABA PLAYOFF RECORD

Season Team	G	Min.	2-POINT FGM	FGA	Pct.	3-POINT FGM	FGA	Pct.	FTM	FTA	Pct.	Reb.	Ast.	Pts.	AVERAGES RPG	APG	PPG
70-71—Kentucky	19	670	207	408	.507	0	0	...	123	141	.872	221	28	536	11.6	1.5	28.2
71-72—Kentucky	6	269	47	113	.416	0	1	.000	38	50	.760	54	5	132	9.0	0.8	22.0
72-73—Kentucky	19	821	197	392	.503	1	6	.167	124	156	.795	225	28	521	11.8	1.5	27.4
73-74—Kentucky	8	311	60	135	.444	0	0	...	28	33	.848	87	14	148	10.9	1.8	18.5
74-75—Kentucky	15	578	122	261	.467	0	0	...	60	74	.811	119	29	304	7.9	1.9	20.3
75-76—Denver	13	470	111	226	.491	0	1	.000	44	56	.786	156	32	266	12.0	2.5	20.5
Totals	80	3119	744	1535	.485	1	8	.125	417	510	.818	862	136	1907	10.8	1.7	23.8

ABA ALL-STAR GAME RECORD

NOTES: ABA All-Star Game Most Valuable Player (1972).

Season Team	Min.	2-POINT FGM	FGA	Pct.	3-POINT FGM	FGA	Pct.	FTM	FTA	Pct.	Reb.	Ast.	Pts.
1971—Kentucky	34	8	15	.533	0	0	...	5	8	.625	11	0	21
1972—Kentucky	23	9	13	.692	0	0	...	3	4	.750	9	5	21
1973—Kentucky	29	6	14	.429	0	0	...	2	2	1.000	7	4	14
1974—Kentucky	26	10	15	.667	0	0	...	1	1	1.000	4	1	21
1975—Kentucky	20	3	6	.500	0	0	...	1	2	.500	7	1	7
1976—Denver	31	6	16	.375	0	0	...	7	9	.778	9	5	19
Totals	163	42	79	.532	0	0	...	19	26	.731	47	16	103

NBA REGULAR-SEASON RECORD

HONORS: J. Walter Kennedy Citizenship Award (1985).

Season Team	G	Min.	FGM	FGA	Pct.	FTM	FTA	Pct.	REBOUNDS Off.	Def.	Tot.	Ast.	St.	Blk.	TO	Pts.	AVERAGES RPG	APG	PPG
76-77—Denver	79	2507	660	1282	.515	445	558	.798	211	485	696	177	91	29	...	1765	8.8	2.2	22.3
77-78—Denver	82	2851	659	1287	.512	428	547	.782	253	577	830	304	100	41	259	1746	10.1	3.7	21.3
78-79—Denver	81	2742	532	1030	.517	316	419	.754	240	498	738	255	61	46	171	1380	9.1	3.1	17.0
79-80—Denver	82	2938	715	1416	.505	517	667	.775	236	483	719	198	88	54	163	1951	8.8	2.4	23.8
80-81—Denver	80	2641	614	1220	.503	519	684	.759	229	447	676	158	83	53	130	1749	8.5	2.0	21.9
81-82—Denver	81	2472	651	1236	.527	546	655	.834	174	434	608	179	67	55	169	1852	7.5	2.2	22.9
82-83—Denver	80	2431	661	1296	.510	400	479	.835	151	445	596	223	83	43	174	1726	7.5	2.8	21.6
83-84—Denver	76	2076	569	1153	.494	364	428	.850	112	401	513	173	60	44	122	1506	6.8	2.3	19.8
84-85—Denver	77	1684	363	791	.459	257	319	.806	80	251	331	137	65	31	93	984	4.3	1.8	12.8
Totals	718	22342	5424	10711	.506	3792	4756	.797	1686	4021	5707	1804	698	396	1281	14659	7.9	2.5	20.4

Three-point field goals: 1979-80, 4-for-12 (.333). 1980-81, 2-for-12 (.167). 1981-82, 4-for-6 (.667). 1982-83, 4-for-19 (.211). 1983-84, 4-for-19 (.211). 1984-85, 1-for-7 (.143). Totals, 19-for-75 (.253).

Personal fouls/disqualifications: 1976-77, 246/7. 1977-78, 279/5. 1978-79, 233/6. 1979-80, 190/1. 1980-81, 249/6. 1981-82, 245/4. 1982-83, 227/0. 1983-84, 182/2. 1984-85, 171/1. Totals, 2022/32.

NBA PLAYOFF RECORD

Season Team	G	Min.	FGM	FGA	Pct.	FTM	FTA	Pct.	REBOUNDS Off.	Def.	Tot.	Ast.	St.	Blk.	TO	Pts.	AVERAGES RPG	APG	PPG
76-77—Denver	6	222	49	96	.510	34	45	.756	18	40	58	17	5	4	...	132	9.7	2.8	22.0
77-78—Denver	13	460	103	212	.486	56	65	.862	41	93	134	53	7	3	39	262	10.3	4.1	20.2
78-79—Denver	3	109	24	45	.533	25	31	.806	7	21	28	10	0	0	9	73	9.3	3.3	24.3
81-82—Denver	3	103	32	60	.533	12	12	1.000	8	13	21	5	3	1	7	76	7.0	1.7	25.3
82-83—Denver	8	227	69	136	.507	25	29	.862	13	45	58	25	9	5	10	163	7.3	3.1	20.4
83-84—Denver	5	153	52	102	.510	32	39	.821	10	30	40	8	6	6	15	137	8.0	1.6	27.4
84-85—Denver	15	325	73	159	.459	39	48	.813	14	40	54	27	12	5	13	186	3.6	1.8	12.4
Totals	53	1599	402	810	.496	223	269	.829	111	282	393	145	42	24	93	1029	7.4	2.7	19.4

Three-point field goals: 1982-83, 0-for-1. 1983-84, 1-for-2 (.500). 1984-85, 1-for-1. Totals, 2-for-4 (.500).

Personal fouls/disqualifications: 1976-77, 20/0. 1977-78, 43/1. 1978-79, 15/0. 1981-82, 10/0. 1982-83, 18/0. 1983-84, 15/0. 1984-85, 36/0. Totals, 157/1.

NBA ALL-STAR GAME RECORD

Season	Team	Min.	FGM	FGA	Pct.	FTM	FTA	Pct.	REBOUNDS Off.	Def.	Tot.	Ast.	PF	Dq.	St.	Blk.	TO	Pts.
1977	—Denver..............	10	0	3	.000	0	0	...	1	0	1	0	0	0	0	0	...	0

COMBINED ABA AND NBA REGULAR-SEASON RECORDS

	G	Min.	FGM	FGA	Pct.	FTM	FTA	Pct.	REBOUNDS Off.	Def.	Tot.	Ast.	Stl.	Blk.	TO	Pts.	AVERAGES RPG	APG	PPG
Totals	1218	41786	10431	20964	.498	6591	8315	.793	...	...	11133	2907	...	...	...	27482	9.1	2.4	22.6

Three-point field goals: 29-for-132 (.220).
Personal fouls/disqualifications: 3504.

NBA COACHING RECORD

Season	Team	REGULAR SEASON W	L	Pct.	Finish	PLAYOFFS W	L	Pct.
92-93	—Denver.....................................	36	46	.439	4th/Midwest Division	—	—	—
93-94	—Denver.....................................	42	40	.512	4th/Midwest Division	6	6	.500
94-95	—Denver.....................................	18	16	.529		—	—	—
99-00	—Denver.....................................	35	47	.427	5th/Midwest Division	—	—	—
00-01	—Denver.....................................	40	42	.488	6th/Midwest Division	—	—	—
Totals (5 years).................................		171	191	.472	Totals (1 year)........	6	6	.500

NOTES:
1994—Defeated Seattle, 3-2, in Western Conference First Round; lost to Utah, 4-3, in Western Conference Semifinals.
1995—Resigned as Denver head coach (January 15); replaced by Gene Littles with club in fourth place.

JACKSON, PHIL   LAKERS

PERSONAL: Born September 17, 1945, in Deer Lodge, Mont. ... 6-8/230. (2,03/104,3). ... Full name: Philip D. Jackson.
HIGH SCHOOL: Williston (N.D.).
COLLEGE: North Dakota.
TRANSACTIONS/CAREER NOTES: Selected by New York Knicks in second round (17th pick overall) of 1967 NBA Draft. ... Traded by Knicks with future draft choice to New Jersey Nets for future draft choices (June 8, 1978). ... Waived by Nets (October 11, 1978). ... Re-signed as free agent by Nets (November 10, 1978). ... Waived by Nets (October 12, 1979). ... Re-signed as free agent by Nets (February 15, 1980).
MISCELLANEOUS: Member of NBA championship team (1973).

COLLEGIATE RECORD

Season Team	G	Min.	FGM	FGA	Pct.	FTM	FTA	Pct.	Reb.	Ast.	Pts.	AVERAGES RPG	APG	PPG
63-64—North Dakota‡..............	...	...	...	...	...	...	...	...	...	...	...	...	...	24.3
64-65—North Dakota.................	31	...	129	307	.420	107	156	.686	361	...	365	11.6	...	11.8
65-66—North Dakota.................	29	...	238	439	.542	155	203	.764	374	...	631	12.9	...	21.8
66-67—North Dakota.................	26	...	252	468	.538	208	278	.748	374	...	712	14.4	...	27.4
Varsity totals.........................	86	...	619	1214	.510	470	637	.738	1109	...	1708	12.9	...	19.9

NBA REGULAR-SEASON RECORD

HONORS: NBA All-Rookie team (1968).
NOTES: Led NBA with 330 personal fouls (1975).

Season Team	G	Min.	FGM	FGA	Pct.	FTM	FTA	Pct.	Reb.	Ast.	PF	Dq.	Pts.	AVERAGES RPG	APG	PPG
67-68 —New York........................	75	1093	182	455	.400	99	168	.589	338	55	212	3	463	4.5	0.7	6.2
68-69 —New York........................	47	924	126	294	.429	80	119	.672	246	43	168	6	332	5.2	0.9	7.1
69-70 —New York........................						Did not play—injured.										
70-71 —New York........................	71	771	118	263	.449	95	133	.714	238	31	169	4	331	3.4	0.4	4.7
71-72 —New York........................	80	1273	205	466	.440	167	228	.732	326	72	224	4	577	4.1	0.9	7.2
72-73 —New York........................	80	1393	245	553	.443	154	195	.790	344	94	218	2	644	4.3	1.2	8.1

Season Team	G	Min.	FGM	FGA	Pct.	FTM	FTA	Pct.	REBOUNDS Off.	Def.	Tot.	Ast.	St.	Blk.	TO	Pts.	AVERAGES RPG	APG	PPG
73-74—New York	82	2050	361	757	.477	191	246	.776	123	355	478	134	42	67	...	913	5.8	1.6	11.1
74-75—New York	78	2285	324	712	.455	193	253	.763	137	463	600	136	84	53	...	841	7.7	1.7	10.8
75-76—New York	80	1461	185	387	.478	110	150	.733	80	263	343	105	41	20	...	480	4.3	1.3	6.0
76-77—N Y Knicks	76	1033	102	232	.440	51	71	.718	75	154	229	85	33	18	...	255	3.0	1.1	3.4
77-78—New York	63	654	55	115	.478	43	56	.768	29	81	110	46	31	15	47	153	1.7	0.7	2.4
78-79—New Jersey	59	1070	144	303	.475	86	105	.819	59	119	178	85	45	22	78	374	3.0	1.4	6.3
79-80—New Jersey	16	194	29	46	.630	7	10	.700	12	12	24	12	5	4	9	65	1.5	0.8	4.1
Totals	807	14201	2076	4583	.453	1276	1734	.736	...	...	3454	898	281	199	134	5428	4.3	1.1	6.7

Three-point field goals: 1979-80, 0-for-2.
Personal fouls/disqualifications: 1973-74, 277/7. 1974-75, 330/10. 1975-76, 275/3. 1976-77, 184/4. 1977-78, 106/0. 1978-79, 168/7. 1979-80, 35/1. Totals, 2366/51.

NBA PLAYOFF RECORD

Season Team	G	Min.	FGM	FGA	Pct.	FTM	FTA	Pct.	Reb.	Ast.	PF	Dq.	Pts.	AVERAGES RPG	APG	PPG
67-68 —New York........................	6	90	10	35	.286	4	5	.800	25	2	23	0	24	4.2	0.3	4.0
68-69 —New York........................						Did not play—injured.										
70-71 —New York........................	5	30	4	14	.286	1	1	1.000	10	2	8	0	9	2.0	0.4	1.8
71-72 —New York........................	16	320	57	120	.475	42	57	.737	82	15	51	1	156	5.1	0.9	9.8
72-73 —New York........................	17	338	60	120	.500	28	38	.737	72	24	59	3	148	4.2	1.4	8.7

Season Team	G	Min.	FGM	FGA	Pct.	FTM	FTA	Pct.	REBOUNDS Off.	Def.	Tot.	Ast.	St.	Blk.	TO	Pts.	AVERAGES RPG	APG	PPG
73-74—New York	12	297	54	116	.466	27	30	.900	15	42	57	15	10	5	...	135	4.8	1.3	11.3
74-75—New York	3	78	10	21	.476	7	8	.875	5	20	25	2	4	3	...	27	8.3	0.7	9.0
77-78—New York	6	50	4	8	.500	4	6	.667	4	6	10	3	3	0	4	12	1.7	0.5	2.0
78-79—New Jersey	2	20	1	3	.333	2	2	1.000	2	1	3	0	1	0	0	4	1.5	0.0	2.0
Totals	67	1223	200	437	.458	115	147	.782	...	...	284	63	18	8	4	515	4.2	0.9	7.7

Personal fouls/disqualifications: 1973-74, 40/0. 1974-75, 15/0. 1977-78, 11/0. 1978-79, 1/0. Totals, 208/4.

HEAD COACHING RECORD

BACKGROUND: Player/assistant coach, New Jersey Nets (1978-79 and 1979-80). ... Assistant coach, Nets (1980-81). ... Broadcaster, Nets (1981-82). ... Assistant coach, Chicago Bulls (1987-88 and 1988-89).

HONORS: NBA Coach of the Year (1996). ... One of the Top 10 Coaches in NBA History (1996). ... CBA Coach of the Year (1985).

RECORDS: Holds NBA regular season record for highest winning percentage—.746. ... Holds NBA playoff record for highest winning percentage (minimum 25 games)—.738.

CBA COACHING RECORD

Season Team	REGULAR SEASON W	L	Pct.	Finish	PLAYOFFS W	L	Pct.
82-83 —Albany	8	11	.421	4th/Eastern Division	—	—	—
83-84 —Albany	25	19	.568	2nd/Eastern Division	9	5	.643
84-85 —Albany	34	14	.708	1st/Eastern Division	5	5	.500
85-86 —Albany	24	24	.500	4th/Eastern Division	3	4	.429
86-87 —Albany	26	22	.542	T2nd/Eastern Division	4	4	.500
Totals (5 years)........................	117	90	.565	Totals (4 years).......	21	18	.538

NBA COACHING RECORD

Season Team	REGULAR SEASON W	L	Pct.	Finish	PLAYOFFS W	L	Pct.
89-90 —Chicago	55	27	.671	2nd/Central Division	10	6	.625
90-91 —Chicago	61	21	.744	1st/Central Division	15	2	.882
91-92 —Chicago	67	15	.817	1st/Central Division	15	7	.682
92-93 —Chicago	57	25	.695	1st/Central Division	15	4	.789
93-94 —Chicago	55	27	.671	2nd/Central Division	6	4	.600
94-95 —Chicago	47	35	.573	2nd/Central Division	5	5	.500
95-96 —Chicago	72	10	.878	1st/Central Division	15	3	.833
96-97 —Chicago	69	13	.841	1st/Central Division	15	4	.789
97-98 —Chicago	62	20	.756	1st/Central Division	15	6	.714
99-00 —Los Angeles Lakers	67	15	.817	1st/Pacific Division	15	8	.652
00-01 —Los Angeles Lakers	56	26	.817	1st/Pacific Division	15	1	.938
Totals (11 years)........................	612	208	.746	Totals (11 years).....	141	50	.738

NOTES:

1983—Replaced Dean Meminger (8-15) and player/interim coach Sam Worthen (0-2) as Albany Patroons head coach (January 29), with record of 8-17.

1984—Defeated Bay State, 3-2, in Eastern semifinals; defeated Puerto Rico, 3-1, in Eastern finals; defeated Wyoming, 3-2, in CBA Championship Series.

1985—Defeated Toronto, 3-2, in Eastern semifinals; lost to Tampa Bay, 3-2, in Eastern finals.

1986—Lost to Tampa Bay in Eastern semifinals.

1987—Defeated Mississippi, 4-0, in Eastern semifinals; lost to Rapid City, 4-0, in Eastern finals.

1990—Defeated Milwaukee, 3-1, in Eastern Conference first round; defeated Philadelphia, 4-1, in Eastern Conference semifinals; lost to Detroit, 4-3, in Eastern Conference finals.

1991—Defeated New York, 3-0, in Eastern Conference first round; defeated Philadelphia, 4-1, in Eastern Conference semifinals; defeated Detroit, 4-0, in Eastern Conference finals; defeated Los Angeles Lakers, 4-1, in NBA Finals.

1992—Defeated Miami, 3-0, in Eastern Conference first round; defeated New York, 4-3, in Eastern Conference semifinals; defeated Cleveland, 4-2, in Eastern Conference finals; defeated Portland, 4-2, in NBA Finals.

1993—Defeated Atlanta, 3-0, in Eastern Conference first round; defeated Cleveland, 4-0, in Eastern Conference semifinals; defeated New York, 4-2, in Eastern Conference finals; defeated Phoenix, 4-2, in NBA Finals.

1994—Defeated Cleveland, 3-0, in Eastern Conference first round; lost to New York, 4-3, in Eastern Conference semifinals.

1995—Defeated Charlotte, 3-1, in Eastern Conference first round; lost to Orlando, 4-2, in Eastern Conference semifinals.

1996—Defeated Miami, 3-0, in Eastern Conference first round; defeated New York, 4-1, in Eastern Conference semifinals; defeated Orlando, 4-0, in Eastern Conference finals; defeated Seattle, 4-2, in NBA Finals.

1997—Defeated Washington, 3-0, in Eastern Conference first round; defeated Atlanta, 4-1, in Eastern Conference semifinals; defeated Miami, 4-1, in Eastern Conference finals; defeated Utah, 4-2, in NBA Finals.

1998—Defeated New Jersey, 3-0, in Eastern Conference first round; defeated Charlotte, 4-1, in Eastern Conference semifinals; defeated Indiana, 4-3, in Eastern Conference finals; defeated Utah, 4-2, in NBA Finals.

2000—Defeated Sacramento, 3-2, in Western Conference first round; defeated Phoenix, 4-1, in Western Conference semifinals; defeated Portland, 4-3, in Western Conference finals; defeated Indiana, 4-2, in NBA Finals.

2001—Defeated Portland, 3-0, in Western Conference first round; defeated Sacramento, 4-0, in Western Conference semifinals; defeated San Antonio, 4-0, in Western Conference finals; defeated Philadelphia, 4-1, in NBA Finals.

KARL, GEORGE   BUCKS

PERSONAL: Born May 12, 1951, in Penn Hills, Pa. ... 6-2/190. (1,88/86,2). ... Full name: George Matthew Karl.
HIGH SCHOOL: Penn Hills (Pa.).
COLLEGE: North Carolina.
TRANSACTIONS/CAREER NOTES: Selected by New York Knicks in fourth round of 1973 NBA Draft. ... Signed as free agent by San Antonio Spurs of American Basketball Association (1973). ... Spurs franchise became part of NBA for 1976-77 season.

COLLEGIATE RECORD

Season Team	G	Min.	FGM	FGA	Pct.	FTM	FTA	Pct.	Reb.	Ast.	Pts.	AVERAGES		
												RPG	APG	PPG
69-70—North Carolina‡	6	...	56	97	.577	20	23	.870	29	...	132	4.8	...	22.0
70-71—North Carolina	32	...	150	286	.524	92	115	.800	104	78	392	3.3	2.4	12.3
71-72—North Carolina	29	...	125	241	.519	89	113	.788	72	124	339	2.5	4.3	11.7
72-73—North Carolina	33	...	219	437	.501	124	163	.761	103	192	562	3.1	5.8	17.0
Varsity totals	94	...	494	964	.512	305	391	.780	279	394	1293	3.0	4.2	13.8

ABA REGULAR-SEASON RECORD

Season Team	G	Min.	2-POINT			3-POINT			FTM	FTA	Pct.	Reb.	Ast.	Pts.	AVERAGES		
			FGM	FGA	Pct.	FGM	FGA	Pct.							RPG	APG	PPG
73-74—San Antonio	74	1339	228	480	.475	8	22	.364	94	113	.832	126	160	574	1.7	2.2	7.8
74-75—San Antonio	82	1629	257	511	.503	4	23	.174	137	177	.774	155	334	663	1.9	4.1	8.1
75-76—San Antonio	75	1200	150	325	.462	0	9	.000	81	106	.764	66	250	381	0.9	3.3	5.1
Totals	231	4168	635	1316	.483	12	54	.222	312	396	.788	347	744	1618	1.5	3.2	7.0

ABA PLAYOFF RECORD

Season Team	G	Min.	2-POINT			3-POINT			FTM	FTA	Pct.	Reb.	Ast.	Pts.	AVERAGES		
			FGM	FGA	Pct.	FGM	FGA	Pct.							RPG	APG	PPG
73-74—San Antonio	7	141	13	27	.481	0	1	.000	2	5	.400	15	23	28	2.1	3.3	4.0
74-75—San Antonio	4	40	1	7	.143	0	1	.000	3	4	.750	3	5	5	0.8	1.3	1.3
75-76—San Antonio	6	64	10	21	.476	0	1	.000	6	9	.667	4	17	26	0.7	2.8	4.3
Totals	17	245	24	55	.436	0	3	.000	11	18	.611	22	45	59	1.3	2.6	3.5

NBA REGULAR-SEASON RECORD

Season Team	G	Min.	FGM	FGA	Pct.	FTM	FTA	Pct.	REBOUNDS			Ast.	St.	Blk.	TO	Pts.	AVERAGES		
									Off.	Def.	Tot.						RPG	APG	PPG
76-77—San Antonio ..	29	251	25	73	.342	29	42	.690	4	13	17	46	10	0	...	79	0.6	1.6	2.7
77-78—San Antonio ..	4	30	2	6	.333	2	2	1.000	0	5	5	5	1	0	4	6	1.3	1.3	1.5
Totals	33	281	27	79	.342	31	44	.705	4	18	22	51	11	0	4	85	0.7	1.5	2.6

Personal fouls/disqualifications: 1976-77, 36/0. 1977-78, 6/0. Totals, 42/0.

NBA PLAYOFF RECORD

Season Team	G	Min.	FGM	FGA	Pct.	FTM	FTA	Pct.	REBOUNDS			Ast.	St.	Blk.	TO	Pts.	AVERAGES		
									Off.	Def.	Tot.						RPG	APG	PPG
76-77—San Antonio ..	1	1	0	0	...	0	0	...	0	0	0	0	0	0	...	0	0.0	0.0	0.0

COMBINED ABA AND NBA REGULAR-SEASON RECORDS

	G	Min.	FGM	FGA	Pct.	FTM	FTA	Pct.	REBOUNDS			Ast.	Stl.	Blk.	TO	Pts.	AVERAGES		
									Off.	Def.	Tot.						RPG	APG	PPG
Totals	264	4449	674	1449	.465	343	440	.780	105	264	369	795	232	20	...	1703	1.4	3.0	6.5

Three-point field goals: 12-for-54 (.222).
Personal fouls/disqualifications: 559.

HEAD COACHING RECORD

BACKGROUND: Assistant coach, San Antonio Spurs (1978-79 and 1979-80). ... Director of player acquisition, Cleveland Cavaliers (1983-84). ... Head coach, Real Madrid of Spanish League (1989-90 and 1991-January 1992).

HONORS: CBA Coach of the Year (1981, 1983, 1991).

CBA COACHING RECORD

Season Team	REGULAR SEASON				PLAYOFFS		
	W	L	Pct.	Finish	W	L	Pct.
80-81 —Montana	27	15	.643	1st/Western Division	5	5	.500
81-82 —Montana	30	16	.652	2nd/Western Division	2	3	.400
82-83 —Montana	33	11	.750	1st/Western Division	6	5	.545
88-89 —Albany	36	18	.667	1st/Eastern Division	2	4	.333
90-91 —Albany	50	6	.893	1st/Eastern Division	5	6	.455
Totals (5 years)	176	66	.727	Totals (5 years)	20	23	.465

NBA COACHING RECORD

Season Team	REGULAR SEASON				PLAYOFFS		
	W	L	Pct.	Finish	W	L	Pct.
84-85 —Cleveland	36	46	.439	4th/Central Division	1	3	.250
85-86 —Cleveland	25	42	.373	—	—	—	—
86-87 —Golden State	42	40	.512	3rd/Pacific Division	4	6	.400
87-88 —Golden State	16	48	.250	—	—	—	—
91-92 —Seattle	27	15	.643	4th/Pacific Division	4	5	.444
92-93 —Seattle	55	27	.671	2nd/Pacific Division	10	9	.526
93-94 —Seattle	63	19	.768	1st/Pacific Division	2	3	.400
94-95 —Seattle	57	25	.695	2nd/Pacific Division	1	3	.250
95-96 —Seattle	64	18	.780	1st/Pacific Division	13	8	.619
96-97 —Seattle	57	25	.695	1st/Pacific Division	6	6	.500
97-98 —Seattle	61	21	.744	1st/Pacific Division	4	6	.400
98-99 —Milwaukee	28	22	.560	4th/Central Division	0	3	.000
99-00 —Milwaukee	42	40	.512	T-5th/Central Division	2	3	.400
00-01 —Milwaukee	52	30	.634	1st/Central Division	10	8	.556
Totals (14 years)	625	418	.599	Totals (12 years)	57	63	.475

NOTES:

1981—Defeated Alberta, 2-0, in Western semifinals; defeated Billings, 3-1, in Western finals; lost to Rochester, 4-0, in CBA Championship Series.
1982—Lost to Billings in Western finals.
1983—Defeated Wyoming, 3-1, in Western finals; lost to Detroit, 4-3, in CBA Championship Series.
1985—Lost to Boston in Eastern Conference first round.
1986—Replaced as Cleveland head coach by Gene Littles (March 16).
1987—Defeated Utah, 3-2, in Western Conference first round; lost to Los Angeles Lakers, 4-1, in Western Conference semifinals.
1988—Resigned as Golden State head coach (March 23).
1989—Lost to Wichita Falls in Eastern semifinals.
1991—Defeated Grand Rapids, 3-2, in National Conference first round; lost to Wichita Falls, 4-2, in National Conference finals.
1992—Replaced K.C. Jones (18-18) and Bob Kloppenburg (2-2) as Seattle head coach (January 23), with record of 20-20 and club in fifth place. Defeated Golden State, 3-1, in Western Conference first round; lost to Utah, 4-1, in Western Conference semifinals.
1993—Defeated Utah, 3-2, in Western Conference first round; defeated Houston, 4-3, in Western Conference semifinals; lost to Phoenix, 4-3, in Western Conference finals.
1994—Lost to Denver in Western Conference first round.
1995—Lost to Los Angeles Lakers in Western Conference first round.
1996—Defeated Sacramento, 3-1, in Western Conference first round; defeated Houston, 4-0, in Western Conference semifinals; defeated Utah, 4-3, in Western Conference finals; lost to Chicago, 4-2, in NBA Finals.
1997—Defeated Phoenix, 3-2, in Western Conference first round; lost to Houston, 4-3, in Western Conference semifinals.
1998—Defeated Minnesota, 3-2, in Western Conference first round; lost to Los Angeles Lakers, 4-1, in Western Conference semifinals.
1999—Lost to Indiana in Eastern Conference first round.
2000—Lost to Indiana in Eastern Conference first round.
2001—Defeated Orlando, 3-1, in Eastern Conference first round; defeated Charlotte, 4-3, in Eastern Conference semifinals; lost to Philadelphia, 4-3, in Eastern Conference finals.

KRUGER, LON   HAWKS

PERSONAL: Born August 19, 1952, in Topeka, Kan.. ... Full Name: Lonnie D. Kruger.
HIGH SCHOOL: Silver Lake (Kan.).
COLLEGE: Kansas State University (degree in business), then Pittsburg State University (master's degree in physical education).
TRANSACTIONS/CAREER NOTES: Selected by Atlanta Hawks in ninth round (151st pick overall) of 1974 NBA Draft.

COLLEGIATE RECORD

Season Team	G	Min.	FGM	FGA	Pct.	FTM	FTA	Pct.	Reb.	Ast.	Pts.	RPG	APG	PPG
70-71—Kansas State						Freshman team statistics unavailable.								
71-72—Kansas State	28	...	83	206	.403	111	146	.760	83	...	277	3.0	...	9.9
72-73—Kansas State	25	...	111	220	.505	90	105	.857	47	...	312	1.9	...	12.5
73-74—Kansas State	27	...	176	364	.484	122	140	.871	77	...	474	2.9	...	17.6
Totals	80	...	370	790	.468	323	391	.826	207	...	1063	2.6	...	13.3

RECORD AS BASEBALL PLAYER

MISCELLANEOUS: Threw right, batted right. ... Selected by Houston Astros organization in 12th round of free-agent draft (June 4, 1970); did not sign. ... Selected by St. Louis Cardinals organization in 21st round of free-agent draft (June 5, 1974).

Year Team (League)	W	L	Pct.	ERA	G	GS	CG	ShO	Sv.	IP	H	R	ER	BB	SO
1974—Sarasota (GCL)	0	0	...	1.29	3	3	0	0	0	14	7	2	2	4	13
—St. Petersburg (FSL)	1	6	.143	3.24	8	8	2	0	0	50	46	29	18	20	27

HEAD COACHING RECORD

NOTES: Assistant coach, Pittsburg State University (1976-77). ... Graduate assistant coach, Kansas State University (1977-78). ... Assistant coach, Kansas State University (1978-79 through 1981-82). ... Athletic Director, Pan American University (1982-83 through 1984-85).

COLLEGIATE COACHING RECORD

Season Team	W	L	Pct.	Finish
82-83 —Pan American (Tex.)	7	21	.250	—
83-84 —Pan American (Tex.)	13	14	.481	—
84-85 —Pan American (Tex.)	12	16	.429	—
85-86 —Pan American (Tex.)	20	8	.714	—
86-87 —Kansas State	20	11	.645	4th/Big Eight Conference
87-88 —Kansas State	25	9	.735	2nd/Big Eight Conference
88-89 —Kansas State	19	11	.633	3rd/Big Eight Conference
89-90 —Kansas State	17	15	.531	4th/Big Eight Conference
90-91 —Florida	11	17	.393	6th/Southeastern Conference
91-92 —Florida	19	14	.576	2nd/Southeastern Conference (East)
92-93 —Florida	16	12	.571	3rd/Southeastern Conference (East)
93-94 —Florida	29	8	.784	T1st/Southeastern Conference (East)
94-95 —Florida	17	13	.567	3rd/Southeastern Conference (East)
95-96 —Florida	12	16	.429	5th/Southeastern Conference (East)
96-97 —Illinois	22	10	.688	T4th/Big Ten Conference
97-98 —Illinois	23	10	.697	T1st/Big Ten Conference
98-99 —Illinois	14	18	.438	11th/Big Ten Conference
99-00 —Illinois	21	9	.700	4th/Big Ten Conference
Totals (18 years)	317	232	.577	

HEAD COACHES

NBA COACHING RECORD

Season Team		REGULAR SEASON				PLAYOFFS		
	W	L	Pct.	Finish		W	L	Pct.
00-01 —Atlanta	25	57	.305	7th/Central Division		—	—	—

NOTES:
1987—Defeated Georgia, 82-79, in NCAA Tournament first round; lost to UNLV, 80-61, in second round.
1988—Defeated LaSalle, 66-53, in NCAA Tournament first round; defeated DePaul, 66-58, in second round; defeated Purdue, 73-70, in regional semifinals; lost to Kansas, 71-58, in regional finals.
1989—Lost to Minnesota, 86-75, in NCAA Tournament second round.
1990—Lost to Xavier, 87-79, in NCAA Tournament first round.
1992—Defeated Richmond, 66-52, in NIT Tournament first round; defeated Pittsburgh, 77-74, in second round; defeated Purdue, 74-67, in third round; lost to Virginia, 62-56, in fourth round; lost to Utah, 81-78, in fifth round.
1993—Lost to Minnesota, 74-66, in NIT Tournament first round.
1994—Defeated James Madison, 64-62, in NCAA Tournament first round; defeated Pennsylvania, 70-58, in second round; defeated Connecticut, 69-60 (OT), in regional semifinals; defeated Boston College, 74-66, in regional finals; lost Duke, 70-65, in semifinals.
1995—Lost to Iowa State, 64-61, in NCAA Tournament first round.
1997—Defeated Southern California, 90-77, in NCAA Tournament first round; lost to Tennessee-Chattanooga, 75-63, in second round.
1998—Defeated South Alabama, 64-51, in NCAA Tournament first round; lost to Maryland, 67-61, in second round.
2000—Defeated Pennsylvania, 68-58, in NCAA Tournament first round; lost to Florida, 93-76, in second round.

LOWE, SIDNEY   GRIZZLIES

PERSONAL: Born January 21, 1960, in Washington, D.C. ... 6-0/195. (1,83/88,5). ... Full Name: Sidney Rochell Lowe.
HIGH SCHOOL: DeMatha (Hyattsville, Md.).
COLLEGE: North Carolina State.
TRANSACTIONS/CAREER NOTES: Selected by Chicago Bulls in second round (25th pick overall) of 1983 NBA Draft. ... Draft rights traded by Bulls with 1984 second-round draft choice to Indiana Pacers for draft rights to G Mitchell Wiggins (June 28, 1983). ... Played in Continental Basketball Association with Tampa Bay Thrillers (1984-85 and 1985-86), Albany Patroons (1987-88) and Rapid City Thrillers (1988-89). ... Waived by Pacers (October 4, 1984). ... Signed by Detroit Pistons (October 12, 1984). ... Waived by Pistons (November 11, 1984). ... Signed by Atlanta Hawks (November 28, 1984). ... Waived by Hawks (December 18, 1984). ... Re-signed by Hawks to 10-day contract (December 20, 1984). ... Re-signed by Hawks to 10-day contract (January 16, 1985). ... Did not play basketball (1986-87). ... Played in World Basketball League with Calgary 88's (1988). ... Signed by Charlotte Hornets to first of two consecutive 10-day contracts (March 27, 1989). ... Re-signed by Hornets for remainder of season (April 16, 1989). ... Signed as free agent by Minnesota Timberwolves (August 3, 1989).

COLLEGIATE RECORD
NOTES: Member of NCAA Division I championship team (1983).

Season Team	G	Min.	FGM	FGA	Pct.	FTM	FTA	Pct.	Reb.	Ast.	Pts.	AVERAGES		
												RPG	APG	PPG
79-80—North Carolina State.......	28	...	43	97	.443	74	105	.705	53	125	160	1.9	4.5	5.7
80-81—North Carolina State.......	24	...	67	148	.453	75	96	.781	80	184	209	3.3	7.7	8.7
81-82—North Carolina State.......	32	...	97	188	.516	79	105	.752	85	182	273	2.7	5.7	8.5
82-83—North Carolina State.......	36	...	136	295	.461	90	116	.776	134	271	406	3.7	7.5	11.3
Totals	120	...	343	728	.471	318	422	.754	352	762	1048	2.9	6.4	8.7

Three-point field goals: 1982-83, 44-for-115 (.383).

NBA REGULAR-SEASON RECORD

Season Team	G	Min.	FGM	FGA	Pct.	FTM	FTA	Pct.	REBOUNDS			Ast.	St.	Blk.	TO	Pts.	AVERAGES		
									Off.	Def.	Tot.						RPG	APG	PPG
83-84—Indiana	78	1238	107	259	.413	108	139	.777	30	92	122	269	93	5	106	324	1.6	3.4	4.2
84-85—Det.-Atlanta....	21	190	10	27	.370	8	8	1.000	4	12	16	50	11	0	13	28	0.8	2.4	1.3
88-89—Charlotte.......	14	250	8	25	.320	7	11	.636	6	28	34	93	14	0	9	23	2.4	6.6	1.6
89-90—Minnesota......	80	1744	73	229	.319	39	54	.722	41	122	163	337	73	4	63	187	2.0	4.2	2.3
Totals	193	3422	198	540	.367	162	212	.764	81	254	335	749	191	9	191	562	1.7	3.9	2.9

Three-point field goals: 1983-84, 2-for-18 (.111). 1984-85, 0-for-1. 1988-89, 0-for-2. 1989-90, 2-for-9 (.222). Totals, 4-for-30 (.133).
Personal fouls/disqualifications: 1983-84, 112/0. 1984-85, 28/0. 1988-89, 28/0. 1989-90, 114/0. Totals, 282/0.

CBA REGULAR-SEASON RECORD
NOTES: Led CBA with 2.8 steals per game (1988). ... Led CBA with 139 steals (1988). ... CBA All-League first team (1988). ... CBA All-Defensive first team (1986, 1988).

Season Team	G	Min.	FGM	FGA	Pct.	FTM	FTA	Pct.	Reb.	Ast.	Pts.	AVERAGES		
												RPG	APG	PPG
84-85—Tampa Bay.....................	18	494	34	76	.447	30	37	.811	42	152	99	2.3	8.4	5.5
85-86—Tampa Bay.....................	43	1629	90	224	.402	87	113	.770	158	406	270	3.7	9.4	6.3
87-88—Albany	50	1842	94	216	.435	64	99	.646	140	437	260	2.8	8.7	5.2
88-89—Rapid City.....................	8	271	15	47	.319	11	16	.688	31	77	41	3.9	9.6	5.1
Totals	119	4236	233	563	.414	192	265	.725	371	1072	670	3.1	9.0	5.6

Three-point field goals: 1984-85, 1-for-6 (.167). 1985-86, 3-for-13 (.231). 1987-88, 8-for-26 (.308). 1988-89, 0-for-2. Totals, 12-for-47 (.255).

HEAD COACHING RECORD
NOTES: Broadcaster, Minnesota Timberwolves (1990-91). ... Assistant coach, Timberwolves (1991-92 through January 11, 1993 and 1999-2000). ... Assistant coach, Cleveland Cavaliers (1994-95 through 1998-99). ... Grizzlies franchise moved to Memphis for 2001-02 season.

HEAD COACHES

NBA COACHING RECORD

Season Team	W	L	Pct.	Finish	W	L	Pct.
					PLAYOFFS		
	REGULAR SEASON						
92-93 —Minnesota	13	40	.245	5th/Midwest Division	—	—	—
93-94 —Minnesota	20	62	.244	5th/Midwest Division	—	—	—
00-01 —Vancouver	23	59	.280	7th/Midwest Division	—	—	—
Totals (3 years)	56	161	.258				

NOTES:
1993—Replaced Jimmy Rodgers as head coach (January 11), with record 6-23 and club in fifth place.

LUCAS, JOHN   CAVALIERS

PERSONAL: Born October 31, 1953, in Durham, N.C. ... 6-3/185. (1,91/83,9). ... Full Name: John Harding Lucas Jr.
HIGH SCHOOL: Hillside (Durham, N.C.).
COLLEGE: Maryland.
TRANSACTIONS/CAREER NOTES: Selected by Houston Rockets in first round (first pick overall) of 1976 NBA Draft. ... Awarded by Rockets with cash to Golden State Warriors as compensation for earlier signing of veteran free agent F Rick Barry (September 5, 1978). ... Traded by Warriors to Washington Bullets for 1982 and 1984 second-round draft choices (October 19, 1981). ... Waived by Bullets (January 25, 1983). ... Signed as free agent by Cleveland Cavaliers (August 29, 1983). ... Waived by Cavaliers (September 21, 1983). ... Played in Continental Basketball Association with Lancaster Lightning (1983-84). ... Signed as free agent by San Antonio Spurs (December 4, 1983). ... Traded by Spurs with 1985 third-round draft choice to Rockets for F James Bailey, 1985 second-round draft choice and cash (October 4, 1984). ... Waived by Rockets (December 10, 1984). ... Re-signed as free agent by Rockets (February 19, 1985). ... Waived by Rockets (March 14, 1986). ... Signed as free agent by Milwaukee Bucks (January 17, 1987). ... Signed as free agent by Seattle SuperSonics (September 19, 1988). ... Signed as unrestricted free agent by Rockets (August 17, 1989). ... Traded by Rockets with F/C Tim McCormick to Atlanta Hawks for G Kenny Smith and G Roy Marble (September 27, 1990).
MISCELLANEOUS: Played World Team Tennis with Golden Gaters and New Orleans Nets (1977, 1978).

COLLEGIATE RECORD
NOTES: THE SPORTING NEWS All-America first team (1975, 1976). ... THE SPORTING NEWS All-America second team (1974).

Season Team	G	Min.	FGM	FGA	Pct.	FTM	FTA	Pct.	Reb.	Ast.	Pts.	RPG	APG	PPG
												AVERAGES		
72-73—Maryland	30	...	190	353	.538	45	64	.703	83	178	425	2.8	5.9	14.2
73-74—Maryland	28	...	253	495	.511	58	77	.753	82	159	564	2.9	5.7	20.1
74-75—Maryland	24	...	186	339	.549	97	116	.836	100	91	469	4.2	3.8	19.5
75-76—Maryland	28	...	233	456	.511	91	117	.778	109	86	557	3.9	3.1	19.9
Totals	110	...	862	1643	.525	291	374	.778	374	514	2015	3.4	4.7	18.3

NBA REGULAR-SEASON RECORD
RECORDS: Holds single-game record for most assists in one quarter—14 (April 15, 1984, vs. Denver).
HONORS: NBA All-Rookie team (1977).

Season Team	G	Min.	FGM	FGA	Pct.	FTM	FTA	Pct.	Off.	Def.	Tot.	Ast.	St.	Blk.	TO	Pts.	RPG	APG	PPG
									REBOUNDS								**AVERAGES**		
76-77—Houston	82	2531	388	814	.477	135	171	.789	55	164	219	463	125	19	...	911	2.7	5.6	11.1
77-78—Houston	82	2933	412	947	.435	193	250	.772	51	204	255	768	160	9	...	1017	3.1	9.4	12.4
78-79—Golden State	82	3095	530	1146	.462	264	321	.822	65	182	247	762	152	9	255	1324	3.0	9.3	16.1
79-80—Golden State	80	2763	388	830	.467	222	289	.768	61	159	220	602	138	3	184	1010	2.8	7.5	12.6
80-81—Golden State	66	1919	222	506	.439	107	145	.738	34	120	154	464	83	2	185	555	2.3	7.0	8.4
81-82—Washington	79	1940	263	618	.426	138	176	.784	40	126	166	551	95	6	156	666	2.1	7.0	8.4
82-83—Washington	35	386	62	131	.473	21	42	.500	8	21	29	102	25	1	47	145	0.8	2.9	4.1
83-84—San Antonio	63	1807	275	595	.462	120	157	.764	23	157	180	673	92	5	147	689	2.9	10.7	10.9
84-85—Houston	47	1158	206	446	.462	103	129	.798	21	64	85	318	62	2	102	536	1.8	6.8	11.4
85-86—Houston	65	2120	365	818	.446	231	298	.775	33	110	143	571	77	5	149	1006	2.2	8.8	15.5
86-87—Milwaukee	43	1358	285	624	.457	137	174	.787	29	96	125	290	71	6	89	753	2.9	6.7	17.5
87-88—Milwaukee	81	1766	281	631	.445	130	162	.802	29	130	159	392	88	3	125	743	2.0	4.8	9.2
88-89—Seattle	74	842	119	299	.398	54	77	.701	22	57	79	260	60	1	66	310	1.1	3.5	4.2
89-90—Houston	49	938	109	291	.375	42	55	.764	19	71	90	238	45	2	85	286	1.8	4.9	5.8
Totals	928	25556	3905	8696	.449	1897	2446	.776	490	1661	2151	6454	1273	73	1803	9951	2.3	7.0	10.7

Three-point field goals: 1979-80, 12-for-42 (.286). 1980-81, 4-for-24 (.167). 1981-82, 2-for-22 (.091). 1982-83, 0-for-5. 1983-84, 19-for-69 (.275). 1984-85, 21-for-66 (.318). 1985-86, 45-for-146 (.308). 1986-87, 46-for-126 (.365). 1987-88, 51-for-151 (.338). 1988-89, 18-for-68 (.265). 1989-90, 26-for-87 (.299). Totals, 244-for-806 (.303).
Personal fouls/disqualifications: 1976-77, 174/0. 1977-78, 208/1. 1978-79, 229/1. 1979-80, 196/2. 1980-81, 140/1. 1981-82, 105/0. 1982-83, 18/0. 1983-84, 123/1. 1984-85, 78/0. 1985-86, 124/0. 1986-87, 82/0. 1987-88, 102/1. 1988-89, 53/0. 1989-90, 59/0. Totals, 1691/7.

NBA PLAYOFF RECORD

Season Team	G	Min.	FGM	FGA	Pct.	FTM	FTA	Pct.	Off.	Def.	Tot.	Ast.	St.	Blk.	TO	Pts.	RPG	APG	PPG
									REBOUNDS								**AVERAGES**		
76-77—Houston	12	430	75	139	.540	26	34	.765	4	29	33	83	24	4	...	176	2.8	6.9	14.7
81-82—Washington	7	74	14	26	.538	2	3	.667	0	8	8	20	3	1	4	31	1.1	2.9	4.4
84-85—Houston	5	152	26	80	.325	14	22	.636	7	14	21	27	6	0	7	68	4.2	5.4	13.6
86-87—Milwaukee	12	362	68	150	.453	39	48	.813	4	21	25	62	14	1	20	187	2.1	5.2	15.6
87-88—Milwaukee	5	80	10	27	.370	6	9	.667	5	3	8	19	5	0	6	29	1.6	3.8	5.8
88-89—Seattle	4	37	5	17	.294	1	2	.500	0	1	1	8	0	0	2	11	0.3	2.0	2.8
Totals	45	1135	198	439	.451	88	118	.746	20	76	96	219	52	6	39	502	2.1	4.9	11.2

Three-point field goals: 1981-82, 1-for-3 (.333). 1984-85, 2-for-14 (.143). 1986-87, 12-for-36 (.333). 1987-88, 3-for-13 (.231). 1988-89, 0-for-3. Totals, 18-for-69 (.261).
Personal fouls/disqualifications: 1976-77, 33/1. 1981-82, 6/0. 1984-85, 14/0. 1986-87, 17/0. 1987-88, 5/0. 1988-89, 5/0. Totals, 80/1.

CBA REGULAR-SEASON RECORD

Season Team	G	Min.	FGM	FGA	Pct.	FTM	FTA	Pct.	Reb.	Ast.	Pts.	AVERAGES RPG	APG	PPG
83-84—Lancaster......................	2	48	12	18	.667	6	6	1.000	1	8	31	0.5	4.0	15.5

Three-point field goals: 1983-84, 1-for-1.

HEAD COACHING RECORD

NOTES: Owner, Miami Tropics of United States Basketball League (1992-93). ... Head coach, Miami Tropics (1992, 1993). ... Head coach/general manager Philadelphia 76ers (1994-95 and 1995-96).

NBA COACHING RECORD

	REGULAR SEASON				PLAYOFFS		
Season Team	W	L	Pct.	Finish	W	L	Pct.
92-93 —San Antonio...	39	22	.639	2nd/Midwest Division	5	5	.500
93-94 —San Antonio...	55	27	.671	2nd/Midwest Division	3	4	.429
94-95 —Philadelphia..	24	58	.293	6th/Atlantic Division	—	—	—
95-96 —Philadelphia..	18	64	.220	7th/Atlantic Division	—	—	—
Totals (4 years)...	136	171	.443	Totals (2 years).......	8	9	.471

NOTES:

1993—Replaced Jerry Tarkanian (9-11) and interim coach Rex Hughes (1-0) as San Antonio head coach (December 18), with 10-11 record and club in third place; defeated Portland, 3-1, in Western Conference first round; lost to Phoenix, 4-2, in Western Conference semifinals.
1994—Lost to Utah in Western Conference first round.

McMILLAN, NATE   SUPERSONICS

PERSONAL: Born August 3, 1964, in Raleigh, N.C. ... 6-5/200. (1,96/90,7). ... Full Name: Nathaniel McMillan.
HIGH SCHOOL: Enloe (Raleigh, N.C.).
JUNIOR COLLEGE: Chowan College (N.C.).
COLLEGE: North Carolina State.
TRANSACTIONS/CAREER NOTES: Selected by Seattle SuperSonics in second round (30th pick overall) of 1986 NBA Draft. ... Announced retirement to become assistant coach of SuperSonics (September 29, 1998).

COLLEGIATE RECORD

Season Team	G	Min.	FGM	FGA	Pct.	FTM	FTA	Pct.	Reb.	Ast.	Pts.	AVERAGES RPG	APG	PPG
82-83—Chowan College.............	27	...	101	174	.580	64	92	.696	134	191	266	5.0	7.1	9.9
83-84—Chowan College.............	35	...	180	331	.544	100	130	.769	342	411	460	9.8	11.7	13.1
84-85—North Carolina State.......	33	973	94	207	.454	64	95	.674	189	169	252	5.7	5.1	7.6
85-86—North Carolina State.......	34	1208	127	262	.485	66	90	.733	155	233	320	4.6	6.9	9.4
Junior College Totals.................	62	...	281	505	.556	164	222	.739	476	602	726	7.7	9.7	11.7
4-Year-College Totals	67	2181	221	469	.471	130	185	.703	344	402	572	5.1	6.0	8.5

NBA REGULAR-SEASON RECORD

RECORDS: Shares single-game record for most assists by a rookie—25 (February 23, 1987, vs. Los Angeles Clippers).
HONORS: NBA All-Defensive second team (1994, 1995).
NOTES: Led NBA with 2.96 steals per game (1994).

Season Team	G	Min.	FGM	FGA	Pct.	FTM	FTA	Pct.	REBOUNDS Off.	Def.	Tot.	Ast.	St.	Blk.	TO	Pts.	AVERAGES RPG	APG	PPG
86-87—Seattle...........	71	1972	143	301	.475	87	141	.617	101	230	331	583	125	45	155	373	4.7	8.2	5.3
87-88—Seattle...........	82	2453	235	496	.474	145	205	.707	117	221	338	702	169	47	189	624	4.1	8.6	7.6
88-89—Seattle...........	75	2341	199	485	.410	119	189	.630	143	245	388	696	156	42	211	532	5.2	9.3	7.1
89-90—Seattle...........	82	2338	207	438	.473	98	153	.641	127	276	403	598	140	37	187	523	4.9	7.3	6.4
90-91—Seattle...........	78	1434	132	305	.433	57	93	.613	71	180	251	371	104	20	122	338	3.2	4.8	4.3
91-92—Seattle...........	72	1652	177	405	.437	54	84	.643	92	160	252	359	129	29	112	435	3.5	5.0	6.0
92-93—Seattle...........	73	1977	213	459	.464	95	134	.709	84	222	306	384	173	33	139	546	4.2	5.3	7.5
93-94—Seattle...........	73	1887	177	396	.447	31	55	.564	50	233	283	387	*216	22	126	437	3.9	5.3	6.0
94-95—Seattle...........	80	2070	166	397	.418	34	58	.586	65	237	302	421	165	53	126	419	3.8	5.3	5.2
95-96—Seattle...........	55	1261	100	238	.420	29	41	.707	41	169	210	197	95	18	75	275	3.8	3.6	5.0
96-97—Seattle...........	37	798	61	149	.409	19	29	.655	15	103	118	140	58	6	32	169	3.2	3.8	4.6
97-98—Seattle...........	18	279	23	67	.343	1	1	1.000	14	27	40	55	14	4	12	62	2.2	3.1	3.4
Totals	796	20462	1833	4136	.443	769	1183	.650	919	2303	3222	4893	1544	356	1486	4733	4.0	6.1	5.9

Three-point field goals: 1986-87, 0-for-7. 1987-88, 9-for-24 (.375). 1988-89, 15-for-70 (.214). 1989-90, 11-for-31 (.355). 1990-91, 17-for-48 (.354). 1991-92, 27-for-98 (.276). 1992-93, 25-for-65 (.385). 1993-94, 52-for-133 (.391). 1994-95, 53-for-155 (.342). 1995-96, 46-for-121 (.380). 1996-97, 28-for-84 (.333). 1997-98, 15-for-34 (.441). Totals, 298-for-870 (.343).
Personal fouls/disqualifications: 1986-87, 238/4. 1987-88, 238/1. 1988-89, 236/3. 1989-90, 289/7. 1990-91, 211/6. 1991-92, 218/4. 1992-93, 240/6. 1993-94, 201/1. 1994-95, 275/8. 1995-96, 143/3. 1996-97, 78/0. 1997-98, 41/0. Totals, 2408/43.

NBA PLAYOFF RECORD

Season Team	G	Min.	FGM	FGA	Pct.	FTM	FTA	Pct.	REBOUNDS Off.	Def.	Tot.	Ast.	St.	Blk.	TO	Pts.	AVERAGES RPG	APG	PPG
86-87—Seattle...........	14	356	27	62	.435	17	24	.708	13	41	54	112	14	10	26	71	3.9	8.0	5.1
87-88—Seattle...........	5	127	12	35	.343	9	14	.643	6	15	21	33	2	3	8	33	4.2	6.6	6.6
88-89—Seattle...........	8	200	19	40	.475	16	25	.640	9	16	25	63	10	5	19	54	3.1	7.9	6.8
90-91—Seattle...........	5	95	6	23	.261	2	4	.500	6	12	18	22	6	1	3	14	3.6	4.4	2.8
91-92—Seattle...........	9	246	35	83	.422	10	14	.714	14	19	33	63	16	3	22	86	3.7	7.0	9.6
92-93—Seattle...........	19	415	35	103	.340	16	30	.533	21	46	67	103	40	11	25	91	3.5	5.4	4.8
93-94—Seattle...........	5	109	8	25	.320	1	4	.250	6	10	16	10	6	1	5	21	3.2	2.0	4.2
94-95—Seattle...........	4	113	8	23	.348	2	2	1.000	7	11	18	29	10	2	7	19	4.5	7.3	4.8
95-96—Seattle...........	19	385	28	69	.406	9	14	.643	13	57	70	52	23	5	20	84	3.7	2.7	4.4
96-97—Seattle...........	3	41	0	2	.000	0	0	...	1	4	5	3	1	0	2	0	1.7	1.0	0.0
97-98—Seattle...........	7	99	6	18	.333	2	2	1.000	2	14	16	15	3	2	2	16	2.3	2.1	2.3
Totals	98	2186	184	483	.381	84	133	.632	98	245	343	505	131	43	139	489	3.5	5.2	5.0

HEAD COACHES

Three-point field goals: 1987-88, 0-for-1. 1988-89, 0-for-2. 1990-91, 0-for-2. 1991-92, 6-for-26 (.231). 1992-93, 5-for-24 (.208). 1993-94, 4-for-11 (.364). 1994-95, 1-for-8 (.125). 1995-96, 19-for-40 (.475). 1996-97, 0-for-2. 1997-98, 2-for-12 (.167). Totals, 37-for-128 (.289).

Personal fouls/disqualifications: 1986-87, 42/1. 1987-88, 11/0. 1988-89, 21/0. 1990-91, 15/0. 1991-92, 35/1. 1992-93, 54/2. 1993-94, 18/1. 1994-95, 13/0. 1995-96, 34/0. 1996-97, 11/0. 1997-98, 17/0. Totals, 271/5.

HEAD COACHING RECORD
NOTES: Assistant coach, Seattle SuperSonics (1998-99 through November 27, 2000).

NBA COACHING RECORD

| Season Team | REGULAR SEASON | | | | PLAYOFFS | | |
	W	L	Pct.	Finish	W	L	Pct.
00-01 —Seattle	38	29	.567	5th Pacific Division	—	—	—

NOTES:
2001—Replaced Paul Westphal as Seattle head coach (November 27), with record of 6-9 and club in fifth place.

NELSON, DON   MAVERICKS

PERSONAL: Born May 15, 1940, in Muskegon, Mich. ... 6-6/210. (1,98/95,3). ... Full name: Don Arvid Nelson.
HIGH SCHOOL: Rock Island (Ill.).
COLLEGE: Iowa.
TRANSACTIONS: Selected by Chicago Zephyrs in third round (19th pick overall) of 1962 NBA Draft. ... Zephyrs franchise moved from Chicago to Baltimore and renamed Bullets for 1963-64 season. ... Contract sold by Bullets to Los Angeles Lakers (September 6, 1963). ... Waived by Lakers (October 21, 1965). ... Signed as free agent by Boston Celtics (October 28, 1965).
MISCELLANEOUS: Member of NBA championship team (1966, 1968, 1969, 1974, 1976). ... Head coach of gold-medal-winning 1994 USA Basketball World Championship Team.

COLLEGIATE RECORD

| Season Team | G | Min. | FGM | FGA | Pct. | FTM | FTA | Pct. | Reb. | Ast. | Pts. | AVERAGES | | |
												RPG	APG	PPG
58-59—Iowa‡						Freshman team did not play intercollegiate schedule.								
59-60—Iowa	24	...	140	320	.438	100	155	.645	241	...	380	10.0	...	15.8
60-61—Iowa	24	...	197	377	.523	176	268	.657	258	...	570	10.8	...	23.8
61-62—Iowa	24	...	193	348	.555	186	264	.705	285	...	572	11.9	...	23.8
Varsity totals	72	...	530	1045	.507	462	687	.672	784	...	1522	10.9	...	21.1

NBA REGULAR-SEASON RECORD

| Season Team | G | Min. | FGM | FGA | Pct. | FTM | FTA | Pct. | Reb. | Ast. | PF | Dq. | Pts. | AVERAGES | | |
														RPG	APG	PPG
62-63 —Chicago	62	1071	129	293	.440	161	221	.729	279	72	136	3	419	4.5	1.2	6.8
63-64 —Los Angeles	80	1406	135	323	.418	149	201	.741	323	76	181	1	419	4.0	1.0	5.2
64-65 —Los Angeles	39	238	36	85	.424	20	26	.769	73	24	40	1	92	1.9	0.6	2.4
65-66 —Boston	75	1765	271	618	.439	223	326	.684	403	79	187	1	765	5.4	1.1	10.2
66-67 —Boston	79	1202	227	509	.446	141	190	.742	295	65	143	0	595	3.7	0.8	7.5
67-68 —Boston	82	1498	312	632	.494	195	268	.728	431	103	178	1	819	5.3	1.3	10.0
68-69 —Boston	82	1773	374	771	.485	201	259	.776	458	92	198	2	949	5.6	1.1	11.6
69-70 —Boston	82	2224	461	920	.501	337	435	.775	601	148	238	3	1259	7.3	1.8	15.4
70-71 —Boston	82	2254	412	881	.468	317	426	.744	565	153	232	2	1141	6.9	1.9	13.9
71-72 —Boston	82	2086	389	811	.480	356	452	.788	453	192	220	3	1134	5.5	2.3	13.8
72-73 —Boston	72	1425	309	649	.476	159	188	.846	315	102	155	1	777	4.4	1.4	10.8

| Season Team | G | Min. | FGM | FGA | Pct. | FTM | FTA | Pct. | REBOUNDS | | | Ast. | Stl. | Blk. | TO | Pts. | AVERAGES | | |
									Off.	Def.	Tot.						RPG	APG	PPG
73-74 —Boston	82	1748	364	717	.508	215	273	.788	90	255	345	162	19	13	...	943	4.2	2.0	11.5
74-75 —Boston	79	2052	423	785	*.539	263	318	.827	127	342	469	181	32	15	...	1109	5.9	2.3	14.0
75-76 —Boston	75	943	175	379	.462	127	161	.789	56	126	182	77	14	7	...	477	2.4	1.0	6.4
Totals	1053	21685	4017	8373	.480	2864	3744	.765	...	...	5192	1526	65	35	...	10898	4.9	1.4	10.3

NBA PLAYOFF RECORD

| Season Team | G | Min. | FGM | FGA | Pct. | FTM | FTA | Pct. | Reb. | Ast. | PF | Dq. | Pts. | AVERAGES | | |
														RPG	APG	PPG
63-64 —Los Angeles	5	56	7	13	.538	3	3	1.000	13	2	11	1	17	2.6	0.4	3.4
64-65 —Los Angeles	11	212	24	53	.453	19	25	.760	59	19	31	0	67	5.4	1.7	6.1
65-66 —Boston	17	316	50	118	.424	42	52	.808	85	13	50	0	142	5.0	0.8	8.4
66-67 —Boston	9	142	27	59	.458	10	17	.588	42	9	12	0	64	4.7	1.0	7.1
67-68 —Boston	19	468	91	175	.520	55	74	.743	143	32	49	0	237	7.5	1.7	12.5
68-69 —Boston	18	348	87	168	.518	50	60	.833	83	21	51	0	224	4.6	1.2	12.4
71-72 —Boston	11	308	52	99	.525	41	48	.854	61	21	30	0	145	5.5	1.9	13.2
72-73 —Boston	13	303	47	101	.465	49	56	.875	38	15	29	0	143	2.9	1.2	11.0

| Season Team | G | Min. | FGM | FGA | Pct. | FTM | FTA | Pct. | REBOUNDS | | | Ast. | Stl. | Blk. | TO | Pts. | AVERAGES | | |
									Off.	Def.	Tot.						RPG	APG	PPG
73-74 —Boston	18	467	82	164	.500	41	53	.774	25	72	97	35	8	3	...	205	5.4	1.9	11.4
74-75 —Boston	11	274	66	117	.564	37	41	.902	18	27	45	26	2	2	...	169	4.1	2.4	15.4
75-76 —Boston	18	315	52	108	.481	60	69	.870	17	36	53	17	3	2	...	164	2.9	0.9	9.1
Totals	150	3209	585	1175	.498	407	498	.817	...	...	719	210	13	7	...	1577	4.8	1.4	10.5

HEAD COACHING RECORD
BACKGROUND: Assistant coach, Milwaukee Bucks (September 9-November 22, 1976). ... Head coach/director of player personnel, Bucks (November 22, 1976 through 1985). ... Head coach/vice president of basketball operations, Bucks (1985-May 27, 1987). ... Executive vice president, Golden State Warriors (1987-88). ... Head coach/general manager, Warriors (1988-89 to February 13, 1995). ... General manager, Dallas Mavericks (February 7, 1997 to present).
HONORS: NBA Coach of the Year (1983, 1985, 1992). ... One of the Top 10 Coaches in NBA History (1996).

NBA COACHING RECORD

Season	Team	REGULAR SEASON				PLAYOFFS		
		W	L	Pct.	Finish	W	L	Pct.
76-77	—Milwaukee	27	37	.422	6th/Midwest Division	—	—	—
77-78	—Milwaukee	44	38	.537	2nd/Midwest Division	5	4	.556
78-79	—Milwaukee	38	44	.463	4th/Midwest Division	—	—	—
79-80	—Milwaukee	49	33	.598	1st/Midwest Division	3	4	.429
80-81	—Milwaukee	60	22	.732	1st/Central Division	3	4	.429
81-82	—Milwaukee	55	27	.671	1st/Central Division	2	4	.333
82-83	—Milwaukee	51	31	.622	1st/Central Division	5	4	.556
83-84	—Milwaukee	50	32	.610	1st/Central Division	8	8	.500
84-85	—Milwaukee	59	23	.720	1st/Central Division	3	5	.375
85-86	—Milwaukee	57	25	.695	1st/Central Division	7	7	.500
86-87	—Milwaukee	50	32	.610	3rd/Central Division	6	6	.500
88-89	—Golden State	43	39	.524	4th/Pacific Division	4	4	.500
89-90	—Golden State	37	45	.451	5th/Pacific Division	—	—	—
90-91	—Golden State	44	38	.537	4th/Pacific Division	4	5	.444
91-92	—Golden State	55	27	.671	2nd/Pacific Division	1	3	.250
92-93	—Golden State	34	48	.415	6th/Pacific Division	—	—	—
93-94	—Golden State	50	32	.610	3rd/Pacific Division	0	3	.000
94-95	—Golden State	14	31	.311		—	—	—
95-96	—New York	34	25	.576		—	—	—
97-98	—Dallas	16	50	.242	5th/Midwest Division	—	—	—
98-99	—Dallas	19	31	.380	4th/Midwest Division	—	—	—
99-00	—Dallas	40	42	.488	4th/Midwest Division	—	—	—
00-01	—Dallas	53	29	.646	T2nd/Midwest Division	4	6	.400
Totals (23 years)		**960**	**750**	**.561**		**55**	**67**	**.451**

Totals (14 years) ...... 55 67 .451

WORLD CHAMPIONSHIP COACHING RECORD

Season	Team	REGULAR SEASON			
		W	L	Pct.	Finish
1994	—Team USA	8	0	1.000	Gold medal

NOTES:

1976—Replaced Larry Costello as Milwaukee head coach (November 22), with record of 3-15 and club in sixth place.

1978—Defeated Phoenix, 2-0, in Western Conference first round; lost to Denver, 4-3, in Western Conference semifinals.

1980—Lost to Seattle in Western Conference semifinals.

1981—Lost to Philadelphia in Eastern Conference semifinals.

1982—Lost to Philadelphia in Eastern Conference semifinals.

1983—Defeated Boston, 4-0, in Eastern Conference semifinals; lost to Philadelphia, 4-1, in Eastern Conference finals.

1984—Defeated Atlanta, 3-2, in Eastern Conference first round; defeated New Jersey, 4-2, in Eastern Conference semifinals; lost to Boston, 4-1, in Eastern Conference finals.

1985—Defeated Chicago, 3-1, in Eastern Conference first round; lost to Philadelphia, 4-0, in Eastern Conference semifinals.

1986—Defeated New Jersey, 3-0, in Eastern Conference first round; defeated Philadelphia, 4-3, in Eastern Conference semifinals; lost to Boston, 4-0, in Eastern Conference finals.

1987—Defeated Philadelphia, 3-2, in Eastern Conference first round; lost to Boston, 4-3, in Eastern Conference semifinals.

1989—Defeated Utah, 3-0, in Western Conference first round; lost to Phoenix, 4-1, in Western Conference semifinals.

1991—Defeated San Antonio, 3-1, in Western Conference first round; lost to Los Angeles Lakers, 4-1, in Western Conference semifinals.

1992—Lost to Seattle in Western Conference first round.

1994—Lost to Phoenix in Western Conference first round.

1995—Replaced as Golden State head coach by Bob Lanier (February 13) with club in sixth place.

1996—Replaced as New York head coach by Jeff Van Gundy (March 8) with club in second place.

1997—Replaced Jim Cleamons as Dallas head coach (December 4), with record of 4-12 and club in sixth place.

2001—Defeated Utah, 3-2, in Western Conference first round; lost to San Antonio, 4-1, in Western Conference semifinals.

O'BRIEN, JIM   CELTICS

PERSONAL: Born February 11, 1952, in Philadelphia. ... 6-0/190. (1,83/86,2). ... Full name: James F. X. O'Brien.
HIGH SCHOOL: Roman Catholic (Philadelphia).
COLLEGE: St. Joseph's.

COLLEGIATE RECORD

Season Team	G	Min.	FGM	FGA	Pct.	FTM	FTA	Pct.	Reb.	Ast.	Pts.	RPG	APG	PPG
70-71—St. Joseph's‡	23	...	115	287	.401	128	181	.707	63	88	358	2.7	3.8	15.6
71-72—St. Joseph's	26	...	59	182	.324	74	92	.804	84	115	192	3.2	4.4	7.4
72-73—St. Joseph's	28	837	68	189	.360	30	44	.682	77	106	166	2.8	3.8	5.9
73-74—St. Joseph's	30	969	117	251	.466	92	112	.821	97	152	326	3.2	5.1	10.9
Totals	**84**	...	**244**	**622**	**.392**	**196**	**248**	**.790**	**258**	**373**	**684**	**3.1**	**4.4**	**8.1**

HEAD COACHING RECORD

NOTES: Assistant coach, Wheeling Jesuit College (1974-75). ... Assistant coach, Pembroke State College (1975-76). ... Assistant coach, University of Maryland (1976-77). ... Assistant coach, St. Joseph's University (1977-78). ... Assistant coach, University of Oregon (1978-79 through 1981-82). ... Assistant coach, New York Knicks (1987-88 and 1988-89). ... Assistant coach, University of Kentucky (1994-95 through 1996-97). ... Assistant coach, Boston Celtics (1997-98 through January 8, 2001).

COLLEGIATE COACHING RECORD

Season	Team	W	L	Pct.	Finish
82-83	—Wheeling Jesuit	17	14	.548	—
83-84	—Wheeling Jesuit	13	15	.464	—
84-85	—Wheeling Jesuit	13	15	.464	—
85-86	—Wheeling Jesuit	18	10	.643	—
86-87	—Wheeling Jesuit	13	15	.464	—

Season Team	W	L	Pct.	Finish
89-90 —Dayton	22	10	.688	2nd/Midwestern Collegiate Conference
90-91 —Dayton	14	15	.483	T3rd/Midwestern Collegiate Conference
91-92 —Dayton	15	15	.500	4th/Midwestern Collegiate Conference
92-93 —Dayton	4	26	.133	T7th/Midwestern Collegiate Conference
93-94 —Dayton	5	21	.192	7th/Great Midwest Conference
Totals(10 years)	134	156	.462	

NOTES:

1990—Defeated Illinois, 88-86, in NCAA Tournament first round; lost to Arkansas, 86-84, in second round.

NBA COACHING RECORD

		REGULAR SEASON				PLAYOFFS		
Season Team	W	L	Pct.	Finish		W	L	Pct.
00-01 —Boston	24	24	.500	5th Atlantic Division		—	—	—

NOTES:

2001—Replaced Rick Pitino as Boston head coach (January 8), with record of 12-22 and club in fifth place.

POPOVICH, GREGG — SPURS

PERSONAL: Born January 28, 1949, in East Chicago, Ind. ... 6-2/200. (1,88/90,7). ... Full name: Gregg Charles Popovich.
HIGH SCHOOL: Merrillville (Ind.).
COLLEGE: Air Force, then Denver.
CAREER NOTES: Executive vice president of basketball operations/general manager, Spurs (1994-95 to present).

COLLEGIATE RECORD

												AVERAGES		
Season Team	G	Min.	FGM	FGA	Pct.	FTM	FTA	Pct.	Reb.	Ast.	Pts.	RPG	APG	PPG
68-69—Air Force	19	...	38	79	.481	26	40	.650	36	...	102	1.9	...	5.4
69-70—Air Force	24	...	132	236	.559	78	98	.796	109	...	342	4.5	...	14.3
Varsity totals	43	...	170	315	.540	104	138	.754	145	...	444	3.4	...	10.3

COLLEGIATE COACHING RECORD

Season Team	W	L	Pct.	Finish
79-80 —Pomona-Pitzer	2	22	.083	T6th/Southern California I.A.C.
80-81 —Pomona-Pitzer	10	15	.400	6th/Southern California I.A.C.
81-82 —Pomona-Pitzer	9	17	.346	4th/Southern California I.A.C.
82-83 —Pomona-Pitzer	12	13	.480	5th/Southern California I.A.C.
83-84 —Pomona-Pitzer	9	17	.346	T4th/Southern California I.A.C.
84-85 —Pomona-Pitzer	11	14	.440	4th/Southern California I.A.C.
85-86 —Pomona-Pitzer	16	12	.571	1st/Southern California I.A.C.
Totals (7 years)	69	110	.385	

NBA COACHING RECORD

BACKGROUND: Assistant coach, Air Force (1972-73 through 1977-78). ... Assistant coach, San Antonio Spurs (1988-89 through 1991-92). ... Assistant coach, Golden State Warriors (1992-93 and 1993-94).

		REGULAR SEASON				PLAYOFFS		
Season Team	W	L	Pct.	Finish		W	L	Pct.
96-97—San Antonio	17	47	.266	6th/Midwest Division		—	—	—
97-98—San Antonio	56	26	.683	2nd/Midwest Division		4	5	.444
98-99—San Antonio	37	13	.740	T1st/Midwest Division		15	2	.882
99-00—San Antonio	53	29	.646	2nd/Midwest Division		1	3	.250
00-01—San Antonio	58	24	.707	1st/Midwest Division		7	6	.539
Totals (5 years)	221	139	.614		Totals (4 years)	27	16	.628

NOTES:

1996—Replaced Bob Hill as San Antonio head coach (December 10), with record of 3-15 and club in seventh place.

1998—Defeated Phoenix, 3-1, in Western Conference first round; lost to Utah, 4-1, in Western Conference semifinals.

1999—Defeated Minnesota, 3-1, in Western Conference first round; defeated Los Angeles Lakers, 4-0, in Western Conference semifinals; defeated Portland, 4-0, in Western Conference finals; defeated New York, 4-1, in NBA Finals.

2000—Lost to Phoenix in Western Conference first round.

2001—Defeated Minnesota, 3-1, in Western Conference first round; defeated Dallas, 4-1, in Western Conference semifinals; lost to Los Angeles Lakers, 4-0, in Western Conference finals.

RILEY, PAT — HEAT

PERSONAL: Born March 20, 1945, in Rome, N.Y. ... 6-4/205. (1,93/93,0). ... Full name: Patrick James Riley. ... Son of Leon Riley, outfielder/catcher with Philadelphia Phillies (1944) and minor league manager; and brother of Lee Riley, defensive back with Detroit Lions, Philadelphia Eagles and New York Giants (1955-1960) and New York Titans of American Football League (1961 and 1962).
HIGH SCHOOL: Linton (Schenectady, N.Y.).
COLLEGE: Kentucky.
TRANSACTIONS/CAREER NOTES: Selected by San Diego Rockets in first round (seventh pick overall) of 1967 NBA Draft. ... Selected by Portland Trail Blazers from Rockets in NBA expansion draft (May 11, 1970). ... Contract sold by Trail Blazers to Los Angeles Lakers (October 9, 1970). ... Traded by Lakers to Phoenix Suns for draft rights to G John Roche and 1976 second-round draft choice (November 3, 1975).
CAREER NOTES: Broadcaster, Los Angeles Lakers (1977-78 and 1978-79). ... Broadcaster, NBC Sports (1990-91). ... President, Miami Heat (1995-96 to present).
MISCELLANEOUS: Member of NBA championship team (1972). ... Selected by Dallas Cowboys in 11th round of 1967 NFL Draft.

COLLEGIATE RECORD

												AVERAGES		
Season Team	G	Min.	FGM	FGA	Pct.	FTM	FTA	Pct.	Reb.	Ast.		Pts.	RPG	APG	PPG
63-64—Kentucky‡	16	...	120	259	.463	93	146	.637	235	...		333	14.7	...	20.8
64-65—Kentucky	25	825	160	370	.432	55	89	.618	212	27		375	8.5	1.1	15.0
65-66—Kentucky	29	1078	265	514	.516	107	153	.699	259	64		637	8.9	2.2	22.0
66-67—Kentucky	26	953	165	373	.442	122	156	.782	201	68		452	7.7	2.6	17.4
Varsity totals..........................	80	2856	590	1257	.469	284	398	.714	672	159		1464	8.4	2.0	18.3

NBA REGULAR-SEASON RECORD

													AVERAGES		
Season Team	G	Min.	FGM	FGA	Pct.	FTM	FTA	Pct.	Reb.	Ast.	PF	Dq.	Pts.	RPG	APG	PPG
67-68 —San Diego......................	80	1263	250	660	.379	128	202	.634	177	138	205	1	628	2.2	1.7	7.9
68-69 —San Diego......................	56	1027	202	498	.406	90	134	.672	112	136	146	1	494	2.0	2.4	8.8
69-70 —San Diego......................	36	474	75	180	.417	40	55	.727	57	85	68	0	190	1.6	2.4	5.3
70-71 —Los Angeles..................	54	506	105	254	.413	56	87	.644	54	72	84	0	266	1.0	1.3	4.9
71-72 —Los Angeles..................	67	926	197	441	.447	55	74	.743	127	75	110	0	449	1.9	1.1	6.7
72-73 —Los Angeles..................	55	801	167	390	.428	65	82	.793	65	81	126	0	399	1.2	1.5	7.3

									REBOUNDS							AVERAGES		
Season Team	G	Min.	FGM	FGA	Pct.	FTM	FTA	Pct.	Off.	Def.	Tot.	Ast.	St.	Blk.	TO	Pts.	RPG	APG	PPG
73-74—Los Angeles ..	72	1361	287	667	.430	110	144	.764	38	90	128	148	54	3	...	684	1.8	2.1	9.5
74-75—Los Angeles ..	46	1016	219	523	.419	69	93	.742	25	60	85	121	36	4	...	507	1.8	2.6	11.0
75-76—L.A.-Phoenix.	62	813	117	301	.389	55	77	.714	16	34	50	57	22	6	...	289	0.8	0.9	4.7
Totals	528	8187	1619	3914	.414	668	948	.705	...	...	855	913	112	13	...	3906	1.6	1.7	7.4

Personal fouls/disqualifications: 1973-74, 173/1. 1974-75, 128/0. 1975-76, 112/0. Totals, 1152/3.

NBA PLAYOFF RECORD

													AVERAGES		
Season Team	G	Min.	FGM	FGA	Pct.	FTM	FTA	Pct.	Reb.	Ast.	PF	Dq.	Pts.	RPG	APG	PPG
68-69 —San Diego......................	5	76	16	37	.432	5	6	.833	11	2	13	0	37	2.2	0.4	7.4
70-71 —Los Angeles..................	7	135	29	69	.420	8	11	.727	15	14	12	0	66	2.1	2.0	9.4
71-72 —Los Angeles..................	15	244	33	99	.333	12	16	.750	29	14	37	0	78	1.9	0.9	5.2
72-73 —Los Angeles..................	7	53	9	27	.333	0	0	...	5	7	10	0	18	0.7	1.0	2.6

									REBOUNDS							AVERAGES		
Season Team	G	Min.	FGM	FGA	Pct.	FTM	FTA	Pct.	Off.	Def.	Tot.	Ast.	St.	Blk.	TO	Pts.	RPG	APG	PPG
73-74—Los Angeles ..	5	106	18	50	.360	3	4	.750	3	3	6	10	4	0	...	39	1.2	2.0	7.8
75-76—Phoenix.........	5	27	6	15	.400	1	1	1.000	0	0	5	5	0	0	...	13	0.0	1.0	2.6
Totals	44	641	111	297	.374	29	38	.763	...	...	66	52	4	0	...	251	1.5	1.2	5.7

Personal fouls/disqualifications: 1973-74, 11/0. 1975-76, 3/0. Totals, 86/0.

HEAD COACHING RECORD

BACKGROUND: Assistant coach, Lakers (1979-80 to November 19, 1981).
HONORS: NBA Coach of the Year (1990, 1993 and 1997). ... One of the Top 10 Coaches in NBA History (1996).
RECORDS: Holds NBA career record for most playoff wins—155.

NBA COACHING RECORD

	REGULAR SEASON				PLAYOFFS		
Season Team	W	L	Pct.	Finish	W	L	Pct.
81-82 —Los Angeles...	50	21	.704	1st/Pacific Division	12	2	.857
82-83 —Los Angeles...	58	24	.707	1st/Pacific Division	8	7	.533
83-84 —Los Angeles...	54	28	.659	1st/Pacific Division	14	7	.667
84-85 —Los Angeles Lakers	62	20	.756	1st/Pacific Division	15	4	.789
85-86 —Los Angeles Lakers	62	20	.756	1st/Pacific Division	8	6	571
86-87 —Los Angeles Lakers	65	17	.793	1st/Pacific Division	15	3	.833
87-88 —Los Angeles Lakers	62	20	.756	1st/Pacific Division	15	9	.625
88-89 —Los Angeles Lakers	57	25	.695	1st/Pacific Division	11	4	.733
89-90 —Los Angeles Lakers	63	19	.768	1st/Pacific Division	4	5	.444
91-92 —New York...	51	31	.622	T1st/Atlantic Division	6	6	.500
92-93 —New York...	60	22	.732	1st/Atlantic Division	9	6	.600
93-94 —New York...	57	25	.695	1st/Atlantic Division	14	11	.560
94-95 —New York...	55	27	.671	2nd/Atlantic Division	6	5	.545
95-96 —Miami..	42	40	.512	3rd/Atlantic Division	0	3	.000
96-97 —Miami..	61	21	.744	1st/Atlantic Division	8	9	.471
97-98 —Miami..	55	27	.671	1st/Atlantic Division	2	3	.400
98-99 —Miami..	33	17	.660	T1st/Atlantic Division	2	3	.400
99-00 —Miami..	52	30	.634	1st/Atlantic Division	6	4	.600
00-01 —Miami..	50	32	.610	2nd/Atlantic Division	0	3	.000
Totals (19 years)...	**1049**	**466**	**.692**	**Totals (19 years)**.......	**155**	**100**	**.608**

NOTES:

1981—Replaced Paul Westhead as Los Angeles head coach (November 19), with record of 7-4 and club in second place.

1982—Defeated Phoenix, 4-0, in Western Conference semifinals; defeated San Antonio, 4-0, in Western Conference finals; defeated Philadelphia, 4-2, in NBA Finals.

1983—Defeated Portland, 4-1, in Western Conference semifinals; defeated San Antonio, 4-2, in Western Conference finals; lost to Philadelphia, 4-0, in NBA Finals.

1984—Defeated Kansas City, 3-0, in Western Conference first round; defeated Dallas, 4-1, in Western Conference semifinals; defeated Phoenix, 4-2, in Western Conference finals; lost to Boston, 4-3, in NBA Finals.

1985—Defeated Phoenix, 3-0, in Western Conference first round; defeated Portland, 4-1, in Western Conference semifinals; defeated Denver, 4-1, in Western Conference finals; defeated Boston, 4-2, in NBA Finals.

HEAD COACHES

1986—Defeated San Antonio, 3-0, in Western Conference first round; defeated Dallas, 4-2, in Western Conference semifinals; lost to Houston, 4-1, in Western Conference finals.

1987—Defeated Denver, 3-0, in Western Conference first round; defeated Golden State, 4-1, in Western Conference semifinals; defeated Seattle, 4-0, in Western Conference finals; defeated Boston, 4-2, in NBA Finals.

1988—Defeated San Antonio, 3-0, in Western Conference first round; defeated Utah, 4-3, in Western Conference semifinals; defeated Dallas, 4-3, in Western Conference finals; defeated Detroit, 4-3, in NBA Finals.

1989—Defeated Portland, 3-0, in Western Conference first round; defeated Seattle, 4-0, in Western Conference semifinals; defeated Phoenix, 4-0, in Western Conference finals; lost to Detroit, 4-0, in NBA Finals.

1990—Defeated Houston, 3-1, in Western Conference first round; lost to Phoenix, 4-1, in Western Conference semifinals.

1992—Defeated Detroit, 3-2, in Eastern Conference first round; lost to Chicago, 4-3, in Eastern Conference semifinals.

1993—Defeated Indiana, 3-1, in Eastern Conference first round; defeated Charlotte, 4-1, in Eastern Conference semifinals; lost to Chicago, 4-2, in Eastern Conference finals.

1994—Defeated New Jersey, 3-1, in Eastern Conference first round; defeated Chicago, 4-3, in Eastern Conference semifinals; defeated Indiana, 4-3, in Eastern Conference finals; lost to Houston, 4-3, in NBA Finals.

1995—Defeated Cleveland, 3-1, in Eastern Conference first round; lost to Indiana, 4-3, in Eastern Conference semifinals.

1996—Lost to Chicago in Eastern Conference first round.

1997—Defeated Orlando, 3-2, in Eastern Conference first round; defeated New York, 4-3, in Eastern Conference semifinals; lost to Chicago, 4-1, in Eastern Conference finals.

1998—Lost to New York in Eastern Conference first round.

1999—Lost to New York in Eastern Conference first round.

2000—Defeated Detroit, 3-0, in Eastern Conference first round; lost to New York, 4-3, in Eastern Conference semifinals.

2001—Lost to Charlotte in Eastern Conference first round.

RIVERS, DOC   MAGIC

PERSONAL: Born October 13, 1961, in Chicago. ... 6-4/210. (1,93/95,3). ... Full name: Glenn Anton Rivers. ... Nephew of Jim Brewer, forward with Cleveland Cavaliers, Detroit Pistons, Portland Trail Blazers and Los Angeles Lakers (1973-74 through 1981-82); cousin of Byron Irvin, guard with Portland Trail Blazers and Washington Bullets (1989-90, 1990-91 and 1992-93); and cousin of Ken Singleton, outfielder/designated hitter with New York Mets, Montreal Expos and Baltimore Orioles (1970 through 1984).

HIGH SCHOOL: Proviso East (Maywood, Ill.).

COLLEGE: Marquette.

TRANSACTIONS: Selected after junior season by Atlanta Hawks in second round (31st pick overall) of 1983 NBA Draft. ... Traded by Hawks to Los Angeles Clippers for 1991 first-round draft choice and 1993 and 1994 second-round draft choices (June 26, 1991). ... Traded by Clippers with C/F Charles Smith and G Bo Kimble to New York Knicks in three-way deal in which Clippers received G Mark Jackson and 1995 second-round draft choice from Knicks and C Stanley Roberts from Orlando Magic and Magic received 1993 first-round draft choice from Knicks and 1994 first-round draft choice from Clippers (September 22, 1992). ... Waived by Knicks (December 15, 1994). ... Signed as free agent by San Antonio Spurs (December 26, 1994). ... Announced retirement (July 11, 1996).

CAREER NOTES: Broadcaster, Turner Sports (1998-99).

MISCELLANEOUS: Atlanta Hawks franchise all-time assists leader with 3,866 (1983-84 through 1990-91).

COLLEGIATE RECORD

Season Team	G	Min.	FGM	FGA	Pct.	FTM	FTA	Pct.	Reb.	Ast.	Pts.	RPG	APG	PPG
80-81—Marquette	31	921	182	329	.553	70	119	.588	99	113	434	3.2	3.6	14.0
81-82—Marquette	29	987	173	382	.453	70	108	.648	99	170	416	3.4	5.9	14.3
82-83—Marquette	29	1012	163	373	.437	58	95	.611	94	126	384	3.2	4.3	13.2
Totals	89	2920	518	1084	.478	198	322	.615	292	409	1234	3.3	4.6	13.9

NBA REGULAR-SEASON RECORD

HONORS: J. Walter Kennedy Citizenship Award (1990).

Season Team	G	Min.	FGM	FGA	Pct.	FTM	FTA	Pct.	Off.	Def.	Tot.	Ast.	St.	Blk.	TO	Pts.	RPG	APG	PPG
83-84—Atlanta	81	1938	250	541	.462	255	325	.785	72	148	220	314	127	30	174	757	2.7	3.9	9.3
84-85—Atlanta	69	2126	334	701	.476	291	378	.770	66	148	214	410	163	53	176	974	3.1	5.9	14.1
85-86—Atlanta	53	1571	220	464	.474	172	283	.608	49	113	162	443	120	13	141	612	3.1	8.4	11.5
86-87—Atlanta	82	2590	342	758	.451	365	441	.828	83	216	299	823	171	30	217	1053	3.6	10.0	12.8
87-88—Atlanta	80	2502	403	890	.453	319	421	.758	83	283	366	747	140	41	210	1134	4.6	9.3	14.2
88-89—Atlanta	76	2462	371	816	.455	247	287	.861	89	197	286	525	181	40	158	1032	3.8	6.9	13.6
89-90—Atlanta	48	1526	218	480	.454	138	170	.812	47	153	200	264	116	22	98	598	4.2	5.5	12.5
90-91—Atlanta	79	2586	444	1020	.435	221	262	.844	47	206	253	340	148	47	125	1197	3.2	4.3	15.2
91-92—L.A. Clippers	59	1657	226	533	.424	163	196	.832	23	124	147	233	111	19	92	641	2.5	3.9	10.9
92-93—New York	77	1886	216	494	.437	133	162	.821	26	166	192	405	123	9	114	604	2.5	5.3	7.8
93-94—New York	19	499	55	127	.433	14	22	.636	4	35	39	100	25	5	29	143	2.1	5.3	7.5
94-95—N.Y.-S.A.	63	989	108	302	.358	60	82	.732	15	94	109	162	65	21	60	321	1.7	2.6	5.1
95-96—San Antonio	78	1235	108	290	.372	48	64	.750	30	108	138	123	73	21	57	311	1.8	1.6	4.0
Totals	864	23567	3295	7416	.444	2426	3093	.784	634	1991	2625	4889	1563	351	1651	9377	3.0	5.7	10.9

Three-point field goals: 1983-84, 2-for-12 (.167). 1984-85, 15-for-36 (.417). 1985-86, 10-for-16. 1986-87, 4-for-21 (.190). 1987-88, 9-for-33 (.273). 1988-89, 43-for-124 (.347). 1989-90, 24-for-66 (.364). 1990-91, 88-for-262 (.336). 1991-92, 26-for-92 (.283). 1992-93, 39-for-123 (.317). 1993-94, 19-for-52 (.365). 1994-95, 45-for-127 (.354). 1995-96, 47-for-137 (.343). Totals, 361-for-1101 (.328).

Personal fouls/disqualifications: 1983-84, 286/8. 1984-85, 250/7. 1985-86, 185/2. 1986-87, 287/5. 1987-88, 272/3. 1988-89, 263/6. 1989-90, 151/2. 1990-91, 216/2. 1991-92, 166/2. 1992-93, 215/2. 1993-94, 44/0. 1994-95, 150/2. 1995-96, 175/0. Totals, 2660/41.

NBA PLAYOFF RECORD

NOTES: Shares single-game playoff record for most assists in one half—15 (May 16, 1988, vs. Boston).

Season Team	G	Min.	FGM	FGA	Pct.	FTM	FTA	Pct.	Off.	Def.	Tot.	Ast.	St.	Blk.	TO	Pts.	RPG	APG	PPG
									REBOUNDS								**AVERAGES**		
83-84—Atlanta	5	130	16	32	.500	36	41	.878	7	3	10	16	12	4	9	68	2.0	3.2	13.6
85-86—Atlanta	9	262	40	92	.435	31	42	.738	10	32	42	78	18	0	26	114	4.7	8.7	12.7
86-87—Atlanta	8	245	18	47	.383	26	52	.500	6	21	27	90	9	3	25	62	3.4	11.3	7.8
87-88—Atlanta	12	409	71	139	.511	39	43	.907	8	51	59	115	25	2	25	188	4.9	9.6	15.7
88-89—Atlanta	5	191	22	57	.386	17	24	.708	4	20	24	34	7	2	12	67	4.8	6.8	13.4
90-91—Atlanta	5	173	30	64	.469	17	19	.895	6	14	20	15	5	2	4	78	4.0	3.0	15.6
91-92—L.A. Clippers ...	5	187	25	56	.446	22	27	.815	4	15	19	21	6	0	3	76	3.8	4.2	15.2
92-93—New York	15	458	48	106	.453	46	60	.767	6	33	39	86	29	1	30	153	2.6	5.7	10.2
94-95—San Antonio	15	318	37	95	.389	26	31	.839	3	26	29	24	14	9	18	117	1.9	1.6	7.8
95-96—San Antonio	2	20	1	3	.333	0	0	...	0	1	1	0	0	0	1	3	0.5	0.0	1.5
Totals	81	2393	308	691	.446	260	339	.767	54	216	270	479	125	23	153	926	3.3	5.9	11.4

Three-point field goals: 1983-84, 0-for-3. 1985-86, 3-for-6 (.500). 1987-88, 7-for-22 (.318). 1988-89, 6-for-19 (.316). 1990-91, 1-for-11 (.091). 1991-92, 4-for-8 (.500). 1992-93, 11-for-31 (.355). 1994-95, 17-for-46 (.370). 1995-96, 1-for-2 (.500). Totals, 50-for-148 (.338).

Personal fouls/disqualifications: 1983-84, 16/0. 1985-86, 38/2. 1986-87, 32/0. 1987-88, 40/1. 1988-89, 22/2. 1990-91, 14/0. 1991-92, 16/0. 1992-93, 44/0. 1994-95, 40/0. 1995-96, 3/0. Totals, 265/5.

NBA ALL-STAR GAME RECORD

Season Team	Min.	FGM	FGA	Pct.	FTM	FTA	Pct.	Off.	Def.	Tot.	Ast.	PF	Dq.	St.	Blk.	TO	Pts.
								REBOUNDS									
1988 —Atlanta...............	16	2	4	.500	5	11	.455	0	3	3	6	3	0	0	0	3	9

NBA COACHING RECORD

HONORS: NBA Coach of the Year (2000).

Season Team	W	L	Pct.	Finish	W	L	Pct.
	REGULAR SEASON				**PLAYOFFS**		
99-00 —Orlando	41	41	.500	4th/Atlantic Division	—	—	—
00-01 —Orlando	43	39	.524	4th/Atlantic Division	1	3	.250
Totals (19 years).....................................	84	80	.512	Totals (1 year)........	1	3	.250

NOTES:
2001—Lost to Milwaukee in Eastern Conference first round.

SAUNDERS, FLIP   TIMBERWOLVES

PERSONAL: Born February 23, 1955, in Cleveland. ... 5-11/175. (1,81/79,4). ... Full name: Philip D. Saunders.
HIGH SCHOOL: Cuyahoga Heights (Ohio).
COLLEGE: Minnesota.
CAREER NOTES: General manager, Minnesota Timberwolves (1994-95 to present).

COLLEGIATE RECORD

Season Team	G	Min.	FGM	FGA	Pct.	FTM	FTA	Pct.	Reb.	Ast.	Pts.	RPG	APG	PPG
												AVERAGES		
73-74—Minnesota	24	...	93	209	.445	53	61	.869	93	...	239	3.9	...	9.9
74-75—Minnesota	26	...	67	154	.435	54	74	.730	74	...	188	2.8	...	7.2
75-76—Minnesota	26	...	99	209	.474	47	55	.854	95	95	245	3.8	3.7	9.4
76-77—Minnesota	27	...	77	172	.448	16	20	.800	103	107	170	3.8	4.0	6.3
Varsity totals........................	103	...	336	744	.452	170	210	.810	365	...	842	3.5	...	8.2

HEAD COACHING RECORD

BACKGROUND: Assistant coach, University of Minnesota (1981-82 through 1985-86). ... Assistant coach, University of Tulsa (1986-87 and 1987-88).
HONORS: CBA Coach of the Year (1990, 1992).

COLLEGIATE COACHING RECORD

Season Team	W	L	Pct.
77-78 —Golden Valley Lutheran College................	19	5	.792
78-79 —Golden Valley Lutheran College................	21	4	.840
79-80 —Golden Valley Lutheran College................	23	2	.920
80-81 —Golden Valley Lutheran College................	28	2	.933
Totals (4 years)...	91	13	.875

CBA COACHING RECORD

Season Team	W	L	Pct.	Finish	W	L	Pct.
	REGULAR SEASON				**PLAYOFFS**		
88-89 —Rapid City...	38	16	.704	1st/Western Division	6	5	.545
89-90 —La Crosse	42	14	.750	1st/Central Division	11	4	.733
90-91 —La Crosse	32	24	.571	2nd/Central Division	2	3	.400
91-92 —La Crosse	40	16	.714	2nd/Midwest Division	10	6	.625
92-93 —La Crosse	32	24	.571	3rd/Mideast Division	2	3	.400
93-94 —La Crosse	35	21	.625	1st/Mideast Division	3	3	.500
94-95 —Sioux Falls	34	22	.607	2nd/Western Division	1	2	.333
Totals (7 years)...	253	137	.649	Totals (7 years).......	35	26	.574

NBA COACHING RECORD

		REGULAR SEASON					PLAYOFFS		
Season Team	W	L	Pct.	Finish			W	L	Pct.
95-96 —Minnesota	20	42	.323	T5th/Midwest Division			—	—	—
96-97 —Minnesota	40	42	.488	3rd/Midwest Division			0	3	.000
97-98 —Minnesota	45	37	.549	3rd/Midwest Division			2	3	.400
98-99 —Minnesota	25	25	.500	4th/Midwest Division			1	3	.250
99-00 —Minnesota	50	32	.610	3rd/Midwest Division			1	3	.250
00-01 —Minnesota	47	35	.573	4th/Midwest Division			1	3	.250
Totals (6 years)	227	213	.516	Totals (5 years)			5	15	.250

NOTES:

1989—Defeated Cedar Rapids, 4-1, in Western semifinals; lost to Rockford, 4-2, in Western finals.

1990—Defeated Quad City, 3-0, in American semifinals; defeated Albany, 4-3, in American finals; defeated Rapid City, 4-1, in CBA Championship Series.

1991—Lost to Quad City, 3-2, in American first round.

1992—Defeated Grand Rapids, 3-1, in American second round; defeated Quad City, 3-2, in American finals; defeated Rapid City, 4-3, in CBA Championship Series.

1993—Lost to Rockford, 3-2, in American first round.

1994—Defeated Rockford, 3-0, in American first round; lost to Quad City, 3-0, in American finals.

1995—Lost to Omaha, 2-1, in National first round. Replaced Bill Blair as Minnesota head coach (December 18), with record of 6-14 and club in sixth place.

1997—Lost to Houston in Western Conference first round.

1998—Lost to Seattle in Western Conference first round.

1999—Lost to San Antonio in Western Conference first round.

2000—Lost to Portland in Western Conference first round.

2001—Lost to San Antonio in Western Conference first round.

HEAD COACHES

SCOTT, BYRON   NETS

PERSONAL: Born March 28, 1961, in Ogden, Utah. ... 6-4/200. (1,93/90,7). ... Full Name: Byron Antom Scott.
HIGH SCHOOL: Morningside (Inglewood, Calif.).
COLLEGE: Arizona State.
TRANSACTIONS/CAREER NOTES: Selected by San Diego Clippers in first round (fourth pick overall) of 1983 NBA Draft. ... Draft rights traded by Clippers with C Swen Nater to Los Angeles Lakers for G Norm Nixon, G Eddie Jordan and 1986 and 1987 second-round draft choices (October 10, 1983). ... Signed as free agent by Indiana Pacers (December 6, 1993). ... Selected by Vancouver Grizzlies from Pacers in NBA Expansion Draft (June 24, 1995). ... Waived by Grizzlies (July 22, 1996). ... Signed as free agent by Lakers (September 30, 1996). ... Played in Greece (1997-98).
MISCELLANEOUS: Member of NBA championship team (1985, 1987, 1988).

COLLEGIATE RECORD

													AVERAGES		
Season Team	G	Min.	FGM	FGA	Pct.	FTM	FTA	Pct.	Reb.	Ast.	Pts.		RPG	APG	PPG
79-80—Arizona State	29	936	166	332	.500	63	86	.733	79	65	395		2.7	2.2	13.6
80-81—Arizona State	28	1003	197	390	.505	70	101	.693	106	78	464		3.8	2.8	16.6
81-82—Arizona State					Did not play—academic and personal reasons.										
82-83—Arizona State	33	1206	283	552	.513	147	188	.782	177	140	713		5.4	4.2	21.6
Totals	90	3145	646	1274	.507	280	375	.747	362	283	1572		4.0	3.1	17.5

HONORS: NBA All-Rookie team (1984).
NOTES: Led NBA with .433 three-point field goal percentage (1985).

NBA REGULAR-SEASON RECORD

									REBOUNDS								AVERAGES		
Season Team	G	Min.	FGM	FGA	Pct.	FTM	FTA	Pct.	Off.	Def.	Tot.	Ast.	St.	Blk.	TO	Pts.	RPG	APG	PPG
83-84—Los Angeles	74	1637	334	690	.484	112	139	.806	50	114	164	177	81	19	116	788	2.2	2.4	10.6
84-85—L.A. Lakers	81	2305	541	1003	.539	187	228	.820	57	153	210	244	100	17	138	1295	2.6	3.0	16.0
85-86—L.A. Lakers	76	2190	507	989	.513	138	176	.784	55	134	189	164	85	15	110	1174	2.5	2.2	15.4
86-87—L.A. Lakers	82	2729	554	1134	.489	224	251	.892	63	223	286	281	125	18	144	1397	3.5	3.4	17.0
87-88—L.A. Lakers	81	3048	710	1348	.527	272	317	.858	76	257	333	335	155	27	161	1754	4.1	4.1	21.7
88-89—L.A. Lakers	74	2605	588	1198	.491	195	226	.863	72	230	302	231	114	27	157	1448	4.1	3.1	19.6
89-90—L.A. Lakers	77	2593	472	1005	.470	160	209	.766	51	191	242	274	77	31	122	1197	3.1	3.6	15.5
90-91—L.A. Lakers	82	2630	501	1051	.477	118	148	.797	54	192	246	177	95	21	85	1191	3.0	2.2	14.5
91-92—L.A. Lakers	82	2679	460	1005	.458	244	291	.838	74	236	310	226	105	28	119	1218	3.8	2.8	14.9
92-93—L.A. Lakers	58	1677	296	659	.449	156	184	.848	27	107	134	157	55	13	70	792	2.3	2.7	13.7
93-94—Indiana	67	1197	256	548	.467	157	195	.805	19	91	110	133	62	9	103	696	1.6	2.0	10.4
94-95—Indiana	80	1528	265	583	.455	193	227	.850	18	133	151	108	61	13	119	802	1.9	1.4	10.0
95-96—Vancouver	80	1894	271	676	.401	203	243	.835	40	152	192	123	63	22	100	819	2.4	1.5	10.2
96-97—L.A. Lakers	79	1440	163	379	.430	127	151	.841	21	97	118	99	46	16	53	526	1.5	1.3	6.7
Totals	1073	30152	5918	12268	.482	2486	2985	.833	677	2310	2987	2729	1224	276	1597	15097	2.8	2.5	14.1

Three-point field goals: 1983-84, 8-for-34 (.235). 1984-85, 26-for-60 (.433). 1985-86, 22-for-61 (.361). 1986-87, 65-for-149 (.436). 1987-88, 62-for-179 (.346). 1988-89, 77-for-193 (.399). 1989-90, 93-for-220 (.423). 1990-91, 71-for-219 (.324). 1991-92, 54-for-157 (.344). 1992-93, 44-for-135 (.326). 1993-94, 27-for-74 (.365). 1994-95, 79-for-203 (.389). 1995-96, 74-for-221 (.335). 1996-97, 73-for-188 (.388). Totals, 775-for-2093 (.370).

Personal fouls/disqualifications: 1983-84, 174/0. 1984-85, 197/1. 1985-86, 167/0. 1986-87, 163/0. 1987-88, 204/2. 1988-89, 181/1. 1989-90, 180/2. 1990-91, 146/0. 1991-92, 140/0. 1992-93, 98/0. 1993-94, 80/0. 1994-95, 123/1. 1995-96, 126/0. 1996-97, 72/0. Totals, 2051/7.

NBA PLAYOFF RECORD

Season Team	G	Min.	FGM	FGA	Pct.	FTM	FTA	Pct.	Off.	Def.	Tot.	Ast.	St.	Blk.	TO	Pts.	RPG	APG	PPG
83-84—Los Angeles....	20	404	74	161	.460	21	35	.600	11	26	37	34	18	2	26	171	1.9	1.7	8.6
84-85—L.A. Lakers.....	19	585	138	267	.517	35	44	.795	16	36	52	50	41	4	24	321	2.7	2.6	16.9
85-86—L.A. Lakers.....	14	470	90	181	.497	38	42	.905	15	40	55	42	19	2	30	224	3.9	3.0	16.0
86-87—L.A. Lakers.....	18	608	103	210	.490	53	67	.791	20	42	62	57	19	4	25	266	3.4	3.2	14.8
87-88—L.A. Lakers.....	24	897	178	357	.499	90	104	.865	26	74	100	60	34	5	47	470	4.2	2.5	19.6
88-89—L.A. Lakers.....	11	402	79	160	.494	46	55	.836	10	35	45	25	18	2	20	219	4.1	2.3	19.9
89-90—L.A. Lakers.....	9	325	49	106	.462	10	13	.769	7	30	37	23	20	3	13	121	4.1	2.6	13.4
90-91—L.A. Lakers.....	18	678	95	186	.511	27	34	.794	13	44	57	29	23	4	17	237	3.2	1.6	13.2
91-92—L.A. Lakers.....	4	148	22	44	.500	24	27	.889	3	7	10	14	6	1	5	75	2.5	3.5	18.8
92-93—L.A. Lakers.....	5	177	21	42	.500	18	23	.783	0	11	11	9	5	0	4	68	2.2	1.8	13.6
93-94—Indiana..........	16	239	38	96	.396	40	51	.784	10	23	33	20	12	2	25	125	2.1	1.3	7.8
94-95—Indiana..........	17	298	32	94	.340	30	34	.882	5	20	25	16	10	1	22	103	1.5	0.9	6.1
96-97—L.A. Lakers.....	8	134	15	33	.455	17	19	.895	0	12	12	11	1	0	8	51	1.5	1.4	6.4
Totals	183	5365	934	1937	.482	449	548	.819	136	400	536	390	226	30	266	2451	2.9	2.1	13.4

Three-point field goals: 1983-84, 2-for-10 (.200). 1984-85, 10-for-21 (.476). 1985-86, 6-for-17 (.353). 1986-87, 7-for-34 (.206). 1987-88, 24-for-55 (.436). 1988-89, 15-for-39 (.385). 1989-90, 13-for-34 (.382). 1990-91, 20-for-38 (.526). 1991-92, 7-for-12 (.583). 1992-93, 8-for-15 (.533). 1993-94, 9-for-19 (.474). 1994-95, 9-for-34 (.265). 1996-97, 4-for-11 (.364). Totals, 134-for-339 (.395).

Personal fouls/disqualifications: 1983-84, 39/1. 1984-85, 47/0. 1985-86, 38/0. 1986-87, 52/0. 1987-88, 65/0. 1988-89, 31/0. 1989-90, 32/1. 1990-91, 53/0. 1991-92, 10/0. 1992-93, 11/0. 1993-94, 22/0. 1994-95, 30/0. 1996-97, 15/0. Totals, 445/2.

HEAD COACHING RECORD

NOTES: Assistant coach, Sacramento Kings (1998-99 and 1999-2000).

NBA COACHING RECORD

		REGULAR SEASON				PLAYOFFS		
Season Team	W	L	Pct.	Finish		W	L	Pct.
00-01—New Jersey................	26	56	.317	6th/Atlantic Division		—	—	—

SILAS, PAUL   HORNETS

PERSONAL: Born July 12, 1943, in Prescott, Ark. ... 6-7/230. (2,00/104,3). ... Full name: Paul Theron Silas.
HIGH SCHOOL: McClymonds (Oakland, Calif.).
COLLEGE: Creighton.
TRANSACTIONS: Selected by St. Louis Hawks in second round (12th pick overall) of 1964 NBA Draft. ... Played in Eastern Basketball League with Wilkes-Barre Barons (1965-66). ... Hawks franchise moved from St. Louis to Atlanta for 1968-69 season. ... Traded by Hawks to Phoenix Suns for F Gary Gregor (May 8, 1969). ... Traded by Suns to Boston Celtics (September 19, 1972) to complete deal in which Suns acquired draft rights to G Charlie Scott (March 14, 1972). ... Traded by Celtics to Denver Nuggets in three-way deal, in which F Curtis Rowe was traded by Detroit Pistons to Celtics, and G Ralph Simpson was traded by Nuggets to Pistons (October 20, 1976). ... Traded by Nuggets with F Willie Wise and C Marvin Webster to Seattle SuperSonics for C Tom Burleson, G/F Bob Wilkerson and 1977 second-round draft choice (May 24, 1977). ... Signed as veteran free agent by San Diego Clippers (May 21, 1980); SuperSonics received 1985 second-round draft choice as compensation.
MISCELLANEOUS: Member of NBA championship team (1974, 1976, 1979).

COLLEGIATE RECORD

NOTES: Led NCAA Division I with 20.6 rebounds per game (1963). ... Holds NCAA record for most rebounds in three-year career—1,751.

Season Team	G	Min.	FGM	FGA	Pct.	FTM	FTA	Pct.	Reb.	Ast.	Pts.	RPG	APG	PPG
60-61—Creighton‡	21	...	225	...	...	96	119	.807	568	...	546	27.0	...	26.0
61-62—Creighton	25	...	213	524	.406	125	215	.581	563	...	551	22.5	...	22.0
62-63—Creighton	27	...	220	531	.414	133	228	.583	557	...	573	20.6	...	21.2
63-64—Creighton	29	...	210	529	.397	117	194	.603	631	...	537	21.8	...	18.5
Varsity totals	81	...	643	1584	.406	375	637	.589	1751	...	1661	21.6	...	20.5

NBA REGULAR-SEASON RECORD

HONORS: NBA All-Defensive first team (1975, 1976). ... NBA All-Defensive second team (1971, 1972, 1973).

Season Team	G	Min.	FGM	FGA	Pct.	FTM	FTA	Pct.	Reb.	Ast.	PF	Dq.	Pts.	RPG	APG	PPG
64-65—St. Louis	79	1243	140	375	.373	83	164	.506	576	48	161	1	363	7.3	0.6	4.6
65-66—St. Louis	46	586	70	173	.405	35	61	.574	236	22	72	0	175	5.1	0.5	3.8
66-67—St. Louis	77	1570	207	482	.429	113	213	.531	669	74	208	4	527	8.7	1.0	6.8
67-68—St. Louis	82	2652	399	871	.458	299	424	.705	958	162	243	4	1097	11.7	2.0	13.4
68-69 Atlanta	79	1853	241	575	.419	204	333	.613	745	140	166	0	686	9.4	1.8	8.7
69-70—Phoenix	78	2836	373	804	.464	250	412	.607	916	214	266	5	996	11.7	2.7	12.8
70-71—Phoenix	81	2944	338	789	.428	285	416	.685	1015	247	227	3	961	12.5	3.0	11.9
71-72—Phoenix	80	3082	485	1031	.470	433	560	.773	955	343	201	2	1403	11.9	4.3	17.5
72-73—Boston	80	2618	400	851	.470	266	380	.700	1039	251	197	1	1066	13.0	3.1	13.3

Season Team	G	Min.	FGM	FGA	Pct.	FTM	FTA	Pct.	Off.	Def.	Tot.	Ast.	St.	Blk.	TO	Pts.	RPG	APG	PPG
73-74—Boston	82	2599	340	772	.440	264	337	.783	334	581	915	334	63	20	...	944	11.2	2.3	11.5
74-75—Boston	82	2661	312	749	.417	244	344	.709	348	677	1025	224	60	22	...	868	12.5	2.7	10.6
75-76—Boston	81	2662	315	740	.426	236	333	.709	*365	660	1025	203	56	33	...	866	12.7	2.5	10.7
76-77—Denver	81	1959	206	572	.360	170	255	.667	236	370	606	132	58	23	...	582	7.5	1.6	7.2
77-78—Seattle	82	2172	184	464	.397	109	186	.586	289	377	666	145	65	16	152	477	8.1	1.8	5.8
78-79—Seattle	82	1957	170	402	.423	116	194	.598	259	316	575	115	31	19	98	456	7.0	1.4	5.6
79-80—Seattle	82	1595	113	299	.378	89	136	.654	204	232	436	66	25	5	83	315	5.3	0.8	3.8
Totals	1254	34989	4293	9949	.432	3196	4748	.673	...	...	12357	2572	358	138	333	11782	9.9	2.1	9.4

Personal fouls/disqualifications: 1973-74, 246/3. 1974-75, 229/4. 1975-76, 227/4. 1976-77, 183/0. 1977-78, 182/0. 1978-79, 177/3. 1979-80, 120/0. Totals, 3105/32.

NBA PLAYOFF RECORD

Season Team	G	Min.	FGM	FGA	Pct.	FTM	FTA	Pct.	Reb.	Ast.	PF	Dq.	Pts.	RPG	APG	PPG
														AVERAGES		
64-65 —St. Louis	4	42	4	10	.400	3	4	.750	18	1	6	0	11	4.5	0.3	2.8
65-66 —St. Louis	7	80	5	18	.278	8	11	.727	34	2	11	0	18	4.9	0.3	2.6
66-67 —St. Louis	8	122	9	36	.250	11	18	.611	52	6	17	0	29	6.5	0.8	3.6
67-68 —St. Louis	6	178	22	51	.431	27	38	.711	57	21	17	0	71	9.5	3.5	11.8
68-69 —Atlanta	11	258	21	58	.362	19	37	.514	92	21	32	0	61	8.4	1.9	5.5
69-70 —Phoenix	7	286	46	109	.422	21	32	.656	111	30	29	1	113	15.9	4.3	16.1
72-73 —Boston	13	512	47	120	.392	31	50	.620	196	39	39	0	125	15.1	3.0	9.6

Season Team	G	Min.	FGM	FGA	Pct.	FTM	FTA	Pct.	Off.	Def.	Tot.	Ast.	St.	Blk.	TO	Pts.	RPG	APG	PPG
									REBOUNDS								AVERAGES		
73-74 —Boston	18	574	50	126	.397	44	53	.830	53	138	191	47	13	9	...	144	10.6	2.6	8.0
74-75 —Boston	11	405	42	92	.457	16	25	.640	46	84	130	40	12	2	...	100	11.8	3.6	9.1
75-76 —Boston	18	741	69	154	.448	56	69	.812	78	168	246	42	24	6	...	194	13.7	2.3	10.8
76-77 —Denver	6	141	14	33	.424	13	24	.542	16	24	40	16	2	4	...	41	6.7	2.7	6.8
77-78 —Seattle	22	605	33	94	.351	41	60	.683	73	114	187	36	12	6	28	107	8.5	1.6	4.9
78-79 —Seattle	17	418	21	54	.389	31	46	.674	40	58	98	19	9	5	34	73	5.8	1.1	4.3
79-80 —Seattle	15	257	13	43	.302	11	13	.846	33	42	75	15	9	2	9	37	5.0	1.0	2.5
Totals	163	4619	396	998	.397	332	480	.692	...	...	1527	335	81	34	71	1124	9.4	2.1	6.9

Personal fouls/disqualifications: 1973-74, 51/2. 1974-75, 45/1. 1975-76, 67/1. 1976-77, 23/1. 1977-78, 59/0. 1978-79, 44/1. 1979-80, 29/0. Totals, 469/7.

NBA ALL-STAR GAME RECORD

Season Team	Min.	FGM	FGA	Pct.	FTM	FTA	Pct.	Reb	Ast.	PF	Dq.	Pts.
1972 —Phoenix	15	0	6	.000	2	3	.667	9	1	1	0	2

Season Team	Min.	FGM	FGA	Pct.	FTM	FTA	Pct.	Off.	Def.	Tot.	Ast.	PF	Dq.	St.	Blk.	TO	Pts.
								REBOUNDS									
1975 —Boston	15	2	4	.500	2	2	1.000	0	2	2	2	2	0	4	0	...	6
Totals	30	2	10	.200	4	5	.800	...	...	11	3	3	0	4	0	...	8

EBL REGULAR-SEASON RECORD

Season Team	G	Min.	FGM	FGA	Pct.	FTM	FTA	Pct.	Reb.	Ast.	PF	Dq.	Pts.	RPG	APG	PPG
														AVERAGES		
65-66 —Wil.-Barre	5	...	...	25	...	13	21	.619	85	9	...	...	63	17.0	1.8	12.6

NBA COACHING RECORD

BACKGROUND: Assistant coach, New Jersey Nets (1988-89 and 1992-93 through 1994-95). ... Assistant coach, New York Knicks (1989-90 through 1991-92). ... Assistant coach, Phoenix Suns (1995-96 and 1996-97). ... Assistant coach, Charlotte Hornets (1997-98 through March 7, 1999).

Season Team	REGULAR SEASON				PLAYOFFS		
	W	L	Pct.	Finish	W	L	Pct.
80-81 —San Diego	36	46	.439	5th/Pacific Division	—	—	—
81-82 —San Diego	17	65	.207	6th/Pacific Division	—	—	—
82-83 —San Diego	25	57	.305	6th/Pacific Division	—	—	—
98-99 —Charlotte	22	13	.629	5th/Central Division	—	—	—
99-00 —Charlotte	49	33	.598	2nd/Central Division	1	3	.250
00-01 —Charlotte	46	36	.561	3rd/Central Division	6	4	.600
Totals (6 years)	195	240	.438	**Totals (2 years)**	7	7	.500

NOTES:

1999—Replaced Dave Cowens as head coach (March 7), with record of 4-11 and club in seventh place.
2000—Lost to Philadelphia in Eastern Conference first round.
2001—Defeated Miami, 3-0, in Eastern Conference first round; lost to Milwaukee, 4-3, in Eastern Conference finals.

SKILES, SCOTT — SUNS

PERSONAL: Born March 5, 1964, in LaPorte, Ind. ... 6-1/180. (1,85/81,6). ... Full Name: Scott Allen Skiles.
HIGH SCHOOL: Plymouth (Ind.).
COLLEGE: Michigan State.
TRANSACTIONS/CAREER NOTES: Selected by Milwaukee Bucks in first round (22nd pick overall) of 1986 NBA Draft. ... Traded by Bucks to Indiana Pacers for second-round draft choice (June 22, 1987). ... Selected by Orlando Magic from Pacers in NBA Expansion Draft (June 15, 1989). ... Traded by Magic with 1996 first-round draft choice and future considerations to Washington Bullets for 1996 second-round draft choice and future considerations (July 29, 1994). ... Signed by Philadelphia 76ers for remainder of season (December 12, 1995). ... Announced retirement (January 6, 1996).
MISCELLANEOUS: Orlando Magic all-time assists leader with 2,776 (1989-90 through 1993-94).

COLLEGIATE RECORD

NOTES: THE SPORTING NEWS All-America first team (1986).

Season Team	G	Min.	FGM	FGA	Pct.	FTM	FTA	Pct.	Reb.	Ast.	Pts.	RPG	APG	PPG
												AVERAGES		
82-83—Michigan State	30	1023	141	286	.493	69	83	.831	63	146	376	2.1	4.9	12.5
83-84—Michigan State	28	983	153	319	.480	99	119	.832	62	128	405	2.2	4.6	14.5
84-85—Michigan State	29	1107	212	420	.505	90	114	.789	93	168	514	3.2	5.8	17.7
85-86—Michigan State	31	1172	331	598	.554	188	209	.900	135	203	850	4.4	6.5	27.4
Totals	118	4285	837	1623	.516	446	525	.850	353	645	2145	3.0	5.5	18.2

Three-point field goals: 1982-83, 25-for-50 (.500).

NBA REGULAR-SEASON RECORD

RECORDS: Holds single-game record for most assists—30 (December 30, 1990, vs. Denver).
HONORS: NBA Most Improved Player (1991).

Season Team	G	Min.	FGM	FGA	Pct.	FTM	FTA	Pct.	REBOUNDS Off.	Def.	Tot.	Ast.	St.	Blk.	TO	Pts.	AVERAGES RPG	APG	PPG
86-87—Milwaukee	13	205	18	62	.290	10	12	.833	6	20	26	45	5	1	21	49	2.0	3.5	3.8
87-88—Indiana...........	51	760	86	209	.411	45	54	.833	11	55	66	180	22	3	76	223	1.3	3.5	4.4
88-89—Indiana...........	80	1571	198	442	.448	130	144	.903	21	128	149	390	64	2	177	546	1.9	4.9	6.8
89-90—Orlando.........	70	1460	190	464	.409	104	119	.874	23	136	159	334	36	4	90	536	2.3	4.8	7.7
90-91—Orlando.........	79	2714	462	1039	.445	340	377	.902	57	213	270	660	89	4	252	1357	3.4	8.4	17.2
91-92—Orlando.........	75	2377	359	868	.414	248	277	.895	36	166	202	544	74	5	233	1057	2.7	7.3	14.1
92-93—Orlando.........	78	3086	416	891	.467	289	324	.892	52	238	290	735	86	2	267	1201	3.7	9.4	15.4
93-94—Orlando.........	82	2303	276	644	.429	195	222	.878	42	147	189	503	47	2	193	815	2.3	6.1	9.9
94-95—Washington ..	62	2077	265	583	.455	179	202	.886	26	133	159	452	70	6	172	805	2.6	7.3	13.0
95-96—Philadelphia	10	236	20	57	.351	8	10	.800	1	15	16	38	7	0	16	63	1.6	3.8	6.3
Totals	600	16789	2290	5259	.435	1548	1741	.889	275	1251	1526	3881	500	29	1497	6652	2.5	6.5	11.1

Three-point field goals: 1986-87, 3-for-14 (.214). 1987-88, 6-for-20 (.300). 1988-89, 20-for-75 (.267). 1989-90, 52-for-132 (.394). 1990-91, 93-for-228 (.408). 1991-92, 91-for-250 (.364). 1992-93, 80-for-235 (.340). 1993-94, 68-for-165 (.412). 1994-95, 96-for-228 (.421). 1995-96, 15-for-34 (.441). Totals, 524-for-1381 (.379).

Personal fouls/disqualifications: 1986-87, 18/0. 1987-88, 97/0. 1988-89, 151/1. 1989-90, 126/0. 1990-91, 192/2. 1991-92, 188/0. 1992-93, 244/4. 1993-94, 171/1. 1994-95, 135/2. 1995-96, 21/0. Totals, 1343/10.

NBA PLAYOFF RECORD

Season Team	G	Min.	FGM	FGA	Pct.	FTM	FTA	Pct.	REBOUNDS Off.	Def.	Tot.	Ast.	St.	Blk.	TO	Pts.	AVERAGES RPG	APG	PPG
93-94—Orlando..........	2	23	4	8	.500	1	1	1.000	1	0	1	3	0	0	5	9	0.5	1.5	4.5

Three-point field goals: 1993-94, 0-for-2.
Personal fouls/disqualifications: 1993-94, 2/0.

HEAD COACHING RECORD

NOTES: Assistant coach, Phoenix Suns (1997-98 through December 13, 1999).

NBA COACHING RECORD

Season Team	REGULAR SEASON W	L	Pct.	Finish	PLAYOFFS W	L	Pct.
99-00 —Phoenix	40	22	.645	3rd/Pacific Division	4	5	.444
00-01 —Phoenix	51	31	.622	3rd/Pacific Division	1	3	.250
Totals (2 years)..	91	53	.632	Totals (2 years).......	5	8	.385

NOTES:

2000—Replaced Danny Ainge as head coach (December 13), with a record of 13-7 and club in fourth place. Defeated San Antonio, 3-1, in Western Conference first round; lost to Los Angeles Lakers, 4-1, in Western Conference semifinals.

2001—Lost to Sacramento in Western Conference first round.

SLOAN, JERRY — JAZZ

PERSONAL: Born March 28, 1942, in McLeansboro, Ill. ... 6-5/200. (1,96/90,7). ... Full name: Gerald Eugene Sloan.
HIGH SCHOOL: McLeansboro (Ill.).
COLLEGE: Illinois, then Evansville.
TRANSACTIONS/CAREER NOTES: Selected by Baltimore Bullets in third round of 1964 NBA Draft. ... Selected by Bullets in second round of 1965 NBA Draft. ... Selected by Chicago Bulls from Bullets in NBA expansion draft (April 30, 1966).
CAREER NOTES: Scout, Chicago Bulls (1976-77). ... Scout, Utah Jazz (1983-84).

COLLEGIATE RECORD

NOTES: Left Illinois before 1961 basketball season. ... Outstanding Player in NCAA College Division Tournament (1964, 1965). ... The Sporting News All-America second team (1965).

Season Team	G	Min.	FGM	FGA	Pct.	FTM	FTA	Pct.	Reb.	Ast.	Pts.	AVERAGES RPG	APG	PPG
61-62—Evansville						Did not play—transfer student.								
62-63—Evansville	27	...	152	446	.341	103	151	.682	293	...	407	10.9	...	15.1
63-64—Evansville	29	...	160	385	.416	84	114	.737	335	...	404	11.6	...	13.9
64-65—Evansville	29	...	207	458	.452	95	126	.754	425	...	509	14.7	...	17.6
Totals	85	...	519	1289	.403	282	391	.721	1053	...	1320	12.4	...	15.5

NBA REGULAR-SEASON RECORD

HONORS: NBA All-Defensive first team (1969, 1972, 1974, 1975). ... NBA All-Defensive second team (1970, 1971).

Season Team	G	Min.	FGM	FGA	Pct.	FTM	FTA	Pct.	Reb.	Ast.	PF	Dq.	Pts.	AVERAGES RPG	APG	PPG
65-66 —Baltimore	59	952	120	289	.415	98	139	.705	230	110	176	7	338	3.9	1.9	5.7
66-67 —Chicago	80	2942	525	1214	.432	340	427	.796	726	170	293	7	1390	9.1	2.1	17.4
67-68 —Chicago	77	2454	369	959	.385	280	386	.725	591	229	291	11	1027	7.7	3.0	13.3
68-69 —Chicago	78	2939	488	1179	.414	333	447	.745	619	276	313	6	1309	7.9	3.5	16.8
69-70 —Chicago	53	1822	310	737	.421	207	318	.651	372	165	179	3	827	7.0	3.1	15.6
70-71 —Chicago	80	3140	592	1342	.441	278	389	.715	701	281	289	5	1462	8.8	3.5	18.3
71-72 —Chicago	82	3035	535	1206	.444	258	391	.660	691	211	309	8	1328	8.4	2.6	16.2
72-73 —Chicago	69	2412	301	733	.411	94	133	.707	475	151	235	5	696	6.9	2.2	10.1

Season Team	G	Min.	FGM	FGA	Pct.	FTM	FTA	Pct.	REBOUNDS Off.	Def.	Tot.	Ast.	St.	Blk.	TO	Pts.	AVERAGES RPG	APG	PPG
73-74—Chicago..........	77	2860	412	921	.447	194	273	.711	150	406	556	149	183	10	...	1018	7.2	1.9	13.2
74-75—Chicago..........	78	2577	380	865	.439	193	258	.748	177	361	538	161	171	17	...	953	6.9	2.1	12.2
75-76—Chicago..........	22	617	84	210	.400	55	78	.705	40	76	116	22	27	5	...	223	5.3	1.0	10.1
Totals	755	25750	4116	9655	.426	2330	3239	.719	...	...	5615	1925	381	32	...	10571	7.4	2.5	14.0

Personal fouls/disqualifications: 1973-74, 273/3. 1974-75, 265/5. 1975-76, 77/1. Totals, 2700/61.

NBA PLAYOFF RECORD

Season Team	G	Min.	FGM	FGA	Pct.	FTM	FTA	Pct.	Reb.	Ast.	PF	Dq.	Pts.	AVERAGES		
														RPG	APG	PPG
65-66 —Baltimore	2	34	5	12	.417	3	4	.750	16	6	6	1	13	8.0	3.0	6.5
66-67 —Chicago	3	71	12	31	.387	6	9	.667	10	1	7	0	30	3.3	0.3	10.0
67-68 —Chicago	5	137	12	37	.324	19	25	.760	32	12	19	0	43	6.4	2.4	8.6
69-70 —Chicago	5	190	29	74	.392	16	25	.640	39	11	18	0	74	7.8	2.2	14.8
70-71 —Chicago	7	284	51	117	.436	17	23	.739	63	17	25	1	119	9.0	2.4	17.0
71-72 —Chicago	4	170	26	64	.406	11	19	.579	35	10	18	1	63	8.8	2.5	15.8
72-73 —Chicago	7	292	45	103	.437	14	19	.737	59	14	31	1	104	8.4	2.0	14.9

Season Team	G	Min.	FGM	FGA	Pct.	FTM	FTA	Pct.	REBOUNDS			Ast.	St.	Blk.	TO	Pts.	AVERAGES		
									Off.	Def.	Tot.						RPG	APG	PPG
73-74—Chicago	6	240	39	88	.443	22	29	.759	18	44	62	12	7	1	...	100	10.3	2.0	16.7
74-75—Chicago	13	470	75	163	.460	20	36	.556	24	72	96	26	20	0	...	170	7.4	2.0	13.1
Totals	52	1888	294	689	.427	128	189	.677	...	...	412	109	27	1	...	716	7.9	2.1	13.8

Personal fouls/disqualifications: 1973-74, 17/0. 1974-75, 46/0. Totals, 187/4.

NBA ALL-STAR GAME RECORD

Season Team	Min.	FGM	FGA	Pct.	FTM	FTA	Pct.	Reb	Ast.	PF	Dq.	Pts.
1967 —Chicago	22	4	9	.444	0	0	...	4	4	5	0	8
1969 —Chicago	18	2	8	.250	0	1	.000	3	0	5	0	4
Totals	40	6	17	.353	0	1	.000	7	4	10	0	12

HEAD COACHING RECORD

BACKGROUND: Assistant coach, Bulls (1977-78 and 1978-79). ... Head coach, Evansville Thunder of CBA (1984-November 19, 1984; no record). ... Assistant coach, Jazz (November 19, 1984-December 9, 1988).

NBA COACHING RECORD

Season Team	REGULAR SEASON				PLAYOFFS		
	W	L	Pct.	Finish	W	L	Pct.
79-80 —Chicago	30	52	.366	4th/Midwest Division	—	—	—
80-81 —Chicago	45	37	.549	2nd/Central Division	2	4	.333
81-82 —Chicago	19	32	.373		—	—	—
88-89 —Utah	40	25	.615	1st/Midwest Division	0	3	.000
89-90 —Utah	55	27	.671	2nd/Midwest Division	2	3	.400
90-91 —Utah	54	28	.659	2nd/Midwest Division	4	5	.444
91-92 —Utah	55	27	.671	1st/Midwest Division	9	7	.563
92-93 —Utah	47	35	.573	3rd/Midwest Division	2	3	.400
93-94 —Utah	53	29	.646	3rd/Midwest Division	8	8	.500
94-95 —Utah	60	22	.732	2nd/Midwest Division	2	3	.400
95-96 —Utah	55	27	.671	2nd/Midwest Division	10	8	.556
96-97 —Utah	64	18	.780	1st/Midwest Division	13	7	.650
97-98 —Utah	62	20	.756	1st/Midwest Division	13	7	.650
98-99 —Utah	37	13	.740	T1st/Midwest Division	5	6	.455
99-00 —Utah	55	27	.671	1st/Midwest Division	4	6	.400
00-01 —Utah	53	29	.646	2nd/Midwest Division	2	3	.400
Totals (16 years)	784	448	.636	Totals (14 years)	76	73	.510

NOTES:

1981—Defeated New York, 2-0, in Eastern Conference first round; lost to Boston, 4-0, in Eastern Conference semifinals.

1982—Replaced as Chicago head coach by Rod Thorn (February 17).

1988—Replaced retiring Utah head coach Frank Layden (December 9), with record of 11-6.

1989—Lost to Golden State in Western Conference first round.

1990—Lost to Phoenix in Western Conference first round.

1991—Defeated Phoenix, 3-1, in Western Conference first round; lost to Portland, 4-1, in Western Conference semifinals.

1992—Defeated Los Angeles Clippers, 3-2, in Western Conference first round; defeated Seattle, 4-1, in Western Conference semifinals; lost to Portland, 4-2, in Western Conference finals.

1993—Lost to Seattle in Western Conference first round.

1994—Defeated San Antonio, 3-1, in Western Conference first round; defeated Denver, 4-3, in Western Conference semifinals; lost to Houston, 4-1, in Western Conference finals.

1995—Lost to Houston in Western Conference first round.

1996—Defeated Portland, 3-2, in Western Conference first round; Defeated San Antonio, 4-2, in Western Conference semifinals; lost to Seattle, 4-3, in Western Conference finals.

1997—Defeated Los Angeles Clippers, 3-0, in Western Conference first round; defeated Los Angeles Lakers, 4-1, in Western Conference semifinals; defeated Houston, 4-2, in Western Conference finals; lost to Chicago, 4-2, in NBA Finals.

1998—Defeated Houston, 3-2, in Western Conference first round; defeated San Antonio, 4-1, in Western Conference semifinals; defeated Los Angeles Lakers, 4-0, in Western Conference finals; lost to Chicago, 4-2, in NBA Finals.

1999—Defeated Sacramento, 3-2, in Western Conference first round; lost to Portland, 4-2, in Western Conference semifinals.

2000—Defeated Seattle, 3-2, in Western Conference first round; lost to Portland, 4-1, in Western Conference semifinals.

2001—Lost to Dallas in Western Conference first round.

HEAD COACHES

THOMAS, ISIAH   PACERS

PERSONAL: Born April 30, 1961, in Chicago. ... 6-1/182. (1,85/82,6). ... Full name: Isiah Lord Thomas III.
HIGH SCHOOL: St. Joseph's (Westchester, Ill.).
COLLEGE: Indiana.
TRANSACTIONS: Selected after sophomore season by Detroit Pistons in first round (second pick overall) of 1981 NBA Draft. ... Announced retirement (May 11, 1994).
CAREER NOTES: Vice president, (May 24, 1994-Nov. 20, 1997) and part owner, Toronto Raptors. ... Broadcaster, NBC Sports (Nov. 25, 1997-June 2000). ... Majority owner, Continental Basketball Association (1999-2000).
CAREER HONORS: One of the 50 Greatest Players in NBA History (1996).
MISCELLANEOUS: Member of NBA championship team (1989, 1990). ... Member of U.S. Olympic team (1980). ... Detroit Pistons franchise all-time leading scorer with 18,822 points, all-time assists leader with 9,061 and all-time steals leader with 1,861 (1981-82 through 1993-94). ... Elected to Naismith Memorial Basketball Hall of Fame (2000).

COLLEGIATE RECORD

NOTES: Member of NCAA Division I championship team (1981). ... NCAA Division I Tournament Most Outstanding Player (1981). ... THE SPORTING NEWS All-America first team (1981).

| | | | | | | | | | | | AVERAGES | | |
Season Team	G	Min.	FGM	FGA	Pct.	FTM	FTA	Pct.	Reb.	Ast.	Pts.	RPG	APG	PPG
79-80—Indiana	29	986	154	302	.510	115	149	.772	116	159	423	4.0	5.5	14.6
80-81—Indiana	34	1190	212	383	.554	121	163	.742	105	197	545	3.1	5.8	16.0
Totals	63	2176	366	685	.534	236	312	.756	221	356	968	3.5	5.7	15.4

NBA REGULAR-SEASON RECORD

HONORS: All-NBA first team (1984, 1985, 1986). ... All-NBA second team (1983, 1987). ... NBA All-Rookie team (1982). ... J. Walter Kennedy Citizenship Award (1987).

| | | | | | | | | | REBOUNDS | | | | | | | | AVERAGES | | |
Season Team	G	Min.	FGM	FGA	Pct.	FTM	FTA	Pct.	Off.	Def.	Tot.	Ast.	St.	Blk.	TO	Pts.	RPG	APG	PPG
81-82—Detroit	72	2433	453	1068	.424	302	429	.704	57	152	209	565	150	17	†299	1225	2.9	7.8	17.0
82-83—Detroit	81	*3093	725	1537	.472	368	518	.710	105	223	328	634	199	29	*326	1854	4.0	7.8	22.9
83-84—Detroit	82	3007	669	1448	.462	388	529	.733	103	224	327	†914	204	33	307	1748	4.0	11.1	21.3
84-85—Detroit	81	3089	646	1410	.458	399	493	.809	114	247	361	*1123	187	25	302	1720	4.5	*13.9	21.2
85-86—Detroit	77	2790	609	1248	.488	365	462	.790	83	194	277	830	171	20	289	1609	3.6	10.8	20.9
86-87—Detroit	81	3013	626	1353	.463	400	521	.768	82	237	319	813	153	20	343	1671	3.9	10.0	20.6
87-88—Detroit	81	2927	621	1341	.463	305	394	.774	64	214	278	678	141	17	273	1577	3.4	8.4	19.5
88-89—Detroit	80	2924	569	1227	.464	287	351	.818	49	224	273	663	133	20	298	1458	3.4	8.3	18.2
89-90—Detroit	81	2993	579	1322	.438	292	377	.775	74	234	308	765	139	19	*322	1492	3.8	9.4	18.4
90-91—Detroit	48	1657	289	665	.435	179	229	.782	35	125	160	446	75	10	185	776	3.3	9.3	16.2
91-92—Detroit	78	2918	564	1264	.446	292	378	.772	68	179	247	560	118	15	252	1445	3.2	7.2	18.5
92-93—Detroit	79	2922	526	1258	.418	278	377	.737	71	161	232	671	123	18	284	1391	2.9	8.5	17.6
93-94—Detroit	58	1750	318	763	.417	181	258	.702	46	113	159	399	68	6	202	856	2.7	6.9	14.8
Totals	979	35516	7194	15904	.452	4036	5316	.759	951	2527	3478	9061	1861	249	3682	18822	3.6	9.3	19.2

Three-point field goals: 1981-82, 17-for-59 (.288). 1982-83, 36-for-125 (.288). 1983-84, 22-for-65 (.338). 1984-85, 29-for-113 (.257). 1985-86, 26-for-84 (.310). 1986-87, 19-for-98 (.194). 1987-88, 30-for-97 (.309). 1988-89, 33-for-121 (.273). 1989-90, 42-for-136 (.309). 1990-91, 19-for-65 (.292). 1991-92, 25-for-86 (.291). 1992-93, 61-for-198 (.308). 1993-94, 39-for-126 (.310). Totals, 398-for-1373 (.290).
Personal fouls/disqualifications: 1981-82, 253/2. 1982-83, 318/8. 1983-84, 324/8. 1984-85, 288/8. 1985-86, 245/9. 1986-87, 251/5. 1987-88, 217/0. 1988-89, 209/0. 1989-90, 206/0. 1990-91, 118/4. 1991-92, 194/2. 1992-93, 193-94, 126/0. Totals, 2971/48.

NBA PLAYOFF RECORD

NOTES: NBA Finals Most Valuable Player (1990). ... Holds NBA Finals single-game records for most points in one quarter—25 (June 19, 1988, vs. Los Angeles Lakers); and most field goals in one quarter—11 (June 19, 1988, vs. Los Angeles Lakers). ... Shares NBA Finals single-game record for most field goals in one half—14 (June 19, 1988, vs. Los Angeles Lakers).

| | | | | | | | | | REBOUNDS | | | | | | | | AVERAGES | | |
Season Team	G	Min.	FGM	FGA	Pct.	FTM	FTA	Pct.	Off.	Def.	Tot.	Ast.	St.	Blk.	TO	Pts.	RPG	APG	PPG
83-84—Detroit	5	198	39	83	.470	27	35	.771	7	12	19	55	13	6	23	107	3.8	11.0	21.4
84-85—Detroit	9	355	83	166	.500	47	62	.758	11	36	47	101	19	4	30	219	5.2	11.2	24.3
85-86—Detroit	4	163	41	91	.451	24	36	.667	8	14	22	48	9	3	17	106	5.5	12.0	26.5
86-87—Detroit	15	562	134	297	.451	83	110	.755	21	46	67	130	39	4	42	361	4.5	8.7	24.1
87-88—Detroit	23	911	183	419	.437	125	151	.828	26	81	107	201	66	8	85	504	4.7	8.7	21.9
88-89—Detroit	17	633	115	279	.412	71	96	.740	24	49	73	141	27	4	43	309	4.3	8.3	18.2
89-90—Detroit	20	758	148	320	.463	81	102	.794	21	88	109	163	43	7	72	409	5.5	8.2	20.5
90-91—Detroit	13	436	60	149	.403	50	69	.725	13	41	54	111	13	2	41	176	4.2	8.5	13.5
91-92—Detroit	5	200	22	65	.338	22	28	.786	3	23	26	37	5	0	16	70	5.2	7.4	14.0
Totals	111	4216	825	1869	.441	530	689	.769	134	390	524	987	234	38	369	2261	4.7	8.9	20.4

Three-point field goals: 1983-84, 2-for-6 (.333). 1984-85, 6-for-15 (.400). 1985-86, 0-for-5. 1986-87, 10-for-33 (.303). 1987-88, 13-for-44 (.295). 1988-89, 8-for-30 (.267). 1989-90, 32-for-68 (.471). 1990-91, 6-for-22 (.273). 1991-92, 4-for-11 (.364). Totals, 81-for-234 (.346).
Personal fouls/disqualifications: 1983-84, 22/1. 1984-85, 39/2. 1985-86, 17/0. 1986-87, 51/1. 1987-88, 71/2. 1988-89, 39/0. 1989-90, 65/1. 1990-91, 41/1. 1991-92, 18/0. Totals, 363/8.

NBA ALL-STAR GAME RECORD

NOTES: NBA All-Star Game Most Valuable Player (1984, 1986).

| | | | | | | | | REBOUNDS | | | | | | | | | |
Season Team	Min.	FGM	FGA	Pct.	FTM	FTA	Pct.	Off.	Def.	Tot.	Ast.	PF	Dq.	St.	Blk.	TO	Pts.
1982 —Detroit	17	5	7	.714	2	4	.500	1	0	1	4	1	0	3	0	1	12
1983 —Detroit	29	9	14	.643	1	1	1.000	3	1	4	7	0	0	4	0	5	19
1984 —Detroit	39	9	17	.529	3	3	1.000	3	2	5	15	4	0	4	0	6	21
1985 —Detroit	25	9	14	.643	1	1	1.000	1	1	2	5	2	0	2	0	1	22
1986 —Detroit	36	11	19	.579	8	9	.889	0	1	1	10	2	0	5	0	5	30
1987 —Detroit	24	4	6	.667	8	9	.889	2	1	3	9	3	0	0	0	5	16
1988 —Detroit	28	4	10	.400	0	0	...	1	1	2	15	1	0	1	0	6	8

Season Team	Min.	FGM	FGA	Pct.	FTM	FTA	Pct.	Off.	Def.	Tot.	Ast.	PF	Dq.	St.	Blk.	TO	Pts.
1989 —Detroit	33	7	13	.538	4	6	.667	1	1	2	14	2	0	4	0	6	19
1990 —Detroit	27	7	12	.583	0	0		1	1	2	9	0	0	3	0	1	15
1991 —Detroit						Selected, did not play—injured.											
1992 —Detroit	28	7	14	.500	0	0	...	0	1	1	5	0	0	3	0	3	15
1993 —Detroit	32	4	7	.571	0	2	.000	0	2	2	4	2	0	2	0	2	8
Totals	318	76	133	.571	27	35	.771	13	14	27	97	17	0	31	0	41	185

Three-point field goals: 1984, 0-for-2. 1985, 3-for-4 (.750). 1986, 0-for-1. 1989, 1-for-3 (.333). 1990, 1-for-1. 1992, 1-for-3 (.333). 1993, 0-for-1. Totals, 6-for-15 (.400).

NBA COACHING RECORD

Season Team	REGULAR SEASON				PLAYOFFS		
	W	L	Pct.	Finish	W	L	Pct.
00-01 —Indiana	42	42	.500	4th/Central Division	1	3	.250

NOTES:
2001—Lost to Philadelphia in Eastern Conference first round.

TOMJANOVICH, RUDY — ROCKETS

PERSONAL: Born November 24, 1948, in Hamtramck, Mich. ... 6-8/220. (2,03/99,8). ... Full name: Rudolph Tomjanovich. ... Name pronounced Tom-JOHN-a-vitch.
HIGH SCHOOL: Hamtramck (Mich.).
COLLEGE: Michigan.
TRANSACTIONS/CAREER NOTES: Selected by San Diego Rockets in first round (second pick overall) of 1970 NBA Draft. ... Rockets franchise moved from San Diego to Houston for 1971-72 season.
MISCELLANEOUS: Head coach of bronze-medal-winning 1998 USA Basketball World Championship Team. ... Head coach of gold-medal-winning 2000 U.S. Olympic Team.

COLLEGIATE RECORD

NOTES: THE SPORTING NEWS All-America first team (1970). ... THE SPORTING NEWS All-America second team (1969).

Season Team	G	Min.	FGM	FGA	Pct.	FTM	FTA	Pct.	Reb.	Ast.	Pts.	RPG	APG	PPG
66-67—Michigan‡	3	...	28	...	...	6	15	.400	...	...	62	...	...	20.7
67-68—Michigan	24	...	210	446	.471	49	78	.628	323	...	469	13.5	...	19.5
68-69—Michigan	24	...	269	541	.497	79	131	.603	340	...	617	14.2	...	25.7
69-70—Michigan	24	...	286	604	.474	150	200	.750	376	...	722	15.7	...	30.1
Varsity totals	72	...	765	1591	.481	278	409	.680	1039	...	1808	14.4	...	25.1

NBA REGULAR-SEASON RECORD

Season Team	G	Min.	FGM	FGA	Pct.	FTM	FTA	Pct.	Reb.	Ast.	PF	Dq.	Pts.	RPG	APG	PPG
70-71—San Diego	77	1062	168	439	.383	73	112	.652	381	73	124	0	409	4.9	0.9	5.3
71-72—Houston	78	2689	500	1010	.495	172	238	.723	923	117	193	2	1172	11.8	1.5	15.0
72-73—Houston	81	2972	655	1371	.478	250	335	.746	938	178	225	1	1560	11.6	2.2	19.3

Season Team	G	Min.	FGM	FGA	Pct.	FTM	FTA	Pct.	Off.	Def.	Tot.	Ast.	St.	Blk.	TO	Pts.	RPG	APG	PPG
73-74—Houston	80	3227	788	1470	.536	385	454	.848	230	487	717	250	89	66	...	1961	9.0	3.1	24.5
74-75—Houston	81	3134	694	1323	.525	289	366	.790	184	429	613	236	76	24	...	1677	7.6	2.9	20.7
75-76—Houston	79	2912	622	1202	.517	221	288	.767	167	499	666	188	42	19	...	1465	8.4	2.4	18.5
76-77—Houston	81	3130	733	1437	.510	287	342	.839	172	512	684	172	57	27	...	1753	8.4	2.1	21.6
77-78—Houston	23	849	217	447	.485	61	81	.753	40	98	138	32	15	5	38	495	6.0	1.4	21.5
78-79—Houston	74	2641	620	1200	.517	168	221	.760	170	402	572	137	44	18	138	1408	7.7	1.9	19.0
79-80—Houston	62	1834	370	778	.476	118	147	.803	144	226	358	109	32	10	98	880	5.8	1.8	14.2
80-81—Houston	52	1264	263	563	.467	65	82	.793	78	130	208	81	19	6	58	603	4.0	1.6	11.6
Totals	768	25714	5630	11240	.501	2089	2666	.784	...	...	6198	1573	374	175	332	13383	8.1	2.0	17.4

Three-point field goals: 1979-80, 22-for-79 (.278). 1980-81, 12-for-51 (.235). Totals, 34-for-130 (.262).
Personal fouls/disqualifications: 1973-74, 230/0. 1974-75, 230/1. 1975-76, 206/1. 1976-77, 198/1. 1977-78, 63/0. 1978-79, 186/0. 1979-80, 161/2. 1980-81, 121/0. Totals, 1937/8.

NBA PLAYOFF RECORD

Season Team	G	Min.	FGM	FGA	Pct.	FTM	FTA	Pct.	Off.	Def.	Tot.	Ast.	St.	Blk.	TO	Pts.	RPG	APG	PPG
74-75—Houston	8	304	72	128	.563	40	48	.833	22	42	64	23	1	4	...	184	8.0	2.9	23.0
76-77—Houston	12	457	107	212	.505	29	37	.784	24	41	65	24	7	3	...	243	5.4	2.0	20.3
78-79—Houston	2	64	9	23	.391	2	5	.400	7	7	14	2	1	1	1	20	7.0	1.0	10.0
79-80—Houston	7	185	24	64	.375	9	13	.692	12	28	40	10	2	0	14	58	5.7	1.4	8.3
80-81—Houston	8	31	1	9	.111	4	6	.667	2	4	6	0	0	0	2	6	0.8	0.0	0.8
Totals	37	1041	213	436	.489	84	109	.771	67	122	189	59	11	8	17	511	5.1	1.6	13.8

Three-point field goals: 1979-80, 1-for-7 (.143). 1980-81, 0-for-3. Totals, 1-for-10 (.100).
Personal fouls/disqualifications: 1974-75, 17/0. 1976-77, 36/0. 1978-79, 1/0. 1979-80, 21/1. 1980-81, 3/0. Totals, 78/1.

NBA ALL-STAR GAME RECORD

Season Team	Min.	FGM	FGA	Pct.	FTM	FTA	Pct.	Off.	Def.	Tot.	Ast.	PF	Dq.	St.	Blk.	TO	Pts.
1974 —Houston	17	2	5	.400	0	0	...	2	3	5	0	1	0	0	0	...	4
1975 —Houston	14	0	3	.000	0	0	...	1	2	3	0	3	0	0	0	...	0
1976 —Houston	12	1	2	.500	0	0	...	1	2	3	0	2	0	0	0	...	2
1977 —Houston	22	3	9	.333	0	0	...	2	8	10	1	1	0	1	1	...	6
1979 —Houston	24	6	13	.462	0	0	...	4	2	6	1	2	0	0	0	0	12
Totals	89	12	32	.375	0	0	...	10	17	27	2	9	0	1	1	0	24

HEAD COACHES

HEAD COACHING RECORD

BACKGROUND: Scout, Houston Rockets (1981-82 and 1982-83). ... Assistant coach, Rockets (1983-84 to February 18, 1992).

NBA COACHING RECORD

Season Team	W	L	Pct.	Finish		W	L	Pct.
				REGULAR SEASON			PLAYOFFS	
91-92 —Houston	16	14	.533	3rd/Midwest Division		—	—	—
92-93 —Houston	55	27	.671	1st/Midwest Division		6	6	.500
93-94 —Houston	58	24	.707	1st/Midwest Division		15	8	.652
94-95 —Houston	47	35	.573	3rd/Midwest Division		15	7	.682
95-96 —Houston	48	34	.585	2nd/Midwest Division		3	5	.375
96-97 —Houston	57	25	.695	2nd/Midwest Division		9	7	.563
97-98 —Houston	41	41	.500	4th/Midwest Division		2	3	.400
98-99 —Houston	31	19	.620	3rd/Midwest Division		1	3	.250
99-00 —Houston	34	48	.415	6th/Midwest Division		—	—	—
00-01 —Houston	45	37	.549	5th/Midwest Division		—	—	—
Totals (10 years)	**432**	**304**	**.587**		**Totals (7 years)**	**51**	**39**	**.567**

WORLD CHAMPIONSHIP RECORD

Season Team	W	L	Pct.	Finish
			REGULAR SEASON	
1998—Team USA	7	2	.778	Bronze medal

OLYMPIC RECORD

Season Team	W	L	Pct.	Finish
			REGULAR SEASON	
2000—Team USA	8	0	1.000	Gold medal

NOTES:

1992—Replaced Don Chaney as Houston head coach (February 18), with record of 26-26 and club in third place.

1993—Defeated L.A. Clippers, 3-2, in Western Conference first round; lost to Seattle, 4-3, in Western Conference semifinals.

1994—Defeated Portland, 3-1, in Western Conference first round; defeated Phoenix, 4-3, in Western Conference semifinals; defeated Utah, 4-1, in Western Conference finals; defeated New York, 4-3, in NBA Finals.

1995—Defeated Utah, 3-2, in Western Conference first round, defeated Phoenix, 4-3, in Western Conference semifinals; defeated San Antonio, 4-2, in Western Conference finals; defeated Orlando, 4-0, in NBA Finals.

1996—Defeated Los Angeles Lakers, 3-1, in Western Conference first round; lost to Seattle, 4-0, in Western Conference semifinals.

1997—Defeated Minnesota, 3-0, in Western Conference first round; defeated Seattle, 4-3, in Western Conference semifinals; lost to Utah, 4-2, in Western Conference finals.

1998—Lost to Utah in Western Conference first round.

1999—Lost to Los Angeles Lakers in Western Conference first round.

VAN GUNDY, JEFF   KNICKS

PERSONAL: Born January 19, 1962, in Hemet, Calif. ... 5-9/150. (1,76/68,0). ... Brother of Stan Van Gundy, assistant coach, Miami Heat.
HIGH SCHOOL: Brockport (N.Y.).
JUNIOR COLLEGE: Menlo Junior College (Palo Alto, Calif.).
COLLEGE: SUNY-Brockport (N.Y.), then Nazareth (Rochester, N.Y.).

COLLEGIATE RECORD

Season Team	G	Min.	FGM	FGA	Pct.	FTM	FTA	Pct.	Reb.	Ast.	Pts.	RPG	APG	PPG
													AVERAGES	
81-82—Menlo Junior College							Statistics unavailable.							
82-83—SUNY-Brockport	24	...	125	222	.536	57	78	.731	80	85	307	3.3	3.5	12.8
83-84—Nazareth	28	...	84	146	.575	41	48	.854	42	118	209	1.5	4.2	7.5
84-85—Nazareth	26	...	88	156	.564	91	104	.875	64	133	267	2.5	5.1	10.3
Varsity totals	**54**	**...**	**172**	**302**	**.570**	**132**	**152**	**.868**	**106**	**251**	**476**	**2.0**	**4.6**	**8.8**

HEAD COACHING RECORD

BACKGROUND: Head coach, McQuaid Jesuit (Rochester, N.Y.) High School (1985-86). ... Graduate assistant, Providence College (1986-87). ... Assistant coach, Providence (1987-88). ... Assistant coach, Rutgers University (1988-89). ... Assistant coach, New York Knicks (1989-90 to March 8, 1996).

NBA COACHING RECORD

Season Team	W	L	Pct.	Finish		W	L	Pct.
				REGULAR SEASON			PLAYOFFS	
95-96 —New York	13	10	.565	2nd/Atlantic Division		4	4	.500
96-97 —New York	57	25	.695	2nd/Atlantic Division		6	4	.600
97-98 —New York	43	39	.524	2nd/Atlantic Division		4	6	.400
98-99 —New York	27	23	.540	4th/Atlantic Division		12	8	.600
99-00 —New York	50	32	.610	2nd/Atlantic Division		9	7	.563
00-01 —New York	48	34	.585	3rd/Atlantic Division		2	3	.400
Totals (6 years)	**238**	**163**	**.594**		**Totals (6 years)**	**37**	**32**	**.536**

NOTES:

1996—Replaced Don Nelson as New York Knicks head coach (March 8), with record of 34-26 and club in second place. Defeated Cleveland, 3-0, in Eastern Conference first round; lost to Chicago, 4-1, in Eastern Conference semifinals.

1997—Defeated Charlotte, 3-0, in Eastern Conference first round; lost to Miami, 4-3, in Eastern Conference semifinals.

1998—Defeated Miami, 3-2, in Eastern Conference first round; lost to Indiana, 4-1, in Eastern Conference semifinals.
1999—Defeated Miami, 3-2, in Eastern Conference first round; defeated Atlanta, 4-0, in Eastern Conference semifinals; defeated Indiana, 4-2, in Eastern Conference finals; lost to San Antonio, 4-1, in NBA Finals.
2000—Defeated Toronto, 3-0, in Eastern Conference first round; defeated Miami, 4-3, in Eastern Conference semifinals; lost to Indiana, 4-2, in Eastern Conference finals.
2001—Lost to Toronto in Eastern Conference first round.

WILKENS, LENNY — RAPTORS

PERSONAL: Born October 28, 1937, in Brooklyn, N.Y. ... 6-1/180. (1,85/81,6). ... Full name: Leonard Randolph Wilkens.
HIGH SCHOOL: Boys (Brooklyn, N.Y.).
COLLEGE: Providence.
TRANSACTIONS/CAREER NOTES: Selected by St. Louis Hawks in first round of 1960 NBA Draft. ... Hawks franchise moved from St. Louis to Atlanta for 1968-69 season. ... Traded by Hawks to Seattle SuperSonics for G Walt Hazzard (October 12, 1968). ... Player/head coach, SuperSonics (1969-70 through 1971-72). ... Traded by SuperSonics with F Barry Clemens to Cleveland Cavaliers for G Butch Beard (August 23, 1972). ... Playing rights transferred from Cavaliers to Portland Trail Blazers for cash (October 7, 1974).
CAREER NOTES: Director of player personnel, SuperSonics (May 13-November 1977). ... Vice president/general manager, SuperSonics (1985-86).
CAREER HONORS: Elected to Naismith Memorial Basketball Hall of Fame as player (1988) and head coach (1998). ... One of the 50 Greatest Players in NBA History (1996). ... One of the Top 10 Coaches in NBA History (1996).
MISCELLANEOUS: Head coach, 1996 gold-medal-winning U.S. Olympic Team.

COLLEGIATE RECORD

NOTES: THE SPORTING NEWS All-America second team (1960).

Season Team	G	Min.	FGM	FGA	Pct.	FTM	FTA	Pct.	Reb.	Ast.	Pts.	RPG	APG	PPG
56-57—Providence‡	23	...	...	...	...	...	...	...	...	...	488	...	...	21.2
57-58—Providence	24	...	137	316	.434	84	130	.646	190	...	358	7.9	...	14.9
58-59—Providence	27	...	167	390	.428	89	144	.618	188	...	423	7.0	...	15.7
59-60—Providence	29	...	157	362	.434	98	140	.700	205	...	412	7.1	...	14.2
Varsity totals	80	...	461	1068	.432	271	414	.655	583	...	1193	7.3	...	14.9

NBA REGULAR-SEASON RECORD

Season Team	G	Min.	FGM	FGA	Pct.	FTM	FTA	Pct.	Reb.	Ast.	PF	Dq.	Pts.	RPG	APG	PPG
60-61—St. Louis	75	1898	333	783	.425	214	300	.713	335	212	215	5	880	4.5	2.8	11.7
61-62—St. Louis	20	870	140	364	.385	84	110	.764	131	116	63	0	364	6.6	5.8	18.2
62-63—St. Louis	75	2569	333	834	.399	222	319	.696	403	381	256	6	888	5.4	5.1	11.8
63-64—St. Louis	78	2526	334	808	.413	270	365	.740	335	359	287	7	938	4.3	4.6	12.0
64-65—St. Louis	78	2854	434	1048	.414	416	558	.746	365	431	283	7	1284	4.7	5.5	16.5
65-66—St. Louis	69	2692	411	954	.431	422	532	.793	322	429	248	4	1244	4.7	6.2	18.0
66-67—St. Louis	78	2974	448	1036	.432	459	583	.787	412	442	280	6	1355	5.3	5.7	17.4
67-68—St. Louis	82	3169	546	1246	.438	546	711	.768	438	679	255	3	1638	5.3	8.3	20.0
68-69—Seattle	82	3463	644	1462	.441	547	710	.770	511	674	294	8	1835	6.2	8.2	22.4
69-70—Seattle	75	2802	448	1066	.420	438	556	.788	378	*683	212	5	1334	5.0	9.1	17.8
70-71—Seattle	71	2641	471	1125	.419	461	574	.803	319	654	201	3	1403	4.5	9.2	19.8
71-72—Seattle	80	2989	479	1027	.466	480	620	.774	338	*766	209	4	1438	4.2	9.6	18.0
72-73—Cleveland	75	2973	572	1275	.449	394	476	.828	346	628	221	2	1538	4.6	8.4	20.5

Season Team	G	Min.	FGM	FGA	Pct.	FTM	FTA	Pct.	Off.	Def.	Tot.	Ast.	St.	Blk.	TO	Pts.	RPG	APG	PPG
73-74—Cleveland	74	2483	462	994	.465	289	361	.801	80	197	277	522	97	17	...	1213	3.7	7.1	16.4
74-75—Portland	65	1161	134	305	.439	152	198	.768	38	82	120	235	77	9	...	420	1.8	3.6	6.5
Totals	1077	38064	6189	14327	.432	5394	6973	.774	...	...	5030	7211	174	26	...	17772	4.7	6.7	16.5

Personal fouls/disqualifications: 1973-74, 165/2. 1974-75, 96/1. Totals, 3285/51.

NBA PLAYOFF RECORD

Season Team	G	Min.	FGM	FGA	Pct.	FTM	FTA	Pct.	Reb.	Ast.	PF	Dq.	Pts.	RPG	APG	PPG
60-61—St. Louis	12	437	63	166	.380	44	58	.759	72	42	51	4	170	6.0	3.5	14.2
62-63—St. Louis	11	400	57	154	.370	37	49	.755	69	69	51	2	151	6.3	6.3	13.7
63-64—St. Louis	12	413	64	143	.448	44	58	.759	60	64	42	0	172	5.0	5.3	14.3
64-65—St. Louis	4	147	20	57	.351	24	29	.828	12	15	14	0	64	3.0	3.8	16.0
65-66—St. Louis	10	391	57	143	.399	57	83	.687	54	70	43	0	171	5.4	7.0	17.1
66-67—St. Louis	9	378	58	145	.400	77	90	.856	68	65	34	0	193	7.6	7.2	21.4
67-68—St. Louis	6	237	40	91	.440	30	40	.750	38	47	23	1	110	6.3	7.8	18.3
Totals	64	2403	359	899	.399	313	407	.769	373	372	258	7	1031	5.8	5.8	16.1

NBA ALL-STAR GAME RECORD

NOTES: NBA All-Star Game Most Valuable Player (1971).

Season Team	Min.	FGM	FGA	Pct.	FTM	FTA	Pct.	Reb	Ast.	PF	Dq.	Pts.
1963—St. Louis	25	2	7	.286	0	1	.000	2	3	0	0	4
1964—St. Louis	14	1	5	.200	1	1	1.000	0	0	3	0	3
1965—St. Louis	20	2	6	.333	4	4	1.000	3	3	3	0	8
1967—St. Louis	16	2	6	.333	2	3	.667	2	6	2	0	6

Season	Team	Min.	FGM	FGA	Pct.	FTM	FTA	Pct.	Reb	Ast.	PF	Dq.	Pts.
1968	—St. Louis	22	4	10	.400	6	8	.750	3	3	1	0	14
1969	—Seattle	24	3	15	.200	4	5	.800	7	5	3	0	10
1970	—Seattle	17	5	7	.714	2	3	.667	2	4	1	0	12
1971	—Seattle	20	8	11	.727	5	5	1.000	1	1	1	0	21
1973	—Cleveland	24	3	8	.375	1	2	.500	2	1	1	0	7
Totals		182	30	75	.400	25	32	.781	22	26	15	0	85

HEAD COACHING RECORD

BACKGROUND: Player/head coach, Seattle SuperSonics (1969-70 through 1971-72). ... Player/head coach, Portland Trail Blazers (1974-75). ... Head coach/director of player personnel, SuperSonics (November 1977 through 1984-85). ... Assistant coach, U.S. Olympic team (1992).
HONORS: NBA Coach of the Year (1994). ... One of the Top 10 Coaches in NBA History (1996).
RECORDS: Holds NBA career record for most wins—1,226.

NBA COACHING RECORD

Season Team	REGULAR SEASON				PLAYOFFS		
	W	L	Pct.	Finish	W	L	Pct.
69-70 —Seattle	36	46	.439	5th/Western Division	—	—	—
70-71 —Seattle	38	44	.463	4th/Pacific Division	—	—	—
71-72 —Seattle	47	35	.573	3rd/Pacific Division	—	—	—
74-75 —Portland	38	44	.463	3rd/Pacific Division	—	—	—
75-76 —Portland	37	45	.451	5th/Pacific Division	—	—	—
77-78 —Seattle	42	18	.700	3rd/Pacific Division	13	9	.591
78-79 —Seattle	52	30	.634	1st/Pacific Division	12	5	.706
79-80 —Seattle	56	26	.683	2nd/Pacific Division	7	8	.467
80-81 —Seattle	34	48	.415	6th/Pacific Division	—	—	—
81-82 —Seattle	52	30	.634	2nd/Pacific Division	3	5	.375
82-83 —Seattle	48	34	.585	3rd/Pacific Division	0	2	.000
83-84 —Seattle	42	40	.512	3rd/Pacific Division	2	3	.400
84-85 —Seattle	31	51	.378	4th/Pacific Division	—	—	—
86-87 —Cleveland	31	51	.378	6th/Central Division	—	—	—
87-88 —Cleveland	42	40	.512	T4th/Central Division	2	3	.400
88-89 —Cleveland	57	25	.695	2nd/Central Division	2	3	.400
89-90 —Cleveland	42	40	.512	T4th/Central Division	2	3	.400
90-91 —Cleveland	33	49	.402	6th/Central Division	—	—	—
91-92 —Cleveland	57	25	.695	2nd/Central Division	9	8	.529
92-93 —Cleveland	54	28	.659	2nd/Central Division	3	6	.333
93-94 —Atlanta	57	25	.695	1st/Central Division	5	6	.455
94-95 —Atlanta	42	40	.512	5th/Central Division	0	3	.000
95-96 —Atlanta	46	36	.561	4th/Central Division	4	6	.400
96-97 —Atlanta	56	26	.683	2nd/Central Division	4	6	.400
97-98 —Atlanta	50	32	.610	4th/Central Division	1	3	.250
98-99 —Atlanta	31	19	.620	2nd/Central Division	3	6	.333
99-00 —Atlanta	28	54	.341	7th/Central Division	—	—	—
00-01 —Toronto	47	35	.573	2nd/Central Division	6	6	.500
Totals (28 years)	1226	1016	.547	Totals (18 years)	78	91	.462

OLYMPIC RECORD

Season Team	REGULAR SEASON			
	W	L	Pct.	Finish
1996 —Team USA	8	0	1.000	Gold medal

NOTES:
1977—Replaced Bob Hopkins as Seattle head coach (November), with record of 5-17.
1978—Defeated Los Angeles Lakers, 2-1, in Western Conference first round; defeated Portland, 4-2, in Western Conference semifinals; defeated Denver, 4-2, in Western Conference finals; lost to Washington, 4-3, in NBA Finals.
1979—Defeated Los Angeles Lakers, 4-1, in Western Conference semifinals; defeated Phoenix, 4-3, in Western Conference finals; defeated Washington, 4-1, in NBA Finals.
1980—Defeated Portland, 2-1, in Western Conference first round; defeated Milwaukee, 4-3, in Western Conference semifinals; lost to Los Angeles Lakers, 4-1, in Western Conference finals.
1982—Defeated Houston, 2-1, in Western Conference first round; lost to San Antonio, 4-1, in Western Conference semifinals.
1983—Lost to Portland in Western Conference first round.
1984—Lost to Dallas in Western Conference first round.
1988—Lost to Chicago in Eastern Conference first round.
1989—Lost to Chicago in Eastern Conference first round.
1990—Lost to Philadelphia in Eastern Conference first round.
1992—Defeated New Jersey, 3-1, in Eastern Conference first round; defeated Boston, 4-3, in Eastern Conference semifinals; lost to Chicago, 4-2, in Eastern Conference finals.
1993—Defeated New Jersey, 3-2, in Eastern Conference first round; lost to Chicago, 4-0, in Eastern Conference semifinals.
1994—Defeated Miami, 3-2, in Eastern Conference first round; lost to Indiana, 4-2, in Eastern Conference semifinals.
1995—Lost to Indiana in Eastern Conference first round.
1996—Defeated Indiana, 3-2, in Eastern Conference first round; lost to Orlando, 4-1, in Eastern Conference semifinals.
　　　Team USA defeated Argentina, 96-68; Angola, 87-54; Lithuania, 104-82; China, 133-70; and Croatia, 102-71, in preliminary round. Defeated Brazil, 98-75, in medal round quarterfinals; defeated Australia, 101-73, in semifinals; defeated Yugoslavia, 95-69, in gold-medal game.
1997—Defeated Detroit, 3-2, in Eastern Conference first round; lost to Chicago, 4-1, in Eastern Conference semifinals.
1998—Lost to Charlotte in Eastern Conference first round.
1999—Defeated Detroit, 3-2, in Eastern Conference first round; lost to New York, 4-0, in Eastern Conference semifinals.
2001—Defeated New York, 3-2, in Eastern Conference first round; lost to Milwaukee, 4-3, in Eastern Conference semifinals.

ABDUL-JABBAR, KAREEM C

PERSONAL: Born April 16, 1947, in New York. ... 7-2/267 (2,18/121,1). ... Full name: Kareem Abdul-Jabbar. ... Formerly known as Lew Alcindor.
HIGH SCHOOL: Power Memorial (New York).
COLLEGE: UCLA.
TRANSACTIONS: Selected by Milwaukee Bucks in first round (first pick overall) of 1969 NBA Draft. ... Traded by Bucks with C Walt Wesley to Los Angeles Lakers for C Elmore Smith, G/F Brian Winters, F Dave Meyers and F/G Junior Bridgeman (June 16, 1975).
CAREER HONORS: Elected to Naismith Memorial Basketball Hall of Fame (1995). ... NBA 35th Anniversary All-Time Team (1980) and One of the 50 Greatest Players in NBA History (1996).
MISCELLANEOUS: Member of NBA championship team (1971, 1980, 1982, 1985, 1987, 1988). ... Milwaukee Bucks all-time leading scorer with 14,211 points and all-time leading rebounder with 7,161 (1969-70 through 1974-75). ... Los Angeles Lakers franchise all-time blocked shots leader with 2,694 (1975-76 through 1988-89).
CAREER NOTES: Assistant coach, Los Angeles Clippers (February 18, 2000-July 1, 2000).

COLLEGIATE RECORD

NOTES: Member of NCAA championship team (1967, 1968, 1969). ... THE SPORTING NEWS College Player of the Year (1967, 1969). ... Naismith Award winner (1969). ... THE SPORTING NEWS All-America first team (1967, 1968, 1969). ... NCAA Tournament Most Outstanding Player (1967, 1968, 1969). ... Led NCAA Division I with .667 field goal percentage (1967) and .635 field goal percentage (1969).

Season Team	G	Min.	FGM	FGA	Pct.	FTM	FTA	Pct.	Reb.	Ast.	Pts.	AVERAGES RPG	APG	PPG
65-66—UCLA‡	21	...	295	432	.683	106	179	.592	452	...	696	21.5	...	33.1
66-67—UCLA	30	...	346	519	.667	178	274	.650	466	...	870	15.5	...	29.0
67-68—UCLA	28	...	294	480	.613	146	237	.616	461	...	734	16.5	...	26.2
68-69—UCLA	30	...	303	477	.635	115	188	.612	440	...	721	14.7	...	24.0
Varsity totals	88	...	943	1476	.639	439	699	.628	1367	...	2325	15.5	...	26.4

NBA REGULAR-SEASON RECORD

RECORDS: Holds career records for most minutes played—57,446; most points—38,387; most field goals made—15,837; most field goals attempted—28,307. ... Holds single-season record for most defensive rebounds—1,111 (1976). ... Holds single-game record for most defensive rebounds—29 (December 14, 1975, vs. Detroit).
HONORS: NBA Most Valuable Player (1971, 1972, 1974, 1976, 1977, 1980). ... NBA Rookie of the Year (1970). ... All-NBA first team (1971, 1972, 1973, 1974, 1976, 1977, 1980, 1981, 1984, 1986). ... All-NBA second team (1970, 1978, 1979, 1983, 1985). ... NBA All-Defensive first team (1974, 1975, 1979, 1980, 1981). ... NBA All-Defensive second team (1970, 1971, 1976, 1977, 1978, 1984). ... NBA All-Rookie team (1970).
NOTES: Led NBA with 3.26 blocked shots per game (1975), 4.12 blocked shots per game (1976), 3.95 blocked shots per game (1979) and 3.41 blocked shots per game (1980).

Season Team	G	Min.	FGM	FGA	Pct.	FTM	FTA	Pct.	Reb.	Ast.	PF	Dq.	Pts.	AVERAGES RPG	APG	PPG
69-70—Milwaukee	82	3534	*938	1810	.518	485	743	.653	1190	337	283	8	*2361	14.5	4.1	28.8
70-71—Milwaukee	82	3288	*1063	1843	.577	470	681	.690	1311	272	264	4	*2596	16.0	3.3	*31.7
71-72—Milwaukee	81	3583	*1159	*2019	.574	504	732	.689	1346	370	235	1	*2822	16.6	4.6	*34.8
72-73—Milwaukee	76	3254	982	1772	.554	328	460	.713	1224	379	208	0	2292	16.1	5.0	30.2

Season Team	G	Min.	FGM	FGA	Pct.	FTM	FTA	Pct.	REBOUNDS Off.	Def.	Tot.	Ast.	St.	Blk.	TO	Pts.	AVERAGES RPG	APG	PPG
73-74—Milwaukee	81	3548	*948	1759	.539	295	420	.702	287	891	1178	386	112	283	...	2191	14.5	4.8	27.0
74-75—Milwaukee	65	2747	812	1584	.513	325	426	.763	194	718	912	264	65	212	...	1949	14.0	4.1	30.0
75-76—Los Angeles	82	*3379	914	1728	.529	447	636	.703	272	*1111	*1383	413	119	*338	...	2275	*16.9	5.0	27.7
76-77—Los Angeles	82	3016	*888	1533	*.579	376	536	.702	266	*824	*1090	319	101	*261	...	2152	13.3	3.9	26.2
77-78—Los Angeles	62	2265	663	1205	.550	274	350	.783	186	615	801	269	103	185	208	1600	12.9	4.3	25.8
78-79—Los Angeles	80	3157	777	1347	.577	349	474	.736	207	818	1025	431	76	*316	282	1903	12.8	5.4	23.8
79-80—Los Angeles	82	3143	835	1383	.604	364	476	.765	190	696	886	371	81	*280	297	2034	10.8	4.5	24.8
80-81—Los Angeles	80	2976	836	1457	.574	423	552	.766	197	624	821	272	59	228	249	2095	10.3	3.4	26.2
81-82—Los Angeles	76	2677	753	1301	.579	312	442	.706	172	487	659	225	63	207	230	1818	8.7	3.0	23.9
82-83—Los Angeles	79	2554	722	1228	.588	278	371	.749	167	425	592	200	61	170	200	1722	7.5	2.5	21.8
83-84—Los Angeles	80	2622	716	1238	.578	285	394	.723	169	418	587	211	55	143	221	1717	7.3	2.6	21.5
84-85—L.A. Lakers	79	2630	723	1207	.599	289	395	.732	162	460	622	249	63	162	197	1735	7.9	3.2	22.0
85-86—L.A. Lakers	79	2629	755	1338	.564	336	439	.765	133	345	478	280	67	130	203	1846	6.1	3.5	23.4
86-87—L.A. Lakers	78	2441	560	993	.564	245	343	.714	152	371	523	203	49	97	186	1366	6.7	2.6	17.5
87-88—L.A. Lakers	80	2308	480	903	.532	205	269	.762	118	360	478	135	48	92	159	1165	6.0	1.7	14.6
88-89—L.A. Lakers	74	1695	313	659	.475	122	165	.739	103	231	334	74	38	85	95	748	4.5	1.0	10.1
Totals	1560	57446	15837	28307	.559	6712	9304	.721	...	...	17440	5660	1160	3189	2527	38387	11.2	3.6	24.6

Three-point field goals: 1979-80, 0-for-1. 1980-81, 0-for-1. 1981-82, 0-for-3. 1982-83, 0-for-2. 1983-84, 0-for-1. 1984-85, 0-for-1. 1985-86, 0-for-2. 1986-87, 1-for-3 (.333). 1987-88, 0-for-1. 1988-89, 0-for-3. Totals, 1-for-18 (.056).
Personal fouls/disqualifications: 1973-74, 238/2. 1974-75, 205/2. 1975-76, 292/6. 1976-77, 262/4. 1977-78, 182/1. 1978-79, 230/3. 1979-80, 216/2. 1980-81, 244/4. 1981-82, 224/0. 1982-83, 220/1. 1983-84, 211/1. 1984-85, 238/3. 1985-86, 248/2. 1986-87, 245/2. 1987-88, 216/1. 1988-89, 196/1. Totals, 4657/104.

NBA PLAYOFF RECORD

NOTES: NBA Finals Most Valuable Player (1971, 1985). ... Holds career playoff records for most seasons played—18; most games played—237; most minutes played—8,851; most field goals made—2,356; most blocked shots—476; and most personal fouls—797.

Season Team	G	Min.	FGM	FGA	Pct.	FTM	FTA	Pct.	Reb.	Ast.	PF	Dq.	Pts.	AVERAGES RPG	APG	PPG
69-70—Milwaukee	10	435	139	245	.567	74	101	.733	168	41	25	1	352	16.8	4.1	35.2
70-71—Milwaukee	14	577	152	295	.515	68	101	.673	238	35	45	0	372	17.0	2.5	26.6
71-72—Milwaukee	11	510	139	318	.437	38	54	.704	200	56	35	0	316	18.2	5.1	28.7
72-73—Milwaukee	6	276	59	138	.428	19	35	.543	97	17	26	0	137	16.2	2.8	22.8

Season Team	G	Min.	FGM	FGA	Pct.	FTM	FTA	Pct.	Off.	Def.	Tot.	Ast.	St.	Blk.	TO	Pts.	RPG	APG	PPG
73-74—Milwaukee	16	758	224	402	.557	67	91	.736	67	186	253	78	20	39	...	515	15.8	4.9	32.2
76-77—Los Angeles....	11	467	147	242	.607	87	120	.725	51	144	195	45	19	38	...	381	17.7	4.1	34.6
77-78—Los Angeles ...	3	134	38	73	.521	5	9	.556	14	27	41	11	2	12	14	81	13.7	3.7	27.0
78-79—Los Angeles ..	8	367	88	152	.579	52	62	.839	18	83	101	38	8	33	29	228	12.6	4.8	28.5
79-80—Los Angeles ..	15	618	198	346	.572	83	105	.790	51	130	181	46	17	58	55	479	12.1	3.1	31.9
80-81—Los Angeles ..	3	134	30	65	.462	20	28	.714	13	37	50	12	3	8	11	80	16.7	4.0	26.7
81-82—Los Angeles ..	14	493	115	221	.520	55	87	.632	33	86	119	51	14	45	41	285	8.5	3.6	20.4
82-83—Los Angeles ..	15	588	163	287	.568	80	106	.755	25	90	115	42	17	55	50	406	7.7	2.8	27.1
83-84—Los Angeles ..	21	767	206	371	.555	90	120	.750	56	117	173	79	23	45	45	502	8.2	3.8	23.9
84-85—L.A. Lakers	19	610	168	300	.560	80	103	.777	50	104	154	76	23	36	52	416	8.1	4.0	21.9
85-86—L.A. Lakers	14	489	157	282	.557	48	61	.787	26	57	83	49	15	24	42	362	5.9	3.5	25.9
86-87—L.A. Lakers	18	559	124	234	.530	97	122	.795	39	84	123	36	8	35	40	345	6.8	2.0	19.2
87-88—L.A. Lakers	24	718	141	304	.464	56	71	.789	49	82	131	36	15	37	46	338	5.5	1.5	14.1
88-89—L.A. Lakers	15	351	68	147	.463	31	43	.721	13	46	59	19	5	11	22	167	3.9	1.3	11.1
Totals	237	8851	2356	4422	.533	1050	1419	.740	...	...	2481	767	189	476	447	5762	10.5	3.2	24.3

Three-point field goals: 1982-83, 0-for-1. 1986-87, 0-for-1. 1987-88, 0-for-2. 1988-89, 0-for-1. Totals, 0-for-5.
Personal fouls/disqualifications: 1973-74, 41/0. 1976-77, 42/0. 1977-78, 14/1. 1978-79, 26/0. 1979-80, 51/0. 1980-81, 14/0. 1981-82, 45/0. 1982-83, 61/1. 1983-84, 71/2. 1984-85, 67/1. 1985-86, 54/0. 1986-87, 56/0. 1987-88, 81/1. 1988-89, 43/0. Totals, 797/7.

NBA ALL-STAR GAME RECORD

NOTES: Holds career records for most games played—18; most minutes played—449; most field goals made—105; most field goals attempted—213; most points—251; most blocked shots—31; and most personal fouls—57. ... Holds single-game record for most blocked shots—6 (1980, OT).

Season	Team	Min.	FGM	FGA	Pct.	FTM	FTA	Pct.	Reb.	Ast.	PF	Dq.	Pts.
1970	—Milwaukee	18	4	8	.500	2	2	1.000	11	4	6	1	10
1971	—Milwaukee	30	8	16	.500	3	4	.750	14	1	2	0	19
1972	—Milwaukee	19	5	10	.500	2	2	1.000	7	2	0	0	12
1973	—Milwaukee							Selected, did not play.					

Season	Team	Min.	FGM	FGA	Pct.	FTM	FTA	Pct.	Off.	Def.	Tot.	Ast.	PF	Dq.	St.	Blk.	TO	Pts.
1974	—Milwaukee	23	7	11	.636	0	0	...	1	7	8	6	2	0	1	1	...	14
1975	—Milwaukee	19	3	10	.300	1	2	.500	5	5	10	3	2	0	0	1	...	7
1976	—Los Angeles	36	9	16	.563	4	4	1.000	2	13	15	3	3	0	0	3	...	22
1977	—Los Angeles	23	8	14	.571	5	6	.833	3	1	4	2	1	0	0	1	...	21
1979	—Los Angeles	28	5	12	.417	1	2	.500	1	7	8	3	4	0	1	1	3	11
1980	—Los Angeles	30	6	17	.353	5	6	.833	5	11	16	9	5	0	0	6	9	17
1981	—Los Angeles	23	6	9	.667	3	3	1.000	2	4	6	4	3	0	0	4	3	15
1982	—Los Angeles	22	1	10	.100	0	0	...	1	2	3	1	3	0	0	2	1	2
1983	—Los Angeles	32	9	12	.750	2	3	.667	2	4	6	5	1	0	1	4	1	20
1984	—Los Angeles	37	11	19	.579	3	4	.750	5	8	13	2	5	0	0	1	4	25
1985	—L.A. Lakers	23	5	10	.500	1	2	.500	0	6	6	1	5	0	1	1	1	11
1986	—L.A. Lakers	32	9	15	.600	3	4	.750	2	5	7	2	4	0	2	2	5	21
1987	—L.A. Lakers	27	4	9	.444	2	2	1.000	2	6	8	3	5	0	0	2	1	10
1988	—L.A. Lakers	14	4	9	.444	2	2	1.000	2	2	4	0	3	0	0	0	0	10
1989	—L.A. Lakers	13	1	6	.167	2	2	1.000	0	3	3	0	3	0	0	2	0	4
Totals..........................		449	105	213	.493	41	50	.820	...	...	149	51	57	1	6	31	28	251

Three-point field goals: 1989, 0-for-1.

AGUIRRE, MARK   F

PERSONAL: Born December 10, 1959, in Chicago. ... 6-6/232 (1,98/105,2). ... Full name: Mark Anthony Aguirre. ... Name pronounced a-GWIRE.
HIGH SCHOOL: Austin (Chicago), then Westinghouse Vocational (Chicago).
COLLEGE: DePaul.
TRANSACTIONS: Selected after junior season by Dallas Mavericks in first round (first pick overall) of 1981 NBA Draft. ... Traded by Mavericks to Detroit Pistons for F Adrian Dantley and 1991 first-round draft choice (February 15, 1989). ... Waived by Pistons (October 7, 1993). ... Signed as free agent by Los Angeles Clippers (October 25, 1993). ... Waived by Clippers (February 1, 1994).
CAREER NOTES: Director of player development and scouting, Dallas Mavericks (1996-97).
MISCELLANEOUS: Member of NBA championship team (1989, 1990). ... Member of U.S. Olympic team (1980).

COLLEGIATE RECORD

NOTES: The Sporting News College Player of the Year (1981). ... Naismith Award winner (1980). ... The Sporting News All-America first team (1980, 1981).

Season Team	G	Min.	FGM	FGA	Pct.	FTM	FTA	Pct.	Reb.	Ast.	Pts.	RPG	APG	PPG
78-79—DePaul.........................	32	1206	302	581	.520	163	213	.765	244	86	767	7.6	2.7	24.0
79-80—DePaul.........................	28	1049	281	520	.540	187	244	.766	213	77	749	7.6	2.8	26.8
80-81—DePaul.........................	29	1069	280	481	.582	106	137	.774	249	131	666	8.6	4.5	23.0
Totals	89	3324	863	1582	.546	456	594	.768	706	294	2182	7.9	3.3	24.5

NBA REGULAR-SEASON RECORD

Season Team	G	Min.	FGM	FGA	Pct.	FTM	FTA	Pct.	Off.	Def.	Tot.	Ast.	St.	Blk.	TO	Pts.	RPG	APG	PPG
81-82—Dallas.............	51	1468	381	820	.465	168	247	.680	89	160	249	164	37	22	135	955	4.9	3.2	18.7
82-83—Dallas.............	81	2784	767	1589	.483	429	589	.728	191	317	508	332	80	26	261	1979	6.3	4.1	24.4
83-84—Dallas.............	79	2900	*925	*1765	.524	465	621	.749	161	308	469	358	80	22	285	2330	5.9	4.5	29.5
84-85—Dallas.............	80	2699	794	1569	.506	440	580	.759	188	289	477	249	60	24	253	2055	6.0	3.1	25.7
85-86—Dallas.............	74	2501	668	1327	.503	318	451	.705	177	268	445	339	62	14	252	1670	6.0	4.6	22.6
86-87—Dallas.............	80	2663	787	1590	.495	429	557	.770	181	246	427	254	84	30	217	2056	5.3	3.2	25.7

Season Team	G	Min.	FGM	FGA	Pct.	FTM	FTA	Pct.	REBOUNDS Off.	Def.	Tot.	Ast.	St.	Blk.	TO	Pts.	AVERAGES RPG	APG	PPG
87-88—Dallas	77	2610	746	1571	.475	388	504	.770	182	252	434	278	70	57	203	1932	5.6	3.6	25.1
88-89—Dallas-Det.	80	2597	586	1270	.461	288	393	.733	146	240	386	278	45	36	208	1511	4.8	3.5	18.9
89-90—Detroit	78	2005	438	898	.488	192	254	.756	117	188	305	145	34	19	121	1099	3.9	1.9	14.1
90-91—Detroit	78	2006	420	909	.462	240	317	.757	134	240	374	139	47	20	128	1104	4.8	1.8	14.2
91-92—Detroit	75	1582	339	787	.431	158	230	.687	67	169	236	126	51	11	105	851	3.1	1.7	11.3
92-93—Detroit	51	1056	187	422	.443	99	129	.767	43	109	152	105	16	7	68	503	3.0	2.1	9.9
93-94—L.A. Clippers	39	859	163	348	.468	50	72	.694	28	88	116	104	21	8	70	413	3.0	2.7	10.6
Totals	923	27730	7201	14865	.484	3664	4964	.741	1704	2874	4578	2871	687	296	2306	18458	5.0	3.1	20.0

Three-point field goals: 1981-82, 25-for-71 (.352). 1982-83, 16-for-76 (.211). 1983-84, 15-for-56 (.268). 1984-85, 27-for-85 (.318). 1985-86, 16-for-56 (.286). 1986-87, 53-for-150 (.353). 1987-88, 52-for-172 (.302). 1988-89, 51-for-174 (.293). 1989-90, 31-for-93 (.333). 1990-91, 24-for-78 (.308). 1991-92, 15-for-71 (.211). 1992-93, 30-for-83 (.361). 1993-94, 37-for-93 (.398). Totals, 392-for-1258 (.312).

Personal fouls/disqualifications: 1981-82, 152/0. 1982-83, 247/5. 1983-84, 246/5. 1984-85, 250/3. 1985-86, 229/6. 1986-87, 243/4. 1987-88, 223/1. 1988-89, 229/2. 1989-90, 201/2. 1990-91, 209/2. 1991-92, 171/0. 1992-93, 101/1. 1993-94, 98/2. Totals, 2599/33.

NBA PLAYOFF RECORD

Season Team	G	Min.	FGM	FGA	Pct.	FTM	FTA	Pct.	REBOUNDS Off.	Def.	Tot.	Ast.	St.	Blk.	TO	Pts.	AVERAGES RPG	APG	PPG
83-84—Dallas	10	350	88	184	.478	44	57	.772	21	55	76	32	5	5	27	220	7.6	3.2	22.0
84-85—Dallas	4	164	44	89	.494	27	32	.844	16	14	30	16	3	0	15	116	7.5	4.0	29.0
85-86—Dallas	10	345	105	214	.491	35	55	.636	21	50	71	54	9	0	23	247	7.1	5.4	24.7
86-87—Dallas	4	130	31	62	.500	23	30	.767	11	13	24	8	8	0	9	85	6.0	2.0	21.3
87-88—Dallas	17	558	147	294	.500	60	86	.698	34	66	100	56	14	9	41	367	5.9	3.3	21.6
88-89—Detroit	17	462	89	182	.489	28	38	.737	26	49	75	28	8	3	20	214	4.4	1.6	12.6
89-90—Detroit	20	439	86	184	.467	39	52	.750	31	60	91	27	10	3	30	219	4.6	1.4	11.0
90-91—Detroit	15	397	90	178	.506	42	51	.824	17	44	61	29	12	1	20	234	4.1	1.9	15.6
91-92—Detroit	5	113	16	48	.333	12	16	.750	4	5	9	12	2	1	13	45	1.8	2.4	9.0
Totals	102	2958	696	1435	.485	310	417	.743	181	356	537	262	71	22	198	1747	5.3	2.6	17.1

Three-point field goals: 1983-84, 0-for-5. 1984-85, 1-for-2 (.500). 1985-86, 2-for-6 (.333). 1986-87, 0-for-4. 1987-88, 13-for-34 (.382). 1988-89, 8-for-29 (.276). 1989-90, 8-for-24 (.333). 1990-91, 12-for-33 (.364). 1991-92, 1-for-5 (.200). Totals, 45-for-142 (.317).

Personal fouls/disqualifications: 1983-84, 34/2. 1984-85, 16/1. 1985-86, 28/1. 1986-87, 15/1. 1987-88, 49/0. 1988-89, 38/0. 1989-90, 51/0. 1990-91, 41/0. 1991-92, 9/0. Totals, 281/5.

NBA ALL-STAR GAME RECORD

Season Team	Min.	FGM	FGA	Pct.	FTM	FTA	Pct.	REBOUNDS Off.	Def.	Tot.	Ast.	PF	Dq.	St.	Blk.	TO	Pts.
1984 —Dallas	13	5	8	.625	3	4	.750	1	0	1	2	1	0	1	1	2	13
1987 —Dallas	17	3	6	.500	2	3	.667	1	1	2	1	1	0	0	0	2	9
1988 —Dallas	12	5	10	.500	3	3	1.000	1	0	1	1	3	0	1	0	3	14
Totals	42	13	24	.542	8	10	.800	2	2	4	4	5	0	2	1	7	36

Three-point field goals: 1987, 1-for-2 (.500). 1988, 1-for-3 (.333). Totals, 2-for-5 (.400).

ARCHIBALD, NATE   G

PERSONAL: Born September 2, 1948, in New York. ... 6-1/160 (1,85/72,6). ... Full name: Nathaniel Archibald. ... Nickname: Tiny.

HIGH SCHOOL: DeWitt Clinton (Bronx, N.Y.).

JUNIOR COLLEGE: Arizona Western College.

COLLEGE: Texas-El Paso.

TRANSACTIONS: Selected by Cincinnati Royals in second round (19th pick overall) of 1970 NBA Draft. ... Royals franchise moved from Cincinnati to Kansas City/Omaha and renamed Kings for 1972-73 season. ... Kings franchise moved from Kansas City/Omaha to Kansas City for 1975-76 season. ... Traded by Kings to New York Nets for G Brian Taylor, G Jim Eakins and 1977 and 1978 first-round draft choices (September 10, 1976). ... Nets franchise moved from New York to New Jersey for 1977-78 season. ... Traded by Nets to Buffalo Braves for C George Johnson and 1979 first-round draft choice (September 1, 1977). ... Braves franchise moved from Buffalo to San Diego and renamed Clippers for 1978-79 season. ... Traded by Clippers with F Marvin Barnes, F/G Billy Knight and 1981 and 1983 second-round draft choices to Boston Celtics for F Kermit Washington, C Kevin Kunnert, F Sidney Wicks and draft rights to G Freeman Williams (August 4, 1978). ... Waived by Celtics (July 22, 1983). ... Signed as free agent by Milwaukee Bucks (August 1, 1983).

CAREER HONORS: Elected to Naismith Memorial Basketball Hall of Fame (1991). ... One of the 50 Greatest Players in NBA History (1996).

MISCELLANEOUS: Member of NBA championship team (1981).

CAREER NOTES: Head coach, Fayetteville Patriots (NBDL).

COLLEGIATE RECORD

Season Team	G	Min.	FGM	FGA	Pct.	FTM	FTA	Pct.	Reb.	Ast.	Pts.	AVERAGES RPG	APG	PPG
66-67—Arizona Western College	27	...	303	...	...	190	...	...	...	...	796	...	...	29.5
67-68—Texas-El Paso	23	...	131	281	.466	102	140	.729	81	...	364	3.5	...	15.8
68-69—Texas-El Paso	25	...	199	374	.532	161	194	.830	69	...	559	2.8	...	22.4
69-70—Texas-El Paso	25	...	180	351	.513	176	225	.782	66	...	536	2.6	...	21.4
Junior college totals	27	...	303	...	...	190	...	...	...	...	796	...	...	29.5
4-year-college totals	73	...	510	1006	.507	439	559	.785	216	...	1459	3.0	...	20.0

NBA REGULAR-SEASON RECORD

HONORS: All-NBA first team (1973, 1975, 1976). ... All-NBA second team (1972, 1981).

Season Team	G	Min.	FGM	FGA	Pct.	FTM	FTA	Pct.	Reb.	Ast.	PF	Dq.	Pts.	AVERAGES RPG	APG	PPG
70-71—Cincinnati	82	2867	486	1095	.444	336	444	.757	242	450	218	2	1308	3.0	5.5	16.0
71-72—Cincinnati	76	3272	734	1511	.486	*677	*824	.822	222	701	198	3	2145	2.9	9.2	28.2
72-73—K.C./Omaha	80	*3681	*1028	*2106	.488	*663	*783	.847	223	*910	207	2	*2719	2.8	*11.4	*34.0

Season Team	G	Min.	FGM	FGA	Pct.	FTM	FTA	Pct.	Off.	Def.	Tot.	Ast.	St.	Blk.	TO	Pts.	RPG	APG	PPG
									REBOUNDS								AVERAGES		
73-74—K.C./Omaha	35	1272	222	492	.451	173	211	.820	21	64	85	266	56	7	...	617	2.4	7.6	17.6
74-75—K.C./Omaha	82	3244	759	1664	.456	*652	748	.872	48	174	222	557	119	7	...	2170	2.7	6.8	26.5
75-76—Kansas City....	78	3184	717	1583	.453	501	625	.802	67	146	213	615	126	15	...	1935	2.7	7.9	24.8
76-77—N.Y. Nets......	34	1277	250	560	.446	197	251	.785	22	58	80	254	59	11	...	697	2.4	7.5	20.5
77-78—Buffalo					Did not play—torn Achilles' tendon.														
78-79—Boston	69	1662	259	573	.452	242	307	.788	25	78	103	324	55	6	197	760	1.5	4.7	11.0
79-80—Boston	80	2864	383	794	.482	361	435	.830	59	138	197	671	106	10	242	1131	2.5	8.4	14.1
80-81—Boston	80	2820	382	766	.499	342	419	.816	36	140	176	618	75	18	265	1106	2.2	7.7	13.8
81-82—Boston	68	2167	308	652	.472	236	316	.747	25	91	116	541	52	3	178	858	1.7	8.0	12.6
82-83—Boston	66	1811	235	553	.425	220	296	.743	25	66	91	409	38	4	163	695	1.4	6.2	10.5
83-84—Milwaukee	46	1038	136	279	.487	64	101	.634	16	60	76	160	33	0	78	340	1.7	3.5	7.4
Totals	876	31159	5899	12628	.467	4664	5760	.810	...	...	2046	6476	719	81	1123	16481	2.3	7.4	18.8

Three-point field goals: 1979-80, 4-for-18 (.222). 1980-81, 0-for-9. 1981-82, 6-for-16 (.375). 1982-83, 5-for-24 (.208). 1983-84, 4-for-18 (.222). Totals, 19-for-85 (.224).

Personal fouls/disqualifications: 1973-74, 76/0. 1974-75, 187/0. 1975-76, 169/0. 1976-77, 77/1. 1978-79, 132/2. 1979-80, 218/2. 1980-81, 201/1. 1981-82, 131/1. 1982-83, 110/1. 1983-84, 78/0. Totals, 2002/15.

NBA PLAYOFF RECORD

Season Team	G	Min.	FGM	FGA	Pct.	FTM	FTA	Pct.	Off.	Def.	Tot.	Ast.	St.	Blk.	TO	Pts.	RPG	APG	PPG
									REBOUNDS								AVERAGES		
74-75—K.C./Omaha	6	242	43	118	.364	35	43	.814	2	9	11	32	4	0	...	121	1.8	5.3	20.2
79-80—Boston	9	332	45	89	.506	37	42	.881	3	8	11	71	10	0	38	128	1.2	7.9	14.2
80-81—Boston	17	630	95	211	.450	76	94	.809	6	22	28	107	13	0	50	266	1.6	6.3	15.6
81-82—Boston	8	277	30	70	.429	25	28	.893	1	16	17	52	5	2	23	85	2.1	6.5	10.6
82-83—Boston	7	161	22	68	.324	22	29	.759	3	7	10	44	2	0	11	67	1.4	6.3	9.6
Totals	47	1642	235	556	.423	195	236	.826	15	62	77	306	34	2	122	667	1.6	6.5	14.2

Three-point field goals: 1979-80, 1-for-2 (.500). 1980-81, 0-for-5. 1981-82, 0-for-4. 1982-83, 1-for-6 (.167). Totals, 2-for-17 (.118).

Personal fouls/disqualifications: 1974-75, 18/0. 1979-80, 28/1. 1980-81, 39/0. 1981-82, 21/0. 1982-83, 12/0. Totals, 118/1.

NBA ALL-STAR GAME RECORD

NOTES: NBA All-Star Game Most Valuable Player (1981).

Season Team	Min.	FGM	FGA	Pct.	FTM	FTA	Pct.	Reb.	Ast.	PF	Dq.	Pts.
1973 —Kansas City/Omaha	27	6	12	.500	5	5	1.000	1	5	1	0	17

Season Team	Min.	FGM	FGA	Pct.	FTM	FTA	Pct.	Off.	Def.	Tot.	Ast.	PF	Dq.	St.	Blk.	TO	Pts.
								REBOUNDS									
1975 —K.C./Omaha	36	10	15	.667	7	8	.875	1	1	2	6	2	0	3	1	...	27
1976 —Kansas City	30	5	13	.385	3	3	1.000	2	3	5	7	0	0	2	0	...	13
1980 —Boston............	21	0	8	.000	2	3	.667	1	2	3	6	1	0	2	0	2	2
1981 —Boston............	25	4	7	.571	1	3	.333	0	5	5	9	3	0	3	0	2	9
1982 —Boston............	23	2	5	.400	2	2	1.000	1	1	2	7	3	0	1	0	2	6
Totals..................	162	27	60	.450	20	24	.833	...	...	18	40	10	0	11	1	6	74

ARIZIN, PAUL   F

PERSONAL: Born April 9, 1928, in Philadelphia. ... 6-4/200 (1,93/90,7). ... Full name: Paul Joseph Arizin.
HIGH SCHOOL: La Salle (Philadelphia).
COLLEGE: Villanova.
TRANSACTIONS: Selected by Philadelphia Warriors in first round of 1950 NBA Draft. ... Played in Eastern Basketball League with Camden Bullets (1962-63 through 1964-65).
CAREER HONORS: Elected to Naismith Memorial Basketball Hall of Fame (1978). ... NBA 25th Anniversary All-Time Team (1970) and One of the 50 Greatest Players in NBA History (1996).
MISCELLANEOUS: Member of NBA championship team (1956).

COLLEGIATE RECORD

NOTES: The Sporting News College Player of the Year (1950). ... The Sporting News All-America first team (1950). ... Led NCAA Division I with 25.3 points per game (1950).

Season Team	G	Min.	FGM	FGA	Pct.	FTM	FTA	Pct.	Reb.	Ast.	Pts.	RPG	APG	PPG
												AVERAGES		
46-47—Villanova........................							Did not play.							
47-48—Villanova........................	24	...	101	...	...	65	...	...	...	...	267	...	...	11.1
48-49—Villanova........................	27	...	210	...	...	174	233	.747	...	...	594	...	...	22.0
49-50—Villanova........................	29	...	260	527	.493	215	277	.776	...	...	735	...	...	25.3
Totals	80	...	571	...	...	454	...	...	...	...	1596	...	...	20.0

NBA REGULAR-SEASON RECORD

HONORS: All-NBA first team (1952, 1956, 1957). ... All-NBA second team (1959).

Season Team	G	Min.	FGM	FGA	Pct.	FTM	FTA	Pct.	Reb.	Ast.	PF	Dq.	Pts.	RPG	APG	PPG
														AVERAGES		
50-51 —Philadelphia	65	...	352	864	.407	417	526	.793	640	138	284	18	1121	9.8	2.1	17.2
51-52 —Philadelphia	66	*2939	*548	1222	*.448	*578	*707	.818	745	170	250	5	*1674	11.3	2.6	*25.4
52-53 —Philadelphia					Did not play—in military service.											
53-54 —Philadelphia					Did not play—in military service.											
54-55 —Philadelphia	72	*2953	*529	*1325	.399	454	585	.776	675	210	270	5	1512	9.4	2.9	21.0
55-56 —Philadelphia	72	2724	617	1378	.448	507	626	.810	539	189	282	11	1741	7.5	2.6	24.2
56-57 —Philadelphia	71	2767	613	1451	.422	591	*713	.829	561	150	274	13	*1817	7.9	2.1	*25.6
57-58 —Philadelphia	68	2377	483	1229	.393	440	544	.809	503	135	235	7	1406	7.4	2.0	20.7
58-59 —Philadelphia	70	2799	632	1466	.431	587	722	.813	637	119	264	7	1851	9.1	1.7	26.4
59-60 —Philadelphia	72	2618	593	1400	.424	420	526	.798	621	165	263	6	1606	8.6	2.3	22.3
60-61 —Philadelphia	79	2935	650	1529	.425	532	639	.833	681	188	*335	11	1832	8.6	2.4	23.2
61-62 —Philadelphia	78	2785	611	1490	.410	484	601	.805	527	201	307	18	1706	6.8	2.6	21.9
Totals................................	713	...	5628	13354	.421	5010	6189	.810	6129	1665	2764	101	16266	8.6	2.3	22.8

NBA PLAYOFF RECORD

Season Team	G	Min.	FGM	FGA	Pct.	FTM	FTA	Pct.	Reb.	Ast.	PF	Dq.	Pts.	AVERAGES RPG	APG	PPG
50-51 —Philadelphia	2	...	14	27	.519	13	16	.813	20	3	10	1	41	10.0	1.5	20.5
51-52 —Philadelphia	3	120	24	53	.453	29	33	.879	38	8	17	2	77	12.7	2.7	25.7
55-56 —Philadelphia	10	409	103	229	.450	83	99	.838	84	29	31	1	289	8.4	2.9	28.9
56-57 —Philadelphia	2	22	3	8	.375	3	5	.600	8	1	3	0	9	4.0	0.5	4.5
57-58 —Philadelphia	8	309	66	169	.391	56	72	.778	62	16	26	1	188	7.8	2.0	23.5
59-60 —Philadelphia	9	371	84	195	.431	69	79	.873	86	33	29	0	237	9.6	3.7	26.3
60-61 —Philadelphia	3	125	22	67	.328	23	33	.697	26	12	17	2	67	8.7	4.0	22.3
61-62 —Philadelphia	12	459	95	253	.376	88	102	.863	80	26	44	1	278	6.7	2.2	23.2
Totals	49	...	411	1001	.411	364	439	.829	404	128	177	8	1186	8.2	2.6	24.2

NBA ALL-STAR GAME RECORD

NOTES: NBA All-Star Game Most Valuable Player (1952).

Season Team	Min.	FGM	FGA	Pct.	FTM	FTA	Pct.	Reb	Ast.	PF	Dq.	Pts.
1951 —Philadelphia	...	7	12	.583	1	2	.500	7	0	2	0	15
1952 —Philadelphia	32	9	13	.692	8	8	1.000	6	0	1	0	26
1955 —Philadelphia	23	4	9	.444	1	2	.500	2	2	5	0	9
1956 —Philadelphia	28	5	13	.385	3	5	.600	7	1	6	1	13
1957 —Philadelphia	26	6	13	.462	1	2	.500	5	0	2	0	13
1958 —Philadelphia	29	11	17	.647	2	2	1.000	8	2	3	0	24
1959 —Philadelphia	30	4	15	.267	8	9	.889	8	0	2	0	16
1960 —Philadelphia					Selected, did not play—injured.							
1961 —Philadelphia	17	6	12	.500	5	6	.833	2	1	4	0	17
1962 —Philadelphia	21	2	12	.167	0	0		2	0	4	0	4
Totals	...	54	116	.466	29	36	.806	47	6	29	1	137

EBL REGULAR-SEASON RECORD

NOTES: Eastern Basketball League Most Valuable Player (1963). ... EBL All-Star first team (1963, 1964). ... EBL All-Star second team (1965).

Season Team	G	Min.	FGM	FGA	Pct.	FTM	FTA	Pct.	Reb.	Ast.	PF	Dq.	Pts.	AVERAGES RPG	APG	PPG
62-63 —Camden	28	...	264	...	...	196	249	.787	203	42	...	...	724	7.3	1.5	25.9
63-64 —Camden	27	...	261	...	...	174	218	.798	226	52	...	...	696	8.4	1.9	25.8
64-65 —Camden	28	...	226	...	...	196	244	.803	164	50	...	...	657	5.9	1.8	23.5
Totals	83	...	751	...		566	711	.796	593	144	...	...	2077	7.1	1.7	25.0

BARKLEY, CHARLES   F

PERSONAL: Born February 20, 1963, in Leeds, Ala. ... 6-6/252. (1.98 m/114 kg). ... Full Name: Charles Wade Barkley.
HIGH SCHOOL: Leeds (Ala.).
COLLEGE: Auburn.
TRANSACTIONS/CAREER NOTES: Selected after junior season by Philadelphia 76ers in first round (fifth pick overall) of 1984 NBA Draft. ... Traded by 76ers to Phoenix Suns for G Jeff Hornacek, F Tim Perry and C Andrew Lang (June 17, 1992). ... Traded by Suns with 1999 second-round draft choice to Houston Rockets for G Sam Cassell, F Chucky Brown, F Robert Horry and F Mark Bryant (August 19, 1996).
CAREER HONORS: NBA 50th Anniversary All-Time Team (1996).
MISCELLANEOUS: Member of gold-medal-winning U.S. Olympic teams (1992, 1996).

COLLEGIATE RECORD

Season Team	G	Min.	FGM	FGA	Pct.	FTM	FTA	Pct.	Reb.	Ast.	Pts.	AVERAGES RPG	APG	PPG
81-82—Auburn	28	746	144	242	.595	68	107	.636	275	30	356	9.8	1.1	12.7
82-83—Auburn	28	782	161	250	.644	82	130	.631	266	49	404	9.5	1.8	14.4
83-84—Auburn	28	794	162	254	.638	99	145	.683	265	58	423	9.5	2.1	15.1
Totals	84	2322	467	746	.626	249	382	.652	806	137	1183	9.6	1.6	14.1

NBA REGULAR-SEASON RECORD

RECORDS: Holds single-game records for most offensive rebounds in one quarter—11; and most offensive rebounds in one half—13 (March 4, 1987, vs. New York).
HONORS: NBA Most Valuable Player (1993). ... IBM Award, for all-around contributions to team's success (1986, 1987, 1988). ... All-NBA first team (1988, 1989, 1990, 1991, 1993). ... All-NBA second team (1986, 1987, 1992, 1994, 1995). ... All-NBA third team (1996). ... NBA All-Rookie team (1985).
NOTES: Led NBA with 333 personal fouls (1986).

Season Team	G	Min.	FGM	FGA	Pct.	FTM	FTA	Pct.	REBOUNDS Off.	Def.	Tot.	Ast.	St.	Blk.	TO	Pts.	AVERAGES RPG	APG	PPG
84-85—Philadelphia	82	2347	427	783	.545	293	400	.733	266	437	703	155	95	80	209	1148	8.6	1.9	14.0
85-86—Philadelphia	80	2952	595	1041	.572	396	578	.685	354	672	1026	312	173	125	*350	1603	12.8	3.9	20.0
86-87—Philadelphia	68	2740	557	937	.594	429	564	.761	*390	604	994	331	119	104	322	1564	*14.6	4.9	23.0
87-88—Philadelphia	80	3170	753	1283	.587	714	*951	.751	*385	566	951	254	100	103	304	2264	11.9	3.2	28.3
88-89—Philadelphia	79	3088	700	1208	.579	602	799	.753	*403	583	986	325	126	67	254	2037	12.5	4.1	25.8
89-90—Philadelphia	79	3085	706	1177	.600	557	744	.749	361	548	909	307	148	50	243	1989	11.5	3.9	25.2
90-91—Philadelphia	67	2498	665	1167	.570	475	658	.722	258	422	680	284	110	33	210	1849	10.1	4.2	27.6
91-92—Philadelphia	75	2881	622	1126	.552	454	653	.695	271	559	830	308	136	44	235	1730	11.1	4.1	23.1
92-93—Phoenix	76	2859	716	1376	.520	445	582	.765	237	691	928	385	119	74	233	1944	12.2	5.1	25.6
93-94—Phoenix	65	2298	518	1046	.495	318	452	.704	198	529	727	296	101	37	206	1402	11.2	4.6	21.6
94-95—Phoenix	68	2382	554	1141	.486	379	507	.748	203	553	756	276	110	45	150	1561	11.1	4.1	23.0
95-96—Phoenix	71	2632	580	1160	.500	440	566	.777	243	578	821	262	114	56	218	1649	11.6	3.7	23.2
96-97—Houston	53	2009	335	692	.484	288	415	.694	212	504	716	248	69	25	151	1016	13.5	4.7	19.2
97-98—Houston	68	2243	361	744	.485	296	397	.746	241	553	794	217	71	28	147	1036	11.7	3.2	15.2
98-99—Houston	42	1526	240	502	.478	192	267	.719	167	349	516	192	43	13	100	676	12.3	4.6	16.1
99-00—Houston	20	620	106	222	.477	71	110	.645	71	138	209	63	14	4	44	289	10.5	3.2	14.5
Totals	1073	39330	8435	15605	.541	6349	8643	.735	4260	8286	12546	4215	1648	888	3376	23757	11.7	3.9	22.1

Three-point field goals: 1984-85, 1-for-6 (.167). 1985-86, 17-for-75 (.227). 1986-87, 21-for-104 (.202). 1987-88, 44-for-157 (.280). 1988-89, 35-for-162 (.216). 1989-90, 20-for-92 (.217). 1990-91, 44-for-155 (.284). 1991-92, 32-for-137 (.234). 1992-93, 67-for-220 (.305). 1993-94, 48-for-178 (.270). 1994-95, 74-for-219 (.338). 1995-96, 49-for-175 (.280). 1996-97, 58-for-205 (.283). 1997-98, 18-for-84 (.214). 1998-99, 4-for-25 (.160). 1999-00, 6-for-26 (.231). Totals, 538-for-2020 (.266).

Personal fouls/disqualifications: 1984-85, 301/5. 1985-86, 333/8. 1986-87, 252/5. 1987-88, 278/6. 1988-89, 262/3. 1989-90, 250/2. 1990-91, 173/2. 1991-92, 196/2. 1992-93, 196/0. 1993-94, 160/1. 1994-95, 201/3. 1995-96, 208/3. 1996-97, 153/2. 1997-98, 187/2. 1998-99, 89/0. 1999-00, 48/0. Totals, 3287/44.

NBA PLAYOFF RECORD

NOTES: Shares single-game playoff records for most free throws made in one half—19 (June 5, 1993, vs. Seattle); and most field goals made in one half—15 (May 4, 1994, at Golden State).

Season Team	G	Min.	FGM	FGA	Pct.	FTM	FTA	Pct.	REBOUNDS Off.	Def.	Tot.	Ast.	St.	Blk.	TO	Pts.	AVERAGES RPG	APG	PPG
84-85—Philadelphia....	13	408	139	.540	40	63	.635	52	92	144	26	23	15	35	194	11.1	2.0	14.9	
85-86—Philadelphia....	12	497	104	180	.578	91	131	.695	60	129	189	67	27	15	65	300	15.8	5.6	25.0
86-87—Philadelphia....	5	210	43	75	.573	36	45	.800	27	36	63	12	4	8	22	123	12.6	2.4	24.6
88-89—Philadelphia....	3	135	29	45	.644	22	31	.710	8	27	35	16	5	2	11	81	11.7	5.3	27.0
89-90—Philadelphia....	10	419	88	162	.543	65	108	.602	66	89	155	43	8	7	30	247	15.5	4.3	24.7
90-91—Philadelphia....	8	326	74	125	.592	49	75	.653	31	53	84	48	15	3	25	199	10.5	6.0	24.9
92-93—Phoenix	24	1026	230	482	.477	168	218	.771	93	233	326	102	39	25	50	638	13.6	4.3	26.6
93-94—Phoenix	10	425	110	216	.509	42	55	.764	34	96	130	48	25	9	27	276	13.0	4.8	27.6
94-95—Phoenix	10	390	91	182	.500	66	90	.733	39	95	134	32	13	11	25	257	13.4	3.2	25.7
95-96—Phoenix	4	164	31	70	.443	37	47	.787	18	36	54	15	4	4	6	102	13.5	3.8	25.5
96-97—Houston	16	605	86	198	.434	103	134	.769	64	128	192	54	19	7	43	286	12.0	3.4	17.9
97-98—Houston	4	87	12	23	.522	12	21	.571	5	16	21	4	5	0	6	36	5.3	1.0	9.0
98-99—Houston	4	157	36	68	.529	20	30	.667	13	42	55	16	5	2	8	94	13.8	3.8	23.5
Totals	123	4849	1009	1965	.513	751	1048	.717	510	1072	1582	482	193	108	353	2833	12.9	3.9	23.0

Three-point field goals: 1984-85, 4-for-6 (.667). 1985-86, 1-for-15 (.067). 1988-89, 1-for-5 (.200). 1989-90, 6-for-18 (.333). 1990-91, 2-for-20 (.100). 1992-93, 10-for-45 (.222). 1993-94, 14-for-40 (.350). 1994-95, 9-for-35 (.257). 1995-96, 3-for-12 (.250). 1996-97, 11-for-38 (.289). 1997-98, 0-for-2. 1998-99, 2-for-7 (.286). Totals, 63-for-243 (.259).

Personal fouls/disqualifications: 1984-85, 49/0. 1985-86, 52/2. 1988-89, 9/0. 1989-90, 36/0. 1990-91, 23/0. 1992-93, 73/0. 1993-94, 26/0. 1994-95, 28/0. 1995-96, 15/0. 1996-97, 52/1. 1997-98, 12/1. 1998-99, 12/0. Totals, 408/4.

NBA ALL-STAR GAME RECORD

NOTES: NBA All-Star Game Most Valuable Player (1991).

Season Team	Min.	FGM	FGA	Pct.	FTM	FTA	Pct.	REBOUNDS Off.	Def.	Tot.	Ast.	PF	Dq.	St.	Blk.	TO	Pts.
1987 —Philadelphia......	16	2	6	.333	3	6	.500	1	3	4	1	2	0	1	0	0	7
1988 —Philadelphia......	15	1	4	.250	2	2	1.000	1	2	3	0	2	0	1	1	3	4
1989 —Philadelphia......	20	6	11	.545	5	8	.625	3	2	5	0	0	0	2	1	1	17
1990 —Philadelphia......	22	7	12	.583	2	3	.667	2	2	4	0	1	0	1	1	2	17
1991 —Philadelphia......	35	7	15	.467	3	6	.500	8	14	22	4	5	0	1	1	3	17
1992 —Philadelphia......	28	6	14	.429	0	0	...	2	7	9	1	3	0	0	0	3	12
1993 —Phoenix	34	5	11	.455	5	7	.714	0	4	4	7	3	0	4	0	4	16
1994 —Phoenix								Selected, did not play—injured.									
1995 —Phoenix	23	7	12	.583	0	0	...	5	4	9	2	1	0	2	0	2	15
1996 —Phoenix	16	4	6	.667	0	0	...	0	0	0	1	1	0	0	0	2	8
1997 —Houston								Selected, did not play—injured.									
Totals	209	45	91	.495	20	32	.625	22	38	60	16	18	0	12	4	20	113

Three-point field goals: 1987, 0-for-2. 1988, 0-for-1. 1990, 1-for-1. 1992, 0-for-2. 1993, 1-for-2 (.500). 1995, 1-for-4 (.250). Totals, 3-for-12 (.250)

BARRY, RICK   F

PERSONAL: Born March 28, 1944, in Elizabeth, N.J. ... 6-7/220 (2,00/99,8). ... Full name: Richard Francis Dennis Barry III. ... Father of Jon Barry, guard with Sacramento Kings; father of Brent Barry, guard with Seattle SuperSonics; and father of Drew Barry, guard with Atlanta Hawks.

HIGH SCHOOL: Roselle Park (N.J.).

COLLEGE: Miami (Fla.).

TRANSACTIONS: Selected by San Francisco Warriors in first round of 1965 NBA Draft. ... Signed as free agent by Oakland Oaks of American Basketball Association (1967); court order required him to sit out option season with Warriors (1967-68). ... Oaks franchise moved to Washington and renamed Capitols for 1969-70 season. ... Capitols franchise moved from Washington to Virginia and renamed Squires for 1970-71 season. ... Traded by Squires to New York Nets for first-round draft choice and cash (August 1970). ... Returned to NBA with Golden State Warriors for 1972-73 season. ... Signed as veteran free agent by Houston Rockets (June 17, 1978); Warriors waived their right of first refusal in exchange for G John Lucas and cash.

CAREER HONORS: Elected to Naismith Memorial Basketball Hall of Fame (1987). ... One of the 50 Greatest Players in NBA History (1996).

MISCELLANEOUS: Member of NBA championship team (1975).

COLLEGIATE RECORD

NOTES: THE SPORTING NEWS All-America second team (1965). ... Led NCAA Division I with 37.4 points per game (1965).

Season Team	G	Min.	FGM	FGA	Pct.	FTM	FTA	Pct.	Reb.	Ast.	Pts.	AVERAGES RPG	APG	PPG
61-62—Miami (Fla.)‡..............	17	...	208	...	...	73	...	...	...	...	489	...	...	28.8
62-63—Miami (Fla.)...................	24	...	162	341	.475	131	158	.829	351	...	455	14.6	...	19.0
63-64—Miami (Fla.)...................	27	...	314	572	.549	242	287	.843	448	...	870	16.6	...	32.2
64-65—Miami (Fla.)...................	26	...	340	651	.522	293	341	.859	475	...	973	18.3	...	37.4
Varsity totals	77	...	816	1564	.522	666	786	.847	1274	...	2298	16.5	...	29.8

NBA REGULAR-SEASON RECORD

RECORDS: Shares single-game record for most free throws made in one quarter—14 (December 6, 1966, vs. New York).

HONORS: NBA Rookie of the Year (1966). ... All-NBA first team (1966, 1967, 1974, 1975, 1976). ... All-NBA second team (1973). ... NBA All-Rookie team (1966).

NOTES: Led NBA with 2.85 steals per game (1975).

Season Team	G	Min.	FGM	FGA	Pct.	FTM	FTA	Pct.	Reb.	Ast.	PF	Dq.	Pts.	AVERAGES RPG	APG	PPG
65-66 —San Francisco	80	2990	745	1698	.439	569	660	.862	850	173	297	2	2059	10.6	2.2	25.7
66-67 —San Francisco	78	3175	*1011	*2240	.451	*753	852	.884	714	282	258	1	*2775	9.2	3.6	*35.6
72-73 —Golden State	82	3075	737	1630	.452	358	397	*.902	728	399	245	2	1832	8.9	4.9	22.3

Season Team	G	Min.	FGM	FGA	Pct.	FTM	FTA	Pct.	REBOUNDS Off.	Def.	Tot.	Ast.	St.	Blk.	TO	Pts.	AVERAGES RPG	APG	PPG
73-74—Golden State	80	2918	796	1746	.456	417	464	.899	103	437	540	484	169	40	...	2009	6.8	6.1	25.1
74-75—Golden State	80	3235	1028	*2217	.464	394	436	*.904	92	364	456	492	*228	33	...	2450	5.7	6.2	30.6
75-76—Golden State	81	3122	707	1624	.435	287	311	*.923	74	422	496	496	202	27	...	1701	6.1	6.1	21.0
76-77—Golden State	79	2904	682	1551	.440	359	392	.916	73	349	422	475	172	58	...	1723	5.3	6.0	21.8
77-78—Golden State	82	3024	760	1686	.451	378	409	*.924	75	374	449	446	158	45	224	1898	5.5	5.4	23.1
78-79—Houston	80	2566	461	1000	.461	160	169	*.947	40	237	277	502	95	38	198	1082	3.5	6.3	13.5
79-80—Houston	72	1816	325	771	.422	143	153	*.935	53	183	236	268	80	28	152	866	3.3	3.7	12.0
Totals	794	28825	7252	16163	.449	3818	4243	.900	...	...	5168	4017	1104	269	574	18395	6.5	5.1	23.2

Three-point field goals: 1979-80, 73-for-221 (.330).
Personal fouls/disqualifications: 1973-74, 265/4. 1974-75, 225/0. 1975-76, 215/1. 1976-77, 194/2. 1977-78, 188/1. 1978-79, 195/0. 1979-80, 182/0.
Totals, 2264/13.

NBA PLAYOFF RECORD

NOTES: NBA Finals Most Valuable Player (1975). ... Holds NBA Finals single-game records for most field goals attempted—48 (April 18, 1967, vs. Philadelphia); and most field goals attempted in one quarter—17 (April 14, 1967, vs. Philadelphia). ... Shares NBA Finals single-game record for most field goals made—22 (April 18, 1967, vs. Philadelphia). ... Holds single-game playoff record for most field goals attempted in one quarter—17 (April 14, 1967, vs. Philadelphia).

Season Team	G	Min.	FGM	FGA	Pct.	FTM	FTA	Pct.	Reb.	Ast.	PF	Dq.	Pts.	AVERAGES RPG	APG	PPG
66-67 —San Francisco	15	614	197	489	.403	127	157	.809	113	58	49	0	521	7.5	3.9	34.7
72-73 —Golden State	11	292	65	164	.396	50	55	.909	54	24	41	1	180	4.9	2.2	16.4

Season Team	G	Min.	FGM	FGA	Pct.	FTM	FTA	Pct.	REBOUNDS Off.	Def.	Tot.	Ast.	St.	Blk.	TO	Pts.	AVERAGES RPG	APG	PPG
74-75—Golden State	17	726	189	426	.444	101	110	.918	22	72	94	103	50	15	...	479	5.5	6.1	28.2
75-76—Golden State	13	532	126	289	.436	60	68	.882	20	64	84	84	38	14	...	312	6.5	6.5	24.0
76-77—Golden State	10	415	122	262	.466	40	44	.909	25	34	59	47	17	7	...	284	5.9	4.7	28.4
78-79—Houston	2	65	8	25	.320	8	8	1.000	2	6	8	9	0	2	2	24	4.0	4.5	12.0
79-80—Houston	6	79	12	33	.364	6	6	1.000	0	6	6	15	1	1	10	33	1.0	2.5	5.5
Totals	74	2723	719	1688	.426	392	448	.875	...	...	418	340	106	39	12	1833	5.6	4.6	24.8

Three-point field goals: 1979-80, 3-for-12 (.250).
Personal fouls/disqualifications: 1974-75, 51/1. 1975-76, 40/1. 1976-77, 32/0. 1978-79, 8/0. 1979-80, 11/0. Totals, 232/3.

NBA ALL-STAR GAME RECORD

NOTES: NBA All-Star Game Most Valuable Player (1967). ... Holds single-game records for most field goals attempted—27 (1967); and most steals—8 (1975).

Season Team	Min.	FGM	FGA	Pct.	FTM	FTA	Pct.	Reb	Ast.	PF	Dq.	Pts.
1966 —San Francisco	17	4	10	.400	2	4	.500	2	2	6	1	10
1967 —San Francisco	34	16	27	.593	6	8	.750	6	3	5	2	38
1973 —Golden State				Selected, did not play—injured.								

Season Team	Min.	FGM	FGA	Pct.	FTM	FTA	Pct.	REBOUNDS Off.	Def.	Tot.	Ast.	PF	Dq.	St.	Blk.	TO	Pts.
1974 —Golden State	19	3	6	.500	2	2	1.000	1	3	4	3	3	0	1	0	...	8
1975 —Golden State	38	11	20	.550	0	0	...	1	4	5	4	0	0	8	1	...	22
1976 —Golden State	28	6	15	.400	5	5	1.000	2	2	4	2	5	0	2	0	...	17
1977 —Golden State	29	7	16	.438	4	4	1.000	1	3	4	8	1	0	2	0	...	18
1978 —Golden State	30	7	17	.412	1	1	1.000	2	2	4	5	6	1	3	0	5	15
Totals	195	54	111	.486	20	24	.833	...	...	29	31	30	2	16	1	5	128

ABA REGULAR-SEASON RECORD

NOTES: Member of ABA championship team (1969). ... ABA All-Star first team (1969, 1970, 1971, 1972).

Season Team	G	Min.	2-POINT FGM	FGA	Pct.	3-POINT FGM	FGA	Pct.	FTM	FTA	Pct.	Reb.	Ast.	Pts.	AVERAGES RPG	APG	PPG
67-68—						Did not play—sat out option year.											
68-69—Oakland	35	1361	389	757	.514	3	10	.300	403	454	*.888	329	136	*1190	9.4	3.9	*34.0
69-70—Washington	52	1849	509	907	.561	8	39	.205	400	463	.864	363	178	1442	7.0	3.4	27.7
70-71—New York	59	2502	613	1262	.486	19	86	.221	451	507	*.890	401	294	1734	6.8	5.0	29.4
71-72—New York	80	3616	829	1732	.479	73	237	.308	*641	730	*.878	602	327	2518	7.5	4.1	31.5
Totals	226	9328	2340	4658	.502	103	372	.277	1895	2154	.880	1695	935	6884	7.5	4.1	30.5

ABA PLAYOFF RECORD

Season Team	G	Min.	2-POINT FGM	FGA	Pct.	3-POINT FGM	FGA	Pct.	FTM	FTA	Pct.	Reb.	Ast.	Pts.	AVERAGES RPG	APG	PPG
69-70—Washington	7	302	105	194	.541	3	9	.333	62	68	.912	70	23	281	10.0	3.3	40.1
70-71—New York	6	287	46	108	.426	14	27	.519	48	59	.814	70	24	202	11.7	4.0	33.7
71-72—New York	18	749	180	368	.489	23	61	.377	125	146	.856	117	69	554	6.5	3.8	30.8
Totals	31	1338	331	670	.494	40	97	.412	235	273	.861	257	116	1037	8.3	3.7	33.5

ABA ALL-STAR GAME RECORD

Season Team	Min.	2-POINT FGM	FGA	Pct.	3-POINT FGM	FGA	Pct.	FTM	FTA	Pct.	Reb.	Ast.	Pts.
1968—Oakland	12	3	9	.333	0	0	...	4	5	.800	3	1	10
1969—Washington	27	7	12	.583	0	0	...	2	2	1.000	7	7	16
1970—New York	17	4	6	.667	0	0	...	6	6	1.000	2	2	14
1971—New York	26	2	10	.200	0	0	...	0	1	.000	12	8	4
Totals	82	16	37	.432	0	0	...	12	14	.857	24	18	44

COMBINED ABA AND NBA REGULAR-SEASON RECORDS

	G	Min.	FGM	FGA	Pct.	FTM	FTA	Pct.	REBOUNDS Off.	Def.	Tot.	Ast.	Stl.	Blk.	TO	Pts.	AVERAGES RPG	APG	PPG
Totals	1020	38153	9695	21193	.457	5713	6397	.893	...	...	6863	4952	...	...	...	25279	6.7	4.9	24.8

Three-point field goals: 176-for-593 (.297).
Personal fouls/disqualifications: 3028.

CBA COACHING RECORD

	REGULAR SEASON				PLAYOFFS		
Season Team	W	L	Pct.	Finish	W	L	Pct.
92-93—Fort Wayne..	11	16	.407	4th/Eastern Division	—	—	—
93-94—Fort Wayne..	14	30	.318				
Totals (2 years)...	25	46	.352				

USBL COACHING RECORD

	REGULAR SEASON				PLAYOFFS		
Season Team	W	L	Pct.	Finish	W	L	Pct.
97-98 —New Jersey..	14	12	.538	3rd/Mid-Atlantic Division	1	1	.500
98-99 —New Jersey..	23	6	.793	1st/Mid-Atlantic Division	3	0	1.000
99-00 —Florida...	16	14	.533	3rd/Southern Division	0	1	.000
Totals (3 years)..	53	32	.624	Totals (3 years).......	4	2	.667

NOTES:
1998—Defeated Tampa Bay in play-in game; lost to Jacksonville in quarterfinals.
1999—Defeated Tampa Bay in quarterfinals; defeated Pennsylvania in semifinals; defeated Connecticut in USBL Finals.
2000—Lost to Kansas in quarterfinals.

BAYLOR, ELGIN   F

PERSONAL: Born September 16, 1934, in Washington, D.C. ... 6-5/225 (1,96/102,1). ... Full name: Elgin Gay Baylor.
HIGH SCHOOL: Phelps Vocational (Washington, D.C.), then Spingarn (Washington, D.C.).
COLLEGE: The College of Idaho, then Seattle.
TRANSACTIONS: Selected after junior season by Minneapolis Lakers in first round (first pick overall) of 1958 NBA Draft.
... Lakers franchise moved to Los Angeles for 1960-61 season.
CAREER HONORS: Elected to Naismith Memorial Basketball Hall of Fame (1977). ... NBA 35th Anniversary All-Time Team
(1980) and One of the 50 Greatest Players in NBA History (1996).
CAREER NOTES: Vice president of basketball operations, Los Angeles Clippers (1986 to present).
MISCELLANEOUS: Los Angeles Lakers franchise all-time leading rebounder with 11,463 (1958-59 through 1971-72).

COLLEGIATE RECORD

NOTES: The Sporting News All-America first team (1958). ... NCAA University Division Tournament Most Valuable Player (1958). ... Led NCAA
Division I with .235 rebound average (1957), when championship was determined by highest individual recoveries as percentage of total
recoveries by both teams in all games. ... Played for Westside Ford (AAU team in Seattle) averaging 34 points per game (1955-56).

												AVERAGES		
Season Team	G	Min.	FGM	FGA	Pct.	FTM	FTA	Pct.	Reb.	Ast.	Pts.	RPG	APG	PPG
54-55—The College of Idaho	26	...	332	651	.510	150	232	.647	492	...	814	18.9	...	31.3
55-56—Seattle						Did not play—transfer student.								
56-57—Seattle	25	...	271	555	.488	201	251	.801	508	...	743	20.3	...	29.7
57-58—Seattle	29	...	353	697	.506	237	308	.769	559	...	943	19.3	...	32.5
Totals	80	...	956	1903	.502	588	791	.743	1559	...	2500	19.5	...	31.3

NBA REGULAR-SEASON RECORD

HONORS: NBA Rookie of the Year (1959). ... All-NBA first team (1959, 1960, 1961, 1962, 1963, 1964, 1965, 1967, 1968, 1969).

														AVERAGES		
Season Team	G	Min.	FGM	FGA	Pct.	FTM	FTA	Pct.	Reb.	Ast.	PF	Dq.	Pts.	RPG	APG	PPG
58-59 —Minneapolis	70	2855	605	1482	.408	532	685	.777	1050	287	270	4	1742	15.0	4.1	24.9
59-60 —Minneapolis	70	2873	755	1781	.424	564	770	.732	1150	243	234	2	2074	16.4	3.5	29.6
60-61 —Los Angeles	73	3133	931	2166	.430	676	863	.783	1447	371	279	3	2538	19.8	5.1	34.8
61-62 —Los Angeles	48	2129	680	1588	.428	476	631	.754	892	222	155	1	1836	18.6	4.6	38.3
62-63 —Los Angeles	80	3370	1029	2273	.453	661	790	.837	1146	386	226	1	2719	14.3	4.8	34.0
63-64 —Los Angeles	78	3164	756	1778	.425	471	586	.804	936	347	235	1	1983	12.0	4.4	25.4
64-65 —Los Angeles	74	3056	763	1903	.401	483	610	.792	950	280	235	0	2009	12.8	3.8	27.1
65-66 —Los Angeles	65	1975	415	1034	.401	249	337	.739	621	224	157	0	1079	9.6	3.4	16.6
66-67 —Los Angeles	70	2706	711	1658	.429	440	541	.813	898	215	211	1	1862	12.8	3.1	26.6
67-68 —Los Angeles	77	3029	757	1709	.443	488	621	.786	941	355	232	0	2002	12.2	4.6	26.0
68-69 —Los Angeles	76	3064	730	1632	.447	421	567	.743	805	408	204	0	1881	10.6	5.4	24.8
69-70 —Los Angeles	54	2213	511	1051	.486	276	357	.773	559	292	132	1	1298	10.4	5.4	24.0
70-71 —Los Angeles	2	57	8	19	.421	4	6	.667	11	2	6	0	20	5.5	1.0	10.0
71-72 —Los Angeles	9	239	42	97	.433	22	27	.815	57	18	20	0	106	6.3	2.0	11.8
Totals.....................................	846	33863	8693	20171	.431	5763	7391	.780	11463	3650	2596	14	23149	13.5	4.3	27.4

NBA PLAYOFF RECORD

NOTES: Holds NBA Finals single-game records for most points—61; and most field goals attempted in one half—25 (April 14, 1962, vs.
Boston). ... Shares NBA Finals single-game record for most field goals made—22 (April 14, 1962, vs. Boston). ... Shares single-game playoff record for most field goals attempted in one half—25 (April 14, 1962, vs. Boston).

														AVERAGES		
Season Team	G	Min.	FGM	FGA	Pct.	FTM	FTA	Pct.	Reb.	Ast.	PF	Dq.	Pts.	RPG	APG	PPG
58-59 —Minneapolis	13	556	122	303	.403	87	113	.770	156	43	52	0	331	12.0	3.3	25.5
59-60 —Minneapolis	9	408	111	234	.474	79	94	.840	127	31	38	0	301	14.1	3.4	33.4
60-61 —Los Angeles	12	540	170	362	.470	117	142	.824	183	55	44	1	457	15.3	4.6	38.1
61-62 —Los Angeles	13	571	186	425	.438	130	168	.774	230	47	45	1	502	17.7	3.6	38.6
62-63 —Los Angeles	13	562	160	362	.442	104	126	.825	177	58	48	0	424	13.6	4.5	32.6
63-64 —Los Angeles	5	221	45	119	.378	31	40	.775	58	28	17	0	121	11.6	5.6	24.2
64-65 —Los Angeles	1	5	0	2	.000	0	0	...	0	1	0	0	0	0.0	1.0	0.0
65-66 —Los Angeles	14	586	145	328	.442	85	105	.810	197	52	38	0	375	14.1	3.7	26.8

ALL-TIME GREAT PLAYERS

	G	Min.	FGM	FGA	Pct.	FTM	FTA	Pct.	Reb.	Ast.	PF	Dq.	Pts.	RPG	APG	PPG
...Angeles	3	121	28	76	.368	15	20	.750	39	9	6	0	71	13.0	3.0	23.7
...Angeles	15	633	176	376	.468	76	112	.679	218	60	41	0	428	14.5	4.0	28.5
...Angeles	18	640	107	278	.385	63	97	.649	166	74	56	0	277	9.2	4.1	15.4
...Angeles	18	667	138	296	.466	60	81	.741	173	83	50	1	336	9.6	4.6	18.7
Totals	134	5510	1388	3161	.439	847	1098	.771	1724	541	435	3	3623	12.9	4.0	27.0

NBA ALL-STAR GAME RECORD

NOTES: NBA All-Star Game co-Most Valuable Player (1959). ... Holds career record for most free throws made—78. ... Shares career record for most free throws attempted—98. ... Shares single-game record for most free throws made—12 (1962).

Season	Team	Min.	FGM	FGA	Pct.	FTM	FTA	Pct.	Reb	Ast.	PF	Dq.	Pts.
1959	—Minneapolis	32	10	20	.500	4	5	.800	11	1	3	0	24
1960	—Minneapolis	28	10	18	.556	5	7	.714	13	3	4	0	25
1961	—Los Angeles	27	3	11	.273	9	10	.900	10	4	5	0	15
1962	—Los Angeles	37	10	23	.435	12	14	.857	9	4	2	0	32
1963	—Los Angeles	36	4	15	.267	9	13	.692	14	7	0	0	17
1964	—Los Angeles	29	5	15	.333	5	11	.455	8	5	1	0	15
1965	—Los Angeles	27	5	13	.385	8	8	1.000	7	0	4	0	18
1967	—Los Angeles	20	8	14	.571	4	4	1.000	5	5	2	0	20
1968	—Los Angeles	27	8	13	.615	6	7	.857	6	1	5	0	22
1969	—Los Angeles	32	5	13	.385	11	12	.917	9	5	2	0	21
1970	—Los Angeles	26	2	9	.222	5	7	.714	7	3	3	0	9
Totals		321	70	164	.427	78	98	.796	99	38	31	0	218

NBA COACHING RECORD

BACKGROUND: Assistant coach, New Orleans Jazz (1974-75 and 1975-76).

		REGULAR SEASON				PLAYOFFS		
Season	Team	W	L	Pct.	Finish	W	L	Pct.
74-75	—New Orleans	0	1	.000		—	—	—
76-77	—New Orleans	21	35	.375	5th/Central Division	—	—	—
77-78	—New Orleans	39	43	.476	5th/Central Division	—	—	—
78-79	—New Orleans	26	56	.317	6th/Central Division	—	—	—
Totals (4 years)		86	135	.389				

NOTES:

1974—Replaced Scotty Robertson as New Orleans head coach (November), with record of 1-14; replaced as New Orleans head coach by Bill van Breda Kolff (November).

1976—Replaced Bill van Breda Kolff as New Orleans head coach (December), with record of 14-12.

BELLAMY, WALT   C

PERSONAL: Born July 24, 1939, in New Bern, N.C. ... 6-11/245 (2,11/111). ... Full name: Walter Jones Bellamy. ... Nickname: Bells.

HIGH SCHOOL: J.T. Barber (New Bern, N.C.).

COLLEGE: Indiana.

TRANSACTIONS: Selected by Chicago Packers in first round (first pick overall) of 1961 NBA Draft. ... Packers franchise renamed Zephyrs for 1962-63 season. ... Zephyrs franchise moved to Baltimore and renamed Bullets for 1963-64 season. ... Traded by Bullets to New York Knicks for F John Green, G John Egan, F/C Jim Barnes and cash (November 2, 1965). ... Traded by Knicks with G Howard Komives to Detroit Pistons for F Dave DeBusschere (December 19, 1968). ... Traded by Pistons to Atlanta Hawks for future considerations (February 1, 1970); Pistons received G John Arthurs from Milwaukee Bucks to complete deal. ... Selected by New Orleans Jazz from Hawks in NBA Expansion Draft (May 20, 1974). ... Waived by Jazz (October 18, 1974).

CAREER HONORS: Elected to Naismith Memorial Basketball Hall of Fame (1993).

MISCELLANEOUS: Member of gold-medal-winning U.S. Olympic Team (1960).

COLLEGIATE RECORD

NOTES: The Sporting News All-America second team (1961).

												AVERAGES		
Season Team	G	Min.	FGM	FGA	Pct.	FTM	FTA	Pct.	Reb.	Ast.	Pts.	RPG	APG	PPG
57-58—Indiana‡					Freshman team did not play intercollegiate schedule.									
58-59—Indiana	22	...	148	289	.512	86	141	.610	335	...	382	15.2	...	17.4
59-60—Indiana	24	...	212	396	.535	113	161	.702	324	...	537	13.5	...	22.4
60-61—Indiana	24	...	195	389	.501	132	204	.647	428	...	522	17.8	...	21.8
Varsity totals	70	...	555	1074	.517	331	506	.654	1087	...	1441	15.5	...	20.6

NBA REGULAR-SEASON RECORD

RECORDS: Holds single-season record for most games played—88 (1969).

HONORS: NBA Rookie of the Year (1962).

														AVERAGES		
Season Team	G	Min.	FGM	FGA	Pct.	FTM	FTA	Pct.	Reb.	Ast.	PF	Dq.	Pts.	RPG	APG	PPG
61-62 —Chicago	79	3344	973	1875	*.519	549	853	.644	1500	210	281	6	2495	19.0	2.7	31.6
62-63 —Chicago	80	3306	840	1595	.527	553	821	.674	1309	233	283	7	2233	16.4	2.9	27.9
63-64 —Baltimore	80	3394	811	1582	.513	537	825	.651	1361	126	300	7	2159	17.0	1.6	27.0
64-65 —Baltimore	80	3301	733	1441	.509	515	752	.685	1166	191	260	2	1981	14.6	2.4	24.8
65-66 —Balt.-N.Y.	80	3352	695	1373	.506	430	689	.624	1254	235	294	9	1820	15.7	2.9	22.8
66-67 —New York	79	3010	565	1084	.521	369	580	.636	1064	206	275	5	1499	13.5	2.6	19.0
67-68 —New York	82	2695	511	944	.541	350	529	.662	961	164	259	3	1372	11.7	2.0	16.7
68-69 —N.Y.-Detroit	88	3159	563	1103	.510	401	618	.649	1101	176	320	5	1527	12.5	2.0	17.4
69-70 —Detroit-Atl.	79	2028	351	671	.523	215	373	.576	707	143	260	5	917	8.9	1.8	11.6
70-71 —Atlanta	82	2908	433	879	.493	336	556	.604	1060	230	271	4	1202	12.9	2.8	14.7
71-72 —Atlanta	82	3187	593	1089	.545	340	585	.581	1049	262	255	2	1526	12.8	3.2	18.6
72-73 —Atlanta	74	2802	455	901	.505	283	526	.538	964	179	244	1	1193	13.0	2.4	16.1

ALL-TIME GREAT PLAYERS

Season Team	G	Min.	FGM	FGA	Pct.	FTM	FTA	Pct.	REBOUNDS Off.	Def.	Tot.	Ast.	St.	Blk.	TO	Pts.	AVERAGES RPG	APG	PPG
73-74—Atlanta	77	2440	389	801	.486	233	383	.608	264	476	740	189	52	48	...	1011	9.6	2.5	13.1
74-75—New Orleans	1	14	2	2	1.000	2	2	1.000	0	5	5	0	0	0	...	6	5.0	0.0	6.0
Totals	1043	38940	7914	15340	.516	5113	8088	.632	...	...	14241	2544	52	48	...	20941	13.7	2.4	20.1

Personal fouls/disqualifications: 1973-74, 232/2. 1974-75, 2/0. Totals, 3536/58.

NBA PLAYOFF RECORD

Season Team	G	Min.	FGM	FGA	Pct.	FTM	FTA	Pct.	Reb.	Ast.	PF	Dq.	Pts.	AVERAGES RPG	APG	PPG
64-65 —Baltimore	10	427	74	158	.468	61	92	.663	151	34	38	0	209	15.1	3.4	20.9
66-67 —New York	4	157	28	54	.519	17	29	.586	66	12	15	0	73	16.5	3.0	18.3
67-68 —New York	6	277	45	107	.421	30	48	.625	96	21	22	0	120	16.0	3.5	20.0
69-70 —Atlanta	9	368	59	126	.468	33	46	.717	140	35	32	0	151	15.6	3.9	16.8
70-71 —Atlanta	5	216	41	69	.594	22	29	.759	72	10	16	0	104	14.4	2.0	20.8
71-72 —Atlanta	6	247	42	86	.488	27	43	.628	82	11	20	0	111	13.7	1.8	18.5
72-73 —Atlanta	6	247	34	86	.395	14	31	.452	73	13	17	0	82	12.2	2.2	13.7
Totals	46	1939	323	686	.471	204	318	.642	680	136	160	0	850	14.8	3.0	18.5

NBA ALL-STAR GAME RECORD

Season Team	Min.	FGM	FGA	Pct.	FTM	FTA	Pct.	Reb	Ast.	PF	Dq.	Pts.
1962 —Chicago	29	10	18	.556	3	8	.375	17	1	6	1	23
1963 —Chicago	14	1	4	.250	0	2	.000	1	2	3	0	2
1964 —Baltimore	23	4	11	.364	3	5	.600	7	0	3	0	11
1965 —Baltimore	17	4	5	.800	4	4	1.000	5	1	3	0	12
Totals	83	19	38	.500	10	19	.526	30	4	15	1	48

BING, DAVE   G

PERSONAL: Born November 24, 1943, in Washington, D.C. ... 6-3/185 (1,90/84). ... Full name: David Bing.
HIGH SCHOOL: Spingarn (Washington, D.C.).
COLLEGE: Syracuse.
TRANSACTIONS: Selected by Detroit Pistons in first round (second pick overall) of 1966 NBA Draft. ... Traded by Pistons with 1977 first-round draft choice to Washington Bullets for G Kevin Porter (August 28, 1975). ... Waived by Bullets (September 20, 1977). ... Signed as free agent by Boston Celtics (September 28, 1977).
CAREER HONORS: Elected to Naismith Memorial Basketball Hall of Fame (1990). ... One of the 50 Greatest Players in NBA History (1996).

COLLEGIATE RECORD

NOTES: THE SPORTING NEWS All-America first team (1966).

Season Team	G	Min.	FGM	FGA	Pct.	FTM	FTA	Pct.	Reb.	Ast.	Pts.	AVERAGES RPG	APG	PPG
62-63—Syracuse‡	17	...	170	341	.499	97	131	.740	192	...	437	11.3	...	25.7
63-64—Syracuse	25	...	215	460	.467	126	172	.733	206	...	556	8.2	...	22.2
64-65—Syracuse	23	...	206	444	.464	121	162	.747	277	...	533	12.0	...	23.2
65-66—Syracuse	28	...	308	569	.541	178	222	.802	303	...	794	10.8	...	28.4
Varsity totals	76	...	729	1473	.495	425	556	.764	786	...	1883	10.3	...	24.8

NBA REGULAR-SEASON RECORD

HONORS: NBA Rookie of the Year (1967). ... All-NBA first team (1968, 1971). ... All-NBA second team (1974). ... NBA All-Rookie team (1967). ... J. Walter Kennedy Citizenship Award (1977).

Season Team	G	Min.	FGM	FGA	Pct.	FTM	FTA	Pct.	Reb.	Ast.	PF	Dq.	Pts.	AVERAGES RPG	APG	PPG
66-67 —Detroit	80	2762	664	1522	.436	273	370	.738	359	330	217	2	1601	4.5	4.1	20.0
67-68 —Detroit	79	3209	*835	*1893	.441	472	668	.707	373	509	254	2	*2142	4.7	6.4	*27.1
68-69 —Detroit	77	3039	678	1594	.425	444	623	.713	382	546	256	3	1800	5.0	7.1	23.4
69-70 —Detroit	70	2334	575	1295	.444	454	580	.783	299	418	196	0	1604	4.3	6.0	22.9
70-71 —Detroit	82	3065	799	1710	.467	*615	*772	.797	364	408	228	4	2213	4.4	5.0	27.0
71-72 —Detroit	45	1936	369	891	.414	278	354	.785	186	317	138	3	1016	4.1	7.0	22.6
72-73 —Detroit	82	3361	692	1545	.448	456	560	.814	298	637	229	1	1840	3.6	7.8	22.4

Season Team	G	Min.	FGM	FGA	Pct.	FTM	FTA	Pct.	REBOUNDS Off.	Def.	Tot.	Ast.	St.	Blk.	TO	Pts.	AVERAGES RPG	APG	PPG
73-74—Detroit	81	3124	582	1336	.436	356	438	.813	108	173	281	555	109	17	...	1520	3.5	6.9	18.8
74-75—Detroit	79	3222	578	1333	.434	343	424	.009	80	200	286	610	116	26	...	1499	3.6	7.7	19.0
75-76—Washington	82	2945	497	1113	.447	332	422	.787	94	143	237	492	118	23	...	1326	2.9	6.0	16.2
76-77—Washington	64	1516	271	597	.454	136	176	.773	54	89	143	275	61	5	...	678	2.2	4.3	10.6
77-78—Boston	80	2256	422	940	.449	244	296	.824	76	136	212	300	79	18	216	1088	2.7	3.8	13.6
Totals	901	32769	6962	15769	.441	4403	5683	.775	...	...	3420	5397	483	89	216	18327	3.8	6.0	20.3

Personal fouls/disqualifications: 1973-74, 216/1. 1974-75, 222/3. 1975-76, 262/0. 1976-77, 150/1. 1977-78, 247/2. Totals, 2615/22.

NBA PLAYOFF RECORD

Season Team	G	Min.	FGM	FGA	Pct.	FTM	FTA	Pct.	REBOUNDS Off.	Def.	Tot.	Ast.	St.	Blk.	TO	Pts.	AVERAGES RPG	APG	PPG
67-68—Detroit	6	254	68	166	.410	33	45	.733	...	...	24	29	...	...	...	169	4.0	4.8	28.2
73-74—Detroit	7	312	55	131	.420	22	30	.733	6	20	26	42	3	1	...	132	3.7	6.0	18.9
74-75—Detroit	3	134	20	47	.426	8	13	.615	3	8	11	29	5	0	...	48	3.7	9.7	16.0
75-76—Washington	7	209	34	76	.447	28	35	.800	6	12	18	28	7	2	...	96	2.6	4.0	13.7
76-77—Washington	8	55	14	32	.438	4	4	1.000	3	3	6	5	0	1	...	32	0.8	0.6	4.0
Totals	31	964	191	452	.423	95	127	.748	...	...	85	133	15	4	...	477	2.7	4.3	15.4

Personal fouls/disqualifications: 1967-68, 21/0. 1973-74, 20/0. 1974-75, 12/0. 1975-76, 18/0. 1976-77, 5/0. Totals, 76/0.

NOTES: NBA All-Star Game Most Valuable Player (1976).

Season	Team	Min.	FGM	FGA	Pct.	FTM	FTA	Pct.	Reb	Ast.	PF	Dq.	Pts.
1968	—Detroit	20	4	7	.571	1	1	1.000	2	4	3	0	9
1969	—Detroit	13	1	3	.333	1	1	1.000	0	3	0	0	3
1971	—Detroit	19	2	7	.286	0	0	...	2	2	1	0	4
1973	—Detroit	19	0	4	.000	2	2	1.000	3	0	1	0	2

									REBOUNDS							
Season	Team	Min.	FGM	FGA	Pct.	FTM	FTA	Pct.	Off.	Def.	Tot.	Ast.	PF	Dq.	St.	Blk.	TO	Pts.
1974	—Detroit	16	2	9	.222	1	1	1.000	1	5	6	2	1	0	0	0	...	5
1975	—Detroit	12	0	2	.000	2	2	1.000	0	0	0	1	0	0	0	0	...	2
1976	—Washington	26	7	11	.636	2	2	1.000	1	2	3	4	1	0	0	0	...	16
Totals		125	16	43	.372	9	9	1.000	...	...	16	16	7	0	0	0	...	41

BIRD, LARRY

PERSONAL: Born December 7, 1956, in West Baden, Ind. ... 6-9/220 (2,05/99,8). ... Full name: Larry Joe Bird.
HIGH SCHOOL: Springs Valley (French Lick, Ind.).
COLLEGE: Indiana, then Northwood Institute (Ind.), then Indiana State.
TRANSACTIONS: Selected after junior season by Boston Celtics in first round (sixth pick overall) of 1978 NBA Draft. ... Announced retirement (August 18, 1992).
CAREER HONORS: Elected to Naismith Memorial Basketball Hall of Fame (1998). ... One of the 50 Greatest Players in NBA History (1996).
MISCELLANEOUS: Member of NBA championship team (1981, 1984, 1986). ... Member of gold-medal-winning U.S. Olympic team (1992). ... Boston Celtics all-time steals leader with 1,556 (1979-80 through 1991-92).

COLLEGIATE RECORD

NOTES: THE SPORTING NEWS College Player of the Year (1979). ... Naismith Award winner (1979). ... Wooden Award winner (1979). ... THE SPORTING NEWS All-America first team (1978, 1979).

												AVERAGES		
Season Team	G	Min.	FGM	FGA	Pct.	FTM	FTA	Pct.	Reb.	Ast.	Pts.	RPG	APG	PPG
74-75—Indiana						Did not play.								
75-76—Indiana State						Did not play—transfer student.								
76-77—Indiana State	28	1033	375	689	.544	168	200	.840	373	122	918	13.3	4.4	32.8
77-78—Indiana State	32	...	403	769	.524	153	193	.793	369	125	959	11.5	3.9	30.0
78-79—Indiana State	34	...	376	707	.532	221	266	.831	505	187	973	14.9	5.5	28.6
Totals	94	...	1154	2165	.533	542	659	.822	1247	434	2850	13.3	4.6	30.3

NBA REGULAR-SEASON RECORD

HONORS: NBA Most Valuable Player (1984, 1985, 1986). ... NBA Rookie of the Year (1980). ... All-NBA first team (1980, 1981, 1982, 1983, 1984, 1985, 1986, 1987, 1988). ... All-NBA second team (1990). ... NBA All-Defensive second team (1982, 1983, 1984). ... NBA All-Rookie team (1980). ... Long Distance Shootout winner (1986, 1987, 1988).

									REBOUNDS								AVERAGES		
Season Team	G	Min.	FGM	FGA	Pct.	FTM	FTA	Pct.	Off.	Def.	Tot.	Ast.	St.	Blk.	TO	Pts.	RPG	APG	PPG
79-80—Boston	82	2955	693	1463	.474	301	360	.836	216	636	852	370	143	53	263	1745	10.4	4.5	21.3
80-81—Boston	82	3239	719	1503	.478	283	328	.863	191	704	895	451	161	63	289	1741	10.9	5.5	21.2
81-82—Boston	77	2923	711	1414	.503	328	380	.863	200	637	837	447	143	66	254	1761	10.9	5.8	22.9
82-83—Boston	79	2982	747	1481	.504	351	418	.840	193	677	870	458	148	71	240	1867	11.0	5.8	23.6
83-84—Boston	79	3028	758	1542	.492	374	421 *.888		181	615	796	520	144	69	237	1908	10.1	6.6	24.2
84-85—Boston	80	3161	918	1760	.522	403	457	.882	164	678	842	531	129	98	248	2295	10.5	6.6	28.7
85-86—Boston	82	3113	796	1606	.496	441	492 *.896		190	615	805	557	166	51	266	2115	9.8	6.8	25.8
86-87—Boston	74	3005	786	1497	.525	414	455 *.910		124	558	682	566	135	70	240	2076	9.2	7.6	28.1
87-88—Boston	76	2965	881	1672	.527	415	453	.916	108	595	703	467	125	57	213	2275	9.3	6.1	29.9
88-89—Boston	6	189	49	104	.471	18	19	.947	1	36	37	29	6	5	11	116	6.2	4.8	19.3
89-90—Boston	75	2944	718	1517	.473	319	343 *.930		90	622	712	562	106	61	243	1820	9.5	7.5	24.3
90-91—Boston	60	2277	462	1017	.454	163	183	.891	53	456	509	431	108	58	187	1164	8.5	7.2	19.4
91-92—Boston	45	1662	353	758	.466	150	162	.926	46	388	434	306	42	33	125	908	9.6	6.8	20.2
Totals	897	34443	8591	17334	.496	3960	4471	.886	1757	7217	8974	5695	1556	755	2816	21791	10.0	6.3	24.3

Three-point field goals: 1979-80, 58-for-143 (.406). 1980-81, 20-for-74 (.270). 1981-82, 11-for-52 (.212). 1982-83, 22-for-77 (.286). 1983-84, 18-for-73 (.247). 1984-85, 56-for-131 (.427). 1985-86, 82-for-194 (.423). 1986-87, 90-for-225 (.400). 1987-88, 98-for-237 (.414). 1989-90, 65-for-195 (.333). 1990-91, 77-for-198 (.389). 1991-92, 52-for-128 (.406). Totals, 649-for-1727 (.376).

Personal fouls/disqualifications: 1979-80, 279/4. 1980-81, 239/2. 1981-82, 244/0. 1982-83, 197/0. 1983-84, 197/0. 1984-85, 208/0. 1985-86, 182/0. 1986-87, 185/3. 1987-88, 157/0. 1988-89, 18/0. 1989-90, 173/2. 1990-91, 118/0. 1991-92, 82/0. Totals, 2279/11.

NBA PLAYOFF RECORD

NOTES: NBA Finals Most Valuable Player (1984, 1986). ... Holds career playoff record for most defensive rebounds—1,323.

									REBOUNDS								AVERAGES		
Season Team	G	Min.	FGM	FGA	Pct.	FTM	FTA	Pct.	Off.	Def.	Tot.	Ast.	St.	Blk.	TO	Pts.	RPG	APG	PPG
79-80—Boston	9	372	83	177	.469	22	25	.880	22	79	101	42	14	8	33	192	11.2	4.7	21.3
80-81—Boston	17	750	147	313	.470	76	85	.894	49	189	238	103	39	17	62	373	14.0	6.1	21.9
81-82—Boston	12	490	88	206	.427	37	45	.822	33	117	150	67	23	17	38	214	12.5	5.6	17.8
82-83—Boston	6	240	49	116	.422	24	29	.828	20	55	75	41	13	3	19	123	12.5	6.8	20.5
83-84—Boston	23	961	229	437	.524	167	190	.879	62	190	252	136	54	27	87	632	11.0	5.9	27.5
84-85—Boston	20	815	196	425	.461	121	136	.890	53	129	182	115	34	19	57	520	9.1	5.8	26.0
85-86—Boston	18	770	171	331	.517	101	109	.927	34	134	168	148	37	11	47	466	9.3	8.2	25.9
86-87—Boston	23	1015	216	454	.476	176	193	.912	41	190	231	165	27	19	71	622	10.0	7.2	27.0
87-88—Boston	17	763	152	338	.450	101	113	.894	29	121	150	115	36	14	49	417	8.8	6.8	24.5
89-90—Boston	5	207	44	99	.444	29	32	.906	7	39	46	44	5	5	18	122	9.2	8.8	24.4
90-91—Boston	10	396	62	152	.408	44	51	.863	8	64	72	65	13	3	19	171	7.2	6.5	17.1
91-92—Boston	4	107	21	42	.500	3	4	.750	2	16	18	21	1	2	6	45	4.5	5.3	11.3
Totals	164	6886	1458	3090	.472	901	1012	.890	360	1323	1683	1062	296	145	506	3897	10.3	6.5	23.8

Three-point field goals: 1979-80, 4-for-15 (.267). 1980-81, 3-for-8 (.375). 1981-82, 1-for-6 (.167). 1982-83, 1-for-4 (.250). 1983-84, 7-for-17 (.412). 1984-85, 7-for-25 (.280). 1985-86, 23-for-56 (.411). 1986-87, 14-for-41 (.341). 1987-88, 12-for-32 (.375). 1989-90, 5-for-19 (.263). 1990-91, 3-for-21 (.143). 1991-92, 0-for-5. Totals, 80-for-249 (.321).

Personal fouls/disqualifications: 1979-80, 30/0. 1980-81, 53/0. 1981-82, 43/0. 1982-83, 15/0. 1983-84, 71/0. 1984-85, 54/0. 1985-86, 55/0. 1986-87, 55/1. 1987-88, 45/0. 1989-90, 10/0. 1990-91, 28/0. 1991-92, 7/0. Totals, 466/1.

NBA ALL-STAR GAME RECORD

NOTES: NBA All-Star Game Most Valuable Player (1982).

								REBOUNDS									
Season Team	Min.	FGM	FGA	Pct.	FTM	FTA	Pct.	Off.	Def.	Tot.	Ast.	PF	Dq.	St.	Blk.	TO	Pts.
1980 —Boston.............	23	3	6	.500	0	0	...	3	3	6	7	1	0	1	0	3	7
1981 —Boston.............	18	1	5	.200	0	0	...	1	3	4	3	1	0	1	0	2	2
1982 —Boston.............	28	7	12	.583	5	8	.625	0	12	12	5	3	0	1	1	4	19
1983 —Boston.............	29	7	14	.500	0	0	...	3	10	13	7	4	0	2	0	5	14
1984 —Boston.............	33	6	18	.333	4	4	1.000	1	6	7	3	1	0	2	0	2	16
1985 —Boston.............	31	8	16	.500	5	6	.833	5	3	8	2	3	0	1	4	21
1986 —Boston.............	35	8	18	.444	5	6	.833	2	6	8	5	5	0	7	0	4	23
1987 —Boston.............	35	7	18	.389	4	4	1.000	2	4	6	5	5	0	2	0	2	18
1988 —Boston.............	32	2	8	.250	2	2	1.000	0	7	7	1	4	0	4	1	2	6
1990 —Boston.............	23	3	8	.375	2	2	1.000	2	6	8	3	1	0	3	0	3	8
1991 —Boston							Selected, did not play—injured.										
1992 —Boston							Selected, did not play—injured.										
Totals...........................	287	52	123	.423	27	32	.844	19	60	79	41	28	0	23	3	31	134

Three-point field goals: 1980, 1-for-2 (.500). 1983, 0-for-1. 1985, 0-for-1. 1986, 2-for-4 (.500). 1987, 0-for-3. 1988, 0-for-1. 1990, 0-for-1. Totals, 3-for-13 (.231).

HEAD COACHING RECORD

BACKGROUND: Special assistant, Boston Celtics (1992-93 through 1996-97).

NBA COACHING RECORD

HONORS: NBA Coach of the Year (1998).

	REGULAR SEASON				PLAYOFFS		
Season Team	W	L	Pct.	Finish	W	L	Pct.
97-98 —Indiana	58	24	.707	2nd/Central Division	10	6	.625
98-99 —Indiana	33	17	.660	1st/Central Division	9	4	.692
99-00 —Indiana	56	26	.683	1st/Central Division	13	10	.565
Totals (3 years)......................................	147	67	.687	Totals (3 years).......	32	20	.615

NOTES:
1998—Defeated Cleveland, 3-1, in Eastern Conference First Round; defeated New York, 4-1, in Eastern Conference Semifinals; lost to Chicago, 4-3, in Eastern Conference Finals.

1999—Defeated Milwaukee, 3-0, in Eastern Conference First Round; defeated Philadelphia, 4-0, in Eastern Conference Semifinals; lost to New York, 4-2, in Eastern Conference Finals.

2000—Defeated Milwaukee, 3-2, in Eastern Conference First Round; defeated Philadelphia, 4-2, in Eastern Conference Semifinals; defeated New York, 4-2, in Eastern Conference Finals; lost to Los Angeles Lakers, 4-2, in NBA Finals.

BLACKMAN, ROLANDO   G

PERSONAL: Born February 26, 1959, in Panama City, Panama. ... 6-6/206 (1,98/93,4). ... Full name: Rolando Antonio Blackman. ... Name pronounced roll-ON-doe.
HIGH SCHOOL: William E. Grady Vocational Technical School (Brooklyn, N.Y.).
COLLEGE: Kansas State.
TRANSACTIONS: Selected by Dallas Mavericks in first round (ninth pick overall) of 1981 NBA Draft. ... Traded by Mavericks to New York Knicks for 1995 first-round draft choice (June 24, 1992). ... Waived by Knicks (July 4, 1994). ... Played in Greece (1994-95). ... Played in Italy (1995-96).
CAREER NOTES: Player development, Dallas Mavericks (2000-01-present).
MISCELLANEOUS: Member of U.S. Olympic team (1980). ... Dallas Mavericks all-time leading scorer with 16,643 points (1981-82 through 1991-92).

COLLEGIATE RECORD

NOTES: THE SPORTING NEWS All-America first team (1981).

													AVERAGES		
Season Team	G	Min.	FGM	FGA	Pct.	FTM	FTA	Pct.	Reb.	Ast.	Pts.		RPG	APG	PPG
77-78—Kansas State	29	967	127	269	.472	61	93	.656	187	45	315		6.4	1.6	10.9
78-79—Kansas State	28	1056	200	392	.510	83	113	.735	110	79	483		3.9	2.8	17.3
79-80—Kansas State	31	1103	226	419	.539	100	145	.690	145	97	552		4.7	3.1	17.8
80-81—Kansas State	33	1239	202	380	.532	90	115	.783	165	102	494		5.0	3.1	15.0
Totals	121	4365	755	1460	.517	334	466	.717	607	323	1844		5.0	2.7	15.2

NBA REGULAR-SEASON RECORD

									REBOUNDS								AVERAGES		
Season Team	G	Min.	FGM	FGA	Pct.	FTM	FTA	Pct.	Off.	Def.	Tot.	Ast.	St.	Blk.	TO	Pts.	RPG	APG	PPG
81-82—Dallas.............	82	1979	439	855	.513	212	276	.768	97	157	254	105	46	30	113	1091	3.1	1.3	13.3
82-83—Dallas.............	75	2349	513	1042	.492	297	381	.780	108	185	293	185	37	29	118	1326	3.9	2.5	17.7
83-84—Dallas.............	81	3025	721	1320	.546	372	458	.812	124	249	373	288	56	37	169	1815	4.6	3.6	22.4
84-85—Dallas.............	81	2834	625	1230	.508	342	413	.828	107	193	300	289	61	16	162	1598	3.7	3.6	19.7
85-86—Dallas.............	82	2787	677	1318	.514	404	483	.836	88	203	291	271	79	25	189	1762	3.5	3.3	21.5
86-87—Dallas.............	80	2758	626	1264	.495	419	474	.884	96	182	278	266	64	21	174	1676	3.5	3.3	21.0
87-88—Dallas.............	71	2580	497	1050	.473	331	379	.873	82	164	246	262	64	18	144	1325	3.5	3.7	18.7
88-89—Dallas.............	78	2946	594	1249	.476	316	370	.854	70	203	273	288	65	20	165	1534	3.5	3.7	19.7
89-90—Dallas.............	80	2934	626	1256	.498	287	340	.844	88	192	280	289	77	21	174	1552	3.5	3.6	19.4
90-91—Dallas.............	80	2965	634	1316	.482	282	326	.865	63	193	256	301	69	19	159	1590	3.2	3.8	19.9
91-92—Dallas.............	75	2527	535	1161	.461	239	266	.899	78	161	239	204	50	22	153	1374	3.2	2.7	18.3
92-93—New York........	60	1434	239	539	.443	71	90	.789	23	79	102	157	22	10	65	580	1.7	2.6	9.7
93-94—New York........	55	969	161	369	.436	48	53	.906	23	70	93	76	25	6	44	400	1.7	1.4	7.3
Totals	980	32087	6887	13969	.493	3620	4309	.840	1047	2231	3278	2981	715	274	1829	17623	3.3	3.0	18.0

Three-point field goals: 1981-82, 1-for-4 (.250). 1982-83, 3-for-15 (.200). 1983-84, 1-for-11 (.091). 1984-85, 6-for-20 (.300). 1985-86, 4-for-29 (.138). 1986-87, 5-for-15 (.333). 1987-88, 0-for-5. 1988-89, 30-for-85 (.353). 1989-90, 13-for-43 (.302). 1990-91, 40-for-114 (.351). 1991-92, 65-for-169 (.385). 1992-93, 31-for-73 (.425). 1993-94, 30-for-84 (.357). Totals, 229-for-667 (.343).

Personal fouls/disqualifications: 1981-82, 122/0. 1982-83, 116/0. 1983-84, 127/0. 1984-85, 96/0. 1985-86, 138/0. 1986-87, 142/0. 1987-88, 112/0. 1988-89, 137/0. 1989-90, 128/0. 1990-91, 153/0. 1991-92, 134/0. 1992-93, 129/1. 1993-94, 100/0. Totals, 1634/1.

NBA PLAYOFF RECORD

Season Team	G	Min.	FGM	FGA	Pct.	FTM	FTA	Pct.	REBOUNDS Off.	Def.	Tot.	Ast.	St.	Blk.	TO	Pts.	AVERAGES RPG	APG	PPG
83-84—Dallas	10	397	93	175	.531	53	63	.841	15	26	41	40	6	4	24	239	4.1	4.0	23.9
84-85—Dallas	4	169	47	92	.511	36	38	.947	11	15	26	19	2	2	14	131	6.5	4.8	32.8
85-86—Dallas	10	371	83	167	.497	42	53	.792	15	20	35	32	8	1	20	208	3.5	3.2	20.8
86-87—Dallas	4	153	36	73	.493	22	24	.917	4	10	14	17	2	0	8	94	3.5	4.3	23.5
87-88—Dallas	17	672	126	261	.483	55	62	.887	26	29	55	77	15	3	25	307	3.2	4.5	18.1
89-90—Dallas	3	127	24	54	.444	10	10	1.000	2	7	9	13	6	2	13	60	3.0	4.3	20.0
92-93—New York	15	214	22	64	.344	15	18	.833	4	13	17	16	3	2	21	63	1.1	1.1	4.2
93-94—New York	6	34	3	11	.273	0	0	...	1	2	3	3	0	0	1	8	0.5	0.5	1.3
Totals	69	2137	434	897	.484	233	268	.869	78	122	200	217	42	14	126	1110	2.9	3.1	16.1

Three-point field goals: 1984-85, 1-for-2 (.500). 1985-86, 0-for-1. 1986-87, 0-for-1. 1987-88, 0-for-3. 1989-90, 2-for-5 (.400). 1992-93, 4-for-15 (.267). 1993-94, 2-for-4 (.500). Totals, 9-for-31 (.290).

Personal fouls/disqualifications: 1983-84, 15/0. 1984-85, 8/0. 1985-86, 26/1. 1986-87, 7/0. 1987-88, 28/0. 1989-90, 7/0. 1992-93, 22/0. 1993-94, 6/0. Totals, 119/1.

NBA ALL-STAR GAME RECORD

Season Team	Min.	FGM	FGA	Pct.	FTM	FTA	Pct.	REBOUNDS Off.	Def.	Tot.	Ast.	PF	Dq.	St.	Blk.	TO	Pts.
1985 —Dallas	23	7	14	.500	1	2	.500	1	2	3	2	1	0	1	1	0	15
1986 —Dallas	22	6	11	.545	0	0	...	1	3	4	8	1	0	2	1	1	12
1987 —Dallas	22	9	15	.600	11	13	.846	1	3	4	1	2	0	0	0	2	29
1990 —Dallas	21	7	9	.778	1	1	1.000	1	1	2	2	1	0	2	0	2	15
Totals	88	29	49	.592	13	16	.813	4	9	13	13	5	0	5	2	5	71

GREEK LEAGUE RECORD

Season Team	G	Min.	FGM	FGA	Pct.	FTM	FTA	Pct.	Reb.	Ast.	Pts.	AVERAGES RPG	APG	PPG
94-95—A.E.K.	14	...	69	150	.460	55	63	.873	...	19	265	...	1.4	18.9

ITALIAN LEAGUE RECORD

Season Team	G	Min.	FGM	FGA	Pct.	FTM	FTA	Pct.	Reb.	Ast.	Pts.	AVERAGES RPG	APG	PPG
95-96—Stefanel Milano	24	...	...	...	...	...	...	...	62	19	383	2.6	0.8	15.9

BOONE, RON   G

PERSONAL: Born September 6, 1946, in Oklahoma City. ... 6-2/200 (1,88/90,7). ... Full name: Ronald Bruce Boone.
HIGH SCHOOL: Tech (Omaha, Neb.).
JUNIOR COLLEGE: Iowa Western Community College.
COLLEGE: Idaho State.
TRANSACTIONS: Selected by Phoenix Suns in 11th round (147th pick overall) of 1968 NBA Draft. ... Selected by Dallas Chaparrals in eighth round of 1968 ABA Draft. ... Traded by Chaparrals with G Glen Combs to Utah Stars for G Donnie Freeman and C Wayne Hightower (January 8, 1971). ... Contract sold by Stars to Spirits of St. Louis (December 2, 1975). ... Selected by Kansas City Kings of NBA from Spirits in ABA dispersal draft (August 5, 1976). ... Traded by Kings with 1979 second-round draft choice to Denver Nuggets for F Darnell Hillman and draft rights to G Mike Evans (June 26, 1978). ... Traded by Nuggets with two 1979 second-round draft choices to Los Angeles Lakers for G Charlie Scott (June 26, 1978). ... Traded by Lakers to Utah Jazz for 1981 third-round draft choice (October 25, 1979). ... Waived by Jazz (January 26, 1981).

COLLEGIATE RECORD

Season Team	G	Min.	FGM	FGA	Pct.	FTM	FTA	Pct.	Reb.	Ast.	Pts.	AVERAGES RPG	APG	PPG
64-65—Iowa Western C.C.	9	...	...	...	...	...	...	...	...	...	227	...	...	25.2
65-66—Idaho State	10	...	46	119	.387	17	26	.654	95	...	109	9.5	...	10.9
66-67—Idaho State	25	...	199	416	.478	160	215	.744	128	...	558	5.1	...	22.3
67-68—Idaho State	26	...	223	519	.430	108	159	.679	110	...	554	4.2	...	21.3
Junior college totals	9	...	...	...	...	...	...	...	...	...	227	...	...	25.2
4-year-college totals	61	...	468	1054	.444	285	400	.713	333	...	1221	5.5	...	20.0

ABA REGULAR-SEASON RECORD

NOTES: ABA All-Star first team (1975). ... ABA All-Star second team (1974). ... ABA All-Rookie team (1969). ... Member of ABA championship team (1971).

Season Team	G	Min.	2-POINT FGM	FGA	Pct.	3-POINT FGM	FGA	Pct.	FTM	FTA	Pct.	Reb.	Ast.	Pts.	AVERAGES RPG	APG	PPG
68-69—Dallas	78	2682	518	1182	.438	2	15	.133	436	537	.812	394	279	1478	5.1	3.6	18.9
69-70—Dallas	84	2340	406	925	.439	17	55	.309	300	382	.785	366	272	1163	4.4	3.2	13.8
70-71—Dallas-Utah	86	2476	561	1257	.446	49	138	.355	278	357	.779	564	256	1547	6.6	3.0	18.0
71-72—Utah	84	2040	391	897	.436	13	65	.200	271	341	.795	393	233	1092	4.7	2.8	13.0
72-73—Utah	84	2585	556	1096	.507	10	40	.250	415	479	.866	423	353	1557	5.0	4.2	18.5
73-74—Utah	84	3098	581	1162	.500	6	26	.231	300	343	.875	435	417	1480	5.2	5.0	17.6
74-75—Utah	84	3414	862	1743	.495	10	33	.303	363	422	.860	406	372	2117	4.8	4.4	25.2
75-76—Utah-St. Louis	78	2961	697	1424	.489	16	43	.372	277	318	.871	319	387	1719	4.1	5.0	22.0
Totals	662	21596	4572	9686	.472	123	415	.296	2640	3179	.830	3300	2569	12153	5.0	3.9	18.4

ABA PLAYOFF RECORD

| Season Team | G | Min. | 2-POINT | | | 3-POINT | | | FTM | FTA | Pct. | Reb. | Ast. | Pts. | AVERAGES | | |
			FGM	FGA	Pct.	FGM	FGA	Pct.							RPG	APG	PPG
68-69—Dallas	7	196	38	81	.469	0	4	.000	21	25	.840	22	27	97	3.1	3.9	13.9
69-70—Dallas	6	193	43	89	.483	3	8	.375	15	21	.714	27	27	110	4.5	4.5	18.3
70-71—Utah	18	569	104	229	.454	9	27	.333	74	86	.860	110	94	309	6.1	5.2	17.2
71-72—Utah	11	209	49	100	.490	1	5	.200	25	29	.862	24	26	126	2.2	2.4	11.5
72-73—Utah	10	360	68	132	.515	0	3	.000	33	34	.971	43	47	169	4.3	4.7	16.9
73-74—Utah	18	747	137	282	.486	0	7	.000	34	37	.919	108	109	308	6.0	6.1	17.1
74-75—Utah	6	219	54	127	.425	0	0	...	34	38	.895	24	41	142	4.0	6.8	23.7
Totals	76	2493	493	1040	.474	13	54	.241	236	270	.874	358	371	1261	4.7	4.9	16.6

ABA ALL-STAR GAME RECORD

| Season Team | Min. | 2-POINT | | | 3-POINT | | | FTM | FTA | Pct. | Reb. | Ast. | Pts. |
		FGM	FGA	Pct.	FGM	FGA	Pct.						
1971—Utah	4	2	4	.500	0	0	...	2	3	.667	2	0	6
1974—Utah	24	6	11	.545	1	2	.500	0	0	...	3	5	15
1975—Utah	23	4	8	.500	0	0	...	2	2	1.000	2	2	10
1976—St. Louis	16	5	11	.455	0	0	...	0	0	...	3	2	10
Totals	67	17	34	.500	1	2	.500	4	5	.800	10	9	41

NBA REGULAR-SEASON RECORD

| Season Team | G | Min. | FGM | FGA | Pct. | FTM | FTA | Pct. | REBOUNDS | | | Ast. | St. | Blk. | TO | Pts. | AVERAGES | | |
									Off.	Def.	Tot.						RPG	APG	PPG
76-77—Kansas City	82	3021	747	1577	.474	324	384	.844	128	193	321	338	119	19	...	1818	3.9	4.1	22.2
77-78—Kansas City	82	2653	563	1271	.443	322	377	.854	112	157	269	311	105	11	303	1448	3.3	3.8	17.7
78-79—Los Angeles	82	1583	259	569	.455	90	104	.865	53	92	145	154	66	11	147	608	1.8	1.9	7.4
79-80—L.A.-Utah	81	2392	405	915	.443	175	196	.893	54	173	227	309	97	3	197	1004	2.8	3.8	12.4
80-81—Utah	52	1146	160	371	.431	75	94	.798	17	67	84	161	33	8	111	406	1.6	3.1	7.8
Totals	379	10795	2134	4703	.454	986	1155	.854	364	682	1046	1273	420	52	758	5284	2.8	3.4	13.9

Three-point field goals: 1979-80, 19-for-50 (.380). 1980-81, 11-for-39 (.282). Totals, 30-for-89 (.337).
Personal fouls/disqualifications: 1976-77, 258/1. 1977-78, 233/3. 1978-79, 171/1. 1979-80, 232/3. 1980-81, 126/0. Totals, 1020/8.

NBA PLAYOFF RECORD

| Season Team | G | Min. | FGM | FGA | Pct. | FTM | FTA | Pct. | REBOUNDS | | | Ast. | St. | Blk. | TO | Pts. | AVERAGES | | |
									Off.	Def.	Tot.						RPG	APG	PPG
78-79—Los Angeles	8	226	37	77	.481	20	21	.952	7	8	15	14	9	0	14	94	1.9	1.8	11.8

Personal fouls/disqualifications: 1978-79, 28/0.

COMBINED ABA AND NBA REGULAR-SEASON RECORDS

| | G | Min. | FGM | FGA | Pct. | FTM | FTA | Pct. | REBOUNDS | | | Ast. | Stl. | Blk. | TO | Pts. | AVERAGES | | |
									Off.	Def.	Tot.						RPG	APG	PPG
Totals	1041	32391	6829	14804	.461	3626	4334	.837	...	...	4346	3842	...	...	...	17437	4.2	3.7	16.8

Three-point field goals: 153-for-504 (.304).

BRIAN, FRANK   G

PERSONAL: Born May 1, 1923, in Zachary, La. ... 6-1/180 (1,85/81,6). ... Full name: Frank Sands Brian. ... Nickname: Flash.
HIGH SCHOOL: Zachary (La.).
COLLEGE: Louisiana State.
TRANSACTIONS: Signed by Anderson of National Basketball League (1947). ... Selected by Chicago from Anderson in NBL dispersal draft (April 25, 1950). ... Traded by Chicago to Tri-Cities (1950). ... Traded by Tri-Cities to Fort Wayne for C/F Howie Schultz, F/C/G Dick Mehen and cash (May 31, 1951).
MISCELLANEOUS: Member of NBL championship team (1949).

COLLEGIATE RECORD

| Season Team | G | Min. | FGM | FGA | Pct. | FTM | FTA | Pct. | Reb. | Ast. | Pts. | AVERAGES | | |
												RPG	APG	PPG
42-43—Louisiana State	15	...	77	...	...	56	...	...	...	...	210	...	...	14.0
43-44—Louisiana State			Did not play—military service.											
44-45—Louisiana State			Did not play—military service.											
45-46—Louisiana State			Did not play—in military service.											
46-47—Louisiana State	21	...	127	...	...	86	...	...	...	...	340	...	...	16.2
Totals	36	...	204	...	...	142	...	...	...	...	550	...	...	15.3

NBL AND NBA REGULAR-SEASON RECORD

HONORS: All-NBA second team (1950, 1951). ... All-NBL first team (1949). ... All-NBL second team (1948).

| Season Team | G | Min. | FGM | FGA | Pct. | FTM | FTA | Pct. | Reb. | Ast. | PF | Dq. | Pts. | AVERAGES | | |
														RPG	APG	PPG
47-48—And. (NBL)	59	...	248	...	...	155	210	.738	...	...	148	...	651	...	...	11.0
48-49—And. (NBL)	64	...	216	...	...	201	256	.785	...	...	144	...	633	...	...	9.9
49-50—Anderson	64	...	368	1156	.318	402	488	*.824	...	189	192	...	1138	...	3.0	17.8
50-51—Tri-Cities	68	...	363	1127	.322	418	508	.823	244	266	215	4	1144	3.6	3.9	16.8
51-52—Fort Wayne	66	2672	342	972	.352	367	433	.848	232	233	220	6	1051	3.5	3.5	15.9
52-53—Fort Wayne	68	1910	245	699	.351	236	297	.795	133	142	205	8	726	2.0	2.1	10.7
53-54—Fort Wayne	64	973	132	352	.375	137	182	.753	79	92	100	2	401	1.2	1.4	6.3
54-55—Fort Wayne	71	1381	237	623	.380	217	255	.851	127	142	133	0	691	1.8	2.0	9.7
55-56—Fort Wayne	37	680	78	263	.297	72	88	.818	88	74	62	0	228	2.4	2.0	6.2
Totals	561	...	2229	...	...	2205	2717	.812	...	...	1419	...	6663	...	...	11.9

NBL AND NBA PLAYOFF RECORD

Season Team	G	Min.	FGM	FGA	Pct.	FTM	FTA	Pct.	Reb.	Ast.	PF	Dq.	Pts.	RPG	APG	PPG
47-48 —And. (NBL)	6	...	18	...	...	11	16	.688	...	...	...	...	47	...	...	7.8
48-49 —And. (NBL)	7	...	26	...	...	27	32	.844	...	...	...	...	79	...	...	11.3
49-50 —Anderson	8	...	26	96	.271	43	48	.896	...	19	24	...	95	...	2.4	11.9
51-52 —Fort Wayne	2	81	6	24	.250	5	6	.833	6	9	10	0	17	3.0	4.5	8.5
52-53 —Fort Wayne	8	146	13	42	.310	19	25	.760	9	11	23	1	45	1.1	1.4	5.6
53-54 —Fort Wayne	4	106	15	36	.417	11	16	.688	12	10	7	0	41	3.0	2.5	10.3
54-55 —Fort Wayne	11	269	48	120	.400	31	38	.816	22	27	26	0	127	2.0	2.5	11.5
55-56 —Fort Wayne	10	166	26	68	.382	17	21	.810	12	17	15	0	69	1.2	1.7	6.9
Totals	56	...	178	...	...	164	202	.812	...	...	...	...	520	...	...	9.3

NBA ALL-STAR GAME RECORD

Season Team	Min.	FGM	FGA	Pct.	FTM	FTA	Pct.	Reb	Ast.	PF	Dq.	Pts.
1951 —Tri-Cities	...	5	14	.357	4	5	.800	6	3	2	...	14
1952 —Fort Wayne	25	4	10	.400	5	6	.833	7	4	2	...	13
Totals	...	9	24	.375	9	11	.818	13	7	4	...	27

BRIDGES, BILL   F

PERSONAL: Born April 4, 1939, in Hobbs, N.M. ... 6-6/235 (1,98/106,6). ... Full name: William C. Bridges.
HIGH SCHOOL: Hobbs (N.M.).
COLLEGE: Kansas.
TRANSACTIONS: Selected by Chicago Packers in third round (32nd pick overall) of 1961 NBA Draft. ... Played in American Basketball League with Kansas City Steers (1961-62 and 1962-63). ... Draft rights traded by Packers with G Ralph Davis to St. Louis Hawks for G Al Ferrari and F Shellie McMillion (June 14, 1962). ... Hawks franchise moved to Atlanta for 1968-69 season. ... Traded by Hawks to Philadelphia 76ers for F/C Jim Washington (November 19, 1971). ... Traded by 76ers with C/F Mel Counts to Los Angeles Lakers for F/C Leroy Ellis and F John Q. Trapp (November 2, 1972). ... Waived by Lakers (December 6, 1974). ... Signed as free agent by Golden State Warriors (March 1, 1975).
MISCELLANEOUS: Member of NBA championship team (1975).

COLLEGIATE RECORD

Season Team	G	Min.	FGM	FGA	Pct.	FTM	FTA	Pct.	Reb.	Ast.	Pts.	RPG	APG	PPG
57-58—Kansas‡					Freshman team did not play intercollegiate schedule.									
58-59—Kansas	25	...	117	307	.381	74	129	.574	343	...	308	13.7	...	12.3
59-60—Kansas	28	...	112	293	.382	94	142	.662	385	...	318	13.8	...	11.4
60-61—Kansas	25	...	146	334	.437	110	155	.710	353	...	402	14.1	...	16.1
Varsity totals	78	...	375	934	.401	278	426	.653	1081	...	1028	13.9	...	13.2

ABL REGULAR-SEASON RECORD

ABL: ABL All-Star first team (1962). ... Holds single-game record for most points—55 (December 9, 1962, vs. Oakland).

Season Team	G	Min.	FGM	FGA	Pct.	FTM	FTA	Pct.	Reb.	Ast.	Pts.	RPG	APG	PPG
61-62—Kansas City	79	3259	638	1400	.456	412	587	.702	*1059	181	1697	13.4	2.3	21.5
62-63—Kansas City	29	1185	312	606	.515	225	289	.779	*437	87	*849	15.1	3.0	29.3
Totals	108	4444	950	2006	.474	637	876	.727	1496	268	2546	13.9	2.5	23.6

NBA REGULAR-SEASON RECORD

HONORS: NBA All-Defensive second team (1969, 1970).

Season Team	G	Min.	FGM	FGA	Pct.	FTM	FTA	Pct.	Reb.	Ast.	PF	Dq.	Pts.	RPG	APG	PPG
62-63 —St. Louis	27	374	66	160	.413	32	51	.627	144	23	58	0	164	5.3	0.9	6.1
63-64 —St. Louis	80	1949	268	675	.397	146	224	.652	680	181	269	6	682	8.5	2.3	8.5
64-65 —St. Louis	79	2362	362	938	.386	186	275	.676	853	187	276	3	910	10.8	2.4	11.5
65-66 —St. Louis	78	2677	377	927	.407	257	364	.706	951	208	333	11	1011	12.2	2.7	13.0
66-67 —St. Louis	79	3130	503	1106	.455	367	523	.702	1190	222	325	12	1373	15.1	2.8	17.4
67-68 —St. Louis	82	3197	466	1009	.462	347	484	.717	1102	253	*366	12	1279	13.4	3.1	15.6
68-69 —Atlanta	80	2930	351	775	.453	239	353	.677	1132	298	290	3	941	14.2	3.7	11.8
69-70 —Atlanta	82	3269	443	932	.475	331	451	.734	1181	345	292	6	1217	14.4	4.2	14.8
70-71 —Atlanta	82	3140	382	834	.458	211	330	.639	1233	240	317	7	975	15.0	2.9	11.9
71-72 —Atl.-Phil.	78	2756	379	779	.487	222	316	.703	1051	198	269	6	980	13.5	2.5	12.6
72-73 —Phil.-L.A.	82	2867	333	722	.461	179	255	.702	904	219	296	3	845	11.0	2.7	10.3

Season Team	G	Min.	FGM	FGA	Pct.	FTM	FTA	Pct.	Off.	Def.	Tot.	Ast.	St.	Blk.	TO	Pts.	RPG	APG	PPG
73-74—Los Angeles	65	1812	216	513	.421	116	164	.707	193	306	499	148	58	31	...	548	7.7	2.3	8.4
74-75—L.A.-G.S.	32	415	35	93	.376	17	34	.500	64	70	134	31	11	5	...	87	4.2	1.0	2.7
Totals	926	30878	4181	9463	.442	2650	3824	.693	...	...	11054	2553	69	36	...	11012	11.9	2.8	11.9

Personal fouls/disqualifications: 1973-74, 219/3. 1974-75, 65/1. Totals, 3375/73.

NBA PLAYOFF RECORD

Season Team	G	Min.	FGM	FGA	Pct.	FTM	FTA	Pct.	Reb.	Ast.	PF	Dq.	Pts.	RPG	APG	PPG
62-63 —St. Louis	11	204	41	96	.427	20	27	.741	86	9	31	0	102	7.8	0.8	9.3
63-64 —St. Louis	12	240	26	83	.313	12	19	.632	84	24	40	0	64	7.0	2.0	5.3
64-65 —St. Louis	4	145	21	59	.356	10	15	.667	67	9	19	1	52	16.8	2.3	13.0
65-66 —St. Louis	10	421	86	170	.506	31	43	.721	149	28	47	2	203	14.9	2.8	20.3
66-67 —St. Louis	9	369	48	128	.375	45	67	.672	169	22	36	2	141	18.8	2.4	15.7
67-68 —St. Louis	6	216	38	75	.507	18	25	.720	77	14	23	0	94	12.8	2.3	15.7

Season Team	G	Min.	FGM	FGA	Pct.	FTM	FTA	Pct.	Reb.	Ast.	PF	Dq.	Pts.	AVERAGES RPG	APG	PPG
68-69 —Atlanta	11	442	69	156	.442	34	48	.708	178	37	48	2	172	16.2	3.4	15.6
69-70 —Atlanta	9	381	44	110	.400	16	27	.593	154	29	37	1	104	17.1	3.2	11.6
70-71 —Atlanta	5	229	23	58	.397	3	9	.333	104	5	17	0	49	20.8	1.0	9.8
72-73 —Los Angeles	17	582	57	136	.419	38	49	.776	158	29	68	2	152	9.3	1.7	8.9

Season Team	G	Min.	FGM	FGA	Pct.	FTM	FTA	Pct.	REBOUNDS Off.	Def.	Tot.	Ast.	St.	Blk.	TO	Pts.	AVERAGES RPG	APG	PPG
73-74 —Los Angeles	5	144	12	41	.293	6	13	.462	14	16	30	6	7	0	...	30	6.0	1.2	6.0
74-75 —Golden State	14	148	10	23	.435	2	7	.286	13	36	49	7	9	4	...	22	3.5	0.5	1.6
Totals	113	3521	475	1135	.419	235	349	.673	...	...	1305	219	16	4	...	1185	11.5	1.9	10.5

Personal fouls/disqualifications: 1973-74, 19/0. 1974-75, 23/0. Totals, 408/10.

NBA ALL-STAR GAME RECORD

Season Team	Min.	FGM	FGA	Pct.	FTM	FTA	Pct.	Reb	Ast.	PF	Dq.	Pts.
1967 —St. Louis	17	4	5	.800	0	2	.000	3	3	1	0	8
1968 —St. Louis	21	7	9	.778	1	4	.250	7	1	4	0	15
1970 —Atlanta	15	2	2	1.000	1	5	.200	4	2	1	0	5
Totals	53	13	16	.813	2	11	.182	14	6	6	0	28

CERVI, AL   G

PERSONAL: Born February 12, 1917, in Buffalo. ... 5-11/185 (1,80/83,9). ... Full name: Alfred Nicholas Cervi. ... Nickname: Digger.
HIGH SCHOOL: East (Buffalo).
COLLEGE: Did not attend college.
TRANSACTIONS: Played with independent teams (1935-36, 1936-37 and 1938-39 through 1944-45 seasons). ... Syracuse Nationals franchise became part of NBA for 1949-50 season.
CAREER HONORS: Elected to Naismith Memorial Basketball Hall of Fame (1985).
MISCELLANEOUS: Member of NBL championship team (1946).

NBL AND NBA REGULAR-SEASON RECORD

HONORS: All-NBA second team (1950). ... All-NBL first team (1947, 1948, 1949). ... All-NBL second team (1946).

Season Team	G	Min.	FGM	FGA	Pct.	FTM	FTA	Pct.	Reb.	Ast.	PF	Dq.	Pts.	AVERAGES RPG	APG	PPG
37-38 —Buff. (NBL)	9	...	19	...	...	6	...	...	...	...	...	...	44	...	...	4.9
45-46 —Roc. (NBL)	28	...	112	...	...	76	108	.704	...	...	21	...	300	...	...	10.7
46-47 —Roc. (NBL)	44	...	228	...	...	176	236	.746	...	...	127	...	*632	...	...	14.4
47-48 —Roc. (NBL)	49	...	234	...	...	187	242	.773	...	...	118	...	655	...	...	13.4
48-49 —Syr. (NBL)	57	...	204	...	...	287	382	.751	...	...	170	...	695	...	...	12.2
49-50 —Syracuse	56	...	143	431	.332	287	346	.829	...	264	223	...	573	...	4.7	10.2
50-51 —Syracuse	53	...	132	346	.382	194	237	.819	152	220	180	9	458	2.9	3.9	8.6
51-52 —Syracuse	55	850	99	280	.354	219	248	.883	87	148	176	7	417	1.6	2.7	7.6
52-53 —Syracuse	38	301	31	71	.437	81	100	.810	22	28	90	2	143	0.6	0.7	3.8
Totals	389	...	1202	...	...	1513	...	...	...	...	...	...	3917	...	...	10.1

NBL AND NBA PLAYOFF RECORD

Season Team	G	Min.	FGM	FGA	Pct.	FTM	FTA	Pct.	Reb.	Ast.	PF	Dq.	Pts.	AVERAGES RPG	APG	PPG
45-46 —Roc. (NBL)	7	...	23	...	...	24	30	.800	...	...	21	...	70	...	...	10.0
46-47 —Roc. (NBL)	11	...	49	...	...	50	68	.735	...	...	41	...	148	...	...	13.5
47-48 —Roc. (NBL)	6	...	18	...	...	14	19	.737	13	...	...	...	50	2.2	...	8.3
48-49 —Syr. (NBL)	6	...	12	...	...	22	30	.733	...	...	23	...	46	...	...	7.7
49-50 —Syracuse	11	...	23	68	.338	38	46	.826	...	52	36	...	84	...	4.7	7.6
50-51 —Syracuse	7	...	17	56	.304	44	50	.880	33	38	31	1	78	4.7	5.4	11.1
51-52 —Syracuse	7	88	7	30	.233	22	23	.957	10	15	23	1	36	1.4	2.1	5.1
52-53 —Syracuse	2	...	3	5	.600	12	15	.800	0	1	12	1	18	0.0	0.5	9.0
Totals	57	...	152	...	...	226	281	.804	...	...	...	...	530	...	...	9.3

HEAD COACHING RECORD

HONORS: NBL Coach of the Year (1949).

NBL AND NBA COACHING RECORD

Season Team	REGULAR SEASON W	L	Pct.	Finish	PLAYOFFS W	L	Pct.
48-49 —Syracuse (NBL)	40	23	.635	2nd/Eastern Division	3	3	.500
49-50 —Syracuse	51	13	.797	1st/Eastern Division	6	5	.545
50-51 —Syracuse	32	34	.485	4th/Eastern Division	4	3	.571
51-52 —Syracuse	40	26	.606	1st/Eastern Division	3	4	.429
52-53 —Syracuse	47	24	.662	2nd/Eastern Division	0	2	.000
53-54 —Syracuse	42	30	.583	3rd/Eastern Division	9	4	.692
54-55 —Syracuse	43	29	.597	1st/Eastern Division	7	4	.636
55-56 —Syracuse	35	37	.493	3rd/Eastern Division	5	4	.555
56-57 —Syracuse	4	8	.333		—	—	—
58-59 —Philadelphia	32	40	.444	4th/Eastern Division	—	—	—
Totals (10 years)	366	264	.581	Totals (8 years)	37	29	.561

NOTES:
1949—Defeated Hammond, 2-0, in Eastern Division First Round; lost to Anderson, 3-1, in Eastern Division Finals.
1950—Defeated Philadelphia, 2-0, in Eastern Division Semifinals; defeated New York, 2-1, in Eastern Division Finals; lost to Minneapolis, 4-2, in NBA Finals.
1951—Defeated Philadelphia, 2-0, in Eastern Division Semifinals; lost to New York, 3-2, in Eastern Division Finals.
1952—Defeated Philadelphia, 2-1, in Eastern Division Semifinals; lost to New York, 3-1, in Eastern Division Finals.

ALL-TIME GREAT PLAYERS

1953—Lost to Boston in Eastern Division Semifinals.
1954—Defeated Boston, 96-95 (OT); defeated New York, 75-68; defeated New York, 103-99; and defeated Boston, 98-85, in Eastern Division round robin; defeated Boston, 2-0, in Eastern Division Finals; lost to Minneapolis, 4-3, in World Championship Series.
1955—Defeated Boston, 3-1, in Eastern Division Finals; defeated Fort Wayne, 4-3, in World Championship Series.
1956—Defeated New York, 82-77, in Eastern Division third-place game; defeated Boston, 2-1, in Eastern Division Semifinals; lost to Philadelphia, 3-2, in Eastern Division Finals. Replaced as Syracuse head coach by Paul Seymour (November).

CHAMBERLAIN, WILT   C

PERSONAL: Born August 21, 1936, in Philadelphia. ... Died October 12, 1999. ... 7-1/275 (2,16/124,7). ... Full name: Wilton Norman Chamberlain. ... Nickname: Wilt the Stilt and The Big Dipper.
HIGH SCHOOL: Overbrook (Philadelphia).
COLLEGE: Kansas.
TRANSACTIONS: Played with Harlem Globetrotters during 1958-59 season. ... Selected by Philadelphia Warriors in 1959 NBA Draft (territorial pick). ... Warriors franchise moved from Philadelphia to San Francisco for 1962-63 season. ... Traded by Warriors to Philadelphia 76ers for G Paul Neumann, C/F Connie Dierking, F Lee Shaffer and cash (January 15, 1965). ... Traded by 76ers to Los Angeles Lakers for F Jerry Chambers, G Archie Clark and C Darrall Imhoff (July 9, 1968).
CAREER HONORS: Elected to Naismith Memorial Basketball Hall of Fame (1978). ... NBA 35th Anniversary All-Time Team (1980) and One of the 50 Greatest Players in NBA History (1996).
MISCELLANEOUS: Member of NBA championship team (1967, 1972). ... Golden State Warriors franchise all-time leading scorer with 17,783 points (1959-60 through 1964-65).

COLLEGIATE RECORD

NOTES: THE SPORTING NEWS All-America first team (1958).

Season Team	G	Min.	FGM	FGA	Pct.	FTM	FTA	Pct.	Reb.	Ast.	Pts.	RPG	APG	PPG
55-56—Kansas‡					Freshman team did not play intercollegiate schedule.									
56-57—Kansas	27	...	275	588	.468	250	399	.627	510	...	800	18.9	...	29.6
57-58—Kansas	21	...	228	482	.473	177	291	.608	367	...	633	17.5	...	30.1
Varsity totals	48	...	503	1070	.470	427	690	.619	877	...	1433	18.3	...	29.9

NBA REGULAR-SEASON RECORD

RECORDS: Holds career records for most games with 50 or more points—118; most seasons leading league in field goal percentage—9; most free throws attempted—11,862; most rebounds—23,924; and highest rebounds-per-game average (minimum 400 games)—22.9. ... Shares career records for most consecutive seasons leading league in scoring—7 (1959-60 through 1965-66). ... Holds single-season records for most games with 50 or more points—45 (1962); most minutes played—3,882 (1962); most points—4,029 (1962); highest points-per-game average—50.4 (1962); most points by a rookie—2,707 (1960); most field goals made—1,597 (1962); most consecutive field goals made—35 (February 17 through February 28, 1967); most field goals attempted—3,159 (1962); highest field goal percentage—.727 (1973); most free throws attempted—1,363 (1962); most rebounds—2,149 (1961); most rebounds by a rookie—1,941 (1960); and highest rebounds-per-game average—27.2 (1961). ... Holds single-game records for most points—100; most points in one half—59; most field goals made—36; most field goals made in one half—22; most field goals attempted—63; most field goals attempted in one half—37; and most field goals attempted in one quarter—21 (March 2, 1962, vs. New York at Hershey, Pa.). ... Holds single-game records for most points by a rookie—58 (January 25, 1960, vs. Detroit); highest field goal percentage (minimum 15 made)—1.000 (January 20, 1967, vs. Los Angeles, 15-for-15; February 24, 1967, vs. Baltimore, 18-for-18; and March 19, 1967, vs. Baltimore, 16-for-16); most rebounds—55 (November 24, 1960, vs. Boston); and most rebounds by a rookie—45 (February 6, 1960, vs. Syracuse). ... Shares single-game record for most free throws made—28 (March 2, 1962, vs. New York at Hershey, Pa.).
HONORS: NBA Most Valuable Player (1960, 1966, 1967, 1968). ... NBA Rookie of the Year (1960). ... All-NBA first team (1960, 1961, 1962, 1964, 1966, 1967, 1968). ... All-NBA second team (1963, 1965, 1972). ... NBA All-Defensive first team (1972, 1973).

Season Team	G	Min.	FGM	FGA	Pct.	FTM	FTA	Pct.	Reb.	Ast.	PF	Dq.	Pts.	RPG	APG	PPG
59-60—Philadelphia	72	†3338	*1065	*2311	.461	577	*991	.582	*1941	168	150	0	*2707	*27.0	2.3	*37.6
60-61—Philadelphia	79	*3773	*1251	*2457	*.509	531	*1054	.504	*2149	148	130	0	3033	*27.2	1.9	*38.4
61-62—Philadelphia	80	*3882	*1597	*3159	.506	*835	*1363	.613	*2052	192	123	0	*4029	*25.7	2.4	*50.4
62-63—San Francisco	80	*3806	*1463	*2770	*.528	660	*1113	.593	*1946	275	136	0	*3586	*24.3	3.4	*44.8
63-64—San Francisco	80	*3689	*1204	*2298	.524	540	*1016	.532	1787	403	182	0	*2948	22.3	5.0	*36.9
64-65—S.F.-Phil.	73	3301	*1063	*2083	*.510	408	*880	.464	1673	250	146	0	*2534	22.9	3.4	*34.7
65-66—Philadelphia	79	*3737	*1074	*1990	*.540	501	976	.513	*1943	414	171	0	*2649	*24.6	5.2	*33.5
66-67—Philadelphia	81	*3682	785	1150	*.683	386	*875	.441	*1957	630	143	0	1956	*24.2	7.8	24.1
67-68—Philadelphia	82	*3836	819	1377	*.595	354	*932	.380	*1952	*702	160	0	1992	*23.8	8.6	24.3
68-69—Los Angeles	81	3669	641	1099	*.583	382	*857	.446	*1712	366	142	0	1664	*21.1	4.5	20.5
69-70—Los Angeles	12	505	129	227	.568	70	157	.446	221	49	31	0	328	18.4	4.1	27.3
70-71—Los Angeles	82	3630	668	1226	.545	360	669	.538	*1493	352	174	0	1696	*18.2	4.3	20.7
71-72—Los Angeles	82	3469	496	764	*.649	221	524	.422	*1572	329	196	0	1213	*19.2	4.0	14.8
72-73—Los Angeles	82	3542	426	586	*.727	232	455	.510	*1526	365	191	0	1084	*18.6	4.5	13.2
Totals	1045	47859	12681	23497	.540	6057	11862	.511	23924	4643	2075	0	31419	22.9	4.4	30.1

NBA PLAYOFF RECORD

NOTES: NBA Finals Most Valuable Player (1972). ... Holds NBA Finals single-game record for most rebounds in one half—26 (April 16, 1967, vs. San Francisco). ... Holds single-series playoff record for highest rebounds-per-game average—32.0 (1967). ... Holds single-game playoff records for most rebounds—41 (April 5, 1967, vs. Boston); most rebounds in one half—26 (April 16, 1967, vs. San Francisco); and most points by a rookie—53 (March 14, 1960, vs. Syracuse). ... Shares single-game playoff records for most field goals made—24 (March 14, 1960, vs. Syracuse); most field goals attempted—48 (March 22, 1962, vs. Syracuse); and most field goals attempted in one half—25 (March 22, 1962, vs. Syracuse).

Season Team	G	Min.	FGM	FGA	Pct.	FTM	FTA	Pct.	Reb.	Ast.	PF	Dq.	Pts.	RPG	APG	PPG
59-60—Philadelphia	9	415	125	252	.496	49	110	.445	232	19	17	0	299	25.8	2.1	33.2
60-61—Philadelphia	3	144	45	96	.469	21	38	.553	69	6	10	0	111	23.0	2.0	37.0
61-62—Philadelphia	12	576	162	347	.467	96	151	.636	319	37	27	0	420	26.6	3.1	35.0
63-64—San Francisco	12	558	175	322	.543	66	139	.475	302	39	27	0	416	25.2	3.3	34.7
64-65—Philadelphia	11	536	123	232	.530	76	136	.559	299	48	29	0	322	27.2	4.4	29.3
65-66—Philadelphia	5	240	56	110	.509	28	68	.412	151	15	10	0	140	30.2	3.0	28.0
66-67—Philadelphia	15	718	132	228	.579	62	160	.388	437	135	37	0	326	29.1	9.0	21.7
67-68—Philadelphia	13	631	124	232	.534	60	158	.380	321	85	29	0	308	24.7	6.5	23.7
68-69—Los Angeles	18	832	96	176	.545	58	148	.392	444	46	56	0	250	24.7	2.6	13.9
69-70—Los Angeles	18	851	158	288	.549	82	202	.406	399	81	42	0	398	22.2	4.5	22.1

ALL-TIME GREAT PLAYERS

Season Team	G	Min.	FGM	FGA	Pct.	FTM	FTA	Pct.	Reb.	Ast.	PF	Dq.	Pts.	RPG	APG	PPG
70-71 —Los Angeles	12	554	85	187	.455	50	97	.515	242	53	33	0	220	20.2	4.4	18.3
71-72 —Los Angeles	15	703	80	142	.563	60	122	.492	315	49	47	0	220	21.0	3.3	14.7
72-73 —Los Angeles	17	801	64	116	.552	49	98	.500	383	60	48	0	177	22.5	3.5	10.4
Totals	160	7559	1425	2728	.522	757	1627	.465	3913	673	412	0	3607	24.5	4.2	22.5

NBA ALL-STAR GAME RECORD

NOTES: NBA All-Star Game Most Valuable Player (1960). ... Holds career record for most rebounds—197. ... Holds single-game records for most points—42 (1962); most free throws attempted—16 (1962); and most field goals made in one half—10 (1962). ... Shares single-game records for most field goals made—17 (1962); and most rebounds in one half—16 (1960).

Season Team	Min.	FGM	FGA	Pct.	FTM	FTA	Pct.	Reb	Ast.	PF	Dq.	Pts.
1960 —Philadelphia	30	9	20	.450	5	7	.714	25	2	1	0	23
1961 —Philadelphia	38	2	8	.250	8	15	.533	18	5	1	0	12
1962 —Philadelphia	37	17	23	.739	8	16	.500	24	1	4	0	42
1963 —San Francisco	35	7	11	.636	3	7	.429	19	0	2	0	17
1964 —San Francisco	37	4	14	.286	11	14	.786	20	1	2	0	19
1965 —San Francisco	31	9	15	.600	2	8	.250	16	1	4	0	20
1966 —Philadelphia	25	8	11	.727	5	9	.556	9	3	2	0	21
1967 —Philadelphia	39	6	7	.857	2	5	.400	22	4	1	0	14
1968 —Philadelphia	25	3	4	.750	1	4	.250	7	6	2	0	7
1969 —Los Angeles	27	2	3	.667	0	1	.000	12	2	2	0	4
1971 —Los Angeles	18	1	1	1.000	0	0	...	8	5	0	0	2
1972 —Los Angeles	24	3	3	1.000	2	8	.250	10	3	2	0	8
1973 —Los Angeles	22	1	2	.500	0	0	...	7	3	0	0	2
Totals	388	72	122	.590	47	94	.500	197	36	23	0	191

ABA COACHING RECORD

Season Team	REGULAR SEASON					PLAYOFFS		
	W	L	Pct.	Finish		W	L	Pct.
73-74 —San Diego	37	47	.440	T4th/Western Division		2	4	.333

NOTES:
1974—Lost to Utah in Western Division Semifinals.

CHAMBERS, TOM   F

PERSONAL: Born June 21, 1959, in Ogden, Utah. ... 6-10/230 (2,08/104,3). ... Full name: Thomas Doane Chambers.
HIGH SCHOOL: Fairview (Boulder, Colo.).
COLLEGE: Utah.
TRANSACTIONS: Selected by San Diego Clippers in first round (eighth pick overall) of 1981 NBA Draft. ... Traded by Clippers with F Al Wood, 1987 second-round draft choice and future third-round draft choice to Seattle SuperSonics for C James Donaldson, F Greg Kelser, G Mark Radford, 1984 first-round draft choice and 1985 second-round draft choice (August 18, 1983). ... Signed as unrestricted free agent by Phoenix Suns (July 5, 1988). ... Signed as unrestricted free agent by Utah Jazz (August 12, 1993). ... Played in Israel (1995-96). ... Signed as free agent by Charlotte Hornets (January 30, 1997). ... Waived by Hornets (April 8, 1997). ... Signed as free agent by Suns (August 22, 1997). ... Traded by Suns to Philadelphia 76ers for G/F Marko Milic (November 21, 1997). ... Announced retirement (December 11, 1997).
CAREER NOTES: Community relations representative, Phoenix Suns (1997-present).

COLLEGIATE RECORD

Season Team	G	Min.	FGM	FGA	Pct.	FTM	FTA	Pct.	Reb.	Ast.	Pts.	RPG	APG	PPG
77-78—Utah	28	355	69	139	.496	40	64	.625	104	7	178	3.7	0.3	6.4
78-79—Utah	30	853	206	379	.544	69	127	.543	266	28	481	8.9	0.9	16.0
79-80—Utah	28	792	195	359	.543	92	129	.713	244	23	482	8.7	0.8	17.2
80-81—Utah	30	959	221	372	.594	115	155	.742	262	24	557	8.7	0.8	18.6
Totals	116	2959	691	1249	.553	316	475	.665	876	82	1698	7.6	0.7	14.6

NBA REGULAR-SEASON RECORD

HONORS: All-NBA second team (1989, 1990).

Season Team	G	Min.	FGM	FGA	Pct.	FTM	FTA	Pct.	REBOUNDS			Ast.	St.	Blk.	TO	Pts.	AVERAGES		
									Off.	Def.	Tot.						RPG	APG	PPG
81-82—San Diego	81	2682	554	1056	.525	284	458	.620	211	350	561	146	58	46	220	1392	6.9	1.8	17.2
82-83—San Diego	79	2665	519	1099	.472	353	488	.723	218	301	519	192	79	57	234	1391	6.6	2.4	17.6
83-84—Seattle	82	2570	554	1110	.499	375	469	.800	219	313	532	133	47	51	192	1483	6.5	1.6	18.1
84-85—Seattle	81	2923	629	1302	.483	475	571	.832	164	415	579	209	70	57	260	1739	7.1	2.6	21.5
85-86—Seattle	66	2019	432	928	.466	346	414	.836	126	305	431	132	55	37	194	1223	6.5	2.0	18.5
86-87—Seattle	82	3018	660	1446	.456	535	630	.849	163	382	545	245	81	50	268	1909	6.6	3.0	23.3
87-88—Seattle	82	2680	611	1364	.448	419	519	.807	135	355	490	212	87	53	209	1674	6.0	2.6	20.4
88-89—Phoenix	81	3002	774	1643	.471	509	598	.851	143	541	684	231	87	55	231	2085	8.4	2.9	25.7
89-90—Phoenix	81	3046	810	1617	.501	547	647	.861	121	450	571	190	88	47	218	2201	7.0	2.3	27.2
90-91—Phoenix	76	2475	556	1271	.437	379	459	.826	104	386	490	194	65	52	177	1511	6.4	2.6	19.9
91-92—Phoenix	69	1948	426	989	.431	258	311	.830	86	315	401	142	57	37	103	1128	5.8	2.1	16.3
92-93—Phoenix	73	1723	320	716	.447	241	288	.837	96	249	345	101	43	23	92	892	4.7	1.4	12.2
93-94—Utah	80	1838	329	748	.440	221	281	.786	87	239	326	79	40	32	89	893	4.1	1.0	11.2
94-95—Utah	81	1240	195	427	.457	109	135	.807	66	147	213	73	25	30	52	503	2.6	0.9	6.2
95-96—								Played in Israel.											
96-97—Charlotte	12	83	7	31	.226	3	4	.750	3	11	14	4	1	0	9	19	1.2	0.3	1.6
97-98—Philadelphia	1	10	2	2	1.000	2	2	1.000	0	2	2	0	2	0	1	6	2.0	0.0	6.0
Totals	1107	33922	7378	15749	.468	5066	6274	.807	1942	4761	6703	2283	885	627	2549	20049	6.1	2.1	18.1

Three-point field goals: 1981-82, 0-for-2. 1982-83, 0-for-8. 1983-84, 0-for-12. 1984-85, 6-for-22 (.273). 1985-86, 13-for-48 (.271). 1986-87, 54-for-145 (.372). 1987-88, 33-for-109 (.303). 1988-89, 28-for-86 (.326). 1989-90, 24-for-86 (.279). 1990-91, 20-for-73 (.274). 1991-92, 18-for-49 (.367). 1992-93, 11-for-28 (.393). 1993-94, 14-for-45 (.311). 1994-95, 4-for-24 (.167). 1996-97, 2-for-3 (.667). Totals, 227-for-740 (.307).

Personal fouls/disqualifications: 1981-82, 341/17. 1982-83, 333/15. 1983-84, 309/8. 1984-85, 312/4. 1985-86, 248/6. 1986-87, 307/9. 1987-88, 297/4. 1988-89, 271/2. 1989-90, 260/1. 1990-91, 235/3. 1991-92, 196/1. 1992-93, 212/2. 1993-94, 232/2. 1994-95, 173/1. 1996-97, 14/0. 1997-98, 2/0. Totals, 3742/75.

NBA PLAYOFF RECORD

Season Team	G	Min.	FGM	FGA	Pct.	FTM	FTA	Pct.	REBOUNDS Off.	Def.	Tot.	Ast.	St.	Blk.	TO	Pts.	RPG	APG	PPG
83-84—Seattle	5	191	28	59	.475	12	18	.667	4	29	33	8	5	3	9	68	6.6	1.6	13.6
86-87—Seattle	14	498	118	263	.449	80	99	.808	32	58	90	32	12	13	34	322	6.4	2.3	23.0
87-88—Seattle	5	168	50	91	.549	29	35	.829	8	23	31	11	3	1	13	129	6.2	2.2	25.8
88-89—Phoenix	12	495	118	257	.459	67	78	.859	22	109	131	46	13	15	39	312	10.9	3.8	26.0
89-90—Phoenix	16	612	117	275	.425	116	132	.879	20	87	107	31	7	7	49	355	6.7	1.9	22.2
90-91—Phoenix	4	142	27	66	.409	14	19	.737	2	21	23	10	7	5	12	68	5.8	2.5	17.0
91-92—Phoenix	7	194	39	85	.459	27	32	.844	8	23	31	19	2	5	15	109	4.4	2.7	15.6
92-93—Phoenix	24	376	64	165	.388	44	54	.815	23	42	65	12	6	10	26	174	2.7	0.5	7.3
93-94—Utah	16	325	35	97	.361	23	29	.793	16	29	45	12	5	9	8	93	2.8	0.8	5.8
94-95—Utah	5	60	11	22	.500	9	13	.692	3	10	13	2	2	0	3	32	2.6	0.4	6.4
Totals	108	3061	607	1380	.440	421	509	.827	138	431	569	183	62	68	208	1662	5.3	1.7	15.4

Three-point field goals: 1983-84, 0-for-1. 1986-87, 6-for-17 (.353). 1987-88, 0-for-2. 1988-89, 9-for-22 (.409). 1989-90, 5-for-19 (.263). 1990-91, 0-for-5. 1991-92, 4-for-7 (.571). 1992-93, 2-for-5 (.400). 1993-94, 0-for-7. 1994-95, 1-for-3 (.333). Totals, 27-for-88 (.307).

Personal fouls/disqualifications: 1983-84, 23/0. 1986-87, 51/0. 1987-88, 24/1. 1988-89, 44/0. 1989-90, 54/0. 1990-91, 12/1. 1991-92, 25/1. 1992-93, 58/0. 1993-94, 50/1. 1994-95, 18/1. Totals, 359/5.

NBA ALL-STAR GAME RECORD

NOTES: NBA All-Star Game Most Valuable Player (1987).

Season Team	Min.	FGM	FGA	Pct.	FTM	FTA	Pct.	REBOUNDS Off.	Def.	Tot.	Ast.	PF	Dq.	St.	Blk.	TO	Pts.
1987 —Seattle	29	13	25	.520	6	9	.667	3	1	4	2	5	0	4	0	3	34
1989 —Phoenix	16	4	8	.500	6	6	1.000	2	3	5	1	3	0	0	0	2	14
1990 —Phoenix	21	8	12	.667	5	7	.714	2	1	3	1	0	0	1	0	3	21
1991 —Phoenix	18	4	11	.364	0	0	...	2	2	4	1	3	0	1	0	4	8
Totals	84	29	56	.518	17	22	.773	9	7	16	5	11	0	6	0	12	77

Three-point field goals: 1987, 2-for-3 (.667). 1990, 0-for-1. 1991, 0-for-1. Totals, 2-for-5 (.400).

CHEEKS, MAURICE   G

See Head Coaches, page 305.

COSTELLO, LARRY   G

See All-Time Great Coaches, page 449.

COUSY, BOB   G

PERSONAL: Born August 9, 1928, in New York. ... 6-1/175 (1,85/79,4). ... Full name: Robert Joseph Cousy. ... Nickname: Houdini of the Hardwood.

HIGH SCHOOL: Andrew Jackson (Queens, N.Y.).

COLLEGE: Holy Cross.

TRANSACTIONS: Selected by Tri-Cities Blackhawks in first round of 1950 NBA Draft. ... Traded by Blackhawks to Chicago Stags for F/G Gene Vance (1950). ... NBA rights drawn out of a hat by Boston Celtics in dispersal of Stags franchise (1950). ... Traded by Celtics to Cincinnati Royals for F Bill Dinwiddie (November 18, 1969).

CAREER HONORS: Elected to Naismith Memorial Basketball Hall of Fame (1971). ... NBA 25th Anniversary All-Time Team (1970), 35th Anniversary All-Time Team (1980) and One of the 50 Greatest Players in NBA History (1996).

MISCELLANEOUS: Member of NBA championship team (1957, 1959, 1960, 1961, 1962, 1963). ... Commissioner of American Soccer League (1975 through mid-1980 season). ... Boston Celtics all-time assists leader with 6,945 (1950-51 through 1962-63).

COLLEGIATE RECORD

NOTES: Member of NCAA championship team (1947). ... THE SPORTING NEWS All-America first team (1950). ... THE SPORTING NEWS All-America second team (1949).

Season Team	G	Min.	FGM	FGA	Pct.	FTM	FTA	Pct.	Reb.	Ast.	Pts.	AVERAGES RPG	APG	PPG
46-47—Holy Cross	30	...	91	...	...	45	...	...	...	...	227	...	...	7.6
47-48—Holy Cross	30	...	207	...	...	72	108	.667	...	...	486	...	...	16.2
48-49—Holy Cross	27	...	195	...	...	90	134	.672	...	...	480	...	...	17.8
49-50—Holy Cross	30	...	216	659	.328	150	199	.754	...	...	582	...	...	19.4
Totals	117	...	709	...	...	357	...	...	...	...	1775	...	...	15.2

NBA REGULAR-SEASON RECORD

RECORDS: Holds single-game record for most assists in one half—19 (February 27, 1959, vs. Minneapolis).

HONORS: NBA Most Valuable Player (1957). ... All-NBA first team (1952, 1953, 1954, 1955, 1956, 1957, 1958, 1959, 1960, 1961). ... All-NBA second team (1962, 1963).

Season Team	G	Min.	FGM	FGA	Pct.	FTM	FTA	Pct.	Reb.	Ast.	PF	Dq.	Pts.	AVERAGES RPG	APG	PPG
50-51 —Boston	69	...	401	1138	.352	276	365	.756	474	341	185	2	1078	6.9	4.9	15.6
51-52 —Boston	66	2681	512	1388	.369	409	506	.808	421	441	190	5	1433	6.4	6.7	21.7
52-53 —Boston	71	2945	464	*1320	.352	479	587	.816	449	*547	227	4	1407	6.3	*7.7	19.8
53-54 —Boston	72	2857	486	1262	.385	411	522	.787	394	*518	201	3	1383	5.5	*7.2	19.2
54-55 —Boston	71	2747	522	1316	.397	460	570	.807	424	*557	165	1	1504	6.0	*7.8	21.2
55-56 —Boston	72	2767	440	1223	.360	476	564	.844	492	*642	206	2	1356	6.8	*8.9	18.8

Season Team	G	Min.	FGM	FGA	Pct.	FTM	FTA	Pct.	Reb.	Ast.	PF	Dq.	Pts.	AVERAGES RPG	APG	PPG
56-57 —Boston	64	2364	478	1264	.378	363	442	.821	309	*478	134	0	1319	4.8	*7.5	20.6
57-58 —Boston	65	2222	445	1262	.353	277	326	.850	322	*463	136	1	1167	5.0	*7.1	18.0
58-59 —Boston	65	2403	484	1260	.384	329	385	.855	359	*557	135	0	1297	5.5	*8.6	20.0
59-60 —Boston	75	2588	568	1481	.384	319	403	.792	352	*715	146	2	1455	4.7	*9.5	19.4
60-61 —Boston	76	2468	513	1382	.371	352	452	.779	331	587	196	0	1378	4.4	7.7	18.1
61-62 —Boston	75	2114	462	1181	.391	333	333	.754	261	584	135	0	1175	3.5	7.8	15.7
62-63 —Boston	76	1975	392	988	.397	219	298	.735	193	515	175	0	1003	2.5	6.8	13.2
69-70 —Cincinnati	7	34	1	3	.333	3	3	1.000	5	10	11	0	5	0.7	1.4	0.7
Totals	924	...	6168	16468	.375	4624	5756	.803	4786	6955	2242	20	16960	5.2	7.5	18.4

NBA PLAYOFF RECORD

NOTES: Shares NBA Finals single-game record for most assists in one quarter—8 (April 9, 1957, vs. St. Louis). ... Holds single-game play-off record for most free throws made—30 (March 21, 1953, vs. Syracuse).

Season Team	G	Min.	FGM	FGA	Pct.	FTM	FTA	Pct.	Reb.	Ast.	PF	Dq.	Pts.	AVERAGES RPG	APG	PPG
50-51 —Boston	2	...	9	42	.214	10	12	.833	15	12	8	...	28	7.5	6.0	14.0
51-52 —Boston	3	138	26	65	.400	41	44	.932	12	19	13	1	93	4.0	6.3	31.0
52-53 —Boston	6	270	46	120	.383	61	73	.836	25	37	21	0	153	4.2	6.2	25.5
53-54 —Boston	6	259	33	116	.284	60	75	.800	32	38	20	0	126	5.3	6.3	21.0
54-55 —Boston	7	299	53	139	.381	46	48	.958	43	65	26	0	152	6.1	9.3	21.7
55-56 —Boston	3	124	28	56	.500	23	25	.920	24	26	4	0	79	8.0	8.7	26.3
56-57 —Boston	10	440	67	207	.324	68	91	.747	61	93	27	0	202	6.1	9.3	20.2
57-58 —Boston	11	457	67	196	.342	64	75	.853	71	82	20	0	198	6.5	7.5	18.0
58-59 —Boston	11	460	72	221	.326	70	94	.745	76	119	28	0	214	6.9	10.8	19.5
59-60 —Boston	13	468	80	262	.305	39	51	.765	48	116	27	0	199	3.7	8.9	15.3
60-61 —Boston	10	337	50	147	.340	67	88	.761	43	91	33	1	167	4.3	9.1	16.7
61-62 —Boston	14	474	86	241	.357	52	76	.684	64	123	43	0	224	4.6	8.8	16.0
62-63 —Boston	13	393	72	204	.353	39	47	.830	32	116	44	2	183	2.5	8.9	14.1
Totals	109	...	689	2016	.342	640	799	.801	546	937	314	...	2018	5.0	8.6	18.5

NBA ALL-STAR GAME RECORD

NOTES: NBA All-Star Game Most Valuable Player (1954, 1957).

Season Team	Min.	FGM	FGA	Pct.	FTM	FTA	Pct.	Reb	Ast.	PF	Dq.	Pts.
1951 —Boston	...	2	12	.167	4	5	.800	9	8	3	0	8
1952 —Boston	33	4	14	.286	1	2	.500	4	13	3	0	9
1953 —Boston	36	4	11	.364	7	7	1.000	5	3	1	0	15
1954 —Boston	34	6	15	.400	8	8	1.000	11	4	1	0	20
1955 —Boston	35	7	14	.500	6	7	.857	9	5	1	0	20
1956 —Boston	24	2	8	.250	3	4	.750	7	2	6	1	7
1957 —Boston	28	4	14	.286	2	2	1.000	5	7	0	0	10
1958 —Boston	31	8	20	.400	4	6	.667	5	10	0	0	20
1959 —Boston	32	4	8	.500	5	6	.833	5	4	0	0	13
1960 —Boston	26	1	7	.143	0	0	...	5	8	2	0	2
1961 —Boston	33	2	11	.182	0	0	...	3	8	6	1	4
1962 —Boston	31	4	13	.308	3	4	.750	6	8	2	0	11
1963 —Boston	25	4	11	.364	0	0	...	4	6	2	0	8
Totals	...	52	158	.329	43	51	.843	78	86	27	2	147

COLLEGIATE COACHING RECORD

Season Team	W	L	Pct.
63-64 —Boston College	10	11	.476
64-65 —Boston College	22	7	.759
65-66 —Boston College	21	5	.808
66-67 —Boston College	23	3	.885
67-68 —Boston College	17	8	.680
68-69 —Boston College	24	4	.857
Totals (6 years)	117	38	.755

NBA COACHING RECORD

Season Team	REGULAR SEASON W	L	Pct.	Finish	PLAYOFFS W	L	Pct.
69-70 —Cincinnati	36	46	.439	5th/Eastern Division	—	—	—
70-71 —Cincinnati	33	49	.402	3rd/Central Division	—	—	—
71-72 —Cincinnati	30	52	.366	3rd/Central Division	—	—	—
72-73 —Kansas City/Omaha	36	46	.439	4th/Midwest Division	—	—	—
73-74 —Kansas City/Omaha	6	16	.273		—	—	—
Totals (5 years)	141	209	.403				

NOTES:

1965—Lost to St. John's, 114-92, in NIT first round.

1966—Defeated Louisville, 96-90 (3 OT), in NIT first round; lost to Villanova, 86-85, in quarterfinals.

1967—Defeated Connecticut, 48-42, in NCAA Tournament first round; defeated St. John's, 63-62, in regional semifinal; lost to North Carolina, 96-80, in regional final.

1968—Lost to St. Bonaventure, 102-93, in NCAA Tournament first round.

1969—Defeated Kansas, 78-62, in NIT first round; defeated Louisville, 88-83, in quarterfinals; defeated Army, 73-61, in semifinals; lost to Temple 89-76, in championship game.

1973—Replaced as Kansas City/Omaha head coach by Draff Young (November).

COWENS, DAVE

See Head Coaches, page 307.

PERSONAL: Born March 15, 1961, in Chicago. ... 6-9/250. (2.06 m/113 kg). ... Full Name: Robert Terrell Cummings.
HIGH SCHOOL: Carver (Chicago).
COLLEGE: DePaul.
TRANSACTIONS/CAREER NOTES: Selected after junior season by San Diego Clippers in first round (second pick overall) of 1982 NBA Draft. ... Clippers franchise moved from San Diego to Los Angeles for 1984-85 season. ... Traded by Clippers with G Craig Hodges and G/F Ricky Pierce to Milwaukee Bucks for F Marques Johnson, C/F Harvey Catchings, G/F Junior Bridgeman and cash (September 29, 1984). ... Traded by Bucks with future considerations to San Antonio Spurs for G Alvin Robertson, F/C Greg Anderson and future considerations (May 28, 1989). ... Signed as unrestricted free agent by Milwaukee Bucks (November 2, 1995). ... Signed as free agent by Seattle SuperSonics (January 13, 1997). ... Signed as free agent by Philadelphia 76ers (September 4, 1997). ... Traded by 76ers to New York Knicks for F Ronnie Grandison and C Herb Williams (February 19, 1998). ... Traded by Knicks with G John Starks and F Chris Mills to Golden State Warriors for G Latrell Sprewell (January 21, 1999). ... Announced retirement (October 2, 2000).

COLLEGIATE RECORD

NOTES: The Sporting News All-America first team (1982).

Season Team	G	Min.	FGM	FGA	Pct.	FTM	FTA	Pct.	Reb.	Ast.	Pts.	RPG	APG	PPG
												AVERAGES		
79-80—DePaul	28	861	154	303	.508	89	107	.832	263	40	397	9.4	1.4	14.2
80-81—DePaul	29	994	151	303	.498	75	100	.750	260	47	377	9.0	1.6	13.0
81-82—DePaul	28	1031	244	430	.567	136	180	.756	334	57	624	11.9	2.0	22.3
Totals	85	2886	549	1036	.530	300	387	.775	857	144	1398	10.1	1.7	16.4

NBA REGULAR-SEASON RECORD

HONORS: NBA Rookie of the Year (1983). ... All-NBA second team (1985). ... All-NBA third team (1989). ... NBA All-Rookie team (1983).

Season Team	G	Min.	FGM	FGA	Pct.	FTM	FTA	Pct.	Off.	Def.	Tot.	Ast.	St.	Blk.	TO	Pts.	RPG	APG	PPG
									REBOUNDS								AVERAGES		
82-83—San Diego	70	2531	684	1309	.523	292	412	.709	303	441	744	177	129	62	204	1660	10.6	2.5	23.7
83-84—San Diego	81	2907	737	1491	.494	380	528	.720	323	454	777	139	92	57	218	1854	9.6	1.7	22.9
84-85—Milwaukee	79	2722	759	1532	.495	343	463	.741	244	472	716	228	117	67	190	1861	9.1	2.9	23.6
85-86—Milwaukee	82	2669	681	1438	.474	265	404	.656	222	472	694	193	121	51	191	1627	8.5	2.4	19.8
86-87—Milwaukee	82	2770	729	1426	.511	249	376	.662	214	486	700	229	129	81	172	1707	8.5	2.8	20.8
87-88—Milwaukee	76	2629	675	1392	.485	270	406	.665	184	369	553	181	78	46	170	1621	7.3	2.4	21.3
88-89—Milwaukee	80	2824	730	1563	.467	362	460	.787	281	369	650	198	106	72	201	1829	8.1	2.5	22.9
89-90—San Antonio	81	2821	728	1532	.475	343	440	.780	226	451	677	219	110	52	202	1818	8.4	2.7	22.4
90-91—San Antonio	67	2195	503	1039	.484	164	240	.683	194	327	521	157	61	30	131	1177	7.8	2.3	17.6
91-92—San Antonio	70	2149	514	1053	.488	177	249	.711	247	384	631	102	58	34	115	1210	9.0	1.5	17.3
92-93—San Antonio	8	76	11	29	.379	5	10	.500	6	13	19	4	1	1	2	27	2.4	0.5	3.4
93-94—San Antonio	59	1133	183	428	.428	63	107	.589	132	165	297	50	31	13	59	429	5.0	0.8	7.3
94-95—San Antonio	76	1273	224	464	.483	72	123	.585	138	240	378	59	36	19	95	520	5.0	0.8	6.8
95-96—Milwaukee	81	1777	270	584	.462	104	160	.650	162	283	445	89	56	30	69	645	5.5	1.1	8.0
96-97—Seattle	45	828	155	319	.486	57	82	.695	70	113	183	39	33	7	45	370	4.1	0.9	8.2
97-98—Phil.-New York	74	1185	200	428	.467	67	98	.684	97	186	283	47	38	10	51	467	3.8	0.6	6.3
98-99—Golden State	50	1011	186	424	.439	81	114	.711	95	160	255	58	46	10	58	454	5.1	1.2	9.1
99-00—Golden State	22	398	76	177	.429	32	39	.821	45	62	107	21	13	8	27	184	4.9	1.0	8.4
Totals	1183	33898	8045	16628	.484	3326	4711	.706	3183	5447	8630	2190	1255	650	2200	19460	7.3	1.9	16.4

Three-point field goals: 1982-83, 0-for-1. 1983-84, 0-for-3. 1984-85, 0-for-1. 1985-86, 0-for-2. 1986-87, 0-for-3. 1987-88, 1-for-3 (.333). 1988-89, 7-for-15 (.467). 1989-90, 19-for-59 (.322). 1990-91, 7-for-33 (.212). 1991-92, 5-for-13 (.385). 1993-94, 0-for-2. 1995-96, 1-for-7 (.143). 1996-97, 3-for-5 (.600). 1997-98, 0-for-1. 1998-99, 1-for-1. Totals, 44-for-149 (.295).

Personal fouls/disqualifications: 1982-83, 294/10. 1983-84, 298/6. 1984-85, 264/4. 1985-86, 283/4. 1986-87, 296/3. 1987-88, 274/6. 1988-89, 265/5. 1989-90, 286/1. 1990-91, 225/5. 1991-92, 210/4. 1993-94, 137/0. 1995-96, 263/2. 1996-97, 113/0. 1997-98, 181/1. 1998-99, 168/4. Totals, 3836/56.

NBA PLAYOFF RECORD

Season Team	G	Min.	FGM	FGA	Pct.	FTM	FTA	Pct.	Off.	Def.	Tot.	Ast.	St.	Blk.	TO	Pts.	RPG	APG	PPG
									REBOUNDS								AVERAGES		
84-85—Milwaukee	8	311	86	149	.577	48	58	.828	21	49	70	20	12	7	26	220	8.8	2.5	27.5
85-86—Milwaukee	14	510	130	253	.514	43	62	.694	33	105	138	42	20	16	39	303	9.9	3.0	21.6
86-87—Milwaukee	12	443	105	215	.488	57	83	.687	29	66	95	28	12	13	15	267	7.9	2.3	22.3
87-88—Milwaukee	5	193	50	89	.562	29	44	.659	12	27	39	13	9	3	12	129	7.8	2.6	25.8
88-89—Milwaukee	5	124	25	69	.362	14	16	.875	19	14	33	7	3	0	4	64	6.6	1.4	12.8
89-90—San Antonio	10	375	103	195	.528	42	52	.808	31	63	94	22	7	4	19	249	9.4	2.2	24.9
90-91—San Antonio	4	124	25	49	.510	9	18	.500	14	23	37	4	3	2	9	59	9.3	1.0	14.8
91-92—San Antonio	3	122	34	66	.515	10	20	.500	15	19	34	7	4	4	7	78	11.3	2.3	26.0
92-93—San Antonio	10	138	31	70	.443	5	8	.625	17	22	39	5	3	1	8	67	3.9	0.5	6.7
93-94—San Antonio	4	72	11	22	.500	10	12	.833	10	15	25	2	5	3	4	32	6.3	0.5	8.0
94-95—San Antonio	15	135	18	48	.375	22	30	.733	12	19	31	4	5	1	7	58	2.1	0.3	3.9
96-97—Seattle	12	292	45	92	.489	16	24	.667	28	44	72	14	11	6	14	106	6.0	1.2	8.8
97-98—New York	8	120	15	34	.441	2	8	.250	11	24	35	5	4	2	7	32	4.4	0.6	4.0
Totals	110	2959	678	1351	.502	307	435	.706	252	490	742	173	98	62	171	1664	6.7	1.6	15.1

Three-point field goals: 1984-85, 0-for-1. 1988-89, 0-for-1. 1989-90, 1-for-5 (.200). 1990-91, 0-for-1. 1991-92, 0-for-1. 1992-93, 0-for-1. 1994-95, 0-for-1. Totals, 1-for-11 (.091).

Personal fouls/disqualifications: 1984-85, 33/1. 1988-89, 16/0. 1989-90, 39/0. 1990-91, 13/0. 1991-92, 9/0. 1992-93, 27/0. 1994-95, 25/0. Totals, 353/3.

NBA ALL-STAR GAME RECORD

Season Team	Min.	FGM	FGA	Pct.	FTM	FTA	Pct.	Off.	Def.	Tot.	Ast.	PF	Dq.	St.	Blk.	TO	Pts.
								REBOUNDS									
1985 —Milwaukee	16	7	17	.412	3	4	.750	4	3	7	0	1	0	0	1	0	17
1989 —Milwaukee	19	4	9	.444	2	2	1.000	2	3	5	1	4	0	3	1	0	10
Totals	35	11	26	.423	5	6	.833	6	6	12	1	5	0	3	2	0	27

CUNNINGHAM, BILLY   F

See All-Time Great Coaches, page 450.

DANIELS, MEL   C

PERSONAL: Born July 20, 1944, in Detroit. ... 6-9/225 (2,06/102,1). ... Full name: Melvin Joe Daniels.
HIGH SCHOOL: Pershing (Detroit).
JUNIOR COLLEGE: Burlington (Iowa) Junior College.
COLLEGE: New Mexico.
TRANSACTIONS: Selected by Minnesota Muskies in first round of 1967 ABA draft. ... Traded by Muskies to Indiana Pacers for 1969 first-round draft choice, G James Dawson, F Ron Kozlicki and cash (May 1968). ... Traded by Pacers with G Freddie Lewis to Memphis Sounds for F Charlie Edge and cash (July 26, 1974). ... Memphis franchise transferred to Baltimore and renamed Claws for 1975-76 season. ... Baltimore franchise folded prior to 1975-76 season. ... Signed as free agent by New York Nets of NBA (October 19, 1976). ... Waived by Nets (December 13, 1976).
CAREER NOTES: Scout, Pacers (1984-85 to 1995-96). ... Director of player personnel (1996 to present).
MISCELLANEOUS: Indiana Pacers franchise all-time leading rebounder with 7,643 (1986-74).

COLLEGIATE RECORD

Season Team	G	Min.	FGM	FGA	Pct.	FTM	FTA	Pct.	Reb.	Ast.	Pts.	RPG	APG	PPG
63-64—Burlington County J.C. ...	34	...	334	...	...	100	...	...	...	...	768	...	...	22.6
64-65—New Mexico	27	...	178	366	.486	111	182	.610	302	...	467	11.2	...	17.3
65-66—New Mexico	23	...	191	394	.485	107	145	.738	238	...	489	10.3	...	21.3
66-67—New Mexico	27	...	225	468	.481	131	191	.686	313	...	581	11.6	...	21.5
Totals	111	...	928	...	...	449	...	...	...	...	2305	...	...	20.8

ABA REGULAR-SEASON RECORD

NOTES: ABA Most Valuable Player (1969, 1971). ... ABA Rookie of the Year (1968). ... All-ABA first team (1968, 1969, 1970, 1971). ... All-ABA second team (1973). ... ABA All-Rookie team (1968). ... Member of ABA championship team (1970, 1972, 1973).

Season Team	G	Min.	2-POINT			3-POINT			FTM	FTA	Pct.	Reb.	Ast.	Pts.	AVERAGES		
			FGM	FGA	Pct.	FGM	FGA	Pct.							RPG	APG	PPG
67-68—Minnesota	78	2938	669	1640	.408	1	5	.200	390	678	.575	1213	109	1729	*15.6	1.4	22.2
68-69—Indiana	76	2934	712	1496	.476	0	4	.000	400	662	.604	1256	116	1824	*16.5	1.5	24.0
69-70—Indiana	83	3039	613	1295	.473	0	2	.000	330	489	.675	1462	131	1556	17.6	1.6	18.7
70-71—Indiana	82	3170	698	1357	.514	1	13	.077	326	480	.679	1475	178	1723	*18.0	2.2	21.0
71-72—Indiana	79	2971	598	1184	.505	0	6	.000	317	451	.703	1297	176	1513	16.4	2.2	19.2
72-73—Indiana	81	3103	587	1217	.482	1	4	.250	322	446	.722	1247	177	1497	15.4	2.2	18.5
73-74—Indiana	78	2539	492	1117	.440	0	0	...	217	287	.756	906	120	1201	11.6	1.5	15.4
74-75—Memphis	71	1646	290	644	.450	0	0	...	116	183	.634	638	125	696	9.0	1.8	9.8
Totals	628	22340	4659	9950	.468	3	34	.088	2418	3676	.658	9494	1132	11739	15.1	1.8	18.7

ABA PLAYOFF RECORD

Season Team	G	Min.	2-POINT			3-POINT			FTM	FTA	Pct.	Reb.	Ast.	Pts.	AVERAGES		
			FGM	FGA	Pct.	FGM	FGA	Pct.							RPG	APG	PPG
67-68—Minnesota	10	409	98	226	.434	0	0	...	54	94	.574	161	19	253	16.1	1.9	25.3
68-69—Indiana	17	570	127	300	.423	0	1	.000	79	130	.608	237	22	333	13.9	1.3	19.6
69-70—Indiana	15	533	108	242	.446	0	1	.000	74	111	.667	265	15	290	17.7	1.0	19.3
70-71—Indiana	11	457	94	194	.485	0	0	...	47	63	.746	211	16	235	19.2	1.5	21.4
71-72—Indiana	20	744	121	249	.486	0	3	.000	64	85	.753	302	28	306	15.1	1.4	15.3
72-73—Indiana	18	636	112	238	.471	0	0	...	62	81	.765	248	40	286	13.8	2.2	15.9
73-74—Indiana	14	498	69	172	.401	0	0	...	33	43	.767	160	27	171	11.4	1.9	12.2
74-75—Indiana	4	54	11	22	.500	0	0	...	5	9	.556	24	1	27	6.0	0.3	6.8
Totals	109	3901	740	1643	.450	0	5	.000	418	616	.679	1608	168	1901	14.8	1.5	17.4

ABA ALL-STAR GAME RECORD

NOTES: ABA All-Star Game Most Valuable Player (1971).

Season Team	Min.	2-POINT			3-POINT			FTM	FTA	Pct.	Reb.	Ast.	Pts.
		FGM	FGA	Pct.	FGM	FGA	Pct.						
1968—Minnesota	29	9	18	.500	0	0	...	4	11	.364	15	0	22
1969—Indiana	31	5	16	.313	0	0	...	7	10	.700	10	2	17
1970—Indiana	26	6	14	.429	0	0	...	1	3	.333	12	1	13
1971—Indiana	30	12	19	.632	0	0	...	5	7	.714	13	3	29
1972—Indiana	28	8	14	.571	U	0	...	5	8	.625	9	1	21
1973—Indiana	33	8	19	.421	0	0	...	9	12	.750	11	1	25
1974—Indiana	20	2	11	.182	0	0	...	1	2	.500	7	0	5
Totals	195	50	111	.450	0	0	...	32	53	.604	77	8	132

NBA REGULAR-SEASON RECORD

Season Team	G	Min.	FGM	FGA	Pct.	FTM	FTA	Pct.	REBOUNDS			Ast.	St.	Blk.	TO	Pts.	AVERAGES		
									Off.	Def.	Tot.						RPG	APG	PPG
76-77—N.Y. Nets	11	126	13	35	.371	13	23	.565	10	24	34	6	3	11	...	39	3.1	0.5	3.5

Personal fouls/disqualifications: 1976-77, 29/0.

COMBINED ABA AND NBA REGULAR-SEASON RECORDS

	G	Min.	FGM	FGA	Pct.	FTM	FTA	Pct.	REBOUNDS			Ast.	Stl.	Blk.	TO	Pts.	AVERAGES		
									Off.	Def.	Tot.						RPG	APG	PPG
Totals	639	22466	4675	10019	.467	2431	3699	.657	...	...	9528	1138	...	...	...	11778	14.9	1.8	18.4

Three-point field goals: 3-for-34 (.088).
Personal fouls/disqualifications: 2309.

HEAD COACHING RECORD

BACKGROUND: Assistant coach, Indiana State (1978-79 through 1981-82). ... Assistant coach, Indiana Pacers (1984-85 through 1988-89 and 1991-92 and 1992-93).
HONORS: USBL Coach of the Year (1993).

NBA COACHING RECORD

		REGULAR SEASON				PLAYOFFS		
Season Team	W	L	Pct.	Finish		W	L	Pct.
88-89 —Indiana	0	2	.000	—		—	—	—

NOTES:
1988—Replaced Jack Ramsay as Indiana head coach (November 17), with record of 0-7 and club in sixth place. Replaced as Indiana interim coach by George Irvine (November 21).

DANTLEY, ADRIAN   F/G

PERSONAL: Born February 28, 1956, in Washington, D.C. ... 6-5/210 (1,96/95,3). ... Full name: Adrian Delano Dantley.
HIGH SCHOOL: DeMatha Catholic (Hyattsville, Md.).
COLLEGE: Notre Dame.
TRANSACTIONS: Selected after junior season by Buffalo Braves in first round (sixth pick overall) of 1976 NBA Draft. ... Traded by Braves with F Mike Bantom to Indiana Pacers for G/F Billy Knight (September 1, 1977). ... Traded by Pacers with C/F Dave Robisch to Los Angeles Lakers for C James Edwards, G Earl Tatum and cash (December 13, 1977). ... Traded by Lakers to Utah Jazz for F Spencer Haywood (September 13, 1979). ... Traded by Jazz with 1987 and 1990 second-round draft choices to Detroit Pistons for F Kelly Tripucka and F/C Kent Benson (August 21, 1986). ... Traded by Pistons with 1991 first-round draft choice to Dallas Mavericks for F Mark Aguirre (February 15, 1989). ... Waived by Mavericks (April 2, 1990). ... Signed as free agent by Milwaukee Bucks (April 2, 1991). ... Played in Italy (1991-92).
MISCELLANEOUS: Member of gold-medal-winning U.S. Olympic team (1976).

COLLEGIATE RECORD

NOTES: THE SPORTING NEWS All-America first team (1975, 1976).

Season Team	G	Min.	FGM	FGA	Pct.	FTM	FTA	Pct.	Reb.	Ast.	Pts.	AVERAGES RPG	APG	PPG
73-74—Notre Dame..................	28	795	189	339	.558	133	161	.826	255	40	511	9.1	1.4	18.3
74-75—Notre Dame..................	29	1091	315	581	.542	253	314	.806	296	47	883	10.2	1.6	30.4
75-76—Notre Dame..................	29	1056	300	510	.588	229	294	.779	292	49	829	10.1	1.7	28.6
Totals	86	2942	804	1430	.562	615	769	.800	843	136	2223	9.8	1.6	25.8

NBA REGULAR-SEASON RECORD

RECORDS: Shares single-game records for most free throws made—28 (January 4, 1984, vs. Houston); and most free throws made in one quarter—14 (December 10, 1986, vs. Sacramento).
HONORS: NBA Rookie of the Year (1977). ... All-NBA second team (1981, 1984). ... NBA All-Rookie team (1977). ... NBA Comeback Player of the Year (1984).

Season Team	G	Min.	FGM	FGA	Pct.	FTM	FTA	Pct.	REBOUNDS Off.	Def.	Tot.	Ast.	St.	Blk.	TO	Pts.	AVERAGES RPG	APG	PPG
76-77—Buffalo	77	2816	544	1046	.520	476	582	.818	251	336	587	144	91	15	...	1564	7.6	1.9	20.3
77-78—Ind.-L.A.	79	2933	578	1128	.512	*541	680	.796	265	355	620	253	118	24	228	1697	7.8	3.2	21.5
78-79—Los Angeles....	60	1775	374	733	.510	292	342	.854	131	211	342	138	63	12	155	1040	5.7	2.3	17.3
79-80—Utah..............	68	2674	730	1267	.576	443	526	.842	183	333	516	191	96	14	233	1903	7.6	2.8	28.0
80-81—Utah..............	80	*3417	*909	1627	.559	*632	784	.806	192	317	509	322	109	18	282	*2452	6.4	4.0	*30.7
81-82—Utah..............	81	3222	904	1586	.570	*648	818	.792	231	283	514	324	95	14	†299	2457	6.3	4.0	30.3
82-83—Utah..............	22	887	233	402	.580	210	248	.847	58	82	140	105	20	0	81	676	6.4	4.8	30.7
83-84—Utah..............	79	2984	802	1438	.558	*813	*946	.859	179	269	448	310	61	4	263	*2418	5.7	3.9	*30.6
84-85—Utah..............	55	1971	512	964	.531	438	545	.804	148	175	323	186	57	8	171	1462	5.9	3.4	26.6
85-86—Utah..............	76	2744	818	1453	.563	*630	796	.791	178	217	395	264	64	4	231	2267	5.2	3.5	29.8
86-87—Detroit	81	2736	601	1126	.534	539	664	.812	104	228	332	162	63	7	181	1742	4.1	2.0	21.5
87-88—Detroit	69	2144	444	863	.514	492	572	.860	84	143	227	171	39	10	135	1380	3.3	2.5	20.0
88-89—Detroit-Dal.......	73	2422	470	954	.493	460	568	.810	117	200	317	171	43	13	163	1400	4.3	2.3	19.2
89-90—Dallas............	45	1300	231	484	.477	200	254	.787	78	94	172	80	20	7	75	662	3.8	1.8	14.7
90-91—Milwaukee	10	126	19	50	.380	18	26	.692	8	5	13	9	5	0	6	57	1.3	0.9	5.7
Totals	955	34151	8169	15121	.540	6832	8351	.818	2207	3248	5455	2830	944	150	2503	23177	5.7	3.0	24.3

Three-point field goals: 1979-80, 0-for-2. 1980-81, 2-for-7 (.286). 1981-82, 1-for-3 (.333). 1983-84, 1-for-4 (.250). 1985-86, 1-for-11 (.091). 1986-87, 1-for-6 (.167). 1987-88, 0-for-2. 1988-89, 0-for-1. 1989-90, 0-for-2. 1990-91, 1-for-3 (.333). Totals, 7-for-41 (.171).
Personal fouls/disqualifications: 1976-77, 215/2. 1977-78, 233/2. 1978-79, 162/0. 1979-80, 211/2. 1980-81, 245/1. 1981-82, 252/1. 1982-83, 62/2. 1983-84, 201/0. 1984-85, 133/0. 1985-86, 206/2. 1986-87, 193/1. 1987-88, 144/0. 1988-89, 186/1. 1989-90, 99/0. 1990-91, 8/0. Totals, 2550/14.

NBA PLAYOFF RECORD

Season Team	G	Min.	FGM	FGA	Pct.	FTM	FTA	Pct.	REBOUNDS Off.	Def.	Tot.	Ast.	St.	Blk.	TO	Pts.	AVERAGES RPG	APG	PPG
77-78—Los Angeles....	3	104	20	35	.571	11	17	.647	9	16	25	11	5	3	6	51	8.3	3.7	17.0
78-79—Los Angeles....	8	236	50	89	.562	41	52	.788	10	23	33	11	6	1	19	141	4.1	1.4	17.6
83-84—Utah..............	11	454	117	232	.504	120	139	.863	37	46	83	46	10	1	38	354	7.5	4.2	32.2
84-85—Utah..............	10	398	79	151	.523	95	122	.779	25	50	75	20	16	0	36	253	7.5	2.0	25.3
85-86—Utah..............							Did not play—injured.												
86-87—Detroit	15	500	111	206	.539	86	111	.775	29	39	68	35	13	0	33	308	4.5	2.3	20.5
87-88—Detroit	23	804	153	292	.524	140	178	.787	37	70	107	46	19	1	51	446	4.7	2.0	19.4
90-91—Milwaukee	3	19	1	7	.143	3	4	.750	2	2	4	0	0	0	2	5	1.3	0.0	1.7
Totals	73	2515	531	1012	.525	496	623	.796	149	246	395	169	69	6	185	1558	5.4	2.3	21.3

Three-point field goals: 1984-85, 0-for-1. 1987-88, 0-for-2. Totals, 0-for-3.
Personal fouls/disqualifications: 1977-78, 9/0. 1978-79, 24/0. 1983-84, 30/0. 1984-85, 39/1. 1986-87, 36/0. 1987-88, 50/0. Totals, 188/1.

NBA ALL-STAR GAME RECORD

Season	Team	Min.	FGM	FGA	Pct.	FTM	FTA	Pct.	REBOUNDS Off.	REBOUNDS Def.	REBOUNDS Tot.	Ast.	PF	Dq.	St.	Blk.	TO	Pts.
1980	—Utah	30	8	15	.533	7	8	.875	4	1	5	2	1	0	2	0	2	23
1981	—Utah	21	3	9	.333	2	2	1.000	2	3	5	0	1	0	1	0	0	8
1982	—Utah	21	6	8	.750	0	1	.000	1	1	2	0	2	0	0	0	1	12
1984	—Utah	18	1	8	.125	0	0	...	0	2	2	1	4	0	1	0	1	2
1985	—Utah	23	2	6	.333	6	6	1.000	0	2	2	1	4	0	1	0	2	10
1986	—Utah	17	3	8	.375	2	2	1.000	1	6	7	3	1	0	1	0	0	8
Totals		130	23	54	.426	17	19	.895	8	15	23	7	13	0	6	0	6	63

ITALIAN LEAGUE RECORD

Season Team	G	Min.	FGM	FGA	Pct.	FTM	FTA	Pct.	Reb.	Ast.	Pts.	AVERAGES RPG	AVERAGES APG	AVERAGES PPG
91-92—Breeze Milan	27	906	253	427	.593	179	221	.810	152	10	721	5.6	0.4	26.7

DAVIES, BOB   G

PERSONAL: Born January 15, 1920, in Harrisburg, Pa. ... Died April 22, 1990. ... 6-1/175 (1,85/79,4). ... Full name: Robert Edris Davies. ... Nickname: The Harrisburg Houdini.
HIGH SCHOOL: John Harris (Harrisburg, Pa.).
COLLEGE: Franklin & Marshall (Pa.), then Seton Hall.
TRANSACTIONS: Played with Great Lakes (Ill.) Naval Training Station during 1942-43 season (led team in scoring—269 points, 114 field goals and 41 free throws). ... In military service during 1942-43, 1943-44 and 1944-45 seasons. ... Played in American Basketball League with Brooklyn Indians (1943-44) and New York Gothams (1944-45). ... Signed as free agent by Rochester Royals of National Basketball League (1945). ... Royals franchise transferred to Basketball Association of America for 1948-49 season.
CAREER HONORS: Elected to Naismith Memorial Basketball Hall of Fame (1970). ... NBA 25th Anniversary All-Time Team (1970).
MISCELLANEOUS: Member of NBA championship team (1951). ... Member of NBL championship team (1946).

COLLEGIATE RECORD

Season Team	G	Min.	FGM	FGA	Pct.	FTM	FTA	Pct.	Reb.	Ast.	Pts.	AVERAGES RPG	AVERAGES APG	AVERAGES PPG
37-38—Frank. & Marshall‡					Freshman team statistics unavailable.									
38-39—Seton Hall‡					Freshman team statistics unavailable.									
39-40—Seton Hall	18	...	78	...	...	56	...	...	...	...	212	...	...	11.8
40-41—Seton Hall	22	...	91	...	...	42	...	...	...	...	224	...	...	10.2
41-42—Seton Hall	19	...	81	...	...	63	...	...	...	...	225	...	...	11.8
Varsity totals	59	...	250	...	...	161	...	...	...	...	661	...	...	11.2

ABL REGULAR-SEASON RECORD

Season Team	G	Min.	FGM	FGA	Pct.	FTM	FTA	Pct.	Reb.	Ast.	Pts.	AVERAGES RPG	AVERAGES APG	AVERAGES PPG
43-44—Brooklyn	4	...	8	...	...	8	...	...	...	...	24	...	...	6.0
44-45—New York	5	...	21	...	...	21	...	...	...	...	63	...	...	12.6
Totals	9	...	29	...	...	29	...	...	...	...	87	...	...	9.7

NBL AND NBA REGULAR-SEASON RECORD

HONORS: All-NBA first team (1950, 1951, 1952). ... All-NBA second team (1953). ... All-BAA first team (1949). ... NBL Most Valuable Player (1947). ... All-NBL first team (1947). ... All-NBL second team (1948).

Season Team	G	Min.	FGM	FGA	Pct.	FTM	FTA	Pct.	Reb.	Ast.	PF	Dq.	Pts.	RPG	APG	PPG
45-46 —Rochester (NBL)	27	...	86	...	...	70	103	.680	...	...	85	...	242	...	...	9.0
46-47 —Rochester (NBL)	32	...	166	...	...	130	166	.783	...	...	90	...	462	...	...	14.4
47-48 —Rochester (NBL)	48	...	176	...	...	120	160	.750	...	...	111	...	472	...	...	9.8
48-49 —Rochester (BAA)	60	...	317	871	.364	270	348	.776	...	*321	197	...	904	...	*5.4	15.1
49-50 —Rochester	64	...	317	887	.357	261	347	.752	...	294	187	...	895	...	4.6	14.0
50-51 —Rochester	63	...	326	877	.372	303	381	.795	197	287	208	7	955	3.1	4.6	15.2
51-52 —Rochester	65	2394	379	990	.383	294	379	.776	189	390	269	10	1052	2.9	6.0	16.2
52-53 —Rochester	66	2216	339	880	.385	351	466	.753	195	280	261	7	1029	3.0	4.2	15.6
53-54 —Rochester	72	2137	288	777	.371	311	433	.718	194	323	224	4	887	2.7	4.5	12.3
54-55 —Rochester	72	1870	326	785	.415	220	293	.751	205	355	220	2	872	2.8	4.9	12.1
Totals	569	...	2720	...	...	2330	3076	.757	...	...	1852	..	7770	...	...	13.7

NBL AND NBA PLAYOFF RECORD

Season Team	G	Min.	FGM	FGA	Pct.	FTM	FTA	Pct.	Reb.	Ast.	PF	Dq.	Pts.	RPG	APG	PPG
45-46 —Rochester (NBL)	7	...	28	...	...	30	41	.732	...	...	17	...	86	...	...	12.3
46-47 —Rochester (NBL)	11	...	54	...	...	43	63	.683	...	...	30	...	151	...	...	13.7
47-48 —Rochester (NBL)	11	...	56	...	...	49	64	.766	...	...	24	...	161	...	...	14.6
48-49 —Rochester (BAA)	4	...	19	51	.373	10	13	.769	...	13	11	...	48	...	3.3	12.0
49-50 —Rochester	2	...	4	17	.235	7	8	.875	...	9	11	...	15	...	4.5	7.5
50-51 —Rochester	14	...	79	234	.338	64	80	.800	43	75	45	1	222	3.1	5.4	15.9
51-52 —Rochester	6	233	37	92	.402	45	55	.818	13	28	18	0	119	2.2	4.7	19.8
52-53 —Rochester	3	91	6	29	.207	14	20	.700	4	14	11	0	26	1.3	4.7	8.7
53-54 —Rochester	6	172	17	52	.327	17	23	.739	12	14	16	0	51	2.0	2.3	8.5
54-55 —Rochester	3	75	11	33	.333	3	4	.750	6	9	11	0	25	2.0	3.0	8.3
Totals	67	...	311	...	...	282	371	.760	...	...	194	...	904	...	...	13.5

NBA ALL-STAR GAME RECORD

Season Team	Min.	FGM	FGA	Pct.	FTM	FTA	Pct.	Reb	Ast.	PF	Dq.	Pts.
1951 —Rochester	...	4	6	.667	5	5	1.000	5	5	3	0	13
1952 —Rochester	27	4	11	.364	0	0	...	0	5	4	0	8
1953 —Rochester	17	3	7	.429	3	6	.500	3	2	2	0	9
1954 —Rochester	31	8	16	.500	2	3	.667	5	5	4	0	18
Totals	...	19	40	.475	10	14	.714	13	17	13	0	48

COLLEGIATE COACHING RECORD

Season Team	W	L	Pct.
46-47 —Seton Hall	24	3	.889
55-56 —Gettysburg	11	17	.393
56-57 —Gettysburg	7	18	.280
Totals (3 years)	42	38	.525

DAVIS, WALTER   G

PERSONAL: Born September 9, 1954, in Pineville, N.C. ... 6-6/200 (1,98/90,7). ... Full name: Walter Paul Davis. ... Uncle of Hubert Davis, guard with Dallas Mavericks.
HIGH SCHOOL: South Mecklenburg (Charlotte).
COLLEGE: North Carolina.
TRANSACTIONS: Selected by Phoenix Suns in first round (fifth pick overall) of 1977 NBA Draft. ... Signed as unrestricted free agent by Denver Nuggets (July 6, 1988). ... Traded by Nuggets to Portland Trail Blazers in three-way deal in which Trail Blazers sent G Drazen Petrovic to New Jersey Nets, Nets sent F Greg Anderson to Nuggets, and Nuggets sent F Terry Mills to Nets (January 23, 1991); Nuggets also received 1992 first-round draft choice from Nets and 1993 second-round draft choice from Trail Blazers and Trail Blazers also received 1992 second-round draft choice from Nuggets. ... Waived by Trail Blazers (October 29, 1991). ... Signed as free agent by Nuggets (November 1, 1991).
MISCELLANEOUS: Member of gold-medal-winning U.S. Olympic team (1976). ... Phoenix Suns all-time leading scorer with 15,666 points (1977-78 through 1987-88).

COLLEGIATE RECORD

Season Team	G	Min.	FGM	FGA	Pct.	FTM	FTA	Pct.	Reb.	Ast.	Pts.	AVERAGES RPG	APG	PPG
73-74—North Carolina	27	...	161	322	.500	65	82	.793	126	72	387	4.7	2.7	14.3
74-75—North Carolina	31	...	200	396	.505	98	130	.754	195	137	498	6.3	4.4	16.1
75-76—North Carolina	29	...	190	351	.541	101	130	.777	166	96	481	5.7	3.3	16.6
76-77—North Carolina	32	...	203	351	.578	91	117	.778	183	104	497	5.7	3.3	15.5
Totals	119	...	754	1420	.531	355	459	.773	670	409	1863	5.6	3.4	15.7

NBA REGULAR-SEASON RECORD

HONORS: NBA Rookie of the Year (1978). ... All-NBA second team (1978, 1979). ... NBA All-Rookie team (1978).

Season Team	G	Min.	FGM	FGA	Pct.	FTM	FTA	Pct.	REBOUNDS Off.	Def.	Tot.	Ast.	St.	Blk.	TO	Pts.	AVERAGES RPG	APG	PPG
77-78—Phoenix	81	2590	786	1494	.526	387	466	.830	158	326	484	273	113	20	283	1959	6.0	3.4	24.2
78-79—Phoenix	79	2437	764	1362	.561	340	409	.831	111	262	373	339	147	26	293	1868	4.7	4.3	23.6
79-80—Phoenix	75	2309	657	1166	.563	299	365	.819	75	197	272	337	114	19	242	1613	3.6	4.5	21.5
80-81—Phoenix	78	2182	593	1101	.539	209	250	.836	63	137	200	302	97	12	222	1402	2.6	3.9	18.0
81-82—Phoenix	55	1182	350	669	.523	91	111	.820	21	82	103	162	46	3	112	794	1.9	2.9	14.4
82-83—Phoenix	80	2491	665	1289	.516	184	225	.818	63	134	197	397	117	12	188	1521	2.5	5.0	19.0
83-84—Phoenix	78	2546	652	1274	.512	233	270	.863	38	164	202	429	107	12	213	1557	2.6	5.5	20.0
84-85—Phoenix	23	570	139	309	.450	64	73	.877	6	29	35	98	18	0	50	345	1.5	4.3	15.0
85-86—Phoenix	70	2239	624	1287	.485	257	305	.843	54	149	203	361	99	3	219	1523	2.9	5.2	21.8
86-87—Phoenix	79	2646	779	1515	.514	288	334	.862	90	154	244	364	96	5	226	1867	3.1	4.6	23.6
87-88—Phoenix	68	1951	488	1031	.473	205	231	.887	32	127	159	278	86	3	126	1217	2.3	4.1	17.9
88-89—Denver	81	1857	536	1076	.498	175	199	.879	41	110	151	190	72	5	132	1267	1.9	2.3	15.6
89-90—Denver	69	1635	497	1033	.481	207	227	.912	46	133	179	155	59	9	102	1207	2.6	2.2	17.5
90-91—Den.-Port.	71	1483	403	862	.468	107	117	.915	71	110	181	125	80	3	88	924	2.5	1.8	13.0
91-92—Denver	46	741	185	403	.459	82	94	.872	20	50	70	68	29	1	45	457	1.5	1.5	9.9
Totals	1033	28859	8118	15871	.511	3128	3676	.851	889	2164	3053	3878	1280	133	2541	19521	3.0	3.8	18.9

Three-point field goals: 1979-80, 0-for-4. 1980-81, 7-for-17 (.412). 1981-82, 3-for-16 (.188). 1982-83, 7-for-23 (.304). 1983-84, 20-for-87 (.230). 1984-85, 3-for-10 (.300). 1985-86, 18-for-76 (.237). 1986-87, 21-for-81 (.259). 1987-88, 36-for-96 (.375). 1988-89, 20-for-69 (.290). 1989-90, 6-for-46 (.130). 1990-91, 11-for-34 (.306). 1991-92, 5-for-16 (.313). Totals, 157-for-571 (.272).

Personal fouls/disqualifications: 1977-78, 242/2. 1978-79, 250/5. 1979-80, 202/2. 1980-81, 192/3. 1981-82, 104/1. 1982-83, 186/2. 1983-84, 202/0. 1984-85, 42/0. 1985-86, 153/1. 1986-87, 184/1. 1987-88, 131/0. 1988-89, 187/1. 1989-90, 160/1. 1990-91, 150/2. 1991-92, 69/0. Totals, 2454/21.

NBA PLAYOFF RECORD

Season Team	G	Min.	FGM	FGA	Pct.	FTM	FTA	Pct.	REBOUNDS Off.	Def.	Tot.	Ast.	St.	Blk.	TO	Pts.	AVERAGES RPG	APG	PPG
77-78—Phoenix	2	66	19	40	.475	12	16	.750	4	13	17	8	3	0	6	50	8.5	4.0	25.0
78-79—Phoenix	15	490	127	244	.521	78	96	.813	24	45	69	79	26	5	66	332	4.6	5.3	22.1
79-80—Phoenix	8	245	69	137	.504	28	38	.737	9	14	23	35	4	1	20	166	2.9	4.4	20.8
80-81—Phoenix	7	199	51	106	.481	10	17	.588	7	12	19	22	7	1	17	112	2.7	3.1	16.0
81-82—Phoenix	7	173	52	116	.448	22	24	.917	5	17	22	30	5	1	12	127	3.1	4.3	18.1
82-83—Phoenix	3	113	30	69	.435	17	21	.810	5	10	15	13	6	5	5	78	5.0	4.3	26.0
83-84—Phoenix	17	623	175	327	.535	70	78	.897	15	31	46	109	29	3	43	423	2.7	6.4	24.9
88-89—Denver	3	94	31	60	.517	15	15	1.000	2	3	5	4	3	0	8	77	1.7	1.3	25.7
89-90—Denver	3	70	18	45	.400	6	6	1.000	4	5	9	6	1	0	5	42	3.0	2.0	14.0
90-91—Portland	13	111	19	48	.396	5	6	.833	7	8	15	6	4	0	7	43	1.2	0.5	3.3
Totals	78	2184	591	1192	.496	263	317	.830	82	158	240	312	88	16	189	1450	3.1	4.0	18.6

Three-point field goals: 1979-80, 0-for-3. 1980-81, 0-for-1. 1981-82, 1-for-3 (.333). 1982-83, 1-for-2 (.500). 1983-84, 3-for-11 (.273). 1988-89, 0-for-4. 1989-90, 0-for-1. 1990-91, 0-for-1. Totals, 5-for-26 (.192).

Personal fouls/disqualifications: 1977-78, 8/0. 1978-79, 41/0. 1979-80, 20/0. 1980-81, 17/0. 1981-82, 19/0. 1982-83, 6/0. 1983-84, 55/0. 1988-89, 11/0. 1989-90, 4/0. 1990-91, 5/0. Totals, 186/0.

NBA ALL-STAR GAME RECORD

Season	Team	Min.	FGM	FGA	Pct.	FTM	FTA	Pct.	Off.	Def.	Tot.	Ast.	PF	Dq.	St.	Blk.	TO	Pts.
									REBOUNDS									
1978	—Phoenix	15	3	6	.500	4	4	1.000	0	1	1	6	1	0	1	0	0	10
1979	—Phoenix	19	4	9	.444	0	0	...	1	3	4	4	0	0	1	0	2	8
1980	—Phoenix	23	5	10	.500	2	2	1.000	2	2	4	2	2	0	4	0	3	12
1981	—Phoenix	22	5	9	.556	2	2	1.000	1	6	7	1	2	0	0	0	1	12
1984	—Phoenix	15	5	9	.556	0	0	...	0	2	2	1	0	0	1	0	0	10
1987	—Phoenix	15	3	12	.250	0	0	...	2	0	2	1	0	0	0	0	0	7
	Totals	109	25	55	.455	8	8	1.000	6	14	20	15	5	0	7	0	6	59

Three-point field goals: 1987, 1-for-1.

DeBUSSCHERE, DAVE   F

PERSONAL: Born October 16, 1940, in Detroit. ... 6-6/235 (1,98/106,6). ... Full name: David Albert DeBusschere.
HIGH SCHOOL: Austin Catholic (Detroit).
COLLEGE: Detroit.
TRANSACTIONS: Selected by Detroit Pistons in 1962 NBA Draft (territorial pick). ... Traded by Pistons to New York Knicks for C Walt Bellamy and G Howard Komives (December 19, 1968).
CAREER HONORS: Elected to Naismith Memorial Basketball Hall of Fame (1983). ... One of the 50 Greatest Players in NBA History (1996).
CAREER NOTES: General manager, New York Knicks (May 1982 through January 1986).
MISCELLANEOUS: Member of NBA championship team (1970, 1973).

COLLEGIATE RECORD

Season Team	G	Min.	FGM	FGA	Pct.	FTM	FTA	Pct.	Reb.	Ast.	Pts.	RPG	APG	PPG
												AVERAGES		
58-59—Detroit‡	15	...	144	306	.471	68	101	.673	305	...	356	20.3	...	23.7
59-60—Detroit	27	...	288	665	.433	115	196	.587	540	...	691	20.0	...	25.6
60-61—Detroit	27	...	256	636	.403	86	155	.555	514	...	598	19.0	...	22.1
61-62—Detroit	26	...	267	616	.433	162	242	.669	498	...	696	19.2	...	26.8
Varsity totals	80	...	811	1917	.423	363	593	.612	1552	...	1985	19.4	...	24.8

NBA REGULAR-SEASON RECORD

HONORS: All-NBA second team (1969). ... NBA All-Defensive first team (1969, 1970, 1971, 1972, 1973, 1974). ... NBA All-Rookie team (1963).

Season Team	G	Min.	FGM	FGA	Pct.	FTM	FTA	Pct.	Reb.	Ast.	PF	Dq.	Pts.	RPG	APG	PPG
														AVERAGES		
62-63 —Detroit	80	2352	406	944	.430	206	287	.718	694	207	247	2	1018	8.7	2.6	12.7
63-64 —Detroit	15	304	52	133	.391	25	43	.581	105	23	32	1	129	7.0	1.5	8.6
64-65 —Detroit	79	2769	508	1196	.425	306	437	.700	874	253	242	5	1322	11.1	3.2	16.7
65-66 —Detroit	79	2696	524	1284	.408	249	378	.659	916	209	252	5	1297	11.6	2.6	16.4
66-67 —Detroit	78	2897	531	1278	.416	361	512	.705	924	216	297	7	1423	11.8	2.8	18.2
67-68 —Detroit	80	3125	573	1295	.442	289	435	.664	1081	181	304	3	1435	13.5	2.3	17.9
68-69 —Detroit-N.Y.	76	2943	506	1140	.444	229	328	.698	888	191	290	6	1241	11.7	2.5	16.3
69-70 —New York	79	2627	488	1082	.451	176	256	.688	790	194	244	2	1152	10.0	2.5	14.6
70-71 —New York	81	2891	523	1243	.421	217	312	.696	901	220	237	2	1263	11.1	2.7	15.6
71-72 —New York	80	3072	520	1218	.427	193	265	.728	901	291	219	1	1233	11.3	3.6	15.4
72-73 —New York	77	2827	532	1224	.435	194	260	.746	787	259	215	1	1258	10.2	3.4	16.3

Season Team	G	Min.	FGM	FGA	Pct.	FTM	FTA	Pct.	Off.	Def.	Tot.	Ast.	St.	Blk.	TO	Pts.	RPG	APG	PPG
									REBOUNDS								AVERAGES		
73-74—New York	71	2699	559	1212	.461	164	217	.756	134	623	757	253	67	39	...	1282	10.7	3.6	18.1
Totals	875	31202	5722	13249	.432	2609	3730	.699	...	...	9618	2497	67	39	...	14053	11.0	2.9	16.1

Personal fouls/disqualifications: 1973-74, 222/2.

NBA PLAYOFF RECORD

Season Team	G	Min.	FGM	FGA	Pct.	FTM	FTA	Pct.	Reb.	Ast.	PF	Dq.	Pts.	RPG	APG	PPG
														AVERAGES		
62-63 —Detroit	4	159	25	59	.424	30	44	.682	63	6	14	1	80	15.8	1.5	20.0
67-68 —Detroit	6	263	45	106	.425	26	45	.578	97	13	23	0	116	16.2	2.2	19.3
68-69 —New York	10	419	61	174	.351	41	50	.820	148	33	43	0	163	14.8	3.3	16.3
69-70 —New York	19	701	130	309	.421	45	68	.662	220	46	63	1	305	11.6	2.4	16.1
70-71 —New York	12	488	84	202	.416	29	44	.659	156	22	40	1	197	13.0	1.8	16.4
71-72 —New York	16	616	109	242	.450	48	64	.750	193	37	51	2	266	12.1	2.3	16.6
72-73 —New York	17	632	117	265	.442	31	40	.775	179	58	57	0	265	10.5	3.4	15.6

Season Team	G	Min.	FGM	FGA	Pct.	FTM	FTA	Pct.	Off.	Def.	Tot.	Ast.	St.	Blk.	TO	Pts.	RPG	APG	PPG
									REBOUNDS								AVERAGES		
73-74—New York	12	404	63	166	.380	18	29	.621	25	74	99	38	7	4	...	144	8.3	3.2	12.0
Totals	96	3682	634	1523	.416	268	384	.698	...	...	1155	253	...	...	...	1536	12.0	2.6	16.0

Personal fouls/disqualifications: 1973-74, 36/0.

NBA ALL-STAR GAME RECORD

NOTES: Shares single-game record for most field goals made in one quarter—8 (1967).

Season	Team	Min.	FGM	FGA	Pct.	FTM	FTA	Pct.	Reb	Ast.	PF	Dq.	Pts.
1966	—Detroit	22	1	14	.071	2	2	1.000	6	1	1	0	4
1967	—Detroit	25	11	17	.647	0	0	...	6	0	1	0	22
1968	—Detroit	12	0	3	.000	0	0	...	4	0	1	0	0
1970	—New York	14	5	10	.500	0	0	...	7	2	1	0	10
1971	—New York	19	4	7	.571	0	0	...	7	3	3	0	8
1972	—New York	26	4	8	.500	0	0	...	11	0	2	0	8
1973	—New York	25	4	8	.500	1		.500	7	2	1	0	9

Season	Team	Min.	FGM	FGA	Pct.	FTM	FTA	Pct.	Off.	Def.	Tot.	Ast.	PF	Dq.	St.	Blk.	TO	Pts.
									REBOUNDS									
1974	—New York	24	8	14	.571	0	0	...	2	1	3	3	2	0	1	0	...	16
	Totals	167	37	81	.457	3	4	.750	...	...	51	11	12	0	1	0	...	77

NBA COACHING RECORD

BACKGROUND: Player/head coach, Detroit Pistons (November 1964 to March 1967).
MISCELLANEOUS: Youngest coach in NBA history.

Season Team	W	L	Pct.	Finish		W	L	Pct.
		REGULAR SEASON					PLAYOFFS	
64-65 —Detroit	29	40	.420	4th/Western Division		—	—	—
65-66 —Detroit	22	58	.275	5th/Western Division		—	—	—
66-67 —Detroit	28	45	.384			—	—	—
Totals (3 years)..................................	**79**	**143**	**.356**					

NOTES:
1964—Replaced Charles Wolf as Detroit head coach (November), with record of 2-9.
1967—Replaced as Detroit head coach by Donnis Butcher (March).

RECORD AS BASEBALL PLAYER

TRANSACTIONS: Signed by Chicago White Sox (April 1, 1962). ... On disabled list (June 4-20, 1964). ... On restricted list (September 7, 1965-December 19, 1968). ... Released by White Sox organization (December 23, 1968).

Year Team (League)	W	L	Pct.	ERA	G	GS	CG	ShO	Sv.	IP	H	R	ER	BB	SO
1962—Chicago (A.L.)	0	0	...	2.00	12	0	0	0	...	18	5	7	4	23	8
Savannah (S. Atl.)	10	1	.909	2.49	15	14	7	2	...	94	62	35	26	53	93
1963—Chicago (A.L.)	3	4	.429	3.11	24	10	1	1	...	84	80	35	29	34	53
1964—Indianapolis (PCL).............	15	8	.652	3.93	32	30	10	2	...	174	173	88	76	66	126
1965—Indianapolis (PCL).............	15	12	.556	3.65	35	*34	10	1	...	*244	*255	120	99	66	176
Major league totals (2 years) ...	**3**	**4**	**.429**	**2.91**	**36**	**10**	**1**	**1**	**...**	**102**	**85**	**42**	**33**	**57**	**61**

DREXLER, CLYDE   G

PERSONAL: Born June 22, 1962, in New Orleans. ... 6-7/222 (2,00/100,7). ... Full name: Clyde Austin Drexler.
HIGH SCHOOL: Sterling (Houston).
COLLEGE: Houston.
TRANSACTIONS: Selected after junior season by Portland Trail Blazers in first round (14th pick overall) of 1983 NBA Draft. ... Traded by Trail Blazers with F Tracy Murray to Houston Rockets for F Otis Thorpe, rights to F Marcelo Nicola and 1995 first-round draft choice (February 14, 1995). ... Announced retirement, effective with the conclusion of 1997-98 season (March 18, 1998).
CAREER HONORS: One of the 50 Greatest Players in NBA History (1996).
MISCELLANEOUS: Member of NBA championship team (1995). ... Member of gold-medal-winning U.S. Olympic team (1992). ... Portland Trail Blazers all-time leading scorer with 18,040 points, all-time leading rebounder with 5,339 and all-time steals leader with 1,795 (1983-84 through 1994-95).
CAREER NOTES: Head coach, University of Houston (1998-99 to 1999-2000).

COLLEGIATE RECORD

Season Team	G	Min.	FGM	FGA	Pct.	FTM	FTA	Pct.	Reb.	Ast.	Pts.	RPG	APG	PPG
													AVERAGES	
80-81—Houston	30	992	153	303	.505	50	85	.588	314	78	356	10.5	2.6	11.9
81-82—Houston	32	1077	206	362	.569	73	120	.608	336	96	485	10.5	3.0	15.2
82-83—Houston	34	1186	236	440	.536	70	95	.737	298	129	542	8.8	3.8	15.9
Totals	**96**	**3255**	**595**	**1105**	**.538**	**193**	**300**	**.643**	**948**	**303**	**1383**	**9.9**	**3.2**	**14.4**

NBA REGULAR-SEASON RECORD

HONORS: All-NBA first team (1992). ... All-NBA second team (1988, 1991). ... All-NBA third team (1990, 1995).

Season Team	G	Min.	FGM	FGA	Pct.	FTM	FTA	Pct.	Off.	Def.	Tot.	Ast.	St.	Blk.	TO	Pts.	RPG	APG	PPG
										REBOUNDS								AVERAGES	
83-84—Portland.........	82	1408	252	559	.451	123	169	.728	112	123	235	153	107	29	123	628	2.9	1.9	7.7
84-85—Portland.........	80	2555	573	1161	.494	223	294	.759	217	259	476	441	177	68	223	1377	6.0	5.5	17.2
85-86—Portland.........	75	2576	542	1142	.475	293	381	.769	171	250	421	600	197	46	282	1389	5.6	8.0	18.5
86-87—Portland.........	82	3114	707	1408	.502	357	470	.760	227	291	518	566	204	71	253	1782	6.3	6.9	21.7
87-88—Portland.........	81	3060	849	1679	.506	476	587	.811	261	272	533	467	203	52	236	2185	6.6	5.8	27.0
88-89—Portland.........	78	3064	829	1672	.496	438	548	.799	289	326	615	450	213	54	250	2123	7.9	5.8	27.2
89-90—Portland.........	73	2683	670	1357	.494	333	430	.774	208	299	507	432	145	51	191	1703	6.9	5.9	23.3
90-91—Portland.........	82	2852	645	1338	.482	416	524	.794	212	334	546	493	144	60	232	1767	6.7	6.0	21.5
91-92—Portland.........	76	2751	694	1476	.470	401	505	.794	166	334	500	512	178	70	240	1903	6.6	6.7	25.0
92-93—Portland.........	49	1671	350	816	.429	245	292	.839	126	183	309	278	95	37	115	976	6.3	5.7	19.9
93-94—Portland.........	68	2334	473	1105	.428	286	368	.777	154	291	445	333	98	34	167	1303	6.5	4.9	19.2
94-95—Port.-Hou.......	76	2728	571	1238	.461	364	442	.824	152	328	480	362	136	45	186	1653	6.3	4.8	21.8
95-96—Houston.........	52	1997	331	764	.433	265	338	.784	97	276	373	302	105	24	134	1005	7.2	5.8	19.3
96-97—Houston.........	62	2271	397	899	.442	201	268	.750	118	255	373	354	119	36	156	1114	6.0	5.7	18.0
97-98—Houston.........	70	2473	452	1059	.427	277	346	.801	105	241	346	382	126	42	189	1287	4.9	5.5	18.4
Totals	**1086**	**37537**	**8335**	**17673**	**.472**	**4698**	**5962**	**.788**	**2615**	**4062**	**6677**	**6125**	**2207**	**719**	**2977**	**22195**	**6.1**	**5.6**	**20.4**

Three-point field goals: 1983-84, 1-for-4 (.250). 1984-85, 8-for-37 (.216). 1985-86, 12-for-60 (.200). 1986-87, 11-for-47 (.234). 1987-88, 11-for-52 (.212). 1988-89, 27-for-104 (.260). 1989-90, 30-for-106 (.283). 1990-91, 61-for-191 (.319). 1991-92, 114-for-338 (.337). 1992-93, 31-for-133 (.233). 1993-94, 71-for-219 (.324). 1994-95, 147-for-408 (.360). 1995-96, 78-for-235 (.332). 1996-97, 119-for-335 (.355). 1997-98, 106-for-334 (.317). Totals, 827-for-2603 (.318).

Personal fouls/disqualifications: 1983-84, 209/2. 1984-85, 265/3. 1985-86, 270/8. 1986-87, 281/7. 1987-88, 250/2. 1988-89, 269/2. 1989-90, 222/1. 1990-91, 226/2. 1991-92, 229/2. 1992-93, 159/1. 1993-94, 202/2. 1994-95, 206/1. 1995-96, 153/0. 1996-97, 151/0. 1997-98, 193/0. Totals, 3285/33.

NBA PLAYOFF RECORD

NOTES: Holds single-game playoff record for most points in an overtime period—13 (April 29, 1992, vs. Los Angeles Lakers).

Season Team	G	Min.	FGM	FGA	Pct.	FTM	FTA	Pct.	REBOUNDS Off.	Def.	Tot.	Ast.	St.	Blk.	TO	Pts.	AVERAGES RPG	APG	PPG
83-84—Portland	5	85	15	35	.429	6	7	.857	7	10	17	8	5	1	7	36	3.4	1.6	7.2
84-85—Portland	9	339	55	134	.410	38	45	.844	27	28	55	83	23	9	29	150	6.1	9.2	16.7
85-86—Portland	4	145	26	57	.456	18	23	.783	9	16	25	26	6	3	19	72	6.3	6.5	18.0
86-87—Portland	4	153	36	79	.456	23	29	.793	16	14	30	15	7	3	6	96	7.5	3.8	24.0
87-88—Portland	4	170	32	83	.386	21	29	.724	12	16	28	21	12	2	12	88	7.0	5.3	22.0
88-89—Portland	3	128	35	71	.493	13	17	.765	13	7	20	25	6	2	12	83	6.7	8.3	27.7
89-90—Portland	21	853	172	390	.441	96	124	.774	63	88	151	150	53	18	67	449	7.2	7.1	21.4
90-91—Portland	16	633	128	269	.476	76	98	.776	40	89	129	129	34	16	61	347	8.1	8.1	21.7
91-92—Portland	21	847	198	425	.466	138	171	.807	60	95	155	147	31	20	58	553	7.4	7.0	26.3
92-93—Portland	3	116	18	43	.419	16	20	.800	8	11	19	14	5	3	3	57	6.3	4.7	19.0
93-94—Portland	4	157	31	73	.425	19	23	.826	10	31	41	22	8	2	9	84	10.3	5.5	21.0
94-95—Houston	22	849	155	322	.481	110	140	.786	45	109	154	111	33	15	45	450	7.0	5.0	20.5
95-96—Houston	8	292	49	118	.415	26	34	.765	15	47	62	40	21	4	20	133	7.8	5.0	16.6
96-97—Houston	16	623	105	241	.436	42	54	.778	25	64	89	77	26	7	36	290	5.6	4.8	18.1
97-98—Houston	5	182	21	68	.309	28	37	.757	9	18	27	23	8	3	13	75	5.4	4.6	15.0
Totals	145	5572	1076	2408	.447	670	851	.787	359	643	1002	891	278	108	397	2963	6.9	6.1	20.4

Three-point field goals: 1983-84, 0-for-1. 1984-85, 2-for-7 (.286). 1985-86, 2-for-5 (.400). 1986-87, 1-for-4 (.250). 1987-88, 3-for-6 (.500). 1988-89, 0-for-2. 1989-90, 9-for-41 (.220). 1990-91, 15-for-56 (.268). 1991-92, 19-for-81 (.235). 1992-93, 5-for-12 (.417). 1993-94, 3-for-13 (.231). 1994-95, 30-for-99 (.303). 1995-96, 9-for-34 (.265). 1996-97, 38-for-102 (.373). 1997-98, 5-for-26 (.192). Totals, 141-for-489 (.288).

Personal fouls/disqualifications: 1983-84, 11/0. 1984-85, 37/0. 1985-86, 19/1. 1986-87, 16/1. 1987-88, 14/0. 1988-89, 11/0. 1989-90, 72/2. 1990-91, 56/0. 1991-92, 77/2. 1992-93, 9/0. 1993-94, 7/0. 1994-95, 68/1. 1995-96, 22/0. 1996-97, 52/0. 1997-98, 15/0. Totals, 486/7.

NBA ALL-STAR GAME RECORD

NOTES: Teamed with Cynthia Cooper to win inaugural Nestlé Crunch All-Star 2ball championship (1998).

Season Team	Min.	FGM	FGA	Pct.	FTM	FTA	Pct.	REBOUNDS Off.	Def.	Tot.	Ast.	PF	Dq.	St.	Blk.	TO	Pts.
1986 —Portland	15	5	7	.714	0	0	...	0	4	4	4	3	0	3	1	3	10
1988 —Portland	15	3	5	.600	6	6	1.000	2	3	5	0	3	0	1	0	1	12
1989 —Portland	25	7	19	.368	0	0	...	6	6	12	4	3	0	2	0	6	14
1990 —Portland	19	2	6	.333	2	2	1.000	4	0	4	2	1	0	1	1	1	7
1991 —Portland	19	4	9	.444	4	4	1.000	2	2	4	2	3	0	1	1	0	12
1992 —Portland	28	10	15	.667	0	0	...	2	7	9	6	2	0	0	2	1	22
1993 —Portland	11	1	3	.333	0	0	...	1	0	1	1	3	0	0	0	2	2
1994 —Portland	15	3	7	.429	0	0	...	0	3	3	1	1	0	1	1	1	6
1996 —Houston	19	5	8	.625	0	0	...	0	2	2	3	0	0	3	0	3	11
1997 —Houston							Selected, did not play—injured.										
Totals	166	40	79	.506	12	12	1.000	17	27	44	23	19	0	12	6	18	96

Three-point field goals: 1986, 0-for-1. 1988, 0-for-1. 1990, 1-for-1. 1992, 2-for-4 (.500). 1993, 0-for-1. 1994, 0-for-2. 1996, 1-for-4 (.250). Totals, 4-for-14 (.286).

COLLEGIATE COACHING RECORD

Season Team	W	L	Pct.	
98-99—Houston	10	17	.370	6th/National Division/Conference USA
99-00—Houston	9	22	.290	6th/National Division/Conference USA

DUMARS, JOE   G

PERSONAL: Born May 24, 1963, in Shreveport, La. ... 6-3/195 (1,90/88,5). ... Full name: Joe Dumars III.
HIGH SCHOOL: Natchitoches (La.) Central.
COLLEGE: McNeese State.
TRANSACTIONS/CAREER NOTES: Selected by Detroit Pistons in first round (18th pick overall) of 1985 NBA Draft. ... Announced retirement (April 28, 1999).
MISCELLANEOUS: Member of NBA championship team (1989, 1990).
CAREER NOTES: Vice President of Player Personnel, Detroit Pistons (1999-2000). ... President of Basketball Operations, Detroit Pistons (June 6, 2000-present).

COLLEGIATE RECORD

NOTES: The Sporting News All-America second team (1985).

Season Team	G	Min.	FGM	FGA	Pct.	FTM	FTA	Pct.	Reb.	Ast.	Pts.	AVERAGES RPG	APG	PPG
81-82—McNeese State	29	...	206	464	.444	115	160	.719	64	80	527	2.2	2.8	18.2
82-83—McNeese State	29	...	212	487	.435	140	197	.711	128	64	569	4.4	2.2	19.6
83-84—McNeese State	31	...	276	586	.471	267	324	.824	164	80	819	5.3	2.6	26.4
84-85—McNeese State	27	...	248	501	.495	201	236	.852	132	106	697	4.9	3.9	25.8
Totals	116	...	942	2038	.462	723	917	.788	488	330	2012	4.2	2.8	22.5

Three-point field goals: 1982-83, 5-for-8 (.625).

NBA REGULAR-SEASON RECORD

HONORS: J. Walter Kennedy Citizenship Award (1994). ... NBA Sportsmanship Award (1996). ... All-NBA second team (1993). ... All-NBA third team (1990, 1991). ... NBA All-Defensive first team (1989, 1990, 1992, 1993). ... NBA All-Defensive second team (1991). ... NBA All-Rookie team (1986).

Season Team	G	Min.	FGM	FGA	Pct.	FTM	FTA	Pct.	REBOUNDS Off.	Def.	Tot.	Ast.	St.	Blk.	TO	Pts.	AVERAGES RPG	APG	PPG
85-86—Detroit	82	1957	287	597	.481	190	238	.798	60	59	119	390	66	11	158	769	1.5	4.8	9.4
86-87—Detroit	79	2439	369	749	.493	184	246	.748	50	117	167	352	83	5	171	931	2.1	4.5	11.8
87-88—Detroit	82	2732	453	960	.472	251	308	.815	63	137	200	387	87	15	172	1161	2.4	4.7	14.2
88-89—Detroit	69	2408	456	903	.505	260	306	.850	57	115	172	390	63	5	178	1186	2.5	5.7	17.2
89-90—Detroit	75	2578	508	1058	.480	297	330	.900	60	152	212	368	63	2	145	1335	2.8	4.9	17.8
90-91—Detroit	80	3046	622	1292	.481	371	417	.890	62	125	187	443	89	7	189	1629	2.3	5.5	20.4
91-92—Detroit	82	3192	587	1311	.448	412	475	.867	82	106	188	375	71	12	193	1635	2.3	4.6	19.9
92-93—Detroit	77	3094	677	1454	.466	343	397	.864	63	85	148	308	78	7	138	1809	1.9	4.0	23.5
93-94—Detroit	69	2591	505	1118	.452	276	330	.836	35	116	151	261	63	4	159	1410	2.2	3.8	20.4

Season Team	G	Min.	FGM	FGA	Pct.	FTM	FTA	Pct.	REBOUNDS Off.	Def.	Tot.	Ast.	St.	Blk.	TO	Pts.	AVERAGES RPG	APG	PPG
94-95—Detroit	67	2544	417	970	.430	277	344	.805	47	111	158	368	72	7	219	1214	2.4	5.5	18.1
95-96—Detroit	67	2193	255	598	.426	162	197	.822	28	110	138	265	43	3	97	793	2.1	4.0	11.8
96-97—Detroit	79	2923	385	875	.440	222	256	.867	38	153	191	318	57	1	128	1158	2.4	4.0	14.7
97-98—Detroit	72	2326	329	791	.416	127	154	.825	14	90	104	253	44	2	84	943	1.4	3.5	13.1
98-99—Detroit	38	1116	144	350	.411	51	61	.836	12	56	68	134	23	2	53	428	1.8	3.5	11.3
Totals	1018	35139	5994	13026	.460	3423	4059	.843	671	1532	2203	4612	902	83	2084	16401	2.2	4.5	16.1

Three-point field goals: 1985-86, 5-for-16 (.313). 1986-87, 9-for-22 (.409). 1987-88, 4-for-19 (.211). 1988-89, 14-for-29 (.483). 1989-90, 22-for-55 (.400). 1990-91, 14-for-45 (.311). 1991-92, 49-for-120 (.408). 1992-93, 112-for-299 (.375). 1993-94, 124-for-320 (.388). 1994-95, 103-for-338 (.305). 1995-96, 121-for-298 (.406). 1996-97, 166-for-384 (.432). 1997-98, 158-for-426 (.371). 1998-99, 89-for-221 (.403). Totals, 990-for-2592 (.382).

Personal fouls/disqualifications: 1985-86, 200/1. 1986-87, 194/1. 1987-88, 155/1. 1988-89, 103/1. 1989-90, 129/1. 1990-91, 135/0. 1991-92, 145/0. 1992-93, 141/0. 1993-94, 118/0. 1994-95, 153/0. 1995-96, 106/0. 1996-97, 97/0. 1997-98, 99/0. 1998-99, 51/0. Totals, 1826/5.

NBA PLAYOFF RECORD

NOTES: NBA Finals Most Valuable Player (1989).

Season Team	G	Min.	FGM	FGA	Pct.	FTM	FTA	Pct.	REBOUNDS Off.	Def.	Tot.	Ast.	St.	Blk.	TO	Pts.	AVERAGES RPG	APG	PPG
85-86—Detroit	4	147	25	41	.610	10	15	.667	6	7	13	25	4	0	7	60	3.3	6.3	15.0
86-87—Detroit	15	473	78	145	.538	32	41	.780	8	11	19	72	12	1	27	190	1.3	4.8	12.7
87-88—Detroit	23	804	113	247	.457	56	63	.889	18	32	50	112	13	2	40	284	2.2	4.9	12.3
88-89—Detroit	17	620	106	233	.455	87	101	.861	11	33	44	96	12	1	31	300	2.6	5.6	17.6
89-90—Detroit	20	754	130	284	.458	99	113	.876	18	26	44	95	22	0	54	364	2.2	4.8	18.2
90-91—Detroit	15	588	105	245	.429	82	97	.845	21	29	50	62	16	1	17	309	3.3	4.1	20.6
91-92—Detroit	5	221	32	68	.471	15	19	.789	5	3	8	16	5	1	7	84	1.6	3.2	16.8
95-96—Detroit	3	123	16	35	.457	4	4	1.000	5	8	13	11	0	0	7	41	4.3	3.7	13.7
96-97—Detroit	5	214	22	61	.361	19	20	.950	2	7	9	10	5	0	6	69	1.8	2.0	13.8
98-99—Detroit	5	153	19	39	.487	3	3	1.000	1	6	7	13	2	0	9	51	1.4	2.6	10.2
Totals	112	4097	646	1398	.462	407	476	.855	95	162	257	512	91	6	205	1752	2.3	4.6	15.6

Three-point field goals: 1986-87, 2-for-3 (.667). 1987-88, 2-for-6 (.333). 1988-89, 1-for-12 (.083). 1989-90, 5-for-19 (.263). 1990-91, 17-for-42 (.405). 1991-92, 5-for-10 (.500). 1995-96, 5-for-14 (.357). 1996-97, 6-for-23 (.261). 1998-99, 10-for-19 (.526). Totals, 53-for-148 (.358).

Personal fouls/disqualifications: 1985-86, 16/0. 1986-87, 26/0. 1987-88, 50/1. 1988-89, 31/0. 1989-90, 37/0. 1990-91, 33/1. 1991-92, 11/0. 1995-96, 5/0. 1996-97, 9/0. 1998-99, 9/0. Totals, 227/2.

NBA ALL-STAR GAME RECORD

Season Team	Min.	FGM	FGA	Pct.	FTM	FTA	Pct.	REBOUNDS Off.	Def.	Tot.	Ast.	PF	Dq.	St.	Blk.	TO	Pts.
1990 —Detroit	18	3	4	.750	1	2	.500	0	1	1	5	0	0	0	0	3	9
1991 —Detroit	15	1	4	.250	0	0	...	1	1	2	1	1	0	0	0	4	2
1992 —Detroit	17	2	7	.286	0	0	...	0	1	1	3	0	0	0	0	2	4
1993 —Detroit	17	2	8	.250	0	0	...	0	2	2	4	1	0	0	0	1	5
1995 —Detroit	21	5	8	.625	0	0	...	0	0	0	6	1	0	1	0	1	11
1997 —Detroit	10	1	4	.250	0	0	...	0	1	1	1	0	0	0	0	0	3
Totals	98	14	35	.400	1	2	.500	1	6	7	20	3	0	1	0	11	34

Three-point field goals: 1990, 2-for-2. 1991, 0-for-1. 1992, 0-for-2. 1993, 1-for-4 (.250). 1995, 1-for-2 (.500). 1997, 1-for-4 (.250). Totals, 5-for-15 (.333).

ELLIS, DALE   G/F

PERSONAL: Born August 6, 1960, in Marietta, Ga. ... 6-7/215. (2.01 m/98 kg).
HIGH SCHOOL: Marietta (Ga.).
COLLEGE: Tennessee.
TRANSACTIONS/CAREER NOTES: Selected by Dallas Mavericks in first round (ninth pick overall) of 1983 NBA Draft. ... Traded by Mavericks to Seattle SuperSonics for G/F Al Wood (July 23, 1986). ... Traded by SuperSonics to Milwaukee Bucks for G/F Ricky Pierce (February 15, 1991). ... Traded by Bucks to San Antonio Spurs for draft rights to F Tracy Murray (July 1, 1992). ... Signed as free agent by Denver Nuggets (October 4, 1994). ... Traded by Nuggets to SuperSonics for G Greg Graham, C Steve Scheffler, 1998 second-round draft choice and 1999 or 2002 conditional second-round draft choice (October 2, 1997). ... Became a free agent when SuperSonics did not exercise option for 1998-99 season (June 30, 1998). ... Re-signed as free agent by SuperSonics (January 21, 1999). ... Traded by SuperSonics with F/G Billy Owens, F Don MacLean and draft rights to F Corey Maggette to Orlando Magic for F Horace Grant and 2001 and 2002 second-round draft choices (June 30, 1999). ... Traded by Magic with F/C Danny Manning to Milwaukee Bucks for F/C Chris Gatling and F Armen Gilliam (August 19, 1999). ... Traded by Bucks to Charlotte Hornets for 2000 and 2001 second-round draft choices (January 18, 2000). ... Traded by Hornets with G Eddie Jones, F Anthony Mason and G Ricky Davis to Miami Heat for F P.J. Brown, F Jamal Mashburn, F/C Otis Thorpe, F Tim James and G/F Rodney Buford (August 1, 2000). ... Waived by Heat (October 30, 2000).

COLLEGIATE RECORD

NOTES: THE SPORTING NEWS All-America first team (1983).

Season Team	G	Min.	FGM	FGA	Pct.	FTM	FTA	Pct.	Reb.	Ast.	Pts.	AVERAGES RPG	APG	PPG
79-80—Tennessee	27	573	81	182	.445	31	40	.775	96	34	193	3.6	1.3	7.1
80-81—Tennessee	29	1057	215	360	.597	83	111	.748	185	21	513	6.4	0.7	17.7
81-82—Tennessee	30	1134	257	393	.654	121	152	.796	189	22	635	6.3	0.7	21.2
82-83—Tennessee	32	1179	279	464	.601	166	221	.751	209	32	724	6.5	1.0	22.6
Totals	118	3943	832	1399	.595	401	524	.765	679	109	2065	5.8	0.9	17.5

NBA REGULAR-SEASON RECORD

RECORDS: Holds single-game record for most minutes played—69 (November 9, 1989, vs. Milwaukee, 5 OT).
HONORS: NBA Most Improved Player (1987). ... Long Distance Shootout winner (1989). ... All-NBA third team (1989).
NOTES: Led NBA with .464 three-point field goal percentage (1998).

Season Team	G	Min.	FGM	FGA	Pct.	FTM	FTA	Pct.	Off.	Def.	Tot.	Ast.	St.	Blk.	TO	Pts.	RPG	APG	PPG
									REBOUNDS								**AVERAGES**		
83-84—Dallas	67	1059	225	493	.456	87	121	.719	106	144	250	56	41	9	78	549	3.7	0.8	8.2
84-85—Dallas	72	1314	274	603	.454	77	104	.740	100	138	238	56	46	7	58	667	3.3	0.8	9.3
85-86—Dallas	72	1086	193	470	.411	59	82	.720	86	82	168	37	40	9	38	508	2.3	0.5	7.1
86-87—Seattle	82	3073	785	1520	.516	385	489	.787	187	260	447	238	104	32	238	2041	5.5	2.9	24.9
87-88—Seattle	75	2790	764	1519	.503	303	395	.767	167	173	340	197	74	11	172	1938	4.5	2.6	25.8
88-89—Seattle	82	3190	857	1710	.501	377	462	.816	156	186	342	164	108	22	218	2253	4.2	2.0	27.5
89-90—Seattle	55	2033	502	1011	.497	193	236	.818	90	148	238	110	59	7	119	1293	4.3	2.0	23.5
90-91—Seattle-Mil.	51	1424	340	718	.474	120	166	.723	66	107	173	95	49	8	81	857	3.4	1.9	16.8
91-92—Milwaukee	81	2191	485	1034	.469	164	212	.774	92	161	253	104	57	18	119	1272	3.1	1.3	15.7
92-93—San Antonio	82	2731	545	1092	.499	157	197	.797	81	231	312	107	78	18	111	1366	3.8	1.3	16.7
93-94—San Antonio	77	2590	478	967	.494	83	107	.776	70	185	255	80	66	11	75	1170	3.3	1.0	15.2
94-95—Denver	81	1996	351	774	.453	110	127	.866	56	166	222	57	37	9	81	918	2.7	0.7	11.3
95-96—Denver	81	2626	459	959	.479	136	179	.760	88	227	315	139	57	7	98	1204	3.9	1.7	14.9
96-97—Denver	82	2940	477	1151	.414	215	263	.817	99	194	293	165	60	7	146	1361	3.6	2.0	16.6
97-98—Seattle	79	1939	348	700	.497	111	142	.782	51	133	184	89	60	5	74	934	2.3	1.1	11.8
98-99—Seattle	48	1232	174	395	.441	53	70	.757	25	90	115	38	25	3	45	495	2.4	0.8	10.3
99-00—Mil.-Charlotte.	42	564	66	159	.415	9	13	.692	13	43	56	14	13	0	20	178	1.3	0.3	4.2
Totals	1209	34778	7323	15275	.479	2639	3365	.784	1533	2668	4201	1746	974	183	1771	19004	3.5	1.4	15.7

Three-point field goals: 1983-84, 12-for-29 (.414). 1984-85, 42-for-109 (.385). 1985-86, 63-for-173 (.364). 1986-87, 86-for-240 (.358). 1987-88, 107-for-259 (.413). 1988-89, 162-for-339 (.478). 1989-90, 96-for-256 (.375). 1990-91, 57-for-157 (.363). 1991-92, 138-for-329 (.419). 1992-93, 119-for-297 (.401). 1993-94, 131-for-332 (.395). 1994-95, 106-for-263 (.403). 1995-96, 150-for-364 (.412). 1996-97, 192-for-528 (.364). 1997-98, 127-for-274 (.464). 1998-99, 94-for-217 (.433). 1999-00, 37-for-100 (.370). Totals, 1719-for-4266 (.403).

Personal fouls/disqualifications: 1983-84, 118/0. 1984-85, 131/1. 1985-86, 78/0. 1986-87, 267/2. 1987-88, 221/1. 1988-89, 197/0. 1989-90, 124/3. 1990-91, 112/1. 1991-92, 151/0. 1992-93, 179/0. 1993-94, 141/0. 1994-95, 142/0. 1995-96, 191/1. 1996-97, 178/0. 1997-98, 128/0. 1998-99, 77/1. 1999-00, 45/0. Totals, 2480/10.

NBA PLAYOFF RECORD

Season Team	G	Min.	FGM	FGA	Pct.	FTM	FTA	Pct.	Off.	Def.	Tot.	Ast.	St.	Blk.	TO	Pts.	RPG	APG	PPG
									REBOUNDS								**AVERAGES**		
83-84—Dallas	8	178	26	80	.325	6	8	.750	19	23	42	4	10	2	5	59	5.3	0.5	7.4
84-85—Dallas	4	68	10	23	.435	1	2	.500	4	3	7	3	4	0	4	23	1.8	0.8	5.8
85-86—Dallas	7	67	9	22	.409	5	5	1.000	3	4	7	2	2	2	4	30	1.0	0.3	4.3
86-87—Seattle	14	530	148	304	.487	44	54	.815	37	53	90	37	10	6	33	353	6.4	2.6	25.2
87-88—Seattle	5	172	40	83	.482	21	29	.724	11	12	23	15	3	2	12	104	4.6	3.0	20.8
88-89—Seattle	8	304	72	160	.450	24	33	.727	14	18	32	10	11	1	21	183	4.0	1.3	22.9
92-93—San Antonio	10	305	51	113	.451	13	16	.813	9	26	35	11	4	0	10	125	3.5	1.1	12.5
93-94—San Antonio	4	114	17	43	.395	3	5	.600	3	7	10	1	3	0	4	42	2.5	0.3	10.5
94-95—Denver	3	73	10	28	.357	12	13	.923	6	8	14	3	2	1	2	36	4.7	1.0	12.0
97-98—Seattle	10	170	20	53	.377	5	6	.833	4	9	13	6	2	0	2	56	1.3	0.6	5.6
Totals	73	1981	403	909	.443	134	171	.784	110	163	273	92	51	14	97	1011	3.7	1.3	13.8

Three-point field goals: 1983-84, 1-for-12 (.083). 1984-85, 2-for-5 (.400). 1985-86, 7-for-12 (.583). 1986-87, 13-for-36 (.361). 1987-88, 3-for-12 (.250). 1988-89, 15-for-37 (.405). 1992-93, 10-for-32 (.313). 1993-94, 5-for-17 (.294). 1994-95, 4-for-13 (.308). 1997-98, 11-for-26 (.423). Totals, 71-for-202 (.351).

Personal fouls/disqualifications: 1983-84, 17/0. 1984-85, 3/0. 1985-86, 6/0. 1986-87, 54/1. 1987-88, 17/0. 1988-89, 19/1. 1992-93, 25/0. 1993-94, 6/0. 1994-95, 6/0. 1997-98, 10/0. Totals, 163/2.

NBA ALL-STAR GAME RECORD

Season Team	Min.	FGM	FGA	Pct.	FTM	FTA	Pct.	Off.	Def.	Tot.	Ast.	PF	Dq.	St.	Blk.	TO	Pts.
								REBOUNDS									
1989 —Seattle	26	12	16	.750	2	2	1.000	3	3	6	2	2	0	0	0	2	27
Totals	26	12	16	.750	2	2	1.000	3	3	6	2	2	0	0	0	2	27

Three-point field goals: 1989, 1-for-1. Totals, 1-for-1 (1.000).

ENGLISH, ALEX   F

PERSONAL: Born January 5, 1954, in Columbia, S.C. ... 6-7/190 (2,00/86,2). ... Full name: Alexander English.
HIGH SCHOOL: Dreher (Columbia, S.C.).
COLLEGE: South Carolina.
TRANSACTIONS: Selected by Milwaukee Bucks in second round (23rd pick overall) of 1976 NBA Draft. ... Signed as veteran free agent by Indiana Pacers (June 8, 1978); Bucks waived their right of first refusal in exchange for 1979 first-round draft choice (October 3, 1978). ... Traded by Pacers with 1980 first-round draft choice to Denver Nuggets for F George McGinnis (February 1, 1980). ... Signed as unrestricted free agent by Dallas Mavericks (August 15, 1990). ... Played in Italy (1991-92).
CAREER HONORS: Elected to Naismith Memorial Basketball Hall of Fame (1997).
MISCELLANEOUS: Denver Nuggets franchise all-time leading scorer with 21,645 points and all-time assists leader with 3,679 (1979-80 through 1989-90).
CAREER NOTES: Head coach, North Charleston Lowgators (NBDL).

COLLEGIATE RECORD

Season Team	G	Min.	FGM	FGA	Pct.	FTM	FTA	Pct.	Reb.	Ast.	Pts.	RPG	APG	PPG
												AVERAGES		
72-73—South Carolina	29	1037	189	368	.514	44	70	.629	306	25	422	10.6	0.9	14.6
73-74—South Carolina	27	1007	209	395	.529	75	112	.670	237	28	493	8.8	1.0	18.3
74-75—South Carolina	28	1024	199	359	.554	49	77	.636	244	30	447	8.7	1.1	16.0
75-76—South Carolina	27	1045	258	468	.551	94	134	.702	277	27	610	10.3	1.0	22.6
Totals	111	4113	855	1590	.538	262	393	.667	1064	110	1972	9.6	1.0	17.8

NBA REGULAR-SEASON RECORD

HONORS: All-NBA second team (1982, 1983, 1986). ... J. Walter Kennedy Citizenship Award (1988).

ALL-TIME GREAT PLAYERS

Season Team	G	Min.	FGM	FGA	Pct.	FTM	FTA	Pct.	REBOUNDS Off.	Def.	Tot.	Ast.	St.	Blk.	TO	Pts.	AVERAGES RPG	APG	PPG
76-77—Milwaukee	60	648	132	277	.477	46	60	.767	68	100	168	25	17	18	...	310	2.8	0.4	5.2
77-78—Milwaukee	82	1552	343	633	.542	104	143	.727	144	251	395	129	41	55	137	790	4.8	1.6	9.6
78-79—Indiana...........	81	2696	563	1102	.511	173	230	.752	253	402	655	271	70	78	196	1299	8.1	3.3	16.0
79-80—Ind.-Denver.....	78	2401	553	1113	.497	210	266	.789	269	336	605	224	73	62	214	1318	7.8	2.9	16.9
80-81—Denver...........	81	3093	768	1555	.494	390	459	.850	273	373	646	290	106	100	241	1929	8.0	3.6	23.8
81-82—Denver...........	82	3015	855	1553	.551	372	443	.840	210	348	558	433	87	120	261	2082	6.8	5.3	25.4
82-83—Denver...........	82	2988	*959	*1857	.516	406	490	.829	263	338	601	397	116	126	263	*2326	7.3	4.8	*28.4
83-84—Denver...........	82	2870	907	1714	.529	352	427	.824	216	248	464	406	83	95	222	2167	5.7	5.0	26.4
84-85—Denver...........	81	2924	*939	1812	.518	383	462	.829	203	255	458	344	101	46	251	2262	5.7	4.2	27.9
85-86—Denver...........	81	3024	*951	1888	.504	511	593	.862	192	213	405	320	73	29	249	*2414	5.0	4.0	29.8
86-87—Denver...........	82	3085	965	1920	.503	411	487	.844	146	198	344	422	73	21	214	2345	4.2	5.1	28.6
87-88—Denver...........	80	2818	843	1704	.495	314	379	.829	166	207	373	377	70	23	181	2000	4.7	4.7	25.0
88-89—Denver...........	82	2990	924	1881	.491	325	379	.858	148	178	326	383	66	12	198	2175	4.0	4.7	26.5
89-90—Denver...........	80	2211	635	1293	.491	161	183	.880	119	167	286	225	51	23	93	1433	3.6	2.8	17.9
90-91—Dallas...........	79	1748	322	734	.439	119	146	.850	108	146	254	105	40	25	101	763	3.2	1.3	9.7
Totals	1193	38063	10659	21036	.507	4277	5141	.832	2778	3760	6538	4351	1067	833	2821	25613	5.5	3.6	21.5

Three-point field goals: 1979-80, 2-for-6 (.333). 1980-81, 3-for-5 (.600). 1981-82, 0-for-5. 1982-83, 2-for-12 (.167). 1983-84, 1-for-7 (.143). 1984-85, 1-for-5 (.200). 1985-86, 1-for-5 (.200). 1986-87, 4-for-15 (.267). 1987-88, 0-for-6. 1988-89, 2-for-8 (.250). 1989-90, 2-for-5 (.400). 1990-91, 0-for-1. Totals, 18-for-83 (.217).

Personal fouls/disqualifications: 1976-77, 78/0. 1977-78, 178/1. 1978-79, 241/3. 1979-80, 206/0. 1980-81, 255/2. 1981-82, 261/2. 1982-83, 235/1. 1983-84, 252/3. 1984-85, 259/1. 1985-86, 235/1. 1986-87, 216/0. 1987-88, 189/0. 1988-89, 174/0. 1989-90, 130/0. 1990-91, 141/0. Totals, 3027/15.

NBA PLAYOFF RECORD

Season Team	G	Min.	FGM	FGA	Pct.	FTM	FTA	Pct.	REBOUNDS Off.	Def.	Tot.	Ast.	St.	Blk.	TO	Pts.	AVERAGES RPG	APG	PPG
77-78—Milwaukee	9	208	48	78	.615	25	32	.781	16	26	42	13	6	7	12	121	4.7	1.4	13.4
81-82—Denver...........	3	118	26	55	.473	6	7	.857	8	15	23	17	3	3	4	58	7.7	5.7	19.3
82-83—Denver...........	7	270	67	150	.447	47	53	.887	20	24	44	42	4	7	21	181	6.3	6.0	25.9
83-84—Denver...........	5	203	60	102	.588	25	28	.893	16	24	40	28	3	2	7	145	8.0	5.6	29.0
84-85—Denver...........	14	536	163	304	.536	97	109	.890	36	56	92	63	17	5	30	423	6.6	4.5	30.2
85-86—Denver...........	10	394	106	229	.463	61	71	.859	18	17	35	52	4	4	28	273	3.5	5.2	27.3
86-87—Denver...........	3	76	25	49	.510	6	7	.857	10	4	14	10	0	0	8	56	4.7	3.3	18.7
87-88—Denver...........	11	438	116	255	.455	35	43	.814	31	28	59	48	7	3	16	267	5.4	4.4	24.3
88-89—Denver...........	3	108	32	62	.516	14	16	.875	8	5	13	11	1	0	14	78	4.3	3.7	26.0
89-90—Denver...........	3	76	25	44	.568	9	11	.818	3	6	9	9	2	1	2	59	3.0	3.0	19.7
Totals	68	2427	668	1328	.503	325	377	.862	166	205	371	293	47	32	142	1661	5.5	4.3	24.4

Three-point field goals: 1982-83, 0-for-2. 1983-84, 0-for-1. 1984-85, 0-for-1. 1985-86, 0-for-1. 1987-88, 0-for-3. Totals, 0-for-8.

Personal fouls/disqualifications: 1977-78, 20/0. 1981-82, 6/0. 1982-83, 21/0. 1983-84, 17/0. 1984-85, 40/1. 1985-86, 29/0. 1986-87, 9/1. 1987-88, 34/0. 1988-89, 6/0. 1989-90, 6/0. Totals, 188/2.

NBA ALL-STAR GAME RECORD

Season Team	Min.	FGM	FGA	Pct.	FTM	FTA	Pct.	REBOUNDS Off.	Def.	Tot.	Ast.	PF	Dq.	St.	Blk.	TO	Pts.
1982 —Denver............	12	2	6	.333	0	0	...	2	3	5	1	2	0	1	0	1	4
1983 —Denver............	23	7	14	.500	0	1	.000	2	2	4	0	2	0	1	2	2	14
1984 —Denver............	19	6	8	.750	1	1	1.000	0	0	0	2	2	0	1	1	3	13
1985 —Denver............	14	0	3	.000	0	0	...	1	1	2	1	1	0	0	0	2	0
1986 —Denver............	16	8	12	.667	0	0	...	1	0	1	2	0	0	0	1	1	16
1987 —Denver............	13	0	6	.000	0	0	...	0	0	0	1	1	0	0	2	0	0
1988 —Denver............	22	5	10	.500	0	0	...	2	1	3	4	0	0	1	0	0	10
1989 —Denver............	29	8	13	.615	0	0	...	1	2	3	4	0	0	2	0	3	16
Totals..........................	148	36	72	.500	1	2	.500	9	9	18	15	8	0	6	4	14	73

ITALIAN LEAGUE RECORD

Season Team	G	Min.	FGM	FGA	Pct.	FTM	FTA	Pct.	Reb.	Ast.	Pts.	AVERAGES RPG	APG	PPG
91-92—Depi Napoli..................	18	566	103	214	.481	44	55	.800	86	5	251	4.8	0.3	13.9

ERVING, JULIUS   F

PERSONAL: Born February 22, 1950, in Roosevelt, N.Y. ... 6-7/210 (2,00/95,3). ... Full name: Julius Winfield Erving II. ... Cousin of Mark Williams, linebacker with four NFL teams (1994-96). ... Nickname: Dr. J.
HIGH SCHOOL: Roosevelt (N.Y.).
COLLEGE: Massachusetts.
TRANSACTIONS: Signed as free agent after junior season by Virginia Squires of American Basketball Association (April 6, 1971). ... Selected by Milwaukee Bucks in first round (12th pick overall) of 1972 NBA draft. ... Traded by Squires with C Willie Sojourner to New York Nets for F George Carter, draft rights to F/C Kermit Washington and cash (August 1, 1973). ... Nets franchise became part of NBA for 1976-77 season. ... Contract sold by Nets to Philadelphia 76ers (October 20, 1976).
CAREER NOTES: Executive vice president, Orlando Magic (1997-98 to present).
CAREER HONORS: Elected to Naismith Memorial Basketball Hall of Fame (1993). ... NBA 35th Anniversary All-Time Team (1980) and One of the 50 Greatest Players in NBA History (1996).
MISCELLANEOUS: Member of NBA championship team (1983). ... Philadelphia 76ers franchise all-time blocked shots leader with 1,293 (1976-77 through 1986-87).

COLLEGIATE RECORD

Season Team	G	Min.	FGM	FGA	Pct.	FTM	FTA	Pct.	Reb.	Ast.	Pts.	AVERAGES RPG	APG	PPG
68-69—Massachusetts‡	15	...	112	216	.519	49	81	.605	214	...	273	14.3	...	18.2
69-70—Massachusetts	25	969	238	468	.509	167	230	.726	522	89	643	20.9	3.6	25.7
70-71—Massachusetts	27	1029	286	609	.470	155	206	.752	527	99	727	19.5	3.7	26.9
Varsity totals	52	1998	524	1077	.487	322	436	.739	1049	188	1370	20.2	3.6	26.3

ABA REGULAR-SEASON RECORD

NOTES: ABA Most Valuable Player (1974, 1976). ... ABA co-Most Valuable Player (1975). ... ABA All-Star first team (1973, 1974, 1975, 1976). ... ABA All-Star second team (1972). ... ABA All-Defensive team (1976). ... ABA All-Rookie team (1972). ... Member of ABA championship team (1974, 1976). ... Holds career record for highest points-per-game average (minimum 250 games)—28.7.

| Season Team | G | Min. | 2-POINT | | | 3-POINT | | | FTM | FTA | Pct. | Reb. | Ast. | Pts. | AVERAGES | | |
			FGM	FGA	Pct.	FGM	FGA	Pct.							RPG	APG	PPG
71-72—Virginia	84	3513	907	1810	.501	3	16	.188	467	627	.745	1319	335	2290	15.7	4.0	27.3
72-73—Virginia	71	2993	889	1780	.499	5	24	.208	475	612	.776	867	*2268	12.2	4.2	*31.9
73-74—New York	84	3398	897	1742	.515	17	43	.395	454	593	.766	899	434	*2299	10.7	5.2	*27.4
74-75—New York	84	3402	885	1719	.515	29	87	.333	486	608	.799	914	462	2343	10.9	5.5	27.9
75-76—New York	84	3244	915	1770	.517	34	103	.330	530	662	.801	925	423	*2462	11.0	5.0	*29.3
Totals	407	16550	4493	8821	.509	88	273	.322	2412	3102	.778	4924	1952	11662	12.1	4.8	28.7

ABA PLAYOFF RECORD

NOTES: ABA Playoff Most Valuable Player (1974, 1976).

| Season Team | G | Min. | 2-POINT | | | 3-POINT | | | FTM | FTA | Pct. | Reb. | Ast. | Pts. | AVERAGES | | |
			FGM	FGA	Pct.	FGM	FGA	Pct.							RPG	APG	PPG
71-72—Virginia	11	504	146	280	.521	1	4	.250	71	85	.835	224	72	366	20.4	6.5	33.3
72-73—Virginia	5	219	59	109	.541	0	3	.000	30	40	.750	45	16	148	9.0	3.2	29.6
73-74—New York	14	579	156	294	.531	5	11	.455	63	85	.741	135	67	390	9.6	4.8	27.9
74-75—New York	5	211	55	113	.487	0	8	.000	27	32	.844	49	28	137	9.8	5.6	27.4
75-76—New York	13	551	156	286	.545	4	14	.286	127	158	.804	164	64	451	12.6	4.9	34.7
Totals	48	2064	572	1082	.529	10	40	.250	318	400	.795	617	247	1492	12.9	5.1	31.1

ABA ALL-STAR GAME RECORD

| Season Team | Min. | 2-POINT | | | 3-POINT | | | FTM | FTA | Pct. | Reb. | Ast. | Pts. |
		FGM	FGA	Pct.	FGM	FGA	Pct.						
1972—Virginia	25	9	15	.600	0	0	...	2	2	1.000	6	3	20
1973—Virginia	30	8	16	.500	0	0	...	6	8	.750	5	1	22
1974—New York	27	6	15	.400	0	0	...	2	2	1.000	11	8	14
1975—New York	27	5	11	.455	1	1	1.000	8	10	.800	7	7	21
1976—New York	25	9	12	.750	0	1	.000	5	7	.714	7	5	23
Totals	134	37	69	.536	1	2	.500	23	29	.793	36	24	100

NBA REGULAR-SEASON RECORD

HONORS: NBA Most Valuable Player (1981). ... All-NBA first team (1978, 1980, 1981, 1982, 1983). ... All-NBA second team (1977, 1984). ... J. Walter Kennedy Citizenship Award (1983).

| Season Team | G | Min. | FGM | FGA | Pct. | FTM | FTA | Pct. | REBOUNDS | | | Ast. | St. | Blk. | TO | Pts. | AVERAGES | | |
									Off.	Def.	Tot.						RPG	APG	PPG
76-77—Philadelphia	82	2940	685	1373	.499	400	515	.777	192	503	695	306	159	113	...	1770	8.5	3.7	21.6
77-78—Philadelphia	74	2429	611	1217	.502	306	362	.845	179	302	481	279	135	97	238	1528	6.5	3.8	20.6
78-79—Philadelphia	78	2802	715	1455	.491	373	501	.745	198	366	564	357	133	100	315	1803	7.2	4.6	23.1
79-80—Philadelphia	78	2812	838	1614	.519	420	534	.787	215	361	576	355	170	140	284	2100	7.4	4.6	26.9
80-81—Philadelphia	82	2874	794	1524	.521	422	536	.787	244	413	657	364	173	147	266	2014	8.0	4.4	24.6
81-82—Philadelphia	81	2789	780	1428	.546	411	539	.763	220	337	557	319	161	141	214	1974	6.9	3.9	24.4
82-83—Philadelphia	72	2421	605	1170	.517	330	435	.759	173	318	491	263	112	131	196	1542	6.8	3.7	21.4
83-84—Philadelphia	77	2683	678	1324	.512	364	483	.754	190	342	532	309	141	139	230	1727	6.9	4.0	22.4
84-85—Philadelphia	78	2535	610	1236	.494	338	442	.765	172	242	414	233	135	109	208	1561	5.3	3.0	20.0
85-86—Philadelphia	74	2474	521	1085	.480	289	368	.785	169	201	370	248	113	82	214	1340	5.0	3.4	18.1
86-87—Philadelphia	60	1918	400	850	.471	191	235	.813	115	149	264	191	76	94	158	1005	4.4	3.2	16.8
Totals	836	28677	7237	14276	.507	3844	4950	.777	2067	3534	5601	3224	1508	1293	2323	18364	6.7	3.9	22.0

Three-point field goals: 1979-80, 4-for-20 (.200). 1980-81, 4-for-18 (.222). 1981-82, 3-for-11 (.273). 1982-83, 2-for-7 (.286). 1983-84, 7-for-21 (.333). 1984-85, 3-for-14 (.214). 1985-86, 9-for-32 (.281). 1986-87, 14-for-53 (.264). Totals, 46-for-176 (.261).
Personal fouls/disqualifications: 1976-77, 251/1. 1977-78, 207/0. 1978-79, 207/0. 1979-80, 208/0. 1980-81, 233/0. 1981-82, 229/1. 1982-83, 202/1. 1983-84, 217/3. 1984-85, 199/0. 1985-86, 196/3. 1986-87, 137/0. Totals, 2286/9.

NBA PLAYOFF RECORD

| Season Team | G | Min. | FGM | FGA | Pct. | FTM | FTA | Pct. | REBOUNDS | | | Ast. | St. | Blk. | TO | Pts. | AVERAGES | | |
									Off.	Def.	Tot.						RPG	APG	PPG
76-77—Philadelphia	19	758	204	390	.523	110	134	.821	41	81	122	85	41	23	...	518	6.4	4.5	27.3
77-78—Philadelphia	10	358	88	180	.489	42	56	.750	40	57	97	40	15	18	35	218	9.7	4.0	21.8
78-79—Philadelphia	9	372	89	172	.517	51	67	.761	29	41	70	53	18	17	38	229	7.8	5.9	25.4
79-80—Philadelphia	18	694	165	338	.488	108	136	.794	31	105	136	79	36	37	56	440	7.6	4.4	24.4
80-81—Philadelphia	16	592	143	301	.475	81	107	.757	52	62	114	54	22	41	55	367	7.1	3.4	22.9
81-82—Philadelphia	21	780	168	324	.519	124	165	.752	57	99	156	99	37	37	67	461	7.4	4.7	22.0
82-83—Philadelphia	13	493	95	211	.450	49	68	.721	32	67	99	44	15	27	39	239	7.6	3.4	18.4
83-84—Philadelphia	5	194	36	76	.474	19	22	.864	9	23	32	25	8	6	21	91	6.4	5.0	18.2
84-85—Philadelphia	13	434	84	187	.449	54	63	.857	29	44	73	48	25	11	37	222	5.6	3.7	17.1
85-86—Philadelphia	12	433	81	180	.450	48	65	.738	26	44	70	50	11	16	39	212	5.8	4.2	17.7
86-87—Philadelphia	5	180	34	82	.415	21	25	.840	14	11	25	17	7	6	9	91	5.0	3.4	18.2
Totals	141	5288	1187	2441	.486	707	908	.779	360	634	994	594	235	239	396	3088	7.0	4.2	21.9

Three-point field goals: 1979-80, 2-for-9 (.222). 1980-81, 0-for-1. 1981-82, 1-for-6 (.167). 1982-83, 0-for-1. 1983-84, 0-for-1. 1984-85, 0-for-1. 1985-86, 2-for-11 (.182). 1986-87, 2-for-6 (.333). Totals, 7-for-36 (.194).
Personal fouls/disqualifications: 1976-77, 45/0. 1977-78, 30/0. 1978-79, 22/0. 1979-80, 56/0. 1980-81, 54/0. 1981-82, 55/0. 1982-83, 42/1. 1983-84, 14/0. 1984-85, 34/0. 1985-86, 32/0. 1986-87, 19/0. Totals, 403/1.

NBA ALL-STAR GAME RECORD

NOTES: NBA All-Star Game Most Valuable Player (1977, 1983). ... Holds single-game record for most free throws attempted in one quarter—11 (1978). ... Shares single-game record for most free throws made in one quarter—9 (1978).

Season Team	Min.	FGM	FGA	Pct.	FTM	FTA	Pct.	REBOUNDS Off.	Def.	Tot.	Ast.	PF	Dq.	St.	Blk.	TO	Pts.
1977 —Philadelphia......	30	12	20	.600	6	6	1.000	5	7	12	3	2	0	4	1	...	30
1978 —Philadelphia......	27	3	14	.214	10	12	.833	2	6	8	3	1	0	0	1	2	16
1979 —Philadelphia......	39	10	22	.455	9	12	.750	6	2	8	5	4	0	2	0	1	29
1980 —Philadelphia......	20	4	12	.333	3	4	.750	2	3	5	2	5	0	2	1	2	11
1981 —Philadelphia......	29	6	15	.400	6	7	.857	3	0	3	2	2	0	2	1	2	18
1982 —Philadelphia......	32	7	16	.438	2	4	.500	3	5	8	2	4	0	1	2	4	16
1983 —Philadelphia......	28	11	19	.579	3	3	1.000	3	3	6	3	1	0	1	2	2	25
1984 —Philadelphia......	36	14	22	.636	6	8	.750	4	4	8	5	4	0	2	2	1	34
1985 —Philadelphia......	23	5	15	.333	2	2	1.000	2	2	4	3	3	0	1	0	1	12
1986 —Philadelphia......	19	4	10	.400	0	2	.000	1	3	4	2	2	0	2	0	2	8
1987 —Philadelphia......	33	9	13	.692	3	3	1.000	3	1	4	5	3	0	1	1	2	22
Totals..........................	316	85	178	.478	50	63	.794	34	36	70	35	31	0	18	11	19	221

Three-point field goals: 1987, 1-for-1.

COMBINED ABA AND NBA REGULAR-SEASON RECORDS

	G	Min.	FGM	FGA	Pct.	FTM	FTA	Pct.	REBOUNDS Off.	Def.	Tot.	Ast.	Stl.	Blk.	TO	Pts.	AVERAGES RPG	APG	PPG
Totals...........	1243	45227	11818	23370	.506	6256	8052	.777	...	...	10525	5176	...	...	...	30026	8.5	4.2	24.2

Three-point field goals: 134-for-449 (.298).
Personal fouls/disqualifications: 3494.

FLOYD, SLEEPY   G

PERSONAL: Born March 6, 1960, in Gastonia, N.C. ... 6-3/185 (1,90/83,9). ... Full name: Eric Augustus Floyd.
HIGH SCHOOL: Hunter Huss (Gastonia, N.C.).
COLLEGE: Georgetown.
TRANSACTIONS: Selected by New Jersey Nets in first round (13th pick overall) of 1982 NBA Draft. ... Traded by Nets with F Mickey Johnson to Golden State Warriors for G Micheal Ray Richardson (February 6, 1983). ... Traded by Warriors with C Joe Barry Carroll to Houston Rockets for C Ralph Sampson and G Steve Harris (December 12, 1987). ... Waived by Rockets (August 2, 1993). ... Signed as free agent by San Antonio Spurs (August 13, 1993). ... Signed as free agent by Nets (October 6, 1994).

COLLEGIATE RECORD

NOTES: The Sporting News All-America second team (1982).

Season Team	G	Min.	FGM	FGA	Pct.	FTM	FTA	Pct.	Reb.	Ast.	Pts.	AVERAGES RPG	APG	PPG
78-79—Georgetown..................	29	975	177	388	.456	126	155	.813	119	78	480	4.1	2.7	16.6
79-80—Georgetown..................	32	1052	246	444	.554	106	140	.757	98	95	598	3.1	3.0	18.7
80-81—Georgetown..................	32	1115	237	508	.467	133	165	.806	133	83	607	4.2	2.6	19.0
81-82—Georgetown..................	37	1200	249	494	.504	121	168	.720	127	99	619	3.4	2.7	16.7
Totals	130	4342	909	1834	.496	486	628	.774	477	355	2304	3.7	2.7	17.7

NBA REGULAR-SEASON RECORD

Season Team	G	Min.	FGM	FGA	Pct.	FTM	FTA	Pct.	REBOUNDS Off.	Def.	Tot.	Ast.	St.	Blk.	TO	Pts.	AVERAGES RPG	APG	PPG
82-83—N.J.-G.S..........	76	1248	226	527	.429	150	180	.833	56	81	137	138	58	17	106	612	1.8	1.8	8.1
83-84—Golden State ...	77	2555	484	1045	.463	315	386	.816	87	184	271	269	103	31	196	1291	3.5	3.5	16.8
84-85—Golden State ...	82	2873	610	1372	.445	336	415	.810	62	140	202	406	134	41	251	1598	2.5	5.0	19.5
85-86—Golden State ...	82	2764	510	1007	.506	351	441	.796	76	221	297	746	157	18	290	1410	3.6	9.1	17.2
86-87—Golden State ...	82	3064	503	1030	.488	462	537	.860	56	212	268	848	146	18	280	1541	3.3	10.3	18.8
87-88—G.S.-Hou......	77	2514	420	969	.433	301	354	.850	77	219	296	544	95	12	223	1155	3.8	7.1	15.0
88-89—Houston..........	82	2788	396	893	.443	261	309	.845	48	258	306	709	124	11	253	1162	3.7	8.6	14.2
89-90—Houston..........	82	2630	362	803	.451	187	232	.806	46	152	198	600	94	11	204	1000	2.4	7.3	12.2
90-91—Houston..........	82	1850	386	939	.411	185	246	.752	52	107	159	317	95	17	140	1005	1.9	3.9	12.3
91-92—Houston..........	82	1662	286	704	.406	135	170	.794	34	116	150	239	57	21	128	744	1.8	2.9	9.1
92-93—Houston..........	52	867	124	305	.407	81	102	.794	14	72	86	132	32	6	64	345	1.7	2.5	6.6
93-94—San Antonio	53	737	70	209	.335	52	78	.667	10	60	70	101	12	8	61	200	1.3	1.9	3.8
94-95—New Jersey	48	831	71	212	.335	30	43	.698	8	46	54	126	13	6	51	197	1.1	2.6	4.1
Totals	957	26383	4448	10015	.444	2846	3493	.815	626	1868	2494	5175	1120	215	2251	12260	2.6	5.4	12.8

Three-point field goals: 1982-83, 10-for-25 (.400). 1983-84, 8-for-45 (.178). 1984-85, 42-for-143 (.294). 1985-86, 39-for-119 (.328). 1986-87, 73-for-190 (.384). 1987-88, 14-for-72 (.194). 1988-89, 109-for-292 (.373). 1989-90, 89-for-234 (.380). 1990-91, 48-for-176 (.273). 1991-92, 37-for-123 (.301). 1992-93, 16-for-56 (.286). 1993-94, 8-for-36 (.222). 1994-95, 25-for-88 (.284). Totals, 518-for-1599 (.324).
Personal fouls/disqualifications: 1982-83, 134/3. 1983-84, 216/0. 1984-85, 226/1. 1985-86, 199/2. 1986-87, 199/1. 1987-88, 190/1. 1988-89, 196/1. 1989-90, 159/0. 1990-91, 122/0. 1991-92, 128/0. 1992-93, 59/0. 1993-94, 70/0. 1994-95, 73/0. Totals, 1972/9.

NBA PLAYOFF RECORD

NOTES: Holds single-game playoff records for most points in one half—39; most points in one quarter—29; and most field goals in one quarter—12 (May 10, 1987, vs. Los Angeles Lakers). ... Shares single-game playoff record for most field goals made in one half—15 (May 10, 1987, vs. Los Angeles Lakers).

Season Team	G	Min.	FGM	FGA	Pct.	FTM	FTA	Pct.	REBOUNDS Off.	Def.	Tot.	Ast.	St.	Blk.	TO	Pts.	AVERAGES RPG	APG	PPG
86-87—Golden State ...	10	414	77	152	.507	47	51	.922	9	21	30	102	18	2	35	214	3.0	10.2	21.4
87-88—Houston..........	4	154	26	61	.426	19	22	.864	3	4	7	34	8	0	12	75	1.8	8.5	18.8
88-89—Houston..........	4	160	22	46	.478	10	14	.714	3	15	18	26	8	1	10	62	4.5	6.5	15.5
89-90—Houston..........	4	172	30	64	.469	11	17	.647	7	8	15	41	5	1	15	74	3.8	10.3	18.5
90-91—Houston..........	3	41	8	24	.333	0	0	...	0	2	2	7	2	1	7	16	0.7	2.3	5.3
92-93—Houston..........	7	60	6	19	.316	7	10	.700	1	3	4	8	2	0	9	20	0.6	1.1	2.9
93-94—San Antonio	4	37	2	8	.250	2	4	.500	0	1	1	1	0	0	4	6	0.3	0.3	1.5
Totals	36	1038	171	374	.457	96	118	.814	23	54	77	219	43	5	92	467	2.1	6.1	13.0

Three-point field goals: 1986-87, 13-for-28 (.464). 1987-88, 4-for-8 (.500). 1988-89, 8-for-15 (.533). 1989-90, 3-for-12 (.250). 1990-91, 0-for-4. 1992-93, 1-for-3 (.333). Totals, 29-for-70 (.414).

Personal fouls/disqualifications: 1986-87, 24/0. 1987-88, 10/0. 1988-89, 10/0. 1989-90, 5/0. 1990-91, 4/0. 1992-93, 2/0. 1993-94, 3/0. Totals, 58/0.

NBA ALL-STAR GAME RECORD

Season	Team	Min.	FGM	FGA	Pct.	FTM	FTA	Pct.	REBOUNDS Off.	REBOUNDS Def.	REBOUNDS Tot.	Ast.	PF	Dq.	St.	Blk.	TO	Pts.
1987	—Golden State......	19	4	7	.571	5	7	.714	2	3	5	1	2	0	1	0	2	14

Three-point field goals: 1987, 1-for-3 (.333).

FOUST, LARRY   C/F

PERSONAL: Born June 24, 1928, in Painesville, Ohio. ... Died October 27, 1984. ... 6-9/250 (2,06/113,4). ... Full name: Lawrence Michael Foust.

HIGH SCHOOL: South Catholic (Philadelphia).

COLLEGE: La Salle.

TRANSACTIONS: Selected by Chicago Stags in first round of 1950 NBA Draft. ... Draft rights selected by Fort Wayne Pistons in dispersal of Stags franchise (1950). ... Pistons franchise moved from Fort Wayne to Detroit for 1957-58 season. ... Traded by Pistons with cash to Minneapolis Lakers for C Walt Dukes (September 12, 1957). ... Traded by Lakers to St. Louis Hawks for C Charlie Share, draft rights to G Nick Mantis, G Willie Merriweather and cash (February 1, 1960).

COLLEGIATE RECORD

NOTES: THE SPORTING NEWS All-America fifth team (1950).

Season Team	G	Min.	FGM	FGA	Pct.	FTM	FTA	Pct.	Reb.	Ast.	Pts.	AVERAGES RPG	AVERAGES APG	AVERAGES PPG
46-47—La Salle	26	...	103	...	...	49	...	...	...	...	255	...	...	9.8
47-48—La Salle	24	...	157	...	...	87	...	...	...	...	401	...	...	16.7
48-49—La Salle	28	...	177	...	...	99	164	.604	...	...	453	...	...	16.2
49-50—La Salle	25	...	136	...	...	83	122	.680	...	...	355	...	...	14.2
Totals	103	...	573	...	...	318	...	...	...	...	1464	...	...	14.2

NBA REGULAR-SEASON RECORD

HONORS: All-NBA first team (1955). ... All-NBA second team (1952).

Season Team	G	Min.	FGM	FGA	Pct.	FTM	FTA	Pct.	Reb.	Ast.	PF	Dq.	Pts.	AVERAGES RPG	AVERAGES APG	AVERAGES PPG
50-51 —Fort Wayne	68	...	327	944	.346	261	396	.659	681	90	247	6	915	10.0	1.3	13.5
51-52 —Fort Wayne	66	2615	390	989	.394	267	394	.678	†880	200	245	10	1047	13.3	3.0	15.9
52-53 —Fort Wayne	67	2303	311	865	.360	336	465	.723	769	151	267	16	958	11.5	2.3	14.3
53-54 —Fort Wayne	72	2693	376	919	.409	338	475	.712	967	161	258	4	1090	13.4	2.2	15.1
54-55 —Fort Wayne	70	2264	398	818	*.487	393	513	.766	700	118	264	9	1189	10.0	1.7	17.0
55-56 —Fort Wayne	72	2024	367	821	.447	432	555	.778	648	127	263	7	1166	9.0	1.8	16.2
56-57 —Fort Wayne	61	1533	243	617	.394	273	380	.718	555	71	221	7	759	9.1	1.2	12.4
57-58 —Minneapolis	72	2200	391	982	.398	428	566	.756	876	108	299	11	1210	12.2	1.5	16.8
58-59 —Minneapolis	72	1933	301	771	.390	280	366	.765	627	91	233	5	882	8.7	1.3	12.3
59-60 —Minn.-St.L.	72	1964	312	766	.407	253	320	.791	621	96	241	7	877	8.6	1.3	12.2
60-61 —St. Louis	68	1208	194	489	.397	164	208	.788	389	77	165	0	552	5.7	1.1	8.1
61-62 —St. Louis	57	1153	204	433	.471	145	178	.815	328	78	186	2	553	5.8	1.4	9.7
Totals	817	...	3814	9414	.405	3570	4816	.741	8041	1368	2889	84	11198	9.8	1.7	13.7

NBA PLAYOFF RECORD

Season Team	G	Min.	FGM	FGA	Pct.	FTM	FTA	Pct.	Reb.	Ast.	PF	Dq.	Pts.	AVERAGES RPG	AVERAGES APG	AVERAGES PPG
50-51 —Fort Wayne	3	...	14	45	.311	8	10	.800	37	5	5	...	36	12.3	1.7	12.0
51-52 —Fort Wayne	2	77	12	23	.522	6	7	.857	30	5	8	1	30	15.0	2.5	15.0
52-53 —Fort Wayne	8	332	48	121	.397	57	68	.838	111	6	34	2	153	13.9	0.8	19.1
53-54 —Fort Wayne	4	129	11	41	.268	19	25	.760	38	7	21	2	41	9.5	1.8	10.3
54-55 —Fort Wayne	11	331	60	152	.395	52	73	.712	107	26	43	0	172	9.7	2.4	15.6
55-56 —Fort Wayne	10	289	49	130	.377	70	89	.787	127	14	38	2	168	12.7	1.4	16.8
56-57 —Fort Wayne	2	64	13	23	.565	19	23	.826	25	6	10	0	45	12.5	3.0	22.5
58-59 —Minneapolis	13	404	56	134	.418	41	50	.820	136	12	47	2	153	10.5	0.9	11.8
59-60 —St. Louis	12	205	29	74	.392	20	25	.800	68	11	36	0	78	5.7	0.9	6.5
60-61 —St. Louis	8	89	9	20	.450	8	14	.571	28	2	13	0	26	3.5	0.3	3.3
Totals....................	73	...	301	763	.394	300	384	.781	707	94	255	...	902	9.7	1.3	12.4

NBA ALL-STAR GAME RECORD

Season	Team	Min.	FGM	FGA	Pct.	FTM	FTA	Pct.	Reb.	Ast.	PF	Dq.	Pts.
1951	—Fort Wayne...............	...	1	6	.167	0	0	...	5	2	3	0	2
1952	—Fort Wayne...............					Selected. did not play—injured.							
1953	—Fort Wayne...............	18	5	7	.714	0	0	...	6	0	4	0	10
1954	—Fort Wayne...............	27	1	9	.111	1	1	1.000	15	0	1	0	3
1955	—Fort Wayne...............	24	3	10	.300	1	1	1.000	7	1	1	0	7
1956	—Fort Wayne...............	20	3	9	.333	3	4	.750	4	0	1	0	9
1958	—Minneapolis...............	13	1	4	.250	8	8	1.000	3	0	3	0	10
1959	—Minneapolis...............	16	3	9	.333	2	2	1.000	9	0	3	0	8
Totals	...	17	54	.315	15	16	.938	49	3	16	0	49	

FRAZIER, WALT G

PERSONAL: Born March 29, 1945, in Atlanta. ... 6-4/205 (1,93/93,0). ... Full name: Walter Frazier Jr. ... Nickname: Clyde.
HIGH SCHOOL: David Howard (Atlanta).
COLLEGE: Southern Illinois.
TRANSACTIONS: Selected by New York Knicks in first round (fifth pick overall) of 1967 NBA Draft. ... Acquired by Cleveland Cavaliers as compensation for Knicks signing veteran free agent G Jim Cleamons (October 7, 1977). ... Waived by Cavaliers (October 19, 1979).
CAREER HONORS: Elected to Naismith Memorial Basketball Hall of Fame (1987). ... One of the 50 Greatest Players in NBA History (1996).
MISCELLANEOUS: Member of NBA championship team (1970, 1973). ... New York Knicks all-time assists leader with 4,791 (1967-68 through 1976-77).

COLLEGIATE RECORD

NOTES: The Sporting News All-America second team (1967).

												AVERAGES		
Season Team	G	Min.	FGM	FGA	Pct.	FTM	FTA	Pct.	Reb.	Ast.	Pts.	RPG	APG	PPG
63-64—Southern Illinois‡	14	...	133	225	.591	52	85	.612	129	...	318	9.2	...	22.7
64-65—Southern Illinois	24	...	161	353	.456	88	111	.793	221	...	410	9.2	...	17.1
65-66—Southern Illinois	Did not play—ineligible.													
66-67—Southern Illinois	26	...	192	397	.484	90	126	.714	310	...	474	11.9	...	18.2
Varsity totals	50	...	353	750	.471	178	237	.751	531	...	884	10.6	...	17.7

NBA REGULAR-SEASON RECORD

HONORS: All-NBA first team (1970, 1972, 1974, 1975). ... All-NBA second team (1971, 1973). ... NBA All-Defensive first team (1969, 1970, 1971, 1972, 1973, 1974, 1975). ... NBA All-Rookie team (1968).

														AVERAGES		
Season Team	G	Min.	FGM	FGA	Pct.	FTM	FTA	Pct.	Reb.	Ast.	PF	Dq.	Pts.	RPG	APG	PPG
67-68 —New York	74	1588	256	568	.451	154	235	.655	313	305	199	2	666	4.2	4.1	9.0
68-69 —New York	80	2949	531	1052	.505	341	457	.746	499	635	245	2	1403	6.2	7.9	17.5
69-70 —New York	77	3040	600	1158	.518	409	547	.748	465	629	203	1	1609	6.0	8.2	20.9
70-71 —New York	80	3455	651	1317	.494	434	557	.779	544	536	240	1	1736	6.8	6.7	21.7
71-72 —New York	77	3126	669	1307	.512	450	557	.808	513	446	185	0	1788	6.7	5.8	23.2
72-73 —New York	78	3181	681	1389	.490	286	350	.817	570	461	186	0	1648	7.3	5.9	21.1

								REBOUNDS								AVERAGES		
Season Team	G	Min.	FGM	FGA	Pct.	FTM	FTA	Pct.	Off.	Def.	Tot.	Ast.	St.	Blk.	TO	Pts.	RPG	APG	PPG
73-74—New York	80	3338	674	1429	.472	295	352	.838	120	416	536	551	161	15	...	1643	6.7	6.9	20.5
74-75—New York	78	3204	672	1391	.483	331	400	.828	90	375	465	474	190	14	...	1675	6.0	6.1	21.5
75-76—New York	59	2427	470	969	.485	186	226	.823	79	321	400	351	106	9	...	1126	6.8	5.9	19.1
76-77—N.Y. Knicks	76	2687	532	1089	.489	259	336	.771	52	241	293	403	132	9	...	1323	3.9	5.3	17.4
77-78—Cleveland	51	1664	336	714	.471	153	180	.850	54	155	209	209	77	9	113	825	4.1	4.1	16.2
78-79—Cleveland	12	279	54	122	.443	21	27	.778	7	13	20	32	13	2	22	129	1.7	2.7	10.8
79-80—Cleveland	3	27	4	11	.364	2	2	1.000	1	2	3	8	2	1	4	10	1.0	2.7	3.3
Totals	825	30965	6130	12516	.490	3321	4226	.786	...	...	4830	5040	681	59	139	15581	5.9	6.1	18.9

Three-point field goals: 1979-80, 0-for-1.

Personal fouls/disqualifications: 1973-74, 212/2. 1974-75, 205/2. 1975-76, 163/1. 1976-77, 194/0. 1977-78, 124/1. 1978-79, 22/0. 1979-80, 2/0. Totals, 2180/12.

NBA PLAYOFF RECORD

														AVERAGES		
Season Team	G	Min.	FGM	FGA	Pct.	FTM	FTA	Pct.	Reb.	Ast.	PF	Dq.	Pts.	RPG	APG	PPG
67-68 —New York	4	119	12	33	.364	14	18	.778	22	25	12	0	38	5.5	6.3	9.5
68-69 —New York	10	415	89	177	.503	34	57	.597	74	91	30	0	212	7.4	9.1	21.2
69-70 —New York	19	834	118	247	.478	68	89	.764	149	156	53	0	304	7.8	8.2	16.0
70-71 —New York	12	501	108	204	.529	55	75	.733	70	54	45	0	271	5.8	4.5	22.6
71-72 —New York	16	704	148	276	.536	92	125	.736	112	98	48	0	388	7.0	6.1	24.3
72-73 —New York	17	765	150	292	.514	73	94	.777	124	106	52	1	373	7.3	6.2	21.9

								REBOUNDS								AVERAGES		
Season Team	G	Min.	FGM	FGA	Pct.	FTM	FTA	Pct.	Off.	Def.	Tot.	Ast.	St.	Blk.	TO	Pts.	RPG	APG	PPG
73-74—New York	12	491	113	225	.502	44	49	.898	21	74	95	48	21	4	...	270	7.9	4.0	22.5
74-75—New York	3	124	29	46	.630	13	16	.813	3	17	20	21	11	0	...	71	6.7	7.0	23.7
Totals	93	3953	767	1500	.511	393	523	.751	...	...	666	599	32	4	...	1927	7.2	6.4	20.7

Personal fouls/disqualifications: 1973-74, 41/1. 1974-75, 4/0. Totals, 285/2.

NBA ALL-STAR GAME RECORD

NOTES: NBA All-Star Game Most Valuable Player (1975).

Season Team	Min.	FGM	FGA	Pct.	FTM	FTA	Pct.	Reb	Ast.	PF	Dq.	Pts.
1970 —New York	24	3	7	.429	1	2	.500	3	4	2	0	7
1971 —New York	26	3	9	.333	0	0	...	6	5	2	0	6
1972 —New York	25	7	11	.636	1	2	.500	3	5	2	0	15
1973 —New York	26	5	15	.333	0	0	...	6	2	1	0	10

								REBOUNDS									
Season Team	Min.	FGM	FGA	Pct.	FTM	FTA	Pct.	Off.	Def.	Tot.	Ast.	PF	Dq.	St.	Blk.	TO	Pts.
1974 —New York	28	5	12	.417	2	2	1.000	1	1	2	5	1	0	3	0	...	12
1975 —New York	35	10	17	.588	10	11	.909	0	5	5	2	2	0	4	0	...	30
1976 —New York	19	2	7	.286	4	4	1.000	0	2	2	3	0	0	2	0	...	8
Totals	183	35	78	.449	18	21	.857	...	...	27	26	10	0	9	0	...	88

FREE, WORLD B. G

PERSONAL: Born December 9, 1953, in Atlanta. ... 6-3/190 (1,90/86,2). ... Formerly known as Lloyd Free.
HIGH SCHOOL: Canarsie (Brooklyn, N.Y.).
COLLEGE: Guilford (N.C.).
TRANSACTIONS: Selected after junior season by Philadelphia 76ers in second round (23rd pick overall) of 1975 NBA Draft. ... Traded by 76ers to San Diego Clippers for 1984 first-round draft choice (October 12, 1978). ... Traded by Clippers to Golden State Warriors for G Phil Smith and 1984 first-round draft choice (August 28, 1980). ... Traded by Warriors to Cleveland Cavaliers for G Ron Brewer (December 15, 1982). ... Signed as veteran free agent by 76ers (December 30, 1986); Cavaliers waived their right of first refusal in exchange for 1990 second-round draft choice. ... Waived by 76ers (March 4, 1987). ... Played in United States Basketball League with Miami Tropics (1987). ... Signed as free agent by Houston Rockets (October 1, 1987).
CAREER NOTES: Named strength and conditioning coach of Philadelphia 76ers (September 28, 1994). ... Community relations player representative, Philadelphia 76ers (1996-97 to present).

COLLEGIATE RECORD

NOTES: Member of NAIA championship team (1973). ... Most Valuable Player in NAIA tournament (1973).

Season Team	G	Min.	FGM	FGA	Pct.	FTM	FTA	Pct.	Reb.	Ast.	Pts.	AVERAGES RPG	APG	PPG
72-73—Guilford (N.C.)	33	...	272	572	.476	153	217	.705	191	...	697	5.8	...	21.1
73-74—Guilford (N.C.)	24	...	216	456	.474	165	225	.733	200	...	597	8.3	...	24.9
74-75—Guilford (N.C.)	28	...	247	486	.508	218	291	.749	163	...	712	5.8	...	25.4
Totals	85	...	735	1514	.485	536	733	.731	554	...	2006	6.5	...	23.6

NBA REGULAR-SEASON RECORD

HONORS: All-NBA second team (1979).

Season Team	G	Min.	FGM	FGA	Pct.	FTM	FTA	Pct.	REBOUNDS Off.	Def.	Tot.	Ast.	St.	Blk.	TO	Pts.	AVERAGES RPG	APG	PPG
75-76—Philadelphia	71	1121	239	533	.448	112	186	.602	64	61	125	104	37	6	...	590	1.8	1.5	8.3
76-77—Philadelphia	78	2253	467	1022	.457	334	464	.720	97	140	237	266	75	25	...	1268	3.0	3.4	16.3
77-78—Philadelphia	76	2050	390	857	.455	411	562	.731	92	120	212	306	68	41	200	1191	2.8	4.0	15.7
78-79—San Diego	78	2954	795	1653	.481	*654	*865	.756	127	174	301	340	111	35	297	2244	3.9	4.4	28.8
79-80—San Diego	68	2585	737	1556	.474	*572	760	.753	129	109	238	283	81	32	228	2055	3.5	4.2	30.2
80-81—Golden State	65	2370	516	1157	.446	528	649	.814	48	111	159	361	85	11	195	1565	2.4	5.6	24.1
81-82—Golden State	78	2796	650	1448	.449	479	647	.740	118	130	248	419	71	8	208	1789	3.2	5.4	22.9
82-83—G.S.-Clev.	73	2638	649	1423	.456	430	583	.738	92	109	201	290	97	15	209	1743	2.8	4.0	23.9
83-84—Cleveland	75	2375	626	1407	.445	395	504	.784	89	128	217	226	94	8	154	1669	2.9	3.0	22.3
84-85—Cleveland	71	2249	609	1328	.459	308	411	.749	61	150	211	320	75	16	139	1597	3.0	4.5	22.5
85-86—Cleveland	75	2535	652	1433	.455	379	486	.780	72	146	218	314	91	19	172	1754	2.9	4.2	23.4
86-87—Philadelphia	20	285	39	123	.317	36	47	.766	5	14	19	30	5	4	18	116	1.0	1.5	5.8
87-88—Houston	58	682	143	350	.409	80	100	.800	14	30	44	60	20	3	49	374	0.8	1.0	6.4
Totals	886	26893	6512	14294	.456	4718	6264	.753	1008	1422	2430	3319	910	223	1869	17955	2.7	3.7	20.3

Three-point field goals: 1975-76, 9-for-25 (.360). 1976-77, 5-for-31 (.161). 1981-82, 10-for-56 (.179). 1982-83, 5-for-45 (.333). 1983-84, 22-for-69 (.319). 1984-85, 71-for-193 (.368). 1985-86, 71-for-169 (.420). 1986-87, 2-for-9 (.222). 1987-88, 8-for-35 (.229). Totals, 213-for-632 (.337).
Personal fouls/disqualifications: 1975-76, 107/0. 1976-77, 207/2. 1977-78, 199/0. 1978-79, 253/8. 1979-80, 195/0. 1980-81, 183/1. 1981-82, 222/1. 1982-83, 241/4. 1983-84, 214/2. 1984-85, 163/0. 1985-86, 186/1. 1986-87, 26/0. 1987-88, 74/2. Totals, 2270/21.

NBA PLAYOFF RECORD

Season Team	G	Min.	FGM	FGA	Pct.	FTM	FTA	Pct.	REBOUNDS Off.	Def.	Tot.	Ast.	St.	Blk.	TO	Pts.	AVERAGES RPG	APG	PPG
75-76—Philadelphia	3	62	11	28	.393	10	13	.769	1	0	1	5	3	0	...	32	0.3	1.7	10.7
76-77—Philadelphia	15	281	63	170	.371	53	77	.688	10	22	32	29	12	8	...	179	2.1	1.9	11.9
77-78—Philadelphia	10	268	51	124	.411	59	81	.728	10	21	31	37	4	6	26	161	3.1	3.7	16.1
84-85—Cleveland	4	150	41	93	.441	23	25	.920	4	6	10	31	6	0	6	105	2.5	7.8	26.3
87-88—Houston	2	12	0	2	.000	0	0	...	1	1	2	1	0	0	3	0	1.0	0.5	0.0
Totals	34	773	166	417	.398	145	196	.740	26	50	76	103	25	14	35	477	2.2	3.0	14.0

Three-point field goals: 1984-85, 0-for-4. 1987-88, 0-for-1. Totals, 0-for-5.
Personal fouls/disqualifications: 1975-76, 6/0. 1976-77, 33/0. 1977-78, 26/0. 1984-85, 12/0. 1987-88, 2/0. Totals, 79/0.

NBA ALL-STAR GAME RECORD

Season Team	Min.	FGM	FGA	Pct.	FTM	FTA	Pct.	REBOUNDS Off.	Def.	Tot.	Ast.	PF	Dq.	St.	Blk.	TO	Pts.
1980 —San Diego	21	7	13	.538	0	1	.000	1	2	3	5	1	0	0	1	5	14

FULKS, JOE F/C

PERSONAL: Born October 26, 1921, in Birmingham, Ky. ... Died March 21, 1976. ... 6-5/190 (1,96/86,2). ... Full name: Joseph Franklin Fulks. ... Nickname: Jumpin' Joe.
HIGH SCHOOL: Birmingham (Ky.), then Kuttawa (Ky.).
COLLEGE: Murray State.
TRANSACTIONS: In military service (1943-44 through 1945-46 seasons). ... Signed by Philadelphia Warriors of Basketball Association of America (1946).
CAREER HONORS: Elected to Naismith Memorial Basketball Hall of Fame (1978). ... NBA 25th Anniversary All-Time Team (1970).
MISCELLANEOUS: Member of BAA championship team (1947).

COLLEGIATE RECORD

NOTES: Elected to NAIA Basketball Hall of Fame (1952).

Season Team	G	Min.	FGM	FGA	Pct.	FTM	FTA	Pct.	Reb.	Ast.	Pts.	AVERAGES RPG	APG	PPG
41-42—Murray State	22	...	117	...	...	50	76	.658	...	...	284	...	...	12.9
42-43—Murray State	25	...	135	...	...	67	100	.670	...	...	337	...	...	13.5
Totals	47	...	252	...	...	117	176	.665	...	...	621	...	...	13.2

NBA REGULAR-SEASON RECORD

HONORS: All-NBA second team (1951). ... All-BAA first team (1947, 1948, 1949).

Season Team	G	Min.	FGM	FGA	Pct.	FTM	FTA	Pct.	Reb.	Ast.	PF	Dq.	Pts.	AVERAGES RPG	APG	PPG
46-47 —Philadelphia (BAA)............	60	...	*475	*1557	.305	*439	*601	.730	...	25	199	...	*1389	...	0.4	*23.2
47-48 —Philadelphia (BAA)............	43	...	326	*1258	.259	*297	390	.762	...	26	162	...	949	...	0.6	*22.1
48-49 —Philadelphia (BAA)............	60	...	529	*1689	.313	502	638	.787	...	74	262	...	1560	...	1.2	26.0
49-50 —Philadelphia................	68	...	336	1209	.278	293	421	.696	...	56	240	...	965	...	0.8	14.2
50-51 —Philadelphia................	66	...	429	1358	.316	378	442	*.855	523	117	247	8	1236	7.9	1.8	18.7
51-52 —Philadelphia................	61	1904	336	1078	.312	250	303	.825	368	123	255	13	922	6.0	2.0	15.1
52-53 —Philadelphia................	70	2085	332	960	.346	168	231	.727	387	138	319	20	832	5.5	2.0	11.9
53-54 —Philadelphia................	61	501	61	229	.266	28	49	.571	101	28	90	0	150	1.7	0.5	2.5
Totals....................	489	...	2824	9338	.302	2355	3075	.766	...	587	1774	...	8003	...	1.2	16.4

NBA PLAYOFF RECORD

Season Team	G	Min.	FGM	FGA	Pct.	FTM	FTA	Pct.	Reb.	Ast.	PF	Dq.	Pts.	AVERAGES RPG	APG	PPG
46-47 —Philadelphia (BAA)............	10	...	74	257	.288	74	94	.787	...	3	32	...	222	...	0.3	22.2
47-48 —Philadelphia (BAA)............	13	...	92	380	.242	98	121	.810	...	3	55	...	282	...	0.2	21.7
48-49 —Philadelphia (BAA)............	1	...	0	0	...	0	0	...	...	0	1	0	0	...	0.0	0.0
49-50 —Philadelphia................	2	...	5	26	.192	5	10	.500	...	2	10	...	15	...	1.0	7.5
50-51 —Philadelphia................	2	...	16	49	.327	20	27	.741	16	1	9	0	52	8.0	0.5	26.0
51-52 —Philadelphia................	3	70	5	33	.152	7	9	.778	12	2	13	1	17	4.0	0.7	5.7
Totals....................	31	...	192	745	.258	204	261	.782	...	11	120	...	588	...	0.4	19.0

NBA ALL-STAR GAME RECORD

Season Team	Min.	FGM	FGA	Pct.	FTM	FTA	Pct.	Reb	Ast.	PF	Dq.	Pts.
1951 —Philadelphia...............	...	6	15	.400	7	9	.778	7	3	5	0	19
1952 —Philadelphia...............	9	3	7	.429	0	1	.000	5	2	2	0	6
Totals.....................	...	9	22	.409	7	10	.700	12	5	7	0	25

GALLATIN, HARRY   F/C

PERSONAL: Born April 26, 1927, in Roxana, Ill. ... 6-6/215 (1,98/97,5). ... Full name: Harry Junior Gallatin. ... Nickname: The Horse.
HIGH SCHOOL: Roxana (Ill.).
COLLEGE: Northeast Missouri State Teachers College.
TRANSACTIONS: Selected by New York Knicks in first round of 1948 BAA Draft. ... Knicks franchise became part of NBA for 1949-50 season. ... Traded by Knicks with G Dick Atha and C/F Nat Clifton to Detroit Pistons for F Mel Hutchins and first-round draft choice (April 3, 1957).
CAREER HONORS: Elected to Naismith Memorial Basketball Hall of Fame (1991).

COLLEGIATE RECORD

NOTES: Elected to NAIA Basketball Hall of Fame (1957).

Season Team	G	Min.	FGM	FGA	Pct.	FTM	FTA	Pct.	Reb.	Ast.	Pts.	AVERAGES RPG	APG	PPG
46-47—NE Missouri St..............	31	...	149	...	...	53	89	.596	...	...	351	...	...	11.3
47-48—NE Missouri St..............	31	...	178	465	.383	109	162	.673	...	...	465	...	...	15.0
Totals....................	62	...	327			162	251	.645	...	...	816	...	...	13.2

NBA REGULAR-SEASON RECORD

HONORS: All-NBA first team (1954). ... All-NBA second team (1955).

Season Team	G	Min.	FGM	FGA	Pct.	FTM	FTA	Pct.	Reb.	Ast.	PF	Dq.	Pts.	AVERAGES RPG	APG	PPG
48-49 —New York (BAA).................	52	...	157	479	.328	120	169	.710	...	63	127	...	434	...	1.2	8.3
49-50 —New York................	68	...	263	664	.396	277	366	.757	...	56	215	...	803	...	0.8	11.8
50-51 —New York................	66	...	293	705	.416	259	354	.732	800	180	244	4	845	12.1	2.7	12.8
51-52 —New York................	66	1931	233	527	.442	275	341	.806	661	115	223	5	741	10.0	1.7	11.2
52-53 —New York................	70	2333	282	635	.444	301	430	.700	916	126	224	6	865	13.1	1.8	12.4
53-54 —New York................	72	2690	258	639	.404	433	552	.784	*1098	153	208	2	949	*15.3	2.1	13.2
54-55 —New York................	72	2548	330	859	.384	393	483	.814	995	176	206	5	1053	13.8	2.4	14.6
55-56 —New York................	72	2378	322	834	.386	358	455	.787	740	168	220	6	1002	10.3	2.3	13.9
56-57 —New York................	72	1943	332	817	.406	415	519	.800	725	85	202	1	1079	10.1	1.2	15.0
57-58 —Detroit................	72	1990	340	898	.379	392	498	.787	749	86	217	5	1072	10.4	1.2	14.9
Totals....................	682	...	2810	7057	.398	3223	4167	.773	...	1208	2086	...	8843	...	1.8	13.0

NBA PLAYOFF RECORD

Season Team	G	Min.	FGM	FGA	Pct.	FTM	FTA	Pct.	Reb.	Ast.	PF	Dq.	Pts.	AVERAGES RPG	APG	PPG
48-49 —New York (BAA)..............	6	...	20	56	.357	32	39	.821	...	10	31	...	72	...	1.7	12.0
49-50 —New York................	5	...	20	52	.385	25	32	.781	...	6	23	...	65	...	1.2	13.0
50-51 —New York................	14	...	49	140	.350	67	87	.770	163	26	57	3	165	11.6	1.9	11.8
51-52 —New York................	14	471	50	122	.410	51	66	.773	134	19	45	1	151	9.6	1.4	10.8
52-53 —New York................	11	303	36	86	.419	44	59	.746	120	15	29	0	116	10.9	1.4	10.5
53-54 —New York................	4	151	16	35	.457	22	31	.710	61	6	12	0	54	15.3	1.5	13.5
54-55 —New York................	3	108	19	42	.452	17	22	.773	44	7	11	0	55	14.7	2.3	18.3
57-58 —Detroit................	7	182	32	87	.368	26	37	.703	70	11	27	1	90	10.0	1.6	12.9
Totals....................	64	...	242	620	.390	284	373	.761	...	100	235	...	768	...	1.6	12.0

NBA ALL-STAR GAME RECORD

Season	Team	Min.	FGM	FGA	Pct.	FTM	FTA	Pct.	Reb	Ast.	PF	Dq.	Pts.
1951	—New York	...	2	4	.500	1	1	1.000	5	2	4	0	5
1952	—New York	22	3	5	.600	1	4	.250	9	3	3	0	7
1953	—New York	19	1	4	.250	1	2	.500	3	2	1	0	3
1954	—New York	28	0	2	.000	5	6	.833	18	3	0	0	5
1955	—New York	36	4	7	.571	5	5	1.000	14	3	2	0	13
1956	—New York	30	5	12	.417	6	7	.857	5	2	4	0	16
1957	—New York	24	4	7	.571	0	2	.000	11	1	3	0	8
Totals		...	19	41	.463	19	27	.704	65	16	17	0	57

HONORS: NBA Coach of the Year (1963).

HEAD COACHING RECORD

COLLEGIATE COACHING RECORD

Season	Team	W	L	Pct.	Finish
58-59	—Southern Illinois-Carbondale	17	10	.630	2nd/Interstate Intercollegiate Athletic Conference
59-60	—Southern Illinois-Carbondale	20	9	.690	T1st/Interstate Intercollegiate Athletic Conference
60-61	—Southern Illinois-Carbondale	21	6	.778	1st/Interstate Intercollegiate Athletic Conference
61-62	—Southern Illinois-Carbondale	21	10	.677	1st/Interstate Intercollegiate Athletic Conference
67-68	—Southern Ill.-Edwardsville	5	5	.500	
68-69	—Southern Ill.-Edwardsville	7	10	.412	
69-70	—Southern Ill.-Edwardsville	7	16	.304	
Totals (7 years)		98	66	.598	

NBA COACHING RECORD

		REGULAR SEASON				PLAYOFFS		
Season	Team	W	L	Pct.	Finish	W	L	Pct.
62-63	—St. Louis	48	32	.600	2nd/Western Division	6	5	.545
63-64	—St. Louis	46	34	.575	2nd/Western Division	6	6	.500
64-65	—St. Louis	17	16	.515		—	—	—
	—New York	19	23	.452	4th/Eastern Division	—	—	—
65-66	—New York	6	15	.286		—	—	—
Totals (4 years)		136	120	.531	Totals (2 years)	12	11	.522

NOTES:

1959—Defeated Wittenberg, 90-80, in NCAA College Division Tournament regional semifinal; lost to Belmont Academy, 79-70, in regional final.

1960—Defeated McKendree, 97-71, in NCAA College Division Tournament regional; lost to Oklahoma Baptist, 75-71, in semifinal.

1961—Defeated Trinity (Tex.), 96-84, in NCAA College Division Tournament regional semifinal; lost to Southeast Missouri, 87-84, in regional final.

1962—Defeated Union, 78-56, in NCAA College Division Tournament regional semifinal; defeated Evansville, 88-83, in regional final; defeated Northeastern, 73-57, in quarterfinal; lost to Mount St. Mary's, 58-57, in semifinals; defeated Nebraska Wesleyan 98-81, in third-place game.

1963—Defeated Detroit, 3-1, in Western Division Semifinals; lost to Los Angeles, 4-3, in Western Division Finals.

1964—Defeated Los Angeles, 3-2, in Western Division Semifinals; lost to San Francisco, 4-3, in Western Division Finals. Replaced as St. Louis head coach by Richie Guerin (November).

1965—Replaced Eddie Donovan as New York head coach (January), with record of 12-26. Replaced as New York head coach by Dick McGuire (November 29).

RECORD AS BASEBALL PLAYER

TRANSACTIONS: Signed by Erwin (Tenn.) of Appalachian League (January 1945). ... On military service list (July 1945-February 24, 1949). ... Placed on suspended list (July 13, 1950). ... Released (September 29, 1950).

Year	Team (League)	W	L	Pct.	ERA	G	GS	CG	ShO	Sv.	IP	H	R	ER	BB	SO
1949	—Decatur (Three I)	7	9	.438	4.28	32	...	10	1	...	166	171	88	79	85	78

GERVIN, GEORGE   G/F

PERSONAL: Born April 27, 1952, in Detroit. ... 6-7/185 (2,00/83,9). ... Full name: George Gervin. ... Nickname: Iceman. ... Brother of Derrick Gervin, guard with New Jersey Nets (1989-90 and 1990-91).
HIGH SCHOOL: Martin Luther King (Detroit).
COLLEGE: Long Beach State, then Eastern Michigan.
TRANSACTIONS: Selected after sophomore season by Virginia Squires in first round of 1973 ABA special circumstance draft. ... Selected by Phoenix Suns in third round (40th pick overall) of 1974 NBA Draft. ... Contract sold by Squires to San Antonio Spurs (January 30, 1974). ... Spurs franchise became part of NBA for 1976-77 season. ... Traded by Spurs to Chicago Bulls for F David Greenwood (October 24, 1985). ... Played in Italy (1986-87). ... Played with Quad City Thunder of Continental Basketball Association (1989-90).
CAREER HONORS: Elected to Naismith Memorial Basketball Hall of Fame (1996). ... One of the 50 Greatest Players in NBA History (1996).
MISCELLANEOUS: San Antonio Spurs franchise all-time leading scorer with 19,383 points (1976-77 through 1984-85).
CAREER NOTES: Assistant coach, San Antonio Spurs (1992-93 and 1993-94). ... Community relations representative, Spurs (1993-94 to 1999-2000). ... Head coach, Detroit Dogs (ABA 2000).

COLLEGIATE RECORD

NOTES: Left Long Beach State before the start of 1969-70 season.

													AVERAGES		
Season Team	G	Min.	FGM	FGA	Pct.	FTM	FTA	Pct.	Reb.	Ast.	Pts.	RPG	APG	PPG
70-71 —Eastern Mich.	9	300	65	123	.528	28	39	.718	104	29	158	11.6	3.2	17.6
71-72 —Eastern Mich.	30	1098	339	571	.594	208	265	.785	458	103	886	15.3	3.4	29.5
Totals	39	1398	404	694	.582	236	304	.776	562	132	1044	14.4	3.4	26.8

ABA REGULAR-SEASON RECORD

NOTES: ABA All-Star second team (1975, 1976). ... ABA All-Rookie team (1973).

Season Team	G	Min.	2-POINT			3-POINT			FTM	FTA	Pct.	Reb.	Ast.	Pts.	AVERAGES		
			FGM	FGA	Pct.	FGM	FGA	Pct.							RPG	APG	PPG
72-73—Virginia	30	689	155	315	.492	6	26	.231	96	118	.814	128	34	424	4.3	1.1	14.1
73-74—Virginia-San Antonio	74	2511	664	1370	.485	8	56	.143	378	464	.815	624	142	1730	8.4	1.9	23.4
74-75—San Antonio	84	3113	767	1600	.479	17	55	.309	380	458	.830	697	207	1965	8.3	2.5	23.4
75-76—San Antonio	81	2748	692	1359	.509	14	55	.255	342	399	.857	546	201	1768	6.7	2.5	21.8
Totals	269	9061	2278	4644	.491	45	192	.234	1196	1439	.831	1995	584	5887	7.4	2.2	21.9

ABA PLAYOFF RECORD

Season Team	G	Min.	2-POINT			3-POINT			FTM	FTA	Pct.	Reb.	Ast.	Pts.	AVERAGES		
			FGM	FGA	Pct.	FGM	FGA	Pct.							RPG	APG	PPG
72-73—Virginia	5	200	33	72	.458	1	5	.200	23	34	.676	38	8	93	7.6	1.6	18.6
73-74—San Antonio	7	226	56	114	.491	1	1	1.000	29	31	.935	52	19	144	7.4	2.7	20.6
74-75—San Antonio	6	276	76	159	.478	3	12	.250	43	52	.827	84	8	204	14.0	1.3	34.0
75-76—San Antonio	7	288	67	125	.536	0	3	.000	56	69	.812	64	19	190	9.1	2.7	27.1
Totals	25	990	232	470	.494	5	21	.238	151	186	.812	238	54	631	9.5	2.2	25.2

ABA ALL-STAR GAME RECORD

Season Team	Min.	2-POINT			3-POINT			FTM	FTA	Pct.	Reb.	Ast.	Pts.
		FGM	FGA	Pct.	FGM	FGA	Pct.						
1974—Virginia	21	3	8	.375	0	1	.000	3	4	.750	5	3	9
1975—San Antonio	30	8	14	.571	0	1	.000	7	8	.875	6	3	23
1976—San Antonio	16	3	13	.231	0	0	...	1	2	.500	6	1	8
Totals	67	14	35	.400	0	2	.000	11	14	.786	17	7	40

NBA REGULAR-SEASON RECORD

RECORDS: Holds single-game record for most points in one quarter—33 (April 9, 1978, vs. New Orleans).
HONORS: All-NBA first team (1978, 1979, 1980, 1981, 1982). ... All-NBA second team (1977, 1983).

Season Team	G	Min.	FGM	FGA	Pct.	FTM	FTA	Pct.	REBOUNDS			Ast.	St.	Blk.	TO	Pts.	AVERAGES		
									Off.	Def.	Tot.						RPG	APG	PPG
76-77—San Antonio	82	2705	726	1335	.544	443	532	.833	134	320	454	238	105	104	...	1895	5.5	2.9	23.1
77-78—San Antonio	82	2857	*864	1611	.536	504	607	.830	118	302	420	302	136	110	306	*2232	5.1	3.7	*27.2
78-79—San Antonio	80	2888	*947	*1749	.541	471	570	.826	142	258	400	219	137	91	286	*2365	5.0	2.7	*29.6
79-80—San Antonio	78	2934	*1024	*1940	.528	505	593	.852	154	249	403	202	110	79	254	*2585	5.2	2.6	*33.1
80-81—San Antonio	82	2765	850	1729	.492	512	620	.826	126	293	419	260	94	56	251	2221	5.1	3.2	27.1
81-82—San Antonio	79	2817	*993	*1987	.500	555	642	.864	138	254	392	187	77	45	210	*2551	5.0	2.4	*32.3
82-83—San Antonio	78	2830	757	1553	.487	517	606	.853	111	246	357	264	88	67	247	2043	4.6	3.4	26.2
83-84—San Antonio	76	2584	765	1561	.490	427	507	.842	106	207	313	220	79	47	224	1967	4.1	2.9	25.9
84-85—San Antonio	72	2091	600	1182	.508	324	384	.844	79	155	234	178	66	48	198	1524	3.3	2.5	21.2
85-86—Chicago	82	2065	519	1100	.472	283	322	.879	78	137	215	144	49	23	161	1325	2.6	1.8	16.2
Totals	791	26536	8045	15747	.511	4541	5383	.844	1186	2421	3607	2214	941	670	2137	20708	4.6	2.8	26.2

Three-point field goals: 1979-80, 32-for-102 (.314). 1980-81, 9-for-35 (.257). 1981-82, 10-for-36 (.278). 1982-83, 12-for-33 (.364). 1983-84, 10-for-24 (.417). 1984-85, 0-for-10. 1985-86, 4-for-19 (.211). Totals, 77-for-259 (.297).

Personal fouls/disqualifications: 1976-77, 286/12. 1977-78, 255/3. 1978-79, 275/5. 1979-80, 208/0. 1980-81, 212/4. 1981-82, 215/2. 1982-83, 243/5. 1983-84, 219/3. 1984-85, 208/2. 1985-86, 210/4. Totals, 2331/40.

NBA PLAYOFF RECORD

Season Team	G	Min.	FGM	FGA	Pct.	FTM	FTA	Pct.	REBOUNDS			Ast.	St.	Blk.	TO	Pts.	AVERAGES		
									Off.	Def.	Tot.						RPG	APG	PPG
76-77—San Antonio	2	62	19	44	.432	12	15	.800	5	6	11	3	1	2	...	50	5.5	1.5	25.0
77-78—San Antonio	6	227	78	142	.549	43	56	.768	11	23	34	19	6	16	19	199	5.7	3.2	33.2
78-79—San Antonio	14	513	158	295	.536	84	104	.808	33	49	82	35	27	14	40	400	5.9	2.5	28.6
79-80—San Antonio	3	122	37	74	.500	26	30	.867	9	11	20	12	5	3	9	100	6.7	4.0	33.3
80-81—San Antonio	7	274	77	154	.500	36	45	.800	9	26	35	24	5	5	20	190	5.0	3.4	27.1
81-82—San Antonio	9	373	103	228	.452	59	71	.831	19	47	66	41	10	4	31	265	7.3	4.6	29.4
82-83—San Antonio	11	437	108	208	.519	61	69	.884	21	53	74	37	12	4	46	277	6.7	3.4	25.2
84-85—San Antonio	5	183	42	79	.532	27	34	.794	3	15	18	14	3	3	20	111	3.6	2.8	22.2
85-86—Chicago	2	11	0	1	.000	0	0	...	0	1	1	1	0	0	2	0	0.5	0.5	0.0
Totals	59	2202	622	1225	.508	348	424	.821	110	231	341	186	69	51	187	1592	5.8	3.2	27.0

Three-point field goals: 1979-80, 0-for-2. 1980-81, 0-for-3. 1981-82, 0-for-3. 1982-83, 0-for-2. 1984-85, 0-for-3. Totals, 0-for-13.

Personal fouls/disqualifications: 1976-77, 9/1. 1977-78, 23/0. 1978-79, 51/1. 1979-80, 8/0. 1980-81, 19/1. 1981-82, 36/1. 1982-83, 39/1. 1984-85, 19/0. 1985-86, 3/0. Totals, 207/5.

NBA ALL-STAR GAME RECORD

NOTES: NBA All-Star Game Most Valuable Player (1980).

Season Team	Min.	FGM	FGA	Pct.	FTM	FTA	Pct.	REBOUNDS			Ast.	PF	Dq.	St.	Blk.	TO	Pts.
								Off.	Def.	Tot.							
1977 —San Antonio	12	0	6	.000	0	0	...	0	1	1	0	1	0	0	1	...	0
1978 —San Antonio	18	4	11	.364	1	3	.333	1	1	2	1	2	0	2	1	2	9
1979 —San Antonio	34	8	16	.500	10	11	.909	2	4	6	2	4	0	1	1	3	26
1980 —San Antonio	40	14	26	.538	6	9	.667	4	6	10	3	2	0	3	0	3	34
1981 —San Antonio	24	5	9	.556	1	2	.500	1	2	3	0	3	0	2	1	2	11
1982 —San Antonio	27	5	14	.357	2	2	1.000	1	5	6	1	3	0	3	0	0	12
1983 —San Antonio	14	3	8	.375	2	2	1.000	0	0	0	3	3	0	2	0	0	8
1984 —San Antonio	21	5	6	.833	3	3	1.000	0	2	2	1	5	0	0	1	6	13
1985 —San Antonio	25	10	12	.833	3	4	.750	0	3	3	1	2	0	1	4	4	23
Totals	215	54	108	.500	28	36	.778	9	24	33	12	25	0	16	9	20	137

COMBINED ABA AND NBA REGULAR-SEASON RECORDS

	G	Min.	FGM	FGA	Pct.	FTM	FTA	Pct.	REBOUNDS			Ast.	Stl.	Blk.	TO	Pts.	AVERAGES		
									Off.	Def.	Tot.						RPG	APG	PPG
Totals	1060	35597	10368	20583	.504	5737	6822	.841	...	...	5602	2798	...	...	...	26595	5.3	2.6	25.1

Three-point field goals: 122-for-451 (.271).
Personal fouls/disqualifications: 3250.

ITALIAN LEAGUE RECORD

												AVERAGES		
Season Team	G	Min.	FGM	FGA	Pct.	FTM	FTA	Pct.	Reb.	Ast.	Pts.	RPG	APG	PPG
86-87—Banco Roma..................	27	893	263	525	.501	159	190	.837	134	9	704	5.0	0.3	26.1

CBA REGULAR-SEASON RECORD

												AVERAGES		
Season Team	G	Min.	FGM	FGA	Pct.	FTM	FTA	Pct.	Reb.	Ast.	Pts.	RPG	APG	PPG
89-90—Quad City......................	14	391	115	235	.489	54	73	.740	91	20	284	6.5	1.4	20.3

ABA 2000 COACHING RECORD

	REGULAR SEASON				PLAYOFFS		
Season Team	W	L	Pct.	Finish	W	L	Pct.
00-01 —Detroit	21	20	.512	1st	3	0	1.000

NOTES:
2001—Defeated Tampa Bay in Eastern Division Semifinals; defeated Indiana in Eastern Division Finals; defeated Chicago in ABA 2000 Finals.

GILMORE, ARTIS   C

PERSONAL: Born September 21, 1949, in Chipley, Fla. ... 7-2/265 (2,18/120,2). ... Full name: Artis Gilmore.
HIGH SCHOOL: Roulhac (Chipley, Fla.), then Carver (Dothan, Ala.).
JUNIOR COLLEGE: Gardner-Webb Junior College (N.C.).
COLLEGE: Jacksonville.
TRANSACTIONS: Selected by Chicago Bulls in seventh round (117th pick overall) of 1971 NBA Draft. ... Selected by Kentucky Colonels in first round of 1971 ABA draft. ... Selected by Bulls from Colonels in ABA dispersal draft (August 5, 1976). ... Traded by Bulls to San Antonio Spurs for C Dave Corzine, F Mark Olberding and cash (July 22, 1982). ... Traded by Spurs to Bulls for 1988 second-round draft choice (June 22, 1987). ... Waived by Bulls (December 26, 1987). ... Signed as free agent by Boston Celtics (January 8, 1988). ... Played in Italy (1988-89).
MISCELLANEOUS: Chicago Bulls all-time blocked shots leader with 1,017 (1976-77 through 1981-82 and 1987-88).

COLLEGIATE RECORD

NOTES: THE SPORTING NEWS All-America first team (1971). ... THE SPORTING NEWS All-America second team (1970). ... Holds NCAA career record for average rebounds per game—22.7. ... Led NCAA Division I with 22.2 rebounds per game (1970) and 23.2 rebounds per game (1971).

												AVERAGES		
Season Team	G	Min.	FGM	FGA	Pct.	FTM	FTA	Pct.	Reb.	Ast.	Pts.	RPG	APG	PPG
67-68—Gardner-Webb J.C.........	31	...	296	...	...	121	...	...	...	...	713	...	...	23.0
68-69—Gardner-Webb J.C.........	36	...	326	...	...	140	...	...	...	...	792	...	...	22.0
69-70—Jacksonville...................	28	...	307	529	.580	128	202	.634	621	51	742	22.2	1.8	26.5
70-71—Jacksonville...................	26	...	229	405	.565	112	188	.596	603	42	570	23.2	1.6	21.9
Junior college totals	67	...	622	...	...	261	...	...	...	...	1505	...	...	22.5
4-year-college totals	54	...	536	934	.574	240	390	.615	1224	93	1312	22.7	1.7	24.3

ABA REGULAR-SEASON RECORD

NOTES: ABA Most Valuable Player (1972). ... ABA Rookie of the Year (1972). ... ABA All-Star first team (1972, 1973, 1974, 1975, 1976). ... ABA All-Defensive team (1973, 1974, 1975, 1976). ... ABA All-Rookie team (1972). ... Member of ABA championship team (1975). ... Holds single-game record for most rebounds—40 (February 3, 1974, vs. New York). ... Holds single-season record for most blocked shots—422 (1972). ... Led ABA with 341 personal fouls (1972).

			2-POINT			3-POINT									AVERAGES		
Season Team	G	Min.	FGM	FGA	Pct.	FGM	FGA	Pct.	FTM	FTA	Pct.	Reb.	Ast.	Pts.	RPG	APG	PPG
71-72—Kentucky..................	84	*3666	806	1348	*.598	0	0	...	391	605	.646	*1491	230	2003	*17.8	2.7	23.8
72-73—Kentucky..................	84	3502	686	1226	*.560	1	2	.500	368	572	.643	*1476	295	1743	*17.6	3.5	20.8
73-74—Kentucky..................	84	*3502	621	1257	.494	0	3	.000	326	489	.667	*1538	329	1568	*18.3	3.9	18.7
74-75—Kentucky..................	84	*3493	783	1348	.580	1	2	.500	412	592	.696	*1361	208	1981	16.2	2.5	23.6
75-76—Kentucky..................	84	3286	773	1401	.552	0	0	...	521	*764	.682	*1303	211	2067	*15.5	2.5	24.6
Totals	420	17449	3669	6581	.558	2	7	.286	2018	3022	.668	7169	1273	9362	17.1	3.0	22.3

ABA PLAYOFF RECORD

NOTES: ABA Playoff Most Valuable Player (1975).

			2-POINT			3-POINT									AVERAGES		
Season Team	G	Min.	FGM	FGA	Pct.	FGM	FGA	Pct.	FTM	FTA	Pct.	Reb.	Ast.	Pts.	RPG	APG	PPG
71-72—Kentucky..................	6	285	52	90	.578	0	1	.000	27	38	.711	106	25	131	17.7	4.2	21.8
72-73—Kentucky..................	19	780	142	261	.544	0	0	...	77	123	.626	260	75	361	13.7	3.9	19.0
73-74—Kentucky..................	8	344	71	127	.559	0	0	...	38	66	.576	149	28	180	18.6	3.5	22.5
74-75—Kentucky..................	15	679	132	245	.539	0	0	...	98	127	.772	264	38	362	17.6	2.5	24.1
75-76—Kentucky..................	10	390	93	153	.608	0	0	...	56	74	.757	152	19	242	15.2	1.9	24.2
Totals	58	2478	490	876	.559	0	1	.000	296	428	.692	931	185	1276	16.1	3.2	22.0

ABA ALL-STAR GAME RECORD

NOTES: ABA All-Star Game Most Valuable Player (1974).

		2-POINT			3-POINT								
Season Team	Min.	FGM	FGA	Pct.	FGM	FGA	Pct.	FTM	FTA	Pct.	Reb.	Ast.	Pts.
1972—Kentucky..................................	27	4	5	.800	0	0	...	6	10	.600	10	2	14
1973—Kentucky..................................	31	3	8	.375	0	0	...	4	8	.500	16	0	10
1974—Kentucky..................................	27	8	12	.667	0	0	...	2	3	.667	13	1	18
1975—Kentucky..................................	28	4	8	.500	0	0	...	3	7	.429	13	2	11
1976—Kentucky..................................	27	5	7	.714	0	0	...	4	6	.667	7	1	14
Totals	140	24	40	.600	0	0	...	19	34	.559	59	6	67

ALL-TIME GREAT PLAYERS

NBA REGULAR-SEASON RECORD

RECORDS: Holds career record for highest field goal percentage (minimum 2,000 made)—.599.

HONORS: NBA All-Defensive second team (1978).

Season Team	G	Min.	FGM	FGA	Pct.	FTM	FTA	Pct.	REBOUNDS Off.	Def.	Tot.	Ast.	St.	Blk.	TO	Pts.	AVERAGES RPG	APG	PPG
76-77—Chicago	82	2877	570	1091	.522	387	586	.660	313	757	1070	199	44	203	...	1527	13.0	2.4	18.6
77-78—Chicago	82	3067	704	1260	.559	471	*669	.704	318	753	1071	263	42	181	*366	1879	13.1	3.2	22.9
78-79—Chicago	82	3265	753	1310	.575	434	587	.739	293	750	1043	274	50	156	310	1940	12.7	3.3	23.7
79-80—Chicago	48	1568	305	513	.595	245	344	.712	108	324	432	133	29	59	133	855	9.0	2.8	17.8
80-81—Chicago	82	2832	547	816	*.670	375	532	.705	220	608	828	172	47	198	236	1469	10.1	2.1	17.9
81-82—Chicago	82	2796	546	837	*.652	424	552	.768	224	611	835	136	49	220	227	1517	10.2	1.7	18.5
82-83—San Antonio	82	2797	556	888	*.626	367	496	.740	299	685	984	126	40	192	254	1479	12.0	1.5	18.0
83-84—San Antonio	64	2034	351	556	*.631	280	390	.718	213	449	662	70	36	132	149	982	10.3	1.1	15.3
84-85—San Antonio	81	2756	532	854	.623	484	646	.749	231	615	846	131	40	173	241	1548	10.4	1.6	19.1
85-86—San Antonio	71	2395	423	684	.618	338	482	.701	166	434	600	102	39	108	186	1184	8.5	1.4	16.7
86-87—San Antonio	82	2405	346	580	.597	242	356	.680	185	394	579	150	39	95	178	934	7.1	1.8	11.4
87-88—Chi.-Boston	71	893	99	181	.547	67	128	.523	69	142	211	21	15	30	67	265	3.0	0.3	3.7
Totals	909	29685	5732	9570	.599	4114	5768	.713	2639	6522	9161	1777	470	1747	2347	15579	10.1	2.0	17.1

Three-point field goals: 1981-82, 1-for-1. 1982-83, 0-for-6. 1983-84, 0-for-3. 1984-85, 0-for-2. 1985-86, 1-for-13 (.077).

Personal fouls/disqualifications: 1976-77, 266/4. 1977-78, 261/4. 1978-79, 280/2. 1979-80, 167/5. 1980-81, 295/2. 1981-82, 287/4. 1982-83, 273/4. 1983-84, 229/4. 1984-85, 306/4. 1985-86, 239/3. 1986-87, 235/2. 1987-88, 148/0. Totals, 2986/38.

NBA PLAYOFF RECORD

Season Team	G	Min.	FGM	FGA	Pct.	FTM	FTA	Pct.	REBOUNDS Off.	Def.	Tot.	Ast.	St.	Blk.	TO	Pts.	AVERAGES RPG	APG	PPG
76-77—Chicago	3	126	19	40	.475	18	23	.783	15	24	39	6	3	8	...	56	13.0	2.0	18.7
80-81—Chicago	6	247	35	59	.593	38	55	.691	24	43	67	12	6	17	17	108	11.2	2.0	18.0
82-83—San Antonio	11	401	76	132	.576	32	46	.696	37	105	142	18	9	34	27	184	12.9	1.6	16.7
84-85—San Antonio	5	185	29	52	.558	31	45	.689	10	40	50	7	2	7	23	89	10.0	1.4	17.8
85-86—San Antonio	3	107	16	24	.667	8	14	.571	7	11	18	3	7	1	10	40	6.0	1.0	13.3
87-88—Boston	14	86	4	8	.500	7	14	.500	4	16	20	1	0	4	4	15	1.4	0.1	1.1
Totals	42	1152	179	315	.568	134	197	.680	97	239	336	47	27	71	81	492	8.0	1.1	11.7

Personal fouls/disqualifications: 1976-77, 9/0. 1980-81, 15/0. 1982-83, 46/1. 1984-85, 18/0. 1985-86, 11/0. 1987-88, 14/0. Totals, 113/1.

NBA ALL-STAR GAME RECORD

Season Team	Min.	FGM	FGA	Pct.	FTM	FTA	Pct.	REBOUNDS Off.	Def.	Tot.	Ast.	PF	Dq.	St.	Blk.	TO	Pts.
1978 —Chicago	13	2	4	.500	6	8	.750	0	2	2	0	1	0	1	2	1	10
1979 —Chicago	15	3	4	.750	2	2	1.000	1	0	1	2	1	0	0	0	1	8
1981 —Chicago	22	5	7	.714	1	2	.500	1	5	6	2	4	0	1	0		11
1982 —Chicago	16	3	6	.500	1	1	1.000	1	2	3	2	4	0	0	1	2	7
1983 —San Antonio	16	2	4	.500	1	2	.500	1	4	5	1	4	0	1	0	1	5
1986 —San Antonio	13	3	4	.750	4	4	1.000	1	1	2	1	4	0	2	0	0	10
Totals	95	18	29	.621	15	19	.789	5	14	19	8	18	0	4	4	5	51

COMBINED ABA AND NBA REGULAR-SEASON RECORDS

	G	Min.	FGM	FGA	Pct.	FTM	FTA	Pct.	REBOUNDS Off.	Def.	Tot.	Ast.	Stl.	Blk.	TO	Pts.	AVERAGES RPG	APG	PPG
Totals	1329	33356	9403	16158	.582	6132	8790	.698	...	...	16330	3050	...	...	...	24041	12.3	2.3	18.1

Three-point field goals: 3-for-20 (.150).

Personal fouls/disqualifications: 4529.

ITALIAN LEAGUE RECORD

Season Team	G	Min.	FGM	FGA	Pct.	FTM	FTA	Pct.	Reb.	Ast.	Pts.	AVERAGES RPG	APG	PPG
88-89—Bologna Arimo	35	1101	166	270	.615	97	147	.660	386	21	429	11.0	0.6	12.3

GOODRICH, GAIL   G

PERSONAL: Born April 23, 1943, in Los Angeles. ... 6-1/175 (1,85/79,4). ... Full name: Gail Charles Goodrich Jr.

HIGH SCHOOL: Los Angeles Polytechnic.

COLLEGE: UCLA.

TRANSACTIONS: Selected by Los Angeles Lakers in 1965 NBA Draft (territorial pick). ... Selected by Phoenix Suns from Lakers in NBA Expansion Draft (May 6, 1968). ... Traded by Suns to Lakers for F Mel Counts (May 20, 1970). ... Signed as veteran free agent by New Orleans Jazz (July 19, 1976); Lakers received 1977 and 1979 first-round draft choices and 1980 second-round draft choice as compensation; Jazz received 1977 second-round draft choice to complete transaction (October 6, 1976).

CAREER HONORS: Elected to Naismith Memorial Basketball Hall of Fame (1996).

MISCELLANEOUS: Member of NBA championship team (1972).

COLLEGIATE RECORD

NOTES: THE SPORTING NEWS All-America first team (1965). ... Member of NCAA Division I championship team (1964, 1965).

Season Team	G	Min.	FGM	FGA	Pct.	FTM	FTA	Pct.	Reb.	Ast.	Pts.	AVERAGES RPG	APG	PPG
61-62—UCLA‡	20	...	189	385	.491	110	155	.710	122	...	488	6.1	...	24.4
62-63—UCLA	29	...	117	280	.418	66	103	.641	101	...	300	3.5	...	10.3
63-64—UCLA	30	...	243	530	.459	160	225	.711	156	...	646	5.2	...	21.5
64-65—UCLA	30	...	277	528	.525	190	265	.717	158	...	744	5.3	...	24.8
Varsity totals	89	...	637	1338	.476	416	593	.702	415	...	1690	4.7	...	19.0

NBA REGULAR-SEASON RECORD

HONORS: All-NBA first team (1974).

Season Team	G	Min.	FGM	FGA	Pct.	FTM	FTA	Pct.	Reb.	Ast.	PF	Dq.	Pts.	RPG	APG	PPG
65-66 —Los Angeles	65	1008	203	503	.404	103	149	.691	130	103	103	1	509	2.0	1.6	7.8
66-67 —Los Angeles	77	1780	352	776	.454	253	337	.751	251	210	194	3	957	3.3	2.7	12.4
67-68 —Los Angeles	79	2057	718	812	.486	302	392	.770	199	205	228	2	1092	2.5	2.6	13.8
68-69 —Phoenix	81	3236	718	1746	.411	495	663	.747	437	518	253	3	1931	5.4	6.4	23.8
69-70 —Phoenix	81	3234	568	1251	.454	488	604	.808	340	605	251	3	1624	4.2	7.5	20.0
70-71 —Los Angeles	79	2808	558	1174	.475	264	343	.770	260	380	258	3	1380	3.3	4.8	17.5
71-72 —Los Angeles	82	3040	826	1695	.487	475	559	.850	295	365	210	0	2127	3.6	4.5	25.9
72-73 —Los Angeles	76	2697	750	1615	.464	314	374	.840	263	332	193	1	1814	3.5	4.4	23.9

Season Team	G	Min.	FGM	FGA	Pct.	FTM	FTA	Pct.	Off.	Def.	Tot.	Ast.	St.	Blk.	TO	Pts.	RPG	APG	PPG
73-74—Los Angeles....	82	3061	784	1773	.442	*508	*588	.864	95	155	250	427	126	12	...	2076	3.0	5.2	25.3
74-75—Los Angeles	72	2668	656	1429	.459	318	378	.841	96	123	219	420	102	6	...	1630	3.0	5.8	22.6
75-76—Los Angeles	75	2646	583	1321	.441	293	346	.847	94	120	214	421	123	17	...	1459	2.9	5.6	19.5
76-77—New Orleans ...	27	609	136	305	.446	68	85	.800	25	36	61	74	22	2	...	340	2.3	2.7	12.6
77-78—New Orleans	81	2553	520	1050	.495	264	332	.795	75	102	177	388	82	22	205	1304	2.2	4.8	16.1
78-79—New Orleans	74	2130	382	850	.449	174	204	.853	68	115	183	357	90	13	185	938	2.5	4.8	12.7
Totals	1031	33527	7431	16300	.456	4319	5354	.807	...	...	3279	4805	545	72	390	19181	3.2	4.7	18.6

Personal fouls/disqualifications: 1973-74, 227/3. 1974-75, 214/1. 1975-76, 238/3. 1976-77, 43/0. 1977-78, 186/0. 1978-79, 177/1. Totals, 2775/24.

NBA PLAYOFF RECORD

Season Team	G	Min.	FGM	FGA	Pct.	FTM	FTA	Pct.	Reb.	Ast.	PF	Dq.	Pts.	RPG	APG	PPG
65-66 —Los Angeles	11	290	43	92	.467	29	43	.674	42	33	35	0	115	3.8	3.0	10.5
66-67 —Los Angeles	3	81	11	31	.355	11	18	.611	9	10	5	0	33	3.0	3.3	11.0
67-68 —Los Angeles	10	100	23	47	.489	14	18	.778	14	14	10	0	60	1.4	1.4	6.0
69-70 —Phoenix	7	265	56	118	.475	30	35	.857	32	38	21	0	142	4.6	5.4	20.3
70-71 —Los Angeles	12	518	105	247	.425	95	113	.841	38	91	38	0	305	3.2	7.6	25.4
71-72 —Los Angeles	15	575	130	292	.445	97	108	.898	38	50	50	0	357	2.5	3.3	23.8
72-73 —Los Angeles	17	604	139	310	.448	62	79	.785	61	67	53	1	340	3.6	3.9	20.0

Season Team	G	Min.	FGM	FGA	Pct.	FTM	FTA	Pct.	Off.	Def.	Tot.	Ast.	St.	Blk.	TO	Pts.	RPG	APG	PPG
73-74—Los Angeles....	5	189	35	90	.389	28	33	.848	7	9	16	30	7	1	...	98	3.2	6.0	19.6
Totals	80	2622	542	1227	.442	366	447	.819	...	...	250	333	7	1	...	1450	3.1	4.2	18.1

Personal fouls/disqualifications: 1973-74, 7/0.

NBA ALL-STAR GAME RECORD

Season Team	Min.	FGM	FGA	Pct.	FTM	FTA	Pct.	Reb	Ast.	PF	Dq.	Pts.
1969 —Phoenix	6	2	4	.500	1	2	.500	1	1	1	0	5
1972 —Los Angeles	14	2	7	.286	0	0	...	1	2	2	0	4
1973 —Los Angeles	16	1	7	.143	0	0	...	2	1	2	0	2

Season Team	Min.	FGM	FGA	Pct.	FTM	FTA	Pct.	Off.	Def.	Tot.	Ast.	PF	Dq.	St.	Blk.	TO	Pts.
1974 —Los Angeles	26	9	16	.563	0	0	...	1	3	4	6	2	0	1	0	...	18
1975 —Los Angeles	15	2	4	.500	0	0	...	0	1	1	4	1	0	0	0	...	4
Totals	77	16	38	.421	1	2	.500	...	...	9	14	8	0	1	0	...	33

GREER, HAL   G

PERSONAL: Born June 26, 1936, in Huntington, W.Va. ... 6-2/175 (1,88/79,4). ... Full name: Harold Everett Greer.
HIGH SCHOOL: Douglass (Huntington, W.Va.).
COLLEGE: Marshall.
TRANSACTIONS: Selected by Syracuse Nationals in second round (14th pick overall) of 1958 NBA Draft. ... Nationals franchise moved from Syracuse to Philadelphia and renamed 76ers for 1963-64 season.
CAREER HONORS: Elected to Naismith Memorial Basketball Hall of Fame (1982). ... One of the 50 Greatest Players in NBA History (1996).
MISCELLANEOUS: Member of NBA championship team (1967). ... Philadelphia 76ers franchise all-time leading scorer with 21,586 points (1958-59 through 1972-73).

COLLEGIATE RECORD

Season Team	G	Min.	FGM	FGA	Pct.	FTM	FTA	Pct.	Reb.	Ast.	Pts.	RPG	APG	PPG
54-55—Marshall‡	...	...	...	...	...	...	...	...	...	...	...	...	...	18.0
55-56—Marshall	23	...	128	213	.601	101	145	.697	153	...	357	6.7	...	15.5
56-57—Marshall	24	...	167	329	.508	119	156	.763	332	...	453	13.8	...	18.9
57-58—Marshall	24	...	236	432	.546	95	114	.833	280	...	567	11.7	...	23.6
Varsity totals	71	...	531	974	.545	315	415	.759	765	...	1377	10.8	...	19.4

NBA REGULAR-SEASON RECORD

HONORS: All-NBA second team (1963, 1964, 1965, 1966, 1967, 1968, 1969).

Season Team	G	Min.	FGM	FGA	Pct.	FTM	FTA	Pct.	Reb.	Ast.	PF	Dq.	Pts.	RPG	APG	PPG
58-59 —Syracuse	68	1625	308	679	.454	137	176	.778	196	101	189	1	753	2.9	1.5	11.1
59-60 —Syracuse	70	1979	388	815	.476	148	189	.783	303	188	208	4	924	4.3	2.7	13.2
60-61 —Syracuse	79	2763	623	1381	.451	305	394	.774	455	302	242	0	1551	5.8	3.8	19.6
61-62 —Syracuse	71	2705	644	1442	.447	331	404	.819	524	313	252	2	1619	7.4	4.4	22.8
62-63 —Syracuse	80	2631	600	1293	.464	362	434	.834	457	275	286	4	1562	5.7	3.4	19.5
63-64 —Philadelphia	80	3157	715	1611	.444	435	525	.829	484	374	291	6	1865	6.1	4.7	23.3
64-65 —Philadelphia	70	2600	539	1245	.433	335	413	.811	355	313	254	7	1413	5.1	4.5	20.2
65-66 —Philadelphia	80	3326	703	1580	.445	413	514	.804	473	384	315	6	1819	5.9	4.8	22.7

Season Team	G	Min.	FGM	FGA	Pct.	FTM	FTA	Pct.	Reb.	Ast.	PF	Dq.	Pts.	RPG	APG	PPG
66-67 —Philadelphia	80	3086	699	1524	.459	367	466	.788	422	303	302	5	1765	5.3	3.8	22.1
67-68 —Philadelphia	82	3263	777	1626	.478	422	549	.769	444	372	289	6	1976	5.4	4.5	24.1
68-69 —Philadelphia	82	3311	732	1595	.459	432	543	.796	435	414	294	8	1896	5.3	5.0	23.1
69-70 —Philadelphia	80	3024	705	1551	.455	352	432	.815	375	405	300	8	1762	4.7	5.1	22.0
70-71 —Philadelphia	81	3060	591	1371	.431	326	405	.805	364	369	289	4	1508	4.5	4.6	18.6
71-72 —Philadelphia	81	2410	389	866	.449	181	234	.774	271	316	268	10	959	3.3	3.9	11.8
72-73 —Philadelphia	38	848	91	232	.392	32	39	.821	106	111	76	1	214	2.8	2.9	5.6
Totals	1122	39788	8504	18811	.452	4578	5717	.801	5665	4540	3855	72	21586	5.0	4.0	19.2

NBA PLAYOFF RECORD

Season Team	G	Min.	FGM	FGA	Pct.	FTM	FTA	Pct.	Reb.	Ast.	PF	Dq.	Pts.	RPG	APG	PPG
58-59 —Syracuse	9	277	39	93	.419	26	32	.813	47	20	35	2	104	5.2	2.2	11.6
59-60 —Syracuse	3	84	22	43	.512	3	4	.750	14	10	5	0	47	4.7	3.3	15.7
60-61 —Syracuse	8	232	41	106	.387	33	40	.825	33	19	32	1	115	4.1	2.4	14.4
61-62 —Syracuse	1	5	0	0	...	0	0	...	0	0	1	0	0	0.0	0.0	0.0
62-63 —Syracuse	5	214	44	87	.506	29	35	.829	27	21	21	1	117	5.4	4.2	23.4
63-64 —Philadelphia	5	211	37	95	.389	33	39	.846	28	30	19	1	107	5.6	6.0	21.4
64-65 —Philadelphia	11	505	101	222	.455	69	87	.793	81	55	45	2	271	7.4	5.0	24.6
65-66 —Philadelphia	5	226	32	91	.352	18	23	.783	36	21	21	0	82	7.2	4.2	16.4
66-67 —Philadelphia	15	688	161	375	.429	94	118	.797	88	79	55	1	416	5.9	5.3	27.7
67-68 —Philadelphia	13	553	120	278	.432	95	111	.856	79	55	49	1	335	6.1	4.2	25.8
68-69 —Philadelphia	5	204	26	81	.321	28	36	.778	30	23	23	0	80	6.0	4.6	16.0
69-70 —Philadelphia	5	178	33	74	.446	11	13	.846	17	27	16	0	77	3.4	5.4	15.4
70-71 —Philadelphia	7	265	49	112	.438	27	36	.750	25	33	35	4	125	3.6	4.7	17.9
Totals	92	3642	705	1657	.425	466	574	.812	505	393	357	13	1876	5.5	4.3	20.4

NBA ALL-STAR GAME RECORD

NOTES: NBA All-Star Game Most Valuable Player (1968).

Season Team	Min.	FGM	FGA	Pct.	FTM	FTA	Pct.	Reb	Ast.	PF	Dq.	Pts.
1961 —Syracuse	18	7	11	.636	0	0	...	6	2	2	0	14
1962 —Syracuse	24	3	14	.214	2	7	.286	10	9	3	0	8
1963 —Syracuse	15	3	7	.429	0	0	...	3	2	4	0	6
1964 —Philadelphia	20	5	10	.500	3	4	.750	3	4	1	0	13
1965 —Philadelphia	21	5	11	.455	3	4	.750	4	1	2	0	13
1966 —Philadelphia	23	4	13	.308	1	1	1.000	5	1	4	0	9
1967 —Philadelphia	31	5	16	.313	7	8	.875	4	1	5	0	17
1968 —Philadelphia	17	8	8	1.000	5	7	.714	3	3	2	0	21
1969 —Philadelphia	17	0	1	.000	4	5	.800	3	2	2	0	4
1970 —Philadelphia	21	7	11	.636	1	1	1.000	4	3	4	0	15
Totals	207	47	102	.461	26	37	.703	45	28	29	0	120

CBA COACHING RECORD

Season Team	REGULAR SEASON				PLAYOFFS		
	W	L	Pct.	Finish	W	L	Pct.
80-81 —Philadelphia	17	23	.425	3rd/Eastern Division	3	3	.500

NOTES:
1981—Defeated Atlantic City, 2-1, in Eastern Division Semifinals; lost to Rochester, 2-1, in Eastern Division Finals.

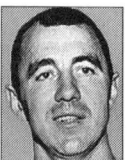

GUERIN, RICHIE   G

PERSONAL: Born May 29, 1932, in New York. ... 6-4/210 (1,93/95,3). ... Full name: Richard V. Guerin.
HIGH SCHOOL: Mount St. Michael Academy (Bronx, N.Y.).
COLLEGE: Iona.
TRANSACTIONS: Selected by New York Knicks in second round of 1954 NBA Draft. ... In military service during 1954-55 and 1955-56 seasons; played with Quantico Marines and Marine All-Star teams. ... Traded by Knicks to St. Louis Hawks for cash and second-round draft choice (October 18, 1963). ... Selected by Seattle SuperSonics from Hawks in NBA Expansion Draft (1967). ... Traded by SuperSonics to Atlanta Hawks for Dick Smith (November 15, 1968).

COLLEGIATE RECORD

Season Team	G	Min.	FGM	FGA	Pct.	FTM	FTA	Pct.	Reb.	Ast.	Pts.	RPG	APG	PPG
50-51—Iona‡						Freshman team statistics unavailable.								
51-52—Iona	27	...	159	...	...	146	...	...	...	...	464	...	...	17.2
52-53—Iona	21	...	139	283	.491	114	172	.663	...	...	392	...	...	18.7
53-54—Iona	21	...	171	405	.422	177	249	.711	...	...	519	...	...	24.7
Varsity totals	69	...	469	...	...	437	...	...	...	...	1375	...	...	19.9

HONORS: All-NBA second team (1959, 1960, 1962).

NBA REGULAR-SEASON RECORD

Season Team	G	Min.	FGM	FGA	Pct.	FTM	FTA	Pct.	Reb.	Ast.	PF	Dq.	Pts.	RPG	APG	PPG
56-57 —New York	72	1793	257	699	.368	181	292	.620	334	182	186	3	695	4.6	2.5	9.7
57-58 —New York	63	2368	344	973	.354	353	511	.691	489	317	202	3	1041	7.8	5.0	16.5
58-59 —New York	71	2558	443	1046	.424	405	505	.802	518	364	255	1	1291	7.3	5.1	18.2
59-60 —New York	74	2429	579	1379	.420	457	591	.773	505	468	242	3	1615	6.8	6.3	21.8
60-61 —New York	79	3023	612	1545	.396	496	626	.792	628	503	310	3	1720	7.9	6.4	21.8
61-62 —New York	78	3348	839	1897	.442	625	762	.820	501	539	299	3	2303	6.4	6.9	29.5
62-63 —New York	79	2712	596	1380	.432	509	600	.848	331	348	228	2	1701	4.2	4.4	21.5

Season Team	G	Min.	FGM	FGA	Pct.	FTM	FTA	Pct.	Reb.	Ast.	PF	Dq.	Pts.	RPG	APG	PPG
63-64 —N.Y.-St.L.	80	2366	351	846	.415	347	424	.818	256	375	276	4	1049	3.2	4.7	13.1
64-65 —St. Louis	57	1678	295	662	.446	231	301	.767	149	271	193	1	821	2.6	4.8	14.4
65-66 —St. Louis	80	2363	414	998	.415	362	446	.812	314	388	256	4	1190	3.9	4.9	14.9
66-67 —St. Louis	80	2275	394	904	.436	304	416	.731	192	345	247	2	1092	2.4	4.3	13.7
67-68 —						Did not play—retired.										
68-69 —Atlanta	27	472	47	111	.423	57	74	.770	59	99	66	0	151	2.2	3.7	5.6
69-70 —Atlanta	8	64	3	11	.273	1	1	1.000	2	12	9	0	7	0.3	1.5	0.9
Totals	848	27449	5174	12451	.416	4328	5549	.780	4278	4211	2769	29	14676	5.0	5.0	17.3

NBA PLAYOFF RECORD

Season Team	G	Min.	FGM	FGA	Pct.	FTM	FTA	Pct.	Reb.	Ast.	PF	Dq.	Pts.	RPG	APG	PPG
58-59 —New York	2	9	35	.257		12	14	.857	18	15	11	1	30	9.0	7.5	15.0
63-64 —St. Louis	12	428	75	169	.444	67	85	.788	50	49	54	1	217	4.2	4.1	18.1
64-65 —St. Louis	4	125	25	65	.385	19	25	.760	8	21	14	0	69	2.0	5.3	17.3
65-66 —St. Louis	10	399	72	159	.453	62	76	.816	37	79	41	0	206	3.7	7.9	20.6
66-67 —St. Louis	9	228	36	86	.419	24	30	.800	23	39	23	0	96	2.6	4.3	10.7
68-69 —Atlanta	3	32	1	4	.250	1	2	.500	5	7	8	0	3	1.7	2.3	1.0
69-70 —Atlanta	2	56	13	21	.619	7	7	1.000	8	4	6	0	33	4.0	2.0	16.5
Totals	42	1345	231	539	.429	192	239	.803	149	214	157	2	654	3.5	5.1	15.6

NBA ALL-STAR GAME RECORD

Season	Team	Min.	FGM	FGA	Pct.	FTM	FTA	Pct.	Reb	Ast.	PF	Dq.	Pts.
1958	—New York	22	2	10	.200	3	4	.750	8	7	3	0	7
1959	—New York	22	1	7	.143	3	5	.600	3	3	1	0	5
1960	—New York	22	5	11	.455	2	2	1.000	4	4	4	0	12
1961	—New York	15	3	8	.375	5	6	.833	0	2	1	0	11
1962	—New York	27	10	17	.588	3	6	.500	3	1	6	1	23
1963	—New York	14	2	3	.667	1	3	.333	1	1	2	0	5
Totals		122	23	56	.411	17	26	.654	19	18	17	1	63

NBA COACHING RECORD

HONORS: NBA Coach of the Year (1968).

	REGULAR SEASON				PLAYOFFS		
Season Team	W	L	Pct.	Finish	W	L	Pct.
64-65 —St. Louis	28	19	.596	2nd/Western Division	1	3	.250
65-66 —St. Louis	36	44	.450	3rd/Western Division	6	4	.600
66-67 —St. Louis	39	42	.481	2nd/Western Division	5	4	.556
67-68 —St. Louis	56	26	.683	1st/Western Division	2	4	.333
68-69 —Atlanta	48	34	.585	2nd/Western Division	5	6	.455
69-70 —Atlanta	48	34	.585	1st/Western Division	4	5	.444
70-71 —Atlanta	36	46	.439	2nd/Central Division	1	4	.200
71-72 —Atlanta	36	46	.439	2nd/Central Division	2	4	.333
Totals (8 years)	327	291	.529	Totals (8 years)	26	34	.433

NOTES:

1964—Replaced Harry Gallatin as St. Louis head coach (November), with record of 17-16.

1965—Lost to Baltimore in Western Division Semifinals.

1966—Defeated Baltimore, 3-0, in Western Division Semifinals; lost to Los Angeles, 4-3, in Western Division Finals.

1967—Defeated Chicago, 3-0, in Western Division Semifinals; lost to San Francisco, 4-2, in Western Division Finals.

1968—Lost to San Francisco in Western Division Semifinals. Hawks franchise moved to Atlanta for 1968-69 season.

1969—Defeated San Diego, 4-2, in Western Division Semifinals; lost to Los Angeles, 4-1, in Western Division Finals.

1970—Defeated Chicago, 4-1, in Western Division Semifinals; lost to Los Angeles, 4-0, in Western Division Finals.

1971—Lost to New York in Eastern Conference Semifinals.

1972—Lost to Boston in Eastern Conference Semifinals.

HAGAN, CLIFF   F

PERSONAL: Born December 9, 1931, in Owensboro, Ky. ... 6-4/215 (1,93/97,5). ... Full name: Clifford Oldham Hagan. ... Nickname: Li'l Abner.
HIGH SCHOOL: Owensboro (Ky.).
COLLEGE: Kentucky.
TRANSACTIONS: Selected by Boston Celtics in third round of 1953 NBA Draft. ... In military service during 1954-55 and 1955-56 seasons; played at Andrews Air Force Base. ... Draft rights traded by Celtics with C/F Ed Macauley to St. Louis Hawks for draft rights to C Bill Russell (April 29, 1956). ... Signed as player/head coach by Dallas Chaparrals of American Basketball Association (June 1967).
CAREER HONORS: Elected to Naismith Memorial Basketball Hall of Fame (1978).
MISCELLANEOUS: Member of NBA championship team (1958).

COLLEGIATE RECORD

NOTES: Member of NCAA championship team (1951).

Season Team	G	Min.	FGM	FGA	Pct.	FTM	FTA	Pct.	Reb.	Ast.	Pts.	RPG	APG	PPG
49-50—Kentucky‡	12	...	114	244	.467	42	58	.724	...	...	270	...	...	22.5
50-51—Kentucky	20	...	69	188	.367	45	61	.738	169	...	183	8.5	...	9.2
51-52—Kentucky	32	...	264	633	.417	164	235	.698	528	...	692	16.5	...	21.6
52-53—Kentucky					Did not play—team suspended for season.									
53-54—Kentucky	25	...	234	514	.455	132	191	.691	338	...	600	13.5	...	24.0
Varsity totals	77	...	567	1335	.425	341	487	.700	1035	...	1475	13.4	...	19.2

NBA REGULAR-SEASON RECORD

HONORS: All-NBA second team (1958, 1959).

Season Team	G	Min.	FGM	FGA	Pct.	FTM	FTA	Pct.	Reb.	Ast.	PF	Dq.	Pts.	RPG	APG	PPG
56-57 —St. Louis	67	971	134	371	.361	100	145	.690	247	86	165	3	368	3.7	1.3	5.5
57-58 —St. Louis	70	2190	503	1135	.443	385	501	.768	707	175	267	9	1391	10.1	2.5	19.9
58-59 —St. Louis	72	2702	646	1417	.456	415	536	.774	783	245	275	10	1707	10.9	3.4	23.7
59-60 —St. Louis	75	2798	719	1549	.464	421	524	.803	803	299	270	4	1859	10.7	4.0	24.8
60-61 —St. Louis	77	2701	661	1490	.444	383	467	.820	715	381	286	9	1705	9.3	4.9	22.1
61-62 —St. Louis	77	2784	701	1490	.470	362	439	.825	633	370	282	8	1764	8.2	4.8	22.9
62-63 —St. Louis	79	1716	491	1055	.465	244	305	.800	341	193	211	2	1226	4.3	2.4	15.5
63-64 —St. Louis	77	2279	572	1280	.447	269	331	.813	377	193	273	4	1413	4.9	2.5	18.4
64-65 —St. Louis	77	1739	393	901	.436	214	268	.799	276	136	182	0	1000	3.6	1.8	13.0
65-66 —St. Louis	74	1851	419	942	.445	176	206	.854	234	164	177	1	1014	3.2	2.2	13.7
Totals	745	21731	5239	11630	.450	2969	3722	.798	5116	2242	2388	50	13447	6.9	3.0	18.0

NBA PLAYOFF RECORD

Season Team	G	Min.	FGM	FGA	Pct.	FTM	FTA	Pct.	Reb.	Ast.	PF	Dq.	Pts.	RPG	APG	PPG
56-57 —St. Louis	10	319	62	143	.434	46	63	.730	112	28	47	3	170	11.2	2.8	17.0
57-58 —St. Louis	11	418	111	221	.502	83	99	.838	115	37	48	3	305	10.5	3.4	27.7
58-59 —St. Louis	6	259	63	123	.512	45	54	.833	72	16	21	0	171	12.0	2.7	28.5
59-60 —St. Louis	14	544	125	296	.422	89	109	.817	138	54	54	1	339	9.9	3.9	24.2
60-61 —St. Louis	12	455	104	235	.443	56	69	.812	118	54	45	1	264	9.8	4.5	22.0
62-63 —St. Louis	11	255	83	179	.464	37	53	.698	55	34	42	4	203	5.0	3.1	18.5
63-64 —St. Louis	12	392	75	175	.429	45	54	.833	74	57	34	0	195	6.2	4.8	16.3
64-65 —St. Louis	4	123	34	75	.453	6	12	.500	26	7	14	0	74	6.5	1.8	18.5
65-66 —St. Louis	10	200	44	97	.454	25	27	.926	34	18	15	0	113	3.4	1.8	11.3
Totals	90	2965	701	1544	.454	432	540	.800	744	305	320	12	1834	8.3	3.4	20.4

NBA ALL-STAR GAME RECORD

Season Team	Min.	FGM	FGA	Pct.	FTM	FTA	Pct.	Reb	Ast.	PF	Dq.	Pts.
1958 —St. Louis					Selected, did not play—injured.							
1959 —St. Louis	22	6	12	.500	3	3	1.000	8	3	5	0	15
1960 —St. Louis	21	1	9	.111	0	0	...	3	2	1	0	2
1961 —St. Louis	13	0	2	.000	2	2	1.000	2	0	1	0	2
1962 —St. Louis	9	1	3	.333	0	0	...	2	1	1	0	2
Totals	65	8	26	.308	5	5	1.000	15	6	8	0	21

ABA REGULAR-SEASON RECORD

| Season Team | G | Min. | 2-POINT | | | 3-POINT | | | FTM | FTA | Pct. | Reb. | Ast. | Pts. | AVERAGES | | |
			FGM	FGA	Pct.	FGM	FGA	Pct.							RPG	APG	PPG
67-68—Dallas	56	1737	371	756	.491	0	3	.000	277	351	.789	334	276	1019	6.0	4.9	18.2
68-69—Dallas	35	579	132	258	.512	0	1	.000	123	144	.854	102	122	387	2.9	3.5	11.1
69-70—Dallas	3	27	8	12	.667	0	1	.000	1	2	.500	3	6	17	1.0	2.0	5.7
Totals	94	2343	511	1026	.498	0	5	.000	401	497	.807	439	404	1423	4.7	4.3	15.1

ABA PLAYOFF RECORD

| Season Team | G | Min. | 2-POINT | | | 3-POINT | | | FTM | FTA | Pct. | Reb. | Ast. | Pts. | AVERAGES | | |
			FGM	FGA	Pct.	FGM	FGA	Pct.							RPG	APG	PPG
67-68—Dallas	3	70	14	37	.378	0	0	...	9	13	.692	13	9	37	4.3	3.0	12.3
68-69—Dallas	2	45	5	14	.357	0	0	...	8	10	.800	6	14	18	3.0	7.0	9.0
Totals	5	115	19	51	.373	0	0	...	17	23	.739	19	23	55	3.8	4.6	11.0

ABA ALL-STAR GAME RECORD

| Season Team | Min. | 2-POINT | | | 3-POINT | | | FTM | FTA | Pct. | Reb. | Ast. | Pts. |
		FGM	FGA	Pct.	FGM	FGA	Pct.						
1968—Dallas	24	4	11	.364	0	0	...	2	2	1.000	0	5	10

COMBINED ABA AND NBA REGULAR-SEASON RECORDS

| | G | Min. | FGM | FGA | Pct. | FTM | FTA | Pct. | REBOUNDS | | | Ast. | Stl. | Blk. | TO | Pts. | AVERAGES | | |
									Off.	Def.	Tot.						RPG	APG	PPG
Totals	839	24074	5750	12661	.454	3370	4219	.799	...	...	5555	2646	...	...	...	14870	6.6	3.2	17.7

Three-point field goals: 0-for-5.
Personal fouls/disqualifications: 2678/58.

ABA COACHING RECORD

BACKGROUND: Player/head coach, Dallas Chaparrals of American Basketball Association (1967-68 to January 1970).

| Season Team | REGULAR SEASON | | | | PLAYOFFS | | |
	W	L	Pct.	Finish	W	L	Pct.
67-68 —Dallas	46	32	.590	2nd/Western Division	4	4	.500
68-69 —Dallas	41	37	.526	4th/Western Division	3	4	.426
69-70 —Dallas	22	21	.512		—	—	—
Totals (3 years)	109	90	.548	Totals (2 years)	7	8	.467

NOTES:
1968—Defeated Houston, 3-0, in Western Division Semifinals; lost to New Orleans, 4-1, in Western Division Finals.
1969—Lost to New Orleans in Western Division Semifinals.
1970—Replaced as Dallas head coach by Max Williams (January).

HARPER, DEREK　　　G

PERSONAL: Born October 13, 1961, in Elberton, Ga. ... 6-4/206 (1,93/93,4). ... Full name: Derek Ricardo Harper.
HIGH SCHOOL: North Shore (West Palm Beach, Fla.).
COLLEGE: Illinois.
TRANSACTIONS/CAREER NOTES: Selected after junior season by Dallas Mavericks in first round (11th pick overall) of 1983 NBA Draft. ... Traded by Mavericks to New York Knicks for G/F Tony Campbell and 1997 first-round draft choice (January 6, 1994). ... Signed as free agent by Mavericks (July 26, 1996). ... Traded by Mavericks with F Ed O'Bannon to Orlando Magic for G Dennis Scott and cash (September 24, 1997). ... Signed as free agent by Los Angeles Lakers (January 21, 1999). ... Traded by Lakers to Detroit Pistons for draft rights to G Melvin Levett (September 21, 1999). ... Placed on suspension by Pistons (did not report) (October 5, 1999). ... Announced retirement (January 30, 2000).
CAREER NOTES: Vice president of business relations, Dallas Mavericks (February through April, 2000).
MISCELLANEOUS: Dallas Mavericks all-time assists leader with 5,111 and all-time steals leader with 1,551 (1983-84 through 1993-94 and 1996-97).

COLLEGIATE RECORD

Season Team	G	Min.	FGM	FGA	Pct.	FTM	FTA	Pct.	Reb.	Ast.	Pts.	AVERAGES RPG	APG	PPG
80-81—Illinois	29	934	104	252	.413	33	46	.717	75	156	241	2.6	5.4	8.3
81-82—Illinois	29	1059	105	230	.457	34	45	.756	133	145	244	4.6	5.0	8.4
82-83—Illinois	32	1182	198	369	.537	83	123	.675	112	118	492	3.5	3.7	15.4
Totals	90	3175	407	851	.478	150	214	.701	320	419	977	3.6	4.7	10.9

Three-point field goals: 1982-83, 13-for-24 (.542).

NBA REGULAR-SEASON RECORD

HONORS: NBA All-Defensive second team (1987, 1990).

Season Team	G	Min.	FGM	FGA	Pct.	FTM	FTA	Pct.	REBOUNDS Off.	Def.	Tot.	Ast.	St.	Blk.	TO	Pts.	AVERAGES RPG	APG	PPG
83-84—Dallas	82	1712	200	451	.443	66	98	.673	53	119	172	239	95	21	111	469	2.1	2.9	5.7
84-85—Dallas	82	2218	329	633	.520	111	154	.721	47	152	199	360	144	37	123	790	2.4	4.4	9.6
85-86—Dallas	79	2150	390	730	.534	171	229	.747	75	151	226	416	153	23	144	963	2.9	5.3	12.2
86-87—Dallas	77	2556	497	993	.501	160	234	.684	51	148	199	609	167	25	138	1230	2.6	7.9	16.0
87-88—Dallas	82	3032	536	1167	.459	261	344	.759	71	175	246	634	168	35	190	1393	3.0	7.7	17.0
88-89—Dallas	81	2968	538	1127	.477	229	284	.806	46	182	228	570	172	41	205	1404	2.8	7.0	17.3
89-90—Dallas	82	3007	567	1161	.488	250	315	.794	54	190	244	609	187	26	207	1473	3.0	7.4	18.0
90-91—Dallas	77	2879	572	1226	.467	286	391	.731	59	174	233	548	147	14	177	1519	3.0	7.1	19.7
91-92—Dallas	65	2252	448	1011	.443	198	261	.759	49	121	170	373	101	17	154	1152	2.6	5.7	17.7
92-93—Dallas	62	2108	393	939	.419	239	316	.756	42	81	123	334	80	16	136	1126	2.0	5.4	18.2
93-94—Dallas-N.Y.	82	2204	303	744	.407	112	163	.687	20	121	141	334	125	8	135	791	1.7	4.1	9.6
94-95—New York	80	2716	337	756	.446	139	192	.724	31	163	194	458	79	10	151	919	2.4	5.7	11.5
95-96—New York	82	2893	436	939	.464	156	205	.757	32	170	202	352	131	5	178	1149	2.5	4.3	14.0
96-97—Dallas	75	2210	299	674	.444	95	128	.742	30	107	137	321	92	12	132	753	1.8	4.3	10.0
97-98—Orlando	66	1761	226	542	.417	55	79	.696	23	80	103	233	72	10	101	566	1.6	3.5	8.6
98-99—L.A. Lakers	45	1120	120	291	.412	26	32	.813	13	54	67	187	44	4	52	309	1.5	4.2	6.9
Totals	1199	37786	6191	13384	.463	2554	3426	.745	696	2188	2884	6577	1957	304	2334	16006	2.4	5.5	13.3

Three-point field goals: 1983-84, 3-for-26 (.115). 1984-85, 21-for-61 (.344). 1985-86, 12-for-51 (.235). 1986-87, 76-for-212 (.358). 1987-88, 60-for-192 (.313). 1988-89, 99-for-278 (.356). 1989-90, 89-for-240 (.371). 1990-91, 89-for-246 (.362). 1991-92, 58-for-186 (.312). 1992-93, 101-for-257 (.393). 1993-94, 73-for-203 (.360). 1994-95, 106-for-292 (.363). 1995-96, 121-for-325 (.372). 1996-97, 60-for-176 (.341). 1997-98, 59-for-164 (.360). 1998-99, 43-for-117 (.368). Totals, 1070-for-3026 (.354).

Personal fouls/disqualifications: 1983-84, 143/0. 1984-85, 194/1. 1985-86, 166/1. 1986-87, 195/0. 1987-88, 164/0. 1988-89, 219/3. 1989-90, 224/1. 1990-91, 222/1. 1991-92, 150/0. 1992-93, 145/1. 1993-94, 163/0. 1994-95, 219/0. 1995-96, 201/0. 1996-97, 144/0. 1997-98, 140/0. 1998-99, 66/0. Totals, 2755/8.

NBA PLAYOFF RECORD

NOTES: Shares NBA Finals single-series record for most three-point field goals made—17 (1994, vs. Houston).

Season Team	G	Min.	FGM	FGA	Pct.	FTM	FTA	Pct.	REBOUNDS Off.	Def.	Tot.	Ast.	St.	Blk.	TO	Pts.	AVERAGES RPG	APG	PPG
83-84—Dallas	10	226	21	54	.389	5	7	.714	8	12	20	28	11	2	6	50	2.0	2.8	5.0
84-85—Dallas	4	132	10	21	.476	5	7	.714	1	11	12	20	6	1	4	26	3.0	5.0	6.5
85-86—Dallas	10	348	57	107	.533	12	16	.750	13	6	19	76	23	0	23	134	1.9	7.6	13.4
86-87—Dallas	4	123	20	40	.500	24	30	.800	2	10	12	27	7	0	5	66	3.0	6.8	16.5
87-88—Dallas	17	602	89	202	.441	43	59	.729	11	32	43	121	32	5	32	230	2.5	7.1	13.5
89-90—Dallas	3	119	21	48	.438	11	16	.688	2	6	8	23	4	0	12	58	2.7	7.7	19.3
93-94—New York	23	750	99	231	.429	36	56	.643	13	41	54	103	42	1	41	263	2.3	4.5	11.4
94-95—New York	11	388	56	109	.514	18	24	.750	5	33	38	62	11	1	26	157	3.5	5.6	14.3
95-96—New York	8	293	29	82	.354	11	15	.733	0	17	17	38	10	1	14	80	2.1	4.8	10.0
98-99—L.A. Lakers	7	113	13	31	.419	3	6	.500	1	9	10	15	2	0	4	30	1.4	2.1	4.3
Totals	97	3094	415	925	.449	168	236	.712	56	177	233	513	148	11	167	1094	2.4	5.3	11.3

Three-point field goals: 1983-84, 3-for-8 (.375). 1984-85, 1-for-3 (.333). 1985-86, 8-for-14 (.571). 1986-87, 2-for-9 (.222). 1987-88, 9-for-36 (.250). 1989-90, 5-for-16 (.313). 1993-94, 29-for-85 (.341). 1994-95, 27-for-47 (.574). 1995-96, 11-for-35 (.314). 1998-99, 1-for-10 (.100). Totals, 96-for-263 (.365).

Personal fouls/disqualifications: 1983-84, 16/0. 1984-85, 12/0. 1985-86, 27/0. 1986-87, 7/0. 1987-88, 44/0. 1989-90, 13/0. 1993-94, 63/1. 1994-95, 29/0. 1995-96, 24/0. 1998-99, 2/0. Totals, 237/1.

HAVLICEK, JOHN　　　F/G

PERSONAL: Born April 8, 1940, in Martins Ferry, Ohio. ... 6-5/205 (1,96/93,0). ... Full name: John J. Havlicek. ... Nickname: Hondo.
HIGH SCHOOL: Bridgeport (Ohio).
COLLEGE: Ohio State.
TRANSACTIONS: Selected by Boston Celtics in first round of 1962 NBA Draft.
CAREER HONORS: Elected to Naismith Memorial Basketball Hall of Fame (1984). ... NBA 35th Anniversary All-Time Team (1980) and One of the 50 Greatest Players in NBA History (1996).

ALL-TIME GREAT PLAYERS

MISCELLANEOUS: Member of NBA championship team (1963, 1964, 1965, 1966, 1968, 1969, 1974, 1976). ... Selected as wide receiver by Cleveland Browns in seventh round of 1962 National Football League draft. ... Boston Celtics all-time leading scorer with 26,395 points (1962-63 through 1977-78).

COLLEGIATE RECORD

NOTES: THE SPORTING NEWS All-America second team (1962). ... Member of NCAA championship team (1960).

Season Team	G	Min.	FGM	FGA	Pct.	FTM	FTA	Pct.	Reb.	Ast.	Pts.	AVERAGES RPG	APG	PPG
58-59—Ohio State‡					Freshman team did not play intercollegiate schedule.									
59-60—Ohio State	28	...	144	312	.462	53	74	.716	205	...	341	7.3	...	12.2
60-61—Ohio State	28	...	173	321	.539	61	87	.701	244	...	407	8.7	...	14.5
61-62—Ohio State	28	...	196	377	.520	83	109	.761	271	...	475	9.7	...	17.0
Varsity totals	84	...	513	1010	.508	197	270	.730	720	...	1223	8.6	...	14.6

NBA REGULAR-SEASON RECORD

HONORS: All-NBA first team (1971, 1972, 1973, 1974). ... All-NBA second team (1964, 1966, 1968, 1969, 1970, 1975, 1976). ... NBA All-Defensive first team (1972, 1973, 1974, 1975, 1976). ... NBA All-Defensive second team (1969, 1970, 1971).

Season Team	G	Min.	FGM	FGA	Pct.	FTM	FTA	Pct.	Reb.	Ast.	PF	Dq.	Pts.	AVERAGES RPG	APG	PPG
62-63—Boston	80	2200	483	1085	.445	174	239	.728	534	179	189	2	1140	6.7	2.2	14.3
63-64—Boston	80	2587	640	1535	.417	315	422	.746	428	238	227	1	1595	5.4	3.0	19.9
64-65—Boston	75	2169	570	1420	.401	235	316	.744	371	199	200	2	1375	4.9	2.7	18.3
65-66—Boston	71	2175	530	1328	.399	274	349	.785	423	210	158	1	1334	6.0	3.0	18.8
66-67—Boston	81	2602	684	1540	.444	365	441	.828	532	278	210	0	1733	6.6	3.4	21.4
67-68—Boston	82	2921	666	1551	.429	368	453	.812	546	384	237	2	1700	6.7	4.7	20.7
68-69—Boston	82	3174	692	1709	.405	387	496	.780	570	441	247	0	1771	7.0	5.4	21.6
69-70—Boston	81	3369	736	1585	.464	488	578	.844	635	550	211	1	1960	7.8	6.8	24.2
70-71—Boston	81	*3678	892	1982	.450	554	677	.818	730	607	200	0	2338	9.0	7.5	28.9
71-72—Boston	82	*3698	897	1957	.458	458	549	.834	672	614	183	1	2252	8.2	7.5	27.5
72-73—Boston	80	3367	766	1704	.450	370	431	.858	567	529	195	1	1902	7.1	6.6	23.8

Season Team	G	Min.	FGM	FGA	Pct.	FTM	FTA	Pct.	REBOUNDS Off.	Def.	Tot.	Ast.	St.	Blk.	TO	Pts.	AVERAGES RPG	APG	PPG
73-74—Boston	76	3091	685	1502	.456	346	416	.832	138	349	487	447	95	32	...	1716	6.4	5.9	22.6
74-75—Boston	82	3132	642	1411	.455	289	332	.870	154	330	484	432	110	16	...	1573	5.9	5.3	19.2
75-76—Boston	76	2598	504	1121	.450	281	333	.844	116	198	314	278	97	29	...	1289	4.1	3.7	17.0
76-77—Boston	79	2913	580	1283	.452	235	288	.816	109	273	382	400	84	18	...	1395	4.8	5.1	17.7
77-78—Boston	82	2797	546	1217	.449	230	269	.855	93	239	332	328	90	22	204	1322	4.0	4.0	16.1
Totals	1270	46471	10513	23930	.439	5369	6589	.815	...	...	8007	6114	476	117	204	26395	6.3	4.8	20.8

Personal fouls/disqualifications: 1973-74, 196/1. 1974-75, 231/2. 1975-76, 204/1. 1976-77, 208/4. 1977-78, 185/2. Totals, 3281/21.

NBA PLAYOFF RECORD

NOTES: NBA Finals Most Valuable Player (1974). ... Shares NBA Finals single-game record for most points in an overtime period—9 (May 10, 1974, vs. Milwaukee). ... Shares single-game playoff record for most field goals made—24 (April 1, 1973, vs. Atlanta).

Season Team	G	Min.	FGM	FGA	Pct.	FTM	FTA	Pct.	Reb.	Ast.	PF	Dq.	Pts.	AVERAGES RPG	APG	PPG
62-63—Boston	11	254	56	125	.448	18	27	.667	53	17	28	1	130	4.8	1.5	11.8
63-64—Boston	10	289	61	159	.384	35	44	.795	43	32	26	0	157	4.3	3.2	15.7
64-65—Boston	12	405	88	250	.352	46	55	.836	88	29	44	1	222	7.3	2.4	18.5
65-66—Boston	17	719	153	374	.409	95	113	.841	154	70	69	2	401	9.1	4.1	23.6
66-67—Boston	9	330	95	212	.448	57	71	.803	73	28	30	0	247	8.1	3.1	27.4
67-68—Boston	19	862	184	407	.452	125	151	.828	164	142	67	1	493	8.6	7.5	25.9
68-69—Boston	18	850	170	382	.445	118	138	.855	179	100	58	2	458	9.9	5.6	25.4
71-72—Boston	11	517	108	235	.460	85	99	.859	92	70	35	1	301	8.4	6.4	27.4
72-73—Boston	12	479	112	235	.477	61	74	.824	62	65	24	0	285	5.2	5.4	23.8

Season Team	G	Min.	FGM	FGA	Pct.	FTM	FTA	Pct.	REBOUNDS Off.	Def.	Tot.	Ast.	St.	Blk.	TO	Pts.	AVERAGES RPG	APG	PPG
73-74—Boston	18	811	199	411	.484	89	101	.881	28	88	116	108	24	6	...	487	6.4	6.0	27.1
74-75—Boston	11	464	83	192	.432	66	76	.868	18	39	57	51	16	1	...	232	5.2	4.6	21.1
75-76—Boston	15	505	80	180	.444	38	47	.809	18	38	56	51	12	5	...	198	3.7	3.4	13.2
76-77—Boston	9	375	62	167	.371	41	50	.820	15	34	49	62	8	4	...	165	5.4	6.9	18.3
Totals	172	6860	1451	3329	.436	874	1046	.836	...	...	1186	825	60	16	...	3776	6.9	4.8	22.0

Personal fouls/disqualifications: 1973-74, 43/0. 1974-75, 38/1. 1975-76, 22/0. 1976-77, 33/0. Totals, 517/9.

NBA ALL-STAR GAME RECORD

Season Team	Min.	FGM	FGA	Pct.	FTM	FTA	Pct.	Reb	Ast.	PF	Dq.	Pts.
1966—Boston	25	6	16	.375	6	6	1.000	6	1	2	0	18
1967—Boston	17	7	14	.500	0	0	...	2	1	1	0	14
1968—Boston	22	9	15	.600	8	11	.727	5	4	0	0	26
1969—Boston	31	6	14	.429	2	2	1.000	7	2	2	0	14
1970—Boston	29	7	15	.467	3	3	1.000	5	7	2	0	17
1971—Boston	24	6	12	.500	0	2	.000	3	2	3	0	12
1972—Boston	24	5	13	.385	5	5	1.000	3	2	2	0	15
1973—Boston	22	6	10	.600	2	5	.400	3	5	1	0	14

Season Team	Min.	FGM	FGA	Pct.	FTM	FTA	Pct.	REBOUNDS Off.	Def.	Tot.	Ast.	PF	Dq.	St.	Blk.	TO	Pts.
1974—Boston	18	5	10	.500	0	2	.000	0	0	0	2	2	0	1	0	...	10
1975—Boston	31	7	12	.583	2	2	1.000	1	5	6	1	2	0	2	0	...	16
1976—Boston	21	3	10	.300	3	3	1.000	1	1	2	2	0	0	1	0	...	9
1977—Boston	17	2	5	.400	0	0	...	0	1	1	1	1	0	0	0	...	4
1978—Boston	22	5	8	.625	0	0	...	0	3	3	1	2	0	0	0	4	10
Totals	303	74	154	.481	31	41	.756	...	...	46	31	20	0	4	0	4	179

HAWKINS, CONNIE   F/C

PERSONAL: Born July 17, 1942, in Brooklyn, N.Y. ... 6-8/215 (2,03/97,5). ... Full name: Cornelius L. Hawkins.
HIGH SCHOOL: Boys (Brooklyn, N.Y.).
COLLEGE: Iowa.
TRANSACTIONS: Signed after freshman season by Pittsburgh Rens of American Basketball League (1961). ... ABL ceased operations (December 31, 1962). ... Played with Harlem Globetrotters (1963-64 through 1966-67) ... Signed by Pittsburgh Pipers of the American Basketball Association (1967). ... Pipers franchise transferred to Minnesota (1968). ... Signed as free agent by Phoenix Suns of NBA (June 20, 1969). ... Traded by Suns to Los Angeles Lakers for Keith Erickson and second-round draft choice (October 30, 1973). ... Traded by Lakers to Atlanta Hawks for draft choices (August 8, 1975). ... Waived by Hawks (1976).
CAREER NOTES: Community relations representative, Phoenix Suns (1992-93 to present).

COLLEGIATE RECORD

Season Team	G	Min.	FGM	FGA	Pct.	FTM	FTA	Pct.	Reb.	Ast.	Pts.	RPG	APG	PPG
60-61—Iowa					Freshman team did not play intercollegiate schedule.									

ABL REGULAR-SEASON RECORD

ABL: ABL Most Valuable Player (1962). ... ABL All-Star first team (1962).

Season Team	G	Min.	FGM	FGA	Pct.	FTM	FTA	Pct.	Reb.	Ast.	Pts.	RPG	APG	PPG
61-62—Pittsburgh	78	3349	760	1490	.510	622	787	.790	1038	183	2145	13.3	2.3	*27.5
62-63—Pittsburgh	16	668	160	326	.491	127	165	.770	205	42	447	12.8	2.6	27.9
Totals	94	4017	920	1816	.507	749	952	.787	1243	225	2592	13.2	2.4	27.6

ABL PLAYOFF RECORD

Season Team	G	Min.	FGM	FGA	Pct.	FTM	FTA	Pct.	Reb.	Ast.	Pts.	RPG	APG	PPG
61-62—Pittsburgh	1	53	14	23	.609	13	14	.929	17	4	41	17.0	4.0	41.0

ABA REGULAR-SEASON RECORD

NOTES: ABA Most Valuable Player (1968). ... ABA All-Star first team (1968 and 1969). ... Member of ABA championship team (1968). ... Led ABA in scoring with 26.79 average (1968).

Season Team	G	Min.	2-POINT FGM	FGA	Pct.	3-POINT FGM	FGA	Pct.	FTM	FTA	Pct.	Reb.	Ast.	Pts.	RPG	APG	PPG
67-68—Pittsburgh	70	3146	633	1214	.521	2	9	.222	603	789	.764	945	320	1875	13.5	4.6	*26.8
68-69—Minnesota	47	1852	493	949	.520	3	22	.136	425	554	.767	534	184	1420	11.4	3.9	30.2
Totals	117	4998	1126	2163	.521	5	31	.161	1028	1343	.765	1479	504	3295	12.6	4.3	28.2

ABA PLAYOFF RECORD

Season Team	G	Min.	2-POINT FGM	FGA	Pct.	3-POINT FGM	FGA	Pct.	FTM	FTA	Pct.	Reb.	Ast.	Pts.	RPG	APG	PPG
67-68—Pittsburgh	14	616	145	244	.594	0	0	...	129	177	.729	172	64	419	12.3	4.6	29.9
68-69—Minnesota	7	320	61	164	.372	4	8	.500	40	62	.645	86	27	174	12.3	3.9	24.9
Totals	21	936	206	408	.505	...	4	...	169	239	.707	258	91	593	12.3	4.3	28.2

NBA REGULAR-SEASON RECORD

HONORS: All-NBA first team (1970).

Season Team	G	Min.	FGM	FGA	Pct.	FTM	FTA	Pct.	Reb.	Ast.	PF	Dq.	Pts.	RPG	APG	PPG
69-70—Phoenix	81	3312	709	1447	.490	577	741	.779	846	391	287	4	1995	10.4	4.8	24.6
70-71—Phoenix	71	2662	512	1181	.434	457	560	.816	643	322	197	2	1481	9.1	4.5	20.9
71-72—Phoenix	76	2798	571	1244	.459	456	565	.807	633	296	235	2	1598	8.3	3.9	21.0
72-73—Phoenix	75	2768	441	920	.479	322	404	.797	641	304	229	5	1204	8.5	4.1	16.1

Season Team	G	Min.	FGM	FGA	Pct.	FTM	FTA	Pct.	REBOUNDS Off.	Def.	Tot.	Ast.	St.	Blk.	TO	Pts.	RPG	APG	PPG
73-74—Pho-Lakers	79	2761	404	807	.501	191	251	.761	176	389	565	407	113	81	...	999	7.2	5.2	12.6
74-75—Los Angeles	43	1026	139	324	.429	68	99	.687	54	144	198	120	51	23	...	346	4.6	2.8	8.0
75-76—Atlanta	74	1907	237	530	.447	136	191	.712	102	343	445	212	80	46	...	610	6.0	2.9	8.2
Totals	499	17234	3013	6453	.467	2207	2811	.785	...	...	3971	2052	...	...	...	8233	8.0	4.1	16.5

Personal fouls/disqualifications: 1973-74, 223/1. 1974-75, 116/1. 1975-76, 172/2. Totals, 1459/17.

NBA PLAYOFF RECORD

Season Team	G	Min.	FGM	FGA	Pct.	FTM	FTA	Pct.	Reb.	Ast.	PF	Dq.	Pts.	RPG	APG	PPG
69-70—Phoenix	7	328	62	150	.413	54	66	.818	97	41	22	0	178	13.9	5.9	25.4

Season Team	G	Min.	FGM	FGA	Pct.	FTM	FTA	Pct.	REBOUNDS Off.	Def.	Tot.	Ast.	St.	Blk.	TO	Pts.	RPG	APG	PPG
73-74—Los Angeles	5	172	21	60	.350	12	15	.800	14	26	40	16	7	1	...	54	8.0	3.2	10.8
Totals	12	500	83	210	.395	66	81	.815	...	...	137	57	7	1	...	232	11.4	4.8	19.3

Personal fouls/disqualifications: 1973-74, 13/0.

NBA ALL-STAR GAME RECORD

Season Team	Min.	FGM	FGA	Pct.	FTM	FTA	Pct.	Reb	Ast.	PF	Dq.	Pts.
1970—Phoenix	19	2	4	.500	6	6	1.000	4	2	3	...	10
1971—Phoenix	1	0	0	...	0	0	...	0	0	0	...	0
1972—Phoenix	14	5	7	.714	3	4	.750	4	0	1	0	13
1973—Phoenix	11	1	5	.200	0	0	...	2	3	1	0	2
Totals	45	8	16	.500	9	10	.900	10	5	5	...	25

COMBINED ABA AND NBA REGULAR-SEASON RECORDS

	G	Min.	FGM	FGA	Pct.	FTM	FTA	Pct.	REBOUNDS Off.	Def.	Tot.	Ast.	Stl.	Blk.	TO	Pts.	RPG	APG	PPG
Totals	616	22232	4144	8647	.479	3235	4154	.779	...	...	5450	2556	...	...	...	11528	8.8	4.1	18.7

Three-point field goals: 5-for-31 (.161).
Personal fouls/disqualifications: 1873/22.

HAYES, ELVIN   F/C

PERSONAL: Born November 17, 1945, in Rayville, La. ... 6-9/235 (2,06/106,6). ... Full name: Elvin Ernest Hayes.
HIGH SCHOOL: Eula D. Britton (Rayville, La.).
COLLEGE: Houston.
TRANSACTIONS: Selected by San Diego Rockets in first round (first pick overall) of 1968 NBA Draft. ... Rockets franchise moved from San Diego to Houston for 1971-72 season. ... Traded by Rockets to Baltimore Bullets for F Jack Marin and future considerations (June 23, 1972). ... Bullets franchise moved from Baltimore to Washington and renamed Capital Bullets for 1973-74 season. ... Bullets franchise renamed Washington Bullets for 1974-75 season. ... Traded by Bullets to Rockets for 1981 and 1983 second-round draft choices (June 8, 1981).
CAREER HONORS: Elected to Naismith Memorial Basketball Hall of Fame (1990). ... One of the 50 Greatest Players in NBA History (1996).
MISCELLANEOUS: Member of NBA championship team (1978). ... Washington Wizards franchise all-time leading scorer with 15,551 points and all-time blocked shots leader with 1,558 (1973-74 through 1980-81).

COLLEGIATE RECORD

NOTES: THE SPORTING NEWS College Player of the Year (1968). ... THE SPORTING NEWS All-America first team (1967, 1968). ... THE SPORTING NEWS All-America second team (1966).

Season Team	G	Min.	FGM	FGA	Pct.	FTM	FTA	Pct.	Reb.	Ast.	Pts.	RPG	APG	PPG
64-65—Houston‡	21	...	217	478	.454	93	176	.528	500	43	527	23.8	2.0	25.1
65-66—Houston	29	946	323	570	.567	143	257	.556	490	6	789	16.9	0.2	27.2
66-67—Houston	31	1119	373	750	.497	135	227	.595	488	33	881	15.7	1.1	28.4
67-68—Houston	33	1270	519	945	.549	176	285	.618	624	59	1214	18.9	1.8	36.8
Varsity totals	93	3335	1215	2265	.536	454	769	.590	1602	98	2884	17.2	1.1	31.0

AVERAGES

NBA REGULAR-SEASON RECORD

RECORDS: Holds single-season record for most minutes played by a rookie—3,695 (1969).
HONORS: All-NBA first team (1975, 1977, 1979). ... All-NBA second team (1973, 1974, 1976). ... NBA All-Defensive second team (1974, 1975). ... NBA All-Rookie team (1969).

Season Team	G	Min.	FGM	FGA	Pct.	FTM	FTA	Pct.	Reb.	Ast.	PF	Dq.	Pts.	RPG	APG	PPG
68-69—San Diego	82	*3695	*930	*2082	.447	467	746	.626	1406	113	266	2	*2327	17.1	1.4	*28.4
69-70—San Diego	82	*3665	914	*2020	.452	428	622	.688	*1386	162	270	5	2256	16.9	2.0	27.5
70-71—San Diego	82	3633	948	*2215	.428	454	676	.672	1362	186	225	1	2350	16.6	2.3	28.7
71-72—Houston	82	3461	832	1918	.434	399	615	.649	1197	270	233	1	2063	14.6	3.3	25.2
72-73—Baltimore	81	3347	713	1607	.444	291	434	.671	1177	127	232	3	1717	14.5	1.6	21.2

| | | | | | | | | | | REBOUNDS | | | | | | | | AVERAGES | | |

Season Team	G	Min.	FGM	FGA	Pct.	FTM	FTA	Pct.	Off.	Def.	Tot.	Ast.	St.	Blk.	TO	Pts.	RPG	APG	PPG
73-74—Capital	81	*3602	689	1627	.423	357	495	.721	*354	*1109	*1463	163	86	240	...	1735	18.1	2.0	21.4
74-75—Washington	82	3465	739	1668	.443	409	534	.766	221	783	1004	206	158	187	...	1887	12.2	2.5	23.0
75-76—Washington	80	2975	649	1381	.470	287	457	.628	210	668	878	121	104	202	...	1585	11.0	1.5	19.8
76-77—Washington	82	*3364	760	1516	.501	422	614	.687	289	740	1029	158	87	220	...	1942	12.5	1.9	23.7
77-78—Washington	81	3246	636	1409	.451	326	514	.634	335	740	1075	149	96	159	229	1598	13.3	1.8	19.7
78-79—Washington	82	3105	720	1477	.487	349	534	.654	312	682	994	143	75	190	235	1789	12.1	1.7	21.8
79-80—Washington	81	3183	761	1677	.454	334	478	.699	269	627	896	129	62	189	215	1859	11.1	1.6	23.0
80-81—Washington	81	2931	584	1296	.451	271	439	.617	235	554	789	98	68	171	189	1439	9.7	1.2	17.8
81-82—Houston	82	3032	519	1100	.472	280	422	.664	267	480	747	144	62	104	208	1318	9.1	1.8	16.1
82-83—Houston	81	2302	424	890	.476	196	287	.683	199	417	616	158	50	81	200	1046	7.6	2.0	12.9
83-84—Houston	81	994	158	389	.406	86	132	.652	87	173	260	71	16	28	82	402	3.2	0.9	5.0
Totals	1303	50000	10976	24272	.452	5356	7999	.670	...	16279	2398	864	1771	1358	27313	12.5	1.8	21.0

Three-point field goals: 1979-80, 3-for-13 (.231). 1980-81, 0-for-10. 1981-82, 0-for-5. 1982-83, 2-for-4 (.500). 1983-84, 0-for-2. Totals, 5-for-34 (.147).
Personal fouls/disqualifications: 1973-74, 252/1. 1974-75, 238/0. 1975-76, 293/5. 1976-77, 312/1. 1977-78, 313/7. 1978-79, 308/5. 1979-80, 309/9. 1980-81, 300/6. 1981-82, 287/4. 1982-83, 232/2. 1983-84, 123/1. Totals, 4193/53.

NBA PLAYOFF RECORD

NOTES: Shares NBA Finals single-game record for most offensive rebounds—11 (May 27, 1979, vs. Seattle).

Season Team	G	Min.	FGM	FGA	Pct.	FTM	FTA	Pct.	Reb.	Ast.	PF	Dq.	Pts.	RPG	APG	PPG
68-69—San Diego	6	278	60	114	.526	35	53	.660	83	5	21	0	155	13.8	0.8	25.8
72-73—Baltimore	5	228	53	105	.505	23	33	.697	57	5	16	0	129	11.4	1.0	25.8

| | | | | | | | | | | REBOUNDS | | | | | | | | AVERAGES | | |

Season Team	G	Min.	FGM	FGA	Pct.	FTM	FTA	Pct.	Off.	Def.	Tot.	Ast.	St.	Blk.	TO	Pts.	RPG	APG	PPG
73-74—Capital	7	323	76	143	.531	29	41	.707	31	80	111	21	5	15	...	181	15.9	3.0	25.9
74-75—Washington	17	751	174	372	.468	86	127	.677	46	140	186	37	26	39	...	434	10.9	2.2	25.5
75-76—Washington	7	305	54	122	.443	32	55	.582	16	72	88	10	5	28	...	140	12.6	1.4	20.0
76-77—Washington	9	405	74	173	.428	41	59	.695	29	93	122	17	10	22	...	189	13.6	1.9	21.0
77-78—Washington	21	868	189	385	.491	79	133	.594	103	176	279	43	32	52	58	457	13.3	2.0	21.8
78-79—Washington	19	786	170	396	.429	87	130	.669	94	172	266	38	17	52	56	427	14.0	2.0	22.5
79-80—Washington	2	92	16	41	.390	8	10	.800	10	12	22	6	0	4	4	40	11.0	3.0	20.0
81-82—Houston	3	124	17	50	.340	8	15	.533	7	23	30	3	2	10	6	42	10.0	1.0	14.0
Totals	96	4160	883	1901	.464	428	656	.652	...	...	1244	185	77	222	124	2194	13.0	1.9	22.9

Personal fouls/disqualifications: 1973-74, 23/0. 1974-75, 70/3. 1975-76, 24/0. 1976-77, 39/0. 1977-78, 86/2. 1978-79, 79/3. 1979-80, 8/0. 1981-82, 12/0. Totals, 378/8.

NBA ALL-STAR GAME RECORD

Season Team	Min.	FGM	FGA	Pct.	FTM	FTA	Pct.	Reb	Ast.	PF	Dq.	Pts.
1969 —San Diego	21	4	9	.444	3	3	1.000	5	0	4	0	11
1970 —San Diego	35	9	21	.429	6	12	.500	15	1	1	0	24
1971 —San Diego	19	4	13	.308	2	3	.667	4	2	1	0	10
1972 —Houston	11	1	6	.167	2	2	1.000	2	0	2	0	4
1973 —Baltimore	16	4	13	.308	2	2	1.000	12	0	0	0	10

Season	Team	Min.	FGM	FGA	Pct.	FTM	FTA	Pct.	REBOUNDS			Ast.	PF	Dq.	St.	Blk.	TO	Pts.
									Off.	Def.	Tot.							
1974	—Capital	35	5	13	.385	2	3	.667	4	11	15	6	4	0	0	1	...	12
1975	—Washington	17	2	6	.333	0	0	...	0	5	5	2	1	0	1	0	...	4
1976	—Washington	31	6	14	.429	0	2	.000	3	7	10	1	5	0	1	0	...	12
1977	—Washington	11	6	6	1.000	0	0	...	0	2	2	1	5	0	0	0	...	12
1978	—Washington	11	1	7	.143	0	0	...	3	1	4	0	4	0	1	0	1	2
1979	—Washington	28	5	11	.455	3	5	.600	4	9	13	0	5	0	1	1	1	13
1980	—Washington	29	5	10	.500	2	2	1.000	2	3	5	4	5	0	1	4	3	12
Totals		264	52	129	.403	22	34	.647	...	...	92	17	37	0	5	6	5	126

HAYWOOD, SPENCER   F/C

PERSONAL: Born April 22, 1949, in Silver City, Miss. ... 6-9/225 (2,05/102,1). ... Full name: Spencer Haywood.

HIGH SCHOOL: Pershing (Detroit).

JUNIOR COLLEGE: Trinidad State Junior College (Colo.).

COLLEGE: Detroit.

TRANSACTIONS: Signed as free agent after sophomore season by Denver Rockets of American Basketball Association (August 16, 1969). ... Selected by Buffalo Braves in second round (30th pick overall) of 1971 NBA Draft. ... Terminated contract with Rockets and signed by Seattle SuperSonics (1971). ... Traded by SuperSonics to New York Knicks for cash and the option of F Eugene Short or future draft choice (October 24, 1975). ... Traded by Knicks to New Orleans Jazz for C Joe C. Meriweather (January 5, 1979). ... Jazz franchise moved from New Orleans to Utah for 1979-80 season. ... Traded by Jazz to Los Angeles Lakers for F Adrian Dantley (September 13, 1979). ... Waived by Lakers (August 19, 1980). ... Played in Italy (1980-81 and 1981-82). ... Signed as free agent by Washington Bullets (October 24, 1981). ... Waived by Bullets (March 9, 1983).

MISCELLANEOUS: Member of NBA championship team (1980). ... Member of gold-medal-winning U.S. Olympic team (1968).

COLLEGIATE RECORD

NOTES: THE SPORTING NEWS All-America first team (1969). ... Led NCAA Division I with 22.1 rebounds per game (1969).

Season Team	G	Min.	FGM	FGA	Pct.	FTM	FTA	Pct.	Reb.	Ast.	Pts.	AVERAGES		
												RPG	APG	PPG
67-68—Trinidad State J.C.	30	...	358	675	.530	129	195	.662	663	...	845	22.1	...	28.2
68-69—Detroit	24	...	288	508	.567	195	254	.768	530	...	771	22.1	...	32.1
Junior college totals	30	...	358	675	.530	129	195	.662	663	...	845	22.1	...	28.2
4-year-college totals	24	...	288	508	.567	195	254	.768	530	...	771	22.1	...	32.1

ABA REGULAR-SEASON RECORD

NOTES: ABA Most Valuable Player (1970). ... ABA Rookie of the Year (1970). ... ABA All-Star first team (1970). ... ABA All-Rookie team (1970). ... Holds single-season records for most minutes played—3,808; most field goals made—986; most rebounds—1,637; and highest rebounds-per-game average—19.5 (1970).

Season Team	G	Min.	2-POINT			3-POINT			FTM	FTA	Pct.	Reb.	Ast.	Pts.	AVERAGES		
			FGM	FGA	Pct.	FGM	FGA	Pct.							RPG	APG	PPG
69-70—Denver	84	*3808	*986	1987	.496	0	11	.000	547	705	.776	*1637	190	*2519	*19.5	2.3	*30.0

ABA PLAYOFF RECORD

Season Team	G	Min.	2-POINT			3-POINT			FTM	FTA	Pct.	Reb.	Ast.	Pts.	AVERAGES		
			FGM	FGA	Pct.	FGM	FGA	Pct.							RPG	APG	PPG
69-70—Denver	12	568	185	362	.511	1	5	.200	69	83	.831	237	39	440	19.8	3.3	36.7

ABA ALL-STAR GAME RECORD

NOTES: ABA All-Star Game Most Valuable Player (1970).

Season Team	Min.	2-POINT			3-POINT			FTM	FTA	Pct.	Reb.	Ast.	Pts.
		FGM	FGA	Pct.	FGM	FGA	Pct.						
1970—Denver	39	10	19	.526	0	0	...	3	4	.750	19	2	23

NBA REGULAR-SEASON RECORD

HONORS: All-NBA first team (1972, 1973). ... All-NBA second team (1974, 1975).

Season Team	G	Min.	FGM	FGA	Pct.	FTM	FTA	Pct.	Reb.	Ast.	PF	Dq.	Pts.	AVERAGES		
														RPG	APG	PPG
70-71—Seattle	33	1162	260	579	.449	160	218	.734	396	48	84	1	680	12.0	1.5	20.6
71-72—Seattle	73	3167	717	1557	.461	480	586	.819	926	148	208	0	1914	12.7	2.0	26.2
72-73—Seattle	77	3259	889	1868	.476	473	564	.039	995	196	213	2	2251	12.9	2.5	29.2

Season Team	G	Min.	FGM	FGA	Pct.	FTM	FTA	Pct.	REBOUNDS			Ast.	St.	Blk.	TO	Pts.	AVERAGES		
									Off.	Def.	Tot.						RPG	APG	PPG
73-74—Seattle	75	3039	694	1520	.457	373	458	.814	318	689	1007	240	65	106	...	1761	13.4	3.2	23.5
74-75—Seattle	68	2529	608	1325	.459	309	381	.811	198	432	630	137	54	108	...	1525	9.3	2.0	22.4
75-76—New York	78	2892	605	1360	.445	339	448	.757	234	644	878	92	53	80	...	1549	11.3	1.2	19.9
76-77—N.Y. Knicks	31	1021	202	449	.450	109	131	.832	77	203	280	50	14	29	...	513	9.0	1.6	16.5
77-78—New York	67	1765	412	852	.484	96	135	.711	141	301	442	126	37	72	140	920	6.6	1.9	13.7
78-79—N.Y.-N.O.	68	2361	595	1205	.494	231	292	.791	172	361	533	127	40	82	200	1421	7.8	1.9	20.9
79-80—Los Angeles	76	1544	288	591	.487	159	206	.772	132	214	346	93	35	57	134	736	4.6	1.2	9.7
81-82—Washington	76	2086	395	829	.476	219	260	.842	144	278	422	64	45	68	175	1009	5.6	0.8	13.3
82-83—Washington	38	775	125	312	.401	63	87	.724	77	106	183	30	12	27	67	313	4.8	0.8	8.2
Totals	760	25600	5790	12447	.465	3011	3766	.800	...	...	7038	1351	355	629	716	14592	9.3	1.8	19.2

Three-point field goals: 1979-80, 1-for-4 (.250). 1981-82, 0-for-3. 1982-83, 0-for-1. Totals, 1-for-8 (.125).

Personal fouls/disqualifications: 1973-74, 198/2. 1974-75, 173/1. 1975-76, 255/1. 1976-77, 97/0. 1977-78, 188/1. 1978-79, 236/8. 1979-80, 197/2. 1981-82, 249/6. 1982-83, 94/2. Totals, 2167/26.

NBA PLAYOFF RECORD

Season Team	G	Min.	FGM	FGA	Pct.	FTM	FTA	Pct.	REBOUNDS			Ast.	St.	Blk.	TO	Pts.	AVERAGES		
									Off.	Def.	Tot.						RPG	APG	PPG
74-75—Seattle	9	337	47	131	.359	47	61	.771	20	61	81	18	7	11	...	141	9.0	2.0	15.7
77-78—New York	6	177	43	85	.506	11	11	1.000	19	23	42	12	2	5	10	97	7.0	2.0	16.2
79-80—Los Angeles....	11	145	25	53	.472	13	16	.813	14	12	26	4	0	6	20	63	2.4	0.4	5.7
81-82—Washington	7	231	57	115	.496	26	35	.743	16	23	39	7	4	14	15	140	5.6	1.0	20.0
Totals	33	890	172	384	.448	97	123	.789	69	119	188	41	13	36	45	441	5.7	1.2	13.4

Three-point field goals: 1979-80, 0-for-1.
Personal fouls/disqualifications: 1974-75, 29/0. 1977-78, 24/1. 1979-80, 17/0. 1981-82, 28/0. Totals, 98/1.

NBA ALL-STAR GAME RECORD

Season Team	Min.	FGM	FGA	Pct.	FTM	FTA	Pct.	Reb	Ast.	PF	Dq.	Pts.
1972 —Seattle	25	4	10	.400	3	4	.750	7	1	2	0	11
1973 —Seattle	22	5	10	.500	2	2	1.000	10	0	5	0	12

Season Team	Min.	FGM	FGA	Pct.	FTM	FTA	Pct.	REBOUNDS			Ast.	PF	Dq.	St.	Blk.	TO	Pts.
								Off.	Def.	Tot.							
1974 —Seattle	33	10	17	.588	3	3	1.000	2	9	11	5	5	0	0	3	...	23
1975 —Seattle	17	1	9	.111	0	0	...	1	2	3	0	1	0	0	0	...	2
Totals	97	20	46	.435	8	9	.889	...	...	31	6	13	0	0	3	...	48

COMBINED ABA AND NBA REGULAR-SEASON RECORDS

	G	Min.	FGM	FGA	Pct.	FTM	FTA	Pct.	REBOUNDS			Ast.	Stl.	Blk.	TO	Pts.	AVERAGES		
									Off.	Def.	Tot.						RPG	APG	PPG
Totals	844	29408	6776	14445	.470	3558	4471	.796	...	...	8675	1541	...	...	...	17111	10.3	1.8	20.3

Three-point field goals: 1-for-19 (.053).
Personal fouls/disqualifications: 2388/27.

ITALIAN LEAGUE RECORD

Season Team	G	Min.	FGM	FGA	Pct.	FTM	FTA	Pct.	Reb.	Ast.	Pts.	AVERAGES		
												RPG	APG	PPG
80-81—Venezia..........................	34	...	334	601	.556	132	179	.737	354	...	800	10.4	...	23.5
81-82—Carrera	5	175	63	100	.630	24	32	.750	37	...	150	7.4	...	30.0
Totals	39	...	397	701	.566	156	211	.739	391	...	950	10.0	...	24.4

HEINSOHN, TOM   F

See All-Time Great Coaches, page 457.

HORNACEK, JEFF   G

PERSONAL: Born May 3, 1963, in Elmhurst, Ill. ... 6-4/190. (1.93 m/86 kg). ... Full Name: Jeffrey John Hornacek. ... Name pronounced HORN-a-sek.
HIGH SCHOOL: Lyons Township (La Grange, Ill.).
COLLEGE: Iowa State.
TRANSACTIONS/CAREER NOTES: Selected by Phoenix Suns in second round (46th pick overall) of 1986 NBA Draft. ... Traded by Suns with C Andrew Lang and F Tim Perry to Philadelphia 76ers for F Charles Barkley (June 17, 1992). ... Traded by 76ers with G Sean Green and 1995 or 1996 second-round draft choice to Utah Jazz for G Jeff Malone and 1994 conditional first-round draft choice (February 24, 1994). ... Announced retirement effective at end of 1999-2000 season.

COLLEGIATE RECORD

Season Team	G	Min.	FGM	FGA	Pct.	FTM	FTA	Pct.	Reb.	Ast.	Pts.	AVERAGES		
												RPG	APG	PPG
81-82—Iowa State					Did not play—redshirted.									
82-83—Iowa State	27	583	57	135	.422	32	45	.711	62	82	146	2.3	3.0	5.4
83-84—Iowa State	29	1065	104	208	.500	83	105	.790	101	198	291	3.5	6.8	10.0
84-85—Iowa State	34	1224	172	330	.521	81	96	.844	122	166	425	3.6	4.9	12.5
85-86—Iowa State	33	1229	177	370	.478	97	125	.776	127	219	451	3.8	6.6	13.7
Totals	123	4101	510	1043	.489	293	371	.790	412	665	1313	3.3	5.4	10.7

NBA REGULAR-SEASON RECORD

RECORDS: Shares single-game record for most three-point field goals without a miss—8 (November 23, 1994, vs. Seattle).
HONORS: Long Distance Shootout winner (1998 and 2000).

Season Team	G	Min.	FGM	FGA	Pct.	FTM	FTA	Pct.	REBOUNDS			Ast.	St.	Blk.	TO	Pts.	AVERAGES		
									Off.	Def.	Tot.						RPG	APG	PPG
86-87—Phoenix	80	1561	159	350	.454	94	121	.777	41	143	184	361	70	5	153	424	2.3	4.5	5.3
87-88—Phoenix	82	2243	306	605	.506	152	185	.822	71	191	262	540	107	10	156	781	3.2	6.6	9.5
88-89—Phoenix	78	2487	440	889	.495	147	178	.826	75	191	266	465	129	8	111	1054	3.4	6.0	13.5
89-90—Phoenix	67	2278	483	901	.536	173	202	.856	86	227	313	337	117	14	125	1179	4.7	5.0	17.6
90-91—Phoenix	80	2733	544	1051	.518	201	224	.897	74	247	321	409	111	16	130	1350	4.0	5.1	16.9
91-92—Phoenix	81	3078	635	1240	.512	279	315	.886	106	301	407	411	158	31	170	1632	5.0	5.1	20.1
92-93—Philadelphia ...	79	2860	582	1239	.470	250	289	.865	84	258	342	548	131	21	222	1511	4.3	6.9	19.1
93-94—Phil.-Utah	80	2820	472	1004	.470	260	296	.878	60	219	279	419	127	13	171	1274	3.5	5.2	15.9
94-95—Utah..............	81	2696	482	937	.514	284	322	.882	53	157	210	347	129	17	145	1337	2.6	4.3	16.5
95-96—Utah..............	82	2588	442	880	.502	259	290	.893	62	147	209	340	106	20	127	1247	2.5	4.1	15.2
96-97—Utah..............	82	2592	413	856	.482	293	326	.899	60	181	241	361	124	26	134	1191	2.9	4.4	14.5
97-98—Utah..............	80	2460	399	828	.482	285	322	.885	65	205	270	349	109	15	132	1139	3.4	4.4	14.2
98-99—Utah..............	48	1435	214	449	.477	125	140	.893	33	127	160	192	52	14	82	587	3.3	4.0	12.2
99-00—Utah..............	77	2133	358	728	.492	171	180	*.950	49	133	182	202	66	16	113	953	2.4	2.6	12.4
Totals	1077	33964	5929	11957	.496	2973	3390	.877	919	2727	3646	5281	1536	226	1971	15659	3.4	4.9	14.5

Three-point field goals: 1986-87, 12-for-43 (.279). 1987-88, 17-for-58 (.293). 1988-89, 27-for-81 (.333). 1989-90, 40-for-98 (.408). 1990-91, 61-for-146 (.418). 1991-92, 83-for-189 (.439). 1992-93, 97-for-249 (.390). 1993-94, 70-for-208 (.337). 1994-95, 89-for-219 (.406). 1995-96, 104-for-223 (.466). 1996-97, 72-for-195 (.369). 1997-98, 56-for-127 (.441). 1998-99, 34-for-81 (.420). 1999-00, 66-for-138 (.478). Totals, 828-for-2055 (.403).

Personal fouls/disqualifications: 1986-87, 130/0. 1987-88, 151/0. 1988-89, 188/0. 1989-90, 144/2. 1990-91, 185/1. 1991-92, 218/1. 1992-93, 203/2. 1993-94, 186/0. 1994-95, 181/1. 1995-96, 171/1. 1996-97, 188/1. 1997-98, 175/1. 1998-99, 95/0. 1999-00, 149/1. Totals, 2364/11.

NBA PLAYOFF RECORD

									REBOUNDS								AVERAGES		
Season Team	G	Min.	FGM	FGA	Pct.	FTM	FTA	Pct.	Off.	Def.	Tot.	Ast.	St.	Blk.	TO	Pts.	RPG	APG	PPG
88-89—Phoenix	12	374	74	149	.497	21	25	.840	25	44	69	62	16	3	18	169	5.8	5.2	14.1
89-90—Phoenix	16	583	112	219	.511	68	73	.932	13	49	62	73	24	0	34	298	3.9	4.6	18.6
90-91—Phoenix	4	145	22	51	.431	26	28	.929	3	22	25	8	3	2	3	73	6.3	2.0	18.3
91-92—Phoenix	8	343	62	128	.484	31	34	.912	12	39	51	42	14	2	19	163	6.4	5.3	20.4
93-94—Utah	16	558	85	179	.475	62	68	.912	11	28	39	64	24	6	28	247	2.4	4.0	15.4
94-95—Utah	5	178	26	51	.510	11	14	.786	3	3	6	20	8	1	7	70	1.2	4.0	14.0
95-96—Utah	18	644	104	207	.502	73	82	.890	22	43	65	60	19	3	27	315	3.6	3.3	17.5
96-97—Utah	20	704	90	208	.433	92	105	.876	22	67	89	73	21	4	36	291	4.5	3.7	14.6
97-98—Utah	20	636	74	178	.416	55	65	.846	7	43	50	64	20	4	32	217	2.5	3.2	10.9
98-99—Utah	11	304	49	106	.462	29	33	.879	9	32	41	26	11	0	12	134	3.7	2.4	12.2
99-00—Utah	10	297	43	102	.422	20	24	.833	9	21	30	33	10	0	15	115	3.0	3.3	11.5
Totals	140	4766	741	1578	.470	488	551	.886	136	391	527	525	170	25	231	2092	3.8	3.8	14.9

Three-point field goals: 1988-89, 0-for-7. 1989-90, 6-for-24 (.250). 1990-91, 3-for-6 (.500). 1991-92, 8-for-17 (.471). 1993-94, 15-for-34 (.441). 1994-95, 7-for-13 (.538). 1995-96, 34-for-58 (.586). 1996-97, 19-for-53 (.358). 1997-98, 14-for-30 (.467). 1998-99, 7-for-18 (.389). 1999-00, 9-for-22 (.409). Totals, 122-for-282 (.433).

Personal fouls/disqualifications: 1988-89, 34/0. 1989-90, 43/1. 1990-91, 13/0. 1991-92, 23/0. 1993-94, 45/0. 1994-95, 19/1. 1995-96, 41/1. 1996-97, 53/1. 1997-98, 51/1. 1998-99, 34/1. 1999-00, 28/0. Totals, 384/6.

NBA ALL-STAR GAME RECORD

								REBOUNDS								
Season Team	Min.	FGM	FGA	Pct.	FTM	FTA	Pct.	Off.	Def.	Tot.	Ast.	PF	Dq.	St.	Blk.	TO	Pts.
1992 —Phoenix	24	5	7	.714	0	0	...	1	1	2	3	0	0	1	0	0	11
Totals	24	5	7	.714	0	0	...	1	1	2	3	0	0	1	0	0	11

Three-point field goals: 1992, 1-for-2 (.500). Totals, 1-for-2 (.500).

HOWELL, BAILEY   F

PERSONAL: Born January 20, 1937, in Middleton, Tenn. ... 6-7/220 (2,00/99,8). ... Full name: Bailey E. Howell.
HIGH SCHOOL: Middleton (Tenn.).
COLLEGE: Mississippi State.
TRANSACTIONS: Selected by Detroit Pistons in first round of 1959 NBA Draft. ... Traded by Pistons with C/F Bob Ferry, G Don Ohl, G Wali Jones and F Les Hunter to Baltimore Bullets for F/G Terry Dischinger, F Don Kojis and G Rod Thorn (June 18, 1964). ... Traded by Bullets to Boston Celtics for F/C Mel Counts (September 1, 1966). ... Selected by Buffalo Braves from Celtics in NBA Expansion Draft (May 11, 1970). ... Traded by Braves to Philadelphia 76ers for C Bob Kauffman and cash or future draft choice (May 11, 1970).
CAREER HONORS: Elected to Naismith Memorial Basketball Hall of Fame (1997).
MISCELLANEOUS: Member of NBA championship team (1968, 1969).

COLLEGIATE RECORD

NOTES: THE SPORTING NEWS All-America first team (1959). ... Led NCAA major college division with .568 field goal percentage (1957).

											AVERAGES		
Season Team	G	Min.	FGM	FGA	Pct.	FTM	FTA	Pct.	Reb.	Ast.	Pts.	RPG	APG	PPG
55-56—Mississippi State‡						Freshman team statistics unavailable.								
56-57—Mississippi State	25	...	217	382	.568	213	285	.747	492	...	647	19.7	...	25.9
57-58—Mississippi State	25	...	226	439	.515	243	315	.771	406	...	695	16.2	...	27.8
58-59—Mississippi State	25	...	231	464	.498	226	292	.774	379	...	688	15.2	...	27.5
Varsity totals	75	...	674	1285	.525	682	892	.765	1277	...	2030	17.0	...	27.1

HONORS: All-NBA second team (1963).

NBA REGULAR-SEASON RECORD

														AVERAGES		
Season Team	G	Min.	FGM	FGA	Pct.	FTM	FTA	Pct.	Reb.	Ast.	PF	Dq.	Pts.	RPG	APG	PPG
59-60 —Detroit	75	2346	510	1119	.456	312	422	.739	790	63	282	13	1332	10.5	0.8	17.8
60-61 —Detroit	77	2952	607	1293	.469	601	798	.753	1111	196	297	10	1815	14.4	2.5	23.6
61-62 —Detroit	79	2857	553	1193	.464	470	612	.768	996	186	317	10	1576	12.6	2.4	19.9
62-63 —Detroit	79	2771	637	1235	.516	519	650	.798	910	232	300	9	1793	11.5	2.9	22.7
63-64 —Detroit	77	2700	598	1267	.472	470	581	.809	776	205	200	9	1666	10.1	2.7	21.6
64-65 —Baltimore	80	2975	515	1040	.495	504	629	.801	869	208	*345	10	1534	10.9	2.6	19.2
65 66 —Baltimore	78	2328	481	986	.488	402	551	.730	773	155	306	12	1364	9.9	2.0	17.5
66-67 —Boston	81	2503	636	1242	.512	349	471	.741	677	103	296	4	1621	8.4	1.3	20.0
67-68 —Boston	82	2801	643	1336	.481	335	461	.727	805	133	285	4	1621	9.8	1.6	19.8
68-69 —Boston	78	2527	612	1257	.487	313	426	.735	685	137	285	3	1537	8.8	1.8	19.7
69-70 —Boston	82	2078	399	931	.429	235	308	.763	550	120	261	4	1033	6.7	1.5	12.6
70-71 —Philadelphia	82	1589	324	686	.472	230	315	.730	441	115	234	2	878	5.4	1.4	10.7
Totals	950	30627	6515	13585	.480	4740	6224	.762	9383	1853	3498	90	17770	9.9	2.0	18.7

NBA PLAYOFF RECORD

														AVERAGES		
Season Team	G	Min.	FGM	FGA	Pct.	FTM	FTA	Pct.	Reb.	Ast.	PF	Dq.	Pts.	RPG	APG	PPG
59-60 —Detroit	2	72	14	41	.341	6	8	.750	17	3	8	0	34	8.5	1.5	17.0
60-61 —Detroit	5	144	20	57	.351	16	23	.696	46	22	22	1	56	9.2	4.4	11.2
61-62 —Detroit	10	378	69	163	.423	62	75	.827	96	23	48	3	200	9.6	2.3	20.0
62-63 —Detroit	4	163	24	64	.375	23	27	.852	42	11	19	1	71	10.5	2.8	17.8
64-65 —Baltimore	9	350	67	130	.515	53	70	.757	105	19	38	3	187	11.7	2.1	20.8

Season Team	G	Min.	FGM	FGA	Pct.	FTM	FTA	Pct.	Reb.	Ast.	PF	Dq.	Pts.	RPG	APG	PPG
65-66 —Baltimore	3	94	23	50	.460	8	11	.727	30	2	13	1	54	10.0	0.7	18.0
66-67 —Boston	9	241	59	122	.484	20	30	.667	66	5	35	2	138	7.3	0.6	15.3
67-68 —Boston	19	597	135	264	.511	74	107	.692	146	22	84	6	344	7.7	1.2	18.1
68-69 —Boston	18	551	112	229	.489	46	64	.719	118	19	84	3	270	6.6	1.1	15.0
70-71 —Philadelphia	7	122	19	45	.422	9	18	.500	31	4	25	1	47	4.4	0.6	6.7
Totals	86	2712	542	1165	.465	317	433	.732	697	130	376	21	1401	8.1	1.5	16.3

NBA ALL-STAR GAME RECORD

Season Team	Min.	FGM	FGA	Pct.	FTM	FTA	Pct.	Reb	Ast.	PF	Dq.	Pts.
1961 —Detroit	16	5	10	.500	3	4	.750	3	3	4	0	13
1962 —Detroit	8	1	2	.500	0	0	...	0	1	1	0	2
1963 —Detroit	11	2	3	.667	0	0	...	1	1	2	0	4
1964 —Detroit	6	1	3	.333	0	0	...	2	0	0	0	2
1966 —Baltimore	26	3	11	.273	1	2	.500	2	2	4	0	7
1967 —Boston	14	1	4	.250	2	2	1.000	2	1	1	0	4
Totals	81	13	33	.394	6	8	.750	10	8	12	0	32

HUDSON, LOU — F/G

PERSONAL: Born July 11, 1944, in Greensboro, N.C. ... 6-5/210 (1,96/95,3). ... Full name: Louis Clyde Hudson. ... Nickname: Sweet Lou.
HIGH SCHOOL: Dudley Senior (Greensboro, N.C.).
COLLEGE: Minnesota.
TRANSACTIONS: Selected by St. Louis Hawks in first round (fourth pick overall) of 1966 NBA Draft. ... Hawks franchise moved from St. Louis to Atlanta for 1968-69 season. ... Traded by Hawks to Los Angeles Lakers for F Ollie Johnson (September 30, 1977).

COLLEGIATE RECORD

Season Team	G	Min.	FGM	FGA	Pct.	FTM	FTA	Pct.	Reb.	Ast.	Pts.	RPG	APG	PPG
62-63 —Minnesota‡					Freshman team did not play intercollegiate schedule.									
63-64 —Minnesota	24	...	191	435	.439	53	85	.624	191	...	435	8.0	...	18.1
64-65 —Minnesota	24	...	231	463	.499	96	123	.780	247	...	558	10.3	...	23.3
65-66 —Minnesota	17	...	143	303	.472	50	77	.649	138	...	336	8.1	...	19.8
Varsity totals	65	...	565	1201	.470	199	285	.698	576	...	1329	8.9	...	20.4

NBA REGULAR-SEASON RECORD

HONORS: All-NBA second team (1970). ... NBA All-Rookie team (1967).

Season Team	G	Min.	FGM	FGA	Pct.	FTM	FTA	Pct.	Reb.	Ast.	PF	Dq.	Pts.	RPG	APG	PPG
66-67 —St. Louis	80	2446	620	1328	.467	231	327	.706	435	95	277	3	1471	5.4	1.2	18.4
67-68 —St. Louis	46	966	227	500	.454	120	164	.732	193	65	113	2	574	4.2	1.4	12.5
68-69 —Atlanta	81	2869	716	1455	.492	338	435	.777	533	216	248	0	1770	6.6	2.7	21.9
69-70 —Atlanta	80	3091	830	1564	.531	371	450	.824	373	276	225	1	2031	4.7	3.5	25.4
70-71 —Atlanta	76	3113	829	1713	.484	381	502	.759	386	257	186	0	2039	5.1	3.4	26.8
71-72 —Atlanta	77	3042	775	1540	.503	349	430	.812	385	309	225	0	1899	5.0	4.0	24.7
72-73 —Atlanta	75	3027	816	1710	.477	397	481	.825	467	258	197	1	2029	6.2	3.4	27.1

Season Team	G	Min.	FGM	FGA	Pct.	FTM	FTA	Pct.	Off.	Def.	Tot.	Ast.	St.	Blk.	TO	Pts.	RPG	APG	PPG
73-74 —Atlanta	65	2588	678	1356	.500	295	353	.836	126	224	350	213	160	29	...	1651	5.4	3.3	25.4
74-75 —Atlanta	11	380	97	225	.431	48	57	.842	14	33	47	40	13	2	...	242	4.3	3.6	22.0
75-76 —Atlanta	81	2558	569	1205	.472	237	291	.814	104	196	300	214	124	17	...	1375	3.7	2.6	17.0
76-77 —Atlanta	58	1745	413	905	.456	142	169	.840	48	81	129	155	67	19	...	968	2.2	2.7	16.7
77-78 —Los Angeles	82	2283	493	992	.497	137	177	.774	80	108	188	193	94	14	150	1123	2.3	2.4	13.7
78-79 —Los Angeles	78	1686	329	636	.517	110	124	.887	64	76	140	141	58	17	99	768	1.8	1.8	9.8
Totals	890	29794	7392	15129	.489	3156	3960	.797	...	...	3926	2432	516	98	249	17940	4.4	2.7	20.2

Personal fouls/disqualifications: 1973-74, 205/3. 1974-75, 33/1. 1975-76, 241/3. 1976-77, 160/2. 1977-78, 196/0. 1978-79, 133/1. Totals, 2439/17.

NBA PLAYOFF RECORD

Season Team	G	Min.	FGM	FGA	Pct.	FTM	FTA	Pct.	Reb.	Ast.	PF	Dq.	Pts.	RPG	APG	PPG
66-67 —St. Louis	9	317	77	179	.430	49	68	.721	48	15	35	1	203	5.3	1.7	22.6
67-68 —St. Louis	6	181	44	99	.444	42	47	.894	43	14	21	0	130	7.2	2.3	21.7
68-69 —Atlanta	11	424	101	216	.468	40	52	.769	59	32	43	1	242	5.4	2.9	22.0
69-70 —Atlanta	9	360	78	187	.417	41	50	.820	40	33	34	2	197	4.4	3.7	21.9
70-71 —Atlanta	5	213	49	108	.454	29	39	.744	35	15	19	0	127	7.0	3.0	25.4
71-72 —Atlanta	6	266	63	139	.453	24	29	.828	33	21	13	0	150	5.5	3.5	25.0
72-73 —Atlanta	6	255	76	166	.458	26	29	.897	47	17	16	0	178	7.8	2.8	29.7

Season Team	G	Min.	FGM	FGA	Pct.	FTM	FTA	Pct.	Off.	Def.	Tot.	Ast.	St.	Blk.	TO	Pts.	RPG	APG	PPG
77-78 —Los Angeles	3	93	14	38	.368	7	8	.875	7	2	9	9	5	0	5	35	3.0	3.0	11.7
78-79 —Los Angeles	6	90	17	32	.531	4	4	1.000	1	3	4	8	1	0	5	38	0.7	1.3	6.3
Totals	61	2199	519	1164	.446	262	326	.804	...	...	318	164	6	0	10	1300	5.2	2.7	21.3

Personal fouls/disqualifications: 1977-78, 9/0. 1978-79, 6/0. Totals, 196/4.

NBA ALL-STAR GAME RECORD

Season	Team	Min.	FGM	FGA	Pct.	FTM	FTA	Pct.	Reb	Ast.	PF	Dq.	Pts.
1969	—Atlanta	20	6	13	.462	1	1	1.000	1	1	0	0	13
1970	—Atlanta	18	5	12	.417	5	5	1.000	1	0	1	0	15
1971	—Atlanta	17	6	13	.462	2	3	.667	3	1	3	0	14
1972	—Atlanta	18	2	7	.286	2	2	1.000	3	3	3	0	6
1973	—Atlanta	9	2	8	.250	2	2	1.000	2	0	2	0	6

									REBOUNDS							
Season	Team	Min.	FGM	FGA	Pct.	FTM	FTA	Pct.	Off.	Def.	Tot.	Ast.	PF	Dq.	St.	Blk.	TO	Pts.
1974	—Atlanta	17	5	8	.625	2	2	1.000	1	2	3	1	2	0	0	1	...	12
Totals		99	26	61	.426	14	15	.933	...	...	13	6	11	0	0	1	...	66

ISSEL, DAN

See Head Coaches, page 309.

JEANNETTE, BUDDY   G

PERSONAL: Born September 15, 1917, in New Kensington, Pa. ... Died March 11, 1998. ... 5-11/175 (1,81/79,4). ... Full name: Harry Edward Jeannette.
HIGH SCHOOL: New Kensington (Pa.).
COLLEGE: Washington & Jefferson (Pa.).
TRANSACTIONS: Warren Penns franchise transferred to Cleveland and renamed White Horses (February 10, 1939). ... Played in New York-Penn League with Elmira in 1939 and New York State League with Saratoga in 1942.
CAREER HONORS: Elected to Naismith Memorial Basketball Basketball Hall of Fame (1994).
MISCELLANEOUS: Member of BAA championship team (1948). ... Member of NBL championship team (1943, 1944, 1945).

COLLEGIATE RECORD

												AVERAGES		
Season Team	G	Min.	FGM	FGA	Pct.	FTM	FTA	Pct.	Reb.	Ast.	Pts.	RPG	APG	PPG
34-35—Wash. & Jefferson	14	...	62	...	...	35	...	...	...	...	159	...	...	11.4
35-36—Wash. & Jefferson	20	...	92	...	...	42	...	...	...	...	226	...	...	11.3
36-37—Wash. & Jefferson	18	...	92	...	...	56	...	...	...	...	240	...	...	13.3
37-38—Wash. & Jefferson	20	...	...	...	...	...	...	...	...	...	240	...	...	12.0
Totals	72	...	...	...	...	...	...	...	...	...	865	...	...	12.0

NBL AND NBA REGULAR-SEASON RECORD

HONORS: All-BAA second team (1948). ... All-NBL first team (1941, 1944, 1945, 1946). ... All-NBL second team (1943).

														AVERAGES		
Season Team	G	Min.	FGM	FGA	Pct.	FTM	FTA	Pct.	Reb.	Ast.	PF	Dq.	Pts.	RPG	APG	PPG
38-39—W-Cl (NBL)	26	...	54	...	...	65	...	...	...	...	57	...	173	...	...	6.7
39-40—Det. (NBL)	25	...	45	...	...	52	80	.650	...	...	62	...	142	...	...	5.7
40-41—Det. (NBL)	23	...	75	...	...	54	86	.628	...	...	56	...	204	...	...	8.9
42-43—Shb. (NBL)	4	...	24	...	...	14	17	.824	...	...	8	...	62	...	...	15.5
43-44—F.W. (NBL)	22	...	68	...	...	48	65	.738	...	...	46	...	184	...	...	8.4
44-45—F.W. (NBL)	27	...	85	...	...	82	111	*.739	...	...	67	...	252	...	...	9.3
45-46—F.W. (NBL)	34	...	99	...	...	105	136	.772	...	...	184	...	303	...	...	8.9
47-48—Baltimore (BAA)	46	...	150	430	.349	191	252	.758	...	70	147	...	491	...	1.5	10.7
48-49—Baltimore (BAA)	56	...	73	199	.367	167	213	.784	...	124	157	...	313	...	2.2	5.6
49-50—Baltimore	37	...	42	148	.284	109	133	.820	...	93	82	...	193	...	2.5	5.2
Totals	300	...	715	...	...	887	...	...	...	...	866	...	2317	...	...	7.7

NBL AND NBA PLAYOFF RECORD

														AVERAGES		
Season Team	G	Min.	FGM	FGA	Pct.	FTM	FTA	Pct.	Reb.	Ast.	PF	Dq.	Pts.	RPG	APG	PPG
39-40—Det. (NBL)	3	...	6	...	...	8	...	...	...	...	...	...	20	...	...	6.7
40-41—Det. (NBL)	3	...	8	...	...	5	...	...	...	...	...	...	21	...	...	7.0
42-43—Shb. (NBL)	5	...	16	...	...	17	...	...	...	...	...	...	49	...	...	9.8
43-44—F.W. (NBL)	5	...	12	...	...	10	...	...	...	...	...	...	34	...	...	6.8
44-45—F.W. (NBL)	7	...	22	...	...	23	...	...	...	...	...	...	67	...	...	9.6
45-46—F.W. (NBL)	4	...	7	...	...	5	6	.833	...	...	...	...	19	...	...	4.8
47-48—Baltimore (BAA)	11	...	30	61	.492	37	42	.881	...	12	45	...	97	...	1.1	8.8
48-49—Baltimore (BAA)	3	...	2	13	.154	4	4	1.000	...	5	11	...	8	...	1.7	2.7
Totals	41	...	103	...	...	109	...	...	...	...	...	...	315	...	...	7.7

ABL REGULAR-SEASON RECORD

												AVERAGES		
Season Team	G	Min.	FGM	FGA	Pct.	FTM	FTA	Pct.	Reb.	Ast.	Pts.	RPG	APG	PPG
46-47—Baltimore	29	...	113	...	...	118	...	...	...	...	344	...	...	11.9

HEAD COACHING RECORD

BACKGROUND: Player/head coach, Baltimore Bullets of ABL (1946-47). ... Assistant coach, Pittsburgh Condors of ABA (1970-71).

ABL COACHING RECORD

		REGULAR SEASON				PLAYOFFS		
Season Team	W	L	Pct.	Finish	W	L	Pct.
46-47—Baltimore	31	3	.912	1st/Southern Division	2	1	.667

COLLEGIATE COACHING RECORD

Season Team	W	L	Pct.
52-53—Georgetown	13	7	.650
53-54—Georgetown	11	18	.379
54-55—Georgetown	12	13	.480
55-56—Georgetown	13	11	.542
Totals (4 years)	49	49	.500

ALL-TIME GREAT PLAYERS

NBA COACHING RECORD

Season Team	W	L	Pct.	Finish	W	L	Pct.
				REGULAR SEASON		PLAYOFFS	
47-48 —Baltimore (BAA)	28	20	.583	2nd/Western Division	9	3	.750
48-49 —Baltimore (BAA)	29	31	.483	3rd/Eastern Division	1	2	.333
49-50 —Baltimore	25	43	.368	5th/Eastern Division	—	—	—
50-51 —Baltimore	14	23	.378				
64-65 —Baltimore	37	43	.463	3rd/Western Division	5	5	.500
66-67 —Baltimore	3	13	.188		—	—	—
Totals (6 years)	136	173	.440	Totals (3 years)	15	10	.600

EBL COACHING RECORD

Season Team	W	L	Pct.	Finish	W	L	Pct.
				REGULAR SEASON		PLAYOFFS	
59-60 —Baltimore	20	8	.714	2nd	2	2	.500
60-61 —Baltimore	19	9	.679	1st	2	0	1.000
Totals (2 years)	39	17	.696	Totals (2 years)	4	2	.667

ABA COACHING RECORD

Season Team	W	L	Pct.	Finish	W	L	Pct.
				REGULAR SEASON		PLAYOFFS	
69-70 —Pittsburgh	15	30	.333	5th/Eastern Division	—	—	—

NOTES:
1948—Defeated Chicago, 75-72, in Western Division tiebreaker; defeated New York, 2-1, in quarterfinals; defeated Chicago, 2-0, in semifinals; defeated Philadelphia, 4-2, in NBA Finals.
1949—Lost to New York in Eastern Division Semifinals.
1951—Replaced as Baltimore head coach by Walt Budko (January).
1960—Defeated Allentown, 103-89, in semifinal; lost to Easton, 2-1, in EBL Finals.
1961—Defeated Scranton, 132-107, in semifinal; defeated Allentown, 119-104, in EBL Final.
1965—Defeated St. Louis, 3-1, in Western Division Semifinals; lost to Los Angeles, 4-2, in Western Division Finals.
1966—Replaced Michael Farmer as Baltimore head coach, with record of 1-8 (November). Replaced as Baltimore head coach by Gene Shue (December).

JOHNSON, DENNIS   G

PERSONAL: Born September 18, 1954, in San Pedro, Calif. ... 6-4/202 (1,93/91,6). ... Full name: Dennis Wayne Johnson. ... Nickname: D.J.
HIGH SCHOOL: Dominquez (Compton, Calif.).
JUNIOR COLLEGE: Los Angeles Harbor Junior College.
COLLEGE: Pepperdine.
TRANSACTIONS: Selected after junior season by Seattle SuperSonics in second round (29th pick overall) of 1976 NBA Draft. ... Traded by SuperSonics to Phoenix Suns for G Paul Westphal (June 4, 1980). ... Traded by Suns with 1983 first- and third-round draft choices to Boston Celtics for F/C Rick Robey and two 1983 second-round draft choices (June 27, 1983).
CAREER NOTES: Assistant coach, Boston Celtics (1993-94 through 1996-97). ... Head coach, La Crosse Catbirds of CBA (1999-February 3, 2000). ... Assistant coach, Los Angeles Clippers (February 4, 2000 to present).
MISCELLANEOUS: Member of NBA championship team (1979, 1984, 1986).

COLLEGIATE RECORD

Season Team	G	Min.	FGM	FGA	Pct.	FTM	FTA	Pct.	Reb.	Ast.	Pts.	RPG	APG	PPG
												AVERAGES		
73-74—Los Angeles Harbor J.C.	...	699	103	191	.539	45	82	.549	230	...	251	...	...	...
74-75—Los Angeles Harbor J.C.	28	967	...	...	...	...	...	...	336	...	511	12.0	...	18.3
75-76—Pepperdine	27	930	181	378	.479	63	112	.563	156	88	425	5.8	3.3	15.7
Junior college totals	...	1666	...	...	...	...	...	...	566	...	762	...	...	...
4-year-college totals	27	930	181	378	.479	63	112	.563	156	88	425	5.8	3.3	15.7

NBA REGULAR-SEASON RECORD

HONORS: All-NBA first team (1981). ... All-NBA second team (1980). ... NBA All-Defensive first team (1979, 1980, 1981, 1982, 1983, 1987). ... NBA All-Defensive second team (1984, 1985, 1986).

Season Team	G	Min.	FGM	FGA	Pct.	FTM	FTA	Pct.	Off.	Def.	Tot.	Ast.	St.	Blk.	TO	Pts.	RPG	APG	PPG
									REBOUNDS								AVERAGES		
76-77—Seattle	81	1667	285	566	.504	179	287	.624	161	141	302	123	123	57	...	749	3.7	1.5	9.2
77-78—Seattle	81	2209	367	881	.417	297	406	.732	152	142	294	230	118	51	164	1031	3.6	2.8	12.7
78-79—Seattle	80	2717	482	1110	.434	306	392	.781	146	228	374	280	100	97	191	1270	4.7	3.5	15.9
79-80—Seattle	81	2937	574	1361	.422	380	487	.780	173	241	414	332	144	82	227	1540	5.1	4.1	19.0
80-81—Phoenix	79	2615	532	1220	.436	411	501	.820	160	203	363	291	136	61	208	1486	4.6	3.7	18.8
81-82—Phoenix	80	2937	577	1228	.470	399	495	.806	142	268	410	369	105	55	233	1565	5.1	4.6	19.5
82-83—Phoenix	77	2551	398	861	.462	292	369	.791	92	243	335	388	97	39	204	1093	4.4	5.0	14.2
83-84—Boston	80	2665	384	878	.437	281	330	.852	87	193	280	338	93	57	172	1053	3.5	4.2	13.2
84-85—Boston	80	2976	493	1066	.462	261	306	.853	91	226	317	543	96	39	212	1254	4.0	6.8	15.7
85-86—Boston	78	2732	482	1060	.455	243	297	.818	69	199	268	456	110	35	173	1213	3.4	5.8	15.6
86-87—Boston	79	2933	423	953	.444	209	251	.833	45	216	261	594	87	38	177	1062	3.3	7.5	13.4
87-88—Boston	77	2670	352	803	.438	255	298	.856	62	178	240	598	93	29	195	971	3.1	7.8	12.6
88-89—Boston	72	2309	277	638	.434	160	195	.821	31	159	190	472	94	21	175	721	2.6	6.6	10.0
89-90—Boston	75	2036	206	475	.434	118	140	.843	48	153	201	485	81	14	117	531	2.7	6.5	7.1
Totals	1100	35954	5832	13100	.445	3791	4754	.797	1459	2790	4249	5499	1477	675	2448	15535	3.9	5.0	14.1

Three-point field goals: 1979-80, 12-for-58 (.207). 1980-81, 11-for-51 (.216). 1981-82, 8-for-42 (.190). 1982-83, 5-for-31 (.161). 1983-84, 4-for-32 (.125). 1984-85, 7-for-26 (.269). 1985-86, 6-for-42 (.143). 1986-87, 7-for-62 (.113). 1987-88, 12-for-46 (.261). 1988-89, 7-for-50 (.140). 1989-90, 1-for-24 (.042). Totals, 80-for-464 (.172).

Personal fouls/disqualifications: 1976-77, 221/3. 1977-78, 213/2. 1978-79, 209/2. 1979-80, 267/6. 1980-81, 244/2. 1981-82, 253/6. 1982-83, 204/1. 1983-84, 251/6. 1984-85, 224/2. 1985-86, 206/3. 1986-87, 201/0. 1987-88, 204/0. 1988-89, 211/3. 1989-90, 179/2. Totals, 3087/38.

NOTES: NBA Finals Most Valuable Player (1979).

Season Team	G	Min.	FGM	FGA	Pct.	FTM	FTA	Pct.	Off.	Def.	Tot.	Ast.	St.	Blk.	TO	Pts.	RPG	APG	PPG
77-78—Seattle	22	827	121	294	.412	112	159	.704	47	54	101	72	23	23	56	354	4.6	3.3	16.1
78-79—Seattle	17	681	136	302	.450	84	109	.771	44	60	104	69	28	26	51	356	6.1	4.1	20.9
79-80—Seattle	15	582	100	244	.410	52	62	.839	25	39	64	57	27	10	43	257	4.3	3.8	17.1
80-81—Phoenix	7	267	52	110	.473	32	42	.762	7	26	33	20	9	9	19	137	4.7	2.9	19.6
81-82—Phoenix	7	271	63	132	.477	30	39	.769	13	18	31	32	15	4	25	156	4.4	4.6	22.3
82-83—Phoenix	3	108	22	48	.458	10	12	.833	6	17	23	17	5	2	8	54	7.7	5.7	18.0
83-84—Boston	22	808	129	319	.404	104	120	.867	30	49	79	97	25	7	53	365	3.6	4.4	16.6
84-85—Boston	21	848	142	319	.445	80	93	.860	24	60	84	154	31	9	72	364	4.0	7.3	17.3
85-86—Boston	18	715	109	245	.445	67	84	.798	23	53	76	107	39	5	51	291	4.2	5.9	16.2
86-87—Boston	23	964	168	361	.465	96	113	.850	24	67	91	205	16	8	44	435	4.0	8.9	18.9
87-88—Boston	17	702	91	210	.433	82	103	.796	15	62	77	139	24	8	45	270	4.5	8.2	15.9
88-89—Boston	3	59	4	15	.267	0	0		2	2	4	9	3	0	3	8	1.3	3.0	2.7
89-90—Boston	5	162	30	62	.484	7	7	1.000	2	12	14	28	2	2	10	69	2.8	5.6	13.8
Totals	180	6994	1167	2661	.439	756	943	.802	262	519	781	1006	247	113	480	3116	4.3	5.6	17.3

Three-point field goals: 1979-80, 5-for-15 (.333). 1980-81, 1-for-5 (.200). 1981-82, 0-for-4. 1982-83, 0-for-1. 1983-84, 3-for-7 (.429). 1984-85, 0-for-14. 1985-86, 6-for-16 (.375). 1986-87, 3-for-26 (.115). 1987-88, 6-for-16 (.375). 1989-90, 2-for-6 (.333). Totals, 26-for-110 (.236).

Personal fouls/disqualifications: 1977-78, 63/0. 1978-79, 63/0. 1979-80, 48/2. 1980-81, 18/0. 1981-82, 28/2. 1982-83, 9/0. 1983-84, 75/1. 1984-85, 66/0. 1985-86, 58/2. 1986-87, 71/0. 1987-88, 51/0. 1988-89, 8/0. 1989-90, 17/1. Totals, 575/8.

NBA ALL-STAR GAME RECORD

Season Team	Min.	FGM	FGA	Pct.	FTM	FTA	Pct.	Off.	Def.	Tot.	Ast.	PF	Dq.	St.	Blk.	TO	Pts.
1979 —Seattle	27	5	7	.714	2	2	1.000	1	0	1	3	3	0	0	1	1	12
1980 —Seattle	20	7	13	.538	5	6	.833	2	2	4	1	3	0	2	1	2	19
1981 —Phoenix	24	5	8	.625	9	10	.900	1	1	2	1	1	0	3	0	2	19
1982 —Phoenix	15	0	2	.000	1	2	.500	2	3	5	1	1	0	0	2	3	1
1985 —Boston	12	3	7	.429	2	2	1.000	1	5	6	3	2	0	0	0	1	8
Totals	98	20	37	.541	19	22	.864	7	11	18	9	10	0	5	4	9	59

CBA COACHING RECORD

Season Team	W	L	Pct.	Finish	W	L	Pct.
99-00 —La Crosse	14	22	.389		—	—	—

NOTES:
2000—Named assistant coach by Los Angeles Clippers (February 4).

JOHNSON, EDDIE   G/F

PERSONAL: Born May 1, 1959, in Chicago. ... 6-7/215 (2,00/97,5). ... Full name: Edward Arnet Johnson.
HIGH SCHOOL: Westinghouse Vocational (Chicago).
COLLEGE: Illinois.
TRANSACTIONS/CAREER NOTES: Selected by Kansas City Kings in second round (29th pick overall) of 1981 NBA Draft. ... Kings franchise moved from Kansas City to Sacramento for 1985-86 season. ... Traded by Kings to Phoenix Suns for F Ed Pinckney and 1988 second-round draft choice (June 21, 1987). ... Traded by Suns with 1991 first-round draft choice and 1993 or 1994 first-round draft choice to Seattle SuperSonics for F Xavier McDaniel (December 7, 1990). ... Traded by SuperSonics with G Dana Barros and option to switch 1994 first-round draft choices to Charlotte Hornets for G Kendall Gill (September 1, 1993). ... Played in Greece (1994-95). ... Signed as free agent by Indiana Pacers (October 3, 1995). ... Traded by Pacers with G Vincent Askew and 1997 and 1998 second-round draft choices to Denver Nuggets for F/C LaSalle Thompson and G Mark Jackson (February 20, 1997). ... Waived by Nuggets (February 27, 1997). ... Signed by Houston Rockets for remainder of season (March 3, 1997).

COLLEGIATE RECORD

Season Team	G	Min.	FGM	FGA	Pct.	FTM	FTA	Pct.	Reb.	Ast.	Pts.	RPG	APG	PPG
77-78—Illinois	27	469	100	234	.427	20	27	.741	84	16	220	3.1	0.6	8.1
78-79—Illinois	30	786	168	405	.415	26	49	.531	170	52	362	5.7	1.7	12.1
79-80—Illinois	35	1215	266	576	.462	78	119	.655	310	71	610	8.9	2.0	17.4
80-81—Illinois	29	1009	219	443	.494	62	82	.756	267	70	500	9.2	2.4	17.2
Totals	121	3479	753	1658	.454	186	277	.671	831	209	1692	6.9	1.7	14.0

NBA REGULAR-SEASON RECORD

HONORS: NBA Sixth Man Award (1989).

Season Team	G	Min.	FGM	FGA	Pct.	FTM	FTA	Pct.	Off.	Def.	Tot.	Ast.	St.	Blk.	TO	Pts.	RPG	APG	PPG
81-82—Kansas City	74	1517	295	643	.459	99	149	.664	128	194	322	109	50	14	97	690	4.4	1.5	9.3
82-83—Kansas City	82	2933	677	1370	.494	247	317	.779	191	310	501	216	70	20	181	1621	6.1	2.6	19.8
83-84—Kansas City	82	2920	753	1552	.485	268	331	.810	165	290	455	296	76	21	213	1794	5.5	3.6	21.9
84-85—Kansas City	82	3029	769	1565	.491	325	373	.871	151	256	407	273	83	22	225	1876	5.0	3.3	22.9
85-86—Sacramento	82	2514	623	1311	.475	280	343	.816	173	246	419	214	54	17	191	1530	5.1	2.6	18.7
86-87—Sacramento	81	2457	606	1309	.463	267	322	.829	146	207	353	251	42	19	163	1516	4.4	3.1	18.7
87-88—Phoenix	73	2177	533	1110	.480	204	240	.850	121	197	318	180	33	9	139	1294	4.4	2.5	17.7
88-89—Phoenix	70	2043	608	1224	.497	217	250	.868	91	215	306	162	47	7	122	1504	4.4	2.3	21.5
89-90—Phoenix	64	1811	411	907	.453	188	205	.917	69	177	246	107	32	10	108	1080	3.8	1.7	16.9
90-91—Phoe.-Seattle	81	2085	543	1122	.484	229	257	.891	107	164	271	111	58	9	122	1354	3.3	1.4	16.7
91-92—Seattle	81	2366	534	1164	.459	291	338	.861	118	174	292	161	55	11	130	1386	3.6	2.0	17.1
92-93—Seattle	82	1869	463	991	.467	234	257	.911	124	148	272	135	36	4	134	1177	3.3	1.6	14.4
93-94—Charlotte	73	1460	339	738	.459	99	127	.780	80	144	224	125	36	8	84	836	3.1	1.7	11.5
95-96—Indiana	62	1002	180	436	.413	70	79	.886	45	108	153	69	20	4	56	475	2.5	1.1	7.7
96-97—Ind.-Hou.	52	913	160	362	.442	55	68	.809	27	111	138	52	15	2	47	424	2.7	1.0	8.2
97-98—Houston	75	1490	227	544	.417	113	136	.831	50	103	153	88	32	3	62	633	2.0	1.2	8.4
98-99—Houston	3	18	6	13	.462	0	0		0	2	2	1	0	0	2	12	0.7	0.3	4.0
Totals	1199	32604	7727	16361	.472	3186	3792	.840	1786	3046	4832	2550	739	180	2076	19202	4.0	2.1	16.0

ALL-TIME GREAT PLAYERS

Three-point field goals: 1981-82, 1-for-11 (.091). 1982-83, 20-for-71 (.282). 1983-84, 20-for-64 (.313). 1984-85, 13-for-54 (.241). 1985-86, 4-for-20 (.200). 1986-87, 37-for-118 (.314). 1987-88, 24-for-94 (.255). 1988-89, 71-for-172 (.413). 1989-90, 70-for-184 (.380). 1990-91, 39-for-120 (.325). 1991-92, 27-for-107 (.252). 1992-93, 17-for-56 (.304). 1993-94, 59-for-150 (.393). 1995-96, 45-for-128 (.352). 1996-97, 49-for-131 (.374). 1997-98, 66-for-198 (.333). 1998-99, 0-for-1. Totals, 562-for-1679 (.335).

Personal fouls/disqualifications: 1981-82, 210/6. 1982-83, 259/3. 1983-84, 266/4. 1984-85, 237/2. 1985-86, 237/0. 1986-87, 218/4. 1987-88, 190/0. 1988-89, 198/0. 1989-90, 174/4. 1990-91, 181/0. 1991-92, 199/0. 1992-93, 173/0. 1993-94, 143/2. 1995-96, 104/1. 1996-97, 81/0. 1997-98, 89/0. 1998-99, 3/0. Totals, 2962/26.

NBA PLAYOFF RECORD

Season Team	G	Min.	FGM	FGA	Pct.	FTM	FTA	Pct.	Off.	Def.	Tot.	Ast.	St.	Blk.	TO	Pts.	RPG	APG	PPG
83-84—Kansas City.....	3	107	21	48	.438	7	7	1.000	4	6	10	12	3	1	2	51	3.3	4.0	17.0
85-86—Sacramento	3	96	24	55	.436	8	9	.889	10	11	21	4	3	1	6	56	7.0	1.3	18.7
88-89—Phoenix	12	392	85	206	.413	30	39	.769	28	59	87	25	12	2	18	213	7.3	2.1	17.8
89-90—Phoenix	16	337	72	160	.450	37	47	.787	15	42	57	17	10	4	20	196	3.6	1.1	12.3
90-91—Seattle	5	171	46	89	.517	24	29	.828	12	9	21	7	7	1	8	120	4.2	1.4	24.0
91-92—Seattle	9	247	65	137	.474	32	34	.941	8	19	27	8	3	3	15	166	3.0	0.9	18.4
92-93—Seattle	19	382	82	210	.390	29	31	.935	17	28	45	17	3	1	19	205	2.4	0.9	10.8
95-96—Indiana...........	1	9	0	5	.000	0	0	...	0	0	0	1	0	0	0	0	0.0	1.0	0.0
96-97—Houston.........	16	284	48	117	.410	23	24	.958	15	21	36	10	5	0	7	133	2.3	0.6	8.3
97-98—Houston.........	5	89	9	27	.333	7	8	.875	4	4	8	1	0	0	3	28	1.6	0.2	5.6
Totals	**89**	**2114**	**452**	**1054**	**.429**	**197**	**228**	**.864**	**113**	**199**	**312**	**102**	**46**	**13**	**98**	**1168**	**3.5**	**1.1**	**13.1**

Three-point field goals: 1983-84, 2-for-5 (.400). 1985-86, 0-for-3. 1988-89, 13-for-38 (.342). 1989-90, 15-for-38 (.395). 1990-91, 4-for-15 (.267). 1991-92, 4-for-22 (.182). 1992-93, 12-for-36 (.333). 1995-96, 0-for-2. 1996-97, 14-for-47 (.298). 1997-98, 3-for-10 (.300). Totals, 67-for-216 (.310).

Personal fouls/disqualifications: 1983-84, 8/0. 1985-86, 7/0. 1988-89, 41/1. 1989-90, 40/0. 1990-91, 13/0. 1991-92, 19/0. 1992-93, 44/2. 1996-97, 17/0. 1997-98, 10/0. Totals, 199/3.

GREEK LEAGUE RECORD

Season Team	G	Min.	FGM	FGA	Pct.	FTM	FTA	Pct.	Reb.	Ast.	Pts.	RPG	APG	PPG
94-95—Olympiakos S.F.P.	25	829	188	419	.449	92	109	.844	122	48	527	4.9	1.9	21.1

JOHNSON, GUS   F

PERSONAL: Born December 13, 1938, in Akron, Ohio. ... Died April 29, 1987. ... 6-6/235 (1,98/106,6). ... Full name: Gus Johnson Jr. ... Nickname: Honeycomb.
HIGH SCHOOL: Central Hower (Akron, Ohio).
JUNIOR COLLEGE: Boise (Idaho) Junior College.
COLLEGE: Akron, then Idaho.
TRANSACTIONS: Selected by Baltimore Bullets in second round (11th pick overall) of 1963 NBA Draft. ... Traded by Bullets to Phoenix Suns for second-round draft choice (April 10, 1972). ... Waived by Suns (December 1, 1972). ... Signed as free agent by Indiana Pacers of American Basketball Association (December 15, 1972).

COLLEGIATE RECORD

NOTES: Left Akron before start of 1959-60 basketball season.

Season Team	G	Min.	FGM	FGA	Pct.	FTM	FTA	Pct.	Reb.	Ast.	Pts.	RPG	APG	PPG
62-63—Idaho.............................	23	...	188	438	.429	62	105	.590	466	...	438	20.3	...	19.0

NBA REGULAR-SEASON RECORD

HONORS: All-NBA second team (1965, 1966, 1970, 1971). ... NBA All-Defensive first team (1970, 1971). ... NBA All-Rookie team (1964).

Season Team	G	Min.	FGM	FGA	Pct.	FTM	FTA	Pct.	Reb.	Ast.	PF	Dq.	Pts.	RPG	APG	PPG
63-64 —Baltimore	78	2847	571	1329	.430	210	319	.658	1064	169	321	†11	1352	13.6	2.2	17.3
64-65 —Baltimore	76	2899	577	1379	.418	261	386	.676	988	270	258	4	1415	13.0	3.6	18.6
65-66 —Baltimore	41	1284	273	661	.413	131	178	.736	546	114	136	3	677	13.3	2.8	16.5
66-67 —Baltimore	73	2626	620	1377	.450	271	383	.708	855	194	281	7	1511	11.7	2.7	20.7
67-68 —Baltimore	60	2271	482	1033	.467	180	270	.667	782	159	223	7	1144	13.0	2.7	19.1
68-69 —Baltimore	49	1671	359	782	.459	160	223	.717	568	97	176	1	878	11.6	2.0	17.9
69-70 —Baltimore	78	2919	578	1282	.451	197	272	.724	1086	264	269	6	1353	13.9	3.4	17.3
70-71 —Baltimore	66	2538	494	1090	.453	214	290	.738	1128	192	227	4	1202	17.1	2.9	18.2
71-72 —Baltimore	39	668	103	269	.383	43	63	.683	226	51	91	0	249	5.8	1.3	6.4
72-73 —Phoenix	21	417	69	181	.381	25	36	.694	136	31	55	0	163	6.5	1.5	7.8
Totals................................	**581**	**20140**	**4126**	**9383**	**.440**	**1692**	**2420**	**.699**	**7379**	**1541**	**2037**	**43**	**9944**	**12.7**	**2.7**	**17.1**

NBA PLAYOFF RECORD

Season Team	G	Min.	FGM	FGA	Pct.	FTM	FTA	Pct.	Reb.	Ast.	PF	Dq.	Pts.	RPG	APG	PPG
64-65 —Baltimore	10	377	62	173	.358	34	46	.739	111	34	38	1	158	11.1	3.4	15.8
65-66 —Baltimore	1	8	1	4	.250	0	0	...	0	0	1	0	2	0.0	0.0	2.0
69-70 —Baltimore	7	298	51	111	.459	27	34	.794	80	9	20	0	129	11.4	1.3	18.4
70-71 —Baltimore	11	365	54	128	.422	35	47	.745	114	30	34	0	143	10.4	2.7	13.0
71-72 —Baltimore	5	77	9	30	.300	2	2	1.000	25	3	17	0	20	5.0	0.6	4.0
Totals................................	**34**	**1125**	**177**	**446**	**.397**	**98**	**129**	**.760**	**330**	**76**	**110**	**1**	**452**	**9.7**	**2.2**	**13.3**

NBA ALL-STAR GAME RECORD

Season Team	Min.	FGM	FGA	Pct.	FTM	FTA	Pct.	Reb	Ast.	PF	Dq.	Pts.
1965 —Baltimore....................	25	7	13	.538	11	13	.846	8	2	2	0	25
1968 —Baltimore....................	16	3	9	.333	1	2	.500	6	1	2	0	7
1969 —Baltimore....................	18	4	10	.400	5	8	.625	10	0	3	0	13

	G				Pct.	FGM	FGA	Pct.	FTM	FTA	Pct.	Reb.	Ast.	Pts.		RPG		PPG
1970 —Baltimore	17	5	12	.417	0	0	...		7	1	2	0	10
1971 —Baltimore	23	5	12	.417	2	2	1.000		4	2	3	0	12
Totals	99	24	56	.429	19	25	.760		35	6	12	0	67

ABA REGULAR-SEASON RECORD

NOTES: Member of ABA championship team (1973).

			2-POINT			3-POINT									AVERAGES		
Season Team	G	Min.	FGM	FGA	Pct.	FGM	FGA	Pct.	FTM	FTA	Pct.	Reb.	Ast.	Pts.	RPG	APG	PPG
72-73—Indiana	50	753	128	278	.460	4	21	.190	31	42	.738	245	62	299	4.9	1.2	6.0

ABA PLAYOFF RECORD

			2-POINT			3-POINT									AVERAGES		
Season Team	G	Min.	FGM	FGA	Pct.	FGM	FGA	Pct.	FTM	FTA	Pct.	Reb.	Ast.	Pts.	RPG	APG	PPG
72-73—Indiana	17	184	15	56	.268	0	3	.000	12	16	.750	69	15	42	4.1	0.9	2.5

COMBINED ABA AND NBA REGULAR-SEASON RECORDS

								REBOUNDS								AVERAGES		
	G	Min.	FGM	FGA	Pct.	FTM	FTA	Pct.	Off.	Def.	Tot.	Ast.	Stl.	Blk.	TO	Pts.	RPG	APG	PPG
Totals	631	20893	4258	9682	.440	1723	2462	.700	...	...	7624	1603	...	...		10243	12.1	2.5	16.2

Three-point field goals: 4-for-21 (.190).
Personal fouls/disqualifications: 2150.

JOHNSON, KEVIN   G

PERSONAL: Born March 4, 1966, in Sacramento. ... 6-1/190. (1.85 m/86 kg). ... Full Name: Kevin Maurice Johnson. ... Nickname: K.J.
HIGH SCHOOL: Sacramento.
COLLEGE: California.
TRANSACTIONS/CAREER NOTES: Selected by Cleveland Cavaliers in first round (seventh pick overall) of 1987 NBA Draft. ... Traded by Cavaliers with G/F Tyrone Corbin, F/C Mark West, 1988 first- and second-round draft choices and 1989 second-round draft choice to Phoenix Suns for F Larry Nance, F Mike Sanders and 1988 second-round draft choice (February 25, 1988). ... Announced retirement (October 12, 1999). ... Activated from retirement (March 25, 2000). ... Announced retirement (August 8, 2000).
MISCELLANEOUS: Member of gold-medal winning U.S. World Championship team (1994). ... Phoenix Suns all-time assists leader with 6,518 (1987-88 through 1997-98 and 1999-2000).

COLLEGIATE RECORD

												AVERAGES		
Season Team	G	Min.	FGM	FGA	Pct.	FTM	FTA	Pct.	Reb.	Ast.	Pts.	RPG	APG	PPG
83-84—California	28	773	98	192	.510	75	104	.721	83	65	271	3.0	2.3	9.7
84-85—California	27	902	127	282	.450	94	142	.662	104	111	348	3.9	4.1	12.9
85-86—California	29	1024	164	335	.490	123	151	.815	104	175	451	3.6	6.0	15.6
86-87—California	34	1115	212	450	.471	113	138	.819	132	170	585	3.9	5.0	17.2
Totals	118	3814	601	1259	.477	405	535	.757	423	521	1655	3.6	4.4	14.0

Three-point field goals: 1986-87, 48-for-124 (.387).

NBA REGULAR-SEASON RECORD

HONORS: NBA Most Improved Player (1989). ... All-NBA second team (1989, 1990, 1991, 1994). ... All-NBA third team (1992).

									REBOUNDS								AVERAGES		
Season Team	G	Min.	FGM	FGA	Pct.	FTM	FTA	Pct.	Off.	Def.	Tot.	Ast.	St.	Blk.	TO	Pts.	RPG	APG	PPG
87-88—Cle.-Phoenix	80	1917	275	596	.461	177	211	.839	36	155	191	437	103	24	146	732	2.4	5.5	9.2
88-89—Phoenix	81	3179	570	1128	.505	508	576	.882	46	294	340	991	135	24	&322	1650	4.2	12.2	20.4
89-90—Phoenix	74	2782	578	1159	.499	501	598	.838	42	228	270	846	95	14	263	1665	3.6	11.4	22.5
90-91—Phoenix	77	2772	591	1145	.516	519	616	.843	54	217	271	781	163	11	269	1710	3.5	10.1	22.2
91-92—Phoenix	78	2899	539	1125	.479	448	555	.807	61	231	292	836	116	23	272	1536	3.7	10.7	19.7
92-93—Phoenix	49	1643	282	565	.499	226	276	.819	30	74	104	384	85	19	151	791	2.1	7.8	16.1
93-94—Phoenix	67	2449	477	980	.487	380	464	.819	55	112	167	637	125	10	235	1340	2.5	9.5	20.0
94-95—Phoenix	47	1352	246	523	.470	234	289	.810	32	83	115	360	47	18	105	730	2.4	7.7	15.5
95-96—Phoenix	56	2007	342	674	.507	342	398	.859	42	179	221	517	82	13	170	1047	3.9	9.2	18.7
96-97—Phoenix	70	2658	441	890	.496	439	515	.852	54	199	253	653	102	12	217	1410	3.6	9.3	20.1
97-98—Phoenix	50	1290	155	347	.447	162	186	.871	35	129	164	245	27	8	101	476	3.3	4.9	9.5
99-00—Phoenix	6	113	16	28	.571	7	7	1.000	0	16	16	24	2	0	7	40	2.7	4.0	6.7
Totals	735	25061	4512	9160	.493	3943	4691	.841	487	1917	2404	6711	1082	176	2258	13127	3.3	9.1	17.9

Three-point field goals: 1987-88, 5-for-24 (.208). 1988-89, 2-for-22 (.091). 1989-90, 8-for-41 (.195). 1990-91, 9-for-44 (.205). 1991-92, 10-for-46 (.217). 1992-93, 1-for-8 (.125). 1993-94, 6-for-27 (.222). 1994-95, 4-for-26 (.154). 1995-96, 21-for-57 (.368). 1996-97, 89-for-202 (.441). 1997-98, 4-for-26 (.154). 1999-00, 1 for 1. Totals, 160-for-524 (.305).
Personal fouls/disqualifications: 1987-88, 155/1. 1988-89, 226/1. 1989-90, 143/0. 1990-91, 174/0. 1991-92, 180/0. 1992-93, 100/0. 1993-94, 127/1. 1994-95, 88/0. 1995-96, 144/0. 1996-97, 141/0. 1997-98, 57/0. 1999-00, 6/0. Totals, 1541/3.

NBA PLAYOFF RECORD

NOTES: Holds NBA Finals single-game record for most minutes played—62 (June 13, 1993, at Chicago, 3 OT).

									REBOUNDS								AVERAGES		
Season Team	G	Min.	FGM	FGA	Pct.	FTM	FTA	Pct.	Off.	Def.	Tot.	Ast.	St.	Blk.	TO	Pts.	RPG	APG	PPG
88-89—Phoenix	12	494	90	182	.495	102	110	.927	12	39	51	147	19	5	55	285	4.3	12.3	23.8
89-90—Phoenix	16	582	123	257	.479	92	112	.821	9	44	53	170	25	0	62	340	3.3	10.6	21.3
90-91—Phoenix	4	146	16	53	.302	18	30	.600	2	11	13	39	2	1	12	51	3.3	9.8	12.8
91-92—Phoenix	8	335	62	128	.484	62	72	.861	8	25	33	93	12	2	25	189	4.1	11.6	23.6
92-93—Phoenix	23	914	143	298	.480	124	156	.795	10	52	62	182	35	13	84	410	2.7	7.9	17.8
93-94—Phoenix	10	427	97	212	.458	69	81	.852	10	25	35	96	10	1	34	266	3.5	9.6	26.6
94-95—Phoenix	10	371	86	150	.573	71	84	.845	7	34	41	93	9	4	34	248	4.1	9.3	24.8
95-96—Phoenix	4	151	27	57	.474	14	17	.824	2	15	17	43	2	2	11	69	4.3	10.8	17.3
96-97—Phoenix	5	208	26	88	.295	29	33	.879	8	14	22	30	13	0	18	84	4.4	6.0	16.8

Season Team	G	Min.	FGM	FGA	Pct.	FTM	FTA	Pct.	Off.	Def.	Tot.	Ast.	St.	Blk.	TO	Pts.	RPG	APG	PPG
97-98—Phoenix	4	122	23	42	.548	8	12	.667	2	7	9	19	2	1	6	55	2.3	4.8	13.8
99-00—Phoenix	9	129	12	37	.324	5	6	.833	0	13	13	23	3	1	13	29	1.4	2.6	3.2
Totals	105	3879	705	1504	.469	594	713	.833	70	279	349	935	132	30	354	2026	3.3	8.9	19.3

Three-point field goals: 1988-89, 3-for-10 (.300). 1989-90, 2-for-11 (.182). 1990-91, 1-for-7 (.143). 1991-92, 3-for-6 (.500). 1992-93, 0-for-3. 1993-94, 3-for-10 (.300). 1994-95, 5-for-10 (.500). 1995-96, 1-for-4 (.250). 1996-97, 3-for-22 (.136). 1997-98, 1-for-4 (.250). 1999-00, 0-for-3. Totals, 22-for-90 (.244).

Personal fouls/disqualifications: 1988-89, 28/0. 1989-90, 28/0. 1990-91, 9/0. 1991-92, 24/1. 1992-93, 57/1. 1993-94, 23/0. 1994-95, 25/0. 1995-96, 8/0. 1996-97, 15/1. 1997-98, 6/0. 1999-00, 10/0. Totals, 233/3.

NBA ALL-STAR GAME RECORD

Season Team	Min.	FGM	FGA	Pct.	FTM	FTA	Pct.	REBOUNDS Off.	Def.	Tot.	Ast.	PF	Dq.	St.	Blk.	TO	Pts.
1990 —Phoenix	14	1	1	1.000	0	0	...	0	0	0	4	2	0	0	0	3	2
1991 —Phoenix	23	2	5	.400	1	2	.500	1	1	2	7	2	0	3	1	3	5
1994 —Phoenix	14	3	6	.500	0	1	.000	0	1	1	2	1	0	1	0	2	6
Totals	51	6	12	.500	1	3	.333	1	2	3	13	5	0	4	1	8	13

JOHNSON, MAGIC   G

PERSONAL: Born August 14, 1959, in Lansing, Mich. ... 6-9/255 (2,05/115,7). ... Full name: Earvin Johnson Jr.
HIGH SCHOOL: Everett (Lansing, Mich.).
COLLEGE: Michigan State.
TRANSACTIONS: Selected after sophomore season by Los Angeles Lakers in first round (first pick overall) of 1979 NBA Draft. ... On voluntarily retired list (November 7, 1991-January 29, 1996). ... Activated from retirement by Lakers (January 29, 1996). ... Announced retirement (May 14, 1996). ... Rights renounced by Lakers (July 16, 1996).
CAREER NOTES: Broadcaster, NBC Sports (1992 through 1994). ... Vice president, Los Angeles Lakers (1994-95 to present).
CAREER HONORS: One of the 50 Greatest Players in NBA History (1996).
MISCELLANEOUS: Member of NBA championship team (1980, 1982, 1985, 1987, 1988). ... Member of gold-medal-winning U.S. Olympic team (1992). ... Los Angeles Lakers franchise all-time assists leader with 10,141 and all-time steals leader with 1,724 (1979-80 through 1990-91 and 1995-96).

COLLEGIATE RECORD

NOTES: Member of NCAA championship team (1979). ... NCAA Division I Tournament Most Outstanding Player (1979). ... THE SPORTING NEWS All-America first team (1979).

Season Team	G	Min.	FGM	FGA	Pct.	FTM	FTA	Pct.	Reb.	Ast.	Pts.	AVERAGES RPG	APG	PPG
77-78—Michigan State	30	...	175	382	.458	161	205	.785	237	222	511	7.9	7.4	17.0
78-79—Michigan State	32	1159	173	370	.468	202	240	.842	234	269	548	7.3	8.4	17.1
Totals	62	...	348	752	.463	363	445	.816	471	491	1059	7.6	7.9	17.1

NBA REGULAR-SEASON RECORD

RECORDS: Holds career record for highest assists-per-game average—11.2. ... Shares career record for most consecutive seasons leading league in steals—2.
HONORS: NBA Most Valuable Player (1987, 1989, 1990). ... IBM Award, for all-around contributions to team's success (1984). ... All-NBA first team (1983, 1984, 1985, 1986, 1987, 1988, 1989, 1990, 1991). ... All-NBA second team (1982). ... NBA All-Rookie team (1980). ... J. Walter Kennedy Citizenship Award (1992).
NOTES: Led NBA with 3.43 steals per game (1981) and 2.67 steals per game (1982).

Season Team	G	Min.	FGM	FGA	Pct.	FTM	FTA	Pct.	REBOUNDS Off.	Def.	Tot.	Ast.	St.	Blk.	TO	Pts.	AVERAGES RPG	APG	PPG
79-80—Los Angeles	77	2795	503	949	.530	374	462	.810	166	430	596	563	187	41	305	1387	7.7	7.3	18.0
80-81—Los Angeles	37	1371	312	587	.532	171	225	.760	101	219	320	317	127	27	143	798	8.6	8.6	21.6
81-82—Los Angeles	78	2991	556	1036	.537	329	433	.760	252	499	751	743	208	34	286	1447	9.6	9.5	18.6
82-83—Los Angeles	79	2907	511	933	.548	304	380	.800	214	469	683	*829	176	47	301	1326	8.6	*10.5	16.8
83-84—Los Angeles	67	2567	441	780	.565	290	358	.810	99	392	491	875	150	49	306	1178	7.3	*13.1	17.6
84-85—L.A. Lakers	77	2781	504	899	.561	391	464	.843	90	386	476	968	113	25	305	1406	6.2	12.6	18.3
85-86—L.A. Lakers	72	2578	483	918	.526	378	434	.871	85	341	426	*907	113	16	273	1354	5.9	*12.6	18.8
86-87—L.A. Lakers	80	2904	683	1308	.522	535	631	.848	122	382	504	*977	138	36	300	1909	6.3	*12.2	23.9
87-88—L.A. Lakers	72	2637	490	996	.492	417	489	.853	88	361	449	858	114	13	269	1408	6.2	11.9	19.6
88-89—L.A. Lakers	77	2886	579	1137	.509	513	563	*.911	111	496	607	988	138	22	312	1730	7.9	12.8	22.5
89-90—L.A. Lakers	79	2937	546	1138	.480	567	637	.890	128	394	522	907	132	34	289	1765	6.6	11.5	22.3
90-91—L.A. Lakers	79	2933	466	976	.477	519	573	.906	105	446	551	989	102	17	*314	1531	7.0	12.5	19.4
91-92—L.A. Lakers						Did not play—retired.													
92-93—L.A. Lakers						Did not play—retired.													
93-94—L.A. Lakers						Did not play—retired.													
94-95—L.A. Lakers						Did not play—retired.													
95-96—L.A. Lakers	32	958	137	294	.466	172	201	.856	40	143	183	220	26	13	103	468	5.7	6.9	14.6
Totals	906	33245	6211	11951	.520	4960	5850	.848	1601	4958	6559	10141	1724	374	3506	17707	7.2	11.2	19.5

Three-point field goals: 1979-80, 7-for-31 (.226). 1980-81, 3-for-17 (.176). 1981-82, 6-for-29 (.207). 1982-83, 0-for-21. 1983-84, 6-for-29 (.207). 1984-85, 7-for-37 (.189). 1985-86, 10-for-43 (.233). 1986-87, 8-for-39 (.205). 1987-88, 11-for-56 (.196). 1988-89, 59-for-188 (.314). 1989-90, 106-for-276 (.384). 1990-91, 80-for-250 (.320). 1995-96, 22-for-58 (.379). Totals, 325-for-1074 (.303).

Personal fouls/disqualifications: 1979-80, 218/1. 1980-81, 100/0. 1981-82, 223/1. 1982-83, 200/1. 1983-84, 169/1. 1984-85, 155/0. 1985-86, 133/0. 1986-87, 168/0. 1987-88, 147/0. 1988-89, 172/0. 1989-90, 167/1. 1990-91, 150/0. 1995-96, 48/0. Totals, 2050/5.

NBA PLAYOFF RECORD

NOTES: NBA Finals Most Valuable Player (1980, 1982, 1987). ... Holds career playoff record for most assists—2,346. ... Holds NBA Finals single-series records for highest assists-per-game average—14.0 (1985); and highest assists-per-game average by a rookie—8.7 (1980). ... Holds NBA Finals single-game records for most points by a rookie—42 (May 16, 1980, vs. Philadelphia); most assists—21 (June 3, 1984, vs. Boston); most assists by a rookie—11 (May 7, 1980, vs. Philadelphia); and most assists in one half—14 (June 19, 1988, vs. Detroit). ... Shares NBA Finals single-game record for most assists in one quarter—8 (four times). ... Holds single-series playoff record for highest assists-per-game average—17.0 (1985). ... Shares single-game playoff records for most free throws made in one half—19 (May 8, 1991, vs. Golden State); most assists—24 (May 15, 1984, vs. Phoenix); and most assists in one half—15 (May 3, 1985, vs. Portland).

REBOUNDS	AVERAGES

Season Team	G	Min.	FGM	FGA	Pct.	FTM	FTA	Pct.	Off.	Def.	Tot.	Ast.	St.	Blk.	TO	Pts.	RPG	APG	PPG
79-80—Los Angeles....	16	658	103	199	.518	85	106	.802	52	116	168	151	49	6	65	293	10.5	9.4	18.3
80-81—Los Angeles....	3	127	19	49	.388	13	20	.650	8	33	41	21	8	3	11	51	13.7	7.0	17.0
81-82—Los Angeles....	14	562	83	157	.529	77	93	.828	54	104	158	130	40	3	44	243	11.3	9.3	17.4
82-83—Los Angeles....	15	643	100	206	.485	68	81	.840	51	77	128	192	34	12	64	268	8.5	12.8	17.9
83-84—Los Angeles....	21	837	151	274	.551	80	100	.800	26	113	139	284	42	20	79	382	6.6	13.5	18.2
84-85—L.A. Lakers	19	687	116	226	.513	100	118	.847	19	115	134	289	32	4	76	333	7.1	15.2	17.5
85-86—L.A. Lakers	14	541	110	205	.537	82	107	.766	21	79	100	211	27	1	45	302	7.1	15.1	21.6
86-87—L.A. Lakers	18	666	146	271	.539	98	118	.831	28	111	139	219	31	7	51	392	7.7	12.2	21.8
87-88—L.A. Lakers	24	965	169	329	.514	132	155	.852	32	98	130	303	34	4	83	477	5.4	12.6	19.9
88-89—L.A. Lakers	14	518	85	174	.489	78	86	.907	15	68	83	165	27	3	53	258	5.9	11.8	18.4
89-90—L.A. Lakers	9	376	76	155	.490	70	79	.886	12	45	57	115	11	1	36	227	6.3	12.8	25.2
90-91—L.A. Lakers	19	823	168	268	.440	157	178	.882	23	131	154	240	23	0	77	414	8.1	12.6	21.8
95-96—L.A. Lakers	4	135	15	39	.385	28	33	.848	8	26	34	26	0	0	12	61	8.5	6.5	15.3
Totals	190	7538	1291	2552	.506	1068	1274	.838	349	1116	1465	2346	358	64	696	3701	7.7	12.3	19.5

Three-point field goals: 1979-80, 2-for-8 (.250). 1981-82, 0-for-4. 1982-83, 0-for-11. 1983-84, 0-for-7. 1984-85, 1-for-7 (.143). 1985-86, 0-for-11. 1986-87, 2-for-10 (.200). 1987-88, 7-for-14 (.500). 1988-89, 10-for-35 (.286). 1989-90, 5-for-25 (.200). 1990-91, 21-for-71 (.296). 1995-96, 3-for-9 (.333). Totals, 51-for-212 (.241).

Personal fouls/disqualifications: 1979-80, 47/1. 1980-81, 14/1. 1981-82, 50/0. 1982-83, 49/0. 1983-84, 71/0. 1984-85, 48/0. 1985-86, 43/0. 1986-87, 37/0. 1987-88, 61/0. 1988-89, 30/1. 1989-90, 28/0. 1990-91, 43/0. 1995-96, 3/0. Totals, 524/3.

NBA ALL-STAR GAME RECORD

NOTES: NBA All-Star Game Most Valuable Player (1990, 1992). ... Holds career records for most assists—127; and most three-point field goals made—10. ... Holds single-game record for most assists—22 (1984, OT).

								REBOUNDS								
Season	Team	Min.	FGM	FGA	Pct.	FTM	FTA	Pct.	Off.	Def.	Tot.	Ast.	PF	Dq.	St.	Blk.	TO	Pts.
1980	—Los Angeles	24	5	8	.625	2	2	1.000	2	0	2	4	3	0	3	2	2	12
1982	—Los Angeles	23	5	9	.556	6	7	.857	3	1	4	7	5	0	0	1	1	16
1983	—Los Angeles	33	7	16	.438	3	4	.750	3	2	5	16	2	0	5	0	7	17
1984	—Los Angeles	37	6	13	.462	2	2	1.000	4	5	9	22	3	0	3	2	4	15
1985	—L.A. Lakers	31	7	14	.500	7	8	.875	2	3	5	15	2	0	1	0	3	21
1986	—L.A. Lakers	28	1	3	.333	4	4	1.000	0	4	4	15	4	0	1	0	9	6
1987	—L.A. Lakers	34	4	10	.400	1	2	.500	1	6	7	13	2	0	4	0	1	9
1988	—L.A. Lakers	39	4	15	.267	9	9	1.000	1	5	6	19	2	0	2	2	8	17
1989	—L.A. Lakers							Selected, did not play—injured.										
1990	—L.A. Lakers	25	9	15	.600	0	0	...	1	5	6	4	1	0	0	1	3	22
1991	—L.A. Lakers	28	7	16	.438	0	0	...	1	3	4	3	1	0	0	0	3	16
1992	—L.A. Lakers	29	9	12	.750	4	4	1.000	3	2	5	9	0	0	2	0	7	25
Totals		331	64	131	.489	38	42	.905	21	36	57	127	25	0	21	7	48	176

Three-point field goals: 1980, 0-for-1. 1983, 0-for-1. 1984, 1-for-3 (.333). 1986, 0-for-1. 1988, 0-for-1. 1990, 4-for-6 (.667). 1991, 2-for-5 (.400). 1992, 3-for-3. Totals, 10-for-21 (.476).

NBA COACHING RECORD

	REGULAR SEASON				PLAYOFFS		
Season Team	W	L	Pct.	Finish	W	L	Pct.
93-94 —L.A. Lakers	5	11	.313	5th/Pacific Division	—	—	—

NOTES:

1994—Replaced Randy Pfund (27-37) and Bill Bertka (1-1) as Los Angeles Lakers head coach (March 27), with record of 28-38 and club in fifth place.

JOHNSTON, NEIL   C

PERSONAL: Born February 4, 1929, in Chillicothe, Ohio. ... Died September 27, 1978. ... 6-8/210 (2,03/95,3). ... Full name: Donald Neil Johnston. ... Nickname: Gabby.
HIGH SCHOOL: Chillicothe (Ohio).
COLLEGE: Ohio State.
TRANSACTIONS: Signed as free agent by Philadelphia Warriors (1951). ... Signed as player/head coach by Pittsburgh Rens of American Basketball League (1961).
CAREER HONORS: Elected to Naismith Memorial Basketball Hall of Fame (1990).
MISCELLANEOUS: Member of NBA championship team (1956).

COLLEGIATE RECORD

NOTES: Signed pro baseball contract in 1948 and became ineligible for his final two years at Ohio State.

												AVERAGES		
Season Team	G	Min.	FGM	FGA	Pct.	FTM	FTA	Pct.	Reb.	Ast.	Pts.	RPG	APG	PPG
46-47—Ohio State	7	...	5	...	...	3	8	.375	...	...	13	...	...	1.9
47-48—Ohio State	20	...	67	219	.306	46	87	.529	...	...	180	...	...	9.0
Totals	27	...	72	...	...	49	95	.516	...	...	193	...	...	7.1

NBA REGULAR-SEASON RECORD

HONORS: All-NBA first team (1953, 1954, 1955, 1956). ... All-NBA second team (1957).

														AVERAGES		
Season Team	G	Min.	FGM	FGA	Pct.	FTM	FTA	Pct.	Reb.	Ast.	PF	Dq.	Pts.	RPG	APG	PPG
51-52 —Philadelphia	64	993	141	299	.472	100	151	.662	342	39	154	5	382	5.3	0.6	6.0
52-53 —Philadelphia	70	*3166	*504	1114	*.452	*556	*794	.700	976	197	248	6	*1564	13.9	2.8	*22.3
53-54 —Philadelphia	72	*3296	*591	*1317	.449	*577	*772	.747	797	203	259	7	*1759	11.1	2.8	*24.4
54-55 —Philadelphia	72	2917	521	1184	.440	*589	*769	.766	*1085	215	255	4	*1631	*15.1	3.0	*22.7
55-56 —Philadelphia	70	2594	499	1092	*.457	549	685	.801	872	225	251	8	1547	12.5	3.2	22.1
56-57 —Philadelphia	69	2531	520	1163	*.447	535	648	.826	855	203	231	2	1575	12.4	2.9	22.8
57-58 —Philadelphia	71	2408	473	1102	.429	442	540	.819	790	166	233	4	1388	11.1	2.3	19.5
58-59 —Philadelphia	28	393	54	164	.329	69	88	.784	139	21	50	0	177	5.0	0.8	6.3
Totals	516	18298	3303	7435	.444	3417	4447	.768	5856	1269	1681	36	10023	11.3	2.5	19.4

NBA PLAYOFF RECORD

Season Team	G	Min.	FGM	FGA	Pct.	FTM	FTA	Pct.	Reb.	Ast.	PF	Dq.	Pts.	AVERAGES RPG	APG	PPG
51-52 —Philadelphia	3	32	5	10	.500	6	8	.750	10	1	8	0	16	3.3	0.3	5.3
55-56 —Philadelphia	10	397	69	169	.408	65	92	.707	143	51	41	0	203	14.3	5.1	20.3
56-57 —Philadelphia	2	84	17	53	.321	4	6	.667	35	9	9	0	38	17.5	4.5	19.0
57-58 —Philadelphia	8	189	30	78	.385	27	33	.818	69	14	18	0	87	8.6	1.8	10.9
Totals	23	702	121	310	.390	102	139	.734	257	75	76	0	344	11.2	3.3	15.0

NBA ALL-STAR GAME RECORD

Season Team	Min.	FGM	FGA	Pct.	FTM	FTA	Pct.	Reb.	Ast.	PF	Dq.	Pts.
1953 —Philadelphia	27	5	13	.385	1	2	.500	12	0	2	0	11
1954 —Philadelphia	20	2	9	.222	2	4	.500	7	2	1	0	6
1955 —Philadelphia	15	1	7	.143	1	1	1.000	6	1	0	0	3
1956 —Philadelphia	25	5	9	.556	7	11	.636	10	1	3	0	17
1957 —Philadelphia	23	8	12	.667	3	3	1.000	9	1	2	0	19
1958 —Philadelphia	22	6	13	.462	2	2	1.000	8	1	5	0	14
Totals	132	27	63	.429	16	23	.696	52	6	13	0	70

ABL REGULAR-SEASON RECORD

Season Team	G	Min.	FGM	FGA	Pct.	FTM	FTA	Pct.	Reb.	Ast.	Pts.	AVERAGES RPG	APG	PPG
61-62—Pittsburgh	5	106	15	37	.405	24	16	1.500	18	10	49	3.6	2.0	9.8

HEAD COACHING RECORD

BACKGROUND: Player/head coach, Pittsburgh Rens of American Basketball League (1961-62).

NBA COACHING RECORD

Season Team	REGULAR SEASON W	L	Pct.	Finish		PLAYOFFS W	L	Pct.
59-60 —Philadelphia	49	26	.653	2nd/Eastern Division		4	5	.444
60-61 —Philadelphia	46	33	.582	2nd/Eastern Division		0	3	.000
Totals (2 years)	95	59	.617		Totals (2 years)	4	8	.333

ABL COACHING RECORD

Season Team	W	L	Pct.	Finish		W	L	Pct.
61-62 —Pittsburgh	41	40	.506	2nd/Eastern Division		0	1	.000
62-63 —Pittsburgh	12	10	.545	3rd		—	—	—
Totals (2 years)	53	50	.515		Totals (1 year)	0	1	.000

EBL COACHING RECORD

Season Team	W	L	Pct.	Finish		W	L	Pct.
64-65 —Wilmington	12	16	.429	5th		—	—	—
65-66 —Wilmington	20	8	.714	1st/Eastern Division		4	2	.667
Totals (2 years)	32	24	.571		Totals (1 year)	4	2	.667

NOTES:
1960—Defeated Syracuse, 2-1, in Eastern Division Semifinals; lost to Boston, 4-2, in Eastern Division Finals.
1961—Lost to Syracuse in Eastern Division Semifinals.
1962—ABL disbanded (December 31).
1966—Defeated Trenton, 2-1, in Eastern Finals; defeated Wilkes-Barre, 2-1, in EBL Finals.

RECORD AS BASEBALL PLAYER

TRANSACTION/CAREER NOTES: Signed by Philadelphia Phillies organization (August 1948). ... Released by Phillies organization (June 1, 1952).

Year Team (League)	G	W	L	Pct.	ERA	Sv.	IP	H	R	ER	BB	SO
1949—Terre Haute (Three I)	29	10	12	.455	3.14	...	166	159	85	58	73	129
1950—Terre Haute (Three I)	28	11	12	.478	2.89	...	168	132	78	54	102	126
1951—Wilmington (Inter-State)	27	3	9	.250	5.40	...	115	126	76	69	79	104

JONES, BOBBY   F

PERSONAL: Born December 18, 1951, in Charlotte. ... 6-9/210 (2,05/95,3). ... Full name: Robert Clyde Jones.
HIGH SCHOOL: South Mecklenburg (Charlotte).
COLLEGE: North Carolina
TRANSACTIONS: Selected by Carolina Cougars in second round of 1973 ABA special circumstance draft. ... Cougars franchise moved to St. Louis and renamed Spirits of St. Louis for 1974-75 season. ... Draft rights traded by Spirits of St. Louis to Denver Nuggets for draft rights to Marvin Barnes (1974). ... Nuggets franchise became part of NBA for 1976-77 season. ... Traded by Nuggets with Ralph Simpson to Philadelphia 76ers for F George McGinnis (August 16, 1978).
MISCELLANEOUS: Member of NBA championship team (1983). ... Member of silver-medal-winning U.S. Olympic team (1972).

COLLEGIATE RECORD

Season Team	G	Min.	FGM	FGA	Pct.	FTM	FTA	Pct.	Reb.	Ast.	Pts.	AVERAGES RPG	APG	PPG
70-71—North Carolina	16	...	136	237	.574	86	113	.761	236	...	358	14.8	...	22.4
71-72—North Carolina	31	...	127	190	.668	62	95	.653	195	75	316	6.3	2.4	10.2
72-73—North Carolina	33	...	206	343	.601	84	128	.656	348	130	496	10.5	3.9	15.0
73-74—North Carolina	28	...	189	326	.580	74	120	.617	274	80	452	9.8	2.9	16.1
Totals	108	...	658	1096	.600	306	456	.671	1053	...	1622	9.8	...	15.0

ABA REGULAR-SEASON RECORD

NOTES: ABA All-Star second team (1976). ... ABA All-Defensive Team (1975 and 1976). ... ABA All-Rookie team (1975). ... Holds ABA single-season record for highest field goal percentage—.605 (1975).

Season Team	G	Min.	2-POINT FGM	FGA	Pct.	3-POINT FGM	FGA	Pct.	FTM	FTA	Pct.	Reb.	Ast.	Pts.	AVERAGES RPG	APG	PPG
74-75—Denver	84	2706	529	875	*.605	0	1	.000	187	269	.695	692	303	1245	8.2	3.6	14.8
75-76—Denver	83	2845	510	878	*.581	0	0	...	215	308	.698	791	331	1235	9.5	4.0	14.9
Totals	167	5551	1039	1753	.593	0	1	.000	402	577	.697	1483	634	2480	8.9	3.8	14.9

ABA PLAYOFF RECORD

Season Team	G	Min.	2-POINT FGM	FGA	Pct.	3-POINT FGM	FGA	Pct.	FTM	FTA	Pct.	Reb.	Ast.	Pts.	AVERAGES RPG	APG	PPG
74-75—Denver	13	428	69	128	.539	0	1	.000	31	40	.775	111	38	169	8.5	2.9	13.0
75-76—Denver	13	433	74	127	.583	0	0	...	30	41	.732	112	59	178	8.6	4.5	13.7
Totals	26	861	143	255	.561	0	1	.000	61	81	.753	223	97	347	8.6	3.7	13.3

ABA ALL-STAR GAME RECORD

Season Team	Min.	2-POINT FGM	FGA	Pct.	3-POINT FGM	FGA	Pct.	FTM	FTA	Pct.	Reb.	Ast.	Pts.
1976—Denver	29	8	12	.667	0	0	...	8	11	.727	10	3	24

NBA REGULAR-SEASON RECORD

HONORS: NBA Sixth Man Award (1983). ... NBA All-Defensive first team (1977, 1978, 1979, 1980, 1981, 1982, 1983, 1984) ... NBA All-Defensive second team (1985).

Season Team	G	Min.	FGM	FGA	Pct.	FTM	FTA	Pct.	REBOUNDS Off.	Def.	Tot.	Ast.	St.	Blk.	TO	Pts.	AVERAGES RPG	APG	PPG
76-77—Denver	82	2419	501	879	.570	236	329	.717	174	504	678	264	186	162	...	1238	8.3	3.2	15.1
77-78—Denver	75	2440	440	761	*.578	208	277	.751	164	472	636	252	137	126	194	1088	8.5	3.4	14.5
78-79—Philadelphia	80	2304	378	704	.537	209	277	.755	199	332	531	201	107	96	165	965	6.6	2.5	12.1
79-80—Philadelphia	81	2125	398	748	.532	257	329	.781	152	298	450	146	102	118	146	1053	5.6	1.8	13.0
80-81—Philadelphia	81	2046	407	755	.539	282	347	.813	142	293	435	226	95	74	149	1096	5.4	2.8	13.5
81-82—Philadelphia	76	2181	416	737	.564	263	333	.790	109	284	393	189	99	112	145	1095	5.2	2.5	14.4
82-83—Philadelphia	74	1749	250	460	.543	165	208	.793	102	242	344	142	85	91	109	665	4.6	1.9	9.0
83-84—Philadelphia	75	1761	226	432	.523	167	213	.784	92	231	323	187	107	103	101	619	4.3	2.5	8.3
84-85—Philadelphia	80	1633	207	385	.538	186	216	.861	105	192	297	155	84	50	118	600	3.7	1.9	7.5
85-86—Philadelphia	70	1519	189	338	.559	114	145	.786	49	120	169	126	48	50	90	492	2.4	1.8	7.0
Totals	774	20177	3412	6199	.550	2087	2674	.780	1288	2968	4256	1888	1050	982	1217	8911	5.5	2.4	11.5

Three-point field goals: 1979-80, 0-for-3. 1980-81, 0-for-3. 1981-82, 0-for-3. 1982-83, 0-for-1. 1983-84, 0-for-1. 1984-85, 0-for-4. 1985-86, 0-for-1. Totals, 0-for-16.

Personal fouls/disqualifications: 1976-77, 238/3. 1977-78, 221/2. 1978-79, 245/2. 1979-80, 223/3. 1980-81, 226/2. 1981-82, 211/3. 1982-83, 199/4. 1983-84, 199/1. 1984-85, 183/2. 1985-86, 159/0. Totals, 2104/22.

NBA PLAYOFF RECORD

Season Team	G	Min.	FGM	FGA	Pct.	FTM	FTA	Pct.	REBOUNDS Off.	Def.	Tot.	Ast.	St.	Blk.	TO	Pts.	AVERAGES RPG	APG	PPG
76-77—Denver	6	187	31	64	.484	10	17	.588	11	24	35	21	17	14	...	72	5.8	3.5	12.0
77-78—Denver	13	390	66	116	.569	34	46	.739	36	66	102	35	16	9	24	166	7.8	2.7	12.8
78-79—Philadelphia	9	260	48	87	.552	22	26	.846	12	31	43	19	5	4	15	118	4.8	2.1	13.1
79-80—Philadelphia	18	470	90	172	.523	53	62	.855	29	57	86	31	21	32	23	233	4.8	1.7	12.9
80-81—Philadelphia	16	443	81	160	.506	73	88	.830	35	53	88	33	18	21	32	235	5.5	2.1	14.7
81-82—Philadelphia	21	589	94	174	.540	68	81	.840	37	62	99	52	15	22	33	256	4.7	2.5	12.2
82-83—Philadelphia	12	324	43	78	.551	17	20	.850	19	39	58	34	15	18	18	103	4.8	2.8	8.6
83-84—Philadelphia	5	130	15	31	.484	18	19	.947	9	14	23	9	3	7	8	48	4.6	1.8	9.6
84-85—Philadelphia	13	309	46	78	.590	14	20	.700	22	26	48	16	12	15	19	106	3.7	1.2	8.2
85-86—Philadelphia	12	329	39	74	.527	38	50	.760	9	23	32	34	10	14	15	116	2.7	2.8	9.7
Totals	125	3431	553	1034	.535	347	429	.809	219	395	614	284	132	156	187	1453	4.9	2.3	11.6

Three-point field goals: 1979-80, 0-for-1. 1982-83, 0-for-1. 1985-86, 0-for-1. Totals, 0-for-3.

Personal fouls/disqualifications: 1976-77, 25/1. 1977-78, 42/1. 1978-79, 30/0. 1979-80, 56/1. 1980-81, 60/1. 1981-82, 69/0. 1982-83, 29/0. 1983-84, 12/0. 1984-85, 38/0. 1985-86, 39/0. Totals, 400/4.

NBA ALL-STAR GAME RECORD

Season Team	Min.	FGM	FGA	Pct.	FTM	FTA	Pct.	REBOUNDS Off.	Def.	Tot.	Ast.	PF	Dq.	St.	Blk.	TO	Pts.
1977 —Denver	14	1	4	.250	0	0	...	0	0	0	3	0	0	1	...		2
1978 —Denver	18	1	3	.333	0	0	...	1	5	6	2	4	0	1	1		2
1981 —Philadelphia	16	5	11	.455	1	1	1.000	1	3	4	0	2	0	1	1	0	11
1982 —Philadelphia	14	2	5	.400	1	2	.500	1	3	4	1	2	0	1	0	0	5
Totals	62	9	23	.391	2	3	.667	3	11	14	6	8	0	2	3	1	20

COMBINED ABA AND NBA REGULAR SEASON RECORDS

	G	Min.	FGM	FGA	Pct.	FTM	FTA	Pct.	REBOUNDS Off.	Def.	Tot.	Ast.	Stl.	Blk.	TO	Pts.	AVERAGES RPG	APG	PPG
Totals	941	25728	4451	7953	.560	2489	3251	.766	1759	3980	5739	2522	1387	1319	1683	11391	6.1	2.7	12.1

Three-point field goals: 0-for-17.
Personal fouls/disqualifications: 2620.

JONES, CALDWELL   F/C

PERSONAL: Born August 4, 1950, in McGehee, Ark. ... 6-11/225 (2,10/102,1). ... Full name: Caldwell Jones. ... Brother of Charles Jones, forward/center with five NBA teams (1983-84 through 1997-98); brother of Major Jones, forward/center with Houston Rockets (1979-80 through 1983-84) and Detroit Pistons (1984-85); and brother of Wilbert Jones, forward with three ABA teams (1969-70 through 1975-76) and Indiana Pacers (1976-77) and Buffalo Braves of the NBA (1977-78).
HIGH SCHOOL: Desha Central (Rohwer, Ark.).
COLLEGE: Albany State College

TRANSACTIONS: Selected by Virginia Squires in third round of 1973 ABA draft. ... Selected by Philadelphia 76ers in second round (32nd pick overall) of 1973 NBA draft. ... Signed by San Diego Conquistadors; G Larry Miller sent by Conquistadors to Squires as compensation (October 29, 1973). ... Signed by 76ers (for future services) (February 25, 1975). ... Purchased by Kentucky Colonels from disbanded San Diego franchise (Nomemeber 14, 1975). ... Traded by Kentucky Colonels to St. Louis for F Maurice Lucas (December 17, 1975). ... Traded by 76ers with 1983 first-round draft choice to Houston Rockets for C Moses Malone (September 15, 1982). ... Traded by Rockets to Chicago Bulls for G Mitchell Wiggins and 1985 second- and third-round draft choices (August 10, 1984). ... Signed by Portland Trail Blazers as veteran free agent (October 1, 1985); Bulls agreed not to exercise its right of first refusal in exchange for 1987 second-round draft choice. ... Signed by San Antonio Spurs as unrestricted free agent (July 20, 1989).

COLLEGIATE RECORD

Season Team	G	Min.	FGM	FGA	Pct.	FTM	FTA	Pct.	Reb.	Ast.	Pts.	RPG	APG	PPG
69-70—Albany (Ga.) State	25	...	185	367	.504	80	108	.741	440	...	450	17.6	...	18.0
70-71—Albany (Ga.) State	27	...	206	437	.471	76	137	.555	576	...	488	21.3	...	18.1
71-72—Albany (Ga.) State	28	...	288	539	.534	156	219	.712	567	...	732	20.3	...	26.1
72-73—Albany (Ga.) State	29	...	238	470	.506	91	134	.679	633	...	567	21.8	...	19.6
Totals	109	...	917	1813	.506	403	598	.674	2216	...	2237	20.3	...	20.5

ABA REGULAR-SEASON RECORD

NOTES: Shares ABA single-game record for most blocks—12 (January 6, 1974, vs. Carolina). ... Led ABA with 4.00 blocked shots per game (1974) and 3.24 blocked shots per game (1975).

Season Team	G	Min.	2-POINT			3-POINT			FTM	FTA	Pct.	Reb.	Ast.	Pts.	AVERAGES		
			FGM	FGA	Pct.	FGM	FGA	Pct.							RPG	APG	PPG
73-74—San Diego	79	2929	505	1083	.466	2	8	.250	171	230	.743	1095	144	1187	13.9	1.8	15.0
74-75—San Diego	76	3004	603	1229	.491	3	11	.273	264	335	.788	1074	162	1479	14.1	2.1	19.5
75-76—SD-Kty.-St.L.	76	2674	423	893	.474	0	7	.000	140	186	.753	853	147	986	11.2	1.9	13.0
Totals	231	8607	1531	3205	.478	5	26	.192	575	751	.766	3022	453	3652	13.1	2.0	15.8

ABA PLAYOFF RECORD

Season Team	G	Min.	2-POINT			3-POINT			FTM	FTA	Pct.	Reb.	Ast.	Pts.	AVERAGES		
			FGM	FGA	Pct.	FGM	FGA	Pct.							RPG	APG	PPG
73-74—San Diego	6	277	36	88	.409	0	0	...	11	16	.688	94	15	83	15.7	2.5	13.8

ABA ALL-STAR GAME RECORD

Season Team	Min.	2-POINT			3-POINT			FTM	FTA	Pct.	Reb.	Ast.	Pts.
		FGM	FGA	Pct.	FGM	FGA	Pct.						
1975—San Diego	15	2	4	.500	0	0	...	1	1	1.000	4	0	5

NBA REGULAR-SEASON RECORD

NOTES: NBA All-Defensive first team (1981, 1982).

Season Team	G	Min.	FGM	FGA	Pct.	FTM	FTA	Pct.	REBOUNDS			Ast.	St.	Blk.	TO	Pts.	AVERAGES		
									Off.	Def.	Tot.						RPG	APG	PPG
76-77—Philadelphia	82	2023	215	424	.507	64	116	.552	190	476	666	92	43	200	...	494	8.1	1.1	6.0
77-78—Philadelphia	80	1636	169	359	.471	96	153	.627	165	405	570	92	26	127	...	434	7.1	1.2	5.4
78-79—Philadelphia	78	2171	302	637	.474	121	162	.747	177	570	747	151	39	157	...	725	9.6	1.9	9.3
79-80—Philadelphia	80	2771	232	532	.436	124	178	.697	219	731	950	164	43	162	...	588	11.9	2.1	7.4
80-81—Philadelphia	81	2639	218	485	.449	148	193	.767	200	613	813	122	53	134	168	584	10.0	1.5	7.2
81-82—Philadelphia	81	2446	231	465	.497	179	219	.817	164	544	708	100	38	146	155	641	8.7	1.2	7.9
82-83—Houston	82	2440	307	677	.453	162	206	.786	222	446	668	138	46	131	171	776	8.1	1.7	9.5
83-84—Houston	81	2506	318	633	.502	164	196	.837	168	414	582	156	46	80	158	801	7.2	1.9	9.9
84-85—Chicago	42	885	53	115	.461	36	47	.766	49	162	211	34	12	31	40	142	5.0	0.8	3.4
85-86—Portland	80	1437	126	254	.496	124	150	.827	105	250	355	74	38	61	102	376	4.4	0.9	4.7
86-87—Portland	78	1578	111	224	.496	97	124	.782	114	341	455	64	23	77	87	319	5.8	0.8	4.1
87-88—Portland	79	1778	128	263	.487	78	106	.736	105	303	408	81	29	99	82	334	5.2	1.0	4.2
88-89—Portland	72	1279	77	183	.421	48	61	.787	88	212	300	59	24	85	83	202	4.2	0.8	2.8
89-90—San Antonio	72	885	67	144	.465	38	54	.704	76	154	230	20	20	27	48	173	3.2	0.3	2.4
Totals	1068	26474	2554	5395	.473	1479	1965	.753	2042	5621	7663	1347	480	1517	...	6589	7.2	1.3	6.2

Three-point field goals: 1979-80, 0-for-1. 1981-82, 0-for-3. 1982-83, 0-for-2. 1983-84, 1-for-3 (.333). 1984-85, 0-for-2. 1985-86, 0-for-7. 1986-87, 0-for-2. 1987-88, 0-for-4. 1988-89, 0-for-1. 1989-90, 1-for-5 (.200). Totals, 2-for-31 (.065).

Personal fouls/disqualifications: 1976-77, 301/3. 1977-78, 281/4. 1978-79, 303/10. 1979-80, 298/5. 1980-81, 271/2. 1981-82, 301/3. 1982-83, 278/2. 1983-84, 335/7. 1984-85, 125/3. 1985-86, 244/2. 1986-87, 227/5. 1987-88, 251/0. 1988-89, 166/0. 1989-90, 146/2. Totals, 3527/48.

NBA PLAYOFF RECORD

Season Team	G	Min.	FGM	FGA	Pct.	FTM	FTA	Pct.	REBOUNDS			Ast.	St.	Blk.	TO	Pts.	AVERAGES		
									Off.	Def.	Tot.						RPG	APG	PPG
76-77—Philadelphia	19	513	37	73	.507	18	30	.600	38	112	150	20	9	40	...	92	7.9	1.1	4.8
77-78—Philadelphia	10	301	28	56	.500	8	10	.800	22	84	106	14	5	30	...	64	10.6	1.4	6.4
78-79—Philadelphia	9	320	43	89	.483	28	36	.778	37	84	121	21	4	22	...	114	13.4	2.3	12.7
79-80—Philadelphia	18	639	58	129	.450	42	52	.808	50	135	185	34	13	37	...	158	10.3	1.9	8.8
80-81—Philadelphia	16	580	54	95	.568	31	42	.738	37	118	155	27	7	31	...	139	9.7	1.7	8.7
81-82—Philadelphia	21	679	74	160	.463	35	41	.854	52	137	189	19	11	40	...	183	9.0	0.9	8.7
84-85—Chicago	2	18	5	6	.833	0	0	...	1	4	5	0	0	1	...	10	2.5	0.0	5.0
85-86—Portland	4	73	6	17	.353	2	4	.500	9	10	19	3	0	2	...	14	4.8	0.8	3.5
86-87—Portland	4	129	5	12	.417	5	6	.833	9	22	31	6	0	6	...	15	7.8	1.5	3.8
87-88—Portland	4	98	6	16	.375	1	2	.500	4	13	17	1	2	8	...	13	4.3	0.3	3.3
88-89—Portland	3	50	2	3	.667	0	0	...	2	6	8	0	0	3	...	4	2.7	0.0	1.3
89-90—San Antonio	9	66	4	9	.444	0	1	.000	6	7	13	2	0	3	...	8	1.4	0.2	0.9
Totals	119	3466	322	665	.484	170	224	.759	267	732	999	147	51	223	...	814	8.4	1.2	6.8

Three-point field goals: 1979-80, 0-for-3. 1984-85, 0-for-1. Totals, 0-for-4.

Personal fouls/disqualifications: 1976-77, 81/4. 1977-78, 36/2. 1978-79, 36/0. 1979-80, 75/1. 1980-81, 53/0. 1981-82, 77/1. 1984-85, 7/1. 1985-86, 13/0. 1986-87, 15/0. 1987-88, 17/0. 1988-89, 6/0. 1989-90, 10/0. Totals, 426/9.

COMBINED ABA AND NBA REGULAR-SEASON RECORDS

	G	Min.	FGM	FGA	Pct.	FTM	FTA	Pct.	REBOUNDS			Ast.	Stl.	Blk.	TO	Pts.	AVERAGES		
									Off.	Def.	Tot.						RPG	APG	PPG
Totals	1299	35081	4090	8626	.474	2054	2716	.756	2921	7764	10685	1800	685	2297	...	10241	8.2	1.4	7.9

JONES, SAM   G

PERSONAL: Born June 24, 1933, in Wilmington, N.C. ... 6-4/205 (1,93/93,0). ... Full name: Samuel Jones.
HIGH SCHOOL: Laurinburg Institute (N.C.).
COLLEGE: North Carolina Central.
TRANSACTIONS: Selected by Boston Celtics in first round (eighth pick overall) of 1957 NBA Draft.
CAREER HONORS: Elected to Naismith Memorial Basketball Hall of Fame (1984). ... NBA 25th Anniversary All-Time Team (1970) and One of the 50 Greatest Players in NBA History (1996).
MISCELLANEOUS: Member of NBA championship team (1959, 1960, 1961, 1962, 1963, 1964, 1965, 1966, 1968, 1969).

COLLEGIATE RECORD

NOTES: Elected to NAIA Basketball Hall of Fame (1962).

Season Team	G	Min.	FGM	FGA	Pct.	FTM	FTA	Pct.	Reb.	Ast.	Pts.	RPG	APG	PPG
51-52—North Carolina Central....	22	...	126	263	.479	48	78	.615	150	...	300	6.8	...	13.6
52-53—North Carolina Central....	24	...	169	370	.457	115	180	.639	248	...	453	10.3	...	18.9
53-54—North Carolina Central....	27	...	208	432	.481	98	137	.715	223	...	514	8.3	...	19.0
54-55—						Did not play—in military service.								
55-56—						Did not play—in military service.								
56-57—North Carolina Central....	27	...	174	398	.437	155	202	.767	288	...	503	10.7	...	18.6
Totals	100	...	677	1463	.463	416	597	.697	909	...	1770	9.1	...	17.7

NBA REGULAR-SEASON RECORD

HONORS: All-NBA second team (1965, 1966, 1967).

Season Team	G	Min.	FGM	FGA	Pct.	FTM	FTA	Pct.	Reb.	Ast.	PF	Dq.	Pts.	RPG	APG	PPG
57-58 —Boston	56	594	100	233	.429	60	84	.714	160	37	42	0	260	2.9	0.7	4.6
58-59 —Boston	71	1466	305	703	.434	151	196	.770	428	101	102	0	761	6.0	1.4	10.7
59-60 —Boston	74	1512	355	782	.454	168	220	.764	375	125	101	1	878	5.1	1.7	11.9
60-61 —Boston	78	2028	480	1069	.449	211	268	.787	421	217	148	1	1171	5.4	2.8	15.0
61-62 —Boston	78	2388	596	1284	.464	243	297	.818	458	232	149	0	1435	5.9	3.0	18.4
62-63 —Boston	76	2323	621	1305	.476	257	324	.793	396	241	162	1	1499	5.2	3.2	19.7
63-64 —Boston	76	2381	612	1359	.450	249	318	.783	349	202	192	1	1473	4.6	2.7	19.4
64-65 —Boston	80	2885	821	1818	.452	428	522	.820	411	223	176	0	2070	5.1	2.8	25.9
65-66 —Boston	67	2155	626	1335	.469	325	407	.799	347	216	170	0	1577	5.2	3.2	23.5
66-67 —Boston	72	2325	638	1406	.454	318	371	.857	338	217	191	1	1594	4.7	3.0	22.1
67-68 —Boston	73	2408	621	1348	.461	311	376	.827	357	216	181	0	1553	4.9	3.0	21.3
68-69 —Boston	70	1820	496	1103	.450	148	189	.783	265	182	121	0	1140	3.8	2.6	16.3
Totals	871	24285	6271	13745	.456	2869	3572	.803	4305	2209	1735	5	15411	4.9	2.5	17.7

NBA PLAYOFF RECORD

Season Team	G	Min.	FGM	FGA	Pct.	FTM	FTA	Pct.	Reb.	Ast.	PF	Dq.	Pts.	RPG	APG	PPG
57-58 —Boston	8	75	10	22	.455	11	16	.688	24	4	7	0	31	3.0	0.5	3.9
58-59 —Boston	11	192	40	108	.370	33	39	.846	63	17	14	0	113	5.7	1.5	10.3
59-60 —Boston	13	197	45	117	.385	17	21	.810	41	18	15	0	107	3.2	1.4	8.2
60-61 —Boston	10	258	50	112	.446	31	35	.886	54	22	22	0	131	5.4	2.2	13.1
61-62 —Boston	14	504	123	277	.444	42	60	.700	99	44	30	0	288	7.1	3.1	20.6
62-63 —Boston	13	450	120	248	.484	69	83	.831	81	32	42	1	309	6.2	2.5	23.8
63-64 —Boston	10	356	91	180	.506	50	68	.735	47	23	24	0	232	4.7	2.3	23.2
64-65 —Boston	12	495	135	294	.459	73	84	.869	55	30	39	1	343	4.6	2.5	28.6
65-66 —Boston	17	602	154	343	.449	114	136	.838	86	53	65	1	422	5.1	3.1	24.8
66-67 —Boston	9	326	95	207	.459	50	58	.862	46	28	30	1	240	5.1	3.1	26.7
67-68 —Boston	19	685	162	367	.441	66	84	.786	64	50	58	0	390	3.4	2.6	20.5
68-69 —Boston	18	514	124	296	.419	55	69	.797	58	37	45	1	303	3.2	2.1	16.8
Totals	154	4654	1149	2571	.447	611	753	.811	718	358	391	5	2909	4.7	2.3	18.9

NBA ALL-STAR GAME RECORD

Season Team	Min.	FGM	FGA	Pct.	FTM	FTA	Pct.	Reb	Ast.	PF	Dq.	Pts.
1962 —Boston	14	1	8	.125	0	1	.000	1	0	1	0	2
1964 —Boston	27	8	20	.400	0	0	...	4	3	2	0	16
1965 —Boston	24	2	12	.167	2	2	1.000	5	3	2	0	6
1966 —Boston	22	5	11	.455	2	2	1.000	2	5	0	0	12
1968 —Boston	15	2	5	.400	1	1	1.000	2	4	1	0	5
Totals	102	18	56	.321	5	6	.833	14	15	6	0	41

HEAD COACHING RECORD

BACKGROUND: Athletic director/head coach, Federal City College, Washington, D.C. (1969-1973). ... Assistant coach, New Orleans Jazz (1974-75).

COLLEGIATE COACHING RECORD

Season Team	W	L	Pct.	Finish
69-70 —Federal City College	5	8	.385	
70-71 —Federal City College	12	9	.571	
71-72 —Federal City College	11	9	.550	
72-73 —Federal City College	11	13	.458	
73-74 —North Carolina Central	5	16	.238	7th/Mid-Eastern Athletic Conference
Totals (5 years)	44	55	.444	

JORDAN, MICHAEL　　　　G

PERSONAL: Born February 17, 1963, in Brooklyn, N.Y. ... 6-6/216 (1,98/98,0). ... Full name: Michael Jeffrey Jordan.
HIGH SCHOOL: Emsley A. Laney (Wilmington, N.C.).
COLLEGE: North Carolina.
TRANSACTIONS/CAREER NOTES: Selected after junior season by Chicago Bulls in first round (third pick overall) of 1984 NBA Draft. ... On voluntarily retired list (October 6, 1993-March 18, 1995). ... Activated from retirement (March 18, 1995). ... Announced retirement (January 13, 1999).
CAREER HONORS: One of the 50 Greatest Players in NBA History (1996).
CAREER NOTES: President of Basketball Operations, Washington Wizards and minority owner, Washington Wizards Sports and Entertainment (January 19, 2000 to present).
MISCELLANEOUS: Member of NBA championship team (1991, 1992, 1993, 1996, 1997, 1998). ... Member of gold-medal-winning U.S. Olympic team (1984, 1992). ... Chicago Bulls all-time leading scorer with 29,277 points, all-time leading rebounder with 5,836, all-time assists leader with 5,012 and all-time steals leader with 2,306 (1984-85 through 1992-93 and 1994-95 through 1997-98).

COLLEGIATE RECORD

NOTES: Member of NCAA Division I championship team (1982). ... THE SPORTING NEWS College Player of the Year (1983, 1984). ... Naismith Award winner (1984). ... Wooden Award winner (1984). ... THE SPORTING NEWS All-America first team (1983, 1984).

Season Team	G	Min.	FGM	FGA	Pct.	FTM	FTA	Pct.	Reb.	Ast.	Pts.	AVERAGES RPG	APG	PPG
81-82—North Carolina	34	1079	191	358	.534	78	108	.722	149	61	460	4.4	1.8	13.5
82-83—North Carolina	36	1113	282	527	.535	123	167	.737	197	56	721	5.5	1.6	20.0
83-84—North Carolina	31	915	247	448	.551	113	145	.779	163	64	607	5.3	2.1	19.6
Totals	101	3107	720	1333	.540	314	420	.748	509	181	1788	5.0	1.8	17.7

Three-point field goals: 1982-83, 34-for-76 (.447).

NBA REGULAR-SEASON RECORD

RECORDS: Holds career record for most seasons leading league in scoring—10; highest points-per-game average (minimum 400 games or 10,000 points)—31.5; most seasons leading league in field goals made—10; and most seasons leading league in field goals attempted—9. ... Shares career records for most seasons leading league in steals—3; and most consecutive seasons leading league in scoring—7 (1986-87 through 1992-93). ... Holds single-game records for most free throws made in one half—20 (December 30, 1992, at Miami); and most free throws attempted in one half—23 (December 30, 1992, at Miami). ... Shares single-game records for most free throws made in one quarter—14 (November 15, 1989, vs. Utah and December 30, 1992, at Miami); and most free throws attempted in one quarter—16 (December 30, 1992, at Miami).
HONORS: NBA Most Valuable Player (1988, 1991, 1992, 1996, 1998). ... NBA Defensive Player of the Year (1988). ... NBA Rookie of the Year (1985). ... IBM Award, for all-around contribution to team's success (1985, 1989). ... Slam Dunk championship winner (1987, 1988). ... All-NBA first team (1987, 1988, 1989, 1990, 1991, 1992, 1993, 1996, 1997, 1998). ... All-NBA second team (1985). ... NBA All-Defensive first team (1988, 1989, 1990, 1991, 1992, 1993, 1996, 1997, 1998). ... NBA All-Rookie team (1985).
NOTES: Led NBA with 3.16 steals per game (1988), 2.77 steals per game (1990) and 2.83 steals per game (1993).

Season Team	G	Min.	FGM	FGA	Pct.	FTM	FTA	Pct.	REBOUNDS Off.	Def.	Tot.	Ast.	St.	Blk.	TO	Pts.	AVERAGES RPG	APG	PPG
84-85—Chicago	82	3144	837	1625	.515	630	746	.845	167	367	534	481	196	69	291	*2313	6.5	5.9	28.2
85-86—Chicago	18	451	150	328	.457	105	125	.840	23	41	64	53	37	21	45	408	3.6	2.9	22.7
86-87—Chicago	82	*3281	*1098	*2279	.482	*833	*972	.857	166	264	430	377	236	125	272	*3041	5.2	4.6	*37.1
87-88—Chicago	82	*3311	*1069	1998	.535	*723	860	.841	139	310	449	485	*259	131	252	*2868	5.5	5.9	*35.0
88-89—Chicago	81	*3255	*966	1795	.538	674	793	.850	149	503	652	650	234	65	290	*2633	8.0	8.0	*32.5
89-90—Chicago	82	3197	*1034	*1964	.526	593	699	.848	143	422	565	519	*227	54	247	*2753	6.9	6.3	*33.6
90-91—Chicago	82	3034	*990	*1837	.539	571	671	.851	118	374	492	453	223	83	202	*2580	6.0	5.5	*31.5
91-92—Chicago	80	3102	*943	*1818	.519	491	590	.832	91	420	511	489	182	75	200	*2404	6.4	6.1	*30.1
92-93—Chicago	78	3067	*992	*2003	.495	476	569	.837	135	387	522	428	*221	61	207	*2541	6.7	5.5	*32.6
93-94—Chicago—					Did not play—retired.														
94-95—Chicago	17	668	166	404	.411	109	136	.801	25	92	117	90	30	13	35	457	6.9	5.3	26.9
95-96—Chicago	82	3090	*916	*1850	.495	548	657	.834	148	395	543	352	180	42	197	*2491	6.6	4.3	*30.4
96-97—Chicago	82	3106	*920	*1892	.486	480	576	.833	113	369	482	352	140	44	166	*2431	5.9	4.3	*29.6
97-98—Chicago	82	3181	*881	*1893	.465	565	721	.784	130	345	475	283	141	45	185	*2357	5.8	3.5	*28.7
Totals	930	35887	10962	21686	.505	6798	8115	.838	1547	4289	5836	5012	2306	828	2589	29277	6.3	5.4	31.5

Three-point field goals: 1984-85, 9-for-52 (.173). 1985-86, 3-for-18 (.167). 1986-87, 12-for-66 (.182). 1987-88, 7-for-53 (.132). 1988-89, 27-for-98 (.276). 1989-90, 92-for-245 (.376). 1990-91, 29-for-93 (.312). 1991-92, 27-for-100 (.270). 1992-93, 81-for-230 (.352). 1994-95, 16-for-32 (.500). 1995-96, 111-for-260 (.427). 1996-97, 111-for-297 (.374). 1997-98, 30-for-126 (.238). Totals, 555-for-1670 (.332).

Personal fouls/disqualifications: 1984-85, 285/4. 1985-86, 46/0. 1986-87, 237/0. 1987-88, 270/2. 1988-89, 247/2. 1989-90, 241/0. 1990-91, 229/1. 1991-92, 201/1. 1992-93, 188/0. 1994-95, 47/0. 1995-96, 195/0. 1996-97, 156/0. 1997-98, 151/0. Totals, 2493/10.

NBA PLAYOFF RECORD

NOTES: NBA Finals Most Valuable Player (1991, 1992, 1993, 1996, 1997, 1998). ... Holds NBA Finals career records for most three-point field goals made—42; and most consecutive games with 20 or more points—35 (June 2, 1991-June 14, 1998). ... Holds NBA Finals single-series record for highest points-per-game average—41.0 (1993). ... Holds NBA Finals single-game record for most points in one half—35 (June 3, 1992, vs. Portland). ... Shares NBA Finals single-game records for most field goals made in one half—14; most three-point field goals made in one half—6 (June 3, 1992, vs. Portland) and most free throws made in one quarter—9 (June 11, 1997, vs. Utah). ... Holds career playoff record for most points—5,987; highest points-per-game average (minimum 25 games or 625 points)—33.4; most field goals attempted—4,497; most free throws made—1,463; most free throws attempted—1,766; and most steals—376. ... Holds single-game play-off records for most points—63 (April 20, 1986, at Boston). ... Shares single-game playoff records for most field goals made—24 (May 1, 1988, vs. Cleveland); most field goals attempted in one half—25 (May 1, 1988, vs. Cleveland).

Season Team	G	Min.	FGM	FGA	Pct.	FTM	FTA	Pct.	REBOUNDS Off.	Def.	Tot.	Ast.	St.	Blk.	TO	Pts.	AVERAGES RPG	APG	PPG
84-85—Chicago	4	171	34	78	.436	48	58	.828	7	16	23	34	11	4	15	117	5.8	8.5	29.3
85-86—Chicago	3	135	48	95	.505	34	39	.872	5	14	19	17	7	4	14	131	6.3	5.7	43.7
86-87—Chicago	3	128	35	84	.417	35	39	.897	7	14	21	18	6	7	8	107	7.0	6.0	35.7
87-88—Chicago	10	427	138	260	.531	86	99	.869	23	48	71	47	24	11	39	363	7.1	4.7	36.3

Season Team	G	Min.	FGM	FGA	Pct.	FTM	FTA	Pct.	Off.	Def.	Tot.	Ast.	St.	Blk.	TO	Pts.	RPG	APG	PPG
									REBOUNDS								**AVERAGES**		
88-89—Chicago	17	718	199	390	.510	183	229	.799	26	93	119	130	42	13	68	591	7.0	7.6	34.8
89-90—Chicago	16	674	219	426	.514	133	159	.836	24	91	115	109	45	14	56	587	7.2	6.8	36.7
90-91—Chicago	17	689	197	376	.524	125	148	.845	18	90	108	142	40	23	43	529	6.4	8.4	31.1
91-92—Chicago	22	920	290	581	.499	162	189	.857	37	100	137	127	44	16	81	759	6.2	5.8	34.5
92-93—Chicago	19	783	251	528	.475	136	169	.805	32	96	128	114	39	17	45	666	6.7	6.0	35.1
94-95—Chicago	10	420	120	248	.484	64	79	.810	20	45	65	45	23	14	41	315	6.5	4.5	31.5
95-96—Chicago	18	733	187	407	.459	153	187	.818	31	58	89	74	33	6	42	552	4.9	4.1	30.7
96-97—Chicago	19	804	227	498	.456	123	148	.831	42	108	150	91	30	17	49	590	7.9	4.8	31.1
97-98—Chicago	21	872	243	526	.462	181	223	.812	33	74	107	74	32	12	45	680	5.1	3.5	32.4
Totals	179	7474	2188	4497	.487	1463	1766	.828	305	847	1152	1022	376	158	546	5987	6.4	5.7	33.4

Three-point field goals: 1984-85, 1-for-8 (.125). 1985-86, 1-for-1. 1986-87, 2-for-5 (.400). 1987-88, 1-for-3 (.333). 1988-89, 10-for-35 (.286). 1989-90, 16-for-50 (.320). 1990-91, 10-for-26 (.385). 1991-92, 17-for-44 (.386). 1992-93, 28-for-72 (.389). 1994-95, 11-for-30 (.367). 1995-96, 25-for-62 (.403). 1996-97, 13-for-67 (.194). 1997-98, 13-for-43 (.302). Totals, 148-for-446 (.332).

Personal fouls/disqualifications: 1984-85, 15/0. 1985-86, 13/1. 1986-87, 11/0. 1987-88, 38/1. 1988-89, 65/1. 1989-90, 54/0. 1990-91, 53/0. 1991-92, 62/0. 1992-93, 58/0. 1994-95, 30/0. 1995-96, 49/0. 1996-97, 46/0. 1997-98, 47/0. Totals, 541/3.

NBA ALL-STAR GAME RECORD

NOTES: NBA All-Star Game Most Valuable Player (1988, 1996, 1998). ... Holds career record for highest points-per-game average—21.3; and most steals—33. ... Recorded only triple-double in All-Star Game history (February 9, 1997).

Season	Team	Min.	FGM	FGA	Pct.	FTM	FTA	Pct.	Off.	Def.	Tot.	Ast.	PF	Dq.	St.	Blk.	TO	Pts.
									REBOUNDS									
1985	—Chicago	22	2	9	.222	3	4	.750	3	3	6	2	4	0	3	1	1	7
1986	—Chicago								Selected, did not play—injured.									
1987	—Chicago	28	5	12	.417	1	2	.500	0	0	0	4	2	0	2	0	5	11
1988	—Chicago	29	17	23	.739	6	6	1.000	3	5	8	3	5	0	4	4	2	40
1989	—Chicago	33	13	23	.565	2	4	.500	1	1	2	3	1	0	5	0	4	28
1990	—Chicago	29	8	17	.471	0	0	...	1	4	5	2	1	0	5	1	5	17
1991	—Chicago	36	10	25	.400	6	7	.857	3	2	5	5	2	0	2	0	10	26
1992	—Chicago	31	9	17	.529	0	0	...	1	0	1	5	2	0	2	0	1	18
1993	—Chicago	36	10	24	.417	9	13	.692	3	1	4	5	5	0	4	0	6	30
1996	—Chicago	22	8	11	.727	4	4	1.000	1	3	4	1	1	0	1	0	0	20
1997	—Chicago	26	5	14	.357	4	7	.571	3	8	11	11	4	0	2	0	3	14
1998	—Chicago	32	10	18	.556	2	3	.667	1	5	6	8	0	0	3	0	2	23
Totals		324	97	193	.503	37	50	.740	20	32	52	49	27	0	33	6	39	234

Three-point field goals: 1985, 0-for-1. 1987, 0-for-1. 1989, 0-for-1. 1990, 1-for-1. 1991, 0-for-2. 1993, 1-for-2 (.500). 1998, 1-for-1. Totals, 3-for-9 (.333).

RECORD AS BASEBALL PLAYER

TRANSACTIONS/CAREER NOTES: Threw right, batted right. ... Signed as non-drafted free agent by Chicago White Sox organization (February 7, 1994). ... On voluntarily retired list (March 25, 1995).

Year	Team (League)	Pos.	G	AB	R	H	2B	3B	HR	RBI	Avg.	BB	SO	SB	PO	A	E	Avg.
											BATTING				**FIELDING**			
1994	—Birm. (South.)	OF	127	436	46	88	17	1	3	51	.202	51	114	30	213	6	†11	.952

KERR, RED   C

PERSONAL: Born July 17, 1932, in Chicago. ... 6-9/230 (2,05/104,3). ... Full name: John G. Kerr.

HIGH SCHOOL: Tilden Technical School (Chicago).

COLLEGE: Illinois.

TRANSACTIONS: Selected by Syracuse Nationals in first round (sixth pick overall) of 1954 NBA Draft. ... Nationals franchise moved from Syracuse to Philadelphia and renamed 76ers for 1963-64 season. ... Traded by 76ers to Baltimore Bullets for G Wali Jones (September 22, 1965). ... Selected by Chicago Bulls from Bullets in NBA Expansion Draft (April 30, 1966).

MISCELLANEOUS: Member of NBA championship team (1955).

COLLEGIATE RECORD

Season Team	G	Min.	FGM	FGA	Pct.	FTM	FTA	Pct.	Reb.	Ast.	Pts.	RPG	APG	PPG
												AVERAGES		
50-51—Illinois‡					Freshman team did not play intercollegiate schedule.									
51-52—Illinois	26	...	143	365	.392	71	124	.573	...	...	357	...	...	13.7
52-53—Illinois	22	...	153	397	.385	80	123	.650	...	...	386	...	...	17.5
53-54—Illinois	22	...	210	520	.404	136	214	.636	...	...	556	...	...	25.3
Varsity totals	70	...	506	1282	.395	287	461	.623	...	...	1299	...	...	18.6

NBA REGULAR-SEASON RECORD

Season Team	G	Min.	FGM	FGA	Pct.	FTM	FTA	Pct.	Reb.	Ast.	PF	Dq.	Pts.	RPG	APG	PPG
														AVERAGES		
54-55 —Syracuse	72	1529	301	718	.419	152	223	.682	474	80	165	2	754	6.6	1.1	10.5
55-56 —Syracuse	72	2114	377	935	.403	207	316	.655	607	84	168	3	961	8.4	1.2	13.3
56-57 —Syracuse	72	2191	333	827	.403	225	313	.719	807	90	190	3	891	11.2	1.3	12.4
57-58 —Syracuse	72	2384	407	1020	.399	280	422	.664	963	88	197	4	1094	13.4	1.2	15.2
58-59 —Syracuse	72	2671	502	1139	.441	281	367	.766	1008	142	183	1	1285	14.0	2.0	17.8
59-60 —Syracuse	75	2372	436	1111	.392	233	310	.752	913	167	207	4	1105	12.2	2.2	14.7
60-61 —Syracuse	79	2676	419	1056	.397	218	299	.729	951	199	230	4	1056	12.0	2.5	13.4
61-62 —Syracuse	80	2768	541	1220	.443	222	302	.735	1176	243	272	7	1304	14.7	3.0	16.3
62-63 —Syracuse	80	2561	507	1069	.474	241	320	.753	1039	214	208	3	1255	13.0	2.7	15.7
63-64 —Philadelphia	80	2938	536	1250	.429	268	357	.751	1017	275	187	2	1340	12.7	3.4	16.8
64-65 —Philadelphia	80	1810	264	714	.370	126	181	.696	551	197	132	1	654	6.9	2.5	8.2
65-66 —Baltimore	71	1770	286	692	.413	209	272	.768	586	225	148	0	781	8.3	3.2	11.0
Totals	905	27784	4909	11751	.418	2662	3682	.723	10092	2004	2287	34	12480	11.2	2.2	13.8

NBA PLAYOFF RECORD

Season Team	G	Min.	FGM	FGA	Pct.	FTM	FTA	Pct.	Reb.	Ast.	PF	Dq.	Pts.	AVERAGES RPG	APG	PPG
54-55 —Syracuse	11	363	59	151	.391	34	61	.557	118	13	27	0	152	10.7	1.2	13.8
55-56 —Syracuse	8	213	37	77	.481	15	33	.455	68	10	23	0	89	8.5	1.3	11.1
56-57 —Syracuse	5	162	28	65	.431	20	29	.690	69	6	7	0	76	13.8	1.2	15.2
57-58 —Syracuse	3	116	18	55	.327	14	18	.778	61	3	5	0	50	20.3	1.0	16.7
58-59 —Syracuse	9	312	50	142	.352	30	33	.909	108	24	20	0	130	12.0	2.7	14.4
59-60 —Syracuse	3	104	15	51	.294	11	12	.917	25	9	9	0	41	8.3	3.0	13.7
60-61 —Syracuse	8	210	30	88	.341	16	23	.696	99	20	18	0	76	12.4	2.5	9.5
61-62 —Syracuse	5	193	41	109	.376	6	8	.750	80	10	15	0	88	16.0	2.0	17.6
62-63 —Syracuse	5	187	26	60	.433	16	21	.762	75	9	12	0	68	15.0	1.8	13.6
63-64 —Philadelphia	5	185	40	83	.482	15	20	.750	69	16	12	0	95	13.8	3.2	19.0
64-65 —Philadelphia	11	181	24	67	.358	15	21	.714	38	28	20	0	63	3.5	2.5	5.7
65-66 —Baltimore	3	49	2	11	.182	1	2	.500	17	4	5	0	5	5.7	1.3	1.7
Totals	76	2275	370	959	.386	193	281	.687	827	152	173	0	933	10.9	2.0	12.3

NBA ALL-STAR GAME RECORD

Season Team	Min.	FGM	FGA	Pct.	FTM	FTA	Pct.	Reb	Ast.	PF	Dq.	Pts.
1956 —Syracuse	16	2	4	.500	0	1	.000	8	0	2	0	4
1959 —Syracuse	21	3	14	.214	1	2	.500	9	2	0	0	7
1963 —Syracuse	11	0	4	.000	2	2	1.000	2	1	3	0	2
Totals	48	5	22	.227	3	5	.600	19	3	5	0	13

NBA COACHING RECORD

HONORS: NBA Coach of the Year (1967).

Season Team	REGULAR SEASON W	L	Pct.	Finish	PLAYOFFS W	L	Pct.
66-67 —Chicago	33	48	.407	4th/Western Division	0	3	.000
67-68 —Chicago	29	53	.354	4th/Western Division	1	4	.200
68-69 —Phoenix	16	66	.195	7th/Western Division	—	—	—
69-70 —Phoenix	15	23	.395		—	—	—
Totals (4 years)	93	190	.329	**Totals (2 years)**	1	7	.125

NOTES:
1967—Lost to St. Louis in Western Division Semifinals.
1968—Lost to Los Angeles in Western Division Semifinals.
1970—Resigned as Phoenix head coach (January 2); replaced by Jerry Colangelo.

KING, BERNARD　　　　F

PERSONAL: Born December 4, 1956, in Brooklyn, N.Y. ... 6-7/205 (2,00/93,0). ... Brother of Albert King, guard/forward with New Jersey Nets, Philadelphia 76ers, San Antonio Spurs and Washington Bullets (1981-82 through 1988-89 and 1991-92).
HIGH SCHOOL: Fort Hamilton (Brooklyn, N.Y.).
COLLEGE: Tennessee.
TRANSACTIONS: Selected after junior season by New Jersey Nets in first round (seventh pick overall) of 1977 NBA Draft. ... Traded by Nets with C/F John Gianelli and G Jim Boylan to Utah Jazz for C Rich Kelley (October 2, 1979). ... Traded by Jazz to Golden State Warriors for C/F Wayne Cooper and 1981 second-round draft choice (September 11, 1980). ... Signed as veteran free agent by New York Knicks (September 28, 1982); Warriors matched offer and traded King to Knicks for G Micheal Ray Richardson and 1984 fifth-round draft choice (October 22, 1982). ... Signed as free agent by Washington Bullets (October 16, 1987). ... Waived by Bullets (January 22, 1993). ... Signed as free agent by New Jersey Nets (February 6, 1993).

COLLEGIATE RECORD

NOTES: The Sporting News All-America second team (1977). ... Led NCAA Division I with .622 field goal percentage (1975).

Season Team	G	Min.	FGM	FGA	Pct.	FTM	FTA	Pct.	Reb.	Ast.	Pts.	AVERAGES RPG	APG	PPG
74-75—Tennessee	25	...	273	439	.622	115	147	.782	308	39	661	12.3	1.6	26.4
75-76—Tennessee	25	...	260	454	.573	109	163	.669	325	40	629	13.0	1.6	25.2
76-77—Tennessee	26	...	278	481	.578	116	163	.712	371	82	672	14.3	3.2	25.8
Totals	76	...	811	1374	.590	340	473	.719	1004	161	1962	13.2	2.1	25.8

NBA REGULAR-SEASON RECORD

HONORS: NBA Comeback Player of the Year (1981). ... All-NBA first team (1984, 1985). ... All-NBA second team (1982). ... All-NBA third team (1991). ... NBA All-Rookie team (1978).

Season Team	G	Min.	FGM	FGA	Pct.	FTM	FTA	Pct.	REBOUNDS Off.	Def.	Tot.	Ast.	St.	Blk.	TO	Pts.	AVERAGES RPG	APG	PPG
77-78—New Jersey	79	3092	798	1665	.479	313	462	.677	265	486	751	193	122	36	311	1909	9.5	2.4	24.2
78-79—New Jersey	82	2859	710	1359	.522	349	619	.564	251	418	669	295	118	39	323	1769	8.2	3.6	21.6
79-80—Utah	19	419	71	137	.518	34	63	.540	24	64	88	52	7	4	50	176	4.6	2.7	9.3
80-81—Golden State	81	2914	731	1244	.588	307	437	.703	178	373	551	287	72	34	265	1771	6.8	3.5	21.9
81-82—Golden State	79	2861	740	1307	.566	352	499	.705	140	329	469	282	78	23	267	1833	5.9	3.6	23.2
82-83—New York	68	2207	603	1142	.528	280	388	.722	99	227	326	195	90	13	197	1486	4.8	2.9	21.9
83-84—New York	77	2667	795	1391	.572	437	561	.779	123	271	394	164	75	17	197	2027	5.1	2.1	26.3
84-85—New York	55	2063	691	1303	.530	426	552	.772	114	203	317	204	71	15	204	1809	5.8	3.7	*32.9
85-86—New York						Did not play—injured.													
86-87—New York	6	214	52	105	.495	32	43	.744	13	19	32	19	2	0	15	136	5.3	3.2	22.7
87-88—Washington	69	2044	470	938	.501	247	324	.762	86	194	280	192	49	10	211	1188	4.1	2.8	17.2

Season Team	G	Min.	FGM	FGA	Pct.	FTM	FTA	Pct.	REBOUNDS Off.	Def.	Tot.	Ast.	St.	Blk.	TO	Pts.	AVERAGES RPG	APG	PPG
88-89—Washington	81	2559	654	1371	.477	361	441	.819	133	251	384	294	64	13	227	1674	4.7	3.6	20.7
89-90—Washington	82	2687	711	1459	.487	412	513	.803	129	275	404	376	51	7	248	1837	4.9	4.6	22.4
90-91—Washington	64	2401	713	1511	.472	383	485	.790	114	205	319	292	56	16	255	1817	5.0	4.6	28.4
91-92—Washington.....							Did not play—injured.												
92-93—New Jersey	32	430	91	177	.514	39	57	.684	35	41	76	18	11	3	21	223	2.4	0.6	7.0
Totals	874	29417	7830	15109	.518	3972	5444	.730	1704	3356	5060	2863	866	230	2791	19655	5.8	3.3	22.5

Three-point field goals: 1980-81, 2-for-6 (.333). 1981-82, 1-for-5 (.200). 1982-83, 0-for-6. 1983-84, 0-for-4. 1984-85, 1-for-10 (.100). 1987-88, 1-for-6 (.167). 1988-89, 5-for-30 (.167). 1989-90, 3-for-23 (.130). 1990-91, 8-for-37 (.216). 1992-93, 2-for-7 (.286). Totals, 23-for-134 (.172).

Personal fouls/disqualifications: 1977-78, 302/5. 1978-79, 326/10. 1979-80, 66/3. 1980-81, 304/5. 1981-82, 285/6. 1982-83, 233/5. 1983-84, 273/2. 1984-85, 191/3. 1986-87, 14/0. 1987-88, 202/3. 1988-89, 219/1. 1989-90, 230/1. 1990-91, 187/1. 1992-93, 53/0. Totals, 2885/45.

NBA PLAYOFF RECORD

Season Team	G	Min.	FGM	FGA	Pct.	FTM	FTA	Pct.	REBOUNDS Off.	Def.	Tot.	Ast.	St.	Blk.	TO	Pts.	AVERAGES RPG	APG	PPG
78-79—New Jersey	2	81	21	42	.500	10	24	.417	5	6	11	7	4	0	6	52	5.5	3.5	26.0
82-83—New York	6	184	56	97	.577	28	35	.800	8	16	24	13	2	0	10	141	4.0	2.2	23.5
83-84—New York	12	477	162	282	.574	93	123	.756	28	46	74	36	14	6	31	417	6.2	3.0	34.8
87-88—Washington	5	168	26	53	.491	17	21	.810	3	8	11	9	3	0	14	69	2.2	1.8	13.8
92-93—New Jersey	3	24	4	7	.571	0	0	...	1	0	1	0	1	0	1	8	0.3	0.0	2.7
Totals	28	934	269	481	.559	148	203	.729	45	76	121	65	24	6	62	687	4.3	2.3	24.5

Three-point field goals: 1982-83, 1-for-3 (.333). 1983-84, 0-for-1. Totals, 1-for-4 (.250).

Personal fouls/disqualifications: 1978-79, 10/0. 1982-83, 16/0. 1983-84, 48/0. 1987-88, 17/0. 1992-93, 3/0. Totals, 94/0.

NBA ALL-STAR GAME RECORD

Season Team	Min.	FGM	FGA	Pct.	FTM	FTA	Pct.	REBOUNDS Off.	Def.	Tot.	Ast.	PF	Dq.	St.	Blk.	TO	Pts.
1982 —Golden State......	14	2	7	.286	2	2	1.000	0	4	4	1	2	0	3	1	2	6
1984 —New York..........	22	8	13	.615	2	5	.400	2	1	3	4	2	0	0	0	0	18
1985 —New York..........	22	6	10	.600	1	2	.500	4	3	7	1	5	0	0	0	1	13
1991 —Washington	26	2	8	.250	4	4	1.000	2	1	3	3	1	0	0	1	1	8
Totals	84	18	38	.474	9	13	.692	8	9	17	9	10	0	3	2	4	45

LAIMBEER, BILL   C

PERSONAL: Born May 19, 1957, in Boston. ... 6-11/260 (2,10/117,9). ... Full name: William Laimbeer Jr. ... Name pronounced lam-BEER.
HIGH SCHOOL: Palos Verdes (Calif.).
JUNIOR COLLEGE: Owens Technical (Ohio).
COLLEGE: Notre Dame.
TRANSACTIONS: Selected by Cleveland Cavaliers in third round (65th pick overall) of 1979 NBA Draft. ... Played in Italy (1979-80). ... Traded by Cavaliers with F Kenny Carr to Detroit Pistons for F Phil Hubbard, C Paul Mokeski and 1982 first- and second-round draft choices (February 16, 1982). ... Announced retirement (December 1, 1993).
MISCELLANEOUS: Member of NBA championship team (1989, 1990). ... Detroit Pistons franchise all-time leading rebounder with 9,430 (1981-82 through 1993-94).

COLLEGIATE RECORD

Season Team	G	Min.	FGM	FGA	Pct.	FTM	FTA	Pct.	Reb.	Ast.	Pts.	AVERAGES RPG	APG	PPG
76-77—Owens Tech...................							Did not play.							
75-76—Notre Dame..................	10	190	32	65	.492	18	23	.783	79	10	82	7.9	1.0	8.2
77-78—Notre Dame..................	29	654	97	175	.554	42	62	.677	190	31	236	6.6	1.1	8.1
78-79—Notre Dame..................	30	614	78	145	.538	35	50	.700	164	30	191	5.5	1.0	6.4
Totals	69	1458	207	385	.538	95	135	.704	433	71	509	6.3	1.0	7.4

ITALIAN LEAGUE RECORD

Season Team	G	Min.	FGM	FGA	Pct.	FTM	FTA	Pct.	Reb.	Ast.	Pts.	AVERAGES RPG	APG	PPG
79-80—Brescia	29	...	258	465	.555	97	124	.782	363	...	613	12.5	...	21.1

NBA REGULAR-SEASON RECORD

Season Team	G	Min.	FGM	FGA	Pct.	FTM	FTA	Pct.	REBOUNDS Off.	Def.	Tot.	Ast.	St.	Blk.	TO	Pts.	AVERAGES RPG	APG	PPG
80-81—Cleveland	81	2460	337	670	.503	117	153	.765	266	427	693	216	56	78	132	791	8.6	2.7	9.8
81-82—Clev.-Det.........	80	1829	265	536	.494	184	232	.793	234	383	617	100	39	64	121	718	7.7	1.3	9.0
82-83—Detroit	82	2871	436	877	.497	245	310	.790	282	711	993	203	51	118	176	1119	12.1	3.2	13.6
83-84—Detroit	82	2864	553	1044	.530	316	365	.866	329	674*1003		149	49	84	151	1422	12.2	1.8	17.3
84-85—Detroit	82	2892	595	1177	.506	244	306	.797	295	718	1013	154	69	71	129	1438	12.4	1.9	17.5
85-86—Detroit	82	2891	545	1107	.492	266	319	.834	305	*770*1075		146	59	65	133	1360	*13.1	1.8	16.6
86-87—Detroit	82	2854	506	1010	.501	245	274	.894	243	712	955	151	72	69	120	1263	11.6	1.8	15.4
87-88—Detroit	82	2897	455	923	.493	187	214	.874	165	667	832	199	66	78	136	1110	10.1	2.4	13.5
88-89—Detroit	81	2640	449	900	.499	178	212	.840	138	638	776	177	51	100	129	1106	9.6	2.2	13.7
89-90—Detroit	81	2675	380	785	.484	164	192	.854	166	614	780	171	57	84	98	981	9.6	2.1	12.1
90-91—Detroit	82	2668	372	778	.478	123	140	.879	173	564	737	157	38	56	98	904	9.0	1.9	11.0
91-92—Detroit	81	2234	342	727	.470	67	75	.893	104	347	451	160	51	54	102	783	5.6	2.0	9.7
92-93—Detroit	79	1933	292	574	.509	93	104	.894	110	309	419	127	46	40	59	687	5.3	1.6	8.7
93-94—Detroit	11	248	47	90	.522	11	13	.846	9	47	56	14	6	4	10	108	5.1	1.3	9.8
Totals	1068	33956	5574	11198	.498	2440	2916	.837	2819	7581	10400	2184	710	965	1594	13790	9.7	2.0	12.9

Three-point field goals: 1981-82, 4-for-13 (.308). 1982-83, 2-for-13 (.154). 1983-84, 0-for-11. 1984-85, 4-for-18 (.222). 1985-86, 4-for-14 (.286). 1986-87, 6-for-21 (.286). 1987-88, 13-for-39 (.333). 1988-89, 30-for-86 (.349). 1989-90, 57-for-158 (.361). 1990-91, 37-for-125 (.296). 1991-92, 32-for-85 (.376). 1992-93, 10-for-27 (.370). 1993-94, 3-for-9 (.333). Totals, 202-for-619 (.326).

Personal fouls/disqualifications: 1980-81, 332/14. 1981-82, 296/5. 1982-83, 320/9. 1983-84, 273/4. 1984-85, 308/4. 1985-86, 291/4. 1986-87, 283/4. 1987-88, 284/6. 1988-89, 259/2. 1989-90, 278/4. 1990-91, 242/3. 1991-92, 225/0. 1992-93, 212/4. 1993-94, 30/0. Totals, 3633/63.

NBA PLAYOFF RECORD

NOTES: Shares NBA Finals single-game record for most points in an overtime period—9 (June 7, 1990, vs. Portland).

Season Team	G	Min.	FGM	FGA	Pct.	FTM	FTA	Pct.	REBOUNDS Off.	Def.	Tot.	Ast.	St.	Blk.	TO	Pts.	AVERAGES RPG	APG	PPG
83-84—Detroit	5	165	29	51	.569	18	20	.900	14	48	62	12	4	3	12	76	12.4	2.4	15.2
84-85—Detroit	9	325	48	107	.449	36	51	.706	36	60	96	15	7	7	16	132	10.7	1.7	14.7
85-86—Detroit	4	168	34	68	.500	21	23	.913	20	36	56	1	2	3	8	90	14.0	0.3	22.5
86-87—Detroit	15	543	84	163	.515	15	24	.625	30	126	156	37	15	12	20	184	10.4	2.5	12.3
87-88—Detroit	23	779	114	250	.456	40	45	.889	43	178	221	44	18	19	30	273	9.6	1.9	11.9
88-89—Detroit	17	497	66	142	.465	25	31	.806	26	114	140	31	6	8	19	172	8.2	1.8	10.1
89-90—Detroit	20	667	91	199	.457	25	29	.862	41	170	211	28	23	18	16	222	10.6	1.4	11.1
90-91—Detroit	15	446	66	148	.446	27	31	.871	42	80	122	19	5	12	17	164	8.1	1.3	10.9
91-92—Detroit	5	145	17	46	.370	5	5	1.000	5	28	33	8	4	1	5	41	6.6	1.6	8.2
Totals	113	3735	549	1174	.468	212	259	.819	257	840	1097	195	84	83	143	1354	9.7	1.7	12.0

Three-point field goals: 1984-85, 0-for-2. 1985-86, 1-for-1. 1986-87, 1-for-5 (.200). 1987-88, 5-for-17 (.294). 1988-89, 15-for-42 (.357). 1989-90, 15-for-43 (.349). 1990-91, 5-for-17 (.294). 1991-92, 2-for-10 (.200). Totals, 44-for-137 (.321).

Personal fouls/disqualifications: 1983-84, 23/2. 1984-85, 32/1. 1985-86, 19/1. 1986-87, 53/2. 1987-88, 77/2. 1988-89, 55/1. 1989-90, 77/3. 1990-91, 54/0. 1991-92, 18/1. Totals, 408/13.

NBA ALL-STAR GAME RECORD

Season Team	Min.	FGM	FGA	Pct.	FTM	FTA	Pct.	REBOUNDS Off.	Def.	Tot.	Ast.	PF	Dq.	St.	Blk.	TO	Pts.
1983 —Detroit	6	1	1	1.000	0	0		1	0	1	0	1	0	0	0	1	2
1984 —Detroit	17	6	8	.750	1	1	1.000	1	4	5	0	3	0	1	2	0	13
1985 —Detroit	11	2	4	.500	1	2	.500	1	2	3	1	1	0	0	0	0	5
1987 —Detroit	11	4	7	.571	0	0		0	2	2	1	2	0	1	0	0	8
Totals	45	13	20	.650	2	3	.667	3	8	11	2	7	0	2	2	1	28

LANIER, BOB   C

PERSONAL: Born September 10, 1948, in Buffalo. ... 6-11/265 (2,10/120,2). ... Full name: Robert Jerry Lanier Jr.
HIGH SCHOOL: Bennett (Buffalo).
COLLEGE: St. Bonaventure.
TRANSACTIONS: Selected by Detroit Pistons in first round (first pick overall) of 1970 NBA Draft. ... Traded by Pistons to Milwaukee Bucks for C Kent Benson and 1980 first-round draft choice (February 4, 1980).
CAREER NOTES: Chairman, NBA Stay in School Program (1989-94). ... Special assistant to the Commissioner/ Chairman, NBA Team-Up Program (1996-present).
CAREER HONORS: Elected to Naismith Memorial Basketball Hall of Fame (1992).

COLLEGIATE RECORD

NOTES: THE SPORTING NEWS All-America first team (1970).

Season Team	G	Min.	FGM	FGA	Pct.	FTM	FTA	Pct.	Reb.	Ast.	Pts.	AVERAGES RPG	APG	PPG
66-67—St. Bonaventure‡	15	...	...	...		...	...		...	...	450	...	...	30.0
67-68—St. Bonaventure	25	...	272	466	.584	112	175	.640	390	...	656	15.6	...	26.2
68-69—St. Bonaventure	24	...	270	460	.587	114	181	.630	374	...	654	15.6	...	27.3
69-70—St. Bonaventure	26	...	308	549	.561	141	194	.727	416	...	757	16.0	...	29.1
Varsity totals	75	...	850	1475	.576	367	550	.667	1180	...	2067	15.7	...	27.6

NBA REGULAR-SEASON RECORD

HONORS: NBA All-Rookie team (1971). ... J. Walter Kennedy Citizenship Award (1978).

Season Team	G	Min.	FGM	FGA	Pct.	FTM	FTA	Pct.	Reb.	Ast.	PF	Dq.	Pts.	AVERAGES RPG	APG	PPG
70-71—Detroit	82	2017	504	1108	.455	273	376	.726	665	146	272	4	1281	8.1	1.8	15.6
71-72—Detroit	80	3092	834	1690	.494	388	505	.768	1132	248	297	6	2056	14.2	3.1	25.7
72-73—Detroit	81	3150	810	1654	.490	307	397	.773	1205	260	278	4	1927	14.9	3.2	23.8

Season Team	G	Min.	FGM	FGA	Pct.	FTM	FTA	Pct.	REBOUNDS Off.	Def.	Tot.	Ast.	St.	Blk.	TO	Pts.	AVERAGES RPG	APG	PPG
73-74—Detroit	81	3047	748	1483	.504	326	409	.797	269	805	1074	343	110	247	...	1822	13.3	4.2	22.5
74-75—Detroit	76	2987	731	1433	.510	361	450	.802	225	689	914	350	75	172	...	1823	12.0	4.6	24.0
75-76—Detroit	64	2363	541	1017	.532	284	370	.768	217	529	746	217	79	86	...	1366	11.7	3.4	21.3
76-77—Detroit	64	2446	678	1269	.534	260	318	.818	200	545	745	214	70	126	...	1616	11.6	3.3	25.3
77-78—Detroit	63	2311	622	1159	.537	298	386	.772	197	518	715	216	82	93	225	1542	11.3	3.4	24.5
78-79—Detroit	53	1835	489	950	.515	275	367	.749	164	330	494	140	50	75	175	1253	9.3	2.6	23.6
79-80—Detroit-Mil.	63	2131	466	867	.537	277	354	.782	152	400	552	184	74	89	162	1210	8.8	2.9	19.2
80-81—Milwaukee	67	1753	376	716	.525	208	277	.751	128	285	413	179	73	81	139	961	6.2	2.7	14.3
81-82—Milwaukee	74	1986	407	729	.558	182	242	.752	92	296	388	219	72	56	166	996	5.2	3.0	13.5
82-83—Milwaukee	39	978	163	332	.491	91	133	.684	58	142	200	105	34	24	82	417	5.1	2.7	10.7
83-84—Milwaukee	72	2007	392	685	.572	194	274	.708	141	314	455	186	58	51	163	978	6.3	2.6	13.6
Totals	959	32103	7761	15092	.514	3724	4858	.767	...	9698	3007	777	1100	1112	19248	10.1	3.1	20.1

Three-point field goals: 1979-80, 1-for-6 (.167). 1980-81, 1-for-1. 1981-82, 0-for-2. 1982-83, 0-for-1. 1983-84, 0-for-3. Totals, 2-for-13 (.154).

Personal fouls/disqualifications: 1973-74, 273/7. 1974-75, 237/1. 1975-76, 203/2. 1976-77, 174/0. 1977-78, 185/2. 1978-79, 181/5. 1979-80, 200/3. 1980-81, 184/0. 1981-82, 211/3. 1982-83, 125/2. 1983-84, 228/8. Totals, 3048/47.

NBA PLAYOFF RECORD

Season Team	G	Min.	FGM	FGA	Pct.	FTM	FTA	Pct.	REBOUNDS Off.	Def.	Tot.	Ast.	St.	Blk.	TO	Pts.	AVERAGES RPG	APG	PPG
73-74—Detroit	7	303	77	152	.507	30	38	.789	26	81	107	21	4	14	...	184	15.3	3.0	26.3
74-75—Detroit	3	128	26	51	.510	9	12	.750	5	27	32	19	4	12	...	61	10.7	6.3	20.3
75-76—Detroit	9	359	95	172	.552	45	50	.900	39	75	114	30	8	21	...	235	12.7	3.3	26.1

Season Team	G	Min.	FGM	FGA	Pct.	FTM	FTA	Pct.	REBOUNDS Off.	Def.	Tot.	Ast.	St.	Blk.	TO	Pts.	AVERAGES RPG	APG	PPG
76-77—Detroit	3	118	34	54	.630	16	19	.842	13	37	50	6	3	7	...	84	16.7	2.0	28.0
79-80—Milwaukee	7	256	52	101	.515	31	42	.738	17	48	65	31	7	8	17	135	9.3	4.4	19.3
80-81—Milwaukee	7	236	50	85	.588	23	32	.719	12	40	52	28	12	8	15	123	7.4	4.0	17.6
81-82—Milwaukee	6	212	41	80	.513	14	25	.560	18	27	45	22	8	5	14	96	7.5	3.7	16.0
82-83—Milwaukee	9	250	51	89	.573	21	35	.600	17	46	63	23	5	14	21	123	7.0	2.6	13.7
83-84—Milwaukee	16	499	82	171	.480	39	44	.886	32	85	117	55	11	10	38	203	7.3	3.4	12.7
Totals	67	2361	508	955	.532	228	297	.768	179	466	645	235	62	99	105	1244	9.6	3.5	18.6

Three-point field goals: 1981-82, 0-for-1.

Personal fouls/disqualifications: 1973-74, 28/1. 1974-75, 10/0. 1975-76, 34/1. 1976-77, 10/0. 1979-80, 23/0. 1980-81, 18/0. 1981-82, 21/2. 1982-83, 32/2. 1983-84, 57/1. Totals, 233/7.

NBA ALL-STAR GAME RECORD

NOTES: NBA All-Star Game Most Valuable Player (1974).

Season	Team	Min.	FGM	FGA	Pct.	FTM	FTA	Pct.	Reb.	Ast.	PF	Dq.	Pts.
1972	—Detroit.....................	5	0	2	.000	2	3	.667	3	0	0	0	2
1973	—Detroit.....................	12	5	9	.556	0	0	...	6	0	1	0	10

Season	Team	Min.	FGM	FGA	Pct.	FTM	FTA	Pct.	REBOUNDS Off.	Def.	Tot.	Ast.	PF	Dq.	St.	Blk.	TO	Pts.
1974	—Detroit..............	26	11	15	.733	2	2	1.000	2	8	10	2	1	0	0	2	...	24
1975	—Detroit..............	12	1	4	.250	0	0	...	2	5	7	2	3	0	2	0	...	2
1977	—Detroit..............	20	7	8	.875	3	3	1.000	5	5	10	4	3	0	1	1	...	17
1978	—Detroit..............	4	0	0		1	2	.500	2	0	2	0	0	0	0	0	1	1
1979	—Detroit..............	31	5	10	.500	0	0	...	1	3	4	4	4	0	1	1	0	10
1982	—Milwaukee........	11	3	7	.429	2	2	1.000	2	1	3	0	3	0	0	1	1	8
Totals...........................		121	32	55	.582	10	12	.833	...	45	12	15	0	4	5	2	74

NBA COACHING RECORD

BACKGROUND: Assistant coach, Golden State Warriors (beginning of 1994-95 season-February 13, 1995).

Season Team	REGULAR SEASON W	L	Pct.	Finish	PLAYOFFS W	L	Pct.
94-95 —Golden State..	12	25	.324	6th/Pacific Division	—	—	—

NOTES:
1995—Replaced Don Nelson as head coach (February 13), with record of 14-31 and club in sixth place.

LUCAS, JERRY   F/C

PERSONAL: Born March 30, 1940, in Middletown, Ohio. ... 6-8/235 (2,03/106,6). ... Full name: Jerry Ray Lucas. ... Nickname: Luke.
HIGH SCHOOL: Middletown (Ohio).
COLLEGE: Ohio State.
TRANSACTIONS: Selected by Cincinnati Royals in 1962 NBA Draft (territorial pick). ... Signed by Cleveland Pipers of American Basketball League (1962); Pipers dropped out of ABL prior to 1962-63 season. ... Did not play pro basketball (1962-63). ... Traded by Royals to San Francisco Warriors for G Jim King and F Bill Turner (October 25, 1969). ... Traded by Warriors to New York Knicks for F Cazzie Russell (May 7, 1971).
CAREER HONORS: Elected to Naismith Memorial Basketball Hall of Fame (1980). ... One of the 50 Greatest Players in NBA History (1996).
MISCELLANEOUS: Member of NBA championship team (1973). ... Member of gold-medal-winning U.S. Olympic team (1960).

COLLEGIATE RECORD

NOTES: THE SPORTING NEWS College Player of the Year (1961, 1962). ... THE SPORTING NEWS All-America first team (1960, 1961, 1962). ... Member of NCAA championship team (1960). ... Led NCAA Division I with .637 field-goal percentage (1960), .623 field-goal percentage (1961) and .611 field-goal percentage (1962). ... Led NCAA Division I with .198 rebound average (1960-61) and .211 rebound average (1961-62), when championship was determined by highest individual recoveries as percentage of total recoveries by both teams in all games.

Season Team	G	Min.	FGM	FGA	Pct.	FTM	FTA	Pct.	Reb.	Ast.	Pts.	AVERAGES RPG	APG	PPG
58-59—Ohio State‡					Freshman team did not play intercollegiate schedule.									
59-60—Ohio State	27	...	283	444	.637	144	187	.770	442	...	710	16.4	...	26.3
60-61—Ohio State	27	...	256	411	.623	159	208	.764	470	...	671	17.4	...	24.9
61-62—Ohio State	28	...	237	388	.611	135	169	.799	499	...	609	17.8	...	21.8
Varsity totals	82	...	776	1243	.624	438	564	.777	1411	...	1990	17.2	...	24.3

NBA REGULAR-SEASON RECORD

HONORS: NBA Rookie of the Year (1964). ... All-NBA first team (1965, 1966, 1968). ... All-NBA second team (1964, 1967). ... NBA All-Rookie team (1964).

Season Team	G	Min.	FGM	FGA	Pct.	FTM	FTA	Pct.	Reb.	Ast.	PF	Dq.	Pts.	AVERAGES RPG	APG	PPG
63-64 —Cincinnati........................	79	3273	545	1035	*.527	310	398	.779	1375	204	300	6	1400	17.4	2.6	17.7
64-65 —Cincinnati........................	66	2864	558	1121	.498	298	366	.814	1321	157	214	1	1414	20.0	2.4	21.4
65-66 —Cincinnati........................	79	3517	690	1523	.453	317	403	.787	1668	213	274	5	1697	21.1	2.7	21.5
66-67 —Cincinnati........................	81	3558	577	1257	.459	284	359	.791	1547	268	280	2	1438	19.1	3.3	17.8
67-68 —Cincinnati........................	82	3619	707	1361	.519	346	445	.778	1560	251	243	3	1760	19.0	3.1	21.5
68-69 —Cincinnati........................	74	3075	555	1007	.551	247	327	.755	1360	306	206	0	1357	18.4	4.1	18.3
69-70 —Cin.-San Francisco	67	2420	405	799	.507	200	255	.784	951	173	166	2	1010	14.2	2.6	15.1
70-71 —San Francisco	80	3251	623	1250	.498	289	367	.787	1265	293	197	0	1535	15.8	3.7	19.2
71-72 —New York	77	2926	543	1060	.512	197	249	.791	1011	318	218	1	1283	13.1	4.1	16.7
72-73 —New York	71	2001	312	608	.513	80	100	.800	510	317	157	0	704	7.2	4.5	9.9

Season Team	G	Min.	FGM	FGA	Pct.	FTM	FTA	Pct.	REBOUNDS Off.	Def.	Tot.	Ast.	St.	Blk.	TO	Pts.	AVERAGES RPG	APG	PPG
73-74—New York....	73	1627	194	420	.462	67	96	.698	62	312	374	230	28	24	...	455	5.1	3.2	6.2
Totals	829	32131	5709	11441	.499	2635	3365	.783	...	...	12942	2730	28	24	...	14053	15.6	3.3	17.0

Personal fouls/disqualifications: 1973-74, 134/0.

NBA PLAYOFF RECORD

Season Team	G	Min.	FGM	FGA	Pct.	FTM	FTA	Pct.	Reb.	Ast.	PF	Dq.	Pts.	AVERAGES RPG	APG	PPG
63-64 —Cincinnati	10	370	48	123	.390	26	37	.703	125	34	37	1	122	12.5	3.4	12.2
64-65 —Cincinnati	4	195	38	75	.507	17	22	.773	84	9	12	0	93	21.0	2.3	23.3
65-66 —Cincinnati	5	231	40	85	.471	27	35	.771	101	14	14	0	107	20.2	2.8	21.4
66-67 —Cincinnati	4	183	24	55	.436	2	2	1.000	77	8	15	0	50	19.3	2.0	12.5
70-71 —San Francisco	5	171	39	77	.507	11	16	.688	50	16	14	0	89	10.0	3.2	17.8
71-72 —New York	16	737	119	238	.500	59	71	.831	173	85	49	1	297	10.8	5.3	18.6
72-73 —New York	17	368	54	112	.482	20	23	.870	85	39	47	0	128	5.0	2.3	7.5

Season Team	G	Min.	FGM	FGA	Pct.	FTM	FTA	Pct.	REBOUNDS Off.	Def.	Tot.	Ast.	St.	Blk.	TO	Pts.	AVERAGES RPG	APG	PPG
73-74 —New York	11	115	5	21	.238	0	0	...	6	16	22	9	4	0	...	10	2.0	0.8	0.9
Totals	72	2370	367	786	.467	162	206	.786	...	...	717	214	4	0	...	896	10.0	3.0	12.4

Personal fouls/disqualifications: 1973-74, 9/0.

NBA ALL-STAR GAME RECORD

NOTES: NBA All-Star Game Most Valuable Player (1965).

Season Team	Min.	FGM	FGA	Pct.	FTM	FTA	Pct.	Reb	Ast.	PF	Dq.	Pts.
1964 —Cincinnati	36	3	6	.500	5	6	.833	8	0	5	0	11
1965 —Cincinnati	35	12	19	.632	1	1	1.000	10	1	2	0	25
1966 —Cincinnati	23	4	11	.364	2	2	1.000	19	0	2	0	10
1967 —Cincinnati	22	3	5	.600	1	1	1.000	7	2	3	0	7
1968 —Cincinnati	21	6	9	.667	4	4	1.000	5	4	3	0	16
1969 —Cincinnati	17	2	5	.400	4	5	.800	6	1	3	0	8
1971 —San Francisco	29	5	9	.556	2	2	1.000	9	4	2	0	12
Totals	183	35	64	.547	19	21	.905	64	12	20	0	89

MACAULEY, ED   C/F

PERSONAL: Born March 22, 1928, in St. Louis. ... 6-8/190 (2,03/86,2). ... Full name: Charles Edward Macauley Jr. ... Nickname: Easy Ed.
HIGH SCHOOL: St. Louis University High School (St. Louis).
COLLEGE: St. Louis.
TRANSACTIONS: Selected by St. Louis Bombers in 1949 Basketball Association of America Draft (territorial pick). ... Selected by Boston Celtics in NBA dispersal draft (April 25, 1950). ... Traded by Celtics with draft rights to F/G Cliff Hagan to St. Louis Hawks for draft rights to C Bill Russell (April 29, 1956).
CAREER HONORS: Elected to Naismith Memorial Basketball Hall of Fame (1960).
MISCELLANEOUS: Member of NBA championship team (1958).

COLLEGIATE RECORD

NOTES: The Sporting News All-America first team (1949). ... Led NCAA Division I with .524 field-goal percentage (1949).

Season Team	G	Min.	FGM	FGA	Pct.	FTM	FTA	Pct.	Reb.	Ast.	Pts.	AVERAGES RPG	APG	PPG
45-46—St. Louis	23	...	94	...	...	71	...	...	...	...	259	...	...	11.3
46-47—St. Louis	28	...	141	...	...	104	...	...	...	...	386	...	...	13.8
47-48—St. Louis	27	...	132	324	.407	104	159	.654	...	...	368	...	...	13.6
48-49—St. Louis	26	...	144	275	.524	116	153	.758	...	...	404	...	...	15.5
Totals	104	...	511	...	...	395	...	...	...	...	1417	...	...	13.6

NBA REGULAR-SEASON RECORD

HONORS: All-NBA first team (1951, 1952, 1953). ... All-NBA second team (1954).

Season Team	G	Min.	FGM	FGA	Pct.	FTM	FTA	Pct.	Reb.	Ast.	PF	Dq.	Pts.	AVERAGES RPG	APG	PPG
49-50—St. Louis	67	...	351	882	.398	379	528	.718	...	200	221	...	1081	...	3.0	16.1
50-51—Boston	68	...	459	985	.466	466	614	.759	616	252	205	4	1384	9.1	3.7	20.4
51-52—Boston	66	2631	384	888	.432	496	621	.799	529	232	174	0	1264	8.0	3.5	19.2
52-53—Boston	69	2902	451	997	.452	500	667	.750	629	280	188	0	1402	9.1	4.1	20.3
53-54—Boston	71	2792	462	950 *	.486	420	554	.758	571	271	168	1	1344	8.0	3.8	18.9
54-55—Boston	71	2706	403	951	.424	442	558	.792	600	275	171	0	1248	8.5	3.9	17.6
55-56—Boston	71	2354	420	995	.422	400	504	.794	422	211	158	2	1240	5.9	3.0	17.5
56-57—St. Louis	72	2582	414	987	.419	359	479	.749	440	202	206	2	1187	6.1	2.8	16.5
57-58—St. Louis	72	1908	376	879	.428	267	369	.724	478	143	156	2	1019	6.6	2.0	14.2
58-59—St. Louis	14	196	22	75	.293	21	35	.600	40	13	20	1	65	2.9	0.9	4.6
Totals	641	...	3742	8589	.436	3750	4929	.761	...	2079	1667	...	11234	...	3.2	17.5

NBA PLAYOFF RECORD

Season Team	G	Min.	FGM	FGA	Pct.	FTM	FTA	Pct.	Reb.	Ast.	PF	Dq.	Pts.	AVERAGES RPG	APG	PPG
50-51—Boston	2	...	17	36	.472	10	16	.625	18	8	4	0	44	9.0	4.0	22.0
51-52—Boston	3	129	27	49	.551	16	19	.842	33	11	11	1	70	11.0	3.7	23.3
52-53—Boston	6	278	31	71	.437	39	54	.722	58	21	23	2	101	9.7	3.5	16.8
53-54—Boston	5	127	8	22	.364	9	13	.692	21	21	14	0	25	4.2	4.2	5.0
54-55—Boston	7	283	43	93	.462	41	54	.759	52	32	21	0	127	7.4	4.6	18.1
55-56—Boston	3	73	12	30	.400	7	11	.636	15	5	6	0	31	5.0	1.7	10.3
56-57—St. Louis	10	297	44	109	.404	54	74	.730	62	22	39	3	142	6.2	2.2	14.2
57-58—St. Louis	11	227	36	89	.405	36	50	.720	62	18	23	0	108	5.6	1.6	9.8
Totals	47	...	218	499	.437	212	291	.729	321	138	141	6	648	6.8	2.9	13.8

NBA ALL-STAR GAME RECORD

NOTES: NBA All-Star Game Most Valuable Player (1951).

Season	Team	Min.	FGM	FGA	Pct.	FTM	FTA	Pct.	Reb	Ast.	PF	Dq.	Pts.
1951	—Boston	...	7	12	.583	6	7	.857	6	1	3	0	20
1952	—Boston	28	3	7	.429	9	9	1.000	7	3	2	0	15
1953	—Boston	35	5	12	.417	8	8	1.000	7	3	2	0	18
1954	—Boston	25	4	11	.364	5	6	.833	1	3	2	0	13
1955	—Boston	27	1	5	.200	4	5	.800	4	2	1	0	6
1956	—Boston	20	1	9	.111	2	4	.500	2	3	3	0	4
1957	—St. Louis	19	3	6	.500	1	2	.500	5	3	0	0	7
Totals		...	24	62	.387	35	41	.854	32	18	13	0	83

NBA COACHING RECORD

		REGULAR SEASON					PLAYOFFS		
Season	Team	W	L	Pct.	Finish		W	L	Pct.
58-59	—St. Louis	43	19	.694	1st/Western Division		2	4	.333
59-60	—St. Louis	46	29	.613	1st/Western Division		7	7	.500
Totals (2 years)		89	48	.650		Totals (2 years)	9	11	.450

NOTES:
1958—Replaced Andy Phillip as St. Louis head coach (November), with record of 6-4.
1959—Lost to Minneapolis in Western Division Finals.
1960—Defeated Minneapolis, 4-3, in Western Division Finals; lost to Boston, 4-3, in NBA Finals.

MALONE, JEFF   G

PERSONAL: Born June 28, 1961, in Mobile, Ala. ... 6-4/205 (1,93/93,0). ... Full name: Jeffrey Nigel Malone.
HIGH SCHOOL: Southwest (Macon, Ga.).
COLLEGE: Mississippi State.
TRANSACTIONS: Selected by Washington Bullets in first round (10th pick overall) of 1983 NBA Draft. ... Traded by Bullets to Utah Jazz in three-way deal in which Sacramento Kings sent F Pervis Ellison to Bullets and Jazz sent G Bob Hansen, F/C Eric Leckner and 1990 first- and second-round draft choices to Kings (June 25, 1990); Jazz also received 1990 second-round draft choice from Kings and Kings also received 1991 second-round draft choice from Bullets. ... Traded by Jazz with 1994 conditional first-round draft choice to Philadelphia 76ers for G Jeff Hornacek and G Sean Green (February 24, 1994). ... Waived by 76ers (January 4, 1996). ... Signed by Miami to first of two consecutive 10-day contracts (February 12, 1996). ... Re-signed by Heat for remainder of season (March 3, 1996). ... Played in Greece (1996-97).
CAREER NOTES: Head coach, Columbus Riverdragons (NBDL).

COLLEGIATE RECORD

NOTES: The Sporting News All-America first team (1983).

												AVERAGES		
Season Team	G	Min.	FGM	FGA	Pct.	FTM	FTA	Pct.	Reb.	Ast.	Pts.	RPG	APG	PPG
79-80—Mississippi State	27	781	139	303	.459	42	51	.824	90	39	320	3.3	1.4	11.9
80-81—Mississippi State	27	999	219	447	.490	105	128	.820	113	43	543	4.2	1.6	20.1
81-82—Mississippi State	27	1001	225	410	.549	52	70	.743	111	20	502	4.1	0.7	18.6
82-83—Mississippi State	29	1070	323	608	.531	131	159	.824	106	66	777	3.7	2.3	26.8
Totals	110	3851	906	1768	.512	330	408	.809	420	168	2142	3.8	1.5	19.5

NBA REGULAR-SEASON RECORD

HONORS: NBA All-Rookie team (1984).

									REBOUNDS								AVERAGES		
Season Team	G	Min.	FGM	FGA	Pct.	FTM	FTA	Pct.	Off.	Def.	Tot.	Ast.	St.	Blk.	TO	Pts.	RPG	APG	PPG
83-84—Washington	81	1976	408	918	.444	142	172	.826	57	98	155	151	23	13	110	982	1.9	1.9	12.1
84-85—Washington	76	2613	605	1213	.499	211	250	.844	60	146	206	184	52	9	107	1436	2.7	2.4	18.9
85-86—Washington	80	2992	735	1522	.483	322	371	.868	66	222	288	191	70	12	168	1795	3.6	2.4	22.4
86-87—Washington	80	2763	689	1509	.457	376	425	.885	50	168	218	298	75	13	182	1758	2.7	3.7	22.0
87-88—Washington	80	2655	648	1360	.476	335	380	.882	44	162	206	237	51	13	172	1641	2.6	3.0	20.5
88-89—Washington	76	2418	677	1410	.480	296	340	.871	55	124	179	219	39	14	165	1651	2.4	2.9	21.7
89-90—Washington	75	2567	781	1592	.491	257	293	.877	54	152	206	243	48	6	125	1820	2.7	3.2	24.3
90-91—Utah	69	2466	525	1034	.508	231	252	.917	36	170	206	143	50	6	108	1282	3.0	2.1	18.6
91-92—Utah	81	2922	691	1353	.511	256	285	.898	49	184	233	180	56	5	140	1639	2.9	2.2	20.2
92-93—Utah	79	2558	595	1205	.494	236	277	.852	31	142	173	128	42	4	125	1429	2.2	1.6	18.1
93-94—Utah-Phil.	77	2560	525	1081	.486	205	247	.830	51	148	199	125	40	5	85	1262	2.6	1.6	16.4
94-95—Philadelphia	19	660	144	284	.507	51	59	.864	11	44	55	29	15	0	29	350	2.9	1.5	18.4
95-96—Phil.-Miami	32	510	76	168	.452	29	32	.906	8	32	40	26	16	0	22	186	1.3	0.8	5.8
Totals	905	29660	7099	14674	.484	2947	3383	.871	572	1792	2364	2154	577	100	1538	17231	2.6	2.4	19.0

Three-point field goals: 1983-84, 24-for-74 (.324). 1984-85, 15-for-72 (.208). 1985-86, 3-for-17 (.176). 1986-87, 4-for-26 (.154). 1987-88, 10-for-24 (.417). 1988-89, 1-for-19 (.053). 1989-90, 1-for-6 (.167). 1990-91, 1-for-6 (.167). 1991-92, 1-for-12 (.083). 1992-93, 3-for-9 (.333). 1993-94, 7-for-12 (.583). 1994-95, 11-for-28 (.393). 1995-96, 5-for-16 (.313). Totals, 86-for-321 (.268).
Personal fouls/disqualifications: 1983-84, 162/1. 1984-85, 176/1. 1985-86, 180/2. 1986-87, 154/0. 1987-88, 198/1. 1988-89, 155/0. 1989-90, 116/1. 1990-91, 128/0. 1991-92, 126/1. 1992-93, 117/0. 1993-94, 123/0. 1994-95, 35/0. 1995-96, 25/0. Totals, 1695/7.

NBA PLAYOFF RECORD

									REBOUNDS								AVERAGES		
Season Team	G	Min.	FGM	FGA	Pct.	FTM	FTA	Pct.	Off.	Def.	Tot.	Ast.	St.	Blk.	TO	Pts.	RPG	APG	PPG
83-84—Washington	4	71	12	26	.462	0	0	...	2	3	5	2	1	0	3	24	1.3	0.5	6.0
84-85—Washington	4	126	27	56	.482	10	13	.769	3	3	6	8	5	0	4	65	1.5	2.0	16.3
85-86—Washington	5	197	42	103	.408	26	29	.897	4	12	16	17	7	3	11	110	3.2	3.4	22.0
86-87—Washington	3	105	17	46	.370	11	11	1.000	1	6	7	9	1	0	11	45	2.3	3.0	15.0
87-88—Washington	5	199	50	97	.515	28	37	.757	3	14	17	11	5	5	14	128	3.4	2.2	25.6
90-91—Utah	9	351	71	144	.493	44	48	.917	7	28	35	29	9	1	12	186	3.9	3.2	20.7
91-92—Utah	16	610	134	275	.487	62	72	.861	12	27	39	31	8	2	26	331	2.4	1.9	20.7
92-93—Utah	5	150	29	65	.446	9	13	.692	3	13	16	3	3	1	9	67	3.2	0.6	13.4
Totals	51	1809	382	812	.470	190	223	.852	35	106	141	110	39	12	90	956	2.8	2.2	18.7

Three-point field goals: 1983-84, 0-for-1. 1984-85, 1-for-3 (.333). 1985-86, 0-for-2. 1987-88, 0-for-1. 1990-91, 0-for-2. 1991-92, 1-for-3 (.333). Totals, 2-for-12 (.167).
Personal fouls/disqualifications: 1983-84, 6/0. 1984-85, 14/1. 1985-86, 13/0. 1986-87, 8/0. 1987-88, 16/0. 1990-91, 22/0. 1991-92, 33/0. 1992-93, 11/0. Totals, 123/1.

ALL-TIME GREAT PLAYERS

NBA ALL-STAR GAME RECORD

Season Team	Min.	FGM	FGA	Pct.	FTM	FTA	Pct.	REBOUNDS Off.	Def.	Tot.	Ast.	PF	Dq.	St.	Blk.	TO	Pts.
1986 —Washington	12	3	5	.600	0	0	...	0	1	1	4	0	0	1	0	0	6
1987 —Washington	13	3	5	.600	0	0	...	1	1	2	2	1	0	0	0	1	6
Totals	25	6	10	.600	0	0	...	1	2	3	6	1	0	1	0	1	12

Three-point field goals: 1987, 0-for-1.

GREEK LEAGUE RECORD

Season Team	G	Min.	FGM	FGA	Pct.	FTM	FTA	Pct.	Reb.	Ast.	Pts.	AVERAGES RPG	APG	PPG
96-97—VAO	12	423	65	165	.394	35	46	.761	29	12	175	2.4	1.0	14.6

MALONE, MOSES C

PERSONAL: Born March 23, 1955, in Petersburg, Va. ... 6-10/260 (2,08/117,9). ... Full name: Moses Eugene Malone.
HIGH SCHOOL: Petersburg (Va.).
COLLEGE: Did not attend college.
TRANSACTIONS: Selected out of high school by Utah Stars in third round of 1974 American Basketball Association Draft. ... Contract sold by Stars to Spirits of St. Louis (December 2, 1975). ... Selected by Portland Trail Blazers of NBA from Spirits in ABA dispersal draft (August 5, 1976). ... Traded by Trail Blazers to Buffalo Braves for 1978 first-round draft choice (October 18, 1976). ... Traded by Braves to Houston Rockets for 1977 and 1978 first-round draft choices (October 24, 1976). ... Signed as veteran free agent by Philadelphia 76ers (September 2, 1982); Rockets matched offer and traded Malone to 76ers for F/C Caldwell Jones and 1983 first-round draft choice (September 15, 1982). ... Traded by 76ers with F Terry Catledge and 1986 and 1988 first-round draft choices to Washington Bullets for C/F Jeff Ruland and F Cliff Robinson (June 16, 1986). ... Signed as unrestricted free agent by Atlanta Hawks (August 16, 1988). ... Signed as unrestricted free agent by Milwaukee Bucks (July 10, 1991). ... Signed as free agent by 76ers (August 12, 1993). ... Waived by 76ers (June 17, 1994). ... Signed as free agent by San Antonio Spurs (August 10, 1994).
CAREER HONORS: Elected to the Naismith Memorial Basketball Hall of Fame (2001). ... One of the 50 Greatest Players in NBA History (1996).
MISCELLANEOUS: Member of NBA championship team (1983).
NOTES: ABA All-Rookie team (1975).

ABA REGULAR-SEASON RECORD

Season Team	G	Min.	2-POINT FGM	FGA	Pct.	3-POINT FGM	FGA	Pct.	FTM	FTA	Pct.	Reb.	Ast.	Pts.	AVERAGES RPG	APG	PPG
74-75—Utah	83	3205	591	1034	.572	0	1	.000	375	591	.635	1209	82	1557	14.6	1.0	18.8
75-76—St. Louis	43	1168	251	488	.514	0	2	.000	112	183	.612	413	58	614	9.6	1.3	14.3
Totals	126	4373	842	1522	.553	0	3	.000	487	774	.629	1622	140	2171	12.9	1.1	17.2

ABA PLAYOFF RECORD

Season Team	G	Min.	2-POINT FGM	FGA	Pct.	3-POINT FGM	FGA	Pct.	FTM	FTA	Pct.	Reb.	Ast.	Pts.	AVERAGES RPG	APG	PPG
74-75—Utah	6	235	51	80	.638	0	0	...	34	51	.667	105	9	136	17.5	1.5	22.7

ABA ALL-STAR GAME RECORD

Season Team	Min.	2-POINT FGM	FGA	Pct.	3-POINT FGM	FGA	Pct.	FTM	FTA	Pct.	Reb.	Ast.	Pts.
1975—Utah	20	2	3	.667	0	0	...	2	5	.400	10	0	6

NBA REGULAR-SEASON RECORD

RECORDS: Holds career records for most consecutive games without a disqualification—1,212 (January 7, 1978 through 1994-95 season); and most offensive rebounds—6,731. ... Holds single-season record for most offensive rebounds—587 (1979). ... Holds single-game record for most offensive rebounds—21 (February 11, 1982, vs. Seattle).
HONORS: NBA Most Valuable Player (1979, 1982, 1983). ... All-NBA first team (1979, 1982, 1983, 1985). ... All-NBA second team (1980, 1981, 1984, 1987). ... NBA All-Defensive first team (1983). ... NBA All-Defensive second team (1979).

Season Team	G	Min.	FGM	FGA	Pct.	FTM	FTA	Pct.	REBOUNDS Off.	Def.	Tot.	Ast.	St.	Blk.	TO	Pts.	AVERAGES RPG	APG	PPG
76-77—Buff.-Houston	82	2506	389	810	.480	305	440	.693	*437	635	1072	89	67	181	...	1083	13.1	1.1	13.2
77-78—Houston	59	2107	413	828	.499	318	443	.718	*380	506	886	31	48	76	220	1144	15.0	0.5	19.4
78-79—Houston	82	*3390	716	1325	.540	599	811	.739	*587	*857	*1444	147	79	119	326	2031	*17.6	1.8	24.8
79-80—Houston	82	3140	778	1549	.502	563	*783	.719	*573	617	1190	147	80	107	300	2119	14.5	1.8	25.8
80-81—Houston	80	3245	806	1545	.522	*804	.757	*474	706	*1180	141	83	150	*308	2222	*14.8	1.8	27.8
81-82—Houston	81	*3398	945	1822	.519	630	*827	.762	*558	630	*1188	142	76	125	294	2520	*14.7	1.8	31.1
82-83—Philadelphia	78	2922	654	1305	.501	*600	*788	.761	*445	*749	*1194	101	89	157	264	1908	*15.3	1.3	24.5
83-84—Philadelphia	71	2613	532	1101	.483	545	727	.750	352	598	950	96	71	110	250	1609	*13.4	1.4	22.7
84-85—Philadelphia	79	2957	602	1284	.469	*737	*904	.815	385	646	*1031	130	67	123	286	1941	*13.1	1.6	24.6
85-86—Philadelphia	74	2706	571	1246	.458	*617	*784	.787	339	533	872	90	67	71	261	1759	11.8	1.2	23.8
86-87—Washington	73	2488	595	1311	.454	570	692	.824	340	484	824	120	59	92	202	1760	11.3	1.6	24.1
87-88—Washington	79	2692	531	1090	.487	543	689	.788	372	512	884	112	59	72	249	1607	11.2	1.4	20.3
88-89—Atlanta	81	2878	538	1096	.491	561	710	.789	386	570	956	112	79	100	245	1637	11.8	1.4	20.2
89-90—Atlanta	81	2735	517	1077	.480	493	631	.781	*364	448	812	130	47	84	232	1528	10.0	1.6	18.9
90-91—Atlanta	82	1912	280	598	.468	309	372	.831	271	396	667	68	30	74	137	869	8.1	0.8	10.6
91-92—Milwaukee	82	2511	440	929	.474	396	504	.786	320	424	744	93	54	64	150	1279	9.1	1.1	15.6
92-93—Milwaukee	11	104	13	42	.310	24	31	.774	22	24	46	7	1	8	10	50	4.2	0.6	4.5
93-94—Philadelphia	55	618	102	232	.440	90	117	.769	106	120	226	34	11	17	59	294	4.1	0.6	5.3
94-95—San Antonio	17	149	13	35	.371	22	32	.688	20	26	46	6	2	3	11	49	2.7	0.4	2.9
Totals	1329	45071	9435	19225	.491	8531	11090	.769	6731	9481	16212	1796	1089	1733	3804	27409	12.2	1.4	20.6

Three-point field goals: 1979-80, 0-for-6. 1980-81, 1-for-3 (.333). 1981-82, 0-for-6. 1982-83, 0-for-1. 1983-84, 0-for-4. 1984-85, 0-for-2. 1985-86, 0-for-1. 1986-87, 0-for-11. 1987-88, 2-for-7 (.286). 1988-89, 0-for-12. 1989-90, 1-for-9 (.111). 1990-91, 0-for-7. 1991-92, 3-for-8 (.375). 1993-94, 0-for-1. 1994-95, 1-for-2 (.500). Totals, 8-for-80 (.100).

Personal fouls/disqualifications: 1976-77, 275/3. 1977-78, 179/2. 1978-79, 223/0. 1979-80, 210/0. 1980-81, 223/0. 1981-82, 208/0. 1982-83, 206/0. 1983-84, 188/0. 1984-85, 216/0. 1985-86, 194/0. 1986-87, 139/0. 1987-88, 160/0. 1988-89, 154/0. 1989-90, 158/0. 1990-91, 134/0. 1991-92, 136/0. 1992-93, 6/0. 1993-94, 52/0. 1994-95, 15/0. Totals, 3076/5.

NBA PLAYOFF RECORD

NOTES: NBA Finals Most Valuable Player (1983). ... Holds single-game playoff record for most offensive rebounds—15 (April 21, 1977, vs. Washington).

Season Team	G	Min.	FGM	FGA	Pct.	FTM	FTA	Pct.	Off.	Def.	Tot.	Ast.	St.	Blk.	TO	Pts.	RPG	APG	PPG
76-77—Houston.........	12	518	81	162	.500	63	91	.692	84	119	203	7	13	21	...	225	16.9	0.6	18.8
78-79—Houston.........	2	78	18	41	.439	13	18	.722	25	16	41	2	1	8	8	49	20.5	1.0	24.5
79-80—Houston.........	7	275	74	138	.536	33	43	.767	42	55	97	7	4	16	22	181	13.9	1.0	25.9
80-81—Houston.........	21	955	207	432	.479	148	208	.712	125	180	305	35	13	34	59	562	14.5	1.7	26.8
81-82—Houston.........	3	136	29	67	.433	14	15	.933	28	23	51	10	2	2	6	72	17.0	3.3	24.0
82-83—Philadelphia	13	524	126	235	.536	86	120	.717	70	136	206	20	19	25	40	338	15.8	1.5	26.0
83-84—Philadelphia	5	212	38	83	.458	31	32	.969	20	49	69	7	3	11	21	107	13.8	1.4	21.4
84-85—Philadelphia	13	505	90	212	.425	82	103	.796	36	102	138	24	17	22	23	262	10.6	1.8	20.2
86-87—Washington	3	114	21	47	.447	20	21	.952	15	23	38	5	0	3	8	62	12.7	1.7	20.7
87-88—Washington	5	198	30	65	.462	33	40	.825	22	34	56	7	3	4	15	93	11.2	1.4	18.6
88-89—Atlanta	5	197	32	64	.500	40	51	.784	27	33	60	9	7	4	11	105	12.0	1.8	21.0
90-91—Atlanta	5	84	4	20	.200	13	14	.929	16	15	31	3	2	1	2	21	6.2	0.6	4.2
Totals	94	3796	750	1566	.479	576	756	.762	510	785	1295	136	84	151	215	2077	13.8	1.4	22.1

Three-point field goals: 1979-80, 0-for-1. 1980-81, 0-for-2. 1982-83, 0-for-1. 1984-85, 0-for-1. 1987-88, 0-for-1. 1988-89, 1-for-1. Totals, 1-for-7 (.143). Personal fouls/disqualifications: 1976-77, 42/0. 1978-79, 5/0. 1979-80, 18/0. 1980-81, 54/0. 1981-82, 8/0. 1982-83, 40/0. 1983-84, 15/0. 1984-85, 39/0. 1986-87, 5/0. 1987-88, 9/0. 1988-89, 5/0. 1990-91, 4/0. Totals, 244/0.

NBA ALL-STAR GAME RECORD

Season	Team	Min.	FGM	FGA	Pct.	FTM	FTA	Pct.	Off.	Def.	Tot.	Ast.	PF	Dq.	St.	Blk.	TO	Pts.
1978	—Houston	14	1	1	1.000	2	4	.500	1	3	4	1	1	0	1	0	0	4
1979	—Houston	17	2	2	1.000	4	5	.800	2	5	7	1	0	0	1	0	1	8
1980	—Houston	31	7	12	.583	6	12	.500	6	6	12	2	4	0	1	2	5	20
1981	—Houston	22	3	8	.375	2	4	.500	2	4	6	3	3	0	1	0	1	8
1982	—Houston	20	5	11	.455	2	6	.333	5	6	11	0	2	0	1	1	3	12
1983	—Philadelphia	24	3	8	.375	4	6	.667	2	6	8	3	1	0	0	1	1	10
1984	—Philadelphia							Selected, did not play—injured.										
1985	—Philadelphia	33	2	10	.200	3	6	.500	5	7	12	1	4	0	0	0	3	7
1986	—Philadelphia	34	5	12	.417	6	9	.667	5	8	13	0	4	0	1	0	1	16
1987	—Washington	35	11	19	.579	5	6	.833	7	11	18	2	4	0	2	1	1	27
1988	—Washington	22	2	6	.333	3	6	.500	5	4	9	2	2	0	0	0	2	7
1989	—Atlanta	19	3	9	.333	3	3	1.000	4	4	8	0	1	0	1	1	1	9
Totals	....	271	44	98	.449	40	67	.597	44	64	108	15	26	0	9	6	19	128

COMBINED ABA AND NBA REGULAR-SEASON RECORDS

	G	Min.	FGM	FGA	Pct.	FTM	FTA	Pct.	Off.	Def.	Tot.	Ast.	Stl.	Blk.	TO	Pts.	RPG	APG	PPG
Totals	1455	49444	10277	20750	.495	9018	11864	.760	7382	10452	17834	1936	1199	1889	4264	29580	12.3	1.3	20.3

Three-point field goals: 8-for-83 (.096).

MARAVICH, PETE   G

PERSONAL: Born June 22, 1947, in Aliquippa, Pa. ... Died January 5, 1988. ... 6-5/200 (1,96/90,7). ... Full name: Peter Press Maravich. ... Nickname: Pistol Pete. ... Son of Press Maravich, former college coach; and guard with Youngstown Bears of National Basketball League (1945-46) and Pittsburgh Ironmen of Basketball Association of America (1946-47).
HIGH SCHOOL: Daniel (Clemson, S.C.), then Needham Broughton (Raleigh, N.C.), then Edwards Military Institute (Salemburg, N.C.).
COLLEGE: Louisiana State.
TRANSACTIONS: Selected by Atlanta Hawks in first round (third pick overall) of 1970 NBA Draft. ... Traded by Hawks to New Orleans Jazz for G Dean Meminger, C/F Bob Kauffman, 1974 and 1975 first-round draft choices and 1975 and 1976 second-round draft choices (May 3, 1974). ... Jazz franchise moved from New Orleans to Utah for 1979-80 season. ... Waived by Jazz (January 17, 1980). ... Signed as free agent by Boston Celtics (January 22, 1980).
CAREER HONORS: Elected to Naismith Memorial Basketball Hall of Fame (1987). ... One of the 50 Greatest Players in NBA History (1996).

COLLEGIATE RECORD

NOTES: THE SPORTING NEWS College Player of the Year (1970). ... Naismith Award winner (1970). ... THE SPORTING NEWS All-America first team (1968, 1969, 1970). ... Holds NCAA career records for most points—3667; highest points-per-game average—44.2; most field goals made—1387; most field goals attempted—3166; most free throws made (three-year career)—893; most free throws attempted (three-year career)—1152; and most games scoring at least 50 points—28. ... Holds NCAA single-season records for most points—1381; highest points-per-game average—44.5; most field goals made—522; most field goals attempted—1168; and most games scoring at least 50 points—10 (1970). ... Holds NCAA single-game record for most free throws made—30 (December 22, 1969, vs. Oregon State in 31 attempts). ... Led NCAA Division I with 43.8 points per game (1968), 44.2 points per game (1969) and 44.5 points per game (1970).

Season Team	G	Min.	FGM	FGA	Pct.	FTM	FTA	Pct.	Reb.	Ast.	Pts.	RPG	APG	PPG
66-67—Louisiana State‡...........	17	...	273	604	.452	195	234	.833	176	124	741	10.4	7.3	43.6
67-68—Louisiana State..............	26	...	432	1022	.423	274	338	.811	195	105	1138	7.5	4.0	43.8
68-69—Louisiana State..............	26	...	433	976	.444	282	378	.746	169	128	1148	6.5	4.9	44.2
69-70—Louisiana State..............	31	...	522	1168	.447	337	436	.773	164	192	1381	5.3	6.2	44.5
Varsity totals	83	...	1387	3166	.438	893	1152	.775	528	425	3667	6.4	5.1	44.2

NBA REGULAR-SEASON RECORD

RECORDS: Shares single-game records for most free throws made in one quarter—14 (November 28, 1973, vs. Buffalo); and most free throws attempted in one quarter—16 (January 2, 1973, vs. Chicago).
HONORS: All-NBA first team (1976, 1977). ... All-NBA second team (1973, 1978). ... NBA All-Rookie team (1971).

ALL-TIME GREAT PLAYERS

Season Team	G	Min.	FGM	FGA	Pct.	FTM	FTA	Pct.	Reb.	Ast.	PF	Dq.	Pts.	RPG	APG	PPG
70-71 —Atlanta	81	2926	738	1613	.458	404	505	.800	298	355	238	1	1880	3.7	4.4	23.2
71-72 —Atlanta	66	2302	460	1077	.427	355	438	.811	256	393	207	0	1275	3.9	6.0	19.3
72-73 —Atlanta	79	3089	789	1788	.441	485	606	.800	346	546	245	1	2063	4.4	6.9	26.1

Season Team	G	Min.	FGM	FGA	Pct.	FTM	FTA	Pct.	Off.	Def.	Tot.	Ast.	St.	Blk.	TO	Pts.	RPG	APG	PPG
73-74 —Atlanta	76	2903	819	*1791	.457	469	568	.826	98	276	374	396	111	13	...	2107	4.9	5.2	27.7
74-75 —New Orleans	79	2853	655	1562	.419	390	481	.811	93	329	422	488	120	18	...	1700	5.3	6.2	21.5
75-76 —New Orleans	62	2373	604	1316	.459	396	488	.811	46	254	300	332	87	23	...	1604	4.8	5.4	25.9
76-77 —New Orleans	73	3041	886	*2047	.433	*501	600	.835	90	284	374	392	84	22	...	*2273	5.1	5.4	*31.1
77-78 —New Orleans	50	2041	556	1253	.444	240	276	.870	49	129	178	335	101	8	248	1352	3.6	6.7	27.0
78-79 —New Orleans	49	1824	436	1035	.421	233	277	.841	33	88	121	243	60	18	200	1105	2.5	5.0	22.6
79-80 —Utah-Boston	43	964	244	543	.449	91	105	.867	17	61	78	83	24	6	82	589	1.8	1.9	13.7
Totals	658	24316	6187	14025	.441	3564	4344	.820	...	...	2747	3563	587	108	530	15948	4.2	5.4	24.2

Three-point field goals: 1979-80, 10-for-15 (.667).
Personal fouls/disqualifications: 1973-74, 261/4. 1974-75, 227/4. 1975-76, 197/3. 1976-77, 191/1. 1977-78, 116/1. 1978-79, 104/2. 1979-80, 79/1. Totals, 1865/18.

NBA PLAYOFF RECORD

Season Team	G	Min.	FGM	FGA	Pct.	FTM	FTA	Pct.	Reb.	Ast.	PF	Dq.	Pts.	RPG	APG	PPG
70-71 —Atlanta	5	199	46	122	.377	18	26	.692	26	24	14	0	110	5.2	4.8	22.0
71-72 —Atlanta	6	219	54	121	.446	58	71	.817	32	28	24	0	166	5.3	4.7	27.7
72-73 —Atlanta	6	234	65	155	.419	27	34	.794	29	40	24	1	157	4.8	6.7	26.2

Season Team	G	Min.	FGM	FGA	Pct.	FTM	FTA	Pct.	Off.	Def.	Tot.	Ast.	St.	Blk.	TO	Pts.	RPG	APG	PPG
79-80 —Boston	9	104	25	51	.490	2	3	.667	0	8	8	6	3	0	9	54	0.9	0.7	6.0
Totals	26	756	190	449	.423	105	134	.784	...	...	95	98	3	0	9	487	3.7	3.8	18.7

Three-point field goals: 1979-80, 2-for-6 (.333).
Personal fouls/disqualifications: 1979-80, 12/0.

NBA ALL-STAR GAME RECORD

Season Team	Min.	FGM	FGA	Pct.	FTM	FTA	Pct.	Reb	Ast.	PF	Dq.	Pts.
1973 —Atlanta	22	4	8	.500	0	0	...	3	5	4	0	8

Season Team	Min.	FGM	FGA	Pct.	FTM	FTA	Pct.	Off.	Def.	Tot.	Ast.	PF	Dq.	St.	Blk.	TO	Pts.
1974 —Atlanta	22	4	15	.267	7	9	.778	1	2	3	4	2	0	0	0	...	15
1977 —New Orleans	21	5	13	.385	0	0	...	0	0	0	4	1	0	4	0	...	10
1978 —New Orleans						Selected, did not play—injured.											
1979 —New Orleans	14	5	8	.625	0	0	...	0	2	2	2	1	0	0	0	4	10
Totals	79	18	44	.409	7	9	.778	...	...	8	15	8	0	4	0	4	43

MARTIN, SLATER   G

PERSONAL: Born October 22, 1925, in Houston. ... 5-10/170 (1,78/77,1). ... Full name: Slater Nelson Martin Jr. ... Nickname: Dugie.
HIGH SCHOOL: Jefferson Davis (Houston).
COLLEGE: Texas.
TRANSACTIONS: Selected by Minneapolis Lakers in 1949 Basketball Association of America Draft. ... Traded by Lakers with F Jerry Bird and player to be named later to New York Knicks for C Walter Dukes and draft rights to F/C Burdette Haldorson (October 26, 1956). ... Traded by Knicks to St. Louis Hawks for F Willie Naulls (December 10, 1956).
CAREER HONORS: Elected to Naismith Memorial Basketball Hall of Fame (1982).
MISCELLANEOUS: Member of NBA championship team (1950, 1952, 1953, 1954, 1958).

COLLEGIATE RECORD

NOTES: The Sporting News All-America fifth team (1949).

Season Team	G	Min.	FGM	FGA	Pct.	FTM	FTA	Pct.	Reb.	Ast.	Pts.	RPG	APG	PPG
43-44—Texas	14	...	75	...	...	34	...	...	...	...	184	...	...	13.1
44-45—					Did not play—in military service.									
45-46—					Did not play—in military service.									
46-47—Texas	27	...	109	...	...	37	...	...	...	...	255	...	...	9.4
47-48—Texas	25	...	126	...	...	65	85	.765	...	...	317	...	...	12.7
48-49—Texas	24	...	165	...	...	54	...	...	...	...	384	...	...	16.0
Totals	90	...	475	...	...	190	...	...	...	...	1140	...	...	12.7

NBA REGULAR-SEASON RECORD

HONORS: All-NBA second team (1954, 1956, 1957, 1958, 1959).

Season Team	G	Min.	FGM	FGA	Pct.	FTM	FTA	Pct.	Reb.	Ast.	PF	Dq.	Pts.	RPG	APG	PPG
49-50 —Minneapolis	67	...	106	302	.351	59	93	.634	...	148	162	...	271	...	2.2	4.0
50-51 —Minneapolis	68	...	227	627	.362	121	177	.684	246	235	199	3	575	3.6	3.5	8.5
51-52 —Minneapolis	66	2480	237	632	.375	142	190	.747	228	249	226	9	616	3.5	3.8	9.3
52-53 —Minneapolis	70	2556	260	634	.410	224	287	.780	186	250	246	4	744	2.7	3.6	10.6
53-54 —Minneapolis	69	2472	254	654	.388	176	243	.724	166	253	198	3	684	2.4	3.7	9.9
54-55 —Minneapolis	72	2784	350	919	.381	276	359	.769	260	427	221	7	976	3.6	5.9	13.6

Season Team	G	Min.	FGM	FGA	Pct.	FTM	FTA	Pct.	Reb.	Ast.	PF	Dq.	Pts.	AVERAGES RPG	APG	PPG
55-56 —Minneapolis	72	*2838	309	863	.358	329	395	.833	260	445	202	2	947	3.6	6.2	13.2
56-57 —N.Y.-St.L.	66	2401	244	736	.332	230	291	.790	288	269	193	1	718	4.4	4.1	10.9
57-58 —St. Louis	60	2098	258	768	.336	206	276	.746	228	218	187	0	722	3.8	3.6	12.0
58-59 —St. Louis	71	2504	245	706	.347	197	254	.776	253	336	230	8	687	3.6	4.7	9.7
59-60 —St. Louis	64	1756	142	383	.371	113	155	.729	187	330	174	2	397	2.9	5.2	6.2
Totals	745	...	2632	7224	.364	2073	2720	.762	...	3160	2238	...	7337	...	4.2	9.8

NBA PLAYOFF RECORD

Season Team	G	Min.	FGM	FGA	Pct.	FTM	FTA	Pct.	Reb.	Ast.	PF	Dq.	Pts.	AVERAGES RPG	APG	PPG
49-50 —Minneapolis	12	...	21	50	.420	14	24	.583	...	25	35	...	56	...	2.1	4.7
50-51 —Minneapolis	7	...	18	51	.353	14	27	.519	42	25	20	...	50	6.0	3.6	7.1
51-52 —Minneapolis	13	523	38	110	.345	41	56	.732	37	56	64	4	117	2.8	4.3	9.0
52-53 —Minneapolis	12	453	41	103	.398	39	51	.765	31	43	49	1	121	2.6	3.6	10.1
53-54 —Minneapolis	13	533	37	112	.330	52	70	.743	29	60	52	1	126	2.2	4.6	9.7
54-55 —Minneapolis	7	315	28	94	.298	40	49	.816	28	31	23	0	96	4.0	4.4	13.7
55-56 —Minneapolis	3	121	17	37	.459	20	24	.833	7	15	9	0	54	2.3	5.0	18.0
56-57 —St. Louis	10	439	55	155	.355	56	74	.757	42	49	39	2	166	4.2	4.9	16.6
57-58 —St. Louis	11	416	44	137	.321	39	63	.619	48	40	40	1	127	4.4	3.6	11.5
58-59 —St. Louis	1	18	4	5	.800	0	0	...	3	2	2	0	8	3.0	2.0	8.0
59-60 —St. Louis	3	58	1	13	.077	1	4	.250	3	8	9	0	3	1.0	2.7	1.0
Totals	92	...	304	867	.351	316	442	.715	...	354	342	...	924	...	3.8	10.0

NBA ALL-STAR GAME RECORD

Season Team	Min.	FGM	FGA	Pct.	FTM	FTA	Pct.	Reb	Ast.	PF	Dq.	Pts.
1953 —Minneapolis	26	2	10	.200	1	1	1.000	2	1	2	0	5
1954 —Minneapolis	23	1	5	.200	0	0	...	0	3	3	0	2
1955 —Minneapolis	23	2	5	.400	1	2	.500	2	5	3	0	5
1956 —Minneapolis	29	3	7	.429	3	3	1.000	1	7	5	0	9
1957 —St. Louis	31	4	11	.364	0	0	...	2	3	1	0	8
1958 —St. Louis	26	2	9	.222	2	4	.500	2	8	3	0	6
1959 —St. Louis	22	2	6	.333	1	2	.500	6	1	2	0	5
Totals	180	16	53	.302	8	12	.667	15	28	19	0	40

NBA COACHING RECORD

BACKGROUND: Player/head coach, St. Louis Hawks (1957). ... Head coach/general manager, Houston Mavericks of ABA (1967-68).

	REGULAR SEASON				PLAYOFFS		
Season Team	W	L	Pct.	Finish	W	L	Pct.
56-57 —St. Louis	5	3	.625		—	—	—

ABA COACHING RECORD

	REGULAR SEASON				PLAYOFFS		
Season Team	W	L	Pct.	Finish	W	L	Pct.
67-68 —Houston	29	49	.372	4th/Western Division	0	3	.000
68-69 —Houston	3	9	.250		—	—	—
Totals (2 years)	32	58	.356		Totals (1 year)........ 0	3	.000>

NOTES:

1957—Replaced Red Holzman as St. Louis head coach (January), with record of 14-19; replaced as St. Louis head coach by Alex Hannum (January).

1968—Lost to Dallas in Western Division Semifinals. Replaced as Houston head coach by Jim Weaver (November).

McADOO, BOB   C/F

PERSONAL: Born September 25, 1951, in Greensboro, N.C. ... 6-9/225 (2,05/102,1). ... Full name: Robert Allen McAdoo Jr.

HIGH SCHOOL: Ben Smith (Greensboro, N.C.).

JUNIOR COLLEGE: Vincennes (Ind.).University.

COLLEGE: North Carolina.

TRANSACTIONS: Selected after junior season by Buffalo Braves in first round (second pick overall) of 1972 NBA Draft. ... Traded by Braves with C/F Tom McMillen to New York Knicks for C/F John Gianelli and cash (December 9, 1976). ... Traded by Knicks to Boston Celtics for three 1979 first-round draft choices and player to be named later (February 12, 1979). ... Knicks acquired C Tom Barker to complete deal (February 14, 1979). ... Acquired by Detroit Pistons for two 1980 first-round draft choices to complete compensation for Celtics signing of veteran free agent F/G M.L. Carr (September 6, 1979). ... Waived by Pistons (March 11, 1981). ... Signed as free agent by New Jersey Nets (March 13, 1981). ... Traded by Nets to Los Angeles Lakers for 1983 second-round draft choice and cash (December 24, 1981). ... Signed as veteran free agent by Philadelphia 76ers (January 31, 1986); Lakers waived their right of first refusal. ... Played in Italy (1986-87 through 1992-93).

CAREER HONORS: Elected to Naismith Memorial Basketball Hall of Fame (2000).

CAREER NOTES: Assistant coach, Miami Heat (September 20, 1995 to present).

MISCELLANEOUS: Member of NBA championship team (1982, 1985).

COLLEGIATE RECORD

NOTES: THE SPORTING NEWS All-America first team (1972).

Season Team	G	Min.	FGM	FGA	Pct.	FTM	FTA	Pct.	Reb.	Ast.	Pts.	AVERAGES RPG	APG	PPG
69-70—Vincennes University	32	...	258	...	...	101	134	.754	320	...	617	10.0	...	19.3
70-71—Vincennes University	27	...	273	...	...	129	164	.787	297	...	675	11.0	...	25.0
71-72—North Carolina	31	...	243	471	.516	118	167	.707	312	72	604	10.1	2.3	19.5
Junior college totals	59	...	531	...	...	230	298	.772	617	...	1292	10.5	...	21.9
4-year-college totals	31	...	243	471	.516	118	167	.707	312	72	604	10.1	2.3	19.5

NBA REGULAR-SEASON RECORD

HONORS: NBA Most Valuable Player (1975). ... NBA Rookie of the Year (1973). ... All-NBA first team (1975). ... All-NBA second team (1974). ... NBA All-Rookie team (1973).

Season Team	G	Min.	FGM	FGA	Pct.	FTM	FTA	Pct.	Reb.	Ast.	PF	Dq.	Pts.	AVERAGES RPG	APG	PPG
72-73—Buffalo	80	2562	585	1293	.452	271	350	.774	728	139	256	6	1441	9.1	1.7	18.0

Season Team	G	Min.	FGM	FGA	Pct.	FTM	FTA	Pct.	REBOUNDS Off.	Def.	Tot.	Ast.	St.	Blk.	TO	Pts.	AVERAGES RPG	APG	PPG
73-74—Buffalo	74	3185	901	1647	*.547	459	579	.793	281	836	1117	170	88	246	...	*2261	15.1	2.3	*30.6
74-75—Buffalo	82	*3539	*1095	2138	.512	641	*796	.805	307	848	*1155	179	92	174	...	*2831	14.1	2.2	*34.5
75-76—Buffalo	78	3328	*934	*1918	.487	*559	*734	.762	241	724	965	315	93	160	...	*2427	12.4	4.0	*31.1
76-77—Buff-Knicks	72	2798	740	1445	.512	381	516	.738	199	727	926	205	77	99	...	1861	12.9	2.8	25.8
77-78—New York	79	3182	814	1564	.520	469	645	.727	236	774	1010	298	105	126	346	2097	12.8	3.8	26.5
78-79—N.Y.-Boston	60	2231	596	1127	.529	295	450	.656	130	390	520	168	74	67	217	1487	8.7	2.8	24.8
79-80—Detroit	58	2097	492	1025	.480	235	322	.730	100	367	467	200	73	65	238	1222	8.1	3.4	21.1
80-81—Detroit-N.J.	16	321	68	157	.433	29	41	.707	17	50	67	30	17	13	32	165	4.2	1.9	10.3
81-82—Los Angeles	41	746	151	330	.458	90	126	.714	45	114	159	32	22	36	51	392	3.9	0.8	9.6
82-83—Los Angeles	47	1019	292	562	.520	119	163	.730	76	171	247	39	40	40	68	703	5.3	0.8	15.0
83-84—Los Angeles	70	1456	352	748	.471	212	264	.803	82	207	289	74	42	50	127	916	4.1	1.1	13.1
84-85—L.A. Lakers	66	1254	284	546	.520	122	162	.753	79	216	295	67	18	53	95	690	4.5	1.0	10.5
85-86—Philadelphia	29	609	116	251	.462	62	81	.765	25	78	103	35	10	18	49	294	3.6	1.2	10.1
Totals	852	28327	7420	14751	.503	3944	5229	.754	...	...	8048	1951	751	1147	1223	18787	9.4	2.3	22.1

Three-point field goals: 1979-80, 3-for-24 (.125). 1980-81, 0-for-5. 1981-82, 0-for-5. 1982-83, 0-for-1. 1983-84, 0-for-5. 1984-85, 0-for-1. Totals, 3-for-37 (.081).

Personal fouls/disqualifications: 1973-74, 252/3. 1974-75, 278/3. 1975-76, 298/5. 1976-77, 262/3. 1977-78, 297/6. 1978-79, 189/3. 1979-80, 178/3. 1980-81, 38/0. 1981-82, 109/1. 1982-83, 153/2. 1983-84, 182/0. 1984-85, 170/0. 1985-86, 64/0. Totals, 2726/35.

NBA PLAYOFF RECORD

Season Team	G	Min.	FGM	FGA	Pct.	FTM	FTA	Pct.	REBOUNDS Off.	Def.	Tot.	Ast.	St.	Blk.	TO	Pts.	AVERAGES RPG	APG	PPG
73-74—Buffalo	6	271	76	159	.478	38	47	.809	14	68	82	9	6	13	...	190	13.7	1.5	31.7
74-75—Buffalo	7	327	104	216	.481	54	73	.740	25	69	94	10	6	19	...	262	13.4	1.4	37.4
75-76—Buffalo	9	406	97	215	.451	58	82	.707	31	97	128	29	7	18	...	252	14.2	3.2	28.0
77-78—New York	6	238	61	126	.484	21	35	.600	11	47	58	23	7	12	23	143	9.7	3.8	23.8
81-82—Los Angeles	14	388	101	179	.564	32	47	.681	21	74	95	22	10	21	35	234	6.8	1.6	16.7
82-83—Los Angeles	8	166	37	84	.440	11	14	.786	15	31	46	5	11	10	14	87	5.8	0.6	10.9
83-84—Los Angeles	20	447	111	215	.516	57	81	.704	30	78	108	12	12	27	39	279	5.4	0.6	14.0
84-85—L.A. Lakers	19	398	91	193	.472	35	47	.745	25	61	86	15	9	26	32	217	4.5	0.8	11.4
85-86—Philadelphia	5	73	20	36	.556	14	16	.875	8	6	14	2	4	5	2	54	2.8	0.4	10.8
Totals	94	2714	698	1423	.491	320	442	.724	180	531	711	127	72	151	145	1718	7.6	1.4	18.3

Three-point field goals: 1982-83, 2-for-6 (.333). 1983-84, 0-for-1. 1984-85, 0-for-1. Totals, 2-for-8 (.250).

Personal fouls/disqualifications: 1973-74, 25/1. 1974-75, 29/1. 1975-76, 37/3. 1977-78, 19/0. 1981-82, 43/2. 1982-83, 23/0. 1983-84, 63/0. 1984-85, 66/2. 1985-86, 13/0. Totals, 318/9.

NBA ALL-STAR GAME RECORD

Season Team	Min.	FGM	FGA	Pct.	FTM	FTA	Pct.	REBOUNDS Off.	Def.	Tot.	Ast.	PF	Dq.	St.	Blk.	TO	Pts.
1974—Buffalo	13	3	4	.750	5	8	.625	1	2	3	1	4	0	0	1	...	11
1975—Buffalo	26	4	9	.444	3	3	1.000	4	2	6	2	4	0	0	0	...	11
1976—Buffalo	29	10	14	.714	2	4	.500	2	5	7	1	5	0	0	0	...	22
1977—N.Y. Knicks	38	13	23	.565	4	4	1.000	3	7	10	2	3	0	3	1	...	30
1978—New York	20	7	14	.500	0	0	...	3	1	4	0	2	0	1	0	3	14
Totals	126	37	64	.578	14	19	.737	13	17	30	6	18	0	4	2	3	88

ITALIAN LEAGUE RECORD

Season Team	G	Min.	FGM	FGA	Pct.	FTM	FTA	Pct.	Reb.	Ast.	Pts.	AVERAGES RPG	APG	PPG
86-87—Tracer Milan	38	1320	387	730	.530	205	268	.765	388	54	991	10.2	1.4	26.1
87-88—Tracer Milan	39	1398	422	730	.578	236	293	.805	333	71	1097	8.5	1.8	28.1
88-89—Philips Milano	38	1195	334	610	.548	161	200	.805	299	60	861	7.9	1.6	22.7
89-90—Philips Milano	33	1014	329	587	.560	178	215	.828	248	41	851	7.5	1.2	25.8
90-91—Filanto	23	858	278	490	.567	179	225	.796	219	28	759	9.5	1.2	33.0
91-92—Filanto Forli	20	700	199	399	.499	129	159	.811	188	20	538	9.4	1.0	26.9
92-93—Team system Fabriano	2	58	14	27	.519	12	17	.706	13	2	44	6.5	1.0	22.0
Totals	193	6543	1963	3573	.549	1100	1377	.799	1688	276	5141	8.7	1.4	26.6

McGINNIS, GEORGE   F

PERSONAL: Born August 12, 1950, in Indianapolis. ... 6-8/235 (2,03/106,6). ... Full name: George F. McGinnis.
HIGH SCHOOL: George Washington (Indianapolis).
COLLEGE: Indiana.
TRANSACTIONS: Signed as free agent after sophomore season by Indiana Pacers of American Basketball Association in lieu of 1972 first-round draft choice (1971). ... Selected by Philadelphia 76ers in second round (22nd pick overall) of 1973 NBA Draft. ... Invoked proviso to buy his way out of contract with Pacers. ... Signed by 76ers (July 10, 1975) after Commissioner Larry O'Brien revoked contract McGinnis had signed with New York Knicks (May 30, 1975). ... Traded by 76ers to Denver Nuggets for F Bobby Jones and G Ralph Simpson (August 16, 1978). ... Traded by Nuggets to Pacers for F Alex English and 1980 first-round draft choice (February 1, 1980). ... Waived by Pacers (October 27, 1982).

COLLEGIATE RECORD

Season Team	G	Min.	FGM	FGA	Pct.	FTM	FTA	Pct.	Reb.	Ast.	Pts.	RPG	APG	PPG
												AVERAGES		
69-70—Indiana‡						Did not play—ineligible.								
70-71—Indiana	24	...	283	615	.460	153	249	.614	352	66	719	14.7	2.8	30.0
Varsity totals	24	...	283	615	.460	153	249	.614	352	66	719	14.7	2.8	30.0

ABA REGULAR-SEASON RECORD

NOTES: ABA co-Most Valuable Player (1975). ... ABA All-Star first team (1974, 1975). ... ABA All-Star second team (1973). ... ABA All-Rookie team (1972). ... Member of ABA championship team (1972, 1973).

Season Team	G	Min.	2-POINT			3-POINT			FTM	FTA	Pct.	Reb.	Ast.	Pts.	AVERAGES		
			FGM	FGA	Pct.	FGM	FGA	Pct.							RPG	APG	PPG
71-72—Indiana....................	73	2179	459	961	.478	6	38	.158	298	462	.645	711	137	1234	9.7	1.9	16.9
72-73—Indiana....................	82	3347	860	1723	.499	8	32	.250	517	*778	.665	1022	205	2261	12.5	2.5	27.6
73-74—Indiana....................	80	3266	784	1652	.475	5	34	.147	488	*715	.683	1197	267	2071	15.0	3.3	25.9
74-75—Indiana....................	79	3193	811	1759	.461	62	175	.354	*545	*753	.724	1126	495	*2353	14.3	6.3	*29.8
Totals	314	11985	2914	6095	.478	81	279	.290	1848	2708	.682	4056	1104	7919	12.9	3.5	25.2

ABA PLAYOFF RECORD

NOTES: ABA Playoff Most Valuable Player (1973).

Season Team	G	Min.	2-POINT			3-POINT			FTM	FTA	Pct.	Reb.	Ast.	Pts.	AVERAGES		
			FGM	FGA	Pct.	FGM	FGA	Pct.							RPG	APG	PPG
71-72—Indiana....................	20	633	102	246	.415	4	15	.267	94	150	.627	227	52	310	11.4	2.6	15.5
72-73—Indiana....................	18	731	161	352	.457	0	5	.000	109	149	.732	222	39	431	12.3	2.2	23.9
73-74—Indiana....................	14	585	117	254	.461	2	7	.286	96	129	.744	166	47	336	11.9	3.4	24.0
74-75—Indiana....................	18	731	190	382	.497	23	73	.315	132	192	.688	286	148	581	15.9	8.2	32.3
Totals	70	2680	570	1234	.462	29	100	.290	431	620	.695	901	286	1658	12.9	4.1	23.7

ABA ALL-STAR GAME RECORD

Season Team	Min.	2-POINT			3-POINT			FTM	FTA	Pct.	Reb.	Ast.	Pts.
		FGM	FGA	Pct.	FGM	FGA	Pct.						
1972—Indiana	34	10	14	.714	0	1	.000	3	6	.500	15	2	23
1973—Indiana	30	7	21	.333	0	0	...	0	0	...	11	1	14
1974—Indiana	32	6	13	.462	0	1	.000	6	11	.545	12	5	18
Totals	96	23	48	.479	0	2	.000	9	17	.529	38	8	55

NBA REGULAR-SEASON RECORD

HONORS: All-NBA first team (1976). ... All-NBA second team (1977).

NOTES: Tied for NBA lead with 12 disqualifications (1980).

Season Team	G	Min.	FGM	FGA	Pct.	FTM	FTA	Pct.	REBOUNDS			Ast.	St.	Blk.	TO	Pts.	AVERAGES		
									Off.	Def.	Tot.						RPG	APG	PPG
75-76—Philadelphia	77	2946	647	1552	.417	475	642	.740	260	707	967	359	198	41	...	1769	12.6	4.7	23.0
76-77—Philadelphia	79	2769	659	1439	.458	372	546	.681	324	587	911	302	163	37	...	1690	11.5	3.8	21.4
77-78—Philadelphia	78	2533	588	1270	.463	411	574	.716	282	528	810	294	137	27	312	1587	10.4	3.8	20.3
78-79—Denver	76	2552	603	1273	.474	509	765	.665	256	608	864	283	129	52	*346	1715	11.4	3.7	22.6
79-80—Denver-Ind.......	73	2208	400	886	.451	270	488	.553	222	477	699	333	101	23	281	1072	9.6	4.6	14.7
80-81—Indiana...........	69	1845	348	768	.453	207	385	.538	164	364	528	210	99	28	221	903	7.7	3.0	13.1
81-82—Indiana...........	76	1341	141	378	.373	72	159	.453	93	305	398	204	96	28	131	354	5.2	2.7	4.7
Totals	528	16194	3386	7566	.448	2316	3559	.651	1601	3576	5177	1985	923	236	1291	9090	9.8	3.8	17.2

Three-point field goals: 1979-80, 2-for-15 (.133). 1980-81, 0-for-7. 1981-82, 0-for-3. Totals, 2-for-25 (.080).
Personal fouls/disqualifications: 1975-76, 334/13. 1976-77, 299/4. 1977-78, 287/6. 1978-79, 321/16. 1979-80, 303/12. 1980-81, 242/3. 1981-82, 98/4. Totals, 1884/58.

NBA PLAYOFF RECORD

Season Team	G	Min.	FGM	FGA	Pct.	FTM	FTA	Pct.	REBOUNDS			Ast.	St.	Blk.	TO	Pts.	AVERAGES		
									Off.	Def.	Tot.						RPG	APG	PPG
75-76—Philadelphia	3	120	29	61	.475	11	18	.611	9	32	41	12	1	4	...	69	13.7	4.0	23.0
76-77—Philadelphia	19	603	102	273	.374	65	114	.570	62	136	198	69	23	6	...	269	10.4	3.6	14.2
77-78—Philadelphia	10	273	53	125	.424	41	49	.837	24	54	78	30	15	1	38	147	7.8	3.0	14.7
80-81—Indiana...........	2	39	3	15	.200	4	8	.500	2	8	10	7	2	0	5	10	5.0	3.5	5.0
Totals	34	1035	187	474	.395	121	189	.640	97	230	327	118	41	11	43	495	9.6	3.5	14.6

Personal fouls/disqualifications: 1975-76, 14/1. 1976-77, 83/2. 1977-78, 40/1. 1980-81, 6/0. Totals, 143/4.

NBA ALL-STAR GAME RECORD

Season	Team	Min.	FGM	FGA	Pct.	FTM	FTA	Pct.	REBOUNDS			Ast.	PF	Dq.	St.	Blk.	TO	Pts.
									Off.	Def.	Tot.							
1976	—Philadelphia.......	19	4	9	.444	2	4	.500	1	6	7	2	2	0	0	0	...	10
1977	—Philadelphia.......	26	2	9	.222	0	2	.000	5	2	7	2	3	0	4	0	...	4
1979	—Denver..............	25	5	12	.417	6	11	.545	2	4	6	3	4	0	5	0	0	16
Totals..........................		70	11	30	.367	8	17	.471	8	12	20	7	9	0	9	0	0	30

COMBINED ABA AND NBA REGULAR-SEASON RECORDS

	G	Min.	FGM	FGA	Pct.	FTM	FTA	Pct.	REBOUNDS			Ast.	Stl.	Blk.	TO	Pts.	AVERAGES		
									Off.	Def.	Tot.						RPG	APG	PPG
Totals	842	28179	6381	13940	.458	4164	6267	.664	...	...	9233	3089	1448	332	...	17009	11.0	3.7	20.2

Three-point field goals: 83-for-304 (.273).
Personal fouls/disqualifications: 3220.

McGUIRE, DICK   G

PERSONAL: Born January 25, 1926, in New York City. ... 6-0/180 (1,83/81,6). ... Full name: Richard Joseph McGuire. ... Brother of Al McGuire, guard with New York Knicks (1951-52 through 1953-54) and Baltimore Bullets (1954-55); and head coach, Belmont Abbey (1957-58 through and 1963-64) and Marquette University (1964-65 through 1976-77). ... Nickname: Tricky Dick.
HIGH SCHOOL: LaSalle Academy (New York).
COLLEGE: St. John's and Dartmouth.
TRANSACTIONS: Selected by New York Knicks in first round of 1949 Basketball Association of America Draft. ... Traded by Knicks to Detroit Pistons for 1958 first-round draft choice (April 3, 1957).
CAREER NOTES: Director of scouting, New York Knicks (1967-68 to present).
CAREER HONORS: Elected to Naismith Memorial Basketball Hall of Fame (1993).

COLLEGIATE RECORD

NOTES: THE SPORTING NEWS All-America second team (1944).

Season Team	G	Min.	FGM	FGA	Pct.	FTM	FTA	Pct.	Reb.	Ast.	Pts.	RPG	APG	PPG
43-44—St. John's	16	...	43	...	...	20	...	...	...	...	106	...	...	6.6
44-45—						Did not play—in military service.								
45-46—						Did not play—in military service.								
46-47—St. John's	21	...	63	...	...	37	...	...	...	...	163	...	...	7.8
47-48—St. John's	22	...	75	...	...	72	115	.626	...	...	222	...	...	10.1
48-49—St. John's	25	...	121	...	...	72	125	.576	...	...	314	...	...	12.6
Totals	84	...	302	...	...	201	...	...	...	...	805	...	...	9.6

NBA REGULAR-SEASON RECORD

HONORS: All-NBA second team (1951).

Season Team	G	Min.	FGM	FGA	Pct.	FTM	FTA	Pct.	Reb.	Ast.	PF	Dq.	Pts.	RPG	APG	PPG
49-50 —New York	68	...	190	563	.337	204	313	.652	...	*386	160	...	584	...	5.7	8.6
50-51 —New York	64	...	179	482	.371	179	276	.649	334	400	154	2	537	5.2	†6.3	8.4
51-52 —New York	64	2018	204	474	.430	183	290	.631	332	388	181	4	591	5.2	6.1	9.2
52-53 —New York	61	1783	142	373	.381	153	269	.569	280	296	172	3	437	4.6	4.9	7.2
53-54 —New York	68	2343	201	493	.408	220	345	.638	310	354	199	3	622	4.6	5.2	9.1
54-55 —New York	71	2310	226	581	.389	195	303	.644	322	542	143	0	647	4.5	7.6	9.1
55-56 —New York	62	1685	152	438	.347	121	193	.627	220	362	146	0	425	3.5	5.8	6.9
56-57 —New York	72	1191	140	366	.383	105	163	.644	146	222	103	0	385	2.0	3.1	5.3
57-58 —Detroit	69	2311	203	544	.373	150	225	.667	291	454	178	0	556	4.2	6.6	8.1
58-59 —Detroit	71	2063	232	543	.427	191	258	.740	285	443	147	1	655	4.0	6.2	9.2
59-60 —Detroit	68	1466	179	402	.445	124	201	.617	264	358	112	0	482	3.9	5.3	7.1
Totals	738	...	2048	5259	.389	1825	2836	.644	...	4205	1695	...	5921	...	5.7	8.0

NBA PLAYOFF RECORD

Season Team	G	Min.	FGM	FGA	Pct.	FTM	FTA	Pct.	Reb.	Ast.	PF	Dq.	Pts.	RPG	APG	PPG
49-50 —New York	5	...	22	52	.423	19	26	.731	...	27	21	...	63	...	5.4	12.6
50-51 —New York	14	...	25	80	.313	24	53	.453	83	78	50	1	74	5.9	5.6	5.3
51-52 —New York	14	546	48	107	.449	49	86	.570	71	90	46	1	145	5.1	6.4	10.4
52-53 —New York	11	360	24	59	.407	35	55	.636	63	70	25	0	83	5.7	6.4	7.5
53-54 —New York	4	68	4	16	.250	3	5	.600	4	5	12	0	11	1.0	1.3	2.8
54-55 —New York	3	75	6	19	.316	8	12	.667	9	12	7	0	20	3.0	4.0	6.7
57-58 —Detroit	7	236	25	60	.417	17	24	.708	33	40	13	0	67	4.7	5.7	9.6
58-59 —Detroit	3	109	20	32	.625	7	11	.636	17	19	10	0	47	5.7	6.3	15.7
59-60 —Detroit	2	42	5	12	.417	1	3	.333	4	9	3	0	11	2.0	4.5	5.5
Totals	63	...	179	437	.410	163	275	.593	...	350	187	...	521	...	5.6	8.3

NBA ALL-STAR GAME RECORD

Season Team	Min.	FGM	FGA	Pct.	FTM	FTA	Pct.	Reb	Ast.	PF	Dq.	Pts.
1951 —New York	...	3	4	.750	0	0	...	5	10	2	0	6
1952 —New York	18	0	0	...	1	3	.333	1	4	0	0	1
1954 —New York	24	2	5	.400	0	0	...	4	2	1	0	4
1955 —New York	25	1	2	.500	1	2	.500	3	6	1	0	3
1956 —New York	29	2	9	.222	2	5	.400	0	3	1	0	6
1958 —Detroit	31	2	4	.500	0	0	...	7	10	4	0	4
1959 —Detroit	24	2	7	.286	1	2	.500	3	3	2	0	5
Totals	...	12	31	.387	5	12	.417	23	38	11	0	29

NBA COACHING RECORD

BACKGROUND: Player/head coach, Detroit Pistons (December 28, 1959-remainder of season).

		REGULAR SEASON				PLAYOFFS		
Season Team	W	L	Pct.	Finish		W	L	Pct.
59-60 —Detroit	17	24	.415	2nd/Western Division		0	2	.000
60-61 —Detroit	34	45	.430	3rd/Western Division		2	3	.400
61-62 —Detroit	37	43	.463	3rd/Western Division		5	5	.500
62-63 —Detroit	34	46	.425	3rd/Western Division		1	3	.250
65-66 —New York	24	35	.407	4th/Eastern Division		—	—	—
66-67 —New York	36	45	.444	4th/Eastern Division		1	3	.250
67-68 —New York	15	22	.405			—	—	—
Totals (7 years)	197	260	.431	**Totals (5 years)**		9	16	.360

NOTES:
1959—Replaced Detroit head coach Red Rocha (December 28), with record of 13-21.
1960—Lost to Minneapolis in Western Division Semifinals.
1961—Lost to Los Angeles in Western Division Semifinals.
1962—Defeated Cincinnati, 3-1, in Western Division Semifinals; lost to Los Angeles, 4-2, in Western Division Finals.
1963—Lost to St. Louis in Western Division Semifinals.
1965—Replaced Harry Gallatin as New York head coach (November 29), with record of 6-15 and in fourth place.
1967—Lost to Boston in Eastern Division Semifinals. Replaced as New York head coach by Red Holzman (December).

McHALE, KEVIN · F/C

PERSONAL: Born December 19, 1957, in Hibbing, Minn. ... 6-10/225 (2,08/102,1). ... Full name: Kevin Edward McHale.
HIGH SCHOOL: Hibbing (Minn.).
COLLEGE: Minnesota.
TRANSACTIONS: Selected by Boston Celtics in first round (third pick overall) of 1980 NBA Draft.
CAREER NOTES: Assistant general manager, Minnesota Timberwolves (1994-95). ... Vice president of basketball operations, Timberwolves (May 1995 to present).
CAREER HONORS: One of the 50 Greatest Players in NBA History (1996). ... Elected to Naismith Memorial Basketball Hall of Fame (1999).
MISCELLANEOUS: Member of NBA championship team (1981, 1984, 1986).

COLLEGIATE RECORD

Season Team	G	Min.	FGM	FGA	Pct.	FTM	FTA	Pct.	Reb.	Ast.	Pts.	RPG	APG	PPG
76-77—Minnesota	27	...	133	241	.552	58	77	.753	218	36	324	8.1	1.3	12.0
77-78—Minnesota	26	...	143	242	.591	54	77	.701	192	27	340	7.4	1.0	13.1
78-79—Minnesota	27	...	202	391	.517	79	96	.823	259	33	483	9.6	1.2	17.9
79-80—Minnesota	32	...	236	416	.567	85	107	.794	281	28	557	8.8	0.9	17.4
Totals	112	...	714	1290	.553	276	357	.773	950	124	1704	8.5	1.1	15.2

NBA REGULAR-SEASON RECORD

HONORS: NBA Sixth Man Award (1984, 1985). ... All-NBA first team (1987). ... NBA All-Defensive first team (1986, 1987, 1988). ... NBA All-Defensive second team (1983, 1989, 1990). ... NBA All-Rookie team (1981).

									REBOUNDS							AVERAGES		
Season Team	G	Min.	FGM	FGA	Pct.	FTM	FTA	Pct.	Off.	Def.	Tot.	Ast.	St.	Blk.	TO	Pts.	RPG	APG	PPG
80-81—Boston	82	1645	355	666	.533	108	159	.679	155	204	359	55	27	151	110	818	4.4	0.7	10.0
81-82—Boston	82	2332	465	875	.531	187	248	.754	191	365	556	91	30	185	137	1117	6.8	1.1	13.6
82-83—Boston	82	2345	483	893	.541	193	269	.717	215	338	553	104	34	192	159	1159	6.7	1.3	14.1
83-84—Boston	82	2577	587	1055	.556	336	439	.765	208	402	610	104	23	126	150	1511	7.4	1.3	18.4
84-85—Boston	79	2653	605	1062	.570	355	467	.760	229	483	712	141	28	120	157	1565	9.0	1.8	19.8
85-86—Boston	68	2397	561	978	.574	326	420	.776	171	380	551	181	29	134	148	1448	8.1	2.7	21.3
86-87—Boston	77	3060	790	1307	*.604	428	512	.836	247	516	763	198	38	172	197	2008	9.9	2.6	26.1
87-88—Boston	64	2390	550	911	*.604	346	434	.797	159	377	536	171	27	92	141	1446	8.4	2.7	22.6
88-89—Boston	78	2876	661	1211	.546	436	533	.818	223	414	637	172	26	97	196	1758	8.2	2.2	22.5
89-90—Boston	82	2722	648	1181	.549	393	440	.893	201	476	677	172	30	157	183	1712	8.3	2.1	20.9
90-91—Boston	68	2067	504	912	.553	228	275	.829	145	335	480	126	25	146	140	1251	7.1	1.9	18.4
91-92—Boston	56	1398	323	634	.509	134	163	.822	119	211	330	82	11	59	82	780	5.9	1.5	13.9
92-93—Boston	71	1656	298	649	.459	164	195	.841	95	263	358	73	16	59	92	762	5.0	1.0	10.7
Totals	971	30118	6830	12334	.554	3634	4554	.798	2358	4764	7122	1670	344	1690	1893	17335	7.3	1.7	17.9

Three-point field goals: 1980-81, 0-for-2. 1982-83, 0-for-1. 1983-84, 1-for-3 (.333). 1984-85, 0-for-6. 1986-87, 0-for-4. 1988-89, 0-for-4. 1989-90, 23-for-69 (.333). 1990-91, 15-for-37 (.405). 1991-92, 0-for-13. 1992-93, 2-for-18 (.111). Totals, 41-for-157 (.261).

Personal fouls/disqualifications: 1980-81, 260/3. 1981-82, 264/1. 1982-83, 241/3. 1983-84, 243/5. 1984-85, 234/3. 1985-86, 192/2. 1986-87, 240/1. 1987-88, 179/1. 1988-89, 223/2. 1989-90, 250/3. 1990-91, 194/2. 1991-92, 112/1. 1992-93, 126/0. Totals, 2758/27.

NBA PLAYOFF RECORD

									REBOUNDS							AVERAGES		
Season Team	G	Min.	FGM	FGA	Pct.	FTM	FTA	Pct.	Off.	Def.	Tot.	Ast.	St.	Blk.	TO	Pts.	RPG	APG	PPG
80-81—Boston	17	296	61	113	.540	23	36	.639	29	30	59	14	4	25	15	145	3.5	0.8	8.5
81-82—Boston	12	344	77	134	.575	40	53	.755	41	44	85	11	5	27	16	194	7.1	0.9	16.2
82-83—Boston	7	177	34	62	.548	10	18	.556	15	27	42	5	3	7	10	78	6.0	0.7	11.1
83-84—Boston	23	702	123	244	.504	94	121	.777	62	81	143	27	3	35	38	340	6.2	1.2	14.8
84-85—Boston	21	837	172	303	.568	121	150	.807	74	134	208	32	13	46	60	465	9.9	1.5	22.1
85-86—Boston	18	715	168	290	.579	112	141	.794	51	104	155	48	8	43	48	448	8.6	2.7	24.9
86-87—Boston	21	827	174	298	.584	96	126	.762	66	128	194	39	7	30	54	444	9.2	1.9	21.1
87-88—Boston	17	716	158	262	.603	115	137	.839	55	81	136	40	7	30	39	432	8.0	2.4	25.4
88-89—Boston	3	115	20	41	.488	17	23	.739	7	17	24	9	1	2	4	57	8.0	3.0	19.0
89-90—Boston	5	192	42	69	.609	25	29	.862	8	31	39	13	2	10	14	110	7.8	2.6	22.0
90-91—Boston	11	376	78	148	.527	66	80	.825	18	54	72	20	5	14	14	228	6.5	1.8	20.7
91-92—Boston	10	306	65	126	.516	35	44	.795	21	46	67	13	5	5	9	165	6.7	1.3	16.5
92-93—Boston	4	113	32	55	.582	12	14	.857	9	20	29	3	2	7	5	76	7.3	0.8	19.0
Totals	169	5716	1204	2145	.561	766	972	.788	456	797	1253	274	65	281	326	3182	7.4	1.6	18.8

Three-point field goals: 1982-83, 0-for-1. 1983-84, 0-for-3. 1985-86, 0-for-1. 1987-88, 1-for-1. 1989-90, 1-for-3 (.333). 1990-91, 6-for-11 (.545). 1991-92, 0-for-1. Totals, 8-for-21 (.381).

Personal fouls/disqualifications: 1980-81, 51/1. 1981-82, 44/0. 1982-83, 16/0. 1983-84, 75/1. 1984-85, 73/3. 1985-86, 64/0. 1986-87, 71/2. 1987-88, 65/1. 1988-89, 13/0. 1989-90, 17/0. 1990-91, 42/0. 1991-92, 34/0. 1992-93, 6/0. Totals, 571/8.

NBA ALL-STAR GAME RECORD

							REBOUNDS								
Season Team	Min.	FGM	FGA	Pct.	FTM	FTA	Pct.	Off.	Def.	Tot.	Ast.	PF	Dq.	St.	Blk.	TO	Pts.
1984 —Boston	11	3	7	.429	4	6	.667	2	3	5	0	1	0	0	0	2	10
1986 —Boston	20	3	8	.375	2	2	1.000	3	7	10	2	4	0	4	0	0	8
1987 —Boston	30	7	11	.636	2	2	1.000	4	3	7	2	5	0	4	0	0	16
1988 —Boston	14	0	1	.000	2	2	1.000	0	1	1	1	2	0	2	2	2	2
1989 —Boston	16	5	7	.714	0	0	...	1	2	3	0	3	0	0	2	1	10
1990 —Boston	20	6	11	.545	0	0	...	2	6	8	1	4	0	0	0	0	13
1991 —Boston	14	0	3	.000	2	2	1.000	1	2	3	2	2	0	1	0	0	2
Totals	125	24	48	.500	12	14	.857	13	24	37	8	21	0	1	12	5	61

Three-point field goals: 1990, 1-for-1. 1991, 0-for-1. Totals, 1-for-2 (.500).

MIKAN, GEORGE   C

PERSONAL: Born June 18, 1924, in Joliet, Ill. ... 6-10/245 (2,08/111,1). ... Full name: George Lawrence Mikan Jr. ... Brother of Ed Mikan, forward/center with Chicago Stags of Basketball Association of America (1948-49) and six NBA teams (1949-50 through 1953-54); and father of Larry Mikan, forward with Cleveland Cavaliers (1970-71).
HIGH SCHOOL: Joliet (Ill.) Catholic, then Quigley Prep (Chicago).
COLLEGE: DePaul.
TRANSACTIONS: Signed by Chicago Gears of National Basketball League (March 16, 1946). ... Gears dropped out of NBL and entered Professional Basketball League of America for 1947-48 season. ... PBLA disbanded (November 13, 1947); Chicago was refused a franchise in the NBL and Mikan was awarded to Minneapolis Lakers at NBL meeting (November 17, 1947). Mikan scored 193 points in the eight PBLA games played by Gears before the league folded and led the league in total points and scoring average. ... Signed by Minneapolis Lakers of NBL (November 1947). ... Lakers franchise transferred to Basketball Association of America for 1948-49 season. ... Lakers franchise became part of NBA upon merger of BAA and NBL for 1949-50 season.
CAREER HONORS: Elected to Naismith Memorial Basketball Hall of Fame (1959). ... NBA 25th Anniversary All-Time Team (1970), 35th Anniversary All-Time Team (1980) and One of the 50 Greatest Players in NBA History (1996).
MISCELLANEOUS: Member of NBA championship team (1950, 1952, 1953, 1954). ... Member of BAA championship team (1949). ... Member of NBL championship team (1947, 1948).

COLLEGIATE RECORD

NOTES: THE SPORTING NEWS All-America first team (1944, 1945).

Season Team	G	Min.	FGM	FGA	Pct.	FTM	FTA	Pct.	Reb.	Ast.	Pts.	RPG	APG	PPG
41-42—DePaul‡						Freshman team statistics unavailable.								
42-43—DePaul	24	...	97	...	...	77	111	.694	...	...	271	...	...	11.3
43-44—DePaul	26	...	188	...	...	110	169	.651	...	...	486	...	...	18.7
44-45—DePaul	24	...	218	...	...	122	199	.613	...	...	558	...	...	23.3
45-46—DePaul	24	...	206	...	...	143	186	.769	...	...	555	...	...	23.1
Varsity totals	98	...	709	...	...	452	665	.680	...	...	1870	...	...	19.1

NBL AND NBA REGULAR-SEASON RECORD

HONORS: All-NBA first team (1950, 1951, 1952, 1953, 1954). ... NBL Most Valuable Player (1948). ... All-NBL first team (1947, 1948). ... All-BAA first team (1949).

Season Team	G	Min.	FGM	FGA	Pct.	FTM	FTA	Pct.	Reb.	Ast.	PF	Dq.	Pts.	RPG	APG	PPG
46-47—Chicago (NBL)	25	...	147	...	...	119	164	.726	...	...	90	...	413	...	...	*16.5
47-48—Minneapolis. (NBL)	56	...	*406	...	...	*383	*509	.752	...	...	210	...	*1195	...	...	*21.3
48-49—Minneapolis (BAA)	60	...	*583	1403	.416	*532	*689	.772	...	218	260	...	*1698	...	3.6	*28.3
49-50—Minneapolis	68	...	*649	*1595	.407	*567	*728	.779	...	197	*297	...	*1865	...	2.9	*27.4
50-51—Minneapolis	68	...	*678	*1584	.428	*576	*717	.803	958	208	*308	14	*1932	14.1	3.1	*28.4
51-52—Minneapolis	64	2572	545	*1414	.385	433	555	.780	866	194	*286	14	1523	*13.5	3.0	*23.8
52-53—Minneapolis	70	2651	500	1252	.399	442	567	.780	*1007	201	290	12	1442	*14.4	2.9	20.6
53-54—Minneapolis	72	2362	441	1160	.380	424	546	.777	1028	174	268	4	1306	14.3	2.4	18.1
54-55—						Did not play—retired.										
55-56—Minneapolis	37	765	148	375	.395	94	122	.771	308	53	153	6	390	8.3	1.4	10.5
Totals	520	...	4097	...	...	3570	4597	.777	...	...	2162	...	11764	...	...	22.6

NBL AND NBA PLAYOFF RECORD

Season Team	G	Min.	FGM	FGA	Pct.	FTM	FTA	Pct.	Reb.	Ast.	PF	Dq.	Pts.	RPG	APG	PPG
46-47—Chi. (NBL)	11	...	72	...	...	73	104	.702	...	...	48	...	217	...	...	19.7
47-48—Minn. (NBL)	10	...	88	...	...	68	97	.701	...	...	37	...	244	...	...	24.4
48-49—Minneapolis (BAA)	10	...	103	227	.454	97	121	.802	...	21	44	...	303	...	2.1	30.3
49-50—Minneapolis	12	...	121	316	.383	134	170	.788	...	36	47	...	376	...	3.0	31.3
50-51—Minneapolis	7	...	62	152	.408	44	55	.800	74	9	25	1	168	10.6	1.3	24.0
51-52—Minneapolis	13	553	99	261	.379	109	138	.790	207	36	63	3	307	15.9	2.8	23.6
52-53—Minneapolis	12	463	78	213	.366	82	112	.732	185	23	56	5	238	15.4	1.9	19.8
53-54—Minneapolis	13	424	87	190	.458	78	96	.813	171	25	56	1	252	13.2	1.9	19.4
55-56—Minneapolis	3	60	13	35	.371	10	13	.769	28	5	14	0	36	9.3	1.7	12.0
Totals	91	...	723	...	...	695	906	.767	...	...	390	...	2141	...	...	23.5

NBA ALL-STAR GAME RECORD

NOTES: NBA All-Star Game Most Valuable Player (1953).

Season Team	Min.	FGM	FGA	Pct.	FTM	FTA	Pct.	Reb	Ast.	PF	Dq.	Pts.
1951 —Minneapolis	...	4	17	.235	4	6	.667	11	3	2	0	12
1952 —Minneapolis	29	9	19	.474	8	9	.889	15	1	5	0	26
1953 —Minneapolis	40	9	26	.346	4	4	1.000	16	2	2	0	22
1954 —Minneapolis	31	6	18	.333	6	8	.750	9	1	5	0	18
Totals	...	28	80	.350	22	27	.815	51	7	14	0	78

NBA COACHING RECORD

Season Team	REGULAR SEASON			PLAYOFFS		
	W	L	Pct.	W	L	Pct.
57-58—Minneapolis	9	30	.231	—	—	—

NOTES:
1958—Resigned as Minneapolis head coach and replaced by John Kundla (January).

MIKKELSEN, VERN　　F/C

PERSONAL: Born October 21, 1928, in Fresno, Calif. ... 6-7/230 (2,00/104,3). ... Full name: Arild Verner Agerskov Mikkelsen.
HIGH SCHOOL: Askov (Minn.).
COLLEGE: Hamline University (Minn.).
TRANSACTIONS: Selected by Minneapolis Lakers in first round of 1949 NBA Draft.
CAREER HONORS: Elected to Naismith Memorial Basketball Hall of Fame (1995).
MISCELLANEOUS: Member of NBA championship team (1950, 1952, 1953, 1954).

COLLEGIATE RECORD

NOTES: THE SPORTING NEWS All-America fourth team (1949). ... Inducted into NAIA Basketball Hall of Fame (1956). ... Led NCAA Division II with .538 field-goal percentage (1949).

Season Team	G	Min.	FGM	FGA	Pct.	FTM	FTA	Pct.	Reb.	Ast.	Pts.	AVERAGES RPG	APG	PPG
45-46—Hamline University	17	...	49	...	...	25	...	...	...	...	123	...	...	7.2
46-47—Hamline University	26	...	102	...	...	52	...	...	...	...	256	...	...	9.8
47-48—Hamline University	31	...	199	...	...	119	...	...	...	...	517	...	...	16.7
48-49—Hamline University	30	...	203	377	.538	113	177	.638	...	...	519	...	...	17.3
Totals	104	...	553			309	...	...	...	...	1415	...	...	13.6

NBA REGULAR-SEASON RECORD

RECORDS: Holds career record for most disqualifications—127.
HONORS: All-NBA second team (1951, 1952, 1953, 1955).

Season Team	G	Min.	FGM	FGA	Pct.	FTM	FTA	Pct.	Reb.	Ast.	PF	Dq.	Pts.	AVERAGES RPG	APG	PPG
49-50 —Minneapolis	68	...	288	722	.399	215	286	.752	...	123	222	...	791		1.8	11.6
50-51 —Minneapolis	64	...	359	893	.402	186	275	.676	655	181	260	13	904	10.2	2.8	14.1
51-52 —Minneapolis	66	2345	363	866	.419	283	372	.761	681	180	282	16	1009	10.3	2.7	15.3
52-53 —Minneapolis	70	2465	378	868	.435	291	387	.752	654	148	289	14	1047	9.3	2.1	15.0
53-54 —Minneapolis	72	2247	288	771	.374	221	298	.742	615	119	264	7	797	8.5	1.7	11.1
54-55 —Minneapolis	71	2559	440	1043	.422	447	598	.748	722	145	*319	14	1327	10.2	2.0	18.7
55-56 —Minneapolis	72	2100	317	821	.386	328	408	.804	608	173	*319	†17	962	8.4	2.4	13.4
56-57 —Minneapolis	72	2198	322	854	.377	342	424	.807	630	121	*312	*18	986	8.8	1.7	13.7
57-58 —Minneapolis	72	2390	439	1070	.410	370	471	.786	805	166	299	*20	1248	11.2	2.3	17.3
58-59 —Minneapolis	72	2139	353	904	.390	286	355	.806	570	159	246	8	992	7.9	2.2	13.8
Totals	699	...	3547	8812	.403	2969	3874	.766	...	1515	2812	...	10063	...	2.2	14.4

NBA PLAYOFF RECORD

Season Team	G	Min.	FGM	FGA	Pct.	FTM	FTA	Pct.	Reb.	Ast.	PF	Dq.	Pts.	AVERAGES RPG	APG	PPG
49-50 —Minneapolis	12	...	55	149	.369	46	60	.767	...	18	52	...	156	...	1.5	13.0
50-51 —Minneapolis	7	...	39	96	.406	31	47	.660	67	17	35	3	109	9.6	2.4	15.6
51-52 —Minneapolis	13	496	60	139	.432	53	64	.828	110	20	66	4	173	8.5	1.5	13.3
52-53 —Minneapolis	12	400	44	133	.331	56	66	.848	104	24	59	3	144	8.7	2.0	12.0
53-54 —Minneapolis	13	375	51	111	.459	31	36	.861	73	17	52	1	133	5.6	1.3	10.2
54-55 —Minneapolis	7	209	30	85	.353	36	46	.783	78	13	36	4	96	11.1	1.9	13.7
55-56 —Minneapolis	3	90	11	26	.423	18	20	.900	17	2	14	2	40	5.7	0.7	13.3
56-57 —Minneapolis	5	162	33	83	.398	22	34	.647	43	17	29	4	88	8.6	3.4	17.6
58-59 —Minneapolis	13	371	73	177	.412	56	73	.767	93	24	54	3	202	7.2	1.8	15.5
Totals	85	...	396	999	.396	349	446	.783	...	152	397	...	1141	...	1.8	13.4

NBA ALL-STAR GAME RECORD

Season Team	Min.	FGM	FGA	Pct.	FTM	FTA	Pct.	Reb	Ast.	PF	Dq.	Pts.
1951 —Minneapolis..............	...	4	11	.364	3	4	.750	9	1	3	0	11
1952 —Minneapolis..............	23	5	8	.625	2	2	1.000	10	0	2	0	12
1953 —Minneapolis..............	19	3	13	.231	0	0	...	6	3	3	0	6
1955 —Minneapolis..............	25	7	15	.467	2	3	.667	9	1	5	0	16
1956 —Minneapolis..............	22	5	13	.385	6	7	.857	9	2	4	0	16
1957 —Minneapolis..............	21	3	10	.300	0	4	.000	9	1	3	0	6
Totals	...	27	70	.386	13	20	.650	52	8	20	0	67

ABA COACHING RECORD

BACKGROUND: General manager, Minnesota Pipers of ABA (1968-69).

Season Team	REGULAR SEASON W	L	Pct.	Finish	PLAYOFFS W	L	Pct.
68-69 —Minnesota	6	7	.462		—	—	—

NOTES:

1969—Replaced Jim Harding as Minnesota head coach (January), with record of 20-12; later replaced by Gus Young.

MONCRIEF, SIDNEY　　　　G

PERSONAL: Born September 21, 1957, in Little Rock, Ark. ... 6-3/183 (1,90/83,0). ... Full name: Sidney A. Moncrief. ... Nickname: The Squid.
HIGH SCHOOL: Hall (Little Rock, Ark.).
COLLEGE: Arkansas.
TRANSACTIONS: Selected by Milwaukee Bucks in first round (fifth pick overall) of 1979 NBA Draft. ... Signed as unrestricted free agent by Atlanta Hawks (October 4, 1990). ... Rights renounced by Hawks (September 29, 1991).
CAREER NOTES: Head coach, University of Arkansas-Little Rock (1999-2000). ... Assistant coach, Dallas Mavericks (2000-present).

COLLEGIATE RECORD

NOTES: THE SPORTING NEWS All-America second team (1979). ... Led NCAA Division I with .665 field goal percentage (1976).

Season Team	G	Min.	FGM	FGA	Pct.	FTM	FTA	Pct.	Reb.	Ast.	Pts.	RPG	APG	PPG
75-76—Arkansas	28	...	149	224	.665	56	77	.727	213	59	354	7.6	2.1	12.6
76-77—Arkansas	28	997	157	242	.649	117	171	.684	235	41	431	8.4	1.5	15.4
77-78—Arkansas	36	1293	209	354	.590	203	256	.793	278	60	621	7.7	1.7	17.3
78-79—Arkansas	30	1157	224	400	.560	212	248	.855	289	80	660	9.6	2.7	22.0
Totals	122	...	739	1220	.606	588	752	.782	1015	240	2066	8.3	2.0	16.9

NBA REGULAR-SEASON RECORD

HONORS: NBA Defensive Player of the Year (1983, 1984). ... All-NBA first team (1983). ... All-NBA second team (1982, 1984, 1985, 1986). ... NBA All-Defensive first team (1983, 1984, 1985, 1986). ... NBA All-Defensive second team (1982).

Season Team	G	Min.	FGM	FGA	Pct.	FTM	FTA	Pct.	Off.	Def.	Tot.	Ast.	St.	Blk.	TO	Pts.	RPG	APG	PPG
79-80—Milwaukee	77	1557	211	451	.468	232	292	.795	154	184	338	133	72	16	117	654	4.4	1.7	8.5
80-81—Milwaukee	80	2417	400	739	.541	320	398	.804	186	220	406	264	90	37	145	1122	5.1	3.3	14.0
81-82—Milwaukee	80	2980	556	1063	.523	468	573	.817	221	313	534	382	138	22	208	1581	6.7	4.8	19.8
82-83—Milwaukee	76	2710	606	1156	.524	499	604	.826	192	245	437	300	113	23	197	1712	5.8	3.9	22.5
83-84—Milwaukee	79	3075	560	1125	.498	529	624	.848	215	313	528	358	108	27	217	1654	6.7	4.5	20.9
84-85—Milwaukee	73	2734	561	1162	.483	454	548	.828	149	242	391	382	117	39	184	1585	5.4	5.2	21.7
85-86—Milwaukee	73	2567	470	962	.489	498	580	.859	115	219	334	357	103	18	174	1471	4.6	4.9	20.2
86-87—Milwaukee	39	992	158	324	.488	136	162	.840	57	70	127	121	27	10	63	460	3.3	3.1	11.8
87-88—Milwaukee	56	1428	217	444	.489	164	196	.837	58	122	180	204	41	12	86	603	3.2	3.6	10.8
88-89—Milwaukee	62	1594	261	532	.491	205	237	.865	46	126	172	188	65	13	94	752	2.8	3.0	12.1
89-90—								Did not play—retired.											
90-91—Atlanta	72	1096	117	240	.488	82	105	.781	31	97	128	104	50	9	66	337	1.8	1.4	4.7
Totals	767	23150	4117	8198	.502	3587	4319	.831	1424	2151	3575	2793	924	226	1551	11931	4.7	3.6	15.6

Three-point field goals: 1979-80, 0-for-1. 1980-81, 2-for-9 (.222). 1981-82, 1-for-14 (.071). 1982-83, 1-for-10 (.100). 1983-84, 5-for-18 (.278). 1984-85, 9-for-33 (.273). 1985-86, 33-for-103 (.320). 1986-87, 8-for-31 (.258). 1987-88, 5-for-31 (.161). 1988-89, 25-for-73 (.342). 1990-91, 21-for-64 (.328). Totals, 110-for-387 (.284).

Personal fouls/disqualifications: 1979-80, 106/0. 1980-81, 156/1. 1981-82, 205/3. 1982-83, 180/1. 1983-84, 204/2. 1984-85, 197/1. 1985-86, 178/1. 1986-87, 73/0. 1987-88, 109/0. 1988-89, 114/1. 1990-91, 112/0. Totals, 1635/10.

NBA PLAYOFF RECORD

Season Team	G	Min.	FGM	FGA	Pct.	FTM	FTA	Pct.	Off.	Def.	Tot.	Ast.	St.	Blk.	TO	Pts.	RPG	APG	PPG
79-80—Milwaukee	7	182	30	51	.588	27	31	.871	17	14	31	11	5	1	14	87	4.4	1.6	12.4
80-81—Milwaukee	7	277	30	69	.435	38	51	.745	19	28	47	20	12	3	21	98	6.7	2.9	14.0
81-82—Milwaukee	6	252	31	74	.419	30	38	.789	15	15	30	24	9	2	12	92	5.0	4.0	15.3
82-83—Milwaukee	9	377	62	142	.437	46	61	.754	28	32	60	33	18	3	27	170	6.7	3.7	18.9
83-84—Milwaukee	16	618	99	191	.518	106	134	.791	44	67	111	68	28	9	61	305	6.9	4.3	19.1
84-85—Milwaukee	8	319	55	99	.556	70	75	.933	10	24	34	40	5	4	20	184	4.3	5.0	23.0
85-86—Milwaukee	9	327	52	122	.426	44	63	.698	15	26	41	44	5	5	21	152	4.6	4.9	16.9
86-87—Milwaukee	12	426	78	165	.473	73	90	.811	21	33	54	36	13	6	24	233	4.5	3.0	19.4
87-88—Milwaukee	5	173	24	50	.480	26	27	.963	6	13	19	26	3	1	11	75	3.8	5.2	15.0
88-89—Milwaukee	9	184	19	48	.396	15	16	.938	8	18	26	13	5	2	11	55	2.9	1.4	6.1
90-91—Atlanta	5	91	11	22	.500	13	16	.813	6	10	16	2	3	0	3	36	3.2	0.4	7.2
Totals	93	3226	491	1033	.475	488	602	.811	189	280	469	317	106	36	225	1487	5.0	3.4	16.0

Three-point field goals: 1981-82, 0-for-1. 1982-83, 0-for-1. 1983-84, 1-for-4 (.250). 1984-85, 4-for-10 (.400). 1985-86, 4-for-14 (.286). 1986-87, 4-for-14 (.286). 1987-88, 1-for-1. 1988-89, 2-for-7 (.286). 1990-91, 1-for-6 (.167). Totals, 17-for-58 (.293).

Personal fouls/disqualifications: 1979-80, 14/0. 1980-81, 24/0. 1981-82, 22/1. 1982-83, 25/1. 1983-84, 54/1. 1984-85, 26/0. 1985-86, 30/0. 1986-87, 43/0. 1987-88, 14/0. 1988-89, 17/0. 1990-91, 16/0. Totals, 285/3.

NBA ALL-STAR GAME RECORD

Season	Team	Min.	FGM	FGA	Pct.	FTM	FTA	Pct.	Off.	Def.	Tot.	Ast.	PF	Dq.	St.	Blk.	TO	Pts.
1982	—Milwaukee	22	3	11	.273	0	2	.000	3	1	4	1	2	0	1	0	1	6
1983	—Milwaukee	23	8	14	.571	4	5	.800	3	2	5	4	1	0	6	1	1	20
1984	—Milwaukee	26	3	6	.500	2	2	1.000	1	4	5	2	3	0	5	0	4	8
1985	—Milwaukee	22	1	5	.200	6	6	1.000	2	3	5	4	1	0	0	0	2	8
1986	—Milwaukee	26	4	11	.364	7	7	1.000	3	0	3	1	0	0	0	1	0	16
Totals		119	19	47	.404	19	22	.864	12	10	22	12	7	0	12	2	8	58

Three-point field goals: 1986, 1-for-1.

HEAD COACHING RECORD

Season Team	W	L	Pct.	Finish	W	L	Pct.
	REGULAR SEASON				**PLAYOFFS**		
99-00 —Arkansas-Little Rock	4	23	.148	9th/Sun Belt Conference	—	—	—

MONROE, EARL　　　　　G

PERSONAL: Born November 21, 1944, in Philadelphia. ... 6-3/190 (1,90/86,2). ... Full name: Vernon Earl Monroe. ... Nickname: The Pearl.
HIGH SCHOOL: John Bartram (Philadelphia).
COLLEGE: Winston-Salem (N.C.) State.
TRANSACTIONS: Selected by Baltimore Bullets in first round (second pick overall) of 1967 NBA Draft. ... Traded by Bullets to New York Knicks for F Dave Stallworth, G Mike Riordan and cash (November 10, 1971).
CAREER HONORS: Elected to Naismith Memorial Basketball Hall of Fame (1990). ... One of the 50 Greatest Players in NBA History (1996).
MISCELLANEOUS: Member of NBA championship team (1973).

COLLEGIATE RECORD

NOTES: The Sporting News All-America first team (1966). ... Holds NCAA Division II single-season record for most points—1329 (1967). ... Inducted into NAIA Basketball Hall of Fame (1975). ... NCAA College Division and NAIA Leading Scorer (1967). ... Outstanding Player in NCAA College Division Tournament (1967). ... Member of NCAA College Division tournament championship team (1967). ... Led NCAA Division II with 41.5 points per game (1967).

Season Team	G	Min.	FGM	FGA	Pct.	FTM	FTA	Pct.	Reb.	Ast.	Pts.	RPG	APG	PPG
63-64—Winst.-Salem State	23	...	71	...	...	21	...	...	...	...	163	...	...	7.1
64-65—Winst.-Salem State	30	...	286	...	...	125	176	.710	211	...	697	7.0	...	23.2
65-66—Winst.-Salem State	25	...	292	519	.563	162	187	.866	167	...	746	6.7	...	29.8
66-67—Winst.-Salem State	32	...	509	839	.607	311	391	.795	218	...	1329	6.8	...	41.5
Totals	110	...	1158	...	...	619	...	...	...	...	2935	...	...	26.7

NBA REGULAR-SEASON RECORD

HONORS: NBA Rookie of the Year (1968). ... All-NBA first team (1969). ... NBA All-Rookie team (1968).

Season Team	G	Min.	FGM	FGA	Pct.	FTM	FTA	Pct.	Reb.	Ast.	PF	Dq.	Pts.	RPG	APG	PPG
67-68 —Baltimore	82	3012	742	1637	.453	507	649	.781	465	349	282	3	1991	5.7	4.3	24.3
68-69 —Baltimore	80	3075	809	1837	.440	447	582	.768	280	392	261	1	2065	3.5	4.9	25.8
69-70 —Baltimore	82	3051	695	1557	.446	532	641	.830	257	402	258	3	1922	3.1	4.9	23.4
70-71 —Baltimore	81	2843	663	1501	.442	406	506	.802	213	354	220	3	1732	2.6	4.4	21.4
71-72 —Balt.-N.Y.	63	1337	287	662	.434	175	224	.781	100	142	139	1	749	1.6	2.3	11.9
72-73 —New York	75	2370	496	1016	.488	171	208	.822	245	288	195	1	1163	3.3	3.8	15.5

Season Team	G	Min.	FGM	FGA	Pct.	FTM	FTA	Pct.	Off.	Def.	Tot.	Ast.	St.	Blk.	TO	Pts.	RPG	APG	PPG
73-74—New York	41	1194	240	513	.468	93	113	.823	22	99	121	110	34	19	...	573	3.0	2.7	14.0
74-75—New York	78	2814	668	1462	.457	297	359	.827	56	271	327	270	108	29	...	1633	4.2	3.5	20.9
75-76—New York	76	2889	647	1354	.478	280	356	.787	48	225	273	304	111	22	...	1574	3.6	4.0	20.7
76-77—N.Y. Knicks	77	2656	613	1185	.517	307	366	.839	45	178	223	366	91	23	...	1533	2.9	4.8	19.9
77-78—New York	76	2369	556	1123	.495	242	291	.832	47	135	182	361	60	19	179	1354	2.4	4.8	17.8
78-79—New York	64	1393	329	699	.471	129	154	.838	26	48	74	189	48	6	98	787	1.2	3.0	12.3
79-80—New York	51	633	161	352	.457	56	64	.875	16	20	36	67	21	3	28	378	0.7	1.3	7.4
Totals	926	29636	6906	14898	.464	3642	4513	.807	...	...	2796	3594	473	121	305	17454	3.0	3.9	18.8

Personal fouls/disqualifications: 1973-74, 97/0. 1974-75, 200/0. 1975-76, 209/1. 1976-77, 197/0. 1977-78, 189/0. 1978-79, 123/0. 1979-80, 46/0. Totals, 2416/13.

NBA PLAYOFF RECORD

Season Team	G	Min.	FGM	FGA	Pct.	FTM	FTA	Pct.	Reb.	Ast.	PF	Dq.	Pts.	RPG	APG	PPG
68-69 —Baltimore	4	171	44	114	.386	25	31	.806	21	16	10	0	113	5.3	4.0	28.3
69-70 —Baltimore	7	299	74	154	.481	48	60	.800	23	28	23	0	196	3.3	4.0	28.0
70-71 —Baltimore	18	671	145	356	.407	107	135	.793	64	74	56	0	397	3.6	4.1	22.1
71-72 —New York	16	429	76	185	.411	45	57	.789	45	47	41	0	197	2.8	2.9	12.3
72-73 —New York	16	504	111	211	.526	36	48	.750	51	51	39	0	258	3.2	3.2	16.1

Season Team	G	Min.	FGM	FGA	Pct.	FTM	FTA	Pct.	Off.	Def.	Tot.	Ast.	St.	Blk.	TO	Pts.	RPG	APG	PPG
73-74—New York	12	407	81	165	.491	47	55	.855	8	40	48	25	8	9	...	209	4.0	2.1	17.4
74-75—New York	3	89	12	45	.267	18	22	.818	1	8	9	6	4	2	...	42	3.0	2.0	14.0
77-78—New York	6	145	24	62	.387	11	18	.611	1	4	5	17	6	0	6	59	0.8	2.8	9.8
Totals	82	2715	567	1292	.439	337	426	.791	...	...	266	264	18	11	6	1471	3.2	3.2	17.9

Personal fouls/disqualifications: 1973-74, 26/0. 1974-75, 6/0. 1977-78, 15/0. Totals, 216/0.

NBA ALL-STAR GAME RECORD

Season Team	Min.	FGM	FGA	Pct.	FTM	FTA	Pct.	Reb	Ast.	PF	Dq.	Pts.
1969 —Baltimore	27	6	15	.400	9	12	.750	4	4	4	0	21
1971 —Baltimore	18	3	9	.333	0	0	...	5	2	3	0	6

Season Team	Min.	FGM	FGA	Pct.	FTM	FTA	Pct.	Off.	Def.	Tot.	Ast.	PF	Dq.	St.	Blk.	TO	Pts.
1975 —New York	25	3	8	.375	3	5	.600	0	3	3	2	2	0	1	0	...	9
1977 —N.Y. Knicks	15	2	7	.286	0	0	...	0	0	0	3	1	0	0	0	...	4
Totals	85	14	39	.359	12	17	.706	...	...	12	11	10	0	1	0	...	40

MURPHY, CALVIN　　　　　G

PERSONAL: Born May 9, 1948, in Norwalk, Conn. ... 5-9/165 (1,76/74,8). ... Full name: Calvin Jerome Murphy.
HIGH SCHOOL: Norwalk (Conn.).
COLLEGE: Niagara.
TRANSACTIONS: Selected by San Diego Rockets in second round (18th pick overall) of 1970 NBA Draft. ... Rockets franchise moved from San Diego to Houston for 1971-72 season.

CAREER NOTES: Community services adviser, Houston Rockets (1989-90 to present).
CAREER HONORS: Elected to Naismith Memorial Basketball Hall of Fame (1993).
MISCELLANEOUS: Houston Rockets franchise all-time assists leader with 4,402 (1970-71 through 1982-83).

COLLEGIATE RECORD

NOTES: THE SPORTING NEWS All-America second team (1969, 1970).

Season Team	G	Min.	FGM	FGA	Pct.	FTM	FTA	Pct.	Reb.	Ast.	Pts.	RPG	APG	PPG
66-67—Niagara‡	19	...	364	719	.506	201	239	.841	102	...	929	5.4	...	48.9
67-68—Niagara	24	...	337	772	.437	242	288	.840	118	...	916	4.9	...	38.2
68-69—Niagara	24	...	294	700	.420	190	230	.826	87	...	778	3.6	...	32.4
69-70—Niagara	29	...	316	692	.457	222	252	.881	103	...	854	3.6	...	29.4
Varsity totals	77	...	947	2164	.438	654	770	.849	308	...	2548	4.0	...	33.1

NBA REGULAR-SEASON RECORD

RECORDS: Holds single-season record for highest free-throw percentage—.958 (1981).
HONORS: NBA All-Rookie team (1971). ... J. Walter Kennedy Citizenship Award (1979).

Season Team	G	Min.	FGM	FGA	Pct.	FTM	FTA	Pct.	Reb.	Ast.	PF	Dq.	Pts.	RPG	APG	PPG
70-71—San Diego	82	2020	471	1029	.458	356	434	.820	245	329	263	4	1298	3.0	4.0	15.8
71-72—Houston	82	2538	571	1255	.455	349	392	.890	258	393	298	6	1491	3.1	4.8	18.2
72-73—Houston	77	1697	381	820	.465	239	269	.888	149	262	211	3	1001	1.9	3.4	13.0

| | | | | | | | | | REBOUNDS | | | | | | | AVERAGES | | |
Season Team	G	Min.	FGM	FGA	Pct.	FTM	FTA	Pct.	Off.	Def.	Tot.	Ast.	St.	Blk.	TO	Pts.	RPG	APG	PPG
73-74—Houston	81	2922	671	1285	.522	310	357	.868	51	137	188	603	157	4	...	1652	2.3	7.4	20.4
74-75—Houston	78	2513	557	1152	.484	341	386	.883	52	121	173	381	128	4	...	1455	2.2	4.9	18.7
75-76—Houston	82	2995	675	1369	.493	372	410	.907	52	157	209	596	151	6	...	1722	2.5	7.3	21.0
76-77—Houston	82	2764	596	1216	.490	272	307	.886	54	118	172	386	144	8	...	1464	2.1	4.7	17.9
77-78—Houston	76	2900	852	*1737	.491	245	267	.918	57	107	164	259	112	3	173	1949	2.2	3.4	25.6
78-79—Houston	82	2941	707	1424	.496	246	265	.928	78	95	173	351	117	6	187	1660	2.1	4.3	20.2
79-80—Houston	76	2676	624	1267	.493	271	302	.897	68	82	150	299	143	9	162	1520	2.0	3.9	20.0
80-81—Houston	76	2014	528	1074	.492	206	215	*.958	33	54	87	222	111	6	129	1266	1.1	2.9	16.7
81-82—Houston	64	1204	277	648	.427	100	110	.909	20	41	61	163	43	1	82	655	1.0	2.5	10.2
82-83—Houston	64	1423	337	754	.447	138	150	*.920	34	40	74	158	59	4	89	816	1.2	2.5	12.8
Totals	1002	30607	7247	15030	.482	3445	3864	.892	...	...	2103	4402	1165	51	822	17949	2.1	4.4	17.9

Three-point field goals: 1979-80, 1-for-25 (.040). 1980-81, 4-for-17 (.235). 1981-82, 1-for-16 (.063). 1982-83, 4-for-14 (.286). Totals, 10-for-72 (.139).
Personal fouls/disqualifications: 1973-74, 310/8. 1974-75, 281/8. 1975-76, 294/3. 1976-77, 281/6. 1977-78, 241/4. 1978-79, 288/5. 1979-80, 269/3. 1980-81, 209/0. 1981-82, 142/0. 1982-83, 163/3. Totals, 3250/53.

NBA PLAYOFF RECORD

| | | | | | | | | | REBOUNDS | | | | | | | AVERAGES | | |
Season Team	G	Min.	FGM	FGA	Pct.	FTM	FTA	Pct.	Off.	Def.	Tot.	Ast.	St.	Blk.	TO	Pts.	RPG	APG	PPG
74-75—Houston	8	305	72	156	.462	51	57	.895	9	10	19	45	14	1	...	195	2.4	5.6	24.4
76-77—Houston	12	420	102	213	.479	28	30	.933	7	12	19	75	19	2	...	232	1.6	6.3	19.3
78-79—Houston	2	73	9	31	.290	8	9	.889	2	1	3	6	8	1	2	26	1.5	3.0	13.0
79-80—Houston	7	265	58	108	.537	13	13	1.000	4	6	10	26	11	0	16	131	1.4	3.7	18.7
80-81—Houston	19	540	142	287	.495	58	60	.967	7	17	24	57	26	0	42	344	1.3	3.0	18.1
81-82—Houston	3	57	5	22	.227	7	8	.875	2	1	3	4	1	0	4	17	1.0	1.3	5.7
Totals	51	1660	388	817	.475	165	177	.932	31	47	78	213	79	4	64	945	1.5	4.2	18.5

Three-point field goals: 1979-80, 2-for-4 (.500). 1980-81, 2-for-7 (.286). 1981-82, 0-for-3. Totals, 4-for-14 (.286).
Personal fouls/disqualifications: 1974-75, 36/2. 1976-77, 47/1. 1978-79, 9/0. 1979-80, 29/1. 1980-81, 68/0. 1981-82, 7/0. Totals, 197/4.

NBA ALL-STAR GAME RECORD

| | | | | | | | | REBOUNDS | | | | | | | | |
Season Team	Min.	FGM	FGA	Pct.	FTM	FTA	Pct.	Off.	Def.	Tot.	Ast.	PF	Dq.	St.	Blk.	TO	Pts.
1979—Houston	15	3	5	.600	0	0	...	0	1	1	5	4	0	2	0	4	6

NIXON, NORM   G

PERSONAL: Born October 10, 1955, in Macon, Ga. ... 6-2/175 (1,88/79,4). ... Full name: Norman Ellard Nixon.
HIGH SCHOOL: Southwest (Macon, Ga.).
COLLEGE: Duquesne.
TRANSACTIONS: Selected by Los Angeles Lakers in first round (22nd pick overall) of 1977 NBA Draft. ... Traded by Lakers with G Eddie Jordan and 1986 and 1987 second-round draft choices to San Diego Clippers for C Swen Nater and draft rights to G Byron Scott (October 10, 1983). ... Played in Italy (1988-89).
MISCELLANEOUS: Member of NBA championship team (1980, 1982).

COLLEGIATE RECORD

Season Team	G	Min.	FGM	FGA	Pct.	FTM	FTA	Pct.	Reb.	Ast.	Pts.	RPG	APG	PPG
73-74—Duquesne	24	...	113	257	.440	31	45	.689	99	144	257	4.1	6.0	10.7
74-75—Duquesne	25	...	147	282	.521	69	92	.750	88	105	363	3.5	4.2	14.5
75-76—Duquesne	25	...	214	434	.493	96	127	.756	105	150	524	4.2	6.0	21.0
76-77—Duquesne	30	1106	279	539	.518	103	138	.746	119	178	661	4.0	5.9	22.0
Totals	104	...	753	1512	.498	299	402	.744	411	577	1805	4.0	5.5	17.4

NBA REGULAR-SEASON RECORD

HONORS: NBA All-Rookie team (1978).

| | | | | | | | | | REBOUNDS | | | | | | | AVERAGES | | |
Season Team	G	Min.	FGM	FGA	Pct.	FTM	FTA	Pct.	Off.	Def.	Tot.	Ast.	St.	Blk.	TO	Pts.	RPG	APG	PPG
77-78—Los Angeles	81	2779	496	998	.497	115	161	.714	41	198	239	553	138	7	251	1107	3.0	6.8	13.7
78-79—Los Angeles	82	3145	623	1149	.542	158	204	.775	48	183	231	737	201	17	231	1404	2.8	9.0	17.1
79-80—Los Angeles	82	*3226	624	1209	.516	197	253	.779	52	177	229	642	147	14	288	1446	2.8	7.8	17.6
80-81—Los Angeles	79	2962	576	1210	.476	196	252	.778	64	168	232	696	146	11	285	1350	2.9	8.8	17.1
81-82—Los Angeles	82	3024	628	1274	.493	181	224	.808	38	138	176	652	132	7	238	1440	2.1	8.0	17.6
82-83—Los Angeles	79	2711	533	1123	.475	125	168	.744	61	144	205	566	104	4	237	1191	2.6	7.2	15.1
83-84—San Diego	82	3053	587	1270	.462	206	271	.760	56	147	203	914	94	4	257	1391	2.5	11.1	17.0

Season Team	G	Min.	FGM	FGA	Pct.	FTM	FTA	Pct.	REBOUNDS Off.	Def.	Tot.	Ast.	St.	Blk.	TO	Pts.	AVERAGES RPG	APG	PPG
84-85—L.A. Clippers...	81	2894	596	1281	.465	170	218	.780	55	163	218	711	95	4	273	1395	2.7	8.8	17.2
85-86—L.A. Clippers...	67	2138	403	921	.438	131	162	.809	45	135	180	576	84	3	190	979	2.7	8.6	14.6
87-88—L.A. Clippers...						Did not play—Achilles' tendon injury.													
88-89—L.A. Clippers...	53	1318	153	370	.414	48	65	.738	13	65	78	339	46	0	118	362	1.5	6.4	6.8
Totals...	768	27250	5219	10805	.483	1527	1978	.772	473	1518	1991	6386	1187	71	2368	12065	2.6	8.3	15.7

Three-point field goals: 1979-80, 1-for-8 (.125). 1980-81, 2-for-12 (.167). 1981-82, 3-for-12 (.250). 1982-83, 0-for-13. 1983-84, 11-for-46 (.239). 1984-85, 33-for-99 (.333). 1985-86, 42-for-121 (.347). 1988-89, 8-for-29 (.276). Totals, 100-for-340 (.294).

Personal fouls/disqualifications: 1977-78, 259/3. 1978-79, 250/6. 1979-80, 241/1. 1980-81, 226/2. 1981-82, 264/3. 1982-83, 176/1. 1983-84, 180/1. 1984-85, 175/2. 1985-86, 143/0. 1988-89, 69/0. Totals, 1983/19.

NBA PLAYOFF RECORD

Season Team	G	Min.	FGM	FGA	Pct.	FTM	FTA	Pct.	REBOUNDS Off.	Def.	Tot.	Ast.	St.	Blk.	TO	Pts.	AVERAGES RPG	APG	PPG
77-78—Los Angeles....	3	92	11	24	.458	2	3	.667	4	5	9	16	4	1	5	24	3.0	5.3	8.0
78-79—Los Angeles....	8	327	56	119	.471	11	15	.733	6	22	28	94	11	0	24	123	3.5	11.8	15.4
79-80—Los Angeles....	16	648	114	239	.477	41	51	.804	13	43	56	125	32	3	49	270	3.5	7.8	16.9
80-81—Los Angeles....	3	133	25	49	.510	8	10	.800	1	10	11	26	1	1	5	58	3.7	8.7	19.3
81-82—Los Angeles....	14	549	121	253	.478	43	57	.754	13	30	43	114	23	2	34	286	3.1	8.1	20.4
82-83—Los Angeles....	14	538	113	237	.477	37	50	.740	13	35	48	89	18	1	34	266	3.4	6.4	19.0
Totals	58	2287	440	921	.478	142	186	.763	50	145	195	464	89	8	151	1027	3.4	8.0	17.7

Three-point field goals: 1979-80, 1-for-5 (.200). 1981-82, 1-for-3 (.333). 1982-83, 3-for-7 (.429). Totals, 5-for-15 (.333).

Personal fouls/disqualifications: 1977-78, 13/0. 1978-79, 37/1. 1979-80, 59/0. 1980-81, 9/0. 1981-82, 43/0. 1982-83, 40/0. Totals, 201/1.

NBA ALL-STAR GAME RECORD

Season Team	Min.	FGM	FGA	Pct.	FTM	FTA	Pct.	REBOUNDS Off.	Def.	Tot.	Ast.	PF	Dq.	St.	Blk.	TO	Pts.
1982 —Los Angeles	19	7	14	.500	0	0	...	0	0	0	2	0	0	1	0	0	14
1985 —L.A. Clippers	19	5	7	.714	1	2	.500	0	2	2	8	0	0	1	0	1	11
1987 —L.A. Clippers						Did not play—Achilles' tendon injury.											
Totals........................	38	12	21	.571	1	2	.500	0	2	2	10	0	0	2	0	1	25

ITALIAN LEAGUE RECORD

Season Team	G	Min.	FGM	FGA	Pct.	FTM	FTA	Pct.	Reb.	Ast.	Pts.	AVERAGES RPG	APG	PPG
88-89—Scavolini Pesaro............	7	217	37	75	.493	4	7	.571	15	19	87	2.1	2.7	12.4

PARISH, ROBERT   C

PERSONAL: Born August 30, 1953, in Shreveport, La. ... 7-1/244 (2,16/110,7). ... Full name: Robert Lee Parish. ... Second cousin of Larry Robinson, forward/guard with seven NBA teams (1990-91 through 2000-01). ... Nickname: Chief.

HIGH SCHOOL: Woodlawn (Shreveport, La.).

COLLEGE: Centenary (La.).

TRANSACTIONS/CAREER NOTES: Selected by Golden State Warriors in first round (eighth pick overall) of 1976 NBA Draft. ... Traded by Warriors with 1980 first-round draft choice to Boston Celtics for two 1980 first-round draft choices (June 9, 1980). ... Signed as unrestricted free agent by Charlotte Hornets (August 4, 1994). ... Signed as free agent by Chicago Bulls (September 25, 1996). ... Announced retirement (August 25, 1997).

CAREER HONORS: One of the 50 Greatest Players in NBA History (1996).

MISCELLANEOUS: Member of NBA championship team (1981, 1984, 1986, 1997). ... Boston Celtics all-time blocked shots leader with 1,703 (1980-81 through 1993-94).

CAREER NOTES: Head coach, Maryland Mustangs (USBL).

COLLEGIATE RECORD

NOTES: THE SPORTING NEWS All-America first team (1976).

Season Team	G	Min.	FGM	FGA	Pct.	FTM	FTA	Pct.	Reb.	Ast.	Pts.	AVERAGES RPG	APG	PPG
72-73—Centenary	27	885	285	492	.579	50	82	.610	505	25	620	18.7	0.9	23.0
73-74—Centenary	25	841	224	428	.523	49	78	.628	382	34	497	15.3	1.4	19.9
74-75—Centenary	29	900	237	423	.560	74	112	.661	447	43	548	15.4	1.5	18.9
75-76—Centenary	27	939	288	489	.589	93	134	.694	486	48	669	18.0	1.8	24.8
Totals	108	3565	1034	1832	.564	266	406	.655	1820	150	2334	16.9	1.4	21.6

NBA REGULAR-SEASON RECORD

RECORDS: Holds career records for most seasons played—21; most games played—1,611; and most defensive rebounds—10,117.

HONORS: All-NBA second team (1982). ... All-NBA third team (1989).

Season Team	G	Min.	FGM	FGA	Pct.	FTM	FTA	Pct.	REBOUNDS Off.	Def.	Tot.	Ast.	St.	Blk.	TO	Pts.	AVERAGES RPG	APG	PPG
76-77—Golden State ...	77	1384	288	573	.503	121	171	.708	201	342	543	74	55	94	...	697	7.1	1.0	9.1
77-78—Golden State ...	82	1969	430	911	.472	165	264	.625	211	469	680	95	79	123	201	1025	8.3	1.2	12.5
78-79—Golden State ...	76	2411	554	1110	.499	196	281	.698	265	651	916	115	100	217	233	1304	12.1	1.5	17.2
79-80—Golden State ...	72	2119	510	1006	.507	203	284	.715	247	536	783	122	58	115	225	1223	10.9	1.7	17.0
80-81—Boston	82	2298	635	1166	.545	282	397	.710	245	532	777	144	81	214	191	1552	9.5	1.8	18.9
81-82—Boston	80	2534	669	1235	.542	252	355	.710	288	578	866	140	68	192	221	1590	10.8	1.8	19.9
82-83—Boston	78	2459	619	1125	.550	271	388	.698	260	567	827	141	79	148	185	1509	10.6	1.8	19.3
83-84—Boston	80	2867	623	1140	.546	274	368	.745	243	614	857	139	55	116	184	1520	10.7	1.7	19.0
84-85—Boston	79	2850	551	1016	.542	292	393	.743	263	577	840	125	56	101	186	1394	10.6	1.6	17.6
85-86—Boston	81	2567	530	966	.549	245	335	.731	246	524	770	145	65	116	187	1305	9.5	1.8	16.1
86-87—Boston	80	2995	588	1057	.556	227	309	.735	254	597	851	173	64	144	191	1403	10.6	2.2	17.5
87-88—Boston	74	2312	442	750	.589	177	241	.734	173	455	628	115	55	84	154	1061	8.5	1.6	14.3
88-89—Boston	80	2840	596	1045	.570	294	409	.719	342	654	996	175	79	116	200	1486	12.5	2.2	18.6

Season Team	G	Min.	FGM	FGA	Pct.	FTM	FTA	Pct.	REBOUNDS Off.	Def.	Tot.	Ast.	St.	Blk.	TO	Pts.	AVERAGES RPG	APG	PPG
89-90—Boston............	79	2396	505	871	.580	233	312	.747	259	537	796	103	38	69	169	1243	10.1	1.3	15.7
90-91—Boston............	81	2441	485	811	.598	237	309	.767	271	585	856	66	66	103	153	1207	10.6	0.8	14.9
91-92—Boston............	79	2285	468	874	.535	179	232	.772	219	486	705	70	68	97	131	1115	8.9	0.9	14.1
92-93—Boston............	79	2146	416	777	.535	162	235	.689	246	494	740	61	57	107	120	994	9.4	0.8	12.6
93-94—Boston............	74	1987	356	725	.491	154	208	.740	141	401	542	82	42	96	108	866	7.3	1.1	11.7
94-95—Charlotte.........	81	1352	159	372	.427	71	101	.703	93	257	350	44	27	36	66	389	4.3	0.5	4.8
95-96—Charlotte.........	74	1086	120	241	.498	50	71	.704	89	214	303	29	21	54	50	290	4.1	0.4	3.9
96-97—Chicago..........	43	406	70	143	.490	21	31	.677	42	47	89	22	6	19	28	161	2.1	0.5	3.7
Totals	1611	45704	9614	17914	.537	4106	5694	.721	4598	10117	14715	2180	1219	2361	3183	23334	9.1	1.4	14.5

Three-point field goals: 1979-80, 0-for-1. 1980-81, 0-for-1. 1982-83, 0-for-1. 1986-87, 0-for-1. 1987-88, 0-for-1. 1990-91, 0-for-1. Totals, 0-for-6.
Personal fouls/disqualifications: 1976-77, 224/7. 1977-78, 291/10. 1978-79, 303/10. 1979-80, 248/6. 1980-81, 310/9. 1981-82, 267/5. 1982-83, 222/4. 1983-84, 266/7. 1984-85, 223/2. 1985-86, 215/3. 1986-87, 266/5. 1987-88, 198/5. 1988-89, 209/2. 1989-90, 189/2. 1990-91, 197/1. 1991-92, 172/2. 1992-93, 201/3. 1993-94, 190/3. 1994-95, 132/0. 1995-96, 80/0. 1996-97, 40/0. Totals, 4443/86.

NBA PLAYOFF RECORD

NOTES: Holds career playoff record for most offensive rebounds—571.

Season Team	G	Min.	FGM	FGA	Pct.	FTM	FTA	Pct.	REBOUNDS Off.	Def.	Tot.	Ast.	St.	Blk.	TO	Pts.	AVERAGES RPG	APG	PPG
76-77—Golden State...	10	239	52	108	.481	17	26	.654	43	60	103	11	7	11	...	121	10.3	1.1	12.1
80-81—Boston...........	17	492	108	219	.493	39	58	.672	50	96	146	19	21	39	44	255	8.6	1.1	15.0
81-82—Boston...........	12	426	102	209	.488	51	75	.680	43	92	135	18	5	48	39	255	11.3	1.5	21.3
82-83—Boston...........	7	249	43	89	.483	17	20	.850	21	53	74	9	5	9	17	103	10.6	1.3	14.7
83-84—Boston...........	23	869	139	291	.478	64	99	.646	76	172	248	27	23	41	45	342	10.8	1.2	14.9
84-85—Boston...........	21	803	136	276	.493	87	111	.784	57	162	219	31	21	34	50	359	10.4	1.5	17.1
85-86—Boston...........	18	591	106	225	.471	58	89	.652	52	106	158	25	9	30	44	270	8.8	1.4	15.0
86-87—Boston...........	21	734	149	263	.567	79	103	.767	59	139	198	28	18	35	38	377	9.4	1.3	18.0
87-88—Boston...........	17	626	100	188	.532	50	61	.820	51	117	168	21	11	19	38	250	9.9	1.2	14.7
88-89—Boston...........	3	112	20	44	.455	7	9	.778	6	20	26	6	4	2	6	47	8.7	2.0	15.7
89-90—Boston...........	5	170	31	54	.574	17	18	.944	23	27	50	13	5	7	12	79	10.0	2.6	15.8
90-91—Boston...........	10	296	58	97	.598	42	61	.689	33	59	92	6	8	7	16	158	9.2	0.6	15.8
91-92—Boston...........	10	335	50	101	.495	20	28	.714	38	59	97	14	7	15	9	120	9.7	1.4	12.0
92-93—Boston...........	4	146	31	57	.544	6	7	.857	13	25	38	5	1	6	6	68	9.5	1.3	17.0
94-95—Charlotte.........	4	71	6	11	.545	2	5	.400	4	5	9	1	0	3	1	14	2.3	0.3	3.5
96-97—Chicago..........	2	18	1	7	.143	0	0	...	2	2	4	0	0	3	0	2	2.0	0.0	1.0
Totals	184	6177	1132	2239	.506	556	770	.722	571	1194	1765	234	145	309	365	2820	9.6	1.3	15.3

Three-point field goals: 1986-87, 0-for-1.
Personal fouls/disqualifications: 1976-77, 42/1. 1980-81, 74/2. 1981-82, 47/1. 1982-83, 18/0. 1983-84, 100/6. 1984-85, 68/0. 1985-86, 47/1. 1986-87, 79/4. 1987-88, 42/0. 1988-89, 5/0. 1989-90, 21/0. 1990-91, 34/1. 1991-92, 22/0. 1992-93, 14/0. 1994-95, 2/0. 1996-97, 2/0. Totals, 617/16.

NBA ALL-STAR GAME RECORD

Season Team	Min.	FGM	FGA	Pct.	FTM	FTA	Pct.	REBOUNDS Off.	Def.	Tot.	Ast.	PF	Dq.	St.	Blk.	TO	Pts.
1981 —Boston..............	25	5	18	.278	6	6	1.000	6	4	10	2	3	0	0	2	1	16
1982 —Boston..............	20	9	12	.750	3	4	.750	0	7	7	1	2	0	0	2	1	21
1983 —Boston..............	18	5	6	.833	3	4	.750	0	3	3	0	2	0	1	1	1	13
1984 —Boston..............	28	5	11	.455	2	4	.500	4	11	15	2	1	0	3	0	4	12
1985 —Boston..............	10	2	5	.400	0	0	...	3	3	6	1	0	0	0	0	0	4
1986 —Boston..............	7	0	0	...	0	2	.000	0	1	1	0	0	0	0	1	1	0
1987 —Boston..............	8	2	3	.667	0	0	...	0	3	3	0	1	0	0	1	1	4
1990 —Boston..............	21	7	11	.636	0	1	.000	2	2	4	2	4	0	0	1	1	14
1991 —Boston..............	5	1	2	.500	0	0	...	1	3	4	0	2	0	0	0	1	2
Totals............................	142	36	68	.529	14	21	.667	16	37	53	8	15	0	4	8	10	86

USBL COACHING RECORD

NOTES: USBL Coach of the Year (2001).

Season Team	REGULAR SEASON W	L	Pct.	Finish	PLAYOFFS W	L	Pct.
00-01 —Maryland	19	11	.633	1st	0	1	.000

NOTES:
2001—Lost to Dodge City in quarterfinals.

PETTIT, BOB   F/C

PERSONAL: Born December 12, 1932, in Baton Rouge, La. ... 6-9/215 (2,05/97,5). ... Full name: Robert Lee Pettit Jr.
HIGH SCHOOL: Baton Rouge (La.).
COLLEGE: Louisiana State.
TRANSACTIONS: Selected by Milwaukee Hawks in first round of 1954 NBA Draft. ... Hawks franchise moved from Milwaukee to St. Louis for 1955-56 season.
CAREER HONORS: Elected to Naismith Memorial Basketball Hall of Fame (1970). ... NBA 25th Anniversary All-Time Team (1970), 35th Anniversary All-Time Team (1980) and One of the 50 Greatest Players in NBA History (1996).
MISCELLANEOUS: Member of NBA championship team (1958). ... Atlanta Hawks franchise all-time leading rebounder with 12,851 (1954-55 through 1964-65).

COLLEGIATE RECORD

Season Team	G	Min.	FGM	FGA	Pct.	FTM	FTA	Pct.	Reb.	Ast.	Pts.	AVERAGES RPG	APG	PPG
50-51—Louisiana State‡............	10	...	...	...	...	...	...	...	...	...	270	...	...	27.0
51-52—Louisiana State..............	23	...	237	549	.432	115	192	.599	315	...	589	13.7	...	25.6
52-53—Louisiana State..............	21	...	193	394	.490	133	215	.619	263	...	519	12.5	...	24.7
53-54—Louisiana State..............	25	...	281	573	.490	223	308	.724	432	...	785	17.3	...	31.4
Varsity totals	69	...	711	1516	.469	471	715	.659	1010	...	1893	14.6	...	27.4

NBA REGULAR-SEASON RECORD

HONORS: NBA Most Valuable Player (1956, 1959). ... NBA Rookie of the Year (1955). ... All-NBA first team (1955, 1956, 1957, 1958, 1959, 1960, 1961, 1962, 1963, 1964). ... All-NBA second team (1965).

													AVERAGES		
Season Team	G	Min.	FGM	FGA	Pct.	FTM	FTA	Pct.	Reb.	Ast.	PF	Dq.	Pts.	RPG	APG	PPG
54-55 —Milwaukee	72	2659	520	1279	.407	426	567	.751	994	229	258	5	1466	13.8	3.2	20.4
55-56 —St. Louis	72	2794	*646	*1507	.429	*557	*757	.736	*1164	189	202	1	*1849	16.2	2.6	*25.7
56-57 —St. Louis	71	2491	*613	*1477	.415	529	684	.773	1037	133	181	1	1755	14.6	1.9	24.7
57-58 —St. Louis	70	2528	581	1418	.410	557	744	.749	1216	157	222	6	1719	17.4	2.2	24.6
58-59 —St. Louis	72	2873	*719	1640	.438	*667	*879	.759	1182	221	200	3	*2105	16.4	3.1	*29.2
59-60 —St. Louis	72	2896	669	1526	.438	544	722	.753	1221	257	204	0	1882	17.0	3.6	26.1
60-61 —St. Louis	76	3027	769	1720	.447	582	804	.724	1540	262	217	0	2120	20.3	3.4	27.9
61-62 —St. Louis	78	3282	867	1928	.450	695	901	.771	1457	289	296	4	2429	18.7	3.7	31.1
62-63 —St. Louis	79	3090	778	1746	.446	*685	885	.774	1195	245	282	8	2241	15.1	3.1	28.4
63-64 —St. Louis	80	3296	791	1708	.463	608	771	.789	1224	259	300	3	2190	15.3	3.2	27.4
64-65 —St. Louis	50	1754	396	923	.429	332	405	.820	621	128	167	0	1124	12.4	2.6	22.5
Totals	792	30690	7349	16872	.436	6182	8119	.761	12851	2369	2529	32	20880	16.2	3.0	26.4

NBA PLAYOFF RECORD

NOTES: Holds NBA Finals single-game record for most free throws made—19 (April 9, 1958, vs. Boston). ... Shares NBA Finals record for most free throws attempted in one quarter—11 (April 9, 1958, vs. Boston).

													AVERAGES		
Season Team	G	Min.	FGM	FGA	Pct.	FTM	FTA	Pct.	Reb.	Ast.	PF	Dq.	Pts.	RPG	APG	PPG
55-56 —St. Louis	8	274	47	128	.367	59	70	.843	84	18	20	0	153	10.5	2.3	19.1
56-57 —St. Louis	10	430	98	237	.414	102	133	.767	168	25	33	0	298	16.8	2.5	29.8
57-58 —St. Louis	11	430	90	230	.391	86	118	.729	181	20	31	0	266	16.5	1.8	24.2
58-59 —St. Louis	6	257	58	137	.423	51	65	.785	75	14	20	0	167	12.5	2.3	27.8
59-60 —St. Louis	14	576	129	292	.442	107	142	.754	221	52	43	1	365	15.8	3.7	26.1
60-61 —St. Louis	12	526	117	284	.412	109	144	.757	211	38	42	0	343	17.6	3.2	28.6
62-63 —St. Louis	11	463	119	259	.459	112	144	.778	166	33	34	0	350	15.1	3.0	31.8
63-64 —St. Louis	12	494	93	226	.412	66	79	.835	174	33	44	0	252	14.5	2.8	21.0
64-65 —St. Louis	4	95	15	41	.366	16	20	.800	24	8	10	0	46	6.0	2.0	11.5
Totals	88	3545	766	1834	.418	708	915	.774	1304	241	277	1	2240	14.8	2.7	25.5

NBA ALL-STAR GAME RECORD

NOTES: NBA All-Star Game Most Valuable Player (1956, 1958, 1962). ... NBA All-Star Game co-Most Valuable Player (1959). ... Holds single-game records for most rebounds—27; and most rebounds in one quarter—10 (1962). ... Shares single-game record for most rebounds in one half—16 (1962).

Season Team	Min.	FGM	FGA	Pct.	FTM	FTA	Pct.	Reb	Ast.	PF	Dq.	Pts.
1955 —Milwaukee	27	3	14	.214	2	4	.500	9	2	0	0	8
1956 —St. Louis	31	7	17	.412	6	7	.857	24	7	4	0	20
1957 —St. Louis	31	8	18	.444	5	6	.833	11	2	2	0	21
1958 —St. Louis	38	10	21	.476	8	10	.800	26	1	1	0	28
1959 —St. Louis	34	8	21	.381	9	9	1.000	16	5	1	0	25
1960 —St. Louis	28	4	15	.267	3	6	.500	14	2	2	0	11
1961 —St. Louis	32	13	22	.591	3	7	.429	9	0	2	0	29
1962 —St. Louis	37	10	20	.500	5	5	1.000	27	2	5	0	25
1963 —St. Louis	32	7	16	.438	11	12	.917	13	0	1	0	25
1964 —St. Louis	36	6	15	.400	7	9	.778	17	2	3	0	19
1965 —St. Louis	34	5	14	.357	3	5	.600	12	0	4	0	13
Totals	360	81	193	.420	62	80	.775	178	23	25	0	224

NBA COACHING RECORD

	REGULAR SEASON				PLAYOFFS		
Season Team	W	L	Pct.	Finish	W	L	Pct.
61-62 —St. Louis	4	2	.667	4th/Western Division	—	—	—

NOTES:
1962—Replaced Paul Seymour (5-9) and Andrew Levane (20-40) as St. Louis head coach (March), with record of 25-49.

POLLARD, JIM   F

PERSONAL: Born July 9, 1922, in Oakland. ... Died January 22, 1993. ... 6-5/185 (1,96/83,9). ... Full name: James Clifford Pollard. ... Nickname: The Kangaroo Kid.
HIGH SCHOOL: Oakland Technical.
COLLEGE: Stanford.
TRANSACTIONS: Signed by Minneapolis Lakers of National Basketball League (1947). ... Lakers franchise transferred to Basketball Association of America for 1948-49 season.
CAREER HONORS: Elected to Naismith Memorial Basketball Hall of Fame (1977).
MISCELLANEOUS: Member of NBA championship team (1950, 1952, 1953, 1954). ... Member of BAA championship team (1949). ... Member of NBL championship team (1948).

COLLEGIATE RECORD

NOTES: Member of NCAA Division I championship team (1942). ... In military service during 1942-43, 1943-44 and 1944-45 seasons; played with Alameda, Calif. Coast Guard team.

												AVERAGES		
Season Team	G	Min.	FGM	FGA	Pct.	FTM	FTA	Pct.	Reb.	Ast.	Pts.	RPG	APG	PPG
40-41—Stanford‡					Freshman team statistics unavailable.									
41-42—Stanford	23	...	103	...	...	35	48	.729	...	...	241	...	...	10.5
Varsity totals	23	...	103	...	...	35	48	.729	...	...	241	...	...	10.5

ABL REGULAR-SEASON RECORD

												AVERAGES		
Season Team	G	Min.	FGM	FGA	Pct.	FTM	FTA	Pct.	Reb.	Ast.	Pts.	RPG	APG	PPG
45-46—San Diego Dons	15	...	84	...	...	55	...	...	...	...	*223	...	...	14.9
46-47—Oakland Bittners	20	...	113	...	...	53	...	...	...	...	*279	...	...	14.0
Totals	35	...	197	...	...	108	...	...	...	...	502	...	...	14.3

NBL AND NBA REGULAR-SEASON RECORD

HONORS: All-NBL first team (1950). ... All-NBA second team (1952, 1954). ... All-BAA first team (1949).

Season Team	G	Min.	FGM	FGA	Pct.	FTM	FTA	Pct.	Reb.	Ast.	PF	Dq.	Pts.	AVERAGES RPG	APG	PPG
47-48 —Minneapolis (NBL)	59	...	310	...	...	140	207	.676	...	...	147	...	760	...	...	12.9
48-49 —Minneapolis (BAA)	53	...	314	792	.396	156	227	.687	...	142	144	...	784	...	2.7	14.8
49-50 —Minneapolis	66	...	394	1140	.346	185	242	.764	...	252	143	...	973	...	3.8	14.7
50-51 —Minneapolis	54	...	256	728	.352	117	156	.750	484	184	157	4	629	9.0	3.4	11.6
51-52 —Minneapolis	65	2545	411	1155	.356	183	260	.704	593	234	199	4	1005	9.1	3.6	15.5
52-53 —Minneapolis	66	2403	333	933	.357	193	251	.769	452	231	194	3	859	6.8	3.5	13.0
53-54 —Minneapolis	71	2483	326	882	.370	179	230	.778	500	214	161	0	831	7.0	3.0	11.7
54-55 —Minneapolis	63	1960	265	749	.354	151	186	.812	458	160	147	3	681	7.3	2.5	10.8
Totals	497	...	2609	...	...	1304	1759	.741	...	...	1292	...	6522	...	...	13.1

NBL AND NBA PLAYOFF RECORD

Season Team	G	Min.	FGM	FGA	Pct.	FTM	FTA	Pct.	Reb.	Ast.	PF	Dq.	Pts.	AVERAGES RPG	APG	PPG
47-48 —Minn. (NBL)	10	...	48	...	...	27	41	.659	...	...	...	...	123	...	...	12.3
48-49 —Minneapolis (BAA)	10	...	43	147	.293	44	62	.710	...	39	31	...	130	...	3.9	13.0
49-50 —Minneapolis	12	...	50	175	.286	44	62	.710	...	56	36	...	144	...	4.7	12.0
50-51 —Minneapolis	7	...	35	108	.324	25	30	.833	62	27	27	1	95	8.9	3.9	13.6
51-52 —Minneapolis	11	469	70	173	.405	37	50	.740	71	33	34	1	177	6.5	3.0	16.1
52-53 —Minneapolis	12	455	62	167	.371	48	62	.774	86	49	37	2	172	7.2	4.1	14.3
53-54 —Minneapolis	13	543	56	155	.361	48	60	.800	110	41	27	0	160	8.5	3.2	12.3
54-55 —Minneapolis	7	257	33	104	.317	33	46	.717	78	14	13	0	99	11.1	2.0	14.1
Totals	82	...	397	...	...	306	413	.741	...	...	...	...	1100	...	...	13.4

NBA ALL-STAR GAME RECORD

Season Team	Min.	FGM	FGA	Pct.	FTM	FTA	Pct.	Reb	Ast.	PF	Dq.	Pts.
1951 —Minneapolis	...	2	11	.182	0	0	...	4	5	1	0	4
1952 —Minneapolis	29	2	17	.118	0	0	...	11	5	3	0	4
1954 —Minneapolis	41	10	22	.455	3	5	.600	3	3	3	0	23
1955 —Minneapolis	27	7	19	.368	3	3	1.000	4	0	1	0	17
Totals	...	21	69	.304	6	8	.750	22	13	8	0	48

COLLEGIATE COACHING RECORD

Season Team	W	L	Pct.
55-56 —LaSalle	15	10	.600
56-57 —LaSalle	17	9	.654
57-58 —LaSalle	16	9	.640
Totals (3 years)	48	28	.632

NBA COACHING RECORD

Season Team	REGULAR SEASON W	L	Pct.	Finish		PLAYOFFS W	L	Pct.
59-60 —Minneapolis	14	25	.359	3rd/Western Division		5	4	.556
61-62 —Chicago	18	62	.225	5th/Western Division		—	—	—
Totals (2 years)	32	87	.269		Totals (1 year)	5	4	.556

ABA COACHING RECORD

Season Team	REGULAR SEASON W	L	Pct.	Finish		PLAYOFFS W	L	Pct.
67-68 —Minnesota	50	28	.641	2nd/Eastern Division		4	6	.400
68-69 —Miami	43	35	.551	2nd/Eastern Division		5	7	.417
69-70 —Miami	5	15	.250			—	—	—
Totals (3 years)	98	78	.557		Totals (2 years)	9	13	.409

NOTES:

1960—Replaced John Castellani as Minneapolis head coach (January 2), with 11-25 record. Defeated Detroit, 2-0, in Western Division Semifinals; lost to St. Louis, 4-3, in Western Division Finals.

1968—Defeated Kentucky, 3-2, in Eastern Division Semifinals; lost to Pittsburgh, 4-1, in Eastern Division Finals. Minnesota Muskies franchise moved to Miami and renamed the Floridians for 1968-69 season.

1969—Defeated Minnesota, 4-3, in Eastern Division Semifinals; lost to Indiana, 4-1, in Eastern Division Finals. Replaced as Miami head coach by Hal Blitman (November).

PRICE, MARK   G

PERSONAL: Born February 15, 1964, in Bartlesville, Okla. ... 6-0/180 (1,83/81,6). ... Full name: William Mark Price. ... Brother of Brent Price, guard with Sacramento Kings.
HIGH SCHOOL: Enid (Okla.).
COLLEGE: Georgia Tech.
TRANSACTIONS/CAREER NOTES: Selected by Dallas Mavericks in second round (25th pick overall) of 1986 NBA Draft. ... Draft rights traded by Mavericks to Cleveland Cavaliers for 1989 second-round draft choice and cash (June 17, 1986). ... Traded by Cavaliers to Washington Bullets for 1996 first-round draft choice (September 27, 1995). ... Signed as free agent by Golden State Warriors (July 21, 1996). ... Traded by Warriors to Orlando Magic for G Brian Shaw and F David Vaughn (October 28, 1997). ... Waived by Magic (June 30, 1998).
MISCELLANEOUS: Cleveland Cavaliers all-time assists leader with 4,206 and all-time steals leader with 734 (1986-87 through 1994-95).

COLLEGIATE RECORD

Season Team	G	Min.	FGM	FGA	Pct.	FTM	FTA	Pct.	Reb.	Ast.	Pts.	AVERAGES		
												RPG	APG	PPG
82-83—Georgia Tech	28	1020	201	462	.435	93	106	.877	105	91	568	3.8	3.3	20.3
83-84—Georgia Tech	29	1078	191	375	.509	70	85	.824	61	121	452	2.1	4.2	15.6
84-85—Georgia Tech	35	1302	223	462	.483	137	163	.840	71	150	583	2.0	4.3	16.7
85-86—Georgia Tech	34	1204	233	441	.528	124	145	.855	94	148	590	2.8	4.4	17.4
Totals	126	4604	848	1740	.487	424	499	.850	331	510	2193	2.6	4.0	17.4

Three-point field goals: 1982-83, 73-for-166 (.440).

NBA REGULAR-SEASON RECORD

RECORDS: Holds career record for highest free throw percentage (minimum 1,200 made)—.904.

HONORS: Long Distance Shootout winner (1993, 1994). ... All-NBA first team (1993). ... All-NBA third team (1989, 1992, 1994).

Season Team	G	Min.	FGM	FGA	Pct.	FTM	FTA	Pct.	REBOUNDS			Ast.	St.	Blk.	TO	Pts.	AVERAGES		
									Off.	Def.	Tot.						RPG	APG	PPG
86-87—Cleveland	67	1217	173	424	.408	95	114	.833	33	84	117	202	43	4	105	464	1.7	3.0	6.9
87-88—Cleveland	80	2626	493	974	.506	221	252	.877	54	126	180	480	99	12	184	1279	2.3	6.0	16.0
88-89—Cleveland	75	2728	529	1006	.526	263	292	.901	48	178	226	631	115	7	212	1414	3.0	8.4	18.9
89-90—Cleveland	73	2706	489	1066	.459	300	338	.888	66	185	251	666	114	5	214	1430	3.4	9.1	19.6
90-91—Cleveland	16	571	97	195	.497	59	62	.952	8	37	45	166	42	2	56	271	2.8	10.4	16.9
91-92—Cleveland	72	2138	438	897	.488	270	285	*.947	38	135	173	535	94	12	159	1247	2.4	7.4	17.3
92-93—Cleveland	75	2380	477	986	.484	289	305	*.948	37	164	201	602	89	11	196	1365	2.7	8.0	18.2
93-94—Cleveland	76	2386	480	1005	.478	238	268	.888	39	189	228	589	103	11	189	1316	3.0	7.8	17.3
94-95—Cleveland	48	1375	253	612	.413	148	162	.914	25	87	112	335	35	4	142	757	2.3	7.0	15.8
95-96—Washington	7	127	18	60	.300	10	10	1.000	1	6	7	18	6	0	10	56	1.0	2.6	8.0
96-97—Golden State	70	1876	263	589	.447	155	171	*.906	36	143	179	342	67	3	161	793	2.6	4.9	11.3
97-98—Orlando	63	1430	229	531	.431	87	103	.845	24	105	129	297	53	5	162	597	2.0	4.7	9.5
Totals	722	21560	3939	8345	.472	2135	2362	.904	409	1439	1848	4863	860	76	1790	10989	2.6	6.7	15.2

Three-point field goals: 1986-87, 23-for-70 (.329). 1987-88, 72-for-148 (.486). 1988-89, 93-for-211 (.441). 1989-90, 152-for-374 (.406). 1990-91, 18-for-53 (.340). 1991-92, 101-for-261 (.387). 1992-93, 122-for-293 (.416). 1993-94, 118-for-297 (.397). 1994-95, 103-for-253 (.407). 1995-96, 10-for-30 (.333). 1996-97, 112-for-283 (.396). 1997-98, 52-for-155 (.335). Totals, 976-for-2428 (.402).

Personal fouls/disqualifications: 1986-87, 75/1. 1987-88, 119/1. 1988-89, 98/0. 1989-90, 89/0. 1990-91, 23/0. 1991-92, 113/0. 1992-93, 105/0. 1993-94, 93/0. 1994-95, 50/0. 1995-96, 7/0. 1996-97, 100/0. 1997-98, 92/0. Totals, 964/2.

NBA PLAYOFF RECORD

NOTES: Holds career playoff record for highest free throw percentage (minimum 100 made)—.944.

Season Team	G	Min.	FGM	FGA	Pct.	FTM	FTA	Pct.	REBOUNDS			Ast.	St.	Blk.	TO	Pts.	AVERAGES		
									Off.	Def.	Tot.						RPG	APG	PPG
87-88—Cleveland	5	205	38	67	.567	24	25	.960	3	15	18	38	3	0	8	105	3.6	7.6	21.0
88-89—Cleveland	4	158	22	57	.386	14	15	.933	4	9	13	22	3	0	19	64	3.3	5.5	16.0
89-90—Cleveland	5	192	32	61	.525	30	30	1.000	0	14	14	44	9	1	15	100	2.8	8.8	20.0
91-92—Cleveland	17	603	118	238	.496	66	73	.904	10	32	42	128	24	4	56	327	2.5	7.5	19.2
92-93—Cleveland	9	288	43	97	.443	23	24	.958	1	18	19	55	15	0	33	117	2.1	6.1	13.0
93-94—Cleveland	3	102	15	43	.349	13	14	.929	1	5	6	14	4	0	9	45	2.0	4.7	15.0
94-95—Cleveland	4	143	12	40	.300	32	33	.970	2	10	12	26	6	0	18	60	3.0	6.5	15.0
Totals	47	1691	280	603	.464	202	214	.944	21	103	124	327	64	5	158	818	2.6	7.0	17.4

Three-point field goals: 1987-88, 5-for-12 (.417). 1988-89, 6-for-16 (.375). 1989-90, 6-for-17 (.353). 1991-92, 25-for-69 (.362). 1992-93, 8-for-26 (.308). 1993-94, 2-for-9 (.222). 1994-95, 4-for-17 (.235). Totals, 56-for-166 (.337).

Personal fouls/disqualifications: 1987-88, 11/1. 1988-89, 3/0. 1989-90, 9/0. 1991-92, 34/0. 1992-93, 13/0. 1993-94, 6/0. 1994-95, 5/0. Totals, 81/1.

NBA ALL-STAR GAME RECORD

Season	Team	Min.	FGM	FGA	Pct.	FTM	FTA	Pct.	REBOUNDS			Ast.	PF	Dq.	St.	Blk.	TO	Pts.
									Off.	Def.	Tot.							
1989	—Cleveland	20	3	9	.333	2	2	1.000	1	2	3	1	2	0	2	0	2	9
1992	—Cleveland	15	1	5	.200	4	4	1.000	0	0	0	3	1	0	1	0	3	6
1993	—Cleveland	23	6	11	.545	1	2	.500	0	1	1	4	5	0	1	0	3	19
1994	—Cleveland	22	8	10	.800	2	2	1.000	0	2	2	5	1	0	1	1	0	20
Totals		80	18	35	.514	9	10	.900	1	5	6	13	9	0	5	1	8	54

Three-point field goals: 1989, 1-for-4 (.250). 1992, 0-for-3. 1993, 6-for-9 (.667). 1994, 2-for-3 (.667). Totals, 9-for-19 (.474).

REED, WILLIS   C/F

PERSONAL: Born June 25, 1942, in Hico, La. ... 6-10/240 (2,08/108,4). ... Full name: Willis Reed Jr.

HIGH SCHOOL: West Side (Lillie, La.).

COLLEGE: Grambling State.

TRANSACTIONS: Selected by New York Knicks in second round (10th pick overall) of 1964 NBA Draft.

CAREER HONORS: Elected to Naismith Memorial Basketball Hall of Fame (1982). ... One of the 50 Greatest Players in NBA History (1996).

CAREER NOTES: General manager/vice president of basketball operations, New Jersey Nets (1988-89 to 1995-96). ... Senior vice president, Nets (1996-97 to present).

MISCELLANEOUS: Member of NBA championship team (1970, 1973).

COLLEGIATE RECORD

NOTES: Member of NAIA championship team (1961). ... Elected to NAIA Basketball Hall of Fame (1970).

Season Team	G	Min.	FGM	FGA	Pct.	FTM	FTA	Pct.	Reb.	Ast.	Pts.	AVERAGES		
												RPG	APG	PPG
60-61—Grambling State	35	...	146	239	.611	86	122	.705	312	...	378	8.9	...	10.8
61-62—Grambling State	26	...	189	323	.585	80	102	.784	380	...	458	14.6	...	17.6
62-63—Grambling State	33	...	282	489	.577	135	177	.763	563	...	699	17.1	...	21.2
63-64—Grambling State	28	...	301	486	.619	143	199	.719	596	...	745	21.3	...	26.6
Totals	122	...	918	1537	.597	444	600	.740	1851	...	2280	15.2	...	18.7

NBA REGULAR-SEASON RECORD

HONORS: NBA Most Valuable Player (1970). ... NBA Rookie of the Year (1965). ... All-NBA first team (1970). ... All-NBA second team (1967, 1968, 1969, 1971). ... NBA All-Defensive first team (1970). ... NBA All-Rookie team (1965).

														AVERAGES		
Season Team	G	Min.	FGM	FGA	Pct.	FTM	FTA	Pct.	Reb.	Ast.	PF	Dq.	Pts.	RPG	APG	PPG
64-65 —New York	80	3042	629	1457	.432	302	407	.742	1175	133	339	14	1560	14.7	1.7	19.5
65-66 —New York	76	2537	438	1009	.434	302	399	.757	883	91	323	13	1178	11.6	1.2	15.5
66-67 —New York	78	2824	635	1298	.489	358	487	.735	1136	126	293	9	1628	14.6	1.6	20.9
67-68 —New York	81	2879	659	1346	.490	367	509	.721	1073	159	343	12	1685	13.2	2.0	20.8
68-69 —New York	82	3108	704	1351	.521	325	435	.747	1191	190	314	7	1733	14.5	2.3	21.1
69-70 —New York	81	3089	702	1385	.507	351	464	.756	1126	161	287	2	1755	13.9	2.0	21.7
70-71 —New York	73	2855	614	1330	.462	299	381	.785	1003	148	228	1	1527	13.7	2.0	20.9
71-72 —New York	11	363	60	137	.438	27	39	.692	96	22	30	0	147	8.7	2.0	13.4
72-73 —New York	69	1876	334	705	.474	92	124	.742	590	126	205	0	760	8.6	1.8	11.0

								REBOUNDS								AVERAGES		
Season Team	G	Min.	FGM	FGA	Pct.	FTM	FTA	Pct.	Off.	Def.	Tot.	Ast.	St.	Blk.	TO	Pts.	RPG	APG	PPG
73-74 —New York	19	500	84	184	.457	42	53	.792	47	94	141	30	12	21	...	210	7.4	1.6	11.1
Totals	650	23073	4859	10202	.476	2465	3298	.747	...	...	8414	1186	12	21	...	12183	12.9	1.8	18.7

Personal fouls/disqualifications: 1973-74, 49/0.

NBA PLAYOFF RECORD

NOTES: NBA Finals Most Valuable Player (1970, 1973).

													AVERAGES		
Season Team	G	Min.	FGM	FGA	Pct.	FTM	FTA	Pct.	Reb.	Ast.	PF	Dq.	Pts.	RPG	APG	PPG
66-67 —New York	4	148	43	80	.538	24	25	.960	55	7	19	1	110	13.8	1.8	27.5
67-68 —New York	6	210	53	98	.541	22	30	.733	62	11	24	1	128	10.3	1.8	21.3
68-69 —New York	10	429	101	198	.510	55	70	.786	141	19	40	1	257	14.1	1.9	25.7
69-70 —New York	18	732	178	378	.471	70	95	.737	248	51	60	0	426	13.8	2.8	23.7
70-71 —New York	12	504	81	196	.413	26	39	.667	144	27	41	0	188	12.0	2.3	15.7
72-73 —New York	17	486	97	208	.466	18	21	.857	129	30	65	1	212	7.6	1.8	12.5

								REBOUNDS								AVERAGES		
Season Team	G	Min.	FGM	FGA	Pct.	FTM	FTA	Pct.	Off.	Def.	Tot.	Ast.	St.	Blk.	TO	Pts.	RPG	APG	PPG
73-74 —New York	11	132	17	45	.378	3	5	.600	4	18	22	4	2	0	...	37	2.0	0.4	3.4
Totals	78	2641	570	1203	.474	218	285	.765	...	...	801	149	2	0	...	1358	10.3	1.9	17.4

Personal fouls/disqualifications: 1973-74, 26/0.

NBA ALL-STAR GAME RECORD

NOTES: NBA All-Star Game Most Valuable Player (1970).

Season Team	Min.	FGM	FGA	Pct.	FTM	FTA	Pct.	Reb	Ast.	PF	Dq.	Pts.
1965 —New York	25	3	11	.273	1	2	.500	5	1	2	0	7
1966 —New York	23	7	11	.636	2	2	1.000	8	1	3	0	16
1967 —New York	17	2	6	.333	0	0	...	9	1	0	0	4
1968 —New York	25	7	14	.500	2	3	.667	8	1	4	0	16
1969 —New York	14	5	8	.625	0	0	...	4	2	2	0	10
1970 —New York	30	9	18	.500	3	3	1.000	11	0	6	1	21
1971 —New York	27	5	16	.313	4	6	.667	13	1	3	0	14
Totals	161	38	84	.452	12	16	.750	58	7	20	1	88

HEAD COACHING RECORD

BACKGROUND: Volunteer assistant, St. John's University (1980-81). ... Assistant coach, Atlanta Hawks (1985-86 and 1986-87). ... Assistant coach, Sacramento Kings (1987-88).

NBA COACHING RECORD

	REGULAR SEASON				PLAYOFFS		
Season Team	W	L	Pct.	Finish	W	L	Pct.
77-78 —New York	43	39	.524	2nd/Atlantic Division	2	4	.333
78-79 —New York	6	8	.429		—	—	—
87-88 —New Jersey	7	21	.250	5th/Atlantic Division	—	—	—
88-89 —New Jersey	26	56	.317	5th/Atlantic Division	—	—	—
Totals (4 years)	82	124	.398	Totals (1 year)	2	4	.333

COLLEGIATE COACHING RECORD

Season Team	W	L	Pct.	Finish
81-82 —Creighton	7	20	.259	8th/Missouri Valley Conference
82-83 —Creighton	8	19	.296	10th/Missouri Valley Conference
83-84 —Creighton	17	14	.548	4th/Missouri Valley Conference
84-85 —Creighton	20	11	.645	4th/Missouri Valley Conference
Totals (4 years)	52	64	.448	

NOTES:

1978—Defeated Cleveland, 2-0, in Eastern Conference First Round; lost to Philadelphia, 4-0, in Eastern Conference Semifinals. Replaced as New York head coach by Red Holzman (November).

1984—Lost to Nebraska, 56-54, in NIT first round.

1988—Replaced interim head coach Bob MacKinnon as New Jersey head coach (February 29), with record of 12-42.

ROBERTSON, OSCAR   G

PERSONAL: Born November 24, 1938, in Charlotte, Tenn. ... 6-5/220 (1,96/99,8). ... Full name: Oscar Palmer Robertson. ... Nickname: Big O.

HIGH SCHOOL: Crispus Attucks (Indianapolis).

COLLEGE: Cincinnati.

TRANSACTIONS: Selected by Cincinnati Royals in 1960 NBA Draft (territorial pick). ... Traded by Royals to Milwaukee Bucks for G Flynn Robinson and F Charlie Paulk (April 21, 1970).

CAREER HONORS: Elected to Naismith Memorial Basketball Hall of Fame (1980). ... NBA 35th Anniversary All-Time Team (1980) and One of the 50 Greatest Players in NBA History (1996).

MISCELLANEOUS: Member of NBA championship team (1971). ... Member of gold-medal-winning U.S. Olympic team (1960). ... Sacramento Kings franchise all-time leading scorer with 22,009 points and all-time assists leader with 7,731 (1960-61 through 1969-70).

COLLEGIATE RECORD

NOTES: The Sporting News College Player of the Year (1958, 1959, 1960). ... The Sporting News All-America first team (1958, 1959, 1960). ... Led NCAA Division I with 35.1 points per game (1958), 32.6 points per game (1959) and 33.7 points per game (1960).

Season Team	G	Min.	FGM	FGA	Pct.	FTM	FTA	Pct.	Reb.	Ast.	Pts.	AVERAGES RPG	APG	PPG
56-57—Cincinnati‡	13	...	151	...	...	127	178	.713	...	...	429	...	...	33.0
57-58—Cincinnati	28	1085	352	617	.571	280	355	.789	425	...	984	15.2	...	35.1
58-59—Cincinnati	30	1172	331	650	.509	316	398	.794	489	206	978	16.3	6.9	32.6
59-60—Cincinnati	30	1155	369	701	.526	273	361	.756	424	219	1011	14.1	7.3	33.7
Varsity totals	88	3412	1052	1968	.535	869	1114	.780	1338	...	2973	15.2	...	33.8

NBA REGULAR-SEASON RECORD

RECORDS: Shares single-game record for most free throws attempted in one quarter—16 (December 27, 1964, vs. Baltimore).

HONORS: NBA Most Valuable Player (1964). ... NBA Rookie of the Year (1961). ... All-NBA first team (1961, 1962, 1963, 1964, 1965, 1966, 1967, 1968, 1969). ... All-NBA second team (1970, 1971).

Season Team	G	Min.	FGM	FGA	Pct.	FTM	FTA	Pct.	Reb.	Ast.	PF	Dq.	Pts.	AVERAGES RPG	APG	PPG
60-61 —Cincinnati	71	3012	756	1600	.473	653	794	.822	716	*690	219	3	2165	10.1	*9.7	30.5
61-62 —Cincinnati	79	3503	866	1810	.478	700	872	.803	985	*899	258	1	2432	12.5	*11.4	30.8
62-63 —Cincinnati	80	3521	825	1593	.518	614	758	.810	835	758	293	1	2264	10.4	9.5	28.3
63-64 —Cincinnati	79	3559	840	1740	.483	*800	938	*.853	783	*868	280	3	2480	9.9	*11.0	31.4
64-65 —Cincinnati	75	3421	807	1681	.480	*665	793	.839	674	*861	205	2	2279	9.0	*11.5	30.4
65-66 —Cincinnati	76	3493	818	1723	.475	742	881	.842	586	*847	227	1	2378	7.7	*11.1	31.3
66-67 —Cincinnati	79	3468	838	1699	.493	736	843	.873	486	845	226	2	2412	6.2	*10.7	30.5
67-68 —Cincinnati	65	2765	660	1321	.500	*576	660	*.873	391	633	199	2	1896	6.0	*9.7	*29.2
68-69 —Cincinnati	79	3461	656	1351	.486	*643	767	.838	502	*772	231	2	1955	6.4	*9.8	24.7
69-70 —Cincinnati	69	2865	647	1267	.511	454	561	.809	422	558	175	1	1748	6.1	8.1	25.3
70-71 —Milwaukee	81	3194	592	1193	.496	385	453	.850	462	668	203	0	1569	5.7	8.2	19.4
71-72 —Milwaukee	64	2390	419	887	.472	276	330	.836	323	491	116	0	1114	5.0	7.7	17.4
72-73 —Milwaukee	73	2737	446	983	.454	238	281	.847	360	551	167	0	1130	4.9	7.5	15.5

Season Team	G	Min.	FGM	FGA	Pct.	FTM	FTA	Pct.	REBOUNDS Off.	Def.	Tot.	Ast.	St.	Blk.	TO	Pts.	AVERAGES RPG	APG	PPG
73-74—Milwaukee	70	2477	338	772	.438	212	254	.835	71	208	279	446	77	4	...	888	4.0	6.4	12.7
Totals	1040	43866	9508	19620	.485	7694	9185	.838	...	...	7804	9887	77	4	...	26710	7.5	9.5	25.7

Personal fouls/disqualifications: 1973-74, 132/0.

NBA PLAYOFF RECORD

Season Team	G	Min.	FGM	FGA	Pct.	FTM	FTA	Pct.	Reb.	Ast.	PF	Dq.	Pts.	AVERAGES RPG	APG	PPG
61-62 —Cincinnati	4	185	42	81	.519	31	39	.795	44	44	18	1	115	11.0	11.0	28.8
62-63 —Cincinnati	12	570	124	264	.470	133	154	.864	156	108	41	0	381	13.0	9.0	31.8
63-64 —Cincinnati	10	471	92	202	.455	109	127	.858	89	84	30	0	293	8.9	8.4	29.3
64-65 —Cincinnati	4	195	38	89	.427	36	39	.923	19	48	14	0	112	4.8	12.0	28.0
65-66 —Cincinnati	5	224	49	120	.408	61	68	.897	38	39	20	1	159	7.6	7.8	31.8
66-67 —Cincinnati	4	183	33	64	.516	33	37	.892	16	45	9	0	99	4.0	11.3	24.8
70-71 —Milwaukee	14	520	102	210	.486	52	69	.754	70	124	39	0	256	5.0	8.9	18.3
71-72 —Milwaukee	11	380	57	140	.407	30	36	.833	64	83	29	0	144	5.8	7.5	13.1
72-73 —Milwaukee	6	256	48	96	.500	31	34	.912	28	45	21	1	127	4.7	7.5	21.2

Season Team	G	Min.	FGM	FGA	Pct.	FTM	FTA	Pct.	REBOUNDS Off.	Def.	Tot.	Ast.	St.	Blk.	TO	Pts.	AVERAGES RPG	APG	PPG
73-74—Milwaukee	16	689	90	200	.450	44	52	.846	15	39	54	149	15	4	...	224	3.4	9.3	14.0
Totals	86	3673	675	1466	.460	560	655	.855	...	...	578	769	15	4	...	1910	6.7	8.9	22.2

Personal fouls/disqualifications: 1973-74, 46/0.

NBA ALL-STAR GAME RECORD

NOTES: NBA All-Star Game Most Valuable Player (1961, 1964, 1969). ... Shares career record for most free throws attempted—98. ... Shares single-game record for most free throws made—12 (1965).

Season Team	Min.	FGM	FGA	Pct.	FTM	FTA	Pct.	Reb.	Ast.	PF	Dq.	Pts.
1961 —Cincinnati	34	8	13	.615	7	9	.778	9	14	5	0	23
1962 —Cincinnati	37	9	20	.450	8	14	.571	7	13	3	0	26
1963 —Cincinnati	37	9	15	.600	3	4	.750	3	6	5	0	21
1964 —Cincinnati	42	10	23	.435	6	10	.600	14	8	4	0	26
1965 —Cincinnati	40	8	18	.444	12	13	.923	6	8	5	0	28
1966 —Cincinnati	25	6	12	.500	5	6	.833	10	8	0	0	17
1967 —Cincinnati	34	9	20	.450	8	10	.800	2	5	4	0	26
1968 —Cincinnati	22	7	9	.778	4	7	.571	1	5	2	0	18
1969 —Cincinnati	32	8	16	.500	8	8	1.000	6	5	3	0	24
1970 —Cincinnati	29	9	11	.818	3	4	.750	6	4	3	0	21
1971 —Milwaukee	24	2	6	.333	1	3	.333	2	2	3	0	5
1972 —Milwaukee	24	3	9	.333	5	10	.500	3	3	4	0	11
Totals	380	88	172	.512	70	98	.714	69	81	41	0	246

ALL-TIME GREAT PLAYERS

RODGERS, GUY   G

PERSONAL: Born September 1, 1935, in Philadelphia. Died February 19, 2001. ... 6-0/185 (1,83/83,9). ... Full name: Guy William Rodgers Jr.
HIGH SCHOOL: Northeast (Philadelphia).
COLLEGE: Temple.
TRANSACTIONS: Selected by Philadelphia Warriors in 1958 NBA Draft (territorial pick). ... Warriors franchise moved from Philadelphia to San Francisco for 1962-63 season. ... Traded by Warriors to Chicago Bulls for draft choice, cash and two players to be named later (September 7, 1966); G Jim King and G Jeff Mullins sent to Warriors to complete deal. ... Traded by Bulls to Cincinnati Royals for G Flynn Robinson, cash and two future draft choices (October 20, 1967). ... Selected by Milwaukee Bucks from Royals in NBA Expansion Draft (May 6, 1968).
MISCELLANEOUS: Golden State Warriors franchise all-time assists leader with 4,855 (1958-59 through 1965-66).

COLLEGIATE RECORD

NOTES: THE SPORTING NEWS All-America first team (1958).

Season Team	G	Min.	FGM	FGA	Pct.	FTM	FTA	Pct.	Reb.	Ast.	Pts.	AVERAGES RPG	APG	PPG
54-55—Temple‡	15	...	...	...	...	...	...	...	...	...	278	...	...	18.5
55-56—Temple	31	...	243	552	.440	87	155	.561	186	...	573	6.0	...	18.5
56-57—Temple	29	...	216	565	.382	159	224	.710	202	...	591	7.0	...	20.4
57-58—Temple	30	...	249	564	.441	105	171	.614	199	...	603	6.6	...	20.1
Varsity totals	90	...	708	1681	.421	351	550	.638	587	...	1767	6.5	...	19.6

NBA REGULAR-SEASON RECORD

Season Team	G	Min.	FGM	FGA	Pct.	FTM	FTA	Pct.	Reb.	Ast.	PF	Dq.	Pts.	AVERAGES RPG	APG	PPG
58-59—Philadelphia	45	1565	211	535	.394	61	112	.545	281	261	132	1	483	6.2	5.8	10.7
59-60—Philadelphia	68	2483	338	870	.389	111	181	.613	391	482	196	3	787	5.8	7.1	11.6
60-61—Philadelphia	78	2905	397	1029	.386	206	300	.687	509	677	262	3	1000	6.5	8.7	12.8
61-62—Philadelphia	80	2650	267	749	.356	121	182	.665	348	643	312	12	655	4.4	8.0	8.2
62-63—San Francisco	79	3249	445	1150	.387	208	286	.727	394	*825	296	7	1098	5.0	*10.4	13.9
63-64—San Francisco	79	2695	337	923	.365	198	280	.707	328	556	245	4	872	4.2	7.0	11.0
64-65—San Francisco	79	2699	465	1225	.380	223	325	.686	323	565	256	4	1153	4.1	7.2	14.6
65-66—San Francisco	79	2902	586	1571	.373	296	407	.727	421	846	241	6	1468	5.3	10.7	18.6
66-67—Chicago	81	3063	538	1377	.391	383	475	.806	346	*908	243	1	1459	4.3	*11.2	18.0
67-68—Chicago-Cincinnati	79	1546	148	426	.347	107	133	.805	150	380	167	1	403	1.9	4.8	5.1
68-69—Milwaukee	81	2157	325	862	.377	184	232	.793	226	561	207	2	834	2.8	6.9	10.3
69-70—Milwaukee	64	749	68	191	.356	67	90	.744	74	213	73	1	203	1.2	3.3	3.2
Totals	892	28663	4125	10908	.378	2165	3003	.721	3791	6917	2630	45	10415	4.3	7.8	11.7

NBA PLAYOFF RECORD

Season Team	G	Min.	FGM	FGA	Pct.	FTM	FTA	Pct.	Reb.	Ast.	PF	Dq.	Pts.	AVERAGES RPG	APG	PPG
59-60—Philadelphia	9	370	49	136	.360	20	36	.556	77	54	39	3	118	8.6	6.0	13.1
60-61—Philadelphia	3	121	21	57	.368	11	20	.550	21	15	16	2	53	7.0	5.0	17.7
61-62—Philadelphia	13	482	52	145	.359	35	55	.636	7	88	57	3	139	0.5	6.8	10.7
63-64—San Fran.	12	419	57	173	.329	33	47	.702	58	90	46	1	147	4.8	7.5	12.3
66-67—Chicago	3	97	15	40	.375	4	5	.800	6	18	11	0	34	2.0	6.0	11.3
69-70—Milwaukee	7	68	4	14	.286	9	12	.750	4	21	7	0	17	0.6	3.0	2.4
Totals	47	1557	198	565	.350	112	175	.640	173	286	176	9	508	3.7	6.1	10.8

NBA ALL-STAR GAME RECORD

Season Team	Min.	FGM	FGA	Pct.	FTM	FTA	Pct.	Reb	Ast.	PF	Dq.	Pts.
1963 —San Francisco	17	3	6	.500	1	2	.500	2	4	2	0	7
1964 —San Francisco	22	3	6	.500	0	0	...	2	2	4	0	6
1966 —San Francisco	34	4	11	.364	0	0	...	7	11	4	0	8
1967 —Chicago	28	0	4	.000	1	1	1.000	2	8	3	0	1
Totals	101	10	27	.370	2	3	.667	13	25	13	0	22

RODMAN, DENNIS   F

PERSONAL: Born May 13, 1961, in Trenton, N.J. ... 6-7/228. (2.01 m/103 kg). ... Full Name: Dennis Keith Rodman. ... Nickname: Worm.
HIGH SCHOOL: South Oak Cliff (Dallas), did not play basketball.
JUNIOR COLLEGE: Cooke County (Texas) Junior College.
COLLEGE: Southeastern Oklahoma State.
TRANSACTIONS/CAREER NOTES: Selected by Detroit Pistons in second round (27th pick overall) of 1986 NBA Draft. ... Traded by Pistons to San Antonio Spurs for F Sean Elliott and F David Wood (October 1, 1993). ... Traded by Spurs to Chicago Bulls for C Will Perdue (October 2, 1995). ... Signed as free agent by Los Angeles Lakers (February 23, 1999). ... Waived by Lakers (April 16, 1999). ... Signed as free agent by Dallas Mavericks (February 3, 2000). ... Waived by Mavericks (March 8, 2000).
MISCELLANEOUS: Member of NBA championship team (1989, 1990, 1996, 1997, 1998).

COLLEGIATE RECORD

NOTES: Led NAIA with 15.9 rebounds per game (1985) and 17.8 rebounds per game (1986).

Season Team	G	Min.	FGM	FGA	Pct.	FTM	FTA	Pct.	Reb.	Ast.	Pts.	AVERAGES RPG	APG	PPG
82-83—Cooke County J.C.	16	...	114	185	.616	53	91	.582	212	...	281	13.3	0.0	17.6
83-84—SE Oklahoma State	30	...	303	490	.618	173	264	.655	392	23	779	13.1	0.8	26.0
84-85—SE Oklahoma State	32	...	353	545	.648	151	267	.566	510	12	857	15.9	0.4	26.8
85-86—SE Oklahoma State	34	...	332	515	.645	165	252	.655	605	26	829	17.8	0.8	24.4
Junior College Totals	16	...	114	185	.616	53	91	.582	212	...	281	13.3	0.0	17.6
4-Year-College Totals	96	...	988	1550	.637	489	783	.625	1507	61	2465	15.7	0.6	25.7

NBA REGULAR-SEASON RECORD

RECORDS: Holds career records for most consecutive seasons leading league in rebounds—7; and most seasons leading league in defensive rebounds—3.

HONORS: NBA Defensive Player of the Year (1990, 1991). ... IBM Award, for all-around contributions to team's success (1992). ... All-NBA third team (1992, 1995). ... NBA All-Defensive first team (1989, 1990, 1991, 1992, 1993, 1995, 1996). ... NBA All-Defensive second team (1994).

								REBOUNDS								AVERAGES		
Season Team	G	Min.	FGM	FGA	Pct.	FTM	FTA	Pct.	Off.	Def.	Tot.	Ast.	St.	Blk.	TO	Pts.	RPG	APG	PPG
86-87—Detroit	77	1155	213	391	.545	74	126	.587	163	169	332	56	38	48	93	500	4.3	0.7	6.5
87-88—Detroit	82	2147	398	709	.561	152	284	.535	318	397	715	110	75	45	156	953	8.7	1.3	11.6
88-89—Detroit	82	2208	316	531	*.595	97	155	.626	327	445	772	99	55	76	126	735	9.4	1.2	9.0
89-90—Detroit	82	2377	288	496	.581	142	217	.654	336	456	792	72	52	60	90	719	9.7	0.9	8.8
90-91—Detroit	82	2747	276	560	.493	111	176	.631	*361	665	1026	85	65	55	94	669	12.5	1.0	8.2
91-92—Detroit	82	3301	342	635	.539	84	140	.600	*523	*1007	*1530	191	68	70	140	800	*18.7	2.3	9.8
92-93—Detroit	62	2410	183	429	.427	87	163	.534	*367	765	*1132	102	48	45	103	468	*18.3	1.6	7.5
93-94—San Antonio ..	79	2989	156	292	.534	53	102	.520	*453	*914	*1367	184	52	32	138	370	*17.3	2.3	4.7
94-95—San Antonio ..	49	1568	137	240	.571	75	111	.676	274	549	823	97	31	23	98	349	*16.8	2.0	7.1
95-96—Chicago	64	2088	146	304	.480	56	106	.528	*356	596	952	160	36	27	138	351	*14.9	2.5	5.5
96-97—Chicago	55	1947	128	286	.448	50	88	.568	*320	563	883	170	32	19	111	311	*16.1	3.1	5.7
97-98—Chicago	80	2856	155	360	.431	61	111	.550	421	*780	*1201	230	47	18	147	375	*15.0	2.9	4.7
98-99—L.A. Lakers	23	657	16	46	.348	17	39	.436	62	196	258	30	10	12	31	49	11.2	1.3	2.1
99-00—Dallas.............	12	389	12	31	.387	10	14	.714	48	123	171	14	2	1	19	34	14.3	1.2	2.8
Totals	911	28839	2766	5310	.521	1069	1832	.584	4329	7625	11954	1600	611	531	1484	6683	13.1	1.8	7.3

Three-point field goals: 1986-87, 0-for-1. 1987-88, 5-for-17 (.294). 1988-89, 6-for-26 (.231). 1989-90, 1-for-9 (.111). 1990-91, 6-for-30 (.200). 1991-92, 32-for-101 (.317). 1992-93, 15-for-73 (.205). 1993-94, 5-for-24 (.208). 1994-95, 0-for-2. 1995-96, 3-for-27 (.111). 1996-97, 5-for-19 (.263). 1997-98, 4-for-23 (.174). 1998-99, 0-for-1. 1999-00, 0-for-1. Totals, 82-for-354 (.232).

Personal fouls/disqualifications: 1986-87, 166/1. 1987-88, 273/5. 1988-89, 292/4. 1989-90, 276/2. 1990-91, 281/7. 1991-92, 248/0. 1992-93, 201/0. 1993-94, 229/0. 1994-95, 159/1. 1995-96, 196/1. 1996-97, 172/1. 1997-98, 238/2. 1998-99, 71/0. 1999-00, 41/2. Totals, 2843/26.

NBA PLAYOFF RECORD

NOTES: Shares NBA Finals single-game record for most offensive rebounds—11 (June 7, 1996, vs. Seattle; and June 16, 1996, vs. Seattle).

								REBOUNDS								AVERAGES		
Season Team	G	Min.	FGM	FGA	Pct.	FTM	FTA	Pct.	Off.	Def.	Tot.	Ast.	St.	Blk.	TO	Pts.	RPG	APG	PPG
86-87—Detroit	15	245	40	74	.541	18	32	.563	32	39	71	3	6	17	17	98	4.7	0.2	6.5
87-88—Detroit	23	474	71	136	.522	22	54	.407	51	85	136	21	14	14	31	164	5.9	0.9	7.1
88-89—Detroit	17	409	37	70	.529	24	35	.686	56	114	170	16	6	12	24	98	10.0	0.9	5.8
89-90—Detroit	19	560	54	95	.568	18	35	.514	55	106	161	17	9	13	31	126	8.5	0.9	6.6
90-91—Detroit	15	495	41	91	.451	10	24	.417	67	110	177	14	11	10	13	94	11.8	0.9	6.3
91-92—Detroit	5	156	16	27	.593	4	8	.500	16	35	51	9	4	2	7	36	10.2	1.8	7.2
93-94—San Antonio	3	114	12	24	.500	1	6	.167	24	24	48	2	6	4	6	25	16.0	0.7	8.3
94-95—San Antonio	14	459	52	96	.542	20	35	.571	69	138	207	18	12	0	25	124	14.8	1.3	8.9
95-96—Chicago	18	620	50	103	.485	35	59	.593	98	149	247	37	14	8	41	135	13.7	2.1	7.5
96-97—Chicago	19	535	30	81	.370	15	26	.577	59	101	160	27	10	4	28	79	8.4	1.4	4.2
97-98—Chicago	21	722	39	105	.371	23	38	.605	99	149	248	41	14	13	35	102	11.8	2.0	4.9
Totals	169	4789	442	902	.490	190	352	.540	626	1050	1676	205	106	97	258	1081	9.9	1.2	6.4

Three-point field goals: 1987-88, 0-for-2. 1988-89, 0-for-4. 1990-91, 2-for-9 (.222). 1991-92, 0-for-2. 1993-94, 0-for-5. 1994-95, 0-for-5. 1996-97, 4-for-16 (.250). 1997-98, 1-for-4 (.250). Totals, 7-for-47 (.149).

Personal fouls/disqualifications: 1987-88, 87/1. 1988-89, 58/0. 1990-91, 55/1. 1991-92, 17/0. 1993-94, 14/0. 1994-95, 51/1. 1996-97, 74/3. 1997-98, 88/4. Totals, 630/12.

NBA ALL-STAR GAME RECORD

								REBOUNDS								
Season Team	Min.	FGM	FGA	Pct.	FTM	FTA	Pct.	Off.	Def.	Tot.	Ast.	PF	Dq.	St.	Blk.	TO	Pts.
1990 —Detroit..............	11	2	4	.500	0	0	...	3	1	4	1	1	0	0	1	2	4
1992 —Detroit..............	25	2	7	.286	0	0	...	7	6	13	0	1	0	1	0	2	4
Totals............................	36	4	11	.364	0	0	...	10	7	17	1	2	0	1	1	4	8

RUSSELL, BILL   C

PERSONAL: Born February 12, 1934, in Monroe, La. ... 6-10/220 (2,08/99,8). ... Full name: William Felton Russell.

HIGH SCHOOL: McClymonds (Oakland, Calif.).

COLLEGE: San Francisco.

TRANSACTIONS: Selected by St. Louis Hawks in first round (third pick overall) of 1956 NBA Draft. ... Draft rights traded by Hawks to Boston Celtics for F/C Ed Macauley and draft rights to F Cliff Hagan (April 29, 1956).

CAREER HONORS: Elected to Naismith Memorial Basketball Hall of Fame (1975). ... Declared Greatest Player in the History of the NBA by Professional Basketball Writers' Association of America (1980). ... NBA 25th Anniversary All-Time Team (1970), 35th Anniversary All-Time Team (1980) and One of the 50 Greatest Players in NBA History (1996).

MISCELLANEOUS: Member of NBA championship team (1957, 1959, 1960, 1961, 1962, 1963, 1964, 1965, 1966, 1968, 1969). ... Member of gold-medal-winning U.S. Olympic team (1956). ... Boston Celtics all-time leading rebounder with 21,620 (1956-57 through 1968-69).

COLLEGIATE RECORD

NOTES: NCAA Tournament Most Outstanding Player (1955). ... Member of NCAA championship team (1955, 1956).

											AVERAGES		
Season Team	G	Min.	FGM	FGA	Pct.	FTM	FTA	Pct.	Reb.	Ast.	Pts.	RPG	APG	PPG
52-53—San Francisco‡..............	23	...	...	...	...	...	...	...	...	...	461	...	...	20.0
53-54—San Francisco................	21	...	150	309	.485	117	212	.552	403	...	417	19.2	...	19.9
54-55—San Francisco................	29	...	229	423	.541	164	278	.590	594	...	622	20.5	...	21.4
55-56—San Francisco................	29	...	246	480	.513	105	212	.495	609	...	597	21.0	...	20.6
Varsity totals	79	...	625	1212	.516	386	702	.550	1606	...	1636	20.3	...	20.7

NBA REGULAR-SEASON RECORD

RECORDS: Holds single-game record for most rebounds in one half—32 (November 16, 1957, vs. Philadelphia).

HONORS: NBA Most Valuable Player (1958, 1961, 1962, 1963, 1965). ... All-NBA first team (1959, 1963, 1965). ... All-NBA second team (1958, 1960, 1961, 1962, 1964, 1966, 1967, 1968). ... NBA All-Defensive first team (1969).

Season Team	G	Min.	FGM	FGA	Pct.	FTM	FTA	Pct.	Reb.	Ast.	PF	Dq.	Pts.	AVERAGES RPG	APG	PPG
56-57 —Boston	48	1695	277	649	.427	152	309	.492	943	88	143	2	706	*19.6	1.8	14.7
57-58 —Boston	69	2640	456	1032	.442	230	443	.519	*1564	202	181	2	1142	*22.7	2.9	16.6
58-59 —Boston	70	*2979	456	997	.457	256	428	.598	*1612	222	161	3	1168	*23.0	3.2	16.7
59-60 —Boston	74	3146	555	1189	.467	240	392	.612	1778	277	210	0	1350	24.0	3.7	18.2
60-61 —Boston	78	3458	532	1250	.426	258	469	.550	1868	268	155	0	1322	23.9	3.4	16.9
61-62 —Boston	76	3433	575	1258	.457	286	481	.595	1790	341	207	3	1436	23.6	4.5	18.9
62-63 —Boston	78	3500	511	1182	.432	287	517	.555	1843	348	189	1	1309	23.6	4.5	16.8
63-64 —Boston	78	3482	466	1077	.433	236	429	.550	*1930	370	190	0	1168	*24.7	4.7	15.0
64-65 —Boston	78	*3466	429	980	.438	244	426	.573	*1878	410	204	1	1102	*24.1	5.3	14.1
65-66 —Boston	78	3386	391	943	.415	223	405	.551	1779	371	221	4	1005	22.8	4.8	12.9
66-67 —Boston	81	3297	395	870	.454	285	467	.610	1700	472	258	4	1075	21.0	5.8	13.3
67-68 —Boston	78	2953	365	858	.425	247	460	.537	1451	357	242	2	977	18.6	4.6	12.5
68-69 —Boston	77	3291	279	645	.433	204	388	.526	1484	374	231	2	762	19.3	4.9	9.9
Totals	963	40726	5687	12930	.440	3148	5614	.561	21620	4100	2592	24	14522	22.5	4.3	15.1

NBA PLAYOFF RECORD

NOTES: Holds career playoff record for most rebounds—4,104. ... Holds NBA Finals records for highest rebounds-per-game average—29.5 (1959); and highest rebounds-per-game average by a rookie—22.9 (1957). ... Shares NBA Finals single-game records for most rebounds—40 (March 29, 1960, vs. St. Louis and April 18, 1962, vs. Los Angeles); most rebounds by a rookie—32 (April 13, 1957, vs. St. Louis); and most rebounds in one quarter—19 (April 18, 1962, vs. Los Angeles).

Season Team	G	Min.	FGM	FGA	Pct.	FTM	FTA	Pct.	Reb.	Ast.	PF	Dq.	Pts.	AVERAGES RPG	APG	PPG
56-57 —Boston	10	409	54	148	.365	31	61	.508	244	32	41	1	139	24.4	3.2	13.9
57-58 —Boston	9	355	48	133	.361	40	66	.606	221	24	24	0	136	24.6	2.7	15.1
58-59 —Boston	11	496	65	159	.409	41	67	.612	305	40	28	1	171	27.7	3.6	15.5
59-60 —Boston	13	572	94	206	.456	53	75	.707	336	38	38	1	241	25.8	2.9	18.5
60-61 —Boston	10	462	73	171	.427	45	86	.523	299	48	24	0	191	29.9	4.8	19.1
61-62 —Boston	14	672	116	253	.459	82	113	.726	370	70	49	0	314	26.4	5.0	22.4
62-63 —Boston	13	617	96	212	.453	72	109	.661	326	66	36	0	264	25.1	5.1	20.3
63-64 —Boston	10	451	47	132	.356	37	67	.552	272	44	33	0	131	27.2	4.4	13.1
64-65 —Boston	12	561	79	150	.527	40	76	.526	302	76	43	2	198	25.2	6.3	16.5
65-66 —Boston	17	814	124	261	.475	76	123	.618	428	85	60	0	324	25.2	5.0	19.1
66-67 —Boston	9	390	31	86	.360	33	52	.635	198	50	32	1	95	22.0	5.6	10.6
67-68 —Boston	19	869	99	242	.409	76	130	.585	434	99	73	1	274	22.8	5.2	14.4
68-69 —Boston	18	829	77	182	.423	41	81	.506	369	98	65	1	195	20.5	5.4	10.8
Totals	165	7497	1003	2335	.430	667	1106	.603	4104	770	546	8	2673	24.9	4.7	16.2

NBA ALL-STAR GAME RECORD

NOTES: NBA All-Star Game Most Valuable Player (1963).

Season Team	Min.	FGM	FGA	Pct.	FTM	FTA	Pct.	Reb	Ast.	PF	Dq.	Pts.
1958 —Boston	26	5	12	.417	1	3	.333	11	2	5	0	11
1959 —Boston	27	3	10	.300	1	1	1.000	9	1	4	0	7
1960 —Boston	27	3	7	.429	0	2	.000	8	3	1	0	6
1961 —Boston	28	9	15	.600	6	8	.750	11	1	2	0	24
1962 —Boston	27	5	12	.417	2	3	.667	12	2	2	0	12
1963 —Boston	37	8	14	.571	3	4	.750	24	5	3	0	19
1964 —Boston	42	6	13	.462	1	2	.500	21	2	4	0	13
1965 —Boston	33	7	12	.583	3	9	.333	13	5	6	1	17
1966 —Boston	23	1	6	.167	0	0	...	10	2	2	0	2
1967 —Boston	22	1	2	.500	0	0	...	5	5	2	0	2
1968 —Boston	23	2	4	.500	0	0	...	9	8	5	0	4
1969 —Boston	28	1	4	.250	1	2	.500	6	3	1	0	3
Totals	343	51	111	.459	18	34	.529	139	39	37	1	120

NBA COACHING RECORD

BACKGROUND: Player/head coach, Boston Celtics (1966-67 through 1968-69). ... Head coach/general manager, Seattle Supersonics (1973-74 through 1976-77).

Season Team	REGULAR SEASON W	L	Pct.	Finish	PLAYOFFS W	L	Pct.
66-67 —Boston	60	21	.741	2nd/Eastern Division	4	5	.444
67-68 —Boston	54	28	.659	2nd/Eastern Division	12	7	.632
68-69 —Boston	48	34	.585	4th/Eastern Division	12	6	.667
73-74 —Seattle	36	46	.439	3rd/Pacific Division	—	—	—
74-75 —Seattle	43	39	.524	2nd/Pacific Division	4	5	.444
75-76 —Seattle	43	39	.524	2nd/Pacific Division	2	4	.333
76-77 —Seattle	40	42	.488	4th/Pacific Division	—	—	—
87-88 —Sacramento	17	41	.293		—	—	—
Totals (8 years)	341	290	.540	Totals (5 years)	34	27	.557

NOTES:

1967—Defeated New York, 3-1, in Eastern Division Semifinals; lost to Philadelphia, 4-1, in Eastern Division Finals.

1968—Defeated Detroit, 4-2, in Eastern Division Semifinals; defeated Philadelphia, 4-3, in Eastern Division Finals; defeated Los Angeles, 4-2, in NBA Finals.

1969—Defeated Philadelphia, 4-1, in Eastern Division Semifinals; defeated New York, 4-2, in Eastern Division Finals; defeated Los Angeles, 4-3, in NBA Finals.

1975—Defeated Detroit, 2-1, in Western Conference First Round; lost to Golden State, 4-2, in Western Conference Semifinals.

1976—Lost to Phoenix in Western Conference Semifinals.

1988—Replaced as Sacramento head coach by Jerry Reynolds (March 7).

SCHAYES, DOLPH F/C

PERSONAL: Born May 19, 1928, in New York. ... 6-8/220 (2,03/99,8). ... Full name: Adolph Schayes. ... Father of Dan Schayes, center with seven NBA teams (1981-82 through 1998-99).
HIGH SCHOOL: DeWitt Clinton (Bronx, N.Y.).
COLLEGE: New York University.
TRANSACTIONS: Selected by Tri-Cities Hawks in 1948 National Basketball League Draft. ... NBL draft rights obtained from Hawks by Syracuse Nationals (1948). ... Nationals franchise became part of NBA for 1949-50 season. ... Nationals franchise moved from Syracuse to Philadelphia and renamed 76ers for 1963-64 season.
CAREER HONORS: Elected to Naismith Memorial Basketball Hall of Fame (1973). ... NBA 25th Anniversary All-Time Team (1970) and One of the 50 Greatest Players in NBA History (1996).
MISCELLANEOUS: Member of NBA championship team (1955). ... Philadelphia 76ers franchise all-time leading rebounder with 11,256 (1948-49 through 1963-64).

COLLEGIATE RECORD

Season Team	G	Min.	FGM	FGA	Pct.	FTM	FTA	Pct.	Reb.	Ast.	Pts.	RPG	APG	PPG
44-45—New York U.	11	...	46	...	...	23	...	...	...	...	115	...	...	10.5
45-46—New York U.	22	...	54	...	...	41	...	...	...	...	149	...	...	6.8
46-47—New York U.	21	...	66	...	...	63	...	...	...	...	195	...	...	9.3
47-48—New York U.	26	...	124	...	...	108	...	...	...	...	356	...	...	13.7
Totals	80	...	290	...	...	235	...	...	...	...	815	...	...	10.2

NBL AND NBA REGULAR-SEASON RECORD

HONORS: All-NBA first team (1952, 1953, 1954, 1955, 1957, 1958). ... All-NBA second team (1950, 1951, 1956, 1959, 1960, 1961). ... NBL Rookie of the Year (1949).

Season Team	G	Min.	FGM	FGA	Pct.	FTM	FTA	Pct.	Reb.	Ast.	PF	Dq.	Pts.	RPG	APG	PPG
48-49 —Syr. (NBL)	63	...	271	...	...	267	370	.722	...	...	232	...	809	...	...	12.8
49-50 —Syracuse	64	...	348	903	.385	376	486	.774	...	259	225	...	1072	...	4.0	16.8
50-51 —Syracuse	66	...	332	930	.357	457	608	.752	*1080	251	271	9	1121	*16.4	3.8	17.0
51-52 —Syracuse	63	2004	263	740	.355	342	424	.807	773	182	213	5	868	12.3	2.9	13.8
52-53 —Syracuse	71	2668	375	1002	.374	512	619	.827	920	227	271	9	1262	13.0	3.2	17.8
53-54 —Syracuse	72	2655	370	973	.380	488	590	.827	870	214	232	4	1228	12.1	3.0	17.1
54-55 —Syracuse	72	2526	422	1103	.383	489	587	.833	887	213	247	6	1333	12.3	3.0	18.5
55-56 —Syracuse	72	2517	465	1202	.387	542	632	.858	891	200	251	9	1472	12.4	2.8	20.4
56-57 —Syracuse	72	*2851	496	1308	.379	*625	691	.904	1008	229	219	5	1617	14.0	3.2	22.5
57-58 —Syracuse	72	*2918	581	1458	.399	629	696	*.904	1022	224	244	6	1791	14.2	3.1	24.9
58-59 —Syracuse	72	2645	504	1304	.387	526	609	.864	962	178	280	9	1534	13.4	2.5	21.3
59-60 —Syracuse	75	2741	578	1440	.401	533	597	*.893	959	256	263	10	1689	12.8	3.4	22.5
60-61 —Syracuse	79	3007	594	1595	.372	*680	783	.868	960	296	296	9	1868	12.2	3.7	23.6
61-62 —Syracuse	56	1480	268	751	.357	286	319	*.897	439	120	167	4	822	7.8	2.1	14.7
62-63 —Syracuse	66	1438	223	575	.388	181	206	.879	375	175	177	2	627	5.7	2.7	9.5
63-64 —Philadelphia	24	350	44	143	.308	46	57	.807	110	48	76	3	134	4.6	2.0	5.6
Totals	1059	...	6134	...	...	6979	8274	.843	...	...	3664	...	19247	...	...	18.2

NBL AND NBA PLAYOFF RECORD

Season Team	G	Min.	FGM	FGA	Pct.	FTM	FTA	Pct.	Reb.	Ast.	PF	Dq.	Pts.	RPG	APG	PPG
48-49 —Syr. (NBL)	6	...	27	...	...	32	42	.762	...	...	26	...	86	...	...	14.3
49-50 —Syracuse	11	...	57	148	.385	74	101	.733	...	28	43	...	188	14.6	2.5	17.1
50-51 —Syracuse	7	...	47	105	.448	49	64	.766	102	20	28	2	143	14.6	2.9	20.4
51-52 —Syracuse	7	248	41	91	.451	60	78	.769	90	15	34	2	142	12.9	2.1	20.3
52-53 —Syracuse	2	58	4	16	.250	10	13	.769	17	1	7	0	18	8.5	0.5	9.0
53-54 —Syracuse	13	374	64	140	.457	80	108	.741	136	24	40	1	208	10.5	1.8	16.0
54-55 —Syracuse	11	363	60	167	.359	89	106	.840	141	40	48	3	209	12.8	3.6	19.0
55-56 —Syracuse	8	310	52	142	.366	73	83	.880	111	27	27	0	177	13.9	3.4	22.1
56-57 —Syracuse	5	215	29	95	.305	49	55	.891	90	14	18	0	107	18.0	2.8	21.4
57-58 —Syracuse	3	131	25	64	.391	30	36	.833	45	6	10	0	80	15.0	2.0	26.7
58-59 —Syracuse	9	351	78	195	.400	98	107	.916	117	41	36	0	254	13.0	4.6	28.2
59-60 —Syracuse	3	126	30	66	.455	28	30	.933	48	8	10	0	88	16.0	2.7	29.3
60-61 —Syracuse	8	308	51	152	.336	63	70	.900	91	21	32	2	165	11.4	2.6	20.6
61-62 —Syracuse	5	95	24	66	.364	9	13	.692	35	5	21	0	57	7.0	1.0	11.4
62-63 —Syracuse	5	108	20	44	.455	11	12	.917	28	7	17	0	51	5.6	1.4	10.2
Totals	103	...	609	...	...	755	918	.822	...	...	397	...	1973	...	...	19.2

NBA ALL-STAR GAME RECORD

Season Team	Min.	FGM	FGA	Pct.	FTM	FTA	Pct.	Reb	Ast.	PF	Dq.	Pts.
1951 —Syracuse	...	7	10	.700	1	2	.500	14	3	1	0	15
1952 —Syracuse				Selected, did not play—injured.								
1953 —Syracuse	26	2	7	.286	4	4	1.000	13	3	3	0	8
1954 —Syracuse	24	1	3	.333	4	6	.667	12	1	1	0	6
1955 —Syracuse	29	6	12	.500	3	3	1.000	13	1	4	0	15
1956 —Syracuse	25	4	8	.500	6	10	.600	4	2	2	0	14
1957 —Syracuse	25	4	6	.667	1	1	1.000	10	1	1	0	9
1958 —Syracuse	39	6	15	.400	6	6	1.000	9	2	4	0	18
1959 —Syracuse	22	3	14	.214	7	8	.875	13	1	6	1	13
1960 —Syracuse	27	8	19	.421	3	3	1.000	10	0	3	0	19
1961 —Syracuse	27	7	15	.467	7	7	1.000	6	3	4	0	21
1962 —Syracuse	4	0	0	...	0	0	...	1	0	3	0	0
Totals	...	48	109	.440	42	50	.840	105	17	32	1	138

NBA COACHING RECORD

BACKGROUND: Player/head coach, Philadelphia 76ers (1963-64).
HONORS: NBA Coach of the Year (1966).

ALL-TIME GREAT PLAYERS

Season Team	REGULAR SEASON W	L	Pct.	Finish	PLAYOFFS W	L	Pct.
63-64 —Philadelphia	34	46	.425	3rd/Eastern Division	2	3	.400
64-65 —Philadelphia	40	40	.500	3rd/Eastern Division	6	5	.545
65-66 —Philadelphia	55	25	.688	1st/Eastern Division	1	4	.200
70-71 —Buffalo	22	60	.268	4th/Atlantic Division	—	—	—
71-72 —Buffalo	0	1	.000		—	—	—
Totals (5 years)	151	172	.467	Totals (3 years)	9	12	.429

NOTES:
1964—Lost to Cincinnati in Eastern Division Semifinals.
1965—Defeated Cincinnati, 3-1, in Eastern Division Semifinals; lost to Boston, 4-3, in Eastern Division Finals.
1966—Lost to Boston in Eastern Division Finals.
1971—Replaced as Buffalo head coach by John McCarthy (October).

SHARMAN, BILL   G

PERSONAL: Born May 25, 1926, in Abilene, Texas. ... 6-1/190 (1,85/86). ... Full name: William Walton Sharman.
HIGH SCHOOL: Narbonne (Lomita, Calif.), then Porterville (Calif.).
COLLEGE: Southern California.
TRANSACTIONS: Selected by Washington Capitols in second round of 1950 NBA Draft. ... Selected by Fort Wayne Pistons in 1951 NBA Dispersal Draft of Capitols franchise (did not report to Fort Wayne). ... Traded by Pistons with F Bob Brannum to Boston Celtics for NBA rights to C Charlie Share (1951). ... Signed as player/head coach by Los Angeles Jets of American Basketball League (1961).
CAREER HONORS: Elected to Naismith Memorial Basketball Hall of Fame (1976). ... NBA 25th Anniversary All-Time Team (1970) and One of the 50 Greatest Players in NBA History (1996).
CAREER NOTES: General manager, Los Angeles Lakers (1975-76 through 1981-82). ... President, Lakers (1982-83 through 1989-90). ... Consultant, Lakers (1990-91 to present).
MISCELLANEOUS: Member of NBA championship team (1957, 1959, 1960, 1961).

COLLEGIATE RECORD

NOTES: THE SPORTING NEWS All-America first team (1950). ... THE SPORTING NEWS All-America third team (1949). ... In military service during 1944-45 and 1945-46 seasons.

Season Team	G	Min.	FGM	FGA	Pct.	FTM	FTA	Pct.	Reb.	Ast.	Pts.	AVERAGES RPG	APG	PPG
46-47—Southern Cal	10	...	16	...	...	9	12	.750	...	...	41	...	...	4.1
47-48—Southern Cal	24	...	100	...	...	38	44	.864	...	...	238	...	...	9.9
48-49—Southern Cal	24	...	142	...	...	98	125	.784	...	...	382	...	...	15.9
49-50—Southern Cal	24	...	171	421	.406	104	129	.806	...	...	446	...	...	18.6
Totals	82	...	429	...	...	249	310	.803	...	...	1107	...	...	13.5

NBA REGULAR-SEASON RECORD

HONORS: All-NBA first team (1956, 1957, 1958, 1959). ... All-NBA second team (1953, 1955, 1960).

Season Team	G	Min.	FGM	FGA	Pct.	FTM	FTA	Pct.	Reb.	Ast.	PF	Dq.	Pts.	AVERAGES RPG	APG	PPG
50-51 —Washington	31	...	141	361	.391	96	108	.889	96	39	86	3	378	3.1	1.3	12.2
51-52 —Boston	63	1389	244	628	.389	183	213	.859	221	151	181	3	671	3.5	2.4	10.7
52-53 —Boston	71	2333	403	925	.436	341	401	*.850	288	191	240	7	1147	4.1	2.7	16.2
53-54 —Boston	72	2467	412	915	.450	331	392	*.844	255	229	211	4	1155	3.5	3.2	16.0
54-55 —Boston	68	2453	453	1062	.427	347	387	*.897	302	280	212	2	1253	4.4	4.1	18.4
55-56 —Boston	72	2698	538	1229	.438	358	413	*.867	259	339	197	1	1434	3.6	4.7	19.9
56-57 —Boston	67	2403	516	1241	.416	381	421	*.905	286	236	188	1	1413	4.3	3.5	21.1
57-58 —Boston	63	2214	550	1297	.424	302	338	.894	295	167	156	3	1402	4.7	2.7	22.3
58-59 —Boston	72	2382	562	1377	.408	342	367	*.932	292	179	173	1	1466	4.1	2.5	20.4
59-60 —Boston	71	1916	559	1225	.456	252	291	.866	262	144	154	2	1370	3.7	2.0	19.3
60-61 —Boston	61	1538	383	908	.422	210	228	*.921	223	146	127	0	976	3.7	2.4	16.0
Totals	711	...	4761	11168	.426	3143	3559	.883	2779	2101	1925	27	12665	3.9	3.0	17.8

NBA PLAYOFF RECORD

Season Team	G	Min.	FGM	FGA	Pct.	FTM	FTA	Pct.	Reb.	Ast.	PF	Dq.	Pts.	AVERAGES RPG	APG	PPG
51-52 —Boston	1	27	7	12	.583	1	1	1.000	3	7	4	0	15	3.0	7.0	15.0
52-53 —Boston	6	201	20	60	.333	30	32	.938	15	15	26	1	70	2.5	2.5	11.7
53-54 —Boston	6	206	35	81	.432	43	50	.860	25	10	29	2	113	4.2	1.7	18.8
54-55 —Boston	7	290	55	110	.500	35	38	.921	38	38	24	1	145	5.4	5.4	20.7
55-56 —Boston	3	119	18	46	.391	16	17	.941	7	12	7	0	52	2.3	4.0	17.3
56-57 —Boston	10	377	75	197	.381	61	64	.953	35	29	23	1	211	3.5	2.9	21.1
57-58 —Boston	11	406	90	221	.407	52	56	.929	54	25	28	0	232	4.9	2.3	21.1
58-59 —Boston	11	322	82	193	.425	57	59	.966	36	28	35	0	221	3.3	2.5	20.1
59-60 —Boston	13	364	88	209	.421	43	53	.811	45	20	22	1	219	3.5	1.5	16.8
60-61 —Boston	10	261	68	133	.511	32	36	.889	27	17	22	0	168	2.7	1.7	16.8
Totals	78	2573	538	1262	.426	370	406	.911	285	201	220	6	1446	3.7	2.6	18.5

NBA ALL-STAR GAME RECORD

NOTES: NBA All-Star Game Most Valuable Player (1955). ... Holds single-game record for most field goals attempted in one quarter—12 (1960).

Season		Min.	FGM	FGA	Pct.	FTM	FTA	Pct.	Reb	Ast.	PF	Dq.	Pts.
1953 —Boston		26	5	8	.625	1	1	1.000	4	0	2	0	11
1954 —Boston		30	6	9	.667	2	4	.500	2	3	3	0	14
1955 —Boston		18	5	10	.500	5	5	1.000	4	2	4	0	15
1956 —Boston		22	2	8	.250	3	5	.600	2	1	2	1	7
1957 —Boston		23	5	17	.294	2	2	1.000	6	5	1	0	12
1958 —Boston		25	6	19	.316	3	3	1.000	4	3	2	0	15
1959 —Boston		24	3	12	.250	5	6	.833	2	0	1	0	11
1960 —Boston		26	8	21	.381	1	1	1.000	6	2	1	0	17
Totals		194	40	104	.385	22	27	.815	31	16	16	1	102

ABL REGULAR-SEASON RECORD

Season Team	G	Min.	FGM	FGA	Pct.	FTM	FTA	Pct.	Reb.	Ast.	Pts.	RPG	APG	PPG
												AVERAGES		
61-62—Los Angeles..................	19	346	35	80	.438	37	34	1.088	43	37	107	2.3	1.9	5.6

HEAD COACHING RECORD

BACKGROUND: Player/head coach, Los Angeles Jets of American Basketball League (1961-62). ... Assistant coach, New Orleans Jazz (1974-75 and 1975-76).

HONORS: NBA Coach of the Year (1972). ... ABA co-Coach of the Year (1970).

COLLEGIATE COACHING RECORD

Season Team	W	L	Pct.	Finish
62-63 —Cal State-Los Angeles	10	12	.455	4th/California Collegiate Athletic Association
63-64 —Cal State-Los Angeles	17	8	.680	2nd/California Collegiate Athletic Association
Totals (2 years)...	27	20	.574	

ABL COACHING RECORD

Season Team	REGULAR SEASON				PLAYOFFS		
	W	L	Pct.	Finish	W	L	Pct.
61-62 —Los Angeles-Cleveland	43	26	.623		5	2	.714

NBA COACHING RECORD

Season Team	REGULAR SEASON				PLAYOFFS		
	W	L	Pct.	Finish	W	L	Pct.
66-67 —San Francisco..	44	37	.543	1st/Western Division	9	6	.600
67-68 —San Francisco..	43	39	.524	3rd/Western Division	4	6	.400
71-72 —Los Angeles...	69	13	.841	1st/Pacific Division	12	3	.800
72-73 —Los Angeles...	60	22	.732	1st/Pacific Division	9	8	.529
73-74 —Los Angeles...	47	35	.573	1st/Pacific Division	1	4	.200
74-75 —Los Angeles...	30	52	.366	5th/Pacific Division	—	—	—
75-76 —Los Angeles...	40	42	.488	4th/Pacific Division	—	—	—
Totals (7 years)...	333	240	.581	Totals (5 years).......	35	27	.565

ABA COACHING RECORD

Season Team	REGULAR SEASON				PLAYOFFS		
	W	L	Pct.	Finish	W	L	Pct.
68-69 —Los Angeles...	33	45	.423	5th/Western Division	—	—	—
69-70 —Los Angeles...	43	41	.512	4th/Western Division	10	7	.588
70-71 —Utah..	57	27	.679	2nd/Western Division	12	6	.667
Totals (3 years)...	133	113	.541	Totals (2 years).......	22	13	.629

NOTES:

1962—Los Angeles Jets had 24-15 record when they folded after first half of season (January 10); Sharman then replaced John McLendon, who resigned as Cleveland Pipers head coach (January 28), and guided Pipers to ABL Championship.

1967—Defeated Los Angeles, 3-0, in Western Division Semifinals; defeated St. Louis, 4-2, in Western Division Finals; lost to Philadelphia, 4-2, in World Championship Series.

1968—Defeated St. Louis, 4-2, in Western Division Semifinals; lost to Los Angeles, 4-0, in Western Division Finals.

1970—Defeated Dallas, 4-2, in Western Division Semifinals; defeated Denver, 4-1, in Western Division Finals; lost to Indiana, 4-2, in ABA Finals.

1971—Defeated Texas, 4-0, in Western Division Semifinals; defeated Indiana, 4-3, in Western Division Finals; defeated Kentucky, 4-3, in ABA Finals.

1972—Defeated Chicago, 4-0, in Western Conference Semifinals; defeated Milwaukee, 4-2, in Western Conference Finals; defeated New York, 4-1, in World Championship Series.

1973—Defeated Chicago, 4-3, in Western Conference Semifinals; defeated Golden State, 4-1, in Western Conference Finals; lost to New York, 4-1, in World Championship Series.

1974—Lost to Milwaukee in Western Conference First Round.

RECORD AS BASEBALL PLAYER

Year	Team (League)	Pos.	G	BATTING									FIELDING			
				AB	R	H	2B	3B	HR	RBI	Avg.	BB	SO	SB	PO	A	E	Avg.
1950—Elmira (Eastern).........	OF	10	38	5	11	2	0	1	11	.289	0	5	0	17	0	1	.944
—Pueblo (Western)	OF	111	427	65	123	22	8	11	70	.288	42	47	11	214	16	10	.958
1951—Fort Worth (Texas)......	OF	157	570	84	163	18	5	8	53	.286	57	44	23	254	11	2	.993
1952—St. Paul (A.A.)	OF	137	411	63	121	16	4	10	77	.294	29	32	2	215	15	3	.987
1953—Mobile (South.)	OF	90	228	21	48	8	1	5	17	.211	30	26	0	136	6	2	.986
1954—						Out of organized baseball.										
1955—St. Paul (A.A.)............	OF-3B	133	424	59	124	15	0	11	58	.292	34	33	3	183	100	11	.963

SIKMA, JACK C/F

PERSONAL: Born November 14, 1955, in Kankakee, Ill. ... 7-0/250 (2,13/113,4). ... Full name: Jack Wayne Sikma.

HIGH SCHOOL: St. Anne (Ill.).

COLLEGE: Illinois Wesleyan.

TRANSACTIONS: Selected by Seattle SuperSonics in first round (eighth pick overall) of 1977 NBA Draft. ... Traded by SuperSonics with 1987 and 1989 second-round draft choices to Milwaukee Bucks for C Alton Lister and 1987 and 1989 first-round draft choices (July 1, 1986).

MISCELLANEOUS: Member of NBA championship team (1979). ... Seattle SuperSonics all-time leading rebounder with 7,729 (1977-78 through 1985-86).

ALL-TIME GREAT PLAYERS

COLLEGIATE RECORD

Season Team	G	Min.	FGM	FGA	Pct.	FTM	FTA	Pct.	Reb.	Ast.	Pts.	AVERAGES		
												RPG	APG	PPG
73-74—Illinois Wesleyan	21	...	148	306	.484	28	37	.757	223	...	324	10.6	...	15.4
74-75—Illinois Wesleyan	30	...	265	537	.493	80	112	.714	415	...	610	13.8	...	20.3
75-76—Illinois Wesleyan	25	...	204	385	.530	93	126	.738	290	...	501	11.6	...	20.0
76-77—Illinois Wesleyan	31	...	302	324	.932	189	235	.804	477	...	837	15.4	...	27.0
Totals	107	...	919	1552	.592	390	510	.765	1405	...	2272	13.1	...	21.2

NBA REGULAR-SEASON RECORD

HONORS: NBA All-Defensive second team (1982). ... NBA All-Rookie team (1978).

NOTES: Tied for NBA lead with 11 disqualifications (1988).

Season Team	G	Min.	FGM	FGA	Pct.	FTM	FTA	Pct.	REBOUNDS			Ast.	St.	Blk.	TO	Pts.	AVERAGES		
									Off.	Def.	Tot.						RPG	APG	PPG
77-78—Seattle	82	2238	342	752	.455	192	247	.777	196	482	678	134	68	40	186	876	8.3	1.6	10.7
78-79—Seattle	82	2958	476	1034	.460	329	404	.814	232	781	1013	261	82	67	253	1281	12.4	3.2	15.6
79-80—Seattle	82	2793	470	989	.475	235	292	.805	198	710	908	279	68	77	202	1175	11.1	3.4	14.3
80-81—Seattle	82	2920	595	1311	.454	340	413	.823	184	668	852	248	78	93	201	1530	10.4	3.0	18.7
81-82—Seattle	82	3049	581	1212	.479	447	523	.855	223	*815	1038	277	102	107	213	1611	12.7	3.4	19.6
82-83—Seattle	75	2564	484	1043	.464	400	478	.837	213	645	858	233	87	65	190	1368	11.4	3.1	18.2
83-84—Seattle	82	2993	576	1155	.499	411	480	.856	225	*686	911	327	95	92	236	1563	11.1	4.0	19.1
84-85—Seattle	68	2402	461	943	.489	335	393	.852	164	559	723	285	83	91	160	1259	10.6	4.2	18.5
85-86—Seattle	82	2790	508	1100	.462	355	411	.864	146	602	748	301	92	73	214	1371	9.4	3.8	17.1
86-87—Milwaukee	82	2536	390	842	.463	265	313	.847	208	614	822	203	88	90	160	1045	10.0	2.5	12.7
87-88—Milwaukee	82	2923	514	1058	.486	321	348	*.922	195	514	709	279	93	80	157	1352	8.6	3.4	16.5
88-89—Milwaukee	80	2587	360	835	.431	266	294	.905	141	482	623	289	85	61	145	1068	7.8	3.6	13.4
89-90—Milwaukee	71	2250	344	827	.416	230	260	.885	109	383	492	229	76	48	139	986	6.9	3.2	13.9
90-91—Milwaukee	77	1940	295	691	.427	166	197	.843	108	333	441	143	65	64	130	802	5.7	1.9	10.4
Totals	1107	36943	6396	13792	.464	4292	5053	.849	2542	8274	10816	3488	1162	1048	2586	17287	9.8	3.2	15.6

Three-point field goals: 1979-80, 0-for-1. 1980-81, 0-for-5. 1981-82, 2-for-13 (.154). 1982-83, 0-for-8. 1983-84, 0-for-2. 1984-85, 2-for-10 (.200). 1985-86, 0-for-13. 1986-87, 0-for-2. 1987-88, 3-for-14 (.214). 1988-89, 82-for-216 (.380). 1989-90, 68-for-199 (.342). 1990-91, 46-for-135 (.341). Totals, 203-for-618 (.328).

Personal fouls/disqualifications: 1977-78, 300/6. 1978-79, 295/4. 1979-80, 232/5. 1980-81, 282/5. 1981-82, 268/5. 1982-83, 263/4. 1983-84, 301/6. 1984-85, 239/1. 1985-86, 293/4. 1986-87, 328/14. 1987-88, 316/11. 1988-89, 300/6. 1989-90, 244/5. 1990-91, 218/4. Totals, 3879/80.

NBA PLAYOFF RECORD

Season Team	G	Min.	FGM	FGA	Pct.	FTM	FTA	Pct.	REBOUNDS			Ast.	St.	Blk.	TO	Pts.	AVERAGES		
									Off.	Def.	Tot.						RPG	APG	PPG
77-78—Seattle	22	701	115	247	.466	71	91	.780	50	128	178	27	18	11	35	301	8.1	1.2	13.7
78-79—Seattle	17	655	102	224	.455	48	61	.787	39	160	199	43	16	24	40	252	11.7	2.5	14.8
79-80—Seattle	15	534	65	163	.399	46	54	.852	30	96	126	55	17	5	35	176	8.4	3.7	11.7
81-82—Seattle	8	315	57	128	.445	50	58	.862	21	76	97	24	9	8	16	164	12.1	3.0	20.5
82-83—Seattle	2	75	11	31	.355	8	12	.667	6	20	26	11	2	2	5	30	13.0	5.5	15.0
83-84—Seattle	5	193	49	98	.500	12	14	.857	11	40	51	5	3	7	9	110	10.2	1.0	22.0
86-87—Milwaukee	12	426	73	150	.487	48	49	.980	33	97	130	23	15	10	18	194	10.8	1.9	16.2
87-88—Milwaukee	5	190	35	76	.461	25	30	.833	24	38	62	13	2	4	15	95	12.4	2.6	19.0
88-89—Milwaukee	9	301	37	94	.394	23	28	.821	9	41	50	30	8	4	21	105	5.6	3.3	11.7
89-90—Milwaukee	4	117	6	23	.261	6	8	.750	0	14	14	7	2	4	12	20	3.5	1.8	5.0
90-91—Milwaukee	3	51	6	15	.400	1	2	.500	3	9	12	6	5	1	31	14	4.0	2.0	4.7
Totals	102	3558	556	1249	.445	338	407	.830	226	719	945	244	97	80	237	1461	9.3	2.4	14.3

Three-point field goals: 1979-80, 0-for-2. 1982-83, 0-for-1. 1983-84, 0-for-1. 1986-87, 0-for-1. 1987-88, 0-for-3. 1988-89, 8-for-28 (.286). 1989-90, 2-for-7 (.286). 1990-91, 1-for-2 (.500). Totals, 11-for-45 (.244).

Personal fouls/disqualifications: 1977-78, 101/7. 1978-79, 70/2. 1979-80, 55/1. 1981-82, 34/1. 1982-83, 7/0. 1983-84, 22/1. 1986-87, 56/3. 1987-88, 23/0. 1988-89, 41/2. 1989-90, 19/0. 1990-91, 4/0. Totals, 432/17.

NBA ALL-STAR GAME RECORD

Season Team	Min.	FGM	FGA	Pct.	FTM	FTA	Pct.	REBOUNDS			Ast.	PF	Dq.	St.	Blk.	TO	Pts.
								Off.	Def.	Tot.							
1979 —Seattle	18	4	5	.800	0	0	...	1	3	4	0	1	0	0	0	0	8
1980 —Seattle	28	4	10	.400	0	0	...	2	6	8	4	5	0	2	3	3	8
1981 —Seattle	21	2	5	.400	2	2	1.000	1	3	4	4	5	0	1	1	1	6
1982 —Seattle	21	5	11	.455	0	0	...	2	7	9	1	2	0	2	1	1	10
1983 —Seattle	17	4	6	.667	0	0	...	1	2	3	1	2	0	1	1	1	5
1984 —Seattle	30	5	12	.417	5	6	.833	5	7	12	1	4	0	3	0	0	15
1985 —Seattle	12	0	2	.000	0	0	...	0	2	2	0	1	0	0	1	1	0
Totals............................	147	24	51	.471	7	8	.875	12	30	42	11	20	0	9	7	7	52

Three-point field goals: 1980, 0-for-1. 1981, 0-for-1. Totals, 0-for-2.

SILAS, PAUL   F/C

See Head Coaches, page 325.

THEUS, REGGIE   G

PERSONAL: Born October 13, 1957, in Inglewood, Calif. ... 6-7/213 (2,00/96,6). ... Full name: Reggie Wayne Theus. ... Name pronounced THEE-us.
HIGH SCHOOL: Inglewood (Calif.).
COLLEGE: UNLV.
TRANSACTIONS: Selected after junior season by Chicago Bulls in first round (ninth pick overall) of 1978 NBA Draft. ... Traded by Bulls to Kansas City Kings for C Steve Johnson, 1984 second-round draft choice and two 1985 second-round draft choices (February 15, 1984). ... Kings franchise moved from Kansas City to Sacramento for 1985-86 season. ... Traded by Kings with 1988 third-round draft choice and future considerations to Atlanta Hawks for G/F Randy Wittman and 1988 first-round draft choice (June 27, 1988). ... Selected by Orlando Magic from Hawks in NBA Expansion Draft (June 15, 1989). ... Traded by Magic to New Jersey Nets for 1993 and 1995 second-round draft choices (June 25, 1990). ... Waived by Nets (August 15, 1991). ... Played in Italy (1991-92).
CAREER NOTES: Broadcaster, Turner Sports (1994-2000).

COLLEGIATE RECORD

Season Team	G	Min.	FGM	FGA	Pct.	FTM	FTA	Pct.	Reb.	Ast.	Pts.	RPG	APG	PPG
75-76—UNLV	31	496	68	163	.417	48	60	.800	53	139	184	1.7	4.5	5.9
76-77—UNLV	32	814	178	358	.497	108	132	.818	145	136	464	4.5	4.3	14.5
77-78—UNLV	28	990	181	389	.465	167	207	.807	191	126	529	6.8	4.5	18.9
Totals	91	2300	427	910	.469	323	399	.810	389	401	1177	4.3	4.4	12.9

NBA REGULAR-SEASON RECORD

HONORS: NBA All-Rookie team (1979).

Season Team	G	Min.	FGM	FGA	Pct.	FTM	FTA	Pct.	REBOUNDS Off.	Def.	Tot.	Ast.	St.	Blk.	TO	Pts.	AVERAGES RPG	APG	PPG
78-79—Chicago	82	2753	537	1119	.480	264	347	.761	92	136	228	429	93	18	303	1338	2.8	5.2	16.3
79-80—Chicago	82	3029	566	1172	.483	500	597	.838	143	186	329	515	114	20	301	1660	4.0	6.3	20.2
80-81—Chicago	82	2820	543	1097	.495	445	550	.809	124	163	287	426	122	20	259	1549	3.5	5.2	18.9
81-82—Chicago	82	2838	560	1194	.469	363	449	.808	115	197	312	476	87	16	277	1508	3.8	5.8	18.4
82-83—Chicago	82	2856	749	1565	.478	434	542	.801	91	209	300	484	143	17	321	1953	3.7	5.9	23.8
83-84—Chi.-K.C.	61	1498	262	625	.419	214	281	.762	50	79	129	352	50	12	156	745	2.1	5.8	12.2
84-85—Kansas City	82	2543	501	1029	.487	334	387	.863	106	164	270	656	95	18	307	1341	3.3	8.0	16.4
85-86—Sacramento	82	2919	546	1137	.480	405	490	.827	73	231	304	788	112	20	327	1503	3.7	9.6	18.3
86-87—Sacramento	79	2872	577	1223	.472	429	495	.867	86	180	266	692	78	16	289	1600	3.4	8.8	20.3
87-88—Sacramento	73	2653	619	1318	.470	320	385	.831	72	160	232	463	59	16	234	1574	3.2	6.3	21.6
88-89—Atlanta	82	2517	497	1067	.466	285	335	.851	86	156	242	387	108	16	194	1296	3.0	4.7	15.8
89-90—Orlando	76	2350	517	1178	.439	378	443	.853	75	146	221	407	60	12	226	1438	2.9	5.4	18.9
90-91—New Jersey	81	2955	583	1247	.468	292	343	.851	69	160	229	378	85	15	252	1510	2.8	4.7	18.6
Totals	1026	34603	7057	14973	.471	4663	5644	.826	1182	2167	3349	6453	1206	236	3493	19015	3.3	6.3	18.5

Three-point field goals: 1979-80, 28-for-105 (.267). 1980-81, 18-for-90 (.200). 1981-82, 25-for-100 (.250). 1982-83, 21-for-91 (.231). 1983-84, 7-for-42 (.167). 1984-85, 5-for-38 (.132). 1985-86, 6-for-35 (.171). 1986-87, 17-for-78 (.218). 1987-88, 16-for-59 (.271). 1988-89, 17-for-58 (.293). 1989-90, 26-for-105 (.248). 1990-91, 52-for-144 (.361). Totals, 238-for-945 (.252).

Personal fouls/disqualifications: 1978-79, 270/2. 1979-80, 262/4. 1980-81, 258/1. 1981-82, 243/1. 1982-83, 281/6. 1983-84, 171/3. 1984-85, 250/0. 1985-86, 231/3. 1986-87, 208/3. 1987-88, 173/0. 1988-89, 236/0. 1989-90, 194/1. 1990-91, 231/0. Totals, 3008/24.

NBA PLAYOFF RECORD

Season Team	G	Min.	FGM	FGA	Pct.	FTM	FTA	Pct.	REBOUNDS Off.	Def.	Tot.	Ast.	St.	Blk.	TO	Pts.	AVERAGES RPG	APG	PPG
80-81—Chicago	6	232	40	90	.444	37	43	.860	7	14	21	38	9	0	15	119	3.5	6.3	19.8
83-84—Kansas City	3	81	17	43	.395	9	10	.900	4	7	11	16	5	0	9	43	3.7	5.3	14.3
85-86—Sacramento	3	102	18	46	.391	9	12	.750	3	5	8	19	3	2	14	45	2.7	6.3	15.0
88-89—Atlanta	5	127	14	38	.368	9	12	.750	3	4	7	24	1	0	10	37	1.4	4.8	7.4
Totals	17	542	89	217	.410	64	77	.831	17	30	47	97	18	2	48	244	2.8	5.7	14.4

Three-point field goals: 1980-81, 2-for-9 (.222). 1983-84, 0-for-3. 1985-86, 0-for-1. 1988-89, 0-for-2. Totals, 2-for-15 (.133).
Personal fouls/disqualifications: 1980-81, 22/0. 1983-84, 9/0. 1985-86, 9/0. 1988-89, 18/1. Totals, 58/1.

NBA ALL-STAR GAME RECORD

Season Team	Min.	FGM	FGA	Pct.	FTM	FTA	Pct.	REBOUNDS Off.	Def.	Tot.	Ast.	PF	Dq.	St.	Blk.	TO	Pts.
1981 —Chicago	19	4	7	.571	0	0	...	0	1	1	3	0	0	2	0	4	8
1983 —Chicago	8	0	5	.000	0	0	...	1	0	1	1	1	0	0	0	0	0
Totals	27	4	12	.333	0	0	...	1	1	2	4	1	0	2	0	4	8

ITALIAN LEAGUE RECORD

Season Team	G	Min.	FGM	FGA	Pct.	FTM	FTA	Pct.	Reb.	Ast.	Pts.	RPG	APG	PPG
91-92—Ranger Varese	30	1151	268	572	.469	288	340	.847	118	161	878	3.9	5.4	29.3

THOMAS, ISIAH

See Head Coaches, page 329.

THURMOND, NATE C/F

PERSONAL: Born July 25, 1941, in Akron, Ohio. ... 6-11/235 (2,10/106,6). ... Full name: Nathaniel Thurmond.
HIGH SCHOOL: Central Hower (Akron, Ohio).
COLLEGE: Bowling Green State.
TRANSACTIONS: Selected by San Francisco Warriors in first round of 1963 NBA Draft. ... Warriors franchise renamed Golden State Warriors for 1971-72 season. ... Traded by Warriors to Chicago Bulls for C Clifford Ray, cash and 1975 first-round draft choice (September 3, 1974). ... Traded by Bulls with F Rowland Garrett to Cleveland Cavaliers for C/F Steve Patterson and F Eric Fernsten (November 27, 1975).
CAREER HONORS: Elected to Naismith Memorial Basketball Hall of Fame (1985). ... One of the 50 Greatest Players in NBA History (1996).
CAREER NOTES: Community Relations Director, Golden State Warriors (1981-82 through 1994-95) ... Community Relations Ambassador, Warriors (1995-96-present).
MISCELLANEOUS: Golden State Warriors franchise all-time leading rebounder with 12,771 (1963-64 through 1973-74).

COLLEGIATE RECORD

NOTES: The Sporting News All-America first team (1963).

Season Team	G	Min.	FGM	FGA	Pct.	FTM	FTA	Pct.	Reb.	Ast.	Pts.	RPG	APG	PPG
59-60—Bowling Green‡	17	...	...	...	...	...	...	...	208	...	225	12.2	...	13.2
60-61—Bowling Green	24	...	170	427	.398	87	129	.674	449	...	427	18.7	...	17.8
61-62—Bowling Green	25	...	163	358	.455	67	113	.593	394	...	393	15.8	...	15.7
62-63—Bowling Green	27	...	206	466	.442	124	197	.629	452	...	536	16.7	...	19.9
Varsity totals	76	...	539	1251	.431	278	439	.633	1295	...	1356	17.0	...	17.8

NBA REGULAR-SEASON RECORD

RECORDS: Holds single-game record for most rebounds in one quarter—18 (February 28, 1965, vs. Baltimore).
HONORS: NBA All-Defensive first team (1969, 1971). ... NBA All-Defensive second team (1972, 1973, 1974). ... NBA All-Rookie team (1964).

Season Team	G	Min.	FGM	FGA	Pct.	FTM	FTA	Pct.	Reb.	Ast.	PF	Dq.	Pts.	RPG	APG	PPG
63-64—San Francisco	76	1966	219	554	.395	95	173	.549	790	86	184	2	533	10.4	1.1	7.0
64-65—San Francisco	77	3173	519	1240	.419	235	357	.658	1395	157	232	3	1273	18.1	2.0	16.5
65-66—San Francisco	73	2891	454	1119	.406	280	428	.654	1312	111	223	7	1188	18.0	1.5	16.3
66-67—San Francisco	65	2755	467	1068	.437	280	445	.629	1382	166	183	3	1214	21.3	2.6	18.7
67-68—San Francisco	51	2222	382	929	.411	282	438	.644	1121	215	137	1	1046	22.0	4.2	20.5
68-69—San Francisco	71	3208	571	1394	.410	382	621	.615	1402	253	171	0	1524	19.7	3.6	21.5
69-70—San Francisco	43	1919	341	824	.414	261	346	.754	762	150	110	1	943	17.7	3.5	21.9
70-71—San Francisco	82	3351	623	1401	.445	395	541	.730	1128	257	192	1	1641	13.8	3.1	20.0
71-72—Golden State	78	3362	628	1454	.432	417	561	.743	1252	230	214	1	1673	16.1	2.9	21.4
72-73—Golden State	79	3419	517	1159	.446	315	439	.718	1349	280	240	2	1349	17.1	3.5	17.1

Season Team	G	Min.	FGM	FGA	Pct.	FTM	FTA	Pct.	Off.	Def.	Tot.	Ast.	St.	Blk.	TO	Pts.	RPG	APG	PPG
73-74—Golden State	62	2463	308	694	.444	191	287	.666	249	629	878	165	41	179	...	807	14.2	2.7	13.0
74-75—Chicago	80	2756	250	686	.364	132	224	.589	259	645	904	328	46	195	...	632	11.3	4.1	7.9
75-76—Chi.-Clev.	78	1393	142	337	.421	62	123	.504	115	300	415	94	22	98	...	346	5.3	1.2	4.4
76-77—Cleveland	49	997	100	246	.407	68	106	.642	121	253	374	83	16	81	...	268	7.6	1.7	5.5
Totals	964	35875	5521	13105	.421	3395	5089	.667	...	...	14464	2575	125	553	...	14437	15.0	2.7	15.0

Personal fouls/disqualifications: 1973-74, 179/4. 1974-75, 271/6. 1975-76, 160/1. 1976-77, 128/2. Totals, 2624/34.

NBA PLAYOFF RECORD

Season Team	G	Min.	FGM	FGA	Pct.	FTM	FTA	Pct.	Reb.	Ast.	PF	Dq.	Pts.	RPG	APG	PPG
63-64—San Francisco	12	410	42	98	.429	36	53	.679	148	12	46	0	120	12.3	1.0	10.0
66-67—San Francisco	15	690	93	215	.433	52	91	.571	346	47	52	1	238	23.1	3.1	15.9
68-69—San Francisco	6	263	40	102	.392	20	34	.588	117	28	18	0	100	19.5	4.7	16.7
70-71—San Francisco	5	192	36	97	.371	16	20	.800	51	15	20	0	88	10.2	3.0	17.6
71-72—Golden State	5	230	53	122	.434	21	28	.750	89	26	12	0	127	17.8	5.2	25.4
72-73—Golden State	11	460	64	161	.398	32	40	.800	145	40	30	1	160	13.2	3.6	14.5

Season Team	G	Min.	FGM	FGA	Pct.	FTM	FTA	Pct.	Off.	Def.	Tot.	Ast.	St.	Blk.	TO	Pts.	RPG	APG	PPG
74-75—Chicago	13	254	14	38	.368	18	37	.486	24	63	87	31	5	21	...	46	6.7	2.4	3.5
75-76—Cleveland	13	375	37	79	.468	13	32	.406	38	79	117	28	6	29	...	87	9.0	2.2	6.7
76-77—Cleveland	1	0	0	0	...	0	0	...	0	1	1	0	0	1	...	0	1.0	0.0	0.0
Totals	81	2875	379	912	.416	208	335	.621	...	...	1101	227	11	51	...	966	13.6	2.8	11.9

Personal fouls/disqualifications: 1974-75, 36/0. 1975-76, 52/2. Totals, 266/4.

NBA ALL-STAR GAME RECORD

Season Team	Min.	FGM	FGA	Pct.	FTM	FTA	Pct.	Reb	Ast.	PF	Dq.	Pts.
1965 —San Francisco	10	0	2	.000	0	0	...	3	0	1	0	0
1966 —San Francisco	33	3	16	.188	1	3	.333	16	1	1	0	7
1967 —San Francisco	42	7	16	.438	2	4	.500	18	0	1	0	16
1968 —San Francisco					Selected, did not play—injured.							
1970 —San Francisco					Selected, did not play—injured.							
1973 —Golden State	14	2	5	.400	0	0	...	4	1	2	0	4

Season Team	Min.	FGM	FGA	Pct.	FTM	FTA	Pct.	Off.	Def.	Tot.	Ast.	PF	Dq.	St.	Blk.	TO	Pts.
1974 —Golden State	5	2	4	.500	0	1	.000	1	2	3	0	0	0	0	0	...	4
Totals	104	14	43	.326	3	8	.375	...	...	44	2	5	0	0	0	...	31

ALL-TIME GREAT PLAYERS

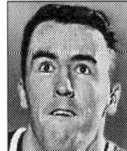

TWYMAN, JACK F/G

PERSONAL: Born May 11, 1934, in Pittsburgh. ... 6-6/210 (1,98/95,3). ... Full name: John Kennedy Twyman.
HIGH SCHOOL: Pittsburgh Central Catholic.
COLLEGE: Cincinnati.
TRANSACTIONS: Selected by Rochester Royals in second round (10th pick overall) of 1955 NBA Draft. ... Royals franchise moved from Rochester to Cincinnati for 1957-58 season.
CAREER HONORS: Elected to Naismith Memorial Basketball Hall of Fame (1983).

COLLEGIATE RECORD

Season Team	G	Min.	FGM	FGA	Pct.	FTM	FTA	Pct.	Reb.	Ast.	Pts.	RPG	APG	PPG
51-52—Cincinnati	16	...	27	83	.325	13	27	.481	55	...	67	3.4	...	4.2
52-53—Cincinnati	24	716	136	323	.421	89	143	.622	362	...	361	15.1	...	15.0
53-54—Cincinnati	21	777	174	443	.393	110	145	.759	347	...	458	16.5	...	21.8
54-55—Cincinnati	29	1097	285	628	.454	142	192	.740	478	...	712	16.5	...	24.6
Totals	90	...	622	1477	.421	354	507	.698	1242	...	1598	13.8	...	17.8

NBA REGULAR-SEASON RECORD

HONORS: All-NBA second team (1960, 1962).

Season Team	G	Min.	FGM	FGA	Pct.	FTM	FTA	Pct.	Reb.	Ast.	PF	Dq.	Pts.	RPG	APG	PPG
55-56—Rochester	72	2186	417	987	.423	204	298	.685	466	171	239	4	1038	6.5	2.4	14.4
56-57—Rochester	72	2338	449	1023	.439	276	363	.760	354	123	251	4	1174	4.9	1.7	16.3
57-58—Cincinnati	72	2178	465	1028	*.452	307	396	.775	464	110	224	3	1237	6.4	1.5	17.2
58-59—Cincinnati	72	2713	710	*1691	.420	437	558	.783	653	209	277	6	1857	9.1	2.9	25.8
59-60—Cincinnati	75	3023	870	2063	.422	*598	762	.785	664	260	275	10	2338	8.9	3.5	31.2
60-61—Cincinnati	79	2920	796	1632	.488	405	554	.731	672	225	279	5	1997	8.5	2.8	25.3
61-62—Cincinnati	80	2991	739	1542	.479	353	435	.812	638	215	323	5	1831	8.0	2.7	22.9
62-63—Cincinnati	80	2623	641	1335	.480	304	375	.811	598	214	286	7	1586	7.5	2.7	19.8
63-64—Cincinnati	68	1996	447	993	.450	189	228	.829	364	137	267	7	1083	5.4	2.0	15.9
64-65—Cincinnati	80	2236	479	1081	.443	198	239	.828	383	137	239	4	1156	4.8	1.7	14.5
65-66—Cincinnati	73	943	224	498	.450	95	117	.812	168	60	122	1	543	2.3	0.8	7.4
Totals	823	26147	6237	13873	.450	3366	4325	.778	5424	1861	2782	56	15840	6.6	2.3	19.2

NBA PLAYOFF RECORD

Season Team	G	Min.	FGM	FGA	Pct.	FTM	FTA	Pct.	Reb.	Ast.	PF	Dq.	Pts.	RPG	APG	PPG
57-58—Cincinnati	2	74	15	45	.333	7	12	.583	22	1	6	0	37	11.0	0.5	18.5
61-62—Cincinnati	4	149	34	78	.436	8	8	1.000	29	12	18	0	76	7.3	3.0	19.0
62-63—Cincinnati	12	410	92	205	.449	65	77	.844	98	30	47	1	249	8.2	2.5	20.8
63-64—Cincinnati	10	354	83	176	.472	29	49	.592	87	16	41	1	205	8.7	1.6	20.5
64-65—Cincinnati	4	97	19	48	.396	11	11	1.000	17	3	16	0	49	4.3	0.8	12.3
65-66—Cincinnati	2	11	2	4	.500	1	2	.500	2	0	3	0	5	1.0	0.0	2.5
Totals	34	1095	245	556	.441	121	159	.761	255	62	131	2	621	7.5	1.8	18.3

NBA ALL-STAR GAME RECORD

Season Team	Min.	FGM	FGA	Pct.	FTM	FTA	Pct.	Reb	Ast.	PF	Dq.	Pts.
1957—Rochester	17	1	8	.125	1	3	.333	0	1	1	0	3
1958—Cincinnati	25	8	13	.615	2	2	1.000	3	0	3	0	18
1959—Cincinnati	23	8	12	.667	2	4	.500	8	3	4	0	18
1960—Cincinnati	28	11	17	.647	5	8	.625	5	1	4	0	27
1962—Cincinnati	8	4	6	.667	3	3	1.000	1	2	0	0	11
1963—Cincinnati	16	6	12	.500	0	0	...	4	1	2	0	12
Totals	117	38	68	.559	13	20	.650	21	8	14	0	89

UNSELD, WES C/F

PERSONAL: Born March 14, 1946, in Louisville, Ky. ... 6-7/245 (2,00/111,1). ... Full name: Westley Sissel Unseld.
HIGH SCHOOL: Seneca (Louisville, Ky.).
COLLEGE: Louisville.
TRANSACTIONS: Selected by Baltimore Bullets in first round (second pick overall) of 1968 NBA Draft. ... Bullets franchise moved from Baltimore to Washington and renamed Capital Bullets for 1973-74 season. ... Bullets franchise renamed Washington Bullets for 1974-75 season.
CAREER HONORS: Elected to Naismith Memorial Basketball Hall of Fame (1988). ... One of the 50 Greatest Players in NBA History (1996).
MISCELLANEOUS: Member of NBA championship team (1978). ... Washington Wizards franchise all-time leading rebounder with 13,769 and all-time assists leader with 3,822 (1968-69 through 1980-81).
CAREER NOTES: Vice president, Washington Bullets (1981-82 to 1995-96). ... Executive vice president/general manager, Washington Bullets (1996-97 season to present). ... Bullets franchise renamed Washington Wizards for 1997-98 season.

COLLEGIATE RECORD

NOTES: THE SPORTING NEWS All-America second team (1967, 1968).

Season Team	G	Min.	FGM	FGA	Pct.	FTM	FTA	Pct.	Reb.	Ast.	Pts.	RPG	APG	PPG
64-65—Louisville‡	14	...	214	312	.686	73	124	.589	331	...	501	23.6	...	35.8
65-66—Louisville	26	...	195	374	.521	128	202	.634	505	...	518	19.4	...	19.9
66-67—Louisville	28	...	201	374	.537	121	177	.684	533	...	523	19.0	...	18.7
67-68—Louisville	28	...	234	382	.613	177	275	.644	513	...	645	18.3	...	23.0
Varsity totals	82	...	630	1130	.558	426	654	.651	1551	...	1686	18.9	...	20.6

NBA REGULAR-SEASON RECORD

HONORS: NBA Most Valuable Player (1969). ... NBA Rookie of the Year (1969). ... All-NBA first team (1969). ... NBA All-Rookie team (1969). ... J. Walter Kennedy Citizenship Award (1975).
NOTES: Led NBA with .561 field goal percentage (1976).

														AVERAGES		
Season Team	G	Min.	FGM	FGA	Pct.	FTM	FTA	Pct.	Reb.	Ast.	PF	Dq.	Pts.	RPG	APG	PPG
68-69—Baltimore	82	2970	427	897	.476	277	458	.605	1491	213	276	4	1131	18.2	2.6	13.8
69-70—Baltimore	82	3234	526	1015	.518	273	428	.638	1370	291	250	2	1325	16.7	3.5	16.2
70-71—Baltimore	74	2904	424	846	.501	199	303	.657	1253	293	235	2	1047	16.9	4.0	14.1
71-72—Baltimore	76	3171	409	822	.498	171	272	.629	1336	278	218	1	989	17.6	3.7	13.0
72-73—Baltimore	79	3085	421	854	.493	149	212	.703	1260	347	168	0	991	15.9	4.4	12.5

									REBOUNDS						AVERAGES		
Season Team	G	Min.	FGM	FGA	Pct.	FTM	FTA	Pct.	Off.	Def.	Tot.	Ast.	St.	Blk.	TO	Pts.	RPG	APG	PPG
73-74—Capital	56	1727	146	333	.438	36	55	.655	152	365	517	159	56	16	...	328	9.2	2.8	5.9
74-75—Washington	73	2904	273	544	.502	126	184	.685	318	759	1077	297	115	68	...	672	*14.8	4.1	9.2
75-76—Washington	78	2922	318	567	*.561	114	195	.585	271	765	1036	404	84	59	...	750	13.3	5.2	9.6
76-77—Washington	82	2860	270	551	.490	100	166	.602	243	634	877	363	87	45	...	640	10.7	4.4	7.8
77-78—Washington	80	2644	257	491	.523	93	173	.538	286	669	955	326	98	45	173	607	11.9	4.1	7.6
78-79—Washington	77	2406	346	600	.577	151	235	.643	274	556	830	315	71	37	156	843	10.8	4.1	10.9
79-80—Washington	82	2973	327	637	.513	139	209	.665	334	760	1094	366	65	61	153	794	13.3	4.5	9.7
80-81—Washington	63	2032	225	429	.524	55	86	.640	207	466	673	170	52	36	97	507	10.7	2.7	8.0
Totals	984	35832	4369	8586	.509	1883	2976	.633	...	...	13769	3822	628	367	579	10624	14.0	3.9	10.8

Three-point field goals: 1979-80, 1-for-2 (.500). 1980-81, 2-for-4 (.500). Totals, 3-for-6 (.500).
Personal fouls/disqualifications: 1973-74, 121/1. 1974-75, 180/1. 1975-76, 203/3. 1976-77, 253/5. 1977-78, 234/2. 1978-79, 204/2. 1979-80, 249/5. 1980-81, 171/1. Totals, 2762/29.

NBA PLAYOFF RECORD

NOTES: NBA Finals Most Valuable Player (1978).

														AVERAGES		
Season Team	G	Min.	FGM	FGA	Pct.	FTM	FTA	Pct.	Reb.	Ast.	PF	Dq.	Pts.	RPG	APG	PPG
68-69—Baltimore	4	165	30	57	.526	15	19	.789	74	5	14	0	75	18.5	1.3	18.8
69-70—Baltimore	7	289	29	70	.414	15	19	.789	165	24	25	1	73	23.6	3.4	10.4
70-71—Baltimore	18	759	96	208	.462	46	81	.568	339	69	60	0	238	18.8	3.8	13.2
71-72—Baltimore	6	266	32	65	.492	10	19	.526	75	25	22	0	74	12.5	4.2	12.3
72-73—Baltimore	5	201	20	48	.417	9	19	.474	76	17	12	0	49	15.2	3.4	9.8

									REBOUNDS						AVERAGES		
Season Team	G	Min.	FGM	FGA	Pct.	FTM	FTA	Pct.	Off.	Def.	Tot.	Ast.	St.	Blk.	TO	Pts.	RPG	APG	PPG
73-74—Capital	7	297	31	63	.492	9	15	.600	22	63	85	27	4	1	...	71	12.1	3.9	10.1
74-75—Washington	17	734	71	130	.546	40	61	.656	65	211	276	64	15	20	...	182	16.2	3.8	10.7
75-76—Washington	7	310	18	39	.462	13	24	.542	26	59	85	28	6	4	...	49	12.1	4.0	7.0
76-77—Washington	9	368	30	54	.556	7	12	.583	24	81	105	44	8	6	...	67	11.7	4.9	7.4
77-78—Washington	18	677	71	134	.530	27	46	.587	72	144	216	79	17	7	36	169	12.0	4.4	9.4
78-79—Washington	19	736	78	158	.494	39	64	.609	90	163	253	64	17	14	30	195	13.3	3.4	10.3
79-80—Washington	2	87	7	14	.500	4	6	.667	7	21	28	7	0	3	3	18	14.0	3.5	9.0
Totals	119	4889	513	1040	.493	234	385	.608	...	...	1777	453	67	55	69	1260	14.9	3.8	10.6

Three-point field goals: 1979-80, 0-for-1.
Personal fouls/disqualifications: 1973-74, 15/0. 1974-75, 39/0. 1975-76, 19/0. 1976-77, 32/0. 1977-78, 62/2. 1978-79, 66/2. 1979-80, 5/0. Totals, 371/5.

NBA ALL-STAR GAME RECORD

Season Team	Min.	FGM	FGA	Pct.	FTM	FTA	Pct.	Reb	Ast.	PF	Dq.	Pts.
1969 —Baltimore	14	5	7	.714	1	3	.333	8	1	3	0	11
1971 —Baltimore	21	4	9	.444	0	0	...	10	2	2	0	8
1972 —Baltimore	16	1	5	.200	0	0	...	7	1	3	0	2
1973 —Baltimore	11	2	4	.500	0	0	...	5	1	0	0	4

							REBOUNDS							
Season Team	Min.	FGM	FGA	Pct.	FTM	FTA	Pct.	Off.	Def.	Tot.	Ast.	PF	Dq.	St.	Blk.	TO	Pts.
1975 —Washington	15	2	3	.667	2	2	1.000	2	4	6	1	2	0	2	0	...	6
Totals	77	14	28	.500	3	5	.600	...	...	36	6	10	0	2	0	...	31

NBA COACHING RECORD

BACKGROUND: Assistant coach, Bullets (1987-January 3, 1988).

	REGULAR SEASON				PLAYOFFS		
Season Team	W	L	Pct.	Finish	W	L	Pct.
87-88 —Washington	30	25	.545	T2nd/Atlantic Division	2	3	.400
88-89 —Washington	40	42	.488	4th/Atlantic Division	—	—	—
89-90 —Washington	31	51	.378	4th/Atlantic Division	—	—	—
90-91 —Washington	30	52	.366	4th/Atlantic Division	—	—	—
91-92 —Washington	25	57	.305	6th/Atlantic Division	—	—	—
92-93 —Washington	22	60	.268	7th/Atlantic Division	—	—	—
93-94 —Washington	24	58	.293	7th/Atlantic Division	—	—	—
Totals (7 years)	202	345	.369		Totals (1 year) 2	3	.400

NOTES:
1988—Replaced Kevin Loughery as Washington head coach (January 3), with record of 8-19. Lost to Detroit in Eastern Conference First Round.

WALKER, CHET   F/G

PERSONAL: Born February 22, 1940, in Benton Harbor, Mich. ... 6-7/220 (2,00/99,8). ... Full name: Chester Walker. ... Nickname: The Jet.
HIGH SCHOOL: Benton Harbor (Mich.).
COLLEGE: Bradley.
TRANSACTIONS: Selected by Syracuse Nationals in second round (14th pick overall) of 1962 NBA Draft. ... Nationals franchise moved from Syracuse to Philadelphia and renamed 76ers for 1963-64 season. ... Traded by 76ers with F Shaler Halimon to Chicago Bulls for F Jim Washington and player to be named later (September 2, 1969).
MISCELLANEOUS: Member of NBA championship team (1967).

COLLEGIATE RECORD

NOTES: THE SPORTING NEWS All-America first team (1962). ... THE SPORTING NEWS All-America second team (1961).

													AVERAGES		
Season Team	G	Min.	FGM	FGA	Pct.	FTM	FTA	Pct.	Reb.	Ast.		Pts.	RPG	APG	PPG
58-59—Bradley‡	15	...	146	264	.553	56	93	.602	246	...		348	16.4	...	23.2
59-60—Bradley	29	...	244	436	.560	144	234	.615	388	...		632	13.4	...	21.8
60-61—Bradley	26	...	238	423	.563	180	250	.720	327	...		656	12.6	...	25.2
61-62—Bradley	26	...	268	500	.536	151	236	.640	321	...		687	12.3	...	26.4
Varsity totals	81	...	750	1359	.552	475	720	.660	1036	...		1975	12.8	...	24.4

NBA REGULAR-SEASON RECORD

HONORS: NBA All-Rookie team (1963).

														AVERAGES		
Season Team	G	Min.	FGM	FGA	Pct.	FTM	FTA	Pct.	Reb.	Ast.	PF	Dq.	Pts.	RPG	APG	PPG
62-63—Syracuse	78	1992	352	751	.469	253	362	.699	561	83	220	3	957	7.2	1.1	12.3
63-64—Philadelphia	76	2775	492	1118	.440	330	464	.711	784	124	232	3	1314	10.3	1.6	17.3
64-65—Philadelphia	79	2187	377	936	.403	288	388	.742	528	132	200	2	1042	6.7	1.7	13.2
65-66—Philadelphia	80	2603	443	982	.451	335	468	.716	636	201	238	3	1221	8.0	2.5	15.3
66-67—Philadelphia	81	2691	561	1150	.488	445	581	.766	660	188	232	4	1567	8.1	2.3	19.3
67-68—Philadelphia	82	2623	539	1172	.460	387	533	.726	607	157	252	3	1465	7.4	1.9	17.9
68-69—Philadelphia	82	2753	554	1145	.484	369	459	.804	640	144	244	0	1477	7.8	1.8	18.0
69-70—Chicago	78	2726	596	1249	.477	483	568	.850	604	192	203	1	1675	7.7	2.5	21.5
70-71—Chicago	81	2927	650	1398	.465	480	559	*.859	588	179	187	2	1780	7.3	2.2	22.0
71-72—Chicago	78	2588	619	1225	.505	481	568	.847	473	178	171	0	1719	6.1	2.3	22.0
72-73—Chicago	79	2455	597	1248	.478	376	452	.832	395	179	166	1	1570	5.0	2.3	19.9

									REBOUNDS							AVERAGES		
Season Team	G	Min.	FGM	FGA	Pct.	FTM	FTA	Pct.	Off.	Def.	Tot.	Ast.	St.	Blk.	TO	Pts.	RPG	APG	PPG
73-74—Chicago	82	2661	572	1178	.486	439	502	.875	131	275	406	200	68	4	...	1583	5.0	2.4	19.3
74-75—Chicago	76	2452	524	1076	.487	413	480	.860	114	318	432	169	49	6	...	1461	5.7	2.2	19.2
Totals	1032	33433	6876	14628	.470	5079	6384	.796	...	...	7314	2126	117	10	...	18831	7.1	2.1	18.2

Personal fouls/disqualifications: 1973-74, 201/1. 1974-75, 181/0. Totals, 2727/23.

NBA PLAYOFF RECORD

														AVERAGES		
Season Team	G	Min.	FGM	FGA	Pct.	FTM	FTA	Pct.	Reb.	Ast.	PF	Dq.	Pts.	RPG	APG	PPG
62-63—Syracuse	5	130	27	53	.509	22	30	.733	47	9	8	0	76	9.4	1.8	15.2
63-64—Philadelphia	5	190	30	77	.390	34	46	.739	52	13	15	0	94	10.4	2.6	18.8
64-65—Philadelphia	11	469	83	173	.480	57	75	.760	79	18	38	0	223	7.2	1.6	20.3
65-66—Philadelphia	5	181	24	64	.375	25	31	.806	37	15	18	0	73	7.4	3.0	14.6
66-67—Philadelphia	15	551	115	246	.467	96	119	.807	114	32	44	0	326	7.6	2.1	21.7
67-68—Philadelphia	13	485	86	210	.410	76	112	.679	96	24	44	1	248	7.4	1.8	19.1
68-69—Philadelphia	4	109	23	43	.535	8	12	.667	23	8	5	0	54	5.8	2.0	13.5
69-70—Chicago	5	178	35	83	.422	27	33	.818	42	11	14	0	97	8.4	2.2	19.4
70-71—Chicago	7	234	44	100	.440	17	24	.708	50	22	20	0	105	7.1	3.1	15.0
71-72—Chicago	4	97	16	38	.421	13	16	.813	14	4	7	0	45	3.5	1.0	11.3
72-73—Chicago	7	229	42	121	.347	33	37	.892	62	14	15	0	117	8.9	2.0	16.7

									REBOUNDS							AVERAGES		
Season Team	G	Min.	FGM	FGA	Pct.	FTM	FTA	Pct.	Off.	Def.	Tot.	Ast.	St.	Blk.	TO	Pts.	RPG	APG	PPG
73-74—Chicago	11	403	81	159	.509	68	79	.861	26	35	61	18	10	1	...	230	5.5	1.6	20.9
74-75—Chicago	13	432	81	164	.494	66	75	.880	10	50	60	24	13	1	...	228	4.6	1.8	17.5
Totals	105	3688	687	1531	.449	542	689	.787	...	...	737	212	23	2	...	1916	7.0	2.0	18.2

Personal fouls/disqualifications: 1973-74, 26/0. 1974-75, 32/2. Totals, 286/3.

NBA ALL-STAR GAME RECORD

Season Team	Min.	FGM	FGA	Pct.	FTM	FTA	Pct.	Reb	Ast.	PF	Dq.	Pts.
1964 —Philadelphia	12	2	5	.400	0	0	...	0	0	1	0	4
1966 —Philadelphia	25	3	10	.300	2	3	.667	6	4	2	0	8
1967 —Philadelphia	22	6	9	.667	3	4	.750	4	1	2	0	15
1970 —Chicago	17	1	3	.333	2	2	1.000	2	1	2	0	4
1971 —Chicago	19	3	9	.333	4	5	.800	3	1	1	0	10
1973 —Chicago	16	1	5	.200	2	2	1.000	1	0	2	0	4

								REBOUNDS								
Season Team	Min.	FGM	FGA	Pct.	FTM	FTA	Pct.	Off.	Def.	Tot.	Ast.	PF	Dq.	St.	Blk.	TO	Pts.
1974 —Chicago	14	4	5	.800	4	4	1.000	0	2	2	1	1	0	0	0	...	12
Totals	125	20	46	.435	17	20	.850	...	...	18	8	11	0	0	0	...	57

WALTON, BILL   C

PERSONAL: Born November 5, 1952, in La Mesa, Calif. ... 6-11/235 (2,10/106,6). ... Full name: William Theodore Walton III. ... Brother of Bruce Walton, offensive lineman with Dallas Cowboys (1973-75).

HIGH SCHOOL: Helix (La Mesa, Calif.).

COLLEGE: UCLA.

TRANSACTIONS: Selected by Portland Trail Blazers in first round (first pick overall) of 1974 NBA Draft. ... Signed as veteran free agent by San Diego Clippers (May 13, 1979); Trail Blazers received C Kevin Kunnert, F Kermit Washington, 1980 first-round draft choice and cash as compensation (September 18, 1979). ... Clippers franchise moved from San Diego to Los Angeles for 1984-85 season. ... Traded by Clippers to Boston Celtics for F Cedric Maxwell, 1986 first-round draft choice and cash (September 6, 1985).

CAREER HONORS: Elected to Naismith Memorial Basketball Hall of Fame (1993). ... One of the 50 Greatest Players in NBA History (1996).
MISCELLANEOUS: Member of NBA championship team (1977, 1986).
CAREER NOTES: Broadcaster, NBC Sports (1992-present).

COLLEGIATE RECORD

NOTES: THE SPORTING NEWS College Player of the Year (1972, 1973, 1974). ... Naismith Award winner (1972, 1973, 1974). ... THE SPORTING NEWS All-America first team (1972, 1973, 1974). ... NCAA Division I Tournament Most Outstanding Player (1972, 1973). ... Member of NCAA Division I championship team (1972, 1973). ... Holds NCAA tournament career record for highest field goal percentage (minimum of 60 made)—68.6 percent, 109-of-159 (1972 through 1974). ... Holds NCAA tournament single-season record for highest field goal percentage (minimum of 40 made)—76.3 percent, 45-of-59 (1973).

Season Team	G	Min.	FGM	FGA	Pct.	FTM	FTA	Pct.	Reb.	Ast.	Pts.	RPG	APG	PPG
70-71—UCLA‡	20	...	155	266	.583	52	82	.634	321	74	362	16.1	3.7	18.1
71-72—UCLA	30	...	238	372	.640	157	223	.704	466	...	633	15.5	...	21.1
72-73—UCLA	30	...	277	426	.650	58	102	.569	506	168	612	16.9	5.6	20.4
73-74—UCLA	27	...	232	349	.665	58	100	.580	398	148	522	14.7	5.5	19.3
Varsity totals	87	...	747	1147	.651	273	425	.642	1370	...	1767	15.7	...	20.3

AVERAGES: RPG, APG, PPG columns.

NBA REGULAR-SEASON RECORD

HONORS: NBA Most Valuable Player (1978). ... NBA Sixth Man Award (1986). ... All-NBA first team (1978). ... All-NBA second team (1977). ... NBA All-Defensive first team (1977, 1978).
NOTES: Led NBA with 3.25 blocked shots per game (1977).

Season Team	G	Min.	FGM	FGA	Pct.	FTM	FTA	Pct.	Off.	Def.	Tot.	Ast.	St.	Blk.	TO	Pts.	RPG	APG	PPG
74-75—Portland	35	1153	177	345	.513	94	137	.686	92	349	441	167	29	94	...	448	12.6	4.8	12.8
75-76—Portland	51	1687	345	732	.471	133	228	.583	132	549	681	220	49	82	...	823	13.4	4.3	16.1
76-77—Portland	65	2264	491	930	.528	228	327	.697	211	723	934	245	66	211	...	1210	*14.4	3.8	18.6
77-78—Portland	58	1929	460	882	.522	177	246	.720	118	648	766	291	60	146	206	1097	13.2	5.0	18.9
78-79—Portland								Did not play—injured.											
79-80—San Diego	14	337	81	161	.503	32	54	.593	28	98	126	34	8	38	37	194	9.0	2.4	13.9
80-81—San Diego								Did not play—injured.											
81-82—San Diego								Did not play—injured.											
82-83—San Diego	33	1099	200	379	.528	65	117	.556	75	248	323	120	34	119	105	465	9.8	3.6	14.1
83-84—San Diego	55	1476	288	518	.556	92	154	.597	132	345	477	183	45	88	177	668	8.7	3.3	12.1
84-85—L.A. Clippers	67	1647	269	516	.521	138	203	.680	168	432	600	156	50	140	174	676	9.0	2.3	10.1
85-86—Boston	80	1546	231	411	.562	144	202	.713	136	408	544	165	38	106	151	606	6.8	2.1	7.6
86-87—Boston	10	112	10	26	.385	8	15	.533	11	20	31	9	1	10	15	28	3.1	0.9	2.8
87-88—Boston								Did not play—injured.											
Totals	468	13250	2552	4900	.521	1111	1683	.660	1103	3820	4923	1590	380	1034	865	6215	10.5	3.4	13.3

REBOUNDS: Off., Def., Tot. columns. AVERAGES: RPG, APG, PPG columns.

Three-point field goals: 1983-84, 0-for-2. 1984-85, 0-for-2. Totals, 0-for-4.
Personal fouls/disqualifications: 1974-75, 115/4. 1975-76, 144/3. 1976-77, 174/5. 1977-78, 145/3. 1979-80, 37/0. 1982-83, 113/0. 1983-84, 153/1. 1984-85, 184/0. 1985-86, 210/1. 1986-87, 23/0. Totals, 1298/17.

NBA PLAYOFF RECORD

NOTES: NBA Finals Most Valuable Player (1977). ... Holds NBA Finals single-game record for most defensive rebounds—20 (June 3, 1977, vs. Philadelphia; and June 5, 1977, vs. Philadelphia). ... Shares NBA Finals single-game record for most blocked shots—8 (June 5, 1977, vs. Philadelphia). ... Shares single-game NBA playoff record for most defensive rebounds—20 (June 3, 1977, vs. Philadelphia; and June 5, 1977, vs. Philadelphia).

Season Team	G	Min.	FGM	FGA	Pct.	FTM	FTA	Pct.	Off.	Def.	Tot.	Ast.	St.	Blk.	TO	Pts.	RPG	APG	PPG
76-77—Portland	19	755	153	302	.507	39	57	.684	56	232	288	104	20	64	...	345	15.2	5.5	18.2
77-78—Portland	2	49	11	18	.611	5	7	.714	5	17	22	4	3	3	6	27	11.0	2.0	13.5
85-86—Boston	16	291	54	93	.581	19	23	.826	25	78	103	27	6	12	22	127	6.4	1.7	7.9
86-87—Boston	12	102	12	25	.480	5	14	.357	9	22	31	10	3	4	8	29	2.6	0.8	2.4
Totals	49	1197	230	438	.525	68	101	.673	95	349	444	145	32	83	36	528	9.1	3.0	10.8

REBOUNDS: Off., Def., Tot. columns. AVERAGES: RPG, APG, PPG columns.

Three-point field goals: 1985-86, 0-for-1.
Personal fouls/disqualifications: 1976-77, 80/3. 1977-78, 1/0. 1985-86, 45/1. 1986-87, 23/0. Totals, 149/4.

NBA ALL-STAR GAME RECORD

Season Team	Min.	FGM	FGA	Pct.	FTM	FTA	Pct.	Off.	Def.	Tot.	Ast.	PF	Dq.	St.	Blk.	TO	Pts.
1977 —Portland						Selected, did not play—injured.											
1978 —Portland	31	6	14	.429	3	3	1.000	2	8	10	2	3	0	3	2	4	15
Totals	31	6	14	.429	3	3	1.000	2	8	10	2	3	0	3	2	4	15

REBOUNDS: Off., Def., Tot. columns.

WEST, JERRY   G

PERSONAL: Born May 28, 1938, in Chelyan, W.Va. ... 6-2/185 (1,88/83,9). ... Full name: Jerry Alan West.
HIGH SCHOOL: East Bank (W.Va.).
COLLEGE: West Virginia.
TRANSACTIONS: Selected by Minneapolis Lakers in first round (second pick overall) of 1960 NBA Draft. ... Lakers franchise moved from Minneapolis to Los Angeles for 1960-61 season.
    CAREER HONORS: Elected to Naismith Memorial Basketball Hall of Fame (1980). ... NBA 35th Anniversary All-Time Team (1980) and One of the 50 Greatest Players in NBA History (1996).
CAREER NOTES: Consultant, Los Angeles Lakers (1979-80 through 1981-82). ... General manager, Lakers (1982-83 through 1993-94). ... Executive vice president, basketball operations, Lakers (1994-95 to 1999-2000).
MISCELLANEOUS: Member of NBA championship team (1972). ... Member of gold-medal-winning U.S. Olympic team (1960). ... Los Angeles Lakers franchise all-time leading scorer with 25,192 points (1960-61 through 1973-74).

COLLEGIATE RECORD

NOTES: THE SPORTING NEWS All-America first team (1959, 1960). ... NCAA Tournament Most Outstanding Player (1959).

Season Team	G	Min.	FGM	FGA	Pct.	FTM	FTA	Pct.	Reb.	Ast.	Pts.	AVERAGES RPG	APG	PPG
56-57—West Virginia‡	17	...	114	...	...	104	...	...	...	...	332	...	...	19.5
57-58—West Virginia	28	799	178	359	.496	142	194	.732	311	41	498	11.1	1.5	17.8
58-59—West Virginia	34	1210	340	656	.518	223	320	.697	419	86	903	12.3	2.5	26.6
59-60—West Virginia	31	1129	325	645	.504	258	337	.766	510	134	908	16.5	4.3	29.3
Varsity totals	93	3138	843	1660	.508	623	851	.732	1240	261	2309	13.3	2.8	24.8

NBA REGULAR-SEASON RECORD

RECORDS: Holds single-season record for most free throws made—840 (1966).
HONORS: All-NBA first team (1962, 1963, 1964, 1965, 1966, 1967, 1970, 1971, 1972, 1973). ... All-NBA second team (1968, 1969). ... NBA All-Defensive first team (1970, 1971, 1972, 1973). ... NBA All-Defensive second team (1969).

Season Team	G	Min.	FGM	FGA	Pct.	FTM	FTA	Pct.	Reb.	Ast.	PF	Dq.	Pts.	AVERAGES RPG	APG	PPG
60-61—Los Angeles	79	2797	529	1264	.419	331	497	.666	611	333	213	1	1389	7.7	4.2	17.6
61-62—Los Angeles	75	3087	799	1795	.445	712	926	.769	591	402	173	4	2310	7.9	5.4	30.8
62-63—Los Angeles	55	2163	559	1213	.461	371	477	.778	384	307	150	1	1489	7.0	5.6	27.1
63-64—Los Angeles	72	2906	740	1529	.484	584	702	.832	443	403	200	2	2064	6.2	5.6	28.7
64-65—Los Angeles	74	3066	822	1655	.497	648	789	.821	447	364	221	2	2292	6.0	4.9	31.0
65-66—Los Angeles	79	3218	818	1731	.473	*840	*977	.860	562	480	243	1	2476	7.1	6.1	31.3
66-67—Los Angeles	66	2670	645	1389	.464	602	686	.878	392	447	160	1	1892	5.9	6.8	28.7
67-68—Los Angeles	51	1919	476	926	.514	391	482	.811	294	310	152	1	1343	5.8	6.1	26.3
68-69—Los Angeles	61	2394	545	1156	.471	490	597	.821	262	423	156	1	1580	4.3	6.9	25.9
69-70—Los Angeles	74	3106	831	1673	.497	*647	*785	.824	338	554	160	3	2309	4.6	7.5	*31.2
70-71—Los Angeles	69	2845	667	1351	.494	525	631	.832	320	655	180	0	1859	4.6	9.5	26.9
71-72—Los Angeles	77	2973	735	1540	.477	515	633	.814	327	747	209	0	1985	4.2	*9.7	25.8
72-73—Los Angeles	69	2460	618	1291	.479	339	421	.805	289	607	138	0	1575	4.2	8.8	22.8

Season Team	G	Min.	FGM	FGA	Pct.	FTM	FTA	Pct.	REBOUNDS Off.	Def.	Tot.	Ast.	St.	Blk.	TO	Pts.	AVERAGES RPG	APG	PPG
73-74—Los Angeles	31	967	232	519	.447	165	198	.833	30	86	116	206	81	23	...	629	3.7	6.6	20.3
Totals	932	36571	9016	19032	.474	7160	8801	.814	...	...	5376	6238	81	23	...	25192	5.8	6.7	27.0

Personal fouls/disqualifications: 1973-74, 80/0.

NBA PLAYOFF RECORD

NOTES: NBA Finals Most Valuable Player (1969). ... Holds single-series playoff record for highest points-per-game average—46.3 (1965).

Season Team	G	Min.	FGM	FGA	Pct.	FTM	FTA	Pct.	Reb.	Ast.	PF	Dq.	Pts.	AVERAGES RPG	APG	PPG
60-61—Los Angeles	12	461	99	202	.490	77	106	.726	104	63	39	0	275	8.7	5.3	22.9
61-62—Los Angeles	13	557	144	310	.465	121	150	.807	88	57	38	0	409	6.8	4.4	31.5
62-63—Los Angeles	13	538	144	286	.504	74	100	.740	106	61	34	0	362	8.2	4.7	27.8
63-64—Los Angeles	5	206	57	115	.496	42	53	.792	36	17	20	0	156	7.2	3.4	31.2
64-65—Los Angeles	11	470	155	351	.442	137	154	.890	63	58	37	0	447	5.7	5.3	40.6
65-66—Los Angeles	14	619	185	357	.518	109	125	.872	88	79	40	0	479	6.3	5.6	34.2
66-67—Los Angeles	1	1	0	0	...	0	0	...	1	0	0	0	0	1.0	0.0	0.0
67-68—Los Angeles	15	622	165	313	.527	132	169	.781	81	82	47	0	462	5.4	5.5	30.8
68-69—Los Angeles	18	757	196	423	.463	164	204	.804	71	135	52	1	556	3.9	7.5	30.9
69-70—Los Angeles	18	830	196	418	.469	170	212	.802	66	151	55	1	562	3.7	8.4	31.2
71-72—Los Angeles	15	608	128	340	.376	88	106	.830	73	134	39	0	344	4.9	8.9	22.9
72-73—Los Angeles	17	638	151	336	.449	99	127	.780	76	132	49	1	401	4.5	7.8	23.6

Season Team	G	Min.	FGM	FGA	Pct.	FTM	FTA	Pct.	REBOUNDS Off.	Def.	Tot.	Ast.	St.	Blk.	TO	Pts.	AVERAGES RPG	APG	PPG
73-74—Los Angeles	1	14	2	9	.222	0	0	...	0	2	2	1	0	0	...	4	2.0	1.0	4.0
Totals	153	6321	1622	3460	.469	1213	1506	.805	...	...	855	970	0	0	...	4457	5.6	6.3	29.1

Personal fouls/disqualifications: 1973-74, 1/0.

NBA ALL-STAR GAME RECORD

NOTES: NBA All-Star Game Most Valuable Player (1972).

Season Team	Min.	FGM	FGA	Pct.	FTM	FTA	Pct.	Reb	Ast.	PF	Dq.	Pts.
1961—Los Angeles‡	25	2	8	.250	5	6	.833	2	4	3	0	9
1962—Los Angeles	31	7	14	.500	4	6	.667	3	1	2	0	18
1963—Los Angeles	32	5	15	.333	3	4	.750	7	5	1	0	13
1964—Los Angeles	42	8	20	.400	1	1	1.000	4	5	3	0	17
1965—Los Angeles	40	8	16	.500	4	6	.667	5	6	2	0	20
1966—Los Angeles	11	1	5	.200	2	2	1.000	1	0	2	0	4
1967—Los Angeles	30	6	11	.545	4	4	1.000	3	6	3	0	16
1968—Los Angeles	32	7	17	.412	3	4	.750	6	6	4	0	17
1969—Los Angeles	Selected, did not play—injured.											
1970—Los Angeles	31	7	12	.583	8	12	.667	5	5	3	0	22
1971—Los Angeles	20	2	4	.500	1	3	.333	1	9	1	0	5
1972—Los Angeles	27	6	9	.667	1	2	.500	6	5	2	0	13
1973—Los Angeles	20	3	6	.500	0	0	...	4	3	2	0	6
1974—Los Angeles	Selected, did not play—injured.											
Totals	341	62	137	.453	36	50	.720	47	55	28	0	160

NBA COACHING RECORD

Season Team	REGULAR SEASON					PLAYOFFS		
	W	L	Pct.	Finish		W	L	Pct.
76-77 —Los Angeles	53	29	.646	1st/Pacific Division		4	7	.364
77-78 —Los Angeles	45	37	.549	4th/Pacific Division		1	2	.333
78-79 —Los Angeles	47	35	.573	3rd/Pacific Division		3	5	.375
Totals (3 years)	145	101	.589	Totals (3 years)		8	14	.364

NOTES:

1977—Defeated Golden State, 4-3, in Western Conference Semifinals; lost to Portland, 4-0, in Western Conference Finals.
1978—Lost to Seattle in Western Conference First Round.
1979—Defeated Denver, 2-1, in Western Conference First Round; lost to Seattle, 4-1, in Western Conference Semifinals.

WESTPHAL, PAUL

PERSONAL: Born November 30, 1950, in Torrance, Calif. ... 6-4/195 (1,93/88,4). ... Full name: Paul Douglas Westphal.
HIGH SCHOOL: Aviation (Redondo Beach, Calif.).
COLLEGE: Southern California.
TRANSACTIONS: Selected by Boston Celtics in first round (10th pick overall) of 1972 NBA Draft. ... Traded by Celtics with 1975 and 1976 second-round draft choices to Phoenix Suns for G Charlie Scott (May 23, 1975). ... Traded by Suns to Seattle SuperSonics for G Dennis Johnson (June 4, 1980). ... Signed as veteran free agent by New York Knicks (March 12, 1982). ... Waived by Knicks (June 20, 1983). ... Signed by Suns (September 27, 1983). ... Waived by Suns (October 12, 1984).
MISCELLANEOUS: Member of NBA championship team (1974).

COLLEGIATE RECORD

NOTES: THE SPORTING NEWS All-America second team (1972).

Season Team	G	Min.	FGM	FGA	Pct.	FTM	FTA	Pct.	Reb.	Ast.	Pts.	AVERAGES		
												RPG	APG	PPG
68-69—Southern Cal‡	19	...	134	262	.511	87	119	.731	106	...	355	5.6	...	18.7
69-70—Southern Cal	26	...	147	277	.531	84	110	.764	68	45	378	2.6	1.7	14.5
70-71—Southern Cal	26	...	157	328	.479	109	150	.727	84	84	423	3.2	3.2	16.3
71-72—Southern Cal	14	...	106	219	.484	72	95	.758	74	71	284	5.3	5.1	20.3
Varsity totals	66	...	410	824	.498	265	355	.746	226	200	1085	3.4	3.0	16.4

NBA REGULAR-SEASON RECORD

HONORS: NBA Comeback Player of the Year (1983). ... All-NBA first team (1977, 1979, 1980). ... All-NBA second team (1978).

Season Team	G	Min.	FGM	FGA	Pct.	FTM	FTA	Pct.	REBOUNDS			Ast.	St.	Blk.	TO	Pts.	AVERAGES		
									Off.	Def.	Tot.						RPG	APG	PPG
72-73—Boston	60	482	89	212	.420	67	86	.779	...	...	67	69	...	...	...	245	1.1	1.2	4.1
73-74—Boston	82	1165	238	475	.501	112	153	.732	49	143	171	39	34	...	...	588	1.7	2.1	7.2
74-75—Boston	82	1581	342	670	.510	119	156	.763	44	119	163	235	78	33	...	803	2.0	2.9	9.8
75-76—Phoenix	82	2960	657	1329	.494	365	440	.830	74	185	259	440	210	38	...	1679	3.2	5.4	20.5
76-77—Phoenix	81	2600	682	1317	.518	362	439	.825	57	138	190	459	134	21	...	1726	2.3	5.7	21.3
77-78—Phoenix	80	2481	809	1568	.516	396	487	.813	41	123	164	437	138	31	280	2014	2.1	5.5	25.2
78-79—Phoenix	81	2641	801	1496	.535	339	405	.837	35	124	159	529	111	26	232	1941	2.0	6.5	24.0
79-80—Phoenix	82	2665	692	1317	.525	382	443	.862	46	141	187	416	119	35	207	1792	2.3	5.1	21.9
80-81—Seattle	36	1078	221	500	.442	153	184	.832	11	57	68	148	46	14	78	601	1.9	4.1	16.7
81-82—New York	18	451	86	194	.443	36	47	.766	9	13	22	100	19	8	47	210	1.2	5.6	11.7
82-83—New York	80	1978	318	693	.459	148	184	.804	19	96	115	439	87	16	196	798	1.4	5.5	10.0
83-84—Phoenix	59	865	144	313	.460	117	142	.824	8	35	43	148	41	6	77	412	0.7	2.5	7.0
Totals	823	20947	5079	10084	.504	2596	3166	.820	...	...	1580	3591	1022	262	1117	12809	1.9	4.4	15.6

Three-point field goals: 1979-80, 26-for-93 (.280). 1980-81, 6-for-25 (.240). 1981-82, 2-for-8 (.250). 1982-83, 14-for-48 (.292). 1983-84, 7-for-26 (.269). Totals, 55-for-200 (.275).
Personal fouls/disqualifications: 1972-73, 88/0. 1973-74, 173/1. 1974-75, 192/0. 1975-76, 218/3. 1976-77, 171/1. 1977-78, 162/0. 1978-79, 159/1. 1979-80, 162/0. 1980-81, 70/0. 1981-82, 61/1. 1982-83, 180/1. 1983-84, 69/0. Totals, 1705/8.

NBA PLAYOFF RECORD

Season Team	G	Min.	FGM	FGA	Pct.	FTM	FTA	Pct.	REBOUNDS			Ast.	St.	Blk.	TO	Pts.	AVERAGES		
									Off.	Def.	Tot.						RPG	APG	PPG
72-73—Boston	11	109	19	39	.487	5	7	.714	...	...	7	9	...	...	...	43	0.6	0.8	3.9
73-74—Boston	18	241	46	100	.460	11	15	.733	6	15	21	31	8	2	...	103	1.2	1.7	5.7
74-75—Boston	11	183	38	81	.469	12	18	.667	5	8	13	32	6	2	...	88	1.2	2.9	8.0
75-76—Phoenix	19	685	165	323	.511	71	93	.763	14	33	47	96	34	9	...	401	2.5	5.1	21.1
77-78—Phoenix	2	66	22	47	.468	8	9	.889	3	3	6	19	1	0	5	52	3.0	9.5	26.0
78-79—Phoenix	15	534	142	287	.495	52	66	.788	7	26	33	64	15	5	38	336	2.2	4.3	22.4
79-80—Phoenix	8	253	69	142	.486	28	32	.875	2	8	10	31	11	3	15	167	1.3	3.9	20.9
82-83—New York	6	156	22	50	.440	10	13	.769	0	8	8	34	2	2	9	57	1.3	5.7	9.5
83-84—Phoenix	17	222	30	80	.375	28	32	.875	3	5	8	37	12	0	24	90	0.5	2.2	5.3
Totals	107	2449	553	1149	.481	225	285	.789	...	...	153	353	89	23	89	1337	1.4	3.3	12.5

Three-point field goals: 1979-80, 1-for-12 (.083). 1982-83, 3-for-8 (.375). 1983-84, 2-for-9 (.222). Totals, 6-for-29 (.207).
Personal fouls/disqualifications: 1972-73, 24/1. 1973-74, 37/0. 1974-75, 21/0. 1975-76, 61/1. 1977-78, 4/0. 1978-79, 38/0. 1979-80, 20/0. 1982-83, 13/0. 1983-84, 23/0. Totals, 241/2.

NBA ALL-STAR GAME RECORD

Season Team	Min.	FGM	FGA	Pct.	FTM	FTA	Pct.	REBOUNDS			Ast.	PF	Dq.	St.	Blk.	TO	Pts.
								Off.	Def.	Tot.							
1977 —Phoenix	31	10	16	.625	0	0	...	0	1	1	6	2	0	3	2	...	20
1978 —Phoenix	24	9	14	.643	2	5	.400	0	0	0	5	4	0	1	1	3	20
1979 —Phoenix	21	8	12	.667	1	2	.500	0	1	1	5	0	0	0	0	1	17
1980 —Phoenix	27	8	14	.571	5	6	.833	1	0	1	5	5	0	2	1	3	21
1981 —Seattle	25	8	12	.667	3	3	1.000	2	2	4	3	3	0	0	1	4	19
Totals	128	43	68	.632	11	16	.688	3	4	7	24	14	0	6	5	11	97

Three-point field goals: 1980, 0-for-2.

ALL-TIME GREAT PLAYERS

HEAD COACHING RECORD

BACKGROUND: Assistant coach, Phoenix Suns (1988-89 through 1991-92).

COLLEGIATE COACHING RECORD

Season Team		REGULAR SEASON		
	W	L	Pct.	Finish
85-86 —S'western Baptist Bible Coll.	21	9	.700	
86-87 —Grand Canyon College (Ariz.)	26	12	.684	NAIA Independent
87-88 —Grand Canyon College (Ariz.)	37	6	.860	NAIA Independent
Totals (3 years)	84	27	.757	

NBA COACHING RECORD

Season Team	REGULAR SEASON				PLAYOFFS		
	W	L	Pct.	Finish	W	L	Pct.
92-93 —Phoenix	62	20	.756	1st/Pacific Division	13	11	.542
93-94 —Phoenix	56	26	.683	2nd/Pacific Division	6	4	.600
94-95 —Phoenix	59	23	.720	1st/Pacific Division	6	4	.600
95-96 —Phoenix	14	19	.424		—	—	—
98-99 —Seattle	25	25	.500	5th/Pacific Division	—	—	—
99-00 —Seattle	45	37	.549	4th/Pacific Division	2	3	.400
00-01 —Seattle	6	9	.400		—	—	—
Totals (7 years)	273	168	.619	**Totals (4 years)**	27	22	.551

NOTES:

1987—Defeated Fort Lewis College (Colo.), 94-87, in NAIA District 7 first round; lost to Western State College (Colo.), 74-69, in NAIA District 7 championship.

1988—Defeated Southern Colorado, 68-62, in NAIA District 7 first round; defeated Colorado School of Mines, 113-79, in District 7 championship; defeated Hastings College (Neb.), 103-75, in NAIA Tournament first round; defeated Fort Hays State (Kan.), 101-95, in second round; defeated College of Idaho, 99-96 (OT), in third round; defeated Waynesburg State (Pa.), 108-106, in fourth round; defeated Auburn-Montgomery (Ala.), 88-86 (OT), in NAIA championship game.

1993—Defeated Los Angeles Lakers, 3-2, in Western Conference first round; defeated San Antonio, 4-2, in Western Conference semifinals; defeated Seattle, 4-3, in Western Conference finals; lost to Chicago, 4-2, in NBA Finals.

1994—Defeated Golden State, 3-0, in Western Conference first round; lost to Houston, 4-3, in Western Conference semifinals.

1995—Defeated Portland, 3-0, in Western Conference first round; lost to Houston, 4-3, in Western Conference semifinals.

1996—Replaced as Phoenix head coach by Cotton Fitzsimmons (January 16), with club in fifth place.

2000—Lost to Utah in Western Conference first round. Replaced as Seattle head coach by Nate McMillan (November 27) with club in fifth place.

WHITE, JO JO   G

PERSONAL: Born November 16, 1946, in St. Louis. ... 6-3/190 (1,90/86,2). ... Full name: Joseph Henry White.
HIGH SCHOOL: Vashon (St. Louis), then McKinley (St. Louis).
COLLEGE: Kansas.
TRANSACTIONS: Selected by Boston Celtics in first round (ninth pick overall) of 1969 NBA Draft. ... Traded by Celtics to Golden State Warriors for 1979 first-round draft choice (January 30, 1979). ... Contract sold by Warriors to Kansas City Kings (September 10, 1980). ... Played in Continental Basketball Association with Topeka Sizzlers (1987-88).
CAREER NOTES: Director of special projects, Boston Celtics (2000-present).
MISCELLANEOUS: Member of NBA championship team (1974, 1976). ... Member of gold-medal-winning U.S. Olympic team (1968).

COLLEGIATE RECORD

NOTES: The Sporting News All-America first team (1968, 1969).

Season Team	G	Min.	FGM	FGA	Pct.	FTM	FTA	Pct.	Reb.	Ast.	Pts.	AVERAGES		
												RPG	APG	PPG
64-65—Kansas‡	2	...	11	34	.324	11	15	.733	25	...	33	12.5	...	16.5
65-66—Kansas‡	6	...	35	88	.398	18	27	.667	32	...	88	5.3	...	14.7
65-66—Kansas	9	...	44	112	.393	14	26	.538	68	...	102	7.6	...	11.3
66-67—Kansas	27	...	170	416	.409	59	72	.819	150	...	399	5.6	...	14.8
67-68—Kansas	30	...	188	462	.407	83	115	.722	150	...	459	3.6	...	15.3
68-69—Kansas	18	...	134	286	.469	58	79	.734	84	...	326	4.7	...	18.1
Varsity totals	84	...	536	1276	.420	214	292	.733	409	...	1286	4.9	...	15.3

NBA REGULAR-SEASON RECORD

HONORS: All-NBA second team (1975, 1977). ... NBA All-Rookie team (1970).

Season Team	G	Min.	FGM	FGA	Pct.	FTM	FTA	Pct.	Reb.	Ast.	PF	Dq.	Pts.	AVERAGES		
														RPG	APG	PPG
69-70—Boston	60	1328	309	684	.452	111	135	.822	169	145	132	1	729	2.8	2.4	12.2
70-71—Boston	75	2787	693	1494	.464	215	269	.799	376	361	255	5	1601	5.0	4.8	21.3
71-72—Boston	79	3261	770	1788	.431	285	343	.831	446	416	227	1	1825	5.6	5.3	23.1
72-73—Boston	82	3250	717	1665	.431	178	228	.781	414	498	185	2	1612	5.0	6.1	19.7

Season Team	G	Min.	FGM	FGA	Pct.	FTM	FTA	Pct.	REBOUNDS			Ast.	St.	Blk.	TO	Pts.	AVERAGES		
									Off.	Def.	Tot.						RPG	APG	PPG
73-74—Boston	82	3238	649	1445	.449	190	227	.837	100	251	351	448	105	25	...	1488	4.3	5.5	18.1
74-75—Boston	82	3220	658	1440	.457	186	223	.834	84	227	311	458	128	17	...	1502	3.8	5.6	18.3
75-76—Boston	82	3257	670	1492	.449	212	253	.838	61	252	313	445	107	20	...	1552	3.8	5.4	18.9
76-77—Boston	82	3333	638	1488	.429	333	383	.869	87	296	383	492	118	22	...	1609	4.7	6.0	19.6
77-78—Boston	46	1641	289	690	.419	103	120	.858	53	127	180	209	49	7	117	681	3.9	4.5	14.8
78-79—Boston-G.S.	76	2338	404	910	.444	139	158	.880	42	158	200	347	80	7	212	947	2.6	4.6	12.5
79-80—Golden State	78	2052	336	706	.476	97	114	.851	42	139	181	239	88	13	157	770	2.3	3.1	9.9
80-81—Kansas City	13	236	36	82	.439	11	18	.611	3	18	21	37	11	1	18	83	1.6	2.8	6.4
Totals	837	29941	6169	13884	.444	2060	2471	.834	...	...	3345	4095	686	112	504	14399	4.0	4.9	17.2

Three-point field goals: 1979-80, 1-for-6 (.167).
Personal fouls/disqualifications: 1973-74, 185/1. 1974-75, 207/1. 1975-76, 183/2. 1976-77, 193/5. 1977-78, 109/2. 1978-79, 173/1. 1979-80, 186/0. 1980-81, 21/0. Totals, 2056/21.

ALL-TIME GREAT PLAYERS

NBA PLAYOFF RECORD

NOTES: NBA Finals Most Valuable Player (1976).

														AVERAGES		
Season Team	G	Min.	FGM	FGA	Pct.	FTM	FTA	Pct.	Reb.	Ast.	PF	Dq.	Pts.	RPG	APG	PPG
71-72—Boston	11	432	109	220	.495	40	48	.833	59	58	31	0	258	5.4	5.3	23.5
72-73—Boston	13	583	135	300	.450	49	54	.907	64	83	44	2	319	4.9	6.4	24.5

									REBOUNDS						AVERAGES		
Season Team	G	Min.	FGM	FGA	Pct.	FTM	FTA	Pct.	Off.	Def.	Tot.	Ast.	St.	Blk.	TO	Pts.	RPG	APG	PPG
73-74—Boston	18	765	132	310	.426	34	46	.739	17	58	75	98	15	2	...	298	4.2	5.4	16.6
74-75—Boston	11	462	100	227	.441	27	33	.818	18	32	50	63	11	4	...	227	4.5	5.7	20.6
75-76—Boston	18	791	165	371	.445	78	95	.821	12	59	71	98	23	1	...	408	3.9	5.4	22.7
76-77—Boston	9	395	91	201	.453	28	33	.848	10	29	39	52	14	0	...	210	4.3	5.8	23.3
Totals	80	3428	732	1629	.449	256	309	.828	...	...	358	452	63	7	...	1720	4.5	5.7	21.5

Personal fouls/disqualifications: 1973-74, 56/1. 1974-75, 32/0. 1975-76, 51/0. 1976-77, 27/0. Totals, 241/3.

NBA ALL-STAR GAME RECORD

Season Team	Min.	FGM	FGA	Pct.	FTM	FTA	Pct.	Reb.	Ast.	PF	Dq.	Pts.
1971 —Boston	22	5	10	.500	0	0	...	9	2	2	0	10
1972 —Boston	18	6	15	.400	0	2	.000	4	3	1	0	12
1973 —Boston	18	3	7	.429	0	0	...	5	5	0	0	6

								REBOUNDS							
Season Team	Min.	FGM	FGA	Pct.	FTM	FTA	Pct.	Off.	Def.	Tot.	Ast.	PF	Dq.	St.	Blk.	TO	Pts.
1974 —Boston	22	6	12	.500	1	3	.333	2	4	6	4	1	0	2	1	...	13
1975 —Boston	13	1	2	.500	5	6	.833	0	1	1	4	1	0	0	0	...	7
1976 —Boston	16	3	7	.429	0	0	...	0	1	1	1	1	0	2	0	...	6
1977 —Boston	15	5	7	.714	0	0	...	0	1	1	2	0	0	0	0	...	10
Totals	124	29	60	.483	6	11	.545	...	...	27	21	6	0	4	1	...	64

CBA REGULAR-SEASON RECORD

												AVERAGES		
Season Team	G	Min.	FGM	FGA	Pct.	FTM	FTA	Pct.	Reb.	Ast.	Pts.	RPG	APG	PPG
87-88—Topeka	5	122	12	30	.400	4	6	.667	6	21	28	1.2	4.2	5.6

Three-point field goals: 1987-88, 0-for-3.

WILKENS, LENNY

See Head Coaches, page 332.

WILKINS, DOMINIQUE   F/G

PERSONAL: Born January 12, 1960, in Paris, France. ... 6-8/224 (2,03/101,6). ... Full name: Jacques Dominique Wilkins. ... Brother of Gerald Wilkins, guard/forward with New York Knicks (1985-86 through 1991-92), Cleveland Cavaliers (1992-93 through 1994-95), Vancouver Grizzlies (1995-96) and Orlando Magic (1996-97 through 1998-99).
HIGH SCHOOL: Washington (N.C.).
COLLEGE: Georgia.
TRANSACTIONS/CAREER NOTES: Selected after junior season by Utah Jazz in first round (third pick overall) of 1982 NBA Draft. ... Draft rights traded by Jazz to Atlanta Hawks for F John Drew, G Freeman Williams and cash (September 2, 1982). ... Traded by Hawks with 1994 conditional first-round draft choice to Los Angeles Clippers for F Danny Manning (February 24, 1994). ... Signed as unrestricted free agent by Boston Celtics (July 25, 1994). ... Played in Greece (1995-96). ... Signed as free agent by San Antonio Spurs (October 4, 1996). ... Played in Italy (1997-98). ... Signed as free agent by Orlando Magic (February 5, 1999). ... Waived by Magic (June 14, 1999).
MISCELLANEOUS: Atlanta Hawks franchise all-time leading scorer with 23,292 points (1982-83 through 1993-94).

NOTES: The Sporting News All-America second team (1981, 1982).

COLLEGIATE RECORD

												AVERAGES		
Season Team	G	Min.	FGM	FGA	Pct.	FTM	FTA	Pct.	Reb.	Ast.	Pts.	RPG	APG	PPG
79-80—Georgia	16	508	135	257	.525	27	37	.730	104	23	297	6.5	1.4	18.6
80-81—Georgia	31	1157	310	582	.533	112	149	.752	234	52	732	7.5	1.7	23.6
81-82—Georgia	31	1083	278	526	.529	103	160	.644	250	41	659	8.1	1.3	21.3
Totals	78	2748	723	1365	.530	242	346	.699	588	116	1688	7.5	1.5	21.6

NBA REGULAR-SEASON RECORD

RECORDS: Holds single-game record for most free throws made without a miss—23 (December 8, 1992, vs. Chicago).
HONORS: Slam Dunk championship winner (1985, 1990). ... All-NBA first team (1986). ... All-NBA second team (1987, 1988, 1991, 1993). ... All-NBA third team (1989, 1994). ... NBA All-Rookie team (1983).

									REBOUNDS								AVERAGES		
Season Team	G	Min.	FGM	FGA	Pct.	FTM	FTA	Pct.	Off.	Def.	Tot.	Ast.	St.	Blk.	TO	Pts.	RPG	APG	PPG
82-83—Atlanta	82	2697	601	1220	.493	230	337	.682	226	252	478	129	84	63	180	1434	5.8	1.6	17.5
83-84—Atlanta	81	2961	684	1429	.479	382	496	.770	254	328	582	126	117	87	215	1750	7.2	1.6	21.6
84-85—Atlanta	81	3023	853	*1891	.451	486	603	.806	226	331	557	200	135	54	225	2217	6.9	2.5	27.4
85-86—Atlanta	78	3049	888	*1897	.468	577	705	.818	261	357	618	206	138	49	251	2366	7.9	2.6	*30.3
86-87—Atlanta	79	2969	828	1787	.463	607	742	.818	210	284	494	261	117	51	215	2294	6.3	3.3	29.0
87-88—Atlanta	78	2948	909	1957	.464	541	655	.826	211	291	502	224	103	47	218	2397	6.4	2.9	30.7
88-89—Atlanta	80	2997	814	1756	.464	442	524	.844	256	297	553	211	117	52	181	2099	6.9	2.6	26.2
89-90—Atlanta	80	2888	810	1672	.484	459	569	.807	217	304	521	200	126	47	174	2138	6.5	2.5	26.7
90-91—Atlanta	81	3078	770	1640	.470	476	574	.829	261	471	732	265	123	65	201	2101	9.0	3.3	25.9
91-92—Atlanta	42	1601	424	914	.464	294	352	.835	103	192	295	158	52	24	122	1179	7.0	3.8	28.1
92-93—Atlanta	71	2647	741	1584	.468	519	627	.828	187	295	482	227	70	27	184	2121	6.8	3.2	29.9
93-94—Atl.-L.A.C.	74	2635	698	1588	.440	442	522	.847	182	299	481	169	92	30	172	1923	6.5	2.3	26.0
94-95—Boston	77	2423	496	1169	.424	266	340	.782	157	244	401	166	61	14	173	1370	5.2	2.2	17.8
96-97—San Antonio	63	1945	397	953	.417	281	350	.803	169	233	402	119	39	31	135	1145	6.4	1.9	18.2
98-99—Orlando	27	252	50	132	.379	29	42	.690	30	41	71	16	4	1	23	134	2.6	0.6	5.0
Totals	1074	38113	9963	21589	.461	6031	7438	.811	2950	4219	7169	2677	1378	642	2669	26668	6.7	2.5	24.8

Three-point field goals: 1982-83, 2-for-11 (.182). 1983-84, 0-for-11. 1984-85, 25-for-81 (.309). 1985-86, 13-for-70 (.186). 1986-87, 31-for-106 (.292). 1987-88, 38-for-129 (.295). 1988-89, 29-for-105 (.276). 1989-90, 59-for-183 (.322). 1990-91, 85-for-249 (.341). 1991-92, 37-for-128 (.289). 1992-93, 120-for-316 (.380). 1993-94, 85-for-295 (.288). 1994-95, 112-for-289 (.388). 1996-97, 70-for-239 (.293). 1998-99, 5-for-19 (.263). Totals, 711-for-2231 (.319).

Personal fouls/disqualifications: 1982-83, 210/1. 1983-84, 197/1. 1984-85, 170/0. 1985-86, 170/0. 1986-87, 149/0. 1987-88, 162/0. 1988-89, 138/0. 1989-90, 141/0. 1990-91, 156/0. 1991-92, 77/0. 1992-93, 116/0. 1993-94, 126/0. 1994-95, 130/0. 1996-97, 100/0. 1998-99, 19/0. Totals, 2061/2.

NBA PLAYOFF RECORD

Season Team	G	Min.	FGM	FGA	Pct.	FTM	FTA	Pct.	REBOUNDS Off.	Def.	Tot.	Ast.	St.	Blk.	TO	Pts.	AVERAGES RPG	APG	PPG
82-83—Atlanta	3	109	17	42	.405	12	14	.857	8	7	15	1	2	1	10	47	5.0	0.3	15.7
83-84—Atlanta	5	197	35	84	.417	26	31	.839	21	20	41	11	12	1	15	96	8.2	2.2	19.2
85-86—Atlanta	9	360	94	217	.433	68	79	.861	20	34	54	25	9	2	30	257	6.0	2.8	28.6
86-87—Atlanta	9	360	86	210	.410	66	74	.892	27	43	70	25	16	8	26	241	7.8	2.8	26.8
87-88—Atlanta	12	473	137	300	.457	96	125	.768	37	40	77	34	16	6	30	374	6.4	2.8	31.2
88-89—Atlanta	5	212	52	116	.448	27	38	.711	10	17	27	17	4	8	12	136	5.4	3.4	27.2
90-91—Atlanta	5	195	35	94	.372	32	35	.914	6	26	32	13	9	5	11	104	6.4	2.6	20.8
92-93—Atlanta	3	113	32	75	.427	23	30	.767	12	4	16	9	3	1	10	90	5.3	3.0	30.0
94-95—Boston	4	150	26	61	.426	16	18	.889	17	26	43	8	2	3	9	76	10.8	2.0	19.0
98-99—Orlando..........	1	3	1	2	.500	0	0		0	0	0	0	0	0	2	2	0.0	0.0	2.0
Totals	56	2172	515	1201	.429	366	444	.824	158	217	375	143	73	35	153	1423	6.7	2.6	25.4

Three-point field goals: 1982-83, 1-for-1. 1983-84, 0-for-1. 1985-86, 1-for-5 (.200). 1986-87, 3-for-10 (.300). 1987-88, 4-for-18 (.222). 1988-89, 5-for-17 (.294). 1990-91, 2-for-15 (.133). 1992-93, 3-for-12 (.250). 1994-95, 8-for-17 (.471). Totals, 27-for-96 (.281).

Personal fouls/disqualifications: 1982-83, 9/0. 1983-84, 13/0. 1985-86, 24/0. 1986-87, 25/0. 1987-88, 24/0. 1988-89, 5/0. 1990-91, 8/0. 1992-93, 8/0. 1994-95, 7/0. Totals, 123/0.

NBA ALL-STAR GAME RECORD

Season Team	Min.	FGM	FGA	Pct.	FTM	FTA	Pct.	REBOUNDS Off.	Def.	Tot.	Ast.	PF	Dq.	St.	Blk.	TO	Pts.
1986 —Atlanta..............	17	6	15	.400	1	2	.500	2	1	3	2	2	0	0	1	1	13
1987 —Atlanta..............	24	3	9	.333	4	7	.571	3	2	5	1	2	0	0	1	2	10
1988 —Atlanta..............	30	12	22	.545	5	6	.833	1	4	5	0	3	0	0	1	0	29
1989 —Atlanta..............	15	3	8	.375	3	3	1.000	1	1	2	0	0	0	3	0	2	9
1990 —Atlanta..............	16	5	10	.500	2	2	1.000	0	0	0	4	1	0	1	0	0	13
1991 —Atlanta..............	22	3	11	.273	6	8	.750	3	0	3	4	2	0	1	1	2	12
1992 —Atlanta..............							Selected, did not play—injured.										
1993 —Atlanta..............	18	2	11	.182	4	4	1.000	4	3	7	0	2	0	1	0	1	9
1994 —Atlanta..............	17	4	9	.444	3	6	.500	2	0	2	4	1	0	0	0	0	11
Totals..........................	159	38	95	.400	28	38	.737	16	11	27	15	13	0	6	4	8	106

Three-point field goals: 1990, 1-for-1. 1991, 0-for-2. 1993, 1-for-3 (.333). 1994, 0-for-2. Totals, 2-for-8 (.250).

GREEK LEAGUE RECORD

Season Team	G	Min.	FGM	FGA	Pct.	FTM	FTA	Pct.	Reb.	Ast.	Pts.	AVERAGES RPG	APG	PPG
95-96—Panathinaikos................	14	...	...	...	...	...	...	...	95	19	292	6.8	1.4	20.9

WILLIAMS, BUCK   F

PERSONAL: Born March 8, 1960, in Rocky Mount, N.C. ... 6-8/225 (2,03/102,1). ... Full name: Charles Linwood Williams.

HIGH SCHOOL: Rocky Mount (N.C.).

COLLEGE: Maryland.

TRANSACTIONS/CAREER NOTES: Selected after junior season by New Jersey Nets in first round (third pick overall) of 1981 NBA Draft. ... Traded by Nets to Portland Trail Blazers for C Sam Bowie and 1989 first-round draft choice (June 24, 1989). ... Rights renounced by Trail Blazers (July 23, 1996). ... Signed as free agent by New York Knicks (July 26, 1996). ... Announced retirement (January 27, 1999).

MISCELLANEOUS: Member of U.S. Olympic team (1980). ... New Jersey Nets franchise all-time leading scorer with 10,440 points and all-time leading rebounder with 7,576 (1981-82 through 1988-89).

COLLEGIATE RECORD

Season Team	G	Min.	FGM	FGA	Pct.	FTM	FTA	Pct.	Reb.	Ast.	Pts.	AVERAGES RPG	APG	PPG
78-79—Maryland	30	906	120	206	.583	60	109	.550	323	18	300	10.8	0.6	10.0
79-80—Maryland	24	872	143	236	.606	85	128	.664	242	27	371	10.1	1.1	15.5
80-81—Maryland	31	1080	183	283	.647	116	182	.637	363	31	482	11.7	1.0	15.5
Totals	85	2858	446	725	.615	261	419	.623	928	76	1153	10.9	0.9	13.6

NBA REGULAR-SEASON RECORD

HONORS: NBA Rookie of the Year (1982). ... All-NBA second team (1983). ... NBA All-Defensive first team (1990, 1991). ... NBA All-Defensive second team (1988, 1992). ... NBA All-Rookie team (1982).

Season Team	G	Min.	FGM	FGA	Pct.	FTM	FTA	Pct.	REBOUNDS Off.	Def.	Tot.	Ast.	St.	Blk.	TO	Pts.	AVERAGES RPG	APG	PPG
81-82—New Jersey	82	2825	513	881	.582	242	388	.624	347	658	1005	107	84	84	235	1268	12.3	1.3	15.5
82-83—New Jersey	82	2961	536	912	.588	324	523	.620	365	662	1027	125	91	110	246	1396	12.5	1.5	17.0
83-84—New Jersey	81	3003	495	926	.535	284	498	.570	*355	645	1000	130	81	125	237	1274	12.3	1.6	15.7
84-85—New Jersey	82	*3182	577	1089	.530	336	538	.625	323	682	1005	167	63	110	238	1491	12.3	2.0	18.2
85-86—New Jersey	82	3070	500	956	.523	301	445	.676	329	657	986	131	73	96	244	1301	12.0	1.6	15.9
86-87—New Jersey	82	2976	521	936	.557	430	588	.731	322	701	1023	129	78	91	280	1472	12.5	1.6	18.0
87-88—New Jersey	70	2637	466	832	.560	346	518	.668	298	536	834	109	68	44	189	1279	11.9	1.6	18.3
88-89—New Jersey	74	2446	373	702	.531	213	320	.666	249	447	696	78	61	36	142	959	9.4	1.1	13.0

Season Team	G	Min.	FGM	FGA	Pct.	FTM	FTA	Pct.	Off.	Def.	Tot.	Ast.	St.	Blk.	TO	Pts.	RPG	APG	PPG
89-90—Portland	82	2801	413	754	.548	288	408	.706	250	550	800	116	69	39	168	1114	9.8	1.4	13.6
90-91—Portland	80	2582	358	595	*.602	217	308	.705	227	524	751	97	47	47	137	933	9.4	1.2	11.7
91-92—Portland	80	2519	340	563	*.604	221	293	.754	260	444	704	108	62	41	130	901	8.8	1.4	11.3
92-93—Portland	82	2498	270	528	.511	138	214	.645	232	458	690	75	81	61	101	678	8.4	0.9	8.3
93-94—Portland	81	2636	291	524	.555	201	296	.679	315	528	843	80	58	47	111	783	10.4	1.0	9.7
94-95—Portland	82	2422	309	604	.512	138	205	.673	251	418	669	78	67	69	119	757	8.2	1.0	9.2
95-96—Portland	70	1672	192	384	.500	125	187	.668	159	245	404	42	40	47	90	511	5.8	0.6	7.3
96-97—New York	74	1496	175	326	.537	115	179	.642	166	231	397	53	40	38	79	465	5.4	0.7	6.3
97-98—New York	41	738	75	149	.503	52	71	.732	78	105	183	21	17	15	38	202	4.5	0.5	4.9
Totals	1307	42464	6404	11661	.549	3971	5979	.664	4526	8491	13017	1646	1080	1100	2784	16784	10.0	1.3	12.8

Three-point field goals: 1981-82, 0-for-1. 1982-83, 0-for-4. 1983-84, 0-for-4. 1984-85, 1-for-4 (.250). 1985-86, 0-for-2. 1986-87, 0-for-1. 1987-88, 1-for-1. 1988-89, 0-for-3. 1989-90, 0-for-1. 1991-92, 0-for-1. 1992-93, 0-for-1. 1993-94, 0-for-1. 1994-95, 1-for-2 (.500). 1995-96, 2-for-3 (.667). 1996-97, 0-for-1. Totals, 5-for-30 (.167).

Personal fouls/disqualifications: 1981-82, 285/5. 1982-83, 270/4. 1983-84, 298/3. 1984-85, 293/7. 1985-86, 294/9. 1986-87, 315/8. 1987-88, 266/5. 1988-89, 223/0. 1989-90, 285/4. 1990-91, 247/2. 1991-92, 244/4. 1992-93, 270/0. 1993-94, 239/1. 1994-95, 254/2. 1995-96, 187/1. 1996-97, 204/2. 1997-98, 93/1. Totals, 4267/58.

NBA PLAYOFF RECORD

Season Team	G	Min.	FGM	FGA	Pct.	FTM	FTA	Pct.	Off.	Def.	Tot.	Ast.	St.	Blk.	TO	Pts.	RPG	APG	PPG
81-82—New Jersey	2	79	14	26	.538	7	15	.467	11	10	21	3	1	2	4	35	10.5	1.5	17.5
82-83—New Jersey	2	85	11	22	.500	16	20	.800	9	14	23	4	2	2	5	38	11.5	2.0	19.0
83-84—New Jersey	11	473	63	130	.485	45	81	.556	57	98	155	16	15	17	29	171	14.1	1.5	15.5
84-85—New Jersey	3	123	26	40	.650	22	30	.733	14	18	32	1	3	5	6	74	10.7	0.3	24.7
85-86—New Jersey	3	126	21	29	.724	20	26	.769	12	19	31	2	6	1	6	62	10.3	0.7	20.7
89-90—Portland	21	776	101	199	.508	71	105	.676	67	126	193	39	13	6	41	273	9.2	1.9	13.0
90-91—Portland	16	572	65	130	.500	35	58	.603	53	90	143	14	10	4	24	165	8.9	0.9	10.3
91-92—Portland	21	758	66	130	.508	69	91	.758	61	118	179	22	27	17	45	201	8.5	1.0	9.6
92-93—Portland	4	119	11	23	.478	13	19	.684	12	17	29	1	1	3	6	35	7.3	0.3	8.8
93-94—Portland	4	125	19	28	.679	13	15	.867	14	21	35	2	4	2	8	51	8.8	0.5	12.8
94-95—Portland	3	103	9	15	.600	7	11	.636	8	11	19	1	4	2	4	25	6.3	0.3	8.3
95-96—Portland	5	133	9	23	.391	5	7	.714	13	12	25	1	1	4	5	24	5.0	0.2	4.8
96-97—New York	10	193	17	35	.486	9	17	.529	13	27	40	6	3	4	4	43	4.0	0.6	4.3
97-98—New York	3	45	4	9	.444	6	8	.750	7	9	16	1	0	1	3	14	5.3	0.3	4.7
Totals	108	3710	436	839	.520	338	503	.672	351	590	941	113	90	70	190	1211	8.7	1.0	11.2

Three-point field goals: 1995-96, 1-for-2 (.500).

Personal fouls/disqualifications: 1981-82, 7/0. 1982-83, 12/2. 1983-84, 44/2. 1984-85, 12/0. 1985-86, 15/1. 1989-90, 74/1. 1990-91, 55/1. 1991-92, 73/1. 1992-93, 12/1. 1993-94, 11/0. 1994-95, 14/1. 1995-96, 18/0. 1996-97, 34/0. 1997-98, 5/0. Totals, 386/10.

NBA ALL-STAR GAME RECORD

Season Team	Min.	FGM	FGA	Pct.	FTM	FTA	Pct.	Off.	Def.	Tot.	Ast.	PF	Dq.	St.	Blk.	TO	Pts.
1982 —New Jersey	22	2	7	.286	0	2	.000	1	9	10	1	3	0	0	2	3	4
1983 —New Jersey	19	3	4	.750	2	4	.500	3	4	7	1	0	0	1	0	0	8
1986 —New Jersey	20	5	8	.625	3	5	.600	3	4	7	4	0	0	0	0	1	13
Totals	61	10	19	.526	5	11	.455	7	17	24	6	3	0	1	2	4	25

WORTHY, JAMES   F

PERSONAL: Born February 27, 1961, in Gastonia, N.C. ... 6-9/225 (2,05/102,1). ... Full name: James Ager Worthy.
HIGH SCHOOL: Ashbrook (Gastonia, N.C.).
COLLEGE: North Carolina.
TRANSACTIONS: Selected after junior season by Los Angeles Lakers in first round (first pick overall) of 1982 NBA Draft. ... Announced retirement (November 10, 1994).
CAREER HONORS: One of the 50 Greatest Players in NBA History (1996).
MISCELLANEOUS: Member of NBA championship team (1985, 1987, 1988).

COLLEGIATE RECORD

NOTES: Member of NCAA Division I championship team (1982). ... NCAA Division I Tournament Most Outstanding Player (1982). ... The Sporting News All-America first team (1982).

Season Team	G	Min.	FGM	FGA	Pct.	FTM	FTA	Pct.	Reb.	Ast.	Pts.	RPG	APG	PPG
79-80—North Carolina	14	396	74	126	.587	27	45	.600	104	26	175	7.4	1.9	12.5
80-81—North Carolina	36	1214	208	416	.500	96	150	.640	301	100	512	8.4	2.8	14.2
81-82—North Carolina	34	1178	203	354	.573	126	187	.674	215	82	532	6.3	2.4	15.6
Totals	84	2788	485	896	.541	249	382	.652	620	208	1219	7.4	2.5	14.5

NBA REGULAR-SEASON RECORD

HONORS: All-NBA third team (1990, 1991). ... NBA All-Rookie team (1983).

Season Team	G	Min.	FGM	FGA	Pct.	FTM	FTA	Pct.	Off.	Def.	Tot.	Ast.	St.	Blk.	TO	Pts.	RPG	APG	PPG
82-83—Los Angeles	77	1970	447	772	.579	138	221	.624	157	242	399	132	91	64	178	1033	5.2	1.7	13.4
83-84—Los Angeles	82	2415	495	890	.556	195	257	.759	157	358	515	207	77	70	181	1185	6.3	2.5	14.5
84-85—L.A. Lakers	80	2696	610	1066	.572	190	245	.776	169	342	511	201	87	67	198	1410	6.4	2.5	17.6
85-86—L.A. Lakers	75	2454	629	1086	.579	242	314	.771	136	251	387	201	82	77	149	1500	5.2	2.7	20.0
86-87—L.A. Lakers	82	2819	651	1207	.539	292	389	.751	158	308	466	226	108	83	168	1594	5.7	2.8	19.4
87-88—L.A. Lakers	75	2655	617	1161	.531	242	304	.796	129	245	374	289	72	55	155	1478	5.0	3.9	19.7

<table>
<tr></tr>
</table>

Season Team	G	Min.	FGM	FGA	Pct.	FTM	FTA	Pct.	Off.	Def.	Tot.	Ast.	St.	Blk.	TO	Pts.	RPG	APG	PPG
88-89—L.A. Lakers	81	2960	702	1282	.548	251	321	.782	169	320	489	288	108	56	182	1657	6.0	3.6	20.5
89-90—L.A. Lakers	80	2960	711	1298	.548	248	317	.782	160	318	478	288	99	49	160	1685	6.0	3.6	21.1
90-91—L.A. Lakers	78	3008	716	1455	.492	212	266	.797	107	249	356	275	104	35	127	1670	4.6	3.5	21.4
91-92—L.A. Lakers	54	2108	450	1007	.447	166	204	.814	98	207	305	252	76	23	127	1075	5.6	4.7	19.9
92-93—L.A. Lakers	82	2359	510	1142	.447	171	211	.810	73	174	247	278	92	27	137	1221	3.0	3.4	14.9
93-94—L.A. Lakers	80	1597	340	838	.406	100	135	.741	48	133	181	154	45	18	97	812	2.3	1.9	10.2
Totals	926	30001	6878	13204	.521	2447	3184	.769	1561	3147	4708	2791	1041	624	1859	16320	5.1	3.0	17.6

Three-point field goals: 1982-83, 1-for-4 (.250). 1983-84, 0-for-6. 1984-85, 0-for-7. 1985-86, 0-for-13. 1986-87, 0-for-13. 1987-88, 2-for-16 (.125). 1988-89, 2-for-23 (.087). 1989-90, 15-for-49 (.306). 1990-91, 26-for-90 (.289). 1991-92, 9-for-43 (.209). 1992-93, 30-for-111 (.270). 1993-94, 32-for-111 (.288). Totals, 117-for-486 (.241).

Personal fouls/disqualifications: 1982-83, 221/2. 1983-84, 244/5. 1984-85, 196/0. 1985-86, 195/0. 1986-87, 206/0. 1987-88, 175/1. 1988-89, 175/0. 1989-90, 190/0. 1990-91, 117/0. 1991-92, 89/0. 1992-93, 87/0. 1993-94, 80/0. Totals, 1975/8.

NBA PLAYOFF RECORD

NOTES: NBA Finals Most Valuable Player (1988).

Season Team	G	Min.	FGM	FGA	Pct.	FTM	FTA	Pct.	Off.	Def.	Tot.	Ast.	St.	Blk.	TO	Pts.	RPG	APG	PPG
83-84—Los Angeles....	21	708	164	274	.599	42	69	.609	36	69	105	56	27	11	39	371	5.0	2.7	17.7
84-85—L.A. Lakers	19	626	166	267	.622	75	111	.676	35	61	96	41	17	13	26	408	5.1	2.2	21.5
85-86—L.A. Lakers	14	539	121	217	.558	32	47	.681	22	43	65	45	16	10	36	274	4.6	3.2	19.6
86-87—L.A. Lakers	18	681	176	298	.591	73	97	.753	31	70	101	63	28	22	40	425	5.6	3.5	23.6
87-88—L.A. Lakers	24	896	204	390	.523	97	128	.758	53	86	139	106	33	19	55	506	5.8	4.4	21.1
88-89—L.A. Lakers	15	600	153	270	.567	63	80	.788	37	64	101	42	18	16	33	372	6.7	2.8	24.8
89-90—L.A. Lakers	9	366	90	181	.497	36	43	.837	11	39	50	27	14	3	22	218	5.6	3.0	24.2
90-91—L.A. Lakers	18	733	161	346	.465	53	72	.736	25	48	73	70	19	2	40	379	4.1	3.9	21.1
92-93—L.A. Lakers	5	148	32	86	.372	3	5	.600	7	10	17	13	5	0	7	69	3.4	2.6	13.8
Totals	143	5297	1267	2329	.544	474	652	.727	257	490	747	463	177	96	298	3022	5.2	3.2	21.1

Three-point field goals: 1983-84, 1-for-2 (.500). 1984-85, 1-for-2 (.500). 1985-86, 0-for-4. 1986-87, 0-for-2. 1987-88, 1-for-9 (.111). 1988-89, 3-for-8 (.375). 1989-90, 2-for-8 (.250). 1990-91, 4-for-24 (.167). 1992-93, 2-for-8 (.250). Totals, 14-for-67 (.209).

Personal fouls/disqualifications: 1983-84, 57/0. 1984-85, 53/1. 1985-86, 43/0. 1986-87, 42/1. 1987-88, 58/0. 1988-89, 36/0. 1989-90, 18/0. 1990-91, 34/0. 1992-93, 11/0. Totals, 352/2.

NBA ALL-STAR GAME RECORD

Season	Team	Min.	FGM	FGA	Pct.	FTM	FTA	Pct.	Off.	Def.	Tot.	Ast.	PF	Dq.	St.	Blk.	TO	Pts.
1986	—L.A. Lakers	28	10	19	.526	0	0	...	2	1	3	2	3	0	0	2	1	20
1987	—L.A. Lakers	29	10	14	.714	2	2	1.000	6	2	8	3	3	0	1	0	2	22
1988	—L.A. Lakers	13	2	8	.250	0	1	.000	1	2	3	1	1	0	0	1	0	4
1989	—L.A. Lakers	18	4	7	.571	0	0	...	0	2	2	2	0	0	2	0	0	8
1990	—L.A. Lakers	19	1	11	.091	0	0	...	3	1	4	0	1	0	1	0	1	2
1991	—L.A. Lakers	21	3	11	.273	3	4	.750	0	2	2	0	2	0	2	1	0	9
1992	—L.A. Lakers	14	4	7	.571	1	2	.500	0	4	4	1	0	0	1	0	0	9
Totals		142	34	77	.442	6	9	.667	12	14	26	9	10	0	7	4	4	74

Three-point field goals: 1986, 0-for-2. 1989, 0-for-1. Totals, 0-for-3.

YARDLEY, GEORGE   F

PERSONAL: Born November 23, 1928, in Hollywood, Calif. ... 6-5/195 (1,96/88,4). ... Full name: George Harry Yardley III.
HIGH SCHOOL: Newport Harbor (Calif.).
COLLEGE: Stanford.
TRANSACTIONS: Selected by Fort Wayne Pistons in first round of 1950 NBA Draft. ... Played with the San Francisco Stewart Chevrolets in the National Industrial Basketball League, an Amateur Athletic Union League, during 1950-51 season (finished third in the league in scoring with a 13.1 point average on 104 field goals and 53 free throws for 261 points in 20 games). ... In military service during 1951-52 and 1952-53 seasons. ... Signed by Pistons (1953). ... Pistons franchise moved from Fort Wayne to Detroit for 1957-58 season. ... Traded by Pistons to Syracuse Nationals for F/G Ed Conlin (February 13, 1959). ... Played in American Basketball League with Los Angeles Jets (1961-62).
CAREER HONORS: Elected to Naismith Memorial Basketball Hall of Fame (1996).

COLLEGIATE RECORD

Season Team	G	Min.	FGM	FGA	Pct.	FTM	FTA	Pct.	Reb.	Ast.	Pts.	RPG	APG	PPG
46-47—Stanford‡						Freshman team statistics unavailable.								
47-48—Stanford	18	...	22	...	...	8	20	.400	...	...	52	...	...	2.9
48-49—Stanford	28	...	126	377	.334	93	131	.710	...	...	345	...	...	12.3
49-50—Stanford	25	...	164	452	.363	95	130	.731	...	...	423	...	...	16.9
Varsity totals	71	...	312	...	...	196	281	.698	...	...	820	...	...	11.5

NBA REGULAR-SEASON RECORD

HONORS: All-NBA first team (1958). ... All-NBA second team (1957).

Season Team	G	Min.	FGM	FGA	Pct.	FTM	FTA	Pct.	Reb.	Ast.	PF	Dq.	Pts.	RPG	APG	PPG
53-54—Fort Wayne	63	1489	209	492	.425	146	205	.712	407	99	166	3	564	6.5	1.6	9.0
54-55—Fort Wayne	60	2150	363	869	.418	310	416	.745	594	126	205	7	1036	9.9	2.1	17.3
55-56—Fort Wayne	71	2353	434	1067	.407	365	492	.742	686	159	212	2	1233	9.7	2.2	17.4
56-57—Fort Wayne	72	2691	522	1273	.410	503	639	.787	755	147	231	2	1547	10.5	2.0	21.5
57-58—Detroit	72	2843	673	*1624	.414	*655	*808	.811	768	97	226	3	*2001	10.7	1.3	*27.8
58-59—Det.-Syr.	61	1839	446	1042	.428	317	407	.779	431	65	159	2	1209	7.1	1.1	19.8
59-60—Syracuse	73	2402	546	1205	.453	381	467	.816	579	122	227	3	1473	7.9	1.7	20.2
Totals	472	15767	3193	7572	.422	2677	3434	.780	4220	815	1426	22	9063	8.9	1.7	19.2

ALL-TIME GREAT PLAYERS

NBA PLAYOFF RECORD

Season Team	G	Min.	FGM	FGA	Pct.	FTM	FTA	Pct.	Reb.	Ast.	PF	Dq.	Pts.	RPG	APG	PPG
														AVERAGES		
53-54 —Fort Wayne	4	107	16	33	.485	10	12	.833	24	3	10	0	42	6.0	0.8	10.5
54-55 —Fort Wayne	11	420	57	143	.399	60	79	.760	99	36	37	2	174	9.0	3.3	15.8
55-56 —Fort Wayne	10	406	77	183	.421	76	98	.776	139	26	25	0	230	13.9	2.6	23.0
56-57 —Fort Wayne	2	85	24	53	.453	9	11	.818	19	8	7	0	57	9.5	4.0	28.5
57-58 —Detroit	7	254	52	127	.409	60	67	.896	72	17	26	0	164	10.3	2.4	23.4
58-59 —Syracuse	9	333	83	189	.439	60	70	.857	87	21	29	0	226	9.7	2.3	25.1
59-60 —Syracuse	3	88	15	39	.385	10	12	.833	17	1	9	0	40	5.7	0.3	13.3
Totals	46	1693	324	767	.422	285	349	.817	457	112	143	2	933	9.9	2.4	20.3

NBA ALL-STAR GAME RECORD

Season Team	Min.	FGM	FGA	Pct.	FTM	FTA	Pct.	Reb	Ast.	PF	Dq.	Pts.
1955 —Fort Wayne	22	4	11	.364	3	4	.750	4	2	2	0	11
1956 —Fort Wayne	19	3	7	.429	2	3	.667	6	1	1	0	8
1957 —Fort Wayne	25	4	10	.400	1	1	1.000	9	0	2	0	9
1958 —Detroit	32	8	15	.533	3	5	.600	9	1	1	0	19
1959 —Detroit	17	2	8	.250	2	2	1.000	4	0	3	0	6
1960 —Syracuse	16	5	9	.556	1	2	.500	3	0	4	0	11
Totals	131	26	60	.433	12	17	.706	35	4	13	0	64

ABL REGULAR-SEASON RECORD

Season Team	G	Min.	FGM	FGA	Pct.	FTM	FTA	Pct.	Reb.	Ast.	Pts.	RPG	APG	PPG
												AVERAGES		
61-62—Los Angeles	25	948	159	378	.421	148	122	1.213	172	65	482	6.9	2.6	19.3

ZASLOFSKY, MAX   G/F

PERSONAL: Born December 7, 1925, in Brooklyn, N.Y. ... Died October 15, 1985. ... 6-2/170 (1,88/77,1). ... Full name: Max Zaslofsky.
HIGH SCHOOL: Thomas Jefferson (Brooklyn, N.Y.).
COLLEGE: St. John's.
TRANSACTIONS: Signed after freshman season as free agent by Chicago Stags of Basketball Association of America (1946). ... Name drawn out of hat by New York Knicks in dispersal of Stags franchise (1950). ... Traded by Knicks to Baltimore Bullets for G/F Jim Baechtold (1953). ... Traded by Bullets to Milwaukee Hawks (November 1953). ... Traded by Hawks to Fort Wayne Pistons (December 1953).

COLLEGIATE RECORD

NOTES: In military service (1944-45 season).

Season Team	G	Min.	FGM	FGA	Pct.	FTM	FTA	Pct.	Reb.	Ast.	Pts.	RPG	APG	PPG
												AVERAGES		
45-46—St. John's	18	...	59	...	...	22	38	.579	...	...	140	...	...	7.8

NBA REGULAR-SEASON RECORD

HONORS: All-NBA first team (1950). ... All-BAA first team (1947, 1948, 1949).

Season Team	G	Min.	FGM	FGA	Pct.	FTM	FTA	Pct.	Reb.	Ast.	PF	Dq.	Pts.	RPG	APG	PPG
														AVERAGES		
46-47 —Chicago (BAA)	61	...	336	1020	.329	205	278	.737	...	40	121	...	877	...	0.7	14.4
47-48 —Chicago (BAA)	48	...	*373	1156	.323	261	333	.784	...	29	125	...	*1007	...	0.6	*21.0
48-49 —Chicago (BAA)	58	...	425	1216	.350	347	413	.840	...	149	156	...	1197	...	2.6	20.6
49-50 —Chicago	68	...	397	1132	.351	321	381	*.843	...	155	185	...	1115	...	2.3	16.4
50-51 —New York	66	...	302	853	.354	231	298	.775	228	136	150	3	835	3.5	2.1	12.7
51-52 —New York	66	...	322	958	.336	287	380	.755	194	156	183	5	931	2.9	2.4	14.1
52-53 —New York	29	...	123	320	.384	98	142	.690	75	55	81	1	344	2.6	1.9	11.9
53-54 —Bal-Mil-FW	65	...	278	756	.368	255	357	.714	160	154	142	1	811	2.5	2.4	12.5
54-55 —Fort Wayne	70	...	269	821	.328	247	352	.702	191	203	130	0	785	2.7	2.9	11.2
55-56 —Fort Wayne	9	...	29	81	.358	30	35	.857	16	16	18	1	88	1.8	1.8	9.8
Totals	540	...	2854	8313	.343	2282	2969	.769	...	1093	1291	...	7990	...	2.0	14.8

NBA PLAYOFF RECORD

Season Team	G	Min.	FGM	FGA	Pct.	FTM	FTA	Pct.	Reb.	Ast.	PF	Dq.	Pts.	RPG	APG	PPG
														AVERAGES		
46-47 —Chicago (BAA)	11	...	60	199	.302	29	44	.659	...	4	26	...	149	...	0.4	13.5
47-48 —Chicago (BAA)	5	...	30	88	.341	37	47	.787	...	0	17	...	97	...	0.0	19.4
48-49 —Chicago (BAA)	2	...	15	49	.306	14	18	.778	...	6	3	0	44	...	3.0	22.0
49-50 —Chicago	2	...	15	32	.469	15	18	.833	...	6	7	...	45	...	3.0	22.5
50-51 —New York	14	...	88	217	.406	74	100	.740	58	38	43	...	250	4.1	2.7	17.9
51-52 —New York	14	...	69	185	.373	89	110	.809	44	23	51	...	227	3.1	1.6	16.2
53-54 —Fort Wayne	4	...	11	36	.306	13	15	.867	3	6	7	...	35	0.8	1.5	8.8
54-55 —Fort Wayne	11	...	18	44	.409	16	20	.800	16	18	20	...	52	1.5	1.6	4.7
Totals	63	...	306	850	.360	287	372	.772	...	101	174	...	899	...	1.6	14.3

NBA ALL-STAR GAME RECORD

Season Team	Min.	FGM	FGA	Pct.	FTM	FTA	Pct.	Reb	Ast.	PF	Dq.	Pts.
1952 —New York	...	3	7	.429	5	5	1.000	4	2	0	0	11

ABA COACHING RECORD

Season Team	REGULAR SEASON				PLAYOFFS		
	W	L	Pct.	Finish	W	L	Pct.
67-68 —New Jersey	36	42	.462	T4th/Eastern Division	—	—	—
67-68 —New York	17	61	.218	5th/Eastern Division	—	—	—
Totals (2 years)	53	103	.340				

ATTLES, AL

PERSONAL: Born November 7, 1936, in Newark, N.J. ... 6-0/185 (1,83/83,9). ... Full name: Alvin A. Attles.
HIGH SCHOOL: Weequahic (Newark, N.J.).
COLLEGE: North Carolina A&T.
TRANSACTIONS: Selected by Philadelphia Warriors in fifth round (39th pick overall) of 1960 NBA Draft. ... Warriors franchise moved from Philadelphia to San Francisco for 1962-63 season.
CAREER NOTES: Vice president/assistant general manager, Golden State Warriors (1987-88 to present).

COLLEGIATE RECORD

Season Team	G	Min.	FGM	FGA	Pct.	FTM	FTA	Pct.	Reb.	Ast.	Pts.	RPG	APG	PPG
56-57 —North Carolina A&T.......						Statistics unavailable.								
57-58 —North Carolina A&T.......						Statistics unavailable.								
58-59 —North Carolina A&T.......	29	...	105	225	.467	56	91	.615	...	...	266	...	...	9.2
59-60 —North Carolina A&T.......	24	...	190	301	.631	47	71	.662	80	...	427	3.3	...	17.8
Totals	53	...	295	526	.561	103	162	.636	...	...	.693	...	...	13.1

NBA REGULAR-SEASON RECORD

Season Team	G	Min.	FGM	FGA	Pct.	FTM	FTA	Pct.	Reb.	Ast.	PF	Dq.	Pts.	RPG	APG	PPG
60-61 —Philadelphia.....................	77	1544	222	543	.409	97	162	.599	214	174	235	5	541	2.8	2.3	7.0
61-62 —Philadelphia	75	2468	343	724	.474	158	267	.592	355	333	279	8	844	4.7	4.4	11.3
62-63 —San Francisco...................	71	1876	301	630	.478	133	206	.646	205	184	253	7	735	2.9	2.6	10.4
63-64 —San Francisco	70	1883	289	640	.452	185	275	.673	236	197	249	4	763	3.4	2.8	10.9
64-65 —San Francisco	73	1733	254	662	.384	171	274	.624	239	205	242	7	679	3.3	2.8	9.3
65-66 —San Francisco	79	2053	364	724	.503	154	252	.611	322	225	265	7	882	4.1	2.8	11.2
66-67 —San Francisco	70	1764	212	467	.454	88	151	.583	321	269	265	13	512	4.6	3.8	7.3
67-68 —San Francisco	67	1992	252	540	.467	150	216	.694	276	390	284	9	654	4.1	5.8	9.8
68-69 —San Francisco	51	1516	162	359	.451	95	149	.638	181	306	183	3	419	3.5	6.0	8.2
69-70 —San Francisco	45	676	78	202	.386	75	113	.664	74	142	103	0	231	1.6	3.2	5.1
70-71 —San Francisco.	34	321	22	54	.407	24	41	.585	40	58	59	2	68	1.2	1.7	2.0
Totals....................	712	17826	2499	5545	.451	1330	2106	.632	2463	2483	2417	65	6328	3.5	3.5	8.9

NBA PLAYOFF RECORD

Season Team	G	Min.	FGM	FGA	Pct.	FTM	FTA	Pct.	Reb.	Ast.	PF	Dq.	Pts.	RPG	APG	PPG
60-61 —Philadelphia.....................	3	110	12	26	.462	5	14	.357	12	9	14	0	29	4.0	3.0	9.7
61-62 —Philadelphia	12	338	28	76	.368	17	31	.548	55	27	54	4	73	4.6	2.3	6.1
63-64 —San Francisco	12	386	58	144	.403	30	56	.536	37	30	54	5	146	3.1	2.5	12.2
66-67 —San Francisco	15	237	20	46	.435	6	16	.375	62	38	45	1	46	4.1	2.5	3.1
67-68 —San Francisco	10	277	25	62	.403	23	30	.767	53	70	49	2	73	5.3	7.0	7.3
68-69 —San Francisco.	6	109	7	21	.333	1	4	.250	18	21	17	0	15	3.0	3.5	2.5
70-71 —San Francisco.	4	47	4	7	.571	4	7	.571	8	11	13	0	12	2.0	2.8	3.0
Totals..................	62	1504	154	382	.403	86	158	.544	245	206	246	12	394	4.0	3.3	6.4

HEAD COACHING RECORD

BACKGROUND: Assistant coach, Warriors (February 13, 1995-remainder of season).

NBA COACHING RECORD

Season Team	REGULAR SEASON				PLAYOFFS		
	W	L	Pct.	Finish	W	L	Pct.
69-70 —San Francisco.............................	8	22	.267	6th/Western Division	—	—	—
70-71 —San Francisco.............................	41	41	.500	2nd/Pacific Division	1	4	.200
71-72 —Golden State.............................	51	31	.622	2nd/Pacific Division	1	4	.200
72-73 —Golden State.............................	47	35	.573	2nd/Pacific Division	5	6	.455
73-74 —Golden State.............................	44	38	.537	2nd/Pacific Division	—	—	—
74-75 —Golden State.............................	48	34	.585	1st/Pacific Division	12	5	.706
75-76 —Golden State.............................	59	23	.720	1st/Pacific Division	7	6	.538
76-77 —Golden State.............................	46	36	.561	3rd/Pacific Division	5	5	.500
77-78 —Golden State.............................	43	39	.524	5th/Pacific Division	—	—	—
78-79 —Golden State.............................	38	44	.463	6th/Pacific Division	—	—	—
79-80 —Golden State.............................	18	43	.295	6th/Pacific Division	—	—	—
80-81 —Golden State.............................	39	43	.476	4th/Pacific Division	—	—	—
81-82 —Golden State.............................	45	37	.549	4th/Pacific Division	—	—	—
82-83 —Golden State.............................	30	52	.366	5th/Pacific Division	—	—	—
Totals (14 years)................................	557	518	.518	**Totals (6 years)**	31	30	.508

NOTES:
1970—Replaced George Lee as San Francisco head coach with record of 22-30.
1971—Lost to Milwaukee in Western Conference Semifinals.
1972—Lost to Milwaukee in Western Conference Semifinals.
1973—Defeated Milwaukee, 4-2, in Western Conference Semifinals; lost to Los Angeles, 4-1, in Western Conference Finals.
1975—Defeated Seattle, 4-2, in Western Conference Semifinals; defeated Chicago, 4-3, in Western Conference Finals; defeated Washington, 4-0, in NBA Finals.
1976—Defeated Detroit, 4-2, in Western Conference Semifinals; lost to Phoenix, 4-3, in Western Conference Finals.
1977—Defeated Detroit, 2-1, in Western Conference First Round; lost to Los Angeles, 4-3, in Western Conference Semifinals.
1980—Missed final 21 games of season due to injury; replaced by assistant coach John Bach (6-15) for remainder of season.

AUERBACH, RED

PERSONAL: Born September 20, 1917, in Brooklyn, N.Y. ... 5-10/170 (1,78/77,1). ... Full name: Arnold Jacob Auerbach. ... Name pronounced HOUR-back.
HIGH SCHOOL: Eastern District (Brooklyn, N.Y.).
JUNIOR COLLEGE: Seth Low Junior College (N.Y.).
COLLEGE: George Washington.
CAREER NOTES: Vice president, Boston Celtics (1950-51 through 1963-64). ... Vice president and general manager, Celtics (1964-65). ... Executive vice president and general manager, Celtics (1965-66 through 1969-70). ... President and general manager, Celtics (1970-71 through 1983-84). ... President, Celtics (1984-85 through 1996-97). .. Vice chairman of the board, Celtics (1997-98 to present).
CAREER HONORS: Elected to Naismith Memorial Basketball Hall of Fame (1968). ... One of the Top 10 Coaches in NBA History (1996).

COLLEGIATE RECORD

Season Team	G	Min.	FGM	FGA	Pct.	FTM	FTA	Pct.	Reb.	Ast.	Pts.	RPG	APG	PPG
36-37—Seth Low J.C.						Statistics unavailable.								
37-38—George Washington	17	...	22	...	...	8	12	.667	...	...	52	...	...	3.1
38-39—George Washington	20	...	54	...	...	12	19	.632	...	...	120	...	...	6.0
39-40—George Washington	19	...	69	...	...	24	39	.615	...	...	162	...	...	8.5
4-year-college totals	56	...	145	...	...	44	70	.629	...	...	334	...	...	6.0

HEAD COACHING RECORD

BACKGROUND: Head coach, St. Alban's Prep (Washington, D.C.). ... Head coach, Roosevelt High School (Washington, D.C.). ... Assistant coach, Duke University (1949-50).
HONORS: NBA Coach of the Year (1965). ... NBA 25th Anniversary All-Time team coach (1970). ... NBA Executive of the Year (1980). ... Selected as the "Greatest Coach in the History of the NBA" by the Professional Basketball Writers' Association of America (1980).

NBA COACHING RECORD

		REGULAR SEASON				PLAYOFFS		
Season Team	W	L	Pct.	Finish		W	L	Pct.
46-47 —Washington (BAA)	49	11	.817	1st/Eastern Division		2	4	.333
47-48 —Washington (BAA)	28	20	.583	T2nd/Western Division		0	1	.000
48-49 —Washington (BAA)	38	22	.633	1st/Eastern Division		6	5	.545
49-50 —Tri-Cities	28	29	.491	3rd/Western Division		1	2	.333
50-51 —Boston	39	30	.565	2nd/Eastern Division		0	2	.000
51-52 —Boston	39	27	.591	2nd/Eastern Division		1	2	.333
52-53 —Boston	46	25	.648	3rd/Eastern Division		3	3	.500
53-54 —Boston	42	30	.583	T2nd/Eastern Division		2	4	.333
54-55 —Boston	36	36	.500	3rd/Eastern Division		3	4	.429
55-56 —Boston	39	33	.542	2nd/Eastern Division		1	2	.333
56-57 —Boston	44	28	.611	1st/Eastern Division		7	3	.700
57-58 —Boston	49	23	.681	1st/Eastern Division		6	5	.545
58-59 —Boston	52	20	.722	1st/Eastern Division		8	3	.727
59-60 —Boston	59	16	.787	1st/Eastern Division		8	5	.615
60-61 —Boston	57	22	.722	1st/Eastern Division		8	2	.800
61-62 —Boston	60	20	.750	1st/Eastern Division		8	6	.571
62-63 —Boston	58	22	.725	1st/Eastern Division		8	5	.615
63-64 —Boston	59	21	.738	1st/Eastern Division		8	2	.800
64-65 —Boston	62	18	.775	1st/Eastern Division		8	4	.667
65-66 —Boston	54	26	.675	2nd/Eastern Division		11	6	.647
Totals (20 years)	938	479	.662	**Totals (20 years)**		99	70	.586

NOTES:
1947—Lost to Chicago in BAA Semifinals.
1948—Lost to Chicago, 74-70, in Western Division tiebreaker.
1949—Defeated Philadelphia, 2-0, in Eastern Division Semifinals; defeated New York, 2-1, in Eastern Division Finals; lost to Minneapolis, 4-2, in NBA Finals. Replaced Roger Potter as Tri-Cities head coach with record of 1-6.
1950—Lost to Anderson in Western Division Semifinals.
1951—Lost to New York in Eastern Division Semifinals.
1952—Lost to New York in Eastern Division Semifinals.
1953—Defeated Syracuse, 2-0, in Eastern Division Semifinals; lost to New York, 3-1, in Eastern Division Finals.
1954—Defeated New York, 93-71; lost to Syracuse, 96-95 (OT); defeated New York, 79-78; lost to Syracuse, 98-85, in Eastern Division round robin; lost to Syracuse, 2-0, in Eastern Division Finals.
1955—Defeated New York, 2-1, in Eastern Division Semifinals; lost to Syracuse, 3-1, in Eastern Division Finals.
1956—Lost to Syracuse in Eastern Division Semifinals.
1957—Defeated Syracuse, 3-0, in Eastern Division Finals; defeated St. Louis, 4-3, in NBA Finals.
1958—Defeated Philadelphia, 4-1, in Eastern Division Finals; lost to St. Louis, 4-2, in NBA Finals.
1959—Defeated Syracuse, 4-3, in Eastern Division Finals; defeated Minneapolis, 4-0, in NBA Finals.
1960—Defeated Philadelphia, 4-2, in Eastern Division Finals; defeated St. Louis, 4-3, in NBA Finals.
1961—Defeated Syracuse, 4-1, in Eastern Division Finals; defeated St. Louis, 4-1, in NBA Finals.
1962—Defeated Philadelphia, 4-3, in Eastern Division Finals; defeated Los Angeles, 4-3, in NBA Finals.
1963—Defeated Cincinnati, 4-3, in Eastern Division Finals; defeated Los Angeles, 4-2, in NBA Finals.
1964—Defeated Cincinnati, 4-1, in Eastern Division Finals; defeated San Francisco, 4-1, in NBA Finals.
1965—Defeated Philadelphia, 4-3, in Eastern Division Finals; defeated Los Angeles, 4-1, in NBA Finals.
1966—Defeated Cincinnati, 3-2 in Eastern Division Semifinals; defeated Philadelphia, 4-1, in Eastern Division Finals; defeated Los Angeles, 4-3, in NBA Finals.

COSTELLO, LARRY

PERSONAL: Born July 2, 1931, in Minoa, N.Y. ... 6-1/188 (1,85/85,3). ... Full name: Lawrence Ronald Costello.
HIGH SCHOOL: Minoa (N.Y.).
COLLEGE: Niagara.
TRANSACTIONS: Selected by Philadelphia Warriors in second round of 1954 NBA Draft. ... Sold by Warriors to Syracuse Nationals (October 10, 1957). ... Nationals franchise moved from Syracuse to Philadelphia and renamed 76ers for 1963-64 season. ... Played in Eastern Basketball League with Wilkes-Barre Barons (1965-66). ... Drafted by Milwaukee Bucks from 76ers in NBA Expansion Draft (May 6, 1968).
MISCELLANEOUS: Member of NBA championship team (1967).

COLLEGIATE RECORD

Season Team	G	Min.	FGM	FGA	Pct.	FTM	FTA	Pct.	Reb.	Ast.	Pts.	RPG	APG	PPG
50-51—Niagara‡						Freshman team statistics unavailable.								
51-52—Niagara	28	...	131	...	...	58	87	.667	...	...	320	...	...	11.4
52-53—Niagara	28	...	185	...	...	140	194	.722	...	...	510	...	...	18.2
53-54—Niagara	29	...	160	...	...	125	152	.822	...	...	445	...	...	15.3
Varsity totals	85	...	476	...	...	323	433	.746	...	...	1275	...	...	15.0

NBA REGULAR-SEASON RECORD

HONORS: All-NBA second team (1961).

Season Team	G	Min.	FGM	FGA	Pct.	FTM	FTA	Pct.	Reb.	Ast.	PF	Dq.	Pts.	RPG	APG	PPG
54-55 —Philadelphia	19	463	46	139	.331	26	32	.813	49	78	37	0	118	2.6	4.1	6.2
55-56 —Philadelphia						Did not play—in military service.										
56-57 —Philadelphia	72	2111	186	497	.374	175	222	.788	323	236	182	2	547	4.5	3.3	7.6
57-58 —Syracuse	72	2746	378	888	.426	320	378	.847	378	317	246	3	1076	5.3	4.4	14.9
58-59 —Syracuse	70	2750	414	948	.437	280	349	.802	365	379	263	7	1108	5.2	5.4	15.8
59-60 —Syracuse	71	2469	372	822	.453	249	289	.862	388	449	234	4	993	5.5	6.3	14.0
60-61 —Syracuse	75	2167	407	844	.482	270	338	.799	292	413	286	9	1084	3.9	5.5	14.5
61-62 —Syracuse	63	1854	310	726	.427	247	295	.837	245	359	220	5	867	3.9	5.7	13.8
62-63 —Syracuse	78	2066	285	660	.432	288	327	*.881	237	334	263	4	858	3.0	4.3	11.0
63-64 —Philadelphia	45	1137	191	408	.468	147	170	.865	105	167	150	3	529	2.3	3.7	11.8
64-65 —Philadelphia	64	1967	309	695	.445	243	277	*.877	169	275	242	10	861	2.6	4.3	13.5
66-67 —Philadelphia	49	976	130	293	.444	120	133	.902	103	140	141	2	380	2.1	2.9	7.8
67-68 —Philadelphia	28	492	67	148	.453	67	81	.827	51	68	62	0	201	1.8	2.4	7.2
Totals	706	21198	3095	7068	.438	2432	2891	.841	2705	3215	2326	49	8622	3.8	4.6	12.2

NBA PLAYOFF RECORD

Season Team	G	Min.	FGM	FGA	Pct.	FTM	FTA	Pct.	Reb.	Ast.	PF	Dq.	Pts.	RPG	APG	PPG
56-57 —Philadelphia	2	16	3	8	.375	0	1	.000	5	2	3	0	6	2.5	1.0	3.0
57-58 —Syracuse	3	134	10	34	.294	14	14	1.000	25	12	6	0	34	8.3	4.0	11.3
58-59 —Syracuse	9	361	54	121	.446	51	61	.836	53	54	40	2	159	5.9	6.0	17.7
59-60 —Syracuse	3	122	20	47	.426	10	12	.833	14	20	15	1	50	4.7	6.7	16.7
60-61 —Syracuse	8	269	42	103	.408	47	55	.855	35	52	39	3	131	4.4	6.5	16.4
61-62 —Syracuse	5	167	22	51	.431	29	33	.879	16	28	21	0	73	3.2	5.6	14.6
62-63 —Syracuse	5	134	16	37	.432	19	23	.826	4	23	27	2	51	0.8	4.6	10.2
63-64 —Philadelphia	5	36	3	14	.214	10	10	1.000	3	4	14	1	16	0.6	0.8	3.2
64-65 —Philadelphia	10	207	22	53	.415	11	16	.688	12	20	43	2	55	1.2	2.0	5.5
66-67 —Philadelphia	2	25	6	8	.750	5	5	1.000	4	3	2	0	17	2.0	1.5	8.5
Totals	52	1471	198	476	.416	196	230	.852	171	218	210	11	592	3.3	4.2	11.4

NBA ALL-STAR GAME RECORD

Season Team	Min.	FGM	FGA	Pct.	FTM	FTA	Pct.	Reb.	Ast.	PF	Dq.	Pts.
1958 —Syracuse	17	0	6	.000	1	1	1.000	1	4	2	0	1
1959 —Syracuse	18	3	8	.375	1	1	1.000	3	3	1	0	7
1960 —Syracuse	20	5	9	.556	0	0	...	4	2	1	0	10
1961 —Syracuse	5	1	2	.500	0	0	...	0	0	2	0	2
1962 —Syracuse					Selected, did not play—injured.							
1965 —Philadelphia	11	2	7	.286	0	0	...	1	2	2	0	4
Totals	71	11	32	.344	2	2	1.000	9	11	8	0	24

EBL REGULAR-SEASON RECORD

Season Team	G	Min.	FGM	FGA	Pct.	FTM	FTA	Pct.	Reb.	Ast.	PF	Dq.	Pts.	RPG	APG	PPG
65-66 —Wilkes-Barre	12	...	54	...	...	53	59	.898	22	83	...	.	167	1.8	6.9	13.9

HEAD COACHING RECORD

BACKGROUND: Head coach, Minoa High School, N.Y. (1965-66). ... Head coach, Milwaukee Does of Women's Professional Basketball League (1979-80).

NBA COACHING RECORD

	REGULAR SEASON				PLAYOFFS		
Season Team	W	L	Pct.	Finish	W	L	Pct.
68-69 —Milwaukee	27	55	.329	7th/Eastern Division	—	—	—
69-70 —Milwaukee	56	26	.683	2nd/Eastern Division	5	5	.500
70-71 —Milwaukee	66	16	.805	1st/Midwest Division	12	2	.857
71-72 —Milwaukee	63	19	.768	1st/Midwest Division	6	5	.545

ALL-TIME GREAT COACHES

Season Team	REGULAR SEASON				PLAYOFFS		
	W	L	Pct.	Finish	W	L	Pct.
72-73 —Milwaukee	60	22	.732	1st/Midwest Division	2	4	.333
73-74 —Milwaukee	59	23	.720	1st/Midwest Division	11	5	.688
74-75 —Milwaukee	38	44	.463	4th/Midwest Division	—	—	—
75-76 —Milwaukee	38	44	.463	1st/Midwest Division	1	2	.333
76-77 —Milwaukee	3	15	.167		—	—	—
78-79 —Chicago	20	36	.357		—	—	—
Totals (10 years)	430	300	.589	Totals (6 years)	37	23	.617

COLLEGIATE COACHING RECORD

Season Team	W	L	Pct.	Finish
80-81 —Utica	13	12	.520	Independent
81-82 —Utica	4	22	.154	Independent
82-83 —Utica	11	15	.423	Independent
83-84 —Utica	11	15	.423	Independent
84-85 —Utica	15	12	.556	Independent
85-86 —Utica	13	14	.481	Independent
86-87 —Utica	10	16	.385	Independent
Totals (7 years)	77	106	.421	

NOTE:

1970—Defeated Philadelphia, 4-1, in Eastern Division Semifinals; lost to New York, 4-1, in Eastern Division Finals.

1971—Defeated San Francisco, 4-1, in Western Conference Semifinals; defeated Los Angeles, 4-1, in Western Conference Finals; defeated Baltimore, 4-0, in NBA Finals.

1972—Defeated Golden State, 4-1, in Western Conference Semifinals; lost to Los Angeles, 4-2, in Western Conference Finals.

1973—Lost to Golden State in Western Conference Semifinals.

1974—Defeated Los Angeles, 4-1, in Western Conference Semifinals; defeated Chicago, 4-0, in Western Conference Finals; lost to Boston, 4-3, in NBA Finals.

1976—Lost to Detroit in Western Conference First Round. Resigned as Milwaukee head coach and replaced by Don Nelson (November 22).

1979—Replaced as Chicago head coach by Scotty Robertson (February 16).

CUNNINGHAM, BILLY

PERSONAL: Born June 3, 1943, in Brooklyn, N.Y. ... 6-7/210 (2,00/95,3). ... Full name: William John Cunningham.
HIGH SCHOOL: Erasmus Hall (Brooklyn, N.Y.).
COLLEGE: North Carolina.
TRANSACTIONS: Selected by Philadelphia 76ers in first round of 1965 NBA Draft. ... Signed as free agent by Carolina Cougars of American Basketball Association (August 1969). ... Signed as free agent by 76ers (1969). ... Suspended by NBA (1972). ... Restored by NBA (1974). ... Returned to 76ers (1974).
CAREER HONORS: Elected to Naismith Memorial Basketball Hall of Fame (1986). ... One of the 50 Greatest Players in NBA History (1996).
CAREER NOTES: Part owner, Miami Heat (1987-88 to 1994-95).
MISCELLANEOUS: Member of NBA championship team (1967).

NOTES: THE SPORTING NEWS All-America second team (1965).

COLLEGIATE RECORD

Season Team	G	Min.	FGM	FGA	Pct.	FTM	FTA	Pct.	Reb.	Ast.	Pts.	AVERAGES		
												RPG	APG	PPG
61-62—North Carolina‡	10	...	81	162	.500	45	78	.577	127	...	207	12.7	...	20.7
62-63—North Carolina	21	...	186	380	.489	105	170	.618	339	...	477	16.1	...	22.7
63-64—North Carolina	24	...	233	526	.443	157	249	.631	379	...	623	15.8	...	26.0
64-65—North Carolina	24	...	237	481	.493	135	213	.634	344	...	609	14.3	...	25.4
Varsity totals	69	...	656	1387	.473	397	632	.628	1062	...	1709	15.4	...	24.8

NBA REGULAR-SEASON RECORD

HONORS: All-NBA first team (1969, 1970, 1971). ... All-NBA second team (1972). ... NBA All-Rookie team (1966).

Season Team	G	Min.	FGM	FGA	Pct.	FTM	FTA	Pct.	Reb.	Ast.	PF	Dq.	Pts.	AVERAGES		
														RPG	APG	PPG
65-66 —Philadelphia	80	2134	431	1011	.426	281	443	.634	599	207	301	12	1143	7.5	2.6	14.3
66-67 —Philadelphia	81	2168	556	1211	.459	383	558	.686	589	205	260	2	1495	7.3	2.5	18.5
67-68 —Philadelphia	74	2076	516	1178	.438	368	509	.723	562	187	260	3	1400	7.6	2.5	18.9
68-69 —Philadelphia	82	3345	739	1736	.426	556	754	.737	1050	287	*329	10	2034	12.8	3.5	24.8
69-70 —Philadelphia	81	3194	802	1710	.469	510	700	.729	1101	352	331	15	2114	13.6	4.3	26.1
70-71 —Philadelphia	81	3090	702	1519	.462	455	620	.734	946	395	328	5	1859	11.7	4.9	23.0
71-72 —Philadelphia	75	2900	658	1428	.461	428	601	.712	918	443	295	12	1744	12.2	5.9	23.3

Season Team	G	Min.	FGM	FGA	Pct.	FTM	FTA	Pct.	REBOUNDS			Ast.	Stl.	Blk.	TO	Pts.	AVERAGES		
									Off.	Def.	Tot.						RPG	APG	PPG
74-75 —Philadelphia	80	2859	609	1423	.428	345	444	.777	130	596	726	442	91	35	...	1563	9.1	5.5	19.5
75-76 —Philadelphia	20	640	103	251	.410	68	88	.773	29	118	147	107	24	10	...	274	7.4	5.4	13.7
Totals	654	22406	5116	11467	.446	3394	4717	.720	...	...	6638	2625	115	45	...	13626	10.1	4.0	20.8

Personal fouls/disqualifications: 1974-75. 270/4. 1975-76, 57/1. Totals, 2431/64.

NBA PLAYOFF RECORD

Season Team	G	Min.	FGM	FGA	Pct.	FTM	FTA	Pct.	Reb.	Ast.	PF	Dq.	Pts.	AVERAGES		
														RPG	APG	PPG
65-66 —Philadelphia	4	69	5	31	.161	11	13	.846	18	10	11	0	21	4.5	2.5	5.3
66-67 —Philadelphia	15	339	83	221	.376	59	90	.656	93	33	53	1	225	6.2	2.2	15.0
67-68 —Philadelphia	3	86	24	43	.558	14	17	.824	22	10	16	1	62	7.3	3.3	20.7
68-69 —Philadelphia	5	217	49	117	.419	24	38	.632	63	12	24	1	122	12.6	2.4	24.4
69-70 —Philadelphia	5	205	61	123	.496	24	36	.667	52	20	19	0	146	10.4	4.0	29.2
70-71 —Philadelphia	7	301	67	142	.472	47	67	.701	108	40	28	0	181	15.4	5.7	25.9
Totals	39	1217	289	677	.427	179	261	.686	356	125	151	3	757	9.1	3.2	19.4

NBA ALL-STAR GAME RECORD

Season	Team	Min.	FGM	FGA	Pct.	FTM	FTA	Pct.	Reb.	Ast.	PF	Dq.	Pts.
1969	—Philadelphia	22	5	10	.500	0	0	...	5	1	3	0	10
1970	—Philadelphia	28	7	13	.538	5	5	1.000	4	2	3	0	19
1971	—Philadelphia	19	2	8	.250	1	2	.500	4	3	1	0	5
1972	—Philadelphia	24	4	13	.308	6	8	.750	10	3	4	0	14
Totals		93	18	44	.409	12	15	.800	23	9	11	0	48

ABA REGULAR-SEASON RECORD

NOTES: ABA Most Valuable Player (1973). ... ABA All-Star first team (1973).

				2-POINT			3-POINT							AVERAGES		
Season	Team	G	Min.	FGM	FGA	Pct.	FGM	FGA	Pct.	FTM	FTA	Pct.	Reb.	Ast.	Pts.	RPG	APG	PPG
72-73—	Carolina	84	3248	757	1534	.493	14	49	.286	472	598	.789	1012	530	2028	12.0	6.3	24.1
73-74—	Carolina	32	1190	252	529	.476	1	8	.125	149	187	.797	331	150	656	10.3	4.7	20.5
Totals		116	4438	1009	2063	.489	15	57	.263	621	785	.791	1343	680	2684	11.6	5.9	23.1

ABA PLAYOFF RECORD

				2-POINT			3-POINT							AVERAGES		
Season	Team	G	Min.	FGM	FGA	Pct.	FGM	FGA	Pct.	FTM	FTA	Pct.	Reb.	Ast.	Pts.	RPG	APG	PPG
72-73—	Carolina	12	472	111	219	.507	1	4	.250	57	83	.687	142	61	282	11.8	5.1	23.5
73-74—	Carolina	3	61	9	29	.310	0	2	.000	4	5	.800	16	6	22	5.3	2.0	7.3
Totals		15	533	120	248	.484	1	6	.167	61	88	.693	158	67	304	10.5	4.5	20.3

ABA ALL-STAR GAME RECORD

			2-POINT			3-POINT								
Season	Team	Min.	FGM	FGA	Pct.	FGM	FGA	Pct.	FTM	FTA	Pct.	Reb.	Ast.	Pts.
1973	—Carolina	20	9	11	.818	0	1	.000	0	0	...	6	4	18

COMBINED ABA AND NBA REGULAR-SEASON RECORDS

								REBOUNDS							AVERAGES		
	G	Min.	FGM	FGA	Pct.	FTM	FTA	Pct.	Off.	Def.	Tot.	Ast.	Stl.	Blk.	TO	Pts.	RPG	APG	PPG
Totals	770	26844	6140	13587	.452	4015	5502	.730	...	...	7981	3305	...	...	...	16310	10.4	4.3	21.2

Three-point field goals: 15-for-57 (.263).
Personal fouls: 2845.

NBA COACHING RECORD

		REGULAR SEASON				PLAYOFFS		
Season	Team	W	L	Pct.	Finish	W	L	Pct.
77-78	—Philadelphia	53	23	.697	1st/Atlantic Division	6	4	.600
78-79	—Philadelphia	47	35	.573	2nd/Atlantic Division	5	4	.556
79-80	—Philadelphia	59	23	.720	2nd/Atlantic Division	12	6	.667
80-81	—Philadelphia	62	20	.756	T1st/Atlantic Division	9	7	.563
81-82	—Philadelphia	58	24	.707	2nd/Atlantic Division	12	9	.571
82-83	—Philadelphia	65	17	.793	1st/Atlantic Division	12	1	.923
83-84	—Philadelphia	52	30	.634	2nd/Atlantic Division	2	3	.400
84-85	—Philadelphia	58	24	.707	2nd/Atlantic Division	8	5	.615
Totals (8 years)		454	196	.698	**Totals (8 years)**	66	39	.629

NOTES:

1977—Replaced Gene Shue as Philadelphia head coach (November 4), with record of 2-4.

1978—Defeated New York, 4-0, in Eastern Conference Semifinals; lost to Washington, 4-2, in Eastern Conference Finals.

1979—Defeated New Jersey, 2-0, in Eastern Conference First Round; lost to San Antonio, 4-3, in Eastern Conference Semifinals.

1980—Defeated Washington, 2-0, in Eastern Conference First Round; defeated Atlanta, 4-1, in Eastern Conference Semifinals; defeated Boston, 4-1, in Eastern Conference Finals; lost to Los Angeles, 4-2, in NBA Finals.

1981—Defeated Indiana, 2-0, in Eastern Conference First Round; defeated Milwaukee, 4-3, in Eastern Conference Semifinals; lost to Boston, 4-3, in Eastern Conference Finals.

1982—Defeated Atlanta, 2-0, in Eastern Conference First Round; defeated Milwaukee, 4-2, in Eastern Conference Semifinals; defeated Boston, 4-3, in Eastern Conference Finals; lost to Los Angeles, 4-2, in NBA Finals.

1983—Defeated New York, 4-0, in Eastern Conference Semifinals; defeated Milwaukee, 4-1, in Eastern Conference Finals; defeated Los Angeles, 4-0, in NBA Finals.

1984—Lost to New Jersey in Eastern Conference First Round.

1985—Defeated Washington, 3-1, in Eastern Conference First Round; defeated Milwaukee, 4-0, in Eastern Conference Semifinals; lost to Boston, 4-1, in Eastern Conference Finals.

DALY, CHUCK

PERSONAL: Born July 20, 1930, in St. Mary's, Pa. ... 6-2/180 (1,88/81,6). ... Full name: Charles Jerome Daly.

HIGH SCHOOL: Kane Area (Pa.).

COLLEGE: St. Bonaventure, then Bloomsburg (Pa.) State.

CAREER NOTES: Broadcaster, 76ers (1982-83). ... Broadcaster, Turner Sports (1994-95 through 1996-97). ... Special consultant to the president, Vancouver Grizzlies (May 10, 2000-present). ... Vancouver franchise moved to Memphis for 2001-02 season.

MISCELLANEOUS: Head coach, gold-medal-winning U.S. Olympic team (1992).

CAREER HONORS: Elected to Naismith Memorial Basketball Hall of Fame (1994). ... One of the Top 10 Coaches in NBA History (1996).

COLLEGIATE RECORD

												AVERAGES		
Season	Team	G	Min.	FGM	FGA	Pct.	FTM	FTA	Pct.	Reb.	Ast.	Pts.	RPG	APG	PPG
48-49—St. Bonaventure‡					Freshman team statistics unavailable.										
49-50—Bloomsburg State					Did not play—transfer student.										
50-51—Bloomsburg State		16	...	...	...	...	...	...	...	...	...	215	...	...	13.4
51-52—Bloomsburg State		16	...	...	...	...	...	...	...	...	...	203	...	...	12.7
Varsity totals		32	...	...	...	...	...	...	...	...	...	418	...	...	13.1

HEAD COACHING RECORD

BACKGROUND: Head coach, Punxsutawney High School, Pa (1955-56 through 1962-63; record: 111-70, .613). ... Assistant coach, Duke University (1963-64 through 1968-69). ... Assistant coach, Philadelphia 76ers (1978-December 4, 1981).

COLLEGIATE COACHING RECORD

Season Team	W	L	Pct.	Finish
69-70 —Boston College	11	13	.458	Independent
70-71 —Boston College	15	11	.577	Independent
71-72 —Pennsylvania	25	3	.893	1st/Ivy League
72-73 —Pennsylvania	21	7	.750	1st/Ivy League
73-74 —Pennsylvania	21	6	.778	1st/Ivy League
74-75 —Pennsylvania	23	5	.821	1st/Ivy League
75-76 —Pennsylvania	17	9	.654	2nd/Ivy League
76-77 —Pennsylvania	18	8	.692	2nd/Ivy League
Totals (8 years)	151	62	.709	

NBA COACHING RECORD

Season Team	REGULAR SEASON				PLAYOFFS		
	W	L	Pct.	Finish	W	L	Pct.
81-82 —Cleveland	9	32	.220		—	—	—
83-84 —Detroit	49	33	.598	2nd/Central Division	2	3	.400
84-85 —Detroit	46	36	.561	2nd/Central Division	5	4	.556
85-86 —Detroit	46	36	.561	3rd/Central Division	1	3	.250
86-87 —Detroit	52	30	.634	2nd/Central Division	10	5	.667
87-88 —Detroit	54	28	.659	1st/Central Division	14	9	.609
88-89 —Detroit	63	19	.768	1st/Central Division	15	2	.882
89-90 —Detroit	59	23	.720	1st/Central Division	15	5	.750
90-91 —Detroit	50	32	.610	2nd/Central Division	7	8	.467
91-92 —Detroit	48	34	.585	3rd/Central Division	2	3	.400
92-93 —New Jersey	43	39	.524	3rd/Atlantic Division	2	3	.400
93-94 —New Jersey	45	37	.549	3rd/Atlantic Division	1	3	.250
97-98 —Orlando	41	41	.500	5th/Atlantic Division	—	—	—
98-99 —Orlando	33	17	.660	T1st/Atlantic Division	1	3	.250
Totals (14 years)	638	437	.593	**Totals (12 years)**	75	51	.595

OLYMPIC RECORD

Season Team	W	L	Pct.	Finish
1992 —Team USA	8	0	1.000	Gold medal

NOTES:

1972—Defeated Providence, 76-60, in NCAA Tournament first round; defeated Villanova, 78-67, in second round; lost to North Carolina, 73-59, in regional final.

1973—Defeated St. John's, 62-61, in NCAA Tournament first round; lost to Providence, 87-65, in second round; lost to Syracuse, 69-68, in regional consolation game.

1974—Lost to Providence, 84-69, in NCAA Tournament first round.

1975—Lost to Kansas State, 69-62, in NCAA Tournament first round.

1981—Replaced Don Delaney (4-13) and Bob Kloppenburg (0-1) as Cleveland head coach (December 4), with record of 4-14.

1982—Replaced as Cleveland head coach by Bill Musselman (February), with record of 13-46.

1984—Lost to New York in Eastern Conference First Round.

1985—Defeated New Jersey, 3-0, in Eastern Conference First Round; lost to Boston, 4-2, in Eastern Conference Semifinals.

1986—Lost to Atlanta in Eastern Conference First Round.

1987—Defeated Washington, 3-0, in Eastern Conference First Round; defeated Atlanta, 4-1, in Eastern Conference Semifinals; lost to Boston, 4-3, in Eastern Conference Finals.

1988—Defeated Washington, 3-2, in Eastern Conference First Round; defeated Chicago, 4-1, in Eastern Conference Semifinals; defeated Boston, 4-2, in Eastern Conference Finals; lost to Los Angeles Lakers, 4-3, in NBA Finals.

1989—Defeated Boston, 3-0, in Eastern Conference First Round; defeated Milwaukee, 4-0, in Eastern Conference Semifinals; defeated Chicago, 4-2, in Eastern Conference Finals; defeated Los Angeles Lakers, 4-0, in NBA Finals.

1990—Defeated Indiana, 3-0, in Eastern Conference First Round; defeated New York, 4-1, in Eastern Conference Semifinals; defeated Chicago, 4-3, in Eastern Conference Finals; defeated Portland, 4-1, in NBA Finals.

1991—Defeated Atlanta, 3-2, in Eastern Conference First Round; defeated Boston, 4-2, in Eastern Conference Semifinals; lost to Chicago, 4-0, in Eastern Conference Finals.

1992—Lost to New York in Eastern Conference First Round.
Team USA defeated Angola, 116-48; Croatia, 103-70; Germany, 111-68; Brazil, 127-83; and Spain, 122-81, in preliminary round. Defeated Puerto Rico, 115-77, in medal round quarterfinals; defeated Lithuania, 127-76, in semifinals; defeated Croatia, 117-85, in gold-medal game.

1993—Lost to Cleveland in Eastern Conference First Round.

1994—Lost to New York in Eastern Conference First Round.

1999—Lost to Philadelphia in Eastern Conference First Round.

FITCH, BILL

PERSONAL: Born May 19, 1934, in Davenport, Iowa. ... 6-2/205 (1,88/93,0). ... Full name: Billy Charles Fitch.
HIGH SCHOOL: Cedar Rapids (Iowa).
COLLEGE: Coe College (Iowa).
CAREER HONORS: One of the Top 10 Coaches in NBA History (1996).

COLLEGIATE RECORD

Season Team	G	Min.	FGM	FGA	Pct.	FTM	FTA	Pct.	Reb.	Ast.	Pts.	AVERAGES		
												RPG	APG	PPG
50-51—Coe College						Freshman team statistics unavailable.								
51-52—Coe College	20	...	63	...	...	50	...	...	...	...	176	...	...	8.8
52-53—Coe College	19	...	83	...	...	72	...	...	...	...	238	...	...	12.5
53-54—Coe College	22	...	123	...	...	92	...	...	...	...	338	...	...	15.4
Totals	61	...	269	...	...	214	...	...	...	...	752	...	...	12.3

HEAD COACHING RECORD

BACKGROUND: Head baseball coach and assistant basketball coach, Creighton University (1956-57 and 1957-58).
HONORS: NBA Coach of the Year (1976, 1980).

COLLEGIATE COACHING RECORD

Season	Team	W	L	Pct.	Finish
58-59	—Coe College	11	9	.550	6th/Midwest Collegiate Athletic Conference
59-60	—Coe College	12	9	.571	T5th/Midwest Collegiate Athletic Conference
60-61	—Coe College	10	12	.455	T4th/Midwest Collegiate Athletic Conference
61-62	—Coe College	11	10	.524	T6th/Midwest Collegiate Athletic Conference
62-63	—North Dakota	14	13	.519	3rd/North Central Intercollegiate Athletic Conference
63-64	—North Dakota	10	16	.385	T3rd/North Central Intercollegiate Athletic Conference
64-65	—North Dakota	26	5	.839	1st/North Central Intercollegiate Athletic Conference
65-66	—North Dakota	24	5	.828	1st/North Central Intercollegiate Athletic Conference
66-67	—North Dakota	20	6	.769	1st/North Central Intercollegiate Athletic Conference
67-68	—Bowling Green	18	7	.720	1st/Mid-American Conference
68-69	—Minnesota	12	12	.500	T5th/Big Ten Conference
69-70	—Minnesota	13	11	.542	5th/Big Ten Conference
	Totals (12 years)	181	115	.611	

NBA COACHING RECORD

		REGULAR SEASON				PLAYOFFS		
Season	Team	W	L	Pct.	Finish	W	L	Pct.
70-71	—Cleveland	15	67	.183	4th/Central Division	—	—	—
71-72	—Cleveland	23	59	.280	4th/Central Division	—	—	—
72-73	—Cleveland	32	50	.390	4th/Central Division	—	—	—
73-74	—Cleveland	29	53	.354	4th/Central Division	—	—	—
74-75	—Cleveland	40	42	.488	3rd/Central Division	—	—	—
75-76	—Cleveland	49	33	.598	1st/Central Division	6	7	.462
76-77	—Cleveland	43	39	.524	4th/Central Division	1	2	.538
77-78	—Cleveland	43	39	.524	3rd/Central Division	0	2	.000
78-79	—Cleveland	30	52	.366	T4th/Central Division	—	—	—
79-80	—Boston	61	21	.744	1st/Atlantic Division	5	4	.556
80-81	—Boston	62	20	.756	T1st/Atlantic Division	12	5	.706
81-82	—Boston	63	19	.768	1st/Atlantic Division	7	5	.583
82-83	—Boston	56	26	.683	2nd/Atlantic Division	2	5	.286
83-84	—Houston	29	53	.354	6th/Midwest Division	—	—	—
84-85	—Houston	48	34	.585	2nd/Midwest Division	2	3	.400
85-86	—Houston	51	31	.622	1st/Midwest Division	13	7	.650
86-87	—Houston	42	40	.512	3rd/Midwest Division	5	5	.500
87-88	—Houston	46	36	.561	4th/Midwest Division	1	3	.250
89-90	—New Jersey	17	65	.207	6th/Atlantic Division	—	—	—
90-91	—New Jersey	26	56	.317	5th/Atlantic Division	—	—	—
91-92	—New Jersey	40	42	.489	3rd/Atlantic Division	1	3	.250
94-95	—L.A. Clippers	17	65	.207	7th/Pacific Division	—	—	—
95-96	—L.A. Clippers	29	53	.354	7th/Pacific Division	—	—	—
96-97	—L.A. Clippers	36	46	.439	5th/Pacific Division	0	3	.000
97-98	—L.A. Clippers	17	65	.207	7th/Pacific Division	—	—	—
	Totals (25 years)	944	1106	.460	**Totals (13 years)**	55	54	.505

NOTES:

1965—Defeated Minnesota-Duluth, 67-57, in College Division Tournament first round; defeated Moorhead (Minn.) State in second round; defeated Seattle Pacific, 97-83, in national quarterfinals; lost to Southern Illinois, 97-64, in national semifinals; defeated St. Michael's (Vt.), 94-86, in national third-place game.

1966—Defeated Northern Colorado, 84-71, in College Division Tournament regional semifinals; defeated Valparaiso, 112-82, in regional finals; defeated Abilene Christian, 63-62, in national quarterfinals; lost to Southern Illinois, 69-61, in national semifinals; lost to Akron, 76-71, in national third-place game.

1967—Lost to Louisiana Tech, 86-77, in College Division Tournament regional semifinals; defeated Parsons (Ia.), 107-56, in regional third-place game.

1968—Lost to Marquette, 72-71, in NCAA Tournament first round.

1976—Defeated Washington, 4-3, in Eastern Conference Semifinals; lost to Boston, 4-2, in Eastern Conference Finals.

1977—Lost to Washington in Eastern Conference First Round.

1978—Lost to New York in Eastern Conference First Round.

1980—Defeated Houston, 4-0, in Eastern Conference Semifinals; lost to Philadelphia, 4-1, in Eastern Conference Finals.

1981—Defeated Chicago, 4-0, in Eastern Conference Semifinals; defeated Philadelphia, 4-3, in Eastern Conference Finals; defeated Houston, 4-2, in NBA Finals.

1982—Defeated Washington, 4-1, in Eastern Conference Semifinals; lost to Philadelphia, 4-3, in Eastern Conference Finals.

1983—Defeated Atlanta, 2-1, in Eastern Conference First Round; lost to Milwaukee, 4-0, in Eastern Conference Semifinals.

1985—Lost to Utah in Western Conference First Round.

1986—Defeated Sacramento, 3-0, in Western Conference First Round; defeated Denver, 4-2, in Western Conference Semifinals; defeated Los Angeles Lakers, 4-1, in Western Conference Finals; lost to Boston, 4-2, in NBA Finals.

1987—Defeated Portland, 3-1, in Western Conference First Round; lost to Seattle, 4-2, in Western Conference Semifinals.

1988—Lost to Dallas in Western Conference First Round.

1992—Lost to Cleveland in Eastern Conference First Round.

1997—Lost to Utah in Western Conference First Round.

DID YOU KNOW . . .

. . . that when neither Karl Malone or John Stockton scored 10 points in Utah's 103-77 loss to the Clippers last March 27 it marked the first time since November 21, 1987 that neither player reached double figures in the same game?

ALL-TIME GREAT COACHES

FITZSIMMONS, COTTON

PERSONAL: Born October 7, 1931, in Hannibal, Mo. ... 5-7/160 (1,70/72,6). ... Full name: Lowell Fitzsimmons. ... Father of Gary Fitzsimmons, assistant general manager/basketball operations with Golden State Warriors.
HIGH SCHOOL: Bowling Green (Mo.).
COLLEGE: Hannibal (Mo.)-LaGrange, then Midwestern State (Texas).
CAREER NOTES: Director of player personnel, Golden State Warriors (1976-77). ... Director of player personnel, Phoenix Suns (1987-88). ... Head coach/director of player personnel, Suns (1988-89 through 1991-92). ... Senior executive vice president, Suns (1992-93 through January 16, 1996 and November 15, 1996 through present).

COLLEGIATE RECORD

Season Team	G	Min.	FGM	FGA	Pct.	FTM	FTA	Pct.	Reb.	Ast.	Pts.	AVERAGES RPG	APG	PPG
52-53—Hann.-LaGrange‡	33	...	...	...	...	...	...	...	...	...	838	...	...	25.4
53-54—Midwestern State	27	...	53	161	.329	128	173	.740	...	...	234	...	...	8.7
54-55—Midwestern State	27	...	118	258	.457	162	210	.771	...	...	398	...	...	14.7
55-56—Midwestern State	28	...	148	319	.464	164	223	.735	...	...	460	...	...	16.4
Varsity totals	82	...	319	738	.432	454	606	.749	...	...	1092	...	...	13.3

HEAD COACHING RECORD

BACKGROUND: Assistant coach, Kansas State University (1967-68).
HONORS: NBA Coach of the Year (1979, 1989).

COLLEGE COACHING RECORD

Season Team	W	L	Pct.	Finish
58-59 —Moberly J.C. (Mo.)	16	15	.516	
59-60 —Moberly J.C. (Mo.)	19	8	.704	
60-61 —Moberly J.C. (Mo.)	26	5	.839	
61-62 —Moberly J.C. (Mo.)	26	9	.743	
62-63 —Moberly J.C. (Mo.)	26	6	.813	
63-64 —Moberly J.C. (Mo.)	24	5	.828	
64-65 —Moberly J.C. (Mo.)	25	5	.833	
65-66 —Moberly J.C. (Mo.)	29	5	.853	
66-67 —Moberly J.C. (Mo.)	31	2	.939	
68-69 —Kansas State	14	12	.538	T2nd/Big Eight Conference
69-70 —Kansas State	20	8	.714	1st/Big Eight Conference
Junior college totals (9 years)	222	60	.787	
4-year college totals (2 years)	34	20	.630	

NBA COACHING RECORD

Season Team	REGULAR SEASON W	L	Pct.	Finish	PLAYOFFS W	L	Pct.
70-71 —Phoenix	48	34	.585	3rd/Midwest Division	—	—	—
71-72 —Phoenix	49	33	.598	3rd/Midwest Division	—	—	—
72-73 —Atlanta	46	36	.561	2nd/Central Division	2	4	.333
73-74 —Atlanta	35	47	.427	2nd/Central Division	—	—	—
74-75 —Atlanta	31	51	.378	4th/Central Division	—	—	—
75-76 —Atlanta	28	46	.378		—	—	—
77-78 —Buffalo	27	55	.329	4th/Atlantic Division	—	—	—
78-79 —Kansas City	48	34	.585	1st/Midwest Division	1	4	.200
79-80 —Kansas City	47	35	.573	2nd/Midwest Division	1	2	.333
80-81 —Kansas City	40	42	.488	T2nd/Midwest Division	7	8	.467
81-82 —Kansas City	30	52	.366	4th/Midwest Division	—	—	—
82-83 —Kansas City	45	37	.549	T2nd/Midwest Division	—	—	—
83-84 —Kansas City	38	44	.463	T3rd/Midwest Division	0	3	.000
84-85 —San Antonio	41	41	.500	T4th/Midwest Division	2	3	.400
85-86 —San Antonio	35	47	.427	6th/Midwest Division	0	3	.000
88-89 —Phoenix	55	27	.671	2nd/Pacific Division	7	5	.583
89-90 —Phoenix	54	28	.659	3rd/Pacific Division	9	7	.563
90-91 —Phoenix	55	27	.671	3rd/Pacific Division	1	3	.250
91-92 —Phoenix	53	29	.646	3rd/Pacific Division	4	4	.500
95-96 —Phoenix	27	22	.551	4th/Pacific Division	1	3	.250
96-97 —Phoenix	0	8	.000		—	—	—
Totals (21 years)	832	775	.518	**Totals (12 years)**	35	49	.417

NOTES:

1966—Won National Junior College Athletic Association national tournament.
1967—Won National Junior College Athletic Association national tournament.
1970—Lost to New Mexico, 70-66, in NCAA Tournament regional semifinal.
1973—Lost to Boston in Eastern Conference Semifinals.
1976—Replaced as Atlanta head coach by Gene Tormohlen (March) with club in fifth place.
1979—Lost to Phoenix in Western Conference Semifinals.
1980—Lost to Phoenix in Western Conference First Round.
1981—Defeated Portland, 2-1, in Western Conference First Round; defeated Phoenix, 4-3, in Western Conference Semifinals; lost to Houston, 4-1, in Western Conference Finals.
1984—Lost to Los Angeles Lakers in Western Conference First Round.
1985—Lost to Denver in Western Conference First Round.

ALL-TIME GREAT COACHES

1986—Lost to Los Angeles Lakers in Western Conference First Round.

1989—Defeated Denver, 3-0, in Western Conference First Round; defeated Golden State, 4-1, in Western Conference Semifinals; lost to Los Angeles Lakers, 4-0, in Western Conference Finals.

1990—Defeated Utah, 3-2, in Western Conference First Round; defeated Los Angeles Lakers, 4-1, in Western Conference Semifinals; lost to Portland, 4-2, in Western Conference Finals.

1991—Lost to Utah in Western Conference First Round.

1992—Defeated San Antonio, 3-0, in Western Conference First Round; lost to Portland, 4-1, in Western Conference Semifinals.

1996—Replaced Paul Westphal as Phoenix head coach (January 16) with record of 14-19 and club in sixth place. Lost to San Antonio in Western Conference First Round. Replaced as Phoenix head coach by Danny Ainge with record of 0-8 and club in seventh place (November 15).

FRATELLO, MIKE

PERSONAL: Born February 24, 1947, in Hackensack, N.J. ... 5-7/150 (1,70/68,0). ... Full name: Michael Robert Fratello.
HIGH SCHOOL: Hackensack (N.J.).
COLLEGE: Montclair (N.J.) State College, then graduate work at Rhode Island.

HEAD COACHING RECORD

BACKGROUND: Football and basketball coach, Hackensack (N.J.) High (1969-70). ... Assistant coach/freshman coach, University of Rhode Island (1970-71 and 1971-72). ... Assistant coach, James Madison University (1972-73 through 1974-75). ... Assistant coach, Villanova University (1975-76 through 1977-78). ... Assistant coach, Atlanta Hawks (1978-79 through 1981-82). ... Assistant coach, New York Knicks (1982-83). ... Vice president/head coach, Hawks (1986-87 through 1989-90).
CAREER NOTES: Broadcaster, NBC Sports (1990-91 through 1992-93). ... Broadcaster, Turner Sports (1999 to present).
HONORS: NBA Coach of the Year (1986).

NBA COACHING RECORD

Season Team	REGULAR SEASON				PLAYOFFS		
	W	L	Pct.	Finish	W	L	Pct.
80-81—Atlanta	0	3	.000	4th/Central Division	—	—	—
83-84—Atlanta	40	42	.488	3rd/Central Division	2	3	.400
84-85—Atlanta	34	48	.415	5th/Central Division	—	—	—
85-86—Atlanta	50	32	.610	2nd/Central Division	4	5	.444
86-87—Atlanta	57	25	.695	1st/Central Division	4	5	.444
87-88—Atlanta	50	32	.610	T2nd/Central Division	6	6	.500
88-89—Atlanta	52	30	.634	3rd/Central Division	2	3	.400
89-90—Atlanta	41	41	.500	6th/Central Division	—	—	—
93-94—Cleveland	47	35	.573	T3rd/Central Division	0	3	.000
94-95—Cleveland	43	39	.524	4th/Central Division	1	3	.250
95-96—Cleveland	47	35	.573	3rd/Central Division	0	3	.000
96-97—Cleveland	42	40	.512	5th/Central Division	—	—	—
97-98—Cleveland	47	35	.573	5th/Central Division	1	3	.250
98-99—Cleveland	22	28	.440	7th/Central Division	—	—	—
Totals (14 years)	**572**	**465**	**.552**	**Totals (9 years)**	**20**	**34**	**.370**

NOTES:

1981—Replaced Hubie Brown as Atlanta head coach (March 26), with record of 31-48 and club in fourth place. Served as interim co-head coach with Brendan Suhr for remainder of season.

1984—Lost to Milwaukee in Eastern Conference First Round.

1986—Defeated Detroit, 3-1, in Eastern Conference First Round; lost to Boston, 4-1, in Eastern Conference Semifinals.

1987—Defeated Indiana, 3-1, in Eastern Conference First Round; lost to Detroit, 4-1, in Eastern Conference Semifinals.

1988—Defeated Milwaukee, 3-2, in Eastern Conference First Round; lost to Boston, 4-3, in Eastern Conference Semifinals.

1989—Lost to Milwaukee in Eastern Conference First Round.

1994—Lost to Chicago in Eastern Conference First Round.

1995—Lost to New York in Eastern Conference First Round.

1996—Lost to New York in Eastern Conference First Round.

1998—Lost to Indiana in Eastern Conference First Round.

HANNUM, ALEX

PERSONAL: Born July 19, 1923, in Los Angeles. ... 6-7/225 (2,00/102,1). ... Full name: Alexander Murray Hannum.
HIGH SCHOOL: Hamilton (Los Angeles).
COLLEGE: Southern California.
TRANSACTIONS: Played for Los Angeles Shamrocks, an Amateur Athletic Union team and averaged 9.8 points per game (1945-46). ... Signed by Oshkosh All-Stars of National Basketball League (1948). ... Sold by Oshkosh of NBL to Syracuse Nationals of NBA (1949). ... Traded by Nationals with Fred Scolari to Baltimore Bullets for Red Rocha (1951). ... Sold by Bullets to Rochester Royals during 1951-52 season. ... Sold by Royals to Milwaukee Hawks (1954). ... Hawks franchise moved from Milwaukee to St. Louis for 1955-56 season. ... Released by Hawks (1956). ... Signed by Fort Wayne Pistons (1956). ... Released by Pistons (December 12, 1956). ... Signed by Hawks (December 17, 1956).
CAREER HONORS: Elected to Naismith Memorial Basketball Hall of Fame (1998).

COLLEGIATE RECORD

NOTES: In military service (1943-44 through 1945-46).

Season Team	G	Min.	FGM	FGA	Pct.	FTM	FTA	Pct.	Reb.	Ast.	Pts.	AVERAGES		
												RPG	APG	PPG
41-42—Southern California‡					Freshman team statistics unavailable.									
42-43—Southern California	15	...	23	...	...	9	20	.450	...	...	55	...	...	3.7
46-47—Southern California	24	...	...	...	...	...	...	...	...	...	251	...	...	10.5
47-48—Southern California	23	...	108	...	...	...	...	...	...	...	263	...	...	11.4
Varsity totals	**62**	...	...	...	...	...	...	...	...	...	**569**	...	...	**9.2**

ALL-TIME GREAT COACHES

NBL AND NBA REGULAR-SEASON RECORD

Season Team	G	Min.	FGM	FGA	Pct.	FTM	FTA	Pct.	Reb.	Ast.	PF	Dq.	Pts.	AVERAGES RPG	APG	PPG
48-49 —Oshkosh (NBL)................	62	...	126	...	...	113	191	.592	...	...	188	...	365	...	...	5.9
49-50 —Syracuse...........................	64	...	177	488	.363	128	186	.688	...	129	264	...	482	...	2.0	7.5
50-51 —Syracuse...........................	63	...	182	494	.368	107	197	.543	301	119	271	16	471	4.8	1.9	7.5
51-52 —Balt.-Roch.......................	66	1508	170	462	.368	98	138	.710	336	133	271	16	438	5.1	2.0	6.6
52-53 —Rochester........................	68	1288	129	360	.358	88	133	.662	279	81	258	18	346	4.1	1.2	5.1
53-54 —Rochester........................	72	1707	175	503	.348	102	164	.622	350	105	279	11	452	4.9	1.5	6.3
54-55 —Milwaukee	53	1088	126	358	.352	61	107	.570	245	105	206	9	313	4.6	2.0	5.9
55-56 —St. Louis........................	71	1480	146	453	.322	93	154	.604	344	157	271	10	385	4.8	2.2	5.4
56-57 —Fort Wayne-St. Louis........	59	642	77	223	.345	37	56	.661	158	28	135	2	191	2.7	0.5	3.2
Totals..............................	578	...	1308	...	...	827	1326	.624	...	...	2143	...	3443	...	...	6.0

NBL AND NBA PLAYOFF RECORD

Season Team	G	Min.	FGM	FGA	Pct.	FTM	FTA	Pct.	Reb.	Ast.	PF	Dq.	Pts.	AVERAGES RPG	APG	PPG
48-49 —Oshkosh (NBL)................	7	...	12	...	...	16	26	.615	...	...	...	...	40	...	...	5.7
49-50 —Syracuse...........................	11	...	38	86	.442	17	34	.500	...	10	50	...	93	...	0.9	8.5
50-51 —Syracuse...........................	7	...	17	39	.436	8	10	.800	47	17	37	3	42	6.7	2.4	6.0
51-52 —Rochester........................	6	146	16	42	.381	8	13	.615	26	8	30	3	40	4.3	1.3	6.7
52-53 —Rochester........................	3	52	4	10	.400	3	8	.375	4	2	16	1	11	1.3	0.7	3.7
53-54 —Rochester........................	6	107	12	29	.414	15	24	.625	22	5	28	3	39	3.7	0.8	6.5
55-56 —St. Louis........................	8	159	21	66	.318	19	35	.543	29	10	36	3	61	3.6	1.3	7.6
56-57 —St. Louis........................	2	6	0	2	.000	0	0	...	0	0	2	0	0	0.0	0.0	0.0
Totals..............................	50	...	120	...	...	86	150	.573	...	...	...	...	326	...	...	6.5

HEAD COACHING RECORD

HONORS: NBA Coach of the Year (1964). ... ABA Coach of the Year (1969).

NBA COACHING RECORD

Season Team	REGULAR SEASON W	L	Pct.	Finish	PLAYOFFS W	L	Pct.
56-57 —St. Louis...............	15	16	.484	T1st/Western Division	8	4	.667
57-58 —St. Louis...............	41	31	.569	1st/Western Division	8	3	.727
60-61 —Syracuse	38	41	.481	3rd/Eastern Division	4	4	.500
61-62 —Syracuse	41	39	.513	3rd/Eastern Division	2	3	.400
62-63 —Syracuse	48	32	.600	2nd/Eastern Division	2	3	.400
63-64 —San Francisco	48	32	.600	1st/Western Division	5	7	.417
64-65 —San Francisco	17	63	.215	5th/Western Division	—	—	—
65-66 —San Francisco	35	45	.438	4th/Western Division	—	—	—
66-67 —Philadelphia	68	13	.840	1st/Eastern Division	11	4	.733
67-68 —Philadelphia	62	20	.756	1st/Eastern Division	7	6	.538
69-70 —San Diego	18	38	.321	7th/Western Division	—	—	—
70-71 —San Diego	40	42	.488	3rd/Pacific Division	—	—	—
Totals (12 years)...................	471	412	.533	Totals (8 years)	47	34	.580

ABA COACHING RECORD

Season Team	REGULAR SEASON W	L	Pct.	Finish	PLAYOFFS W	L	Pct.
68-69 —Oakland	60	18	.769	1st/Western Division	12	4	.750
71-72 —Denver	34	50	.405	4th/Western Division	3	4	.429
72-73 —Denver	47	37	.560	3rd/Western Division	1	4	.200
73-74 —Denver	37	47	.440	T4th/Western Division	—	—	—
Totals (4 years)...................	178	152	.539	Totals (3 years)	16	12	.571

NOTES:

1957—Replaced Red Holzman (14-19) and Slater Martin (5-3) as St. Louis head coach (January), with record of 19-22. Defeated Fort Wayne, 115-103, and Minneapolis, 114-111, in Western Division tiebreakers; defeated Minneapolis, 3-0, in Western Division Finals; lost to Boston, 4-3, in NBA Finals.

1958—Defeated Detroit, 4-1, in Western Division Finals; defeated Boston, 4-2, in NBA Finals.

1961—Defeated Philadelphia, 3-0, in Eastern Division Semifinals; lost to Boston, 4-1, in Eastern Division Finals.

1962—Lost to Philadelphia in Eastern Division Semifinals.

1963—Lost to Cincinnati in Eastern Division Semifinals.

1964—Defeated St. Louis, 4-3, in Western Division Finals; lost to Boston, 4-1, in NBA Finals.

1967—Defeated Cincinnati, 3-1, in Eastern Division Semifinals; defeated Boston, 4-1, in Eastern Division Finals; defeated San Francisco, 4-2, in NBA Finals.

1968—Defeated New York, 4-2, in Eastern Division Semifinals; lost to Boston, 4-3, in Eastern Division Finals.

1969—Defeated Denver, 4-3, in Western Division Semifinals; defeated New Orleans, 4-0, in Western Division Finals; defeated Indiana, 4-1, in ABA Finals. Replaced Jack McMahon as San Diego head coach (December), with record of 9-17.

1972—Lost to Indiana in Western Division Semifinals.

1973—Lost to Indiana in Western Division Semifinals.

HARRIS, DEL

PERSONAL: Born June 18, 1937, in Plainfield, Ind. ... 6-4/205 (1,93/93,0). ... Full name: Delmer W. Harris.
HIGH SCHOOL: Plainfield (Ind.).
COLLEGE: Milligan College (Tenn.).
CAREER NOTES: Vice president, Bucks (1987 through 1992). ... Consultant, Sacramento Kings (1993-94).

COLLEGIATE RECORD

NOTES: Field goal attempts for five games and rebounds for 13 games are unavailable.

Season Team	G	Min.	FGM	FGA	Pct.	FTM	FTA	Pct.	Reb.	Ast.	Pts.	AVERAGES RPG	APG	PPG
55-56—Milligan College.............	24	...	101	232	.435	89	126	.706	122	...	291	5.1	...	12.1
56-57—Milligan College.............	24	...	162	375	.432	141	197	.716	165	...	465	6.9	...	19.4
57-58—Milligan College.............	22	...	167	378	.442	119	149	.799	240	...	453	10.9	...	20.6
58-59—Milligan College.............	21	...	136	306	.444	158	202	.782	338	...	430	16.1	...	20.5
Totals	91	...	566	1291	.438	507	674	.752	865	...	1639	9.5	...	18.0

HEAD COACHING RECORD

BACKGROUND: Head coach, Superior League, Puerto Rico (1969 through 1975). ... Assistant coach, Utah Stars of ABA (1975-76). ... Assistant coach, Houston Rockets (1976-77 through 1978-79). ... Scout, Milwaukee Bucks (1983 through 1986). ... Assistant coach, Bucks (1986-87). ... Assistant coach, Dallas Mavericks (2000-present).

HONORS: NBA Coach of the Year (1995).

COLLEGIATE COACHING RECORD

Season Team	W	L	Pct.	Finish
65-66 —Earlham College	14	8	.636	Hoosier Collegiate Conference
66-67 —Earlham College	15	9	.625	4th/Hoosier Collegiate Conference
67-68 —Earlham College	25	3	.893	1st/Hoosier Collegiate Conference
68-69 —Earlham College	18	8	.692	2nd/Hoosier Collegiate Conference
69-70 —Earlham College	22	8	.733	1st/Hoosier Collegiate Conference
70-71 —Earlham College	24	5	.828	1st/Hoosier Collegiate Conference
71-72 —Earlham College	21	9	.700	1st/Hoosier Collegiate Conference
72-73 —Earlham College	17	11	.607	3rd/Hoosier Collegiate Conference
73-74 —Earlham College	19	9	.679	3rd/Hoosier Collegiate Conference
Totals (9 years)...................	175	70	.714	

NBA COACHING RECORD

Season Team	REGULAR SEASON W	L	Pct.	Finish	PLAYOFFS W	L	Pct.
79-80 —Houston................	41	41	.500	T2nd/Central Division	2	5	.286
80-81 —Houston................	40	42	.488	T2nd/Midwest Division	12	9	.571
81-82 —Houston................	46	36	.561	T2nd/Midwest Division	1	2	.333
82-83 —Houston................	14	68	.171	6th/Midwest Division	—	—	—
87-88 —Milwaukee	42	40	.512	T4th/Central Division	2	3	.400
88-89 —Milwaukee	49	33	.598	4th/Central Division	3	6	.333
89-90 —Milwaukee	44	38	.537	3rd/Central Division	1	3	.250
90-91 —Milwaukee	48	34	.585	3rd/Central Division	0	3	.000
91-92 —Milwaukee	8	9	.471		—	—	—
94-95 —L.A. Lakers	48	34	.585	3rd/Pacific Division	5	5	.500
95-96 —L.A. Lakers	53	29	.646	2nd/Pacific Division	1	3	.250
96-97 —L.A. Lakers	56	26	.683	2nd/Pacific Division	4	5	.444
97-98 —L.A. Lakers	61	21	.744	T1st/Pacific Division	7	6	.538
98-99 —L.A. Lakers	6	6	.500				
Totals (14 years)...................	556	457	.549	Totals (11 years).....	38	50	.432

NOTES:

1968—Posted 1-1 record in NAIA District Tournament.

1969—Posted 0-1 record in NAIA District Tournament.

1970—Posted 1-1 record in NAIA District Tournament.

1971—Posted 2-0 record in NAIA District Tournament; posted 1-1 record in NAIA National Tournament.

1972—Posted 1-1 record in NAIA District Tournament.

1973—Posted 2-1 record in NAIA District Tournament.

1980—Defeated San Antonio, 2-1, in Eastern Conference First Round; lost to Boston, 4-0, in Eastern Conference Semifinals.

1981—Defeated Los Angeles Lakers, 2-1, in Western Conference First Round; defeated San Antonio, 4-3, in Western Conference Semifinals; defeated Kansas City, 4-1, in Western Conference Finals; lost to Boston, 4-2, in NBA Finals.

1982—Lost to Seattle in Western Conference First Round.

1988—Lost to Atlanta in Eastern Conference First Round.

1989—Defeated Atlanta, 3-2, in Eastern Conference First Round; lost to Detroit, 4-0, in Eastern Conference Semifinals.

1990—Lost to Chicago in Eastern Conference First Round.

1991—Lost to Philadelphia in Eastern Conference First Round. Replaced as Milwaukee head coach by Frank Hamblen (December 4) with club in third place.

1995—Defeated Seattle, 3-1, in Western Conference First Round; lost to San Antonio, 4-2, in Western Conference Semifinals.

1996—Lost to Houston in Western Conference First Round.

1997—Defeated Portland, 3-1, in Western Conference First Round; lost to Utah, 4-1, in Western Conference Semifinals.

1998—Defeated Portland, 3-1, in Western Conference First Round; defeated Seattle, 4-1, in Western Conference Semifinals; lost to Utah, 4-0, in Western Conference Finals.

1999—Replaced as head coach on an interim basis by Kurt Rambis (February 24) with club in fourth place.

HEINSOHN, TOM

PERSONAL: Born August 26, 1934, in Jersey City, N.J. ... 6-7/218 (2,00/98,9). ... Full name: Thomas William Heinsohn.

HIGH SCHOOL: St. Michael's (Union City, N.J.).

COLLEGE: Holy Cross.

TRANSACTIONS: Selected by Boston Celtics in 1956 NBA Draft (territorial pick).

CAREER HONORS: Elected to Naismith Memorial Basketball Hall of Fame (1986).

MISCELLANEOUS: Member of NBA championship team (1957, 1959, 1960, 1961, 1962, 1963, 1964, 1965).

COLLEGIATE RECORD

Season Team	G	Min.	FGM	FGA	Pct.	FTM	FTA	Pct.	Reb.	Ast.	Pts.	AVERAGES RPG	APG	PPG
52-53—Holy Cross‡...................	15	...	97	...	...	70	...	...	...	...	264	...	...	17.6
53-54—Holy Cross...................	28	...	175	364	.481	94	142	.662	300	...	444	10.7	...	15.9
54-55—Holy Cross...................	26	...	232	499	.465	141	215	.656	385	...	605	14.8	...	23.3
55-56—Holy Cross...................	27	...	254	630	.403	232	304	.763	569	...	740	21.1	...	27.4
Varsity totals.........................	81	...	661	1493	.443	467	661	.707	1254	...	1789	15.5	...	22.1

– 457 –

ALL-TIME GREAT COACHES

NBA REGULAR-SEASON RECORD

HONORS: NBA Rookie of the Year (1957). ... All-NBA second team (1961, 1962, 1963, 1964).

Season Team	G	Min.	FGM	FGA	Pct.	FTM	FTA	Pct.	Reb.	Ast.	PF	Dq.	Pts.	RPG	APG	PPG
56-57 —Boston	72	2150	446	1123	.397	271	343	.790	705	117	304	12	1163	9.8	1.6	16.2
57-58 —Boston	69	2206	468	1226	.382	294	394	.746	705	125	274	6	1230	10.2	1.8	17.8
58-59 —Boston	66	2089	465	1192	.390	312	391	.798	638	164	271	11	1242	9.7	2.5	18.8
59-60 —Boston	75	2420	673	1590	.423	283	386	.733	794	171	275	8	1629	10.6	2.3	21.7
60-61 —Boston	74	2256	627	1566	.400	325	424	.767	732	141	260	7	1579	9.9	1.9	21.3
61-62 —Boston	79	2383	692	1613	.429	358	437	.819	747	165	280	2	1742	9.5	2.1	22.1
62-63 —Boston	76	2004	550	1300	.423	340	407	.835	569	95	270	4	1440	7.5	1.3	18.9
63-64 —Boston	76	2040	487	1223	.398	283	342	.827	460	183	268	3	1257	6.1	2.4	16.5
64-65 —Boston	67	1706	365	954	.383	182	229	.795	399	157	252	5	912	6.0	2.3	13.6
Totals	654	19254	4773	11787	.405	2648	3353	.790	5749	1318	2454	58	12194	8.8	2.0	18.6

NBA PLAYOFF RECORD

Season Team	G	Min.	FGM	FGA	Pct.	FTM	FTA	Pct.	Reb.	Ast.	PF	Dq.	Pts.	RPG	APG	PPG
56-57 —Boston	10	370	90	231	.390	49	69	.710	117	20	40	1	229	11.7	2.0	22.9
57-58 —Boston	11	349	68	194	.351	56	72	.778	119	18	52	3	192	10.8	1.6	17.5
58-59 —Boston	11	348	91	220	.414	37	56	.661	98	32	41	0	219	8.9	2.9	19.9
59-60 —Boston	13	423	112	267	.419	60	80	.750	126	27	53	2	284	9.7	2.1	21.8
60-61 —Boston	10	291	82	201	.408	33	43	.767	99	20	36	1	197	9.9	2.0	19.7
61-62 —Boston	14	445	116	291	.399	58	76	.763	115	34	58	4	290	8.2	2.4	20.7
62-63 —Boston	13	413	123	270	.456	75	98	.765	116	15	55	2	321	8.9	1.2	24.7
63-64 —Boston	10	308	70	180	.389	34	42	.810	80	26	36	0	174	8.0	2.6	17.4
64-65 —Boston	12	276	66	181	.365	20	32	.625	84	23	46	1	152	7.0	1.9	12.7
Totals	104	3223	818	2035	.402	422	568	.743	954	215	417	14	2058	9.2	2.1	19.8

NBA ALL-STAR GAME RECORD

Season Team	Min.	FGM	FGA	Pct.	FTM	FTA	Pct.	Reb.	Ast.	PF	Dq.	Pts.
1957 —Boston	23	5	17	.294	2	2	1.000	7	0	3	0	12
1961 —Boston	19	2	16	.125	0	0	...	6	1	4	0	4
1962 —Boston	13	4	11	.364	2	2	1.000	2	1	4	0	10
1963 —Boston	21	6	11	.545	3	4	.750	2	1	4	0	15
1964 —Boston	21	5	12	.417	0	0	...	3	0	5	0	10
1965 —Boston	Selected, did not play—injured.											
Totals	97	22	67	.328	7	8	.875	20	3	20	0	51

HEAD COACHING RECORD

NOTES: NBA Coach of the Year (1973).

NBA COACHING RECORD

Season Team	REGULAR SEASON				PLAYOFFS		
	W	L	Pct.	Finish	W	L	Pct.
69-70 —Boston	34	48	.415	6th/Eastern Division	—	—	—
70-71 —Boston	44	38	.537	3rd/Atlantic Division	—	—	—
71-72 —Boston	56	26	.683	1st/Atlantic Division	5	6	.455
72-73 —Boston	68	14	.829	1st/Atlantic Division	7	6	.538
73-74 —Boston	56	26	.683	1st/Atlantic Division	12	6	.667
74-75 —Boston	60	22	.732	1st/Atlantic Division	6	5	.545
75-76 —Boston	54	28	.659	1st/Atlantic Division	12	6	.667
76-77 —Boston	44	38	.537	2nd/Atlantic Division	5	4	.556
77-78 —Boston	11	23	.324		—	—	—
Totals (9 years)	427	263	.619	Totals (6 years)	47	33	.588

NOTES:

1972—Defeated Atlanta, 4-2, in Eastern Conference Semifinals; lost to New York, 4-1, in Eastern Conference Finals.

1973—Defeated Atlanta, 4-2, in Eastern Conference Semifinals; lost to New York, 4-3, in Eastern Conference Finals.

1974—Defeated Buffalo, 4-2, in Eastern Conference Semifinals; defeated New York, 4-1, in Eastern Conference Finals; defeated Milwaukee, 4-3, in NBA Finals.

1975—Defeated Houston, 4-1, in Eastern Conference Semifinals; lost to Washington, 4-2, in Eastern Conference Finals.

1976—Defeated Buffalo, 4-2, in Eastern Conference Semifinals; defeated Cleveland, 4-2, in Eastern Conference Finals; defeated Phoenix, 4-2, in NBA Finals.

1977—Defeated San Antonio, 2-0, in Eastern Conference First Round; lost to Philadelphia, 4-3, in Eastern Conference Semifinals.

1978—Replaced as Boston head coach by Tom Sanders with club in third place (January 3).

HOLZMAN, RED

PERSONAL: Born August 10, 1920, in Brooklyn, N.Y. ... Died November 13, 1998. ... 5-10/175 (1,78/79,4). ... Full name: William Holzman.

HIGH SCHOOL: Franklin K. Lane (Brooklyn, N.Y.).

COLLEGE: Baltimore, then City College of New York.

TRANSACTIONS: Played in New York State League with Albany (1941-42). ... In military service during 1942-43, 1943-44 and 1944-45 seasons; played at Norfolk, Va., Naval Training Station and scored 305 points in 1942-43 and 258 points in 1943-44. ... Signed by Rochester Royals of National Basketball League (1945). ... Played in American Basketball League with New York (1945-46). ... Royals franchise transferred to Basketball Association of America for 1948-49 season. ... Royals franchise became part of NBA for 1949-50 season. ... Acquired from Royals by Milwaukee Hawks (1953).

CAREER NOTES: Basketball consultant, New York Knicks (1991 to 1998).
CAREER HONORS: Elected to Naismith Memorial Basketball Hall of Fame (1986). ... One of the Top 10 Coaches in NBA History (1996).
MISCELLANEOUS: Member of NBL championship team (1946). ... Member of NBA championship team (1951).

COLLEGIATE RECORD

Season Team	G	Min.	FGM	FGA	Pct.	FTM	FTA	Pct.	Reb.	Ast.	Pts.	RPG	APG	PPG
												AVERAGES		
38-39—Baltimore......................						Statistics unavailable.								
39-40—City College. (N.Y.)						Did not play—transfer student.								
40-41—City College. (N.Y.)	21	...	96	...	...	37	...	...	...	...	229	...	...	10.9
41-42—City College. (N.Y.)	18	...	87	...	...	51	...	...	...	...	225	...	...	12.5
Totals	39	...	183	...	...	88	...	...	...	...	454	...	...	11.6

ABL REGULAR-SEASON RECORD

Season Team	G	Min.	FGM	FGA	Pct.	FTM	FTA	Pct.	Reb.	Ast.	Pts.	RPG	APG	PPG
												AVERAGES		
45-46—New York......................	4	...	18	...	...	12	...	...	...	...	48	...	...	12.0

NBL AND NBA REGULAR-SEASON RECORD

HONORS: All-NBL first team (1946, 1948). ... All-NBL second team (1947).

Season Team	G	Min.	FGM	FGA	Pct.	FTM	FTA	Pct.	Reb.	Ast.	PF	Dq.	Pts.	RPG	APG	PPG
														AVERAGES		
45-46 —Rochester (NBL)...............	34	...	144	...	...	77	115	.670	...	...	54	...	365	...	...	10.7
46-47 —Rochester (NBL)...............	44	...	227	...	...	74	139	.532	...	...	68	...	528	...	...	12.0
47-48 —Rochester (NBL)...............	60	...	246	...	...	117	182	.643	...	...	58	...	609	...	...	10.2
48-49 —Rochester (BAA)...............	60	...	225	691	.326	96	157	.611	...	149	93	...	546	...	2.5	9.1
49-50 —Rochester	68	...	206	625	.330	144	210	.686	...	200	67	...	556	...	2.9	8.2
50-51 —Rochester	68	...	183	561	.326	130	179	.726	152	147	94	0	496	2.2	2.2	7.3
51-52 —Rochester	65	1065	104	372	.280	61	85	.718	106	115	95	1	269	1.6	1.8	4.1
52-53 —Rochester	46	392	38	149	.255	27	38	.711	40	35	56	2	103	0.9	0.8	2.2
53-54 —Milwaukee	51	649	74	224	.330	48	73	.658	46	75	73	1	196	0.9	1.5	3.8
Totals................................	496	...	1447	...	...	774	1178	.657	...	...	658	...	3668	...	...	7.4

NBL AND NBA PLAYOFF RECORD

Season Team	G	Min.	FGM	FGA	Pct.	FTM	FTA	Pct.	Reb.	Ast.	PF	Dq.	Pts.	RPG	APG	PPG
														AVERAGES		
45-46 —Rochester (NBL)...............	7	...	30	...	...	21	31	.677	...	...	10	...	81	...	...	11.6
46-47 —Rochester (NBL)...............	11	...	42	...	...	22	29	.759	...	...	22	...	106	...	...	9.6
47-48 —Rochester (NBL)...............	10	...	35	...	...	10	15	.667	...	...	6	...	80	...	...	8.0
48-49 —Rochester (BAA)...............	4	...	18	40	.450	5	6	.833	...	13	3	...	41	...	3.3	10.3
49-50 —Rochester	2	...	3	9	.333	1	2	.500	...	0	3	...	7	...	0.0	3.5
50-51 —Rochester	14	...	31	76	.408	23	34	.676	19	20	14	0	85	1.4	1.4	6.1
51-52 —Rochester	6	65	3	15	.200	1	6	.167	6	2	3	0	7	1.0	0.3	1.2
52-53 —Rochester	2	14	1	5	.200	1	4	.250	1	1	4	0	3	0.5	0.5	1.5
Totals................................	56	...	163	...	...	84	127	.661	...	...	65	...	410	...	...	7.3

HEAD COACHING RECORD

BACKGROUND: Chief scout, New York Knicks (1959-60 through 1966-67).
HONORS: NBA Coach of the Year (1970).

NBA COACHING RECORD

Season Team	REGULAR SEASON				PLAYOFFS		
	W	L	Pct.	Finish	W	L	Pct.
53-54 —Milwaukee	10	16	.385	4th/Western Division	—	—	—
54-55 —Milwaukee	26	46	.361	4th/Western Division	—	—	—
55-56 —St. Louis	33	39	.458	T2nd/Western Division	4	5	.444
56-57 —St. Louis	14	19	.424		—	—	—
67-68 —New York	28	17	.622	3rd/Eastern Division	2	4	.333
68-69 —New York	54	28	.659	3rd/Eastern Division	6	4	.600
69-70 —New York	60	22	.732	1st/Eastern Division	12	7	.632
70-71 —New York	52	30	.634	1st/Atlantic Division	7	5	.583
71-72 —New York	48	34	.585	2nd/Atlantic Division	9	7	.563
72-73 —New York	57	25	.695	2nd/Atlantic Division	12	5	.706
73-74 —New York	49	33	.598	2nd/Atlantic Division	5	7	.417
74-75 —New York	40	42	.488	3rd/Atlantic Division	1	2	.333
75-76 —New York	38	44	.463	4th/Atlantic Division	—	—	—
76-77 —New York	40	42	.488	3rd/Atlantic Division	—	—	—
78-79 —New York	25	43	.368	4th/Atlantic Division	—	—	—
79-80 —New York	39	43	.476	T3rd/Atlantic Division	—	—	—
80-81 —New York	50	32	.610	3rd/Atlantic Division	0	2	.000
81-82 —New York	33	49	.402	5th/Atlantic Division	—	—	—
Totals (18 years).............................	696	604	.535	Totals (10 years)	58	48	.547

NOTES:
1954—Replaced Fuzzy Levane as Milwaukee head coach with record of 11-35.
1955—Milwaukee franchise transferred to St. Louis.
1956—Lost to Minneapolis, 103-97, in Western Division 2nd place game; defeated Minneapolis, 2-1, in Western Division Semifinals; lost to Fort Wayne, 3-2, in Western Division Finals.
1957—Replaced as St. Louis head coach by Slater Martin (January).
1967—Replaced Dick McGuire as New York head coach (December), with record of 15-22 and in fifth place.

ALL-TIME GREAT COACHES

1968—Lost to Philadelphia in Eastern Division Semifinals.
1969—Defeated Baltimore, 4-0, in Eastern Division Semifinals; lost to Boston, 4-2, in Eastern Division Finals.
1970—Defeated Baltimore, 4-3, in Eastern Division Semifinals; defeated Milwaukee, 4-1, in Eastern Division Finals; defeated Los Angeles, 4-3, in NBA Finals.
1971—Defeated Atlanta, 4-1, in Eastern Conference Semifinals; lost to Baltimore, 4-3, in Eastern Conference Finals.
1972—Defeated Baltimore, 4-2, in Eastern Conference Semifinals; defeated Boston, 4-1, in Eastern Conference Finals; lost to Los Angeles, 4-1, in NBA Finals.
1973—Defeated Baltimore, 4-1, in Eastern Conference Semifinals; defeated Boston, 4-3, in Eastern Conference Finals; defeated Los Angeles, 4-1, in NBA Finals.
1974—Defeated Capital, 4-3, in Eastern Conference Semifinals; lost to Boston, 4-1, in Eastern Conference Finals.
1975—Lost to Houston in Eastern Conference First Round.
1978—Replaced Willis Reed as New York head coach (November) with record of 6-8.
1981—Lost to Chicago in Eastern Conference First Round.

JONES, K.C.

PERSONAL: Born May 25, 1932, in Taylor, Texas. ... 6-1/200 (1,85/90,7).
HIGH SCHOOL: Commerce (San Francisco).
COLLEGE: San Francisco.
TRANSACTIONS: Selected by Boston Celtics in second round of 1956 NBA Draft. ... In military service (1956-57 and 1957-58); played at Fort Leonard Wood, Mo.; named to Amateur Athletic Union All-America team as a member of 1957-58 Fort Leonard Wood team. ... Played in Eastern Basketball League with Hartford Capitols (1967-68).
CAREER HONORS: Elected to Naismith Memorial Basketball Hall of Fame (1989).
MISCELLANEOUS: Member of NBA championship team (1959, 1960, 1961, 1962, 1963, 1964, 1965, 1966). ... Selected by Los Angeles Rams in 30th round of 1955 National Football League Draft. ... Member of gold-medal-winning U.S. Olympic team (1956).

COLLEGIATE RECORD

NOTES: Underwent appendectomy after one game of the 1953-54 season and was granted an extra year of eligibility by the University of San Francisco; however, he was ineligible for the 1955-56 NCAA tournament because he was playing his fifth season of college basketball. ... Member of NCAA championship team (1955).

Season Team	G	Min.	FGM	FGA	Pct.	FTM	FTA	Pct.	Reb.	Ast.	Pts.	AVERAGES RPG	APG	PPG
51-52—San Francisco‡	24	...	44	128	.344	46	64	.719	...	...	134	...	...	5.6
52-53—San Francisco	23	...	63	159	.396	81	149	.544	...	...	207	...	...	9.0
53-54—San Francisco	1	...	3	12	.250	2	2	1.000	3	...	8	3.0	...	8.0
54-55—San Francisco	29	...	105	293	.358	97	144	.674	148	...	307	5.1	...	10.6
55-56—San Francisco	25	...	76	208	.365	93	142	.655	130	...	245	5.2	...	9.8
Totals	78	...	247	672	.368	273	437	.625	...	...	767	...	...	9.8

NBA REGULAR-SEASON RECORD

Season Team	G	Min.	FGM	FGA	Pct.	FTM	FTA	Pct.	Reb.	Ast.	PF	Dq.	Pts.	AVERAGES RPG	APG	PPG
58-59—Boston	49	609	65	192	.339	41	68	.603	127	70	58	0	171	2.6	1.4	3.5
59-60—Boston	74	1274	169	414	.408	128	170	.753	199	189	109	1	466	2.7	2.6	6.3
60-61—Boston	78	1607	203	601	.338	186	320	.581	279	253	200	3	592	3.6	3.2	7.6
61-62—Boston	79	2023	289	707	.409	145	231	.628	291	339	204	2	723	3.7	4.3	9.2
62-63—Boston	79	1945	230	591	.389	112	177	.633	263	317	221	3	572	3.3	4.0	7.2
63-64—Boston	80	2424	283	722	.392	88	168	.524	372	407	253	0	654	4.7	5.1	8.2
64-65—Boston	78	2434	253	639	.396	143	227	.630	318	437	263	5	649	4.1	5.6	8.3
65-66—Boston	80	2710	240	619	.388	209	303	.690	304	503	243	4	689	3.8	6.3	8.6
66-67—Boston	78	2446	182	459	.397	119	189	.630	239	389	273	7	483	3.1	5.0	6.2
Totals	675	17472	1914	4944	.387	1171	1853	.632	2392	2904	1824	25	4999	3.5	4.3	7.4

NBA PLAYOFF RECORD

Season Team	G	Min.	FGM	FGA	Pct.	FTM	FTA	Pct.	Reb.	Ast.	PF	Dq.	Pts.	AVERAGES RPG	APG	PPG
58-59—Boston	8	75	5	20	.250	5	5	1.000	12	10	8	0	15	1.5	1.3	1.9
59-60—Boston	13	232	27	80	.338	17	22	.773	45	14	28	0	71	3.5	1.1	5.5
60-61—Boston	9	103	9	30	.300	7	14	.500	19	15	17	0	25	2.1	1.7	2.8
61-62—Boston	14	329	44	102	.431	38	53	.717	56	55	50	1	126	4.0	3.9	9.0
62-63—Boston	13	250	19	64	.297	21	30	.700	36	37	42	1	59	2.8	2.8	4.5
63-64—Boston	10	312	25	72	.347	13	25	.520	37	68	40	0	63	3.7	6.8	6.3
64-65—Boston	12	396	43	104	.413	35	45	.778	39	74	49	1	121	3.3	6.2	10.1
65-66—Boston	17	543	45	109	.413	39	57	.684	52	75	65	0	129	3.1	4.4	7.6
66-67—Boston	9	254	24	75	.320	11	18	.611	24	48	36	1	59	2.7	5.3	6.6
Totals	105	2494	241	656	.367	186	269	.691	320	396	335	4	668	3.0	3.8	6.4

EBL REGULAR-SEASON RECORD

Season Team	G	Min.	FGM	FGA	Pct.	FTM	FTA	Pct.	Reb.	Ast.	PF	Dq.	Pts.	AVERAGES RPG	APG	PPG
67-68—Hartford	6	...	15	...	...	9	18	.500	24	41	...	...	39	4.0	6.8	6.5

HEAD COACHING RECORD

BACKGROUND: Assistant coach, Harvard University (1970-71). ... Assistant coach, Los Angeles Lakers (1971-72). ... Assistant coach, Milwaukee Bucks (1976-77). ... Assistant coach, Boston Celtics (1978-79 through 1982-83 and 1996-97). ... Vice president/basketball operations, Celtics (1988-89). ... Assistant coach, Seattle SuperSonics (1989-90). ... Assistant coach, Detroit Pistons (1994-95). ... Assistant coach, Celtics (1996-97).

COLLEGIATE COACHING RECORD

Season Team	W	L	Pct.
67-68 —Brandeis	11	10	.524
68-69 —Brandeis	12	9	.571
69-70 —Brandeis	11	13	.458
Totals (3 years)	34	32	.515

ABA COACHING RECORD

Season Team	REGULAR SEASON				PLAYOFFS		
	W	L	Pct.	Finish	W	L	Pct.
72-73 —San Diego	30	54	.357	4th/Western Division	0	4	.000

ABL COACHING RECORD

Season Team	REGULAR SEASON				PLAYOFFS		
	W	L	Pct.	Finish	W	L	Pct.
97-98 —New England	24	20	.545	2nd/Eastern Conference	0	2	.000
98-99 —New England	3	10	.231		—	—	—
Totals (2 years)	27	30	.474				

NBA COACHING RECORD

Season Team	REGULAR SEASON				PLAYOFFS		
	W	L	Pct.	Finish	W	L	Pct.
73-74 —Capital	47	35	.573	1st/Central Division	3	4	.429
74-75 —Washington	60	22	.732	1st/Central Division	8	9	.471
75-76 —Washington	48	34	.585	2nd/Central Division	3	4	.429
83-84 —Boston	62	20	.756	1st/Atlantic Division	15	8	.652
84-85 —Boston	63	19	.768	1st/Atlantic Division	13	8	.619
85-86 —Boston	67	15	.817	1st/Atlantic Division	15	3	.833
86-87 —Boston	59	23	.720	1st/Atlantic Division	13	10	.565
87-88 —Boston	57	25	.695	1st/Atlantic Division	9	8	.529
90-91 —Seattle	41	41	.500	5th/Pacific Division	2	3	.400
91-92 —Seattle	18	18	.500		—	—	—
Totals (10 years)	522	252	.674	Totals (9 years)	81	57	.587

NOTES:
1973—Lost to Utah in Western Division Semifinals.
1974—Lost to New York in Eastern Conference Semifinals.
1975—Defeated Buffalo, 4-3, in Eastern Conference Semifinals; defeated Boston, 4-2, in Eastern Conference Finals; lost to Golden State, 4-0, in NBA Finals.
1976—Lost to Cleveland in Eastern Conference Semifinals.
1984—Defeated Washington, 3-1, in Eastern Conference First Round; defeated New York, 4-3, in Eastern Conference Semifinals; defeated Milwaukee, 4-1, in Eastern Conference Finals; defeated Los Angeles, 4-3, in NBA Finals.
1985—Defeated Cleveland, 3-1, in Eastern Conference First Round; defeated Detroit, 4-2, in Eastern Conference Semifinals; defeated Philadelphia, 4-1, in Eastern Conference Finals; lost to Los Angeles Lakers, 4-2, in NBA Finals.
1986—Defeated Chicago, 3-0, in Eastern Conference First Round; defeated Atlanta, 4-1, in Eastern Conference Semifinals; defeated Milwaukee, 4-0, in Eastern Conference Finals; defeated Houston, 4-2, in NBA Finals.
1987—Defeated Chicago, 3-0, in Eastern Conference First Round; defeated Milwaukee, 4-3, in Eastern Conference Semifinals; defeated Detroit, 4-3, in Eastern Conference Finals; lost to Los Angeles Lakers, 4-2, in NBA Finals.
1988—Defeated New York, 3-1, in Eastern Conference First Round; defeated Atlanta, 4-3, in Eastern Conference Semifinals; lost to Detroit, 4-2, in Eastern Conference Finals.
1991—Lost to Portland in Western Conference First Round.
1992—Replaced as Seattle head coach by interim coach Bob Kloppenburg with club in sixth place (January 15).

KUNDLA, JOHN

PERSONAL: Born July 3, 1916, in Star Junction, Pa. ... 6-2/180 (1,88/81,6). ... Full name: John Albert Kundla.
HIGH SCHOOL: Central (Minneapolis).
COLLEGE: Minnesota.
CAREER HONORS: Elected to Naismith Memorial Basketball Hall of Fame (1995). ... One of the Top 10 Coaches in NBA History (1996).

COLLEGIATE RECORD

Season Team	G	Min.	FGM	FGA	Pct.	FTM	FTA	Pct.	Reb.	Ast.	Pts.	AVERAGES		
												RPG	APG	PPG
35-36—Minnesota‡						Freshman team statistics unavailable.								
36-37—Minnesota	15	...	53	...	...	34	53	.642	...	...	140	...	...	9.3
37-38—Minnesota	20	...	62	...	...	41	77	.532	...	...	165	...	...	8.3
38-39—Minnesota	17	...	71	...	...	40	63	.635	...	...	182	...	...	10.7
Varsity totals	52	...	186	...	...	115	193	.596	...	...	487	...	...	9.4

HEAD COACHING RECORD

BACKGROUND: Head coach, De La Salle High School (Minn.).

COLLEGIATE COACHING RECORD

Season Team	W	L	Pct.	Finish
46-47 —St. Thomas (Minn.)	11	11	.500	
59-60 —Minnesota	12	12	.500	T3rd/Big Ten Conference
60-61 —Minnesota	10	13	.435	T4th/Big Ten Conference
61-62 —Minnesota	10	14	.417	7th/Big Ten Conference
62-63 —Minnesota	12	12	.500	T4th/Big Ten Conference

Season Team	W	L	Pct.	Finish
63-64 —Minnesota	17	7	.708	3rd/Big Ten Conference
64-65 —Minnesota	19	5	.792	2nd/Big Ten Conference
65-66 —Minnesota	14	10	.583	T5th/Big Ten Conference
66-67 —Minnesota	9	15	.375	9th/Big Ten Conference
67-68 —Minnesota	7	17	.292	T9th/Big Ten Conference
Totals (10 years)	121	116	.511	

NBL COACHING RECORD

Season Team	REGULAR SEASON W	L	Pct.	Finish	PLAYOFFS W	L	Pct.
47-48 —Minneapolis	43	17	.717	1st/Western Division	8	2	.800

NBA COACHING RECORD

Season Team	REGULAR SEASON W	L	Pct.	Finish	PLAYOFFS W	L	Pct.
48-49 —Minneapolis	44	16	.733	2nd/Western Division	8	2	.800
49-50 —Minneapolis	51	17	.750	T1st/Central Division	10	2	.833
50-51 —Minneapolis	44	24	.647	1st/Western Division	3	4	.429
51-52 —Minneapolis	40	26	.606	2nd/Western Division	9	4	.692
52-53 —Minneapolis	48	22	.686	1st/Western Division	9	3	.750
53-54 —Minneapolis	46	26	.639	1st/Western Division	9	4	.692
54-55 —Minneapolis	40	32	.556	2nd/Western Division	3	4	.429
55-56 —Minneapolis	33	39	.458	T2nd/Western Division	1	2	.333
56-57 —Minneapolis	34	38	.472	T1st/Western Division	2	3	.400
57-58 —Minneapolis	10	23	.303	4th/Western Division	—	—	—
58-59 —Minneapolis	33	39	.458	2nd/Western Division	6	7	.462
Totals (11 years)	423	302	.583	Totals (10 years)	60	35	.632

NOTES:

1948—Defeated Oshkosh, 3-1, in NBL playoffs; defeated Tri-Cities, 2-0, in NBL semifinals; defeated Rochester, 3-1, in NBL championship series.

1949—Defeated Chicago, 2-0, in Western Division Semifinals; defeated Rochester, 2-0, in Western Division Finals; defeated Washington, 4-2, in NBA Finals.

1950—Defeated Rochester, 78-76, in Central Division first-place game; defeated Chicago, 2-0, in Central Division Semifinals; defeated Fort Wayne, 2-0, in Central Division Finals; defeated Anderson, 2-0, in NBA Semifinals; defeated Syracuse, 4-2, in NBA Finals.

1951—Defeated Indianapolis, 2-1, in Western Division Semifinals; lost to Rochester, 3-1, in Western Division Finals.

1952—Defeated Indianapolis, 2-0, in Western Division Semifinals; defeated Rochester, 3-1, in Western Division Finals; defeated New York, 4-3, in NBA Finals.

1953—Defeated Indianapolis, 2-0, in Western Division Semifinals; defeated Fort Wayne, 3-2, in Western Division Finals; defeated New York, 4-1, in NBA Finals.

1954—Defeated Rochester, 109-88; Fort Wayne, 90-85; and Fort Wayne, 78-73, in Western Division round robin; defeated Rochester, 2-1, in Western Division Semifinals; defeated Syracuse, 4-3, in NBA Finals.

1955—Defeated Rochester, 2-1, in Western Division Semifinals; lost to Fort Wayne, 3-1, in Western Division Finals.

1956—Defeated St. Louis, 103-97, in Western Division second-place game; lost to St. Louis, 2-1, in Western Division Semifinals.

1957—Lost to St. Louis, 114-111, in Western Division tiebreaker; defeated Fort Wayne, 2-0, in Western Division Semifinals; lost to St. Louis, 3-0, in Western Division Finals.

1958—Replaced George Mikan as Minneapolis head coach (January 14), with record of 9-30 and in fourth place.

1959—Defeated Detroit, 2-1, in Western Division Semifinals; defeated St. Louis, 4-2, in Western Division Finals; lost to Boston, 4-0, in NBA Finals.

LAPCHICK, JOE

PERSONAL: Born April 12, 1900, in Yonkers, N.Y. ... Died August 10, 1970. ... 6-5/185 (1,96/83,9). ... Full name: Joseph Bohomiel Lapchick.

TRANSACTIONS: Played with independent teams, including the Original Celtics (1917 through 1920, 1924 through 1926, 1932 through 1936).

CAREER HONORS: Elected to Naismith Memorial Basketball Hall of Fame (1966).

MISCELLANEOUS: Did not play high school or college basketball.

PRO RECORD

Season Team	League	G	FGM	FTM	Pts.	Avg.
20-21 —Holyoke	IL	11	14	40	68	6.2
Schenectady	NYSL	5	2	10	14	2.8
21-22 —Schenectady-Troy	NYSL	32	12	95	119	3.7
Holyoke	MBL	10	6	20	32	3.2
	IL	16	13	40	66	4.1
22-23 —Brooklyn	MBL	33	34	109	177	5.4
Troy	NYSL	24	13	59	85	3.5
Holyoke	IL			Statistics unavailable.		
26-27 —Brooklyn	ABL	32	35	131	201	6.3
New York	NBL	17	20	66	106	6.2
27-28 —New York	ABL	47	103	110	316	6.7
28-29 —Cleveland	ABL	39	51	86	188	4.8
29-30 —Cleveland	ABL	52	47	92	186	3.6
30-31 —Cleveland-Toledo	ABL	30	22	49	93	3.1
32-33 —Yonkers	MBL	1	0	0	0	0.0
33-34 —Plymouth	PSL	1	1	3	5	5.0
ABL pro totals		200	258	468	984	4.9
MBL pro totals		44	40	129	209	4.8

COLLEGIATE COACHING RECORD

Season Team	W	L	Pct.	Finish
36-37 —St. John's	12	7	.632	Independent
37-38 —St. John's	15	4	.789	Independent
38-39 —St. John's	18	4	.818	Independent
39-40 —St. John's	15	5	.750	Independent
40-41 —St. John's	11	6	.647	Independent
41-42 —St. John's	16	5	.762	Independent
42-43 —St. John's	21	3	.875	Independent
43-44 —St. John's	18	5	.783	Independent
44-45 —St. John's	21	3	.875	Independent
45-46 —St. John's	17	6	.739	Independent
46-47 —St. John's	16	7	.696	Independent
56-57 —St. John's	14	9	.609	Independent
57-58 —St. John's	18	8	.692	Independent
58-59 —St. John's	20	6	.769	Independent
59-60 —St. John's	17	8	.680	Independent
60-61 —St. John's	20	5	.800	Independent
61-62 —St. John's	21	5	.808	Independent
62-63 —St. John's	9	15	.375	Independent
63-64 —St. John's	14	11	.560	Independent
64-65 —St. John's	21	8	.724	Independent
Totals (20 years)	**334**	**130**	**.720**	

ABL COACHING RECORD

Season Team	REGULAR SEASON				PLAYOFFS		
	W	L	Pct.	Finish	W	L	Pct.
61-62—Cleveland	6	6	.500		—	—	—

NBA COACHING RECORD

Season Team	REGULAR SEASON				PLAYOFFS		
	W	L	Pct.	Finish	W	L	Pct.
47-48 —New York (BAA)	26	22	.542	2nd/Eastern Division	1	2	.333
48-49 —New York (BAA)	32	28	.533	2nd/Eastern Division	3	3	.500
49-50 —New York	40	28	.588	2nd/Eastern Division	3	2	.600
50-51 —New York	36	30	.545	3rd/Eastern Division	8	6	.571
51-52 —New York	37	29	.561	3rd/Eastern Division	8	6	.571
52-53 —New York	47	23	.671	1st/Midwest Division	6	5	.545
53-54 —New York	44	28	.611	1st/Eastern Division	0	4	.000
54-55 —New York	38	34	.528	2nd/Eastern Division	1	2	.333
55-56 —New York	26	25	.510		—	—	—
Totals (9 years)	**326**	**247**	**.569**	**Totals (8 years)**	**30**	**30**	**.500**

NOTES:

1939—Defeated Roanoke, 71-47, in NIT quarterfinals; lost to Loyola, 51-46, in semifinals; lost to Bradley, 40-35, in third-place game.

1940—Lost to Duquesne, 38-31, in NIT quarterfinals.

1943—Defeated Rice, 51-49, in NIT quarterfinals; defeated Fordham, 69-43, in semifinals; defeated Toledo, 48-27, in finals.

1944—Defeated Bowling Green, 44-40, in NIT quarterfinals; defeated Kentucky, 48-45, in semifinals; defeated DePaul, 47-39, in finals.

1945—Defeated Muhlenberg, 34-33, in NIT quarterfinals; lost to Bowling Green, 57-44, in semifinals; lost to Rhode Island, 64-57, in third-place game.

1946—Lost to West Virginia, 70-58, in NIT quarterfinals.

1947—Lost to North Carolina State, 61-55, in NIT quarterfinals.

1948—Lost to Baltimore in quarterfinals.

1949—Defeated Baltimore, 2-1, in Eastern Division Semifinals; lost to Washington, 2-1, in Eastern Division Finals.

1950—Defeated Washington, 2-0, in Eastern Division Semifinals; lost to Syracuse, 2-1, in Eastern Division Finals.

1951—Defeated Boston, 2-0, in Eastern Division Semifinals; defeated Syracuse, 3-2, in Eastern Division Finals; lost to Rochester, 4-3, in NBA Finals.

1952—Defeated Boston, 2-1, in Eastern Division Semifinals; defeated Syracuse, 3-1, in Eastern Division Finals; lost to Minneapolis, 4-3, in NBA Finals.

1953—Defeated Baltimore, 2-0, in Eastern Division Semifinals; defeated Boston, 3-1, in Eastern Division Finals; lost to Minneapolis, 4-1, in NBA Finals.

1954—Lost to Boston, 93-71; Syracuse, 75-68; Boston, 79-78; and Syracuse, 103-99, in Eastern Division round robin.

1955—Lost to Boston in Eastern Division Semifinals.

1956—Resigned as New York head coach.

1958—Defeated Butler, 76-69, in NIT first round; defeated Utah, 71-70, in quarterfinals; lost to Dayton, 80-56, in semifinals; lost to St. Bonaventure, 84-69, in third-place game.

1959—Defeated Villanova, 75-67, in NIT first round; defeated St. Bonaventure, 82-74, in quarterfinals; defeated Providence, 76-55, in semifinals; defeated Bradley, 76-71 (OT), in finals.

1960—Lost to St. Bonaventure, 106-71, in NIT quarterfinals.

1961—Lost to Wake Forest, 97-74, in NCAA Tournament first round.

1962—Defeated Holy Cross, 80-74, in NIT quarterfinals; defeated Duquesne, 76-65, in semifinals; lost to Dayton, 73-67, in finals.

1965—Defeated Boston College, 114-92, in NIT first round; defeated New Mexico, 61-54, in quarterfinals; defeated Army, 67-60, in semifinals; defeated Villanova, 55-51, in finals.

ALL-TIME GREAT COACHES

DID YOU KNOW . . .

. . . that Fred Roberts was the only player to be an NBA teammate of both Magic Johnson and Larry Bird?

LOUGHERY, KEVIN

PERSONAL: Born March 28, 1940, in Brooklyn, N.Y. ... 6-3/190 (1,90/86,2). ... Full name: Kevin Michael Loughery.
HIGH SCHOOL: Cardinal Hayes (Bronx, N.Y.).
COLLEGE: Boston College, then St. John's.
TRANSACTIONS: Selected by Detroit Pistons in second round (13th pick overall) of 1962 NBA Draft. ... Traded by Pistons to Baltimore Bullets for Larry Staverman (October 28, 1963). ... Traded by Bullets with Fred Carter to Philadelphia 76ers for Archie Clark and future draft choice (October 18, 1971).
CAREER NOTES: Broadcaster (1988-89 and 1989-90). ... Scout, Miami Heat (1988-89 and 1989-90). ... Vice president/director of player personnel, Heat (February 1995 to 1995-96) ... Vice president/consultant, Heat (1996-97).

COLLEGIATE RECORD

Season Team	G	Min.	FGM	FGA	Pct.	FTM	FTA	Pct.	Reb.	Ast.	Pts.	AVERAGES		
---	---	---	---	---	---	---	---	---	---	---	---	RPG	APG	PPG
57-58—Boston College‡	19	...	133	...	...	55	...	...	...	...	321	...	...	16.9
58-59—Boston College	19	...	128	...	...	65	...	...	...	...	321	...	...	16.9
59-60—St. John's					Did not play—transfer student.									
60-61—St. John's	25	...	106	252	.421	54	77	.701	116	...	266	4.6	...	10.6
61-62—St. John's	26	...	169	378	.447	65	76	.855	151	...	403	5.8	...	15.5
Varsity totals	70	...	403	...	...	184	...	...	...	...	990	...	...	14.1

NBA REGULAR-SEASON RECORD

Season Team	G	Min.	FGM	FGA	Pct.	FTM	FTA	Pct.	Reb.	Ast.	PF	Dq.	Pts.	AVERAGES		
---	---	---	---	---	---	---	---	---	---	---	---	---	---	RPG	APG	PPG
62-63—Detroit	57	845	146	397	.368	71	100	.710	109	104	135	1	363	1.9	1.8	6.4
63-64—Det.-Balt.	66	1459	236	631	.374	126	177	.712	138	182	175	2	598	2.1	2.8	9.1
64-65—Baltimore	80	2417	406	957	.424	212	281	.754	235	296	320	13	1024	2.9	3.7	12.8
65-66—Baltimore	74	2455	526	1264	.416	297	358	.830	227	356	273	8	1349	3.1	4.8	18.2
66-67—Baltimore	76	2577	520	1306	.398	340	412	.825	349	288	294	10	1380	4.6	3.8	18.2
67-68—Baltimore	77	2297	458	1127	.406	305	392	.778	247	256	301	13	1221	3.2	3.3	15.9
68-69—Baltimore	80	3135	717	1636	.438	372	463	.803	266	384	299	3	1806	3.3	4.8	22.6
69-70—Baltimore	55	2037	477	1082	.441	253	298	.849	168	292	183	3	1207	3.1	5.3	21.9
70-71—Baltimore	82	2260	481	1193	.403	275	331	.831	219	301	246	2	1237	2.7	3.7	15.1
71-72—Balt.-Phil.	76	1771	341	809	.422	263	320	.822	183	196	213	3	945	2.4	2.6	12.4
72-73—Philadelphia	32	955	169	427	.396	107	130	.823	113	148	104	0	445	3.5	4.6	13.9
Totals	755	22208	4477	10829	.413	2621	3262	.803	2254	2803	2543	58	11575	3.0	3.7	15.3

NBA PLAYOFF RECORD

Season Team	G	Min.	FGM	FGA	Pct.	FTM	FTA	Pct.	Reb.	Ast.	PF	Dq.	Pts.	AVERAGES		
---	---	---	---	---	---	---	---	---	---	---	---	---	---	RPG	APG	PPG
62-63—Detroit	2	26	1	10	.100	1	1	1.000	0	4	3	0	3	0.0	0.0	1.5
64-65—Baltimore	10	297	53	137	.387	34	38	.895	34	30	36	0	140	3.4	3.0	14.0
65-66—Baltimore	3	27	3	7	.429	3	6	.500	1	1	4	0	9	0.3	0.3	3.0
68-69—Baltimore	4	173	29	79	.367	23	35	.657	18	21	16	0	81	4.5	5.3	20.3
69-70—Baltimore	7	153	26	77	.338	15	21	.714	16	8	24	0	67	2.3	1.1	9.6
70-71—Baltimore	17	500	84	212	.396	64	85	.753	38	52	57	2	232	2.2	3.1	13.6
Totals	43	1176	196	522	.375	140	186	.753	107	116	140	2	532	2.5	2.7	12.4

HEAD COACHING RECORD

BACKGROUND: Player/head coach, Philadelphia 76ers (February 1973-remainder of 1972-73 season). ... Assistant coach, Atlanta Hawks (1990-91).

NBA COACHING RECORD

Season Team	REGULAR SEASON				PLAYOFFS		
	W	L	Pct.	Finish	W	L	Pct.
72-73 —Philadelphia	5	26	.161	4th/Atlantic Division	—	—	—
76-77 —New York Nets	22	60	.268	5th/Atlantic Division	—	—	—
77-78 —New Jersey	24	58	.293	5th/Atlantic Division	—	—	—
78-79 —New Jersey	37	45	.451	3rd/Atlantic Division	0	2	.000
79-80 —New Jersey	34	48	.415	5th/Atlantic Division	—	—	—
80-81 —New Jersey	12	23	.343		—	—	—
81-82 —Atlanta	42	40	.512	2nd/Central Division	0	2	.000
82-83 —Atlanta	43	39	.524	2nd/Central Division	1	2	.333
83-84 —Chicago	27	55	.329	5th/Central Division	—	—	—
84-85 —Chicago	38	44	.463	3rd/Central Division	1	3	.250
85-86 —Washington	7	6	.538	T3rd/Atlantic Division	2	3	.400
86-87 —Washington	42	40	.512	3rd/Atlantic Division	0	3	.000
87-88 —Washington	8	19	.296		—	—	—
91-92 —Miami	38	44	.463	4th/Atlantic Division	0	3	.000
92-93 —Miami	36	46	.439	5th/Atlantic Division	—	—	—
93-94 —Miami	42	40	.512	4th/Atlantic Division	2	3	.400
94-95 —Miami	17	29	.370	5th/Atlantic Division	—	—	—
Totals (17 years)	474	662	.417	Totals (8 years)	6	21	.222

ABA COACHING RECORD

Season Team	REGULAR SEASON				PLAYOFFS		
	W	L	Pct.	Finish	W	L	Pct.
73-74 —New York Nets	55	29	.655	1st/Eastern Division	12	2	.857
74-75 —New York Nets	58	26	.690	T1st/Eastern Division	1	4	.200
75-76 —New York Nets	55	29	.655	2nd	8	5	.615
Totals (3 years)	168	84	.667	Totals (3 years)	21	11	.656

NOTES:
1973—Replaced Roy Rubin as Philadelphia head coach (February), with record of 4-47.
1974—Defeated Virginia, 4-1, in Eastern Division Semifinals; defeated Kentucky, 4-0, in Eastern Division Finals; defeated Utah, 4-1, in ABA Finals.
1975—Lost to St. Louis in Eastern Division Semifinals.
1976—Defeated San Antonio, 4-3, in semifinals; defeated Denver, 4-2, in ABA Finals.
1979—Lost to Philadelphia in Eastern Conference First Round.
1980—Resigned as New Jersey head coach (December); replaced by Bob MacKinnon with club in fifth place.
1982—Lost to Philadelphia in Eastern Conference First Round.
1983—Lost to Boston in Eastern Conference First Round.
1985—Lost to Milwaukee in Eastern Conference First Round.
1986—Replaced Gene Shue as Washington head coach (March 19), with record of 32-37. Lost to Philadelphia in Eastern Conference First Round.
1987—Lost to Detroit in Eastern Conference First Round.
1988—Replaced as Washington head coach by Wes Unseld (January 3) with club in fourth place.
1992—Lost to Chicago in Eastern Conference First Round.
1994—Lost to Atlanta in Eastern Conference First Round.
1995—Replaced as Miami head coach by Alvin Gentry (February 14) with club in fifth place.

MacLEOD, JOHN

PERSONAL: Born October 3, 1937, in New Albany, Ind. ... 6-0/170 (1,83/77,1). ... Full name: John Matthew MacLeod.
HIGH SCHOOL: New Providence (Clarksville, Ind.).
COLLEGE: Bellarmine (Ky.).
CAREER NOTES: Head coach, Oklahoma (1967-68 through 1972-73). ... Head coach, Notre Dame (1991-92 to 1998-99).

COLLEGIATE RECORD

Season Team	G	Min.	FGM	FGA	Pct.	FTM	FTA	Pct.	Reb.	Ast.	Pts.	RPG	APG	PPG
55-56—Bellarmine					Freshman team statistics unavailable.									
56-57—Bellarmine	10	...	0	...	...	1	...	...	...	...	1	...	...	0.1
57-58—Bellarmine	8	...	2	...	...	3	10	.300	...	...	7	...	...	0.9
58-59—Bellarmine	5	...	2	...	...	4	...	...	...	...	8	...	...	1.6
Totals	23	...	4	...	...	8	...	...	...	...	16	...	...	0.7

HEAD COACHING RECORD

BACKGROUND: Assistant coach, DeSales High School, Ky. (1959-60 through 1961-62). ... Head coach, Smithville High School, Ind. (1963-64 and 1964-65; record: 16-24). ... Assistant coach, Cathedral High School, Ind. (1965-66). ... Assistant coach, University of Oklahoma (1966-67).

COLLEGIATE COACHING RECORD

Season Team	W	L	Pct.	Finish
67-68 —Oklahoma	13	13	.500	T3rd/Big Eight Conference
68-69 —Oklahoma	7	19	.269	8th/Big Eight Conference
69-70 —Oklahoma	19	9	.679	3rd/Big Eight Conference
70-71 —Oklahoma	19	8	.704	2nd/Big Eight Conference
71-72 —Oklahoma	14	12	.538	3rd/Big Eight Conference
72-73 —Oklahoma	18	8	.692	4th/Big Eight Conference
91-92 —Notre Dame	18	15	.545	Independent
92-93 —Notre Dame	9	18	.333	Independent
93-94 —Notre Dame	12	17	.414	Independent
94-95 —Notre Dame	15	12	.555	Independent
95-96 —Notre Dame	9	18	.333	13th/Big East Conference
96-97 —Notre Dame	16	14	.533	T4th/Big East Six Division/Big East Conference
97-98 —Notre Dame	13	14	.481	5th/Big East Six Division/Big East Conference
98-99 —Notre Dame	14	16	.467	4th/Big East Six Division/Big East Conference
Totals (14 years)..............................	196	193	.504	

NBA COACHING RECORD

	REGULAR SEASON				PLAYOFFS		
Season Team	W	L	Pct.	Finish	W	L	Pct.
73-74 —Phoenix	30	52	.396	4th/Pacific Division	—	—	—
74-75 —Phoenix	32	50	.390	4th/Pacific Division	—	—	—
75-76 —Phoenix	42	40	.512	3rd/Pacific Division	10	9	.526
76-77 —Phoenix	34	48	.415	5th/Pacific Division	—	—	—
77-78 —Phoenix	49	33	.598	2nd/Pacific Division	0	2	.000
78-79 —Phoenix	50	32	.610	2nd/Pacific Division	9	6	.600
79-80 —Phoenix	55	27	.671	3rd/Pacific Division	3	5	.375
80-81 —Phoenix	57	25	.695	1st/Pacific Division	3	4	.429
81-82 —Phoenix	46	36	.561	3rd/Pacific Division	2	5	.286
82-83 —Phoenix	53	29	.646	2nd/Pacific Division	1	2	.333
83-84 —Phoenix	41	41	.500	4th/Pacific Division	9	8	.529
84-85 —Phoenix	36	46	.439	3rd/Pacific Division	0	3	.000
85-86 —Phoenix	32	50	.390	T3rd/Pacific Division	—	—	—
86-87 —Phoenix	22	34	.393		—	—	—
87-88 —Dallas	53	29	.646	2nd/Midwest Division	10	7	.588
88-89 —Dallas	38	44	.463	4th/Midwest Division	—	—	—
89-90 —Dallas	5	6	.455		—	—	—
90-91 —New York.................................	32	35	.478	3rd/Atlantic Division	0	3	.000
Totals (18 years)...............................	707	657	.518	Totals (11 years)	47	54	.465

NOTES:

1970—Defeated Louisville, 74-73, in NIT first round; lost to Louisiana State, 97-94, in quarterfinals.

1971—Lost to Hawaii, 87-86 (2 OT), in NIT first round.

1976—Defeated Seattle, 4-2, in Western Conference Semifinals; defeated Golden State, 4-3, in Western Conference Finals; lost to Boston, 4-2, in NBA Finals.

1978—Lost to Milwaukee in Western Conference First Round.

1979—Defeated Portland, 2-1, in Western Conference First Round; defeated Kansas City, 4-1, in Western Conference Semifinals; lost to Seattle, 4-3, in Western Conference Finals.

1980—Defeated Kansas City, 2-1, in Western Conference First Round; lost to Los Angeles Lakers, 4-1, in Western Conference Semifinals.

1981—Lost to Kansas City in Western Conference Semifinals.

1982—Defeated Denver, 2-1, in Western Conference Semifinals; lost to Los Angeles Lakers, 4-0, in Western Conference Finals.

1983—Lost to Denver in Western Conference First Round.

1984—Defeated Portland, 3-2, in Western Conference First Round; defeated Utah, 4-2, in Western Conference Semifinals; lost to Los Angeles Lakers, 4-2, in Western Conference Finals.

1985—Lost to Los Angeles Lakers in Western Conference First Round.

1987—Replaced as Phoenix head coach by Dick Van Arsdale (February 26).

1988—Defeated Houston, 3-1, in Western Conference First Round; defeated Denver, 4-2, in Western Conference Semifinals; lost to Los Angeles Lakers, 4-3, in Western Conference Finals.

1989—Replaced as Dallas head coach by Richie Adubato (November 29).

1990—Replaced Stu Jackson as New York head coach (December 3) with record of 7-8.

1991—Lost to Chicago in Eastern Conference First Round.

1992—Defeated Western Michigan, 63-56, in NIT first round; defeated Kansas State, 64-47, in second round; defeated Manhattan, 74-58, in quarterfinals; defeated Utah, 58-55, in semifinals; lost to Virginia, 81-76, in final.

1997—Defeated Oral Roberts, 74-58, in NIT first round; defeated TCU, 82-72, in NIT second round; lost to Michigan, 67-66, in NIT quarter finals.

MOE, DOUG

PERSONAL: Born September 21, 1938, in Brooklyn, N.Y. ... 6-5/220 (1,96/99,8). ... Full name: Douglas Edwin Moe.

HIGH SCHOOL: Erasmus Hall (Brooklyn, N.Y.), then Bullis Prep School (Silver Springs, Md.).

COLLEGE: North Carolina, then Elon College (N.C.).

TRANSACTIONS: Selected by Chicago Packers in second round (22nd pick overall) of 1961 NBA Draft. ... Signed by Packers (1961); Packers later refused to honor contract when Moe was implicated in college point-shaving scandal; Moe was exonerated but did not play basketball from 1961-62 through 1964-65. ... Played with Padua, Italy (1965-66 and 1966-67). ... Signed by New Orleans Buccaneers of American Basketball Association (1967). ... Traded by Buccaneers with Larry Brown to Oakland Oaks for Steve Jones, Ron Franz and Barry Leibowitz (June 18, 1968). ... Traded by Oaks to Carolina Cougars in three-way deal in which Cougars sent Stew Johnson to Pittsburgh Pipers and Pipers sent Frank Card to Oaks (June 12, 1969). ... Traded by Cougars to Washington Capitols for Gary Bradds and Ira Harge (July 24, 1970). ... Capitols franchise moved from Washington to Virginia and renamed Squires for 1970-71 season.

COLLEGIATE RECORD

NOTES: The Sporting News All-America second team (1959, 1961).

Season Team	G	Min.	FGM	FGA	Pct.	FTM	FTA	Pct.	Reb.	Ast.	Pts.	RPG	APG	PPG
												AVERAGES		
57-58—North Carolina‡						Freshman team statistics unavailable.								
58-59—North Carolina	25	...	106	265	.400	104	164	.634	179	67	316	7.2	2.7	12.6
59-60—North Carolina	12	...	60	144	.417	82	113	.726	135	...	202	11.3	...	16.8
60-61—North Carolina	23	...	163	401	.406	143	207	.691	321	...	469	14.0	...	20.4
Totals	60	...	329	810	.406	329	484	.680	635	...	987	10.6	...	16.5

ABA REGULAR-SEASON RECORD

NOTES: Member of ABA championship team (1969). ... ABA All-Star first team (1968). ... ABA All-Star second team (1969).

Season Team	G	Min.	2-POINT			3-POINT			FTM	FTA	Pct.	Reb.	Ast.	Pts.	AVERAGES		
			FGM	FGA	Pct.	FGM	FGA	Pct.							RPG	APG	PPG
67-68— New Orleans	78	3113	662	1588	.417	3	22	.136	551	693	.795	795	202	1884	10.2	2.6	24.2
68-69— Oakland	75	2528	524	1213	.432	5	14	.357	360	444	.811	614	151	1423	8.2	2.0	19.0
69-70— Carolina	80	2671	527	1220	.432	8	34	.235	304	399	.762	437	425	1382	5.5	5.3	17.3
70-71— Virginia	78	2297	395	861	.459	2	10	.200	221	259	.853	473	270	1017	6.1	3.5	13.0
71-72— Virginia	67	1472	174	406	.429	1	9	.111	104	129	.806	241	149	455	3.6	2.2	6.8
Totals	378	12081	2282	5288	.432	19	89	.213	1540	1924	.800	2560	1197	6161	6.8	3.2	16.3

ABA PLAYOFF RECORD

Season Team	G	Min.	2-POINT			3-POINT			FTM	FTA	Pct.	Reb.	Ast.	Pts.	AVERAGES		
			FGM	FGA	Pct.	FGM	FGA	Pct.							RPG	APG	PPG
67-68— New Orleans	17	715	140	335	.418	4	11	.364	107	149	.718	169	40	399	9.9	2.4	23.5
68-69— Oakland	16	593	115	280	.411	0	4	.000	87	111	.784	124	31	317	7.8	1.9	19.8
69-70— Carolina	4	168	25	72	.347	0	4	.000	12	16	.750	26	25	62	6.5	6.3	15.5
70-71— Virginia	12	421	89	174	.511	1	3	.333	31	41	.756	57	37	212	4.8	3.1	17.7
71-72— Virginia	11	245	37	84	.440	0	1	.000	22	25	.880	43	27	96	3.9	2.5	8.7
Totals	60	2142	406	945	.430	5	23	.217	259	342	.757	419	160	1086	7.0	2.7	18.1

ABA ALL-STAR GAME RECORD

Season Team	Min.	2-POINT			3-POINT			FTM	FTA	Pct.	Reb.	Ast.	Pts.
		FGM	FGA	Pct.	FGM	FGA	Pct.						
1968 —New Orleans	29	7	12	.583	0	1	.000	3	5	.600	7	5	17
1969 —Oakland	26	6	13	.462	0	0	...	5	8	.625	6	6	17
1970 —Carolina	36	0	5	.000	0	0	...	2	3	.667	8	6	2
Totals	91	13	30	.433	0	1	.000	10	16	.625	21	17	36

HEAD COACHING RECORD

BACKGROUND: Assistant coach, Elon College, N.C. (1963-64 and 1964-65). ... Assistant coach/director of player personnel, Carolina Cougars of ABA (1972-73 and 1973-74). ... Assistant coach/director of player personnel, Denver Nuggets of ABA (1974-75 and 1975-76). ... Assistant coach, Nuggets (1980).
HONORS: NBA Coach of the Year (1988).

NBA COACHING RECORD

Season	Team	REGULAR SEASON				PLAYOFFS		
		W	L	Pct.	Finish	W	L	Pct.
76-77	—San Antonio	44	38	.537	3rd/Central Division	0	2	.000
77-78	—San Antonio	52	30	.634	1st/Central Division	2	4	.333
78-79	—San Antonio	48	34	.585	1st/Central Division	7	7	.500
79-80	—San Antonio	33	33	.500		—	—	—
80-81	—Denver	26	25	.510	4th/Midwest Division	—	—	—
81-82	—Denver	46	36	.561	T2nd/Midwest Division	1	2	.333
82-83	—Denver	45	37	.549	T2nd/Midwest Division	3	5	.375
83-84	—Denver	38	44	.463	T3rd/Midwest Division	2	3	.400
84-85	—Denver	52	30	.634	1st/Midwest Division	8	7	.533
85-86	—Denver	47	35	.573	2nd/Midwest Division	5	5	.500
86-87	—Denver	37	45	.451	4th/Midwest Division	0	3	.000
87-88	—Denver	54	28	.659	1st/Midwest Division	5	6	.455
88-89	—Denver	44	38	.537	3rd/Midwest Division	0	3	.000
89-90	—Denver	43	39	.524	4th/Midwest Division	0	3	.000
92-93	—Philadelphia	19	37	.339		—	—	—
Totals (15 years)		**628**	**529**	**.543**	**Totals (12 years)**	**33**	**50**	**.398**

NOTES:
1977—Lost to Boston in Eastern Conference First Round.
1978—Lost to Washington in Eastern Conference Semifinals.
1979—Defeated Philadelphia, 4-3, in Eastern Conference Semifinals; lost to Washington, 4-3, in Eastern Conference Finals.
1980—Replaced as San Antonio head coach by Bob Bass (March 1). Replaced Donnie Walsh as Denver head coach (December), with record of 11-20.
1982—Lost to Phoenix in Western Conference First Round.
1983—Defeated Phoenix, 2-1, in Western Conference First Round; lost to San Antonio, 4-1, in Western Conference Semifinals.
1984—Lost to Utah in Western Conference First Round.
1985—Defeated San Antonio, 3-2, in Western Conference First Round; defeated Utah, 4-1, in Western Conference Semifinals; lost to Los Angeles Lakers, 4-1, in Western Conference Finals.
1986—Defeated Portland, 3-1, in Western Conference First Round; lost to Houston, 4-2, in Western Conference Semifinals.
1987—Lost to Los Angeles Lakers in Western Conference First Round.
1988—Defeated Seattle, 3-2, in Western Conference First Round; lost to Dallas, 4-2, in Western Conference Semifinals.
1989—Lost to Phoenix in Western Conference First Round.
1990—Lost to San Antonio, 3-0, in Western Conference First Round.
1993—Replaced as Philadelphia head coach by Fred Carter (March 7) with club in sixth place.

MOTTA, DICK

PERSONAL: Born September 3, 1931, in Midvale, Utah. ... 5-10/170 (1,78/77,1). ... Full name: John Richard Motta.
HIGH SCHOOL: Jordan (Utah); did not play varsity basketball.
COLLEGE: Utah State (did not play basketball).

HEAD COACHING RECORD

BACKGROUND: Head coach, Grace Junior High School (1954-55). ... Head coach, Grace High School (1955-56 through 1959-60). ... Head coach, Weber Junior College (1960-61 and 1961-62). ... Broadcaster, Detroit Pistons (1988 through January 1990). ... Consultant, Dallas Mavericks (1990). ... Assistant coach, Denver Nuggets (July 19-November 26, 1996).
HONORS: NBA Coach of the Year (1971).

COLLEGIATE COACHING RECORD

Season	Team	W	L	Pct.	Finish
62-63	—Weber State	22	4	.846	Independent
63-64	—Weber State	17	8	.680	2nd/Big Sky Conference
64-65	—Weber State	22	3	.880	1st/Big Sky Conference
65-66	—Weber State	20	5	.765	2nd/Big Sky Conference
66-67	—Weber State	18	7	.720	3rd/Big Sky Conference
67-68	—Weber State	21	6	.778	1st/Big Sky Conference
Totals (6 years)		**120**	**33**	**.784**	

NBA COACHING RECORD

Season	Team	REGULAR SEASON				PLAYOFFS		
		W	L	Pct.	Finish	W	L	Pct.
68-69	—Chicago	33	49	.402	5th/Western Division	—	—	—
69-70	—Chicago	39	43	.476	T3rd/Western Division	1	4	.250
70-71	—Chicago	51	31	.622	2nd/Midwest Division	3	4	.429
71-72	—Chicago	57	25	.695	2nd/Midwest Division	0	4	.000
72-73	—Chicago	51	31	.622	2nd/Midwest Division	3	4	.429
73-74	—Chicago	54	28	.659	2nd/Midwest Division	4	7	.364
74-75	—Chicago	47	35	.573	T1st/Midwest Division	7	6	.538

Season Team	REGULAR SEASON W	L	Pct.	Finish	PLAYOFFS W	L	Pct.
75-76 —Chicago	24	58	.293	4th/Midwest Division	—	—	—
76-77 —Washington	48	34	.585	2nd/Central Division	4	5	.444
77-78 —Washington	44	38	.537	2nd/Central Division	14	7	.666
78-79 —Washington	54	28	.659	1st/Atlantic Division	9	10	.474
79-80 —Washington	39	43	.476	3rd/Atlantic Division	0	2	.000
80-81 —Dallas	15	67	.183	6th/Midwest Division	—	—	—
81-82 —Dallas	28	54	.341	5th/Midwest Division	—	—	—
82-83 —Dallas	38	44	.463	4th/Midwest Division	—	—	—
83-84 —Dallas	43	39	.524	2nd/Midwest Division	4	6	.400
84-85 —Dallas	44	38	.537	3rd/Midwest Division	1	3	.250
85-86 —Dallas	44	38	.537	3rd/Midwest Division	5	5	.500
86-87 —Dallas	55	27	.671	1st/Midwest Division	1	3	.250
89-90 —Sacramento	16	38	.296	7th/Pacific Division	—	—	—
90-91 —Sacramento	25	57	.305	7th/Pacific Division	—	—	—
91-92 —Sacramento	7	18	.280		—	—	—
94-95 —Dallas	36	46	.439	5th/Midwest Division	—	—	—
95-96 —Dallas	26	56	.317	T5th/Midwest Division	—	—	—
96-97 —Denver	17	52	.246	5th/Midwest Division	—	—	—
Totals (25 years)	**935**	**1017**	**.479**	**Totals (14 years)**	**56**	**70**	**.444**

NOTES:

1970—Lost to Atlanta in Western Division First Round.

1971—Lost to Los Angeles in Western Conference First Round.

1972—Lost to Los Angeles in Western Conference First Round.

1973—Lost to Los Angeles in Western Conference First Round.

1974—Defeated Detroit, 4-3, in Western Conference First Round; lost to Milwaukee, 4-0, in Western Conference Semifinals.

1975—Defeated Kansas City/Omaha, 4-2, in Western Conference First Round; lost to Golden State, 4-3, in Western Conference Semifinals.

1977—Defeated Cleveland, 2-1, in Eastern Conference First Round; lost to Houston, 4-2, in Eastern Conference Semifinals.

1978—Defeated Atlanta, 2-0, in Eastern Conference First Round; defeated San Antonio, 4-2, in Eastern Conference Semifinals; defeated Philadelphia, 4-2, in Eastern Conference Finals; defeated Seattle, 4-3, in NBA Finals.

1979—Defeated Atlanta, 4-3, in Eastern Conference Semifinals; defeated San Antonio, 4-3, in Eastern Conference Finals; lost to Seattle, 4-1, in NBA Finals.

1980—Lost to Philadelphia in Eastern Conference First Round.

1984—Defeated Seattle, 3-2, in Western Conference First Round; lost to Los Angeles Lakers, 4-1, in Western Conference Semifinals.

1985—Lost to Portland in Western Conference First Round.

1986—Defeated Utah, 3-1, in Western Conference First Round; lost to Los Angeles Lakers, 4-2, in Western Conference Semifinals.

1987—Lost to Seattle in Western Conference First Round.

1990—Replaced Jerry Reynolds as Sacramento head coach (January 4) with record of 7-21 and club in seventh place.

1991—Replaced as Sacramento head coach by Rex Hughes (December 24) with club in seventh place.

1996—Replaced Bernie Bickerstaff as Denver head coach (November 26) with record of 4-9 and club in fourth place.

RAMSAY, JACK

PERSONAL: Born February 21, 1925, in Philadelphia. ... 6-1/180 (1,85/81,6). ... Full name: John T. Ramsay.
HIGH SCHOOL: Upper Darby Senior (Pa.).
COLLEGE: St. Joseph's, then Villanova, then Pennsylvania.
TRANSACTIONS: Played with San Diego Dons, an Amateur Athletic Union team (1945-46). ... Played in Eastern Basketball League with Harrisburg and Sunbury (1949-50 through 1954-55).
CAREER HONORS: Elected to Naismith Memorial Basketball Hall of Fame (1992). ... One of the Top 10 Coaches in NBA History (1996).

COLLEGIATE RECORD

Season Team	G	Min.	FGM	FGA	Pct.	FTM	FTA	Pct.	Reb.	Ast.	Pts.	AVERAGES RPG	APG	PPG
42-43—St. Joseph's‡						Freshman team statistics unavailable.								
43-44						Did not play—in military service.								
44-45						Did not play—in military service.								
45-46						Did not play—in military service.								
46-47—St. Joseph's	21	...	72	214	.336	20	32	.625	...	...	164	...	...	7.8
47-48—St. Joseph's	14	...	60	...	...	38	...	...	...	...	158	...	...	11.3
48-49—St. Joseph's	23	...	75	...	...	52	...	...	...	...	202	...	...	8.8
Varsity totals	**58**	...	**207**	...	...	**110**	...	...	...	...	**524**	...	...	**9.0**

EBL REGULAR-SEASON RECORD

Season Team	G	Min.	FGM	FGA	Pct.	FTM	FTA	Pct.	Reb.	Ast.	PF	Dq.	Pts.	AVERAGES RPG	APG	PPG
49-50 —Harrisburg	25	...	134	...	...	68	...	...	...	...	...	...	336	...	...	13.4
50-51 —Harrisburg	20	...	96	...	...	43	...	...	...	...	...	...	235	...	...	11.8
51-52 —Sunbury	26	...	159	...	...	86	...	...	...	...	...	...	404	...	...	15.5
52-53 —Sunbury	21	...	116	...	...	97	...	...	...	...	...	...	329	...	...	15.7
53-54 —Sunbury	28	...	112	...	...	101	...	...	...	...	...	...	325	...	...	11.6
54-55 —Sunbury	30	...	164	...	...	155	...	...	...	...	...	...	483	...	...	16.1
Totals	**130**	...	**685**	...	...	**507**	...	...	...	...	...	...	**1877**	...	...	**14.4**

HEAD COACHING RECORD

BACKGROUND: Head coach, St. James High School (Pa.) and later head coach, Mount Pleasant High School, Del. (1949-1955). ... General manager, Philadelphia 76ers (1966-67 and 1967-68). ... Head coach/general manager, 76ers (1968-69 and 1969-70).

COLLEGIATE COACHING RECORD

Season	Team	W	L	Pct.	Finish
55-56	—St. Joseph's	23	6	.793	Independent
56-57	—St. Joseph's	17	7	.708	Independent
57-58	—St. Joseph's	18	9	.667	2nd/Middle Atlantic Conference
58-59	—St. Joseph's	22	5	.815	1st/Middle Atlantic Conference
59-60	—St. Joseph's	20	7	.741	1st/Middle Atlantic Conference
60-61	—St. Joseph's	25	5	.833	1st/Middle Atlantic Conference
61-62	—St. Joseph's	18	10	.643	1st/Middle Atlantic Conference
62-63	—St. Joseph's	23	5	.821	1st/Middle Atlantic Conference
63-64	—St. Joseph's	18	10	.643	T2nd/Middle Atlantic Conference
64-65	—St. Joseph's	26	3	.897	1st/Middle Atlantic Conference
65-66	—St. Joseph's	24	5	.828	1st/Middle Atlantic Conference
Totals (11 years)		**234**	**72**	**.765**	

NBA COACHING RECORD

		REGULAR SEASON				PLAYOFFS		
Season	Team	W	L	Pct.	Finish	W	L	Pct.
68-69	—Philadelphia	55	27	.671	2nd/Eastern Division	1	4	.200
69-70	—Philadelphia	42	40	.512	4th/Eastern Division	1	4	.200
70-71	—Philadelphia	47	35	.573	2nd/Atlantic Division	3	4	.429
71-72	—Philadelphia	30	52	.366	3rd/Atlantic Division	—	—	—
72-73	—Buffalo	21	61	.256	3rd/Atlantic Division	—	—	—
73-74	—Buffalo	42	40	.512	3rd/Atlantic Division	2	4	.333
74-75	—Buffalo	49	33	.598	2nd/Atlantic Division	3	4	.429
75-76	—Buffalo	46	36	.561	T2nd/Atlantic Division	4	5	.444
76-77	—Portland	49	33	.598	2nd/Pacific Division	14	5	.737
77-78	—Portland	58	24	.707	1st/Pacific Division	2	4	.333
78-79	—Portland	45	37	.549	4th/Pacific Division	1	2	.333
79-80	—Portland	38	44	.463	4th/Pacific Division	1	2	.333
80-81	—Portland	45	37	.549	3rd/Pacific Division	1	2	.333
81-82	—Portland	42	40	.512	5th/Pacific Division	—	—	—
82-83	—Portland	46	36	.561	4th/Pacific Division	3	4	.429
83-84	—Portland	48	34	.585	2nd/Pacific Division	2	3	.400
84-85	—Portland	42	40	.512	2nd/Pacific Division	4	5	.444
85-86	—Portland	40	42	.488	2nd/Pacific Division	1	3	.250
86-87	—Indiana	41	41	.500	4th/Central Division	1	3	.250
87-88	—Indiana	38	44	.463	6th/Central Division	—	—	—
88-89	—Indiana	0	7	.000		—	—	—
Totals (21 years)		**864**	**783**	**.525**	**Totals (16 years)**	**44**	**58**	**.431**

NOTES:

1956—Defeated Seton Hall, 74-65, in NIT quarterfinals; lost to Louisville, 89-79, in semifinals; defeated St. Francis-New York, 93-82, in third-place game.

1958—Defeated St. Peter's, 83-72, in NIT first round; lost to St. Bonaventure, 79-75, in quarterfinals.

1959—Lost to West Virginia, 95-92, in NCAA Tournament first round; lost to Navy, 70-59, in regional consolation game.

1960—Lost to Duke, 58-56, in NCAA Tournament first round; lost to West Virginia, 106-100, in regional consolation game.

1961—Defeated Princeton, 72-67, in NCAA Tournament regional semifinal; defeated Wake Forest, 96-86, in regional final; lost to Ohio State, 95-69, in national semifinal; defeated Utah, 127-120 (4 OT), in consolation game.

1962—Lost to Wake Forest, 96-85 (OT), in NCAA Tournament regional semifinal; lost to New York University, 94-85, in regional consolation game.

1963—Defeated Princeton, 82-81, in NCAA Tournament first round; defeated West Virginia, 97-88, in regional semifinal; lost to Duke, 73-59, in regional final.

1964—Defeated Miami (Fla.), 86-76, in NIT first round; lost to Bradley, 83-81, in quarterfinals.

1965—Defeated Connecticut, 67-61, in NCAA Tournament first round; lost to Providence, 81-73 (OT), in regional semifinal; lost to North Carolina State, 103-81, in regional consolation game.

1966—Defeated Providence, 65-48, in NCAA Tournament first round; lost to Duke, 76-74, in regional semifinal; defeated Davidson, 92-76, in regional consolation game.

1969—Lost to Boston in Eastern Division Semifinals.

1970—Lost to Milwaukee in Eastern Division Semifinals.

1971—Lost to Baltimore in Eastern Conference Semifinals.

1974—Lost to Boston in Eastern Conference Semifinals

1975—Lost to Washington in Eastern Conference Semifinals.

1976—Defeated Philadelphia, 2-1, in Eastern Conference First Round; lost to Boston, 4-2, in Eastern Conference Semifinals.

1977—Defeated Chicago, 2-1, in Western Conference First Round; defeated Denver, 4-2, in Western Conference Semifinals; defeated Los Angeles Lakers, 4-0, in Western Conference Finals; defeated Philadelphia, 4-2, in NBA Finals.

1978—Lost to Seattle in Western Conference Semifinals.

1979—Lost to Phoenix in Western Conference First Round.

1980—Lost to Seattle in Western Conference First Round.

1981—Lost to Kansas City in Western Conference First Round.

1983—Defeated Seattle, 2-0, in Western Conference First Round; lost to Los Angeles Lakers, 4-1, in Western Conference Semifinals.

1984—Lost to Phoenix in Western Conference First Round.

1985—Defeated Dallas, 3-1, in Western Conference First Round; lost to Los Angeles Lakers, 4-1, in Western Conference Semifinals.

1986—Lost to Denver in Western Conference First Round.

1987—Lost to Atlanta in Eastern Conference First Round.

1988—Resigned as Indiana head coach (November 17); replaced by Mel Daniels with club in sixth place.

ALL-TIME GREAT COACHES

SHUE, GENE

PERSONAL: Born December 18, 1931, in Baltimore. ... 6-2/175 (1,88/79,4).
COLLEGE: Maryland.
TRANSACTIONS: Selected by Philadelphia Warriors in first round (third pick overall) of 1954 NBA Draft. ... Contract sold by Warriors to New York Knicks (November 29, 1954). ... Traded by Knicks to Fort Wayne Pistons for rights to G Ron Sobieszcyk (April 30, 1956). ... Pistons moved from Fort Wayne to Detroit for 1957-58 season. ... Traded by Pistons to Knicks for C Darrall Imhoff and cash (August 29, 1962). ... Traded by Knicks with C Paul Hogue to Baltimore Bullets for G/F Bill McGill (October 30, 1963).
CAREER NOTES: General manager, Philadelphia 76ers (1990-91 and 1991-92). ... Director of player personnel, 76ers (1992-93 through 1996-97).

COLLEGIATE RECORD

Season Team	G	Min.	FGM	FGA	Pct.	FTM	FTA	Pct.	Reb.	Ast.	Pts.	RPG	APG	PPG
50-51—Maryland‡	14	...	...	...	...	...	...	...	...	...	181	...	...	12.9
51-52—Maryland	22	...	91	243	.374	53	75	.707	...	...	205	...	...	9.3
52-53—Maryland	23	...	176	375	.469	156	223	.700	...	...	508	...	...	22.1
53-54—Maryland	30	...	237	469	.505	180	228	.789	...	...	654	...	...	21.8
Varsity totals	75	...	504	1087	.464	389	526	.740	...	...	1367	...	...	18.2

NBA REGULAR-SEASON RECORD

HONORS: All-NBA first team (1960). ... All-NBA second team (1961).

Season Team	G	Min.	FGM	FGA	Pct.	FTM	FTA	Pct.	Reb.	Ast.	PF	Dq.	Pts.	RPG	APG	PPG
54-55—Phil.-N.Y.	62	947	100	289	.346	59	78	.756	154	89	64	0	259	2.5	1.4	4.2
55-56—New York	72	1750	240	625	.384	181	237	.764	212	179	111	0	661	2.9	2.5	9.2
56-57—Fort Wayne	72	2470	273	710	.385	241	316	.763	421	238	137	0	787	5.8	3.3	10.9
57-58—Detroit	63	2333	353	919	.384	276	327	.844	333	172	150	1	982	5.3	2.7	15.6
58-59—Detroit	72	2745	464	1197	.388	338	421	.803	335	231	129	1	1266	4.7	3.2	17.6
59-60—Detroit	75	†3338	620	1501	.413	472	541	.872	409	295	146	2	1712	5.5	3.9	22.8
60-61—Detroit	78	3361	650	1545	.421	465	543	.856	334	530	207	1	1765	4.3	6.8	22.6
61-62—Detroit	80	3143	580	1422	.408	362	447	.810	372	465	192	1	1522	4.7	5.8	19.0
62-63—New York	78	2288	354	894	.396	208	302	.689	191	259	171	0	916	2.4	3.3	11.7
63-64—Baltimore	47	963	81	276	.293	36	61	.590	94	150	98	2	198	2.0	3.2	4.2
Totals	699	23338	3715	9378	.396	2638	3273	.806	2855	2608	1405	8	10068	4.1	3.7	14.4

NBA PLAYOFF RECORD

Season Team	G	Min.	FGM	FGA	Pct.	FTM	FTA	Pct.	Reb.	Ast.	PF	Dq.	Pts.	RPG	APG	PPG
54-55—New York	3	49	8	17	.471	6	7	.857	12	4	5	0	22	4.0	1.3	7.3
56-57—Fort Wayne	2	79	14	27	.519	4	4	1.000	7	8	3	0	32	3.5	4.0	16.0
57-58—Detroit	7	281	45	123	.366	40	43	.930	46	33	15	0	130	6.6	4.7	18.6
58-59—Detroit	3	118	28	60	.467	27	33	.818	14	10	7	0	83	4.7	3.3	27.7
59-60—Detroit	2	89	15	38	.395	18	20	.900	12	6	5	0	48	6.0	3.0	24.0
60-61—Detroit	5	186	35	72	.486	23	29	.793	12	22	11	0	93	2.4	4.4	18.6
61-62—Detroit	10	369	62	151	.411	37	48	.771	30	49	29	0	161	3.0	4.9	16.1
Totals	32	1171	207	488	.424	155	184	.842	133	132	75	0	569	4.2	4.1	17.8

NBA ALL-STAR GAME RECORD

Season Team	Min.	FGM	FGA	Pct.	FTM	FTA	Pct.	Reb	Ast.	PF	Dq.	Pts.
1958—Detroit	25	8	11	.727	2	3	.667	2	0	3	0	18
1959—Detroit	31	6	12	.500	1	2	.500	4	3	4	0	13
1960—Detroit	34	6	13	.462	1	2	.500	6	6	0	0	13
1961—Detroit	23	6	10	.600	3	4	.750	3	6	1	0	15
1962—Detroit	17	3	6	.500	1	1	1.000	5	4	3	0	7
Totals	130	29	52	.558	8	12	.667	20	19	11	0	66

HEAD COACHING RECORD

HONORS: NBA Coach of the Year (1969, 1982).

NBA COACHING RECORD

Season Team	REGULAR SEASON				PLAYOFFS		
	W	L	Pct.	Finish	W	L	Pct.
66-67 —Baltimore	16	40	.286	5th/Eastern Division	—	—	—
67-68 —Baltimore	36	46	.439	6th/Eastern Division	—	—	—
68-69 —Baltimore	57	25	.695	1st/Eastern Division	0	4	.000
69-70 —Baltimore	50	32	.610	3rd/Central Division	3	4	.429
70-71 —Baltimore	42	40	.512	1st/Central Division	8	10	.444
71-72 —Baltimore	38	44	.463	1st/Central Division	2	4	.333
72-73 —Baltimore	52	30	.634	1st/Central Division	1	4	.200
73-74 —Philadelphia	25	57	.305	4th/Atlantic Division	—	—	—
74-75 —Philadelphia	34	48	.415	4th/Atlantic Division	—	—	—
75-76 —Philadelphia	46	36	.561	T2nd/Atlantic Division	1	2	.333
76-77 —Philadelphia	50	32	.610	1st/Atlantic Division	10	9	.526
77-78 —Philadelphia	2	4	.333		—	—	—
78-79 —San Diego	43	39	.524	5th/Pacific Division	—	—	—
79-80 —San Diego	35	47	.427	5th/Pacific Division	—	—	—
80-81 —Washington	39	43	.476	4th/Atlantic Division	—	—	—
81-82 —Washington	43	39	.524	4th/Atlantic Division	3	4	.429

Season	Team	REGULAR SEASON				PLAYOFFS		
		W	L	Pct.	Finish	W	L	Pct.
82-83	—Washington	42	40	.512	5th/Atlantic Division	—	—	—
83-84	—Washington	35	47	.427	5th/Atlantic Division	1	3	.250
84-85	—Washington	40	42	.488	4th/Atlantic Division	1	3	.250
85-86	—Washington	32	37	.464				
87-88	—L.A. Clippers	17	65	.207	6th/Pacific Division	—	—	—
88-89	—L.A. Clippers	10	28	.263				
Totals (22 years)		**784**	**861**	**.477**	**Totals (10 years)**	**30**	**47**	**.390**

NOTES:

1966—Replaced Mike Farmer (1-8) and Buddy Jeannette (3-13) as Baltimore head coach (December) with record of 4-21.

1969—Lost to New York in Eastern Division Semifinals.

1970—Lost to New York in Eastern Division Semifinals.

1971—Defeated Philadelphia, 4-3, in Eastern Conference Semifinals; defeated New York, 4-3, in Eastern Conference Finals; lost to Milwaukee, 4-0, in NBA Finals.

1972—Lost to New York in Eastern Conference Semifinals.

1973—Lost to New York in Eastern Conference Semifinals.

1976—Lost to Buffalo in Eastern Conference First Round.

1977—Defeated Boston, 4-3, in Eastern Conference Semifinals; defeated Houston, 4-2, in Eastern Conference Finals; lost to Portland, 4-2, in NBA Finals. Replaced as Philadelphia head coach by Billy Cunningham (November 4).

1982—Defeated New Jersey, 2-0, in Eastern Conference First Round; lost to Boston, 4-1, in Eastern Conference Semifinals.

1984—Lost to Boston in Eastern Conference First Round.

1985—Lost to Philadelphia in Eastern Conference First Round.

1986—Replaced as Washington head coach by Kevin Loughery (March 19).

1989—Replaced as L.A. Clippers head coach by Don Casey (January 19).

POINTS

(minimum 70 games or 1,400 points)

	G	FGM	FTM	Pts.	Avg.
Allen Iverson, Philadelphia	71	762	585	2207	31.1
Jerry Stackhouse, Detroit	80	774	666	2380	29.8
Shaquille O'Neal, L.A. Lakers	74	813	499	2125	28.7
Kobe Bryant, L.A. Lakers	68	701	475	1938	28.5
Vince Carter, Toronto	75	762	384	2070	27.6
Chris Webber, Sacramento	70	786	324	1898	27.1
Tracy McGrady, Orlando	77	788	430	2065	26.8
Paul Pierce, Boston	82	687	550	2071	25.3
Antawn Jamison, Gold. St.	82	800	382	2044	24.9
Stephon Marbury, New Jersey	67	563	362	1598	23.9

REBOUNDS

(minimum 70 games or 800 rebounds)

	G	Off.	Def.	Tot.	Avg.
Dikembe Mutombo, Atl.-Phi.	75	307	708	1015	13.5
Ben Wallace, Detroit	80	303	749	1052	13.2
Shaquille O'Neal, L.A. Lakers	74	291	649	940	12.7
Tim Duncan, San Antonio	82	259	738	997	12.2
Antonio McDyess, Denver	70	240	605	845	12.1
Kevin Garnett, Minnesota	81	219	702	921	11.4
Chris Webber, Sacramento	70	179	598	777	11.1
Shawn Marion, Phoenix	79	220	628	848	10.7
Antonio Davis, Toronto	78	274	513	787	10.1
Elton Brand, Chicago	74	285	461	746	10.1

FIELD GOALS

(minimum 300 made)

	FGM	FGA	Pct.
Shaquille O'Neal, L.A. Lakers	813	1422	.572
Bonzi Wells, Portland	387	726	.533
Marcus Camby, New York	304	580	.524
Kurt Thomas, New York	314	614	.511
Wally Szczerbiak, Minnesota	469	920	.510
Darius Miles, L.A. Clippers	318	630	.505
John Stockton, Utah	328	651	.504
Donyell Marshall, Utah	427	849	.503
Corliss Williamson, Tor.-Det.	325	647	.502
Clarence Weatherspoon, Cleve.	347	692	.501
Rasheed Wallace, Portland	590	1178	.501

STEALS

(minimum 70 games or 125 steals)

	G	No.	Avg.
Allen Iverson, Philadelphia	71	178	2.51
Mookie Blaylock, Golden State	69	163	2.36
Doug Christie, Sacramento	81	183	2.26
Jason Kidd, Phoenix	77	166	2.16
Baron Davis, Charlotte	82	170	2.07
Terrell Brandon, Minnesota	78	161	2.06
Ron Artest, Chicago	76	152	2.00
Darrell Armstrong, Orlando	75	135	1.80
Steve Francis, Houston	80	141	1.76
Antoine Walker, Boston	81	138	1.70

FREE THROWS

(minimum 125 made)

	FTM	FTA	Pct.
Reggie Miller, Indiana	323	348	.928
Allan Houston, New York	279	307	.909
Doug Christie, Sacramento	280	312	.897
Steve Nash, Dallas	231	258	.895
Mitch Richmond, Washington	143	160	.894
Steve Smith, Portland	309	347	.890
Ray Allen, Milwaukee	348	392	.888
Darrell Armstrong, Orlando	220	249	.884
Eric Piatkowski, L.A. Clippers	158	181	.873
Terrell Brandon, Minnesota	195	224	.871

BLOCKED SHOTS

(minimum 70 games or 100 blocked shots)

	G	No.	Avg.
Theo Ratliff, Philadelphia	50	187	3.74
Jermaine O'Neal, Indiana	81	228	2.81
Shawn Bradley, Dallas	82	228	2.78
Shaquille O'Neal, L.A. Lakers	74	204	2.76
Dikembe Mutombo, Atl.-Phi.	75	203	2.71
Adonal Foyle, Golden State	58	156	2.69
Raef LaFrentz, Denver	78	206	2.64
David Robinson, San Antonio	80	197	2.46
Tim Duncan, San Antonio	82	192	2.34
Ben Wallace, Detroit	80	186	2.33

ASSISTS

(minimum 70 games or 400 assists)

	G	No.	Avg.
Jason Kidd, Phoenix	77	753	9.8
John Stockton, Utah	82	713	8.7
Nick Van Exel, Denver	71	600	8.5
Mike Bibby, Vancouver	82	685	8.4
Gary Payton, Seattle	79	642	8.1
Andre Miller, Cleveland	82	657	8.0
Mark Jackson, Tor.-N.Y.	83	661	8.0
Sam Cassell, Milwaukee	76	580	7.6
Stephon Marbury, New Jersey	67	506	7.6
Terrell Brandon, Minnesota	78	583	7.5

THREE-POINT FIELD GOALS

(minimum 55 made)

	FGM	FGA	Pct.
Brent Barry, Seattle	109	229	.476
John Stockton, Utah	61	132	.462
Shammond Williams, Seattle	61	133	.459
Hubert Davis, Dal.-Was.	78	171	.456
Danny Ferry, San Antonio	70	156	.449
Toni Kukoc, Phi.-Atl.	70	157	.446
Pat Garrity, Orlando	97	224	.433
Ray Allen, Milwaukee	202	467	.433
Rashard Lewis, Seattle	123	285	.432
Dell Curry, Toronto	62	145	.428